HOOVER'S HANDBOOK of AMERICAN COMPANIES

1996

EDITED BY
PATRICK J. SPAIN
& JAMES R. TALBOT

*Hoover's Handbook*s are intended to provide their readers with accurate and authoritative information about the enterprises profiled in them. The Reference Press asked all profiled companies and organizations to provide information for this book. Many did so; a number did not. The information contained herein is as accurate as we could reasonably make it. In many cases we have relied on third-party material that we believe to be trustworthy but were unable to verify independently. We do not warrant that the book is absolutely accurate or without any errors. Readers should not rely on any information contained herein where such reliance might cause loss or damage. The editors and publisher and their data suppliers specifically disclaim all warranties, including the implied warranties of merchantability and fitness for a specific purpose. This book is sold with the understanding that neither the editors nor the publisher is engaged in providing investment, financial, accounting, legal, or other professional advice.

The financial data (How Much section) in this book are from a variety of sources. Media General Financial Services, Inc., provided selected financial data for the How Much section for a number of the publicly traded companies. For private companies and for historical information on public companies prior to their becoming public, we obtained information directly from the companies or from trade sources deemed to be reliable. The Reference Press, Inc., is solely responsible for the presentation of all data.

Many of the names of products and services mentioned in this book are the trademarks or service marks of the companies manufacturing or selling them and are subject to protection under US law. Space has not permitted us to indicate which names are subject to such protection, and readers are advised to consult with the owners of such marks regarding their use. Hoover's Handbook® is a registered trademark of The Reference Press, Inc.

The Reference Press, Inc. ™

10 9 8 7 6 5 4 3 2 1

Publisher Cataloging-In-Publication Data

Hoover's Handbook of American Companies 1996. Edited by Patrick J. Spain and James R. Talbot

Includes indexes.
1. Business enterprises — Directories. 2. Corporations — Directories.
HF3010   338.7

*Hoover's Handbook*s are also available on America Online, Bloomberg Financial Network, CompuServe, Dow Jones News Retrieval, eWorld, LEXIS-NEXIS, Microsoft Network, NlightN, and on the Internet at Hoover's Online (http://www.hoovers.com), Pathfinder (http://pathfinder.com), InfoSeek (http://www.infoseek.com), PAWWS Financial Network (http://www.pawws.com), and Farcast (http://www.farcast.com).

ISBN 1-878753-87-8 trade paper

This book was produced by The Reference Press on Apple Macintosh computers using Aldus Corporation's PageMaker 4.2 software and Adobe System, Inc.'s fonts from the Clearface and Futura families. Graphs were created using DeltaGraph, a product of DeltaPoint, Inc. Cover design is by Kristin M. Jackson, of Austin, Texas. Electronic prepress and printing was done by Courier Corporation at Westford, Massachusetts, USA. Text paper is 60# Postmark White. Cover stock is 10 point, coated one side, film laminated.

Published in association with Warner Books, Inc.

*Hoover's Handbook*s are available in bookstores in the US and Canada, in most European countries, through all major US book distributors and library jobbers, and directly from The Reference Press. The following companies are authorized distributors of *Hoover's Handbook*s:

US AND WORLD DIRECT SALES
The Reference Press, Inc.
6448 Highway 290 E., Suite E-104
Austin, Texas 78723
Phone: 512-454-7778
Fax: 512-454-9401
e-mail: refpress6@aol.com

EUROPE
William Snyder Publishing
5, Five Mile Drive
Oxford, 0X2 8HT
England
Phone & fax: +44(01)86-551-3186
e-mail: 100072.2511@compuserve.com

US BOOKSELLERS AND JOBBERS
Little, Brown and Co.
200 West Street
Waltham, Massachusetts 02154
Phone: 800-759-0190
Fax: 617-890-0875

US WHOLESALER ORDERS
Warner Publisher Services Book Div.
9210 King Palm Drive
Tampa, Florida 33619
Phone: 800-873-BOOK
Fax: 813-664-8193

CANADIAN BOOKSELLERS AND WHOLESALER ORDERS
H. B. Fenn and Company Ltd.
1090 Lorimar Drive
Mississauga, Ontario L5S 1R7, Canada
Phone: 905-670-FENN
Fax: 905-670-3422

THE REFERENCE PRESS

The Reference Press Mission Statement

1. To produce business information products and services of the highest quality, accuracy, and readability.

2. To make that information available whenever, wherever, and however our customers want it through mass distribution at affordable prices.

3. To continually expand our range of products and services and our markets for those products and services.

4. To reward our employees, suppliers, and shareholders based on their contributions to the success of our enterprise.

5. To hold to the highest ethical business standards, erring on the side of generosity when in doubt.

ABBREVIATIONS

AFL-CIO – American Federation of Labor and Congress of Industrial Organizations

AMA – American Medical Association

AMEX – American Stock Exchange

ARM – adjustable rate mortgage

ATM – asynchronous transfer mode

CAD/CAM – computer-aided design/computer-aided manufacturing

CASE – computer-aided software engineering

CD-ROM – compact disc – read-only memory

CEO – chief executive officer

CFO – chief financial officer

CISC – complex instruction set computer

CMOS – complimentary metal oxide silicon

COO – chief operating officer

DAT – digital audio tape

DOD – Department of Defense

DOE – Department of Energy

DOS – disk operating system

DOT – Department of Transportation

DRAM – dynamic random-access memory

EPA – Environmental Protection Agency

EPROM – erasable programmable read-only memory

EPS – earnings per share

ESOP – employee stock ownership plan

EU – European Union

EVP – executive vice-president

FCC – Federal Communications Commission

FDA – Food and Drug Administration

FDIC – Federal Deposit Insurance Corporation

FTC – Federal Trade Commission

FTP – file transfer protocol

GATT – General Agreement on Tariffs and Trade

GDP – gross domestic product

GUI – graphical user interface

HMO – health maintenance organization

HR – human resources

HTML – hypertext markup language

ICC – Interstate Commerce Commission

IPO – initial public offering

IRS – Internal Revenue Service

ISDN – Integrated Services Digital Network

LAN – local-area network

LBO – leveraged buyout

LCD – liquid crystal display

LNG – liquefied natural gas

LP – limited partnership

Ltd. – limited

MIPS – million instructions per second

NAFTA – North American Free Trade Agreement

NASA – National Aeronautics and Space Administration

Nasdaq – National Association of Securities Dealers Automated Quotations

NATO – North Atlantic Treaty Organization

NYSE – New York Stock Exchange

OCR – optical character recognition

OECD – Organization for Economic Cooperation and Development

OEM – original equipment manufacturer

OPEC – Organization of Petroleum Exporting Countries

OS – operating system

OSHA – Occupational Safety and Health Administration

OTC – over the counter

PBX – private branch exchange

PCMCIA – Personal Computer Memory Card International Association

P/E – price to earnings ratio

RAM – random access memory

R&D – research and development

RBOC – Regional Bell Operating Company

RISC – reduced instruction set computer

ROA – return on assets

ROE – return on equity

ROI – return on investment

ROM – read-only memory

S&L – savings and loan

SEC – Securities and Exchange Commission

SEVP – senior executive vice-president

SIC – Standard Industrial Classification

SPARC – scalable processor architecture

SVP – senior vice-president

VAR – value-added remarketer

VAT – value-added tax

VC – vice-chairman

VP – vice-president

WAN – wide-area network

www – world wide web

Contents

List of Lists

Companies Profiled

Schlumberger N.V.	762	The Travelers Inc.	852
SCI Systems, Inc.	764	Tribune Company	854
Scott Paper Company	766	TRW Inc.	856
Seagate Technology, Inc.	768	Turner Broadcasting System, Inc.	858
Sears, Roebuck and Co.	770	Tyco International Ltd.	860
Service Merchandise Company, Inc.	772	Tyson Foods, Inc.	862
The Sherwin-Williams Company	774	UAL Corporation	864
Silicon Graphics, Inc.	776	Unicom Corporation	866
Smithsonian Institution*	778	Union Carbide Corporation	868
The Southern Company	780	Union Pacific Corporation	870
Southern Pacific Rail Corporation	782	Unisys Corporation	872
The Southland Corporation	784	United HealthCare Corporation*	874
Southwest Airlines Co.	786	United Parcel Service of America, Inc.	876
Spiegel, Inc.	788	United States Postal Service*	878
Springs Industries, Inc.	790	United Technologies Corporation	880
Sprint Corporation	792	Universal Corporation	882
The Stanley Works	794	Unocal Corporation	884
State Farm Mutual Automobile Insurance		The Upjohn Company	886
Company	796	U S WEST, Inc.	888
Steelcase Inc.*	798	USAA	890
Stone Container Corporation	800	USAir Group, Inc.	892
Storage Technology Corporation	802	USF&G Corporation	894
Student Loan Marketing Association	804	USX–Marathon Group	896
Sun Company, Inc.	806	USX–U.S. Steel Group	898
Sun Microsystems, Inc.	808	V. F. Corporation	900
SunTrust Banks, Inc.	810	Viacom Inc.	902
SUPERVALU Inc.	812	The Vons Companies, Inc.	904
SYSCO Corporation	814	Walgreen Co.	906
Tandem Computers Incorporated	816	Wal-Mart Stores, Inc.	908
Tandy Corporation	818	The Walt Disney Company	910
Teachers Insurance and Annuity Association	820	Warner-Lambert Company	912
Tele-Communications, Inc.	822	The Washington Post Company	914
Teledyne, Inc.	824	Wells Fargo & Company	916
Tenet Healthcare Corporation	826	Westinghouse Electric Corporation	918
Tenneco Inc.	828	Weyerhaeuser Company	920
Tennessee Valley Authority*	830	Whirlpool Corporation	922
Texaco Inc.	832	Whitman Corporation	924
Texas Instruments Incorporated	834	Wm. Wrigley Jr. Company	926
Texas Utilities Company	836	Winn-Dixie Stores, Inc.	928
Textron Inc.	838	WMX Technologies, Inc.	930
Time Warner Inc.	840	Woolworth Corporation	932
The Times Mirror Company	842	W. R. Grace & Co.	934
The TJX Companies, Inc.	844	Xerox Corporation	936
Toys "R" Us, Inc.	846	Yellow Corporation	938
Trans World Airlines, Inc.	848	Young & Rubicam Inc.	940
Transamerica Corporation	850	Zenith Electronics Corporation	942

COMPANY NAME CHANGES SINCE *HOOVER'S HANDBOOK OF AMERICAN BUSINESS 1995*

American Financial Group (was American Financial Corporation)
American Standard Companies (was American Standard Inc.)
ARAMARK (was The ARA Group Inc.)
Ashland Inc. (was Ashland Oil, Inc.)
Hughes Electronics Corp. (was GM Hughes Electronics Corporation)
Lockheed Martin Corp. (was Lockheed Corporation and Martin Marietta Corporation)
The McGraw Hill Companies, Inc. (was McGraw-Hill, Inc.)
SBC Communications, Inc. (was Southwestern Bell Corporation)
Tenet Healthcare Corporation (was National Medical Enterprises, Inc.)

*Companies added to *Hoover's Handbook of American Companies 1996*

ABOUT HOOVER'S HANDBOOK OF AMERICAN BUSINESS

I n 1990 The Reference Press published *Hoover's Handbook 1991: Profiles of Over 500 Major Corporations*. That book, the first of our series of reasonably priced business references, was an immediate success. As we expanded our coverage, we split it into 2 volumes: *Hoover's Handbook of American Business* and *Hoover's Handbook of World Business*. We also published a number of other volumes, including *Hoover's Handbook of Emerging Companies, Hoover's Guide to Private Companies, Hoover's Guide to Computer Companies, Hoover's MasterList of America's Top 2,500 Employers*, and a series of regional *Hoover's Guides*. In addition we made our company profiles and other information available electronically on diskette and CD-ROM and on on-line services (e.g., America Online and CompuServe) and the Internet (e.g., Hoover's Online at http://www.hoovers.com).

The book you hold in your hands represents the next step in the evolution of *Hoover's Handbooks*. This year we've split it into 2 separate editions to meet the differing needs of our audience. This edition, entitled *Hoover's Handbook of American Companies*, profiles 450 companies in paperback and is intended for those who found that our existing book met their information needs. In late 1995 we will publish *Hoover's Handbook of American Business*, a 2-volume hardcover book that will profile over 750 companies. That edition is aimed at individuals and institutions who need more information than we could provide in the traditional paperback format.

We believe that anyone who buys from, sells to, invests in, lends to, competes with, interviews with, or works for a company should know about that enterprise. Taken together, this book and the other *Hoover's Handbooks* and *Hoover's Guides* represent the most complete source of basic corporate information readily available to the general public. We have endeavored to provide you with a concise, accurate, and useful guide to the companies that affect our lives.

Hoover's Handbook of American Companies 1996 covers 450 of the largest and most influential companies in America. From the largest (General Motors, at $155 billion) to the smallest (The Green Bay Packers, at $62 million), each company has been chosen because of its unique and important role in American business. More detail on how these companies were selected is included in the section of this book entitled "Using the Profiles."

This book consists of 4 components:

1. The first section, "Using the Profiles," describes the contents of the profiles and explains the ways in which we gather and compile our data.

2. Next we have included "A List-Lover's Compendium," which contains lists of the largest companies in the book and selected lists from other sources to provide you with different viewpoints.

3. The third and most important part of the book is the profiles themselves — 450 profiles of major U.S. enterprises, arranged alphabetically.

4. The book concludes with 3 indexes: (1) the companies organized by industry groupings, (2) the companies organized by headquarters location, and (3) the main index of the book, containing the names of all brands, companies, and people mentioned in the profiles.

As an added feature we've included software that will enable you to access America Online, the fastest-growing on-line service in the US, and use the service for free for 10 hours. Once on America Online, use the keyword "Hoovers" to access the full range of our company information, including over 1,600 company profiles and 8,000 capsule profiles, and to get full access to the World Wide Web. This diskette is only for computers running Windows. You can obtain a DOS or Macintosh disk by calling 800-827-6364, ext. 17592. For more details see the last page of the book.

As always, we hope you find our books useful. We invite your comments via phone (512-454-7778), fax (512-454-9401), mail (6448 Hwy. 290 East, Ste. E-104, Austin, TX 78723), or e-mail (refpress3@aol.com).

The Editors
Austin, Texas
August 1995

USING THE PROFILES

Selection of the Companies Profiled

The 450 enterprises profiled in this book include mutual and cooperative organizations (owned by customers; e.g., Prudential Insurance and Associated Milk Producers) and a number of large private corporations (such as UPS, Mars, and Cargill), as well as a few other nonpublic enterprises (e.g., the Smithsonian Institution and the Tennessee Valley Authority). However, over 380 of the entities profiled are publicly held corporations.

In selecting these companies, our foremost question was "What companies will our readers be most interested in?" Our goal was to answer as many questions as we could in one book, in effect trying to anticipate your curiosity. This approach resulted in 4 general criteria for selecting companies for inclusion in the book:

1. **Size.** The 400 or so largest American companies, measured by sales and by number of employees, are included in the book. In general, these companies have sales in excess of $2 billion, and they are the ones you will have heard of and the ones you will want to know about. These are the companies at the top of the various *FORTUNE*, *Forbes*, and *Business Week* lists. We have made sure to include the top private companies in this number.

2. **Growth.** We believe that relatively few readers will be going to work for, or investing in, the savings and loan industry. Therefore, only a few S&Ls and a handful of forest products companies (which, while very large, are not growing rapidly) are in the book. On the other hand, we have included a number of computer and peripheral makers and numerous other electronics and software firms.

3. **Visibility.** Most readers will have heard of Hilton Hotels, Irvin Feld & Kenneth Feld Productions (Ringling Brothers and Barnum & Bailey Circuses), Turner Broadcasting, and Wm. Wrigley. Their consumer or service natures make them household names, even though they are not among the corporate giants in terms of sales and employment.

4. **Breadth of coverage.** To show the diversity of economic activity, we've included two professional sports teams, one ranch, one agricultural cooperative, the Big Six accounting firms, the 3 principal US stock exchanges, etc. We feel that these businesses are important enough — and interesting enough — to enjoy at least "token" representation. While we might not emphasize certain industries, the industry leaders are present.

Organization of the Profiles

The profiles are presented in alphabetical order. This alphabetization is generally word by word, which means that Advance Publications precedes Advanced Micro Devices. We have shown the full legal name of the enterprise at the top of each page, unless it is too long, in which case you will find it above the address in the Where section of the profile. If a company name starts with a person's first name, like Arthur Andersen or Walt Disney, it will be alphabetized under the first name; if the company name starts with initials, like J. C. Penney or H. J. Heinz, look for it under the initials (in the above examples, JC and HJ, respectively). All company names (past and present) used in the profiles are indexed in the last index in the book.

Certain pieces of basic data are listed at the top left of the second page of each profile: where the company's stock is traded if it is public, the ticker symbol used by the stock exchange, and the company's fiscal year-end.

The annual financial information contained in the profiles is current through fiscal year-ends occurring as late as April 1995. We have included nonfinancial developments, such as officer changes, through July 1995.

Overview

In this section we have tried to give a thumbnail description of the company and what it does. The description will usually include information on the company's strategy, reputation, and ownership. We recommend that you read this section first.

When

This longer section reflects our belief that every enterprise is the sum of its history, and that you have to know where you came from in order to know where you are going. While some companies have very little historical awareness and were unable to help us much, and other companies are just plain boring, we think the vast majority of the enterprises in the book have colorful backgrounds. When we could find information, we tried to focus on the people who made the enterprise what it is today. We have found these histories to be full of twists and ironies; they can make for some fascinating, quick reading.

Who

Here we list the names of the people who run the company, insofar as space allows. In the case of public companies, we have shown the ages and pay levels of key officers. In some cases the published data are for last year although the company has announced promotions or retirements since year-end. We have tried to show current officers, with their pay for the latest year available. The pay represents cash compensation, including bonuses, but excludes stock option programs.

While companies are free to structure their management titles any way they please, most modern corporations follow standard practices. The ultimate power in any corporation lies with the shareholders, who elect a board of directors, usually including officers or "insiders" as well as individuals from outside the company. The chief officer, the person on whose desk the buck stops, is usually called the chief executive officer (CEO). Normally, he or she is also the chairman of the board. As corporate management has become more complex, it is common for the CEO to have a "right-hand person" who oversees the day-to-day operations of the company, allowing the CEO plenty of time to focus on strategy and long-term issues. This right-hand person is usually designated the chief operating officer (COO) and is often the president of the company. In other cases one person is both chairman and president.

A multitude of other titles exists, including chief financial officer (CFO), chief administrative officer, and vice-chairman (VC). We have always tried to include the CFO, the chief legal officer, and the chief personnel or human resources officer. Our best advice is that officers' pay levels are clear indicators of who the board of directors thinks are most important on the management team. The Who section also includes the name of the company's auditing (accounting) firm.

The people named in the profiles are indexed at the back of the book.

Where

Here we include the company's headquarters street address and phone and fax numbers as available. The back of the book includes an index of companies by headquarters locations.

We have also included as much information as we could gather and fit on the geographical distribution of the company's business, including sales and profit data. Note that these profit numbers, like those in the What section below, are usually operating or pretax profits rather than net profits. Operating profits are generally those before financing costs (interest income and payments) and before taxes, which are considered costs attributable to the whole company rather than to one division or part of the world. For this reason the net income figures (in the How Much section) are usually much lower, since they are after interest and taxes. Pretax profits are after interest but before taxes. When sales and operating profits by region were not available or were not appropriate, we have published other measures of geographic diversity. For example, for regional retailers we have listed the number of stores by state.

What

This section lists as many of the company's products, services, brand names, divisions, subsidiaries, and joint ventures as we could fit. We have tried to include all its major lines and all familiar brand names. The nature of this section varies by industry, company, and the amount of information available. If the company publishes sales and profit information by type of business, we have included it. The brand, division, and subsidiary names are listed in the last index in the book.

Key Competitors

In this section we have listed those other companies that compete with the profiled company. This feature is included as a quick way to locate similar companies and compare them. The universe of key competitors includes all public companies and all private companies with sales in excess of $500 million. In a few instances we have identified smaller private companies as key competitors. All the companies in the book are listed by broad industry groups in the first index at the back of the book.

How Much

Here we have tried to present as much data about each enterprise's financial performance as we could compile in the allocated space. While the information varies somewhat from industry to industry, and is less complete in the case of private companies that do not release these data (though we have always tried to provide annual sales and employment), the following information is generally present.

A 10-year table, with relevant annualized compound growth rates, covering:
- Fiscal year sales (year-end assets for most financial companies)
- Fiscal year net income (before accounting changes)
- Fiscal year net income as a percent of sales (as a percent of assets for most financial firms)
- Fiscal year Earnings Per Share (EPS) (fully diluted unless italicized)
- Calendar year stock price high, low, and close
- Calendar year high and low Price/Earnings ratio (P/E)
- Fiscal year dividends per share
- Fiscal year-end book value (shareholders' equity per share)
- Fiscal year-end or average number of employees

All revenue numbers are as reported by the company in its annual report.

The 10-year information on the number of employees is intended to aid the reader interested in knowing whether a company has a long-term trend of increasing or decreasing employment. As far as we know, we are the only company that publishes this information in print format.

The year at the top of each column in the How Much section is the year in which the company's fiscal year actually ends. Thus a company with a February 28, 1995, year-end is shown as 1995. Stock price information for companies with year-ends between January and April is for the last trading day of the prior calendar year and is so footnoted on the chart.

Key year-end statistics in this section generally show the financial strength of the enterprise, including:

- Debt ratio (total debt as a percent of combined total debt and shareholders' equity)
- Return on Average Equity (net income divided by the average of beginning shareholders' equity and ending shareholders' equity) for the fiscal year
- Cash and marketable securities on hand at the end of the fiscal year
- Current ratio at fiscal year-end (ratio of current assets to current liabilities)
- Total long-term debt (excluding capital lease obligations) at year-end
- Number of shares of common stock outstanding at year-end
- Dividend yield (fiscal year dividends per share divided by the calendar year-end closing stock price)
- Dividend payout (fiscal year dividends divided by fiscal year EPS)

- Market value at calendar year-end (calendar year-end closing stock price multiplied by fiscal year-end number of shares outstanding)

For financial institutions and insurance companies, we have also included annual sales in this section.

Per share data have been adjusted for stock splits. The data for some public companies (and private companies with public debt) have been provided to us by Media General Financial Services, Inc. Other public company information was compiled by The Reference Press, which takes full responsibility for the content of this section.

In the case of private companies that do not publicly disclose financial information, we usually did not have access to such standardized data. We have gathered estimates of sales and other statistics from numerous sources; among the most helpful were trade publications such as *Advertising Age* and *Forbes*'s list of the largest private companies. ▲

A LIST-LOVER'S COMPENDIUM

100 Largest Companies by Sales in *Hoover's Handbook of American Companies 1996*

Rank	Company	Sales ($ mil.)
1	General Motors Corporation	154,951
2	Ford Motor Company	128,439
3	Exxon Corporation	113,904
4	Wal-Mart Stores, Inc.	82,494
5	AT&T Corp.	75,094
6	Mobil Corporation	67,383
7	Philip Morris Companies Inc.	65,125
8	International Business Machines	64,052
9	General Electric Company	60,109
10	Sears, Roebuck and Co.	54,559
11	Chrysler Corporation	52,224
12	Cargill, Incorporated	51,000
13	United States Postal Service	49,252
14	The Prudential Insurance Company of America	43,557
15	E. I. du Pont de Nemours	39,333
16	Chevron Corporation	35,854
17	Kmart Corporation	34,313
18	Texaco Inc.	32,540
19	Citicorp	31,650
20	Amoco Corporation	30,362
21	The Procter & Gamble Company	30,296
22	Metropolitan Life Insurance Company	29,983
23	PepsiCo, Inc.	28,472
24	State Farm	25,598
25	Hewlett-Packard Company	24,991
26	Koch Industries, Inc.	23,725
27	ITT Corporation	23,620
28	ConAgra, Inc.	23,512
29	The Kroger Co.	22,959
30	American International Group, Inc.	22,442
31	Motorola, Inc.	22,245
32	The Boeing Company	21,924
33	The Allstate Corporation	21,464
34	Dayton Hudson Corporation	21,311
35	United Technologies Corporation	21,197
36	J. C. Penney Company, Inc.	20,380
37	The Dow Chemical Company	20,015
38	GTE Corporation	19,944
39	United Parcel Service of America, Inc.	19,576
40	Federal National Mortgage Association	18,573
41	The Travelers Inc.	18,465
42	CIGNA Corporation	18,392
43	American Stores Company	18,355
44	Merrill Lynch & Co., Inc.	18,233
45	Xerox Corporation	17,837
46	Aetna Life and Casualty Company	17,534
47	Atlantic Richfield Company	17,199
48	BellSouth Corporation	16,845
49	SUPERVALU Inc.	16,564
50	BankAmerica Corporation	16,531
51	Nationwide Insurance Enterprise	16,507
52	Price/Costco, Inc.	16,481
53	The Coca-Cola Company	16,172
54	AMR Corporation	16,137
55	New York Life Insurance Company	15,807
56	Fleming Companies, Inc.	15,753
57	Johnson & Johnson	15,734
58	Safeway Inc.	15,627
59	Sara Lee Corporation	15,536
60	RJR Nabisco Holdings Corp.	15,366
61	Minnesota Mining and Manufacturing	15,079
62	Merck & Co., Inc.	14,970
63	International Paper Company	14,966
64	Caltex Petroleum Corporation	14,751
65	Caterpillar Inc.	14,328
66	American Express Company	14,282
67	Hughes Electronics Corp.	14,099
68	Continental Grain Company	14,000
69	UAL Corporation	13,950
70	Bell Atlantic Corporation	13,791
71	Anheuser-Busch Companies, Inc.	13,734
72	Eastman Kodak Company	13,687
73	Loews Corporation	13,515
74	Digital Equipment Corporation	13,451
75	MCI Communications Corporation	13,338
76	NYNEX Corporation	13,307
77	McKesson Corporation	13,189
78	McDonnell Douglas Corporation	13,176
79	American Brands, Inc.	13,147
80	Lockheed Martin Corporation	13,130
81	AlliedSignal Inc.	12,817
82	USX–Marathon Group	12,757
83	Georgia-Pacific Corporation	12,738
84	Chemical Banking Corporation	12,685
85	Sprint Corporation	12,662
86	Ameritech Corporation	12,570
87	Mars, Inc.	12,500
88	The Home Depot, Inc.	12,477
89	NationsBank Corporation	12,470
90	Phillips Petroleum Company	12,367
91	Delta Air Lines, Inc.	12,359
92	The Goodyear Tire & Rubber Company	12,288
93	Kaiser Foundation Health Plan, Inc.	12,268
94	The May Department Stores Company	12,223
95	Tenneco Inc.	12,174
96	IBP, inc.	12,075
97	Bristol-Myers Squibb Company	11,984
98	J.P. Morgan & Co. Incorporated	11,915
99	Albertson's, Inc.	11,895
100	The Chase Manhattan Corporation	11,817

100 Most Profitable Companies in *Hoover's Handbook of American Companies 1996*

Rank	Company	Net Income ($ mil.)	Rank	Company	Net Income ($ mil.)
1	General Motors Corporation	5,338	51	ITT Corporation	1,033
2	Ford Motor Company	5,308	52	ITT Industries	1,033
3	Exxon Corporation	5,100	53	Anheuser-Busch Companies, Inc.	1,032
4	General Electric Company	4,726	54	Merrill Lynch & Co., Inc.	1,017
5	Philip Morris Companies Inc.	4,725	55	Pacific Gas and Electric Company	1,008
6	AT&T Corp.	4,710	56	Banc One Corporation	1,005
7	Chrysler Corporation	3,713	57	The Southern Company	989
8	Citicorp	3,422	58	Hughes Electronics Corp.	956
9	Merck & Co., Inc.	2,997	59	Caterpillar Inc.	955
10	International Business Machines Corporation	2,937	60	United Parcel Service of America, Inc.	943
11	E. I. du Pont de Nemours and Company	2,727	61	The Dow Chemical Company	931
12	Wal-Mart Stores, Inc.	2,681	62	First Union Corporation	925
13	The Coca-Cola Company	2,554	63	Schering-Plough Corporation	922
14	GTE Corporation	2,451	64	Atlantic Richfield Company	919
15	Intel Corporation	2,288	65	Texaco Inc.	910
16	The Procter & Gamble Company	2,211	66	Emerson Electric Co.	904
17	American International Group, Inc.	2,176	67	Sprint Corporation	888
18	BankAmerica Corporation	2,176	68	Compaq Computer Corporation	867
19	BellSouth Corporation	2,160	69	The Boeing Company	856
20	Federal National Mortgage Association	2,132	70	Wells Fargo & Company	841
21	Johnson & Johnson	2,006	71	KeyCorp	837
22	Bristol-Myers Squibb Company	1,842	72	Electronic Data Systems Corporation	822
23	Amoco Corporation	1,789	73	Kaiser Foundation Health Plan, Inc.	816
24	PepsiCo, Inc.	1,784	74	MCI Communications Corporation	795
25	Mobil Corporation	1,759	75	Xerox Corporation	794
26	Chevron Corporation	1,693	76	NYNEX Corporation	793
27	NationsBank Corporation	1,690	77	WMX Technologies, Inc.	784
28	United HealthCare Corporation	1,665	78	The May Department Stores Company	782
29	SBC Communications Inc.	1,649	79	AlliedSignal Inc.	759
30	Hewlett-Packard Company	1,599	80	Dean Witter, Discover & Co.	741
31	Motorola, Inc.	1,560	81	The Bank of New York Company, Inc.	736
32	American Home Products Corporation	1,528	82	American Brands, Inc.	734
33	Abbott Laboratories	1,517	83	First Interstate Bancorp	734
34	Sears, Roebuck and Co.	1,454	84	Kellogg Company	705
35	U S WEST, Inc.	1,426	85	Consolidated Edison Company of New York, Inc.	699
36	American Express Company	1,413	86	The Gillette Company	698
37	Bell Atlantic Corporation	1,402	87	The Mead Corporation	696
38	The Travelers Inc.	1,326	88	Warner-Lambert Company	694
39	Minnesota Mining and Manufacturing	1,322	89	Texas Instruments Incorporated	691
40	Pfizer Inc.	1,298	90	First Chicago Corporation	690
41	Chemical Banking Corporation	1,294	91	Caltex Petroleum Corporation	689
42	Eli Lilly and Company	1,286	92	SCEcorp	681
43	McDonald's Corporation	1,224	93	Capital Cities/ABC, Inc.	680
44	J.P. Morgan & Co. Incorporated	1,215	94	Public Service Enterprise Group	679
45	The Chase Manhattan Corporation	1,205	95	Cargill, Incorporated	671
46	Ameritech Corporation	1,170	96	Norfolk Southern Corporation	668
47	Pacific Telesis Group	1,159	97	General Re Corporation	665
48	Microsoft Corporation	1,146	98	CSX Corporation	652
49	The Walt Disney Company	1,110	99	Duke Power Company	639
50	J. C. Penney Company, Inc.	1,057	100	Rockwell International Corporation	634

100 Most Valuable Public Companies in *Hoover's Handbook of American Companies 1996*

Rank	Company	Market Value ($ mil.)	Rank	Company	Market Value ($ mil.)
1	General Electric Company	87,004	51	AMP Incorporated	15,251
2	AT&T Corp.	78,843	52	Viacom Inc.	14,972
3	Exxon Corporation	75,452	53	BankAmerica Corporation	14,662
4	The Coca-Cola Company	65,711	54	American Express Company	14,628
5	Philip Morris Companies Inc.	49,039	55	Emerson Electric Co.	13,947
6	Wal-Mart Stores, Inc.	48,811	56	Hughes Electronics Corp.	13,947
7	Merck & Co., Inc.	47,573	57	Schering-Plough Corporation	13,765
8	General Motors Corporation	46,388	58	Time Warner Inc.	13,323
9	International Business Machines	43,197	59	Capital Cities/ABC, Inc.	13,133
10	The Procter & Gamble Company	42,430	60	The Southern Company	13,131
11	E. I. du Pont de Nemours	38,221	61	NationsBank Corporation	13,126
12	Microsoft Corporation	35,514	62	Columbia/HCA Healthcare Corporation	13,121
13	Johnson & Johnson	35,205	63	Anheuser-Busch Companies, Inc.	13,090
14	Motorola, Inc.	34,104	64	Kellogg Company	12,886
15	Mobil Corporation	33,362	65	WMX Technologies, Inc.	12,645
16	American International Group, Inc.	30,952	66	Oracle Corporation	12,636
17	Bristol-Myers Squibb Company	29,362	67	Tele-Communications, Inc.	12,529
18	Amoco Corporation	29,352	68	MCI Communications Corporation	12,498
19	GTE Corporation	29,319	69	Schlumberger N.V.	12,204
20	Chevron Corporation	29,088	70	Sara Lee Corporation	12,134
21	PepsiCo, Inc.	28,634	71	Pacific Telesis Group	12,086
22	Ford Motor Company	28,559	72	Caterpillar Inc.	11,050
23	BellSouth Corporation	26,862	73	Campbell Soup Company	10,912
24	Intel Corporation	26,380	74	PPG Industries, Inc.	10,788
25	Abbott Laboratories	26,211	75	The Allstate Corporation	10,657
26	Hewlett-Packard Company	25,452	76	Archer-Daniels-Midland Company	10,631
27	SBC Communications Inc.	24,595	77	J.P. Morgan & Co. Incorporated	10,536
28	Pfizer Inc.	24,274	78	Xerox Corporation	10,493
29	The Walt Disney Company	24,104	79	Pacific Gas and Electric Company	10,489
30	Berkshire Hathaway Inc.	24,024	80	Warner-Lambert Company	10,364
31	Minnesota Mining and Manufacturing Company	22,406	81	Compaq Computer Corporation	10,311
32	Ameritech Corporation	22,268	82	The Travelers Inc.	10,249
33	Bell Atlantic Corporation	21,700	83	J. C. Penney Company, Inc.	10,131
34	The Home Depot, Inc.	20,885	84	General Re Corporation	10,111
35	McDonald's Corporation	20,291	85	Banc One Corporation	10,076
36	Federal National Mortgage Association	19,880	86	Sprint Corporation	9,632
37	American Home Products Corporation	19,200	87	AlliedSignal Inc.	9,626
38	Eli Lilly and Company	19,160	88	International Paper Company	9,490
39	The Dow Chemical Company	18,637	89	ITT Corporation	9,365
40	Electronic Data Systems Corporation	18,485	90	Union Pacific Corporation	9,345
41	Chrysler Corporation	17,400	91	The Dun & Bradstreet Corporation	9,337
42	U S WEST, Inc.	16,723	92	Colgate-Palmolive Company	9,152
43	The Gillette Company	16,581	93	General Mills, Inc.	9,054
44	Atlantic Richfield Company	16,357	94	Chemical Banking Corporation	8,773
45	Citicorp	16,348	95	Toys "R" Us, Inc.	8,604
46	Eastman Kodak Company	16,223	96	Phillips Petroleum Company	8,569
47	Sears, Roebuck and Co.	16,178	97	The May Department Stores Company	8,384
48	The Boeing Company	16,021	98	Automatic Data Processing, Inc.	8,231
49	NYNEX Corporation	15,567	99	Norfolk Southern Corporation	8,072
50	Texaco Inc.	15,541	100	Kimberly-Clark Corporation	8,070

100 Largest Employers in *Hoover's Handbook of American Companies 1996*

Rank	Company	Number of Employees	Rank	Company	Number of Employees
1	Manpower Inc.	1,507,400	51	Publix Super Markets, Inc.	90,000
2	United States Postal Service	728,944	52	Flagstar Companies, Inc.	90,000
3	General Motors Corporation	692,800	53	Xerox Corporation	87,600
4	Kelly Services, Inc.	665,000	54	AlliedSignal Inc.	87,500
5	Wal-Mart Stores, Inc.	622,000	55	ConAgra, Inc.	87,000
6	PepsiCo, Inc.	471,000	56	Exxon Corporation	86,000
7	Sears, Roebuck and Co.	399,800	57	Minnesota Mining and Manufacturing	85,166
8	Kmart Corporation	348,000	58	H&R Block, Inc.	85,000
9	Ford Motor Company	337,778	59	Kaiser Foundation Health Plan, Inc.	84,845
10	United Parcel Service	320,000	60	Westinghouse Electric Corporation	84,400
11	AT&T Corp.	304,500	61	Digital Equipment Corporation	82,800
12	General Electric Company	221,000	62	Citicorp	82,600
13	International Business Machines	219,839	63	Lockheed Martin Corporation	82,500
14	J. C. Penney Company, Inc.	202,000	64	Beverly Enterprises, Inc.	82,000
15	The Kroger Co.	200,000	65	Johnson & Johnson	81,500
16	Dayton Hudson Corporation	194,000	66	UAL Corporation	77,900
17	McDonald's Corporation	183,000	67	Hughes Electronics Corp.	77,100
18	United Technologies Corporation	171,500	68	KPMG Peat Marwick LLP	76,200
19	Philip Morris Companies Inc.	165,000	69	Albertson's, Inc.	76,000
20	Marriott International, Inc.	163,440	70	WMX Technologies, Inc.	74,400
21	Columbia/HCA Healthcare	157,000	71	American Home Products Corporation	74,009
22	Sara Lee Corporation	145,900	72	Emerson Electric Co.	73,900
23	ARAMARK Corporation	133,000	73	Cargill, Incorporated	73,300
24	Motorola, Inc.	132,000	74	Arthur Andersen & Co, SC	72,722
25	General Mills, Inc.	125,700	75	American Express Company	72,412
26	Chrysler Corporation	121,000	76	Bell Atlantic Corporation	72,300
27	The May Department Stores	119,000	77	Rockwell International Corporation	71,891
28	Woolworth Corporation	119,000	78	Delta Air Lines, Inc.	71,412
29	American Stores Company	118,000	79	RJR Nabisco Holdings Corp.	70,600
30	The Boeing Company	117,000	80	State Farm Mutual Automobile Insurance Company	70,220
31	Melville Corporation	117,000	81	International Paper Company	70,000
32	Domino's Pizza, Inc.	115,000	82	Electronic Data Systems Corporation	70,000
33	Winn-Dixie Stores, Inc.	112,000	83	Viacom Inc.	70,000
34	Federated Department Stores, Inc.	111,700	84	Meijer, Inc.	70,000
35	GTE Corporation	111,000	85	Coopers & Lybrand L.L.P.	68,360
36	ITT Corporation	110,000	86	V.F. Corporation	68,000
37	Safeway Inc.	110,000	87	The Home Depot, Inc.	67,300
38	AMR Corporation	109,800	88	McDonnell Douglas Corporation	65,760
39	Darden Restaurants, Inc.	107,500	89	NYNEX Corporation	65,400
40	E. I. du Pont de Nemours	107,000	90	The Walt Disney Company	65,000
41	The Limited, Inc.	105,600	91	Food Lion, Inc.	64,840
42	Federal Express Corporation	101,000	92	TRW Inc.	64,200
43	The Prudential Insurance Company of America	99,386	93	Ameritech Corporation	63,594
44	BankAmerica Corporation	98,556	94	Carlson Companies, Inc.	62,500
45	Hewlett-Packard Company	98,400	95	Walgreen Co.	61,900
46	The Procter & Gamble Company	96,500	96	Aluminum Company of America	61,700
47	Eastman Kodak Company	96,300	97	U S WEST, Inc.	61,505
48	BellSouth Corporation	92,100	98	NationsBank Corporation	61,484
49	The Great Atlantic & Pacific Tea Co.	92,000	99	Ernst & Young LLP	61,287
50	The Goodyear Tire & Rubber Co.	90,712	100	Raytheon Company	60,200

40 Fastest Growing Companies by Sales in *Hoover's Handbook of American Companies 1996*

Rank	Company	Annual % Change		Rank	Company	Annual % Change
1	Gateway 2000, Inc.	191.8		21	The Home Depot, Inc.	37.7
2	Columbia/HCA Healthcare Corporation	150.5		22	AST Research, Inc.	37.0
3	Office Depot, Inc.	99.8		23	Viacom Inc.	36.6
4	Intelligent Electronics, Inc.	82.9		24	Seagate Technology, Inc.	36.3
5	CompUSA Inc.	82.4		25	Foundation Health Corporation	35.7
6	Dell Computer Corporation	67.2		26	Computer Associates International, Inc.	33.8
7	Oracle Corporation	64.2		27	The Vons Companies, Inc.	32.9
8	Amgen Inc.	60.7		28	Manpower Inc.	31.4
9	Silicon Graphics, Inc.	60.0		29	Reebok International Ltd.	30.1
10	Packard Bell Electronics, Inc.	58.7		30	Wal-Mart Stores, Inc.	28.8
11	Novell, Inc.	57.2		31	Price/Costco, Inc.	27.6
12	Conner Peripherals, Inc.	54.4		32	Ingram Industries Inc.	27.5
13	Best Buy Co., Inc.	52.6		33	Genentech, Inc.	27.4
14	Sun Microsystems, Inc.	51.0		34	NationsBank Corporation	27.0
15	United HealthCare Corporation	49.5		35	The Charles Schwab Corporation	26.7
16	Merisel, Inc.	48.2		36	Intel Corporation	26.7
17	Microsoft Corporation	47.6		37	Banc One Corporation	26.4
18	Quantum Corporation	44.7		38	Loral Corporation	26.4
19	PacifiCare Health Systems, Inc.	42.6		39	Turner Broadcasting System, Inc.	26.0
20	Compaq Computer Corporation	40.7		40	Circuit City Stores, Inc.	25.8

Note: Growth rates (compounded and annualized) are based on the sales histories detailed in each profile's HOW MUCH section; most, but not all, growth rates are for 9-year periods. These rates reflect acquisitions and divestitures.

40 Fastest Growing Companies by Employment in *Hoover's Handbook of American Companies 1996*

Rank	Company	Annual % Change		Rank	Company	Annual % Change
1	Gateway 2000, Inc.	142.6		21	Seagate Technology, Inc.	30.9
2	Columbia/HCA Healthcare Corporation	127.1		22	Reebok International Ltd.	30.7
3	CompUSA Inc.	70.5		23	Sun Microsystems, Inc.	30.3
4	Intelligent Electronics, Inc.	64.9		24	Quantum Corporation	29.8
5	Office Depot, Inc.	54.0		25	Price/Costco, Inc.	27.2
6	Foundation Health Corporation	52.2		26	Compaq Computer Corporation	25.6
7	Novell, Inc.	47.7		27	MacAndrews & Forbes Holdings, Inc.	25.0
8	United HealthCare Corporation	43.2		28	Circuit City Stores, Inc.	23.9
9	Best Buy Co., Inc.	42.5		29	Tele-Communications, Inc.	23.7
10	Packard Bell Electronics, Inc.	41.4		30	Conner Peripherals, Inc.	23.5
11	Oracle Corporation	40.9		31	NationsBank Corporation	22.4
12	Microsoft Corporation	38.1		32	Borders Group, Inc.	22.3
13	Amgen Inc.	38.0		33	Student Loan Marketing Association	22.1
14	Silicon Graphics, Inc.	38.0		34	Wal-Mart Stores, Inc.	22.0
15	Viacom Inc.	37.8		35	Banc One Corporation	21.3
16	PacifiCare Health Systems, Inc.	36.1		36	The Gap, Inc.	19.6
17	AST Research, Inc.	33.1		37	Lands' End, Inc.	18.7
18	Dell Computer Corporation	32.6		38	Computer Associates International, Inc.	18.5
19	The Home Depot, Inc.	32.4		39	KeyCorp	17.8
20	Merisel, Inc.	31.9		40	Ingram Industries Inc.	17.7

Note: Growth rates (compounded and annualized) are based on the employees histories detailed in each profile's HOW MUCH section; most, but not all, growth rates are for 9-year periods. These rates reflect acquisitions and divestitures.

40 Shrinking Companies by Sales in *Hoover's Handbook of American Companies 1996*

Rank	Company	Annual % Change	Rank	Company	Annual % Change
1	Occidental Petroleum Corporation	-14.3	21	CBS Inc.	-2.5
2	General Dynamics Corporation	-10.3	22	Safeway Inc.	-2.5
3	Pacific Enterprises	-6.9	23	The Columbia Gas System, Inc.	-2.4
4	Union Carbide Corporation	-6.6	24	Tenneco Inc.	-2.4
5	Sun Company, Inc.	-6.5	25	USX–U.S. Steel Group	-2.3
6	Burlington Northern Inc.	-5.9	26	Pathmark Stores, Inc.	-2.2
7	Whitman Corporation	-5.5	27	Westinghouse Electric Corporation	-2.1
8	Unocal Corporation	-4.2	28	Amerada Hess Corporation	-1.6
9	Case Corporation	-3.8	29	Trans World Airlines, Inc.	-1.4
10	Texaco Inc.	-3.8	30	Zenith Electronics Corporation	-1.1
11	Teledyne, Inc.	-3.4	31	American Financial Group, Inc.	-1.0
12	Atlantic Richfield Company	-3.2	32	Honeywell Inc.	-1.0
13	ITT Industries	-3.1	33	Bethlehem Steel Corporation	-0.7
14	Lehman Brothers Holdings Inc.	-3.1	34	McDermott International, Inc.	-0.7
15	Litton Industries, Inc.	-3.1	35	Enron Corp.	-0.6
16	Burlington Industries, Inc.	-3.0	36	Transamerica Corporation	-0.5
17	The LTV Corporation	-3.0	37	Union Pacific Corporation	-0.3
18	The Southland Corporation	-2.7	38	Ralston Purina Group	-0.2
19	Chevron Corporation	-2.6	39	Tenet Healthcare Corporation	-0.2
20	Phillips Petroleum Company	-2.6	40	W. R. Grace & Co.	-0.2

Note: Growth rates (compounded and annualized) are based on the sales histories detailed in each profile's HOW MUCH section; most, but not all, growth rates are for 9-year periods. These rates reflect acquisitions and divestitures.

40 Shrinking Companies by Employment in *Hoover's Handbook of American Companies 1996*

Rank	Company	Annual % Change	Rank	Company	Annual % Change
1	Lehman Brothers Holdings Inc.	-25.3	21	Litton Industries, Inc.	-7.4
2	Union Carbide Corporation	-20.2	22	Monsanto Company	-6.9
3	General Dynamics Corporation	-14.9	23	Burlington Industries, Inc.	-6.8
4	CBS Inc.	-14.4	24	International Business Machines Corp.	-6.6
5	The LTV Corporation	-12.8	25	Ralston Purina Group	-6.6
6	Pacific Enterprises	-11.9	26	Honeywell Inc.	-6.5
7	Whitman Corporation	-10.9	27	Household International, Inc.	-6.5
8	Mobil Corporation	-10.8	28	Texaco Inc.	-6.5
9	Bechtel Group, Inc.	-10.6	29	Pathmark Stores, Inc.	-6.3
10	Case Corporation	-10.3	30	Southern Pacific Rail Corporation	-6.2
11	Teledyne, Inc.	-10.2	31	Tenet Healthcare Corporation	-6.2
12	Sun Company, Inc.	-10.1	32	Tribune Company	-6.2
13	W. R. Grace & Co.	-9.6	33	Champion International Corporation	-6.0
14	The Southland Corporation	-9.4	34	Tennessee Valley Authority	-6.0
15	Bethlehem Steel Corporation	-8.6	35	Enron Corp.	-5.8
16	Occidental Petroleum Corporation	-8.3	36	Rockwell International Corporation	-5.8
17	American Brands, Inc.	-8.1	37	Exxon Corporation	-5.7
18	Hercules Incorporated	-8.0	38	National Semiconductor Corporation	-5.5
19	RJR Nabisco Holdings Corp.	-7.9	39	AlliedSignal Inc.	-5.4
20	Tenneco Inc.	-7.5	40	GTE Corporation	-5.4

Note: Growth rates (compounded and annualized) are based on the employees histories detailed in each profile's HOW MUCH section; most, but not all, growth rates are for 9-year periods. These rates reflect acquisitions and divestitures.

The *FORTUNE* 500 Largest US Corporations

Rank	Company	1994 Revenues ($ mil.)	Rank	Company	1994 Revenues ($ mil.)
1	General Motors	154,951.2	51	Fleming	15,754.0
2	Ford Motor	128,439.0	52	Johnson & Johnson	15,734.0
3	Exxon	101,459.0	53	Atlantic Richfield	15,682.0
4	Wal-Mart Stores	83,412.4	54	Safeway	15,627.0
5	AT&T	75,094.0	55	American Express	15,593.0
6	General Electric	64,687.0	56	Sara Lee	15,536.0
7	Intl. Business Machines	64,052.0	57	RJR Nabisco Holdings	15,366.0
8	Mobil	59,621.0	58	Minnesota Mining & Mfg.	15,079.0
9	Sears, Roebuck	54,559.0	59	Merck	14,970.0
10	Philip Morris	53,776.0	60	International Paper	14,966.0
11	Chrysler	52,224.0	61	Caterpillar	14,328.0
12	State Farm Group	38,850.1	62	UAL	13,950.0
13	Prudential Ins. Co. of America	36,946.0	63	Bell Atlantic	13,791.4
14	E. I. du Pont de Nemours	34,968.0	64	Loews	13,515.2
15	Kmart	34,313.0	65	Digital Equipment	13,450.8
16	Texaco	33,768.0	66	MCI Communications	13,338.0
17	Citicorp	31,650.0	67	NYNEX	13,307.0
18	Chevron	31,064.0	68	Tenneco	13,222.0
19	Procter & Gamble	30,296.0	69	McDonnell Douglas	13,176.0
20	PepsiCo	28,472.1	70	Lockheed	13,130.0
21	Amoco	26,953.0	71	NationsBank Corp.	13,126.0
22	Hewlett-Packard	24,991.0	72	AlliedSignal	12,817.0
23	ITT	23,767.0	73	Georgia-Pacific	12,738.0
24	ConAgra	23,512.2	74	Chemical Banking Corp.	12,685.0
25	Kroger	22,959.1	75	Sprint	12,662.0
26	American International Group	22,386.0	76	Ameritech	12,570.0
27	Metropolitan Life Insurance	22,258.0	77	Home Depot	12,477.0
28	Motorola	22,245.0	78	McKesson	12,428.2
29	Boeing	21,924.0	79	Phillips Petroleum	12,367.0
30	Dayton Hudson	21,311.0	80	Delta Air Lines	12,359.0
31	United Technologies	21,197.0	81	Goodyear Tire & Rubber	12,288.2
32	J. C. Penney	21,082.0	82	May Department Stores	12,223.0
33	Dow Chemical	20,015.0	83	IBP	12,075.4
34	GTE	19,944.3	84	New York Life Insurance	12,067.0
35	United Parcel Service	19,576.0	85	Anheuser-Busch	12,054.0
36	Fed. Natl. Mortgage Assn.	18,572.4	86	Bristol-Myers Squibb	11,984.0
37	Travelers Inc.	18,465.0	87	J.P. Morgan & Co.	11,915.0
38	CIGNA	18,392.0	88	Albertson's	11,895.0
39	American Stores	18,355.1	89	SBC Communications	11,619.0
40	Merrill Lynch	18,233.1	90	Intel	11,521.0
41	Xerox	17,837.0	91	US WEST	11,506.0
42	Aetna Life & Casualty	17,525.0	92	Archer-Daniels-Midland	11,374.4
43	Eastman Kodak	16,862.0	93	Melville	11,286.0
44	BellSouth	16,845.0	94	Rockwell International	11,205.0
45	USX	16,799.0	95	Chase Manhattan Corp.	11,187.0
46	BankAmerica Corp.	16,531.0	96	Nationwide Ins. Enterprise	11,183.1
47	Price/Costco	16,481.0	97	Columbia/HCA Healthcare	11,132.0
48	Coca-Cola	16,172.0	98	Winn-Dixie Stores	11,082.2
49	AMR	16,137.0	99	SYSCO	10,943.0
50	SUPERVALU	15,937.0	100	Compaq Computer	10,866.0

The *FORTUNE* 500 Largest US Corporations (continued)

Rank	Company	1994 Revenues ($ mil.)	Rank	Company	1994 Revenues ($ mil.)
101	Teachers Ins. & Annuity Assn.	10,550.8	151	Sun Co.	7,792.0
102	Pacific Gas & Electric	10,447.4	152	Ralston Purina	7,705.3
103	Weyerhaeuser	10,398.0	153	Viacom	7,636.6
104	ALCOA	10,391.5	154	Colgate-Palmolive	7,587.9
105	Great Atlantic & Pacific Tea	10,384.1	155	Bankers Trust New York Corp.	7,503.0
106	Texas Instruments	10,315.0	156	Bergen Brunswig	7,483.8
107	WMX Technologies	10,097.3	157	CPC International	7,425.4
108	Walt Disney	10,055.1	158	Unisys	7,399.7
109	Raytheon	10,012.9	159	Time Warner	7,396.0
110	Coastal	10,012.7	160	Kimberly-Clark	7,364.2
111	Martin Marietta	9,873.7	161	Limited	7,320.8
112	Textron	9,683.0	162	Supermarkets Genl. Hldgs.	7,226.5
113	CSX	9,608.0	163	Unocal	7,072.0
114	Northwestern Mutual Life Ins.	9,581.4	164	H. J. Heinz	7,046.7
115	Ashland, Inc.	9,505.3	165	Eli Lilly	7,000.8
116	Pacific Telesis Group	9,494.0	166	USAir Group	6,997.2
117	Occidental Petroleum	9,416.0	167	Lincoln National	6,984.4
118	Morgan Stanley Group	9,376.0	168	Federal Home Loan Morgage	6,923.0
119	Baxter International	9,324.0	169	Johnson Controls	6,870.5
120	Walgreen	9,235.0	170	Dana	6,740.5
121	Westinghouse Electric	9,208.0	171	Northrop Grumman	6,711.0
122	Lehman Brothers	9,190.0	172	Amerada Hess	6,698.8
123	Apple Computer	9,188.7	173	Campbell Soup	6,690.5
124	Abbott Laboratories	9,156.0	174	Farmland Industries	6,677.9
125	Northwest Airlines	9,142.9	175	Dean Witter, Discover	6,602.6
126	TRW	9,087.0	176	Kellogg	6,562.0
127	Deere	9,029.8	177	Borden	6,494.8
128	Liberty Mutual Ins. Group	8,985.5	178	Equitable	6,447.3
129	Enron	8,983.7	179	Warner-Lambert	6,416.8
130	American Home Products	8,966.2	180	W. R. Grace	6,381.0
131	Toys "R" Us	8,745.6	181	Capitol Cities/ABC	6,379.2
132	Publix Super Markets	8,742.5	182	Tosco	6,365.8
133	Emerson Electric	8,607.2	183	PPG Industries	6,331.2
134	Fluor	8,556.3	184	Salomon	6,278.0
135	General Mills	8,516.9	185	Unicom	6,277.5
136	Federal Express	8,479.5	186	Cooper Industries	6,258.0
137	American Brands	8,441.5	187	First Union Corp.	6,253.6
138	Marriott International	8,415.0	188	Consolidated Edison of New York	6,239.6
139	SCEcorp	8,345.0	189	United Services Automobile Assn.	6,181.4
140	McDonald's	8,320.8	190	Guardian Life Ins. Co. of America	6,133.8
141	Federated Department Stores	8,315.9	191	AFLAC	6,110.8
142	Southern	8,297.0	192	Lowe's	6,110.5
143	Woolworth	8,293.0	193	Levi Strauss Associates	6,074.3
144	Pfizer	8,281.3	194	Gillette	6,070.2
145	Monsanto	8,272.0	195	Honeywell	6,057.0
146	Union Pacific	8,140.0	196	Eaton	6,052.0
147	Whirlpool	8,104.0	197	Norwest Corp.	6,032.0
148	Principal Mutual Life Insurance	8,006.7	198	Reynolds Metals	6,013.2
149	Alco Standard	7,996.1	199	Coca-Cola Enterprises	6,011.0
150	Banc One Corp.	7,857.1	200	Entergy	5,963.3

The *FORTUNE* 500 Largest US Corporations (continued)

Rank	Company	1994 Revenues ($ mil.)	Rank	Company	1994 Revenues ($ mil.)
201	Quaker Oats	5,955.0	251	Household International	4,603.3
202	Public Service Enterprise Group	5,915.8	252	Panhandle Eastern	4,585.1
203	Cardinal Health	5,790.4	253	Norfolk Southern	4,581.3
204	Stone Container	5,748.7	254	Roadway Services	4,572.0
205	Halliburton	5,740.5	255	Eckerd	4,549.0
206	Dillard Department Stores	5,728.6	256	Bank of Boston Corp.	4,546.8
207	Chubb	5,709.5	257	Litton Industries	4,535.3
208	Continental Airlines	5,669.9	258	LTV	4,529.2
209	John Hancock Mutual Life Ins.	5,669.1	259	Ingersoll-Rand	4,507.5
210	Texas Utilities	5,663.5	260	PACCAR	4,499.1
211	American Electric Power	5,504.7	261	Inland Steel Industries	4,497.0
212	FPL Group	5,422.7	262	Dominion Resources	4,491.1
213	James River Corp. of VA	5,417.3	263	Duke Power	4,488.9
214	Foxmeyer Health	5,409.4	264	Masco	4,468.0
215	KeyCorp	5,372.7	265	American Standard	4,457.5
216	Transamerica	5,354.5	266	Crown Cork & Seal	4,452.2
217	Navistar International	5,337.0	267	Fleet Financial Group	4,445.0
218	Massachusetts Mut. Life Ins.	5,332.5	268	Rite Aid	4,331.9
219	Dresser Industries	5,330.7	269	Eastman Chemical	4,329.0
220	Champion International	5,318.2	270	Avon Products	4,324.6
221	Black & Decker	5,248.3	271	Browning-Ferris Industries	4,314.5
222	Continental	5,164.1	272	AmeriSource Distribution	4,301.8
223	ARAMARK	5,161.6	273	Manpower	4,296.4
224	Mead	5,122.7	274	Office Depot	4,266.2
225	Tyson Foods	5,110.3	275	Bank of New York Co.	4,251.0
226	First Chicago Corp.	5,094.6	276	First Interstate Bancorp	4,246.3
227	Merisel	5,018.7	277	Aon	4,156.9
228	Vons	4,996.6	278	Niagara Mohawk Power	4,152.0
229	Burlington Northern	4,995.0	279	Boise Cascade	4,141.8
230	V.F. Corp.	4,971.7	280	Circuit City Stores	4,130.4
231	Wells Fargo & Co.	4,965.0	281	FMC	4,051.3
232	Tandy	4,943.7	282	Service Merchandise	4,050.4
233	Tele-Communications	4,936.0	283	Peco Energy	4,040.6
234	Dun & Bradstreet	4,895.7	284	Bindley Western	4,037.4
235	R.R. Donnelley & Sons	4,888.8	285	AMP	4,027.5
236	Union Carbide	4,865.0	286	Loral	4,008.7
237	Genuine Parts	4,858.4	287	Houston Industries	4,001.9
238	American General	4,840.5	288	Mutual of Omaha Insurance	3,981.6
239	Bethlehem Steel	4,819.4	289	Paine Webber Group	3,964.1
240	Corning	4,799.2	290	Chiquita Brands International	3,961.7
241	Cummins Engine	4,737.2	291	Mellon Bank Corp.	3,957.0
242	Scott Paper	4,726.4	292	Nordstrom	3,894.5
243	St. Paul Cos.	4,701.3	293	Lyondell Petrochemical	3,857.0
244	Sun Microsystems	4,689.9	294	Times Mirror	3,855.5
245	Ryder System	4,685.6	295	Berkshire Hathaway	3,847.5
246	PNC Bank Corp.	4,684.5	296	TJX	3,842.8
247	Consolidated Freightways	4,680.5	297	Dole Food	3,841.6
248	Schering-Plough	4,657.1	298	General Re	3,826.1
249	Arrow Electronics	4,649.2	299	Gannett	3,824.5
250	Microsoft	4,649.0	300	Pitney Bowes	3,822.9

The *FORTUNE* 500 Largest US Corporations (continued)

Rank	Company	1994 Revenues ($ mil.)	Rank	Company	1994 Revenues ($ mil.)
301	Nike	3,789.7	351	Jefferson Smurfit	3,233.3
302	Stop & Shop	3,789.0	352	USF&G	3,221.0
303	United Healthcare	3,768.9	353	Centex	3,214.5
304	Conrail	3,733.0	354	Mattel	3,205.0
305	Gap	3,722.9	355	Lear Seating	3,147.5
306	CBS	3,711.9	356	Southern Pacific Rail	3,142.6
307	General Dynamics	3,702.0	357	Fred Meyer	3,128.4
308	Humana	3,654.0	358	Intelligent Electronics	3,126.7
309	Owens-Illinois	3,652.9	359	Sherwin-Williams	3,100.1
310	Waban	3,650.3	360	Barnett Banks	3,097.5
311	General Public Untilities	3,649.5	361	Dover	3,085.3
312	Northeast Utilities	3,642.7	362	Long Island Lighting	3,067.3
313	Harcourt General	3,640.0	363	Hormel Foods	3,064.8
314	UNUM	3,623.7	364	MAPCO	3,059.3
315	Central and South West	3,622.6	365	Student Loan Marketing Assn.	3,057.1
316	CMS Energy	3,619.0	366	Reliance Group Holdings	3,047.1
317	Hershey Foods	3,606.3	367	Louisiana-Pacific	3,039.5
318	Giant Food	3,567.5	368	Consolidated Natural Gas	3,036.0
319	Upjohn	3,565.9	369	W. W. Grainger	3,023.1
320	Avnet	3,552.5	370	Agway	3,017.0
321	SAFECO	3,551.6	371	Spiegel	3,016.0
322	Dial	3,546.8	372	Willamette Industries	3,007.9
323	Rohm & Haas	3,534.0	373	Best Buy	3,006.5
324	Flagstar	3,525.7	374	Great Western Financial Corp.	2,997.6
325	Detroit Edison	3,519.3	375	Peter Kiewit Sons'	2,991.0
326	Associated Insurance	3,511.2	376	ServiceMaster	2,985.2
327	PacifiCorp	3,506.5	377	Beverly Enterprises	2,983.8
328	Seagate Technology	3,500.1	378	Smith's Food & Drug Centers	2,981.4
329	Air Products and Chemicals	3,485.3	379	Nucor	2,975.6
330	Dell Computer	3,475.3	380	Universal	2,975.1
331	Illinois Tool Works	3,461.3	381	U.S. Healthcare	2,974.5
332	NBD Bancorp	3,461.0	382	Wachovia Corp.	2,970.0
333	Premark International	3,450.8	383	HealthTrust	2,970.0
334	Natl. Medical Enterprises	3,443.0	384	ALLTEL	2,961.7
335	Bear Stearns	3,441.1	385	Providian	2,959.1
336	Marsh & McLennan	3,435.0	386	Sante Fe Pacific	2,954.6
337	Trans World Airlines	3,407.7	387	Temple-Inland	2,937.5
338	Union Camp	3,395.8	388	CINergy	2,924.2
339	H.F. Ahmanson	3,381.4	389	National City Corp.	2,905.2
340	Maytag	3,372.5	390	PacifCare Health Systems	2,893.3
341	Kerr-McGee	3,353.4	391	Carolina Power & Light	2,876.6
342	Owens-Corning Fiberglas	3,351.0	392	Yellow	2,867.5
343	Thrifty PayLess Holdings	3,346.7	393	Avery Dennison	2,856.7
344	Penn Traffic	3,333.2	394	Morton International	2,849.6
345	Harris	3,326.1	395	Brunswick	2,835.6
346	Phelps Dodge	3,289.2	396	Bruno's	2,834.7
347	Reebok	3,287.6	397	Columbia Gas System	2,833.4
348	Allmerica Financial	3,273.3	398	Nash Finch	2,832.0
349	Tyco International	3,262.8	399	Hercules	2,821.0
350	SunTrust Banks	3,252.3	400	Mercantile Stores	2,819.8

The FORTUNE 500 Largest US Corporations (continued)

Rank	Company	1994 Revenues ($ mil.)	Rank	Company	1994 Revenues ($ mil.)
401	Transco Energy	2,816.2	451	CoreStates Finan. Corp.	2,497.1
402	Turner Broadcasting	2,809.1	452	Northern States Power	2,486.5
403	Reader's Digest Association	2,806.4	453	Grand Union Holdings	2,477.3
404	Noram Energy	2,801.4	454	Ultramar	2,475.4
405	American President	2,793.5	455	FHP International	2,473.0
406	Shaw Industries	2,788.5	456	Automatic Data Proc.	2,469.0
407	Cyprus Amax Minerals	2,788.0	457	Roundy's	2,465.4
408	Baltimore Gas & Electric	2,783.0	458	Hechinger	2,454.0
409	Florida Progress	2,771.5	459	Allegheny Power System	2,451.7
410	Provident Life and Accident Ins.	2,762.2	460	Dean Foods	2,431.2
411	McGraw-Hill	2,760.9	461	Caremark International	2,426.0
412	Alumax	2,754.5	462	York International	2,421.9
413	Armstrong World Industries	2,752.7	463	Centerior Energy	2,421.0
414	Caldor	2,748.6	464	Tech Data	2,418.4
415	Aid Association for Lutherans	2,733.8	465	Progressive	2,415.3
416	Payless Cashways	2,733.2	466	Owens & Minor	2,395.8
417	Pennsylvania Power & Light	2,725.1	467	Teledyne	2,391.2
418	GEICO	2,716.0	468	Engelhard	2,385.8
419	Praxair	2,711.0	469	American Medical Holdings	2,381.7
420	Pacific Enterprises	2,702.0	470	First Bank System	2,375.1
421	Gateway 2000	2,701.2	471	Fleetwood Enterprises	2,369.4
422	Williams	2,672.9	472	Ohio Edison	2,368.2
423	Hasbro	2,670.3	473	AST Research	2,367.3
424	Pittston	2,667.3	474	Conner Peripherals	2,365.2
425	Whitman	2,658.8	475	Graybar Electric	2,364.5
426	Olin	2,658.1	476	Kelly Services	2,362.6
427	Knight-Ridder	2,649.0	477	New York Times	2,357.6
428	Turner Corp.	2,638.6	478	Ace Hardware	2,326.1
429	EG&G	2,632.6	479	Shawmut National Corp.	2,316.4
430	Diamond Shamrock	2,621.1	480	Polaroid	2,312.5
431	Westvaco	2,613.2	481	Health Systems Intl.	2,306.2
432	United States Shoe	2,598.3	482	Sonoco Products	2,300.1
433	Ball	2,594.7	483	Fruit of the Loom	2,297.8
434	Southwest Airlines	2,591.9	484	National Semiconductor	2,295.4
435	Food 4 Less Supermarkets	2,585.2	485	Boatmen's Bancshares	2,294.2
436	Computer Sciences	2,582.7	486	Hannaford Bros.	2,291.8
437	Parker Hannifin	2,576.3	487	USG	2,290.0
438	Cotter	2,574.4	488	Foster Wheeler	2,271.1
439	Pennzoil	2,562.9	489	Olsten	2,260.3
440	Manville	2,560.3	490	Phoenix Home Life Mutual Ins.	2,254.4
441	Republic New York Corp.	2,559.7	491	New England Electric Sys.	2,243.0
442	Becton Dickinson	2,559.5	492	New England Mutual Life Ins.	2,238.3
443	Comerica	2,558.6	493	Witco	2,234.7
444	Long Drug Stores	2,558.3	493	Echlin	2,229.5
445	First Fidelity Bancorp.	2,553.1	495	International Multifoods	2,224.7
446	Varity	2,520.9	496	Lutheran Brotherhood	2,222.7
447	Stanley Works	2,510.9	497	MicroAge	2,220.8
448	Baker Hughes	2,504.8	498	LDDS Communications	2,220.8
449	Revco D.S.	2,504.0	499	First Financial Management	2,207.5
450	Morrison Knudsen	2,500.0	500	Dow Corning	2,204.6

Source: *FORTUNE*; May 15, 1995

Top 100 Companies from the *Business Week* 1000

Rank	Company	1995 Market Value ($ mil.)	Rank	Company	1995 Market Value ($ mil.)
1	General Electric	93,402	51	Boeing	15,724
2	AT&T	81,000	52	Chrysler	15,401
3	Exxon	79,298	53	Columbia/HCA Healthcare	15,024
4	Coca-Cola	70,176	54	Emerson Electric	14,766
5	Wal-Mart Stores	54,202	55	Time Warner	14,643
6	Merck	52,877	56	Anheuser-Busch	14,601
7	Philip Morris	52,317	57	Schering-Plough	14,578
6	Procter & Gamble	45,619	58	NationsBank	13,788
9	International Business Machines	44,261	59	Schlumberger	13,777
10	DuPont	38,211	60	MCI Communications	13,685
11	Microsoft	36,603	61	Capital Cities/ABC	13,632
12	Johnson & Johnson	36,490	62	Oracle Systems	13,482
13	Mobil	34,452	63	Southern	13,466
14	Motorola	33,810	64	Airtouch Communications	13,386
15	Intel	33,048	65	WMX Technologies	13,091
16	American International Group	32,792	66	Tele-Communications	12,992
17	GTE	32,210	67	Pacific Telesis Group	12,722
18	General Motors	32,124	68	Sara Lee	12,631
19	Bristol-Myers Squibb	31,388	69	Allstate	12,357
20	Chevron	31,036	70	Travelers	12,304
21	PepsiCo	31,007	71	J.P. Morgan	12,107
22	Amoco	29,473	72	Kellogg	12,006
23	Hewlett-Packard	29,325	73	Xerox	11,729
24	BellSouth	29,214	74	Banc One	11,612
25	Abbott Laboratories	28,680	75	Campbell Soup	11,276
26	Walt Disney	27,974	76	Pacific Gas & Electric	11,025
27	Ford Motor	26,595	77	AlliedSignal	10,724
28	Berkshire Hathaway	26,240	78	Union Pacific	10,716
29	Pfizer	26,127	79	General Re	10,664
30	SBC Communications	25,354	80	Federal Home Loan Mortgage	10,484
31	Ameritech	23,644	81	Caterpillar	10,348
32	Bell Atlantic	23,402	82	ITT	10,303
33	McDonald's	23,066	83	Warner-Lambert	10,297
34	Minnesota Mining & Mfg.	22,984	84	Sprint	10,194
35	American Home Products	21,865	85	Chemical Banking	9,806
36	Fannie Mae	21,040	86	Archer Daniels Midland	9,740
37	Home Depot	20,345	87	J. C. Penney	9,733
38	Eli Lilly	19,364	88	H. J. Heinz	9,713
39	Dow Chemical	18,579	89	General Mills	9,566
40	U S WEST	18,187	90	International Paper	9,547
41	Atlantic Richfield	17,891	91	Colgate-Palmolive	9,314
42	BankAmerica	17,863	92	Raytheon	9,276
43	CitiCorp	17,779	93	Amgen	9,171
44	Gillette	17,494	94	Computer Associates International	9,160
45	Eastman Kodak	17,328	95	May Department Stores	9,066
46	Sears, Roebuck	17,323	96	Compaq Computer	9,005
47	American Express	16,675	97	Monsanto	8,876
48	NYNEX	16,625	98	Cisco Systems	8,817
49	Texaco	16,431	99	Norfolk Southern	8,803
50	Viacom	15,953	100	Baxter International	8,787

Source: *Business Week*; March 27, 1995; Market value calculated as of February 28, 1995.

Top 100 from the *Forbes* 500 Largest Private US Companies

Rank	Company	Revenues ($ mil.)	Rank	Company	Revenues ($ mil.)
1	Cargill	47,135	51	Schwan's Sales Enterprises	**2,100
2	Koch Industries	**23,725	52	J.R. Simplot Co.	2,100
3	United Parcel Service	17,782	53	Graybar Electric	2,033
4	Continental Grain	**12,600	54	Lefrak Organization	**2,000
5	Mars	**12,500	55	Metromedia	**2,000
6	Goldman Sachs Group	**11,440	56	Giant Eagle	**1,985
7	Publix Super Markets	7,473	57	Enterprise Rent-A-Car	1,975
8	Bechtel Group	7,337	58	Core-Mark International*	**1,900
9	Montgomery Ward & Co.	**6,802	59	Morse Operations	1,887
10	Arthur Andersen & Co, SC	6,738	60	Phar-Mor	1,850
11	KPMG Peat Marwick	**6,414	61	C&S Wholesale Grocers	1,837
12	Ernst & Young LLP	**6,271	62	Wegmans Food Markets	1,813
13	RH Macy & Co.	6,163	63	Carlson Cos.	**1,800
14	Ingram Industries	6,163	64	Lexmark International	1,800
15	Levi Strauss & Co.	5,893	65	Raley's	1,800
16	Coopers & Lybrand	**5,612	66	Belk Services	**1,750
17	Deloitte & Touche	**5,429	67	Menards*	**1,750
18	Meijer	**5,160	68	Gulf States Toyota	**1,743
19	ARAMARK	**5,119	69	Trump Organization	**1,723
20	H.E.Butt Grocery	4,850	70	Science Applications International	1,671
21	Advance Publications	**4,637	71	TLC Beatrice International Holdings	1,656
22	Thrifty PayLess Holdings*	4,565	72	Gulf Oil LP*	**1,650
23	Marmon Group	4,319	73	Southern Wine & Spirits*	**1,620
24	Amway	**4,309	74	Kohler	**1,604
25	AmeriSource	4,300	75	Polo/Ralph Lauren	**1,600
26	Pathmark Stores	4,207	76	Renco Group	1,600
27	Price Waterhouse	3,976	77	Brown Automotive Group	**1,550
28	American Standard	3,831	78	Parsons Corp.	1,547
29	S.C. Johnson & Son	**3,800	79	Hendrick Automotive Group	**1,537
30	JM Family Enterprises	3,500	80	Stater Bros. Markets	**1,537
31	Hallmark Cards	3,400	81	Consolidated Electrical Dist.*	**1,500
32	Penske	3,287	82	Perdue Farms	1,500
33	Huntsman Cos.	3,140	83	Del Monte Foods	1,499
34	Edward J. DeBartolo	**3,043	84	Eby-Brown Cos.	1,450
35	MacAndrews & Forbes Holdings	3,030	85	Grocers Supply Co.	**1,450
36	Estée Lauder Cos.	**2,770	86	US Foodservice	1,443
37	American Financial	2,721	87	Hillman	1,429
38	Milliken & Co.	**2,706	88	Avis	1,400
39	Cox Enterprises	2,675	89	DeMoulas Super Markets	**1,400
40	Fidelity Investments	2,660	90	VT	1,356
41	Food 4 Less Supermarkets	2,585	91	Sammons Enterprises	**1,350
42	Dominick's Finer Foods	**2,500	92	Gates Corp.	1,340
43	Red Apple Group	2,500	93	Jordan Motors	1,338
44	Global Petroleum	2,484	94	Transammonia	1,330
45	Hy-Vee Food Stores	2,480	95	Walter Industries	1,307
46	Grand Union Holdings	2,477	96	Southwire	1,300
47	Randall's Food Markets	2,321	97	21 International Holdings	1,300
48	Steelcase	**2,300	98	Dunavant Enterprises	1,291
49	Hearst	**2,200	99	Lennox International	**1,290
50	Peter Kiewit Sons'	2,179	100	Schreiber Foods	**1,282

Source: *Forbes*; December 5, 1994
*New in 1994
**Estimate

The *Datamation* North American 100

Rank	Company	1994 Information Technology Revenues ($ mil.)	Rank	Company	1994 Information Technology Revenues ($ mil.)
1	IBM	64,052	51	Sybase	826
2	Hewlett-Packard	19,200	52	Wang	821
3	Digital	13,500	53	Cabletron Systems	811
4	AT&T	11,459	54	Kingston Technology	802
5	Compaq	10,866	55	Newbridge Networks	737
6	EDS	10,052	56	Adobe Systems	598
7	Apple	9,549	57	Coopers & Lybrand	591
8	Unisys	6,216	58	Stratus	577
9	Sun Microsystems	5,348	59	Computervision	574
10	Microsoft	4,650	60	Ernst & Young	557
11	Xerox	3,983	61	Control Data	524
12	Dell	3,500	62	LEGENT	509
13	Seagate	3,500	63	Diebold	493
14	Quantum	3,286	64	Sterling Software	490
15	Computer Sciences	3,085	65	SAS Institute	482
16	Gateway 2000	2,700	66	Informix Software	469
17	Packard Bell	2,600	67	Autodesk	465
18	Computer Associates	2,455	68	Compuware	464
19	Andersen Consulting	2,452	69	AMS	460
20	Conner Peripherals	2,400	70	Ceridian	458
21	Oracle	2,377	71	Sequent	451
22	Motorola	2,372	72	Cadence	429
23	AST Research	2,311	73	Tektronix	422
24	Intel	2,304	74	D&B Software	406
25	KPMG Peat Marwick	2,300	75	Attachmate	390
26	Tandem	2,108	76	Dynatech	386
27	Lockheed Martin	2,070	77	Exabyte	382
28	Novell	1,998	78	ISM	381
29	Western Digital	1,900	79	U.S. Robotics	379
30	Amdahl	1,639	80	Wyse	350
31	Silicon Graphics	1,631	81	Mentor Graphics	348
32	StorageTek	1,625	82	Micropolis	347
33	Cisco Systems	1,500	83	System Software Associates	345
34	EMC	1,378	84	Exide	327
35	Lexmark	1,350	85	Radius	324
36	Entex	1,300	86	Computer Task Group	302
37	Texas Instruments	1,238	87	QMS	293
38	Bay Networks	1,200	88	BMC Software	289
39	Data General	1,142	89	Hayes Microcomputer	270
40	Intergraph	1,041	90	National Computer Systems	270
41	Deloitte & Touche	1,041	91	Network Equipment Tech.	269
42	Price Waterhouse	1,020	92	Chipcom	268
43	3Com	1,014	93	Symantec	267
44	Lotus	971	94	ZEOS	266
45	Memorex Telex	934	95	Standard Microsystems	259
46	Cray Research	922	96	Borland	250
47	Maxtor	891	97	Information Builders	243
48	General Electric	889	98	J.D. Edwards	241
49	SHL Systemhouse	860	99	GENICOM	234
50	Bell Atlantic	828	100	General DataComm	221

Source: *DATAMATION*; June 1, 1995. Information technology revenue only; total company revenue may be higher.

10 Largest Computer Services Companies

Rank	Company	1994 Revenues ($ mil.)
1	IBM	16,653.5
2	EDS	10,052.4
3	Digital	6,345.0
4	Hewlett-Packard	4,608.0
5	Unisys	3,108.0
6	Computer Sciences	3,085.0
7	KPMG Peat Marwick	2,300.0
8	Andersen Consulting	2,206.8
9	Entex	1,300.0
10	Deloitte & Touche	1,041.0

Source: *DATAMATION*; June 1, 1995

10 Largest Computer Peripherals Manufacturers

Rank	Company	1994 Revenues ($ mil.)
1	IBM	8,583.0
2	Hewlett-Packard	6,336.0
3	Seagate	3,465.0
4	Quantum	3,286.0
5	Xerox	3,126.8
6	Conner Periperals	2,352.0
7	Western Digital	1,900.0
8	Digital	1,620.0
9	Lexmark	1,215.0
10	StorageTek	1,121.2

Source: *DATAMATION*; June 1, 1995

10 Largest Personal Computer Manufacturers

Rank	Company	1994 Revenues ($ mil.)
1	Compaq	9,018.8
2	IBM	8,775.1
3	Apple	7,161.8
4	Dell	2,870.0
5	Gateway 2000	2,700.0
6	Packard Bell	2,600.0
7	AST Research	2,311.0
8	AT&T GIS	1,718.9
9	Digital	1,350.0
10	Hewlett-Packard	1,152.0

Source: *DATAMATION*; June 1, 1995

10 Largest Software Companies

Rank	Company	1994 Revenues ($ mil.)
1	IBM	11,529.4
2	Microsoft	4,464.0
3	Computer Associates	2,454.7
4	Novell	1,918.1
5	Oracle	1,901.6
6	Lockheed Martin	1,242.0
7	Digital	1,215.0
8	AT&T	916.7
9	Lotus	873.6
10	Unisys	683.8

Source: *DATAMATION*; June 1, 1995

10 Largest Midrange/Server Manufacturers

Rank	Company	1994 Revenues ($ mil.)
1	IBM	5,764.7
2	AT&T GIS	5,042.0
3	Hewlett-Packard	2,688.0
4	Tandem	1,538.9
5	Digital	1,174.5
6	Motorola	616.8
7	Data General	536.5
8	Sun Microsystems	534.8
9	Unisys	497.3
10	Apple	477.5

Source: *DATAMATION*; June 1, 1995

10 Largest Workstation Manufacturers

Rank	Company	1994 Revenues ($ mil.)
1	Sun Microsystems	3,262.0
2	IBM	3,206.6
3	Hewlett-Packard	2,880.0
4	Silicon Graphics	1,223.2
5	Digital	1,080.0
6	Intergraph	833.1
7	Motorola	593.1
8	Unisys	435.1
9	Control Data	31.5
10	Data General	22.8

Source: *DATAMATION*; June 1, 1995

US New-Car and Light-Truck Sales — 1994

Make	Cars Sold (thou.)	Light Trucks Sold (thou.)	Total (thou.)	Market Share % 1994	Market Share % 1993
Chevrolet/Geo	1,004	1,454	2,458	16.3	17.0
Pontiac	586	35	621	4.1	4.1
Buick	547	—	547	3.6	3.6
Oldsmobile	424	25	449	3.0	2.9
GMC	—	444	444	2.9	2.8
Saturn	286	—	286	1.9	1.6
Cadillac	211	—	211	1.4	1.5
General Motors	**3,058**	**1,958**	**5,016**	**33.2**	**33.5**
Ford	1,369	1,802	3,172	21.0	20.9
Mercury	390	77	467	3.1	3.5
Lincoln	179	—	179	1.2	1.2
Ford	**1,939**	**1,879**	**3,818**	**25.3**	**25.6**
Dodge	354	711	1,065	7.1	6.7
Jeep	—	436	436	2.9	2.9
Plymouth	198	211	409	2.7	3.0
Chrysler	197	33	231	1.5	1.6
Eagle	62	—	62	0.4	0.5
Chrysler	**812**	**1,392**	**2,204**	**14.6**	**14.7**
Toyota	678	323	1,001	6.6	6.7
Lexus	87	—	87	0.6	0.7
Toyota/Lexus	**765**	**323**	**1,088**	**7.2**	**7.4**
Honda	650	26	676	4.5	4.4
Acura	112	—	112	0.7	0.8
Honda/Acura	**762**	**26**	**788**	**5.1**	**4.9**
Nissan	486	237	723	4.8	4.6
Infiniti	51	—	51	0.3	0.4
Nissan/Infiniti	**537**	**237**	**774**	**5.1**	**4.9**
Volkswagon	92	5	97	0.6	0.4
Audi	13	—	13	0.1	0.1
Volkswagon/Audi	**105**	**5**	**110**	**0.6**	**0.4**
Mazda	283	93	375	2.5	2.5
Mitsubishi	201	29	230	1.5	1.4
Hyundai	126	—	126	0.8	0.8
Isuzu	0	117	117	0.8	0.8
Subaru	101	—	101	0.7	0.7
BMW	85	—	85	0.6	0.6
Volvo	82	—	82	0.5	0.5
Mercedes	73	—	73	0.5	0.4
Suzuki	7	27	34	0.2	0.2
Saab	22	—	22	0.1	0.1
Jaguar	15	—	15	0.1	0.1
Porsche	6	—	6	0.0	0.0
Others	14	12	26	0.2	0.0
Total	**8,991**	**6,098**	**15,089**	**100.0**	**100.0**

Source: *Automotive News*; May 24, 1995
Note: Totals may not add because of rounding.

Top 10 Vehicles in the US — 1994

Rank	Vehicle	Number Sold	Rank	Vehicle	Number Sold
1	Ford F-series pickups	646,039	6	Ford Escort	336,967
2	Chevrolet C/K pickups	580,445	7	Toyota Camry	321,979
3	Ford Taurus	397,037	8	Saturn	286,003
4	Honda Accord	367,615	9	Ford Explorer	278,065
5	Ford Ranger	344,744	10	Dodge Caravan	268,013

Source: *Automotive News*; May 24, 1995

30 Largest Law Firms in the US

Rank	Firm	1994 Revenues ($ mil.)	Rank	Firm	1994 Revenues ($ mil.)
1	Skadden Arps, Slate, Meagher & Flom	582.0	16	Fulbright & Jaworski	227.0
2	Baker & McKenzie	546.0	17	Simpson Thacher & Bartlett	216.0
3	Jones, Day. Reavis & Pogue	384.0	18	Kirkland & Ellis	215.0
4	Weil, Gotshal & Manges	311.0	19	Pillsbury Madison & Sutro	211.0
5	Sullivan & Cromwell	298.0	19	Vinson & Elkins	211.0
6	Gibson, Dunn & Crutcher	278.0	21	McDermott, Will & Emery	208.5
7	Shearman & Sterling	268.0	22	Morrison & Foerster	200.0
8	Cleary, Gottlieb, Steen & Hamilton	265.0	23	Cravath, Swaine & Moore	186.0
9	Latham & Watkins	263.0	24	Debevoise & Plimpton	181.5
9	Mayer, Brown & Platt	263.0	25	Paul, Weiss, Rifkind, Wharton & Garrison	175.5
11	O'Melveny & Myers	257.0	26	Milbank, Tweed, Hadley & McCloy	172.5
12	Sidley & Austin	254.5	27	Willkie Farr & Gallagher	172.0
13	Davis Polk & Wardwell	254.0	28	Baker & Botts	171.0
14	Morgan, Lewis & Bockius	241.5	29	Proskauer Rose Goetz & Mendelsohn	169.0
15	White & Case	232.5	30	Dewey Ballantine	164.0

Source: *The American Lawyer*, July/August 1995

40 Largest Management Consulting Firms in the US

Rank	Company	1994 Revenues ($ mil.)	Rank	Company	1994 Revenues ($ mil.)
1	Ernst & Young	830.0	21	The Boston Consulting Group	155.0
2	McKinsey & Co.	600.0	22	Bain & Company	150.0
3	Mercer Consulting Group	553.0	23	Milliman & Robertson	143.7
4	Andersen Consulting	518.8	24	Buck Consultants	140.0
5	Towers Perrin	510.4	25	A Foster Higgins & Co.	134.0
6	Arthur Andersen	503.6	26	Arthur D. Little	130.0
7	Deloitte & Touche	491.0	27	Alexander Consulting Group	119.9
8	Coopers & Lybrand Consulting	480.0	28	Godwins International	118.8
9	KPMG Peat Marwick	410.0	29	The Hay Group	93.0
10	Hewitt Associates LLC	384.6	30	RCG International	85.1
11	Booz-Allen & Hamilton	340.0	31	Sedgwick Noble Lowndes	73.6
12	Watson Wyatt Worldwide	330.0	32	Monitor Company	69.0
13	Gemini Consulting	260.0	33	The Segal Co.	69.0
14	CSC Consulting Group	200.0	34	Proudfoot PLC	58.0
15	IBM Consulting Group	198.0	35	Kurt Salmon Associates	49.0
16	A T Kearney	195.0	36	George S. May International Co.	46.0
17	American Management Systems	190.0	37	Oracle Corporation	40.0
18	Unisys Corporation	189.0	38	Grant Thornton	38.9
19	Price Waterhouse	180.0	39	AT&T Solutions	30.0
20	EDS Management Consulting	160.0	40	Marakon Associates	25.0

Source: *Consultant News*, July/August 1995. US management consulting revenues only; total revenues may be higher.

Top 20 in CEO Compensation

Rank	CEO Name	Company	1994 Total Compensation ($ thou.)
1	Charles Locke	Morton International	25,928
2	James Donald	DSC Communications	23,826
3	Carl Reichardt	Wells Fargo	16,612
4	Reuben Mark	Colgate-Palmolive	15,770
5	Eckhard Pfeiffer	Compaq Computer	14,692
6	James Cayne	Bear Stearns	14,572
7	Hugh McColl	NationsBank	13,725
8	Lawrence Bossidy	AlliedSignal	12,389
9	Louis Gerstner	IBM	12,353
10	Sanford Weill	Travelers	12,169
11	Maurice Greenberg	American International Group	12,080
12	Roberto Goizueta	Coca-Cola	12,054
13	Warren Batts	Premark International	11,977
14	Charles Knight	Emerson Electric	11,753
15	James Mellor	General Dynamics	11,224
16	Michael Eisner	Walt Disney	10,657
17	Robert Kidder	Duracell International	10,629
18	W. J. Sanders III	Advanced Micro Devices	10,433
19	Kenneth Lay	Enron	10,139
20	Steven Walske	Parametric Technology	8,905

Source: *Business Week*; April 24, 1995

20 Greatest US Fortunes

Rank	Name	Net Worth ($ bil.)
1	Walton family	21.7
2	Mars family	10.0
3	du Pont (Pierre Samuel II) family	10.0
4	Williams Henry Gates III	9.4
5	Warren Edward Buffett	9.2
6	Richard Marvin DeVos & Jay Van Andel	9.0
7	Samuel I. Newhouse Jr. & Donald Edward Newhouse	8.0
8	Rockefeller (John D.) family	6.0
9	John Werner Kluge	5.9
10	Barbara Cox Anthony, Ann Cox Chambers & family	5.8
11	Edward Crosby Johnson III & family	5.1
12	Mellon family	5.0
13	Ronald Owen Perelman	4.5
14	Jay Arthur Pritzker & Robert Alan Pritzker	4.4
15	Keith Rupert Murdoch	4.0
16	Sumner Murray Redstone	4.0
17	Paul G. Allen	3.9
18	Sid Richardson Bass & Lee Marshall Bass	3.3
19	Lawrence J. Ellison	2.9
20	Walter Hubert Annenberg	2.8

Source: *Forbes*; October 17, 1994

Top 20 CPA Firms in the US

Rank	Company	1994 US Net Revenues ($ mil.)
1	Arthur Andersen & Co., SC	2,922.0
2	Ernst & Young	2,351.0
3	Deloitte & Touche	2,055.0
4	KPMG Peat Marwick	1,907.0
5	Coopers & Lybrand	1,640.0
6	Price Waterhouse	1,430.0
7	Grant Thornton	224.0
8	McGladrey & Pullen	208.9
9	BDO Seidman	201.0
10	Kenneth Leventhal & Co.	193.0
11	Baird, Kurtz & Dobson	67.8
12	Crowe, Chizek & Co.	*64.4
13	Plante & Moran	57.0
14	Clifton, Gunderson & Co.	51.6
15	Moss Adams	48.0
16	Altshuler, Melvoin and Glasser	40.0
17	Geo. S. Olive & Co., LLC	38.8
18	Richard A. Eisner & Co.	38.2
19	Friedman, Eisenstein, Raemer & Schwartz	33.7
20	Larson, Allen, Weishair & Co.	27.7

Source: *Public Accounting Report*; August 31, 1994
* Estimate

20 Most Advertised Brands in the US

Rank	Brand	Parent Company	1994 Ad Spending ($ mil.)
1	AT&T telephone services	AT&T Corp.	698.6
2	Ford cars & trucks	Ford Motor Co.	549.3
3	Sears stores	Sears, Roebuck & Co.	491.7
4	Kellogg's cereals	Kellogg Co.	483.7
5	McDonald's restaurants	McDonald's Corp.	425.8
6	Chevrolet cars & trucks	General Motors Corp.	420.0
7	Toyota cars & trucks	Toyota Motor Corp.	374.5
8	MCI telephone services	MCI Communications Corp.	325.4
9	Circuit City stores	Circuit City Stores	311.3
10	Chrysler cars & trucks	Chrysler Corp.	295.0
11	General Mills cereals	General Mills	280.8
12	J.C. Penney stores	J. C. Penney Co.	276.9
13	Disney entertainment	Walt Disney Co.	275.6
14	Nissan cars & trucks	Nissan Motor Co.	264.9
15	Dodge cars & trucks	Chrysler Corp.	234.8
16	Honda cars, trucks & power equipment	Honda Motor Co.	232.6
17	Mazda cars & trucks	Mazda Motor Corp.	225.8
18	Columbia movies & recordings	Sony Corp.	209.0
19	Budweiser beer	Anheuser-Busch Cos.	203.5
20	Burger King restaurants	Grand Metropolitan	203.5

Source: *Advertising Age*; May 1, 1995

20 Largest Advertising Agencies in the US

Rank	Company	City	1994 Sales ($ mil.)
1	McCann-Erickson Worldwide	New York	1,076.1
2	Young & Rubicam	New York	985.5
3	BBDO Worldwide	New York	917.7
4	J. Walter Thompson Co.	New York	915.7
5	DDB Needham Worldwide	New York	875.7
6	Ogilvy & Mather Worldwide	New York	768.7
7	Lintas Worldwide	New York	760.5
8	Grey Advertising	New York	749.8
9	Saatchi & Saatchi Advertising	New York	690.5
10	Leo Burnett Co.	Chicago	677.5
11	True North Communications	Chicago	619.0
12	D'Arcy Masius Benton & Bowles	New York	587.9
13	Bates Worldwide	New York	516.7
14	Lowe Group	New York	374.4
15	Bozell Worldwide	New York	299.6
16	TBWA	New York	182.5
17	TMP Worldwide	New York	127.1
18	Campbell Mithun Esty	Minneapolis	125.1
19	Chiat/Day	Venice, CA	122.9
20	N W Ayer & Partners	New York	101.0

Source: Advertising Age; April 10, 1995

25 Largest Magazines in the US

Rank	Magazine	1993 Revenues ($ mil.)	Paid Circulation	Parent Company
1	TV Guide	$1,037.0	14,037,062	News Corp.
2	People	762.7	3,424,858	Time Warner
3	Sports Illustrated	653.8	3,252,641	Time Warner
4	Time	638.6	4,063.1	Time Warner
5	Reader's Digest	477.8	15,126,664	Reader's Digest Assn.
6	Parade	447.7	37,610,000	Advance
7	Newsweek	427.7	3,158,617	Washington Post Co.
8	Better Homes & Gardens	353.5	7,613,661	Meredith Corp.
9	PC Magazine	325.7	1,051,381	Ziff-Davis
10	Good Housekeeping	315.3	5,223,935	Hearst
11	U.S. News & World Report	315.0	2,240,710	Mortimer Zuckerman
12	Business Week	279.2	880,357	McGraw-Hill
13	Family Circle	261.0	5,005,301	Bertelsmann
14	Woman's Day	245.2	4,724,500	Lagardère
15	Ladies' Home Journal	242.5	5,048,081	Meredith Corp.
16	Forbes	235.9	777,353	Forbes Inc.
17	National Enquirer	221.2	3,066,032	American Media
18	Cosmopolitan	220.4	2,527,928	Hearst Corp.
19	USA Weekend	218.1	19,026,254	Gannett Co.
20	National Geographic	212.6	7,837,993	National Geographic Society
21	FORTUNE	208.9	750,971	Time Warner
22	PC Week	194.6	6,169	Ziff-Davis
23	Star Magazine	189.0	2,752,280	American Media
24	McCall's	188.9	4,611,848	Bertelsmann
25	Money	178.6	1,994,237	Time Warner

Source: *Advertising Age*; May 8, 1995

20 Largest Newspapers in the US

Rank	Newspaper	Average Weekday Circulation	Parent Company
1	Wall Street Journal	1,823,207	Dow Jones
2	USA Today	1,570,624	Gannett
3	New York Times	1,170,869	The New York Times Co.
4	Los Angeles Times	1,058,498	Times Mirror
5	Washington Post	840,232	Washington Post Co.
6	New York Daily News	725,599	Mortimer Zuckerman
7	Chicago Tribune	691,283	Tribune Co.
8	Newsday	669,739	Times Mirror
9	Dallas Morning News	539,114	A. H. Belo Corporation
10	Detroit Free Press	531,825	Knight-Ridder
11	Chicago Sun-Times	500,969	Sun Times Corp.
12	Boston Globe	500,587	The New York Times Co.
13	San Francisco Chronicle	499,526	Chronicle Publishing
14	Philadelphia Inquirer	470,693	Knight-Ridder
15	Newark Star-Ledger	450,316	Advance Publications
16	Houston Chronicle	413,717	Hearst
17	New York Post	408,204	News Corp.
18	Minneapolis-St. Paul Star Tribune	404,757	Cowles Media
19	Cleveland Plain Dealer	404,400	Advance Publications
20	Arizona Republic	399,702	Phoenix Newspapers

Source: *Advertising Age*; May 8, 1995

Professional Football Teams

Rank	Team	1994 Revenues ($ mil.)
1	Dallas Cowboys	98.2
2	Miami Dolphins	72.3
3	San Francisco 49ers	69.6
4	Philadelphia Eagles	68.7
5	New York Giants	66.5
6	Chicago Bears	65.1
7	Kansas City Chiefs	64.4
8	Cleveland Browns	64.0
9	Buffalo Bills	63.3
10	New Orleans Saints	62.6
11	New England Patriots	60.5
12	San Diego Chargers	60.3
13	Denver Broncos	59.9
14	Arizona Cardinals	59.7
15	Green Bay Packers	59.0
16	Minnesota Vikings	58.3
17	Houston Oilers	58.1
18	Washington Redskins	58.1
19	Atlanta Falcons	57.6
20	Los Angeles Rams	57.4
21	Los Angeles Raiders	57.3
22	Pittsburgh Steelers	57.2
23	Seattle Seahawks	56.9
24	New York Jets	56.2
25	Tampa Bay Buccaneers	56.2
26	Detroit Lions	56.1
27	Cincinnati Bengals	54.0
28	Indianapolis Colts	52.0

Source: *Financial World*; May 9, 1995

Professional Baseball Teams

Rank	Team	1994 Revenues ($ mil.)
1	New York Yankees	71.5
2	Toronto Blue Jays	56.4
3	Atlanta Braves	55.8
4	Chicago Cubs	53.8
5	Baltimore Orioles	53.1
6	Texas Rangers	50.1
7	Boston Red Sox	49.9
8	Los Angeles Dodgers	49.5
9	Chicago White Sox	45.5
10	New York Mets	45.0
11	Colorado Rockies	43.5
12	San Francisco Giants	43.1
13	Philadelphia Phillies	41.1
14	Cleveland Indians	41.0
15	Florida Marlins	40.9
16	St. Louis Cardinals	39.3
17	Oakland Athletics	36.7
18	Houston Astros	34.3
19	Detroit Tigers	33.0
20	Kansas City Royals	31.9
21	Cincinnati Reds	30.6
22	California Angels	30.0
23	Seattle Mariners	27.4
24	Minnesota Twins	26.2
25	Milwaukee Brewers	26.0
26	Montreal Expos	25.8
27	Pittsburgh Pirates	25.6
28	San Diego Padres	25.0

Source: *Financial World*; May 9, 1995

Sports Franchises That Increased the Most in Value

Rank	Team (League)	1994–95 Change in Value (%)
1	Phoenix Suns (NBA)	45
2	Tampa Bay Lightning (NHL)	41
3	New York Rangers (NHL)	33
4	Utah Jazz (NBA)	29
5	Sacramento Kings (NBA)	29
6	Denver Nuggets (NBA)	27
7	Chicago Black Hawks (NHL)	27
8	Vancouver Canucks (NHL)	27
9	New York Knickerbockers (NBA)	27
10	Baltimore Orioles (MLB)	27

Source: *Financial World*; May 9, 1995

Sports Franchises That Decreased the Most in Value

Rank	Team (League)	1994–95 Change in Value (%)
1	Milwaukee Brewers (MLB)	-22
2	San Diego Padres (MLB)	-13
3	Pittsburgh Pirates (MLB)	-11
4	Oakland Athletics (MLB)	-11
5	Edmonton Oilers (NHL)	-10
6	New York Mets (MLB)	-9
7	Detroit Tigers (MLB)	-7
8	Hartford Whalers (NHL)	-6
9	California Angels (MLB)	-5
10	Indianapolis Colts (NFL)	-5

Source: *Financial World*; May 9, 1995

Professional Basketball Teams

Rank	Team	1994 Revenues ($ mil.)
1	New York Knickerbockers	77.7
2	Los Angeles Lakers	72.4
3	Detroit Pistons	66.9
4	Phoenix Suns	66.4
5	Chicaco Bulls	57.5
6	Utah Jazz	53.8
7	San Antonio Spurs	50.5
8	Cleveland Cavaliers	49.9
9	Boston Celtics	47.5
10	Orlando Magic	46.3
11	Portland Trailblazers	46.0
12	Charlotte Hornets	45.2
13	Houston Rockets	44.7
14	Seattle Supersonics	44.3
15	New Jersey Nets	41.8
16	Sacramento Kings	41.4
17	Minnesota Timberwolves	40.9
18	Golden State Warriors	39.8
19	Denver Nuggets	39.4
20	Miami Heat	38.7
21	Washington Bullets	38.2
22	Milwaukee Bucks	38.1
23	Atlanta Hawks	37.3
24	Los Angeles Clippers	35.5
25	Dallas Mavericks	35.0
26	Indiana Pacers	33.2
27	Philadelphia 76ers	30.7

Source: *Financial World*; May 9, 1995

Professional Hockey Teams

Rank	Team	1994 Revenues ($ mil.)
1	New York Rangers	55.7
2	Detroit Red Wings	50.1
3	Toronto Maple Leafs	46.2
4	Anaheim Mighty Ducks	45.1
5	Boston Bruins	44.0
6	Chicago Black Hawks	42.6
7	San Jose Sharks	40.5
8	Vancouver Canucks	37.1
9	Los Angeles Kings	35.9
10	Philadelphia Flyers	35.5
11	Pittsburgh Penguins	35.0
12	Dallas Stars	31.1
13	Montreal Canadiens	31.1
14	New Jersey Devils	26.7
15	Washington Capitals	26.4
16	New York Islanders	25.8
17	St. Louis Blues	25.3
18	Buffalo Sabres	23.9
19	Calgary Flames	23.9
20	Tampa Bay Lightning	23.0
21	Florida Panthers	22.2
22	Ottawa Senators	21.7
23	Hartford Whalers	19.6
24	Quebec Nordiques	18.9
25	Edmonton Oilers	15.9
26	Winnipeg Jets	14.2

Source: *Financial World*; May 9, 1995

15 Top-Paid Professional Athletes — 1994

Rank	Athlete	Sport	1994 Total Pay ($ mil.)
1	Michael Jordan	Minor League Baseball	30.0
2	Shaquille O'Neal	Basketball	16.7
3	Jack Nicklaus	Golf	14.8
4	Arnold Palmer	Golf	13.6
5	Gerhard Berger	Auto Racing	13.5
6	Wayne Gretzky	Hockey	13.5
7	Michael Moorer	Boxing	12.1
8	Evander Holyfield	Boxing	12.0
9	Andre Agassi	Tennis	11.4
10	Nigel Mansell	Auto Racing	11.3
11	Pete Sampras	Tennis	10.6
12	Joe Montana	Football	10.3
13	Charles Barkley	Basketball	9.3
14	Greg Norman	Golf	8.8
15	George Foreman	Boxing	8.5

Source: *Forbes*; December 19, 1994

100 Best Companies to Work For

Company	City	Company	City
Acipco	Birmingham, AL	Lowe's	North Wilkesboro, NC
Advanced Micro Devices	Sunnyvale, CA	Lyondell Petrochemical	Houston
Alagasco	Birmingham, AL	Marquette Electronics	Milwaukee
Anheuser-Busch	St. Louis	Mary Kay Cosmetics	Dallas
Apogee Enterprises	Minneapolis	McCormick	Hunt Valley, MD
Armstrong	Lancaster, PA	Merck	Whitehouse Station, NJ
Avis	Garden City, NY	Methodist Hospital	Houston
Baptist Hospital of Miami	Miami	Microsoft	Redmond, WA
BE&K	Birmingham, AL	Herman Miller	Zeeland, MI
Ben & Jerry's Homemade	Waterbury, VT	3M	St. Paul
Beth Israel Hospital Boston*	Boston	Moog	East Aurora, NY
Leo Burnett	Chicago	J.P. Morgan	New York
Chaparral Steel	Midlothian, TX	Morrison & Foerster	San Francisco
Compaq Computer	Houston	Motorola	Schaumburg, IL
Cooper Tire	Findlay, OH	Nissan Motor Manufacturing	Smyrna, TN
Corning	Corning, NY	Nordstrom	Seattle
Cray Research	Eagan, MN	Northwestern Mutual Life	Milwaukee
Cummins Engine	Columbus, IN	Odetics	Anaheim, CA
Dayton Hudson	Minneapolis	Patagonia	Ventura, CA
John Deere	Moline, IL	J. C. Penney	Plano, TX
Delta Air Lines*	Atlanta	Physio-Control	Redmond, WA
Donnelly*	Holland, MI	Pitney Bowes	Stamford, CT
DuPont	Wilmington, DE	Polaroid	Cambridge, MA
A. G. Edwards	St. Louis	Preston Trucking	Preston, MD
Erie Insurance	Erie, PA	Procter & Gamble	Cincinnati
Federal Express*	Memphis	Publix Super Markets*	Lakeland, FL
Fel-Pro*	Skokie, IL	Quad/Graphics	Pewaukee, WI
First Federal Bank of California	Santa Monica	Reader's Digest	Pleasantville, NY
H. B. Fuller	St. Paul, MN	REI	Seattle
General Mills	Minneapolis	Rosenbluth International*	Philadelphia
Goldman Sachs	New York	SAS Institute	Cary, NC
W. L. Gore & Associates	Newark, DE	J. M. Smucker	Orrville, OH
Great Plains Software	Fargo, ND	Southwest Airlines*	Dallas
Hallmark Cards*	Kansas City, MO	Springfield ReManufacturing	Springfield, MO
Haworth	Holland, MI	Springs	Fort Mill, SC
Hershey Foods	Hershey, PA	Steelcase	Grand Rapids
Hewitt Associates	Lincolnshire, IL	Syntex	Palo Alto, CA
Hewlett-Packard	Palo Alto, CA	Tandem	Cupertino, CA
Honda of America Mfg.	Marysville, OH	TDIndustries	Dallas
IBM	Armonk, NY	Tennant	Minneapolis
Inland Steel	Chicago	UNUM	Portland, ME
Intel	Santa Clara, CA	USAA*	San Antonio
Johnson & Johnson	New Brunswick, NJ	U S WEST	Englewood, CO
SC Johnson Wax	Racine, WI	Valassis Communications	Livonia, MI
Kellogg	Battle Creek, MI	Viking Freight System	San Jose
Knight-Ridder	Miami	Wal-Mart	Bentonville, AR
Lands' End	Dodgeville, WI	Wegmans	Rochester, NY
Lincoln Electric	Cleveland	Weyerhaeuser	Tacoma, WA
Los Angeles Dodgers	Los Angeles	Worthington Industries	Columbus, OH
Lotus Development	Cambridge, MA	Xerox	Stamford, CT

Source: Levering, Robert and Moskowitz, Milton. *The 100 Best Companies to Work For in America*. New York: Doubleday, 1993.

*Indicates one of Top Ten

America's 100 Most Admired Companies

Rank	Company	Rank	Company
1	Rubbermaid	50	SYSCO
2	Microsoft	52	Wal-Mart Stores
3	Coca-Cola	53	Capital Cities/ABC
4	Motorola	53	Mobil
5	Home Depot	55	Sara Lee
6	Intel	56	Northwestern Mutual Life
7	Procter & Gamble	56	Walgreen
8	3M	58	Deere
9	United Parcel Service	59	PacifiCare Health Systems
10	Hewlett-Packard	59	Roadway Services
11	United HealthCare	61	Compaq Computer
12	Gillette	62	American International Group
13	Boeing	62	Armstrong World Industries, Inc.
14	General Electric	62	Federal Express
15	Albertson's	62	Golden West Financial
16	Levi Strauss Associates	66	Abbott Laboratories
17	Johnson & Johnson	66	Banc One
18	Corning	66	Illinois Tool Works
19	AT&T	66	Morgan Stanley Group
20	Fluor	70	Exxon
20	Pfizer	71	Washington Mutual Savings Bank
22	J.P. Morgan	72	PepsiCo
23	Oracle Systems	72	SBC Communications
24	Merck	74	AlliedSignal
25	Walt Disney	75	Centex
25	Herman Miller	75	Martin Marietta
25	NIKE	77	McKesson
28	U.S. Healthcare	78	International Flavors & Fragrances Inc.
29	Du Pont	79	Chevron
29	Publix Super Markets	79	Schering-Plough
31	Kimberly-Clark	81	Chrysler
32	Toys "R" Us	82	Xerox
33	General Mills	83	Colgate-Palmolive
34	Electronic Data Systems	83	Viacom
35	Leggett & Platt	85	CSX
35	Union Pacific	85	UST
37	Enron	85	V.F.
38	Dow Chemical	88	Automatic Data Processing
38	Shell Oil	88	Bankers Trust New York
40	Goodyear Tire & Rubber	88	Merrill Lynch
41	Shaw Industries	91	Caterpillar
42	Norfolk Southern	92	Dow Jones
42	Southwest Airlines	92	Reader's Digest Association
44	Columbia/HCA Healthcare	92	Time Warner
44	Ford Motor	95	Anheuser-Busch
46	Berkshire Hathaway	96	ConAgra
47	Amoco	96	HON Industries
47	Nucor	98	MCI Communications
49	Unifi	99	Burlington Resources
50	Emerson Electric	100	Springs Industries

Source: *FORTUNE*; March 6, 1995

Top 20 Businesses Controlled by Women

Rank	Company	Primary Owner	1994 Revenues ($ mil.)
1	TLC Beatrice	Loida N. Lewis	1,820
2	Raley's	Joyce Raley Teel	1,800
3	Roll International	Lynda Resnick	1,400
4	Little Caesar Enterprises	Marian Ilitch	1,000
5	Axel Johnson	Antonia Axson Johnson	815
6	Minyard Food Stores	Liz Minyard and Gretchen Minyard Williams	800
7	Warnaco	Linda Wachner	789
8	Donna Karan	Donna Karan	465
9	Jockey International	Donna Wolf Steigerwaldt	450
10	Copley Press	Helen Copley	380
11	Jenny Craig	Jenny Craig	376
12	Carole Little	Carole Little	375
13	Troy Motors	Irma Elder	364
14	Owen Healthcare	Dian Graves Owen	320
15	Esprit de Corp.	Susie Tompkins	300
16	Lundy Packing	Annabelle Lundy Fetterman	299
17	Tootsie Roll Industries	Ellen Gordon	298
18	Chas. Levy	Barbara Levy Kipper	285
19	Columbia Sportswear	Gertrude Boyle	265
20	Resort Condominiums International	Christel DeHaan	259

Source: *Working Woman*, May 1995

Top 20 Black-Owned Businesses

Rank	Company	1994 Revenues ($ mil.)
1	TLC Beatrice International	1,800.0
2	Johnson Publishing Co. Inc.	306.6
3	Philadelphia Coca-Cola Bottling	305.0
4	H.J. Russell & Co.	154.7
5	Pulsar Data Systems Inc.	137.0
6	RMS Technologies Inc.	121.0
7	The Anderson-Dubose Co.	118.0
8	Gold Line Refining Ltd.	108.6
9	Uniworld Group Inc.	104.1
10	Bet Holdings Inc.	97.5
11	Soft Sheen Products Inc.	97.2
12	Envirotest Systems Corp.	96.4
13	The Bing Group	93.5
14	Mays Chemical Co. Inc.	88.9
15	Midwest Stamping Inc.	83.0
16	Burrell Communications Group	80.8
17	Essence Communications Inc.	77.5
18	Granite Broadcasting Corp.	76.2
19	Marco International Inc.	75.0
20	Stop Shop and Save	68.0

Source: *Black Enterprise,* June 1995

Top 20 Hispanic-Owned Businesses

Rank	Company	1994 Revenues ($ mil.)
1	Goya Foods Inc.	527.0
2	Burt Enterprises	423.0
3	Troy Ford Inc.	364.7
4	de la Cruz Cos.	266.6
5	Ancira Interprises Inc.	257.8
6	Sedano's Supermarkets	253.4
7	Galeana Van Dyke Dodge	202.4
8	The Vincam Group Inc.	193.1
9	International Bancshares Corp.	181.7
10	Normac Foods Inc.	158.2
11	CTA Incorporated	156.6
12	Precision Trading Corp.	150.0
13	MasTec Inc.	142.0
14	United Poultry Corp.	134.3
15	Capital Bancorp.	126.5
16	Mexican Industries in Michigan Inc.	121.3
17	Avanti/Case-Hoyt	120.0
18	Bella Automotive Group Ltd.	108.9
19	Colsa Corp.	105.0
20	Lloyd A. Wise Cos.	104.0

Source: *Hispanic Business*, June 1995

THE COMPANY PROFILES

2

ABBOTT LABORATORIES

OVERVIEW

Based in a northern suburb of Chicago, Abbott Labs is a diversified health care company that develops, manufactures, and sells diagnostic, therapeutic, and nutritional products. The company is the world leader in the production of the antibiotic erythromycin, and its baby formula Similac commands the #1 position in the US baby-formula market. Abbott is a worldwide leader in in-vitro diagnostic products such as thyroid tests, cancer monitoring tests, and tests for detecting hepatitis and AIDS antibodies, among others.

Abbott has 2 divisions: pharmaceutical and nutritional products (including chemical and agricultural products), and hospital and laboratory products (anesthetics, drug delivery systems, diagnostic systems). The traditionally lean and efficient company's R&D department is adept at developing niche products (such as nutritional supplements) and finding new uses for already developed drugs. Its pipeline has many products in all stages of investigation.

Abbott is committed to expanding its growing overseas markets. It sells products in about 130 countries, and almost 40% of its sales take place outside the US. The company has manufacturing plants in North America, Europe, and Japan. Abbott is carefully adapting its products for the developing markets in Latin America and Asia.

WHEN

Family physician Wallace Abbott founded the Abbott Alkaloidal Company in a Chicago suburb in 1888 to sell his improved form of the dosimetric granule (a pill that supplied uniform quantities of drugs). By 1900 sales were $125,000. The AMA criticized Dr. Abbott for his aggressive marketing, but the doctor successfully defended himself, receiving support from much of the medical profession.

During WWI Abbott scientists discovered techniques for synthesizing anesthetics and sedatives previously available only from some German companies. In 1922 the company improved its research capacity by buying Dermatological Research Laboratories. In 1928 Abbott acquired John T. Milliken of St. Louis, which brought Abbott well-trained salesmen.

Abbott went public in 1929. Flamboyant salesman DeWitt Clough became president in 1933; the Abbott magazine *What's New*, prepared by Clough's promotional staff, was a significant new corporate marketing tool. The company began to operate internationally in the mid-1930s, opening branches in Argentina, Brazil, Cuba, Mexico, and the UK.

Abbott was one of several drug companies that increased penicillin production during WWII. After the war, the company introduced new forms of penicillin. Research toward other antibiotics yielded Erythrocin (1952), Abbott's form of the antibiotic erythromycin. In the 1960s the company added consumer products (Selsun shampoo, Murine) and infant and nutritional formulas (such as Similac), but drugs and hospital products remained its mainstay. The FDA banned artificial sweetener Sucaryl (introduced in 1950) in 1970 after tests indicated it might be carcinogenic. In 1971 millions of intravenous solutions were recalled following contamination reports.

In 1981 Abbott introduced a hospital nutritional support service. In the early 1980s the company was licensed to sell Japanese-developed pharmaceuticals in the US. Profits increased steadily after 1979, when Robert Schoellhorn became CEO. Schoellhorn cut R&D and fired several top managers; in 1990 he was laid off.

In 1990 Abbott received FDA approval to market ProSom (an insomnia drug). The company came under legal fire from children of women who, in the 1950s, took DES, a synthetic hormone that may cause cancer. In 1992 Abbott exchanged rights to its controversial HIVIG (HIV immune globulin) product, which may fight AIDS, to North American Biologicals for 16% of the company.

The FTC brought suit for price fixing against Abbott, Bristol-Myers Squibb, and American Home Products in 1992. The other 2 settled out of court, but Abbott fought the allegations. By the end of 1992, Abbott had paid about $140 million in settlements.

In 1993 Hytrin, a hypertension drug, received FDA approval for the treatment of enlarged prostates. Also in 1993 the company strengthened its lead in the US anesthesia market by introducing generic inhalation agents isoflurane and enflurane.

In late 1994 the company purchased the nutritional business of the Spanish concern Puleva. In 1995 the FDA approved Abbott's new ulcer treatment, Prevacid, and expanded treatment uses for 2 drugs: Depakote (an anticonvulsant) for manic depression, and Lupron (a prostate cancer treatment) for anemia due to fibroid tumors.

WHO

Chairman and CEO: Duane L. Burnham, age 53, $1,594,269 pay
President and COO: Thomas R. Hodgson, age 53, $1,219,438 pay
SVP Finance and CFO: Gary P. Coughlan, age 50, $786,923 pay
SVP Strategic Improvement Processes: David A. Thompson, age 53, $752,692 pay
SVP Pharmaceutical Operations: Paul N. Clark, age 48, $732,692 pay
SVP Hospital Products: John G. Kringel, age 55
SVP, Secretary, and General Counsel: Jose M. de Lasa, age 53
SVP Chemical and Agricultural Products: Robert L. Parkinson Jr., age 44
SVP Chief Scientific Officer: David V. Milligan, age 54
SVP Diagnostic Operations: Miles D. White, age 39
SVP Human Resources: Robert N. Beck, age 54
Auditors: Arthur Andersen & Co, SC

WHERE

HQ: 100 Abbott Park Rd., Abbott Park, IL 60064-3500
Phone: 708-937-6100
Fax: 708-937-1511

	1994 Sales		1994 Operating Income	
	$ mil.	% of total	$ mil.	% of total
US	5,758	63	1,558	70
Europe, Africa & Middle East	1,662	18	352	6
Pacific, Far East & Canada	1,246	14	182	16
Latin America	490	5	131	8
Adjustments	—	—	(20)	—
Total	**9,156**	**100**	**2,203**	**100**

WHAT

	1994 Sales		1994 Operating Income	
	$ mil.	% of total	$ mil.	% of total
Pharmaceutical & nutritional prods.	4,951	54	1,385	63
Hospital & lab prods.	4,205	46	818	37
Total	**9,156**	**100**	**2,203**	**100**

Selected Brand Names

Agricultural Products
ProGibb (plant growth regulator)
VectoBac (larvacide)
XenTari (insecticide)

Consumer Products
Murine (eye and ear drops)
Selsun Blue (dandruff shampoo)

Hospital Products
ADD-Vantage (IV system)
ADx (drug testing equipment)
IMx (immunoassay testing system)
LifeShield (needleless IV system)
Opticath (monitor)
Transpac (blood pressure monitor)

Nutritional Supplements
Advera (nutrition for AIDS patients)
Ensure (adult nutrition)
PediaSure (infant formula)

Prescription Drugs
Abbokinase (blood clot dissolver)
Biaxin (antibiotic)
Depakote (anticonvulsant)
Hytrin (hypertension and prostate treatment)
Lupron (cancer drug)
Survanta (treatment for premature infant respiratory distress)

KEY COMPETITORS

ALZA
American Home Products
Bausch & Lomb
Baxter
Becton, Dickinson
Biogen
Bristol-Myers Squibb
Chiron Corp.

C. R. Bard
Diagnostic Products
Dow Chemical
DuPont
Genentech
Genzyme
Hoechst
Johnson & Johnson

Medtronic
Nellcor
Nestlé
Procter & Gamble
Purepac
St. Jude Medical
Unilever

HOW MUCH

	9-Year Growth	1985	1986	1987	1988	1989	1990	1991	1992	1993	1994
Sales ($ mil.)	11.8%	3,360	3,808	4,388	4,937	5,380	6,159	6,877	7,852	8,408	9,156
Net income ($ mil.)	14.0%	465	541	633	752	860	966	1,089	1,239	1,399	1,517
Income as % of sales	—	13.8%	14.2%	14.4%	15.2%	16.0%	15.7%	15.8%	15.8%	16.6%	16.6%
Earnings per share ($)	16.0%	0.49	0.58	0.70	0.84	0.97	1.11	1.28	1.47	1.69	1.87
Stock price – high ($)	—	9.00	13.75	16.75	13.09	17.59	23.19	34.88	34.19	30.88	34.00
Stock price – low ($)	—	4.98	7.92	10.00	10.72	11.56	15.63	19.63	26.13	22.63	25.38
Stock price – close ($)	16.0%	8.55	11.41	12.06	12.03	17.00	22.50	34.44	30.38	29.63	32.63
P/E – high	—	18	24	24	16	18	21	27	23	18	18
P/E – low	—	10	14	14	13	12	14	15	18	13	14
Dividends per share ($)	17.8%	0.17	0.21	0.24	0.29	0.34	0.40	0.48	0.58	0.66	0.74
Book value per share ($)	11.1%	1.96	1.94	2.31	2.74	3.08	3.30	3.77	4.00	4.48	5.04
Employees	4.0%	34,742	35,754	37,828	38,751	40,249	43,770	45,694	48,118	49,659	49,464

1994 Year-end:
Debt ratio: 20.7%
Return on equity: 39.3%
Cash (mil.): $315
Current ratio: 1.12
Long-term debt (mil.): $287
No. of shares (mil.): 803
Dividends
  Yield: 2.3%
  Payout: 39.6%
Market value (mil.): $26,211

Stock Price History
High/Low 1985–94

ADOLPH COORS COMPANY

OVERVIEW

Adolph Coors, the US's 3rd largest brewer, is pouring new ideas into the saturated beer market. Long known as a single-product, regional beer maker, in 1994 Coors introduced 8 new products, bringing its roster to a rainbow of 22 amber, brown, gold, red, and even clear brews.

Coors Brewing (the company's principal subsidiary) has opened its first non-US breweries: a joint venture in South Korea with Jinro Ltd. that will supply the Asian market and a wholly owned 425,000-barrel facility in Spain that will export to the rest of Europe. The Korean plant, opened in mid-1994, has already captured 10% of that beer market.

Coors is also thinking innovatively to cut overhead and improve sales. With aluminum

sheet costs up more than 50%, in 1995 Coors expanded its joint venture with American National Can Co. The previous year the company created 8 decentralized sales regions to help local sales organizations provide faster service.

Coors — whose top label, Coors Light, accounts for about 2/3 of sales — continues to test new products after the successful 1994 launch of Zima Clearmalt. In 1995 Zima Gold, George Killian's Irish Brown Ale, and a pair of "ice" brews joined the Coors family. The company spent over 20% of 1994 revenues on advertising, including sponsorship of the Silver Bullets, the only women's professional baseball team in the US.

The heirs of founder Adolph Coors own 100% of the company's voting stock.

WHEN

Adolph Coors landed in Baltimore in 1868, a 21-year-old stowaway fleeing Germany's military draft. He worked his way west to Denver, where he bought a bottling company in 1872 and became partners with Jacob Schueler, a local merchant, in 1873. The partners built a brewery in Golden, Colorado, a small town in the nearby Rocky Mountain foothills. In 1880 Coors became sole owner of the company. For most of its history, Coors confined sales to western states. The cost of nationwide distribution was prohibitive because Coors used a single brewery, natural brewing methods, and no preservatives; Coors beer was made, transported, and stored under refrigeration, with a shelf life of only one month.

Coors survived Prohibition (1919–33) by making near-beer and malted milk and by entering cement and porcelain chemicalware production. By this time Coors's 3 sons worked in the business. After repeal, beer sales grew steadily in Coors's 11-state market. By the 1960s Coors beer had achieved national popularity, as thousands of loyal customers from outside the market area packed it home.

By 1975 Coors beer was the top seller in 10 of its 11 state markets (the company sometimes restricted distributors to selling its beer exclusively). The brand's meteoric rise was blunted by continuing sales declines through 1978, the result of campaigns for new "light" and "superpremium" beers introduced by Miller and Anheuser-Busch. Coors responded by introducing light and superpremium brands, removing distribution restrictions, and expanding its market area to 16 states.

During the 1970s Joe Coors, grandson of Adolph, financed ultraconservative projects to express strong family opposition to the era's liberal movements. In the late 1970s and 1980s, Coors began rapid expansion while enduring boycotts and strikes due to alleged discriminatory labor practices. Coors eventually developed progressive employment policies.

To meet increasing demand, in 1990 Coors bought Stroh's Memphis brewery. Coors spun off its aluminum making and packaging operations in 1992 to form a new company, ACX Technologies. That same year a nasty advertising fight began when Anheuser-Busch claimed that the Coors Light sold in the Northeast mixed water from Virginia with its legendary "Rocky Mountain spring water." Also in 1992 Coors introduced Zima, a high-priced, clear, malt-based alcohol beverage that became a surprise hit. Zima went national in 1994.

In 1993 Leo Kiely, a former president at Frito-Lay, became president and COO (the first nonfamily member to be in that office). Also, Coors cut its work force by nearly 700; the severance program cost $70 million and resulted in Coors's first loss in over 10 years.

Coors introduced its version of ice beer, Coors Artic Ice, in 1994, hoping to catch up with Anheuser-Busch's and Miller's entries in the category. That year the company signed an agreement to create a microbrewery, the SandLot Brewery, at Coors Field, the new stadium of the Colorado Rockies baseball team. In 1995 Coors instituted a 1% price hike to offset higher costs; the increase was limited by the market's strong competition.

Nasdaq symbol: ACCOB
Fiscal year ends: Last Sunday in December

WHO

Chairman and President: William K. Coors, age 78, $277,734 pay
VC: Joseph Coors, age 77
VC and CEO, Coors Brewing Co.: Peter H. Coors, age 48, $764,590 pay
President and COO, Coors Brewing Co.: W. Leo Kiely III, age 48, $615,258 pay
SVP Operations and Technology, Coors Brewing Co.: Alvin C. Babb, age 62, $422,766 pay
SVP Marketing, Coors Brewing Co.: William H. Weintraub, age 52, $400,304 pay
SVP and Chief International Officer, Coors Brewing Co.: Michael A. Marranzino, age 47
SVP Corporate Development, Coors Brewing Co.: Robert D. Klugman, age 47
SVP Human Resources, Coors Brewing Co.: Robert W. Ehret, age 50
VP, Treasurer, and CFO; SVP and CFO, Coors Brewing Co.: Timothy V. Wolf, age 41
VP; VP and Chief Legal Officer, Coors Brewing Co.: M. Caroline Turner, age 45
VP Public Affairs, Coors Brewing Co.: Marvin D. Johnson
VP Research and Development, Coors Brewing Co.: Hugo Patiño
Auditors: Price Waterhouse LLP

WHERE

HQ: Golden, CO 80401
Phone: 303-279-6565
Fax: 303-277-6564

Coors has production facilities in Golden, Colorado; Memphis, Tennessee; Elkton, Virginia; and Zaragoza, Spain. The company exports its products to Asia, Australasia, the Caribbean, Central America, Europe, and the Middle East.

WHAT

	1994 Production
	Barrels (mil.)
Coors Light	12.8
Original Coors	2.4
Coors Extra Gold	0.3
Coors Artic Ice	0.2
Coors Dry	0.1
Other brands	4.4
Total	**20.2**

Selected Brand Names

Coors Artic Ice	Keystone Amber Light
Coors Cutter	Keystone Dry
Coors Dry	Keystone Ice
Coors Extra Gold	Keystone Light
Coors Light	Original Coors
Coors Red Light	Shulers Lager
George Killian's	Shulers Light
Irish Brown Ale	Steinlager
George Killian's	Winterfest
Irish Red Lager	Zima Clearmalt
Keystone	Zima Gold

Selected Subsidiaries
Coors Brewing Ibérica SA (Spain-based beer production)
Coors Distributing Co. (beer distributor)
Coors Energy Co. (gas pipelines)
Jinro-Coors Brewing Co. (33%, South Korea)
The Rocky Mountain Water Co. (water processing)
The Wannamaker Ditch Co. (water processing)

KEY COMPETITORS

Allied Domecq	Danone	John Labatt
Anchor Brewing	Foster's Brewing	Kirin
Anheuser-Busch	Genessee	Philip Morris
Boston Beer	Guinness	San Miguel
Canandaigua	Heileman	S&P
Wine Co.	Heineken	Stroh
Carlsberg		

HOW MUCH

	9-Year Growth	1985	1986	1987	1988	1989	1990	1991	1992	1993	1994
Sales ($ mil.)	2.9%	1,281	1,315	1,351	1,522	1,764	1,863	1,917	1,551	1,582	1,663
Net income ($ mil.)	1.0%	53	59	48	47	13	39	24	6	(42)	58
Income as % of sales	—	4.2%	4.5%	3.6%	3.1%	0.7%	2.1%	1.3%	0.4%	—	3.5%
Earnings per share ($)	0.0%	1.52	1.65	1.32	1.28	0.36	1.05	0.64	0.17	(1.10)	1.52
Stock price – high ($)	—	22.00	31.63	29.75	20.75	23.75	27.38	24.25	22.88	22.63	20.88
Stock price – low ($)	—	14.50	20.38	16.38	17.75	17.50	17.13	17.38	15.50	15.00	14.75
Stock price – close ($)	(2.8%)	21.63	24.00	16.88	20.00	19.75	20.50	21.00	16.50	16.25	16.75
P/E – high	—	15	19	23	16	66	26	38	135	—	14
P/E – low	—	10	12	12	14	49	16	27	91	—	10
Dividends per share ($)	2.5%	0.40	0.50	0.50	0.50	0.50	0.50	0.50	0.50	0.50	0.50
Book value per share ($)	(10.1%)	26.46	27.41	28.19	28.96	28.75	29.20	29.33	18.17	16.54	10.10
Employees	(4.3%)	9,400	9,820	9,900	10,500	10,600	10,700	11,800	7,100	6,200	6,300

1994 Year-end:
Debt ratio: 31.9%
Return on equity: 31.1%
Cash (mil.): $27
Current ratio: 0.93
Long-term debt (mil.): $131
No. of shares (mil.): 37
Dividends
  Yield: 3.0%
  Payout: 32.9%
Market value (mil.): $621

Stock Price History
High/Low 1985–94

ADVANCE PUBLICATIONS, INC.

OVERVIEW

New York City–based Advance Publications is the holding company for one of the largest media groups in the US. Its holdings include books (Random House), magazines (Condé Nast), newspapers, and cable TV. Advance is owned by Si and Donald Newhouse, sons of the founder, who are known for their tight-lipped control of the company's operations.

Random House is the #1 consumer book publisher in the US, controlling the publishers Knopf, Ballantine, and Vintage, among others. Condé Nast is one of the leading US magazine publishers, with 15 titles, including *Vogue*, the *New Yorker*, and *Details*. Newhouse Newspapers publishes more than 20 newspapers,

including the Cleveland *Plain Dealer* and the New Orleans *Times-Picayune*.

In 1995 Advance formed a joint venture with Time Warner, combining Newhouse Broadcasting's cable systems, which serve 1.4 million subscribers, with Time Warner's systems in New York, North Carolina, and Florida. The deal comes as the cable industry is undergoing consolidation and preparing to compete with phone companies in the race to provide interactive television and other advanced communication services. Advance has also formed joint ventures to put many of its magazines and newspapers on-line.

WHEN

Solomon Neuhaus (who later became Samuel I. Newhouse) dropped out of school at age 13 because of family poverty. He went to work for a lawyer who received the *Bayonne* (New Jersey) *Times* as payment for a debt. At age 16 in 1911, Newhouse was put in charge of the failing newspaper; he turned the company around. In 1922 he bought the Staten Island *Advance*, the core of Advance Publications.

Newhouse used profits from the *Advance* to buy newspapers throughout the New York area, operating out of a briefcase rather than a headquarters suite. He purchased the *Long Island Press* (1932), the Newark *Star-Ledger* (1933), the *Long Island Star-Journal* (1938), and the *Syracuse Journal* (1939). He later acquired the *Syracuse Herald-Standard* (1941), the *Jersey Journal* (1945), and the Harrisburg *Patriot* (1948). In 1955 he expanded into the South by buying the *Birmingham News* and the *Huntsville Times*.

In 1959 Newhouse entered magazine publishing when he bought Condé Nast (*Vogue, Bride's, House & Garden*) as an anniversary gift for his wife, Mitzi (joking that she had asked for a fashion magazine, so he bought her *Vogue*). Continuing to build his newspaper empire, in 1962 he paid $42 million for the New Orleans *Times-Picayune* and *New Orleans States-Item*, a record price broken by his 1967 purchase of the Cleveland *Plain Dealer* for $54 million. By 1967 Newhouse had also established NewChannels, which owned several cable systems (10,000 subscribers). Newhouse set yet another newspaper purchase record in 1976 by buying the Booth chain of 8 Michigan newspapers for $304 million.

Newhouse died in 1979, leaving his sons Si and Donald as trustees of the company's 10

shares of voting stock. They claimed that the estate was worth $181.9 million, taxable at $48.7 million. The IRS contested that figure. When the case — the largest ever at the time — was decided in 1990, the IRS lost.

Meanwhile, the sons continued to expand Advance Publications. They entered book publishing by buying Random House, at that time the largest general-interest US book publisher, from RCA in 1980. Random House began in 1925 when Bennett Cerf bought the Modern Library from his boss. In 1927 Cerf and his partner, Donald Klopfer, began publishing luxury editions (chosen "at Random") in addition to the inexpensive Modern Library books. In 1966 RCA bought Random, but bureaucratic RCA and genteel Random did not mesh.

Advance resurrected *Vanity Fair* in 1983 and bought the *New Yorker* in 1985. In 1989 Advance bought Crown Publishing. In 1992 Si Newhouse moved *Vanity Fair* editor Tina Brown to the *New Yorker*, hoping to give an edge to the eccentric weekly. In 1993 Condé Nast bought Knapp Publications (*Architectural Digest, Bon Appetit*).

Also in 1993 the company joined with Brøderbund Software to create children's multimedia software and bought the electronic publishing division of Bantam Doubleday Dell. That year it also offered $500 million to QVC, backing its bid for Paramount (which QVC later lost to Viacom). The company acquired 25% of *Wired*, a leading multimedia magazine, in 1994. In 1995 Random House signed a deal with Planeta Internacional (the #1 book publisher in the Spanish-speaking world) to distribute Spanish-language books in the US and Canada, and Advance agreed to buy American City Business Journals for $269 million.

Private company
Fiscal year ends: December 31

WHO

Chairman and CEO: Samuel I. "Si" Newhouse Jr.,
age 66
President: Donald E. Newhouse, age 64
Publisher: Richard Diamond
Chairman, President, and CEO, Random House:
Alberto Vitale
President, Condé Nast Publications: Steven T. Florio
President, Newhouse Newspapers Metro-Suburbia:
Edwin F. Russell
Editorial Director, Condé Nast Publications Inc.: James
Truman

WHERE

HQ: 950 Fingerboard Rd., Staten Island, NY 10305
Phone: 718-981-1234
Fax: 718-981-1415

Advance Publications has newspapers and cable TV
groups in the US and book and magazine operations in
New York and Europe.

WHAT

The Condé Nast Publications Inc.
Allure
Architectural Digest
Bon Appetit
Bride's
Condé Nast Traveler
Details
Glamour
Gourmet
GQ
Mademoiselle
The New Yorker
Parade
Self
Vanity Fair
Vogue

Newhouse Broadcasting
Cable television (1.4 million subscribers)

Newhouse Newspapers Metro-Suburbia (Selected)

Alabama
  Birmingham News
  Birmingham Post-Herald
  The Mobile Press
  The Mobile Press
   Register
  The Mobile Register
Louisiana
  The Times-Picayune (New
   Orleans)
Massachusetts
  Union-News & Sunday
   Republican (Springfield)
Michigan
  The Ann Arbor News
  The Flint Times
  The Grand Rapids
   Press
  Kalamazoo Gazette
  The Saginaw News
  *Times (*Bay City*)*
Mississippi
  Mississippi Press (Pascagoula)
  Mississippi Press
   Register (Pascagoula)

New Jersey
  Jersey Journal (Jersey
   City)
  Star-Ledger (Newark)
  Times (Trenton)
New York
  Herald-American
   (Syracuse)
  The Post-Standard
   (Syracuse)
  Syracuse Herald-
   Journal
Ohio
  Plain Dealer (Cleveland)
Oregon
  The Oregonian
   (Portland)
Pennsylvania
  The Patriot-News
   (Harrisburg)

Random House, Inc.

Alfred A. Knopf
Ballantine Books
Beginner Books
Crown Publishers
Fawcett Books
Fodor's Travel Publications
Modern Library

Orion
Pantheon Books
Random Century (UK)
Times Books
Villard Books
Vintage Books

KEY COMPETITORS

ADVO
American Express
Bertelsmann
Cablevision
Capital Cities/ABC
Comcast
Cox
Electronic Arts
E. W. Scripps
Gannett

Harcourt General
Hearst
Houghton Mifflin
Knight-Ridder
Lagardère
McGraw-Hill
New York Times
News Corp.
Pearson
Reader's Digest

Scholastic
TCI
Thomson Corp.
Time Warner
Times Mirror
Tribune
Universal Press
  Syndicate
Viacom
Washington Post

HOW MUCH

	9-Year Growth	1985	1986	1987	1988	1989	1990	1991	1992	1993	1994
Estimated sales ($ mil.)	—	2,030	2,200	2,482	2,655	2,882	3,040	3,095	4,287	4,416	4,690
Newspaper revenues ($ mil.)	—	—	1,407	1,601	1,470	1,745	1,797	1,748	1,800	1,800	1,926
Newspapers	—	26	27	26	36	26	30	32	28	26	29
Magazine revenues ($ mil.)	—	—	544	678	745	842	845	941	975	970	1,008
Cable TV revenue ($ mil.)	—	—	186	203	229	295	398	440	467	496	526
Employees	—	917	1,027	1,098	1,078	1,147	1,242	1,301	—	1,350	1,400
Cable subscribers (thou.)	0.3%	18,500	18,500	19,000	19,000	19,500	19,500	19,000	19,000	19,000	19,000

Estimated Sales ($ mil.) 1985–94

RANDOM HOUSE

ADVANCED MICRO DEVICES, INC.

OVERVIEW

Not everyone drives a Cadillac, and not every PC user drives a Pentium microprocessor. That leaves plenty of room for midpriced chips like Advanced Micro Devices's AM486. While the faster Pentium has won over many PC users, the 486 is still in demand in budget-minded markets such as education. To keep up with demand — AMD ships about 10 million chips a year — in 1995 the company opened a $1.2 billion wafer "megafab" in Austin, Texas.

California-based AMD, the US's #4 maker of integrated circuits, also manufactures memory products, programmable logic devices, and circuits for telecommunications and networking applications. The company is preparing to release a 586 chip, called the K5, that will compete with Pentium and PowerPC chips.

Flash memories used in cellular phones, SCSI disk drives, and networking equipment are another growth area for AMD. In 1994 the company began production of flash memory products at its new Japanese plant, a joint venture with Fujitsu.

AMD spent over 13% of 1994 revenues on R&D. Late that year the company started using 0.5-micron technology, a miniaturized production standard that increased Am486 production capacity by more than 50%.

After nearly a decade of legal wrangling over intellectual property rights, in early 1995 AMD and Intel (the #1 chip maker) settled their differences. Each side agreed to pay damages, and AMD won a perpetual license to the microcode in Intel's 386 and 486 chips.

WHEN

A new management team at Silicon Valley powerhouse Fairchild Camera pushed aside 30-year-old marketing whiz Jerry Sanders, reportedly firing him for wearing a pink shirt while making a sales call on IBM. After considering his options, in 1969 he decided to start up a semiconductor company, just as his former boss, Intel founder Robert Noyce, had done a year earlier.

Unlike Noyce, Sanders had no general management experience and was unable to raise the large amounts of capital required to engage in semiconductor R&D. So he built AMD by securing 2nd-source agreements (licenses to manufacture products designed by other chip makers) and by employing his marketing flair. The company went public in 1972 and received a $30 million cash infusion in 1977 when Siemens, anxious to get its foot in the door of the US semiconductor market, bought nearly 20% of AMD. In 1982 the company inked a 2nd-source deal with Intel, enabling AMD to manufacture exact copies of Intel's iAPX86 line of microprocessors, the "brains" of IBM and IBM-compatible PCs.

Aided by soaring demand for semiconductors in the mid-1980s, AMD became one of the nation's fastest-growing companies and began developing its own chips.

But AMD was slow to adopt key new products and technologies, including customizable gate array chips and CMOS (complementary metal oxide semiconductor) production technology, and was set back further when a group of CMOS engineers left to start Cypress Semiconductor in 1982. When prices for its old Intel microprocessor clones fell, the company

initiated a series of plant closures and announced its first layoffs in 1986. The next year AMD bought programmable logic chip maker Monolithic Memories and began legal action against Intel for breaking the 1982 agreement for AMD to 2nd-source Intel's new 386 chips.

In 1990 Intel sued for copyright infringement when AMD introduced a version of Intel's 287 math coprocessor. Taking a swipe at Intel, Sanders sent prospective buyers Monopoly game sets as AMD released a 386 clone of its own design the following year, prompting Intel to sue for copyright infringement. AMD released its 486 clone in 1993, triggering another lawsuit by Intel.

In 1992, to finance the construction of a chip production facility in Austin, Texas, AMD sold its 5.5% stake in Xilinx.

AMD signed a technology pact to develop microprocessors with Hewlett-Packard in 1993. The company also formed a joint venture with Fujitsu to develop, produce, and market flash memory devices. As part of the deal, Fujitsu and AMD acquired minority stakes in each other's companies.

In 1994 a federal jury handed down a decision in AMD's favor in the 287 math coprocessor case. That same year AMD agreed to sell its Am486 chip to Compaq (one of Intel's biggest microchip customers).

In 1995 AMD and Cyrix codeveloped a proposed industry standard that makes it easier to manufacture computers based on microprocessors made by different companies. The new "programmable interrupt controller technology" would replace the patented Intel standard now widely used.

WHO

Chairman and CEO: W. Jeremiah "Jerry" Sanders III, age 58, $2,856,675 pay
VC: Anthony B. Holbrook, age 55, $1,278,823 pay
President and COO: Richard Previte, age 60, $1,856,250 pay
SVP and Chief Marketing Executive: Stephen J. Zelencik, age 60, $963,091 pay
SVP, CFO, and Treasurer: Marvin D. Burkett, age 52, $862,129 pay
SVP Operations: Eugene D. Conner, age 51, $841,425 pay
SVP Human Resources: Stanley Winvick, age 55
Group VP, Microprocessor Products: John Bourgoin
Group VP, Non-Volatile Memory and Programmable Logic: Richard Forte
Group VP, Applications Solutions Products: Terryll R. Smith
VP, General Counsel, and Secretary: Thomas M. McCoy, age 44
Auditors: Ernst & Young LLP

WHERE

HQ: One AMD Place, Sunnyvale, CA 94088-3453
Phone: 408-732-2400
Fax: 408-982-6164

AMD has US manufacturing facilities in California and Texas and overseas manufacturing facilities in Japan, Malaysia, Singapore, Thailand, and the UK.

	1994 Sales		1994 Operating Income	
	$ mil.	% of total	$ mil.	% of total
US	1,524	71	467	91
Europe	484	23	16	3
Asia	127	6	30	6
Total	**2,135**	**100**	**513**	**100**

WHAT

Selected Products

CPU and Embedded Microprocessors
Am386 series (clone of Intel 386 microprocessor) CPU
Am486 series (clone of Intel 486 microprocessor) CPU
Am29000 reduced instruction set computer (RISC) microprocessor
Am29200 RISC series microcontroller
AMD K5 (Windows-compatible superscalar RISC microprocessor)

Network and Voice/Data Communications Products
Ethernet local-area network (LAN) devices
PCnet-ISA controller chip for Ethernet LANs
PhoX controller chip for digital cordless telephones
SLAC analog/digital converters for telephone voice signals
SLIC telephone digital switching interface

Nonvolatile Memory Devices
Erasable programmable read-only memories (EPROMs), from 64k to 4 megabits
ExpressROM
FLASH (nonvolatile read/write) memories
One-time programmable EPROMs

Programmable Logic Devices
MACH series of high-speed, high-density programmable logic devices

KEY COMPETITORS

Altera	IBM	NEC
Apple	Intel	Oki
Atmel	LG Group	Philips
Chips and	LSI Logic	Samsung
Technologies	Matsushita	Sharp
Cirrus Logic	Micron	Texas
Cyrix	Technology	Instruments
Daewoo	Mitsubishi	Toshiba
Fujitsu	Motorola	VLSI Technology
Hitachi	National	Xilinx
Hyundai	Semiconductor	Zilog

HOW MUCH

	9-Year Growth	1985	1986	1987	1988	1989	1990	1991	1992	1993	1994
Sales ($ mil.)	15.7%	576	632	997	1,126	1,105	1,059	1,227	1,515	1,648	2,135
Net income ($ mil.)	—	(37)	(96)	(48)	19	46	(54)	145	245	229	295
Income as % of sales	—	—	—	—	1.7%	4.2%	—	11.8%	16.2%	13.9%	13.8%
Earnings per share ($)	—	(0.65)	(1.66)	(0.72)	0.11	0.44	(0.78)	1.52	2.49	2.24	2.92
Stock price – high ($)	—	36.38	33.50	24.88	16.88	10.50	11.38	17.75	21.50	32.88	31.75
Stock price – low ($)	—	22.13	12.88	7.50	7.13	7.13	3.63	4.00	7.38	17.00	16.75
Stock price – close ($)	(1.7%)	29.00	13.75	9.88	8.63	7.88	4.88	17.50	18.13	17.75	24.88
P/E – high	—	—	—	—	154	24	—	12	9	15	11
P/E – low	—	—	—	—	65	16	—	3	3	8	6
Dividends per share ($)	—	0.00	0.00	0.00	0.00	0.00	0.00	0.00	0.75	0.00	0.00
Book value per share ($)	11.5%	6.81	8.11	8.41	8.07	8.51	7.73	9.32	11.86	14.63	18.19
Employees	(2.9%)	15,299	13,689	10,597	14,817	13,072	11,997	11,254	11,554	12,065	11,793

1994 Year-end:
Debt ratio: 7.3%
Return on equity: 19.1%
Cash (mil.): $378
Current ratio: 1.67
Long-term debt (mil.): $76
No. of shares (mil.): 95
Dividends
  Yield: —
  Payout: —
Market value (mil.): $2,374

Stock Price History High/Low 1985–94

AETNA LIFE AND CASUALTY COMPANY

OVERVIEW

Aetna has returned to the black after years of falling earnings that ended in a 1993 loss. But much of the improvement is the result of stringent cost control measures rather than increased business in the company's primary lines of business.

Aetna sells life, group health, and property/casualty insurance and financial services, including pension management, to corporations, public and private organizations, and individuals. It has exited such diverse areas as auto insurance (in many states), individual health insurance, and reinsurance.

Aetna's health and medical plans are the brightest part of the company's financial picture and represent an area earmarked for further development. The company is acquiring medical practices in order to build a network of HMOs.

Property/casualty results, on the other hand, have been lackluster for years because of both the pitfalls of writing auto insurance and the great number of natural disasters such as floods, hurricanes, and earthquakes (liabilities due to the Northridge earthquake of 1994 continue to build as previously undiscovered structural damage to buildings is reported). In addition, Aetna has been increasing its loss reserves for asbestos and other potential environmental liabilities.

WHEN

Hartford businessman and judge Eliphalet Bulkeley started Connecticut Mutual Life Insurance, a mutual company owned by policyholders, in 1846. The next year he was overthrown by agents who gained control of the company.

In 1853 Bulkeley and a group of Hartford businessmen founded Aetna Life Insurance as a spinoff of Aetna Fire Insurance. Aetna's early growth is attributed to Dr. Thomas Lacey, a former Aetna medical examiner, who became known in the late 1800s as the "father" of Aetna's system for enlisting agents around the US to sell policies.

In the 1860s Aetna expanded by offering a participating life policy (developed by Aetna's 2nd president, Thomas Enders), which returned dividends to policyholders based on investment earnings. This policy allowed the company to compete with mutual life insurance companies. In 1868 Aetna was the first company to offer renewable-term life policies.

Morgan Bulkeley, son of Eliphalet, became president in 1879 and served for 43 years. Aetna began to offer multiple lines by introducing accident insurance in 1891, health insurance in 1899, workers' compensation in 1902, and automobile and other property insurance in 1907. Bulkeley increased Aetna's visibility by serving as mayor of Hartford, as governor of Connecticut, and as a US senator, all the while remaining Aetna's president (which would now be considered unethical).

By 1920 Aetna had added ocean marine and inland marine insurance, and by 1922 it was the largest multiple-line insurance group in the nation. Aetna's non–life insurance companies, particularly the automobile line, expanded too fast during the 1920s, threatening Aetna's solvency. The company survived the Depression by restricting underwriting and reestablishing sufficient reserves.

After World War II the company expanded into group life, health, and accident insurance. In 1967 it reorganized into a holding company, Aetna Life and Casualty.

In the 1960s and 1970s Aetna continued to expand its multiple lines of insurance. In the 1980s it caught the M&A fever, making such ill-advised purchases as oil-services firm Geosource (1982; sold at a loss in 1984) and Federated Investors (1982; sold in 1989 to Federated management) and investing heavily in commercial real estate. Then the boom went bust.

Since 1991 Aetna has continuously reorganized itself and has also withdrawn from some lines of insurance. In 1992 the company paid Massachusetts $87 million for the privilege of abandoning its auto insurance business there. It has withdrawn from auto insurance in 28 states because the business is too costly. Aetna also sold its profitable American Reinsurance Co. to KKR, but the sale yielded less than anticipated.

By 1993 the company had begun to see savings from the elimination of more than 4,000 jobs since 1990. But it was not enough, and the next year saw another 4,000 jobs cut.

In 1994 Aetna closed a long chapter by agreeing to pay customers $31 million in rebates and refunds demanded by the state of California after the 1988 approval of Proposition 103, which called for rate rollbacks.

As part of Aetna's effort to boost its pension services, in 1995 Aetna received permission to set up a bank, AE Trust Co., which will allow the bank to act as a pension trustee.

NYSE symbol: AET
Fiscal year ends: December 31

WHO

Chairman, President, and CEO: Ronald E. Compton, age 62, $1,075,000 pay
VC Strategy and Finance: Richard L. Huber, age 58
EVP Investments/Financial Services: Daniel P. Kearney, age 55, $700,000 pay
EVP Health/Group Life: James W. McLane, age 56, $700,000 pay
EVP Property/Casualty: Gary G. Benanav, age 49, $580,000 pay
SVP and General Counsel: Zoë Baird, age 42, $575,000 pay
SVP Finance and Corporate Controller: Robert E. Broatch, age 46
SVP Federal Government Relations: Vanda B. McMurtry, age 45
SVP Human Resources: Mary Ann Champlin, age 47
VP and Senior Corporate Actuary: Brian E. Scott
Auditors: KPMG Peat Marwick LLP

WHERE

HQ: 151 Farmington Ave., Hartford, CT 06156
Phone: 203-273-0123
Fax: 203-275-2677

WHAT

	1994 Assets	
	$ mil.	% of total
Cash & equivalents	2,954	3
Government securities	12,556	13
Mortgage-backed securities	6,722	7
Corporate bonds	13,689	15
Mortgage & policy loans	12,377	13
Separate accounts	24,123	26
Other	21,752	23
Total	**94,173**	**100**

	1994 Sales		1994 Net Income	
	$ mil.	% of total	$ mil.	% of total
Health plans	7,139	41	342	50
Property/casualty	5,339	31	58	9
Pensions	2,355	13	54	8
International	1,297	7	71	10
Life & annuity	1,404	8	159	23
Other	—	—	(218)	—
Total	**17,534**	**100**	**468**	**100**

Product Lines
Annuities
Life, health, and disability insurance
Managed health care
Pension plan services
Property/casualty insurance

KEY COMPETITORS

AFLAC	Lincoln National
Allianz	Lloyd's of London
Allstate	Loews
American Financial	MassMutual
B.A.T	MetLife
Berkshire Hathaway	Nationwide Insurance
Blue Cross	New York Life
Chubb	Northwestern Mutual
CIGNA	Oxford Health Plans
Equitable	PacifiCare
Farmers Group	Prudential
Foundation	Qual-Med
Health	Sierra Health Services
GEICO	State Farm
General Electric	Teachers Insurance
General Re	Textron
Guardian Life Insurance	Tokio Marine and Fire
ITT Hartford	Transamerica
John Hancock	Travelers
Kaiser Foundation	UniHealth America
Health Plan	USAA
Liberty Mutual	USF&G

HOW MUCH

	9-Year Growth	1985	1986	1987	1988	1989	1990	1991	1992	1993	1994
Assets ($ mil.)	5.5%	58,294	66,830	72,754	81,415	87,099	89,301	91,988	89,928	100,037	94,173
Net income ($ mil.)	0.9%	430	714	867	699	639	614	505	169	(588)	468
Income as % of assets	—	0.7%	1.1%	1.2%	0.9%	0.7%	0.7%	0.5%	0.2%	—	0.5%
Earnings per share ($)	0.8%	3.84	6.18	7.48	6.12	5.69	5.52	4.59	1.18	(5.30)	4.14
Stock price – high ($)	—	53.50	66.25	68.25	52.50	62.50	58.38	49.13	48.88	66.25	65.75
Stock price – low ($)	—	36.13	52.25	43.75	39.50	46.63	29.00	31.88	38.00	43.38	42.25
Stock price – close ($)	(1.4%)	53.50	56.38	45.25	47.25	56.50	39.00	44.00	46.50	60.38	47.13
P/E – high	—	14	11	9	9	11	11	11	41	—	16
P/E – low	—	9	9	6	7	8	5	7	32	—	10
Dividends per share ($)	0.5%	2.64	2.64	2.73	2.76	2.76	2.76	2.76	2.76	2.76	2.76
Book value per share ($)	1.8%	41.52	48.81	53.56	58.11	61.94	64.23	67.09	65.64	62.77	48.85
Employees	0.0%	41,000	45,100	43,900	45,100	45,500	47,100	48,300	43,000	42,600	40,900

1994 Year-end:
Equity as % of assets: 5.8%
Return on assets: 0.5%
Return on equity: 7.5%
Long-term debt (mil.): $1,115
No. of shares (mil.): 113
Dividends
  Yield: 5.9%
  Payout: 66.7%
Market value (mil.): $5,310
Sales (mil.): $17,534

**Stock Price History
High/Low 1985–94**

AFLAC INCORPORATED

OVERVIEW

AFLAC is the leading seller of supplemental medical insurance in both the US and Japan, with more than 38 million policyholders. The Columbus, Georgia–based company sells policies designed to take up the slack in other insurance policies when the insured needs intensive care, long-term (nursing home) care, in-home care, or simply a Medicare supplement. But the company's underlying philosophy, "All insurance is sold on fear," applies particularly to its first (and for 30 years only) product — cancer insurance. It also owns 7 TV stations, in smaller markets in the US, that are leaders in their areas.

Although AFLAC is based in the US, it does most of its business (84% in 1994) in Japan. AFLAC's primary sales tool there is an agency system in which a corporation forms a subsidiary to sell AFLAC's insurance to its employees. Its US approach, known as cluster selling, is similar in that it sells to individuals through their places of employment and may deduct premiums from the payroll.

Since the mid-1980s AFLAC has attempted to increase its US business, offering a wider variety of products (covering intensive care and long-term care) and embarking on a national advertising campaign.

WHEN

American Family Life Assurance Co. (AFLAC) was founded in Columbus, Georgia, in 1955 by brothers William, John, and Paul Amos to sell life, health, and accident insurance. In the mid-1950s, with Americans expanding into the suburbs, competition was fierce, and the little company did poorly.

With the company nearing bankruptcy, the brothers looked for a special niche. Taking their cue from the polio scares of the 1940s and 1950s, which had spawned specialty insurance against that disease, the Amoses decided to sell cancer insurance. In 1958 they introduced the world's first cancer expense policy. It was a hit; by 1959 the company had written nearly a million dollars in premiums and expanded across state lines.

The company grew quickly during the 1960s, especially after developing its cluster selling approach, in which it made presentations to groups of employees at their workplaces. The advantage of this system was that the employer was usually willing to make payroll deductions, thus saving AFLAC the expense of billing and processing individual payments. By 1971 the company was operating in 42 states.

While traveling in Japan in 1970, John decided to market his supplemental cancer coverage to the Japanese, whose national health care plan left them exposed to considerable expense from cancer treatment. Becoming licensed to sell insurance in Japan took 4 years, but the company was ultimately successful, in part because it did not represent a threat to any existing market in Japan and also because the Amoses found backing from notables in the Japanese insurance and medical industries. In 1974 AFLAC received an

8-year monopoly on cancer insurance, thus becoming the 2nd non-Japanese company to sell insurance there.

In 1973 AFLAC reorganized as a holding company and began buying television stations in the South and Midwest.

The 1980s were marked by US and state government inquiries into dread disease insurance, which many believed to be of poor value, being too expensive in relation to its benefits and covering only one disease. Yet demand for such insurance increased, bringing other companies into the US market. As AFLAC's US sales flattened in the 1980s, they grew in Japan; soon Japanese sales accounted for most of the company's revenues. Attempts to sell the insurance in the UK and Australia failed.

The company avoided the common insurance pitfall of the 1980s — making risky investments — and kept its US operations well capitalized. Meanwhile, it developed expertise in the Japanese financial markets to increase its reserves in Japan.

In 1990 John Amos died of cancer and was replaced as CEO by his nephew Dan. In 1992 the company officially renamed itself AFLAC (partly because Dan planned to increase the company's US profile and was advised that hundreds of insurance companies began with the word "American").

AFLAC has fought falling interest in cancer insurance by introducing new products and improving old ones in order to encourage policyholders to add on or trade up.

The dollar's fall against the yen in 1995 meant that AFLAC could get more dollars for its Japanese profits (when it repatriated the money), which it then invested in the more buoyant US financial markets.

WHO

Chairman: Paul S. Amos, age 68, $1,862,670 pay
VC and CEO: Daniel P. Amos, age 43, $1,725,820 pay
Chairman, AFLAC Japan; VC, AFLAC International, Inc.: Yoshiki Otake, age 55, $964,260 pay
EVP, CFO, and Treasurer: Kriss Cloninger III, age 47, $554,007 pay
EVP: E. Stephen Purdom, age 47
President, AFLAC Japan: Hidefumi Matsui, age 50, $525,549 pay
President, AFLAC International, Inc.: Minoru Nakai, age 53
President, AFLAC Broadcast Division: Thomas L. Paul, age 65
SVP, General Counsel, and Corporate Secretary: Joey M. Loudermilk, age 41
VP Human Resources: Ann B. Henderson
Auditors: KPMG Peat Marwick LLP

WHERE

HQ: 1932 Wynnton Rd., Columbus, GA 31999
Phone: 706-323-3431
Fax: 706-324-6330

AFLAC conducts business throughout the US and its territories and in Canada, Japan, and Taiwan.

	1994 Sales $ mil.	% of total	1994 Pretax Income $ mil.	% of total
Insurance in Japan	5,150	84	471	82
Insurance in US	875	14	89	16
Other operations	123	2	13	2
Adjustments	(37)	—	(69)	—
Total	**6,111**	**100**	**504**	**100**

WHAT

	1994 Assets $ mil.	% of total
Cash & equivalents	18	0
¥-based: Govt. securities	6,703	33
Utility bonds	2,723	13
Corporate bonds	4,166	21
US $–based: govt. bonds	482	2
Corporate bonds	1,434	7
Other investments	1,000	5
Deferred assets	2,403	12
Other	1,358	7
Total	**20,287**	**100**

	1994 Sales $ mil.	% of total
Premiums	5,181	84
Net investments	839	14
Other	91	2
Total	**6,111**	**100**

Insurance Products
Cancer expense insurance
Life insurance
Long-term care insurance
Supplemental care insurance
Supplemental medical expense plans

Television Stations
KFVS (Cape Girardeau, MO)
KWWL (Waterloo, IA)
WAFB (Baton Rouge, LA)
WAFF (Huntsville, AL)
WITN (Washington, NC)
WTOC (Savannah, GA)
WTVM (Columbus, GA)

KEY COMPETITORS

Aetna
American Medical Security
Capitol American Financial
CIGNA
Equitable
John Hancock
MassMutual
MetLife
Nationwide Insurance
New York Life
Northwestern Mutual
Prudential
Transamerica
United HealthCare

HOW MUCH

	9-Year Growth	1985	1986	1987	1988	1989	1990	1991	1992	1993	1994
Assets ($ mil.)	27.5%	2,271	3,302	5,031	6,074	6,515	8,035	10,145	11,901	15,423	20,287
Net income ($ mil.)	20.7%	54	78	93	109	81	117	149	183	244	293
Income as % of assets	—	2.4%	2.4%	1.9%	1.8%	1.2%	1.5%	1.5%	1.5%	1.6%	1.4%
Earnings per share ($)	20.3%	0.54	0.78	0.93	1.08	0.80	1.15	1.46	1.79	2.32	2.84
Stock price – high ($)	—	9.35	14.95	14.80	13.60	18.00	15.40	24.90	27.90	34.00	36.13
Stock price – low ($)	—	4.58	8.30	7.90	9.20	10.70	9.70	14.30	19.20	24.75	25.25
Stock price – close ($)	16.2%	8.30	10.40	11.30	11.00	14.40	15.30	23.90	27.60	28.50	32.00
P/E – high	—	17	19	16	13	23	13	17	16	15	13
P/E – low	—	9	11	9	9	13	8	10	11	11	9
Dividends per share ($)	13.9%	0.14	0.17	0.18	0.20	0.23	0.26	0.30	0.34	0.39	0.45
Book value per share ($)	20.0%	3.40	4.44	5.43	6.34	6.91	7.77	9.03	10.48	13.20	17.58
Employees	5.8%	2,600	—	3,247	3,259	3,005	3,150	3,318	3,618	3,902	4,321

1994 Year-end:
Equity as % of assets: 8.6%
Return on assets: 1.6%
Return on equity: 18.8%
Long-term debt (mil.): $185
No. of shares (mil.): 100
Dividends
 Yield: 1.4%
 Payout: 15.7%
Market value (mil.): $3,189
Sales (mil.): $6,111

Stock Price History High/Low 1985–94

ALBERTSON'S, INC.

OVERVIEW

Like a runaway shopping cart, Albertson's capital expenditure machine continues to roll. The Boise, Idaho–based supermarket chain — the nation's 4th largest food and drug retailer — opened 55 new stores in 1994, spending $473 million on its expansion plans. The 720-store company plans even more such spending in 1995 and intends to pony up $3.4 billion for new stores, remodeling, upgraded distribution and information systems, and better store equipment by the year 2000, when it hopes to have more than 1,000 stores.

Albertson's operates 588 combination food and drug stores (35,000–75,000 square feet), 88 conventional grocery stores (15,000–35,000 square feet), and 44 warehouse stores (up to 73,000 square feet) in 19 western, midwestern, and southern states. The warehouse stores, most of which are named Max Food and Drug, are no-frills stores that emphasize discounted meat and produce.

By having its stores spread out over so many states, the company has achieved geographical diversity, which insulates it from regional troubles such as natural disasters, price wars, and labor strife. Albertson's has 11 distribution centers throughout its operating area. The company's stores are organized into 14 geographical divisions. With Albertson's entering the greater Houston area with 8 stores and a distribution center in 1995, the retailer's South Texas division (currently with 34 stores) is making a major expansion push.

J. B. Scott and 86-year-old Kathryn Albertson, company founder Joe Albertson's grandson and widow, own 11% of the company's stock. German investor Markus Stiftung owns about 11.5%.

WHEN

J. A. "Joe" Albertson left his position as district manager for Safeway in 1939 and opened his first food store, Albertson's Food Center, in Boise, Idaho. The store differed from others in that it covered 10,000 square feet — 8 times the competitors' average — and had plenty of free parking, an in-store butcher shop, a bakery, and an ice cream shop. With these innovations Joe Albertson was a key developer of the "supermarket" concept in food retailing.

Albertson's refined its supermarket concept further by opening its first combination food and drug store (1951), a 60,000-square-foot superstore, and by locating stores in growing suburban areas. Jonathan Scott, who became president of Albertson's in 1955, married Joe's daughter Barbara; though they divorced, Scott remained president until 1975. Albertson's went public to raise expansion capital in 1959 and by 1960 had 62 stores in Idaho, Washington, Oregon, and Utah. Albertson's acquired Greater All American Markets (1964), a grocery chain based in Downey, California, and Semrau & Sons (1965) of Oakland, which aided the company's thrust into the California market.

Salt Lake City–based drugstore chain Skaggs (now part of rival American Stores) and Albertson's formed a partnership in 1969 to jointly operate large Skaggs Albertson's food-and-drug combination stores.

In 1973 the company built its first full-line distribution facility in Brea, California, and opened an even larger facility in Salt Lake City in 1976. Albertson's and Skaggs dissolved their partnership in 1977, with each taking half of the units in the jointly owned chain. By 1986 the company had reached $5 billion in sales, a fivefold increase over 1975. Albertson's added a distribution facility in Denver in 1982 and its first mechanized distribution center, in Portland, Oregon, in 1988.

In 1990 the company started the HOPE (Helping Our Planet's Ecology) line of environmentally friendly paper products.

In 1992 the company made the largest acquisition in its history, purchasing 74 Jewel Osco combination food and drug stores (mostly in Arkansas, Florida, Oklahoma, and Texas) from American Stores. The company's founder, Joe Albertson, died in 1993 at age 86. In 1994, with the Plant City, Florida, distribution center becoming fully operational, Albertson's began servicing each of its retail stores from its own distribution centers.

Albertson's in 1995 signed a $1 billion, 5-year contract with pharmaceutical distributor McKesson. The contract covers both the supply and warehousing of products for Albertson's 455 pharmacies. Also in 1995 the company inked a 5-year pact with American Express's MoneyGram money wiring service, which will enable shoppers to send money to more than 17,500 locations in 80 countries. Albertson's initially tested the service in Denver, Las Vegas, and Southern California stores.

The company saw its 25th consecutive year of increased sales and earnings in 1995, as well as its 24th straight year of higher dividends for its stockholders.

WHO

Chairman and CEO: Gary G. Michael, age 54,
$983,100 pay
President and COO: John B. Carley, age 61,
$877,877 pay
Chairman of the Executive Committee: Warren E.
McCain, age 69, $500,000 pay
EVP Store Development: Michael F. Reuling, age 48
EVP Administration and General Counsel: Thomas R.
Saldin, age 48
SVP and Regional Manager: Ronald D. Walk, age 51,
$410,366 pay
SVP Corporate Merchandising: Carl W. Pennington,
age 57, $365,462 pay
SVP Finance and CFO: A. Craig Olson, age 53
SVP Distribution: Thomas E. Brother, age 53
SVP and Regional Manager: Richard L. King, age 45
SVP and Regional Manager: Allen R. Rowland, age 50
SVP Information Systems and Technology: Patrick S.
Steele, age 45
SVP Human Resources: Steven D. Young, age 46
Auditors: Deloitte & Touche LLP

WHERE

HQ: 250 Parkcenter Blvd., PO Box 20, Boise, ID 83726
Phone: 208-385-6200
Fax: 208-385-6349

The company operates 720 stores in 19 states in the
West, South, and Midwest. The chain has combination
food-drug stores located in all 19 states, conventional
stores located in 10 states, and warehouse stores located
in 6 states. Albertson's has 2 distribution centers in
Boise, Idaho, and one each in Brea, California; Denver;
Fort Worth, Texas; Phoenix; Plant City, Florida; Ponca
City, Oklahoma; Portland, Oregon; Sacramento,
California; and Salt Lake City.

	1995 Stores
	No.
California	161
Texas	128
Florida	82
Washington	71
Colorado	46
Oregon	46
Utah	33
Idaho	28
Arizona	24
Other states	101
Total	**720**

WHAT

	No. of Stores
Combination food & drug stores	588
Conventional supermarkets	88
Warehouse stores	44
Total	**720**

Selected Specialty Departments

Bakery	Pharmacy
Floral	Service delicatessen
Liquor	Service seafood and meat
Lobby/Video	

KEY COMPETITORS

American Stores	Kash n' Karry	Rite Aid
Associated Grocers	Food Stores	Safeway
Bruno's	Kmart	Smith's Food &
Certified Grocers	Kroger	Drug
Fiesta Mart	Longs	Stater Bros.
Eckerd	Melville	Thrifty PayLess
Fleming	Price/Costco	Vons
Food Lion	Publix	Walgreen
Fred Meyer	Pueblo Xtra	Wal-Mart
Giant Food	Raley's	Winn-Dixie
Great A&P	Randall's	Yucaipa
H. E. Butt	Revco	

HOW MUCH

	9-Year Growth	1986	1987	1988	1989	1990	1991	1992	1993	1994	1995
Sales ($ mil.)	10.0%	5,060	5,380	5,869	6,773	7,423	8,219	8,681	10,174	11,284	11,895
Net income ($ mil.)	19.3%	85	100	125	163	197	234	258	276	340	417
Income as % of sales	—	1.7%	1.9%	2.1%	2.4%	2.6%	2.8%	3.0%	2.7%	3.0%	3.5%
Earnings per share ($)[1]	19.6%	0.33	0.38	0.47	0.61	0.74	0.88	0.97	1.05	1.34	1.65
Stock price – high ($)[1]	—	4.16	6.19	8.50	9.69	15.06	18.88	25.69	26.69	29.69	30.88
Stock price – low ($)[1]	—	3.30	3.81	5.06	6.00	9.16	12.19	16.31	18.38	23.38	25.13
Stock price – close ($)[1]	24.4%	4.06	5.38	6.34	9.47	13.88	18.25	19.63	25.25	26.75	29.00
P/E – high	—	13	16	18	16	20	22	27	25	22	19
P/E – low	—	10	10	11	10	12	14	17	18	17	15
Dividends per share ($)	17.3%	0.10	0.11	0.12	0.14	0.19	0.23	0.27	0.31	0.35	0.42
Book value per share ($)	14.6%	1.95	2.22	2.51	2.99	3.47	4.06	4.54	5.25	5.48	6.65
Employees	8.3%	37,000	40,000	43,000	50,000	55,000	58,000	60,000	71,000	75,000	76,000

1995 Year-end:
Debt ratio: 29.9%
Return on equity: 27.1%
Cash (mil.): $50
Current ratio: 1.09
Long-term debt (mil.): $512
No. of shares (mil.): 254
Dividends
  Yield: 1.4%
  Payout: 25.5%
Market value (mil.): $7,366

**Stock Price History[1]
High/Low 1986–95**

[1] Stock prices are for the prior calendar year.

ALCO STANDARD CORPORATION

OVERVIEW

Alco Standard packs a one-two punch of wholesale paper distribution and specialty paper conversion, and the sale, lease, and servicing of office equipment.

Its paper division, Unisource Worldwide, is the largest wholesale paper distribution network in the US and sells papers for printing, industrial, and food service applications. It accounts for almost 72% of Alco's sales and just under half of its operating income. Alco Office Products sells and leases copiers, fax machines, and other office equipment in the US and Canada. A European subsidiary, Erskine House, is the largest independent copier dealer in Great Britain.

Alco Standard has a voracious appetite for acquiring other companies. In 1994 its office products division swallowed up 45 North American companies representing more than $200 million in annual revenues. Erskine House got into the shopping spree in Europe, buying 2 UK companies which, together with companies in Denmark, France, and Germany, pushed Alco's European office products business to more than $150 million in annual revenues.

The company's office products growth, particularly that of its servicing operations, is also being driven by the price decline in photocopiers (making them more available to a larger consumer base) and by the growing popularity of fax machines.

Unisource is no slouch when it comes to acquisitions either. Having paused in 1994 to assimilate the 25 separate companies that it had acquired in recent years, Unisource for 1995 has earmarked for acquisition companies worth $350 million in annual revenues.

WHEN

Tinkham Veale II, a mechanical engineer from Cleveland, Ohio, in 1941 married the daughter of A. C. Ernst of the Ernst & Ernst accounting firm. Ernst helped Veale buy a stake in an engineered goods manufacturer, which prospered during WWII. Veale retired at age 37 to breed and race horses. He invested his earnings, became a millionaire by 1951, and joined the board of Alco Oil and Chemical (formerly Rainbow Production Company). In 1960 Veale and his associates formed a holding company, V & V Associates, and bought a large minority share in Alco.

Alco (renamed Alco Chemical in 1962) acquired 4 fertilizer companies and in 1965 (renamed Alco Standard) merged with V & V, which had bought stakes in several machinery producers. Veale then implemented the partnership strategy that would serve the company for 25 years: he bought small, privately owned companies, usually in exchange for cash and Alco Standard stock, and let the owners continue to run them. By 1968 Alco Standard had bought 52 companies in this way and had branched into electrical, metallurgical, and distribution businesses.

Alco Standard expanded into coal mining in the 1970s by acquiring several Appalachian coal properties. The company bought several paper distributors in the 1970s and formed a national paper distributor called Unisource. The division's profitability prompted Alco Standard to enter other distribution businesses, including pharmaceuticals, hospital supplies, steel products, auto parts, food service equipment, and liquor. By 1981 distribution provided 60% of the company's earnings and 75% of sales.

Veale had also acquired several manufacturers (plastics, machinery, rubber, and chemicals), but they had not grown as rapidly as the distribution businesses. In 1984 he merged the manufacturers into Alco Industries and sold the new company to its managers while retaining a minority stake. Alco Standard continued to buy distributors, such as Saxon Industries (1984), an international paper seller valued at $378 million.

In 1986 Ray Mundt (Veale's successor as chairman) switched the company's focus to office products and paper distribution, cutting 7 divisions, including health services and ice cream.

In August 1993 John Stuart succeeded Mundt as CEO. In June 1994 Stuart assumed additional duties as acting president of Unisource, overseeing a restructuring that is expected to be completed by the fall of 1996. Although a 1992 joint venture with European company IMM Office Systems (IMMOS) didn't work out, Alco did not walk away empty-handed; the dissolution agreement gave it 2 IMMOS subsidiaries, Denmark-based Eskofot and France-based STR.

In 1995 Alco Standard made a $129 million offer to acquire Southern Business Group PLC, a copier-distribution and service company based in the UK.

WHO

Chairman: Ray B. Mundt, age 66, $1,640,000 pay
VC: William F. Drake Jr., age 62
President and CEO: John E. Stuart, age 50, $1,400,000 pay
EVP: Hugh G. Moulton, age 61, $600,000 pay
EVP and CFO: Kurt Dinkelacker, age 41, $600,000 pay
VP; President, Alco Office Products: James E. Head, age 49, $600,000 pay
VP Finance: O. Gordon Brewer Jr., age 57
VP and Treasurer: Kathleen M. Burns, age 42
VP, General Counsel, and Secretary: J. Kenneth Croney, age 52
VP and Controller: Michael J. Dillon, age 41
VP Tax: Stephen K. Deay, age 47
VP Financial Operations Support: William M. Laughlin, age 52
VP EVP Canadian Operations, Unisource: Raymond A. Peterson
Director, Corporate Management Information Systems and Human Resources: Elizabeth H. Barrett
Auditors: Ernst & Young LLP

WHERE

HQ: PO Box 834, Valley Forge, PA 19482
Phone: 610-296-8000
Fax: 610-296-8419

Alco Standard has operations in 47 states, Canada, and Europe.

	1994 Sales		1994 Operating Income	
	$ mil.	% of total	$ mil.	% of total
US	7,154	89	333	92
International	843	11	29	8
Adjustments	(1)	—	—	—
Total	**7,996**	**100**	**362**	**100**

WHAT

	1994 Sales		1994 Operating Income	
	$ mil.	% of total	$ mil.	% of total
Paper products	5,757	72	163	45
Office products	2,240	28	199	55
Adjustments	(1)	—	—	—
Total	**7,996**	**100**	**362**	**100**

Paper Products (Unisource)
Copy paper
Envelopes
Food-service paper and plastic
Industrial, janitorial, and packaging paper
Packaging tape and tape-dispensing equipment
Printing and publishing paper
Writing paper

Office Products and Services (Alco)
Facsimile machine sales, rental, and leasing
Office equipment service and supplies
Photocopier sales, rental, and leasing
Photocopying facilities management

Major Subsidiaries
Alco Office Products
Unisource

KEY COMPETITORS

Boise Cascade
Canadian Pacific
Champion International
Copifax
Eastman Kodak
Fletcher Challenge
Fuji Photo
Georgia-Pacific
Harris Corp.
James River
Kimberly-Clark
Matsushita
3M
Minolta
Office Depot
Office Max
Pitney Bowes
Scott
Staples
Stone Container
Weyerhaeuser
Xerox

HOW MUCH

	9-Year Growth	1985	1986	1987	1988	1989	1990	1991	1992	1993	1994
Sales ($ mil.)	8.5%	3,823	4,323	3,633	3,817	4,146	4,320	4,758	4,921	6,445	7,996
Net income ($ mil.)	3.6%	51	57	80	110	171	106	118	96	(9)	59
Income as % of sales	—	1.3%	1.3%	2.2%	2.9%	4.1%	2.5%	2.5%	2.0%	—	0.7%
Earnings per share ($)	(0.3%)	1.13	1.28	1.68	2.29	3.91	2.56	2.61	2.04	(0.20)	1.10
Stock price – high ($)	—	19.50	23.38	30.00	28.00	36.63	37.88	35.88	42.63	54.75	69.50
Stock price – low ($)	—	15.06	17.75	15.25	20.25	25.38	27.63	29.00	33.13	35.75	49.50
Stock price – close ($)	14.2%	19.06	20.94	20.38	27.88	34.50	33.13	34.25	36.38	54.75	62.75
P/E – high	—	17	18	18	12	9	15	14	21	—	60
P/E – low	—	13	14	9	9	7	11	11	16	—	45
Dividends per share ($)	5.8%	0.60	0.62	0.64	0.68	0.76	0.84	0.88	0.92	0.96	1.00
Book value per share ($)	8.3%	10.45	10.48	12.78	14.01	14.76	16.77	18.40	18.73	17.52	21.44
Employees	5.8%	18,400	18,700	17,300	17,300	19,800	20,900	18,800	23,500	28,500	30,600

1994 Year-end:
Debt ratio: 24.6%
Return on equity: 4.9%
Cash (mil.): $53
Current ratio: 1.62
Long-term debt (mil.): $341
No. of shares (mil.): 54
Dividends
　Yield: 1.6%
　Payout: 90.0%
Market value (mil.): $3,417

**Stock Price History
High/Low 1985–94**

ALLIEDSIGNAL INC.

OVERVIEW

AlliedSignal finally has it together, thanks to CEO Lawrence Bossidy, who took over in 1991. Bossidy (*Financial World's* 1994 CEO of the year) trimmed unprofitable businesses while slashing employee and supplier rosters. For the first time in 7 years, in 1994 each of the Morristown, New Jersey–based company's 3 segments — Aerospace, Automotive, and Engineered Materials — had increased sales.

In 1994 and 1995 Allied continued to grow its core businesses through acquisitions and joint ventures. Acquisitions in 1994 included Ford Motor Company's UK spark plug operations and Textron's Lycoming Turbine Engine Division. The following year the company added Fiat Auto's braking business in Poland and the wheel and brake division of the Budd

Co. Joint ventures include an airline maintenance center with TAECO (Hong Kong), manufacturing agreements for auto safety equipment with Jay Bharat Group (India), an auto safety radar system with Amerigon (US), and civilian aircraft parts with Aviation Corp. Rubin (Russia).

Attracted by Asia's high-growth potential, in 1994 Allied began building a $27 million truck engine turbocharger plant in Shanghai and pledged $100 million in investments in China. The following year Allied agreed to form a joint venture with China's 2nd largest car maker to produce hydraulic braking systems.

Nearly $9 million in stock options pushed Bossidy's salary to $12.4 million in 1994, making him the 6th-highest-paid CEO in the US.

WHEN

During WWI Germany controlled much of the world's chemical industry, causing shortages of such commodities as dyes and drugs. In response, in 1920 *Washington Post* publisher Eugene Meyer and scientist William Nichols organized the Allied Chemical & Dye Corporation from 5 existing companies.

In 1928 Allied opened a synthetic ammonia plant near Hopewell, Virginia, becoming the world's leading producer of ammonia. This represented the company's earliest venture into new markets. After WWII Allied began manufacturing other new products, including nylon 6 (for making everything from tires to clothes) and refrigerants. In 1958 it became Allied Chemical Corporation.

In 1962 Allied bought Union Texas Natural Gas, which owned oil and gas properties throughout the Americas. Allied regarded it mainly as a supplier of raw materials for its chemical products, but this changed in the early 1970s when CEO John Connor (secretary of commerce under Lyndon Johnson) sold many of Allied's unprofitable businesses and invested in oil and gas exploration. By 1979, when Edward Hennessy Jr. became CEO, Union Texas produced 80% of Allied's income.

Through purchases directed by Hennessy, Allied entered new fields, including electronics (Eltra, 1979; Bunker Ramo, 1981) and health and scientific products (Fisher Scientific, 1981). Under its new name, Allied Corporation (1981), the company went on to buy the Bendix Corporation, an aerospace and automotive company, in 1983. By 1984 Bendix generated 50% of Allied's income, while oil and gas generated 38%.

In 1985 Allied merged with the Signal Companies to form Allied-Signal (which changed its name to AlliedSignal in 1993). Founded by Sam Mosher in 1922 as the Signal Gasoline Company, Signal originally produced gasoline from natural gas. In 1928 the company changed its name to Signal Oil & Gas, entering into oil production the same year. Signal merged with the Garrett Corporation, a Los Angeles–based aerospace company, in 1964; acquired Mack Trucks in 1967 (spun off 1983); and in 1968 adopted the Signal Companies as its corporate name. Signal bought the Ampex Corporation in 1981.

The addition of Signal's Garrett division to Bendix made aerospace Allied's largest business sector. In 1985 the company sold 50% of Union Texas, and in 1986 it spun off 35 mostly unprofitable chemical and engineering businesses. Hennessy sold 7 more businesses in 1987, leaving Allied in aerospace, auto parts, and chemicals.

In 1992 Allied bought Westinghouse Electric's copper-laminates business and sold its 39% stake in Union Texas through a public offering. The following year the company signed a deal with the Russian government to help convert weapons-grade uranium from Russia's surplus missiles. Allied constructed a new laminates plant in Thailand in 1994.

In 1994 and 1995 the company scored several major contracts, including advanced systems and products for Boeing's 777s, radar warning systems for Singapore Airlines, avionics and maintenance contracts for Southwest Airlines, and turbofan engines for Raytheon's Hawker aircraft.

NYSE symbol: ALD
Fiscal year ends: December 31

WHO

Chairman and CEO: Lawrence A. Bossidy, age 59,
$3,625,000 pay
EVP; President, AlliedSignal Engineered Materials:
Frederic M. Poses, age 52, $975,000 pay
EVP; President, AlliedSignal Aerospace:
Daniel P. Burnham, age 48, $806,670 pay
EVP; AlliedSignal Automotive: John W. Barter, age 48,
$802,500 pay (prior to promotion)
SVP and CFO: Richard Wallman, age 43
SVP, General Counsel, and Secretary: Peter M.
Kreindler, age 49, $725,000 pay
SVP and Chief Technology Officer: Isaac R. Barpal,
age 55
SVP International: Paul R. Schindler, age 53
SVP Quality and Productivity: James E. Sierk, age 56
SVP Public Affairs: David G. Powell, age 61
SVP Human Resources: Donald J. Redlinger,
age 50
VP Manufacturing: Richard P. Schroeder, age 43
VP Materials Management: Raymond C. Stark, age 52
Auditors: Price Waterhouse LLP

WHERE

HQ: 101 Columbia Rd., PO Box 4000, Morristown, NJ
07962-2497
Phone: 201-455-2000
Fax: 201-455-4807

AlliedSignal has 383 facilities in 40 countries.

	1994 Sales		1994 Net Income	
	$ mil.	% of total	$ mil.	% of total
US	9,739	76	654	86
Europe	2,283	18	65	9
Canada	202	1	23	3
Other regions	593	5	17	2
Total	**12,817**	**100**	**759**	**100**

WHAT

	1994 Sales		1994 Net Income	
	$ mil.	% of total	$ mil.	% of total
Aerospace	4,623	36	260	32
Automotive	4,922	38	223	27
Engineered Matls.	3,272	26	331	41
Adjustments	—	—	(55)	—
Total	**12,817**	**100**	**759**	**100**

Principal Business Areas

Aerospace
Aerospace Equipment Systems
AlliedSignal Engines
Commercial Avionics Systems
Government Electronic Systems

Automotive
Automotive aftermarket
Braking systems
Engine components
Safety restraint systems

Engineered Materials
Fibers
Fluorine Products
Laminate Systems
Performance Materials
Plastics

KEY COMPETITORS

American Standard	General Electric	Rockwell
BASF	Hercules	Rolls-Royce
Borg-Warner	Hexcel	Teledyne
Automotive	Hoechst	Tenneco
Coltec	Honeywell	Textron
Dana	ITT Industries	TRW
DuPont	Litton Industries	United
Eaton	Monsanto	Technologies
AB Electrolux	Morton	Westinghouse
Formosa Plastics	Robert Bosch	

HOW MUCH

	9-Year Growth	1985	1986	1987	1988	1989	1990	1991	1992	1993	1994
Sales ($ mil.)	3.9%	9,115	11,794	11,116	11,909	11,942	12,343	11,831	12,042	11,827	12,817
Net income ($ mil.)	—	(279)	605	518	463	528	462	(273)	535	656	759
Income as % of sales	—	—	5.1%	4.7%	3.9%	4.4%	3.7%	—	4.4%	5.5%	5.9%
Earnings per share ($)	—	(1.64)	1.63	1.55	1.55	1.78	1.68	(1.00)	1.90	2.31	2.68
Stock price – high ($)	—	21.66	24.53	24.63	18.44	20.19	18.94	22.50	31.00	40.06	40.69
Stock price – low ($)	—	18.91	18.38	13.00	14.00	15.88	12.44	12.94	20.44	28.75	30.38
Stock price – close ($)	5.5%	21.03	20.06	14.13	16.25	17.44	13.50	21.94	30.25	39.50	34.00
P/E – high	—	—	15	16	12	11	11	—	16	17	15
P/E – low	—	—	11	8	9	9	7	—	11	12	11
Dividends per share ($)	(3.2%)	0.90	0.90	0.90	0.90	0.90	0.90	0.80	0.50	0.58	0.65
Book value per share ($)	(5.0%)	16.65	10.52	10.43	11.04	11.77	12.55	10.80	7.93	8.42	10.53
Employees	(5.4%)	143,800	137,200	115,300	109,550	107,100	105,800	98,300	89,300	86,400	87,500

1994 Year-end:
Debt ratio: 34.2%
Return on equity: 28.3%
Cash (mil.): $508
Current ratio: 1.35
Long-term debt (mil.): $1,424
No. of shares (mil.): 283
Dividends
  Yield: 1.9%
  Payout: 24.3%
Market value (mil.): $9,626

**Stock Price History
High/Low 1985–94**

THE ALLSTATE CORPORATION

OVERVIEW

Allstate's fate is in its own good hands now. In 1995 Sears won approval to spin off its 80% share of the insurance company that has been a part of the retailer since 1931.

Allstate is the 2nd largest home and auto insurer in the US (after State Farm), with about a 12% market share. It also offers life insurance and annuity and pension products and sells property/liability insurance to small businesses. The company operates in Canada, Japan, and South Korea and is a worldwide reinsurer through its Allstate Reinsurance Co., based in London.

The move to independence is changing the way the company does business. It is moving to strengthen its nonproperty lines, especially its life, annuity, and pension products.

Allstate has traditionally sold its products through its own network of 14,500 agents in the US and Canada. The company also accepts business from over 2,000 independent agents, primarily in rural areas, where they wouldn't compete with Allstate's own agencies.

To facilitate its sales plans, Allstate is using its database to target existing customers for additional sales. It is also concentrating on areas that are less vulnerable to natural disasters than California and other coastal areas.

Allstate is starting out with one of its worst earnings years ever, mainly because of losses (over $1 billion and still rising) due to the Northridge earthquake in California.

WHEN

Allstate, the "good hands" company, had its origins in a friendly game of bridge played in 1930 on a Chicago-area commuter train between Sears president Robert Wood and a friend, insurance broker Carl Odell. Odell suggested that Sears sell auto insurance through the mail. Woods liked the idea, financed the company, and in 1931 put Odell in charge (making that hand of bridge a very good one for Odell). The company was named Allstate, after one of Sears's brands of tires.

Allstate was born just as Sears was beginning its push into retailing, and Allstate went with it, selling insurance out of all the new Sears stores.

Growth was slow during the Great Depression and World War II, but the postwar boom was a gold mine for Sears and for Allstate. The growth of suburban developments made it necessary to have a car, 1950s prudence made it necessary to insure the car, and Sears made it easy to buy the insurance, at their stores and, increasingly, at free-standing agencies. In the late 1950s Allstate added home and other property/casualty insurance lines as well as life insurance. Allstate's life insurance in force zoomed from zero to $1 billion in 6 years, the fastest growth ever in the life insurance industry.

In 1960 Sears formed Allstate Enterprises as an umbrella for all its noninsurance operations. In 1970 Allstate Enterprises bought its first S&L. The insurance company continued to acquire other S&Ls and to add subsidiaries throughout the 1970s and 1980s.

This strategy dovetailed neatly with Sears's own plan, which was to become a diversified financial services company. In 1985 Sears introduced the Discover Card through Allstate's Greenwood Trust Company.

In the late 1980s it was obvious that Sears would never be a financial services giant. Moreover, it was losing so much in retailing that by 1987 Allstate was the major contributor to corporate net income. Sears began to dismantle its financial empire in the 1990s.

Allstate had its own problems to contend with. Beginning in 1989 it changed its relations with its sales force, including the imposition of de facto sales quotas (said to have hurt underwriting standards).

Allstate suffered from a backlash against high insurance rates. When Massachusetts instituted no-fault insurance in 1989, Allstate stopped writing new auto insurance there. Later Allstate settled a suit with California over rate rollbacks called for under 1988's Proposition 103 by agreeing to refund $110 million to affected customers.

Some of Allstate's underwriting practices have brought regulatory investigations and fines. Georgia fined the company $3.5 million for failing to tell people why their auto policies were canceled (while at the same time offering them more expensive policies). Texas assessed an $850,000 fine against Allstate for discriminating against unmarried drivers or those who did not buy other Allstate insurance products by refusing to insure them or by placing them in high-risk, high-rate categories. In Washington, state regulators investigated the company's practice of using credit history as an underwriting criterion.

In 1995 Allstate announced its plan to take PMI, its mortgage insurance unit, public.

WHO

Chairman and CEO: Jerry D. Choate, age 56,
$528,421 pay (prior to promotion)
President and COO: Edward M. Liddy, age 49,
$200,000 pay (prior to promotion)
President, Business Insurance Unit: John D. Callahan,
$416,258 pay
President, Allstate Life Insurance: Louis G. Lower II,
age 49, $416,000 pay
SVP and Treasurer: Myron J. Resnick, age 63,
$313,500 pay
SVP and CFO: Thomas J. Wilson, age 37
SVP and Chief Information Officer: Frank W. Pollard
SVP, Secretary, and General Counsel: Robert W. Pike
SVP Human Resources: Joan M. Crockett, age 44
Auditors: Deloitte & Touche LLP

WHERE

HQ: Allstate Plaza, Northbrook, IL 60062
Phone: 708-402-5000
Fax: 708-402-0045

Allstate sells life and property/casualty insurance in the
US, Puerto Rico, and Canada; it also operates in Japan
and Korea and sells reinsurance worldwide.

WHAT

	1994 Assets	
	$ mil.	% of total
Treasury & agency securities	2,091	3
Mortgage-backed securities	6,220	10
Municipal bonds	16,294	27
Corporate bonds	12,905	21
Mortgage loans	3,234	5
Other investments	7,434	12
Cash & other assets	13,191	22
Total	**61,369**	**100**

	1994 Sales		1994 Net Income	
	$ mil.	% of total	$ mil.	% of total
Personal property/ casualty ins.	16,462	77	(172)	—
Business ins.	1,687	8	145	28
Life insurance	2,857	13	312	59
Mortgage guaranty insurance	387	2	70	13
Corporate	1	0	(61)	—
Other	70	0	(67)	—
Total	**21,464**	**100**	**227**	**100**

Selected Subsidiaries
Allstate Life Insurance Co.
Forestview Mortgage Insurance Co.
Glenbrook Life and Annuity Co.
Glenbrook Life Insurance Co.
Lincoln Benefit Life Company
Northbrook Indemnity Company
Northbrook Life Insurance Co.
Northbrook National Insurance Co.
Northbrook Property and Casualty Insurance Co.
Surety Life Insurance Company
Tech-Cor, Inc. (auto safety testing)

KEY COMPETITORS

20th Century Industries
Allmerica Property
American Financial
American General
Berkshire Hathaway
Chubb
CIGNA
Cincinnati Financial
CNA Financial
Continental Corp.
GEICO
Home Holdings
ITT Hartford
Kemper National Insurance

Liberty Mutual
Lincoln National
Lloyd's of London
Loews
Mutual of Omaha
Nationwide Insurance
Ohio Casualty
Old Republic
Progressive Corp.
Prudential
SAFECO
St. Paul Cos.
State Farm
Travelers
USF&G

HOW MUCH

	Annual Growth	1985	1986	1987	1988	1989	1990	1991	1992	1993	1994
Assets ($ mil.)	14.8%	17,740	21,417	25,608	31,030	35,583	41,478	43,378	52,098	59,358	61,369
Net income ($ mil.)	(2.3%)	596	738	946	768	815	701	723	(500)	1,302	484
Income as % of assets	—	3.4%	3.4%	3.7%	2.5%	2.7%	1.7%	1.5%	—	2.2%	0.8%
Earnings per share ($)	(63.9%)	—	—	—	—	—	—	—	—	2.99	1.08
Stock price – high ($)	—	—	—	—	—	—	—	—	—	34.25	29.88
Stock price – low ($)	—	—	—	—	—	—	—	—	—	27.13	22.63
Stock price – close ($)	(19.5%)	—	—	—	—	—	—	—	—	29.50	23.75
P/E – high	—	—	—	—	—	—	—	—	—	11	28
P/E – low	—	—	—	—	—	—	—	—	—	9	21
Dividends per share ($)	100.0%	—	—	—	—	—	—	—	—	0.36	0.72
Book value per share ($)	(18.0%)	—	—	—	—	—	—	—	—	22.89	18.78
Employees	(2.8%)	—	—	—	55,003	55,789	57,232	54,144	51,515	49,000	46,300

1994 Year-end:
Equity as % of assets: 13.7%
Return on assets: 0.8%
Return on equity: 5.2%
Long-term debt (mil.): $869
No. of shares (mil.): 449
Dividends
  Yield: 3.0%
  Payout: 66.7%
Market value (mil.): $10,657
Sales (mil.): $21,464

Stock Price History
High/Low 1993–94

ALUMINUM COMPANY OF AMERICA

OVERVIEW

Aluminum Company of America (Alcoa) pioneered the development of the aluminum industry more than 100 years ago. Today it is still the world's top aluminum producer. Operating in 26 countries, Alcoa and its subsidiaries produce primary aluminum, alumina-based chemicals, and semifinished and finished aluminum products for the packaging, automotive, construction, and aerospace industries.

Voluntary cutbacks in production and a tenuous international agreement have reduced the world's stockpiles of aluminum and boosted Alcoa's bottom line. Under chairman Paul O'Neill the company reorganized in 1991,

cut debt, lowered operating costs, and explored new markets. In 1994 years of dwindling profits were reversed with the increased demand that resulted from growing economies in Asia, Europe, and the Americas and from higher aluminum prices.

Alcoa is supplying more parts to the automobile industry. The company was selected in 1994 to produce components for Mercedes-Benz and Chrysler. It also teamed up with CMI International to make engine cylinder blocks and opened a new plant in Germany to make parts for Audi. Alcoa announced in early 1995 that it is building a plant in Ohio to mass-produce automobile frames.

WHEN

In 1886, 2 chemists, one in France and one in the US, simultaneously discovered an inexpensive process for aluminum production. The American, Charles Martin Hall, pursued commercial applications. In 1888, with an investor group led by Captain Alfred Hunt, Hall formed the Pittsburgh Reduction Company. Its first salesman, Arthur Vining Davis, secured an initial order for 2,000 cooking pots.

In 1889 the Mellon Bank loaned the company $4,000. In 1891 Alcoa recapitalized as a million-dollar corporation, with the Mellons holding 12% of the stock. By the 1920s the Mellons had raised their stake to 33%.

Hunt died in 1899, and Davis led the company until 1957, remaining on the board until his death in 1962 at age 95. Alcoa, the first industrial user of Niagara Falls (1893), introduced aluminum foil (1910) and found applications for aluminum in emerging industries (e.g., airplanes and automobiles). The present name was adopted in 1907.

By the end of WWI, Alcoa had integrated backward into bauxite mining and forward into end-use production. Alcoa transferred most foreign properties to Aluminium Ltd., a Canadian subsidiary, in 1928.

The government and Alcoa debated antitrust issues in court for years after the smelting patent expired in 1912. Finally, a 1946 federal ruling forced Alcoa to sell many operations built during WWII as well as its Canadian subsidiary (today called Alcan, its largest competitor).

In the competitive aluminum industry of the 1960s, Alcoa relied on its laboratories (established 1919) and entrepreneurship. The company devised lower-cost production methods and seized market shares, especially

in beverage cans. Alcoa reentered the international arena, establishing 23 locations in 13 countries between 1959 and 1965.

In the 1970s Alcoa diversified, focusing on new products such as aerospace components. In the 1980s Alcoa doubled R&D expenditures and invested heavily in acquisitions, joint ventures, and plant modernization.

CEO Paul O'Neill arrived in 1987 and shifted the company back to aluminum. Sales and earnings set records in 1988 and 1989 but plunged afterward, reflecting a weak global economy and record-low aluminum prices. Alcoa agreed with Audi in 1991 to mass-produce aluminum car frames.

In 1992 Alcoa sold its 44% stake in a Mexican affiliate (Grupo Aluminio) and its Venezuelan investments. The company laid off 2,000 employees, its first major layoff in 6 years.

O'Neill looked worldwide for new uses and new growth opportunities for aluminum. The company acquired 4 bottle cap plants in Latin America and opened another in Bahrain in 1993. That same year, as part of a joint venture with Kobe Steel, Alcoa started commercial operations of a new mill, Japan's largest, which produces aluminum sheet for beverage cans. Also that year Alcoa supported a move to reduce global stockpiles of aluminum.

In early 1994 Alcoa voluntarily cut its production as part of a 2-year international accord. That same year the company agreed to pool its alumina and chemical operations with Australia's Western Mining Corp., which will own 40% of the new enterprise.

In early 1995 Alcoa formed a joint venture with Shanghai Aluminum Fabrication Plant in China and was reported to be exploring a sizable investment in Russia.

NYSE symbol: AA
Fiscal year ends: December 31

WHO

Chairman and CEO: Paul H. O'Neill, age 59,
$1,450,200 pay
EVP: Alain J. P. Belda, age 51, $673,500 pay
EVP and Chairman's Counsel: Richard L. Fischer,
age 58, $530,400 pay
EVP Human Resources, Quality, and Communications:
Ronald R. Hoffman, age 60, $530,400 pay
EVP and CFO: Jan H. M. Hommen, age 51, $490,800 pay
EVP and Chief Technical Officer: Peter R. Bridenbaugh,
age 54
Auditors: Coopers & Lybrand L.L.P.

WHERE

HQ: Alcoa Bldg., 425 Sixth Ave., Pittsburgh, PA
15219-1850
Phone: 412-553-4545
Fax: 412-553-4498

	1994 Sales $ mil.	% of total	1994 Operating Income $ mil.	% of total
US	5,574	56	(65)	—
Pacific	1,670	17	291	51
Other Americas	1,362	14	239	41
Europe	1,298	13	48	8
Total	**9,904**	**100**	**513**	**100**

WHAT

	1994 Sales $ mil.	% of total	1994 Operating Income $ mil.	% of total
Aluminum procs.	6,477	66	145	28
Nonaluminum products	1,919	19	91	18
Alumina & chem.	1,508	15	277	54
Total	**9,904**	**100**	**513**	**100**

1994 Revenues by Market

	$ mil.	% of total
Packaging	2,830	29
Transportation	1,671	17
Alumina & chemicals	1,494	15
Building & construction	1,391	14
Aluminum ingot	948	9
Distributor & other	1,570	16
Total	**9,904**	**100**

Major Subsidiaries and Affiliates

Alcoa Alumina & Chemicals, L.L.C. (60%; a pooling of
bauxite, alumina, and industrial chemical operations
in Guinea, India, Jamaica, Japan, Liberia, Singapore,
Suriname, and the US; joint venture with Western
Mining Corp., Australia)
Alcoa Brazil Holdings Co.
Alcoa Aluminio SA (59%; aluminum mining, refining,
smelting, and fabrication; Brazil)
Alcoa Composites, Inc. (aerospace parts)
Alcoa International Holdings Co. (Australia, Hong Kong
Hungary, Japan, Mexico, the Netherlands, Norway,
and Switzerland)
Alcoa Properties, Inc. (real estate development, Florida
and South Carolina)
Alcoa Securities Corp.
Alcoa Fujikura Ltd. (51%, wiring systems, Germany)
KSL Alcoa Aluminum Co., Ltd. (50%, joint
venture with Kobe Steel; aluminum sheet; Japan)

KEY COMPETITORS

Alcan	FMC	Northrop
Alumina Partners	Inco	Grumman
Anglo American	Inland Steel	Ormet
ASARCO	Kyocera	Phelps Dodge
Broken Hill	MAXXAM	Reynolds
Corning	Mitsubishi	Metals
Crown, Cork	Mitsui	RTZ
& Seal	Nippon Steel	Thyssen
Cyprus Amax	Norsk Hydro	

HOW MUCH

	9-Year Growth	1985	1986	1987	1988	1989	1990	1991	1992	1993	1994
Sales ($ mil.)	4.6%	6,600	6,431	7,767	9,795	10,910	10,710	9,884	9,492	9,056	9,904
Net income ($ mil.)	—	(17)	254	200	861	945	295	63	27	5	375
Income as % of sales	—	—	4.0%	2.6%	8.8%	8.7%	2.8%	0.6%	0.3%	0.1%	3.8%
Earnings per share ($)	—	(0.12)	1.48	1.13	4.87	5.34	1.70	0.36	0.15	0.02	2.10
Stock price – high ($)	—	20.38	23.19	32.38	28.69	39.82	38.63	36.57	40.32	39.19	45.13
Stock price – low ($)	—	14.88	16.32	16.88	19.32	27.63	24.82	26.88	30.50	29.50	32.13
Stock price – close ($)	22.5%	19.25	16.94	23.38	28.00	37.50	28.82	32.19	35.82	34.69	43.31
P/E – high	—	—	16	29	6	7	23	—	—	—	21
P/E – low	—	—	11	15	4	5	15	—	—	—	15
Dividends per share ($)	3.2%	0.60	0.60	0.60	0.65	1.36	1.53	0.89	0.80	0.80	0.80
Book value per share ($)	1.1%	19.92	21.00	21.81	25.88	29.71	30.10	28.82	20.70	19.96	22.07
Employees	1.3%	55,000	54,000	55,000	59,000	60,600	63,700	65,600	63,600	63,400	61,700

1994 Year-end:
Debt ratio: 24.7%
Return on equity: 10.0%
Cash (mil.): $625
Current ratio: 1.63
Long-term debt (mil.): $1,030
No. of shares (mil.): 179
Dividends
  Yield: 1.8%
  Payout: 38.1
Market value (mil.): $7,740

Stock Price History
High/Low 1985–94

AMDAHL CORPORATION

OVERVIEW

Luckily for Amdahl, reports of the death of mainframe computing have been greatly exaggerated. Amdahl, which manufactures IBM-compatible mainframes, is among the top 10 makers of large computers. The company also supplies UNIX servers and software, applications development and production software, and data communications products.

With many corporations choosing to keep their mainframe computers rather than migrate to smaller systems, the mainframe market has recovered from its slump. That market revival and a concerted effort by the company to cut inventory and operating costs have returned Amdahl to profitability.

To reduce its dependence on mainframe sales, Amdahl is expanding into software and services such as systems integration and consulting. In 1995 it released a new version of its Huron applications development and production software for Hewlett-Packard, IBM, and Sun workstation and server platforms.

Amdahl is also forging alliances with other technology firms, including Fujitsu, which owns 44% of the company and is a major supplier of its computer components. In 1994 Amdahl introduced the XPlorer 2000 database server in an alliance with Oracle, nCUBE, and Information Builders. The next year the company began marketing Cray's high-end servers.

WHEN

In the 1960s Gene Amdahl was the principal architect of IBM's popular family of mainframe computers, the System 360. After his idea for a more advanced computer was rejected, Amdahl quit IBM in 1970 and started his own company to manufacture IBM-compatible mainframes. In view of previous failures by others, investors were reluctant to back a company challenging IBM's market dominance. But Amdahl's strategy — to make its system faster, cheaper, and with high capacity, yet compatible with IBM software and peripherals — was unique, and it persuaded investors to supply enough capital to start the company. Fujitsu was one of the earliest investors. In 1975, with $47 million poured into R&D, Amdahl introduced the 470V/6, a computer compatible with IBM's largest 370 mainframe, the Model 168. IBM users could transfer to the less-expensive Amdahl V/6 and continue to use their existing software and peripherals.

Amdahl's strategy of building IBM clones with better performance for less money succeeded, and the company went public in 1976. Amdahl followed its 470V/6 with the V/7 in 1977 and a V/8 model in 1978. As Amdahl prospered by outperforming and underselling IBM, Big Blue struck back by cutting prices and announcing impending technological improvements. Potential Amdahl customers delayed purchases, drying up cash flow. By 1979 Fujitsu's interest was 34% and Gene Amdahl was gone. Seeking to diversify and bolstered by funds from a 1980 stock offering, new president Eugene White bought Tran Telecommunications (data communications products, 1980) and sought to buy Memorex (1979) and Storage Technology Corporation (1980), but Fujitsu stopped both transactions.

In 1983 Amdahl Corporation's revenues shot up 68% from the previous year to $778 million following shipments of its new 5860 mainframe and diversification into disk drives. Sales flattened in 1984, however, because of bugs in the new computer. Amdahl bounced back in 1985 with its 5890 family of computers (comparable to IBM's 3090 series). As the US mainframe computer market matured in the 1980s, Amdahl looked toward Europe, where profit derived not merely from sales but also from a declining dollar. The company bought Key Computer Labs (scalar computing) in 1989 and launched the 5995 mainframe series in 1990.

Amdahl released Huron, an applications software development package, in 1991. That same year Amdahl licensed Sun Microsystems's SPARC (RISC) technology to further its movement toward open systems. The company formed a joint venture, Antares Alliance Group, with Electronic Data Systems (EDS, a unit of General Motors) in 1993 to develop software capable of running on both mainframes and smaller computers. Amdahl owns 80% and EDS owns 20% of the venture.

After heavy losses in 1993 due to the slow mainframe market, Amdahl rebounded in 1994 and posted its first yearly profit since 1991. In a major reorganization, it cut manufacturing capacity in half and employment by 1/3 and wrote off about $200 million in surplus plants and equipment.

In 1995 Amdahl formed a technology education consortium, called KnowledgePool, with subsidiaries of Fujitsu and UK computer company ICL to provide technology training programs to corporations. Also that year Silicon Graphics licensed Amdahl's HTML editor technology for its WebForce product line.

AMEX symbol: AMH
Fiscal year ends: Last Friday in December

WHO

Chairman: John C. Lewis, age 59, $910,036 pay
President and CEO: E. Joseph Zemke, age 54,
$1,544,361 pay
SVP, CFO, and Corporate Secretary: Bruce J. Ryan,
age 51
SVP Human Resources and Corporate Services:
Anthony M. Pozos, age 54
VP and General Manager, Worldwide Field Operations:
David B. Wright, age 45, $581,823 pay
VP and General Manager, Compatible Systems: David L.
Anderson, age 47, $555,426 pay
VP and General Manager, Worldwide Field Operations:
Orval J. Nutt, age 54, $514,650 pay
Auditors: Arthur Andersen & Co, SC

WHERE

HQ: 1250 E. Arques Ave., Sunnyvale, CA 94088-3470
Phone: 408-746-6000
Fax: 408-746-6468

Amdahl markets its products in Asia, Canada, Europe,
and the US. The company's products are also marketed
by Fujitsu and other distributors in parts of Africa, Asia,
Europe, the Middle East, and South America. The
company has manufacturing facilities in Sunnyvale,
California, and Dublin, Ireland.

	1994 Sales		1994 Operating Income	
	$ mil.	% of total	$ mil.	% of total
US	955	58	50	81
Europe	507	31	3	5
Canada	62	4	4	7
Pacific Basin & other	115	7	4	7
Adjustments	—	—	3	—
Total	**1,639**	**100**	**64**	**100**

WHAT

	1994 Sales	
	$ mil.	% of total
Processors	802	49
Storage products	203	12
Communications products	45	3
Equipment lease, maintenance & other	589	36
Total	**1,639**	**100**

Computers
5995A series (mainframe)
5995M series (mainframe)
XPlorer 2000 (database server)

Storage Subsystems
6100 storage processor
6390 series disk storage units (7.5 to 45 gigabytes)

Communications Products
4655 series UNIX network processors
4745 series communications processors

Software
A-UMA (open system management)
Huron (applications development and production)
OpenTune (open system management)
UTS (UNIX) operating system

Customer Services
Consulting services
Training and maintenance

KEY COMPETITORS

AT&T	IBM	Siemens
Control Data	Intel	Silicon Graphics
Systems	Intergraph	Storage
Cray Research	Machines Bull	Technology
Data General	NEC	Stratus
DEC	Olivetti	Computer
Digital	Pyramid	Tandem
Hewlett-Packard	Technology	Unisys
Hitachi	Sequent	Wang

HOW MUCH

	9-Year Growth	1985	1986	1987	1988	1989	1990	1991	1992	1993	1994
Sales ($ mil.)	7.4%	862	966	1,505	1,802	2,101	2,159	1,703	2,525	1,681	1,639
Net income ($ mil.)	13.5%	24	39	142	214	153	184	4	(7)	(589)	75
Income as % of sales	—	2.8%	4.1%	9.4%	11.9%	7.3%	8.5%	0.3%	—	—	4.6%
Earnings per share ($)	10.3%	0.26	0.41	1.37	1.99	1.39	1.66	0.04	(0.06)	(5.17)	0.63
Stock price – high ($)	—	9.06	12.88	25.06	28.00	23.38	18.88	17.88	20.63	8.50	11.13
Stock price – low ($)	—	5.06	6.75	9.56	14.06	10.75	10.00	11.63	6.63	4.38	5.25
Stock price – close ($)	4.6%	7.31	11.69	17.63	20.25	14.38	14.13	15.75	7.25	6.00	11.00
P/E – high	—	35	31	18	14	17	11	—	—	—	18
P/E – low	—	20	17	7	7	8	6	—	—	—	8
Dividends per share ($)	(100.0%)	0.10	0.10	0.10	0.10	0.10	0.10	0.10	0.10	0.05	0.00
Book value per share ($)	5.1%	4.82	5.19	7.32	9.51	10.80	12.44	12.38	12.12	6.90	7.51
Employees	(2.4%)	7,000	7,200	7,650	8,150	8,200	8,950	9,400	8,769	5,552	5,600

1994 Year-end:
Debt ratio: 13.6%
Return on equity: 9.0%
Cash (mil.): $699
Current ratio: 2.04
Long-term debt (mil.): $130
No. of shares (mil.): 117
Dividends
  Yield: —
  Payout: —
Market value (mil.): $1,283

Stock Price History
High/Low 1985–94

AMERADA HESS CORPORATION

OVERVIEW

After 50 years of running oil and gas operations, 81-year-old Leon Hess turned over the reins of oil and gas giant Amerada Hess in 1995 to his son John. The younger Hess might count himself fortunate — Leon's father had stayed on the job until his death at age 92. The company president, 70-year-old Robert Wright, also stepped down as part of the company's 1995 reorganization.

The New York–based company has reserves of 670 million barrels of oil and 2.65 trillion cubic feet of natural gas. Its exploration activities are located primarily in the US, Canada, Gabon, and the North Sea. Amerada Hess refines an average of more than 250,000 barrels a day and sells gasoline in 541 HESS stations,

mainly in New York, New Jersey, and Florida. Of these stations, 155 operate HESS MART convenience stores.

Amerada Hess produces oil and gas at 9 major fields in the North Sea. Fifty-one percent of the company's crude oil is produced from these fields, along with 25% of its natural gas. Amerada Hess has updated its St. Croix, Virgin Islands, refinery, one of the largest in the world, spending $1 billion to satisfy the requirements of the Clean Air Act.

The $2.5 billion that management spent on reshaping the company in recent years left Amerada Hess with a heavy debt load. Leon Hess holds 12.9% of the company's stock; John Hess owns 1.7%.

WHEN

It was a logical match — Amerada Petroleum, which had been in the exploration and production business since the early part of the century, and Hess Oil and Chemical, involved in refining since the 1930s.

In 1919 oil entrepreneur Lord Cowdray formed Amerada Corporation to explore for oil in the US, Canada, and Central America. One of the first and most important people Cowdray hired was geophysicist Everette DeGolyer, a pioneer in oil geology research methods. DeGolyer's systematic methods — in a time when guesswork was still the norm — not only helped Amerada find oil deposits faster, but also helped the company pick up fields previously missed by competitors. DeGolyer became president of Amerada in 1929. He left the company in 1932 to work as an independent consultant. Amerada continued to make major discoveries in the US.

After WWII Amerada began exploring overseas, and during the 1950s the company entered into pipelining and refining. Amerada continued its overseas exploration through Oasis, a consortium formed with Marathon, Shell, and Continental to explore in Libya in 1964. At one time Oasis controlled half of Libya's oil production.

Leon Hess began to buy stock in Amerada in 1966. Hess started in the oil business during the Depression, selling "resid" — thick refining leftovers that the refineries thought were useless. Hess bought the resid cheap, kept it warm in heated trucks (so it would flow), and sold it as heating fuel to hotels and later to Public Service Electric & Gas. Hess also began speculating, buying oil cheap in the summer and selling it for a profit in the win-

ter. He also branched out into refining, gasoline retailing, transportation, and exploration.

All that expansion pushed debt up, so in 1962 Hess Oil and Chemical went public by merging with Cletrac Corporation. In 1966 Hess began building a refinery in St. Croix, Virgin Islands. After battling Phillips Petroleum and settling a suit brought by Amerada, Hess acquired Amerada in 1969.

During the 1970s Amerada Hess began drilling on Alaska's North Slope. In 1978 the company was one of 5 oil companies convicted of fixing retail gasoline prices.

The company took a roller coaster ride during the 1980s, posting sales of $10 billion in 1981, which then plunged, as oil prices plummeted, to only $4 billion in 1986, when Amerada Hess posted a loss of $219 million. Takeover rumors circulated as oilman T. Boone Pickens bought up a chunk of Amerada Hess's stock. However, the company rebounded, and Hess was able to fight off any takeover.

In 1989 Hurricane Hugo knocked out the company's refinery in St. Croix, which took a year to rebuild.

In 1993 Amerada Hess completed work on the Central Area Transmission System pipeline. The company owns 18% of the pipeline, which carries natural gas from the North Sea to the UK. In 1994 Amerada Hess's UK subsidiary began production in the South Scott oil field in the North Sea. Also that year the company began a consolidation of its US exploration and production operations in Houston, resulting in reduced staffing levels.

In 1995 Amerada Hess successfully met the federal guidelines regarding the sale of reformulated gasoline in the US.

NYSE symbol: AHC
Fiscal year ends: December 31

WHO

Chairman of the Executive Committee: Leon Hess, age 81, $300,000 pay
Chairman and CEO: John B. Hess, age 40, $735,000 pay (prior to promotion)
President and COO: W. Sam H. Laidlaw, age 39, $575,000 pay (prior to promotion)
EVP and CFO: John Y. Schreyer, age 55, $550,000 pay
EVP Refining and Marketing: Michael W. Press, age 47
EVP and General Counsel: J. Barclay Collins II, age 50
SVP: Alan A. Bernstein, age 50
SVP: Marco B. Bianchi, age 55
SVP: James F. Cassidy, age 67
SVP: F. Lamar Clark, age 61
SVP: Charles H. Norz, age 57
SVP: Benedict J. O'Bryan, age 57
SVP: Rene L. Sagebien, age 54
SVP Human Resources: Neal Gelfand, age 50
Auditors: Ernst & Young LLP

WHERE

HQ: 1185 Avenue of the Americas, New York, NY 10036
Phone: 212-997-8500
Fax: 212-536-8390

Amerada Hess explores for oil and natural gas in the US, Canada, Denmark, Egypt, Gabon, Namibia, Thailand, and the North Sea. It has refineries in the US Virgin Islands and in New Jersey and retail stations in the US.

	1994 Sales		1994 Operating Income	
	$ mil.	% of total	$ mil.	% of total
US	5,437	82	66	14
Europe	907	14	303	63
Other regions	258	4	112	23
Adjustments	97	—	—	—
Total	**6,699**	**100**	**481**	**100**

WHAT

	1994 Sales		1994 Operating Income	
	$ mil.	% of total	$ mil.	% of total
Refining & marketing	4,154	63	83	17
Exploration & production	2,263	34	368	77
Other	185	3	30	6
Adjustments	97	—	—	—
Total	**6,699**	**100**	**481**	**100**

Lines of Business
Marketing of refined products
Oil and gas exploration and production
Petroleum refining
Transportation of refined products

Selected Subsidiaries
Amerada Hess Canada Ltd.
Amerada Hess Ltd. (UK)
Amerada Hess Norge A/S (Norway)
Hess Oil Virgin Islands Corp.

KEY COMPETITORS

Amoco	Panhandle Eastern
Ashland, Inc.	PDVSA
Atlantic Richfield	PEMEX
British Petroleum	Pennzoil
Broken Hill	Petrobrás
Chevron	Petrofina
Circle K	Phillips Petroleum
Coastal	Repsol
Elf Aquitaine	Royal Dutch/Shell
Exxon	Sinclair Oil
Imperial Oil	Southland
Koch	Sun Company
Lyondell Petrochemical	Texaco
Mobil	TOTAL
Occidental	Unocal
Oryx	USX–Marathon

HOW MUCH

	9-Year Growth	1985	1986	1987	1988	1989	1990	1991	1992	1993	1994
Sales ($ mil.)	(1.6%)	7,723	4,062	4,785	4,264	5,679	7,081	6,416	5,970	5,873	6,699
Net income ($ mil.)	—	(260)	(219)	230	124	476	483	84	8	(298)	74
Income as % of sales	—	—	—	4.8%	2.9%	8.4%	6.8%	1.3%	0.1%	—	1.1%
Earnings per share ($)	—	(3.08)	(2.60)	2.73	1.51	5.87	5.96	1.04	0.09	(3.22)	0.79
Stock price – high ($)	—	34.00	29.00	41.88	33.25	51.88	56.00	59.13	51.25	56.38	52.63
Stock price – low ($)	—	22.75	16.50	21.50	22.50	31.00	42.88	42.50	36.63	42.38	43.75
Stock price – close ($)	5.9%	27.25	23.75	24.88	31.50	48.75	46.38	47.50	46.00	45.13	45.63
P/E – high	—	—	—	15	22	9	9	57	—	—	67
P/E – low	—	—	—	8	15	5	7	41	—	—	55
Dividends per share ($)	(6.5%)	1.10	0.28	0.60	0.30	0.60	0.60	0.75	0.45	0.75	0.45	0.60
Book value per share ($)	2.3%	27.22	24.68	26.29	27.02	31.69	38.34	38.63	36.59	32.71	33.33
Employees	1.9%	8,290	7,776	7,890	8,151	16,638	9,645	10,317	10,263	10,173	9,858

1994 Year-end:
Debt ratio: 52.5%
Return on equity: 2.4%
Cash (mil.): $53
Current ratio: 1.43
Long-term debt (mil.): $3,235
No. of shares (mil.): 93
Dividends
Yield: 1.3%
Payout: 75.9
Market value (mil.): $4,243

**Stock Price History
High/Low 1985–94**

AMERICAN BRANDS, INC.

OVERVIEW

If American Brands isn't swallowed by an even bigger fish, and if it doesn't exit the tobacco business altogether (as some analysts predict), the Connecticut-based conglomerate should change its name: About 47% of the company's 1994 sales came from its UK-based subsidiary, Gallaher Tobacco, the #1 British tobacco company. American Brands sold its American Tobacco subsidiary, including the Pall Mall and Lucky Strike brands, to B.A.T Industries for $1 billion in late 1994.

American Brands is focusing on its non-tobacco subsidiaries, all makers of leading consumer brands, including Jim Beam, the #2 US producer of distilled spirits; top pro golf equipment brands Titleist and Foot-Joy; ACCO office products; and faucet maker Moen.

The company continues to shed noncore operations. It gained $1.17 billion in early 1995 by selling Franklin Life Insurance to American General and announced it would sell its Forbuoys retail outlet chain and Prestige cookware, both based in the UK.

With proceeds from recent sales, the company has retired $1 billion in debt. It is also expected to buy back outstanding shares and make strategic acquisitions, possibly in the highly profitable distilled spirits division.

WHEN

American Brands began in 1864 as W. Duke and Sons, a small tobacco company started by Washington Duke, a North Carolina farmer. James Buchanan Duke joined his father's business at age 14 (1870) and by age 25 was its president. James Duke was the first to use the Bonsack cigarette rolling machine, which produced substantially cheaper cigarettes and allowed him to undercut competitors' prices. He advertised to expanding markets, bought rival tobacco firms, and by 1904 controlled the industry. That year he merged all the competitive groups as American Tobacco Company.

In a 1911 antitrust suit, the US Supreme Court dissolved American Tobacco into its original competitive firms, ordering them to operate independently.

Duke left American Tobacco in 1912 but remained president of British American Tobacco Company (now B.A.T, which he had founded in 1902). He also continued his work with Southern Power Company, which he had started in North Carolina in 1905. He later merged that company with Duke Power and Light. Duke established a $100 million trust fund, composed mainly of holdings in Duke Power and Light, for the local Trinity College, which became Duke University in 1924.

American Tobacco merely drifted under Duke's successor Percival Hill, but it found a dynamic new leader in George Washington Hill, who succeeded his father as president in 1925. For the next 19 years until his death, Hill proved himself a consummate ad man, pushing Lucky Strike, Pall Mall, and Tareyton cigarettes to top sales.

Research first linked cigarette smoking to lung cancer in 1953, and smokers switched to filter-tipped cigarettes in record numbers. American Tobacco, however, ignored the trend and continued to rely on its popular filterless brands until the mid-1960s.

American Tobacco remained solely in the tobacco business until 1966, when it purchased Sunshine Biscuits (sold in 1988) and Jim Beam Distillery. Later came Swingline (office supplies, 1970) and Master Lock (1970). Reflecting its increasing diversity, the company became American Brands in 1970.

Threatened by a takeover by E-II Holdings (a conglomerate of brands split from Beatrice), American Brands bought E-II for $1.1 billion in 1988. The company kept 5 of E-II's companies — Day-Timers (time management products), Aristokraft (cabinets), Waterloo (tool storage), Twentieth Century (plumbing supplies), and Vogel Peterson (office partitions) — and sold the rest (Culligan and Samsonite) to Riklis Family Corporation.

Acquisitions in 1990 included Moen (faucets) and Whyte & Mackay (distillers). In 1991 the company bought 7 liquor brands from Seagram, including Kessler (whiskey), Ronrico (rum), and Leroux (cordials). Whyte & Mackay became the world's 3rd largest scotch whiskey producer in 1993 with the acquisition of the Invergordon Distillers Group.

In 1994 American Brands sold Dollond & Aitchison, its UK-based optical group. It also sold the rubber divison of Acushnet (leisure products) to members of that unit's top management. That same year it settled a false advertising charge filed by the FTC regarding American Tobacco's claim that its Carlton brand cigarettes deliver less tar and nicotine to smokers.

In 1995 Jim Beam, the top-selling bourbon in the world, celebrated its 200th birthday. The previous year over 5 million cases of the whiskey were sold.

NYSE symbol: AMB
Fiscal year ends: December 31

WHO

Chairman and CEO: Thomas C. Hays, age 59,
$1,089,400 pay (prior to promotion)
President and COO: John T. Ludes, age 58,
$696,600 pay (prior to promotion)
SVP and CFO: Dudley L. Bauerlein Jr., age 48
SVP and Chief Accounting Officer: Robert L. Plancher,
age 63
SVP and General Counsel: Gilbert L. Klemann II, age 44
SVP and Chief Administrative Officer: Steven C.
Mendenhall, age 46
Chairman and CEO, Gallaher Tobacco Limited: Peter
M. Wilson, age 53, $839,219 pay
Chairman and CEO, Jim Beam Brands Co.: Barry M.
Berish
President and CEO, Acco World Corp.: Norman H.
Wesley
President and CEO, Acushnet Co.: Walter R. Uihlein
President and CEO, Masterbrand Industries: Randall W.
Larrimore
Auditors: Coopers & Lybrand L.L.P.

WHERE

HQ: 1700 E. Putnam Ave., PO Box 811, Old Greenwich,
CT 06870-0811
Phone: 203-698-5000
Fax: 203-637-2580

American Brands is a holding company with subsidiaries
operating in Asia, Australia, Europe (principally the UK),
and North America.

	1994 Sales		1994 Operating Income	
	$ mil.	% of total	$ mil.	% of total
Europe	8,074	61	586	45
US	4,677	36	671	51
Other regions	396	3	55	4
Total	**13,147**	**100**	**1,312**	**100**

WHAT

	1994 Sales		1994 Operating Income	
	$ mil.	% of total	$ mil.	% of total
Tobacco products	7,764	59	765	58
Hardware & home imprvmt. prods.	1,271	10	176	13
Distilled spirits	1,268	10	221	17
Office products	1,050	8	75	6
Other businesses	1,794	13	75	6
Total	**13,147**	**100**	**1,312**	**100**

Selected Brands

Tobacco Products	Kamchatka
Amber Leaf	Lord Calvert
Benson & Hedges (UK)	Old Grand-Dad
Berkeley	Ronrico
Old Holborn	Windsor Canadian
Samson	Wolfschmidt
Silk Cut	

Hardware and Home Improvement	**Office Products**
	ACCO
	Day-Timers
Aristokraft (cabinets)	Kensington Microware
Master Lock (hardware)	Perma Products
Moen (faucets)	Swingline
Waterloo (tool boxes)	Wilson Jones

Distilled Spirits	**Other Products**
Gilbey's	Foot-Joy (golf shoes)
Jim Beam	Titleist (golf equipment)

KEY COMPETITORS

Allied Domecq	Eastern Co.	Loews
American Standard	Franklin Quest	Masco
Bacardi	Grand Metropolitan	Philip Morris
B.A.T	Guinness	RJR Nabisco
Black & Decker	Hanson	Seagram
Brown-Forman	Hillenbrand	Stanley
Brunswick	Ingersoll-Rand	Todhunter Intl.
Day Runner	Kohler	Waxman

HOW MUCH

	9-Year Growth	1985	1986	1987	1988	1989	1990	1991	1992	1993	1994
Sales ($ mil.)	6.7%	7,308	8,470	9,153	11,980	11,921	13,781	14,064	14,623	13,701	13,147
Net income ($ mil.)	6.4%	421	365	523	580	631	596	806	884	668	734
Income as % of sales	—	5.8%	4.3%	5.7%	4.8%	5.3%	4.3%	5.7%	6.0%	4.9%	5.6%
Earnings per share ($)	8.6%	1.80	1.56	2.24	2.76	3.04	2.84	3.74	4.13	3.23	3.77
Stock price – high ($)	—	17.50	26.25	30.00	35.88	40.94	41.63	47.63	49.88	40.63	38.38
Stock price – low ($)	—	13.31	15.66	18.25	21.13	30.63	30.88	35.63	39.00	28.50	29.38
Stock price – close ($)	9.6%	16.50	21.25	22.25	32.75	35.50	41.50	45.00	40.50	33.25	37.50
P/E – high	—	10	17	13	13	14	15	13	12	13	10
P/E – low	—	7	10	8	8	10	11	10	9	9	8
Dividends per share ($)	8.2%	0.98	1.02	1.06	1.16	1.26	1.41	1.59	1.81	1.97	1.99
Book value per share ($)	8.7%	10.86	11.57	13.32	13.34	15.03	18.13	20.42	21.14	21.09	22.93
Employees	(8.1%)	74,600	78,900	78,600	48,900	47,300	49,000	47,600	46,220	46,660	34,820

1994 Year-end:
Debt ratio: 32.4%
Return on equity: 16.5%
Cash (mil.): $110
Current ratio: 1.50
Long-term debt (mil.): $1,512
No. of shares (mil.): 202
Dividends
  Yield: 5.3%
  Payout: 52.8%
Market value (mil.): $7,560

Stock Price History
High/Low 1985–94

AMERICAN ELECTRIC POWER COMPANY

OVERVIEW

American Electric Power (AEP) is one of the largest investor-owned utilities in the US. Through 7 operating utilities, the Columbus, Ohio–based holding company provides power to 7 million people throughout 3,250 communities in parts of 7 midwestern and Appalachian states. AEP's subsidiaries operate an integrated network of 38 coal-fired, nuclear, hydroelectric, and gas turbine generating units. The AEP System is managed by AEP Service Corporation, which provides administrative, engineering, legal, and other services.

AEP's profits rebounded in 1994 following a drop of nearly 25% in 1993 after the Ohio Supreme Court upheld a decision disallowing AEP's inclusion of part of the construction costs of a coal-fired plant in its rate base.

Like every other electric utility in the US, AEP is preparing for the deregulation of the power industry. CEO Linn Draper has compared AEP to a battleship that will take time to change course, but he is already spinning the wheel. The company recently won a 15-year wholesale power contract to supply 200 megawatts of power to the North Carolina Electric Membership Corporation, and it convinced Steel Dynamics to build a $500 million steel mini-mill in its Indiana service area.

WHEN

Late in 1906 Richard Breed, Sidney Mitchell, and Henry Doherty set up American Gas & Electric (AG&E) in New York to buy 23 utilities from Philadelphia's Electric Company of America. With properties scattered in 7 states between Illinois and the East Coast, AG&E set out to consolidate operations along geographic lines by acquiring and then merging small, sometimes competing, electric properties. The result was the creation of the predecessors of Ohio Power (1911), Kentucky Power (1919), and Appalachian Power (1926). During this period AG&E also bought the predecessor of Indiana Michigan Power (1922).

By 1926 AG&E was serving communities in Michigan, Indiana, Kentucky, West Virginia, and Ohio. In 1935 AG&E engineer Philip Sporn, who had pioneered research on the effects of lightning on power lines (and was later known as the Henry Ford of power), introduced his high-voltage, super-fast circuit breaker. AG&E added Kingsport Power to its list of operating companies in 1938.

After becoming AG&E's president in 1947, Sporn started an ambitious building program that continued through the 1960s. During this period, plants designed by AG&E (renamed American Electric Power in 1958) were among the world's most efficient, and electric rates stayed 25–38% below the national average.

AEP bought Michigan Power in 1967 — 6 years after Donald Cook succeeded Sporn as president. Cook, who refused to attach scrubbers (devices used to decrease sulfur dioxide emissions) to the smokestacks of AEP's coal-fired plants, came under fire in the early 1970s from environmentalists concerned about acid rain. Coal had long been AEP's primary fuel, and Cook, who believed that scrubbers were unproven and unnecessary, chose instead to increase the height of chimneys to dilute the harmful emissions. AEP's first nuclear plant (named in Cook's honor) went on-line in Michigan in 1975.

AEP moved its headquarters from New York to Columbus, Ohio, in 1980 after buying what is now Columbus Southern Power. It set up AEP Generating Company in 1982 to provide power to its other operating units.

Conversion of AEP's 2nd nuclear facility (Zimmer) to a coal-fired plant began in 1984 after the Nuclear Regulatory Commission halted construction of the plant for failure to keep adequate records. The company's Tidd Plant became operational in 1990, making AEP the first US operator of a pressurized fluidized bed combustion (PFBC) facility. In 1991 AEP's Columbus Southern Power unit filed for a rate increase to cover the costs of the Zimmer transformation, but in 1992 it received approval for only a partial increase. Columbus Southern filed an appeal with the Ohio Supreme Court, but in 1993 the court upheld the earlier decision.

Despite its former aversion to coal scrubbers, in 1992 AEP began installing scrubbers costing $815 million at its coal-fired Gavin plant in Ohio after being ordered to comply with the Clean Air Act.

In 1994 AEP bought interactive communications and home automation systems for 25,000 of its residential customers. The devices allow users to program appliances, such as air conditioning units, to avoid use during peak periods, when electricity rates are higher.

In 1995 AEP announced plans to plant 15 million trees to help counteract the effects of greenhouse gas emissions.

WHO

Chairman, President, and CEO: E. Linn Draper Jr.,
age 53, $829,436 pay
**Treasurer; EVP Administration and Chief Accounting
Officer, AEP Service Corp.:** Peter J. DeMaria, age 60,
$408,029 pay
VP and Secretary; EVP and CFO, AEP Service Corp.:
Gerald P. Maloney, age 62, $401,340 pay
EVP, AEP Service Corp.: William J. Lhota, age 55,
$374,584 pay
**EVP Engineering and Construction, AEP Service
Corp.:** James J. Markowsky, age 50, $357,193 pay
SVP Human Resources, AEP Service Corp.: Ronald A.
Petti
Auditors: Deloitte & Touche LLP

WHERE

HQ: American Electric Power Company, Inc.,
One Riverside Plaza, Columbus, OH 43215
Phone: 614-223-1000
Fax: 614-223-1823

AEP serves portions of Indiana, Kentucky, Michigan,
Ohio, Tennessee, Virginia, and West Virginia.

WHAT

	1994 Electricity Sales	
	$ mil.	% of total
Residential	1,835	33
Industrial	1,579	29
Commercial	1,218	22
Resales	714	13
Miscellaneous retail	65	1
Other	94	2
Total	**5,505**	**100**

1994 Fuel Sources	
	% of total
Coal	89
Nuclear	7
Purchased power	3
Hydroelectric & other	1
Total	**100**

Generating Facilities

Coal	Hydroelectric
Beckjord (OH)	Berrien Springs (MI)
Big Sandy (KY)	Buchanan (MI)
Cardinal (OH)	Buck (VA)
Clinch River (VA)	Byllesby (VA)
Conesville (OH)	Claytor (VA)
Gen. James M. Gavin (OH)	Constantine (MI)
Glen Lyn (VA)	Elkhart (IN)
John E. Amos (WV)	Leesville (VA)
Kammer (WV)	London (WV)
Kanawha River (WV)	Marmet (WV)
Mitchell (WV)	Mottville (MI)
Mountaineer (WV)	Niagara (VA)
Muskingum River (OH)	Racine (OH)
Philip Sporn (WV)	Reusens (VA)
Picway (OH)	Smith Mountain (VA)
Rockport (IN)	Twin Branch (IN)
Stuart (OH)	Winfield (WV)
Tanners Creek (IN)	
Zimmer (OH, 25.4%)	**Nuclear**
	Donald C. Cook (MI)
Gas Turbine	
Fourth Street (IN)	**Pumped Storage**
	Smith Mountain (VA)

Selected Subsidiaries

AEP Energy Services, Inc.
AEP Generating Co.
AEP Service Corp.
Appalachian Power Co.
Columbus Southern Power Co.
Indiana Michigan Power Co.
Kentucky Power Co.
Kingsport Power Co.
Ohio Power Co.
Wheeling Power Co.

HOW MUCH

	9-Year Growth	1985	1986	1987	1988	1989	1990	1991	1992	1993	1994
Sales ($ mil.)	1.4%	4,848	4,843	4,788	4,841	5,140	5,168	5,047	5,045	5,269	5,505
Net income ($ mil.)	0.3%	485	507	503	627	629	496	498	468	354	500
Income as % of sales	—	10.0%	10.5%	10.5%	13.0%	12.2%	9.6%	9.9%	6.7%	6.7%	9.1%
Earnings per share ($)	0.7%	2.54	2.62	2.60	3.24	3.25	2.65	2.70	2.54	1.92	2.71
Stock price – high ($)	—	24.88	31.50	31.63	29.75	33.38	33.13	34.25	35.25	40.38	37.38
Stock price – low ($)	—	19.88	22.75	17.50	25.88	25.75	26.00	26.63	30.38	32.00	27.25
Stock price – close ($)	3.7%	23.63	27.50	26.25	27.25	33.00	28.00	34.25	33.13	37.13	32.88
P/E – high	—	10	12	12	9	10	13	13	14	21	14
P/E – low	—	8	9	7	8	8	10	10	12	17	10
Dividends per share ($)	0.7%	2.26	2.26	2.34	2.34	2.36	2.40	2.40	2.40	2.40	2.40
Book value per share ($)	1.3%	20.35	20.71	20.94	21.84	22.71	22.58	22.88	23.01	22.50	22.83
Employees	(1.9%)	23,413	23,315	22,987	22,886	22,700	22,798	22,136	20,841	20,007	19,660

1994 Year-end:
Debt ratio: 55.6%
Return on equity: 11.9%
Cash (mil.): $63
Current ratio: 0.70
Long-term debt (mil.): $4,687
No. of shares (mil.): 185
Dividends
  Yield: 7.3%
  Payout: 88.6%
Market value (mil.): $6,091

**Stock Price History
High/Low 1985–94**

AMERICAN EXPRESS COMPANY

OVERVIEW

American Express, one of the US's largest financial services companies and the largest corporate travel agency, is continuing the drastic makeover it began in 1994 with the spinoff of Lehman Brothers.

Chairman Harvey Golub has trimmed the company to 3 units — Travel Related Services (TRS), American Express Financial Advisors (formerly IDS), and American Express Bank — and is now concentrating on wringing maximum performance from them by expanding services while cutting up to 6,000 jobs.

Though it is best known for American Express cards and Travelers Cheques, TRS operates a worldwide travel agency, with locations in 160 countries. It also publishes lifestyle and travel magazines and sells life insurance through AMEX Life Assurance. American Express Financial Services sells life and property/casualty insurance, annuities, investment funds, and financial advisory services. American Express Bank has offices in 37 countries.

In the 1980s American Express fell to a distant 3rd in the competition of the cards, behind Visa and MasterCard. It is now attempting to grow this business again, particularly in the areas of corporate travel and purchasing. After years of denigrating revolving credit cards, it has revamped its money-losing Optima card and plans to add up to 15 other credit card products to its lineup. But American Express has an uphill battle because of the proliferation of credit cards, its small merchant base, and its inexperience in credit underwriting.

The company has also reemphasized its travel agency services, which enjoy a tremendous synergy with its card products.

Warren Buffett controls 9.8% of American Express. In 1995 he applied for SEC permission to increase his interest to above 10%.

WHEN

In 1850 Henry Wells and his 2 main competitors combined delivery services to form American Express. When company directors refused to expand to California in 1852, Wells and VP William Fargo, while remaining at American Express, started Wells Fargo.

American Express merged with Merchants Union Express in 1868 and developed a money order to compete with the government's postal money order. Fargo's difficulty in cashing letters of credit in Europe led to the offering of Travelers Cheques in 1891. Services for US travelers overseas followed.

In WWI the US government nationalized and consolidated all express delivery services, compensating the owners. After the war American Express incorporated as an overseas freight (sold 1970) and financial services and exchange provider.

In 1958 the company introduced the American Express charge card (users had no credit limits and had to pay off balances each month). In 1968 the company bought Fireman's Fund American Insurance (sold gradually, 1985–89) and Equitable Securities.

James Robinson (CEO, 1977–93) expanded the company through acquisitions that included half of Warner Cable Communications (Warner Amex Cable, 1979; sold 1986), Shearson Loeb Rhoades (brokerage, 1981), the Boston Company (banking, 1981), Balcor (real estate, 1982; in liquidation), Lehman Brothers Holding Company and Investors Diversified Services (brokerage, 1984), and E.F. Hutton (brokerage, 1987). In 1987 the company introduced Optima, a revolving credit card, to compete with MasterCard and Visa. The financial units (except IDS) were combined as Shearson Lehman Brothers (SLB).

In 1989 American Express issued a public apology for having investigated and spread rumors about Edmond Safra, former chairman of American Express Bank. In connection with this settlement, the company paid $8 million to Safra's favorite charities. This action sparked a shareholder suit against management. Later that year the company acquired Lifeco Services Corporation, the 5th largest travel agency in the US. In 1993 American Express sold 3 magazines and turned over management of the rest of its magazines to Time Inc. The company also began an ad campaign for its Optima credit cards, lambasting Visa for its high interest rates, as Visa had lambasted American Express for its small merchant base. But the card was a failure because it was poorly underwritten.

American Express spun off Lehman Brothers in 1994 with a dowry of $1.1 billion to ensure its credit rating. The cultures had never fused, and Lehman had a way of snatching fiscal defeat from the jaws of victory. Also in 1994 the company bought the US offices and international accounts of Thomas Cook.

In 1995 American Express, in cooperation with America Online, set up ExpressNet, which allows users to pay bills and make travel reservations by computer.

WHO

Chairman and CEO: Harvey Golub, age 56,
$2,840,000 pay
VC: Jonathan S. Linen, age 51, $1,400,000 pay
VC; President, U.S.A.-Travel Related Services: Kenneth
I. Chenault, age 43, $1,260,000 pay
President: Jeffrey E. Stiefler, age 48, $2,003,000 pay
President and CEO, American Express Financial: David
R. Hubers, age 52, $1,060,000 pay
President, International Travel Related Services:
R. Craig Hoenshell, age 50
Chairman and CEO, American Express Bank: Steven D.
Goldstein, age 43
EVP, CFO, and Treasurer: Michael P. Monaco, age 47
EVP and General Counsel: Louise M. Parent, age 44
EVP and Chief Information Officer: Allan Z. Loren,
age 56
EVP Quality and Human Resources: Joseph W. Keilty,
age 57
Auditors: Ernst & Young LLP

WHERE

HQ: American Express Tower, World Financial Center,
New York, NY 10285
Phone: 212-640-2000
Fax: 212-619-9802

American Express operates throughout the US and in
more than 160 countries.

	1994 Sales		1994 Pretax Income	
	$ mil.	% of total	$ mil.	% of total
US	10,801	73	1,150	61
Europe	1,858	12	364	19
Asia/Pacific	1,220	8	225	12
Other regions	1,028	7	152	8
Adjustments	(625)	—	—	—
Total	**14,282**	**100**	**1,891**	**100**

WHAT

	1994 Sales		1994 Pretax Income	
	$ mil.	% of total	$ mil.	% of total
Travel Related Svcs.	10,256	71	1,396	65
American Express Financial Advisors	3,270	23	631	29
American Express Bank	652	5	119	6
Other	188	1	(255)	—
Adjustments	(84)	—	—	—
Total	**14,282**	**100**	**1,891**	**100**

Selected Services
American Express Cards
American Express
  Travelers Cheques
Banking services
Corporate cards
Financial planning services
Property/casualty insurance
Revolving credit
  cards (Optima)
Travel planning

Magazines
Departures
Food & Wine
Travel & Leisure
Your Company

Selected Subsidiaries
American Express Bank
American Express
  Financial Advisors
AMEX Life Assurance Co.
Travel Related Services

KEY COMPETITORS

Advance Publications
Aetna
Allstate
AT&T
Barclays
Carlson
Chase Manhattan
Chemical Banking
Citicorp
Dean Witter, Discover
First Chicago
Hearst
Household Intl.

John Hancock
Lagardère
Maritz Travel
MasterCard
MetLife
New York Times
Prudential
Rosenbluth Intl.
Thomas Cook
Thomson Corp.
Visa
World Travel

HOW MUCH

	9-Year Growth	1985	1986	1987	1988	1989	1990	1991	1992	1993	1994
Sales ($ mil.)	2.1%	11,850	14,652	17,626	23,132	25,047	24,332	25,763	26,961	14,173	14,282
Net income ($ mil.)	6.4%	810	1,110	533	1,038	1,157	338	789	436	1,478	1,413
Income as % of sales	—	6.8%	7.6%	3.0%	4.5%	4.6%	1.4%	3.1%	1.6%	10.4%	9.9%
Earnings per share ($)	5.0%	1.78	2.46	1.20	2.43	2.70	0.69	1.59	0.83	2.92	2.75
Stock price – high ($)	—	27.50	35.06	40.63	30.38	39.38	35.25	30.38	25.38	36.63	33.13
Stock price – low ($)	—	17.94	25.25	20.75	22.88	26.38	17.50	20.00	22.38	22.38	25.25
Stock price – close ($)	1.2%	26.50	28.31	22.88	26.63	34.88	20.63	20.50	24.88	30.88	29.50
P/E – high	—	15	15	47	13	15	17	14	19	13	12
P/E – low	—	10	11	24	9	10	8	9	15	8	9
Dividends per share ($)	4.3%	0.65	0.68	0.75	0.76	0.84	0.92	0.94	1.00	1.00	0.95
Book value per share ($)	1.1%	11.41	12.60	10.11	11.39	12.90	13.21	14.43	14.58	17.42	12.57
Employees	0.3%	70,536	78,747	84,278	100,188	107,542	106,836	110,728	114,352	64,654	72,412

1994 Year-end:
Debt ratio: 77.4%
Return on equity: 19.1%
Cash (mil.): $3,433
Long-term debt (mil.): $7,162
No. of shares (mil.): 496
Dividends
  Yield: 3.2%
  Payout: 34.2%
Market value (mil.): $14,628
Assets (mil.): $97,006

**Stock Price History
High/Low 1985–94**

AMERICAN FINANCIAL GROUP, INC.

OVERVIEW

Yes, they do have bananas, but the Lindners are splitting things up a whole new way these days. Cincinnati-based American Financial Group was created in 1995 after the Lindner family reshuffled their holdings to take public their private holding company, American Financial Corporation. In the shake-up, American Premier, a publicly traded insurance company 43% owned by the Lindner family, acquired American Financial Corp. When the transaction was completed — after 3 name changes and 9 lawsuits (since settled) — American Financial Group became the 51%-family-owned holding company for a group of businesses focused primarily on insurance.

American Financial Group's insurance holdings include Great American Insurance Group (multiline property and casualty

insurance), American Annuity Group (property and casualty insurance), and American Premier Underwriters (nonstandard auto insurance and California workers' compensation). Other holdings include Chiquita Brands International (production, processing, marketing, and distribution of bananas and other foods), Citicasters (radio and TV station ownership), and *Financial World* magazine.

American Financial remains a family affair. It is headed by 76-year-old Carl Lindner, and his 3 sons are all on the board. Some analysts complain that the Lindners restructured their holdings so they could shift their high debt payments to the publicly traded company. However, others say the new setup will more solidly align family management interests with shareholders.

WHEN

Carl Lindner, who had built his family's dairy business into the 220-unit United Dairy Farmers ice cream store chain, formed Henthy Realty (1955) and bought 3 S&Ls (1959). In 1960 the company's name became American Financial Corp. (AFC) to reflect the diversified financial services it offered. After a 1961 IPO, American Financial bought United Liberty Life Insurance (1963) and Provident Bank (1966).

American Financial then diversified into several new areas. American Financial Leasing & Services Company was formed in 1968 to lease airplanes, computers, and other equipment to corporate customers, and in 1969 AFC acquired Phoenix developer Rubenstein Construction, renaming it American Continental. In 1971 American Financial bought several life, casualty, and mortgage insurance companies and entered publishing by purchasing a 95% stake in the *Cincinnati Enquirer*. In 1973 it bought National General, which owned the Great American Insurance Group; paperback publisher Bantam Books; and hardback publisher Grosset & Dunlap.

American Financial suffered during the mid-1970s, when inflation grew faster than regulated insurance rates. In addition to selling its book publishers (1974), AFC sold the *Enquirer* and American Continental (1975). The insurance companies were consolidated as Great American Insurance Company in 1976. AFC spun off Provident Bank as a special dividend to shareholders in 1980.

Lindner took AFC private in 1981. That year subsidiary American Financial Enterprises

acquired a 20% interest in Penn Central, the former railroad that had emerged from a 1970 bankruptcy as an industrial manufacturer. In 1984 American Financial sold convenience store chain UtoteM to Circle K for a minority interest in Circle K. Also that year, AFC increased its holdings in United Brands (later renamed Chiquita Brands International) from 29% to 45%; Lindner installed himself as CEO and reversed that company's losses. In 1990, after Circle K went bankrupt, AFC wrote off most of its investment in that company. AFC has since divested many holdings, including Hunter S&L, Kings Island amusement park, and its interest in Scripps Howard Broadcasting.

In part, the divestitures were to raise money to keep Great American Communications (formerly Taft Communications, acquired in 1987) afloat. The company fared poorly because of the recession but also because Lindner loaded it up with debt when he bought large portions of its stock in a $1.5 billion takeover. The company entered bankruptcy in 1992 but emerged the next year with a new focus (broadcasting to metropolitan markets) and a new name (Citicasters Inc.) to reflect that focus.

AFC left the TV show production business in 1993 by swapping its 48% investment in Spelling Entertainment for stock in Blockbuster Entertainment. In 1995, as part of the merger and reorganization, members of the Lindner family and their associates received about $50 million in management bonuses.

WHO

Chairman and CEO: Carl H. Lindner, age 76,
$1,781,250 pay
VC: S. Craig Lindner, age 40
VC: Keith E. Lindner, age 35
President and COO: Carl H. Lindner III, age 41,
$1,810,897 pay
SVP: Neil M. Hahl, age 46, $932,897 pay
SVP, General Counsel, and Secretary: Robert W. Olson,
age 49, $762,431 pay
President, Non-Standard Automobile Insurance Group:
Michael D. Krause, age 42, $591,250 pay
VP and Treasurer: Fred J. Runk
VP Human Resources: Lawrence Otto
Auditors: Ernst & Young LLP

WHERE

HQ: One E. 4th St., Cincinnati, OH 45202
Phone: 513-579-6600
Fax: 513-579-2580

WHAT

	1994 Sales		1994 Operating Income	
	$ mil.	% of total	$ mil.	% of total
Auto liability & physical damage	436	20	(14)	—
Property & multiple peril	382	18	(41)	—
Annuities	378	18	59	20
Workers' comp. & other liability	375	18	39	13
Investment & other income	315	15	199	67
Other property & casualty insurance	186	9	(18)	—
Other	48	2	—	—
Adjustments	(17)	—	(181)	—
Total	**2,103**	**100**	**44**	**100**

1994 Assets		
	$ mil.	% of total
Cash & equivalents	171	2
Treasury & agency securities	293	3
Foreign governments' securities	58	1
Utility bonds	767	7
Mortgage-backed securities	1,624	15
State & municipal bonds	60	1
Corporate bonds	3,585	34
Stocks	314	3
Other investments	833	8
Loans receivable	642	6
Reinsurance recoverables & prepaid premiums	902	8
Goodwill	176	2
Other assets	971	9
Total	**10,550**	**100**

Subsidiaries and Affiliates
American Annuity Group (80%)
American Financial Enterprises (83%)
American Premier Underwriters (51%)
Chiquita Brands International (46%)
Citicasters Inc. (55%)
Great American Insurance Group

Other Holdings
FW magazine
The Golf Center at Kings Island
Provident Travel Corp.

KEY COMPETITORS

Aetna	Liberty Mutual
Allstate	McGraw-Hill
CIGNA	MetLife
Dole	New York Life
Equitable	Northwestern Mutual
FMR	Prudential
Forbes	State Farm
GEICO	Time Warner
Kemper	Transamerica

HOW MUCH

	9-Year Growth	1985	1986	1987	1988	1989	1990	1991	1992	1993	1994
Sales ($ mil.)	(1.0%)	2,310	2,791	2,588	6,814	7,038	7,761	5,219	3,929	2,721	2,103
Net income ($ mil.)	—	(23)	184	127	102	3	(6)	57	(162)	220	2
Income as % of sales	—	—	6.6%	4.9%	1.5%	0.0%	—	1.1%	—	0.8%	0.1%
Employees	2.0%	45,800	44,300	52,800	52,000	53,000	54,000	54,000	69,200	60,790	54,840

1994 Year-end:
Equity as % of assets: 3.8%
Return on equity: 0.4%
Cash (mil.): $171
Long-term debt (mil.): $1,107
Assets (mil.): $10,550

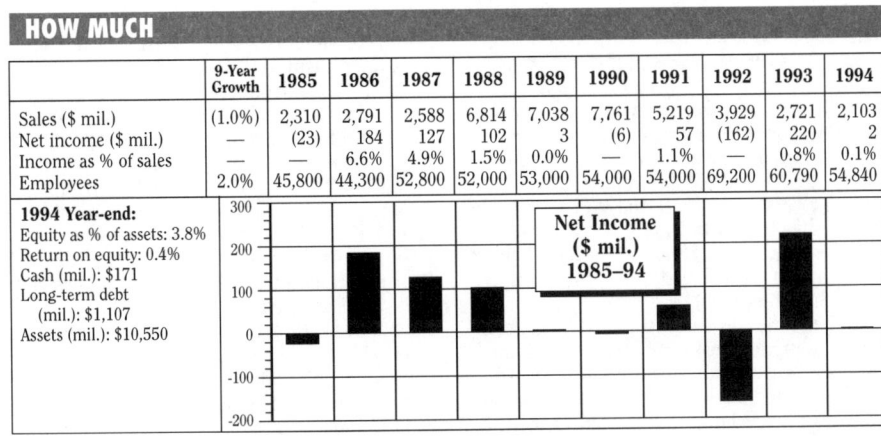

Net Income ($ mil.) 1985–94

AMERICAN HOME PRODUCTS CORP.

OVERVIEW

Madison, New Jersey–based American Home Products (AHP) is a large diversified concern that is growing larger. Its major units produce pharmaceutical, consumer health care, animal health, agricultural, and food products, as well as medical supplies and diagnostics. In 1994 American Cyanamid, after initial resistance, merged with AHP in a deal valued at $9.6 billion to form the world's 4th largest pharmaceutical company with expected sales of about $13 billion in 1995.

The combination broadens and diversifies the company's products and improves the company's standing in such areas as biotechnology, generics, and agricultural products. It also beefs up R&D, which will expand the long-term pipeline for new products.

The company boasts the leading US prescription drug company, by number of prescriptions dispensed, in its subsidiary Wyeth-Ayerst Laboratories. AHP's well-known divisional names include Whitehall Labs (Advil, Anacin) and A. H. Robins (Robitussin).

AHP maintains a leadership position in women's health care products. The company's lineup includes Premarin, an estrogen drug that is made from pregnant mares' urine and is the most prescribed drug in America. Use of Premarin for the treatment of symptoms of menopause and osteoporosis will continue to grow as the baby boomers age.

American Cyanamid brings to the merger its status as the largest US producer of childhood vaccines and its prominent Centrum multivitamins. Although the merger will be expensive, the company expects restructuring (including 4,000 job cuts) to result eventually in economies of scale.

WHEN

Incorporated in 1926, American Home Products consolidated several small companies that made proprietary medicinals such as Hill's Cascara Quinine and St. Jacob's Oil. AHP's history is one of continuous acquisitions.

During the Great Depression AHP bought over 30 food and drug companies. A sunburn oil acquired in 1935 became the hemorrhoid treatment Preparation H. Anacin was also acquired in the 1930s; Chef Boyardee was added in 1946. AHP purchased Canadian company Ayerst Laboratories in 1943 (cod liver oil, vitamins, and Premarin). Ayerst made penicillin for the Canadian armed forces in WWII.

In alliance with the British drug company Imperial Chemical Industries (ICI), Ayerst developed Inderal (1968), the first of the beta-blocker class of antihypertensives. AHP acquired Sherwood Medical Group (medical supplies) in 1982 and Bristol-Myers's animal health division in 1987. In 1988 it took over A. H. Robins, the company bankrupted by suits over the Dalkon Shield contraceptive device. In 1989, within 5 years of its introduction, Advil (AHP's OTC version of ibuprofen) outsold Bristol-Myers's Nuprin. In the 1980s AHP sold its non–health care businesses. In 1990 it completed integrating A. H. Robins, strengthening AHP's line of medical, veterinary, and consumer health products.

In 1993 the company expanded its generic drug making. In 1994 AHP began selling the antidepressant Effexor, claiming it has fewer side effects and works better than other antidepressants; it also bought American Cyanamid.

When Frank Washburn learned of a German process that extracted nitrogen, lime, and carbide to make cyanamid, a basic component of fertilizer, he bought the North American process rights, founded American Cyanamid in 1907, and began producing calcium cyanamide, the world's first synthetic fertilizer.

Washburn died in 1922, and his assistant, William Bell, became president. The company, which sold cyanide to the mining industry for extracting minerals from ore, diversified in the 1920s by buying chemical concerns.

During WWII American Cyanamid supplied US troops with typhus vaccine, dried blood plasma, and surgical sutures. In 1948 subsidiary Lederle discovered Aureomycin, an antibiotic. It diversified into consumer-related businesses in the 1950s and 1960s, buying Shulton (fragrances) in 1971. (It sold all its consumer businesses by 1990.)

In 1988 it introduced Novantrone (an anticancer drug). In 1992 it created an autonomous unit for its chemical operations, Cytec Industries (spun off in 1994). Also in 1992 it merged its oncology business with cancer drug maker Immunex. American Cyanamid paid $350 million and received 53.5% of Immunex. In 1994 it joined with Progenics Pharmaceuticals to develop drugs that destroy cells infected with HIV.

In 1995 AHP agreed to sell its Latin American oral health business (Kolynos) to Colgate-Palmolive for $1 billion and its Acufex Microsurgical unit to Smith & Nephew plc for $141 million.

NYSE symbol: AHP
Fiscal year ends: December 31

WHO

Chairman, President, and CEO: John R. Stafford,
age 57, $1,668,750 pay
EVP: Robert G. Blount, age 56, $814,875 pay
SVP: Fred Hassan, age 49, $738,000 pay
SVP: Stanley F. Barshay, age 55, $598,125 pay
SVP and General Counsel: Louis L. Hoynes Jr., age 59,
$564,038 pay
SVP: Joseph J. Carr, age 52
President, Wyeth-Ayerst Laboratories: Robert Essner
President, American Home Food Products: Charles E.
LaRosa
VP Finance (Principal Accounting Officer): John R.
Considine, age 44
VP Human Resources: René R. Lewin, age 48
VP Taxes: Thomas M. Nee, age 55
VP: E. Thomas Corcoran, age 47
VP: David Lilley, age 48
VP: William J. Murray, age 49
Auditors: Arthur Andersen & Co, SC

WHERE

HQ: American Home Products Corporation,
Five Giralda Farms, Madison, NJ 07940-0874
Phone: 201-660-5000
Fax: 201-660-6048

	1994 Sales		1994 Pretax Income	
	$ mil.	% of total	$ mil.	% of total
US	5,908	66	1,346	66
Europe & Africa	1,423	16	300	15
Canada & Latin America	1,022	11	271	13
Asia & Australia	613	7	113	6
Total	**8,966**	**100**	**2,030**	**100**

WHAT

	1994 Sales		1994 Pretax Income	
	$ mil.	% of total	$ mil.	% of total
Health care prod.	7,886	88	1,840	91
Food products	997	11	156	7
Agricultural prod.	83	1	17	1
Adjustments	—	—	17	1
Total	**8,966**	**100**	**2,030**	**100**

Selected Brands

Agricultural Products
Counter (insecticide)
Delan (fungicide)
Pursuit (herbicide)

Consumer Products
Advil
Anacin
Centrum (multivitamins)
Chef Boyardee
Denorex (shampoo)
Gulden's (mustard)
Jiffy Pop
Polaner (fruit spread)

Preparation H
Robitussin

Selected Pharmaceuticals
Cordarone (cardiovascular)
Effexor (antidepressant)
ISMO (angina treatment)
Minocin (antibiotic)
Norplant (contraceptive)
Orudis (anti-inflammatory)
Pipracil (antibiotic)
Premarin (estrogen
replacement)
Vaccines

KEY COMPETITORS

Abbott Labs	DuPont	PepsiCo
ALZA	Eli Lilly	Pfizer
Amgen	FMC	Procter & Gamble
BASF	Genentech	Quaker Oats
Baxter	Glaxo	Rhône-Poulenc
Bayer	Heinz	Roche
Becton, Dickinson	Hoechst	St. Jude Medical
Block Drug	ICN	Sandoz
Bristol-Myers	Pharmaceuticals	Schering-Plough
Squibb	Imperial Chemical	Siemens
Carter-Wallace	Johnson	SmithKline
Chiron Corp.	& Johnson	Beecham
Ciba-Geigy	Merck	Upjohn
ConAgra	Nestlé	U.S. Surgical
C. R. Bard	Novo Nordisk	Warner-Lambert

HOW MUCH

	9-Year Growth	1985	1986	1987	1988	1989	1990	1991	1992	1993	1994
Sales ($ mil.)	5.9%	5,358	5,684	5,850	6,401	6,747	6,775	7,079	7,874	8,305	8,966
Net income ($ mil.)	7.2%	818	866	928	996	1,102	1,231	1,375	1,151	1,469	1,528
Income as % of sales	—	15.2%	15.2%	15.9%	15.6%	16.3%	18.2%	19.4%	14.6%	17.7%	17.0%
Earnings per share ($)	7.7%	2.54	2.73	2.98	3.22	3.54	3.92	4.36	3.66	4.73	4.97
Stock price – high ($)	—	33.44	47.44	48.38	42.88	54.69	55.13	86.25	84.25	69.00	67.25
Stock price – low ($)	—	25.06	30.63	31.00	35.19	39.88	43.00	46.50	63.25	55.50	55.38
Stock price – close ($)	8.0%	31.44	38.44	36.38	41.63	53.75	52.63	84.63	67.50	64.75	62.75
P/E – high	—	14	18	17	13	15	14	20	23	15	14
P/E – low	—	11	12	11	11	11	11	11	17	12	11
Dividends per share ($)	8.2%	1.45	1.55	1.67	1.80	1.95	2.15	2.38	2.66	2.86	2.94
Book value per share ($)	7.0%	7.59	8.03	8.71	10.18	6.30	8.52	10.46	11.38	12.49	13.90
Employees	3.7%	53,337	49,896	50,623	51,464	50,816	48,700	47,938	50,653	51,399	74,009

1994 Year-end:
Debt ratio: 70.3%
Return on equity: 37.6%
Cash (mil.): $1,944
Current ratio: 1.69
Long-term debt (mil.): $9,973
No. of shares (mil.): 306
Dividends
  Yield: 4.7%
  Payout: 59.2%
Market value (mil.): $19,200

Stock Price History
High/Low 1985–94

AMERICAN INTERNATIONAL GROUP, INC.

OVERVIEW

American International Group (AIG) is the US's largest public property/casualty insurer and one of the largest insurance companies in the world. With a well-diversified product line (it specializes in property/casualty in the US but also has strong life insurance operations overseas, where it makes 52% of its money), AIG was able to withstand the natural disasters of the early 1990s better than many of its competitors. And its savvy investment strategy helped the company weather the US bond market collapse of 1994.

AIG has been branching into other lines in recent years, including personal auto (through its investment in 20th Century Industries, California's most efficient, though troubled, auto insurer), insurance brokerage (through the purchase of part of Alexander & Alexander), and health care (with new workers' compensation and health care management operations developed in-house).

The company is also continuing to expand overseas by adding commercial insurance operations in Russia and Uzbekistan, returning to Pakistan after a 20-year absence, and expanding its operations in China (where AIG was born and where it is the first US life insurer to be licensed since the 1950s).

WHEN

Former ice cream parlor owner Cornelius Starr founded casualty and property insurer C. V. Starr & Co. in Shanghai in 1919. For a few years Starr underwrote business for other insurers. Then in 1921 he began selling life insurance to the Chinese. In 1926 he opened a New York office to solicit insurance business on risks incurred outside the US by American companies. As WWII approached, Starr moved his base to the US; when the war in Europe cut off business there, he concentrated on Latin America. In the 1950s he developed an international benefits pool that provided disability, health, and life insurance and portable pension plans for employees who moved from country to country.

In 1967 Starr chose his successor, attorney Maurice Greenberg, and died the following year. By 1972 Greenberg had established American International Group as a holding company for Starr's worldwide collection of insurance companies. Greenberg is widely regarded as the true genius behind AIG.

AIG has always taken risks its competitors shun. During the mid-1970s AIG insured offshore oil rigs when other insurers would not, charging annual premiums as high as 10% of value. The company uses reinsurers around the world to help leverage otherwise risky ventures. AIG accepts larger single risks than most other insurers and therefore is the largest user of reinsurance in the US.

By 1975 it was the largest foreign life insurer in Hong Kong, Japan, Malaysia, the Philippines, Singapore, and Taiwan and the only insurer with sales and support facilities operating throughout the world.

From 1979 to 1984 the property/casualty business suffered heavy price competition that cost the industry almost $21 billion in under-writing losses, but during this period AIG outperformed all rivals in terms of its combined ratio (expenses plus losses divided by premiums). In 1986 the company again leveraged its international presence by offering services to foreign manufacturers interested in the American market.

The next year the company finally succeeded in cracking the Korean market, becoming only the 2nd US-owned company to do so (CIGNA was the first).

In the 1980s AIG began investment operations in Asia, increased its presence in health care, and formed a financial services group. In 1990 it bought International Lease Finance Corp., which leases and remarkets jets to airlines. AIG also became the first US insurer licensed to operate in Poland and Hungary (both joint ventures). In 1991 AIG began operating in Estonia.

The company resumed its Chinese operations in 1993 after triumphing over stiff opposition from local state monopolies. AIG is once again sending commissioned Chinese salespeople door-to-door to sell life insurance to their compatriots.

In 1994, a year in which many insurers suffered from the Northridge earthquake in California and other natural disasters, AIG enjoyed double-digit earnings growth. Its 1995 results will suffer little from the Kobe earthquake because earthquake insurance is not used in Japan.

AIG (along with most of the US insurance industry) welcomed the probusiness Republican landslide of 1994, which in 1995 resulted in the appointment of more sympathetic state insurance commissioners. It is expected to lead to relaxation of environmental liability regulations, particularly Superfund rules.

WHO

Chairman and CEO: Maurice R. Greenberg, age 69, $3,750,000 pay
VC Finance: Edward E. Matthews, age 63, $766,924 pay
VC Life Insurance: Ernest E. Stempel, age 78, $475,000 pay
President: Thomas R. Tizzio, age 57, $716,239 pay
EVP Life Insurance: Edmund S. W. Tse, $470,834 pay
EVP: Evan Greenberg
SVP Domestic General-Brokerage: Kevin H. Kelley
SVP Life Insurance: R. Kendall Nottingham
SVP Administration: Lawrence W. English
SVP Worldwide Claims: John G. Hughes
SVP and Chief Investment Officer: Win J. Neuger
SVP Financial Services: Petros K. Sabatacakis
SVP and Comptroller: Howard I. Smith
SVP Senior Casualty Actuary and Senior Claims Officer: Robert M. Sandler
SVP: Stephen Y. N. Tse
SVP Human Resources: Axel I. Freudmann
General Counsel: Florence A. Davis
Auditors: Coopers & Lybrand L.L.P

WHERE

HQ: 70 Pine St., New York, NY 10270
Phone: 212-770-7000
Fax: 212-943-1125

AIG's property/casualty subsidiaries operate in all 50 states and approximately 130 countries.

	1994 Sales		1994 Pretax Income	
	$ mil.	% of total	$ mil.	% of total
US & Canada	10,806	48	1,420	48
Asia	8,374	37	1,193	40
Other regions	3,262	15	339	12
Total	**22,442**	**100**	**2,952**	**100**

WHAT

	1994 Assets	
	$ mil.	% of total
Cash & equivalents	76	0
State & municipal bonds	15,398	14
Corporate bonds	14,082	12
Foreign gov't securities	6,528	6
Stocks	5,658	5
Receivables & reinsurance	25,092	22
Mortgages & real estate	7,218	6
Flight equipment	10,723	9
Other	29,571	26
Total	**114,346**	**100**

	1994 Sales		1994 Pretax Income	
	$ mil.	% of total	$ mil.	% of total
General insurance	11,774	50	1,635	42
Life insurance	8,559	37	952	24
Financial services	1,866	8	405	10
Agency & svc. fees	238	1	54	1
Corporate	900	4	900	23
Adjustments	(895)	—	(994)	—
Total	**22,442**	**100**	**2,952**	**100**

Selected Subsidiaries
AIG Europe S.A.
American Home Assurance Co.
American International Assurance Co., Ltd.
American Life Insurance Co.
Lexington Insurance Co.
Nan Shan Life Insurance Co., Ltd.
National Union Fire Insurance Co.
Philippine American Life Insurance Co.

KEY COMPETITORS

Aetna	General Re	Prudential
Allianz	John Hancock	Tokio Marine
Allstate	Kemper National	and Fire
Chubb	Lloyd's of London	Transamerica
CIGNA	Loews	Travelers
Equitable	New York Life	USF&G

HOW MUCH

	9-Year Growth	1985	1986	1987	1988	1989	1990	1991	1992	1993	1994
Assets ($ mil.)	24.6%	15,845	21,473	29,555	37,317	46,037	58,202	69,389	92,722	101,015	114,346
Net income ($ mil.)	20.1%	420	791	1,033	1,209	1,367	1,442	1,553	1,625	1,918	2,176
Income as % of assets	—	2.7%	3.7%	3.5%	3.2%	3.0%	2.5%	2.2%	1.8%	1.9%	1.9%
Earnings per share ($)	18.7%	1.47	2.59	3.35	3.92	4.42	4.61	4.86	5.10	6.04	6.87
Stock price – high ($)	—	29.33	38.27	44.67	36.67	59.73	56.47	68.00	80.92	100.25	100.75
Stock price – low ($)	—	17.33	27.73	28.53	26.13	35.33	38.00	48.00	54.67	73.38	81.75
Stock price – close ($)	14.8%	28.27	32.60	32.00	36.13	55.20	51.25	65.59	77.33	87.75	98.00
P/E – high	—	22	18	15	10	14	12	14	16	17	15
P/E – low	—	13	13	9	7	8	8	10	11	12	12
Dividends per share ($)	15.2%	0.12	0.12	0.14	0.19	0.23	0.27	0.31	0.35	0.39	0.43
Book value per share ($)	17.7%	12.03	15.35	18.22	22.23	26.90	30.65	35.53	39.79	47.93	51.99
Employees	2.3%	26,100	28,000	31,000	31,000	33,000	33,000	33,600	32,000	33,000	32,000

1994 Year-end:
Equity as % of assets: 14.4%
Return on assets: 13.7%
Return on equity: 13.7%
Long-term debt (mil.): $13,730
No. of shares (mil.): 316
Dividends
  Yield: 0.4%
  Payout: 6.3%
Market value (mil.): $30,952
Sales (mil.): $22,442

Stock Price History
High/Low 1985–94

AMERICAN PRESIDENT COMPANIES, LTD.

OVERVIEW

American President offers an integrated system of ocean, rail, and truck transportation linking points in North America, Asia, and the Middle East. The Oakland-based company's shipping line (American President Lines) operates 21 containerships (4 more are expected in the near future) and a network of feeder vessels serving 58 ports in the Pacific and Indian Oceans and the Persian Gulf. In its intra-Asia market it serves about 425 ports. Because the containers are intermodal, freight can be taken off a ship, loaded on a truck or railcar in the same container, and sent onward.

Most of American President's domestic long-haul cargo is moved in double-stack rail-cars. Strong growth in its stack-train services has increased departures, leading it to acquire 1,800 domestic containers and lease 149 double-stack cars. The company has increased its presence in China and Mexico and started services in Latin America and Europe.

The US government is the company's single largest customer for international transportation, accounting for 3% of 1994 revenue. However, as more US foreign military bases are closed, military cargo traffic will decrease and business from the US government will likely decrease. American President's Asian services suffered from the 1995 earthquake in Kobe, Japan.

WHEN

In 1848 New York merchant William Aspinwall launched the first shipping line between Panama and California — the Pacific Mail Steamship Company. The company's first steamers left New York later that year and arrived in San Francisco Bay in 1849.

In 1866 Pacific Mail bought Atlantic Mail (owned by Cornelius Vanderbilt) while Vanderbilt went on to take over the New York Central Railroad. In 1867 Pacific Mail pioneered trade to Asia.

During the recession of 1873, Pacific Mail narrowly averted bankruptcy brought on by an overambitious construction program. Jay Gould gained control of the company in 1874, and by 1885 Gould's Union Pacific Railroad owned a majority share of Pacific Mail.

C. P. Huntington of the Central Pacific and Southern Pacific Railroads bought Pacific Mail in 1893. Upon Huntington's death in 1900, Southern Pacific bought the company. Edward Harriman took over Southern Pacific in 1902, operating it and Pacific Mail until his death in 1909. W. R. Grace bought Pacific Mail in 1915, and then in 1926 it was acquired by the Dollar Steamship Company.

Founded by Robert Dollar, the Dollar Company had conducted transpacific trade since 1902. However, weakened by strikes, the company faced bankruptcy by the mid-1930s. In 1938 the Maritime Commission forced the Dollar family to transfer control of the company to the government, reorganizing it as American President Lines.

From 1940 to 1952 the Dollar family tried to regain the company, which, by court order, was put up for sale. Venture capitalists led by Ralph Davies (formerly of Standard Oil) bought American President in 1952. Davies'

Natomas Company (offshore oil) bought the company in 1956. Bruce Seaton (SVP Finance, Natomas) became president of American President in 1977, emphasizing transpacific trade by intermodal container.

After buying Natomas in 1983, Diamond Shamrock spun off American President to the public. The company introduced double-stack intermodal railcars in the US in 1984. In 1988 American President invested about $6 million in Amtech (electronic tracking of intermodal containers). However, operating costs and interest expenses led to an 86% decline in earnings between 1988 and 1989. A $109 million restructuring charge sent the company into red ink in 1990, but military transport contracts for Operation Desert Storm boosted its bottom line in 1991 (as well as 1992–94).

Also in 1991 the company began rail service between the US and Mexico City and formed a joint venture with Orient Overseas Container (Hong Kong) to share vessel space. In 1992 it sold 61% of its interest in Amtech.

During 1994 the company sold its remaining real estate in California and began direct all-water service from Asia to Mexico. In late 1994 the shipping line received a waiver from the US Maritime Administration that will allow it to operate its new ships under foreign flags with foreign crews and still receive US government subsidies. American President requested the waiver because Congress took no action to reinstate the subsidies shipping companies had received for US-flagged vessels. The shipping lines have contended the subsidies are necessary because of costs associated with US labor requirements. In 1995 the merchant marine unions brought suit to repeal the waiver.

NYSE symbol: APS
Fiscal year ends: Last Friday in December

WHO

Chairman, President, and CEO: John M. Lillie, age 58, $870,548 pay
President and CEO, American President Lines: Joji Hayashi, age 55, $542,422 pay
President and CEO, APL Land Transport Services: Timothy J. Rhein, age 53, $542,422 pay
SVP and Chief Information Officer: James S. Marston, age 61, $425,250 pay
EVP and CFO: L. Dale Crandall, age 53
EVP, General Counsel, and Secretary: Maryellen B. Cattani, age 51
EVP, American President Lines: Michael Diaz, age 46
EVP, American President Lines: John G. Burgess, age 50
VP Human Resources: Nancy Williams
Auditors: Arthur Andersen & Co, SC

WHERE

HQ: 1111 Broadway, Oakland, CA 94607
Phone: 510-272-8000
Fax: 510-272-7941

The company maintains offices and agents in 45 countries.

Country of origin	1994 Ocean Transportation Sales % of total
US	26
Hong Kong	14
China	10
Japan	9
Taiwan	9
India	5
South Korea	4
Other	23
Total	**100**

	1994 Sales		1994 Operating Income	
	$ mil.	% of total	$ mil.	% of total
Intl. trans.	2,016	72	114	93
North American trans.	761	27	—	—
Other	16	1	9	7
Total	**2,793**	**100**	**123**	**100**

WHAT

	1994 Sales		1994 Operating Income	
	$ mil.	% of total	$ mil.	% of total
Transportation	2,777	99	114	93
Real estate	16	1	9	7
Total	**2,793**	**100**	**123**	**100**

Transportation
American Consolidation Services, Ltd.
American President Lines, Ltd. (ocean carrier)
APL Land Transport Services, Inc.
Eagle Marine Services, Ltd. (stevedoring and terminal services)

KEY COMPETITORS

Alexander & Baldwin
Crowley Maritime
CSX
Evergreen Marine
General Steamship
Kawasaki
Mitsubishi
Mitsui
Navix
Orient Overseas

HOW MUCH

	9-Year Growth	1985	1986	1987	1988	1989	1990	1991	1992	1993	1994
Sales ($ mil.)	10.1%	1,171	1,440	1,825	2,131	2,234	2,270	2,449	2,505	2,594	2,793
Net income ($ mil.)	7.6%	39	18	79	81	11	(60)	64	78	80	74
Income as % of sales	—	3.3%	1.3%	4.3%	3.8%	0.5%	—	2.6%	3.1%	3.1%	2.7%
Earnings per share ($)	10.6%	0.93	0.36	1.62	1.63	0.12	(1.73)	1.83	2.34	2.50	2.30
Stock price – high ($)	—	14.50	14.50	25.50	17.94	20.44	14.56	21.69	24.00	30.25	34.00
Stock price – low ($)	—	6.94	8.44	10.81	11.31	13.38	5.19	7.88	15.13	18.56	19.00
Stock price – close ($)	11.6%	9.44	13.06	14.75	17.00	14.06	7.75	20.63	19.38	28.63	25.25
P/E – high	—	16	40	16	11	—	—	12	10	12	15
P/E – low	—	8	23	7	7	—	—	4	7	7	8
Dividends per share ($)	8.6%	0.19	0.25	0.25	0.25	0.29	0.30	0.30	0.30	0.30	0.40
Book value per share ($)	4.9%	12.94	12.98	14.43	15.26	14.86	13.24	15.42	15.25	17.72	19.82
Employees	3.5%	3,687	3,970	3,975	4,508	4,994	5,117	5,232	5,209	5,437	5,025

1994 Year-end:
Debt ratio: 41.9%
Return on equity: 14.6%
Cash (mil.): $255
Current ratio: 1.51
Long-term debt (mil.): $386
No. of shares (mil.): 27
Dividends
  Yield: 1.6%
  Payout: 17.4%
Market value (mil.): $690

Stock Price History High/Low 1985–94

AMERICAN STANDARD COMPANIES INC.

OVERVIEW

While American Standard's profits have been in the toilet for years and its $2.1 billion debt has threatened to put the brakes on its breakneck expansion, investors have not cooled on the diversified manufacturer. The reasons? Piscataway, New Jersey–based American Standard — which makes plumbing products, braking systems for heavy trucks and buses, and air conditioning systems — is a globally diversified company with 94 plants in 32 countries, its sales are steadily rising, and its businesses are 1st or 2nd in each of its markets.

Its plumbing products unit offers a wide selection of products designed to fit the consumer tastes of individual countries. Its air-conditioning products unit makes products under the Trane brand name and emphasizes servicing, repair, and replacement over new construction. Its transportation products unit makes air brakes primarily for the commercial vehicle industries of Europe and Brazil.

The company's shift to demand flow technology (an improved version of just-in-time technology that greatly reduces product delivery time and improves product quality) has proved expensive to implement but should pay off in coming years.

The newly public company is controlled by Kelso ASI Partners (the firm that bought the company in 1988 and holds 59% of its stock). American Standard's employees own 14% through a stock ownership plan.

WHEN

In 1881 American Radiator was created in Buffalo to make steam and water heating equipment. J. P. Morgan acquired the company along with almost every other US heating equipment firm, consolidating them under the American Radiator name in 1899.

That same year Louisville-based Ahrens & Ott joined with Pittsburgh-based Standard Manufacturing to create Standard Sanitary, which produced enameled cast-iron plumbing parts and developed the one-piece lavatory, built-in bathtubs, and single taps for hot and cold running water.

Both American Radiator and Standard Sanitary grew through numerous acquisitions in the early decades of the 20th century. In 1929 the 2 companies merged to form American Radiator & Standard Sanitary, headquartered in New York City, which later that year bought CF Church (toilet seats). During the next 3 decades, the company expanded its operations across North and South America and into Europe. By the 1960s American Radiator & Standard Sanitary was the world's largest manufacturer of plumbing fixtures.

In 1967 the company changed its name to American Standard and then diversified out of the bathroom, acquiring a number of companies, the most important of which was Westinghouse Air Brake (WABCO, 1968). WABCO traces its history to Union Switch and Signal, begun in 1882. In 1917 Union Switch was bought by Westinghouse Air Brake. George Westinghouse had invented the airbrake before turning his attention to electrical products. Union Switch merged with its parent company and adopted the WABCO corporate name in 1951.

During the 1970s and 1980s American Standard consolidated its operations and sold off numerous businesses. It purchased Clayton Dewandre (truck brakes, 1977) and Queroy (faucets and fittings, 1982). In 1984 the company purchased Trane (air conditioners). In 1988 American Standard fought off a hostile takeover attempt by Black & Decker and then agreed to be purchased by ASI Holding (formed by the leveraged buyout firm Kelso & Co.) for $3 billion and taken private.

The transaction left American Standard deeply in debt. To raise cash in 1988, the company sold its Manhattan headquarters, its railway signal business ($105 million), and its Steelcraft division (steel doors, to Masco for $126 million). In 1989 the sale of American Standard's pneumatic controls business raised $102 million. The company sold its railway brake products operations to a group led by Investment AB Cardo (Sweden) in 1990. In 1991 it sold Tyler Refrigeration (refrigerated display cases) to a Kelso & Co. affiliate for $82 million, losing $22 million in the deal.

California's attorney general filed suit against American Standard in 1992 for allegedly violating EPA lead limits. In 1993 Dan Quayle joined American Standard's board.

In 1994 American Standard, in a joint venture agreement, acquired 70% of German manufacturer Deutsche Perrot-Bremsen's brake business. That same year it expanded its plumbing manufacturing business in China. The setting up of 6 joint ventures made the company the #1 full-line supplier of plumbing products in that country.

In February 1995 the company went public again through an IPO.

NYSE symbol: ASD
Fiscal year ends: December 31

WHO

Chairman, President, and CEO: Emmanuel A.
Kampouris, age 60, $1,200,000 pay
SVP Plumbing Products: George H. Kerckhove, age 57,
$491,000 pay
SVP Automotive Products: Horst Hinrichs, age 62,
$469,394 pay
VP and CFO: Fred A. Allardyce, age 53, $381,000 pay
VP; Group Executive, Plumbing Products, Europe:
Luigi Gandini, age 56, $368,369 pay
**VP; Group Executive, Air Conditioning Products,
Europe, Middle East, and Africa:** Daniel Hilger,
age 54
**VP; Group Executive, Plumbing Products, Worldwide
Fittings:** Wilfried Delker, age 54
VP; Group Executive, Plumbing Products, PRC: Gary A.
Brogoch, age 44
VP; Group Executive, Plumbing Products, Americas:
Alexander A. Apostolopoulos, age 52
**VP; Group Executive, Air Conditioning Products,
International:** William A. Klug, age 62
VP Air Conditioning Products, Compressor Business:
Bruce R. Schiller, age 50
VP, General Counsel, and Secretary: Richard A.
Kalaher, age 54
VP Systems and Technology: Cyril Gallimore, age 65
VP Human Resources: Adrian B. Deshotel, age 49
Auditors: Ernst & Young LLP

WHERE

HQ: One Centennial Ave., PO Box 6820, Piscataway,
NJ 08855-6820
Phone: 908-980-6000
Fax: 908-980-6120

The company operates 94 manufacturing facilities in 32
countries.

	1994 Sales		1994 Operating Income	
	$ mil.	% of total	$ mil.	% of total
US	2,465	54	168	47
Europe	1,572	34	144	41
Other regions	550	12	43	12
Adjustments	(130)	—	—	—
Total	**4,457**	**100**	**355**	**100**

WHAT

	1994 Sales		1994 Operating Income	
	$ mil.	% of total	$ mil.	% of total
Air-conditioning	2,480	56	182	51
Plumbing	1,218	27	111	31
Automotive	759	17	62	18
Total	**4,457**	**100**	**355**	**100**

Products

Plumbing
Bathroom and kitchen fittings and fixtures
Bathtubs

Automotive
Air brake and related systems

Air-Conditioning
Applied systems (custom-engineered and field-installed
components)
Mini-split systems (small unitary systems operating
without air ducts and generally used in residences)
Unitary systems (factory-assembled in one to 2 units for
residential and commercial use)

Major Brand Names

Plumbing
AMERICAN-STANDARD
IDEAL-STANDARD
STANDARD

Automotive
CLAYTON DEWANDRE
PERROT
WABCO
WABCO WESTINGHOUSE

Air-Conditioning
AMERICAN-STANDARD
TRANE

KEY COMPETITORS

AlliedSignal	Lennox
American Brands	Masco
Black & Decker	Tecumseh Products
Eaton	United Technologies
AB Electrolux	Watsco
Eljer Industries	Whitman
Fedders	York International
Kohler	

HOW MUCH

	9-Year Growth	1985	1986	1987	1988	1989	1990	1991	1992	1993	1994
Sales ($ mil.)	4.8%	2,912	2,998	3,400	3,716	3,334	3,637	3,595	3,792	3,830	4,457
Net income ($ mil.)	—	(3)	110	133	(26)	(34)	(54)	(111)	(57)	(209)	(86)
Income as % of sales	—	—	3.7%	3.9%	—	—	—	—	—	—	—
Employees	(0.6%)	40,000	38,900	39,300	34,100	33,300	32,900	32,000	33,500	36,000	38,000

1994 Year-end:
Debt ratio: 100.0%
Cash (mil.): $93
Current ratio: 0.99
Long-term debt (mil.): $2,152
Total assets (mil.): $3,156

American Standard Inc.

Net Income
($ mil.)
1985–94

AMERICAN STORES COMPANY

OVERVIEW

With no stores in Utah but about 1,600 in 26 other states, Salt Lake City–based American Stores is the 2nd largest US food retailer (behind Kroger). The holding company also owns one of the biggest drugstore chains in the country. American Stores, previously a decentralized operation, currently is trying to better integrate its businesses.

The company operates its food stores under the names Lucky, Super Saver, Jewel, and Acme and its drugstores under the Osco and Sav-on monikers; 149 stores are Jewel Osco combinations. American Stores ranks at or near the top of its markets in several major cities. Its food stores are #1 or #2 in Chicago, Oakland, Orange County, Philadelphia, and San Diego, while its drugstores hold the same distinction in Chicago, Indianapolis, Kansas City, Los Angeles, and Phoenix.

Capital spending by American Stores reached $565 million in 1994; the company opened 49 stores and remodeled 166 while investing $79 million in technological improvements. About 17% of American Stores's sales come from higher-margin products under private labels such as Acme, American Premier, Jewel, Lady Lee, Lancaster Brand, Osco, President's Choice, and Value Wise; the company wants 1/4 of its sales to come from private-label merchandise by the year 2000.

American Stores has begun 2 new ventures related to its drugstore business. Osco Home Health Care stores offer such items as wheelchairs and sleep monitors, while RxAmerica manages pharmacy benefits through contracts with 35,000 drugstores.

L. S. Skaggs, chairman of American Stores, owns 17% of the company.

WHEN

Leonard S. Skaggs, one of 6 sons of Safeway founder Marion Skaggs, bought Pay Less Drug Stores in Salt Lake City in 1939 with his Safeway stock proceeds. L. S. Skaggs, the current chairman, took over after his father's death in 1950. In 1965, when the business had 69 locations, it incorporated as Skaggs Drug Centers and went public. In 1969 the company formed a joint venture with Albertson's, a grocery store operator in the West, to develop combination food/drug stores under the name Skaggs Albertson's. Skaggs and Albertson's dissolved their venture in 1977, with each receiving half of the jointly owned locations.

Skaggs merged in 1979 with American Stores of Philadelphia. (American was formed in 1917 by the combination of 5 grocers, including Acme Tea [founded 1885], and operated stores throughout the mid-Atlantic states.) Skaggs then changed its name to American Stores and continued to operate as a holding company, with stores under local names. After acquiring American Stores, which had owned the Alpha Beta stores in Southern California since the 1940s, the company applied the name Skaggs Alpha Beta to the stores left over from the joint venture with Albertson's.

American sold Alphy's Restaurants to Denny's in 1983 and in 1984 sold several of its Arizona Alpha Beta food stores, Houston Sav-on drugstores, and another drug chain, Rea & Derick. Also in 1984 American acquired Chicago-based Jewel Companies. Jewel, originally the Jewel Tea Company, had begun in

Chicago in 1899 as a route-delivery grocery operation and had opened grocery stores in the 1930s. It operated stores under the names of Jewel, Jewel Osco, Star Market (sold 1994), Buttrey's, and Osco Drug. Jewel unleashed a torrent of legal activity in 1985 when it inadvertently produced milk contaminated by salmonella.

American bought Lucky Stores, a major California-based chain, in 1988, but antitrust considerations kept it from integrating the Southern California store operations of Lucky Stores and Alpha Beta. The company sold its 44 Buttrey Food & Drug stores and support facilities (1990), its Alpha Beta Stores in Southern California, and 51 of its Osco Drug Stores (1991). In 1992 American bought 63 CVS pharmacies and operating rights to 22 CVS health and beauty aids stores from Melville. That year it sold 74 Jewel Osco stores and agreed to pay $90 million to women the company had allegedly discriminated against.

In 1993 American debuted a price-cutting program in recession-battered Southern California with the slogan "Times are tough and Lucky just got tougher," which has increased its customer base. In 1994 American sold its Boston-area Star Market to an Investcorp-formed investment group.

The company sold 45 Acme Supermarkets in New York and Pennsylvania to Penn Traffic for $94 million in early 1995. Soon after, American Stores bought 17-store Clark Drugs for $35 million; Clark had been founded in 1959 by former Sav-on executive Alton Clark.

NYSE symbol: ASC
Fiscal year ends: Saturday closest to January 31

WHO

Chairman: L. S. Skaggs, age 71, $726,510 pay
President and CEO: Victor L. Lund, age 47,
$1,089,764 pay
COO, Procurement and Logistics: Robert P. Hermanns,
age 51, $694,055 pay (prior to promotion)
COO: David L. Maher, age 56, $653,859 pay (prior to
promotion)
COO, Markets: William J. Bolton, age 48, $373,589 pay
(prior to promotion)
CFO: Teresa Beck, age 40
Chief Strategy Officer: Kent T. Anderson, age 41
Chief Planning Officer: James R. Clark, age 51
COO, Retail: Martin A. Scholtens, age 52
Chief Human Resources Officer: Stephen L.
Mannschreck, age 49
Auditors: Ernst & Young LLP

WHERE

HQ: 709 E. South Temple, PO Box 27447, Salt Lake City,
UT 84127-0447
Phone: 801-539-0112
Fax: 801-531-0768

American Stores operates 1,597 retail food and drug
stores in 26 states.

	1995 Stores
	By State
California	636
Illinois	393
Pennsylvania	84
New Jersey	81
Indiana	71
Arizona	64
Other	268
Total	**1,597**

WHAT

	1995 Sales		1995 Operating Profit	
	$ mil.	**% of total**	**$ mil.**	**% of total**
Western Food	7,002	38	246	34
Eastern Food	5,957	33	258	35
Drug Store	4,544	24	229	31
Adjustments	852	5	(83)	—
Total	**18,355**	**100**	**650**	**100**

Western Food Operations
Jewel Osco–New Mexico
Lucky Stores Northern California
Lucky Stores Southern California
Super Saver

Eastern Food Operations
Acme Markets
Jewel Food Stores

Drug Stores
Osco Drug
Sav-on

Home Health Care Supply Stores
Osco Home Health Care

Pharmacy Benefit Management
RxAmerica

KEY COMPETITORS

ABCO Markets	IGA	Rite Aid
Albertson's	J Sainsbury	Safeway
Bruno's	Kmart	Smith's Food &
Eckerd	Kroger	Drug
George Weston	Longs	Stater Bros.
Limited	Meijer	Stop & Shop
Giant Eagle	Pathmark	Thrifty PayLess
Giant Food	Penn Traffic	Vons
Grand Union	Price/Costco	Walgreen
Great A&P	Raley's	Wal-Mart
Hughes Markets	Revco	Yucaipa

HOW MUCH

	9-Year Growth	1986	1987	1988	1989	1990	1991	1992	1993	1994	1995
Sales ($ mil.)	3.1%	13,890	14,022	14,272	18,478	22,004	22,156	20,823	19,051	18,763	18,355
Net income ($ mil.)	9.3%	155	145	154	98	118	182	240	206	247	345
Income as % of sales	—	1.1%	1.0%	1.1%	0.5%	0.5%	0.8%	1.2%	1.1%	1.3%	1.9%
Earnings per share ($)	9.5%	1.03	0.95	1.05	0.64	0.87	1.32	1.74	1.47	1.69	2.33
Stock price – high ($)[1]	—	17.06	17.81	21.56	16.63	18.13	17.88	23.09	23.50	24.63	27.75
Stock price – low ($)[1]	—	9.69	12.91	10.38	11.91	13.25	10.66	13.00	15.25	18.13	20.88
Stock price – close ($)[1]	5.8%	16.19	13.59	12.63	14.47	14.13	13.72	16.94	21.88	21.50	26.88
P/E – high	—	17	19	21	26	21	14	13	16	15	12
P/E – low	—	9	14	10	19	15	8	8	10	11	9
Dividends per share ($)	11.5%	0.18	0.21	0.21	0.24	0.25	0.28	0.32	0.37	0.40	0.48
Book value per share ($)	9.9%	6.11	6.74	7.35	7.63	8.72	9.78	10.94	11.93	12.23	14.34
Employees	(0.3%)	121,000	129,000	130,000	165,000	170,400	163,900	148,000	133,000	127,000	118,000

1995 Year-end:
Debt ratio: 51.8%
Return on equity: 18.2%
Cash (mil.): $196
Current ratio: 1.10
Long-term debt (mil.): $2,064
No. of shares (mil.): 143
Dividends
  Yield: 1.8%
  Payout: 20.6%
Market value (mil.): $3,843

**Stock Price History[1]
High/Low 1986–95**

[1] Stock prices are for the prior calendar year.

AMERITECH CORPORATION

OVERVIEW

Ameritech has stayed out of the merger mania among telephone and cable companies and has passed up offers to form national wireless communications networks. Instead, the company is focusing on core telecommunications services in its own 5-state Great Lakes region. CEO Richard Notebaert continues to promote opening its local telecommunications market to competition in exchange for entering the long distance and cable television markets. Major competitors, including AT&T and Teleport Communications, have already begun to offer some forms of local telecommunications services.

In transforming itself into a full-service communications company, Ameritech reorganized its operations along customer groups, including consumer and business customers and pay phone, cellular, advertising, and leasing customers. The company is also developing for its customers such new services as long distance and interactive services. Ameritech has investments in foreign telecommunications companies, including Telecom Corp. of New Zealand and Centertel of Poland.

With the recommendation of the Justice Department, Ameritech has requested permission from a federal judge to enter the long distance market (for the first time in 11 years) on a trial basis in Chicago and in Grand Rapids, Michigan, in 1996. In exchange, AT&T would be allowed to compete in the local telephone markets in these areas.

WHEN

Ameritech began as an arm of AT&T. From 1880 to 1885 the Bell System consolidated small, individual telephone companies into larger companies that, under franchise agreements, could construct long distance lines to other Bell exchanges. Gradually the long distance lines became AT&T Long Lines; local operations were retained by the Bell Operating Companies. Illinois Bell, now Ameritech's largest operating company, was originally known as Chicago Telephone and operated between 1881 and 1920.

In the late 1870s E. T. Gilliland Company of Indianapolis, long part of Ameritech's Indiana Bell company, was considered Bell's most innovative manufacturer. In 1881 Gilliland sold 61% of its operations to Western Electric, at that time controlled by Bell's chief rival, Western Union. The purchase could have destroyed Bell and changed the history of US telephony, but Bell regained Gilliland through an outside investor named Jay Gould, who bought shares quietly.

A century later, in 1984, AT&T spun off its local operating subsidiaries as part of its antitrust settlement. Ameritech, which began operations that same year, received 5 of AT&T's 22 telephone subsidiaries, Ameritech Mobile Communications (cellular service provider), and a share in Bell Communications Research (Bellcore, the R&D arm shared by the Bell companies).

Since divestiture Ameritech has expanded its paging services by purchasing existing operations. It also began offering electronic mail and information services by starting iNet (1987) with Bell Canada and Telenet. In 1990 Ameritech was chosen, along with Bell Atlantic, to acquire an interest in New Zealand's public phone system for $2.5 billion. The following year it joined France Telecom and the Polish government to create a national cellular phone system in Poland.

Back in the US, in 1991 Ameritech bought CyberTel, one of the 2 cellular firms in St. Louis (the other is Southwestern Bell); Knowledge Data Systems (data processing systems); and NOTIS (library information software systems). In 1992 then-CEO William Weiss held a fateful meeting in which he asked each top executive to write a "profile" of Ameritech as envisioned in 1995. Afterward only 4 executives who shared Weiss's enthusiasm for radical corporate change (current CEO Notebaert among them) joined him in planning the company's future in video, long distance, and wireless services. In the same year Ameritech and Singapore Telecom acquired a 49.9% interest in Norway's NetCom GSM (cellular services). In 1993 Ameritech bought 15% of MATAV, Hungary's telephone company.

In 1994 Ameritech signed a memorandum of understanding with Walt Disney, BellSouth, and SBC Communications to develop and deliver video programming to consumers. Ameritech also made an investment in General Electric Information Services (electronic business services). In 1995 Ameritech, along with the other 6 Bell companies, announced plans to sell Bellcore.

NYSE symbol: AIT
Fiscal year ends: December 31

WHO

Chairman, President, and CEO: Richard C. Notebaert, age 47, $1,463,783 pay
EVP Corporate Strategy and Business Development: W. Patrick Campbell, age 48, $722,092 pay
EVP and General Counsel: Thomas P. Hester, age 57, $662,700 pay
EVP International: Walter S. Catlow, age 50
EVP and CFO: Oren G. Shaffer, age 52
SVP Corporate Communications: Rita P. Wilson, age 48
SVP State and Government Affairs: Thomas J. Reiman, age 45
SVP Human Resources: Walter M. Oliver, age 49
Auditors: Arthur Andersen & Co, SC

WHERE

HQ: 30 S. Wacker Dr., Chicago, IL 60606
Phone: 312-750-5000
Fax: 312-207-1601

WHAT

	1994 Sales	
	$ mil.	% of total
Local service	5,337	42
Interstate access	2,218	18
Long distance	1,456	12
Intrastate access	612	5
Directory, cellular & other	2,947	23
Total	**12,570**	**100**

Selected Affiliates
Centertel (24.5%, cellular services, Poland)
MATÁV (15%, long distance and cellular services, Hungary)
NetCom (25%, cellular services, Norway)
Telecom Corporation of New Zealand, Ltd. (24.8%)
Wer liefert was? (publisher of business purchasing guides, Germany)
Worldview Systems Corp. (40%, electronic travel information)

Selected Services
Advertising services
Cellular and other wireless services
Billing and collection services
Interactive services
Leasing services
Local and toll services
Long distance services
Network access services
Paging services

Telephone Companies
Illinois Bell Telephone Co.
Indiana Bell Telephone Co., Inc.
Michigan Bell Telephone Co.
The Ohio Bell Telephone Co.
Wisconsin Bell, Inc.

KEY COMPETITORS

AirTouch	MCI
American Business Information	NYNEX
	Pacific Telesis
AT&T	SBC Communications
Bell Atlantic	Sprint
BellSouth	TCI Intl.
BT	Telephone and Data Systems
Cable & Wireless	Teleport Communications
Century Telephone	Time Warner
Contel Cellular	U.S. Long Distance
GTE	U.S. Signal
LDDS Communications	U S WEST

HOW MUCH

	9-Year Growth	1985	1986	1987	1988	1989	1990	1991	1992	1993	1994
Sales ($ mil.)	3.8%	9,021	9,362	9,536	9,903	10,211	10,663	10,818	11,153	11,710	12,570
Net income ($ mil.)	0.9%	1,078	1,138	1,188	1,237	1,238	1,254	1,166	1,346	1,513	1,170
Income as % of sales	—	11.9%	12.2%	12.5%	12.5%	12.1%	11.8%	10.8%	12.1%	12.9%	9.3%
Earnings per share ($)	1.6%	1.84	1.97	2.12	2.28	2.30	2.37	2.20	2.51	2.78	2.13
Stock price – high ($)	—	17.77	25.39	24.97	24.47	48.06	34.88	34.88	37.25	45.56	43.13
Stock price – low ($)	—	12.42	16.34	18.50	20.50	24.00	26.25	27.88	28.13	35.00	36.25
Stock price – close ($)	9.5%	17.77	22.09	21.16	23.94	34.00	33.38	31.75	35.63	38.38	40.38
P/E – high	—	10	13	12	11	21	15	16	15	33	20
P/E – low	—	7	8	9	9	10	11	13	11	25	17
Dividends per share ($)	6.6%	1.08	1.16	1.25	1.35	1.46	1.58	1.70	1.76	1.86	1.92
Book value per share ($)	(1.7%)	12.76	13.33	13.86	14.57	14.25	14.63	15.18	12.94	14.41	10.98
Employees	(1.8%)	74,885	77,538	78,510	77,334	77,326	75,780	73,967	71,300	67,192	63,594

1994 Year-end:
Debt ratio: 51.2%
Return on equity: 16.8%
Cash (mil.): $74
Current ratio: 0.56
Long-term debt (mil.): $4,448
No. of shares (mil.): 551
Dividends
 Yield: 4.8%
 Payout: 90.1%
Market value (mil.): $22,268

Stock Price History
High/Low 1985–94

AMGEN INC.

Amgen, based in Thousand Oaks, California (near Los Angeles), is one of the world's largest biotechnology companies. Amgen's current success is attributable to 2 products developed using recombinant DNA technology (popularly known as "gene splicing"). EPOGEN is a red blood cell stimulator used to treat anemia in renal dialysis patients. NEUPOGEN stimulates production of infection-fighting white blood cells in chemotherapy patients. It also has been approved by the FDA for bone marrow transplant patients and for those with chronic neutropenia (a rare blood disorder). Although the company has no new products on the market, NEUPOGEN and EPOGEN sales are growing and it does have products in clinical trials.

The company's therapeutics are based on advances in cellular and molecular biology. Amgen's research concentrates on hemato-poiesis (blood cell formation), neurobiology, inflammation, and soft tissue repair and regeneration. The company headquarters is strategically located near such important research centers as the California Institute of Technology, UCLA, and UC Santa Barbara.

Amgen has joint ventures with Roche to sell NEUPOGEN, with Johnson & Johnson to promote EPOGEN for conditions other than dialysis anemia, and with Kirin to research neurotrophic diseases like Alzheimer's. With Regeneron Pharmaceuticals the company is researching brain-derived neurotrophic factor (BDNF) and Neurotropin-3 (NT-3).

The acquisition of Synergen in 1994 added another research facility, allowing for an accelerated research pace and expanding the number of products in various stages of research and clinical trials.

WHEN

Amgen was formed as Applied Molecular Genetics in 1980 by a group of scientists and venture capitalists to develop health care products based on molecular biological technology. George Rathmann, a VP at Abbott Laboratories who was doing research at UCLA, became the company's CEO and first employee. Rathmann decided to develop a few potentially profitable products rather than conduct general research. The company initially raised $19 million.

Amgen operated close to bankruptcy until 1983, when company scientist Fu-Kuen Lin cloned the human protein erythropoietin (EPO), which stimulates red blood cell production in the body. Amgen made its first public stock offering, of 2.4 million shares, that same year.

The company formed a joint venture with Kirin Brewery (Japan) in 1984 to develop and market EPO. The 2 companies also collaborated on recombinant human granulocyte colony stimulating factor (G-CSF), a human protein that stimulates the body's immune system to combat bacterial infection.

In 1985 Amgen established a marketing agreement with Ortho Pharmaceutical Corporation, a subsidiary of Johnson & Johnson. In 1988 Amgen created a tie with Roche Holdings. Company fortunes soared in 1989 when the FDA granted Amgen a license to produce EPOGEN (the brand name of EPO) to treat anemia.

In 1991 Amgen received approval to market NEUPOGEN, the brand name of G-CSF, to chemotherapy patients. That same year a federal court denied permission to Genetics Institute to market its version of EPO, giving Amgen a US monopoly on the product. A 1992 patent dispute with Genetics Institute's partner, Chugai Pharmaceutical, favored Amgen. Chugai had to renounce its US patents for its version of G-CSF and assign its US license rights to Amgen.

In 1992 Johnson & Johnson had to pay Amgen about $90 million in lost royalties concerning unfulfilled research obligations. Also in 1992 Amgen hired Kevin Sharer away from MCI as president, reflecting the growing company's need to concentrate as much on business management as pharmaceutical development. In 1993 Europe, Canada, and Australia expanded NEUPOGEN's therapies to include treatment of severe chronic neutropenia.

With the markets for its 2 major products beginning to mature and with increasing US efforts to minimize health costs, Amgen's phenomenal revenue growth is expected to slow to merely low double digits — around 15%. BDNF and Infergen (hepatitis C treatment) appear likely to be the company's next important products.

In 1993 Amgen became the first biotechnology company to establish a presence in China, reaching an agreement with Kirin Pharmaceuticals to sell NEUPOGEN (under the name Gran) and EPOGEN there. In 1995 Amgen received FDA permission for human clinical trials on a new blood-clotting drug (MGDF).

Nasdaq symbol: AMGN
Fiscal year ends: December 31

WHO

Chairman and CEO: Gordon M. Binder, age 59,
$1,256,648 pay
President and COO: Kevin W. Sharer, age 46,
$813,680 pay
SVP Finance and Corporate Development: Robert S.
Attiyeh, age 60, $798,000 pay
SVP Research: Daniel Vapnek, age 56, $711,076 pay
SVP Development: N. Kirby Alton, age 44, $497,036 pay
SVP Operations: Dennis M. Fenton, age 43
SVP Asia Pacific: Daryl D. Hill, age 49
VP Corporate Controller and Chief Accounting Officer:
Larry A. May, age 45
VP, Secretary, and General Counsel: Thomas E.
Workman Jr., age 67
VP Quality Assurance: Linda R. Wudl, age 49
VP Human Resources: Edward Garrnett
Auditors: Ernst & Young LLP

WHERE

HQ: 1840 Dehavilland Dr., Thousand Oaks, CA
91320-1789
Phone: 805-447-1000
Fax: 805-499-9315

Amgen has offices in Australia, Canada, China, Japan,
the US, and several European countries.

	1994 Sales		1994 Operating Profit	
	$ mil.	% of total	$ mil.	% of total
US	1,334	86	624	93
Europe	193	13	50	7
Other regions	23	1	(26)	—
Adjustments	98	—	(3)	—
Total	**1,648**	**100**	**645**	**100**

WHAT

	1994 Sales	
	$ mil.	% of total
Product sales	1,550	94
Other revenues	98	6
Total	**1,648**	**100**

Products
EPOGEN
NEUPOGEN

Products in Clinical Trials
Brain-derived neurotro-
phic factor (BDNF)
Hepatitis B vaccine
Infergen (interferon)
Interleukin-2 (IL-2)
Megakaryocyted growth
and development
factor (MGDF)

Neurotrophin-3 (NT-3)
Stem cell factor (SCF)

Key Strategic Alliances
AmCell
Johnson & Johnson
Kirin Brewery Co.
Regeneron Pharma-
ceuticals, Inc.
Roche Holdings
Rockefeller University

KEY COMPETITORS

Abbott Labs	Creative	Monsanto
Alpha-Beta	Biomolecules	Novo Nordisk
Technology	Cytel	Pfizer
American Home	Dow Chemical	Purepac
Products	DuPont	Regeneron
AMRAD	Eli Lilly	Pharmaceuticals
Bayer	Genentech	Rhône-Poulenc
Biogen	Glaxo	Roche
Bristol-Myers	Wellcome	Sandoz
Squibb	Glycomed	Schering-Plough
Cephalon	Hoechst	Scios Nova
Chiron Corp.	ICOS	SmithKline
Chugai	Immunex	Beecham
Pharmaceutical	Johnson	Upjohn
Ciba-Geigy	& Johnson	U.S. Bioscience
	Merck	Warner-Lambert

HOW MUCH

	9-Year Growth	1985[1]	1986[1]	1987[1]	1988[1]	1989[1]	1990[1]	1991	1992	1993	1994
Sales ($ mil.)	60.7%	23	35	53	78	199	381	682	1,093	1,374	1,648
Net income ($ mil.)	105.0%	1	1	2	(8)	19	34	98	358	375	320
Income as % of sales	—	2.3%	3.3%	3.2%	—	9.6%	9.0%	14.3%	32.7%	27.3%	19.4%
Earnings per share ($)	82.7%	0.01	0.01	0.01	(0.08)	0.18	0.24	0.66	2.42	2.60	2.27
Stock price – high ($)	—	2.43	4.74	7.41	5.95	9.99	21.14	76.00	78.25	71.75	60.25
Stock price – low ($)	—	0.77	2.06	2.71	4.29	5.31	7.16	18.81	49.25	31.00	34.75
Stock price – close ($)	43.8%	2.25	3.68	5.16	5.62	8.16	20.73	75.75	70.63	49.50	59.00
P/E – high	—	243	474	741	—	56	88	115	32	28	27
P/E – low	—	77	206	271	—	30	30	29	20	12	15
Dividends per share ($)	—	0.00	0.00	0.00	0.00	0.00	0.00	0.00	0.00	0.00	0.00
Book value per share ($)	34.0%	0.69	0.71	1.39	1.38	1.80	3.14	4.03	6.85	8.73	9.63
Employees	38.0%	195	265	353	537	721	1,179	1,723	2,335	3,100	3,546

1994 Year-end:
Debt ratio: 18.2%
Return on equity: 26.1%
Cash (mil.): $796
Current ratio: 2.08
Long-term debt (mil.): $183
No. of shares (mil.): 132
Dividends
  Yield: —
  Payout: —
Market value (mil.): $7,807

Stock Price History
High/Low 1985–94

[1] Figures (except stock prices) are for year ended March 31 of the following year.

AMOCO CORPORATION

OVERVIEW

Chicago-based Amoco is North America's largest natural gas producer and one of the world's largest integrated oil and chemical companies, with confirmed oil reserves of 2.2 billion barrels and gas reserves of 18.2 trillion cubic feet.

Amoco's 3 main businesses are refining and marketing (Amoco Oil), oil and gas exploration and production (Amoco Production), and chemical production (Amoco Chemical). A major restructuring in 1994 redistributed the operating duties of those 3 subsidiaries among 17 business groups.

Since 1991 Amoco has shed weak product lines (including its oil well chemicals business) and has invested $1.7 billion to beef up its faster-growing and profitable businesses. One such profit center Amoco has developed is its polyester chemical business. It holds 40% of the world market in paraxylene and purified terephthalic acid, both used in the production of polyester. To support the booming demand for polyester in the growing economies in Asia, Amoco and its partners in Indonesia, Singapore, and Taiwan are investing $2 billion to expand the manufacturing capacity for these chemicals.

Despite a sluggish worldwide market for crude oil, Amoco's gas sales were up approximately 5% in volume in 1994.

WHEN

John D. Rockefeller organized the Standard Oil Trust in 1882. In 1886 he risked buying and storing Lima (Ohio) oil, a high-sulphur crude. Rockefeller anticipated the discovery of a sulphur-removing process, which, indeed, was patented in 1887 by chemist Herman Frasch. Certain that his copper oxide process would work on a commercial scale, Frasch persuaded the company to try it on the Lima crude. Its success assured the company a continued oil supply.

In 1889 Standard Oil organized Standard Oil of Indiana as its upper midwestern subsidiary, complete with a new refinery in Whiting, Indiana. The subsidiary built a strong retail marketing organization, including company-owned service stations and a research laboratory at the refinery — innovations at the time.

In 1911 the Supreme Court ordered Standard Oil to split up because of antitrust violations; the split-up created 33 new independent oil companies. The decision left Standard (Indiana) with 2 operations, oil refining and domestic marketing, and its exclusive right to the Standard name in the Midwest. The company purchased its crude oil and transportation from former Standard sisters Prairie Oil & Gas and Prairie Pipe Line.

In 1917 Standard (Indiana) began buying crude oil production companies; in 1925 it purchased controlling interest (81% by 1929) in Pan American Petroleum and Transport, one of the world's largest crude producers, with production facilities in Mexico and Venezuela. In 1923 Pan American bought a 50% interest in American Oil, founded in 1922 by Louis Blaustein. He had introduced antiknock gasoline, marketed under the Amoco name. Standard (Indiana), recognizing the additional value of oil converted to chemicals, began Amoco Chemicals in 1945. The company purchased Utah Oil Refining (1956), along with other refineries in the 1950s and 1960s.

In 1978 the supertanker *Amoco Cadiz* ran aground, dumping 120,000 tons of oil (6 times more than the 1989 *Exxon Valdez* spill) off the French coast, resulting in a $128 million judgment against Amoco in 1990.

Standard (Indiana) bought Cyprus Mines (copper and industrial minerals) in 1979, but in 1985 it spun off its industrial minerals business as Cyprus Minerals (now Cyprus Amax). Standard (Indiana) changed its name to Amoco in 1985. In 1988 Amoco bought debt-ridden but resource-rich Dome Petroleum of Canada, making Amoco the largest private owner of North American natural gas reserves.

In 1992 a consortium led by Amoco finished laying a 255-mile natural gas pipeline in the North Sea. Also in 1992 the company signed agreements for drilling exploration wells in Romania and for exploration rights in China, making Amoco the first foreign oil company to explore the Chinese mainland.

In 1994 Amoco and Norsk Hydro agreed to jointly evaluate oil and gas exploration opportunities off the Russian coast. The company made 2 significant natural gas discoveries off Trinidad in 1994 as well as major oil discoveries in the Gulf of Mexico, the North Sea, and Colombia.

After a profitable year in polypropylene production in Europe in 1994, Amoco announced plans to build a 440 million pounds-per-year polymer plant in Geel, Belgium, due to begin operations in 1996.

In 1995 Amoco teamed up with Shell and Exxon to develop a deep-water oil platform.

NYSE symbol: AN
Fiscal year ends: December 31

WHO

Chairman, President, and CEO: H. Laurance Fuller, age 56, $1,678,865 pay
VC: Lawrason D. Thomas, age 60, $960,799 pay
EVP Exploration and Production Sector: William G. Lowrie, age 51, $724,053 pay
EVP Chemical Sector: James E. Fligg, age 58, $657,504 pay
EVP Petroleum Products Sector: W. Douglas Ford, age 51
EVP and CFO: John L. Carl, age 47
SVP Shared Services: L. Richard Flury, age 47
SVP and General Counsel: George S. Spindler, age 57
SVP Human Resources: R. Wayne Anderson, age 53
VP and Controller: John R. Reid, age 52
Auditors: Price Waterhouse LLP

WHERE

HQ: 200 E. Randolph Dr., Chicago, IL 60601
Phone: 312-856-6111
Fax: 312-856-2460

Amoco conducts operations in approximately 40 countries. Foreign exploration activities are carried out primarily in the Arabian Peninsula, Argentina, Australia, Canada, China, Colombia, the Gulf of Suez, New Zealand, the Nile Delta (Egypt), the North Sea, Poland, Romania, Trinidad, Venezuela, and West Africa.

	1994 Sales		1994 Operating Income	
	$ mil.	% of total	$ mil.	% of total
US	24,003	80	1,836	70
Canada	2,555	9	349	13
Europe	1,403	5	47	2
Other regions	1,899	6	380	15
Adjustments	502	—	—	—
Total	**30,362**	**100**	**2,612**	**100**

WHAT

	1994 Sales		1994 Operating Income	
	$ mil.	% of total	$ mil.	% of total
Refining, mktg. & transportation	23,531	68	1,585	55
Exploration & production	6,460	19	591	21
Chemicals	4,662	13	684	24
Other	144	—	(248)	—
Adjustments	(4,435)	—	—	—
Total	**30,362**	**100**	**2,612**	**100**

Lines of Business
Chemical manufacturing
Marketing of refined products and chemicals
Oil and gas exploration and production
Petroleum refining

Other Operations
Amoco Technology Co. (lasers, solar power, biotechnology)
AmProp, Inc. (real estate)
Ecova Corporation (hazardous waste disposal)

KEY COMPETITORS

Amerada Hess	Elf Aquitaine	PEMEX
Ashland, Inc.	Enron	Pennzoil
Atlantic Richfield	Exxon	Petrobrás
BASF	Hercules	Petrofina
Bayer	Hoechst	Phillips
British Gas	Imperial Oil	Petroleum
British Petroleum	Koch	Repsol
Broken Hill	Lyondell	Royal Dutch/Shell
Chevron	Petrochemical	Sinclair Oil
Coastal	Mobil	Sun Company
Columbia Gas	Norsk Hydro	Tenneco
Diamond	Occidental	Texaco
Shamrock	Oryx	TOTAL
Dow Chemical	Panhandle	Union Carbide
DuPont	Eastern	Unocal
	PDVSA	USX–Marathon

HOW MUCH

	9-Year Growth	1985	1986	1987	1988	1989	1990	1991	1992	1993	1994
Sales ($ mil.)	0.6%	28,873	20,231	22,388	23,919	26,760	31,581	28,296	26,219	28,617	30,362
Net income ($ mil.)	(1.0%)	1,953	747	1,360	2,063	1,610	1,913	1,173	850	1,820	1,789
Income as % of sales	—	6.7%	3.7%	6.1%	9.4%	8.6%	6.6%	6.1%	3.2%	6.4%	5.9%
Earnings per share ($)	(0.3%)	3.71	1.46	2.66	4.00	3.12	3.77	2.36	1.71	3.66	3.60
Stock price – high ($)	—	35.13	36.06	45.13	40.13	55.75	60.38	55.00	53.75	59.25	64.13
Stock price – low ($)	—	25.13	26.56	28.50	33.81	36.81	49.25	45.63	41.75	48.13	50.88
Stock price – close ($)	7.5%	30.94	32.63	34.50	37.50	54.63	52.38	49.13	48.75	52.88	59.13
P/E – high	—	10	25	17	10	18	16	23	31	16	18
P/E – low	—	7	18	11	9	12	13	19	24	13	14
Dividends per share ($)	3.2%	1.65	1.65	1.65	1.75	1.90	2.04	2.20	2.20	2.20	2.20
Book value per share ($)	2.9%	22.39	22.14	23.50	25.80	26.75	28.03	28.52	26.11	27.53	28.97
Employees	(1.5%)	49,545	46,775	46,774	53,423	53,653	54,524	54,120	46,994	46,317	43,205

1994 Year-end:
Debt ratio: 24.4%
Return on equity: 12.8%
Cash (mil.): $1,789
Current ratio: 1.32
Long-term debt (mil.): $4,387
No. of shares (mil.): 496
Dividends
Yield: 3.7%
Payout: 61.1%
Market value (mil.): $29,352

Stock Price History
High/Low 1985–94

AMP INCORPORATED

OVERVIEW

AMP is the world's leading manufacturer of electronic connectors — vital components in all electrical products, from cars to computers and from aircraft to washing machines. The company sells over 100,000 kinds of products and has a 20% market share worldwide.

A 3-pronged attack is at the heart of AMP's global growth strategy. First, the company is expanding its manufacturing facilities, with $550 million in capital expenditures budgeted for 1995. Plans include a new warehouse in Japan, a manufacturing plant in the Czech Republic, and construction or enlargement of over a dozen facilities in Europe.

AMP is also pursuing new markets in developing economies, including China, Eastern Europe, and India. The weak US dollar continues to boost overseas revenues.

The potentially most important element of AMP's global expansion is the development of new kinds of products; the company spends nearly 12% of revenues on R&D.

AMP gained access to the wireless communications market in 1995 when it acquired M/A-COM, a maker of wireless data and telecommunications interconnection components. M/A-COM's coaxial cable operations will be merged with AMP's own cable business as the Global Wireless Products Group.

In 1996 AMP plans to enter the fast-growing networking market with new ATM (asynchronous transfer mode) products.

WHEN

U. A. Whitaker founded Aircraft-Marine Products of Elizabeth, New Jersey, in 1941, just 2 months before the attack on Pearl Harbor. As a manufacturer of parts for aircraft, ships, and radios, AMP (pronounced "amp," not A-M-P) grew rapidly during WWII. In 1943 the company moved to Harrisburg, Pennsylvania. A preinsulated electrical terminal and a special crimping tool invented in 1943 would later become AMP's mainstay.

The company nearly failed in its transition to a peacetime economy, with profits dropping sharply in 1946. Focusing on commercial markets, primarily for its electrical terminal, the company was doing well again by the 1950s. In 1956 the company went public, shortening its name to AMP.

AMP began international expansion in the 1950s, forming 10 subsidiaries in other countries, including Canada, Japan, France, and West Germany. AMP's success is partially attributed to a policy of rapidly building plants wherever it had a market for its products and carefully adapting to foreign requirements. When Fiat needed electrical connectors for its cars, the company built a plant in Italy in 1959. AMP entered the ranks of the *FORTUNE* 500 in 1966 with sales of $142 million.

In the 1970s and 1980s, AMP developed new connecting devices for computers, telecommunications equipment, and home entertainment systems. Its electrical components were used in the high-speed French TGV railroad and the Washington Metro. The company invested in plant modernization in the mid-1980s and spent $100 million developing fiber-optic technology. AMP also introduced new cable and data communication connectors, now standard on local area networks such as Ethernet and IBM's Token-Ring. New products in the late 1980s were "smart" connectors and under-carpet flat cables for offices.

Expansion into the Far East continued in 1987 with the opening of plants in Taiwan, South Korea, and Singapore. AMP entered several new markets through acquisitions (including Matrix Science, 1988; Garry Screw Machine, 1989; Switzerland's Decolletage S.A. St-Maurice, 1989; and Kaptron, 1990) and through a joint venture with Akzo of the Netherlands (1990). In 1991 AMP bought Precision Interconnect (specialty cables and cable assemblies) and a minority interest in Broad-Band Technologies (fiber loop networking).

AMP continued international expansion in 1992, building plants in Brazil, France, Germany, India, Italy, Japan, and Taiwan. That same year the company acquired Electro Optics Products (intelligent hubs and networking products) and Optical Fiber Technologies (metal ferrule fiber-optic connectors).

During 1993 AMP made several minor acquisitions, including Elf Atochem Sensors (piezoelectric plastic film sensors), the microwave electronics business of COMSAT Laboratories, and the ATM chips and network adapters business of Fischer and Porter.

In 1994 AMP launched marketing operations in the Czech Republic, Indonesia, the Philippines, Poland, and Vietnam. That same year the company opened new plants in Hungary, India, Ireland, and South Korea. In the US, AMP began construction on an engineering facility in Pennsylvania, while operations began at plants in North Carolina (automotive products) and Texas (panel assembly).

NYSE symbol: AMP
Fiscal year ends: December 31

WHO

Chairman: James E. Marley, age 59, $811,000 pay
President and CEO: William J. Hudson Jr., age 60, $1,022,400 pay
VP Global Interconnection Systems Businesses: Javad K. Hassan, age 54, $356,862 pay
VP Europe: John E. Gurski, age 54, $354,780 pay
VP Americas: Dennis Horowitz, age 48
VP Asia/Pacific: Herbert M. Cole, age 58
VP Global Marketing: Ted L. Dalrymple, age 62
VP Technology: Howard R. Peiffer
VP US Sales and Marketing: Dean Hooper
VP: Jean Gorjat, age 64
VP and CFO: Robert Ripp, age 53
VP and General Legal Counsel: Charles W. Goonrey, age 58
VP Global Human Resources: Philip G. Guarneschelli, age 62
Auditors: Arthur Andersen & Co, SC

WHERE

HQ: PO Box 3608, Harrisburg, PA 17105-3608
Phone: 717-564-0100
Fax: 717-780-6130

AMP has 185 manufacturing and sales facilities in the US and 35 foreign countries.

	1994 Sales		1994 Net Income	
	$ mil.	% of total	$ mil.	% of total
US	2,067	46	182	48
Europe	1,281	28	120	32
Asia/Pacific	947	21	63	17
Other Americas	228	5	12	3
Adjustments	(496)	—	(8)	—
Total	**4,027**	**100**	**369**	**100**

WHAT

	1994 Sales
Market	% of total
Transportation/electrical	25
Computer/office	19
Communications	17
Industrial/commercial	16
Consumer goods	8
Aerospace/military	3
Distribution, construction, other	12
Total	**100**

Selected Products
Cable and board assemblies
Cable and cabling systems
Cable connectors and assemblies
Connectorized printed circuit boards
Fiber-optic connectors and assemblies
Flexible circuitry–based connectors and sensors
LAN and WAN products and systems
Microwave and millimeter wave components
Printed circuit board connectors and assemblies
Sensors
Signal conditioning products
Specialized machinery and tools for applying and installing AMP products
Terminals
Wireless telephone and frequency interconnection components

KEY COMPETITORS

Altron
Augat
Cherry Corp.
General Microproducts
Methode Electronics
Molex
Parlex
Robinson Nugent
Siemens
Texas Instruments
Thomas & Betts

HOW MUCH

	9-Year Growth	1985	1986	1987	1988	1989	1990	1991	1992	1993	1994
Sales ($ mil.)	10.5%	1,636	1,933	2,318	2,670	2,797	3,044	3,095	3,337	3,451	4,027
Net income ($ mil.)	14.6%	108	164	250	319	281	287	260	290	297	369
Income as % of sales	—	6.6%	8.5%	10.8%	12.0%	10.0%	9.4%	8.4%	8.7%	8.6%	9.2%
Earnings per share ($)	15.0%	0.50	0.75	1.16	1.48	1.32	1.35	1.23	1.38	1.41	1.76
Stock price – high ($)	—	18.94	22.50	35.75	27.13	24.69	27.63	30.00	34.38	33.63	39.66
Stock price – low ($)	—	13.75	16.44	17.07	20.25	20.00	18.94	20.44	26.32	27.32	28.81
Stock price – close ($)	8.1%	18.00	18.07	23.38	22.25	22.25	21.75	29.32	29.00	31.57	36.38
P/E – high	—	38	30	31	18	19	20	24	25	24	23
P/E – low	—	28	22	15	14	15	14	17	19	19	16
Dividends per share ($)	9.9%	0.36	0.37	0.43	0.50	0.60	0.68	0.72	0.76	0.80	0.84
Book value per share ($)	10.3%	4.62	5.25	6.27	7.08	7.24	8.46	9.02	9.26	9.80	11.14
Employees	3.2%	22,800	21,800	22,000	24,100	24,400	24,700	25,000	25,100	26,900	30,400

1994 Year-end:
Debt ratio: 14.2%
Return on equity: 16.8%
Cash (mil.): $395
Current ratio: 1.99
Long-term debt (mil.): $211
No. of shares (mil.): 210
Dividends
  Yield: 1.2%
  Payout: 47.7%
Market value (mil.): $15,251

Stock Price History
High/Low 1985–94

AMR CORPORATION

OVERVIEW

American Airlines, the #1 US airline, is flying high again. Its improved economic performance helped lift Fort Worth–based AMR, American's holding company, to its first annual profit in 5 years in 1994. A combination of an expanding economy and cost-cutting measures have lifted the company's sales and productivity. The carrier has cut jet service to 30 cities, removed more than 90 jet aircraft from its fleet, and drastically reduced its payroll.

AMR also owns American Eagle, a group of 4 small regional airlines; operates the SABRE reservations system; and manages airport ground services, consulting, information, and telemarketing systems.

The air carrier is focusing on expanding its services to more than 20 key markets that cater to the business traveler, and it is increasing its services to Chicago, Dallas/Fort Worth, and Miami.

AMR ended 1994 on a down note with 2 fatal crashes of American Eagle planes, due in part to wing icing on its ATR planes. Under FAA restrictions AMR redeployed its ATR fleet to southern routes. American Airlines itself extended its safety record to 15 years and over 10 million flights since its last fatal accident.

In 1995 AMR planned to break into the large Chinese aviation market by selling travel-related services and technology to Chinese airlines.

WHEN

In 1929 Sherman Fairchild's Fairchild Aviation Corporation created a New York City holding company called the Aviation Corporation (AVCO). By 1930 AVCO owned about 85 small airlines, which together formed an unconnected coast-to-coast network. Hoping to consolidate this route structure, AVCO created American Airways in 1930.

In 1934 new postal regulations forced AVCO to split up its aircraft-making and transportation concerns. American Airlines was formed as a result, and, through an exchange of stock, it bought American Airways.

With former AVCO manager C. R. Smith at the helm, American surpassed United as the leading US airline in the late 1930s. The Douglas DC-3, built to Smith's specifications, was introduced into service by American in 1936 and was the first commercial airliner to pay its way on passenger revenues alone.

After WWII, American bought American Export Airlines (renamed American Overseas Airlines), with flights to northern Europe, but it sold this division to Pan Am in 1950. American formed subsidiary Americana Hotels in 1963 and introduced SABRE, the industry's first automated reservations system, in 1964. In 1968 Smith left American to serve President Johnson as secretary of commerce.

American bought Trans Caribbean Airlines in 1971, gaining routes to the Caribbean. In 1977 Americana Hotels bought the Howard Corporation's hotel properties and by 1978 operated 21 hotels and resorts in the US, Latin America, and Korea. Within 10 years most of the hotels were sold.

In 1979 American moved its headquarters from New York to Dallas/Fort Worth. Former

CFO Bob Crandall became president in 1980 and, using SABRE to keep track of mileage, introduced the industry's first frequent flyer program (AAdvantage) in 1981. In 1982 American created AMR Corporation as its holding company. After acquiring Nashville Eagle (commuter airline) in 1987, AMR established AMR Eagle to operate commuter services as American Eagle, buying 4 new commuter services in 1988 and 1989.

In 1989 AMR weathered an unsolicited takeover bid by Donald Trump and bought Eastern Air Lines's Latin American routes from Texas Air (now Continental Airlines). In 1991 AMR bought TWA's US–London routes and won DOT approval to fly to Manchester, England. AMR also bought Continental's Seattle–Tokyo route and Midway Airlines's gates at LaGuardia and Washington National airports. The new routes did not bring the expected financial results, and AMR scaled back its expansion.

In 1993, despite taking steps toward profitability, AMR asked its flight attendants for concessions. The resulting strike took the airline into the red and tied up Thanksgiving weekend travel; it ended when President Clinton persuaded the parties to go to arbitration. Most of the attendants' pay and labor issues were resolved in a 1995 agreement.

Reflecting its growing business activities in China, AMR opened an office in Beijing in 1994. The air carrier also announced a frequent flyer relationship with Japan Airlines.

A freak hail storm that swept through Dallas/Fort Worth International Airport in 1995 damaged 55 planes belonging to American Airlines and caused several days of canceled flights and high repair costs.

NYSE symbol: AMR
Fiscal year ends: December 31

WHO

Chairman and CEO: Robert L. Crandall, age 59,
$600,000 pay
EVP; President, American Airlines: Donald J. Carty,
age 48, $540,000 pay
EVP Operations, American Airlines: Robert W. Baker,
age 50, $540,000 pay
SVP Marketing, American Airlines: Michael W. Gunn,
age 49, $400,000 pay
SVP and CFO: Gerard J. Arpey, age 36
**SVP Florida, Caribbean and Latin America, American
Airlines:** Peter J. Dolara
SVP International, American Airlines: Hans Mirka
SVP and General Counsel: Anne H. McNamara, age 47
President, AMR Eagle Inc.: Daniel P. Garton, age 38
VP Corporate Real Estate, American Airlines: A. Jaynne
Allison
VP Employee Relations, American Airlines: Jane G.
Allen
VP Human Resources, American Airlines: Mary B.
Jordan
Corporate Secretary: Charles D. MarLett, age 40
Auditors: Ernst & Young LLP

WHERE

HQ: 4333 Amon Carter Blvd., Fort Worth, TX 76155
Phone: 817-963-1234
Fax: 817-967-9641
Reservations: 800-433-7300

American serves more than 170 worldwide destinations.
American Eagle serves cities in the US, the Bahamas,
and the Caribbean.

Hub Locations
Chicago, IL
Dallas/Fort Worth, TX
Miami, FL
Nashville, TN
San Juan, Puerto Rico

WHAT

	1994 Sales	
	$ mil.	% of total
Air Transport Group		
Passenger	13,616	80
Cargo	657	4
Other	622	4
SABRE Group	1,542	9
AMR Management Svcs.	535	3
Adjustments	(835)	—
Total	**16,137**	**100**

	1994 Aircraft	
	Owned	Leased
Airbus A300	10	25
Boeing 727	49	39
Boeing 757	40	41
Boeing 767	29	38
Fokker 100	66	9
McDonnell Douglas DC-10	19	5
McDonnell Douglas MD-11	17	—
McDonnell Douglas MD-80	119	141
Total	**349**	**298**

Selected Subsidiaries and Affiliates
American Airlines, Inc.
AMR Eagle, Inc. (commuter services)
AMR Investment Services (investment management)
AMR Services Corp. (ground services)
SABRE Computer Services (data processing)
SABRE Decision Technologies (consulting to travel and
other industries)
SABRE Travel Information Network (reservations)

KEY COMPETITORS

Air France	Galileo Intl.	Southwest
America West	IRI	Airlines
British Airways	JAL	TWA
Continental	KLM	UAL
Airlines	Lufthansa	USAir Group
Delta	Northwest Airlines	Virgin Group

HOW MUCH

	9-Year Growth	1985	1986	1987	1988	1989	1990	1991	1992	1993	1994
Sales ($ mil.)	11.4%	6,131	6,018	7,198	8,824	10,480	11,720	12,887	14,396	15,816	16,137
Net income ($ mil.)	(0.1%)	346	279	198	477	455	(40)	(240)	(475)	(170)	343
Income as % of sales	—	5.6%	4.6%	2.8%	5.4%	4.3%	—	—	—	—	2.1%
Earnings per share ($)	(2.9%)	5.88	4.63	3.28	7.66	7.15	(0.64)	(3.54)	(6.35)	(2.23)	4.51
Stock price – high ($)	—	50.75	62.13	65.50	55.00	107.25	70.25	71.13	80.25	72.88	72.75
Stock price – low ($)	—	33.50	39.25	26.75	32.63	52.13	39.75	44.25	54.38	55.50	48.13
Stock price – close ($)	2.8%	41.38	53.63	35.25	53.63	58.00	48.38	70.50	67.50	67.00	53.25
P/E – high	—	9	13	20	7	15	—	—	—	—	16
P/E – low	—	6	9	8	4	7	—	—	—	—	11
Dividends per share ($)	—	0.00	0.00	0.00	0.00	0.00	0.00	0.00	0.00	0.00	0.00
Book value per share ($)	1.8%	37.17	42.30	45.58	53.50	60.54	59.83	55.50	44.41	42.17	43.50
Employees	8.6%	52,100	54,300	65,100	77,100	89,000	102,809	116,300	119,300	118,900	109,800

1994 Year-end:
Debt ratio: 71.8%
Return on equity: 10.6%
Cash (mil.): $777
Current ratio: 0.63
Long-term debt (mil.): $7,878
No. of shares (mil.): 76
Dividends
  Yield: —
  Payout: —
Market value (mil.): $4,042

**Stock Price History
High/Low 1985–94**

ANHEUSER-BUSCH COMPANIES, INC.

OVERVIEW

Anheuser-Busch, the St. Louis–based "King of Beers," is out to conquer the world. The company is the world's largest beer maker, but with only 9% of the international market it sees plenty of room for growth. Since 1993 Anheuser-Busch has spread its global reach via partnerships in Brazil (Companhia Antárctica Paulista, 10%), China (Tsingtao Brewery, 5%; Zhongde Brewery, 80%), and India (Shaw Wallace, distribution agreement), among others. In 1995 Anheuser-Busch and UK-based Courage Ltd. (a subsidiary of Foster's Brewing) formed a joint venture to operate London's Stag Brewery.

In the US, Anheuser-Busch remains the largest brewer, with 44% of the market. More than half the company's sales come from its Budweiser brand. The company is countering flat domestic beer sales with new products, such as the Elk Mountain and Red Wolf brands and Crossroads, a wheat-based beer.

While Bud, Busch, Michelob, and a freezer full of other beer brands account for 75% of Anheuser-Busch's revenues, the company is also the world's 2nd largest theme park operator, with 10 facilities, including the Sea World and Busch Gardens parks. Anheuser-Busch also owns the St. Louis Cardinals baseball team, and its Campbell Taggart subsidiary is the US's #2 baked goods company.

Budweiser brand manager August Busch IV is in line to become the 5th generation from that family to lead the company. The Busch family controls 8% of company stock.

WHEN

George Schneider founded the Bavarian Brewery in St. Louis in 1852. Unable to turn a profit, Schneider sold the brewery to Eberhard Anheuser in 1860. Anheuser's son-in-law Adolphus Busch joined the company in 1865 and in 1876 assisted restaurateur Carl Conrad in creating Budweiser, a light beer like those brewed in the Bohemian town of Budweis. The brewery's rapid growth was based in part on the popularity of Budweiser over heavier, darker beers.

When Adolphus died in 1913, his son August took over the company, which was renamed Anheuser-Busch, Inc., in 1919. When beer vats lay dry during Prohibition (1920–33), August saved the company by selling yeast, refrigeration units, truck bodies, syrup, and soft drinks. When repeal came in 1933, Busch quickly resumed brewing, delivering a case of Budweiser to President Franklin Roosevelt in a carriage drawn by Clydesdale horses, which became Anheuser-Busch's symbol. However, the tribulations of Prohibition had damaged August Busch's health, and he killed himself in 1934.

In 1953 Anheuser-Busch acquired the St. Louis Cardinals and 4 years later knocked Schlitz out of first place among US brewers. In 1959 the company established its Busch Entertainment theme park division.

In 1970 Miller held 7th place in the industry, but tobacco giant Philip Morris acquired it and began a long, fierce challenge to Budweiser's leadership. By 1978 Miller had passed Schlitz and Pabst to take 2nd place, but Anheuser-Busch triumphed, becoming the first brewer to sell 40 million barrels a year. By 1980 the 2 foes produced over 50% of the beer sold in America.

In 1982 Anheuser-Busch bought Campbell Taggart (baked goods) and created its Eagle snack foods unit. In 1989 the company acquired Sea World from Harcourt Brace Jovanovich.

To counter rival Miller's successful Miller Genuine Draft (introduced in 1986), the company launched several draft beers, including Michelob Golden Draft, introduced in 1991.

In 1993 the beer maker bought 18% of Modelo, Mexico's top brewer. The agreement came with an option for Anheuser-Busch to acquire up to 35% of Modelo, which produces Corona, the #1 beer in Mexico.

In April 1993, following years of opposition, the brewer became the first since Prohibition to list alcohol content on its beers. That year Anheuser-Busch took a $565 million charge related to restructuring and enticed 10% of its work force into retirement.

A new beer, Ice Draft (now Bud Ice), was introduced with success in 1994. Also that year Japan's Kirin Brewery announced that it would begin buying beer cans and beer (brewed in California but sold in Japan under the Kirin banner) from Anheuser-Busch. In late 1994 the company acquired 25% of Redhook Ale Brewery and the right to distribute Redhook products in new US markets.

In 1995 Anheuser-Busch won a $5 million judgment from Canadian brewer John Labatt in a countersuit regarding use of the designation "ice beer." That same year the company announced it would raise beer prices 3.5% and spin off its Campbell Taggart baking unit.

NYSE symbol: BUD
Fiscal year ends: December 31

WHO

Chairman and President: August A. Busch III, age 57, $2,172,000 pay
EVP, CFO, and Chief Administrative Officer: Jerry E. Ritter, age 60, $1,091,000 pay
Chairman and SVP Europe, Anheuser-Busch Europe: Jaime Iglesias, age 64
VP and Group Executive; Chairman and CEO, Anheuser-Busch Investment Capital Corp.: Patrick T. Stokes, age 52, $1,023,000 pay
VP and Group Executive; Chairman and CEO, Campbell Taggart and Eagle Snacks: Barry H. Beracha, age 53, $636,000 pay
VP and Group Executive; Chairman and CEO, Anheuser-Busch International: John H. Purnell, age 53, $615,000 pay
VP and General Counsel: Ellis W. McCracken Jr.
VP Corporate Human Resources: William L. Rammes, age 53
Auditors: Price Waterhouse LLP

WHERE

HQ: One Busch Place, St. Louis, MO 63118
Phone: 314-577-2000
Fax: 314-577-2900

Anheuser-Busch sells its beer in more than 70 countries.

WHAT

	1994 Sales		1994 Operating Income	
	$ mil.	% of total	$ mil.	% of total
Beer & beer prods.	9,232	76	1,786	94
Food products	2,132	18	44	2
Entertainment	742	6	69	4
Adjustments	1,628	—	—	—
Total	**13,734**	**100**	**1,899**	**100**

Selected Beverages

Bud Ice	King Cobra
Budweiser	Michelob
Busch	Natural Light
Carlsberg (imported)	Natural Pilsner
Crossroads	O'Doul's (nonalcoholic)
Elephant (imported)	Red Wolf
Elk Mountain	ZiegenBock (only in Texas)

Food and Snacks
Campbell Taggart (baked goods)
Eagle Snacks (chips and nuts)

Busch Entertainment Corp.
Adventure Island (water park, Tampa)
Baseball City Sports Complex (Orlando)
Busch Gardens (theme parks, Florida and Virginia)
Cypress Gardens (Winter Haven, Florida)
Port Aventura (20%, joint venture with UK's Pearson PLC, Spain)
St. Louis Cardinals (major league baseball)
Sea World (theme parks; California, Florida, Ohio, and Texas)
Sesame Place (educational play park, Philadelphia)
Water Country U.S.A. (Williamsburg, Virginia)

Selected Other Businesses
Anheuser-Busch International, Inc. (foreign licensing)
Anheuser-Busch Recycling Corporation
Busch Agricultural Resources, Inc. (grain processing)
Busch Creative Services Corp. (communications)
Busch Properties, Inc. (real estate development)
Metal Container Corporation (beverage containers)

KEY COMPETITORS

Adolph Coors	Danone	MCA
Allied Domecq	Foster's Brewing	Molson
Anchor Brewing	Genessee	PepsiCo
Bass	Grand	Philip Morris
Borden	Metropolitan	RJR Nabisco
Boston Beer	Guinness	S&P
Campbell Soup	Heileman	Six Flags
ConAgra	Heineken	Stroh
CPC	Interstate Bakeries	Walt Disney

HOW MUCH

	9-Year Growth	1985	1986	1987	1988	1989	1990	1991	1992	1993	1994
Sales ($ mil.)	6.0%	7,757	8,479	9,110	9,705	10,239	11,612	12,634	13,062	13,185	13,734
Net income ($ mil.)	9.8%	444	518	615	716	767	842	940	994	595	1,032
Income as % of sales	—	5.7%	6.1%	6.7%	7.4%	7.5%	7.3%	7.4%	7.6%	4.5%	7.5%
Earnings per share ($)	11.9%	1.42	1.69	2.04	2.45	2.68	2.95	3.25	3.46	2.17	3.91
Stock price – high ($)	—	22.88	29.06	40.13	34.38	46.00	45.25	62.00	60.75	60.25	55.38
Stock price – low ($)	—	11.81	19.75	18.25	29.00	30.63	34.00	39.25	51.75	43.00	47.13
Stock price – close ($)	10.3%	21.13	26.13	33.38	31.50	38.50	43.00	61.50	58.50	49.13	50.88
P/E – high	—	16	17	20	14	17	15	19	18	28	14
P/E – low	—	8	12	9	12	11	12	12	15	20	12
Dividends per share ($)	17.0%	0.37	0.44	0.54	0.66	0.80	0.94	1.06	1.24	1.36	1.52
Book value per share ($)	9.1%	7.84	8.61	9.87	10.95	10.95	13.03	15.57	16.60	15.94	17.16
Employees	0.8%	39,769	41,805	41,541	41,118	46,608	45,432	44,386	44,790	43,345	42,622

1994 Year-end:
Debt ratio: 41.1%
Return on equity: 23.8%
Cash (mil.): $156
Current ratio: 1.12
Long-term debt (mil.): $3,078
No. of shares (mil.): 257
Dividends
  Yield: 3.0%
  Payout: 38.9%
Market value (mil.): $13,090

Stock Price History
High/Low 1985–94

APPLE COMPUTER, INC.

OVERVIEW

After some rotten times, Apple, the world's #2 computer maker (after IBM), spent 1994 reinventing itself. The company has reorganized its operations to target business, education, government, and home computing. It is also releasing several innovative new products, among them a set-top box that allows Apple CD-ROM software to run on television sets.

In 1994 Apple rolled out its Power Mac computer, which features the "neutral" PowerPC microchip (developed with IBM and Motorola). PowerPC allows computers to run software designed for Mac OS, Windows NT, OS/2, and AIX platforms. Demand for Power Macs has been so strong the company has had trouble meeting demand.

Also, after years of discouraging clones of its computers by refusing to license its operating system, the company did an about-face in 1994, licensing Power Computing, Pioneer Electronic Corp., and Radius to build Macintosh-compatible machines (other licenses will follow). Apple hopes a flurry of clones will boost the amount of software written for the Mac, eventually boosting Mac sales.

In early 1995 Apple sued Microsoft, alleging that the software giant misappropriated software for displaying video images on PC screens. The next month Microsoft filed a countersuit accusing Apple of conducting a disinformation campaign regarding Microsoft's *Video for Windows* software.

Also in 1995, Apple CEO Michael Spindler denied continuing rumors that Apple is a takeover target (AT&T, IBM, and Motorola have been mentioned as potential buyers).

WHEN

Two college dropouts, Steven Jobs and Stephen Wozniak, founded Apple in 1976 in the Santa Clara Valley. Their original plan to sell circuit boards changed to selling fully assembled microcomputers after Jobs's first sales call brought an order for 50 units. They built the Apple I in Jobs's garage and sold it without a monitor, keyboard, or casing.

The demand for the Apple I made Jobs aware of the market for small computers. The choice of the Apple name (reminiscent of the time Jobs spent on an Oregon farm) and the computer's "user-friendly" appearance set it apart from other companies' computers, appealing even to nontechnical buyers.

By 1977 Wozniak, who invented the Apple I, had substantially improved it by adding a keyboard, color monitor, and 8 slots for peripheral devices. The latter feature gave the new machine, the Apple II, considerable versatility and inspired numerous 3rd-party add-on devices and software programs.

By 1980 over 130,000 Apple II units had been sold. Revenues jumped from $7.8 million in 1978 to $117 million in 1980, the year Apple went public. By 1983 Wozniak had left and Jobs had hired John Sculley from PepsiCo to succeed Mike Markkula as Apple's president. (After a tumultuous power struggle, Jobs left in 1985 and started NeXT with 5 former Apple employees.) Following the failure of the Apple III and Lisa computers (1983), Apple roared back in 1984 with the revolutionary Macintosh. Its introduction was preceded by an intriguing commercial, aired only once, during the Super Bowl, that challenged chief rival IBM. Advertised as the computer "For the Rest of Us," Macintosh incorporated a graphical user interface inspired by Xerox's Alto computer. In 1986 Apple moved into the office market with the Mac Plus and the LaserWriter printer, a combination that ushered in the desktop-publishing revolution.

In 1992 Apple lost a key ruling in its suit against Microsoft and Hewlett-Packard in which it had claimed copyright protection for the "look and feel" of the Macintosh user interface. After it experienced an 84% drop in net income in 1993, the company made some major changes, including upgrading its technology and trimming its work force. That same year Sculley stepped down (or, according to some, was forced out) as head of Apple. Michael Spindler became CEO, and Markkula returned as chairman.

In 1994 Hewlett-Packard bought a 15% stake in Taligent, an Apple-IBM joint venture. The partnership is developing an object-oriented operating environment to challenge Microsoft. That same year Apple introduced a new on-line service called eWorld, which focuses on business customers. Service providers include Dow Jones, Reuters, and The Reference Press (publisher of this profile).

After disappointing sales of the original version, in 1995 Apple launched an upgraded version of its Newton MessagePad hand-held computer. Also that year Apple settled a lawsuit by a user claiming repetitive stress injury when the company's law firm failed to provide the plaintiff's lawyers with required documents (the law firm paid the damages).

Nasdaq symbol: AAPL
Fiscal year ends: Last Friday in September

WHO

Chairman: Armas C. "Mike" Markkula Jr., age 52
President and CEO: Michael H. Spindler, age 52, $934,442 pay
EVP and CFO: Joseph A. Graziano, age 51, $514,461 pay
SVP; President, Apple USA: James J. Buckley, age 44, $493,504 pay
SVP; President and CEO, Claris Corp.: Daniel L. Eilers, age 39, $470,994 pay
SVP, Apple Online Services: Peter H. Friedman
SVP, Macintosh Desktop, PowerBook, and Imaging: Howard F. Lee
SVP Worldwide Operations: G. Frederick Forsyth, age 50
SVP; General Manager, AppleSoft Division: David C. Nagel, age 49
SVP Human Resources: Kevin J. Sullivan, age 53
VP, General Counsel, and Secretary: Edward B. Stead, age 47
VP Corporate Development: Robert A. Lauridsen
Auditors: Ernst & Young LLP

WHERE

HQ: One Infinite Loop, Cupertino, CA 95014
Phone: 408-996-1010
Fax: 408-996-0275

The company has manufacturing facilities in California, Colorado, Ireland, and Singapore and does business worldwide.

	1994 Sales		1994 Operating Income	
	$ mil.	% of total	$ mil.	% of total
US	4,983	54	45	9
Europe	2,096	23	263	50
Other regions	2,110	23	220	41
Adjustments	—	—	(6)	—
Total	**9,189**	**100**	**522**	**100**

WHAT

Computers
Apple II
Macintosh Classic
Macintosh LC
Macintosh Performa
Macintosh PowerBook
Macintosh Quadra
Power Mac PC

Personal Digital Assistant
Newton MessagePad

Software
AppleScript
AppleTalk
A/UX
FileMaker Pro
HyperCard
Mac OS
MultiFinder
OpenDoc
QuickDraw
QuickTime

Printers
ImageWriter
LaserWriter
StyleWriter

Other Peripheral Products
CD-ROM drives
Monitors
Network interfaces
Scanners

On-line Service
eWorld

Subsidiaries and Affiliates
Claris Corp. (software)
General Magic (11.3%, communications software)
Kaleida (multimedia joint venture with IBM)
Taligent (software joint venture with Hewlett-Packard and IBM)

KEY COMPETITORS

Acer	Gateway 2000	NEC
America Online	GE Information	Novell
Artisoft	Services	Oki
AST	Harris Computer	Olivetti
AT&T	Hewlett-Packard	Philips
Canon	Hitachi	Power Computing
Casio	Hyundai	Prodigy
Compaq	IBM	Radius
CompuAdd	Intel	Samsung
CompuServe	Iomega	Sharp
Daewoo	LG Group	Siemens
Data General	Machines Bull	Silicon Graphics
DEC	Matsushita	Sony
Dell	Micron Technology	Sun Microsystems
Delphi Internet	Microsoft	Tandem
Fujitsu	Mitsubishi	Toshiba

HOW MUCH

	9-Year Growth	1985	1986	1987	1988	1989	1990	1991	1992	1993	1994
Sales ($ mil.)	19.0%	1,918	1,902	2,661	4,071	5,284	5,558	6,309	7,087	7,977	9,189
Net income ($ mil.)	19.8%	61	154	218	400	454	475	310	530	87	310
Income as % of sales	—	3.2%	8.1%	8.2%	9.8%	8.6%	8.5%	4.9%	7.5%	1.1%	3.4%
Earnings per share ($)	20.2%	0.50	1.20	1.65	3.08	3.53	3.77	2.58	4.33	0.73	2.61
Stock price – high ($)	—	15.31	21.88	59.25	47.25	49.63	47.75	73.25	70.00	65.25	43.75
Stock price – low ($)	—	7.13	10.88	20.44	36.13	33.75	24.25	40.25	41.50	22.00	24.63
Stock price – close ($)	15.1%	11.00	20.25	42.00	40.25	35.25	43.00	56.38	59.75	29.25	39.00
P/E – high	—	31	18	36	15	14	13	28	16	89	17
P/E – low	—	14	9	12	12	10	6	16	10	30	9
Dividends per share ($)	—	0.00	0.00	0.12	0.32	0.40	0.44	0.48	0.48	0.48	0.48
Book value per share ($)	18.1%	4.45	5.54	6.63	8.17	11.77	12.54	14.92	18.46	17.45	19.94
Employees	13.8%	4,561	5,586	7,228	10,836	14,517	14,528	14,432	14,798	14,938	14,592

1994 Year-end:
Debt ratio: 20.0%
Return on equity: 14.1%
Cash (mil.): $1,258
Current ratio: 2.30
Long-term debt (mil.): $304
No. of shares (mil.): 120
Dividends
  Yield: 1.2%
  Payout: 18.4%
Market value (mil.): $4,662

Stock Price History High/Low 1985–94

ARAMARK CORPORATION

OVERVIEW

The year 1994 marked the end of an "ara." ARA, the Philadelphia-based diversified service company, became ARAMARK. The name change was accompanied by the unification of most of its dozens of businesses. The company hopes this move will give it stronger recognition in its many markets and facilitate cross-selling among its different business groups. The company's new logo, the "star person," is intended to establish ARAMARK's identity among its patrons, who may not have been aware of who was serving the hotdogs at sports arenas, national parks, schools, businesses, and prisons.

Other businesses that the privately owned company engages in include textile and uniform rental and maintenance, health service management, child care, and book and magazine distribution.

ARAMARK increased its presence at public parks with the 1994 purchase of Flagstar's TW Recreational Services. In 1995 the company was awarded the food services management contract for the 1996 Atlanta Olympics.

WHEN

In 1959 Davidson Automatic Merchandising, owned by Davre Davidson of California, merged with a Chicago vending company owned by William Fishman. The 2 had become friends through their individual roles as vending machine suppliers to local Douglas aircraft factories during WWII. Davidson became chairman and CEO and Fishman became president of the new company, Automatic Retailers of America.

ARA serviced mainly candy, beverage, and cigarette machines and by 1961 operated in 38 states and ranked first in sales among vending companies. ARA moved into food vending in the early 1960s, with clients such as the Southern Pacific Railway. Between 1959 and 1963 ARA acquired 150 food service companies, including Slater Systems in 1961, which gave ARA a top spot in operating cafeterias at colleges, hospitals, and work sites. Davidson and Fishman eased ARA into manual vending, despite the slimmer profit margins, because it was less capital-intensive and more responsive to price changes than machines, which required nickel increases. The company (which officially became ARA in 1969) grew so rapidly that the FTC stepped in, and the company agreed to restrict future vending acquisitions.

In 1968 ARA provided food service at the Mexico City Olympics. The company has provided service and management at a total of 9 Olympiads (Atlanta, 1996, will make 10).

ARA began diversifying into other service businesses, such as publication distribution, in 1968 and in 1970 expanded into janitorial and maintenance services by buying Ground Services (airline cleaning and loading services, sold 1990).

In 1973 ARA bought National Living Centers (now Living Centers of America), which operated residential communities for the elderly. This acquisition also led to ARA's entry into emergency care, for which the company provides emergency room staff. A high percentage of revenues for the emergency care segment comes from Medicare and Medicaid. A 1976 joint venture with Mitsui & Company introduced ARA food services to Japan. ARA bought Work Wear in 1977 and National Child Care Centers in 1980.

In 1984 a former director, William Siegel, and 2 Texas-based partners offered chairman Joseph Neubauer $722 million for the company. Neubauer refused and, to avoid a hostile takeover, took the company private in a $1.2 billion management buyout. Since then ARA has repurchased shares from other investors (investment banks and employee-benefit plans) to increase management's stake to more than 90%. Stock ownership is an incentive award for managers and employees. ARA is known for the loyalty it inspires in its employees.

The company acquired Szabo (correctional food services, 1986), Cory Food Services (1986), and Children's World Learning Centers (1987). In 1990 ARA divested its airport ground handling service and won the hospitality concessions for Olympic National Park.

In the 1990s ARA also expanded its textile rental and German food services operations. With sales slowing, ARA sold its retirement home business in 1993. That year the company bought Coordinated Health Services, a medical billing service, and introduced the ProSpect database, which has information on 550,000 practicing physicians and which ARA uses to recruit doctors for its medical services.

The next year ARAMARK introduced a learning program, *Quest 4 Fun*, at its child care centers.

The company scored a great coup in 1995 when it received the contract to manage food services at Disney World in Orlando.

Private company
Fiscal year ends: Friday nearest September 30

WHO

Chairman, President, and CEO: Joseph Neubauer,
age 53
**EVP; President, ARAMARK Food & Support Services
Group:** William Leonard, age 46
**EVP; President, ARAMARK Leisure/International
Services Group:** Richard H. Vent, age 53
**EVP; President, ARAMARK Health and Education
Services Group:** Julian L. Carr Jr., age 48
EVP; President ARAMARK Uniform Services Group:
L. Frederick Sutherland, age 42
EVP; Chairman, ARAMARK Global Food Service: John
R. Farquharson, age 56
EVP Finance and Personnel and CFO: James E.
Ksansnak, age 54
EVP, General Counsel, and Secretary: Martin W.
Spector, age 56
SVP Corporate Communications: Brian J. Gail, age 48
VP Human Resources: Brian G. Mulvaney, age 38
Auditors: Arthur Andersen & Co, SC

WHERE

HQ: 1101 Market St., Philadelphia, PA 19107
Phone: 215-238-3000
Fax: 215-238-3333

Most of ARAMARK's operations are located in the US.
The company also operates in Belgium, Canada, the
Czech Republic, Germany, Hungary, Japan, Korea,
Mexico, Spain, and the UK.

	1994 Sales	1994 Operating Income
	% of total	% of total
US	85	91
Other countries	15	9
Total	**100**	**100**

WHAT

	1994 Sales		1994 Operating Income	
	$ mil.	% of total	$ mil.	% of total
Food, leisure & support services	3,274	63	138	46
Uniform services	811	16	96	32
Health & education	673	13	37	13
Distributive services	404	8	27	9
Total	**5,162**	**100**	**298**	**100**

Subsidiaries
ARAMARK Business Dining Services
ARAMARK Campus Services
ARAMARK Correctional Services
ARAMARK Facility Services
ARAMARK Healthcare Support Services
ARAMARK International Services
ARAMARK Leisure Services
ARAMARK Magazine & Book Services
ARAMARK Refreshment Services
ARAMARK School Nutrition Services
ARAMARK Uniform Services
Children's World Learning Centers
GMARA
Spectrum Healthcare Services
WearGuard

Selected Foreign Operations
AIM Services (Japan)
ARAKOR (Korea)
ARAMARK/Germany
ARAMARK/UK
Husa S.L. (Spain)

KEY COMPETITORS

Accor	Helmsley
Amoskeag	Host Marriott
Angelica	Jim Pattison Group
Berkshire Hathaway	Koor
CareLine	Lagardère
Carlson	McDonald's
Cintas	Ogden
Corrections Corp. of America	PepsiCo
	Schwan's
Delaware North	Sterling Healthcare
Dial	Uno Restaurant
EmCare	W. R. Grace
G&K Services	

HOW MUCH

	Annual Growth	1985[1]	1986	1987	1988	1989	1990	1991	1992	1993	1994
Sales ($ mil.)	4.1%	2,652	3,749	4,019	3,917	4,244	4,596	4,774	4,865	4,891	5,162
Net income ($ mil.)	23.6%	6	16	22	5	39	52	64	67	77	87
Income as % of sales	—	0.2%	0.4%	0.5%	0.1%	0.9%	1.1%	1.3%	1.4%	1.6%	1.7%
Employees	1.8%	112,000	115,000	119,000	120,000	125,000	134,000	135,000	124,000	131,000	133,000

1994 Year-end:
Debt ratio: 84.6%
Return on equity: 57.0%
Cash (mil.): $44
Current ratio: 1.06%
Long-term debt (mil.): $982
Shareholder equity (mil.):
$183

Net Income ($ mil.)
1985–94

[1] 9-month fiscal year

ARCHER-DANIELS-MIDLAND COMPANY

OVERVIEW

Archer-Daniels-Midland (ADM) has a "mature business" — the company has been processing raw grain and seed for over 50 years. But the agri-giant continues to grow by creating new products from, and new markets for, its core corn, grain, and vegetable processing business.

"Bioproducts" such as vitamins and soy-based proteins, used in food for both humans and animals, are one growth market for ADM. The company opened a new plant to process natural vitamin E in 1994 (the vitamin will be marketed by Eastman Chemical). It also sells biotin, lecithin, riboflavin, and corn products such as lysine, xanthan gum, tryptophan, and vitamin C. ADM plans to produce 10 vitamins by the year 2000. In 1994 the company purchased Premiere Agri-Technologies, a leading

developer of cattle feeds with 52 plants worldwide, to expand its bioproduct business.

Encouraged by NAFTA and GATT, the company is finding international markets another route for expansion. ADM has a high-fructose corn syrup joint venture in Hungary and corn processing and wheat milling operations in Mexico. In 1994 it began shipping vegetable oil to China and soy-based products to Armenia, Russia, and South Africa.

In 1995 the US government began an investigation into charges of criminal price-fixing after an ADM BioProducts Division executive "blew the whistle" on his employer. The government is looking into whether ADM and others colluded to fix prices on citric acid, high-fructose corn syrup, and lysine.

WHEN

In 1878 John Daniels started crushing flaxseed to produce linseed oil, and in 1902 he formed Daniels Linseed Company in Minneapolis. George Archer, another experienced flaxseed crusher, joined the company in 1903. In 1923 the company bought Midland Linseed Products and became Archer-Daniels-Midland. During the 1920s ADM started to conduct research (an uncommon practice at the time) on the chemical composition of linseed oil and acquired several other linseed oil companies.

ADM entered the flour milling business in 1930 when it bought Commander-Larabee (then the #3 flour miller in the US). In the 1930s the company discovered a method for extracting lecithin (a food additive used in candy and other products) from soybean oil.

After WWII, ADM went through a period of rapid growth. By 1949 the company was the leading processor of linseed oil and soybeans in the US and was 4th in flour milling. During the early 1950s the company entered a period of foreign expansion. In 1954 it bought the resin division of US Industrial Chemicals.

ADM encountered financial difficulties in the early 1960s because of fluctuating commodities prices and losses in the chemical division. In 1966 the company's leadership passed to Dwayne Andreas, a former Cargill executive who had purchased a block of Archer family stock. He sold the chemical division and in 1967 purchased Fleischmann Malting, a producer of malt for beer and other uses.

Andreas, aware of the potential of the soybean (which is about 50% protein once processed), prompted the company's effort to produce textured vegetable protein. In 1969 he

established a plant in Decatur, Illinois, to produce edible soy protein.

Andreas's restructuring paved the way for productivity and expansion. In 1971 the company acquired Corn Sweeteners (glutens, high fructose syrups), which today also produces ethanol. Other acquisitions included Supreme Sugar (1973), Tabor (grain, 1975), and Columbian Peanut (1981); the latter made ADM the leading domestic sheller of peanuts.

The company continued to expand its global presence in the early 1990s through the purchases of Collingwood Grain (Kansas) and Pfizer's Citric Acid division. In 1991 ADM sold its White Lily Foods unit to Windmill Corporation and in 1992 bought Ogilvie Mills from John Labatt. That same year ADM formed a flour milling joint venture with Pillsbury.

During the 1992 presidential race the Andreas family made substantial donations to both parties in the hope that whoever won would support the use of ethanol in gasoline. Major midwestern flooding in 1993 dampened ADM's sales by about $40 million.

In 1994 the EPA approved a requirement that 1/10 of all gas sold in the US be blended with ethanol. That same year Andreas paid $9.5 million to buy 10% of the nonvoting shares of American Publishing Co., owner of the *Chicago Sun-Times* and 340 other newspapers. Also in 1994 the company began expanding its Harvest Burger production facilities to meet the growing demand for the Pillsbury-marketed meatless burger.

ADM purchased a minority stake in Savannah Foods & Industries, a refiner of cane and beet sugar, in 1995.

WHO

Chairman and CEO: Dwayne O. Andreas, age 76,
$2,972,630 pay
VC and EVP: Michael D. Andreas, age 45, $942,015 pay
President: James R. Randall, age 69, $1,461,641 pay
Chairman and CEO, ADM Milling: H. D. Hale, age 69,
$800,993 pay
SVP: Martin L. Andreas, age 55
Group VP: Burnell D. Kraft, age 62, $614,128 pay
Group VP: Charles T. Bayless, age 59
Group VP: Howard E. Buoy, age 67
VP; CEO, Europe: John G. Reed Jr., age 64
VP; President, Protein Specialties: Larry H.
Cunningham, age 50
VP; President, ADM Investor Services: Paul L. Krug Jr.,
age 50
VP, Secretary, and General Counsel: Richard P. Reising,
age 50
VP, Controller, and CFO: Douglas J. Schmalz, age 48
VP Employee Relations: Martin Reed
Auditors: Ernst & Young LLP

WHERE

HQ: 4666 Faries Pkwy., Box 1470, Decatur, IL 62525
Phone: 217-424-5200
Fax: 217-424-5839 (Public Relations)

ADM operates 200 plants, including 8 multipurpose
refineries, that process 150,000 tons of grain, seed, and
vegetable products each day.

	1994 Sales		1994 Operating Income	
	$ mil.	% of total	$ mil.	% of total
US	8,365	74	704	92
Other countries	3,009	26	62	8
Total	**11,374**	**100**	**766**	**100**

WHAT

	1994 Sales
	% of total
Oilseed products	50
Corn products	26
Wheat & other milled products	13
Other products & services	11
Total	**100**

Selected Divisions and Subsidiaries
ADM Agri Industries (oilseed products)
ADM BioProducts Division
ADM Corn Processing Division (corn products and ethanol)
ADM Europoort BV (oilseed products)
ADM Far East Ltd.
ADM Investor Services, Inc. (commodity hedging)
ADM Malting Division (barley malts)
ADM Milling Co. (wheat, corn, rice, oats, and barley)
ADM Processing Division (soybean products, cotton, and
canola)
ADM Protein Specialties Division
ADM/GROWMARK
Agrinational Insurance Co.
American River Transportation Co. (barges)
Archer Daniels Midland Shipping Co.
The British Arkady Co. Ltd. (vegetarian foods)
Collingwood Grain, Inc.
Gooch Foods, Inc. (pasta)
Hickory Point Bank and Trust (banking)
Southern Cotton Oil Co.

KEY COMPETITORS

Ag Processing	ConAgra	International
Ajinomoto	Continental Grain	Multifoods
American	Countrymark	Kyowa Hakko
Maize-Products	Co-op	Midwest Grain
Anderson Grain	CPC	Products
Bartlett & Co.	CSX	Riceland Foods
Bayer	Farmland Industries	Scoular
Borden	Harvest States	Tate & Lyle
Cargill	Co-ops	Universal Corp.

HOW MUCH

	9-Year Growth	1985	1986	1987	1988	1989	1990	1991	1992	1993	1994
Sales ($ mil.)	10.2%	4,739	5,336	5,775	6,798	7,929	7,751	8,468	9,232	9,811	11,374
Net income ($ mil.)	12.8%	164	236	265	353	425	484	467	504	535	484
Income as % of sales	—	3.5%	4.3%	4.6%	5.2%	5.4%	6.2%	5.5%	5.5%	5.4%	4.3%
Earnings per share ($)	13.2%	0.31	0.43	0.49	0.65	0.79	0.89	0.86	0.93	0.99	0.93
Stock price – high ($)	—	5.16	7.03	8.77	7.34	12.28	14.19	19.14	18.86	17.53	21.13
Stock price – low ($)	—	3.34	4.67	5.27	5.89	6.80	9.53	10.63	12.89	13.30	14.13
Stock price – close ($)	17.1%	4.97	5.53	6.72	6.92	12.08	12.48	19.08	16.03	14.44	20.63
P/E – high	—	17	16	18	11	15	16	22	20	18	23
P/E – low	—	11	11	11	9	9	11	12	14	13	15
Dividends per share ($)	9.4%	0.03	0.03	0.03	0.03	0.03	0.05	0.05	0.06	0.06	0.06
Book value per share ($)	12.5%	3.38	4.01	4.34	4.92	5.64	6.58	7.26	8.32	9.06	9.79
Employees	6.0%	9,446	10,386	10,573	9,631	10,214	11,861	13,049	13,524	14,168	16,013

1994 Year-end:
Debt ratio: 28.8%
Return on equity: 9.8%
Cash (mil.): $1,335
Current ratio: 3.47
Long-term debt (mil.): $2,021
No. of shares (mil.): 515
Dividends
  Yield: 0.3%
  Payout: 6.4%
Market value (mil.): $10,631

**Stock Price History
High/Low 1985–94**

ARMSTRONG WORLD INDUSTRIES, INC.

OVERVIEW

Armstrong has managed to avoid strong-arm tactics to maintain its profitability, but it has been cutting costs, shedding employees, and closing plants. The Lancaster, Pennsylvania–based manufacturer of floor coverings (ceramic tile and resilient flooring), furniture, and building products is committed to divesting its nonstrategic and underperforming businesses as part of its growth strategy.

Armstrong World Industries (which also manufactures specialty products for the building, automotive, and textile industries) is benefiting from the strong growth in housing sales over the past 3 years. Sales to the residential repair and remodeling markets accounted for more than 48% of 1994 revenues. Sales to overseas markets accounted for about 1/4 of Armstrong's 1994 revenues.

The company is looking to expand its business through acquisitions, alliances, and joint ventures. In 1994 Armstrong formed an alliance with Holmsund Golv AB, a Swedish manufacturer of resilient flooring. That year the company announced plans to build a ceiling plant in Shanghai, China, its first in Asia. The plant is earmarked to begin operation in 1996 to support the sales expansion of RH90, ceiling materials resistant to the high humidity common in China and other Asian countries.

The company's Thomasville Furniture subsidiary also expanded internationally in 1994. Armstrong increased its sales to a leading retail chain in Japan and opened new Thomasville Home Furnishings Stores in Taipei and Mexico City.

WHEN

Thomas Armstrong and John Glass started the Armstrong Brothers cork-cutting shop in Pittsburgh in 1860. Armstrong carved the corks by hand, stamped his name on each one, and made his first deliveries in a wheelbarrow.

Concerned with fairness to his customers, Armstrong rejected the maxim of "let the buyer beware" and put a written guarantee in each burlap sack of corks before shipping. By the mid-1890s Armstrong Brothers was the largest cork company in the world. In 1895 the company changed its name to Armstrong Cork.

To compensate for decreasing cork markets near the turn of the century (which was due to the invention of Mason jars and spring bottle stoppers), Armstrong found new uses for its cork in insulated corkboard and brick. In 1906 Armstrong turned its attention to linoleum (which then was made with cork powder) and started building a new factory in Lancaster, Pennsylvania. Thomas Armstrong died in 1908, a year before the company's linoleum hit the market.

Armstrong continued to produce mainly flooring and insulating materials through the 1950s while establishing foreign operations, primarily in Canada, Europe, and Australia. During the 1960s the company expanded its line to include home furnishings by purchasing E. & B. Carpet Mills (1967) and Thomasville Furniture Industries (1968). In 1969 the company sold its packaging materials operations.

In 1980 the company changed its name to Armstrong World Industries. During the 1980s

Armstrong rapidly expanded through acquisitions, buying Applied Color Systems (computerized color systems, 1981; sold in 1989), Chemline Industries (chemicals, 1985), the W. W. Henry Co. (adhesives and powder products, 1986), and American Olean (ceramic tile, 1988). Armstrong sold its carpet operations in 1989; 11 months later a hostile takeover attempt by Canada's Belzberg family failed.

Armstrong formed a joint venture in 1990 with Internacional de Cerámica to make ceramic tile in Mexico. In 1992 Armstrong and Worthington Industries combined their suspended-ceiling businesses, and Armstrong sold its 50% interest in ArmStar (marble flooring tiles).

In 1993 the company's Building Products Operations was recognized as a finalist for the Malcolm Baldrige National Quality Award, making it the 2nd Armstrong unit within 2 years to share that coveted distinction. Armstrong also created a new wholly owned trading company, Armstrong World Industries (China), to distribute floor and ceiling products in China.

By the end of 1994 the company's building products division had cut its worldwide work force to 75% of its 1990 level. Armstrong's North American sheet flooring unit introduced 166 new products in 1994, representing nearly 30% of its sheet flooring line.

In 1995 Armstrong purchased a gasket and specialty papers manufacturing facility from Brattleboro, Vermont–based Specialty Paperboard for an undisclosed price.

NYSE symbol: ACK
Fiscal year ends: December 31

WHO

Chairman, President, and CEO: George A. Lorch, age 53, $671,284 pay
EVP: E. Allen Deaver, age 59, $487,618 pay
President, Thomasville Furniture Industries: Frederick B. Starr, age 62, $404,794 pay
President, Worldwide Floor Products Operations: Dennis M. Draeger, age 54, $376,078 pay
President, Worldwide Building Products Operations: Henry A. Bradshaw, age 59, $318,372 pay
President, Corporate Retail Accounts Division: Stephen E. Stockwell, age 49
President, American Olean Tile: Robert J. Shannon Jr., age 46
SVP, Secretary, and General Counsel: Larry A. Pulkrabek, age 55
SVP and CFO: Frank A. Riddick III
VP and Director Asian Operations: Alan L. Burnaford
VP and Director Human Resources: John N. Jordin
Auditors: KPMG Peat Marwick LLP

WHERE

HQ: 313 W. Liberty St., PO Box 3001, Lancaster, PA 17604-3001
Phone: 717-397-0611
Fax: 717-396-2126

The company produces and markets its products worldwide, operating 56 manufacturing facilities in the US and 18 in 10 other countries.

	1994 Sales		1994 Operating Income	
	$ mil.	% of total	$ mil.	% of total
US	2,091	76	274	77
Europe	483	18	75	21
Other regions	179	6	8	2
Adjustments	—	—	(24)	—
Total	**2,753**	**100**	**333**	**100**

WHAT

	1994 Sales		1994 Operating Income	
	$ mil.	% of total	$ mil.	% of total
Floor coverings	1,284	47	190	53
Building products	630	23	87	24
Furniture	527	19	39	11
Industry products	312	11	41	12
Adjustments	—	—	(24)	—
Total	**2,753**	**100**	**333**	**100**

	1994 US Sales
	% of total
Residential improvement	48
Nonresidential improvement	23
New nonresidential	14
New residential	12
Industrial	3
Total	**100**

Selected Products
Industrial (adhesives, gasket materials, pipe insulation, textile mill supplies)
Nonresidential building and improvement (adhesives, ceramic tile, ceiling and wall systems, furniture, pipe insulation, resilient flooring)
Residential building and improvement (adhesives, ceramic tile, ceiling systems, furniture, pipe insulation, resilient flooring)

Selected Subsidiaries
American Olean Tile Company, Inc.
Armstrong World Industries (China) Ltd.
Thomasville Furniture Industries, Inc.
The W. W. Henry Company

KEY COMPETITORS

American Biltrite	Ladd Furniture	Mohasco
Bassett Furniture	Leggett & Platt	Owens-
Color Tile	Manville	Corning
Dal-Tile	Masco	Premark
INTERCO	3M	USG

HOW MUCH

	9-Year Growth	1985	1986	1987	1988	1989	1990	1991	1992	1993	1994
Sales ($ mil.)	5.6%	1,679	1,920	2,365	2,680	2,513	2,531	2,439	2,550	2,525	2,753
Net income ($ mil.)	8.5%	101	122	150	163	166	144	57	(62)	64	210
Income as % of sales	—	6.0%	6.4%	6.4%	6.1%	6.6%	5.7%	2.3%	—	2.5%	7.6%
Earnings per share ($)	9.2%	2.10	2.54	3.18	3.51	3.27	2.88	1.00	(2.03)	1.26	4.64
Stock price – high ($)	—	22.63	35.00	47.38	44.00	50.88	38.75	34.50	37.50	55.25	57.50
Stock price – low ($)	—	15.19	19.81	22.50	29.50	33.38	18.00	22.88	24.50	28.88	36.00
Stock price – close ($)	6.3%	22.31	29.88	32.25	35.00	37.25	25.00	29.25	31.88	53.25	38.50
P/E – high	—	11	14	15	13	16	14	35	—	44	12
P/E – low	—	7	8	7	8	10	6	23	—	23	8
Dividends per share ($)	7.8%	0.64	0.73	0.89	0.98	1.05	1.14	1.19	1.20	1.20	1.26
Book value per share ($)	(1.8%)	14.94	16.76	19.40	21.73	16.72	17.01	16.65	7.98	8.21	12.70
Employees	(0.1%)	20,781	21,667	24,121	25,941	25,607	25,200	24,066	23,500	21,682	20,583

1994 Year-end:
Debt ratio: 52.3%
Return on equity: 54.0%
Cash (mil.): $12
Current ratio: 1.78
Long-term debt (mil.): $483
No. of shares (mil.): 37
Dividends
  Yield: 3.3%
  Payout: 27.2%
Market value (mil.): $1,435

**Stock Price History
High/Low 1985–94**

ARTHUR ANDERSEN & CO, SC

OVERVIEW

Chicago-based Arthur Andersen is the biggest of the Big 6 accounting firms and the most diversified. Although all 6 firms offer management consulting, Andersen's consulting business is the largest and most developed, contributing almost half of the Big 6's total sales. The firm has a reputation for strict adherence to procedures and rules and conformity among its professional staff that has earned them the sobriquet "Arthur Androids."

Arthur Andersen is composed of 2 distinct units (coordinated by a Swiss entity, Arthur Andersen & Co, SC): Arthur Andersen & Co., which provides auditing, business advisory services, tax services, and specialty consulting services; and Andersen Consulting, which provides strategic services and technology consulting.

Andersen, along with the rest of the Big 6, has been stung in recent years by litigation arising from disappointing performances of IPOs and from wrongdoing by the management of companies it has audited. As a result, the firm has begun to shy away from doing audits for IPO companies and to drop clients.

Arthur Andersen's computer technology expertise is an important part of its consulting practice. In 1995 the firm made a pact with PeopleSoft to develop client/server software for manufacturing companies.

WHEN

Arthur Andersen, an orphan of Norwegian parents, worked in the Chicago office of Price Waterhouse in 1907. In 1908 at 23, after becoming the youngest CPA in Illinois, he began teaching accounting at Northwestern University. Following a brief period in 1911 as controller at Schlitz Brewing, Andersen became head of the accounting department at Northwestern. In 1913 at age 28, he formed a public accounting firm, Andersen, DeLany & Company, with Clarence DeLany.

Establishment of the Federal Reserve and implementation of the federal income tax in 1913 aided the firm's early growth by increasing the demand for accounting services. The company gained large clients, including ITT, Briggs & Stratton, Colgate-Palmolive, and Parker Pen, during the period between 1913 and 1920. In 1915 it opened a branch office in Milwaukee. After DeLany's departure in 1918, the firm adopted its present name.

Andersen grew rapidly during the 1920s and added to its list of services financial investigations, which formed the basis for its future strength in management consulting. The firm opened 6 offices in the 1920s, including ones in New York (1921), Kansas City (1923), and Los Angeles (1926).

When Samuel Insull's empire collapsed in 1932, Andersen was appointed the bankers' representative and guarded the assets during the refinancing. Andersen opened additional offices in Boston and Houston (1937) and in Atlanta and Minneapolis (1940).

Andersen's presence dominated the firm during his life. Upon his death in 1947, it found new leadership in Leonard Spacek. During Spacek's tenure, which continued until 1963, the firm opened 18 new US offices and began a period of foreign expansion with the establishment of a Mexico City office, followed by 25 more in other countries.

Andersen has been an innovator among the major accounting firms. The company opened Andersen University, its Center for Professional Education, in the early 1970s on a campus in St. Charles, Illinois, and provided the first worldwide annual report in 1973. To broaden its scope, it transferred its headquarters to Geneva in 1977.

During the 1970s Andersen increased its consulting business, which accounted for 21% of revenues by 1979; by 1988 consulting fees made up 40% of revenues, making Andersen the world's largest consulting firm. Tension between the consultants and the auditors eventually forced a 1989 restructuring, which established Arthur Andersen and Andersen Consulting as distinct entities.

A rash of megamergers among the then–Big 8 accounting firms led Andersen and Price Waterhouse to flirt briefly with a merger (1989), but discussions broke down.

In 1992 the RTC sued Arthur Andersen for $400 million, alleging negligence in auditing failed Benjamin Franklin Savings. The firm paid the RTC $65 million in 1993 to settle the case as part of a "global" settlement, exempting it from any possible future government charges for its earlier role as auditor of failed US savings and loans.

In 1994 Arthur Andersen and Deloitte & Touche were named in a $1.1 billion suit brought by investors who claim the 2 firms and Prudential Securities inflated the prices of several limited partnerships. Also that year the #8 UK accounting firm, Binder Hamlyn, was merged into Arthur Andersen.

International partnership
Fiscal year ends: August 31

WHO

Chairman, Managing Partner, and CEO: Lawrence A. Weinbach
Managing Partner, Arthur Andersen: Richard L. Measelle
Managing Partner, Andersen Consulting: George T. Shaheen
CFO: John D. Lewis
General Counsel: Jon N. Ekdahl
Manager Human Resources: Peter Pesce
CEO, Arthur Andersen & Co. (US): James Kackley

WHERE

HQ: 18, quai Général-Guisan, 1211 Geneva 3, Switzerland
Phone: +41-22-214444
Fax: +41-22-214418
US HQ: Arthur Andersen & Co., SC, 69 W. Washington St., Chicago, IL 60602-3094
US Phone: 312-580-0069
US Fax: 312-507-2548

Arthur Andersen & Co, SC, maintains over 350 offices in 74 countries.

	1994 Sales	
	$ mil.	% of total
Arthur Andersen		
Americas	1,919	29
Europe, India, Africa & Middle East	1,110	16
Asia/Pacific	489	7
Subtotal	**3,518**	**52**
Andersen Consulting		
Americas	1,801	27
Europe, India, Africa & Middle East	1,113	16
Asia/Pacific	306	5
Subtotal	**3,220**	**48**
Total	**6,738**	**100**

Worldwide Personnel		
	No.	% of total
Americas	37,382	51
Europe, India, Africa & Middle East	23,676	33
Asia/Pacific	11,664	16
Total	**72,722**	**100**

WHAT

Operating Units

Arthur Andersen
Auditing
Business advisory and corporate specialty services
Tax services

Andersen Consulting
Application software products
Business process management
Change management services
Client/server–based solutions
Object-oriented technology
Strategic services
Systems integration services
Technology services

Selected Representative Clients

American Express
Cadbury Schweppes
Chemical Bank
First Chicago
Inland Steel
KLM
New South Wales Police Service
NYNEX
Pacific Bell

KEY COMPETITORS

Bain & Co.
Booz, Allen
Boston Consulting Group
Control Data Systems
Coopers & Lybrand
DEC
Deloitte & Touche
EDS

Ernst & Young
H&R Block
IBM
KPMG
Marsh & McLennan
Perot Systems
Price Waterhouse
SHL Systemhouse

HOW MUCH

	9-Year Growth	1985	1986	1987	1988	1989	1990	1991	1992	1993	1994
Sales ($ mil.)	17.5%	1,574	1,924	2,316	2,820	3,382	4,160	4,948	5,577	6,017	6,738
Offices	5.8%	215	219	226	231	243	299	307	318	324	358
Partners	4.9%	1,630	1,847	1,957	2,016	2,134	2,292	2,393	2,454	2,487	2,517
Employees	11.1%	28,172	36,117	39,645	45,918	51,414	56,801	59,797	62,134	66,478	72,722

1994 Year-end:
Sales per partner: $2,676,996

ARTHUR ANDERSEN & CO.

Sales ($ mil.)
1985–94

ASARCO INCORPORATED

OVERVIEW

With world metals prices at new highs, ASARCO's prospects are very bright these days. The New York–based company is one of the world's leading producers of copper — as well as lead, zinc, silver, and gold. During years of depressed metals prices, ASARCO reorganized, sold noncore businesses, boosted earnings from nonmetal operations, and quadrupled its domestic copper production. Greater efficiencies, lower operating costs, and shrewd investments paid off in 1994 when metals prices surged.

Since 1985 ASARCO has evolved from a custom smelter and refiner to a major integrated mining company. Through its mines in the US, Peru, Australia, and Mexico, ASARCO and its affiliates in 1994 accounted for about 13% of the copper mined in the Western

world, 12% of the silver, 19% of the lead, and 9% of the zinc. To a lesser extent the company also provides environmental services and produces specialty chemicals (for treating metals) and construction aggregate.

ASARCO, a comparatively high-cost producer, is continuing to pare operating costs. During 1994 it also accelerated the development of 2 key Arizona copper mines and boosted its stake from 52.3% to 63% in Southern Peru Copper, which has some of the world's largest copper deposits.

Higher metals prices also spurred ASARCO in 1995 to form a 50/50 joint venture (Silver Valley Resources) with Coeur d'Alene Mines, a leading silver and gold producer, to redevelop silver mines in Idaho idled since 1990 by low silver prices.

WHEN

Henry Rogers, who helped create the Standard Oil Trust, tried to duplicate that effort in the US nonferrous metals industry by founding the American Smelting and Refining Company in 1899 (officially renamed ASARCO in 1975). Rogers began with 23 companies, 16 smelters, 18 refineries, and some mines. The major holdout, and later a major competitor, was M. Guggenheim's Sons, the smelting and refining business of Colorado's Guggenheim family (later well known as philanthropists).

Competition from the Guggenheims and labor strikes against the company forced ASARCO to merge with Guggenheim in 1901, but the Guggenheims and their allies held the controlling interest and several board positions. ASARCO became a public company when the Guggenheims sold all but 10% of their stock following the 1907 panic.

ASARCO expanded, acquiring 5 Mexican mines (1901), Federal Mining and Smelting in Idaho (1903), and a controlling interest in US Zinc (1903). In 1910 ASARCO bought copper mines in Arizona; it began its first open-pit copper mine there in 1954. In the 1920s the company started manufacturing products using its metals, later buying an interest in Michigan Copper and Brass (1928; later Revere Copper and Brass, makers of Revere Ware; sold 1982).

ASARCO expanded overseas to Peru in 1921. In 1930 it invested in Mount Isa Mines (now M.I.M. Holdings), an Australian silver, lead, zinc, and copper mining company; 20 years later it was discovered to have a huge copper strike. After WWII ASARCO diversified by

producing secondary metals from its ores, and in the 1950s the company expanded into asbestos and increased the size of its copper mining operations in Peru (Southern Peru Copper). By the 1970s copper accounted for almost 2/3 of its earnings.

ASARCO increased its copper holdings during the 1980s by buying properties in Arizona from Amoco (1985), the Ray mine from British Petroleum (1986), and the Eisenhower mine from a joint venture of Anaconda and Amax (1987). ASARCO continued to diversify, buying chemical companies OMI International (1988) and IMASA Group (1989). Although ASARCO ended its asbestos mining in 1989, the company and 2 subsidiaries were defendants in hundreds of asbestos-related lawsuits by 1992; most of these cases were dismissed or settled by late 1994.

A drop in metals prices in 1992 forced ASARCO to suspend operations at its Galena, Idaho, silver mine (1992) and its Troy, Montana, silver and copper mine (1993). In 1993 ASARCO converted its stake in poorly performing Mexico Desarrollo Industrial Minero (copper, lead, and zinc) to a 23.6% stake in Mexico's largest nonferrous metals mining company, Grupo Mexico. That same year it completed a $1 billion modernization and expansion program, its largest to date.

In 1994 ASARCO completed the divestiture, begun in 1993, of its principal gold mining operations, ASARCO Australia. Also that year ASARCO sold its PVC and asbestos pipe company (Capco Pipe) and announced it would sell its share of Grupo Mexico in 1996.

NYSE symbol: AR
Fiscal year ends: December 31

WHO

Chairman, President, and CEO: Richard de J. Osborne, age 60, $1,093,800 pay
EVP Copper Operations: Francis R. McAllister, age 52, $511,600 pay
VP Finance and CFO: Kevin R. Morano, age 41, $378,600 pay
VP Lead, Zinc, Silver, and Mineral Operations: Robert M. Novotny, age 46, $350,600 pay
VP Government and Public Affairs: Robert J. Muth, age 61, $334,100 pay
VP, General Counsel, and Secretary: Augustus B. Kinsolving, age 55
VP Commercial: James J. Kerr, age 64
VP Environmental Operations: Michael O. Varner, age 53
VP Exploration: Gerald D. Van Voorhis, age 56
Treasurer: Thomas J. Findley Jr., age 47
VP Human Resources: David B. Woodbury, age 54
Auditors: Coopers & Lybrand L.L.P.

WHERE

HQ: 180 Maiden Ln., New York, NY 10038
Phone: 212-510-2000
Fax: 212-510-1855

ASARCO's principal US mines are located in Arizona, Colorado, Idaho, Missouri, Montana, and Tennessee. Major foreign mines are located in Argentina, Australia, Canada, Mexico, and Peru.

	1994 Sales		1994 Operating Income	
	$ mil.	% of total	$ mil.	% of total
US	1,867	92	17	100
Other countries	165	8	—	—
Total	**2,032**	**100**	**17**	**100**

WHAT

	1994 Sales		1994 Operating Income	
	$ mil.	% of total	$ mil.	% of total
Metals	1,675	82	(9)	—
Specialty chemicals	278	14	13	50
Aggregates	43	2	7	27
Other	36	2	6	23
Total	**2,032**	**100**	**17**	**100**

Mining, Refining, and Smelting
Antimony oxide
Copper
Gold
Lead
Molybdenum
Palladium
Platinum
Silver
Zinc

Major Subsidiaries and Affiliates
American Limestone Co., Inc. (building materials)
Enthone–OMI, Inc. (specialty chemicals)
Grupo Mexico (23.6%)
M.I.M. Holdings Ltd. (15.4%, mining, Australia)
Silver Valley Resources (50%, silver mining)
Southern Peru Copper Corp. (63%)

KEY COMPETITORS

Alcan	FMC	Newmont Gold
Alcoa	Freeport-McMoRan	Phelps Dodge
Anglo American	Homestake Mining	Placer Dome
Broken Hill	Horsehead Industries	Reynolds
Codelco	Inco	Metals
Cyprus Amax	Koch	RTZ
Dow Chemical	Lyondell	Union Carbide
DuPont	Petrochemical	Vulcan
Echo Bay Mines	Magma Copper	Materials
Essex Group		

HOW MUCH

	9-Year Growth	1985	1986	1987	1988	1989	1990	1991	1992	1993	1994
Sales ($ mil.)	6.4%	1,167	1,057	1,355	1,988	2,211	2,209	1,910	1,909	1,736	2,032
Net income ($ mil.)	—	(62)	9	208	207	231	149	46	(29)	(71)	64
Income as % of sales	—	—	0.9%	15.4%	10.4%	10.5%	6.8%	2.4%	—	—	3.1%
Earnings per share ($)	—	(2.87)	(0.46)	4.88	4.92	5.50	3.60	1.12	(0.70)	(1.70)	1.53
Stock price – high ($)	—	27.75	22.88	34.25	29.50	35.88	34.13	30.50	31.75	28.63	34.88
Stock price – low ($)	—	15.75	10.00	14.88	19.38	26.13	22.25	18.25	19.75	16.25	21.38
Stock price – close ($)	5.0%	18.38	14.88	28.50	27.38	29.88	27.13	21.38	25.00	22.88	28.50
P/E – high	—	—	—	—	7	6	7	10	27	—	—	23
P/E – low	—	—	—	3	4	5	6	16	—	—	14
Dividends per share ($)	—	0.00	0.00	0.10	0.70	1.50	1.60	1.60	0.80	0.40	0.40
Book value per share ($)	6.8%	20.02	20.33	28.49	31.67	34.56	36.78	36.24	32.74	35.27	36.04
Employees	0.3%	7,800	7,000	7,600	8,500	9,000	9,300	9,055	8,900	8,500	8,000

1994 Year-end:
Debt ratio: 38.1%
Return on equity: 4.3%
Cash (mil.): $18
Current ratio: 1.61
Long-term debt (mil.): $915
No. of shares (mil.): 42
Dividends
  Yield: 1.4%
  Payout: 26.1%
Market value (mil.): $1,200

Stock Price History
High/Low 1985–94

ASHLAND, INC.

Russell, Kentucky–based Ashland refined more than oil in recent months; it changed its corporate name from Ashland Oil to Ashland, Inc. While Ashland remains one of the nation's largest independent petroleum refiners, it continues to reap the rewards of strong performances by its nonrefining energy and chemical businesses, which account for 60% of total revenues. Ashland Chemical is the largest distributor of industrial chemicals and plastics in the US. Its Valvoline subsidiary makes one of the US's leading motor oils, and Ashland's construction business, APAC, is the largest highway contractor in the US.

In 1995 the company increased its holdings in Ashland Coal from 39% to 54%, prompting Ashland to change its name to reflect its broad energy and chemical interests.

Ashland's oil and gas exploration subsidiary has more than doubled its natural gas production over the past 5 years, and it is developing a major gas field in the Gulf of Mexico. In 1994 the company made a promising oil discovery in the first well sunk in a multiwell exploratory project in Nigeria.

Ashland's 3 refineries provide gasoline to the company's 600 SuperAmerica convenience stores in the Ohio Valley and upper Midwest as well as to independent marketers. It plans to add up to 200 SuperAmerica stores over the next 5 years.

Despite the growing role of the firm's chemical and energy segments, refining remains the cornerstone of Ashland's business. The company planned to invest over $165 million in Ashland Petroleum during 1995.

WHEN

J. Fred Miles sold his Oklahoma oil drilling company in 1917 to wheel and deal in Kentucky. He attracted Chicago backers and prominent Kentuckians to invest in his Swiss Oil Company drilling venture.

In 1924 Swiss bought a troubled refinery in Catlettsburg, then a rough river town near sedate Ashland, and created the Ashland Refining subsidiary. Miles battled Swiss directors for control, lost, and resigned in 1927.

Swiss expanded by buying Tri-State Refining (1930) and Cumberland Pipeline's eastern Kentucky network (1931). Swiss changed its name to Ashland Oil and Refining in 1936.

Following WWII, CEO Paul Blazer spurred Ashland on to acquire small independent oil firms (Allied Oil in 1948, Aetna Oil in 1950). When Ashland bought Freedom-Valvoline in 1950, it acquired the venerable Valvoline name. The firm bought Frontier Oil of Buffalo and National Refining of Cleveland in 1950.

Blazer passed the torch to Orin Atkins in 1965. Ashland formed its Ashland Chemical subsidiary in 1967 after acquiring Anderson-Prichard Oil (1958), United Carbon (1963), and ADM Chemical (1967). The firm added its SuperAmerica retail marketing chain in 1970 and began exploring Nigeria for oil in 1973.

In 1975 Atkins admitted ordering Ashland executives to make illegal contributions to the Nixon campaign. Atkins was deposed in 1981 after Ashland made questionable payments to highly placed "consultants" with connections to oil-rich Middle Eastern governments. In one payment Ashland had bankrolled a

consultant's scheme to make reusable sausage casings.

Atkins was arrested in 1988 for attempting to fence purloined documents regarding litigation between Ashland and the National Iranian Oil Company (NIOC). Ashland, which launched the federal investigation that led to Atkins's arrest, settled with NIOC for $325 million in 1989. Atkins pleaded guilty to charges related to the documents and, after cooperating in other proceedings, received a probated sentence.

Even without Atkins as a lightning rod, Ashland faced challenges. Chairman John Hall had to fend off a takeover by the Belzberg family of Canada in 1986.

Ashland bought Permian (crude oil gathering and marketing) in 1991 and merged it into its Scurlock Oil. In 1992 Ashland Chemical acquired most of Unocal's chemical distribution business. Ashland sold its barge operations to Dixie Carriers and its Florida SuperAmerica stores to Shell Oil in 1993.

In 1994 Ashland Chemical acquired 2 companies that produce chemicals for the semiconductor industry: Eurobase (Italy) and ACT Inc. (Pennsylvania). Also in 1994 Ashland sold its Arizona highway construction business to Kiewit Construction Group. The company's APAC construction unit posted record earnings of $70 million in 1994, and made 4 small acquisitions during the year.

In 1995 Ashland completed the purchase of certain assets of Waco Oil and Gas Co., giving it ownership of an additional 1,200 natural gas wells in West Virginia.

NYSE symbol: ASH
Fiscal year ends: September 30

WHO

Chairman and CEO: John R. Hall, age 62,
$1,634,003 pay
President and COO: Paul W. Chellgren, age 51,
$1,083,200 pay
**SVP; Group Operating Officer, Ashland Chemical,
Valvoline, and SuperAmerica:** John A. Brothers,
age 54, $718,694 pay
**SVP; Group Operating Officer, APAC, Ashland
Exploration, Ashland Services, and Arch Mineral:**
James R. Boyd, age 48, $677,277 pay
SVP; President, Ashland Chemical: David J. D'Antoni,
age 49, $606,917 pay
**SVP; Group Operating Officer, Ashland Petroleum and
South Point Ethanol; President, Ashland Petroleum:**
Robert E. Yancey Jr., age 49
SVP; President, Ashland Exploration: G. Thomas
Wilkinson, age 56
SVP and CFO: J. Marvin Quin, age 47
SVP, General Counsel, and Secretary: Thomas L.
Feazell, age 57
Administrative VP and Controller: Kenneth L. Aulen,
age 45
Administrative VP Human Resources: Philip W. Block,
age 47
Auditors: Ernst & Young LLP

WHERE

HQ: 1000 Ashland Dr., Russell, KY 41169
Phone: 606-329-3333
Fax: 606-329-5274

Ashland's 3 refineries are located in Canton, Ohio;
Catlettsburg, Kentucky; and St. Paul, Minnesota. It
explores for oil and natural gas in Australia, Morocco,
Nigeria, and the US. Valvoline's products and services
are sold in more than 140 countries. Ashland Chemical
has manufacturing facilities in 10 states and 17 foreign
countries.

WHAT

	1994 Sales		1994 Operating Income	
	$ mil.	% of total	$ mil.	% of total
Petroleum	4,666	40	113	25
Chemical	2,885	25	125	28
SuperAmerica	1,706	15	59	13
Construction	1,101	9	70	16
Valvoline	1,000	9	52	12
Exploration	199	2	28	6
Adjustments	(1,175)	—	(80)	—
Total	**10,382**	**100**	**367**	**100**

Selected Subsidiaries
APAC Group (construction)
Arch Mineral Corp. (50%, coal)
Ashland Chemical Co. (chemicals)
Ashland Coal, Inc. (54%, coal)
Ashland Exploration (oil and gas producer and marketer)
Ashland Petroleum (refining, transportation)
SuperAmerica Group (retailing)
The Valvoline Company (auto products and services)

KEY COMPETITORS

Amerada Hess	Halliburton	Petrobrás
Amoco	Hanson	Petrofina
Atlantic Richfield	Koch	Phillips
Bechtel	Lyondell	Petroleum
British Petroleum	Petrochemical	Quaker State
Broken Hill	Martin Oil	Repsol
Chevron	Marketing	Royal Dutch/
Circle K	McDermott	Shell
Coastal	Mobil	Southland
Cyprus Amax	Occidental	Sun Company
Diamond Shamrock	Oryx	Texaco
Dow Chemical	PDVSA	TOTAL
DuPont	PEMEX	Union Pacific
Elf Aquitaine	Pennzoil	Unocal
Exxon	Peter Kiewit	USX–Marathon
Fluor	Sons'	Vulcan Materials

HOW MUCH

	9-Year Growth	1985	1986	1987	1988	1989	1990	1991	1992	1993	1994
Sales ($ mil.)	2.6%	8,238	7,374	7,311	8,269	8,536	9,048	9,923	10,251	10,256	10,382
Net income ($ mil.)	3.3%	147	209	133	184	86	182	145	(68)	142	197
Income as % of sales	—	1.8%	2.8%	1.8%	2.2%	1.0%	2.0%	1.5%	—	1.4%	1.9%
Earnings per share ($)	3.4%	2.06	3.08	2.14	3.29	1.55	3.20	2.54	(1.18)	2.20	2.79
Stock price – high ($)	—	19.69	32.13	35.88	38.13	43.00	40.13	35.25	34.00	35.63	44.50
Stock price – low ($)	—	12.00	17.75	23.25	26.38	33.13	26.38	26.13	22.50	24.25	31.25
Stock price – close ($)	7.0%	18.69	28.00	28.88	33.50	40.00	27.25	29.88	26.38	34.13	34.50
P/E – high	—	10	10	17	12	28	13	14	—	16	16
P/E – low	—	6	6	11	8	21	8	10	—	11	11
Dividends per share ($)	2.5%	0.80	0.85	0.90	0.95	1.00	1.00	1.00	1.00	1.00	1.00
Book value per share ($)	3.0%	16.37	14.92	17.17	19.06	19.62	22.14	24.11	18.12	19.35	21.34
Employees	(0.4%)	32,800	34,400	42,000	37,600	37,800	33,400	33,000	33,700	31,800	31,600

1994 Year-end:
Debt ratio: 48.9%
Return on equity: 16.0%
Cash (mil.): $40
Current ratio: 1.29
Long-term debt (mil.): $1,391
No. of shares (mil.): 61
Dividends
  Yield: 2.9%
  Payout: 35.8%
Market value (mil.): $2,105

**Stock Price History
High/Low 1985–94**

ASSOCIATED MILK PRODUCERS, INC.

OVERVIEW

Membership is slipping and so is market share, but you won't find AMPI crying over spilt milk — especially not when its farmers collect 15.5 billion pounds of the stuff. San Antonio–based Associated Milk Producers, Inc., the largest US milk cooperative, was responsible for 10% of the nation's milk supply in 1994, down 2% from the year before. AMPI had a 9% slice of the US cheese production and churned out 143 million pounds of butter. The cooperative's products can be found in grocery stores, convenience stores, restaurants, delis, and other food service operations.

AMPI's 12,698 member farms (down 48% in the past 10 years) are located in 20 states and organized into 3 operating regions, each of which manufactures, processes, and markets dairy items. Morning Glory Farms includes operations primarily in Illinois, Indiana, and Wisconsin and specializes in cheese production. The North Central and Southern Regions, meanwhile, produce a broader range of dairy products, including milk, cheese, butter, whey, ice cream, cottage cheese, sour cream, and yogurt.

While demand for dairy products has increased 19% in the past decade, milk prices have declined, brought down by oversupply despite sometimes drastic measures instituted by the US government. There are fewer than 190,000 dairy farms in the US, down from more than one million in the early 1960s.

AMPI's political action committee, C-TAPE (Committee for Thorough Agricultural Political Education), saw victories by 86% of the 284 US congressional candidates it backed in 1994. That year, the cooperative awarded more than $18 million in rebates to its members.

WHEN

In 1969, faced with declining income and milk consumption, about 100 dairy cooperatives in the Midwest and the South merged to form Associated Milk Producers, Inc. The membership elected John Butterbrodt, from a Wisconsin cooperative, as the first president and established headquarters in San Antonio, home of the largest cooperative, Milk Producers Association. Cooperatives throughout the central US clamored to join, and AMPI became the largest US dairy cooperative within 2 years of its formation.

Almost from the beginning AMPI became embroiled in the 2 main controversies involving dairy cooperatives: monopolistic practices and political contributions. In 1972 consumer advocate Ralph Nader alleged that the 3 main dairy cooperatives — AMPI, Dairymen, and Mid-America Dairymen — had illegally contributed $422,000 to President Nixon's reelection campaign in an attempt to obtain higher price supports (enacted in 1971) and an agreement that the administration would drop antitrust suits against the cooperatives. Watergate investigators subpoenaed Nixon's tapes, and AMPI was accused of bribery, destruction of evidence, and attempting to achieve "complete market dominance." In 1974 AMPI pleaded guilty to making illegal political contributions in 1968, 1970, and 1972. By 1975, 3 former AMPI employees had been convicted of various charges and Butterbrodt had resigned.

AMPI spent the last half of the 1970s quietly reorganizing; during this time it estab-lished its current regional management structure. In 1982 a suit for monopolistic practices, originally filed in 1971 by the National Farmers' Organization (NFO), finally reached the federal courts. The case was decided in favor of AMPI and 2 other large cooperatives, but before the year was out an appeals court reversed the decision, saying AMPI and its codefendants had conspired to eliminate competitive sellers of milk. In 1983 Congress rejected a bill to cut price supports for dairy farmers and instead adopted a program to pay farmers not to produce milk. Industry critics charged that the 3 major milk cooperatives had bought the legislation through large political contributions.

AMPI extended its dominance of the industry in 1985 by merging its central region, then called the Mid-States Region, with 2,200 members of Shawano, Wisconsin–based Morning Glory Farms Cooperative. In 1989 the US Supreme Court upheld the appeals court ruling in the NFO antitrust case.

In 1990 business soured for AMPI: it posted a $27 million loss. In 1991 dissatisfied Arkansas farmers threatened to bolt AMPI. AMPI successfully lobbied the Department of Agriculture to strengthen dairy price supports in 1992.

The cooperative in 1994 became one of the first targets of a lawsuit stemming from the Family Leave Act. The Labor Department filed a suit on behalf of a truck driver in New Mexico who was fired a week after he missed work while his wife was in early labor with triplets.

Mutual company
Fiscal year ends: December 31

President: Irvin J. Elkin
General Manager: Noble Anderson
President, Morning Glory Farms Region: Robert Thompson
President, North Central Region: Mel Kunstleben
President, Southern Region: Bill Thornton
Manager, Morning Glory Farms Region: Jim Kasten
Manager, North Central Region: Mark Furth
Manager, Southern Region: Jim Carroll
Corporate Controller: Terry Krueger
Manager Human Resources: Charlie Warren
Auditors: Deloitte & Touche LLP

WHERE

HQ: 6609 Blanco Rd., PO Box 790287, San Antonio, TX 78279-0287
Phone: 210-340-9100
Fax: 210-340-9158

AMPI is divided into 3 regions. The Morning Glory Farms Region serves customers in Illinois, Indiana, Michigan, Ohio, and Wisconsin. The North Central Region serves customers in Iowa, Minnesota, Missouri, Nebraska, South Dakota, and Wisconsin. The Southern Region serves customers in Arkansas, Colorado, Kansas, Kentucky, Louisiana, Mississippi, Missouri, Nebraska, New Mexico, Oklahoma, Tennessee, and Texas.

	1994 Membership	
Regions	No. of members	% of total
North Central	6,125	48
Morning Glory Farms	3,333	26
Southern	3,240	26
Total	**12,698**	**100**

	1994 Production	
Regions	Lbs. mil.	% of total
Southern	8,100	52
North Central	4,500	29
Morning Glory Farms	2,900	19
Total	**15,500**	**100**

WHAT

	1994 Sales	
	$ mil.	% of total
Milk products	2,587	98
Hauling & other	42	2
Total	**2,629**	**100**

	1994 Production
	Lbs. mil.
Unprocessed milk	15,500
Cheese	576
Dried whey	243
Nonfat dry milk	185
Butter	143

Dairy Activities
Grade A milk production
Production and packaging of dairy products, canned cheese sauces, and other milk-based goods under the Morning Glory, New Holstein, State Brand, and other labels

Major Subsidiaries, Affiliates, and Investments
Farm Credit System Banks
Land O'Lakes, Inc.
Northland Foods Cooperative
Prairie Farms Dairy, Inc.

Membership Services
AMPI Investment Corp. (investment subsidiary of the Southern Region)
Member insurance

Political Activities
Committee for Thorough Agricultural Political Education (C-TAPE)
State political committees in the Southern Region

KEY COMPETITORS

Alpine Lace	Mid-America Dairymen
Borden	MorningStar Group
Dairyman's Co-op Creamery	Philip Morris
Dairymen	Schreiber Foods
Danone	Shamrock Foods
Darigold	Southern Foods
Dean Foods	Specialty Foods
John Labatt	Universal Foods
Michael Foods	Wisconsin Dairies

HOW MUCH

	Annual Growth	1985	1986	1987	1988	1989	1990	1991	1992	1993	1994
Sales ($ mil.)	0.9%	2,416	2,489	2,710	2,777	2,987	3,063	2,768	2,835	2,692	2,629
Operating income ($ mil.)	(24.3%)	—	—	7	4	12	(27)	1	(13)	11	1
Member farms	(6.5%)	23,300	23,500	22,400	20,800	19,400	18,478	16,321	14,729	13,403	12,698
Milk deliveries (lbs. mil.)	(0.1%)	15,700	15,900	17,200	17,700	17,300	17,700	17,100	16,500	15,700	15,500
Employees	1.4%	—	—	—	—	—	4,200	4,500	4,319	4,364	4,199	4,500

Sales ($ mil.)
1985–94

3,500
3,000
2,500
2,000
1,500
1,000
500
0

AST RESEARCH, INC.

OVERVIEW

AST Research is ailing and Samsung has the cure. Samsung Electronics, the world's #1 maker of memory chips and part of the Korea-based Samsung Group, has agreed to acquire a 40.25% stake in California-based AST, the world's 6th largest maker of personal computers. Samsung will get an immediate presence in the world PC market; AST will get an infusion of $250 million plus a reliable source for critical parts. As part of the deal, Samsung will supply computer components and collaborate on product design, and the 2 companies will trade technology.

AST, which early on established a reputation for quality and innovation, has been struggling since its 1993 acquisition of Tandy's PC operations for $112 million. The company was also slow to get its Pentium-based products to consumers and was forced to close some plants and cut its work force.

The alliance with Samsung is expected to boost AST's PC output by a third. The company manufactures a broad line of desktop and notebook computers, servers, and monitors, as well as connectivity, graphics, and memory enhancement products. The company spends less than 2% of revenues on R&D, depending on alliances with top hardware and software developers such as IBM, Intel, Microsoft, and Novell for product development.

Chairman Safi Qureshey, one of the company's founders, owns about 9.7% of AST.

WHEN

In 1979 friends Albert Wong, Safi Qureshey, and Tom Yuen started a high-tech consulting firm, drawing lots to see who would be president. They called the Orange County–based venture AST Associates after the initials of their first names. In 1980 they incorporated as AST Research, Inc., and the 3 Asia-born engineers, working from Yuen's garage, set out to make computer enhancement and peripheral products.

Their timing couldn't have been better. Only 4 months after IBM came out with its PC in 1981, AST had a memory enhancer. In 1983 sales reached $12 million, and in 1984 AST went public, raising over $13 million.

As PCs became more sophisticated, with more software features built in, demand for enhancement products matured. AST responded by introducing its own PC, the Premium/286 (based on Intel's 286 chip), in 1986. But it fell behind in introducing a machine based on the 386 chip in 1987.

In 1988, after Wong left to start his own company, Qureshey and Yuen reorganized AST, selling divisions that made enhancement boards for Apple and Digital Equipment and cutting staff. The company was in trouble: its former marketing complacency had led to financial woes, and its first loss was reported in fiscal 1989.

By mid-year AST was back on track with 2 new 386-based computers. In 1989 the company introduced a line of PCs with the microprocessor on a separate board, allowing users to upgrade without having to buy a complete new motherboard. It also began emphasizing overseas business, establishing subsidiaries in Europe and the Far East.

In 1990 AST introduced 12 new computers, including a notebook PC priced 30–50% lower than its competitors. The company also unveiled the first PC to run both NEC 9801 (the de facto standard in Japan) and MS-DOS operating systems, making it a potential contender in the hard-to-crack Japanese market. That same year AST and IBM announced a 5-year patent cross-licensing accord. AST launched a CAD (computer-aided design) workstation in 1991 and a multiprocessor computer in 1992. Fierce competition slowed AST's growth in 1992, forcing the company to restructure. In a surprising move cofounder Yuen abruptly left the company that same year.

In 1993 AST started a new subsidiary in Singapore and launched its Pentium-based Manhattan servers and its Premmia 486-based computers. It also acquired Tandy's PC manufacturing operations in a deal that expanded AST's manufacturing capacity by 40% and gave it new distribution outlets via Tandy's Radio Shack, Computer City, and Incredible Universe retail stores.

In 1994 AST formed subsidiaries in Ireland, Korea, Malaysia, and Norway, as well as a sales and manufacturing operation in China. The company closed its plant in Scotland (acquired in the Tandy deal) and opened a facility in Ireland. Also that year AST introduced its Ascentia line of notebook computers and a new line of Advantage PCs that feature user interface software (AST Works).

To maintain its share of the PC market, in 1995 AST cut prices on some servers by as much as 22% and bundled Novell's Netware operating system with some servers to make them more attractive.

Nasdaq symbol: ASTA
Fiscal year ends: Saturday nearest June 30

WHO

Chairman and CEO: Safi U. Qureshey, age 43,
$859,297 pay
President and COO: James T. Schraith, age 37,
$444,200 pay
EVP Finance and CFO: Bruce C. Edwards, age 40,
$377,474 pay
SVP Worldwide Operations: James L. Forquer, age 44,
$338,613 pay
SVP Administration (HR): Richard P. Ottaviano, age 48,
$287,551 pay
VP and General Manager Server Products: Scott A.
Smith, age 39
VP Corporate Development: Wai S. Szeto, age 46
VP Legal and Treasury Operations and Secretary:
Dennis R. Leibel, age 50
Auditors: Ernst & Young LLP

WHERE

HQ: 16215 Alton Pkwy., PO Box 57005, Irvine, CA
92619-7005
Phone: 714-727-4141
Fax: 714-727-8584 (Investor Relations)

AST has plants in the US (California and Texas), Hong
Kong, China, Ireland, and Taiwan and sales offices in
over 30 countries. Its products are sold in more than 100
countries.

	1994 Sales		1994 Operating Income	
	$ mil.	% of total	$ mil.	% of total
Americas	1,546	66	83	—
Europe	533	23	(42)	—
Pacific	261	11	37	—
Adjustments	27	—	9	—
Total	**2,367**	**100**	**87**	**—**

WHAT

	1994 Sales	
	$ mil.	% of total
486-based desktop systems	1,500	63
Notebook computers	519	22
80386 & 80386SX-based PCs	90	4
Other	258	11
Total	**2,367**	**100**

Computer Product Lines
Advantage!
Ascentia (notebook computers)
Bravo
GRiD (palmtop and pen-based systems)
Manhattan SMP (multiprocessor line for minicomputer/
superserver marketplace)
PowerExec (notebook computer)
Premmia (desktops and servers)
Victor (desktops, Europe)

Other Products
ASTVision color monitors
Graphics adapters
Memory and multifunction boards

KEY COMPETITORS

Acer	Hewlett-Packard	Radius
Apple	Hitachi	Sanyo
AT&T	Hyundai	SCI Systems
Atari	IBM	Sharp
Canon	Intel	Silicon Graphics
Compaq	LG Group	Sony
Creative	Machines Bull	Sun
Technology	Matsushita	Microsystems
Daewoo	Media Vision	Tatung
Data General	Micron	Texas
DEC	Technology	Instruments
Dell	NEC	Toshiba
Fujitsu	Olivetti	Unisys
Gateway 2000	Packard Bell	

HOW MUCH

	9-Year Growth	1985	1986	1987	1988	1989	1990	1991	1992	1993	1994
Sales ($ mil.)	37.0%	139	172	206	413	457	534	689	944	1,412	2,367
Net income ($ mil.)	5.6%	19	27	13	15	(8)	35	65	69	(54)	31
Income as % of sales	—	13.7%	15.8%	6.3%	3.7%	—	6.6%	9.4%	7.3%	—	2.3%
Earnings per share ($)	(0.5%)	0.99	1.17	0.57	0.64	(0.32)	1.21	2.13	2.16	(1.72)	0.95
Stock price – high ($)	—	16.00	15.63	10.88	8.50	5.50	18.88	32.75	24.50	25.50	33.00
Stock price – low ($)	—	4.25	5.31	3.25	3.63	3.38	5.19	14.50	11.25	12.57	10.38
Stock price – close ($)	(0.6%)	15.38	6.44	3.69	3.94	5.19	18.63	16.75	21.00	22.75	14.63
P/E – high	—	16	13	19	13	—	16	15	11	—	35
P/E – low	—	4	5	6	6	—	4	7	5	—	11
Dividends per share ($)	—	0.00	0.00	0.00	0.00	0.00	0.00	0.00	0.00	0.00	0.00
Book value per share ($)	17.9%	2.54	3.79	4.34	5.01	4.68	6.34	9.34	11.80	10.09	11.19
Employees	33.1%	532	800	1,350	2,242	2,281	2,312	2,960	3,560	4,509	6,977

1994 Year-end:
Debt ratio: 37.4%
Return on equity: 9.2%
Cash (mil.): $153
Current ratio: 2.01
Long-term debt (mil.): $215
No. of shares (mil.): 32
Dividends
  Yield: —
  Payout: —
Market value (mil.): $473

**Stock Price History
High/Low 1985–94**

AT&T CORP.

OVERVIEW

Based in New York City, AT&T plans to take advantage of the emerging global information business by combining communications, computers, and network products and services. AT&T has the largest long distance network in the US and has stabilized its market share in this highly competitive market. With its $11.5 billion purchase in 1994 of McCaw Cellular, the nation's #1 cellular service, AT&T has gained a major share in a high-growth sector of the telecommunications industry. As the only phone company that also manufactures equipment, AT&T also offers both computer and network products and services. In 1994 network and equipment revenue increased by 19% on the basis of large orders from Bell Atlantic, Pacific Telesis, and Saudi Arabia. AT&T has also won contracts to provide telecommunications equipment to India ($21 million) and Russia ($200 million).

AT&T has moved far from its Ma Bell roots to become a global company. The company created WorldPartners, an international consortium of telephone companies, and joined forces with Nippon Telegraph and Telephone (the world's 2nd largest telephone company after AT&T) in long distance service on a 6-month trial basis.

WHEN

"Mr. Watson. Come here. I want you."

Alexander Graham Bell's legendary summons, the first words on a telephone, came as he was perfecting his invention in 1876. As demand for the new device spread, Bell's backers, fathers of deaf students he was tutoring, founded Bell Telephone (1877) and New England Telephone (1878), which were consolidated as National Bell Telephone in 1879.

After several years of litigation, National Bell barred rival Western Union from the telephone business in 1879. Western Union had tried to market Elisha Gray's competing patent, filed just hours after Bell's. In 1882 the Bell company wrested control of Western Electric, the US's #1 electrical equipment manufacturer, from Western Union.

Bell's patents expired in the 1890s, and independent phone companies raced into the market. Bell struggled to compete. After changing its name to American Telephone and Telegraph and relocating the headquarters from Boston to New York in 1899, AT&T shifted its focus to swallowing smaller companies. AT&T also blocked independents from access to Bell System phone lines.

J. P. Morgan and his allies gained control of AT&T and installed Theodore Vail as president in 1907. AT&T won control of Western Union in 1909; however, the Wilson administration threatened antitrust action. In the 1913 Kingsbury Commitment, AT&T agreed to sell Western Union, buy no more independent phone companies without regulatory approval, and grant independents access to its networks. Bell Labs, the heralded research and development division, was formed in 1925.

In 1949 the Justice Department sued to force AT&T to sell Western Electric. A 1956 settlement allowed AT&T to keep Western Electric but prohibited it from entering non-regulated businesses. FCC rulings stripped AT&T of its telephone equipment monopoly (1968) and allowed specialized carriers, such as MCI, to hook their microwave-based systems to the phone network (1969), injecting competition into the long distance arena.

A government suit led to the 1982 settlement that, in 1984, spun off the 7 regional Bell companies. AT&T kept long distance services and Western Electric. Since the breakup, CEO Robert Allen has cut levels of management and eliminated jobs in order to remain competitive. In 1990 AT&T offered a consumer credit card (Universal Card) and also acquired Western Union's business services group (electronic mail, telex). In 1991 AT&T acquired computer makers Teradata and NCR. The purchase of NCR made AT&T the world's 7th largest computer maker and gave the company a presence in more than 120 countries.

In 1994 AT&T proposed opening local telecommunications markets in Illinois and gave up on its wireless communicator, shuttering the operation. Also in that year the company formally adopted the name AT&T Corp. and relabeled its NCR unit AT&T Global Information Solutions.

In 1994 the company acquired Interchange Network Company, an on-line service, from Ziff-Davis Publishing. In 1995 AT&T announced it would pay $3.3 billion for the 48% of cellular communications company LIN Broadcasting that it did not already own. (It had acquired 52% of LIN when it bought McCaw Cellular.) AT&T also decided to sell its remaining stake in video game creator 3DO to focus on other computer segments, such as wireless communications, and closed EO, a developer of pen-based mobile computers.

NYSE symbol: T
Fiscal year ends: December 31

Chairman and CEO: Robert E. Allen, age 59,
$3,362,600 pay
EVP; Chairman, Global Operations Team: Victor A.
Pelson, age 57, $1,657,600 pay
EVP; CEO, Communications Services: Alex J. Mandl,
age 51, $1,482,100 pay
EVP; CEO, Multimedia Products: William B. Marx Jr.,
age 55, $1,428,400 pay
CEO, AT&T GIS: Lars Nyberg, age 43
EVP; CEO, Network Systems: Richard A. McGinn,
age 48
EVP and CFO: Richard W. Miller, age 54
SVP General Counsel and Government Affairs: John D.
Zeglis, age 47
SVP Human Resources: Harold W. Burlingame, age 54
Auditors: Coopers & Lybrand L.L.P.

WHERE

HQ: 32 Avenue of the Americas, New York, NY
10013-2412
Phone: 212-387-5400
Fax: 212-841-4715 (Public Relations)

AT&T provides communications, computer, and network
services and products as well as financial and leasing
services worldwide. AT&T operates 92 manufacturing
facilities worldwide.

	1994 Sales		1994 Operating Income	
	$ mil.	% of total	$ mil.	% of total
US	67,769	90	6,841	91
Other countries	7,325	10	677	9
Total	**75,094**	**100**	**7,518**	**100**

WHAT

	1994 Sales	
	$ mil.	% of total
Telecommunication services	43,425	58
Products & systems	21,161	28
Rentals & other services	7,391	10
Financial services & leasing	3,117	4
Total	**75,094**	**100**

Financial Services and Leasing
AT&T Capital (leasing, financing)
AT&T Universal Card Services (consumer credit card)

Global Information Movement and Management
AT&T Global Information Solutions Group (information
systems)
Communications Services Group
AT&T Solutions
Multimedia Products Group (equipment)
AT&T Microelectronics
AT&T Ventures
Network Systems Group (switching systems)

Other Operations
AT&T Bell Laboratories
International (alliances, including WorldPartners;
ventures; manufacturing facilities; and investments)
Wireless Services (McCaw Cellular)

KEY COMPETITORS

ACC	Cable & Wireless	NEC
AirTouch	Cray Research	NYNEX
ALC Comm.	EDS	Pacific Telesis
ALLTEL	Ericsson	SBC
Alcatel Alsthom	Fujitsu	Communications
American Express	GTE	Siemens
Ameritech	Hitachi	Sprint
BCE	IBM	U.S. Long Distance
Bell Atlantic	MCI	U S WEST
BellSouth	MFS	Visa
BT	Communications	WorldCom

HOW MUCH

	9-Year Growth	1985	1986	1987	1988	1989	1990	1991	1992	1993	1994
Sales ($ mil.)	8.9%	34,910	34,087	33,598	35,210	36,112	37,285	63,089	64,904	67,156	75,094
Net income ($ mil.)	13.1%	1,557	314	2,044	(1,669)	2,697	2,735	522	3,807	3,974	4,710
Income as % of sales	—	4.5%	0.9%	6.1%	—	7.5%	7.3%	0.8%	5.9%	5.9%	6.3%
Earnings per share ($)	9.1%	1.37	0.21	1.88	(1.55)	2.50	2.51	0.40	2.86	2.94	3.01
Stock price – high ($)	—	25.38	27.88	35.88	30.38	47.38	46.63	41.25	53.13	65.00	57.13
Stock price – low ($)	—	19.00	20.88	20.00	24.13	28.13	29.00	29.00	36.63	50.13	47.25
Stock price – close ($)	8.1%	25.00	25.00	27.00	28.75	45.50	30.13	39.13	51.00	52.50	50.25
P/E – high	—	19	133	19	—	19	19	103	19	22	19
P/E – low	—	14	99	11	—	11	12	73	13	17	16
Dividends per share ($)	1.1%	1.20	1.20	1.20	1.20	1.20	1.29	1.32	1.32	1.32	1.32
Book value per share ($)	(2.0%)	13.68	12.64	13.46	10.68	11.84	12.90	12.39	14.12	10.24	11.42
Employees	(3.0%)	399,600	378,900	365,000	364,700	339,500	328,900	317,100	312,700	308,700	304,500

1994 Year-end:
Debt ratio: 38.8%
Return on equity: 30.1%
Cash (mil.): $1,208
Current ratio: 1.22
Long-term debt (mil.):
$11,358
No. of shares (mil.): 1,569
Dividends
Yield: 2.6%
Payout: 43.9%
Market value (mil.): $78,843

**Stock Price History
High/Low 1985–94**

ATLANTIC RICHFIELD COMPANY

OVERVIEW

Atlantic Richfield Company (ARCO), the 6th largest US oil company, was once swimming in oil. Today it is standing in the shallows. One of the largest gas retailers on the West Coast, Los Angeles–based ARCO is a fully integrated petroleum company, engaged in everything from exploration, development, and production to refining, transportation, and marketing of petroleum products. But its primary source of wealth over the past 20 years — cheap Alaskan crude — is being depleted at a faster rate than new sources of oil are being found.

ARCO also mines coal, manufactures chemicals, manages convenience stores and auto emissions testing services, and owns 49.9% of Lyondell Petrochemical (one of the US's largest petrochemical firms) and 83.3% of ARCO Chemical.

Mike Bowlin (who became CEO in 1994 and chairman in 1995) is adopting a cautious approach to exploration and development. With roughly 90% of ARCO's overseas production coming from Indonesia and the North Sea, the company is shunning the megaprojects in Asia and the former Soviet Union favored by some of its rivals in favor of cost cutting and asset building. ARCO has axed 16% of its work force (4,500) over the past 3 years.

WHEN

In 1866 Charles Lockhart and other pioneers in the Pennsylvania oil industry formed Atlantic Petroleum Storage, changing its name to Atlantic Refining in 1870 after buying a small refinery. It became a secret affiliate of Standard Oil in 1874 and was spun off by order of the US Supreme Court in 1911.

In the 1920s Atlantic Refining explored for oil in Iraq and in the 1930s designed the first all-welded ship. Through the 1950s and 1960s, it bought oil and plastics companies. In 1963 Atlantic Refining bought Hondo Oil & Gas (New Mexico) from oilman Robert Anderson, who became the company's #1 shareholder and was elected chairman in 1965.

Under Anderson, Atlantic Refining grew from a small East Coast oil refiner to a large West Coast integrated oil leader. In 1966 it purchased Richfield Oil (founded as Rio Grande; California, 1905) and adopted Atlantic Richfield (ARCO) as its name. Richfield's assets included an exploration program on Alaska's North Slope at Prudhoe Bay.

In 1968 ARCO, exploring on the North Slope in partnership with Humble Oil (later Exxon), drilled into the largest oil deposit in North America. To transport the oil to the lower 48 states, 8 oil companies formed the Trans Alaska Pipeline System (TAPS). ARCO owns 21.3% of TAPS. The oil field began production in 1977, and the completed pipeline began transporting oil from Prudhoe Bay to the ice-free coastal waters of Valdez, 800 miles away.

ARCO bought Sinclair Oil, a midwestern integrated oil company (1969), and in 1972 ARCO moved its main offices to Los Angeles. To diversify, it bought Anaconda (1977), a Montana copper and uranium mining company. In 1986 Anderson retired, and Lodwrick Cook, a Louisianan who had started out pumping gas at a family store, took the helm.

In 1985 ARCO authorized a stock repurchase of up to $4 billion to make itself a less appealing takeover target. It sold or closed its weak, noncore businesses, including Anaconda, and buttressed its energy and chemical concerns.

In 1989 ARCO spun off 50.1% of its Houston subsidiary Lyondell Petrochemical, created in 1988. To stem a decline of reserves, ARCO bought oil and gas properties in California (from Tenneco, 1988, and Oryx, 1990) and Oklahoma (USX's TXO Production, 1990).

Lowered gas prices and the economic recession led to a 1991 net earnings drop of 58% from 1990's record-setting levels. In response, ARCO cut 2,100 jobs.

ARCO signed an agreement in 1992 to develop its South China Sea gas field to provide gas for electrical power generation in Hong Kong. In 1993 the company added to its Alaskan properties when it acquired 130,000 acres of leases near Cook Inlet in a partnership with Phillips Petroleum.

In 1994 ARCO sold approximately $1 billion in debt securities tied to Lyondell Petrochemical's stock. The offering, which ARCO can pay off in cash or Lyondell stock, was delayed after Lyondell's senior management was charged with violating environmental regulations. Also that year, ARCO acquired a 9.9% stake in China's Zhenhai Refining and Chemical Company, near Shanghai.

During 1994 ARCO completed extensive refinery modifications to meet the EPA's emission control regulations, and in 1995 it introduced a new product mix in conjunction with a range of reformulated oils.

WHO

Chairman, President and CEO: Mike R. Bowlin, age 52,
$1,315,731 pay (prior to promotion)
EVP and CFO: Ronald J. Arnault, age 51, $1,154,654 pay
EVP: William E. Wade Jr., age 52, $925,000 pay
EVP: Anthony G. Fernandes, age 49, $639,141 pay
**SVP; President, ARCO Exploration and Production
Technology:** H. L. Bilhartz
SVP; President, ARCO Asia-Pacific: E. Kent Damon Jr.
SVP External Affairs: Kenneth R. Dickerson
SVP; President, ARCO International Oil and Gas:
Marlan W. Downey
SVP; President, ARCO Transportation: Marie L.
Knowles
SVP; President, ARCO Coal: Stephen R. Mut
SVP; President, ARCO Products: William C. Rusnak
SVP, General Counsel, and Corporate Secretary: Bruce
G. Whitmore
VP Human Resources: John H. Kelly
Auditors: Coopers & Lybrand L.L.P.

WHERE

HQ: 515 S. Flower St., Los Angeles, CA 90071
Phone: 213-486-3511
Fax: 213-486-2063

ARCO drills for oil and gas in China, Dubai, Indonesia,
the UK, and the US, and mines for coal in Australia and
the US. It owns service stations in Arizona, California,
Nevada, Oregon, and Washington.

	1994 Sales	
	$ mil.	% of total
US	13,947	84
Other countries	2,605	16
Adjustments	647	—
Total	**17,199**	**100**

WHAT

	1994 Sales		1994 Net Income	
	$ mil.	% of total	$ mil.	% of total
Oil & gas	7,969	40	405	33
Refining & mktg.	6,529	33	195	16
Intermediate chemicals & specialty prods.	3,423	17	265	22
Transportation	897	4	172	14
Coal	663	3	70	6
Other	677	3	111	9
Adjustments	(2,959)	—	(299)	—
Total	**17,199**	**100**	**919**	**100**

Major Operations
Chemical manufacturing
Coal mining
Convenience stores (am/pm minimarkets)
Emissions testing services (SMOGPROS)
Oil and gas exploration and production
Petroleum refining
Service station operations (ARCO)
Transportation of crude and refined products

KEY COMPETITORS

Amerada Hess	Hanson	Petrofina
Amoco	Imperial Oil	Phillips
ASARCO	Ingram	Petroleum
Ashland, Inc.	Kerr-McGee	Pittston Minerals
Bethlehem Steel	Koch	Repsol
British Petroleum	Kroger	Royal Dutch/
Broken Hill	Mobil	Shell
Chevron	NERCO	Sinclair Oil
Circle K	Norsk Hydro	Southland
Coastal	Occidental	Sun Company
Cyprus Amax	Oryx	Texaco
Dow Chemical	PDVSA	TOTAL
DuPont	PEMEX	Union Pacific
Elf Aquitaine	Pennzoil	Unocal
Exxon	Petrobrás	USX–Marathon

HOW MUCH

	9-Year Growth	1985	1986	1987	1988	1989	1990	1991	1992	1993	1994
Sales ($ mil.)	(3.2%)	23,080	15,774	17,608	18,868	16,815	19,896	18,922	19,248	19,183	17,199
Net income ($ mil.)	—	(202)	615	1,224	1,583	1,953	1,688	709	1,193	269	919
Income as % of sales	—	—	3.8%	6.9%	8.47%	11.6%	8.5%	3.8%	6.2%	1.4%	5.3%
Earnings per share ($)	—	(0.97)	3.38	6.68	8.78	11.26	10.20	4.39	7.39	1.66	5.63
Stock price – high ($)	—	67.88	64.38	99.13	90.88	114.38	142.25	135.75	121.75	127.75	112.38
Stock price – low ($)	—	42.00	45.25	58.75	67.50	80.38	105.50	99.13	98.13	100.50	92.50
Stock price – close ($)	5.3%	63.75	60.00	69.00	80.63	111.38	123.63	106.75	114.75	105.25	101.75
P/E – high	—	—	19	15	10	10	14	31	17	77	20
P/E – low	—	—	13	9	8	7	10	23	13	61	16
Dividends per share ($)	4.3%	3.75	4.00	4.00	4.00	4.50	5.00	5.50	5.50	5.50	5.50
Book value per share ($)	2.7%	30.62	29.62	33.07	36.32	39.96	44.98	43.34	42.28	38.30	39.05
Employees	(3.3%)	31,300	26,600	25,800	27,200	26,600	27,300	27,700	26,800	25,100	23,200

1994 Year-end:
Debt ratio: 43.5%
Return on equity: 14.8%
Cash (mil.): $4,385
Current ratio: 1.52
Long-term debt (mil.): $7,198
No. of shares (mil.): 161
Dividends
  Yield: 5.4%
  Payout: 97.7%
Market value (mil.): $16,357

**Stock Price History
High/Low 1985–94**

AUTOMATIC DATA PROCESSING, INC.

OVERVIEW

With 275,000 accounts, Automatic Data Processing (ADP) is the #1 payroll and tax filing processor in the US. Its tax processing services to employers accounted for 58% of total revenues in 1994; ADP filed 9.5 million payroll tax returns with 2,000 different taxing authorities. ADP's Brokerage Services — front-office quotation workstations and back-office record keeping, order entry, and proxy services for brokerage firms — accounted for 24% of sales. The firm's Dealer Services unit provides accounting, inventory, and other management services to 9,500 auto and truck dealers in North America and Europe. Other services include accounting and auto collision esti-

mates for insurers. Sales outside North America are less than 5% of total revenue.

Effective management and a focused strategy have steered ADP to double-digit per-share earnings growth for 132 consecutive quarters, along with strong cash flow. The company has also been buoyed by the growing US economy and the trend toward outsourcing by American corporations. The Dealer Services division is the company's fastest-growing area, with sales up 22% last year. The trend away from mainframes has benefited the data processing giant as corporations have outsourced payroll, administrative, and human resource tasks to the company.

WHEN

In 1949, 22-year-old Henry Taub started Automatic Payrolls, a manual payroll preparation service, in Paterson, New Jersey. Taub's business had 8 accounts that created gross revenues of around $2,000 that year. In 1952 Taub's brother Joe joined the company, as did a childhood friend, Frank Lautenberg, who took a pay cut to become the company's first salesman. During the 1950s the company continued selling its payroll services to new clients and grew steadily.

In 1961 the company went public and changed its name to Automatic Data Processing (ADP). The next year ADP offered back-office services to brokerage houses and bought its first computer, beginning the automation of the company's manual accounting business. In 1962 ADP's revenues reached $1 million.

During the 1970s ADP bought more than 30 companies in the US, Brazil, and the UK, all involved in data and payroll processing, shareholder services, computer networks, inventory control, or automated banking. ADP stock began trading on the NYSE (1970), revenues reached $50 million (1971), and the company started data centers in Florida (1972) and Connecticut (1973). In 1975 Lautenberg became CEO.

ADP bought more than 25 additional businesses during the 1980s in the US, Canada, and Germany, mainly in data and information services. ADP's purchases of stock information provider GTE Telenet (1983) and Bunker Ramo's information system business (1986) brought the company 45,000 stock quote terminals in brokerages such as E.F. Hutton, Dean Witter, and Prudential-Bache. When Lautenberg resigned as CEO to become one of

New Jersey's US senators in 1983, Josh Weston, who had joined the company as VP of planning in 1970, replaced him.

By 1985 ADP revenues had climbed to $1 billion. Soon after, founder Taub retired as chairman. In 1986 the company sold the German data processing firm it had bought in 1981, as well as the US banking operations ADP had bought earlier in 1986 as part of Bunker Ramo. ADP installed 15,000 computer workstations at brokerages in 1986 and in 1989 began installing more than 38,000 new integrated workstations at Merrill Lynch and Shearson Lehman. ADP shed units, including its Canadian stock quote and Brazilian businesses, in 1989 and 1990.

Deterred from major acquisitions by the inflated prices of the late 1980s, ADP made several strategic purchases during the early 1990s. These included the 1992 purchase of BankAmerica Corp.'s 17,000-client Business Services Division. In 1993 ADP bought Industry Software Corporation's back-office and international equities business from Quotron.

In 1994 ADP purchased Peachtree Software (accounting and payroll software for small companies), National Bio Systems (medical bill auditing), and V-Crest (auto dealership management systems). It also agreed to acquire the Application Group, a leading client/server applications business.

In 1995 the company signed a deal with Hewlett-Packard to deliver its client/server human resource management system on HP's UNIX-based database servers. The company also acquired Williams, Thatcher & Rand, an employee-benefits consultant and 401(k) processor.

NYSE symbol: AUD
Fiscal year ends: June 30

WHO

Chairman and CEO: Josh S. Weston, age 65,
$1,068,750 pay
President and COO: Arthur F. Weinbach, age 51,
$615,833 pay
President, Brokerage Services Group: Robert J. Casale,
age 55, $541,923 pay
President, Employer Services Group: Glenn W.
Marschel, age 48, $537,500 pay
President, Dealer Services Group: Gary C. Butler,
age 47, $466,250 pay
President, Claims Services: John R. Gaulding, age 49
SVP, Secretary, and Counsel: Fred S. Lafer, age 65
VP and CFO: Fred D. Anderson Jr., age 50
VP and Controller: Richard J. Haviland, age 48
VP and Treasurer: Joseph B. Pirret, age 53
VP Corporate Development: Michael W. Reece, age 49
VP Human Resources: Michael Holmes, age 36
Auditors: Deloitte & Touche LLP

WHERE

HQ: One ADP Blvd., Roseland, NJ 07068-1728
Phone: 201-994-5000
Fax: 201-994-5387

The company has 53 regional processing centers in the
US, one in Canada, and 2 in Europe.

WHAT

	1994 Sales	
	$ mil.	% of total
Employer services	1,424	58
Brokerage services	606	24
Dealer services	334	13
Other	105	5
Total	**2,469**	**100**

Employer Services

401(k) record keeping and reporting
Human resource record keeping and reporting
Payroll processing and tax filing
Unemployment compensation management

Brokerage Services

On-line inquiry and data collection
On-line trading
Order matching
Portfolio reporting
Stock loan accounting
Trade processing

Dealer Services

Computer systems sales
Data processing
Hardware maintenance
Manufacturer/dealer data communications networks
Software licensing/support
Vehicle registration services

Claims Services

Audatex (collision repair estimating)
Parts Exchange (parts identification, location, and
pricing)
Vehicle valuation (replacement valuation)

Selected Subsidiaries

ADP Credit Corp. (computer leasing and financing)
Peachtree Software Inc. (accounting software)

KEY COMPETITORS

American Management	H&R Block
AutoInfo	Hewitt Associates
BankAmerica	Intuit
Bertelsmann	Knight-Ridder
BHC Financial	Microsoft
Bloomberg	Paychex
Ceridian	PeopleSoft
Citicorp	Perot Systems
CompuCom	Platinum Software
Dow Jones	Reuters
Dun & Bradstreet	Technology Solutions
General Electric	Vanstar

HOW MUCH

	9-Year Growth	1985	1986	1987	1988	1989	1990	1991	1992	1993	1994
Sales ($ mil.)	10.2%	1,030	1,204	1,384	1,549	1,678	1,714	1,772	1,941	2,223	2,469
Net income ($ mil.)	16.0%	88	106	132	170	188	212	228	256	294	334
Income as % of sales	—	8.5%	8.8%	9.5%	11.0%	11.2%	12.4%	12.9%	13.2%	13.2%	13.5%
Earnings per share ($)	16.1%	0.62	0.70	0.84	1.07	1.23	1.44	1.63	1.84	2.08	2.37
Stock price – high ($)	—	15.00	19.38	27.25	23.63	25.38	30.13	46.38	55.63	56.88	59.75
Stock price – low ($)	—	9.63	14.00	16.13	17.31	17.88	22.63	25.00	38.75	46.88	47.63
Stock price – close ($)	16.5%	14.75	17.63	22.44	19.38	24.50	26.81	45.50	53.13	55.25	58.50
P/E – high	—	24	28	32	22	21	21	29	30	27	25
P/E – low	—	16	20	19	16	15	16	16	21	23	20
Dividends per share ($)	14.5%	0.16	0.17	0.19	0.22	0.26	0.30	0.35	0.40	0.46	0.54
Book value per share ($)	13.4%	3.89	4.52	5.64	6.36	6.53	7.63	7.62	9.25	10.59	12.02
Employees	1.9%	18,500	20,000	21,000	23,000	21,000	19,000	19,000	20,500	21,000	22,000

1994 Year-end:
Debt ratio: 18.2%
Return on equity: 21.0%
Cash (mil.): $591
Current ratio: 2.06
Long-term debt (mil.): $373
No. of shares (mil.): 141
Dividends
  Yield: 0.9%
  Payout: 22.8%
Market value (mil.): $8,231

Stock Price History
High/Low 1985–94

AVIS, INC.

Avis is the 2nd largest car rental and leasing company in the US (after Ford's Hertz unit) and one of the largest employee-owned companies in the US. The company's employees own 71%, and General Motors owns 29%.

Although sales have risen, profits of the Garden City, New York–based company have fallen. Avis has been hurt by more expensive fleet costs and stiffer competition as aggressive upstarts, such as Alamo Rent A Car, have eaten away at Avis's market share by undercutting the company on price. In addition, Avis has had trouble judging rental car demand. For

example, the company raised its prices 10% in the summer of 1994, thinking Hertz would do the same, but Hertz kept prices steady, drawing away Avis customers.

CEO Joseph Vittoria says the company is working on improving its pricing system. Avis is also upgrading its technology to provide better service to customers. Cars in selected areas are being outfitted with electronic navigation devices, and the company is also providing return agents with handheld computers that can provide customers with up-to-the-minute flight information.

Young Detroit car dealer Warren Avis noticed that no car rental agencies, including Hertz, had airport operations. A former army pilot, Avis believed air travel was the way of the future. In 1946 he invested his savings and $75,000 of borrowed funds to open Avis Airlines Rent-A-Car System outlets at Detroit's Willow Run Airport and Miami International Airport. Avis's idea was a success, and in 1948 his company opened inner-city locations to serve hotels and office buildings.

By 1954 Avis had expanded to Mexico, Canada, and Europe. That year Warren Avis sold the company to Richard Robie, a Boston-based car rental agent, for $8 million. Robie planned to have a nationwide system of one-way car rentals and a company charge card but ran out of money and sold Avis to Boston investors in 1956. After forming a holding company (Avis, Inc.) with Avis Rent-A-Car System as its main subsidiary, the new owners instituted car leasing. In 1962 they sold Avis to investment bankers Lazard Frères, who named Robert Townsend (author of *Up the Organization: How to Stop the Organization from Stifling People and Strangling Profits*) president and moved Avis's headquarters to Garden City, New York. That was the year Avis first used the slogan "We're only No. 2. We try harder."

ITT bought Avis in 1965. Winston Morrow Jr. replaced Townsend as CEO and focused on overseas expansion. A headquarters serving Africa, Europe and the Middle East (now Avis Europe) was established in the UK. In 1972 Avis pioneered use of the Wizard System, now the industry's oldest and largest computer reservation system. That year, as part of an antitrust settlement, ITT sold 48% of the company to the public; the rest was held by a court-appointed trustee. Avis again became privately owned in 1977: Norton Simon

bought it for $174 million. In 1979 Avis's fleet started to feature GM cars.

Former Hertz executive Joseph Vittoria became president in 1982 and took 15 people with him when he went to Avis.

Avis was again passed from owner to owner: Esmark bought Norton Simon in 1983 and in turn was bought by Beatrice in 1984. Kohlberg Kravis Roberts took Beatrice private through an LBO in 1985 and sold Avis to William Simon's Wesray Capital Corporation (an investment partnership) in 1986. That year Avis sold its leasing operations to PHH Group and most of Avis Europe to the public (on the London Exchange).

In 1987 Avis's employees, led by Vittoria, established an Employee Stock Ownership Plan (ESOP) and bought the company for $1.79 billion. Also in 1987 Avis established WizCom International, a subsidiary to sell the Wizard System to other industries. Avis then joined General Motors and Lease International to form Cilva Holdings, which bought Avis Europe in 1989.

Hertz filed a lawsuit against Avis in 1991, alleging false advertising claims on the basis of a survey Hertz believed used questionable methods. The suit was settled in early 1992 in Hertz's favor, but Avis paid no damages.

Avis promoted a sweepstakes ("Win Your Own Travel Agency") in 1993 that caused established travel agencies to complain. Avis legally had to continue the contest but advised contestants, "do anything . . . but don't open your own agency."

In 1994 the Justice Department ended an investigation of Avis under the Americans with Disabilities Act after Avis agreed to provide more hand controls for the disabled in its cars.

In 1995 Avis paid off the last of its ESOP acquisition debt.

Private company
Fiscal year ends: Last day of February

WHO

Chairman and CEO: Joseph V. Vittoria, age 59
EVP and CFO: Lawrence Ferezy
EVP: Charles A. Bovino
EVP: James E. Collins
EVP, Systems Development and Marketing; President, WizCom International: David P. McNicholas
SVP and General Manager: F. Robert Salerno
SVP Human Resources and Secretary to the Board: Donald L. Korn
VP and Tax Counsel: Steven L. Greenberger
VP and Treasurer: Gerard J. Kennell
VP and Assistant Secretary: James R. B. Fitzsimmons
VP, General Counsel, and Corporate Secretary: John J. Lynch
VP Corporate Communications: Russell L. James
Auditors: Price Waterhouse LLP

WHERE

HQ: 900 Old Country Rd., Garden City, NY 11530
Phone: 516-222-3000
Fax: 516-222-4381
Reservations: 800-331-1212

Avis has operations at 4,800 locations in 140 countries around the world.

WHAT

Major Subsidiaries and Affiliates

Avis Europe
WizCom Europe

Avis International
Avis Australia
Avis Canada

Avis Rent A Car System, Inc.
International Division
US Rent A Car Division
WizCom International, Ltd.

Services

Avis Cares (safety and security services)
In-car Computer Navigation Systems (selected areas)
Panic Button (Miami, emergency police-call system)

Wizard System
Inside Availability hotel reservations access
Preferred Service rental checkouts
Roving Rapid Return procedures
Wizard Number customer profiles
Wizard on Wheels computer terminal

Worldwide Reservation Center (Tulsa, OK)
Tulsa Advanced Function Terminal

KEY COMPETITORS

Accor
Agency Rent-a-Car
Alamo Rent A Car
Budget Rent a Car
Chrysler
Enterprise Rent-A-Car
Ford
Mitsubishi
National Car Rental
Sears
Snappy Rent A Car
Volvo

HOW MUCH

	9-Year Growth	1986	1987	1988	1989	1990	1991	1992	1993	1994	1995
Sales ($ mil.)	7.1%	916	813	1,060	1,100	1,159	1,205	1,234	1,300	1,400	1,700
Employees	2.2%	10,500	10,500	14,000	14,000	13,000	13,000	13,000	13,500	14,000	12,800

AVIS

Sales ($ mil.) 1986–95

AVON PRODUCTS, INC.

OVERVIEW

Avon is calling on its traditional means of selling beauty products — direct sales — for its expansion into emerging markets. Based in New York City, Avon is the world's leading direct seller of beauty and related products, with 1.9 million independent representatives. Avon sold its Giorgio Beverly Hills retail subsidiary to Procter & Gamble for $150 million to focus on its global direct-selling business.

Since many emerging markets don't have developed infrastructures and distribution systems, Avon hires representatives to sell its products in such hard-to-reach locales as the Amazon basin. Avon now has 478,000 "beauty consultants" in Brazil and has more than doubled its Chinese sales force from 12,000 at the beginning of 1994 to 25,000 at year-end.

However, Avon has had difficulty competing with retail chains like Wal-Mart in the US and hypermarkets in Western Europe, which sell similar products at discount prices. In both markets, Avon has appointed new management to reinvigorate sales and marketing efforts. Avon is also improving its product line and cutting costs. The company began marketing a line of intimate and casual wear clothing through a brochure called Avon Style. It is mailing copies to its 415,000 representatives in the US and has recorded impressive sales of $120 million since the line's introduction. In its first-ever worldwide product launch, in 1994 Avon introduced Far Away, a women's fragrance, in all of its more than 100 markets.

WHEN

In the 1880s book salesman David McConnell gave small bottles of perfume to New York housewives who listened to his sales pitch. The perfume was more popular than the books, so in 1886 McConnell created the California Perfume Company (renamed Avon in 1950 after the Avon River in England) and hired women to sell door-to-door. Through the 1950s these women, mostly housewives seeking extra income, made Avon a major force in the cosmetics industry. The company still relies heavily on direct sales.

From the 1960s until the mid-1980s, Avon was the world's largest cosmetics company, known for its appeal to middle-class homemakers. Avon hit hard times in 1974, when recession made many of its products too pricey for blue-collar customers. Women were also leaving home for the work force, making door-to-door sales less viable. Avon discovered that its traditional products had little appeal for younger women. In response, president David Mitchell began to diversify and overhaul Avon's product line, introducing the Colorworks line for teenagers with the slogan "It's not your mother's makeup" and ads picturing active young women.

Avon acquired the Tiffany jewelry company to help improve the company's image in 1979, then sold it in 1984. The company also expanded into the health care field; acquisitions included Mallinckrodt (hospital supply and chemical company, 1982), Foster Medical (1984), and 60 other medical suppliers. The health care field soon proved unprofitable because of stricter reimbursement policies set by Medicare. Avon sold Mallinckrodt in 1986 and

continued to sell off its remaining health care companies through 1990.

To boost profits Avon entered the retail prestige fragrances business by launching a joint venture with Liz Claiborne (1985) and buying Giorgio (1987). When Avon bought Parfums Stern, a Claiborne competitor, in 1987 (sold in 1990), Claiborne dissolved the joint venture. That same year Avon sold 40% of Avon Japan (started in 1969) to the Japanese public for $218 million.

The company introduced Avon Color cosmetics in 1988 and sleepwear, preschool toys, and videos in 1989, the same year that Amway and Irwin Jacobs made an unsuccessful attempt to buy Avon. In 1990 the company expanded into Eastern Europe and China, and in 1991 it branched into direct mail in an attempt to boost domestic sales. Also in 1991 it reached a peaceful settlement with Chartwell Associates, ending the latter's 18-month attempt to gain control of Avon. Under the agreement Chartwell may not increase its Avon holdings beyond 4.9%.

Avon continued to expand its global reach in 1992 when it began direct sales in Poland. It also opened a showroom and service center in downtown Tokyo. That same year Avon introduced its highly successful new skin-care product called Anew Perfecting Complex, which uses alpha hydroxy acids to improve skin softness and smoothness. Avon expanded into Russia in 1993.

In 1995 Avon signed a joint licensing agreement with designer Diane Von Furstenberg to create a budget-to-moderate line of casual sportswear.

NYSE symbol: AVP
Fiscal year ends: December 31

WHO

Chairman and CEO: James E. Preston, age 61,
$1,050,412 pay
President and COO: Edward J. Robinson, age 54,
$1,038,300 pay
EVP Asia/Pacific: John I. Novosad, age 54, $398,832 pay
SVP; President, Avon US: Christina A. Gold, age 47,
$482,280 pay
SVP and CFO: Edwina D. Woodbury, age 43,
$406,520 pay
SVP, General Counsel, and Secretary: Ward M.
Miller Jr., age 62
SVP and Chief Information Officer: Ronald D.
Mastrogiovanni
SVP Global Human Resources and Corporate Affairs:
Marcia L. Worthing, age 52
President, Continental Europe: Alfredo Cuello, age 47
Group VP Taxes and Treasurer: Robert J. Corti, age 45
Auditors: Coopers & Lybrand L.L.P.

WHERE

HQ: 9 West 57th St., New York, NY 10019-2683
Phone: 212-546-6015
Fax: 212-546-6136

Avon makes beauty and related products in 18
manufacturing laboratories around the world. The
company operates subsidiaries in 40 countries and
distributes its products in 80 additional countries.

	1994 Sales		1994 Operating Income	
	$ mil.	% of total	$ mil.	% of total
US	1,535	36	201	35
Other Americas	1,416	33	274	47
Pacific	664	16	90	15
Europe	652	15	15	3
Adjustments	—	—	(146)	—
Total	**4,267**	**100**	**434**	**100**

WHAT

	1994 Sales	
	$ mil.	% of total
Cosmetics, fragrances & toiletries	2,604	61
Gift & decorative	769	18
Apparel	480	11
Fashion jewelry & accessories	413	10
Total	**4,267**	**100**

Selected Domestic and International Brands
Anew (skin care)
Avon Color (cosmetics)
Avon Fashions (lingerie and apparel)
Avon Life (vitamin and nutritional supplements)
Avon Style (lingerie and casual wear)
BioAdvance (skin care)
Boutique (jewelry and lingerie)
Daily Revival (skin care)
Far Away (fragrance)
Parfums Créatifs (fragrance)
Skin-So-Soft (lotion)
Triumph (cologne)

KEY COMPETITORS

Alberto-Culver	General Nutrition	Maybelline
Allou	Hasbro	MEM
American	Helene Curtis	Nature's
Home	Herbalife Intl.	Sunshine
Products	J. C. Penney	Nordstrom
Amway	Jean Philippe	Perrigo
Chattem	Fragrances	Pfizer
Colgate-	Johnson & Johnson	Premark
Palmolive	Johnson Publishing	Procter &
Dep	The Limited	Gamble
Dillard	L'Oréal	Sandoz
Estée Lauder	LVMH	Shiseido
Forever Living	Mary Kay	Toys "R" Us
Frederick's of	Mattel	Unilever
Hollywood		

HOW MUCH

	9-Year Growth	1985	1986	1987	1988	1989	1990	1991	1992	1993	1994
Sales ($ mil.)	6.3%	2,470	2,883	2,763	3,063	3,300	3,454	3,593	3,810	4,008	4,267
Net income ($ mil.)	4.4%	163	159	183	96	55	195	136	175	240	241
Income as % of sales	—	6.6%	5.5%	6.6%	3.1%	1.7%	5.7%	3.8%	4.6%	6.0%	5.6%
Earnings per share ($)	5.8%	2.05	2.23	2.59	1.29	0.37	2.60	1.89	2.43	3.32	3.41
Stock price – high ($)	—	29.00	36.38	38.63	28.38	41.25	38.13	49.00	60.25	64.38	63.63
Stock price – low ($)	—	17.88	25.75	19.25	18.63	19.50	22.75	26.13	44.00	47.63	48.38
Stock price – close ($)	8.9%	27.63	27.00	25.75	19.50	36.88	29.38	46.00	55.38	48.63	59.75
P/E – high	—	14	16	15	22	—	15	26	25	19	19
P/E – low	—	9	12	7	14	—	9	14	18	14	14
Dividends per share ($)	(0.6%)	2.00	2.00	2.00	1.52	1.00	1.00	4.40	1.50	1.70	1.90
Book value per share ($)	(15.1%)	11.69	9.76	10.66	4.11	3.72	6.60	3.51	4.31	4.36	2.69
Employees	0.8%	28,200	28,500	28,600	28,800	30,100	30,300	30,500	29,700	29,800	30,400

1994 Year-end:
Debt ratio: 48.9%
Return on equity: 96.5%
Cash (mil.): $215
Current ratio: 1.01
Long-term debt (mil.): $117
No. of shares (mil.): 69
Dividends
  Yield: 3.2%
  Payout: 55.7%
Market value (mil.): $4,127

Stock Price History
High/Low 1985–94

BAKER HUGHES INCORPORATED

OVERVIEW

Baker Hughes serves the oil industry through 2 industry segments — Baker Hughes Oilfield Operations (drill bits, drilling fluids, and other equipment used in the drilling process; equipment and services involved in the completion and repair of oil and gas wells) and Baker Hughes Process Equipment Operations (process equipment for mining and other industries).

As Baker Hughes is the world's leading maker of rock drilling bits and the #1 provider of drilling services, its fortunes are tied to the state of the oil industry. Unfortunately, 1994

was not a good year for oil exploration and production, as industrywide the number of operating oil and gas rigs hovered around 700 (only about 100 more than 1993's all-time low and a far cry from 1981's peak of 4,500).

To provide oil companies with a "one-stop shop" of oil field equipment and services, Baker Hughes has reorganized in order to concentrate on its oil, gas, and process businesses. It has sold several business units to pay down debt. In 1994 it sold EnviroTech Measurement & Controls to Thermo Electron for $134 million.

WHEN

Howard Hughes Sr., developed the first oil well drill bit for rock in 1909. Hughes and partner Walter Sharp opened a plant in Houston, and Sharp & Hughes soon had a near monopoly on rock bits. When Sharp died in 1912, Hughes bought his half of the company, incorporating as Hughes Tool. Hughes held 73 patents when he died in 1924; the company passed to Howard Hughes Jr.

It is estimated that between 1924 and 1972 the tool company provided Hughes Jr. with $745 million in pretax profits, which he used to diversify into movies (RKO), airlines (TWA), and Las Vegas casinos. In 1972 Hughes sold the tool division of Hughes Tool to the public for $150 million. After 1972 the company expanded into above-ground oil production tools.

In 1913 oil well drilling contractor Carl Baker organized the Baker Casing Shoe Company in California to collect royalties on his 3 oil tool inventions. In 1918 Baker began to manufacture his own products. During the 1920s Baker expanded nationwide, began international sales, and formed Baker Oil Tools (1928). Sales increased sixfold between 1933 and 1941. In the late 1940s and the 1950s, Baker grew as oil drilling boomed.

During the 1960s Baker prospered despite fewer US well completions. Foreign sales increased from 19% to 33% of total revenues. Baker bought Kobe (oil field pumping equipment) in 1963 and diversified into mining equipment with the purchase of Galigher (1969) and Ramsey Engineering (1974). The company bought Reed Tool (oil well drill hits) in 1975. In 1979 revenues topped $1 billion for the first time.

Between 1982 and 1986, US expenditures for oil services fell from $40 billion to $9 billion. In 1987, when both Baker and

Hughes faced declining revenues and Hughes had large debts from expansion, the 2 companies merged to form Baker Hughes. By closing plants and combining operations, the company cut annual expenses by $80 million and was profitable by the end of fiscal 1988. Several small acquisitions in 1989 included Bird Machine (process centrifuges) and EDECO Petroleum Services (pumps). The company bought Eastman Christensen (world leader in directional and horizontal drilling equipment) and acquired the instrumentation unit of Tracor Holdings in 1990.

In 1991 Baker Hughes spun off BJ Services (pumping services) to the public. That same year it sold the Eastern Hemisphere operations of Baker Hughes Tubular Services (BHTS) to Tuboscope. It sold Western Hemisphere operations of BHTS to ICO in 1992.

Also in 1992 Baker Hughes bought Teleco Oilfield Services, a pioneer in sophisticated directional drilling techniques, from Sonat Inc. for $350 million. In 1993 the company consolidated its drilling technologies businesses into a single unit, named Baker Hughes INTEQ, to package services more efficiently for its clients in the oil industry.

In 1994 Baker Performance Chemicals opened a new office in Seoul, South Korea; formed a new joint venture in Indonesia; and set up a new company in Peru. In that year Baker Hughes also reorganized its operations; it streamlined its geographical operating business units from 5 to 3 and merged its 4 technology groups into one cohesive unit.

In 1995 Baker Hughes completed the sale of EnviroTech Pumpsystems, which provides specialized pumps to the mining, chemical, and petrochemical markets, to the Weir Group of Glasgow, Scotland, for $210 million.

NYSE symbol: BHI
Fiscal year ends: September 30

WHO

Chairman, President, and CEO: James D. Woods,
age 63, $1,417,835 pay
EVP; President, Baker Hughes Oilfield Operations: Max
L. Lukens, age 46, $738,560 pay
SVP and General Counsel: Franklin Myers, age 42,
$461,042 pay
SVP and CFO: Eric L. Mattson, age 43, $436,566 pay
**VP; President, Baker Hughes Process Equipment
Operations:** Timothy J. Probert, age 43, $318,238 pay
**VP; VP Technology and Market Development, Baker
Hughes Oilfield Operations:** Roger P. Herbert, age 48
VP Government Affairs: Arthur T. Downey, age 57
VP Investor Relations: Scott B. Gill, age 35
VP Human Resources: Phillip A. Rice, age 59
Controller: James E. Braun, age 35
Auditors: Deloitte & Touche LLP

WHERE

HQ: 3900 Essex Ln., Houston, TX 77027-5177
Phone: 713-439-8600
Fax: 713-439-8699

Baker Hughes operates 72 manufacturing plants around
the world, of which 43 are located in the US.

	1994 Sales		1994 Operating Income	
	$ mil.	% of total	$ mil.	% of total
US	1,272	52	60	28
Europe	479	19	39	16
Other Western Hemisphere	362	14	60	28
Other regions	392	15	60	28
Total	**2,505**	**100**	**219**	**100**

WHAT

	1994 Sales		1994 Operating Income	
	$ mil.	% of total	$ mil.	% of total
Oilfield	2,111	84	158	72
Process	298	12	22	10
Disposed businesses	96	4	39	18
Total	**2,505**	**100**	**219**	**100**

Divisions and Selected Subsidiaries

Baker Hughes Oilfield Operations
Baker Hughes INTEQ (technical service, project
management)
Baker Oil Tools (completion, production, workover, and
fishing equipment and services)
Baker Performance Chemicals Inc. (specialty chemicals)
Centrilift (pumps, drives, speed controls, and cabling)
Hughes Christensen Co. (drill bits)

Baker Hughes Process Equipment Operations
Baker Hughes Process Systems (designs and supplies
processing systems for water injection)
Bird Machine Company, Inc.(centrifugal and filtration
equipment)
EIMCO Process Equipment Co. (separation technology
and equipment)

KEY COMPETITORS

Alfa-Laval	Kaneb Services
Bechtel	Klockner-Humbollt-Deutch
Camco	LTV
Cooper Industries	McDermott
Dorr-Oliver	Michael Baker
Dresser	Nabors Industries
Energy Service	Outokumpu
Fluor	Pearson
FMC	Sala
Halliburton	Schlumberger
Ingersoll-Rand	Serck Baker
Ingram	Smith International

HOW MUCH

	9-Year Growth	1985[1]	1986[1]	1987	1988	1989	1990	1991	1992	1993	1994
Sales ($ mil.)	3.8%	1,904	1,557	1,924	2,316	2,328	2,614	2,828	2,539	2,702	2,505
Net income ($ mil.)	(0.1%)	88	(19)	(255)	59	83	142	174	5	59	87
Income as % of sales	—	4.6%	—	—	2.6%	3.6%	5.4%	6.1%	0.2%	2.2%	3.5%
Earnings per share ($)	(8.9%)	1.25	(0.27)	(2.22)	0.45	0.64	1.06	1.26	0.00	0.34	0.54
Stock price – high ($)	—	18.88	17.88	27.38	19.88	27.63	34.75	31.00	25.38	29.63	22.13
Stock price – low ($)	—	14.13	8.88	11.13	12.13	13.63	21.75	17.88	15.88	18.50	17.00
Stock price – close ($)	0.2%	17.88	11.88	13.63	14.00	25.50	25.63	19.25	19.63	20.00	18.25
P/E – high	—	15	—	—	44	43	33	25	—	87	41
P/E – low	—	11	—	—	27	21	21	14	—	54	31
Dividends per share ($)	(7.4%)	0.92	0.81	0.23	0.46	0.46	0.46	0.46	0.46	0.46	0.46
Book value per share ($)	(2.4%)	14.43	9.67	7.78	8.10	8.31	10.36	11.17	11.84	11.44	11.60
Employees	(3.7%)	20,600	14,900	24,482	21,500	20,400	20,900	21,300	19,600	18,400	14,700

1994 Year-end:
Debt ratio: 28.5%
Return on equity: 5.4%
Cash (mil.): $69
Current ratio: 2.57
Long-term debt (mil.): $638
No. of shares (mil.): 141
Dividends:
  Yield: 2.5%
  Payout: 85.2%
Market value (mil.): $2,571

Stock Price History
High/Low 1985–94

[1] Note: Figures are for Baker International Corporation only.

BANC ONE CORPORATION

OVERVIEW

Banc One's 26-year streak of ever-increasing annual earnings ended in 1994 with a 10% earnings decline. This decline was largely attributable to rising interest rates, which played havoc with the company's investment portfolio (including significant investments in money-losing interest rate swaps). In response, the company sold some of its long-term securities (resulting in a $170 million charge) to make new short-term investments.

Otherwise the Columbus, Ohio–based bank did reasonably well with its strategy of avoiding high-risk loans and geographic concentration of loans. It also diversified its income by acquiring other banks, primarily in the Mid-west and Southwest, and by unifying their product offerings nationally.

Banc One customarily avoids wholesale firings, using incumbent expertise on local conditions to target consumers and small to medium-sized businesses. However, this practice has led to widespread duplication and redundancy in operations. Shocked from its complacency by the earnings decline of 1994, the company began a restructuring that will unify its back-office operations in a small number of locations and trim staff.

In 1995 Banc One intends to continue reducing costs by consolidating its subsidiary banks along state lines.

WHEN

Banc One traces its origins to 1868 when F. C. Session opened a bank in Columbus, Ohio. He later combined his operations with those of J. A. Jeffrey and Orange Johnson to form Commercial Bank, later Commercial National.

In 1929 Commercial National and City National Bank of Commerce combined to form City National Bank and Trust. In 1935 John H. McCoy became the bank's president, beginning a family dynasty.

John G. McCoy succeeded his father in 1958, and in the 1960s City National began to break with tradition. The bank hired a housewife-turned-comic from Lima, Ohio, for radio and TV commercials. Both Phyllis Diller and City National were on their way.

In 1966 the bank introduced the first Visa (then BankAmericard) credit card service outside of California. McCoy formed the First Banc Group of Ohio in 1967, folding in City National. In its first foray outside Columbus, the company bought Farmers Savings and Trust of Mansfield, Ohio (1968).

While growing through acquisitions, First Banc scored a coup in 1977 when Merrill Lynch hired it to handle the Cash Management Account, a package combining a brokerage account with checking and a debit card.

In 1979 First Banc Group changed its name to Banc One, and all affiliated banks included Bank One — with a "k" — in their names. John Bonnet McCoy, the 3rd generation of bankers, succeeded his father as CEO in 1984 as barriers to interstate bank owner ship were falling. Banc One expanded rapidly westward into Indiana (buying Indiana's 2nd largest bank, American Fletcher, in 1986), Kentucky, Michigan, and Wisconsin. In 1989 Banc One moved into the troubled Texas market with the announcement that it was acquiring, with a large dose of federal aid, 20 failed MCorp bank branches. Banc One paid $34 million for $11 billion in assets, including $2.5 billion in problem loans managed by Banc One but guaranteed by the government. Banc One then added to its Texas holdings 2 failed Dallas-based firms, Bright Banc Savings (1990) and Team Bancshares (1992).

In 1991 Banc One added Illinois banks, acquiring Marine Corporation and First Illinois, and in 1992 Banc One moved into Arizona and Utah with the acquisition of Valley National with a $1.2 billion stock swap.

Wherever it has gone, Banc One has taken its distinctive philosophy of "branding," which it uses to help market its growing list of services and service "products." This strategy has proved itself to be successful in drawing customers from other banks, even though some of Banc One's products are more expensive.

In 1992 Banc One formed a development alliance with Banco Nacional de Mexico and received a 5-year FDIC contract to liquidate $944 million in loans and foreclosures.

A 1993 plan to buy FirsTier Financial (Nebraska) foundered in early 1994 when investor concern about Banc One's exposure in the derivatives market (interest rate swaps) drove down the company's stock price. The deal collapsed when Banc One refused to increase the amount of stock it would pay for FirsTier.

Banc One has plenty of experience in harmonizing new operations, but in 1994 the company stumbled in its purchase of First Illinois Corp., its first foray into the metropolitan Chicago market. In addition to overpaying, Banc One badly underestimated the costs of operating in such a large urban area.

NYSE symbol: ONE
Fiscal year ends: December 31

WHO

Chairman and CEO: John B. McCoy, age 51,
$1,505,000 pay
President: Richard J. Lehmann, age 50, $787,500 pay
(prior to promotion)
Chairman and CEO, Banc One Ohio Corp.: Thomas E.
Hoaglin, age 45, $655,800 pay
Chairman and CEO, Banc One Indiana Corp.: Joseph
D. Barnette Jr., age 55, $624,300 pay
SEVP: William P. Boardman, age 53
EVP and General Counsel: Steven A. Bennett
EVP Finance: Michael J. McMennamin, age 47
Chief Communication Officer: John A. Russell
SVP: Julia F. Johnson, age 43
SVP Personnel Administration: Michael W. Hager
Auditors: Coopers & Lybrand L.L.P.

WHERE

HQ: 100 E. Broad St., Columbus, OH 43271
Phone: 614-248-5944
Fax: 614-248-5624

Banc One operates 1,418 bank branches in 13 states.

	1994 Assets
	% of total
Ohio	24
Texas	21
Arizona	13
Indiana	10
Wisconsin	9
Kentucky	8
Illinois	5
Colorado	4
West Virginia	3
Other states	3
Total	**100**

WHAT

	1994 Assets	
	$ mil.	% of total
Cash & equivalents	8,613	10
Government securities	6,768	7
Other securities	8,175	9
Net loans	61,096	69
Other	4,271	5
Total	**88,923**	**100**

	1994 Sales	
	$ mil.	% of total
Interest & fees on loans & leases	5,375	66
Other interest	1,062	13
Loan processing & servicing	484	6
Service charges on deposits	484	6
Other	713	9
Total	**8,118**	**100**

Selected Services
Brokerage services
Consumer finance
Equipment leasing
Leases
Loans
Money market accounts
Mortgage banking
Retail and commercial banking
Trust services

Selected Affiliates
Banc One Capital Corp.
Banc One Funds Management Co.
Banc One Insurance Services Group
Banc One Investment Advisors Corp.
Banc One Mortgage Corp.
Banc One Securities Corp.

KEY COMPETITORS

BankAmerica
Bank of Montreal
Chase Manhattan
Chemical Banking
Citicorp
CNB Bancshares
Cullen/Frost Bankers
First Chicago
First Indiana
First Interstate
Fleet
General Electric
H.F. Ahmanson
Household Intl.
KeyCorp
NationsBank
PNC

HOW MUCH

	9-Year Growth	1985	1986	1987	1988	1989	1990	1991	1992	1993	1994
Assets ($ mil.)	26.4%	10,824	17,372	18,730	25,274	26,552	30,336	46,293	61,417	79,919	88,923
Net income ($ mil.)	25.5%	130	200	209	340	363	423	530	781	1,121	1,005
Income as % of assets	—	1.2%	1.2%	1.1%	1.3%	1.4%	1.4%	1.1%	1.3%	1.4%	1.1%
Earnings per share ($)	9.2%	1.10	1.16	1.19	1.56	1.66	1.83	2.12	2.38	2.93	2.42
Stock price – high ($)	—	13.84	18.10	16.11	16.61	22.23	21.90	34.87	38.91	44.72	38.00
Stock price – low ($)	—	8.28	11.67	9.69	12.85	13.37	12.56	16.44	30.63	32.27	24.13
Stock price – close ($)	7.9%	12.79	12.48	13.10	13.37	19.46	18.34	34.79	38.63	35.56	25.38
P/E – high	—	13	16	14	11	13	12	16	16	15	16
P/E – low	—	8	10	8	8	8	7	8	13	11	10
Dividends per share ($)	14.4%	0.36	0.43	0.48	0.55	0.61	0.67	0.75	0.85	1.02	1.21
Book value per share ($)	12.0%	6.62	7.51	8.27	9.36	10.35	11.97	13.96	15.52	17.82	18.43
Employees	21.3%	8,595	12,654	13,865	16,870	17,800	19,300	27,500	32,700	45,300	48,800

1994 Year-end:
Equity as % of assets: 8.5%
Return on assets: 1.2%
Return on equity: 14.3%
Long-term debt (mil.): $1,866
No. of shares (mil.): 397
Dividends
  Yield: 4.8%
  Payout: 50.0%
Market value (mil.): $10,076
Sales (mil.): $8,118

Stock Price History High/Low 1985–94

BANK OF BOSTON CORPORATION

OVERVIEW

Bank of Boston had the urge to merge in 1995 but just couldn't get it together. And after CEO Ira Stepanian passed up an opportunity with Mellon Bank only to have talks break down with CoreStates Financial, Bank of Boston suddenly had the urge to purge. In July Stepanian resigned and was replaced by president Charles Gifford.

The bank operates 3 core lines: Corporate Banking (finance and real estate), Global Banking (investment banking), and Personal Banking (consumer finance, mortgages, and other retail services). However, the bank's operating environments are changing, particularly in New England, following Fleet's acquisition of Shawmut National Bank (which Bank

of Boston had once considered buying). This union gives Fleet an advantage over Bank of Boston in terms of the number of branches. In response, Bank of Boston is shrinking its branch system in northern New England and focusing on the Massachusetts area and on activities such as mortgage banking that can be carried on nationwide without branches.

Bank of Boston is also New England's only global bank. Although this caused problems when Brazil and Argentina defaulted on their debts in 1987, Bank of Boston stuck it out. Now that the region's economy is improving, the bank is carving a place for itself as a retail and commercial bank, dealing with individuals and businesses rather than governments.

WHEN

William Phillips and 5 other Boston merchants founded the Massachusetts Bank in 1784 to avoid having to use British banks. Profitable from the beginning (because it was the only bank in town for 8 years), the bank maintained strict credit requirements, which both made enemies and encouraged competition. The bank helped finance the lucrative China trade of the early 19th century. In 1864 the bank became Massachusetts National Bank, reluctantly joining the national bank system after other Boston banks.

Massachusetts National was almost terminally hidebound by the end of the 19th century, refusing to change, and therefore losing business, until new management came in. Deposits grew from $1 million to over $6 million between 1900 and 1903, when the bank merged with the First National Bank of Boston (founded in 1859) and took its name.

The new First National of Boston opened branches in Argentina (1917) and Cuba (1923). By 1927 the bank had representative offices in Europe and was a leader in financing foreign trade.

In 1929 the bank acquired Old Colony Trust Co. Then, in 1931, nearly at the bottom of the Depression, it bought Jamaica Plain Trust Company. Three years later, in compliance with the Banking Act of 1933, it spun off its investment banking business into a new corporation, The First Boston Corp.

In 1945 the bank opened a Brazilian office. In the late 1940s it became the first US bank to offer a full factoring service (loans on accounts receivable); in the 1960s the factoring operation went international.

In 1970 the bank organized a holding company, First National Boston Corp., which changed its name to Bank of Boston Corp. in 1983. In the 1970s and 1980s the bank became the largest in New England, purchasing banks in Massachusetts, Maine, Connecticut, Vermont, and Rhode Island. In the late 1970s and early 1980s, the bank increased its lending to foreign governments, many of which were unable to keep up with their loan payments. Increased loss provisions dropped profits by 91% between 1986 and 1987.

The bank's 1988 record profit was a breather before the New England real estate bust. During the boom it had relaxed its commercial loan underwriting standards and was left holding subordinated liens on properties whose values had dropped below their loan amounts. Income dropped 64% in 1989.

Bank of Boston bit the bullet, shored up its capital, and in 1991 took control of First Mutual Bank for Savings in Boston. Expansion continued in 1992 and 1993 with Society for Savings Bancorp in Hartford; Multibank Financial Corp. of Dedham, Massachusetts; and Bank Worcester Corporation. The bank also affirmed its policy of divesting noncore lines with the sale to Bank of New York of its US factoring operations.

In 1994 Bank of Boston opened its first Chinese office, in Shanghai. Although Bank of Boston's Latin American operations are growing, the bank announced in 1995 that it was discontinuing its Canadian operations. The remains of that business are being merged into the Bank of New York Financial Corporation.

WHO

Chairman, CEO, and President: Charles K. Gifford, age 52, $1,604,807 pay (prior to promotion)
VC: Edward A. O'Neal, age 50, $918,269 pay
VC, CFO, and Treasurer: William J. Shea, age 47, $850,576 pay
Executive Director Mergers and Acquisitions: Peter J. Manning, age 56, $455,000 pay
Executive Director External Affairs: Ira A. Jackson, age 46
Executive Director Credit and Loan Review: Paul F. Hogan, age 50
General Counsel and Clerk: Gary A. Spiess, age 54
Chief Technology Officer: Michael R. Lezenski, age 47
Executive Director Human Resources: Helen G. Drinan, age 47
Auditors: Coopers & Lybrand L.L.P.

WHERE

HQ: 100 Federal St., Boston, MA 02110
Phone: 617-434-2200
Fax: 617-575-2232

Bank of Boston conducts banking and related operations at 272 branches in New England, 26 other states, and 23 foreign countries.

	1994 Pretax Income	
	$ mil.	% of total
US	591	75
Latin America	149	19
Europe	32	4
Asia/Pacific	16	2
Other regions	3	0
Total	**791**	**100**

WHAT

	1994 Assets	
	$ mil.	% of total
Cash & equivalents	5,105	12
US Treasurys	1,499	3
Foreign bonds	507	1
Mortgage-backed securities	2,215	5
Other securities	1,215	3
Net loans & leases	30,325	68
Other	3,764	8
Total	**44,630**	**100**

	1994 Sales	
	$ mil.	% of total
Interest from loans & leases	2,606	57
Other interest	1,112	24
Service & trust fees	597	14
Other	231	5
Total	**4,546**	**100**

Financial Services
Consumer finance
Corporate lending and finance
Leasing
Mortgage services
Real estate
Retail and commercial banking
Securities and payments services
Trust services

Major Bank Subsidiaries
Bank of Boston Connecticut
The First National Bank of Boston
Rhode Island Hospital Trust National Bank

KEY COMPETITORS

Abington Savings
Barnett Banks
BayBanks
Chase Manhattan
Chemical Banking
Citicorp
Fleet
H.F. Ahmanson
Household International
KeyCorp
PNC Bank
State Street Boston

HOW MUCH

	9-Year Growth	1985	1986	1987	1988	1989	1990	1991	1992	1993	1994
Assets ($ mil.)	5.2%	28,296	34,045	34,117	36,061	39,178	32,529	32,700	32,346	40,588	44,630
Net income ($ mil.)	10.7%	174	233	20	322	70	(438)	(34)	192	275	435
Income as % of assets	—	0.6%	0.7%	0.1%	0.9%	0.2%	—	—	0.6%	0.7%	1.0%
Earnings per share ($)	3.0%	2.82	3.49	0.10	4.43	0.80	(6.21)	(0.53)	2.02	2.22	3.67
Stock price – high ($)	—	20.84	29.94	38.00	30.00	30.63	20.00	12.88	26.38	29.13	29.25
Stock price – low ($)	—	13.22	19.31	17.88	20.88	15.75	6.00	3.00	11.25	20.25	22.13
Stock price – close ($)	2.4%	20.84	26.59	22.50	23.63	19.00	6.38	11.50	25.50	23.00	25.88
P/E – high	—	7	9	—	7	38	—	—	13	13	8
P/E – low	—	5	6	—	5	20	—	—	6	9	6
Dividends per share ($)	1.7%	0.80	0.88	1.00	1.08	1.24	1.03	0.20	0.10	0.40	0.93
Book value per share ($)	1.5%	21.54	24.47	23.62	27.02	26.51	19.63	18.69	21.15	22.71	24.72
Employees	(0.9%)	20,000	20,000	20,200	22,462	21,733	20,339	18,752	19,459	18,644	18,355

1994 Year-end:
Equity as % of assets: 5.9%
Return on assets: 1.0%
Return on equity: 17.5%
Long-term debt (mil.): $2,169
No. of shares (mil.): 107
Dividends
  Yield: 3.6%
  Payout: 25.3%
Market value (mil.): $2,757
Sales (mil.): $4,546

Stock Price History
High/Low 1985–94

THE BANK OF NEW YORK CO., INC.

OVERVIEW

The Bank of New York Company is continuing its strategy of business diversity and regional specialization by dominating the suburban New York and New Jersey retail banking market (with no immediate plans to expand its geographical territory), solidifying its role as an important US corporate and multinational banker, and increasing its role in several fee-generating specialty niches. Among these are factoring, securities transaction processing, trust services, and credit cards.

Other business lines include investment management, financial market services, investment banking, and international leasing. The Bank of New York Company is also one of the largest US sponsors of ADRs and a leader in government securities and international funds clearance.

All of these businesses have helped reduce the company's former dependence on loan income (which caused problems in the late 1980s and early 1990s).

In 1994, to ensure an orderly executive transition, chairman Carter Bacot announced that president and COO Thomas Renyi would succeed him upon his retirement in 1997.

WHEN

In 1784 Alexander Hamilton (at 27 already a Revolutionary War hero and early economic theorist) and a group of New York merchants and lawyers founded New York City's first bank, the Bank of New York. Hamilton saw a need to institute a credit system to finance the nation's growth and to establish credibility for the new nation's chaotic monetary system.

Hamilton became US secretary of the treasury in 1789 and soon negotiated the new US government's first loan, issued by Bank of New York for $200,000 (this would now be considered a highly suspect transaction). The bank also helped finance the War of 1812, by offering $16 million in subscription books, and the Civil War, by loaning the government $150 million (the strength of the returns for this latter transaction helped the bank raise its dividends to 5% in 1865). In 1878 the bank became a US Treasury depository for the sale of government bonds.

With its reputation for probity and conservative fiscal policies, the bank weathered numerous panics during the 19th century, but because Bank of New York emphasized commercial banking to select customers rather than competing for size with other banks, by 1904 it was no longer one of the largest in the US. In 1922 the bank merged with New York Life Insurance and Trust Co. (formed in 1830 by many of Bank of New York's directors) to form Bank of New York and Trust Co. and began to develop trust and investment services. The bank weathered the crash of 1929 and remained profitable, paying dividends throughout the Depression. In 1938 it changed its name back to Bank of New York.

In 1948 the bank acquired the Fifth Avenue Bank to get a mid-Manhattan location and to expand trust services. In 1966 it acquired Empire Trust Co., which specialized in lending to developing industries. The Bank of New York Co., Inc., a holding company created in 1968, expanded statewide. In 1980 the bank bought Empire National Bank (Newburgh), the #2 state branch network outside New York City.

In the 1980s, under the leadership of chairman and president J. Carter Bacot, Bank of New York relaxed its conservative lending policies to cash in on the economic boom. The bank bought New York competitor Irving Bank in a 1988 hostile takeover for $1.4 billion and in 1990 bought the credit card portfolios of First City Bancorp. of Texas and of Dreyfus Consumer Bank's Gold MasterCard. Bank of New York (Delaware), which manages these portfolios, is one of the US's largest credit card operations, specializing in low rate cards whose interest clock begins ticking at purchase rather than in the following month, and affinity cards, such as one for the AFL-CIO. Also in the late 1980s, Bank of New York began building up its fee-for-service side, beefing up its ADR business through direct solicitation of European companies, and going after government securities business as well.

As the economy cooled in the early 1990s, the bank suffered from its portfolio of highly leveraged transactions and nonperforming loans; in 1991 nonperforming assets peaked at $1.8 billion. Since then loan sales have reduced its nonperforming assets.

In 1994 and 1995 the company went on a very specialized buying spree, acquiring, among others, BankAmerica's securities processing business and the municipal bond administration business of Frost Bank (Texas). One business the bank is exiting, however, is mortgage servicing (although it will continue to originate mortgage loans in its home region); in 1995 it sold California-based mortgage servicing company ARCS Mortgage.

WHO

Chairman and CEO: J. Carter Bacot, age 62,
$2,700,000 pay
VC: Samuel F. Chevalier, age 61, $1,245,193 pay
VC: Alan R. Griffith, age 53, $783,846 pay
President; President and COO, The Bank of New York:
Thomas A. Renyi, age 49, $878,846 pay
SEVP; SEVP and CFO, The Bank of New York: Deno D.
Papageorge, age 56, $1,057,693 pay
**EVP Investment Co. Services and Operations, The
Bank of New York:** Thomas J. Perna
EVP: Richard D. Field, age 54
**SVP Public and Investor Relations, The Bank of New
York:** Paul J. Leyden
SVP Personnel, The Bank of New York: Frank L.
Peterson
Secretary and Chief Legal Officer: Phebe C. Miller,
age 45
Auditors: Deloitte & Touche LLP

WHERE

HQ: The Bank of New York Company, Inc., 48 Wall St.,
New York, NY 10286
Phone: 212-495-1784
Fax: 212-495-1398

The Bank of New York operates retail branch banks in
the Northeast with other businesses throughout the US
and in 24 countries.

	1994 Sales		1994 Pretax income	
	$ mil.	% of total	$ mil.	% of total
US	3,735	88	1,089	91
Asia	211	5	94	8
Europe	124	3	6	0
Other regions	181	4	9	1
Total	**4,251**	**100**	**1,198**	**100**

WHAT

	1994 Assets	
	$ mil.	% of total
Cash & equivalents	6,914	14
Treasurys	2,854	6
State & municipal bonds	776	2
Derivatives	522	1
Other securities	1,439	3
Net loans	32,291	66
Other	4,083	8
Total	**48,879**	**100**

	1994 Sales	
	$ mil.	% of total
Loan interest	2,405	57
Other interest	557	13
Trust & service charges	591	14
Processing fees	530	12
Other	168	4
Total	**4,251**	**100**

Selected Subsidiaries

The Bank of New York
(retail and corporate
banking, trusts and
investments, securities
processing)
The Bank of New York
(Delaware) (credit cards)

The Bank of New York
Mortgage Co.
BNY Associates, Inc.
(investment banking)
BNY Financial
Corp. (factoring)
BNY Leasing Corp.

KEY COMPETITORS

ADVANTA	Chemical Banking	HSBC
AT&T	Citicorp	J.P. Morgan
BankAmerica	Crédit Lyonnais	KeyCorp
Bankers Trust	Dai-Ichi Kangyo	Mellon Bank
Barclays	Deutsche Bank	NatWest
Bell Bancorp	First Chicago	Royal Bank of
BFS Bankorp	First Interstate	Canada
Canadian Imperial	Fleet	Union Bank of
Chase Manhattan	General Motors	Switzerland

HOW MUCH

	9-Year Growth	1985	1986	1987	1988	1989	1990	1991	1992	1993	1994
Assets ($ mil.)	11.4%	18,486	20,709	23,065	47,388	48,857	45,390	39,426	40,909	45,546	48,879
Net income ($ mil.)	21.2%	130	155	103	213	51	308	122	369	534	736
Income as % of assets	—	0.7%	0.7%	0.4%	0.4%	0.1%	0.7%	0.3%	0.9%	1.2%	1.5%
Earnings per share ($)	7.0%	2.01	2.27	1.41	2.61	0.14	1.99	0.64	2.12	2.72	3.70
Stock price – high ($)	—	17.47	23.39	22.94	18.63	27.50	20.88	18.06	27.31	31.25	33.25
Stock price – low ($)	—	11.63	16.42	12.25	12.94	18.38	6.63	8.25	15.00	25.31	24.94
Stock price – close ($)	6.3%	17.14	19.44	12.88	18.50	20.13	8.88	15.44	26.94	28.50	29.77
P/E – high	—	9	10	16	7	—	11	28	13	12	9
P/E – low	—	6	7	9	5	—	3	13	7	9	7
Dividends per share ($)	5.2%	0.70	0.78	0.86	0.92	0.99	1.06	0.84	0.76	0.86	1.10
Book value per share ($)	5.1%	14.20	15.88	16.83	18.67	17.44	17.96	17.93	19.26	20.18	22.26
Employees	8.2%	7,616	9,304	10,249	17,776	17,083	15,847	15,139	16,167	15,621	15,477

1994 Year-end:
Equity as % of assets: 8.5%
Return on assets: 3.0%
Return on equity: 18.5%
Long-term debt (mil.): $1,774
No. of shares (mil.): 188
Dividends
  Yield: 3.7%
  Payout: 29.7%
Market value (mil.): $5,586
Sales (mil.): $4,251

**Stock Price History
High/Low 1985–94**

BANKAMERICA CORPORATION

OVERVIEW

San Francisco–based BankAmerica has traditionally followed a strategy of growth through acquisition. Now, however, the US's 2nd largest banking company after Citicorp (and the West Coast's largest) has shifted gears to emphasize growth of its individual business lines.

These include retail and corporate banking, credit cards, investment products, and mortgage lending (an increasingly important business for the bank). BankAmerica also has a significant international presence, with offices in 36 countries and a particular interest in the Pacific Rim.

The company hopes to build these businesses through increased attention to providing customers with services (cross-selling products) across departmental lines. It is beginning to target small businesses, which generate most economic growth in the US.

BankAmerica is also gearing up for the brave new world of postmodern banking by experimenting with self-service branches, in-store branches, and electronic banking. BankAmerica has an Internet site and in 1995 acquired (with NationsBank) H&R Block's MECA unit, which makes financial software.

WHEN

Amadeo Giannini, son of Italian immigrants, founded the Bank of Italy in San Francisco in 1904. Two years later he saved the bank's cash, gold, and notes before it was destroyed by fire after the 1906 earthquake. Giannini soon reopened in a temporary site on a pier and made loans to finance reconstruction.

Giannini circumvented a 1921 federal ruling prohibiting branch banking by acquiring the Bank of America of Los Angeles, which had 21 branches. In 1928, dreaming of a nationwide system of banks, Giannini formed a holding company, Transamerica Corp., to manage his banks and other businesses. By 1930 Bank of Italy and Bank of America were operating as Bank of America (BofA). In the 1930s Giannini was hounded by regulatory investigations, and in 1937 Transamerica was forced to divest 58% of Bank of America.

By the end of 1945 Bank of America had passed Chase Manhattan to become the largest US bank. But by 1953 dogged SEC action had resulted in Transamerica's divestiture of all Bank of America stock.

During the 1950s BofA decentralized; the company encouraged local managers to make decisions based on local conditions. BofA also expanded internationally; by 1970 it was one of the largest international lenders in the US. It was also an early pioneer in consumer credit, introducing the BankAmericard (which became VISA in 1977) in 1958.

BankAmerica Corp., a holding company, was formed in 1968. In the late 1960s and early 1970s, BofA's size and wealth made it a target for social protest groups, and it made efforts to increase its minority hiring and widen the scope of its lending policies.

In 1970 A. W. Clausen became CEO. Under his leadership the bank expanded in energy, agricultural and foreign loans, and real estate. Earnings and assets quadrupled during the inflationary 1970s but decreased in the early 1980s as interest rates declined. The bank suffered losses due to the fall and eventual collapse of energy prices, low agricultural commodities prices, and arrearages in foreign loans. At the end of 1980, Citicorp passed BankAmerica as the largest US bank.

In 1981 Clausen became head of the World Bank and was replaced at BofA by Samuel Armacost, who continued expansion. In 1983 the company acquired Seafirst (Seattle–First National Bank) and Charles Schwab (discount brokerage, sold back to Schwab in 1987). By 1985 losses had forced Armacost to lay off employees for the first time in company history. In 1986 Armacost resigned under fire, and the board reappointed Clausen as CEO.

After reducing costs and US problem loans, the bank became profitable again in 1988 after 3 years of losses. In 1990 Clausen retired, and president Richard Rosenberg, a 22-year Wells Fargo veteran, became CEO. The company began 1990 with banking operations in 3 states and ended the year in 7, through 8 thrift acquisitions. In 1992 BankAmerica acquired Security Pacific in the largest US banking merger to date, and embarked on a new round of cost-cutting.

Expansion continued with the 1993 acquisition of First Gibralter (Texas). In 1994 and 1995 BankAmerica began seriously targeting the mortgage origination business, acquiring United Mortgage (Minnesota) and Arbor National Holdings (New York) and bolstering the company's nationwide presence. Internationally, BankAmerica opened commercial banking offices in Dubai and Hanoi. VC David Coulter — chosen as president in 1995 over CFO and front-runner Lewis Coleman — is expected to replace Rosenberg as CEO in 1996.

NYSE symbol: BAC
Fiscal year ends: December 31

WHO

Chairman and CEO: Richard M. Rosenberg, age 64, $3,141,667 pay
VC and President: David A. Coulter, age 48, $1,091,667 pay (prior to promotion)
VC and CFO: Lewis W. Coleman, age 53, $1,750,000 pay
VC: Michael E. Rossi, age 50, $1,040,000 pay
VC: Thomas E. Peterson, age 59, $1,025,000 pay
VC: Martin A. Stein, age 54, $1,022,500 pay
VC and Personnel Relations Officer: : Kathleen J. Burke, age 43
Group EVP, Corporate Relations, Bank of America: Julia Chang Bloch
Group EVP, Technology Support Services, Bank of America: Bruce Fadem
Group EVP and General Counsel, Bank of America: Michael J. Halloran
Auditors: Ernst & Young

WHERE

HQ: Bank of America Center, San Francisco, CA 94104
Phone: 415-622-3530
Fax: 415-622-7915

BankAmerica provides banking or other services in all 50 states and does business in 36 nations worldwide.

	1994 Sales		1994 Pretax Income	
	$ mil.	% of total	$ mil.	% of total
US	13,262	80	3,156	85
Asia	1,317	8	283	8
Europe, the Middle East & Africa	1,299	8	108	3
Latin America & the Caribbean	561	3	83	2
Canada	92	1	87	2
Total	**16,531**	**100**	**3,717**	**100**

WHAT

	1994 Assets	
	$ mil.	% of total
Cash & equivalents	25,848	12
Mortgage-backed securities	10,026	4
Other securities	14,931	7
Net loans	137,222	64
Other	27,448	13
Total	**215,475**	**100**

	1994 Sales	
	$ mil.	% of total
Loan interest & fees	9,806	60
Other interest	2,578	15
Deposit account fees	1,201	7
Credit card fees	343	2
Other fees & commissions	1,111	7
Other	1,492	9
Total	**16,531**	**100**

Selected Services
Bank credit cards
Consumer and commercial banking
Credit-related insurance
Investment banking

Selected Subsidiaries
Bank of America Community Development Bank
Bank of America NT&SA
Bank of America, FSB
Seattle-First National Bank

KEY COMPETITORS

American Express
AT&T
Banc One
Bank of Boston
Bank of Montreal
Bank of New York
Canadian Imperial
Chase Manhattan
Chemical Banking
Citicorp
Countrywide Credit
Crédit Lyonnais
CS Holding
Dai-Ichi Kangyo
First Chicago
First Interstate
Fleet
General Electric
Golden State
Great Western
H.F. Ahmanson
Household International
J.P. Morgan
KeyCorp
NationsBank
NatWest
Wells Fargo

HOW MUCH

	9-Year Growth	1985	1986	1987	1988	1989	1990	1991	1992	1993	1994
Assets ($ mil.)	6.9%	118,541	104,189	92,833	94,647	98,764	110,728	115,509	180,646	186,933	215,475
Net income ($ mil.)	—	(337)	(518)	(955)	547	820	877	1,124	1,492	1,954	2,176
Income as % of assets	—	—	—	—	0.6%	0.8%	0.8%	1.0%	0.8%	1.0%	1.0%
Earnings per share ($)	—	(2.68)	(3.74)	(6.43)	2.77	3.74	3.84	4.78	4.21	4.76	5.33
Stock price – high ($)	—	22.75	18.75	15.38	19.13	36.38	33.50	44.75	49.75	55.50	50.25
Stock price – low ($)	—	12.88	9.50	5.25	6.75	17.00	17.50	23.13	35.38	40.38	38.38
Stock price – close ($)	10.9%	15.63	14.63	6.88	17.63	26.75	26.50	35.88	46.50	46.38	39.50
P/E – high	—	—	—	—	7	10	9	9	12	12	9
P/E – low	—	—	—	—	2	5	5	5	8	9	7
Dividends per share ($)	3.6%	1.16	0.00	0.00	0.00	0.60	1.00	1.00	1.20	1.30	1.60
Book value per share ($)	6.1%	25.11	21.49	15.12	18.43	23.32	27.21	30.78	35.88	39.58	42.63
Employees	1.9%	83,299	73,465	65,151	61,020	63,075	65,190	62,609	99,184	96,428	98,556

1994 Year-end:
Equity as % of assets: 7.3%
Return on assets: 1.1%
Return on equity: 14.5%
Long-term debt (mil.): $15,428
No. of shares (mil.): 371
Dividends
  Yield: 4.1%
  Payout: 30.0%
Market value (mil.): $14,662
Sales (mil.): $16,531

Stock Price History High/Low 1985–94

BANKERS TRUST NEW YORK

OVERVIEW

Bankers Trust (BT) has had a few "difficulties." These included the crash of the US bond market in early 1994, which helped send income diving by 43%; lawsuits relating to derivatives BT sold to 2 long-time clients, Gibson Greetings and Procter & Gamble; a written supervisory agreement imposed by the Fed that restricts some of BT's sales activities; and a $10 million fine imposed by the SEC and the Commodity Futures Trading Commission.

Yet Bankers Trust remains committed to its specialty of risk management — using derivatives and other strategies to shield itself and its clients from the worst vagaries of the market. It also shields itself from the worst vagaries of the risk management market with other businesses, such as trading, loan syndications, currency trading, and international merchant banking. The fees BT earns from these activities help offset declines from derivatives and from proprietary trading (which in 1994 accounted for 11% of net earnings, down from 53% in 1993). BT has also begun trying to cultivate customer relationships and to improve communications between departments (to facilitate cross-selling).

Bankers Trust was clobbered by the collapse of the Mexican peso in late 1994 and the subsequent decline of some other Latin American investments.

WHEN

Bankers Trust Co. (BT) was founded in 1903 by a group of bankers led by Henry Davison to handle trust business for commercial banks. Within 5 years BT began building a network of correspondent banks in other countries to handle international trust business. It soon began to expand domestically, acquiring Mercantile Trust (1911), Manhattan Trust (1912), and Astor Trust (1917). The 1913 Federal Reserve Act (which allowed all banks to offer trust services) eliminated BT's competitive edge. So in 1917 Bankers Trust joined the Federal Reserve System and began offering a variety of banking services. In 1919 BT's securities department (started in 1916) began underwriting and distributing securities. In 1928 it became a subsidiary, but with the 1931 passage of the Glass-Steagall Act (which separated investment banking from commercial banking) the subsidiary was discontinued.

After WWII Bankers Trust ventured into retail banking, offering savings and checking accounts and home improvement, auto, and unsecured business loans.

In 1950 BT bought Lawyers Trust, Title Guaranty & Trust's banking division, and Flushing National Bank. By 1965 it had added 22 branches and bought several more banks.

By 1967 Bankers Trust had 89 offices in New York and 2 in London; within 8 years there were 200 offices. International operations expanded in the 1970s to more than 30 countries, and BT's network of correspondent banks had grown to more than 1,200 banks in over 120 countries.

In the early 1980s the company sold its consumer banking business in order to focus on corporate services, particularly international commercial and merchant banking. It had not done much to cultivate traditional corporate clients, however, and gravitated to the high-risk, high-profit LBO arena, where it became a favorite of dealmakers like KKR. When the 1980s LBO craze faded, bad loan expenses rose as interest rates dropped. The bank lost money in 1989. A diminished customer base and a need for profits drove the bank deeper into proprietary trading and risk management.

Risk management involves hedging positions with derivatives, which can be as simple as "plain vanilla" options, but which can also be very complex (with names like "the ratio swap," "Spreadlock 1 and 2," and "Wedding Band 3 and 6") and contain multiple leveraging factors that vastly increase the potential for profit (and, as it turned out in 1994, for loss). These instruments were often stunningly profitable in 1993, when interest rates were falling, but many turned mean when rates rose in 1994.

Some of BT's clients, suffering losses, turned against their bank, and 2 clients sued (although Gibson Greetings, facing a loss of $17.5 million, was unable to resist a last desperate gamble that added another $10 million to the tab). Later in 1994 the bank settled with Gibson (accepting only $6 million from the greeting card company instead of the $14 million BT said it was owed) after a tape of 2 of BT's employees discussing methods of concealing the extent of Gibson's losses was discovered. These problems have contributed to BT's loss of share of a much subdued derivatives market.

Several top BT executives announced their resignations in 1995, including CEO Charles Sanford and CFO Timothy Yates, both of whom plan to retire in 1996.

NYSE symbol: BT
Fiscal year ends: December 31

WHO

Chairman and CEO: Charles S. Sanford Jr., age 59, $757,100 pay
VC: George J. Vojta, age 59, $507,100 pay
President: Eugene B. Shanks Jr., age 48, $507,100 pay
EVP and Chief Credit Officer: Joseph A. Manganello Jr., age 59, $832,100
EVP and General Counsel: James J. Baechle, age 62, $757,100 pay
EVP, CFO, and Controller: Timothy T. Yates, age 48, $269,600 pay
Managing Director Corporate Human Resources: Mark Bieler
Auditors: Ernst & Young LLP

WHERE

HQ: Bankers Trust New York Corporation, 280 Park Ave., New York, NY 10017
Phone: 212-250-2500
Fax: 212-454-1704 (Public Relations)

Bankers Trust operates globally.

	1994 Sales		1994 Pretax Income	
	$ mil.	% of total	$ mil.	% of total
US	4,210	50	364	42
UK	1,546	18	144	17
Asia & the Pacific	1,167	14	218	25
Other Americas	896	11	103	12
Other countries	597	7	40	4
Adjustments	(913)	—	—	—
Total	**7,503**	**100**	**869**	**100**

WHAT

	1994 Assets	
	$ mil.	% of total
Cash & equivalents	24,059	25
Treas. & agency securities	13,314	14
Foreign govt. securities	9,828	10
Derivatives	14,071	15
Other securities	17,776	18
Net loans	11,249	11
Other	6,719	7
Total	**97,016**	**100**

	1994 Sales	
	$ mil.	% of total
Interest	5,030	67
Trading	465	6
Fiduciary & funds mgmt.	740	10
Fees & commissions	756	10
Other	512	7
Total	**7,503**	**100**

Financial Services	Selected Subsidiaries
Commercial banking	American Bank in Poland
Corporate finance	Bankers Trust Australia Ltd.
Fiduciary and securities services	BT Bank of Canada
	Didier Philippe SA (France)
Global operating and information services	TISCO Securities Hong Kong Ltd.
International merchant banking	Turk Merchant Bank AS
	United Bank for Africa Ltd.
Investment management	The WM Company PLC (UK)

KEY COMPETITORS

Bank of New York	Deutsche Bank	J.P. Morgan
BankAmerica	First Chicago	Merrill Lynch
Bear Stearns	Fleet	Morgan Stanley
Chemical Banking	General Electric	NatWest
Citicorp	Goldman Sachs	Paine Webber
Crédit Lyonnais	HSBC	Salomon
CS Holding	Industrial Bank of	Union Bank of
Dai-Ichi Kangyo	Japan	Switzerland

HOW MUCH

	9-Year Growth	1985	1986	1987	1988	1989	1990	1991	1992	1993	1994
Assets ($ mil.)	7.5%	50,581	56,420	56,521	57,942	55,658	63,596	63,959	72,448	92,082	97,016
Net income ($ mil.)	6.2%	371	428	1	648	(987)	634	633	731	1,047	587
Income as % of assets	—	0.7%	0.8%	0.0%	1.1%	—	1.0%	1.0%	1.0%	1.1%	0.6%
Earnings per share ($)	3.2%	5.39	6.01	0.02	8.09	(12.10)	7.80	7.75	8.82	12.29	7.17
Stock price – high ($)	—	37.88	52.50	55.25	41.25	58.25	46.75	68.00	70.13	83.50	84.63
Stock price – low ($)	—	26.88	33.38	26.25	29.63	34.50	28.50	39.50	50.00	65.75	54.75
Stock price – close ($)	4.7%	36.75	45.25	31.75	35.00	41.38	43.38	63.75	68.50	79.13	55.38
P/E – high	—	7	9	—	5	—	6	9	10	7	12
P/E – low	—	5	6	—	4	—	4	5	7	5	8
Dividends per share ($)	11.9%	1.35	1.48	1.71	1.92	2.14	2.38	2.61	2.88	3.24	3.70
Book value per share ($)	5.4%	34.32	38.78	37.39	43.14	26.28	31.19	35.33	39.93	53.15	55.19
Employees	3.6%	10,543	11,069	12,292	12,558	13,485	13,315	12,088	12,917	13,571	14,529

1994 Year-end:
Equity as % of assets: 4.4%
Return on assets: 0.6%
Return on equity: 13.7%
Long-term debt (mil.): $6,455
No. of shares (mil.): 78
Dividends
  Yield: 6.7%
  Payout: 51.6%
Market value (mil.): $4,323
Sales (mil.): $7,503

Stock Price History
High/Low 1985–94

BARNES & NOBLE, INC.

OVERVIEW

The superstar on Barnes & Noble's roster these days is the superstore. Like other retailers, such as Toys "R" Us and Home Depot, the company is building bigger and bigger stores. Barnes & Noble's superstores offer between 60,000 and 175,000 titles and feature wood fixtures, antique-style chairs and tables, and, at some locations, coffee bars. Headquartered in New York City, the company also runs one of the nation's largest direct-mail bookselling businesses, operates a chain of mall stores, and has its own publishing business. The mall bookstores are operated under the names B. Dalton Bookseller, Doubleday Book Shops, and Scribner's Bookstore and the superstores under the names Barnes & Noble Booksellers, Bookstop, and Bookstar.

Not only is Barnes & Noble the #1 bookseller in the US, it is also the fastest growing as it continues to add more superstores. Its expansion plans call for the addition of about 200 superstores over the next 3 years. In 1994 the company added CD-ROMs and enlarged its selection of recorded music. Same-store sales at its superstores were up 12.6% in fiscal 1995. The company also plans to increase its publishing, which currently accounts for 1.4% of its product mix.

Barnes & Noble's mall stores have not fared as well. Same-store sales were down 2.3% in fiscal 1995. The company closed a net 36 mall stores in 1994. CEO Leonard Riggio owns approximately 24% of the company and Dutch retailer Vendex International owns 9.3%.

WHEN

The son of a prizefighter, Leonard Riggio worked in a New York University bookstore as a sales clerk to help pay for night school. He was studying engineering, but he got the itch for book retailing. In 1965, at the age of 24, he borrowed $5,000 and opened a college bookstore of his own in Greenwich Village called Student Book Exchange NYC. Beginning in the late 1960s, he expanded by buying other college bookstores.

He entered the general bookstore business in 1971 when he paid $1.2 million for the Barnes & Noble Bookstore (founded in 1873), a large, money-losing bookstore in New York City. With the acquisition of Marboro Books in 1979, the company entered the mail order and publishing business.

In 1986 Riggio and Dutch retailer Vendex International bought the 754 stores of the B. Dalton mall bookstore chain from Dayton Hudson for about $275 million. Founded in 1966, B. Dalton was created to tap into a growing market of better-educated, more affluent customers. It focused at first on the shopping malls that were beginning to spring up all over the US. It eventually shifted its strategy and began placing its stores in other heavily trafficked areas such as office complexes.

In 1984 B. Dalton created Software Etc. to sell software within the bookstores. When Riggio and Vendex bought B. Dalton, they got Software Etc. as well, and in 1987 they spun the software retailer off as a separate company.

In 1989 both Barnes & Noble and competitor Waldenbooks came under heavy criticism when they pulled Salman Rushdie's *Satanic*

Verses from their shelves. After public outcry, both began selling the book again.

Also in 1989 the company acquired the Scribner's Bookstore trade name from Macmillan Publishing and Rizzoli International. That same year it beat out Crown Books to buy Bookstop, a chain of 23 Bookstop and Bookstar superstores founded in 1982 by entrepreneur Gary Hoover. With the acquisition of Bookstop, the first book superstore chain, Barnes & Noble began its shift to superstore format. It also began streamlining its operations to integrate Bookstop and Doubleday (acquired in 1990) into its existing business.

Barnes & Noble had planned a public offering for 1992 but withdrew after it got a tepid response from Wall Street because of the company's debt load. Instead, Barnes & Noble raised $100 million in financing from Riggio, Vendex, and private investors. The company also eased its debt burden by refinancing about $508 million in debt. It then embarked on a major expansion of its superstore operation.

In 1993, with sales at its superstores booming, the company made a 2nd try at going public. This time it had no trouble getting Wall Street's attention. Its share price rose to more than $29 the first day, after opening at $20. In 1994 Riggio sold an additional 1.5 million shares from his holdings to the public. Also in 1994 the company opened 70 new superstores.

In 1995 Stephen Riggio, Leonard's younger brother, was named COO.

NYSE symbol: BKS
Fiscal year ends: Saturday nearest January 31

WHO

Chairman and CEO: Leonard Riggio, age 54, $1,170,000 pay
COO: Stephen Riggio, age 40, $520,000 pay (prior to promotion)
EVP; President, Barnes & Noble Superstores: Mitchell S. Klipper, age 37, $600,000 pay
EVP Finance and CFO: Irene Miller, age 42, $472,000 pay
VP Real Estate: Jeffrey L. Berk, age 39, $249,835 pay
VP; President, B. Dalton Bookseller: Thomas Tolworthy, age 43
VP and General Merchandise Manager: Maureen H. Golden, age 44
Secretary: Michael N. Rosen, age 54
VP Human Resources: Don Lapp
Auditors: BDO Seidman

WHERE

HQ: 122 Fifth Ave., New York, NY 10011
Phone: 212-633-3300
Fax: 212-675-0413

	1995 Stores	
	Mall bookstores	Superstores
California	97	45
Texas	52	35
Florida	41	23
New York	38	23
Michigan	34	6
Minnesota	29	10
Ohio	29	8
Pennsylvania	28	7
Illinois	27	11
New Jersey	24	10
Other states	299	90
Total	**698**	**268**

WHAT

	1995 Sales	
	$ mil.	% of total
Superstores	953	58
Mall stores	647	40
Other	23	2
Total	**1,623**	**100**

Superstores
Barnes & Noble Booksellers
Bookstar
Bookstop

Mall Bookstores
B. Dalton Bookseller
Doubleday Book Shops
Scribner's Bookstore

Mail Order Business
Marboro Books Corp. (Barnes & Noble mail order business)

Publishing
Barnes & Noble Books

KEY COMPETITORS

Books-A-Million
Borders
Crown Books
Half Price Books
Hastings Books
Lauriat's
MTS
Oxford Books
Price/Cosco
Tattered Cover
Taylor's
Toys "R" Us
Wal-Mart
W. H. Smith

HOW MUCH

	Annual Growth	1986	1987	1988	1989	1990	1991	1992	1993	1994	1995
Sales ($ mil.)	18.7%	—	412	661	669	749	880	921	1,087	1,337	1,623
Net income ($ mil.)	—	—	(22)	(2)	3	11	7	(5)	(6)	(3)	25
Income as % of sales	—	—	—	—	0.4%	1.5%	0.8%	—	—	—	1.6%
Earnings per share ($)	—	—	—	—	—	—	—	—	—	(0.11)	0.81
Stock price – high ($)[1]	—	—	—	—	—	—	—	—	—	34.00	31.38
Stock price – low ($)[1]	—	—	—	—	—	—	—	—	—	22.63	20.00
Stock price – close ($)[1]	25.6%	—	—	—	—	—	—	—	—	24.88	31.25
P/E – high	—	—	—	—	—	—	—	—	—	—	39
P/E – low	—	—	—	—	—	—	—	—	—	—	25
Dividends per share ($)	—	—	—	—	—	—	—	—	—	0.00	0.00
Book value per share ($)	8.1%	—	—	—	—	—	—	—	—	11.01	11.91
Employees	16.7%	—	—	—	—	—	—	12,600	17,000	14,700	20,000

1995 Year-end:
Debt ratio: 34.7%
Return on equity: 7.4%
Cash (mil.): $55
Current ratio: 1.34
Long-term debt (mil.): $190
No. of shares (mil.): 30
Dividends
    Yield: —
    Payout: —
Market value (mil.): $940

Stock Price History[1]
High/Low 1994–95

(chart with scale 0 to 35)

[1] Stock prices are for the prior calendar year.

BARNETT BANKS, INC.

OVERVIEW

Barnett Banks is hustling. After a decade of sitting and waiting for business to come to it (after all, wasn't everyone moving to Florida?), the Jacksonville-based company has begun looking for new ways to make money, finally jumping aboard the financial services train (many of its competitors, including out-of-state First Union, have been following the diversity strategy for years).

In recent years Barnett has dug itself out of the hole created by overinvestment in local commercial real estate, but most of its growth has come from cost cutting rather than new

business. Now the company has chosen to specialize in mortgage banking (both retail and wholesale), beefed up its credit card operations, and announced plans to enter the leasing business.

Barnett is also instilling a new corporate culture in its employees, emphasizing sales of fee- or commission-generating income (like investment products). As part of this effort, the company is using its database to target existing customers for new products. It is also redoubling its efforts to attract small- and middle-market business customers.

WHEN

William Barnett, a Kansas banker, and his family moved to Jacksonville, Florida, in 1877 for his wife's health. That same year he started the National Bank of Jacksonville.

In 1930 the Barnetts formed Barnett National Securities Corp., a bank holding company, which soon acquired and reopened 3 banks that had failed after the 1929 stock market crash (in Cocoa, DeLand, and St. Augustine). The day before President Franklin Roosevelt's bank holiday during the Depression in 1933, Barnett opened every teller window and had tellers slowly count money for withdrawals using nothing larger than a $20 bill; this strategy prevented a run on the bank because many people in line were reassured and went home.

Jacksonville attorney Guy Botts, who joined the bank as president in 1963, wanted it to become a statewide banking institution and a leader in every market. He began a program of acquisitions, and in 1966 Barnett bought First National Bank of Winter Park; by 1969 the holding company had purchased 7 other banks throughout Florida. To clarify its identity, the company in 1969 changed its name to Barnett Banks of Florida (then to Barnett Banks, Inc., in 1987).

In the 1970s Barnett established Florida's first credit card franchise. Barnett was the first southeastern banking company to be listed on the New York Stock Exchange.

The company survived the Florida real estate crash of the mid-1970s, and when state law changed to allow banks to open branch offices, it began branching left and right. By the end of the decade, Barnett had bought 29 more banks.

Barnett continued to acquire banks and add branches in the 1980s. After Florida's approval of regional interstate banking, the company

moved into Georgia in 1986 by buying First National Bank of Cobb County; it bought several more small Georgia and Florida banks in 1989 and 1990.

In 1990 Barnett was sued in a class action alleging that Barnett Equity Securities had misstated or failed to disclose material facts to investors. The case was settled out of court in 1992 with the issuance of $1.25 million in common stock to the plaintiff class.

As the economy cooled again in the early 1990s, Barnett found itself with sharply increased levels of nonperforming assets and loan charge-offs. Since then the company has reduced these liabilities through loan restructuring and sales and has cut back on commercial real estate lending. The company has also stabilized its credit quality by restructuring its credit operations.

In 1992 Barnett bought, among others, First Florida Banks, Florida's last large independent bank. Also that year the company bought CSX Corp.'s student loan business, which became BTI Services, but sold it in 1993 because it was insufficiently profitable. Also in 1993 Barnett swapped its Atlanta banks for Bank South Corporation's Pensacola bank.

Barnett continued its acquisition program in 1994 with the purchase of Glendale (California) Federal's Florida deposits.

In 1994, in keeping with its new strategy of becoming a mortgage banking powerhouse, Barnett bought Loan America Financial Corp. (a mortgage wholesaler, which buys loans from brokers) and EquiCredit (which specializes in consumer loans secured by first and 2nd mortgages). In 1995 it took steps to enter the nationwide retail mortgage field by agreeing to acquire BancPLUS, which originates, sells, and services home mortgages.

NYSE symbol: BBI
Fiscal year ends: December 31

WHO

Chairman and CEO: Charles E. Rice, age 59,
$1,707,500 pay
President and COO: Allen L. Lastinger Jr., age 52,
$911,250 pay
EVP: Hinton F. Nobles Jr., age 49, $491,400 pay
CFO: Charles W. Newman, age 45, $491,400 pay
Chief Credit Policy Executive: Richard C. Brewer,
age 53, $479,780 pay
Chief Legal Executive: Judy S. Beaubouef, age 48
Regional Banking Executive/South: James F. Mondello,
age 51
Regional Banking Executive/North: Lee H. Chaplin Jr.,
age 55
Chief Marketing Executive: Susan S. Blaser, age 45
Chief Retail Banking and Technology Executive:
Jonathan J. Palmer, age 51
Chief Corporate Banking Executive: Douglas K.
Freeman, age 44
Chief Human Resources Executive: Paul T. Kerins,
age 51
Auditors: Arthur Andersen & Co, SC

WHERE

HQ: 50 N. Laura St., Jacksonville, FL 32202-3638
PO Box 40789, 32203-0789
Phone: 904-791-7720
Fax: 904-791-7166

Barnett Banks operates banks in Florida and Georgia
and operates 9 nonbank subsidiaries in Florida.

	1994 Locations
	No. of offices
Florida	610
Georgia	18
Total	**628**

WHAT

	1994 Assets	
	$ mil.	% of total
Cash & equivalents	2,908	7
US Treasurys	3,139	8
Mortgage-backed securities	2,396	6
Other securities	2,148	5
Net loans	28,020	68
Other	2,667	6
Total	**41,278**	**100**

	1994 Sales	
	$ mil.	% of total
Loan interest	2,164	70
Other interest	391	13
Service charges & fees	332	11
Credit card discounts & fees	54	1
Other income	156	5
Total	**3,097**	**100**

Selected Services
Insurance
Mutual funds
Retail and commercial
banking

Nonbanking Subsidiaries
Barnett Banks Insurance,
Inc. (reinsurance of
policies on affiliates'
loans)

Barnett Banks Trust Co.,
N.A. (trust management)
Barnett Card Services Corp.
Barnett Mortgage Co.
Barnett Recovery Corp.
(loan collections)
Barnett Securities, Inc.
(brokerage)
Barnett Technologies, Inc.
(information processing)

KEY COMPETITORS

BancFlorida Financial
BankAmerica
BankAtlantic
Central and Southern
Holding
Charles Schwab
Citicorp

FF Bancorp
First Union
Florida Bank
General Electric
H.F. Ahmanson
Merrill Lynch
Mid-State Federal

NationsBank
Paine Webber
Republic
Savings
SunTrust

HOW MUCH

	9-Year Growth	1985	1986	1987	1988	1989	1990	1991	1992	1993	1994
Assets ($ mil.)	12.0%	14,829	20,229	23,451	25,748	29,007	32,214	32,721	39,465	38,331	41,278
Net income ($ mil.)	16.0%	128	162	196	226	257	101	124	208	421	488
Income as % of assets	—	0.9%	0.8%	0.8%	0.9%	0.9%	0.3%	0.4%	0.5%	1.1%	1.2%
Earnings per share ($)	6.8%	2.57	2.96	3.25	3.75	4.07	1.61	1.71	1.98	4.01	4.66
Stock price – high ($)	—	30.00	40.88	41.75	37.38	40.00	37.75	36.38	43.63	50.38	48.13
Stock price – low ($)	—	18.69	25.69	27.13	29.00	32.25	14.13	15.50	31.00	37.38	37.25
Stock price – close ($)	2.9%	29.84	31.25	28.38	34.00	36.13	18.88	33.50	41.25	41.50	38.50
P/E – high	—	12	14	13	10	10	23	21	22	13	10
P/E – low	—	7	9	8	8	8	9	9	16	9	9
Dividends per share ($)	10.1%	0.65	0.75	0.86	0.98	1.12	1.26	1.32	1.32	1.38	1.54
Book value per share ($)	7.4%	16.35	19.07	21.97	24.37	26.79	24.84	26.83	25.14	28.21	31.05
Employees	3.3%	14,107	16,902	18,743	18,533	18,983	19,300	18,750	22,179	18,649	18,929

1994 Year-end:
Equity as % of assets: 7.6%
Return on assets: 1.2%
Return on equity: 17.5%
Long-term debt (mil.): $777
No. of shares (mil.): 94
Dividends
  Yield: 4.0%
  Payout: 33.0%
Market value (mil.): $3,619
Sales (mil.): $3,097

Stock Price History
High/Low 1985–94

BAXTER INTERNATIONAL INC.

OVERVIEW

Baxter International's 2 main product segments are medical specialties (products for blood processing, dialysis systems, and cardiovascular devices) and medical/laboratory products and distribution (anesthetics, surgery supplies and products, intravenous systems, and sales and distribution services). The medical/laboratory products and distribution segment is the leading US manufacturer and distributor of health care products. Baxter distributes its 200,000 health care–related products in 100 countries. After a poor year in 1993, its net income rebounded dramatically in 1994.

Baxter, based in Deerfield, Illinois, a northern suburb of Chicago, is concentrating more on its medical specialties segment — 2/3 of each of its capital and R&D budgets are going

toward improving and expanding that segment because of worldwide growth potential.

The company is creating alliances with foreign firms to fuel international growth. Baxter has alliances in Brazil, Hungary, Mexico, the Philippines, Taiwan, Thailand, and Turkey. Product lines in these markets are IV solutions and nutritional and disposable medical products. In China the company, in conjunction with a local alliance, is building a renal products manufacturing plant and planning another.

Baxter is becoming a player in the transplant niche of the biotech industry. Nextran, a company created by Baxter and DNX in 1994, has on the market its first product, a monitoring kit to test organ donor and recipient compatibility.

WHEN

Idaho surgeon Ralph Falk, his brother Harry, and California physician Donald Baxter formed the Don Baxter Intravenous Products Corporation in 1931 to distribute the intravenous (IV) solutions Baxter made in Los Angeles. Two years later the company opened its first manufacturing plant in Glenview, Illinois. Ralph Falk bought Baxter's interest in 1935 and began R&D efforts leading to the first sterilized vacuum-type blood collection device (1939), which could store blood for 21 days instead of a few hours. Demand for Baxter's products during WWII spurred sales above $1.5 million by 1945.

In 1949 the company created Travenol Laboratories to make and sell drugs. Baxter went public in 1951 and began an acquisition program the following year. Failing health caused both Falks in 1953 to give company control to William Graham, a manager since 1945. Graham continued the acquisition program, absorbing 5 US companies: Hyland Labs (1952), Wallerstein Company (1957), Fenwal Labs (1959), Flint, Eaton (1959), and Dayton Flexible Products (1967).

In 1975 Baxter moved its headquarters to Deerfield, Illinois. The company had $1 billion in sales in 1978, the same year it introduced the first portable dialysis machine. In 1985 Baxter acquired American Hospital Supply, a Baxter distributor from 1932 until 1962. American's sales were 65% higher than Baxter's, but American distributed more lower-margin products than Baxter, which manufactured most of its own items. The

merger made Baxter the world's largest hospital supply company.

Offering more than 120,000 products and an electronic order-entry system that connected customers with over 1,500 vendors, Baxter captured nearly 25% of the US hospital supply market in 1988. That same year the company changed its name to Baxter International.

In 1992 Baxter spun off Caremark (home infusion therapy and mail-order drugs), which was competing directly with hospitals, Baxter's main source of revenues. Baxter retained Caremark's renal division, which had a 75% world market share in dialysis machines.

Baxter pleaded guilty in 1993 to paying Syria a bribe (in the form of deeply discounted medical supplies) in an effort to be removed from an Arab blacklist of companies doing business in Israel and apologized for the "unintentional violation." A 4-month suspension from doing business with the Veterans Administration followed. Also in 1993 the company centralized its gene therapy research. President James Tobin's sudden departure in December 1993 (he had been appointed in March 1992) capped a difficult year for Baxter.

In 1994 Baxter signed an 8-year agreement with giant Columbia/HCA Healthcare to supply intravenous products and services and some diagnostic products to its 195 hospitals and 100 surgery centers throughout the US. Also in 1994 Baxter sold its medical diagnostic test businesses to Bain Capital.

In 1995 Bio-Plexus, maker of patented self-blunting blood collection needles, announced Baxter would begin distributing its needles.

NYSE symbol: BAX
Fiscal year ends: December 31

WHO

Senior Chairman: William B. Graham, age 83
Chairman and CEO: Vernon R. Loucks Jr., age 60,
$1,380,100 pay
EVP: Tony L. White, age 48, $727,950 pay
EVP: Lester B. Knight, age 36, $724,938 pay
SVP and CFO: Harry M. Jansen Kraemer Jr., age 40,
$474,615 pay
SVP, Secretary, and General Counsel: Arthur F.
Staubitz, age 55
SVP Human Resources: Herbert E. Walker, age 60
Group VP Baxter World Trade Corporation: Manuel A.
Baez, age 53, $478,007 pay
Group VP Corporate Research and Development: Dale
A. Smith, age 63
VP Government Affairs: David J. Aho, age 45
VP Corporate Development and Strategy: John F.
Gaither Jr., age 45
VP Manufacturing, Operations, and Strategy: James H.
Taylor Jr., age 56
Auditors: Price Waterhouse LLP

WHERE

HQ: One Baxter Pkwy., Deerfield, IL 60015
Phone: 708-948-2000
Fax: 708-948-2887

Baxter sells products in about 100 countries. Baxter has
71 manufacturing plants in 21 countries, 149 distribution centers, and 25 research facilities worldwide.

	1994 Sales		1994 Pretax Income	
	$ mil.	% of total	$ mil.	% of total
US	6,831	74	453	41
Europe	1,245	13	251	23
Other regions	1,248	13	393	36
Adjustments	—	—	(296)	—
Total	**9,324**	**100**	**801**	**100**

WHAT

	1994 Sales		1994 Pretax Income	
	$ mil.	% of total	$ mil.	% of total
Medical/lab prods. & distribution	5,767	62	474	43
Medical specialties	3,557	38	621	57
Adjustments	—	—	(294)	—
Total	**9,324**	**100**	**801**	**100**

Selected Products
Artificial heart valves
Blood-handling equipment
Cardiac catheters
Cardiac monitoring and bypass systems
Dialysis products and services
Electromechanical heart assist systems
Gammagard S/D (immune system disorder treatment)
Intravenous therapy products
Laboratory apparatus and supplies
Nutritional supplies
Peritoneal dialysis products (home dialysis)
Surgical instruments and supplies

KEY COMPETITORS

Abbott Labs
American Home
  Products
Amgen
Ballard Medical
Bayer
Bergen Brunswig
Ciba-Geigy
C. R. Bard
Diagnostic Products
Eli Lilly
Genentech
Hoechst

Johnson & Johnson
Medtronic
Merck
Mitek Surgical
Northfield Labs
Novo Nordisk
Pfizer
Roche
St. Jude Medical
Somatogen
Thermo Electron
U.S. Surgical
Vital Signs

HOW MUCH

	9-Year Growth	1985	1986	1987	1988	1989	1990	1991	1992	1993	1994
Sales ($ mil.)	16.5%	2,355	5,543	6,223	6,861	7,399	8,100	8,921	8,471	8,879	9,324
Net income ($ mil.)	17.7%	137	219	323	388	446	40	591	606	(268)	596
Income as % of sales	—	5.8%	4.0%	5.2%	5.7%	6.0%	0.5%	6.6%	7.2%	—	6.4%
Earnings per share ($)	11.0%	0.83	0.79	1.09	1.30	1.49	(0.05)	2.00	2.13	(0.97)	2.13
Stock price – high ($)	—	16.88	21.25	29.25	26.13	25.88	29.50	40.88	40.50	32.75	28.88
Stock price – low ($)	—	12.38	15.13	15.50	16.25	17.50	20.50	25.63	30.50	20.00	21.63
Stock price – close ($)	6.7%	15.75	19.25	22.75	17.63	25.00	27.88	40.00	32.38	24.38	28.25
P/E – high	—	20	27	27	20	17	—	20	19	—	14
P/E – low	—	15	19	14	13	12	—	13	14	—	10
Dividends per share ($)	12.1%	0.36	0.39	0.43	0.49	0.55	0.62	0.72	0.83	0.97	1.01
Book value per share ($)	3.3%	9.86	11.57	11.79	12.61	13.49	13.45	14.45	13.59	11.52	13.18
Employees	(1.3%)	60,000	60,000	60,000	61,500	61,000	60,600	60,400	61,300	60,400	53,500

1994 Year-end:
Debt ratio: 43.6%
Return on equity: 17.3%
Cash (mil.): $471
Current ratio: 1.57
Long-term debt (mil.): $2,341
No. of shares (mil.): 282
Dividends
  Yield: 3.6%
  Payout: 47.4%
Market value (mil.): $7,975

Stock Price History
High/Low 1985–94

THE BEAR STEARNS COMPANIES INC.

OVERVIEW

Bear Stearns is one of the US's leading securities trading, investment banking, and brokerage firms. It serves an elite clientele of corporations, financial institutions, governments, and individuals.

It also has a major presence overseas, particularly in Latin America, where it holds a 66% share of equity offerings underwriting. It has operated in Europe for 40 years but arrived late in Asia. However, in the 1990s it has made great strides, especially in Japan. As the Chinese economy has opened, Bear Stearns has kept pace, expanding its Hong Kong office to full branch status and opening representative offices in Beijing and Shanghai. Bear Stearns diversifies its income by performing trade clearing services.

The company is known not only for its aggressive trading but also for its dedication to conforming to trading rules (it employs a staff of "ferrets" to look for infractions and imposes swift punishment on the guilty).

Bear Stearns was hurt by the interest rate increases of 1994. The company saw decreased income of $241 million (from $3.8 billion in sales) in fiscal 1995.

WHEN

As the 1920s roared onto Wall Street, a fledgling brokerage firm opened in 1923 with $500,000 in capital. The partners were Joseph Ainslee Bear, Robert Stearns, and Harold Mayer. Their firm was Bear, Stearns & Co.

The firm grew rapidly and weathered the 1929 stock market crash with no layoffs. In the New Deal era, Bear Stearns aggressively promoted government bonds. Its arbitrage department, created in 1938, dealt in the securities of New York City transit systems.

In 1940 Bear Stearns opened its first branch office, in Chicago. The company's international department was created in 1948, and in 1955 Bear Stearns opened an office in Amsterdam. Other branches followed in Geneva (1963), San Francisco (1965), Paris (1967), and Los Angeles (1968).

Bear Stearns was guided in the 1950s and 1960s by colorful trader Salim "Cy" Lewis. Lewis began his career as a runner for Salomon Brothers. At Bear Stearns he climbed the ladder to chairman, becoming a Wall Street legend as the hard-charging, Scotch-drinking taskmaster of "The Bear," as the firm came to be known. During the 1950s Lewis originated block (large-scale) trading.

In 1973, after Bear Stearns moved to new headquarters, it found itself with additional space. It recruited independent brokers and gave them free rent if they would use the company for clearing — processing stock trades . Clearing grew to be a major contributor to the company's bottom line.

When Lewis died in 1978, Alan Greenberg became CEO and not only maintained his predecessor's reputation for aggressive trading but surpassed it. Greenberg, Kansas-born and Oklahoma-reared, had worked his way up from the risk arbitrage desk, to which he was assigned at the age of 25.

Under Greenberg the firm formed the government securities department (1979), the mortgage-backed securities department (1981), and Bear Stearns Asset Management and Custodial Trust, a New Jersey bank and trust company (1984).

In 1985 Bear Stearns formed a holding company called the Bear Stearns Companies Inc., which it took public. In the late 1980s Bear Stearns moved further into investment banking with hopes of becoming a leading US firm. In Latin America Bear Stearns became the leading equity underwriter in 1991. The firm also created Bear Stearns Securities Corporation to clear transactions for the company and for correspondent brokerages.

In 1992 Bear Stearns extended its industry coverage to include biotech, capital industry, and machinery stocks.

Along with the advantages of success and high visibility came difficulties. The company's volume of underwritings also prompted a deluge of lawsuits relating to junk bonds and hot IPOs that fizzled (matters still pending include suits relating to In-Store Advertising and Jenny Craig).

Bear Stearns has upgraded and expanded its information processing capabilities to provide all its locations with the most efficient systems possible.

In 1994 the company hired former Federal Reserve governor Wayne Angell as its chief economist. His experience with the Fed has been presumed to provide him with insight into the actions of that body (which was responsible for the 6 interest rate increases that produced the turmoil of 1994).

Also, Bear Stearns has become active in M&As, advising on deals like Raytheon's acquisition of E-Systems and the Martin Marietta/Lockheed merger in 1995.

NYSE symbol: BSC
Fiscal year ends: June 30

WHO

Chairman: Alan C. Greenberg, age 67, $10,981,310 pay
President and CEO: James E. Cayne, age 60, $7,665,620 pay
COO and CFO: William J. Montgoris, age 47
EVP: John C. Sites Jr., age 42, $7,152,000 pay
EVP: Warren J. Spector, age 36, $7,034,000 pay
EVP: Michael L. Tarnopol, age 58, $5,700,560 pay
EVP: Vincent J. Mattone, age 49, $4,161,120 pay
EVP: Alan D. Schwartz, age 44, $4,148,870 pay
Managing Director of Personnel: Stephen A. Lacoff
Auditors: Deloitte & Touche LLP

WHERE

HQ: 245 Park Ave., New York, NY 10167
Phone: 212-272-2000
Fax: 212-272-8239 (Investor Relations)

Bear Stearns has offices in Atlanta, Boca Raton (Florida), Boston, Chicago, Dallas, Los Angeles, New York, Philadelphia, Princeton (New Jersey), San Francisco, and Washington, DC. It also has offices in Beijing, Buenos Aires, Frankfurt, Geneva, Hong Kong, Karachi, London, Paris, Sao Paulo, Shanghai, and Tokyo.

WHAT

	1994 Sales	
	$ mil.	**% of total**
Commissions	483	14
Principal transactions	1,132	33
Investment banking	494	14
Interest & dividends	1,304	38
Other income	28	1
Total	**3,441**	**100**

Selected Services
Asset management
Brokerage
Clearing and custody services
Fiduciary services
Financing for securities transactions
Investment banking
Securities lending
Securities trading
Trust services

Selected Subsidiaries
Bear Stearns Argentina, Inc.
Bear Stearns Asia, Ltd. (Hong Kong)
Bear Stearns Bank GmbH (Germany)
Bear Stearns do Brasil Ltda.
Bear Stearns Fiduciary Services, Inc.
Bear, Stearns International Ltd. (UK)
Bear Stearns Jahangir Siddiqui Ltd. (Pakistan)
Bear Stearns (Japan), Ltd.
Bear Stearns Mortgage Capital Corp.
Bear Stearns S.A. (France)
Bear, Stearns Securities Corp.
Custodial Trust Co.

KEY COMPETITORS

AIG
American Express
Bankers Trust
Brown Brothers Harriman
Canadian Imperial
Charles Schwab
CS Holding
Dai-Ichi Kangyo
Dean Witter, Discover
Deutsche Bank
Edward Jones
Equitable
General Electric
Goldman Sachs
Industrial Bank of Japan
KKR
Lehman Brothers
Merrill Lynch
Morgan Stanley
Nomura Securities
Paine Webber
Prudential
Royal Bank of Canada
Safeguard Scientifics
Salomon
Travelers
Union Bank of Switzerland

HOW MUCH

	Annual Growth	1985	1986	1987	1988	1989	1990	1991	1992	1993	1994
Sales ($ mil.)	15.2%	961	1,410	1,774	1,888	2,365	2,386	2,380	2,677	2,857	3,441
Net income ($ mil.)	17.9%	88	132	177	143	172	119	143	295	362	387
Income as % of sales	—	8.6%	9.3%	9.9%	7.5	7.3%	5.0%	6.0%	11.0%	12.7%	11.2%
Earnings per share ($)	19.1%	0.60	0.89	1.20	0.91	1.14	0.78	1.07	2.33	2.72	2.89
Stock price – high ($)	—	—	8.70	14.79	12.69	11.23	10.28	14.48	17.58	24.75	23.56
Stock price – low ($)	—	—	6.78	7.86	4.67	7.22	5.58	6.98	12.19	14.27	14.75
Stock price – close ($)	8.3%	—	8.15	9.15	6.05	8.57	7.54	13.96	15.75	20.83	15.38
P/E – high	—	—	10	12	14	10	13	14	8	9	8
P/E – low	—	—	8	7	5	6	7	7	5	5	5
Dividends per share ($)	24.0%	—	0.10	0.25	0.28	0.38	0.36	0.43	0.52	0.53	0.56
Book value per share ($)	17.0%	—	—	5.37	6.07	6.74	7.06	7.68	9.56	11.93	15.24
Employees	6.4%	4,186	4,927	5,784	6,012	5,994	5,732	5,612	5,873	6,036	7,321

1994 Year-end:
Debt ratio: 94.6%
Return on equity: 24.4%
Cash (mil.): $2,991
Long-term debt (mil.): $3,408
No. of shares (mil.): 113
Dividends
  Yield: 3.6%
  Payout: 19.4%
Market value (mil.): $1,745
Assets (mil.): $67,392

**Stock Price History
High/Low 1986–94**

BECHTEL GROUP, INC.

OVERVIEW

Bechtel has a yuan for China. The megabuilder is one of the first foreign construction companies licensed to do business under its own name in China (before 1995 its Chinese projects were joint ventures, usually with government entities).

San Francisco–based Bechtel designs and builds facilities in such fields as power, petroleum, chemicals, mining and metals, pipelines, surface transportation, aviation, space facilities, telecommunications, water management, environmental and pollution control, hazardous waste cleanup, and industrial and commercial construction. The company is a leading environmental consultant in the US.

Bechtel will draw on most of these skills for its plum Chinese project — Daxie — a 12-square-mile island that China wants to redevelop as a major deepwater port. In addition to harbor facilities, the $5 billion joint venture with the Chinese government includes the development of an entire town on the sparsely populated island. The project is intended to provide deeper harbor facilities than nearby Shanghai can offer.

The fiercely competitive international construction business has experienced a slowdown in the 1990s. To help offset the effects of the slowdown, the company has streamlined its facilities and cut costs.

WHEN

In 1898, 26-year-old Warren Bechtel left his Kansas farm to grade railroads in the Oklahoma Indian territories, where he soon founded his own company. After Bechtel settled in Oakland, California, his engineering and management skills brought him large projects such as the Northern California Highway and the Bowman Dam. By the time of its incorporation in 1925, Bechtel was the West's largest construction company.

Stephen Bechtel (president after his father's death in 1933) weathered the Depression with huge projects like the Hoover Dam (where Bechtel supervised 8 companies) and the San Francisco Bay Bridge. WWII meant full recovery, with the company winning many contracts, including one to build 570 ships in Bechtel-built yards in California.

In the postwar years Bechtel expanded overseas, building pipelines (TransArabian, 1947; Canada's TransMountain, 1954; Australia's first, 1964) and numerous power projects, including one that doubled South Korea's energy output (1948). By the time Stephen Bechtel Jr. became CEO in 1960 (when his father moved to chairman), the company was operating on 6 continents.

Bechtel built many nuclear power plants in the next 2 decades, including the world's first large one to be privately financed (Dresden, Illinois; opened 1960) and Canada's first (1962). Large transportation projects included San Francisco's Bay Area Rapid Transit system (BART, 1961–74) and Washington, DC's subway system (early 1970s). Work on Canada's James Bay hydroelectric project was begun in 1972 and completed in the mid-1980s; it supplies energy to 8 million people. Bechtel's Jubail project in Saudi Arabia, begun in 1976,

is raising from the Arabian desert a city of 275,000.

With the attractions of nuclear power fading in the wake of the Three Mile Island accident (which Bechtel won the right to clean up, starting in 1979), Bechtel began concentrating on other markets such as mining in New Guinea (gold and copper, 1981–84) and in China (coal, 1984). However, the company also sees work ahead in the decommissioning of aging nuclear plants.

Bechtel reeled under the recession and rising developing-world debt of the early 1980s. It cut its work force by 22,000 (almost half the total) and stemmed losses by taking on plant modernizations and other small projects.

Under 4th-generation family member Riley Bechtel (CEO since 1990), the company has won contracts for numerous projects, including the controversial new Hong Kong airport, a subway system for Athens, project management of the channel tunnel between Britain and France, and the Boston Central Artery/Tunnel project.

Over the years Bechtel has built over half a billion miles of oil pipeline. In 1992 and 1993 Bechtel signed deals to expand the former Soviet Union's crude oil pipeline network, to operate a series of new pipelines in Canada (with Interprovincial Pipe Line of Canada), and for a natural gas pipeline in Algeria.

In 1995, the company won the 3-year, $18 million assignment from the Agency for International Development to help restructure the energy sectors of 11 countries in eastern Europe. This will involve working with the individual governments to develop new laws and regulations governing local electric, gas, and oil development.

Private company
Fiscal year ends: December 31

WHO

Chairman Emeritus: Stephen D. Bechtel Jr., age 70
President and CEO: Riley P. Bechtel, age 43
EVP: William L. Friend, age 60
EVP: Don J. Gunther, age 56
EVP: Cordell W. Hull, age 61
EVP: John Neerhout Jr., age 64
EVP: Fred Gluck
SVP, CFO, Treasurer, and Controller: V. Paul Unruh, age 46
VP, Manager of Human Resources: Shirley Gaufin, age 49
Counsel: John W. Weiser, age 63
Auditors: Coopers & Lybrand L.L.P.

WHERE

HQ: 50 Beale St., San Francisco, CA 94105-1895
Phone: 415-768-1234
Fax: 415-768-0263 (Public Relations)

Bechtel operates worldwide with 4 regional offices in the US (Gaithersburg, MD; Houston; Los Angeles; and San Francisco) and offices in a number of other nations.

	1994 Offices	
	No.	**% of total**
Asia & Australia	13	28
US	13	28
Europe	7	14
Middle East	6	13
Latin America	5	11
Canada	2	4
Africa	1	2
Total	**47**	**100**

WHAT

Principal Operations
Bechtel Civil Co. (planning, design, and construction management for transportation, water resources, and building and infrastructure sectors)
Bechtel Construction Operations Inc.
  Bechtel Builders International
  Bechtel Construction Co.
  Becon Construction Co.
  Construction Resources and Technologies (provides construction equipment and technical resources to the construction companies)
Bechtel Enterprises, Inc. (project development, financing and ownership)
  North West Water
  United Infrastructure Co.
  US Generating Co. (independent power producer)
Bechtel Environmental, Inc. (hazardous waste remediation)
Bechtel National, Inc. (systems engineering and design, construction management, and environmental remediation services)
Bechtel Petroleum, Chemical & Industrial Co. (engineering, procurement, construction, and start-up for petroleum, chemical, and pharmaceutical industries)
Bechtel Power Corp. (design, construction, and development of power plants)
Bechtel Technology Group (cutting-edge technologies)
Mining & Metals (mineral exploration, development, and processing services)

KEY COMPETITORS

ABB	Michael Baker Corp.
Ashland, Inc.	Mid-American Waste
Baker Hughes	Morrison Knudsen
British Aerospace	Parsons Corp.
CBI Industries	Perini
Conrail	Peter Kiewit Sons'
Dresser	Raytheon
Duke Power	Safety-Kleen
Fluor	TRW
Halliburton	Union Pacific
Jacobs Engineering	USA Waste Services
McCarthy Building	Westinghouse
McDermott	WMX Technologies

HOW MUCH

	9-Year Growth	1985	1986	1987	1988	1989	1990	1991	1992	1993	1994
Sales ($ mil.)	1.5%	6,891	6,679	4,501	4,472	5,096	5,631	7,526	7,774	7,337	7,885
New work booked ($ mil.)	5.0%	4,982	3,675	3,537	4,486	5,427	4,787	7,248	8,396	9,445	7,741
Number of clients	(2.4%)	750	—	800	900	950	900	850	750	600	600
No. of active projects	(1.4%)	1,300	—	1,350	1,450	1,600	1,700	1,750	1,400	1,100	1,150
Employees	(10.6%)	80,000	50,000	43,000	36,000	27,800	32,500	30,900	30,900	29,400	29,200

Sales ($ mil.)
1985–94

Bechtel Group, Inc.

BECTON, DICKINSON AND COMPANY

OVERVIEW

Becton, Dickinson manufactures and sells medical supplies and devices and diagnostic systems worldwide. The company, headquartered in Franklin Lakes, New Jersey, has an extensive product line that includes hypodermic needles and syringes, blood collecting equipment, gloves, IV catheters (Becton, Dickinson is the world's #1 supplier), tissue culture labware, and immunodiagnostic test kits. It is a leader in clinical diagnostic products for infectious diseases (including AIDS testing), advanced cellular analysis, and physicians' office and real-time testing.

Becton, Dickinson maintains its leadership position by continually beating its competitors in decreasing costs and introducing and patenting products in demand. Becton, Dickinson is also modifying its products to make them

more efficient, safe, and cost-effective. For example, it produces catheters that can stay in blood vessels longer (thus requiring fewer per patient during a hospital stay). The company also makes products that improve or accelerate disease diagnosis such as those that evaluate immune system status. Efforts to improve testing and to protect health care workers from infected blood have fostered demand for the company's products, including its SAFETY-LOK syringes, blood collection systems (VACUTAINER is the market leader), the BACTEC 9000 series blood culturing systems, and INTERLINK needleless injection systems.

The company has expanded its overseas operations. Sales growth has been particularly strong in Japan and the Asia/Pacific region. R&D continues to be about 5.6% of sales.

WHEN

Maxwell Becton and Fairleigh Dickinson established a medical supply firm in New York in 1897. In 1907 the company moved to East Rutherford, New Jersey, and became one of the first US firms to manufacture hypodermic needles.

During WWI Becton, Dickinson manufactured all-glass syringes and introduced the all-cotton elastic (ACE) bandage. After the war researchers designed an improved stethoscope and created specialized hypodermic needles.

During WWII the company received an award for supplying medical equipment to the armed forces, and Becton and Dickinson helped establish Fairleigh Dickinson Junior College (now Fairleigh Dickinson University). The company continued to develop products such as the VACUTAINER blood collection apparatus, its first medical laboratory aid.

After the deaths of Dickinson (1948) and Becton (1951), their sons Fairleigh Dickinson Jr. and Henry Becton took over the company. Disposable hypodermic syringes developed by the company in 1961 virtually replaced reusable syringes in the US by 1987. The company went public in 1963 to raise money for manufacturing, packaging, and distribution facilities. In the 1960s Becton, Dickinson opened plants in Brazil, Canada, France, and Ireland and diversified into nonmedical businesses, purchasing Edmont (industrial gloves, 1966) and Spear (computer systems, 1968).

Wesley Howe, successor to Fairleigh Dickinson Jr., began expanding the company's foreign sales. From 1976 to 1980 the company added new medical products through internal

research and purchases such as Johnston Laboratories (automated bacteriology, 1979).

In 1978 the company thwarted a takeover bid by the Sun Company, which had purchased 32.5% of the company's stock. Howe began to sell the company's nonmedical businesses in 1983, ending with the 1989 sale of Edmont. The company acquired Deseret Medical (IV catheters, surgical gloves and masks) for $230 million in 1986.

In 1991 the company agreed to manufacture and market Baxter's InterLink needleless injection system, which greatly reduces the risk of accidental needle sticks.

In 1993 the company formed a joint venture with NeXagen, Inc., to make and market in vitro diagnostics. As tuberculosis has re-emerged in the US as a serious health threat, the company has improved its TB detection and drug resistance test systems (BACTEC 460 TB), which reduce testing time from 5–7 weeks to less than 2 weeks. The US Centers for Disease Control recommended this methodology of TB testing as the method of choice for detection.

In June 1994, after 18 years with Becton, Dickinson, chairman and CEO Raymond Gilmartin jumped ship to take the helm at Merck, then the world's #1 drug company.

The company signed a letter of intent to form a joint venture with Suzhou Pharmaceutical General in China. The venture, effected through Becton's Singapore subsidiary, will make various medication delivery devices for the region beginning in 1996.

NYSE symbol: BDX
Fiscal year ends: September 30

WHO

Chairman, President, and CEO: Clateo Castellini, age 59, $756,042 pay
VC and General Counsel: John W. Galiardo, age 60, $508,375 pay
Sector President, Infectious Disease Diagnostics: Walter M. Miller, age 51, $481,667 pay
Sector President, Drug Delivery: Mark C. Throdahl, age 43
Sector President, Technique Products: Vincent L. De Caprio, age 44
Sector President, Cellular Analysis Diagnostics: Kenneth R. Weisshaar, age 44
VP Strategic Management: E. Ralph Biggadike
VP Finance and Controller: William L. Nichols, age 41
VP Taxes: Mark H. Borofsky
VP R&D: Donald S. Hetzel
VP and Secretary: Raymond P. Ohlmuller
VP Medical Affairs: Thomas A. Reichert
VP Human Resources: Rosemary Mede
Chief Information Officer: Alfred J. Battaglia
Auditors: Ernst & Young LLP

WHERE

HQ: One Becton Dr., Franklin Lakes, NJ 07417-1880
Phone: 201-847-6800
Fax: 201-847-6475

	1994 Sales		1994 Operating Income	
	$ mil.	% of total	$ mil.	% of total
US	1,423	55	264	69
Europe	704	28	82	21
Other regions	432	17	39	10
Adjustments	—	—	(89)	—
Total	**2,559**	**100**	**296**	**100**

WHAT

	1994 Sales		1994 Operating Income	
	$ mil.	% of total	$ mil.	% of total
Medical Supplies & Devices	1,421	56	274	71
Diagnostic Systems	1,138	44	111	29
Adjustments	—	—	(89)	—
Total	**2,559**	**100**	**296**	**100**

Selected Medical Supplies and Devices
Acute care/surgical products
Diabetes care products
Drug infusion systems
Elastic support products
General hospital and consumer supplies
Hypodermic products
Pharmaceutical systems
Thermometers
Vascular access/specialty needles

Selected Diagnostic Systems
Blood collection products
Cellular analysis equipment
Hematology instruments
Immunodiagnostic test kits
Real-time diagnosis products
Tissue culture labware

KEY COMPETITORS

Abbott Labs	Johnson & Johnson
ALZA	Medtronic
American Home Products	Merck
Ballard Medical	Mitek Surgical
Baxter	Novo Nordisk
Bristol-Myers Squibb	Pfizer
Cordis	PPG
C. R. Bard	St. Jude Medical
Diagnostic Products	SCIMED Life
EG&G	Siemens
Eli Lilly	U.S. Surgical
Hewlett-Packard	Vital Signs

HOW MUCH

	9-Year Growth	1985	1986	1987	1988	1989	1990	1991	1992	1993	1994
Sales ($ mil.)	9.4%	1,144	1,312	1,582	1,709	1,812	2,013	2,172	2,365	2,465	2,559
Net income ($ mil.)	11.1%	88	112	142	162	169	182	190	201	213	227
Income as % of sales	—	7.7%	8.5%	9.0%	9.5%	9.3%	9.1%	8.7%	8.5%	8.6%	8.9%
Earnings per share ($)	12.6%	1.05	1.31	1.71	2.01	2.14	2.34	2.43	2.58	2.71	3.05
Stock price – high ($)	—	16.50	30.63	34.50	31.06	31.13	38.38	40.75	42.06	40.75	49.88
Stock price – low ($)	—	9.88	15.47	21.13	23.25	24.19	27.88	29.00	32.19	32.63	34.00
Stock price – close ($)	13.4%	15.50	25.00	25.50	26.00	30.94	37.25	34.25	39.31	35.75	48.00
P/E – high	—	16	23	20	16	15	16	17	16	15	16
P/E – low	—	9	12	12	12	11	12	12	13	12	11
Dividends per share ($)	10.6%	0.30	0.33	0.37	0.43	0.50	0.54	0.58	0.60	0.66	0.74
Book value per share ($)	10.7%	8.45	9.81	10.37	11.88	13.53	15.68	17.34	20.22	18.72	21.08
Employees	1.1%	16,900	19,300	19,900	20,600	18,800	18,500	18,600	19,100	19,000	18,600

1994 Year-end:
Debt ratio: 36.2%
Return on equity: 15.4%
Cash (mil.): $179
Current ratio: 1.96
Long-term debt (mil.): $669
No. of shares (mil.): 70.3
Dividends
  Yield: 1.5%
  Payout: 24.3%
Market value (mil.): $3,373

Stock Price History
High/Low 1985–94

BELL ATLANTIC CORPORATION

OVERVIEW

Bell Atlantic continues to pursue other lines of communication with its customers, but it has put on hold its ambitious plans to provide them with interactive video services. Based in Philadelphia, Bell Atlantic provides local telephone service to a 6-state area (plus the District of Columbia) with approximately 11 million households. Bell Atlantic has formed 2 partnerships with NYNEX, U S WEST, and AirTouch Communications. PCS PrimeCo, the first partnership, successfully acquired licenses for personal communications services (PCS) in 11 markets. Following the merger of Bell Atlantic's and NYNEX's cellular telephone operations, the company plans to form a partnership with these companies to develop a national wireless company.

Bell Atlantic has requested a suspension of its application with the FCC to offer video services and plans to re-examine its technical strategy to upgrade its telephone network. This request followed a decision by Bell Atlantic to cancel, because of concerns over project control, its agreement with AT&T as the primary contractor to build its interactive video network. Despite these events, Bell Atlantic continues to pursue other avenues for distributing TV programming. Along with NYNEX, Bell Atlantic plans to invest $100 million in a wireless cable company called CAI Wireless that would enable Bell Atlantic to offer video programming by 1996.

Bell Atlantic has increased its involvement in the international telecommunications marketplace by forming a joint venture, InfoStrada SpA, with Olivetti to offer telecommunications services to business customers in Italy. Bell Atlantic owns 33% of the venture.

WHEN

Bell Atlantic's current telephone operations are rooted in the AT&T/Bell System, which began in the 1870s. After 1900, local telephone traffic and service quality grew steadily until the Depression. Following WWII, telephone traffic continued to increase. Local telephone service is now a mature market with a relatively slow growth rate.

In 1984 Bell Atlantic was spun off from AT&T in a now-historic antitrust settlement. The settlement gave Bell Atlantic local phone service rights in 6 states and Washington, DC; Bell Atlantic Mobile Systems (cellular service); and 1/7 of the R&D subsidiary, Bell Communications Research, jointly owned by the 7 regional Bell operating companies (RBOC).

Given the maturity of local telephone services, Bell Atlantic pursued growth opportunities in nonregulated services such as its cellular and paging operations, electronic mail and other on-line services, directory publishing, and sales of computer and office supplies via catalog. Bell Atlantic also invested heavily in data transport markets to supplement existing voice services. The company introduced a data network known as PDN (1986); began testing integrated voice/data network services known as ISDN (1987); bought 3 computer-maintenance vendors (by 1987); acquired ESS (1986), a computer parts sales-and-repair organization; and bought computer parts distributor Camex (1987). Yet Bell Atlantic did not ignore its mainstream revenue base. It introduced new custom-calling features to residences in 1987. The company began testing service delivery through fiber-optic cable in Virginia in 1990.

The company also expanded internationally. Bell Atlantic assisted in a modernization program for Spain's telephone network in 1988. In 1990 Bell Atlantic was selected, along with Ameritech, to buy New Zealand's public phone system for about $2.5 billion. In 1991 Bell Atlantic, along with U S WEST, began offering cellular services in 3 Czechoslovak cities. In 1992 the company acquired Metro Mobile, at the time the 2nd biggest independent cellular radio telecommunications provider in the US. The acquisition gave Bell Atlantic the most extensive cellular phone coverage on the East Coast.

In 1993 Bell Atlantic bought 23% of Grupo Iusacell (Mexico) and joined 4 other RBOCs in a petition to the FCC to allow them to offer long distance services.

In 1994 the company announced plans to wire 8 million homes for interactive TV by 1998; agreed to work with Oracle to create Stargazer, an interactive shopping, entertainment, and information service; and received FCC approval to offer interactive TV to 38,000 homes in New Jersey. In late 1994 Bell Atlantic canceled its planned acquisition of Tele-Communications (TCI), the largest cable company in the US, because of cable rate reductions required by the FCC.

In 1995 Bell Atlantic, along with the other 6 RBOCs, announced plans to sell Bell Communications Research (BellCore), its jointly owned research lab.

WHO

Chairman and CEO: Raymond W. Smith, age 57, $1,609,900 pay
VC: James G. Cullen, age 52, $768,200 pay
VC: Lawrence T. Babbio Jr., age 50, $594,000 pay
Group President Large Business and Information Services, Bell Atlantic Network Services, Inc.: Stuart C. Johnson, age 52, $554,900 pay
Group President Consumer and Small Business Services, Bell Atlantic Network Services, Inc.: Bruce S. Gordon, age 49
EVP and CFO: William O. Albertini, age 51, $549,200 pay
VP Strategic Planning: Joseph T. Ambrozy, age 55
VP Corporate Secretary and Counsel: P. Alan Bulliner, age 51
VP Finance, Controller, and Treasurer: Barbara L. Connor, age 44
VP Corporate Cost Reduction: Charles W. Crist Jr., age 51
SVP Corporate Resources and Performance Assurance: John F. Gamba, age 56
VP Mergers and Acquisitions and Associate General Counsel: Thomas R. McKeough, age 48
VP Corporate Development: Brian D. Oliver, age 39
VP General Counsel: James R. Young, age 43
VP Human Resources: Kevin Pennington
Auditors: Coopers & Lybrand L.L.P.

WHERE

HQ: 1717 Arch St., Philadelphia, PA 19103
Phone: 215-963-6000
Fax: 215-963-6470 (Investor Relations)

Bell Atlantic provides local telephone services in Delaware, Maryland, New Jersey, Pennsylvania, Virginia, Washington, D.C., and West Virginia and cellular services in many metropolitan and rural areas of the United States.

WHAT

	1994 Sales	
	$ mil.	% of total
Transport services	9,106	66
Ancillary services	1,524	11
Value-added services	1,284	9
Wireless services	1,060	8
Other services	817	6
Total	**13,791**	**100**

Major Subsidiaries and Affiliates
Bell Atlantic Business Systems Services, Inc.
Bell Atlantic - Delaware, Inc.
Bell Atlantic International, Inc.
  Grupo Iusacell, SA de CV (42%)
  Infostrada SpA (33%)
  Telecom Corporation of New Zealand Ltd. (24.5%)
Bell Atlantic - Maryland, Inc.
Bell Atlantic Mobile
Bell Atlantic - New Jersey, Inc.
Bell Atlantic Paging, Inc.
Bell Atlantic - Pennsylvania, Inc.
Bell Atlantic - Virginia, Inc.
Bell Atlantic - Washington, D.C., Inc.
Bell Atlantic - West Virginia, Inc.
Bell Communications Research, Inc. (1/7)

KEY COMPETITORS

Ameritech	R. R. Donnelley
AT&T	SBC Communications
BellSouth	Sprint
Cable & Wireless	TCI International
EDS	Telephone and
GTE	Data Systems
MCI	Time Warner
MFS Communications	U.S. Long Distance
NYNEX	U S WEST
Pacific Telesis	WorldCom

HOW MUCH

	9-Year Growth	1985	1986	1987	1988	1989	1990	1991	1992	1993	1994
Sales ($ mil.)	4.7%	9,084	9,921	10,298	10,880	11,449	12,298	12,280	12,647	12,990	13,791
Net income ($ mil.)	2.8%	1,093	1,167	1,240	1,317	1,075	1,313	1,332	1,382	1,423	1,402
Income as % of sales	—	12.0%	11.8%	12.0%	12.1%	9.4%	10.7%	10.8%	10.9%	11.4%	10.2%
Earnings per share ($)	1.8%	2.74	2.93	3.12	3.33	2.72	3.38	3.41	3.23	3.23	3.21
Stock price – high ($)	—	26.84	38.50	39.88	37.25	56.13	57.13	54.13	53.88	69.13	59.63
Stock price – low ($)	—	19.44	25.00	30.25	31.13	34.69	39.50	43.00	40.25	49.63	48.38
Stock price – close ($)	7.2%	26.63	33.75	32.50	35.56	55.63	53.63	48.25	51.25	59.25	49.75
P/E – high	—	10	13	13	11	21	17	16	17	20	19
P/E – low	—	7	9	10	9	13	12	13	13	15	15
Dividends per share ($)	5.6%	1.68	1.78	1.89	2.01	2.16	2.32	2.48	2.58	2.66	2.74
Book value per share ($)	(3.8%)	19.83	20.83	22.07	23.29	21.78	22.71	19.77	18.01	18.85	13.94
Employees	(1.0%)	79,285	80,185	80,950	81,000	79,100	81,600	75,700	71,400	73,600	72,300

1994 Year-end:
Debt ratio: 59.1%
Return on equity: 19.6%
Cash (mil.): $143
Current ratio: 0.68
Long-term debt (mil.): $6,806
No. of shares (mil.): 436
Dividends
  Yield: 5.5%
  Payout: 85.4%
Market value (mil.): $21,700

**Stock Price History
High/Low 1985–94**

BELLSOUTH CORPORATION

OVERVIEW

BellSouth continues to invest large amounts of money on the future of wireless communications. With its cumulative investment of $500 million, BellSouth has had both positive and negative results. Its cellular and paging businesses rank 2nd in the nation with 2.2 million and 1.4 million customers, respectively. However, besides its paging business, BellSouth's foray into wireless data services, including its RAM Mobile Data and Cellular Data services, has yet to bear fruit.

Atlanta-based BellSouth's strategy is to buy large segments of the radio spectrum and offer a wide array of wireless communication services. As the highest bidder ($47.5 million) in the FCC auction of the broad-band radio spectrum, BellSouth is planning to build one of the first personal communications systems in the US with Northern Telecom.

BellSouth is also forming ventures to provide applications and hardware for its data services. BellSouth is working with Lotus, Microsoft, and Oracle to develop e-mail and database products. A phone/computer product called Simon (jointly developed with IBM) is another example of its efforts.

Along with Walt Disney, Ameritech, and SBC Communications, BellSouth is also planning to develop and deliver interactive video programming to consumers.

WHEN

In the beginning, executives of Boston-based National Bell struggled as they tried to market Alexander Graham Bell's telephone throughout the nation. In 1878 general manager Theodore Vail recruited agent James Merrill Ormes to target the South. Ormes created Bell exchanges throughout the region, but growth was hampered by competition with Western Union. In 1879 Ormes hammered out an agreement with Western Union that ended telephone competition in the South and created Southern Bell Telephone and Telegraph. Western Union dropped its own telephone enterprise in exchange for a controlling interest in Southern Bell, and National Bell granted a license for the use of telephones. The agreement was the forerunner of a nationwide truce between National Bell and Western Union.

In the 1890s, after the Bell organization had acquired controlling interest in Southern Bell, Bell's original telephone patents expired, and a slew of competitors entered the business. Southern Bell president Edward Hall upgraded quality, undercut competition, and, when necessary, bought out rivals.

In 1912 the Atlanta-based company relinquished its Virginia and West Virginia territory, and AT&T arranged Southern Bell's merger with Cumberland Telephone and Telegraph, which served Kentucky, Louisiana, Mississippi, Tennessee, and parts of Illinois and Indiana. Illinois and Indiana franchises were later redistributed within the Bell system. Revenues fell during the Depression, but growth resumed in the post-WWII boom.

In 1957 Southern Bell was structured into 2 divisions, a prelude to the 1968 split of the company into Birmingham-based South Central Bell (Alabama, Kentucky, Louisiana, Mississippi, and Tennessee) and Atlanta-based Southern Bell (Florida, Georgia, North Carolina, and South Carolina). The division was short-lived. The 1982 settlement in the landmark antitrust case required AT&T to spin off 7 regional holding companies in 1984. BellSouth, reuniting Southern Bell and South Central Bell, was the largest.

BellSouth bought L. M. Berry, a directory publisher (1986), and MCCA, a paging and mobile communications firm (1989). In 1990 it agreed to buy Graphic Scanning Corp. (cellular, paging). Its bid for LIN Broadcasting, with extensive cellular telephone holdings, was thwarted by McCaw Cellular in 1989, but BellSouth bought 18 midwestern cellular systems from McCaw in 1991. Later in 1991 the company agreed to form a venture with RAM Broadcasting to provide wireless data network services in the US and abroad.

In 1993 the company announced plans to invest $250 million in Las Vegas–based cable operator Prime Management, while in 1994 BellSouth continued its overseas investments with the approval to provide long distance services in Chile. BellSouth also posted record revenues and earnings of $16.8 billion and $2.2 billion, respectively, in 1994.

BellSouth, which had already planned to slash its workforce by 5,000 during 1995, announced in mid-year that it would make another 9,000 to 11,000 cuts in the next 2 years.

NYSE symbol: BLS
Fiscal year ends: December 31

WHO

Chairman, President, and CEO: John L. Clendenin, age 60, $1,468,900 pay
VC and COO: F. Duane Ackerman, age 52, $851,500 pay (prior to promotion)
EVP and General Counsel: Walter H. Alford, age 56, $587,200 pay
EVP Corporate Relations: H. C. Henry Jr., age 50, $538,800 pay
President, BellSouth Enterprises, Inc.: Earle Mauldin, age 54, $517,500 pay (prior to promotion)
President and CEO, BellSouth Telecommunications, Inc.: Jere A. Drummond, age 55
President, International: Charles C. Miller III, age 42
SVP Strategic Planning: C. Sidney Boren, age 51
VP, CFO, and Comptroller: Ronald M. Dykes, age 48
VP Corporate Development: Mark L. Feidler, age 38
VP and Associate General Counsel: John F. Beasley, age 55
VP Corporate Responsibility and Compliance: J. Robert Fitzgerald, age 55
VP Governmental Affairs: David J. Markey, age 54
VP, Secretary, and Treasurer: Arlen G. Yokley, age 57
Director Human Resources: Laura Walker
Auditors: Coopers & Lybrand L.L.P.

WHERE

HQ: 1155 Peachtree St. NE, Atlanta, GA 30309-3610
Phone: 404-249-2000
Fax: 404-249-5599

BellSouth Telecommunications provides services in Alabama, Florida, Georgia, Kentucky, Louisiana, Mississippi, North Carolina, South Carolina, and Tennessee.

WHAT

	1994 Sales	
	$ mil.	% of total
Local service	6,863	41
Interstate access	3,127	19
Wireless communications	2,067	12
Directory advertising & publishing	1,556	9
Tolls	1,190	7
Intrastate access	908	5
Other services	1,134	7
Total	**16,845**	**100**

BellSouth Enterprises, Inc.
Broad-band services
Directory advertising and publishing
Domestic cellular operations
Equipment sales, leasing, and maintenance
International cellular operations
Mobile data communications
Paging operations
Personal communications services

KEY COMPETITORS

American Business Information
Ameritech
AT&T
Bell Atlantic
Century Telephone
Comcast
Contel Cellular
GTE
IBM
MCI
MFS Communications
Motorola
Nextel
NYNEX
Pacific Telesis
R. R. Donnelley
SBC Communications
Sprint
TCI Intl.
Telephone and Data Systems
Time Warner
U.S. Long Distance
U S WEST
Viacom
WorldCom

HOW MUCH

	9-Year Growth	1985	1986	1987	1988	1989	1990	1991	1992	1993	1994
Sales ($ mil.)	4.6%	11,273	12,086	12,950	10,532	13,996	14,345	14,446	15,202	15,880	16,845
Net income ($ mil.)	4.8%	1,418	1,589	1,665	1,666	1,695	1,632	1,507	1,658	1,034	2,160
Income as % of sales	—	12.6%	13.1%	12.9%	15.8%	12.1%	11.4%	10.4%	10.9%	6.5%	12.8%
Earnings per share ($)	3.7%	3.13	3.38	3.46	3.51	3.55	3.38	3.11	3.38	2.08	4.35
Stock price – high ($)	—	32.84	46.03	44.28	43.88	58.13	59.25	55.00	55.50	63.88	63.50
Stock price – low ($)	—	21.59	30.00	28.75	35.75	39.00	49.00	45.38	43.38	50.38	50.50
Stock price – close ($)	5.8%	32.69	38.53	36.38	39.88	57.88	54.75	51.75	51.38	58.00	54.13
P/E – high	—	11	14	13	13	16	18	18	16	31	15
P/E – low	—	7	9	8	10	11	15	15	13	24	12
Dividends per share ($)	4.7%	1.83	1.99	2.16	2.32	2.48	2.64	2.74	2.76	2.76	2.76
Book value per share ($)	2.5%	23.09	23.84	25.13	26.78	27.21	26.28	27.01	28.03	27.20	28.95
Employees	(0.1%)	92,500	96,900	98,700	100,300	101,230	101,945	96,084	97,112	95,084	92,100

1994 Year-end:
Debt ratio: 39.7%
Return on equity: 15.5%
Cash (mil.): $607
Current ratio: 0.73
Long-term debt (mil.): $7,435
No. of shares (mil.): 496
Dividends
  Yield: 5.1%
  Payout: 63.4%
Market value (mil.): $26,862

Stock Price History
High/Low 1985–94

BERGEN BRUNSWIG CORPORATION

OVERVIEW

Pharmaceutical distributor Bergen Brunswig stocks about 19% of the nation's medicine cabinets (2nd only to McKesson), including those of Columbia/HCA, the biggest hospital chain in the US. The Orange, California–based company's freshly inked contracts with Columbia, Safeway, and other major customers promise Bergen $5 billion in business over the next 5 years — a prescription for continued corporate health.

Bergen gets 51% of its sales from hospitals and other managed care facilities, with the remainder coming from retail outlets such as chain drug stores and independent pharmacies. Two particular areas of sales growth for Bergen are generic prescription drugs and medical-surgical products, both of which offer higher margins than do name-brand prescription medications.

The company distributes its products from 33 locations in 23 states but is increasingly emphasizing highly automated regional distribution; an 8th regional facility opened in 1995 near Boston. Bergen expects AccuSource, an electronic drug information, ordering, and distribution system it developed with Apple Computer, to be used by 5,000 retail pharmacies by the end of 1995.

A rumored takeover bid for Bergen Brunswig by Cardinal Health, the nation's #3 drug distributor, boosted Bergen's stock in 1995. However, industry analysts expected that antitrust concerns would keep such a deal from materializing.

WHEN

Doctor's son and Frenchman Lucien Napoleon Brunswig immigrated to America in 1871 to seek his fortune. He opened a drugstore 4 years later, followed by another in Fort Worth, Texas, which was so successful that he was offered a job at a New Orleans–based wholesale drug company in 1882. Brunswig took over in 1885 upon his boss's death.

Several years later Brunswig expanded the company westward to Los Angeles. He moved there in 1903, and in 1907 he renamed the business Brunswig Drug Company. Lucien Brunswig died in 1943, but the company continued to grow.

Brunswig Drug merged with New Jersey's Bergen Drug Company in 1969, forming Bergen Brunswig Corporation. Bergen had been founded in Hackensack in 1947 by Emil Martini (and named after the county in which it was headquartered). Emil Jr. took the helm after his father's death in 1956.

In the 1970s Bergen acquired a large number of businesses and pioneered the use of automated order-entry systems. Between 1975 and 1990 sales per employee skyrocketed from $200,000 to $1.6 million. In the 1980s these advances and an aging population spurred tremendous growth. The company diversified into videocassette distribution in 1982 with the purchase of Commtron. In 1986 Bergen began replacing and consolidating outdated distribution centers with state-of-the-art automated facilities. In 1988 and 1989 Bergen introduced 2 advanced order-entry systems.

A stock recapitalization plan, which eventually left control of the company in the public's hands, was implemented in 1989, and the Martinis saw their voting stake fall to about 13%. Also that year Bergen unveiled an ad campaign for pharmacies associated with its Good Neighbor Pharmacy program, which gives independent pharmacists the buying power of a chain. By 1990 about 900 pharmacies had joined the program; enrollment is now 3,000.

By 1991 the company had captured about 16% of the US pharmaceutical products distribution market. In 1992 Emil Martini, who had been running the company for 36 years, died. His brother Robert, a pharmacist, took over.

Bergen sold its videocassette wholesaler, Commtron, to Ingram Industries in 1992 and agreed to buy Healthcare Distributors of Indiana. A bidding war with Cardinal Distribution (now Cardinal Health) for Durr-Fillauer Medical ended in Bergen's favor in 1992. Bergen paid $406 million for the company.

In 1994 Bergen announced the formation of the Managed Care Access Alliance with Pharmaceutical Care Network, which seeks to give retail pharmacies improved access to health insurance plans. Bergen also signed a 5-year, exclusive supplier contract with ShopKo, which has 122 stores in 15 states, and received 6 drug contracts from the Department of Defense. In 1995 the company bought Biddle & Crowther, a medical-surgical supplies distributor, which gave Bergen an entry into the Alaskan market.

Bergen's directors responded to rumors of a hostile takeover attempt by rival Cardinal Health in 1995 by altering the corporate bylaws to give the company more time to react to and discourage such an effort.

NYSE symbol: BBC
Fiscal year ends: September 30

WHO

Chairman and CEO: Robert E. Martini, age 62,
$884,808 pay
President and COO: Dwight A. Steffensen, age 51,
$699,808 pay
EVP and CFO: Neil F. Dimick, age 45, $408,654 pay
EVP Supplier Relations and Operations: Phillip R.
Engle, age 54, $374,231 pay
EVP, Chief Legal Officer, and Secretary: Milan A.
Sawdei, age 48, $265,478 pay
EVP and Chief Information Officer: Denny W. Steele,
age 51
EVP Sales and Marketing: Michael J. Quinn
EVP Distribution Technology: James L. Cody
EVP Human Resources: Carol E. Scherman
VP and Controller: John P. Naughton, age 56
Auditors: Deloitte & Touche LLP

WHERE

HQ: 4000 Metropolitan Dr., Orange, CA 92668-3510
Phone: 714-385-4000
Fax: 714-385-1442

Bergen Brunswig ships pharmaceutical products from
33 locations in 23 states to 13,000 customers (hospital
pharmacies, managed care facilities, health maintenance
organizations [HMOs], independent retail pharmacies,
pharmacy chains, food retailers, and other retailers) in
more than 44 states, Guam, and Mexico.

WHAT

	1994 Sales
	% of total
Managed care	51
Retail	49
Total	**100**

Products Distributed
Cosmetics
Home health care supplies and equipment
Personal health products
Pharmaceuticals
Proprietary medicines
Sundries
Toiletries

Services
Advertising
Delivery
Information
In-store merchandising programs
Inventory management
Marketing assistance
Order-entry systems
Pharmacy computers
Point-of-sale systems
Private-label products
Promotion
Shelf management systems

Selected Subsidiaries
Biddle & Crowther Co.
Durr Medical Corp.
Professional Medical Supply Co.
Southeastern Hospital Supply Corp.

KEY COMPETITORS

Affiliated Foods	McKesson
AmeriSource	Merck
Behrens	Moore Medical
Bindley Western	Owens & Minor
Cardinal Health	Physician Sales
Core-Mark	& Service
D & K Wholesale	Quality King
FoxMeyer Health	Russ Berrie
Gulf South Medical Supply	Topco Associates

HOW MUCH

	9-Year Growth	1985	1986	1987	1988	1989	1990	1991	1992	1993	1994[1]
Sales ($ mil.)	13.3%	2,435	3,066	3,376	3,486	3,923	4,442	4,838	5,048	6,824	7,484
Net income ($ mil.)	9.8%	24	21	16	33	48	63	64	57	29	56
Income as % of sales	—	1.0%	0.7%	0.5%	0.9%	1.2%	1.4%	1.3%	1.1%	0.4%	0.7%
Earnings per share ($)	6.7%	0.85	0.70	0.56	1.04	1.33	1.40	1.44	1.44	0.79	1.52
Stock price – high ($)	—	14.53	17.40	12.85	15.75	21.80	23.70	26.20	22.25	24.38	20.88
Stock price – low ($)	—	9.73	7.65	6.73	9.00	14.40	16.40	16.00	16.63	14.13	13.75
Stock price – close ($)	4.3%	14.25	9.65	9.40	14.65	19.50	22.90	18.50	22.13	17.88	20.88
P/E – high	—	17	25	23	15	16	17	18	16	31	14
P/E – low	—	11	11	12	9	11	12	11	12	18	9
Dividends per share ($)	16.7%	0.14	0.14	0.14	0.17	0.22	0.27	0.32	0.40	0.40	0.56
Book value per share ($)	9.2%	5.64	6.23	6.60	7.67	9.43	10.72	10.76	11.32	11.74	12.41
Employees	0.7%	4,000	4,300	4,000	3,600	3,600	3,800	3,700	3,500	4,250	4,250

1994 Year-end:
Debt ratio: 41.1%
Return on equity: 12.8%
Cash (mil.): $5
Current ratio: 1.21
Long-term debt (mil.): $321
No. of shares (mil.): 37
Dividends
  Yield: 2.7%
  Payout: 36.8%
Market value (mil.): $777

Stock Price History
High/Low 1985–94

[1] 13-month fiscal year

BERKSHIRE HATHAWAY INC.

OVERVIEW

Based in Omaha, Berkshire Hathaway is a holding company and investment vehicle for the 2nd-richest man in the world — Warren Buffett. According to *Forbes*, Buffett is worth an estimated $10.7 billion (preceded only by Bill Gates of Microsoft). Buffett is a legend among many investors for his folksy behavior. Although he owns a 41% ($10 billion) stake in Berkshire, Buffett draws an annual salary of just $100,000 as chairman and CEO.

Berkshire operates its property and casualty insurance and reinsurance business through 13 subsidiaries, including National Indemnity and Cypress Insurance. Equity investments held by these subsidiaries include Capital Cities/ABC (13%), Coca-Cola (8%), and Gillette (11%). Berkshire also oversees a diverse array of businesses, including publishing (*Buffalo News* and

World Book), shoes (H. H. Brown, Lowell, and Dexter), and candy (See's Candies).

Although Berkshire's investments performed better than the overall market in 1994, all did not go exactly Buffett's way. He has admitted that his $358 million investment in USAir (written down to $89.5 million) was a mistake. Buffett is also facing difficulties with the $1 billion investment in Salomon, the parent of troubled Salomon Brothers investment bank.

In 1995 Berkshire agreed to pay $2.3 billion for the 49% of auto insurer GEICO it didn't already own. Also in 1995 Berkshire invested over $350 million for a 4.9% stake in Gannett, the publisher of *USA TODAY*. To date, the company has also accumulated a 9.8% stake in American Express ($1.6 billion) and an 8.3% share of PNC Bank ($504 million).

WHEN

Warren Buffett began his career at age 11 by purchasing 3 shares of Cities Service. In the 1950s Buffett attended Columbia to study under famed value investor Benjamin Graham. Buffett absorbed the master's teachings: Use quantitative analysis to discover companies whose intrinsic worth exceeds their stock prices; popularity is irrelevant; and the market will eventually vindicate the patient investor.

In 1956 Buffett, then 25, founded Buffett Partnership, Ltd. The $105,000 in initial assets grew quickly, making possible such bargain purchases as Berkshire Hathaway (textiles, 1965) and National Indemnity (insurance, 1967). Believing that stocks were overvalued, Buffett dissolved the partnership (1969); the initial value per share had grown thirtyfold, and net assets were over $100 million.

Buffett had become disenchanted with businesses with intrinsically poor economics (like textile albatross Berkshire Hathaway, closed in 1985). He adopted the Berkshire name for his new investment firm and began searching for solid businesses with strong management. In 1972 Berkshire bought See's Candies; between 1976 and 1981 Berkshire invested $45 million in GEICO (worth more than $1.9 million in mid-1995).

Buffett liked media-based companies that capital-intensive industries (e.g., car and chemical manufacturers) needed as advertising conduits. During the stock market slump of 1973 and 1974, Buffett bought stakes in advertising agencies (Interpublic, Ogilvy & Mather) and newspapers (*Washington Post*,

Boston Globe), followed by the *Buffalo News* (1977) and Capital Cities/ABC (1985).

In the 1980s Berkshire bought majority interests in Nebraska Furniture Mart (1983) and Fechheimer Brothers (uniform makers, 1986) and full ownership of Scott Fetzer (*World Book* encyclopedias and Kirby vacuum cleaners, 1986). Berkshire sold its stake in the *Boston Globe* in 1986 and spent billions to buy holdings in Salomon (investment banking, 1987), Gillette (1989), USAir Group (1989), Champion International (1990), and American Express (1991).

Berkshire bought RJR Nabisco junk bonds (1989–90) and stakes in Coca-Cola (1988–89), Borsheim's jewelry store (1989), Wells Fargo (1989–91), and General Dynamics (1992). In 1991 Berkshire acquired H. H. Brown Shoe Company, the leading North American shoe manufacturer, which in turn purchased Lowell Shoe Company. The next year Berkshire bought 82% of Central States Indemnity, a credit insurance company. In 1993 Berkshire received FTC permission to raise its stake in Salomon to 25%. Also in 1993 Berkshire expanded its shoe operations by purchasing Dexter Shoe in a stock swap.

In 1995 Berkshire purchased and merged R.C. Willey Home Furnishings and Helzberg's Diamond Shops into the company. R.C. Willey is a furniture retailer with 7 stores in Utah. Helzberg's operates 148 jewelry stores in 23 states. Berkshire also bought stakes in Suntrust Banks, Federal National Mortgage Association, and First Interstate Bancorp.

NYSE symbol: BRK
Fiscal year ends: December 31

WHO

Chairman and CEO: Warren E. Buffett, age 64,
$100,000 pay
VC: Charles T. Munger, age 71, $100,000 pay
VP and CFO: Marc D. Hamburg, age 45, $205,000 pay
Secretary: Forrest N. Krutter
Auditors: Deloitte & Touche LLP

WHERE

HQ: 1440 Kiewit Plaza, Omaha, NE 68131
Phone: 402-346-1400
Fax: 402-536-3030

Berkshire Hathaway is a holding company owning
subsidiaries engaged in diverse business activities, most
importantly insurance and investing activities conducted
primarily in the US.

WHAT

	1994 Sales $ mil.	1994 Sales % of total	1994 Operating Income $ mil.	1994 Operating Income % of total
Insurance	1,437	37	639	70
Shoes	609	16	76	8
Home furnishings	245	6	17	2
Candy	216	6	47	5
Home cleaning systems	208	5	44	5
Encyclopedias & reference materials	191	5	24	3
Newspaper	151	4	54	6
Uniform mfg. & distribution	151	4	13	1
Other	639	17	(192)	—
Adjustments	—	—	(60)	—
Total	**3,847**	**100**	**662**	**100**

Insurance
Central States Indemnity (82%)
National Indemnity Co.

Selected Operations
Adalet (conduit fittings)
Berkshire Hathaway Credit Corp.
BHR (real estate)
Blue Chip Stamps
Borsheim's (85%, jewelry)
Buffalo News (daily newspaper)
Dexter Shoe Co.
Fechheimer Bros. Co. (uniforms)
France (appliance controls)
GEICO Corp.
Halex (electrical fittings)
Helzberg's Diamond Shops Inc.
H. H. Brown Shoe Co.
Kirby (home cleaning systems)
Lowell Shoe, Inc.
Nebraska Furniture Mart
Northland (fractional horsepower motors)
Precision (steel service center)
Quikut (cutlery)
R.C. Willey Home Furnishings
Scott Fetzer Financial Group (consumer finance)
ScottCare (cardiopulmonary rehabilitation equipment)
See's Candies
Wayne (furnace burners and pumps)
Wesco Financial Insurance Co.
World Book (encyclopedias)

Major Equity Investments
American Express (9.8%)
Capital Cities/ABC (13.0%)
Coca-Cola (7.8%)
Federal Home Loan Mortgage Corp. (6.3%)
Gannett Co. (4.9%)
Gillette (10.8%)
PNC Bank (8.3%)
Washington Post Co. (15.2%)
Wells Fargo & Co. (13.3%)

KEY COMPETITORS

Advance Publications
Allstate
ARAMARK
Brown Group
Cadbury Schweppes
Campbell Soup
CIGNA
Cintas
AB Electrolux
Encyclopædia Britannica
Equitable
Forschner Group
Fred Meyer
Great Western
Hershey
H.F. Ahmanson
Lagardère
Lincoln National
Loews
Mars
Maytag
Merrill Lynch
Nestlé
Nine West
Prudential
Raytheon
Royal Appliance
Tiffany
Timberland
Tootsie Roll
Travelers
V. F.
Wolverine World Wide
Zale

HOW MUCH

	Annual Growth	1985	1986	1987	1988	1989	1990	1991	1992	1993	1994
Sales ($ mil.)	11.3%	1,464	2,452	2,432	2,465	2,484	2,660	3,105	3,029	3,654	3,847
Net income ($ mil.)	1.4%	436	282	235	399	448	394	440	407	759	495
Income as % of sales	—	29.8%	11.5%	9.6%	16.2%	18.0%	14.8%	8.0%	13.4%	20.8%	12.9%
Earnings per share ($)	1.1%	379.99	246.19	204.51	348.23	390.01	344.00	384.00	355.24	656.00	420.00
Stock price – high ($)	—	1,990	3,250	4,250	5,000	8,875	7,425	9,125	11,750	17,800	20,800
Stock price – low ($)	—	1,725	2,220	2,470	3,000	4,625	5,500	6,550	8,575	11,350	15,150
Stock price – close ($)	29.5%	1,990	2,820	2,950	4,700	8,675	6,675	9,050	11,750	16,325	20,400
P/E – high	—	5	13	21	14	23	22	24	33	27	50
P/E – low	—	5	9	12	9	12	16	17	24	17	36
Dividends per share ($)	—	0.00	0.00	0.00	0.00	0.00	0.00	0.00	0.00	0.00	0.00
Book value per share ($)	22.4%	1,639	2,068	2,471	2,965	4,283	4,612	6,440	7,743	8,853	10,083
Employees	1.6%	—	—	—	20,000	20,000	20,000	22,000	22,000	22,000	22,000

1994 Year-end:
Debt ratio: 6.4%
Return on equity: 4.4%
Cash (mil.): $274
Current ratio: —
Long-term debt (mil.): $811
No. of shares (mil.): 1
Dividends
  Yield: —
  Payout: —
Market value (mil.): $24,024

Stock Price History
High/Low 1985–94

BEST BUY CO., INC.

OVERVIEW

Running neck and neck with archrival Circuit City for the title of #1 consumer electronics retailer in the US, Best Buy has grown like a weed the past few years. CEO Richard Schulze has modeled his Eden Prairie, Minnesota–based company's operations on another fast-growing retailer, Arkansas retailing behemoth, Wal-Mart.

Like Wal-Mart, Schulze has focused on keeping prices low by constantly working to improve efficiency. One way he has cut costs is to use salaried (rather than commissioned) salespeople. Best Buy believes its customers don't need a lot of hand-holding (and don't want a lot of sales pressure) when they are shopping. Best Buy's laid-back approach re-

quires fewer employees, cutting payroll costs. However, with the growing importance of computers to its product mix, the company has begun to offer incentives (such as promotions) to employees who sell higher-end PCs. The company hopes the new compensation package will attract a more computer-literate staff.

With same-store sales up nearly 20% in fiscal 1995, Best Buy continues to grow rapidly. The company plans to add 47 new stores in 1995. Looking to stay ahead of the retailing curve, in late 1994 Best Buy introduced the first of its Concept III stores: larger outlets featuring amenities such as interactive answer center kiosks and CD listening posts.

WHEN

Richard Schulze and a partner founded Sound of Music, a home and car stereo store, in Minnesota in 1966. In 1971 Schulze bought out his partner and began to expand the chain.

While chairing a local school board, Schulze saw declining enrollment and realized that his target customer group, 15- to 18-year-old males, was shrinking. In the early 1980s he began to broaden his product line, offering appliances and VCRs and targeting older, more affluent customers. In 1983 he changed the company's name to Best Buy and began to open larger "superstores." The company went public in 1985.

Buoyed by the format change and the fast-rising popularity of the VCR, the company grew rapidly. Between 1984 and 1987 it expanded from 8 stores to 24, and sales jumped from $29 million to $240 million. The next year it opened another 16 stores, and sales jumped by 84%. However, by 1987 Best Buy was beginning to butt heads with a number of other rapidly expanding consumer electronics retailers, and its profits took a beating. Rumors floated that Schulze was considering selling the company to Sears.

Instead, Schulze decided he needed to set his company apart from his competitors. In 1988 he and his managers began to develop a retail concept that was more "consumer driven," based on successful models like Toys "R" Us and the Home Depot.

In 1989 Schulze introduced the Concept II store format. He believed that his customers could buy his products without a lot of sales help. Schulze took sales staff off commission, relieving customers of a salesperson's pressure, and he reduced the number of employees

per store by about 1/3, cutting payroll costs. The new format also allowed customers to buy products in just one step: customers needed only take goods from the aisle to the cash register. The concept proved to be such a hit in Best Buy's home base, Minneapolis–St. Paul, that it drove major competitor Highland Appliance out of town.

While the change proved to be a big hit with customers, many of Best Buy's suppliers were not so happy. Many of its vendors felt their products couldn't be sold without some sales help, and they also didn't like the warehouse atmosphere of the new stores. Mitsubishi, Onkyo, and Harmon/Kardon all pulled their products from company stores. The losses didn't seem to hurt Best Buy, though. The company continued to expand rapidly.

That same year Best Buy entered the competitive Chicago market successfully, with a strong 14-store blitz. In late 1992 the company entered the Houston and Denver markets. With rapid expansion came troubles with distribution. In 1993 the company's Ardmore, Oklahoma, distribution center became overwhelmed trying to keep up with demand from Best Buy's rapidly expanding roster of new stores. To ease the burden, the company nearly doubled the size of the facility.

In 1994 Whirlpool said it would stop selling its higher-priced Whirlpool line of appliances through Best Buy, although it will continue to sell its lower-priced Roper line. Best Buy was also subpoenaed in a Justice Department probe to determine if Whirlpool used cooperative advertising relationships to illegally fix prices. In 1995 Best Buy agreed to sell Cambridge Soundworks's line of stereo speakers.

NYSE symbol: BBY
Fiscal year ends: Saturday nearest the last day in Feb.

WHO

Chairman and CEO: Richard M. Schulze, age 54, $727,528 pay
President and COO: Bradbury H. Anderson, age 46, $548,317 pay
EVP and CFO: Allen U. Lenzmeier, age 51, $421,760 pay
SVP Sales: Wade R. Fenn, age 36, $294,873 pay
SVP Marketing: Lee H. Schoenfeld, age 42, $274,214 pay
VP Human Resources and General Counsel: Joseph M. Joyce
Auditors: Ernst & Young LLP

WHERE

HQ: 7075 Flying Cloud Dr., Eden Prairie, MN 55344
Phone: 612-947-2000
Fax: 612-947-2422

	1995 Stores
	No.
Texas	32
Illinois	31
Minnesota	15
Michigan	14
Ohio	12
Wisconsin	11
Missouri	10
Georgia	9
Indiana	8
Arizona	7
California	7
Colorado	6
Iowa	5
Kansas	5
Virginia	5
Maryland	4
Other states	23
Total	**204**

WHAT

	1995 Sales
	% of total
Home office	37
Video	20
Audio	14
Entertainment software	14
Appliances	8
Other	7
Total	**100**

Selected Products

Home office (answering machines, computers and peripherals, copiers, fax machines, telephones)
Video (camcorders, televisions, VCRs)
Audio (audio systems and components, car stereos, keyboards, mobile electronics, portable audio products)
Entertainment software (audio- and videocassettes, compact discs, computer software)
Appliances (air conditioners, dishwashers, dryers, freezers, microwave ovens, ranges, refrigerators, vacuum cleaners)

KEY COMPETITORS

Blockbuster	Musicland
Camelot	NeoStar
Circuit City	Office Depot
CompuCom	REX Stores
CompUSA	Sears
Dayton Hudson	Staples
Dell	Sun Television & Appliances
Egghead	Tandy
ELEK-TEK	Toys "R" Us
Fretter	Trans World Music
Gateway 2000	Ultimate Electronics
Good Guys	Venture Stores
Kmart	Viking Office Products
Montgomery Ward	Wal-Mart
MTS	Wherehouse Entertainment

HOW MUCH

	9-Year Growth	1986	1987	1988	1989	1990	1991	1992	1993	1994	1995
Sales ($ mil.)	52.6%	113	240	439	507	513	665	930	1,620	3,007	5,080
Net income ($ mil.)	34.6%	4	8	3	2	6	5	10	20	42	58
Income as % of sales	—	3.6%	3.2%	0.6%	0.4%	1.1%	0.7%	1.0%	1.2%	1.4%	1.1%
Earnings per share ($)	21.5%	0.23	0.33	0.12	0.09	0.23	0.19	0.34	0.57	1.01	1.33
Stock price – high ($)[1]	—	3.22	7.15	7.75	5.13	3.84	4.21	11.80	13.34	31.44	45.25
Stock price – low ($)[1]	—	2.11	3.00	1.92	2.21	1.88	1.50	1.75	4.71	10.75	19.00
Stock price – close ($)[1]	28.7%	3.22	5.28	2.75	2.79	2.00	1.88	5.50	13.00	23.25	31.25
P/E – high	—	14	22	64	57	17	22	35	23	31	34
P/E – low	—	5	9	16	25	8	8	5	8	11	14
Dividends per share ($)	—	0.00	0.00	0.00	0.00	0.00	0.00	0.00	0.00	0.00	0.00
Book value per share ($)	31.1%	0.78	2.25	2.36	2.44	2.67	2.28	4.69	5.42	7.46	8.91
Employees	42.5%	1,047	2,200	3,411	3,533	3,900	4,300	5,500	9,600	15,200	25,300

1995 Year-end:
Debt ratio: 46.2%
Return on equity: 16.8%
Cash (mil.): $145
Current ratio: 1.96
Long-term debt (mil.): $227
No. of shares (mil.): 42.2
Dividends
  Yield: —
  Payout: —
Market value (mil.): $1,319

**Stock Price History[1]
High/Low 1986–95**

[1] Stock prices are for the prior calendar year.

BETHLEHEM STEEL CORPORATION

OVERVIEW

Big Steel has made a comeback. In 1994 Bethlehem Steel — the 2nd largest US steel producer (after USX–U.S. Steel), the largest steel supplier to the construction industry, and a major supplier to the automotive industry and railroads — made its first profit in 5 years. Competition in the 1980s from foreign steelmakers and low-cost US minimills forced Bethlehem to pare expenses and employees and concentrate on steelmaking; the company invested over $4 billion to modernize its plants and sold its nonsteel operations. A growing world economy in 1994 helped sales and production to grow 12%, and Bethlehem made an $81 million profit, reversing 1993's

$266 million loss. The company produced 9.8 million tons of steel in 1994 (10% of US production).

Bethlehem has completed an $80 million modernization of its Pennsylvania Steel Technologies division, the US's largest rail producer. Its Sparrows Point and Burns Harbor facilities already are 2 of the world's most efficient steel mills. The company has also changed its product mix. To supply a growing market in light construction, it opened a new steel coating plant in Mississippi in 1994 and announced that its Bethlehem Structural Production division will discontinue iron, steel, and heavy-beam production.

WHEN

Bethlehem Steel began as Saucona Iron in South Bethlehem, Pennsylvania, in 1857, rolling iron railroad rails. It changed its name to Bethlehem Rolling Mills & Iron in 1859, then to Bethlehem Iron in 1861, when it began producing forging for electric generators and armor plate for US navy ships. In 1899 it became Bethlehem Steel.

In the first years of the 20th century, the president of United States Steel, Charles Schwab, personally bought (1901), sold (1902), and again bought (1902) Bethlehem Steel. He then transferred Bethlehem to a new venture, United States Shipbuilding. This venture failed in 1903, and Bethlehem Steel was spun off in 1904 with Schwab as president. Bethlehem's assets then included a steel plant, shipbuilding yards on both US coasts, and iron ore mines in Cuba.

Schwab saw the potential in Henry Grey's one-piece, wide-flange steel beams for building construction and built a structural mill at Saucon, Pennsylvania. He bought Grey's patents and found a commercial market in the construction industry.

In 1912 Schwab bought the Tofo Iron Mines in Chile, a cheap source of superior-grade iron ore. Bethlehem grew with the purchases of Pennsylvania Steel and Maryland Steel in 1916. With shipbuilding facilities, steel manufacturing plants, and good sources of ore and coal, Bethlehem was well prepared for the steel and shipbuilding needs of WWI.

In 1930 Bethlehem bought Pacific Coast Steel as well as Southern California Iron & Steel. In 1931 it entered bridge and building construction by buying the fabricating business of McClintic-Marshall Construction and made the steelwork for structures such as the

Golden Gate Bridge, Rockefeller Center, and the US Supreme Court building. During WWII Bethlehem built 1,121 ships.

In the 1960s Bethlehem developed products such as tin-free steel for cans. In the face of growing US imports in the 1970s and 1980s, Bethlehem reduced production, sold some steel plants, and sold off nonsteel operations that included mines and shipyards. In 1981 the company initiated a major modernization of its steel plants and in 1986 began building new facilities. In 1989 Bethlehem bought an interest in Walbridge Coatings (electro-galvanized, corrosion-resistant steel sheets).

A slimmer Bethlehem faced an industry-wide slump in demand and the recession of 1990–91. The company subsequently sold its Freight Car Division (1991) and a Pennsylvania coal mine (1992) and closed its bar, rod, and wire operations (1992; sold in 1994).

In 1993 Bethlehem and Lafayette Steel formed a joint venture (Precision Blank Welding) to produce steel blanks for creating custom auto parts; in 1994 Precision was chosen by Chrysler as a supplier for its 1995 compacts, Dodge Stratus and Chrysler Cirrus. Also in 1994 Bethlehem announced it would stop producing jumbo steel beams, which it had made since 1908, to focus on a growing market for lighter and smaller beams. Following a price hike by USX–U.S. Steel, Bethlehem raised its steel prices late in the year.

In 1994 Bethlehem teamed up with USX–U.S. Steel to conduct research on basic ironmaking and steelmaking technologies. About 1,850 people will be laid off in 1995 when Bethlehem shuts down the blast furnace at its Bethlehem Structural Products Corp.

NYSE symbol: BS
Fiscal year ends: December 31

WHO

Chairman and CEO: Curtis H. Barnette, age 60,
$671,000 pay
President and COO: Roger P. Penny, age 58,
$555,100 pay
EVP and CFO: Gary L. Millenbruch, age 57,
$488,000 pay
SVP Administration (HR): John A. Jordan Jr., age 59,
$394,267 pay
SVP Commercial: David P. Post, age 61, $329,400 pay
VP Law, General Counsel, and Secretary: William H.
Graham, age 49
VP and Controller: Lonnie A. Arnett, age 49
VP Planning: Carl F. Meitzner, age 55
VP Union Relations: John L. Kluttz, age 52
**Chief Technology Officer and President, Services
Division:** Walter N. Bargeron, age 52
Auditors: Price Waterhouse LLP

WHERE

HQ: 1170 Eighth Ave., Bethlehem, PA 18016-7699
Phone: 610-694-2424
Fax: 610-694-1509

Major Plants
Bethlehem, PA (structural steel shapes, piling)
Burns Harbor, IN (rolled and coated sheet, steel plate)
Sparrows Point, MD (steel plate, rolled sheet, tin plate,
Galvalume sheet)
Steelton, PA (rail products, flat bars, pipe)

Bethlehem owns or operates coal mines and coal
processing plants in Pennsylvania and West Virginia.
The company also owns 5 shortline railroads, 2
shipyards, a flat-bed trucking company, and stakes in 3
iron mines (Minnesota, Canada, and Brazil).

WHAT

	1994 Sales % of total
Sheets & tin mill products	66
Plates	14
Other steel products	12
Other	8
Total	**100**

	1994 Shipments % of total
Service centers, processors & converters	46
Transportation (including automotive)	24
Construction	15
Containers	6
Machinery & other	9
Total	**100**

Steel Operations
Bethlehem Structural Products Corporation
(continuously cast steel)
Double G Coatings Company, LP (joint venture,
galvanized and Galvalume sheets)
Pennsylvania Steel Technologies, Inc. (railroad rails,
specialty blooms, flat bars, and pipe)

Steel-Related Operations
BethForge, Inc. (forgings and castings)
BethShip Division (shipyards and repair facilities)
CENTEC (centrifugally cast rolls)

KEY COMPETITORS

AK Steel	Hyundai	Nippon Steel
Anglo American	Inland Steel	Nucor
Armco	IRI	Oregon Steel
Broken Hill	LTV	Mills
Cargill	Mitsubishi	Thyssen
Fluor	Mitsui	USX–U.S. Steel
Friedrich Krupp	National Steel	Weirton Steel

HOW MUCH

	9-Year Growth	1985	1986	1987	1988	1989	1990	1991	1992	1993	1994
Sales ($ mil.)	(0.7%)	5,118	4,333	4,621	5,489	5,251	4,899	4,318	4,008	4,323	4,819
Net income ($ mil.)	—	(196)	(153)	104	392	246	(464)	(767)	(199)	(266)	81
Income as % of sales	—	—	—	2.2%	7.1%	4.7%	—	—	—	—	1.7%
Earnings per share ($)	—	(4.37)	(3.37)	1.48	4.77	2.86	(6.45)	(10.41)	(2.73)	(3.37)	0.35
Stock price – high ($)	—	21.13	22.00	21.50	25.50	28.50	21.13	18.50	17.25	21.00	24.25
Stock price – low ($)	—	12.50	4.63	6.38	15.25	15.25	10.63	10.75	10.00	12.88	16.25
Stock price – close ($)	1.6%	15.63	6.25	16.75	23.25	18.50	14.75	14.00	16.00	20.38	18.00
P/E – high	—	—	—	15	5	10	—	—	—	—	69
P/E – low	—	—	—	4	3	5	—	—	—	—	46
Dividends per share ($)	(100%)	0.30	0.00	0.00	0.00	0.20	0.40	0.40	0.00	0.00	0.00
Book value per share ($)	(4.1%)	15.13	11.98	14.74	19.59	22.37	15.56	8.71	8.72	7.46	10.39
Employees	(8.6%)	44,500	37,500	34,400	32,900	30,500	29,600	27,500	24,900	20,700	19,900

1994 Year-end:
Debt ratio: 49.8%
Return on equity: 8.8%
Cash (mil.): $160
Current ratio: 1.55
Long-term debt (mil.): $668
No. of shares (mil.): 110
Dividends
Yield: —
Payout: —
Market value (mil.): $1,978

**Stock Price History
High/Low 1985–94**

BEVERLY ENTERPRISES, INC.

OVERVIEW

Coming off the most profitable year in its history, Beverly Enterprises is spinning off one of its best moneymakers. The Fort Smith, Arkansas–based nursing home chain — the largest in the US — plans to set up its Pharmacy Corp. of America (PCA) institutional pharmacy subsidiary as a separate company. The move will allow Beverly to focus more on its 727-unit nursing home business, which has greater sales but lower profit margins.

Over 1/3 of Beverly's 1994 revenues came from specialty operations such as pharmacy services, retirement homes, rehabilitation services, and acute nursing care (for patients with highly specialized needs). The company has created a new subsidiary, Hospice

Preferred Choice, to provide care in homes and nursing facilities to terminally ill patients; 12 hospice programs are planned by the end of 1996. It also intends to buy more acute-care facilities like the American Transitional Hospitals it acquired in 1994.

Beverly expects to have 70 outpatient rehabilitation centers built by the end of 1995, which would complement the workers' compensation business, Pharmacy Management Services, that it acquired for $148.5 million the year before. Also in the works for Beverly is AdviNet, a nationwide referral system to help individuals, families, employers, and insurance companies select providers of long-term and other types of care.

WHEN

In 1963 a Utah accountant, Roy Christensen, founded Beverly as 3 convalescent hospitals in Southern California. The development of Medicare and Medicaid in the mid-1960s attracted entrepreneurs to the nursing home field, and Beverly expanded rapidly. The company also dealt with such diverse products as mirrors, plastics, real estate, and printing. Beverly went public in 1966.

By the early 1970s the nursing home industry had overexpanded. With Beverly losing money, Robert Van Tuyle came in as a director. Van Tuyle stuck with the growth prospects of long-term nursing care and sold the unrelated businesses. In 1977 Beverly doubled in size with the purchase of Leisure Lodges, a chain of nursing homes. The chairman of Leisure Lodges, David Banks, became president of Beverly in 1979. Beverly continued to grow through acquisitions during the late 1970s and early 1980s. Centralized management and large-scale operations allowed the company to be more profitable than single-site facilities and small chains. By 1983 Beverly had become the #1 nursing home operator in the US.

The rest of the 1980s saw Beverly caught between shrinking Medicaid-Medicare payments and rising labor unrest. Legislative changes in the method of Medicaid-Medicare reimbursements during 1983 made the health care industry more cost conscious. States in which Beverly operated took from 18 months to 3 years to make Medicaid payments. Since most of Beverly's employees earned only 50¢ more an hour than they could earn in an entry-level fast-food job, employee turnover was high, reaching 78% in the late 1980s.

Compounding Beverly's problems were allegations of patient neglect and unfair labor practices. The state of California alleged that Beverly was responsible for the deaths of 9 patients, and Minnesota accused it of being responsible for the deaths of 8 more. Beverly reeled under the onslaught of bad publicity, heavy fines, falling occupancy rates, and state authorities' revocation, suspension, and probation of its operating licenses.

After *Financial World* magazine branded the company one of the 10 worst-managed US companies in 1988, Beverly began a major restructuring. Management was decentralized and assets were sold to cut Beverly's $1.1 billion debt. Forty-one Iowa nursing homes were bought in 1989 by a Texas banker who quickly sold them for a hefty profit in a deal backed by tax-exempt bonds. The deal was shepherded by cronies and White House appointees of future President Bill Clinton. In 1990 Van Tuyle retired as chairman of Beverly and the company moved its headquarters to Arkansas.

Also in 1990, after a judge ruled that Beverly had committed unfair labor practices at 33 nursing homes in 12 states, the National Labor Relations Board determined in 1993 that the company had committed more than 130 violations of labor laws to stifle workers' efforts to unionize. In 1994 the New York federal appeals court scaled back the labor board's decision that had extended its findings companywide.

Beverly's PCA subsidiary — the largest institutional pharmacy services provider in the US — expanded in 1994 through the purchases of Insta-Care Holdings and Synetic's pharmacy subsidiaries.

NYSE symbol: BEV
Fiscal year ends: December 31

Chairman, President, and CEO: David R. Banks, age 58,
$712,554 pay
**EVP; President, Beverly Health and Rehabilitation
Services:** Boyd W. Hendrickson, age 50, $404,414 pay
EVP; President, Pharmacy Corporation of America:
Ronald C. Kayne, age 56, $367,905 pay
EVP; President, Beverly Managed Care: T. Jerald Moore,
age 54, $341,488 pay
EVP Development: Bobby W. Stephens, age 50
EVP Finance and CFO: Robert D. Woltil, age 40
EVP, General Counsel, and Secretary: Robert W.
Pommerville, age 54
VP Human Resources: Carol Johansen
Auditors: Ernst & Young LLP

WHERE

HQ: 5111 Rogers Ave., Ste. 40 A, Fort Smith, AR 72919
Phone: 501-452-6712
Fax: 501-452-5131

Beverly operates 727 nursing homes, 65 pharmacies, 40
retirement and congregate living projects, 6 transitional
hospitals, and 4 home health care centers in 36 states
and the District of Columbia.

	Facilities by State		
	Nursing	Retirement	Pharmacy
California	78	2	6
Indiana	72	2	2
Florida	66	7	8
Texas	52	—	11
Pennsylvania	42	3	2
Arkansas	38	3	1
Minnesota	37	2	1
Other states	342	21	34
Total	**727**	**40**	**65**

WHAT

	1994 Patient Census
	% of total
Medicaid	68
Private	20
Medicare	12
Total	**100**

	1994 Revenues
	% of total
Nursing Home Care	64
Rehabilitation Services	15
High-Acuity Nursing Care	11
Pharmacy Services	9
Other	1
Total	**100**

Operations

Home health centers	Retirement living centers
Hospice care	Transitional hospitals
Institutional pharmacies	Workers compensation
Nursing homes	pharmacy management
Rehabilitation centers	

KEY COMPETITORS

Arbor Health	Geriatric &	Manor Care
Care	Medical Cos.	Mid Atlantic
Assisted Living	Health Care and	Medical
Caremark	Retirement	National
Columbia/HCA	Corp.	HealthCare
Continental	Hillhaven	Regency
Medical	Homedco Group	Health
Evergreen	Horizon	Services
Healthcare	Healthcare	Sun Healthcare
Foundation	Host Marriott	TheraTech
Health	Life Care Centers	Vitalink
Genesis Health	Living Centers of	Pharmacy
Ventures	America	Services

HOW MUCH

	9-Year Growth	1985	1986	1987	1988	1989	1990	1991	1992	1993	1994
Sales ($ mil.)	6.5%	1,691	2,019	2,094	2,025	2,104	2,113	2,301	2,597	2,871	2,969
Net income ($ mil.)	2.5%	60	52	(33)	(24)	(104)	13	29	4	60	75
Income as % of sales	—	3.5%	2.6%	—	—	—	0.6%	1.3%	0.2%	2.1%	2.5%
Earnings per share ($)	(3.2%)	1.02	0.77	(0.55)	(0.45)	(1.87)	0.18	0.35	0.04	0.45	0.76
Stock price – high ($)	—	19.10	21.42	17.97	7.50	9.52	8.45	11.78	12.50	14.04	15.88
Stock price – low ($)	—	14.46	13.45	6.31	3.57	4.76	3.57	6.55	6.78	8.81	11.75
Stock price – close ($)	(2.0%)	17.31	15.59	6.66	5.95	5.71	8.21	8.45	12.38	12.61	14.38
P/E – high	—	19	28	—	—	—	47	34	—	31	21
P/E – low	—	14	18	—	—	—	20	19	—	20	15
Dividends per share ($)	(100.0%)	0.15	0.19	0.19	0.05	0.00	0.00	0.00	0.00	0.00	0.00
Book value per share ($)	(1.9%)	9.37	9.83	8.61	8.20	6.34	6.03	6.71	6.58	7.19	7.91
Employees	(2.7%)	105,000	116,000	110,000	106,000	96,000	92,000	93,000	93,000	89,000	82,000

1994 Year-end:
Debt ratio: 54.2%
Return on equity: 12.1%
Cash (mil.): $68
Current ratio: 1.59
Long-term debt (mil.): $918
No. of shares (mil.): 86
Dividends
  Yield: —
  Payout:—
Market value (mil.): $1,232

**Stock Price History
High/Low 1985–94**

THE BLACK & DECKER CORPORATION

OVERVIEW

Black & Decker is the world's largest producer of power tools and accessories, and electric lawn and garden tools. The company is also the world leader in specialty fastening systems, glass container–making equipment, steel golf club shafts, and security hardware (locksets, deadbolts, electronic locks), and it's the largest full-line supplier of small household appliances in North America.

The Towson, Maryland–based company has a stable of well-known brands including Alligator, Black & Decker, DeWalt, Dynalite, and Dustbuster. The company's DeWalt and Elu professional power tools continue to push up Black & Decker's global sales. International sales were up over 11% in 1994. Black & Decker is also investing in innovative product lines such as the award-winning SnakeLight flexible flashlight.

Still bearing a heavy debt load from its 1989 Emhart acquisition, Black & Decker remains focused on paying down debt through refinancing and divestitures.

The company's plumbing products have been making steady gains in the North American market in the past 10 years.

WHEN

In 1910, when Duncan Black and Alonzo Decker opened the Black & Decker Manufacturing Company in Baltimore with a $1,200 investment, they began a partnership that would last over 40 years. Starting with milk-bottle–cap machines and candy dippers, the partners introduced their first major tool in 1917 — a portable 1/2" electric drill with patented pistol grip and trigger switch, which can now be viewed at the Smithsonian.

Also in 1917 the company built its first manufacturing plant, which would become the company headquarters, in rural Towson, Maryland. Sales passed $1 million in 1919, and the company added a 20,000-square-foot factory. Black & Decker quickly established itself in international markets. It had sales representatives in Russia, Japan, and Australia by 1919, and in 1922 Black & Decker Ltd., a Canadian subsidiary, opened as its first facility outside the US.

Black & Decker produced tools that defined the power-tool industry — the first portable screwdriver (1922), the 1/2" BB special drill (1923), the first electric hammer (1936), portable electric drills for do-it-yourself home repair (1946), finishing sanders and jigsaws (1953), and the Dustbuster hand-held vacuum (1979). The original founders led Black & Decker until they died — Black in 1951 and Decker in 1956.

In 1984 Black & Decker acquired the General Electric housewares operations, replacing GE's trademark with the Black & Decker hexagonal trademark on such items as toaster ovens, can openers, and irons.

In the mid-1980s Black & Decker lost market share. Administrative and production costs were high, and product quality was suffering. The company's manufacturing network was inefficient, its management was fat, and customer service was faltering.

Nolan Archibald, the company's 3rd CEO unrelated to the Black or Decker families, joined the company in 1985 and began a major restructuring. Black & Decker closed 5 plants, streamlined distribution systems, consolidated overseas facilities, and cut payroll 10%. The company's 1987 net earnings showed a 100% increase over 1986.

In 1989 Black & Decker acquired Emhart (formerly American Hardware), but the purchase caused earnings to fall. To service its debt Black & Decker sold off pieces of its acquisition: Emhart's Bostik adhesives, Arcotronics capacitors, True Temper Hardware, the Medic division of PRC information systems, GardenAmerica lawn products, and North American Mallory Controls.

In 1992 the company announced a plan to sell Emhart's PRC unit (now part of Information Systems and Services) in an IPO. The plan was later withdrawn because of weakness in defense-related stocks. After Black & Decker removed PRC from the auction block, the unit won a $1.7 billion contract with the Defense Department to provide a super minicomputer.

In 1993 Black & Decker sold the architectural hardware business of Corbin Russwin and the through-hole machinery business of Dynapert (a maker of printed circuit board assembly equipment). The divestitures raised $108 million, which was used to reduce the company's debt.

In 1994 the company closed a number of plants, including a glass container making equipment factory in Sweden, a household iron facility in Singapore, and a power tool plant in Germany. In 1995 it sold its PRC Realty Systems for $60 million.

NYSE symbol: BDK
Fiscal year ends: December 31

WHO

Chairman, President, and CEO: Nolan D. Archibald, age 51, $1,565,000 pay
Group VP; President, Power Tools and Accessories: Gary T. DiCamillo, age 44, $585,000 pay
EVP; President, Commercial and Industrial Group: Raymond A. DeVita, age 58, $540,000 pay
EVP; President, Security Hardware Group: Dennis G. Heiner, age 51, $530,000 pay
Group VP; President, Eastern Hemisphere: Roger H. Thomas, age 52, $501,215 pay
President and CEO, PRC Inc.: James J. Leto, age 51
VP; President, North American Power Tools: Joseph Galli, age 36
VP; President, Europe: Anton van Schijndel, age 51
VP and Treasurer: Kathleen W. Hyle, age 36
VP Public Affairs and Corporate Secretary: Barbara B. Lucas, age 49
VP and CFO: Thomas M. Schoewe, age 42
VP and General Counsel: Charles E. Fenton, age 46
VP Human Resources: Leonard A. Strom, age 49
Auditors: Ernst & Young LLP

WHERE

HQ: 701 E. Joppa Rd., Towson, MD 21286
Phone: 410-716-3900
Fax: 410-716-2933 (Investor Relations)

Black & Decker products are marketed in more than 100 countries.

	1994 Sales		1994 Operating Income	
	$ mil.	% of total	$ mil.	% of total
US	3,292	63	254	66
Europe	1,279	24	115	30
Other regions	677	13	15	4
Adjustments	—	—	10	—
Total	**5,248**	**100**	**394**	**100**

WHAT

	1994 Sales	
	$ mil.	% of total
Power tools	1,632	31
Information systems & svcs.	883	17
Household products	745	14
Commercial & industrial	591	11
Security hardware	512	10
Accessories	356	7
Outdoor products	311	6
Plumbing	218	4
Total	**5,248**	**100**

Selected Brand Names

Power Tools	Appliances	Fastening Systems
Air Station	Brew 'N Go	Gripco
Alligator	Dustbuster	HeliCoil
CarVac	HandyChopper	Parker-Kalon
Cyclone	Spacemaker	POP NUT
DeWalt	Sure Steam	
Elu	Toast-R-Oven	**Outdoor**
Proline		Dynalite
Quantum	**Security Hardware**	Dynamic
Quattro	Corbin Co.	Dynamic Gold
VersaPak	DOM	Groom'N'Edge
Plumbing	Kwikset	Leafbuster
Price Pfister	Lane	True Temper
	Titan	Vac'N'Mulch

KEY COMPETITORS

Actava	Hillenbrand	Premark
Aldila	Huffy	Robert Bosch
American Brands	Illinois Tool	Royal Appliance
American Standard	Works	Sears
Amway	Ingersoll-Rand	Snap-on Tools
Arthur Andersen	Kohler	Stanley Works
Cooper Industries	Masco	Sunbeam
EDS	Matsushita	Textron
Emerson	Mr. Coffee	Toro
Gillette	Newell Co.	

HOW MUCH

	9-Year Growth	1985	1986	1987	1988	1989	1990	1991	1992	1993	1994
Sales ($ mil.)	13.1%	1,732	1,791	1,935	2,281	3,190	4,832	4,637	4,780	4,882	5,248
Net income ($ mil.)	11.7%	47	28	56	97	30	51	53	(73)	95	127
Income as % of sales	—	2.7%	1.5%	2.9%	4.3%	0.9%	1.1%	1.1%	—	1.9%	2.4%
Earnings per share ($)	4.5%	0.92	0.49	0.95	1.65	0.51	0.84	0.81	(1.11)	1.00	1.37
Stock price – high ($)	—	26.88	25.25	26.50	24.75	25.25	20.13	19.63	26.88	22.25	25.75
Stock price – low ($)	—	17.25	14.50	13.00	17.13	18.13	8.00	8.50	14.63	16.63	17.00
Stock price – close ($)	1.1%	21.50	16.25	18.88	23.13	19.50	9.38	17.00	18.13	19.75	23.75
P/E – high	—	29	52	28	15	50	24	24	—	22	19
P/E – low	—	19	30	14	10	36	10	11	—	17	12
Dividends per share ($)	(5.1%)	0.64	0.58	0.40	0.40	0.40	0.40	0.40	0.40	0.40	0.40
Book value per share ($)	2.3%	9.94	10.62	11.12	12.38	12.23	14.94	14.18	11.08	10.72	12.16
Employees	5.3%	22,400	21,700	19,700	20,800	38,600	43,400	38,600	38,800	37,300	35,800

1994 Year-end:
Debt ratio: 67.2%
Return on equity: 13.2%
Cash (mil.): $66
Current ratio: 0.98
Long-term debt (mil.): $1,723
No. of shares (mil.): 84
Dividends
  Yield: 1.7%
  Payout: 29.2%
Market value (mil.): $1,991

**Stock Price History
High/Low 1985–94**

THE BOEING COMPANY

OVERVIEW

"We have been technically excellent but process poor, and we have to change," says Frank Shrontz, CEO of Boeing. In the past, process poor has worked. The Seattle-based company has been the world's #1 commercial aircraft maker for more than 30 years, and it is one of the US's largest exporters. However, with airlines cutting back on orders and European consortium Airbus bringing stiff competition, Shrontz knows process poor won't work anymore. Boeing sales have dropped more than 1/4 over the past 2 years.

Taking cues from vehicle manufacturers, including Toyota and PACCAR, Boeing is switching to "just-in-time" inventory control, opening up lines of communication with its employees, and giving more responsibility to middle management and workers on the shop floor. The once supersecretive company is also allowing its customers in on the design process. To lower its costs, Boeing has cut its work force by more than 40,000 since 1990, and it plans to cut another 12,000 positions.

In 1995 Boeing introduced its newest plane, the 777, a wide-body twin-engine jet designed to challenge the Airbus A330 and the A340. Boeing got a boost when the FAA certified the jet for long routes over the ocean, a process that usually takes years of service.

Boeing's Defense & Space Group has also worked to streamline its operations to compete more effectively in the shrinking defense market. The group builds a variety of aircraft, including the F-22 fighter (with Lockheed Martin), and it is the prime contractor for the space station *Alpha*.

WHEN

Bill Boeing built his first airplane in 1916 with navy officer Conrad Westervelt. His Seattle factory, at first called Pacific Aero Products Company, changed its name to Boeing Airplane Company the following year.

During WWI Boeing built training planes for the US Navy and afterward, when military sales evaporated, began the first international airmail service, between Seattle and Victoria, British Columbia, using the newly designed B-1 flying boat. Another key airmail route (from San Francisco to Chicago) followed in 1927, and Boeing established an airline subsidiary, Boeing Air Transport.

The airline's success was helped along by Boeing's Model 40A, the first plane using Frederick Rentschler's new air-cooled engine, the Wasp. (Rentschler went on to become the head of engine-maker Pratt & Whitney.) In 1927 Boeing bought Pacific Air Transport and in 1928 formed a holding company, Boeing Airplane and Transport Corporation, for its manufacturing and transportation concerns. In 1929 Rentschler and Boeing combined their companies as United Aircraft and Transport. United soon owned a number of aviation-related businesses, including Sikorsky Aviation, Stout Air Services, and Clement Keys' National Air Transport.

The company introduced the first all-metal airliner in 1933. In 1934 new airmail rules forced United (the predecessor of today's UAL) to sell its airline operations, leaving Boeing Airplane (as it was known until 1961) with the manufacturing concerns.

Between 1935 and 1965 Boeing built many successful planes, including the Model 314 Clipper (flying boats) used by Pan Am; the Model 307 Stratoliner (the first aircraft with a pressurized cabin); the B-17, B-29, and B-52 bombers; and the 707 and 727 jetliners.

In the 1960s Boeing built the first stage of the rockets used in the Apollo space program. It delivered the first of the best-selling 737s in 1967; the 747 (the first jumbo jet) also went into production in the late 1960s.

World fuel shortages and concern over aircraft noise prompted Boeing to design the efficient and quiet 757 and 767 late in the 1970s. Meanwhile, the company expanded its information services and aerospace capabilities by establishing Boeing Computer Services (data communications services, 1970). It bought an equity interest in Carnegie Group (artificial intelligence, 1984) and ARGOSystems (defense electronics, 1987).

In 1990 Boeing announced plans to build the 777, its first new commercial aircraft in 11 years. (The 777 made its first commercial flight, for United Airlines, in 1995.) Boeing exited the turboprop commuter aircraft business in 1992 by selling de Havilland to Bombardier. In 1994 Boeing paid $75 million to settle a case in which it was accused of overcharging the US government millions of dollars for R&D costs.

In 1995 the company beat out archrival McDonnell Douglas for a 55-plane order from Scandinavian Airlines. It also won a 28-plane, $4.2 billion order from air carrier Saudia.

NYSE symbol: BA
Fiscal year ends: December 31

Chairman and CEO: Frank A. Shrontz, age 63,
$1,468,828 pay
President: Philip M. Condit, age 53, $811,714 pay
SVP and CFO: Boyd E. Givan, age 58, $551,824 pay
SVP: Douglas P. Beighle, age 62, $530,615 pay
SVP; President, Defense and Space Group: C. Gerald
King, age 60, $505,243 pay
SVP; President, Commercial Airplane Group: Ronald B.
Woodard, age 51, $446,676 pay
SVP Operations: Deane D. Cruze, age 64
SVP Planning and International Development:
Lawrence W. Clarkson, age 56
SVP Human Resources: Larry G. McKean, age 59
VP Engineering and Technology: Robert A. Davis,
age 61
VP and General Counsel: Theodore J. Collins
Auditors: Deloitte & Touche LLP

WHERE

HQ: 7755 E. Marginal Way South, Seattle, WA 98108
Phone: 206-655-2121
Fax: 206-655-7004

Boeing has operations worldwide. Its plants are located
in 11 US states and 2 Canadian provinces.

	1994 Sales	
	$ mil.	% of total
US	10,080	46
Asia	7,403	33
Europe	3,277	15
Oceania	887	4
Africa	135	1
Western Hemisphere	142	1
Total	**21,924**	**100**

WHAT

	1994 Sales		1994 Operating Income	
	$ mil.	% of total	$ mil.	% of total
Commercial				
aircraft	16,851	76	1,022	77
Defense & space	4,742	22	303	23
Other industries	331	2	2	0
Total	**21,924**	**100**	**1,327**	**100**

Commercial Transport
737 (short-to-medium-range 2-engine jet; 108 to 146
seats)
747 (long-range 4-engine jet; 420 to 566 seats)
757 (short-to-medium-range 2-engine jet; 180 to 230
seats)
767 (medium-to-long-range 2-engine jet; 210 to 250
seats)
777 (long-range 2-engine jet; 305 to 440 seats)

Defense and Space Products
B-2 bomber
CH-47 Chinook helicopter
E-3 Airborne Warning and Control System (AWACS)
F-22 fighter program
RAH-66 Comanche helicopter
Space station *Alpha*
V-22 Osprey tiltrotor aircraft

Other Industries
Information systems
Management services

KEY COMPETITORS

Airbus	Lockheed Martin	Orbital Sciences
British Aerospace	Loral	Raytheon
Daimler-Benz	McDonnell	Rockwell
FlightSafety	Douglas	Textron
General	Northrop	Thiokol
Dynamics	Grumman	Thomson SA

HOW MUCH

	9-Year Growth	1985	1986	1987	1988	1989	1990	1991	1992	1993	1994
Sales ($ mil.)	5.4%	13,636	16,341	15,355	16,962	20,276	27,595	29,314	30,184	25,438	21,924
Net income ($ mil.)	4.7%	566	665	480	614	675	1,385	1,567	1,554	1,244	856
Income as % of sales	—	4.2%	4.1%	3.1%	3.6%	3.3%	5.0%	5.3%	5.1%	4.9%	3.9%
Earnings per share ($)	4.9%	1.63	1.90	1.38	1.79	1.96	4.01	4.56	4.57	3.66	2.51
Stock price – high ($)	—	23.47	28.87	24.37	30.08	41.27	61.88	53.00	54.63	44.75	50.13
Stock price – low ($)	—	16.09	20.34	12.80	16.63	25.74	37.77	41.25	32.13	33.38	42.13
Stock price – close ($)	8.1%	23.24	22.74	16.47	26.97	39.60	45.38	47.75	40.13	43.25	47.00
P/E – high	—	14	15	18	17	21	15	12	12	12	20
P/E – low	—	10	11	9	9	13	9	9	7	9	17
Dividends per share ($)	9.0%	0.46	0.53	0.62	0.69	0.78	0.95	1.00	1.00	1.00	1.00
Book value per share ($)	9.6%	12.51	13.84	14.57	15.69	17.74	20.30	23.71	23.73	26.41	28.46
Employees	1.3%	104,000	124,196	143,100	153,000	163,900	160,500	155,700	142,000	123,000	117,000

1994 Year-end:
Debt ratio: 21.2%
Return on equity: 9.2%
Cash (mil.): $2,643
Current ratio: 1.53
Long-term debt (mil.): $2,603
No. of shares (mil.): 341
Dividends
　Yield: 2.1%
　Payout: 39.8%
Market value (mil.): $16,021

**Stock Price History
High/Low 1985–94**

BOISE CASCADE CORPORATION

OVERVIEW

Boise Cascade's income has been cascading downward in the 1990s, but resurgent paper prices in 1994 have begun to lift the company out of the red. The Boise, Idaho–based company is the 9th largest pulp and paper producer in the US and a leading seller of wood, building supplies, office equipment, furniture, and paper. It operates 7 paper mills and 26 office supply distribution centers in the US.

The company's core paper products unit (39% of 1994 sales) includes uncoated business, printing, forms, and photocopier papers; coated magazine paper; newsprint; and pulp.

In 1994 John Fery retired from his 22-year stint as CEO. New CEO George Harad, a 23-year company man who became president and COO in 1991, used his financial skills to help

Boise Cascade issue convertible preferred stock to reduce its $2 billion debt.

The company completed a 1994 IPO of its former Canadian subsidiary, Rainy River Forest Products. Following the sale, which helped reduce parent company debt by $330 million, Boise Cascade held a 49% voting interest in the new company.

Boise Cascade, the #3 distributor of full-line building products in the US, is expanding its laminated veneer lumber mills in Oregon and Louisiana. Building product sales have doubled in the past 5 years, and the company plans further expansion of its distribution channels, primarily in the western US.

The company's 3rd line, office products, accounted for 22% of 1994 revenue.

WHEN

Boise Cascade got its start in 1957 with the merger of 2 small lumber companies — Boise Payette Lumber Company (Boise, Idaho) and Cascade Lumber Company (Yakima, Washington). The company diversified in the 1960s under the leadership of Robert Hansberger, moving into office products distribution in 1964. A number of acquisitions followed, including that of Ebasco Industries (1969), which had started out as a holding company (Electric Bond & Share) and, over time, had expanded into a consulting, engineering, and construction firm. By 1970 Boise Cascade had made more than 30 acquisitions to diversify into building materials, paper products, real estate, recreational vehicles, and publishing.

In the early 1970s the company's reliance on public timberlands for raw timber, in lieu of a strong reforestation program, led to a timber shortage. Concurrent plans to develop recreational communities in Hawaii, Washington, and California met opposition from residents, causing the company to scrap all but 6 of the 29 projects. Costs related to the remaining projects were higher than originally planned. In 1972, $1 billion in debt, Boise Cascade lost $171 million.

John Fery, who replaced Hansberger as president in 1972, responded to the crisis by centralizing authority and selling most of Hansberger's acquisitions not directly related to Boise Cascade's core forest products operations. Among those sold were the recreational vehicle businesses (1972), the engineering and construction businesses (Chemical Construction Corporation, 1973),

and the publishing companies (Communications/Research/Machines and George Macy Companies, 1973). Boise Cascade sold Ebasco in 1973 and later sold some of the Latin American investments obtained through the Ebasco purchase. It bought 348,000 acres of New England timberland in 1980.

Since the late 1980s the company has sold more nonstrategic operations, including its Specialty Paperboard Division (1989) and its 50% interest in a European corrugated container factory (1991). In 1992 Boise Cascade sold its 11 corrugated container plants (located east of the Rocky Mountains). These sales reflect the company's decision to focus on manufacturing forest products and distributing building materials and office supplies. Capital investment totaled $2.2 billion from 1989 to 1993.

Boise Cascade sold its wholesale office products business in 1992 to focus on direct sales to big buyers such as IBM and Boeing. In 1994 the company entered direct-mail distribution by agreeing to buy the direct-mail business of Reliable Corporation, a Chicago-based national office products supplier. Boise Cascade also bought a 10% stake in Reliable's 18 retail stores, located mostly in the Midwest.

In 1995, in a move into the international paper market, Boise Cascade signed a joint venture agreement with Shenzhen Leasing to form Zhuhai Hiwin Boise Cascade, a manufacturer of carbonless paper. Boise Cascade sees this firm as its springboard to further Asian projects. The venture will become the largest producer of carbonless paper in China in 1996.

NYSE symbol: BCC
Fiscal year ends: December 31

WHO

Chairman: John B. Fery, age 65, $1,095,833 pay
President and CEO: George J. Harad, age 50, $881,539 pay
EVP and General Manager, Office Products Distribution: Peter G. Danis Jr., age 63, $557,345 pay
SVP and General Manager, Paper Division: N. David Spence, age 59, $391,999 pay
SVP Human Resources and Corporate Relations: Alice E. Hennessey, age 58, $390,383 pay
SVP Building Products: Richard B. Parrish, age 56, $369,096 pay
SVP Manufacturing, Paper: A. Ben Groce, age 53
SVP Marketing and Sales, Paper: Terry R. Lock, age 53
SVP and CFO: Theodore Crumley, age 49
VP Operations, Timber and Wood Products: John C. Bender, age 54
VP Building Materials Distribution and Engineered Wood Products, Sales and Marketing: Stanley R. Bell, age 48
VP and General Manager, Containerboard Sales and Converting Paper: H. John Leusner, age 59
VP and General Counsel: John W. Holleran, age 40
Auditors: Arthur Andersen & Co, SC

WHERE

HQ: 1111 W. Jefferson St., PO Box 50, Boise, ID 83728-0001
Phone: 208-384-6161
Fax: 208-384-7298

The company operates 12 plywood mills, 12 lumber mills, and 2 other specialty mills.

Owned or Leased Timberland	Acres (thou.)
Northwest	1,364
South	710
New England	665
Midwest	308
Total	**3,047**

WHAT

	1994 Sales		1994 Operating Income	
	$ mil.	% of total	$ mil.	% of total
Paper	1,630	39	(38)	—
Building products	1,590	38	151	76
Office products	907	22	42	21
Other	13	0	5	3
Adjustments	—	—	(66)	—
Total	**4,140**	**100**	**92**	**100**

Paper Products	
Coated magazine and catalog paper	Fiberboard siding
	Gypsum board
Containerboard	Insulation
Copy paper	Laminated veneer lumber
Corrugated containers	Lumber
Envelope and label paper	Molding
Market pulp	Paneling
Newsprint	Particleboard
Offset-printing paper	Plywood
Writing paper	Roofing
	Windows

Building Products	Office Products Distribution
Building hardware	Copy paper
Ceiling tile	Office furniture
Doors	Office supplies
Engineered wood products	

KEY COMPETITORS

Alco Standard
Andersen Corp.
Buhrmann-Tetterode
Canadian Pacific
Champion International
Fletcher Challenge
Georgia-Pacific
Home Depot
International Paper
James River
Jefferson Smurfit
Kimberly-Clark
Manville
Masco
Mead
Moore
Newell Co.
Owens-Corning
Pella
Scott
Stone Container
USG
Weyerhaeuser
Willamette Industries

HOW MUCH

	9-Year Growth	1985	1986	1987	1988	1989	1990	1991	1992	1993	1994
Sales ($ mil.)	1.1%	3,737	3,740	3,821	4,095	4,338	4,186	3,951	3,716	3,958	4,140
Net income ($ mil.)	—	104	102	183	289	268	75	(80)	(154)	(77)	(63)
Income as % of sales	—	2.8%	2.7%	4.8%	7.1%	6.2%	1.8%	—	—	—	—
Earnings per share ($)	—	2.07	1.99	3.70	6.15	5.70	1.62	(2.46)	(4.79)	(3.17)	(3.08)
Stock price – high ($)	—	30.59	38.94	52.13	50.00	48.00	46.25	29.25	25.38	27.50	30.50
Stock price – low ($)	—	22.34	26.69	28.81	36.00	39.75	19.75	18.38	16.38	19.50	19.00
Stock price – close ($)	(0.6%)	28.19	35.84	40.81	41.25	44.38	26.00	22.25	21.13	23.50	26.75
P/E – high	—	15	20	14	8	8	29	—	—	—	—
P/E – low	—	11	13	8	6	7	12	—	—	—	—
Dividends per share ($)	(6.9%)	1.14	1.14	1.14	1.20	1.50	1.52	1.52	0.60	0.60	0.60
Book value per share ($)	(3.5%)	29.90	30.34	32.41	37.34	41.23	41.07	37.49	29.95	25.92	21.78
Employees	(3.4%)	22,690	23,333	20,244	19,835	19,539	19,810	19,619	17,222	17,362	16,618

1994 Year-end:
Debt ratio: 59.1%
Return on equity: —
Cash (mil.): $29
Current ratio: 1.40
Long-term debt (mil.): $1,856
No. of shares (mil.): 38
Dividends
  Yield: 2.2%
  Payout: —
Market value (mil.): $1,024

Stock Price History High/Low 1985–94

BORDEN, INC.

If news of a new Borden CEO and corporate restructuring sounds familiar, it should. Amid the turmoil surrounding the dairy goods, pasta, and chemical producer's takeover by Kohlberg Kravis Roberts & Co. (KKR) in late 1994 and early 1995, Borden booted chief executive Ervin Shames after barely a year on the job. And for the 4th time since 1989, Columbus, Ohio–based Borden reorganized itself, this time into separate divisions for consumer packaged products, dairy products, and packaging and industrial products.

In December 1994 KKR bought 63.5% of Borden, paying for its acquisition with $2 billion in RJR Nabisco stock. As a result of other moves in the months before and after that purchase, affiliates of KKR now own 100% of Borden's outstanding common stock. Borden had seen its market value fall by nearly 2/3 since 1991, despite the company's status as the leading pasta producer in the US, one of the US's premier dairy companies, and the leader in several niche grocery and nonfood categories.

Among the challenges faced by new chairman and CEO Robert Kidder (formerly head of KKR-controlled Duracell) are stabilizing sagging income in the pasta division and unloading poorly performing dairy operations in the eastern US. Brands recently sold by Borden include Campfire (marshmallows), Coco Lopez (drink mixes), Accent (paints), and Country Colors (paints). The company has discontinued its Hobby Craft line of glue.

Galveston resident Gail Borden Jr., founder of one of Texas's first newspapers (the *Telegraph and Texas Register*, in which Borden headlined the phrase "Remember the Alamo"), was also an inventor whose innovations included a portable bathhouse, an oar-driven steamboat, and a nonperishable meat biscuit.

Returning from London in 1851 after accepting an award for the meat biscuit, Borden witnessed infant deaths from putrefied milk and decided to make nonperishable milk. His process required condensation in a vacuum to preserve the milk. It took 4 efforts (1856) and a personal commendation from Sam Houston before the patent was approved.

Borden located his business in Burrville, Connecticut, as Gail Borden, Jr., and Company in 1857 and formed New York Condensed Milk with grocer Jeremiah Milbank in 1858. A big break came with the Civil War, when the US Army ordered 500 pounds of condensed milk. Condensed milk was later carried on Peary's North Pole and Annapurna expeditions. At the time of Borden's death in 1874, the company was the leading milk condenser in the US. The company sold condensed milk door-to-door in New York City and soon added fresh milk.

The company incorporated in 1899, taking the name the Borden Company in 1919. Between 1928 and 1929, Borden doubled in size, purchasing more than 90 companies and gaining operations in ice cream, cheese, and powdered milk. By 1929 it was one of the nation's largest food companies and had diversified through the purchase of glue maker Casein.

The company had expanded internationally by 1937 and branched into synthetic adhesives. By the end of WWII, Borden was well positioned internationally and in the chemicals market. As part of a plan to reduce its dependence on dairy revenues, Borden expanded its chemical operations by buying Columbus Coated Fabrics (1961) and Smith-Douglass (1964). Expansion into snacks began in 1964 with the purchase of Wise Foods and Cracker Jack. In 1979 Borden bought Buckeye and Guy's Food potato chip manufacturers. The company shored up its specialty chemicals operations to balance a depressed mid-1980s petrochemical market.

In the 1980s the company spent $1.9 billion on 91 acquisitions, mainly regional snack food and pasta makers, but the lack of a centralized manufacturing and selling network slowed growth tremendously and resulted in lost market share for many of the company's best-known products. Acquisitions included Meadow Gold (dairies, 1986), Moore's (snack foods, 1989), Catelli (pasta, 1989), and American Original (clam products, 1991).

Talks of a buyout by Hanson PLC broke down in late 1993 when the UK firm refused to offer as much as Borden's board was asking. Around that time, Borden axed CEO Anthony D'Amato. Under D'Amato's leadership the company's market value had dropped 50% in 2 years, to $2.4 billion.

In 1994 Borden sold its $225 million-in-annual-sales food service unit to Heinz. That year, the company also sold its Japanese ice cream, clam products, and Bennett's sauces divisions.

Private company
Fiscal year ends: December 31

WHO

Chairman and CEO: C. Robert Kidder, age 50
EVP; President, Packaging and Industrial Products:
Joseph M. Saggese, age 63, $364,000 pay
EVP and CFO: William H. Carter, age 41
EVP Corporate Strategy and Development: Richard L. de Ney, age 45
EVP; President, Dairy Products: Robert W. Allan, age 51
SVP and General Counsel: Allan L. Miller, age 62, $345,000 pay
SVP Human Resources and Corporate Affairs: Randy D. Kautto, age 50, $229,167 pay
SVP Operations and Technology, Consumer Packaged Products: Craig G. Hammond, age 49
VP and General Controller: P. Michael Morton, age 49
VP Public Affairs: Nicholas R. Iammartino, age 47
VP and Treasurer: David A. Kelly, age 56
Auditors: Deloitte & Touche LLP

WHERE

HQ: 180 E. Broad St., Columbus, OH 43215
Phone: 614-225-4000
Fax: 614-225-3410

Borden operates 42 dairy processing facilities in 22 states, 36 packaging and industrial manufacturing and processing facilities in 19 states, and 21 consumer packaged-product manufacturing and processing facilities in 13 states and Puerto Rico. Also, Borden operates 58 foreign packaging and industrial manufacturing and processing facilities, principally in Brazil, Canada, the Far East, and Western Europe. In addition, the company has 45 food manufacturing and processing facilities in foreign countries, primarily in Canada, Latin America, and Western Europe.

	1994 Sales		1994 Operating Income	
	$ mil.	% of total	$ mil.	% of total
US	3,695	66	(299)	—
Europe	908	16	76	—
Other countries	1,023	18	107	—
Total	**5,626**	**100**	**(116)**	**—**

WHAT

	1994 Sales		1994 Operating Income	
	$ mil.	% of total	$ mil.	% of total
Consumer packaged prods.	2,332	41	107	—
Packaging & industrial prods.	2,017	36	202	—
Dairy products	1,277	23	(425)	—
Total	**5,626**	**100**	**(116)**	**—**

Selected US Brands

Dairy
Borden
Crazy Milk
Eagle Brand
Lite-Line
Meadow Gold
Mountain High

Pasta and Sauces
Anthony's
Aunt Millie's
Bravo
Classico
Creamette
Dutch Maid
Gioia
Globe A-1
Goodman's
Luxury
Merlino's
New Mill
Pennsylvania Dutch
Prince

R&F
Red Cross
Ronco
Silver Award
Vimco

Other Foods
Cary's
Ched-O-Mate
Cracker Jack
Cremora
Frosticks
Juice Stix
Kava
La Famous
MacDonald's
Magnolia
Maple Orchards
MBT
Mississippi Mud
Moore's
Mrs. Grass
New York Deli
None Such

Pizza-Mate
ReaLemon
ReaLime
Salad-Mate
Sandwich-Mate
Soup Starter
Steero
Taco-Mate
Thirstee Smash
Viva
Wise
Wyler's

Nonfoods
Aron Alpha
Elmer's
Fill 'N Finish
Glucolors
Krazy Glue
Slide-All
Sun-Tex
Wall-Tex

KEY COMPETITORS

ADM
Anheuser-Busch
Associated Milk Producers
Barilla
Ben & Jerry's
Campbell Soup
ConAgra
CPC
Danone

Dreyer's
General Mills
Georgia-Pacific
Grand Metropolitan
Hershey
Kellogg
Luchetti
Mars
Mid-America Dairymen

Nestlé
PepsiCo
Philip Morris
Procter & Gamble
Quaker Oats
RJR Nabisco
Sara Lee
Tekfen

HOW MUCH

	9-Year Growth	1985	1986	1987	1988	1989	1990	1991	1992	1993	1994
Sales ($ mil.)	2.0%	4,716	5,002	6,514	7,244	7,593	7,633	7,235	7,143	5,506	5,626
Net income ($ mil.)	—	194	223	267	312	(61)	364	295	(211)	(613)	(598)
Income as % of sales	—	4.1%	4.5%	4.1%	4.3%	—	4.8%	4.1%	—	—	—
Employees	(0.1%)	32,700	33,800	39,400	45,400	46,500	46,300	44,400	41,900	41,900	32,300

1994 Year-end:
Debt ratio: 100%
Return on equity: —
Cash (mil.): $125
Current ratio: 1.06
Long-term debt (mil.): $1,379

Net Income
($ mil.)
1985–94

BORDERS GROUP, INC.

OVERVIEW

Borders Group began writing a new page in its history in 1995 when it was spun off by discount retailer Kmart. The Ann Arbor, Michigan–based company operates 3 specialty retail chains: Waldenbooks (the US's #1 mall-based bookstore chain), Borders (a fast-growing book superstore chain), and the Planet Music chain (formerly CD Superstore). Once the largest bookstore operator in the US, the company was bumped to 2nd place in 1992 by Barnes & Noble. Borders operates more than 1,100 stores in 50 states. Kmart sold the group to raise money for its flagging discount stores.

The group continues to downsize Waldenbooks but maintain its presence in malls. Borders is focusing on its superstores, which include trained staff, a huge selection, and a pleasing ambience. It plans to open 30 to 35 book and music superstores in the next 2 years. In a nod to ever-changing technology, the group is adding multimedia software sections to many of its Borders superstores.

WHEN

Named for the Massachusetts pond that inspired Thoreau, Waldenbooks was founded in 1933 by Larry Hoyt, who opened a book rental library and rented books for 3¢ a day. By 1948 the company had 250 outlets. That same year it began selling books. In 1968 the company opened its first all-retail bookstore in Pittsburgh.

In 1969 the chain was acquired by Carter Hawley Hale (now Broadway Stores). During the 1970s Waldenbooks took advantage of the growing number of shopping malls sprouting up across the US to expand rapidly. By 1979 the company had nearly 550 stores. That same year it hired Harry Hoffman, a former executive with Procter & Gamble, to run the company. Hoffman drew the ire of traditionalists in the book retailing industry because he focused on best-sellers, leaving little space for literary works. Hoffman also added nonbook items, including audio tapes, greeting cards, and stuffed toys, to the stores' merchandise mix. Hoffman continued the chain's rapid expansion. In 1981 Waldenbooks became the first bookseller to operate in all 50 states.

In 1984 Carter Hawley Hale was looking to raise cash for a stock buyback to fight off a takeover attempt by the Limited. It sold Waldenbooks to Kmart for $295 million. That same year Waldenbooks founded its Longmeadow Press publishing operations, which published 5 financial guides.

During the 1980s the company branched out into other retailing concepts, including Waldenbooks & More, larger stores that featured books and gifts. It also opened Waldenkids children's bookstores and Walden Software. By 1988 the company had more than 1,300 stores and sold about 100 million books annually.

In an effort to improve customer loyalty, Waldenbooks introduced a Preferred Reader Program in 1990. The program offered customers who paid a $10 yearly fee a 10% discount on their book purchases. In 1991 Hoffman retired and was replaced by Charles Cumello.

In 1992 Kmart, Waldenbooks's parent, expanded its bookselling business with the acquisition of Book Inventory Systems, owner of superstore chain Borders Books.

Brothers Louis and Tom Borders founded their first bookstore in Ann Arbor, Michigan, in 1971. The store originally sold only used books, but it soon began to include new books in the mix. As the store added new titles, Louis developed systems to keep track of the growing inventory. In the mid-1970s the Borders brothers formed Book Inventory Systems to market Louis's buying and inventory system to other independent bookstores and to run Borders.

The brothers focused on building the service part of their business through the late 1970s and early 1980s, but by the mid-1980s they were having trouble finding enough large, independent bookstores that wanted to buy their services. So they began concentrating on running bookstores again. They opened their 2nd store, in Birmingham, Michigan, in 1985. By 1988 they had 3 stores in Michigan, one in Atlanta, and one in Indianapolis. That same year they hired Hickory Farms president Robert DiRomualdo to run Borders Books. DiRomualdo continued the expansion, and when Kmart acquired the company in 1992 Borders Books had 19 superstores.

In 1994 Kmart acquired CD Superstore, which was founded by Paul Mayer in 1986. The company's name was changed to Planet Music.

Kmart spun off Borders Group to the public in 1995. It originally planned to retain 48% of the company but ended up selling all but 13%. Later in the year Borders announced that it would buy Kmart's remaining stake in the company.

NYSE symbol: BGP
Fiscal year ends: Saturday nearest January 31

WHO

Chairman and CEO: Robert F. DiRomualdo, age 50, $450,000 pay
VC, President, and CFO: George R. Mrkonic, age 42, $643,349 pay
President and COO, Walden Book Company: Bruce A. Quinnell, age 46, $438,527 pay
Chairman and CEO, Planet Music: Paul B. Mayer, age 33, $256,105 pay
President and COO, Borders: Richard L. Flanagan, age 42, $250,000 pay
VP and General Counsel: Thomas D. Carney, age 48
VP Group Planning and Resource Management: Cedric J. Vanzura, age 31
VP Human Resources: Kevin Mahoney
Auditors: Price Waterhouse LLP

WHERE

HQ: 500 E. Washington St., Ann Arbor, MI 48104
Phone: 313-913-1100
Fax: 313-913-1965

Borders operates bookstores in 50 states and 10 Planet Music stores in Maryland, North Carolina, Tennessee, Texas, and Virginia.

	1995 Stores	
	Mall bookstores	Borders
California	112	7
Texas	74	4
Florida	65	2
Pennsylvania	60	7
New York	58	8
Ohio	48	5
Illinois	46	6
Virginia	35	3
North Carolina	33	1
Michigan	32	6
Georgia	28	1
New Jersey	27	5
Indiana	25	1
Maryland	25	2
Massachusetts	24	2
Missouri	24	—
Washington	24	2
Other states	313	19
Total	**1,053**	**81**

WHAT

Stores
Borders Book Shop (superstore with coffee bar)
Borders Books & Music (superstore with books, videos, and multimedia products)
Brentano's (upscale mall bookstore)
Planet Music (music superstore)
Walden & More (books and gifts)
Walden Software (video games and software)
Waldenbooks (basic bookstore)
Waldenkids (children's bookstore)

	1995 Stores
	No.
Walden mall bookstores	1,053
Borders superstores	81
CD Superstores/Planet Music superstores	10
Total	**1,144**

	1995 Sales	
	$ mil.	% of total
Mall bookstores	1,085	72
Superstores	426	28
Total	**1,511**	**100**

KEY COMPETITORS

Barnes & Noble
Best Buy
Books-A-Million
Camelot Music
Crown Books
Hastings Books
Lauriat's
MTS
Musicland
Oxford Books
Price/Costco
Stacey's
Taylor's
Toys "R" Us
Trans World Entertainment
Virgin Group
Wal-Mart
W. H. Smith

HOW MUCH

	Annual Growth	1986	1987	1988	1989	1990	1991	1992	1993	1994	1995
Sales ($ mil.)	9.2%	—	—	—	—	—	1,064	1,140	1,183	1,370	1,511
Net income ($ mil.)	53.6%	—	—	—	—	—	2	17	23	(38)	9
Income as % of sales	—	—	—	—	—	—	0.2%	1.5%	1.9%	—	0.6%
Employees	22.3%	—	—	—	—	—	—	—	—	13,650	16,700

Net Income
($ mil.)
1991–95

BOSTON CELTICS LIMITED PARTNERSHIP

OVERVIEW

Boston Celtics Limited is going one-on-one with its basketball operations. Of course, basketball is nothing new to the tradition-rich Celtics. The team boasts 16 NBA titles, 17 Hall-of-Famers (with former players Larry Bird, Kevin McHale, and Robert Parish likely candidates), and 15 Most Valuable Players. The company sold its radio station (WEEI) and announced plans to sell its television station (WFXT) to Fox in 1994.

Don Gaston, Alan Cohen, and Paul Dupee Jr. own a corporation that serves as the general partner. Approximately 80,000 other investors, 50,000 of whom possess one share each, own 40% of the partnership units.

The team generates its revenues through home-game ticket sales; licensing of the rights to Celtics games for TV, cable, and radio; and merchandising of the Celtics' name. The Celtics played their final game at the historic Boston Garden in 1995. The team will move across the street to the Shawmut Center for the 1995–96 season. Although fans must now wait 15 years for season tickets to become available, the team makes it a practice to sell about 2,000 tickets on a per-game basis.

WHEN

Walter Brown founded the Boston Celtics basketball team (so named partially because of Brown's Irish background) in 1946. After 4 initial losing seasons, Brown hired Arnold "Red" Auerbach as head coach in 1950.

Auerbach quickly turned the Celtics into a competitive organization by acquiring such players as Bob Cousy, Chuck Cooper (the first black player in the NBA), Bill Sharman, and Frank Ramsey. Although the Celtics greatly improved during Auerbach's first 6 years as coach, they were unable to win an NBA title. The turning point came in 1956, when Auerbach traded 2 players to the St. Louis Hawks for a first-round draft pick that turned out to be Bill Russell. Around Russell's gifted play Auerbach created the greatest dynasty in basketball history, winning 9 NBA championships (8 in a row) from 1957 through 1966. Auerbach left coaching to become the team's general manager in 1966. Russell took over and, as the first black NBA coach, led the team to 2 more titles in 1968 and 1969.

During the early 1970s, under coach Tom Heinsohn, the team was restructured and, with the talents of players like John Havlicek, Don Nelson, Jo Jo White, and Dave Cowens, won NBA titles in 1974 and 1976. By the late 1970s, however, the team had slipped into last place, and Brown sold his interest to Harry Mangurian. During the 1979–80 season the team registered another major turnaround, due largely to the efforts of 1978 draft choice Larry Bird. With the assistance of players like Kevin McHale and Robert Parish, the Celtics won their 14th title in 1981.

In 1983 Mangurian sold control of the team to a triumvirate consisting of Don Gaston, Paul Dupee, and Alan Cohen. K. C. Jones became head coach in 1983 and led the team to titles in 1984 and 1986.

In 1986 the Celtics drafted Len Bias, a former counselor at Auerbach's summer basketball camp. Before the next season, though, Bias died of cocaine intoxication.

In late 1986 the 3 owners established a limited partnership and offered units to the public (a first for a pro franchise). The offering yielded gains of over $44 million for the 3 principal shareholders.

In 1989 the Celtics purchased WFXT-TV and WEEI-AM, Boston stations with rights to Celtics games. In 1990 the Celtics fired coach Jim Rodgers and replaced him with Chris Ford. In the same year the company spun off its broadcast properties in a rights offering but bought them back in 1992. Also in 1992 the company named Paul Gaston (Don's son) chairman and Stephen Schram president (Auerbach continued as basketball president).

During the 1993 NBA playoffs, the team's captain and leading scorer, Reggie Lewis, collapsed from heart disease. While shooting baskets that summer, Lewis died. Even before this tragedy, the Celtics had said goodbye to 2 champions when legend Larry Bird retired before the 1992–93 season began and 7-time All-Star Kevin McHale retired at season's end.

In 1995 a *Wall Street Journal* article quoted cardiologists who said Lewis's heart condition was consistent with cocaine use. The article said the possible link to drug use may not have been fully investigated for several reasons, including fear of public scandal and loss of a $15 million insurance policy. The team threatened to file a $100 million libel suit against the *Journal*. After reviewing the autopsy, the Massachusetts Medical Examiner's office said Lewis's death was not caused by cocaine, but the *Journal* stood by its story.

Also in 1995 M. L. Carr replaced Ford as head coach.

NYSE symbol: BOS
Fiscal year ends: June 30

Chairman and CEO: Paul E. Gaston, age 37, $1,549,000 pay
VC: David R. Gavitt, age 56, $600,000 pay
VC: Paul R. Dupee Jr., age 51
President: Stephen C. Schram, age 37, $1,549,000 pay
President: Arnold "Red" Auerbach, age 77, $250,000 pay
EVP, CFO, and Treasurer: Thomas M. Bartlett Jr., age 68, $375,000 pay
EVP and General Manager: Jan Volk, age 47
EVP Basketball Operations and Head Coach: Michael L. "M. L." Carr, age 44
VP, Controller, and Secretary: Richard G. Pond, age 34
VP Planning and Special Events: Stuart Layne
VP Marketing and Communications: Tod Rosensweig
VP Sales: Stephen Riley
Special Assistant: Larry J. Bird, age 39
Auditors: Ernst & Young LLP

WHERE

HQ: 151 Merrimac St., Boston, MA 02114
Phone: 617-523-6050
Fax: 617-523-5949

The team is a member of the Atlantic Division of the Eastern Conference of the National Basketball Association.

WHAT

	1994 Sales	
	$ mil.	% of total
TV & radio stations	39	47
Basketball team		
Ticket sales	20	24
TV, cable & radio broadcast rights fees	19	23
Advertising & other	5	6
Total	**83**	**100**

Basketball
Celtics LP (99%)
Boston Celtics

Boston Facilities
Shawmut Center (more than 18,000 seats; leased; to open for 1995–96 season)

KEY COMPETITORS

Boston Bruins
Boston Red Sox
Comcast
Hartford Whalers
Hearst
New England Patriots
New Jersey Nets
New York Giants
New York Jets
New York Knicks
Philadelphia 76ers
Tribune
Washington Bullets

HOW MUCH

	Annual Growth	1985	1986	1987	1988	1989	1990	1991	1992	1993	1994
Sales ($ mil.)	20.9%	—	—	22	28	27	30	41	46	81	83
Net income ($ mil.)	21.9%	—	—	6	10	12	8	11	8	5	24
Income as % of sales	—	—	—	29.5%	36.3%	44.5%	26.8%	27.0%	16.8%	6.5%	28.7%
Earnings per share ($)	20.1%	—	—	1.00	1.59	1.88	1.23	1.69	1.19	0.80	3.61
Stock price – high ($)	—	—	—	16.13	15.75	19.50	19.13	20.88	23.88	21.63	24.13
Stock price – low ($)	—	—	—	10.38	11.63	13.50	14.50	16.13	16.25	16.38	18.50
Stock price – close ($)	9.5%	—	—	11.50	13.75	18.13	17.88	20.00	17.00	19.00	21.75
P/E – high	—	—	—	16	10	10	16	12	20	27	7
P/E – low	—	—	—	10	7	7	12	10	14	20	5
Dividends per share ($)	19.9%	—	—	0.35	1.60	1.60	1.70	1.40	2.25	1.25	1.25
Book value per share ($)	—	—	—	0.47	0.45	0.73	0.62	0.92	(0.17)	(4.32)	(1.06)
Employees	11.6%	—	52	35	38	39	43	43	42	173	125

1994 Year-end:
Debt ratio: 100.0%
Return on equity: —
Cash (mil.): $60
Current ratio: 3.41
Long-term debt (mil.): $60
No. of shares (mil.): 6
Dividends
  Yield: 5.7%
  Payout: 34.6%
Market value (mil.): $139

**Stock Price History
High/Low 1987–94**

BRISTOL-MYERS SQUIBB COMPANY

OVERVIEW

Bristol-Myers Squibb, based in New York City, is one of the largest pharmaceutical companies in the US; 58% of revenues come from its pharmaceutical division. The division concentrates on cardiovascular, anti-infective, and anticancer drugs. The company also has a consumer health products division (nutritional products), a medical devices division, and a toiletries and beauty aids division.

With the US and German patents for the company's prominent heart drug, Capoten (with about $1.5 billion in sales), expiring in 1995, Bristol-Myers hopes that sales of Pravachol, its cholesterol fighter, and TAXOL, an anticancer agent, will counteract this giant loss. The company's short-term drug pipeline is not flush with products, so it has begun licensing drugs in the final stages of development from other companies, including sorivudine, a SmithKline Beecham drug that combats shingles.

Since 1990 the company has cut employment by 8,500 workers. To improve company relations with managed care entities, the pharmaceutical division's 12 regional business units receive support from centralized managed care operations and marketing units. Unlike many large drug companies, Bristol-Myers has refrained from spending big bucks on a big drug benefit manager (such as Merck's purchase of Medco) that has the potential to influence drug choice and cost for large insurers.

WHEN

Bristol-Myers Squibb is a merger of 2 rivals. Squibb was founded by Dr. Edward Squibb in New York City in 1858. Squibb developed techniques for making pure ether and chloroform. He headed the business most of his life, turning it over to his sons in 1891. Theodore Weicker, one of Merck's founders, bought a major interest in Squibb in 1905.

Sales of $414,000 in 1904 grew to $13 million by 1928. Squibb supplied penicillin and morphine during WWII. In 1952 the company was bought by Mathieson Chemical, which in turn was bought by Olin Industries in 1953, forming Olin Mathieson Chemical. (Squibb maintained its separate identity.)

From 1968 to 1971 the company went through a series of reorganizations and changed its name to the Squibb Corporation. By 1975 sales had reached $1 billion. Capoten and Corgard, 2 major cardiovascular drugs, were introduced in the late 1970s. Capoten was the first drug engineered to attack a specific disease-causing mechanism rather than developed by the traditional method of trial and error. Squibb formed a joint venture with Denmark's Novo in 1982 to sell insulin.

William Bristol and John Myers founded Clinton Pharmaceutical in Clinton, New York, in 1887 (renamed Bristol-Myers in 1900) to sell bulk pharmaceuticals. Bristol-Myers made antibiotics after the 1943 purchase of Cheplin Biological Labs.

The company began overseas expansion in the 1950s with the purchase of English and German companies. Bristol-Myers bought Clairol (1959), Mead Johnson (drugs, infant and nutritional formula; 1967), and Zimmer (orthopedic implants, 1972). The company introduced new drugs for treating cancer (Platinol, 1978) and a new antianxiety drug (BuSpar, 1986). In 1986 the company acquired the biotech companies Oncogen and Genetic Systems. Bristol-Myers purchased Squibb in 1989 for $12.7 billion. In 1990 the company bought Concept (arthroscopy products, US), Orthoplant (implants, Germany), and an interest in Rueil-Malmaison (drugs, France). Bristol-Myers bought Astel Group, a producer of hip implants, in 1991.

In 1993 company scientists developed a compound that killed certain cancer cells in rats and mice. Also that year Bristol-Myers sold the Drackett Company, its household goods business, for $1.15 billion and joined Eastman Kodak and Elf Aquitaine in developing 2 new heart drugs. Demand for recently introduced drugs VIDEX (AIDS treatment) and TAXOL (anticancer) indicates that they will be substantial producers for the company. In August 1993 Bristol-Myers announced a 5-year sales agreement with American Healthcare Systems, an alliance of over 1,000 nonprofit hospitals. Also in 1993 Axion Pharmaceuticals, a cancer treatment distributor, and Bristol-Myers formed a joint distribution venture.

President and CEO Charles Heimbold also took on the position of chairman of the board in 1995. Bristol Myers made Serzone, a new antidepressant with a low incidence of side effects, widely available in 1995. The company is being responsive to managed care providers and consumers by offering the new drug at a cost 10% to 20% below that of similar drugs used for the same purpose.

NYSE symbol: BMY
Fiscal year ends: December 31

WHO

Chairman, President, and CEO: Charles A. Heimbol Jr., age 61, $1,909,642 pay (prior to promotion)
EVP: Michael E. Autera, age 56, $1,092,851 pay
EVP; President, Pharmaceutical Group: Kenneth E. Weg, age 56, $933,502 pay (prior to promotion)
President, Pharmaceutical Research Institute: L. E. Rosenberg, age 62, $799,073 pay
President, Worldwide Consumer Medicines: Stephen E. Bear, age 43
President, Bristol-Myers Squibb Pharmaceuticals US: Samuel L. Barker, age 52
President, Bristol-Myers Squibb Pharmaceuticals Intercontinental: Samuel A. Hamad, age 53
President, Mead Johnson Nutritional Group: Peter R. Dolan, age 39
SVP and CFO: Michael F. Mee, age 52
SVP Human Resources: Charles G. Tharp, age 43
SVP and General Counsel: John L. McGoldrick, age 54
SVP Corporate Development: George P. Kooluris, age 50
SVP: E. Lynn Johnson, age 50
Auditors: Price Waterhouse LLP

WHERE

HQ: 345 Park Ave., New York, NY 10154-0037
Phone: 212-546-4000
Fax: 212-546-4020

	1994 Sales	
	$ mil.	% of total
US	7,846	59
Europe, Middle East & Africa	3,139	23
Pacific	1,320	10
Other Western Hemisphere	1,039	8
Adjustments	(1,360)	—
Total	**11,984**	**100**

WHAT

	1994 Sales	
	$ mil.	% of total
Prescription drugs	6,970	58
Consumer health	2,043	17
Medical devices	1,685	14
Toiletries/beauty aids	1,286	11
Total	**11,984**	**100**

Selected Pharmaceuticals
Azactam (antibiotic)
Capoten (cardiovascular)
Corgard (cardiovascular)
Glucophage (antidiabetic)
Monopril (cardiovascular)
Platinol (cancer drug)
Pravachol (cardiovascular)
Questran (cholesterol reducer)
Stadol (analgesic)
TAXOL (cancer drug)
VePesid (cancer drug)
VIDEX (AIDS treatment)

Selected Medical Devices
Minimally invasive surgery products
Orthopedic and surgical instruments

Consumer Health
Bufferin   Excedrin
Comtrex   Nuprin

Toiletries and Beauty Aids
Ban   Nice 'n Easy
Keri   Theragran
Miss Clairol   Vavoom

KEY COMPETITORS

Abbott Labs
American Home Products
Amgen
Ballard Medical
Bayer
Biogen
Biomet
Chiron Corp.
Ciba-Geigy
Danek Group
Dial
Dow Chemical
DuPont
Eli Lilly
Genentech
Glaxo Wellcome
Glycomed
Hoechst
Immunex
Johnson & Johnson
L'Oréal
Merck
Mitek Surgical
Monsanto
Novo Nordisk
Pfizer
Procter & Gamble
Rhône-Poulenc
Roche
St. Jude Medical
Sandoz
Schering-Plough
SmithKline Beecham
Upjohn
U.S. Surgical
Warner-Lambert

HOW MUCH

	9-Year Growth	1985	1986	1987	1988	1989	1990	1991	1992	1993	1994
Sales ($ mil.)	11.7%	4,444	4,836	5,401	5,973	9,189	10,300	11,159	11,156	11,413	11,984
Net income ($ mil.)	14.8%	531	590	710	829	747	1,748	2,056	1,603	1,959	1,842
Income as % of sales	—	12.0%	12.2%	13.1%	13.9%	8.1%	17.0%	18.4%	14.4%	17.2%	15.4%
Earnings per share ($)	7.2%	1.93	2.03	2.43	2.85	1.43	3.33	3.95	3.09	3.80	3.62
Stock price – high ($)	—	34.25	44.25	55.81	46.50	58.00	68.00	68.00	89.38	90.13	67.25	61.00
Stock price – low ($)	—	24.50	30.13	28.25	38.13	44.00	50.50	61.13	60.00	50.88	50.00
Stock price – close ($)	7.1%	31.13	41.31	41.63	45.25	56.00	67.00	88.25	67.38	58.25	57.88
P/E – high	—	18	18	23	16	41	20	23	29	18	17
P/E – low	—	13	15	12	13	31	15	16	19	13	14
Dividends per share ($)	13.4%	0.94	1.06	1.40	1.68	2.00	2.12	2.40	2.76	2.88	2.92
Book value per share ($)	2.7%	8.84	9.91	11.20	12.31	9.68	10.34	11.15	11.62	11.60	11.24
Employees	3.3%	35,700	34,900	34,100	35,200	54,100	52,900	53,500	52,600	49,500	47,700

1994 Year-end:
Debt ratio: 19.4%
Return on equity: 31.6%
Cash (mil.): $2,423
Current ratio: 1.57
Long-term debt (mil.): $644
No. of shares (mil.): 507
Dividends
　Yield: 5.0%
　Payout: 80.7%
Market value (mil.): $29,362

**Stock Price History
High/Low 1985–94**

BROWN-FORMAN CORPORATION

If you get no kick from champagne, maybe a boilermaker will work. Either way, you can get all the fixings from Brown-Forman. The Kentucky-based maker of Jack Daniel's and Southern Comfort has added beer (now brewed at its Lynchburg, Tennessee, distillery and tested in Nashville) to its lineup. The company also produces and sells all the accoutrements of fine dining (Lenox, Dansk, and Gorham) and travel (Hartmann luggage).

Brown-Forman (still controlled by members of the founding family) is one of the US's leading producers and distributors of spirits and wine. But in recent years sales and earnings have been flat, in part because of a decline in the popularity of hard liquor in the US. In response, the company has fortified its sales with varietal wines (a growing market), single malt whiskeys like Glenmorangie, and novelties like Tropical Freezes (premixed drinks that come in handy freezer pouches).

Brown-Forman is also shaking up its sales by concentrating on overseas sales. It is focusing not only on tried-and-true markets like Germany and Japan (where sales declined in 1994) and the UK, but also on new markets in Europe, Africa, and Asia. These new markets comprise 75% of the world's liquor market.

In 1870 George Brown and John Forman opened the Brown-Forman Distillery in Louisville, Kentucky, to produce Old Forester brand bourbon. Old Forester sold well through the end of the century, in part because of the company's innovative packaging (safety seals and quality guarantees on the bottles). Forman sold his interest in the company to the Brown family (which still controls Brown-Forman today) in 1902.

Old Forester continued to be successful under the Brown family. The company went public just before Prohibition in 1920 and obtained government approval to produce alcohol for medicinal purposes. In 1923 it made its first acquisition, Early Times. The company reestablished the Old Forester image as an alcoholic beverage after Prohibition.

During WWII the government greatly curtailed alcoholic beverage production (alcohol was needed for the war effort). The company compensated by providing alcohol for wartime rubber and gunpowder production. In 1941 Brown-Forman correctly predicted that the war would be over by 1945 and started the 4-year aging process for its bourbon. As a result Early Times dominated the bourbon market after the war.

In 1956 Brown-Forman expanded beyond Old Forester by purchasing Lynchburg, Tennessee–based Jack Daniel's (sour mash whiskey). The company retained the simple, black Jack Daniel's label and promoted the image of a small Tennessee distillery. Today the brand sells 4 million cases a year and is known worldwide.

Brown-Forman continued to expand its alcohol line during the 1960s and 1970s, acquiring Korbel (champagne and brandy, 1965), Quality Importers (Ambassador Scotch, Ambassador Gin, and Old Bushmills Irish Whiskey; 1967), Bolla and Cella (wines, 1968), and Canadian Mist (blended whiskey, 1971). In 1979 Brown-Forman purchased Southern Comfort (a top-selling liqueur).

Brown-Forman acquired Lenox (a leading US maker of fine china, crystal, gifts, and Hartmann luggage) in 1983. In 1990 the company bought Kirk Stieff (silver and pewter), and in 1991 it purchased Dansk International Designs, a producer of china, crystal, and silver, including the high-quality Gorham line. The company has been focusing on selling its Lenox and Hartmann products in Europe, Japan, Australia, and Hong Kong.

In 1991 Brown-Forman acquired the US distribution rights to Glenmorangie scotch and Fontanafredda Italian wines and acquired wine maker Jekel Vineyards. In 1992 it bought the family-owned Fetzer Vineyards in Mendocino County, California.

In 1993 Owsley Brown II succeeded his brother Lee as CEO. That same year the company introduced Southern Comfort Cocktails — an effort to mimic the success of the Jack Daniel's line of Country Cocktails, introduced earlier in the year.

As sales continued to lag in 1994 despite the introduction of new drink products for the popular market, the company reorganized its beverage operations to facilitate foreign sales. The wisdom of this effort began to be apparent in 1995 when the company agreed to form a 50/50 joint venture with India's Jagatjit Industries to bring Brown-Forman's products to that country's potentially large market.

After Moore County, Tennessee, voters approved a referendum in 1995, whiskey sales were allowed in Lynchburg (home of Jack Daniel's) for the first time since Prohibition.

WHO

Chairman, President, and CEO: Owsley Brown II,
age 52, $1,655,682 pay (prior to promotion)
VC: Owsley Brown Frazier, age 59, $768,645 pay
**President and CEO, Brown-Forman Beverages
Worldwide:** William M. Street, age 56, $1,208,266 pay
EVP and CFO: Steven B. Ratoff, age 52
Chairman and CEO, Lenox, Inc.: Malcolm Jozoff,
age 55, $1,031,518 pay
SVP: John P. Bridenhall, age 45
SVP: Lois Mateus, age 48
SVP, General Counsel, and Secretary: Michael B.
Crutcher, age 51
**SVP; Executive Director, Human Resources and
Information Services:** Russell Buzby, age 61
Auditors: Coopers & Lybrand L.L.P.

WHERE

HQ: 850 Dixie Hwy., PO Box 1080, Louisville,
KY 40201-1080
Phone: 502-585-1100
Fax: 502-774-7876

The Wines and Spirits segment operates 18 facilities in
the US, 2 in Canada, 2 in the US Virgin Islands, and one
in Ireland. Consumer Durables operates 19 facilities in
the US and 86 domestic retail stores.

	1995 Sales	
	$ mil.	% of total
US	1,459	87
Other countries	221	13
Total	**1,680**	**100**

WHAT

	1995 Sales		1995 Operating Income	
	$ mil.	% of total	$ mil.	% of total
Wines & Spirits	1,138	68	244	87
Consumer Durables	542	32	38	13
Other	—	—	(14)	—
Total	**1,680**	**100**	**268**	**100**

Selected Brands

Spirits	Wines
Black Bush (whiskey)	Bel Arbors
Canadian Mist (whiskey)	Bolla
Gentleman Jack (whiskey)	Brolio
Glenmorangie (scotch)	Carmen Vineyards
Jack Daniel's (whiskey)	Cella
Jack Daniel's Country	Fetzer Vineyards
Cocktails	Fontana Candida
Korbel (brandy)	Fontanafredda
Old Forester (bourbon)	Jekel Vineyards
Pepe Lopez (tequila)	Korbel Champagnes
Southern Comfort	Noilly Prat Vermouths
(liqueur)	
Southern Comfort	**Consumer Durables**
Cocktails	Dansk (china, crystal)
Tropical Freezes	Gorham (china, crystal,
Usher's (scotch)	flatware)
	Hartmann (luggage, leather
Beer	goods)
Jack Daniel's Classic	Lenox (china, crystal,
1866 Amber Lager Beer	giftware)

KEY COMPETITORS

Allied Domecq	Grand Metropolitan	Oneida
American Brands	Guinness	Robert Mondavi
Anheuser-Busch	Kendall-Jackson	Royal Doulton
Canandaigua Wine	Libbey	Samsonite
Carlsberg	LVMH	Sara Lee
Corning	Mikasa	Seagram
Dunhill	Nestlé	Waterford
Gallo	Noritake	Wedgewood

HOW MUCH

	9-Year Growth	1986	1987	1988	1989	1990	1991	1992	1993	1994	1995
Sales ($ mil.)	6.0%	995	1,098	1,067	1,006	1,017	1,119	1,260	1,692	1,665	1,680
Net income ($ mil.)	6.3%	86	90	103	145	81	145	146	156	161	149
Income as % of sales	—	8.7%	8.2%	9.7%	14.4%	8.0%	13.0%	11.6%	9.2%	9.7%	8.9%
Earnings per share ($)	10.3%	0.89	0.93	1.08	1.72	0.96	1.74	1.76	1.88	2.04	2.15
Stock price – high ($)[1]	—	10.67	14.33	18.46	19.33	29.42	30.58	28.17	30.00	29.58	32.50
Stock price – low ($)[1]	—	6.81	9.94	8.88	11.29	18.75	18.67	21.58	24.00	24.33	26.13
Stock price – close ($)[1]	12.8%	10.33	13.47	11.75	19.21	29.42	23.25	27.42	27.50	29.08	30.50
P/E – high	—	12	15	17	11	31	18	16	16	15	15
P/E – low	—	8	11	8	7	20	11	12	13	12	12
Dividends per share ($)	17.9%	0.22	0.30	0.41	0.51	0.63	0.72	0.78	0.86	0.93	0.97
Book value per share ($)	4.2%	5.36	6.00	5.27	6.48	6.95	7.97	8.89	9.75	6.55	7.74
Employees	0.8%	6,800	6,600	5,600	5,500	5,400	5,600	6,900	6,700	7,100	7,300

1995 Year-end:
Debt ratio: 36.1%
Return on equity: 30.1%
Cash (mil.): $62
Current ratio: 2.44
Long-term debt (mil.): $247
No. of shares (mil.): 69
Dividends
  Yield: 3.2%
  Payout: 45.1%
Market value (mil.): $2,104

**Stock Price History[1]
High/Low 1986–95**

[1]Stock prices are for the prior calendar year.

BROWNING-FERRIS INDUSTRIES, INC.

OVERVIEW

Like the Pac-Man of garbage, Browning-Ferris Industries (BFI) is gobbling up smaller waste disposal firms — 113 in 1994 alone — as that industry becomes increasingly consolidated. Among the company's 1994 purchases were UK-based Attwoods plc, the US's #4 waste company (won in a hostile takeover) and a 50% stake in Otto Waste Services, one of Germany's top trash haulers. Despite BFI's appetite, the Houston-based company remains the world's #2 waste management firm, after WMX Technologies.

BFI's fleet of 12,400 trucks collects solid waste in 45 states and 11 foreign countries. The company operates 110 waste transfer stations (50 company-owned), nearly 150 landfills, 28 medical-waste treatment facilities, and 136 recycling facilities worldwide.

BFI's fastest-growing business is recycling, an industry BFI veterans discounted when William Ruckelshaus became CEO in 1988. Anticipating increasing government regulation, Ruckelshaus nurtured BFI's recycling segment and its revenues soared from $9.6 million in 1990 to $359 million in 1994.

In 1995 BFI began an aggressive ad campaign that targeted the company's rivals in the New York City refuse industry. BFI entered that city's market in 1993 and is now its largest waste collection company.

WHEN

Accountant Tom Fatjo and Harvard MBA Louis Waters founded American Refuse Systems in 1967 with a single truck, providing garbage collection to a Houston neighborhood. They saw that the 1960s clean-air laws created opportunities for large garbage businesses with the resources to comply with changing environmental regulations. In 1969 the company acquired construction equipment distributor Browning-Ferris Machinery and changed its name to Browning-Ferris Industries. BFI acquired a total of 157 waste disposal firms by 1973. That year BFI signed its first foreign contract to provide trash service in parts of Spain. Although it continued to expand its international presence, concentrating on Europe and the Far East, it lagged behind rival Waste Management, which picked up most of the lucrative international contracts.

BFI moved into a variety of peripheral businesses during the 1970s, including wastepaper recycling. In 1975 revenues and profits fell 18%, partly because of decreased demand for wastepaper, which had previously provided nearly half of the company's revenues. BFI spun off its wastepaper subsidiary, Consolidated Fibres, in 1976. In 1976 and 1977 BFI hiked prices across its entire operation, resulting in a 37% rise in earnings in 1977.

By 1980 BFI had become the 2nd largest US waste disposal company. It acquired 508 companies from 1981 to 1988, including hazardous-waste disposer CECOS International (1983). It formed a joint venture to market trash-burning power plants (1984) and entered the medical-waste field by buying 2 small firms (1986).

BFI paid fines of $1.35 million after pleading guilty to price fixing in 1987 and paid $2.5 million in 1988 and $1.55 million in 1990 to settle suits arising from environmental violations at Louisiana hazardous-waste sites. To improve its image, in 1988 BFI recruited William Ruckelshaus, a former EPA administrator, to take over as CEO. (As a US deputy attorney general, Ruckelshaus had resigned rather than follow Richard Nixon's directive to fire Watergate special prosecutor Archibald Cox.)

After the EPA denied BFI permits to restart 2 hazardous-waste operations in 1990, the company discontinued such operations altogether, writing off $295 million in the process. The company reserved another $246.5 million in 1991 for projected landfill closure and postclosure management costs resulting from new EPA regulations.

In 1993 BFI spent almost $140 million to buy more than 100 companies. It had announced plans to acquire rival Western Waste but backed out of the deal after it decided that the $400 million price tag was too high.

In 1994 the SEC accused BFI's former general counsel, Howard Hoover, of insider trading because he had sold about half his shares in the company a week before it announced lower earnings projections in 1991. BFI had fired Hoover several weeks after the sale was revealed in 1991.

BFI took garbage collection high-tech in 1995 when it contracted with MapInfo Corp. and software provider RoTec, to develop new collection routes to improve productivity and cut costs. That same year BFI Europe acquired Swiss waste collection and transport company Fritz Erismann AG. The company's Sunshine Canyon landfill near metropolitan Los Angeles was being readied for a fall 1995 opening.

WHO

Chairman and CEO: William D. Ruckelshaus, age 62,
$1,143,546 pay
VC and Chief Marketing Officer: Norman A. Myers,
age 58, $639,096 pay
President and COO: Bruce E. Ranck, age 45,
$657,638 pay
Chairman and President, BFI International, Inc.: Louis
A. Waters, age 56, $510,298 pay
President, Browning-Ferris Industries Europe, Inc.:
Eric A. Black
SVP and CFO: Jeffrey E. Curtiss, age 46, $361,197 pay
SVP Disposal Operations: Hugh J. Dillingham III,
age 45
SVP Corporate Development: J. Gregory Muldoon,
age 40
SVP and General Counsel: Rufus Wallingford, age 54
VP Sales and Marketing: Edward H. Hamlett
VP, Controller, and Chief Accounting Officer: David R.
Hopkins, age 51
VP Human Resources and Employee Relations:
Susan J. Piller
Auditors: Arthur Andersen & Co, SC

WHERE

HQ: 757 N. Eldridge, Houston, TX 77079
Phone: 713-870-8100
Fax: 713-870-7844

BFI operates in 650 locations in Asia, Australia, Europe,
the Middle East, New Zealand, and North America.

	1994 Sales		1994 Operating Income	
	$ mil.	% of total	$ mil.	% of total
US & Puerto Rico	3,294	76	427	78
Other countries	1,021	24	117	22
Total	**4,315**	**100**	**544**	**100**

WHAT

	1994 Sales	
	$ mil.	% of total
North America		
Solid waste collection	2,360	50
Solid waste transfer & disposal	885	19
Recycling	359	8
Medical waste	161	3
Other services	83	2
International	859	18
Adjustments	(392)	—
Total	**4,315**	**100**

Solid Waste Services
Collection (commercial/governmental/industrial/
residential collection)
Transfer and disposal (operation of 110 transfer stations
and 146 landfills)
Medical waste (collection and disposal, including 28
waste treatment sites)
Recycling (service for residential and commercial
customers, including collection, organic waste
treatment, and tire recycling)
Other services (including portable restroom services and
street and parking lot sweeping services)

KEY COMPETITORS

Allied Waste
American Waste
Bechtel
Canadian Pacific
Conrail
EnviroSource
Integrated Waste
 Services
International
 Technology

Mid-American Waste
Norcal Waste
Safety-Kleen
Sanifill
TRW
Union Pacific
USA Waste Services
Western Waste
WMX Technologies

HOW MUCH

	9-Year Growth	1985	1986	1987	1988	1989	1990	1991	1992	1993	1994
Sales ($ mil.)	15.9%	1,145	1,328	1,657	2,067	2,551	2,968	3,183	3,288	3,495	4,315
Net income ($ mil.)	10.9%	112	137	172	227	263	250	65	176	197	284
Income as % of sales	—	9.8%	10.3%	10.4%	11.0%	10.3%	8.4%	2.0%	5.3%	5.6%	6.6%
Earnings per share ($)	7.4%	0.80	0.95	1.15	1.51	1.74	1.64	0.42	1.11	1.15	1.52
Stock price – high ($)	—	16.00	23.69	35.75	29.25	42.75	49.25	30.75	27.13	28.63	32.88
Stock price – low ($)	—	9.16	15.13	17.50	20.88	26.88	20.00	16.88	19.50	20.88	24.25
Stock price – close ($)	6.6%	16.00	22.38	28.00	27.38	38.75	22.25	21.75	26.13	25.75	28.38
P/E – high	—	20	25	31	19	25	30	73	24	25	22
P/E – low	—	12	16	15	14	15	12	40	18	18	16
Dividends per share ($)	10.8%	0.27	0.31	0.38	0.46	0.54	0.62	0.67	0.68	0.68	0.68
Book value per share ($)	13.3%	3.95	5.11	5.93	7.05	8.33	7.61	7.29	8.66	8.83	12.18
Employees	8.8%	17,300	18,000	18,200	21,500	25,500	25,200	27,000	29,400	31,600	37,000

1994 Year-end:
Debt ratio: 38.7%
Return on equity: 14.5%
Cash (mil.): $141
Current ratio: 1.01
Long-term debt (mil.): $1,459
No. of shares (mil.): 196
Dividends
 Yield: 2.4%
 Payout: 44.7%
Market value (mil.): $5,572

**Stock Price History
High/Low 1985–94**

BRUNSWICK CORPORATION

OVERVIEW

Brunswick's business is leisure. The 150-year-old Illinois-based company is the leading US maker of recreation and leisure products as well as the world's leading manufacturer of pleasure boats and equipment. It operates one of North America's largest bowling chains (Brunswick Recreation Centers) as well as restaurants (Circus World Pizza) and manufactures bowling equipment (Brunswick), fishing rods and reels (Zebco and Browning), golf equipment, and billiard tables (Brunswick). Almost 3/4 of the company's revenues comes from its marine operations, which include a variety of outboard motors (for example, Mercury, Mariner, and Force); boats designed for sport fishing (Robalo), pleasure (Bayliner),

performance (Astro), and yachting (Sea Ray), among others; and trailers and accessories.

Despite a surge in profits, Brunswick has been in choppy waters of late. Earnings in 1994 were up 240%, but the company's prospects were clouded by federal investigations into its defense business and personal conflicts among executives (causing president John Reilly to jump ship after 9 months on the job). The government dropped its case, and the company sold most of its military operations in 1995.

In May 1995 former Johnson & Johnson executive Peter Larson was brought on board to succeed chairman Jack Reichert, who is retiring October 1, 1995.

WHEN

Swiss immigrant woodworker John Brunswick built his first billiard table in 1845 in Cincinnati. In 1874 he formed a partnership with Julius Balke, and in 1884 they teamed with H. W. Collender, forming the Brunswick-Balke-Collender Company.

Following Brunswick's death, son-in-law Moses Bensinger became president and diversified into bowling equipment in the 1880s. His son B. E. followed as president (1904) and led the company into wood and rubber products, phonographs, and records. (Al Jolson recorded "Sonny Boy" on a Brunswick label.) Brunswick went public after WWI.

By 1930 Brunswick had sold many businesses to concentrate on bowling and billiards, sports that had acquired bad reputations during the 1920s and 1930s. When B. E. died in 1935, his son Bob became CEO and launched a massive promotional campaign to make the sports more respectable.

Bob Bensinger moved to chairman in 1954, and his brother Ted succeeded him as CEO. Rival A.M.F. introduced the first automatic pinsetter in 1952, and Brunswick followed in 1956. By 1958 Brunswick had captured the industry lead, as bowling equipment sales rose 650% between 1956 and 1961. Under Ted, Brunswick diversified, adding MacGregor (sporting goods, 1958), Aloe (medical supplies, 1959), Mercury (marine products, 1961), and Zebco (fishing equipment, 1961). The company adopted its present name in 1960.

By 1963 bowling sales had plummeted, and in 1965 Brunswick lost $76.9 million. The company sold many unprofitable enterprises, intensified research on an automatic scorer

and metal fiber technology (for industrial and defense applications), and emphasized health products through subsidiary Sherwood Medical Industries. In 1978 Brunswick added Oxford Laboratories (medical diagnostics) and the Vapor Corporation (energy and transportation products). To foil a takeover by Whittaker Corporation in 1982, Brunswick sold Sherwood to American Home Products. CEO Jack Reichert, a former pin boy who became chairman in 1983, cut corporate staff 59% and promoted the marine business.

In 1986 Brunswick sparked an industry-wide consolidation trend by spending $774 million to buy boat builders Bayliner and Ray Industries.

A marine industry slump led to a $71 million loss in 1989. The company restructured and cut costs, which enabled it to post a profit in 1990. Brunswick bought Kiekhaefer Aeromarine (marine propulsion engines, 1990) and Martin Reel Company (fly reels, 1991). In 1992 Brunswick and Tracker Marine (Missouri-based boat manufacturer) agreed to form a partnership to manufacture boats and marine equipment.

That same year the company acquired the Browning line of rods and reels. In 1993 the company announced plans to sell its Technical Group (aerospace, defense, electronics, machinery, automotive, aircraft, and oil and gas products); the sale went through once the federal investigation was closed.

In 1995 Brunswick's Mercury division formed a joint venture with Orbital Engine (Australia) to design and make fuel systems for small, 2-cycle engines to meet stricter EPA emission standards.

NYSE symbol: BC
Fiscal year ends: December 31

WHO

Chairman: Jack F. Reichert, age 64, $1,735,000 pay
President and CEO: Peter N. Larson, age 55
EVP; Group President, Brunswick Marine: John M.
Charvat, age 64, $684,197 pay
VP; President, Mercury Marine Division: David D.
Jones, age 52, $588,384 pay (prior to promotion)
VP; President, Brunswick Division: Frederick J.
Florjancic Jr., age 48, $476,301 pay
VP; President, Zebco Division: Jim W. Dawson, age 60
President, US Marine Division: Robert C. Steinway,
age 43
President, Sea Ray Division: William J. Barrington,
age 44
VP Administration: Dianne M. Yaconetti, age 48
VP Finance: William R. McManaman, age 47
Controller: Thomas K. Erwin, age 45
General Counsel: Robert T. McNaney, age 60
Director Human Resources: Patrick J. Gannon
Auditors: Arthur Andersen & Co, SC

WHERE

HQ: One N. Field Ct., Lake Forest, IL 60045-4811
Phone: 708-735-4700
Fax: 708-735-4765

Brunswick operates approximately 35 US plants, 5
foreign plants, and 7 pizza restaurants. Of its 126
bowling centers, 117 are in North America and 9 in
Germany and Austria.

	1994 Sales		1994 Operating Income	
	$ mil.	% of total	$ mil.	% of total
US	2,213	82	205	79
Other countries	487	18	53	21
Total	**2,700**	**100**	**258**	**100**

WHAT

	1994 Sales		1994 Operating Income	
	$ mil.	% of total	$ mil.	% of total
Marine	1,991	74	175	68
Recreation	709	26	83	32
Total	**2,700**	**100**	**258**	**100**

Selected Brand Names

Boats

Astro	Fisher	Procraft	Ski Ray
Bayliner	Jazz	Quantum	Spectrum
Ciera	Laguna	Robalo	Starcraft
Cobra	Maxum	Sea Ray	Trophy
Escort (trailers)	MonArk	Sea Rayder	US Marine

Boat Motors

Force	MotorGuide	Stealth
Mariner	Quicksilver Marine	Thruster
MerCruiser	(parts/accessories)	
Mercury Marine		

Recreation Centers/Restaurants
Brunswick Recreation Centers
Circus World Pizza

Sporting Goods
Bowling (Anvilane, Armor Plate 3000, AS-90, BallWall,
BowlerVision, Brunswick, Colorvision, GS-10,
Guardian, Leiserv, Perry-Austen, Rhino, Systems
2000)
Billiards (Brunswick)
Golf (Brunswick Golf, Precision FCM)
Fishing (Classic, Martin, Pro Staff, Quantum, Zebco)

KEY COMPETITORS

Anthony	Harley-Davidson	Outboard Marine
Industries	Honda	ShowBiz Pizza
Callaway Golf	Johnson	Time
Fountain	Worldwide	Suzuki
Powerboat	MacAndrews	Volvo
Genmar	& Forbes	Yamaha

HOW MUCH

	9-Year Growth	1985	1986	1987	1988	1989	1990	1991	1992	1993	1994
Sales ($ mil.)	6.4%	1,539	1,717	3,086	3,282	2,826	2,478	2,088	2,059	2,207	2,700
Net income ($ mil.)	2.9%	100	110	169	193	(71)	71	(24)	38	38	129
Income as % of sales	—	6.5%	6.4%	5.5%	5.9%	—	2.9%	—	1.8%	1.7%	4.8%
Earnings per share ($)	1.6%	1.17	1.32	1.90	2.20	(0.81)	0.80	(0.27)	0.41	0.39	1.35
Stock price – high ($)	—	11.38	19.69	30.25	24.13	21.50	16.13	16.38	17.75	18.50	25.38
Stock price – low ($)	—	7.75	10.81	6.75	14.50	13.00	6.38	8.00	12.13	12.50	17.00
Stock price – close ($)	6.3%	10.91	16.94	14.75	16.88	14.13	9.00	13.88	16.25	18.00	18.88
P/E – high	—	10	15	16	11	—	20	—	43	47	19
P/E – low	—	7	8	4	7	—	8	—	30	32	13
Dividends per share ($)	6.5%	0.25	0.28	0.30	0.40	0.44	0.44	0.44	0.44	0.44	0.44
Book value per share ($)	4.8%	6.23	7.80	9.52	10.97	8.82	9.33	8.79	8.65	8.44	9.54
Employees	1.2%	18,700	26,800	28,400	28,500	25,700	20,500	19,500	17,000	18,000	20,800

1994 Year-end:
Debt ratio: 26.4%
Return on equity: 15.0%
Cash (mil.): $203
Current ratio: 1.70
Long-term debt (mil.): $319
No. of shares (mil.): 95
Dividends
  Yield: 2.3%
  Payout: 32.6%
Market value (mil.): $1,802

**Stock Price History
High/Low 1985–94**

BURLINGTON INDUSTRIES, INC.

OVERVIEW

After several years of losses, Burlington Industries is back in the black again, posting profits for 2 straight years. The Greensboro, North Carolina–based company has restructured since a 1987 LBO (it went public again in 1992), selling a number of assets and consolidating operations.

Burlington makes a variety of finished fabrics for the apparel industry and is the nation's #1 maker of specialty denim. It also manufactures synthetic yarns and home furnishing products, including fabrics for draperies, mattresses, and upholstery (Burlington House), as well as blinds, area rugs, and commercial and residential carpeting (Lees Carpets).

The company is focusing on improving its time-to-market to best its competition. To improve its ability to quickly provide its customers with new products, the company has worked to improve product development and production time.

In 1994 George Henderson was named CEO. He succeeded Frank Greenberg, who helped engineer the company's restructuring.

WHEN

Spencer Love, who had entered the milling business after WWI, moved his North Carolina cotton mill from Gastonia to Burlington in 1923. In order to finance the new mill, he convinced the citizens of Burlington to help him sell stock in a new company, Burlington Mills. In 1924, when the mill was struggling due to waning demand for its cotton products, Love switched from cotton milling to rayon.

When textile prices dropped during the Great Depression, many mills went out of business, especially in the North, where labor was more expensive. Burlington bought several of these failed businesses. Corporate headquarters moved to Greensboro in 1935. Burlington started producing hosiery in 1940. It continued to expand in the 1950s, buying Pacific Mills and Klopman Mills, and changed its name to Burlington Industries in 1955.

Burlington further diversified into consumer products with the acquisitions of Charm Tred Mills, a scatter-rug manufacturer (1959), and Philadelphia carpet producer James Lees & Company (1960). The company bought Globe Furniture in 1966 and made several other acquisitions in the furniture business throughout the 1970s. William Klopman, son of Klopman Mills's founder, became CEO in 1976. He focused on renovating the company's plants and moving Burlington into consumer products and clothing fabrics in response to increasing foreign competition in its traditional textiles markets.

By 1980 Burlington was by far the world's largest textile producer. Most of its profits came from consumer products sold under private labels and Burlington's brand names. The company's inability to move beyond the commodity textiles business led to several years of poor profits and a takeover attempt by Montreal-based Dominion Textile, a former Burlington partner in the rayon business.

Chairman Frank Greenberg led management in an LBO (financed primarily by Morgan Stanley), taking the company private in 1987. Burlington subsequently sold off its foreign operations (except in North America) and focused on repaying its acquisition debt.

The company continued to sell businesses not related to its core product lines, including its automotive interior carpet and trim manufacturing subsidiary (C. H. Masland & Sons) in 1991. Burlington went public in 1992 with a $629 million stock offering. The company, renamed Burlington Industries Equity, continued cost-cutting efforts by restructuring its residential carpet division.

In 1992 the US Department of Labor started an investigation of Burlington's administration of its ESOP. Later that year 2 company employees representing the 20,000-member ESOP sued Burlington management and Morgan Stanley. The suit alleged breach of fiduciary duty and other violations of the ESOP following the LBO. The ESOP, which formerly controlled 49% of Burlington's stock, saw its ownership shrink to less than 3%. In November 1992 Burlington was granted a change of venue by a US District Court judge.

In 1994 the federal labor department completed its investigation and found nothing wrong. Also that year the court dismissed in whole or in part 10 of the plaintiffs' 18 complaints, although their basic elements remain in effect. Also in 1994 the company sold its decorative prints business to Galey & Lord, and stockholders voted to reinstate the old Burlington Industries name.

In 1995 Burlington acquired Bacova Guild, a maker of rugs, welcome mats, and kitchen and bath accessories. That same year the company signed a joint venture agreement with Mafatlal Industries, India's largest textile producer, to make and market denim in India.

NYSE symbol: BUR
Fiscal year ends: Saturday nearest September 30

WHO

Chairman: Frank S. Greenberg, age 65, $1,750,004 pay
VC: Bernard A. Leventhal, age 61, $745,000 pay
President and CEO: George W. Henderson III, age 46, $830,008 pay (prior to promotion)
EVP; President and COO, Burlington Interior Furnishings Group: Abraham B. Stenberg, age 59, $800,008 pay
EVP: Gary P. Welchman, age 51
SVP Finance and Law and CFO: John D. Englar, age 47
Group VP: George C. Waldrep Jr., age 55
VP Finance and Investor Relations: James H. Clippard Jr., age 57
VP and Controller: Agustin J. Diodati, age 56
VP and General Counsel: Peter D. W. Heberling, age 43
VP Human Resources and Public Relations: J. Kenneth Lesley, age 58
Treasurer: Park R. Davidson, age 60
Auditors: Ernst & Young LLP

WHERE

HQ: 3330 W. Friendly Ave., Greensboro, NC 27410
Phone: 910-379-2000
Fax: 910-379-4504

Burlington has 41 plants in 9 states and 3 plants in Mexico.

WHAT

	1994 Sales		1994 Operating Income	
	$ mil.	% of total	$ mil.	% of total
Apparel products	1,331	63	152	72
Interior furnishings products	796	37	60	28
Adjustments	—	—	(8)	—
Total	**2,127**	**100**	**204**	**100**

Apparel Products

Denim Fabrics

Knitted Fabrics (cotton and cotton/polyester blends)

Synthetic Yarns (Burlington Madison Yarn Co.)
Filament yarns
Spun synthetic yarns

Wool Worsted and Worsted Blend Fabrics (Menswear)

Woven Synthetic Fabrics (Klopman Fabrics)
Lightweight, reusable, protective barrier fabrics (Maxima)
Lightweight polyester and polyester blend fabrics
Waterproof, water-repellent, breathable, and other coated synthetic fabrics (Ultrex)
Woven polyester and nylon fabrics

Interior Furnishings Products

Carpets
Area rugs (tufted) and bath rugs
Commercial carpet and carpet tiles (Lees)
Custom carpet samples (Colorfax)
Permanently stain-resistant residential carpeting (Lees for Life)
Stain-resistant commercial carpeting (Duracolor)

Fabrics
Burlington House Fabrics and Burlington House American Lifestyle
Bedroom ensembles
Draperies (ready-made and made-to-measure)
Mattress ticking
Upholstery fabrics (woven jacquard and textured fabrics)
Window coverings

KEY COMPETITORS

Avondale Mills
Dunavant Enterprises
DuPont
Fieldcrest Cannon
Fruit of the Loom
Greenwood Mills
Guilford Mills
JPS Textile
Milliken
Mohawk Industries
Newell Co.
R.B. Pamplin
Shaw Industries
Springs Industries
Unifi
WestPoint Stevens

HOW MUCH

	Annual Growth	1985	1986	1987	1988	1989	1990	1991	1992	1993	1994
Sales ($ mil.)	(3.0%)	2,802	2,778	3,279	2,452	2,181	2,043	1,926	2,066	2,058	2,127
Net income ($ mil.)	24.7%	13	48	22	(33)	(36)	(117)	(92)	(89)	90	95
Income as % of sales	—	—	1.7%	0.7%	—	—	—	—	—	4.4%	4.5%
Earnings per share ($)	—	—	—	—	—	—	—	—	(2.42)	1.31	1.40
Stock price – high ($)	—	—	—	—	—	—	—	—	15.00	16.88	17.13
Stock price – low ($)	—	—	—	—	—	—	—	—	10.88	12.63	9.25
Stock price – close ($)	(16.0%)	—	—	—	—	—	—	—	14.00	15.50	9.88
P/E – high	—	—	—	—	—	—	—	—	—	13	12
P/E – low	—	—	—	—	—	—	—	—	—	10	7
Dividends per share ($)	—	—	—	—	—	—	—	—	0.00	0.00	0.00
Book value per share ($)	10.5%	—	—	—	—	—	—	—	6.96	8.22	8.51
Employees	(6.8%)	45,000	43,000	44,000	28,000	27,500	28,000	24,000	23,400	23,600	23,800

1994 Year-end:
Debt ratio: 61.3%
Return on equity: 16.7%
Cash (mil.): $41
Current ratio: 2.33
Long-term debt (mil.): $858
No. of shares (mil.): 68
Dividends
  Yield: —
  Payout: —
Market value (mil.): $667

Stock Price History
High/Low 1992–94

BURLINGTON NORTHERN INC.

OVERVIEW

Burlington Northern (BN) operates one of the longest freight rail systems in North America, a 24,300-mile system of main and secondary track in 25 states and 2 Canadian provinces. With track from the Florida Panhandle to British Columbia, Fort Worth–based BN serves some of the continent's richest coal-, grain-, and timber-producing regions. Its intermodal business (train-to-truck, train-to-ship, or truck-to-ship) is 15% of revenue. BN has access to both Mexico and Canada.

In 1995 BN and Santa Fe Pacific Corporation received ICC approval to merge. The path to the merger was not always a smooth one: in

1994 rival Union Pacific (UP) made a hostile bid for Santa Fe but withdrew its offer for legal reasons in early 1995. Santa Fe's tough CEO, Rob Krebs, will likely become CEO of the newly combined railroad, with revenues near $8 billion and almost 31,000 track miles. While that will make it the nation's biggest railroad, the company may not hold the title for long: in mid-1995 UP announced its intention to buy the Southern Pacific, thereby creating a railroad with 35,000 miles of track.

BN lately has improved performance by reducing its job force and instituting state-of-the-art technology into its operations.

WHEN

Burlington Northern is largely the creation of James Hill, who began his railroad empire in 1878 by acquiring the St. Paul & Pacific Railroad in Minnesota. By 1893 Hill had completed the Great Northern Railway, which extended from St. Paul to Seattle. The following year he gained control of Northern Pacific (chartered in 1864), which had been constructed between Duluth, Minnesota, and Tacoma, Washington, with extensions to Portland, Oregon, and St. Paul. With the help of J. P. Morgan, in 1901 Hill acquired the Chicago, Burlington & Quincy (Burlington), whose routes included Chicago–St. Paul, Chicago–Denver, Omaha–Billings, and Billings–Denver–Fort Worth–Houston. To give Great Northern an entrance to Oregon, Hill created the Spokane, Portland & Seattle Railway (SP&S), completed in 1908.

Hill intended to merge Great Northern, Northern Pacific, SP&S, and Burlington under his Morgan-backed Northern Securities Company, but in 1904 the Supreme Court found that Northern Securities had violated the Sherman Anti-Trust Act. Although the Court dissolved the holding company, Hill kept control of the individual railroads until his death in 1916.

Meanwhile, Jim Hill's railroads produced some of America's best-known passenger trains. Great Northern's Empire Builder began service between Chicago and Seattle in 1929; it is operated today by Amtrak. The 1934 Burlington Zephyr was the nation's first streamlined passenger diesel.

After several years of deliberation by the ICC, Great Northern and Northern Pacific were allowed to merge in 1970 along with jointly owned subsidiaries Burlington and

SP&S. The new company, Burlington Northern (BN), acquired the St. Louis–San Francisco Railway (Frisco) in 1980. The Frisco, with lines stretching from St. Louis to such cities as Dallas, Oklahoma City, Kansas City, and Pensacola, added more than 4,650 miles to the BN rail network.

The company formed Burlington Motor Carriers (BMC) in 1985 to manage 5 trucking companies it had acquired. As a result of its decision to focus only on railroads, BN in 1988 sold BMC and spun off Burlington Resources, an independent holding company for its nonrailroad businesses (primarily natural gas, oil, minerals, construction, and forest products, including 1.8 million acres of land). This left Burlington Northern Railroad and BN Leasing as its principal subsidiaries.

In 1989 BN hired an outside director as CEO: Gerald Grinstein, a former Western Airlines CEO with a knack for labor relations but with no experience running a railroad. In 1991 BN built a link into Mexico through a rail-barge joint venture with Mexican industrial firm Grupo Protexa. In 1992 it cut 4 levels of field management; a systemwide control center was opened in Fort Worth the same year.

In 1993 BN's service was disrupted by midwestern summer flooding, one of the worst natural disasters to affect US railroads. In 1994 BN put into operation the first of its new 350 high-tech locomotives, which run on alternating current and are significantly more powerful than most others (3 of the new ones can pull a payload that would need 5 of the older ones).

In 1995 the company opened its 180,000-square-foot, high-tech Network Operations Center, the nerve center of the entire railroad.

NYSE symbol: BNI
Fiscal year ends: December 31

Chairman and CEO: Gerald Grinstein, age 62,
$1,482,527 pay
**EVP Safety and Corporate Support, Burlington
Northern Railroad Co.:** John T. Chain Jr., age 60,
$572,220 pay
EVP and CFO: David C. Anderson, age 53, $558,333 pay
EVP Law and Secretary: Edmund W. Burke, age 46,
$497,125 pay
EVP Coal Business Group: John Q. Anderson, age 43,
$484,167 pay
**EVP Merchandise Business, Burlington Northern
Railroad Co.:** Ronald A. Rittenmeyer, age 47
**EVP Intermodal Business, Burlington Northern
Railroad Co.:** Gregory T. Swienton, age 45
EVP Employee Relations: James B. Dagnon, age 55
**SVP Corporate Development, Burlington Northern
Railroad Co.:** Richard L. Lewis, age 54
SVP and Treasurer: Robert F. McKenney, age 41
Auditors: Coopers & Lybrand L.L.P.

WHERE

HQ: 3800 Continental Plaza, 777 Main St., Fort Worth,
TX 76102-5384
Phone: 817-333-2000
Fax: 817-878-2377

Principal Cities Served

Billings, MT	Omaha, NE
Birmingham, AL	Pensacola, FL
Chicago, IL	Portland, OR
Dallas, TX	St. Louis, MO
Denver, CO	Seattle, WA
Fargo, ND	Tulsa, OK
Fort Worth, TX	Vancouver, British Columbia,
Houston, TX	Canada
Kansas City, MO	Winnipeg, Manitoba,
Memphis, TN	Canada
Minneapolis–St. Paul, MN	

WHAT

	1994 Sales	
Items Transported	$ mil.	% of total
Coal	1,669	33
Agricultural commodities	830	16
Intermodal containers	772	15
Forest products	498	10
Chemicals	412	8
Metals	277	5
Consumer products	267	5
Mineral processors	208	4
Vehicles & machinery	190	4
Shortlines & other	(128)	—
Total	**4,995**	**100**

	Equipment
	No.
Freight cars	44,435
Locomotives	1,156
Total	**45,591**

Subsidiaries
BN Leasing Corp. (acquires railcars and other
equipment)
Burlington Northern Railroad Co.

KEY COMPETITORS

American Freightways	J.B. Hunt
American President	Leaseway
Arkansas Best	Transportation
Canadian Pacific	Norfolk Southern
C.H. Robinson	Roadway
Conrail	Schneider National
Consolidated	Southern Pacific Rail
Freightways	TNT Freightways
CSX	Union Pacific
Illinois Central	Yellow Corp.
Ingram	

HOW MUCH

	9-Year Growth	1985	1986	1987	1988	1989	1990	1991	1992	1993	1994
Sales ($ mil.)	(5.9%)	8,651	6,941	6,621	4,700	4,606	4,674	4,559	4,630	4,699	4,995
Net income ($ mil.)	(4.7%)	658	(525)	369	264	243	222	(306)	299	296	426
Income as % of sales	—	7.6%	—	5.6%	5.6%	5.3%	4.7%	—	6.5%	6.3%	8.5%
Earnings per share ($)	(6.5%)	8.03	(7.53)	4.93	3.49	3.19	2.89	(3.96)	3.35	3.06	4.38
Stock price – high ($)	—	72.63	82.38	84.25	80.38	32.38	39.25	41.88	47.38	58.88	66.63
Stock price – low ($)	—	46.25	46.50	40.00	56.00	21.38	22.25	25.25	33.25	42.00	46.50
Stock price – close ($)	(3.8%)	68.25	53.25	62.75	79.00	31.50	28.75	40.50	43.50	57.88	48.13
P/E – high	—	9	—	17	23	10	14	—	14	19	15
P/E – low	—	6	—	8	16	7	8	—	10	14	11
Dividends per share ($)	(0.9%)	1.30	1.55	2.00	2.20	1.45	1.20	1.20	1.20	1.20	1.20
Book value per share ($)	(11.4%)	63.13	47.84	50.80	12.31	14.30	16.29	13.76	15.80	17.82	21.29
Employees	(4.2%)	45,022	44,200	42,300	32,400	32,900	32,905	31,760	31,204	30,502	30,711

1994 Year-end:
Debt ratio: 44.8%
Return on equity: 24.5%
Cash (mil.): $27
Current ratio: 0.70
Long-term debt (mil.): $1,697
No. of shares (mil.): 89
Dividends
  Yield: 2.5%
  Payout: 27.4%
Market value (mil.): $4,294

Stock Price History
High/Low 1985–94

CALTEX PETROLEUM CORPORATION

OVERVIEW

Dallas-based Caltex Petroleum is a 50-50 joint venture between Texaco and Chevron. Its subsidiaries and affiliates have operations in 61 countries, primarily in Africa, Australasia, Asia, and the Middle East. Caltex markets products through more than 18,000 retail outlets in 31 countries (including Australia, Japan, the Philippines, South Africa, and South Korea), fuels aircraft at 41 airports, and provides marine fuels and lubricants at 103 ports in 22 countries. Caltex boasts average market shares of 18% in motor fuels in the markets it serves.

With the growing economies in countries in the Asia/Pacific region, demand for petroleum products is expected to grow at 6–8% a year, and Caltex is focusing on increasing its refining and retailing capacity in that area. It is planning to invest over $8 billion in the next 5 years in the region, where it already sells more gasoline, diesel, and other refined products than any other Western oil company.

In 1994 Caltex launched a major study to assess a potential joint venture in China with Sinopec, the Chinese national petroleum body, to upgrade Sinopec's Nanjing Refinery. Caltex is expanding its retail service network in China and is building a $1.7 billion, 130,000-barrel-a-day refinery in Thailand (scheduled to commence full production in 1996).

WHEN

In the 1930s Standard Oil of California (Socal) had a problem most oil companies would only wish upon themselves: it had oil reserves in Bahrain with a potential 30,000-barrel-a-day production capacity. The problem was that Socal didn't have the marketing or refining network to sell the oil profitably.

While Socal's oil sat idly in the Bahrain soil, Texaco had its own problems. It had a large marketing network in Asia and Africa but lacked a crude supply in the eastern hemisphere; it was shipping its products from the US. Enter James Forrestal, head of the investment bank Dillon, Read, with plans for a little matchmaking. Forrestal brought together the 2 companies, and in 1936 they formed the California-Texas Oil Company.

The new company had barely taken its first steps when WWII disrupted operations. Caltex had moved drilling equipment into a promising field in Sumatra, but, after the war started, the Japanese took over the field and struck oil using Caltex's equipment.

Following the war, Caltex grew rapidly as oil demand began to climb. It formed companies in Malaysia, Thailand, and Yemen. Caltex also increased its refining capacity in Bahrain (1945), began a refinery construction and expansion program in other areas (1946), and bought Texaco's European and North African marketing facilities (1947).

In 1951 the company formed the Nippon Petroleum Refining Company as a joint venture with Nippon Oil to refine crude oil, supplied by Caltex, in Japan. Caltex also bought 50% of Japan's Koa Oil Company.

Caltex sold its European operations, which it had served from Saudi Arabia, to Socal and Texaco in 1967, allowing it to concentrate on building its presence in Africa, Asia, and Australasia. In 1968 Caltex entered Korea and formed the Honam Oil Refinery Company in a partnership with Lucky Chemical.

During the 1970s several of Caltex's Arab holdings were nationalized as an OPEC-spawned upheaval shook the oil industry, and in 1978 the Indian government nationalized Caltex Oil Refining (India) Ltd.

In 1982 the company moved its offices to Dallas from New York. In 1986 the company began a major modernization program of its refineries in Australia, the Philippines, and Singapore. That same year Caltex entered the real estate development business in Hong Kong when it began construction of a $176 million condominium and shopping complex on the site of a former petroleum products terminal. In 1988 the company created Caltex Services Corporation to provide technical support to Caltex companies.

P. T. Caltex Pacific Indonesia signed an agreement with the Indonesian government in 1992 to extend its production-sharing agreement in Sumatra through 2021.

In 1993, 3 Japanese refiners pulled out of a $9.5 billion joint venture with Caltex and Saudi Aramco, apparently because it would take at least 12 years to profit from the planned 3-refinery project. That same year Caltex formed a lubricants blending and marketing joint venture with Indian oil company IBP.

In 1994 the company built its first service station in Laos and opened offices in Vietnam and Indonesia.

In 1995 Caltex veteran David Law-Smith succeeded Patrick Ward as chairman and CEO.

Joint venture
Fiscal year ends: December 31

Chairman and CEO: David Law-Smith, age 55
SVP and CFO: Malcolm J. McAuley, age 57
SVP: John McPhail
SVP: G. J. Camarata
SVP: Matt W. Saunders
VP and General Counsel: Frank W. Blue
VP Human Resources: E. M. Schmidt
Auditors: KPMG Peat Marwick LLP

WHERE

HQ: 125 E. John Carpenter Fwy., PO Box 619500,
Irving, TX 75602-2750
Phone: 214-830-1000
Fax: 214-830-1156

Caltex has operations in 61 countries, primarily in
Africa, Asia, Australasia, and the Middle East. The
company markets products through more than 18,000
retail outlets in 31 countries, fuels aircraft at 41 airports,
and provides marine fuels and lubricants at 103 ports in
22 countries.

**International Supply
and Trading Offices**
Bahrain
Cape Town
Dallas
London
Singapore (HQ)
Tokyo

Refineries
Bahrain (40%)
Batangas (the Philippines)
Cape Town (South Africa)
Karachi (Pakistan, 12%)
Kurnell (Australia, 75%)
Marifu (Japan, 50%)
Mombasa (Kenya, 11.75%)
Muroran (Japan, 50%)
Negishi (Japan, 50%)
Osaka (Japan, 50%)
Pualau Merilimau (Singapore, 33.3%)
Sriracha (Thailand, 4.75%)
Whangarei (New Zealand, 8.57%)
Yocheon (South Korea, 50%)

WHAT

Real Estate Holdings
Riviera Gardens (apartments, shopping, restaurants;
Hong Kong)

Selected Subsidiaries and Affiliates
American Overseas Petroleum Ltd.
(coordinates activities of P. T. Caltex Pacific Indonesia)
Amoseas Indonesia Inc. (manages holdings in Indonesia)
Caltex Australia
Caltex Oil South Africa (refining and marketing)
Caltex Services Corp. (technical services to group
companies)
Caltex Services Private, Ltd. (tanker operations,
Singapore)
Honam Oil Refinery Company, Ltd. (refining and
marketing, Korea)
Honam Tanker Co.
Korea Tanker Co.
Koa Oil Company, Ltd. (refining, Japan)
Nippon Petroleum Refining Company, Ltd.
(refining, Japan)
P. T. Caltex Pacific Indonesia (oil and gas
exploration)
Singapore Refining Co.

KEY COMPETITORS

Amerada Hess	Mobil
Amoco	Nippon Seiro
Ashland, Inc.	Norsk Hydro
Atlantic Richfield	Occidental
British Petroleum	PDVSA
Broken Hill	PEMEX
Coastal	Pennzoil
Cosmo Oil	Petrobrás
Elf Aquitaine	Petrofina
ENI	Phillips Petroleum
Exxon	Repsol
Hutchison Whampoa	Royal Dutch/Shell
Idemitsu Kosan	Showa Shell Sekiyu
Imperial Oil	Swire Pacific
Jardine Matheson	TOTAL
Kerr-McGee	Unocal
Koch	USX–Marathon
Mitsubishi	YPF

HOW MUCH

	Annual Growth	1985	1986	1987	1988	1989	1990	1991	1992	1993	1994
Sales ($ mil.)	0.0%	14,784	9,526	10,186	10,277	11,507	15,147	15,445	17,281	15,409	14,751
Net income ($ mil.)	(0.2%)	701	568	472	471	609	601	839	720	720	689
Income as % of sales	—	4.7%	5.7%	4.6%	4.6%	5.3%	4.0%	5.4%	4.2%	4.7%	4.7%
Employees	1.0%	—	—	—	—	—	7,700	7,700	7,600	7,800	8,000

1994 Year-end:
Debt ratio: 15.6%
Return on equity: 15.3%
Cash (mil.): $251
Current ratio: 0.79
Long-term debt (mil.): $715

Net Income ($ mil.)
1985–94

900
800
700
600
500
400
300
200
100
0

CAMPBELL SOUP COMPANY

OVERVIEW

New Jersey–based Campbell, the 126-year-old soup company, believes brands are the name of the game in food retailing. That's one reason it was hot to purchase Pace, the top-selling salsa. Campbell completed the Pace acquisition in early 1995 for $1.1 billion, its biggest purchase to date. Now it hopes to leverage the Pace name into an extended line of Mexican-style food products.

Acquisitions are fueling Campbell's self-styled global crusade. In late 1994 the company purchased the food business of UK-based Albert Fisher Group, while its Pepperidge Farms division acquired Greenfield Healthy Foods, a maker of low-fat brownies and popcorn. The following year Campbell upped its stake in Arnotts, an Australia-based cookie and biscuit maker, to 64%.

Another avenue for Campbell's international growth is strategic partnerships. In late 1994 the company joined with Benihana National Corp. to develop a line of frozen stir-fry products under the Benihana name; it also formed a joint venture with Nakano Vinegar to market Campbell soups in Japan. In 1995 Campbell signed a licensing agreement to develop canned pasta brands based on Gargoyles and Shnookums, syndicated Disney cartoon characters.

Meanwhile, Campbell continues to sell off noncore businesses as it refocuses on shelf-stable products. In 1994 it sold Mallow Foods (Ireland), Campbell Chilled Foods (UK), and Laforest Perigord (France).

Heirs of Arthur Dorrance, an early owner, control about 45% of Campbell's stock.

WHEN

Campbell Soup Company began in Camden, New Jersey, in 1869 as a canning and preserving business. The company's founders, icebox maker Abram Anderson and fruit merchant Joseph Campbell, quickly established Campbell's enduring reputation for quality. Anderson left in 1876, and Arthur Dorrance took his place. The Dorrance family assumed control after Campbell retired in 1894.

Arthur Dorrance's nephew, John Dorrance, joined Campbell in 1897. The talented chemist soon found a way to condense soup by removing most of its water, a discovery crucial to the company's success. Without the heavy bulk of water-filled cans, Campbell rapidly gained a wider, less costly distribution than its competitors, and its products spread nationally.

In 1904 the company introduced its Campbell Kids to help sell soup. Entering the California market in 1911, Campbell became one of the first American companies to achieve national distribution of a food brand. It bought Franco-American, the first American soup maker, in 1915.

Campbell's ubiquity in American kitchens made its soup can an American pop culture icon, illustrated by Andy Warhol's 1960s print, and brought great wealth and social prestige to the Dorrance family. When John Dorrance died in 1930, he left the 3rd largest estate recorded at that time — $115 million. His son John Jr. became chairman in 1962.

Campbell built a reputation as a conservatively managed concern and cautiously began to diversify beyond soups. It acquired V8 juice (1948), Swanson (1955), Vlasic pickles (1978),

and Mrs. Paul's seafood (1982) and formed Godiva Chocolatier (1966) to sell chocolates in the US. It introduced Prego spaghetti sauce and LeMenu frozen dinners in the early 1980s.

In 1989 Robert Vlasic, who became chairman in 1988, made a bid to merge with Quaker Oats. The deal died, but 3 disenchanted Dorrance heirs pressed for the sale of the company until new CEO David Johnson restructured Campbell for more profits.

Campbell prospered in the recession of the 1990s by targeting moderately priced lines and controlling costs.

In 1993 the company absorbed a $300 million restructuring charge for the planned closing and consolidation of various operations. That year the company sold Produce Partners (dry mixes), Win Schuler (cheese), and St. Mary's Ontario (frozen foods). Also in 1993 Bennett Dorrance, grandson of early owner Arthur Dorrance, took up the role of VC as the first family member to take a senior executive position in 10 years.

In 1994 Campbell realigned its businesses into 3 divisions: Campbell USA, Campbell International, and Campbell Biscuit and Bakery. That year the company sponsored Olympic skater Nancy Kerrigan. Also in 1994 the firm offered early retirement to 10% of its HQ staff.

Campbell's Prego spaghetti sauce won a court ruling in 1995 against rival Ragu (made and marketed by Unilever) protecting Prego's claim to be the thicker sauce. Also in 1995 Campbell began producing its V8 vegetable juice in Korea, its first product manufactured in that country.

NYSE symbol: CPB
Fiscal year ends: Sunday nearest July 31

WHO

Chairman, President, and CEO: David W. Johnson,
age 62, $1,809,541 pay
VC: Bennett Dorrance, age 48
SVP Bakery and Confectionery: Frank E. Weise III,
age 50, $599,773 pay
SVP Law and Public Affairs: John M. Coleman, age 44,
$526,150 pay
SVP Finance: Robert Subin, age 56, $519,689 pay
**SVP Research and Development and Quality Assurance;
President, Campbell Institute for Research and
Technology:** James R. Kirk, age 52
VP; President, Confectionery Group: David L. Albright
VP; President, Frozen Foods Group: Kathleen
MacDonnell, age 46
VP; President, International Grocery: Robert F.
Bernstock, age 43
VP; President, Meal Enhancement Group: Alfred Poe,
age 45
VP; President, Pepperidge Farm North America:
Charles V. McCarthy, age 44
VP; President, US Soup: F. Martin Thrasher, age 43
VP Human Resources: Edward F. Walsh, age 53
Auditors: Price Waterhouse LLP

WHERE

HQ: Campbell Place, Camden, NJ 08103-1799
Phone: 609-342-4800
Fax: 609-342-3878

	1994 Sales		1994 Operating Income	
	$ mil.	% of total	$ mil.	% of total
US	4,639	68	854	80
Europe	1,041	15	64	6
Australia	507	8	81	7
Other regions	604	9	73	7
Adjustments	(101)	—	—	—
Total	**6,690**	**100**	**1,072**	**100**

WHAT

	1994 Sales		1994 Operating Income	
	$ mil.	% of total	$ mil.	% of total
Campbell USA	3,961	59	783	73
Campbell Intl.	1,555	23	136	13
Campbell Biscuit & Bakery	1,236	18	153	14
Adjustments	(62)	—	—	—
Total	**6,690**	**100**	**1,072**	**100**

Selected Brand Names

US

Campbell's	Prego	Imperial
Chunky	SpaghettiOs	Kattus
Franco-American	Swanson	Kwatta
Godiva	Vlasic	La Patrona
Goldfish		Lacroix
Great Starts	**International**	Leo
Healthy Request	Arnott's	Lutti
Healthy Treasures	Beeck	MacFarms
Home Cookin'	Candy Man	Pleyben
Hungry-Man	Delacre	Probare
LeMenu	Exeter	Roll Up
Marie's	Freshbake	Royal Mail
Mrs. Paul's	Granny's	Swift
Open Pit	Groko	Tubble Gum
Pepperidge Farm	Habitant	

KEY COMPETITORS

ADM	Continental	Mars
Allied Domecq	Grain	Nestlé
Anheuser-Busch	CPC	PepsiCo
Associated Milk	Danone	Philip Morris
Producers	General Mills	Quaker Oats
Borden	Grand	RJR Nabisco
Cadbury	Metropolitan	Sara Lee
Schweppes	Heinz	Smithfield Foods
Cargill	Hershey	Specialty Foods
Chiquita Brands	Hormel	TLC Beatrice
ConAgra	Kellogg	Unilever

HOW MUCH

	9-Year Growth	1985	1986	1987	1988	1989	1990	1991	1992	1993	1994
Sales ($ mil.)	5.9%	3,989	4,379	4,490	4,869	5,672	6,206	6,204	6,263	6,586	6,690
Net income ($ mil.)	13.7%	198	223	247	242	13	4	402	491	257	630
Income as % of sales	—	5.0%	5.1%	5.5%	5.0%	0.2%	0.1%	6.5%	7.8%	3.9%	9.4%
Earnings per share ($)	14.0%	0.77	0.87	0.96	0.94	0.05	0.02	1.58	1.95	1.02	2.51
Stock price – high ($)	—	14.53	17.13	17.69	17.63	30.31	31.00	43.88	45.25	45.38	46.00
Stock price – low ($)	—	7.55	11.00	11.38	3.94	15.25	21.88	27.06	31.50	35.25	34.25
Stock price – close ($)	15.2%	12.34	14.25	13.94	15.75	29.31	29.25	42.50	42.13	41.00	44.00
P/E – high	—	19	20	18	19	—	—	28	23	44	18
P/E – low	—	10	13	12	4	—	—	17	16	35	14
Dividends per share ($)	14.6%	0.31	0.33	0.36	0.41	0.45	0.49	0.56	0.52	0.91	1.06
Book value per share ($)	4.6%	5.35	6.21	6.98	7.34	6.86	6.54	7.06	8.07	6.76	8.02
Employees	(0.1%)	44,716	46,976	49,226	48,389	55,412	49,941	44,934	43,256	46,920	44,378

1994 Year-end:
Debt ratio: 33.3%
Return on equity: 34.1%
Cash (mil.): $94
Current ratio: 0.96
Long-term debt (mil.): $560
No. of shares (mil.): 248
Dividends
  Yield: 2.4%
  Payout: 42.2%
Market value (mil.): $10,912

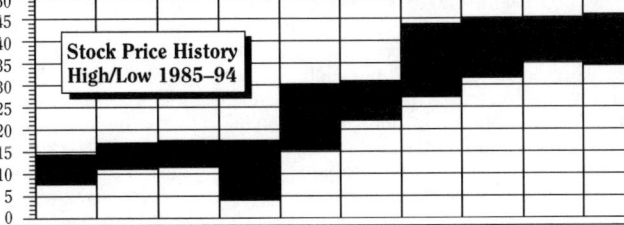

Stock Price History
High/Low 1985–94

CAPITAL CITIES/ABC, INC.

Capital Cities/ABC joined the Mickey Mouse Club in 1995. The New York City–based communications giant — with substantial interests in TV, radio, and publishing — agreed to be bought by Walt Disney for $19 billion, creating the biggest media company in the world. Capital Cities brings to the party the ABC TV network; 8 TV stations and 21 radio stations in several major metropolitan areas (including New York, Los Angeles, Houston, and Chicago); the country's largest radio network; stakes in various cable TV interests (such as ESPN, the A&E Network, and Lifetime TV); and newspapers, shopping guides, and specialized publications (including *Los Angeles*, *Institutional Investor*, and *W*). Warren Buffett's Berkshire Hathaway holding company owns 13% of the company's stock.

The company's broadcasting operations account for the bulk of revenues. The ABC network, which became the top-rated broadcast network in 1994–95 for the first time in 15 years, carried 5 of the top 10 TV series, including *Home Improvement*, *Monday Night Football*, *NYPD Blue*, and *Roseanne*. The network had 225 affiliated stations in 1994 and reached 99.9% of all households.

Unlike its chief rivals, Capital Cities is committed to programming. After FCC rules governing network ownership of programs were eased in 1994, the company pledged $100 million toward the creation of a TV studio with Steven Spielberg, David Geffen, and disgruntled ex-Disney executive Jeffrey Katzenberg, who will develop various types of programming; Capital Cities and DreamWorks SKG will share advertising and syndication revenues. Capital Cities invested another $100 million in a joint venture with Brillstein/Grey Entertainment to develop sitcoms.

WHEN

Capital Cities/ABC resulted from the 1986 acquisition of the American Broadcasting Companies by much smaller Capital Cities Communications in the largest media merger at the time. The youngest of 3 major networks, ABC began as a spinoff from RCA's Blue Network in 1943; it was sold that year to LifeSavers candy promoter Edward J. Noble when the FCC prohibited any company from owning more than one network.

In the 1940s and 1950s, ABC was in 3rd place, with 5 TV stations and no daytime programming. Buyout attempts by CBS and 20th Century Fox failed, but ABC and United Paramount Theatres merged in 1953. Leonard Goldenson of United Paramount hired Disney Studios to produce a series for ABC's 1954–55 season. Soon other studios, including Warner Brothers, were producing ABC shows (*Ozzie and Harriet* and *Wyatt Earp*, 1955). Goldenson also was behind the decision in 1954 to broadcast for 36 days the complete Senate hearings staged by Senator Joseph McCarthy.

That same year Hudson Valley Broadcasting hired Thomas Murphy (today chairman and CEO of Capital Cities/ABC) to bail out its struggling TV station in Albany, New York. In 1957 Hudson Valley bought a Raleigh, North Carolina, station and went public, becoming Capital Cities Communications. While Capital Cities founder Frank Smith bought and sold TV and radio stations and publications, Murphy ran the company.

Smith died in 1966. In 1968 Capital Cities, under Murphy, bought Fairchild Publications (*Women's Wear Daily*). In 1970 the company bought Walter Annenberg's Triangle Publications (*TV Guide*), now owned by Rupert Murdoch's News Corp.

Meanwhile, still in 3rd place in the 1960s, ABC fended off takeover attempts by Norton Simon, General Electric, and Howard Hughes. Programming whiz Fred Silverman defected from CBS, joining ABC in 1975. In 1976 ABC was the #1 network, and it stayed on top until 1979, the year after Silverman went to NBC.

In the 1980s Capital Cities bought cable systems, then sold them in 1986. ABC bought cable sports channel ESPN in 1984. In 1986 Capital Cities, backed by Berkshire Hathaway, bought ABC for $3.5 billion.

In 1990 Daniel Burke, formerly president, replaced Murphy as Capital Cities/ABC CEO.

In 1993 ESPN launched ESPN2, which spotlights sports entertainment for young adults. That year ABC and NBC won the rights to broadcast major league baseball for 6 years; in 1995 the 2 networks canceled the agreement, effective at the close of the season.

Burke retired in 1994 and Murphy once again became CEO as well as chairman. Also that year ABC TV Network head Robert Iger was promoted to Capital Cities/ABC president and COO. The company agreed to purchase 2 more TV stations (WJRT, Flint, MI; and WTVG, Toledo, OH) and bought a 14% stake in Young Broadcasting, an owner of 5 TV stations.

NYSE symbol: CCB
Fiscal year ends: December 31

WHO

Chairman and CEO: Thomas S. Murphy, age 69, $1,259,200 pay
President and COO: Robert A. Iger, age 44, $1,217,300 pay (prior to promotion)
EVP; Chairman, Fairchild Publications: John B. Fairchild, age 68
SVP and CFO: Ronald J. Doerfler, age 53, $975,000 pay
SVP; President, Broadcast Group: Michael P. Mallardi, age 61, $950,000 pay
SVP; President, Multimedia Group: Stephen A. Weiswasser, age 54, $840,000 pay
SVP; President, ABC Television Network Group: David Westin, age 42
SVP; President, Cable and International Broadcast Group: Herbert A. Granath, age 66
SVP; President, Publishing Group: Phillip J. Meek, age 57
VP and General Counsel: Alan N. Braverman, age 47
VP and Executive Assistant to the Chairman (HR): William J. Wilkinson
Auditors: Ernst & Young LLP

WHERE

HQ: 77 W. 66th St., New York, NY 10023-6298
Phone: 212-456-7777
Fax: 212-456-6850 (Public Relations)

WHAT

	1994 Sales		1994 Operating Income	
	$ mil.	% of total	$ mil.	% of total
Broadcasting	5,277	83	1,127	88
Publishing	1,102	17	155	12
Adjustments	—	—	(43)	—
Total	**6,379**	**100**	**1,239**	**100**

Selected Holdings

Broadcast Group
ABC Radio Networks
Radio stations
  KABC (AM)/KLOS (FM)/
    KMPC (AM), Los
    Angeles
  KGO (AM)/KSFO (AM),
    San Francisco
  KQRS (AM/FM)/KEGE
    (FM), Minneapolis–
    St. Paul
  KSCS (FM)/WBAP (AM),
    Dallas–Fort Worth
  WABC (AM)/WPLJ (FM),
    New York
  WHYT (FM)/WJR (AM),
    Detroit
  WKHX (AM/FM)/WYAY
    (FM), Atlanta
  WLS (AM/FM), Chicago
  WMAL (AM)/WRQX
    (FM), Washington, DC
Television stations
  KABC-TV, Los Angeles
  KFSN-TV, Fresno
  KGO-TV, San Francisco
  KTRK-TV, Houston
  WABC-TV, New York
  WLS-TV, Chicago
  WPVI-TV, Philadelphia
  WTVD-TV, Raleigh–
    Durham

Cable and International Broadcast Group
ABC Distribution
A&E Network (37.5%)
DIC Animation City
  (children's programs)
ESPN (80%)
Lifetime (50%)

Multimedia Group
Capital Cities/ABC Video Publishing

Publishing Group
Diversified publishing (agricultural publishing, Chilton Publications, Grupo Editorial Expansión, *Los Angeles* magazine, NILS Publishing Co.)
Fairchild Publications (*W*, *Women's Wear Daily*, other publications)
Financial services and medical (*Institutional Investor*, International Medical News Group)
Fort Worth Star-Telegram
The Kansas City (MO) *Star*
Other newspapers and publications in 11 states

KEY COMPETITORS

Advance	General Electric	Time Warner
Publications	Hearst	Times Mirror
Bertelsmann	Knight-Ridder	Tribune
CBS	Lagardère	Turner
Cox	News Corp.	Broadcasting
Dow Jones	TCI	Viacom
Gannett	Thomson Corp.	Washington Post

HOW MUCH

	9-Year Growth	1985	1986	1987	1988	1989	1990	1991	1992	1993	1994
Sales ($ mil.)	22.6%	1,021	4,124	4,440	4,774	4,957	5,386	5,382	5,344	5,674	6,379
Net income ($ mil.)	19.0%	142	182	279	387	486	478	375	389	467	680
Income as % of sales	—	13.9%	4.4%	6.3%	8.1%	9.8%	8.9%	7.0%	7.3%	8.2%	10.7%
Earnings per share ($)	16.8%	1.09	1.12	1.65	2.23	2.73	2.77	2.23	2.35	2.85	4.42
Stock price – high ($)	—	22.88	28.00	45.00	37.00	56.75	63.25	50.38	52.13	64.38	86.50
Stock price – low ($)	—	15.25	20.88	26.75	29.75	35.25	38.00	35.75	41.00	47.60	60.25
Stock price – close ($)	16.0%	22.50	26.75	34.50	36.25	56.38	45.88	43.38	50.75	62.00	85.25
P/E – high	—	21	25	27	17	21	23	23	22	23	20
P/E – low	—	14	19	16	13	13	14	16	17	17	14
Dividends per share ($)	26.0%	0.02	0.02	0.02	0.02	0.02	0.02	0.02	0.02	0.02	0.16
Book value per share ($)	16.9%	6.84	12.08	13.74	16.81	18.77	20.10	21.97	23.14	23.22	27.84
Employees	0.3%	19,700	19,960	20,120	19,720	19,860	20,100	19,650	19,250	19,250	20,200

1994 Year-end:
Debt ratio: 12.5%
Return on equity: 17.3%
Cash (mil.): $1,019
Current ratio: 2.60
Long-term debt (mil.): $611
No. of shares (mil.): 154.1
Dividends
  Yield: 0.2%
  Payout: 3.6%
Market value (mil.): $13,133

**Stock Price History
High/Low 1985–94**

CARGILL, INCORPORATED

Cargill, the monolith of Minnetonka, Minnesota, has a hand in the production, processing, transport, and trade of goods ranging from finished steel to fruit concentrate. One of the nation's biggest food companies and the single largest private US company, Cargill gets the greatest percentage of its profits from corn milling, followed by financial services such as futures trading and life insurance.

Descendants of Cargill's founder still control the company, but the family's reign inside the executive offices has ended. In 1995 Ernest Micek, a chemical engineer named president the year before, was named Cargill's CEO. Micek's background has suggested to some

that he will increase the company's emphasis on new products and biotechnology.

The planet's biggest grain trader, Cargill is responsible for 1/4 of US grain exports. Lately, the company has been flexing its muscles in other agricultural areas. Cargill announced in 1995 that it would substantially increase its production capacity for corn syrups, specialty starches, and corn sweeteners. Also, the company plans to capitalize on the popularity of canola oil by opening a major processing plant and refinery in western Canada in time for the 1996 crop.

Cargill's results were boosted in 1995 by record harvests of corn and soybeans in 1994.

William Cargill, the son of a Scottish immigrant sea captain, bought his first grain elevator in Conover, Iowa, shortly after the Civil War. He and his brother Sam bought grain elevators all along the Southern Minnesota Railroad in 1870, a time when Minnesota was becoming an important shipping route for grain. Sam and another brother, James, expanded the elevator operations while William worked with the railroads to monopolize grain transport to markets and coal transport back to the farmers.

Around the turn of the century, William's son, also named William, invested in a Montana irrigation project and other ill-fated ventures. William Sr. went to Montana and found that his name had been used to finance these undertakings; shortly afterward, he died of pneumonia. Cargill's creditors started pressing for repayment, which threatened to bankrupt the company. John MacMillan, who had married William Sr.'s daughter Edna, took control and rebuilt Cargill. By the time the company recovered in 1916, it had been stripped of timber holdings and land in Mexico and Canada that William Sr. had collected. MacMillan opened offices in New York (1922) and Argentina (1929), expanding Cargill's grain trading and transport operations.

During the Depression Cargill built the river barges necessary to transport its products. When the grain fields turned into the Dust Bowl, Cargill bought up all the corn futures on the Chicago exchange, prompting the Board of Trade to kick Cargill's broker off the floor. During WWII Cargill used its barge-building facilities to build ships for the navy.

After WWII, North American wheat became an increasingly important product because of

the ravages of war and a growing world population. In 1945 Cargill bought Nutrena Mills (animal feed) and entered soybean processing; corn processing began soon after and has grown with the demand for corn sweeteners. In 1954 the US began lending money to help developing countries buy American grain, and Cargill was one of the main beneficiaries of the policy. Subsidiary Tradax, established in 1955, quickly became one of the largest grain traders in Europe. In 1965 Cargill entered sugar trading by buying sugar and molasses in the Philippines and selling it abroad.

As a requirement for a takeover bid of Missouri Portland Cement (the bid was unsuccessful), Cargill made its finances public in 1973, revealing itself as one of the US's largest companies ($5.2 billion in sales). In the 1970s it expanded into coal, steel, and waste disposal and became a major force in metals processing, beef, and salt production. In the early 1990s Cargill started selling branded meats and packaged foods directly to supermarkets.

The company sold employees 17% of its stock in 1991. In 1993 then-CEO Whitney MacMillan was named by Senator Bob Dole and Representative Richard Gephardt to a panel shaping final US negotiations of the GATT agreement, which could provide up to $10 billion in US agricultural exports in the next decade. In 1994 Cargill lost $100 million on derivative holdings in its Minnetonka Fund.

A year after Nelson Mandela's inauguration as South African president, Cargill in 1995 resumed trading in that country through the creation of Cargill South Africa (PTY) Limited. In July 1995 Cargill sold its US chicken operations to Tyson Foods.

Private company
Fiscal year ends: May 31

WHO

Chairman: Whitney MacMillan, age 65
VC: Gerald M. Mitchell, age 65
CEO and President: Ernest S. Micek, age 59
President, Trading Sector: David W. Raisbeck, age 45
President, Financial Markets: David W. Rogers
President, Food Sector: Guillame Bastiaens
SVP and CFO: Robert L. Lumpkins, age 51
SVP Human Resources: Everett MacLennan
VP, General Counsel, and Secretary: James D. Moe
Auditors: KPMG Peat Marwick LLP

WHERE

HQ: PO Box 5625, 15407 McGinty Rd., Minnetonka, MN
55440-5625
Phone: 612-742-6000
Fax: 612-742-7393

Cargill and its roughly 50 subsidiaries and affiliates have
about 800 plants, 500 US offices, and 300 foreign offices
in 60 countries.

Regional US Sales Offices
North Atlantic Region (Watkins Glen, NY)
Central Atlantic Region (Baltimore)
Southern Region (Breaux Bridge, LA)
Mideast Region (Cincinnati)
Northern and Central Region (Minneapolis)
Midwest Region (Hutchinson, KS)
Northwest Region (Portland, OR)
Northern California (Newark, CA)
Southern California (Vernon, CA)

WHAT

Agricultural Products
Animal feeds (Nutrena)
Feed supplements
Seed and fertilizer

Commodities Trading and Transport
Barges and vessels (Cargo Carriers, Inc.)
Coffee and cocoa
Cotton (Hohenberg Bros.)
Fertilizers
Grain and oilseeds
Iron and finished steel
Juice and fruit concentrates
Molasses and sugar
Oceangoing vessels
Petroleum products and petrochemicals
Rubber
Tallow

Financial Operations
Equipment leasing
Futures trading and foreign exchange
Life insurance
Risk management

Food Production and Processing
Animal by-products
Beef and pork processing and packaging
Bulk commodities
Citric acid
Corn syrup sweeteners
Ethanol
Flour and corn milling
Salt (Leslie)
Starches

Industrial Products
Industrial chemicals
Scrap steel yards (Magnimet)
Steel and wire
Steel minimills (North Star)

KEY COMPETITORS

ADM	Heinz	Morton
Akzo Nobel	Hormel	Nippon Steel
BASF	IBP	Nucor
Bethlehem Steel	Ingram	Occidental
Broken Hill	Inland Steel	Philip Morris
Chiquita Brands	IRI	Prudential
ConAgra	Koch	Ralston Purina
Continental Grain	LTV	Group
CPC	Lyondell	Salomon
CSX	Petrochemical	Sara Lee
Dole	MetLife	Thyssen
DuPont	Mitsubishi	Tyson Foods
General Mills	Mitsui	USX–U.S. Steel
Harvest States Co-ops	Monsanto	W. R. Grace

HOW MUCH

	Annual Growth	1986	1987	1988	1989	1990	1991	1992	1993	1994	1995
Sales ($ mil.)	5.2%	32,280	32,400	38,200	43,000	44,000	49,100	46,800	47,100	47,135	51,000
Net income ($ mil.)	12.5%	—	—	—	—	372	382	450	358	571	671
Income as % of sales	—	—	—	—	—	0.8%	0.8%	1.0%	0.8%	1.2%	1.3%
Total employees	5.2%	46,351	51,600	55,020	53,710	55,200	60,000	63,500	70,000	70,700	73,300

Net Income
($ mil.)
1990–95

CARGILL

CARLSON COMPANIES, INC.

OVERVIEW

Minneapolis-based Carlson Companies operates in 3 segments: travel, hospitality, and marketing and motivation. Most of the company's sales come from the Travel Group, which is the US's 2nd largest travel services provider, after American Express. Looking to expand its international presence, Carlson entered into a 50-50 alliance with Accor's Wagonlit Travel of Paris in 1994. The deal created Carlson Wagonlit Travel and gives Carlson a presence in more than 4,000 locations in 125 countries.

Carlson Hospitality Worldwide operates and franchises more than 350 Radisson Hotels and Country Inns. The company owns only 2 hotels outright. It also oversees 240 Country Kitchens and 310 T.G.I. Friday's restaurants. Carlson Marketing Group is one of the largest motivational companies in the world, serving most of the *FORTUNE* 500 companies by providing employee training and incentives programs. In 1994 Carlson had system-wide sales (including franchisees) of $10.4 billion.

Carlson and its competitors in the travel industry got a shock in 1995 when US airlines put a cap on the commissions they will pay to travel agents for booking US flights. Carlson has switched to fee-based service and expects sales to drop by $100 million.

The company is concentrating on building its hospitality business, adding restaurants in the US and overseas, and expanding its international hotel operations.

Founder, CEO, and owner Curtis Carlson, who has been criticized for his brusque management style, has announced plans to retire by the end of 1996 and hand the reins to his daughter Marilyn Carlson Nelson.

WHEN

Curtis Carlson, the son of Swedish immigrants, graduated from the University of Minnesota in 1937 and went to work as a Procter & Gamble soap salesman in the Minneapolis/St. Paul area. In 1938 he borrowed $50 and formed Gold Bond Stamp Company to sell trading stamps to grocery stores in his spare time. His wife, Arleen, dressed as a drum majorette and twirled a baton to promote the concept. By 1941 the company had 200 accounts. In 1952 a large local chain, SUPERVALU, started using the stamps, boosting Gold Bond's sales to $2.4 million. By 1960 the trading stamps were generating so much capital that Carlson began investing in other enterprises: Ardan catalog and jewelry showrooms, travel agencies, and business promotion and employee motivation programs.

In 1962 Carlson bought the original Radisson Hotel in Minneapolis. He followed with 7 more hotels throughout the state and in 1970 expanded the Radisson chain outside Minnesota, buying the future Radisson Denver from Hyatt. By 1976 the majority of Radisson rooms were outside Minnesota. Carlson diversified into restaurants by buying the 11-unit T.G.I. (Thank God It's) Friday's, a dining and singles-bar chain, and Country Kitchen International (family restaurants).

By 1978 Radisson had 19 hotel properties, including one in the West Indies. Many of the Radissons were older hotels remodeled by Contract Services Associates, another Carlson company. In 1978 Carlson bought his first travel agency, Ask Mr. Foster (now Carlson Wagonlit Travel). In 1979 he bought Colony Resorts (hotel/condominium management company) from its founder, Peter Ueberroth, who later served as baseball commissioner.

Carlson Companies slowed the pace of its acquisitions in the 1980s. In 1984 Carlson hired Juergen Bartels to head its hospitality division. Bartels changed the division's growth strategy from one of building and owning hotels to one of franchising and managing them. This helped the company avoid the worst consequences of the 1980s hotel overbuilding boom. Carlson took T.G.I. Friday's public in 1983 (retaining 76% of the stock) to fund expansion of the chain but reacquired all outstanding shares in 1990. That year and the next year Carlson bought 2 UK travel agencies, A.T. Mays (1990) and Smith Travel (1991). The company entered the cruise ship business in 1992, launching the luxury liner SSC *Radisson Diamond*.

In the 1990s Carlson began to be dogged by rumors that Curtis Carlson's health was failing and that there was a high turnover rate among its officers. In 1990 Carlson's son-in-law and heir-apparent, Edwin Gage, quit Carlson Marketing, taking with him a significant share of business. The company signed a joint venture with Hospitality Franchise Systems in 1992 to open a T.G.I. Friday's or Country Kitchen restaurant adjacent to each of its partner's hotels.

In 1995 the company announced plans to open a sales office in Hong Kong and add 6 franchised or managed Radisson Hotels in the Asia/Pacific region by the end of the year.

Private company
Fiscal year ends: December 31

WHO

Chairman, President, and CEO: Curtis L. Carlson, age 80
VC: Marilyn Carlson Nelson, age 55
CFO: Martyn Redgrave
President, Radisson Hospitality Worldwide: John Norlander
President, Radisson Hospitality Development Worldwide: Peter Blyth
President, Friday's Hospitality Worldwide: Wally Doolin
President, Country Hospitality Worldwide: Curtis Nelson
President, Marketing Group: James Ryan
EVP; President, Travel Group: Travis Tanner
VP and Treasurer: John M. Diracles, Jr.
VP Public Relations/Public Affairs: Thomas D. Jardine
VP Legal, Secretary, and General Counsel: Lee Bearmon
VP Human Resources: Terry M. Butorac
Auditors: Arthur Andersen & Co, SC

WHERE

HQ: Carlson Pkwy., PO Box 59159, Minneapolis, MN 55459
Phone: 612-540-5000
Fax: 612-540-5832
Reservations (Radisson Hotels International): 800-333-3333

The company operates or franchises more than 350 hotels in 39 countries and operates 550 restaurants in 17 countries. It also has more than 4,000 travel agency locations around the world and operates 3 cruise ships.

	1994 Sales % of total
US	67
Other countries	33
Total	**100**

WHAT

Cruise Ships
MS *Hanseatic*
Radisson Song of Flower
SSC *Radisson Diamond*

	1994 Sales % of total
Travel	65
Hospitality	30
Marketing	5
Total	**100**

Carlson Travel Group
A.T. Mays (UK)
Carlson Wagonlit Travel
P. Lawson Travel (Canada)

Carlson Hospitality Worldwide
Colony Hotels & Resorts
Country Hospitality Corp.
  Country Kitchen International
Radisson Hotels International
T.G.I. Friday's Inc.

Carlson Marketing Group
Collateral distribution
Database management/learning systems
Direct marketing/direct mail/telemarketing
Event marketing and management
Frequency and partnership marketing
Marketing consultation and strategic planning
Meeting, convention, and trade show planning
Motivational programs
Quality service and productivity programs
Retail promotions/promotional merchandise

Carlson Real Estate Company

Carlson Investment Group

KEY COMPETITORS

American Express
Bass
Brinker
Carnival Hotels
  and Casinos
Cracker Barrel
Edward J. DeBartolo
Flagstar
Hilton
Hyatt
ITT Corp.

IVI Travel
Maritz
Marriott Intl.
Northwestern Travel
Rank
Reed Elsevier
Ritz-Carlton
Rosenbluth International
Tennessee Restaurant
Thomson Corp.
Westin Hotel

HOW MUCH

	Annual Growth	1985	1986	1987	1988	1989	1990	1991	1992	1993	1994
Estimated sales ($ mil.)	11.0%	900	1,300	1,500	1,800	2,000	2,200	2,300	2,900	2,295	2,300
Hotels and motels	18.5%	75	135	160	195	223	270	315	336	340	345
Hotel rooms	16.7%	20,000	32,000	38,000	47,000	50,000	60,000	69,000	76,000	73,000	80,000
Employees	(2.1%)	—	—	—	—	—	68,000	70,000	49,350	41,000	62,500

Estimated Sales ($ mil.) 1985–94

(bar chart, values ranging 0 to 3,000)

CARNIVAL CORPORATION

OVERVIEW

Miami-based Carnival Corporation is the world's #1 overnight cruise operator, with a 30% share of the North American market.

The company's Carnival Cruise Lines (9 ships) caters to budget-minded travelers, while its Holland America Line and Windstar Cruises (7 and 3 ships, respectively) appeal to well-heeled clients. Carnival's cruise/tour business (Holland America Westours) conducts bus, train, and cruise tours of Alaska and Canada, where it owns or operates 16 hotels. Carnival also owns a 25% stake in the ultraluxury cruise line Seabourn (2 ships).

Hoping to attract a huge untapped market (only about 7% of the American public has taken a cruise), Carnival has an ambitious shipbuilding program. It launched 2 new ships in 1994 (the *Fascination* and the *Ryndam*), and it plans to spend $2.5 billion over the next 5 years to build 8 new ships. To attract passengers, Carnival stresses the shipboard experience rather than the destination, enticing clients with casinos, nightclubs, entertainment, pampered service, and unlimited food.

Founder Ted Arison and his son Micky own a controlling interest in the company.

WHEN

In 1972 Ted Arison (formerly attached to Norwegian Caribbean Lines) persuaded old friend Meshulam Riklis to bankroll Arison's $6.5 million purchase of the *Empress of Canada*. Riklis owned (among other things) the Boston-based American International Travel Service (AITS). Setting up Carnival Cruise Lines as an AITS subsidiary, Arison renamed his ship the *Mardi Gras*. Unfortunately, she ran aground on her maiden voyage, sending Carnival into red ink for 3 years.

Arison in 1974 bought out Riklis for $1 and assumed Carnival's $5 million debt. Envisioning a cruise line that offered affordable vacation packages to young middle-class consumers, Arison invented a new type of cruise ship that featured live music, gambling, and other entertainment on board. Within a month Carnival was profitable. By the end of 1975, Arison had paid off Carnival's debt and bought its 2nd ship, the *Carnivale*.

In 1977 Arison bought the *Festivale*, which set sail for the Caribbean in 1978. That year (when shipbuilding costs and fuel prices were very high) Arison stunned the cruise industry by announcing that Carnival would build a new ship. The *Tropicale* set sail in 1982 from Los Angeles to Mexico's west coast.

The *Tropicale's* overwhelming success led Micky Arison, who had succeeded his father as CEO in 1979, to build 3 more ships — the *Holiday* (1985), the *Jubilee* (1986), and the *Celebration* (1987). The success of these ships made Carnival the world's #1 cruise operator, and in 1987 the Arisons sold 20% of Carnival's shares to the public.

In the meantime Carnival had added 3- and 4-day short cruises to the Bahamas, and in 1988 it opened Carnival's Crystal Palace Resort in the Bahamas. The company started offering luxury cruises in 1989 after buying Holland America Line for $635 million. Holland America operated cruises to Alaska and the Caribbean (Holland America Cruises) and to the Caribbean and the South Pacific (Windstar Cruises) and ran the Westours brand tours and the Westmark hotel chain.

The Carnival Cruise ship *Fantasy* set sail in 1990, followed by the *Ecstasy* in 1991. Carnival bought Premier Cruise Lines in 1991 and in 1992 formed a joint venture with Seabourn Cruise Lines. The company sold one Crystal Palace hotel to the government-owned Hotel Corporation of the Bahamas and put the rest of the resort up for sale in 1992.

In 1993 the *Statendam* and *Maasdam* were added to Holland America's fleet, and the *Sensation* joined Carnival Cruise Lines. That same year Carnival created the FiestaMarina cruise line for Latin fun-seekers. However, the venture's startup was rocky because of marketing obstacles and equipment problems. FiestaMarina's itinerary was discontinued in 1994.

In 1994 Carnival changed its name to Carnival Corporation to reflect its diverse operations and announced that it would merge its land-based gaming interests with The Continental Companies to form a new company, Carnival Hotels and Casinos. Ownership of the new entity was equally divided between the 2 parent companies.

Also in 1994 the company sold its 81% of the Crystal Palace hotel/casino resort in Nassau, the Bahamas, to the Ruffin Hotel Group for $80 million.

In 1995 Carnival Hotels and Casinos signed a deal with Irvin and Kenneth Feld Productions to design and manage an entertainment complex for a casino and theme park proposed for construction by the Wampanoag Tribe in New Bedford, Massachusetts.

NYSE symbol: CCL
Fiscal year ends: November 30

Chairman and CEO: M. Micky Arison, age 45,
$911,000 pay
VC and CFO: Howard S. Frank, age 53, $628,000 pay
**President and CEO, Holland America Line —
Westours, Inc.:** A. Kirk Lanterman, age 63,
$1,035,000 pay
President and COO, Carnival Cruise Lines: Robert H.
Dickinson, age 52, $738,000 pay
SVP Operations, Carnival Cruise Lines: Meshulam
Zonis, age 61, $529,000 pay
Director Employee Policies and Benefits (HR): Susan
Herrmann
Auditors: Price Waterhouse LLP

WHERE

HQ: 3655 NW 87th Ave., Miami, FL 33178-2428
Phone: 305-599-2600
Fax: 305-471-4700

Hotels	Location	No. of rooms
The Baranof	Alaska	194
Westmark Anchorage	Alaska	198
Westmark Cape Fox	Alaska	72
Westmark Fairbanks	Alaska	238
Westmark Inn (Anchorage)	Alaska	90
Westmark Inn (Beaver Creek)	Canada	174
Westmark Inn (Dawson)	Canada	131
Westmark Inn (Fairbanks)	Alaska	173
Westmark Inn Skagway	Alaska	209
Westmark Juneau	Alaska	105
Westmark Klondike Inn	Canada	99
Westmark Kodiak	Alaska	81
Westmark Shee Atika	Alaska	101
Westmark Tok	Alaska	92
Westmark Valdez	Alaska	97
Westmark Whitehorse	Canada	181
Total		**2,235**

HOW MUCH

WHAT

Cruise Ships	Areas of Operation	Capacity
Carnival Cruise Lines		
Celebration	Caribbean	1,486
Ecstasy	Caribbean	2,040
Fantasy	Bahamas	2,044
Fascination	Caribbean	2,040
Festivale	Caribbean	1,146
Holiday	Mexico	1,452
Jubilee	Mexico	1,486
Sensation	Caribbean	2,040
Tropicale	Caribbean	1,022
Holland America Line		
Maasdam	Caribbean, Europe	1,266
Nieuw Amsterdam	Alaska, Caribbean	1,214
Noordam	Alaska, Caribbean	1,214
Rotterdam	Alaska, Hawaii	1,075
Ryndam	Alaska, Caribbean	1,266
Statendam	Alaska, Caribbean	1,266
Westerdam	Caribbean	1,494
Windstar Cruises		
Wind Song	South Pacific	148
Wind Spirit	Caribbean, Mediterranean	148
Wind Star	Caribbean, Mediterranean	148
Total		**23,995**

	1994 Sales		1994 Operating Income	
	$ mil.	% of total	% mil.	% of total
Cruise	1,623	88	426	96
Tour	228	12	18	4
Adjustments	(45)	—	—	—
Total	**1,806**	**100**	**444**	**100**

KEY COMPETITORS

Accor	Cunard	Seabourn
American Classic	Epirotiki	Sea Containers
Voyages	Peninsular & Oriental	Thomson Corp
Carlson	Royal Caribbean	Vard
Club Med	Cruises	

	Annual Growth	1985	1986	1987	1988	1989	1990	1991	1992	1993	1994
Sales ($ mil.)	20.0%	—	421	564	600	1,148	1,391	1,405	1,474	1,557	1,806
Net income ($ mil.)	18.5%	—	98	153	196	194	206	85	282	318	382
Income as % of sales	—	—	23.2%	27.1%	32.7%	16.9%	14.8%	6.1%	19.1%	20.4%	21.1%
Earnings per share ($)	11.0%	—	—	0.65	0.73	0.72	0.77	0.31	1.00	1.13	1.35
Stock price – high ($)	—	—	—	8.75	7.75	13.19	12.44	14.63	17.00	25.00	26.13
Stock price – low ($)	—	—	—	4.07	5.63	7.44	5.38	6.06	12.00	15.13	19.13
Stock price close ($)	19.8%	—	—	6.00	7.75	9.94	7.19	13.13	16.38	23.63	21.25
P/E – high	—	—	—	14	11	18	16	47	17	22	19
P/E – low	—	—	—	6	8	10	7	20	12	13	14
Dividends per share ($)	—	—	—	0.00	0.15	0.37	0.23	0.24	0.28	0.28	0.29
Book value per share ($)	14.4%	—	—	2.36	2.80	3.28	3.80	4.17	4.91	5.77	6.06
Employees	16.8%	—	—	5,800	7,300	14,450	15,500	16,000	14,870	15,650	17,250

1994 Year-end:
Debt ratio: 39.3%
Return on equity: 21.5%
Cash (mil.): $124
Current ratio: 0.43
Long-term debt (mil.): $1,162
No. of shares (mil.): 228
Dividends
  Yield: 1.3%
  Payout: 21.1%
Market value (mil.): $4,836

**Stock Price History
High/Low 1987–94**

CASE CORPORATION

Racine, Wisconsin–based Case Corp. is North America's 2nd largest maker of farm equipment (after Caterpillar) and the world's largest manufacturer of small and medium-sized construction equipment. The company manufactures more than 100 models of farm machinery and implements (47% of 1994 sales), including tractors, combines, plows, field cultivators, and soil conditioning equipment. Case also makes a broad range of construction equipment, such as excavators, wheel tractors, loaders, and bulldozers. Through subsidiaries in the US and Canada, Case offers wholesale financing to dealers and limited retail financing to customers. Equipment and replacement parts are sold worldwide in more than 150 countries; 43% of 1994 revenues were from international sales.

Case was a subsidiary of Tenneco from 1970 to 1994. It has undergone a renaissance from a 1991 company restructuring; in 1994 Case had record earnings. The company intends to continue cutting manufacturing costs, improving product lines, shedding excess capacity, streamlining its distribution process, and selling company-owned stores.

WHEN

In 1842 Jerome I. Case moved to Rochester, Wisconsin, with a crude mechanized thresher, which Case modified to separate straw from grain. He moved to Racine in 1844 and 3 years later started manufacturing his separator-thresher as the Jerome Increase Case Machinery Co. The company's name was changed to Racine Threshing Machine Works in 1848; by the early 1850s the company was a leading employer in the area.

During the Civil War, Case established J.I. Case & Co. with 3 partners. In 1876 the company introduced its first self-propelled steam traction engine and began to make a line of road machinery. In 1880 the company's name was changed again to J.I. Case Threshing Machine Co.; each partner received 2,500 shares of stock.

Case died in 1891. One of Case's partners, Stephen Bull, took over management of the company; he and 3 others bought all the stock from the Case family. By WWI the company was listed on the New York Stock Exchange.

Between 1893 and 1924 the company diversified and expanded into Canada and overseas. A former John Deere executive, Leon Clausen, became president in 1924 when Case was losing sales to competitors such as John Deere.

Clausen, who remained president until 1948, improved designs, expanded the line, modernized Case's factories, and built the company's network of dealerships. Following a reorganization in 1928, the company's name was changed to J.I. Case Co., which was used until 1994.

In the 1920s and 1930s the company acquired Emerson-Brantingham (binders, mowers, reapers, and corn planters) and the Rock Island Plow Co. (drills, spreaders, and plows). Case was one of the top 3 manufacturers of farm equipment by 1937.

During WWII Case made tractors, shells, and other equipment for the military. A 440-day strike at Case from 1945 to 1947 — the longest in US history at the time — hurt the company's relationships with unions, dealers, and customers and forced Clausen to step down as president although he remained chairman until 1958.

In the 1950s Case lost market share with outmoded products and conservative management. The company merged with American Tractor (tractors, backhoes, and crawlers) in 1957, expanding its product line, but by 1959 Case had a huge debt load.

By 1962 Case was unable to meet its debt payments. The company reorganized and refinanced, finding a majority buyer (Kern County Land) in 1964. Tenneco, a Houston-based holding company, bought Kern in 1967 and acquired the rest of Case in 1970.

Case prospered during the 1970s as it focused on overseas markets and construction equipment. The company bought a stake in Poclain (hydraulic excavators) in France and set up a joint venture with Cummins Engine to build a diesel engine for Case equipment.

A recession in agriculture in the early 1980s hurt domestic sales and caused the industry to consolidate. In 1985 Case bought International Harvester's farm equipment operations and became the #2 manufacturer of agricultural equipment. But despite a brief upturn, Case's overall losses forced the company to close factories and slash employment.

Tenneco restructured Case in 1991. In 1994 Tenneco began the process of divesting Case, rejuvenated by rebounding agricultural and construction markets, via a public offering of 29% of Case shares. Later that year Tenneco reduced its stake to 45%. In 1995 Case signed a 3-year labor agreement with the UAW.

NYSE symbol: CSE
Fiscal year ends: December 31

WHO

Chairman: Dana G. Mead, age 58
President and CEO: Jean-Pierre Rosso, age 54,
$832,142 pay
EVP and COO: Steven G. Lamb, age 38, $631,464 pay
SVP Operations: Thomas E. Evans, age 43, $450,479 pay
SVP Product Management and Strategic Planning:
Richard M. Christman, age 44, $430,723 pay
SVP and CFO: Theodore R. French, age 40,
$392,792 pay
SVP Product Development and Engineering: R. Gary
Diaz, age 38
General Counsel and Secretary: Richard S. Brennan,
age 56
VP Human Resources: Marc J. Castor
Auditors: Arthur Andersen & Co, SC

WHERE

HQ: 700 State St., Racine, Wisconsin 53404
Phone: 414-636-6011
Fax: 414-636-0483

Case products are sold through a network of about 4,100
independent dealers and 113 company-owned retail
stores located in all 50 states and about 150 countries.
Case has manufacturing plants in Brazil, Canada,
France, Germany, the UK, and the US.

	1994 Sales		1994 Pretax Income	
	$ mil.	% of total	$ mil.	% of total
US	2,847	57	175	51
Europe	1,442	29	97	29
Canada	432	9	47	14
Other regions	274	5	20	6
Adjustments	(590)	—	(81)	—
Total	**4,405**	**100**	**258**	**100**

WHAT

	1994 Sales	
	$ mil.	% of total
Agricultural equipment	2,008	47
Construction equipment	1,328	31
Parts	926	22
Adjustments	143	—
Total	**4,405**	**100**

Agricultural Equipment
Chisel plows
Combines
Cotton pickers
Disk harrows
Field cultivators
Hay and forage equipment
Moldboard plows
Planters
Seeders
Soil conditioners
Tractors (4-wheel
drive & utility)

Construction Equipment
Crawler dozers
Excavators

Loader/backhoes
Skid steer loaders
Trenchers
Wheel loaders

Trademarks
Axial-Flow
BuyRite
Case
Case IH
Case Poclain
Cotton Express
Cyclo Air
LeaseRite
Magnum
Maxxum
Uni-Loader

Subsidiaries and Affiliates
Case Credit Corp. (financing, leasing, and insurance)
Case Credit Ltd. (financing, leasing, and insurance;
Canada)
Consolidated Diesel Co. (50%, diesel engines)
Hay and Forage Industries (50%, hay and forage
equipment)

KEY COMPETITORS

AGCO	Hitachi	Pearce
BTR	Ingersoll-Rand	Industries
Caterpillar	Isuzu	Peterson Tractor
Deere	Komatsu	Portec
Fiat	Kubota	Samsung
Ford	Mustang Tractor	Volvo

HOW MUCH

	Annual Growth	1985	1986	1987	1988	1989	1990	1991	1992	1993	1994
Sales ($ mil.)	(3.8%)	—	—	—	—	5,343	5,715	4,763	4,150	3,995	4,405
Net income ($ mil.)	11.9%	—	—	—	—	90	41	(985)	(1,107)	(22)	158
Income as % of sales	—	—	—	—	—	0.7%	0.7%	—	—	—	3.6%
Earnings per share ($)	—	—	—	—	—	—	—	—	—	(0.31)	2.26
Stock price – high ($)	—	—	—	—	—	—	—	—	—	—	21.50
Stock price – low ($)	—	—	—	—	—	—	—	—	—	—	18.25
Stock price – close ($)	—	—	—	—	—	—	—	—	—	—	21.50
P/E – high	—	—	—	—	—	—	—	—	—	—	10
P/E – low	—	—	—	—	—	—	—	—	—	—	8
Dividends per share ($)	—	—	—	—	—	—	—	—	—	—	0.10
Book value per share ($)	—	—	—	—	—	—	—	—	—	—	16.74
Employees	(10.3%)	—	—	—	—	29,100	28,500	24,200	18,500	17,100	16,900

1994 Year-end:
Debt ratio: 61.0%
Return on equity: 13.4%
Cash (mil.): $68
Current ratio: 1.39
Long-term debt (mil.): $1,443
No. of shares (mil.): 71
Dividends
  Yield: 0.5%
  Payout: 4.4%
Market value (mil.): $1,517

Net Income ($ mil.)
1989–94

CATERPILLAR INC.

Illinois-based Caterpillar (Cat), the world's #1 maker of earthmoving machinery, builds and maintains the world's infrastructure. Renowned for the durability of its products, Cat designs and makes a variety of construction, mining, and agricultural machinery as well as diesel and gas engines for trucks, locomotives, and electrical power generation systems. The company also provides financing and insurance for dealers and customers. With 38 manufacturing plants around the world, Cat is an international company; 49% of its 1994 sales were outside the US.

Cat completed a $1.8 billion modernization program in 1993 that automated many of its factories, reduced the size of its labor force, and helped protect the company from organized labor, with which Cat has uneasy relations. The company has been embroiled in a

bitter fight with some of its union workers, who have been working without a contract since 1991. Almost 2/3 of Cat's UAW employees at 8 plants in Colorado, Illinois, and Pennsylvania have been on strike since June 1994 over unfair labor charges.

Cat's management, as tough as its machines, swiftly retaliated to the strike by shifting office workers to factory jobs, recalling retired employees, hiring temporary, contract, and permanent workers, and using its foreign factories to help fill orders. With employees working long hours and weekends and markets improving worldwide, Cat reported record sales and profits in 1994 — and boasted that the strike has had no impact.

In early 1995 both sides agreed to federally mediated contract talks in hopes of ending the strike.

In 1904 in Stockton, California, combine-maker Benjamin Holt modified the farming tractor by substituting a gas engine for steam and replacing iron wheels with crawler tracks. This improved the tractor's mobility over dirt by making it lighter and distributing its weight more evenly.

In 1915 the British adapted the "caterpillar" (Holt's nickname for the tractor) design to the armored tank. Following WWI the US Army donated tanks to local governments for construction work. The caterpillar's efficiency surprised Holt and spurred the development of earthmoving and construction equipment.

Holt merged with another California company, Best Tractor, in 1925. In 1928 the new organization, named Caterpillar (Cat), moved to its present Peoria, Illinois, headquarters.

In the 1930s Cat expanded into foreign markets, forming a worldwide dealer network, and phased out combine production to concentrate on construction and road equipment.

Sales volume more than tripled during WWII when Cat supplied the military with earthmoving equipment. Returning servicemen touted its durability and quality, and the company enjoyed continued high demand during postwar years. Cat emerged in solid first place in the industry, far ahead of 2nd-place International Harvester.

In 1951 Cat established its first overseas plant, in England. In 1963 it entered one of the first 50-50 joint ventures in Japan, with Mitsubishi. Sales increased steadily, reaching almost $9.2 billion by 1981. That year Cat

bought Solar Turbines (gasoline engines) for $505 million. However, 50 consecutive years of profits ended when Cat ran up $953 million in losses between 1982 and 1984 as equipment demand fell and competition from foreign firms — Komatsu in particular — intensified.

Cat doubled its product line between 1984 and 1989. The "Plant with a Future" (PWAF) program, introduced in 1985, shifted production toward smaller equipment, cut the work force, and enabled Cat to recoup lost market share. In 1987 the company began a $1.8 billion factory modernization program.

In 1990 CEO Donald Fites reorganized Cat along product lines. Cat picked up Barber-Greene's asphalt paving operations in 1991. Later in 1991 Cat clashed with the UAW over wage and health benefits, which resulted in a strike, and the company reported its first annual loss since 1984. Most of Cat's 12,500 striking employees had returned to work without a contract by May 1992.

Cat formed 3 joint ventures with Mitsubishi in 1992 to design and make equipment and related parts in the US, Asia, and Europe, with Cat retaining a 20% interest in each.

In 1994 Cat formed 2 joint ventures in Russia (one with Kirovsky Zavod and one with AMO-ZiL) and another in China. Also that year Cat formed an alliance with Shanghai Diesel Engine, China's largest diesel engine maker.

In 1995 Fites, who had restructured the company and taken on the UAW in his 5 years at the helm, was named CEO of the year by *Financial World* magazine.

NYSE symbol: CAT
Fiscal year ends: December 31

WHO

Chairman and CEO: Donald V. Fites, age 61,
$1,572,800 pay
Group President: Glen A. Barton, age 55, $649,800 pay
Group President: Gerald S. Flaherty, age 56,
$649,800 pay
Group President: Richard L. Thompson, age 55
Group President: James W. Owens, age 48
VP Engine Division: Gerald L. Shaheen, age 50
VP Engine Operations: Donald G. Western, 46
VP; President, Caterpillar Financial Services Corp.:
James S. Beard, age 53
VP, General Counsel, and Secretary: R. Rennie
Atterbury III, age 57
VP Corporate Services and CFO: Douglas Oberhelman,
age 41
VP Human Resources: Wayne M. Zimmerman, age 59
Auditors: Price Waterhouse LLP

WHERE

HQ: 100 NE Adams St., Peoria, IL 61629
Phone: 309-675-1000
Fax: 309-675-5948

Caterpillar has 38 plants in 12 countries and 187
dealerships in 128 countries.

	1994 Sales	
	$ mil.	% of total
US	7,008	51
Europe	2,078	15
Asia/Pacific	1,964	14
Latin America	1,151	8
Canada	909	7
Africa/Middle East	753	5
Adjustments	465	—
Total	**14,328**	**100**

WHAT

	1994 Sales		1994 Operating Income	
	$ mil.	% of total	$ mil.	% of total
Machinery	10,164	71	1,099	73
Engines	3,699	26	348	23
Financial services	465	3	64	4
Total	**14,328**	**100**	**1,511**	**100**

Products

Agricultural tractors and
forest machines
Backhoe loaders
Compactors
Diesel engines
Emergency power systems
Excavators
Gas turbines
Integrated toolcarriers
Loaders
Mining shovels
Motor graders
Paving products
Pipelayers
Power generation
systems
Scrapers

Tractors
Trucks
Turbine engines

Brand Names
Barber-Greene
Cat
Caterpillar
Solar

Financial Subsidiaries
Caterpillar Financial
Services Corporation
Caterpillar Insurance
Services Corporation

KEY COMPETITORS

AGCO
Allied Products
Case
Core Industries
Cummins Engine
Daimler-Benz
Deere
Dresser
Fiat
FMC

Ford
Harnischfeger
Hitachi
Hyundai
Ingersoll-Rand
Isuzu
Komatsu
Kubota
Navistar
Penske

Peterson
Tractor
Peugeot
Rolls-Royce
Stewart &
Stevenson
Terex
Volvo

HOW MUCH

	9-Year Growth	1985	1986	1987	1988	1989	1990	1991	1992	1993	1994
Sales ($ mil.)	8.8%	6,725	7,321	8,180	10,435	11,126	11,436	10,182	10,194	11,615	14,328
Net income ($ mil.)	19.1%	198	76	319	616	497	210	(404)	(218)	681	955
Income as % of sales	—	2.9%	1.0%	3.9%	5.9%	4.5%	1.8%	—	—	5.9%	6.7%
Earnings per share ($)	18.6%	1.01	0.39	1.60	3.04	2.45	1.04	(2.00)	(1.08)	3.36	4.70
Stock price – high ($)	—	21.56	27.69	37.38	34.25	34.50	34.25	28.81	31.06	46.56	60.75
Stock price – low ($)	—	14.50	18.31	19.94	26.94	26.44	19.06	18.81	20.63	26.94	44.38
Stock price – close ($)	11.3%	21.00	20.06	31.00	31.81	28.94	23.50	21.94	26.81	44.50	55.13
P/E – high	—	21	71	23	11	14	33	—	—	14	13
P/E – low	—	14	47	13	9	11	18	—	—	8	9
Dividends per share ($)	6.7%	0.25	0.25	0.25	0.38	0.60	0.60	0.60	0.30	0.30	0.45
Book value per share ($)	(0.8%)	15.59	15.93	17.57	20.28	22.06	22.50	20.04	7.80	10.79	14.52
Employees	(0.4%)	55,815	54,024	53,770	57,954	60,784	59,662	55,950	52,340	50,443	53,986

1994 Year-end:
Debt ratio: 67.0%
Return on equity: 37.4%
Cash (mil.): $419
Current ratio: 1.35
Long-term debt (mil.): $4,270
No. of shares (mil.): 200
Dividends
  Yield: 0.8%
  Payout: 9.6%
Market value (mil.): $11,050

Stock Price History
High/Low 1985–94

CBS INC.

OVERVIEW

Many a potential suitor had an eye on CBS in 1995, and despite its denials the world's 2nd oldest broadcasting network was often rumored to be for sale. The rumors proved true that summer when CBS announced it would be bought by Westinghouse for $5.4 billion. (The announcement was overshadowed by rival Capital Cities/ABC's monumental, $19 billion deal with Disney the day before.) Westinghouse, whose Group W broadcasting unit owns TV and radio stations, had already teamed up with CBS in 1994 in the joint ownership of several TV stations.

Based in New York City, CBS owns 6 TV stations and 21 radio stations, most located in the country's major metropolitan areas; its 206 TV and 585 radio affiliates give the company a nationwide reach. CBS is both producer and distributor of a wide range of programming, dishing out news, public affairs, entertainment, and sports programs via TV and radio.

CBS has languished among its competitors. The network has been plagued by a loss of top executives, key station affiliates, and NFL broadcast rights. The latest ratings put CBS 3rd among the major networks and 4th behind Fox with younger viewers. In 1995 one of CBS's 2 top institutional investors gave a no-confidence vote to chairman Laurence Tisch, whose Loews Corp. owns 18% of CBS stock.

WHEN

In 1925 William Paley (age 23) was plugging his father's Philadelphia-based La Palina cigars in radio advertisements. Sensing an opportunity, in 1928 he bought control of the year-old Columbia Broadcasting System radio network, which had 16 affiliates but no stations of its own.

Paley changed the face of broadcasting, set industry standards, and gave the company its reputation as a first-class network. He promoted daytime dramas; raided stars from NBC such as George Burns, Gracie Allen, and Jack Benny; and built a strong news organization. Local affiliates grew from 22 in 1928 to 97 in 1935. Edward R. Murrow, who was at CBS from 1930 to 1960, broke new ground in news broadcasting.

In 1938 CBS bought American Recording (renamed CBS Records). CBS had hired scientist Peter Carl Goldmark in 1936; he invented the long-playing record in 1948. Goldmark worked on a color TV system, but the FCC approved RCA/NBC's color system in 1953.

From 1955 to 1968 CBS was #1 in entertainment ratings. But CBS lost ratings and revenues in the early 1970s because its programs were not geared to younger viewers. From the 1960s to the 1980s, CBS bought and sold the New York Yankees, Fender guitars, Steinway pianos, and other famous US corporate names in an effort to diversify.

CBS bought cable companies in the 1960s, but the FCC soon prohibited network ownership of cable systems. Viacom was formed in a 1970 forced divestiture. In 1982 CBS and Twentieth Century Fox-Video formed CBS/Fox to distribute videocassettes, and in 1983 CBS, HBO, and CPI Film Holdings formed Tri-Star Pictures (sold, 1985).

During the mid-1980s CBS was hurt financially from takeover attempts and a tumble in ratings after trusted news anchor Walter Cronkite retired. Paley's inability to pick a successor left CBS leaderless between 1971 and 1986. Ted Turner announced his intention to take over the company in 1985 but was blocked by CBS. That year Loews Corp., led by Laurence Tisch, began buying CBS stock with the broadcaster's blessing; Tisch joined the CBS board.

In 1987 Tisch became CEO of CBS. He sold CBS Records (to Sony) and the remaining book and magazine businesses in 1988. When Paley died in 1990, Tisch became chairman as well. Despite higher ratings — CBS jumped to #1 in 1991 — the company was losing money.

In 1993 CBS lured late-night host David Letterman away from NBC (for $14 million a year) and added Connie Chung as co-anchor to its evening news, which was languishing with longtime anchor Dan Rather. (Chung was removed as co-anchor in 1995 amid accusations of sex discrimination.)

The broadcasting company was stunned in 1994 when the Fox network outbid CBS for National Football Conference games (after 38 years) and when key affiliates owned by New World Communications Group switched from CBS to Fox. In one season CBS tumbled from the top network ranking, which it had for 3 years, to 3rd place. Also in 1994 QVC (TV shopping) started talks to merge with CBS, but negotiations fell through. Tisch denied the company was for sale.

Prior to the 1995 deal with Westinghouse, CBS had been the last independent US broadcasting network. Ted Turner had also talked about buying CBS that year.

NYSE symbol: CBS
Fiscal year ends: December 31

WHO

Chairman, President, and CEO: Laurence A. Tisch, age 72, $1,000,000 pay
VP; President, CBS/Broadcast Group: Peter A. Lund, age 54, $898,458 pay (prior to promotion)
EVP CBS Operations and Administration: Edward Grebow, age 45
EVP and CFO: Peter W. Keegan, age 50
EVP, General Counsel, and Secretary: Ellen Oran Kaden, age 43
SVP Human Resources: Joan Showalter
President, CBS News Division: Eric W. Ober, age 53, $750,769 pay
President, CBS Television Network: James A. Warner, age 41
President, CBS Entertainment Division: Leslie Moonves, age 45
President, CBS Sports Division: David Kenin, age 53
President, CBS Radio Division: Nancy C. Widmann, age 52
Auditors: Coopers & Lybrand L.L.P.

WHERE

HQ: 51 W. 52nd St., New York, NY 10019-6188
Phone: 212-975-4321
Fax: 212-975-7133

CBS has local and network broadcast, production, and cable interests nationwide.

WHAT

Top-rated CBS TV Programs, 1994–95 Season

Prime Time	Daytime
60 Minutes	*The Young and the Restless*
Murder, She Wrote	*The Price Is Right*
	The Bold and the Beautiful
	As the World Turns
	Guiding Light

Selected Holdings

CBS Radio Stations

KCBS (AM)/KRQR (FM), San Francisco
KCBS (FM)/KNX (AM), Los Angeles
KKRW (FM), Houston-Galveston
KLOU (FM)/KMOX (AM), St. Louis
KRRW (FM)/KTXQ (FM), Dallas–Fort Worth
WARW (FM), Washington, DC
WBBM (AM/FM), Chicago
WCBS (AM/FM), New York
WCCO (AM)/WLTE (FM), Minneapolis–St. Paul
WODS (FM), Boston
WOGL (FM)/WGMP (AM), Philadelphia
WYST(FM)/WWJ (AM), Detroit

CBS Television Stations

KCBS-TV, Los Angeles
WBBM-TV, Chicago
WCBS-TV, New York
WCCO-TV, Minneapolis–St. Paul
WFRV-TV, Green Bay–Appleton, WI
WGPR-TV, Detroit

Other Selected Holdings

CBS Americas (Spanish-language radio news service)
CBS Broadcast International (overseas TV program sales)
CBS Enterprises (program distributor)
CBS Entertainment (TV programming)
CBS Video (50%, videocassette distributorship)
Midwest Sports Channel (cable programming)
Radford Studio Center Inc. (production studio)
Station Partners (50%, TV stations, Westinghouse)
Teleport Minnesota (cable programming)

KEY COMPETITORS

BET	Infinity	Sony
Blockbuster	Broadcasting	Time Warner
Capital Cities/ABC	Intl. Family	Tribune
Comcast	Entertainment	Turner
Cox	King World	Broadcasting
DreamWorks SKG	MacAndrews &	Viacom
Gannett	Forbes	Walt Disney
General Electric	News Corp.	Washington Post
Hearst	Seagram	

HOW MUCH

	9-Year Growth	1985	1986	1987	1988	1989	1990	1991	1992	1993	1994
Sales ($ mil.)	(2.5%)	4,677	4,646	2,762	2,778	2,962	3,261	3,035	3,503	3,510	3,712
Net income ($ mil.)	29.5%	27	389	453	283	297	112	(86)	163	326	282
Income as % of sales	—	0.6%	8.4%	16.4%	10.2%	10.0%	3.4%	—	4.6%	9.3%	7.6%
Earnings per share ($)	41.9%	0.16	3.21	3.55	2.20	2.31	0.87	(1.06)	2.10	4.08	3.74
Stock price – high ($)	—	25.25	30.30	45.25	36.55	44.20	41.25	37.68	44.10	65.30	72.20
Stock price – low ($)	—	14.18	22.00	25.50	29.20	33.20	30.30	25.63	27.20	37.23	50.00
Stock price – close ($)	10.1%	23.18	25.40	31.40	34.10	37.60	34.53	28.50	37.60	57.70	55.25
P/E – high	—	158	9	13	17	19	47	—	21	16	19
P/E – low	—	89	7	7	13	14	35	—	13	9	13
Dividends per share ($)	(4.4%)	0.60	0.60	0.60	0.67	0.88	0.88	0.20	0.20	0.25	0.40
Book value per share ($)	1.1%	4.11	6.86	10.17	18.71	20.24	20.20	5.37	6.64	14.28	4.52
Employees	(14.4%)	26,000	18,300	7,025	6,500	6,750	6,650	6,160	6,500	6,500	6,400

1994 Year-end:
Debt ratio: 70.4%
Return on equity: 39.8%
Cash (mil.): $102
Current ratio: 1.20
Long-term debt (mil.): $507
No. of shares (mil.): 61
Dividends
  Yield: 0.7%
  Payout: 10.7%
Market value (mil.): $3,387

Stock Price History
High/Low 1985–94

CENTEX CORPORATION

OVERVIEW

The housing business, like land itself, is uneven. To be successful, a housing company has to find a way to smooth things out.

Dallas-based Centex Corporation, the US's largest home builder, smooths things out with a strategy of diversification that has helped keep it in business through the boom and bust cycles of the housing market for nearly 50 years. The company builds single-family houses in 44 major markets in every region of the continental US. Its other lines of business include mortgage banking, land ownership, commercial real estate development (through its 3333 Holding Corp.), and construction supply manufacturing (through its 49% interest in Centex Construction Products, which went public in 1995).

The company also entered into joint ventures in 1995 with the Charles Church Group to build luxury houses in the UK and with Kensington Cottages Corp. to build 2 living centers for people suffering from Alzheimer's disease and memory disorders.

Although the company's strategy of geographical diversification protects it from regional downturns, Centex was helpless in the face of the repeated interest rate increases of 1994. Without the gain the company received from Centex Construction Products, 1995 earnings would have declined even further than they did. But Centex sees good prospects for the construction products company in sales of cement, of which there is an incipient shortage, and wallboard for home renovations.

WHEN

Centex was founded in 1950 by Tom Lively and Ira Rupley, whose association in home construction had begun informally 5 years earlier. In 1949 they built their first large subdivision near Dallas. They named their company Centex and were soon ready to operate nationally. Their first out-of-state project was Elk Grove Village, a development of 7,000 houses near Chicago. By 1960 the company had built 25,000 houses.

Centex's involvement in construction products began in 1963 when it built its first cement plant. Its Fernley, Nevada, cement kiln was started up in 1964 (3 other plants were established nationwide in the next 24 years).

In 1966 Centex expanded into the commercial construction business with the purchase of J. W. Bateson Co. (now called Centex Bateson Construction Co.), a construction and contracting company that had operated in Dallas since 1936. Centex moved into mortgage banking in 1973, allowing it to combine home building with home financing. Also during the 1970s, when oil prices seemed destined to rise forever, the company invested in petroleum, forming a new subsidiary, Cenergy.

Centex expanded its contracting and construction segment in 1978 by acquiring Frank J. Rooney, Inc., a large general contractor in Florida, and later acquiring other contractors in California and Washington, DC.

Centex's early geographical focus was narrow. In 1979, 72% of the company's 9,600 homes were built in Texas. And by 1980 the company was leveraged to the hilt.

Larry Hirsch, a New York–reared lawyer who had been at the helm of a Houston cement and energy company, became COO in 1984 (and CEO in 1988). In that year, after oil prices had begun to decline but before the collapse in 1986, Centex sold Cenergy. The early 1980s were a boom time for Texas real estate because deregulation left many S&L officers desperate to make loans, any loans. The market became overbuilt, and when credit began to dry up in 1986–87 after the spectacular failure of several Texas S&Ls, the Texas real estate market crashed. Centex was pinched, but because its fixed costs (personnel and leased equipment) were elastic, it survived on the sales from less depressed areas of the US. The Texas market began rebounding after 1991.

Centex Development Company (CDC) was established in 1987 as a custodian for $75.9 million worth of land that the company could not develop during the bust and whose carrying costs were a burden on its balance sheet. Centex also created a new subsidiary, Centex-Rodgers Construction, in Nashville, which focused on medical construction, then a growth area. In the 1990s Centex continued to diversify its building operations and to expand its mortgage banking operations.

In 1994 the company took its construction products division public, retaining a 49% interest. But it was a dicey year for home builders as increases in interest rates frightened many buyers off, so response to the IPO was notably subdued. Also in 1994 Centex announced plans to buy Vista Properties, a bankrupt Dallas-based land developer.

After a 7-year experiment with thrift management, Centex sold off its S&Ls in 1994.

NYSE symbol: CTX
Fiscal year ends: March 31

Chairman and CEO: Laurence E. Hirsch, age 49,
$790,000 pay
**President and COO; Chairman, President, and CEO,
Centex Construction Group:** William J. Gillilan III,
age 49, $575,000 pay
President, CEO, and COO, Centex Real Estate:
Timothy R. Eller, age 46, $575,000 pay
CEO, CTX Mortgage: Carl N. Hearne
President, Nova Mortgage Credit: Richard L. Smith
EVP and CFO: David W. Quinn, age 53, $560,000 pay
**VP, Chief Legal Officer, General Counsel, and
Secretary:** Raymond G. Smerge, age 51, $345,500 pay
VP Finance and Controller: Michael S. Albright, age 47
VP Tax: Richard C. Harvey
VP Corporate Communications: Sheila E. Gallagher
Auditors: Arthur Andersen & Co, SC

HQ: 3333 Lee Pkwy., Ste. 1200, Dallas, TX 75219
Phone: 214-559-6500
Fax: 214-559-6750

Centex builds houses in 44 markets in California,
Florida, Georgia, Illinois, Minnesota, New Mexico, North
Carolina, Ohio, South Carolina, Texas, Washington, and
the District of Columbia.

	1995 Houses Completed	
	No.	% of total
Southwest	3,674	28
East	2,921	23
Southeast	2,632	20
West	2,454	19
Midwest	1,283	10
Total	**12,964**	**100**

	1995 Sales		1995 Operating Income	
	$ mil.	% of total	$ mil.	% of total
Home building	2,111	65	112	93
Contracting & construction services	1,060	32	(2)	—
Financial services	107	3	9	7
Total	**3,278**	**100**	**119**	**100**

Selected Subsidiaries
Centex Construction Group, Inc.
Centex Escrow Co.
Centex Insurance Agencies
Centex Real Estate
Centex Roofing Co.
Centex Senior Services
Centex Title Co.
CTX Commercial Loan Division
CTX Mortgage Co.
Metropolitan Title and Guaranty Co.
Nova Mortgage Credit Corp.

Beazer Homes
Del Webb
Fleetwood
Kaufman and Broad
NVR
Pulte
Ryland
US Home
Weekley Homes

	9-Year Growth	1986	1987	1988	1989	1990	1991	1992	1993	1994	1995
Sales ($ mil.)	1.9%	2,767	2,530	2,884	3,632	4,039	4,404	2,166	2,503	3,214	3,278
Net income ($ mil.)	7.5%	48	44	24	40	62	44	35	61	85	92
Income as % of sales	—	1.7%	1.7%	0.8%	1.1%	1.5%	1.0%	1.6%	2.4%	2.7%	2.8%
Earnings per share ($)	9.8%	1.31	1.24	0.75	1.32	2.01	1.42	1.11	1.91	2.60	3.04
Stock price – high ($)[1]	—	13.44	20.25	17.81	14.75	20.94	22.13	23.31	32.88	45.25	45.75
Stock price – low ($)[1]	—	10.25	12.00	7.56	8.25	13.63	9.63	14.00	19.88	26.75	20.13
Stock price – close ($)[1]	6.7%	12.69	15.63	8.63	14.63	15.44	14.94	22.44	32.00	42.00	22.75
P/E – high	—	10	16	24	11	10	16	21	17	17	15
P/E – low	—	8	10	10	6	7	7	13	10	10	7
Dividends per share ($)	4.9%	0.13	0.13	0.13	0.13	0.20	0.20	0.20	0.20	0.20	0.20
Book value per share ($)	11.2%	9.17	10.23	12.12	13.28	14.85	16.07	16.99	18.57	21.12	23.80
Employees	3.7%	4,600	4,500	4,200	4,700	5,100	5,300	5,500	6,500	8,430	6,395

1995 Year-end:
Debt ratio: 54.4%
Return on equity: 13.8%
Cash (mil.): $24
Current ratio: —
Long-term debt (mil.): $223
No. of shares (mil.): 28
Dividends
  Yield: 0.9%
  Payout: 6.6%
Market value (mil.): $639

**Stock Price History[1]
High/Low 1986–95**

[1] Stock prices are for the prior calendar year.

CHAMPION INTERNATIONAL

OVERVIEW

Champion International's timing has finally improved. The company, one of the US's largest manufacturers of paper and wood products, began modernizing its facilities and selling nonessential assets in the mid-1980s; however, expenses peaked in 1989, just as the US and European economies declined and paper prices fell. Finally, in mid-1994 rebounding paper prices and improving economies converged with Champion's newly streamlined operations, pulling the company out of a 5-year earnings slump. A year later Champion used its new-found profits to retire nearly $400 million in debt and to buy back nearly 10% of its outstanding shares.

With more than 5 million acres of timberland, Champion is one of the largest landholders in the US. The company produced over 6 million tons of packaging, paper, and pulp products in 1994, including newsprint, magazine papers, printing and writing papers, and beverage cartons. That same year the company produced over 2 million board feet of lumber and nearly 1.5 million square feet of plywood. Champion also has forests and pulp production operations in Brazil and Canada.

High demand had Champion's paper mills running close to full capacity in 1995. The modernization efforts begun in the mid-1980s have increased production capacity by 30%.

CEO Andrew Sigler, who orchestrated Champion's capital improvements program, is set to retire in 1996. The Loews Corp. owns about 15% of the company.

WHEN

Champion International was formed by the 1967 merger of US Plywood and Champion Paper & Fibre. US Plywood, founded in New York by Lawrence Ottinger in 1919, started out selling glue and WWI surplus plywood. By 1932 the company had started manufacturing its own products, and it consolidated operations with Aircraft Plywood in 1937.

Champion Paper & Fibre, the other party in the merger, was created when Reuben Robertson, who founded Champion Fibre in Ohio in 1906, married the daughter of the founder of similarly named Champion Coated Paper, incorporated in Ohio in 1893.

The first years for US Plywood–Champion Paper, the name of the company resulting from the 1967 merger, were marked by internal quarrels between the paper and plywood divisions over such issues as allocation of the company's timber resources. During that same period the company diversified, buying Drexel Enterprises (furniture, 1968; sold in 1977), Trend Industries (carpet, 1969; sold in 1978), Path Fork Harlan Coal (to power the company's pulp and paper mills, 1970), and AW Securities (carpets, 1974; sold in 1980). It adopted its present name in 1972.

In 1974 director Karl Bendetson, who disapproved of plans to diversify Champion into chemicals, persuaded the board to fire CEO Thomas Willers. Andrew Sigler replaced Willers and quickly turned the company's focus back to forest products by selling more than a dozen nonforest businesses.

In 1977 Champion International bought Hoerner Waldorf, the 4th largest American producer of paper packaging products such as grocery bags and cardboard boxes. Hoerner Waldorf traces its roots back to the 1966 merger of Hoerner Boxes (formed in Keokuk, Iowa, in 1920) and Waldorf Paper (originated in St. Paul as part of Baker-Collins in 1886).

With the company's $1.8 billion acquisition of St. Regis in 1984, Champion narrowed its focus to pulp and paper production. The company sold its office products businesses (1984); 55 corrugated container plants, packaging plants, and paperboard mills (1986); and 2 Texas mills and its Columbus, Ohio, specialty paper plant (1987, 1988). In 1991 and 1992 Champion sold large tracts of its western timberlands that were not easily accessible to the company's pulp and paper mills.

Champion was a defendant in a $5 billion class-action lawsuit alleging the company's Canton, North Carolina, mill had discharged dioxins and other pollutants into the Pigeon River, but a mistrial was declared in 1992. In 1993 a judge approved a settlement calling for Champion to pay $6.5 million in restitution.

Also in 1993 Champion sold 870,000 acres of Montana woods to Plum Creek Timber and 2 wood products mills to Stimson Lumber.

In 1994 Champion lobbied the city of Houston to expand its recycling program to help the company feed its new Texas newsprint plant. Also in 1994 Champion announced a breakthrough in bleach filtrate recycling (BFR) technology that substantially reduces the waste of bleached pulp mills. Wheelabrator Technologies acquired exclusive licensing rights to the BFR process in 1995. That same year, continuing high demand allowed Champion to raise paper prices several times.

WHO

Chairman and CEO: Andrew C. Sigler, age 63,
$1,525,000 pay
VC: Kenwood C. Nichols, age 55, $750,000 pay
President and COO: L. C. Heist, age 63, $950,000 pay
EVP: William H. Burchfield, age 59, $557,000 pay
EVP: Richard E. Olson, age 57, $541,000 pay
SVP and General Counsel: Marvin H. Ginsky, age 64
**SVP Organizational Development and Human
Resources:** Mark V. Childers, age 42
President and CEO, Weldwood of Canada, Ltd.: Graham
I. Bender
Managing Director, Champion Papel e Celulose Ltda.:
Odair A. Garcia
Auditors: Arthur Andersen & Co, SC

WHERE

HQ: Champion International Corporation,
One Champion Plaza, Stamford, CT 06921
Phone: 203-358-7000
Fax: 203-358-2975

Champion's manufacturing facilities are located in
Brazil, Canada, and the US.

Owned or Leased Timberlands	Acres (thou.)
Champion US	5,070
Champion Papel e Celulose	229
Total	**5,299**

	1994 Sales		1994 Operating Income	
	$ mil.	% of total	$ mil.	% of total
US	4,370	82	125	40
Canada	694	13	134	43
Brazil	254	5	54	17
Adjustments	—	—	(47)	—
Total	**5,318**	**100**	**266**	**100**

WHAT

	1994 Sales		1994 Operating Income	
	$ mil.	% of total	$ mil.	% of total
Paper	4,217	79	71	23
Wood products	1,101	21	242	77
Adjustments	—	—	(47)	—
Total	**5,318**	**100**	**266**	**100**

Selected Products

Paper and Board
Coated free sheet
Coated groundwood
Kraft paper
Linerboard
Liquid packaging board
Newsprint
Recycled fiber
Uncoated free sheet

Pulp
Bleached pulp
Groundwood/thermo-mechanical pulp
Unbleached pulp

Wood Chemicals
Tall oil
Turpentine

Wood Products
Chips
Lumber/studs
Plywood
Veneer
Waferboard

Major Subsidiaries and Affiliates

Cariboo Pulp & Paper Co. (50/50 joint venture of
Weldwood and Daishowa-Marubeni International Ltd.)
Champion Papel e Celulose Ltda. (99%, pulp and paper,
Brazil)
Weldwood of Canada Ltd. (84%, bleached softwood
kraft pulp)

KEY COMPETITORS

Akzo Nobel
Alco Standard
Boise Cascade
Canadian Pacific
Consolidated
Papers
Fletcher
Challenge

Fort Howard
Georgia-Pacific
International
Paper
James River
Manville
Mead
Potlatch

Rayonier
Reynolds Metals
Scott
Stone Container
Temple-Inland
Union Camp
Weyerhaeuser

HOW MUCH

	9-Year Growth	1985	1986	1987	1988	1989	1990	1991	1992	1993	1994
Sales ($ mil.)	(0.1%)	5,770	4,388	4,615	5,129	5,163	5,090	4,786	4,926	5,069	5,318
Net income ($ mil.)	(10.0%)	163	201	382	456	432	223	40	14	(149)	63
Income as % of sales	—	2.8%	4.6%	8.3%	8.9%	8.4%	4.4%	0.8%	0.3%	—	1.2%
Earnings per share ($)	(14.7%)	1.59	2.05	3.92	4.65	4.43	2.08	0.14	(0.15)	(1.90)	0.38
Stock price – high ($)	—	25.38	34.00	44.63	38.13	37.75	33.75	30.63	30.25	34.63	40.00
Stock price – low ($)	—	20.00	22.50	23.25	29.50	28.88	23.13	22.25	23.50	27.13	28.00
Stock price – close ($)	4.4%	24.88	30.75	34.50	32.13	32.00	25.63	24.00	28.75	33.38	36.50
P/E – high	—	16	17	11	8	9	16	—	—	—	105
P/E – low	—	13	11	6	6	7	11	—	—	—	74
Dividends per share ($)	(8.2%)	0.43	0.52	0.65	0.90	1.08	1.10	0.43	0.20	0.20	0.20
Book value per share ($)	2.1%	26.34	27.52	30.82	35.06	38.60	39.58	39.51	34.01	31.71	31.74
Employees	(6.0%)	43,000	32,200	30,700	30,400	29,500	28,500	27,500	27,300	25,250	24,615

1994 Year-end:
Debt ratio: 52.6%
Return on equity: 2.1%
Cash (mil.): $91
Current ratio: 1.14
Long-term debt (mil.): $2,889
No. of shares (mil.): 93.3
Dividends
  Yield: 0.5%
  Payout: 52.6%
Market value (mil.): $3,405

**Stock Price History
High/Low 1985–94**

THE CHARLES SCHWAB CORPORATION

Charles Schwab beat the Street in 1994. While many other brokerage houses saw significant earnings declines because of rising interest rates and the bond market crash (which gave the industry its worst year since 1990), San Francisco–based Schwab had a banner year despite lower sales overall. It gained clients and assets, along with management fees that helped offset lower commission earnings, thanks to its growing mutual funds business.

Schwab's main business is discount brokerage: making trades for clients who make their own investment decisions. The company differs from the legion of discount brokers in the amount of information it provides (offering materials that help clients decide the direction of their investment programs without making specific recommendations) and in its level of technology, including a touch-tone phone trading system and various software offerings. Schwab has 208 offices that maintain a human connection with clients; this is especially helpful because people prefer to open accounts in person. The company also works closely with independent financial advisors.

Founder Charles Schwab owns 23.3% of the company, and another 10.7% is held by the Schwab ESOP.

WHEN

After graduating from Stanford, Charles Schwab managed personal investment portfolios and published a newsletter in the 1960s for the First Commander Corporation, his California investment firm. The firm became Charles Schwab & Company, Inc., in 1971.

Initially a full-service broker, Schwab became a discount brokerage service in May 1975 after the SEC outlawed fixed commissions. While most brokers raised commissions, Schwab cut its rates steeply.

From 1977 to 1983 Schwab's client list increased thirtyfold while revenues grew from $4.6 million to $126.5 million, enabling the firm to automate its operations and develop cash-management account systems.

To gain capital for expansion, Charles sold the company to BankAmerica for $55 million in 1983. Schwab grew, but expansion into mutual funds and services like telephone trading was prevented by federal regulations prohibiting banks from acting as brokerages.

In 1987 Charles repurchased his company in a $280 million leveraged buyout and took it public. When the stock market crashed later in the year, trading volume fell by nearly half, from 17,900 per day. Revenues dropped from $465 million in 1987 to $392 million in 1988.

Stung by the stock crash, Schwab increased its efforts to diversify, offering new services and accounts to increase income from other sources. Commission contributions to revenues fell from 64% in early 1987 to 39% in 1990. By 1994, however, a long bull market had pushed commissions to 52% of sales.

The company has spent heavily on communications and computer systems. In 1989 the company introduced TeleBroker, its touch-tone telephone trading service. It has opened several communications centers to facilitate round-the-clock trading orders nationwide. Schwab continues to spend heavily on computer and telecommunications systems. It now has the capacity to page clients with market information on a prearranged basis (if a client wants to make a transaction when a stock reaches a certain price, for example).

Schwab has acquired other discount brokerages and in 1991 bought Mayer & Schweitzer (M&S), an OTC stock wholesaler that accounts for 6% of all Nasdaq trades. In 1995 the SEC was investigating Nasdaq's bid/ask system for price fixing, and M&S, as a major market maker, fell under scrutiny. But Schwab policy is to make transactions on only the most advantageous terms for its clients.

The company continues to open branch offices as well (it opened 10 new offices in 1994, fewer than planned), believing that its best long-term strategy for growth is to increase its customer base and that this is best accomplished in person. Schwab also spends heavily on advertising, much of it using Charles's trustworthy, avuncular face.

Although Schwab's clientele take responsibility for their own decisions, some court rulings involving Schwab clients have concluded that discount brokers must protect unqualified clients from the results of bad trading.

Schwab has continued to diversify, offering execution and back office services to independent financial advisors. In 1993 Schwab opened its first overseas office, in London. But it did not manage to crack the London Stock Exchange and was relegated to trading only in dollar-denominated stocks. This situation will be remedied by the consummation of its 1995 agreement to buy ShareLink, the UK's largest discount brokerage.

NYSE symbol: SCH
Fiscal year ends: December 31

WHO

Chairman and CEO: Charles R. Schwab, age 57, $3,272,731 pay
VC: Lawrence J. Stupski, age 49, $940,789 pay
President and COO: David S. Pottruck, age 46, $1,321,298 pay
EVP: Ronald W. Readmond, age 52, $722,864 pay
EVP Finance and CFO: A. John Gambs, age 49, $643,991 pay
EVP and Chief Information Officer: Dawn Gould Lepore, age 41
EVP Mutual Funds: Elizabeth Gibson Sawi, age 43
EVP Retail Brokerage: Tom D. Seip, age 45
EVP Capital Markets and Trading: John N. Tognino, age 56
EVP Human Resources: Luis E. Valencia, age 50
Auditors: Deloitte & Touche LLP

WHERE

HQ: 101 Montgomery St., San Francisco, CA 94104
Phone: 415-627-7000
Fax: 415-627-8538

Schwab has 208 branch offices in 46 states, the District of Columbia, Puerto Rico, and the UK.

WHAT

	1994 Sales	
	$ mil.	% of total
Commissions	546	52
Interest	165	15
Principal transactions	163	15
Mutual fund service fees	157	15
Other	34	3
Total	**1,065**	**100**

Investment Choices
Equities and Options
Fixed Income Investments
Mutual Fund Marketplace
Schwab International FundSource Service
Schwab Mutual Fund OneSource
SchwabFunds

Investor Information
The Charles Schwab Guides
The Equalizer for DOS
Investor Seminars
Schwab Investment Reports Service
Schwab Mutual Fund Select List
StreetSmart for Windows

Selected Accounts and Services
The Charles Schwab Trust Company
Company Retirement Account
Custodial Account
Schwab Automatic Investment Plan
Schwab Brokerage Account
Schwab Individual Retirement Account
Schwab Keogh Account
Schwab MoneyLink Transfer Service (automatic funds transfer)
Schwab One Brokerage Account with Checking and VISA debit card
Schwab One International Account with Checking
Schwab TeleBroker Services (touch-tone phone stock quotes and orders)
SchwabLink (software for financial advisors)
Trust Brokerage Account

KEY COMPETITORS

Citicorp	John Hancock	T. Rowe Price
Dean Witter,	Merrill Lynch	Transamerica
Discover	Paine Webber	Travelers
Edward Jones	Piper Jaffray	Waterhouse
Equitable	Prudential	Securities
FMR	Quick & Reilly	
Interstate/Johnson	Raymond James	
Lane	Financial	

HOW MUCH

	Annual Growth	1985	1986	1987	1988	1989	1990	1991	1992	1993	1994
Sales ($ mil.)	26.7%	203	308	465	392	553	625	795	909	1,097	1,065
Net income ($ mil.)	32.1%	11	15	8	7	19	17	50	81	118	135
Income as % of sales	—	5.4%	4.8%	1.7%	1.9%	3.4%	2.7%	6.2%	8.9%	10.8%	12.7%
Earnings per share ($)	47.9%	—	—	0.10	0.08	0.20	0.18	0.57	0.93	1.39	1.55
Stock price – high ($)	—	—	—	5.04	2.86	5.04	5.30	14.24	16.79	25.60	24.68
Stock price – low ($)	—	—	—	1.71	1.74	2.00	3.15	3.38	7.40	11.07	15.84
Stock price – close ($)	44.4%	—	—	1.78	2.00	4.12	3.38	13.51	11.62	21.59	23.26
P/E – high	—	—	—	50	36	25	29	25	18	18	16
P/E – low	—	—	—	17	22	10	18	6	8	8	10
Dividends per share ($)	—	—	—	0.00	0.00	0.03	0.04	0.05	0.10	0.13	0.19
Book value per share ($)	17.7%	—	—	1.75	1.86	2.01	1.87	2.31	3.05	4.37	5.47
Employees	13.9%	—	—	2,611	2,211	2,700	2,900	3,800	4,500	6,500	6,500

1994 Year-end:
Debt ratio: 38.2%
Return on equity: 32.0%
Cash (mil.): $4,587
Long-term debt (mil.): $289
No. of shares (mil.): 85
Dividends
  Yield: 0.8%
  Payout: 12.3%
Market value (mil.): $1,988
Assets (mil.): $7,918

Stock Price History
High/Low 1987–94

THE CHASE MANHATTAN CORPORATION

OVERVIEW

Chase Manhattan got considerably closer to its goal of becoming the best financial services company in the world when it announced its $10 billion merger with Chemical Banking in August 1995. The 2 powerhouses would shed about 12,000 jobs in forming the biggest US bank, which would take the Chase name.

Chase is now primarily a regional consumer bank with strong foreign exchange, derivatives, mutual funds, and underwriting operations in other countries (particularly in Latin America, which was hit by the fallout of the Mexican peso crash of 1994; Chase has less of a presence in the stable European and the fast-growing Asian markets).

Although Chase operates nationwide in the US, offering credit cards, mortgages, auto finance, and insurance, it maintains a branch network only in the Northeast.

These new business emphases have evolved since Chase began restructuring in 1990. But the most difficult restructuring has been in the hearts and minds of its executives. Whereas Chase's departments were formerly independent and its culture encouraged territoriality, the company has started to change, attempting to instill principles of cooperation and collegiality (and cross-selling) in formerly uncommunicative employees. One avenue for change has been a series of executive retreats.

WHEN

Chase Manhattan traces its roots to a water utility founded in 1799. The Manhattan Company was created by the New York legislature to bring pure water to the city, but investor Aaron Burr, later US vice president and the man who killed Alexander Hamilton (founder of Bank of New York) in a duel, lobbied to allow the company to use surplus funds for other services. The Bank of the Manhattan Company was the result, and, after the city bought the water company in 1808, it survived as the Bank of Manhattan.

In 1877 John Thompson formed Chase National Bank, named for Abraham Lincoln's secretary of the treasury, Salmon P. Chase. Chase National grew to prominence under Albert Wiggin, who became president in 1911.

Wiggin engineered Chase's merger with John D. Rockefeller Jr.'s Equitable Trust (1930), and Chase became the world's largest bank in assets. After retiring in 1932 Wiggin was implicated in a scandal involving speculation with bank funds.

In 1932 Rockefeller's brother-in-law Winthrop Aldrich led the bank. Aldrich expanded the bank to Germany and Japan, and he recruited his eventual successor — nephew David Rockefeller. In 1955 Chase merged with the Bank of Manhattan.

Rockefeller became co–chief executive in 1960 and chairman in 1969. His globe-trotting brought the bank both prestige and controversy (arising from his involvement in foreign policy issues).

Rockefeller retired in 1981, leaving Willard Butcher to face the consequences of the 1982 twin failures of Drysdale Government Securities and the Penn Square Bank, an Oklahoma

City bank bloated by bad oil loans. In 1993 litigation arising from this failure was settled with the awarding to Chase of $4 million in accounting services by Peat Marwick, Penn Square's auditor.

Chase formed a Delaware subsidiary in 1982 to market consumer credit instruments across state lines. In 1984 it bought Lincoln First of upstate New York, as well as operations in Ohio, Maryland, and Arizona.

In 1989 Chase was forced to absorb massive charges due to the Latin American debt crisis. Then the US commercial real estate market crashed. In the 2nd quarter of 1990, past-due real estate loans and foreclosures rose 52%. As the situation worsened, Butcher retired and Thomas Labrecque became CEO.

By the end of 1991, Labrecque had cut 6,000 from the payroll, raised capital, sold $6 billion in assets, and bought 2 banks for deposit strength. Chase's financial picture improved in 1992, but the bloodletting went on. Chase sold off its noncore banks and trimmed noncore foreign operations, including retail banking — a field in which it chose not to compete outside the US.

In 1993 Chase bought Troy & Nichols, a consumer mortgage company, as well as other mortgage portfolios, with a total value of $17 billion. It also continued reducing its retail banking operations overseas, closing banks in Singapore and Chile and selling credit card operations in Singapore and Hong Kong. The next year it teamed with Microsoft to offer PC-based on-line banking services to individuals and small businesses. In 1995, after moving its back-office operations from Manhattan, Chase began trying to sell some of its office facilities.

NYSE symbol: CMB
Fiscal year ends: December 31

WHO

Chairman and CEO: Thomas G. Labrecque, age 56, $3,420,000 pay
VC Global Financial Services: E. Michel Kruse, age 51, $1,075,000 pay (prior to promotion)
VC and Senior Loan and Investment Officer: Richard J. Boyle, age 51, $1,000,000 pay
VC Regional Banking: Donald L. Boudreau, age 54, $857,500 pay (prior to promotion)
SEVP National Consumer Products: Robert D. Hunter, age 51
EVP and General Counsel: L. Edward Shaw Jr., age 50, $856,667 pay
EVP and Treasurer: Deborah L. Duncan, age 39
EVP Corporate Communications: A. Wright Elliott, age 59
EVP and CFO: Arjun K. Mathrani, age 50
EVP Corporate Human Resources: John J. Farrell, age 43
Auditors: Price Waterhouse LLP

WHERE

HQ: One Chase Manhattan Plaza, New York, NY 10081-0001
Phone: 212-552-2222
Fax: 212-552-5005

Chase has operations in more than 50 countries.

	1994 Pretax Income	
	$ mil.	% of total
US	982	55
Other Western Hemisphere	579	33
Europe, the Middle East & Africa	156	9
Asia	53	3
Total	**1,770**	**100**

WHAT

	1994 Assets	
	$ mil.	% of total
Cash & equivalents	18,784	16
US gov't. securities	4,082	4
Foreign gov't. securities	5,407	5
Other securities	3,676	3
Derivative contracts	8,276	7
Net loans	62,511	55
Other	11,302	10
Total	**114,038**	**100**

	1994 Sales	
	$ mil.	% of total
Interest & fees on loans	5,270	47
Other interest	2,864	26
Fees & commissions	1,876	17
Other	1,177	10
Total	**11,187**	**100**

Selected Services	Selected Subsidiaries
Asset management	American Residential
Consumer loans	Holding
Corporate finance	Chase Auto Finance
Credit cards	Chase BankCard Services
Custodial services	Chase InfoServe
Foreign exchange services	Chase Manhattan Mortgage
Residential and	Holdings, Inc.
commercial real estate	Troy & Nichols, Inc.
loans	

KEY COMPETITORS

ADVANTA	Citicorp	First Chicago
American Express	CoreStates	First USA
Bank of Boston	Financial	Fleet
Bank of New York	Countrywide	General Electric
BankAmerica	Credit	General Motors
Bankers Trust	Crédit Lyonnais	J.P Morgan
Barclays	CS Holding	KeyCorp
Canadian Imperial	Dime Bancorp	NatWest

HOW MUCH

	9-Year Growth	1985	1986	1987	1988	1989	1990	1991	1992	1993	1994
Assets ($ mil.)	3.0%	87,685	94,766	99,133	97,455	107,369	98,064	98,197	95,862	102,103	114,038
Net income ($ mil.)	8.8%	565	585	(895)	1,059	(665)	(334)	520	639	466	1,205
Income as % of assets	—	0.6%	0.6%	—	1.1%	—	—	0.5%	0.7%	0.5%	1.1%
Earnings per share ($)	(0.5%)	6.15	6.50	(11.56)	11.48	(7.94)	(3.31)	3.12	3.46	1.89	5.87
Stock price – high ($)	—	36.63	49.50	46.25	30.75	44.88	35.75	21.88	30.38	38.00	40.00
Stock price – low ($)	—	23.25	34.00	19.38	20.88	28.00	9.75	10.25	17.25	27.38	30.38
Stock price – close ($)	(0.6%)	36.31	35.63	22.13	28.63	34.75	10.50	17.25	28.50	33.88	34.38
P/E – high	—	6	8	—	3	—	—	7	9	20	7
P/E – low	—	4	5	—	2	—	—	3	5	14	5
Dividends per share ($)	(2.9%)	1.90	2.05	2.16	2.16	2.36	2.16	1.20	1.20	1.20	1.46
Book value per share ($)	(2.5%)	49.19	52.95	38.70	47.19	36.40	29.54	30.62	32.25	36.48	39.28
Employees	(2.9%)	46,450	47,480	42,390	41,570	41,610	39,480	36,210	34,540	34,390	35,774

1994 Year-end:
Equity as % of assets: 6.1%
Return on assets: 2.1%
Return on equity: 17.6%
Long-term debt (mil.): $5,070
No. of shares (mil.): 177
Dividends
    Yield: 4.2%
    Payout: 24.9%
Market value (mil.): $6,090
Sales (mil.): $11,187

Stock Price History High/Low 1985–94

CHEMICAL BANKING CORPORATION

Chemical Banking experienced the thrill of the Chase in 1995 when it agreed to a $10 billion merger with Chase Manhattan. By joining forces, the 2 banks expect to save $1.5 billion a year. New York–based Chemical had planned to cut 3,700 jobs in 1995; the merger would result in 12,000 job cuts between the 2 parties.

Chemical has been refining its business lines — abandoning some (such as its bid to become a retail banking powerhouse in south and central New Jersey) and expanding others (mortgage banking, credit cards, and private banking). In addition to its retail, credit card, and mortgage activities, Chemical has strong overseas operations, particularly in foreign currency and corporate financing. Other businesses include corporate equity and debt underwriting (it is one of the few US banks currently permitted to do this). It also owns Texas Commerce Bank, which has one of that state's largest banking networks.

Chemical's problem loan portfolio has shrunk because of aggressive write-downs and sales, and in 1994 the bank sold a package of its risky loans and 80 pieces of property to Morgan Stanley's real estate fund. Many of the company's problems continue to stem from its 1991 merger with Manufacturers Hanover, which created a large number of operational redundancies in the organization.

WHEN

Balthazar Melick, Mark Spenser, and Geradus Post founded the New York Chemical Manufacturing Company in 1823, largely in order to be able to open a bank (the New York legislature was reluctant to grant charters to banks unaffiliated with businesses). In 1824 they opened Chemical Bank. In 1844 the chemical firm was liquidated, and the company continued as a bank.

Chemical Bank was a founder (1853) of the New York Clearing House, which expedited the exchange and settlement of funds among New York City banks. In 1865 the bank took a national charter and issued bank notes backed by federal bonds. Chemical survived repeated recessions in the 1800s by keeping large reserves of specie for note redemption.

Building on the business of acting as agent for other banks, Chemical grew to be one of the largest and strongest US banks by 1900. There followed a period of drifting, in which Chemical lost clientele and market share, but this was remedied during WWI by new management and a general upturn in business.

In 1920 the bank began to diversify into other services, such as trusts, and acquired Citizens National Bank in the first of several mergers with New York institutions. Chemical opened its first branch in 1923 and its first foreign office in London in 1929. That same year Chemical converted to a state charter to gain more trust powers and facilitate a merger with United States Mortgage & Trust.

Chemical grew even in the Depression; by 1941 assets were $1 billion. In 1968 Chemical formed a bank holding company and bought consumer loan, mortgage banking, and factoring firms. The 1960s also saw the growth of Chemical's international business.

Chemical is a technological innovator. It introduced BankLink (1977), a computerized cash management system, and Pronto, the first electronic home banking service (1982).

Chemical grew through mergers in the 1980s, buying troubled Texas Commerce Bancshares (1987), one of Texas's largest banks, and Horizon Bancorp of New Jersey (1989; in 1995, unable to gain a significant share of the market outside the New York metropolitan area, it sold 60 branches to PNC and folded the rest into its metro-area operations). In the late 1980s Chemical was hit by foreign loan losses, particularly those in Brazil and Argentina.

In 1991 Chemical (then the 6th largest US bank) merged with Manufacturers Hanover (which was the 9th largest). Although the merger was touted as a merger of equals and the new company's management was resolutely divided between the parties, there remained some friction at lower levels.

Chemical continued to add to its Texas operations. In 1992 Texas Commerce bought branches of the defunct First City banks. The next year it added 4 of First City's banks and Ameritrust Texas Corporation.

In 1993 Chemical received permission to deal in and underwrite corporate securities, which allowed the company to offer more financing options to its business customers.

In 1995 the company sold its interest in the Far East Bank & Trust Company of the Philippines. It was also revealed that one of the bank's currency traders (since fired) had made unauthorized trades in the Mexican peso before and during the peso collapse of 1994–95. This forced Chemical to take a $70 million pretax charge for losses.

NYSE symbol: CHL
Fiscal year ends: December 31

Chairman and CEO: Walter V. Shipley, age 59,
$2,496,154 pay
VC: William B. Harrison Jr., age 51, $1,746,154 pay
President: Edward D. Miller, age 54, $1,871,154 pay
**Chairman, President, and CEO, Texas Commerce Bank
National Association:** Marc J. Shapiro
SEVP: Michael Hegarty
SEVP: Donald H. Layton
SEVP: William H. Turner
EVP and CFO: Peter J. Tobin, $923,077 pay
EVP and Chief Credit Risk Policy Officer: William C.
Langley, $825,000 pay
EVP and General Counsel: William H. McDavid
EVP and Director Human Resources: Martin H.
Zuckerman
Auditors: Price Waterhouse LLP

WHERE

HQ: 270 Park Ave., New York, NY 10017
Phone: 212-270-6000
Fax: 212-270-2613

Chemical Banking and its subsidiaries operate
throughout the US and in 35 other nations.

	1994 Sales		1994 Pretax Income	
	$ mil.	% of total	$ mil.	% of total
US	9,530	75	1,470	66
Europe	1,638	13	348	16
Latin America & Caribbean	831	7	228	10
Asia & Pacific	567	4	167	8
Middle East & Africa	79	1	5	0
Other regions	40	0	(6)	—
Total	**12,685**	**100**	**2,212**	**100**

WHAT

	1994 Assets	
	$ mil.	% of total
Cash & equivalents	27,278	16
Treasury & agency securities	8,741	5
Foreign investments	7,720	5
Mortgage-backed securities & CMOs	16,325	9
Unrealized derivatives gains	17,709	10
Net loans	76,287	45
Other	17,363	10
Total	**171,423**	**100**

	1994 Sales	
	$ mil.	% of total
Loans	5,730	45
Securities interest	1,715	14
Other interest	1,643	13
Service & management fees	2,274	18
Trading account	645	5
Other	678	5
Total	**12,685**	**100**

Selected Subsidiaries
Chemical Bank
CIT (40%)
Geoserve, Inc.

Texas Commerce Bank
National Association

KEY COMPETITORS

American Express	Crédit Lyonnais	J.P. Morgan
Banc One	CS Holding	Merrill Lynch
Bank of New York	Deutsche Bank	Morgan Stanley
BankAmerica	Dime Anchor	NationsBank
Bankers Trust	First Chicago	NatWest
Barclays	First Fidelity	Royal Bank of
Bear Stearns	First Interstate	Canada
Canadian Imperial	Fleet	Salomon
Citicorp	General Electric	Union Bank of
Club Corp.	HSBC	Switzerland
Countrywide Credit		

HOW MUCH

	9-Year Growth	1985	1986	1987	1988	1989	1990	1991	1992	1993	1994
Assets ($ mil.)	13.0%	56,990	60,564	78,189	67,349	71,513	73,019	138,930	139,655	149,888	171,423
Net income ($ mil.)	14.2%	390	402	(854)	754	(482)	291	154	1,086	1,569	1,294
Income as % of assets	—	0.7%	0.7%	—	1.1%	—	0.4%	0.1%	0.8%	1.0%	0.8%
Earnings per share ($)	(4.7%)	7.15	7.42	(16.68)	12.02	(8.29)	2.38	0.11	3.90	5.63	4.64
Stock price – high ($)	—	46.25	56.25	49.50	33.88	41.13	31.38	30.13	39.50	46.38	42.13
Stock price – low ($)	—	33.13	40.75	20.25	20.00	28.50	9.63	10.50	21.88	35.00	33.63
Stock price – close ($)	(2.6%)	45.38	42.25	21.38	31.00	29.88	10.75	21.25	38.63	40.13	35.88
P/E – high	—	7	8	—	3	—	13	—	10	8	9
P/E – low	—	5	6	—	2	—	4	96	6	6	7
Dividends per share ($)	(4.8%)	2.45	2.57	2.69	2.72	2.72	2.72	1.00	1.20	1.29	1.58
Book value per share ($)	(3.3%)	51.17	56.14	25.96	31.31	24.32	24.25	26.28	32.43	37.61	37.88
Employees	8.8%	19,691	20,993	28,597	27,225	49,173	45,636	43,169	39,687	41,567	42,130

1994 Year-end:
Equity as % of assets: 6.2%
Return on assets: 0.8%
Return on equity: 13.8%
Long-term debt (mil.): $7,991
No. of shares (mil.): 245
Dividends
  Yield: 4.4%
  Payout: 34.1%
Market value (mil.): $8,773
Sales (mil.): $12,685

Stock Price History
High/Low 1985–94

CHEVRON CORPORATION

OVERVIEW

One of the largest US-based international oil and gas companies, San Francisco–based Chevron has net reserves of 4.2 billion barrels of oil and 10 trillion cubic feet of gas. A fully integrated oil and gas company, Chevron has operations ranging from exploration to refining to distribution. Chevron is the largest oil refiner in the US and the 2nd largest natural gas producer. It is also the leading US marketer of refined products, including gasoline, diesel, and lubricants, and operates 7,900 service stations in the US, 500 in the UK, and 200 in Canada. As a 50%-owner of Caltex Petroleum (half-owned by Texaco), it supplies products to more than 18,000 outlets in

Africa, the Middle East, Asia, Australia, and New Zealand. Chevron operates chemical plants in Brazil, France, Japan, and the US and mines coal in 6 states in the US. It also invests in domestic real estate.

A sluggish oil market in the past few years depressed prices and forced Chevron, like its competitors in the oil business, to cut costs and improve operational efficiency. It has cut nearly 10,000 employees (approaching 20% of the total) from its payroll in the past 4 years. But the company is also pursuing an aggressive exploration and production strategy outside the US. Non-US projects accounted for 70% of Chevron's capital budget in 1994.

WHEN

Thirty years after the California Gold Rush, a small company started selling a different product from the ground — oil. The crude came from wildcatter Frederick Taylor's well north of Los Angeles. In 1879 Taylor and other oil marketers in the area formed Pacific Coast Oil.

Pacific Coast's debut wasn't as earthshaking an event as Sutter's Mill, but it attracted the attention of John D. Rockefeller's Standard Oil. The 2 companies competed fiercely until Standard bought Pacific Coast in 1900.

When the Supreme Court ordered the breakup of Standard Oil in 1911, West Coast operations became the stand-alone Standard Oil Company (California), the only former subsidiary considered a truly integrated petroleum firm, with production, refining, pipelines, and marketing. All its former Standard stablemates were running on fewer than those 4 legs.

The San Francisco–based company, nicknamed Socal and marketing products under the Chevron name, found itself at a different kind of golden gate when it won drilling concessions on the island of Bahrain and in Saudi Arabia in the 1930s. The desert oil trove proved so vast that Socal summoned Texaco to help market the crude. They formed Caltex — the California Texas Oil Company — as equal partners. In 1948 Socony (later Mobil) and Jersey Standard (later Exxon) bought 40% of Caltex's Saudi operations, and the Saudi arm became Aramco (Arabian American Oil Company).

Socal exploration pushed into Louisiana and the Gulf of Mexico in the 1940s. In 1961 it bought Standard Oil Company of Kentucky (Kyso) to acquire southern service stations.

Caltex suffered nationalization of some Arab holdings in the OPEC-spawned upheaval of the 1970s. In 1980 Aramco became part of the

Saudi Arabian government, and in the mid-1980s the company had to abandon a nearly $1 billion investment in Sudan when guerrillas attacked construction sites.

In 1984 Socal renamed itself Chevron (assuming its brand name) and doubled its oil and gas reserves with a record $13.3 billion purchase of Gulf Corporation.

Gulf had begun in the 1901 Spindletop gusher in Texas as J. M. Guffey Petroleum, bankrolled by the Mellon family of Pittsburgh. Founder Guffey was unseated by William Larimer Mellon (1902), and the company's name was changed to Gulf (1907). Spurred by strikes in Louisiana and Oklahoma, Gulf became an oil power by developing Kuwaiti concessions. In the 1970s oil cutbacks in Kuwait and reports of government payoffs at home and abroad hobbled Gulf.

Chevron paid $2.5 billion for Tenneco's Gulf of Mexico oil and gas properties in 1988, which helped make it a leader in US natural gas production.

In 1992 Chevron exchanged interests in 266 oil and gas fields, valued at $1.1 billion, for 15.7 million shares of Chevron stock owned by Pennzoil. The tax-free trade cut Pennzoil's holdings in Chevron from 9.7% to 5.3%.

Chevron announced an agreement in 1993 to sell its petroleum marketing businesses in El Salvador, Guatemala, and Nicaragua to the Royal Dutch/Shell group.

Chevron sold its Philadelphia refinery to the Sun Company in 1994 and its Port Arthur, Texas, refinery to Clark Refining & Marketing a year later. In late 1994 Chevron and rival Conoco received permission from UK authorities to develop the Britannia Field, the largest unexploited natural gas field in the North Sea.

NYSE symbol: CHV
Fiscal year ends: December 31

Chairman and CEO: Kenneth T. Derr, age 58, $1,700,000 pay
VC: J. Dennis Bonney, age 64, $995,000 pay
VC: James N. Sullivan, age 57, $923,000 pay
VP and CFO: Martin R. Klitten, age 50, $589,250 pay
VP; President, Chevron U.S.A. Production Company: Raymond E. Galvin, age 63, $564,000 pay
VP, Chevron U.S.A. Products Company: David J. O'Reilly, age 48
VP; President, Chevron Overseas Petroleum: Richard H. Matzke, age 58
VP; President, Chevron Chemical Company: John E. Peppercorn, age 57
VP and General Counsel: Harvey D. Hinman, age 54
VP Public Affairs: Roderick L. Hartung, age 59
VP and Comptroller: Donald G. Henderson, age 55
VP Strategic Planning and Quality: Peter J. Robertson, age 48
VP Human Resources: Ronald C. Kiskis, age 46
Auditors: Price Waterhouse LLP

WHERE

HQ: 225 Bush St., San Francisco, CA 94104
Phone: 415-894-7700
Fax: 415-894-0593

Chevron conducts integrated petroleum operations in the US and about 100 other countries.

	1994 Sales		1994 Net Income	
	$ mil.	% of total	$ mil.	% of total
US	24,540	70	1,132	38
Other countries	10,570	30	1,832	62
Adjustments	744	—	(1,271)	—
Total	**35,854**	**100**	**1,693**	**100**

WHAT

	1994 Sales		1994 Operating Income	
	$ mil.	% of total	$ mil.	% of total
Petroleum	31,613	88	1,336	79
Chemicals	3,081	9	206	12
Minerals	416	1	111	7
Other	744	2	40	2
Total	**35,854**	**100**	**1,693**	**100**

Selected Major Subsidiaries and Affiliates
Caltex Petroleum Corp. (50%, refining and marketing)
Chevron Chemical Co. (industrial chemicals, consumer products)
Chevron International Oil Co., Inc. (trading and marketing)
Chevron Overseas Petroleum Inc.
Chevron Pipe Line Co.
Chevron Transport Corp. (marine transportation)
Chevron U.S.A. Production Co.
Chevron U.S.A. Products Co.
Gulf Oil (Great Britain) Limited
The Pittsburg & Midway Coal Mining Co.

KEY COMPETITORS

Amerada Hess	Exxon	Petrobrás
Amoco	Hanson	Petrofina
Ashland, Inc.	Huntsman	Phillips Petroleum
Atlantic	Chemical	Repsol
Richfield	Kerr-McGee	Royal Dutch/Shell
British	Lyondell	Sinclair Oil
Petroleum	Petrochemical	Southland
Broken Hill	Mobil	Sun Company
Coastal	Norsk Hydro	Texaco
Cyprus Amax	Occidental	TOTAL
DuPont	Oryx	Union Carbide
Eastman	PDVSA	Unocal
Chemical	PEMEX	USX–Marathon
Elf Aquitaine	Pennzoil	

HOW MUCH

	9-Year Growth	1985	1986	1987	1988	1989	1990	1991	1992	1993	1994
Sales ($ mil.)	(2.6%)	45,325	27,131	29,097	28,857	32,785	42,566	40,945	42,893	37,082	35,854
Net income ($ mil.)	1.0%	1,547	715	1,007	1,768	251	2,157	1,293	2,210	1,265	1,693
Income as % of sales	—	3.4%	2.6%	3.5%	6.1%	0.8%	5.5%	3.5%	5.8%	3.4%	4.7%
Earnings per share ($)	1.6%	2.26	1.05	1.47	2.59	0.37	3.05	1.85	3.26	1.95	2.60
Stock price – high ($)	—	20.38	24.06	32.31	26.00	36.75	40.81	40.06	37.69	49.38	49.19
Stock price – low ($)	—	14.63	17.00	16.00	19.50	22.69	31.56	31.75	30.06	33.69	39.88
Stock price – close ($)	9.9%	19.06	22.69	19.81	22.88	33.88	36.31	34.50	34.75	43.56	44.63
P/E – high	—	9	23	22	10	99	13	22	12	25	19
P/E – low	—	7	16	11	8	61	10	17	9	17	15
Dividends per share ($)	4.9%	1.20	1.20	1.20	1.28	1.40	1.48	1.63	1.65	1.75	1.85
Book value per share ($)	(0.2%)	22.73	22.64	23.06	21.61	19.69	21.15	21.25	21.11	21.48	22.40
Employees	(3.1%)	60,845	51,095	51,697	53,675	54,826	54,208	55,123	49,245	47,576	45,758

1994 Year-end:
Debt ratio: 35.8%
Return on equity: 11.8%
Cash (mil.): $1,306
Current ratio: 0.81
Long-term debt (mil.): $4,128
No. of shares (mil.): 652
Dividends
  Yield: 4.1%
  Payout: 71.2%
Market value (mil.): $29,088

Stock Price History
High/Low 1985–94

CHIQUITA BRANDS INTERNATIONAL, INC.

OVERVIEW

A trade war has broken out over bananas, and Chiquita is caught in the split. In Europe the EU is restricting banana imports from Latin America, while some Latin American countries (Colombia, Costa Rica, Nicaragua, and Venezuela) are taxing banana exports. Calling the trade practices unfair, in 1994 Chiquita asked the US government to intervene on its behalf.

Chiquita is a leading producer of fruits and vegetables worldwide. Bananas, the "world's perfect food," accounts for 60% of its income.

Chiquita has a bunch of excuses for its 3-year run of red ink, including low prices resulting from high crop yields, labor strikes in Honduras, a slowdown in the company's Japanese operations, and the ongoing banana imbroglio. Meanwhile, Dole is squeezing Chiquita's bananas out of some Midwestern grocery chains by undercutting its prices.

As market realities change, Chiquita is moving to streamline its operations. In 1994 the company completed a long-term program to replace leased assets, including ships and production facilities, with company-owned properties. It also scaled back operations in Honduras and Japan. Chiquita is still trying to sell its meat subsidiaries (including the Rath Black Hawk and John Morrell brands), which have been on the market since 1992.

Carl Lindner, chairman and CEO, controls 46% of Chiquita's common stock. His son Keith is president and COO.

WHEN

In 1870 Lorenzo Baker sailed into Jersey City with 160 bunches of Jamaican bananas. Finding the new fruit profitable, Baker arranged to sell bananas through Boston produce agent Andrew Preston. With the support of Preston's partners, the 2 men formed the Boston Fruit Company in 1885. In 1899 Boston Fruit merged with 3 other banana importers and incorporated as United Fruit Company. Soon the company was importing bananas from numerous Central American plantations for expanded distribution in the US.

The company entered the Cuban sugar trade (Fidel Castro worked on a United Fruit sugar plantation) with the purchase of Nipe Bay (1907) and Saetia Sugar (1912). In 1930 the company bought Samuel Zemurray's Cuyamel Fruit Company, leaving Zemurray as the largest shareholder. Zemurray, who had masterminded the overthrow of the Honduran government in 1905 to establish a government favorable to his business, forcibly established himself as United Fruit's president in 1933. Because of the company's broad influence throughout Honduran politics and society, Hondurans called it the "Octopus."

In 1954, when leftist Guatemalan leader Jacobo Arbenz threatened to seize United Fruit holdings, the company convinced Congress and the American public that Arbenz was a communist threat and provided ships to transport CIA-backed troops and ammunition for his ultimate overthrow. In 1961 United Fruit provided 2 ships for the ill-fated Bay of Pigs invasion of Cuba. The term "banana republic" originates from United Fruit's involvement in establishing Central American regimes friendly to its operations.

During the 1950s the company introduced its catchy calypso-style Chiquita Banana ad campaign and in the 1960s diversified, buying A&W (restaurants and root beer, 1966) and Baskin-Robbins (ice cream, 1967).

Eli Black, founder of AMK (which included the Morrell meat company), bought United Fruit in 1970 and changed its name to United Brands. In 1975, after Hurricane Fifi had destroyed much of the Honduran banana crop and the news leaked that he had bribed the Honduran president, Black killed himself.

During the 1970s and 1980s, United Brands sold many of its holdings, including Baskin-Robbins (1973), Foster Grant (sunglasses, 1974), and A&W (restaurants, 1982; soft drinks, 1987). Financier Carl Lindner's American Financial took a key interest in United Brands in 1987.

The company became Chiquita Brands International in 1990. The following year it entered new markets in Eastern Europe, South Korea, and Iran; created a French joint venture; and bought T&P Custom Marketing (ingredients for processed fruits and vegetables).

In 1992 Chiquita exchanged 2.7 million shares for Friday Canning Corporation, one of the US's largest private-label vegetable processors. The company also began to divest its meat division units.

The company sold its specialty meat operations for about $53 million in 1994. It also raised $310 million to retire high-cost debt by selling senior notes and preferred stock. In 1995 Chiquita licensee Connor Foods began test marketing ready-to-bake banana muffins and chocolate-dipped banana ice cream bars under the Chiquita label.

NYSE symbol: CQB
Fiscal year ends: December 31

WHO

Chairman and CEO: Carl H. Lindner, age 75,
$415,000 pay
**President and COO; President, Chiquita Banana Group
(Worldwide):** Keith E. Lindner, age 35, $1,030,000 pay
SEVP Chiquita Banana Group (Worldwide): Robert F.
Kistinger, age 42, $550,000 pay
EVP, Chief Administrative Officer, and CFO: Steven G.
Warshaw, age 41, $630,000 pay
President, Chiquita Banana North America Division:
Jos P. Stalenhoef, age 53, $407,500 pay
President, Chiquita Processed Foods: Anthony D.
Battaglia
President and CEO, Meat Division: Joseph B. Sebring
VP, General Counsel, and Secretary: Charles R. Morgan,
age 48
VP and Controller: William A. Tsacalis, age 51
VP Human Resources: Jean B. Lapointe
VP: Fred J. Runk, age 52
VP: Thomas E. Mischell, age 47
Auditors: Ernst & Young LLP

WHERE

HQ: 250 E. Fifth St., Cincinnati, OH 45202
Phone: 513-784-8011
Fax: 513-784-8030

Chiquita distributes its fruit and vegetable products
worldwide.

	1994 Sales		1994 Operating Income	
	$ mil.	% of total	$ mil.	% of total
North America	2,680	67	30	25
Latin America	180	5	19	15
Europe & other regions	1,102	28	74	60
Adjustments	—	—	(13)	—
Total	**3,962**	**100**	**110**	**100**

WHAT

	1994 Sales		1994 Operating Income	
	$ mil.	% of total	$ mil.	% of total
Chiquita produce operations	2,506	63	71	65
Meat division	1,456	37	39	35
Total	**3,962**	**100**	**110**	**100**

Selected Products

Fruit Brands	Other Brands
Amigo	Chiquita (cookies, baked
Chico	goods, and fruit juices)
Chiquita	Clover (shortening,
Consul	margarine, and vegetable
Frupac	oil products)
Premium	Club Chef (salads)
	Friday (processed fruits and
Meat Brands	vegetables)
Dinner Bell	Naked Foods (salads)
John Morrell	Numar (shortening,
Kretschmar	margarine, and vegetable
Rath Black Hawk	oil products)
Rodeo	Saratoga (spices)
Tobin's First Prize	

KEY COMPETITORS

Borden	Ocean Spray
Cadbury Schweppes	PepsiCo
Coca-Cola	Philip Morris
ConAgra	Procter & Gamble
CPC	Quaker Oats
Danone	RJR Nabisco
Del Monte	Sara Lee
Dole	Seagram
Ferolito, Vultaggio	TLC Beatrice
Fresh America	Tri Valley Growers
General Mills	United Foods
Goya	Universal Foods
Grand Metropolitan	Veryfine
National Grape Co-op	

HOW MUCH

	9-Year Growth	1985	1986	1987	1988	1989	1990	1991	1992	1993	1994
Sales ($ mil.)	6.3%	2,288	3,307	3,268	3,503	3,823	4,273	4,627	2,723	2,533	3,962
Net income ($ mil.)	—	23	54	61	60	68	94	129	(284)	(51)	(72)
Income as % of sales	—	1.0%	1.6%	1.9%	1.7%	1.8%	2.2%	2.8%	—	—	—
Earnings per share ($)	—	0.46	1.09	1.30	1.45	1.67	2.20	2.52	(5.48)	(0.99)	(1.51)
Stock price – high ($)	—	9.28	12.31	16.66	19.88	17.63	32.13	50.75	40.13	17.75	19.38
Stock price – low ($)	—	3.50	7.38	9.31	13.75	12.88	16.00	29.38	15.25	10.00	11.25
Stock price – close ($)	4.4%	9.25	11.06	15.19	16.38	17.38	32.00	40.00	17.25	11.50	13.63
P/E – high	—	20	11	13	14	11	15	20	—	—	—
P/E – low	—	8	7	7	10	8	7	12	—	—	—
Dividends per share ($)	29.2%	0.02	0.02	0.15	0.19	0.20	0.35	0.55	0.66	0.44	0.20
Book value per share ($)	2.0%	7.69	8.81	10.91	10.38	11.94	15.21	19.39	12.93	11.33	9.21
Employees	0.0%	40,000	39,000	40,000	42,000	44,000	46,000	50,000	45,000	45,000	40,000

1994 Year-end:
Debt ratio: 71.1%
Return on equity: —
Cash (mil.): $179
Current ratio: 1.40
Long-term debt (mil.): $1,365
No. of shares (mil.): 49
Dividends
  Yield: 1.5%
  Payout: —
Market value (mil.): $672

Stock Price History
High/Low 1985-94

CHRYSLER CORPORATION

OVERVIEW

Chrysler, the #3 US automaker after General Motors and Ford, designs and produces cars, trucks, minivans, and sport-utility vehicles under 5 nameplates for customers in more than 100 countries. It is the world's lowest-cost automaker, and it has the highest profit margin among the major US automakers. Chrysler also owns the Dollar and Thrifty car rental agencies and, like other automakers, offers an array of financial, leasing, and insurance services to dealers and customers.

Since 1989 the company has ruthlessly cut costs, reorganized, and pared the development time for launching new car models. Chrysler has squirreled away more than $7 billion as a cushion against the next inevitable downturn in the auto industry. The automaker has announced its intentions to sell off its other rental-car operations; in 1994 Chrysler sold its Snappy Car Rental unit for about $10 million.

Chrysler is under siege by its largest shareholder, Kirk Kerkorian, who owns over 10% of the company. The Las Vegas billionaire, with support from former Chrysler chairman Lee Iacocca, made a surprise $20 billion hostile takeover bid for Chrysler in April 1995 but was emphatically rebuffed. Although Kerkorian withdrew his bid in May, the gambling tycoon continues to badger Chrysler's board to increase its dividend and stock price. In response, the beleaguered automaker began a $1 billion stock repurchase program.

Chrysler lost out to Mercedes-Benz in 1995 on a $1 billion minivan joint venture in China.

WHEN

When the Maxwell Motor Car Company entered receivership in 1920, a bankers' syndicate hired Walter Chrysler, former Buick president and General Motors VP, to reorganize it. Chrysler became president in 1923 and in 1924 introduced his own car, the Chrysler, which borrowed from WWI aircraft in the design of its 6-cylinder engine. In 1925 Chrysler took over Maxwell and renamed it after himself.

In 1928 Chrysler acquired Dodge and introduced the low-priced Plymouth and the luxurious DeSoto. The Chrysler R&D budget never decreased during the Great Depression, and innovations included overdrive and a 3-point engine suspension on rubber mountings. In 1933 Chrysler's sales surpassed Ford's, and in 1935 Walter Chrysler retired.

To minimize costs, Chrysler kept the same car models from 1942 until 1953, while other manufacturers were making yearly style modifications. Chrysler lost market share and slipped to 3rd place by 1950.

Chrysler misjudged customer demands in the 1960s when it introduced small cars and in the 1970s when it maintained production of large cars. Steadily declining market share led to losses of over $1 billion in 1979 and 1980. Facing the prospect of bankruptcy, Chrysler negotiated $1.5 billion in loan guarantees from the federal government and brought in Lee Iacocca, former Ford president (and the man behind the immensely popular Ford Mustang), as CEO in 1978.

Iacocca became one of the most visible CEOs ever, appearing in TV commercials, publishing his autobiography, and making an issue of Japanese trading practices. The company reorganized, closed several plants, and cut its work force. Chrysler cut production costs by using the K-car chassis for several models. By 1983 the company had repaid all guaranteed loans, 7 years ahead of schedule. In 1984 Chrysler introduced the first minivan.

In 1985 Chrysler began to diversify, buying Gulfstream Aerospace (corporate jets, sold in 1990), E.F. Hutton Credit, and Finance America for a total of $1.2 billion. In 1986 Chrysler created a joint venture with Mitsubishi (Diamond-Star) to sell Mitsubishi cars in the US (sold 1993), and in 1987 it purchased American Motors. Between 1989 and 1991 Chrysler bought Thrifty, Snappy, Dollar, and General car rental agencies.

In 1990 corporate raider Kirk Kerkorian bought 9.8% of Chrysler at bargain prices. The company skidded into red ink the following year because of the recession and weak consumer demand. Also in 1991 Chrysler joined Austria's Steyr-Daimler-Puch Fahrzeugtechnik to form Eurostar, a joint venture that manufactures Chrysler minivans for the European market. An economic downturn in 1992 forced Chrysler to sell nonautomotive assets worth $3 billion. Iacocca stepped down as chairman in late 1992. He was replaced by GM's head of European operations, Robert Eaton.

In 1994 the company suffered through a series of embarrassing recalls, including that of 115,000 1993 Jeep Cherokees because of flaws in the steering column. In 1995 Chrysler became the 2nd automaker to seek a joint venture in Vietnam, where it wants to build an assembly plant.

NYSE symbol: C
Fiscal year ends: December 31

WHO

Chairman and CEO: Robert J. Eaton, age 54,
$3,263,750 pay
VC and Chief Administrative Officer: Thomas G.
Denomme, age 55, $1,496,250 pay
President and COO: Robert A. Lutz, age 62,
$2,408,750 pay
EVP and CFO: Gary C. Valade, age 52, $1,137,500 pay
EVP Sales and Marketing; General Manager, Minivans:
Theodor R. Cunningham, age 48, $1,112,500 pay
EVP Manufacturing: Dennis K. Pawley, age 53
VP; Chairman, Chrysler Financial: Thomas W. Sidlik,
age 45
VP Chrysler Technologies and Rental Car Operations:
Joseph E. Cappy, age 60
VP, General Counsel, and Secretary: William J. O'Brien,
age 51
VP Corporate Personnel: Kathleen M. Oswald, age 45
Chairman and President, Chrysler Technologies: Paul
E. Wright
Auditors: Deloitte & Touche LLP

WHERE

HQ: 12000 Chrysler Dr., Highland Park, MI 48288-0001
Phone: 313-956-5741
Fax: 313-956-3747

Chrysler has manufacturing and assembly plants in
Alabama, Delaware, Illinois, Indiana, Michigan, Missouri,
New York, Ohio, Texas, and Wisconsin in the US and
overseas in Austria and Venezuela.

	1994 Sales		1994 Pretax Income	
	$ mil.	% of total	$ mil.	% of total
US	45,655	88	5,239	90
Canada	3,877	7	208	3
Other countries	2,692	5	383	7
Total	**52,224**	**100**	**5,830**	**100**

WHAT

	1994 Sales		1994 Pretax Income	
	$ mil.	% of total	$ mil.	% of total
Cars & trucks	50,381	96	5,515	95
Financial services	1,843	4	315	5
Total	**52,224**	**100**	**5,830**	**100**

Nameplates
Chrysler   Jeep
Dodge   Plymouth
Eagle

Selected Subsidiaries and Affiliates
American Motors Pan American Corp.
Automotive Financial Services, Inc.
Chrysler Canada Ltd.
Chrysler Capital Corp. (financial services)
Chrysler de México SA (99.9%)
Chrysler Financial Corp.
Chrysler Insurance Co.
Chrysler Motors de Venezuela, SA
Chrysler Pentastar Aviation, Inc. (commercial aviation)
Chrysler Technologies Corp. (defense electronics)
Pentastar Transportation Group, Inc. (auto leasing)
  Dollar (Rent A Car) Systems, Inc.
  Scamp Auto Rental I, Inc.
  Thrifty Rent-A-Car System, Inc.

KEY COMPETITORS

Alamo Rent A Car
Avis
Banc One
BankAmerica
BMW
Budget Rent A Car
Chase Manhattan
Citicorp
Daimler-Benz
Enterprise
  Rent-A-Car
Fiat
Ford
General Motors
Honda
Household Intl.
Hyundai
Isuzu
KeyCorp
Kia Motors
Mazda
Mitsubishi
National Car
  Rental
NationsBank
Nissan
Peugeot
Renault
Saab-Scania
Suzuki
Toyota
Volkswagen
Volvo

HOW MUCH

	9-Year Growth	1985	1986	1987	1988	1989	1990	1991	1992	1993	1994
Sales ($ mil.)	10.5%	21,256	22,586	26,277	35,473	34,922	30,620	29,370	36,897	43,600	52,224
Net income ($ mil.)	9.5%	1,635	1,404	1,290	1,050	359	68	(538)	505	2,415	3,713
Income as % of sales	—	7.7%	6.2%	4.9%	3.0%	1.0%	0.2%	—	1.4%	5.5%	7.1%
Earnings per share ($)	4.3%	6.22	6.32	5.90	4.66	1.55	0.30	(2.22)	1.49	6.77	9.10
Stock price – high ($)	—	20.91	31.44	48.00	27.88	29.63	20.38	15.88	33.88	58.38	63.50
Stock price – low ($)	—	13.31	18.13	19.63	20.50	18.13	9.13	9.75	11.50	31.75	42.25
Stock price – close ($)	10.0%	20.75	24.69	22.13	25.75	19.00	12.63	11.75	32.00	53.25	49.00
P/E – high	—	3	5	8	6	19	68	—	23	9	7
P/E – low	—	2	3	3	4	12	30	—	8	5	5
Dividends per share ($)	8.0%	0.45	0.68	0.98	1.00	1.15	1.20	0.75	0.60	0.60	0.90
Book value per share ($)	5.6%	18.51	24.67	29.39	32.52	32.42	30.47	20.90	25.47	19.41	30.11
Employees	1.3%	107,850	115,074	122,745	145,000	121,947	124,000	124,000	128,000	128,000	121,000

1994 Year-end:
Debt ratio: 55.1%
Return on equity: 42.4%
Cash (mil.): $8,371
Current ratio: 0.92
Long-term debt (mil.): $7,650
No. of shares (mil.): 355
Dividends
  Yield: 1.8%
  Payout: 9.9%
Market value (mil.): $17,400

Stock Price History
High/Low 1985–94

THE CHUBB CORPORATION

Chubb Corporation wants to grow through consolidation. It intends to become one of the 10 largest property/casualty insurers (by underwriting profit) in the US by the year 2000, and, because the US market is mature, it is targeting markets overseas for further growth. By 1994 it had almost attained its goal of deriving 25% of its sales from foreign business (it operates in most major markets in Europe, Asia, and Latin America).

As part of this effort, Chubb has been streamlining its operations by consolidating administrative offices in New York and Los Angeles and cutting the number of life insurance offices from 40 to 20. In the process the company is upgrading its technical systems and improving its customer services. Under the new system, customers will have one con-

tact within the company, rather than having different contacts for every type of insurance.

Chubb's products, aimed at businesses and affluent individuals, include traditional property/casualty insurance as well as niche property products (like the winery coverage it offers in France) and life and health insurance (both group and individual). Its Chubb & Son subsidiary offers insurance company management services, and its Bellemead Development Corp. develops real estate.

In 1994 some of Chubb's segments showed lackluster results. Property/casualty was hit by losses due to the Northridge earthquake. Its employee benefits business (part of life and health) suffered from New York State's imposition of community ratings premiums, and Chubb's real estate units performed poorly.

Thomas Caldecot Chubb and his son Percy formed Chubb & Son in New York in 1882 to underwrite cargo and ship insurance. The company soon became the US manager for Sea Insurance Co. of England and cofounded New York Marine Underwriters (NYMU). In 1901 NYMU became Chubb's chief property and casualty affiliate, Federal Insurance Co.

Chubb expanded in the 1920s, opening a Chicago office (1923) and, just before the 1929 crash, organizing Associated Aviation Underwriters. Growth slowed during the Depression, but Chubb recovered enough by 1939 to buy Vigilant Insurance Co.

Chubb bought Colonial Life in 1959 and Pacific Indemnity (which had written insurance for Fibreboard Corporation, later a major defendant in asbestos-related damage litigation) in 1967. In that year Chubb Corp. was formed as a holding company, with Chubb & Son as the manager of the property and casualty insurance businesses. In 1969 a takeover attempt by New York's First National City Corp. — predecessor of Citicorp — was foiled by federal regulators.

Chubb acquired Bellemead Development (1970) to expand its real estate portfolio. Following a strategy of insuring in specialty niches, in the 1970s Chubb launched insurance packages for the entertainment industry, including films and Broadway shows. After the Tylenol poisonings of 1982, Chubb developed insurance against product tampering and contamination (which it no longer offers).

In 1984 Chubb acquired Chattanooga-based Volunteer State Life. In this period Chubb

focused on specialized property and casualty insurance lines and in 1985 retreated from medical malpractice insurance.

In 1988 Chubb authorized Good Weather International to write up to $30 million in drought insurance. Chubb discovered too late that Good Weather wrote more than 10 times that amount. Chubb promptly settled the matter, paying any claims that would have been due if the customers had received their policies.

In 1991 Chubb combined 3 subsidiaries into Chubb Life Insurance Co. of America. The next year Chubb subsidiary Pacific Indemnity settled a suit over Fibreboard Corp.'s asbestos liability (the settlement was revised in 1993 and extended in 1995). This resulted in a 1993 payment of $538 million into an escrow account set up to settle future asbestos-related damage claims. This contributed to a total charge for asbestos-related losses of $675 million and led to an earnings decrease in 1993.

Taking advantage of Lloyd's of London's financial problems and subsequent relaxation of rules relating to doing business with nonmembers, Chubb in 1993 opened an office at Lloyd's. It has also extended its insurance of the affluent to the UK by forming a joint venture with Sun Alliance. Chubb opened a new underwriting office at the Institute of London Underwriters in 1994.

In 1994 Chubb bought Personal Lines Insurance Brokerage and the personal lines business of Alexander & Alexander. In 1995 it opened offices in Munich and Hamburg and increased its holdings in Mexico.

NYSE symbol: CB
Fiscal year ends: December 31

WHO

Chairman: Dean R. O'Hare, age 52, $1,393,492 pay
VC and CFO: Percy Chubb III, age 60, $615,777 pay
VC and General Counsel: John J. Degnan, age 50
President: Robert P. Crawford Jr., age 53, $558,560 pay
EVP: George T. Van Gilder, age 51, $431,369 pay
EVP: Edward Dunlop, age 54
EVP: David S. Fowler, age 49
EVP: Frederick L. Hyer Jr.
EVP: Charles M. Luchs
SVP and Treasurer: Philip J. Sempier
Auditors: Ernst & Young LLP

WHERE

HQ: 15 Mountain View Rd., PO Box 1615, Warren, NJ
07061-1615
Phone: 908-903-2000
Fax: 908-580-2027

Chubb operates in all 50 US states and the District of
Columbia, Puerto Rico, and the Virgin Islands. It has 36
offices in 25 other countries.

WHAT

	1994 Assets	
	$ mil.	% of total
Cash & equivalents	6	0
Tax-exempt securities	5,680	28
Taxable bonds	3,376	16
Mortgage-backed securities	1,648	8
Real estate	1,740	8
Receivables & recoverables	2,768	13
Other	5,505	27
Total	**20,723**	**100**

	1994 Sales		1994 Operating Income	
	$ mil.	% of total	$ mil.	% of total
Life & health ins.	1,055	18	28	4
Real estate	205	4	(67)	—
Property/casualty insurance	4,402	77	607	94
Corporate	48	1	10	2
Total	**5,710**	**100**	**639**	**100**

Selected Subsidiaries and Affiliates

Associated Aviation
  Underwriters, Inc.
Bellemead Development
  Corp.
Chubb Asset
  Managers, Inc.
Chubb Capital Corp.
Chubb Customer
  Center, Inc.
Chubb de Colombia
  Compañía de
  Seguros, SA
Chubb de México,
  Compañía Afianzadora
  SA de SV

Chubb de México,
  Compañía de
  Seguros SA de SV
Chubb Programmer
  Resources, Inc.
Chubb Securities Corp.
Chubb Services Corp.
The Colonial Life
  Insurance Co. of America
Federal Insurance Co.
Great Northern Ins. Co.
Northwestern Pacific
  Indemnity Co.
Pacific Indemnity Co.
Seguros La Federación, CA
Texas Pacific Indemnity Co.
Vigilant Insurance Co.

KEY COMPETITORS

Aetna	General Re	Northwestern
AIG	ITT Hartford	Mutual
Allianz	John Hancock	Prudential
Allstate	Kolonia Conzern	State Farm
Axa	Liberty Mutual	Teachers
CIGNA	Lincoln National	Insurance
CNA Financial	Lloyd's of London	Tokio Marine
Commercial Union	MassMutual	and Fire
Equitable	MetLife	Travelers
GEICO	New York Life	USF&G

HOW MUCH

	9-Year Growth	1985	1986	1987	1988	1989	1990	1991	1992	1993	1994
Assets ($ mil.)	13.2%	6,802	8,487	10,167	11,507	13,385	14,511	16,164	17,559	19,437	20,723
Net income ($ mil.)	25.0%	71	268	330	360	421	522	552	617	344	528
Income as % of assets	—	1.0%	3.2%	3.2%	3.1%	3.1%	3.6%	3.4%	3.5%	1.8%	2.6%
Earnings per share ($)	22.5%	0.96	3.53	3.97	4.27	4.91	6.07	6.32	6.96	3.91	5.95
Stock price – high ($)	—	28.81	39.06	36.75	31.69	49.75	54.75	78.00	91.00	95.75	83.18
Stock price – low ($)	—	16.58	27.00	25.44	25.63	28.81	34.63	50.00	62.38	76.63	68.63
Stock price – close ($)	12.2%	27.44	29.63	27.94	29.00	47.63	54.25	77.00	88.88	77.88	77.38
P/E – high	—	30	11	9	7	10	9	12	13	24	14
P/E – low	—	17	8	6	6	6	6	8	9	20	12
Dividends per share ($)	10.3%	0.76	0.80	0.89	1.08	1.16	1.32	1.48	1.60	1.72	1.84
Book value per share ($)	14.1%	14.88	20.06	23.85	27.54	30.84	35.19	40.74	45.18	47.84	48.92
Employees	2.5%	9,000	9,600	9,800	9,800	10,100	10,100	10,100	10,000	10,500	11,200

1994 Year-end:
Equity as % of assets: 20.5%
Return on assets: 2.6%
Return on equity: 12.5%
Long term debt (mil.): $1,268
No. of shares (mil.): 87
Dividends
  Yield: 2.4%
  Payout: 30.9%
Market value (mil.): $6,718
Sales (mil.): $5,710

Stock Price History
High/Low 1985–94

CIGNA CORPORATION

OVERVIEW

Philadelphia-based CIGNA is one of the US's foremost insurance companies, offering property/casualty insurance; managed, individual, and group health plans; life and disability insurance; and related financial service products. These include pension and retirement savings and investment products as well as institutional investment management.

CIGNA's results have been less than sterling in recent years, primarily because of losses in its property/casualty and reinsurance operations. Some of the losses have been due to an unprecedented string of natural disasters and manmade catastrophes, but some have been attributable to inefficient operations. In 1993 the company began streamlining its direct property/casualty operations, and in 1995 it decided to exit property/casualty reinsurance altogether, agreeing to sell these operations to the St. Paul Companies and Employers Reassurance.

In contrast, CIGNA's health and financial services operations remained robust. Its HealthCare subsidiary covers some 19 million people, both individually and under employee benefit plans. Its investment operations are poised to benefit by the graying of the baby boomers as they prepare for retirement.

WHEN

In 1982 Connecticut General and INA merged to form CIGNA. INA, the older of the 2, formed as Insurance Co. of North America by a group of Philadelphia businessmen in 1792, was both the US's first stock insurance company and its first marine insurance company.

In 1794 INA issued its first life insurance policy, became the first US issuer of fire insurance outside city limits, and was the first to insure building contents against fire. In 1808 it appointed independent agents in 5 states, thus originating the American Agency System. INA grew internationally in the late 1800s, appointing an agent for marine insurance in Canada (1873) and adding agents in London and Vienna (1887) and in Shanghai (1897); it was the first US company to write insurance in China.

In 1942 INA provided accident and health insurance for the US Army's 30 men working on the Manhattan Project, the effort to develop the atom bomb. In 1950 it introduced the homeowner's policy, the first homeowner coverage with broad availability. In 1978 INA bought HMO International, the largest publicly owned prepaid health care provider in the US.

Connecticut General, the other half of CIGNA, was formed in 1865 as a life insurer. Connecticut General formed an accident department to offer health insurance (1912); wrote its first group insurance, for the *Hartford Courant* newspaper (1913); and wrote the first individual regular accident coverage for airline passengers (1926).

In the late 1930s Connecticut General was an industry leader in developing group medical and surgical insurance. Connecticut General offered the first group medical coverage for general use in 1952 and in 1964 introduced group dental insurance.

After the merger of INA and Connecticut General in 1982, CIGNA bought Crusader Insurance (UK, 1983; sold in 1991) and AFIA (1984). CIGNA sold its individual insurance products division to InterContinental Life (Jackson, Mississippi; 1988) and its Horace Mann Cos. (individual financial services) to an investor group (1989) in order to begin positioning itself as one of the foremost providers of managed health care to the commercial market. To this end, in 1990 CIGNA bought EQUICOR, an HMO started by Hospital Corporation of America and the Equitable insurance company. The company also began to withdraw from the personal property/casualty business in order to focus on small- and medium-sized commercial clients in the US. In the early 1990s CIGNA reduced its property/casualty business by cutting sales overseas (combining them with life and health operations) and exited areas such as airline insurance and surety bonds.

CIGNA also sought to diversify its financial services income by offering service products, such as its ProFiles software, which helps employers project their employees' retirement income.

CIGNA returned to China in 1993, 43 years after its 1950 departure, opening an office in Beijing to prepare for the company's eventual reentry into the Chinese market. In 1994 the company increased its exposure in Asia by buying 60% of an Indonesian insurance company affiliated with Bank Niaga. More than 30 million people in Indonesia now have incomes large enough to need financial planning.

Continuing its Asian expansion in 1995, CIGNA entered into a mutual cooperation agreement with Vietnam's state insurance company, Baoviet.

NYSE symbol: CI
Fiscal year ends: December 31

WHO

Chairman and CEO: Wilson H. Taylor, age 51, $1,722,900 pay
President, CIGNA Property & Casualty: Gerald A. Isom, age 56, $993,300 pay
President, CIGNA HealthCare: Lawrence P. English, age 54, $986,500 pay
President, CIGNA Investment Management: Arthur C. Reeds III, age 50, $700,000 pay
President, CIGNA Individual Insurance: Thomas C. Jones, age 48
President, CIGNA Group Insurance: John K. Leonard, age 46
EVP and CFO: James G. Stewart, age 52, $996,900 pay
EVP and General Counsel: Thomas J. Wagner, age 55
EVP Human Resources and Services: Donald M. Levinson, age 49
Auditors: Price Waterhouse LLP

WHERE

HQ: One Liberty Place, Philadelphia, PA 19192-1550
Phone: 215-761-1000
Fax: 215-761-5515

CIGNA operates in the US, Europe, Latin America, and Asia.

	1994 Sales		1994 Operating Income	
	$ mil.	% of total	$ mil.	% of total
US prop./cas.	2,871	16	(417)	—
Intl. prop./cas.	2,610	14	76	5
Individual financial services	1,637	9	210	15
Life & health	8,650	47	829	60
Retirement	1,935	10	287	20
Other	689	4	(180)	—
Total	**18,392**	**100**	**805**	**100**

WHAT

	1994 Assets	
	$ mil.	% of total
Cash & equivalents	1,693	2
Government securities	4,887	5
Asset-backed securities	6,890	8
Corporate bonds	19,040	22
Mortgage & policy loans	15,325	18
Receivables & recoverables	11,472	13
Other investments	3,030	4
Separate account assets	14,551	17
Other	9,214	11
Total	**86,102**	**100**

Financial Services	Principal Subsidiaries
Group life, health, accident, and disability insurance	Connecticut General Life Insurance Co.
Health care services	Insurance Company of North America
Individual life and health insurance	
Pension and retirement services	
Property/casualty ins.	

KEY COMPETITORS

Aetna	Kemper National Insurance
Allianz	Liberty Mutual
Allstate	Lloyd's of London
American Express	MassMutual
American Financial	Mellon Bank
Berkshire Hathaway	Merck
Blue Cross	Merrill Lynch
Charles Schwab	MetLife
Chubb	New York Life
CNA Financial	Northwestern Mutual
Equitable	Oxford Health Plans
ITT Hartford	Prudential
John Hancock	Sierra Health Services
Kaiser Foundation Health Plan	State Farm
	Travelers

HOW MUCH

	9-Year Growth	1985	1986	1987	1988	1989	1990	1991	1992	1993	1994
Assets ($ mil.)	7.5%	44,736	50,016	53,495	55,825	57,779	63,691	66,737	69,827	84,975	86,102
Net income ($ mil.)	—	(855)	535	686	472	562	330	453	337	234	554
Income as % of assets	—		1.1%	1.3%	0.8%	1.0%	0.5%	0.7%	0.5%	0.3%	0.6%
Earnings per share ($)	—	(12.46)	6.34	8.11	5.68	7.00	4.36	6.34	4.70	3.25	7.66
Stock price – high ($)	—	64.25	77.25	69.50	55.38	66.75	60.63	61.75	60.88	68.38	74.00
Stock price – low ($)	—	43.50	51.13	41.25	42.75	45.88	33.25	36.00	47.13	56.50	57.00
Stock price – close ($)	(0.1%)	64.25	55.00	43.88	47.13	59.50	40.88	61.13	58.63	62.75	63.63
P/E – high	—	—	12	9	10	10	14	10	13	21	10
P/E – low	—	—	8	5	8	7	8	6	10	17	7
Dividends per share ($)	1.8%	2.60	2.60	2.75	2.92	2.96	3.02	3.04	3.04	3.04	3.04
Book value per share ($)	5.0%	51.84	58.85	61.33	64.34	70.59	73.51	81.93	80.09	91.33	80.69
Employees	(0.3%)	49,431	50,056	48,427	48,615	47,677	56,973	55,961	52,255	50,600	48,300

1994 Year-end:
Equity as % of assets: 6.7%
Return on assets: 0.6%
Return on equity: 8.9%
Long-term debt (mil.): $1,389
No. of shares (mil.): 72
Dividends
  Yield: 4.8%
  Payout: 39.7%
Market value (mil.): $4,582
Sales (mil.): $18,392

Stock Price History
High/Low 1985–94

THE CIRCLE K CORPORATION

OVERVIEW

Something's afoot at Circle K. After years of not-so-excellent adventures — several annual losses, a journey through Chapter 11, the closing or selling of 45% of its stores, and a moratorium on buying or building new stores — the Phoenix–based convenience store operator has turned a corner. In 1995 Circle K re-emerged as a public company and began making deals faster than you can nuke a burrito.

Circle K operates 2,458 stores in 28 states, mostly in the Sunbelt; only Southland Corp., owner of 7-Eleven, has more US convenience stores. The company also licenses 831 Circle K stores in 19 other countries. In 1994 the company derived nearly half of its sales from the 1.5 billion gallons of gas it sold in the US. Other key items sold at Circle K include beer, cigarettes, soft drinks, and dairy products.

Within weeks of going public the company entered its first franchising agreement ever, through which Massachusetts-based Gibbs Oil will operate 83 Circle K stores, and formed a joint venture with Southguard Corp. to operate 164 stores in Texas and Oklahoma. The company plans further such ventures.

Renovations at most Circle K stores have created a new store format called Shoppers Express, which consists of distinct departments for sales and service, beverages, groceries, prepared food, snacks, and auto care products. The company also is testing Blimpie and Taco Bell franchises in its stores, adding pay-at-the-pump credit card readers, and test marketing its own brand of gasoline, Performazene Z2000. The Bahrain-based investment firm, Investcorp., still owns 29.6% of the company.

WHEN

Fred Hervey, a 2-term mayor of El Paso, Texas, bought the 3 locations of Kay's Food Stores in El Paso in 1951 and soon extended the chain to 10 locations. In 1957 he expanded into Arizona, renamed the stores Circle K, and adopted the company's distinctive, western-style logo.

Circle K went public in 1963. During the 1960s and 1970s, the company expanded into New Mexico, California, Colorado, Montana, Idaho, and Oregon. In 1979 Circle K licensed UNY of Japan to operate Circle K stores there. UNY currently operates more than 1,586 Circle K stores in Japan. (In 1993 Circle K sold all Japanese rights to its name and trademark to UNY for $22 million.)

The corporation became a holding company in 1980, with its Circle K chain as a subsidiary, and began expanding through acquisitions. That year the company bought 13% of Nucorp Energy, an oil and gas developer. Nucorp filed for bankruptcy in 1982, and Circle K sold its remaining interest in 1983 at a large loss. Also in 1983 Circle K nearly doubled its size by acquiring the 960-store UtoteM chain from American Financial, headed by Cincinnati financier Carl Lindner. Lindner's friend Karl Eller became Circle K's chairman and CEO.

Eller initiated an aggressive growth plan aimed at quadrupling the number of stores by 1990. Through acquisitions Circle K grew from 1,221 stores in 1983 to 5,751 by the end of 1989, increasing its long-term debt from $40.5 million to $1.1 billion. In its buying frenzy of the 1980s, Circle K bought several stores that turned out to be across the street from each other. Founder Hervey left the company's board of directors in 1988.

Circle K began having financial problems in 1989, owing in part to $96 million in annual interest payments. It put itself up for sale, but no buyers emerged. Lindner, whose American Financial owned 15% of Circle K's common stock (sold 1991) and was a major creditor, brought in Robert Dearth from his Chiquita Brands as Circle K's president in 1990. Soon after, Eller left the company "to pursue personal business opportunities." Prices were cut and store managers were given more buying authority, but in May 1990 Circle K declared bankruptcy. In June 1991 Dearth resigned.

In 1993, after losing nearly $1.3 billion since 1990, Circle K was sold to Investcorp S.A. (led by former Iraqi political prisoner Nemir Kirdar) for $400 million, becoming a private operation. The money went to pay off creditors, leaving many shareholders grumbling. Shortly after Circle K emerged from bankruptcy, Bart Brown resigned as CEO (although remaining as chairman), and John Antioco, formerly COO, assumed this role.

Also in 1993 Circle K reached an agreement in federal court over contamination from leaking underground gasoline tanks and agreed to pay about $30 million in fines to 29 states. In 1994 rising crime against convenience stores prompted Circle K to begin staffing all of its stores with 2 clerks at all times. Circle K and National Convenience Stores swapped several stores in 1994 so that each company could focus on markets key to its strategy. Circle K offered to buy all 661 National stores in 1995.

NYSE symbol: CRK
Fiscal year ends: April 30

WHO

Chairman: Bart A. Brown Jr., age 63, $553,860 pay
President and CEO: John F. Antioco, age 45, $1,353,747 pay
EVP and CFO: Larry Zine, age 40, $788,112 pay
EVP and COO: Mitchel E. Telson, age 52, $578,605 pay
EVP: Bruce Krysiak, age 44
President, Arizona Division: David C. Moore, $317,580 pay (prior to promotion)
SVP and General Counsel: Gehl P. Babinec, age 52
VP Human Resources: Terry S. Broekemeier
Auditors: Coopers & Lybrand L.L.P.

WHERE

HQ: 3003 N. Central Ave., Ste. 1600, Phoenix, AZ 85012
Phone: 602-530-5001
Fax: 602-530-5278

Circle K operates 2,458 convenience stores in 28 US states, primarily in the Sunbelt, and 831 stores in 19 other countries.

	US Stores	
Location	No. of stores	% of total
Arizona	541	22
Florida	428	18
California	293	12
Texas	263	11
Louisiana	180	7
Georgia	126	5
Oklahoma	85	3
North Carolina	66	3
Other US	476	19
Total	**2,458**	**100**

	Total Stores	
Location	No. of stores	% of total
US	2,458	74
Canada	192	6
South Korea	184	6
Taiwan	172	5
Hong Kong	97	3
Other countries	186	6
Total	**3,289**	**100**

WHAT

	1995 Sales
	% of total
Gasoline	47
Cigarettes	14
Beer	11
Soda	5
Candy	3
Chips	2
Fountain	2
Dairy	2
Other	14
Total	**100**

Merchandising Departments

Beverage Depot (beer, soda, juices, teas, bottled waters, isotonics, liquor, wine)
Car Care (oil, transmission fluid, other automotive supplies)
Food Court (soft drinks, coffee, hot dogs, sandwiches, frozen carbonated beverages)
Grocery Express (groceries, frozen food, dairy products, bakery products)
Sales & Service (tobacco products, lottery tickets, money orders, magazines, newspapers, ATMs)
Snack World (candy bars, bulk candy, gum, children's novelties, jerky, seeds, nuts, chips, healthy snacks)

KEY COMPETITORS

ABCO Markets	H. E. Butt	Raley's
Albertson's	Hughes Markets	Randall's
American Stores	IGA	Royal Dutch/
Amoco	J Sainsbury	Shell
Atlantic Richfield	Kash n' Karry	Safeway
Bashas'	Kroger	Save Mart
British Petroleum	Megafoods	Supermarkets
Brookshire	Minyard Food	Schwegmann
Grocery	Stores	Sedano's
Bruno's	Mobil	Supermarkets
Chevron	National	Southland
Cumberland	Convenience	Stater Bros.
Farms	Stores	Texaco
Exxon	Phillips Petroleum	Thrifty Oil
EZ Mart Stores	Publix	Unocal
Fiesta	Pueblo Xtra	Vons
Food Lion	QuikTrip	Wawa
George Weston	Racetrac	Winn-Dixie
Great A&P	Petroleum	Yucaipa

HOW MUCH

	9-Year Growth	1986	1987	1988	1989	1990	1991	1992	1993	1994	1995
Sales ($ mil.)	5.9%	2,129	2,317	2,657	3,495	3,737	3,599	2,904	3,089	3,320	3,566
Net income ($ mil.)	(7.9%)	40	49	60	15	(773)	(307)	(197)	(60)	21	19
Income as % of sales	—	1.9%	2.1%	2.3%	0.4%	—	—	—	—	0.6%	0.5%
Employees	0.7%	19,342	20,983	24,544	27,264	25,942	23,377	21,487	20,000	21,000	20,566

Net Income ($ mil.) 1986–95

CIRCUIT CITY STORES, INC.

OVERVIEW

Richmond, Virginia–based Circuit City is the nation's largest retailer of major appliances and brand-name consumer electronics. The company operates more than 350 stores in 33 states and the District of Columbia.

Most units are Circuit City Superstores, which average between 16,000 square feet and 42,000 square feet. Lately the company has been emphasizing the larger stores in an effort to compete in large metropolitan areas. The company also operates electronics-only stores and mall stores.

While consumer electronics (such as TVs, VCRs, stereos, and compact disc players) and appliances (such as washers, dryers, and refrigerators) remain the mainstays of the company's product mix, computers are gaining importance. Sales of home office products, including PCs, peripherals, and fax machines, accounted for 20% of sales in fiscal 1995, up from 5% in fiscal 1992.

To compete in the fierce consumer electronics market, Circuit City focuses on both price and service. Its commissioned salespeople go through 2 weeks of training before starting work and also receive ongoing training. The company continues to expand aggressively. It plans to add 180 stores in the next 3 years and reach $10 billion in sales by the year 2000.

WHEN

While on vacation in Richmond, Virginia, in 1949, Samuel Wurtzel learned from a local barber that the first TV station in the South was about to go on the air. Wurtzel immediately decided to launch a southern TV retailing operation and founded Wards Company (an acronym for family names Wurtzel, Alan, Ruth, David, and Samuel) in Richmond that same year, gradually diversifying into small appliances. Wards went public in 1961.

Throughout the 1960s and early 1970s, Wards expanded by acquiring several appliance retailers, including Murmic (Delaware, 1965), Custom Electronics (Washington, DC; 1969), Certified TV & Appliance (Virginia, 1969), and Woodville Appliances (Ohio, 1970). Samuel's son Alan joined the business in 1966, when the company was focused on selling stereos. Predicting the end of the stereo boom, Alan Wurtzel converted the stores into full-line electronics specialty retailers.

The company took its boldest step in 1975 when it spent half of its net worth to open an electronics superstore in Richmond. It was an immediate success, and in 1981 Alan, then president, made the decision to branch into the New York market with the purchase of Lafayette Radio Electronics. In New York the company found itself unable to compete with exuberant competitors like Crazy Eddie (which has since gone out of business) and abandoned the market. From its experiences in New York, Wards developed the strategy of blitzing single markets in the South and the West with a high number of stores. (Now entrenched in these areas, the company has lately been entering the Northeast once again.) In 1984 the company changed its name to Circuit City.

In 1986 Alan Wurtzel stepped down as CEO to spend more time with his family, and company leadership passed to Richard Sharp, a former computer consultant who had designed Circuit City's advanced computerized sales system. Sharp made it a company priority to maintain one of the most efficient distribution and records systems in the industry.

Earnings slipped in 1990 as consumer spending dropped and the electronics industry was slow to introduce new blockbuster products. During this time Circuit City expanded to mall settings by opening the first of its Impulse stores.

In 1991 Circuit City became the first superstore retailer to offer the IBM PS/1 computer, and the company entered the Texas market by opening superstores in Dallas, Houston, and Austin. The Houston and Austin stores used a new format that offered electronic office products such as computers, copiers, fax machines, and software.

Circuit City began selling recorded music in its superstores in 1992. In 1993 the company ended its relationship with Mitsubishi, saying that the company's products were uncompetitive in pricing and technology. That same year Circuit City entered Chicago (archrival Best Buy's largest market) with 18 stores.

Also in 1993 Circuit City began experimenting with used car sales through its CarMax dealership in Richmond, Virginia. In 1994 it opened a 2nd CarMax, in Raleigh, North Carolina, and announced plans to open 2 more in the Southeast. That same year it renamed its Impulse stores Circuit City Express.

In 1995 Hewlett-Packard granted Circuit City an exclusive contract to sell its new line of retail PCs for 90 days.

WHO

Chairman, President, and CEO: Richard L. Sharp,
  age 48, $1,626,747 pay
VC: Alan L. Wurtzel, age 61
EVP Operations: Richard S. Birnbaum, age 42,
  $838,572 pay
SVP Administration: John A. Fitzsimmons, age 52,
  $672,045 pay
SVP, CFO, and Secretary: Michael T. Chalifoux, age 48,
  $588,170 pay
SVP Merchandising: W. Alan McCollough, age 45
SVP Corporate Planning and Automotive: W. Austin
  Ligon, age 44
SVP and General Counsel: W. Stephen Cannon, age 43
SVP Human Resources: William E. Zierden, age 56
Auditors: KPMG Peat Marwick LLP

WHERE

HQ: 9950 Mayland Dr., Richmond, VA 23233
Phone: 804-527-4000
Fax: 804-527-4164

	1995 Stores No.
California	70
Florida	33
Texas	32
Illinois	27
Virginia	23
Maryland	17
Massachusetts	16
Georgia	13
North Carolina	11
Arizona	10
Minnesota	10
Missouri	10
Other states	84
Total	**356**

WHAT

Product Category	1995 % of Sales
Audio	20
Home office	20
TV	19
Appliances	15
VCR/Camcorders	14
Other	12
Total	**100**

	1995 Stores No.
Superstores	318
Circuit City Express (mall stores)	33
Circuit City (electronics only)	5
Total	**356**

Selected Major Suppliers

General Electric	Panasonic
Hitachi	Sony
JVC	Thomson
Kenwood	Whirlpool
Packard Bell	Zenith

KEY COMPETITORS

Ames	J. C. Penney	Sharper Image
Anam Group	Kmart	Sound Advice
Best Buy	Mid-Atlantic Cars	Staples
Blockbuster	Montgomery Ward	Sun Television
Cellstar Corp.	MTS	& Appliances
CompuCom	Musicland	Tandy
CompUSA	NeoStar	Tops Appliance
Egghead	Office Depot	City
Fretter	Price/Costco	Wal-Mart
Fry's Electronics	REX Stores	
Good Guys	Sears	
J&R Music	Service Merchandise	

HOW MUCH

	9-Year Growth	1986	1987	1988	1989	1990	1991	1992	1993	1994	1995
Sales ($ mil.)	25.8%	706	1,011	1,350	1,722	2,097	2,367	2,790	3,270	4,130	5,583
Net income ($ mil.)	25.3%	22	35	50	70	78	57	78	110	132	168
Income as % of sales	—	3.1%	3.5%	3.7%	4.0%	3.7%	2.4%	2.8%	3.4%	3.2%	3.0%
Earnings per share ($)	23.9%	0.25	0.40	0.57	0.77	0.85	0.61	0.83	1.15	1.36	1.72
Stock price – high ($)[1]	—	3.88	8.56	10.41	11.31	13.50	14.50	13.00	26.13	33.88	27.50
Stock price – low ($)[1]	—	2.33	2.94	4.25	4.66	8.84	4.50	5.63	11.13	19.75	16.50
Stock price – close ($)[1]	24.4%	3.11	7.66	4.59	8.84	10.88	6.38	11.56	25.88	21.75	22.25
P/E – high	—	16	21	18	15	16	24	16	23	25	16
P/E – low	—	9	7	8	6	10	7	7	10	15	10
Dividends per share ($)	19.6%	0.02	0.02	0.02	0.03	0.04	0.05	0.05	0.06	0.08	0.10
Book value per share ($)	24.5%	1.27	1.68	2.25	3.02	3.92	3.96	4.77	6.02	7.39	9.10
Employees	23.9%	4,554	5,922	7,219	10,481	13,092	14,982	16,635	20,107	23,625	31,413

1995 Year-end:
Debt ratio: 17.1%
Return on equity: 21.1%
Cash (mil.): $47
Current ratio: 1.96
Long-term debt (mil.): $179
No. of shares (mil.): 96
Dividends
  Yield: 0.4%
  Payout: 5.8%
Market value (mil.): $2,147

**Stock Price History[1]
High/Low 1986–95**

[1] Stock prices are for the prior calendar year.

CITICORP

OVERVIEW

Citicorp is the largest US banking company and the world's only global full-service consumer bank. It has more than 3,400 locations worldwide, including some 1,205 retail branches (complete with greeters) that are designed to look and perform uniformly. And Citicorp continues to expand. In 1994–95 it opened offices in South Africa, Kazakhstan, Tanzania, and Vietnam and brought its brand of consumer banking to Budapest.

Citicorp is still beating its way back from the problems it had in the early 1990s, when it fell victim to bad loans and management bloat. Poor results brought a loss in 1991 and a subsequent decline in credit rating that the company is still working to improve.

As part of this effort, the bank is increasing its specialization, focusing on global retail banking (including, increasingly, the sale of financial services products such as mutual funds and annuities); credit card issuance and servicing (both for its own cards and many private-label cards); and the extremes of business banking (small business, which it defines as up to $20 million in sales, and giant international companies). Two areas it has decided to de-emphasize, however, are middle-market business and mortgage servicing.

WHEN

Colonel Samuel Osgood, first commissioner of the US Treasury, founded City Bank of New York in 1812 to serve cotton, sugar, metal, and coal merchants.

Opening offices in London and Shanghai in 1902 and in Buenos Aires in 1914, the bank (by then renamed National City Bank of New York) was a pioneer in expanding overseas. It moved into retail (consumer) banking in the 1920s and became the first commercial bank to make personal loans. In the 1920s and 1930s the bank's international operations grew. By 1939 it had 100 foreign offices.

James Rockefeller, who expanded the bank's retail banking in the late 1940s and early 1950s, became president in 1952. In 1955 the bank merged with First National (New York) to become First National City Bank. In 1961 the bank, under VP Walter Wriston, invented the certificate of deposit (CD), paying a higher interest rate on funds deposited for a specified period. CDs allowed the bank to compete against US government securities for funds. Wriston led the bank to international prominence (and into the morass of overseas debt markets) as president (1967–70) and as chairman (1970–84).

In 1968 First National City Corp. (renamed Citicorp in 1974) was created as a holding company; Citibank also passed Chase Manhattan as the largest New York City bank.

Citibank became a major issuer of VISA and MasterCard in the 1970s and acquired Carte Blanche in 1978 and Diners Club in 1981. In 1977 Citibank became the US's largest credit card issuer (it is still the market leader). It was the first bank to introduce automated teller machines (ATMs) on a large scale. John Reed, who developed the ATM and consumer banking markets, became chairman in 1984.

At the end of 1980, the bank passed BankAmerica to become the largest US bank. In the 1980s Citibank's acquisitions included institutions in San Francisco, Chicago, Miami, and Washington, DC. Under Reed, management jobs multiplied like cancer cells.

The bank's loans to other countries, particularly Brazil and Argentina, became a problem in the late 1980s, forcing Citicorp to make large loan loss provisions of $4 billion in 1987 and 1989. Then came the US's slide into recession and with it the collapse of the glutted commercial real estate market.

Hemorrhaging from real estate losses and the economic slowdown, Citicorp recapitalized in 1991 and 1992, raising $2.6 billion, 1/4 of it from Saudi prince al-Waleed bin Talal (who in 1995 held rights to over 9% of Citicorp stock). The company also sold assets and eliminated dividends. In 1992 Citibank was placed under regulatory supervision, limiting its ability to make loans.

Citicorp resisted selling nonperforming real estate assets, hoping instead to manage them until the boom returned, but in 1993 it sold $600 million worth of them (about 62% of the portfolio's face value).

In 1994 friends of Reed and Citibank Argentina's president were found to have profited from the 1992 sale of shares in a stock fund created by a swap of Argentine government bonds for stocks in Argentine companies. Citicorp contended that this was not improper because the stocks might have proven worthless. No legal action was taken.

As part of its stress on customer services, Citicorp has upgraded its communications systems and is entering the electronic banking age, offering home computer banking systems in New York, Chicago, and Washington.

NYSE symbol: CCI
Fiscal year ends: December 31

WHO

Chairman: John S. Reed, age 56, $4,275,000 pay
VC: William R. Rhodes, age 59, $1,650,000 pay
VC: Christopher J. Steffen, age 53, $1,650,000 pay
VC: H. Onno Ruding, age 55, $1,415,000 pay
VC: Pei-yuan Chia, age 56, $1,415,000 pay
VC: Paul J. Collins, age 58, $1,225,000 pay
EVP and Principal Financial Officer: Thomas E. Jones, age 56
EVP Legal Affairs: John J. Roche, age 59
EVP Bankcards Europe and North America: Roberta J. Arena, age 46
EVP Asia/Pacific Global Finance: Shaukat Aziz, age 45
EVP North America Global Finance: Alan S. MacDonald, age 52
EVP European Global Finance: Ernst W. Brutsche, age 57
EVP Latin America Global Finance: Dionisio R. Martin, age 51
Senior Human Resources Officer: Lawrence R. Phillips, age 55
Auditors: KPMG Peat Marwick LLP

WHERE

HQ: 399 Park Ave., New York, NY 10043
Phone: 800-285-3000
Fax: 212-527-3277

Citicorp operates in the US and 93 other countries.

	1994 Sales % of total
US	51
Western Europe	16
Asia/Pacific	14
Latin America	13
Canada & Japan	3
Other regions	3
Total	**100**

WHAT

	1994 Assets	
	$ mil.	% of total
Cash & equivalents	20,327	8
US & foreign gov't. securities	19,077	8
Other securities	19,957	8
Unrealized derivatives gains	20,544	8
Net loans	147,265	59
Other	23,319	9
Total	**250,489**	**100**

	1994 Sales	
	$ mil.	% of total
Interest & fees on loans	16,241	52
Other interest	7,572	24
Fees & commissions	5,155	16
Other	2,682	8
Total	**31,650**	**100**

Selected Services
Asset management
Corporate finance
Credit cards
Foreign exchange
Retail and corporate banking
Securities trading

Selected Subsidiaries
Aspiration, Inc.

Citibank Mexico, S.A.
Grupo Financiero
Citibank
Citibank Overseas
Investment Corporation
Citibank Privatkunden A.G.
Citicorp Holdings, Inc.
Citicorp Mortgage, Inc.
Citicorp North America, Inc.
Court Square Capital Ltd.

KEY COMPETITORS

American Express
Bank of New York
BankAmerica
Bankers Trust
Barclays
Canadian Imperial
Charles Schwab
Chase Manhattan
Chemical Banking
Crédit Lyonnais
CS Holding
Dai-Ichi Kangyo
Dean Witter, Discover
Deutsche Bank
First Chicago
First Fidelity
Fleet
General Electric
Great Western
HSBC
Industrial Bank of Japan
J.P. Morgan
NatWest
SunTrust

HOW MUCH

	9-Year Growth	1985	1986	1987	1988	1989	1990	1991	1992	1993	1994
Assets ($ mil.)	4.2%	173,597	196,124	203,607	207,666	230,643	216,986	216,922	213,701	216,574	250,489
Net income ($ mil.)	14.7%	998	1,058	(1,138)	1,698	498	318	(914)	722	1,919	3,422
Income as % of assets	—	0.6%	0.5%	—	0.8%	0.2%	0.1%	—	0.3%	1.0%	1.4%
Earnings per share ($)	6.7%	3.56	3.57	(4.26)	4.87	1.16	0.57	(3.22)	1.35	3.53	6.40
Stock price – high ($)	—	25.88	31.88	34.19	27.00	35.50	29.63	17.50	22.50	39.75	47.75
Stock price – low ($)	—	18.44	23.44	15.88	18.00	24.63	10.75	8.50	10.38	20.50	36.00
Stock price – close ($)	5.9%	24.69	26.50	18.63	25.88	28.88	12.63	10.38	22.25	36.88	41.38
P/E – high	—	7	9	—	6	31	52	—	17	11	8
P/E – low	—	5	7	—	4	21	19	—	8	6	6
Dividends per share ($)	(9.5%)	1.11	1.21	1.32	1.45	1.59	1.74	0.75	0.00	0.00	0.45
Book value per share ($)	3.5%	25.31	27.96	22.83	25.93	25.36	24.34	21.22	21.74	26.04	34.38
Employees	0.2%	81,300	88,500	90,000	89,000	92,000	95,000	86,000	81,000	81,500	82,600

1994 Year-end:
Equity as % of assets: 7.1%
Return on assets: 1.5%
Return on equity: 15.3%
Long-term debt (mil.): $17,894
No. of shares (mil.): 395
Dividends
 Yield: 1.1%
 Payout: 7.0%
Market value (mil.): $16,348
Sales ($ mil.): $31,650

**Stock Price History
High/Low 1985–94**

THE CLOROX COMPANY

OVERVIEW

CEO Craig Sullivan has steered Clorox safely back to its core business with the help of S.O.S. Based in Oakland, California, Clorox manufactures mainly household consumer products, including Clorox bleach, Kingsford charcoal, and Hidden Valley Ranch dressing.

With the divestiture of its frozen food and bottled water operations in 1993, Clorox is focusing on businesses that it knows well, such as cleaning products. Clorox has bought S.O.S. soap pads from Miles Inc. and introduced S.O.S. Junior soap pads for one-time use. In addition, the company has restructured its retail divisions into Food Products (dressings and sauces), Household Products (laundry and cleaning products), and Kingsford Products

(charcoal, insecticides, and cat litter). Clorox is consolidating its manufacturing operations, too. The company has agreed to sell its plant in Dyersburg, Tennessee, to Huish Detergents and plans to cut the work force at its S.O.S. plant in Bedford Park, Illinois, by 30–50 jobs.

Internationally, Clorox formed a joint venture to produce and sell bleach with Yuhan Corp. of South Korea. The company has also bought 2 bleach businesses in Chile, reached an agreement to purchase the leading scrubber pad and stain remover business in Argentina, and opened a plant for Combat roach killer in China. Henkel, the German consumer products giant, owns nearly 29% of Clorox.

WHEN

Known in its first few years as the Electro-Alkaline Company, Clorox was founded in 1913 by 5 Oakland investors to make bleach using water from salt ponds around San Francisco Bay. The next year the company registered the brand name Clorox and its diamond-shaped trademark; the name is believed to have come from the product's 2 main ingredients, chlorine and sodium hydroxide. At first the company sold only industrial-strength bleach, but in 1916 it formulated a less-concentrated household solution.

With the establishment of a Philadelphia distributor in 1921, Clorox began a national expansion. The company went public in 1928. In the late 1930s Clorox built 2 more plants, in Chicago and New Jersey; in the late 1940s and early 1950s, it opened 9 more plants throughout the country. In 1957 Procter & Gamble (P&G) bought Clorox. Antitrust questions were raised by the FTC, and litigation ensued over the next decade. P&G was ordered to divest Clorox, and in 1969 Clorox again became an independent company.

Following its split with P&G, Clorox added new products, mostly household consumer goods and foods, acquiring the brands Liquid-Plumr (drain opener, 1969), Formula 409 (spray cleaner, 1970), Litter Green (cat litter, 1971), and Hidden Valley Ranch (salad dressings, 1972). In 1970 the company introduced Clorox 2, a nonchlorine bleach to compete with the new enzymatic cleaners, Clorox entered the specialty food products business by buying Grocery Store Products (Kitchen Bouquet, 1971), Martin-Brower (food products and equipment, 1972), and Kingsford (charcoal briquettes, 1973).

In 1974 Henkel, a large West German maker of cleansers and detergents, purchased 15% of Clorox stock as part of an agreement to share research. The agreement was later expanded to include joint manufacturing and marketing. Beginning in 1977, Clorox sold off subsidiaries and brands such as Country Kitchen Foods (1979) to focus on household goods, particularly those sold through grocery stores. Also in 1977 Clorox introduced Soft Scrub, the first liquid cleanser in the US.

During the 1980s the company launched a variety of new products, including Match Light (instant-lighting charcoal, 1980), Tilex (stain remover, 1981), and Fresh Step (cat litter, 1984). In 1990 the company bought American Cyanamid's household products group, which included Pine-Sol cleaner and Combat insecticide, for $465 million.

In 1991 Clorox pulled out of the laundry detergent business (entered in 1988) after it was battered by heavyweights Procter & Gamble and Unilever. In 1993 Clorox increased its holding in Argentina's largest bleach company, Progar S.A., from 51% to 90%. Clorox also bought Chilean cleaning products maker Sánchez Compañía Limitada. In 1994 Clorox introduced a toilet bowl cleaner under the Clorox name. The company also began marketing its liquid bleach in Hungary through a Henkel subsidiary.

In 1995 Clorox announced plans to purchase Brita International Holdings, a manufacturer of water filtration systems based in Brampton, Ontario. Clorox has marketed Brita products in the US since 1988 and plans to expand the business throughout North America.

NYSE symbol: CLX
Fiscal year ends: June 30

Chairman, CEO, and President: G. Craig Sullivan, age 54, $974,206 pay
Group VP, US Operations: Neil P. DeFeo, age 48, $518,494 pay
Group VP and CFO: William F. Ausfahl, age 54, $466,550 pay
Group VP Technical: Ramon A. Llenado, age 47, $406,665 pay
Group VP: Peter N. Louras Jr., age 44, $404,650 pay
SVP, General Counsel, and Secretary: Edward A. Cutter, age 55
VP Manufacturing, Engineering, and Distribution: Anthony W. Biebl, age 44
VP Corporate Affairs: James O. Cole, age 53
VP International: Richard T. Conti, age 39
VP International Manufacturing: Lee Griffey, age 58
VP Kingsford Products: Gerald E. Johnston, age 47
VP Clorox Professional Products: Robert C. Klaus, age 49
VP Household Products: Donald C. Murray, age 58
VP Food Products: Jack D. M. Robertson, age 42
VP Treasurer: Karen M. Rose, age 45
VP Controller: Henry J. Salvo Jr., age 46
VP Research and Development: Barry A. Sudbury, age 47
VP Human Resources: Janet M. Brady, age 40
Auditors: Deloitte & Touche LLP

WHERE

HQ: 1221 Broadway, Oakland, CA 94612-1888
Phone: 510-271-7000
Fax: 510-465-8875

Clorox sells its products in more than 90 countries and produces them in more than 35 plants in Argentina, Canada, Chile, Mexico, Puerto Rico, South Korea, and the US.

WHAT

Selected Brands
BBQ Bag (charcoal briquettes)
Brita (water filter systems)
Clorox (liquid bleach)
Clorox 2 (all-fabric bleach)
Clorox Clean-Up (household cleaner)
Combat (insecticide)
Control (cat litter)
Formula 409 (spray cleaner)
Fresh Step (cat litter)
Hidden Valley Ranch (salad dressings)
Hidden Valley Ranch Salad Crispins (seasoned mini-croutons)
K.C. Masterpiece (barbecue sauce)
Kingsford (charcoal briquettes and lighter)
Kitchen Bouquet (seasoning sauce)
Liquid-Plumr (drain opener)
Litter Green (cat litter)
Match Light (instant-lighting charcoal briquettes)
Pine-Sol (cleaner)
Scoop Fresh (cat litter)
Soft Scrub (liquid cleanser)
S.O.S. (steel wool soap pads and cleaning products)
S.O.S. Junior (one-time steel wool soap pads)
Stain Out (stain remover)
SuperBait (roach killer)
Tackle (household cleaner/disinfectant)
Tilex (mildew stain remover)
Tuffy (mesh scrubber)

KEY COMPETITORS

Abbott Labs	Church & Dwight	3M
American Home	Colgate-Palmolive	NCH
Products	Dial	PepsiCo
Amway	Dow Chemical	Philip Morris
Bayer	Eastman Kodak	Procter & Gamble
Bristol-Myers	First Brands	RJR Nabisco
Squibb	FMC	S.C. Johnson
Carter-Wallace	Heinz	Unilever

HOW MUCH

	9-Year Growth	1985	1986	1987	1988	1989	1990	1991	1992	1993	1994
Sales ($ mil.)	6.4%	1,055	1,089	1,126	1,260	1,356	1,484	1,647	1,717	1,634	1,837
Net income ($ mil.)	10.5%	86	96	105	133	124	154	53	118	167	212
Income as % of sales	—	8.2%	8.8%	9.3%	10.5%	9.2%	10.4%	3.2%	6.9%	10.2%	11.5%
Earnings per share ($)	10.6%	1.59	1.75	1.90	2.40	2.24	2.80	0.98	2.17	3.05	3.94
Stock price – high ($)	—	25.25	30.19	36.00	33.75	44.50	45.38	42.38	52.00	55.38	59.50
Stock price – low ($)	—	13.75	22.00	23.50	26.13	30.13	32.13	35.00	39.50	44.00	47.00
Stock price – close ($)	10.6%	23.81	25.31	27.75	31.00	42.00	37.75	42.38	46.50	54.25	58.88
P/E – high	—	16	17	19	14	20	16	43	24	18	15
P/E – low	—	9	13	12	11	14	12	36	18	14	12
Dividends per share ($)	12.6%	0.62	0.70	0.79	0.92	1.09	1.29	1.47	1.59	1.71	1.80
Book value per share ($)	7.1%	9.18	10.31	11.51	13.19	14.19	15.00	14.47	14.92	16.03	17.04
Employees	(1.6%)	5,600	5,100	4,500	4,800	5,300	5,500	6,100	5,800	4,700	4,850

1994 Year-end:
Debt ratio: 22.2%
Return on equity: 23.7%
Cash (mil.): $116
Current ratio: 1.34
Long-term debt (mil.): $216
No. of shares (mil.): 53
Dividends
  Yield: 3.1%
  Payout: 45.7%
Market value (mil.): $3,143

**Stock Price History
High/Low 1985–94**

CNA FINANCIAL CORPORATION

OVERVIEW

CNA Financial is part of Loews Corp. (which owns 84% of CNA), the wide-ranging empire of the Tisch family that also includes Bulova Corp. (watches), CBS, Loews Hotels, and Lorillard (cigarettes). The company is the umbrella organization for a wide range of insurance companies, including Continental Casualty Co. and Continental Assurance.

In May 1995, after receiving shareholder approval, CNA welcomed another Continental to its family: Continental Corp. (CNA already owned 16% of that company). As part of the transaction, Continental Corp. merged with CNA's Chicago Acquisition Corp. and became a wholly owned subsidiary of CNA Financial. The merger cost approximately $1.1 billion (at $20 per share) and brought CNA into the top 10 of US insurance companies. The business lines of the 2 companies are primarily prop-

erty/casualty insurance. Continental Corp. will bring investment management operations to CNA, which also has significant group life operations.

Both CNA and Continental Corp. have been hard hit in the 1990s by natural and man-made disasters such as hurricanes, storms, floods, and riots. However, CNA has withstood them better because financial support and, more important, investment skills provided by Loews helped CNA survive its underwriting losses. Both companies were hit by rising interest rates in 1994.

After the 1995 merger, CNA began consolidating operations to produce significant cost savings. About 5,000 of the combined 20,000 jobs were to be eliminated in the year after the merger, many of them at Continental Corp.'s metropolitan New York–area offices.

WHEN

CNA merged with its elder, if not its better, in 1995. Continental Corp. was founded in 1852 as the Continental Insurance Co. because merchant Henry Bowen could not find a company offering the type of fire insurance he wanted. Bowen assembled a group of investors and started out with about $500,000 in capital. The company grew westward with the railroads.

In 1882 Continental added marine insurance and tornado insurance. In 1889 the company made Francis Moore, developer of the Universal Mercantile Schedule (a system of assessing fire hazards in buildings), president.

About the time Continental was writing the book on fire insurance, several midwestern investors were having trouble assessing risk in their own insurance field — disability. In 1897, after 2 earlier attempts had failed for lack of adequate capitalization, this group founded the Continental Casualty Co. in Hammond, Indiana. In the early years its primary clients were railroads providing disability insurance to their employees (railroading being a fairly hazardous profession then). Continental Casualty soon merged with other companies in the field. By 1904 the company was writing business in 41 states and territories, and by the next year it had branch offices in 9 states and Hawaii.

Both Continentals added new insurance lines in 1911: Continental Insurance went into personal auto, and Continental Casualty formed Continental Assurance, a subsidiary, to sell life insurance. Continental Insurance continued growing, partly through acquisi-

tions. By 1915 it had 4 primary companies, which — spurred by the growing patriotism of the immediate prewar era — it called the America Fore Group.

Both companies rose to the challenges presented by the world wars and the Depression, and they entered the 1950s ready for new growth. Both made new acquisitions in insurance, and in the 1960s they began to diversify into other fields as well.

Continental Insurance added interests in Diners Club and Capital Financial Services, and in 1968 it formed a holding company, Continental Corp. Continental Assurance (which formed CNA Financial, its own holding company) went even farther afield, adding mutual funds companies, consumer finance companies, nursing homes, and a home builder.

By the early 1970s, setbacks in the housing business and the recession had CNA on the ropes. After merger negotiations with Gulf Oil failed, Robert and Laurence Tisch bought most of CNA in 1974 and cut costs ruthlessly. Continental Corp. had its own problems in the 1970s, including an Iranian joint venture that got caught up in the revolution.

Both companies suffered losses arising from Hurricane Andrew in 1992, but CNA, having gone through its housecleaning in the 1970s, was better able to deal with the blow than Continental, which came out of the 1980s in need of restructuring. Although the company had been streamlining itself, in 1994 it threw in the towel and took the CNA merger offer.

WHO

Chairman: Edward J. Noha, age 67
CEO: Laurence A. Tisch, age 72
SVP and CFO: Peter E. Jokiel
SVP, General Counsel, and Secretary: Donald M. Lowry
Chairman and CEO, CNA Insurance Cos.: Dennis H. Chookaszian, age 51, $1,242,091 pay
President, CNA Insurance Cos.: Philip L. Engel, age 54, $825,539 pay
SVP, CNA Insurance Cos.: Carolyn L. Murphy, $558,333 pay
SVP, CNA Insurance Cos.: Jae L. Wittlich, $464,842 pay
SVP Human Resources: Floyd E. Brady
Auditors: Deloitte & Touche LLP

WHERE

HQ: CNA Plaza, Chicago, IL 60685
Phone: 312-822-5000
Fax: 312-822-6419

WHAT

	1994 Assets	
	$ mil.	% of total
Cash & equivalents	5,184	12
Treasury & agency securities	10,782	24
State & municipal bonds	3,769	9
Corporate & other bonds	3,284	7
Asset-backed securities	2,563	6
Stocks	1,184	3
Receivables & recoverables	7,274	16
Separate account assets	6,080	14
Other	4,200	9
Total	**44,320**	**100**

	1994 Sales	
	$ mil.	% of total
Commercial property/casualty	6,562	58
Group life	2,443	22
Other property/casualty	1,687	15
Individual life	596	5
Other & adjustments	(288)	—
Total	**11,000**	**100**

Selected Subsidiaries
1897 Corp.
1911 Corp.
Agency Management Services, Inc.
American Casualty Co.
Cinema Completions International, Inc. (50%)
CNA Automation, Inc.
CNA (Bermuda) Services, Ltd.
CNA Management Co. Ltd. (UK)
CNA Management (International) Ltd. (Jersey Channel Islands)
Continental Assurance Co.
Continental Casualty Co.
Galway Insurance Co.
Larwin Developments, Inc.
National Fire Insurance Co. of Hartford
Transcontinental Insurance Co.
Transcontinental Technical Services, Inc.
Transportation Insurance Co.
Valley Forge Insurance Co.
Viaticus, Inc.

KEY COMPETITORS

20th Century Industries	GEICO	Nationwide Insurance
AARP	Guardian Life Insurance	New York Life
Aetna	ITT Hartford	Pacific Mutual Life
Allstate	John Hancock	Prudential
American Financial	Liberty Mutual	State Farm
Chubb	MassMutual	Travelers
CIGNA	MetLife	USAA
	Mutual of Omaha	USF&G

HOW MUCH

	9-Year Growth	1985	1986	1987	1988	1989	1990	1991	1992	1993	1994
Assets ($ mil.)	13.6%	14,116	16,678	19,563	22,941	28,682	31,089	35,673	36,680	41,912	44,320
Net income ($ mil.)	(20.9%)	305	404	393	546	614	367	613	(267)	268	37
Income as % of assets	—	2.2%	2.4%	2.0%	2.4%	2.1%	1.25	1.7%	—	0.6%	0.1%
Earnings per share ($)	(22.6%)	5.11	6.25	6.96	8.59	9.73	5.77	9.80	(10.79)	4.26	0.51
Stock price – high ($)	—	65.13	75.00	66.50	66.13	108.75	100.00	99.25	104.50	101.00	82.25
Stock price – low ($)	—	31.50	47.25	47.00	51.00	57.63	49.63	62.75	78.50	74.25	60.00
Stock price – close ($)	0.1%	64.50	53.75	55.63	60.50	98.00	68.63	98.00	98.00	77.50	64.88
P/E – high	—	13	12	11	8	11	17	10	—	24	161
P/E – low	—	6	8	8	6	6	9	6	—	17	118
Dividends per share ($)	—	0.00	0.00	0.00	0.00	0.00	0.00	0.00	0.00	0.00	0.00
Book value per share ($)	8.8%	33.24	40.37	46.40	65.87	64.74	70.23	80.24	75.07	84.59	71.08
Employees	2.2%	12,800	14,000	15,000	15,900	16,700	17,200	17,800	17,200	16,800	15,600

1994 Year-end:
Equity as % of assets: 9.9%
Return on assets: 0.1%
Return on equity: 0.8%
Long-term debt (mil.): $912
No. of shares (mil.): 62
Dividends
  Yield: —
  Payout: —
Market value (mil.): $4,012
Sales ($ mil.): $11,000

Stock Price History High/Low 1985–94

THE COASTAL CORPORATION

OVERVIEW

Diversified energy giant Coastal Corporation has $10 billion in assets but is not coasting into the future. The Houston-based company has operations in natural gas marketing, transmission, and storage; petroleum refining, marketing, and distribution; oil and gas exploration; coal mining; chemicals; independent power production; and trucking.

Coastal's most profitable business is the interstate transmission of natural gas. Through its ANR Pipeline subsidiary it operates 2 major pipeline systems (over 19,000 miles in total length), one in the Midwest and one in the Rocky Mountain region and Kansas.

Through subsidiary Coastal Mart and branded marketers, Coastal conducts retail marketing in 37 states through 1,457 Coastal branded outlets. The company is investing $150 million to upgrade its 3 wholly owned refineries in Aruba, New Jersey, and Texas in order to increase their capacity to produce middle distillates, such as gasoline.

Coastal is also increasing its international operations. In 1994 and 1995 it signed deals to develop tracts in central Peru and the South China Sea. It also set up a 1995 joint venture agreement to construct and operate an electric plant in Wuxi City, China.

WHEN

After spending boyhood summers working in the oil fields, serving as a bomber pilot in WWII, and earning a mechanical engineering degree from Texas A&M, Oscar Wyatt started a small natural gas gathering business in 1951 in Corpus Christi, Texas.

In 1955 the company became Coastal States Gas Producing Company. It collected and distributed natural gas from oil fields in southern Texas. In 1962 Coastal purchased Sinclair Oil's Corpus Christi refinery and pipeline network. Also in the early 1960s, a Coastal subsidiary, Lo-Vaca Gathering, supplied natural gas to Texas cities and utilities. During the energy crisis of the early 1970s, Lo-Vaca curtailed its natural gas supplies and then raised prices. Unhappy customers sued Coastal, and regulators in 1977 ordered Lo-Vaca to refund $1.6 billion. To finance the settlement, Coastal spun off Lo-Vaca as Valero Energy.

Meanwhile, the combative Wyatt, who would earn a reputation as one of the swashbuckling corporate raiders of the 1980s, had been expanding Coastal through a series of deals. Coastal won Rio Grande Valley Gas, a small South Texas pipeline (1968), and then in 1973 mounted a successful $182 million hostile bid for Colorado Interstate Gas and changed its name to Coastal States Gas Corporation. With aggressive acquisitions, Coastal moved into low-sulfur Utah coal (Southern Utah Fuel, 1973), New England pipelines (Union Petroleum, 1973), California refining (Pacific Refining, 1976), and Florida petroleum marketing and transportation (Belcher Oil, 1977; renamed in 1990). In 1980 Coastal adopted its present name. Wyatt tried to snare Texas Gas Resources (1983) and Houston Natural Gas (1984). These bids were thwarted, but when the companies bought back stock

owned by Coastal to defend themselves, Coastal made money.

In 1985 Coastal purchased American Natural Resources in a $2.5 billion hostile takeover. In 1989, just before Wyatt stepped down as CEO, Coastal bid $2.6 billion for Texas Eastern, but that company sold out to white knight Panhandle Eastern.

Before the 1991 Gulf War, Wyatt courted the Iraqis, attempting to trade Coastal's refining and marketing assets for a steady supply of Iraq's crude oil. Wyatt and Coastal director John B. Connally, former US secretary of the treasury, met with Saddam Hussein and flew hostages out of Baghdad. Wyatt's statements against Operation Desert Storm drew harsh US criticism. In 1992 Coastal cut staff and inventory and closed a Kansas refinery after its Refining and Marketing Group posted a $192 million operating loss.

In 1993 Coastal announced plans to build the 600-mile SunShine Pipeline in Florida. Coastal also signed contracts with Peoples Gas System and Florida Power Corporation to supply Florida with natural gas. That same year construction was completed on the Empire State Pipeline. The 156-mile pipeline system, in which Coastal holds a 45% interest, runs from Niagara Falls to Syracuse, New York.

In 1994 the company announced a $100 million expansion of its refinery complex in Aruba, in the Caribbean.

In 1995 Coastal agreed to buy Maverick Markets, a chain of 102 gasoline-selling convenience stores in South Texas. The largest concentration of these stores (35) is in Corpus Christi. Also that year, Coastal signed a project development agreement with Habibullah Energy to build and manage a 140-megawatt power plant in the Pakistani city of Quetta.

WHO

Chairman and CEO: Oscar S. Wyatt Jr., age 70,
$1,049,093 pay
VC: Harold Burrow, age 80
President, COO, and CFO: David A. Arledge, age 50,
$703,873 pay
EVP Natural Gas: James F. Cordes, age 54, $722,223 pay
EVP Refining, Engineering, and Chemicals: James A.
King, age 55, $418,823 pay
EVP Crude Oil Supply and Marketing: Sam F.
Willson Jr., age 65, $409,062 pay
SVP and General Counsel: Carl A. Corrallo, age 51
SVP: Jeffrey A. Connelly, age 48
SVP Finance: Donald H. Gullquist, age 51
SVP and Controller: Coby C. Hesse, age 47
SVP Coal: James L. Van Lanen, age 50
SVP Exploration and Production: Jerry D. Bullock,
age 65
SVP Marketing: Dan J. Hill, age 54
SVP Retail Marketing: Jack C. Pester, age 60
SVP Special Projects: Kenneth O. Johnson, age 74
SVP and Secretary: Austin M. O'Toole, age 59
VP Product Supply and Transportation: Edward A.
Moré, age 46
VP Crude Oil Supply and Marketing: Thomas M. Wade,
age 42
VP Employee Relations: E. C. Simpson, age 59
Auditors: Deloitte & Touche LLP

WHERE

HQ: Coastal Tower, 9 Greenway Plaza, Houston, TX
77046-0995
Phone: 713-877-1400
Fax: 713-877-6754

Coastal conducts marketing and distribution operations
around the world. The company and its branded
marketers operate 1,457 Coastal outlets in 37 states.

WHAT

	1994 Sales		1994 Operating Income	
	$ mil.	% of total	$ mil.	% of total
Refining & marketing	6,459	62	153	21
Natural gas	3,076	29	431	59
Coal	451	4	98	13
Exploration & production	299	3	42	6
Other	208	2	9	1
Adjustments	(278)	—	—	—
Total	**10,215**	**100**	**733**	**100**

Selected Subsidiaries

Refining, Marketing, and Distribution
Coastal Fuels Marketing, Inc.
Coastal Refining & Marketing, Inc.

Natural Gas
ANR Pipeline Co.
ANR Storage Co.
Coastal Gas Services Co.
Colorado Interstate Gas Co.

Coal
ANR Coal Co.
Coastal States Energy Co.

Exploration and Production
ANR Production Co.
CIG Exploration, Inc.
Coastal Oil & Gas Corp.

Other
ANR Freight System, Inc.
Coastal Power Production Co.

KEY COMPETITORS

Amerada Hess
Amoco
Ashland, Inc.
Atlantic Richfield
British Petroleum
Broken Hill
Chevron
Columbia Gas
Diamond Shamrock
DuPont
Elf Aquitaine
Enron

Exxon
Kaneb Services
Koch
Mobil
Natural Gas
Occidental
Oryx
Panhandle Eastern
PDVSA
PEMEX
Pennzoil

Petrofina
Phillips Petroleum
Royal Dutch/Shell
Sonat, Inc.
Southland
Sun Company
Tenneco
Texaco
TOTAL
Unocal
USX-Marathon
Valero Energy

HOW MUCH

	9-Year Growth	1985	1986	1987	1988	1989	1990	1991	1992	1993	1994
Sales ($ mil.)	3.8%	7,275	6,668	7,429	8,187	8,271	9,381	9,549	10,063	10,136	10,215
Net income ($ mil.)	5.6%	142	72	113	157	170	226	96	(127)	116	233
Income as % of sales	—	2.0%	1.1%	1.5%	1.9%	2.1%	2.4%	1.0%	—	1.2%	2.3%
Earnings per share ($)	2.7%	1.61	0.56	1.40	1.80	1.81	2.15	0.92	(1.23)	1.02	2.05
Stock price – high ($)	—	17.47	16.03	25.69	22.50	33.09	39.63	36.75	30.00	31.38	33.75
Stock price – low ($)	—	12.47	12.72	14.03	19.84	22.00	29.25	23.75	22.00	23.50	24.75
Stock price – close ($)	4.4%	17.41	15.56	17.34	22.84	33.09	32.25	24.63	23.88	28.25	25.75
P/E – high	—	11	29	18	13	18	18	40	—	31	17
P/E – low	—	8	23	10	11	12	14	26	—	23	12
Dividends per share ($)	11.5%	0.15	0.18	0.22	0.27	0.27	0.40	0.40	0.40	0.40	0.40
Book value per share ($)	8.0%	11.71	11.75	12.84	14.25	17.36	19.21	19.67	19.33	21.77	23.43
Employees	0.1%	16,200	16,500	17,800	19,000	13,100	13,900	16,500	16,600	16,000	16,300

1994 Year-end:
Debt ratio: 61.7%
Return on equity: 9.8%
Cash (mil.): $74
Current ratio: 0.97
Long-term debt (mil.): $3,720
No. of shares (mil.): 105
Dividends
  Yield: 1.6%
  Payout: 19.5%
Market value (mil.): $2,697

Stock Price History
High/Low 1985–94

THE COCA-COLA COMPANY

The 109-year-old Coca-Cola Company isn't resting on its laurels. The world's largest soft-drink company with the world's most recognizable brand (its products are sold in over 195 countries) is keeping up with consumer tastes of the 1990s. Sassy advertising, new-age products, and increased visibility are moving Coke into new markets at home and abroad. Coca-Cola still dominates the global soft-drink market. Four of its brands — Coca-Cola Classic, Diet Coke, Caffeine-free Diet Coke, and Sprite — are among the US's 10 best-selling soft drinks. Coke has 41% of the US soft-drink market and 50% of the rest of the world's.

To keep up with lifestyle changes and the decline in cola consumption, the company's products have been diversified. To attract younger consumers, Coke introduced

Fruitopia "alternative" fruit drinks to compete with Snapple's new-age drinks; the quirky, Generation X–inspired OK soda; and Powerade, a sports drink challenging the leading Gatorade brand. In 1995 Coke bought root beer maker Barq's, its first purchase of a US beverage maker in over 3 decades; the company also planned to add more flavors to the Fruitopia and Nestea lines.

As part of a campaign to boost sales, Coke sponsored the 1994 World Cup and will help publicize the 1996 Olympics in Atlanta. It is also expanding its operations in other countries, such as Mexico (1993) and Egypt (1994), through joint ventures with bottlers.

Billionaire investor Warren Buffett, Coke's largest shareholder, has upped his stake in the company to 100 million shares.

WHEN

Atlanta pharmacist John S. Pemberton invented Coke in 1886. His bookkeeper, Frank Robinson, named the product after 2 ingredients, coca leaves (later cleaned of narcotics) and kola nuts. By 1891 druggist Asa Candler had bought the company for $2,300. By 1895 the soda fountain drink was available in all states, entering Canada and Mexico by 1898.

Candler sold most US bottling rights in 1899 to Benjamin Thomas and John Whitehead of Chattanooga for $1.00. With the backing of John Lupton, these men developed the regional franchise bottling system, creating over 1,000 bottlers within 20 years. The bottlers used the contoured bottle designed by the C. J. Root Glass Company in 1916.

In 1916 Candler retired to become Atlanta's mayor; his family sold the company to Atlanta banker Ernest Woodruff for $25 million in 1919, the same year Coca-Cola went public. In 1923 Woodruff appointed his son Robert president. Robert continued as chairman until 1942 and remained influential until his death in 1985 at age 95.

Robert Woodruff's contributions were in advertising and overseas expansion. He introduced "The Pause that Refreshes" (1929) and "It's the Real Thing" (1941), adding to the "Delicious and Refreshing" slogan used in the early days. During WWII Woodruff decreed that every soldier would have access to a 5-cent bottle of Coke. With government assistance Coca-Cola built 64 overseas bottling plants during WWII. Also during this period (1941), the company accepted "Coke" as an official brand name.

Coca-Cola bought Minute Maid in 1960 and introduced Sprite (now the world's #1 lemon-lime soft drink) in 1961, TAB in 1963, and Diet Coke in 1982.

Woodruff, who headed the company for over 60 years, saw to it that he was succeeded by his protégé, Roberto Goizueta, in 1981. A Yale-educated chemical engineer who gradually rose through the ranks, Goizueta is credited with refocusing and rejuvenating the company. Coke has dabbled in several industries; the largest of these diversifications, the acquisition of Columbia Pictures in 1982, was followed by other entertainment purchases. All were sold to Sony in 1989.

In 1986 the company consolidated the US bottling operations it owned into Coca-Cola Enterprises (CCE) and sold 51% of the new company to the public. In 1990 Coke introduced Powerade, its entry in the rapidly growing sports drink market. In 1992 the company formed Coca-Cola Refreshments–Moscow (CCRM), established a separate operation for Africa, and announced its return to India (Coke had exited the country in 1977 after a dispute with the Indian government). Also that year Coke switched its advertising to Creative Artists Agency (CAA).

In 1993 Coke entered a joint venture with FEMSA, Mexico's largest beverage company. In 1994 the company introduced a contoured plastic container shaped like Coke's trademark glass bottle. Under the Americans with Disabilities Act, a US district court jury in 1995 decided Coke should pay $7.1 million to an alcoholic executive the company had fired.

NYSE symbol: KO
Fiscal year ends: December 31

WHO

Chairman and CEO: Roberto C. Goizueta, age 63,
$4,371,167 pay
President and COO: M. Douglas Ivester, age 47,
$1,167,500 pay
EVP and Principal Operating Officer/International:
John Hunter, age 57, $862,500 pay
SVP; President, Coca-Cola USA: Jack L. Stahl, age 41,
$640,140 pay
SVP and Chief Marketing Officer: Sergio Zyman,
age 49, $583,333 pay
SVP and CFO: James Chestnut, age 44
SVP; President, Latin America Group: Weldon H.
Johnson, age 57
SVP; President, Greater Europe Group: E. Neville
Isdell, age 51
VP; President, Middle and Far East Group: Douglas N.
Daft, age 51
SVP and General Counsel: Joseph R. Gladden Jr., age 52
VP Human Resources: Michael W. Walters
Auditors: Ernst & Young LLP

WHERE

HQ: One Coca-Cola Plaza NW, Atlanta, GA 30313
Phone: 404-676-2121
Fax: 404-676-6792

	1994 Sales		1994 Operating Income	
	$ mil.	% of total	$ mil.	% of total
US	5,092	32	869	21
EC	4,255	26	984	24
Pacific & Canada	3,463	22	1,213	30
Latin America	1,928	12	713	17
Africa	522	3	182	4
Other regions	880	5	184	4
Adjustments	32	—	(437)	—
Total	**16,172**	**100**	**3,708**	**100**

WHAT

	1994 Sales		1994 Operating Income	
	$ mil.	% of total	$ mil.	% of total
Soft drinks	14,412	89	4,022	97
Juices & foods	1,728	11	123	3
Corporate	32	0	(437)	—
Total	**16,172**	**100**	**3,708**	**100**

Brand Names

Soft Drinks		Juices and Foods
Aquarius	OK soda	Bacardi Tropical
Barq's	Sprite	Fruit Mixers
Cherry Coke	Thums Up	Bright & Early
Coca-Cola	(India)	Five Alive
Coca-Cola Classic	TAB	Fruitopia (fruit
Coca-Cola Light		juices and teas)
Diet Coke		Georgia (coffee)
Fanta		Hi-C
Fresca		Minute Maid
Iron Brew		Nestea
(South Africa)		Powerade
Limca (India)		Seiryusabo
Mello Yello		(Japan)
Mr. PiBB		

KEY COMPETITORS

Anheuser-Busch	Dole	Procter &
Borden	Ferolito, Vultaggio	Gamble
Brown-Forman	Grand	Quaker Oats
Cadbury	Metropolitan	Seagram
Schweppes	Kirin	Starbucks
Celestial	National Beverage	Triarc
Seasonings	National Grape	Unilever
Chiquita Brands	Co-op	Veryfine
Citrus World	Ocean Spray	Whitman
Clearly Canadian	PepsiCo	Wrigley
Cott	Philip Morris	

HOW MUCH

	9-Year Growth	1985	1986	1987	1988	1989	1990	1991	1992	1993	1994
Sales ($ mil.)	8.3%	7,904	8,669	7,658	8,338	8,966	10,236	11,572	13,074	13,957	16,172
Net income ($ mil.)	15.1%	722	934	916	1,045	1,214	1,382	1,618	1,884	2,188	2,554
Income as % of sales	—	9.1%	10.8%	12.0%	12.5%	13.5%	13.5%	14.0%	14.4%	15.7%	15.8%
Earnings per share ($)	17.6%	0.46	0.61	0.61	0.72	1.24	1.02	1.22	1.43	1.68	1.98
Stock price – high ($)	—	7.34	11.22	13.28	11.31	20.25	24.50	40.88	45.38	45.13	53.50
Stock price – low ($)	—	4.95	6.39	7.25	8.75	10.84	16.31	21.31	35.56	37.50	38.88
Stock price – close ($)	24.8%	7.03	9.44	9.53	11.16	19.31	23.25	40.13	41.88	44.63	51.50
P/E – high	—	16	18	22	16	16	24	34	32	27	27
P/E – low	—	11	11	12	12	9	16	18	25	22	20
Dividends per share ($)	13.5%	0.25	0.26	0.28	0.30	0.34	0.40	0.48	0.56	0.68	0.78
Book value per share ($)	8.7%	1.93	2.28	2.16	2.15	2.36	2.82	3.33	2.98	3.53	4.10
Employees	(1.7%)	38,520	28,030	17,400	18,700	20,960	24,000	28,900	31,300	34,000	33,000

1994 Year-end:
Debt ratio: 40.1%
Return on equity: 52%
Cash (mil.): $1,386
Current ratio: 0.84
Long-term debt (mil.): $1,426
No. of shares (mil.): 1,276
Dividends
  Yield: 1.5%
  Payout: 39.4%
Market value (mil.): $65,711

Stock Price History High/Low 1985–94

COLGATE-PALMOLIVE COMPANY

OVERVIEW

Colgate-Palmolive is being squeezed in the US market but is swallowing more market share in Latin America and Asia. Based in New York, Colgate-Palmolive is a leading global consumer products company in the oral, personal, and household care and pet food markets.

While Colgate is #1 in toothbrushes and liquid soaps and #2 in toothpastes, many of Colgate's brands are trailing the competition in the US market. As retailers shrink store size and carry only the leading and private-label brands, Colgate has had to become more aggressive in the home market. Colgate is in-

creasing product development and advertising in higher-margin businesses like oral care.

With 2/3 of its revenues from outside the US, Colgate-Palmolive is an old pro in the international consumer market. In 1995 Colgate purchased Kolynos, a leading South American oral hygiene business, from American Home Products for $1 billion. With the purchase Colgate increases its share of the oral care market in Latin America from 54% to 79%. The company also bought Ciba-Geigy's oral hygiene business in India, increasing its share of that toothpaste market to 68%.

WHEN

In 1806 William Colgate founded the Colgate Company in Manhattan to produce soap, candles, and starch. The company moved to Jersey City in 1847. William Colgate died 10 years later, and the company passed to his son Samuel, who renamed it Colgate and Company. In 1877 the company introduced Colgate Dental Cream, which it began selling in a tube in 1890. By 1906 Colgate was making 160 kinds of soap, 625 perfumes, and 2,000 other products. The company went public in 1908.

In 1898 a Milwaukee soap maker, B. J. Johnson Soap Company (founded in 1864), introduced Palmolive, a soap made of palm and olive oils. It became so popular that the firm changed its name to the Palmolive company in 1917. In 1927 Palmolive merged with Peet Brothers, a Kansas City soap maker founded in 1872. Palmolive-Peet merged with Colgate in 1928, forming Colgate-Palmolive-Peet (shortened to Colgate-Palmolive in 1953). The stock market crash of 1929 prevented a planned merger of the company with Hershey and Kraft.

During the 1930s the company purchased French and German soap makers and opened branches in Europe. After WWII the Ajax, Colgate, and Palmolive brands were outselling rivals in Europe. The company expanded to the Far East in the 1950s, and by 1961 foreign sales were 52% of the total.

Colgate-Palmolive introduced several new products in the 1960s, including Cold Power detergent, Palmolive dishwashing liquid, Ultra Brite toothpaste, and Colgate with MFP. During the 1960s and 1970s, the company diversified by buying approximately 70 other companies, including Helena Rubenstein (1973), Ram Golf (1974), and Maui Divers

(1977). But the strategy failed, and most of these businesses were sold in the 1980s.

In the late 1980s the company launched a reorganization to focus on building Colgate-Palmolive's core businesses (personal care and household products), taking a $145 million charge against earnings in 1987 to cover reorganization costs.

Products introduced during the 1980s include Palmolive automatic dishwasher detergent (1986), Colgate Tartar Control toothpaste (1986), and Fab 1-Shot laundry detergent (1987). The company strengthened its hold on the global bleach market through its purchases of Cotelle (France, 1988), Klorin (Scandinavia, 1988), Unisol (Portugal, 1990), and Javex (Canada's #1 bleach producer, 1990). Other recent acquisitions include McKesson's veterinary distribution business (1989), Vipont Pharmaceutical (1990), the dental therapeutics unit of Scherer Laboratories (1990), and Murphy-Phoenix (maker of Murphy Oil Soap, 1991).

In 1992 Colgate expanded its presence in personal care products by paying $670 million for Mennen, maker of the leading US deodorant, Speed Stick. In 1993 Colgate-Europe purchased S.C. Johnson Wax's liquid soap products, becoming the global leader in liquid soap. In 1994 Colgate shifted from its traditional special-promotion pricing to everyday low pricing, resulting in a basic philosophy shift for its US retailers from promotion-induced purchases to actual-need purchases. As of the end of 1994, Colgate priced 50% of its business on an everyday low-price basis.

In 1995 Colgate continued its purchases of South American oral hygiene companies by buying 94% of the Argentinean dental care company Odol Saic.

WHO

Chairman and CEO: Reuben Mark, age 56,
$2,358,500 pay
President and COO: William S. Shanahan,
age 54, $1,296,667 pay
**Chief of Operations, Specialty Marketing and
International Business Development:** William G.
Cooling, age 50, $700,833 pay
SEVP and CFO: Robert M. Agate, age 59, $665,833 pay
President, Colgate-Europe: David A. Metzler, age 52,
$566,325 pay
President, Colgate-USA/Canada/Puerto Rico:
Lois Juliber, age 46
President, Colgate-Asia Pacific: Stephen A. Lister,
age 53
Chief Technological Officer: Craig B. Tate, age 49
SVP, General Counsel, and Secretary: Andrew D.
Hendry, age 47
SVP Human Resources: Douglas M. Reid, age 60
Auditors: Arthur Andersen & Co, SC

WHERE

HQ: 300 Park Ave., New York, NY 10022
Phone: 212-310-2000
Fax: 212-310-3284

Colgate-Palmolive operates 66 facilities in the
US and 235 in over 60 other countries.

	1994 Sales		1994 Operating Income	
	$ mil.	% of total	$ mil.	% of total
North America	2,400	31	306	31
Europe	2,043	27	202	21
Latin America	1,737	23	298	31
Asia & Africa	1,408	19	165	17
Total	**7,588**	**100**	**972**	**100**

WHAT

	1994 Sales
	% of total
Oral care	26
Personal care	24
Fabric care	18
Household surface care	17
Pet dietary care	11
Other	4
Total	**100**

Selected Brand Names

Personal Care	**Laundry Care**
Baby Magic	Ajax
Colgate	Axion
Irish Spring	Fab
Lady Speed Stick	Soupline/Suavitel
Mennen	Sta-Soft
Nouriché	
Optims	**Household Care**
Palmolive	Ajax
Protex	Fab
Skin Bracer	Fabuloso
Softsoap	Palmolive
Speed Stick	**Pet Care**
Total	Hill's Science Diet

KEY COMPETITORS

Abbott Labs	Dial	Mars
American	First Brands	NCH
Home Products	Gillette	Nestlé
Amway	Hanson	Oneida
Avon	Heinz	Pet Ventures
Brown-Forman	Helene Curtis	Procter & Gamble
Carter-Wallace	Henkel	Ralston Purina
Chattem	Johnson &	Group
Church & Dwight	Johnson	S.C. Johnson
Clorox	Libbey	Shiseido
Corning	L'Oréal	Unilever

HOW MUCH

	9-Year Growth	1985	1986	1987	1988	1989	1990	1991	1992	1993	1994
Sales ($ mil.)	9.0%	3,489	3,769	4,366	4,734	5,039	5,691	6,060	7,007	7,141	7,588
Net income ($ mil.)	18.8%	123	115	1	153	280	321	125	477	548	580
Income as % of sales	—	3.5%	3.1%	0.0%	3.2%	5.6%	5.6%	2.1%	6.8%	7.7%	7.6%
Earnings per share ($)	18.5%	0.77	0.81	0.01	1.10	1.90	2.12	0.75	2.74	3.15	3.56
Stock price – high ($)	—	16.69	23.50	26.31	24.75	32.44	37.75	49.13	60.63	67.25	65.38
Stock price – low ($)	—	11.31	15.19	14.00	19.25	22.06	26.38	33.63	45.13	46.75	49.50
Stock price – close ($)	16.2%	16.38	20.44	19.63	23.50	31.75	36.88	48.88	55.75	62.38	63.38
P/E – high	—	16	19	—	22	17	18	66	22	21	18
P/E – low	—	11	12	—	17	12	12	45	16	15	14
Dividends per share ($)	10.1%	0.65	0.68	0.70	0.74	0.78	0.90	1.02	1.15	1.34	1.54
Book value per share ($)	5.0%	6.33	6.91	6.77	8.24	5.30	7.06	9.81	13.74	9.79	9.80
Employees	(2.3%)	40,600	37,900	37,400	24,700	24,100	24,800	24,900	28,800	28,000	32,800

1994 Year-end:
Debt ratio: 51.8%
Return on equity: 40.4%
Cash (mil.): $218
Current ratio: 1.42
Long-term debt (mil.): $1,752
No. of shares (mil.): 144
Dividends
  Yield: 2.4%
  Payout: 43.3%
Market value (mil.): $9,152

Stock Price History
High/Low 1985–94

THE COLUMBIA GAS SYSTEM, INC.

OVERVIEW

Wilmington, Delaware–based Columbia Gas System is a holding company for one of the largest natural gas systems in the US, and it is the parent for subsidiaries with operations from exploration and production to storage and distribution. The company's oil and gas operations hold leases for more than 2.5 million acres; its transmission subsidiaries operate a 23,000-mile pipeline network reaching from the Gulf of Mexico to New York; and its distribution subsidiaries provide service to over 1.9 million customers in Kentucky, Maryland, Ohio, Pennsylvania, and Virginia.

Columbia also develops gas-fired cogeneration facilities (which produce both steam and electricity) through its TriStar Ventures subsidiary, sells propane, provides supply and fuel management services, and owns more than 500 million tons of coal reserves.

Columbia and pipeline subsidiary Columbia Gas Transmission, both of which entered bankruptcy in 1991, filed a reorganization plan in 1995 and could emerge from Chapter 11 by the end of the year. The companies' plans call for Columbia Gas Transmission to pay creditors $1.7 billion and its parent another $2.2 billion and for Columbia Gas System to pay creditors about $3.6 billion. The companies' troubles were brought on by fixed-price supply contracts from the early 1980s.

While it has struggled through bankruptcy, Columbia has also had to adapt to the deregulation of the gas industry. It is spending hundreds of millions of dollars to upgrade its pipeline system and other facilities; Columbia Gas Transmission plans to expand its pipeline system by 250 million cubic feet a day.

WHEN

In 1906, 4 eastern and midwestern businessmen founded Columbia Gas & Electric. Based in Huntington, West Virginia, Columbia managed about 232,000 acres of oil and gas fields in Kentucky and West Virginia and by 1909 operated a 180-mile natural gas pipeline serving 4 cities in Kentucky and Ohio. In 1926 Columbia merged with George Crawford's Ohio Fuel, which provided natural gas to parts of Ohio, Pennsylvania, and West Virginia. With Crawford as chairman, Columbia moved its headquarters to Delaware and was listed on the NYSE in 1926. Purchases over the next 40 years expanded Columbia's service area to the District of Columbia, Maryland, and New York.

In 1931 Columbia completed a 460-mile pipeline linking Washington, DC, to gas fields in Kentucky. After adopting its current name in 1948, the company bought Gulf Interstate Gas in 1958. Gulf operated an 845-mile pipeline linking Louisiana's gas fields to eastern Kentucky, where the gas was distributed. By 1972 Columbia was supplying about 10% of America's gas customers.

With fuel shortages predicted as early as 1970, Columbia explored for gas in Canada (1971) and arranged for delivery of gas from Alaska (1974). Still, supplies ran short, forcing schools and factories to close in company territory during the winter of 1976–77.

Hoping to assure future supplies, Columbia (with Consolidated System LNG) built a liquid natural gas plant at Cove Point, Maryland, in 1978. The plant closed in 1980 because of price disputes with Algerian suppliers, and in 1988

Columbia sold a 50% interest in the plant to Shell Oil. In 1981 Columbia bought Commonwealth Natural Resources, expanding its service area to central and eastern Virginia.

In another effort to secure future gas supplies, Columbia entered into several take-or-pay contracts between 1982 and 1984, agreeing to buy large amounts of gas at the seller's price. These contracts required Columbia to pay for the gas whether or not the company could resell it. Gas supplies rose in the mid-1980s while demand fell, and Columbia faced bankruptcy by 1985, mostly as a result of the take-or-pay contracts. CEO John Croom renegotiated most of the contracts, but to retain distribution customers he cut Columbia's rates to $1 billion below cost over a 2-year period.

The company agreed to sell its New York distribution subsidiary to New York State Electric & Gas for $39 million in 1990. Mild winter weather (1990–91) affected 1990 earnings, which were lower than management had anticipated. The price of gas fell below the company's supply costs and ultimately caused Columbia to enter bankruptcy in 1991. In 1992 the company divested Columbia Gas Development of Canada.

In 1994 Columbia Gas Transmission received approval from the Federal Energy Regulatory Commission to raise its rates by $23 million annually to cover increased costs and construction expenditures.

In 1995 Oliver Richard, CEO of New Jersey Resources, became CEO of Columbia Gas System, replacing Croom, who retired.

WHO

Chairman, President, and CEO: Oliver G. Richard III, age 42
Chairman and CEO, Columbia Distribution Companies: C. Ronald Tilley, age 57, $694,775 pay
Chairman and CEO, Columbia Transmission Companies: James P. Holland, age 46, $295,020 pay
SVP and CFO: Michael W. O'Donnell, age 50, $365,315 pay
SVP, Columbia Gas System Service: Logan W. Wallingford, age 62, $355,595 pay
SVP and Chief Legal Officer: Peter M. Schwolsky, age 49
President, Columbia Gas Development: John P. Bornman Jr.
President and CEO, Columbia Natural Resources and Columbia Coal Gasification: John R. Henning
President, Columbia Atlantic Trading and Columbia LNG: L. Michael Bridges
President, Columbia Energy Services: Anthony Trubisz
President, Columbia Propane and Commonwealth Propane: A. Mason Brent
VP Human Resources: Dennis P. Geran
Auditors: Arthur Andersen & Co, SC

WHERE

HQ: 20 Montchanin Rd., Wilmington, DE 19807-0020
Phone: 302-429-5000
Fax: 302-429-5730

The company's transmission subsidiaries, which operate a pipeline system extending from the Gulf of Mexico to the Northeast, serve customers in 15 states and the District of Columbia. Its distribution subsidiaries provide natural gas service in Kentucky, Maryland, Ohio, Pennsylvania, and Virginia. Columbia Gas explores for oil and gas in 24 US states.

WHAT

	1994 Sales		1994 Operating Income	
	$ mil.	% of total	$ mil.	% of total
Distribution	1,831	65	128	33
Transmission	583	21	205	54
Oil & gas	122	4	31	8
Other	297	10	18	5
Adjustments	—	—	(9)	—
Total	**2,833**	**100**	**373**	**100**

Distribution Companies
Columbia Gas of Kentucky, Inc.
Columbia Gas of Maryland, Inc.
Columbia Gas of Ohio, Inc.
Columbia Gas of Pennsylvania, Inc.
Commonwealth Gas Services, Inc.

Transmission Companies
Columbia Gas Transmission Corp.
Columbia Gulf Transmission Co.
Columbia LNG Corp.

Oil and Gas Exploration
Columbia Gas Development Corp.
Columbia Natural Resources, Inc.

Other Energy Companies
Columbia Coal Gasification Corp.
Columbia Energy Services Corp.
Columbia Propane Corp.
Commonwealth Propane, Inc.
TriStar Ventures Corp. (cogeneration plants)

KEY COMPETITORS

AES	General Electric	Sonat Inc.
British Gas	Kaneb Services	Tejas Gas
Coastal	Koch	Tenneco
Destec Energy	MAPCO Petroleum	Valero Energy
Enron	NGC	Western Gas
ENSERCH Corp.	Occidental	Westinghouse
FPL	Panhandle Eastern	Williams Cos.

HOW MUCH

	9-Year Growth	1985	1986	1987	1988	1989	1990	1991	1992	1993	1994[1]
Sales ($ mil.)	(2.4%)	4,053	3,397	2,798	3,129	3,204	2,358	2,577	2,922	3,391	2,833
Net income ($ mil.)	—	(94)	99	111	119	146	105	(795)	91	152	246
Income as % of sales	—	—	2.9%	4.0%	3.8%	4.6%	4.0%	—	1.8%	4.5%	8.7%
Earnings per share ($)	—	(2.67)	2.12	2.30	2.46	3.21	2.21	(15.72)	1.01	3.01	4.87
Stock price – high ($)	—	40.00	46.00	56.50	44.75	52.75	54.75	47.50	23.88	27.50	30.75
Stock price – low ($)	—	26.75	34.75	35.50	26.88	33.75	41.50	12.88	14.00	18.13	21.50
Stock price – close ($)	(5.6%)	39.50	45.25	40.25	34.50	52.00	46.88	17.25	19.13	22.38	23.50
P/E – high	—	—	22	25	18	16	25	—	13	9	6
P/E – low	—	—	16	15	11	11	19	—	8	6	4
Dividends per share ($)	(100%)	3.18	3.18	3.18	2.30	2.00	2.20	1.16	0.00	0.00	0.00
Book value per share ($)	(2.1%)	35.10	34.06	34.08	34.18	35.50	34.80	19.92	21.26	24.27	29.03
Employees	(0.2%)	10,800	10,583	10,700	10,700	10,800	10,829	10,367	10,172	10,114	10,600

1994 Year-end:[1]
Debt ratio: 0.4%
Return on equity: 18.3%
Cash (mil.): $1,482
Current ratio: 2.89
Long-term debt (mil.): $4
No. of shares (mil.): 51
Dividends
  Yield: —
  Payout: —
Market value (mil.): $1,188

Stock Price History
High/Low 1985–94

[1]Debtor-in-possession

COLUMBIA/HCA HEALTHCARE

OVERVIEW

Columbia/HCA, the quickly growing hospital colossus, has found religion. The latest wrinkle in the Nashville–based company's expansion plans is a series of deals with non-profit, often church-affiliated hospitals happy to say "Amen!" to Columbia's financial base. The health care giant now operates about 320 hospitals in the US, the UK, and Switzerland, up from 196 hospitals at the end of 1993. Columbia's holdings also include outpatient surgery and diagnostic centers, rehabilitation facilities, and home health care agencies.

The company's biggest news in 1995 was the completion of its $3.45 billion takeover of 117-hospital HealthTrust, the largest hospital merger to date in the US. Previous acquisitions include Galen Health Care (1993) and HCA–Hospital Corporation of America (1994). Columbia expects to pick up 30 or 40 more hospitals annually in the near future.

Nationally, Columbia's enormous scale brings big discounts from insurers and medical suppliers; locally, the company buys up multiple medical centers providing several services in a single area. Part of its strategy for local dominance involves the oft-criticized tactic of courting local doctors and selling them stakes (as high as 40%) in the facilities.

WHEN

In 1987 Dallas lawyer Richard Scott and Fort Worth financier Richard Rainwater, a former financial advisor to the Bass family, joined forces and founded Columbia Hospital Corp. to buy 2 hospitals in El Paso for $60 million. The pair began renovating the run-down hospitals, pleasing doctors by responding quickly to their demands and needs. The partners eventually sold 40% of the hospitals to local doctors, hoping that ownership would motivate physicians to increase productivity and efficiency. However, some critics claimed the practice would lead to overcharging.

The company entered the Miami market the next year and by 1990 had 4 hospitals in operation. After merging with Smith Laboratories in 1990, Columbia went public. With the merger Columbia acquired Sutter Laboratories (orthopedic products). By the end of 1990, Columbia had 11 hospitals. Sales grew, driven not only by new hospital revenues, but also by increased same-hospital sales.

In 1992 Columbia entered the Fort Myers, Florida, market with the purchase of Basic America Medical, Inc. (BAMI). BAMI operated 8 hospitals (with a total of 1,203 beds) and owned several peripheral businesses, most of which Columbia eventually divested. Columbia bought additional facilities that year, including several in the Miami area and a psychiatric hospital in El Paso.

In 1993 Columbia merged with Galen Health Care, which operated 73 hospitals. The merger provided Columbia with about 15 new markets and linked Columbia's respected name with Galen's strength in numbers. Galen had been spun off from health plan operator Humana in early 1993. Humana was founded by lawyers David Jones and Wendell Cherry, who bought their first hospital in 1968 and continued buying one a month until 1971. By 1979 they controlled the 2nd largest operator of hospitals in the US. Sales continued to increase, and the company began offering health insurance in the late 1980s. Humana split into 2 when its segments began competing against each other.

In 1994 Columbia and HCA merged. It was Scott's 2nd try at grabbing HCA; he had originally made a bid for it in 1987. HCA was founded in 1968 by Thomas Frist, his son Thomas Frist Jr., and Jack Massey (founder of Kentucky Fried Chicken Corporation) in Nashville. It started with a single Nashville hospital but grew rapidly. By 1973 the company ran 50 hospitals, and by 1983 HCA owned 376 hospitals in the US and 7 foreign countries.

Changes in Medicare reimbursement procedures (paying on fixed schedules rather than a percentage basis) and the advent of HMOs began to cut into hospital occupancy rates. HCA began paring operations in the late 1980s, including selling 102 of its rural hospitals to an employee stock ownership plan. In 1989 Frist Jr. led a $5.1 billion LBO of the company. To pay down debt Frist continued to sell assets, and in 1992 he took the company public once again.

Columbia/HCA in 1994 acquired the US's largest operator of outpatient surgery centers, Dallas-based Medical Care America, for $859 million in stock.

In addition to the purchase of HealthTrust, in 1995 the company agreed to enter into a 50/50 joint venture with HealthONE, the biggest health care provider in Colorado. Columbia/HCA also agreed to enter into a joint venture with or purchase Massachusetts's MetroWest Health, the nonprofit parent company of a teaching hospital system.

NYSE symbol: COL
Fiscal year ends: December 31

WHO

Chairman: Thomas F. Frist Jr., age 56, $1,133,000 pay
President and CEO: Richard L. Scott, age 42, $1,129,574 pay
COO: David T. Vandewater, age 44, $785,000 pay
SVP, CFO, and Treasurer: David C. Colby, age 41, $431,000 pay
SVP and General Counsel: Stephen T. Braun, age 39, $359,000 pay
SVP Financial Operations: Samuel A. Greco, age 43
SVP Marketing/Public Affairs: Lindy B. Richardson, age 48
SVP Development: Joseph D. Moore, age 48
SVP Finance: Richard A. Schweinhart, age 45
SVP Human Resources: Neil D. Hemphill, age 41
SVP: Victor L. Campbell, age 48
Auditors: Ernst & Young LLP

WHERE

HQ: Columbia/HCA Healthcare Corporation,
One Park Plaza, Nashville, TN 37203
Phone: 615-327-9551
Fax: 615-320-2266 (Investor Relations)

Columbia/HCA operates 320 hospitals and more than 125 outpatient centers in 36 US states, Switzerland, and the UK.

WHAT

	Hospitals	
	No.	**% of total**
Acute-care	171	54
Psychiatric	28	9
HealthTrust	117	37
Total	**316**	**100**

WHAT

	1994 Sales
	% of total
Medicare	34
Medicaid	5
Other	61
Total	**100**

	1994 Patient Revenues
	% of total
Inpatient	70
Outpatient	30
Total	**100**

Selected Services

Cardiology	Neurosurgery
Diagnostic services	Obstetrics
Emergency services	Oncology
General surgery	Orthopedics
Home health care	Outpatient surgery
Internal medicine	

KEY COMPETITORS

Adventist Health	Intermountain Health
Allegheny Health,	Care
Ed. & Research	Mayo Foundation
Allina Health	Mercy Health Services
American Medical	Montefiore Medical
Holdings	National Medical
Beverly Enterprises	NovaCare
Catholic Healthcare West	OrNda HealthCorp
Charter Medical	Quorum Health
Detroit Medical Center	Sisters of Charity Health
Franciscan Health	Care
HEALTHSOUTH	SSM Health Care
Holy Cross Health System	Tenet
In Home Health	UniHealth America
Integrated Health Services	Universal Health Services

HOW MUCH

	Annual Growth	1985	1986	1987	1988	1989	1990	1991	1992	1993	1994
Sales ($ mil.)	150.5%	—	—	—	45	153	290	499	807	10,252	11,132
Net income ($ mil.)	160.8%	—	—	—	2	6	10	15	26	507	630
Income as % of sales	—	—	—	—	4.4%	4.1%	3.4%	3.0%	3.2%	4.9%	5.7%
Earnings per share ($)	21.0%	—	—	—	—	—	0.84	0.92	1.18	1.50	1.80
Stock price – high ($)	—	—	—	—	—	—	15.50	18.75	22.00	33.88	45.25
Stock price – low ($)	—	—	—	—	—	—	10.00	9.75	13.75	16.25	33.25
Stock price – close ($)	32.5%	—	—	—	—	—	11.75	17.00	21.25	32.88	36.25
P/E – high	—	—	—	—	—	—	18	20	19	23	25
P/E – low	—	—	—	—	—	—	12	11	12	11	18
Dividends per share ($)	—	—	—	—	—	—	0.00	0.00	0.00	0.12	0.12
Book value per share ($)	47.5%	—	—	—	—	—	2.93	6.40	10.25	10.31	13.87
Employees	127.1%	—	—	—	—	—	5,900	6,300	13,300	131,600	157,000

1994 Year-end:
Debt ratio: 43.9%
Return on equity: 14.8%
Cash (mil.): $13
Current ratio: 1.44
Long-term debt (mil.): $3,853
No. of shares (mil.): 362
Dividends
   Yield: 0.3%
   Payout: 6.7%
Market value (mil.): $13,121

**Stock Price History
High/Low 1990–94**

COMPAQ COMPUTER CORPORATION

OVERVIEW

Compaq, which in 1995 slipped to #2 in the PC market (after Packard Bell), is fighting to regain the top spot. Among the weapons in its arsenal are a low-cost manufacturing agreement with Taiwanese subcontractors and a barrage of new products. Also in 1995 Compaq filed a suit accusing Packard Bell of selling new computers that incorporate used parts (a charge Packard Bell denies).

Despite rapid sales growth in early 1995, Compaq, which sells primarily to corporate clients, is having trouble competing in 2 key areas: low-end home computers and laptop models. Instead of relying on its own highly touted manufacturing, the company has decided to put its name on home models made by Mitac International and laptops made by

Inventec Group (both of Taiwan). Compaq is risking consumer disfavor in return for low cost and a reliable inventory.

It was Compaq's in-house manufacturing that cost the company its top market share in the first place: rivals such as Packard Bell, Dell, and Gateway, which use Pentium-based components made by Intel, introduced the faster machines while Compaq was still relying on 486-based models as the top of its line.

Not to worry. In early 1995 Compaq made its biggest product introduction ever, rolling out more than 100 new items, many with Pentium chips and built-in networking and systems management capabilities. A recent pact with NewGen for Pentium clones should increase Compaq's margins even more.

WHEN

Joseph R. (Rod) Canion and 2 other ex–Texas Instruments engineers started Compaq in Houston in 1982 to manufacture and sell portable IBM-compatible computers. Compaq's first portable was developed from a prototype the 3 sketched on a paper place mat when they first discussed the product idea.

Compaq shipped its first computer in 1982 and in 1983 (the year it went public) recorded sales of $111 million — unprecedented growth for a computer start-up. Compaq's success was due in part to emphasis on leading-edge technology. In 1983 Compaq introduced a portable computer — 18 months before IBM did — and in 1986 it was first out with a computer based on Intel's 386 chip. However, Compaq delayed introduction of its laptop until the prototype's display and battery technologies met engineering specifications. Although introduced late (1988), Compaq's SLT/286 laptop with its crisp display screen became an immediate success.

To sell its products, Compaq capitalized on the extensive base of dealers and suppliers built up around the IBM PC. Rather than establish a large sales force, Compaq gave exclusive rights to dealers for sales and service of its products and by 1990 had a network of 3,800 retailers in 152 countries. The dealer channel proved to be effective. In 1988 Compaq became the first company to exceed the $2 billion sales mark within 6 years of its first product introduction (1982–88). Sales in 1989 rose to $2.9 billion.

In 1989 the company dropped Businessland, its 2nd largest reseller (after ComputerLand), as an authorized dealer after Businessland demanded preferential discounts. Compaq

reauthorized Businessland as a dealer in 1990 after it agreed to abide by Compaq's policies. In 1991 Compaq bought a 13% interest in engineering workstation maker Silicon Graphics and paid $50 million for access to its graphics technology. Compaq also took a lead role in creating a 21-company alliance, Advanced Computer Environment (ACE), to establish a standard for Reduced Instruction Set Computing (RISC) computers to compete with those of Sun and IBM.

Economic recession and stiff price competition slashed Compaq's revenues in 1991. Founder and CEO Canion (an engineer) was forced to resign; he was replaced with Eckhard Pfeiffer (a salesman). The next year Compaq withdrew from ACE and sold back its stake in Silicon Graphics and its 20% interest in Conner Peripherals (bought in 1986) for an $80 million profit. Late in 1992 Compaq introduced the world's fastest PC server, the Compaq SYSTEMPRO/XL. In 1993 Compaq and Microsoft announced a joint venture to develop pen-based PCs, mobile computing, and multiprocessor computers and servers.

By 1994 Compaq had become the world's top manufacturer of personal computers, passing IBM and Apple to take 10% of the market. That same year the company announced a joint venture with video conferencing developer Picturetel Corporation to design and build personal conferencing products.

In 1995 Compaq established a unit to develop multimedia software products. The previous year the company had acquired a 4% stake in pioneering software publisher Books That Work.

NYSE symbol: CPQ
Fiscal year ends: December 31

WHO

Chairman: Benjamin M. Rosen, age 62
President and CEO: Eckhard Pfeiffer, age 53,
$3,550,000 pay
SVP Systems: Gary Stimac, age 43, $1,000,000 pay
SVP Europe, Middle East, and Africa: Andreas Barth,
age 50, $914,298 pay
SVP North America: Ross A. Cooley, age 54,
$890,000 pay
SVP Finance and CFO: Daryl J. White, age 47,
$835,000 pay
SVP Desktop PC Division: John T. Rose
SVP Portable PC Division: Hugh Barnes
SVP Corporate Operations: Gregory E. Petsch, age 44
SVP, General Counsel, and Secretary: Wilson D. Fargo,
age 50
SVP Human Resources: Hans W. Gutsch, age 51
Auditors: Price Waterhouse LLP

WHERE

HQ: 20555 SH 249, Houston, TX 77070
Phone: 713-370-0670
Fax: 713-374-1740

Compaq has manufacturing facilities in Brazil, China,
Scotland, and Singapore. The company sells and
supports its products in more than 100 countries.

	1994 Sales		1994 Operating Income	
	$ mil.	% of total	$ mil.	% of total
US & Canada	5,473	50	533	41
Europe	3,829	35	470	36
Other regions	1,564	15	292	23
Adjustments	—	—	(1)	—
Total	**10,866**	**100**	**1,294**	**100**

WHAT

	1994 Sales
	% of total
Desktop PCs	58
Portable PCs	25
PC systems	17
Total	**100**

Computer Peripherals
COMPAQ ProLiant

Desktop PCs
COMPAQ Deskpro Series
COMPAQ Presario
COMPAQ ProLinea Series

PC Systems
COMPAQ ProSignia
COMPAQ Systempro

Portables
COMPAQ Concerto
COMPAQ Contura
COMPAQ LTE Lite

Software
Rack Builder
TabWorks

KEY COMPETITORS

Advanced	Gateway 2000	Oki
Logic Research	Hewlett-	Olivetti
Apple	Packard	Packard Bell
AST	Hitachi	Philips
AT&T	Hyundai	Sharp
Atari	IBM	Siemens
Canon	Intel	Sun
Casio	Machines Bull	Microsystems
CompuAdd	Matsushita	Tandy
Data General	Micron	Toshiba
DEC	Technology	Unisys
Dell	NEC	Wang
Fujitsu		

HOW MUCH

	9-Year Growth	1985	1986	1987	1988	1989	1990	1991	1992	1993	1994
Sales ($ mil.)	40.7%	504	625	1,224	2,066	2,876	3,599	3,271	4,100	7,191	10,866
Net income ($ mil.)	47.0%	27	43	136	255	333	455	131	213	462	867
Income as % of sales	—	5.3%	6.9%	11.1%	12.4%	11.6%	12.6%	4.0%	5.2%	6.4%	8.0%
Earnings per share ($)	40.5%	0.15	0.22	0.60	1.05	1.29	1.70	0.50	0.84	1.78	3.21
Stock price – high ($)	—	2.37	3.60	13.07	10.95	18.73	22.60	24.73	16.61	25.22	42.13
Stock price – low ($)	—	1.02	1.94	3.21	6.99	9.87	11.82	7.37	7.41	13.90	24.13
Stock price – close ($)	37.8%	2.21	3.21	9.22	9.93	13.24	18.77	8.78	16.23	24.60	39.50
P/E – high	—	16	16	22	10	15	13	50	20	14	13
P/E – low	—	7	9	5	7	8	7	15	9	8	8
Dividends per share ($)	—	0.00	0.00	0.00	0.00	0.00	0.00	0.00	0.00	0.00	0.00
Book value per share ($)	36.4%	0.86	1.13	1.95	3.52	4.97	7.88	7.64	8.37	10.48	14.07
Employees	25.6%	1,850	2,200	4,000	6,900	9,500	11,400	11,600	11,300	10,541	14,372

1994 Year-end:
Debt ratio: 7.5%
Return on equity: 27.4%
Cash (mil.): $471
Current ratio: 2.56
Long-term debt (mil.): $300
No. of shares (mil.): 261
Dividends
  Yield: —
  Payout: —
Market value (mil.): $10,311

Stock Price History
High/Low 1985–94

COMPUSA INC.

Almost counted out by some analysts, Dallas-based CompUSA has risen from the mat and come back fighting. The nation's largest computer retailer, CompUSA posted a $17 million loss in fiscal 1994 after expanding too rapidly.

The company has installed a new management team led by James Halpin and instituted a number of changes designed to transform the company from an entrepreneurial daredevil into a stable, mature corporation. In addition to decreasing the rate of new store openings (and even closing some old stores), changes included a new emphasis on training and customer services, consolidation of inventory and pricing at the corporate level, and a new focus on the home market rather than the hard-core "techie" market. In order to facilitate this change, the company began remodel-ing its stores to make them less intimidating to computer neophytes and adding informational programs and events.

The makeover seems to have helped. CompUSA's sales were up 31%, to $2.8 billion, and its same-store sales rose 10.3% in fiscal 1995. However, CompUSA doesn't have time to rest on its laurels. It faces stiff competition from both computer superstores, including Tandy's Computer City, and consumer electronics chains, including Best Buy and Circuit City.

CompUSA plans to continue to focus on "nontechie" computer buyers. To entice parents it has introduced to many of its stores a CompKids area, which features hundreds of edutainment software titles that kids can try before they buy.

WHEN

CompUSA was founded in 1984, when 23-year-old Mike Henochowicz (a native of South Africa and former Highland Appliance salesman) and 33-year-old Errol Jacobson invested $2,000 to open Soft Warehouse, an 800-square-foot software store near Dallas.

When the business opened, profit margins on computer programs were huge, and deep discounting, with little competition, still offered good profits. Soft Warehouse prospered by offering a wide selection of titles. In 1985 Henochowicz and Jacobson opened their first superstore in Dallas.

While the superstore concept was booming in other retail areas, it was a fairly new concept in the computer world. In the early 1980s buyers often did not know very much about computers and would go to one store to purchase hardware and another to buy software, relying on each store's technical expertise to guide their buying decisions. Soft Warehouse's one-stop-shopping concept coincided with the rise of savvy buyers who knew what they wanted. Soft Warehouse let them explore many options under one roof.

In 1988 the partners opened a 24,000-square-foot store in Atlanta. In 1989 Dubin Clark & Co., a private investment firm, bought a 50% interest in Soft Warehouse and brought in Nathan Morton, a former SVP of Home Depot, as the new COO. With the influx of capital, Morton immediately began an expansion program by opening stores in Houston, Los Angeles, Philadelphia, Miami, San Diego, and Washington, DC — all in 1989. In 1990 Morton became CEO, and Soft Warehouse attempted an IPO but abandoned the effort when the Persian Gulf War dampened the market.

Decisions by Dell in 1990 and Apple in 1991 to sell their products through Soft Warehouse built the company's credibility. Because it was then selling computer hardware as well as software, in 1991 Soft Warehouse adopted the name CompUSA to reflect its broader product lines and national expansion. Also in 1991 CompUSA successfully launched its IPO. The 2 founders left the company about that time to pursue other interests. By 1992 the company operated 31 stores in 21 markets.

To manage its growth, CompUSA restructured in May 1993 and created an international division to service its planned worldwide markets. Morton became chairman, while James Halpin (former president of HomeBase) was named president.

Just 7 months later, Morton resigned amid board dissatisfaction with CompUSA's poor earnings, which analysts blamed on inefficiencies stemming from rapid growth. Under Morton CompUSA had become extremely decentralized — individual stores were responsible for buying and pricing. Halpin became CEO and killed plans for an international division. He also began staff cutbacks and instituted centralized buying (decentralization had resulted in such great inefficiencies that in late 1994 the company had to auction off excess inventory).

In 1995 CompUSA opened its first stand-alone customer training centers, in Boston and Seattle.

WHO

Chairman: Giles H. Bateman
President and CEO: James F. Halpin, age 43,
$451,805 pay
EVP and COO: Harold F. Compton, age 47
EVP Merchandising: Lawrence N. Mondry, age 34,
$236,000 pay
EVP, CFO, and Treasurer: James Skinner, age 41
SVP Services and Administration: Paul Poyfair, age 42
SVP Marketing and Advertising: Ronald Gilmore, age 39
VP, General Counsel, and Secretary: Mark R. Walker,
age 37
VP Direct Sales: Stanley R. Schiller, age 58
VP Real Estate: Ronald D. Strongwater, age 51
VP Human Resources: Mel McCall, age 51
Auditors: Ernst & Young LLP

WHERE

HQ: 14951 N. Dallas Pkwy., Dallas, TX 75240
Phone: 214-383-4000
Fax: 214-383-4276

	1994 Stores
	No.
California	13
Ohio	6
Texas	6
Florida	5
Georgia	4
New Jersey	4
New York	4
Illinois	3
Maryland	3
Massachusetts	3
Michigan	3
Pennsylvania	3
Virginia	3
Other states	16
Total	**76**

WHAT

Selected Products
Connectivity products
Data storage devices
Laptop computers
Microcomputers
Modems
Monitors
Printers

Selected Brands
Apple
Compaq
DEC
Dell
Hewlett-Packard
Sony
Texas Instruments
Toshiba

KEY COMPETITORS

Anam Group	Intelligent Electronics
Barnes & Noble	J&R Music
Best Buy	Kmart
CDW Computer Centers	Micro Warehouse
Circuit City	MicroAge
CompuAdd	Micro Center
CompuCom	Montgomery Ward
Dell	NeoStar
Egghead	Price/Costco
ELEK-TEK	Sears
Entex	Service Merchandise
Fretter	Software Spectrum
Fry's Electronics	Staples
Future Shop	Supercom
Gateway 2000	Tandy
Global Directmail	Tiger Direct
InaCom	Vanstar
Inmac	Wal-Mart

HOW MUCH

	Annual Growth	1985	1986	1987	1988	1989	1990	1991	1992	1993	1994
Sales ($ mil.)	82.4%	—	—	32	67	137	300	544	821	1,342	2,146
Net income ($ mil.)	—	—	—	0	2	2	2	(11)	8	12	(17)
Income as % of sales	—	—	—	0.9%	2.9%	1.2%	0.5%	—	1.0%	0.9%	—
Earnings per share ($)	—	—	—	—	—	0.01	0.16	(1.58)	0.62	0.67	(0.92)
Stock price – high ($)	—	—	—	—	—	—	—	23.75	40.50	37.00	22.25
Stock price – low ($)	—	—	—	—	—	—	—	15.00	19.25	17.88	6.75
Stock price – close ($)	(11.3%)	—	—	—	—	—	—	21.50	28.00	19.88	15.00
P/E – high	—	—	—	—	—	—	—	—	65	55	—
P/E – low	—	—	—	—	—	—	—	—	31	27	—
Dividends per share ($)	—	—	—	—	—	—	—	0.00	0.00	0.00	0.00
Book value per share ($)	—	—	—	—	—	—	—	(2.05)	5.55	8.80	7.91
Employees	70.5%	—	—	—	—	543	1,208	1,782	2,767	5,086	7,819

1994 Year-end:
Debt ratio: 52.0%
Return on equity: —
Cash (mil.): $23
Current ratio: 2.00
Long-term debt (mil.): $153
No. of shares (mil.): 18
Dividends
  Yield: —
  Payout: —
Market value (mil.): $277

Stock Price History
High/Low 1991–94

COMPUTER ASSOCIATES

OVERVIEW

Charles Wang, the founder and CEO of #2 software vendor Computer Associates (CA; Microsoft is #1), has a recipe for success: develop, acquire, integrate. CA took the development step in 1994 when it rewrote its flagship CA-Unicenter systems management software for use on smaller computers as well as mainframes. In 1995 CA agreed to acquire Legent, a rival software developer, for $1.74 billion. CA has acquired over 50 companies since 1976.

Now comes the integration part, with CA trying to keep its mainframe customers happy even as it moves away from that (some say slowing) market.

CA has been using recent acquisitions to shift its focus to midrange computers. In 1994 it bought the ASK Group, a client/server software developer. The following year it introduced *CA-OpenIngres/Desktop*, which integrates ASK's *Ingres* database software with Gupta Corporation's database technology.

In 1995 CA and Microsoft announced an alliance to bring CA software to the Windows NT operating system. The new product will incorporate CA-Unicenter with Microsoft's NT Server and SQL Server runtime.

Wang owns 4.9% of CA. Swiss billionaire Walter Haefner owns 23% of the company.

WHEN

Charles Wang (pronounced "wong") and his family fled Communist China in 1952. After graduating from Queens College (New York), in 1976 Wang started a joint venture with Swiss-owned Computer Associates to sell software in the US. Wang started with 4 employees and one product, a file organizer for IBM storage systems (CA-SORT). It was a great success. In 1980 Wang bought out his Swiss partners.

Wang soon realized that a penetrating distribution and service network, continuously fed by new products, was the key to success; acquiring existing software (and its customers) reduced risky in-house development and moved products to market sooner. CA's buying (of mostly struggling software firms) produced the first independent software company to reach $1 billion in sales (1989).

Wang moved beyond mainframe utilities into microcomputer software, buying the popular *SuperCalc* spreadsheet (from Sorcim, 1984) and *BPI* (accounting software, 1987); data security software, including the *Top Secret* program (1985); and a string of applications vendors, including Software International (financial, 1986) and Integrated Software Systems (graphics, 1986).

CA's 1987 purchase of chief utilities rival UCCEL made CA the world's largest independent software supplier — and gave Swiss billionaire Walter Haefner 20% of CA. CA then had 64% of the tape/disk-management software market and a strong presence in banking applications and in data security.

CA entered the mainframe database software market in 1988 with the purchase of Applied Data Research (ADR) from Ameritech. In 1989, with the $300 million acquisition of Cullinet, CA added the IDMS database line,

software for VAX computers, and banking applications to its product line. But the incompatibility of Cullinet's IDMS software with that of ADR left customers guessing which one CA would ultimately support. This uncertainty and other problems in assimilating Cullinet caused product sales and net income to drop in 1990.

In 1991 CA acquired New Jersey–based On-Line Software, a maker of mainframe debugging software, for $120 million. Soon after, it paid $290 million for Pansophic Systems, a financially troubled maker of AS/400 (IBM minicomputer), information retrieval, and CASE software applications.

In 1994 CA acquired ASK Group, a developer of popular material management software (founded in 1974 by Sandra Kurtzig). ASK had grown by introducing ever more sophisticated software and by entering into alliances with other manufacturing software companies. However, by 1994 ASK's sales were slumping. Wang bought ASK and vowed to turn it around. That same year Wang promoted EVP of operations Sanjay Kumar to president. Also in 1994 CA resolved a legal dispute with GM's Electronic Data Systems in which CA claimed EDS was using its software without the proper licensing. The 2 companies signed a new 12-year contract that could bring CA $100 million annually.

In 1995 MCI said it would use CA-Unicenter to manage its entire enterprise client/server system, and defense electronics manufacturer Thomson-CSF chose CA-CAS/UNIX as the standard for use on over 3,000 of its workstations worldwide. Also in 1995 CA and Fujitsu announced a major alliance to develop database management tools using object-oriented technology.

WHO

Chairman and CEO: Charles B. Wang, age 50
President and COO: Sanjay Kumar, age 33
EVP Research and Development: Russell M. Artzt, age 48
EVP Sales: Richard Chiarello
SVP Finance and CFO: Peter A. Schwartz, age 51
SVP and Secretary: Belden A. Frease, age 56
SVP and Treasurer: Ira Zar, age 33
SVP Human Resources: Lisa Mars
Auditors: Ernst & Young LLP

WHERE

HQ: Computer Associates International, Inc.,
One Computer Associates Plaza, Islandia, NY
11788-7000
Phone: 516-342-5224 (516-DIAL-CAI)
Fax: 516-342-5329 (516-DIAL-FAX)

Computer Associates offers over 300 software products.
The company has over 100 offices in 30 countries.

	1995 Sales		1995 Net Income	
	$ mil.	% of total	$ mil.	% of total
US	1,553	53	277	64
Other countries	1,360	47	155	36
Adjustment	(290)	—	—	—
Total	**2,623**	**100**	**432**	**100**

WHAT

	1995 Sales	
	$ mil.	% of total
Products	1,903	73
Maintenance	720	27
Total	**2,623**	**100**

Selected Products and Licensing Services

Software
Application development
Automated production control
Business decision tools
CASE technologies
COBOL and testing tools
Data center administration
Database management
DB2 tools
Distributed client/server solutions
Enterprise information solutions
Financial management
Graphics tools
Licensing
Manufacturing management
Security, control, and audit
Warehouse management

Licensing
Enterprise licensing (no additional fee for subsidiaries' use of software)
Fixed fee (one-time fee plus annual usage and maintenance fee)
Maintenance Savings (subscription fee in return for guaranteed annual usage and maintenance fee)
Term license (right to use software for specified period from one month to 3 years)

KEY COMPETITORS

American Software	Intuit
Apple	Microsoft
BMC Software	Novell
Borland	OpenVision Technologies
Consilium	Oracle
Data General	PeopleSoft
DEC	PLATINUM technology
Dun & Bradstreet	Progress Software
Fourth Shift	Sterling Software
H&R Block	Sybase
Hewlett-Packard	System Software Associates
Hyperion Software	Tivoli Systems
Informix	Wang

HOW MUCH

	9-Year Growth	1986	1987	1988	1989	1990	1991	1992	1993	1994	1995
Sales ($ mil.)	33.8%	191	309	709	1,030	1,296	1,348	1,509	1,841	2,148	2,623
Net income ($ mil.)	41.5%	19	37	102	164	158	159	163	246	401	432
Income as % of sales	—	9.7%	11.8%	14.4%	15.9%	12.2%	11.8%	10.8%	13.3%	18.7%	16.5%
Earnings per share ($)	32.1%	0.21	0.37	0.63	0.98	0.85	0.86	0.92	1.44	2.34	2.57
Stock price – high ($)[1]	—	4.38	7.72	18.63	16.44	22.13	16.88	11.88	20.75	44.25	50.88
Stock price – low ($)[1]	—	2.28	4.06	6.84	11.94	10.50	4.38	6.25	10.88	20.13	27.38
Stock price – close ($)[1]	30.6%	4.38	6.88	16.00	15.94	12.50	7.75	11.38	20.25	40.00	48.50
P/E – high	—	21	21	30	17	26	20	13	14	19	20
P/E – low	—	11	11	11	12	12	5	7	8	9	11
Dividends per share ($)	—	0.00	0.00	0.00	0.00	0.00	0.10	0.10	0.10	0.14	0.20
Book value per share ($)	21.0%	1.77	2.21	3.15	4.46	5.31	5.99	5.57	6.28	7.62	9.85
Employees	18.5%	1,640	2,700	4,450	6,250	6,900	6,700	7,400	7,200	6,900	7,550

1995 Year-end:
Debt ratio: 15.7%
Return on equity: 30.6%
Cash (mil.): $301
Current ratio: 1.35
Long-term debt (mil.): $50
No. of shares (mil.): 160
Dividends
  Yield: 0.4%
  Payout: 7.8%
Market value (mil.): $7,767

Stock Price History[1]
High/Low 1986–95

[1] Stock prices are for the prior calendar year.

CONAGRA, INC.

OVERVIEW

Omaha-based ConAgra is an international diversified food company with a broad mix of businesses ranging from supplying to farmers feed and fertilizers to producing commodities like grain and beef. It also sells grocery brands such as Wesson (oil), Armour (meats and frozen foods), and County Line (cheeses).

ConAgra is the nation's #2 food company (after Philip Morris), thanks to an an aggressive acquisition strategy, and has seen sales and profits rise for 14 straight years. The company has 18 brands that have yearly retail sales of over $100 million, including its $1 billion flagship brand, Healthy Choice. The chief engine of growth has been the prepared foods segment, which includes shelf foods, frozen foods, and meats and accounts for more than 3/4 of ConAgra's total sales.

The company's agri-products division (feeds, fertilizers) serves agricultural markets, and its trading and processing division (grains, milling, and commodity trading and futures) serves the food industry. Its operations also include more than 200 country general stores and fabric and craft shops, mostly located in agricultural areas.

Conagra is committed to world growth and has joint ventures with Dutch frozen food maker Meijer, Carlsberg beer in Denmark, and malt makers in China and Australia.

WHEN

In 1919, 4 flour mills joined to form Nebraska Consolidated Mills and established headquarters in Omaha. The company did not expand to other states until the 1940s.

In the 1950s the company developed Duncan Hines cake mix (later sold to Procter & Gamble) and in 1957 set up a flour and feed mill in Puerto Rico. The company entered the poultry processing business in the 1960s while continuing to buy flour mills nationwide.

By 1970 the company had opened poultry processing plants in Alabama, Georgia, and Louisiana. In 1971 the company changed its name to ConAgra (which means "in partnership with the land" in Latin). During the 1970s the company expanded into the fertilizer, catfish, and pet accessory businesses.

Bad investments and commodity speculation caused ConAgra severe financial problems until 1974, when Charles M. "Mike" Harper, a former Pillsbury executive, took over. Harper trimmed properties to reduce debt and had the company back on its feet by 1976. In 1977 ConAgra established large-scale grain and feed merchandising operations and in 1978 bought United Agri Products (agricultural chemicals).

In 1980 the company bought Banquet (frozen food) from RCA and within 6 years had introduced almost 90 new products under that label. With the purchases of Singleton Seafood and Sea-Alaska products, ConAgra achieved $1 billion in sales for the first time in 1981. ConAgra bought Peavey (milling and retailing) and Country Pride (chicken) in 1982 and in 1983 acquired Armour Food Company (meats, dairy products, and frozen food).

In 1986 ConAgra bought RJR Nabisco's frozen food business, which included the Chun King, Morton, and Patio brands. The company became a major factor in the red meat market with the 1987 purchases of E. A. Miller (boxed beef), Monfort (beef and lamb), and Swift Independent Packing. Further acquisitions included O'Donnell-Usen (seafood, 1987) and Blue Star (frozen food, 1988).

In 1990 ConAgra bought Beatrice. Formed as a dairy company in 1894, Beatrice grew by acquiring several large food product businesses starting in the 1940s. The purchase brought ConAgra the US's #1 popcorn (Orville Redenbacher's) and #1 tomato sauce (Hunt's).

ConAgra bought Golden Valley Microwave Foods in 1991 and set up a joint venture with Chilewich Partners, an exporter of food to Eastern Europe. In 1992 the company bought food maker Arrow Industries and created Casa de Oro to compete in the tortilla business.

Harper stepped down as CEO in September 1992 but stayed as chairman until May 1993. President Philip Fletcher replaced Harper at both positions. Also in 1993 ConAgra bought kosher products maker National Foods (Hebrew National) — part of $500 million worth of acquisitions or joint ventures (40 in all) approved during the year. That was the first year of new CEO Fletcher's tenure, and ConAgra had modest results as "hostile" fresh meat and frozen food prices undercut the 50% surge in sales of its Healthy Choice brand.

In 1994 the company bought the frozen food unit of Universal Foods and joined with Kellogg to develop 3 Healthy Choice cereals. Also in 1994 ConAgra announced plans to sell noncore assets. In 1995 its beef processing unit pleaded guilty to labor law violations after the death of a worker in a cattle hide processing machine. The company saw record earnings of nearly $496 million in fiscal 1995.

NYSE symbol: CAG
Fiscal year ends: Last Sunday in May

WHO

Chairman and CEO: Philip B. Fletcher, age 61, $1,600,00 pay
EVP and CFO: James P. O'Donnell, age 47
President and COO, Grocery Products Cos.: Albert J. Crosson, age 63, $935,000 pay
President and COO, ConAgra Meat Products Cos.: Leroy O. Lochmann, age 59, $725,000 pay
President and COO, Diversified Products Co.: James D. Watkins, age 46, $601,200 pay
President and COO, ConAgra Trading and Processing Cos.: Thomas L. Manuel, age 47
SVP and Chief Information Officer: Dwight J. Goslee, age 44
SVP, Corporate Secretary, and Risk Officer: L. B. Thomas, age 58
SVP Human Resources: Gerald B. Vernon, age 53
VP and Controller: Kenneth W. DiFonzo, age 42
Auditors: Deloitte & Touche LLP

WHERE

HQ: One ConAgra Dr., Omaha, NE 68102-5001
Phone: 402-595-4000
Fax: 402-595-4595 (Public Relations)

ConAgra has international offices in 27 countries; manufactures private-label groceries; sells meat and potato products; and merchandises beans and grains.

WHAT

	1994 Sales		1994 Operating Income	
	$ mil.	% of total	$ mil.	% of total
Prepared Foods	18,119	77	864	81
Agri-Products	2,967	13	92	9
Trading & Proc.	2,426	10	111	10
Total	**23,512**	**100**	**1,067**	**100**

Prepared Foods (Selected Brands)
Act II
Armour
Banquet
Butterball
Casa de Oro
Chun King
Country Pride
Country Skillet
County Line
Decker
Eckrich
Healthy Choice
Hebrew National
Hunt's
La Choy
Longmont
Manwich
Morton
Orville Redenbacher's
Patio
Peter Pan
Reddi–Wip
Rosarita
Swiss Miss
Taste O'Sea
Wesson

Agri-Products
Animal health care products
Crop protection chemicals
Fertilizer products
Nutrient additives for animal feed

Trading and Processing
Animal feeds
Commodity futures brokerage
Feed ingredient merchandising
Global commodity trading
Grain milling
Spices, seasonings, flavors, and spray-dried food ingredients

General Stores
Anfinson's
Country General
Peavey Ranch and Home
S&S
Sandvig's
Wheelers

Fabric and Craft Stores
Northwest Fabrics & Crafts
Rainbow Bay Crafts

KEY COMPETITORS

ADM	General Mills	Procter
Agway	Grand	& Gamble
Anheuser-Busch	Metropolitan	Quaker Oats
Borden	Heinz	Ralston Purina
Campbell Soup	Hormel	Group
Cargill	IBP	Salomon
Chiquita Brands	Kmart	Sandoz
Continental Grain	Nabisco Holdings	Sara Lee
CPC	Nestlé	Tyson Foods
Danone	Perdue	Unilever
Farmland	Philip Morris	Wal-Mart
Industries		

HOW MUCH

	9-Year Growth	1985	1986	1987	1988	1989	1990	1991	1992	1993	1994
Sales ($ mil.)	17.5%	5,498	5,911	9,002	9,475	11,340	15,501	19,505	21,219	21,519	23,512
Net income ($ mil.)	18.9%	92	105	149	155	198	232	311	372	392	437
Income as % of sales	—	1.7%	1.8%	1.7%	1.6%	1.7%	1.5%	1.6%	1.8%	1.8%	1.9%
Earnings per share ($)	13.3%	0.59	0.67	0.81	0.85	1.08	1.25	1.42	1.50	1.58	1.81
Stock price – high ($)	—	10.51	14.30	16.90	15.13	20.18	25.51	36.25	35.75	33.63	33.13
Stock price – low ($)	—	5.77	8.65	9.30	10.57	12.90	15.17	22.34	24.50	22.75	25.50
Stock price – close ($)	14.2%	9.46	12.74	11.30	12.90	19.01	24.68	35.50	33.13	26.38	31.25
P/E – high	—	18	21	21	18	19	20	26	24	21	18
P/E – low	—	10	13	12	12	12	12	16	16	14	14
Dividends per share ($)	16.3%	0.18	0.21	0.24	0.28	0.32	0.37	0.43	0.50	0.60	0.70
Book value per share ($)	12.6%	3.08	3.43	4.12	4.64	5.25	5.95	8.68	9.62	8.16	8.97
Employees	12.4%	30,410	33,642	42,176	42,993	55,202	58,369	74,718	80,787	83,000	87,000

1994 Year-end:
Debt ratio: 55.2%
Return on equity: 20.4%
Cash (mil.): $166
Current ratio: 1.08
Long-term debt (mil.): $2,207
No. of shares (mil.): 248
Dividends
  Yield: 2.4%
  Payout: 38.4%
Market value (mil.): $7,756

Stock Price History
High/Low 1985–94

CONNER PERIPHERALS, INC.

OVERVIEW

Conner Peripherals is holding onto its leadership position among makers of computer disk and tape drives for OEMs — despite component shortages, engineering problems, an aging inventory, customer defections, and an intensely competitive market. California-based Conner is keeping pace by offering a broader product line to a marketplace that is forever demanding faster, smaller drives with higher storage capacity and lower power consumption.

In 1994 Conner, a storage systems pioneer that spends 5.5% of revenues on R&D, introduced more than 40 new products, including disk array storage systems, data protection software, and 14 new disk drive products. In late 1994 Conner won certification from 3 major computer manufacturers for several prod- ucts, including its advanced 3.5" disk drives. The company began shipments in early 1995.

While manufacturers such as Compaq, Packard Bell, and Sun account for nearly 3/4 of Conner's sales, the company is also courting retail customers. In 1994 its Disk•Stor and Tape•Stor backup systems were being sold through CompUSA, Office Depot, and Wal-Mart stores.

Conner provides software for data storage protection and data management through its Arcada subsidiary. In 1994 Arcada strengthened its product line with the acquisition of Quest Development, a data management software company known for its development of the Norton backup software.

Founder and chairman Finis Conner owns 3.1% of the company's stock.

WHEN

Having cofounded and left computer disk drive manufacturers Shugart Associates and Seagate Technology, Finis Conner created Conner Peripherals in 1985 as a vehicle for yet another disk drive venture. In 1986 he merged his new company with Co-Data Memory, a newly established company owned by John Squires, a disk drive designer and cofounder of Miniscribe, a disk drive manufacturer that had filed for bankruptcy. Conner's search for capital led him to his old friend Rod Canion, the president of Compaq, a company interested in small hard disk drives for its portable microcomputers. Conner sold Canion on Squires's 3.5" drive designs (5.25" drives were standard at the time) and talked him into arranging for Compaq to sink $6 million into his start-up company. Another $6 million injection followed months later.

Conner's first-year sales of $113 million (1987) eclipsed the previous rookie-year record held by Compaq (which, ironically was Conner's biggest customer, accounting for 90% of sales). With a dominant position in high-capacity 3.5" drives and with a design edge that made its drives more reliable and power-efficient than its competitors', Conner began selling to other computer makers, particularly the emerging laptop market.

By 1988 Conner had established its pattern of designing its products in Colorado, beginning pilot production in San Jose, and then transferring volume production to low-cost countries, initially Singapore. In 1988 Conner went public and bought 49% control of a money-losing Olivetti disk drive subsidiary in Italy, renamed Conner Peripherals Europe. Olivetti soon became a major customer.

In 1989 Conner raised its stake in Conner Peripherals Europe to 51% and shipped its first 2.5" disk drives, beating its competition to the market by a year.

Conner bought Domain Technologies' disk coating operations and began building new offshore plants in Malaysia and Scotland in 1990. Sales soared to well over $1 billion.

In 1991 Conner acquired VISqUS (head-to-media technology for flash memory applications) and 6% of Read-Rite (a manufacturer of disk heads). Conner bought 16% of disk head maker Sunward Technologies in 1992. That same year the company released a removable 1.8" drive for palmtops, and it acquired Archive and bought back the 20% interest that Compaq had held in that company.

In 1993 Conner created Arcada Software to develop and market data management software for client/server networks. Following a loss and a restructuring in 1993, Conner returned to profitability in 1994. Although the company said no overtures had been made, late in 1994 it implemented a "poison pill" plan to prevent a takeover.

In 1995 Conner introduced Tape•Stor 4000-IDE, a 4-gigabyte tape backup system for high-end desktop computers and workstations. That same year the company joined with Compaq, Quantum Corp., and Seagate Technology to develop a new advanced diagnostic tool designed to prevent data loss and computer system downtime by warning users of impending drive failures.

NYSE symbol: CNR
Fiscal year ends: Saturday nearest December 31

Chairman and CEO: Finis F. Conner, age 51, $1,071,935 pay
President and COO: David T. Mitchell, age 53, $742,844 pay
EVP and CFO: P. Jackson Bell, age 53, $564,901 pay
EVP Sales and Marketing; President, Tape Division: Donald J. Massaro, age 51, $226,347 pay
EVP; General Manager, Disk Drive Operations: Kenneth F. Potashner, age 37
SVP Engineering and Chief Technical Officer: Michael L. Workman, age 38, $379,442 pay
SVP Corporate Quality and Chief Quality Officer: A. Donald Stratton
VP Human Resources: Greg Goodere
Auditors: Price Waterhouse LLP

WHERE

HQ: 3081 Zanker Rd., San Jose, CA 95134-2128
Phone: 408-456-4500
Fax: 408-456-4501

Conner is a leading supplier of information storage products, including disk drives, tape drives, storage management software, and integrated storage systems. The company has manufacturing facilities in China, Italy, Malaysia, and Singapore.

	1994 Sales		1994 Operating Income	
	$ mil.	% of total	$ mil.	% of total
US	2,143	91	14	9
Asia	142	6	110	66
Europe	80	3	42	25
Total	**2,365**	**100**	**166**	**100**

WHAT

Product Lines

Disk Drives
Filepro (210 to 420 megabytes)
Filepro Advantage (340 to 1080 megabytes)
Filepro Notebook (170 to 340 megabytes)
Filepro Performance (1,060 to 2,120 megabytes)

Tape Drives
DAT drives
Data cartridge drives
Minicartridge tape drives

Software
Backup Exec for NetWare
Backup Exec for Windows NT
Storage Exec
StorView

Storage Systems
CS disk and tape systems
Disk•Stor
HSM and Networker
MS tape systems
RAID (redundant arrays of inexpensive disks)
Tape•Stor

KEY COMPETITORS

Cambex	Micropolis
Cheyenne Software	MiniStor Peripherals
DEC	NEC
EMC	Quantum Corp.
Exabyte	Rexon
Fujitsu	Seagate
Hewlett-Packard	Storage Dimensions
Hitachi	Storage Technology
IBM	SyQuest
Iomega	Toshiba
Komag	Western Digital
Maxtor	

HOW MUCH

	Annual Growth	1985	1986	1987	1988	1989	1990	1991	1992	1993	1994
Sales ($ mil.)	54.4%	—	—	113	257	705	1,338	1,599	2,238	2,152	2,365
Net income ($ mil.)	38.9%	—	—	11	20	41	130	93	121	(445)	110
Income as % of sales	—	—	—	10.1%	7.7%	5.9%	9.7%	5.8%	5.4%	—	4.6%
Earnings per share ($)	22.4%	—	—	0.43	0.58	1.00	2.41	1.54	1.89	(9.03)	1.77
Stock price – high ($)	—	—	—	—	10.00	15.13	31.25	29.75	23.88	25.50	20.50
Stock price – low ($)	—	—	—	—	6.88	6.63	12.25	12.50	15.63	9.00	9.00
Stock price – close ($)	3.2%	—	—	—	7.88	13.13	23.63	15.75	20.75	14.63	9.50
P/E – high	—	—	—	—	17	15	13	19	13	—	12
P/E – low	—	—	—	—	12	7	5	8	8	—	5
Dividends per share ($)	—	—	—	—	0.00	0.00	0.00	0.00	0.00	0.00	0.00
Book value per share ($)	13.1%	—	—	—	3.07	5.04	10.64	12.27	12.96	4.13	6.42
Employees	23.5%	—	—	—	2,898	5,298	9,576	8,284	12,302	9,097	10,290

1994 Year-end:
Debt ratio: 66.3%
Return on equity: 40.2%
Cash (mil.): $443
Current ratio: 3.21
Long-term debt (mil.): $627
No. of shares (mil.): 52
Dividends
  Yield: —
  Payout: —
Market value (mil.): $498

Stock Price History High/Low 1988–94

CONRAIL INC.

OVERVIEW

Conrail Inc. is the holding company for Philadelphia-based Consolidated Rail Corp. (the successor to the bankrupt Penn Central railroad and 5 other failed railroads). Conrail is the dominant freight railroad in the heavily industrialized Northeast. Its 18,951 miles of track stretch from Massachusetts to Illinois, across the Northeast, Midwest, and Quebec, with connections to the rest of the US. The railroad does not provide passenger service; many of its competitors are trucking lines.

The company reorganized 2 departments in 1994 into 4 service groups to transport goods: CORE (petrochemicals, waste, food and agricultural products, metals, and forest products), Intermodal (truck-to-train), Unit Train (coal and ore), and Automotive Service (parts and finished autos).

Conrail dominates the Northeast, but physical growth potential appears limited because of the preponderance of that area's short hauls. The "Big X" long haul routes, from Chicago to New York and East St. Louis to Boston, are good moneymakers. A number of other railroads have coveted "Big X."

In late 1994 merger talks between Conrail and Norfolk Southern broke down. Apparently Norfolk would not pay as much as Conrail expected to receive for its stock. Instead of merging, Conrail would prefer to create additional alliances such as a venture launched with Norfolk Southern in 1993. The 2 rival railroads have a joint intermodal service in the East, giving Conrail access to the South.

WHEN

Conrail's earliest predecessor, the Mohawk & Hudson, opened a line between Albany and Schenectady, New York, in 1831. It merged with 9 other railroads to form the New York Central (NYC) in 1853. Cornelius Vanderbilt acquired NYC in 1867 and merged it with other railroads 2 years later. By 1914 the railroad stretched from New York to Chicago. President Alfred Perlman shifted the railroad's emphasis from passenger traffic to freight operations in the 1950s. He led the company to merge with the rival Pennsylvania Railroad ("the Pennsy") in 1968.

The Pennsy (chartered in 1846 to run from Harrisburg to Philadelphia) for many years led the industry in revenues and tonnage hauled and had an unequaled history of dividend payment until 1946. After WWII it was burdened by an overbuilt system and declining traffic. Pennsy chairman James Symes began planning a merger with NYC in 1957; the merger was completed 11 years later under his successor, Stuart Saunders. The new company was named Penn Central Transportation Company.

Penn Central, hurt by mismanagement and still-dwindling traffic, declared bankruptcy in 1970. After studying the chaotic state of the eastern rail system, in 1976 the US government created Conrail to assume the operations of Penn Central and 5 other failed railroads: Central of New Jersey, Erie Lackawanna, Lehigh & Hudson River, Lehigh Valley, and Reading (Penn Central survives as a diversified holding company). With federal financing of $2.1 billion, Conrail sold its intercity passenger operations to Amtrak and rebuilt its physical plant.

Conrail had lost $1.5 billion by 1981, when former Southern Railway chairman Stanley Crane became CEO. Crane, with the help of labor concessions and legislation, engineered a dramatic turnaround that culminated in a $472 million profit in 1984. In the largest stock offering up to that time in the US, the government sold its 85% stake in Conrail to the public for $1.59 billion in 1987; the other 15% went to the railroad's employees.

Conrail took its first step outside the railroad business in 1989 by forming a joint venture with OHM Corp. (Concord Resources Group) that disposes of solid and hazardous waste. That same year it formed a subsidiary to handle door-to-door intermodal deliveries (Conrail Mercury). In 1990 Conrail bought the remaining 2/3 of coal-hauling Monongahela Railway Company and sold its Pennsylvania Truck Lines subsidiary.

In 1993 Conrail handled 46% of the US Postal Service's rail traffic.

Severe winter weather and an increase in demand for hauling services in 1994 caused long delivery delays. Conrail also sold part of its joint venture, Concord Resources Group, that year and expected to sell the rest during 1995. To handle increased hauling demand and improve service, the company bought 136 new locomotives and hired more than 1,000 new train workers. In 1995 Conrail began contemplating selling or abandoning as much as 1/3 of its rail routes to boost profits.

NYSE symbol: CRR
Fiscal year ends: December 31

WHO

Chairman: James A. Hagen, age 62, $732,985 pay
President and CEO: David M. LeVan, age 49,
$342,708 pay (prior to promotion)
SVP Development: Charles N. Marshall, age 53,
$385,833 pay
SVP Finance and Administration: H. William Brown,
age 56, $294,150 pay
SVP Intermodal Service Group: Cynthia A. Archer,
age 41
SVP Operations: Ronald J. Conway, age 51
SVP Unit Train Service Group: Timothy P. Dwyer,
age 45
SVP CORE Service Group: John P. Sammon, age 44
SVP Law: Bruce B. Wilson, age 59
VP Resource Development (HR): Frank H. Nichols,
age 48
Auditors: Price Waterhouse LLP

WHERE

HQ: 2001 Market St., 2 Commerce Square, Philadelphia,
PA 19101-1417
Phone: 215-209-4000
Fax: 215-209-5567

Principal Cities Served

Albany, NY	Indianapolis, IN
Boston, MA	Lansing, MI
Buffalo, NY	Louisville, KY
Charleston, WV	Montreal, Quebec
Chicago, IL	New York, NY
Cincinnati, OH	Newark, NJ
Cleveland, OH	Peoria, IL
Columbus, OH	Philadelphia, PA
Detroit, MI	Pittsburgh, PA
Dover, DE	St. Louis, MO
Fort Wayne, IN	Syracuse, NY
Harrisburg, PA	Toledo, OH
Hartford, CT	Washington, DC

WHAT

	1994 Sales	
Service Groups	$ mil.	% of total
CORE		
Petrochemicals & waste	603	16
Food & agriculture	362	10
Forest and mfg. products	326	9
Metals	317	8
Intermodal Service Group	752	20
Unit Train Service Group	639	17
Automotive Service Group	565	15
Other	169	5
Total	**3,733**	**100**

Joint Ventures
Concord Resources Group (81%, hazardous waste
handling joint venture with OHM Corp.)
Triple Crown Services (intermodal joint venture with
Norfolk Southern)

KEY COMPETITORS

American Freightways	Ogden
American President	Roadway
Bechtel	Ryder
Browning-Ferris	Safety-Kleen
Canadian Pacific	Schneider National
Consolidated Freightways	Southern Pacific Rail
CSX	TNT Freightways
Heartland Express	TRW
Landstar Systems	Werner
Leaseway Transportation	WMX Technologies
MNX	Yellow Corp.
Norfolk Southern	

HOW MUCH

	Annual Growth	1985	1986	1987	1988	1989	1990	1991	1992	1993	1994
Sales ($ mil.)	1.7%	3,208	3,144	3,247	3,490	3,411	3,372	3,252	3,345	3,453	3,733
Net income ($ mil.)	(1.2%)	361	316	267	306	148	247	(207)	282	234	324
Income as % of sales	—	11.3%	10.1%	8.2%	8.8%	4.3%	7.3%	—	8.4%	6.8%	8.7%
Earnings per share ($)	2.8%	2.78	2.37	1.94	2.22	1.09	2.39	(2.70)	2.99	2.51	3.56
Stock price – high ($)	—	—	—	20.44	17.63	24.63	25.63	42.38	48.38	67.50	69.25
Stock price – low ($)	—	—	—	9.88	13.13	16.00	16.13	18.38	36.25	47.50	48.13
Stock price – close ($)	20.4%	—	—	13.75	16.88	23.88	20.13	42.25	47.50	66.88	50.50
P/E – high	—	—	—	11	8	23	11	—	16	27	19
P/E – low	—	—	—	5	6	15	7	—	12	19	14
Dividends per share ($)	29.2%	—	—	0.25	0.55	0.65	0.75	0.85	1.00	1.20	1.50
Book value per share ($)	3.1%	—	—	27.85	29.76	30.12	32.49	28.90	30.86	31.39	34.39
Employees	(4.1%)	36,332	35,000	33,500	32,600	31,574	27,787	25,852	25,380	25,406	24,833

1994 Year-end:
Debt ratio: 45.2%
Return on equity: 12.6%
Cash (mil.): $43
Current ratio: 0.94
Long-term debt (mil.): $1,940
No. of shares (mil.): 77
Dividends
  Yield: 3.0%
  Payout: 42.1%
Market value (mil.): $3,880

Stock Price History
High/Low 1987–94

CONSOLIDATED EDISON OF NEW YORK

OVERVIEW

Consolidated Edision (Con Ed) is one of the largest publicly owned gas and electric utilities in the US. Headquartered in New York City, the company provides electric power to more than 8 million people in a service area covering most of that city (except for parts of Queens) and most of Westchester County. Con Ed also supplies gas in Manhattan, the Bronx, and parts of Queens and Westchester and steam in part of Manhattan. It sells electricity to government customers through the New York Power Authority.

With deregulation of the electric and gas industries creating increased competition, Con Ed has concentrated on increasing efficiency. In the last decade it has cut employment by about 20%. It is also adding more value-added services and expanding its gas marketing and power purchasing programs.

Con Ed continues to shift the mix of its fuel sources away from oil toward natural gas and other sources. In 1994 oil produced 9% of the company's electricity, down from over 70% in the mid-1970s.

WHEN

A group of New York professionals, led by Timothy Dewey, founded the New York Gas Light Company in 1823 to provide utility service to a limited area of Manhattan. Various companies served other areas of New York City, and, in 1884, 5 of these joined with New York Gas Light to form the Consolidated Gas Company of New York.

This unification occurred on the heels of the introduction of Thomas Edison's incandescent lamp (1879). The Edison Electric Illuminating Company of New York was formed in 1880 to build the world's first commercial electric power station, financed by a group led by J. P. Morgan. Edison supervised this project, known as the Pearl Street Station, and in 1882 New York became the first major city to experience electric lighting.

Realizing that electric lighting would most certainly replace gas, Consolidated Gas began buying New York's electric companies, including Anthony Brady's New York Gas and Electric Light, Heat and Power Company (1900), which consolidated with Edison's Illuminating Company in 1901 to form the New York Edison Company. More than 170 other purchases followed, including that of the New York Steam Company in 1930 to provide a cheap source of steam for the company's electric turbines. In 1936 these utilities combined to form the Consolidated Edison Company of New York.

In 1962 Con Ed opened its first nuclear station at Indian Point. Environmentalists worried that Con Ed's proposed Cornwall pumped-storage plant at the foot of Storm King Mountain would damage the local ecosystem, and they managed to delay construction throughout the 1960s and early 1970s. A federal court ordered Con Ed to cease construction of the plant in 1974. In the meantime Con Ed had had trouble supplying enough power to meet demand. Inflation and the OPEC oil embargo had driven up the price of oil (Con Ed's main energy source), and in 1974 the company skipped a dividend for the first time since 1885. The New York State Power Authority bought 2 of Con Ed's unfinished power plants, saving the company about $200 million.

Con Ed started buying power from various suppliers and in 1984 agreed to a 2-year rate freeze, a boon to New Yorkers, whose electric bills were nearly twice as high as those of most other big-city residents. In 1992 Con Ed formed a partnership with several other companies to build a 47-mile natural gas pipeline from New Jersey to Kennedy International Airport. Also in 1992 the New York State Public Service Commission approved a 3-year, 4.5% rate increase, the first since 1983.

In 1993 Indeck Energy Services, a cogeneration facility operator, filed a breach-of-contract suit against Con Ed after Con Ed refused to buy electricity from a plant being built on a site it had not approved.

Con Ed canceled a long-term power purchase contract with Montreal-based Hydro-Quebec in 1994 after Hydro-Quebec came under fire from environmentalists (and Con Ed drew heat from its shareholders).

In 1995 the Public Service Commission (PSC) refused Con Ed's request for a $429 million electricity rate increase. In a deal struck with the PSC, however, the company will be allowed to defer differences between actual and projected amounts of certain expenses. Also in 1995 Con Ed was fined $2 million and given 3 years of probation after pleading guilty to concealing the fact that a 1989 manhole explosion had released more than 200 pounds of asbestos into a New York residential neighborhood.

NYSE symbol: ED
Fiscal year ends: December 31

WHO

Chairman, President, and CEO: Eugene R. McGrath,
age 53, $839,066 pay
EVP and CFO: Raymond J. McCann, age 60,
$480,776 pay
EVP Customer Service: Charles F. Soutar, age 58,
$391,333 pay
EVP Central Operations: J. Michael Evans, age 49,
$365,666 pay
SVP: Stephen B. Bram, age 52, $316,333 pay
SVP Gas Operations: Mary Jane McCartney, age 46
SVP Financial and Regulatory Matters: Carl W. Greene,
age 59
SVP Public Affairs: Horace S. Webb, age 54
SVP and General Counsel: T. Bowring Woodbury II,
age 57
SVP Central Services (Personnel): Thomas J. Galvin,
age 56
Auditors: Price Waterhouse LLP

WHERE

HQ: Consolidated Edison Company of New York, Inc.,
4 Irving Place, New York, NY 10003
Phone: 212-460-4600
Fax: 212-982-7816

Generating Facilities

Electric – Fossil Fueled
59th Street Station
74th Street Station
Arthur Kill (Staten Island)
Astoria (Queens)
Bowline Point (Orange County, 66.3%)
East River (Manhattan)
Hudson Avenue (Brooklyn)
Ravenswood (Queens)
Roseton (Newburgh, 40%)
Waterside (Manhattan)

Electric – Gas Turbines Gowanus (Brooklyn)
Indian Point (Buchanan)
Narrows (Brooklyn)

Electric – Nuclear
Indian Point (Buchanan)

Steam
59th Street Station
74th Street Station
Hudson Avenue (Brooklyn)
Ravenswood (Queens)

WHAT

	1994 Electricity Sales	
	$ mil.	% of total
Commercial & industrial	3,111	61
Residential	1,680	33
Public authorities	57	1
Sales to other utilities	49	1
Railroads	5	—
Delivery to NY Power Authority	238	4
Total	**5,140**	**100**

	1994 Sales		1994 Operating Income	
	$ mil.	% of total	$ mil.	% of total
Electric	5,140	81	881	85
Gas	890	14	117	11
Steam	343	5	38	4
Total	**6,373**	**100**	**1,036**	**100**

	1994 Fuel Sources
	% of total
Natural gas	34
Nuclear	19
Oil	9
Hydroelectric	5
Refuse	1
Purchased power	32
Total	**100**

HOW MUCH

	9-Year Growth	1985	1986	1987	1988	1989	1990	1991	1992	1993	1994
Sales ($ mil.)	1.7%	5,498	5,198	5,094	5,109	5,551	5,739	5,873	5,933	6,265	6,373
Net income ($ mil.)	3.2%	525	508	512	562	569	534	530	568	623	699
Income as % of sales	—	9.6%	9.8%	10.1%	11.0%	10.2%	9.3%	9.0%	9.6%	9.9%	11.0%
Earnings per share ($)	3.8%	2.13	2.13	2.21	2.47	2.49	2.34	2.32	2.46	2.66	2.98
Stock price – high ($)	—	19.81	26.44	26.00	23.75	29.88	29.25	28.75	32.88	37.75	32.38
Stock price – low ($)	—	14.69	18.81	18.75	20.44	22.19	19.75	22.50	25.00	30.25	23.00
Stock price – close ($)	3.0%	19.75	23.56	20.88	23.25	29.13	23.63	28.63	32.63	32.13	25.75
P/E – high	—	9	12	12	10	12	13	12	13	14	11
P/E – low	—	7	9	8	8	9	8	10	10	11	8
Dividends per share ($)	5.8%	1.20	1.34	1.48	1.60	1.72	1.82	1.86	1.90	1.94	2.00
Book value per share ($)	3.7%	16.35	17.03	17.59	18.44	19.21	19.73	20.18	20.89	21.63	22.62
Employees	(2.3%)	21,076	20,698	20,260	20,108	19,798	19,483	19,087	18,718	17,586	17,097

1994 Year-end:
Debt ratio: 43.5%
Return on equity: 13.5%
Cash (mil.): $245
Current ratio: 1.31
Long-term debt (mil.): $4,078
No. of shares (mil.): 235
Dividends
  Yield: 7.8%
  Payout: 67.1%
Market value (mil.): $6,049

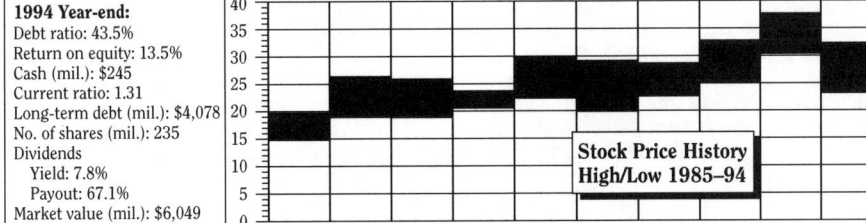

Stock Price History
High/Low 1985–94

CONSOLIDATED FREIGHTWAYS, INC.

OVERVIEW

Palo Alto–based Consolidated Freightways (CF) is a diversified freight and package delivery company with operations in North America and 89 countries elsewhere.

CF's long-haul trucking division (CF MotorFreight) is one of the nation's largest and specializes in less-than-truckload shipments (LTL, less than 10,000 pounds). It also provides international service to countries throughout the world. Con-Way Transportation Services is a regional trucking and full-service truck-loading company that offers overnight and 2nd-day delivery to 75,000 communities in the US, Puerto Rico, Mexico and parts of Canada. Con-Way's intermodal operations (in which freight is shipped by truck, train, or ship in the same container) serves ports in the US and throughout the world. The popularity of Con-Way's less-regulated regional carriers has increased while the unionized CF MotorFreight suffers.

CF's Emery Worldwide carries airfreight to 89 countries with 538 locations. One of Emery's divisions is the #1 US heavy-freight air carrier. Emery has a 10-year contract with the US Postal Service (for $880 million) to carry priority mail. Emery Worldwide's profits quadrupled for 1994.

CF also does contract logistics, customs brokerage, equipment supply, and trailer manufacturing. Logistics clients include AT&T, Coca-Cola, Hewlett-Packard, and Sears.

WHEN

Leland James, co-owner of a Portland, Oregon, bus company, founded Consolidated Truck Lines in 1929. The company offered heavy hauling, moving, and other transportation services in the Pacific Northwest. Operations extended to San Francisco and Idaho by 1934 and to North Dakota by 1936. The company adopted its present name in 1939.

James formed Freightways Manufacturing that year, making CF the only trucking company to design and build its own trucks (Freightliners). Between 1940 and 1950 CF used acquisitions to extend service to Chicago, Minneapolis, and Los Angeles.

CF went public in 1951 and moved to Menlo Park, California, in 1956. More acquisitions (52 between 1955 and 1960) extended operations throughout the US and Canada. When an attempt to coordinate intermodal services with railroads and shipping lines failed, contributing to a loss of $2.7 million in 1960, William White (formerly of the Delaware Lackawanna and Western Railroad) became president. White terminated intermodal operations and decided to focus trucking operations on LTL shipments.

In 1969 CF bought Pacific Far East Lines, a San Francisco shipping line. (This company is now a part of Con-Way Truckload Services, which serves Europe, Australia, and the Pacific Rim.) In 1970 CF formed CF AirFreight to offer air cargo services in the US and Canada. CF used the proceeds from the 1981 sale of Freightways Manufacturing to establish regional trucking operations called Con-Way Transportation Services (1983).

In 1989 the company bought Emery Air Freight, an international air cargo service that now is known as Emery Worldwide. Founded in 1946, Emery Air Freight expanded across the US (and overseas, 1956) by using extra cargo space on scheduled airline flights. The company chartered aircraft in the early 1970s and bought its first plane in 1979. Emery established hubs at Dayton, Ohio (1981), and Maastricht, Holland (1985). After buying Purolator Courier in 1987, Emery had trouble combining the companies. It was further plagued by a 1988 takeover attempt by former Federal Express president Arthur Bass, which resulted in losses of almost $100 million.

CF appointed Bass as Emery's president in 1990, hoping he could turn it around, and financial wizard Donald Moffitt came out of retirement to become CEO. But early in 1991, as Emery's losses dragged CF into red ink, Bass resigned.

In 1993 the company invested $201 million for vehicle and technology improvements and achieved its first net income ($32 million) in 4 years. CF MotorFreight, the long-haul division, decreased expenses by closing 100 terminals during 1992–93.

In 1994 CF MotorFreight suffered its longest strike (18 working days) in history; it reported an operating loss of almost $47 million for the year, most of it related to the Teamster strike. That year CF formed an eastern Europe division to serve the Baltics, the Czech Republic, Hungary, Russia, and Slovakia.

In 1995 Emery won a 4-year extension on its logistics contract with GM's North American operations and a 2-year extension of shipping services for Philips Electronics.

NYSE symbol: CNF
Fiscal year ends: December 31

WHO

Chairman, President, and CEO: Donald E. Moffitt, age 62, $1,179,586 pay
EVP and CFO: Gregory L. Quesnel, age 46, $577,579 pay
SVP; President and CEO, CF MotorFreight: W. Roger Curry, age 56, $783,684 pay
SVP; President and CEO, Con-Way Transportation Services: Robert T. Robertson, age 53, $721,793 pay
SVP; President and CEO, Emery Worldwide: David I. Beatson, age 47
SVP and General Counsel: Eberhard G. H. Schmoller, age 51, $445,968 pay
VP PR and Advertising: James R. Allen
VP Administrative Services (HR): Ronald L. Axon
VP Investor Relations and Corporate Secretary: Maryla R. Boonstoppel
VP Information Systems: Maurice W. Johnson
VP and Treasurer: David F. Morrison
VP Corporate and Government Relations: Henry A. Schmitt
VP and Controller: Gary D. Taliaferro
VP Tax: Howard A. Young
Auditors: Arthur Andersen & Co, SC

WHERE

HQ: 3240 Hillview Ave., Palo Alto, CA 94304
Phone: 415-494-2900
Fax: 415-813-0158

CF has operations in North America and Puerto Rico and in 89 countries elsewhere.

	1994 Sales		1994 Operating Income	
	$ mil.	% of total	$ mil.	% of total
US	3,981	85	115	81
Other countries	699	15	27	19
Total	**4,680**	**100**	**142**	**100**

WHAT

	1994 Sales		1994 Operating Income	
	$ mil.	% of total	$ mil.	% of total
CF MotorFreight	2,094	45	(47)	—
Emery Worldwide	1,568	33	78	41
Con-Way Trans.	1,018	22	111	59
Total	**4,680**	**100**	**142**	**100**

CF, Inc.
Menlo Logistics
Road Systems, Inc. (trailer manufacturer)
Willamette Sales Co. (equipment distributor)

CF MotorFreight
Canadian Freightways
Milne & Craighead Customs Brokers

Con-Way Transportation Services, Inc.
Con-Way Central Express, Inc.
Con-Way Southern Express, Inc.
Con-Way Truckload Services
Con-Way Western Express, Inc.

Emery Worldwide
Emery Customs Brokers
Emery Worldwide Airlines, Inc.
Logistics Worldwide

KEY COMPETITORS

Airborne Freight	Harper Group
American Freightways	J.B. Hunt
American President	Leaseway Transportation
AMR	Lufthansa
Arkansas Best	McGraw-Hill
Burlington Northern	Norfolk Southern
Carolina Freight	Pittston Services
C.H. Robinson	Roadway
Conrail	Southern Pacific Rail
CSX	Union Pacific
DHL Worldwide Express	UPS
FedEx	Yellow Corp.

HOW MUCH

	9-Year Growth	1985	1986	1987	1988	1989	1990	1991	1992	1993	1994
Sales ($ mil.)	10.7%	1,882	2,125	2,297	2,689	3,760	4,209	4,082	4,056	4,192	4,680
Net income ($ mil.)	(8.5%)	79	89	75	113	23	(41)	(53)	(28)	32	36
Income as % of sales	—	4.2%	4.2%	3.2%	4.2%	0.6%	—	—	—	0.8%	0.8%
Earnings per share ($)	(9.2%)	2.07	2.31	1.93	3.00	0.02	(1.16)	(1.52)	(0.58)	0.77	0.87
Stock price – high ($)	—	27.50	36.50	41.25	34.75	37.75	26.88	21.50	19.63	24.00	29.25
Stock price – low ($)	—	18.69	23.69	22.75	25.25	25.25	10.75	9.50	12.50	13.63	17.88
Stock price – close ($)	(1.9%)	26.50	30.00	27.50	33.00	26.50	11.75	15.38	17.63	23.63	22.38
P/E – high	—	13	16	21	12	—	—	—	—	31	34
P/E – low	—	9	10	12	8	—	—	—	—	18	21
Dividends per share ($)	(19.7%)	0.72	0.80	0.88	0.96	1.04	0.53	0.00	0.00	0.00	0.10
Book value per share ($)	(0.8%)	15.69	17.22	18.16	20.32	14.72	13.49	15.30	12.64	13.65	14.58
Employees	7.2%	21,700	24,600	26,300	29,400	40,800	41,300	37,700	37,900	39,100	40,500

1994 Year-end:
Debt ratio: 37.3%
Return on equity: 8.4%
Cash (mil.): $96
Current ratio: 1.09
Long-term debt (mil.): $398
No. of shares (mil.): 36
Dividends
  Yield: 0.4%
  Payout: 11.5%
Market value (mil.): $813

**Stock Price History
High/Low 1985–94**

CONTINENTAL AIRLINES, INC.

OVERVIEW

Good idea, bad result. Continental's bold move to compete with low-cost, no-frills carriers like Southwest, through its CALite short-haul (flights of 2 hours or less) carrier, spun out of control last year. Far from making money, the carrier ran up a 1994 loss of $166.5 million on its CALite service. Continental decided to pull out of the short-haul business in 1995.

CEO Gordon Bethune's other strategies aimed at cutting costs and improving productivity have proved more successful. Continental and its affiliates, which serve over 100 cities in the US and 54 in Asia, Australia, Europe, and Latin America, have been clipping the wings of underperforming flights; the company cut its Munich route in 1994. Con-

centrating on its strengths, the firm expanded its services on core routes in Europe, Micronesia, and Latin America. The airline now offers 164 flights per week to Mexico (and 10 destinations) and 71 weekly flights to Central and South America, more service than any other US carrier. Continental also has a code-sharing deal with Alitalia.

Continental's majority owners include Air Canada (18.7%) and Air Partners (24.8%), a limited partnership, led by Texan David Bonderman, that also has a stake in America West.

Bethune received a bonus of $1.5 million in 1994 as part of a deal to keep him with the carrier after rival United tried to recruit him.

WHEN

Houston-based Trans Texas Airways began serving Texas communities in 1947. It became Texas International in 1968 and served the West Coast and Mexico by 1970. However, the company was unable to compete with major airlines on interstate routes or with commuter airlines in Texas and faced bankruptcy in 1972, when Frank Lorenzo's Jet Capital Corporation gained control. With Lorenzo at the helm, Texas International had netted over $3 million by 1976. In 1980 Lorenzo formed Texas Air, a holding company for Texas International and a newly created New York–Washington, DC, shuttle, New York Air.

In 1981 Texas Air bought 50% of Continental Airlines (founded as Varney Speed Lines in 1934), which operated in the western US, Mexico, and the Pacific. Continental's employees tried to block the takeover, but Texas Air bought the rest of the company in 1982. Continental had lost over $500 million between 1978 and 1983. In 1983, when Lorenzo's efforts to wrest wage concessions from the airline's unions resulted in a strike, Lorenzo maneuvered the airline into Chapter 11, abrogating union contracts. Continental emerged from bankruptcy in 1986 as a nonunion, low-fare carrier with the industry's lowest labor costs.

That year Texas Air bought Eastern Air Lines (founded as Pitcairn Aviation in 1927). WWI ace Eddie Rickenbacker had run Eastern from 1935 until his retirement in 1963. Losses and union disputes in the 1960s and 1970s forced Eastern's CEO, Frank Borman (a former astronaut), to sell in 1986. That year Texas Air also bought People Express Airlines and Frontier Airlines.

In 1988 Lorenzo sold Eastern's Air Shuttle to Donald Trump, but in 1989 mounting losses and a machinists' strike forced Eastern into bankruptcy. In 1990 the bankruptcy court removed Texas Air from Eastern's management, appointing Martin Shugrue as trustee. Texas Air then changed its name to Continental Airlines Holdings. Lorenzo resigned as chairman, president, and CEO after selling his stake in the company to SAS for a substantial premium plus $19.7 million in salary and severance pay. After Lorenzo's resignation, Hollis Harris, former president of Delta Air Lines, was named CEO.

With fuel prices up and traffic down, Continental followed Eastern into bankruptcy late in 1990. Eastern held on until January 1991, when increasing losses forced it to liquidate. Harris, who opposed new cost-cutting efforts, left Continental in 1991 and was replaced by former CFO Robert Ferguson. In 1991 Continental sold its Seattle–Tokyo route to AMR for $145 million.

Out of bankruptcy in 1993, Continental began pursuing the ill-fated strategy of muscling into the short-haul market, with a high level of employee cooperation that would have been unthinkable in earlier years.

Bethune was appointed CEO in late 1994, replacing Ferguson, the chief proponent of the ill-starred CALite strategy. In 1995 Bethune managed to secure a deal with Boeing whereby the airplane maker agreed to defer delivery of 24 jets in 1995 and 1996 (for a savings of $200 million). Continental also persuaded General Electric, its primary lender, to defer principal payments in 1995 and 1996, saving an additional $140 million.

NYSE symbol: CAIB
Fiscal year ends: December 31

WHO

Chairman: David Bonderman, age 52
President and CEO: Gordon M. Bethune, age 53,
$2,221,154 pay
COO: Gregory D. Brenneman, age 33
SVP Strategic Business Units: Daniel P. Garton, age 38,
$349,992 pay
SVP and CFO: Lawrence W. Kellner, age 36
SVP, General Counsel, and Secretary: Jeffery A. Smisek,
age 40
SVP Operations: C. D. McLean, age 54
SVP European Operations: Barry P. Simon, age 52
SVP Airport Services: Mark A. Erwin, age 39
SVP Inflight Service: D. Sam Coats, age 54
SVP Human Resources: David A. Loeser, age 40
President and CEO, Continental Micronesia: Donald J.
Breeding, age 60
President and CEO, Continental Express: Jonathan
Ornstein, age 37
President, System One: William S. Diffenderffer, age 44
VP Reservations: Larry D. Goodwin
VP Marketing and Sales: Bonnie Reitz
VP Route Planning and Scheduling: David N. Siegel
Auditors: Ernst & Young LLP

WHERE

HQ: 2929 Allen Pkwy., Houston, TX 77019
Phone: 713-834-5000
Fax: 713-834-2087
Reservations: 800-525-0280

Continental flies to more than 100 cities in the US and
to 60 destinations in Asia, Australia, Europe, and Latin
America.

Hub Locations
Cleveland
Houston
Newark

WHAT

	1994 Sales	
	$ mil.	% of total
Passenger	5,036	89
Cargo, mail & other	634	11
Total	**5,670**	**100**

Major Affiliate
Continental Micronesia, Inc. (91%, air service in the
Pacific)

	Aircraft	
	Owned	Leased
A300	2	19
Boeing 727	1	64
Boeing 737	32	79
Boeing 747	—	5
Boeing 757	—	11
DC-9	3	28
DC-10	—	19
MD-80	10	57
Total	**48**	**282**

KEY COMPETITORS

Air France
Alaska Air
All Nippon Airways
America West
AMR
British Airways
Delta
Galileo International
IRI
JAL
Kimberly-Clark
Kiwi Air
KLM
Lufthansa
Northwest Airlines
Ogden
SAS
Singapore Airlines
Southwest Airlines
Swire Pacific
TWA
UAL
USAir Group
ValuJet Airlines
Virgin Group

HOW MUCH

	Annual Growth	1985	1986	1987	1988	1989	1990	1991	1992	1993	1994
Sales ($ mil.)	12.6%	1,944	4,407	8,626	8,552	6,650	6,184	5,487	5,494	5,775	5,670
Net income ($ mil.)	—	49	42	(466)	(719)	(908)	(2,403)	(306)	(125)	(1,017)	(619)
Income as % of sales	—	2.5%	1.0%	—	—	—	—	—	—	—	—
Earnings per share ($)	—	—	—	—	—	—	—	—	—	(23.15)	(23.76)
Stock price – high ($)	—	—	—	—	—	—	—	—	—	30.50	27.25
Stock price – low ($)	—	—	—	—	—	—	—	—	—	13.00	7.50
Stock price – close ($)	(54.9%)	—	—	—	—	—	—	—	—	20.50	9.25
P/E – high	—	—	—	—	—	—	—	—	—	—	—
P/E – low	—	—	—	—	—	—	—	—	—	—	—
Dividends per share ($)	—	—	—	—	—	—	—	—	—	0.00	0.00
Book value per share ($)	(86.2%)	—	—	—	—	—	—	—	—	28.23	3.89
Employees	1.0%	—	—	—	35,649	31,400	34,800	36,300	38,300	43,100	37,800

1994 Year-end:
Debt ratio: 94.1%
Return on equity: —
Cash (mil.): $396
Current ratio: 0.41
Long-term debt (mil.): $1,038
No. of shares (mil.): 27
Dividends
  Yield: —
  Payout: —
Market value (mil.): $247

Stock Price History
High/Low 1993–94

CONTINENTAL GRAIN COMPANY

OVERVIEW

One of the world's largest commodities traders and one of the US's biggest private companies, New York City–based Continental Grain racks up about $14 billion in annual sales of grain, cotton, chickens, pigs, and petroleum, among other things. Continental operates in more than 50 countries and is involved in feeding cattle and in milling, brokering, and shipping commodities as well as in financial services. The company's sales have held fairly steady for many years, leaving Continental to squeeze any profits from the same annual revenues derived from low-margin operations.

Continental continues to invest in ventures in China. In 1995 the company announced that it would control 52% of a $60 million venture with Shanghai Petrochemical (China's largest oil company) for the construction and operation of a facility in Shanghai to import and market liquid petroleum gas. When the plant begins operations in 1997, it will be the first of its kind in east China. Meanwhile, Continental controls 40% of a plastic packaging manufacturing plant in China in partnership with Huntsman Chemical.

Eighty-one-year-old chairman emeritus Michel Fribourg (the great-great-grandson of Continental's founder) and his family own the company as well as a stake in Overseas Ship Holding Group, the biggest independent owner and operator of tankers and commodity vessels in the US.

WHEN

In 1813 Simon Fribourg founded a commodity trading business in Belgium. The company operated primarily as a domestic concern until 1848, when a severe drought in Belgium caused the company to buy large stocks in Russian wheat.

As the Industrial Revolution swept across Europe and populations shifted toward the cities, people began consuming more traded grain. In the midst of such rapid changes, the company prospered.

After WWI, Russia, which had been Europe's primary grain supplier, ceased to be a major player in the trading game, and Western Hemisphere countries picked up the slack. Sensing the shift, Jules and René Fribourg reorganized the business as Continental Grain and opened the company's first US office in Chicago in 1921. Seven years later Continental leased a grain elevator in St. Louis (during the Depression the company bought US grain elevators wherever they could find them, often at low prices). In 1930 Continental leased a Galveston terminal from the Southern Pacific Railroad. Through its rapid purchases, the company built an elaborate North American grain network that included such important locations as Kansas City, Nashville, and Toledo.

Meanwhile, in Europe the Fribourgs were forced to weather constant political and economic upheaval, often profiting from it (the Fribourgs supplied food to the Republican forces during the Spanish Civil War). When the Nazis invaded Belgium in 1940, the Fribourgs were forced to flee but reorganized the business in New York City after the war.

During the postwar years, Continental conducted a lucrative grain trade with the Soviets and expanded its international presence. During the 1960s and 1970s, the company went on a buying spree, acquiring Allied Mills (feed milling, 1965) and absorbing several agricultural and transport businesses, including feedlots in Texas, an English soybean producer (sold in 1986), a bakery, and Quaker Oats's agricultural products unit.

During the 1980s the company slimmed down by selling its baking units (Oroweat and Arnold) as well as its commodities brokerage house. Michel Fribourg stepped down as CEO in 1988. Donald Staheli, the first nonfamily member to hold the position, succeeded him. Soon after, Continental realigned its international grain and oilseeds operations into the World Grain and Oilseeds Processing Group under the leadership of Michel's son Paul.

Continental in 1991 agreed with Scoular to enter a grain-handling and -merchandising joint venture. In 1992 Continental and Tosco formed a short-lived company to trade Russian oil. Because Continental uses futures contracts, it was well insulated from price swings caused by Mississippi River basin flooding in 1993. Continental ran into opposition to several proposed Missouri pork-producing plants in 1994. Local citizens, holding signs that read "Continental Grain, Go Home," were wary of land and air pollution and depressed land values.

In 1994 the company named CEO Staheli as chairman and Paul Fribourg, widely seen as the next head of the company, as president and COO. The next year Staheli succeeded Michel Fribourg as chairman of the company's executive committee. Also in 1995 Continental merged its ContiMilling division into its ContiLatin trading unit.

Private company
Fiscal year ends: March 31

WHO

Chairman Emeritus: Michel Fribourg, age 81
Chairman and CEO: Donald L. Staheli, age 63
President and COO: Paul J. Fribourg. age 41
President, Commodity Marketing, The Americas: Vart Adjemian
President, Commodity Marketing, Europe and Far East: Poul Schroeder
President, Milling Group: Dale F. Larson
President, ContiFinancial: James E. Moore
EVP and CFO: James J. Bigham
SVP and Merchandising Manager: John Laesch
SVP: Bernard Steinweg
VP and General Counsel: Lawrence G. Weppler
VP and General Counsel, Commodity Marketing: David G. Friedman
VP Public Affairs: Daryl Natz
VP Human Resources: Dwight Coffin

WHERE

HQ: 277 Park Ave., New York, NY 10172-0002
Phone: 212-207-5100
Fax: 212-207-5181

Continental Grain has offices and facilities in more than 50 countries.

WHAT

Commodity Marketing Group
Astral International Shipping (shipping agents, New Orleans)
ContiCarriers & Terminals (transport, Chicago)
ContiChem (liquefied petroleum gases; Stamford, Connecticut)
ContiCotton (cotton merchandising, Memphis)
ContiLatin (Latin American trading unit, New York)
Continental Grain (Canada)
ContiQuincy Export (soybean merchandising partnership with Quincy Soybean, New York)
Finagrain (European trading unit, Geneva)
North American Grain Division (Chicago)
Rice Division (rice trading, New York)
Stellar Chartering and Brokerage (ocean vessels, Chicago)
World Grain and Oilseeds Merchandising (Chicago)

ContiFinancial
ContiFinancial Services (New York)
ContiMortgage Corp. (Horsham, Pennsylvania)
ContiTrade Services (New York)

Meat Group
Cattle Feeding Division (Chicago)
Dutch Quality House (poultry; Gainesville, GA)
Poultry Division (Atlanta)
Swine Marketing Services Division (Chicago)

Milling Group
Asian Agri Industries (Hong Kong)
Wayne Feed Division (Chicago)

KEY COMPETITORS

ADM
Ag Processing
Agway
BeefAmerica
Cargill
CENEX
Central Soya
ConAgra
Connell Co.
Countrymark Co-op
Farmland Industries
Gold Kist
Harvest States Co-ops
Hudson Foods
IBP
International Multifoods
Keystone Foods
Moorman Manufacturing
Perdue
Pilgrim's Pride
Pioneer Hi-Bred
Ralston Purina Group
Schreiber Foods
Scoular
Seaboard Corp.
Smithfield Foods
Tyson Foods

HOW MUCH

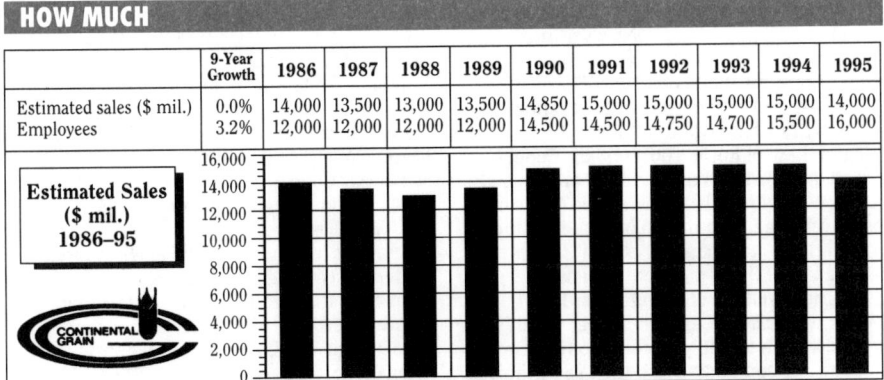

	9-Year Growth	1986	1987	1988	1989	1990	1991	1992	1993	1994	1995
Estimated sales ($ mil.)	0.0%	14,000	13,500	13,000	13,500	14,850	15,000	15,000	15,000	15,000	14,000
Employees	3.2%	12,000	12,000	12,000	12,000	14,500	14,500	14,750	14,700	15,500	16,000

Estimated Sales ($ mil.) 1986–95

16,000
14,000
12,000
10,000
8,000
6,000
4,000
2,000
0

COOPER INDUSTRIES, INC.

OVERVIEW

A corporate tune-up — including the spin-off of Cooper Cameron, its sputtering petroleum equipment segment — has Cooper Industries running smoothly again. The giant manufacturer had suffered from slowdowns in the construction and energy industries, and in 1994 a $313 million write-off for the Cooper Cameron deal negatively affected net income.

Cooper has realigned its numerous subsidiaries into 3 business segments. Its Automotive Products division includes name-brand manufacturers Anco and Champion. In late 1994 Cooper added Abex Friction Products (brake materials) and Zanxx (lighting components) to its auto parts makers.

Cooper's Electrical Products segment includes Buss (fuses) and Halo (lighting fixtures). Its Tools and Hardware unit includes Crescent (wrenches), Kirsch (drapery hardware), and Diamond (pliers and wrenches).

With construction and industrial production both up in early 1995, Cooper's Electrical Products and Tools and Hardware segments showed revenue increases. Auto segment sales were helped by recent acquisitions.

Cooper Cameron, which had accounted for about 1/4 of its parent's revenues, was spun off in early 1995. That spring it won a $72 million Shell Oil contract for North Sea wellhead and production equipment. In mid-1995 Cooper Cameron became an independent company.

A struggle between Cooper and the United Steelworkers continued in 1995 despite a National Labor Relations Board decision ordering Cooper to recognize the union as a bargaining agent for employees at a Pennsylvania plant.

WHEN

In 1833 Charles Cooper sold a horse for $50 and borrowed additional money to open a foundry with his brother Elias in Mount Vernon, Ohio. Known as C. & E. Cooper, the company made plows, hog troughs, maple syrup kettles, stoves, and wagon boxes.

In the 1840s Cooper began making steam engines for use in mills and on farms; it later adapted the engines for wood-burning locomotives. In 1868 the company built its first Corliss steam engine and in 1875 introduced the first steam-powered farm tractor. By 1900 Cooper's steam engines were sold in the US and overseas. In 1909 Cooper introduced an internal combustion engine-compressor for natural-gas pipelines.

In the 1920s Cooper became the biggest seller of compression engines for oil and gas pipeline transmission. A 1929 merger with Bessemer (small gas and diesel engines) created Cooper-Bessemer, whose diesel engines powered marine vessels. Cooper was hurt badly by the Depression; sales fell 90% in 1931. The success of a new turbocharged diesel to power locomotives revived revenues.

Diversification began in the late 1950s with the purchase of Rotor Tools (1959). Cooper adopted its current name in 1965 and moved its headquarters to Houston in 1967. The company went on to acquire 20 other companies, including its "tool basket": Lufkin Rule (measuring tapes, 1967), Crescent (wrenches, 1968), and Weller (soldering tools, 1970).

The purchase of Gardner-Denver in 1979 gave Cooper a strong position in oil-drilling and mining equipment, and the 1981 acquisi-

tion of Crouse-Hinds was a significant diversification into electrical materials. Another 1981 purchase was Kirsch (drapery hardware). The decline in oil prices in the early 1980s caused sales to drop more than 35% between 1981 and 1983, but Cooper remained profitable because of its tools and electrical products.

The electrical segment expanded further with the 1985 purchase of McGraw-Edison, maker of both consumer products (Buss fuses) and heavy transmission gear for electrical utilities. Cooper bought RTE (electrical equipment, 1988), Cameron Iron Works (oil-drilling equipment, 1989), and Ferramentas Belzer do Brasil (hand-tool maker, 1992).

Expanding into automotive parts, Cooper bought Champion Spark Plug (1989) and Moog (auto replacement parts, 1992).

Tough times have forced Cooper to shake out nonessential or underperforming product lines. From 1991 to 1993 the company completed 11 divestitures, using the proceeds to help finance acquisitions of 13 complementary lines and streamline manufacturing.

In 1993 Cooper sold Belden Inc. (electrical wires and cables) through a public offering, keeping a 9.6% share in the company. That same year Cooper made 5 product-line acquisitions, which included Hawker Fusegear of the UK (electrical fuses), Triangle Tool Group (nonpower hand tools), and Fail-Safe Lighting Systems (security lighting).

In 1994 the company spun off Gardner-Denver Industrial Machinery to Cooper shareholders and sold Cameron Forged Products to Wyman-Gordon.

WHO

Chairman and CEO: Robert Cizik, age 64, $895,000 pay
President and COO: H. John Riley Jr., age 54, $487,500 pay
EVP Operations: Michael J. Sebastian, age 64, $377,500 pay
EVP Operations: Ralph E. Jackson Jr., age 53, $285,938 pay
EVP Operations: Larry W. McCurdy, age 59, $275,000 pay
SVP Finance and CFO: D. Bradley McWilliams, age 53
SVP, General Counsel, and Secretary: Diane K. Schumacher, age 41
SVP Human Resources: Carl J. Plesnicher Jr., age 57
Auditors: Ernst & Young LLP

WHERE

HQ: First City Tower, Ste. 4000, Houston, TX 77002
Phone: 713-739-5400
Fax: 713-739-5555

Cooper manufactures and sells automotive and electrical products, hardware, and tools worldwide.

	1994 Sales	
	$ mil.	% of total
US	3,493	77
Other countries	1,062	23
Adjustments	33	—
Total	**4,588**	**100**

	1994 Manufacturing Facilities
	No. of Plants
US	82
Europe	19
Other Americas	18
Other regions	6
Total	**125**

WHAT

	1994 Sales		1994 Operating Income	
	$ mil.	% of total	$ mil.	% of total
Electrical products	2,035	44	326	53
Automotive prods.	1,622	35	190	31
Tools & hardware	898	20	103	16
Other	33	1	(41)	—
Total	**4,588**	**100**	**578**	**100**

Selected Products

Automotive
ACI electric motors
Anco windshield wipers
Belden wire and cable
Champion spark plugs
Everco heating products
Precision universal joints
Wagner lighting products
Zanxx lighting products

Electrical Products
Arrow Hart wiring devices
Buss and Edison fuses
Crouse-Hinds industrial lighting
Edison indoor and outdoor lighting

Halo recessed and track lighting
Kyle distribution switchgear
Metalux fluorescent lighting

Tools and Hardware
Apex impact sockets
Crescent wrenches
Diamond farrier tools
Kirsch drapery hardware
Lufkin measuring tapes
Nicholson files and saws
Plumb hammers
Weller soldering equipment
Wiss cutting products

KEY COMPETITORS

ABB
Arrow Automotive
Baker Hughes
Black & Decker
Borg-Warner Automotive
Dana
Danaher
Dresser
Eaton
Echlin
Emerson

Fastenal
Federal-Mogul
General Electric
General Signal
Hastings Manufacturing
Illinois Tool Works
Ingersoll-Rand
Masco
Newell Co.
PACCAR

Philips
Robert Bosch
Siemens
Snap-on Tools
Standard Products
Stanley Works
Tenneco
Textron
Waxman
Westinghouse

HOW MUCH

	9-Year Growth	1985	1986	1987	1988	1989	1990	1991	1992	1993	1994
Sales ($ mil.)	4.6%	3,067	3,433	3,586	4,258	5,129	6,222	6,163	6,159	6,274	4,588
Net income ($ mil.)	—	135	148	174	224	268	361	393	361	367	(20)
Income as % of sales	—	4.4%	4.3%	4.8%	5.3%	5.2%	5.8%	6.4%	5.9%	5.9%	—
Earnings per share ($)	—	1.39	1.52	1.73	2.20	2.49	2.81	3.01	2.71	2.75	(0.64)
Stock price – high ($)	—	21.19	25.75	37.25	31.38	40.00	46.00	58.00	59.38	54.75	52.25
Stock price – low ($)	—	14.00	17.81	19.50	25.06	26.88	31.25	38.50	41.75	45.63	31.63
Stock price – close ($)	5.5%	21.00	20.69	27.75	27.00	40.00	41.13	57.25	47.38	49.25	34.00
P/E – high	—	15	17	22	14	16	16	19	22	20	—
P/E – low	—	10	12	11	11	11	11	13	15	17	—
Dividends per share ($)	6.3%	0.76	0.79	0.83	0.89	0.98	1.06	1.14	1.22	1.30	1.32
Book value per share ($)	5.3%	14.58	14.66	15.91	17.47	24.75	27.66	29.96	24.99	25.84	23.16
Employees	(1.3%)	46,000	40,200	43,200	46,300	58,100	57,500	53,900	52,900	49,500	40,800

1994 Year-end:
Debt ratio: 36.0%
Return on equity: —
Cash (mil.): $25
Current ratio: 1.58
Long-term debt (mil.): $1,362
No. of shares (mil.): 117
Dividends
  Yield: 3.9%
  Payout: —
Market value (mil.): $3,979

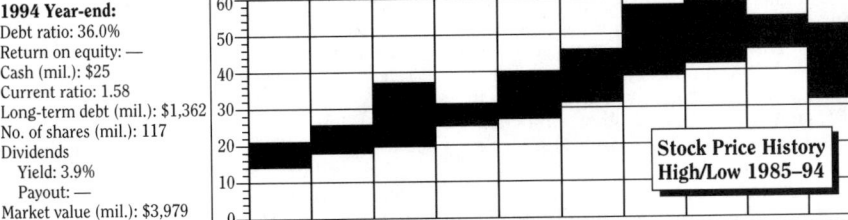

**Stock Price History
High/Low 1985–94**

COOPERS & LYBRAND L.L.P.

OVERVIEW

Coopers & Lybrand is one of the Big 6 accounting firms and, as such, operates on a truly international scale, with offices in 130 countries. Although its primary business through its nearly 100 years of history has been auditing companies, in recent years the firm, like the other members of its fraternity, has been moving into the more lucrative area of business consulting. Not only has auditing become less profitable because of increased price competition (with Coopers & Lybrand a leading price cutter), but in the hyperlitigious 1990s it is becoming downright dangerous.

Coopers & Lybrand is currently involved in a number of legal actions in which investors and government bodies have attempted to hold the firm accountable not only for the form of audited financial statements (which traditionally was all the auditor attested to) but for their veracity as well.

Consolidation of the accounting industry has been a factor in Coopers & Lybrand's international growth, as it has added overseas accounting firms. It also bought a number of consulting firms, including Coppi & Associates (construction management) in 1995.

WHEN

Coopers & Lybrand, the product of a 1957 transatlantic merger, literally wrote the book on auditing. Lybrand, Ross Bros. & Montgomery, as the US ancestor was known, had been formed in 1898 by 4 partners — William Lybrand, Edward Ross, Adam Ross, and Robert Montgomery. In 1912 Montgomery wrote *Montgomery's Auditing*, termed by many as the bible of the accounting profession.

In the early years the accounting firm grew slowly, and the Ross brothers' sister served as secretary, typist, and bookkeeper. In 1902 the company opened a New York office at 25 Broad Street. Other offices across the country followed — Pittsburgh (1908), Chicago (1909), and Boston (1915). WWI focused attention on Washington, DC, and the Lybrand firm opened an office there (1919) and then branched out to the new auto capital of Detroit (1920), to Seattle (1920), and to Baltimore (1924). A merger with the firm of Klink, Bean & Company gave the firm a window on California (1924). Another merger brought the firm into Dallas (1930), with an offshoot office in Houston a year later.

In Europe Lybrand established offices in Berlin (1924, closed in 1938 as WWII loomed), Paris (1926), and London (1929). At the same time the UK firm of Cooper Brothers was also expanding in Europe.

Cooper Brothers had begun in 1854 when William Cooper, the oldest son of a Quaker banker, formed his accountancy at 13 George Street in London. He was quickly joined by his brothers, Arthur, Francis, and Ernest. The firm became Cooper Brothers & Company in 1861. After WWI Cooper Brothers branched out to Liverpool (1920), Brussels (1921), New York (1926), and Paris (1930). After WWII Cooper Brothers acquired 3 venerable firms — Alfred Tongue & Company; Aspell Dunn &

Company; and Rattray Brothers, Alexander & France.

In 1957 Coopers & Lybrand was formed by the amalgamation of the international accounting firms, and by 1973 the affiliated partnerships had largely adopted the Coopers & Lybrand name. In the 1960s the firm expanded into employee benefits consulting and introduced a new auditing method that included evaluating clients' systems of internal control. During the 1970s Coopers & Lybrand focused on integrating computer technology into the auditing process.

During the 1980s Coopers & Lybrand dropped from the top of the Big 8 to 5th in the Big 6 as several of its competitors paired off in a series of mergers. However, the firm unexpectedly benefited from merger mania, becoming a refuge for partners from the other firms. The mergers only increased the cutthroat nature of auditing competitions, and auditing became increasingly price driven.

In 1991 Coopers & Lybrand and IBM formed Meritus, a consulting service for the health care and consumer goods industries. In 1992 the firm agreed to pay $95 million to settle claims of defrauded investors in now-defunct disk drive maker MiniScribe. The next year it hired former SEC chairman Richard Breeden as vice-chairman of its domestic and foreign financial service groups.

Coopers & Lybrand introduced *Telesim*, a management simulation software package for the telecommunications industry, in 1994. *Telesim* was developed with Pacific Telesis, NYNEX, and software maker Thinking Tools.

In 1995 a former vice-chairman, Robert Caruso, was indicted on fraud charges. Caruso had allegedly converted to his own use funds obtained from Coopers & Lybrand for donation to Seton Hall University.

International partnership
Fiscal year ends: September 30

WHO

Chairman and CEO: Nicholas G. Moore
COO: William K. O'Brien
VC, Coopers & Lybrand Consulting: John M. Jacobs
VC, International: James T. Clarke
VC, Learning and Human Resources: Judith A.
  Rosenblum
Director Strategy and Planning: R. Joseph Schlosser
National Director Marketing and Communications: Lee
  S. Pinkard Jr.
CFO: Frank V. Scalia
General Counsel: Harris J. Amhowitz

WHERE

HQ: 1251 Avenue of the Americas, New York, NY 10020
Phone: 212-536-2000
Fax: 212-536-3145

Coopers & Lybrand has offices in 130 countries.

	1994 Revenues	
	$ mil.	% of total
US	1,783	32
Other countries	3,759	68
Total	**5,542**	**100**

WHAT

	1994 US Revenues
	% of total
Accounting & auditing	58
Tax	18
Consulting & other	24
Total	**100**

Representative Clients
American Brands
AT&T
Ford
Johnson & Johnson
The Limited
3M
Philip Morris
Unilever

Selected Services

Business Assurance
ERISA
In-control services
Internal audit services
Regulatory and compliance services
Technology-related services

Coopers & Lybrand Consulting Units
Center for Operations Technology
Financial Management and Business Analysis
Integrated Management Services
Logistics/Systecon
Solutions Thru Technology
Technology Advisory Services

Financial Advisory Services
Business reorganization services
Corporate financial services
Litigation and claims services
Real estate services
Hospitality services

Human Resource Advisory
Communication services
Health care consulting
Human resource management
Human resource technology
Organizational effectiveness and development
Retirement plans
Total compensation services

Tax
Entertainment (Gelfand, Rennert & Feldman)
International tax services
Multistate tax services
Tax process management
Tax technology services
Wealth preservation services

KEY COMPETITORS

Arthur Andersen
Arthur Little
Bain & Co.
Booz, Allen & Hamilton
Boston Consulting
Deloitte & Touche
Delta Consulting
EDS
Ernst & Young
Gemini Consulting
H&R Block
Harcourt General
Hewitt Associates
IBM
KPMG
Marsh & McLennan
McKinsey & Co.
Price Waterhouse
Towers Perrin
Wyatt Co.

HOW MUCH

	Annual Growth	1985	1986	1987	1988	1989	1990	1991	1992	1993	1994
Sales ($ mil.)	16.4%	1,414	1,780	2,076	2,520	2,977	4,136	4,959	5,350	5,220	5,542
Offices	4.3%	518	531	550	580	602	710	735	733	740	758
Partners	3.0%	—	—	—	—	—	—	—	—	5,091	5,243
Employees	7.3%	36,243	38,520	41,134	45,486	50,636	63,300	67,175	66,600	66,300	68,360

1994 Year-end:
Sales per partner:
  $1,057,028

Sales ($ mil.)
1985–94

Coopers
&Lybrand

CORNING INCORPORATED

OVERVIEW

Innovation is the driving force that has maintained small town–based Corning (of Corning, New York) as a world leader in specialty glass materials. Corning is the main producer of glass substrates for flat screens used in personal computers and is a leading maker of optical fiber, as well as one of the world's foremost medical test laboratories. The company also produces specialty materials, including auto pollution control devices and catalytic converters, nose cones for spacecraft, giant mirrors for astronomical telescopes, and projection lenses for high-definition television sets. On the consumer side the company is the world's #1 producer of tableware and cookware, led by its patented Pyrex and Corning Ware heat-resistant oven containers.

Corning invented the fiber-optic cable, a catalyst for the information revolution, over 20 years ago and maintains a technological edge in the market. As telephone and cable firms upgrade their networks, Corning is seeing strong sales of its fiber-optic cables.

However, innovation has its drawbacks. A Corning scientist invented silicone in the 1930s, and Dow Corning, the company's joint venture with Dow Chemical, was a leading maker of breast implants. But after more than 10,000 women opted out of a $4.2 billion payout that Dow Corning and other silicone makers had agreed to in 1994 to settle litigation arising from problems with the implants, Dow Corning sought Chapter 11 bankruptcy protection in 1995.

WHEN

Amory Houghton started Houghton Glass in Massachusetts in 1851 and moved to Corning, New York, in 1868. By 1876 the company, renamed Corning Glass Works, was making several types of technical and pharmaceutical glass. In 1880 Corning supplied the glass for Thomas Edison's first light bulb.

Houghton's son Amory Jr. enlisted the help of a Cornell University physicist in 1877 to improve railroad signals. By using red, yellow, and green lenses, Corning helped to develop the current standard traffic-signal color system.

Corning used borosilicate glass (which can withstand sudden temperature changes) in 1912 to improve the brakeman's lantern; in 1915 it was also used for Pyrex oven and laboratory ware.

Corning has been highly successful at forming joint ventures, which have greatly expanded the company's production and marketing capabilities and have been crucial to its success. Early ones included Pittsburgh Corning (Pittsburgh Plate Glass, 1937, glass construction blocks), Owens-Corning (Owens-Illinois, 1938, fiberglass), and Dow Corning (Dow Chemical, 1943, silicones).

By 1945 Corning's laboratories (established in 1908) had made the company the undisputed leader in the manufacture of specialty glass. Among the applications for Corning's glass technology were the first mass-produced TV tubes, freezer to oven ceramic cookware (Pyroceram, Corning Ware), and car headlights.

After WWII Corning emphasized consumer product sales, which climbed from 12% of total sales in 1953 to 25% in 1963. Corning next expanded globally, nearly tripling foreign sales between 1966 and 1970. In the 1970s the company pioneered the development of optical fiber and auto emission technology, now 2 of Corning's principal products.

Seeing maturing markets for such established products as light bulbs and TV tubes, Corning began to buy higher-growth laboratory services companies (MetPath, 1982; Hazleton, 1987; Enseco, 1989; G.H. Besselaar, 1989). High-tech international joint ventures (e.g., Siemens, Mitsubishi, Samsung) enhanced Corning's solid leadership positions in specialty materials and video glass. In 1988 Corning bought Revere Ware (cookware). Reflecting its broadened orientation, Corning dropped Glass Works from its name in 1989.

In 1993 Corning was chosen by AT&T to provide fiber-optic couplers for its next-generation undersea telecommunications system and developed an electrically heated catalytic converter that beat tough California emissions standards set for 1997. Corning also divested its 49% stake in money-losing Vitro Corning (consumer products in Mexico) and acquired Damon (clinical lab) in 1993. That purchase was followed by the acquisition ($325 million) in 1994 of Nichols Testing, a clinical testing firm that expanded Corning's presence in the western states. That year Corning and Siecor (a joint venture) acquired several fiber and cable businesses from Northern Telecom, expanding the firms' presence in Canada. In 1995 Corning acquired National Packaging Systems, a supplier of packages and services to the drug industry.

NYSE symbol: GLW
Fiscal year ends: Sunday nearest December 31

WHO

Chairman and CEO: James R. Houghton, age 58, $1,521,240 pay
VC and CFO: Van C. Campbell, age 56, $885,465 pay
VC and Chief Technology Officer: David A. Duke, age 59, $787,080 pay
President and COO: Roger G. Ackerman, age 56, $1,146,720 pay
Chairman and CEO, Corning Life Sciences: Randy H. Thurman, age 45, $893,350 pay
EVP Specialty Materials Group: Norman E. Garrity, age 53
EVP; President and CEO, Corning Consumer Products Co.: John W. Loose, age 52
EVP Information Display Group: James M. Ramich, age 49
EVP Opto-Electronics Group: Jan H. Suwinski, age 53
EVP (HR): Kenneth W. Freeman, age 44
SVP and General Counsel: William C. Ughetta, age 62
Auditors: Price Waterhouse LLP

WHERE

HQ: One Riverfront Plaza, Corning, NY 14831
Phone: 607-974-9000
Fax: 607-974-8551

Corning makes 60,000 products, operates 41 plants in 8 countries, and provides lab services in 10 countries.

	1994 Sales		1994 Pretax Income	
	$ mil.	% of total	$ mil.	% of total
US	3,911	82	501	87
Europe	400	8	47	8
Other regions	460	10	31	5
Adjustments	—	—	(119)	—
Total	**4,771**	**100**	**460**	**100**

WHAT

	1994 Sales		1994 Pretax Income	
	$ mil.	% of total	$ mil.	% of total
Laboratory Services	1,687	35	156	22
Communications	1,459	31	346	47
Specialty Materials	846	18	164	23
Consumer Products	779	16	57	8
Adjustments	—	—	(263)	—
Total	**4,771**	**100**	**460**	**100**

Laboratory Services
G.H. Besselaar Associates (pharmaceutical testing)
Hazleton Corp. (life-science lab services)
MetPath Inc. (clinical testing)
SciCor Inc. (clinical research)

Communications
Flat-panel displays
Liquid crystal glass
Optical fiber
Projection-television lenses

Specialty Materials
Auto emission-control substrates

Consumer Products
Corelle (dinnerware)
Corning Ware (cookware)
Pyrex (glassware)
Serengeti (sunglasses)
Steuben (crystal)

Selected Joint Ventures
Cormetech (50%, Mitsubishi)
Corning Asahi Video Products (51%, Asahi Glass)
Dow Corning (50%, Dow Chemical)
Iwaki Corning Malaysia (80%, Iwaki Glass)
Optical Fibres (50%, BICC)
Pittsburgh Corning (50%, PPG)
Samcor Glass (45%, Samtel)
Samsung-Corning (50%, Samsung)
Siecor GmbH (50%, Siemens)

KEY COMPETITORS

Alcoa	Brown-Forman	PharmChem Labs
Allergan	Carlsberg	Pilkington
American Optical	Mikasa	PPG
Baccarat	Noritake	Unilab
Bausch & Lomb	Ogden	Waterford
	Owens-Illinois	Wedgwood

HOW MUCH

	9-Year Growth	1985	1986	1987	1988	1989	1990	1991	1992	1993	1994
Sales ($ mil.)	12.2%	1,691	1,856	2,084	2,122	2,439	2,941	3,259	3,709	4,005	4,771
Net income ($ mil.)	11.3%	108	162	189	292	259	289	311	266	(15)	281
Income as % of sales	—	6.4%	8.7%	9.1%	13.8%	10.6%	9.8%	9.5%	7.2%	—	5.9%
Earnings per share ($)	8.4%	0.64	0.93	1.03	1.63	1.40	1.54	1.66	1.40	(0.09)	1.32
Stock price – high ($)	—	15.72	20.38	19.25	17.47	21.69	25.88	43.13	40.31	39.00	35.06
Stock price – low ($)	—	8.53	11.66	8.69	11.19	16.00	17.38	21.06	28.75	24.00	27.63
Stock price – close ($)	7.6%	15.44	13.72	11.69	17.34	21.50	22.44	38.38	37.50	28.00	29.88
P/E – high	—	25	22	19	11	16	17	26	29	—	27
P/E – low	—	13	13	8	7	11	11	13	21	—	21
Dividends per share ($)	8.9%	0.32	0.35	0.35	0.37	0.50	0.69	0.68	0.62	0.68	0.69
Book value per share ($)	4.1%	6.91	7.83	8.52	8.78	9.08	10.07	10.43	9.30	8.40	9.92
Employees	6.4%	24,600	25,100	25,500	26,300	27,500	28,600	30,700	31,100	39,200	43,000

1994 Year-end:
Debt ratio: 39.1%
Return on equity: 14.2%
Cash (mil.): $161
Current ratio: 1.61
Long-term debt (mil.): $1,406
No. of shares (mil.): 228
Dividends
  Yield: 2.3%
  Payout: 52.3
Market value (mil.): $6,819

Stock Price History
High/Low 1985–94

COX ENTERPRISES, INC.

OVERVIEW

Whether it's by paperboy or satellite dish, Cox Enterprises will find a way to get information to you. The Atlanta-based company is one of the largest media conglomerates in the US, with interests in newspapers, radio, and broadcast and cable television. With the emergence of new technologies such as wireless communications and fiber optics, Cox is finding new ways to deliver the news.

In 1995 Cox completed its acquisition of Times Mirror's cable television operations for $2.3 billion in cash and stock. Cox folded Times Mirror's cable systems and its own into a new, publicly traded company, Cox Communications. Cox controls about 85% of the stock of the new company, which (with some 3.2 mil-

lion subscribers) is one of the largest cable systems in the US. Cox also publishes 18 daily newspapers and 6 weeklies. It owns 6 broadcast TV stations and 16 radio stations. Cox's Manheim Auctions is the US's largest auto auction company.

Cox continues to look for ways to hitch a ride on the growing interest in the information superhighway. In 1994 it formed a partnership with Sprint, TCI, and Comcast to package telephone service, cable television, and other communication services together as a "one-stop shop for customers."

The company is owned by founder James Cox's daughters, Barbara Cox Anthony (mother of CEO Jim Kennedy) and Anne Cox Chambers.

WHEN

James Middleton Cox dropped out of school in 1886 at age 16 and worked as a teacher, reporter, and congressional secretary before buying the *Dayton Daily News* in 1898. He acquired the nearby *Springfield Press–Republican* in 1905 and soon took up politics. Cox served 2 terms in the US Congress (1909–13) and 3 terms as Ohio governor (1913–15; 1917–21). In 1920 he was the Democratic candidate for president, with Franklin D. Roosevelt as his running mate, but he lost to rival Ohio publisher Warren G. Harding. In 1923 Cox bought the *Miami Daily News* and formed WHIO, Dayton's first radio station. He bought Atlanta's WSB ("Welcome South, Brother"), the South's first radio station, in 1939 and expanded it in 1948 by starting WSB-FM and WSB-TV, the first FM and TV stations in the South. In 1949 Cox started WHIO-FM and WHIO-TV, the first FM and TV stations in Dayton. The *Atlanta Constitution*, now the company's flagship paper, joined Cox's collection in 1950. When Cox died in 1957, his company owned 7 newspapers, 3 TV stations, and several radio stations.

Cox Enterprises expanded its broadcasting interests by buying WSOC-AM/FM/TV (Charlotte, 1959) and KTVU-TV (San Francisco–Oakland, 1963). Cox became one of the first major broadcasting companies to enter cable TV when it purchased a system in Lewistown, Pennsylvania (1962). In 1964 the Cox family's broadcast properties were placed in publicly held Cox Broadcasting. In 1968 Cox newspapers in 1968 were placed into privately held Cox Enterprises and the cable holdings became publicly held Cox Cable Communications. By 1969 Cox was the #2 US cable operator. The

broadcasting arm diversified, buying Manheim Services (auto auctions, 1968) and Kansas City Automobile Auction (1969).

Cox Broadcasting bought TeleRep, a TV advertising sales representation firm, in 1972. Cox Cable was in 9 states and had 500,000 subscribers by 1977, when it rejoined Cox Broadcasting. The broadcasting company changed its name to Cox Communications in 1982; the Cox family took the company private again in 1985 and combined it with Cox Enterprises. James Kennedy, the founder's grandson, became chairman in 1987.

In 1991 Cox merged its Manheim unit with the auto auction business of Ford Motor Credit and GE Capital and bought Val-Pak Direct Marketing, a direct mail coupon company. In the same year Discovery Communications, 1/4-owned by Cox, bought The Learning Channel. In 1993 Cox started a cable and satellite television channel targeted at women in the UK called UK Living. BellSouth partnered with Cox in a venture to offer classified advertising and yellow pages–type information by phone, a service to be expanded to PCs and one that may use other technology. Cox also began providing news via a 511 phone number in Atlanta and South Florida.

In 1994 Cox agreed to a $4.9 billion cable television joint venture with Southwestern Bell and supported QVC's bid to buy Paramount. However, both deals fell through: Viacom bought Paramount, and Southwestern Bell (now SBC Communications) and Cox called off their deal after the 2 decided that new FCC rules would eat up profits.

In 1995 Cox sold its 50% stake in its Danish cable business, STOFA A/S, to Telia AB.

Private company
Fiscal year ends: December 31

WHO

Chairman and CEO: James Cox Kennedy
President and COO: David E. Easterly
SVP and CFO: John R. Dillon
VP Legal Affairs and Secretary: Andrew A. Merdek
VP and Controller: John G. Boyette
VP Tax: Preston B. Barnett
VP Planning and Analysis: William L. Killen Jr.
VP Public Policy: Alexander V. Netchvolodoff
VP Corporate Security: Charles W. Rochner
VP Human Resources: Timothy W. Hughes
Auditors: Deloitte & Touche LLP

WHERE

HQ: 1400 Lake Hearn Dr., Atlanta, GA 30319
Phone: 404-843-5000
Fax: 404-843-5142

WHAT

Major Newspapers	Avg. Daily Circulation
The Atlanta Constitution	310,287
Austin American-Statesman	175,617
The Palm Beach Post	169,620
Dayton Daily News	163,758
The Atlanta Journal	139,159

Other Daily Newspapers

Chandler Arizonan Tribune
The Daily Sentinel (Grand
  Junction, CO)
The Daily Sentinel
  (Nacogdoches, TX)
Gilbert Tribune (Arizona)
Longview News-Journal
  (Texas)
The Lufkin Daily News
  (Texas)
Mesa Tribune (Arizona)

Palm Beach Daily News
Scottsdale Progress
  Tribune (Arizona)
Springfield News-Sun
  (Ohio)
Tempe Daily News Tribune
  (Arizona)
Waco Tribune-Herald
  (Texas)
The Yuma Daily Sun
  (Arizona)

Other Cox Newspaper Businesses
Cox Target Media (direct mail advertising)
  Trader Publishing Co. (50%, Virginia)
  Val-Pak Direct Marketing Systems, Inc. (Florida)
InfoVentures of Atlanta (50%)
Longstreet Press (Georgia)

Radio Stations

KACE (FM), Los Angeles
KFI (AM), Los Angeles
KOST (FM), Los Angeles
WCKG (FM), Chicago
WCOF (FM), Tampa
WFLC (FM), Miami
WHIO (AM), Dayton
WHKO (FM), Dayton

WHQT (FM), Miami
WIOD (AM), Miami
WJZF (FM), La Grange, GA
WSB (AM/FM), Atlanta
WSUN (AM), Tampa
WWRM (FM), Tampa
WYSY (FM), Aurora-
  Chicago

Television Stations

KTVU, San Francisco–
  Oakland
WFTV, Orlando
WHIO-TV, Dayton

WPXI, Pittsburgh
WSB-TV, Atlanta
WSOC-TV, Charlotte

Cable and Other Television
Cox Communications, Inc. (85%, 3.2 million cable
  subscribers)
Cox Fibernet (voice, data, video transmission)
Discovery Communications (24%, The Discovery
  Channel)
Harrington, Righter & Parsons (sales representation,
  New York)
Rysher Entertainment (production and distribution,
  Los Angeles)
SBC CableComms UK (50%)
TeleRep, Inc. (sales representation, New York)

Manheim Auctions
52 auto auctions in the US and Canada

Other
Clarendon Farms, Inc. (farming and timber, South
  Carolina)
Hualalai Land Corporation (cattle ranch and flower
  plantation, Hawaii)
Nine Bar Ranch Texas, Inc. (cattle ranch)
Southeast Paper Manufacturing Co. (33%, Georgia)

KEY COMPETITORS

ADT
Advance
  Publications
AT&T
Cablevision
CBS
Comcast
Dow Jones
Dun & Bradstreet
E.W. Scripps

Gannett
General Electric
Hearst
Heritage Media
Knight-Ridder
Media General
New York Times
News Corp.
TCI

Thomson Corp.
Time Warner
Times Mirror
Tribune
Turner
  Broadcasting
Viacom
Walt Disney
Washington Post

HOW MUCH

	9-Year Growth	1985	1986	1987	1988	1989	1990	1991	1992	1993	1994
Sales ($ mil.)	8.0%	1,471	1,569	1,665	1,816	1,973	2,094	2,323	2,495	2,675	2,939
Cable subscribers (thou.)	8.7%	1,511	1,372	1,442	1,442	1,555	1,616	1,678	1,722	1,784	3,192
Daily newspapers	—	19	20	20	20	18	17	17	18	18	18
Daily circulation (thou.)	0.3%	1,210	1,250	1,275	1,310	1,306	1,320	1,283	1,256	1,241	1,245
Employees	10.6%	15,000	20,000	20,766	21,612	22,487	24,864	29,943	30,865	31,000	37,000

COX
ENTERPRISES,INC.

Sales ($ mil.)
1985–94

3,000
2,500
2,000
1,500
1,000
500
0

CPC INTERNATIONAL INC.

OVERVIEW

US sales may be sluggish for CPC, but the rest of the world has developed a taste for great American products like Skippy peanut butter. CPC is a consumer foods giant with over 1,700 trademark brands that include Skippy, Knorr soups, and Hellmann's and Best Foods mayonnaise. (Mayonnaise, in fact, accounted for over 11% of the company's sales in 1994.)

Globalization has been a major thrust of CPC for more than a quarter century, and over 64% of the company's 1994 sales came from international markets. In just the last 3 years CPC has engaged in more than 20 foreign start-ups, acquisitions, and joint ventures. These include new subsidiaries in China, Eastern Europe, and Russia. In 1995 it added Lesieur, one of France's top salad dressing makers.

Analysts blame CPC's slim domestic sales on a growing awareness of dietary fat. The company is countering with such new products as low-fat mayonnaise and reduced-fat peanut butter.

The company, a major corn refiner with operations in 17 countries, produces Mazola corn oil, Karo corn syrup, and a variety of cornstarches, as well as ethanol for fuel. After severe flooding dampened the corn refining segment's business in 1993, new products and supplier relationships boosted 1994 sales.

WHEN

In 1842 Thomas Kingsford developed a technique for separating starch from corn, and by 1890 the corn refining industry had emerged. Competition forced 20 cornstarch and syrup producers to band together as National Starch Manufacturing. The group established quotas and gained 70% of the cornstarch market, but their pool broke down and ruinous pricing competition resumed.

This pattern was typical of the unstable corn refining industry for the next decade. By 1906 price competition had forced Edward Bedford's New York Glucose to merge with Glucose Sugar Refining Company, of which National Starch was by then a part, forming Corn Products Refining Company. CPRC became the first stable corn refining company by improving refinery equipment and processes. In 1906 CPRC controlled 64% of the starch and 100% of the glucose output in the US.

For the first half of this century CPRC dominated corn refining, eliciting several antitrust actions. In 1916 Judge Learned Hand forced CPRC's eventual sale of portions of its business. In 1922 CPRC faced antitrust charges in connection with Karo syrup; the charges were dismissed. Between 1940 and 1942 the FTC filed antitrust charges against CPRC for "phantom freight" prices; to control prices, CPRC charged for shipping from places other than the actual point of origin. Removing phantom freight (1945) reduced industry concentration; by 1954 CPRC had only a 46% share of corn-grinding capacity.

Although the company produced some branded products (Mazola, Karo, Argo, and Kingsford's), CPRC remained largely a corn refinery until 1958. That year the company merged with Best Foods, producers of Hellmann's, Best Foods, Skippy, and Rit brands, and bought C. H. Knorr (soups). During the 1960s CPRC bought 4 educational companies — MIND, the best known of these, made remedial training systems to improve workers' skills — but sold them all by 1980.

In 1969 the company was renamed CPC International to emphasize its international expansion. CPC bought S. B. Thomas (English muffins, 1969), C. F. Mueller (pasta, 1983), and Arnold Foods (crackers, 1986).

In 1986 CPC thwarted a takeover attempt by financier Ronald Perelman (MacAndrews & Forbes) and sold Bosco brand chocolate syrup.

Since 1988 CPC has spent nearly $1 billion to acquire over 50 companies, including Ambrosia (desserts, UK), Conimex (oriental foods, the Netherlands), Milwaukee Seasonings, and Fearn International (soups and sauces, US), as well as a 50% stake in Israel Edible Products (Israel). In 1993 the company acquired Pfanni potato products, the largest such company in Europe, and Henri's salad dressings in the US, as well as new businesses in Costa Rica, Turkey, Denmark, and the Czech Republic.

In 1994 CPC began a 2-year restructuring program aimed at cutting costs. The plan includes consolidation of the company's North American and European operations and reduction of its work force. That same year CPC and General Mills formed a joint venture to market baking and dessert mixes in Latin America.

Also in 1994 CPC and Mexico-based Arancia S.A. de C.V. formed a joint venture for corn refining. CPC CEO Charles Shoemate has targeted the company's Latin American business for expansion in 1995, with development of a high-fructose corn syrup market in Mexico one goal of the Arancia agreement.

WHO

Chairman, President, and CEO: Charles R. Shoemate,
age 55, $1,201,667 pay
EVP: Robert J. Gillespie, age 52, $668,750 pay
EVP; President, CPC Europe Division: Alain Labergère,
age 60, $582,500 pay
SVP and General Counsel: Clifford B. Storms, age 62,
$529,583 pay
SVP and CFO: Konrad Schlatter, age 59, $502,500 pay
**President, Best Foods Grocery Products Group, Best
Foods Division:** Lawrence K. Hathaway
**President, CPC Latin America Consumer Foods
Division:** Gordon F. Granger
President, Corn Refining Business: Bernard H. Kastory
VP; President, Best Foods Division: Axel Krauss, age 50
VP Human Resources: Richard P. Bergeman, age 56
Auditors: KPMG Peat Marwick LLP

WHERE

HQ: International Plaza, PO Box 8000,
Englewood Cliffs, NJ 07632-9976
Phone: 201-894-4000
Fax: 201-894-2186

CPC has 27 operating plants in the US, 8 in Canada, 42
in Europe, 20 in Africa and the Middle East, 32 in Latin
America, and 14 in Asia.

	1994 Sales		1994 Operating Income	
	$ mil.	% of total	$ mil.	% of total
Europe	2,933	40	181	25
North America	2,907	39	344	46
Latin America	1,273	17	166	22
Asia	312	4	49	7
Adjustments	—	—	(28)	—
Total	**7,425**	**100**	**712**	**100**

WHAT

	1994 Sales		1994 Operating Income	
	$ mil.	% of total	$ mil.	% of total
Consumer foods	6,203	84	552	75
Corn refining	1,222	16	188	25
Adjustments	—	—	(28)	—
Total	**7,425**	**100**	**712**	**100**

Major Brand Names

Baked Goods	Maizena	**Mayonnaise**
Arnold	Polly	Best Foods
Bran'nola	Vitamilho	Hellmann's
Brownberry		Telma
Sahara	**Desserts**	
Thomas'	Alsa	**Pasta**
	Ambrosia	Mueller's
Corn Oil	Yabon	Napolina
Mazola		Royal
	Dressings	
Corn Syrup	Henri's	**Peanut Butter**
Karo	Western	Lady's Choice
		Skippy
Cornstarch	**Jams**	
Argo	Fruco	**Soups, Sauces,**
Arrozina	Mateus	**and Bouillons**
Cremogema	Santa Rosa	Knorr
Kingsford's		Pfanni

KEY COMPETITORS

ADM	Continental	Mars
American	Grain	Monsanto
Brands	Danone	Nestlé
Anheuser-Busch	General Mills	PepsiCo
Associated Milk	George Weston	Philip Morris
Producers	Grand	Quaker Oats
Borden	Metropolitan	RJR Nabisco
Campbell Soup	Heinz	Sara Lee
Cargill	Hershey	Tate & Lyle
Chiquita Brands	Hormel	TLC Beatrice
ConAgra	John Labatt	Unilever

HOW MUCH

	9-Year Growth	1985	1986	1987	1988	1989	1990	1991	1992	1993	1994
Sales ($ mil.)	6.5%	4,210	4,549	4,903	4,700	5,103	5,781	6,189	6,599	6,738	7,425
Net income ($ mil.)	10.4%	142	219	355	289	328	374	373	384	454	345
Income as % of sales	—	3.4%	4.8%	7.2%	6.2%	6.4%	6.5%	6.0%	5.8%	6.8%	4.6%
Earnings per share ($)	13.3%	0.73	1.15	2.17	1.84	2.11	2.42	2.40	2.47	2.95	2.25
Stock price – high ($)	—	13.31	22.13	29.25	29.19	36.88	42.38	46.75	51.63	51.13	55.63
Stock price – low ($)	—	9.56	11.63	13.00	19.75	24.69	31.00	36.00	39.75	39.88	44.25
Stock price – close ($)	17.2%	12.75	19.81	20.25	25.94	36.88	41.63	45.25	50.63	47.63	53.25
P/E – high	—	18	19	14	16	18	18	20	21	17	25
P/E – low	—	13	10	6	11	12	13	15	16	14	20
Dividends per share ($)	10.8%	0.55	0.55	0.62	0.74	0.85	0.98	1.08	1.18	1.28	1.38
Book value per share ($)	4.6%	7.05	5.79	6.81	7.62	6.73	8.30	9.46	9.72	10.45	10.60
Employees	1.1%	38,000	38,700	31,400	32,137	33,500	35,542	35,000	38,000	39,000	41,900

1994 Year-end:
Debt ratio: 49.8%
Return on equity: 44.4%
Cash (mil.): $125
Current ratio: 1.06
Long-term debt (mil.): $879
No. of shares (mil.): 146.7
Dividends
  Yield: 2.6%
  Payout: 61.3%
Market value (mil.): $7,813

**Stock Price History
High/Low 1985–94**

CROWN CORK & SEAL COMPANY, INC.

OVERVIEW

Philadelphia-based Crown Cork & Seal (CC&S) lives up to its name, almost. While the firm makes crowns and seals, cork is no longer used as a primary sealant material. CC&S is a leading worldwide producer of crowns and closures for bottles, metal containers, and plastic containers. It is also a leading manufacturer of high-speed filling, handling, and packaging machinery. Recent acquisitions of polyethylene terephthalate (PET) plastic container makers and can-making facilities have made CC&S one of the world's top packaging companies and North America's largest. CC&S's plastics division has grown to 22% of the company's sales.

The company, which operates 152 plants worldwide, sells to the food, citrus, brewing, soft drink, oil, paint, toiletry, drug, antifreeze, chemicals, and pet food industries.

High raw materials prices — including a 40% hike in the price of aluminum can sheet, the material used to make beverage cans —

put the squeeze on CC&S in 1994. The firm reorganized its metal packaging operations that year, a strategy that included closing 10 North American plants and restructuring 3 others.

A key element of CC&S's strategy, in addition to keeping costs low, is overseas expansion. While the domestic market for aluminum cans is losing ground to plastic containers, the demand for beverage cans is growing outside the US. International sales accounted for 33% of the company's total 1994 revenues.

The company is building its aluminum can business through alliances with manufacturers in Latin America and Asia, especially in China, where it has an 80% stake in a Beijing aluminum can operation. In 1995 CC&S announced it would form 2 joint ventures with Brazilian manufacturing company Petropar SA.

The Connelly Foundation, a private charitable foundation named after the company's late president, owns almost 9% of CC&S.

WHEN

Formed as Crown Cork & Seal Co. of Baltimore in 1892, CC&S was consolidated into its present form in 1927 when it merged with New Process Cork and New York Patents. The next year CC&S expanded overseas and formed Crown Cork International.

In 1936 CC&S acquired Acme Can and benefited from the movement at the time from home canning to processed canning. The company, in 1946, was the first to develop the aerosol can.

By 1957 a heavy debt load had CC&S in trouble. Teetering on the brink of bankruptcy, the company hired Irishman John Connelly as president. Connelly immediately stopped can production (sending stockpiled inventory to customers), discontinued unprofitable product lines (ice cube trays), and reduced overhead (25% of CC&S's employees were laid off over a 20-month period). He then directed CC&S to take advantage of new uses for aerosol cans (insecticides, hair spray, and bathroom cleaning supplies) and to expand overseas. CC&S obtained "pioneer rights" between 1955 and 1960 from foreign countries that granted CC&S the first crack at new closure or can business.

The introduction of the pull-tab pop-top in 1963 hit the can-making business like an exploding grenade. Connelly embraced pull-tabs, but he rejected getting into production of 2-piece aluminum cans (first introduced in

the mid-1970s), focusing instead on existing 3-piece can technology. He also resisted the diversification trend then popular in the can-making industry, which later led to the declining performances of competitors Continental Can and American Can. In 1970 CC&S moved into the printing end of the industry and gained the ability to imprint color lithography on its bottle caps and cans through its acquisition of R. Hoe.

Connelly kept CC&S debt free through most of the 1980s, using cash flow to buy back about half of CC&S's stock. In 1989 he picked Bill Avery to succeed him. (Connelly, known as the "Iron Man" for his tight-fisted control of fiscal matters, died in 1990.) With Connelly's blessing, Avery began a buying spree, which doubled the firm's size. CC&S bought the plants of Continental Can in 3 stages, paying $800 million. In 1992 CC&S acquired CONSTAR International, the #1 maker of PET plastic containers.

In 1993 the company acquired another PET provider in Europe (Wellstar Holdings) and a metal-can maker (Van Dorn). In 1994 CC&S acquired the metal can–manufacturing unit of Tri Valley Growers, one of the biggest in the country, for $61 million. Also that year, the Northridge earthquake ruined the company's beverage can plant in Van Nuys, California.

In 1995, in a move that would create the world's largest packaging firm, CC&S offered $3.9 billion for Carnaud Metalbox of Paris.

NYSE symbol: CCK
Fiscal year ends: December 31

Chairman, President, and CEO: William J. Avery,
age 54, $990,600 pay
EVP; President, North American Division: Michael J.
McKenna, age 60, $410,300 pay
EVP Corporate Technologies: Mark W. Hartman,
age 57, $350,300 pay
EVP and CFO: Alan W. Rutherford, age 51, $326,650 pay
EVP; President, Plastics Division: Hans J. Loliger,
age 51, $321,020 pay
EVP; President, International Division: John W.
Conway, age 49
EVP Procurement and Traffic: Ronald R. Thoma,
age 60
EVP, Secretary, and General Counsel: Richard L.
Krzyzanowski, age 62
VP and Treasurer: Craig R. L. Calle, age 35
VP Human Resources: Gary L. Burgess
Financial Controller: Timothy J. Donahue, age 32
Manufacturing Controller: Richard Donohue, age 60
Auditors: Price Waterhouse LLP

WHERE

HQ: 9300 Ashton Rd., Philadelphia, PA 19136
Phone: 215-698-5100
Fax: 215-676-7245 (Human Resources)

Crown operates 82 plants in the US as well as 70 plants
in over 40 countries.

	1994 Sales		1994 Operating Income	
	$ mil.	% of total	$ mil.	% of total
US	2,970	67	179	62
Europe	640	14	48	17
Other Americas	466	11	18	6
Other countries	376	8	44	15
Total	**4,452**	**100**	**289**	**100**

WHAT

	1994 Sales		1994 Operating Income	
	$ mil.	% of total	$ mil.	% of total
Metal pkg. & fabricated machinery	3,494	78	212	73
Plastic packaging	958	22	77	27
Total	**4,452**	**100**	**289**	**100**

Metal Packaging
Aerosol cans
Beer and beverage cans
Closures
Cone-top cans
Crowns
"F" style rectangular cans
Food cans
Motor oil cans
Paint cans

Fabricated Machinery
Bottle and can fillers
Bottle and can warmers
Bottle washers and rinsers
Casers and decasers
Conveyors
Crown dust removal
  equipment
Crowners
Depalletizers
Palletizers
Process equipment

Plastic Packaging
Closures
HDPE containers
PET beverage
  containers
PET dish detergent
  containers
PET food containers
PET personal care
  containers
PET preforms
PET water containers
Polypropylene closures
Polypropylene medical
  disposal devices

KEY COMPETITORS

ACX Technologies
Alcoa
Ball Corp.
Bemis
Brown-Forman
Carlisle Plastics
Continental Can

Cooper Industries
Johnson Controls
Myers Industries
Owens-Illinois
Premark
Reynolds Metals
St.-Gobain

Sealright
Silgan
Sun Coast
  Industries
U.S. Can
Wheaton

HOW MUCH

	9-Year Growth	1985	1986	1987	1988	1989	1990	1991	1992	1993	1994
Sales ($ mil.)	13.0%	1,487	1,619	1,718	1,834	1,910	3,072	3,807	3,781	4,163	4,452
Net income ($ mil.)	6.9%	72	79	88	93	94	107	128	155	181	131
Income as % of sales	—	4.8%	4.9%	5.1%	5.1%	4.9%	3.5%	3.4%	4.1%	4.4%	2.9%
Earnings per share ($)	8.3%	0.72	0.83	0.95	1.12	1.19	1.24	1.48	1.79	2.08	1.47
Stock price – high ($)	—	9.94	12.66	15.52	15.73	18.98	22.31	30.89	41.13	41.88	41.88
Stock price – low ($)	—	4.89	8.56	9.48	10.01	14.61	16.48	18.15	27.39	33.25	33.50
Stock price – close ($)	16.0%	9.94	11.44	11.70	15.40	17.69	18.90	29.89	39.88	41.88	37.75
P/E – high	—	14	15	16	14	16	18	21	23	20	29
P/E – low	—	7	10	10	9	12	13	12	15	16	23
Dividends per share ($)	—	0.00	0.00	0.00	0.00	0.00	0.00	0.00	0.00	0.00	0.00
Book value per share ($)	11.8%	5.60	6.42	7.56	7.99	9.39	10.97	12.44	13.24	14.09	15.28
Employees	6.7%	12,523	12,403	12,354	12,567	14,747	17,205	17,763	20,378	21,254	22,373

1994 Year-end:
Debt ratio: 57.2%
Return on equity: 10.0%
Cash (mil.): $44
Current ratio: 1.08
Long-term debt (mil.): $1,090
No. of shares (mil.): 89
Dividends
  Yield: —
  Payout: —
Market value (mil.): $3,373

Stock Price History
High/Low 1985–94

CSX CORPORATION

OVERVIEW

While other large railroads are merging like mad, CSX Corporation keeps on rolling solo and continues to improve its delivery time. In addition to rail shipping, company services include intermodal (ship-to-truck-to-train) and ocean shipping, trucking, inland barging, and distribution. Subsidiary CSX Transportation is the largest hauler of coal in the US and has the best safety record in the business.

Richmond-based CSX also operates resorts in West Virginia (The Greenbrier) and Wyoming (Grand Teton Lodge), develops real estate (CSX Real Property Inc.), and has a majority stake in Yukon Pacific Corporation, which promotes construction of the Trans-Alaska Gas System.

CSX's 18,759-mile rail system is concentrated in 20 states (in the eastern, midwestern, and southern US) and Ontario. It has extended intermodal operations into the Northeast through a joint effort with rival Norfolk Southern to run the heavily used tracks between Chicago and New York.

CSX's Sea-Land Service, a worldwide leader in container shipping, has 93 container ships serving 120 ports in 80 countries and territories. Sea-Land's growing intermodal shipping business is well placed in the expanding routes between the US and South America, Asia, the Middle East, and Europe, as well as within Asia. Over 1/3 of its worldwide operating revenues come from routes in the Pacific region.

WHEN

CSX Corporation was formed in 1980, when Chessie System and Seaboard Coast Line merged in an effort to reduce costs and improve the efficiency of their railroads.

Chessie was a holding company for several railroads in the Northeast and Midwest. Its oldest, the Baltimore & Ohio (B&O), was chartered in 1827 to help Baltimore compete against New York and Philadelphia for freight traffic. By the late 1800s the railroad served New York, Cincinnati, Chicago, St. Louis, and Washington, DC. Under president Daniel Willard (1910–41), B&O modernized its tracks and equipment and gained a reputation for courteous service. Chesapeake & Ohio (C&O) acquired it in 1962.

C&O originated in Virginia with the Louisa Railroad in 1836. It gained access to Chicago, Cincinnati, and Washington, DC, and was by the mid-1900s a major coal carrier. After B&O and C&O acquired joint control of Baltimore-based Western Maryland Railway (1967), the 3 railroads became subsidiaries of newly formed Chessie System (1973).

One of Seaboard Coast Line's 2 predecessors, Seaboard Air Line Railroad (SAL), grew out of Virginia's Portsmouth & Roanoke Rail Road of 1832. By 1875 the line was controlled by John Robinson, who gave the system its name. SAL eventually acquired routes in Georgia, Florida, and Alabama.

The other predecessor, Atlantic Coast Line Railroad (ACL), took shape between 1869 and 1893 as William Walters acquired several southern railroads. In 1902 ACL acquired the Plant System (railroads in Georgia, Florida, and other southern states) and the Louisville & Nashville (a north-south line connecting

New Orleans, Nashville, St. Louis, Cincinnati, and Chicago), giving ACL the basic form it retained until 1967, when it merged with SAL to form Seaboard Coast Line (SCL). The merger eliminated their duplicate routes.

CSX inherited from Chessie System and SCL a combined rail network of over 27,000 route miles. The company bought Texas Gas Resources (gas pipeline, 1983), American Commercial Lines (Texas Gas's river barge subsidiary, 1984), and Sea-Land Corporation (ocean container shipping, 1986). To improve its market value, CSX sold most of its oil and gas properties, its communications holdings (LightNet), and most of its resort properties (Rockresorts) in 1988 and 1989. In 1991 it sold its only natural gas unit (CSX Energy).

Also in 1991 Sea-Land formed joint ventures to penetrate markets in the former Soviet Union and in South America (Venezuela and Brazil), adding Argentina and Uruguay in 1992. That year American Commercial Lines acquired Valley Line, boosting ACL's barge capacity by more than 1/3.

In 1993 CSX and its unions agreed to have 2-person crews on 99% of CSX trains, and the company ordered 300 locomotives from GE. In 1994 CSX's railroad achieved its highest-ever efficiency rating, and the company had record sales and income. After years of waiting for maritime reform, in 1995 CSX received government permission to begin registering new ships outside the US. The company hopes for federal legislative relief in the future. In 1995 CSX was the first major company to resume service to the port of Kobe, Japan, following the devastating earthquake in January of that year.

NYSE symbol: CSX
Fiscal year ends: Last Friday in December

WHO

Chairman, President, and CEO: John W. Snow, age 55, $1,885,666 pay
President and CEO, CSX Transportation: Alvin R. Carpenter, age 53, $897,098 pay
President and CEO, Sea-Land Service: John P. Clancey, age 50, $687,978 pay
President and CEO, American Commercial Lines: Michael C. Hagan, age 48
President and CEO, Customized Transportation: David G. Kulik, age 46
EVP and COO, CSX Transportation: Gerald L. Nichols, age 59
SVP Finance (Principal Financial Officer): James Ermer, age 52, $614,729 pay
SVP Law and Public Affairs: Mark G. Aron, age 52
SVP Employee Relations, CSX Transportation: Donald D. Davis, age 55
VP General Counsel and Corporate Secretary: Alan A. Rudnick, age 47
Auditors: Ernst & Young LLP

WHERE

HQ: One James Center, 901 E. Cary St., Richmond, VA 23219-4031
Phone: 804-782-1400
Fax: 804-782-1409

CSX's rail system links 20 US states in the East, Midwest, and South, and the District of Columbia and Ontario, Canada.

WHAT

	1994 Sales	
	$ mil.	% of total
Transportation	9,410	98
Nontransportation	198	2
Total	**9,608**	**100**

	1994 Sales	
	$ mil.	% of total
Container shipping	3,492	36
Rail commodities		
Coal	1,465	15
Chemicals	685	7
Automotive	493	5
Forest products	444	5
Minerals	365	4
Agricultural products	318	3
Other	855	9
Intermodal	902	9
Barge	449	5
Nontransportation	198	2
Other/Adjustments	(58)	—
Total	**9,608**	**100**

Major Subsidiaries and Affiliates
American Commercial Lines Inc. (inland marine services)
CSX Intermodal Inc. (transcontinental intermodal services)
CSX Real Property Inc. (real estate development)
CSX Transportation Inc. (rail transportation and distribution services)
Customized Transportation Inc. (contract logistics)
Grand Teton Lodge Co. (resort; Moran, WY)
The Greenbrier (resort; White Sulphur Springs, WV)
Sea-Land Service Inc. (container shipping worldwide)
Yukon Pacific Corp. (promotion of Trans-Alaska Gas System construction)

KEY COMPETITORS

Alexander & Baldwin	Ingram	Orient Overseas
American President	J.B. Hunt	Roadway
Arkansas Best	Kawasaki Kisen	Schneider
C.H. Robinson	Leaseway	National
Conrail	Transportation	TNT
Crowley Maritime	Mitsubishi	Freightways
Evergreen Marine	Mitsui	Yellow
General Steamship	Norfolk	Corporation
	Southern	

HOW MUCH

	9-Year Growth	1985	1986	1987	1988	1989	1990	1991	1992	1993	1994
Sales ($ mil.)	3.1%	7,320	6,428	8,043	7,592	7,745	8,205	8,636	8,734	8,940	9,608
Net income ($ mil.)	—	(118)	418	432	(33)	429	364	(76)	20	359	652
Income as % of sales	—	—	6.5%	5.4%	—	5.5%	4.4%	—	0.2%	4.0%	6.8%
Earnings per share ($)	—	(0.78)	2.73	2.78	(0.30)	4.11	3.62	(0.75)	0.19	3.46	6.23
Stock price – high ($)	—	31.88	37.50	41.75	32.50	38.63	38.13	58.00	73.63	88.13	92.38
Stock price – low ($)	—	22.38	25.63	22.13	24.38	29.75	26.00	29.75	54.50	66.38	63.13
Stock price – close ($)	9.7%	30.25	29.13	29.13	31.75	35.88	31.75	57.88	68.75	81.88	69.63
P/E – high	—	—	14	15	—	9	11	—	—	26	15
P/E – low	—	—	9	8	—	7	7	—	—	19	10
Dividends per share ($)	5.0%	1.13	1.16	1.18	1.29	1.28	1.40	1.43	1.52	1.58	1.76
Book value per share ($)	1.9%	30.15	31.64	31.25	30.39	33.24	35.93	31.08	28.75	30.55	35.63
Employees	(1.4%)	53,200	48,000	51,000	53,968	52,582	50,931	49,883	47,597	47,063	46,747

1994 Year-end:
Debt ratio: 45.6%
Return on equity: 18.9%
Cash (mil.): $535
Current ratio: 0.66
Long-term debt (mil.): $2,618
No. of shares (mil.): 105
Dividends
  Yield: 2.5%
  Payout: 28.3%
Market value (mil.): $7,292

Stock Price History High/Low 1985–94

CUMMINS ENGINE COMPANY, INC.

OVERVIEW

Indiana-based Cummins is the world's largest independent maker of diesel engines. All major North American truck makers (except Mack Trucks) offer Cummins engines as standard or optional equipment. They are under the hoods of Navistar International heavy-duty trucks, Ford's midrange trucks, and Chrysler's popular Dodge Ram. The company also supplies diesel engines for school buses, delivery trucks, recreational vehicles, and urban transit systems. Cummins accounts for about a third of the US heavy-duty and midrange truck engine markets.

The diesel-engine maker is becoming more international and diversified. Over the years

Cummins has extended its reach through alliances with Komatsu of Japan, Wartsila in Finland, and TELCO, India's largest truck maker. In 1994 international sales accounted for 43% of revenues. Cummins is looking for other alliances and acquisitions. In 1994 it expanded its electrical power generation division (the company's 2nd largest market with 22% of sales) with Power Group International, a UK manufacturer of generation equipment, and formed a joint venture with China National Heavy Duty Truck Corp., China's largest maker of heavy-duty trucks. Over the next 5 years, the company plans to revamp all its models and regularly introduce new ones.

WHEN

Chauffeur Clessie Cummins believed that Rudolph Diesel's cumbersome and smoky engine could be improved for use in transportation. Borrowing money and work space from his employer — Columbus, Indiana, banker W. G. Irwin — Cummins founded Cummins Engine in 1919. Irwin eventually invested over $2.5 million in the business, and in the mid-1920s Cummins produced a mobile diesel engine. Truck manufacturers were reluctant to make the switch from gas to diesel, so Cummins used publicity stunts (including racing in the Indianapolis 500) to advertise his engine, and Irwin installed the engines in his California Purity Stores delivery truck fleet.

The company earned its first profit in 1937, the year Irwin's grandnephew, J. Irwin Miller, took over as leader. During WWII the engine was used in trucks transporting large, heavy shipments. Heavy postwar demand caused sales to jump from $20 million in 1946 to over $100 million by 1956. In the 1950s Cummins pioneered a line of 4-stroke diesel engines, started its first overseas plant in Scotland (1956), and bought Atlas Crankshafts (1958). By 1967 it had 50% of the diesel engine market. Two years later General Motors agreed to offer Cummins engines.

In 1970 Cummins acquired businesses not related to diesel engine production, including the K2 Ski Company (fiberglass skis) and Coot Industries (all-terrain vehicles), but had sold them by 1976. After touring Japanese factories, Henry Schacht, CEO since 1973, began a program to modernize company plants. When he learned that some of his customers were testing engines from Japanese firms (e.g., Nissan and Komatsu), he lowered Cummins prices 20–40%.

In the early 1980s Cummins introduced a line of midrange engines developed in a joint venture with Tenneco subsidiary J. I. Case. To remain competitive in manufacturing, Cummins cut costs by 22%, which doubled productivity in its US and UK plants, and spent $1.8 billion to retool its factories. The strategy yielded mixed results. Profits were erratic, and restructuring prevented the company from taking advantage of an industry boom between 1987 and 1988.

Having twice repelled unwelcome foreign suitors in 1989, Cummins sold 27% of its stock, collectively, to Ford, Tenneco, and Japanese tractor maker Kubota for $250 million in 1990, a move that raised much-needed cash and offered Cummins protection against future takeover bids. The next year Cummins joined Russian truck maker KamAZ to form KamDizel, J. E., an engine-manufacturing venture, and in 1992 it agreed to jointly develop an engine based on its high-pressure fuel-injection technology with Sweden's Saab-Scania.

In 1993 Cummins established a joint venture to manufacture its "B series" engines for TELCO vehicles with India's largest heavy-vehicle maker, Tata Engineering & Locomotive. That same year the company entered another joint venture with Japan's leading construction equipment maker, Komatsu, to produce 3.9- and 5.9-liter engines.

In 1994 Cummins introduced a natural-gas engine for school buses and formed a joint venture to produce turbochargers in India.

In 1995 James Henderson, Cummins's #2 executive, succeeded long-time chairman Schacht, who retired but remains on the board.

NYSE symbol: CUM
Fiscal year ends: December 31

WHO

Chairman and CEO: James A. Henderson, age 60,
$1,419,690 pay (prior to promotion)
President and COO: Theodore M. Solso, age 47,
$847,686 pay (prior to promotion)
Group VP Worldwide Operations and Technology:
F. Joseph Loughrey, age 45, $516,763 pay
Group VP Marketing: C. Roberto Cordaro, age 44
VP and CFO: Peter B. Hamilton, age 48, $610,638 pay
VP Law and External Affairs and Secretary: Steven L.
Zeller, age 38
VP and Corporate Controller: John McLachlan, age 62
VP International: John K. Edwards, age 50
**VP Cummins Power Generation Group; President,
Onan Corporation:** Richard B. Stoner Jr., age 48
VP Human Resources: Brenda S. Pitts
Auditors: Arthur Andersen & Co, SC

WHERE

HQ: 500 Jackson St., Box 3005, Columbus, IN
47202-3005
Phone: 812-377-5000
Fax: 812-377-3334

Cummins has manufacturing operations in 14 countries.

	1994 Sales	
	$ mil.	% of total
US	2,712	57
Europe	671	14
Asia, Far East & Australia	626	13
Canada	330	7
Mexico & South America	318	7
Africa & Middle East	80	2
Total	**4,737**	**100**

WHAT

	1994 Sales	
	$ mil.	% of total
Heavy-duty truck	1,410	30
Power generation	1,039	22
Bus & light commercial vehicle	592	12
Industrial products	526	11
Midrange truck	513	11
Marine	78	2
Government	67	1
Other	512	11
Total	**4,737**	**100**

**Heavy-duty and Midrange
Truck**
160–300 HP diesel engines
for mid-range trucks
250–500 HP diesel engines
for heavy-duty trucks

Power Generation
Alternators, engines,
generator sets, and
switches

**Bus and Light
Commercial Vehicle**
Engines for pickup trucks,
school buses, urban
transit buses, delivery
trucks, and recreational
vehicles

Industrial Products
Engines for construction,
logging, mining, and
agricultural, petroleum,
and rail markets

Marine
76–1,400 HP engines for
recreational,
commercial, and
military markets

Government
Engines for military and
civilian applications

Other
Filters, turbochargers,
and electronic systems

KEY COMPETITORS

Allison Engine	Eaton	Navistar
Briggs & Stratton	Fiat	Outboard Marine
Brunswick	General	Penske
Caterpillar	Motors	Renault
Cooper Industries	Hitachi	Rolls-Royce
Daimler-Benz	Isuzu	Tata
Dana	Mitsubishi	Volvo

HOW MUCH

	9-Year Growth	1985	1986	1987	1988	1989	1990	1991	1992	1993	1994
Sales ($ mil.)	9.2%	2,146	2,304	2,767	3,310	3,511	3,462	3,406	3,749	4,248	4,737
Net income ($ mil.)	19.7%	50	(107)	14	(63)	(6)	(165)	(66)	67	177	253
Income as % of sales	—	2.3%	—	0.5%	—	—	—	—	1.8%	4.2%	5.3%
Earnings per share ($)	9.9%	2.61	(5.23)	0.28	(3.36)	(0.76)	(7.24)	(2.48)	1.77	4.63	6.11
Stock price – high ($)	—	44.25	39.38	47.38	34.00	36.13	27.75	27.25	40.44	54.38	57.63
Stock price – low ($)	—	29.13	25.63	20.38	21.56	24.00	15.56	16.25	26.63	37.38	35.88
Stock price – close ($)	2.6%	36.00	33.56	23.63	32.13	25.38	18.63	27.13	39.00	53.75	45.25
P/E – high	—	17	—	169	—	—	—	—	23	12	9
P/E – low	—	11	—	73	—	—	—	—	15	8	6
Dividends per share ($)	(6.0%)	1.10	1.10	1.10	1.10	1.10	1.10	0.35	0.10	0.20	0.63
Book value per share ($)	(3.9%)	37.02	30.94	32.50	27.51	19.89	18.68	17.14	11.21	18.41	25.78
Employees	3.0%	19,624	23,000	24,500	26,100	25,100	24,900	22,900	23,400	23,600	25,600

1994 Year-end:
Debt ratio: 17.8%
Return on equity: 28.4%
Cash (mil.): $147
Current ratio: 1.55
Long-term debt (mil.): $155
No. of shares (mil.): 42
Dividends
  Yield: 1.4%
  Payout: 10.2%
Market value (mil.): $1,882

Stock Price History
High/Low 1985–94

CYPRUS AMAX MINERALS COMPANY

OVERVIEW

Colorado-based Cyprus Amax is the US's largest mining company and one of the world's largest natural resource concerns. It is the US's 2nd largest copper producer, a leading coal producer, and the world's biggest supplier of molybdenum (used in steelmaking) and lithium (half of the world's supply; used in plastics, chemicals, and many other products). Cyprus Amax also has significant interests in gold through its 42% stake in Amax Gold. After a year of slashing costs, streamlining, and acquiring strategic properties, the company is aggressively positioning itself to become a major international supplier of key metals and minerals used in the US and world economies.

Cyprus Amax is simultaneously developing several major projects worldwide. It bought majority stakes in 2 "world-class" copper properties in Chile (with Codelco, the world's largest copper producer) and Peru (with Sociedad Minera Cerro Verde); created joint ventures to produce gold in Chile, Alaska, and Russia; boosted the production of low-sulfur export coal; and reopened a molybdenum mine.

WHEN

Cyprus Amax was created in 1993 when Cyprus Minerals Co., a coal and copper producer, merged with AMAX Inc., a diversified metals and energy company.

Berthold Hochschild founded the American Metal Company (Amco for short) to trade in metals for a German banking firm. After severing ties with Germany during WWI, Amco in 1916 formed an independent syndicate to exploit Colorado deposits of molybdenum. In 1957 Amco merged with the syndicate, creating American Metal Climax, which was informally known as AMAX until the name became official in 1974.

AMAX ventured into other mining operations, including tungsten (Canada, 1961), lead (Missouri, 1963), and iron (Australia, 1963). Most important was its 1962 entry into aluminum with the purchase of Kawneer of Michigan and Apex Smelting of Chicago. AMAX added to its holdings by buying California-based Hunter Engineering (1963). Combined under one name as Alumax, the unit later became the US's 3rd largest aluminum company.

AMAX ventured into midwestern coal by acquiring Ayrshire Collieries in 1969 and Wyoming mines in the 1970s. During the 1980s the company branched into gold and sold or wrote off unrelated operations before moving into energy in 1990 with the purchase of Ladd Petroleum. In the early 1990s AMAX was hurt by a weak global economy, low metals prices, and excess imports of aluminum from the former Soviet Union.

The Cyprus Minerals Co. evolved from Amoco Minerals Co., which was a subsidiary created in 1969 to handle mineral rights for the integrated oil company, Amoco Corp. The name was changed in 1979 to Cyprus Minerals when the subsidiary acquired a diversified mining company, dating back to 1916, that explored for minerals on Cyprus and later acquired oil and other minerals in the US and Peru. In 1985 Amoco Minerals was spun off as Cyprus Minerals.

The new publicly traded company went on a buying spree, purchasing coal mines in Utah (1985), Colorado (1985), and Wyoming (1987) and copper mines in Arizona (1986 and 1987) and New Mexico (1987). Also in 1987 Cyprus began mining for gold in Arizona and Australia. The company continued its rapid growth, and sales topped $1 billion by 1988.

Cyprus continued to expand, buying Foote Mineral (lithium, 1988), Windsor Minerals (talc division of Johnson & Johnson, 1989; sold 1992), Sociedad Chilena (lithium, 1989), Reserve Mining (iron ore, 1989), and Warrenton Refining (copper ingot, 1989). Cyprus bought MCR (copper rod, Chicago) in 1990 and the next year entered a coal mining joint venture with Carbones del Zulia (a subsidiary of Petróleos de Venezuela).

The 1993 merger between Cyprus and AMAX consolidated the coal and copper operations of both companies and greatly reduced AMAX's debt. Spun off in the merger were Alumax and Amax Gold, in which the new company acquired a 42% stake.

Cyprus chairman Milton Ward became the CEO and split the chairman's job with Allen Born, AMAX's former chief, who became CEO of Alumax. Ward trimmed jobs, cut costs, and boosted productivity to make the new company a low-cost, high-volume worldwide producer.

In 1994 the AMAX Oil and Gas subsidiary was sold to finance new mining projects in South America; also sold were the company's Minnesota iron ore mine and processing facilities. In 1995 Ward reorganized the company, bringing in new executives for its coal operations and creating a development unit to help the company grow.

NYSE symbol: CYM
Fiscal year ends: December 31

WHO

Co-chairman, President, and CEO: Milton H. Ward, age 62, $1,813,530 pay
Co-chairman; Chairman and CEO, Alumax: Allen Born, age 61
SVP and CFO: Gerald J. Malys, age 50, $505,366 pay
SVP; President, Cyprus Climax Metals Co.: Jeffrey G. Clevenger, age 45, $402,946 pay
SVP; President, Cyprus Amax Coal Co.: Garold R. Spindler, age 47
SVP, General Counsel, and Corporate Secretary: Philip C. Wolf, age 47, $342,440 pay
SVP Exploration: David H. Watkins, age 50
VP; President, Cyprus Amax Engineering and Development Co.: Robin J. Hickson, age 51
VP Investor Relations and Treasurer: Francis J. Kane, age 36
VP Human Resources: Gerard H. Peppard, age 51
Auditors: Price Waterhouse LLP

WHERE

HQ: 9100 E. Mineral Circle, Englewood, CO 80112
Phone: 303-643-5000
Fax: 303-643-5049

Cyprus Amax has operations in 17 states as well as Australia, Chile, the Netherlands, Peru, Sweden, and the UK.

	1994 Sales		1994 Operating Income	
	$ mil.	% of total	$ mil.	% of total
US	2,561	92	311	88
Other countries	227	8	41	12
Total	**2,788**	**100**	**352**	**100**

Mines and Major Production Facilities

Coal	Illinois	Molybdenum
Australia	New Mexico	Colorado
Colorado	Peru	Iowa
Illinois		The Netherlands
Indiana	**Gold**	Sweden
Kentucky	California	UK
Ohio	Chile	
Pennsylvania	Nevada	**Specialty Metals**
Tennessee		**and Chemicals**
Utah	**Lithium**	Illinois
West Virginia	Chile	Louisiana
Wyoming	Nevada	Michigan
	Tennessee	Ohio
Copper	Virginia	Pennsylvania
Arizona		UK
Chile		

WHAT

	1994 Sales		1994 Operating Income	
	$ mil.	% of total	$ mil.	% of total
Copper/molybdenum	1,327	48	206	59
Coal	1,248	45	106	30
Other (minerals)	213	7	40	11
Total	**2,788**	**100**	**352**	**100**

KEY COMPETITORS

Anglo American	FMC	Phelps Dodge
ASARCO	Freeport-McMoRan	Pittston
Ashland Inc.	Copper & Gold	Minerals
Atlantic	Homestake	RTZ
Richfield	Mining	Westmoreland
Broken Hill	Kerr-McGee	Coal
Cleveland-Cliffs	Magma Copper	Zambia
Cominco	Newmont Gold	Copper
CONSOL	Noranda	Zeigler Coal
Energy	Peter Kiewit	
Fluor	Sons'	

HOW MUCH

	9-Year Growth	1985	1986	1987	1988	1989	1990	1991	1992	1993	1994
Sales ($ mil.)	15.7%	749	864	843	1,395	1,790	1,866	1,657	1,641	1,764	2,788
Net income ($ mil.)	—	(452)	21	26	170	250	111	43	(246)	100	175
Income as % of sales	—	—	2.4%	3.1%	12.2%	14.0%	5.9%	2.6%	—	5.7%	6.3%
Earnings per share ($)	—	(11.49)	0.54	0.68	3.98	5.30	2.29	0.72	(6.31)	1.85	1.69
Stock price – high ($)	—	11.59	16.50	19.50	24.00	33.00	28.50	25.38	32.00	36.38	33.38
Stock price – low ($)	—	7.34	9.59	9.66	13.44	21.34	13.88	17.50	18.50	21.25	26.13
Stock price – close ($)	10.0%	11.09	10.84	16.19	21.69	26.50	18.50	22.88	31.50	25.88	26.13
P/E – high	—	—	31	29	6	6	12	35	—	20	20
P/E – low	—	—	18	14	3	4	6	24	—	12	14
Dividends per share ($)	—	0.00	0.00	0.00	0.13	0.63	0.80	0.80	0.85	0.80	0.90
Book value per share ($)	2.3%	20.50	21.35	21.96	25.63	30.92	27.94	28.02	19.52	21.64	25.11
Employees	8.1%	4,723	5,025	5,150	7,400	8,500	8,000	8,100	7,000	10,750	9,500

1994 Year-end:
Debt ratio: 38.5%
Return on equity: 7.7%
Cash (mil.): $139
Current ratio: 1.68
Long-term debt (mil.): $1,155
No. of shares (mil.): 93
Dividends
  Yield: 3.4%
  Payout: 53.3%
Market value (mil.): $2,419

Stock Price History
High/Low 1985–94

DANA CORPORATION

Toledo, Ohio–based Dana Corp. specializes in what you don't see: axles, driveshafts, filters, valves, and piston rings, among many other components and parts used inside and under cars, pickups, vans, medium-weight and heavy trucks, and the popular sport/utility vehicles. Dana sells many of its products to OEMs, including 2 of the Big 3 automakers; Ford, with 16% of 1994 sales, is Dana's biggest customer, and Chrysler accounts for 12%. It also sells to parts distributors (34%). With almost $7 billion in sales, the company is a leading supplier to vehicular and industrial markets in addition to construction and agricultural machinery manufacturers. A subsidiary provides leasing

and financing services. International sales accounted for 25% of 1994 revenues.

Dana is expanding into international markets and boosting parts distribution to offset the cyclical automobile industry. The company wants to boost international sales to 50% of its total revenues by the year 2000. Toward that end in 1994 the company bought 4 related companies in Europe and Mexico and created 2 joint ventures in China and Brazil. In 1995 Dana set up a sales and marketing office in Vietnam as a springboard to Asia and the Pacific. The company also acquired a molded rubber manufacturer in 1995 and most of the stock of Canadian parts maker Hayes-Dana.

WHEN

Clarence Spicer began developing a universal joint and driveshaft for automobiles while studying at Cornell University. Leaving Cornell in 1904, he patented his design and founded Spicer Manufacturing in Plainfield, New Jersey. Spicer marketed the product himself, signing Mack Trucks in 1906 and International Harvester in 1914. Both have been continuous customers.

The company encountered financial trouble in 1913, and in 1914 New York attorney Charles Dana joined, advancing Spicer money to refinance.

Acquisitions after WWI strengthened Spicer's position in the growing truck industry: Chadwick Engine Works (U-joints), Parish Pressed Steel (vehicle frames), Brown-Lipe Gear Company (truck transmissions), Salisbury (axles), and Sheldon (axles).

The company moved to Toledo in 1929 to be nearer the emerging Detroit automotive center. Sales increased 18.4% annually from 1930 to 1940, rising to $19 million. In 1946 the company was renamed in honor of Dana, who became chairman 2 years later. In the 1950s sales topped $150 million.

In the 1960s Dana Corp. adopted a strategy of market penetration and product development, targeting the heavy truck and service industries, and entered a new market in 1963 by purchasing 2 replacement-parts makers, Perfect Circle and Aluminum Industries. In 1966 Dana added Victor Manufacturing and Gasket. Dana also decentralized, giving divisional managers more responsibility. Charles Dana retired in 1966, after more than 50 years of service.

Dana continued to grow throughout the 1970s, reaching its first $1 billion in sales in 1974. Dana bought the Weatherhead Company

(hoses, fittings, and couplings; 1977), the Wix Corporation (filters, 1979), and Tyrone Hydraulics (pumps and motors, 1980). By 1980 sales had exceeded $2.5 billion. During this time Dana branched into financial services.

Dana polished its production and sourcing methods during the 1980s. As a result, sales rose to $4.9 billion by 1988, while employment remained about even. Overall reliance on automotive original equipment decreased from nearly 60% of total sales to 50%. Dana emerged as a leader in mobile fluid power (e.g., pumps, motors, and hoses) and mechanical and electrical industrial equipment.

In 1989 Dana introduced a 9-speed, heavy-duty truck transmission (developed jointly with Navistar), the first all-new design of its type in over 25 years. Sluggish truck markets along with losses in the company's financial segment reduced 1990 and 1991 earnings.

In 1992 Dana sold its mortgage banking business and some other financial services. Also that year Dana acquired Krizman and Delta Automotive, 2 leading automotive aftermarket parts makers and distributors.

Dana's sales topped $5 billion in 1993. That year Dana acquired the Reinz group, German gasket makers. Included in the deal were Reinz subsidiaries in Spain and the US, along with interests in operations in Japan, India, and France.

In 1994 Dana bought Sige, an Italian axle maker; Stieber Heidelberg, a German industrial components manufacturer; Tece, a Dutch auto parts distributor; and Tremec, a Mexican transmission manufacturer. Strong global economies in 1994 boosted sales over $6.7 billion. In 1995 Dana bought the Plumley Companies (automotive sealing products).

NYSE symbol: DCN
Fiscal year ends: December 31

WHO

Chairman, CEO, President, and COO: Southwood J.
Morcott, age 56, $1,923,430 pay
EVP: Carl H. Hirsch, age 60, $909,100 pay
EVP: Borge R. Reimer, age 64, $897,700 pay
VP Finance, Treasurer, and CFO: James E. Ayers,
age 62, $824,400 pay
VP, General Counsel, and Secretary: Martin J. Strobel,
age 54
President, Dana North America Operations: Joseph M.
Magliochetti, age 52, $837,300 pay
President, Dana South American Operations: C. J.
Eterovic, age 60
President, Dana Europe: M. A. Franklin III, age 47
President, Dana Asia/Pacific Operations: J. S. Simpson,
age 54
President, Lease Financing: E. J. Schultz, age 52
Human Resource Manager: Pat Gahagan
Auditors: Price Waterhouse LLP

WHERE

HQ: 4500 Dorr St., Toledo, OH 43615
Phone: 419-535-4500
Fax: 419-535-4643

Dana operates 445 manufacturing, assembly, and
distribution facilities in 27 countries.

	1994 Sales		1994 Operating Income	
	$ mil.	% of total	$ mil.	% of total
US	5,073	75	462	79
Europe	740	11	14	2
Other regions	941	14	113	19
Adjustments	(269)	—	—	—
Total	**6,741**	**100**	**589**	**100**

WHAT

	1994 Sales		1994 Operating Income	
	$ mil.	% of total	$ mil.	% of total
Vehicular prods.	5,299	79	520	88
Industrial prods.	1,309	19	57	10
Financial services	146	2	12	2
Adjustments	(13)	—	—	—
Total	**6,741**	**100**	**589**	**100**

Brand Names

Chassis Products
Perfect Circle
Spicer

Drivetrain Systems
Chelsea
Spicer

Engine Parts
Perfect Circle
Victor Reinz
Warner Electric
Wix

Fluid Power Systems
Boston

Everflex
Gresen
Hyco
Tyrone
Weatherhead

Industrial Power Transmission Products
Boston
Formsprag
Seco
Warner Electric
Wichita

Structural Components
Parish

Selected Subsidiary

Dana Commercial Credit (leasing)

KEY COMPETITORS

AlliedSignal
A. O. Smith
Arvin Industries
Borg-Warner
  Automotive
Caterpillar
Cooper
  Industries
Cummins Engine

Danaher
Eaton
Emerson
General Electric
Mascotech
Navistar
PACCAR
Reliance Electric
Robert Bosch

Rockwell
Siemens
SPX
Tecumseh
  Products
Textron
Thyssen
Western
  Atlas
Westinghouse

HOW MUCH

	9-Year Growth	1985	1986	1987	1988	1989	1990	1991	1992	1993	1994
Sales ($ mil.)	6.5%	3,777	3,960	4,422	5,175	5,134	5,185	4,572	5,011	5,563	6,741
Net income ($ mil.)	3.7%	165	86	141	162	132	76	13	43	129	228
Income as % of sales	—	4.4%	2.2%	3.2%	3.1%	2.6%	1.5%	0.3%	0.9%	2.3%	3.5%
Earnings per share ($)	5.1%	1.48	0.84	1.61	1.90	1.55	0.93	0.17	0.49	1.39	2.31
Stock price – high ($)	—	15.19	18.25	27.13	20.25	21.44	19.06	18.25	24.13	30.13	30.69
Stock price – low ($)	—	11.13	12.75	13.75	16.25	16.50	9.94	12.31	13.38	22.00	19.63
Stock price – close ($)	6.2%	13.63	17.44	17.06	19.44	17.31	14.94	13.88	23.50	29.94	23.50
P/E – high	—	10	22	17	11	14	21	—	49	22	13
P/E – low	—	8	15	9	9	11	11	—	27	16	9
Dividends per share ($)	2.9%	0.64	0.64	0.70	0.77	0.80	0.80	0.80	0.80	0.80	0.83
Book value per share ($)	(2.0%)	11.37	10.70	10.81	11.80	12.47	12.78	12.02	7.70	8.73	9.51
Employees	0.4%	38,200	37,000	37,500	39,500	37,500	33,300	35,000	35,000	36,000	39,500

1994 Year-end:
Debt ratio: 65.3%
Return on equity: 26.2%
Cash (mil.): $112
Current ratio: 1.86
Long-term debt (mil.): $1,187
No. of shares (mil.): 99
Dividends
  Yield: 3.5%
  Payout: 35.9%
Market value (mil.): $2,322

**Stock Price History
High/Low 1985–94**

DARDEN RESTAURANTS, INC.

OVERVIEW

The largest casual-dining restaurant company in the US, Darden Restaurants was served up by General Mills in a 1995 spin-off to its stockholders. Formerly General Mills Restaurant Group, the Orlando-based company operates approximately 700 Red Lobster seafood restaurants and more than 475 Olive Garden Italian restaurants. In August 1995 Darden junked its 51-restaurant China Coast chain. The venture was Darden's failed attempt to enter the popular, highly fragmented Asian restaurant business. Darden had invested $104 million in the chain, the per-restaurant sales of which had been 50% below expectations.

Red Lobster is the US's #1 casual-dining chain, holding a 29% share of the seafood restaurant market. Olive Garden is the nation's largest chain of full-service Italian restaurants, with a 17% market share.

General Mills CEO Bruce Atwater decided to split the company's restaurant business off from its food operations so the 2 groups could focus more effectively on their particular businesses. With the casual-dining business in a slump, Darden is proceeding cautiously. It plans to open 50 to 80 new restaurants in 1995, down from the average of 118 it has opened each of the last 3 years.

WHEN

Bill Darden started in the restaurant business in the late 1930s at age 19 in Waycross, Georgia, with a luncheonette called the Green Frog luncheonette. The 25-seat restaurant, which featured the slogan "Service with a Hop," was a hit, and Darden's restaurant career was born. During the 1950s he owned a variety of restaurants, including several Howard Johnson's, Bonanza restaurants, and Kentucky Fried Chicken outlets.

In 1963 Darden teamed with a group of investors to buy an Orlando restaurant, Gary's Duck Inn. The restaurant became a prototype for Darden's idea for a landlocked, moderately priced, sit-down seafood chain. Darden, at the suggestion of a printer making his menus, decided to name the new chain Red Lobster, a takeoff of the old Green Frog.

The first Red Lobster opened in Lakeland, Florida, in 1968, with Joe Lee, who had worked in one of Darden's other restaurants, as its manager. It was such a success that within a month the restaurant had to be expanded. In 1970, when there were 3 Red Lobsters in operation and 2 under construction in central Florida, General Mills bought the chain, keeping Darden on to run it.

Red Lobster was not General Mills's first foray into the restaurant business. In 1968 the company opened Betty Crocker Tree House Restaurant, and that same year it acquired a fish and chips chain and a barbecue chain. But Red Lobster would be its first success. Rather than franchise the Red Lobster name, it chose to develop the chain on its own. In 1975 Joe Lee was named president of Red Lobster and Darden became chairman of General Mills Restaurants.

While General Mills continued to expand Red Lobster, it also cast around for another concept to complement its seafood chain. Among those that were tried and discarded were a steakhouse, a Mexican restaurant, and a health-food restaurant.

In 1980 the company began to develop an Italian restaurant. After 2 years of marketing questionnaires and recipe tests, General Mills opened a prototype Olive Garden in Orlando. The company eventually spent about $100 million to develop Olive Garden, which featured moderately priced Italian food and a festive atmosphere. General Mills began to add outlets beginning in the mid-1980s, and Olive Garden became one of the success stories of the casual-dining business. Meanwhile, the company began a major remodeling of its Red Lobsters.

In the early 1990s Red Lobster began to run into trouble. It had become one of the highest-priced chains in the casual-dining segment, and when the economy soured, the chain began fighting to keep its head above water. In response Red Lobster introduced a line of menu items under $10.

In 1990 General Mills had begun testing a new Chinese restaurant concept, China Coast, opening its first outlet in Orlando. In 1993 the company announced the official launch of its China Coast chain. Also in 1993 the Olive Garden began to cool off. Same-store sales began to slide as competitors added Italian items to their menus. In 1994 Olive Garden increased its advertising budget, introduced new menu items, and began testing new unit styles, including a smaller cafe-version for malls.

Prior to the 1995 spin-off, it was announced that General Mills Restaurant Group would be renamed Darden Restaurants in honor of Bill Darden, who died in 1994. Darden's net income for fiscal 1995 was $49 million.

NYSE symbol: DRI
Fiscal year ends: Last Sunday in May

WHO

Chairman and CEO: Joe R. Lee, age 54, $524,669 pay
President and COO: Jeffrey J. O'Hara, age 47, $554,300 pay (prior to promotion)
EVP; President, New Business Development: Blaine G. Sweatt, age 47, $318,200 pay
President, Olive Garden North America: Bradley D. Blum, age 41
President, Red Lobster North America: Kirk L. Spresser, age 39
SVP, Secretary, and General Counsel: Clifford L. Whitehill, age 64, $376,885 pay
SVP Finance: James D. Smith, age 52
SVP Corporate Relations: Richard J. Walsh, age 42
SVP Investor Relations: Edward L. Blood, age 49
SVP Personnel: Frank E. Ruble, age 55
Auditors: KPMG Peat Marwick LLP

WHERE

HQ: 5900 Lake Ellenor Dr., PO Box 593330, Orlando, FL 32859-3330
Phone: 407-245-4000
Fax: 407-245-5135

Darden operates about 1,200 restaurants in 49 states and Canada.

	1994 Restaurants
	No.
Florida	125
Texas	121
California	117
Illinois	52
Michigan	48
Pennsylvania	45
New York	44
Indiana	37
Georgia	36
Virginia	34
Tennessee	28
Missouri	27
North Carolina	26
New Jersey	23
Arizona	22
Other states	360
Canada	76
Total	**1,221**

WHAT

	1994 Sales	
	$ mil.	% of total
Red Lobster	1,838	62
Olive Garden	1,098	37
China Coast	27	1
Total	**2,963**	**100**

	1994 Restaurants	
	No.	% of total
Red Lobster	694	57
Olive Garden	477	39
China Coast	50	4
Total	**1,221**	**100**

Selected Menu Items

Red Lobster
Crab
Fresh fish
Lobster
Scallops
Shrimp

Olive Garden
Baked lasagna
Chicken marsala
Fettuccine Alfredo
Manicotti
Tossed salad
Veal piccata

KEY COMPETITORS

Applebee's	Metromedia
Bertucci's	Morrison Restaurants
Brinker	NPC Intl.
Buffets	Outback Steakhouse
Carlson	Pappas Restaurants
Chart House	Ryan's Family Steak
Cracker Barrel	Houses
DAKA	Sizzler
Family Restaurants	Taco Cabana
Landry's Seafood	Tennessee Restaurant
Long John Silver's	Uno Restaurant

HOW MUCH

	Annual Growth	1985	1986	1987	1988	1989	1990	1991	1992	1993	1994
Sales ($ mil.)	11.2%	1,140	1,051	1,249	1,312	1,622	1,928	2,214	2,542	2,737	2,963
Net income ($ mil.)	4.8%	—	—	—	—	—	—	—	112	92	123
Income as % of sales	—	—	—	—	—	—	—	—	4.4%	3.3%	4.2%
Employees	16.3%	29,722	35,502	44,415	52,177	67,814	76,305	85,799	90,626	109,875	115,518

1994 Year-end:
Debt ratio: 20.1%
Return on equity: 9.4%
Cash (mil.): $17
Current ratio: 0.72
Long-term debt (mil.): $4

Net Income ($ mil.)
1992–94

DAYTON HUDSON CORPORATION

OVERVIEW

Breaking up may be hard to do, but that could be what is in store for Dayton Hudson. The Minneapolis-based company has a range of retail formats, including an "upscale discounter" (Target), a mid-range department store (Mervyn's), and upscale department stores (Dayton's, Hudson's, and Marshall Field's). Some analysts have suggested that the proceeds from the sale of Mervyn's or the department store division could fund expansion of Target.

The company's best performer, Target has done well by zeroing in on its own niche. Ostensibly a discount chain, Target offers more upscale prices than discount competitors like Wal-Mart and Kmart, but its prices are still lower than at most department stores. Target accounted for nearly 64% of Dayton Hudson's 1994 sales.

While Target has headed toward a bull's-eye, Mervyn's has been off the mark. The unit has suffered for a number of reasons, including a lack of name-brand merchandise, poor promotion, and a heavy concentration of stores in California, which has been slow to recover from its recession. Dayton Hudson is testing an updated format for Mervyn's that includes bigger luggage and women's shoe departments, a portrait studio, Ticketmaster services, and a buffet restaurant.

WHEN

The panic of 1873 left Joseph Hudson bankrupt. After he had paid his debts at 60 cents on the dollar, he saved enough to open a men's clothing store in Detroit in 1881. Among his innovations were merchandise return privileges and price marking in place of bargaining. By 1891 Hudson's was the largest retailer of men's clothing in America. Hudson repaid his creditors from 1873 in full with interest.

When Hudson died in 1912, 4 nephews took over and expanded the business. In 1928 Hudson's built a new building in downtown Detroit that became the 2nd largest retail store building in the US, eventually growing to 25 stories with 49 acres of floor space.

In 1902 former banker George Dayton established a dry-goods store in Minneapolis on a spot where he had found the most foot traffic. Like Hudson, he offered return privileges and liberal credit. His store grew to a 12-story, full-line department store.

After WWII both companies saw that the future lay in the suburbs. In 1954 Hudson's built Northland in Detroit, then the largest US shopping center. Dayton's built the world's first fully enclosed shopping mall in Edina, a Minneapolis suburb (1956), and opened its first Target discount store (1962) and its first B. Dalton bookstore (1962; sold 1986).

Dayton's went public in 1966, and in 1969 it bought the family-owned Hudson's for stock, forming Dayton Hudson Corporation. The corporation increased its ownership of malls and invested in such specialty areas as consumer electronics (Team Central, Minneapolis, 1970; sold 1979) and hard goods (Lechmere, Boston, 1969; sold 1989).

In 1977 Target became the company's top moneymaker. The company then bought California-based Mervyn's and began selling other operations. In the late 1970s and 1980s, it sold 9 regional malls and several other businesses.

In the late 1980s Dayton Hudson took Target to Los Angeles and the Northwest. In 1991 it started to move Mervyn's into Florida.

In 1990 the company bought Marshall Field's department store, which had grown out of a dry-goods store started in Chicago in 1852 by Potter Palmer. Marshall Field had bought into the store in 1865, building it into one of Chicago's biggest retailers. His motto, "Give the lady what she wants," became the hallmark of customer-oriented retailing.

Looking to improve Mervyn's operations, in 1993 Dayton Hudson introduced a value pricing strategy, reintroduced women's dresses (which had been dropped in 1991), improved customer service, and replaced about 70% of the chain's senior management team. That same year Dayton Hudson entered the world of infomercials, becoming the first major retailer to advertise in that format. The 30-minute program, called "Marshall Field's Presents," aired in 30 national markets.

In 1994 Kenneth Macke retired as chairman and CEO. He was succeeded by Robert Ulrich, formerly chairman and CEO of Target. That same year the company announced plans to revive its catalog business, which it had discontinued in 1990.

In 1995 Dayton Hudson's department store division began testing interactive kiosks that combine a gift registry with an electronic catalog. Using a touch screen, customers can browse a catalog of gifts selected by a registrant. Once a gift is selected, the customer can pay for it with a credit card.

NYSE symbol: DH
Fiscal year ends: Saturday nearest January 31

WHO

Chairman and CEO: Robert J. Ulrich, age 51, $1,731,525 pay
President; Chairman and CEO, Department Store Division: Stephen E. Watson, age 50, $1,062,491 pay
President, Target: Kenneth P. Woodrow, age 50, $842,124 pay
President and COO, Mervyn's: Paul W. Sauser, age 47, $663,750 pay
EVP Merchandising, Target: Gregg W. Steinhafel, age 40, $622,977 pay
EVP Merchandising and Marketing, Mervyn's: Raj Joneja, age 47
SVP, General Counsel, and Secretary: James T. Hale, age 54
SVP and CFO: Douglas A. Scovanner, age 39
SVP Personnel: Edwin H. Wingate, age 62
Auditors: Ernst & Young LLP

WHERE

HQ: 777 Nicollet Mall, Minneapolis, MN 55402-2055
Phone: 612-370-6948
Fax: 612-370-5502

Location	1995 Stores No. of Targets	No. of Mervyn's
Los Angeles area	65	50
Minneapolis/St. Paul	29	—
Chicago	24	—
Detroit	21	9
Dallas/Ft. Worth	20	13
Houston	19	10
San Francisco area	17	22
Phoenix	15	11
Atlanta	14	7
Miami/Ft. Lauderdale	14	14
Other locations	373	150
Total	**611**	**286**

	1995 Stores		
Location	No. of Dayton's	No. of Hudson's	No. of Marshall Field's
Minnesota	12	—	—
North Dakota	3	—	—
Wisconsin	3	—	3
South Dakota	1	—	—
Illinois	—	—	15
Michigan	—	18	—
Indiana	—	2	—
Ohio	—	1	1
Texas	—	—	4
Total	**19**	**21**	**23**

WHAT

	1995 Sales		1995 Operating Income	
	$ mil.	% of total	$ mil.	% of total
Target	13,600	64	732	61
Mervyn's	4,561	21	206	17
Department stores	3,150	15	270	22
Total	**21,311**	**100**	**1,208**	**100**

KEY COMPETITORS

Ames	J. C. Penney	Nine West
Best Products	Kohl's	Nordstrom
Bradlees	Kmart	Price/Costco
Broadway Stores	Lands' End	Sears
Brown Group	The Limited	Service
Caldor	Liz Claiborne	Merchandise
Damark Intl.	May	Spiegel
Dillard	McCrory	Toys "R" Us
Edison Brothers	Melville	Venture Stores
Federated	Men's Wearhouse	Wal-Mart
The Gap	Merry-Go-Round	Woolworth
Harcourt General	Montgomery Ward	

HOW MUCH

	9-Year Growth	1986	1987	1988	1989	1990	1991	1992	1993	1994	1995
Sales ($ mil.)	10.3%	8,793	9,259	10,677	12,204	13,644	14,739	16,115	17,927	19,233	21,311
Net income ($ mil.)	4.8%	284	257	228	287	410	410	301	383	375	434
Income as % of sales	—	3.2%	2.8%	2.1%	2.4%	3.0%	2.8%	1.9%	2.1%	1.9%	2.0%
Earnings per share ($)[1]	7.3%	2.92	2.64	2.41	3.45	5.35	5.17	3.72	4.82	4.77	5.52
Stock price – high ($)[1]	—	48.75	58.50	63.00	45.50	67.00	79.50	80.25	79.25	85.00	86.88
Stock price – low ($)[1]	—	29.38	40.00	21.50	28.25	38.75	46.25	53.75	58.00	62.63	64.88
Stock price – close ($)[1]	4.9%	45.88	42.50	27.63	39.63	63.63	57.25	61.88	75.75	66.63	70.75
P/E – high	—	17	22	26	13	13	15	22	16	18	16
P/E – low	—	10	15	9	8	7	9	14	12	13	12
Dividends per share ($)	9.2%	0.76	0.84	0.92	1.02	1.12	1.32	1.44	1.52	1.62	1.68
Book value per share ($)	8.7%	20.04	22.38	23.15	23.97	24.73	28.82	31.32	34.83	38.27	42.45
Employees	7.9%	98,000	111,000	134,000	128,000	144,000	161,000	168,000	170,000	174,000	194,000

1995 Year-end:
Debt ratio: 60.7%
Return on equity: 15.0%
Cash (mil.): $147
Current ratio: 1.46
Long-term debt (mil.):$4,488
No. of shares (mil.): 72
Dividends
  Yield: 2.4%
  Payout: 30.4%
Market value (mil.): $5,072

Stock Price History[1]
High/Low 1986–95

[1] Stock prices are for the prior calendar year.

DEAN WITTER, DISCOVER & CO.

OVERVIEW

Dean Witter, Discover's watchwords are Profit and Growth. And the company, which was spun off from Allstate Insurance in 1993, pursues its goals with a combination of strict cost controls and market expansion.

The New York–based company's business is almost evenly balanced between its consumer credit operations — the Discover Card — and the financial services it offers through its Dean Witter Reynolds brokerage and investment banking operations.

The Discover Card was launched in 1986 by Sears in an attempt to build a financial services empire. The card's gimmick, cash back on purchases, helped it gain acceptance with 43 million users and an increasing number of merchants — including, as of 1994, the US Postal Service. This unit also includes credit transaction processing for private label cards, home mortgage and equity loans, and a co-branded (with NationsBank) MasterCard, the Prime Option card.

The other half of the business, Dean Witter Reynolds, engages in brokerage, mutual fund sales and management, investment advice, and investment banking. The company also has agreements with Allstate and ITT Hartford to sell their annuity products to its patrons.

WHEN

Dean Witter founded a brokerage in San Francisco in 1924. Witter, a broker of the old school, believed that serving his customers was a sacred trust and managed the firm accordingly for more than 40 years. The firm remained strongly regional, serving primarily wealthy retail customers.

In 1977 the company, under the leadership of Andrew Melton, merged with another regional, primarily retail, brokerage, Reynolds Securities International. Reynolds had been started by Richard Reynolds Jr., son of the founder of Reynolds Metals and grandnephew of the founder of Reynolds Tobacco company.

Melton hoped that the addition of Reynolds, whose retail offices did not compete with Dean Witter's, would provide a springboard for growing the company's investment banking activities. The newly combined company, Dean Witter Reynolds, became the US's 2nd largest brokerage (although it remained based in San Francisco) after Merrill Lynch, with more than 3,550 brokers.

The company then proceeded to transform itself into a full-service financial institution, building up its investment banking and block trading businesses. To do so, it lured brokers and traders away from other firms by offering top-dollar salaries.

In the late 1970s and early 1980s, the US economy was in trouble, interest rates were high, and banks and financial services companies needed new sources of capital. For Dean Witter, that source was Sears, which acquired Dean Witter (then one of the top 10 US investment firms) in 1981. Sears wanted to diversify into financial services and to make Dean Witter into a financial Allstate: an in-store, one-stop shopping center for Middle America's financial and investment needs. It was an ambition that contrasted with Dean Witter's recent successful effort to become a major underwriter. Sears replaced Melton with Robert Gardiner, who was oriented toward retail operations. It also cut staff and costs at Dean Witter in an effort to tailor the firm to fit into its stores. The apparent lack of interest of Sears's management in the investment side led to further staff reductions through resignations and hurt Dean Witter's investment operations, dragging down results.

In 1986 Sears and Dean Witter introduced the Discover Card, which was an almost instant success. Within a year Dean Witter was restructured and on an even keel again; even its investment business picked up.

But by the end of the 1980s, it was obvious that Sears was not going to be a financial giant — it was not even certain that it was going to continue to be a retail giant. Strapped for cash, it sold Allstate, Coldwell Banker, and the newly renamed Dean Witter, Discover.

Dean Witter and NationsBank entered into a brokerage joint venture, NationsSecurities, in 1992, but differences over sales policies led to the breakup of the venture in 1994. Dean Witter, Discover continues to provide services to NationsBank.

The company has fought a long battle to be allowed to issue Visa cards and MasterCards. It received permission (but only in partnership with NationsBank) to issue a MasterCard, Prime Option, in 1993. Access to Visa was denied in 1995, when the US Supreme Court let stand a lower court ruling that Visa's denial of the right to issue cards did not constitute a violation of the Sherman Antitrust Act. Dean Witter had hoped to gain access to the larger merchant base and overseas recognition enjoyed by the 2 major card consortia.

WHO

Chairman and CEO: Philip J. Purcell, age 51, $2,700,000 pay
EVP; President and COO, Dean Witter Capital: Richard M. DeMartini, age 42, $1,760,000 pay
EVP; President and COO, Dean Witter Financial: James F. Higgins, age 46, $1,756,000 pay
EVP; President and COO, Discover Card Services: Thomas R. Butler, age 52, $770,000 pay
EVP and CFO: Thomas C. Schneider, age 57, $1,043,000 pay
EVP and Chief Administrative Officer: Mitchell M. Merin, age 41
EVP, General Counsel, and Secretary: Christine A. Edwards, age 42
SVP Human Resources: Michael Cunningham
Auditors: Deloitte & Touche LLP

WHERE

HQ: 2 World Trade Center, New York, NY 10048
Phone: 212-392-2222
Fax: 212-392-3118

Dean Witter, Discover has 353 offices nationwide, staffed by 8,044 brokers.

WHAT

	1994 Sales		1994 Pretax income	
	$ mil.	% of total	$ mil.	% of total
Credit services	3,460	52	672	45
Securities services	3,143	48	543	55
Total	**6,603**	**100**	**1,215**	**100**

1994 Sales		
	$ mil.	% of total
Interest	2,507	38
Asset management fees	973	15
Merchant & cardmember fees	940	14
Commissions	874	13
Servicing fees	587	9
Principal transactions	422	6
Investment banking	198	3
Other	102	2
Total	**6,603**	**100**

Services	Selected Subsidiaries
Asset management	Dean Witter InterCapital, Inc.
Brokerage services	
Consumer credit services	Dean Witter Realty, Inc.
Home equity loans	Dean Witter Reynolds, Inc.
Information processing	Demeter Management Corp.
Insurance services	Discover Card
Investment banking	Greenwood Trust Company
Mutual funds	NOVUS Financial Corp.
Trust services	Prime Option Services
	SPS Transaction Services, Inc. (74%)

KEY COMPETITORS

A. G. Edwards
Alex. Brown
Allstate Financial
American Express
Bear Stearns
Beneficial
Brown Brothers Harriman
Charles Schwab
Chase Manhattan
Citicorp
Countrywide Credit
Edward Jones
Equitable
FMR
Goldman Sachs

Hambrecht & Quist
Household Intl.
Kemper Corp.
Lehman Brothers
MasterCard
Merrill Lynch
Morgan Stanley
Nomura Securities
Paine Webber
Quick & Reilly
Salomon
T. Rowe Price
Transamerica
Travelers
USAA
Visa

HOW MUCH

	Annual Growth	1985	1986	1987	1988	1989	1990	1991	1992	1993	1994
Sales ($ mil.)	10.0%	—	—	—	3,733	3,942	4,506	4,882	5,184	5,822	6,603
Net income ($ mil.)	43.2%	—	—	—	86	166	233	345	439	604	741
Income as % of sales	—	—	—	—	2.3%	4.2%	5.2%	7.1%	8.5%	10.4%	11.2%
Earnings per share ($)	30.1%	—	—	—	—	—	—	—	2.57	3.54	4.35
Stock price – high ($)	—	—	—	—	—	—	—	—	—	46.50	43.13
Stock price – low ($)	—	—	—	—	—	—	—	—	—	30.63	31.50
Stock price – close ($)	(2.2%)	—	—	—	—	—	—	—	—	34.63	33.88
P/E – high	—	—	—	—	—	—	—	—	—	13	10
P/E – low	—	—	—	—	—	—	—	—	—	8	7
Dividends per share ($)	66.7%	—	—	—	—	—	—	—	—	0.30	0.50
Book value per share ($)	19.3%	—	—	—	—	—	—	—	—	20.38	24.32
Employees	7.2%	—	—	—	—	—	—	—	—	26,564	28,475

1994 Year-end:
Debt ratio: 75.6%
Return on equity: 19.5%
Cash (mil.): $2,829
Long-term debt (mil.): $5,293
No. of shares (mil.): 169
Dividends
  Yield: 1.5%
  Payout: 11.5%
Market value (mil.): $5,721
Assets (mil.): $31,859

**Stock Price History
High/Low 1993–94**

DEERE & COMPANY

OVERVIEW

Illinois-based Deere & Company is the world's largest manufacturer of farm equipment and a leading producer of industrial and lawn care equipment. Deere's wide range of products includes tractors, construction equipment, diesel engines, chain saws, and lawn trimmers. Its farm equipment, painted a signature green, is made in 9 countries and sold in more than 160.

Deere also provides financing and leasing options, as well as a range of insurance coverages, for its customers. Its health care operations, first designed for employees, now serve almost 600 companies and 300,000 people.

Deere is known as an industry innovator. The company recently upgraded its farm equipment models, and improvements in its factories have meant fewer employees are needed to reach production goals.

Deere had record sales and earnings in 1994. International sales (more than 20% of 1994 total sales) are an important part of the company's strategy. The decline in the dollar has hurt Deere in Europe, where it laid off 2,000 employees in 1993. Deere is in the process of restructuring and streamlining its European operations. The company is negotiating 2 joint ventures in China and looking for other sales and manufacturing opportunities in developing markets.

Deere expects to benefit from the NAFTA and GATT agreements, which phase out tariffs on farm, construction, and other equipment, with savings of more than $45 million a year.

WHEN

Vermont-born John Deere moved westward to Grand Detour, Illinois, in 1836 and set up a blacksmith shop. Deere and other pioneers had trouble with the black midwestern soil sticking to the iron plows designed for sandy eastern soils, so in 1837 Deere used a circular steel saw blade to fashion a self-scouring plow that moved so quickly it was nicknamed "the whistling plow." Deere sold only 3 in 1838 but was making 25 a week by 1842.

Deere moved to Moline, Illinois, in 1847. His son Charles joined the firm in 1853, beginning a tradition of family management. All 5 presidents prior to 1982 were related by blood or marriage. Charles Deere set up a system of distribution to independent dealerships and expanded the product line to include wagons, buggies, and corn planters.

Under Charles Deere's son-in-law William Butterworth (1907–28), the company bought other agricultural equipment manufacturers and developed harvesting equipment and tractors with internal combustion engines. Butterworth's nephew Charles Wiman, who became president in 1928, extended credit to farmers during the Great Depression, a policy that won long-term customer loyalty (Deere is one of the oldest suppliers of agricultural credit in the US). In 1931 Deere opened its first foreign plant, in Canada.

William Hewitt, Wiman's son-in-law, became CEO in 1955. In 1958 Deere passed International Harvester to become the largest US producer of agricultural equipment, and by 1963 it had become the largest in the world. Operations abroad expanded to include Mexico, Argentina, France, and Spain; today the company's products are sold worldwide. Deere has used joint ventures abroad (Yanmar, small tractors, 1977; Hitachi, excavators, 1983) and internal research to diversify.

Despite an industrywide sales slump culminating in losses totaling $328 million in 1986 and 1987, Deere was the only major agricultural equipment maker to neither change ownership nor close factories during the 1980s. Deere cut its work force 44% and improved efficiency, lowering the manufacturing break-even point from 70% to 35% of capacity.

Robert Hanson became the first nonfamily CEO in 1982. He poured $2 billion into R&D during the 1980s, and in 1989 Deere introduced its largest new product offering up to that time, including the 9000 series of combines, which had taken 15 years to develop. Deere acquired Funk Manufacturing, a powertrain components manufacturer, for $87 million in 1989. That same year Hans Becherer succeeded Hanson as CEO.

In recent years Deere has rapidly expanded its lawn care equipment business, particularly in Europe. In 1991 it acquired a majority stake in SABO Maschinenfabrik, a German manufacturer of commercial lawn mowers. In 1993 Deere gained distribution rights to Zetor tractors and Brno diesel engines (from the Czech Republic), which the company plans to market in Latin America and the Far East.

By 1994 Deere had replaced its tractor line with all-new models. That same year it bought Homelite, a leading maker of hand-held outdoor power equipment, from Textron. In 1995 Deere agreed to a 3-year contract with the UAW that creates an incentive-pay program.

NYSE symbol: DE
Fiscal year ends: October 31

WHO

Chairman and CEO: Hans W. Becherer, age 59, $1,638,630 pay
President and COO: David H. Stowe Jr., age 58, $1,091,271 pay
EVP Financial Services and Principal Financial Officer: Eugene L. Schotanus, age 57, $745,015 pay
EVP, Worldwide Agricultural Equipment Division: Bernard L. Hardiek, age 54
SVP Engineering, Technology, and Human Resources: Michael S. Plunkett, age 57, $668,873 pay
SVP Finance, Accounting, and CFO: Pierre E. Leroy, age 46
SVP, Worldwide Parts Division: Joseph W. England, age 54
SVP and Managing Director, Europe, Africa, and the Middle East: J. Michael Frank, age 56
SVP, Worldwide Industrial Equipment Division: Ferdinand F. Korndorf, age 45
VP, General Counsel, and Corporate Secretary: Frank S. Cottrell, age 52
Auditors: Deloitte & Touche LLP

WHERE

HQ: John Deere Rd., Moline, IL 61265-8098
Phone: 309-765-8000
Fax: 309-765-5772

The company sells its agricultural equipment in more than 160 countries.

	1994 Sales		1994 Operating Income	
	$ mil.	% of total	$ mil.	% of total
US & Canada	7,131	79	1,002	92
Other countries	1,803	20	83	8
Adjustments	96	1	—	—
Total	**9,030**	**100**	**1,085**	**100**

WHAT

	1994 Sales		1994 Operating Income	
	$ mil.	% of total	$ mil.	% of total
Farm equipment	4,837	51	553	51
Industrial equip.	1,744	19	132	12
Lawn & grounds care equipment	1,305	14	162	15
Insurance & health care	907	10	60	6
Credit	516	5	178	16
Other	96	1	—	—
Adjustments	(375)	—	—	—
Total	**9,030**	**100**	**1,085**	**100**

Selected Products and Services

Farm Equipment
Crop handling equipment
Harvesting machinery
Planting machinery
Soil preparation machinery
Tillers
Tractors

Industrial Equipment
Backhoe loaders
Crawler dozers/loaders
Drivetrain components
Engines
Excavators
Log skidders
Motor graders
Scrapers

Lawn and Grounds Care Equipment
Chain saws
Golf course equipment
Leaf blowers
Mowers and small tractors
Snowblowers
String trimmers

Insurance/Health Care
Heritage National Healthplan (HMO)
Life insurance
Property/casualty insurance

Credit
Customer financing and leasing

KEY COMPETITORS

AGCO
Black & Decker
Caterpillar
Fiat
FMC
Ford
General Electric
Honda
Hyundai
Ingersoll-Rand
Mitsubishi
Navistar
TIC United
Toro
Volvo

HOW MUCH

	9-Year Growth	1985	1986	1987	1988	1989	1990	1991	1992	1993	1994
Sales ($ mil.)	7.6%	4,677	4,196	4,854	6,238	7,220	7,875	7,055	6,961	7,754	9,030
Net income ($ mil.)	39.3%	31	(229)	(99)	287	380	411	(20)	37	184	604
Income as % of sales	—	0.7%	—	—	4.6%	5.3%	5.2%	—	0.5%	2.4%	6.7%
Earnings per share ($)	35.7%	0.45	(3.38)	(1.46)	3.90	5.06	5.42	(0.27)	0.49	2.39	7.01
Stock price – high ($)	—	33.13	35.13	43.00	50.50	64.25	78.38	57.38	54.00	78.38	90.88
Stock price – low ($)	—	24.25	21.50	22.50	33.38	44.00	37.63	39.88	36.75	42.38	61.25
Stock price – close ($)	9.7%	28.75	22.88	34.75	48.00	61.50	46.88	48.00	43.75	74.00	66.25
P/E – high	—	74	—	—	13	13	15	—	110	33	13
P/E – low	—	54	—	—	9	9	7	—	75	18	9
Dividends per share ($)	8.3%	1.00	0.88	0.31	0.51	1.15	1.85	2.00	2.00	2.00	2.05
Book value per share ($)	(1.3%)	33.29	29.46	28.23	32.92	36.76	39.52	37.20	34.73	24.39	29.60
Employees	(1.8%)	40,509	37,481	37,931	38,268	38,949	38,493	36,469	25,250	33,070	34,300

1994 Year-end:
Debt ratio: 64.7%
Return on equity: 26.0%
Cash (mil.): $1,372
Current ratio: 1.74
Long-term debt (mil.): $2,054
No. of shares (mil.): 86
Dividends
  Yield: 3.0%
  Payout: 29.2%
Market value (mil.): $5,725

Stock Price History
High/Low 1985–94

DELL COMPUTER CORPORATION

OVERVIEW

Dell, the world's #7 personal computer maker, is back on track after pulling out of retail stores and reconfiguring its notebook computer operations. The Texas-based company is one of the world's 2 leading mail-order computer vendors (Gateway 2000 is its main rival).

Dell's turnaround came in 1994 after it abandoned Wal-Mart and other retail stores to refocus on its mail-order origins. The company took a $40 million charge in early 1994 to kill its troubled notebook computer line; later that year it released the Latitude notebook to general acclaim. The company offered its first Pentium-based notebook in 1995.

Dell's earnings rose in 1995, partially on the strength of its notebook computers, which jumped to 9% of sales. The company also benefited from its early entry into the Pentium-based PC market and from its introduction of innovative products such as lithium-ion notebook batteries, which last longer than conventional batteries.

Dell is now setting its sights on overseas opportunities (one of the most promising horizons for computer sales). The company is doubling capacity at its Irish plant and building a new facility in Malaysia to serve the Asian market. The company is also expanding the meaning of "mail order" by marketing its wares on the Internet.

The Dell family owns 30% of the company's stock.

WHEN

At the age of 13, Michael Dell was already a successful businessman. From his parents' home in Houston, Dell ran a mail-order stamp trading business that, within a few months, grossed over $2,000. At 16 he sold subscriptions to the *Houston Post* and at 17 bought his first BMW. When he enrolled at the University of Texas in 1983, he was thoroughly bitten by the business bug.

Although Dell started college as a pre-med major, he found time to establish a business selling random-access memory (RAM) chips and disk drives for IBM PCs. Dell bought his products at cost from IBM dealers, who, at the time, were required to order from IBM large monthly quotas of PCs, which frequently exceeded demand. Dell resold his stock through newspapers (and later through national computer magazines) at 10–15% below retail.

By April 1984 Dell's dorm-room computer components business was grossing about $80,000 a month — enough to convince him to drop out of college. At about that time he started making and selling his own IBM clones under the brand name PC's Limited. Drawing on his previous sales experience, Dell sold his machines directly to end-users rather than through retail computer outlets, as most manufacturers did. By eliminating the retail markup, Dell could sell his PCs at about 40% of the price of an IBM.

The company was plagued by management changes during the mid-1980s. Renamed Dell Computer, it added international sales offices in 1987. In 1988 it started selling to government agencies and added a sales force to serve larger customers. That year Dell went public in a $34.2 million offering.

Dell tripped in 1990, reporting a 64% drop in profits. Sales were growing — but so were costs, mostly because of Dell's efforts to design a PC using proprietary components and RISC chips. Also, the company's warehouses were oversupplied. But within a year Dell turned itself around by cutting inventories and coming out with 8 new products.

In 1990 Dell entered the retail arena by allowing Soft Warehouse Superstores (now CompUSA) to sell its PCs at mail-order prices. In 1991 the company struck a similar deal with Staples, an office supply chain. Also that year Dell opened a plant in Limerick, Ireland.

In 1992 Xerox agreed to sell Dell machines in 19 Latin American countries. That same year Dell sold a new line of PCs through Price Club (now Price/Costco). The following year Dell opened subsidiaries in Japan and Austria and began selling PCs through Best Buy's 117 US stores, located in 16 states.

Dell introduced a new line of servers, called PowerEdge, in 1994. That same year Dell suspended sales in retail stores and signed deals with resellers in Indonesia and Korea to sell its products. Late in 1994 Joel Kocher — Dell's wunderkind president of worldwide sales, marketing, and services, who had led the company's marketing efforts since 1987 — left to become COO of Artisoft, maker of networking products such as LANtastic.

In 1995 Dell introduced the OptiPlex DGX system, its first dual-processor desktop computer. It also reduced prices on its workhorse Dimension series PCs. Also that year a suit was filed accusing Dell of selling new computers containing used parts (Compaq has accused rival Packard Bell of a similar tactic).

Nasdaq symbol: DELL
Fiscal year ends: Saturday nearest January 31

WHO

Chairman and CEO: Michael S. Dell, age 30, $818,032 pay
VC: Morton L. Topfer, age 58, $566,015 pay
CFO: Thomas J. Meredith, age 44, $524,308 pay
SVP Product Group: Eric F. Harslem, age 49, $651,153 pay
SVP; General Manager, Dell Americas: Richard N. Snyder, age 50
VP and General Manager — Asia: Phillip E. Kelly, age 37
VP and General Manager — Europe: Martyn R. Ratcliffe, age 33
VP Advanced Systems Group: Terry Klein
VP and Corporate Controller: Catherine P. Thompson
General Counsel and Secretary: Thomas B. Green, age 40
VP Human Resources: Julie A. Sackett, age 51
Auditors: Price Waterhouse LLP

WHERE

HQ: 9505 Arboretum Blvd., Austin, TX 78759-7299
Phone: 512-338-4400
Fax: 512-728-3653

Dell sells 64 computer systems in 7 product families as well as a variety of computer software and peripheral products through the company's DellWare and ReadyWare programs. Dell computer products are sold in more than 125 countries.

	1995 Sales
	% of total
Americas	69
Europe	27
Other regions	4
Total	**100**

WHAT

	1995 Sales
	% of total
Desktop systems	85
Notebooks	9
Servers	6
Total	**100**

Selected Dell Products

Desktop Systems	Servers
Dimension family	Performance family
NetPlex family	PowerEdge family
OptiPlex family	Series family

Notebooks
Latitude family

Third-Party Products

CD-ROM drives	Printers
Modems	Removable storage devices
Monitors	Scanners
Networking hardware	Software
PCMCIA cards	Speakers
Power accessories	Tape backup systems

KEY COMPETITORS

Advanced Logic Research	Gateway 2000	NeoStar
Apple	Hewlett-Packard	Oki
AST	Hitachi	Olivetti
AT&T	Hyundai	Packard Bell
Compaq	IBM	Philips
CompuCom Systems	Machines Bull	Sharp
CompuAdd	Matsushita	Siemens
CompUSA	Micro Warehouse	Stream Intl.
Data General	Micron Technology	Sun Microsystems
DEC	NEC	Tandy
Fujitsu		Toshiba
		Unisys

HOW MUCH

	Annual Growth	1986	1987	1988	1989	1990	1991	1992	1993	1994	1995
Sales ($ mil.)	67.2%	34	70	159	258	389	546	890	2,014	2,873	3,475
Net income ($ mil.)	73.2%	1	2	9	14	5	27	51	102	(36)	140
Income as % of sales	—	2.9%	3.2%	5.9%	5.6%	1.3%	5.0%	5.7%	5.0%	—	4.0%
Earnings per share ($)	58.5%	0.05	0.13	0.48	0.53	0.18	0.91	1.40	2.59	(1.06)	3.15
Stock price – high ($)[1]	—	—	—	—	8.34	6.92	12.59	24.18	48.38	49.88	47.38
Stock price – low ($)[1]	—	—	—	—	5.25	3.42	3.08	10.51	15.00	15.88	19.13
Stock price – close ($)[1]	35.3%	—	—	—	6.67	3.67	12.34	17.09	48.00	22.63	41.00
P/E – high	—	—	—	—	16	38	14	17	19	—	15
P/E – low	—	—	—	—	10	19	3	8	6	—	6
Dividends per share ($)	—	—	—	—	0.00	0.00	0.00	0.00	0.00	0.00	0.00
Book value per share ($)	35.2%	—	—	—	2.69	2.83	3.86	7.66	10.02	12.42	16.42
Employees	32.6%	—	—	—	1,175	1,500	2,050	2,970	4,650	5,980	6,400

1995 Year-end:
Debt ratio: 14.8%
Return on equity: 25.0%
Cash (mil.): $527
Current ratio: 1.96
Long-term debt (mil.): $113
No. of shares (mil.): 40
Dividends
  Yield: —
  Payout: —
Market value (mil.): $1,627

**Stock Price History[1]
High/Low 1989–95**

[1] Stock prices are for the prior calendar year.

DELOITTE TOUCHE TOHMATSU

OVERVIEW

In the daredevil new world of Big 6 accounting, Deloitte Touche Tohmatsu has won some and lost some — court cases, that is. The cases have arisen from the growing tendency to hold auditors responsible for the performances of the entities they audit. In the win column is the case in which Torrance, California, tried to hold the firm responsible for its investment losses. In the loss column, at least for now, is the $81.3 million judgment relating to the 1990 bankruptcy of Jacksonville, Florida–based Koger Properties, an audit client. The firm will appeal. Also in the losses column was the $312 million that the firm paid the US government in 1994 to settle malpractice cases arising from the S&L crisis of the 1980s.

Deloitte Touche Tohmatsu is the product of the 1989 merger of Deloitte Haskins & Sells and Touche Ross (whose Japanese affiliate's name, Ross Tohmatsu, rounds out the firm's name). In an industry that is becoming globally consolidated, the latter union gave the firm a truly international outlook. It still operates as Deloitte & Touche in the US.

Since the firm's original business, auditing, has become more driven by price rather than relationship, Deloitte Touche has branched into consulting and has grown by acquisitions.

In 1995 the firm began to revamp its operations, adopting a regional structure that is intended to make the firm more responsive to clients with far-flung operations.

WHEN

In 1845 William Welch Deloitte opened an accounting office in London. Deloitte's grandfather, Count de Loitte, had fled France during the Reign of Terror (1793–94) and supported himself by teaching French.

At first Deloitte, a former staff member of the Official Assignee in Bankruptcy of the City of London, solicited business from bankrupts. The development of joint stock companies in the mid-19th century fueled the rise of accounting in the UK (and in the US) because of the need for standardized financial reporting. Deloitte moved into the new field.

As the firm grew, it added partners, among them John Griffiths (1869). Griffiths visited the US in 1888, and in 1890 the firm opened a branch on Wall Street. Other branches followed in Cincinnati (1905), Chicago (1912), Montreal (1912), Boston (1930), and Los Angeles (1945). In 1952 the Deloitte firm formed an alliance with the accounting firm of Haskins & Sells, which operated 34 US offices.

Deloitte developed a reputation as a thorough, and therefore expensive, firm. Its aim was to be "the Cadillac, not the Ford" of accounting, but the firm, which became Deloitte Haskins & Sells in 1978, began to lose its conservatism as competition for auditing contracts and for management consulting clients became more intense. When the profession relaxed its restrictions on advertising, Deloitte Haskins & Sells was the first Big 8 firm with aggressive ads extolling its virtues.

In 1984, in a move that foreshadowed the merger mania to come, Deloitte Haskins & Sells tried to merge with Price Waterhouse. However, British partners in Price Waterhouse objected to the deal, and it was dropped.

In the US the Big 8 accounting firms became the Big 6 in 1989. Ernst & Whinney merged with Arthur Young to become Ernst & Young and the staid Deloitte Haskins & Sells teamed up with flamboyant Touche Ross to form Deloitte & Touche. Touche Ross had been founded in New York in 1947 and had a reputation as the hard-charging, bare-knuckled bad boy of the Big 8. The merger was engineered by Deloitte's Michael Cook and Touche's Edward Kangas in part to unite the former firm's US and European strengths with the latter firm's Asian presence (Cook continues to oversee US operations and Kangas presides over international operations). But many affiliates, particularly in the UK, objected to the merger and defected to competing firms.

In 1992 California regulators sued Deloitte & Touche, claiming that it had been the "auditor of choice" of a "daisy chain" linking Drexel Burnham junk-bond king Michael Milken to failed Executive Life. More legal grief came to Deloitte & Touche as the RTC began a series of actions designed to recover some of the losses brought about by the 1980s' S&L debacle.

The firm has been something of a pioneer in audit technology. In 1988 it introduced the A+ Audit Software System, which was largely instrumental in automating the firm's audits. It cut audit time by about 10% (which has the effect of reducing hourly billings, too).

Deloitte & Touche has made a concerted effort to accommodate women, devising a "mommy track" that actually leads to partnership.

In 1995 the SEC chose Michael Sutton, the firm's national director of auditing and accounting practice, as its chief accountant.

International partnership
Fiscal year ends: May 31

WHO

Chairman and CEO, Deloitte Touche Tohmatsu International: Edward A. Kangas
COO, Deloitte Touche Tohmatsu International: J. Thomas Presby
Chairman and CEO, Deloitte & Touche LLP: J. Michael Cook
VC, Deloitte & Touche LLP: John T. Cardis
Managing Partner, Deloitte & Touche LLP: James E. Copeland Jr.
National Managing Director of Finance, Deloitte & Touche LLP: Robert W. Pivik
National Director Marketing and Communications, Deloitte & Touche LLP: Gary Gerard
General Counsel, Deloitte & Touche LLP: Howard J. Krongard
National Director Human Resources, Deloitte & Touche LLP: James H. Wall

WHERE

HQ: Deloitte Touche Tohmatsu International, 1633 Broadway, New York, NY 10019
Phone: 212-492-4000
Fax: 214-492-4001
US HQ: Deloitte & Touche LLP, 10 Westport Rd., Wilton, CT 06897-0820
Phone: 203-761-3000
Fax: 203-834-2200

Deloitte Touche Tohmatsu operates offices in more than 655 cities in 124 countries worldwide.

WHAT

Selected Services
Accounting and auditing
Information technology consulting
Management consulting
Mergers and acquisitions consulting
Tax advice and planning

Representative Clients

Bank of New York	Mayo Foundation
BASF	Merrill Lynch
Boeing	MetLife
Bridgestone	Mitsubishi
Chrysler	Mitsui
Dow Chemical	Monsanto
Flagstar	PPG
General Motors	Procter & Gamble
Great A&P	RJR Nabisco
Litton Industries	Rockwell
Lowes	Sears

Selected Affiliates
Akintola Williams & Co. (Cameroon)
Braxton Associates (US)
C. C. Chokshi & Co. (India)
D&T Corporate Finance Europe Ltd.
Deloitte & Touche Eastern Europe
Goh, Tan & Co. (Brunei)
Hans Tuanakotta & Mustofa (Indonesia)
Nautilus Indemnity Holdings Ltd. (Bermuda)
PROFIT Project (US)
Shawki & Co. (Egypt)
Tohmatsu & Co. (Japan)
Vishnu Prasad & Co. (Fiji)

KEY COMPETITORS

Apogee Research	H&R Block
Arthur Andersen	Hewitt Associates
Arthur Little	IBM
Bain & Co.	KPMG
Booz, Allen	Marsh & McLennan
Boston Consulting Group	McKinsey & Co.
Carlson	Measured Marketing
Coopers & Lybrand	Services
Delta Consulting	Price Waterhouse
EDS	Right Management
Ernst & Young	Consultants
Gemini Consulting	Towers Perrin
Grant Thornton	Wyatt Co.

HOW MUCH

	9-Year Growth	1985	1986	1987	1988	1989	1990	1991	1992	1993	1994
Sales ($ mil.)	11.7%	1,926	2,339	2,950	3,760	3,900	4,200	4,500	4,800	5,000	5,200
Deloitte Haskins & Sells	—	953	1,188	1,500	1,920	—	—	—	—	—	—
Touche Ross	—	973	1,151	1,450	1,840	—	—	—	—	—	—
Offices[1]	14.6%	192	205	195	196	126	630	647	647	653	655
Partners[1]	12.3%	1,619	1,600	1,590	1,600	1,652	4,900	4,700	4,600	4,600	4,600
Employees[1]	14.1%	17,253	17,521	18,252	19,276	19,668	59,700	56,000	56,000	56,000	56,600

Deloitte & Touche

Sales ($ mil.) 1985–94

[1] US only 1985–89

DELTA AIR LINES, INC.

OVERVIEW

Market forces have dealt a cruel blow to Delta in the last few years. The only money loser among the top 4 US airlines (American, United, Delta, and Northwest) in fiscal 1994, the company is struggling to pull out of a 4-year financial tailspin. Delta, which operates 4,900 daily flights to 48 US states and 32 countries, has been buffeted by weak results in Europe and competition from low-cost rivals.

To cut its losses, Delta has reduced transatlantic flights and has code-sharing agreements with foreign airlines (including Aeroflot, Austrian Airlines, Sabena, Swissair, and Virgin) to carry passengers to and from international destinations. The code sharing allowed Delta to reduce international capacity by 6% in 1995, while offering its customers access to more flights through its affiliated airlines.

In order to effectively compete, the airline is implementing a plan aimed at reducing operating costs by $2 billion annually by the end of 1997. To do this, Delta has eliminated 10% of its work force, lowered wages, sped up aircraft turnaround times, introduced "no-frills" service on some flights, and dumped some routes. A bright spot was the growth of its cargo unit in 1994; revenues were up 10%.

The only fly in the curative ointment that Delta management has been applying is the company's inability to reach agreement with its pilot union (8,500 strong) on reducing annual pilot costs by $340 million.

WHEN

Delta was founded in Macon, Georgia, in 1924 as the world's first crop-dusting service, Huff-Daland Dusters, to combat a boll weevil infestation of cotton fields. It moved to Monroe, Louisiana, in 1925. In 1928 field manager C. E. Woolman and 2 partners bought the service and renamed it Delta Air Service after the Mississippi Delta region it served.

In 1929 Delta pioneered passenger service from Dallas to Jackson, Mississippi, operating without a government mail subsidy until 1934, when Delta got a US Postal Service contract from Fort Worth to Charleston, South Carolina, via Atlanta. Delta moved to Atlanta in 1941. Woolman became president in 1945 and managed Delta until he died in 1966.

Delta added flights to Cincinnati and New Orleans in 1943 and from Chicago to Miami in 1945. Its 1952 purchase of Chicago and Southern Airlines added a direct route from Chicago to New Orleans, making Delta the 5th largest US airline, with service to cities in the South, the Midwest, Texas, and the Caribbean. Delta offered its first transcontinental flight in 1961. In 1972 the airline bought Northeast Airlines, thereby expanding service to New England and Canada, and then crossed the Atlantic in 1978 with service to London.

In 1982 Delta's employees pledged $30 million to buy a Boeing 767 jet. Christened *The Spirit of Delta*, this aircraft was a token of appreciation from employees. In fiscal 1983 Delta succumbed to the weak US economy, posting its first loss ever. Delta became profitable again in 1985 and bought Los Angeles–based Western Air Lines in 1986.

Delta began service to Asia in 1987. By 1989 international routes provided 11% of the company's passenger revenues. That year Delta signed agreements with Swissair and Singapore Airlines, allowing the 3 airlines to buy stakes of up to 5% in one another. In 1990 Delta joined TWA and Northwest to form WORLDSPAN, a computer reservation service. Fare discounts and higher fuel and labor costs caused a slump in earnings in 1990.

In 1991 Delta bought gates, planes, and 3 Canadian routes from Eastern, and Pan Am's New York–Boston shuttle, European routes, and Frankfurt hub (for $621 million in cash and $668 million in debt assumption). This made Delta the world's largest airline in terms of profitability and cities served. That same year the weak economy, fare wars, and the cost of acquiring part of Pan Am began taking its toll, and the airline posted its first loss since 1983. After suffering a larger loss in 1992, Delta began several rounds of cost cutting. In 1992 Pan Am and some of its creditors filed a $2.5 billion breach-of-contract lawsuit against the company after Delta backed out of an agreement to fund Pan Am's reorganization. A district court settled the case in 1994, ruling overwhelmingly in Delta's favor .

That year Delta announced plans to reduce its aircraft rental costs by phasing out its fleet of A310 planes by the end of 1995. In addition, the carrier withdrew from a number of short-haul routes, allowing it to redeploy aircraft to more profitable routes. Delta faced the ire of travel agents when it pioneered the placing of caps on agent commissions in 1994, a move copied by other major airlines in 1995.

In 1995 sales rose to $12.2 billion and earnings came in at $408 million, the first profit in 5 years.

NYSE symbol: DAL
Fiscal year ends: June 30

WHO

Chairman, President, and CEO: Ronald W. Allen, age 52, $475,000 pay
EVP Operations: Harry C. Alger, age 56, $261,250 pay
SVP Finance and CFO: Thomas J. Roeck Jr., age 50, $261,250 pay
SVP Technical Operations: Russell H. Heil, age 52, $251,750 pay
SVP Corporate Services: Rex A. McClelland, age 58, $221,667 pay
SVP Marketing: Robert W. Coggin, age 58
SVP General Counsel: Robert S. Harkey, age 53
SVP Personnel: Maurice W. Worth, age 54
Auditors: Arthur Andersen & Co, SC

WHERE

HQ: Hartsfield Atlanta International Airport, Atlanta, GA 30320
Phone: 404-715-2600
Fax: 404-765-2233
Reservations: 800-221-1212

Delta serves the US and 32 other countries.

Hub Locations

Atlanta, GA	New York, NY
Cincinnati, OH	Orlando, FL
Dallas/Ft. Worth, TX	Portland, OR
Frankfurt, Germany	Salt Lake City, UT
Los Angeles, CA	

	1994 Sales % of total
US operations	77
International operations	23
Total	**100**

WHAT

	1994 Sales	
	$ mil.	% of total
Passenger	11,316	92
Cargo	769	6
Other	274	2
Total	**12,359**	**100**

Major Subsidiaries and Affiliates
The Delta Connection (carriers)
  Atlantic Southeast Airlines (23.3%)
  Comair (20.6%)
  SkyWest (13.6%)

Computer Reservation System
WORLDSPAN (38%)

Aircraft	No.	Orders
Airbus 310	13	—
Boeing 727	138	—
Boeing 737	73	52
Boeing 757	84	6
Boeing 767	55	7
L-1011	56	—
MD-11	11	4
MD-88	120	—
MD-90	—	55
Total	**550**	**124**

KEY COMPETITORS

Alaska Air	HAL	SAS
All Nippon	JAL	Singapore
Airways	Kimberly-	Airlines
America West	Clark	Southwest
AMR	KLM	Airlines
British Airways	Lufthansa	Swire Pacific
Continental	Mesa Air	TWA
Airlines	Northwest	UAL
Galileo	Airlines	USAir Group
International	Qantas	ValuJet Airlines

HOW MUCH

	9-Year Growth	1985	1986	1987	1988	1989	1990	1991	1992	1993	1994
Sales ($ mil.)	11.4%	4,684	4,460	5,318	6,915	8,089	8,582	9,171	10,837	11,997	12,359
Net income ($ mil.)	—	259	47	264	307	461	285	(343)	(525)	(1,112)	(519)
Income as % of sales	—	5.5%	1.1%	5.0%	4.4%	5.7%	3.3%	—	—	—	—
Earnings per share ($)	—	6.50	1.18	5.90	6.30	9.37	5.28	(7.73)	(10.60)	(22.32)	(10.32)
Stock price – high ($)	—	52.75	51.88	67.13	55.13	85.75	80.88	78.75	75.25	61.38	57.88
Stock price – low ($)	—	36.13	37.75	32.00	36.00	48.75	52.50	55.50	47.75	45.75	39.50
Stock price – close ($)	2.9%	39.00	48.13	37.13	50.13	68.25	55.75	66.13	50.88	54.63	50.50
P/E – high	—	8	44	11	9	9	15	—	—	—	—
P/E – low	—	6	32	5	6	5	10	—	—	—	—
Dividends per share ($)	(13.0%)	0.70	1.00	1.00	1.20	1.20	1.70	1.20	1.20	0.70	0.20
Book value per share ($)	(1.1%)	32.21	32.45	39.84	44.99	53.18	56.32	49.73	38.11	37.75	29.08
Employees	6.9%	39,047	38,901	51,054	51,381	58,784	61,675	66,512	70,907	73,533	71,412

1994 Year-end:
Debt ratio: 69.7%
Return on equity: —
Cash (mil.): $1,710
Current ratio: 0.91
Long-term debt (mil.): $3,142
No. of shares (mil.): 50.5
Dividends
  Yield: 0.4%
  Payout: —
Market value (mil.): $2,548

Stock Price History High/Low 1985–94

THE DIAL CORP

OVERVIEW

Based in Phoenix, Dial Corp has emerged from the flames of restructuring with a more-focused business portfolio. However, chairman John Teets continues to buy and sell businesses to strengthen Dial's focus on consumer products and service businesses.

In the highly competitive consumer products market, Dial understands its role as a 2nd-tier player in the personal and household categories. As a result, Dial carefully follows market trends (and major competitors) and introduces new products that play to these trends. Recent additions include Moisturizing Dial Plus antibacterial beauty soap and a concentrated version of Purex laundry detergent.

Through its various subsidiaries, Dial also offers airline catering and ground-handling services, convention services, cruises, money orders, Canadian bus service, and food ser-

vices. Dial is making its Aircraft Service International Group (airline fueling and other services) a unit of its Dobbs International Services subsidiary (catering). With airlines such as Delta reducing food service on short-distance flights, Dial plans to bundle services, including cargo warehousing, interior cleaning of aircraft, and supplying potable water, to cost-conscious airlines.

Dial has expanded its convention services business with the purchase of All West Display by its Exhibitgroup subsidiary. Sales at Dial's transportation and cruise operations declined because of the fall in the relative value of the Canadian dollar (which affected Greyhound Lines of Canada), lower levels of Florida tourism, increased competition in the cruise industry, and higher ship-leasing costs (which affected Premier Cruise Lines).

WHEN

Around 1945, the meatpacker Armour & Company set its sights on developing a deodorant soap to gain a larger share of the postwar soap market. A chemist at the company added the germicidal agent AT-7 to soap, which reduced bacteria on the skin by about 95% and thereby limited body odor. The new deodorant soap was named Dial because of its 24-hour protection against bacteria that cause body odor.

In 1948 Armour & Company introduced Dial soap in a full-page advertisement in the *Chicago Tribune*. The ad was printed on paper with scented ink and encouraged its readers to sample its refreshing fragrance by smelling the newspaper. The company adopted the slogan "Aren't you glad you use Dial? Don't you wish everybody did?" in 1953.

In 1970 Greyhound bought Armour & Company and its Dial brand for $400 million. However, Greyhound kept only the meatpacking (Armour Foods) and consumer products operations (Armour-Dial) and sold the rest of Armour's assets for $225 million. With its Armour purchase, Greyhound capped off a decade of diversification. In addition to its core bus operation, it had acquired a food service company (Prophet Company, 1964), a money order business (Traveler's Express, 1966), and ground-handling and janitorial services (Aircraft Services International, 1967). Greyhound's diversification strategy was prompted by the problems in the bus industry, which was declining because more of its customers could afford cars. In 1971 Greyhound moved its headquarters from Chicago to Phoenix.

John Teets was appointed chairman and CEO of Greyhound in 1981 and immediately began selling unprofitable subsidiaries. In 1983 Greyhound divested its Armour Foods subsidiary by buying out the union contract for $50 million, firing its 4,000 employees, and selling Armour's assets to ConAgra for $166 million in cash and stock. Greyhound established Premier Cruise Lines in 1984 and bought Purex with its Brillo brand in 1985. In 1987 Greyhound bought Dobbs International Services (airline catering) and Dobbs Houses (airport concessions, sold 1992). Also that year Greyhound sold all its intercity bus business to a Dallas investment group led by Fred Currey, but it bought GM's bus manufacturing division, Motor Coach Industries. Greyhound also bought the 20 Mule Team division of US Borax & Chemical Corp. (1988) and the Breck trademark and operations (1990).

Greyhound changed its name to Greyhound Dial in 1990 and to Dial in 1991 to reflect its new focus. Dial spun off its financial businesses in 1992. In 1993 Teets completed a major restructuring begun in 1987 by selling Motor Coach Industries to the public, ending Dial's historic involvement in the US bus industry. Also in 1993 Dial bought Renuzit Air Fresheners (from S.C. Johnson) and United Exposition Services (trade shows), and it began acquiring 15 in-flight catering kitchens from United Air Lines for its Dobbs International subsidiary. As a result, Dobbs became #1 in airline catering. In 1995 Dial agreed to purchase 2 leased cruise ships.

NYSE symbol: DL
Fiscal year ends: December 31

WHO

Chairman and CEO: John W. Teets, age 61,
$2,343,000 pay
President and COO: Andrew S. Patti, age 54,
$675,633 pay (prior to promotion)
Chairman and CEO, GES Exposition Services: Norton
D. Rittmaster, age 60, $497,882 pay
President, Dobbs International Services: Frederick J.
Martin, age 60, $524,900 pay
President and CEO, Travelers Express Company:
Robert H. Bohannon, age 50
VP and General Counsel: L. Gene Lemon, age 54,
$574,500 pay
VP and Secretary: Frederick G. Emerson, age 61
VP Finance and Treasurer: Ronald G. Nelson, age 53
VP Human Resources: Joan F. Ingalls, age 46
Auditors: Deloitte & Touche LLP

WHERE

HQ: Dial Tower, Phoenix, AZ 85077
Phone: 602-207-4000
Fax: 602-207-5100

Dial operates offices and other facilities worldwide.

WHAT

	1994 Sales		1994 Operating Income	
	$ mil.	% of total	$ mil.	% of total
Consumer products	1,511	43	160	48
Services				
Airline catering & svcs.	764	21	61	19
Travel/payment	749	21	58	18
Convention	523	15	51	15
Adjustments	—	—	(44)	—
Total	**3,547**	**100**	**286**	**100**

Selected Brands

Armour Star	Liquid Dial	Purex Rinse'n Soft
Bo-Peep	Lunch Bucket	Purex Sta Puf
Borateem	Luron	Purex Toss 'n Soft
Boraxo	Magic	Renuzit
Breck	Moisturizing	Sno Bol
Brillo	Dial Plus	Spirit
Bruce	Parsons	Tone
Cameo	Pure & Natural	Treet
Dial	Purex	Trend
Dutch		

Selected Subsidiaries

Aircraft Service International Group
Brewster Transport Company Ltd. (tour and charter
buses, travel agency, hotels, and recreation services)
Crystal Holidays, Ltd. (tour operator)
Dobbs International Services, Inc. (in-flight catering)
Exhibitgroup Inc. (convention exhibits and displays)
GES Exposition Services, Inc. (convention services)
Greyhound Leisure Services, Inc. (duty-free shops)
Greyhound Lines of Canada Ltd. (intercity bus service)
Premier Cruise Lines, Ltd.
Restaura, Inc. (food services and lodging operations)
Travelers Express Co., Inc. (money orders)

KEY COMPETITORS

Accor	Gillette
American Express	Henkel
American Home Products	Hormel
Amway	Hyatt
ARAMARK	Imasco
Bayer	Lufthansa
Campbell Soup	MasterCard
Carlson	Nestlé
Carnival Corp.	Ogden
Caterair	Philip Morris
Church & Dwight	Procter & Gamble
Clorox	Reed Elsevier
Colgate-Palmolive	Royal Caribbean Cruises
ConAgra	Sara Lee
Dow Chemical	S.C. Johnson
Duty Free Intl.	Unilever
Freeman Cos.	Visa

HOW MUCH

	9-Year Growth	1985	1986	1987	1988	1989	1990	1991	1992	1993	1994
Sales ($ mil.)	3.7%	2,562	2,584	2,274	3,305	3,537	3,519	3,310	3,389	3,000	3,547
Net income ($ mil.)	1.7%	120	186	31	93	109	116	(58)	34	142	140
Income as % of sales	—	4.7%	7.2%	1.4%	1.5%	3.1%	0.5%	—	1.0%	4.7%	4.0%
Earnings per share ($)	3.1%	1.22	2.05	0.39	1.21	1.38	0.19	(0.74)	0.39	1.66	1.61
Stock price – high ($)	—	17.25	19.00	23.00	18.44	18.88	16.13	23.06	25.31	22.25	24.00
Stock price – low ($)	—	11.94	13.56	9.63	12.69	14.38	9.50	12.31	16.69	17.94	19.25
Stock price – close ($)	3.1%	16.19	15.50	12.75	15.00	16.00	12.31	22.88	21.00	20.19	21.25
P/E – high	—	14	9	59	15	14	85	—	65	13	15
P/E – low	—	10	7	25	11	10	50	—	43	11	12
Dividends per share ($)	(0.7%)	0.62	0.66	0.66	0.66	0.66	0.66	0.67	0.70	0.63	0.56	0.58
Book value per share ($)	(7.4%)	11.95	11.31	12.40	13.16	13.50	13.09	11.72	4.16	5.10	5.98
Employees	(2.7%)	36,942	35,922	29,694	36,544	36,233	36,413	32,746	30,112	25,025	28,900

1994 Year-end:
Debt ratio: 57.0%
Return on equity: 27.4%
Cash (mil.): $33
Current ratio: 0.60
Long-term debt (mil.): $722
No. of shares (mil.): 93
Dividends
  Yield: 2.7%
  Payout: 36.0%
Market value (mil.): $1,972

Stock Price History
High/Low 1985–94

HOOVER'S HANDBOOK OF AMERICAN COMPANIES 1996   303

DIGITAL EQUIPMENT CORPORATION

OVERVIEW

After 4 years of heavy losses, DEC — one of the world's top suppliers of networked computer systems and components, software, and services — may again hold a winning hand. The company's trump card is its 64-bit Alpha microprocessor (the industry standard is still 32 bits). Database software alliances with Microsoft and Oracle should boost sales of DEC's Alpha-based servers and workstations.

Robert Palmer, who became CEO in 1992 and chairman in 1995, is the maverick in charge of DEC's drastic restructuring and returning profitability. Since Palmer took over, DEC has reorganized into units based on product lines, sold off noncore businesses, and slashed operating costs.

DEC is betting the future on strategic partnerships and emerging technology. In 1994 DEC introduced its HiNote notebook computer that is one inch thick but has a full-size screen and keyboard. In 1995 it announced a pact with Sybase, a leading developer of client/server software. The companies will codevelop a system for delivering and managing interactive television services. Also in 1995 DEC and AccelGraphics announced an advanced graphics accelerator card that allows 3-D designers to take advantage of DEC's Alpha processor.

WHEN

Two young MIT engineers, Kenneth Olsen and Harlan Anderson, founded DEC in 1957 to venture beyond mainframes into smaller, less-expensive computers that were interactive. DEC's converted woolen mill near Boston soon produced innovations popular with engineers and scientists, including the PDP-1 (the first interactive computer, 1960) and the PDP-5 (dubbed the minicomputer, 1963). The PDP-8 (1965) and later the PDP-11 (1970) provided number-crunching breakthroughs.

Olsen began minicomputer sales in the mid-1960s using the matrix management model (with individuals answerable to both functional and line managers) and sales to OEMs; revenue and profit growth averaged 30% per year for almost 2 decades.

DEC began its networking tradition in 1974, introducing the Digital network architecture (DNA) to link its PDP-11s to local- and wide-area networks (LANs and WANs); the result was DECnet Phase I. DEC engineering whiz Gordon Bell conceived of the VAX line of computers, which allowed easy upgrades from PDPs and virtually unlimited memory; the VAX-11/780 appeared in 1977.

In 1979 Olsen pledged billions to an expanded VAX generation using all DEC-made components. Olsen dispensed with the matrix model and instituted unified marketing during the arduous 5-year undertaking. The company refocused the new VAXes (like the VAX 6000 mini, 1984) on the larger commercial market and extended its DECnet umbrella to provide global company/client/supplier connections. During the VAX glory days, between 1984 and 1988, sales doubled and earnings nearly quadrupled.

By 1988 DEC was embracing open systems and entering alliances to connect PCs to VAXes (Apple, Compaq), to translate VAX software to ULTRIX (DEC's version of UNIX), and to bring popular software to the VAX line (*Lotus 1-2-3, dBase*). DEC also took a 5% stake in MIPS Computer (which provides the RISC chip for the RISC-based DECstation).

DEC reported its first quarterly loss ever in 1990 and a $617 million annual net loss for fiscal 1991. In response the company restructured and reduced its work force. In 1991 it bought Digital Kienzle Computersysteme (computers, Germany), 80% of manufacturing software developer EA Systems, and most of the computer business of Philips.

After Digital posted a loss of more than $2 billion in 1992, Olsen resigned, but he handpicked his successor, Bob Palmer, an expert in semiconductors and cofounder of semiconductor manufacturer Mostek Corp. Known as "GQ Bob" within DEC for his tailored suits and fast cars, Palmer accelerated cost cutting. That same year DEC agreed to buy 10% of Olivetti (office equipment, Italy) and began mail-order PC sales.

Mitsubishi agreed to manufacture DEC's new Alpha chip in 1993. The following year NYNEX and Ameritech picked Digital to supply video-server equipment as the 2 Baby Bells gear up to supply video-on-demand services over their phone lines. In late 1994 the company sold its RDB database software operations to Oracle for $108 million.

In 1995 DEC and Raytheon entered a multiyear, multimillion-dollar cooperative agreement to develop an upgrade of the on-board computer of the Navy's E-2C Hawkeye, a carrier-based aircraft. Fiscal 1995 brought DEC its first profit since 1990. With increased sales of $13.8 billion, the company earned nearly $122 million for the year.

NYSE symbol: DEC
Fiscal year ends: Saturday nearest June 30

Chairman, President, and CEO: Robert B. Palmer, age 54, $900,016 pay
VP and General Manager, Computer Systems Division: Enrico Pesatori, age 53, $569,242 pay
VP and Chief Technical Officer: William D. Strecker, age 50, $427,891 pay
VP and General Manager, Components Division: Charles F. Christ, age 55, $315,016 pay
VP Finance and CFO: Vincent J. Mullarkey, age 46
VP; President, Asia Pacific: Bobby A. F. Choonavala
VP; President, The Americas: Harold D. Copperman
VP and General Manager Accounts Business Unit; President, Digital Europe: Vencenzo Damiani
VP and Chief Information Officer: Robert E. McNulty
VP and General Manager, PC Business Unit: Bernhard Auer
VP Corporate Research: Samuel H. Fuller
VP and General Counsel: Thomas C. Siekman, age 52
VP Human Resources: Savino R. "Sid" Ferrales, age 44
Auditors: Coopers & Lybrand L.L.P.

WHERE

HQ: 146 Main St., Maynard, MA 01754-2571
Phone: 508-493-5111
Fax: 508-493-8780

Digital sells its products in more than 100 countries. The company develops and manufactures its products in the Americas, Europe, and the Pacific Rim.

	1994 Sales		1994 Operating Income	
	$ mil.	% of total	$ mil.	% of total
US	5,177	39	(741)	—
Europe	5,832	43	(1,109)	—
Other regions	2,442	18	(170)	—
Total	**13,451**	**100**	**(2,020)**	**—**

WHAT

	1994 Sales	
	$ mil.	% of total
Products	7,191	54
Services & other	6,260	46
Total	**13,451**	**100**

Selected Products and Services

Computers
Alpha AXP family
RISC/UNIX-based family
VAX family

Peripherals
Network components
Printers
Terminals
Video terminals

Semiconductors
Alpha microprocessor

Services
Education and customer training
Information systems consulting
Network design and support
Systems integration and project management

Software
Networking and communications
Operating system

KEY COMPETITORS

Advanced Logic Research
Amdahl
American Management
Apple
Arthur Andersen
AST
AT&T
Compaq
Computer Sciences
Data General
Dell
Dun & Bradstreet
EDS
Ernst & Young
Fujitsu

Gateway 2000
Hewlett-Packard
Hitachi
IBM
ICL
Intel
Machines Bull
Matsushita
Micron Technology
Microsoft
Motorola
NEC
Novell
Olivetti
Packard Bell

Sequent
Sharp
Siemens
Silicon Graphics
Sony
Storage Technology
Stratus Computer
Sun Microsystems
Tandem
Toshiba
Unisys
Vobis
Wang

HOW MUCH

	9-Year Growth	1985	1986	1987	1988	1989	1990	1991	1992	1993	1994
Sales ($ mil.)	8.1%	6,686	7,590	9,389	11,475	12,742	12,943	13,911	13,931	14,371	13,451
Net income ($ mil.)	—	447	617	1,137	1,306	1,073	74	(617)	(2,310)	(251)	(2,094)
Income as % of sales	—	6.7%	8.1%	12.1%	11.4%	8.4%	0.6%	—	—	—	—
Earnings per share ($)	—	3.71	4.81	8.53	9.90	8.45	0.59	(5.08)	(18.50)	(1.93)	(15.43)
Stock price – high ($)	—	68.38	109.00	199.50	144.75	122.38	95.13	83.00	65.50	49.25	38.13
Stock price – low ($)	—	42.63	65.81	110.00	86.38	56.88	45.50	48.50	30.38	32.75	18.25
Stock price – close ($)	(7.4%)	66.25	104.75	135.00	98.38	82.00	54.88	55.25	33.75	34.25	33.25
P/E – high	—	18	23	23	15	15	161	—	—	—	—
P/E – low	—	12	14	13	9	7	77	—	—	—	—
Dividends per share ($)	—	0.00	0.00	0.00	0.00	0.00	0.00	0.00	0.00	0.00	0.00
Book value per share ($)	(5.5%)	38.43	44.54	49.87	59.47	66.12	66.76	61.17	38.58	36.19	23.02
Employees	(0.8%)	89,000	94,700	110,500	121,500	125,800	124,000	121,000	113,800	94,200	82,800

1994 Year-end:
Debt ratio: 23.6%
Return on equity: —
Cash (mil.): $1,181
Current ratio: 1.36
Long-term debt (mil.): $1,011
No. of shares (mil.): 142
Dividends
Yield: —
Payout: —
Market value (mil.): $4,731

**Stock Price History
High/Low 1985–94**

DILLARD DEPARTMENT STORES, INC.

OVERVIEW

Based in Little Rock, Arkansas, Dillard is among the largest department store chains in the US, operating about 230 stores in 21 Sunbelt and midwestern states. Its stores, which emphasize fashion apparel and home furnishings, cater to middle- to upper-middle-income consumers. The Dillard family owns about 99% of the Class B stock and holds 5 seats on the board.

Although same-store sales were up 5% in fiscal 1995, Dillard's net income growth has slowed lately, hurt by a weak market for women's apparel. Long a favorite among analysts for its merchandising, cost control, and expansion strategies, Dillard has lost favor in some circles for sticking with a marketing strategy it has had since the mid-1980s. Rather than offer frequent, advertised sales (an industry standard), Dillard prefers to build customer loyalty with "everyday-low-pricing." But with the slump in women's apparel, pricing and advertised sales have become increasingly important to the industry.

The company has no plans to change its marketing strategy, but it is working to increase its mix of private-label brands. It also continues to expand aggressively, with plans to build 11 stores in 1995.

WHEN

At age 12 William Dillard began working in his father's general store in Mineral Springs, Arkansas. After he graduated from Columbia University (1937), the 3rd-generation retailer spent 7 months in the Sears, Roebuck manager training program in Tulsa.

With $8,000 borrowed from his father, Dillard opened his first department store in Nashville, Arkansas, in 1938. He sold the store in 1948 to finance a partnership in Wooten's Department Store in Texarkana, Arkansas, later buying out Wooten and establishing Dillard's, Inc., in 1949.

During the 1950s and 1960s the company became a strong regional retailer, developing its strategy of buying well-established downtown stores in small cities — Mayer & Schmidt (Tyler, Texas; 1956), Brown-Dunkin (Tulsa, 1960), Joseph Pfeifer (Little Rock, 1963), and Gus Blass (Little Rock, 1964). Dillard's moved its headquarters to Little Rock after buying Pfeifer. When Dillard (the name was changed to Dillard Department Stores in 1964) went public in 1969, the chain had 15 stores in 3 states, with sales of $65.2 million.

During the early 1960s E. Ray Kemp, vice-chairman until 1992, began computerizing operations to streamline inventory and information management. In 1970 the company added computerized cash registers, which gave management hourly sales figures.

Dillard's acquisitions during the 1970s included 5 Fedways (Southwest, 1971), 5 Leonard's (Dallas–Fort Worth, 1974), and Alden's (Texarkana, 1978).

Acquisitions in the 1980s included 12 Stix, Baer & Fuller stores; 12 Diamond's stores; 5 John A. Brown stores; 12 Macy stores; 27 Joske's stores; 4 Cain-Sloan stores; and 17 D. H. Holmes stores. In a 1988 joint venture with Edward J. DeBartolo, Dillard bought a 50% interest in the 12 Higbee's stores in Ohio (buying the other 50% in 1992, shortly after Higbee's bought 5 former Horne's stores in Ohio). In 1990 Dillard acquired 23 J. B. Ivey stores in South Carolina, North Carolina, and Florida, and in 1991 it bought 8 Maison Blanche Department Stores in central and western Florida.

In 1991 Vendamerica BV, a subsidiary of Vendex International and the only major nonfamily holder of the company's stock, sold its 8.9 million shares of Class A stock (25% of the class) in an underwritten public offering.

In 1992 the company announced that Dillard stores would be the anchors for 5 regional shopping malls slated for development in Mexico. The venture is the company's first foray into the Mexican market.

Looking for help in developing its Mexican stores, Dillard entered a joint venture with Wal-Mart and Mexican retailer Cifra in 1994 to build several stores in Mexico. Dillard holds a 50% stake in the venture and Wal-Mart and Cifra share the other 50%. Also in 1994 the FTC filed a lawsuit against Dillard, claiming the company made it unreasonably difficult for Dillard credit card holders to remove unauthorized charges from their bills. Dillard said its practices were standard within the industry.

In 1995 the company settled a religious discrimination suit brought by the Equal Employment Opportunity Commission. Several job seekers at the company's St. Louis store had claimed they were denied employment because they could not work Saturdays or Sundays because of religious beliefs. That same year, following the devaluation of the peso, Dillard pushed back its Mexican expansion to 1997.

NYSE symbol: DDS
Fiscal year ends: Saturday nearest January 31

WHO

Chairman and CEO: William Dillard, age 80,
$1,900,000 pay
President and COO: William Dillard II, age 50,
$1,600,000 pay
EVP: Alex Dillard, age 45, $1,510,000 pay
EVP: Mike Dillard, age 43, $1,120,000 pay
SVP and CFO: James I. Freeman, age 45, $585,000 pay
SVP, Secretary, and General Counsel: James E. Darr Jr.,
age 51
Director Personnel: Joyce Wisner
Auditors: Deloitte & Touche LLP

WHERE

HQ: 1600 Cantrell Rd., Little Rock, AR 72201
Phone: 501-376-5200
Fax: 501-376-5917

	1995 Stores
	No.
Texas	62
Florida	27
Louisiana	16
Missouri	16
Oklahoma	14
Arizona	13
North Carolina	13
Ohio	13
Tennessee	12
Kansas	9
Arkansas	7
South Carolina	6
Nebraska	4
New Mexico	4
Mississippi	3
Nevada	3
Other	7
Total	**229**

WHAT

	1995 Sales
	% of total
Women's & juniors' clothing	30
Shoes, lingerie & accessories	19
Men's clothing & accessories	18
Cosmetics	13
Home	12
Children's clothing	7
Leased departments	1
Total	**100**

	1995 Sales
	% of total
Branded merchandise	80
Private-label merchandise	20
Total	**100**

KEY COMPETITORS

Belk Stores
Benetton
Best Buy
Bombay Company
Broadway Stores
Brown Group
Carson Pirie Scott
Circuit City
Dayton Hudson
Dunlap
Edison Brothers
Federated
The Gap
Harcourt General
J. Crew
J. C. Penney
Jos. A. Bank
Lands' End
Levitz
The Limited
Liz Claiborne
Luxottica
Marks and Spencer
May
Men's Wearhouse
Mercantile Stores
Merry-Go-Round
Montgomery Ward
Nine West
Nordstrom
Proffitt's
Sears
Spiegel
TJX
Woolworth

HOW MUCH

	9-Year Growth	1986	1987	1988	1989	1990	1991	1992	1993	1994	1995
Sales ($ mil.)	14.8%	1,601	1,851	2,206	2,558	3,049	3,606	4,036	4,714	5,131	5,546
Net income ($ mil.)	15.9%	67	75	91	114	148	183	206	236	241	252
Income as % of sales	—	4.2%	4.0%	4.1%	4.4%	4.9%	5.1%	5.1%	5.0%	4.7%	4.5%
Earnings per share ($)[1]	12.7%	0.76	0.78	0.94	1.18	1.45	1.67	1.84	2.11	2.14	2.23
Stock price – high ($)[1]	—	12.82	15.03	19.15	15.48	24.73	31.97	45.54	51.50	52.75	37.63
Stock price – low ($)[1]	—	6.04	10.66	7.99	8.37	13.65	20.56	27.47	30.00	33.13	25.50
Stock price – close ($)[1]	8.8%	12.49	12.61	8.20	14.11	23.64	29.10	41.13	49.75	38.00	26.75
P/E – high	—	17	19	20	13	17	19	25	24	25	17
P/E – low	—	8	14	9	7	9	12	15	14	16	11
Dividends per share ($)	13.0%	0.03	0.04	0.04	0.05	0.06	0.07	0.07	0.08	0.08	0.09
Book value per share ($)	19.5%	4.12	5.74	6.64	7.79	10.22	12.30	14.18	16.28	18.43	20.55
Employees	10.0%	16,010	18,412	21,168	23,114	26,304	31,786	32,132	33,883	35,536	37,832

1995 Year-end:
Debt ratio: 36.7%
Return on equity: 11.4%
Cash (mil.): $51
Current ratio: 3.33
Long-term debt (mil.): $1,201
No. of shares (mil.): 113
Dividends
 Yield: 0.3%
 Payout: 4.0%
Market value (mil.): $3,024

Stock Price History[1]
High/Low 1986–95

[1]Stock prices are for the prior calendar year.

DOLE FOOD COMPANY, INC.

OVERVIEW

Dole is poised to slice its produce operations from its small but growing real estate business. California-based Dole is one of the world's largest distributors of fresh and processed fruits, vegetables, and nuts. But since David Murdock, who owns 23% of Dole, became CEO in the mid-1980s, the company has had a growing presence in real estate, including upscale residential and commercial developments and 2 posh resorts on the (mostly private) Hawaiian island of Lana'i.

Before it splits its 2 segments, though, Dole is polishing their operations. In 1994 the company purchased Dromedary (dates) and Made in Nature, which represents organic produce growers. In 1995 it acquired Chiquita's New

Zealand produce operations. Early in 1995 Dole sold its juice business for $285 million to Seagram's Tropicana division and its California dried fruit operations to the Sun-Diamond Growers cooperative for $100 million.

On the other (real estate) hand, in 1994 Dole bought 22 acres on eastern Oahu (Hawaii) for a condominium development. In 1995 the company began marketing homes on one of its 2 Lana'i golf courses. Dole also has property under development in Arizona, California, and the southeastern US.

In 1995 Dole had to contend with a continuing quota on fruit imports imposed by the European Union (EU) as well as severe flooding in California's Salinas Valley.

WHEN

Samuel Castle and Amos Cooke, missionaries to Hawaii, formed Castle & Cooke (C&C) in 1851 to manage their church's failing depository, which supplied outlying mission posts with staple goods. Within a year they had added a store in Honolulu, selling goods to the general public. In 1858 they entered the sugar business and within 10 years served as agents for several Hawaiian sugar plantations and the ships that carried their cargoes.

In 1907 C&C became agent and part owner of Matson Navigation, the largest shipping company operating between Hawaii and the mainland. C&C entered another Hawaiian industry in 1932, buying 1/5 of the Hawaiian Pineapple Company, founded by James Dole in 1901. Extensive advertising made Dole pineapples a major product by 1936.

After WWII, labor unions organized and wages improved, almost doubling payrolls at C&C's sugar plantations. The sugar and pineapple industries responded by increasing mechanization in their operations.

In the late 1950s and early 1960s, C&C began the transition to a food and land business. It bought Bumble Bee, an Oregon seafood company (1959), and completed the purchase of Dole Pineapple, including thousands of acres of Hawaiian land (1961). In 1964 C&C became a banana importer with the purchase of Standard Fruit of New Orleans. The company started pineapple and banana farms in the Philippines in the 1960s to supply markets in East Asia.

In the early 1980s the company was heavily in debt and earnings were down. In 1985, following 2 takeover attempts, C&C agreed to merge with Flexi-Van, a container-leasing company headed by David Murdock, who took

over operations. He brought in management talent and capital as well as Flexi-Van's fleet of ships to transport Dole produce. Murdock trimmed operations, selling off Bumble Bee (1986) and Flexi-Van's container-leasing business (1987), leaving C&C with its fruit and real estate operations. In 1987 C&C bought the agricultural operations of Apache Corporation and Tenneco West and in 1988 the raisin operations of Bonner Packing.

In 1991 the company changed its name to Dole Food Company. That year Murdock shocked Hawaiians when he announced that Dole would end its pineapple operations on Lana'i to concentrate on tourist properties there: The Lodge at Koele opened in 1990 and the Manele Bay Hotel in 1991. Among Dole's 1992 acquisitions was SAMICA, a leading European marketer of dried fruits and nuts.

Soft banana prices and the EU's 1993 imposition of quotas on some fruit imports resulted in flat sales in 1993. Dole countered with a cost-cutting campaign that reduced annual operating expenses by $130 million. That same year the company spent $117 million on acquisitions, including Looza, a European juice company.

As the first step toward spinning it off, Dole completed the IPO of 18% of its Castle & Cooke Homes home-building subsidiary in 1993. It repurchased the outstanding shares of C&C the following year because of a lackluster market (higher interest rates had slowed home sales). Among Dole's 1994 acquisitions was an interest in Jamaica Fruit Distributors (UK).

In 1995 a coalition of US labor and consumer groups targeted several companies, including Dole, for buying their products in low-wage countries.

WHO

Chairman and CEO: David H. Murdock, age 71, $1,000,013 pay
EVP; President, International: David A. DeLorenzo, age 48, $500,000 pay
EVP: Gerald W. LaFleur, age 62, $500,000 pay
EVP; President, North America: Ernest W. Townsend, age 49, $500,000 pay
EVP: Alan B. Sellers, age 47
President, Dole Asia: Paul Cuyegkeng
President, Dole Europe SA: William F. Feeney
VP; President and CEO, Castle & Cooke Properties, Inc.: Thomas C. Leppert, age 40, $687,512 pay
VP, Treasurer, and CFO: Michael S. Karsner, age 36
VP and Corporate General Counsel: J. Brett Tibbitts, age 39
VP Human Resources: George R. Horne, age 58
Auditors: Arthur Andersen & Co, SC

WHERE

HQ: 31355 Oak Crest Dr., Westlake Village, CA 91361
Phone: 818-879-6600
Fax: 818-879-6618 (public relations)

Dole has food operations in the Americas, Asia, and Europe. The company markets its products worldwide. Dole also owns and develops real estate in the US and owns 2 resort hotels in Hawaii.

	1994 Sales		1994 Operating Income	
	$ mil.	% of total	$ mil.	% of total
North America	2,277	50	28	15
Asia	842	18	16	9
Europe	777	17	13	7
Latin America	677	15	131	69
Adjustments	(731)	—	(14)	(14)
Total	**3,842**	**100**	**174**	**100**

WHAT

	1994 Sales		1994 Operating Income	
	$ mil.	% of total	$ mil.	% of total
Food products	3,498	91	152	68
Real estate	297	8	73	32
Resorts	47	1	(37)	—
Adjustments	—	—	(14)	—
Total	**3,842**	**100**	**174**	**100**

Selected Products

Food Products
Dates (chopped and pitted)
Dried fruits and nuts (almonds, date nut rolls, pistachios, prunes, raisins, and trail mix)
Fresh fruit (apples, bananas, cherries, grapefruit, grapes, lemons, kiwi, mangos, melons, oranges, pears, pineapples, plums, raspberries, strawberries, and tangelos)
Fresh vegetables (artichokes, asparagus, broccoli, brussels sprouts, carrots, cauliflower, celery, lettuce, and onions)
Organic produce (fruits, vegetables, and packaged fruits and nuts)
Packaged foods (canned fruits and fruit salads, snack bars, and fruit sorbets)

Real estate (commercial, industrial, and residential)

Resorts (The Lodge at Koele, Manele Bay Hotel)

KEY COMPETITORS

Borden	National Grape	United Foods
C Brewer Homes	Co-op	Universal
ConAgra	Ocean Spray	Foods
CPC	Philip Morris	Westin Hotel
Danone	Procter &	
Del Monte	Gamble	
Hilton	RJR Nabisco	
Hyatt	Schuler Homes	
Kamehameha Schools/	Tri Valley	
Bishop Estate	Growers	

HOW MUCH

	9-Year Growth	1985	1986	1987	1988	1989	1990	1991	1992	1993	1994
Sales ($ mil.)	10.2%	1,601	1,738	1,749	2,469	2,718	3,003	3,216	3,376	3,431	3,842
Net income ($ mil.)	—	(29)	44	97	112	95	121	134	65	78	68
Income as % of sales	—	—	2.5%	5.6%	4.5%	3.5%	4.0%	4.2%	1.9%	2.3%	1.8%
Earnings per share ($)	—	(1.47)	0.56	1.60	1.90	1.60	2.03	2.24	1.09	1.30	1.14
Stock price – high ($)	—	16.38	20.25	26.63	29.38	45.25	38.63	48.00	40.00	37.88	35.50
Stock price – low ($)	—	9.88	13.00	12.00	17.25	25.38	26.25	28.00	26.00	25.88	22.50
Stock price – close ($)	6.5%	13.00	19.25	18.50	28.25	34.75	29.38	36.00	32.13	26.75	23.00
P/E – high	—	—	36	17	16	28	19	21	37	29	31
P/E – low	—	—	23	8	9	16	13	13	24	20	20
Dividends per share ($)	—	0.00	0.00	0.00	0.00	0.00	0.00	0.50	0.40	0.40	0.40
Book value per share ($)	8.7%	8.59	9.97	11.22	12.53	14.11	15.67	17.53	16.85	17.70	18.17
Employees	3.1%	35,000	34,600	39,250	42,000	45,000	51,000	50,000	50,000	45,300	46,000

1994 Year-end:
Debt ratio: 59.8%
Return on equity: 6.4%
Cash (mil.): $47
Current ratio: 1.91
Long-term debt (mil.): $1,555
No. of shares (mil.): 59
Dividends
  Yield: 1.7%
  Payout: 35.1%
Market value (mil.): $1,368

Stock Price History High/Low 1985–94

DOMINO'S PIZZA, INC.

OVERVIEW

"Pride goeth before destruction, and a haughty spirit before a fall" is a lesson that Thomas Monaghan, founder of Domino's Pizza, has learned from experience. Ann Arbor–based Domino's still clings to its position as the #1 fast-food delivery company, but it has lost market share to other pizza makers and to indirect competitors like McDonald's, which now delivers in some markets. Part of the reason for the loss of share lies simply in increased competition and part in the company's reluctance to add variety to the menu.

The story of the relative decline and rise of Domino's is closely linked with Monaghan's emergence as a born-again entrepreneur. It was his practice of linking his personal and professional finances that got both founder and company into such dire fiscal straits that no one even wanted to buy the company when he put it up for sale. Monaghan's baseball team, his Frank Lloyd Wright collection, his antique and specialty car collection, and his resort island have all been sold off (some at a loss). Having learned that all is vanity, he now occupies a monastic cell of an office and applies himself to God, family, and his business.

Domino's has added a limited number of new items to its menu, including a new deep dish pizza and buffalo wings. It has also begun a program of repurchasing selected franchises. And although it no longer promises 30-minute delivery, the company emphasizes its delivery experience (to point out delivery errors by its competitors). Domino's continues to expand abroad, particularly in Eastern Europe and in India.

WHEN

Thomas Monaghan's early life was one of hardship. After growing up in an orphanage and numerous foster homes, Monaghan spent his young adult life experimenting, trying everything from a Catholic seminary to a stint in the Marine Corps.

After dropping out of college for financial reasons, in 1960 he borrowed $900 and bought DomiNick's, a failed pizza parlor in Ypsilanti, Michigan, which he operated with the help of his brother James. A year later Monaghan traded a Volkswagen Beetle for his brother's half of the company.

During the next few years, Monaghan learned the pizza business largely by trial and error. After a brief partnership with an experienced restaurateur with whom he later fell out, Monaghan developed a strategy to sell only pizza, to deliver it hot and fresh within 30 minutes, and to locate stores near colleges and military bases. In 1965 the company changed its name to Domino's.

In the 1960s and 1970s, Monaghan endured setbacks that almost killed the growing company. Among these were a 1968 fire that destroyed the Domino's headquarters and a 1975 lawsuit from Amstar Corporation (maker of Domino Sugar) for trademark infringement. But the company won the ensuing legal battles and by 1978 it operated 200 stores.

In the 1980s Domino's grew phenomenally. In 1981 the company created regional offices in 6 cities to oversee its 500 units. Domino's went international 2 years later when it opened a store in Winnipeg, Canada. Between 1981 and 1983 Domino's doubled its number of US stores to 1,000. In 1984 Domino's moved its headquarters to Ann Arbor, Michigan.

The company's growth brought Monaghan a personal fortune. In 1983 he bought the Detroit Tigers baseball team and amassed one of the world's largest collections of Frank Lloyd Wright objects. He also bought real estate and collected classic cars.

Expansion continued in the mid-1980s. Sales topped $1 billion in 1985 and then nearly doubled in only 2 years. In 1989 the company introduced pan pizza, its first new product. Also that year Monaghan put the company up for sale. Unable to find a buyer, Monaghan installed a new management group and retired to pursue lay work for the Catholic Church. His stance against abortion put him at odds with the National Organization for Women, which urged a boycott of Domino's Pizza in the late 1980s.

When company performance began to slide, Monaghan returned, having experienced a religious rebirth. He sold off his private holdings to reinvigorate the company and reorganized management.

An incident in which a driver trying to fulfill the company's 30-minute delivery guarantee ran a red light and collided with another car resulted in a $79 million judgment against the company in 1993. The episode prompted Domino's to alter its delivery policy.

In recent years the company's marketing efforts have been unfocused because of high turnover in the marketing department (3 marketing VPs in as many years). Domino's hopes the current VP, Cheryl Bachelder, will deliver.

Private company
Fiscal year ends: December 31

WHO

Founder, CEO, and President: Thomas S. Monaghan
VP Corporate Operations: Patrick Kelly
VP Franchise Operations: Stuart Mathis
VP; Managing Director, Domino's Pizza International:
Gary McCausland
VP Finance and Administration and CFO: Harry
Silverman
VP Distribution: Mike Soignet
VP Marketing and Product Development: Cheryl A.
Bachelder
Director Human Resources: Ron Woodman
Auditors: Arthur Andersen & Co, SC

WHERE

HQ: 30 Frank Lloyd Wright Dr., PO Box 997,
Ann Arbor, MI 48106-0997
Phone: 313-930-3030
Fax: 313-668-4614

	1994 Stores
	No.
US	4,256
Canada	176
Mexico	119
Japan	117
England	90
Taiwan	44
Korea	33
France	32
Puerto Rico	30
Australia	25
Saudi Arabia	18
Israel	17
Spain	12
Hong Kong	9
The Netherlands	9
Guatemala	8
Venezuela	8
Brazil	6
Chile	6
Panama	6
Other countries	58
Total	**5,079**

	1994 Sales
	% of total
US sales	83
Other countries	17
Total	**100**

WHAT

Major Products

Breadsticks
Buffalo wings
Deep dish pizza
Pan pizza
Salad
Soda
Submarine sandwiches
Thin-crust pizza

Ingredients Used in 1994	Amount
Anchovies	47,500 pounds
Bacon	2 million pounds
Beef	4.4 million pounds
Flour	115 million pounds
Green peppers	3.3 million pounds
Ham	4.5 million pounds
Hot peppers	44 thousand pounds
Mozzarella cheese	110 million pounds
Mushrooms	7 million pounds
Olives	152 thousand cases
Pepperoni	17 million pounds
Pineapple	86 thousand cases
Sausage	11 million pounds
Tomatoes	170 million pounds

KEY COMPETITORS

Accor	Rally's
Checkers Drive-In	Sbarro
Dairy Queen	Schwan's Sales Enterprises
Flagstar	ShowBiz Pizza Time
Grand Metropolitan	Sonic Corp.
Little Caesars	Subway
McDonald's	Triarc
Papa John's	Wendy's
PepsiCo	Whatabuger

HOW MUCH

	Annual Growth	1985	1986	1987	1988	1989	1990	1991	1992	1993	1994
Sales ($ mil.)	9.6%	1,100	1,430	2,000	2,300	2,500	2,600	2,400	2,450	2,200	2,500
Stores	6.7%	2,841	3,610	4,279	4,858	5,185	5,342	5,571	5,264	5,269	5,079
Employees	3.6%	—	—	—	—	—	100,000	—	—	—	115,000

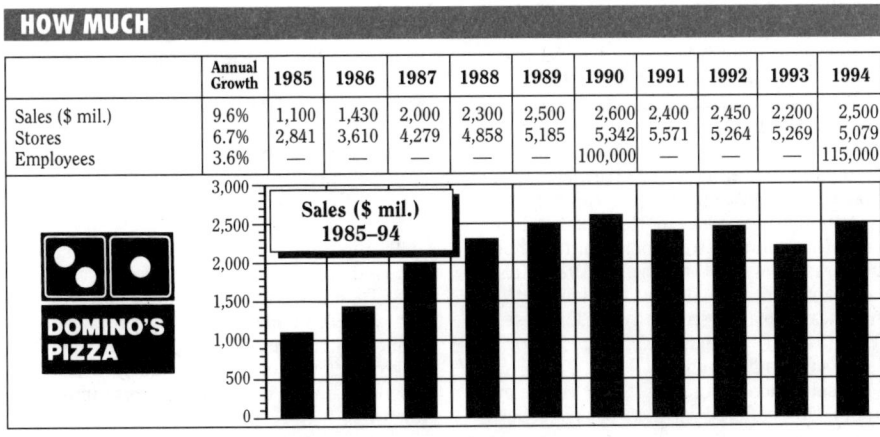

Sales ($ mil.)
1985–94

DOMINO'S PIZZA

THE DOW CHEMICAL COMPANY

Dow Chemical makes and supplies more than 2,500 product families, including chemical and performance products, plastics, hydrocarbons and energy, and consumer specialties (agricultural products and consumer products). The #2 chemical company after DuPont, Dow Chemical manufactures basic chemicals and plastics, including ethylene, butadiene, benzene, caustic soda, polyethylene, and polystyrene. The Midland, Michigan–based company's consumer products business (DowBrands) includes such well-known names as Fantastik, Saran Wrap, Spray'N Wash, Ziploc, Yes, and Vivid. The company manufactures petrochemicals such as olefins and aromatics and also makes agricultural chemicals through DowElanco, a joint venture with Eli Lilly.

Dow Chemical's overall performance has been hurt by the poor performance of its 2 spinoffs (Marion Merrell Dow and Destec) and the litigation facing its Dow Corning joint venture. Its prescription drugs and over-the-counter health care business (Marion Merrell Dow) lost 1/3 of its value since Dow took it public in 1989. The company cut its losses and sold its 71% stake in the drug firm to German pharmaceutical giant Hoechst for $7.1 billion in 1995. Destec Energy, a producer of cogenerated power and steam for the independent power market, has lost 45% of its market value since 1991.

Herbert Dow founded Dow Chemical in 1897 after developing a process that used electricity to extract bromides and chlorides from underground brine deposits around Midland, Michigan. The company's first product was chlorine bleach. Dow sold his products on the world market and eventually overcame British and German monopolies on bleach, bromides, and other chemicals.

In the mid-1920s the company rejected an attempted takeover by DuPont. By 1930, the year of Herbert Dow's death, sales had reached $15 million. Dow began building new plants around the country in the late 1930s. The Freeport, Texas, plant, completed in 1941 to supply magnesium and other products for the military, was the beginning of today's Texas Gulf Coast petrochemical complex.

Dow research yielded new plastics in the 1940s that became leaders in the industry by the 1950s. Saran Wrap (introduced in 1953) was the company's first major consumer product. By 1957 plastics accounted for 32% of Dow's sales, compared with 2% in 1940.

Plastics and silicone products boosted sales through the 1950s and propelled Dow into the top ranks of US firms. In 1964 sales passed $1 billion. Dow entered the pharmaceutical field with the 1960 purchase of Allied Labs.

Although Dow had exported chemicals for years (the diamond trademark on its indigo dyes was known in China before 1920), the company built its first plant outside North America, in partnership with the Japanese, in 1952 (Asahi-Dow) to make plastic nets for the latter's fishing industry.

Despite increasing sales ($10.6 billion by 1980), Dow suffered earnings drops in the recession years from 1981 to 1983 because of drops in chemical prices. To limit the cyclical effect of chemicals on profits, Dow continued to expand other business segments, notably pharmaceuticals (Merrell Drug, 1981) and consumer goods (Texize, household cleaners, 1984). In 1989 Dow merged its pharmaceutical division, Merrell Dow, with the pharmaceutical company Marion Labs, creating Marion Merrell Dow (with combined sales of $2.3 billion at that time). In 1989 Dow formed DowElanco, a joint venture with Eli Lilly to produce agricultural chemicals.

Following allegations that it had put a breast implant on the market without proper testing, Dow Corning, a 50-50 joint venture with Corning and the #1 producer of silicone breast implants, halted production of the devices in 1992. Also in 1992 Dow sold its share in an oil-field services joint venture to its partner, Schlumberger.

In 1993 Dow sold its Freeport, Texas, oil refinery to Phibro Energy, a subsidiary of Salomon, for $200 million. That same year Marion Merrell Dow acquired generic drug maker The Rugby Group.

Dow teamed up with Asahi Chemical again in 1994 when it signed a joint venture agreement with the Japanese chemical giant to market polystyrene in Asia.

Facing hundreds (and potentially thousands) of breast implant litigation cases, in 1995 Dow Corning applied for Chapter 11 bankruptcy. In April 1995 a federal judge granted claimants the right to name Dow Chemical (and not just Dow Corning) as a defendant in the upcoming series of implant lawsuits.

NYSE symbol: DOW
Fiscal year ends: December 31

WHO

Chairman: Frank P. Popoff, age 59, $1,635,004 pay
CEO: William S. Stavropoulos, age 55, $900,008 pay
SVP; President, Dow North America: Enrique J. Sosa, age 54, $744,996 pay
Senior Consultant; Chairman, DowBrands Inc. and DowElanco: Joseph L. Downey, age 58, $711,436 pay
Senior Consultant: Andrew J. Butler, age 60, $632,607 pay
CEO, Dow Corning: Richard A. Hazleton
Group VP: Anthony J. Carbone
Group VP: Michael D. Parker
VP and General Counsel: John G. Scriven
VP; Corporate Director, Environment, Health and Safety, Public Affairs, and Information Systems: David T. Buzzelli
Financial VP and Treasurer: J. Pedro Reinhard
VP and Corporate Director, R&D: Fred P. Corson
VP and Director, Manufacturing and Engineering: Larry F. Wright
VP Human Resources, Chemicals, and Plastics: Larry Washington
Auditors: Deloitte & Touche LLP

WHERE

HQ: 2030 Dow Center, Midland, MI 48674
Phone: 517-636-1000
Fax: 517-636-1830

Dow has 50 manufacturing plants in 16 states and Puerto Rico and 80 plants in 28 foreign countries.

	1994 Sales		1994 Operating Income	
	$ mil.	% of total	$ mil.	% of total
US	9,942	50	1,293	55
Europe	5,320	26	273	12
Other regions	4,753	24	779	33
Total	**20,015**	**100**	**2,345**	**100**

WHAT

	1994 Sales		1994 Operating Income	
	$ mil.	% of total	$ mil.	% of total
Plastic products	7,476	37	1,131	44
Consumer specialties	5,854	29	762	30
Chemicals & performance prods.	4,536	23	592	23
Hydrocarbons & energy	2,043	10	74	3
Other	106	1	(214)	—
Total	**20,015**	**100**	**2,345**	**100**

Selected Products

Plastic Products
Film (Opticite)
Plastic foam (Styrofoam)
Polymer (Insite)
Polystyrene (Stryon)
Resin (Pulse, Sabre)

Consumer Specialties
Bathroom cleaner (Dow)
Hair care (Perma Soft)
Herbicide (Treflan)
Insecticide (Dursban)
Plastic bags (Ziploc)
Plastic wrap (Handi-Wrap, Saran Wrap)
Stain remover (Spray'N Wash)

Chemicals and Performance Products
Calcium chloride (Dowflake, Liquidow)
Chlorinated solvents
Chlorines
Ion exchange resins (Dowex)
Latex coatings
Membrane (Filmtec)

Hydrocarbons and Energy
Aromatics
Destec Energy (76%, power production)
Olefins
Styrene

KEY COMPETITORS

Akzo Nobel
Amway
BASF
Chevron
Clorox
Dial
DuPont
Eastman Chemical
Formosa Plastics
Hercules
Hoechst
Huntsman Chemical
Imperial Chemical
Lyondell Petrochemical
Mobil
Monsanto
Phillips Petroleum
Rhône-Poulenc
Union Carbide
W. R. Grace

HOW MUCH

	9-Year Growth	1985	1986	1987	1988	1989	1990	1991	1992	1993	1994
Sales ($ mil.)	7.4%	10,500	11,113	13,377	16,682	17,600	19,773	18,807	18,971	18,060	20,015
Net income ($ mil.)	36.1%	58	732	1,240	2,398	2,487	1,384	942	276	644	931
Income as % of sales	—	0.6%	6.6%	9.3%	14.4%	14.1%	7.0%	5.0%	1.5%	3.6%	4.7%
Earnings per share ($)	36.9%	0.20	2.55	4.31	8.51	9.20	5.10	3.46	0.99	2.33	3.37
Stock price – high ($)	—	27.92	41.17	73.08	62.67	72.25	75.75	58.00	62.88	62.00	79.25
Stock price – low ($)	—	18.00	26.59	39.17	51.17	55.50	37.00	44.13	51.25	49.00	56.50
Stock price – close ($)	10.5%	27.33	39.00	60.00	58.50	71.38	47.50	53.75	57.25	56.75	67.25
P/E – high	—	—	16	17	7	8	15	17	64	27	24
P/E – low	—	—	10	9	6	6	7	13	52	21	17
Dividends per share ($)	9.0%	1.20	1.27	1.43	1.73	2.37	2.60	2.60	2.60	2.60	2.60
Book value per share ($)	5.2%	18.85	18.05	20.31	26.35	29.55	32.33	34.90	26.69	29.36	29.63
Employees	0.1%	53,200	51,300	53,100	55,500	62,100	62,100	62,200	61,353	55,436	53,730

1994 Year-end:
Debt ratio: 44.5%
Return on equity: 11.5%
Cash (mil.): $1,134
Current ratio: 1.31
Long-term debt (mil.): $5,303
No. of shares (mil.): 277
Dividends
  Yield: 3.9%
  Payout: 77.2%
Market value (mil.): $18,637

Stock Price History
High/Low 1985–94

DOW JONES & COMPANY, INC.

OVERVIEW

Dow Jones, a $2.1 billion multinational media company, specializes in business news and information and dispenses it in print, on-line, and by satellite, radio, TV, pager, and fax.

Dow Jones's many operations are grouped into 3 divisions. Information Services includes Dow Jones Telerate (on-line, real-time business and financial news, quotes, and analytical tools) and Dow Jones News/Retrieval (on-line business and legal news and information). Business Publications includes the company's flagship publication, the 106-year-old daily *Wall Street Journal*; 2 companion editions, the *Asian Wall Street Journal* and the *Wall Street Journal Europe*; and the company's broadcasting operations. Dow also publishes *Barron's* (a weekly newspaper geared toward investors), the *Far Eastern Economic Review* (Asia's leading English-language weekly), and *SmartMoney* (a monthly magazine focusing on personal finance). Community Newspapers

consists of the company's Ottaway Newspapers, 21 general-interest daily newspapers published in 11 states. Dow Jones also invests in information-based ventures, such as international and regional publications (*Texas Monthly* and Germany's *Handelsblatt*), newsprint mills, and satellite broadcasting (U.S. Satellite Broadcasting).

In 1994 Dow Jones began supplying foreign-language business inserts to leading newspapers in Latin America, Poland, and South Korea. It also added coverage of regional issues (*Southeast Journal* and *Florida Journal*), and moved on-line into consumer markets (eWorld and CompuServe). The company is building a worldwide business TV network, and in 1994 it began broadcasting its European Business News network from London.

Heirs of early owner Clarence Barron still own 69% of the voting interest and 47% of all the company's stock.

WHEN

Charles Dow, Edward Jones, and Charles Bergstresser, financial reporters, left the Kiernan News Agency and began Dow Jones & Company in 1882. Working out of an office next door to the NYSE, the company delivered handwritten bulletins of stock and bond trading news to subscribers in New York's financial districts. In 1883 Dow Jones started summarizing the trading day in the *Customers' Afternoon Letter*, which evolved into the *Wall Street Journal* (1889). Dow Jones offered more timely reports through its stock ticker service, acquired in 1897 from Kiernan.

Jones sold out to his partners in 1899; in 1902 Dow and Bergstresser sold the company to Clarence Barron, the company's Boston correspondent. Dow died later in 1902. *Journal* circulation grew from 7,000 in 1902 to over 50,000 in 1928, the year Barron died. In 1921 the company introduced *Barron's National Business and Financial Weekly*.

In 1941 managing editor Bernard Kilgore broadened the *Journal*'s coverage to include news summaries and in-depth business articles; he became president in 1945. By Kilgore's 1966 retirement, the *Journal* had a circulation of one million. In 1962 Dow Jones started the *National Observer*, a general-interest weekly, but the company closed it in 1977 after losing $16.2 million.

In 1975 Dow Jones began to offer same-day service to all US readers by transmitting copy via satellite to regional printing plants.

The *Journal*'s circulation began to drop after peaking in 1983, and the company turned its attention to computerized news delivery to keep pace with a changing marketplace. By the end of 1989, Dow Jones included several publications and an array of electronic news retrieval services, including Telerate, which the company had acquired through a series of stock purchases (1985–90) totaling $1.6 billion. In 1991 Telerate acquired equity interest in Minex, a Japanese consortium developing automated foreign exchange trading information. In 1992 Dow Jones and BellSouth tested a service providing telephone access to Dow Jones reports (discontinued in 1995), and the company and NYNEX entered into a venture to send video over telephone lines.

In 1993 the *Journal* began providing regional news coverage in its Texas edition and introduced *SmartMoney* with Hearst Corp.

In 1994 Dow Jones joined with American City Business Journals to launch *BIZ*, a monthly magazine for small businesses (discontinued 1995). Also in 1994 the company bought a stake in direct broadcast TV (U.S. Satellite Broadcasting) and introduced the PC-based Telerate Workstation.

In 1995 the company added Japan's leading business publisher, Nikkei, to its on-line database and bought Charter Financial Publishing. With ITT Corp., it bought public TV station WNYC for $207 million; the station will become business and sports channel WBIS.

NYSE symbol: DJ
Fiscal year ends: December 31

WHO

**Chairman and CEO; Publisher, *The Wall Street Journal:* Peter R. Kann, age 52, $1,050,000 pay
President and COO: Kenneth L. Burenga, age 50, $765,000 pay
SVP: Carl M. Valenti, age 56, $607,000 pay
SVP, General Counsel, and Secretary: Peter G. Skinner, age 50, $536,000 pay
SVP: James H. Ottaway Jr., age 57, $509,000 pay
VP Finance and CFO: Kevin J. Roche, age 60
VP Employee Relations: James A. Scaduto, age 40
Auditors: Coopers & Lybrand L.L.P.

WHERE

HQ: 200 Liberty St., New York, NY 10281
Phone: 212-416-2000
Fax: 212-732-8356

	1994 Sales		1994 Operating Income	
	$ mil.	% of total	$ mil.	% of total
US	1,489	71	234	62
Europe, Middle East, Africa	330	16	61	16
Asia/Pacific	225	11	78	21
Other regions	47	2	3	1
Adjustments	—	—	(18)	—
Total	**2,091**	**100**	**358**	**100**

WHAT

	1994 Sales		1994 Operating Income	
	$ mil.	% of total	$ mil.	% of total
Information services	977	47	199	53
Business publications	862	41	141	37
Community papers	252	12	36	10
Other	—	—	(18)	—
Total	**2,091**	**100**	**358**	**100**

Selected Information Services
AP-Dow Jones News Service (economic, business, and financial news wire, with the Associated Press)
Dow Jones Asian Equities Report (coverage of 12 Asian/Pacific stock markets)
Dow Jones News Service (business and financial news)
Dow Jones News/Retrieval (on-line business and financial news and information)
Dow Jones Telerate (market information)
DowVision (customized on-line news service)
Federal Filings (government and court news wire)
Personal Journal (electronic publication; personalized business news, world news, weather, and sports)
Professional Investor Report (financial news wire)
SportsTicker (20%, on-line sports information)
The Wall Street Journal Interactive Edition (wire services and on-line extension of the *Wall Street Journal*)
The Wall Street Journal Report (radio and TV programs)

Selected Business Publications
American Demographics
The Asian Wall Street Journal (Hong Kong)
Asian Wall Street Journal Weekly (US)
Barron's
Central European Economic Review (Belgium)
Far Eastern Economic Review (Hong Kong)
National Business Employment Weekly
SmartMoney, The Wall Street Journal Magazine of Personal Business (monthly, with Hearst Corp.)
The Wall Street Journal (1,808,743 daily circulation)
The Wall Street Journal Europe (Belgium)

Community Newspapers
Ottaway Newspapers, Inc. (21 newspapers in 11 states)

KEY COMPETITORS

America Online	McGraw-Hill	Reuters
Bloomberg	Media General	Times Mirror
Dun & Bradstreet	New York Times	Tribune
Forbes	News Corp.	Turner
Gannett	Pearson	Broadcasting
Knight-Ridder	Reed Elsevier	Washington Post

HOW MUCH

	9-Year Growth	1985	1986	1987	1988	1989	1990	1991	1992	1993	1994
Sales ($ mil.)	8.1%	1,040	1,135	1,314	1,603	1,688	1,720	1,725	1,818	1,932	2,091
Net income ($ mil.)	3.0%	139	183	203	228	317	107	72	118	148	181
Income as % of sales	—	13.3%	16.2%	15.4%	14.2%	18.8%	6.2%	4.2%	6.5%	7.6%	8.7%
Earnings per share ($)	2.8%	1.43	1.89	2.10	2.35	3.15	1.06	0.71	1.17	1.48	1.83
Stock price – high ($)	—	33.34	42.13	56.25	36.50	42.50	33.75	30.63	35.38	39.00	41.88
Stock price – low ($)	—	24.50	28.00	28.00	26.75	29.25	18.13	21.63	24.50	26.75	28.13
Stock price – close ($)	(0.2%)	31.50	39.00	29.88	29.50	33.25	24.00	25.88	27.00	35.75	31.00
P/E – high	—	23	22	27	16	14	32	43	30	26	23
P/E – low	—	17	15	13	11	9	17	30	21	18	15
Dividends per share ($)	5.5%	0.52	0.55	0.64	0.68	0.72	0.76	0.76	0.76	0.80	0.84
Book value per share ($)	10.6%	6.21	7.52	8.77	11.95	13.94	14.23	14.21	14.41	14.91	15.33
Employees	4.5%	6,924	7,069	9,014	9,080	9,818	9,677	9,459	9,860	10,006	10,300

1994 Year-end:
Debt ratio: 16.9%
Return on equity: 12.2%
Cash (mil.): $11
Current ratio: 0.58
Long-term debt (mil.): $296
No. of shares (mil.): 96.6
Dividends
  Yield: 2.7%
  Payout: 45.9%
Market value (mil.): $2,995

Stock Price History
High/Low 1985–94

DRESSER INDUSTRIES, INC.

OVERVIEW

With more than 100 manufacturing plants in some 50 countries, Dallas, Texas–based Dresser Industries is one of the largest energy service companies in the world, offering everything from drill bits to gas pumps to pipe coating services. Through joint venture Dresser-Rand, the company makes compressors and other industrial machinery. Engineering and construction services are provided through M. W. Kellogg, whose specialty is liquefied natural gas (LNG) liquefaction facilities and LNG receiving terminals. Approximately 61% of Dresser's sales are to customers outside of North America.

The company has shuffled the deck with recent acquisitions and divestitures in order to improve its position in the highly competitive drilling industry.

The 1994 purchases of Baroid and Wheatley TXT for $930 million allow Dresser's drilling operations to offer more services and equipment to drillers and strengthen its global presence. The divestiture of its stakes in Western Atlas International (a provider of oil and gas services), M-I Drilling Fluids, and IRI International (a manufacturer of mobile drilling rigs) helped raise approximately $720 million in cash that same year.

The company is banking on increased demand for its services from growing oil and gas markets in Asia, the Middle East, Latin America, and Africa.

WHEN

Solomon Dresser arrived in the oil boom town of Bradford, Pennsylvania, in 1878 with a consumptive wife and 4 children. He eked out a living in oil field jobs. He also tinkered with an invention, and in 1880 Dresser was granted a patent for a cap packer, a device that prevents crude oil from mixing with other fluids in a well. In the 1880s and 1890s, he perfected a coupling that used fitted rubber to prevent leaks in pipeline connections.

As the natural gas industry grew, so did demand for the reliable Dresser coupling. The family firm prospered even after Solomon's death in 1911, but his heirs, anxious to pursue other interests, sold the company to W. A. Harriman & Company in 1928, and the investment banker took Dresser public. Soon after, 3 Harriman executives — including Roland Harriman, son of the founder, and Prescott Bush, father of future US president George Bush — were discussing the vacant Dresser presidency. Just then, an old Yale friend, Neil Mallon, dropped by the office, and Harriman tapped Mallon for the top post.

During Mallon's 41-year career with Dresser, the company grew into an oil field conglomerate. Bryant Heating and Manufacturing was the first acquisition (bought in 1933 and sold in 1949). When Dresser tried to develop a high-speed compressor for gas pipelines, it purchased Clark Brothers (compressors, 1937). It later abandoned its compressor research, but Olean, New York–based Clark became a company cornerstone. Dresser moved its headquarters to Dallas in 1950. Acquisitions ranged from Magnet Cove (drilling "mud" lubricant for oil well holes, 1949) to Symington-Wayne (gasoline pumps, 1968).

In 1983, after an oil services boom had peaked, CEO Jack Murphy refocused on the petroleum business, balancing upstream (exploration and production) and downstream (refining and marketing) services and products. In 1986 Dresser formed a joint venture (now 51%-owned) with Ingersoll-Rand called Dresser-Rand (compressors, gas turbines). Dresser bought M. W. Kellogg Company (refinery engineering, 1988) and the diamond drill bit product line of Baker Hughes (1990).

In 1992 Dresser spun off its industrial products and equipment operations as INDRESCO to Dresser's shareholders. That same year Dresser acquired AVA International (oil field safety valves and well-completion equipment) and pooled its pump operations with Ingersoll-Rand to form a minority-held (49%) joint venture, Ingersoll-Dresser Pump. In 1993 Dresser bought Bredero Price Pipe (pipe coating) and TK Valve (oil and gas production ball valves).

In 1994 Dresser sold its 29.5% stake in Western Atlas and acquired Houston, Texas–based Baroid (offshore and drilling services and products). To get the purchase approved by antitrust regulators, in 1994 Dresser sold M-I Drilling Fluids to Smith International and placed the diamond drilling bit business of Baroid unit DBS on the auction block.

In 1995 Dresser was awarded a $300 million contract to provide Statoil, the Norwegian oil and gas company, with external and internal coatings for its new gas pipelines in the North Sea. Also that year Dresser signed a contract to prepare design and engineering work on an LNG project in Oman. The project is 51%-owned by the government of Oman and 34%-owned by Royal Dutch/Shell and others.

WHO

Chairman and CEO: John J. Murphy, age 63, $1,748,700 pay
VC: Bill D. St. John, age 63, $946,360 pay
President and COO: William E. Bradford, age 60, $959,600 pay
SVP Operations; Chairman, President, and CEO, M. W. Kellogg: Donald C. Vaughn, age 58, $890,059 pay
SVP Operations: James L. Bryan, age 58, $541,575 pay
VP: George A. Helland Jr., age 57
VP and General Counsel: Clinton E. Ables, age 55
VP Washington Counsel: Ardon B. Judd Jr., age 58
VP Human Resources: Paul M. Bryant, age 48
VP Tax: David R. Smith, age 48
VP Corporate Counsel and Secretary: Rebecca R. Morris, age 49
Treasurer: Paul W. Willey, age 57
Assistant Treasurer: Richard T. Kernen
Assistant Secretary: Stanley E. McGlothlin
Auditors: Price Waterhouse LLP

WHERE

HQ: 2001 Ross Ave., PO Box 718, Dallas, TX 75221
Phone: 214-740-6000
Fax: 214-740-6584

Dresser operates manufacturing, marketing, and service facilities serving more than 80 countries.

	1994 Sales		1994 Operating Income	
	$ mil.	% of total	$ mil.	% of total
US	1,802	34	171	37
Europe	1,069	20	58	13
Latin America	722	14	53	12
Canada	262	5	31	7
Other regions	1,476	27	147	31
Total	**5,331**	**100**	**460**	**100**

WHAT

	1994 Sales		1994 Operating Income	
	$ mil.	% of total	$ mil.	% of total
Hydrocarbon processing	2,416	45	218	47
Oil field services	1,653	31	157	34
Engineering services	1,265	24	85	19
Adjustments	(3)	—	—	—
Total	**5,331**	**100**	**460**	**100**

Hydrocarbon Processing
Compressors
Control products for process, power, and gas distribution industries
Electric motors
Gas and diesel engines
Gas and steam turbines
Gasoline and diesel fuel dispensing systems
Generators
Pumps

Oil Field Services
Drilling fluid
Drilling services
Offshore services
Oil field and mining rock bits
Pipe coating services
Production tools

Engineering Services
Engineering and construction for hydrocarbon processing industries

Selected Joint Ventures
Dresser-Rand (51%, compressors and turbines)
Ingersoll-Dresser Pump (49%, pumps)

KEY COMPETITORS

ABB
Baker Hughes
Bechtel
BJ Services
Caterpillar
Cooper Industries
Deere
DSI Industries
Fluor
FMC
Friedrich Krupp

General Electric
Halliburton
Keystone Intl.
LTV
McDermott
Nabors Industries
Peter Kiewit Sons'
Raytheon
Schlumberger
Smith Intl.
Western Atlas

HOW MUCH

	9-Year Growth	1985	1986	1987	1988	1989	1990	1991	1992	1993	1994
Sales ($ mil.)	2.9%	4,111	3,661	3,120	3,942	3,956	4,480	4,670	3,797	4,216	5,331
Net income ($ mil.)	—	(196)	1	43	146	163	174	140	35	127	362
Income as % of sales	—	—	0.0%	1.4%	3.7%	4.1%	3.9%	3.0%	0.9%	3.0%	6.8%
Earnings per share ($)	—	(1.29)	0.01	0.29	1.06	1.21	1.29	1.04	0.26	0.92	1.98
Stock price – high ($)	—	12.13	10.19	17.81	17.81	24.00	28.13	28.50	23.63	25.38	24.88
Stock price – low ($)	—	8.38	7.00	8.81	11.25	14.50	16.50	16.25	17.25	17.25	18.50
Stock price – close ($)	8.5%	9.06	9.69	13.13	14.69	22.44	20.88	20.13	18.00	20.75	18.88
P/E – high	—	—	—	61	17	20	22	27	91	28	13
P/E – low	—	—	—	30	11	12	13	16	66	19	9
Dividends per share ($)	5.7%	0.40	0.35	0.20	0.28	0.45	0.55	0.60	0.60	0.60	0.66
Book value per share ($)	(2.2%)	10.80	10.67	10.75	11.19	11.88	13.01	13.11	6.93	6.86	8.88
Employees	(5.0%)	46,200	39,700	30,800	30,700	31,436	33,133	31,839	27,380	25,926	29,200

1994 Year-end:
Debt ratio: 23.4%
Return on equity: 28.1%
Cash (mil.): $515
Current ratio: 1.61
Long-term debt (mil.): $461
No. of shares (mil.): 183
Dividends
  Yield: 3.5%
  Payout: 33.3%
Market value (mil.): $2,681

Stock Price History High/Low 1985–94

DUKE POWER COMPANY

OVERVIEW

Duke Power is one of the largest publicly owned utilities in the US. Based in Charlotte, North Carolina, the company provides electricity to more than 1.7 million customers in a 20,000-square-mile region in North and South Carolina that includes Charlotte, Durham, Greenville, and Winston-Salem. In addition, subsidiary Nantahala Power and Light provides electricity to more than 53,000 customers in 5 counties in western North Carolina.

Through its subsidiaries Duke is engaged in a variety of other businesses, including engineering consulting, power plant design and construction, real estate development and forest management, electrical appliance marketing, and investment management.

Nuclear power plays an important role in Duke's energy generating system, with 60% of the company's total generation coming from its 3 nuclear power plants.

Led by CEO William Grigg, Duke has cut employment to keep costs down as deregulation has brought a more competitive power market. To keep customers happy, Grigg says, "we will not be filing for any rate increases as long as I remain around." Grigg also has his eye on expanding through acquisitions. He plans to buy up smaller utilities that are unable to compete in the deregulated market.

WHEN

In 1899 engineer-turned-surgeon W. Gill Wylie founded the Catawba Power Company and hired engineer W. S. Lee to design the company's first hydroelectric power plant near Fort Mill, South Carolina. Operational by 1904, this plant set the standard for the company's future plants — each one was designed by company engineers and, after 1924, built by company construction teams.

In 1905 the Southern Power Company was formed out of the American Development Company, which had acquired all of Catawba Power's stock. Wylie was installed as president and Lee as chief engineer. James "Buck" Duke (founder of the American Tobacco Company and the W. Duke and Sons tobacco empire), who was instrumental in the formation of the power companies, became president in 1910 and organized Mill-Power Supply to sell heavy electric equipment to the region's textile mills. Duke formed the Southern Public Utility Company (SPUC) in 1913 to buy various Piedmont utilities (gas, water, and electric).

In 1917 Duke established Wateree Electric. Wateree was renamed Duke Power Company in 1924 and by 1935 owned all of the properties formerly held by Southern Power. When Buck died in 1925, about 85% of Duke Power's stock was held by the Duke family, Doris Duke Trust, and Duke Endowment (a trust created in 1924 for Piedmont area colleges, including Trinity College, which was renamed Duke University in 1924 in Buck Duke's honor). When the company's stock was first traded publicly (Curb Exchange, 1950), the Duke family, trust, and endowment still owned 67%. This was diluted to about 15% after the company's 1961 listing on the NYSE.

In 1970 Duke Power bought 3 Kentucky coal mining companies to provide fuel for its steam generators. Oconee, the company's first nuclear plant (designed by Lee's grandson, W. S. Lee III), was operational by 1974. The company bought the electrical systems at Duke University (1975) and the University of North Carolina at Chapel Hill (1976). Its McGuire nuclear plant was operational by 1984, and a 3rd nuclear plant (Catawba) went on-line in 1986.

Duke had begun offering its engineering expertise to outside firms in 1982 and formed a related subsidiary, Duke Engineering & Services, in 1987. In 1988 the company organized the Duke Energy Corporation to develop and finance power projects outside the Piedmont area and bought Nantahala Power and Light. Because it no longer related to the company's long-term strategy, Mill-Power Supply was sold in 1990.

In 1992 Duke/Fluor Daniel began construction of a 385-megawatt coal-fired power plant in South Carolina, and a consortium led by subsidiary Duke Energy Group acquired the Guemes Power Station in Argentina. In 1993 a consortium led by Duke Energy bought 65% of Transener, Argentina's primary electric transmission company.

In 1994 William Grigg succeeded William Lee as chairman and CEO. That same year the company formed DukeNet Communications to market communications services it had developed for its own internal use.

Duke/Fluor Daniel was part of a consortium that includes Mitsui and Toyo Engineering that won a $2.5 billion contract in 1995 to build a power plant in Indonesia.

NYSE symbol: DUK
Fiscal year ends: December 31

WHO

Chairman and CEO: William H. Grigg, age 62,
$661,996 pay
VC and General Counsel: Steve C. Griffith Jr., age 61,
$405,928 pay
President and COO: Richard B. Priory, age 48,
$411,503 pay
President, Associated Enterprises Group: William A.
Coley, age 51, $403,053 pay
SVP and CFO: Richard J. Osborne, age 43, $254,341 pay
VP Organization Effectiveness (HR): Christopher C.
Rolfe
Auditors: Deloitte & Touche LLP

WHERE

HQ: 422 S. Church St., Charlotte, NC 28242-0001
Phone: 704-594-0887
Fax: 704-382-3814 (Investor Relations)

Selected Generating Facilities

Fossil Fuel
Allen (NC)
Belews Creek (NC)
Buck (NC)
Cliffside (NC)
Dan River (NC)
Lee (SC)
Marshall (NC)
Riverbend (NC)

Hydroelectric
Bad Creek (NC)
Bridgewater (NC)
Buzzard Roost (SC)
Cowans Ford (NC)
Dearborn (SC)
Fishing Creek (SC)
Gaston Shoals (NC)
Holliday's Bridge (SC)

Idols (NC)
Jocassee (SC)
Keowee (SC)
Lookout Shoals (NC)
Ninety-Nine Islands (SC)
Oxford (NC)
Rhodhiss (NC)
Rocky Creek (SC)
Saluda (SC)
Turner (NC)
Tuxedo (NC)
Wateree (SC)
Wylie (SC)

Nuclear
Catawba (12.5%, SC)
McGuire (NC)
Oconee (SC)

WHAT

| | 1994 Sales | |
	$ mil.	% of total
Residential	1,380	31
General service	1,031	23
Textile industry	498	11
Other industries	745	16
Wholesale & other energy	540	12
Other revenues	85	2
Affiliates & other	210	5
Total	**4,489**	**100**

| | 1994 Energy Sources |
	% of total
Nuclear	60
Coal	38
Hydroelectric & other	2
Total	**100**

Major Subsidiaries and Activities
Church Street Capital Corp. (funds management)
Crescent Resources, Inc. (forest management and real
estate development)
Duke Energy Group (independent power projects)
Duke Engineering & Services, Inc. (engineering and
consulting services)
Duke Merchandising (appliance and electronics sales
and service)
Duke Water Operations (water service for customers in
South Carolina and North Carolina)
Duke/Fluor Daniel (partnership with Fluor Daniel;
engineering and construction services)
DukeNet Communications Inc. (communications
systems management and development)
Nantahala Power and Light Co. (electric utility serving
about 53,000 customers in western North Carolina)

KEY COMPETITORS

ABB
Bechtel
Entergy
Halliburton
McDermott
NIPSCO Industries
Peter Kiewit
Sons'
Southern Co.

HOW MUCH

	9-Year Growth	1985	1986	1987	1988	1989	1990	1991	1992	1993	1994
Sales ($ mil.)	5.0%	2,899	3,400	3,706	3,620	3,639	3,682	3,817	3,962	4,282	4,489
Net income ($ mil.)	4.3%	438	468	500	448	572	538	584	508	626	639
Income as % of sales	—	15.1%	13.8%	13.5%	12.4%	15.7%	14.6%	15.3%	12.8%	14.6%	14.2%
Earnings per share ($)	5.0%	1.86	2.02	2.20	1.95	2.57	2.40	2.60	2.21	2.80	2.88
Stock price – high ($)	—	18.44	26.00	25.88	24.50	28.25	32.38	35.00	37.50	44.88	43.00
Stock price – low ($)	—	14.25	17.44	19.69	21.13	21.38	25.50	26.75	31.38	35.38	32.88
Stock price – close ($)	8.9%	17.69	22.63	21.44	23.13	28.06	30.63	35.00	36.13	42.38	38.13
P/E – high	—	10	13	12	13	11	14	14	17	16	15
P/E – low	—	8	9	9	11	8	11	10	14	13	11
Dividends per share ($)	4.7%	1.27	1.32	1.37	1.44	1.52	1.60	1.68	1.76	1.84	1.92
Book value per share ($)	4.8%	14.49	15.17	15.98	17.01	18.05	18.84	19.86	20.26	21.17	22.13
Employees	(2.0%)	20,450	20,300	19,600	19,430	19,449	18,187	17,968	18,727	18,274	17,052

1994 Year-end:
Debt ratio: 41.5%
Return on equity: 14.4%
Cash (mil.): $170
Current ratio: 1.38
Long-term debt (mil.): $3,567
No. of shares (mil.): 205
Dividends
  Yield: 5.0%
  Payout: 66.7%
Market value (mil.): $7,811

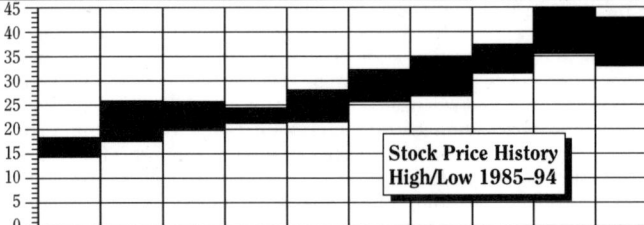

Stock Price History
High/Low 1985–94

THE DUN & BRADSTREET CORPORATION

OVERVIEW

Dun & Bradstreet (D&B) is the world's #1 marketer of information, software, and services for business decision making. It provides services in 5 areas: directory information, marketing information, risk management and business marketing information, software, and business support.

Subsidiary Dun & Bradstreet Information Services is the world's largest credit reporting agency, selling credit information on more than 38 million businesses in over 30 countries. D&B's Moody's Investors Service is a leading publisher of financial information, and IMS International is the #1 provider of marketing services to the health care and pharmaceutical industries. D&B's A.C. Nielsen

measures TV audiences and conducts marketing research in 90 countries. About 75% of Nielsen's revenues come from outside the US. In 1994 Nielsen acquired the #1 supplier of market research information in Asia, the Survey Research Group.

Other divisions offer directory information (R. H. Donnelley's *Yellow Pages*) and sell software and services to various industries.

D&B is pursuing a strategy of "information engineering," the integration of technology, data, and service to provide customized solutions to its clients. In line with this strategy, D&B spent over $300 million on acquisitions in 1994 and launched its integrated client/server product suite, SmartStream 3.0.

WHEN

Dun & Bradstreet originated in Lewis Tappan's Mercantile Agency, established in 1841 in New York City. The Mercantile Agency was one of the first commercial credit reporting agencies, and it supplied wholesalers and importers with information on their customers. Tappan's credit reporters, who prepared written reports on companies, included 4 men who became US presidents (Lincoln, Grant, Cleveland, and McKinley). In the 1840s Tappan opened offices in Boston, Philadelphia, and Baltimore and in 1857 established offices in Montreal and London. In 1859 Robert Dun took over the agency and changed its name to R.G. Dun & Co. The first edition of the *Dun's Book* (1859) contained information on 20,268 businesses; by 1886 the number had risen to over one million. John M. Bradstreet, a rival company founded in Cincinnati in 1849, merged with Dun in 1933; the company adopted the Dun & Bradstreet name in 1939.

In 1961 D&B bought Reuben H. Donnelley Corp., a direct-mail advertiser and publisher of the *Yellow Pages* (first published in 1886) and 10 trade magazines. In 1962 Moody's Investors Service (founded 1900) and Official Airline Guides (guides first published in 1929; sold, 1988) became part of D&B.

D&B's records were first computerized in the 1960s and eventually became the largest private database in the world. By 1975 D&B had a national network with a centralized database. Sales boomed when D&B created new products by repackaging information from its vast database (such as *Dun's Financial Profiles*, first published in 1979).

Since the late 1970s the company has purchased Technical Publishing (trade and profes-

sional publications, 1978), National CSS (computer services, 1979), and McCormack & Dodge (software, 1983). The addition of A.C. Nielsen (1984) and IMS International (pharmaceutical sales data, 1988) made D&B the largest marketing research company in the world. A 1987 attempt to buy Nielsen competitor Information Resources Inc. was nixed by regulators on antitrust grounds. In 1989 D&B bought Management Science America. That year reports surfaced that D&B was overcharging customers for credit reports; a resulting class-action suit was settled in 1994.

In 1990 D&B sold Zytron, Petroleum Information, and Neodata. In 1991 Donnelley Marketing, a direct marketer with an 85-million-household consumer information database, was sold, as were the IMS communications unit and Carol Wright Sales. D&B continued divestments in 1992, selling Datastream International and Information Associates.

Dun & Bradstreet acquired a majority interest in Gartner Group, an international market research firm, in 1993 and also formed D&B HealthCare Information to conduct health research. That same year the company introduced a restructuring program that was designed to improve efficiency in its spread-out information services businesses. It consolidated its 27 data centers worldwide to 4 automated centers and cut its headquarters staffing.

In 1994 Dun & Bradstreet bought Pilot Software (on-line software) for around $35 million. In 1995 D&B sold its Interactive Data Corporation unit (international financial information) to media group Pearson for $201 million.

NYSE symbol: DNB
Fiscal year ends: December 31

Chairman, President, and CEO: Robert E. Weissman, age 54, $1,409,507 pay
EVP; Chairman, Dun & Bradstreet Information Services: Volney Taylor, age 55, $973,922 pay
EVP Finance and CFO: Edwin A. Bescherer Jr., age 61, $809,075 pay
EVP; Chairman, A.C. Nielsen Co.: Robert J. Lievense, age 49
EVP; Chairman, IMS International: William G. Jacobi, age 51
EVP: Dennis G. Sisco, age 48
SVP Communications and Government Affairs: Michael F. Brewer, age 51
SVP: David Fehr, age 59
SVP: Frank R. Noonan, age 52
SVP and Controller: Thomas W. Young, age 56
SVP and General Counsel: Earl H. Doppelt, age 41
SVP Human Resources: Michael P. Connors, age 39
Auditors: Coopers & Lybrand L.L.P.

WHERE

HQ: 187 Danbury Rd., Wilton, CT 06897
Phone: 203-834-4200
Fax: 203-834-4201

	1994 Sales		1994 Operating Income	
	$ mil.	% of total	$ mil.	% of total
US	2,889	59	667	72
Europe	1,354	28	186	20
Other regions	653	13	73	8
Total	**4,896**	**100**	**926**	**100**

WHAT

	1994 Sales		1994 Operating Income	
	$ mil.	% of total	$ mil.	% of total
Marketing info. svcs.	2,043	42	285	26
Risk mgmt. & business mktg.	1,606	33	447	41
Directory info. svcs.	440	9	248	23
Software services	406	8	(4)	—
Business services	401	8	110	10
Adjustments	—	—	(160)	—
Total	**4,896**	**100**	**926**	**100**

Marketing Info. Services
IMS International (health care market research)
A.C. Nielsen (marketing and media research)

Risk Mgmt. and Business Marketing Info. Services
Dun & Bradstreet Information Services (credit information and insurance, receivables management)
Moody's Investors Service, Inc. (financial information, bond rating)

Directory Info. Services
Reuben H. Donnelley

Software Services
Dun & Bradstreet Software Services
Erisco (employee-benefits software and services)
Pilot Software (software solutions for on-line analytical processing)
Sales Technologies (field sales systems)

Business Services
Dataquest (high-tech market research)
Dun & Bradstreet Pension Services (health insurance administration)
Gartner Group (50.6% information technology)
NCH Promotional Services (coupon processing)

KEY COMPETITORS

ADP	Information	PeopleSoft
American Business	Resources	Reed Elsevier
Information	Intelliquest	Reuters
Dow Jones	M/A/R/C	Thomson Corp.
Equifax	McGraw-Hill	TRW
IBM	Pearson	Value Line

HOW MUCH

	9-Year Growth	1985	1986	1987	1988	1989	1990	1991	1992	1993	1994
Sales ($ mil.)	6.5%	2,772	3,114	3,359	4,267	4,322	4,818	4,643	4,751	4,710	4,896
Net income ($ mil.)	8.8%	295	340	393	499	586	508	509	554	429	630
Income as % of sales	—	10.6%	10.9%	11.7%	11.7%	13.6%	10.5%	11.0%	11.7%	9.1%	12.9%
Earnings per share ($)	7.4%	1.94	2.24	2.58	2.67	3.14	2.80	2.85	3.10	2.42	3.70
Stock price – high ($)	—	43.94	60.19	71.75	57.50	60.25	48.63	58.00	59.13	68.50	64.00
Stock price – low ($)	—	31.38	40.38	44.50	45.88	41.25	36.13	39.13	50.63	55.75	51.88
Stock price – close ($)	3.1%	41.88	52.63	54.75	53.63	46.00	42.13	57.50	57.75	61.63	55.00
P/E – high	—	23	27	28	22	19	17	20	19	28	17
P/E – low	—	16	18	17	17	13	13	14	16	23	14
Dividends per share ($)	10.3%	1.06	1.24	1.45	1.68	1.94	2.09	2.15	2.25	2.40	2.56
Book value per share ($)	(1.5%)	8.92	9.79	10.95	11.18	11.80	11.65	12.11	12.10	6.53	7.77
Employees	(2.4%)	58,400	58,352	62,000	69,500	71,500	62,900	58,500	52,400	50,400	47,000

1994 Year-end:
Debt ratio: 27.5%
Return on equity: 51.8%
Cash (mil.): $362
Current ratio: 0.91
Long-term debt (mil.): $0
No. of shares (mil.): 170
Dividends
  Yield: 4.7%
  Payout: 69.2%
Market value (mil.): $9,337

**Stock Price History
High/Low 1985–94**

E. & J. GALLO WINERY

OVERVIEW

E. & J. Gallo is the world's largest wine maker. Based in Modesto, California, and owned by the Gallo family, the company has over 1/4 of the domestic wine market, with flagship brands that include Carlo Rossi and Gallo (as well as the ever-popular Thunderbird). Gallo sells more than 50 types of wine in all price ranges, from fortified wines and wine coolers to a growing number of upscale varietals that can fetch up to $60 a bottle. The company is also a leading brandy producer.

Although spirits and inexpensive wine consumption is declining in much of the US, there is a growing market for fine wines, thanks to the increased sophistication of US wine drinkers. In the last decade Gallo has followed this trend, moving upmarket. In the 1980s the company bought and planted prime land in Sonoma County (its original vineyards were near Modesto and the company used a mix of grapes that included Thompson seedless, a table variety, for some of its wines) and in the mid-1990s these vineyards reached full production for fine varietals.

One of the reasons for Gallo's success is its distribution system, which has given it full market penetration. This has been a particular advantage because of the shift toward grocery stores (which overwhelmingly favor leading brands) over liquor stores as alcoholic beverage outlets. Many grocery stores are cutting back on smaller brands.

WHEN

At first there were Ernest & Julio and Joe, the 3 sons of Joe Gallo. Joe Gallo Sr. left Italy for San Francisco around 1906. He started selling wine and then, after marrying the daughter of a commercial wine maker, began growing grapes. During Prohibition Gallo sent his grapes to Chicago, where Ernest and Julio sold them for use in legal home wine making.

Near the end of Prohibition, Joe Sr. and his wife were found dead in an apparent murder-suicide. In 1933 Ernest and Julio (guardians of their young brother Joe) started their own business, building on their father's estate and selling through the Chicago contacts they had made while selling grapes. Gallo soon became a popular local brand.

Ernest ran the business end, assembling a large distribution network and starting to build a national brand, while Julio made the wine and Joe worked for them. In the early 1940s Gallo opened bottling plants in Los Angeles and New Orleans, using screw-cap bottles, which then seemed more hygienic and modern than corks. The business lagged during the war when alcohol was diverted for the military. Under Julio's supervision, Gallo began upgrading its planting stock and refining its wine making technology.

In the 1950s US wine tastes were generally unsophisticated, and sweet wines like Italian Swiss Colony were the leaders. In an attempt to take this market, the company introduced its own sweet wine, Thunderbird, a fortified wine (with a 20% alcohol content) in 1957.

In the 1960s Gallo spurred its growth by advertising heavily and keeping prices low. In 1964 it introduced Hearty Burgundy, a jug wine. It also introduced Ripple.

Gallo introduced the carbonated, fruit-flavored Boone's Farm Apple Wine in 1969, creating an interest in "pop" wines that lasted for a few years. In 1974 the company introduced its first varietal wines.

In the 1970s Gallo field workers switched unions from the United Farm Workers to the Teamsters. Repercussions included protests and boycotts, but sales were largely unaffected. From 1976 to 1982 Gallo operated under an FTC order limiting its control over wholesalers. The order was lifted after the industry's competitive balance changed.

Through the 1970s and 1980s, Gallo expanded its production of varietals; in 1988 it began adding vintage dates to the wines' labels. But it also kept a hand in the lower levels of the market, introducing Bartles & Jaymes wine coolers (now a declining segment).

Beginning in 1986, the company fought a legal battle with Joe Gallo over the use of the Gallo name. After working for his brothers for years, Joe had been eased out and had started a dairy farm to make cheese. In 1992 he lost the use of his name for commercial purposes. Ernest Gallo died in 1993.

Gallo was unenthusiastic about NAFTA, which took effect in 1994. NAFTA allows Mexican brandy to enter the US freely while Mexico's 20% tariffs on US brandy will be reduced gradually. Also, a pact between Mexico and Chile will open Mexico's infant wine market to Chile while US wine is still subject to tariffs.

In 1995 Heublein, which sells Jose Cuervo tequila, sued Gallo for selling a "margarita" cooler, maintaining that only a drink containing tequila could be called a margarita.

Private company
Fiscal year ends: December 31

WHO

Chairman: Ernest Gallo, age 84
EVP: Albion Fenderson
VP Finance: Louis Freedman
VP: Joseph E. Gallo
VP: Robert J. Gallo
VP: James E. Coleman
VP: David Gallo

WHERE

HQ: PO Box 1130, 600 Yosemite Blvd., Modesto,
CA 95353
Phone: 209-579-3111
Fax: 209-579-3312

Vineyards in California (Counties)
Fresno
Merced
Sonoma
Stanislaus

WHAT

Label Names
Andre
Ballatore
Bartles & Jaymes
Boone's
Carlo Rossi
Cooperidge
E & J Brandy
Eden Roc
Ernest & Julio Gallo
Ernest & Julio Gallo Sonoma
Ernest & Julio Gallo Sonoma Estate
Gallo
Livingston Cellars
Night Train Express
The Reserve Cellars of Ernest & Julio Gallo
Thunderbird
Tott's
Wm. Wycliffe

Subsidiaries and Divisions
E & J Gallo Winery Europe (wholesale distribution in
Europe)
Fairbanks Trucking Inc. (long-distance trucking)
Gallo Glass Co. (glass wine bottles)
Midcal Aluminum Inc. (metal bottle closures)
San Joaquin Valley Express (partnership, agricultural
trucking)
United Packaging Co. (partnership, importer of wine
bottle corks)
US Intermodal Services (partnership, freight brokerage)

KEY COMPETITORS

Adolph Coors
Allied Domecq
American Freightways
Anheuser-Busch
Bacardi
Bass
Bronco Wine Co.
Brown-Forman
Canandaigua Wine
Chalone Wine
Fetzer
Grand Metropolitan
Kendall-Jackson
LVMH
Nestlé
Parducci
Robert Mondavi
Seagram
Sebastiani Vineyards
Sutter Home Winery
Todhunter Intl.
Vintners International
Williamsburg Winery

HOW MUCH

	Annual Growth	1985	1986	1987	1988	1989	1990	1991	1992	1993	1994
Estimated sales ($ mil.)	4.8%	645	750	1,000	1,000	1,000	1,050	1,110	1,000	1,100	980
Wine shipments (gallons mil.)	—	154	169	166	165	169	157	157	153	135	134
Employees	4.5%	2,700	2,700	3,000	3,000	2,950	3,000	3,000	3,000	4,000	4,000

Estimated Sales
($ mil.)
1985–94

EASTMAN CHEMICAL COMPANY

OVERVIEW

Kingsport, Tennessee–based Eastman Chemical is the world leader in polyester plastics for packaging, a major supplier of cellulose acetate filter tow, and a leading supplier of coatings, fine chemicals, and specialty chemicals. The company manufactures polyester plastics such as polyethylene terephthalate (PET), a plastic used worldwide in soft drink, water, and sports drink containers. PET products accounted for about 1/4 of 1994 sales.

The company is also a leading manufacturer of specialty chemicals (used in coatings, inks, and resins) and cellulose (used in acetate yarn and cigarette filters). It makes chemicals used in photographic products and pharmaceuticals, and it makes vitamin E and natural and synthetic food antioxidants.

Eastman Chemical veteran and CEO Earnest Deavenport steered the company through its Kodak moment (when it was spun off from photographic products giant Eastman Kodak in early 1994) and led the new company to record sales. Lifted by an industrywide increase in demand for plastics, coatings, inks and resins, the firm's performance chemicals segment posted a 14% increase in operating income in 1994, while its industrial segment doubled its profits. The extra cash enabled Eastman Chemical to reduce its long-term debt to $1.2 billion.

WHEN

Eastman Chemical became a public company on January 1, 1994, but it traces its roots back to the 19th century. George Eastman, after developing a method for dry-plate photography, established The Eastman Dry Plate and Film Company in 1884 in Rochester, New York (changed to Eastman Kodak in 1892).

In 1886 Eastman hired Henry Reichenbach as his first scientist to help with the creation and manufacture of new photographic chemicals. However, as time passed, Reichenbach and the company's other scientists began to come up with chemicals not directly related to photography or that had uses in addition to photography. During WWI cellulose acetate, which was developed as a base for safety film, was used to coat the wings of airplanes.

In 1920 Eastman bought a wood distillation plant in Kingsport, Tennessee, and formed the Tennessee Eastman Corporation to make methanol and acetone, used as raw materials for the manufacture of the company's photographic chemicals. In the early 1930s the company introduced acetate yarn and Tenite, a cellulose ester plastic. In 1938 Eastman Kodak formed a joint venture with General Mills, called Distillation Products, Inc., to develop a process for molecular distillation, and the firm soon began supplying vitamin E products.

During WWII the company formed Holston Defense to make explosives for the US's armed forces. Kodak began to vertically integrate Eastman Tennessee's operations during the 1950s. In 1950 Kodak acquired A. M. Tenney Associates, Tennessee Eastman's selling agent for its acetate yarn products. Kodak also established Texas Eastman and opened a plant in Longview, Texas, to produce ethyl alcohol and aldehydes, raw materials used in fiber and film production. At the end of 1952 Kodak created Eastman Chemical Products, Inc., to sell alcohols, plastics, and fibers made by Tennessee Eastman and Texas Eastman.

Also in 1952 Tennessee Eastman developed cellulose acetate filter tow, used in cigarette filters. In the late 1950s the company introduced Kodel polyester fiber. In 1968 Kodak created Carolina Eastman Company and opened a plant in Columbia, South Carolina, to produce Kodel and other polyester products. Kodak also created Eastman Chemicals Division to handle its chemical operations.

During the 1970s Kodak established Arkansas Eastman, opening a plant in Batesville, Arkansas, to manufacture specialty chemicals. Eastman Chemicals introduced PET resin, used to make containers, in the late 1970s. In 1987 it acquired biological and molecular instrumentation manufacturer International Biotechnologies.

In 1990 Eastman Chemicals Division became Eastman Chemical Company. The next year Eastman Chemical acquired ARCO's propylene and urethane polyols businesses.

In 1993 the company exited the polyester fiber business, and in 1994 Eastman Chemical agreed to sell its polypropylene business to Huntsman Chemical. However, its PET projects are set to expand. PET production will increase from 1.6 billion pounds to over 2.8 billion pounds by 1998, with the opening of plants in Mexico and Spain in 1996.

When Kodak spun off Eastman Chemical in early 1994, it was saddled with $1.8 billion in debt. The firm is seeking to expand its overseas businesses to boost sales and bring down debt. It plans to increase its overseas assets from 5% in 1994 to 30% by the year 2000.

NYSE symbol: EMN
Fiscal year ends: December 31

WHO

Chairman and CEO: Earnest W. Deavenport Jr., age 56, $1,311,849 pay
VC and EVP: R. Wiley Bourne Jr., age 57, $746,417 pay
SVP Functional Organizations: Tom O. Nethery, age 56, $616,756 pay
SVP Business Organizations: James L. Chitwood, age 52, $614,295 pay
SVP New Business Generation: James W. Giggey, age 63, $493,856 pay
VP Supply and Distribution: B. Fielding Rolston, age 53
VP Quality, Health, Safety, and Environment: Robert C. Joines, age 54
VP, Secretary, and General Counsel: John C. Bracy, age 62
VP and CFO: H. Virgil Stephens, age 57
VP Human Resources, Communications, and Public Affairs: William G. Adams, age 60
Auditors: Price Waterhouse LLP

WHERE

HQ: 100 N. Eastman Rd., Kingsport, TN 37660
Phone: 615-229-2000
Fax: 615-229-1351 (Investor Relations)

Eastman Chemical's main plants are located in Batesville, Arkansas; Columbia, South Carolina; Kingsport, Tennessee; Longview, Texas; Rochester, New York; Toronto; and Hartlepool and Workington, UK.

	1994 Sales		1994 Operating Income	
	$ mil.	% of total	$ mil.	% of total
US	3,393	78	613	97
Europe	629	15	20	3
Other regions	307	7	(5)	—
Adjustments	—	—	8	—
Total	**4,329**	**100**	**636**	**100**

WHAT

	1994 Sales		1994 Operating Income	
	$ mil.	% of total	$ mil.	% of total
Performance chemicals	2,584	60	382	60
Industrial chemicals	1,745	40	254	40
Total	**4,329**	**100**	**636**	**100**

Performance Chemicals
Coatings, inks, and resins
Container plastics
Fine chemicals
Nutrition and formulation products
Performance plastics
Polyester plastics
Polymer modifiers
Specialty packaging plastics

Industrial Chemicals
Fibers
Filter products
Flexible products
Industrial intermediates

Selected Operating Units
Arkansas Eastman
Carolina Eastman
Tennessee Eastman
Texas Eastman

KEY COMPETITORS

Akzo Nobel
Atlantic Richfield
BASF
Bayer
British Petroleum
Chevron
Ciba-Geigy
Dow Chemical
DuPont
Exxon
Formosa Plastics
General Electric
Hanson
Henkel
Hercules

Hoechst
Huntsman Chemical
Imperial Chemical
Lyondell Petrochemical
Mitsubishi
Mobil
Monsanto
Occidental
Phillips Petroleum
PPG
Rhône-Poulenc
Rohm and Haas
Royal Dutch/Shell
Union Carbide
W. R. Grace

HOW MUCH

	Annual Growth	1985	1986	1987	1988	1989	1990	1991	1992	1993	1994
Sales ($ mil.)	7.0%	2,348	2,378	2,600	2,806	3,246	3,433	3,614	3,811	3,903	4,329
Net income ($ mil.)	(2.3%)	—	—	—	387	433	359	336	292	247	336
Income as % of sales	—	—	—	—	13.8%	13.3%	10.5%	9.3%	7.7%	6.3%	7.8%
Earnings per share ($)	—	—	—	—	—	—	3.93	3.72	2.85	2.46	4.05
Stock price – high ($)	—	—	—	—	—	—	—	—	—	—	56.00
Stock price – low ($)	—	—	—	—	—	—	—	—	—	—	39.50
Stock price – close ($)	—	—	—	—	—	—	—	—	—	—	50.50
P/E – high	—	—	—	—	—	—	—	—	—	—	14
P/E – low	—	—	—	—	—	—	—	—	—	—	10
Dividends per share ($)	—	—	—	—	—	—	—	—	—	—	1.60
Book value per share ($)	—	—	—	—	—	—	—	—	—	—	15.59
Employees	0.3%	17,000	17,000	17,000	17,000	17,532	17,561	17,796	18,457	18,043	17,495

1994 Year-end:
Debt ratio: 48.0%
Return on equity: 28.5%
Cash (mil.): $90
Current ratio: 1.59
Long-term debt (mil.): $1,195
No. of shares (mil.): 83
Dividends
  Yield: 3.2%
  Payout: 39.5%
Market value (mil.): $4,196

Net Income ($ mil.) 1988–94

EASTMAN KODAK COMPANY

OVERVIEW

Based in Rochester, New York, Eastman Kodak has refocused its operations on its historic core business — image making. Under the leadership of chairman George Fisher (former CEO of Motorola), Kodak sold its nonimaging businesses and used the $8 billion in proceeds to reduce the company's long-term debt.

With about 70% of the 35-mm US film market, Kodak understands that digital imaging will erode its film sales in the US. Thus, Kodak plans to aggressively grow its digital imaging products and services in the US and its film products in the developing world.

In the US, Kodak is teaming up with partners in the high-tech industry to develop new products for digital imaging. As part of these efforts, the company's partnership with Apple Computer is producing a $750 nonfilm digital camera (under Apple's QuickTake name) that transfers images directly to Macintosh computers.

Kodak has also announced alliances with Microsoft (to develop software for finishing photos on PCs), IBM (to market Photo CD products), Hewlett-Packard (to develop inkjet printers for printing high-quality images), and Sprint (to create a system for storing and sending images over telephone lines). Kodak has restructured its $500 million Digital & Applied Imaging division in order to work more effectively with its high-tech partners. For its digital products Kodak has also developed a new brand name — Kodak Digital Science — and hired former Apple executive John Sculley as a marketing consultant.

Overseas, Kodak plans to focus on marketing its traditional film products in developing countries, such as Brazil, China, India, and Russia. By leveraging its traditional products in international markets, Kodak hopes to pay for the capital investments necessary for its future in digital imaging.

WHEN

George Eastman, after developing a method for dry-plate photography, established the Eastman Dry Plate and Film Company in 1884 in Rochester, New York. The company settled on the name Kodak in 1892, after Eastman tried many combinations of letters starting and ending with "K," which he thought was a "strong, incisive sort of letter."

In 1888 the company introduced its first camera, a small, easy-to-use device that sold for $25, loaded with enough film for 100 pictures. To develop the film, owners mailed the camera to Kodak, which returned it with the pictures and more film. The Brownie followed in 1900. In 1923 Kodak introduced a home-movie camera, projector, and film.

Ailing and concluding that his work was done, Eastman shot and killed himself in 1932. Kodak continued to dominate the photography industry with the introduction of color film (Kodachrome, 1935) and the Brownie hand-held movie camera (1951). Kodak established plants in Tennessee (1920) and Texas (1950) to produce the chemicals, plastics, and fibers used in its film production.

The Instamatic, introduced in 1963, became Kodak's biggest success. The camera, with the film in a foolproof cartridge, eliminated the need for loading in the dark. By 1976 Kodak had sold an estimated 60 million Instamatics, 50 million more cameras than all its competitors combined had sold. Subsequent introductions have included the Kodak instant camera

(1976) and the disc camera, both of which have been discontinued.

In the 1980s Kodak streamlined operations and diversified into electronic publishing, batteries, floppy disks (Verbatim, 1985; sold in 1990), pharmaceuticals (Sterling Drug, sold in 1994), and do-it-yourself and household products (L&F Products, sold in 1994).

Kodak entered a joint R&D project with 4 Japanese photo giants (Canon, Nikon, Minolta, and Fuji Photo) in 1992 to examine silver-halide photographic systems. That same year Kodak introduced the Photo CD, a compact disk capable of storing photographs. At a price of $20 per disk and $500 for the player, the Photo CD failed as a consumer product. However, it later became popular among desktop publishers and other small businesses.

In 1993 Kodak introduced a portable photo-CD player for viewing photo CDs on a television and a $199 zoom-lens camera. Also in 1993 George Fisher became chairman.

In 1994 Kodak sold most of its nonimaging businesses, including Sterling Winthrop, L&F Products, and Clinical Diagnostics (clinical chemistry analyzers).

Kodak relaunched its Photo CD directly to the desktop publishing market in 1995 and will license, for free, its machine standards for converting photos into CDs. Also in 1995 Kodak lodged a trade complaint against Japan, charging that competitor Fuji has an unfair advantage on its home turf.

NYSE symbol: EK
Fiscal year ends: December 31

WHO

Chairman, President, and CEO: George M. C. Fisher,
age 54, $3,860,373 pay
EVP: Leo J. Thomas, age 58, $1,107,009 pay (prior to
promotion)
EVP: Wilbur J. Prezzano, age 54, $1,053,943 pay (prior
to promotion)
EVP and CFO: Harry L. Kavetas, age 57, $935,682 pay
(prior to promotion)
SVP: Richard T. Bourns, age 60, $710,238 pay
SVP, Secretary, and General Counsel: Gary P.
Van Graafeiland, age 48
SVP: James W. Meyer, age 51
SVP and Director, Corporate Human Resources:
Michael P. Morley, age 51
VP and Director, Communications and Public Affairs:
Michael P. Benard, age 47
VP and Director, Corporate Quality: Ronald L. Heidke
VP and Director, Commercial Affairs: Peter Giles
**VP and Director, Corporate Health, Safety, and
Environment:** R. Hays Bell
Auditors: Price Waterhouse LLP

WHERE

HQ: 343 State St., Rochester, NY 14650
Phone: 716-724-4000
Fax: 716-724-0663

	1994 Sales		1994 Operating Income	
	$ mil.	% of total	$ mil.	% of total
US	6,434	48	884	66
Europe	3,670	27	315	24
Canada & Latin America	1,266	9	130	10
Other regions	2,187	16	(17)	—
Adjustments	130	—	(3)	—
Total	**13,687**	**100**	**1,309**	**100**

WHAT

	1994 Sales		1994 Operating Income	
	$ mil.	% of total	$ mil.	% of total
Consumer Imaging	5,919	43	878	67
Commercial Imaging	7,646	56	431	33
Other	130	1	—	—
Adjustments	(8)	—	—	—
Total	**13,687**	**100**	**1,309**	**100**

Selected Products and Services

Consumer Imaging
Cameras
  Fun Saver
Film and papers
  Royal Gold film
Photographic chemicals
Processing services
  Qualex, Inc.
Projectors

Commercial Imaging
Application software
Audiovisual equipment
Copiers
Films
  ClinicSelect x-ray films

Graphic arts films
  Eastman EXR 200T
  Ektachrome 100
Microfilm products
  COM DR microfilm 2467
  Imagelink microfilmer 2200
Photo CDs and players
Photographic chemicals
Photographic papers
Photographic plates
Printers
  LionHeart
  XLS 8600 PS
Processing equipment
Scanners
  Imagelink

KEY COMPETITORS

Alcatel Alsthom
Bayer
Canon
Concord Camera
CPI Corp.
Fuji Photo
General Electric
Harris Corp.
3M

Minolta
Philips
Photo Control
Pitney Bowes
Polaroid
PrimeSource Corp.
Sharp
Siemens
Xerox

HOW MUCH

	9-Year Growth	1985	1986	1987	1988	1989	1990	1991	1992	1993	1994
Sales ($ mil.)	2.8%	10,631	11,550	13,305	17,034	18,398	18,908	19,419	20,183	16,364	13,687
Net income ($ mil.)	5.9%	332	374	1,178	1,397	529	703	17	994	667	557
Income as % of sales	—	3.1%	3.2%	8.9%	8.2%	2.9%	3.7%	0.1%	4.9%	4.1%	4.1%
Earnings per share ($)	5.9%	0.97	1.11	3.52	4.31	1.63	2.17	0.05	2.98	2.02	1.63
Stock price – high ($)	—	35.59	46.69	70.69	53.25	52.38	43.88	49.75	50.75	65.00	56.38
Stock price – low ($)	—	27.38	30.59	41.94	39.13	40.00	33.75	37.63	37.75	40.25	40.69
Stock price – close ($)	3.9%	33.78	45.78	49.00	45.13	41.13	41.63	48.25	40.50	56.25	47.75
P/E – high	—	37	42	20	12	32	20	—	17	32	35
P/E – low	—	28	28	12	9	25	16	—	13	20	25
Dividends per share ($)	0.1%	1.69	1.74	1.68	1.85	2.00	2.00	2.00	2.00	2.00	1.70
Book value per share ($)	(5.4%)	19.39	18.85	18.54	20.90	20.46	20.75	18.79	20.12	10.15	11.82
Employees	(3.2%)	128,950	121,450	124,400	145,300	137,750	134,450	133,200	132,600	110,400	96,300

1994 Year-end:
Debt ratio: 20.4%
Return on equity: 22.3%
Cash (mil.): $2,068
Current ratio: 1.34
Long-term debt (mil.): $660
No. of shares (mil.): 340
Dividends
  Yield: 3.6%
  Payout: 70.2%
Market value (mil.): $16,223

**Stock Price History
High/Low 1985–94**

EATON CORPORATION

OVERVIEW

Cleveland-based Eaton is a global manufacturer of highly engineered products ranging from switches to axles to electrical power grids. One of the US's top 3 makers of automobile components in the 1970s, Eaton has diversified its products and expanded overseas to offset the cyclical swings of its traditional businesses. Over the past decade, Eaton has bought 26 companies. In the largest acquisition in company history, Eaton in 1994 bought the electrical distribution and control business of Westinghouse for $1.1 billion, which tripled the size of its electrical power and controls operation (51% of 1994 revenues). Eaton's 1994 sales set a company record, topping $6

billion for the first time. International business accounted for about 25%.

Eaton has 2 major divisions. Vehicle Components makes original equipment, such as axles, transmissions, and engine components, for automotive, heavy-truck, and off-road vehicles. Electrical and Electronic Controls makes a wide variety of electronic and electromechanical devices used in the appliance, automotive, construction, industrial, aerospace, and military industries. Eaton still makes defense electronics. Eaton is looking to expand into Latin America and the Pacific Rim, manufacture entire systems instead of components, and buy synergistic companies.

WHEN

In 1911 Joseph Eaton and Viggo Torbensen started the Torbensen Gear and Axle Company to manufacture an internal-gear rear axle for trucks patented by Torbensen in 1902. The company moved from Newark, New Jersey, to Cleveland in 1914.

After Republic Motor Truck bought Torbensen (1917), Eaton formed the Eaton Axle Company (1919), repurchased Torbensen (1922), and by 1931 had bought 11 more automotive parts companies (adding bumpers, springs, heaters, and engine parts to its line). In 1932 the company became Eaton Manufacturing.

The Great Depression reduced demand for automobiles, and profits plummeted. Heavy wartime demand helped Eaton recover, and in 1946 the company bought Dynamatic (eddy-current drives). Joseph Eaton died in 1949.

Attempting to diversify, Eaton bought Fuller Manufacturing (truck transmissions, 1958), Cleveland Worm & Gear (1959), Dole Valve (1963), and Yale & Towne Manufacturing (locks and forklift trucks, 1963). The acquisitions augmented Eaton's international business, and foreign sales increased from virtually zero in 1961 to 20% of total sales by 1966. That year the company changed its name to Eaton Yale & Towne; it adopted its present name in 1971.

In 1978 Eaton sold the lock and security business to Scovill Manufacturing and bought Cutler-Hammer (electronics), Kenway (automated storage and retrieval systems), and Samuel Moore (plastics and fluid power). By 1980 Eaton was supplying the space shuttle's landing systems and making traffic control systems for the air and waterways. In 1981 the US government awarded Eaton the $3

billion B-1B bomber defense avionics (radar-jamming) contract. This contract was partially terminated by the government in 1990, resulting in the loss of 1,600 jobs.

Downturns in the truck and automobile industries forced Eaton to close 30 plants and trim 23,000 jobs between 1979 and 1983. In 1982 the company reported its first loss in 50 years. During this time the company decided to diversify as a high-technology company and expand overseas.

From 1984 to 1993 Eaton spent almost $4 billion in capital improvements and R&D that enabled the company to introduce several new products. Eaton continued to buy other companies, acquiring Consolidated Controls (precision instruments); Pacific-Sierra Research (computer and defense systems); and Singer Controls (valves and switches) in 1986. Eaton also put its defense electronics business (AIL Systems) up for sale, but there was no buyer.

In 1991 Eaton bought Nordhauser Ventil (automotive engine valves, Germany), Control Displays (flight deck equipment), and Arrow-Hart's specialty switch businesses. In 1992 Eaton acquired Franz Kirsten (a German maker of automotive switches), Heinemann Electric (a producer of hydraulic-magnetic circuit breakers), and the automotive switch business of Illinois Tool Works.

With the purchase of Westinghouse's electrical equipment business in 1994, Eaton announced intentions to cut hundreds of jobs and eliminate excess capacity. In 1995 it agreed to buy the electrical switchgear and controls business of Email Ltd. (Australia), which gives Eaton a presence in Pacific Rim markets. Chairman William Butler announced his retirement, effective at the end of 1995.

NYSE symbol: ETN
Fiscal year ends: December 31

WHO

Chairman: William E. Butler, age 63, $2,002,550 pay
VC and CEO: Stephen R. Hardis, age 59, $1,096,941 pay (prior to promotion)
President and COO: Alexander M. Cutler, age 43, $1,002,641 pay (prior to promotion)
EVP and General Counsel: Gerald L. Gherlein, age 56, $623,567 pay
SVP Controls and Hydraulics: Robert J. McCloskey, age 56
SVP Automotive Components: Larry M. Oman, age 54
SVP, Cutler-Hammer: Joseph L. Becherer, age 53
SVP Truck Components: Thomas W. O'Boyle, age 52
VP; Chief Financial and Planning Officer: Adrian T. Dillon, age 41
VP International: Patrick X. Donovan, age 59
Secretary and Associate General Counsel: Earl R. Franklin, age 51
VP Human Resources: Susan J. Cook, age 47
Auditors: Ernst & Young LLP

WHERE

HQ: Eaton Center, Cleveland, OH 44114-2584
Phone: 216-523-5000
Fax: 216-523-4787

Eaton has 150 facilities in 18 countries.

	1994 Sales		1994 Operating Income	
	$ mil.	% of total	$ mil.	% of total
US	4,807	75	491	83
Europe	912	14	50	8
Latin America	298	5	9	2
Canada	292	4	30	5
Other regions	103	2	14	2
Adjustments	(360)	—	—	—
Total	**6,052**	**100**	**594**	**100**

WHAT

	1994 Sales		1994 Operating Income	
	$ mil.	% of total	$ mil.	% of total
Electrical & Electronic Controls	3,088	51	239	40
Vehicle Components	2,828	47	354	60
Defense Systems	136	2	1	—
Total	**6,052**	**100**	**594**	**100**

Brand Names	Selected Products
C-H Control	Axles
Challenger	Brakes
Char-Lynn	Controllers
Commander	Cylinders
Cutler-Hammer	Electric drives
Dill	Engine valves
Dole	Fan drives
Durant	Forgings
Dynamatic	Industrial clutches and brakes
Eaton	Materials-handling systems
Fuller	Panels
Golf Pride	Sensors
Heinemann	Starters
Lectron	Switches
L/P	Thermostats
Panelmate	Timers
Roadranger	Transformers
Top Spec	Transmissions

KEY COMPETITORS

AlliedSignal	GTE	Siemens
A. O. Smith	Honeywell	SPX
Arvin Industries	Johnson	Sundstrand
Borg-Warner	Controls	TRINOVA
Automotive	Motorola	TRW
Cooper Industries	PACCAR	United
Cummins Engine	Parker Hannifin	Technologies
Dana	Raytheon	Western Atlas
Emerson	Robert Bosch	Westinghouse
General Signal	Rockwell	

HOW MUCH

	9-Year Growth	1985	1986	1987	1988	1989	1990	1991	1992	1993	1994
Sales ($ mil.)	5.7%	3,675	3,812	3,138	3,469	3,671	3,639	3,381	3,869	4,401	6,052
Net income ($ mil.)	4.2%	138	138	201	230	225	179	74	140	180	333
Income as % of sales	—	6.3%	3.6%	6.4%	6.6%	6.1%	4.9%	2.2%	3.6%	4.1%	5.5%
Earnings per share ($)	7.8%	2.24	1.39	2.34	3.09	3.01	2.53	1.10	2.03	2.57	4.40
Stock price – high ($)	—	21.64	26.64	35.94	28.69	33.75	32.19	33.13	41.63	55.38	62.13
Stock price – low ($)	—	16.52	21.02	18.52	22.34	26.50	20.38	23.31	30.88	38.25	43.88
Stock price – close ($)	9.8%	21.39	24.59	26.44	27.88	28.50	24.94	32.31	40.81	50.50	49.50
P/E – high	—	10	19	15	9	11	13	30	21	22	14
P/E – low	—	7	15	8	7	9	8	21	15	15	10
Dividends per share ($)	11.5%	0.45	0.54	0.64	0.84	1.00	1.05	1.10	1.10	1.22	1.20
Book value per share ($)	4.8%	14.17	14.32	14.26	15.62	15.51	16.81	16.92	13.67	15.50	21.54
Employees	2.4%	41,100	43,438	35,914	43,000	38,734	36,603	35,656	38,000	38,000	51,000

1994 Year-end:
Debt ratio: 39.3%
Return on equity: 23.9%
Cash (mil.): $41
Current ratio: 1.68
Long-term debt (mil.): $1,053
No. of shares (mil.): 78
Dividends
  Yield: 2.4%
  Payout: 27.3%
Market value (mil.): $3,861

Stock Price History
High/Low 1985–94

ECKERD CORPORATION

The medicine seems to be taking effect at Eckerd Corporation. One of the largest drugstore chains in the US, the Largo, Florida–based company has rebounded after spending most of the early 1990s feeling a bit sickly. Eckerd has divested noncore operations, invested in new technology, retooled its merchandising strategy, and increased its focus on 3rd-party marketing and managed care programs. Same-store sales were up 8.2% in fiscal 1995.

Eckerd operates 1,735 drugstores in 13 states, mainly in the Sunbelt. Its primary focus is the sale of prescription and over-the-counter drugs (now about 61% of total sales), but it has expanded its merchandise offerings in many stores to include convenience items, especially soft drinks and snack foods. Eckerd also operates an extensive photo processing operation and is among the top 3 retail photofinishers in the US.

In an effort to cut costs, Eckerd plans to close 90 underperforming stores during 1995. However, as part of an expansion, the company plans to add 90 new stores in 1995 and 100 new stores in 1996.

Merrill Lynch owns 38.3% of the company's stock.

WHEN

In 1898 Jack Eckerd's father, J. Milton Eckerd, started one of the US's first drugstore chains, in Erie, Pennsylvania. Jack worked for his father's company during the Great Depression but left to start his own chain of stores in Florida by buying 3 locations in Tampa and Clearwater in 1952. In a case that he won in the Supreme Court of Florida, he challenged "fair" trade laws that imposed price restrictions that prevented him from underselling competitors.

Eckerd took the company public as Eckerd Drugs of Florida in 1961 and began buying other companies, beginning with Old Dominion Candies in 1966 (sold 1972). In 1968 the company bought Jackson's/Byrons, renamed J. Byrons, a Miami department store chain (sold 1985). The company further expanded in 1969 with its purchases of Gray Security Service and food-service supplier Kurman Company, both sold in 1976.

Jack Eckerd ran unsuccessfully for governor of Florida in 1970 and for US senator from Florida in 1974. He gave $10 million to Florida Presbyterian College, renamed Eckerd College, in 1971. Eckerd joined the Ford administration in 1975 as head of the General Services Administration.

Meanwhile, the company continued to expand its drugstores, buying Brown's Thrift City Wholesale Drugs and Mading-Dugan Drugs in 1970 and Ward Cut-Rate Drug and Eckerd Drugs Eastern in 1973. Finally, Jack Eckerd Drugs bought Eckerd Drugs of Charlotte from Edward O'Herron Jr., son-in-law of Milton Eckerd, bringing all the Eckerd stores under its control in 1977.

In 1986 Eckerd's management turned to Merrill Lynch Capital Partners to handle a $1.2 billion leveraged buyout of the company for which the firm received $14.5 million in fees. That year Eckerd closed 45 stores because of poor performance or potential, sold 11 stores in Tulsa, bought 32 Shoppers Drug Mart stores in Florida, and opened 50 new stores.

Between 1987 and 1989 Jack Eckerd expanded its optical services with 23 Visionworks stores (sold 1994) and its photofinishing business with 79 Express Photo locations. In 1990 the company acquired 220 stores from the bankrupt Ohio drugstore chain Revco. In 1991 Eckerd entered into a fierce bidding war with Rite Aid for the remaining Revco stores. But at the last minute Eckerd dropped out, and Revco emerged from bankruptcy on its own.

The company underwent a massive restructuring in 1992 and 1993 that included the elimination of about 600 jobs and the consolidation of operating divisions. In 1993, 7 years after going private, Eckerd once again went public, selling 15% of its stock in an effort to relieve debt. To reflect its new status, the company designed a new logo and changed its name to Eckerd Corporation.

Eckerd acquired Crown Drugs, a 19-unit chain based in Winston-Salem, North Carolina, in 1994. That same year the company sold Insta-Care (which provides prescription drugs and medical consulting services to long-term health care operations) to Beverly Enterprises for about $94 million.

In 1995 Eckerd agreed to buy 109 Florida drugstores from Rite Aid for $75 million. Also in 1995 the company teamed with Corning to offer medical testing services, including blood and urine sampling, in its drugstores. The program, called Eckerd Life Care Centers, will be conducted by registered nurses and phlebotomists.

NYSE symbol: ECK
Fiscal year ends: Saturday nearest January 31

WHO

Chairman and CEO: Stewart Turley, age 60, $1,133,002 pay
President and COO: Francis A. Newman, age 46, $941,389 pay
EVP Administration and Secretary (HR): James M. Santo, age 53, $340,762 pay
SVP and CFO: Samuel G. Wright, age 44, $334,839 pay
SVP Pharmacy Services: Richard R. Powis, age 47
SVP Store Operations: Kenneth L. Flynn, age 50
SVP Merchandising: Edward W. Kelly, age 49
VP and Treasurer: Martin W. Gladysz, age 42
VP, General Counsel, and Assistant Secretary: Robert E. Lewis, age 34
Auditors: KPMG Peat Marwick LLP

WHERE

HQ: 8333 Bryan Dairy Rd., Largo, FL 34647
Phone: 813-399-6000
Fax: 813-399-6409 (Public Affairs)

	1995 Drugstores
	No.
Florida	553
Texas	490
North Carolina	192
Georgia	164
Louisiana	110
South Carolina	82
Tennessee	35
New Jersey	27
Mississippi	26
Oklahoma	26
Alabama	18
Delaware	11
Maryland	1
Total	**1,735**

WHAT

	Estimated 1995 Sales
	% of total
Pharmacy & OTC drugs	61
Photofinishing & photo-related products	9
Other	30
Total	**100**

Products and Services
Books and magazines
Cosmetics
Food
Fragrances
Greeting cards
Health care products
Household products
Over-the-counter drugs
Prescription drugs
Photofinishing services
Tobacco products
Toys

KEY COMPETITORS

Albertson's	Merck
Big B	National Convenience
Bruno's	Pathmark
Circle K	Price/Costco
Drug Emporium	Publix
Eastman Kodak	Randalls
Eli Lilly	Revco
Food Lion	Rite Aid
Giant Food	Safeway
H. E. Butt	Southland
K&B	Walgreen
Kmart	Wal-Mart
Kroger	Winn-Dixie
Melville	

HOW MUCH

	Annual Growth	1986	1987	1988	1989	1990	1991	1992	1993	1994	1995
Sales ($ mil.)	6.8%	2,508	2,566	2,750	2,875	3,175	3,456	3,740	3,887	4,191	4,549
Net income ($ mil.)	—	—	—	—	—	(17)	(47)	(8)	(15)	(8)	48
Income as % of sales	—	—	—	—	—	—	—	—	—	—	1.1%
Earnings per share ($)	—	—	—	—	—	(0.79)	(1.97)	(0.32)	(0.56)	(0.27)	1.47
Stock price – high ($)[1]	—	—	—	—	—	—	—	—	—	19.25	32.00
Stock price – low ($)[1]	—	—	—	—	—	—	—	—	—	12.75	17.88
Stock price – close ($)[1]	61.5%	—	—	—	—	—	—	—	—	18.50	29.88
P/E – high	—	—	—	—	—	—	—	—	—	—	22
P/E – low	—	—	—	—	—	—	—	—	—	—	12
Dividends per share ($)	—	—	—	—	—	—	—	—	—	0.00	0.00
Book value per share ($)	—	—	—	—	—	—	—	—	—	(5.66)	(3.82)
Employees	2.7%	—	—	35,400	36,400	40,000	40,800	39,800	40,300	43,000	42,700

1995 Year-end:
Debt ratio: 100.0%
Return on equity: —
Cash (mil.): $9
Current ratio: 1.51
Long-term debt (mil.): $786
No. of shares (mil.): 32
Dividends
  Yield: —
  Payout: —
Market value (mil.): $959

Stock Price History[1]
High/Low 1994–95

[1] Stock prices are for the prior calendar year.

E. I. DU PONT DE NEMOURS

OVERVIEW

Like the Teflon products it makes, DuPont has resisted the damage caused by sticking (to underperforming operations and procedures). The country's #1 chemical company has been restructuring its operations over the past 3 years. It has concentrated on reducing costs, cutting almost 37,000 jobs since 1990, and reorganizing into smaller business units. DuPont has shed $1.8 billion in assets over the past few years, selling a number of businesses as it focuses on its competitive and technological strengths. Its connector systems division was sold to Hicks, Muse & Co., and gun maker Remington Arms was sold to investment firm Clayton, Dubilier & Rice.

The Delaware-based company is organized into 5 principal business segments — chemicals (refrigerants, pigments, and polymer intermediates); fibers (Lycra, Tyvek); polymers (elastomers, nylon resins, packaging materials, Teflon); petroleum (Conoco, its largest subsidiary, accounting for $16.8 billion or 43% of 1994 sales); and diversified businesses (agricultural products, electronics, medical products, printing and publishing, and CONSOL Energy).

Following a year of record earnings in 1994 DuPont spent $8.8 billion in 1995 to buy back 23% of its shares from Seagram (originally acquired by Seagram in 1980).

DuPont's Conoco subsidiary plans to begin operating new offshore oilfields in Norway and the UK in 1995. DuPont also plans to enter the women's apparel retail market in 1995 with private-label sportswear designed and manufactured by the firm. Unconventional perhaps, but it will help DuPont promote its big investment in the manufacture of synthetic fibers.

WHEN

Eleuthère Irénée du Pont de Nemours, a Frenchman who had studied gunpowder manufacture under chemist Antoine Lavoisier, fled to America in 1800 after the French Revolution. In 1802, with the help of French capital, he founded E. I. du Pont de Nemours and Company and set up a gunpowder plant on Delaware's Brandywine Creek.

Within a decade the plant (known as DuPont) grew to be the largest of its kind in the US and benefited greatly from government contracts during the War of 1812. After Irénée's death in 1834, his sons Alfred and Henry took over, buying out the other partners to ensure du Pont family control. Under their leadership the company profited from selling gunpowder to the US government during the Mexican-American War (1840s) and to both sides during the Crimean War (1850s). DuPont added dynamite and nitroglycerine (1880) and introduced guncotton (1892) and smokeless powder (1894).

In 1902 du Pont cousins Pierre, Alfred, and Coleman bought DuPont, and in 1903 they instituted a centralized structure with functionally organized departments, an innovation that big business widely adopted. By 1906 DuPont controlled 70% of the US explosives market. A 1912 antitrust decision forced it to dispose of part of the powder business, but the outbreak of WWI in 1914 generated $89 million in earnings for DuPont to use in diversifying into paints, plastics, and dyes.

In 1917 DuPont acquired an interest in General Motors; the stake had increased to 37% by 1922. In 1962, after 13 years of litigation, the US Supreme Court ordered the DuPont-GM connection broken for antitrust violations; DuPont distributed its GM shares to DuPont shareholders. In the 1920s DuPont bought and improved French cellophane technology and began production of rayon. The company's long list of inventions includes neoprene synthetic rubber (1931), Lucite (1937), nylon (1938), Teflon (1938), Orlon, and Dacron. The last du Pont to head the company resigned as chairman in 1972.

In 1981 DuPont acquired Conoco, formerly Continental Oil, for $7.6 billion — one of the largest US acquisitions at that time. DuPont and Merck began a partnership in 1991 to create an independent drug company (DuPont Merck Pharmaceutical Co.) to focus on non-US markets.

In 1993 DuPont bought the nylon business of Imperial Chemical in exchange for its acrylics products business and $356 million. In 1994 a Florida jury decided that DuPont's fungicide Benlate 50 DF did not damage the crops of 5 farmers who had brought suit against the firm. The decision was a major victory for DuPont, which had already paid over $200 million in claims related to Benlate (pulled from the market in 1991).

With an eye to overseas expansion, DuPont announced plans to establish new chemical, fiber, polymer, and electronics joint ventures in China in 1995. By year's end the company will have doubled (to 8) the number of manufacturing facilities operating in that country.

NYSE symbol: DD
Fiscal year ends: December 31

Chairman and CEO: Edgar S. Woolard Jr., age 60,
  $2,025,000 pay
VC; President and CEO, Conoco Inc.:
  Constantine S. Nicandros, age 61, $1,448,000 pay
VC: John A. Krol, age 58, $1,397,000 pay
SVP; President, DuPont Europe: Robert v. d. Luft,
  age 59, $906,000 pay
SVP; EVP, Conoco Inc.: Archie W. Dunham, age 56,
  $904,800 pay
SVP; EVP, Conoco Inc.: Robert E. McKee III, age 49
SVP; President, DuPont Asia Pacific: Charles O.
  Holliday Jr., age 46
SVP DuPont Research and Development: Joseph A.
  Miller Jr., age 53
SVP and CFO: Charles L. Henry, age 53
SVP and General Counsel: Howard J. Rudge, age 59
VP Human Resources: Daniel W. Burger Jr.
Auditors: Price Waterhouse LLP

WHERE

HQ: E. I. du Pont de Nemours and Company,
  1007 Market St., Wilmington, DE 19898
Phone: 302-774-1000
Fax: 302-774-7322

DuPont and its subsidiaries conduct operations in about
70 countries worldwide.

	1994 Sales	
	$ mil.	% of total
US	20,769	53
Europe	14,216	36
Other regions	4,348	11
Total	**39,333**	**100**

WHAT

	1994 Sales		1994 Operating Income	
	$ mil.	% of total	$ mil.	% of total
Petroleum	16,815	43	1,141	26
Fibers	6,767	17	1,083	24
Polymers	6,318	16	1,084	24
Chemicals	3,760	10	536	14
Other businesses	5,673	14	595	12
Total	**39,333**	**100**	**4,439**	**100**

Selected Consumer Product Materials and Brands

Lycra	Teflon
Mylar	Tyvek

Divisions
Chemicals (intermediates, fluorochemicals, specialty
  chemicals, pigments)
Diversified businesses (agricultural herbicides and
  insecticides, electronic materials, medical products,
  printing and publishing products)
Fibers (textiles, nonwovens, nylons, composites)
Petroleum (Conoco – exploration, production, refining,
  marketing, petrochemicals)
Polymers (films, finishes, fluoropolymers, elastomers)

KEY COMPETITORS

Akzo Nobel	Exxon	Occidental
AlliedSignal	Fieldcrest Cannon	PPG
Amoco	FMC	Rhône-Poulenc
BASF	Formosa Plastics	Royal Dutch/
Bayer	Fuji Photo	Shell
Chevron	Hercules	Sherwin-
Ciba-Geigy	Hoechst	Williams
Clorox	Imperial Chemical	Siemens
Dow Chemical	Mobil	Texaco
Eastman	Monsanto	Union Carbide
Chemical	Novo Nordisk	W. R. Grace

HOW MUCH

	9-Year Growth	1985	1986	1987	1988	1989	1990	1991	1992	1993	1994
Sales ($ mil.)	3.3%	29,483	27,148	30,468	32,917	35,534	40,047	38,695	37,799	37,098	39,333
Net income ($ mil.)	10.4%	1,118	1,538	1,786	2,190	2,480	2,310	1,403	975	566	2,727
Income as % of sales	—	3.8%	5.7%	5.9%	6.7%	7.0%	5.8%	3.6%	2.6%	1.5%	6.9%
Earnings per share ($)	11.2%	1.54	2.12	2.46	3.03	3.53	3.40	2.08	1.43	0.83	4.00
Stock price – high ($)	—	23.09	30.81	43.63	30.94	42.13	42.38	50.00	54.88	57.88	62.38
Stock price – low ($)	—	15.84	19.81	24.97	25.22	28.69	31.38	32.75	43.50	44.50	48.25
Stock price – close ($)	10.6%	22.59	27.97	29.09	29.38	40.97	36.75	46.63	47.13	48.25	56.13
P/E – high	—	15	15	18	10	12	13	24	38	65	16
P/E – low	—	10	9	10	8	8	9	16	30	54	12
Dividends per share ($)	6.9%	1.00	1.02	1.10	1.23	1.45	1.62	1.68	1.74	1.76	1.82
Book value per share ($)	0.8%	17.19	18.23	19.53	21.34	22.71	24.16	24.58	17.08	16.22	18.48
Employees	(3.4%)	146,017	141,268	140,145	140,949	145,787	143,961	132,578	124,916	114,000	107,000

1994 Year-end:
Debt ratio: 37.4%
Return on equity: 23.1%
Cash (mil.): $1,109
Current ratio: 1.47
Long-term debt (mil.): $6,376
No. of shares (mil.): 681
Dividends
  Yield: 3.2%
  Payout: 45.5%
Market value (mil.): $38,221

Stock Price History
High/Low 1985–94

ELECTRONIC DATA SYSTEMS CORP.

OVERVIEW

The way to a consultant's heart is through his wallet. In 1995 Electronic Data Systems (EDS), after a year of negotiations, finally found the number that overcame the objections of A.T. Kearney's partners to a merger between the companies. It was $600 million in cash and stock, which works out to over $4.5 million for each of Kearney's approximately 130 partners.

The merger is intended to propel EDS's struggling management consulting business into the major leagues of international consulting. The unit was started in 1993 and has been gobbling up MBAs ever since, but it needed the name recognition and experience that only an established firm like Kearney could provide in order to draw clients.

Plano, Texas–based EDS believes that high-profile consultancy is an important complement to its primary business: the design of data management systems for companies in many fields, including the insurance, automotive, financial, and communications industries, as well as for the government. One of the largest data processing companies in the US, EDS (founded by Ross Perot) has been a wholly owned subsidiary of General Motors since 1984 but is becoming increasingly independent, fueling speculation about a possible spinoff. GM still accounted for 35% of EDS's 1994 revenues (down from 73% in 1986).

EDS has been losing market share in its traditional market of outsourcing and is putting more emphasis on reengineering.

WHEN

After 10 years with Big Blue, disgruntled salesman Ross Perot founded Electronic Data Systems in 1962. IBM executives had pooh-poohed Perot's idea to provide companies with electronic data processing management services, taking computer and data management worries off clients' hands.

It took Perot 5 months to find his first customer, Collins Radio of Cedar Rapids, Iowa. EDS pioneered the long-term, fixed-price contract with Frito-Lay in 1963, writing a 5-year contract instead of the 60- to 90-day contracts usually offered by service companies.

The company entered Medicare and Medicaid claims processing (mid-1960s), insurance company data processing (1963), and data management for banks (1968). EDS went on to become the #1 provider of data management services in all 3 of these markets.

EDS went public in 1968. It bought Wall Street Leasing (computer services) and established Regional Data Centers and central data processing stations, pioneering the concept of distributed processing in the early 1970s.

In 1976 EDS signed its first offshore contract, in Saudi Arabia, and also signed a contract with the government of Iran. But by 1978 Iran was 6 months behind in its payments, and EDS halted operations. When 2 EDS employees were later arrested, amid the disorder of the Islamic revolution, Perot assembled a rescue team to get them out of the country. The 2 employees were eventually released, and the team aided in their flight from Iran.

In the mid-1970s EDS began moving toward the installation of computer systems and away from the management of them.

In 1984, on its 22nd anniversary (and Perot's birthday), General Motors bought EDS for $2.5 billion. GM promised EDS its independence as well as contract work managing its lumbering data processing system. EDS prospered, but the differing managerial styles of Perot and GM chairman Roger Smith resulted in an uneasy alliance that ended in divorce. GM bought Perot's EDS shares in 1986 for over $700 million. Perot formed competitor Perot Systems Corporation in 1988. Perot's company has barely dented EDS's sales.

Lester Alberthal became CEO, and through the rest of the 1980s he lessened EDS's dependence on GM by diversifying widely.

In 1990 EDS bought the UK's SD-Scicon. The next year IBM, facing declining profits (and looking more green than blue), entered the profitable data management industry.

EDS won an FAA contract worth $508 million in 1993, and the next year the company began, on a small scale, selling new housebrand personal computers. Also in 1993 the company launched its management consulting service as a way of leveraging the contacts it makes in its systems business, but it was a slow, money-losing startup.

The company scored a major hit in 1994 when Xerox contracted with EDS to manage most of its information technology needs (worth $3 billion). A bid to move into multimedia communications via an alliance with Sprint collapsed because issues relating to EDS's independence from GM and the value of the company itself were not resolved.

In 1995 EDS acquired, A.T. Kearney and FCI, a securities industry consultant.

NYSE symbol: GME
Fiscal year ends: December 31

WHO

Chairman, President, and CEO: Lester M. Alberthal Jr., age 50
SVP and Secretary: John R. Castle Jr.
SVP and CFO: Joseph M. Grant
SVP: Paul J. Chiapparone
SVP: Gary J. Fernandes
SVP: Jeffrey M. Heller
SVP: Dean Linderman
SVP Personnel: G. Stuart Reeves
VP and General Counsel: D. Gilbert Friedlander
Auditors: KPMG Peat Marwick LLP

WHERE

HQ: Electronic Data Systems Corporation,
5400 Legacy Dr., Plano, TX 75024-3199
Phone: 214-604-6000
Fax: 214-605-6798

EDS has operations in over 30 countries.

| | 1994 Sales | |
	$ mil.	% of total
US	7,376	74
Europe	1,831	18
Other regions	753	8
Adjustments	92	—
Total	**10,052**	**100**

WHAT

| | 1994 Sales | |
	$ mil.	% of total
Systems & other contracts	9,960	99
Interest & other	92	1
Total	**10,052**	**100**

| | 1994 Sales | |
	$ mil.	% of total
Outside customers	6,413	64
GM & subsidiaries	3,547	35
Interest & other	92	1
Total	**10,052**	**100**

Products and Services
Computer Services
  Corporate outsourcing
  Data-center management
  Networking
  Reengineering
Insurance
  Claims underwriting (through National Heritage
    Insurance Company, a wholly owned subsidiary)
Management consulting

Selected Customers
American Express
Apple Computer
Banco Santander
General Motors
Gruppo S&M
Kooperativa Förbundet
Rockwell International
Southland
Spectradyne
USTravel
Xerox

KEY COMPETITORS

ADP
American Software
Arthur Andersen
Arthur D. Little
AT&T
Bain & Co.
Booz, Allen
Cap Gemini
CompuCom
Computer Sciences
Continuum
Coopers & Lybrand
Deloitte & Touche
Ernst & Young
IBM
Intelligent Electronics
MCI
Perot Systems
Policy Management Systems
SHL Systemhouse
System Software Associates

HOW MUCH

	9-Year Growth	1985	1986	1987	1988	1989	1990	1991	1992	1993	1994
Sales ($ mil.)	12.6%	3,442	4,366	4,423	4,844	5,467	6,109	7,099	8,219	8,562	10,052
Net income ($ mil.)	17.7%	190	261	323	384	435	497	563	636	724	822
Income as % of sales	—	5.5%	6.0%	7.3%	7.9%	8.0%	8.1%	7.9%	7.7%	8.5%	8.2%
Earnings per share ($)	17.8%	0.39	0.53	0.67	0.79	0.91	1.04	1.17	1.33	1.51	1.71
Stock price – high ($)	—	11.63	12.38	12.75	11.22	14.41	20.06	33.06	34.00	35.88	39.50
Stock price – low ($)	—	5.13	6.13	6.00	8.38	10.63	12.19	17.50	25.25	26.00	27.50
Stock price – close ($)	15.8%	10.25	6.25	9.63	11.22	13.66	19.31	31.50	32.88	29.25	38.38
P/E – high	—	30	23	19	14	16	19	28	26	24	23
P/E – low	—	13	12	9	11	12	12	15	19	17	16
Dividends per share ($)	28.6%	0.05	0.10	0.13	0.17	0.24	0.28	0.32	0.36	0.40	0.48
Book value per share ($)	26.1%	1.09	1.64	2.16	2.88	3.69	4.56	5.46	6.39	7.52	8.79
Employees	6.4%	40,000	45,000	44,000	47,500	55,000	59,900	65,800	70,500	70,000	70,000

1994 Year-end:
Debt ratio: 22.4%
Return on equity: 20.9%
Cash (mil.): $758
Current ratio: 1.17
Long-term debt (mil.): $1,021
No. of shares (mil.): 482
Dividends
  Yield: 1.3%
  Payout: 28.1%
Market value (mil.): $18,485

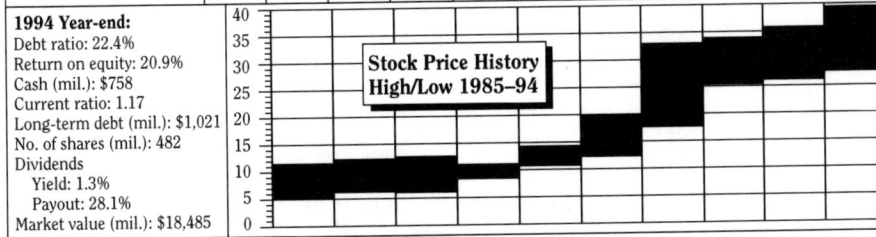

Stock Price History
High/Low 1985–94

ELI LILLY AND COMPANY

OVERVIEW

Eli Lilly researches, produces, and markets pharmaceuticals spanning the entire drug spectrum and the entire globe. Although the Indianapolis-based company is well known for its life-saving insulin, its top-selling drugs are the antidepressant Prozac and the antibiotic Ceclor. Lilly also produces treatments for animal diseases and treatments to improve the efficiency of animal food production.

In 1994 the company combined 5 of its medical device and diagnostic businesses to form Guidant Corporation; then it spun the new corporation off with an IPO of about 20% of its stock. Lilly retains 80% and expects to offer it to Lilly stockholders through a tax-free split-off. Lilly also sold 3 of its other medical device companies and hopes to sell its remaining separate one, Hybritech.

Lilly, recognizing health care market changes, is increasing efforts toward the growing managed care sector. Toward this end, in late 1994 Lilly acquired McKesson's pharmacy benefit management business, PCS Health Systems (the largest drug benefit manager in the country), for $4 billion. Drug benefit managers are hired by employers and insurers to get the best drug prices available for their clients from drug manufacturers.

Before the transaction was final, the FTC required Lilly to sign a consent agreement that allows other drug makers to have access to PCS's list of preferred drugs and prevents Lilly from seeing bids from other drug companies while they are competing to have their drugs on the PCS list.

WHEN

Colonel Eli Lilly, pharmacist and Union officer in the Civil War, started Eli Lilly & Company in Indianapolis in 1876 with $1,300. The Colonel's process of coating pills with gelatin led to 1881 sales of nearly $82,000. Later, the company made gelatin capsules, which it still sells. Lilly died in 1898, and his son and 2 grandsons successively ran Lilly until 1953.

Following intensive research, Lilly introduced insulin in 1923. In those days the pancreas glands of 6,000 cattle or 24,000 hogs were processed to extract one ounce of the substance. Other Lilly products created in the 1920s and 1930s included Merthiolate (an antiseptic), Seconal (a sedative), and treatments for pernicious anemia and heart disease. Sales went from $13 million in 1932 to $72 million by 1945. In 1952 Lilly researchers isolated the antibiotic erythromycin from a species of mold found in the Philippines, and during the 1950s Lilly produced more than 60% of Salk vaccine supplies. In the 1950s and 1960s, the company opened manufacturing plants overseas.

Lilly diversified in the 1970s, buying Elizabeth Arden (cosmetics, 1971) and IVAC (medical instruments, 1977). Lilly's Darvon captured 80% of the prescription analgesic market. Increased R&D spending resulted in new antibiotics, including Ceclor (1979).

Not all Lilly products have been wonder drugs. Since 1974 the company has been involved in litigation over DES (diethylstilbestrol; widely used until 1971, it may have caused cancer and other problems in children whose mothers took the drug). In 1983 Lilly lost a $6 million lawsuit over a death caused by the arthritis drug Oraflex.

In 1982 Lilly became the first company to market a biotechnology product, introducing Humulin (licensed from Genentech), an insulin identical to human insulin. In 1986 Lilly acquired Hybritech, a biotechnology company, for more than $300 million, and the next year the company sold Elizabeth Arden.

In 1988 Lilly introduced Axid (anti-ulcer drug) and Prozac. The Church of Scientology launched a smear campaign against the company, claiming that Prozac triggered psychotic and suicidal reactions in users. The FDA found no evidence to support the allegations. Prozac remains the #1 antidepressant.

Lilly bought drug maker Beiersdorf GmbH and surgical products maker Origin Medsystems in 1992. Also that year the company formed an alliance with struggling biotech firm Centocor to develop and sell Centoxin, a drug to treat septic infections. Well-known antibiotic Ceclor lost most of its patent in late 1992. Also in 1992 the company had its first quarterly loss. The withdrawal of a pacemaker in mid-1992, for FDA safety concerns, bruised revenues and earnings. Lilly also bought 5% of Centocor and formed a venture with Ranbaxy Laboratories to market products in India.

In 1994 the FDA approved Prozac for the treatment of obsessive-compulsive disorder (OCD). It is the only drug marketed in the US to treat both depression and OCD. In 1995 the FDA gave the okay to 2 companies to sell generic versions of Ceclor, which will lead to a drop in Lilly's drug price.

WHO

Chairman and CEO: Randall L. Tobias, age 53, $1,848,995 pay
EVP; President, Pharmaceutical Division: Sidney Taurel, age 46, $1,055,249 pay
President, North American Pharmaceutical Operations: Mitchell E. Daniels Jr., age 45
President, European Pharmaceutical Operations: Gerhard N. Mayr, age 48
President and CEO, Guidant Corporation: Ronald W. Dollens, age 48
VP Finance and CFO: James M. Cornelius, age 51, $895,671 pay
VP Corporate Affairs: Stephen A. Stitle, age 49, $654,065 pay
VP and General Counsel: Rebecca O. Goss, age 47
VP Human Resources: Pedro P. Granadillo, age 47
Auditors: Ernst & Young LLP

WHERE

HQ: Lilly Corporate Center, Indianapolis, IN 46285
Phone: 317-276-2000
Fax: 317-276-2095

The company operates production and/or distribution facilities in 27 countries and sells its products in about 117 countries.

	1994 Sales		1994 Pretax Income	
	$ mil.	% of total	$ mil.	% of total
US	3,282	57	1,067	62
Japan, Middle East & Europe	1,765	31	554	32
Other regions	665	12	103	6
Adjustments	—	—	(26)	—
Total	**5,712**	**100**	**1,699**	**100**

WHAT

	1994 Sales	
	$ mil.	% of total
Central nervous system products	1,836	32
Anti-infectives	1,634	29
Diabetes care	775	14
Gastrointestinal	487	8
Animal health products	464	8
Other products	516	9
Total	**5,712**	**100**

Selected Pharmaceuticals
Axid (anti-ulcer drug)
Ceclor (antibiotic)
Darvocet (analgesic)
Darvon (analgesic)
Dobutrex (cardiovascular)
Humatrope (hormones)
Humulin (insulin)
Iletin (insulin)
Keflex (antibiotic)
Lorabid (antibiotic)
Prozac (antidepressant)
Tazidime (antibiotic)
Tylan (animal antibiotic)
Vancocin (antibiotic)

Subsidiaries and Affiliates
Clinical Pharmaceuticals, Inc.
Guidant Corporation (80%)
Hybritech, Inc.
PCS Health Systems
Sphinx Pharmaceuticals

KEY COMPETITORS

Abbott Labs
ALZA
American Home Products
Amgen
C. R. Bard
Baxter
Bayer
Becton, Dickinson
Bristol-Myers Squibb
Ciba-Geigy

Dow Chemical
DuPont
Genentech
Glaxo Wellcome
Hoechst
Johnson & Johnson
Medtronic
Merck
Monsanto
Novo Nordisk
Pfizer

Rhône-Poulenc
Roche
Sandoz
Schering-Plough
SmithKline Beecham
Upjohn
U.S. Surgical
Warner-Lambert

HOW MUCH

	9-Year Growth	1985	1986	1987	1988	1989	1990	1991	1992	1993	1994
Sales ($ mil.)	6.4%	3,271	3,720	3,644	4,070	4,176	5,192	5,726	6,167	6,452	5,712
Net income ($ mil.)	10.6%	518	558	644	761	940	1,127	1,315	828	491	1,286
Income as % of sales	—	15.8%	15.0%	17.7%	18.7%	22.5%	21.7%	23.0%	13.4%	7.6%	22.5%
Earnings per share ($)	10.2%	1.85	2.01	2.21	2.67	3.20	3.90	4.50	2.81	1.67	4.45
Stock price – high ($)	—	27.97	41.75	53.88	45.88	35.38	42.38	58.75	67.50	62.00	66.25
Stock price – low ($)	—	16.09	25.13	28.88	35.38	42.38	58.75	67.50	57.75	43.63	47.13
Stock price – close ($)	10.0%	27.88	37.13	39.00	42.75	68.50	73.25	83.50	60.75	59.38	65.63
P/E – high	—	15	21	24	17	21	23	19	31	37	15
P/E – low	—	9	13	13	13	13	15	15	21	26	11
Dividends per share ($)	13.5%	0.80	0.90	1.00	1.15	1.35	1.64	2.00	2.20	2.42	2.50
Book value per share ($)	8.8%	8.56	9.85	10.92	11.76	13.48	12.98	16.97	16.71	15.61	18.35
Employees	(1.3%)	28,000	29,100	25,700	26,700	27,800	29,500	30,800	32,200	32,700	24,900

1994 Year-end:
Debt ratio: 43.3%
Return on equity: 25.9%
Cash (mil.): $747
Current ratio: 0.70
Long-term debt (mil.): $2,126
No. of shares (mil.): 292
Dividends
  Yield: 3.8%
  Payout: 56.2%
Market value (mil.): $19,160

Stock Price History
High/Low 1985–94

EMERSON ELECTRIC CO.

OVERVIEW

In an industry squeezed by global competition and rapidly changing technology, Emerson Electric is sticking to the basics, a strategy that has produced record earnings for 37 consecutive years.

Some 88% of Emerson's electrical products are #1 or #2 in their markets. The company's commercial and industrial components segment includes process control systems, industrial motors and machinery, and electronic products; its appliances and construction components segment includes appliance components, HVAC components, and tools.

A calculated strategy of acquisition coupled with product development has fueled Emerson's growth. In 1994 the company added 3 UK-based companies to its 40-plus subsidiaries: F.G. Wilson (generators), Control Techniques (electronic drives), and Switched Reluctance Drives (switched reluctance is a technology for advanced motor design).

Emerson introduced 100 major products in 1994, spending 3.5% on R&D. To boost product innovation, in 1995 the company purchased Intellution, a developer of plant automation and process application software.

WHEN

Emerson was cofounded in St. Louis in 1890 by brothers Alexander and Charles Meston, inventors developing applications for the newly introduced AC electric motor. It was named after former Missouri judge and US marshal John Emerson, who financed the company and became its first president. Emerson's best-known product was an adaptation of the electric motor — the electric fan, introduced in 1892. The company also put its motors to use in player pianos, hair dryers, sewing machines, and water pumps. Between 1910 and 1920 Emerson played a part in developing the first forced-air circulating systems.

The Great Depression and labor problems in the 1930s nearly forced Emerson into bankruptcy. New developments, including a hermetic motor for refrigerators, pulled the company back from the brink, and Emerson's electric motors were adapted to new uses during WWII, particularly in aircraft. Emerson made the gun turret for the B-24 bomber.

The company, having grown dependent on defense business, suffered again in postwar years. Former football coach Wallace Persons took over as president in 1954 and began turning Emerson into a major manufacturer of electrical products.

Starting in the early 1960s, Persons bought a number of smaller companies: White-Rodgers (1962, thermostats and gas controls), Ridge (1966, Ridgid tools), In-Sink-Erator (1968), Browning (1969, power transmission products), Harris (1973, welding and cutting tools), and Louisville Ladder (1973). Persons retired in 1974 after boosting sales from $56 million in 1954 to $800 million in 1973.

Former college football player Chuck Knight, who was only 37 when he became CEO in 1974, changed the company's character again, taking Emerson into high-tech

fields and expanding its hardware segment. Acquisitions included Varec (1975, chemical and petroleum measurement systems), Rosemount (1976, industrial measurement and control systems), Weed Eater (1977), Skil (1979, power tools), Western Forge (1981, Craftsman hand tools), Beckman Industrial (1984, analytical and electrical instruments), Hazeltine (1986, defense electronics), and Liebert (1987, computer support systems).

Anticipating reduced defense spending, Emerson spun off Hazeltine and other businesses in 1990 as ESCO Electronics. That same year Emerson bought European motor makers Leroy-Somer (France) and CESET (Italy), McGill Manufacturing (electric switches, US), and a 47% stake in Hong Kong–based Astec (power supplies), boosting its international presence. The company also formed 2 joint ventures with Robert Bosch of Germany: Vermont American (power tool accessories, 1990) and S-B Power Tool (1992).

In 1992 Emerson became the largest provider of process control equipment with its $1.25 billion purchase of Fisher Controls International (control valves and regulators). That same year the company acquired Buehler International (sample preparation equipment for destructive testing of materials). In 1993 Emerson sold the aerospace business of subsidiary Rosemount to BF Goodrich.

In 1993 and 1994 Emerson continued to expand globally, setting up manufacturing operations and an engineering center in China, forming 5 joint ventures in China and India, and starting 5 manufacturing facilities in Eastern Europe. The company has over 20 joint ventures worldwide.

In 1995 Emerson agreed to sell its 50% stake in S-B Power Tool to joint venture partner Robert Bosch.

WHO

Chairman and CEO: Charles F. Knight, age 58,
$1,975,000 pay
SVC and COO: A. E. Suter, age 59, $975,000 pay
VC; CEO, Emerson-Asia Pacific: Robert W. Staley,
age 59, $535,000 pay
SEVP: William L. Davis
EVP: R. J. Bateman
EVP: James G. Berges
EVP: D. O. Gifford
EVP: J-P. L. Montupet
EVP: R. J. Novello
EVP: L. W. Solley
EVP: G. W. Tamke
SVP Finance and CFO: W. J. Galvin, age 48,
$440,000 pay
SVP, Secretary, and General Counsel: W. W. Withers,
age 54
VP Corporate Sales: G. W. Monken
VP Human Resources: C. T. Kelly
Auditors: KPMG Peat Marwick LLP

WHERE

HQ: 8000 W. Florissant Ave., PO Box 4100,
St. Louis, MO 63136
Phone: 314-553-2000
Fax: 314-553-3527

Emerson has 270 manufacturing facilities worldwide.

	1994 Sales		1994 Pretax Income	
	$ mil.	% of total	$ mil.	% of total
US	5,953	69	956	81
Europe	1,933	23	147	12
Other countries	721	8	85	7
Adjustments	—	—	240	—
Total	**8,607**	**100**	**1,428**	**100**

WHAT

	1994 Sales		1994 Pretax Income	
	$ mil.	% of total	$ mil.	% of total
Commercial & industrial	4,947	57	675	53
Appliance & construction	3,660	43	602	47
Adjustments	—	—	151	—
Total	**8,607**	**100**	**1,428**	**100**

Selected Products
Appliance timers and
controls
Compressors
Diesel generator sets
Fractional horsepower
electric motors
Garbage disposals
Gas control valves
Hand tools
Industrial electric
motors
Mechanical power
transmission products
Temperature sensors
and controls
Variable speed drives
Welding equipment

Selected Subsidiaries
Branson Ultrasonics
Control Techniques
Copeland Compliant Scroll
Digital Appliance Controls
Emerson Motors
Emerson Power
Transmission
F.G. Wilson
Fisher-Rosemount
In-Sink-Erator
Mallory Controls
Skil Corp.
Switched Reluctance Drives
Thermo-O-Disc
U.S. Electrical Motors
Western Forge
White-Rodgers

KEY COMPETITORS

ABB
American Power
Conversion
Black & Decker
Cooper Industries
Dana
Eaton
General Electric
General Signal
Hitachi
Honeywell
Illinois Tool Works
Ingersoll-Rand
Johnson Controls
MagneTek
Mark IV
McDermott
NEC
Raytheon
Rockwell
Rolls-Royce
Siemens
Snap-on Tools
Stanley Works
Tecumseh
Products
Teledyne
United
Technologies
Watsco

HOW MUCH

	9-Year Growth	1985	1986	1987	1988	1989	1990	1991	1992	1993	1994
Sales ($ mil.)	7.1%	4,649	4,953	6,170	6,652	7,071	7,573	7,427	7,706	8,174	8,607
Net income ($ mil.)	9.5%	401	409	467	529	588	613	632	663	708	904
Income as % of sales	—	8.6%	8.3%	7.6%	8.0%	8.3%	8.1%	8.5%	8.6%	8.7%	10.5%
Earnings per share ($)	9.3%	1.81	1.87	2.00	2.31	2.63	2.75	2.83	2.96	3.15	4.04
Stock price – high ($)	—	27.47	30.84	41.88	36.00	39.88	44.38	55.00	58.00	62.38	65.88
Stock price – low ($)	—	22.22	26.03	26.75	27.25	29.50	30.75	36.88	46.75	52.75	56.13
Stock price – close ($)	9.7%	27.06	27.88	34.63	30.38	39.00	37.75	55.00	55.00	60.25	62.38
P/E – high	—	15	17	21	16	15	16	19	20	20	16
P/E – low	—	12	14	13	12	11	11	13	16	17	14
Dividends per share ($)	6.7%	0.87	0.92	0.97	1.00	1.12	1.26	1.32	1.38	1.44	1.56
Book value per share ($)	7.6%	10.02	10.89	11.68	12.51	13.79	13.39	14.47	16.63	17.42	19.42
Employees	1.6%	64,000	62,800	68,700	70,800	72,600	73,700	69,500	69,400	71,600	73,900

1994 Year-end:
Debt ratio: 21.7%
Return on equity: 21.9%
Cash (mil.): $113
Current ratio: 1.28
Long-term debt (mil.): $280
No. of shares (mil.): 224
Dividends
  Yield: 2.5%
  Payout: 38.6%
Market value (mil.): $13,947

Stock Price History
High/Low 1985–94

ENRON CORP.

Houston-based Enron is North America's #1 buyer and seller of natural gas and has a vision of becoming the world's #1 natural gas provider. To accomplish this ambitious task, the company is organized into 5 major subsidiaries. Enron Operations handles about 15% of the natural gas consumed in the US and 4% of the natural gas liquids. It builds and manages worldwide natural gas transportation, power generation, liquids, and clean fuels facilities.

Enron Capital & Trade Resources manages the world's largest portfolio of natural gas–related risk management contracts (futures and swaps) and is the leading supplier of natural gas to the US electric generation industry.

Enron Development and Enron Global Power & Pipelines build and operate power plants and pipelines in such emerging-market economies as China, Guatemala, and the Philippines. The company also operates a natural gas pipeline in Argentina and has signed a deal with Russia's Gazprom to help the state-owned company market gas in Europe. Enron Oil and Gas (80%-owned) is one of the world's largest independent oil and gas exploration companies.

The company currently owns energy facilities in 15 countries and is developing power projects in another 15. Enron employees own approximately 14% of the company.

Enron traces its history through 2 well-established natural gas companies — InterNorth and Houston Natural Gas (HNG).

InterNorth started out in 1930 as Northern Natural Gas, an Omaha, Nebraska, gas pipeline company. By 1950 Northern had doubled its capacity and in 1960 it started processing and transporting natural gas liquids. The company changed its name to InterNorth in 1980. In 1983 it spent $768 million to buy Belco Petroleum, adding 821 billion cubic feet of natural gas and 67 million barrels of oil to its reserves. At the same time the company (with 4 partners) was building the Northern Border Pipeline to link Canadian fields with US markets.

HNG, formed in 1925 as a South Texas natural gas distributor, served more than 55,000 customers by the early 1940s. It started developing oil and gas properties in 1953 and bought Houston Pipe Line Company in 1956. Other major acquisitions included Valley Gas Production, a South Texas natural gas company (1963), and Houston's Bammel Gas Storage Field (1965). In the 1970s the company started developing offshore fields in the Gulf of Mexico, and in 1976 it sold its original gas distribution properties to Entex. In 1984 HNG, faced with a hostile takeover attempt by Coastal Corporation, brought in former Exxon executive Kenneth Lay as CEO. Lay refocused the company on natural gas, selling $632 million worth of unrelated assets. He added Transwestern Pipeline (California) and Florida Gas Transmission, and by 1985 the firm operated the only transcontinental gas pipeline.

In 1985 InterNorth bought HNG for $2.4 billion, creating the US's largest natural gas pipeline system (38,000 miles). Soon after,

Lay became chairman/CEO of newly named Enron (1986), and the company moved its headquarters from Omaha to Houston. Laden with $3.3 billion of debt (most related to the HNG acquisition), Enron sold 50% of Citrus Corporation (owner of Florida Gas Transmission, 1986), 50% of Enron Cogeneration (1988), and 16% of Enron Oil & Gas (1989).

In 1990 the company bought CSX Energy's Louisiana production facilities, which helped to increase Enron's production of natural gas liquids by nearly 33%. In 1991 Enron closed a deal with Tenneco to buy that company's natural gas liquids/petrochemical operations for $632 million.

In 1992 Enron signed a contract with Sithe Energies Group to supply $4 billion worth of natural gas over 20 years to a planned upstate New York cogeneration plant. Also in 1992 Enron and 3 partners acquired a 70% interest in the 3,800-mile Transportadora de Gas del Sur pipeline in Argentina. Enron acquired the Louisiana Resources Company and several other gas businesses, including a 540-mile pipeline, from the Williams Companies for $170 million in 1993.

In 1994 Enron renamed its gas services subsidiary Enron Capital & Trade Resources. Also in 1994 Enron completed a $90 million extension of the Argentinian natural gas pipeline, and in 1995 the $1 billion, 815-mile expansion of the Florida Gas Transmission pipeline was completed, linking the Mobile Bay production field to key consumer markets in southwest Florida. A state government in India in 1995 terminated an Enron-backed, $2.8 billion power plant project already under construction, deeming it too expensive.

WHO

Chairman and CEO: Kenneth L. Lay, age 52, $2,190,000 pay
VC: John A. Urquhart, age 66
President and COO: Richard D. Kinder, age 50, $1,500,044 pay
Managing Director, North American Operations, Enron Capital & Trade Resources: Ronald J. Burns, age 41, $821,000 pay
EVP and Chief of Staff: Edmund P. Segner III, age 41, $650,000 pay
Managing Director, International Operations, Enron Capital & Trade Resources: Rodney L. Gray, age 42, $638,000 pay
SVP and General Counsel: James V. Derrick Jr., age 50
SVP Government Affairs and Public Policy: Terence H. Thorn
SVP Chief Information, Administrative, and Accounting Officer: Jack I. Tomkins, age 45
President, Enron Services Corp.: James G. Barnhart
VP Finance and Treasurer: Kurt S. Huneke, age 41
VP Human Resources: Philip J. Bazelides
Auditors: Arthur Andersen & Co, SC

WHERE

HQ: 1400 Smith St., Houston, TX 77002-7369
Phone: 713-853-6161
Fax: 713-853-3129

Enron operates natural gas pipelines in North and South America and operates energy projects worldwide.

	1994 Sales		1994 Operating Income	
	$ mil.	% of total	$ mil.	% of total
US	7,604	85	609	85
Other countries	1,380	15	107	15
Total	**8,984**	**100**	**716**	**100**

WHAT

	1994 Sales		1994 Operating Income	
	$ mil.	% of total	$ mil.	% of total
Domestic gas & power services	7,166	81	164	22
Trans. & operation	938	10	327	43
International gas & power services	392	4	72	9
Exploration & prod.	488	5	195	26
Adjustments	—	—	(42)	—
Total	**8,984**	**100**	**716**	**100**

Gas Services
Intrastate natural gas pipelines
Natural gas–fired power plants (North America)
Price risk management and financing arrangements
Purchasing and marketing of natural gas, natural gas liquids (NGLs), and power

Transportation and Operation
Crude oil transportation
Natural gas liquid plant and power facility construction, management, and operation

Natural gas transmission
Pipeline construction, management, and operation

International Gas and Power Services
Natural gas liquids marketing
Power plant, NGL facility, and pipeline development (outside North America)

Exploration and Production
Natural gas and crude oil exploration and production

Gas Processing
NGL extraction (North America)

KEY COMPETITORS

British Gas	Natural Gas Pipeline	Sonat
Coastal	NOVA	Tejas Gas
Columbia Gas	Occidental	Tenneco
Gaz de France	Panhandle Eastern	USX–Delhi
Koch	Phillips Petroleum	Valero Energy

HOW MUCH

	9-Year Growth	1985	1986	1987	1988	1989	1990	1991	1992	1993	1994
Sales ($ mil.)	(0.6%)	9,458	7,453	5,916	5,708	9,836	13,165	13,520	6,325	7,972	8,984
Net income ($ mil.)	—	(128)	29	(39)	73	201	177	217	284	316	438
Income as % of sales	—	—	0.4%	—	1.3%	2.0%	1.3%	1.6%	4.5%	4.0%	4.9%
Earnings per share ($)	—	(2.89)	0.66	(0.86)	1.54	3.85	3.44	2.04	2.42	1.25	1.70
Stock price – high ($)	—	13.66	12.66	13.38	10.75	15.25	15.69	19.22	25.06	37.00	34.63
Stock price – low ($)	—	9.75	8.44	7.75	8.72	8.88	12.56	12.41	15.31	22.19	26.75
Stock price – close ($)	11.7%	11.25	9.88	9.78	9.16	14.41	13.69	17.50	23.19	29.00	30.50
P/E – high	—	—	19	—	7	4	5	9	10	30	20
P/E – low	—	—	13	—	6	2	4	6	6	18	16
Dividends per share ($)	2.3%	0.62	0.62	0.62	0.62	0.62	0.62	0.63	0.67	0.71	0.76
Book value per share ($)	5.0%	7.01	5.46	5.02	7.39	7.69	8.02	8.43	9.97	9.93	10.89
Employees	(5.8%)	11,911	7,200	6,900	6,895	6,900	6,962	7,400	7,780	7,100	6,978

1994 Year-end:
Debt ratio: 49.3%
Return on equity: 16.8%
Cash (mil.): $132
Current ratio: 0.83
Long-term debt (mil.): $2,805
No. of shares (mil.): 252
Dividends
  Yield: 2.5%
  Payout: 44.7%
Market value (mil.): $7,676

Stock Price History
High/Low 1985–94

ENTERGY CORPORATION

OVERVIEW

Entergy is one of the nation's largest publicly owned utility holding companies and the #1 electricity supplier in the middle South. The New Orleans–based company provides electricity to about 2.4 million customers. Entergy operates through 5 utilities: Arkansas Power & Light (AP&L), Louisiana Power & Light (LP&L), Mississippi Power & Light (MP&L), New Orleans Public Service Inc. (NOPSI), and Gulf States Utilities (GSU).

Other subsidiaries include Entergy Systems and Services (energy conservation products and services) and Entergy Operations (management of the company's 4 nuclear power plants, which provide about 30% of Entergy's electricity).

Although Entergy's sales got a major power surge from the company's 1993 acquisition of GSU, its profits have dropped, partly due to merger costs, but also because of $183 million in rate reductions mandated by the regulators of the company's various service areas.

Entergy is focusing on cutting costs and improving customer service to compete more effectively in a deregulated power industry. The company is also expanding its independent power business, conducted through its Entergy Power subsidiary. The company plans to spend about $150 million annually on expanding its business, including overseas power projects, with an eye on China, Indonesia, Brazil, and Australia.

WHEN

Little Rock–based AP&L, founded in 1913, consolidated operations with Arkansas Central Power, Arkansas Light & Power, and Pine Company in 1926. That year NOPSI (founded in New Orleans in 1922) merged with 2 of the city's other electric companies (Citizens Light & Power and Consumers Electric Light & Power). LP&L, another New Orleans utility, was founded in 1927 to acquire the assets of 6 Louisiana electric companies. MP&L was also formed in 1927, through the consolidation of 3 Mississippi power companies.

AP&L, LP&L, MP&L, NOPSI, and other utilities were consolidated under a Maine holding company, Electric Power and Light (formed in 1925). That company was dissolved in 1949, and a new holding company, Middle South Utilities, emerged to take over the assets of AP&L, LP&L, MP&L, and NOPSI.

Floyd Lewis, a Middle South employee since 1949, became president in 1970. In 1971 the company bought Arkansas-Missouri Power Company and its affiliate, Associated Natural Gas (both were consolidated with AP&L in 1981). In 1974 Middle South brought its first nuclear plant on-line (near Russellville, Arkansas) and formed Middle South Energy (later System Energy Resources) to finance and construct units 1 and 2 of another nuclear facility (Grand Gulf). Unfortunately, Grand Gulf 1 was completed 6 years behind schedule (in 1985) at a cost of $3.8 billion. When Middle South tried to pass costs related to the plant's construction on to its customers, lawsuits and rate disputes with state regulators ensued. Construction of Grand Gulf 2 was halted, and, as the controversy raged, Lewis retired in 1985. Only 2 years after his replacement, CFO Edwin Lupberger,

took over, losses related to the unsettled rate issues took Middle South to the brink of bankruptcy.

With Lupberger's guidance the company moved to settle the disputes by absorbing a $900 million loss on its $926 million investment in Grand Gulf 2 in 1989. Then, to distance itself from the controversy, it adopted the name Entergy Corporation. It formed 2 new subsidiaries in 1990: Entergy Operations (to streamline operation of its nuclear plants) and Entergy Power (to take advantage of the wholesale electricity market).

In 1991 NOPSI and the City of New Orleans settled a dispute related to rate increases stemming from NOPSI's $135 million Grand Gulf 1 costs. Under the agreement NOPSI was allowed to reinstate $90 million in construction expenses as a deferred cost. Also in 1991 Entergy began a restructuring effort in which it streamlined operations along functional lines. At that time, Entergy began to pool its excess generating capacity to sell to other parts of the country. The company bought 10% of First Pacific Networks (electric service devices), its first acquisition of a nonregulated business, in 1991.

In 1993 a consortium including Entergy acquired a 51% interest in an electric company providing service to Buenos Aires, and in 1994 Entergy Power Asia signed a deal to build 4 coal-fired power plants in Datong, China.

Entergy Power Development bought a 20% interest in the 695-megawatt Dabhol Power Plant (under construction in Maharashtra, India) from Enron Development in 1995. However, later that year an Indian state government announced it was halting the project.

WHO

Chairman and CEO: Edwin Lupberger, age 58,
$900,328 pay
President and COO: Jerry L. Maulden, age 58,
$562,096 pay
EVP and Chief Nuclear Officer: Donald C. Hintz, age 52,
$463,518 pay
EVP Marketing and External Affairs: Jerry D. Jackson,
age 50, $429,866 pay
SVP and CFO: Gerald D. McInvale, age 51, $310,392 pay
SVP, Chief Legal Officer, and Secretary: Michael G.
Thompson, age 54
VP Federal Governmental Affairs: S. M. Henry
Brown Jr., age 56
VP Corporate Communications and Public Relations:
Charles L. Kelly, age 58
VP and Chief Accounting Officer: Lee W. Randall,
age 46
Manager Employee Relations: Joseph Hotard
Auditors: Coopers & Lybrand L.L.P.

WHERE

HQ: 639 Loyola Ave., New Orleans, LA 70113
Phone: 504-529-5262
Fax: 504-569-4265

Entergy provides electric service in Arkansas, Louisiana,
Mississippi, and Texas.

	1994 Electric Customers	
	No.	% of total
Louisiana Power & Light	607,002	26
Arkansas Power & Light	599,702	25
Gulf States Utilities Company	595,348	25
Mississippi Power & Light	367,692	16
New Orleans Public Service	189,836	8
Total	**2,359,580**	**100**

WHAT

	1994 Sales	
	$ mil.	% of total
Electricity		
Residential	2,126	35
Industrial	1,833	30
Commercial	1,499	24
Sales for resale	311	5
Governmental	160	3
Natural gas	119	2
Steam products	47	1
Other	(132)	—
Total	**5,963**	**100**

Utility Companies
Arkansas Power & Light Company
Gulf States Utilities Company
Louisiana Power & Light Company
Mississippi Power & Light Company
New Orleans Public Service Inc.

Other Subsidiaries
Entergy Argentina, S.A. (10%, consortium that owns
51% of electric distribution company that provides
service to Buenos Aires)
Entergy Enterprises, Inc. (nonutility operations)
Entergy Operations, Inc. (nuclear plant management)
Entergy Power, Inc. (produces and wholesales
electricity)
Entergy Services, Inc. (technical support)
Entergy Systems and Service, Inc. (energy management
services)
System Energy Resources, Inc. (owns 90% of Grand Gulf
Nuclear Station)

KEY COMPETITORS

AES	FPL	Pacific Gas and
Destec Energy	General Electric	Electric
Duke Power	NIPSCO Industries	SCEcorp
	Pacific Enterprises	Westinghouse

HOW MUCH

	9-Year Growth	1985	1986	1987	1988	1989	1990	1991	1992	1993	1994
Sales ($ mil.)	7.0%	3,239	3,486	3,454	3,565	3,724	3,982	4,051	4,117	4,485	5,963
Net income ($ mil.)	(1.8%)	401	451	357	411	(473)	478	482	438	458	342
Income as % of sales	—	12.4%	12.9%	10.3%	11.5%	—	12.0%	11.9%	10.6%	10.2%	5.7%
Earnings per share ($)	(3.3%)	2.01	2.21	1.74	2.01	(2.31)	2.44	2.64	2.48	2.62	1.49
Stock price – high ($)	—	15.25	15.00	16.25	16.13	23.25	23.63	29.88	33.63	39.88	37.38
Stock price – low ($)	—	8.13	10.50	7.75	8.50	15.50	18.00	21.88	26.13	32.50	21.25
Stock price – close ($)	8.4%	10.63	13.13	8.25	16.00	23.25	22.38	29.63	33.00	36.00	21.88
P/E – high	—	8	7	9	8	—	10	11	14	15	25
P/E – low	—	4	5	5	4	—	7	8	11	12	14
Dividends per share ($)	3.3%	1.34	0.00	0.00	0.20	0.90	1.05	1.25	1.45	1.65	1.80
Book value per share ($)	4.3%	19.10	21.28	22.13	23.96	20.68	22.34	23.53	24.43	28.27	27.93
Employees	1.8%	13,650	13,650	13,750	13,136	13,190	13,379	12,763	12,457	16,679	16,037

1994 Year-end:
Debt ratio: 55.4%
Return on equity: 5.3%
Cash (mil.): $614
Current ratio: 1.09
Long-term debt (mil.): $7,367
No. of shares (mil.): 227
Dividends
Yield: 8.2%
Payout: 120.8%
Market value (mil.): $4,975

**Stock Price History
High/Low 1985–94**

EQUIFAX INC.

OVERVIEW

Don't play *I've Got a Secret* with Equifax. It already knows. And it's passed your secrets on to the bank, the credit card company, the auto dealer, and the insurance company that you hope to do business with.

Atlanta-based Equifax is the US's largest credit reporting agency. It has compiled financial and other data on more than 119 million people in the US and has recently begun moving overseas, primarily through the purchase of interests in local credit agencies. But for now, the majority of the company's non-US earnings come from Canada because the record-keeping infrastructure required for

Equifax's operations does not exist in much of the world.

Because the sale of credit data is cyclical, falling during recessions, the company is turning increasingly to the insurance and health care records fields, compiling data that are used to underwrite property/casualty and health insurance policies. It is also a major credit card transaction processor.

The power that Equifax (and other credit reporting companies) has over people's lives has aroused the suspicions of consumer advocates, particularly now that it is branching into health and medical data.

WHEN

Brothers Cator and Guy Woolford started Retail Credit Company in Atlanta in 1899. They compiled consumer credit records of local residents into their *Merchants Guide*, which they sold to retailers for $25 a year.

In 1901 the brothers extended their services to the insurance industry, providing background investigations on insurance applicants. The company grew steadily and by 1920 had offices across the US and Canada.

In 1937 the company grouped its many credit reporting agencies into Credit Bureau, which is still its primary consumer credit reporting subsidiary. After several decades of quiet growth, Retail Credit found itself branching into other information sectors through internal diversification and acquisitions, most of which were small, regional concerns.

The company came under scrutiny in 1973, when the FTC filed an antimonopoly suit against its consumer credit division and a complaint against its investigative practices (Retail Credit maintained a small army of field investigators who probed into people's backgrounds). The suit was eventually dropped in 1982. The company changed its name to Equifax (which means "equitability in the gathering and presentation of facts") in 1976.

In the 1980s and 1990s, Equifax continued to acquire small businesses in the US and Europe. The company benefited from the blossoming of the Information Age, finding a growing list of businesses (such as direct mail marketers) clamoring for its services. By the end of the decade, Equifax had passed TRW as the world's largest provider of consumer information. In 1990 it acquired Telecredit, a check and credit card processing company.

Growth did not exempt Equifax from the consumer backlash that began in the late

1980s. Under C. B. Rogers, former IBM executive who became Equifax's president in 1987, the company became more receptive to consumer concerns. As a result the company scrapped Marketplace, a 1991 joint venture with Lotus Development to compile a database of the shopping habits of 100 million Americans, and discontinued the sale of lists to direct marketers. The company does, however, offer marketing databases in Europe.

During the early 1990s Equifax continued to grow, acquiring regional credit and collections firms in Georgia, Florida, and Texas. The company restructured in 1992, merging its US and Canadian operations, cutting the number of field offices, updating some of its automated services, and expanding its international operations. In 1992 and 1993 it settled cases with several states arising from intrusive and inaccurate credit and job reference reports. In 1993 California terminated its lottery gaming system contract with Equifax subsidiary HISI, charging that HISI failed to meet standards. Equifax filed a cross-complaint. The matter was still pending in 1995.

In 1993 Equifax contracted its data processing operation to an IBM subsidiary, a move aimed at reducing the company's capital spending. The company also joined with Dun & Bradstreet Information Services to offer a credit rating system for small businesses to D&B subscribers.

Equifax has continued to slice and dice its information to create "economic value added" products for new clients. It is also growing through acquisitions, making 14 in 1994 and gaining new operations in South America, Europe, Australia, and New Zealand. The company is also developing a variety of paperless record-keeping products.

NYSE symbol: EFX
Fiscal year ends: December 31

WHO

Chairman and CEO: C. B. Rogers Jr., age 65, $522,696 pay
President and COO: D. W. McGlaughlin, age 58, $546,805 pay
EVP and Group Executive, Financial Information Services: Thomas F. Chapman, age 51, $395,318 pay
EVP: D. V. Smith, age 40, $354,434 pay
EVP; Chairman and CEO Equifax Canada: J. C. Chartrand, age 60
SVP (Human Resources): Donald F. Walsh, age 62, $322,367 pay
SVP and CFO: D. U. Hallman, age 53
Corporate VP, General Counsel, and Secretary: T. H. Magis, age 54
Corporate VP and Treasurer: R. F. Haygood, age 47
VP Investor Relations: Marietta E. Zakas
Auditors: Arthur Andersen & Co, SC

WHERE

HQ: PO Box 4081, 1600 Peachtree St. NW, Atlanta, GA 30302
Phone: 404-885-8000
Fax: 404-888-5043

Equifax operates in Australia, Canada, the Caribbean, Europe, Latin America, and the US.

	1994 Sales		1994 Operating Income	
	$ mil.	% of total	$ mil.	% of total
US	1,277	90	228	94
Canada	78	5	16	6
Europe	67	5	(1)	—
Total	**1,422**	**100**	**243**	**100**

WHAT

	1994 Sales		1994 Operating Income	
	$ mil.	% of total	$ mil.	% of total
Credit information	446	32	147	60
Insurance info.	453	32	19	7
Payment svcs.	247	17	57	23
General info. svcs.	133	9	4	2
International ops.	143	10	16	8
Total	**1,422**	**100**	**243**	**100**

Major Business Segments

Financial Information Services Group
Card Svcs.
Check Svcs.
Credit Reporting Svcs.
Decision Svcs.
FBS Software
Mortgage Information Svcs.
Risk Management Svcs.

Insurance Information Services Group
Commercial Specialists
CUE UK
Data Svcs.
Field Svcs.
Osborn Laboratories
Programming Resources Co.

General Information Services Group
Administrative Svcs.
Database Svcs.
EDI Svcs.
Elrick & Lavidge (marketing svcs.)
Government and Special Systems
Market Development Svcs.
National Decision Systems
Patient Satisfaction Svcs.
Quick Test

International Operations Group
AN POST (Ireland)
ASNEF/Equifax (Spain)
DICOM (Chile)
Organizacion Veraz (Argentina)
Telecredit Canada
Transax (intl.)

KEY COMPETITORS

ADP
American Claims Evaluation
Casino & Credit Services
Ceridian
Fair, Isaac
First Data
Hyatt
TRW
Wright Express

HOW MUCH

	9-Year Growth	1985	1986	1987	1988	1989	1990	1991	1992	1993	1994
Sales ($ mil.)	10.8%	564	635	670	743	840	1,079	1,094	1,134	1,217	1,422
Net income ($ mil.)	23.3%	18	26	31	34	36	64	54	85	64	120
Income as % of sales	—	3.2%	4.0%	4.6%	4.6%	4.2%	5.9%	4.9%	7.5%	5.3%	8.5%
Earnings per share ($)	15.9%	0.43	0.60	0.72	0.74	0.73	0.79	0.66	1.04	0.85	1.62
Stock price – high ($)	—	10.13	14.25	15.75	16.44	20.00	22.38	21.13	20.63	27.38	30.50
Stock price – low ($)	—	5.31	9.50	8.75	12.19	13.00	13.50	13.38	14.38	17.38	21.88
Stock price – close ($)	11.5%	9.91	10.94	13.88	13.56	16.00	16.25	15.88	20.63	27.38	26.38
P/E – high	—	24	24	22	22	27	28	32	20	32	19
P/E – low	—	12	16	12	17	18	17	20	14	20	14
Dividends per share ($)	8.6%	0.29	0.32	0.35	0.39	0.54	0.48	0.52	0.52	0.56	0.61
Book value per share ($)	8.8%	2.23	2.55	2.93	4.60	5.03	4.60	4.26	3.40	3.40	4.77
Employees	3.2%	10,667	11,082	10,767	13,500	13,900	14,200	13,400	12,400	12,800	14,200

1994 Year-end:
Debt ratio: 43.2%
Return on equity: 39.1%
Cash (mil.): $79
Current ratio: 1.25
Long-term debt (mil.): $212
No. of shares (mil.): 76
Dividends
  Yield: 2.3%
  Payout: 37.7%
Market value (mil.): $2,002

Stock Price History
High/Low 1985–94

THE EQUITABLE COMPANIES INC.

OVERVIEW

At Equitable, *on parle français*. Because in 1995 French insurance giant Axa exercised its prerogative to convert its preferred stock to common, thus raising its equity stake in the New York–based insurer to 60%.

Axa's $1 billion 1991 investment was responsible for Equitable's Lazarus-like rise from moribund mutual company to profitable public company, and Equitable's new status makes it a partner in Axa's global empire.

Spearheading the company's rise to profitability since its 1992 demutualization has been Equitable Life Assurance Co. Focusing on the retirement and investment needs of baby boomers, the subsidiary has offered investment and annuity products that have reinvigo-

rated Equitable's insurance operations. These products fit well with the company's other operations, which include Alliance Capital Management (mutual funds and cash management, in addition to institutional services) and Donaldson, Lufkin & Jenrette, Equitable's brokerage and investment banking subsidiary (which in 1995, for the first time in years, did not outperform insurance.)

Most of the company's 7,800 insurance agents are also licensed stockbrokers, making them qualified to sell the full range of Equitable's products. The company is also a major manager and developer of commercial real estate (another bright spot after years of poor performance).

WHEN

As a student in Catskill, New York, Henry Hyde was advised by his teacher, General John Johnston (founder of Northwestern Mutual Life Insurance Co. in 1857), to go into life insurance. Hyde joined Mutual Life of New York and left in 1859 at age 25 to found the Equitable Life Assurance Society in New York, a joint stock company named after the Equitable Life Assurance Society of London.

Business boomed during the Civil War, and Equitable expanded to Asia, Europe, South America, and the Middle East. It grew faster than the insurance industry overall and by 1899 was the world's first company to have $1 billion of life insurance in force.

Revelations in 1905 about the company's financial condition led to the resignation of management and, in 1917, its conversion to a mutual company. It was the first company to write group insurance (Montgomery Ward, 1911) and to develop a method for apportioning dividends within a particular group, which was adopted by others in the industry.

After the boom of the 1920s, Equitable weathered the Depression and WWII. It continued to grow in the postwar boom.

The 1970s saw diversification into computers, mining, and real estate. Equitable also pioneered guaranteed investment contracts (GICs) — retirement plans that guaranteed principal and returns of up to 18% and allowed contributions for the life of the contract. This forced the company to pay inflationary rates even after interest rates fell in the 1980s. To cover the difference, the company invested in risky, high-yield junk bonds and real estate. Diversification continued with the acquisition of Donaldson, Lufkin &

Jenrette and the formation of an HMO (Equicor, with Hospital Corp. of America, 1986; sold 1990). When the mid-1980s boom faded in the late 1980s, the company was left with $15 billion in GIC obligations.

In a total management change in May 1990, Richard Jenrette became CEO and began cutting costs, seeking new capital, and investing in new areas. Equitable formed COMPASS (property leasing and management), acquired an interest in Europolis (European property markets), and expanded Capital Management (now owned by subsidiary Alliance Capital Management) to London and Tokyo. By 1991 GIC obligations were down to $10 billion (they were further reduced to under $3 billion in 1993, and by 1994 were less than $2 billion). Yet rumors of Equitable's demise brought a run of policy redemptions, further increasing the need for cash. As a mutual it had no way to raise capital, so Jenrette took it public in 1992.

Since then, cost cutting and an economic upturn have helped turn the tide. But a little asset shuffling hasn't hurt either. In 1993 the parent company capitalized the Life Assurance unit by buying 61% of Donaldson, Lufkin & Jenrette from it, and in 1994 the corporation improved its asset quality by selling (through Alliance) $700 million of collateralized below–investment grade bonds, some of which the company then repurchased.

The Axa transaction improved Equitable's balance sheet, and the company continues to seek ways to improve its financial condition, including continued cost cutting, the sale of assets like shopping malls, and even the announcement in 1995 that it was considering selling Donaldson, Lufkin & Jenrette.

NYSE symbol: EQ
Fiscal year ends: December 31

WHO

Chairman and CEO: Richard H. Jenrette, age 65, $7,730,000 pay
President and COO: Joseph J. Melone, age 62, $2,600,000 pay
SEVP: James M. Benson, age 48, $2,000,000 pay
EVP and CFO: Jerry M. de St. Paer, age 53, $1,350,000 pay
EVP and Chief Administrative Officer: William T. McCaffrey, age 58, $1,025,000 pay
EVP and Chief Investment Officer: Brian S. O'Neil, age 42
EVP and General Counsel: Robert E. Garber, age 45
EVP and Chief Agency Officer: José S. Suquet
SVP and Chief Information Officer: Leon B. Billis
SVP and Chief Marketing Officer: Michael E. Fisher
SVP and Chief Compliance Officer: Richard V. Silver
President, Income Management Group: Jerome Golden
President and CEO, Donaldson, Lufkin & Jenrette: John S. Chalsty
Chairman and CEO, Equitable Real Estate Investment Management: George R. Puskar
Chairman and CEO, Alliance Capital Management: Dave H. Williams
VP Human Resources: Janet Friedman
Auditors: Price Waterhouse LLP

WHERE

HQ: The Equitable Companies Incorporated, 787 Seventh Ave., New York, NY 10019
Phone: 212-554-1234
Fax: 212-315-2825

The Equitable operates throughout the US.

WHAT

	1994 Assets	
	$ mil.	% of total
Cash & equivalents	1,268	1
Corporate bonds	10,349	11
Trading accounts	8,970	9
Other securities	13,321	14
Mortgage loans & real estate	10,078	11
Broker-dealer receivables	13,982	15
Separate accounts	20,470	22
Other	16,202	17
Total	**94,640**	**100**

	1994 Sales		1994 Pretax income	
	$ mil.	% of total	$ mil.	% of total
Individual ins. & annuities	3,111	48	246	43
Investment svcs.	2,908	45	307	54
Group pension	359	5	16	3
Other	111	2	(85)	—
Adjustments	(42)	—	(2)	—
Total	**6,447**	**100**	**482**	**100**

Selected Subsidiaries
Alliance Capital Management L.P. (60%)
Donaldson, Lufkin & Jenrette, Inc.
The Equitable Life Assurance Society of the United States
Equitable Real Estate Investment Management, Inc.
The Equitable Variable Life Insurance Co. (EVLICO)

KEY COMPETITORS

Aetna	Goldman Sachs	Paine Webber
Allstate	JMB Realty	Prudential
Charles Schwab	John Hancock	Salomon
Chubb	Merrill Lynch	State Farm
CIGNA	MetLife	T. Rowe Price
Dean Witter, Discover	New York Life	Transamerica
	Northwestern	Travelers
FMR	Mutual	USF&G

HOW MUCH

	Annual Growth	1985	1986	1987	1988	1989	1990	1991	1992	1993	1994
Assets ($ mil.)	7.1%	51,168	54,577	56,794	60,934	68,574	69,789	74,918	78,869	98,991	94,640
Net income ($ mil.)	9.2%	—	—	—	144	132	(454)	(898)	(148)	169	244
Income as % of sales	—	—	—	—	0.2%	0.2%	—	—	—	0.2%	0.3%
Earnings per share ($)	—	—	—	—	—	—	—	—	(0.08)	1.09	1.38
Stock price – high ($)	—	—	—	—	—	—	—	—	14.38	31.50	30.00
Stock price – low ($)	—	—	—	—	—	—	—	—	7.13	13.38	16.75
Stock price – close ($)	13.8%	—	—	—	—	—	—	—	14.00	27.00	18.13
P/E – high	—	—	—	—	—	—	—	—	—	29	20
P/E – low	—	—	—	—	—	—	—	—	—	12	11
Dividends per share ($)	41.4%	—	—	—	—	—	—	—	0.10	0.20	0.20
Book value per share ($)	(1.1%)	—	—	—	—	—	—	—	14.51	15.78	14.20
Employees	5.2%	—	—	—	—	—	—	—	12,300	13,100	13,600

1994 Year-end:
Equity as % of assets: 2.8%
Return on assets: 0.3%
Return on equity: 10.0%
Long-term debt (mil.): $2,926
No. of shares (mil.): 184
Dividends
 Yield: 1.1%
 Payout: 13.1%
Market value (mil.): $3,330
Sales (mil.): $6,447

Stock Price History
High/Low 1992–94

35
30
25
20
15
10
5
0

ERNST & YOUNG LLP

OVERVIEW

Ernst & Young, one of the Big 6 accounting firms, has an image problem. It doesn't really have an image. One contributing factor has been the long period of consolidation after its 1989 merger. In 1995, Ernst & Young was still closing offices and reassigning people to streamline its operations. The firm has used this process to upgrade its internal communications; it has been integrating its systems to achieve worldwide access to its data.

Like its competitors, Ernst & Young offers accounting and auditing services as well as management, regulatory, human resources services consulting, and other services. Accounting firms have been jolted by the ten-dency to blame auditors for the performance of their clients (in 1992 Ernst & Young paid $400 million to settle claims arising from the S&L debacle). So they have diversified into consulting. But there are perils there, too. In 1995 Ernst & Young was hit with a $42 million judgment relating to its actions as a litigation loss consultant in a California case.

In 1995 the firm took a step to help differentiate it from its competitors, merging with Kenneth Leventhal & Co., a real estate consulting firm. The resulting unit, Ernst & Young Kenneth Leventhal Real Estate Group, will make Ernst & Young one of the preeminent real estate consultancies in the US.

WHEN

While the 1494 publication in Venice of Luca Pacioli's *Summa di Arithmetica* — the first published work dealing with double-entry bookkeeping — boosted the accounting profession, it wasn't until well after the Industrial Revolution in England that accountants developed their craft.

Frederick Whinney joined the UK firm of Harding & Pullein in 1849. R. P. Harding reputedly had been a hat maker whose business ended up in court. The ledgers he produced were so well kept that an official advised him to take up accounting, which was a growth field as stock companies proliferated.

Whinney's name was added to the firm in 1859, and later his sons also became partners. The firm's name changed to Whinney, Smith & Whinney in 1894. The name became the longest-lived of the firm's many incarnations, not yielding until 1965.

After WWII, Whinney, Smith & Whinney formed an alliance with the American firm of Ernst & Ernst. Ernst & Ernst had been founded in Cleveland in 1903 by brothers Alwin and Theodore Ernst. The alliance, which recognized that the accountants' business clients were getting larger and more international in orientation, provided that each firm would operate in the other's behalf within their respective markets.

In 1965 the Whinney firm merged with Brown, Fleming & Murray to become Whinney Murray. The merger also included the fledgling computer department — the harbinger of electronic accounting systems — set up by Brown, Fleming & Murray to serve British Petroleum. Whinney Murray also formed joint ventures with other accounting firms to provide consulting services.

In 1979 Whinney Murray and Turquands Barton Mayhew — itself the product of a merger that began with a cricket match — united with Ernst & Ernst to form Ernst & Whinney, a firm with an international scope.

Ernst & Whinney, a merger melting pot, wasn't finished with its combinations. Having grown to the world's 4th largest accounting firm by 1989, it merged with the 5th largest, Arthur Young. Arthur Young had taken its name from the Scottish immigrant who had founded a partnership with C. U. Stuart in Chicago in 1894. When Stuart withdrew, Young took brother Stanley as a partner. Arthur Young — the firm — was long known as the "old reliable" of the accounting giants. In 1984 the spotlight shone on it as vice-presidential candidate Geraldine Ferraro chose the firm to sort out her tax troubles.

The new firm of Ernst & Young faced a rocky start. At the end of 1990, it was forced to defend itself from rumors of collapse. In 1991 it pared back the payroll, thinning the ranks of partners and others. That same year it agreed to pay the RTC $41 million to settle claims stemming from its involvement with Charles Keating's Lincoln Savings and Loan.

The next year Ernst & Young agreed to pay $400 million for allegedly mishandling the audits of 4 failed S&Ls. In early 1994 a federal judge in Rhode Island ordered Ernst & Young and the state to settle a suit arising from the collapse of the state's credit union system.

In 1994, after these setbacks, Ernst & Young slashed its legal staff by half and replaced its head, Carl Riggio, with Kathryn Oberly. Riggio had built up the department and preferred to fight cases to the end rather than settle with opponents.

International partnership
Fiscal year ends: September 30

WHO

Chairman: Philip A. Laskawy
Co-chairman: William L. Kimsey
CEO, International: Michael A. Henning
VC Finance and Administration: Hilton Dean
VC Human Resources: Bruce J. Mantia
General Counsel: Kathryn A. Oberly

WHERE

HQ: 787 Park Ave., New York, NY 10019
Phone: 212-773-3000
Fax: 212-773-1996

Ernst & Young maintains more than 600 offices in over 100 countries.

	1994 Sales	
	$ mil.	% of total
US	2,540	42
Other countries	3,480	58
Total	**6,020**	**100**

WHAT

	1994 US Sales
	% of total
Accounting & auditing	48
Tax	21
Management consulting	31
Total	**100**

Representative Clients

Apple Computer	McDonald's
BankAmerica	Mobil
Coca-Cola	The Reference Press
Eli Lilly	Time Warner
Hanson	USF&G
Knight-Ridder	Wal-Mart
Martin Marietta	

US Services

Accounting and auditing services	Insurance actuarial services
Capital markets services	Insurance regulatory services
Cash management services	
Continuous improvement	Internal audit functions
Corporate finance services	International services
Corporate real estate advisory services	International tax compliance and consulting services
Corporate tax functions	Investment services
Environmental consulting	Litigation services
Federal and state regulatory risk management	Management consulting
	Organization alignment
Financial and accounting systems	Organizational change management
Financial products services	Outsourcing services
Focused process improvement	Performance measurement
Government relations and contract services	Personal financial counseling
Health care consulting	Regulatory and related services
Health care legislative services	
	Relocation services
Human resources services Actuarial, benefits, and compensation consulting Expatriate tax services	Restructuring and reorganization services
	Special services
	Tax policy and legislative services
Industry services	Tax services
Information technology services	Valuation services

KEY COMPETITORS

Arthur Andersen
Bain & Co.
Booz, Allen
Coopers & Lybrand
Deloitte & Touche
Electronic Data Systems
H&R Block
Hewitt
KPMG
Marsh & McLennan
McKinsey & Co.
Price Waterhouse

HOW MUCH

	Annual Growth	1985	1986	1987	1988	1989	1990	1991	1992	1993	1994
Sales ($ mil.)	11.0%	2,345	2,919	3,480	4,244	4,200	5,006	5,406	5,701	5,839	6,020
Arthur Young	—	1,160	1,427	1,702	2,053	—	—	—	—	—	—
Ernst & Whinney	—	1,185	1,492	1,778	2,191	—	—	—	—	—	—
Offices	1.4%	—	—	—	—	—	642	673	660	663	680
Partners	(1.7%)	—	—	—	—	—	5,609	5,665	5,300	5,318	5,228
Employees	(0.1%)	—	—	—	—	—	61,591	61,173	58,900	58,377	61,287

1994 Year-end:
Sales per partner:
$1,151,492

ΞJ ERNST&YOUNG

Sales ($ mil.)
1985–94

7,000
6,000
5,000
4,000
3,000
2,000
1,000
0

EXXON CORPORATION

OVERVIEW

Exxon is the world's largest publicly owned integrated oil company, with oil reserves of 6.6 billion barrels and gas reserves of 42.2 trillion cubic feet. In addition to conducting worldwide oil and gas exploration and production, it produces and sells petrochemicals, mines coal and other minerals, and owns 60% of a Hong Kong electric power generating station.

The company is continuing to focus on lowering costs and selling nonstrategic assets. It has sold about $1 billion in assets per year since 1990, and staffing levels are half of 1981 levels. Exxon's finances have been buoyed by its chemical division, whose profits more than doubled to $954 million in 1994.

Exxon spends about 1/3 of its refining and retail operations capital on the fast-growing Asia/Pacific region.

Despite slick work in cleaning up the *Exxon Valdez* oil spill, on which it spent approximately $2.5 billion, Exxon was slapped with a $5 billion punitive damage verdict by a federal court in Alaska in 1994, a judgment it plans to appeal.

WHEN

John D. Rockefeller, a commodity trader, started his first oil refinery in 1863 in Cleveland. Realizing that the price of oil at the well would shrink with each new strike, Rockefeller chose to monopolize oil refining and transportation. He raised $1 million in loans and investments and in 1870 formed the Standard Oil Company. In 1882 Rockefeller and his associates created the Standard Oil Trust, which allowed Rockefeller and 8 others to dissolve existing Standard Oil affiliates and set up new, ostensibly independent companies in different states, including the Standard Oil Company of New Jersey (Jersey Standard).

Initially capitalized at $70 million, the Standard Oil Trust controlled 90% of the petroleum industry. In 1911, after 2 decades of political and legal wrangling, the Supreme Court disbanded the trust into 34 companies, the largest of which was Jersey Standard. In that year John Archbold took over as president of Jersey Standard and commenced more active exploration efforts.

Walter Teagle took over the presidency in 1917, secretly bought half of Humble Oil of Texas (1919), and expanded into South America. In 1928 Jersey Standard joined in the Red Line Agreement, which reserved most Middle East oil for a handful of companies. Congressional investigation of a prewar research pact giving Farben of Germany patents for a lead essential to the development of aviation fuel in exchange for a formula for synthetic rubber (never received) led to Teagle's resignation in 1942.

The 1948 purchase of a 30% interest in Arabian American Oil Company for $74 million, combined with a 7% share of Iranian production acquired in 1954, made Jersey Standard the world's largest oil company.

Other US companies still using the Standard Oil name objected to Jersey Standard marketing in their territories as Esso (derived from the initials S.O. for Standard Oil). To end the confusion, Jersey Standard became Exxon in 1972. The name change cost $100 million.

In the 1970s nationalization of oil assets by producing countries reduced Exxon's access to oil. Despite increased exploration in the 1970s and 1980s, Exxon's reserves shrank faster than new reserves could be found.

The oil tanker *Exxon Valdez*, under the command of Joseph Hazelwood, spilled nearly 11 million gallons of oil into Alaska's Prince William Sound in 1989. In 1991 Exxon agreed to settle criminal charges resulting from the spill. Payments to the US government and the state of Alaska totaled $1.1 billion. Exxon spent billions on coastal cleanup operations.

In 1992 Exxon announced a $900 million expansion of its Sriracha refinery in Thailand and an agreement with Mobil to develop an 86-million-acre area in Siberia. Also in 1992 Arthur Seale, a former security official with Exxon, pleaded guilty to the kidnapping and murder of Sidney Reso, president of Exxon's international division. He was sentenced to life plus 125 years in prison.

In 1994 a federal jury in Alaska found that Exxon's "recklessness" caused the grounding of the *Exxon Valdez*.

In that same year Exxon and Pertamina, the Indonesian state oil company, agreed on terms to develop the giant Natuna gas field (50%-owned by Exxon), which contains an estimated 45 trillion cubic feet of natural gas.

In 1995 the company awarded 10 contracts worth approximately $200 million to 6 Malaysian companies to construct natural gas platforms and pipelines. Also that year Exxon signed a $15 billion agreement to develop 3 oil and natural gas fields off Sakhalin Island in Russia. Drilling is expected to get underway sometime in 1996.

NYSE symbol: XON
Fiscal year ends: December 31

WHO

Chairman and CEO: Lee R. Raymond, age 56,
$1,850,000 pay
President: Charles R. Sitter, age 64, $1,285,000 pay
SVP: Robert E. Wilhelm, age 54, $900,000 pay
SVP: H. J. Longwell, age 53, $695,833 pay (prior to
promotion)
SVP: Edwin J. Hess, age 61
VP Investor Relations and Secretary: T. P. Townsend,
age 58
VP and Treasurer: Edgar A. Robinson, age 61
VP Medicine and Occupational Health: T. J. McDonagh,
age 63
VP and Controller: W. B. Cook, age 59
VP and General Counsel: C. W. Matthews Jr., age 50
VP Public Affairs: A. W. Atkiss, age 55
VP Human Resources: Daniel S. Sanders, age 55
General Manager Corporate Planning: S. F. Goldmann,
age 50
Auditors: Price Waterhouse LLP

WHERE

HQ: 225 E. John W. Carpenter Fwy., Irving, TX
75062-2298
Phone: 214-444-1000
Fax: 214-444-1505

Exxon conducts operations in the US and in more than
100 other countries.

	1994 Sales		1994 Net Income	
	$ mil.	% of total	$ mil.	% of total
US	22,651	21	1,560	31
Other Western Hemisphere	16,875	15	370	7
Other regions	70,429	64	3,195	62
Adjustments	3,949	—	(25)	—
Total	**113,904**	**100**	**5,100**	**100**

WHAT

	1994 Sales		1994 Net Income	
	$ mil.	% of total	$ mil.	% of total
Petroleum & natural gas	100,409	89	4,171	81
Chemicals	9,544	8	954	19
Other	3,951	3	(25)	—
Total	**113,904**	**100**	**5,100**	**100**

Petroleum and Natural Gas
Upstream operations
  Oil and gas exploration
   and production
Downstream operations
  Lubricants
  Refining
  Service stations

Chemicals
Aromatics
Fuel and lubricant additives

Performance chemicals
  for oil field operations
Plasticizers
Polyethylene and
  polypropylene plastics
Solvents
Specialty resins
Specialty rubbers

Other Activities
Coal and mineral mining
Power generation

KEY COMPETITORS

Amerada Hess
Amoco
Ashland, Inc.
Atlantic Richfield
British Gas
British Petroleum
Broken Hill
Caltex Petroleum
Chevron
Circle K
Coastal
Diamond Shamrock
Dow Chemical
DuPont
Eastman Chemical
Elf Aquitaine
Enron

Hanson
Huntsman
  Chemical
Imperial Oil
Koch
Lyondell
  Petrochemical
Mobil
Norsk Hydro
NOVA
Occidental
Oryx
Panhandle
  Eastern
PDVSA
PEMEX
Pennzoil

Petrobrás
Petrofina
Phillips
  Petroleum
Repsol
Royal Dutch/
  Shell
Sinclair Oil
Southland
Star Enterprise
Sun Company
Texaco
TOTAL
Union Carbide
Unocal
USX–Marathon
YPF

HOW MUCH

	9-Year Growth	1985	1986	1987	1988	1989	1990	1991	1992	1993	1994
Sales ($ mil.)	2.3%	92,869	76,555	83,335	88,563	96,285	116,940	116,492	117,106	111,211	113,904
Net income ($ mil.)	0.5%	4,870	5,360	4,840	5,260	2,975	5,010	5,600	4,810	5,280	5,100
Income as % of sales	—	5.2%	7.0%	5.8%	5.9%	3.1%	4.3%	4.8%	4.1%	4.7%	4.5%
Earnings per share ($)	2.6%	3.23	3.71	3.43	3.95	2.32	3.96	4.45	3.82	4.21	4.07
Stock price – high ($)	—	27.94	37.06	50.38	47.75	51.63	55.13	61.88	65.50	69.00	67.38
Stock price – low ($)	—	22.06	24.19	30.88	36.63	41.50	44.88	49.63	53.75	57.75	56.13
Stock price – close ($)	9.2%	27.56	35.06	38.13	44.00	50.00	51.75	60.88	61.13	63.13	60.75
P/E – high	—	9	10	15	12	22	14	14	17	16	17
P/E – low	—	7	7	9	9	18	11	11	14	14	14
Dividends per share ($)	5.9%	1.73	1.80	1.90	2.15	2.30	2.47	2.68	2.83	2.88	2.91
Book value per share ($)	4.5%	19.90	22.29	24.38	24.64	23.36	25.78	27.42	26.57	28.02	29.68
Employees	(5.7%)	146,000	102,000	151,000	101,000	104,000	104,000	101,000	95,000	91,000	86,000

1994 Year-end:
Debt ratio: 25.3%
Return on equity: 14.4%
Cash (mil.): $1,775
Current ratio: 0.84
Long-term debt (mil.): $8,831
No. of shares (mil.): 1,242
Dividends
  Yield: 4.8%
  Payout: 71.5%
Market value (mil.): $75,452

Stock Price History
High/Low 1985–94

FARMLAND INDUSTRIES, INC.

OVERVIEW

The next time you wolf down a chili dog in front of the Kremlin, you might be doing Farmland Industries a favor. Based in Kansas City, Farmland is not only the nation's biggest agricultural cooperative but also a growing player in global agribusiness. Nearly 1/10 of its sales now come from foreign countries, especially Japan, Mexico, South Korea, and Russia. Farmland hot dogs are the wieners of choice for many Moscow street vendors.

Farmland is owned by about 8,000 livestock producers and 1,300 smaller co-ops throughout the Midwest. Its operations include providing petroleum, fertilizer, and feed products to help members produce their goods and then processing and marketing the food and grain

grown by co-op members. Information services is another key business area. Sales jumped more than 40% in 1994, mostly because of the acquisitions in recent years of National Beef Packing and Wells-Bowman Trading (grain).

The co-op's $70.6 million rebate to its members in 1994 was Farmland's biggest since 1980. It has been working to diversify its operations by category as well as by location. Now part of 26 business alliances and joint ventures worldwide, Farmland has teamed with Reuters to form Market Communications Group, which provides agriculture market news and information to businesses and other cooperatives.

WHEN

US agriculture has always been sensitive to boom and bust cycles and to the ups and downs of raw commodities prices.

After a golden age of supplying food for a world rent by WWI, US agriculture had a bad time of it during the 1920s. Many solutions were proposed, including the imposition of import/export tariffs. In 1929 the newly elected Herbert Hoover called a special session of Congress to deal with farm issues. The result was the Agricultural Marketing Act, which encouraged the formation of cooperatives. These were widely viewed as anticapitalistic.

One of the cooperatives formed was the Union Oil Company, Farmland's original predecessor. Union Oil was intended to provide petroleum supplies to farmers in a period of rapid agricultural mechanization.

But the Agricultural Marketing Act failed to improve conditions because 1928–29 grain production worldwide reached record levels. The glut ground down prices, and later the Depression (and drought) dried up markets.

In the early 1930s, as the government sought to regulate supply by introducing payments for taking land out of production, Union Oil increased the range of its cooperative activities. It changed its name to Consumers Cooperative Association in 1935.

Farming did not revive until WWII, though price controls and supports remained an important feature of agricultural policy.

Throughout this period, the performance of Consumers Cooperative's growing membership of primary producers and local cooperatives remained tied to raw commodities prices, and the company's sales remained tied to the

provision of fuels and other supplies, particularly fertilizers, to its members.

In 1959, however, to decrease its reliance on commodity prices, Consumers Cooperative bought a pork-processing plant in Denison, Iowa, and began making Farmbest meat products. It was a success, and 4 years later the company opened another plant in Iowa Falls. In 1966 Consumers Cooperative became Farmland Industries. In the 1970s it expanded into beef production also, but when prices and consumption declined, it exited the field.

As Farmland increased its output (production) emphasis, it tried to decrease its input (raw materials) side, especially after the crash of oil prices in 1986 cost the company $90 million and almost bankrupted it. Since then the company has reduced its petroleum and agricultural chemical production assets by selling refineries and other facilities.

Farmland has a flexible approach to marketing. After a period of volatile prices, the company stopped handling grains in 1985 but profitably reentered the market in 1992. In 1993 it resumed beef processing and expanded its pork-processing facilities. Farmland is now the #4 beef packer in the US.

Also in 1993 Farmland paid $10 million to settle a lawsuit alleging that it had defrauded defunct co-ops and their members in several states. A similar suit was brought in 1994 regarding Farmland's 1992 purchase of the Union Equity cooperative. A federal judge held Farmland in contempt of court in 1995 for violating a gag order after publishing "misleading" information about the lawsuits in a co-op newspaper.

Agricultural cooperative
Fiscal year ends: August 31

WHO

Chairman: Albert J. Shivley
President and CEO: H. D. Cleberg
EVP and CFO: John F. Berardi
EVP Ag Input Operations: Robert W. Honse
EVP; Director General, Farmland Industrias, S.A. de C.V.: Stephen P. Dees
SVP Ag Production Marketing/Processing: Gary Evans
VP and Secretary: Bernard L. Sanders
VP and Treasurer: Terry M. Campbell
VP and Controller: Merl Daniel
President, Farmland Foods and VP Farmland Industries: George E. Grazier
VP and General Counsel: Robert B. Terry
VP International/Transportation: William R. Allen Jr.
VP Corporate Administrative Services: Dave Fulton
VP Grain Marketing: Anthony H. Lewis
VP Petroleum Marketing: Ken Otwell
VP Information Services: George H. Richter
VP Crop Production: Stan Riemann
VP Transportation: Fred E. Schrodt
VP Feed Operations: Michael T. Sweat
VP Human Resources: Holly D. McCoy
Auditors: KPMG Peat Marwick LLP

WHERE

HQ: 3315 North Oak Trafficway, Kansas City, MO 64116
Phone: 816-459-6000
Fax: 816-459-6979

Farmland conducts business in all 50 states and in more than 85 foreign countries. Farmland has regional offices in Lewisville, Texas; Lincoln, Nebraska; St. Louis, Missouri; Urbandale, Iowa; and Wichita, Kansas.

WHAT

	1994 Sales		1994 Operating Income	
	$ mil.	$ of total	$ mil.	% of total
Food marketing	2,356	35	21	11
Grain marketing	1,627	24	(34)	—
Crop production	1,163	18	126	66
Petroleum	856	13	27	14
Feed	528	8	17	9
Other	148	2	(2)	—
Total	**6,678**	**100**	**155**	**100**

Selected Subsidiaries and Affiliates

Ceres Realty Corporation (real estate brokerage)
Cooperative Service Company (auditing, insurance, management service)
Double Circle Farm Supply Company (retail petroleum and farm supply)
Environmental and Safety Services, Inc. (consulting)
Equity Country, Inc. (retail grain marketing)
Farmers Chemical Company (fertilizer production)
Farmland Foods, Inc. (pork processing and marketing)
Farmland Hydro, L.P. (fertilizer manufacturing)
Farmland Industrias S.A. de C.V. (marketing support services)
Farmland Industries, Ltd. (foreign sales)
Farmland Insurance Agency, Inc.
Farmland Securities Company (broker-dealer)
Farmland Transportation, Inc. (brokerage)
Heartland Data Services, Inc. (computer services)
Heartland Wheat Growers, L.P. & G.P. (wheat gluten and starch processing)
National Beef Packing Company L.P. & G.P.
National Carriers, Inc. (transportation brokerage)
Penterra, Inc. (petroleum hedging and risk management services)
SF Phosphates, Limited Company (fertilizer manufacturing)
Tradigrain, Inc. (international grain trading)

KEY COMPETITORS

ADM	Hormel
Ag Processing	Hudson Foods
Agway	IBP
American Home Products	IMC Global
	International Multifoods
Campbell Soup	JR Simplot
Cargill	Keystone Foods
ConAgra	Monsanto
Continental Grain	Pennzoil
Freeport-McMoRan	Schreiber Foods
Gold Kist	Specialty Foods
Harvest States Co-ops	Tyson Foods

HOW MUCH

	Annual Growth	1985	1986	1987	1988	1989	1990	1991	1992	1993	1994
Sales ($ mil.)	9.4%	2,967	2,703	2,590	2,817	2,975	3,378	3,638	3,429	4,723	6,678
Net income ($ mil.)	—	(60)	(152)	55	51	99	49	43	62	(30)	79
Members	—	2,269	2,265	2,186	2,123	2,068	2,002	1,820	1500	1500	1500
Employees	4.2%	8,256	7,495	6,246	5,670	6,372	6,691	7,126	7,616	8,155	12,000

1994 Year-end:
Debt ratio: 59.2%
Return on equity: 12.9%
Cash (mil.): $44
Current ratio: 1.36
Long-term debt (mil.): $518
Total assets (mil.): $1,927

Farmland

Net Income
($ mil.)
1985–94

FEDERAL EXPRESS CORPORATION

OVERVIEW

Federal Express (FedEx) has the world's largest fleet of air cargo delivery planes and is a world leader in the package delivery market, providing time-definite deliveries of more than 2.3 million items to 193 countries a night. FedEx, through a joint venture with Network Courier Services, is going head to head with rival UPS for the US market for same-day package delivery service. By focusing on transatlantic service and domestic operations, FedEx rebounded with improved earnings over the last two years.

Memphis-based FedEx has branched into business logistics. It operates a distribution network in Singapore for National Semiconductor and has a contract with Laura Ashley to handle the London-based fashion company's global distribution. In 1995 the company and IA Corporation launched FedEx's Domestic Customer Invoicing System, one of the world's largest client/server-based imaging systems.

FedEx's reputation for high employee morale was jolted by its pilots' 1993 decision to unionize. Unions are campaigning to organize other FedEx employees, a move the company is fighting. Throughout the last half of 1994 FedEx pilots and management were in negotiations with government mediators present. In 1995 the pilots union authorized an initial $1 million to support the FedEx pilots' mediation efforts; additional money was authorized for a legal fight.

Founder and CEO Fred Smith still owns almost 9% of FedEx's stock.

WHEN

FedEx was the inspiration of Fred Smith, who recognized in the late 1960s that the US was becoming a service-oriented economy with a need for reliable, overnight delivery services. Smith presented FedEx's business concept in a Yale term paper — his grade, a "C," now seems ironic. Between 1969 and 1971 Smith found investors willing to contribute $40 million, used $8 million of family money, and received bank financing to total $90 million, making FedEx the largest start-up ever funded by venture capital. Services to 22 US cities started in 1973 with overnight and 2nd-day delivery and a $5-per-package Courier Pak envelope for expediting documents.

Several factors contributed to FedEx's success. Air passenger traffic was growing rapidly, so parcel service became less important to commercial airlines; United Parcel Service union workers struck in 1974, disrupting service; and, finally, competitor REA Express went bankrupt. By fiscal year-end 1975, FedEx had lost $29.3 million; by 1976 it was profitable — but owed creditors $49 million. It went public in 1978.

FedEx has had one fiasco. Believing hardcopy delivery services could be severely eroded by the burgeoning electronic mail market, the company invested heavily in ZapMail, a satellite-based network that provided 2-hour document delivery. Failing to anticipate the impact of low-cost fax machines, FedEx lost over $300 million in 1986 on the now-disbanded ZapMail. Despite heavy ZapMail losses, FedEx remained profitable.

FedEx bought Island Courier Companies and Cansica (1987), SAMIMA (Italy, 1988), and 3 Japanese freight carriers (1988). In 1989 it spent $880 million for Tiger International (Flying Tigers line), doubling overseas revenues and making FedEx the #1 air cargo company. Unfortunately, FedEx inherited Tiger's losses in overseas markets and has yet to make a profit on operations abroad. The company executed an untimely US expansion in the late 1980s.

A new challenge presented itself in 1990 when UPS started offering guaranteed 10:30 a.m. delivery services in the US. In 1991 FedEx introduced EXPRESSfreighter, an international air-express cargo service, and began to explore diversifying into aviation services through a new unit, FEDEX Aeronautics Corporation. Also that year FedEx agreed to sell about half of its UK operations back to the original owner (Littlewoods Organisation).

In late 1991 COO James Barksdale and CFO David Anderson left the company. Their departures (followed by the 1993 resignations of #2 executive Thomas Oliver and SVP Carole Presley) created concerns about a "brain drain."

In 1992 FedEx scrapped its intra-European express delivery, cut 7,000 jobs in Europe, took a $254 million restructuring charge, and lost $114 million. In 1993 it expanded into Bhutan, Brunei, French Guiana, Guyana, Marshall Islands, Micronesia, Palau, and Suriname. In 1994 FedEx signed a contract with GM to be its only express transportation carrier in the US. In 1995 FedEx became the only US express carrier with direct flights to China by buying the route from Evergreen International. In fiscal 1995 sales increased to $9.4 billion and net income was $298 million.

WHO

Chairman, President, and CEO: Frederick W. Smith, age 49, $1,120,121 pay
EVP Worldwide Customer Operations: William J. Razzouk, age 46, $780,076 pay
SVP Air Operations: Theodore L. Weise, age 50, $614,035 pay
SVP Americas and Caribbean: Jeffrey R. Rodek, age 40, $530,061 pay
SVP and General Counsel: Kenneth R. Masterson, age 50, $512,590 pay
SVP and CFO: Alan B. Graf Jr., age 40
SVP and Chief Personnel Officer: James A. Perkins, age 50
Auditors: Arthur Andersen & Co, SC

WHERE

HQ: 2005 Corporate Ave., Memphis, TN 38132
Phone: 901-369-3600
Fax: 901-795-1027

FedEx offers package delivery services in the US and 192 foreign countries. The company operates about 462 aircraft and about 35,000 delivery vehicles.

US Hubs and Major Sorting Facilities

Anchorage	Memphis
Chicago	Newark
Indianapolis	Oakland
Los Angeles	

	1994 Sales		1994 Operating Income	
	$ mil.	% of total	$ mil.	% of total
US	6,200	73	560	—
Other countries	2,279	27	(29)	—
Total	**8,479**	**100**	**531**	**—**

WHAT

	1994 Sales	
Services	$ mil.	% of total
Priority overnight	3,708	44
International priority	1,318	15
Standard overnight	1,167	14
Economy 2-day	1,091	13
International freight	505	6
Other	690	8
Total	**8,479**	**100**

Domestic Overnight Services
FedEx Overnight Freight Service
FedEx Priority Overnight Service
FedEx Standard Overnight Service

International Services
FedEx International Airport-to-Airport Cargo Service
FedEx International EXPRESSfreighter Service
FedEx International MailService
FedEx Logistics Services
International Priority Distribution Service
International Priority Freight Service
International Priority Plus
International Priority Service

	Aircraft
	No.
Boeing B727	159
Cessna	216
DC-10	31
Fokker	32
Other	24
Total	**462**

KEY COMPETITORS

Airborne Freight	TNT Freightways
Consolidated Freightways	UPS
DHL Worldwide Express	U.S. Postal Service
Pittston Services	Yellow Corp.
Roadway	

HOW MUCH

	9-Year Growth	1985	1986	1987	1988	1989	1990	1991	1992	1993	1994
Sales ($ mil.)	17.2%	2,031	2,606	3,178	3,883	5,167	7,015	7,688	7,550	7,808	8,479
Net income ($ mil.)	11.6%	76	132	(66)	188	167	116	6	(114)	110	204
Income as % of sales	—	3.7%	5.1%	—	4.8%	3.2%	1.7%	0.1%	—	1.4%	2.4%
Earnings per share ($)	9.5%	1.61	2.64	(1.27)	3.56	3.18	2.18	0.11	(2.11)	2.01	3.65
Stock price – high ($)	—	61.00	73.75	75.50	51.00	57.88	58.00	44.50	56.13	72.50	80.75
Stock price – low ($)	—	31.38	51.00	35.25	35.38	42.13	29.50	31.38	34.50	44.38	53.50
Stock price – close ($)	(0.1%)	60.63	63.13	39.88	50.63	45.75	33.88	38.75	54.50	70.88	60.25
P/E – high	—	38	28	—	14	18	27	—	—	36	22
P/E – low	—	20	19	—	10	13	14	—	—	22	15
Dividends per share ($)	—	0.00	0.00	0.00	0.00	0.00	0.00	0.00	0.00	0.00	0.00
Book value per share ($)	8.0%	17.27	21.49	20.90	25.42	28.80	31.03	31.11	29.50	30.53	34.43
Employees	16.5%	25,600	32,000	34,000	47,600	58,500	78,500	86,800	91,550	95,000	101,000

1994 Year-end:
Debt ratio: 48.7%
Return on equity: 11.4%
Cash (mil.): $393
Current ratio: 1.15
Long-term debt (mil.): $1,632
No. of shares (mil.): 56
Dividends
  Yield: —
  Payout: —
Market value (mil.): $3,368

Stock Price History
High/Low 1985–94

FEDERAL NATIONAL MORTGAGE ASSN.

OVERVIEW

Fannie Mae (the Federal National Mortgage Association) is "Showing America a New Way Home." This promotional campaign is part of a 6-year, $1 trillion effort to extend home-ownership opportunities to people who do not fit conventional mortgage criteria but who may nevertheless be good bets for home ownership (i.e., people with steady jobs who lack the savings for a down payment).

Fannie Mae, the US's largest financial company, is able to launch such public interest efforts because it is a public/private hybrid (a federally mandated for-profit institution that is publicly traded). It was created to ensure a source of credit for low- and moderate-income home buyers by buying the mortgages

from the originating institutions; it repackages them as securities for sale in the US and, increasingly, abroad. In addition to earning money, Fannie Mae is able to fuel the market by borrowing money at favorable rates because of its government backing. Despite the rising interest rates of 1994, which were responsible for a 25% reduction in new mortgages, Fannie Mae managed to achieve record income for an 8th consecutive year.

In 1995 Fannie Mae's business was threatened when Republican budgeteers suggested that Fannie Mae pay the government fees equal to the interest rate discounts it receives when borrowing money. But support was low because it was viewed as a new tax on the middle class.

WHEN

Fannie Mae was created in 1938 by President Franklin D. Roosevelt as part of the government-owned Reconstruction Finance Corporation to buy FHA (Federal Housing Administration) loans. Fannie Mae began buying VA (Veterans Administration) mortgages in 1948. In 1954 it was rechartered as a partly private, partly governmental "mixed ownership corporation." The Housing Act of 1968 divided the corporation into 2 entities: the Government National Mortgage Association (Ginnie Mae, which, as part of Housing and Urban Development, retained explicit US backing) and Fannie Mae, which went public (with only an implicit US guarantee). Fannie Mae retained its "treasury backstop authority," whereby the secretary of the treasury can purchase up to $2.24 billion of the company's obligations.

Fannie Mae introduced uniform conventional loan mortgage documents in 1970; began to buy conventional, in addition to VA and FHA, mortgages in 1972; and started buying condo and planned unit development mortgages in 1974. By 1976 it was buying more conventional than FHA and VA loans.

As interest rates rose in the 1970s, Fannie Mae's profits declined; by 1981 it was losing more than $1 million a day. Then it began offering mortgage-backed securities (MBSs), which were popular because they were an investment product with an implicit guarantee from the government. By 1982 Fannie Mae funded 14% of US home mortgages.

In 1984 Fannie Mae began borrowing money overseas and buying conventional multifamily and co-op housing loans. In 1985 it tightened its credit rules and began issuing

securities aimed at foreign investors, such as yen-denominated securities. Fannie Mae issued its first real estate mortgage investment conduit (REMIC) securities (shares in mortgage pools of specific maturities and risk classes) and introduced a program to allow small lenders to pool loans with other lenders to create MBSs in 1987.

After David Maxwell's 1991 retirement with a reported $29 million pension package, there were calls to limit the company's executive salaries (squelched by Fannie Mae's powerful Washington lobby). Other attempts to make the company more competitive with private concerns were more successful. A bill that raised Fannie Mae's capital standards, while keeping them below those required of banks, became law in 1992. The bill also required that Fannie Mae lend greater support to inner-city buyers (resulting in a 1994 commitment to provide $1 trillion through the year 2000 for special housing programs) and provide more information to federal regulators.

During the 1980s Fannie Mae struggled to improve its information technology capabilities, pouring more than $100 million into a mainframe data system, called LASER, that was obsolete by the time it came on-line in the late 1980s. In the 1990s LASER was superseded by a more flexible client/server system that was up in time to help meet the deluge of new loans and refinancings that came in 1993. This system is continuing to evolve, and in 1995 Fannie Mae began offering mortgage originators direct links with its own loan underwriting system. The company also ventured onto the Internet with an informational web site at http://www.fanniemae.com.

NYSE symbol: FNM
Fiscal year ends: December 31

WHO

Chairman and CEO: James A. Johnson, age 51,
$1,567,433 pay
VC: Franklin D. Raines, age 46, $852,027 pay
President and COO: Lawrence M. Small, age 53,
$1,020,898 pay
EVP and CFO: J. Timothy Howard, age 46, $509,044 pay
EVP Marketing: Robert J. Levin, age 39, $509,044 pay
EVP and Chief Credit Officer: Ann D. Logan, age 40
EVP and Chief Information Officer: William E. Kelvie,
age 47
EVP, General Counsel, and Secretary: Robert B.
Zoellick, age 41
SVP Administration: Douglas M. Bibby, age 48
SVP Communications: John Buckley, age 38
VP Human Resources: Leon Z. Hollins
Auditors: KPMG Peat Marwick LLP

WHERE

HQ: Federal National Mortgage Association,
3900 Wisconsin Ave. NW, Washington, DC 20016
Phone: 202-752-7000
Fax: 202-752-6099

Fannie Mae operates throughout the US, with 5 regional
offices in Atlanta; Chicago; Dallas; Pasadena, CA; and
Philadelphia.

	1994 Mortgage Portfolio[1]	
	$ mil.	% of total
California	43,038	24
New York	10,358	6
Texas	9,752	5
Illinois	8,455	5
Florida	7,922	4
Other states	98,533	56
Total	**178,058**	**100**

[1] Exclusive of mortgage-backed securities

WHAT

	1994 Assets	
	$ mil.	% of total
Cash & equivalents	231	0
Net mortgage portfolio	220,525	82
Investments	46,335	17
Accrued interest receivable	1,688	0
Other	3,729	1
Total	**272,508**	**100**

	1994 Sales	
	$ mil.	% of total
Mortgage portfolio interest	15,851	85
Other interest	1,496	8
Guaranty fees	1,083	6
Sales of mortgages	(2)	—
Other	145	1
Total	**18,573**	**100**

KEY COMPETITORS

Banc One
BankAmerica
Barnett Banks
Chase Manhattan
Chemical Banking
Citicorp
Countrywide Credit
First American Financial
First Interstate
First Union
Fleet Financial
Great Western
H.F. Ahmanson
Mellon Bank
NationsBank
North American Mortgage
PNC Bank
TELACU
Wells Fargo

HOW MUCH

	Annual Growth	1985	1986	1987	1988	1989	1990	1991	1992	1993	1994
Assets ($ mil.)	11.9%	99,087	100,405	103,459	112,258	124,315	133,113	147,072	180,978	216,979	272,508
Net income ($ mil.)	56.9%	37	183	376	507	807	1,173	1,363	1,623	1,873	2,132
Income as % of assets	—	0.0%	0.2%	0.4%	0.5%	0.7%	0.9%	1.0%	0.9%	0.9%	0.8%
Earnings per share ($)	52.9%	0.17	0.83	1.55	2.11	3.10	4.49	4.98	5.91	6.82	7.77
Stock price – high ($)	—	9.88	14.00	16.13	17.50	46.08	44.63	69.63	77.25	86.13	90.38
Stock price – low ($)	—	4.63	7.63	8.38	9.63	16.71	24.88	32.38	55.13	72.88	68.13
Stock price – close ($)	26.8%	8.63	13.58	10.17	16.92	33.88	35.63	69.00	76.38	78.50	72.88
P/E – high	—	57	17	10	8	15	10	13	13	13	12
P/E – low	—	27	9	5	5	5	6	6	9	11	9
Dividends per share ($)	53.7%	0.05	0.07	0.12	0.24	0.43	0.72	1.04	1.38	1.84	2.40
Book value per share ($)	21.3%	6.14	7.20	7.67	9.58	12.52	16.54	20.32	24.79	29.55	34.97
Employees	7.0%	—	—	—	—	2,500	1,900	2,763	3,000	3,200	3,500

1994 Year-end:
Equity as % of assets: 3.5%
Return on assets: 0.9%
Return on equity: 24.2%
Long-term debt (mil.): $144,628
No. of shares (mil.): 273
Dividends
  Yield: 3.3%
  Payout: 30.9%
Market value (mil.): $19,880
Sales (mil.): $18,573

Stock Price History
High/Low 1985–94

FEDERATED DEPARTMENT STORES, INC.

OVERVIEW

Federated Department Stores has rung up a bill that tops any ever seen in one of its stores. The Cincinnati-based company paid $4.1 billion for bankrupt department store operator R.H. Macy in late 1994, making Federated the largest department store retailer in the US. The acquisition of Macy's adds the venerable chain (founded in the 1850s) to Federated's list of some of the most prestigious names in retailing. Its other stores include Lazarus, the Bon Marché, Bloomingdale's, Jordan Marsh, Stern's, Rich's, Goldsmith's, and Burdines.

Federated operates more than 350 department stores in 35 states as well as 92 Aeropostale and 30 Charter Club specialty stores in 20 of these states.

Now that the acquisition of Macy's is complete, Federated is working to consolidate and streamline its operations. The company has merged its A&S/Jordan Marsh division into its new Macy's East division, discontinuing its Abraham & Straus name.

Federated is also working to develop a common merchandising process for all its chains and is looking to tap its new Macy's buyers (who are highly respected in the industry) for their experience with private labels. The company wants to raise its percentage of sales from private labels (which are more profitable) from 5% to 16% of merchandise. Federated also plans to spend more than $2.8 billion remodeling its stores, primarily Macy's.

WHEN

The story of Federated Department Stores reflects the rise, fall, and rebirth of one of America's great companies. The story begins in 1929 with Fred Lazarus, who controlled Columbus, Ohio's giant F&R Lazarus department store and John Shillito Company (the oldest department store west of the Alleghenies; 1830). That year he met with 3 other great retailers on a yacht in Long Island Sound: Walter Rothschild of Brooklyn-based Abraham & Straus; Louis Kirstein of Boston-based Filene's; and Samuel Bloomingdale, head of Manhattan's Bloomingdale's. Lazarus, Rothschild, and Kirstein agreed to merge into one of the loosest federations in American corporate history to reduce vulnerability to local economic fluctuations. The company had no head office, and its financial statement showed just one column of numbers for each participating company. Bloomingdale's joined the next year.

Though Federated set up a headquarters in Cincinnati in 1945, the company continued to be run by powerful, well-paid merchants in each city where it operated. Under Lazarus's leadership the company was among the first to see the coming of the Sunbelt, acquiring Foley's (Houston, 1945), Burdines (Miami, 1956), Sanger's (Dallas, 1958), Bullock's and I. Magnin (California, 1964), and Rich's (Atlanta, 1976). In addition to extreme autonomy, the hallmarks of Federated were talented people, great training, conservative and profitable financial management, and the best merchandising in the world.

After Fred Lazarus's son Ralph stepped down in 1981, the next 2 CEOs let Federated coast. Growth stopped as May rose to prominence and newcomers like Nordstrom and Dillard came along. Ventures into discounting and small towns were disappointing as well. By 1989 Federated was no longer an innovator or the leader of the pack, although it was still financially strong.

Years before, when Federated was growing and leading the department store industry, #2 was Allied Stores, which had descended from the Hahn chain created in 1929. Allied was an amalgamation of 2nd-place and small-town stores, with a few leaders (Maas Brothers, the Bon Marché, Jordan Marsh). It had a mediocre track record until Thomas Macioce took the helm in 1971. He closed unprofitable stores and downsized others before embarking on an acquisition spree, after which he controlled Washington, DC's Garfinkel's, Brooks Brothers, Ann Taylor, and others.

Robert Campeau bought Allied in 1988 and Federated the next year. Saddled with more than $8 billion in debt, both companies declared bankruptcy in 1990. Allen Questrom became Federated's CEO and oversaw the reorganization. In 1992 the companies emerged from bankruptcy as Federated Department Stores. After being rebuffed in a bid to merge with Macy's, Federated purchased 50% of Macy's unsecured debt from the Prudential Insurance Company of America in 1993, setting the stage for a 1994 merger agreement.

In 1995 Federated was outbid by May Department Stores and J. C. Penney in its effort to acquire several stores from bankrupt retailer Woodward & Lothrop; however, it did reach an agreement to buy beleaguered Broadway Stores. Federated also announced plans to close its 14 Macy's Close-Out stores.

WHO

Chairman and CEO: Allen I. Questrom, age 55,
$1,200,000 pay
VC and CFO: Ronald W. Tysoe, age 42, $942,700 pay
President and COO: James M. Zimmerman, age 51,
$1,319,600 pay
EVP Legal and Human Resources: Thomas G. Cody,
age 53, $798,950 pay
SVP, General Counsel, and Secretary: Dennis J.
Broderick, age 46, $386,800 pay
SVP and Controller: John E. Brown, age 55
Auditors: KPMG Peat Marwick LLP

WHERE

HQ: 7 W. Seventh St., Cincinnati, OH 45202
Phone: 513-579-7000
Fax: 513-579-7555

Federated has operations in 35 states.

WHAT

	1995 Stores
	No.
Aeropostale (specialty stores)	92
Macy's East (department stores)	79
Macy's West/Bullock's (department stores)	57
Lazarus (department stores)	51
Burdines (department stores)	46
The Bon Marché (department stores)	40
Charter Club (specialty stores)	30
Rich's/Goldsmith's (department stores)	25
Stern's (department stores)	22
Jordan Marsh (department stores)	19
Bloomingdale's (department stores)	16
Macy's Close-Out (clearance stores)	14
Total	**491**

	1995 Sales	
	$ mil.	% of total
A&S/Jordan Marsh	1,441	17
Bloomingdale's	1,298	16
Burdines	1,259	15
Lazarus	1,130	14
Rich's/Goldsmith's	1,000	12
The Bon Marché	873	10
Stern's	707	9
Macy's	608	7
Total	**8,316**	**100**

KEY COMPETITORS

Broadway Stores
Carson Pirie Scott
Dayton Hudson
Dillard
Edison Brothers
The Gap
Harcourt General
J. C. Penney
Jos. A. Bank
Kmart
Lands' End
The Limited
Liz Claiborne
Marks and Spencer
May
Melville
Men's Wearhouse
Mercantile Stores
Merry-Go-Round
Montgomery Ward
Nordstrom
Saks
Sears
Service Merchandise
Spiegel
TJX
Woolworth

HOW MUCH

	Annual Growth	1986	1987	1988	1989	1990	1991	1992	1993	1994	1995
Sales ($ mil.)	0.4%	—	—	—	8,136	7,578	7,142	6,932	7,080	7,229	8,316
Net income ($ mil.)	—	—	—	—	(390)	(1,774)	(271)	(1,236)	133	193	188
Income as % of sales	—	—	—	—	—	—	—	—	1.9%	2.7%	2.3%
Earnings per share ($)	8.9%	—	—	—	—	—	—	—	1.19	1.56	1.41
Stock price – high ($)[1]	—	—	—	—	—	—	—	—	20.13	25.00	25.25
Stock price – low ($)[1]	—	—	—	—	—	—	—	—	11.25	17.38	18.00
Stock price – close ($)[1]	(1.3%)	—	—	—	—	—	—	—	19.75	20.75	19.25
P/E – high	—	—	—	—	—	—	—	—	17	16	18
P/E – low	—	—	—	—	—	—	—	—	10	11	13
Dividends per share ($)	—	—	—	—	—	—	—	—	0.00	0.00	0.00
Book value per share ($)	10.1%	—	—	—	—	—	—	—	16.46	18.03	19.94
Employees	9.8%	—	—	—	63,700	60,300	54,200	78,900	73,000	67,300	111,700

1995 Year-end:
Debt ratio: 57.8%
Return on equity: 6.3%
Cash (mil.): $206
Current ratio: 1.91
Long-term debt (mil.): $4,529
No. of shares (mil.): 183
Dividends
  Yield: —
  Payout: —
Market value (mil.): $3,513

Stock Price History[1]
High/Low 1993–95

[1] Stock prices are for the prior calendar year.

FIRST CHICAGO CORPORATION

OVERVIEW

In a move rich in irony, First Chicago Corporation's First National Bank of Chicago imposed a $3 fee for using a teller at the same time it began a "Customer First" program based on its new mission statement. But some customers are more equal than others. "Customer First" applies to corporate and institutional customers. The fee applies to customers without minimum balances and, consumer advocate protests notwithstanding, does not include patrons truly in need of help.

First National Bank is the dominant bank in the Chicago market, with more than 80 branches (thanks to a program of acquiring neighborhood banks and their small personal accounts). It is one of the US's largest credit card issuers and also owns American National Bank, which caters mainly to businesses.

In July 1995 the company neared its goal of becoming one of the top 10 US banks when it announced plans to merge with Detroit's NBD Bancorp. If approved, the $5.1 billion deal would be one of the biggest US bank mergers ever. Prior to the agreement, First Chicago's turbulent recent history had raised speculation that it might be a takeover candidate.

WHEN

In 1863 the US Comptroller of the Currency granted Charter #8 to the First National Bank of Chicago. First National, from its first office on LaSalle Street, grew rapidly. When the Chicago Fire of 1871 leveled much of the city, the bank's "fireproof" building burned too. A cashier named Lyman Gage, who later became the bank's president and William McKinley's secretary of the treasury, found that the bank's documents and money had survived in a vault, and First National resumed operations quickly as the city rebuilt.

The bank bought the Union National Bank in 1900 and Metropolitan National Bank in 1902, almost doubling in size. It then founded a subsidiary called First Trust and Savings Bank, renamed First Union Trust and Savings Bank after a 1929 merger with Union Trust.

As the Depression settled in, First National took over Foreman State Banks (1931), weathered a run on the bank for $50 million (1933), and folded First Union Trust back into First National (1933). WWII spurred the bank's growth. In 1959 it entered the international marketplace with the opening of a London office. A Tokyo office opened in 1962. A 1969 reorganization created First Chicago as the bank's holding corporation.

First Chicago grew rapidly in the early 1970s under chairman Gaylord Freeman. By the end of Freeman's tenure, sloppy underwriting practices had produced a mountain of nonperforming loans, particularly in real estate. Deputy chairman Robert Abboud took over in 1975 to deal with the $2 billion problem and with the threat of a shutdown by federal regulators. Abboud tightened underwriting standards but alienated employees and clients and slowed the bank's growth.

Barry Sullivan, who replaced Abboud, restructured the company and resumed the bank's growth. First Chicago bought enough credit card accounts from other banks to make it the 3rd largest card issuer in the US. Under Sullivan, however, the bank tilted strongly toward energy and commercial real estate.

First Chicago took advantage of the near failure of Continental in 1984 to acquire that bank's $3 billion American National Corp., a holding company for American National Bank and Trust, which concentrates on middle market business clients.

In 1987 First Chicago plunged into the red when several Latin American countries defaulted on their loans. Yet growth continued, and First Chicago added several Chicago-area banks and failed S&Ls in the late 1980s and early 1990s. It bought Continental's personal and small business accounts when that bank discontinued consumer banking operations.

By the early 1990s the company had overinvested in commercial real estate loans, and when the bottom fell out of the market First National found itself with over $2 billion in nonperforming loans and real estate.

Sullivan, under a cloud for his lending policies, was replaced by president Richard Thomas. He focused on reducing the nonperforming loan portfolio. He also began reducing overseas operations (though the bank still has a presence in 10 non-US cities).

First Chicago's forays into other financial services have had spotty results. The company's 1994 earnings decline was largely attributable to its trading, venture capital, and equities operations, which were areas affected by interest rates and the bond market decline of early in the year.

In 1994 First Chicago won a contract from the Treasury Department to develop and install an electronic tax payment system for nationwide use, which will be completed in 1995.

NYSE symbol: FNB
Fiscal year ends: December 31

WHO

Chairman and CEO: Richard L. Thomas, age 64,
$1,760,057 pay
VC: David J. Vitale, age 48, $846,437 pay
President and COO: Leo F. Mullin, age 52, $914,636 pay
EVP: Scott P. Marks Jr., age 48, $820,659 pay
EVP: W. G. Jurgensen, age 43, $754,770 pay
EVP and CFO: Robert A. Rosholt, age 44
EVP Corporate and Institutional Banking: John W. Ballantine, age 48
EVP Corporate and Institutional Banking: Thomas H. Hodges, age 49
EVP Corporate and Institutional Banking: Donald R. Hollis, age 59
EVP, General Counsel, and Secretary: Sherman I. Goldberg, age 52
EVP Human Resources: Marvin James Alef Jr., age 50
Auditors: Arthur Andersen & Co, SC

WHERE

HQ: One First National Plaza, Chicago, IL 60670
Phone: 312-732-4000
Fax: 312-732-5976

First Chicago operates in Australia, the Cayman Islands, China, Hong Kong, Japan, Singapore, South Korea, Taiwan, the UK, and the US.

	1994 Sales		1994 Pretax Income	
	$ mil.	% of total	$ mil.	% of total
US	4,445	87	1,034	96
Europe, Middle East & Africa	387	8	11	1
Asia/Pacific	122	2	(13)	—
Other regions	141	3	31	3
Total	**5,095**	**100**	**1,063**	**100**

WHAT

	1994 Assets	
	$ mil.	% of total
Cash & equivalents	25,633	39
Trading account	4,967	8
Unrealized derivatives gains	4,389	6
Net loans	25,224	38
Other assets	5,687	9
Total	**65,900**	**100**

	1994 Sales	
	$ mil.	% of total
Interest & fees on loans	1,897	38
Other interest	1,323	26
Credit card fees	832	16
Fees, service charges & commissions	621	12
Capital markets income	296	6
Other	126	2
Total	**5,095**	**100**

Selected Services
Credit cards
Debt trading
Leasing
Mortgage servicing
Retail and commercial banking
Trust services

Selected Subsidiaries
American National Corp.
FCC National Bank
First Chicago Capital Markets, Inc.
First Chicago International
First Chicago National Processing Corp.
First National Bank of Chicago

KEY COMPETITORS

ADVANTA	Canadian Imperial	First USA
American Express	Chase Manhattan	H.F. Ahmanson
Banc One	Chemical Banking	KeyCorp
Bank of Montreal	Citicorp	LaSalle/Talman
Bank of New York	CoreStates	MNB
BankAmerica	Financial	NationsBank
Barclays	CS Holding	Northern Trust
Bell Bancorp	Dai-Ichi Kangyo	Travelers

HOW MUCH

	9-Year Growth	1985	1986	1987	1988	1989	1990	1991	1992	1993	1994
Assets ($ mil.)	6.0%	38,893	39,148	44,209	44,432	47,907	50,779	48,963	49,281	52,560	65,900
Net income ($ mil.)	16.9%	169	276	(571)	513	359	249	116	(115)	805	690
Income as % of assets	—	0.4%	0.7%	—	1.2%	0.7%	0.5%	0.2%	—	1.5%	1.0%
Earnings per share ($)	10.3%	2.84	4.70	(10.71)	7.92	4.99	3.32	1.15	(2.08)	8.43	6.88
Stock price – high ($)	—	30.13	34.88	34.00	35.25	49.63	38.25	28.75	37.75	50.63	55.50
Stock price – low ($)	—	20.13	18.88	16.63	18.75	29.25	13.13	15.63	22.88	35.50	41.13
Stock price – close ($)	5.5%	29.50	28.63	18.88	29.63	37.13	16.50	24.63	36.75	43.25	47.75
P/E – high	—	11	7	—	5	10	12	25	—	6	8
P/E – low	—	7	4	—	2	6	4	14	—	4	6
Dividends per share ($)	3.5%	1.32	1.32	1.46	1.50	1.73	1.95	2.00	1.40	1.30	1.80
Book value per share ($)	2.4%	34.10	36.91	19.18	38.32	35.05	36.25	34.90	33.19	43.25	42.14
Employees	2.4%	14,276	13,884	15,108	16,069	18,158	19,068	18,549	16,998	17,355	17,630

1994 Year-end:
Equity as % of assets: 6.9%
Return on assets: 1.2%
Return on equity: 18.9%
Long-term debt (mil.): $9,936
No. of shares (mil.): 90
Dividends
  Yield: 3.8%
  Payout: 26.2%
Market value (mil.): $4,291
Sales (mil.): $5,095

**Stock Price History
High/Low 1985–94**

FIRST DATA CORPORATION

OVERVIEW

In 1995 Hackensack, New Jersey–based First Data Corporation announced its merger with Atlanta's First Financial Management. If approved, the union will bring together the 2 first families of both credit card processing and cash transmission services.

First Data is the largest credit transaction processor in the US. Part of its business is in processing applications, embossing cards, and providing billing services for banks that issue MasterCards and Visas. First Financial, meanwhile, has concentrated on the merchant side, providing transaction authorization and settlement services. While First Data has sometimes contracted with both the issuer and the merchant in credit card transactions, much of its business has come from servicing only part of the transaction. Having First Financial on

board may give First Data the added business of settling the merchant side too. This would eliminate the need (when the 2 parts of the transaction are split) of settling through the card consortia. Some banks do both sides themselves and compete with First Data.

In the merger, First Data will acquire Western Union, the largest cash transfer service in the US (which it had tried to buy in 1994). The addition of this business to its MoneyGram services will make it dominant in the field — and raises red flags for antitrust regulators. The merger will also bring Telecheck, the largest check authorization service in the US and the backbone of First Financial's business, as well as First Financial's data imaging business. First Data also has a major mutual fund transaction settlement operation.

WHEN

Both First Data and First Financial Management developed from in-house data processing operations that became independent profit centers for their parent companies and were then spun off.

First Financial Management is the older of the 2 companies. It arose out of the data processing department of the Georgia Railroad Bank & Trust Co. in 1971. Its goal was to provide small banks (in addition to its parent company) with a variety of data and transaction services. By the time it went public in 1983, it was the largest banking data processor in the Southeast. The company grew rapidly in a consolidating industry, and in 1987 it entered the credit card transaction processing business with the purchase of NaBANCO.

That same year American Express created a separate unit, First Data Resources, for its transaction processing functions under the leadership of Henry Duques. Duques had built up the unit during the 1980s to process a variety of transactions for American Express's charge card processing business and its burgeoning financial services operations, which included the Boston Company, Lehman Brothers, E. F. Hutton, and IDS. Between its founding and its spinoff, the company expanded its 3rd-party transaction business, offering services at low prices made possible by economies of scale that smaller organizations could not achieve.

While First Data was growing, First Financial remained active, buying Georgia Federal Bank in 1989 to facilitate the growth of its bank card business.

As the 1990s dawned, American Express's dreams of a financial services empire were crumbling. The businesses did not fit well with American Express, and its attention was being diverted from its core lines. However, First Data had become the largest bank card processing company in the US and a significant power in mutual funds transactions. In 1992 it was spun off in an IPO that left American Express the owner of 60% of First Data Corp.'s stock (it now owns 20%).

About this time First Financial began sharpening its focus on merchant (rather than bank) services. It bought Telecheck (check authorization) in 1992 and began divesting its banking and banking services holdings.

In 1994 the 2 companies came head-to-head in a battle to acquire Western Union, the leading consumer funds transfer company (founded in 1855). It was on the market after its parent, New Valley Corp., went into bankruptcy. After a bruising bidding war (which also included Forstmann, Little), First Data backed away from matching First Financial's bid of $1.9 billion.

In the next 9 months, both companies continued to make acquisitions, and First Financial took Western Union into China.

Then, in June 1995, First Data announced that it would buy First Financial for $6.5 billion. The merger, which would make First Data the largest in its field, aroused speculation that there might be antitrust obstacles to its closing. The union would give the company a 30% share of a fragmented field that is drawing new competitors like AT&T and IBM.

NYSE symbol: FDC
Fiscal year ends: December 31

WHO

Chairman and CEO: Henry C. Duques, age 51, $419,996 pay
EVP: Walter M. Hoff, age 42, $308,904 pay
EVP: Charles T. Fote, age 46, $260,000 pay
EVP Business Development: Edward C. Nafus, age 54, $258,000 pay
EVP: Robert J. Levenson, age 53, $255,000 pay
EVP and CFO: Lee Adrean, age 43
President, First Data Resources: Aldo J. Tesi
President, Shareholder Services Group: Robert F. Radin
President, Health Systems Group: Larry R. Ferguson
President, ACB Business Services: A. Wayne Johnson
President, First Data InfoSource Group: William Bak
SVP Finance: Larry D. Hain, age 54
SVP Human Resources: Donald F. Crowley
General Counsel: David P. Bailis, age 39
Auditors: Ernst & Young LLP

WHERE

HQ: 401 Hackensack Ave., Hackensack, NJ 07601
Phone: 201-525-4702
Fax: 201-342-0402

First Data operates in Australia, the UK, and the US.

	1994 Sales		1994 Operating Income	
	$ mil.	% of total	$ mil.	% of total
US	1,477	89	361	91
UK	153	9	32	8
Other regions	22	1	4	1
Total	**1,652**	**100**	**397**	**100**

WHAT

	1994 Sales	
	$ mil.	% of total
Net fees	1,406	85
Affiliates' revenues	66	4
Fees on financial instrument sales	180	11
Total	**1,652**	**100**

Selected Subsidiaries
ACB Business Services (accounts receivables management services)
Call Interactive (800 and 900 numbers)
Card Establishment Services (merchant processing services)
Card Product Services (technology and data processing)
Card Program Management (client support services)
Electronic Funds Services (merchant, debit, and private-label card processing)
ENVOY (merchant processing services)
FDR Australia (electronic funds transfers)
FDR Ltd. (UK, bank card processing)
First Data InfoSource (consumer and business information databases)
First Data Resources (3rd party processor of bank card transactions)
Health Systems Group (medical information management systems and services)
Integrated Payment Systems (cash remittance services)
Shareholder Services Group (mutual fund transaction processing)
Teleservices (operator and customer support for MCI)

KEY COMPETITORS

American Express
AT&T
Citicorp
Dial
DST Services
EDS
Equifax
Financial Card Services
Maryland Bank
Thomson Corp.
Total System Services
TRW

HOW MUCH

	Annual Growth	1985	1986	1987	1988	1989	1990	1991	1992	1993	1994
Sales ($ mil.)	23.9%	—	—	—	457	672	845	1,026	1,205	1,490	1,652
Net income ($ mil.)	22.0%	—	—	—	63	98	103	118	141	173	208
Income as % of sales	—	—	—	—	13.8%	14.6%	12.2%	11.55%	11.7%	11.6%	12.6%
Earnings per share ($)	20.5%	—	—	—	0.61	0.94	0.99	1.13	1.30	1.56	1.87
Stock price – high ($)	—	—	—	—	—	—	—	—	34.38	42.25	50.63
Stock price – low ($)	—	—	—	—	—	—	—	—	21.25	31.25	40.50
Stock price – close ($)	17.4%	—	—	—	—	—	—	—	34.38	40.75	47.38
P/E – high	—	—	—	—	—	—	—	—	26	27	27
P/E – low	—	—	—	—	—	—	—	—	16	20	22
Dividends per share ($)	(24.4%)	—	—	—	—	—	—	—	0.21	0.12	0.12
Book value per share ($)	14.3%	—	—	—	—	—	—	—	7.22	8.65	9.43
Employees	6.5%	—	—	—	—	—	—	—	19,400	19,300	22,000

1994 Year-end:
Debt ratio: 41.0%
Return on equity: 21.1%
Cash (mil.): $363
Long-term debt (mil.): $475
No. of shares (mil.): 108
Dividends
  Yield: 0.3%
  Payout: 6.4%
Market value (mil.): $5,100
Assets (mil.): $5,419

**Stock Price History
High/Low 1992–94**

FIRST INTERSTATE BANCORP

OVERVIEW

Los Angeles–based First Interstate continued its solid earnings growth for a 3rd year (between 1987 and 1991 it lost money every other year because of acquisitions, the recession, and its own lending policies). The return to a solid footing has allowed the company to keep acquiring banks (over a dozen in 1994–1995). It also let the bank begin a major restructuring from a position of strength.

Edward Carson, generally credited for the improvement, ceded the duties of chairman and CEO to president William Siart in 1995.

In the past 5 years, First Interstate has repositioned itself as a superregional bank after failing in its efforts to become a major international player. Instead, it has concentrated on expanding its retail and commercial bank operations (adding new services to increase cross-selling) in the West and the Southwest, with particular emphasis on its home state, California, and Texas. First Interstate is reducing the number of separate state subsidiaries, further cutting expenses and consolidating operations. The new interstate banking regulations of 1994 allow states to opt out of the system, however, and resistance in Texas means that First Interstate may be unable to consolidate its Texas operations fully.

WHEN

First Interstate is the descendant of the Bank of Italy, opened in San Francisco in 1904 by Amadeo Peter Giannini. Having made enough money in his stepfather's produce firm to retire by the age of 31, he instead began dabbling in real estate and banking.

Hoping to develop a nationwide bank chain, Giannini formed Transamerica in 1928 as the umbrella company for Bank of Italy and Bank of America. Transamerica acquired banks and insurance companies in several states during the 1930s, despite regulatory investigations and US government–mandated divestitures.

Even before the Bank Holding Company Act of 1956, Transamerica had divested Bank of America; afterward it spun off Firstamerica (23 banks in 11 other western states) and concentrated on insurance. These 2 former siblings became arch-competitors.

Firstamerica bought California Bank (1959) and First Western Bank and Trust (1961), and in 1961 Firstamerica became Western Bancorp. In 1978 Joseph Pinola became chairman and CEO of Western. He centralized policymaking and launched an ambitious program of growth.

In 1981 Western changed its name to First Interstate Bancorp and began franchising its name, advertising, products, and services to locally owned banks (1982). Pinola also reorganized the company. In 1985 he divided the California banking operations into 2 sections, wholesale (banking to other corporations) and retail. The wholesale arm used a London merchant bank bought from Continental Illinois. In the 1980s First Interstate acquired retail banks in, among other places, Denver (1983) and Oklahoma (1986); it even tried, unsuccessfully, to buy Bank of America and its parent company for $3.4 billion (1986).

First Interstate ran into asset problems with the purchase of Texas's troubled Allied Bancshares for $160 million (1988). Other risky ventures included making real estate loans in such declining markets as Colorado and Arizona.

In 1989 First Interstate acquired Alex. Brown Financial Group. That same year it announced a plan to offer an additional $400 million in stock to cover real estate loan losses in Texas and Arizona. Stockholders protested and Pinola resigned in 1990. First Interstate reduced the offering to $276 million in 1990 and sold 40% of the new stock to Kohlberg Kravis Roberts (which owns about 8% of the corporation). At that time First Interstate's weakness made it a prime target for takeover. Pinola's replacement, Edward Carson, sold off some of the smaller banks in troubled locations as well as some noncore businesses, such as NOVA Financial Services (consumer lending), and began aggressively selling nonperforming assets in a program that became an industry model.

Since then the corporation has ruthlessly cut costs by trimming staff and consolidating branches. In 1994 First Interstate announced that it would work to improve its stock price by further cutting costs in order to defend against possible acquisition.

It is also improving its information systems division, which is becoming a profit center by offering cash management services (such as payroll and taxes) to small and medium-sized businesses. Expanding on this business in 1995, First Interstate started a technology banking group and set up an Internet web site. One of its newest initiatives is *Business Express Plus*, a software package that helps small businesses track their banking transactions.

NYSE symbol: I
Fiscal year ends: December 31

WHO

Chairman and CEO: William E. B. Siart, age 48,
$1,559,500 pay (prior to promotion)
President and COO: William S. Randall, age 54,
$939,252 pay (prior to promotion)
VC; CEO, California Region: Bruce G. Willison, age 46,
$944,133 pay
CEO, Northwest Region: James J. Curran, age 55,
$819,604 pay
EVP and General Counsel: William J. Bogaard, age 56
EVP and CFO: Thomas P. Marrie, age 56
EVP Investor Relations: Christine M. McCarthy
EVP Central Marketing: T. Christian Armstrong
EVP Human Resources: Lillian R. Gorman, age 41
SVP Corporate Communications: Shirley T. Hosoi
Auditors: Ernst & Young LLP

WHERE

HQ: 633 W. Fifth St., Los Angeles, CA 90071
Phone: 213-614-3001
Fax: 213-614-3741

First Interstate has 1,100 branches in Alaska, Arizona,
California, Colorado, Idaho, Montana, Nevada, Oregon,
Texas, Utah, Washington, and Wyoming, and operations
in Brazil, the Cayman Islands, Spain, and the UK.

WHAT

	1994 Assets	
	$ mil.	% of total
Cash & equivalents	6,275	11
US Treasurys & agencies	5,703	10
Mortgage-backed securities	7,085	13
Net loans	32,288	58
Other	4,462	8
Total	**55,813**	**100**

	1994 Sales	
	$ mil.	% of total
Loan interest	2,304	54
Other interest	888	21
Trust fees	193	5
Service charges on deposits	562	13
Commissions & fees	132	3
Other	167	4
Total	**4,246**	**100**

Services
Asset management
Bank credit cards
Checking and NOW
  accounts
Commercial financing
International banking
Investment counseling
Mortgage banking
Real estate and
  commercial loans
Savings accounts
Venture capital

Selected Subsidiaries
First Interstate
  Administração e Serviços,
  Ltd. (Brazil)
First Interstate Denver Asset
  Corp.
First Interstate Equity Corp.
First Interstate Insurance
First Interstate Investment
  Services, Inc.
First Interstate Leasing
First Interstate Mortgage Co.
First Interstate Securities
  Co. (UK) Ltd.

KEY COMPETITORS

Banc One
BankAmerica
Boatmen's Bancshares
California Bancshares
Chemical Banking
Citadel Holding
Citicorp
City National
Club Corp.
Coast Savings
Countrywide Credit
CU Bancorp
Cullen/Frost Bankers
Fidelity Savings

First Chicago
First Mortgage
GBC Bancorp
Great Western
H. F. Ahmanson
Household
International
NationsBank
Pacific Bancorporation
Sumitomo
Union Bank
ValliCorp
Wells Fargo
Westcorp Financial

HOW MUCH

	9-Year Growth	1985	1986	1987	1988	1989	1990	1991	1992	1993	1994
Assets ($ mil.)	1.5%	48,957	55,360	50,853	58,194	59,051	51,356	48,922	50,863	51,461	55,813
Net income ($ mil.)	10.3%	304	322	(604)	102	(152)	439	(288)	282	537	734
Income as % of assets	—	0.6%	0.6%	—	0.2%	—	0.9%	—	0.6%	1.1%	1.3%
Earnings per share ($)	3.1%	6.64	6.84	(13.01)	2.03	(3.89)	6.79	(5.24)	3.23	6.36	8.71
Stock price – high ($)	—	55.38	67.38	62.75	53.50	70.38	45.88	42.50	48.25	68.00	85.00
Stock price – low ($)	—	41.50	50.75	35.00	39.13	40.75	15.63	20.00	29.25	44.50	62.38
Stock price – close ($)	2.8%	52.88	52.00	39.25	43.38	41.88	23.50	30.00	46.75	64.13	67.63
P/E – high	—	8	10	—	26	—	7	—	15	11	10
P/E – low	—	6	7	—	19	—	2	—	9	7	7
Dividends per share ($)	1.2%	2.46	2.62	2.77	2.89	2.98	3.00	1.80	1.20	1.60	2.75
Book value per share ($)	(2.9%)	54.42	57.83	42.49	42.56	36.78	39.78	32.57	35.04	41.36	41.59
Employees	(2.6%)	34,303	35,410	36,253	38,270	36,027	35,192	30,281	26,990	26,589	27,000

1994 Year-end:
Equity as % of assets: 5.5%
Return on assets: 1.4%
Return on equity: 23.3%
Long-term debt (mil.): $1,388
No. of shares (mil.): 74
Dividends
  Yield: 4.1%
  Payout: 31.6%
Market value (mil.): $5,018
Sales (mil.): $4,246

**Stock Price History
High/Low 1985–94**

FIRST UNION CORPORATION

OVERVIEW

First Union's chairman and CEO, Edward Crutchfield, sees traditional banks as dinosaurs lumbering inevitably toward extinction. Those that survive are the ones that can evolve into something new — financial services companies. He sees fewer companies (perhaps only 10 to 15), but ones that are leaner and more responsive to their customers. The others will be swallowed up. Crutchfield is determined that his Charlotte, North Carolina–based bank will finish at the top of this Darwinian food chain.

In order to avoid becoming merely part of the geological record, Crutchfield gave a whole new meaning to regional banking by engineering a merger with Newark-based First Fidelity Bancorp. This merger of the Sunbelt and the Rust Belt will put the combined operation in the first rank of US banking, with a branch network running the length of the East Coast.

Through this enlarged network the company will offer a uniform array of financial services and products, including mortgage banking, insurance, trust and brokerage services, mutual funds (through Lieber & Co., which administers the Evergreen family of funds), and derivatives (which it uses to manage risk rather than for profit). With no overlap in operations, widespread job cuts are unlikely, and the managements of the 2 companies are expected to merge amicably.

WHEN

The Union National Bank of Charlotte, North Carolina, was formed in 1908. It chugged along for the next 50 years, weathering wars and depressions, in the shadow of tobacco-banking giant Wachovia, of Winston-Salem. In 1958 the company acquired First National Bank & Trust, of Asheville, and became First Union National Bank of North Carolina.

In 1967 First Union formed a holding company, First Union National Bancorp. In 1971 one of its subsidiaries, Cameron Brown, merged with the Reid-McGee Company, of Mississippi, a mortgage banker. The next year the holding company was renamed Cameron Financial Corporation. But a 1974 reorganization, which shifted Cameron Brown to the jurisdiction of First Union Bank (where it was renamed First Union Mortgage Corp. and, later, First Union Home Equity Corp.), resulted in yet another renaming of the holding company. In 1975 it became First Union Corporation.

Until about 1985 the bank itself continued making acquisitions separately from those of the holding company. That year state regulations were changed to permit regional branch banking, allowing the holding company to move into lucrative markets out of state, especially Florida. Since 1985 the corporation has had a steady diet of acquisitions, the bulk of them in retiree-filled Florida. That state's assets and deposits now dominate the bank's holdings mix. Institutions the corporation acquired there include Central Florida Bank Corporation, First Bankers Corporation, Sarasota Bank & Trust, First State Bank of Pensacola, and Dis-Com Securities of Hallandale. Other regional acquisitions include Georgia State Bancshares, the First Railroad & Banking Company of Georgia, Atlantic Bancor- poration, and Southern Bancorporation.

First Union has reduced its level of nonperforming assets, but they were never an undue burden. Most of First Union's region was not subject to the overheated boom of the 1980s whose end badly hurt banks in many regions of the country. In addition, the Southeast has been a growth area in the 1990s.

First Union kept up the pace of acquisitions in the 1990s. In 1991 it bought the failed Southeast Banks from the FDIC, which reimbursed First Union for 85% of all losses stemming from the non–credit card commercial portfolio and funded all of Southeast Bank's nonperforming assets (i.e., paid the cost of maintaining real estate owned through foreclosure or reversion).

In 1993 First Union took possession of Dominion Bancshares of Washington, DC, with branches in Virginia and Maryland. It also bought First American Metro Corporation, another DC area bank, which had been owned by First American Bankshares. American Metro and First American Bankshares were owned by the notorious Bank of Credit and Commerce International (BCCI), which the US government forced into liquidation.

In 1994 and 1995 First Union assimilated more than 10 banks with its usual ease (First Union is unusual among expansionist banks in that it has uniform data processing systems in all its regions).

First Union is testing the waters of electronic banking, which will allow it to operate nationally without adding branches. It expects to have a full range of services available via the Internet by late 1995.

NYSE symbol: FTU
Fiscal year ends: December 31

WHO

Chairman and CEO: Edward E. Crutchfield, age 53, $1,670,000 pay
VC: B. J. Walker, age 64, $650,000 pay
President: John R. Georgius, age 50, $1,200,000 pay
CEO, First Union National Bank of Florida:
Byron E. Hodnett, $790,000 pay
EVP and CFO: Robert T. Atwood, age 54, $670,000 pay
EVP, Secretary, and General Counsel: Marion A.
Cowell Jr., age 60
EVP Automation and Operations: Austin A. Adams
EVP Human Resources: Don R. Johnson
SVP Corporate Communications and Investor
Relations: Barbara K. Massa
SVP Marketing and Strategic Planning: Alvin T. Sale
Auditors: KPMG Peat Marwick LLP

WHERE

HQ: One First Union Center, Charlotte, NC
28288-0013
Phone: 704-374-6565
Fax: 704-374-2140

First Union Corporation has 1,338 banking offices in the Southeast.

	1994 US Deposits	
	$ mil.	% of total
Florida	25,900	41
North Carolina	18,000	28
Georgia	7,200	11
Virginia	6,200	10
South Carolina	1,900	3
Tennessee	1,700	3
Washington, DC	1,200	2
Maryland	961	2
Total	**63,061**	**100**

WHAT

	1994 Assets	
	$ mil.	% of total
Cash & equivalents	3,741	5
Trading account	1,207	1
Treasury & agency securities	6,164	8
Collateralized mortgage obligations	2,244	3
State & municipal bonds	1,226	1
Net loans	53,051	69
Other	9,681	13
Total	**77,314**	**100**

	1994 Sales	
	$ mil.	% of total
Interest & fees on loans	4,173	67
Other interest	921	15
Deposit account svc. charges	435	7
Capital management	225	4
Service fees & commissions	114	2
Other	386	5
Total	**6,254**	**100**

Selected Services
Credit cards
Home equity loans
Insurance
Investment banking
Mortgage banking
Mutual funds
Retail and commercial banking
Securities brokerage

Selected Subsidiaries
First Union Brokerage Services Inc.
First Union Capital Markets Corp.
First Union Home Equity
First Union Mortgage Corp.
First Union National Banks

KEY COMPETITORS

Bank South
BankAmerica
Barnett Banks
BB&T Financial
Central Fidelity
Charles Schwab

Countrywide Credit
Crestar Financial
First Fidelity
First Virginia
FMR
Mellon Bank

Merrill Lynch
NationsBank
SunTrust
Synovus Financial
Wachovia

HOW MUCH

	9-Year Growth	1985	1986	1987	1988	1989	1990	1991	1992	1993	1994
Assets ($ mil.)	18.7%	16,567	26,820	27,630	28,978	32,131	40,781	46,085	51,327	70,787	77,314
Net income ($ mil.)	20.4%	174	296	283	297	256	304	319	515	818	925
Income as % of assets	—	1.0%	1.1%	1.0%	1.0%	0.8%	0.7%	0.7%	1.0%	1.2%	1.2%
Earnings per share ($)	10.3%	2.16	2.72	2.55	2.76	2.40	2.52	2.55	3.72	4.73	5.22
Stock price – high ($)	—	22.44	29.94	28.88	23.75	27.00	22.00	31.00	44.88	53.13	48.00
Stock price – low ($)	—	17.31	20.56	16.63	19.38	19.63	13.75	13.50	29.13	37.25	39.00
Stock price – close ($)	7.5%	21.50	24.13	19.50	22.13	20.63	15.38	30.00	43.63	41.25	41.38
P/E – high	—	10	11	11	9	11	9	12	12	11	9
P/E – low	—	8	8	7	7	8	6	5	8	8	8
Dividends per share ($)	12.8%	0.58	0.65	0.77	0.86	1.00	1.08	1.12	1.28	1.50	1.72
Book value per share ($)	10.0%	12.96	14.55	16.25	17.98	19.37	23.19	24.62	27.93	30.39	30.66
Employees	11.6%	11,903	19,266	20,284	19,761	17,733	20,521	24,203	23,459	32,861	31,858

1994 Year-end:
Equity as % of assets: 7.0%
Return on assets: 1.2%
Return on equity: 17.5%
Long-term debt (mil.): $3,429
No. of shares (mil.): 176
Dividends
  Yield: 4.2%
  Payout: 33.0%
Market value (mil.): $7,284
Sales (mil.): $6,254

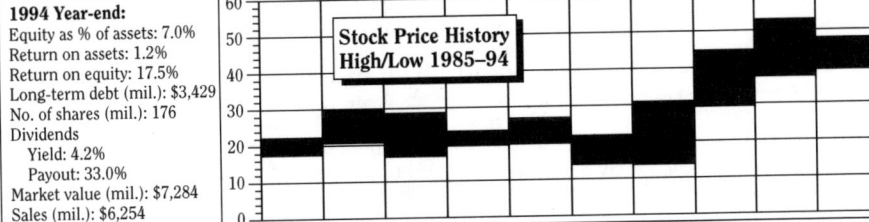

Stock Price History
High/Low 1985–94

FLAGSTAR COMPANIES, INC.

OVERVIEW

These days Flagstar is just trying to put food on the table. One of the largest restaurant companies in the nation, Spartanburg, South Carolina–based Flagstar is focusing on restaurants by selling its nonrestaurant businesses, including its vending, concessions, and recreation services operations.

Through its Flagstar Corporation subsidiary, the company owns and operates or franchises 1,548 Denny's restaurants (full-service family chain), 207 Quincy's restaurants (family steakhouse chain in the Southeast), and 209 El Pollo Loco restaurants (broiled chicken chain). It is also the largest Hardee's franchisee, with 595 units.

Flagstar returned to profitability in 1994 after 5 years of losses, but it is still struggling under more than $2 billion in debt. Its focus on core restaurant business is designed to raise cash from asset sales to pay down debt and update Denny's restaurants, which have been called drab and outdated.

The task of cooking up a healthy future for the company was handed to James Adamson, former CEO of Burger King, who was named CEO of Flagstar in 1995. Adamson succeeds Jerry Richardson, who left to concentrate on his new NFL team, the Carolina Panthers.

Investment firm KKR owns about 61% of the company.

WHEN

In the late 1960s, in an effort to stabilize earnings, Trans World Airlines acquired businesses outside the volatile airline industry. Starting with Hilton International Hotels in 1967, TWA bought Canteen (food services, 1973), Spartan Food Systems (Hardee's and Quincy's restaurants, 1979), and Century 21 (real estate, 1979). The companies were consolidated under holding company Trans World Corporation in 1979. Ironically, the unstable earnings of the airline, which lost $128 million between 1973 and 1980, led Trans World to spin off TWA to its shareholders in 1984. In 1985 the company sold Century 21 to Metropolitan Life for $251 million.

Of the 3 businesses remaining at the end of 1985, Canteen was the largest, generating 46% of sales through food service contracts and vending machines in businesses, recreation areas, schools, and health care facilities. Hilton International, which cannot use the Hilton name in the US, operated 90 hotels in the US (under the name Vista International), Guam, Puerto Rico, and 43 foreign countries. Spartan operated 332 Hardee's restaurant franchises and 216 Quincy's Family Steakhouses in the southeastern US. Trans World sold Hilton, which had an inconsistent earnings record, to UAL (parent of United Air Lines) in 1986 for $835 million and 2.5 million shares of UAL common stock.

That year Trans World bought nursing home operator American Medical Services and became Transworld Services. The company outbid Marriott for Denny's (paying $843 million) in 1987. With the purchase came El Pollo Loco, a Denny's subsidiary. TW Services formed a joint venture (EPL Japan) with

Japan's Mitsui in 1987 to operate El Pollo Loco restaurants in Japan through 1998 (Japanese operation of Denny's restaurants had begun in 1973). By 1988 TW Services was the 4th largest US restaurant company, with food sales of nearly $3.6 billion.

After a 9-month takeover fight, Coniston Partners paid $1.7 billion to increase its ownership of TW Services stock from 19% to 80% in 1989; agreeing to a merger with TW Holdings, a company formed by Coniston especially for the deal, TW Services became a wholly owned subsidiary of TW Holdings. The buyout left TW Holdings with $1.9 billion in debt at the end of 1989. Buyout-related costs contributed to losses in 1989, 1990, 1991, and 1992. In an effort to raise cash to pay off its debt, TW Holdings sold several assets in 1990, including American Medical Services. Flagstar sold a 47.2% stake to Kohlberg Kravis Roberts for $300 million in 1992.

The company changed its name from TW Holdings to Flagstar Companies in 1993. Also in 1993 several suits were filed against Denny's by patrons who claimed they were denied service because of race. Most notable was a suit filed by 6 black US Secret Service agents in Maryland. The suits are pending.

In 1994 the company sold most of its Canteen food and vending unit to London-based Compass Group PLC for $450 million. That same year Flagstar agreed to sell its TW Recreational Services, which provides lodging, food, and guest services for national parks and resorts, including Yellowstone and Mount Rushmore, to ARAMARK for $130 million. However, in 1995 the deal fell through and Flagstar put the unit up for sale again.

WHO

Chairman, President, and CEO: James B. Adamson, age 47
EVP, Flagstar Corp.; President and CEO, Denny's: C. Ronald Petty, age 50, $428,565 pay
EVP Product Development and Distribution, Flagstar Corp.: Samuel H. Maw, age 61, $355,684 pay
EVP and CFO: C. Robert Campbell, age 50
EVP Special Projects, Flagstar Corp.: H. Stephen McManus, age 52
EVP Human Resources and Corporate Affairs, Flagstar Corp.: Edna K. Morris, age 43
SVP, Flagstar Corp.; President and COO, El Pollo Loco: Raymond J. Perry, age 53, $372,339 pay
SVP, Flagstar Corp.; President and COO, Quincy's: Gregory M. Buckley, age 41, $347,979 pay
SVP, Flagstar Corp.; President and COO, Flagstar Enterprises (Hardee's): James P. Kibler, age 40
SVP Corporate Affairs, Flagstar Corp.: Coleman J. Sullivan, age 45
VP and General Counsel: Rhonda J. Parrish, age 38
Auditors: Deloitte & Touche LLP

WHERE

HQ: 203 E. Main St., Spartanburg, SC 29319-9966
Phone: 803-597-8000
Fax: 803-597-8780 (Public Relations)

Flagstar has operations in the US, Canada, and overseas.

	Restaurants by Geographic Area	
	No.	% of total
US	2,472	97
Canada	25	1
Other countries	62	2
Total	**2,559**	**100**

WHAT

	1994 Sales	
	$ mil.	% of total
Denny's	1,548	58
Hardee's	701	26
Quincy's	284	11
El Pollo Loco & other	133	5
Total	**2,666**	**100**

	1994 Restaurants
	No.
Denny's	1,548
Hardee's	595
El Pollo Loco	209
Quincy's	207
Total	**2,559**

KEY COMPETITORS

Accor	Imasco
Allied Domecq	Investor's Management
Applebee's	McDonald's
Bertucci's	PepsiCo
Bob Evans	Rally's
Buffets	Shoney's
Carlson	Sizzler
Checkers Drive-In	Sonic Corp.
CKE Restaurants	Subway
Cracker Barrel	Taco Cabana
Dairy Queen	Tennessee Restuarant
Family Restaurants	Uno Restaurant
Foodmaker	Wendy's
Fresh Choice	Whataburger
IHOP	

HOW MUCH

	Annual Growth	1985	1986	1987	1988	1989	1990	1991	1992	1993	1994
Sales ($ mil.)	3.2%	2,002	2,152	2,492	3,574	3,485	3,682	3,618	3,720	3,970	2,666
Net income ($ mil.)	14.3%	105	16	56	54	(57)	(68)	(68)	(52)	(1,648)	350
Income as % of sales	—	5.2%	0.7%	2.2%	1.5%	—	—	—	—	—	13.1%
Earnings per share ($)	—	—	—	—	—	(8.70)	(3.05)	(3.05)	(2.32)	(39.23)	6.13
Stock price – high ($)	—	—	—	—	—	22.50	29.69	23.13	23.75	20.94	12.75
Stock price – low ($)	—	—	—	—	—	17.81	12.19	10.63	13.44	8.50	5.50
Stock price – close ($)	(20.8%)	—	—	—	—	22.50	14.38	15.00	20.00	9.25	7.00
P/E – high	—	—	—	—	—	—	—	—	—	—	2
P/E – low	—	—	—	—	—	—	—	—	—	—	1
Dividends per share ($)	—	—	—	—	—	0.00	0.00	0.00	0.00	0.00	0.00
Book value per share ($)	—	—	—	—	—	9.41	6.33	3.44	6.81	(33.59)	(25.09)
Employees	(3.6%)	—	—	—	—	108,000	100,000	112,000	116,000	123,000	90,000

1994 Year-end:
Debt ratio: 100.0%
Return on equity: —
Cash (mil.): $67
Current ratio: 0.67
Long-term debt (mil.): $2,068
Number of shares (mil.): 42
Dividends
  Yield: —
  Payout: —
Market value (mil.): $297

**Stock Price History
High/Low 1989–94**

FLEET FINANCIAL GROUP, INC.

OVERVIEW

The race is to the fleet — Fleet Financial, that is, which may have won the race for banking dominance in New England. Through successive acquisitions in the late 1980s and early 1990s, Fleet had positioned itself as one of the 3 major players (with Bank of Boston and Shawmut National). Then, in 1995 (after 14 acquisitions in recent years) it forged ahead of Bank of Boston with the announcement of a planned merger with 159-year-old Shawmut. Investment firm Kohlberg Kravis Roberts owns about 14% of Fleet.

The new institution would so overpower some markets, including Fleet's native Rhode Island, that significant public and governmental opposition has arisen. This opposition is based both on the reduction of banking competition and on the loss of jobs which will occur as the company consolidates redundant operations.

Shawmut brings strong consumer and small- and middle-market business banking operations to Fleet, which also has significant consumer, student, and mortgage loan operations. In 1994–95 the company bolstered its financial services business still more by acquiring Plaza Home Mortgage, a mortgage servicer, and the IBM mutual fund family.

WHEN

Like all good New Englanders, Fleet can trace its roots back to early America — the 1791 founding of the Providence Bank.

The Providence Bank evolved into Fleet National Bank, and in 1968 Fleet became the wholly owned subsidiary of a new bank holding company, Industrial Bancorp, which in 1970 became Industrial National Corp.

The bank's specialty was lending to the jewelry industry in the Northeast. In the 1970s the bank began diversifying beyond its traditional market and overseas. It acquired Southern Discount of Atlanta (consumer finance) in 1973 and Mortgage Associates of Milwaukee (mortgage banking) in 1974.

Terrence Murray became CEO in 1982, the year that Industrial National Corp. changed its name to Fleet Financial Group. The young CEO continued the bank's diversification, acquiring Credico of New Jersey (consumer lending, 1983) and folding it into Atlanta-based Fleet Finance. Fleet also crossed the banking borders after Rhode Island permitted interstate banking in New England in 1984.

In the 1980s Fleet bought 46 companies as its assets rose nearly 700% between 1980 and 1990. Even its failed acquisitions were successes. Fleet was outbid for Massachusetts-based Conifer Group in 1986, but Conifer was saddled with bad real estate loans. The "winner" was the doomed Bank of New England.

In 1988 Fleet bought New York–based Norstar in a $1.3 billion deal, taking the name Fleet/Norstar. Norstar traced its history to the 1803 founding of the State Bank of Albany.

Fleet was not immune to the excesses of its time and place. Its expansion and its own credit policies had given it the same problem that afflicted its competitors: risky loans that turned into nonperforming assets when the

northeastern economy went into recession. Decreased economic activity and high loss provisions took Fleet into the red for 1990, though it remained essentially sound — sound enough to capitalize on other banks' problems. In 1991 Fleet, with the help of out-of-industry Kohlberg Kravis Roberts, bought Bank of New England (except for its bad loan portfolio) and 2 other, smaller banks from the FDIC. However, Fleet received a contract to service the BNE loans through its RECOLL Management Corp.

Fleet/Norstar changed its name to Fleet Financial Group, sold some of its nonperforming loans to raise cash, and made 6 more acquisitions in New England in 1992.

Also in that year Fleet received adverse publicity from a *60 Minutes* investigation of exorbitant home equity interest rates and fees imposed by lenders from whom Fleet Financial had bought loans. As a result, Fleet Financial stopped buying 3rd-party loans. In 1993 the company settled with the State of Georgia, agreeing to pay $30 million in "relief" to affected customers and to contribute $70 million to low-income housing programs. It was, however, cleared of usury charges by the Georgia Supreme Court.

Fleet continued to make acquisitions in 1993 and 1994 while implementing a major restructuring plan designed to cut the fat accumulated during its previous acquisitions.

In 1995 Fleet and Shawmut agreed to merge. Shawmut was founded in 1836 in Boston as the Warren Bank, with ties to the Warren Insurance Company. It was renamed Shawmut (a Native American word associating land and water) in 1837 and joined the national bank system in 1864.

WHO

Chairman, President, and CEO: Terrence Murray, age 55, $1,892,200 pay
VC: H. Jay Sarles, age 49, $862,692 pay
VC: Michael R. Zucchini, age 48, $860,769 pay
VC: Robert J. Higgins, age 49, $855,769 pay
EVP and CFO: Eugene M. McQuade, age 46, $630,769 pay
EVP: John B. Robinson Jr., age 48
SVP: Peter C. Fitts, age 54
SVP: Anne M. Slattery, age 47
SVP, Secretary, and General Counsel: William C. Mutterperl, age 48
SVP Human Resources: M. Anne Szostak, age 44
Auditors: KPMG Peat Marwick LLP

WHERE

HQ: 50 Kennedy Plaza, Providence, RI 02903
Phone: 401-278-5800
Fax: 401-278-5801

Fleet Financial Group, Inc., is a regional bank in the northeastern US, with mortgage and other consumer finance services in 38 states.

	1994 Banking Offices	
	No.	% of total
New York	333	39
Massachusetts	200	23
Connecticut	135	16
Maine	104	12
Rhode Island	57	6
New Hampshire	35	4
Total	**864**	**100**

WHAT

	1994 Assets	
	$ mil.	% of total
Cash & equivalents	5,857	12
US Treasurys & agencies	2,444	5
Mortgage-backed securities	7,465	15
Other securities	1,335	3
Net loans	26,588	55
Other	5,068	10
Total	**48,757**	**100**

	1994 Sales	
	$ mil.	% of total
Loan interest & fees	2,367	53
Other interest	905	21
Mortgage banking	363	8
Banking service charges & fees	321	7
Investment services	175	4
Other	314	7
Total	**4,445**	**100**

Selected Services
Brokerage services
Consumer finance
Consumer retail banking
Investment services
Trust services

Selected Subsidiaries
AFSA Data Corp. (student loans)
The Fleet Banks

Fleet Brokerage Services
Fleet Capital, Inc.
Fleet Credit Corp.
Fleet Finance, Inc.
Fleet Investment Advisors
Fleet Investment Services
Fleet Mortgage Group, Inc.
Fleet Securities, Inc,
Fleet Services Corp.
RECOLL Management

KEY COMPETITORS

Banc One	Chase Manhattan	H.F. Ahmanson
Bank of Boston	Chemical	Mellon Bank
Bank of New York	Banking	National Boston
BankAmerica	Citicorp	Sallie Mae
BayBanks	First Fidelity	State Street
Charles Schwab	First Interstate	Boston

HOW MUCH

	9-year Growth	1985	1986	1987	1988	1989	1990	1991	1992	1993	1994
Assets ($ mil.)	10.6%	19,654	24,354	26,218	29,052	33,441	32,507	45,445	46,939	47,923	48,757
Net income ($ mil.)	12.7%	209	253	200	336	371	(74)	98	280	488	613
Income as % of assets	—	1.1%	2.2%	0.8%	1.2%	1.1%	—	0.2%	0.6%	1.0%	1.3%
Earnings per share ($)	7.4%	1.97	2.37	1.82	3.01	3.30	(0.75)	0.67	1.77	3.01	3.75
Stock price – high ($)	—	21.50	28.13	30.63	27.88	30.88	27.63	26.38	33.88	37.88	41.38
Stock price – low ($)	—	14.25	18.63	17.00	22.38	23.75	10.50	9.63	24.25	28.25	29.88
Stock price – close ($)	5.3%	20.31	23.25	22.75	25.50	26.13	11.00	24.88	32.75	33.38	32.38
P/E – high	—	11	12	17	9	9	—	39	19	13	11
P/E – low	—	7	8	9	7	7	—	14	14	9	8
Dividends per share ($)	8.4%	0.68	0.74	0.88	1.20	1.31	1.25	0.80	0.83	1.03	1.40
Book value per share ($)	6.5%	13.21	14.84	15.83	17.84	19.87	17.65	18.15	19.50	22.84	23.36
Employees	17.0%	5,246	8,410	18,750	20,000	18,500	18,000	25,000	27,500	26,000	21,500

1994 Year-end:
Equity as % of assets: 6.2%
Return on assets: 1.3%
Return on equity: 20.0%
Long-term debt (mil.): $3,457
No. of shares (mil.): 128
Dividends
  Yield: 4.3%
  Payout: 37.3%
Market value (mil.): $4,159
Sales (mil.): $4,445

**Stock Price History
High/Low 1985–94**

FLEETWOOD ENTERPRISES, INC.

OVERVIEW

Fleetwood Enterprises, a Riverside, California–based company, is the nation's largest maker of recreational vehicles. Fleetwood manufactures 3 types of RVs: folding trailers, travel trailers, and motor homes. Brand names include American Dream, American Eagle, Jamboree, Pace Arrow, Savanna, Southwind, and Tioga.

Fleetwood is also the US's #1 maker of manufactured housing. Its Fleetwood Credit Corp. finances recreational vehicle purchases by both wholesale and retail customers, and its building supply operations provide materials both for its own use and for other companies. These operations include 2 fiberglass manufacturing companies and a lumber producer. Fleetwood's insurance subsidiary provides

product liability risk insurancefor the parent company and other subsidiaries.

The company is not content with its market share leads. Its goal is to have a 35% share of the manufactured housing market and a 40% share of the RV market within the next few years. Fleetwood is also looking to Europe for growth opportunities. However, its Germany-based subsidiary, Niesmann & Bischoff, has had large operating losses in the last 2 years, even though management has switched manufacturing away from luxury RVs to more moderately priced motor homes.

CEO and founder John Crean takes one of his company's RVs out on the open road every year for an extended test drive. Crean owns 17.7% of the company.

WHEN

In 1950 John Crean started a business in California to make and sell venetian blinds to the motor home manufacturing industry. This enterprise was the forerunner of Fleetwood, Crean's 1957 entry into the manufactured housing industry, headquartered in Riverside. The company entered the RV market in 1964 by buying a small plant producing the Terry travel trailer. Fleetwood went public in 1965.

In 1969 the company bought Pace Arrow, a motor home producer, expanding Fleetwood's offerings in the rapidly growing RV market. Between 1968 and 1973 Fleetwood's sales grew at a nearly 55% annual rate.

An industrywide recession caused by the 1973 oil shock and subsequent credit crunch dropped Fleetwood's stock from a 1972 high of $49.50 to $3.50 in 1974. Intensive cost cutting helped position Fleetwood for the eventual upturn, and in 1976 the company bought Avion Coach Corporation, a manufacturer of luxury-class travel trailers and motor homes.

COO Glenn F. Kummer succeeded Crean as president in 1982, but Crean remained chairman and CEO. Strong RV sales helped pull Fleetwood out of a mild recession in the mid-1980s, when the company's stock plummeted again, from a 1983 high of $42 to a $9 low in 1985.

In 1987 the company opened a credit office in Southern California to finance customer purchases of RVs, avoiding riskier loans to manufactured housing buyers. Fleetwood Credit Corporation now has offices in California, Oregon, Indiana, Georgia, Massachusetts, and Texas. Fleetwood added to its existing supply operations (fiberglass and lumber) by

purchasing a cabinet door manufacturer (1988) and an aluminum window maker (1989).

In 1989 Fleetwood became the first company to surpass the $1 billion annual sales mark in RVs, increasing market share during an industry slump. Total sales increased 15% to a company-record $1.6 billion, while Fleetwood continued to steer clear of any long-term debt. The company added 2 new motor home models to its RV line: the lower-priced Flair and the curved-wall Cambria.

In 1989 Fleetwood bought Coleman's folding trailer business — the largest in the industry. The next year the company received a Saudi Arabian order for 2,000 manufactured homes. Unfortunately, in 1990 and 1991 recession and the Persian Gulf War inhibited demand for RVs and manufactured housing, even hurting tight-fisted Fleetwood, but sales began to recover by mid-1991. Fleetwood and Ford Motor Credit formed a joint venture in 1991 to offer financing to Fleetwood's manufactured housing dealers.

Fleetwood acquired an 80% interest in Niesmann & Bischoff, a German luxury-priced motor home manufacturer, in 1992. In 1993 the company completed a plant in Tennessee.

In 1994 the company built a new plant near Waco, Texas, bringing that area's total to 5 Fleetwood plants. The travel trailer division introduced a line of lighter-weight products for the customer with limited towing capacity. In 1995 the company began producing manufactured homes in Wichita Falls, Texas, and began construction of a housing manufacturing center in Winchester, Kentucky.

NYSE symbol: FLE
Fiscal year ends: Last Sunday in April

WHO

Chairman and CEO: John C. Crean, age 70,
$1,438,676 pay
President and COO: Glenn F. Kummer, age 61,
$1,260,716 pay
SVP Housing Group: Jon A. Nord, age 55, $631,368 pay
SVP RV Group: Elden L. Smith, age 55, $566,375 pay
SVP; President, Fleetwood Credit Corp.: Lawrence F.
Pittroff, age 60, $452,799 pay
Financial VP, Assistant Secretary, and CFO: Paul M.
Bingham, age 53
VP, General Counsel, and Secretary: William H. Lear,
age 55
VP Travel Trailers: Larry J. Hughes, age 51
VP Motor Homes: Richard E. Parks, age 48
VP Housing Group Operations: Mallory S. Smith,
age 53
VP Supply Subsidiaries: Larry L. Mace, age 52
VP Administration and Human Resources: Robert W.
Graham, age 58
VP Quality: Jerry L. Hewitt, age 51
Auditors: Arthur Andersen & Co, SC

WHERE

HQ: 3125 Myers St., Riverside, CA 92503-5527
Phone: 909-351-3500
Fax: 909-351-3690

Fleetwood operates 22 recreational vehicle and 38
manufactured housing plants in 19 states, Canada,
and Germany.

	1995 Sales	
	$ mil.	% of total
North America	2,803	98
Other regions	53	2
Total	**2,856**	**100**

WHAT

	1995 Sales	
	$ mil.	% of total
Recreational vehicles	1,388	49
Manufactured housing	1,370	48
Finance operations	48	1
Supply operations	50	2
Total	**2,856**	**100**

Selected Recreational Vehicles

American Eagle	Jamboree	Southwind
Avion	Mallard	Terry
Bounder	Pace Arrow	Tioga
Coronado	Prowler	Wilderness
Flair		

Selected Subsidiaries
Buckingham Development Co.
Continental Lumber Products, Inc.
Fleetwood Credit Corp.
Fleetwood Folding Trailers, Inc.
Fleetwood Foreign Sales Corp.
Fleetwood International, Inc.
Gibraltar Insurance Co., Ltd.
Gold Shield, Inc.
GSF Installation Co.
Hauser Lake Lumber Operation, Inc.
Niesmann & Bischoff Clou Mobile
Verwaltungsgesellschaft mbH (80%, Germany)

KEY COMPETITORS

Champion Enterprises	Redman Industries
Clayton Homes	Shelter Components
Coachmen Industries	Skyline
Harley-Davidson	Thor Industries
Oakwood Homes	Winnebago
Palm Harbor Homes	

HOW MUCH

	9-Year Growth	1986	1987	1988	1989	1990	1991	1992	1993	1994	1995
Sales ($ mil.)	9.9%	1,218	1,259	1,406	1,619	1,549	1,401	1,589	1,942	2,369	2,856
Net income ($ mil.)	9.0%	39	40	48	71	55	30	40	57	67	85
Income as % of sales	—	3.2%	3.2%	3.4%	4.4%	3.6%	2.2%	2.5%	2.9%	2.8%	3.0%
Earnings per share ($)	8.8%	0.85	0.85	1.04	1.53	1.21	0.69	0.88	1.23	1.43	1.82
Stock price – high ($)[1]	—	14.38	16.75	16.00	13.31	15.31	14.56	18.38	24.56	26.88	27.25
Stock price – low ($)[1]	—	8.75	10.38	7.00	8.50	11.00	7.88	10.25	12.69	16.50	17.88
Stock price – close ($)[1]	4.9%	12.19	12.69	8.69	12.56	12.00	10.94	17.38	24.25	23.75	18.75
P/E – high	—	17	20	15	9	13	21	21	20	18	15
P/E – low	—	10	12	7	6	9	11	12	10	11	10
Dividends per share ($)	11.5%	0.21	0.25	0.29	0.32	0.37	0.41	0.44	0.46	0.50	0.56
Book value per share ($)	8.8%	6.18	6.78	7.51	8.74	9.51	9.78	10.26	11.01	11.88	13.20
Employees	6.7%	10,000	10,000	10,500	12,000	12,000	11,000	12,000	14,000	16,000	18,000

1995 Year-end:
Debt ratio: 38.8%
Return on equity: 14.7%
Cash (mil.): $198
Current ratio: 1.32
Long-term debt (mil.): $145
No. of shares (mil.): 46
Dividends
  Yield: 3.0%
  Payout: 30.8%
Market value (mil.): $864

Stock Price History[1]
High/Low 1986–95

[1]Stock prices are for the prior calendar year.

FLEMING COMPANIES, INC.

OVERVIEW

Even the biggest kid on the block can have growing pains, and Oklahoma City–based Fleming Companies is experiencing its share. Since buying Scrivner in 1994 and becoming the largest US wholesale grocery distributor, Fleming has seen flat sales and continuing pressures from a changing grocery business. On the bright side, earnings in 1994 bounced back somewhat from dismal 1993 numbers.

Fleming distributes food to more than 10,000 stores and operates 350 stores of its own, which account for 16% of sales. The company is emphasizing its retail operations and hopes to increase revenues from company-owned stores to 25% of total sales. By owning more of the stores it serves,

Fleming stands to get more promotional dollars from manufacturers and have a steadier customer base. (In 1995 bankrupt Arizona grocery chain Megafoods broke a distribution deal that cost Fleming $133 million in sales.)

A massive restructuring program that includes consolidating operations, reducing employment, and selling off underperforming units continues under chairman and CEO Robert Stauth. Other efforts to boost business include increased and accelerated sharing of information between manufacturers and retailers via Fleming, as well as an insistence that retailers serviced by Fleming commit themselves to upgrading and updating technology and in-store features.

WHEN

Lux Mercantile, a Topeka, Kansas, wholesale grocery founded by O. A. Fleming, Gene Wilson, and Sam Lux, was incorporated in 1915. In 1918 the company became Fleming-Wilson Mercantile.

Facing competition from chains, independent wholesalers and grocers banded together in "voluntary groups" to provide competitive mass merchandising, advertising, and efficient store operations. Fleming's son Ned helped establish Fleming-Wilson as the first voluntary wholesaler west of the Mississippi (1927). The company was renamed the Fleming Company, Inc. (1941), and Ned Fleming became president (1945–64) and then chairman and CEO (1964–81). The company went public in 1959, adopted its present name in 1972, and was reincorporated in Oklahoma in 1981.

Since the 1930s Fleming has grown by acquisitions, primarily of midwestern wholesale food distributors and supermarkets. Purchases in the 1930s and 1940s included Hutchinson Wholesale Grocery (1935); Carroll, Brough & Robinson (1941); Ryley-Wilson Grocery (1949); and Golden Wedding Coffee (1948; renamed Certified Brands, 1949). In the 1950s and 1960s, Fleming bought Ruston Bakery (1953, renamed Certified Bakers), Topeka Wholesale Drug (1958, renamed Drug Distributors), Grainger Brothers (1962, renamed the Fleming Company of Nebraska), Inter-State Grocer (1964), and Nelson Davis (1964).

Acquisitions in the 1980s included American-Strevell (1983); an Alpha Beta distribution center (1985); Associated Grocers of Arizona (1985); a wholesale distribution center of Foodland Super Markets (1986); and

Godfrey, with 32 Sentry supermarkets and 4 Sun warehouse markets (1987).

The $600 million purchase of Tennessee-based Malone & Hyde (1988), the 6th largest wholesale food distributor in the US, made Fleming the largest food distributor in the US. That same year the company sold Malone & Hyde's 99-store retail drug subsidiary, M&A Drugs, for $55 million and White Swan (bought in 1982) for $217 million.

When Albertson's completed its own warehouse and Alpha Beta merged with Lucky, Fleming lost them as customers and had to close its Fremont, California, distribution center (1990). The company has worked to make up for that lost business, and in 1991 it bought the warehouse and transportation assets of Furr's, greatly increasing its Texas and New Mexico sales.

Traditionally Fleming has made loans to independent customers, including problem stores, but when bad loans cost the company $20 million in the last quarter of 1993, Fleming decided to lend only to financially healthy clients. Fleming has had to part with another tradition, for a while at least. Lenders who in 1994 financed the $1.09 billion buyout of Scrivner from German company Franz Haniel have put the brakes on new acquisitions until 1997.

In 1995 Fleming jumped on the new "premium private label" bandwagon by offering pinto bean dip, black bean dip, and salsa-flavored ketchup to stores it services. Also that year the company struck a distribution deal with new customer Brown & Cole (Washington and Oregon) worth $36 million in sales.

NYSE symbol: FLM
Fiscal year ends: December 31

WHO

Chairman and CEO: Robert E. Stauth, age 50, $812,859 pay
President and COO: William J. Dowd, age 52
EVP: Gerald G. Austin, age 57, $469,865 pay
EVP: E. Stephen Davis, age 54, $360,148 pay
EVP: Glenn E. Mealman, age 60, $323,062 pay
EVP and CFO: Harry L. Winn Jr., age 50
SVP Retail Operations: Thomas L. Zaricki, age 50, $312,757 pay
SVP, General Counsel, and Secretary: David R. Almond, age 55
SVP General Merchandise: Ronald C. Anderson, age 52
SVP Customer Management: Mark K. Batenic, age 46
SVP Category Marketing: Darreld R. Easter, age 58
SVP Human Resources: Larry A. Wagner, age 48
Auditors: Deloitte & Touche LLP

WHERE

HQ: 6301 Waterford Blvd., PO Box 26647, Oklahoma City, OK 73126-0647
Phone: 405-840-7200
Fax: 405-841-8149

Fleming serves more than 10,000 stores, including 3,700 supermarkets, in 43 states and several foreign countries. The company also operates 350 company-owned stores.

	Distribution Centers
	No.
Texas	6
Pennsylvania	5
Tennessee	5
Wisconsin	5
Kansas	4
Other states	22
Total	**47**

WHAT

	1994 Sales
Store Format	% of total
Conventional	47
Superstore	22
Price impact	19
Combination	12
Total	**100**

	1994 Sales
Customer Type	% of total
Multistore (independent)	32
Corporate chain	30
Single-store (independent)	20
Company-owned	13
Voluntary chain	5
Total	**100**

Selected Licensed Franchise Trade Names

Big Star	IGA	Sentry
Big T	Jamboree Foods	Shop 'n Bag
Buy-for-Less	Jubilee Foods	Shop 'n Kart
Checkers	MEGA MARKET	Super 1 Foods
Festival Foods	Minimax	Super Save
Food 4 Less	Piggly Wiggly	Super Thrift

KEY COMPETITORS

Albertson's	George Weston	Shurfine Intl.
Alex Lee	Great A&P	Spartan Stores
American Stores	Grocers Supply	SUPERVALU
Associated Food	H. E. Butt	Topco Associates
Associated Wholesale Grocers	Kroger	United Grocers
	Meijer	Vendamerica
C&S Wholesale Grocers	Nash-Finch	Vons
	Publix	Wakefern Food
Certified Grocers	Roundy's	Wal-Mart
Di Giorgio	Safeway	Winn-Dixie
Food Lion	Services Group	

HOW MUCH

	9-Year Growth	1985	1986	1987	1988	1989	1990	1991	1992	1993	1994
Sales ($ mil.)	9.3%	7,095	7,653	8,608	10,467	12,045	11,933	12,902	12,938	13,092	15,753
Net income ($ mil.)	(0.7%)	60	39	50	65	80	97	72	119	38	56
Income as % of sales	—	0.8%	0.5%	0.6%	0.6%	0.7%	0.8%	0.6%	0.9%	0.3%	0.4%
Earnings per share ($)	(6.6%)	2.79	1.80	1.86	2.43	2.54	2.93	1.78	3.21	1.02	1.51
Stock price – high ($)	—	41.88	44.88	45.88	35.50	40.00	37.63	40.63	35.13	34.38	30.00
Stock price – low ($)	—	32.00	31.00	22.00	26.50	27.50	28.00	29.88	27.25	23.75	22.63
Stock price – close ($)	(5.6%)	38.88	34.63	27.25	35.00	30.13	35.25	34.38	31.50	24.75	23.25
P/E – high	—	15	25	25	15	16	13	23	11	34	20
P/E – low	—	12	17	12	11	11	10	17	9	23	15
Dividends per share ($)	2.4%	0.97	1.00	1.00	1.00	1.00	1.03	1.14	1.20	1.20	1.20
Book value per share ($)	3.8%	20.56	21.46	19.58	21.79	22.95	25.03	27.01	28.90	28.90	28.78
Employees	9.3%	19,000	19,100	18,600	24,600	22,800	22,900	22,800	22,800	23,300	42,400

1994 Year-end:
Debt ratio: 66.3%
Return on equity: 5.3%
Cash (mil.): $28
Current ratio: 1.38
Long-term debt (mil.): $1,995
No. of shares (mil.): 37
Dividends
  Yield: 5.2%
  Payout: 79.5%
Market value (mil.): $871

Stock Price History
High/Low 1985–94

FLUOR CORPORATION

OVERVIEW

Fluor continues to build its global success on diversification of services and big international projects. Its Fluor Daniel subsidiary, which accounts for over 90% of the parent company's revenues, is one of the world's largest engineering and construction (E&C) firms.

In 1994 CEO Les McCraw reorganized Fluor Daniel into 4 segments, streamlining management and decentralizing operations to capitalize on the company's global presence. A new segment, Diversified Services, was formed to offer E&C services to a broader client base.

Fluor Daniel won $8.1 billion worth of contracts in 1994. The trend continued in 1995

with contracts for a $25 million oil dock and pipeline in South Korea (for Yukong Ltd.) and a $2.5 billion power plant in Indonesia (with Mitsui and Toyo Engineering). In the US, Fluor Daniel will build a $50 million sports and entertainment complex in South Carolina.

In mid-1995 Fluor Daniel agreed to buy Anderson DeBartolo Pan (ADP), a privately held architecture, engineering, and construction management firm. ADP will operate as an independent subsidiary.

Fluor also owns 100% of A. T. Massey, one of the US's top 5 coal mining concerns with 16 mining facilities in the eastern US.

WHEN

The world's largest engineering and construction firm began with a Swiss immigrant carpenter in Santa Ana, California. Si Fluor launched a modest, family-run construction firm in 1912. In 1922 Fluor's company won a contract to build a 10,000-gallon-a-day refinery for Richfield Oil, and in 1930 it won work on a midwestern pipeline.

After WWII Fluor entered the international oil industry with a contract in Saudi Arabia. During the early 1960s, when Si Fluor's grandson Bob Fluor began running the company, Fluor continued to emphasize oil and gas work, acquiring drilling companies to establish a contract-drilling unit.

Despite a slump in the early 1970s, Fluor didn't cut staff, and when the 1973 Arab oil embargo touched off price increases, Fluor was ready. In 1977 the company won a $3 billion contract for a Saudi Arabian petrochemical plant. Also that year, in what would prove to be a masterstroke, Fluor bought Daniel International, a South Carolina E&C firm with over $1 billion in annual revenues.

Daniel International had begun in 1934 when Charlie Daniel quit his lumber company job and opened a contracting firm. The nonunion firm moved to South Carolina in 1942 and became involved in construction for the textile industry. Daniel later branched out to serve the chemical, pharmaceutical, pulp and paper, metals, food, and power industries.

Flush with cash and a backlog of projects, Fluor spent $2.2 billion in 1981 to acquire St. Joe Minerals. In a *Forbes* article that year, analysts projected "a 25% annual revenue and earnings gain for the company throughout the decade." But a drop in oil prices in the early 1980s killed demand for the big projects that had become Fluor's bread and butter. St. Joe

didn't help the bottom line because, along with servicing debt to buy the minerals concern, Fluor also faced declining metals prices. Then Bob Fluor died of lung cancer in 1984.

When David Tappan stepped in as CEO, he faced a $573 million loss his first year. The white-haired son of missionaries to China, Tappan became known as "the Ice Man" as he dumped subsidiaries and halved the payroll. In 1986 Tappan merged Daniel into Fluor's engineering subsidiary, forming Fluor Daniel, and refocused the company away from petroleum megaprojects and toward smaller jobs.

Leslie McCraw succeeded Tappan as chairman and CEO in 1991. The next year Fluor set up a joint venture with Jaakko Poyry, a globally renowned Finnish pulp and paper engineering and design firm.

In 1993 Fluor bought a 49% stake in ICA Industrial, a wholly owned subsidiary of Empresas ICA Sociedad Controladora, the largest E&C firm in Mexico.

Fluor sold its discontinued lead business to the Renco Group in 1994. That same year it won a contract as overall program manager for a new $1 billion petrochemical project in Kuwait; acquired 35% of Prochem S.A., one of Poland's largest E&C companies; and was awarded a contract for developing a North Sea gas field (with Chevron U.K. Ltd.). Also in 1994 McCraw, who had been diagnosed with prostate cancer, received a clean bill of health.

In 1995 Fluor Daniel acquired 10% of a $550 million smelter and refinery under construction in Indonesia (Mitsubishi owns 70% of the project and Freeport-McMoRan Copper & Gold owns 20%). With its equity investment Fluor Daniel will also become the project's primary E&C firm.

NYSE symbol: FLR
Fiscal year ends: October 31

WHO

Chairman and CEO: Leslie G. McCraw, age 60, $1,410,061 pay
VC: Hugh K. Coble, age 60, $690,020 pay
Chairman and CEO, A. T. Massey Coal Co.: Don L. Blankenship, age 44, $578,340 pay
SVP and Chief Administrative Officer: James O. Rollans, age 52, $572,707 pay
SVP Law and Secretary: P. Joseph Trimble, age 64, $500,000 pay
Group President Americas, Fluor Daniel: Dennis G. Bernhart, age 49
Group President Asia/Pacific, Fluor Daniel: Richard D. Carano, age 55
Group President Europe, Africa, and Middle East; Fluor Daniel: Carel J. C. Smeets, age 55
Group President Sales, Marketing, Strategic Planning, and Project Finance, Fluor Daniel: Charles R. Oliver Jr., age 51
VP and CFO: J. Michal Conaway, age 46
VP Human Resources and Administration: Charles J. Bradley Jr., age 59
Auditors: Ernst & Young LLP

WHERE

HQ: 3333 Michelson Dr., Irvine, CA 92730
Phone: 714-975-2000
Fax: 714-975-5271

Fluor has operations in more than 80 countries.

	1994 Sales		1994 Operating Income	
	$ mil.	% of total	$ mil.	% of total
North America	6,358	75	297	84
Europe	1,166	14	23	6
Asia/Pacific	673	8	13	4
Other regions	287	3	21	6
Total	**8,485**	**100**	**354**	**100**

WHAT

	1994 Sales		1994 Operating Income	
	$ mil.	% of total	$ mil.	% of total
Engineering & construction	7,718	91	259	73
Coal	767	9	95	27
Total	**8,485**	**100**	**354**	**100**

Selected Operations

Fluor Constructors (construction, construction management, and maintenance services)

Fluor Daniel (engineering and construction)
Diversified Services (provides construction tools and equipment, environmental services, plant and facility services, and temporary personnel to support Fluor Daniel operating companies)
Industrial (provides services to the automotive and general manufacturing, food and beverage, commercial and industrial facilities, electronics, infrastructure, mining and metals, pharmaceuticals and biotechnology, pulp and paper, and telecommunications industries)
Power and Government (provides services to private power companies and public utilities)
Process (provides services to the petroleum and petrochemicals; production and pipelines; and chemicals, plastics, and fibers industries)

A. T. Massey Coal Co., Inc. (produces, processes, and sells bituminous, low-sulfur coal)

KEY COMPETITORS

ABB	Foster Wheeler	Morrison
Ashland Coal	Halliburton	Knudsen
Baker Hughes	Hyundai	Nippon Steel
Bechtel	ITOCHU	Ogden
CBI Industries	Jacobs	Perini
Clark	Engineering	Peter Kiewit Sons'
Enterprises	Mannesmann	Raytheon
Dresser	Mitsubishi	Samsung

HOW MUCH

	9-Year Growth	1985	1986	1987	1988	1989	1990	1991	1992	1993	1994
Sales ($ mil.)	8.2%	4,168	4,660	3,925	5,133	6,278	7,446	6,742	6,601	7,850	8,485
Net income ($ mil.)	—	(617)	(60)	19	56	109	147	161	39	167	192
Income as % of sales	—	—	—	0.5%	1.1%	1.7%	2.0%	2.4%	0.6%	2.1%	2.3%
Earnings per share ($)	—	(7.80)	(0.76)	0.24	0.71	1.35	1.81	1.97	0.47	2.03	2.32
Stock price – high ($)	—	20.13	19.25	21.63	23.88	37.75	49.25	54.75	48.13	46.13	56.25
Stock price – low ($)	—	13.75	11.13	11.00	12.75	21.63	29.00	32.13	36.63	38.00	40.13
Stock price – close ($)	12.0%	15.50	11.50	13.75	23.38	36.75	36.75	43.75	41.88	40.50	43.13
P/E – high	—	—	—	90	34	28	27	28	102	23	24
P/E – low	—	—	—	46	18	16	16	16	78	19	17
Dividends per share ($)	3.0%	0.40	0.40	0.10	0.02	0.14	0.24	0.32	0.40	0.48	0.52
Book value per share ($)	1.4%	13.06	11.99	6.74	7.54	9.03	10.75	12.58	10.81	12.72	14.79
Employees	4.4%	26,958	22,309	14,351	17,876	20,059	22,188	39,637	43,605	38,532	39,807

1994 Year-end:
Debt ratio: 4.9%
Return on equity: 17.0%
Cash (mil.): $492
Current ratio: 1.23
Long-term debt (mil.): $24
No. of shares (mil.): 83
Dividends
  Yield: 1.2%
  Payout: 22.4%
Market value (mil.): $3,558

Stock Price History
High/Low 1985–94

FMC CORPORATION

OVERVIEW

Chemicals have been the catalyst for FMC's recent record revenues. The Chicago-based conglomerate manufactures chemicals for the agriculture, food, and pharmaceutical markets. It also makes machinery for the defense, energy, food processing, and transportation industries. The company's defense unit makes the Bradley fighting vehicle and its FMC Gold subsidiary develops gold and silver mines.

Once considered a stodgy old conglomerate, FMC has completed a recent restructuring that cut costs by $70 million in 1994. Since 1992 FMC has spent over $275 million to grow its business by acquiring complementary companies and establishing strategic partnerships. In 1995 it bought Moorco, a Houston-based

manufacturer of measurement products for the energy industry.

FMC, the world's top producer of natural soda ash (used in glassmaking), formed a soda ash–mining joint venture in 1995 with Nippon Sheet Glass and Sumitomo Corp., which together paid $150 million for 20% of the project. FMC will spend $45 million to boost capacity at its Green River, Wyoming, soda ash plant by 700,000 tons by 1997.

Agricultural chemicals continue to grow as a source of revenues for FMC. In 1994 the company announced it would build an $88 million plant to manufacture a new herbicide used in soybean and sugarcane farming.

Employees own nearly 22% of FMC.

WHEN

After retiring to California, inventor John Bean developed a pump to deliver a continuous spray of insecticide (1884). This invention led to the Bean Spray Pump Company (1904). In 1928 Bean Spray Pump went public and bought Anderson-Barngrover (food growing and processing equipment). The new company name, John Bean Manufacturing, gave way to Food Machinery Corporation in 1929. The company bought Peerless Pump (agricultural and industrial pumps) in 1933.

During WWII the company started making military equipment. It entered the agricultural chemical field when it purchased Niagara Sprayer & Chemical (1943). After the war it added Westvaco Chemical (1948) and changed its name to Food Machinery & Chemical.

The Bean family ran the company until 1956, when John Bean's grandson, John Crummey, retired as chairman. The company extended its product line, buying such companies as Oil Center Tool (wellhead equipment, 1957), Sunland Industries (fertilizer and insecticides, 1959), and Barrett Equipment (automotive brake equipment, 1961).

In light of its growing diversification, the company changed its name to FMC in 1961. Major purchases in the 1960s included American Viscose (rayon and cellophane, 1963) and Link-Belt (equipment for power transmission and for bulk-material handling, 1967).

To be centrally located FMC moved its headquarters from San Jose to Chicago in 1972. In 1970 it sold its pump and fiber divisions and its 50% interest in Ketchikan Pulp (part of the American Viscose purchase). FMC continued to sell its slow-growing businesses, including the semiconductor division (1979),

the industrial packaging division (1980), the Niagara Seed Operation (1980), and the Power Transmission Group (1981).

In 1979 FMC entered mining in a joint venture with Freeport Minerals for a gold mine in Jerritt Canyon, Nevada (discovered 1973). In the 1980s FMC found more gold near Gabbs, Nevada, and entered the lithium business by buying Lithium Corp. of America (1985). In a 1986 antitakeover move, FMC financed a $2 billion recapitalization, paying shareholders $80 per share and giving employees a larger stake in the company. In 1989 FMC bought the French company Mather et Platt (harvesters, food processing equipment). The next year FMC Gold bought Meridian Gold from Burlington Resources.

In 1992 FMC bought Ciba-Geigy's flame retardants and water treatment businesses and combined its defense operations with Harsco as United Defense (60% FMC-owned). In 1993 the company announced a restructuring plan that cut 1,200 jobs and included a $123 million write-off. FMC also announced that FMC Gold would take a $60 million charge to write down assets at an Idaho gold mine.

FMC's 1994 acquisitions included Abex's Jetway Systems Division, a leading designer of aircraft support systems, Caterpillar's Automated Vehicle Systems group, and the Fluid Control Systems products of National-Oilwell.

Also in 1994 FMC acquired the remaining shares of United Defense. In 1994 and 1995 United Defense won contracts worth nearly $100 million for tank recovery and Command and Control vehicles. It was also awarded a TRW subcontract for computerized battlefield communications.

NYSE symbol: FMC
Fiscal year ends: December 31

WHO

Chairman and CEO: Robert N. Burt, age 57, $1,167,831 pay
President: Larry D. Brady, age 52, $742,550 pay
EVP: William F. Beck, age 56, $553,478 pay
EVP and CFO: Michael J. Callahan, age 55
SVP: William J. Kirby, age 57, $520,790 pay
VP; General Manager, Agricultural Products Group: William H. Schumann III, age 44
VP; General Manager, Food Machinery Group: Charles H. Cannon, age 42
VP; General Manager, Chemical Products Group: Robert I. Harries, age 51
VP; General Manager, Energy and Transportation Equipment Group: Joseph H. Netherland, age 48
VP; President and CEO, United Defense, L.P.: Thomas W. Rabaut, age 46
VP and General Counsel: Patrick J. Head, age 62
VP Communications: William R. Jenkins
VP Human Resources: William W. Murray
Auditors: KPMG Peat Marwick LLP

WHERE

HQ: 200 E. Randolph Dr., Chicago, IL 60601
Phone: 312-861-6000
Fax: 312-861-6176

FMC operates 100 manufacturing facilities and mines in the US and 20 other countries.

	1994 Sales		1994 Operating Income	
	$ mil.	% of total	$ mil.	% of total
US	3,085	77	341	75
Europe	693	17	100	22
Other Americas	160	4	14	3
Other regions	73	2	2	0
Total	**4,011**	**1005**	**457**	**100**

WHAT

	1994 Sales		1994 Operating Income	
	$ mil.	% of total	$ mil.	% of total
Defense systems	1,081	27	160	34
Performance chem.	1,060	26	154	33
Machinery & equip.	973	24	33	7
Industrial chem.	867	21	119	26
Precious metals	61	2	(9)	—
Adjustments	(31)	—	—	—
Total	**4,011**	**100**	**57**	**100**

Business Units

Defense Systems
Armament Systems
Ground Systems
International
Steel Products
United Defense, L.P.

Performance Chemicals
Agricultural Products Group
BioProducts
Food Ingredients Division
Lithium Division
Pharmaceutical Division
Process Additives Division

Machinery
Energy and Transportation
Equipment Group
Food Machinery Group

Industrial Chemicals
Alkali Chemicals Division
FMC Foret, S.A.
Peroxygen Chemicals Division
Phosphorus Chemicals Division

Precious Metals
FMC Gold

KEY COMPETITORS

AGCO	Cyprus Amax	Hoechst
Anglo American	Dow Chemical	Homestake
ASARCO	Dresser	Mining
Baker Hughes	DuPont	Ingersoll-Rand
BASF	Freeport-McMoRan	Kerr-McGee
Berwind	Copper & Gold	Monsanto
British Aerospace	GenCorp	Morton
Broken Hill	General Dynamics	Olin
Cambrex	Halliburton	Pearson
Caterpillar	Hanson	Phelps Dodge
Ciba-Geigy	Hercules	Schlumberger

HOW MUCH

	9-Year Growth	1985	1986	1987	1988	1989	1990	1991	1992	1993	1994
Sales ($ mil.)	2.3%	3,261	3,003	3,139	3,287	3,415	3,722	3,899	3,974	3,754	4,011
Net income ($ mil.)	(1.4%)	197	153	191	129	157	155	173	119	36	173
Income as % of sales	—	5.1%	6.1%	3.9%	4.6%	4.2%	4.4%	3.0%	1.0%	4.3%	4.3%
Earnings per share ($)	15.2%	1.30	1.62	4.52	3.60	4.34	4.30	4.68	3.20	0.98	4.65
Stock price – high ($)	—	12.75	26.38	60.38	39.13	49.00	38.75	51.63	53.25	54.00	65.13
Stock price – low ($)	—	9.50	15.50	24.00	24.38	31.63	25.38	29.50	42.50	41.50	45.50
Stock price – close ($)	19.6%	11.50	25.75	33.75	32.00	35.25	31.88	47.88	49.50	47.13	57.75
P/E – high	—	—	16	13	11	11	9	11	17	55	14
P/E – low	—	—	10	5	7	7	6	6	13	42	10
Dividends per share ($)	(100%)	0.33	0.10	0.00	0.00	0.00	0.00	0.00	0.00	0.00	0.00
Book value per share ($)	4.7%	7.54	(11.25)	(7.60)	(6.53)	(2.05)	4.30	8.78	6.10	5.99	11.41
Employees	(3.0%)	28,064	24,966	24,797	24,342	24,110	23,882	23,150	22,097	20,696	21,344

1994 Year-end:
Debt ratio: 70.8%
Return on equity: 54.8%
Cash (mil.): $98
Current ratio: 1.08
Long-term debt (mil.): $901
No. of shares (mil.): 37
Dividends
  Yield: —
  Payout: —
Market value (mil.): $2,109

**Stock Price History
High/Low 1985–94**

FOOD LION, INC.

OVERVIEW

In the last few years, Food Lion's roar was reduced to a whimper, but the Salisbury, North Carolina–based company is on the comeback. After years of expansion in which it added roughly 100 stores a year, becoming one of the 10 largest grocery store chains in the US, Food Lion was rocked by negative TV publicity in 1992. ABC's *PrimeTime Live* aired a segment accusing the chain of unsanitary food handling, including changing dates on out-of-date foods. The company's income fell 98% the following year. Food Lion quickly set about coaxing its customers back with quality guarantees and the remodeling of many of its stores, which now number 1,039. The grocer finished 1994 with $153 million in income, up from $4 million the previous year.

Food Lion remains committed to its core marketing concept — low prices. However,

the controversy of the early 1990s has forced the company into sharpening its focus on quality and, more importantly, convincing the public of its commitment. Food Lion offered proof in the way of its "Gold Lion Guarantee," a promise to customers to provide only the highest-quality products or their money back. Food Lion also remodeled 65 of its stores in the past year. Most of the remodeling consisted of enlarging stores from 21,000–25,000 square feet to 30,000 square feet and adding a deli/bakery department.

Food Lion is not out of the woods yet. In 1995 the company agreed to a refund request by Consumers United with Employees (CUE), which purchased 1,088 cans of outdated infant formula from the company's stores. Food Lion is over 50%–owned by Delhaize "Le Lion," one of Belgium's largest public companies.

WHEN

Food Lion was formed in 1957 in Salisbury, North Carolina, by 3 former Winn-Dixie employees — Wilson Smith, Ralph Ketner, and Ralph's brother Brown Ketner. They named the market Food Town and peddled stock in the new company at $10 per share to anyone in Salisbury who would buy. One of the store's first employees was bagger Tom Smith, who is now chairman and CEO.

The company struggled through its first 10 years of operation; by the end of 1967 it was foundering. Trading stamps, contests, and drawings failed to attract customers. That year Ralph Ketner pored over 6 months of store receipts and determined that if Food Town lowered the prices on all 3,000 items and sales increased 50%, the company would survive. The strategy paid off, and the company was reborn as a resolute cost cutter. The company's slogan, LFPINC (Lowest Food Prices in North Carolina), soon appeared on bumper stickers.

In 1974 a Belgian grocery company, Delhaize Freres (Lion Brothers, known as "Le Lion"), which used a lion as its symbol, began investing in Food Town. By 1989 it owned 50.3% of the voting stock. Food Town changed its name in 1983 to avoid confusion with another Food Town store in its market area. Ketner adopted the name Food Lion, not only because of the lion symbol of Delhaize Freres, but also because he could save money by replacing only the "t" and the "w" at the company's stores.

In the 1980s Food Lion increased its number of stores from 106 to 663, always following the company's low-price, cost-cutting formula, and built 3 distribution centers.

Food Lion maintained its high growth rate in 1990 by having a net increase of 115 new stores. In 1991 the company broke with its tradition of entering only contiguous states by penetrating the Texas market, opening 41 stores in the Dallas/Ft. Worth area. Food Lion opened 131 new stores in 1992, including its first stores in Oklahoma and Louisiana.

The company planned to open as many as 110 stores in 1993, but the total store count increased by only 84 in the wake of stunted sales growth in 1992.

In 1993 Food Lion agreed to pay more than $16 million in a settlement involving child labor violations and forced "off-the-clock" hours. For 8 months in 1993 and 1994, the FDA inspected 63 Food Lions in 6 southeastern states, for which the company was given an "excellent" rating.

In 1994 the company closed 87 unprofitable stores. Food Lion was particularly unsuccessful in the Southwest, where it closed about 50 stores, mostly in Texas and Oklahoma.

In 1995 Food Lion filed a $30 million lawsuit against ABC News, claiming the network broke the law during its 1992 investigation of Food Lion. The grocer said ABC's news gathering method was deceitful and amounted to fraud and trespassing and should not be protected by the First Amendment.

Nasdaq symbol: FDLNA
Fiscal year ends: Saturday nearest December 31

WHO

Chairman, President, and CEO: Tom E. Smith, age 53, $948,270 pay
SVP Store Operations and COO: John P. Watkins, age 39, $285,173 pay
VP Finance, CFO, and Secretary: Dan A. Boone, $249,808 pay
VP Management Information Systems: A. Edward Benner Jr., $201,289 pay
VP Human Resources: Eugene R. McKinley, $228,071 pay
Auditors: Coopers & Lybrand L.L.P.

WHERE

HQ: 2110 Executive Dr., PO Box 1330, Salisbury, NC 28145-1330
Phone: 704-633-8250
Fax: 704-636-5024

Food Lion operates 1,039 general food supermarkets in 14 states, primarily in the Mid-Atlantic, Southeast, and Southwest.

	1994 Warehouse Space	
	Sq. ft. thou.	% of total
Salisbury, NC	1,630	17
Roanoke, TX	1,254	13
Greencastle, PA	1,236	12
Dunn, NC	1,225	12
Petersburg, VA	1,125	11
Elloree, SC	1,093	11
Green Cove Springs, FL	832	8
Clinton, TN	826	8
Plant City, FL	759	8
Total	**9,980**	**100**

	1994 Store Locations	
	No. of stores	% of total
North Carolina	364	35
Virginia	222	21
Florida	106	10
South Carolina	97	9
Tennessee	70	6
Georgia	52	5
Texas	49	5
Maryland	24	2
West Virginia	15	2
Kentucky	13	1
Oklahoma	8	1
Delaware	7	1
Pennsylvania	7	1
Louisiana	5	1
Total	**1,039**	**100**

WHAT

	1994 Stores	
	No.	% of total
Existing stores	1,009	97
New stores	30	3
Total	**1,039**	**100**

KEY COMPETITORS

Albertson's	Kroger
American Stores	K-VA-T
Bruno's	Melville
H. E. Butt	National Convenience
Circle K	Publix
Delchamps	Pueblo Xtra
Eckerd	Randalls
Fiesta Mart	Rite Aid
Giant Food	Safeway
Great A&P	Southland
Homeland Holding	Walgreen
Kash n' Karry	Wal-Mart
Kmart	Winn-Dixie

HOW MUCH

	9-Year Growth	1985	1986	1987	1988	1989	1990	1991	1992	1993	1994
Sales ($ mil.)	17.4%	1,866	2,407	2,954	3,815	4,717	5,584	6,439	7,196	7,610	7,933
Net income ($ mil.)	13.7%	48	62	86	113	140	173	205	178	4	153
Income as % of sales	—	2.6%	2.6%	2.9%	3.0%	3.0%	3.1%	3.2%	2.5%	0.1%	1.9%
Earnings per share ($)	13.8%	0.10	0.13	0.18	0.23	0.29	0.36	0.42	0.37	0.01	0.32
Stock price – high ($)	—	2.50	6.25	9.75	9.00	9.13	11.13	18.18	18.01	8.13	7.50
Stock price – low ($)	—	1.50	2.25	4.00	6.50	6.38	6.88	8.09	6.25	5.25	5.13
Stock price – close ($)	8.7%	2.42	4.08	8.58	6.67	7.50	9.08	18.18	8.13	6.50	5.13
P/E – high	—	25	48	54	39	32	31	43	49	—	23
P/E – low	—	15	17	22	28	22	19	19	17	—	16
Dividends per share ($)	27.7%	0.01	0.01	0.03	0.04	0.07	0.09	0.10	0.11	0.09	0.09
Book value per share ($)	19.4%	0.43	0.55	0.70	0.89	1.11	1.39	1.71	1.98	1.90	2.12
Employees	16.0%	17,089	20,871	27,033	35,531	40,736	47,276	53,583	59,721	65,494	64,840

1994 Year-end:
Debt ratio: 40.2%
Return on equity: 15.7%
Cash (mil.): $67
Current ratio: 1.62
Long-term debt (mil.): $660
No. of shares (mil.): 487
Dividends
  Yield: 1.8%
  Payout: 28.1%
Market value (mil.): $2,479

Stock Price History High/Low 1985–94

FORD MOTOR COMPANY

OVERVIEW

Change is job one at Ford these days. The world's #2 automaker, Ford is undergoing a thorough restructuring (dubbed "Ford 2000") that will merge its automotive operations, scattered across 5 continents, into a single global organization. The first step is to combine its $94 billion-a-year North American and European operations; those in Asia, Africa, and South America are next. The goals are to cut costs, eliminate duplication, streamline management, and usurp #1-ranked automaker General Motors.

To reach those goals, Ford plans to build a "world car," a family of autos that can be sold around the world and tailored to suit local tastes. The Dearborn, Michigan–based company has spent $6 billion and 6 years on a prototype, known as the Ford Contour and Mercury Mystique in the US and the Mondeo

in Europe. Although a hit in Europe, the car sold poorly in the US. The first products developed under Ford 2000 are due in late 1997.

Ford builds 5 of the top 8 best-selling vehicles in the US, including the #1-selling car (Taurus) and the #1-selling truck (F-Series). Its overall market share in the US is 25.2% and 12.1% in Europe. Ford's 2 core businesses are automotive operations (cars, trucks, and tractors) and financial services (such as Ford Motor Credit and Granite Management).

Ford is positioning itself for the markets outside North America, Europe, and Japan that have most of the world's population but account for a small share of vehicle sales. In 1994 the automaker launched ventures in China, India, and Vietnam, reentered the South African market, and explored manufacturing opportunities in Thailand.

WHEN

Henry Ford began the Ford Motor Company in 1903 in Dearborn, Michigan, hoping to design a car he could mass-produce. In 1908 Ford introduced the Model T, dropping other models in 1909. His business manager, James Couzens, recommended he lower the selling price to $600, so Ford perfected the moving assembly line. Couzens and William Knudsen (later GM president) created the first branch assembly plant system and a national dealer network. By 1916 the cars cost $360; by 1920 60% of all vehicles on the road were Fords.

In 1916 Ford omitted its customary extra dividend. Stockholders sued for payment, and in 1919 Ford bought all outstanding shares for $100 million. It was 1956 before the Fords again allowed outside ownership; the family still retains over 48% of Ford's class B stock.

Ford bought Lincoln in 1922 and discontinued the Model T in 1927. Its replacement, the Model A (1932), was the first low-priced car with a V-8 engine. With Henry Ford's health failing, his son Edsel became president in 1932. Despite the introduction of the Mercury (1938), market share slipped behind GM and Chrysler. After Edsel's sudden death in 1943, the navy released his son, Henry II, to run Ford. Henry II decentralized Ford, then losing $10 million a month, following the GM model. In 1950 Ford recaptured 2nd place.

In the 1950s the company created the Aerospace Division (1956) and introduced the infamous Edsel (1958). In 1964 Ford launched the popular Mustang, created by Ford president Lee Iacocca. In 1979 Henry II retired.

Ford cut its work force by 33% and closed 15 plants during the 1980s. In 1986 Ford earned higher profits than GM (on 33% less revenue) for the first time since 1924. With the purchase of New Holland (1986) and Versatile (1987), Ford became the world's #3 agricultural equipment maker. Ford bought First Nationwide Bank in 1986 (sold 1994) and set up a joint venture with Volkswagen to share supply and manufacturing costs in Brazil and Argentina (dissolved 1995). The 1988 introduction of the Taurus and Sable (both the inspiration of then-CEO Donald Petersen) spurred Ford to its largest US car market share (21.7%) in 10 years. In 1989 Ford bought the Associates (financial services) and Jaguar.

Harold "Red" Poling succeeded Petersen as CEO in 1990, and the company sold Ford Aerospace to Loral. Ford merged New Holland with a Fiat subsidiary in 1991.

In 1992 Ford agreed to jointly build with Volkswagen in Portugal a multipurpose vehicle for the European market. It also took a $7.4 billion charge relating to the future cost of retiree health care benefits.

In 1993 sold its North American automotive seating and trim business for $73 million. Also that year Poling retired and Alex Trotman was named chairman and CEO.

In 1994 Ford acquired Volvo's 26% share in Hertz and Hertz management's 20% share, raising its stake to 100%. That same year Ford's Jaguar operations made a profit for the first time in 6 years.

NYSE symbol: F
Fiscal year ends: December 31

WHO

Chairman, President, and CEO: Alexander J. Trotman, age 61, $3,900,000 pay
VC and Chief Technical Officer: Louis R. Ross, age 63, $1,900,000 pay
EVP; President, Ford Automotive Operations: Edward E. Hagenlocker, age 55, $1,925,000 pay
EVP; President, Ford Financial Services Group: Kenneth Whipple, age 60, $1,700,000 pay
EVP International Automotive Operations: W. Wayne Booker, age 60
EVP Corporate Relations: Peter J. Pestillo, age 57
Group VP and CFO: John M. Devine, age 50
Group VP Product Development: Jacques A. Nasser, age 47
Group VP; Chairman and CEO, Ford Motor Credit Co.: William E. Odom, age 59
Group VP Marketing and Sales Operations: Robert L. Rewey, age 56
Group VP Manufacturing: Robert H. Transou, age 55
VP and General Counsel: John W. Martin Jr., age 58
VP Employee Development: Robert O. Kramer, age 56
Auditors: Coopers & Lybrand L.L.P.

WHERE

HQ: The American Rd., Dearborn, MI 48121-1899
Phone: 313-322-3000
Fax: 313-845-0570

Ford has operations in 34 countries.

	1994 Sales		1994 Net Income	
	$ mil.	% of total	$ mil.	% of total
US	90,364	70	4,159	78
Europe	24,120	19	665	13
Other regions	13,955	11	484	9
Total	**128,439**	**100**	**5,308**	**100**

WHAT

	1994 Sales		1994 Net Income	
	$ mil.	% of total	$ mil.	% of total
Automotive	107,137	83	3,824	72
Financial svcs.	21,302	17	1,484	18
Total	**128,439**	**100**	**5,308**	**100**

Nameplates
Ford
Jaguar
Lincoln
Mercury

Financial Subsidiaries
Ford Credit Europe plc
Ford Holdings, Inc.
  The American Road Insurance Co.
  Associates First Capital Corp.
  USL Capital Corp.
Ford Motor Credit Co.
Granite Management Corp.
The Hertz Corp.

Other Selected Holdings
Mahindra Ltd. (6.5%, autos and tractors, India)
Mazda Motor Corp. (25%)
South African Motor Corp. (pty.) Ltd. (45%, vehicle assembler)

KEY COMPETITORS

Alamo Rent A Car	Daimler-Benz	National Car
Avis	Deere	Rental
Banc One	Enterprise	NationsBank
BankAmerica	Rent-A-Car	Navistar
Beneficial	Fiat	Nissan
BMW	General Motors	Peugeot
British Aerospace	Honda	Renault
Budget Rent	Household Intl.	Saab-Scania
a Car	Hyundai	Suzuki
Caterpillar	Isuzu	Toyota
Chase Manhattan	Kia Motors	Volkswagen
Chrysler	Mitsubishi	Volvo

HOW MUCH

	9-Year Growth	1985	1986	1987	1988	1989	1990	1991	1992	1993	1994
Sales ($ mil.)	10.4%	52,774	62,716	71,643	92,446	96,146	97,650	88,286	100,132	108,521	128,439
Net income ($ mil.)	8.7%	2,515	3,285	4,625	5,300	3,835	860	(2,258)	(502)	2,529	5,308
Income as % of sales	—	4.8%	5.2%	6.5%	5.7%	4.0%	0.9%	—	—	2.3%	4.1%
Earnings per share ($)	8.1%	2.21	3.03	4.46	5.48	4.11	0.93	(2.40)	(0.73)	2.10	4.44
Stock price – high ($)	—	9.86	15.88	28.16	27.50	28.31	24.56	21.50	24.44	33.06	35.06
Stock price – low ($)	—	6.69	8.97	14.22	19.03	20.69	12.50	11.69	13.88	21.50	25.63
Stock price – close ($)	12.5%	9.67	14.06	18.84	25.25	21.81	13.31	14.06	21.44	32.25	27.88
P/E – high	—	5	5	6	5	7	26	—	—	16	8
P/E – low	—	3	3	3	4	5	13	—	—	10	6
Dividends per share ($)	7.1%	0.49	0.56	0.79	1.15	1.50	1.50	0.98	0.80	0.80	0.91
Book value per share ($)	7.5%	10.99	13.84	18.22	21.93	24.04	24.56	23.47	15.07	15.61	21.14
Employees	(0.1%)	369,314	382,274	351,711	358,939	366,641	368,547	331,977	325,333	322,213	337,778

1994 Year-end:
Debt ratio: 85.8%
Return on equity: 28.5%
Cash (mil.): $6,220
Current ratio: 1.03
Long-term debt (mil.): $65,207
No. of shares (mil.): 1,024
Dividends
  Yield: 3.3%
  Payout: 20.5%
Market value (mil.): $28,559

**Stock Price History
High/Low 1985–94**

FOUNDATION HEALTH CORPORATION

OVERVIEW

Like so many other top competitors in the managed care industry, Rancho Cordova, California–based Foundation Health Corporation is rapidly expanding beyond its traditional stomping grounds. While most of its health care facilities are still located in the Golden State, Foundation has entered several other states and the UK in recent years through a variety of start-ups, acquisitions, and government contracts.

Now serving about 3.5 million people, Foundation has numerous subsidiaries offering health maintenance organization (HMO) plans, workers' compensation, life insurance, eye care, and other services. Integrated Pharmaceutical Services, formed by the company in 1994, manages pharmacy benefits for HMOs, preferred provider organizations (PPOs), the government, and other groups.

The sting of losing a major government contract for Hawaii and California in 1993 eased somewhat in 1995 when Foundation won a 5-year, $1.8 billion DOD managed care contract for Oklahoma and parts of Arkansas, Louisiana, and Texas. (That pact, through the Civilian Health and Medical Program of the Uniformed Services, covers 590,000 beneficiaries, compared with the 860,000 covered by the CHAMPUS contract lost 2 years earlier.) In 1994 the company received a smaller military contract for Oregon and Washington.

Hot on the heels of its $720 million purchase in 1994 of Intergroup Healthcare and Thomas-Davis Medical Centers (expected to bring Foundation's revenues to about $2.4 billion), early the next year the company dropped its $1.55 billion offer for Health Systems International.

WHEN

Foundation Health started as the nonprofit Foundation Community Health Plan in the 1960s. In 1984 it was acquired by AmeriCare Health Corporation, a holding company with HMOs in 6 states. As a subsidiary based in northern California, Foundation Health accounted for the bulk of AmeriCare's sales.

Shortly after AmeriCare went public in 1985, it was the nation's 5th largest publicly held HMO. In 1986 a lawsuit by an out-of-state company forced AmeriCare to change its corporate name to Foundation Health Corporation. The company started an aggressive expansion effort that saw the health care provider move into several other states and acquire unrelated businesses, such as commercial real estate, silk flowers, and furniture.

In late 1986 the company was purchased by senior management and other investors in a $140 million LBO, which left it hobbled with debt when the industry was starting to slide. Foundation Health mushroomed in 1988 when it won a 5-year, $3 billion DOD contract to provide health care to 860,000 military retirees and their dependents in California and Hawaii. Despite the contract, Foundation Health was still struggling with its rapid growth, debt load, and another year of losses.

The CEO slot had been vacant a year when Dan Crowley, trained as an accountant, came aboard in May 1989. Crowley, who had a record of turning companies around, met daily with management to review cash flows. He also cut staff, slashed budgets, sold off unrelated and nonperforming units, and personally kicked off a huge sales effort. To satisfy bankers and the DOD, which was threatening to rescind its contract, Crowley refinanced Foundation's debt by issuing notes to company owners and subcontractors. Within a little over a year, Foundation Health had the most profitable year in its history. In 1990 the company went public.

Once it regained its footing, the company began to expand both its services and its markets through acquisitions in order to pool services and become a "one-stop shop" of health services. Key purchases were Western Universal Life Insurance Co. (renamed Foundation Health Benefit Life Insurance Co., 1991), DentiCare (dental HMO, 1991), Apollo Enterprises (pharmacy claims, 1991), Occupational Health Services (employee assistance and substance abuse programs, 1992), Century MediCorp. (hospitals and HMOs, 1992), and California Compensation Insurance Co. (workers' compensation insurance, 1993).

In 1993 the company obtained a license in Louisiana with 75,000 state employees as its first customers, and opened a mail-order pharmacy. That year Foundation lost to Aetna a huge government contract that provided almost half of its revenues. Though Foundation recovered the revenues from other sources, the company protested the decision; the contract was rebid, but to no avail.

In 1994 Foundation acquired Miami-based CareFlorida Health Systems and the next year received a contract to coordinate Medicaid services in Massachusetts.

NYSE symbol: FH
Fiscal year ends: June 30

WHO

Chairman, President, and CEO: Daniel D.
Crowley, age 46, $3,255,288 pay
President and COO, Specialty Services: Steven D.
Tough, age 43, $569,147 pay
President, Intergroup: Rick Barrett
SVP and CFO: Jeffrey L. Elder, age 46, $479,180 pay
**SVP Corporate Development; Acting President and
COO, Foundation Health, a California Health Plan:**
Kirk A. Benson, age 44, $477,123 pay
SVP, General Counsel, and Secretary: Allen J.
Marabito, age 48
SVP Human Resources: Dan Smithson
Auditors: Deloitte & Touche LLP

WHERE

HQ: 3400 Data Dr., Rancho Cordova, CA 95670
Phone: 916-631-5000
Fax: 916-631-5149

Foundation Health offers managed health care in
Alabama, Arizona, Arkansas, California, Colorado,
Florida, Louisiana, Massachusetts, Nebraska, Nevada,
New Jersey, New Mexico, Oklahoma, Oregon, Texas,
Utah, and Washington. The company also provides
health care services in the UK.

WHAT

	1994 Sales	
	$ mil.	% of total
Commercial premiums	726	42
Government contracts	543	32
Specialty services	378	22
Patient services	41	2
Investments & other	29	2
Total	**1,718**	**100**

Selected Services
Behavioral health services
Dental services
Government-sponsored
managed care plans
Individual HMO plans
Medicaid HMO plans
Medicare HMO plans
Pharmaceutical services
Vision services
Workers' compensation
insurance, cost
containment, and
administration

Selected Subsidiaries
Associated Claims Management, Inc. of California
AVP Vision Plans
California Compensation Insurance Co.
DentiCare of California, Inc.
Foundation Health, a California Health Plan
Foundation Health, a Florida Health Plan
Foundation Health, a Louisiana Health Plan
Foundation Health, a Texas Health Plan
Foundation Health, an Oklahoma Health Plan
Foundation Health Benefit Life Insurance Co.
Foundation Health Federal Services, Inc.
Foundation Health Medical Resource Management
Foundation Health National Life Insurance Co.
Foundation Health Preferred Administrators
Foundation Health PsychCare Services, Inc.
Foundation Health Unlimited
Integrated Pharmaceutical Services
Intergroup of Arizona

KEY COMPETITORS

Aetna
AFLAC
Blue Cross
Caremark
CIGNA
Complete Health Services
Equitable
FHP International
Health Systems
Kaiser Foundation
Health Plan
Lifeguard
Maxicare Health Plans
National Medical
Pacific Physician
PacifiCare
Physician Corp. of America
Prudential
Sierra Health Services
Summit Care
Systemed
U.S. Healthcare
WellPoint Health
Networks

HOW MUCH

	Annual Growth	1985	1986	1987	1988	1989	1990	1991	1992	1993	1994
Sales ($ mil.)	35.7%	—	149	189	268	762	895	963	1,143	1,517	1,718
Net income ($ mil.)	45.9%	—	4	(12)	(48)	(3)	11	25	46	62	82
Income as % of sales	—	—	2.7%	—	—	—	1.2%	2.6%	4.0%	4.1%	4.8%
Earnings per share ($)	32.6%	—	—	—	—	—	0.92	1.33	2.02	2.05	2.84
Stock price – high ($)	—	—	—	—	—	—	10.01	23.76	44.75	42.50	46.00
Stock price – low ($)	—	—	—	—	—	—	6.59	7.17	22.43	18.13	29.75
Stock price – close ($)	38.5%	—	—	—	—	—	8.42	23.35	38.50	31.00	31.00
P/E – high	—	—	—	—	—	—	11	18	22	21	16
P/E – low	—	—	—	—	—	—	7	5	11	9	11
Dividends per share ($)	—	—	—	—	—	—	0.00	0.00	0.00	0.00	0.00
Book value per share ($)	—	—	—	—	—	—	(8.84)	15.84	8.44	9.91	12.55
Employees	52.2%	—	—	—	400[1]	1,000[1]	1,100	1,370	1,940	4,400	4,978

1994 Year-end:
Debt ratio: 27.3%
Return on equity: 25.3%
Cash (mil.): $122
Current ratio: 5.95
Long-term debt (mil.): $135
No. of shares (mil.): 29
Dividends
  Yield: —
  Payout: —
Market value (mil.): $889

Stock Price History
High/Low 1990–94

[1] Estimated

FPL GROUP, INC.

OVERVIEW

FPL helps power the Sunshine State. One of the US's largest publicly owned electric utilities, the Juno Beach, Florida–based company, through its Florida Power & Light Company subsidiary, provides electric service to more than 3.4 million customers on Florida's east and lower west coasts (about half of Florida's population), including residents of Miami.

However, electricity is not the only thing that lights FPL's way. Other FPL subsidiaries include ESI Energy (independent energy projects), Turner Foods (one of Florida's largest developers and operators of citrus groves), and Qualtec Quality Services (management consulting and training services). These nonutility operations are managed by FPL Group Capital. As part of a streamlining of its operations, FPL has reduced its investment in cable televison and real estate.

The streamlining comes as the company works to deal with competition brought by deregulation of the power industry. FPL has focused on improving efficiency and cutting costs to hold the line on rate increases.

WHEN

FPL traces its roots back to Florida's land boom during the early 1920s. New homes and businesses were built at an impressive rate, but electric utilities were few and far between, and no transmission lines linked one system to another. In 1925 American Power & Light Company (AP&L), which was already operating utilities throughout the Americas, set up Florida Power & Light (FP&L) to buy and consolidate the state's electric properties. AP&L built transmission lines from Miami to Stuart on the Atlantic Coast and from Arcadia to Punta Gorda on the Gulf Coast, linking 58 communities in the FP&L power system. Besides electric generating and transmission facilities, FP&L's holdings included a limestone quarry; streetcar and telephone companies; a steam laundry; and ice, water, and cold storage companies.

More purchases in 1926 and 1927 nearly doubled FP&L's electric properties. In 1927 the company used an electric pump to demonstrate how swamplands could be drained and cultivated. In the 1940s and 1950s, FP&L sold its nonelectric properties. AP&L ceased operations in 1950 and, as part of its dissolution plan, spun off FP&L to its stockholders. FP&L was listed on the NYSE in 1950. With Florida's population booming, FP&L grew rapidly, and by 1964 it was serving 2.7 million customers.

Marshall McDonald became president of FP&L in 1971. FP&L's first nuclear plant (Turkey Point), located on the mud flats south of Miami, went on-line in 1972. While the plant was under construction (1965–72), FP&L established youth camps, nature trails, shrimp ponds, and a US Air Force Sea Survival School at Turkey Point to illustrate its concern for the area's ecological balance.

In the 1970s and 1980s, the company diversified by forming Fuel Supply Service (1973, oil and uranium acquisition, later renamed Qualtec); W. Flagler Investment (1981, real estate development, later renamed Alandco); and ESI Energy (1985, nonutility fuel sources). FPL Group was created in 1984 as a holding company for Florida Power & Light as it moved into nonutility operations. FPL subsequently acquired Telesat Cablevision (1985, cable television operator); Colonial Penn Group (1985, insurance); and Turner Foods Corporation (1988, citrus grower). FPL sold Praxis Group, a Colonial Penn subsidiary providing information services, in 1988.

In 1981 McDonald, then chairman, began a quality improvement program (QIP), using teams of employees and statistical methods to track and solve company problems. Received with little enthusiasm at first, QIP eventually caught on, with impressive results. In 1989 FPL became the first non-Japanese company to win the Deming Prize, Japan's prestigious international award for quality.

In 1990 FPL took a $752 million charge (related to its decision to get out of insurance, cable TV, and real estate) that greatly contributed to its $391 million loss. That year the company also agreed to buy a stake (17.7%) in Georgia Power's Scherer Unit 4 — its first out-of-state plant. FPL sold its ailing Colonial Penn unit to New York's Leucadia National Corporation for $150 million in 1991.

In 1993 FPL began selling its real estate (Alandco) and cable TV (Telesat) businesses. In 1994 the company slashed its dividend by nearly 1/4 and announced plans to buy back 10 million shares of its stock in hopes of improving shareholder value.

In 1995, in a surprise move, FP&L president Steve Frank resigned. Less than a week later, CFO Paul Evanson was named to replace him, fueling speculation that Frank was forced out.

WHO

Chairman, President, and CEO: James L. Broadhead,
age 59, $1,445,800 pay
President, FP&L: Paul J. Evanson, age 53, $450,000 pay
(prior to promotion)
President, Nuclear Division, FP&L: Jerome H.
Goldberg, age 63, $674,961 pay
General Counsel and Secretary: Dennis P. Coyle, age 56,
$466,673 pay
SVP Power Generation, FP&L: C. O. Woody, age 56
SVP External Affiars, FP&L: J. Thomas Petillo, age 50
VP Finance and CFO: Michael W. Yackira, age 43
Controller and Chief Accounting Officer: K. Michael
Davis, age 48
VP Human Resources: Lawrence J. Kelleher, age 47
Auditors: Deloitte & Touche LLP

WHERE

HQ: 700 Universe Blvd., Juno Beach, FL 33408
Phone: 407-694-4647
Fax: 407-694-6385

Generating Facilities

Coal
St. Johns River Power Park
(20%; Jacksonville, FL)
Scherer (77%, Monroe
County, GA)

Oil and Gas
Cape Canaveral
(Cocoa, FL)
Cutler (Miami, FL)
Fort Myers
(Fort Myers, FL)
Lauderdale (Dania, FL)
Manatee (Parrish, FL)

Martin (Indiantown, FL)
Port Everglades (Port
Everglades, FL)
Putnam (Palatka, FL)
Riviera (Riviera Beach, FL)
Sanford (Lake Monroe, FL)
Turkey Point (Florida
City, FL)

Nuclear
St. Lucie (85%; Hutchinson
Island, FL)
Turkey Point (Florida
City, FL)

WHAT

	1994 Sales
	% of total
Residential	50
Commercial	39
Industrial	5
Interchange power sales	2
Other	4
Total	**100**

	1994 Power Sources
	% of total
Oil	31
Nuclear	26
Natural gas	20
Coal	6
Purchased power	17
Total	**100**

Florida Power & Light Co.

FPL Group Capital, Inc.
ESI Energy, Inc. (energy projects)
Qualtec Quality Services, Inc. (management consulting
and training services)
Turner Foods Corp. (management and operation of
agricultural property)

KEY COMPETITORS

AES
California Energy
Duke Power
General Electric
Lykes Bros.
Ocean Spray
Orange Co. Florida

Pacific Enterprises
Pacific Gas and Electric
SCEcorp
Southern Co.
Sunkist
Westinghouse

HOW MUCH

	9-Year Growth	1985	1986	1987	1988	1989	1990	1991	1992	1993	1994
Sales ($ mil.)	2.5%	4,349	4,092	4,439	5,854	6,180	6,289	5,249	5,193	5,316	5,423
Net income ($ mil.)	3.8%	372	365	403	448	410	(391)	241	467	429	519
Income as % of sales	—	8.6%	8.9%	9.1%	7.7%	6.6%	—	4.6%	9.0%	8.1%	9.6%
Earnings per share ($)	(0.7%)	3.11	2.90	3.10	3.42	3.12	(2.86)	1.48	2.65	2.30	2.91
Stock price – high ($)	—	29.00	38.00	34.88	32.50	36.75	36.50	37.25	38.38	41.00	39.13
Stock price – low ($)	—	20.50	26.38	24.38	27.75	29.00	26.13	28.13	32.00	35.50	26.88
Stock price – close ($)	2.5%	28.25	31.63	28.63	31.13	36.38	29.00	37.00	36.25	39.13	35.13
P/E – high	—	9	13	11	10	12	—	25	15	18	13
P/E – low	—	7	9	8	8	9	—	19	12	15	9
Dividends per share ($)	(0.3%)	1.94	2.02	2.10	2.18	2.26	2.34	2.39	2.43	2.47	1.88
Book value per share ($)	0.6%	21.38	22.99	23.83	24.90	26.11	19.63	19.64	20.99	21.57	22.51
Employees	(3.7%)	17,100	18,700	20,000	19,000	18,800	19,138	14,500	14,530	12,400	12,135

1994 Year-end:
Debt ratio: 48.5%
Return on equity: 12.5%
Cash (mil.): $86
Current ratio: 0.82
Long-term debt (mil.): $4,050
No. of shares (mil.): 186
Dividends
  Yield: 5.4%
  Payout: 64.6%
Market value (mil.): $6,550

**Stock Price History
High/Low 1985–94**

FRED MEYER, INC.

OVERVIEW

In its massive stores in the western US, Fred Meyer, Inc., sells just about everything, from food to jewelry to home improvement products. But the Portland, Oregon–based retail chain had trouble selling its employees on work-scheduling proposals in 1994, resulting in work stoppages lasting 88 days. The strikes — mostly by food workers at stores in the Portland and Vancouver, Washington, areas — cost the company at least $60 million, resulting in a steep drop in net income.

Fred Meyer's strategy is to enable customers to do all their household shopping within its walls. The company operates more than 130 stores, including about 100 "multidepartment" stores (the average size is 141,000 square feet), most of which include food departments. Expansion plans called for 6 new full-size stores and 8 store remodelings in 1995, with a particular emphasis on Utah. In 1996 Fred Meyer expects to concentrate on

Idaho, Oregon, and Washington with 7 new stores and 6 remodelings. Fred Meyer also operates more than 30 small specialty stores, primarily jewelry stores in malls.

Several of the states Fred Meyer operates in are among the fastest-growing in the nation, and the company now faces a variety of new competitors eager to take advantage of the region's growth. To defend itself against the likes of Home Depot, Circuit City, and Wal-Mart's Sam's Club, Fred Meyer is continuing its efforts to upgrade inventory management technology and replenishment programs. But it isn't just national brand-name merchandise that the retailer wants to keep in stock; in recent years the company has increased its focus on lower-price, higher-margin private-label goods under the Fred Meyer, President's Choice, and FMV (Fred Meyer Value) names.

Investment firm Kohlberg Kravis Roberts (KKR) owns 38% of the company's stock.

WHEN

Founder Fred G. Meyer peddled coffee, tea, and spices door-to-door in Portland, Oregon (1909), and opened his first grocery and variety store in downtown Portland (1922). Meyer opened a branch in Hollywood, a Portland suburb, after police banned downtown parking because of traffic problems (1931).

During the next 3 decades, the Fred Meyer Stores spread throughout Oregon and southern Washington state. Fred Meyer's innovations included free parking; fluorescent lights, prepackaged goods; cash-and-carry pricing; self-service; and one-stop shopping, with separate departments under one roof.

In 1960 the 18-store chain went public, posting sales of $56 million. The company added prepared entrees and frozen foods (1968) and home improvement and garden centers (late 1960s). During the 1960s and 1970s, the company purchased several retailers in the northwest and expanded into Idaho, Alaska, and western Montana. Founder Fred Meyer died in 1978.

KKR took the company private in a $420 million management LBO (1981). The company bought the 30-store Grand Central chain (1984), retaining 21 stores in Utah and Idaho, and went public again (1986), selling a 35% stake and raising $63 million to reduce debt. During Fred Meyer's 5 years as a private company, sales increased by 53%, from $1.1 billion to $1.7 billion, and net income increased almost fivefold, from $5 million to $24 million.

In 1988 the company hired Frederick Stevens to modernize the aging chain. Stevens's remodeling and replacing of older stores and the establishment of a computer system that improved inventory tracking and information management contributed to Fred Meyer's 1990 loss of $6.8 million. Strikes at the Seattle stores and a distribution center also negatively affected income. Stevens's abrupt departure in 1991 led to speculation that KKR was preparing to restructure or sell the chain.

In 1992 the company issued 2 million new shares of stock. That same year KKR returned 2 million shares to circulation, reducing its stake in Fred Meyer to about 51.1%.

In 1994, to reduce product handling costs, Fred Meyer opened a 310,000-square-foot, high-tech distribution center for apparel and music products in Chehalis, Washington, between key markets Portland and Seattle. Also in 1994 the company announced that it would leave the northern California market rather than simply end its expansion there as originally planned.

The 88 days of strikes in 1994 resulted from Fred Meyer's refusal to guarantee that 60% of all workers would be full-time employees. As a result of the settlement, employees with seniority were granted the flexibility to ask for more hours.

By mid-1995 sales in Fred Meyer's Portland stores had yet to return to prestrike levels.

WHO

Chairman and CEO: Robert G. Miller, age 50,
$555,481 pay
President and COO: Cyril K. Green, age 63,
$306,258 pay
SVP Food Group: Curt A. Lerew III, age 47,
$255,327 pay
SVP General Group: Mary F. Sammons, age 48,
$251,635 pay
SVP and Chief Information Officer: Ronald J. McEvoy,
age 47, $219,538 pay
SVP Finance and CFO: Kenneth Thrasher, age 45
SVP, General Counsel, and Secretary: Roger A. Cooke,
age 46
SVP Stores: R. Eric Baltzell, age 54
SVP Jewelry Group: Edward A. Dayoob, age 55
SVP Human Resources: Keith W. Lovett, age 51
Auditors: Deloitte & Touche LLP

WHERE

HQ: 3800 SE 22nd Ave., Portland, OR 97202
Phone: 503-232-8844
Fax: 503-797-5609 (Public Affairs)

Fred Meyer operates more than 131 stores in 7 western states.

	1994 Stores		
	No. Full-size	No. Specialty	Total
Oregon	42	9	51
Washington	32	13	45
Utah	11	1	12
Alaska	7	3	10
Idaho	6	2	8
California	1	2	3
Montana	1	1	2
Total	**100**	**31**	**131**

WHAT

	1995 Sales
	% of total
Nonfood sales	62
Food sales	38
Total	**100**

	1994 Stores
	No.
Multidepartment stores	
With food	86
Without food	14
Specialty stores	
Fine jewelry	26
Other formats (grocery, nutrition & other merchandise)	5
Total	**131**

Departments
Apparel (apparel, cosmetics, shoes)
Fine Jewelry
Food
Health and Beauty Aids
The Home (cards and books; garden; home improvement and automotive; housewares, domestics, and home decor; sporting goods; toys; variety and seasonal)
Home Electronics
Pharmacy

KEY COMPETITORS

Albertson's	Good Guys	Price/Costco
American Stores	Home Depot	Safeway
Associated Grocers	J. C. Penney	ShopKo Stores
Carr-Gottstein	Kmart	Tandy
Foods	Lamonts Apparel	Thrifty PayLess
Circuit City	May	Toys "R" Us
Dayton Hudson	Mercantile	Wal-Mart
Eagle Hardware	Stores	Yucaipa
& Garden	Nordstrom	Zale

HOW MUCH

	Annual Growth	1986	1987	1988	1989	1990	1991	1992	1993	1994	1995
Sales ($ mil.)	7.9%	1,584	1,688	1,848	2,074	2,285	2,476	2,703	2,854	2,979	3,128
Net income ($ mil.)	(11.0%)	20	24	32	37	(7)	34	45	61	71	7
Income as % of sales	—	1.2%	1.4%	1.7%	1.8%	—	1.4%	1.7%	2.1%	2.4%	0.2%
Earnings per share ($)	(14.8%)	1.06	1.15	1.31	1.50	(0.28)	1.37	1.80	2.21	2.50	0.25
Stock price – high ($)[1]	—	—	14.50	17.88	16.13	22.88	18.75	26.88	33.38	38.50	42.50
Stock price – low ($)[1]	—	—	12.75	9.63	11.00	16.13	10.00	11.25	22.75	27.88	29.25
Stock price – close ($)[1]	11.2%	—	13.13	10.63	16.13	18.50	12.50	26.75	31.38	36.00	30.75
P/E – high	—	—	13	14	11	—	14	15	15	15	—
P/E – low	—	—	11	7	7	—	7	6	10	11	—
Dividends per share ($)	—	—	0.00	0.00	0.00	0.00	0.00	0.00	0.00	0.00	0.00
Book value per share ($)	11.3%	—	8.61	9.99	11.65	11.31	12.81	14.81	17.80	19.98	20.27
Employees	6.9%	—	15,800	17,000	20,000	22,200	21,700	24,200	24,000	25,000	27,000

1995 Year-end:
Debt ratio: 50.1%
Return on equity: 1.3%
Cash (mil.): $35
Current ratio: 1.64
Long-term debt (mil.): $540
No. of shares (mil.): 27
Dividends
  Yield: —
  Payout: —
Market value (mil.): $817

**Stock Price History[1]
High/Low 1987–95**

[1] Stock prices are for the prior calendar year.

FRUIT OF THE LOOM, INC.

OVERVIEW

Fruit of the Loom did not enjoy the fruits of its labors in 1994. Sales were up 22%, but its net income unraveled, falling sharply. Based in Chicago, the company is the US's #1 maker of underwear and of activewear for imprints.

A number of factors took a bite out of Fruit of the Loom's profits, including higher cotton prices (the company is the nation's #1 cotton buyer) and charges related to acquisitions. Its 1994 acquisitions reflect its strategy of expanding its product lines. To boost its line of women's apparel, it bought jeans maker Gitano, and to build its growing line of licensed sports apparel, it bought Artex and Pro Player.

Besides having licensing agreements with all the major US sports leagues and many universities, the company also has agreements with entertainment companies such as Walt Disney and Time Warner. In 1995 the company expects strong growth from the licensing of characters from the movies *Batman Forever*, *Mighty Morphin Power Rangers*, and *Pocahontas*.

To cut costs, Fruit of the Loom plans to move more of its production outside the US, although it does not plan to close any major US plants. The company also plans to raise prices between 4% and 7%. CEO William Farley owns 33.1% of the company.

WHEN

Jacob Goldfarb, a Polish immigrant, learned the underwear business from the bottom up. He founded his own company, Union Underwear, in 1926. By the mid-1950s Union was the biggest maker of men's briefs in the US. In 1955 Goldfarb, then 60 and worried Union might be liquidated after he died, accepted a cash offer for his company from Philadelphia & Reading Corporation.

In 1955 Philadelphia & Reading was a money-losing coal railroad operating in eastern Pennsylvania. It had started out in 1871 as the coal mining subsidiary of the Philadelphia & Reading Railroad. It remained a producer of anthracite coal until the mid-1950s, when a group of investors led by Howard Newman transformed it into a holding company (Philadelphia & Reading). Newman went on to buy Acme Boot Company (1956), Fruit of the Loom (1961), and Lone Star Steel (1965). In 1968 Philadelphia & Reading was bought by Ben Heineman's Northwest Industries.

Like Newman, Heineman had begun with a railroad — the Chicago-based North Western — in 1956. He wound up selling the railroad to its employees in 1972 and building a conglomerate that included Velsicol Chemical (acquired in 1965) and the assets of Philadelphia & Reading. Then in 1985 Heineman sold Northwest Industries to William Farley for $1.4 billion. Farley, who had already built a reputation as a deal maker, got most of the money from junk bond specialists Drexel Burnham Lambert.

That year Farley spun off Lone Star Steel to offset acquisition debt and changed Northwest's name to Farley/Northwest Industries. In 1987 he changed its name to Fruit of the Loom. That year Farley's own holding company (Farley, Inc.) made a 27-million-share public offering of its Fruit of the Loom stock but kept control of the company.

Under Farley's ownership Fruit of the Loom began to diversify, manufacturing socks (1986), branching into sweatshirts, and increasing production of women's underwear (which it began selling in 1984). But Farley, Inc., ran into trouble in 1989 when it tried to buy West Point–Pepperell through yet another Drexel-financed LBO. The junk bond market collapsed in the middle of the deal, and, trying to keep ahead of debt and interest payments, Farley shed businesses. Its voting stake in Fruit of the Loom dwindled to 33%. In September 1991, after defaulting on $20 million in payments to its bondholders, Farley, Inc., agreed to reorganize. Farley, Inc.'s voting power is now at less than 16%, but Farley himself holds 33% of the Fruit of the Loom vote and the right to appoint 25% of its board.

In 1991 Fruit of the Loom introduced a new line of infants' and toddlers' apparel and agreed to let Warnaco manufacture and sell bras under the Fruit of the Loom name.

In 1993 the company struck a licensing deal with Wilson Sporting Goods to produce and market Wilson athletic wear in the US. Also in 1993 it acquired sports clothing licensee Salem Sportswear. It bought Artex Manufacturing in 1994, which, besides sports leagues, also licenses many popular cartoon characters from Disney, Peanuts, and Looney Tunes.

In 1995 the company announced a stepped-up TV advertising campaign that included the return of "the fruits," a group of men dressed as grapes and apples, who starred in the company's TV ads for more than 10 years before being dropped in 1990.

NYSE symbol: FTL
Fiscal year ends: December 31

WHO

Chairman and CEO: William Farley, age 52,
$1,360,000 pay
VC: Richard C. Lappin, age 50, $700,000 pay
President and COO: John B. Holland, age 62,
$797,500 pay
SEVP Corporate Development: Richard M. Cion, age 51,
$572,438 pay
EVP and CFO: Larry K. Switzer, age 51
EVP Operations: John Wigodsky
EVP Manufacturing: Stan W. Vinson
SVP, General Counsel, and Assistant Secretary: Joyce
M. Russell
SVP Finance: G. William Newton
VP and Treasurer: Earl C. Shanks, age 38, $332,967 pay
VP and Controller: Michael F. Bogacki, age 40
VP Administration (HR): Burgess D. Ridge, age 50
Auditors: Ernst & Young LLP

WHERE

HQ: 5000 Sears Tower, 233 S. Wacker Dr., Chicago, IL
60606
Phone: 312-876-1724
Fax: 312-993-1749

Fruit of the Loom has 61 manufacturing facilities in
Canada, El Salvador, Honduras, Ireland, Jamaica,
Mexico, the UK, and the US.

	1994 Sales		1994 Operating Income	
	$ mil.	% of total	$ mil.	% of total
US	1,972	86	234	91
Other countries	326	14	22	9
Adjustments	—	—	(21)	—
Total	**2,298**	**100**	**235**	**100**

WHAT

Brand Names
Best
Botany 500
BVD
Fruit of the Loom
Funpals
Gitano
John Henry
Kangaroo
Lofteez
Munsingwear
Official Fan
Pro Player
Salem
Salem Sportswear
Screen Stars
Wilson (license)

Products
Active wear
Athletic sportswear

Casual wear
Childrens wear
Hosiery
Sports-licensed apparel
Underwear
    Men and boys
    Women and girls

Licensing Partners
Major League Baseball
National Basketball
    Association
National Football League
National Hockey League
Time Warner
The Walt Disney Company
Warnaco Inc.
Wilson Sporting
    Goods Co.

KEY COMPETITORS

Benetton
Bugle Boy
Esprit
The Gap
Gelmart Industries
Gerber
Guess?
Gymboree
J. Crew
Lands' End
Levi Strauss
Liz Claiborne

L.L. Bean
Nautica
NIKE
Oshkosh B'Gosh
Oxford Industries
Polo/Ralph Lauren
Reebok
Russell Corporation
Sara Lee
Spiegel
Starter
V. F.

HOW MUCH

	Annual Growth	1985	1986	1987	1988	1989	1990	1991	1992	1993	1994
Sales ($ mil.)	16.2%	—	693	870	1,005	1,321	1,427	1,628	1,855	1,884	2,298
Net income ($ mil.)	22.3%	—	12	43	73	72	77	111	189	213	60
Income as % of sales	—	—	1.7%	4.9%	7.3%	5.5%	5.4%	6.8%	10.2%	11.3%	2.6%
Earnings per share ($)	—	—	(0.79)	0.61	1.13	1.11	1.18	1.55	2.48	2.80	0.79
Stock price – high ($)	—	—	—	9.75	7.63	16.00	15.38	28.00	49.63	49.25	33.00
Stock price – low ($)	—	—	—	3.88	4.25	6.13	6.13	7.63	26.50	22.88	23.00
Stock price – close ($)	27.2%	—	—	5.00	6.38	14.88	8.88	27.63	48.63	24.13	27.00
P/E – high	—	—	—	16	7	14	13	18	20	18	42
P/E – low	—	—	—	6	4	6	5	5	11	8	29
Dividends per share ($)	—	—	—	0.00	0.00	0.00	0.00	0.00	0.00	0.00	0.00
Book value per share ($)	24.8%	—	—	3.14	4.19	5.30	6.77	9.21	11.32	13.83	14.84
Employees	10.5%	—	16,800	19,600	23,400	26,000	27,700	26,700	31,100	35,000	37,400

1994 Year-end:
Debt ratio: 56.5%
Return on equity: 5.6%
Cash (mil.): $49
Current ratio: 3.24
Long-term debt (mil.): $1,440
No. of shares (mil.): 76
Dividends
  Yield: 0.0%
  Payout: 0.0%
Market value (mil.): $2,048

Stock Price History
High/Low 1987–94

GANNETT CO., INC.

OVERVIEW

Gannett is the US's largest newspaper publisher. The Arlington, Virginia–based company publishes 84 daily newspapers (and more than 50 nondaily publications) in 34 states, Guam, and the Virgin Islands. It is the company behind USA TODAY, the nation's largest newspaper, whose graphics, use of color, and short stories have been mimicked by other newspapers although critics once dubbed it the journalistic equivalent of fast food ("McPaper"). Available in 50 states, USA TODAY has an international edition that is sold in more than 90 countries. More than 80% of Gannett's 1994 revenues were from newspapers.

The company also has major stakes in broadcasting and billboards. Its 10 TV stations, all network affiliates, include major urban areas (such as Washington, DC; Atlanta; Denver; Minneapolis–St. Paul; and Phoenix) and 2 new NFL cities (Greensboro, North Carolina, and Jacksonville, Florida). The company's radio properties now number 11 (5 AM, 6 FM) stations. Gannett also owns North America's largest billboard group (Mediacom in Canada and Outdoor Network in the US), Louis Harris & Associates polling company, and Gannett News Service, among many other properties.

Like other newspaper publishers, Gannett is going on-line; USA TODAY now offers links to the Internet. Much higher newsprint costs could squeeze the company, but that possibility did not discourage Warren Buffett from buying a 4.9% stake in Gannett, worth more than $350 million, in late 1994.

WHEN

In 1906 Frank Gannett started building a newspaper empire when he and his associates purchased a half-interest in the *Elmira* (New York) *Gazette*. The small company expanded slowly, purchasing 2 additional newspapers by 1912. In 1918 the company moved to Rochester, where it acquired 2 more newspapers, and in 1923 Gannett bought out his associates' interests and formed the Gannett Company. In 1929 Frank Gannett invested in the development of the teletypesetter. Gannett continued to buy small- and medium-size dailies in the Northeast, and by 1947 the company operated 21 newspapers and 7 radio stations. At the time of Gannett's death in 1957, the company had accumulated 30 newspapers.

During the 1960s Gannett continued buying local newspapers, expanding into a national newspaper chain. It was not until 1966, however, that Gannett started its own newspaper, *TODAY*, in Cocoa Beach, Florida. Gannett went public in 1967.

The company went through its greatest expansion during the 1970s and 1980s under the direction of Allen Neuharth, who became CEO in 1973 and chairman in 1979. Gannett captured national attention in 1979 when it merged with Phoenix-based Combined Communications Corporation (CCC), another media conglomerate whose holdings included TV and radio stations, an outdoor advertising business (2nd largest in the US), the Louis Harris polling business, the *Cincinnati Enquirer*, and the *Oakland Tribune*. Gannett's revenues passed the $1 billion mark in 1979.

In 1982 Gannett started *USA TODAY*, a national newspaper whose splashy format and short articles made it an industry novelty. Gannett's largest acquisition came in 1986 when it bought the Evening News Association for $717 million, gaining 5 more newspapers, including the *Detroit News*, and 2 TV stations. In 1989 the *Detroit News* entered into a joint operating agreement with its competition, the *Detroit Free Press*, to publish a Sunday edition.

Neuharth retired as chairman of Gannett in 1989. During his 16-year tenure as the company's leader, the outspoken Neuharth had spent approximately $1.5 billion on acquisitions and increased the combined circulation of Gannett's newspapers to 6.3 million. In 1990 Gannett's string of 89 consecutive quarters of earnings gains was broken.

In 1991 Gannett sold 5 Washington, DC–area newspapers to comply with FCC rules and, after absorbing cumulative losses of $100 million, sold the assets of Little Rock's *Arkansas Gazette* to the *Arkansas Democrat*.

USA TODAY-On-Demand, a fax service for such information as corporate earnings and news, began in 1992. In 1993 *USA TODAY* recorded its first annual profit. That year Gannett sold 4 Missouri radio stations. The company sold its Boston TV station in 1994 but bought another TV station in Little Rock, Arkansas.

In 1995 Gannett agreed to buy the *Daily Commercial* (Leesburg, Florida) from the New York Times Co. and joined the national New Century Network on-line newspaper service. Also, the company agreed in July 1995 to buy cable and program syndication company Multimedia for $1.7 billion.

NYSE symbol: GCI
Fiscal year ends: Last Sunday of the calendar year

WHO

Chairman, President, and CEO: John J. Curley, age 56, $1,362,500 pay
VC, CFO, and Chief Administrative Officer: Douglas H. McCorkindale, age 55, $1,156,250 pay
President, Gannett Newspaper Division: Gary L. Watson, age 49, $657,500 pay
President, Broadcasting Division: Cecil L. Walker, age 58, $500,000 pay
President and Publisher, *USA TODAY*: Thomas Curley, age 46, $481,250 pay
President, Gannett Outdoor Group: Donald W. Davidson, age 56
SVP Personnel: Richard L. Clapp, age 54
VP, General Counsel, and Secretary: Thomas L. Chapple, age 47
Auditors: Price Waterhouse LLP

WHERE

HQ: 1100 Wilson Blvd., Arlington, VA 22234
Phone: 703-284-6000
Fax: 703-558-4697

Gannett has facilities in 41 states, the District of Columbia, Guam, the US Virgin Islands, Canada, Hong Kong, Switzerland, and the UK.

WHAT

	1994 Sales		1994 Operating Income	
	$ mil.	% of total	$ mil.	% of total
Newspapers	3,177	83	734	83
Broadcasting	406	11	129	15
Outdoor advertising	241	6	17	2
Adjustments	—	—	(67)	—
Total	**3,824**	**100**	**813**	**100**

Selected Daily Newspapers
The Cincinnati Enquirer (204,498 daily circulation)
The Courier-Journal (Louisville; 241,084 daily circulation)
The Des Moines Register (184,395 daily circulation)
The Detroit News (355,329 daily circulation)
The Tennessean (Nashville; 147,379 daily circulation)
USA TODAY (2,026,109 daily circulation)
78 other newspapers in 34 states and 2 territories

Selected Nondaily Publications
USA TODAY Baseball Weekly
USA WEEKEND (weekly magazine in 428 newspapers)
Nondaily publications (27 states/District of Columbia)

Television Stations	Radio Stations
KARE-TV, Minneapolis–St. Paul	KCLX (FM), San Diego
KOCO-TV, Oklahoma City	KHKS (FM), Dallas
KPNX-TV, Phoenix	KIIS (AM/FM), Los Angeles
KTHV-TV, Little Rock, AR	KKBQ (AM/FM), Houston
KUSA-TV, Denver	KSDO (AM), San Diego
KVUE-TV, Austin	WDAE (AM), Tampa–St. Petersburg
WFMY-TV, Greensboro, NC	WGCI (AM/FM), Chicago
WTLV-TV, Jacksonville, FL	WUSA (FM), Tampa–St. Petersburg
WUSA-TV, Washington, DC	
WXIA-TV, Atlanta	

Selected Other Businesses
Gannett Community Directories of New Jersey (yellow-pages publishing)
Gannett Direct Marketing Services, Inc.
Gannett Media Technologies International (software and other products for publishing industry)
Gannett News Service
Louis Harris & Associates (opinion research)
USA TODAY Information Network (on-line information)

KEY COMPETITORS

Advance Publications	E.W. Scripps	Reuters
ADVO	Hearst	Thomson Corp.
Cox	Knight-Ridder	Times Mirror
Dow Jones	New York Times	Tribune
Enquirer/Star Group	News Corp.	Washington Post

HOW MUCH

	9-Year Growth	1985	1986	1987	1988	1989	1990	1991	1992	1993	1994
Sales ($ mil.)	6.3%	2,209	2,801	3,079	3,314	3,518	3,442	3,382	3,469	3,642	3,824
Net income ($ mil.)	7.0%	253	276	319	364	398	377	302	312	398	465
Income as % of sales	—	11.5%	9.9%	10.4%	11.0%	11.3%	11.0%	8.9%	9.0%	10.9%	12.1%
Earnings per share ($)	8.3%	1.58	1.71	1.98	2.26	2.47	2.36	2.00	2.40	2.72	3.23
Stock price – high ($)	—	32.88	43.56	55.25	39.50	49.88	44.38	46.63	53.63	58.25	59.00
Stock price – low ($)	—	23.57	29.63	31.75	29.38	34.63	35.75	41.50	46.75	46.13
Stock price – close ($)	6.3%	30.63	36.06	39.13	35.63	43.50	36.13	45.50	50.75	57.25	53.25
P/E – high	—	21	25	28	18	20	19	24	23	21	18
P/E – low	—	15	17	13	13	14	13	18	17	17	14
Dividends per share ($)	6.3%	0.77	0.86	0.94	1.02	1.11	1.21	1.24	1.26	1.30	1.34
Book value per share ($)	5.7%	7.93	8.88	9.94	11.09	12.40	12.98	10.71	10.94	12.98	13.04
Employees	2.0%	30,000	36,000	36,000	37,000	36,650	36,600	36,700	36,700	36,500	36,000

1994 Year-end:
Debt ratio: 29.7%
Return on equity: 25.0%
Cash (mil.): $44
Current ratio: 1.23
Long-term debt (mil.): $767
No. of shares (mil.): 140
Dividends
  Yield: 2.5%
  Payout: 41.5%
Market value (mil.): $7,443

Stock Price History
High/Low 1985–94

THE GAP, INC.

OVERVIEW

Based in San Francisco, the Gap operates 1,508 casual clothing stores in the US, Canada, France, and the UK. Besides the Gap, the company operates GapKids (including the babyGap line of infant and toddler apparel), Banana Republic, and Old Navy Clothing Co. stores. All of the Gap's merchandise is private label.

The company's sales and net income were up in fiscal 1995, thanks primarily to new store openings, but the Gap began to run into trouble in the 2nd half of the year. Its choice of higher-margin women's fashions proved less than successful, and the greater emphasis it placed on these fashions (rather than on basics), coupled with a slump in the women's clothing market, sent the company back to the drawing board. It has broadened its merchandise to appeal to a wider market. Same-store sales rose only 1% in fiscal 1995.

On the plus side, both Banana Republic and GapKids performed well. The company continues to expand. It plans to add between 175 and 200 new stores during 1995. In particular, it's looking for growth from Old Navy, which offers private-label, "Gaplike" clothing at lower prices in warehouse-style stores. However, with the discount clothing market already crowded with competitors, the company will have to work to find a niche for Old Navy.

Founders Donald and Doris Fisher own 23.3% of the company.

WHEN

In 1969 Donald Fisher and his wife, Doris, opened a small store near what is now San Francisco State University. The couple named their store the Gap (after "the generation gap") and concentrated on selling Levi's jeans. The couple opened a 2nd store in San Jose 8 months later, and by the end of 1970 there were 6 Gap stores. In the beginning the Fishers catered almost exclusively to teenagers, but in the 1970s they expanded into active wear that would appeal to a larger spectrum of customers. Nevertheless, by the early 1980s the Gap was still dependent upon its largely teenage customer base.

In a 1983 effort to revamp the company's image, Fisher hired Millard "Mickey" Drexler, a former president of Ann Taylor who had a spotless track record in the apparel industry, as the Gap's new president. Drexler immediately overhauled the motley clothing lines to concentrate on sturdy, brightly colored cotton clothing. He also consolidated the store's many private clothing labels into the Gap brand. As a final touch Drexler ripped out the stores' circular clothing racks and installed white shelving upon which the clothes could be neatly stacked and displayed.

Also in 1983 the company bought Banana Republic, a unique chain of stores that sold safari clothing in a jungle decor. The company expanded the chain, which enjoyed tremendous success in the mid-1980s; however, after the novelty of the stores wore off in the late 1980s, sales went into a slump. Drexler responded by introducing a broader range of clothes (including higher-priced leather items) and playing down the jungle image. By 1990 Banana Republic was again profitable.

In 1985 the company opened its first GapKids after Drexler could not find clothing that he liked for his son. In 1987 the company opened its experimental Hemisphere chain to sell European-style clothing, but the stores were discontinued in 1989.

During the late 1980s and early 1990s, the Gap continued to grow rapidly, opening its first stores in Canada and the UK. In 1990 it introduced babyGap in 25 GapKids stores, featuring miniature versions of its GapKids line. In 1991 the company announced it would no longer sell Levi's (which had fallen to less than 2% of total sales) and would go completely private label.

The Gap's earnings fell in fiscal 1993 because of Gap division losses brought on by low margins and high rents. An unpopular fall merchandise line led the Gap to slash prices again, and much of the new clothing wound up on sales racks. It shuffled management positions and titles as part of a streamlining effort.

The company rebounded in 1994, concentrating more on improving profit margins than increasing sales. Also in 1994 the company launched a chain of discount clothing warehouse outlets called Old Navy Clothing Co., which it had previously tested under the name Gap Warehouse. That same year the company introduced GapScents, a line of personal care products.

In 1995 the company launched a line of body and bath products at Banana Republic. Also in 1995 Banana Republic opened its first 2 stores outside the US, in Edmonton and Toronto in Canada. The company plans to open its first Gap stores in Japan in 1995.

NYSE symbol: GPS
Fiscal year ends: Saturday nearest January 31

WHO

Chairman and CEO: Donald G. Fisher, age 66, $2,165,662 pay
President and COO: Millard S. Drexler, age 50, $2,164,731 pay
EVP and CFO: Robert J. Fisher, age 40, $898,615 pay
EVP and President, Gap Division: Richard M. Lyons, age 38, $869,324 pay
EVP Advertising: Magdalene Gross, age 46
President, Gap Kids: Patricia DeRosa, age 42, $694,305 pay
President, International Division: William S. Fisher, age 38
SVP Finance: Warren R. Hashagen, age 44
SVP General Counsel: Anne B. Gust, age 37
SVP Strategic Planning and Business Development: Charles K. Crovitz
VP Human Resources: Susan L. Cooper
Auditors: Deloitte & Touche LLP

WHERE

HQ: One Harrison, San Francisco, CA 94105
Phone: 415-952-4400
Fax: 415-896-0322

The Gap has stores in 48 states (including the 50 largest metropolitan areas in the US) and in Canada, France, Puerto Rico, and the UK.

Location	No. of Stores
US & Puerto Rico	1,384
Canada	72
UK	49
France	3
Total	**1,508**

WHAT

	No. of Stores
The Gap	892
GapKids	369
Banana Republic	188
Old Navy Clothing	59
Total	**1,508**

Stores
babyGap (infant clothing boutiques within GapKids stores)
Banana Republic (casual clothing)
The Gap (casual and active clothing)
GapKids (clothing for children)
Old Navy Clothing Company (lower-priced family clothing)

KEY COMPETITORS

50-Off Stores	Luxottica
Benetton	May
Broadway Stores	Melville
Brown Group	Mercantile Stores
Dayton Hudson	Merry-Go-Round
Dillard	Montgomery Ward
Donna Karan	NIKE
Edison Brothers	Nordstrom
Federated	Oshkosh B'Gosh
Harcourt General	Reebok
INTERCO	Sears
J. Crew	Spiegel
J. C. Penney	TJX
L.A. Gear	Toys "R" Us
Lands' End	Tweeds
Levi Strauss	V. F.
The Limited	Woolworth
Liz Claiborne	

HOW MUCH

	9-Year Growth	1986	1987	1988	1989	1990	1991	1992	1993	1994	1995
Sales ($ mil.)	21.5%	647	848	1,062	1,252	1,587	1,934	2,519	2,960	3,296	3,723
Net income ($ mil.)	31.3%	28	68	70	74	98	145	230	211	258	320
Income as % of sales	—	4.3%	8.0%	6.6%	5.9%	6.2%	7.5%	9.1%	7.1%	7.8%	8.6%
Earnings per share ($)	29.8%	0.21	0.49	0.49	0.52	0.70	1.02	1.62	1.47	1.78	2.20
Stock price – high ($)[1]	—	3.97	11.47	19.47	10.59	15.38	18.13	56.25	59.38	42.50	49.38
Stock price – low ($)[1]	—	1.28	3.88	4.00	4.63	8.81	9.75	16.50	28.13	25.50	28.88
Stock price – close ($)[1]	25.6%	3.92	8.94	5.06	10.44	12.84	16.56	53.50	33.00	39.38	30.50
P/E – high	—	19	23	40	20	22	18	35	40	24	22
P/E – low	—	6	8	8	9	13	10	10	19	14	13
Dividends per share ($)	35.4%	0.03	0.08	0.13	0.13	0.17	0.22	0.30	0.32	0.40	0.46
Book value per share ($)	27.3%	1.08	1.49	1.90	1.86	2.40	3.30	4.76	6.16	7.76	9.50
Employees	19.6%	11,000	12,000	15,700	19,800	23,000	26,000	32,000	39,000	44,000	55,000

1995 Year-end:
Debt ratio: —
Return on equity: 25.6%
Cash (mil.): $415
Current ratio: 2.11
Long-term debt (mil.): $0
No. of shares (mil.): 145
Dividends
  Yield: 1.5%
  Payout: 20.9%
Market value (mil.): $4,415

**Stock Price History[1]
High/Low 1986–95**

[1]Stock prices are for the prior calendar year.

GATEWAY 2000, INC.

OVERVIEW

Holy cow! Gateway, whose company mascot is a cow and whose headquarters is painted like a Holstein, sold more than one million PCs in 1994. The South Dakota–based manufacturer of IBM-compatible computers also became the world's leading supplier of Pentium-based computers (by early 1995 Pentium machines accounted for 60% of the company's sales, up from 35% in 1994).

Like its chief rival, Dell Computer, Gateway sells directly to the public. In the US over 500 salespeople staff the company phone banks 16 hours a day. Gateway is known for its wild ads and its cowhide-patterned packaging.

In early 1994 Gateway introduced a 90-megahertz microprocessor but was left with a warehouse full of slower microprocessors. The $16.5 million inventory writedown that followed lowered 1994 net income.

With less than 10% of 1994 sales outside the US, Gateway is targeting overseas markets. In 1994 the company expanded its sales operations to France and Germany and began recruiting distributors in Asia and Latin America.

Portable computing, which is gaining in popularity, is another avenue Gateway has marked for growth. In 1995 the company began shipping its ColorBook 2 notebook computers, which include a 16-bit stereo card and other advanced features.

Ted and Norm Waitt own most of Gateway's stock (50.1% and 30.9%, respectively).

WHEN

Apparently, college and billion-dollar PC retailers don't mix. Like his main competitor, Michael Dell, Ted Waitt dropped out of college to get into the computer business. Waitt had gone to Des Moines to see his roommates' band one weekend, met a friend who was working for a computer retailer, liked the sound of the job, and dropped out of school to go to work. After 9 months of on-the-job training, he quit to start his own company.

Using his grandmother's certificate of deposit as collateral, Waitt borrowed $10,000 and set up shop in his father's barn in South Dakota in 1985, founding a company called the TIPC Network with his brother Norm and Mike Hammond. The company sold add-on parts by phone for Texas Instruments PCs. However, Waitt's goal was to sell PCs himself, and in 1987 Waitt and company jumped into the fray. Waitt and Hammond put together a fully configured computer system at a price that was near what other companies were charging for a bare-bones system. In 1988 they changed the company's name to Gateway 2000 (because they believed their computers were the gateway to the 21st century). Sales took off, and the company moved its headquarters to the Livestock Exchange Building in Sioux City, Iowa.

Gateway's customer base was made up of sophisticated buyers who were willing to dig through computer catalogs to find the best price for the exact system they wanted, and much of Gateway's success was rooted in Waitt's ability to predict which standard features customers would want.

Gateway also distinguished itself from competitors with eye-catching ads. Some featured cows; others featured Gateway employees, including one in which Waitt was dressed as Robin Hood. Waitt's idea was to sell the company, to convince potential customers that if they bought a computer, Gateway 2000 would be around in the future to service it. When Gateway's eccentric ads popped up month after month in computer magazines, the company's name stuck in readers' minds.

The company continued to grow at breakneck speed. In 1990 Gateway moved across the state line to North Sioux City, South Dakota, and by the end of the year, sales reached $276 million. In 1991 the company topped the *Inc.* 500 list. That same year Waitt hired Rick Snyder, head of mergers and acquisitions at Coopers & Lybrand's Chicago office, to help him manage a company that was rapidly becoming a major player in the PC wars.

In 1992 Gateway introduced a line of notebook computers and a subnotebook, called Handbook. The company also began offering a CD-ROM product from Sony and created a new division to handle component add-ons.

Gateway made its initial public offering in late 1993. That same year it opened a manufacturing and service facility in Ireland.

Gateway weathered the storm created late in 1994 when many of its Intel-made Pentium chips were found to contain a flaw (corrected by early 1995). Also in late 1994 Waitt said Gateway planned to expand its catalog with software, computer peripherals, and non computer items such as CDs and movies. That same year the company opened a sales and support facility in Kansas City, Missouri.

In 1995 Gateway began installing quad-speed CD-ROM drives on all its PCs.

Nasdaq symbol: GATE
Fiscal year ends: December 31

WHO

Chairman, President, and CEO: Theodore "Ted" W. Waitt, age 32, $654,475 pay
EVP and Secretary: Richard D. Snyder, age 36, $399,800 pay
SVP and CFO: David J. McKittrick, age 49
VP Sales: Todd S. Osborn, age 34, $227,007 pay
VP Technical Services: James Collas, age 34, $185,782 pay
VP: Robert M. Spears, age 35, $146,980 pay
VP: Mike Hammond, age 33
VP Manufacturing: John d'Auguste, age 44
VP and General Counsel: William M. Elliott, age 61
Director Human Resources: Dwayne Rideout
Auditors: Coopers & Lybrand L.L.P.

WHERE

HQ: 610 Gateway Dr., PO Box 2000, North Sioux City, SD 57049-2000
Phone: 605-232-2000
Fax: 605-232-2023

Gateway 2000 has operations in Missouri, South Dakota, and Ireland.

	1994 Sales	
	$ mil.	% of total
US	2,510	93
Other countries	191	7
Total	**2,701**	**100**

WHAT

	1994 Sales
	% of total
Desktop PCs (non-Pentium) & peripherals	57
Pentium products	35
Portable products	8
Total	**100**

Selected Products

Computers
PC systems
  4DX2-66 Integrated System
  DX2-66 Family PC
  P4D-66 PCI Local-Bus System
  P5-60
  P5-60 Family PC
  P5-75
  P5-75 Family PC
  P5-90 Family PC
  P5-100 Best Buy
  P5-100XL
Portable computers
  ColorBook[2]
  Liberty

Other Products
Cache upgrades
CD-ROM drives
Chips
Disk drives
Keyboards
Memory upgrades
Modems
Monitors
Multimedia accessories
Network cards
PCMCIA cards
Printers
Processors and coprocessors
Software and software bundles
Speakers
Tape backup units

KEY COMPETITORS

Advanced Logic Research
Apple
AST
Atari
Compaq
CompuAdd
CompuCom Systems
Damark International
Data General
DEC
Dell
ELEK-TEK
Fry's Electronics
Fujitsu
Hewlett-Packard
Hyundai
IBM
InaCom
Intelligent Electronics
Machines Bull
Matsushita
Micro Warehouse
MicroAge
Micron Technology
NEC
Olivetti
Packard Bell
PCs Compleat
Tandy
Tech Data
Texas Instruments
Toshiba

HOW MUCH

	Annual Growth	1985	1986	1987	1988	1989	1990	1991	1992	1993	1994
Sales ($ mil.)	191.8%	—	—	2	12	71	276	627	1,107	1,732	2,701
Net income ($ mil.)	157.7%	—	—	—	0	4	17	39	70	100	96
Income as % of sales	—	—	—	—	2.8%	5.0%	6.0%	6.3%	6.3%	5.8%	3.6%
Earnings per share ($)	89.4%	—	—	—	—	0.05	0.25	0.59	1.03	1.41	1.22
Stock price – high ($)	—	—	—	—	—	—	—	—	—	21.50	24.75
Stock price – low ($)	—	—	—	—	—	—	—	—	—	16.75	9.25
Stock price – close ($)	10.2%	—	—	—	—	—	—	—	—	19.63	21.63
P/E – high	—	—	—	—	—	—	—	—	—	15	20
P/E – low	—	—	—	—	—	—	—	—	—	12	8
Dividends per share ($)	—	—	—	—	—	—	—	—	—	0.00	0.00
Book value per share ($)	34.1%	—	—	—	—	—	—	—	—	3.87	5.19
Employees	142.6%	—	—	11	40	150	303	657	1,369	2,832	5,442

1994 Year-end:
Debt ratio: 7.6%
Return on equity: 29.2%
Cash (mil.): $244
Current ratio: 1.88
Long-term debt (mil.): $27
No. of shares (mil.): 72
Dividends
  Yield: —
  Payout: —
Market value (mil.): $1,566

Stock Price History High/Low 1993-94

GEICO CORPORATION

OVERVIEW

GEICO is the holding company for Government Employees Insurance Co., one of the US's largest auto insurers. It has traditionally provided auto and other insurance to low-risk demographic groups (such as mature, steadily employed people), but has also begun to target the nonstandard auto market (high-risk individuals who are required by law to buy auto insurance). Longtime GEICO investor Warren Buffett's Berkshire Hathaway Corp. agreed in 1995 to buy the 49% of the company that it didn't already own.

GEICO keeps its costs and premiums low by marketing its products directly to government and military employees and to others via direct mail, word-of-mouth, and, new in 1994, television advertising. Soliciting customers directly eliminates the need for a large and expensive sales or agency force. Its high rate of policyholder retentions also saves costs.

GEICO is one of the few major insurers that still makes auto insurance the backbone of its business. It reinforced this position in 1995 when it decided to phase out its homeowners insurance (which was only a small percentage of its business and had been hit with an unprecedented string of natural disasters in the 1990s) and most of its small, money-losing consumer finance operations ($45 million in loans sold to Litchfield Financial Corp.).

WHEN

Leo Goodwin, an accountant for a San Antonio insurer, believed he could start an auto insurance firm during the Depression by selling to targeted customers without an agent. In 1936 at age 50, he founded Government Employees Insurance Co. in Fort Worth with $100,000 — 75% from Fort Worth banker Cleaves Rhea.

At first Leo and his wife, Lillian, worked 12 hours a day for a combined income of $250 a month. They targeted government employees (mature people with steady incomes in a time of financial uncertainty). In 1937 the company moved to Washington, DC, where the most government workers were.

GEICO had $15,000 net income in 1940, the first of 35 consecutive profitable years. In 1941, after a major hailstorm damaged cars in the Washington area, Goodwin engaged auto repair shops to work 24 hours a day solely for GEICO. Goodwin's policyholders told friends about the service, and business grew by word-of-mouth. GEICO participated in the post-WWII boom by insuring the new homes and autos of veterans. GEICO's new premium income reached $2.5 million in 1946, a 50% increase over 1945.

In 1948 the Rhea family sold its 75% interest to the Graham-Newman Corp., which spun it off to stockholders. In 1949 the profits of newly public GEICO exceeded $1 million, and the company diversified into life insurance and financial services.

The company targeted state, county, and municipal employees in 1952 and nongovernmental professional, technical, and managerial workers in 1958. Goodwin retired from the company in that year.

In the 1970s GEICO was shaken by federal wage and price controls and no-fault insurance. By 1975 these factors, as well as poor management decisions, resulted in an $85 million loss. As GEICO neared insolvency, new management was installed. New CEO John Byrne raised rates, cut costs, reunderwrote all policies, and retained Salomon Brothers to underwrite a $76 million stock offering. One new investor was Berkshire Hathaway. The plan worked and GEICO returned to profitability in 1977.

After moving into financial services and life insurance in the 1980s, GEICO decided in 1988 to focus again on property, casualty, and auto lines. As part of this plan, the company stopped writing reinsurance in 1987 (this business continued to wind down in 1994).

In 1991 the corporation bought Southern Heritage Insurance and Merastar, both of which sell through agents. But by 1993 the company had determined that these agency systems were out of sync with the rest of the organization and sold them.

In 1993 GEICO began to curtail the writing of new homeowner policies in hurricane-prone areas and to raise rates. It also decided not to renew its own reinsurance policies (which may leave it vulnerable to future disasters). In addition, GEICO refunded $21 million in premiums to customers as a result of California's 1988 Proposition 103, which called for auto premium rollbacks.

Following its decision to quit the homeowners insurance business, GEICO arranged for Aetna to take over most of the accounts as they come up for renewal in 1996. In states where Aetna does not do business, GEICO has offered to help its customers make other arrangements. But some consumer advocates fear the new insurers will be too expensive.

NYSE symbol: GEC
Fiscal year ends: December 31

WHO

Chairman, President and CEO: Olza M. Nicely, age 51, $570,074 pay
President and CEO, Capital Operations: Louis A. Simpson, age 58, $500,000 pay
President and CEO, Government Employees Financial Corporation: John M. Avery
EVP and CFO: W. Alvon Sparks Jr., age 59, $370,666 pay
SVP: James M. Hitt, age 50, $249,285 pay
SVP and Chief Information Officer: Simone J. Pace, age 52, $214,698 pay
SVP Human Resources: Marion E. Byrd, age 58
Group VP and Controller: Thomas M. Wells, age 44
VP and General Counsel: Charles R. Davies, age 54
VP and Legislative Counsel: Andrea M. Covell
VP: Rynthia M. Rost
VP: Donald R. Lyns, age 48
VP: David H. Pushman, age 46
VP: David Schindler, age 49
VP: Richard C. VanEssendelft, age 54
Treasurer: Charles G. Schara
Corporate Secretary: Rosalind A. Phillips
Auditors: Coopers & Lybrand L.L.P.

WHERE

HQ: One GEICO Plaza, Washington, DC 20076-0001
Phone: 301-986-2500
Fax: 301-986-2113

GEICO operates in all 50 states and Washington, DC. It has an office serving US military personnel in Germany and agents in Italy, Turkey, and the UK.

WHAT

	1994 Assets	
	$ mil.	% of total
Cash & equivalents	78	2
Treasury & agency securities	842	17
State & municipal bonds	2,293	46
Corporate bonds	97	2
Stocks	760	15
Other securities	61	1
Receivable & recoverables	425	8
Property & equipment	142	3
Other	300	6
Total	**4,998**	**100**

	1994 Sales	
	$ mil.	% of total
Premiums	2,476	91
Net investments	202	7
Gains on investments	13	1
Interest on loans	10	0
Other	15	1
Total	**2,716**	**100**

Insurance Services
Life and health insurance
Personal property/casualty insurance (auto and homeowners insurance)

Selected Subsidiaries
GEICO Casualty Co.
GEICO General Insurance Co.
GEICO Indemnity Co.
Government Employees Insurance Co. (GEICO)

KEY COMPETITORS

20th Century Industries	CNA Financial	Penn America
Allstate	ITT Hartford	Prudential
B.A.T	Liberty Mutual	SAFECO
Chubb	Lincoln National	State Farm
CIGNA	Midland Financial	Travelers
	Nationwide Insurance	

HOW MUCH

	9-Year Growth	1985	1986	1987	1988	1989	1990	1991	1992	1993	1994
Assets ($ mil.)	8.6%	2,378	2,715	2,846	3,061	3,434	3,576	4,086	4,378	4,831	4,998
Net income ($ mil.)	11.6%	78	119	178	134	213	208	196	173	274	209
Income as % of assets	—	3.3%	4.4%	6.3%	4.4%	6.2%	5.8%	4.8%	3.9%	5.7%	4.2%
Earnings per share ($)	15.1%	0.84	1.38	1.80	1.70	2.75	2.73	2.70	2.39	4.01	2.98
Stock price – high ($)	—	17.60	21.10	27.35	26.40	31.20	33.90	39.85	66.00	67.63	57.63
Stock price – low ($)	—	11.43	15.55	18.03	20.30	24.55	25.15	31.30	39.60	47.38	47.63
Stock price – close ($)	12.2%	17.40	19.70	22.10	24.80	30.50	32.43	39.80	65.00	51.38	49.00
P/E – high	—	21	15	15	16	11	12	15	28	17	19
P/E – low	—	14	11	10	12	9	9	12	17	12	16
Dividends per share ($)	19.6%	0.20	0.22	0.27	0.33	0.36	0.40	0.46	0.60	0.68	1.00
Book value per share ($)	15.4%	5.83	7.47	7.84	9.16	11.76	12.78	16.67	18.23	21.66	21.17
Employees	4.9%	5,287	5,989	6,371	6,671	6,716	6,716	7,322	7,003	8,125	8,151

1994 Year-end:
Equity as % of assets: 28.9%
Return on assets: 4.2%
Return on equity: 14.0%
Long-term debt (mil.): $391
No. of shares (mil.): 68
Dividends
  Yield: 2.0%
  Payout: 33.6%
Market value (mil.): $3,346
Sales (mil.): $2,716

Stock Price History
High/Low 1985–94

GENENTECH, INC.

OVERVIEW

South San Francisco–based biotechnology firm Genentech's pharmaceutical pipeline is as wide as it is deep. Genentech has 5 biotech products marketed in various countries and a number in the later stages of development. It sells Protropin (treats children's growth hormone inadequacy), Activase (breaks up blood clots after heart attacks), Actimmune (treats a rare, inherited immune system disorder), Nutropin (similar to Protropin), and Pulmozyme (which is the first new drug to treat cystic fibrosis in 30 years and which may also help chronic bronchitis sufferers).

Other Genentech products in the later stages of development include gp120 (anti-AIDS drug), Auriculin (treatment for acute renal failure), Anti-HER2 (treatment for breast cancer), Anti-IgE (treatment for rhinitis and asthma), IGF-1 (insulin-like growth factor for AIDS and diabetes treatment), and NGF (nerve growth factor). The company spent over 50% of product sales on R&D in 1994.

Swiss drug-giant Roche Holdings helped bring the company back to life by purchasing 60% of Genentech for $2.1 billion. Roche has since increased its holdings in the company to 66% and has a complicated option plan to purchase the rest of the company by 1999. Genentech still operates autonomously.

Aggressive sales tactics have helped the company grow. However, in 1994 a company sales executive was indicted for bribing a Minnesota physician (under the guise of a research grant) to prescribe the company's growth hormone to more children. Also, in 1995 the FDA began a broad investigation of Genentech's marketing practices, citing a "pattern of violative product promotion."

WHEN

Venture capitalist Robert Swanson and molecular biologist Herbert Boyer founded Genentech in 1976 to commercialize genetically engineered products. Boyer held a patent on techniques for splicing genes into microorganisms that could be used as "micro-factories" to produce large amounts of therapeutic substances. Before it even marketed a product, Genentech achieved fame when it went public in 1980. Its market value doubled to $688 million on the first trading day but fell back closer to its issue level within a month. Boyer's initial investment of a few hundred dollars was briefly worth $80 million.

Genentech's first product was a bioengineered human form of insulin; in 1982 it became the first FDA-approved biotech product. The company licensed it to Eli Lilly, which sold it as Humulin. Selling marketing rights in exchange for royalties allowed the company to focus on research, which could run over $100 million per product. The company next developed the human immune system protein alpha interferon and licensed it to Hoffmann-La Roche, who sold the cancer treatment as Roferon-A. The first product to bear the Genentech name was its human growth hormone, Protropin, approved by the FDA in 1985. A charge for R&D expenses resulted in a significant drop in profits and a loss in 1986.

Genentech's Activase (a t-PA clot dissolver to treat heart attacks) had the largest first-year sales of any new drug ($180 million in 1988). In 1988 and 1989 half of the company's sales came from Activase. Genentech won a federal suit to exclusively make and sell Activase in 1990, although UK courts invalidated its t-PA patent. Activase development required $200 million and 5 years. The company anticipated sales of $1 billion by 1990, but expectations dropped after a 1990 announcement that heart attack survival rates were no greater with Activase than with its rival, streptokinase, which costs 1/10 as much. A $55 million study funded by Genentech in 1993 indicated that the survival rate for heart attack patients who use Activase is only one percentage point higher than for patients who use streptokinase. However, sales rebounded following the release of the results.

In 1990 Swiss drug giant Roche Holding bought 60% (it now owns 66%) of Genentech for $2.1 billion, which included nearly $500 million in cash, to be used for research to maintain the company's long-term product pipeline. In 1993 Genentech and Merck scientists developed a compound to stop the Ras oncogene (the gene that turns normal cells into cancer cells in the pancreas, colon, and lung) from becoming activated. That same year the company increased its stake in Glycomed and extended its research agreement.

Genentech began shipping new product Nutropin (a human growth hormone) in early 1994. In 1995 president and CEO Kirk Rabb was ousted after trying to secure a $2 million loan guarantee from Roche. Scientist Arthur Levinson replaced Rabb, which many saw as an indication of Roche's commitment to the R&D side of the business.

NYSE symbol: GNE
Fiscal year ends: December 31

WHO

Chairman: Robert A. Swanson, age 47
President and CEO: Arthur D. Levinson, age 44,
$515,000 pay (prior to promotion)
SVP: William D. Young, age 50, $491,000 pay
SVP and Secretary: John P. McLaughlin, age 43,
$470,000 pay
SVP and CFO: Louis J. Lavigne Jr., age 46,
$462,000 pay
SVP: Richard B. Brewer, age 43
SVP and Chief Medical Officer: Barry M. Sherman,
age 53
VP Corporate Communications: Gregory Baird, age 44
VP Government Affairs: David W. Beier, age 46
VP Quality: Robert Garnick, age 45
VP Research Technology: Dennis J. Henner, age 43
VP and General Manager, Europe: Kurt Kopp, age 46
VP Research Discovery: Hugh D. Niall, age 57
VP and General Counsel: Stephen G. Juelsgaard, age 46
VP Human Resources: Larry Setren, age 43
Auditors: Ernst & Young LLP

WHERE

HQ: 460 Point San Bruno Blvd., South San Francisco,
CA 94080-4990
Phone: 415-225-1000
Fax: 415-225-2021

Genentech sells goods in North America, Europe, and
Japan and licenses products worldwide.

	1994 Sales	
	$ mil.	% of total
US	683	86
Europe	82	10
Asia	20	3
Canada	10	1
Total	**795**	**100**

WHAT

	1994 Sales	
	$ mil.	% of total
Product sales		
Activase	281	36
Protropin & Nutropin	225	28
Pulmozyme	88	11
Actimmune	6	1
Royalties	126	16
Contract & other	26	3
Interest	43	5
Total	**795**	**100**

Products on the Market
Actimmune (treatment of a rare immune system
disorder)
Activase (dissolves clots in heart and lung)
Nutropin (human growth hormone)
Protropin (human growth hormone)
Pulmozyme DNase (treatment for chronic obstructive
pulmonary disease and cystic fibrosis)

Products in Development
Anti-HER2 Antibody (treatment for breast cancer)
Anti-IgE Antibody (treatment for allergic rhinitis and
asthma)
Auriculin (treatment for acute renal failure)
gp120 (immunotherapy for HIV-1 infected patients)
IGF-1 (insulin-like growth factor; treatment for diabetes)
NGF (nerve growth factor; treatment for peripheral
neuropathy)

KEY COMPETITORS

Abbott Labs	Dow Chemical	Monsanto
American Home	DuPont	Novo Nordisk
Products	Eli Lilly	Pfizer
Amgen	Glaxo Wellcome	Rhône-Poulenc
Bayer	Glycomed	Sandoz
Biogen	Hoechst	Schering-
Bristol-Myers	Immunex	Plough
Squibb	Johnson &	SmithKline
Chiron Corp.	Johnson	Beecham
Ciba-Geigy	Merck	Upjohn

HOW MUCH

	9-Year Growth	1985	1986	1987	1988	1989	1990	1991	1992	1993	1994
Sales ($ mil.)	27.4%	90	134	231	335	401	476	516	544	650	795
Net income ($ mil.)	40.1%	6	(353)	42	21	44	(98)	44	21	59	124
Income as % of sales	—	6.8%	—	18.2%	6.3%	11.0%	—	8.5%	3.9%	9.1%	15.6%
Earnings per share ($)	29.7%	0.10	(5.10)	0.50	0.24	0.51	(1.05)	0.39	0.18	0.50	1.04
Stock price – high ($)	—	18.81	49.38	64.75	47.50	23.38	30.88	36.25	39.50	50.50	53.50
Stock price – low ($)	—	8.56	16.44	28.00	14.38	16.00	20.13	20.75	25.88	31.25	41.75
Stock price – close ($)	11.3%	17.44	42.50	42.00	16.00	20.75	22.50	32.25	37.38	50.50	45.68
P/E – high	—	188	—	130	198	46	—	93	219	101	51
P/E – low	—	86	—	56	60	31	—	53	144	63	40
Dividends per share ($)	—	0.00	0.00	0.00	0.00	0.00	0.00	0.00	0.00	0.00	0.00
Book value per share ($)	15.7%	3.09	4.37	4.52	4.82	5.56	8.08	8.53	8.92	9.73	11.50
Employees	13.3%	893	1,168	1,465	1,744	1,790	1,923	2,202	2,331	2,510	2,738

1994 Year-end:
Debt ratio: 10.1%
Return on equity: 10.1%
Cash (mil.): $719
Current ratio: 4.52
Long-term debt (mil.): $150
No. of shares (mil.): 117
Dividends
  Yield: —
  Payout: —
Market value (mil.): $5,355

**Stock Price History
High/Low 1985–94**

GENERAL DYNAMICS CORPORATION

OVERVIEW

Once a defense giant with a range of programs, Falls Church, Virginia–based General Dynamics has sold off a number of its businesses to cope with military downsizing. What's left is a company about 1/3 its former size, with 2 main areas of operation: nuclear submarines and artillery systems. Its Electric Boat division builds the SSN 688–class and Seawolf-class attack submarines and the Trident ballistic missile submarine. Its Land Systems division builds the M1 Series Main Battle Tank and is part of a team developing an advanced artillery system for the US Army.

To pump up Electric Boat's operations, General Dynamics, with about $1.1 billion in

cash from its divestitures, agreed in 1995 to buy surface-ship builder Bath Iron Works for $300 million. While the end of the Cold War has brought many defense cuts, Electric Boat has managed to stay afloat. The Clinton administration has earmarked $1 billion to build a 3rd Seawolf submarine — not because the sub is needed, but because a Pentagon review determined that if the sub were not built and Electric Boat were allowed to go under, vital technological know-how would be lost.

A group led by investor Warren Buffett owns 8.4% of the company, and directors Lester Crown and Charles Goodman and their families own 13.1%.

WHEN

The history of General Dynamics begins with the Electric Boat Company, a New Jersey ship and submarine builder founded by John Holland in 1899. Electric Boat produced large numbers of submarines, ships, and PT boats during WWII. Faced with dwindling orders after the war, the company, under the direction of John Jay Hopkins, began to diversify with the 1947 purchase of Canadian aircraft builder Canadair. Hopkins formed General Dynamics in 1952, merging Electric Boat and Canadair into the new company, and bought California-based Consolidated Vultee Aircraft (Convair), a major producer of military and civilian aircraft, in 1954.

Electric Boat launched the first nuclear submarine, the *Nautilus,* in the mid-1950s. In 1955, at the urging of Howard Hughes, Convair began designing its first commercial jetliners, the Convair 880 and 990. While nuclear subs became a mainstay for General Dynamics, it gave up on jetliners after losses on the aircraft reached $425 million (1961). Meanwhile, weakened by the cost of producing the 880 and 990, General Dynamics merged with Chicago building-materials supplier Material Service Corporation (1959), whose owner, Colonel Henry Crown, received a 20% stake.

During the 1960s General Dynamics developed the controversial F-111 fighter. Despite numerous problems, the aircraft proved financially and militarily successful (F-111s participated in the 1986 US bombing raid on Libya).

Backed by Crown (the company's largest stockholder), David Lewis became CEO in 1970. Under Lewis, General Dynamics won contracts for the navy's 688-class attack submarine (1971), liquefied natural gas tankers for Burmah Oil Company (1972), the Trident

ballistic missile submarine (1974), and the F-16 lightweight fighter aircraft (1975). The company sold Canadair (1976) and bought Chrysler Defense, which had a contract to build the army's new M1 tank, in 1982. Lewis made General Dynamics profitable but retired in 1985 amid federal investigations of overcharges to the government.

CEO Stanley Pace instituted tough ethics rules and cut costs. The company bought Cessna Aircraft in 1986 and sold its Quincy shipyard in 1987. Also in 1987 it won a contract to design and build the Centaur high-energy upper stage for the Titan IV launch vehicle. In 1991 former astronaut William Anders became CEO. With the end of the Cold War leading to defense budget cuts, Anders began selling off pieces of the company, including Cessna Aircraft (1992, to Textron), its missile operations (1992, to Hughes Aircraft), and its electronics business (1993, to the Carlyle Group).

In 1993 General Dynamics sold its Tactical Military Aircraft unit (which had been its most profitable business) to Lockheed for $1.5 billion. That same year the company paid out special dividends totaling about $1.5 billion. Also in 1993 Anders retired as CEO and was succeeded by president James Mellor.

In 1994 the company sold its space systems business to Martin Marietta for $209 million. That same year its Land Systems division won a $116 million contract to build radio systems for the army.

In 1995, 8 former General Dynamics employees sued the company for age discrimination. The former employees claim they were fired so the company could bring in younger, lower-paid workers.

WHO

Chairman and CEO: James R. Mellor, age 64,
$2,270,000 pay
EVP: Nicholas D. Chabraja, age 52, $1,100,000 pay
EVP; President, Electric Boat Division: James E.
Turner Jr., age 60, $831,000 pay
VP; President, Land Systems Division: Roger E.
Tetrault, age 53, $551,000 pay
VP and CFO: Michael J. Manusco, age 52
VP and General Counsel: Edward C. Bruntrager, age 47
VP Government Relations: G. Kent Bankus, age 52
VP International Business Development: Henry J.
Sechler
VP Communications: Paul A. Hesse, age 53
VP Human Resources and Administration: Ralph W.
Kiger, age 49
Staff VP and Corporate Secretary: E. Alan Klobasa,
age 47
Staff VP and Treasurer: David H. Fogg, age 39
Auditors: Arthur Andersen & Co, SC

WHERE

HQ: 3190 Fairview Park Dr., Falls Church, VA
22042-4523
Phone: 703-876-3000
Fax: 703-876-3125

General Dynamics has submarine manufacturing
facilities in Avenel, New Jersey; Groton, Connecticut;
and Quonset Point, Rhode Island; it has tank
manufacturing facilities in Lima, Ohio, and Warren,
Michigan.

	1994 Sales	
	$ mil.	% of total
US	2,336	76
Other countries	722	24
Total	**3,058**	**100**

WHAT

	1994 Sales		1994 Operating Income	
	$ mil.	% of total	$ mil.	% of total
Nuclear subs	1,678	55	173	54
Armored vehicles	1,184	39	140	44
Other	196	6	8	2
Total	**3,058**	**100**	**321**	**100**

	1994 Sales	
	$ mil.	% of total
US government	2,880	94
Other	178	6
Total	**3,058**	**100**

Nuclear Submarines (Electric Boat)
Design and construction
  Seawolf
  SSN 688
  Trident
Engineering support
Overhaul and repairs

Armored Vehicles (Land Systems)
Design and construction
  M1 Series Abrams Main Battle Tank
  Single Channel Ground and Airborne Radio System
  (SINCGARS, with Tadrian Ltd.)
Engineering support
Operation and maintenance training

Other
American Overseas Marine Corp. (ship management
services)
Freeman Energy Corp. (coal mining)
Patriot Shipping Corporations (liquefied natural gas
tanker leasing)

KEY COMPETITORS

FMC	Lockheed Martin	Raytheon
ITT Industries	Loral	Siemens
Litton Industries	Northrop Grumman	Textron

HOW MUCH

	9-Year Growth	1985	1986	1987	1988	1989	1990	1991	1992	1993	1994
Sales ($ mil.)	(10.3%)	8,164	8,892	9,344	9,551	10,043	10,173	8,751	3,472	3,187	3,058
Net income ($ mil.)	(5.3%)	388	(53)	437	379	293	(578)	505	441	885	238
Income as % of sales	—	4.8%	—	4.7%	4.0%	2.9%	—	5.8%	12.7%	27.8%	7.8%
Earnings per share ($)	(2.2%)	4.59	(0.61)	5.13	4.52	3.51	(6.93)	6.04	5.05	13.99	3.75
Stock price – high ($)	—	29.91	31.78	28.13	21.01	21.54	16.42	19.36	38.41	50.38	47.63
Stock price – low ($)	—	22.08	22.88	15.18	15.89	15.13	6.77	7.21	19.01	36.81	38.00
Stock price – close ($)	(6.6%)	24.48	24.13	17.36	18.07	15.98	8.99	19.14	36.90	46.13	43.50
P/E – high	—	7	—	6	5	6	—	3	8	4	13
P/E – low	—	5	—	3	4	4	—	1	4	3	11
Dividends per share ($)	11.7%	0.50	0.50	0.50	0.50	0.50	0.50	0.50	0.73	25.90	1.35
Book value per share ($)	3.2%	15.73	14.73	19.09	23.05	25.56	18.12	23.62	26.18	18.81	20.89
Employees	(14.9%)	103,300	107,877	105,300	102,800	102,200	98,100	80,600	56,800	30,500	24,200

1994 Year-end:
Debt ratio: 13.0%
Return on equity: 19.1%
Cash (mil.): $1,059
Current ratio: 2.87
Long-term debt (mil.): $196
No. of shares (mil.): 63
Dividends
  Yield: 3.1%
  Payout: 36.0%
Market value (mil.): $2,740

Stock Price History
High/Low 1985–94

GENERAL ELECTRIC COMPANY

OVERVIEW

Industrial behemoth General Electric (GE) makes everything from lightbulbs to locomotives, power generators, and jet engines. The manufacturer ranks among the world's 10 largest industrial companies and is #1 among US electronics firms.

Diversity has protected GE's bottom line from recent fluctuations in its primary markets: automobile electronics, aircraft engines, and power generation are down; materials (especially plastics), financial services (GE Capital Corp.), and ad rates at NBC are up. Other GE businesses include appliances, lighting, medical systems, and information services.

Like other international companies, GE is reacting to global competition by reducing its work force and streamlining its operations while expanding its global reach. In 1994 GE Capital acquired Minebea Credit (Japan), and

GE Power Generation acquired 80% of turbine maker Nuovo Pignone (Italy). The company's aircraft engines unit won important orders from Air Canada and Singapore Airlines. In Europe and the Middle East, over 60 million homes tuned in to the NBC Super Channel.

GE's operations hit some turbulence in 1995 when CEO Jack Welch underwent triple bypass surgery, raising questions about the company's line of succession. Later that year delivery of the GE90 engine, used to power British Airways's new Boeing 777s, was delayed when the engine failed to meet FAA testing.

On an up note, in 1994 GE sold scandal-plagued Kidder, Peabody to Paine Webber for a package valued at $670 million. In 1995 the company announced that it had developed a new electric power generator that converts a record 60% of fuel to energy.

WHEN

General Electric was established in 1892 in New York, the result of a merger between the Thomson-Houston Company and the Edison General Electric Company. Charles Coffin was GE's first president and Thomas Edison, who left the company in 1894, one of its directors.

GE's financial strength (backed by the Morgan banking house) and focus on research (it started one of the first corporate research laboratories in 1900) led to the company's success. Products included elevators (1885), trolleys, motors, the lightbulb, and toasters (1905) and other appliances under the GE and Hotpoint labels. In the 1920s GE joined AT&T and Westinghouse in a radio broadcasting joint venture, Radio Corporation of America (RCA). GE sold off its RCA holdings (1930) because of an antitrust ruling (one of 65 antitrust actions against GE between 1911 and 1967).

From 1940 to 1952 annual sales increased sixfold to $2.6 billion. GE entered the computer industry in 1956 but sold the business in 1970 to Honeywell because of operating losses. By 1980 GE's revenues had reached $25 billion from sales of plastics, consumer electronics, nuclear reactors, and jet engines.

In the 1980s GE's strategy was to pursue only high-performance ventures. Between 1980 and 1989 GE sold operations that accounted for 25% of its 1980 sales and focused on medical equipment, financial services, and high-performance plastics and ceramics. GE shed its air-conditioning (1982), housewares (1984), mining (1984), and semiconductor (1988) businesses. It acquired Employers

Reinsurance in 1984 ($1.1 billion); RCA, including NBC, in 1986 ($6.4 billion); investment bankers Kidder, Peabody (completed in 1990); and CGR medical equipment from Thomson of France in 1987 as part of an exchange for GE's consumer electronics division.

GE entered Eastern Europe in 1990, taking a majority interest in the Hungarian lighting company Tungsram. In 1991 GE acquired a stake in THORN Light Source in the UK. The 2 purchases increased GE's European share of the lamp market to 20%. In 1992 GE entered a lighting equipment joint venture with Hitachi, giving GE access to the Japanese company's distribution network. In 1993 GE moved into the mutual fund business, buying mutual fund wholesaler GNA for $525 million and gaining SEC permission to allow GE Investment Management, which runs GE's pension assets, to sell mutual funds to the public.

In 1994 GE fired its top government bond trader for allegedly making phony trades at Kidder, Peabody that led to a $350 million charge. The debacle, which also resulted in the resignation of Kidder CEO Michael Carpenter, reignited rumors that GE would sell off the unit. GE talked with Disney and Turner Broadcasting in 1994 about buying NBC, but neither deal panned out.

The doctor with the first patent for magnetic resonance imaging (MRI) won an $111 million patent infringement award from GE in 1995. GE claimed that it had independently developed MRI technology and said it expected the judgment to be thrown out on appeal.

WHO

Chairman and CEO: John F. (Jack) Welch Jr., age 59, $4,350,000 pay
VC and Executive Officer: Paolo Fresco, age 61, $2,125,000 pay
EVP: Frank P. Doyle, age 64, $1,476,667 pay
SVP Finance: Dennis D. Dammerman, age 49, $1,475,000 pay
SVP, General Counsel, and Secretary: Benjamin W. Heineman Jr., age 51, $1,427,500 pay
SVP GE Asia-Pacific: W. James McNerney Jr., age 45
SVP GE Power Systems: David C. Genever-Watling, age 49
SVP GE Aircraft Engines: Eugene F. Murphy, age 59
SVP GE Lighting: John D. Opie, age 57
SVP GE Plastics: Gary L. Rogers, age 50
SVP GE Appliances: J. Richard Stonesifer, age 58
SVP GE Medical Systems: John M. Trani, age 50
SVP Research and Development: Lewis S. Edelheit, age 52
SVP Human Resources: William J. Conaty, age 49
Auditors: KPMG Peat Marwick LLP

WHERE

HQ: 3135 Easton Tnpk., Fairfield, CT 06431-0001
Phone: 203-373-2211
Fax: 203-373-3131

GE has 145 manufacturing plants in 31 states and Puerto Rico and 113 plants in 25 other countries.

	1994 Sales		1994 Operating Income	
	$ mil.	% of total	$ mil.	% of total
US	49,920	79	8,445	87
Other countries	13,290	21	1,268	13
Adjustments	(3,101)	—	5	—
Total	**60,109**	**100**	**9,718**	**100**

WHAT

	1994 Sales		1994 Operating Income	
	$ mil.	% of total	$ mil.	% of total
GE Capital				
Financing	14,932	24	2,662	25
Other	4,943	8	287	3
Industrial products	9,038	15	1,328	12
Major appliances	5,671	9	683	6
Power generation	5,962	10	1,238	11
Aircraft engines	5,889	9	935	9
Materials	5,638	9	967	9
Technical	4,267	7	787	7
Broadcasting	3,361	5	500	5
Other	2,348	4	1,346	13
Adjustments	(1,940)	—	(2,072)	—
Total	**60,109**	**100**	**8,661**	**100**

Products and Services
Aircraft engines (engines and replacement parts)
Appliances (kitchen and laundry equipment)
Broadcasting (National Broadcasting Co. [NBC])
Industrial products and systems (lighting, electrical distribution, and control equipment)
Materials (plastics, silicones, laminates, and abrasives)
Power generation (products for generating electricity)
Technical products and services (medical and network-based information services)

KEY COMPETITORS

ABB	GTE	Rolls-Royce
Alcatel Alsthom	Hitachi	Siemens
Bear Stearns	Ingersoll-Rand	Time Warner
Capital Cities/ABC	Matsushita	Toshiba
CBS	Maytag	Turner
CS Holding	Mitsubishi	Broadcasting
AB Electrolux	Mitsui	United Technologies
Fried. Krupp	News Corp.	USG
GEC	Philips	Viacom
General Motors	Raytheon	Westinghouse
General Re	Rockwell	Whirlpool

HOW MUCH

	9-Year Growth	1985	1986	1987	1988	1989	1990	1991	1992	1993	1994
Sales ($ mil.)	8.7%	28,285	35,210	39,315	38,793	54,574	58,414	60,236	57,073	60,562	60,109
Net income ($ mil.)	8.1%	2,336	2,492	2,119	3,386	3,939	4,303	4,435	4,725	5,177	4,726
Income as % of sales	—	8.3%	7.1%	5.4%	8.7%	7.2%	7.4%	7.4%	8.3%	8.5%	7.9%
Earnings per share ($)	8.9%	1.29	1.37	1.17	1.88	2.18	2.43	2.55	2.76	3.03	2.77
Stock price – high ($)	—	18.47	22.19	33.19	23.94	32.38	37.75	39.06	43.75	53.50	54.88
Stock price – low ($)	—	13.91	16.63	19.38	19.19	21.75	25.00	26.50	36.38	40.44	45.00
Stock price – close ($)	12.1%	18.19	21.50	22.06	22.38	32.25	28.69	38.25	42.75	52.44	51.00
P/E – high	—	14	16	28	13	15	16	15	16	18	20
P/E – low	—	11	12	17	10	10	10	10	13	13	16
Dividends per share ($)	11.7%	0.55	0.58	0.65	0.70	0.82	0.94	1.02	1.12	1.26	1.49
Book value per share ($)	8.2%	7.62	8.29	9.13	10.23	11.54	12.42	12.55	13.71	15.09	15.47
Employees	(3.5%)	304,000	359,000	302,000	298,000	292,000	298,000	284,000	231,000	222,000	221,000

1994 Year-end:
Debt ratio: 78.0%
Return on equity: 18.1%
Cash (mil.): $2,591
Current ratio: 1.74
Long-term debt (mil.): $36,979
No. of shares (mil.): 1,706
Dividends
  Yield: 2.9%
  Payout: 53.8%
Market value (mil.): $87,004

Stock Price History
High/Low 1985–94

GENERAL MILLS, INC.

OVERVIEW

The maker of Cheerios has said *adios* to the restaurant business. In May 1995 General Mills — the #2 cereal maker in the US (after Kellogg) — spun off its casual dining unit as an independent company (Darden Restaurants). Now with roughly 2/3 the sales it had before the spinoff, Minneapolis-based General Mills can focus on the brands (which include Betty Crocker, Gold Medal, and Yoplait) in its $5.6 billion consumer foods business.

The spinoff fulfilled a strategy, adopted by Bruce Atwater when he took over as CEO in 1981, to separate consumer foods from the restaurant business and other operations. His mission accomplished, Atwater then stepped

down and was replaced as CEO by Steve Sanger. Jeff Rotsch, the new president of General Mills's $2.4 billion cereal business, is charged with restoring a unit that has faltered in recent years. The company lost market share when shortages of its cereals coincided with its reduction of coupon promotions in 1994; it may have some breathing room now that other cereal makers have cut back as well.

Continuing its foreign expansion, General Mills in 1995 announced a joint venture with CPC International to develop a Latin American baking and dessert mix business. Also in 1995 General Mills sold its Gorton's seafood business to Unilever.

WHEN

In 1866 Cadwallader Washburn founded the Washburn Crosby Company. After winning a gold medal for flour at an 1880 exhibition, the company introduced the Gold Medal Flour trademark. In 1921 advertising manager Sam Gale created fictional spokeswoman Betty Crocker so that correspondence to housewives could go out with her signature. The company introduced Wheaties ready-to-eat cereal in 1924. James Bell, made president of Washburn Crosby in 1925, consolidated the company with other mills around the country (including Red Star, Rocky Mountain Elevator, and Kalispell Flour) to form General Mills, the world's largest miller. Although the companies operated independently of one another, corporate headquarters coordinated advertising and merchandising.

General Mills introduced convenience foods such as Bisquick (1930s) and Cheerios (1941) and supported these brands with radio and, later, television advertising. Along with flour these products generated sufficient sales to permit General Mills to keep paying dividends throughout the 1930s and 1940s. During WWII the company produced goods needed for the war, such as ordnance equipment, and developed chemical and electronics divisions.

When Edwin Rawlings became CEO in 1961, he closed down half the flour mills and divested such unprofitable lines as electronics. This cost $200 million in annual sales but freed resources for such acquisitions as the Tom Huston Peanut Company (snack foods, 1966), Kenner Products (toys, 1967), and Parker Brothers (board games, 1968). The Kenner and Parker purchases made General Mills the world's largest toy company. Other acquisitions included Gorton's (frozen sea-

food, 1968), Monet (jewelry, 1968), David Crystal (Izod sportswear, 1969), Red Lobster (restaurants, 1970), Eddie Bauer (outerwear, 1971), Talbots (women's clothing, 1973), Ship 'n Shore (blouses, 1977), Wallpapers to Go (interior decorating supplies, 1977), and the rights to Yoplait yogurt (1977). The restaurant division started The Olive Garden in 1983.

When the toy and fashion divisions' profits fell in 1984, they were spun off as Kenner Parker Toys and Crystal Brands (1985). Reemphasizing food, General Mills sold Wallpapers to Go (1986), Eddie Bauer and Talbots (retail clothing, 1989), and O-Cel-O (sponges, 1990).

In 1989 General Mills mounted a blitzkrieg into the European cereal market by forming with Nestlé the Cereal Partners Worldwide joint venture, now the #2 cereal maker outside North America. China Coast, a 3rd restaurant chain, began in 1990. In 1992 General Mills formed Snack Ventures Europe, an alliance with PepsiCo Foods International that now sells products in 7 European countries.

In 1994 the company said it would cut coupon promotion costs by $175 million while lowering prices on many of its cereals by 30 to 70 cents. But later in the year the FDA found Dursban, an unauthorized pesticide, in General Mills cereal. When General Mills's removal of 50 million boxes from store shelves created a shortage, some retailers declined to pass those lower prices on to consumers. In 1995 the company agreed to issue $10 million in coupons for free cereal to consumers who bought boxes of cereal containing Dursban. General Mills finished fiscal 1995 with over $367 million in net income, which includes the earnings of the now spun-off restaurant operations.

NYSE symbol: GIS
Fiscal year ends: Last Sunday in May

WHO

Chairman and CEO: Stephen W. Sanger, age 49,
$545,825 pay (prior to promotion)
President: Charles W. Gaillard, age 53, $536,510 pay
(prior to promotion)
President, Big G: Jeffrey J. Rotsch, age 44
President, Yoplait: Gary M. Rodkin, age 42
President, Betty Crocker: Christina L. Steiner
President, International Foods: David D. Murphy,
age 42
President, Gold Medal: Michael E. Cushmore, age 54
President, General Mills Snack Products: Y. Marc
Belton
President, Foodservice: Roger W. Rumble
SVP Corporate Finance: Leslie M. Frécon, age 41
SVP Financial Operations: Kenneth L. Thome, age 46
SVP Sales and Distribution: Edward K. Bixby, age 58
SVP Innovation and Technology: Stephen J. Garthwaite,
age 50
SVP Personnel: Michael A. Peel, age 44
Auditors: KPMG Peat Marwick LLP

WHERE

HQ: Number 1 General Mills Blvd., PO Box 1113,
Minneapolis, MN 55440
Phone: 612-540-2311
Fax: 612-540-4925

General Mills has facilities throughout the US and
Canada.

	1994 Sales		1994 Operating Income	
	$ mil.	% of total	$ mil.	% of total
US	8,172	96	875	—
Other countries	345	4	(3)	—
Adjustments	—	—	(119)	—
Total	**8,517**	**100**	**753**	**—**

WHAT

	1994 Sales		1994 Operating Income	
	$ mil.	% of total	$ mil.	% of total
Consumer foods	5,554	65	653	75
Restaurants	2,963	35	219	25
Adjustments	—	—	(119)	—
Total	**8,517**	**100**	**753**	**100**

Selected Brand Names

Cereals
Basic 4
Cheerios
Cinnamon Toast Crunch
Clusters
Cocoa Puffs
Crispy Wheats 'N Raisins
Fiber One
Golden Grahams
Hidden Treasures
Kix
Lucky Charms
Oatmeal Crisp
Raisin Nut Bran
Reese's Peanut Butter Puffs
Ripple Crisp
Sprinkle Spangles
Sun Crunchers
Total
Triples
Trix
Wheaties

Other Foods
Bac*O's
Bisquick
Bugles
Fruit Roll-Ups
Gold Medal
Hamburger Helper
Nature Valley Granola
  Bars
Pop Secret
Potato Buds
Suddenly Salad
Yoplait

KEY COMPETITORS

Anheuser-Busch
Borden
Cadbury
  Schweppes
Campbell Soup
ConAgra
CPC
Danone
Grand
  Metropolitan
Heinz
Hershey
Hormel
Interstate Bakeries
Kellogg
Mars
Nestlé
PepsiCo
PET
Philip Morris
Quaker Oats
Ralcorp
RJR Nabisco
Sara Lee
Specialty Foods
Unilever

HOW MUCH

	9-Year Growth	1985	1986	1987	1988	1989	1990	1991	1992	1993	1994
Sales ($ mil.)	7.9%	4,285	4,587	5,189	5,179	5,621	6,448	7,153	7,778	8,135	8,517
Net income ($ mil.)	—	(73)	184	222	283	484	381	473	516	506	470
Income as % of sales	—	—	4.0%	4.3%	5.5%	8.6%	5.9%	6.6%	6.6%	6.2%	5.5%
Earnings per share ($)	24.5%	0.41	1.03	1.25	1.66	2.96	2.33	2.87	2.99	3.10	2.95
Stock price – high ($)	—	17.31	23.69	31.06	29.00	38.44	52.00	73.63	75.88	74.13	62.25
Stock price – low ($)	—	11.94	14.13	20.38	21.56	25.19	31.38	43.50	58.75	60.50	49.38
Stock price – close ($)	15.8%	15.28	21.56	24.81	25.94	36.19	49.00	73.63	68.50	60.50	57.13
P/E – high	—	42	23	25	18	13	22	26	25	24	21
P/E – low	—	29	14	16	13	9	14	15	20	18	17
Dividends per share ($)	14.4%	0.56	0.57	0.63	0.80	0.94	1.10	1.28	1.48	1.68	1.88
Book value per share ($)	2.6%	5.76	3.81	4.14	3.88	4.48	4.96	6.74	8.28	7.59	7.26
Employees	7.9%	63,162	62,056	65,619	74,453	83,837	97,238	108,077	111,501	121,290	125,700

1994 Year-end:
Debt ratio: 63.1%
Return on equity: 39.6%
Cash (mil.): $0
Current ratio: 0.62
Long-term debt (mil.): $1,417
No. of shares (mil.): 158.5
Dividends
  Yield: 3.3%
  Payout: 63.7%
Market value (mil.): $9,054

Stock Price History
High/Low 1985–94

GENERAL MOTORS CORPORATION

OVERVIEW

The world's biggest industrial enterprise, General Motors is also the world's largest automaker; 80% of its revenues are from automotive products. GM designs, makes, and sells 77 different car and truck models under 8 well-known nameplates that include Buick, Chevrolet, Pontiac, Oldsmobile, and Cadillac. Some of these models are proving to be excess baggage as GM, although still #1, is the choice of only 1 out of every 3 buyers these days. As a result GM is rethinking its strategy. It is also continuing a major downsizing, started in 1992, and dramatic cost-cutting efforts.

In late 1994 CEO John Smith brought in outsider Ronald Zarrella, former president of Bausch & Lomb, as marketing chief to help jump-start the troubled giant. Zarrella wants to reduce the number of chassis used throughout GM, trim the number of dealerships, decentralize product development decisions, hire managers from the outside, clearly differentiate each brand name, and ax some venerable models. First to go: the Cadillac Fleetwood, Chevrolet Impala SS, Buick Roadmaster, and Chevrolet Caprice.

GM already is trimming its Oldsmobile division and converting at least one car assembly plant to boost production of light-duty trucks. In mid-1995 GM agreed to sell its National Car Rental Co. to focus on its core auto businesses.

WHEN

In its early years the automobile industry consisted of hundreds of firms, each producing a few models. William Durant, who bought and reorganized a failing Buick Motors in 1904, reasoned that if several makers united, each would be protected in an off year. Durant formed the General Motors Company in Flint, Michigan, in 1908.

Durant had bought 17 companies (including Oldsmobile, Cadillac, and Pontiac) by 1910, the year a bankers' syndicate forced him to step down. In a 1915 stock swap, Durant regained control through Chevrolet, a company he had formed with race car driver Louis Chevrolet. GM created the GM Acceptance Corporation (auto financing) and acquired a number of companies, including Fisher Body, Frigidaire (sold 1979), and a small bearing company, Hyatt Roller Bearing. With the Hyatt acquisition came Alfred Sloan, an administrative genius who would build GM into a corporate colossus.

Durant resigned in 1920 and sold his stock to DuPont, which had begun buying GM stock in 1917, raising its total stake to 23%. DuPont kept this share until a 1957 Supreme Court antitrust ruling forced it to sell.

Sloan, president from 1923 to 1937, implemented a decentralized management system, now emulated worldwide. (He remained chairman until 1956; his 1963 book, *My Years with General Motors*, is a management classic.) GM competed by offering models ranging from luxury to economy, colors besides black, and yearly style modifications. By 1927 GM had become the industry leader.

The first US company to downsize its cars in response to Japanese imports, GM introduced a line of front wheel–drive compacts in 1979. Under Roger Smith, CEO from 1981 to 1990, GM laid off thousands of workers as part of a massive companywide restructuring and cost cutting program. The workers' plight was depicted in the 1989 documentary film *Roger and Me.*

GM bought Ross Perot's Electronic Data Systems (1984) and Hughes Aircraft (1986). Intense competition from imports and Ford caused GM's market share to drop from 47% in 1979 to 35% by 1989. That year GM bought 50% of Saab Automobile.

In 1990 GM launched Saturn, its first new nameplate since 1926, and wrote off $2.1 billion to cover plant closings. In 1992 GM made the largest stock offering in US history, raising $2.2 billion. GM also underwent a series of boardroom coups, and for much of the year it existed in a kind of limbo, no one knowing quite where the company was headed. Unhappy that costs weren't being cut more quickly and seeking to "end the chaos," the executive board forced CEO Robert Stempel to resign and John Smith took over.

In 1993 NBC apologized for improprieties in its exposé alleging that GM pickups equipped with "sidesaddle" gas tanks tended to explode upon side impact. However, the government still asked GM to recall 4.7 million trucks.

A unanimous federal appeals court in 1995 overturned the settlement of a national class action suit involving GM's side-mounted pickups, which would have given owners a $1,000 voucher to buy a new GM truck and plaintiffs' attorneys $9.5 million in fees.

GM announced in August 1995 that it would go ahead with its long-considered move to spin off Electronic Data Systems, its computer services unit.

NYSE symbol: GM
Fiscal year ends: December 31

WHO

Chairman: John G. Smale, age 67
CEO and President: John F. Smith Jr., age 56,
$3,425,000 pay
EVP; President, Strategic Decision Center: Harry J.
Pearce, age 52, $1,763,000 pay
EVP; President, International Operations: Louis R.
Hughes, age 46, $1,763,000 pay
EVP; President, North American Operations:
G. Richard Wagoner Jr., age 42, $1,763,000 pay
EVP and CFO: J. Michael Losh, age 48
SVP; President, Delphi Automotive Systems: J. T.
Battenberg III
SVP and General Counsel: Thomas A. Gottschalk
VP Personnel, North American Operations: Gerald A.
Knechtel
Auditors: Deloitte & Touche LLP

WHERE

HQ: 3044 W. Grand Blvd., Detroit, MI 48202-3091
Phone: 313-556-5000
Fax: 313-556-5108

GM has approximately 9,200 motor vehicle dealers in
the US and 5,500 outlets overseas. GM has major
manufacturing and assembly operations in Austria,
Belgium, Brazil, Canada, Germany, Mexico, Spain, the
UK, and the US.

	1994 Sales		1994 Net Income	
	$ mil.	% of total	$ mil.	% of total
US	110,910	72	1,362	28
Europe	27,227	18	1,337	27
Canada & Mexico	9,335	6	1,133	23
Latin America	5,717	3	829	17
Other regions	1,762	1	257	5
Adjustments	—	—	420	—
Total	**154,951**	**100**	**5,338**	**100**

WHAT

	1994 Sales		1994 Operating Profit	
	$ mil.	% of total	$ mil.	% of total
Automotive products	123,253	80	6,116	74
Financing & insurance	9,419	6	—	
Other	22,279	14	2,105	26
Total	**154,951**	**100**	**8,221**	**100**

Cars and Trucks

Buick	Oldsmobile
Cadillac	Opel/Vauxhall
Chevrolet	Pontiac
GMC	Saturn

Business Units
Delphi Automotive Systems
General Motors Acceptance Corp. (GMAC)
GM Hughes Electronics Corp.
International Automotive Operations
North American Operations (NAO)

Selected Subsidiaries and Affiliates
Isuzu Motors Ltd. (37.5%)
New United Motor Manufacturing, Inc. (50%, with
Toyota)
Saab Automobile AB (50%)

KEY COMPETITORS

Boeing	Mitsubishi
British Aerospace	Navistar
Chrysler	Nissan
Daimler-Benz	PACCAR
Fiat	Peugeot
Ford	Renault
Honda	Spartan Motors
Hyundai	Suzuki
Kia Motors	Volkswagen
Mazda	Volvo

HOW MUCH

	9-Year Growth	1985	1986	1987	1988	1989	1990	1991	1992	1993	1994
Sales ($ mil.)	4.2%	106,656	115,610	114,870	123,642	126,932	124,705	123,109	132,242	138,220	154,951
Net income ($ mil.)	3.3%	3,987	2,934	3,537	4,830	4,190	(2,024)	(4,523)	(2,927)	2,109	5,338
Income as % of sales	—	3.7%	2.5%	3.1%	3.9%	3.3%	—	—	—	1.5%	3.4%
Earnings per share ($)	0.1%	6.14	4.11	5.03	6.82	6.33	(4.09)	(8.85)	(4.85)	2.13	6.20
Stock price – high ($)	—	42.50	44.31	47.06	44.06	50.50	50.50	44.38	44.38	57.13	65.38
Stock price – low ($)	—	32.13	32.94	25.00	30.00	39.13	33.13	26.75	28.63	32.00	36.13
Stock price – close ($)	2.0%	35.19	33.00	30.69	41.75	42.25	34.38	28.88	32.25	54.88	42.13
P/E – high	—	7	11	9	7	8	—	—	—	27	11
P/E – low	—	5	8	5	4	6	—	—	—	15	6
Dividends per share ($)	(11.9%)	2.50	2.50	2.50	2.50	3.00	3.00	1.60	1.40	0.80	0.80
Book value per share ($)	(14.1%)	45.91	47.74	52.76	58.20	57.37	49.23	43.62	6.62	5.29	11.65
Employees	(1.7%)	811,000	876,000	813,000	765,700	775,100	761,000	756,300	750,000	710,800	692,800

1994 Year-end:
Debt ratio: 85.2%
Return on equity: 58.0%
Cash (mil.): $16,076
Current ratio: 1.02
Long-term debt (mil.): $37,490
No. of shares (mil.): 1,101
Dividends
  Yield: 1.9%
  Payout: 12.9%
Market value (mil.): $46,388

**Stock Price History
High/Low 1985–94**

GENERAL RE CORPORATION

OVERVIEW

Stamford, Connecticut–based General Re is the parent company of General Reinsurance, the largest property/casualty reinsurer in the US and one of the 3 largest in the world.

Primary insurers use reinsurance to cover their own risks. General Re writes most of its business on an excess-of-loss basis, meaning that the company pays only after the primary insurer's losses exceed a specific sum. Most policies are written by the company through direct contact with the purchasing insurers.

In the past 4 years, the insurance business has been shaken by an unprecedented series of natural and man-made disasters. This has made it difficult for General Re to make an underwriting profit (a profit from premium sales alone).

In 1994 the major culprit in its underwriting loss was the Northridge earthquake in California. Fortunately the company's investment income has boosted results.

Other segments of General Re's business include insurance consulting, aviation insurance, securities, and derivatives trading in the US and overseas.

Although the US reinsurance market is mature, there is room for growth in overseas markets, where new business is on the rise. To take advantage of this growing market, in 1995 General Re formed an alliance with Germany's Colonia Konzern (a subsidiary of Union des Assurances de Paris), by forming a joint venture to buy Colonia's subsidiary, Cologne Re.

WHEN

In 1921, when Duncan Reid became president of the newly organized General Casualty and Surety Reinsurance Corp. of New York, the reinsurance field was virtually nonexistent in the US. By 1923 the company's name had changed to General Reinsurance Corp.; Carl Hansen, an underwriting expert, became VP and general manager. By 1925 Hansen and 2 partners controlled the company, which began providing property and casualty reinsurance — its domain to this day.

Reinsurance was a small market, and business grew slowly. It began to take off when, in 1945, the Mellon family united its privately owned Mellon Indemnity with General Re and took over operations. Edward Lowry Jr. was brought in as head in 1946. Reinsurers then paid claims on losses but provided no other services. Lowry, recognizing that reinsurers were the first to know when a branch of the industry was at risk, began offering management consulting services, which remain important to General Re in customer retention.

After the merger General Re held a near monopoly on reinsurance. From 1945 to 1980 General Re was able to charge the highest premiums in the business and was consistently the most profitable US reinsurer.

Lowry retired in 1960. Successor James Cathcart began international expansion in 1962, starting Zurich-based International Reinsurance and buying Stockholm's Swedish Atlas Reinsurance and an interest in Reinsurance Company of Australasia. In the 1960s and 1970s General Re expanded its facultative group (companies that insure against specific risks), started in 1954. Beginning

from a small revenue base, the group contributed half of General Re's premium income by 1978. In the mid-1970s the company also began reinsuring against medical malpractice and equipment leasing losses.

By 1978 General Re was suffering price competition from startups; concurrently, about a dozen senior managers left, some to form competitor Trenwick Re.

In 1980 General Re formed a holding company for its operations and began investing in other insurers such as British-based Trident Insurance Group (sold in 1985) and Monarch Insurance Co. of Ohio (1985).

General Re did not join the 1980s stampede into risky investments. It kept noninvestment grade bonds to under 1% of its portfolio.

General Re's US Aviation subsidiary was the leader of a 15-member syndicate that carried 30% of the insurance on the plane involved in the 1988 Pan Am 103 bombing, about which there was considerable litigation.

In 1993 General Re and the W.R. Berkley Corporation agreed to form a holding company for their respective wholly owned subsidiaries, North Star and Signet Reinsurance. General Re owns 40% of the new company, Signet Star Holdings, Inc.

In accordance with the company's plans to expand overseas, the 1994 acquisition of part of Colonia Konzern's Cologne Re will give General Re easier access to the European reinsurance market.

Cologne Re is the world's oldest reinsurance company. It was founded in 1846 and was the 5th largest reinsurer in the world in 1994.

WHO

Chairman, President, and CEO: Ronald E. Ferguson,
age 53, $1,457,917 pay
VC: John C. Etling, age 59, $1,016,250 pay
President and COO, General Reinsurance Corp.: Tom
N. Kellogg, age 58
Chairman and CEO, General Reinsurance Corp.: James
E. Gustafson, age 48
VP and Chief Investment Officer: Ernest C. Frohboese,
age 54, $564,167 pay
VP and CFO: Joseph P. Brandon, age 36, $410,000 pay
VP, General Counsel, and Secretary: Charles F. Barr,
age 45, $317,258 pay
Controller: Elizabeth A. Monrad, age 40
SVP Information Systems, General Re Services Corp.:
Stephen P. Raye, age 52
SVP Human Resources, General Re Services Corp.:
Theron S. Hoffman Jr., age 47
Auditors: Coopers & Lybrand L.L.P.

WHERE

HQ: 695 E. Main St., PO Box 10351, Stamford, CT
06904-2351
Phone: 203-328-5000
Fax: 203-328-5329

General Re conducts business in the US and in 13 other
countries worldwide.

	1994 Sales		1994 Pretax income	
	$ mil.	% of total	$ mil.	% of total
US	3,381	88	741	93
Other countries	456	12	53	7
Total	**3,837**	**100**	**794**	**100**

WHAT

	1994 Assets	
	$ mil.	% of total
Cash & equivalents	1,274	4
US Treasurys	1,702	6
Foreign govt. securities	5,215	17
State & municipal bonds	5,224	18
Corporate bonds	1,160	4
Stocks	2,977	10
Other securities	4,329	15
Receivables & recoverables	3,488	12
Other assets	4,228	14
Total	**29,597**	**100**

Selected Domestic Subsidiaries
General Re Asset Management, Inc.
General Star Indemnity Co.
General Star National Insurance Co.
Genesis Indemnity Insurance Co.
Genesis Insurance Co.
United States Aviation Underwriters, Inc.

International Operations
General Re-CKAG Reinsurance & Investments SARL
  (Luxembourg)
General Re Compañia de Reaseguros, SA (Argentina)
General Re Correduría de Reaseguros, SA (Spain)
General Re Europe Ltd.
General Re Financial Products (Japan) Inc.
General Re Financial Products, Ltd. (UK)
General Re Financial Securities, Ltd. (UK)
General Re Underwriting Services, Ltd. (Bermuda)
General Reinsurance Australasia Ltd. (Australia,
  New Zealand, Singapore)

KEY COMPETITORS

Aetna
AIG
Allianz
CIGNA
Lloyd's of London

Marsh & McLennan
Prudential
Tokio Marine and Fire
USF&G

HOW MUCH

	9-Year Growth	1985	1986	1987	1988	1989	1990	1991	1992	1993	1994
Assets ($ mil.)	19.4%	6,005	8,078	8,902	9,394	10,390	11,033	12,416	14,700	18,469	29,597
Net income ($ mil.)	19.3%	136	329	511	480	599	614	657	596	697	665
Income as % of assets	—	2.3%	4.0%	5.7%	5.1%	5.8%	5.6%	5.3%	4.1%	3.8%	2.2%
Earnings per share ($)	20.8%	1.45	3.22	5.04	5.04	6.52	6.89	7.46	6.84	8.11	7.97
Stock price – high ($)	—	52.50	68.88	68.38	59.25	95.75	93.00	101.88	123.13	133.38	129.13
Stock price – low ($)	—	30.57	49.44	48.75	45.88	55.00	69.00	84.88	78.63	104.75	101.75
Stock price – close ($)	10.6%	50.06	55.50	55.88	55.25	87.13	93.00	101.88	115.75	107.00	123.50
P/E – high	—	36	21	14	12	15	14	14	18	16	16
P/E – low	—	21	15	10	9	8	10	11	11	13	13
Dividends per share ($)	10.5%	0.78	0.88	1.00	1.20	1.36	1.52	1.68	1.80	1.88	1.92
Book value per share ($)	13.8%	18.48	23.47	26.20	29.04	34.28	37.50	45.14	49.89	56.93	59.32
Employees	0.9%	2,185	2,332	2,426	2,363	2,379	2,496	2,513	2,413	2,397	2,360

1994 Year-end:
Equity as % of assets: 16.4%
Return on assets: 2.8%
Return on equity: 13.8%
Long-term debt (mil.): $157
No. of shares (mil.): 82
Dividends
  Yield: 1.6%
  Payout: 24.1%
Market value (mil.): $10,111
Sales (mil.): $3,837

**Stock Price History
High/Low 1985–94**

GEORGIA-PACIFIC CORPORATION

OVERVIEW

Resurgent pulp and paper prices helped lift Georgia-Pacific out of a slump, enabling it to post a $326 million profit in 1994, its first since 1990. The company controls over 6 million acres of timberland in the US and Canada. Georgia-Pacific has sunk $410 million in capital expenditures (out of a 1994 total of $894 million) to reduce production costs and upgrade its environmental performance. Capital investments are expected to exceed $1 billion by the end of 1995. The firm makes containerboard and packaging, communication papers, market pulp, and tissue at 84 facilities. Its output of 8.7 million tons of pulp, paper, and paperboard is 8% of total US capacity.

The Atlanta-based timber company is the top US manufacturer and distributor of building products and the nation's leading wholesaler of building products. Georgia-Pacific produces plywood, oriented strand board and other wood panels, lumber, gypsum wallboard, chemicals, and other products at 225 facilities in North America, including 2 in Canada and 2 in Mexico. It leads the market in the manufacture of wood panels, accounting for about 20% of domestic capacity. Building products carried the company's bottom line during the pulp and paper slump in the early 1990s, with operating profits in this segment more than doubling in the last 5 years.

CEO Pete Correll is gearing up investments in high-return areas. In 1994 the company launched 2 projects to increase recycled containerboard capacity and lower production costs at its Big Island, Virginia, and Toledo, Oregon, plants, for a cost of $250 million. The building products group is modernizing its plywood plants and lumber mills to enable it to make processed lumber products out of smaller logs and wood chips.

WHEN

Owen Cheatham founded the Georgia Hardwood Lumber Company in Augusta, Georgia, in 1927 to wholesale hardwood lumber (which he bought from others). By 1938 the company was operating 5 southern sawmills, and during WWII it became the largest lumber supplier to the US armed forces.

In 1947 the company bought a plywood mill in Bellingham, Washington. Recognizing the potential of plywood, Cheatham acquired several more plywood mills in the late 1940s.

In 1951 Cheatham began an aggressive land-buying spree that would give the company its first timberlands. The company moved its headquarters to Oregon in 1954, adopting its present name in 1957. That year Georgia-Pacific entered the pulp and paper business by establishing a new mill at Toledo, Oregon, and embarked on a period of explosive growth. By 1960 the company had a million acres of timberland.

In the 1960s the company acquired several competitors and built new facilities that allowed it to diversify into containers, paperboard, tissue, and chemicals and to produce its own chemicals for paper, resin, plywood glue, and other products. In 1972 the FTC forced Georgia-Pacific to sell 20% of its assets to reduce its size. In 1973 the company bought Boise Cascade's wood products operations at Fort Bragg, California, and in 1975 it acquired Exchange Oil and Gas.

In 1976 chairman Robert Flowerree continued the diversification into chemicals and cautiously introduced cheaper substitutes for plywood, like waferboard. Under Flowerree the company acquired timberland in the South and modernized existing paper mills. In 1979 Georgia-Pacific bought Hudson Pulp and Paper and reached $5 billion in sales.

The company returned to Georgia in 1982 and in 1984 decided to sell most chemical operations unrelated to forest products.

In 1988 Georgia-Pacific bought Brunswick Pulp and Paper in Georgia, greatly increasing its southern timber holdings. The 1990 acquisition of Great Northern Nekoosa increased Georgia-Pacific's reliance on pulp and paper. To pay off some of the debt related to the takeover of Nekoosa, Georgia-Pacific sold $1 billion in assets in 1990, including 19 container plants and 540,000 acres of timber.

In 1991, after pleading guilty to charges of tax evasion, Georgia-Pacific paid a $5 million fine. That same year the company sold 80% of Great Northern Paper to Bowater for $300 million and gained the right to require Bowater to buy the remaining 20% of Great Northern after mid-1992.

In 1993 Pete Correll was promoted from president to chairman and CEO. The firm sold its envelope-making business for $115 million to The Sterling Group in 1994. It also sold its roofing manufacturing line that year. In 1995 Georgia-Pacific was actively pursuing a new policy of acquiring timberlands outside the US, particularly in Brazil, Chile, and Argentina, which have abundant softwood forests.

NYSE symbol: GP
Fiscal year ends: December 31

WHO

Chairman and CEO: Alston D. "Pete" Correll, age 53, $1,525,000 pay
EVP Building Products: Davis K. Mortensen, age 62, $749,250 pay
EVP Pulp and Paper: W. E. "Ed" Babin, age 59, $621,000 pay
SVP Law and General Counsel: James F. Kelley, age 53, $466,000 pay
SVP Paper: Lee M. Thomas, age 50, $348,750 pay
SVP Distribution and Millwork: George A. MacConnell, age 47
SVP Pulp, Bleached Board, and Logistics: Clint M. Kennedy, age 45
SVP Containerboard and Packaging: Maurice W. Kring, age 58
SVP Building Products Manufacturing and Sales: Donald L. Glass, age 46
SVP Forest Resources: John F. Rasor, age 51
SVP Administration: David W. Reynolds, age 63
SVP Environmental, Government Affairs and Communications: James E. Bostic Jr., age 47
SVP Finance and CFO: John F. McGovern, age 48
SVP Human Resources: Gerard R. Brandt, age 55
Auditors: Arthur Andersen & Co, SC

WHERE

HQ: 133 Peachtree St. NE, Atlanta, GA 30303
Phone: 404-652-4000
Fax: 404-521-4422

Georgia-Pacific has 221 manufacturing facilities in the US, 2 in Canada, and 2 in Mexico.

Owned or Leased US Timberland	% of Total
South	70
East	20
West	10
Total	**100**

WHAT

	1994 Sales		1994 Operating Income	
	$ mil.	% of total	$ mil.	% of total
Building prods.	7,561	60	989	81
Pulp & paper	5,138	40	171	14
Other	39	0	67	5
Total	**12,738**	**100**	**1,227**	**100**

Building Products	Copy paper
Adhesives	Envelopes
Building product– related chemicals	Market pulp
	Napkins
Doors	Packaging materials
Fiberboard	Paper towels
Gypsum wallboard	Paperboard
Hardboard	Printing paper
Lumber	Writing paper
Particleboard	
Siding	**Paper Products**
Structural wood panels	**(Brand Names)**
	Angel Soft
	Coronet
Pulp and Paper Products	Delta
Bath tissue	MD
Containers	Sparkle

KEY COMPETITORS

Akzo Nobel	Mead
Alco Standard	3M
Boise Cascade	Owens-Corning
Canadian Pacific	Procter & Gamble
Champion International	Scott
Fletcher Challenge	Stone Container
Fort Howard	Stora
International Paper	Union Camp
James River	USG
Jefferson Smurfit	Weyerhaeuser
Kimberly-Clark	Willamette Industries

HOW MUCH

	9-Year Growth	1985	1986	1987	1988	1989	1990	1991	1992	1993	1994
Sales ($ mil.)	7.4%	6,716	7,223	8,603	9,509	10,171	12,665	11,524	11,847	12,330	12,738
Net income ($ mil.)	6.6%	177	296	458	467	661	365	(79)	(60)	(34)	315
Income as % of sales	—	2.6%	4.1%	5.3%	4.9%	6.5%	2.9%	—	—	—	2.5%
Earnings per share ($)	9.8%	1.52	2.64	4.23	4.76	7.42	4.28	(0.92)	(0.69)	(0.39)	3.54
Stock price – high ($)	—	27.38	41.25	52.75	42.88	62.00	52.13	60.25	72.00	75.00	79.00
Stock price – low ($)	—	20.50	24.75	22.75	30.75	36.63	25.38	36.25	48.25	55.00	56.75
Stock price – close ($)	11.7%	26.50	37.00	34.50	36.88	48.50	37.25	53.63	62.38	68.75	71.50
P/E – high	—	18	16	13	9	8	12	—	—	—	22
P/E – low	—	14	9	5	7	5	6	—	—	—	16
Dividends per share ($)	7.7%	0.82	0.85	1.05	1.25	1.45	1.60	1.60	1.60	1.60	1.60
Book value per share ($)	3.7%	20.80	22.84	25.59	27.79	31.40	34.31	31.30	28.46	26.60	28.96
Employees	2.4%	38,000	39,000	42,000	44,000	44,000	48,000	57,000	52,000	50,000	47,000

1994 Year-end:
Debt ratio: 65.7%
Return on equity: 24.0%
Cash (mil.): $53
Current ratio: 0.80
Long-term debt (mil.): $3,904
No. of shares (mil.): 90.5
Dividends
  Yield: 2.2%
  Payout: 45.2%
Market value (mil.): $6,468

Stock Price History
High/Low 1985–94

THE GILLETTE COMPANY

OVERVIEW

Gillette's earnings have been anything but dull. The company, which gets 39% of its sales from blades and razors (69% of profits), had $698 million in net income in 1994, up from $427 million the previous year. Gillette, however, is hoping to become less reliant on shaving tools. Its Braun division, the world leader in coffee makers, makes a number of small appliances and electric shavers. Gillette is also the world's leading producer of dental care products through its Oral-B subsidiary and the #1 seller of writing products (Parker Pen, Paper Mate, and Waterman). The company also makes toiletries and cosmetics, including Right Guard and Dry Idea antiperspirants.

Gillette puts great emphasis on R&D. The company normally has 15 projects in research for every 3 that make it to development. Of those 3, only one makes it to the stores. As a low-cost manufacturer, Gillette believes that if it cannot produce a product at its "target" cost, then there is no point in bringing it to market. The company would rather absorb the cost of developing an unsuccessful product than attempt to sell that product in the marketplace. In 1994 Gillette introduced more than 20 new products, most notably the Braun SuperVolume hair dryer equipped with long plastic fingers designed to add body to hair as it dries.

With about 2/3 of sales generated outside the US, Gillette ranks among the most global of the *FORTUNE* 500 companies. It began producing shavers in China in 1994.

WHEN

In 1895 King C. Gillette, a salesman for the Baltimore Seal Company, originated the idea of a disposable razor blade while shaving with a dull straight razor at his home in Brookline, Massachusetts. For the next 6 years, Gillette developed his idea yet could find neither investors nor toolmakers to back him. Finally in 1901 MIT machinist William Nickerson joined with Gillette and perfected the safety razor. With the financial support of some wealthy friends, the 2 men formed the American Safety Razor Company in Boston.

Gillette put his safety razor on the market in 1903, selling only 51 sets the first year. But the good news spread fast, and in 1904 Gillette sold 90,844 sets. In 1905 he established his first overseas operation in London.

Gillette sold most of his interest in the business in 1910 (he remained president of the company until 1931) to pursue his utopian corporate theories, which he had first published in his 1894 book *The Human Drift*.

During WWI the company sold 3.5 million Service Set shaving kits to the US government. In the 1920s the company distributed free razors through such diverse mediums as banks (via the "Shave and Save" plan) and boxes of Wrigley's gum. The sales tactic brought millions of new customers, who depended on Gillette for the blades.

During the difficult years of the 1930s, Gillette began sponsoring major sporting events. The company's many sponsorships became known as Gillette's "Cavalcade of Sports" and carried its advertising worldwide.

In 1948 the company began diversifying by purchasing Toni (home permanent kits), which became the Personal Care Division in 1971. In the 1950s Gillette adopted its present name, introduced Foamy (shaving cream, 1953), and bought Paper Mate (pens, 1955).

During the 1960s and 1970s, the company expanded its product line further by introducing Right Guard (deodorant, 1960), Trac II (twin-blade razors, 1971), Cricket (disposable lighters, 1972; sold to Swedish Match, 1984), Good News (disposable razors, 1975), and Eraser Mate (erasable pens, 1979) and acquiring Braun (electric shavers and appliances, 1967) and Liquid Paper (correction fluid, 1979). In 1984 Gillette branched into dental products with the purchase of Oral-B.

The 1989–90 purchase of Swedish Match (Wilkinson Sword razors) was problematic, with the US and the UK governments opposing the high market shares it gave Gillette. In 1991 Gillette was ordered to divest the UK portion of Swedish Match, and in 1992 it was ordered by antitrust officials to sell its European holdings in Wilkinson Sword.

In 1992 the company introduced the Gillette Series, a line of men's shaving and skin products. In 1993 the company acquired Parker Pen (writing products) and introduced the SensorExcel in continental Europe and in Canada.

In 1994 Gillette introduced the SensorExcel shaving system in Japan, the UK, and the US. Gillette named Michael Hawley its president in 1995. The post had been vacant since 1991.

NYSE symbol: G
Fiscal year ends: December 31

WHO

Chairman and CEO: Alfred M. Zeien, age 65,
$2,000,000 pay
VC: Joseph E. Mullaney, age 61, $645,000 pay
President and COO: Michael C. Hawley, age 57,
$627,917 pay (prior to promotion)
EVP, North Atlantic Group: Robert J. Murray, age 53,
$825,000 pay
EVP, Diversified Group: Jacques Lagarde, age 56,
$713,750 pay
SVP Finance: Thomas F. Skelly, age 61
SVP Personnel and Administration: Robert E. DiCenso,
age 54
VP and Controller: Anthony S. Lucas, age 62
VP Research and Development: John B. Bush Jr.
VP New Business Development: Kenneth F. Kames
VP Investor Relations: Everett R. Howe
VP Corporate Information Technology: Patrick J.
Zilvitis
Auditors: KPMG Peat Marwick LLP

WHERE

HQ: Prudential Tower Bldg., Boston, MA 02199
Phone: 617-421-7000
Fax: 617-421-7123

Gillette sells its products in more than 200 countries
and territories and manufactures them at 57 locations in
28 countries.

	1994 Sales		1994 Operating Income	
	$ mil.	% of total	$ mil.	% of total
Europe	2,119	35	438	34
US	1,944	32	385	30
Latin America	860	14	229	18
Other regions	1,147	19	225	18
Adjustments	—	—	(51)	—
Total	**6,070**	**100**	**1,227**	**100**

WHAT

	1994 Sales		1994 Operating Income	
	$ mil.	% of total	$ mil.	% of total
Blades & razors	2,351	39	878	69
Braun products	1,348	22	200	16
Toiletries	1,162	19	79	6
Stationery products	807	13	95	7
Oral-B & other	402	7	25	2
Adjustments	—	—	(50)	—
Total	**6,070**	**100**	**1,227**	**100**

Major US Brand Names

Blades and Razors	Stationery Products
Atra	Helit (desk accessories)
Good News	Liquid Paper
Sensor	(correction fluid)
Sensor for Women	Paper Mate (markers and
SensorExcel	pens)
Trac II	Waterman (pens)

Toiletries and Cosmetics
Dry Idea (antiperspirant)
Foamy (shaving cream)
Gillette Series (men's
  toiletries)
Right Guard (deodorant)

Small Appliances
Braun (shavers, blenders,
  juicers, coffee makers)

Dental Products
Oral-B (toothbrushes)

KEY COMPETITORS

Amway	Health O Meter	Premark
A. T. Cross	Products	Procter & Gamble
Avon	Johnson &	Remington
Bausch & Lomb	Johnson	Products
BIC	L'Oréal	Richemont
Black & Decker	MacAndrews &	SmithKline
Carter-Wallace	Forbes	Beecham
Colgate-	Mary Kay	Sunbeam-Oster
Palmolive	Matsushita	Teledyne
Conair	3M	Unilever
Dep	Philips	Wahl Clipper
Dial		Warner-Lambert

HOW MUCH

	9-Year Growth	1985	1986	1987	1988	1989	1990	1991	1992	1993	1994
Sales ($ mil.)	10.9%	2,400	2,818	3,167	3,581	3,819	4,345	4,684	5,163	5,411	6,070
Net income ($ mil.)	17.8%	160	16	230	269	285	368	427	513	427	698
Income as % of sales	—	6.7%	0.6%	7.3%	7.5%	7.5%	8.5%	9.1%	9.9%	7.9%	11.5%
Earnings per share ($)	19.8%	0.62	0.07	1.00	1.23	1.35	1.60	1.94	2.32	1.92	3.14
Stock price – high ($)	—	9.00	17.22	22.94	24.50	24.88	32.63	56.13	61.25	63.75	76.50
Stock price – low ($)	—	6.64	8.59	8.81	14.56	16.50	21.75	28.19	43.88	47.38	57.75
Stock price – close ($)	27.0%	8.69	12.31	14.19	16.63	24.56	31.38	56.13	56.88	59.63	74.88
P/E – high	—	15	—	23	20	18	20	29	26	33	24
P/E – low	—	11	123	9	12	12	14	15	19	25	18
Dividends per share ($)	13.1%	0.33	0.34	0.37	0.43	0.47	0.53	0.60	0.70	0.84	1.00
Book value per share ($)	10.2%	3.63	2.01	2.60	(0.44)	0.36	1.33	5.18	6.35	6.25	8.67
Employees	0.5%	31,400	32,100	30,100	29,600	30,400	30,400	31,200	30,900	33,400	32,800

1994 Year-end:
Debt ratio: 36.2%
Return on equity: 42.3%
Cash (mil.): $46
Current ratio: 1.54
Long-term debt (mil.): $715
No. of shares (mil.): 221.4
Dividends
  Yield: 1.3%
  Payout: 31.8%
Market value (mil.): $16,581

Stock Price History
High/Low 1985–94

THE GOLDMAN SACHS GROUP, L.P.

OVERVIEW

Goldman Sacks! For the first time since the dark days of the late 1980s, Wall Street's last major private partnership laid off staff in 1995. The reason is the bond crash of 1994 and the subsequent decline in new debt issues. The news of layoffs and other cost cutting measures came on the heels of the firm's best year ever and was preceded by a steep increase in new hires and the admission of the largest-ever cohort of new partners (58).

But problems at New York–based Goldman Sachs appear to go deeper than the crash, and may stem from stretching a partnership (an intimate, all-for-one-and-one-for-all form of organization) to globe-straddling size. As it has grown, an important portion of the firm's business has shifted from client-centered investment banking to firm-centered proprietary

trading. Many feel the firm has lost some of its family feeling and become more anonymous.

The 1994 retirement of Stephen Friedman (whom some considered responsible for the company's turmoil) sparked a rash of partner retirements. Because partners can begin to cash out only when they leave, this in turn has raised concerns about the firm's future capital strength and led to rumors that Goldman Sachs might go public.

Goldman Sachs's core areas are research, investment (trading and market making, derivatives), municipal and corporate financing (underwriting debt and equity issues), mergers and acquisitions, foreign exchange and commodities, and real estate.

The Kamehameha Schools/Bishop Estate of Hawaii owns over 20% of Goldman Sachs.

WHEN

Philadelphia retailer Marcus Goldman moved to New York in 1869 and began buying customers' promissory notes from jewelers and reselling them to commercial banks. Samuel Sachs, Goldman's son-in-law, joined the business in 1882, and the firm became Goldman, Sachs & Company in 1885.

In 1887 Goldman Sachs, through British merchant bankers Kleinwort Sons, offered its clients US–UK foreign exchange and currency services. To serve clients like Sears, Roebuck, the firm expanded to Chicago and St. Louis. In 1896 it joined the NYSE.

In the late 1890s and early 1900s, the firm increased its contacts in Europe. Goldman's son Henry made the firm a major source of financing for US industry. In 1906 the firm comanaged its first public offering, $4.5 million for United Cigar Manufacturers (later General Cigar). By 1920 the firm had arranged the IPOs of Sears, May Department Stores, Jewel Tea, B.F. Goodrich, and Merck.

Sidney Weinberg became a partner in 1927 and remained a leader until his death in 1969. In the 1930s the firm started a securities dealer (rather than agent) operation and sales departments. Since WWII it has been a leader in investment banking. It comanaged Ford's IPO (1956). In the 1970s Goldman Sachs was the first firm to buy blocks of stock for resale.

Under Sidney's son, John Weinberg (co–senior partner with John Whitehead beginning in 1976, retired 1991), Goldman Sachs expanded its international operations, became a leader in mergers and acquisitions (M&A), and acquired First Dallas, Ltd. (1982, landed mer-

chant banking). By 1982 it was the largest M&A lead manager with $24.7 billion in mergers, including U.S. Steel–Marathon Oil, Occidental Petroleum–Cities Service, and Connecticut General–INA. Another acquisition, J. Aron Co. (1981), the world's largest coffee trader, gave Goldman a significant presence in precious metals. Contacts made through Aron have been instrumental in Goldman's growth in South America.

In the late 1980s and the 1990s Goldman sought capital, raising over $500 million from Sumitomo for a nonparticipatory 12.5% interest. The Kamehameha Schools/Bishop Estate (a Hawaiian educational trust) has invested approximately $500 million in the firm (most recently in 1994, when Goldman Sachs sought more capital after a bruising year).

In the 1990s the firm expanded rapidly overseas but ran into problems with some of these ventures. An investment project in China fell through after the firm asked for a greater share than the Chinese were willing to grant; the Hong Kong office ballooned to more than 500 employees; and in Russia the company hitched its star to a government official who was booted out of office.

As a partnership, Goldman Sachs is reluctant to divulge its financial results, but offering documents that fell into the hands of the press showed record profits in 1993. Partners' bonuses (a large part of the appeal of working for the firm) were more than $3 million.

In 1995 the company continued to raise capital, borrowing over $250 million in the private debt markets, but at high interest rates.

Private partnership
Fiscal year ends: Last Friday in November

WHO

Senior Partner and Chairman of the Management Committee: Jon S. Corzine, age 48
VC of the Management Committee and COO: Henry M. Paulson Jr., age 48
Chairman, Goldman Sachs International: Peter Sutherland, age 49
Partner and Co–General Counsel: Robert J. Katz
Partner and Co–General Counsel: Gregory K. Palm
Partner, International Comptroller: David W. Blood
Partner, Personnel: Jonathan L. Cohen
Auditors: Coopers & Lybrand L.L.P.

WHERE

HQ: 85 Broad St., New York, NY 10004
Phone: 212-902-1000
Fax: 212-902-1512

Goldman Sachs operates as an equities and fixed income broker and underwriter, investment banker, asset manager, and commodities trader in Belgium, France, Germany, Japan, Singapore, the UK, and the US.

	1994 Offices
	No.
US	11
Asia/Pacific	9
Europe	7
Other	4
Total	**31**

WHAT

Services

Asset Management

Investment Banking
Advisory services
Mergers and acquisitions
Underwriting
  Bonds
  State and municipal issues
  Stocks

Real estate
Mortgage-backed securities
Real estate investment trusts

Research

Trading
Bonds
Commodities
Currency
Derivatives and custom products
Stocks
US Treasury instruments (primary trader)

Selected Subsidiaries

Goldman, Sachs & Co. Finanz GmbH (Frankfurt)
Goldman, Sachs & Co. (Zurich)
Goldman Sachs (Asia) Ltd.
Goldman Sachs (Australia) Ltd
Goldman Sachs International Ltd. (UK)
Goldman Sachs (Japan) Corp.
Goldman Sachs (Singapore) Pte. Ltd

KEY COMPETITORS

AIG
Alex. Brown
Bankers Trust
Bear Stearns
Brown Brothers Harriman
CS Holding
Daiwa Securities
Dean Witter, Discover
Deutsche Bank
Equitable
GE
GM
Hambrecht & Quist
J.P. Morgan
KKR
Lehman Brothers
Merrill Lynch
Morgan Stanley
Nomura Securities
Paine Webber
Prudential
Salomon
Travelers
Yamaichi Securities

HOW MUCH

	Annual Growth	1985	1986	1987	1988	1989	1990	1991	1992	1993	1994
Estimated sales ($ mil.)	15.5%	—	3,600	4,200	4,000	3,400	4,600	5,290	8,500	13,200	11,440
Net income	(7.8%)	—	—	—	—	750	886	1,150	1,500	2,700	500[1]
Net income as % of sales	—	—	—	—	—	22.1%	19.3%	21.7%	17.6%	20.5%	4.4%
Partners' capital ($ mil.)	20.9%	868	1,104	1,656	1,876	2,145	2,477	3,010	3,714	5,008	4,800
Employees	8.0%	4,516	6,049	6,087	6,500	6,400	5,800	6,600	6,733	7,000	9,000

Goldman Sachs

Net Income
($ mil.) 1989–94

[1] Estimated

THE GOODYEAR TIRE & RUBBER COMPANY

OVERVIEW

Goodyear is the world's largest rubber manufacturer. The Akron, Ohio–based company is the US's top tire maker and ranks #3 in the world (after Michelin and Bridgestone). Primarily a maker of car and truck tires (85% of 1994 sales), Goodyear also produces many industrial, consumer, and chemical products from rubber (14%). Through its Celeron subsidiary the company operates the US's longest crude oil pipeline (All American Pipeline), which connects California to Texas. The company oversees 6 rubber plantations in Indonesia and Guatemala.

Goodyear supplies tires to US, European, and Japanese automakers, construction and agricultural equipment makers, and the replacement tire market (about 20% of the worldwide tire market). The company also provides automotive repair services through its network of retail outlets and makes rubber products such as belts and hoses, shoe soles, and gum used in printing.

Outgoing chairman Stanley Gault boosted Goodyear's earnings but antagonized its legion of independent tire dealers by selling Goodyear brands through mass merchandisers. EVP Samir Gibara, named Gault's successor in early 1995, was behind the recent move to offer dealers exclusive tire models that won't be sold in other retail outlets.

WHEN

In 1898 Frank and Charles Seiberling founded a tire and rubber company in Akron, naming it after Charles Goodyear (inventor of the vulcanization process, 1839). Initially producing bicycle and carriage tires, Goodyear soon targeted the fledgling automotive industry. The introduction of the Quick Detachable tire and the Universal Rim (1903) made Goodyear the world's largest tire manufacturer by 1916, the year it introduced the pneumatic truck tire.

Goodyear had begun foreign manufacturing in Canada in 1910 and expanded overseas in the 1920s and 1930s (Australia, Argentina, and the Dutch East Indies). It established its own rubber plantations in Sumatra in 1916, and by 1926 Goodyear had become the world's largest rubber company.

Meanwhile, financial troubles led to reorganization in 1921, and investment bankers Dillon, Read forced the Seiberlings out. Succeeding a caretaker management team, Paul Litchfield began 3 decades as CEO (1926). The company had acquired rights to make zeppelins in 1924, and by the 1930s Goodyear blimps served as advertisements nationwide. In that decade Goodyear opened company stores, acquired Kelly-Springfield (1935), and began producing synthetic rubber tires (1937). After WWII Goodyear was a leader in implementing new technologies such as polyester tire cord (1962) and the bias-belted tire (1967). Goodyear provided the tires used in the Apollo 14 lunar landing in 1971.

Michelin introduced the radial tire in the US in 1966. By 1976 radials accounted for 45% of tire sales, and by 1980, with the introduction of the all-weather Tiempo, the Eagle, and the Arriva, Goodyear led the US market.

Fending off Sir James Goldsmith's takeover attempt in 1986, CEO Robert Mercer raised $1.7 billion by selling nontire businesses (Motor Wheel, Goodyear Aerospace, and Celeron Oil) and by borrowing heavily, accumulating $4.7 billion of debt in a 47% stock buyback.

Recession, overcapacity, and price cutting in 1990 led to hard times worldwide for tire makers. Goodyear's problems were worsened by heavy interest payments (over $1 million per day) on debt incurred in its 1986 takeover defense. After suffering through 1990, its first money-losing year since the Depression, Goodyear lured out of retirement Stanley Gault, the man who had swept Rubbermaid to $1.5 billion in sales.

Gault broke with the tradition of marketing Goodyear tires exclusively through an extensive dealer network by selling tires through Wal-Mart, Kmart, and Sears, and rather than gradually introducing new tires to the market, Gault ordered the simultaneous release of 4 tires. He also cut costs through layoffs (nearly 12,000 workers in 1991 and 1992), plant closures, and capital spending reductions, returning Goodyear to profitability in 1991. *FW* magazine named Gault its CEO of the year in 1992.

In 1993 the company acquired all of the shares of Goodyear Canada that it did not already own. That same year Goodyear announced a joint venture with Indian tire maker Ceat to build a tire plant in western India. In 1994 Goodyear bought a 60% stake in a Chinese automotive hose factory and a 75% stake in a Chinese tire factory (Dalian International Nordic Tire Co.), whose operations should start up in early 1995.

NYSE symbol: GT
Fiscal year ends: December 31

WHO

Chairman and CEO: Stanley C. Gault, age 69,
$2,157,500 pay
President and COO: Samir F. Gibara, age 55,
$612,500 pay (prior to promotion)
EVP: William J. Sharp, age 53, $590,000 pay
EVP: Eugene R. Culler Jr., age 56
EVP and CFO: Robert W. Tieken, age 55
VP Health and Environmental Affairs: Robert M. Hehir,
age 63
VP Original Equipment Sales Worldwide: James W.
Barnett, age 64
VP and Secretary: James Boyazis, age 58
VP and General Counsel: John M. Ross, age 63,
$547,500 pay
VP Human Resources and Total Quality Culture: Mike
L. Burns, age 53
Auditors: Price Waterhouse LLP

WHERE

HQ: 1144 E. Market St., Akron, OH 44316-0001
Phone: 216-796-2121
Fax: 216-796-2222

Goodyear operates 32 plants in the US and 42 plants in
29 other countries. The company operates about 1,800
retail outlets in the US.

	1994 Sales		1994 Operating Income	
	$ mil.	% of total	$ mil.	% of total
US	7,130	58	592	49
Europe	2,280	19	212	18
Latin America	1,512	12	278	23
Asia	712	6	81	7
Canada	654	5	30	3
Total	**12,288**	**100**	**1,193**	**100**

WHAT

	1994 Sales		1994 Operating Income	
	$ mil.	% of total	$ mil.	% of total
Tires & related	10,508	85	1,010	85
General products	1,701	14	171	14
Oil transportation	79	1	12	1
Total	**12,288**	**100**	**1,193**	**100**

**Tires and Related Products
and Services**
Automotive equipment
Automotive repair services
Bias-ply tires
Radial tires
Retreading services
Rubber

General Products
Chemical products
Industrial rubber products
Plastic products
Shoe and graphic products
Vehicle components

Oil Transportation
Gathering
Pipelining
Trading

Major US Tire Brands
Aquatred
Corsa GT
Eagle
Intrepid
Regatta
Tracker ATT
Unisteel
Workhorse
Wrangler

Major Subsidiaries and Affiliates
Brad Ragan, Inc. (74.5%, tire sales and service chain)
Celeron Corp. (oil pipelines)
  All American Pipeline Co.
The Kelly-Springfield Tire Co.
Lee Tire & Rubber Co.

KEY COMPETITORS

Bandag	Hercules	Pep Boys
Bayer	Michelin	Pirelli
Big O Tires	Mobil	Price/Costco
Bridgestone	Monro Muffler	Sears
Chevron	Brake	Sumitomo
Continental AG	Montgomery	Toyo Tire
Cooper Tire &	Ward	Whitman
Rubber	Nokia	
General Motors	Pennzoil	

HOW MUCH

	9-Year Growth	1985	1986	1987	1988	1989	1990	1991	1992	1993	1994
Sales ($ mil.)	2.8%	9,585	9,103	9,905	10,810	10,869	11,273	10,907	11,785	11,643	12,288
Net income ($ mil.)	3.6%	412	124	771	350	189	(38)	75	367	489	567
Income as % of sales	—	4.3%	1.4%	7.8%	3.2%	1.7%	—	0.7%	3.1%	4.2%	4.6%
Earnings per share ($)	7.7%	1.93	0.58	6.37	3.06	1.64	(0.33)	0.62	2.57	3.33	3.75
Stock price – high ($)	—	15.63	25.00	38.25	33.94	29.88	23.19	27.06	38.06	47.25	49.25
Stock price – low ($)	—	12.56	14.50	17.50	23.50	21.06	6.44	8.38	26.00	32.56	31.63
Stock price – close ($)	8.9%	15.63	20.94	30.00	25.56	21.75	9.44	26.75	34.19	45.75	33.63
P/E – high	—	8	43	6	11	18	—	44	15	14	13
P/E – low	—	7	25	3	8	13	—	14	10	10	8
Dividends per share ($)	(0.7%)	0.80	0.80	0.80	0.85	0.90	0.90	0.20	0.28	0.58	0.75
Book value per share ($)	1.5%	16.22	15.46	16.09	17.65	18.54	17.94	19.32	13.36	15.29	18.51
Employees	(4.3%)	134,115	121,586	114,568	114,161	111,489	107,671	99,952	95,712	91,754	90,712

1994 Year-end:
Debt ratio: 32.3%
Return on equity: 22.2%
Cash (mil.): $266
Current ratio: 1.41
Long-term debt (mil.): $1,109
No. of shares (mil.): 151
Dividends
  Yield: 2.2%
  Payout: 20.0%
Market value (mil.): $5,092

**Stock Price History
High/Low 1985–94**

GREAT ATLANTIC & PACIFIC TEA CO.

OVERVIEW

A&P's 1,108 stores — 1,107 of which are not located in New York's Trump Palace — make the Montvale, New Jersey–based chain one of the top food retailers in North America. The company is Ontario's #1 grocer, but don't remind CEO James Wood. Troubles there in 1993 and 1994 included tough, lower-cost competition and a 14-week strike that shut down 63 stores. A&P converted 25 Ontario stores to low-price Super Fresh formats but still finished fiscal 1995 in the red because of its Canadian operations. The company no doubt hopes Trump Palace's swanky Food Emporium is more indicative of its direction.

The company has supermarkets in 22 states, the District of Columbia, and Ontario under 15 names, the best known being A&P. The company is the top grocery chain in New York City and Detroit. Strong markets for A&P in 1994 included Michigan (where the company has spent $123 million in capital improve-ments in the past 5 years) and Atlanta (where the weaker stores obtained in a 1992 acquisition have been unloaded). In 1994 A&P opened 16 stores and renovated 55 while shuttering 87; the company plans to open about 30 stores annually for several years.

The company has been consolidating its variety of private-label brand names under the America's Choice moniker. In addition to the Eight O'Clock, Bokar, and Royale brands of coffee (sold not only by A&P but by other retailers outside its markets), A&P manufactures baked goods, deli products, and ice cream. Private-label products account for over 22% of A&P's sales, not far from the company's goal of 25%.

Tengelmann, a German firm that owns almost 54% of A&P, has been applying the company's name to grocery stores it owns in the Netherlands, where the name has previously been a known product brand.

WHEN

George Gilman and George H. Hartford of Augusta, Maine, set up shop in 1859 on New York City's docks to sell tea at a 50% discount by eliminating middlemen. The Great American Tea Company advertised by drawing a red wagon through the city's streets. By 1869 the company, renamed The Great Atlantic & Pacific Tea Company, had 11 stores offering discounted items.

Gilman retired in 1878, and Hartford brought in his sons George and John. In 1912, when the company had 400 stores, John opened a store on a low-price, cash-and-carry format, without customer credit or premiums, which proved popular. When the company passed to the sons in 1916, A&P had over 1,000 cash-and-carry stores and a strategy of having "a store on every corner."

During the 1920s and 1930s, the company grew to more than 15,000 stores; however, there was a movement by small retailers to restrict chain stores in general and A&P in particular. To improve the company's image, John Hartford initiated innovative marketing and customer service policies. A&P grew in the 1940s by converting its stores to supermarkets, but an antitrust suit in 1949 and the company's reluctance to carry more nonfood items pushed A&P into decline. Management shut stores in California and Washington to shore up the northeastern states.

In 1975, after a long period of poor sales and failed discount format attempts, the board chose a new CEO: former Albertson's president Jonathan Scott (who eventually left A&P to become president and CEO of American Stores). Scott cut costs by closing stores and reducing the work force, but his efforts proved ineffective. The company's 1978 sales increases failed to keep ahead of inflation, and A&P posted a $52 million loss.

In 1979 the Hartford Foundation sold its A&P holdings to the German Tengelmann Group, which appointed English-born James Wood as CEO (1980). A&P has since acquired Super Fresh (1982), Kohl's (1983), Pantry Pride (1984), Borman's (1989), Ontario's Miracle Food Mart (1990), and Atlanta's Big Star (1992).

The company entered the 1990s trying to fend off the effects of the recession and increasing competition from warehouse-type stores. Rivals' larger, newer, and cleaner supermarkets have stripped away market share in New York City, Detroit, and Long Island. In response, A&P has closed hundreds of old stores, planned openings of larger stores, and tried its hand at emphasizing ethnic and gourmet foods and unusual produce.

A&P in 1994 transplanted its Farmer Jack store name from Michigan to Virginia, where it is being used for a new produce-intensive store concept. In 1995 customers of A&P's 6 New York City Food Emporium stores were given the option of ordering their groceries from home via America Online.

NYSE symbol: GAP
Fiscal year ends: Last Saturday in February

WHO

Chairman and CEO: James Wood, age 65,
$1,160,500 pay
VC, CFO, and Treasurer: Fred Corrado, age 55,
$488,500 pay
President and COO: Christian W. E. Haub, age 30
EVP Development and Strategic Planning: Peter J.
O'Gorman, age 56, $374,712 pay
EVP Marketing and Merchandising: Gerald L. Good,
age 52
**Chairman and CEO, The Great Atlantic & Pacific
Company of Canada, Ltd.:** John D. Moffatt, age 47
SVP and Chief Merchandising Officer: George Graham,
age 45, $384,712 pay
SVP and General Counsel: Robert G. Ulrich, age 60
SVP and COO, US Operations: J. Wayne Harris, age 56
SVP and Chief Services Officer: Ivan K. Szathmary,
age 58
SVP Human Resources: H. Nelson "Bud" Lewis
Auditors: Deloitte & Touche LLP

WHERE

HQ: The Great Atlantic & Pacific Tea Company, Inc.,
2 Paragon Dr., Montvale, NJ 07645
Phone: 201-573-9700
Fax: 201-930-8106

A&P operates 1,108 supermarkets in 22 states in the
eastern, southern, and midwestern US, the District of
Columbia, and Ontario.

	1995 Sales		1995 Operating Income	
	$ mil.	% of total	$ mil.	% of total
US	8,541	83	138	—
Canada	1,791	17	(196)	—
Total	**10,332**	**100**	**(58)**	**—**

	No. of Stores
Ontario	235
New York	196
New Jersey	115
Michigan	100
Connecticut	62
Wisconsin	56
Virginia	53
Maryland	51
Pennsylvania	48
Georgia	46
Louisiana	32
North Carolina	29
Massachusetts	28
South Carolina	13
Delaware	9
West Virginia	8
Alabama	7
Mississippi	6
Other states	14
Total	**1,108**

WHAT

Store Names

A&P	Food Bazaar	Miracle Food Mart
Compass Foods	Food Emporium	Sav-A-Center
Dominion	Food Mart	Super Fresh
Family Mart	Futurestore	Ultra Mart
Farmer Jack	Kohl's	Waldbaum's

KEY COMPETITORS

Albertson's	Grand Union	Rite Aid
American Stores	J Sainsbury	Roundy's
Bruno's	Kohl's	Ruddick
DeMoulas Super	Kroger	Safeway
Markets	Meijer	Stop & Shop
Food Lion	Pathmark	Walgreen
George Weston	Penn Traffic	Wegmans Food
Giant Eagle	Publix	Markets
Giant Food	Red Apple Group	Winn-Dixie

HOW MUCH

	9-Year Growth	1986	1987	1988	1989	1990	1991	1992	1993	1994	1995
Sales ($ mil.)	5.1%	6,615	7,835	9,532	10,068	11,148	11,391	11,591	10,500	10,384	10,332
Net income ($ mil.)	—	56	69	103	128	147	151	71	(99)	4	(167)
Income as % of sales	—	0.8%	0.9%	1.1%	1.3%	1.3%	1.3%	0.6%	—	—	—
Earnings per share ($)	—	1.48	1.82	2.71	3.34	3.84	3.95	1.85	(2.58)	0.10	(4.36)
Stock price – high ($)[1]	—	22.00	27.75	46.88	48.13	65.38	61.75	57.75	35.25	35.00	27.38
Stock price – low ($)[1]	—	14.38	19.25	23.63	31.88	44.25	37.75	25.50	21.38	22.50	17.38
Stock price – close ($)[1]	(2.1%)	21.88	23.50	37.50	44.63	58.88	44.13	28.38	23.88	27.00	18.13
P/E – high	—	15	15	17	14	17	16	31	—	—	—
P/E – low	—	10	11	9	10	12	10	14	—	—	—
Dividends per share ($)	23.1%	0.10	0.40	0.48	0.58	0.68	0.78	0.80	0.80	0.80	0.65
Book value per share ($)	1.6%	17.63	19.85	22.32	25.42	28.59	31.96	32.79	27.06	26.02	20.27
Employees	4.9%	60,000	81,500	83,000	92,000	91,000	99,300	94,600	90,000	94,000	92,000

1995 Year-end:
Debt ratio: 53.3%
Return on equity: —
Cash (mil.): $129
Current ratio: 1.09
Long-term debt (mil.): $759
No. of shares (mil.): 38
Dividends
  Yield: 3.6%
  Payout: —
Market value (mil.): $693

Stock Price History[1]
High/Low 1986–95

[1]Stock prices are for the prior calendar year.

GREAT WESTERN FINANCIAL CORP.

OVERVIEW

Chatsworth, California–based Great Western is going back East, hoping to mine the region for a mother lode of mortgage and consumer lending business. After being clobbered by the California recession and the subsequent real estate bust, the bank is diversifying its income geographically (in 1994 mortgage originations from outside Californa rose to 45% of total).

Although Great Western traditionally emphasized savings banking (in which savings accounts provided capital for home mortgages, all, ideally, at low interest rates), in recent years the company has worked hard to increase fee income from checking accounts and the sale of investment products like mutual funds. As Great Western has diversified the types and regional sources of its service income, it has shrunk its out-of-state retail branch network, leaving New York, Washington, Arizona, and, in 1994, western Florida.

In 1995 Great Western joined a movement that is picking up speed among savings banks by applying to change the charters of some of its banks to the national bank system because of the lower deposit insurance rates available to national banks.

WHEN

Great Western began operations in California as a state-licensed savings and loan in 1919.

In 1955 Great Western was merged into a new holding company, Great Western Financial Corp. Within 5 years Great Western Financial acquired Santa Ana Savings (1956), West Coast Savings (Sacramento, 1957), Guaranty Savings (San Jose, 1958), Central Savings (San Luis Obispo, 1959), and First Savings (Oakland, 1959). The company later bought Santa Rosa Savings (1968) and Safety Savings (Los Angeles, 1969).

In 1970 and 1971 Great Western continued expanding by purchasing 4 more California S&Ls. In 1972 Great Western Financial combined its acquired savings subsidiaries into Great Western Savings.

In the 1970s, as inflation rose and interest rates began their nearly decade-long climb, many lenders were caught with outstanding loans at interest rates below their cost of funds. Lenders were challenged with making long-term mortgages in a climate in which interest rates seemed to climb inexorably. Great Western's solution was to offer variable-rate mortgages (VRMs). By 1979, 60% of the company's mortgage loans were variable-rate. In 1981 federal regulators approved adjustable-rate mortgages (which feature rate ceilings and floors), and by the early 1980s all of Great Western's new mortgages were ARMs.

Under James Montgomery, who became CEO in 1979, Great Western grew and diversified. It expanded its consumer finance business in 1983 by buying Aristar and its Blazer Financial Services subsidiary. That year Great Western began lending in Florida by opening a real estate loan office in Boca Raton.

In 1984 Great Western became the first US savings institution to issue floating-rate notes in Europe. By 1987, 75% of the company's fixed-rate and variable-rate mortgage loans were converted to ARMs. The company expanded into Washington and Arizona and bought City Finance (consumer finance, 1987). That year it ceased making new commercial real estate loans and began to focus on single-family mortgages and consumer loans. But the commercial loan portfolio had already begun to drag down earnings.

The company continued to expand in 1990 and 1991, buying, among other things, California's Lincoln Savings Bank (Irvine), former centerpiece of Charles Keating's financial empire, and Capitol Finance Group (consumer finance).

Great Western completed acquisitions of AmeriFirst and Republic Federal S&Ls in 1992. As interest rates fell, the company's Sierra Trust mutual funds gained investors.

In 1992 California remained in recession, especially hard hit by defense cutbacks and falling property values. Yet Great Western held on to its problem loans until 1993, when it began an aggressive sales campaign. As interest rates fell to a 20-year low that year, many of Great Western's ARMs began to hit their floors (the minimum contractual rates, which may now be higher than the going rates) and were refinanced (often elsewhere).

In 1994, operations were particularly affected by the Northridge earthquake because the company has an administration center there. That year's profits, however, quadrupled, thanks to lower loss reserves and the gain on the sale of its 31-branch network on Florida's Gulf Coast (it continues to conduct retail business on the state's east coast).

In 1995 Chairman Montgomery announced that he would pass the office of CEO to Great Western's president, John Maher, at the end of the year.

WHO

Chairman and CEO: James F. Montgomery, age 60, $1,468,700 pay
President and COO: John F. Maher, age 51, $945,750 pay
President, Consumer Finance: Michael M. Pappas, age 62, $586,988 pay
EVP and CFO: Carl F. Geuther, age 49, $491,040 pay
EVP: Eugene A. Crane, age 57, $518,320 pay
EVP: Curtis J. Crivelli, age 52, $491,040 pay
EVP, Secretary, and General Counsel: J. Lance Erikson
SVP Corporate Communications: Ian D. Campbell
SVP Human Resources, Great Western Bank: Patricia A. Benninger
Auditors: Price Waterhouse LLP

WHERE

HQ: Great Western Financial Corporation, 9200 Oakdale Ave., Chatsworth, CA 91311-6519
Phone: 818-775-3411
Fax: 818-775-3434

Great Western has 419 retail branches in California and Florida, 530 consumer finance offices in 24 states, and 258 mortgage loan offices in 23 states.

WHAT

	1994 Sales	
	$ mil.	% of total
Real estate loan interest	1,914	63
Other interest	716	24
Banking fees	141	5
Mortgage sales & serving	86	3
Other	141	5
Total	**2,998**	**100**

	1994 Assets	
	$ mil.	% of total
Cash & equivalents	2,066	5
Mortgage-backed securities	9,269	22
Other investments	927	2
Net loans	28,378	67
Other	1,578	4
Total	**42,218**	**100**

Selected Services
Adjustable-rate mortgages
Commercial and retail banking
Mutual funds
Real estate lending and investing
Securities brokerage

Subsidiaries and Affiliates
Blazer Financial Services
California Reconveyance Company
City Finance Company
Great Western Bank F.S.B.
Great Western Financial Insurance Agency
Great Western Financial Services
Great Western Investment Management Corp.
Great Western Mortgage Corp.

KEY COMPETITORS

BancFlorida Financial
BankAmerica
BankAtlantic
Barnett Banks
CalFed
Citicorp
Coast Savings
Countrywide Credit
Fannie Mae
First American Financial
First Interstate
Fleet
Glendale Federal
Golden West Financial
H.F. Ahmanson
NationsBank
North American Mortgage
SunTrust
TELACU
Wells Fargo

HOW MUCH

	9-Year Growth	1985	1986	1987	1988	1989	1990	1991	1992	1993	1994
Assets ($ mil.)	5.8%	25,471	27,630	28,631	32,815	37,176	39,406	39,600	38,439	38,348	42,218
Net income ($ mil.)	2.4%	202	301	210	248	100	193	298	54	62	251
Income as % of assets	—	0.8%	1.1%	0.7%	0.8%	0.3%	0.5%	0.8%	0.1%	0.2%	0.6%
Earnings per share ($)	(0.6%)	1.78	2.51	1.64	1.95	0.78	1.50	2.24	0.30	0.28	1.69
Stock price – high ($)	—	13.91	19.31	24.38	17.38	25.13	21.13	21.38	20.00	20.88	21.13
Stock price – low ($)	—	9.00	13.25	12.00	12.63	14.63	8.50	11.00	12.50	15.25	15.25
Stock price – close ($)	1.6%	13.84	18.59	15.25	15.00	17.50	12.25	18.00	17.50	20.00	16.00
P/E – high	—	8	8	15	9	32	14	10	—	75	13
P/E – low	—	5	5	7	7	19	6	5	—	55	9
Dividends per share ($)	10.3%	0.38	0.46	0.66	0.75	0.79	0.83	0.87	0.91	0.92	0.92
Book value per share ($)	3.5%	11.93	14.19	14.87	15.48	15.49	16.15	17.01	16.48	16.05	16.30
Employees	6.2%	9,112	12,435	11,547	12,609	12,791	14,057	14,786	16,016	17,029	15,644

1994 Year-end:
Equity as % of assets: 5.9%
Return on assets: 0.6%
Return on equity: 10.2%
Long-term debt (mil.): $2,611
No. of shares (mil.): 134
Dividends
 Yield: 5.8%
 Payout: 54.4%
Market value (mil.): $2,149
Sales (mil.): $2,998

**Stock Price History
High/Low 1985–94**

THE GREEN BAY PACKERS, INC.

OVERVIEW

The Green Bay Packers, Inc., is unlike any other football team. The world-famous team is set up as a nonprofit corporation, which is publicly owned by 1,877 shareholders and governed by 45 directors and a 7-person, unpaid executive committee. Altogether there are 4,632 shares (originally sold at $25 each); these pay no dividends. And if the team is ever liquidated, proceeds will go to build a war memorial in Green Bay, Wisconsin. The organization is also unique in the NFL. Although NFL rules prohibit public ownership of teams, the Packers are older than the rule. As of mid-1995 the Packers were the only team in the NFL with no free agents.

The NFL's oldest franchise survives on proceeds from the NFL's TV contract (63% of its 1993 revenues), which are shared equally among all 28 NFL teams, and on proceeds from the team's stadium and pro shop. To help raise revenues the Packers now play all home games in Lambeau Field at Green Bay (considered the Wrigley Field of football), having ended a long-standing tradition of also playing at Milwaukee.

Packers president Bob Harlan has expanded the team's business staff, greatly boosted marketing operations, and hired a CFO and general counsel. Harlan, who rose through the ranks of the organization, has overseen 2 stadium expansion projects and the building of the team's new indoor practice facility. Also in the works are a new scoreboard, sound system, and 2nd replay board.

WHEN

In 1919 Curly Lambeau and George Calhoun met in the newsroom of the *Green Bay Press-Gazette* to organize a football team. The pair later talked Lambeau's employer — Indian Packing — into buying equipment for the team. To honor the sponsor, the team became known as the Packers.

Fans passed the hat at games. Heartened by early gridiron successes, Lambeau and 2 businessmen in 1921 obtained a franchise from the National Football League. Receipts didn't cover expenses, and the franchise had to be forfeited at the end of the season.

Lambeau and other backers bought the franchise again in 1922 for $250, but the Packers ran afoul of bad weather. The team's insurance company wouldn't pay off on a rained-out game because the rainfall was 1/100th of an inch less than the policy required. Later that year a storm threatened to cancel another game and ruin the team's fiscal health. A. B. Turnbull, a *Press-Gazette* executive who was the first Packers president, convinced merchants in Green Bay to underwrite the team, and the Packers became a corporation.

In 1934 the Packers lost a $5,000 lawsuit filed by a fan who fell from the stands. The club's insurance company went out of business, and the Packers were forced into receivership. Green Bay merchants raised $15,000 to revive the corporation.

With Lambeau as coach, Green Bay developed a reputation for hard-nosed football. Spurred by end Don Hutson, the Packers won championships in 1936, 1939, and 1944. Even though pro football grew in popularity after WWII, Green Bay continued to suffer

financially. A 1949 intrasquad game raised $50,000 to keep the team afloat, and a 1950 stock drive in the community raised another $118,000.

Lambeau resigned from the Packers in 1950. The team's football fortunes dipped in the 1950s until coach Vince Lombardi arrived in 1959. The team immediately began winning again, and Lombardi teams dominated the game, winning back-to-back Super Bowls (1967, 1968). Lombardi left coaching for the front office in 1968, and the team struggled to regain its luster during dismal seasons in the 1970s and 1980s.

In 1982 Judge Robert Parins became the team's first full-time CEO, spurring the corporation to a record $3 million profit (1986). Parins assumed the honorary board chairmanship in 1989, and Bob Harlan, a former sports publicist who joined the Packers as assistant general manager in 1971, became president and CEO that year.

Harlan named Ron Wolf general manager in mid-season 1991. After a subsequent disappointing 4–12 season record, Wolf replaced coach Lindy Infante (named the NFL Coach of the Year in 1989) with Mike Holmgren, the team's 11th head coach. In his first 3 seasons, Holmgren led the Packers to consecutive 9–7 records. The Packers reached the playoffs in the 1993–94 season, the first time in 11 years, and again in the 1994–95 season.

In 1995 star wide receiver Sterling Sharpe, who was seriously injured during the 1994–95 season and subsequently released by the Packers, filed a lawsuit against his former team for $9.6 million.

Private company
Fiscal year ends: March 31

WHO

President and CEO: Robert E. Harlan, age 58
EVP and General Manager: Ron Wolf, age 56
VP and CFO: Michael R. Reinfeldt, age 42
VP: John Fabry
General Legal Counsel: Lance Lopes
Head Coach: Michael G. Holmgren, age 47
Offensive Coordinator: Sherman Lewis
Defensive Coordinator: Fritz Shurmur
Director Pro Personnel: Ted Thompson
Auditors: Wipfli, Ullrich, & Bertelson

WHERE

HQ: 1265 Lombardi Ave., Green Bay, WI 54304
Phone: 414-496-5700
Fax: 414-496-5738

The Green Bay Packers, Inc., fields a professional football team that plays games in Green Bay, Wisconsin, and in the cities of opposing teams. It is assigned to the National Football Conference, Central Division, of the National Football League.

WHAT

| | 1995 Sales | |
	$ mil.	% of total
Ticket & media income		
Television & radio	37.3	60
Home games	8.5	14
Road & postseason games	6.4	10
NFL properties	2.6	4
Expansion fee income	1.8	3
Private box income	1.6	3
Other	4.0	6
Total	**62.2**	**100**

| | 1995 Assets | |
	$ mil.	% of total
Cash & equivalents	6.5	11
Other investments	21.4	38
Net property & equipment	22.4	40
Other	6.3	11
Total	**56.6**	**100**

1995 Regular-Season Schedule
Sept. 3 — St. Louis Rams at Green Bay
Sept. 11 — Chicago Bears at Chicago
Sept. 17 — New York Giants at Green Bay
Sept. 24 — Jacksonville Jaguars at Jacksonville
Oct. 8 — Dallas Cowboys at Dallas
Oct. 15 — Detroit Lions at Green Bay
Oct. 22 — Minnesota Vikings at Green Bay
Oct. 29 — Detroit Lions at Detroit
Nov. 5 — Minnesota Vikings at Minnesota
Nov. 12 — Chicago Bears at Green Bay
Nov. 19 — Cleveland Browns at Cleveland
Nov. 26 — Tampa Bay Buccaneers at Green Bay
Dec. 3 — Cincinnati Bengals at Green Bay
Dec. 10 — Tampa Bay Buccaneers at Tampa Bay
Dec. 16 — New Orleans Saints at New Orleans
Dec. 24 — Pittsburgh Steelers at Green Bay

Offense (1994)
Passing touchdowns (33)
Rushing touchdowns (11)
Return touchdowns (3)
Field goals (19)
Yards gained
  Rushing (1,543)
  Passing (3,773)

Defense (1994)
Interceptions (21)
Quarterback sacks (37)
Yards allowed
  Rushing (1,363)
  Passing (3,401)

KEY COMPETITORS

Chicago Bears
Detroit Lions
Minnesota Vikings
Tampa Bay Buccaneers

HOW MUCH

	9-Year Growth	1986	1987[1]	1988	1989	1990	1991	1992	1993	1994	1995
Sales ($ mil.)	11.0%	24.4	27.4	23.7	28.0	30.1	41.9	44.5	54.0	65.5	62.2
Net income ($ mil.)	0.0%	2.0	3.1	2.8	1.3	0.4	1.9	2.2	0.9	1.9	2.0
Attendance (thou.)[2,3]	1.9%	821	865	697	811	876	906	846	937	968	975
Games won[2]	—	8	4	5	4	10	6	4	9	9	9
Games lost[2]	—	8	12	9	12	6	10	12	7	7	7
Games tied[2]	—	0	0	1	0	0	0	0	0	0	0
Points for[2]	—	337	254	255	240	362	271	273	276	340	382
Points against[2]	—	355	418	300	315	356	347	313	296	282	287
Division finish[2]	—	2	4	3	5	2	2	4	2	2	2
Winning percentage[2]	—	50.0%	25.0%	33.3%	25.0%	62.5%	37.5%	25.0%	56.3%	56.3%	56.3%
Employees (nonplayers)	6.7%	44	44	48	45	51	54	62	72	74	79

1995 Year-end:
Debt ratio: 7.3%
Return on equity: 5.1%
Cash (mil.): $0.7
Current ratio: 0.81
Long-term debt (mil.): $0
No. of shares: 4,632
Est. franchise value (mil.): $154

Net Income 1986–95

Note: All figures are for regular season   [1]Strike-shortened season   [2]Games were played in prior calendar year   [3]Home and away games

GTE CORPORATION

OVERVIEW

Based in Stamford, Connecticut, GTE is the 4th largest publicly owned telecommunications company in the world. It is the leading local telephone company in the US and provides traditional wireline telephone services in 28 states. Through its Mobilnet and Contel Cellular units, GTE is also the #2 cellular provider in the US. It recently purchased the 10% of Contel Cellular that it did not already own.

GTE is now combining wireline and wireless communications by offering Tele-Go, the first personal communications service (PCS) for the US residential market. Tele-Go is a cordless phone that can receive calls over wireline and cellular networks. Through its alliance with SBC Communications, GTE is able to offer both wireline and wireless telecommunications services in its Texas market.

In addition, it is extending its wireless services through its purchase of the broadband spectrum licenses necessary for PCS in Atlanta, Seattle, Cincinnati, and Denver.

The company has received construction approval from the FCC for its video-dialtone networks in 3 initial markets — Ventura County, California; Pasco and Pinellas Counties, Florida; and Honolulu. GTE plans to deliver video programming to 900,000 homes by the end of 1997.

GTE has numerous investments overseas, currently holding stakes in telephone companies in Argentina, Canada, the Dominican Republic, and Venezuela. It has signed an agreement with China United Telecommunications (UNICOM) to develop a 2nd telecommunications network in that country.

WHEN

Two former staff members of the Wisconsin Railroad Commission — Sigurd Odegard and John O'Connell — formed Richland Center Telephone in Wisconsin dairy country in 1918.

With backing from a utilities executive and a Paine Webber partner, Odegard and O'Connell created Associated Telephone Utilities in 1926. That year they bought a Long Beach telephone company, which Odegard, while on a California vacation, had noticed was up for sale. Associated Telephone grew rapidly, but the company was caught with too much debt in the Depression. Lenders took control in 1932 and moved headquarters from Chicago to New York. Still beset by problems, Associated was forced into bankruptcy and emerged as General Telephone (GT) in 1935.

Attorney David Power, named CEO in 1951, guided post-WWII growth as GT acquired Theodore Gary and Company (1955) and Sylvania (1959). When GT purchased Sylvania, which had been founded in 1901 by Frank Poor as a company that refilled burned-out light bulbs, it became a manufacturer and developer of lighting and electronics and was renamed General Telephone and Electronics.

The company, long the largest phone company independent of the Bell group, expanded with the purchase of phone companies in Florida (1957), the Southwest (1964), and Hawaii (1967). GTE sold its US consumer electronics business to North American Philips in 1981, and GTE Mobilnet was formed in 1982 to provide cellular telephone service. Under chairman James (Rocky) Johnson, it sold most of its US Sprint long-distance service, purchased in

1983 from Southern Pacific, to partner United Telecommunications in 1989. Concentrating again on its lucrative local phone businesses, GTE jettisoned PBX (private branch telephone exchange) maker Automatic Electric as AG Communication Systems, creating a joint venture to be owned by AT&T.

In 1991 the company merged with Contel ($3 billion in annual sales), which consisted of 30 telephone companies serving more than 2 million people in 30 states and the Caribbean. The historic merger made GTE the largest US local telephone utility (adding 2.6 million to GTE's 15.1 million lines) and the 2nd largest cellular telephone provider (nearly doubling GTE's cellular properties).

After acquiring about 20% of the Venezuelan phone company in 1991, GTE sold its remaining interest in Sprint in 1992 to United Telecommunications (now Sprint). It sold its electrical products business in 1993 and agreed to sell its GTE Spacenet satellite unit to GE in 1994. In the same year a GTE-led consortium won its bid for Argentinian cellular licenses.

In 1995 GTE chose 15 states, including Florida, Hawaii, and California, for video operations center (VOC) installations to support video-conferencing service for business. It also began selling telephone equipment for the home and office in its newly introduced GTE Phone Mart on CompuServe's on-line Electronic Mall. In addition, GTE Government Systems Corp., Sun Microsystems, and 2 other companies won a $200 million US government contract to provide the army's next generation of computer systems for the battlefield.

NYSE symbol: GTE
Fiscal year ends: December 31

WHO

Chairman and CEO: Charles R. Lee, age 55, $2,004,115 pay
VC; President, GTE Telephone Operations: Kent B. Foster, age 51, $1,525,508 pay
VC: Michael T. Masin, age 50, $1,271,077 pay
EVP Strategic Planning and Group President: Nicholas L. Trivisonno, age 47, $1,062,592 pay
SVP Finance: J. Michael Kelly, age 38
SVP Corporate Planning and Development: Robert C. Calafell, age 53
SVP and General Counsel: William P. Barr, age 44
VP Taxes: John P. Z. Kent, age 54
VP and Treasurer: James Murphy, age 57
VP Public Affairs and Communications: G. Bruce Redditt, age 44
VP Government Affairs: Samuel F. Shawhan Jr., age 62
VP and Controller: Lawrence R. Whitman, age 43
VP Human Resources and Administration: J. Randall MacDonald, age 46
Auditors: Arthur Andersen & Co, SC

WHERE

HQ: One Stamford Forum, Stamford, CT 06904
Phone: 203-965-2000
Fax: 203-965-2277

GTE has telecommunications operations in 28 states, Argentina, Canada, the Dominican Republic, and Venezuela.

	1994 Sales	
	$ mil.	% of total
US	17,363	87
Other countries	2,581	13
Total	**19,944**	**100**

WHAT

	1994 Sales		1994 Operating Income	
	$ mil.	% of total	$ mil.	% of total
Telephone ops.	15,905	80	4,238	87
Telecomm prods. & svcs.	4,039	20	608	13
Total	**19,944**	**100**	**4,846**	**100**

Major Operations

Selected Products and Services	Telephone Operations
GTE Airfone	Local network services
GTE Government Systems	Long-distance services
GTE Information Services	Network access services
Personal Communications Services	

Selected Subsidiaries and Affiliates
AG Communication Systems (20%)
BC TEL (51%)
BELGACOM Directory Services (20%, Belgium)
Compañía de Teléfonos del Interior (26%, Argentina)
Compañía Anónima Nacional Teléfonos de Venezuela (20%)
Compañía Dominicana de Teléfonos, C. por A.
Contel Cellular Inc.
GTE Mobilnet
Québec Telephone (51%)

KEY COMPETITORS

AirTouch	Ericsson	SBC
Ameritech	Goeken Group	Communications
AT&T	Loral	Sprint
BCE	MCI	Telephone and
Bell Atlantic	MFS	Data Systems
BellSouth	Communications	U.S. Long
Cable & Wireless	Motorola	Distance
Century Telephone	NYNEX	U S WEST
Dun & Bradstreet	Pacific Telesis	

HOW MUCH

	9-Year Growth	1985	1986	1987	1988	1989	1990	1991	1992	1993	1994
Sales ($ mil.)	2.7%	15,732	15,112	15,421	16,460	17,424	18,374	19,621	19,984	19,748	19,944
Net income ($ mil.)	—	(161)	1,184	1,119	1,225	1,417	1,541	1,580	1,739	990	2,451
Income as % of sales	—	—	7.8%	7.3%	7.4%	8.1%	8.4%	8.1%	8.7%	5.0%	12.3%
Earnings per share ($)	—	(0.32)	1.72	1.61	1.77	2.08	2.26	1.75	1.90	1.03	2.55
Stock price – high ($)	—	15.47	21.30	22.38	22.94	35.56	36.00	35.00	35.75	39.88	35.25
Stock price – low ($)	—	12.72	15.09	8.81	16.88	21.44	23.50	27.50	28.88	34.13	29.50
Stock price – close ($)	7.9%	15.34	19.47	17.69	22.25	35.00	29.25	34.63	34.63	35.00	30.38
P/E – high	—	—	12	14	13	17	16	20	19	39	14
P/E – low	—	—	9	6	10	10	10	16	15	33	12
Dividends per share ($)	6.9%	1.03	1.06	1.23	1.28	1.37	1.49	1.61	1.73	1.84	1.88
Book value per share ($)	0.1 %	10.75	11.61	11.90	12.45	12.01	12.90	12.21	10.61	10.14	10.86
Employees	(5.4%)	183,033	160,463	161,224	159,000	158,000	177,477	162,000	131,000	117,446	111,000

1994 Year-end:
Debt ratio: 57.3%
Return on equity: 24.4%
Cash (mil.): $323
Current ratio: 0.69
Long-term debt (mil.): $12,163
No. of shares (mil.): 965
Dividends
  Yield: 6.2%
  Payout: 73.7%
Market value (mil.): $29,319

Stock Price History High/Low 1985–94

HALLIBURTON COMPANY

One of the world's biggest energy, engineering, and construction services companies, Dallas-based Halliburton operates 3 business segments. The company's energy services business provides a wide range of equipment, products, and services from drilling equipment for oil exploration to construction and maintenance services for oil refineries. Halliburton's engineering and construction unit, led by Brown & Root, provides services for industrial and government customers, including oil and chemical companies, electric power generators, and manufacturing firms. The company's insurance subsidiary, Highlands Insurance, issues property and casualty insurance.

The company has reorganized itself over the past 2 years, selling noncore assets and streamlining its operations. In 1994 the firm sold its gas-compression unit to Tidewater Compression Service for $205 million and its troubled geophysical business to Western Atlas for $190 million. It is also considering divesting its insurance business, which broke even in 1994 after 2 years of losses.

In 1994 Brown & Root was contracted to provide logistical support to the US military in its peacekeeping mission in Haiti.

WHEN

Erle Halliburton began his oil career in 1916, when he went to work for Perkins Oil Well Cementing. Discharged for suggesting too many new ideas, Halliburton left for Burkburnett, Texas, in 1919 and started his Better Method Oil Well Cementing Company. Halliburton used cement to hold a steel pipe in a well, which kept oil out of the water table. Although his contribution is widely recognized today, it was considered nonessential then. In 1921, the same year he moved to Duncan, Oklahoma, he recorded his first profit — of 50¢. In 1924 he incorporated as Halliburton Oil Well Cementing Company.

Between the 1950s and 1970s, Halliburton built up its oil service business by buying companies with expertise throughout the oil and gas market. It acquired Welex, a well-logging company (1957), and Houston-based Brown & Root construction company (1966), which had expertise in offshore platforms. It bought Ebasco Services, an electric utility engineering company with expertise in nuclear plants (1973), but the Justice Department forced its sale (1976), fearing that Halliburton's 20% share of the utility engineering market would limit competition.

The investments in Welex and Brown & Root left Halliburton well positioned to benefit from the oil boom of the 1970s. Later that decade, as drilling costs surged, Halliburton became the leader in stimulating old and abandoned wells by developing new techniques for fracturing deep formations.

When the oil industry slumped in 1982, Halliburton avoided further energy investments, instead cutting employment by more than half, while rivals Schlumberger and Dresser bought distressed companies at bargain prices. Another Halliburton business was not faring well, either: in 1985 Brown & Root, already suffering a scarcity of new construction projects, settled out of court for $750 million for mismanagement of the South Texas Nuclear Project.

Halliburton began reinvesting in oil and gas services, buying 60% of Texas Instruments's Geophysical Services (GSI), and Geosource, another geophysical service company (1988). Halliburton also bought Gearhart Industries (wireline services) and merged it with Welex to form Halliburton Logging Services. It purchased the remaining interest in GSI in 1991.

Halliburton opened an office in Moscow in 1991 and has since established joint enterprises throughout the former Soviet Union. Also in 1991 Brown & Root was chosen by Tokyo-based Sanpo Land Industrial as the prime contractor for an $8 billion luxury resort to be located near Nagoya, Japan.

In 1993 Halliburton acquired Smith International's directional drilling and services business for $240 million in stock. That same year the firm signed a joint venture deal with China National Petroleum Corporation to provide oil and gas field equipment and services.

In 1994 Brown & Root was named contractor for the Gulf–South Asia Gas Project, a $3.2 billion pipeline stretching from Qatar to Pakistan. In that same year Brown & Root started building a floating production platform for BHP Petroleum in the Dai Hung Field in the waters off Vietnam.

In 1995 Halliburton set the record for the world's deepest horizontal fracture (18,860 feet) at a Mobil well in Germany. Former US defense secretary Dick Cheney was named president and CEO in August 1995.

NYSE symbol: HAL
Fiscal year ends: December 31

WHO

Chairman: Thomas H. Cruikshank, age 63,
$1,200,000 pay
VC and COO: W. Bernard Pieper, age 62, $842,500 pay
VC: Dale P. Jones, age 58, $750,000 pay (prior to
promotion)
President and CEO: Richard B. Cheney, age 54
President and CEO, Halliburton Energy Services:
Kenneth R. LeSuer, age 59, $635,837 pay
President and CEO, Brown & Root, Inc.: Tommy E.
Knight, age 56, $622,500 pay
President and CEO, Highlands Insurance: Harold G.
Duble
EVP and General Counsel: Lester L. Coleman, age 52
VP Finance (CFO): Jerry H. Blurton, age 50
VP Government Relations: George L. Gleason
VP and Corporate Secretary: Susan S. Keith
VP and Treasurer: C. Robert Fielder
VP Legal: Robert M. Kennedy
VP Investor Relations: Guy T. Marcus
VP Administration (Personnel): Karen S. Stuart
Auditors: Arthur Andersen & Co, SC

WHERE

HQ: 3600 Lincoln Plaza, Dallas, TX 75201
Phone: 214-978-2600
Fax: 214-978-2611

Halliburton conducts business in the US and in more
than 100 other countries.

	1994 Sales		1994 Operating Income	
	$ mil.	% of total	$ mil.	% of total
US	3,416	60	172	61
Europe	961	15	(22)	—
Other regions	1,363	25	108	39
Adjustments	—	—	(23)	—
Total	**5,740**	**100**	**235**	**100**

WHAT

	1994 Sales		1994 Operating Income	
	$ mil.	% of total	$ mil.	% of total
Engineering & construction	2,996	52	67	26
Energy services	2,514	44	191	74
Insurance services	230	4	0	—
Adjustments	—	—	(23)	—
Total	**5,740**	**100**	**235**	**100**

Engineering and Construction Services
Construction
Engineering
Environmental services
Facilities operation and maintenance
Project management

Energy Services
Cementing, casing equipment, and water control services
Drilling systems and services

Logging and perforating
Pressure pumping equipment and services
Software
Specialized completion and production equipment and services
Well control
Well testing and reservoir evaluation services

Insurance Services
Casualty
Property

KEY COMPETITORS

ABB	General Electric	Raytheon
Baker Hughes	Jacobs	Schlumberger
Bechtel	Engineering	Siemens
BJ Services	Litton Industries	Turner
Black and Veatch	McDermott	Industries
Camco	Morrison	Union Pacific
CBI Industries	Knudsen	Western Atlas
CSX	Nabors Industries	Westinghouse
Dresser	Ogden	WMX
Duke Power	Perini	Technologies
Fluor	Peter Kiewit	
FMC	Sons'	

HOW MUCH

	9-Year Growth	1985	1986	1987	1988	1989	1990	1991	1992	1993	1994
Sales ($ mil.)	2.1%	4,781	3,527	3,836	4,839	5,661	6,926	7,019	6,566	6,351	5,740
Net income ($ mil.)	22.3%	29	(515)	48	85	134	197	27	(124)	(161)	178
Income as % of sales	—	0.6%	—	1.3%	1.8%	2.4%	2.8%	0.4%	—	—	3.1%
Earnings per share ($)	21.5%	0.27	(4.85)	0.45	0.81	1.26	1.85	0.25	(1.15)	(1.43)	1.56
Stock price – high ($)	—	33.88	28.00	43.13	36.50	44.50	58.75	55.25	36.88	44.00	37.25
Stock price – low ($)	—	24.50	17.38	20.13	24.38	27.50	38.75	25.50	21.75	25.75	27.88
Stock price – close ($)	2.1%	27.50	24.38	24.75	28.00	42.75	45.63	28.50	28.75	31.88	33.13
P/E – high	—	—	—	96	45	35	32	—	—	—	24
P/E – low	—	—	91	45	30	22	21	77	—	—	18
Dividends per share ($)	(6.3%)	1.80	1.20	1.00	1.00	1.00	1.00	1.00	1.00	1.00	1.00
Book value per share ($)	(4.7%)	26.30	20.30	19.77	19.80	19.90	21.04	20.24	17.80	16.55	17.02
Employees	(1.4%)	64,955	46,909	48,600	61,400	65,500	77,000	73,400	69,200	64,700	57,200

1994 Year-end:
Debt ratio: 25.8%
Return on equity: 9.3%
Cash (mil.): $647
Current ratio: 2.42
Long-term debt (mil.): $643
No. of shares (mil.): 114
Dividends
  Yield: 3.0%
  Payout: 64.1%
Market value (mil.): $3,780

Stock Price History
High/Low 1985–94

HALLMARK CARDS, INC.

OVERVIEW

To Hallmark, good taste has meant good business. The world's largest greeting card company, Hallmark designs and makes 21,000 cards (in 20 languages) that are sold in more than 100 countries. The privately held company has dominated the greeting card market for decades, promoting an upscale image with the Hallmark slogan ("When you care enough to send the very best") and specialty card shops that also sell home decorations and wedding gifts from suburban malls.

But the company's share of the market is slipping (most recently to 45%), and Hallmark is having to cut its costs, boost its marketing efforts, and diversify to keep up with the trends of the 1990s. The company is consolidating its Canadian and US operations to lower costs and going on-line to reach other markets. Hallmark is creating new products, marketing cards to mass retailers (where most customers buy cards these days), and selling videocassettes of its *Hallmark Hall of Fame* network TV specials. The company sold its cable operations in 1994 to concentrate on its new subsidiary, Hallmark Entertainment, which is the world's leading maker and distributor of family-oriented TV entertainment. The company intends to create wholesome TV specials and miniseries and market them in the US and abroad.

WHEN

Eighteen-year-old Joyce Hall started selling picture postcards from 2 shoeboxes in his room at the Kansas City, Missouri, YMCA in 1910. His brother Rollie joined him in 1911, and the 2 added greeting cards (made by another company) to their line in 1912. The brothers opened Hall Brothers, a store that sold postcards, gifts, books, and stationery, but it was destroyed in a 1915 fire — just before Valentine's Day. The Halls got a loan, bought an engraving company, and produced their first original cards in time for Christmas.

In 1920 a 3rd brother, William, joined the firm, which started stamping the backs of its cards with the phrase "A Hallmark Card." By 1922 Hall Brothers had salesmen in all 48 states and had begun offering gift wrap. Joyce Hall wrote the company's first national ad for *Ladies' Home Journal* in 1928.

In 1936 Hall Brothers patented the "Eye-Vision" display case for greeting cards (which had previously been kept under counters or in drawers) and sold it to retailers across the country. The company aired its first radio ad in 1938. In 1939 Hall Brothers introduced a friendship card, showing a cart filled with purple pansies. The card became the company's best seller and is still sold. In 1944 a Hallmark executive penned the company's slogan.

After WWII, Hall Brothers grew rapidly. The company opened its first retail store in 1950 and in 1952 broadcast the first production of its *Hallmark Hall of Fame*, which became the longest-running dramatic series on television and has won more Emmy awards than any other TV show. Hall Brothers changed its name to Hallmark Cards in 1954 and 3 years later began selling overseas. Mass merchandising unit Ambassador Cards opened in 1959.

Hallmark introduced a line of paper party products and started putting *Peanuts* characters on cards in 1960. In 1973 Christmas ornaments were added to its product line.

In 1967 the company started constructing Crown Center, a privately financed redevelopment of 85 acres of formerly rundown properties surrounding the company headquarters in Kansas City. In 1981, 2 walkways collapsed at the Crown Center's Hyatt Regency hotel, killing 114 and injuring 225.

In 1982 Joyce Hall died; his son Donald became chairman in 1983. Hallmark acquired Binney & Smith (Crayola Crayons, Magic Marker) in 1984 and the Spanish-language Univision TV network in 1987 (sold 1992). In 1986 the company introduced Shoebox Greetings, a line of nontraditional cards.

In 1990 Hallmark acquired Willitts Designs (collectibles, sold 1993), and in 1991 it entered the cable television industry by creating Crown Media and buying a controlling interest in St. Louis–based Cencom Cable for about $1 billion; both were sold in 1994.

The company teamed up with Information Storage Devices in 1993 to market recordable greeting cards. Hallmark also introduced Touch-Screen Greetings kiosks, which use computers to create cards with personal messages, in grocery and mall stores.

In 1995 the company joined with leading European broadcaster Flextech to create a family-oriented entertainment network (Hallmark Entertainment Network), which plans a 1996 startup in Ireland and the UK. Also that year the company began offering greeting cards through America Online (Hallmark Connections). It intends to offer on-line products through other networks, including Microsoft's.

Private company
Fiscal year ends: December 31

WHO

Chairman: Donald J. Hall, age 67
President and CEO: Irvine O. Hockaday Jr., age 58
CFO: Robert Druten
President and CEO, Hallmark Entertainment: Robert Halmi Jr.
VP Human Resources: Lowell J. Mayone
Auditors: KPMG Peat Marwick LLP

WHERE

HQ: 2501 McGee St., Kansas City, MO 64108
Phone: 816-274-5111
Fax: 816-274-8513

Hallmark has production facilities in 3 cities in Kansas (Lawrence, Leavenworth, and Topeka) and in Kansas City, Missouri. It has distribution centers in Enfield, Connecticut, and Liberty, Missouri. Products are distributed in more than 100 countries.

WHAT

Brand Names

Andrew Brownsword (greeting cards)
Crayola (crayons)
Hallmark (cards and other goods)
Heartline
Liquitex (art supplies)
Magic Marker (markers)
Mahogany (greeting cards)
Party Express
Primor (Spanish-language cards)
Revell-Monogram
Shoebox Greetings (nontraditional cards)
Springbok (jigsaw puzzles)
Touch-Screen Greetings (computer-generated cards)
Tree of Life
Valentines of Dundee
Verkerke

Selected Products

Calendars	Home decorations	Party supplies
Candles	Long-distance	Photo albums
Collectibles	telephone greeting	Ribbons
Gift wrap	cards	Stationery
Holiday ornaments	Mugs	Toys

Subsidiaries and Affiliates

Binney & Smith Inc. (crayons, art products)
Crown Center (Kansas City commercial and residential complex)
Crown Power and Redevelopment Corp. (real estate)
Evenson Card Shops, Inc. (card stores)
Flextech PLC (9.9%, broadcasting, UK)
Hallmark Entertainment (TV programming)
  Hallmark Home Entertainment (home video distributor)
  RHI Entertainment, Inc. (TV miniseries and movies)
  Signboard Hill Productions (TV and film)
Hallmark International (global marketing)
Hallmark Marketing Corp. (sales)
Halls Crown Center (Kansas City)
Halls Merchandising, Inc. (department stores)
Halls Plaza (Kansas City)
Litho-Krome Co. (lithography)
Mundi-Paper (cards, Spain)
Revell-Monogram Inc. (toys and games)
Spanjersberg Group (cards, The Netherlands)
Verkerke Reprodukties (fine art reproductions, The Netherlands)
W.N. Sharpe Holdings (cards, UK)

KEY COMPETITORS

American Greetings
Artistic Greetings
Artistic Impressions
Brøderbund
Deluxe
Gibson Greetings
Gillette
Hasbro
Healthy Planet Products
Marvel
Mattel
Pearson
Rank
Recycled Greetings
Thomas Nelson
United Nations
Walt Disney

HOW MUCH

	9-Year Growth	1985	1986	1987	1988	1989	1990	1991	1992	1993	1994
Sales ($ mil.)	8.4%	1,833	1,882	2,102	2,358	2,487	2,742	2,850	3,100	3,400	3,800
Domestic employees[1]	(0.7%)	13,615	12,988	12,583	13,600	13,213	13,877	13,202	12,487	12,600	12,800

Sales ($ mil.)
1985–94

[1]Does not include all subsidiaries.

H&R BLOCK, INC.

OVERVIEW

There's a new kid on the Block. In 1995, for the first time, H&R Block's CompuServe subsidiary enjoyed higher pretax earnings than the company's flagship tax preparation operations. This has raised speculation that H&R Block may spin off CompuServe, one of the leading computer on-line services (an intention the company has denied). Further questions about the company's future were raised by the 1995 resignation of H&R Block's president, Thomas Bloch (son of cofounder Henry Bloch), who said he would seek a new career that will help serve the public good. Former Ameritech EVP Richard Brown replaced him. The Blochs together own about 5.5% of the

company, and Thomas is expected to remain involved with the company after he leaves.

H&R Block's tax business (which includes both company-owned and franchised locations, many operating in Sears stores) has been flat recently because tax reforms in the US and Canada have simplified tax forms. But with a 12% market share in North America, the tax operation is a cash cow.

In 1995, as competitors vied to provide Americans with on-ramps to the information superhighway, CompuServe bought Spry, a maker of Internet access software. This purchase is expected to enhance its business as the popularity of the Internet grows.

WHEN

Brothers Henry and Richard Bloch opened the United Business Company in Kansas City in 1946 to provide bookkeeping, collection, management, and tax services to businesses.

Tax preparation soon began to monopolize the Blochs' time, and they planned to turn away clients. But one client, a newspaper advertising salesman, suggested they specialize in preparing taxes. The Blochs bought 2 ads, the first of which brought a stampede of clients.

In 1955 the company focused on tax preparation and became H&R Block (the Blochs didn't want customers to read the name as "blotch"). The company based its charges on the number and complexity of forms. That meant low fees and a mass market.

The first tax season was a success, and the brothers tested their formula in New York City (1956), where it was similarly successful. But neither brother wanted to move to New York. Instead, they worked out a franchise-like agreement with local CPAs, the first step toward a nationwide chain.

The Blochs opened offices in Columbia, Missouri, and Topeka, Kansas, in 1957, and in Des Moines, Little Rock, and Oklahoma City in 1958. To assure consistency from office to office, H&R Block began training preparers at H&R Block Income Tax Schools. By 1969, when Richard retired, H&R Block boasted over 3,000 offices in the US and Canada.

In the 1970s Henry Bloch began appearing in commercials. Bloch's avuncular, midwestern-Rotarian manner reassured Americans that they wouldn't have to face their taxes alone.

Fearing market saturation, Bloch pushed the company into new areas. H&R Block

bought Personnel Pool of America in 1978, and in 1980 it bought 80% of Hyatt Legal Services, a pioneer in chains of law offices. Synergies between the tax operations and the legal clinics never developed, and H&R Block sold its stake in 1987 back to a group headed by founder Joel Hyatt. The company also flirted with the management seminar business, buying Path Management (1985, sold 1990).

The 1986 Tax Reform Act brought a deluge of business from perplexed taxpayers.

Since H&R Block bought CompuServe in 1980 the 2 companies' operations have proven compatible, with CompuServe helping to develop H&R Block's tax preparation and electronic filing software. In 1990 CompuServe bought its on-line competitor, the Source, and MicroSolutions, a vendor of computer connectivity products. H&R Block's Personnel Pool of America subsidiary bought Interim Systems (temps) in 1991; it was later found incompatible with H&R Block's new direction, and Interim went public in 1994.

In 1992 Bloch was succeeded as president by his son, Thomas, who actively pursued nontax operations. This helped to distribute income more evenly (it has traditionally been concentrated in the 4th quarter).

In 1993 H&R Block bought MECA Software, a personal finance software company. H&R Block thought that MECA's relationships with banks, based on its refund anticipation loan program, would help develop on-line banking services. But in 1994 the IRS limited this service, and the bank ties became less important. The IRS also narrowed qualifications for electronic filing, reducing the number of on-line filing customers. In 1995 the company sold MECA to BankAmerica and NationsBank.

NYSE symbol: HRB
Fiscal year ends: April 30

WHO

Chairman: Henry W. Bloch, age 71, $608,333 pay
CEO and President: Richard H. Brown, age 48
SVP Corporate Operations: William F. Evans, age 46, $438,178 pay
VP Corporate Development and CFO; President and CEO, Block Financial Corp.: William P. Anderson, age 45, $323,362 pay
VP, Corporate Controller, and Treasurer: Ozzie Wenich, age 51, $171,779 pay
Assistant VP and Director Human Resources: Nicki Gustin
President and CEO, H&R Block Tax Services: Harry W. Buckley
President and CEO, CompuServe: Robert J. Massey
President, Legal Knowledge Systems: Daniel Caine
Auditors: Deloitte & Touche LLP

WHERE

HQ: 4410 Main St., Kansas City, MO 64111
Phone: 816-753-6900
Fax: 816-753-5346

H&R Block operates 9,577 offices in Australia, Canada, Europe, and the US.

WHAT

	1995 Sales	
	$ mil.	% of total
Tax services	730	54
Computer services	583	43
Financial services	39	3
Adjustments	8	—
Total	**1,360**	**100**

Selected Subsidiaries

Access Technology
BFC Investment, Inc.
Block Financial Corp.
Block Investment Corp.
BWA Advertising, Inc.
Capitol Software, Inc.
Companion Insurance, Ltd.
CompuPlex Inc.
CompuServe Inc.
CompuServe Information Services GMBH
Franchise Partner, Inc.
Great American Software, Inc.
H&R Block (Australia) Ltd.
H&R Block Canada, Inc.
H&R Block (Guam) Inc.
H&R Block Tax Services, Inc.
HRB Partners, Inc.
Legal Knowledge Systems, Inc.
Live Free or Die Software, Ltd.
PM Industries, Inc.

KEY COMPETITORS

ADP	GE Information Systems
America Online	IBM
American Business	Intuit
Information	Jackson Hewitt
Apple	KPMG
Arthur Andersen	MCI
AT&T	Microsoft
Bertelsmann	Netcom
Bloomberg	Netscape
Coopers & Lybrand	Oracle
Deloitte & Touche	Price Waterhouse
Delphi Internet	Prodigy
Dow Jones	Reuters
Dun & Bradstreet	Spyglass
Ernst & Young	

HOW MUCH

	9-Year Growth	1986	1987	1988	1989	1990	1991	1992	1993	1994	1995
Sales ($ mil.)	9.7%	591	687	778	877	1,028	1,163	1,337	1,495	1,231	1,360
Net income ($ mil.)	6.6%	60	73	88	100	124	140	162	181	201	107
Income as % of sales	—	10.2%	10.7%	11.3%	11.4%	12.0%	12.0%	12.1%	12.1%	16.3%	7.9%
Earnings per share ($)	5.8%	0.61	0.72	0.86	0.95	1.16	1.31	1.49	1.68	1.88	1.01
Stock price – high ($)[1]	—	9.91	13.22	16.66	17.19	18.69	22.75	38.25	41.13	42.75	48.75
Stock price – low ($)[1]	—	5.52	8.94	10.00	11.38	13.06	15.00	19.94	30.13	40.75	33.00
Stock price – close ($)[1]	16.2%	9.63	11.25	15.50	14.19	18.00	21.63	37.50	39.75	40.75	37.13
P/E – high	—	16	18	19	18	16	17	26	25	23	48
P/E – low	—	9	12	12	12	11	12	13	18	17	33
Dividends per share ($)	15.9%	0.33	0.36	0.42	0.50	0.61	0.75	0.86	0.97	1.09	1.25
Book value per share ($)	9.2%	2.93	3.41	3.69	4.25	4.76	5.39	5.76	6.12	6.67	6.46
Employees	7.1%	46,000	54,800	59,700	66,000	69,000	81,000	89,400	82,000	82,800	85,000

1995 Year-end:
Debt ratio: 6.8%
Return on equity: 15.4%
Cash (mil.): $353
Current ratio: 1.77
Long-term debt (mil.): $0
No. of shares (mil.): 106
Dividends
  Yield: 3.4%
  Payout: 123.8%
Market value (mil.): $3,920

Stock Price History[1]
High/Low 1986–95

[1] Stock prices are for the prior calendar year.

HARLEY-DAVIDSON, INC.

OVERVIEW

To Harley-Davidson, it's not where you go, it's how you get there. The Milwaukee-based company makes the legendary, high-powered Harley motorcycles, which boast record sales because of their mystique, quality, and "look" (created by Willie Davidson, grandson of one of the founders). The only major US maker of motorcycles, Harley-Davidson makes and sells 20 styles of touring and custom motorcycles through a worldwide network of more than 1,000 dealers.

For 9 years Harley-Davidson has been #1 in the US heavyweight motorcycle market; its share in 1994 was limited to 56% only because it lacks the manufacturing capacity to match demand. Motorcycles and accessories represented 75% of 1994 sales; the company also makes a line of commercial delivery vehicles (Utilimaster) for customers such as Federal

Express and Ryder. Other products include premium-priced RVs (Holiday Rambler), contemporary office furniture, and custom cabinetry and plastic-injection moldings for its RVs.

Harley-Davidson sells a lifestyle and the accessories to go with it. Goods licensed with the company name include toys, collectibles, and a line of clothing (MotorClothes). Its 270,000-member Harley Owners Groups (known as H.O.G., also a nickname for its motorcycles) and Holiday Rambler Recreational Vehicle Clubs sponsor rallies, trips, and extended treks.

Harley-Davidson is increasing its annual production of motorcycles to 115,000 by 1997 (compared with 95,800 in 1994 and 81,700 in 1993). It is also boosting sales efforts in Europe, where the Harley ranks #5 in the largest heavyweight motorcycle market in the world.

WHEN

In 1903 William Harley and the Davidson brothers (Walter, William, and Arthur) of Milwaukee sold their first motorcycles, which were essentially motor-assisted bicycles that required pedaling uphill. Demand was high, and most sold before leaving the factory. In 1909 the company introduced its trademark 2-cylinder, V-twin engine (that produced a low rumbling sound), which reached speeds of 60 mph; 4 years later there were 150 competitors.

WWI created a demand for US motorcycles overseas that made foreign sales important. In the 1920s Harley-Davidson was a leader in innovative engineering, introducing models with a front brake and the "teardrop" gas tank that became part of the Harley look.

The Great Depression decimated the motorcycle industry. As one of only 2 remaining companies, Harley-Davidson survived by its exports and by sales to the police and military. To improve sales, the company added styling features like art deco decals and 3-tone paint. The 1936 EL model, with its "knucklehead" engine (named for its odd appearance), was a forerunner of today's models.

During WWII Harley-Davidson prospered from military orders, elevating production to record levels (90,000 cycles were built for the military). After the war it introduced new models that catered to a growing recreational market made up of consumers with money to spend: the K-model (1952), Sportster ("superbike," 1957), and Duo-Glide (1958). By 1953 Harley-Davidson was the last remaining major motorcycle manufacturer in the US.

The company began making golf carts (since discontinued) in the early 1960s. In 1965 it went public, merging with American Machine and Foundry (AMF) in 1969. By the late 1970s sales and quality were slipping; certain that Harley-Davidson would lose to Japanese bikes flooding the market, AMF put the company up for sale. There was no buyer until 1981, when Vaughn Beals and other AMF executives purchased it. Minutes away from bankruptcy in 1985, then-CFO Richard Teerlink convinced lenders to accept a restructuring plan. Despite low demand and Japanese competition, Harley-Davidson made one of the greatest comebacks in US automotive history. Using Japanese management principles, it updated manufacturing methods, improved quality, and expanded the model line. Harley-Davidson again went public in 1986. By 1987 it had acquired 25% of the US heavyweight motorcycle market, up from 16% in 1985.

In 1990 Harley-Davidson opened its first retail mall outlet to sell MotorClothes. In 1993 it acquired a 49% stake in Eagle Credit (financing, insurance, and credit cards for dealers and customers) and a 49% share of Wisconsin-based Buell Motorcycle (gaining a niche in the performance motorcycle market).

In 1995 Harley-Davidson sued Lorillard Tobacco to break its 9-year-old licensing agreement that puts its name on cigarettes, citing concerns that the Harley name would entice children to smoke and fears that the motorcycle maker would be exposed to tobacco liability lawsuits.

NYSE symbol: HDI
Fiscal year ends: December 31

WHO

Chairman: Vaughn L. Beals Jr., age 67
President and CEO: Richard F. Teerlink, age 58,
$1,140,901 pay
EVP; President and COO, Motor Company: Jeffrey L.
Bleustein, age 55, $548,554 pay
VP Continuous Improvement: Thomas A. Gelb, age 59,
$445,673 pay
VP Human Resources: C. William Gray, age 53,
$311,319 pay
VP; President and COO, Holiday Rambler: Martin R.
Snoey, age 51, $308,134 pay
VP and CFO: James L. Ziemer, age 45
VP, Controller, and Treasurer: James M. Brostowitz,
age 43
VP, General Counsel, and Secretary: Timothy K.
Hoelter, age 48
President, Holiday World: James E. Cafmeyer
Assistant Secretary: Michael B. Weiss
Auditors: Ernst & Young LLP

WHERE

HQ: 3700 W. Juneau Ave., Milwaukee, WI 53208
Phone: 414-342-4680
Fax: 414-935-4977

Harley-Davidson operates 6 manufacturing facilities in
Wisconsin, Pennsylvania, and Indiana. There are 1,033
motorcycle dealerships and 120 Holiday Rambler dealers
worldwide.

	1994 Motorcycle Sales
	% of total
US	71
Other countries	29
Total	**100**

WHAT

	1994 Sales		1994 Operating Income	
	$ mil.	% of total	$ mil.	% of total
Motorcycles & accessories	1,159	75	163	96
RVs & commercial vehicles	383	25	7	4
Adjustments	—	—	(10)	—
Total	**1,542**	**100**	**160**	**100**

Model Names

Motorcycles		RVs
Cafe Racer	Softail	Aluma-Lite
Dyna Glide	Sportster	Endeavor
Electra Glide	Super Glide	Imperial
Fat Boy	Tour Glide	Navigator
Low Rider	Wide Glide	Vacationer

Other Businesses

Products	Licensing	Affiliates
Mobile rescue and special-use emergency vehicles	Cigarettes Jewelry Leather goods MotorClothes	Buell Motorcycle Company (49%) Eaglemark
Office furniture	Restaurant	Financial
Parcel delivery vans	(Harley	Services
Standard walk-in vans	Davidson Cafe)	(49%)
Truck bodies	Toys	
Walk-in vans	T-shirts	

KEY COMPETITORS

BMW	Grumman-Olsen	Steelcase
Coachmen Industries	Hanson Herman Miller	Supreme Corp. Suzuki
Chrysler	Honda	Thor Industries
Fleetwood	Kawasaki Motors	Winnebago
Ford	Navistar	Yamaha
General Motors		

HOW MUCH

	Annual Growth	1985	1986	1987	1988	1989	1990	1991	1992	1993	1994
Sales ($ mil.)	20.5%	288	295	685	757	791	865	940	1,105	1,217	1,542
Net income ($ mil.)	50.7%	3	4	18	27	36	38	37	54	18	104
Income as % of sales	—	0.9%	1.5%	2.6%	3.6%	4.6%	4.4%	3.9%	4.9%	1.5%	6.8%
Earnings per share ($)	35.3%	0.09	0.11	0.34	0.43	0.52	0.54	0.52	0.73	0.25	1.37
Stock price – high ($)	—	—	1.73	3.31	3.73	5.38	8.59	15.19	19.38	23.75	29.88
Stock price – low ($)	—	—	0.91	1.16	1.48	3.05	3.34	4.44	10.88	15.75	21.63
Stock price – close ($)	46.6%	—	1.31	1.63	3.17	4.91	4.81	11.19	18.81	22.06	28.00
P/E – high	—	—	16	10	9	10	16	29	27	95	22
P/E – low	—	—	8	3	3	6	6	9	15	63	16
Dividends per share ($)	—	—	0.00	0.00	0.00	0.00	0.00	0.00	0.00	0.06	0.14
Book value per share ($)	33.0%	—	0.58	1.14	1.76	2.24	2.80	3.34	4.43	4.28	5.68
Employees	13.2%	2,200	4,200	4,700	5,000	5,000	5,000	5,300	5,800	6,000	6,700

1994 Year-end:
Debt ratio: 4.1%
Return on equity: 27.5%
Cash (mil.): $59
Current ratio: 1.88
Long-term debt (mil.): $0
No. of shares (mil.): 76
Dividends
  Yield: 0.5%
  Payout: 10.2%
Market value (mil.): $2,137

**Stock Price History
High/Low 1986–94**

HARRIS CORPORATION

OVERVIEW

Defense electronics manufacturer Harris Corporation is no Cold War dinosaur, having diversified early into "infotech" products such as semiconductors, telecommunications systems, and radio and TV broadcasting equipment.

In 1994 and 1995 Florida-based Harris won several important civilian contracts, including orders for an air-to-ground radio system for Hong Kong's new airport and equipment upgrades for the BBC and Mexico's TV Azteca.

Harris's government sales still accounted for nearly 24% of revenues in 1994. Recent 5-year military contracts include secure tactical radios for US Special Operations Forces ($85 million) and technology assistance on a new meteorological satellite for the air force ($49.5 million). But Uncle Sam isn't Harris's only military customer; it will also supply radio communications systems to the Royal Netherlands army worth $40 million.

Harris built its empire on innovation; the company spent nearly 19% of sales on R&D in 1994. Among the 200 new products Harris introduced that year was CyberGuard Firewall, a computer system that protects corporate and governmental computer systems from "hackers" who gain access via public networks such as the Internet. With Chrysler Corporation the company also developed "intelligent-power circuits" that help cars conserve fuel.

Harris has spent the last decade refining its focus, selling noncore businesses and buying complementary ones. In 1994 it spun off its computer unit as Harris Computer Systems, a publicly traded company in which Harris no longer owns an interest. The company's publishing systems subsidiary acquired Baseview Products, a maker of newspaper prepress systems, while Lanier Worldwide acquired medical records transcription provider ML&M.

WHEN

Harris was founded in Niles, Ohio, in 1895 by brothers Alfred and Charles Harris, both jewelers and inventors. Among their inventions was a printing press that became Harris Automatic Press Company's flagship product.

Harris remained a small, family-run company until 1944, when engineer George Dively was hired as general manager. Under Dively, the company began manufacturing bindery, typesetting, and paper-converting equipment while remaining a leading supplier of printing presses. In 1957 Harris merged with Intertype, a typesetter manufacturer, and became known as Harris-Intertype Corporation.

During the 1960s Harris-Intertype expanded its business through several acquisitions. In 1967 it bought electronics and data-processing equipment maker Radiation, a $50 million company heavily dependent upon government contracts, and relocated to Radiation's headquarters in Melbourne, Florida. The company also bought RF Communications (2-way radios, 1969), GE's broadcast equipment line (1972), and UCC-Communications Systems (data-processing equipment, 1972).

The company changed its name to Harris Corporation in 1974. In 1980 Harris bought Farinon, manufacturer of microwave radio systems, and Lanier Business Products, the leading maker of dictating equipment. In 1983 it sold its printing equipment business. In 1986 Harris formed a joint venture with 3M called Harris/3M Document Products to market copiers and fax machines, and in 1989 it acquired the entire operation, which became Lanier Worldwide. Other 1980s acquisitions included Scientific Calculations, a CAD software developer (1986), and GE's Solid State group (1988). Harris sold off its PC, information systems, and data communications businesses in 1989 and 1990.

In 1992 Harris won its largest single contract to date, a $1.7 billion deal with the Federal Aviation Administration (FAA) to modernize voice communications between airports and airplanes. Later that year Harris acquired Westronic, a leading supplier of automated control systems for electric utilities.

The company formed a joint venture with Shenzen Telecom Equipment (China) in 1993 to produce digital microwave radios. That same year Harris withdrew from Sematech, the computer chip research consortium, to conserve its R&D funds. Also in 1993 a California state court ruled against Harris, awarding $66.8 million in damages to PLS, a defunct software company that accused the company of reneging on a license agreement.

Harris won a $140 million contract in 1994 for communications links among the FAA's Alaskan facilities. That same year it began installing the world's largest private digital telephone network along Russia's gas pipeline.

In 1995 Harris said it would spend about $100 million over the next 5 years to upgrade its 20-year-old Malaysian factory and to move its computer chip manufacturing operations to Malaysia from Singapore.

NYSE symbol: HRS
Fiscal year ends: June 30

WHO

Chairman, President, CEO, and COO: Phillip W.
Farmer, age 56, $745,065 pay (prior to promotion)
President, Lanier Worldwide: Wesley E. Cantrell, age 59,
$577,764 pay
President, Communications Sector: Guy W. Numann,
age 62, $544,147 pay
President, Semiconductor Sector: John C. Garrett,
age 51
President, Electronic Systems Sector: Allen S. Henry,
age 54
SVP and CFO: Bryan R. Roub, age 53, $492,545 pay
SVP Administration: Robert E. Sullivan, age 62
SVP: Frank J. Lewis, age 63
VP Corporate Relations: W. Peter Carney, age 62
VP Quality and New Products: John G. Johnson, age 58
VP, General Counsel, and Secretary: Richard L.
Ballantyne, age 54
VP Human Resources: Nick E. Heldreth, age 52
Auditors: Ernst & Young LLP

WHERE

HQ: 1025 W. NASA Blvd., Melbourne, FL 32919
Phone: 407-727-9100
Fax: 407-727-9344

Harris has 29 manufacturing plants and about 400
offices worldwide.

	1994 Sales		1994 Operating Income	
	$ mil.	% of total	$ mil.	% of total
US	2,742	82	138	71
Other countries	594	18	56	29
Total	**3,336**	**100**	**194**	**100**

WHAT

	1994 Sales		1994 Operating Income	
	$ mil.	% of total	$ mil.	% of total
Electronic systems	1,129	34	101	32
Lanier Worldwide	944	28	90	28
Semiconductors	635	19	70	22
Communications	628	19	58	18
Adjustments	—	—	(125)	—
Total	**3,336**	**100**	**194**	**100**

Selected Products

Electronic Systems
Air traffic control
Avionics
Communications
Electronics systems testing
Energy management
Newspaper composition
Mobile radio networks
Space exploration

Lanier Worldwide
Dictation systems
Facsimile units
Information management

Office copiers
Voice recording products
and systems

Semiconductors
Integrated circuits
Semiconductors

Communications
2-way radio
Digital telephone switches
Microwave systems
Radio and television
transmission systems

KEY COMPETITORS

Alco Standard
AM International
AMD
AT&T
Canon
Casio
Eastman Kodak
GEC
General
Dynamics
General Signal
Hitachi
Honeywell

Hyundai
Litton Industries
Minolta
Motorola
National
Semiconductor
NEC
Northrop
Grumman
Pitney Bowes
Raytheon
Rockwell
Sharp

Siemens
Smith Corona
Sony
Sun
Microsystems
Teledyne
Thomson SA
United
Stationers
Viking Office
Products
Xerox

HOW MUCH

	9-Year Growth	1985	1986	1987	1988	1989	1990	1991	1992	1993	1994
Sales ($ mil.)	4.3%	2,281	2,217	2,079	2,063	2,214	3,053	3,040	3,004	3,099	3,336
Net income ($ mil.)	4.8%	80	60	85	65	21	131	20	78	111	122
Income as % of sales	—	3.5%	2.7%	4.1%	3.2%	1.0%	4.3%	0.6%	2.6%	3.6%	3.7%
Earnings per share ($)	4.9%	2.00	1.48	2.05	1.63	0.55	3.30	0.50	2.00	2.82	3.07
Stock price – high ($)	—	35.00	36.88	42.75	33.25	39.50	36.13	28.88	35.50	47.38	52.25
Stock price – low ($)	—	22.25	25.50	22.00	24.25	26.38	13.75	18.25	26.63	33.63	37.75
Stock price – close ($)	5.1%	27.25	29.75	26.00	27.00	33.13	19.88	26.88	33.50	45.50	42.50
P/E – high	—	18	25	21	20	72	11	58	18	17	17
P/E – low	—	11	17	11	15	48	4	37	13	12	12
Dividends per share ($)	2.7%	0.88	0.88	0.88	0.88	0.88	0.96	1.04	1.04	1.04	1.12
Book value per share ($)	3.8%	21.56	22.37	23.64	24.94	24.45	27.02	26.45	27.30	28.82	30.23
Employees	(1.2%)	31,400	26,700	24,300	22,600	35,100	33,400	30,700	28,300	28,300	28,200

1994 Year-end:
Debt ratio: 36.5%
Return on equity: 10.5%
Cash (mil.): $139
Current ratio: 2.11
Long-term debt (mil.): $662
No. of shares (mil.): 39
Dividends
Yield: 2.6%
Payout: 36.5%
Market value (mil.): $1,670

**Stock Price History
High/Low 1985–94**

HASBRO, INC.

Hasbro is transforming its organization and purchasing more companies for its Park Place. Based in Pawtucket, Rhode Island, Hasbro is the #2 toy company in the US, with such popular toys and games as G.I. Joe, Play-Doh, Monopoly, and Trivial Pursuit.

Hasbro merged its 5 toy divisions — Playskool, Playskool Baby, Hasbro Toy, Kid Dimension, and Kenner — into a single Toy Group and its 2 game companies — Milton Bradley and Parker Brothers — into a Games Group. The purpose of the reorganization is to make the company more responsive to large retailers like Wal-Mart, Toys "R" Us, and Target and halve the product development cycle

from a year to 6 months. Hasbro has also purchased John Waddington, a British game maker, and the puzzle and board-game businesses of Western Publishing.

Hasbro is attempting to regain its #1 position in the toy industry from Mattel with a host of new toys based on movies, comic books, and TV shows, including *Batman Forever* and *The Mask*. (Licensing goods from the film and television industry resulted in nearly half of the $17 billion retail toy sales in 1994.) Hasbro will also introduce the interactive version of its Monopoly game in the fall of 1995. Monopoly CD-ROM will feature 3-D animation and will be accessible through the Internet.

WHEN

In 1923 Henry and Hillel Hassenfeld formed Hassenfeld Brothers in Pawtucket, Rhode Island, to distribute fabric remnants. By 1926 the company was manufacturing fabric-covered pencil boxes and shortly thereafter was making the pencils themselves.

Hassenfeld Brothers branched into the toy industry during the 1940s by introducing toy nurse and doctor kits. The company's toy division was the first to use TV to promote a toy product (Mr. Potato Head in 1952).

The company continued to expand both its toy and pencil businesses. In the mid-1960s the company introduced G.I. Joe (an action doll for boys), which quickly became its primary toy line. Hassenfeld Brothers went public in 1968 and changed its name to Hasbro Industries. In 1969 Hasbro bought Romper Room (TV productions).

In the 1970s the toy and pencil divisions, led by different family members, disagreed over the company's finances, future direction, and leadership. The dispute caused the company to split in 1980. The toy division continued to operate as the Hasbro name; the pencil division (Empire Pencil Corporation in Shelbyville, Tennessee), led by Harold Hassenfeld, became a separate corporation.

Hasbro expanded rapidly in the 1980s under new CEO Stephen Hassenfeld, one of the 3rd generation of family members to run the company. Hassenfeld reduced the number of products by 1/3 to concentrate on developing a stable line of toys aimed at specific markets. During the 1980s Hasbro released a number of successful toys, including a newer and smaller version of G.I. Joe (1982), My Little Pony (a horse with brushable hair, 1983), and Transformers (small vehicles that "transform" into

robots, 1984). In 1983 Hasbro acquired from Warner Bros. much of the inventory of Knickerbocker (plush toys). In 1984 the company bought Milton Bradley, a major producer of board games (Chutes and Ladders, Candy Land), puzzles, and preschool toys (Playskool). By the mid-1980s Hasbro had passed Mattel as the world's #1 toymaker. In 1989 the company acquired certain items from Coleco (which went bankrupt in 1988), including Cabbage Patch Kids, Scrabble, and Parcheesi. After Stephen Hassenfeld died in 1989, his brother Alan became CEO.

In 1991 Hasbro bought Tonka for $486 million. The company established operations in Greece, Mexico, and Hungary that same year. In 1992 it bought Japanese toymaker Nomura Toys and acquired majority interest in Asian toy distributor Palmyra. Also in 1992 Hasbro set a marketing precedent by purchasing all commercial time during a 14-hour Thanksgiving weekend cartoon marathon on 3 Turner Broadcasting System networks. Hasbro paid only about $1 million for more than 700 of the 30-second spots.

In April 1993 Hasbro settled a $175,000 deceptive advertising lawsuit with the FTC. Hasbro formed a joint venture with Connector Set Limited Partnership in 1994 to market its K'Nex construction toys outside the US. The company also established operations in Israel in the same year.

In 1995 Hasbro announced a licensing agreement with Viacom International's Nickelodeon cable network to develop toys under the Nickelodeon brand, including indoor-outdoor toys, Milton Bradley novelty toys, and foam sports equipment. The company also canceled its development work on virtual reality games.

ASE symbol: HAS
Fiscal year ends: Last Sunday in December

WHO

Chairman, President, and CEO: Alan G. Hassenfeld, age 46, $1,123,886 pay
VC: Barry J. Alperin, age 54, $516,150 pay
VC: Harold P. Gordon, age 57
COO, Games and International: George R. Ditomassi Jr., age 60, $661,238 pay
COO, Domestic Toy Operations: Alfred J. Verrecchia, age 52, $627,920 pay
EVP and CFO: John T. O'Neill, age 50, $472,205 pay
EVP; President, International: Norman C. Walker, age 56
President, Hasbro Toy Group: Dan D. Owen, age 46
President, Hasbro Games Group: E. David Wilson, age 57
SVP and Controller: Richard B. Holt, age 53
SVP, General Counsel, and Corporate Secretary: Donald M. Robbins, age 59
SVP Employee Relations: Sherry Turner
Auditors: KPMG Peat Marwick LLP

WHERE

HQ: 1027 Newport Ave., Pawtucket, RI 02861
Phone: 401-431-8697
Fax: 401-431-8535

Hasbro designs, manufactures, and markets toy products and related items throughout the world. The company has operations in 10 states and 25 foreign countries.

	1994 Sales		1994 Operating Income	
	$ mil.	% of total	$ mil.	% of total
US	1,531	57	170	57
Foreign	1,139	43	126	43
Total	**2,670**	**100**	**296**	**100**

WHAT

Selected Brand Names

Toys	Games and Puzzles
1-2-3 Baseball	Aggravation
1-2-3 Swing	Battleship
Baby All Gone	Big Ben Puzzles
Batman action figures	Boggle
Easy Bake Oven	Candy Land
Fantastic Flowers	Channel Surfing
Fantastic Sticker Maker	Chutes and Ladders
Fire Truck	Clue
G.I. Joe	Connect Four
Lincoln Logs	The Game of Life
Littlest Pet Shop	Hungry Hungry Hippos
Magic Smoking Grill	Jenga
Magic Tea Party	Lite-Brite
Mr. Potato Head	Monopoly
Musical Dream Screen	Mousetrap
Nerf	Operation
Play-Doh	Ouija
Raggedy Andy	Parcheesi
Ricochet vehicle	Pictionary
Sesame Street figures	Rack-O
Spirograph	Risk
Steady Steps walkers	Rook
Talking Alphie	Scrabble
Talking Barney	Sorry!
Techno Zoids	Trivial Pursuit
Tinkertoy	Trouble
Tonka trucks	Twister
Transformers	Yahtzee

KEY COMPETITORS

3DO	Lewis Galoob Toys	Rubbermaid
Acclaim	Mattel	SEGA
Entertainment	Monarch Avalon	SLM
Action Performance	Nest	International
Dakin	Entertainment	T-HQ
Equity Marketing	Nintendo	Toy Biz
EXX	Philips	Tyco Toys
Just Toys	Pleasant	

HOW MUCH

	9-Year Growth	1985	1986	1987	1988	1989	1990	1991	1992	1993	1994
Sales ($ mil.)	9.0%	1,233	1,330	1,345	1,358	1,410	1,520	2,141	2,541	2,747	2,670
Net income ($ mil.)	6.8%	99	99	48	72	92	89	82	179	200	179
Income as % of sales	—	8.0%	7.5%	3.6%	5.3%	6.5%	5.9%	3.8%	7.0%	7.3%	6.7%
Earnings per share ($)	6.0%	1.19	1.13	0.55	0.83	1.04	1.03	0.94	2.01	2.22	2.01
Stock price – high ($)	—	13.17	20.59	17.68	11.34	16.26	14.34	27.26	35.88	40.50	36.63
Stock price – low ($)	—	7.30	11.05	6.67	8.00	10.17	7.50	10.09	23.13	28.13	27.88
Stock price – close ($)	10.8%	11.59	13.01	8.84	10.42	12.51	10.42	27.01	32.63	36.25	29.13
P/E – high	—	11	18	32	14	16	14	29	18	18	18
P/E – low	—	6	10	12	10	10	7	11	12	13	14
Dividends per share ($)	20.6%	0.05	0.05	0.06	0.08	0.10	0.10	0.13	0.15	0.19	0.23	0.27
Book value per share ($)	13.0%	5.32	6.92	8.03	8.80	9.11	10.25	11.08	12.68	14.54	15.94
Employees	6.7%	7,000	7,800	8,300	8,200	8,200	7,700	10,500	11,000	12,500	12,500

1994 Year-end:
Debt ratio: 14.2%
Return on equity: 13.4%
Cash (mil.): $137
Current ratio: 1.64
Long-term debt (mil.): $150
No. of shares (mil.): 88
Dividends
  Yield: 0.9%
  Payout: 13.4%
Market value (mil.): $2,550

**Stock Price History
High/Low 1985–94**

THE HEARST CORPORATION

OVERVIEW

The Hearst Corporation's presence in newspapers, magazines, books, and broadcasting makes it one of the world's largest diversified media companies. Still controlled by descendants of William Randolph Hearst, the closely held, New York–based company owns 12 daily and 5 weekly newspapers (such as the *San Antonio Express-News* and *San Francisco Examiner*); 15 US consumer magazines (including *Popular Mechanics*, *Good Housekeeping*, and *Redbook*); stakes in 4 cable TV networks; 6 TV and 6 radio stations; and major book and business publishers.

Hearst intends to be a big wheel on the information autobahn. It opened a New Media Center to inspire staff and showcase advanced media. In 1995 it joined 8 other large newspaper companies to create New Century Network, a national on-line array of newspaper services still under development. Hearst is already selling magazine subscriptions, videos, and other products in cyberspace on the Multimedia Newsstand and plans to create on-line editions of 6 magazines and the *Houston Chronicle*. It bought stakes in Netscape Communications (Internet software developer) and KidSoft (educational software company).

Hearst's magazines, which supply almost half of the company's revenues, successfully launched *Marie Claire* in 1994. The company created a new unit to hunt for magazine ideas both inside and outside the company.

WHEN

William Randolph Hearst, son of a California mining magnate, started his empire as a reporter, having been expelled from Harvard in 1884 for playing jokes on professors. He became editor of the *San Francisco Examiner*, which his father had obtained as payment for a gambling debt, in 1887. Hearst's sensationalist style brought financial success to the paper. In 1895 he bought the *New York Morning Journal* and competed against the *New York World*, owned by Joseph Pulitzer, Hearst's first employer. The "yellow journalism" resulting from that rivalry characterized American journalism at the turn of the century. Hearst used his newspapers as a forum for his personal and political views for more than 30 years.

The company branched out into magazines (1903), film (1913), and radio (1928). The Hearst organization owned 13 newspapers and 7 magazines by 1920 and pioneered film journalism throughout the 1920s with the Hearst-Selig News Pictorial. In 1935 the company was at its peak, with newspapers in 19 cities (nearly 14% of total US daily and 24% of Sunday circulation), the largest syndicate (King Features), international news and photo services, 13 magazines, 8 radio stations, and 2 motion picture companies. Two years later Hearst had to relinquish control of the company to avoid bankruptcy. Movie companies, radio stations, magazines, and, later, most of his San Simeon estate were sold to reduce debt. Hearst inspired Orson Welles's 1941 film *Citizen Kane*

When Hearst died in 1951, Richard Berlin, in charge of the company since 1940, became CEO. During his tenure Berlin sold off failing newspapers but also moved into television and acquired more magazines. The Hearst family retained control through a family trust.

Frank Bennack Jr., president and CEO since 1979, expanded the company, acquiring daily and weekly newspapers (in Los Angeles, Houston, and Seattle, among other cities), publishing companies (notably William Morrow, 1981), 3 TV stations (in 1981, 1982, and 1986), magazines (*Redbook*, 1982; *Esquire*, 1986), and 20% of cable sports network ESPN (1991). Hearst branched into video via a joint venture with Capital Cities/ABC (1981) and helped launch the Lifetime and Arts & Entertainment cable channels (1984). It closed the Los Angeles *Herald Examiner* in 1989.

Hearst teamed up with *Izvestia* (1990) to start a newspaper in Russia and with Dow Jones (1992) to publish *SmartMoney*, a personal finance magazine. Also in 1992 Hearst closed the *Light* in San Antonio after buying its competitor, the *Express-News*, and launched a New England news network with Continental Cablevision. Hearst hired former FCC chairman Alfred Sikes, who quickly moved the company onto the information superhighway.

In 1993 Hearst joined with Canadian cable company Le Groupe Vidéotron to experiment in interactive TV; bought a stake in a California electronic publisher to put Hearst magazines on-line; and created an interactive home service (HomeArts). Hearst also bought other companies for their medical databases. That same year founder Hearst's son and namesake, who was chairman of the executive committee, died at age 85.

Hearst planned to launch a weekly magazine with ESPN in 1995 called *Total Sports*.

Private company
Fiscal year ends: December 31

WHO

Chairman: Randolph A. Hearst, age 80
President and CEO: Frank A. Bennack Jr., age 62
EVP and COO: Gilbert C. Maurer, age 66
SVP, CFO, and Chief Legal Officer: Victor F. Ganzi, age 47
VP; General Manager, Hearst Broadcasting: John G. Conomikes
VP; General Manager, Hearst Newspapers: Robert J. Danzig
VP; Group Head, Hearst New Media and Technology: Alfred C. Sikes, age 55
VP and General Counsel: Jon E. Thackeray
VP and Director Human Resources: Kenneth A. Feldman

WHERE

HQ: 959 Eighth Ave., New York, NY 10019
Phone: 212-649-2000
Fax: 212-765-3528 (corporate communications)

Hearst products are available throughout the US and in more than 80 countries.

WHAT

Selected Businesses

US Magazines

Colonial Homes	House Beautiful	Redbook
Cosmopolitan	Marie Claire	SmartMoney
Country Living	Motor Boating	Sports Afield
Esquire	& Sailing	Town &
Good Housekeeping	Popular	Country
Harper's Bazaar	Mechanics	Victoria

Broadcasting

KMBC-TV, Kansas City, MO	WISN-TV, Milwaukee
WBAL (AM) Baltimore	WIYY (FM), Baltimore
WBAL-TV, Baltimore	WLTQ (FM), Milwaukee
WCVA-TV, Boston	WTAE (AM), Pittsburgh
WDTN-TV, Dayton, OH	WTAE-TV, Pittsburgh
WISN (AM), Milwaukee	WVTY (FM), Pittsburgh

Book Publishing
Avon Books
William Morrow & Co.

Business Publishing
American Druggist
Black Book series (auto guides)
HDG International (UK partnership with R.R. Donnelley Co.)
Motor magazine
Official Guides to Walt Disney World/Disneyland
Retirement Advisors Inc.
United Technical Publications

Electronic Publishing
Camdat Corp. (medical information software)
First DataBank (drug database)
N-Squared Computing
Professional Drug Systems

Entertainment and Syndication
Arts & Entertainment Network (37.5%)
ESPN (20%)
Hearst/ABC Video Services (joint venture)
Hearst Entertainment Distribution
Hearst Entertainment Productions

KEY COMPETITORS

Advance Publications	Enquirer/ Star Group	News Corp.
Bertelsmann	E.W. Scripps	Reader's Digest
Bloomberg	Gannett	Reed Elsevier
Capital Cities/ABC	Heritage Media	Time Warner
CBS	Lagardère	Times Mirror
Chronicle Publishing	McGraw-Hill	Tribune
Cox	MediaNews	Viacom
	New York Times	Washington Post

King Features Syndicate
Lifetime Television (50%)
New England Cable News (joint venture)
North America Syndicate

New Media/Technology
Books That Work (minority stake)
Hearst Interactive Canada
Hearst Multimedia Publishing
Hearst New Media Center
HomeArts (on-line home and garden information)
KidSoft, Inc. (29%)
Netscape Communications (minority stake)
New Century Network
UBI (interactive TV, with Le Groupe Vidéotron and 4 others, Canada)

Newspapers (Major)
Albany (NY) Times Union
Houston Chronicle
San Antonio Express-News
San Francisco Examiner
Seattle Post-Intelligencer

Other
Associated Publishing Co. (telephone directories)
Hearst Broadcasting Productions
Hearst Magazines Enterprises

HOW MUCH

	Annual Growth	1985	1986	1987	1988	1989	1990	1991	1992	1993	1994
Sales ($ mil.)	4.6%	1,540	1,529	1,886	1,986	2,094	2,138	1,888	1,973	2,174	2,299
Newspaper revenues ($ mil.)	8.9%	—	390	650	689	700	715	680	701	720	770
Magazine revenues ($ mil.)	5.9%	—	780	873	919	992	1,022	1,002	1,062	1,200	1,236
Broadcast revenues ($ mil.)	0.5%	—	280	262	263	270	290	206	210	254	292
Cable TV revenues ($ mil.)	—	—	9	11	15	21	—	—	—	—	—
Other revenues ($ mil.)	—	—	70	90	100	111	111	—	—	—	—
Employees	1.7%	12,000	12,000	15,000	15,000	14,000	13,950	14,000	13,000	13,500	14,000

The Hearst Corporation

Sales ($ mil.)
1985–94

HERCULES INCORPORATED

OVERVIEW

Hercules rocketed into 1995 with the sale of its aerospace business (which makes solid rocket motor systems, and which accounted for 26% of 1994 sales) to Alliant Techsystems for $440 million in cash and stock. The deal gave Hercules a 30% ownership of Alliant. The aerospace unit sale was the biggest of a series of divestitures made in recent years by Hercules in order to focus on its core chemicals and drug businesses. The company is a worldwide supplier of specialty chemicals, including chemicals used in the papermaking industry; polypropylene fibers used in hygiene products, home furnishings, and automobiles; and resins used in rubber and plastics fabrication,

adhesives, and inks. Hercules manufactures water-soluble polymers and additives used in everything from paints to beverages, and it also makes food gums and aroma chemicals. Tastemaker, Hercules' joint venture with IMCERA, and the world's 5th largest flavor company, makes flavorings for beverages, sweet goods, and oils.

Hercules is pursuing a policy of international expansion. In 1994 the firm announced plans to build a polypropylene fiber plant in Mexico (scheduled to open in 1996) to supply customers in Central and South America. That year it also began production at a $76 million methylcellulose plant in Belgium.

WHEN

A 1912 federal court decision forced DuPont, which controlled 2/3 of US explosives production, to spin off half the business into 2 companies, Hercules Powder and Atlas Powder.

Hercules began operating explosives plants across the US in 1913. Russell Dunham, Hercules' first president, had expanded the company's operations by 1915 into Utah and Missouri. During WWI the company became the largest US producer of TNT, making 71 million pounds for the US military. After WWI Hercules diversified into nonexplosive products, such as nitrocellulose for the manufacture of plastics, lacquers, and films. The 1920 purchase of Yaryan Rosin and Turpentine made Hercules the world's largest producer of steam-distilled rosin and turpentine.

By the late 1920s the company's core business had changed from powders to chemicals, which would be its focus for the next 3 decades. Hercules expanded the marketing of its rosin products to dozens of industries, including the paper industry, the largest user. Hercules also became the largest US producer of nitrocellulose in 1930. In the 1940s the company developed water-soluble polymers.

In the early 1950s Hercules developed a new process for making phenol, used in plastics, paints, and pharmaceuticals. The company's explosives department made important contributions in rocketry, developing propellants for Nike rockets and making motors for Minuteman and Polaris missiles.

By the late 1950s Hercules was making chemical propellants, petrochemical plastics, synthetic fibers, agricultural and paper chemicals, and food additives. In the 1960s and early 1970s, the company, renamed Hercules Inc. in 1966, increased plastic resin and fabricated

plastic production, opening 5 new manufacturing plants.

Hercules also developed foreign markets, doubling export sales between 1962 and 1972. Following the energy crisis of the 1970s, CEO Alexander Giacco decided to reduce dependence on commodity petrochemicals and to expand specialty chemical and defense-related rocket propulsion businesses. In 1987 it sold its interest in the polypropylene resins business (HIMONT) and in 1989 took full ownership of The Aqualon Group, which since 1987 had been a 50-50 joint venture with Germany's Henkel.

In 1989 Hercules had a $96 million loss, taking a $323 million charge to cover cost overruns on Titan IV, Delta II, and SRAM missile contracts. The 1991 explosion of the Titan IV during a test firing led to a suit against development partner Martin Marietta. The suit was dropped in 1993 when the US Air Force and Martin Marietta agreed to reimburse Hercules for its program investments and development costs. Also in 1991 the company sold its Semi-Gas Systems unit and its interests in Orbital Sciences; Devron-Hercules; Texas Alkyls; and Petrocel, SA.

In 1993 Hercules formed a subsidiary, Global Environmental Solutions, to handle the disposal and cleanup of weapons stockpiles. The company completed the divestiture of its Packaging Films and Liquid Molding Resins business units in 1994.

The Vietnam War continues to haunt Hercules. In 1995 the firm appealed to the Supreme Court for government reimbursement of payments made to Vietnam veterans who sued the firm over health problems caused by the Agent Orange defoliant it had produced.

NYSE symbol: HPC
Fiscal year ends: December 31

WHO

Chairman, President, and CEO: Thomas L. Gossage, age 60, $1,502,340 pay
EVP and CFO: R. Keith Elliott, age 53, $744,846 pay
SVP Technology: Vincent J. Corbo, age 51, $502,754 pay (prior to promotion)
Group VP; President, Hercules Chemical Specialties Company: C. Doyle Miller, age 54, $470,496 pay
Group VP; President, Hercules Food & Functional Products Company: Robert J. A. Fraser, age 45
President, Hercules Europe: Herbert K. Pattberg, age 51
VP and General Counsel: Michael B. Keehan, age 59
VP Finance: George MacKenzie, age 45
VP Human Resources: Edward V. Carrington, age 52
Controller: Vikram Jog, age 38
Treasurer: Jan M. King, age 45
Secretary: Israel J. Floyd, age 48
Auditors: Coopers & Lybrand L.L.P.

WHERE

HQ: Hercules Plaza, 1313 N. Market St., Wilmington, DE 19894-0001
Phone: 302-594-5000
Fax: 302-594-5400

Hercules' subsidiaries and/or affiliated companies have major plants in 18 countries.

	1994 Sales		1994 Operating Income	
	$ mil.	% of total	$ mil.	% of total
US	1,921	68	250	60
Europe	709	25	145	35
Other regions	191	7	24	5
Total	**2,821**	**100**	**419**	**100**

WHAT

	1994 Sales		1994 Operating Income	
	$ mil.	% of total	$ mil.	% of total
Chemical specialties	1,081	38	197	45
Food & functional products	945	34	148	33
Aerospace	743	26	98	22
Other	52	2	(24)	—
Total	**2,821**	**100**	**419**	**100**

Chemical Specialties
Fibers (polypropylene nonwoven fibers and polypropylene textile yarns)
Paper technology (defoamers, retention aids, and wax emulsions)
Resins (rosin resins, hydrocarbon resins, and peroxides)

Food and Functional Products
Aqualon (ethylcellulose, nitrocellulose, methylcellulose, and other celluloses)
Electronics and printing products (photopolymer resins for the printing and publishing markets)
Food gums (food gums and aroma chemicals for processed foods and beverages)

Joint Venture
Tastemaker (flavorings, with IMCERA)

KEY COMPETITORS

BASF	Imperial Chemical
Bayer	Monsanto
British Petroleum	Novo Nordisk
Chemfab	Procter & Gamble
Dow Chemical	Rhône-Poulenc
DuPont	Roche
Eastman Chemical	Union Carbide
Elf Aquitaine	Vulcan Materials
Hoechst	W. R. Grace
IFF	Wrigley

HOW MUCH

	9-Year Growth	1985	1986	1987	1988	1989	1990	1991	1992	1993	1994
Sales ($ mil.)	1.0%	2,587	2,615	2,693	2,802	3,092	3,200	2,929	2,865	2,773	2,821
Net income ($ mil.)	8.4%	133	227	821	120	(96)	96	95	168	205	274
Income as % of sales	—	5.1%	8.7%	30.5%	4.3%	—	3.0%	3.2%	5.9%	7.5%	9.7%
Earnings per share ($)	12.4%	0.80	1.34	4.91	0.85	(0.70)	0.68	0.67	1.23	1.62	2.29
Stock price – high ($)	—	13.58	20.00	24.50	18.00	17.42	13.83	16.79	21.25	38.29	40.50
Stock price – low ($)	—	10.38	12.33	13.33	14.21	12.79	8.54	10.58	14.88	21.08	32.13
Stock price – close ($)	12.7%	13.13	16.88	15.67	14.83	13.00	11.21	16.75	21.17	37.83	38.46
P/E – high	—	17	15	5	21	—	20	25	17	24	18
P/E – low	—	13	9	3	17	—	13	16	12	13	14
Dividends per share ($)	3.9%	0.53	0.57	0.61	0.67	0.75	0.75	0.75	0.75	0.75	0.75
Book value per share ($)	2.3%	9.04	10.37	14.96	14.86	13.59	13.78	13.70	13.38	11.17	11.10
Employees	(8.0%)	25,448	25,120	23,152	22,718	23,290	19,867	17,324	15,419	14,083	11,989

1994 Year-end:
Debt ratio: 27.7%
Return on equity: 42.4%
Cash (mil.): $112
Current ratio: 1.50
Long-term debt (mil.): $307
No. of shares (mil.): 117
Dividends
  Yield: 2.0%
  Payout: 32.8%
Market value (mil.): $4,486

**Stock Price History
High/Low 1985–94**

HERSHEY FOODS CORPORATION

OVERVIEW

How sweet it is! Catering to a country of chocoholics, the 100-year-old Hershey Foods is steadily outpacing #2 confectioner Mars in the candy market. In 1994 the company held a 34.5% market share (compared to Mars's 26.0%).

But Hershey is more than Hugs, Kisses, and a cornucopia of other chocolate delights. The company is the #1 retail dry pasta maker in the US; it is a leading nonchocolate confectioner in Italy; and it operates other confectionery businesses in Germany, Belgium, Japan, and the Netherlands.

In 1994 Hershey organized a grocery division to help market the company's full line of chocolate and chocolate-related baking products, ice cream toppings, peanut butter, milk products, and other grocery items. The company's syrup and cocoa lines are #1 in their respective fields.

Product innovation is a key part of Hershey's sales strategy. New products such as Reese's NutRageous bar, Hershey's Nuggets chocolates, and Twizzlers Pull-n-Peel were big sellers in 1994.

Hershey (41.6%-owned by the Hershey Trust) is planning to expand into emerging markets, such as Latin America and China, via acquisitions, joint ventures, or new factories. Buoyed by the popularity of American products, Hershey's sales in Russia have been strong in recent months. By contrast, Hershey's Canadian business has struggled, due in part to overcapacity.

WHEN

Hershey is the legacy of Milton Hershey, of Pennsylvania Dutch origin. Apprenticed in 1872 at age 15 to a candy maker, Hershey started Lancaster Caramel Company at age 30. In 1893 at the Chicago Exposition, he saw a new chocolate-making machine, and in 1900 he sold the caramel operations for $1 million to start a chocolate factory.

The factory was completed in 1905 in Derry Church, Pennsylvania, renamed Hershey in 1906. In 1909 the candy man founded the Milton Hershey School, an orphanage; in 1918 the company was donated to a trust and for years existed solely to fund the school. Although the company is now publicly traded, the school still controls the majority of shareholder votes. Former chairman William Dearden (1976–84) was a Hershey School graduate, as are many Hershey employees.

Concerned more with benevolence than profits, Hershey put people to work during the Depression building a hotel, golf courses, a library, theaters, a museum, a stadium, and other facilities in Hershey.

Hershey pioneered mass-production techniques for chocolates and developed much of the machinery for making and packaging its own products. At one time the company supplied its own sugar cane from Cuba and enlarged the world's almond supply sixfold through nut farm ownership. The Hershey bar became so universally familiar that it was used overseas during WWII as currency.

Hershey had refused to advertise, believing that quality would speak for itself. Even after Hershey's death in 1945, the company contin-

ued his policy. Then, in 1970, facing a sluggish candy market and a diet-conscious public, Hershey lost share to Mars, and management relented.

In the 1970s Hershey diversified in order to stabilize the effects of changing commodity prices. It brought out Big Block (large-sized) bars (1980), bought the Friendly Ice Cream chain (1979, sold in 1988), and ventured into pasta. The company expanded candy operations by buying Cadbury's US candy business (Peter Paul, Cadbury, Caramello; 1988).

In 1990 Hershey formed a joint venture with Fujiya (Tokyo) to distribute Hershey products in Japan and bought Ronzoni's pasta, cheese, and sauce operations. In 1991 Hershey bought its first European manufacturing facility (Gubor Schokoladen, Germany) and then bought its partner's shares of Nacional de Dulces, a Mexican candy maker.

Hershey netted $80 million in 1993 from selling its 18.6% interest in Freia Marabou after being outbid by Philip Morris for the Scandinavian chocolate maker. That same year Hershey introduced Hugs, a white-and-dark chocolate product shaped like Hershey's Kisses. In 1994 the firm conducted a major review of its domestic and international operations as the first step in a restructuring program to reduce costs and improve efficiency.

In a unique combination of telecommunications and chocolate marketing, MCI teamed up with Hershey in 1995 to offer free long-distance calling to consumers who buy an 8-ounce or larger bag of Hershey's Kisses, Hershey's Hugs, or other chocolate products.

NYSE symbol: HSY
Fiscal year ends: December 31

WHO

Chairman and CEO: Kenneth L. Wolfe, age 56, $896,500 pay
President and COO: Joseph P. Viviano, age 56, $678,325 pay
President, Hershey Chocolate North America: Michael F. Pasquale, age 47, $465,378 pay
SVP and CFO: William F. Christ, age 54, $366,000 pay
President, Hershey International: Jay F. Carr, age 50, $293,608 pay
General Manager, Hershey Grocery: Dennis N. Eshleman, age 40
President, Hershey Pasta Group: C. Mickey Skinner, age 61
VP Science and Technology: Barry L. Zoumas, age 52
VP Research and Development: Charles L. Duncan, age 55
VP and General Counsel: Robert M. Reese, age 45
VP and Treasurer: Thomas C. Fitzgerald, age 55
VP Human Resources: Sharon A. Lambly, age 54
Auditors: Arthur Andersen & Co, SC

WHERE

HQ: 100 Crystal A Dr., Hershey, PA 17033
Phone: 717-534-6799
Fax: 717-534-4078

Hershey Foods's main candy-making facilities are located in Hershey and Lancaster, Pennsylvania; Oakdale, California; Stuarts Draft, Virginia; and Smiths Falls, Ontario.

	1994 Sales		1994 Operating Income	
	$ mil.	% of total	$ mil.	% of total
US	3,124	87	446	—
Other countries	482	13	(78)	—
Total	**3,606**	**100**	**368**	**—**

WHAT

Selected Confections and Foods

5th Avenue	Oh Henry!
Amazin' Fruit	Peter Paul Almond Joy
Bar None	Peter Paul Mounds
Cadbury's Creme Eggs	Pot of Gold boxed
Caramello	chocolates
Cookies 'n' Mint	Reese's NutRageous
Golden Almond	Reese's peanut butter cups
Hershey's Kisses	Reese's Pieces
Hershey's Kisses With	Rolo
Almonds	Skor
Hershey's milk	Twizzlers Pull-n-Peel
chocolate bars	Whatchamacallit
Hershey's milk	York peppermint patties
chocolate bars with	
almonds	**Pasta**
Hershey's Miniatures	American Beauty
Hershey's Nuggets	Light 'N Fluffy
Hugs	P&R
Kit Kat	Ronzoni
Mr. Goodbar	San Giorgio
	Skinner

KEY COMPETITORS

ADM	Luchetti
Anheuser-Busch	Mars
Barilla	Monterey Pasta
Berkshire Hathaway	Nestlé
Borden	Pacific Dunlop
Brock Candy	PepsiCo
Cadbury Schweppes	PET
Campbell Soup	Philip Morris
ConAgra	Procter & Gamble
CPC	Quaker Oats
Danone	Ralcorp
Del Monte	RJR Nabisco
General Mills	Tekfen Holding
George Weston	Tootsie Roll
Heinz	World's Finest Chocolate
Kellogg	Wrigley

HOW MUCH

	9-Year Growth	1985	1986	1987	1988	1989	1990	1991	1992	1993	1994
Sales ($ mil.)	6.8%	1,996	2,170	2,434	2,168	2,421	2,716	2,899	3,220	3,488	3,606
Net income ($ mil.)	5.7%	112	133	148	214	171	216	220	243	297	184
Income as % of sales	—	5.6%	6.1%	6.1%	9.9%	7.1%	8.0%	7.6%	7.5%	8.5%	5.1%
Earnings per share ($)	6.6%	1.19	1.42	1.64	2.37	1.90	2.39	2.43	2.69	3.31	2.12
Stock price – high ($)	—	18.31	29.88	37.75	28.63	36.88	39.63	44.50	48.38	55.88	53.50
Stock price – low ($)	—	11.66	15.50	20.75	21.88	24.75	28.25	35.13	38.25	43.50	41.13
Stock price – close ($)	12.2%	17.16	24.63	24.50	26.00	35.88	37.50	44.38	47.00	49.00	48.38
P/E – high	—	15	21	23	12	19	17	18	18	17	25
P/E – low	—	10	11	13	9	13	12	15	14	13	19
Dividends per share ($)	11.2%	0.48	0.52	0.58	0.66	0.74	0.99	0.94	1.03	1.14	1.25
Book value per share ($)	8.9%	7.73	8.07	9.23	11.15	12.39	13.79	14.81	16.25	16.12	16.61
Employees	4.6%	10,380	10,210	10,540	12,100	11,800	12,700	14,000	13,700	14,300	15,600

1994 Year-end:
Debt ratio: 25.1%
Return on equity: 12.9%
Cash (mil.): $27
Current ratio: 1.19
Long-term debt (mil.): $157
No. of shares (mil.): 87
Dividends
  Yield: 2.6%
  Payout: 59.0%
Market value (mil.): $4,196

Stock Price History High/Low 1985–94

HEWLETT-PACKARD COMPANY

OVERVIEW

Hewlett-Packard (HP), already a force in office computing and computer printing, launched its blitz on the home computing market in 1994 with a series of competitively priced, multimedia, Pentium-based PCs.

To grab a share of the home PC market, HP is giving its computers bright colors, sporty lines, and minimal setup times. The company is courting retailer enthusiasm and reducing inventory costs with a new system that manufactures computers to order.

Commercial customers currently make up the core of HP's computer sales — about 1.2 million units in 1994. In 1995 the company formed a financial services unit to supply computer systems to banks, stock brokerages, and other financial institutions. The US government is also a major customer, with about $200 million in purchases expected in 1995.

HP spends about 8% of revenues on R&D and is also a leader in medical and test-and-measurement technology. In 1994 the company introduced its CareVue computerized medical information system and an advanced quality measurement system for the new digital cellular communications standard.

Dave Packard and Bill Hewlett still own nearly 22% of HP.

WHEN

In 1938, 2 Stanford engineers, Bill Hewlett and Dave Packard, encouraged by their professor, Frederick Terman (considered the founder of Silicon Valley), started Hewlett-Packard out of a garage in Palo Alto, California, with $538. Their first product was an audio oscillator. One of HP's first customers was Walt Disney Studios, which bought 8 oscillators to use in the making of *Fantasia*.

Demand for HP's electronic testing equipment during WWII spurred revenue growth from $34,000 (1940) to near $1 million (1943). HP expanded 50–100% each year during the 1950s and opened up European subsidiaries. HP entered the medical field in 1961 by acquiring Sanborn Company, and it entered the analytical instrumentation business in 1965 with the acquisition of F&M Scientific.

In 1972 HP pioneered personal computing with the world's first hand-held scientific calculator (HP-35) and launched the HP 3000 for business computing. By the late 1970s computers accounted for half of HP's sales.

Under the leadership of John Young, the founders' chosen successor (president in 1977, CEO in 1978), HP introduced personal computers (HP-85, 1980; HP Vectra PC, 1985), the first desktop mainframe (HP 9000, 1982), and the LaserJet printer.

Young's 5-year, $250-million open-systems effort (starting in the early 1980s) produced in 1986 a high-performance RISC-based Spectrum line able to run the UNIX operating system. HP licensed its RISC chip to Hitachi and Samsung to increase the availability of Spectrum applications. Hewlett retired in 1987.

HP became a leader in the workstation market with the 1989 purchase of workstation pioneer Apollo Computers for $500 million. Differences in technologies, however, caused problems in integrating the 2 product lines and delayed HP's workstation development. The company's other introductions included *NewWave* software to boost office productivity; the advanced HP 3000 line, which launched HP into mainframe power; and the HP 95LX palmtop PC — a computer the size of a checkbook.

In 1991 HP bought microwave-component manufacturer Avantek. The next year HP took a 5% interest in Convex Computer; as part of the deal, Convex agreed to use HP's RISC technology in its supercomputers. Also in 1992 HP started a joint venture with Sweden's LM Ericsson to develop telecommunications network management systems and announced plans to produce devices enabling TV access to certain services (e.g., home banking). In addition, HP bought Texas Instruments's line of UNIX-based computers.

In 1993 HP cut 2,400 jobs and introduced one of the first personal communicators, the pocket-sized HP 100LX — a PC that can send and receive messages. Also in 1993 HP passed the 10-million sales mark for its DeskJet printer line, converted its entire line of popular laser printers to LaserJet 4 models, and transformed its microwave component division into a video technology shop. That same year HP, AT&T, and Citizen Watch teamed up to make a 1.3" disk drive.

In 1994 HP formed a product development and marketing alliance with Lotus. That same year the company paid about $50 million for a 15% stake in Taligent, an IBM-Apple joint venture to develop a computer operating system that uses object-oriented technology.

In 1995 HP beat out rivals Hughes and DEC for the contract to build a $1.3 billion Tactical Advanced Computer for the US Navy.

NYSE symbol: HWP
Fiscal year ends: October 31

WHO

Chairman, President, and CEO: Lewis E. Platt, age 53, $1,179,388 pay
EVP Finance and Administration and CFO: Robert P. Wayman, age 49, $685,509 pay
SVP and General Manager, Computer Systems Organization: Willem P. Roelandts, age 49, $517,848 pay
SVP and General Manager, Worldwide Customer Support Operations: James L. Arthur
SVP Research and Development: Joel S. Birnbaum, age 57, $498,225 pay
SVP and General Manager, Test and Measurement Organization: Edward W. Barnholt, age 51, $479,890 pay
VP and General Manager, Microwave and Communications Group: Richard W. Anderson
VP Corporate Affairs and General Counsel: S. T. Jack Brigham III, age 55
VP Personnel: F. E. (Pete) Peterson, age 53
Auditors: Price Waterhouse LLP

WHERE

HQ: 3000 Hanover St., Palo Alto, CA 94304
Phone: 415-857-1501
Fax: 415-857-7299

Hewlett-Packard operates facilities in 9 states, Puerto Rico, and 16 countries and has 600 sales and support offices in more than 120 countries.

	1994 Sales		1994 Operating Income	
	$ mil.	% of total	$ mil.	% of total
US	11,469	46	1,472	50
Europe	8,423	34	660	22
Other countries	5,099	20	824	28
Adjustments	—	—	(407)	—
Total	**24,991**	**100**	**2,459**	**100**

WHAT

	1994 Sales	
	$ mil.	% of total
Computers, service & support	19,632	78
Electronic test & measurement equip.	2,722	11
Medical electronics & service	1,141	5
Analytical instrumentation & service	754	3
Electronic components	742	3
Total	**24,991**	**100**

Selected Products

Computer Products
Calculators
Desktop computers
Disk and tape drives
Laptops
Networking products
Printers and plotters
Scanners
Workstations

Computer Services
Data management
Distributed systems
Networks
Software programming

Electronic Test Equipment
Oscilloscopes
Signal generators
Voltmeters

Medical Electronics
Hospital supplies
Software

Analytical Instrumentation
Chromatographs
Mass spectrometers
Spectrophotometers

Electronic Components
Optoelectronic devices
Video servers

KEY COMPETITORS

Apple
AST
AT&T
Becton, Dickinson
Cabletron
Casio
Compaq
CompuAdd
C. R. Bard
Data General
DEC
Dell

Fisher Scientific
Gateway 2000
IBM
Intel
Iomega
LG Group
Machines Bull
NEC
Oki
Olivetti
Philips
Power Computing

Radius
Samsung
Sharp
Silicon Graphics
Sony
Sun Microsystems
SyQuest
Tandem
Texas Instruments
Unisys

HOW MUCH

	9-Year Growth	1985	1986	1987	1988	1989	1990	1991	1992	1993	1994
Sales ($ mil.)	16.1%	6,505	7,102	8,090	9,831	11,899	13,233	14,494	16,410	20,317	24,991
Net income ($ mil.)	14.1%	489	516	644	816	829	739	755	881	1,177	1,599
Income as % of sales	—	7.5%	7.3%	8.0%	8.3%	7.0%	5.6%	5.2%	5.4%	5.8%	6.4%
Earnings per share ($)	13.9%	1.91	2.02	2.50	3.36	3.52	3.06	3.02	3.49	4.65	6.14
Stock price – high ($)	—	38.88	49.63	73.63	65.50	61.50	50.38	57.38	85.00	89.25	102.50
Stock price – low ($)	—	28.75	35.75	35.75	43.75	40.25	24.88	29.88	50.25	64.38	71.88
Stock price – close ($)	11.7%	36.75	41.88	58.25	53.25	47.25	31.88	57.00	69.88	79.00	99.88
P/E – high	—	20	25	30	20	18	17	19	24	19	17
P/E – low	—	15	18	14	13	11	8	10	14	14	12
Dividends per share ($)	19.6%	0.22	0.22	0.23	0.28	0.36	0.42	0.48	0.73	0.90	1.10
Book value per share ($)	10.8%	15.50	17.08	20.02	19.35	22.92	26.07	28.90	29.90	33.68	38.95
Employees	1.8%	84,000	82,000	82,000	87,000	95,000	92,000	89,000	92,600	96,200	98,400

1994 Year-end:
Debt ratio: 23.3%
Return on equity: 17.3%
Cash (mil.): $2,478
Current ratio: 1.52
Long-term debt (mil.): $547
No. of shares (mil.): 255
Dividends
 Yield: 1.1%
 Payout: 17.9%
Market value (mil.): $25,452

Stock Price History
High/Low 1985–94

H.F. AHMANSON & COMPANY

OVERVIEW

H.F. Ahmanson of Irwindale, California, has resolved never to let history repeat itself. Stung by a 1993 loss (due primarily to the sale of over $1.2 billion in nonperforming single-family home loans), the company has decided that the remedy is diversifying its income sources and refining its geographical focus.

Ahmanson's Home Savings of America is the US's largest savings institution and one of the largest mortgage lenders and servicers. The company hopes to add significantly to its nonmortgage income by offering home equity and consumer loans and by increasing sales of

investment products and insurance offered by its Griffin Financial Services subsidiary.

The company will use its mortgage operations to help sell its new products via targeted mailings. It will also sell its financial products through its existing branch network and in independent consumer loan offices.

In 1995 Ahmanson applied to switch some of its thrifts from federally chartered savings associations to state-chartered banks because the fund that insures savings banks charges much lower premiums than the one that insures savings associations.

WHEN

By 1889, when Walter Bonynge organized Home Investment Building and Loan (a type of S&L) in Los Angeles, he already had made a fortune in silver in Nevada and started a fire insurance company in San Antonio. By the early 1900s the company had several locations in Los Angeles. The company became Home Building and Loan Association in 1922. Bonynge remained active in the company until his death in 1924.

In 1947 Howard Ahmanson, a Los Angeles insurance man, bought the company, which then became a subsidiary of H.F. Ahmanson & Co. (founded in 1928). In 1950 Home Building purchased Long Beach Savings and Loan, with offices in Long Beach and Huntington Park. The company changed its name to Home Savings and Loan Association in 1951 and opened a Beverly Hills branch in 1953. Home Savings rode the postwar California boom, and by the end of the decade, the $700 million institution led the S&L industry in assets, deposits, customer base, and mortgage lending. In 1961 Home Savings became the first S&L with assets of $1 billion. Ahmanson remained the company chairman until the late 1960s, and family members, as trustees of the Ahmanson Foundation, are still members of the company's board of directors.

Despite the economic upheavals of the 1970s, which included oil shortages and price rises and rampant inflation, Home Savings flourished, growing to over 100 offices throughout California. Assets were $12 billion by 1980, compared with $2 billion in 1967. It got over the interest rate squeeze of the 1970s by pioneering adjustable rate mortgages and sticking to its core business of residential mortgages, rather than diversifying as many other S&Ls had done. In the 1980s Home Savings continued this strategy by adding new

services, including interest-bearing checking accounts, check guarantee cards, and overdraft protection.

When regulators approved interstate expansion, Home Savings, in a 4-week period in late 1981, moved into Florida, Missouri, Texas, and Illinois. It became Home Savings of America and expanded into New York (1984), Arizona (1985), and Washington (1985). In 1988 Home Savings bought the Bowery Savings Bank.

Ahmanson's annual net income hovered around $200 million in the late 1980s, when many S&Ls were troubled by overexpansion and risky loans. In 1988 the company ceased making commercial real estate loans and began tightening its underwriting practices.

In the early 1990s Ahmanson began an acquisitions spree, acquiring more branches in California as well as banks in New York. In 1991 it moved its headquarters to Irwindale.

By 1993 the recession had caught up with Ahmanson. Besides making a bulk sale of bad loans, it hired a company to help manage its remaining properties. Ahmanson also withdrew from Missouri and Washington in order to concentrate on California, Texas, and New York. Although loan activities were up in 1993, most were due to refinancings because of low interest rates. The company lost business when some ARM mortgage holders refinanced at other banks. The company also began a skip-a-payment program to help its customers through hard times.

Ahmanson's geographical contraction continued in 1994 and 1995, as it announced its plans to concentrate its retail efforts on Texas, Florida, and California. Concurrently it increased its presence in California with the purchase of 53 new branches in 1994 and the acquisition of Household Bank's 52 California branches in 1995.

WHO

Chairman and CEO: Charles R. Rinehart, age 48,
$1,292,446 pay
President and COO: Frederic J. Forster, age 50,
$739,004 pay (prior to promotion)
SEVP and CFO: Kevin M. Twomey, age 48, $535,703 pay
EVP, General Counsel, and Secretary: George G.
Gregory, age 62, $474,316 pay
EVP and Treasurer: Anne-Drue M. Anderson, age 34
First VP and Principal Accounting Officer: George
Miranda, age 47, $292,919 pay
First VP Operations and Controller: Robert L. Stevens
First VP Human Resources: Merrill S. Wall
SVP Investor Relations: Stephen A. Swartz
SVP Public Relations: Mary A. Trigg
SVP and Assistant General Counsel: Tim S. Glassett
SVP Taxes: Linda L. McCall
Auditors: KPMG Peat Marwick LLP

WHERE

HQ: 4900 Rivergrade Rd., Irwindale, CA 91706
Phone: 818-960-6311
Fax: 818-814-3675

H.F. Ahmanson has 357 retail banking offices in 6 states
and 82 loan offices in 12 states.

	1994 Retail Deposits	
	$ mil.	% of total
California	25,133	62
New York	8,195	20
Florida	4,360	11
Texas	2,713	7
Other states	254	0
Total	**40,655**	**100**

WHAT

	1994 Assets	
	$ mil.	% of total
Cash & equivalents	2,047	4
Mortgage-backed securities	12,789	24
FHLB stock	440	1
Net loans	36,002	67
Real estate	475	1
Other	1,973	3
Total	**53,726**	**100**

	1994 Sales	
	$ mil.	% of total
Real estate loan interest	2,265	67
Other interest	830	24
Loan servicing & other fees	185	5
Loan sale losses	(21)	—
Other	122	4
Total	**3,381**	**100**

Financial Services
Annuities
Consumer deposit
  accounts
Consumer loans
Home equity loans
Life insurance
Mortgage loan servicing
Mortgage loans

Mutual funds
Property/casualty insurance
Secondary mortgage loan
  sales

Subsidiaries
Griffin Financial Services
Home Savings of America,
  FSB

KEY COMPETITORS

Banc One
BankAmerica
Barnett Banks
Berkshire Hathaway
California Federal
Chase Manhattan
Chemical Banking
Citicorp

Club Corp.
Countrywide
  Credit
First Chicago
First Interstate
Fleet
Great Western

Golden West
  Financial
Glendale Federal
Mellon Bank
NationsBank
PNC Bank
SunTrust
Wells Fargo

HOW MUCH

	9-Year Growth	1985	1986	1987	1988	1989	1990	1991	1992	1993	1994
Assets ($ mil.)	7.8%	27,229	27,592	30,507	40,258	44,652	51,201	47,226	48,141	50,871	53,726
Net income ($ mil.)	0.8%	221	304	200	203	194	191	246	156	(138)	237
Income as % of assets	—	0.8%	1.1%	0.7%	0.5%	0.4%	0.4%	0.5%	0.3%	—	0.4%
Earnings per share ($)	(5.5%)	2.63	3.22	2.03	2.05	1.95	1.64	2.06	1.19	(1.51)	1.58
Stock price – high ($)	—	16.31	28.75	26.88	18.63	25.00	22.50	20.88	19.50	22.13	22.75
Stock price – low ($)	—	8.13	15.78	13.00	13.75	15.75	10.63	12.00	13.00	16.75	15.25
Stock price – close ($)	(0.1%)	16.31	21.63	16.50	16.38	19.00	13.50	17.38	19.25	19.63	16.13
P/E – high	—	6	9	13	9	13	14	10	16	—	14
P/E – low	—	3	5	6	7	8	7	6	11	—	10
Dividends per share ($)	9.2%	0.40	0.45	0.88	0.88	0.88	0.88	0.88	0.88	0.88	0.88
Book value per share ($)	7.3%	13.42	17.14	18.28	19.11	20.22	20.20	22.85	23.54	25.23	25.31
Employees	1.6%	8,580	9,150	10,500	11,600	10,819	10,879	10,292	10,318	10,479	9,859

1994 Year-end:
Return on equity: 8.0%
Equity as % of assets: 5.4%
Return on assets: 0.9%
Long-term debt (mil.): $6,822
No. of shares (mil.): 117
Dividends
  Yield: 5.5%
  Payout: 55.7%
Market value (mil.): $1,889
Sales (mil.): $3,381

Stock Price History
High/Low 1985–94

HILTON HOTELS CORPORATION

OVERVIEW

Hilton isn't playing games anymore. The company announced in 1995 that it would spin off its gaming operations (which accounted for nearly 60% of sales in 1994) in a tax-free distribution to its shareholders. Based in Beverly Hills, California, Hilton is one of the world's largest hoteliers. It operates, manages, or franchises more than 220 hotels around the globe. Outside the US, Hilton's 4 hotels and 2 hotel-casinos are operated by its subsidiary, Conrad International Hotels.

Hilton's gaming operations include 5 casino hotels in Nevada, a riverboat casino in New Orleans, and other interests in Australia,

Canada, and Turkey. It hopes the spinoff will help its gaming operations and its hotel operations develop and expand more effectively.

Takeover rumors have circulated since 1989, when Hilton announced it was up for sale but failed to attract a bid to its liking. When the company hired investment banker Smith Barney in 1994 to study ways to boost Hilton's value, many analysts speculated the company would be sold, and many believe separation of the company's 2 businesses could be a prelude to a sale.

Barron Hilton, CEO and son of founder Conrad Hilton, owns 24.4% of Hilton Hotels.

WHEN

Conrad Hilton got his start in hotel management by renting rooms in his family's New Mexico home. He served as a state legislator and started a bank before leaving for Texas in 1919, hoping to make his fortune in banking. There Hilton combined his $5,000 savings with a $20,000 loan and $15,000 from partners to buy his first hotel — in Cisco, Texas. Over the next decade he bought 7 more Texas hotels. While scathed by the Great Depression (he had only 5 hotels by 1934), Hilton survived, in part because he had leased land for his hotels instead of borrowing to buy it.

He began buying hotels again, moving into California (1938), New Mexico (1939), and Mexico (1942). In 1942 he met and married Zsa Zsa Gabor, whom he later divorced. He founded Hilton International to manage his foreign business (1948) and realized his ambition to run New York's Waldorf-Astoria (1949), which he called "the greatest of them all." Hilton's first European hotel opened in Madrid in 1953. He paid $111 million for the 10-hotel Statler chain in 1954 in the biggest transaction in hotel history to that date.

The company began franchising in 1965 to capitalize on the best-known name in the hotel business and by 1987 had franchised 225 hotels. Conrad Hilton's son Barron became president in 1966. Barron persuaded his father to sell the 38-hotel Hilton International chain to TWA in 1967 in exchange for TWA stock. In 1970 Barron bought 2 hotels in Las Vegas, creating a gaming division.

Upon Conrad's death in 1979, Barron became chairman. He reentered the overseas hotel business with Conrad International Hotels in 1982 and opened a gaming hotel in Australia in 1985. The company spent $1.2 billion to refurbish and expand its 12 most

glamorous hotels in the 1980s, including the Waldorf-Astoria and Hilton's 2 Las Vegas hotels (making them the 2 largest in the world).

Settlement of his father's will in 1988 gave Barron Hilton control of almost 25% of Hilton's stock. He put the company up for sale in 1989 after foreign investors made high offers for other US hotels, but he took it off the market after 9 months because bids did not meet his expectations. Meanwhile the company opened the first Hilton Suites, hotels that provide only suites, and CrestHil, a chain of moderately priced country inns.

In 1992 Hilton bought Bally's Casino Resort in Reno for $88 million ($142 million less than Bally's paid for it in 1986). That same year Hilton joined forces with competitors Circus Circus and Caesars World to propose a $2 billion Las Vegas–style gambling facility in Chicago, but the project soon ran aground because of opposition from Illinois's governor. The 3 linked up again in 1993 to build a casino in Ontario. Also in 1993 Hilton purchased the Hyatt Regency Waikoloa resort in Hawaii and renamed it Hilton Waikoloa Village.

Hilton acquired the Fort Lee Holiday Inn in New Jersey and began managing the Hotel Millenium in New York City in 1994. That same year it launched the Hilton Queen of New Orleans, its first riverboat casino.

Also in 1994 a jury ordered Hilton to pay former navy lieutenant Paula Coughlin $6.7 million in damages for failing to provide her with adequate protection from sexual attacks during a 1991 party for the Tailhook Association at the Las Vegas Hilton. Hilton is appealing the ruling.

In 1995 the Missouri Gaming Commission approved continuous dockside operations of Hilton's proposed casino in Kansas City.

NYSE symbol: HLT
Fiscal year ends: December 31

WHO

Chairman and CEO: Barron Hilton, age 67,
$1,000,000 pay
VC: Eric M. Hilton, age 61, $443,750 pay
President and COO: Raymond C. Avansino Jr., age 51,
$942,477 pay
EVP; President, Hotel Operations: Dieter H.
Huckestein, age 51, $443,167 pay
EVP; President, Gaming Operations: Floyd M. Celey Jr.,
age 55
EVP Gaming and Hotel Development: F. Michael
O'Brien, age 54
SVP and General Counsel: William C. Lebo Jr., age 51,
$388,583 pay
SVP Finance (Principal Financial Officer): Steve
Krithis, age 65
SVP and Chief Information Officer: Terrence P.
McGowan
SVP Corporate Affairs: Marc A. Grossman
SVP Corporate Development: Robley T. Barber
SVP Franchising and Select Hotels: James R.
Abrahamson
SVP Labor Relations and Personnel Administration:
James M. Anderson
SVP Marketing: Robert E. Dirks
SVP Vacation Ownership Operations: Donald L. Harrill
SVP Europe: Clement J. Barter
SVP Asia: Dario Regazzoni
Auditors: Arthur Andersen & Co, SC

WHERE

HQ: 9336 Civic Center Dr., Beverly Hills, CA 90210
Phone: 310-278-4321
Fax: 310-205-4599
Reservations: 800-445-8667

Hilton owns 23 hotels, manages 40 hotels, and
franchises 160 hotels in the US, Australia, Belgium,
Hong Kong, Ireland, Turkey, and the UK.

WHAT

	1994 Sales		1994 Operating Income	
	$ mil.	% of total	$ mil.	% of total
Gaming	889	59	159	52
Hotels	617	41	146	48
Adjustments	—	—	(28)	—
Total	**1,506**	**100**	**277**	**100**

Selected Owned Hotels and Casinos
Atlanta Airport Hilton
Flamingo Hilton–Las Vegas (hotel/casino)
Flamingo Hilton–Laughlin (hotel/casino; Laughlin, NV)
Flamingo Hilton–Reno (hotel/casino)
Hilton Suites (Auburn Hills, MI)
New Orleans Airport Hilton
Palmer House Hilton (Chicago)
Portland Hilton (Portland, OR)
Reno Hilton
Waldorf-Astoria (New York)

Leased Hotels
Logan Airport Hilton (Boston)
Oakland Airport Hilton
O'Hare Hilton (Chicago)
Pittsburgh Hilton & Towers
San Diego Hilton Beach & Tennis Resort
San Francisco Airport Hilton
Seattle Airport Hilton
Tarrytown Hilton (Tarrytown, New York)

KEY COMPETITORS

Accor	Helmsley	Mirage Resorts
Bally Entertainment	Hospitality	Promus
Bass	Franchise	Rank
Canadian Pacific	Hyatt	Showboat
Carlson	ITT Corp.	Trump
Carnival Corp.	Loews	Westin Hotel
Circus Circus	Marriott	Wyndham
Doubletree	International	Hotel
Four Seasons	MGM Grand	

HOW MUCH

	9-Year Growth	1985	1986	1987	1988	1989	1990	1991	1992	1993	1994
Sales ($ mil.)	8.5%	725	693	779	954	998	1,125	1,113	1,230	1,394	1,506
Net income ($ mil.)	2.2%	100	98	140	131	110	113	84	104	103	122
Income as % of sales	—	13.8%	14.1%	18.0%	13.7%	11.0%	10.0%	7.6%	8.4%	7.4%	8.1%
Earnings per share ($)	2.5%	2.02	1.96	2.80	2.72	2.27	2.34	1.76	2.17	2.14	2.52
Stock price – high ($)	—	36.75	40.13	45.88	55.25	115.50	84.38	49.88	53.25	61.00	74.00
Stock price – low ($)	—	27.88	30.25	27.50	34.00	48.38	26.38	34.25	39.75	41.50	49.75
Stock price – close ($)	8.6%	32.44	33.63	35.50	53.38	82.50	37.25	40.50	43.38	60.75	68.00
P/E – high	—	18	21	16	20	51	36	28	25	29	29
P/E – low	—	14	15	10	13	21	11	20	18	19	20
Dividends per share ($)	3.2%	0.90	0.90	0.90	0.95	1.00	1.40	1.20	1.20	1.20	1.20
Book value per share ($)	6.6%	13.20	14.23	15.79	17.06	18.40	19.44	20.06	21.02	22.11	23.45
Employees	2.9%	34,000	35,000	35,000	38,000	39,000	38,000	40,000	41,000	43,000	44,000

1994 Year-end:
Debt ratio: 53.3%
Return on equity: 11.1%
Cash (mil.): $393
Current ratio: 2.05
Long-term debt (mil.): $1,252
No. of shares (mil.): 48
Dividends
  Yield: 1.8%
  Payout: 47.6%
Market value (mil.): $3,271

Stock Price History
High/Low 1985–94

H. J. HEINZ COMPANY

OVERVIEW

Pittsburgh-based Heinz believes in putting its money where your mouth is. It is one of the world's leading food processing companies, satisfying the appetites of people and their pets. Heinz, which garners more than 90% of its sales from processed food, has strong positions in many US markets, including ketchup (50% market share), frozen potatoes (48%), cat food (26%), and diet food (51%).

The company is also a strong international competitor, deriving an increasing amount of its revenue (43% in 1995) from non-US operations. Indeed, since the 1992 acquisition of Wattie's (New Zealand), sales in the Asia/Pacific area have more than doubled.

Under its globe-trotting CEO, Anthony O'Reilly (the former Irish rugby star, who racks up 500,000 frequent-flyer miles a year),

Heinz is pursuing a 3-pronged strategy for increasing sales: expand institutional food service (that is, sell more ketchup, sauces, and soups to hotels and restaurants); go global, particularly with baby foods; and reinvigorate Weight Watchers. In 1994 the company expanded its baby food business by $200 million in annual sales with acquisitions in India and the UK. The purchases make Heinz's baby food operations a company almost the size of US market leader Gerber.

Improvements in its traditional businesses (including Weight Watchers, which had struggled in 1994) helped lift revenues to over $8 billion in 1995.

The Heinz family controls about 24% of the company stock through trusts. Officers and directors own approximately 8%.

WHEN

In 1852, 8-year-old Henry J. Heinz started selling produce from the family garden to his neighbors in Sharpsburg, Pennsylvania. In 1869 he formed a partnership with his friend L. C. Noble to bottle horseradish sauce, but the business went bankrupt in 1875.

The following year, with the help of his brother John and his cousin Frederick, Heinz created F. & J. Heinz, where he developed tomato ketchup (1876) and sweet pickles (1880). He gained financial control of the firm in 1888 and changed the name to the H. J. Heinz Company.

Heinz developed a reputation as an advertising and marketing genius. At the 1893 World's Fair in Chicago, he had the largest commercial exhibit. Three years later he coined his "57 Varieties" slogan. In 1900 Heinz raised New York City's first large electric advertising sign (a 40-foot green pickle).

By 1905 Heinz was also manufacturing his food products in England. In America his Pittsburgh plants (complete with an indoor gym, swimming pool, hospital, and 3-story stable) became known as a "utopia for working men." Although most of the food industry was opposed to the Pure Food Act in 1906, Heinz sent his son to Washington to campaign for it. While Heinz controlled his company, there was never a strike at his plants. After his death in 1919, the company, under the direction of Heinz's son and later his grandson (whose son, John Heinz, was a US senator who died in a plane crash in 1991), continued to rely on its traditional product lines for the next 4 decades. In 1969 Burt Gookin became CEO as

the first non–family member to hold the top position in the company.

During the 1960s the company began its long program of acquisition, buying Star-Kist (tuna, 1963), Ore-Ida (potatoes, 1965), Tuffy's (pet food, 1971), Weight Watchers (weight reduction programs and products, 1978), and Chico-San (rice cakes, 1984).

Irishman Anthony O'Reilly became CEO in 1979 and focused the company's strategy on international expansion, particularly in Europe and in developing countries.

In 1991 the company sold its Hubinger (corn milling) unit and bought JLFoods (commercial food service supply) for $500 million, as well as several small food companies. In 1992 the company bought Wattie's Limited, New Zealand's largest food processing company. Because Wattie's already has a significant presence in Japan, Heinz is expanding the company into a major manufacturing base for the growing Asian market.

In fiscal 1994 Heinz sold its Italian confectionery business and its Near East specialty rice business ($127 million). Heinz made 3 acquisitions in 1994: Farley's Health Products, the Boots Company's UK line of baby food ($144 million); Glaxo's baby food business in India; and Borden's food service business.

In 1995 Heinz nearly doubled its pet food interests by agreeing to purchase all of Quaker Oats's pet food business in the US and Canada for $725 million. Heinz will add the well-known brand names Gravy Train and Kibbles 'n Bits to its already extensive list of pet food products.

NYSE symbol: HNZ
Fiscal year ends: Wednesday nearest April 30

WHO

Chairman, President, and CEO: Anthony J. F. O'Reilly, age 59
VC; Chairman, Star-Kist Foods: Joseph J. Bogdanovich, age 83
SVP; President and CEO, Star-Kist Foods: William R. Johnson, age 46
SVP; President, Heinz North America: William C. Springer, age 55
SVP General Counsel: Lawrence J. McCabe, age 60
SVP Finance and CFO: David R. Williams, age 52
SVP Europe: Luigi Ribolla, age 58
VP Organization Development and Administration: George C. Greer
Auditors: Coopers & Lybrand L.L.P.

WHERE

HQ: 600 Grant St., Pittsburgh, PA 15219
Phone: 412-456-5700
Fax: 412-237-5377 (Public Relations)

Heinz operates 88 food processing plants in 21 countries.

	1995 Sales		1995 Operating Income	
	$ mil.	% of total	$ mil.	% of total
US	4,629	57	657	57
Europe	1,881	23	283	24
Asia/Pacific	1,006	13	122	11
Canada	354	4	59	5
Other regions	217	3	35	3
Total	**8,087**	**100**	**1,156**	**100**

WHAT

	1995 Sales % of total
Ketchup, sauces & condiments	21
Tuna & other seafood products	9
Baby food	9
Other	61
Total	**100**

Selected Brand Names

Sauces and Condiments
57 Sauce
Heinz ketchup
Heinz pickles
Heinz relish

Food and Beverages
Bagel Bites (frozen appetizer)
Chef Francisco (frozen soup)
Chico-San (rice cakes)
Domani (frozen pasta)
Guloso (tomato products)
Mare D'Oro (seafood)
Marie Elisabeth (sardines)
Misura (dietetic products)
Moore's (coated vegetables)
Nipiol (baby food)
Ore-Ida (frozen potatoes)

Orlando (tomato products)
Petit Navire (fish)
Plasmon (baby food)
Star-Kist (tuna)
Tegel (poultry products)
Tip Top (frozen desserts)
Weight Watchers (foods and diet centers)

Pet Food
9-Lives
Amore
Gravy Train
Kibbles 'n Bits
Meaty Bones
Recipe
Skippy Premium
Vets

KEY COMPETITORS

ADM
Allied Domecq
Campbell Soup
Carter-Wallace
Clorox
Colgate-Palmolive
CPC
Danone
General Mills

Grand Metropolitan
Heico
Hershey
Hormel
Jenny Craig
Kellogg
Mars
Nestlé
Philip Morris

Quaker Oats
Ralcorp
Ralston Purina Group
RJR Nabisco
Sandoz
Slim-Fast Nutritional

HOW MUCH

	9-Year Growth	1986	1987	1988	1989	1990	1991	1992	1993	1994	1995
Sales ($ mil.)	7.1%	4,366	4,640	5,244	5,801	6,086	6,647	6,582	7,103	7,047	8,087
Net income ($ mil.)	7.7%	302	339	386	440	505	568	638	530	603	591
Income as % of sales	—	6.9%	7.3%	7.4%	7.6%	8.3%	8.5%	9.7%	7.5%	8.6%	7.3%
Earnings per share ($)[1]	9.0%	1.10	1.24	1.46	1.67	1.90	2.13	2.40	2.04	2.35	2.38
Stock price – high ($)[1]	—	17.13	24.13	25.88	25.00	35.88	37.00	48.63	45.50	45.25	39.00
Stock price – low ($)[1]	—	10.25	14.63	16.75	18.75	22.50	27.50	31.50	35.13	34.13	30.75
Stock price – close ($)[1]	9.5%	16.19	20.25	20.19	23.38	35.00	34.88	38.88	44.13	35.88	36.75
P/E – high	—	16	20	18	15	19	17	20	22	19	16
P/E – low	—	9	12	12	11	12	13	13	17	15	13
Dividends per share ($)	13.8%	0.44	0.50	0.61	0.70	0.81	0.93	1.05	1.17	1.29	1.41
Book value per share ($)	8.0%	5.09	5.41	6.24	6.91	7.44	8.77	9.32	9.12	9.39	10.15
Employees	1.7%	36,400	37,500	39,000	36,200	37,300	34,100	35,500	37,700	35,700	42,200

1995 Year-end:
Debt ratio: 57.9%
Return on equity: 24.6%
Cash (mil.): $207
Current ratio: 1.10
Long-term debt (mil.): $244
No. of shares (mil.):
Dividends
  Yield: 3.8%
  Payout: 59.2%
Market value (mil.): $8,955

Stock Price History[1]
High/Low 1986–95

[1] Stock prices are for the prior calendar year.

THE HOME DEPOT, INC.

OVERVIEW

The Home Depot is definitely not a homebody. The Atlanta-based company, the largest home center retailer in the US, continues to expand rapidly, adding outlets across the US. The company moved into Canada in 1994, and it is planning moves into Mexico and Central and South America. The Home Depot has nearly 350 stores and plans to more than double that number by 1998.

The typical Home Depot store contains more than 100,000 square feet of space and stocks some 40,000 to 50,000 kinds of home improvement materials, building supplies, and lawn and garden items. The Home Depot caters to do-it-yourselfers as well as professional contractors. It offers product installation services

and professional designers who provide free consultation on home improvement projects. The company's operating strategy stresses superior customer service, low prices, and a broad product assortment.

While competition in home center retailing remains fierce, the Home Depot plans to stay #1 both through geographic expansion and new store formats. In 1994 the company opened its first Expo Design Centers (in San Diego and Atlanta), which offer upscale interior design products and services, and it plans to open its first CrossRoads store in 1995 in Quincy, Illinois. CrossRoads will offer building and home improvement supplies as well as farming and ranching supplies.

WHEN

The Home Depot was founded in 1978 after Bernard Marcus and Arthur Blank lost their executive jobs with Handy Dan Home Improvement Centers in a corporate buyout. They joined Handy Dan co-worker Ronald Brill to launch a new and improved home center for the do-it-yourselfer. In 1979 they opened 3 stores in the Atlanta area, soon expanding to 4 stores (1980).

In 1981 the Home Depot went public, raised more than $4 million, opened 4 stores in southern Florida, and posted sales of $50 million. After opening 2 more Florida stores and making sales of $100 million in 1982, the company was named Retailer of the Year in the home building supply industry.

The chain next entered Louisiana and Arizona, opening 5 stores there, plus 4 more in Florida in 1983. That year sales were more than $250 million. The company also began shifting from manual to computerized information management, installing computerized checkout systems. In 1984 inventory reordering was computerized.

Also in 1984 the Home Depot's stock was listed on the NYSE, and the company acquired 9 Bowater Home Centers in Texas, Louisiana, and Alabama. The company then entered Southern California, Handy Dan's home turf, opening 6 stores. It finished 1985 with 50 stores and sales of $700 million. The Bowater acquisition and rapid internal expansion caused the Home Depot to falter and experience the only dip in earnings in its history.

Back on track in 1986, the Home Depot opened 10 more stores (5 in California), and sales exceeded $1 billion in the 60 stores. The company initiated the current policy of "low

day-in day-out pricing" in 1987, achieving Marcus's dream of eliminating sales events. It also began installing bar code scanning systems, completing the job within 2 years.

With sales of over $2 billion in 96 stores in 1988, the Home Depot was included in the S&P 500. Entering the competitive Northeast market, the company bought 3 Modell's Shoppers World stores on Long Island. In 1989 the company added 22 stores, primarily in California, Florida, and New England, and installed a satellite communication network to enhance its continual-training policy.

The Home Depot's sales rose during the 1990–92 recession. The company opened 25 new stores in 1990 and 30 more in 1991 (including its first units in New Hampshire, Massachusetts, and Maryland). The Home Depot opened 40 more stores in 1992. The company aspires to pass the 500-store mark by the end of 1996, and in 1992 it announced its intention to expand outside of the US.

In 1993 the Home Depot announced plans to acquire 7 stores in the Chicago area from Waban Inc. (owner of HomeBase) after that company decided to leave the Midwest.

The Home Depot acquired a 75% interest in Aikenhead's, a Canadian home improvement retailer, in 1994. That same year several female employees filed an employment discrimination class action lawsuit against the company, claiming female workers are not trained, promoted, or paid on an equal basis with male employees.

In 1995 the Home Depot announced plans to introduce Right at Home, a line of coordinated home furnishings, including textiles, wall coverings, floor tile, and lighting fixtures.

NYSE symbol: HD
Fiscal year ends: Sunday nearest January 31

WHO

Chairman, CEO, and Secretary: Bernard Marcus, age 65, $2,600,000 pay
President and COO: Arthur M. Blank, age 52, $2,600,000 pay
EVP, CFO, and Treasurer: Ronald M. Brill, age 51, $605,385 pay
EVP Strategic Development: James W. Inglis, age 51, $556,923 pay
EVP Merchandising: Bill Hamlin, age 42
SVP Human Resources: Stephen R. Messana
Auditors: KPMG Peat Marwick LLP

WHERE

HQ: 2727 Paces Ferry Rd., Atlanta, GA 30339-4089
Phone: 404-433-8211
Fax: 404-431-2707

	No. of Stores
California	76
Florida	55
Texas	33
Georgia	18
New York	16
New Jersey	13
Canada	12
Arizona	11
Massachusetts	11
North Carolina	10
Connecticut	7
Tennessee	7
Louisiana	7
Maryland	7
Pennsylvania	7
Washington	7
Illinois	6
Other	37
Total	**340**

WHAT

	1995 Sales
	% of total
Building materials, lumber, floor & wall coverings	34
Plumbing, heating, lighting & electrical supplies	28
Seasonal & specialty items	14
Hardware & tools	13
Paint & other	11
Total	**100**

KEY COMPETITORS

84 Lumber
Ace Hardware
BMC West
Cotter & Company
D.I.Y. Home Warehouse
Eagle Hardware & Garden
Foxworth-Galbraith Lumber
Grossman's
Hechinger
Home Hardware Stores
Kmart
Lowe's
McCoy
Menard
Montgomery Ward
National Home Centers
NHD
Orchard Supply Hardware
Payless Cashways
Sears
Servistar
Sherwin-Williams
Waban
Wal-Mart
Wickes Lumber

HOW MUCH

	9-Year Growth	1986	1987	1988	1989	1990	1991	1992	1993	1994	1995
Sales ($ mil.)	37.7%	701	1,012	1,454	2,000	2,759	3,815	5,137	7,148	9,239	12,477
Net income ($ mil.)	61.3%	8	24	54	77	112	163	249	363	457	605
Income as % of sales	—	1.2%	2.4%	3.7%	3.8%	4.1%	4.3%	4.9%	5.1%	5.0%	4.8%
Earnings per share ($)	47.5%	0.04	0.09	0.17	0.23	0.32	0.45	0.60	0.82	1.01	1.32
Stock price – high ($)[1]	—	2.02	2.15	4.17	4.75	8.54	14.51	35.08	51.47	50.91	48.25
Stock price – low ($)[1]	—	1.04	1.06	1.77	2.58	4.27	7.68	11.55	29.76	35.00	36.50
Stock price – close ($)[1]	49.4%	1.24	1.77	2.78	4.69	8.15	12.89	33.70	50.63	39.50	46.00
P/E – high	—	51	24	25	21	27	32	59	63	50	37
P/E – low	—	26	12	10	11	13	17	19	36	35	28
Dividends per share ($)	—	0.00	0.00	0.01	0.02	0.02	0.04	0.06	0.08	0.11	0.15
Book value per share ($)	40.8%	0.35	0.57	0.96	1.15	1.48	1.93	4.01	5.19	6.26	7.59
Employees	32.4%	5,400	6,600	9,100	13,000	17,500	21,500	28,000	38,900	50,600	67,300

1995 Year-end:
Debt ratio: 22.6%
Return on equity: 19.3%
Cash (mil.): $58
Current ratio: 1.76
Long-term debt (mil.): $983
No. of shares (mil.): 453
Dividends
    Yield: 0.3%
    Payout: 11.4%
Market value (mil.): $20,885

Stock Price History[1]
High/Low 1986–95

[1]Stock prices are for the prior calendar year.

HONEYWELL INC.

OVERVIEW

Honeywell is big on control. In fact, it is one of the world's top manufacturers and marketers of control systems and components for use in buildings, homes, industry, space, and aviation. The company (which invented the thermostat) provides integrated systems that can control not only the AC, heat, lights, and TVs in households (TotalHome) but also entire industrial facilities (TotalPlant). The company is among the world's leaders in developing automation and control systems aimed at conserving energy and improving productivity in industrial and residential settings. Honeywell is also one of the world's largest avionic equipment manufacturers and makes switches and sensors used in other products.

But it's not all sweetness and light at Honeywell. The company's 1994 restructuring (its 6th in 8 years) did little to stem the firm's string of mediocre performances, marked by

flat sales growth and shrinking income, of the 1990s. While the company can point to declining orders for commercial jets (down 20% in 1994) and cutbacks in government spending to explain poor military and space sales, critics point to Honeywell's slow-changing corporate culture as a major culprit. Despite its use of state-of-the-art robots, Honeywell still uses US workers for the labor-intensive tasks its competitors are outsourcing to low-wage countries.

CEO Michael Bonsignore is confident that international growth, coupled with new products, could make Honeywell a $10 billion company by the end of the decade. Bonsignore is also committed to the relocation of manufacturing to low-cost countries and has begun to trim its costly European operations, partially by outsourcing some manufacturing activities to Eastern Europe.

WHEN

An invention patented by Al Butz in 1885, the Damper Flapper, led to the building regulation equipment that Honeywell still provides. The Damper Flapper, forerunner of the thermostat, opened furnace vents automatically. Butz formed the Butz Thermo-Electric Regulator Co. to market the product but sold patent rights to investor William Sweatt in 1893. Sweatt led the company for 4 decades. The company eventually began producing a burner-control system for fire protection on oil and gas furnaces. Sweatt persuaded manufacturers to redesign furnaces to accommodate controls, establishing a new market.

In 1927 the chief competitor was Mark Honeywell Heating Specialties Co. (of Indiana). The companies merged that year as Minneapolis-Honeywell Regulator Co. In 1964 the company adopted its present name.

Honeywell developed expertise in precision optics during WWII, when the US military sought its assistance in developing instrumentation and control systems for long-range bombers, including B-17s and B-29s.

In the 1950s Honeywell used computers in control and guidance systems. It formed Datamatic Corporation (1955) with Raytheon to develop and market data processors. In 1970 Honeywell purchased GE's computer division, receiving with it 66% interest in a French company, Machines Bull. Honeywell then bought Xerox's computer business in 1976. The same year it merged its Machines Bull unit with a computer company owned by

the French government, which purchased Honeywell's entire interest (after threatening to nationalize it) in 1982. In 1986 Honeywell bought Sperry Aerospace Group, increasing its avionics market share. In 1987 Honeywell renewed its ties with Bull, creating Honeywell Bull Inc. (in 1991 Honeywell sold its interest in the Bull enterprise).

In 1990 Honeywell obtained a $13.4 million air force contract to upgrade the F-16 navigation system. In 1992 the company acquired the Enviracaire Division of Environmental Air Control (air cleaners) and 2 regional security companies (Security, Washington, DC; and Westco Security, Minneapolis). Honeywell also expanded its European business services with the acquisitions of Comfort Cooling (UK) and Strumentecnica (Italy).

In 1993 a jury found that Honeywell had infringed the patent on an airplane guidance system and awarded a $1.2 billion judgment to Litton Industries. However, in 1995 a judge set aside the judgment.

The company spent $105 million on acquisitions in 1994. Home and Building Control acquired leading European providers of building services, security systems, and water controls. Industrial Control bought 3 companies to expand its TotalPlant range of products and services.

In 1995 Honeywell made plans to build its first manufacturing plant in China, making heating controls for the Asian building market.

NYSE symbol: HON
Fiscal year ends: December 31

WHO

Chairman and CEO: Michael R. Bonsignore, age 53, $1,016,233 pay
President and COO: D. Larry Moore, age 58, $923,155 pay
President, Space and Aviation Control: John R. Dewane, age 60, $409,022 pay
President, Home and Building Control: Brian M. McGourty, age 57
President, Industrial Automation and Control: Markos I. Tambakeras, age 44
EVP: Edward T. Hurd, age 56, $450,078 pay (prior to promotion)
VP and General Counsel: Edward D. Grayson, age 56, $444,109 pay
VP Information Systems: William L. Sanders
VP and CFO: William M. Hjerpe, age 43
VP Technology: Ronald E. Peterson
VP Business Development: James J. Grierson
VP and Controller: Philip M. Palazzari, age 47
VP and Secretary: Sigurd Ueland Jr.
VP Human Resources: James E. Porter
Auditors: Deloitte & Touche LLP

WHERE

HQ: Honeywell Plaza, Minneapolis, MN 55408-1792
Phone: 612-951-1000
Fax: 612-951-0137

Honeywell operates in 95 countries.

	1994 Sales		1994 Operating Income	
	$ mil.	% of total	$ mil.	% of total
US	3,825	63	344	65
Europe	1,528	25	139	27
Other regions	704	12	41	8
Total	**6,057**	**100**	**524**	**100**

WHAT

	1994 Sales		1994 Operating Income	
	$ mil.	% of total	$ mil.	% of total
Home & Building Control	2,665	44	236	45
Industrial Control	1,835	30	207	40
Space & Aviation Control	1,432	24	81	15
Other	125	2	—	—
Total	**6,057**	**100**	**524**	**100**

Selected Products

Home and Building Control
Building automation (EXCEL 5000, TotalHome)
Energy management
Environmental controls
Fire protection and security systems

Industrial Control
Automation and control products ranging from sensors to integrated systems (TotalPlant)
Field instrumentation
Vision-based sensors

Space and Aviation Control
Commercial avionics
Military avionics
Space avionics

KEY COMPETITORS

ABB	Fisher	Omron
ADT	Rosemount	Rockwell
Andover	IBM	Siebe
Banner Aerospace	IRI	Siemens
Cherry Corp.	Johnson Controls	Sprague
Electrowatt	Kaiser Electronics	Telemechanique
Elsag-Bailey	Landis & Gyr	Turck
Emerson	Measurex	Yokogawa

HOW MUCH

	9-Year Growth	1985	1986	1987	1988	1989	1990	1991	1992	1993	1994
Sales ($ mil.)	(1.0%)	6,625	5,378	6,679	7,148	6,059	6,309	6,193	6,223	5,963	6,057
Net income ($ mil.)	0.2%	275	10	254	(435)	604	382	331	400	322	279
Income as % of sales	—	4.2%	0.2%	3.8%	—	10.0%	6.1%	5.3%	6.4%	5.4	4.6%
Earnings per share ($)	4.0%	1.51	0.05	1.44	(2.56)	3.55	2.52	2.35	2.88	2.40	2.15
Stock price – high ($)	—	21.63	21.06	22.63	19.16	22.94	28.09	32.75	37.94	39.38	36.88
Stock price – low ($)	—	13.56	14.56	12.25	13.56	14.88	17.66	20.50	30.19	31.00	28.25
Stock price – close ($)	6.1%	18.53	14.78	13.47	14.94	21.69	22.25	32.56	33.25	34.25	31.50
P/E – high	—	14	—	16	—	7	11	14	13	16	17
P/E – low	—	9	—	9	—	4	7	9	11	13	13
Dividends per share ($)	7.9%	0.49	0.50	0.51	0.53	0.57	0.71	0.77	0.84	0.91	0.97
Book value per share ($)	0.4%	14.02	12.17	13.20	10.04	11.99	11.99	13.25	13.10	13.48	14.57
Employees	(6.5%)	94,022	78,097	78,881	70,400	65,500	60,300	58,200	55,400	52,300	50,800

1994 Year-end:
Debt ratio: 31.7%
Return on equity: 15.4%
Cash (mil.): $275
Current ratio: 1.28
Long-term debt (mil.): $502
No. of shares (mil.): 127
Dividends
  Yield: 3.1%
  Payout: 45.1%
Market value (mil.): $4,009

Stock Price History High/Low 1985–94

HORMEL FOODS CORPORATION

OVERVIEW

Hormel, producer of SPAM canned meat and Dinty Moore stews and one of the US's leading pork processors, is living high on the hog these days. Depressed hog prices have led to increased margins and record earnings. In 1994 the company's revenues exceeded $3 billion for the first time.

Hormel is using these boom times to improve its Minnesota processing plants (spending $80 million in 1995) and to expand in foreign markets. In 1994 the company opened sales offices in Hong Kong and Mexico. In 1995 it formed 2 joint ventures in China and formed Hormel Alimentos in Mexico (with Grupo Herdez).

Branded products have been the key to Hormel's longevity. The company introduced 175 new products in 1994 and continues to push development of shelf-stable, microwaveable entrees, including its Top Shelf, Kid's Kitchen, and Micro-Cup labels.

Hormel heirs own over 40% of company stock through the Hormel Foundation. In late 1994 the family accused the foundation of costing them millions by refusing to lower its stake in the company. The heirs have asked a district court to order foundation trustees to sell some of the company stock. Heirs and trustees have been locked in a battle over the matter since 1992.

WHEN

George Hormel opened his Austin, Minnesota, slaughterhouse in an abandoned creamery in 1891. By 1900 Hormel had expanded and modernized his facilities to compete with larger meat processors who possessed refrigeration units and automated processing lines.

In 1903 Hormel introduced its first brand name (Dairy Brand) and a year later began opening distribution centers nationwide. In 1921 Hormel discovered that an assistant controller had embezzled over $1 million; the scandal almost broke the company. Hormel initiated tighter controls, the company survived, and by 1924 it was processing more than one million hogs annually. Hormel introduced its first canned ham in 1926.

George's son Jay became president in 1929, and under his guidance Hormel introduced some of its most successful products, such as Dinty Moore stew (1936) and SPAM (1937).

In WWII Hormel sold over half of its output to the US government, which supplied SPAM to servicemen. Nikita Khrushchev later claimed that the USSR could not have fed its army without lend-lease SPAM.

After WWII Hormel sponsored a traveling entertainment group, the Hormel Girls, to promote products. In 1959 the company introduced its Little Sizzlers brand of pork sausage and sold its billionth can of SPAM.

New products introduced in the 1960s included those in Hormel's Famous Foods of the World line (1960) and its Cure 81 ham (1963). In 1969 the company realigned into 3 groups: Meat Products, Prepared Foods, and Operations. By the mid-1970s Hormel was producing more than 750 products.

In 1985, feeling the pinch of price instability, Hormel announced a $2-an-hour pay cut

for workers at its Austin processing plant; 1,500 of the unionized workers walked out, sparking a violent, nationally publicized strike. In the end only 500 strikers returned, and all workers accepted lower pay scales.

Seeking to avoid the fate of its failing industry peers, Hormel, under CEO Richard Knowlton (who started working for the company at the age of 16 in the beef kill and gelatin departments), sold its slaughtering operation in 1988.

In the late 1980s Hormel introduced Top Shelf and Light & Lean Franks. In 1990 the company began trading on the NYSE.

In 1992 the Hormel family, beneficiaries of the stock held by the Hormel Foundation, sued their trustees, claiming that concentration of their estate in Hormel stock cost them $175 million in 1991 because of falling stock values. A decision ordering the trustees to divest at least 6% of the shares (worth as much as $213 million) was reversed in 1993.

Hormel bought the House of Tsang and Oriental Deli brands in 1992. The next year it acquired the Dubuque (hams, franks, sausages, and bacon) and Herb-Ox (bouillon and dry soup mix) brands.

After being known as Geo. A. Hormel & Co. for more than 100 years, in 1993 the company began calling itself the Hormel Foods Corporation to reflect its expansion in the fish, poultry, and ethnic foods markets (the name change became official in 1995).

Proving it can take a joke (even if the object is one of the company's mainstays, now nearly 60 years old), Hormel debuted its SPAM catalog in 1994. The 1995 version offers 56 products that feature the SPAM name and likeness, including earrings and a special SPAM cutter.

NYSE symbol: HRL
Fiscal year ends: Last Saturday in October

Chairman: Richard L. Knowlton, age 62
President and CEO: Joel W. Johnson, age 51, $985,100 pay
EVP and CFO: Don J. Hodapp, age 56, $656,900 pay
EVP Operations: Gary J. Ray, age 48, $569,100 pay
SVP Meat Products: Eric A. Brown, age 48
Group VP Prepared Foods: Robert F. Patterson, age 54, $517,500 pay
Group VP Meat Products: Stanley E. Kerber, age 56, $490,900 pay
Group VP Foodservice: James W. Cole, age 60
Group VP International, Planning and Development: David N. Dickson, age 51
Group VP Foodservice: James W. Cole, age 60
VP; President, Hormel International Corp.: Ronald E. Plath, age 60
VP; President and CEO, Jennie-O Foods: James N. Rieth, age 54
VP and General Counsel: Mahlon C. Schneider, age 55
VP and Controller: Richard W. Schlange, age 59
VP Human Resources: James A. Jorgenson, age 49
Auditors: Ernst & Young LLP

WHERE

HQ: One Hormel Place, Austin, MN 55912-3680
Phone: 507-437-5737
Fax: 507-437-5489

Hormel has processing and packaging facilities in 12 states and sells its products in more than 40 countries.

Selected International Markets

Australia	Mexico
Hong Kong	Panama
Japan	Philippines
Korea	UK

WHAT

	1994 Sales
	% of total
Meat products	57
Prepared foods	26
Poultry, fish & other	17
Total	**100**

Selected Food Brands

Black Label	Frank'N Stuff	Old Smokehouse
Bread Ready	Griddlemaster	Old Tyme
Breakfast Combos	Herb-Ox	Parma Brand
Burgermeister	Homeland	Pillow Pack
By George	Hormel	Prima Festa
Chi-Chi's	House of Tsang	Primissimo
Country Brand	Jennie-O	Quick Meal
Cure 81	Kid's Kitchen	Range Brand
Curemaster	Layout Pack	Rosa
Di Lusso	Light & Lean	Rosa Grande
Dinty Moore	Light & Lean 97	San Remo Brand
Dubuque	Little Sizzlers	Sandwich Maker
Eggspressions	Mary Kitchen	SPAM
Farm Fresh	Menumaster	Super Select
Fast'N Easy	Messina Brand	Top Shelf
Fiddler's Wharf	OKC	Wranglers

KEY COMPETITORS

American Foods	Nestlé
Campbell Soup	PET
ConAgra	Philip Morris
CPC	Pilgrim's Pride
Dial	RJR Nabisco
Foster Farms	San Miguel
General Mills	Sara Lee
Goya	Schreiber Foods
Grand Metropolitan	Seaboard Corp.
Heinz	Smithfield Foods
Hudson Foods	Specialty Foods
IBP	Thorn Apple Valley
Keystone Foods	Tyson Foods

HOW MUCH

	9-Year Growth	1985	1986	1987	1988	1989	1990	1991	1992	1993	1994
Sales ($ mil.)	8.2%	1,502	1,960	2,314	2,293	2,341	2,681	2,836	2,814	2,854	3,065
Net income ($ mil.)	13.2%	39	39	46	60	70	77	86	95	101	118
Income as % of sales	—	2.6%	2.0%	2.0%	2.6%	3.0%	2.9%	3.0%	3.4%	3.5%	3.9%
Earnings per share ($)	13.1%	0.51	0.51	0.60	0.79	0.92	1.01	1.13	1.24	1.31	1.54
Stock price – high ($)	—	6.63	8.78	14.69	13.69	16.94	19.75	23.13	24.75	25.50	26.75
Stock price – low ($)	—	3.78	5.53	8.13	8.75	10.06	14.00	16.00	16.75	20.25	18.75
Stock price – close ($)	16.2%	6.41	8.56	10.69	11.00	16.88	19.13	21.38	23.50	22.13	24.75
P/E – high	—	13	17	25	17	18	20	21	20	19	17
P/E – low	—	7	11	14	11	11	14	14	14	15	12
Dividends per share ($)	14.9%	0.14	0.14	0.15	0.18	0.21	0.25	0.29	0.35	0.42	0.49
Book value per share ($)	8.8%	4.05	4.42	4.86	5.45	6.13	6.70	7.61	8.41	7.43	8.62
Employees	3.5%	6,996	5,965	5,428	7,994	8,000	8,300	8,300	8,300	10,800	9,500

1994 Year-end:
Debt ratio: 39.5%
Return on equity: 19.2%
Cash (mil.): $249
Current ratio: 2.67
Long-term debt (mil.): $10
No. of shares (mil.): 77
Dividends
 Yield: 2.0%
 Payout: 31.8%
Market value (mil.): $1,898

Stock Price History High/Low 1985–94

HOUSEHOLD INTERNATIONAL, INC.

OVERVIEW

Household International is cleaning house, sweeping out more of the operations it added in the 1980s in order to return to its original business: consumer loans (and their modern manifestation, credit cards). Prospect Heights, Illinois–based Household's brokerage operations and first mortgage origination business have been left at the curb, along with its chronically unproductive Australian operations and most of its branch banks outside the Midwest. This is a major change of emphasis from 2 years ago, when it aimed to be a national banking powerhouse.

In addition to making secured (home equity) and unsecured consumer loans through its primary subsidiary, Household Finance, the company is one of the top issuers of credit cards in the US. Its credit card business in recent years has blossomed on the strength of private label and affinity cards (like the GM Card, which allows users to earn points toward buying a car). The company also offers life and credit insurance, commercial vehicle and equipment leasing, and commercial loans (a new joint venture with Dominion Resources will provide loans to middle-market companies).

In 1994 Household's UK business improved greatly, but the company decided to discontinue its Australian operations and to consolidate many of its Canadian functions into US operations.

WHEN

Household Finance was founded in Minneapolis in 1878, when Frank Mackey opened a finance company to loan cash to workers between paychecks. In 1894, when the company had 14 offices throughout the Midwest, Mackey moved the headquarters to Chicago (they are now located in a suburb). The company introduced installment payments on loans in 1905.

In 1925 more than 30 such companies across the country, controlled by Mackey and operating under a variety of names, consolidated as Household Finance Corporation (HFC), a public company. That year the company paid its first quarterly dividend (it has never missed a dividend since).

In 1930 HFC set up the Money Management Institute to teach people how to handle credit. One pamphlet showed a family of 5 how to live on $150 a month. In 1931 HFC's banks froze the company's credit, stopping lending, but the freeze was lifted in 1932 and the company weathered the Depression. It made its first non-US purchase in 1933, buying Central Finance, a Canadian company. After WWII the unleashed US demand for goods propelled HFC into the suburbs, and by 1960 it had 1,000 branch offices and was advertising on television.

In the conglomerate-crazed 1960s, HFC, viewing itself broadly as a retailer of money, began to diversify into other kinds of retailing: hardware stores (Coast-to-Coast, 1961), variety chains (Ben Franklin and TG&Y, 1965), vacuum jugs (King-Seeley Thermos, 1968), and car rentals (National, 1969). HFC also bought a savings and loan company, 4 banks, and Alexander Hamilton Life (1977). This diversification strategy benefited the company in the 1970s, when rising inflation rates made Household's traditional short-term, fixed-rate loans less profitable.

The company adopted Household International as its corporate name in 1981. In 1984 chairman Donald Clark thwarted an $8 billion takeover by dissident shareholders by adopting a "poison pill" that, after a takeover, would have let stockholders buy stock in the resulting company for half price. In the mid-1980s Clark refocused the company on financial services, particularly consumer banking, and began divesting its noncore operations, jettisoning retailing, transportation, and manufacturing, including the 1989 spinoff of 3 companies, Eljer, Scotsman, and Schwitzer. Between 1985 and 1988 it bought several finance companies and banks, including BGC Finance in Australia.

In 1993 Household joined a consortium led by Goldman, Sachs that bought ITT's unsecured consumer loan portfolio, which HFC services.

In addition to the divestiture of several businesses, the 1994–95 restructuring included the streamlining of Household's back-office operations, which consolidated its processing operations along business lines. At the same time the company moved most Canadian processing operations to the US and servicing for all HFC-originated loans was moved to a single site in Illinois, while billing, payment, and check processing operations were moved to 4 regional processing centers.

William Aldinger, formerly of Wells Fargo, became president and CEO in 1994, taking over executive duties from Chairman Clark.

WHO

Chairman: Donald C. Clark, age 63, $1,877,119 pay
President and CEO: William F. Aldinger, age 47, $685,770 pay
Group Executive, US BankCard and Household Retail Services: Joseph W. Saunders, age 49, $778,805 pay
Group Executive, US Consumer Finance and Canada: Robert F. Elliott, age 54, $644,371 pay
Group Executive, Household Bank, f.s.b. and HFC Bank (UK): Lawrence N. Bangs, age 58
Chairman, Alexander Hamilton Life Insurance: Richard H. Headlee, age 64
SVP and CFO: David A. Schoenholz, age 43
VP and General Counsel: Kenneth H. Robin, age 48
VP and Chief Information Officer: David B. Barany, age 51
VP Corporate Communications: Michael H. Morgan, age 40
VP Human Resources: Colin P. Kelly, age 52
Auditors: Arthur Andersen & Co, SC

WHERE

HQ: 2700 Sanders Rd., Prospect Heights, IL 60070
Phone: 708-564-5000
Fax: 708-205-7452

Household International operates 759 offices in Canada, the UK, and the US.

	1994 Sales		1994 Operating Income	
	$ mil.	% of total	$ mil.	% of total
US	3,969	86	512	94
Canada	239	5	(17)	—
UK	322	7	31	6
Australia	73	2	2	0
Total	**4,603**	**100**	**528**	**100**

WHAT

	1994 Assets	
	$ mil.	% of total
Cash & equivalents	541	2
Government securities	431	1
Mortgage-backed securities	2,892	8
Corporate bonds	4,502	13
Other securities	819	2
Credit receivables	20,778	61
Mortgage & policy loans	235	1
Other	4,140	12
Total	**34,338**	**100**

	1994 Sales		1994 Operating Income	
	$ mil.	% of total	$ mil.	% of total
Finance & banking	4,012	87	448	85
Individual life insurance	591	13	80	15
Total	**4,603**	**100**	**528**	**100**

Selected Subsidiaries
Alexander Hamilton Life Insurance Co. of America
Household Bank, f.s.b. (full-service consumer banking)
Household Bank, NA (MasterCard and VISA accounts)
Household Commercial Financial Services, Inc.
Household Finance Corp. (consumer credit, home equity loans)
Household Retail Services, Inc. (revolving credit administration for retailers)

KEY COMPETITORS

ADVANTA	CoreStates	First USA
American Express	Financial	Ford
AT&T	Countrywide	General Electric
BankAmerica	Credit	Great Western
Beneficial	Dean Witter,	MBNA
Chase Manhattan	Discover	Prudential
Chemical Banking	Equifax	Transamerica
Citicorp	First Chicago	Wells Fargo

HOW MUCH

	9-Year Growth	1985	1986	1987	1988	1989	1990	1991	1992	1993	1994
Sales ($ mil.)	3.5%	3,383	2,741	3,441	2,637	3,490	4,320	4,594	4,181	4,455	4,603
Net income ($ mil.)	9.1%	168	248	222	310	240	235	150	191	299	368
Income as % of sales	—	5.0%	9.0%	6.5%	11.8%	6.9%	5.4%	3.3%	4.6%	6.7%	8.0%
Earnings per share ($)	10.6%	1.41	2.57	2.66	3.21	3.07	2.88	1.55	1.93	2.85	3.50
Stock price – high ($)	—	21.69	26.25	31.25	30.50	32.75	26.63	31.50	30.25	40.44	39.75
Stock price – low ($)	—	14.19	19.56	16.25	19.75	23.19	9.69	13.75	20.75	26.94	28.50
Stock price – close ($)	6.5%	21.13	23.88	19.94	28.44	25.94	16.44	25.63	29.63	32.63	37.13
P/E – high	—	15	10	12	10	11	9	20	16	14	11
P/E – low	—	10	8	6	6	8	3	9	11	10	8
Dividends per share ($)	3.6%	0.89	0.91	0.95	1.02	1.07	1.08	1.11	1.14	1.17	1.22
Book value per share ($)	4.1%	15.85	14.28	14.47	17.03	16.91	19.02	19.17	19.41	21.92	22.78
Employees	(6.5%)	28,300	21,419	22,029	—	14,500	14,500	14,500	13,397	16,900	15,500

1994 Year-end:
Debt ratio: 91.3%
Return on equity: 17.2%
Cash (mil.): $541
Long-term debt (mil.): $10,274
No. of shares (mil.): 97
Dividends
  Yield: 3.3%
  Payout: 34.9%
Market value (mil.): $3,587
Assets (mil.) $34,338

Stock Price History
High/Low 1985–94

HUGHES ELECTRONICS CORP.

OVERVIEW

Hughes Electronics is high on satellites — the defense and commercial electronics unit of giant automaker General Motors has 15 satellites in orbit and has anted up $1.5 billion to buy more satellite launches from McDonnell Douglas. The "big birds" are at the heart of 2 new businesses that Hughes hopes to ride into the 21st century: DIRECTV and DirecPC.

DIRECTV, a broadcast television system with a high-quality picture and over 150 channels, gained over 400,000 subscribers in its first 10 months, despite an initial cost of over $700 for a satellite dish. As equipment costs come down, subscriber numbers should pick up. In 1996 DIRECTV will begin serving Latin America; the company also has its eye on Asia, Europe, and the Middle East. DirecPC is a

satellite-based, high-speed digital communications service that zaps news, software, video, and other information to PCs; the service uses satellite dishes to bypass hardwired modems.

Hughes's 2 largest segments, defense electronics and automotive electronics, have faltered recently. In 1994 the company consolidated its Hughes Aircraft and Delco Electronics operations, cutting that segment's work force by over 8%. Defense contracts still make up the bulk of Hughes's revenues. In 1995 Hughes Missile Systems won a $2 billion contract from the US Navy for Tomahawk missiles. Hughes Training won several contracts for training and simulation systems.

In 1994 over 50% of Hughes's sales were to other GM companies.

WHEN

GM Hughes Electronics (GMHE) was formed in 1985 after General Motors bought Hughes Aircraft for $5.2 billion and teamed it with its electronics operations.

Hughes Aircraft was founded in 1932 to build experimental airplanes for Howard Hughes, who set a number of world airspeed records with the company's H-1 racer. During WWII the company began building a flying boat that could fly over German U-boats, which were sinking US supply convoys. However, the giant floating plane, dubbed the "Spruce Goose," wasn't completed until 1947, when Hughes took it for its only flight.

Following WWII, the company refurbished DC-3s for corporate customers and also conducted research. It began moving into the growing field of defense electronics and, with help from the military's buildup during the Korean War, the company's sales took off, jumping from $2 million in 1948 to $200 million in 1953. However, in 1953 the company underwent a major shakeup when about 80 of its top engineers walked out, dissatisfied with Howard Hughes, who was becoming more distant and difficult to work with.

The secretary of the air force threatened to cancel the company's contracts because of Hughes's erratic behavior, so Hughes transferred the company's assets to the Howard Hughes Medical Institute (with himself as its sole trustee) and hired former Bendix Aviation executive Lawrence Hyland to run the company. Hyland rebuilt Hughes's research staff; and in 1960 the company produced the first beam of coherent laser light, in 1963 it placed the first communications satellite into geosyn-

chronous orbit, and in 1966 the Hughes-built Surveyor landed on the moon.

When Hughes died in 1976, a board of trustees was created to oversee the medical institute. The company experienced strong growth as the US military budget grew, but in 1984 the DOD canceled several missile contracts because of quality control problems and cost overruns. The company found it difficult to both fund R&D and meet IRS requirements for contributions to the medical institute.

In 1985 General Motors, looking for a way to diversify and to increase its technological know-how, bought the company. GM also reorganized its Delco Electronics unit and put it with Hughes to form GM Hughes Electronics. Founded in 1912, Delco, a maker of car radios and automotive electronics, was acquired by GM in 1936. Following the acquisition, GMHE began a plant modernization program, completed in 1988.

In 1992 the company acquired General Dynamics's missile business for $450 million. That same year GMHE tapped former IBM executive Michael Armstrong as CEO. He immediately began refocusing the company on commercial electronics and began a restructuring that cut employment by 13%. Hughes Aircraft won $114 million in 1994 in a satellite technology patent suit that it had brought against the US government in 1966.

In 1995 GMHE became Hughes Electronics. In that same year its Galaxy Institute, which produces educational programs for DIRECTV, began broadcasts to 450 schools. Also in 1995 the company said it would sell Hughes LAN Systems to Whittaker Corp. for $57.5 million.

NYSE symbol: GMH
Fiscal year ends: December 31

Chairman and CEO: C. Michael Armstrong
VC: Michael T. Smith
SVP; President, Telecommunications and Space:
Steven D. Dorfman
President, Hughes Communications Galaxy: Jerald F.
Farrell
EVP: Gary W. Dickinson
SVP and CFO: Charles H. Noski
SVP: Gareth C.C. Chang
SVP: Arthur N. Chester
SVP: Jack A. Shaw
SVP: W. Scott Walker
SVP, General Counsel, and Secretary: John J. Higgins
SVP Human Resources: Ted G. Westerman
Auditors: Deloitte & Touche LLP

WHERE

HQ: PO Box 80028, Los Angeles, CA 90080-0028
Phone: 310-568-7200
Fax: 310-568-6390

Hughes Electronics has operations worldwide and a fleet
of 15 communications satellites orbiting the earth.

	1994 Sales	
	$ mil.	% of total
US	11,203	79
Canada	876	6
Asia	758	6
Europe	679	5
Middle East	370	3
Latin America	187	1
Africa	26	0
Total	**14,099**	**100**

WHAT

	1994 Sales		1994 Operating Income	
	$ mil.	% of total	$ mil.	% of total
Defense Electronics	5,591	40	584	36
Automotive Electronics	5,267	37	794	48
Telecomm. & Space	2,529	18	267	16
Commercial Tech.	712	5	(125)	—
Adjustments	—	—	(13)	—
Total	**14,099**	**100**	**1,507**	**100**

Selected Products and Services

Defense Electronics
Air defense systems
Airborne radar systems
Communications systems
Guided missiles
Laser range finders
Night vision systems
Sonar systems

Automotive Electronics
Air bag electronics
Antilock brake modules
Audio systems
Climate controls
Engine and transmission
controls
Remote keyless entry

Telecommunications and Space
Broadcasting
Satellites
Satellite-based
telecommunications
systems and services
Telecommunications
networks and services

Commercial Technologies
Air traffic control systems
Airline passenger
communications and
entertainment systems
Database management
systems

KEY COMPETITORS

AlliedSignal	Loral	Raytheon
Boeing	McDonnell	Robert Bosch
British Aerospace	Douglas	Rockwell
Comcast	Motorola	Siemens
Cooper Industries	News Corp.	TCI
Cox	Northrop	Textron
EG&G	Grumman	Thiokol
Hercules	Orbital	Thomson S.A.
Lockheed Martin	Sciences	Time Warner

HOW MUCH

	Annual Growth	1985	1986	1987	1988	1989	1990	1991	1992	1993	1994
Sales ($ mil.)	4.5%	9,469	10,372	10,481	11,244	11,359	11,723	11,541	12,297	13,518	14,099
Net income ($ mil.)	7.7%	489	594	670	802	781	726	559	(922)	798	956
Income as % of sales	—	5.2%	5.7%	6.4%	7.1%	6.9%	6.2%	4.8%	—	5.9%	6.8%
Earnings per share ($)	9.2%	1.22	1.49	1.67	1.78	1.94	1.82	1.26	(0.11)	2.30	2.70
Stock price – high ($)	—	25.00	24.63	25.25	40.63	32.13	25.63	21.00	26.13	42.38	40.38
Stock price – low ($)	—	19.00	16.25	19.38	24.13	23.50	17.00	13.13	14.25	22.88	31.00
Stock price – close ($)	6.9%	19.13	19.31	25.00	25.38	25.50	17.63	14.75	25.75	39.00	34.88
P/E – high	—	20	17	15	23	17	14	17	—	18	15
P/E – low	—	16	11	12	14	12	9	10	—	10	11
Dividends per share ($)	—	0.00	0.30	0.36	0.44	0.72	0.72	0.72	0.72	0.72	0.80
Book value per share ($)	2.5%	15.91	16.72	17.68	18.88	19.75	20.25	20.55	17.04	18.32	19.94
Employees	(0.6%)	—	80,800	77,500	75,700	73,200	93,600	92,900	89,300	78,000	77,100

1994 Year-end:
Debt ratio: 4.2%
Return on equity: 12.5%
Cash (mil.): $1,502
Current ratio: 1.76
Long-term debt (mil.): $354
No. of shares (mil.): 400
Dividends
  Yield: 2.3%
  Payout: 29.6%
Market value (mil.): $13,947

**Stock Price History
High/Low 1985–94**

HYATT CORPORATION

OVERVIEW

Chicago-based Hyatt Corporation is one of the largest hotel operators in the US. Led by CEO Jay Pritzker, the company is a subsidiary of H Group Holding, which is owned by the Pritzker family, one of the US's wealthiest families (with a net worth estimated at $4.4 billion by *Forbes*). Through Hyatt Hotels Corp. the company manages 104 hotels in North America and the Caribbean. Hyatt International runs more than 60 hotels overseas.

Long known for superlative service, Hyatt introduced many amenities (free shampoo, restricted-access floors) that have been copied by other hotels. However, by the early 1990s many of the company's contractees began to complain that Hyatt was concentrating more on adding luxuries than on generating profits. The company began a major restructuring focused on cutting costs. Some of the company's amenities were trimmed. For example, at the Chicago Hyatt Regency if guests want their beds turned down at night, they now have to ask. The change has saved the hotel more than $200,000 a year. The company has also reduced middle management and centralized much of its purchasing. Overall it has saved $100 million annually.

The company is now focusing on expansion. It has begun selectively franchising the Hyatt name, is entering the time-share business, and has some 30 hotel projects in development.

WHEN

In 1881 Nicholas Pritzker left Kiev for Chicago, where he began his progeny's ascent to the ranks of America's wealthiest families.

Nicholas's son A. N. left the family law practice in the 1930s and began investing in a variety of businesses. He turned a 1942 investment (Cory Corporation) worth $25,000 into $23 million by 1967.

After WWII, A. N.'s son Jay followed in his father's wheeling-and-dealing footsteps. In 1953, with the help of his father's banking connections, Jay purchased Colson Company and recruited his brother Bob, an industrial engineer, to restructure a company that made tricycles and navy rockets. By 1990 Jay and Bob had added 60 industrial companies, with annual sales exceeding $3 billion, to the entity they called the Marmon Group.

In 1957 Jay bought a hotel called Hyatt House, located near the Los Angeles airport, from Hyatt von Dehn. Jay had added 5 locations by 1961 and brought his gregarious youngest brother, Donald, to California to manage the hotel company.

In 1967 the Pritzkers took the company public, but the move that opened new vistas for the hotel chain was the purchase of an 800-room hotel in Atlanta that both Hilton and Marriott had turned down. John Portman's design, incorporating a 21-story atrium, a large fountain, and a revolving rooftop restaurant, became a Hyatt trademark.

The Pritzkers formed Hyatt International in 1969 to operate hotels overseas, and the company grew rapidly during the 1970s in the US and abroad. Donald Pritzker died in 1972, and his successor ran up some questionable expenses. This prompted the family to move the corporate offices to Chicago in 1977 and to take the company private in 1979. In 1980 Hyatt built its first Park Hyatt, a European-style super-luxury hotel, near the Water Tower in Chicago. The company opened its next Park Hyatt, in Washington, DC, in 1986.

Much of Hyatt's growth in the 1970s came from contracts to manage, under the Hyatt banner, hotels built by other investors. In the 1980s Hyatt's cut on those contracts shrank, and it launched its own hotel and resort developments under Nick Pritzker, a cousin to Jay and Bob. In 1988, with US and Japanese partners, it built the $360 million Hyatt Regency Waikoloa on Hawaii's Big Island. At the time the resort was, according to *FORTUNE*, the most expensive hotel ever built.

Through Hyatt subsidiaries the Pritzkers bought bedraggled Braniff Airlines in 1983 as it emerged from bankruptcy. After a failed 1987 attempt to merge the airline with Pan Am, the Pritzkers sold Braniff in 1988.

In 1989 Hyatt launched Classic Residence by Hyatt, a group of upscale retirement communities. In 1993 Hyatt sold the majority of its 85% interest in Ticketmaster to Paul Allen, cofounder of Microsoft. That same year Donald Trump sued Hyatt, alleging that the hotelier was trying to squeeze him out of his 50% stake in New York City's Grand Hyatt. In 1994 Hyatt sued Trump, claiming that "The Donald" was trying to lessen his financial woes by blocking renovations on the Grand Hyatt and that he had turned over his share of the hotel to 2 of his creditors.

In 1995 Hyatt signed deals to manage Makkah Hyatt Regency in Saudi Arabia and the Hyatt Regency Baku in Azerbaijan.

Private company
Fiscal year ends: January 31

WHO

Chairman and CEO: Jay A. Pritzker, age 72
President: Thomas V. Pritzker, age 44
SVP and CFO: Ken Posner
SVP Planning and Human Resources: Larry Deans
SVP Sales and Marketing: Jim Evans
Chairman, Hyatt Hotels Corp.: Darryl Hartley-Leonard
President, Hyatt Hotels Corp.: Doug Geoga, age 39
President, Classic Residence: Penny S. Pritzker
President, Marmon Group: Robert Pritzker, age 68
EVP, Hyatt Hotels Corp.: Albert J. Kelly
General Counsel: Michael Evanoff
Auditors: KPMG Peat Marwick LLP

WHERE

HQ: 200 W. Madison, Chicago, IL 60606
Phone: 312-750-1234
Fax: 312-750-8550
Reservations: 800-233-1234

Through its domestic division, Hyatt Corporation operates hotels across the US. Hyatt's international division is responsible for the company's network of foreign-based hotels, found worldwide.

Selected Hotels
Bali Hyatt
Grand Hyatt Hong Kong
Grand Hyatt New York
Grand Hyatt San Francisco
Hyatt Regency Atlanta
Hyatt Regency Austin
Hyatt Regency Baku
Hyatt Regency Belgrade
Hyatt Regency Buenos Aires
Hyatt Regency Casablanca
Hyatt Regency Chicago
Hyatt Regency Dubai
Hyatt Regency Istanbul
Hyatt Regency Jerusalem
Haytt Regency Paris
Hyatt Regency Riyadh
Makkah Hyatt Regency
Park Hyatt Tokyo
UN Plaza-Park Hyatt Hotel

WHAT

Subsidiaries
Hyatt Hotels Corp.
  Classic Residence by Hyatt (upscale retirement communities)
  Grand Hyatt
  Hyatt
  Hyatt Hotels International
  Hyatt Regency
  Park Hyatt
Spectacor Management Group (50%, arena management)

Related Pritzker Businesses
American Medical International (hospitals)
Conwood Co. (tobacco products)
Dalfort Corp. (aircraft maintenance)
Hawthorn Suites (lodging)
Itel Corp. (minority interest, railroad cars)
Marmon Group (over 60 industrial companies)
Penguin Realty Associates LP
Royal Caribbean Cruises Ltd. (50%, cruise line)
Tampa Bay Hockey Group (applicant for National Hockey League franchise)
Ticketmaster Corp. (15%, ticket sales)
Trans Union Corp. (credit reporting service)

KEY COMPETITORS

Accor	Hilton
American Express	ITT
Bally	Loews
Bass	Marriott Intl.
Canadian Pacific	Metromedia
Carlson	Nestlé
Carnival Cruise Lines	Ogden
Circus Circus	Promus
Delaware North	Rank
Dial	Ritz-Carlton
Dole	Trump Organization
Doubletree	TRW
Equifax	Walt Disney
Four Seasons	Westin Hotel
Helmsley	

HOW MUCH

	Annual Growth	1985	1986	1987	1988	1989	1990	1991	1992	1993	1994
Estimated sales ($ mil.)	3.3%	—	2,000	2,300	2,330	2,400	3,101	2,915	2,400[1]	2,500[1]	2,600[1]
Total hotels	10.0%	—	79	85	91	101	158	160	164	164	169
New hotels	—	—	7	6	6	10	57	2	4	—	5
Employees	7.2%	—	30,000	30,000	40,000	40,000	55,195	49,820	51,275	52,275	52,275

Estimated Sales ($ mil.) 1986–94

HYATT
HOTELS & RESORTS

[Bar chart showing Estimated Sales ($ mil.) from 1986 to 1994, scale 0 to 3,500]

[1]Does not include revenue for franchised or managed hotels

IBP, INC.

OVERVIEW

IBP, the world's largest producer of beef and pork, is benefiting from low cattle and swine prices. The depressed livestock market has lowered IBP's costs and enabled the company to operate facilities at nearly 90% of capacity.

In 1994 IBP acquired its first non-US plant when it purchased Lakeside Farm Industries, Canada's 2nd largest slaughterhouse. The purchase broadens the company's scope: the Lakeside operation includes poultry processing. Also in 1994 IBP bought International Multifoods, a New Mexico–based deli meats producer. In 1995 it acquired Western Packing, a Texas-based beef processor.

With help from the GATT accord and improved custom-processing technologies, IBP is beefing up its efforts to lasso foreign markets. In 1995 it reached a 10,000-metric-ton pork production agreement with Nippon Meat Packers, Japan's largest meat processor. The company also began marketing low-cost meats in Eastern Europe and Russia. CEO Robert Peterson may use the recent New Mexico acquisition to expand sales in Mexico and other areas of Latin America.

In the US, a new facility in Iowa came on-line in June, and several existing plants are being expanded to meet rising demand.

WHEN

A. D. Anderson and Currier J. Holman's experiences in the meatpacking business convinced them that the industry needed modernization. In 1960 they formed Iowa Beef Packers and, with their first plant in Denison, Iowa, broke with tradition. To cut costs and save time, IBP built facilities in rural areas where cattle were raised. Carefully monitored demand and more efficient slaughtering kept inventory from building up; almost as soon as a steer walked into a plant, it exited in a considerably less animated manner.

IBP's highly automated plants were manned by local unskilled workers; the company paid better than other meatpackers but offered few fringe benefits. Employees organized and in 1965 walked out over the right to strike. Union relations eroded further in 1967 when IBP began cutting meat into smaller amounts (minus fat and bone) for shipping, thus reducing supermarkets' need for butchers.

By 1969 IBP had 8 plants in the Midwest. Its takeover of 2 Blue Ribbon facilities in Iowa was challenged under antitrust laws, and in 1970 the company was barred from obtaining any plants in South Dakota, Minnesota, Nebraska, or Iowa for the next 10 years.

In 1969 IBP workers in Dakota City, Nebraska, struck over pay reforms. When 3 Iowa plants shut down as well, IBP sued the United Food and Commercial Workers for sabotage and other interference. Vandalism, death threats, shootings, and 56 bombings (one at a company vice-president's home) ensued over the next several months — all over a 20¢ per hour raise. IBP eventually won $2.6 million for damages suffered in the strike.

Union concerns continued to affect the company, which in 1970 changed its name to the more-encompassing Iowa Beef Processors.

In the early 1970s Holman paid a mob-related meat broker almost $1 million to ensure that unions wouldn't interfere with New York City distribution. IBP and Holman were convicted of bribery, but a New York state judge fined the company only $7,000, pinning the blame on the city's corrupt meat trade. In 1975 a son-in-law of the meat broker became an IBP executive, but concerned company bankrollers quickly drove him out.

IBP started operating in new areas (Texas, 1975; Idaho and Washington, 1976; Kansas, 1980; and Illinois, 1983) but couldn't stay out of trouble. In the late 1970s the company was investigated by the government for anticompetitive practices. (The inquiry was allegedly shut down by a USDA head who later became an IBP official.) The company was found guilty in a Brooklyn trial of making price concessions to a grocery chain. In the 1980s IBP was fined $2.6 million by OSHA for unreported worker injuries and received other penalties over the prevalence of a hand disorder caused by meat-cutting techniques.

Armand Hammer's Occidental Petroleum acquired the company in 1981. The following year it changed its name to IBP and entered the pork business. In 1987 49% of IBP was offered to the public. After Hammer's death in 1990, successor Ray Irani spun the meat business off to its shareholders in 1991. In 1993 IBP acquired Heinhold, a major hog marketing firm based in Indiana.

In 1995 IBP gained Department of Agriculture approval to test a new steam vacuum system that removes potentially harmful bacteria and other contaminants from newly processed meat. Also that year, IBP said it would purchase Nebraska-based Gibbon Packing, a privately held meat processor.

NYSE symbol: IBP
Fiscal year ends: Last Saturday in December

Chairman, President, and CEO: Robert L. Peterson, age 62, $4,872,990 pay
EVP Pork Division: Eugene D. Leman, age 52, $552,639 pay
EVP Finance and Administration: Lonnie O. Grigsby, age 55, $410,833 pay
Group VP Beef Sales and Marketing: Richard L. Bond, age 47, $438,902 pay
Group VP Design Products: David C. Layhee, age 50, $392,470 pay
President and CEO, Lakeside Farm Industries: Garnet Altwasser
SVP Hide Division: Kenneth W. Browning Jr., age 45
SVP Logistics Services: Kenneth L. Rose, age 50
SVP Technical Services: James V. Lochner, age 42
VP International Sales: Roel G. M. Andriessen
VP and Chief Information Officer: John R. Coleman
Assistant VP Quality Control: Dean A. Danilson
Assistant VP Personnel: Richard A. Jochum
Auditors: Price Waterhouse LLP

WHERE

HQ: IBP Ave., PO Box 515, Dakota City, NE 68731
Phone: 402-494-2061
Fax: 402-241-2063 (Public Relations)

IBP produces beef, pork, and chicken for worldwide distribution. The company has facilities in 13 states in the US and plants in Canada, Japan, and the UK.

	1994 Sales % of total
Domestic	87
International	13
Total	**100**

WHAT

	1994 Sales % of total
Boxed beef products	66
Pork products	17
Beef & pork allied products	13
Beef carcasses sold to 3rd parties	4
Total	**100**

	Facilities No.
Beef plants	12
Service centers	10
Hide plants	8
Pork plants	7
Cold storage warehouses	6
Tanneries	4
Ham plants	2
Cooked meat & prepared foods plants	2
Lakeside Farm facility	1
Tallow refinery	1
Total	**53**

Products	Uses of Byproducts	
Boxed beef	Animal feed	Luncheon meats
Cooked meats	Cosmetics	Pharmaceuticals
Fresh pork	Gelatin	Sausage
	Leather	

KEY COMPETITORS

American Foods	Keystone Foods
BeefAmerica	L&H Packing
Campbell Soup	Moyer Packing
Cargill	Nippon Meat Packers
ConAgra	Schreiber Foods
Foodbrands America	Seaboard Corp.
GFI America	Smithfield Foods
Gillett Holdings	Specialty Foods
Hormel	Thorn Apple Valley
Hudson Foods	

HOW MUCH

	Annual Growth	1985	1986	1987	1988	1989	1990	1991	1992	1993	1994
Sales ($ mil.)	7.1%	6,509	6,822	7,681	9,066	9,129	10,185	10,388	11,128	11,671	12,075
Net income ($ mil.)	15.2%	51	67	68	62	35	48	1	64	77	182
Income as % of sales	—	0.8%	1.0%	0.9%	0.7%	0.4%	0.5%	0.0%	0.6%	0.7%	1.5%
Earnings per share ($)	18.9%	—	0.95	1.10	1.32	0.74	1.01	0.03	1.34	1.62	3.79
Stock price – high ($)	—	—	—	20.25	15.75	17.75	21.75	26.25	20.63	26.25	35.50
Stock price – low ($)	—	—	—	10.75	11.25	13.50	14.75	12.88	14.50	17.50	22.63
Stock price – close ($)	13.1%	—	—	12.75	15.63	15.38	20.88	14.63	20.13	25.88	30.25
P/E – high	—	—	—	18	12	24	22	—	16	16	9
P/E – low	—	—	—	10	9	18	15	—	11	11	6
Dividends per share ($)	(16.7%)	—	—	—	0.60	0.60	0.60	0.60	0.30	0.20	0.20
Book value per share ($)	7.9%	—	—	9.66	10.36	10.51	10.80	10.20	11.24	12.93	16.45
Employees	6.3%	—	—	20,000	21,700	23,793	25,290	26,500	27,500	29,200	30,700

1994 Year-end:
Debt ratio: 31.7%
Return on equity: 26.2%
Cash (mil.): $161
Current ratio: 1.58
Long-term debt (mil.): $362
No. of shares (mil.): 47
Dividends
  Yield: 0.7%
  Payout: 5.3%
Market value (mil.): $1,435

Stock Price History
High/Low 1987–94

ILLINOIS TOOL WORKS INC.

OVERVIEW

The name is misleading. Illinois Tool Works (ITW) covers more than Illinois and makes more than a single tool. ITW makes an extensive range of equipment for the automotive, construction, food and beverage, and general industrial markets worldwide.

ITW operates in 2 business segments (Engineered Components and Industrial Systems and Consumables), making plastic and metal fastening components and assemblies, fastening tools, gears and switches, adhesives and polymers, packing systems and consumer packaging products, paint finishing and static control systems and products, quality assurance products, and arc welding equipment.

ITW has developed its various business units as small, decentralized structures in order to be responsive to its customers.

The company, which operates 261 units in 33 countries, has seen its sales buoyed by the worldwide resurgence of the automotive and construction markets. These 2 markets accounted for 63% of 1994 revenues in the Engineered Components segment.

The Smith family (descendants of the company founder) owns 37% of ITW.

WHEN

In the early years of the 20th century, Byron Smith, founder of Chicago's Northern Trust Company, recognized that rapid industrialization was outgrowing the capacity of small shops to supply machine tools. Smith encouraged 2 of his 4 sons to launch Illinois Tool Works in 1912.

One Smith brother, Harold C., became president of ITW in 1915 and expanded its product line into automotive parts. WWI boosted company business and profits.

ITW developed the Shakeproof fastener, the first twisted-tooth lock washer, in 1923. When Harold C. died in 1936, the torch passed to his son Harold B., who decentralized the company and exhorted salesmen to learn customers' businesses so well that they could develop solutions even before the customer recognized the problems. As WWII spurred demand for the company's products, Smith plowed profits back into research.

In the 1950s the company began exploring plastics and combination metal-and-plastic fasteners as well as electrical controls and instruments, becoming a leader in miniaturization. Its major breakthrough came in the early 1960s with the development of flexible plastic collars to hold 6-packs of beverage cans. This item, under a new division called Hi-Cone, was ITW's most profitable offering.

Smith gave up his board chairmanship in 1970 and turned the CEO slot over to Silas Cathcart. Smith's son, another Harold B., was president and COO until 1981 (he remains on the board of directors and is chairman of the board's executive committee). By the early 1980s ITW had become bureaucratic and susceptible to foreign competition. It was forced to lower prices to hold on to customers. Wary after the 1982 recession, ITW hired John Nichols as CEO.

After Nichols and his staff analyzed Japanese production methods and studied profiles in business publications, ITW adopted 3 manufacturing concepts — in-lining, the 80/20 rule, and focused factories. In-lining boosts productivity by concentrating the steps of production; the 80/20 rule, recognizing that 20% of customers account for 80% of orders, takes advantage of economies of scale in large orders; and focused factories are decentralized facilities that empower and challenge workers.

Nichols broadened the company's product line and doubled ITW's size by buying 27 companies, the largest being Signode Industries for $524 million (1986). Nichols broke Signode into smaller units, speeding development of 20 new products.

ITW acquired Ransburg Corporation (electrostatic finishing systems, 1989) and the DeVilbiss division of Eagle Industries (1990), merging the 2 to form its Finishing Systems and Products division.

In 1993 ITW acquired ownership of the Miller Group, a maker of arc welding equipment and related systems, through a stock swap. That same year the firm also made a number of small acquisitions, which included Pro/Mark (high-quality, thermally applied graphics) and the Edgeboard product line (pallet packaging items) from Sonoco.

An increased growth in car building in Europe in 1994 (11%) caused revenues of the company's engineered components segment to grow dramatically. That year 76% of ITW's international revenues derived from its European operations.

Following its tradition of promoting from within, ITW in 1995 named president James Farrell as CEO, replacing John Nichols. Nichols will retire from the position of chairman in 1996.

NYSE symbol: ITW
Fiscal year ends: December 31

WHO

Chairman of the Executive Committee: Harold B. Smith, age 61
Chairman: John D. Nichols, age 64, $1,402,067 pay
VC: H. Richard Crowther, age 62, $569,398 pay
President and CEO: W. James Farrell, age 52, $542,050 pay (prior to promotion)
EVP: Robert H. Jenkins, age 52, $432,641 pay
EVP: Frank S. Ptak, age 51, $387,165 pay
EVP: Gunter A. Berlin, age 62
EVP: F. Ronald Seager, age 54
EVP: Russell M. Flaum, age 44
SVP and Controller: Michael W. Gregg, age 59
SVP, General Counsel, and Secretary: Stewart S. Hudnut, age 55
SVP Human Resources: John Karpan, age 54
VP Patents and Technology: Thomas W. Buckman, age 57
VP Research and Advanced Development: Donald L. VanErden, age 59
Auditors: Arthur Andersen & Co, SC

WHERE

HQ: 3600 W. Lake Ave., Glenview, IL 60025-5811
Phone: 708-724-7500
Fax: 708-657-4261

The company operates 172 plants and offices in the US. Major international offices and plants are located in Australia, Belgium, Canada, France, Germany, Ireland, Italy, Japan, Malaysia, Spain, Switzerland, and the UK.

	1994 Sales		1994 Operating Income	
	$ mil.	% of total	$ mil.	% of total
US	2,229	64	361	72
International	1,232	36	138	28
Total	**3,461**	**100**	**499**	**100**

WHAT

	1994 Sales		1994 Operating Income	
	$ mil.	% of total	$ mil.	% of total
Engineered Components	1,828	53	275	55
Industrial Systems & Consumables	1,633	47	224	45
Total	**3,461**	**100**	**499**	**100**

Engineered Components
Adhesives, polymers, and application systems
Arc welding equipment
Automobile exterior door handle assemblies
Collated nails and staples
Fastener systems
Insert molding products
Metal screws

Industrial Systems and Consumables
Electrostatic and conventional, liquid and powder finishing spray guns
Hot stamp imprinters
Metallic foils
Paint curing systems
Paper packaging systems
Plastic multipack ring carriers and application systems
Resealable plastic bags
Strapping machinery

KEY COMPETITORS

Armstrong World
BASF
Black & Decker
Ciba-Geigy
Cooper Industries
DuPont
Emerson
Esstar
Giddings & Lewis
W. R. Grace
Hoechst
Manville
3M
Morton
PPG
Premark
SPS Technologies
Stanley Works
Textron
TriMas
Tyco International
Union Carbide

HOW MUCH

	9-Year Growth	1985	1986	1987	1988	1989	1990	1991	1992	1993	1994
Sales ($ mil.)	21.6%	596	961	1,698	1,930	2,173	2,544	2,640	2,812	3,159	3,461
Net income ($ mil.)	27.2%	32	80	106	140	164	182	181	192	207	278
Income as % of sales	—	5.3%	8.3%	6.3%	7.3%	7.5%	7.2%	6.8%	6.8%	6.5%	8.0%
Earnings per share ($)	25.4%	0.32	0.78	1.03	1.33	1.53	1.68	1.63	1.72	1.83	2.45
Stock price – high ($)	—	9.06	13.38	24.75	21.88	23.75	28.69	34.69	35.31	40.50	45.50
Stock price – low ($)	—	6.81	7.75	12.63	15.13	16.50	19.63	22.81	28.50	32.50	37.00
Stock price – close ($)	19.6%	8.75	12.97	16.50	17.38	22.44	24.13	31.88	32.63	39.00	43.75
P/E – high	—	28	17	24	17	16	17	21	21	22	19
P/E – low	—	21	10	12	11	11	12	14	17	18	15
Dividends per share ($)	15.0%	0.17	0.18	0.20	0.22	0.27	0.33	0.40	0.45	0.49	0.60
Book value per share ($)	14.5%	4.00	4.65	5.87	7.05	8.12	9.95	10.88	11.94	11.12	13.53
Employees	11.5%	7,300	13,700	13,600	14,200	15,700	18,400	18,700	17,800	19,000	19,500

1994 Year-end:
Debt ratio: 18.1%
Return on equity: 36.0%
Cash (mil.): $77
Current ratio: 2.01
Long-term debt (mil.): $273
No. of shares (mil.): 114.0
Dividends
  Yield: 1.4%
  Payout: 24.5%
Market value (mil.): $4,986

Stock Price History High/Low 1985–94

INGERSOLL-RAND COMPANY

OVERVIEW

With 42% of its sales destined for overseas markets in 1994, the Woodcliff Lake, New Jersey–based Ingersoll-Rand Company is poised to take advantage of the growing economies in Asia and Europe. The company is a leading manufacturer of nonelectrical industrial machinery and air compression systems, antifriction bearings, construction equipment, air tools, pumps, and other industrial tools.

Ingersoll-Rand operates 3 major business segments: standard machinery (32% of 1994 sales), which makes air compressors and construction and mining machinery; engineered equipment (21%), which sells pump and processing systems; and bearings, locks, and tools (47%). The firm also owns 49% of Dresser-Rand, which primarily sells compressors.

Ingersoll-Rand places a strong emphasis on technological innovation and invested a record $154.6 million in R&D in 1994. The company has registered 440 US patents in the past 5 years, including 98 in 1994.

Acquisitions have also been a key part of the company's growth strategy. In 1995 the company agreed to shell out $1.5 billion to acquire the $950-million-in-sales Clark Equipment Co. The acquisition makes Ingersoll-Rand a major player in the market for small and medium-sized construction machines, such as those used in road repair.

WHEN

Simon Ingersoll invented the steam-driven rock drill in New York City in 1871. In 1874 he sold the patent to José Francisco de Navarro, who financed the organization of the Ingersoll Rock Drill Company. Three years later the company merged with Sergeant Drill, a company created by Navarro's former foreman, Henry Clark Sergeant.

In 1871, at the same time Ingersoll was inventing his drill, Albert, Jasper, and Addison Rand were forming the Rand Drill Company. Both companies continued to make drills and other equipment through the turn of the century. In 1905 they merged to become Ingersoll-Rand.

During the next several years, Ingersoll-Rand started producing air compressors in addition to its basic line of rock drills. In 1912 the company added centrifugal compressors and turbo blowers to its product line. Further diversification occurred with the purchase of A. S. Cameron Steam Pump Works and Imperial Pneumatic Tool Company (portable air tools). For several decades the company continued to grow as a major manufacturer of compressed-air tools, sold mostly to the mining industry.

After WWII Ingersoll-Rand expanded its operations to Canada, Europe, South America, and Africa. During the 1960s it diversified into new specialized machinery. Acquisitions included Aldrich Pump (high-pressure plunger pumps, 1961), Pendleton Tool (mechanics' service tools, 1964), and Torrington (antifriction bearings and textile machine needles, 1969). Diversification continued during the 1970s and 1980s with the acquisitions of DAMCO (truck-mounted drilling rigs, 1973); Schlage Lock (lock and door hardware,

1974); California Pellet (1974); Western Land Roller (vertical water pumps, 1977); and Fafnir Bearings, the purchase of which made Ingersoll-Rand the largest US bearing manufacturer (1986).

During this time the company developed several new products, including small air compressors and water jet systems capable of cutting steel and concrete. In 1986 Ingersoll-Rand formed a partnership with Dresser Industries (Dresser-Rand, 49%) to produce gas turbines, compressors, and similar equipment. In 1992 the companies combined their pump businesses (Ingersoll-Dresser Pump, 51%). Ingersoll-Rand bought Aro (air-powered tools, 1990) from Todd Shipyards and German ABG (paving-equipment maker, 1990) and sold Schlage Electronics (1991) to Westinghouse.

After 5 years at the company's helm, Theodore Black retired in 1993 and was replaced by 16-year veteran James Perrella. In 1993 Ingersoll-Rand bought the German needle and cylindrical bearing business of FAG Kugelfischer Georg Schäfer for $43 million and agreed to buy a 12% interest in Nuovo Pignone (turbines, compressors, pumps, valves) from Italy's ENI. That same year the company sold its underground coal-mining machinery business to Long-Airdox and its domestic jet engine bearing operation to MPB. In 1994 Ingersoll-Rand agreed to buy ECOAIR, a unit of MAN GHH, and formed a joint venture (50%) with MAN GHH to produce rotary-screw airends.

In 1994 the firm purchased Montabert SA, a French maker of rock-breaking and drilling equipment, for $18.4 million, and French industrial toolmaker SA Charles Maire.

NYSE symbol: IR
Fiscal year ends: December 31

WHO

Chairman, President, and CEO: James E. Perrella, age 59, $1,245,417 pay
EVP; President, Production Equipment Group: J. Frank Travis, age 59, $613,625 pay
EVP: William G. Mulligan, age 64, $516,667 pay
SVP and CFO: Thomas F. McBride, age 59, $466,667
VP; President, Air Compressor Group: Paul L. Bergren, age 45, $436,417 pay
VP; President, Bearing and Components Group: Allen M. Nixon, age 54
VP; President, IDP: Frederick W. Hadfield, age 58
VP; President, Construction and Mining Group: R. Barry Uber, age 49
VP; President, Process Systems Group: Larry H. Pitsch, age 54
VP and Treasurer: William J. Armstrong, age 53
VP and General Counsel: Patricia Nachtigal, age 48
VP Human Resources: Donald H. Rice, age 50
Auditors: Price Waterhouse LLP

WHERE

HQ: 200 Chestnut Ridge Rd., Woodcliff Lake, NJ 07675
Phone: 201-573-0123
Fax: 201-573-3448

The company operates 47 plants in the US, 6 in Canada, 27 in Europe, 5 in the Far East, 5 in Latin America, 2 in Asia, and one in Africa.

	1994 Sales $ mil.	% of total	1994 Operating Income $ mil.	% of total
US	2,810	62	336	81
Europe	1,254	28	43	11
Other regions	444	10	35	8
Adjustments	—	—	(37)	—
Total	**4,508**	**100**	**377**	**100**

WHAT

	1994 Sales $ mil.	% of total	1994 Operating Income $ mil.	% of total
Bearings, locks & tools	2,135	47	257	62
Standard machinery	1,446	32	122	30
Engineered equip.	927	21	35	8
Adjustments	—	—	(37)	—
Total	**4,508**	**100**	**377**	**100**

Selected Products
Air compressors
Air motors
Air tools
Asphalt compactors
Automotive components
Ball and roller bearings
Construction equipment
Door hardware
Engine-starting systems
Fluid-handling equipment
Food-processing equipment
Industrial pumps
Lubrication equipment
Material-handling equip.
Mining machinery
Paving equipment
Pellet mills
Pneumatic valves
Portable generators
Pulp-processing machinery
Road-building machinery
Roller mills
Rotary drills
Rough-terrain forklifts
Separation equipment
Soil compactors
Spray-coating systems
Waterjet cutting systems
Winches

KEY COMPETITORS

AMSTED
Anglo American
Baker Hughes
Black & Decker
Caterpillar
Cooper Industries
Deere
Dover
Eaton
Emerson
Fiat
FMC
Friedrich Krupp
General Signal
Goulds Pumps
Harnischfeger Industries
Honda
Honeywell
ITT Industries
Masco
Newell Co.
Raytheon
Robert Bosch
Rolls-Royce
Stanley Works
Teledyne
Texas Instruments
Thermo Electron
TRINOVA
Willcox & Gibbs

HOW MUCH

	9-Year Growth	1985	1986	1987	1988	1989	1990	1991	1992	1993	1994
Sales ($ mil.)	6.1%	2,637	2,800	2,648	3,021	3,447	3,738	3,586	3,784	4,021	4,508
Net income ($ mil.)	11.4%	80	101	108	162	202	185	151	116	164	211
Income as % of sales	—	3.0%	3.6%	4.1%	5.3%	5.9%	5.0%	4.2%	3.1%	4.1%	4.7%
Earnings per share ($)	11.4%	0.76	0.95	0.99	1.50	1.89	1.78	1.46	1.11	1.56	2.00
Stock price – high ($)	—	11.34	13.78	22.88	22.31	25.13	30.25	27.50	34.25	39.88	41.63
Stock price – low ($)	—	8.84	10.17	11.25	15.50	16.81	14.25	17.50	25.00	28.75	29.50
Stock price – close ($)	12.7%	10.70	11.16	17.75	17.13	25.13	18.63	27.50	29.13	38.25	31.50
P/E – high	—	15	15	23	15	13	17	19	31	26	21
P/E – low	—	12	11	11	10	9	8	12	23	18	15
Dividends per share ($)	3.7%	0.52	0.52	0.52	0.52	0.58	0.63	0.66	0.69	0.70	0.72
Book value per share ($)	3.2%	10.61	11.05	10.98	12.04	13.37	14.53	15.21	12.36	12.82	14.03
Employees	0.4%	34,740	29,857	29,556	30,284	31,623	33,722	31,117	35,308	35,143	35,932

1994 Year-end:
Debt ratio: 17.1%
Return on equity: 14.7%
Cash (mil.): $207
Current ratio: 1.93
Long-term debt (mil.): $316
No. of shares (mil.): 109
Dividends
Yield: 2.3%
Payout: 36.0%
Market value (mil.): $3,437

Stock Price History High/Low 1985–94

INGRAM INDUSTRIES INC.

OVERVIEW

When CEO Bronson Ingram established a plan of succession for Ingram Industries in December 1993, nobody knew it would be needed so soon. But in December 1994 Ingram — Tennessee's only billionaire — was diagnosed with cancer. Six months later, he died.

The Nashville-based company Ingram left behind is the world's #1 independent seller of general-interest books, microcomputer products, and prerecorded videos, with other interests in barging, aggregate supply, oil and gas wellhead equipment, and insurance. Now leading the company is president and new CEO Linwood "Chip" Lacy, Bronson Ingram's handpicked successor, although sons Orrin, John, and David and widow Martha are all involved with the company's operations.

Those operations include Ingram Micro, which distributes 30,000 computer hardware,

software, and accessory products to customers such as Computer City and Micro Warehouse; Ingram Book Company, which provides nearly 200,000 titles from more than 2,000 publishers to the likes of Barnes & Noble and Waldenbooks; and Ingram Entertainment, which sells entertainment products such as videotapes, laser discs, audiocassettes, video games, and musical tapes and CDs. Ingram Entertainment has about 10% of the US videotape wholesale market; indeed, each of Ingram's divisions is a market leader.

Most of Bronson Ingram's $1.3 billion fortune was invested in his company. Although Ingram himself showed no interest in taking his company public, after his death board member Clayton McWhorter (chairman of Columbia/HCA Healthcare) quickly raised the possibility of a public offering.

WHEN

Bronson Ingram's great-grandfather, Orrin Ingram, was a New York farm boy who, in the late 1840s, took a job at a sawmill. He learned the business quickly and at age 21 began designing and operating mills in Ontario, Canada. In 1857 Ingram and 2 partners founded a sawmill (Dole, Ingram & Kennedy) in Eau Claire, Wisconsin, on the Chippewa River, about 50 miles upstream from the Mississippi River. By the 1870s the company (renamed Ingram & Kennedy) was selling lumber as far downstream as Hannibal, Missouri.

Ingram's success was noticed by Frederick Weyerhaeuser, a German immigrant in Rock Island, Illinois, who, like Ingram, had worked in a sawmill before buying one of his own. In 1881 Ingram and 3 other companies formed Empire Lumber, with Orrin Ingram as president. That same year Ingram and Weyerhaeuser negotiated the formation of Chippewa Logging (35%-owned by up-river partners, 65%-owned by down-river interests), which controlled the white pine harvest of the Chippewa Valley. In 1900 Ingram paid $216,000 for 2,160 shares in the newly formed Weyerhaeuser Timber Company. Ingram let his sons and grandsons handle the investment and formed O.H. Ingram Co. to manage the family's interests. He died in 1918.

In 1946 Ingram's descendants founded Ingram Barge, which hauled crude oil to the company's refinery near St. Louis. After buying and then selling other holdings, in 1962 the family formed Ingram Corp., consisting solely of Ingram Barge. Brothers Bronson and

Fritz Ingram bought the company from their father, Hank, before he died in 1963. In 1964 they bought half of a textbook distributing company (Tennessee Book, founded 1935), and in 1970 they formed Ingram Book to sell trade books to bookstores and libraries.

In 1971 Ingram Barge won a $48 million sludge-hauling contract in Chicago, but 4 years later the company was accused of bribing city politicians with $1.2 million in order to land the contract. The brothers stood trial in 1977 for authorizing the bribes; Bronson was acquitted, but the court convicted Fritz on 29 counts. Before Fritz entered prison (he served 16 months of a 4-year sentence), he and his brother split their company. Fritz took the energy operations and went bust in the 1980s. Bronson took the barge and book businesses and formed Ingram Industries.

Ingram Industries formed a computer products distributor (Ingram Computer) in 1982 and between 1985 and 1989 bought all the stock of computer wholesaler Micro D. Ingram Computer and Micro D merged to form Ingram Micro. In 1992 Ingram acquired Commtron, the world's #1 wholesaler of prerecorded videocassettes, and merged it into Ingram Entertainment. In 1994 Ingram Industries made available 20,000 computer-related items (such as 486-based Toshiba notebooks) to PC users who wanted to shop on the Internet. Ingram created its Ingram Publisher Services division in 1995 to oversee the anticipated growth in order-fulfillment services for medium-sized and large publishers.

Private company
Fiscal year ends: December 31

WHO

Chairman and Public Relations Director: Martha Ingram
CEO and President; Co-Chairman, Ingram Micro Inc.: Linwood A. "Chip" Lacy Jr., age 50
Co-Chairman, Ingram Micro Inc.: David Dukes
President and COO, Ingram Micro Inc.: Jeffrey R. Rodek
Chairman and CEO, Ingram Book Co.: Lee Synnott
President, Ingram Book Co.: John Ingram
President, Ingram Publisher Services: Steven Little
EVP; Chairman, Ingram Distribution Group: Philip M. Pfeffer
VP and Treasurer: Thomas H. Lunn
VP Human Resources: W. Michael Head

WHERE

HQ: One Belle Meade Place, 4400 Harding Rd., Nashville, TN 37205-2244
Phone: 615-298-8200
Fax: 615-298-8242

Ingram Book is headquartered in La Vergne, TN, with warehouses in Avon, CT; Denver, CO; Fort Wayne, IN; Petersburg, VA; and Walnut, CA. Ingram Micro is headquartered in Santa Ana, CA, with warehouses in Buffalo Grove, IL; Carrollton, TX; Cheshire, CT; Clarkston, GA; Columbia, MD; and Fremont, CA.

WHAT

Ingram Distribution Group
Ingram Book Co.
  Ingram Publisher Services
    Publisher Resources Inc. (distribution services for publishers, wholesalers, and retailers)
    Tennessee Book Co. (textbook distributor)
    White Bridge Communications (promotional programs)
Ingram Entertainment Inc. (prerecorded videocassette distribution)
Ingram International Inc.
Ingram Library Services Inc.
Ingram Merchandising Services Inc.
Ingram Periodicals Inc.
Ingram Micro Inc. (microcomputer products)
  Ingram Alliance Reseller Co.
  Ingram Dicom S.A. de C.V. (Mexico)
  Ingram Micro Europe
  Ingram Micro Inc. (Canada)

Energy Group
Ingram Cactus Co. (66%; design, manufacture, and installation of petroleum-drilling equipment)
Ingram Coal Co.
Ingram Production Co. (owns a 5% stake in an Indonesian oil field)

Ingram Book Publications and Services
Advance Magazine
Communique
Electronic ordering
Ingram Microfiche Service
Mac D Vision
Paperback Advance
Specialty magazines
Update
The Var Side
Videopedia

Inland Marine Group
Ingram Barge Co. (custom fuel services)
Ingram Materials Co.

Insurance Group
Permanent General Cos. (auto insurance)
Tennessee Insurance Co. (insures Ingram affiliates)

KEY COMPETITORS

Advanced Marketing	InaCom
Atlantic Richfield	Lone Star Technologies
Baker & Taylor	LTV
Baker Hughes	Merisel
Bookazine	MicroAge
Brodart	Navarre
Camco	Occidental
Cargill	Otis Engineering
CIGNA	Pacific Pipeline
Coastal	SOFTBANK
CompuCom	Software Spectrum
Cooper Industries	State Farm
CSX	Stream International
Dresser	Tech Data
East Texas Distributing	USX–Marathon
Halliburton	Wal-Mart
Handleman	

HOW MUCH

	9-Year Growth	1985	1986	1987	1988	1989	1990	1991	1992	1993	1994
Estimated sales ($ mil.)	27.5%	900	1,000	1,170	2,090	2,640	2,677	3,422	4,657	6,163	8,010
Employees	17.7%	2,300	2,400	3,000	3,425	4,600	5,400	6,526	8,407	9,658	10,000

INGRAM

Estimated Sales
($ mil.)
1985–94

INLAND STEEL INDUSTRIES, INC.

OVERVIEW

Inland Steel Industries is a holding company with 3 operating units that make and sell steel (Inland Steel Co.), distribute industrial materials nationally (Inland Materials Distribution Group, Inc.), and trade steel and other industrial materials internationally (Inland International, Inc.).

The US's 5th largest integrated steel manufacturer, Inland Steel Co. produced 5.5% (5.5 million tons) of all US steel in 1994. It is a leading supplier to the automotive, appliance, and office furniture industries. Inland Materials Distribution Group, the nation's largest metals distributor, operates 56 US steel service centers (Joseph T. Ryerson & Son) and metals distribution and processing centers (J.M. Tull Metals Company). As part of a strategy to widen its markets internationally, the parent company created Inland International in 1994

to sell, trade, and distribute steel products and other industrial materials worldwide.

In 1994 an upswing in the US helped Inland earn its first profit in 5 years. The company also has closed unprofitable operations, sold off noncore businesses, and pursued new markets abroad. Now Inland is aggressively seeking growth opportunities in emerging markets around the world. It created a joint venture (Ryerson de México) in 1994 with Altos Hornos de México, Mexico's biggest steel company, and another (Ryerson de China) in 1995 with China's #3 steelmaker, Baoshan Iron and Steel, to set up distribution centers. Inland also has expressed an interest in India. In early 1995 Inland formed a joint venture in Hong Kong with South African Macsteel and Canada's Federal Industries to handle exports of steel and other industrial products.

WHEN

In 1893, 8 partners purchased 40 freight cars of used steel-making machinery from bankrupt Chicago Steel and established Inland Steel in the Chicago Heights area. By 1894 Inland was selling agricultural implements (plows, etc.).

In 1901 the Lake Michigan Land Company offered 50 acres of land at Indiana Harbor to any company that would spend $1 million to develop the land by building an open-hearth steel mill. Inland raised the money and built Indiana Harbor Works and in 1906 bought the Laura Ore iron mine in Minnesota.

Inland grew steadily and then in 1916 began a rapid expansion to meet the WWI demand for steel. By 1920 Inland was producing 2% of American steel. After converting back to peacetime production, Inland began producing rails (1922).

During the Great Depression, Inland turned to the lighter steel (tinplate, sheets) used in consumer goods. In 1931 the company, under chairman L. E. Block, built facilities to make strip, sheet, and plate steel. Inland bought Joseph T. Ryerson & Son (steel warehousing) in 1935 and Wilson & Bennett Manufacturing (later renamed Inland Steel Containers) in 1939. The company introduced Ledloy (a steel/lead alloy machining metal) in 1938.

Inland again turned to wartime production in the 1940s. In 1947 the company expanded the capacity of its rolling mills and introduced its line of galvanized steel sheets (marketed under the TI-CO trade name) in 1951. In 1957 Inland built its skyscraper headquarters (one

of the first constructed using external columns and stainless steel) in Chicago.

Inland became a billion-dollar company in 1966. The 1970s brought a steel boom but when the boom ended in the 1980s, Inland suffered big losses.

In 1986 Inland reorganized as a holding company to separate its steel manufacturing operations from its more profitable steel distribution division. The company also acquired J.M. Tull Metals from Bethlehem Steel. During the late 1980s Inland increasingly turned its attention to the production of custom work (such as painted steel for appliances).

Inland entered into joint ventures with Nippon Steel in 1987 and 1989 to build and operate a cold rolling mill (I/N Tek, 60% owned) and a coating facility (I/N Kote, 50%). The I/N Tek plant began operation in 1990 and I/N Kote in late 1991. Inland's 1991 closure of a structural steel mill removed the company from structural steel manufacturing.

In May 1993 Inland and the United Steelworkers agreed on a 6-year contract with a no-layoff clause. The company also closed a 69-oven facility for producing coke (a material used as fuel for steelmaking) to comply with federal clean air requirements.

In 1994 Inland created a 3rd operating unit, Inland International, and new divisions,among them Inland International Trading and Ryerson de México, to help sell and distribute its products to a wide range of industrial customers worldwide.

NYSE symbol: IAD
Fiscal year ends: December 31

WHO

Chairman, President, and CEO: Robert J. Darnall, age 56, $965,389 pay
EVP; President and CEO, Inland Steel Co.: Maurice S. Nelson Jr., age 57, $772,848 pay
SVP and CFO; President and COO, Inland International Inc.: Earl L. Mason, age 47, $513,881 pay
SVP; President and COO, Inland Materials Distribution Group, Inc.: Neil S. Novich, age 40
VP Corporate Development, General Counsel, and Secretary: David B. Anderson, age 52, $456,333 pay
VP Finance: Jay E. Dittus, age 62
VP Information Technology: H. William Howard, age 60
VP Human Resources: Judd R. Cool, age 59
Auditors: Price Waterhouse LLP

WHERE

HQ: 30 W. Monroe St., Chicago, IL 60603
Phone: 312-346-0300
Fax: 312-899-3197

The company produces all of its raw steel at Indiana Harbor Works in East Chicago, Indiana. It operates 54 steel service centers nationwide.

WHAT

	1994 Sales		1994 Operating Income	
	$ mil.	% of total	$ mil.	% of total
Steel mfg.	2,487	53	149	60
Materials distribution	2,198	47	98	40
Adjustments	(188)	—	2	—
Total	**4,497**	**100**	**249**	**100**

	1994 Shipments
	% of total
Automotive	32
Steel service centers	29
Steel converters/processors	12
Appliance	9
Industrial, electrical & farm machinery	8
Construction & contractors' products	2
Other	8
Total	**100**

Major Subsidiaries and Affiliates

Inland International, Inc. (international marketing, trading, and distribution)
I.M.F. Steel International Ltd. (50%, industrial metals and services)
Inland Industries de México SA de CV
Inland International Trading, Inc. (international purchasing and exporting services)
Ryerson de México (50%, service centers, Mexico)

Inland Materials Distribution Group, Inc.
J.M. Tull Metals Co., Inc. (metals distribution)
Joseph T. Ryerson & Son, Inc. (steel service centers)
Ryerson Coil Processing Co.

Inland Steel Co. (steel production)
I/N Kote (50%, steel finishing)
I/N Tek (60%, steel finishing)
Inland Steel Bar Co. (high-quality steel bars)
Inland Steel Flat Products Co. (sheet and steel plate)

KEY COMPETITORS

AK Steel	Cargill	National Steel
Alcan	Earle Jorgensen	Nucor
Alcoa	Holdings	Oregon Steel
Allegheny Ludlum	Friedrich Krupp	Mills
A.M. Castle	Hyundai	Phelps Dodge
Anglo American	IRI	Reynolds Metals
Armco	LTV	Thyssen
ASARCO	Mitsubishi	USX–U.S. Steel
Bethlehem Steel	Mitsui	Weirton Steel
Broken Hill		

HOW MUCH

	9-Year Growth	1985	1986	1987	1988	1989	1990	1991	1992	1993	1994
Sales ($ mil.)	4.6%	2,999	3,173	3,453	4,068	4,147	3,870	3,405	3,494	3,888	4,497
Net income ($ mil.)	—	(147)	35	112	249	120	(21)	(275)	(159)	(38)	107
Income as % of sales	—	—	1.1%	3.2%	6.1%	2.9%	—	—	—	—	2.4%
Earnings per share ($)	—	(6.14)	0.95	3.09	6.99	3.15	(1.41)	(9.88)	(5.83)	(1.96)	1.70
Stock price – high ($)	—	26.00	28.38	35.25	42.63	48.50	36.38	26.13	27.00	35.00	42.00
Stock price – low ($)	—	19.50	14.50	17.00	27.50	31.38	20.88	17.38	16.25	20.00	29.38
Stock price – close ($)	5.0%	22.63	18.88	30.38	41.50	33.75	24.75	21.63	22.63	33.13	35.13
P/E – high	—	—	30	11	6	15	—	—	—	—	25
P/E – low	—	—	15	6	4	10	—	—	—	—	17
Dividends per share ($)	(100.0%)	0.38	0.00	0.00	0.75	1.40	1.40	0.15	0.00	0.00	0.00
Book value per share ($)	(11.89%)	34.20	32.85	36.15	42.50	43.00	41.27	31.10	6.01	7.79	11.06
Employees	(4.9%)	24,413	22,668	20,740	20,639	20,715	20,154	18,600	17,180	16,200	15,500

1994 Year-end:
Debt ratio: 58.9%
Return on equity: 23.9%
Cash (mil.): $107
Current ratio: 1.91
Long-term debt (mil.): $706
No. of shares (mil.): 45
Dividends
  Yield: —
  Payout: —
Market value (mil.): $1,565

Stock Price History
High/Low 1985–94

INTEL CORPORATION

OVERVIEW

Intel, the #1 maker of integrated circuits with 75% of the market, continues to ride the crest of the desktop computing tidal wave. Profits from the Pentium chip have already risen past those of the company's 486 microprocessor. A 6th-generation Pentium (the P6, with 5.5 million transistors) is ready for release, and the P7 is in the works.

California-based Intel's $475 million charge to replace flawed Pentiums in late 1994 is old news — surging Pentium sales are making up for any costs. And as Pentium sales increase, the price will drop, further boosting sales. Intel inside indeed!

Two sources have geared up to challenge Intel's market dominance. Upstart chip makers such as NexGen and Cyrix as well as old nemesis Advanced Micro Devices (AMD) are forging ahead with their own processor innovations; AMD's forthcoming K-5 chip is being hyped as more powerful than current Pentiums. Also, the faster and cheaper PowerPC microchip developed by Apple, IBM, and Motorola, and now being shipped in Apple's Power Mac computers, may steal sales away from Intel. Some major PC makers, including Compaq and IBM, are beginning to find other sources for their microchips.

Such eager competition is why Intel has earmarked $2.9 billion to expand and update its facilities and equipment. In 1994 the company opened new manufacturing plants in Ireland and New Mexico and broke ground on a $1.3 billion chip factory in Arizona.

Intel spends nearly 10% of revenues on R&D (over $1.1 billion in 1994). The company was instrumental in developing new standards such as PCMCIA, DMI (desktop management interface), and PCI (peripheral component interconnect). The company continues to expand the parameters of desktop computing with LAN management products, videoconferencing, voice communications, and multimedia products, as well as flash memory and RISC chips.

WHEN

In 1968, 3 PhD engineers from Fairchild Semiconductor created Intel (a contraction of their preferred name, Integrated Electronics, which was in use) in Mountain View, California, to realize the potential of large-scale integration (LSI) technology for silicon-based chips. Robert Noyce (co-inventor of the integrated circuit, 1958) and Gordon Moore handled long-range planning, while current CEO Andrew Grove oversaw manufacturing.

Intel started with 12 employees and first-year sales of $2,672 but soon mushroomed as a supplier of semiconductor memory for large computers (DRAM chips, which replaced magnetic core memory storage, 1970; and EPROM chips, which allowed ROM to be erased and reused, 1971). This success funded Intel's microprocessor designs (the 4004 in 1971 and its descendants, the 8008, 8080, and 8088), which revolutionized the electronics industry. When IBM chose the 8088 chip for its PC in 1981, Intel secured its place as the microcomputer standards supplier.

Noyce stepped down from top management in 1979, serving as a director and deputy chairman of the company's board (he was also a founder of the SEMATECH manufacturing consortium) until his death in June 1990.

Cutthroat pricing of DRAMs by Japanese competitors forced Grove (who succeeded Noyce as president and CEO) to close plants, cut the work force by 30%, and withdraw from the DRAM market in 1985.

To regroup, Grove focused on proprietary PC chips. In its drive to become the industry standard, Intel licensed AMD and others to produce clones of the 286, only to see AMD capture 52% of that market by 1990. In response, Intel fiercely protected the technology of its highly successful 386 chip (1985) and 486 chip (1989), leading AMD to sue for breach of contract in 1987. In 1990 and again in 1992, an arbitrator ruled against Intel, validating a 1982 technology exchange deal with AMD. Intel introduced a credit-card-sized, 20MB flash memory card for small PCs (1992) and its 5th-generation Pentium chip (1993).

Over the past few years, Intel has sued AMD for copyright infringement on the microcode of the Intel287 math coprocessor (1990), the 386 (1991), and the 486 (1993). In 1995 the 2 rivals settled their past microcode court cases: AMD got the microcode license; Intel will receive $58 million in past damages. Just as that settlement was reached, the company faced more litigation when Apple sued Microsoft and Intel over code contained in Windows 95 (Intel originally developed the code, but Microsoft claims it has been rewritten). That same year Vinod Dham , who led development of the Pentium, left Intel to become EVP and COO of rival NexGen.

Nasdaq symbol: INTC
Fiscal year ends: Last Saturday in December

WHO

Chairman: Gordon E. Moore, age 66
President and CEO: Andrew S. Grove, age 58, $2,102,400 pay
EVP and COO: Craig R. Barrett, age 55, $1,554,500 pay
SVP; Director, Corporate Strategy: David L. House, age 51, $1,127,400 pay
SVP; General Manager, Intel Products Group: Frank C. Gill, age 51, $1,040,700 pay
SVP; Director, Corporate Business Development: Leslie L. Vadasz, age 58, $993,700 pay
SVP; General Manager, Technology and Manufacturing Group: Gerhard H. Parker, age 51
SVP; Director, Sales: Paul S. Otellini, age 44
VP and CFO: Andy D. Bryant, age 44
VP, General Counsel, and Secretary: F. Thomas Dunlap Jr., age 43
VP; Director, Corporate Marketing Group: Dennis L. Carter
VP; Director, Human Resources: Kirby A. Dyess
Auditors: Ernst & Young LLP

WHERE

HQ: 2200 Mission College Blvd., PO Box 58119, Santa Clara, CA 95052-8119
Phone: 408-765-8080
Fax: 408-765-1402

Intel has manufacturing plants in the US and Puerto Rico, and in Ireland, Israel, Malaysia, and the Philippines.

	1994 Sales		1994 Operating Income	
	$ mil.	% of total	$ mil.	% of total
US	5,826	51	2,742	72
Europe	3,158	27	418	11
Asia/Pacific	2,537	22	279	7
Other regions	—	—	378	10
Adjustments	—	—	(430)	—
Total	**11,521**	**100**	**3,387**	**100**

WHAT

Embedded Products
8-bit MCS51 microcontroller
16-bit 8096 microcontroller
32-bit i960 series
80C196MD controller
386 EX/CX (for embedded control applications)
82078 floppy disk controller

Memory Devices
4MB, 20MB, and 40MB flash memory cards
5MB and 10MB flash memory drive
16MB and 32MB flash memory chips

Microprocessor Peripheral Components
Indeo Video (software compression and decompression)

Microprocessors (CPUs)
486 series
i860 series (for supercomputers)
i960 series (for embedded control applications)
Pentium

Network Products
EtherExpress LAN adapter
FastEthernet cards
NetportExpress print server
StorageExpress backup server

Personal Conferencing & Communications Products
ProShareVideo System 200

Supercomputers
iPSC/860 supercomputer
Paragon XP/S massively parallel supercomputer

KEY COMPETITORS

AMD	IBM
Apple	LG Group
AST	Micron Technology
Atmel	Motorola
Canon	National Semiconductor
Chips and Technologies	NEC
Compaq	NexGen
Cray Research	Oki
Cyrix	Samsung
Data General	SCI Systems
DEC	Siemens
Dell	Silicon Graphics
Fujitsu	Sun Microsystems
Harris Corp.	Texas Instruments
Hewlett-Packard	Thomson SA
Hitachi	Toshiba
Hyundai	Unisys

HOW MUCH

	9-Year Growth	1985	1986	1987	1988	1989	1990	1991	1992	1993	1994
Sales ($ mil.)	26.7%	1,365	1,265	1,907	2,875	3,127	3,921	4,779	5,844	8,782	11,521
Net income ($ mil.)	118.7%	2	(203)	248	453	391	650	819	1,067	2,295	2,288
Income as % of sales	—	0.1%	(14.5%)	9.2%	15.8%	12.5%	16.6%	17.1%	18.3%	26.1%	19.9%
Earnings per share ($)	—	0.00	(0.58)	0.69	1.26	1.04	1.60	1.96	2.49	5.20	5.24
Stock price – high ($)	—	10.75	10.75	21.75	18.63	18.00	26.00	29.58	45.75	74.25	73.50
Stock price – low ($)	—	6.88	5.50	6.88	9.63	11.38	14.00	18.88	23.25	42.75	56.00
Stock price – close ($)	23.2%	9.75	7.00	13.25	11.87	17.25	19.75	29.50	43.50	62.00	63.88
P/E – high	—	—	—	43	15	17	16	15	18	14	14
P/E – low	—	—	—	14	8	11	9	10	9	8	11
Dividends per share ($)	—	0.00	0.00	0.00	0.00	0.00	0.00	0.00	0.05	0.20	0.24
Book value per share ($)	20.9%	4.08	3.52	3.79	5.76	6.91	8.99	10.83	13.00	17.94	22.44
Employees	4.8%	21,300	18,200	19,200	20,800	21,700	23,900	24,600	25,800	29,500	32,600

1994 Year-end:
Debt ratio: 8.9%
Return on equity: 27.3%
Cash (mil.): $2,410
Current ratio: 2.04
Long-term debt (mil.): $392
No. of shares (mil.): 413
Dividends
　Yield: 0.4%
　Payout: 4.6%
Market value (mil.): $26,380

Stock Price History
High/Low 1985–94

INTELLIGENT ELECTRONICS, INC.

OVERVIEW

Intelligent Electronics (IE) is one of the leading wholesaler/resellers of technology products and services in the US. Headquartered in Exton, Pennsylvania, the company sells microcomputer systems, workstations, networking and telecommunications equipment, and software to corporate customers, educational institutions, and government agencies. IE also provides products and services to more than 2,500 network integrators.

The company's network members include Intelligent Systems Group, Entre Computer Centers, Todays Computers Business Centers, and Connecting Point of America. To these and other network members, IE sells products and also provides services such as configuration, promotion, and technical support.

IE's profits sank in fiscal 1995 because of increased competition, a restructuring, litigation costs, and a series of embarrassing outages of the company's own computer system. As competition has increased in the computer industry, IE's suppliers have switched to "open sourcing," dropping long-term proprietary relationships with IE. In response, the company added many more vendors to its roster. The overload of new vendor transactions caused the company's computer system to crash, resulting in inventory losses and lost potential sales. The company is working to improve its computer systems.

In 1995 IE acquired its largest customer, computer sales and consulting company the Future Now.

WHEN

In 1982 Commodore EVP Richard Sanford, 38, retired, having accumulated enough wealth to never work again. After 4 months of relaxing, Sanford, bored to tears, went back to work — not for the money or the prestige, he later said, but for the challenge. Using venture capital, he founded Intelligent Electronics (IE), leasing space from Strawbridge & Clothier's department store in Philadelphia to sell computers under the name Todays Computers Business Centers.

With a little guidance from the department store's head Peter Strawbridge, Sanford enlarged his customer base and acquired salesmanship and public relations savvy. In 1984, after expanding into Pittsburgh, Sanford began franchising out his company's name, products, and services. Targeting smaller "stand-alone" office supply merchants who weren't yet selling computers, Sanford succeeded by passing on bulk-purchase savings and requiring no royalty fee.

By year-end 1985 IE controlled a 45-store network and had begun to establish relationships with key suppliers. The company began selling Compaq computers in 1986 after IBM placed a moratorium on reseller authorizations.

In 1987, the year the company went public, sales reached $81 million. Between 1986 and 1989, IE more than doubled the size of its retail network, to 193 stores. In 1989 the company bought 2 computer resellers, Entre Computer Centers (184 locations) and Connecting Point of America (245 locations), and subsequently became the nation's #1 reseller. The company also began marketing Apple computers that year.

IE entered the retail superstore market in 1991 with the purchase of the 57-store BizMart chain (for $179 million). The company believed that BizMart could generate high computer sales. However, computer sales never really took off, and market competition proved strong. BizMart lost $27 million in 1992. Also in 1992 IE won its first major outsourcing contract, with IBM's EduQuest, to provide computer services to IBM customers in primary and secondary schools.

IE sold BizMart in 1993 to Kmart's OfficeMax for $270 million. In 1994 the company announced the development of Wireless Telecom, Inc., a wholly owned subsidiary, in order to create a specialized sales channel for wireless data communications products and services. Also in 1994 the SEC began an informal investigation of IE's alleged overcharging of suppliers (including Apple, IBM, and Hewlett-Packard) for contributions earmarked for marketing. An article in the *Wall Street Journal* revealed that about half of the company's 1991 operating income came from unused marketing funds, and it raised the question of whether IE's failure to fully report the sources of its profits constituted fraud on its shareholders. Following the article, IE's stock dropped 25%.

In 1995 the company settled a suit filed by former counsel Daniel Shannon, who had been in charge of compliance with the SEC. Shannon had filed a wrongful discharge suit in 1993 after he was fired.

Nasdaq symbol: INEL
Fiscal year ends: Saturday nearest January 31

WHO

Chairman and CEO: Richard D. Sanford, age 51,
$850,000 pay
President and COO: Gregory A. Pratt, age 46,
$530,000 pay
SVP Demand Generation: Mark R. Briggs, age 38,
$363,500 pay
SVP Operational Capacity Planning: Robert P. May,
age 45, $321,875 pay
SVP Fulfillment: Timothy D. Cook, age 34
VP and CFO: Edward A. Meltzer, age 46, $153,712 pay
VP, Secretary, and Treasurer: Stephanie D. Cohen,
age 33
Personnel Administrator: Sherri Haines
Auditors: Price Waterhouse LLP

WHERE

HQ: 411 Eagleview Blvd., Exton, PA 19341
Phone: 610-458-5500
Fax: 610-458-8454

Intelligent Electronics's network consists of more than
2,500 integrators across the US. The company operates 4
leased distribution centers: one in Memphis and 3 in the
Denver area.

WHAT

	1995 Suppliers
	% of total
Compaq	25
Hewlett-Packard	24
IBM	15
Apple	12
Other	24
Total	**100**

**Reseller Network Division Computers System
Specialists and Affiliates**
Connecting Point of America
Entre Computer Centers
The Future Now
Todays Computers Business Centers

Selected Services
Financing programs
Marketing programs
New product evaluation
Preshipment configuration
Product selection
Promotions
Technical support

Selected Suppliers
Apple
AT&T
Compaq
DEC
Epson
Hewlett-Packard
IBM
Microsoft
NEC
Novell
Toshiba

KEY COMPETITORS

ADP
CompuCom
Computers 2000
EDS
Entex
IBM
InaCom
Ingram
Merisel
MicroAge
Robec
Tech Data
Vanstar

HOW MUCH

	Annual Growth	1986	1987	1988	1989	1990	1991	1992	1993	1994	1995
Sales ($ mil.)	82.9%	14	57	81	129	712	1,459	1,914	2,017	2,646	3,208
Net income ($ mil.)	26.0%	1	1	2	5	11	29	38	2	43	8
Income as % of sales	—	3.5%	1.4%	2.7%	4.0%	1.5%	2.0%	2.0%	0.1%	1.6%	0.2%
Earnings per share ($)	41.7%	0.01	0.04	0.16	0.30	0.51	1.05	1.11	0.06	1.18	0.23
Stock price – high ($)[1]	—	—	—	3.13	3.13	8.56	11.88	18.75	30.38	28.00	27.63
Stock price – low ($)[1]	—	—	—	1.50	1.56	2.88	4.81	8.75	6.25	12.00	7.50
Stock price – close ($)[1]	22.4%	—	—	1.94	3.00	6.94	10.75	17.50	12.88	27.38	8.00
P/E – high	—	—	—	20	10	17	11	17	—	24	120
P/E – low	—	—	—	9	5	6	5	8	—	10	33
Dividends per share ($)	—	—	—	0.00	0.00	0.00	0.00	0.00	0.00	2.16	0.38
Book value per share ($)	26.1%	—	—	1.06	1.43	3.26	4.98	7.59	7.75	6.23	5.37
Employees	64.9%	—	—	35	53	765	721	2,669	526	809	1,162

1995 Year-end:
Debt ratio: 0.0%
Return on equity: 4.2%
Cash (mil.): $77
Current ratio: 1.06
Long-term debt: $0
No. of shares (mil.): 31
Dividends
 Yield: 4.8%
 Payout: 165.2%
Market value (mil.): $250

Stock Price History[1]
High/Low 1988–95

[1] Stock prices are for the prior calendar year.

INTERNATIONAL BUSINESS MACHINES

OVERVIEW

Big Blue is back in the pink. IBM, the world's top computer company (hardware and software), showed a profit in 1994 after 3 years of losses totaling more than $15 billion.

IBM agreed to acquire software pioneer Lotus, developer of the *1-2-3* spreadsheet, for $3.52 billion in mid-1995. IBM, which has had trouble selling PC users on its own OS/2 operating system, wants to challenge the dominance of Microsoft Windows in that market with Lotus's *Notes*, which links PCs regardless of operating system. Lotus also gives IBM a commanding presence in desktop software.

The Lotus acquisition is the most flamboyant chapter in IBM's recent effort to recapture slipping market share after a drop in mainframe and minicomputer sales during the early 1990s. Ironically, it was a mid-1990s resurgence in high-end products (mainframes, minicomputers, and data-storage products) that pulled the company back into the black. To boost sales, IBM is also broadening its focus to include PCs, software, networking, and client/server products.

Under Louis Gerstner, who became CEO in 1993, the company has begun cutting costs by shutting plants, selling real estate, and laying off workers. IBM wants to reduce annual expenses by $8 billion by mid-1996.

Gerstner is changing IBM's tone with new products, a growing service unit, and a casual dress code that replaces the long-standard dark suits. The company is cash rich, so more acquisitions could be in store.

WHEN

In 1914 National Cash Register's star salesman, 40-year-old Thomas Watson, left to rescue the flagging Computing-Tabulating-Recording Company. Watson aggressively marketed C-T-R's Hollerith machine (a punch card tabulator) and supplied tabulators to the US government during WWI, tripling C-T-R's revenues to almost $15 million by 1920.

Watson then expanded operations to Europe, Latin America, and the Far East. In 1924 the company became International Business Machines. IBM soon dominated the market for tabulators, time clocks, and electric typewriters, becoming the US's largest office machinery firm by 1940, with sales approaching $50 million.

IBM perfected electromechanical calculation (the Harvard Mark I, 1944) but initially dismissed the potential of computers. When Remington Rand's commercial computer (UNIVAC, 1951) began replacing IBM machines, IBM quickly responded, using its superior R&D and marketing to build a market share near 80% in the 1960s and 1970s; competitors scattered to niches on the periphery.

Triumphs achieved under Thomas Watson Jr. (president in 1952) included IBM's first computer (the 701, 1952), the STRETCH systems (which eliminated vacuum tubes, 1960), and the first compatible family of computers (System/360, 1964; System/370, 1970). Accompanying innovations included the FORTRAN programming language (1957) and floppy disk storage (1971). IBM later moved into midrange systems (System/38, 1978; AS/400, 1988). The IBM PC (1981) spawned entirely new PC-related industries.

The shift to open, smaller systems, along with greater competition in all of IBM's segments, caused wrenching change. After posting profits of $6.6 billion in 1984, IBM began a slow slide. The company began reducing its work force in 1986 and by 1992 cut worldwide employment by 100,000 through attrition and early retirement inducements. IBM also sold many noncomputer businesses, such as its copier division (to Kodak, 1988); Rolm telecommunications (to Siemens, 1988); and its typewriter, keyboard, personal printer, and supplies business (Lexmark, to Clayton & Dubilier, 1991).

IBM restructured in 1991, and in 1992 it set up a European unit to sell low-cost clones of its own computers. Also in 1992 the company formed a joint venture with Sears called Advantis to provide voice-and-data network services. In 1993 IBM and Groupe Bull entered a joint venture to develop software.

In 1994 IBM sold its Federal Systems unit, which provides computer systems and services to the government, to Loral for $1.5 billion. That same year, in a challenge to Intel's dominance of the microprocessor business, IBM agreed to manufacture computer chips designed by Cyrix.

Several of IBM's highest-ranking executives, including chief strategist James Cannavino, left the company in 1995 as Gerstner continued to clean house. Also that year Apple released its first Power Mac computers that use the PowerPC chip developed by Apple, IBM, and Motorola. IBM also acquired Footprint Software, a banking-industry software developer whose programs are sold with OS/2.

NYSE symbol: IBM
Fiscal year ends: December 31

WHO

Chairman and CEO: Louis V. Gerstner Jr., age 53, $4,600,000 pay
SVP and CFO: Jerome B. York, age 56, $1,375,000 pay
SVP and Group Executive, Worldwide Sales and Services: Ned C. Lautenbach, age 51, $1,065,000 pay
SVP and Group Executive, Software Group: John M. Thompson, age 53, $1,008,000 pay
SVP and Group Executive, Personal Computer Group: G. Richard Thoman, age 50
SVP and Group Executive, Technology Group: Patrick A. Toole, age 57
SVP and Group Executive, Server Group: Nicholas M. Donofrio, age 50
SVP Research: James C. McGroddy, age 57
SVP and General Counsel: Lawrence Ricciardi, age 54
SVP Human Resources: J. Thomas Bouchard
Auditors: Price Waterhouse LLP

WHERE

HQ: International Business Machines Corporation, One Old Orchard Rd., Armonk, NY 10504
Phone: 914-765-1900
Fax: 914-288-1147 (HR)

IBM sells its products worldwide.

	1994 Sales		1994 Net Income	
	$ mil.	% of total	$ mil.	% of total
US	24,118	38	969	31
Europe/Middle East/Africa	23,034	36	1,086	35
Asia/Pacific	11,365	18	567	18
Americas	5,535	8	498	16
Adjustments	—	—	(183)	—
Total	**64,052**	**100**	**2,937**	**100**

WHAT

	1994 Sales	
	$ mil.	% of total
Workstations	13,038	21
Software	11,346	18
Processors	9,784	15
Services	9,715	15
Maintenance	7,222	11
Storage & other peripherals	5,557	9
OEM hardware	3,248	5
Financing & other	4,142	6
Total	**64,052**	**100**

Business Units

Application Solutions	Personal Computer Company
AS/400	Personal Software Products
Large Scale Computing	Power Personal Systems
Microelectronics	Printing Systems Company
Networking Hardware	RISC System/6000
Networking Software	Storage Systems

KEY COMPETITORS

AMD	Hewlett-Packard
Amdahl	Hitachi
Apple	Intel
Arthur Andersen	Intergraph
AST	Machines Bull
AT&T	Matsushita
Canon	Microsoft
Ceridian	NEC
Compaq	Oracle
Computer Associates	Packard Bell
Conner Peripherals	Siemens
Cray Research	Silicon Graphics
Cyrix	Storage Technology
Data General	Sun Microsystems
DEC	Tandem
Dell	Texas Instruments
EDS	Toshiba
Fujitsu	Unisys
Gateway 2000	

HOW MUCH

	9-Year Growth	1985	1986	1987	1988	1989	1990	1991	1992	1993	1994
Sales ($ mil.)	2.6%	50,718	52,160	55,256	59,598	62,654	68,931	64,766	64,523	62,716	64,052
Net income ($ mil.)	(8.5%)	6,555	4,789	5,258	5,451	3,722	5,967	(598)	(6,865)	(7,940)	2,937
Income as % of sales	—	13.1%	9.3%	9.7%	9.1%	5.9%	8.7%	—	—	—	4.6%
Earnings per share ($)	(8.0%)	10.67	7.81	8.72	9.20	6.41	10.42	(1.05)	(12.03)	(14.02)	5.02
Stock price – high ($)	—	158.50	161.88	175.88	129.50	130.88	123.13	139.75	100.38	59.88	76.38
Stock price – low ($)	—	117.38	119.25	102.00	104.50	93.38	94.50	83.50	48.75	40.63	51.38
Stock price – close ($)	(8.0%)	155.50	120.00	115.50	121.88	94.13	113.00	89.00	50.38	56.50	73.50
P/E – high	—	15	21	20	14	20	12	—	—	—	15
P/E – low	—	11	15	12	11	14	9	—	—	—	10
Dividends per share ($)	(15.2%)	4.40	4.40	4.40	4.40	4.73	4.84	4.84	4.84	1.58	1.00
Book value per share ($)	(3.4%)	51.98	56.73	64.09	66.99	67.01	76.43	64.20	48.31	33.95	38.00
Employees	(6.6%)	405,535	407,080	389,348	387,112	383,220	373,816	344,396	301,542	256,207	219,839

1994 Year-end:
Debt ratio: 49.8%
Return on equity: 14.3%
Cash (mil.): $10,554
Current ratio: 1.41
Long-term debt (mil.): $12,548
No. of shares (mil.): 599
Dividends
  Yield: 1.4%
  Payout: 19.9%
Market value (mil.): $43,197

Stock Price History
High/Low 1985–94

INTERNATIONAL PAPER COMPANY

OVERVIEW

International Paper is both living up to its name and trying to change its image at the same time. The world's leading producer of forest products and one of the US's largest industrial corporations went on an international shopping spree in 1995, buying a controlling interest in New Zealand's leading forest products company, Carter Holt Harvey, for $1.15 billion and offering to buy Swiss paper distribution firm Holvis for approximately $350 million. At the same time the firm has diversified its business away from overdependence on paper and packaging products (76% of 1986 revenues, 52% of 1994 sales) to a broader product line that includes distribution services, forest products, printing paper, industrial and consumer packaging, and spe-

cialty items ranging from photographic film to oil and natural gas. International Paper is a leading distributor of paper and office supply products.

The company has invested $9.4 billion in capital projects in the past 10 years and has transformed its once inefficient US mills into more competitive ones, with increased energy self-sufficiency and with many plants producing pulp on-site. International Paper has also invested in other overseas acquisitions, buying forest product companies and paper mills in Europe, Canada, and Israel.

The absorption of Carter and Holvis will increase foreign sales to 45% of total revenue and give the firm greater access to markets in South America, Europe, and the Pacific Rim.

WHEN

In 1898, 18 northeastern pulp and paper companies consolidated to lower operating costs. The resulting International Paper Company started with 20 mills in Maine, New Hampshire, Vermont, Massachusetts, and New York.

These mills depended on the forests of the northeastern US and those in neighboring Canada for wood pulp. However, Canadian provinces were enacting legislation to prevent the export of pulpwood, wanting instead to export finished products. Thus in 1919 International Paper formed Canadian International Paper, which bought Riordon (a Canadian paper company) in 1925.

In the 1920s International Paper built a hydroelectric plant on the Hudson River, and between 1928 and 1941 the company called itself International Paper & Power. The company entered the kraft (German for strength) paper market (e.g., paper sacks) in 1925 with the purchase of the Bastrop Pulp & Paper kraft paper mill (Louisiana). Mass production of paper was made possible by the Fourdrinier paper machine, which could make paper in a continuous sheet (patented by Henry and Sealy Fourdrinier in England about 1807). International Paper first mass-produced kraft containerboard in 1931.

During the 1940s and 1950s, International Paper bought Agar Manufacturing (shipping containers, 1940), Single Service Containers (Pure-Pak milk containers, 1946), and Lord Baltimore Press (folding cartons, 1958). The company diversified in the 1960s and 1970s, buying Davol (hospital products, 1968; sold to C. R. Bard in 1980), American Central (land development, 1968; assets sold to developers

in 1974), and General Crude Oil (gas and oil, 1975; sold to Mobil Oil in 1979).

In the 1980s International Paper modernized its plants to change its business mix to less cyclical products and became the industry's low-cost producer. After selling Canadian International Paper in 1981, the company went on a buying spree, starting with Hammermill Paper (office paper, 1986), Arvey (paper manufacturer and distributor, 1987), and Masonite (composite wood products, 1988). In 1989 International Paper entered the European paper market by buying Aussedat Rey (France), Ilford Group (UK), and Zanders (West Germany). The company's 1990 acquisitions included Dixon Paper (paper and graphic arts supply distributor), Nevamar (laminates), and the UK's Cookson Group (printing plates).

In 1991 International Paper enhanced its US distribution network by buying Dillard Paper and Leslie Paper; in Europe it bought Scaldia Papier (the Netherlands). Acquisitions in 1992 included Western Paper; a $258 million investment in Carter Holt Harvey, a New Zealand forest products company; and 11% (up to 12% in 1993) of Israel's Scitex, the world's #1 maker of electronic prepress systems. In 1993 the company began building a paper machine for recycled paper production at its Selma, Alabama, mill.

In 1994 International Paper formed a joint venture to build and operate a liquid packaging plant in China; it also acquired 2 Mexican paper distributing companies.

In 1995 the company acquired the assets of 2 Michigan-based paper distributors, Carpenter Paper and Seaman-Patrick.

NYSE symbol: IP
Fiscal year ends: December 31

WHO

Chairman and CEO: John A. Georges, age 64,
$2,068,750 pay
EVP Packaging: John T. Dillon, age 56, $800,000 pay
EVP Legal and External Affairs and General Counsel:
James P. Melican, age 54, $765,000 pay
EVP Distribution, Forest and Specialty Products: Mark
A. Suwyn, age 52, $708,500 pay
EVP Printing Papers: C. Wesley Smith, age 55,
$668,750 pay
President, International Paper Europe: W. Michael
Amick
SVP Industrial Packaging: Victor A. Casebolt
SVP Specialty Products: Milan J. Turk
SVP and CFO: Robert C. Butler, age 64
Controller: Andrew R. Lessin, age 52
SVP Human Resources: Robert M. Byrnes, age 57
VP Manufacturing Programs: J. Alan Day
Auditors: Arthur Andersen & Co, SC

WHERE

HQ: 2 Manhattanville Rd., Purchase, NY 10577
Phone: 914-397-1500
Fax: 914-397-1596

International Paper has production facilities in 27
countries. The company sells its products in 130
countries.

	1994 Sales		1994 Operating Income	
	$ mil.	% of total	$ mil.	% of total
US	11,965	79	915	89
Europe	2,958	19	97	9
Other regions	354	2	21	2
Adjustments	(311)	—	—	—
Total	**14,966**	**100**	**1,033**	**100**

WHAT

	1994 Sales		1994 Operating Income	
	$ mil.	% of total	$ mil.	% of total
Printing papers	4,400	28	20	2
Distribution	3,470	22	74	7
Packaging	3,375	22	293	28
Specialty products	2,590	17	268	26
Forest products	1,715	11	378	37
Adjustments	(584)	—	—	—
Total	**14,966**	**100**	**1,033**	**100**

Pulp and Paper
Coated publication papers
(Hudson Web, Zanders)
Copy paper (Aussedat Rey,
Springhill, Hammermill)
File folders, posters
Magazine papers (Aerial,
Aussedat Rey)
Market pulp
Printing, writing, and
artistic papers (Beckett,
Strathmore, Ward)

Distribution Businesses
Office products
Packaging and industrial
supplies
Paper

Paperboard and Packaging
Cartons
Containerboard

Food packaging (Akrosil,
Nicolet, Thilmany)
Kraft packaging papers
Linerboards (Pineliner,
ColorBrite)

Specialty Products
Chemicals (Arizona
Chemical)
Nonwoven fabrics (Veratec)
Oil and gas production
Photographic films and
plates (Anitec, Horsell,
Ilford)
Specialty panels (Masonite,
CraftMaster, OmniWood)

Forest Products
Fiberboard
Logs and lumber
Particleboard and siding
Treated poles

KEY COMPETITORS

Alco Standard	Fletcher Challenge	3M
Arjo Wiggins	Georgia-Pacific	Scott
Appleton	James River	Stone Container
Boise Cascade	Jefferson Smurfit	Stora
Canadian Pacific	Kimberly-Clark	Weyerhaeuser
Champion	Mead	
International		

HOW MUCH

	9-Year Growth	1985	1986	1987	1988	1989	1990	1991	1992	1993	1994
Sales ($ mil.)	14.3%	4,502	5,500	7,763	9,533	11,378	12,960	12,703	13,598	13,685	14,966
Net income ($ mil.)	14.2%	131	305	407	754	864	569	399	136	289	432
Income as % of sales	—	3.0%	5.5%	5.2%	7.9%	6.0%	4.4%	3.1%	1.0%	2.1%	2.9%
Earnings per share ($)	13.9%	1.07	2.90	3.68	6.57	7.72	5.21	3.61	1.12	2.34	3.46
Stock price – high ($)	—	28.88	40.06	57.81	49.38	58.75	59.75	78.25	78.50	69.88	80.50
Stock price – low ($)	—	22.13	24.19	27.00	36.50	45.13	42.75	50.50	58.50	56.63	60.63
Stock price – close ($)	12.9%	25.38	37.56	42.25	46.38	56.50	53.50	70.75	66.63	67.75	75.38
P/E – high	—	27	14	16	8	8	12	22	70	30	23
P/E – low	—	21	8	7	6	6	8	14	52	24	18
Dividends per share ($)	3.8%	1.20	1.20	1.23	1.28	1.53	1.68	1.68	1.68	1.68	1.68
Book value per share ($)	5.0%	33.34	35.05	36.35	41.17	47.35	51.34	51.01	50.44	50.24	51.74
Employees	9.1%	32,000	44,000	45,500	55,500	63,500	69,000	70,500	73,000	72,500	70,000

1994 Year-end:
Debt ratio: 50.1%
Return on equity: 6.8%
Cash (mil.): $270
Current ratio: 1.20
Long-term debt (mil.): $4,464
No. of shares (mil.): 126
Dividends
  Yield: 2.2%
  Payout: 48.6%
Market value (mil.): $9,490

**Stock Price History
High/Low 1985–94**

IRVIN FELD & KENNETH FELD

OVERVIEW

He already has the "greatest show on earth," but Kenneth Feld is looking to put more attractions under his big top. Feld owns 82% of Irvin Feld & Kenneth Feld Productions (3 company executives own the rest), which owns Ringling Bros. and Barnum & Bailey Circus. The Virginia-based company also owns Walt Disney on Ice and produces other acts, including the Siegfried & Roy magic show.

Feld continues to add to his business. In 1994 he bought the ice show rights to Wizard of Oz from Turner Entertainment, and he also formed Pachyderm Entertainment with a group of investors to develop television, film, and theater projects. Feld's goal is to reach $1 billion in sales by the year 2000. Although Feld is closemouthed about how much the company takes in, *Forbes* estimated sales at about $570 million in 1994.

Feld is known in the industry for his tight-fisted ways. He reportedly charges his circus performers, many of whom make about $20 a show, $10 a week to stay on the circus train and 25 cents a ride on the shuttle bus from the train to the arena.

The company is looking for growth overseas. Feld plans to add Ringling Bros. touring companies in Latin America and Asia.

WHEN

Legend has it that when 5-year-old Irvin Feld found a $1 bill in 1923 he told his mother, "I'm going to buy a circus." It took him a few more years, and a few more dollars, but he did eventually fulfill his promise. He worked the sideshows of traveling circuses before settling in Washington, DC, in 1938, where he opened a novelty store. In 1940 Feld, who was white, opened the Super Cut-Rate Drugstore in a black section of segregated Washington with the backing of the NAACP.

Feld played gospel and popular music outside the pharmacy to attract customers, and later he began to stock records. In 1944 he opened the Super Music City record store and started his own record company, Super Disc. Feld and his brother Israel also began promoting outdoor concerts by Super Disc acts. When rock-and-roll became popular in the 1950s, Feld promoted Chubby Checker and Fats Domino, among others.

In 1956 Feld began managing the Ringling Brothers and Barnum & Bailey Circus for majority owner John Ringling North. North's circus traced its roots back to promoter P. T. Barnum's circus, founded in 1871. In 1881 Barnum's circus merged with James Bailey's circus, creating Barnum and Bailey. In 1907 Bailey's widow sold Barnum and Bailey to North's uncles, the Ringling brothers, who had started their circus in 1884.

Among Feld's suggestions to North was moving the circus out from under the big top and into air-conditioned arenas, saving $50,000 per week because 1,800 roustabouts (who set up the tents) were no longer needed.

Feld continued to promote music acts, but he suffered a serious blow in 1959 when 3 of his stars — Buddy Holly, Ritchie Valens, and the Big Bopper — died in a plane crash.

Feld's dream of owning a circus came true in 1967 when he and a group of investors paid $8 million for Ringling Brothers. He fired most of the circus's performers and in 1968 opened his Clown College to train new ones. That same year Feld bought a German circus to get animal trainer Gunther Gebel-Williams. In 1969, in one of his most important innovations, Feld split the circus into 2 units so he could book it in 2 parts of the country at the same time and double his profits.

In 1971 Feld and the other investors sold the circus to Mattel for $50 million in stock, but Feld stayed on as manager. He held onto the lucrative concession business, Sells-Floto. In 1979 Feld convinced Mattel to buy the Ice Follies, Holiday on Ice, and the Siegfried & Roy magic show. When Mattel sold the circus back to Feld in 1982 for $22.6 million, he got the ice shows and the magic show, too.

When Irvin Feld died in 1984, his son Kenneth became head of the company. A chip off the old block, Kenneth fired almost all the circus performers when he took over. In 1985 Kenneth drew heat from the ASPCA when he introduced a new act to his circus — the Living Unicorn. Actually there were 2 living unicorns: each a goat with its horns laser-grafted together by a Texas animal breeder.

In 1994 a Ringling Brothers circus train bound for a show in Orlando derailed near Lakeland, Florida; an animal trainer and a clown were killed. Also in 1994 Ringling Bros. sued retailer Bargain Circus for copyright infringement for using the slogan "The Greatest Bargains on Earth."

In 1995 Carnival Hotels and Casinos hired the company to design a $25 million entertainment complex for the casino Carnival is building for the Wampanoag tribe in Massachusetts.

Private company
Fiscal year ends: January 31

WHO

President: Kenneth Feld
SVP; VP and Treasurer, Ringling Brothers: Charles E. Smith
VP Marketing and Sales: Allen J. Bloom
Accounting Finance Manager: Joe Kobylski
Director Human Resources, Ringling Brothers: Jule Bailey

WHERE

HQ: Irvin Feld & Kenneth Feld Productions, Inc., 8607 Westwood Center Dr., Vienna, VA 22182-7506
Phone: 703-448-4000
Fax: 703-448-4100

Irvin Feld & Kenneth Feld Productions's shows are seen around the world by an estimated 25 million people per year.

WHAT

Selected Attractions
American Gladiators Live
Fool Moon (touring Broadway show)
George Lucas's Super Live Adventure
Replica of the Space Shuttle
Ringling Bros. and Barnum & Bailey Circus
Siegfried & Roy magic show
Walt Disney's World on Ice
Wizard of Oz ice show

Selected Circus Acts
Amazing Españas Wheel of Death (motorcycle acrobatics)
Bamboo Balancers from the People's Republic of China
The Boger Buffaloes and Mountain Lions
Chepiakova & Kim (animal trainers)
Chinese Acrobatic Troupe
Crazy Clown Cavalcade
Johnny Peers' Muttville Comix (dogs)
Kaganovitch Flying Trapeze
The Lenz Chimpanzees
Mark Oliver Gebel (animal trainer)
Mednikov Highwire
Royal Bengal Tigers
Vivien Larible-Washington Trapeze

Subsidiaries and Affiliates
Feld Brothers Management (personal management)
Hagenbeck-Wallace (circus equipment)
Klowns Publishing Co. (show programs)
Pachyderm Entertainment (television, film, and theater production)
Sells-Floto (circus concessions)

KEY COMPETITORS

Anheuser-Busch
Capital Cities/ABC
CBS
Cirque du Soleil
Clyde Beatty-Cole Brothers Circus
General Electric
Great American Circus
Hanneford Family Circus
Ice Capades
King World
MCA
Metromedia
Pickle Family Circus
Six Flags
Sony
TCI
Thorn EMI
Time Warner
Turner Broadcasting
Viacom

HOW MUCH

	Annual Growth	1985	1986	1987	1988	1989	1990	1991	1992	1993	1994
Estimated sales ($ mil.)	15.4%	—	—	—	—	—	—	—	—	494	570
Employees	0.0%	—	—	—	—	—	—	—	—	2,500	2,500

Estimated Sales
($ mil.)
1993–94

ITT CORPORATION

OVERVIEW

ITT Corp. has a new destination: profits based on hospitality, gambling, and sports entertainment. When ITT restructures in late 1995 (spinning off its insurance unit and its electronics and defense segment), the parent company will keep its ITT Destinations subsidiary. The 425-hotel Sheraton chain will serve as the centerpiece of the new ITT Corp.

In 1994 ITT Corp. bought the exclusive Phoenician Hotel in Scottsdale, Arizona, and 70% of CIGA SpA, an Italian luxury hotel chain. The company confirmed its commitment to the hospitality industry in 1995 when it paid $1.7 billion for the 3 Caesars World hotel/casinos, including the chain's flagship, the 1,500-room Caesars Palace in Las Vegas.

In 1995 ITT Corp. became a big-league player in the sports entertainment industry when it bought a 50% stake in Madison Square Garden (MSG) from Viacom; Cablevision Systems is co-owner. The $1 billion joint purchase includes the sports and entertainment arena, the 5,600-seat Paramount Theater, the MSG Network (cable sports), and the New York Knicks (basketball) and New York Rangers (hockey) professional sports teams.

ITT Corp.'s Communications and Information (COINS) segment includes ITT World Directories, which creates telephone directories in 9 countries, and ITT Educational Services, which has 20,000 students in 58 trade schools. It sold off about 17% of ITT Educational to the public in 1994.

After orchestrating ITT's breakup, Rand Araskog, who has led the company for 16 years, chose to stay with the hospitality segment.

WHEN

Colonel Sosthenes Behn founded the International Telephone and Telegraph Corp. in 1920, intending to build a global telephone company. Over the next 4 decades ITT grew into an international powerhouse with business and political interests on several continents. During the 1940s the company sold its telephone services to focus on telecommunications equipment manufacturing. Harold Geneen became CEO in 1959 and diversified ITT by buying such companies as Aetna Finance, the Sheraton hotels, and Continental Baking. By the time Rand Araskog took over in 1979, ITT had become a floundering giant, embroiled in political scandals in South America and at home. Araskog sold all or part of 250 companies, including the last of ITT's telecommunications operations.

The Sheraton chain was founded by Harvard classmates Ernest Henderson and Robert Moore, who pooled their WWI war bonuses to invest in real estate. When they bought the Sheraton Hotel in Boston, they decided it would be too costly to replace the electric sign, so they took the name for their company.

Sheraton bought and refurbished hotels along the East Coast, including Boston's famed Copley Plaza (1941). The company introduced several innovations, including a telex reservation network (1948), a centralized electronic reservation system (1958), and a toll-free reservation number (1970). As the US became more mobile after WWII, Sheraton expanded its luxury hotels and its motor inns. It also went international, buying properties in Canada (1949); Israel, Jamaica, and Puerto Rico (1961); and Venezuela (1963). By the 1960s it was the #1 hotel owner in the US. Henderson died in 1967, and ITT acquired the company in 1968. In the 1980s ITT Sheraton opened the first US-based hotels in China and Eastern Europe.

The $1 million grand opening of Jay Sarno's Caesars Palace in 1966 featured champagne and movie stars. Sarno had made his fortune with the Cabana motel chain. In 1969 Caesars was sold to Clifford and Stuart Perlman (originators of Lum's fast-food restaurants) who named the company Caesars World. With the end of Atlantic City's gambling ban, Caesars added the Boardwalk Regency (now Caesars Atlantic City) in 1979; Caesars Tahoe also opened that year. In 1981 Caesars World shareholders bought the Perlmans' 18% stake for twice its value to rid the company of the brothers' questionable contacts.

Madison Square Garden began as P. T. Barnum's Hippodrome in 1874. It took the MSG name in 1879. The current Garden, the 4th, was opened in 1968 and acquired by Gulf + Western in 1987 (that company became Paramount in 1989). During its various incarnations MSG has hosted rodeos, boxing matches, and concert performances by Frank Sinatra, Judy Garland, and Mick Jagger. Paramount abandoned plans to rebuild MSG and instead gave it a $200 million facelift in 1991.

During the early 1990s Sheraton opened its 10th Hawaiian hotel and its 1,500-room Walt Disney World location. The company also entered the gaming industry in 1993 when it bought the Desert Inn in Las Vegas. In 1995 Sheraton said it would convert several hotels to a new, mid-priced brand, Four Points Hotels.

Fiscal year ends: December 31

WHO

Chairman and CEO: Rand V. Araskog, age 63,
$4,030,000 pay
President and COO: Robert A. Bowman, age 40,
$928,000 pay
Chairman and CEO, ITT Sheraton: John Kapioltas,
age 67, $910,417 pay
EVP, General Counsel, and Corporate Secretary:
Richard S. Ward, age 54, $695,624 pay
CFO: Ann N. Reese, age 42
Chairman and CEO, ITT Educational Services: Rene
Champagne, age 53
Chairman and CEO, World Directories: Gerald C.
Crotty, age 43
President and COO, Caesars World: Peter Boynton,
age 52
SVP and Director Human Resources: Ralph W. Pausig
Auditors: Arthur Andersen & Co, SC

WHERE

HQ: 1330 Avenue of the Americas, New York, NY
10019-5490
Phone: 212-258-1000·
Fax: 212-489-5196

WHAT

	1994 Sales		1994 Cash Flow	
	$ mil.	% of total	$ mil.	% of total
ITT Sheraton	3,927	13	258	8
Caesars	1,005	3	193	6
COINS	833	3	181	5
MSG	353	1	12	0
Adjustment	(1,358)	—	(220)	—
Subtotal	**4,760**	**20**	**424**	**21**
Spun-off business	18,860	80	1,595	79
Total	**23,620**	**100**	**2,019**	**100**

Operating Segments

Caesars World (hotel/casinos)
Caesars Atlantic City
Caesars Palace (Las Vegas)
Caesars Tahoe

ITT Communications and Information Services
(COINS)
ITT Educational Services (83%; 58 technical schools in
25 states)
ITT World Directories (telephone directories in the
Caribbean, Europe, Japan, and South Africa)

ITT Sheraton (casinos, hotels, and resorts; 425
properties in 63 countries)

Madison Square Garden (50%, entertainment)
Madison Square Garden (20,000-seat arena)
MSG Network (sports cable network)
New York Knicks (professional basketball team)
New York Rangers (professional hockey team)
Paramount Theater (5,600-seat theater in NYC)

KEY COMPETITORS

Accor	Four Seasons	National
Apollo Group	Harrah's	Education
Aztar	Entertainment	Nestlé
Bally	Helmsley	New Otani
Entertainment	Hilton	Rank
Bass	Hospitality	Resorts Intl.
Boomtown	Franchise	Ritz-Carlton
Boyd Gaming	Hyatt	Sahara Gaming
Canadian Pacific	Loews	Sands Regent
Carlson	Marriott Intl.	Showboat
Carnival Corp.	Mashantucket	Tata Enterprises
Circus Circus	Pequot Gaming	Trump
Computer Learning	MGM Grand	Westin Hotel
Centers	Mirage Resorts	WMS Industries
DeVRY		Wyndham Hotel

HOW MUCH

	9-Year Growth	1985	1986	1987	1988	1989	1990	1991	1992	1993	1994
Sales ($ mil.)	7.9%	11,871	7,596	8,551	19,355	20,005	20,604	20,421	21,651	22,762	23,620
Net income ($ mil.)	15.0%	294	494	1,085	817	922	958	817	(260)	913	1,033
Income as % of sales	—	2.5%	6.5%	12.7%	4.2%	4.6%	4.6%	4.0%	—	4.0%	4.4%%
Earnings per share ($)	17.6%	1.89	3.23	7.20	5.70	6.30	6.85	6.05	(2.19)	6.90	8.11
Stock price – high ($)	—	38.88	59.50	66.38	54.88	64.50	60.88	63.00	72.13	94.88	104.25
Stock price – low ($)	—	28.38	35.38	41.75	43.25	49.75	40.25	44.88	54.75	69.00	77.00
Stock price – close ($)	9.9%	38.00	53.38	44.50	50.38	58.88	48.00	57.75	72.00	91.25	88.63
P/E – high	—	21	217	9	10	10	9	10	—	14	13
P/E – low	—	15	10	6	8	8	6	7	—	10	9
Dividends per share ($)	7.9%	1.00	1.00	1.00	1.25	1.48	1.60	1.72	1.81	1.98	1.98
Book value per share ($)	0.4%	43.75	48.28	55.52	58.05	57.67	66.33	71.72	55.10	58.00	45.46
Employees	8.0%	232,000	123,000	120,000	227,000	119,000	114,000	110,000	106,000	98,000	110,000

1994 Year-end:
Debt ratio: 74.4%
Return on equity: 17.5%
Cash (mil.): $1,136
Current ratio: —
Long-term debt (mil.): $13,940
No. of shares (mil.): 106
Dividends
  Yield: 2.2%
  Payout: 24.4%
Market value (mil.): $9,365

Stock Price History
High/Low 1985–94

ITT HARTFORD GROUP

OVERVIEW

Hartford is going stag. After 25 years as an integral part of ITT Corporation, the 185-year-old insurance company will be on its own again at the end of 1995, when Hartford's parent disbands itself into 3 corporations, to be spun off to shareholders. The other 2 entities are ITT Industries (manufacturing) and the new ITT Corp. (hospitality). ITT decided to take this step because conglomerates are out of fashion and because splitting the companies will allow their managements to concentrate on their respective core businesses.

ITT Hartford, which will be run by the same group that managed it before the spinoff, has been one of parent ITT's strongest groups. Its primary operating company, Hartford Fire Insurance, offers a variety of personal and commercial property/casualty insurance products, including homeowners, auto, and workers' compensation. Hartford Life offers individual and group life insurance, annuities, employee benefits administration, and asset management. In 1993, in a climate of uncertainty in the field, Hartford Life sold its employee health insurance unit. The company also decided several years ago to wind down its property/casualty reinsurance operations.

The company's 1994 purchase of a Spanish multiline company indicates its belief in the growth potential of the less mature insurance markets outside North America and Northern Europe.

WHEN

In 1810 a group of Hartford, Connecticut, businessmen led by Walter Mitchell and Henry Terry founded the Hartford Fire Insurance Co.

Hartford's management had little awareness of the difficulties of assessing risks and setting premiums. So the company was often on the edge of insolvency, thanks to frequent fires in America's wooden cities. It happened so often, in fact, that in 1835 stockholders staged a coup and threw out the management.

After each of the frequent urban conflagrations, which included the Chicago Fire of 1871, Hartford made a special effort to seek out and pay all its policyholders. Learning underwriting under fire, the company used such disasters to refine its rates.

The company's stag logo was once a little deer, as shown on a policy sold to Abraham Lincoln in 1861. A few years later, Hartford began using the magnificent beast (from a Landseer painting) now familiar to customers.

By the 1880s Hartford operated nationwide as well as in Canada and Hawaii. In 1882, an agent named Mrs. Dodds from Osage City, Kansas, asked the company to consider windstorm insurance. Her suggestion was met with disdain, but within a few years Hartford was writing tornado insurance. Other new types of coverage were also added (including auto, travel, and inland marine), particularly after the San Francisco earthquake of 1906.

The company survived both world wars and the Depression but emerged in the 1950s in need of consolidation. It set up new regional offices to coordinate local activities. It also added life insurance, acquiring Columbian National Life (Boston). Founded in 1902, the company became Hartford Life Insurance Co.

In 1969 Hartford was acquired by ITT (formerly International Telephone and Telegraph), whose CEO, Harold Geneen, was an avid conglomerateur. The acquisition was strongly opposed by Ralph Nader, who led a court fight against the merger for years afterward. (Nader viewed the 1995 spinoff as a vindication of his opposition to conglomerates.) Others were unhappy about it, too, as ITT had engineered the merger based on an IRS ruling that Hartford stockholders would not have to pay capital gains taxes on the purchase price of their stock. The ruling was later revoked.

In 1978 the insurance operations were consolidated as the Hartford Life Insurance Co. In the 1980s, as bloated ITT seemed to lurch from disaster to disaster, Hartford remained one of the conglomerate's strongest operations. A conservative investment policy kept Hartford safe from the junk bond and real estate manias of the 1980s.

Hartford reorganized its property/casualty operations along 3 lines in 1986, and in 1992 it streamlined its reinsurance business into one unit. The company faced some liability in relation to Dow Corning's breast implants, but underwriting standards after 1985 reduced its long-term risk.

After 3 years of negotiations, Hartford agreed in 1994 to provide an exclusive line of annuity products to AARP members.

The company was busy in 1995. In addition to its spinoff, Hartford sold its real estate portfolio to the in-house group that had managed it. It also joined with Health Net, a California-based HMO, to design a new workers' compensation management plan.

Fiscal year ends: December 31

WHO

Chairman and CEO: Donald R. Frahm, age 63,
$835,833 pay
President and COO: Ramani Ayer, age 48, $568,333 pay
President and COO, Hartford Life Insurance Cos.:
Lowndes A. Smith, age 55, $533,333 pay
EVP and Chief Investment Officer: Joseph H. Gareau,
age 48, $404,583 pay
SVP Business Development: John F. Donahue, age 59,
$308,333 pay
SVP Corporate Relations and Government Affairs:
Edward L. Morgan, age 52
SVP and Group Controller: James J. Westervelt, age 48
SVP, General Counsel, and Secretary: Michael S.
Wilder, age 53
SVP Human Resources: Helen G. Goodman, age 54
Auditors: Arthur Andersen & Co, SC

WHERE

HQ: Hartford Plaza, Hartford, CT 06115
Phone: 203-547-5000
Fax: 203-547-3799

ITT Hartford operates in Argentina, Bermuda, Canada,
France, Hong Kong, the Netherlands, Spain, Taiwan,
the UK, and the US.

	1994 Premiums	
	$ mil.	% of total
US property/casualty	5,654	56
US life	2,127	21
Foreign property/casualty	1,085	11
Foreign life	1,142	12
Total	**10,008**	**100**

WHAT

	1994 Sales	
	$ mil.	% of total
Property/casualty insurance	6,580	59
Life insurance	2,173	20
Net investment income	2,259	20
Other	90	1
Total	**11,102**	**100**

	1994 Assets	
	$ mil.	% of total
Cash & equivalents	55	0
Government securities	7,535	10
US agency securities	8,545	11
Corporate bonds	6,324	8
Other bonds	5,014	7
Stocks	1,350	2
Receivables & recoverables	14,216	19
Policy loans	2,614	3
Separate account assets	23,255	30
Other	7,857	10
Total	**76,765**	**100**

Lines of Business

Life Insurance
Asset management
Employee benefits
Individual life and annuities

Property/Casualty Insurance
Auto, commercial, and personal
Fire and allied lines
Homeowners
Inland marine
Liability
Workers' compensation

Selected Subsidiaries

American Maturity Life (annuities for AARP members)
Hartford Life Insurance Cos.
Hartford Re Management Co.
ITT Ercos de Seguros y Reaseguros SA (Spain)
ITT London & Edinburgh (UK)
Zwolsche Algemeene (The Netherlands)

KEY COMPETITORS

20th Century
  Industries
Aetna
Allianz
Allstate
American Financial
Berkshire Hathaway
Chubb
CIGNA
Guardian Life Insurance
John Hancock
Liberty Mutual

MassMutual
MetLife
Mutual of Omaha
New York Life
Northwestern Mutual
Prudential
State Farm
Tokio Marine and Fire
USAA
USF&G

HOW MUCH

	Annual Growth	1985	1986	1987	1988	1989	1990	1991	1992	1993	1994
Assets ($ mil.)	20.5%	—	—	20,843	22,787	24,493	32,014	37,771	54,180	66,179	76,765
Net income ($ mil.)	10.0%	—	—	325	435	372	328	431	(274)	537	632
Income as % of assets	—	—	—	1.5%	1.9%	1.5%	1.0%	1.1%	—	0.8%	0.8%
Employees	(1.2%)	—	—	—	—	—	21,000	21,000	21,000	21,000	20,000

1994 Year-end:
Equity as % of assets: 4.1%
Return on assets: 0.9%
Return on equity: 17.6%
Long-term debt (mil.): $596
Sales (mil.): $11,102

Net Income
($ mil.) 1987–94

ITT INDUSTRIES, INC.

OVERVIEW

ITT Industries is one of a trio of companies that will be formed by ITT Corporation's break-up, scheduled for late 1995. ITT Corporation's 3 manufacturing companies — ITT Automotive, ITT Defense & Electronics, and ITT Fluid Technology — will make up ITT Industries.

ITT Automotive, the largest of the 3 companies, is one of the world's leading suppliers of automobile components and systems. The company makes assemblies for antilock brakes, doors, windows, windshield wipers, and car seats. In 1994 ITT Automotive bought General Motors's actuators and motors business, renaming it ITT Automotive Electrical Systems.

ITT Defense & Electronics develops and manufactures high-tech electronics for commercial and defense applications. It is a leading supplier of audio/video signal processors, combat radios, radar, night-vision devices, and air

traffic control systems. The US government accounted for nearly 60% of ITT Defense & Electronics's 1994 sales.

ITT Fluid Technology produces pumps, controls, valves, and other fluid-handling devices for use principally in the construction, manufacturing, and water and wastewater treatment industries.

Each of ITT's manufacturing companies is pursuing growth in emerging markets. In 1994 ITT Automotive established a manufacturing facility in Hungary and became 40% owner of a joint venture with Shanghai Automotive Brake Systems. Also in 1994 ITT Fluid Technology formed joint ventures to manufacture pumps in Brazil and China.

Travis Engen, who studied aeronautics and astronautics at MIT and who had served as CEO of ITT Defense, will head ITT Industries.

WHEN

Colonel Sosthenes Behn founded the International Telephone and Telegraph Corporation (ITT) in 1920 to manage Cuban and Puerto Rican telephone companies. By 1925 Behn had added 3 other small telephone companies. ITT bought International Western Electric (renamed International Standard Electric, or ISE) from AT&T in 1925, making ITT a major international phone equipment manufacturer. In the late 1920s ITT bought Mackay, a US holding company involved in telegraph, cable, radio, and equipment manufacturing. During WWII, ISE scientists who had fled Europe gravitated to the company's New York laboratory. Their work laid the foundation for ITT's high-tech electronics business.

As WWII began to cause losses at ITT's considerable foreign interests (more than 2/3 of company revenues had come from overseas), Behn determined that ITT should rely less on foreign income sources. To increase US opportunities, Behn arranged for a Mackay subsidiary, Federal Telegraph (later Federal Electric), to become part of ITT. Behn took charge of Federal, creating the Federal Telephone & Radio Laboratories. By 1944 Federal had $90 million in sales. Its primary products were radio and telephone systems and military equipment.

By the 1950s ITT was a diverse and unwieldy collection of companies. In the mid-1950s ISE was the company's biggest segment, developing advanced telephone switching equipment. ITT Laboratories pioneered transistor technology, although management failed to capitalize on the lab's products.

In 1956 the aging Behn resigned as chairman of ITT. He died a year later. Former Raytheon executive Harold Geneen took the reins of ITT in 1959.

During the 1960s and 1970s, ITT added several companies that would evolve into ITT Industries. Auto parts makers included Teves (car brakes, West Germany), Ulma (auto trim, Italy), and Altissimo (auto lights and accessories, Italy). Electronics acquisitions included Cannon Electric (a leading manufacturer of electrical connectors) and National Computer Products (electronics for satellite communications). Fluid technology companies included Bell & Gossett (the US's largest maker of commercial and industrial pumps) and Flygt (pumps and mixers, Sweden). When ITT acquired Sheraton in 1968, it also got Thompson Industries, a supplier of auto parts. By 1977 ITT's Engineered Products division consisted of nearly 80 companies making automotive and electrical products.

In the 1980s ITT established itself as a leading supplier of antilock brakes (viewed as the most significant auto safety development of the decade), a top manufacturer of semiconductors and defense electronics, and (with the 1988 purchase of Allis-Chalmers's pump business) an international force in fluid technology. In 1990 ITT Fluid Technology passed the $1 billion sales mark.

During the early 1990s ITT's Defense & Electronics segment earned major military contracts to manufacture equipment for use in the Persian Gulf War.

WHO

Chairman, President, and CEO: D. Travis Engen, age 51, $1,246,583 pay
SVP; President, ITT Automotive: Timothy D. Leuliette, age 45, $785,417 pay
SVP; President, ITT Defense & Electronics: Louis J. Giuliano, age 48, $613,814 pay
SVP; President, ITT Fluid Technology: Bertil T. Nilsson, age 63, $517,100 pay
SVP and Director Human Resources: James P. Smith Jr., age 52, $325,000 pay
SVP and Controller: Richard J. M. Hamilton, age 45
SVP, Secretary, and General Counsel: Vincent A. Maffeo, age 44
VP and Director Corporate Development: Martin Kamber, age 47
Auditors: Arthur Andersen & Co, SC

WHERE

HQ: 1330 Avenue of the Americas, New York, NY 10019-5490
Phone: 212-258-1000
Fax: 212-489-5198

ITT Industries' automotive, defense and electronics, and fluid technology segments operate worldwide.

	1994 Sales
	% of total
US	50
Western Europe	38
Canada	6
Asia/Pacific	3
Other regions	3
Total	**100**

WHAT

	1994 Sales		1994 Operating Income	
	$ mil.	% of total	$ mil.	% of total
Automotive	4,784	62	328	63
Defense & Electronics	1,498	19	96	18
Fluid Technology	1,125	14	99	19
Other	351	5	—	—
Total	**7,758**	**100**	**523**	**100**

Companies & Products

ITT Automotive
Brake and Chassis Systems
  Antilock brakes
  Chassis systems
  Fluid-handling components
  Foundation brake components
  "Koni" brand shock absorbers
  Traction-control systems
Body and Electrical Systems
  Air management systems
  Door and window assemblies
  Fractional horsepower DC motors
  Seat systems
  Switches
  Wiper module assemblies

ITT Defense & Electronics
Electronic warfare systems
Interconnect products
Night-vision devices
Operations and management services
Radar
Space payloads
Tactical communications equipment

ITT Fluid Technology
Controls and instruments
Heat exchangers
Mixers
Pumps
Valves

KEY COMPETITORS

Alliant Techsystems
AlliedSignal
British Aerospace
BW/IP
Core Industries
Crawford Fitting
Dana
Daniel Industries
Echlin
FMC
GenCorp
Hughes Electronics
Johnson Controls
Lear Seating
Litton
Mannesmann
Olin
Raytheon
Rockwell
SCI Systems
Texas Instruments
Thomson SA
Tracor
TRW
Unisys
U.S. Industries
Watts Industries

HOW MUCH

	Annual Growth	1985	1986	1987	1988	1989	1990	1991	1992	1993	1994
Sales ($ mil.)	(3.1%)	10,314	5,870	6,626	7,464	7,741	8,057	7,342	6,845	6,621	7,758
Net income ($ mil.)	—	—	—	—	—	—	—	—	(260)	913	1,033
Income as % of sales	—	—	—	—	—	—	—	—	—	13.8%	13.3%
Employees	—	—	—	—	—	—	—	—	—	—	58,400

1994 Year-end:
Debt ratio: 32.6%
Return on equity: 17.5%
Cash (mil.): $322
Current ratio: 0.99
Long-term debt (mil.): $1,712
No. of shares (mil.): —
Dividends
Yield: —
Payout: —
Market value (mil.): —

Net Income ($ mil.) High/Low 1992–94

JAMES RIVER CORPORATION

OVERVIEW

James River has decided to cut adrift its office-paper business, and possibly its packaging business, in order to allow the company to increase its upstream progress in the consumer paper market. The Richmond-based company is a major international paper manufacturer and one of the top 4 US makers of paper towel and tissue products, competing for market lead with rivals Procter & Gamble, Fort Howard, and Scott Paper. Leading brands include Brawny, Northern, and Nice 'n Soft.

The company is a major producer of paper and plastic beverage and food service products, including Dixie plates and cups. Dixie holds the #1 position in commercial food service, ahead of Sweetheart Cups. James River also makes packaging for the retail food and consumer products market, making cereal boxes, ice cream cartons, potato chip bags, and plastic sandwich wrapping.

The company is bulking up its consumer products operations and is expanding in Europe. In 1994 the company shelled out $575 million to increase to 86% its investment in Jamont, Europe's #3 paper producer (after Scott Paper and Molnycke-PWA), with operations in 12 countries. Jamont makes a number of popular consumer brands, including Lotus bathroom tissue and Vania feminine-hygiene products.

James River's communications papers unit has been losing money for years, but cost reductions and the resurgence of paper prices have restored the division to near profitability.

The company entered the premium, private-label towel, tissue, and table-top product markets in 1994 by selling premium private-label brands to several of its key US customers. James River made plans to spin off its office paper business in June 1995.

WHEN

In 1969, when Ethyl Corporation (Richmond, Virginia) wanted to sell Albemarle Paper's Hollywood Mill (its unprofitable paper maker), Ethyl executives Brenton Halsey and Robert Williams, some Albemarle employees, and a few investors joined forces to buy the mill, located on the James River in Richmond. Halsey was named chairman and CEO and Williams president and COO of the resulting company, James River Paper. In 1973 the company went public and changed its name to James River Corporation of Virginia.

Rather than build new pulp and paper enterprises, James River bought existing ones from other companies. These included 80% of Pepperell Paper (1971), Peninsular Paper (1974), and Weyerhaeuser Massachusetts (1975). In 1977 James River bought Curtis Paper, Rochester Paper, and Riegel Products. The company entered the industrial film products market in 1978 (buying Scott Graphics from Scott Paper) and the wood pulp business in 1980 (buying Brown Paper from Gulf & Western).

The company became the maker of Dixie cups, Northern towels and tissues, and Marathon folding cartons in 1982, when it bought Dixie/Northern paper and forest properties from American Can Company for $455 million. In 1983 James River bought the pulp and papermaking facilities of Diamond International (Vanity Fair products).

James River expanded into Europe in 1984 (GB Papers, Scotland). In 1986 the company

bought the pulp, papermaking, flexible packaging, and distribution businesses of Crown Zellerbach for $1.6 billion. Founded around 1870, Crown was one of the world's largest integrated paper companies, operating mostly in the western US. Its brand names included Nice 'n Soft, Zee, and Spill Mate.

In 1987 James River bought 50% of Kaysersberg, France's leading manufacturer of paper towel and tissue products. In 1990 the company sold its Nonwovens Group and formed a joint venture (Jamont) with Italy's Gruppo Feruzzi and Finland's Nokia Corporation to gain a foothold in the European tissue market.

As part of a restructuring program, James River sold its specialty paper business to AEA Investors (1991). Halsey retired in 1992 and was succeeded as chairman and CEO by co-founder Williams. In 1993 James River bought Occidental Forest's 77% stake in Diamond Occidental Forest for $198 million, gaining 500,000 acres of forest near James River's pulp and paper mills. James River already owned 23% of Diamond Occidental.

In 1994 Williams announced he would retire in early 1996. The company also closed a napkin manufacturing plant in Sandston, Virginia, eliminating 45 jobs.

In 1995 James River announced that it will invest an additional $36 million to upgrade the bathroom tissue converting plant at its mill in Naheola, Alabama.

NYSE symbol: JR
Fiscal year ends: Last Sunday in December

WHO

Chairman: Robert C. Williams, age 65, $1,175,000 pay
President and CEO: Miles L. Marsh, age 48
CEO, Jamont N.V.: Ronald L. Singer, age 50, $698,077 pay
EVP Food and Consumer Packaging: Norman K. Ryan, age 58, $390,000 pay
EVP Consumer Products: James K. Goodwin, age 48, $359,154 pay
SVP Corporate Finance and CFO: Stephen E. Hare, age 41
SVP, General Counsel, and Corporate Secretary: Clifford A. Cutchins IV, age 46
SVP and Group Executive, Flexible Packaging: Richard K. Lee, age 54
SVP Strategic Services: John M. Nevin, age 59
SVP Fiber Business: E. Lee Showalter, age 58
SVP Human Resources: Daniel J. Girvan, age 46
Auditors: Coopers & Lybrand L.L.P.

WHERE

HQ: James River Corporation of Virginia, 120 Tredegar St., Richmond, VA 23219
Phone: 804-644-5411
Fax: 804-649-4428

	1994 Pulp and Paper Mills	
	No. of units	% of total
US	33	55
UK	8	13
France	6	10
Other countries	13	22
Total	**60**	**100**

WHAT

	1994 Sales		1994 Operating Income	
	$ mil.	% of total	$ mil.	% of total
Consumer Prods.	3,053	54	150	60
Food & Consumer Packaging	1,610	29	97	40
Communications Papers	930	17	(36)	—
Adjustments	(176)	—	(65)	—
Total	**5,417**	**100**	**146**	**100**

Selected Product Lines
Bathroom tissue (Chelsea, Compact, Lotus, Marina, Nice 'n Soft, Quilted Northern)
Copy paper (Eureka!)
Cover papers (Curtis, King James)
Facial tissue (Lotus)
Flexible multilayer packaging
Institutional paper products (Dixie/Marathon, Handi-Kup, Canada Cup)
Magazine and catalog paper
Offset printing paper
Paper cups and plates (Dixie)
Paper napkins (Northern, Vanity Fair)
Paper towels (Brawny)
Paperboard cartons
Plastic cups and utensils
Plastic pouches
Printing and publication papers (Graphika!, Curtis)
Specialty packaging papers
Writing papers (Curtis, Retreeve)

KEY COMPETITORS

Alco Standard
Arjo Wiggins Appleton
Boise Cascade
Canadian Pacific
Champion Intl.
Dart Container
Fletcher Challenge
Fort Howard
Georgia-Pacific
International Paper
Jefferson Smurfit
Kimberly-Clark
Mead
Molnycke - PWA
Procter & Gamble
Rayonier
Reynolds Metals
Rubbermaid
Scott
Stone Container
Stora
Sweetheart Cups
Union Camp
Weyerhaeuser

HOW MUCH

	9-Year Growth	1985	1986	1987	1988	1989	1990	1991	1992	1993	1994
Sales ($ mil.)	9.0%	2,492	2,607	4,479	5,098	5,872	5,950	4,562	4,728	4,650	5,417
Net income ($ mil.)	—	101	95	170	209	255	222	78	(122)	(0)	(13)
Income as % of sales	—	4.1%	3.7%	3.8%	4.1%	4.3%	3.7%	1.7%	—	—	—
Earnings per share ($)	—	1.93	1.73	2.03	2.36	2.87	2.45	0.66	(1.82)	(0.40)	(0.72)
Stock price – high ($)	—	23.00	31.12	43.75	39.00	30.75	34.38	29.25	23.38	23.38	24.75
Stock price – low ($)	—	15.63	17.12	22.00	18.50	21.12	22.75	17.00	17.00	16.25	15.63
Stock price – close ($)	1.7%	17.33	30.75	36.00	24.63	28.50	22.88	19.88	18.00	18.50	20.25
P/E – high	—	12	18	22	17	11	14	44	—	—	—
P/E – low	—	8	9	11	9	7	9	26	—	—	—
Dividends per share ($)	5.5%	0.37	0.37	0.40	0.40	0.48	0.60	0.60	0.60	0.60	0.60
Book value per share ($)	3.0%	13.35	14.40	21.22	23.12	25.24	27.14	27.25	20.34	18.55	17.40
Employees	(0.9%)	36,600	35,453	39,000	42,000	46,000	46,000	38,000	38,000	35,000	33,800

1994 Year-end:
Debt ratio: 68.7%
Return on equity: —
Cash (mil.): $59
Current ratio: 1.26
Long-term debt (mil.): $2,668
No. of shares (mil.): 81.7
Dividends
　Yield: 3.0%
　Payout: —
Market value (mil.): $1,654

Stock Price History
High/Low 1985–94

J. C. PENNEY COMPANY, INC.

OVERVIEW

"It is our objective to have the customer think of J. C. Penney first for every category of merchandise we compete in," says new CEO James Oesterreicher. He succeeded William Howell (who remains chairman) at the beginning of 1995 to take the helm of the Plano, Texas–based retailer. Oesterreicher is taking control of a company that has been on something of a roll lately; sales and profits have been on the rise for 3 years.

The new chief is working to boost Penney's market share by cutting costs to keep prices down. He also plans to continue the company's emphasis on private-label products (including Arizona jeans, Stafford men's suits, and Worthington women's business casual clothing), which account for about half its merchandise.

The company is also expanding internationally, looking to develop new markets because it sees the US as "over-stored." It is opening stores in Chile and Mexico and has its eyes on Japan, China, and the Middle East. It already offers mail-order service in Iceland, Brazil, and Russia. Penney also operates drugstores, an insurance company, and a credit bank.

WHEN

In 1902 James Cash Penney and 2 former employers opened The Golden Rule, a dry goods store, in Kemmerer, Wyoming. Penney bought out his partners in 1907 and opened stores that sold high-demand soft goods in small towns. Basing his customer service policy on his Baptist heritage, he held employees (called "associates") to a high moral code. Managers, usually former sales clerks, were offered 1/3 partnerships in the stores.

The company incorporated in Utah in 1913 as the J. C. Penney Company, with headquarters in Salt Lake City, but moved to New York City in 1914 to aid buying and financial operations. In the 1920s the company expanded to nearly 1,400 stores and went public in 1929. The company grew during the Depression on the strength of its reputation for high quality and low prices.

With Penney riding the postwar boom, by 1951 sales in the more than 1,600 stores had surpassed $1 billion. Penney introduced credit plans in 1958. In 1963 the company added hard goods, which, with the purchase of General Merchandise Company (1962, Milwaukee, mail order) allowed it to compete with Sears and Montgomery Ward.

The company bought Treasure Island discount stores in 1962 (sold in 1981) and formed JCPenney Insurance from companies it bought in the mid-1960s. Penney bought Thrift Drug in 1969 and continued to grow. In 1973, 2 years after James Cash Penney's death, there were 2,053 stores.

In the 1970s Penney began its first, ill-fated foray overseas by buying chains in Belgium and Italy in hopes of duplicating its US formula — giant department stores. But there was local resistance to the large stores. The company took until 1987 to extricate itself.

Penney bought First National Bank (Harrington, Delaware; 1983), renamed JCPenney National Bank (1984), to issue MasterCard and Visa cards. The company refocused on soft goods during the 1980s. In 1983 Penney stopped selling automotive services, restaurants, appliances, paint, hardware, and fabrics. In 1987 it discontinued sporting goods, consumer electronics, and photographic equipment.

The company entered the cable television shopping market twice between 1987 and 1991 but was not successful. In 1988 JCPenney Telemarketing was started to take catalog phone orders and provide telemarketing services for other companies. Also in 1988 the company moved its headquarters from New York to Texas.

In the 1980s Penney tried to move upmarket, enlisting Halston to produce a fashion line for the store. The fashion world viewed this as a betrayal; the Penney line failed, and it effectively ended Halston's career. Thereafter, unable to enlist any famous names, the company developed its own, including Hunt Club, St. John's Bay, and Worthington, which have developed considerable cachet abroad.

Penney began a marketing program targeted at minorities in 1993. In 1994 it settled a class action lawsuit that charged Penney had illegally calculated pension benefits. As part of the settlement, the company agreed to change the way it determines benefits for employees and retirees.

After facing many delays (including the devaluation of the peso), Penney opened its first Mexican store in 1995 in the Plaza San Agustin mall in Monterrey. Also that year, the company acquired 7 stores in the Washington, DC, area from bankrupt Woodward & Lothrop.

NYSE symbol: JCP
Fiscal year ends: Last Saturday in January

WHO

Chairman: William R. Howell, age 59, $1,801,644 pay
VC and CEO: James E. Oesterreicher, age 53, $672,277 pay (prior to promotion)
President and COO: W. Barger Tygart, age 59, $602,345 pay
SEVP; Director, Personnel and Company Communications: Gale Duff-Bloom, age 55
President, JCPenney Stores: John T. Cody Jr., age 55, $445,744 pay
President, Merchandising Worldwide: Thomas D. Hutchens, age 54, $439,820 pay
President, Catalog and Distribution: William E. McCarthy, age 53
EVP and CFO: Robert E. Northam, age 64, $680,096 pay
EVP; Director, Support Services: Terry S. Prindiville, age 59
EVP, Secretary, and General Counsel: Charles R. Lotter, age 57
SVP; Director, Financial Services and Government Relations: Ted L. Spurlock, age 56
SVP; Director, Planning and Information Systems: David V. Evans, age 51
VP and Treasurer: Leo A. Gispanski
VP and Controller: Donald A. McKay
VP; Director, Communications: Russell H. Longyear
VP; Director, Personnel: Jay F. Hundley
Auditors: KPMG Peat Marwick LLP

WHERE

HQ: 6501 Legacy Dr., Plano, TX 75024-3698
Phone: 214-431-1000
Fax: 214-431-1977

J. C. Penney operates 1,233 JCPenney retail stores and 526 Thrift Drug drugstores throughout all 50 states and Puerto Rico, as well as 6 distribution centers.

WHAT

| | 1995 Sales | |
	$ mil.	% of total
JCPenney stores	15,023	74
Catalog	3,817	19
Drugstores	1,540	7
Total	**20,380**	**100**

| | 1995 Stores | |
	No.	% of total
JCPenney stores	1,233	70
Drugstores	526	30
Total	**1,759**	**100**

Major Product Lines	Selected Subsidiaries
Accessories	JCPenney Insurance
Family apparel	JCPenney National Bank
Home furnishings	Thrift Drug, Inc.
Jewelry	
Shoes	

KEY COMPETITORS

American Stores	May
Ames	Melville
Broadway Stores	Mercantile Stores
Circuit City	Merck
Clothestime	Montgomery Ward
Dayton Hudson	Nordstrom
Dillard	Paul Harris Stores
Dress Barn	Price/Costco
Eckerd	Rex Stores
Federated	Sears
Fred Meyer	Service Merchandise
Harcourt General	Spiegel
J. Crew	Stein Mart
Kmart	Thrifty PayLess
Lands' End	TJX
The Limited	Venture Stores
L.L. Bean	Walgreen
Longs	Wal-Mart

HOW MUCH

	9-Year Growth	1986	1987	1988	1989	1990	1991	1992	1993	1994	1995
Sales ($ mil.)	4.5%	13,747	14,740	15,332	15,296	16,103	16,365	16,201	18,009	18,983	20,380
Net income ($ mil.)	11.5%	397	530	608	807	802	577	264	777	889	1,057
Income as % of sales	—	2.9%	3.6%	4.0%	5.3%	5.0%	3.5%	1.6%	4.3%	4.7%	5.2%
Earnings per share ($)	13.2%	1.33	1.77	2.06	2.96	2.93	2.17	0.99	4.19	56.38	4.05
Stock price – high ($)[1]	—	14.44	22.09	33.00	27.88	36.63	37.81	29.13	40.19	56.38	59.00
Stock price – low ($)[1]	—	11.16	13.16	17.63	19.00	25.19	18.69	21.25	25.38	35.38	41.13
Stock price – close ($)[1]	13.9%	13.88	18.06	21.69	25.31	36.38	22.13	27.50	38.88	52.63	44.63
P/E – high	—	11	13	16	9	13	17	29	14	16	15
P/E – low	—	8	7	9	6	9	9	22	9	10	10
Dividends per share ($)	11.9%	0.59	0.62	0.71	0.94	1.09	1.32	1.32	1.32	1.41	1.62
Book value per share ($)	6.2%	13.60	14.50	15.10	13.23	17.78	18.29	17.20	19.11	21.59	23.31
Employees	1.5%	177,000	176,000	181,000	190,000	198,000	196,000	185,000	192,000	193,000	202,000

1995 Year-end:
Debt ratio: 49.1%
Return on equity: 20.4%
Cash (mil.): $261
Current ratio: 2.11
Long-term debt (mil.): $3,335
No. of shares (mil.): 227
Dividends
  Yield: 3.6%
  Payout: 40.0%
Market value (mil.): $10,131

Stock Price History[1]
High/Low 1986–95

[1] Stock prices are for the prior calendar year.

JOHN HANCOCK MUTUAL LIFE

OVERVIEW

Boston-based mutual insurer John Hancock is gearing up for the 21st century with a series of initiatives designed to streamline and automate its operations, strengthen its product lines, and add to its presence overseas.

As part of this effort, the company has begun consolidating offices, shedding more than 1,000 agents. In 1995 this effort was brought to the home office with a plan to cut 460 more jobs. These cuts — not simply of organizational fat — are made possible by automation advances that reduce paperwork.

In addition to its traditional life insurance products and annuities, John Hancock also offers health plans, including long-term care plans, and accelerated death benefits options, which are useful in providing income to potentially terminally ill people.

But the area where John Hancock is making the most strides is in financial services. The company has been acquiring investment companies, brokerages, and mutual funds companies since the 1980s; in 1995 it launched a new holding company, John Hancock Asset Management, for these companies and older units such as its timber and agricultural funds. Some analysts believe this may be a prelude to taking the unit public.

WHEN

In 1862 Albert Murdock and other Boston businessmen founded John Hancock Mutual Life Insurance Co., named after a signer of the Declaration of Independence. In 1865 the company added agents in Connecticut, Illinois, Missouri, and Pennsylvania.

In 1866 the company began making annual distributions of surplus to paid-up policyholders. In 1879 John Hancock became the first US mutual life insurance company to offer industrial insurance (weekly premium life insurance in small amounts). The company was also a pioneer in granting dividends and cash surrender values (the amount returned to the policyholder when a policy is canceled) with industrial insurance. In 1902 the company's weekly premium agencies began selling annual premium insurance.

John Hancock added annuities in 1922, group insurance in 1924, and individual health insurance in 1957. In 1968 the company formed John Hancock Advisers (mutual funds) and John Hancock International Group Program (group health and life insurance overseas). In the early 1970s it started property and casualty insurance operations in partnership with Sentry Insurance.

Despite these forays into new areas, John Hancock's mainstay was still whole life insurance, which was traditionally seen as a safe investment. In the late 1970s, as interest rates soared toward 20%, policyholders borrowed on their policies at low rates to invest at higher rates, draining company funds. Though interest rates later declined, the company was convinced that it had to diversify in order to survive and prosper.

Acquisitions included Tucker Anthony & R.L. Day (securities brokerage, Boston, 1982); Gabriele, Hueglin & Cashman (fixed-income

securities, New York, 1985); and Sutro & Co. (investments, California, 1986). New product offerings included equipment leasing (1980), universal life (1983), and credit cards (1985).

Despite the proliferation of products, John Hancock's position in the industry declined throughout the 1980s. In the late 1980s the company became known for unusual investment vehicles. By 1990, of the $2.9 billion in nontraditional assets under management, 31% was in timber funds, 31% in venture capital funds, and the remainder in power, real estate, and agriculture. Because of its relatively large investment in real estate during the 1980s, John Hancock established loss reserves to protect against potential defaults.

Insurers have generally found asset management a successful diversification, and John Hancock aims to become a major player in mutual funds (which, unusually, it sells primarily through stockbrokers rather than insurance agents).

The company expanded overseas by acquiring interests in insurers in Singapore and Thailand. In 1992 its First Signature Bank subsidiary sold its credit card operations to National Westminster Bank (UK) to concentrate on other business segments.

In 1994 John Hancock agreed to pay over $1 million in fines for giving gifts (primarily entertainment items like meals and tickets to sporting events) to Massachusetts state legislators over a period of 6 years. Of that sum, $900,000 was paid to the federal government and $110,000 to the state. In 1995 one of the company's former lobbyists was convicted and sentenced to jail for engaging in banned lobbying practices in connection with the case.

In 1995 John Hancock opened a representative office in Beijing.

Mutual company
Fiscal year ends: December 31

WHO

Chairman and CEO: Stephen L. Brown
VC and Chief Investment Officer: Foster L. Aborn
President and COO: William L. Boyan
CFO: Thomas E. Moloney
SEVP Retail Sector: David F. D'Alessandro
SEVP Business Insurance: George F. Miller
EVP Corporate Sector: Diane M. Capstaff
SVP International Operations: Derek Chilvers
SVP Investment, Technology, and Financial Management: John M. DeCiccio
SVP Retail Service and Systems: Robert A. Marra
SVP Sales Practices: Michael B. O'Toole
SVP Tax Law, Government Relations, and Issues Management: Stuart A. Yoffe
VP Corporate Law and Secretary: Bruce E. Skrine
VP Corporate Communications: Kathleen F. Driscoll
VP Retail Human Resources: David L. Murphy Jr.
VP Corporate Human Resources: A. Page Palmer
General Counsel: Richard S. Scipione
Auditors: Ernst & Young LLP

WHERE

HQ: John Hancock Mutual Life Insurance Company, PO Box 111, Boston, MA 02117
Phone: 617-572-6000
Fax: 617-572-6451

John Hancock is licensed in all 50 states, the District of Columbia, and Canada. It has subsidiaries and affiliates in Belgium, Indonesia, Malaysia, Thailand, and the UK and does business in 46 countries worldwide.

WHAT

	1994 Assets	
	$ mil.	% of total
Cash & equivalents	1,017	2
Bonds	20,713	42
Stocks	1,289	2
Mortgage loans	8,504	17
Real estate	2,179	4
Policy loans	1,826	4
Assets in separate accounts	12,434	25
Other assets	1,843	4
Total	**49,805**	**100**

	1994 Sales	
	$ mil.	% of total
Premiums, annuity considerations & pension fund contributions	8,048	75
Net investment income	2,652	25
Other income	70	0
Total	**10,770**	**100**

Selected Services
Banking services
Group life, accident, and health insurance
Group retirement funds
Guaranteed investment contracts
Life insurance and annuities
Long-term care insurance
Mortgage loans
Mutual funds
Property and casualty insurance
Securities brokerage and investment banking

Selected Subsidiaries
Cost Care, Inc.
Hancock Venture Partners, Inc.
HealthPlan Management Services, Inc.

KEY COMPETITORS

Aetna
Allstate
Blue Cross
Charles Schwab
Chase Manhattan
Chemical Banking
Chubb
CIGNA
Citicorp
Conseco
Dean Witter, Discover
First Chicago
FMR
Lehman Brothers
MassMutual
Merrill Lynch
MetLife
Morgan Stanley
New York Life
Northwestern Mutual
Oxford Health Plans
Prudential
Sierra Health Services
State Farm
T. Rowe Price
Transamerica
Travelers
USF&G

HOW MUCH

	Annual Growth	1985	1986	1987	1988	1989	1990	1991	1992	1993	1994
Assets ($ mil.)	7.2%	26,594	27,808	28,211	29,461	32,344	35,332	38,105	41,242	46,468	49,805
Net income ($ mil.)	6.0%	108	134	132	171	232	224	233	141	199	183
Net income as % of assets	—	0.4%	0.5%	0.5%	0.6%	0.7%	0.6%	0.6%	0.3%	0.4%	0.4%
Employees	0.4%	—	—	—	—	15,655	16,000	16,500	13,903	16,500	16,000

1994 Year-end:
Equity as % of assets: 4.7%
Return on assets: 0.4%
Return on equity: 8.8%
Sales (mil.): $10,770

Net Income ($ mil.) 1985–94

JOHNSON & JOHNSON

OVERVIEW

Johnson & Johnson (J&J), based in New Brunswick, New Jersey, is a company in continual transition. Between 1989 and 1994 J&J acquired 24 businesses, sold 13 others, consolidated 47 units, and closed more than 25 plants. One of the world's largest and most diversified health care products makers, it owns industry-leading products, ranging from a leading pain reliever (Tylenol) to the world's leading contact lens brand (Acuvue).

The company operates in 3 sectors: consumer products (with brands like Band-Aid and Reach toothbrushes), professional products (ranging from surgical instruments to joint replacements), and pharmaceuticals. J&J's ability to discover, develop, or acquire new products and get them to penetrate markets quickly has served it well during world-

wide changes in the health care industry. The company is known for the autonomy it allows its business units. International expansion is an important strategy. In 1994, for the 2nd year in a row, J&J's Xian-Janssen was named the most successful joint venture in China.

Increased private-label competition in consumer products and pressure by managed care organizations and governments to limit price increases continue to limit profit margins and encourage the company to improve productivity. To improve business relations, at the end of 1994 J&J created Johnson and Johnson Health Care Systems to assist its managed care customers in better serving their clients. Also that year the company purchased Eastman Kodak's Clinical Diagnostics segment to advance its diagnostics business position.

WHEN

Brothers James and Edward Mead Johnson founded the medical products company that bears the family name in 1885 in New Brunswick, New Jersey. In 1886 Robert Johnson joined his brothers to make and sell the antiseptic surgical dressings he developed.

In 1897 Edward left to found the drug company Mead Johnson (now a part of Bristol-Myers Squibb). In 1916 J&J bought gauze maker Chicopee Manufacturing. A byproduct of Johnson's dressing, the Band-Aid, was introduced in 1921 along with Johnson's Baby Cream.

In 1932 Robert Johnson Jr. became chairman and served until 1963. An Army general in WWII, he believed in decentralization; managers were given substantial freedom, a principle still used today. Early product lines, now business units, included Ortho (birth-control products) and Ethicon (sutures) in the 1940s. In 1959 J&J bought McNeil Labs, which launched Tylenol (acetaminophen) as an over-the-counter drug in 1960. Foreign acquisitions included Switzerland's Cilag-Chemie (1959) and Belgium's Janssen (1961).

J&J bought Iolab Corporation, a developer of intraocular lenses used in cataract surgery (1980), and Lifescan, a maker of blood glucose monitoring systems for diabetics (1986). J&J's sales had grown to nearly $5 billion by 1980. But there have since been problems: the drug Zomax (for arthritis pain) was linked to 5 deaths and was pulled in 1983. When someone laced Tylenol capsules with cyanide in 1982, killing 8 people, it cost the company $240 mil-

lion in recalls, advertising, and repackaging and cut Tylenol's profits by nearly 50%. J&J's immediate recall of 31 million bottles and its openness in dealing with the problem saved the Tylenol brand. Now sold as tablets and caplets to prevent tampering, Tylenol is still a leader in the over-the-counter analgesic market.

New products in the 1980s included Acuvue (a disposable contact lens), Retin-A (skin treatment), and Eprex (a bioengineered treatment for anemia). In 1989 J&J began a venture with Merck to sell Mylanta and other drugs bought from ICI Americas. In 1990 it entered the Eastern European market.

In late 1991 the company formed a joint venture with Fujisawa to market a new antibiotic. In 1992 J&J took a mandated down charge of over $600 million relating to future pensions. Key products that year included Prepulsid (digestion aid), Eprex (anti-anemia agent), and One Touch II (blood glucose monitor). J&J paid 3M $116 million in 1992 in a patent infringement suit concerning fiberglass tape used in orthopedic casts.

In 1993 the company introduced the first daily-wear, disposable contact lenses and opened its 2nd Chinese production facility in Shanghai. In 1994 J&J purchased soap and skin cream maker Neutrogena to enhance its consumer product line. To diversify its product line and better compete for hospital business, the company acquired Mitek Surgical Products in 1995 through a stock swap worth about $128 million.

NYSE symbol: JNJ
Fiscal year ends: Sunday nearest December 31

WHO

Chairman and CEO: Ralph S. Larsen, age 56,
$1,506,714 pay
VC: Robert N. Wilson, age 54, $1,178,967 pay
Corporate VP: Frank H. Barker
Chairman, Pharmaceutical and Diagnostics Group:
Ronald G. Gelbman, age 47
VP Finance and CFO: Clark H. Johnson, age 59,
$642,087 pay
VP Science and Technology: Robert Z. Gussin
VP and General Counsel: George S. Frazza, age 61
VP Administration (Personnel): Roger S. Fine, age 52
Auditors: Coopers & Lybrand L.L.P.

WHERE

HQ: One Johnson & Johnson Plaza, New Brunswick, NJ
08933
Phone: 908-524-0400
Fax: 908-214-0332

The company has operations in 50 countries and sells
items in more than 175 countries.

	1994 Sales		1994 Operating Income	
	$ mil.	% of total	$ mil.	% of total
US	7,812	50	1,534	52
Europe	4,504	28	1,050	35
Africa & Asia/Pacific	1,907	12	198	7
Canada & Latin America	1,511	10	173	6
Adjustments	—	—	(274)	—
Total	**15,734**	**100**	**2,681**	**100**

WHAT

	1994 Sales		1994 Operating Income	
	$ mil.	% of total	$ mil.	% of total
Professional prods.	5,325	34	843	29
Consumer prods.	5,251	33	443	15
Pharmaceuticals	5,158	33	1,669	56
Other	—	—	(274)	—
Total	**15,734**	**100**	**2,681**	**100**

Consumer Products
Acuvue (contact lens)
Baby Oil
Baby Shampoo
Band-Aid
Clean & Clear (skin care)
Imodium A-D (anti-
diarrheal)
Monistat 7 (yeast infection
treatment)
Mylanta (antacid)
Neutrogena (skin &
hair products)
Reach (toothbrush)
Tylenol (pain reliever)

Pharmaceuticals
Duragesic (analgesic)
Eprex (anti-anemia agent)
Ergamisol (cancer treatment)
Floxin (antibacterial)
Hismanal (antihistamine)
Ortho-Novum (birth control)
Propulsid (digestive aid)
Retin-A (acne cream)
Risperdal (anti-psychotic)

Professional Products
Hepatitis testing systems
Joint replacements
Surgical instruments

KEY COMPETITORS

Abbott Labs
ALZA
American Home
Products
Amgen
Bausch & Lomb
Baxter
Bayer
Becton,
Dickinson
Bristol-Myers
Squibb
Carter-Wallace

Ciba-Geigy
Clorox
Colgate-Palmolive
Dial
Dow Chemical
Eli Lilly
Genentech
Gillette
Glaxo Wellcome
Hoechst
James River
Kimberly-Clark
Medtronic

Merck
3M
Nestlé
Novo Nordisk
Pfizer
Procter & Gamble
Rhône-Poulenc
St. Jude Medical
Sandoz
Unilever
Upjohn
U.S. Surgical

HOW MUCH

	9-Year Growth	1985	1986	1987	1988	1989	1990	1991	1992	1993	1994
Sales ($ mil.)	10.5%	6,421	7,003	8,012	9,000	9,757	11,232	12,447	13,753	14,138	15,734
Net income ($ mil.)	14.1%	614	330	833	974	1,082	1,143	1,461	1,625	1,787	2,006
Income as % of sales	—	9.6%	4.7%	10.4%	10.8%	11.1%	10.2%	11.7%	11.8%	12.6%	12.7%
Earnings per share ($)	15.7%	0.84	0.47	1.21	1.43	1.63	1.72	2.20	2.46	2.74	3.12
Stock price – high ($)	—	13.81	18.56	26.34	22.03	29.75	37.06	58.13	58.69	50.38	56.50
Stock price – low ($)	—	8.78	11.44	13.75	17.31	20.75	25.56	32.69	43.00	35.63	36.00
Stock price – close ($)	17.2%	13.16	16.41	18.72	21.28	29.69	35.88	57.25	50.50	44.88	54.75
P/E – high	—	16	40	22	15	18	22	26	24	18	18
P/E – low	—	11	24	11	12	13	15	15	18	13	12
Dividends per share ($)	15.0%	0.32	0.35	0.41	0.48	0.56	0.66	0.77	0.89	1.01	1.13
Book value per share ($)	10.3%	4.58	4.08	5.06	5.26	6.23	7.36	8.44	7.89	8.66	11.08
Employees	0.9%	74,900	77,100	78,200	81,300	83,100	82,200	82,700	84,900	81,600	81,500

1994 Year-end:
Debt ratio: 54.5%
Return on equity: 31.6%
Cash (mil.): $636
Current ratio: 1.57
Long-term debt (mil.): $2,199
No. of shares (mil.): 643
Dividends
  Yield: 2.1%
  Payout: 36.2%
Market value (mil.): $35,205

**Stock Price History
High/Low 1985–94**

JOHNSON CONTROLS, INC.

OVERVIEW

Johnson Controls is guiding its revenues to new records. The company is a leader in each of its four markets: batteries, facilities management for commercial buildings, plastic containers, and vehicle seating. It provides goods and services to everyone from AutoZone to the Eiffel Tower, Coca-Cola to General Motors.

Johnson scored several gains in 1994, its 48th consecutive year of sales increases. The company made its millionth auto seat for Chrysler and won a seating contract from Rover. The FDA okayed Johnson's Supercycle process for recycling PET (a polyethylene plastic) — good news not only for the company's

container unit but also for its plastics molding machinery business. Also, Johnson's building services unit installed its 7,000th Metasys, an integrated system that controls a facility's energy, environment, and security units.

Award-winning product design and innovative customer programs should keep company sales charged up. In 1995 Johnson won a multiyear battery contract from AutoZone and a contract to manage buildings at 6 British atomic energy plants. The company, which opened 7 auto seating factories in Europe in 1994, said it would invest about $200 million to add 6 more European factories in 1995.

WHEN

Professor Warren Johnson developed the electric telethermoscope in 1880 so janitors at Whitewater, Wisconsin's State Normal School could regulate room temperatures without disturbing classrooms. Johnson's device used mercury to move a heat element that opened and shut a circuit. Milwaukee hotelier William Plankinton, a believer in Johnson's invention, invested $150,000 to begin production.

The men formed Johnson Electric Service Company in 1885; sold off marketing, installation, and service rights to the thermostat; and concentrated on manufacturing. Johnson kept inventing other devices; in the 1890s he worked on the invention for which he is best remembered: tower clocks. Johnson also experimented with the telegraph, forming American Wireless Telegraph in 1900, but this venture was abandoned when Johnson became intrigued with the automobile.

Johnson turned his factory to production of steam-powered cars. He won the US Postal Service's first automotive delivery contract but never gained support for the steamers within his own company and continued to look elsewhere for financing until his death in 1911.

In 1912 the renamed Johnson Services regained full rights to its thermostats, and new president Harry Ellis sold all other businesses. During the Great Depression the company brought out economy systems, which automatically lowered building temperature during off-peak periods. During WWII Johnson Services diversified to aid the war effort, building devices to gather weather data, inspect barrage balloons, and test radar sets.

Beginning in 1960 Johnson Services established an international division and focused on military and research facilities requiring highly reliable control systems. Also in the

1960s Johnson Services began to develop centralized control systems — first introduced in 1967 — for temperature, fire alarm, lighting, and security regulation. In 1968 the company acquired Penn Controls, a maker of water-pump pressure controls.

The company was renamed Johnson Controls in 1974. It acquired automotive battery manufacturer Globe-Union in 1978.

In 1985 the company bought auto seat and plastics manufacturer Hoover Universal and auto seat maker Ferro Manufacturing. It continued its expansion in the controls business through purchase of ITT's European controls group (1982) and Pan Am World Services (1989), a provider of facilities management to the government.

In 1990 Johnson sold its car door components business and bought Varta's Canadian battery plant. In 1991 the company acquired several European car seat component manufacturers, and the following year it bought a Welsh PET (plastic) manufacturer and a Czechoslovakian seat cover producer.

A joint venture involving Johnson Controls and the French car seat maker Bertrand Faure was chosen in 1993 to supply seats for Ford of Europe's 1995 Escort/Orion and 1996 Fiesta.

The battery unit faced a major setback in 1994 when Sears announced that it was dropping Johnson as its battery maker. Sears had accounted for between 5% and 10% of Johnson's total operating income in 1993. Also in 1994 Ameritech hired a Johnson/LaSalle Partners joint venture to manage its 48 million square feet of properties in 5 states.

In 1995 Johnson began negotiations to acquire Roth Freres, a France-based major supplier of automobile seating and interior components.

NYSE symbol: JCI
Fiscal year ends: September 30

WHO

Chairman, President, and CEO: James H. Keyes, age 54, $1,291,060 pay
EVP: John M. Barth, age 48, $635,614 pay
EVP: Joseph W. Lewis, age 59, $537,117 pay
VP and CFO: Stephen A. Roell, age 44, $439,168 pay
VP, Secretary, and General Counsel: John P. Kennedy, age 50, $352,412 pay
VP and General Manager North American Operations, Automotive Systems: Charles D. McClure, age 40
VP and General Manager European Operations, Automotive Systems: Giovanni Fiori, age 50
VP Corporate Technology: Steven J. Bomba, age 57
VP Corporate Development and Strategy: William P. Killian, age 59
VP and General Manager, Battery Group: Michael F. Johnston, age 47
VP Controls Division: Ronald M. Williams, age 59
VP Controls Division: James F. Wilson, age 57
VP Communications: Denise M. Zutz, age 43
VP Human Resources: Susan F. Davis, age 41
Auditors: Price Waterhouse LLP

WHERE

HQ: 5757 N. Green Bay Ave., PO Box 591, Milwaukee, WI 53201
Phone: 414-228-1200
Fax: 414-228-2302

Johnson Controls has operations at more than 500 locations worldwide.

	1994 Sales		1994 Operating Income	
	$ mil.	% of total	$ mil.	% of total
US	5,295	77	316	87
Europe	1,172	17	11	3
Other regions	404	6	38	10
Total	**6,871**	**100**	**365**	**100**

WHAT

	1994 Sales		1994 Operating Income	
	$ mil.	% of total	$ mil.	% of total
Automotive	2,874	42	144	39
Controls	2,260	33	94	26
Plastics	998	14	72	20
Batteries	739	11	55	15
Total	**6,871**	**100**	**365**	**100**

Automotive Segment
Interior trim
Seats and seating components
(Customers include Ford, GM, and other vehicle makers)

Controls Segment
Facility management and control systems
Management of facility operations and maintenance
(Customers include Ameritech, IBM, and over 9,000 schools and hospitals)

Plastics Technology Segment
Automotive components
Blow-molding machinery
Plastic containers
(Customers include Clorox, Coca-Cola, and Ocean Spray)

Battery Segment
Automotive and rechargeable batteries
(Customers include AutoZone, Caterpillar, John Deere, Kmart, and major automakers)

KEY COMPETITORS

Bemis	General Signal	Ralston Purina
Borg-Warner	Hitachi	Group
Automotive	Honeywell	Rayovac
Bridgestone	ITT Industries	Sears
Continental Can	Jason Inc.	Tenneco
Crown, Cork & Seal	Landis & Gyr	Tyco Intl.
Dart Container	Lear Seating	United
Duracell	Lennox	Technologies
Eaton	Ogden	Watsco
Fedders	Owens-Illinois	

HOW MUCH

	9-Year Growth	1985	1986	1987	1988	1989	1990	1991	1992	1993	1994
Sales ($ mil.)	16.1%	1,787	2,639	2,677	3,100	3,684	4,504	4,559	5,157	6,182	6,871
Net income ($ mil.)	8.6%	78	96	90	104	98	92	95	123	138	165
Income as % of sales	—	4.4%	3.6%	3.3%	3.3%	2.6%	2.1%	2.1%	2.4%	2.2%	2.4%
Earnings per share ($)	4.6%	2.40	2.36	2.20	2.71	2.42	2.05	2.11	2.73	2.98	3.60
Stock price – high ($)	—	25.31	36.00	40.00	38.50	46.75	32.25	36.63	46.13	59.13	61.75
Stock price – low ($)	—	19.44	23.88	20.50	24.75	27.88	17.13	21.88	34.63	43.00	44.88
Stock price – close ($)	8.0%	24.50	28.63	25.63	36.63	32.25	25.00	36.00	44.88	53.13	49.00
P/E – high	—	11	15	18	14	19	16	17	17	20	17
P/E – low	—	8	10	9	9	12	8	10	13	14	12
Dividends per share ($)	5.0%	0.93	1.00	1.06	1.10	1.16	1.20	1.24	1.28	1.36	1.44
Book value per share ($)	4.2%	20.45	21.92	20.38	23.10	24.82	21.86	22.47	29.56	26.76	29.55
Employees	7.3%	29,000	26,900	26,900	26,900	42,600	43,500	42,700	46,800	50,100	54,800

1994 Year-end:
Debt ratio: %
Return on equity: 14.5%
Cash (mil.): $133
Current ratio: 1.17
Long-term debt (mil.): $670
No. of shares (mil.): 41
Dividends
  Yield: 2.9%
  Payout: 40.0%
Market value (mil.): $1,995

Stock Price History
High/Low 1985–94

J.P. MORGAN & CO. INCORPORATED

OVERVIEW

One short year after touting its increased investment in people, J.P. Morgan, one of the US's premier international banking companies, embarked in 1995 on a restructuring that would cut costs by cutting jobs. With the possibility of 5–10% staff reductions, this will be J.P. Morgan's first-ever layoff (previous staff reductions have largely been accomplished through attrition). There are 2 factors in the timing of this action, the first being the generally poor year for the financial industry due in part to the decline of the bond market in early 1994. The 2nd is the changing of the guard following the retirement of Dennis Weatherstone and his replacement as chairman and CEO by Douglas Warner.

J.P. Morgan's primary subsidiary is Morgan Guaranty Trust. The company is a primary dealer in government securities and also deals in derivatives and currencies for a worldwide clientele. The bank, traditionally client-centered, has in recent years derived an increasing amount of income from trading for its own account. Over the years, rapid growth has resulted in inefficiencies and duplications. The restructuring is intended to eliminate some of these problems and refocus the bank on relationship banking.

WHEN

J.P. Morgan & Co. was born into international capitalism and has lived there ever since. Junius Spencer Morgan became a partner in Londoner George Peabody's banking house in 1854. Morgan assumed control and renamed the firm J. S. Morgan and Co. when Peabody retired in the early 1860s.

Morgan's son began his own firm, J. Pierpont Morgan and Co., in New York in 1862. Connections on both sides of the Atlantic led to profits and power as the firm funneled European capital into the US. Early in its career the firm came to the rescue of the US government. When Congress bickered over the Hayes-Tilden election in 1877 and didn't get around to paying the army, a Morgan affiliate came up with the funds until Congress reconvened.

After Junius's death in 1890, his son reorganized his businesses in London and New York as J.P. Morgan & Co. The firm had already financed and restructured much of the American railroad network, and J. P. Morgan, who became the personification of Wall Street, helped devise the deals that created U.S. Steel, General Electric, and International Harvester.

In 1907 J.P. Morgan acted as the country's de facto central bank, leading a group of bankers to stop a financial panic. Its influence was pervasive. In 1912 a congressional investigation panel found that Morgan partners held 72 directorships in 47 corporations, with total resources of $10 billion.

Morgan's son J. P. Morgan Jr. became senior partner of the firm upon his father's death in 1913. He yielded day-to-day control to partner Thomas Lamont, who tried in 1929, just as J. P. Morgan Sr. had in 1907, to stem national financial collapse; however, the stock crash overwhelmed the effort.

In 1933 the Glass-Steagall Act forced the company to split its activities. J.P. Morgan remained a commercial bank, and a spinoff entity — Morgan Stanley — became the securities underwriter.

In 1959 J.P. Morgan merged with Guaranty Trust Co. of New York and in 1969 became a holding company. In the 1960s Morgan was the most active trader in government securities and intensified its international efforts. After a 1987 restructuring, the company pushed into mergers and acquisitions.

In 1991 an arm of the Morgan organization, J.P. Morgan Securities, served as underwriter for a $56 million equity issue for Amsco, a health products manufacturer. The event was historic — the first time since the Glass-Steagall Act that an affiliate of a commercial bank was permitted both to trade and to underwrite corporate equities.

J.P. Morgan pushed into the uncharted territory of Eastern Europe in 1993 when it was chosen to advise the Czech Republic on the privatization of its telephone company.

The bank entered 1994 in high spirits, on the heels of its record-breaking performance in 1993. Then in February came the decline of the US bond market as interest rates rose and financing activity declined. In response, J.P. Morgan began tightening its belt, deciding after 1994's earnings decline to lay off workers (which entailed a significant shift of culture for the company). Reporting relationships to the new chairman and CEO were also changed through the creation of regional executives with added responsibilities and autonomy. The bank has opened new offices in Beijing, Shanghai, Prague, Warsaw, and Mexico City and received authorization to begin branch banking operations in Australia.

NYSE symbol: JPM
Fiscal year ends: December 31

WHO

Chairman, President, and CEO: Douglas A. Warner III, age 48, $1,949,600 pay
VC: Roberto G. Mendoza, age 49, $1,778,400 pay
VC: Kurt F. Viermetz, age 55, $1,778,400 pay
VC: Rodney B. Wagner, age 63, $1,504,000 pay
CFO: John Meyer, age 55
Chief Administrative Officer: Michael E. Patterson
Corporate Risk Management: Peter B. Smith
Corporate Risk Management: Stephen G. Thieke
Controller: David H. Sidwell
Technology and Operations: Michael Enthoven
Corporate Services: Ronald H. Menaker
General Counsel: Edward J. Kelly III
Auditor: Edward F. Murphy
Managing Director Human Resources: Herbert J. Hefke
Auditors: Price Waterhouse LLP

WHERE

HQ: 60 Wall St., New York, NY 10260-0060
Phone: 212-483-2323
Fax: 212-648-5193

J.P. Morgan conducts banking and investment operations at offices in 7 US cities and in 35 other cities around the world.

	1994 Sales		1994 Pretax Income	
	$ mil.	% of total	$ mil.	% of total
US	6,485	55	955	51
Europe, the Middle East & Africa	4,432	37	890	48
Asia/Pacific	617	5	(47)	—
Other Western Hemisphere	381	3	27	1
Total	**11,915**	**100**	**1,825**	**100**

WHAT

	1994 Assets	
	$ mil.	% of total
Cash & equivalents	37,049	24
Treasury & agency securities	25,276	16
Foreign investments	21,576	14
Swaps, options & other derivatives	19,495	13
Other securities	13,375	9
Net loans	20,949	14
Other assets	17,197	11
Total	**154,917**	**100**

	1994 Sales	
	$ mil.	% of total
Interest	8,379	70
Trading	1,019	8
Corporate finance	434	4
Fees	1,267	11
Other	816	7
Total	**11,915**	**100**

Services	Selected Subsidiaries
Asset and liability management	J.P. Morgan Benelux S.A.
Asset management and servicing	J.P. Morgan España S.A.
	J.P. Morgan Securities Asia, Ltd. (Singapore)
Equity investments	J.P. Morgan Sterling
Finance and advisory	Securities Ltd. (UK)
Sales and trading	Société de Bourse J.P. Morgan S.A. (France)

KEY COMPETITORS

American Express	Citicorp	Morgan Stanley
BankAmerica	Crédit Lyonnais	NatWest
Bankers Trust	CS Holding	Paine Webber
Barclays	Dai-Ichi Kangyo	Royal Bank of
Bear Stearns	Deutsche Bank	Canada
Canadian Imperial	Goldman Sachs	Salomon
Chase Manhattan	HSBC	Union Bank of
Chemical Banking	Merrill Lynch	Switzerland

HOW MUCH

	9-Year Growth	1985	1986	1987	1988	1989	1990	1991	1992	1993	1994
Assets ($ mil.)	9.3%	69,375	76,039	75,414	83,923	88,964	93,103	103,468	102,941	133,888	154,917
Net income ($ mil.)	6.2%	705	873	83	1,002	(1,275)	775	1,114	1,382	1,723	1,215
Income as % of assets	—	1.0%	1.1%	0.1%	1.2%	—	0.8%	1.1%	1.3%	1.3%	0.8%
Earnings per share ($)	4.9%	3.91	4.74	0.39	5.38	(7.04)	3.99	5.63	6.92	8.48	6.02
Stock price – high ($)	—	33.00	48.00	53.63	40.25	48.13	47.25	70.50	70.50	79.38	72.00
Stock price – low ($)	—	19.13	29.50	27.00	30.75	34.00	29.63	40.50	51.50	59.38	55.13
Stock price – close ($)	6.4%	32.06	41.25	36.25	34.88	44.00	44.38	68.63	65.75	69.38	56.13
P/E – high	—	8	10	—	8	—	12	13	10	9	12
P/E – low	—	5	6	—	6	—	7	7	7	7	9
Dividends per share ($)	10.6%	1.10	1.23	1.36	1.50	1.66	1.82	1.98	2.18	2.40	2.72
Book value per share ($)	8.2%	23.70	27.64	26.32	30.52	21.78	25.29	29.41	34.30	48.50	48.34
Employees	2.6%	13,506	14,518	15,731	15,363	14,207	12,968	13,323	14,368	15,193	17,055

1994 Year-end:
Equity as % of assets: 6.2%
Return on assets: 0.8%
Return on equity: 13.2%
Long-term debt (mil.): $6,802
No. of shares (mil.): 188
Dividends
  Yield: 4.8%
  Payout: 45.2%
Market value (mil.): $10,536
Sales (mil.): $11,915

Stock Price History
High/Low 1985–94

KAISER FOUNDATION, INC.

OVERVIEW

"We need to be growing, and we're not," laments David Lawrence, CEO of the Kaiser Foundation Health Plan, more commonly known as Kaiser Permanente. Oakland, California–based Kaiser consists of the nation's largest HMO as well as the Kaiser Foundation Hospitals, the Permanente Medical Groups, a rehabilitation center, and a research institute. The organization has nearly 6.6 million members (more than 2/3 of whom reside in California), but that number has held steady since the early 1990s despite strong growth by other managed care providers.

Nonprofit Kaiser operates coast-to-coast and in Hawaii; it owns and operates 28 medical centers and employs more than 9,500 doctors. The Kaiser Foundation Health Plan (one of several foundations established by industrialist Henry J. Kaiser) funds the organization's health care and hospital systems.

Kaiser is trying to overcome its flat growth by improving operating efficiency and increasing customer satisfaction. Cost cutting measures — such as decreasing the days patients spend in hospitals — are in the works, and new phone and scheduling systems have been installed to make visits to the doctor as pleasant as possible. A 1995 survey ranked Kaiser's customer satisfaction levels above average in 8 of the 9 markets studied.

WHEN

Henry J. Kaiser, builder of Hoover and Grand Coulee Dams, shipbuilder, war profiteer, and founder of Kaiser Aluminum, was a bootstrap capitalist who did well by doing good.

In 1906 Kaiser, a high school dropout from upstate New York, moved to Spokane and went into road construction. During the Depression he was a leader in his field and headed the consortium that built the great WPA dams.

When WWII broke out, Kaiser moved into shipbuilding and steelmaking (the first steel plant on the West Coast), turning out more than 1,400 Liberty ships during the war. In his drive to turn out cargo ships at the rate of one per day, Kaiser noticed that healthy workers were more efficient and had lower levels of absenteeism. He therefore established clinics at his work sites, funded by the US government (through Kaiser's construction contracts) as part of legitimate operating expenses.

After the war the clinics became war surplus, and Kaiser and his wife bought them, through the newly founded Kaiser Hospital Foundation, at a 99% discount. Kaiser's vision was to provide the public with low-cost, prepaid medical care. To this end, he also created the Health Plan, the self-supporting entity that administers the system, and the Group Medical Organization, Permanente (named after the site of Kaiser's first cement plant). And he started the ball rolling by endowing the Health Plan with $200,000.

From the start, the Kaiser health plan, the first and most classic model of the HMO, was criticized by the medical establishment, which characterized the Kaiser plan as socialized medicine and scoffed at "employee" doctors.

The plan flourished, becoming California's largest system of hospitals and physicians. In 1958 Kaiser retired to Hawaii and started his health plan there. But national growth was limited by physician resistance — HMOs were outlawed in 38 states as late as 1978.

As health care costs rose in the 1980s, federal legislation legalized HMOs in all states. Kaiser began to expand, eventually going almost nationwide. As it expanded outside its traditional geographic areas, Kaiser began contracting for hospital space rather than building new hospitals. But the development of new HMOs and other health plans resulted in increased competition for Kaiser, forcing it to become more cost conscious and slowing its growth rate.

Some health care costs in California began falling in the early 1990s as more medical procedures were performed on an outpatient basis. Also, specialists flooded the state, and as price competition among doctors and hospitals heated up, it allowed many HMOs to land contracts providing great cost savings. But because Kaiser used its own highly paid doctors and was unable to realize the same savings, its prices did not remain as competitive as they had been in the past. Thus, Kaiser's membership stalled in the early 1990s.

In 1993 Kaiser's 30,000 unionized employees charged that Kaiser had cut back health benefits, but a strike was averted. In 1994 Kaiser began letting members pay higher deductibles and premiums in order to choose doctors outside the system in an effort to boost growth by attracting those who are put off by the restriction of a set list of participating physicians.

Kaiser in 1995 announced partnerships with 2 California workers' compensation insurers that will combine health coverage and workers' comp by using the same health care provider for both illnesses and work-related injuries.

Nonprofit organization
Fiscal year ends: December 31

Chairman and CEO: David M. Lawrence
EVP: Richard G. Barnaby
EVP and Regional Manager, Southern California Region: Hugh A. Jones
EVP and Regional Manager, Northern California Region: David G. Pockell
SVP and President, Northwest Region: Michael H. Katcher
SVP and President, Mid-Atlantic States Region: Alan J. Silverstone
SVP General Counsel and Secretary: Kirk E. Miller
SVP Corporate Services and CFO: Susan E. Porth
SVP Strategic Development and Human Resources: James B. Williams
Auditors: Deloitte & Touche LLP

HQ: Kaiser Foundation Health Plan, Inc.,
One Kaiser Plaza, Oakland, CA 94612
Phone: 510-271-5934
Fax: 510-271-5917

	1994 Members		1994 Physicians	
	No.	% of total	No.	% of total
N. California Region	2,442,032	37	3,662	38
S. California Region	2,174,471	32	3,155	33
Northwest	382,071	6	557	6
Mid-Atlantic States Region	342,092	5	452	5
Colorado Region	300,301	4	435	4
Ohio Region	194,462	3	257	3
Hawaii Region	186,996	3	300	3
Georgia Region	175,055	3	186	2
N. Carolina Region	122,910	2	154	2
Texas Region	121,981	2	180	2
Northeast Region	112,461	2	122	1
Kansas City Area	44,211	1	52	1
Total	**6,599,043**	**100**	**9,512**	**100**

	1994 Sales	
	$ mil.	% of total
Members' dues & supplemental charges	9,915	81
Other	2,353	19
Total	**12,268**	**100**

Kaiser Foundation Health Plan, Inc.
  Kaiser Foundation Health Plan of Colorado
  Kaiser Foundation Health Plan of Connecticut, Inc.
  Kaiser Foundation Health Plan of Georgia, Inc.
  Kaiser Foundation Health Plan of Kansas City, Inc.
  Kaiser Foundation Health Plan of Massachusetts, Inc.
  Kaiser Foundation Health Plan of the Mid-Atlantic States, Inc.
  Kaiser Foundation Health Plan of New York
  Kaiser Foundation Health Plan of North Carolina
  Kaiser Foundation Health Plan of the Northwest
  Kaiser Foundation Health Plan of Ohio
  Kaiser Foundation Health Plan of Texas
Kaiser Foundation Hospitals (community hospitals and outpatient facilities)
Kaiser Foundation Rehabilitation Center (Vallejo, California)
Kaiser Foundation Research Institute
Permanente Medical Groups
  Capital Area Permanente Medical Group, P.C.
  The Carolina Permanente Medical Group, P.A.
  Colorado Permanente Medical Group, P.C.
  Hawaii Permanente Medical Group, Inc.
  Northeast Permanente Medical Group
  Northwest Permanente, P.C., Physicians and Surgeons
  Ohio Permanente Medical Group, Inc.
  Permanente Medical Association of Texas
  The Permanente Medical Group, Inc.
  Permanente Medical Group of Mid-America, P.A.
  The Southeast Permanente Medical Group, Inc.
  Southern California Permanente Medical Group

Aetna	FHP International	Prudential
AFLAC	Group Health	Tenet Healthcare
Blue Cross	Co-op of	U.S. Healthcare
CIGNA	Puget Sound	WellPoint Health
Columbia/HCA	PacifiCare	Networks

	Annual Growth	1985	1986	1987	1988	1989	1990	1991	1992	1993	1994
Sales ($ mil.)	13.0%	4,075	4,477	4,862	5,565	6,857	8,443	9,823	11,032	11,930	12,268
Net income ($ mil.)	17.3%	194	198	157	109	159	381	486	796	848	816
Income as % of sales	—	4.8%	4.4%	3.2%	1.2%	2.3%	4.5%	4.9%	7.2%	7.1%	6.7%
Employees	1.2%	—	—	—	—	—	—	—	82,858	84,885	84,845

1994 Year-end
Debt ratio: 22.6%
Cash (mil.): $2,070
Long-term debt (mil.): $1,498

KAISER PERMANENTE

Net Income
($ mil.)
1985–94

900
800
700
600
500
400
300
200
100
0

KELLOGG COMPANY

OVERVIEW

There's hot competition in cold cereal, but Kellogg is holding onto its spot as the world's top ready-to-eat cereal manufacturer, with 12 of the top 15 brands worldwide (General Mills is its chief rival). In 1994 and 1995 the company added 2 new brands, Healthy Choice and Temptations, to capitalize on the continuing interest in healthier foods. The company's Convenience Foods division makes such products as Eggo frozen waffles, Pop-Tarts, and Rice Krispie Treats.

Intense competition and consumer unhappiness with high prices have kept domestic cereal sales growth slow (1% in 1994). However, Kellogg has refused to follow the lead of its competitors, who have cut prices. Now the company is losing market share (down from 42% in 1986 to 34% in 1994), and some analysts feel the market is primed for a cereal price war.

Kellogg is using aggressive global expansion to mitigate flat domestic sales. The company introduced 4 new cereal brands outside the US in 1994 (including Banana Bubbles in the UK and Crispy Sea in France). It opened factories in Russia in 1993 and India in 1994. In 1995 the company added manufacturing facilities in Argentina and China.

To improve profit margins, the company is streamlining its operations and reducing its work force. Kellogg has said it will also cut promotional spending (12% of 1994 revenues).

The W. K. Kellogg Foundation controls over 68% of the company's stock. Financier George Gund III, owner of the San Jose Sharks and Cleveland Cavaliers, owns 11.4% of Kellogg.

WHEN

W. K. Kellogg first made wheat flakes in 1894 while working for his brother, Dr. John Kellogg, at Battle Creek's famed homeopathic sanitarium. While doing an experiment with grains (for patients' diets) the 2 men had been interrupted; by the time they returned to the dough, it had absorbed water. They rolled it anyway, toasted the result, and accidentally created the first flaked cereal. Dr. Kellogg sold the flakes via mail order (1899) in a partnership that W. K. managed. In 1906 W. K. started his own firm to produce corn flakes.

As head of the Battle Creek Toasted Corn Flake Company, W. K. Kellogg competed against 42 cereal companies in Battle Creek (one run by former patient C. W. Post) and became the leader because of his innovative marketing ideas. A 1906 *Ladies Home Journal* ad helped to increase demand from 33 cases a day earlier that year to 2,900 a day by year-end. In 1907 W. K. formed campaigns around his cereal's main ingredient, corn grit, termed "The Sweetheart of the Corn." One ad, then considered risqué, offered a free box of cereal to every woman who winked at her grocer. Kellogg was the first to use full-color magazine ads and widespread consumer sampling.

W. K. continued to introduce new products, such as Bran Flakes (1915), All-Bran (1916), and Rice Krispies (1928). Another innovation was the Waxtite inner lining to keep cereal fresh (1914). International expansion began in Canada (1914) and followed in Australia (1924) and England (1938).

In 1927 George Gund Jr. sold his family's Sanka decaffeinated coffee brand to Kellogg in return for company stock (Sanka was later sold to General Foods).

W. K. Kellogg established the Kellogg Foundation in 1930, giving it the majority of his interest in the company.

Kellogg has diversified little beyond cereal and other breakfast products, but it purchased Eggo waffles and Mrs. Smith's pies in the 1970s and developed Whitney's Foods, a yogurt maker, in 1982. In 1983 Kellogg's US market share hit a low of 36.7% because of strong competition from rival General Mills and others. Kellogg targeted new cereals toward health-conscious adults and aggressively pursued the fast-growing food category in Europe. In 1984 Kellogg repurchased about 20% of its stock from the Kellogg Foundation.

New products introduced in the early 1990s included Rice Krispies Treats, S'More Pop-Tarts, and Low-Fat Granola. In 1993 New York State attorney general Robert Abrams blasted Kellogg and other cereal leaders over soaring prices. The company spent the mid-1990s reengineering itself, creating a USA Convenience Foods Division and selling such noncore assets as its carton container and Argentine snack foods makers (1993) and its Mrs. Smith's frozen pie unit (1994).

In 1994 Kellogg teamed with ConAgra to form a cereal line that will be sold under ConAgra's popular Healthy Choice label.

Cereal pricing again came under fire in 1995 when Rep. Charles Schumer charged Kellogg and other leading cereal makers with colluding to keep prices high and urged Attorney General Janet Reno to investigate.

NYSE symbol: K
Fiscal year ends: December 31

WHO

Chairman, President, and CEO: Arnold G. Langbo,
age 57, $1,488,500 pay
EVP; President, Kellogg North America: Thomas A.
Knowlton, age 48, $634,167 pay
EVP Corporate Services and Technology: Donald W.
Thomason, age 51, $579,600 pay
EVP; President, Kellogg Latin America: William A.
Camstra, age 62, $519,000 pay
EVP; President, Kellogg Europe: Donald G. Fritz,
age 47
EVP; President, Kellogg Asia-Pacific: Carlos M.
Gutierrez, age 41
EVP Operations, Kellogg USA: Arthur A. Byrd
**EVP; General Manager, Convenience Foods Division,
Kellogg USA:** Jonathan D. Wilson
SVP Administration and CFO: John R. Hinton, age 49
SVP, General Counsel, and Secretary: Richard M. Clark,
age 57
SVP Human Resources: Robert L. Creviston, age 53
Auditors: Price Waterhouse LLP

WHERE

HQ: One Kellogg Sq., Battle Creek, MI 49016-3599
Phone: 616-961-2000
Fax: 616-961-2871

Kellogg manufactures its products in 19 countries and
distributes them in 160 countries.

	1994 Sales		1994 Operating Income	
	$ mil.	% of total	$ mil.	% of total
US	3,841	59	709	61
Europe	1,637	25	279	24
Other regions	1,084	16	175	15
Total	**6,562**	**100**	**1,163**	**100**

WHAT

Selected Brands

Cereals

All-Bran	Healthy Choice
Apple Jacks	Just Right
Apple Raisin Crisp	Kenmei
Bran Buds	Low Fat Granola
Cinnamon Mini-Buns	Müeslix
Cocoa Krispies	Nut & Honey Crunch
Common Sense	Nutri-Grain
Complete Bran Flakes	Oatbake
Corn Flakes	Pops
Cracklin' Oat Bran	Product 19
Crispix	Raisin Bran
Double Dip Crunch	Rice Krispies
Froot Loops	Rice Krispies Treats
Frosted Flakes	Smacks
Frosted Krispies	Special K
Frosted Mini-Wheats	Squares
Fruitful Bran	Temptations
Fruity Marshmallow Krispies	

Other Products
Corn Flake Crumbs (breading)
Croutettes (stuffing mix)
Eggo (frozen waffles)
Nutri-Grain Bars (cereal bars)
Pop-Tarts (toaster pastries)
Rice Krispies Treats (cereal bars)

KEY COMPETITORS

Borden	Mars
Cadbury Schweppes	Nestlé
Campbell Soup	Philip Morris
Danone	Quaker Oats
General Mills	Ralcorp
Grand Metropolitan	RJR Nabisco
Grist Mill	Sara Lee
Heinz	

HOW MUCH

	9-Year Growth	1985	1986	1987	1988	1989	1990	1991	1992	1993	1994
Sales ($ mil.)	9.4%	2,930	3,341	3,793	4,349	4,652	5,181	5,787	6,191	6,295	6,562
Net income ($ mil.)	10.7%	281	319	396	480	422	503	606	683	681	705
Income as % of sales	—	9.6%	9.5%	10.4%	11.0%	9.1%	9.7%	10.5%	11.0%	10.8%	10.7%
Earnings per share ($)	11.9%	1.14	1.29	1.60	1.95	1.93	2.08	2.51	2.86	2.94	3.15
Stock price – high ($)	—	18.00	29.38	34.38	34.25	40.81	38.75	67.00	75.38	67.88	60.75
Stock price – low ($)	—	9.63	15.75	18.94	24.50	28.88	29.38	35.00	54.38	47.25	47.38
Stock price – close ($)	14.4%	17.38	25.88	26.19	32.13	33.81	37.94	65.38	67.00	56.75	58.13
P/E – high	—	16	23	22	18	21	19	27	26	23	19
P/E – low	—	8	12	12	13	15	14	14	19	16	15
Dividends per share ($)	13.4%	0.45	0.51	0.65	0.76	0.86	0.96	1.08	1.20	1.32	1.40
Book value per share ($)	12.7%	2.77	3.64	4.91	6.03	6.71	7.88	8.98	8.20	7.52	8.15
Employees	(1.0%)	17,082	17,383	17,762	17,461	17,268	17,239	17,017	16,551	16,151	15,657

1994 Year-end:
Debt ratio: 35.5%
Return on equity: 40.1%
Cash (mil.): $266
Current ratio: 1.21
Long-term debt (mil.): $719
No. of shares (mil.): 222
Dividends
 Yield: 2.4%
 Payout: 44.4%
Market value (mil.): $12,886

Stock Price History
High/Low 1985–94

KELLY SERVICES, INC.

OVERVIEW

Kelly will celebrate its 50th birthday in 1996, so it seems ironic to call this a "temporary service." The Troy, Michigan–based company provides more than 650,000 employees to some 200,000 customers and is one of the Big 3 in the temporary personnel business (with Manpower and Olsten). Founder William Kelly, now nearly 90, is still on the job as the chairman of the board, although his adopted son, Terence Adderley, serves as president and CEO. They own 61% and 28%, respectively, of the company.

Kelly's primary subsidiary, Temporary Services, has benefited from the structural changes in the US (and, increasingly, in the world) economy that have made it preferable for some companies to keep their own employment rolls lean and mean and accommodate

increased demand with temps. Thus, what was once primarily a business dealing with clerical help has expanded to include technical and professional employees, which Kelly provides in addition to light-industry workers. The company is an innovator in providing training in computer and other skills.

Another subsidiary, Kelly Assisted Living Services, provides personal care and daily living assistance to people who need care at home.

Kelly, like any temporary agency, is very sensitive to the ups and downs of the economy because its employees are often, by definition, the last hired and first fired. It suffered in the recession of the late 1980s and early 1990s and has yet to reproduce the earnings results it had achieved in 1989–90.

WHEN

William Russell Kelly, a college dropout and former car salesman, returned from WWII with a knowledge of what business machines could do. In 1946 he set up Russell Kelly Office Services in his Detroit office to provide copying and typing services and to calculate inventory for other businesses. As companies began to acquire their own machines, Kelly learned that they still needed people to work at their offices.

Kelly reincorporated his rapidly expanding business as Personnel Service in 1952. In 1955 the company opened its first branch office in Louisville, Kentucky, and by the end of that year had 35 offices throughout the US. In 1957 the company became Kelly Girl Service, a change motivated by the all-female composition of the company's work force. Kelly Girl went public in 1962, boasting 148 branches. In 1966 the company adopted its present name, Kelly Services. By 1979 there was a Kelly office in every state.

Having offered only office services during the 1960s, Kelly pursued opportunities in other areas needing temporary workers. The company began providing everything from convention hostesses, blue-collar workers, and data processors to door-to-door marketers and drafters. The company's first foreign office was opened in Toronto in 1968, with a Paris office following in 1972 and a London office in 1973.

Employers saw the benefits of hiring "Kelly Girls" to meet seasonal needs and special projects. A tough US economy in the 1970s saw a surge in corporate interest in temporary

employees. Because the cost of hiring and training a permanent employee can run up to 150% of a new recruit's salary, employers began avoiding the risk and expense of hiring, opting for well-trained temps instead.

In 1976 Kelly Services acquired a modest health care services company and used it to form Kelly Home Care (later Kelly Health Care). In the 1980s this division abandoned the Medicaid and Medicare markets and shifted to private-sector care. Renamed Kelly Assisted Living Services in 1984, the unit offered aides to perform various household duties and nurses to conduct home visits for the elderly and disabled. Also in the 1980s Kelly Services began hiring retired people as part of its ENCORE Program to use their experience in temporary positions.

International expansion has been a central focus for Kelly. From 1988 through 1993, 13 international acquisitions expanded the company in Europe, North America, and Australia/New Zealand. However, overseas sales are only 15% of the total. Stateside, Your Staff was acquired in 1994. This 5,000-employee staff leasing company provides companies with entire human resources departments, including benefits and payroll services.

A recent reorganization created 4 corporate divisions — Middle Markets, Major Markets, Metro Markets, and International — that help the company target specific markets.

In 1995 the company introduced a new computer-training CD-ROM, PinPoint, which will help employees learn computer programs.

Nasdaq symbol: KELYA
Fiscal year ends: Sunday nearest December 31

WHO

Chairman: William R. Kelly, age 89
President and CEO: Terence E. Adderley, age 61, $1,121,000 pay
EVP Administration: Robert E. Thompson, $529,334 pay
EVP Operations: Robert G. Barranco, age 54, $529,334 pay
SVP and General Manager, Metro Markets Division: Carolyn R. Fryar, age 52, $317,000 pay
SVP and General Manager, Major Markets Division: Donald A. Bobo, age 53
SVP Information Services: Christopher A. Arnette, age 38
SVP Finance and CFO: Paul K. Geiger, age 61
SVP, General Counsel, and Secretary: Eugene L. Hartwig, age 61
SVP Marketing: Carl T. Camden
SVP Human Resources: Joanne E. Start
Auditors: Price Waterhouse LLP

WHERE

HQ: 999 W. Big Beaver Rd., Troy, MI 48084
Phone: 810-362-4444
Fax: 810-244-4924

Kelly Services operates over 1,000 offices in the US, Australia, Canada, Denmark, France, Ireland, Mexico, the Netherlands, New Zealand, Norway, Puerto Rico, Switzerland, and the UK.

	1994 Sales	
	$ mil.	**% of total**
US	2,006	85
Other	357	15
Total	**2,363**	**100**

WHAT

Selected Operations

US
Kelly Assisted Living Services
Kelly Professional Services
Kelly Properties
Kelly Services
Kelly Temporary Services
Your Staff

Other North America
Kelly Temporary Services (Canada)
Kelly Temporary Services (Mexico)
Lenore Simpson Personnel (Canada)
Les Services Kelly (Canada)

Pacific Rim
Kelly Temporary Services (Australia)
Kelly Temporary Services (New Zealand)

Europe
Karin Lanng Kelly (Denmark)
Kelly Personal Byrået (Norway)
Kelly Services (UK)
Kelly Uitzendburo (the Netherlands)
Kelly Vikarer (Denmark)
Société Services Kelly (France)

KEY COMPETITORS

Adia	Interim Services
Administaff	Mac Temps
Amserv Healthcare	Manpower
Barrett Business Services	Norrell
Career Horizons	Olsten
HealthInfusion	Staff Builders
Hospital Staffing	TAD Resources
Services	Volt Information
In Home Health	Western Temporary Services

HOW MUCH

	9-Year Growth	1985	1986	1987	1988	1989	1990	1991	1992	1993	1994
Sales ($ mil.)	11.6%	876	1,034	1,161	1,269	1,378	1,471	1,438	1,723	1,954	2,363
Net income ($ mil.)	7.2%	33	36	51	60	71	71	39	39	45	61
Income as % of sales	—	3.7%	3.5%	4.3%	4.8%	5.1%	4.8%	2.7%	2.3%	2.3%	2.6%
Earnings per share ($)	7.2%	0.86	0.97	1.34	1.61	1.89	1.90	1.02	1.04	1.18	1.61
Stock price – high ($)	—	19.85	26.05	30.95	30.08	33.60	32.20	33.40	35.00	36.50	32.00
Stock price – low ($)	—	9.05	19.20	18.55	21.45	21.45	21.80	21.60	22.20	22.00	23.00
Stock price – close ($)	3.7%	19.85	20.93	24.95	23.68	31.40	26.20	25.20	35.00	27.75	27.50
P/E – high	—	23	27	23	19	18	17	33	34	31	20
P/E – low	—	11	20	14	13	11	12	21	21	19	14
Dividends per share ($)	12.6%	0.24	0.27	0.45	0.38	0.46	0.53	0.58	0.58	0.63	0.70
Book value per share ($)	14.3%	3.41	3.94	4.91	6.13	7.55	8.98	9.44	9.74	10.23	11.37
Employees	3.7%	478,075	529,600	553,600	558,750	583,900	578,800	553,900	584,000	634,300	665,000

1994 Year-end:
Debt ratio: 0.0%
Return on equity: 14.9%
Cash (mil.): $191.9
Current ratio: 2.50
Long-term debt (mil.): $0
No. of shares (mil.): 38
Dividends
  Yield: 2.5%
  Payout: 43.5%
Market value (mil.): $1,044

Stock Price History
High/Low 1985–94

KERR-MCGEE CORPORATION

OVERVIEW

Kerr-McGee is an international energy and chemicals company. During the 1980s the Oklahoma City–based company narrowed its focus to 3 main businesses: oil and natural gas exploration and production, coal, and inorganic chemicals.

Kerr-McGee explores for and produces oil and natural gas in the US, the UK, and Canada (about 50% of the company's oil was produced in the North Sea) and has low-sulfur coal mining activities in 3 states in the US. It also produces and sells industrial and specialty chemicals, railroad crossties (45% of the US market), and heavy minerals from plants in the US, Australia, and Saudi Arabia. Kerr-McGee — one of only 8 producers of titanium dioxide pigment, a white pigment used in paint, plastics, and paper — had 10% of the US and 5% of the world markets.

In early 1995 the company agreed to sell most of its refining and marketing operations (these accounted for 57% of 1994 sales but only 14% of profits); Kerr-McGee intends to dispose of the rest of these assets later in the year. The company sold its stake in the Abu Al Bu Khoosh oil field in the Arabian Gulf but is boosting oil exploration activities in other areas, especially the South China Sea.

In May 1995 Kerr-McGee named Luke Corbett, formerly a group VP, as president and heir apparent to Frank McPherson, who has been chairman and CEO since 1983.

WHEN

In 1929 partners Robert Kerr and James Anderson founded Anderson & Kerr Drilling Company in Ada, Oklahoma. They moved the business to Oklahoma City the following year and drilled a well near Konawa, Oklahoma, which continuously produced oil until 1969.

The company (renamed A & K Petroleum in 1932) went public in 1935. Anderson felt the company was growing too large and sold his stake in it the following year. A & K (renamed Kerlyn Oil in 1937) recruited Dean McGee, Phillips Petroleum's chief geologist, who in 1938 made a major oil find in Arkansas. Kerr entered Oklahoma politics in 1942 and was elected the state's governor and later its US senator. Kerlyn made a big oil strike in Oklahoma in 1943.

To reduce dependency on crude oil, Kerlyn bought its first refinery in 1945 and began exploring for oil in the Gulf of Mexico. In 1946 the company became Kerr-McGee Oil Industries and in 1947 pioneered offshore drilling along Louisiana's coast.

Kerr-McGee diversified in the early 1950s by acquiring 4 natural gas–processing plants in Oklahoma and Texas. During the Cold War atomic bomb production boosted uranium demand; Kerr-McGee began mining uranium in Arizona (it was the first oil company to enter the uranium industry) and built its first processing plant in New Mexico in 1954, the year McGee became president and CEO. Kerr-McGee became a fully integrated oil company with the 1955 purchase of Deep Rock Oil, which operated service stations in the Midwest, as well as pipeline and refining operations. In 1957 it bought Triangle Refineries and Cato Oil and Grease Company (sold 1995).

By the 1960s Kerr-McGee (renamed Kerr-McGee Corporation in 1965) was doing contract drilling in the US and overseas; it entered the timber and industrial chemicals businesses by acquiring 2 railroad crosstie plants and several fertilizer companies. The 1967 acquisition of American Potash & Chemical gave Kerr-McGee 2 industrial chemical plants and a 13,000-acre California lake from which it extracted brine to make soda ash, boron, sodium sulfate, and potash.

Kerr-McGee began mining coal in 1969. It opened more uranium plants and bought Southwestern Refining Co. in 1974. While it diversified, Kerr-McGee let its oil and gas reserves dwindle, and earnings dropped from $211 million in 1981 to $65 million in 1984.

Problems plagued the company's nuclear program in the 1980s. Karen Silkwood, a plutonium plant employee who had accused the company of many safety breaches, was killed in a mysterious car accident. A 1986 explosion at Kerr-McGee's nuclear fuel plant in Gore, Oklahoma, killed a worker and injured dozens of people.

Chairman Frank McPherson (who succeeded McGee in 1983) sold the company's potash and phosphate mines, uranium interests, and contract drilling operations and focused on expanding its oil and gas, coal, and chemicals businesses.

In 1994 the company launched a new natural gas marketing subsidiary and stopped producing high sulfur coal. In early 1995 Kerr-McGee agreed to sell its 3 oil refineries, a pipeline gathering system and trucking operation, and 41 company-owned retail filling stations.

NYSE symbol: KMG
Fiscal year ends: December 31

WHO

Chairman and CEO: Frank A. McPherson, age 61,
$739,000 pay
President and COO: Luke R. Corbett, age 47,
$371,167 pay (prior to promotion)
SVP and CFO: John C. Linehan, age 55, $335,000 pay
SVP and Corporate Secretary: Tom J. McDaniel, age 56,
$315,000 pay
SVP; President, Kerr-McGee Chemical Corp.: George R.
Hennigan, age 59, $232,308 pay
SVP; President, Kerr-McGee Coal Corp.: Robert C.
Scharp, age 47
VP and General Counsel: Russell G. Horner Jr., age 55
VP and Controller: J. Michael Rauh, age 45
VP and Treasurer: Thomas B. Stephens, age 50
VP Human Resources: Jean B. Wallace, age 40
Auditors: Arthur Andersen & Co, SC

WHERE

HQ: Kerr-McGee Center, Oklahoma City, OK 73125
Phone: 405-270-1313
Fax: 405-270-3029

Kerr-McGee's oil and gas activities are in Canada, the
South China Sea, the Gulf of Mexico, and the North Sea.
The company's coal operations are in Illinois, West
Virginia, and Wyoming.

	1994 Sales		1994 Operating Income	
	$ mil.	% of total	$ mil.	% of total
US	2,958	88	186	73
North Sea	191	6	54	21
Australia (chemicals)	114	3	7	3
Canada	54	2	8	3
Other regions	36	1	(10)	—
Total	**3,353**	**100**	**245**	**100**

WHAT

	1994 Sales		1994 Operating Income	
	$ mil.	% of total	$ mil.	% of total
Refining & marketing	1,893	57	35	14
Chemicals	639	19	92	38
Exploration & production	482	14	74	30
Coal	294	9	45	18
Other	45	1	(1)	—
Total	**3,353**	**100**	**245**	**100**

Selected Subsidiaries and Affiliates
Kerr-McGee Canada Ltd.
Kerr-McGee Chemical Corporation
 KMCC Western Australia Pty. Ltd.
Kerr-McGee Coal Corporation
 Pioneer Fuel Corporation
Kerr-McGee Natural Gas Inc.
Kerr-McGee Oil (UK) PLC

KEY COMPETITORS

Amerada Hess	Imperial Oil
Amoco	Koch
ARCO	Mobil
ASARCO	Occidental
Ashland, Inc.	Oryx
Atlantic Richfield	Panhandle Eastern
British Petroleum	Pennzoil
Broken Hill	Peter Kiewit Sons'
Burlington Resources	Phillips Petroleum
Chevron	Royal Dutch/Shell
Coastal	Sun Energy
CONSOL Energy	Tenneco
Cyprus Amax	Texaco
Exxon	Unocal
FINA	USX–Marathon
Freeport-McMoRan	Zeigler Coal

HOW MUCH

	9-Year Growth	1985	1986	1987	1988	1989	1990	1991	1992	1993	1994
Sales ($ mil.)	0.0%	3,345	2,535	2,608	2,689	3,087	3,683	3,274	3,382	3,281	3,353
Net income ($ mil.)	(4.6%)	137	(292)	84	102	126	150	102	(31)	77	90
Income as % of sales	—	4.1%	—	3.2%	3.8%	4.1%	4.1%	3.1%	—	2.3%	2.7%
Earnings per share ($)	(4.4%)	2.62	(6.01)	1.73	2.11	2.58	3.01	2.10	(0.53)	1.57	1.74
Stock price – high ($)	—	36.00	33.88	46.88	42.88	52.00	53.63	46.88	46.38	56.00	51.00
Stock price – low ($)	—	26.25	23.50	28.13	32.75	37.38	42.38	35.13	35.63	41.75	40.00
Stock price – close ($)	3.5%	34.00	28.13	36.25	37.88	50.75	44.88	38.63	45.00	45.25	46.25
P/E – high	—	14	—	27	20	16	18	22	—	36	29
P/E – low	—	10	—	16	16	12	14	17	—	27	23
Dividends per share ($)	3.7%	1.10	1.10	1.10	1.10	1.10	1.21	1.38	1.48	1.52	1.52
Book value per share ($)	(1.6%)	34.65	27.65	28.25	29.42	29.44	30.77	31.43	27.96	29.27	29.85
Employees	(4.5%)	8,351	7,373	7,670	7,771	7,942	6,756	6,072	5,866	5,812	5,524

1994 Year-end:
Debt ratio: 39.2%
Return on equity: 5.9%
Cash (mil.): $82
Current ratio: 1.08
Long-term debt (mil.): $673
No. of shares (mil.): 52
Dividends
 Yield: 3.3%
 Payout: 87.4%
Market value (mil.): $2,391

Stock Price History
High/Low 1985–94

KEYCORP

OVERVIEW

Cleveland-based KeyCorp is the product of a 1994 merger of equals between 2 banks: the Society Corporation, formerly of Columbus, Ohio, and KeyCorp, of Albany, New York.

The merger joined Society — which concentrated on the Midwest (Ohio, Indiana, and Michigan, with outposts in Florida, Texas, and Pennsylvania) and was active in corporate banking — with KeyCorp, which emphasized retail banking in small towns in the northern tier of states. The firm is one of the US's most geographically diverse banking companies, with branches from Alaska to Florida.

The unification of the 2 companies went smoothly, despite some fears in the industry that the corporate cultures might not meld well. In addition, the lack of overlapping

segments left some industry analysts disapproving of KeyCorp's failure to eliminate nonexistent personnel and office duplications.

Instead, KeyCorp is attempting to improve its results simply by growing the business. The old KeyCorp's small-town roots will help it build its market share in the increasingly attractive small-business lending market. Management believes that Society's roster of investment products, including mutual funds, will find ready takers in small towns that may be underserved by other financial companies.

KeyCorp hopes to boost the percentage of business attributable to fees. To this end, in 1995 it bought investment manager Spears, Benzak, Salomon & Farrell and finance company AutoFinance Group.

WHEN

KeyCorp's history dates from 1825, when its predecessor, Commercial Bank of Albany, was chartered. In 1865 it joined the new national banking system and became National Commercial Bank of Albany. After WWI, National Commercial consolidated with Union National Bank & Trust and was renamed National Commercial Bank and Trust. The bank chugged along, surviving wars, depressions, and recessions, until 1971, when it merged with First Trust and Deposit.

In 1973 Victor Riley became president and CEO. He directed the bank through its successful growth during the 1970s and 1980s and oversaw the merger into Society. Under Riley, National Commercial grew through acquisitions, swallowing more than 25 banks in upstate New York in the 1970s and 1980s. At the time, Riley hoped to establish the bank as a regional powerhouse. This hope was dashed by banking laws in several New England states that aimed at preventing dominance of the region by Manhattan banks.

Instead, the company, renamed Key Bank in 1979, followed Horace Greeley's advice and went west. It also embarked on a new strategy of mostly avoiding big cities and moving into small towns, where there was less competition. Thus situated it prospered, despite entering Alaska just in time for the 1986 oil price collapse.

Meanwhile, back in Cleveland, Society for Savings was following a different path. Founded as a mutual savings bank in Cleveland in 1849, the institution was a success from the start. It survived the Civil War and the postwar economic turmoil and by 1890

had built Cleveland's first skyscraper. It continued to grow, even during the depression, and by 1949 was the largest savings bank outside the Northeast.

In 1955 a holding company, Society National, was formed, and in 1958 it took over all of Society for Savings's assets. Society grew through the acquisitions of smaller banks in Ohio until 1979, when Ohio allowed branch banking in contiguous counties. Thereafter, Society National expanded by opening branches as well.

In the mid-1980s, as the age of superregionals dawned, the renamed Society Corporation began consolidating its operations and continued to add more. In 1990 it began expanding out of state by acquiring a Toledo bank that had offices in Michigan and Indiana.

In 1991 Society bought Cleveland's Ameritrust Corporation, which brought with it trust operations in Texas, Florida, Missouri, Colorado, and Connecticut. After this the company spent some time consolidating and promoting itself.

In 1993 Society and KeyCorp (which had both been looking for alliances) announced plans to merge, which were completed after shareholder approval in 1994. Unifying the companies' operations was simplified by the coincidental fact that the 2 banks happened to have compatible systems and software.

In 1995 KeyCorp made several acquisitions; in addition to an auto finance company and an investment management company, it added banks in Vermont and Colorado. But that same year it sold its mortage-servicing operations to NationsBank.

NYSE symbol: KEY
Fiscal year ends: December 31

WHO

Chairman: Victor J. Riley Jr., age 63, $1,346,936 pay
President and CEO: Robert W. Gillespie, age 50, $1,150,000 pay
COO: Henry L. Meyer III, age 45, $637,250 pay (prior to promotion)
SEVP and Chief Banking Officer: Gary R. Allen, age 46, $655,927 pay
SEVP, Chief Administrative Officer, General Counsel, and Secretary: Roger Noall, age 59, $637,250 pay (prior to promotion)
SEVP and Chief Investment Officer: James W. Wert, age 47, $637,250 pay (prior to promotion)
EVP Credit Administration: Carl C. Heintel Jr., age 51
EVP Credit Policy and Risk Administration: Kevin M. Blakely, age 43
EVP Marketing and Strategic Planning: Stephen A. Cone, age 44
EVP Investment Management: Martin J. Walker, age 43
EVP Corporate Human Resources: Michael L. Evans, age 47
Auditors: Ernst & Young LLP

WHERE

HQ: 127 Public Sq., Cleveland, OH 44114-1306
Phone: 216-689-3000
Fax: 216-689-0519

KeyCorp operates more than 1,300 banking and financial services offices in the US.

	1994 Banking Offices	
	No.	% of total
Northeast	452	34
Great Lakes & Florida	441	33
Northwest	290	22
Rocky Mountains	143	11
Total	**1,326**	**100**

WHAT

	1994 Assets	
	$ mil.	% of total
Cash & equivalents	4,181	6
Bonds	3,120	5
Mortgage-backed securities	9,063	14
Net loans	45,394	68
Other	5,040	7
Total	**66,798**	**100**

	1994 Sales	
	$ mil.	% of total
Loan interest	3,608	68
Other interest	882	16
Trust income	220	4
Service fees & charges	445	8
Other	218	4
Total	**5,373**	**100**

Selected Services	Selected Subsidiaries
Credit card	Key Bank Life Insurance,
Insurance	Ltd.
Investment management	Key Investments Inc.
Leasing	Key Trust Co.
Mortgage banking	KeyCorp Leasing Ltd.
Retail and commercial	Niagara Asset Corp.
banking	Schaenen Wood &
Securities brokerage	Associates, Inc.
Trust services	Society Asset
	Management, Inc.

KEY COMPETITORS

Affiliated Bancshares	Barnett Bank	Mountain West Savings Bank
American Express	Charles Schwab	National
AT&T	Chemical Banking	Bancorp of
Banc One	Citicorp	Alaska
Bank of Boston	Edward Jones	NationsBank
Bank of New York	Fleet	SunTrust
BankAmerica	General Electric	Zions Bancor-
	General Motors	poration
	Merrill Lynch	

HOW MUCH

	9-Year Growth	1985	1986	1987	1988	1989	1990	1991	1992	1993	1994
Assets ($ mil.)	25.3%	8,749	9,061	9,077	10,010	10,903	15,110	15,405	24,978	59,631	66,798
Net income ($ mil.)	34.0%	60	84	91	100	110	155	163	301	692	837
Income as % of assets	—	0.7%	0.9%	1.0%	1.0%	1.0%	1.0%	1.1%	1.2%	1.3%	1.3%
Earnings per share ($)	9.6%	1.51	1.72	1.88	2.10	2.32	2.32	2.45	2.52	2.89	3.45
Stock price – high ($)	—	13.69	17.75	19.88	18.75	20.25	17.63	26.25	33.44	37.25	33.75
Stock price – low ($)	—	8.88	13.50	13.50	15.50	16.63	12.00	15.25	24.25	27.25	23.63
Stock price – close ($)	7.1%	13.50	14.13	16.25	16.63	17.06	16.13	24.75	32.13	29.75	25.00
P/E – high	—	9	10	11	9	9	8	11	13	13	10
P/E – low	—	6	8	7	7	7	5	6	10	9	7
Dividends per share ($)	12.0%	0.46	0.48	0.60	0.68	0.80	0.88	0.92	0.98	1.12	1.28
Book value per share ($)	6.3%	10.90	12.14	13.47	14.98	16.58	15.34	16.90	15.49	17.53	18.88
Employees	17.8%	6,672	6,151	—	6,076	5,935	8,752	7,919	12,451	29,983	29,211

1994 Year-end:
Equity as % of assets: 6.8%
Return on assets: 1.4%
Return on equity: 19.5%
Long-term debt (mil.): $3,570
No. of shares (mil.): 240
Dividends
  Yield: 5.1%
  Payout: 37.1%
Market value (mil.): $6,009
Sales (mil.): $5,373

Stock Price History
High/Low 1985–94

KIMBERLY-CLARK CORPORATION

OVERVIEW

It's women and children first, but Kimberly-Clark is certainly not abandoning ship. Far from it, the Dallas-based company that makes Kotex and New Freedom feminine care products and Huggies disposable diapers (#1 in the US) brought aboard a new first mate in 1995: Scott Paper. In acquiring the competing maker of facial tissue, baby wipes, paper towels, and toilet paper for $7.4 billion, Kimberly-Clark has narrowed the gap between it and the #1 paper products maker, Procter & Gamble.

Kimberly-Clark is gearing up for an expansion of its consumer product tissue lines. Its Kleenex tissue is the #1 US brand, with a 45% market share. Kimberly-Clark also makes Depend incontinence care products and Pull-Ups training pants, and it makes and markets paper towels, industrial wipes, and health care products, including disposable surgical gowns and sterile wrapping for surgical instruments.

The company, which owns about 700,000 acres of timberland, also makes groundwood printing papers and paper specialty products for the tobacco, electronics, and other industries. However, the company's products are not all paper-based. Its K-C Aviation operates the Milwaukee-based airline Midwest Express. Originally set up in the 1980s as a means to transport Kimberly-Clark employees, the airline now operates 260 flights daily.

The company plans to exit its pulp and newsprint mills in Alabama and Ontario, Canada. The peso crisis in Mexico hurt its Mexican subsidiary's performance in 1995.

WHEN

In 1872 John Kimberly, Charles Clark, Havilah Babcock, and Frank Shattuck founded Kimberly, Clark & Company in Neenah, Wisconsin, to manufacture newsprint from rags. After incorporating as Kimberly & Clark Company (1880), the company built a pulp and paper plant on the Fox River (1889). The town of Kimberly, Wisconsin — named in John Kimberly's honor — formed as a result.

In 1914 the company developed cellucotton, a cotton substitute used by the US army as surgical cotton during WWI. Army nurses began using cellucotton pads as disposable sanitary napkins, and in 1920 the company introduced Kotex, the first disposable feminine hygiene product. Kleenex, the first throw-away handkerchief, followed in 1924, and soon many Americans were referring to all sanitary napkins and facial tissues as Kotex and Kleenex, respectively. In 1926 the company joined with The New York Times Company to build a newsprint mill (now Spruce Falls Power and Paper) in Ontario. In 1928 the company adopted its present name and was listed on the NYSE.

Kimberly-Clark expanded internationally during the 1950s, opening plants in Mexico, Germany, and the UK. During the 1960s the company began operations in 17 more foreign locations.

Before retiring in 1971 Guy Minard (CEO since 1968) sold the 4 mills that handled Kimberly-Clark's unprofitable coated-paper business and entered the paper towel and disposable diaper markets. Minard's successor, Darwin Smith, introduced Kimbies diapers in 1968, but they leaked and were withdrawn from the market. An improved version of Kimbies came out in 1976, followed by Huggies, a premium-priced diaper with elastic leg bands, in 1978.

From its corporate flight department, the company formed Midwest Express Airlines in 1984. Smith moved Kimberly-Clark's headquarters from Neenah to Dallas in 1985. From 1988 to 1989 he served as chairman and president of the King Ranch while still acting as chief executive of Kimberly-Clark.

In 1991 Kimberly-Clark, along with The New York Times Company, sold Spruce Falls Power and Paper. Smith retired as chairman in 1992. Wayne R. Sanders, who was largely responsible for designing Huggies Pull-Ups (introduced in 1989) succeeded Smith. Also in 1992 Procter & Gamble (P&G) settled out of court with Kimberly-Clark for an undisclosed sum. P&G had been charged with trying to dominate the US diaper market illegally. In 1994 the company entered into a joint venture with an Argentinian firm to make personal care products in that country. That year the firm also bought the feminine care products units of VP-Schickedanz (Germany) and Handan Comfort and Beauty Group (China).

To save costs, Kimberly-Clark agreed in 1995 to have all its domestic trucking handled by Schneider National Carriers. Also that year the company purchased a 51% stake in the tissue and feminine care assets of Peru based Unicel SA. To compete with Procter & Gamble and the private labels, the company introduced Huggies Supreme diapers with Velcro tabs in 1994.

WHO

Chairman and CEO: Wayne R. Sanders, age 47,
$1,134,384 pay
EVP: James G. Grosklaus, age 59, $542,400 pay
Group President, North American Consumer Products:
Thomas J. Falk, age 36, $476,877 pay
Group President, North American Consumer Products:
Kathi P. Seifert, age 45
EVP: James T. McCauley, age 56, $475,600 pay
**President, European Consumer and Service &
Industrial Operations:** John A. Van Steenberg, age 47
SVP and CFO: John W. Donehower, age 48
SVP Law and Government Affairs: O. George Everbach,
age 56
SVP: Larry M. Farrar
SVP: Robert A. Underhill
VP and Secretary: Donald M. Crook
VP and Controller: Randy J. Vest
VP Human Resources: Bruce J. Olson
Auditors: Deloitte & Touche LLP

WHERE

HQ: PO Box 619100, Dallas, TX 75261-9100
Phone: 214-830-1200
Fax: 214-830-1490

Kimberly-Clark has plants in the US and 25 foreign
countries. Its products are sold in 150 countries.

	1994 Sales		1994 Operating Income	
	$ mil.	% of total	$ mil.	% of total
US	5,439	73	817	88
Europe	1,075	15	(59)	—
Asia/Latin America	544	7	80	9
Canada	388	5	25	3
Adjustments	(82)	—	(44)	—
Total	**7,364**	**100**	**819**	**100**

WHAT

	1994 Sales		1994 Operating Income	
	$ mil.	% of total	$ mil.	% of total
Consumer prods.	5,911	79	656	76
Newsprint & paper	1,099	15	188	22
Air transportation	410	6	19	2
Adjustments	(56)	—	(44)	—
Total	**7,364**	**100**	**819**	**100**

Consumer Products
Baby wipes (Huggies)
Bathroom tissue (Delsey, Kleenex)
Commercial wipes (Kimwipes)
Disposable diapers (Huggies, Pull-Ups, UltraTrim)
Disposable surgical gowns and accessories (Kimguard)
Facial tissue (Kleenex)
Feminine hygiene products (Kotex, New Freedom, Lightdays)
Incontinence products (Depend, Poise)
Paper napkins (Kleenex)
Paper towels (Hi-Dri)
Pulp

Newsprint and Paper
Business and writing papers (Neenah)
Newsprint
Printing papers
Technical papers
Tobacco industry papers

Air Transportation
Midwest Express Airlines

KEY COMPETITORS

America West
AMR
Boise Cascade
Canadian Pacific
Champion International
Drypers
Fletcher Challenge
Fort Howard
Georgia-Pacific
International Paper
James River
Johnson & Johnson
Mead
Midway Airlines
Northwest Airlines
Paragon
Procter & Gamble
Rayonier
Sandoz
Southwest Airlines
Stone Container
Tambrands
Trade Brands
UAL
Union Camp
Weyerhaeuser

HOW MUCH

	9-Year Growth	1985	1986	1987	1988	1989	1990	1991	1992	1993	1994
Sales ($ mil.)	6.8%	4,073	4,303	4,885	5,394	5,734	6,407	6,777	7,091	6,973	7,364
Net income ($ mil.)	9.0%	267	269	325	379	424	432	508	345	511	535
Income as % of sales	—	6.6%	6.3%	6.7%	7.0%	7.4%	6.7%	7.5%	4.9%	7.3%	7.3%
Earnings per share ($)	9.6%	1.46	1.47	1.87	2.36	2.63	2.70	3.18	2.15	3.18	3.33
Stock price – high ($)	—	17.50	23.16	31.63	32.88	37.69	42.88	52.25	63.25	62.00	60.00
Stock price – low ($)	—	11.25	15.84	19.69	23.06	28.69	30.75	38.00	46.25	44.63	47.00
Stock price – close ($)	13.0%	16.75	19.97	25.00	29.13	36.75	42.00	50.69	59.00	51.88	50.38
P/E – high	—	12	16	17	14	14	16	16	29	19	18
P/E – low	—	8	11	11	10	11	11	12	22	14	14
Dividends per share ($)	13.1%	0.58	0.61	0.70	0.78	1.18	1.35	1.45	1.64	1.70	1.75
Book value per share ($)	6.1%	9.52	10.45	9.80	11.60	12.93	14.01	15.74	13.63	15.27	16.20
Employees	1.7%	36,648	36,490	37,357	38,328	39,664	39,954	41,286	42,902	42,131	42,707

1994 Year-end:
Debt ratio: 39.6%
Return on equity: 21.2%
Cash (mil.): $24
Current ratio: 0.88
Long-term debt (mil.): $930
No. of shares (mil.): 160
Dividends
  Yield: 3.5%
  Payout: 52.6%
Market value (mil.): $8,070

**Stock Price History
High/Low 1985–94**

KING RANCH, INC.

OVERVIEW

With 142 years under its Texas-sized belt, 825,000-acre King Ranch is showing that it's not too old to try something new. The fabled ranch, which is larger than Rhode Island and managed from its corporate headquarters in the Woodlands (near Houston), is trying its luck with a new CEO, a new tourism venture, and a new breed of cattle.

Jack Hunt, former CEO of Tejon Ranch (at 270,000 acres, it's California's largest piece of private property), took over as president and top executive of privately held King Ranch in 1995. The spread he now oversees includes not only cattle ranching on 4 noncontiguous ranches in 6 South Texas counties, but also oil

and gas exploration and development as well as diversified farming and other operations.

King Ranch introduced a new breed of beef cattle in 1995. The Santa Cruz, which is 1/4 Gelbvieh, 1/4 Red Angus, and 1/2 Santa Gertrudis, took 7 years to develop and is highly fertile. Undertakings announced in 1994 by King Ranch include "eco-tours" through the ranch (home to more than 200 animal species) and a 1/3 interest in an Ecuadorian oil-and-gas venture with Australia's Broken Hill Proprietary. Plans to build a power plant in Ecuador hit a snag in 1995 when local opponents objected to plans to burn imported diesel instead of Ecuadorian fuel.

WHEN

The King Ranch was founded in 1853 by New York City runaway Richard King, a former steamboat captain, and his wife, Henrietta, the cultivated daughter of a Brownsville missionary. On the advice of his friend Robert E. Lee, King used his profits from steamboating to buy land — miles of flat, brush-filled coastal plain and desert south of Corpus Christi that was valued at pennies an acre.

In 1854 King relocated the residents of an entire drought-ravaged village in Mexico to the ranch and employed them as ranch hands, known ever after as *kiñenos* ("King's men"). In 1858 King and his wife built their homestead at a site recommended by Lee.

King Ranch endured attacks from Union guerrillas during the Civil War and from Mexican bandits after the war. In 1867 the ranch used its famed Running W brand for the first time. After King's death in 1885, Corpus Christi attorney Robert Kleberg, who had married King's daughter Alice, managed the 1.2 million–acre ranch for his mother-in-law.

Henrietta died in 1925, and 3/4 of the ranch was left to Alice. Before Robert's death in 1932, control of the ranch was passed to sons Richard and Bob. In 1933 Bob negotiated an exclusive and lucrative oil-and-gas lease with Houston-based Humble Oil, which later became part of Exxon. In 1935, to protect the ranch, the Klebergs incorporated.

While Richard served in Congress, Bob ran the ranch until his death in 1974. He developed the Santa Gertrudis, the first breed of cattle ever created in the US, by crossing beefy British shorthorn cattle with Indian Brahmas. The new beef breed was better suited to the hot, dry South Texas climate.

Kleberg made King Ranch a leading breeder of quarter horses, used to work cattle, and Thoroughbreds, which he raced. Kleberg bought Kentucky Derby winner Bold Venture (1938) and Idle Hour Stable, a Kentucky breeding farm (1946). In 1946 a King Ranch horse, Assault, won racing's Triple Crown.

When Bob Kleberg died, the family asked Princeton graduate James Clement, husband of one of the founders' great-granddaughters, to become CEO. Bypassed was Robert Shelton, a King relative and orphan whom Kleberg had raised as his own son. Shelton severed ties with the ranch and the family in 1977 over a lawsuit he filed, and partially won, against Exxon, alleging underpayment of royalties. (Clement and Shelton died within days of each other in 1994.)

Under Clement the King Ranch became a multinational corporation. In 1980 it formed King Ranch Oil and Gas to explore for and produce oil and gas in 5 states and the Gulf of Mexico. In 1988 Clement retired, and Kimberly-Clark executive Darwin Smith became CEO, the first unrelated by blood or marriage to the founders. Smith left after only one year, and the reins passed to Roger Jarvis, a petroleum geologist who headed the corporation's oil and gas operations, then to Jack Hunt in 1995.

In 1993 the US Navy announced plans to put transmitter antenna towers on the King Ranch as part of a radar system designed to track drug-carrying aircraft.

The great-great-grandson of a business partner of Richard King sued in 1995 for 15,000 acres of ranch land he said King and Robert Kleberg had swindled from his family in 1883.

Private company
Fiscal year ends: December 31

Chairman: Abraham Zaleznik
President and CEO: Jack Hunt, age 50
VP: Stephen J. "Tio" Kleberg, age 50
VP and Treasurer: Mark Kent
VP, General Counsel, and Secretary: Larry Worden
VP, Controller, and Assistant Secretary: James E. Savage
VP Audit: James B. Spear
Director: James H. Clement Jr.
Director: John D. Alexander
Director: John H. Duncan
Personnel Manager: Rickey Blackman

WHERE

HQ: 10055 Grogan's Mill Rd., Ste. 100, The Woodlands, TX 77380
Phone: 713-367-7300
Fax: 713-367-7332

King Ranch operates ranching and farming interests in South Texas as well as in Arizona, Florida, Kentucky, and Brazil.

US Agricultural Operations
King Ranch — Arizona
King Ranch Farm (Lexington, KY)
King Ranch Farms — Florida (Belle Glade, FL)
King Ranch Feedyard (Kingsville, TX)
King Ranch (Kingsville, TX)

WHAT

Selected Ranch Animals

Cattle
Monkey (foundation sire of the Santa Gertrudis breed)
Running W "A" herd

Quarter Horses
Mr San Peppy
Old Sorrel
Peppy
Peppy San Badger
Wimpy

Thoroughbred Horses
Assault (1946 Triple Crown winner)
Bold Venture
Chicaro
Gallant Bloom
High Gun
Middle Ground (1950 Kentucky Derby and Belmont Stakes winner)

Farming

Citrus
Cotton
Milo
Sod
Sugar cane

Selected Subsidiaries

King Ranch Holdings, Inc.
King Ranch Oil and Gas, Inc.
Kingsville Lumber Co. (retail building material)
Kingsville Publishing Co. (newspaper)
Robstown Hardware Co. (farm equipment)

KEY COMPETITORS

Amerada Hess	K.S.A. Industries
Amoco	Lane Industries
Atlantic Richfield	Lefrak
AZTX Cattle	Louisiana Land
British Petroleum	Mitchell Energy
Broken Hill	Mobil
Burlington Resources	Norsk Hydro
Cactus Feeders	Occidental
Calcot	Oryx
Castle Energy	PDVSA
CENEX	PEMEX
CF Industries	Pennzoil
Chevron	Petrobrás
Elf Aquitaine	Phillips Petroleum
Enron Corp.	Repsol
EOTT Energy Partners	Royal Dutch/Shell
Flying J	Southern States Co-op
Friona Industries	Sunkist
GROWMARK	Tata
Howell Corp.	Tejon Ranch
Imperial Oil	Texaco
International Thoroughbred Breeders	TOTAL
Kerr-McGee	Unocal
Koch	USX–Marathon
	YPF

HOW MUCH

	Annual Growth	1985	1986	1987	1988	1989	1990	1991	1992	1993	1994
Estimated sales ($ mil.)	9.3%	—	—	—	—	160	160	165	330	250	250
Employees	14.9%	—	—	—	—	350	350	350	700	360	700

Estimated Sales ($ mil.) 1989–94

KMART CORPORATION

OVERVIEW

Kmart has been doing some selling lately, but the wares have not been what's in the stores, but the stores themselves. Struggling with more than 2 years of disappointing results, the Troy, Michigan–based retailer has spun off 3 of its specialty retailers to focus on its core discount operations. Gone are OfficeMax, the Sports Authority, and Borders Group bookstores. Also gone is the man who bought them in the first place, Joseph Antonini, who was ousted as CEO in March 1995. In June of that year the company hired Floyd Hall, whose resume includes stints with grocer Grand Union and discount retailer Target.

Hall must right a company that has been listing while archrival Wal-Mart has sailed

by. Kmart's problems stem from years of neglect of the core discount business while Antonini followed a diversification strategy. Meanwhile Kmart's stores got older and more run-down, and business defected to Wal-Mart. In 1990 the company began a renovation program, but updating stores is expensive, and Kmart needed more cash. Thus the sell-offs began.

The company is now focusing on improving the operations of its Kmart discount stores and Builders Square stores, modernizing the stores and fixing an inefficient distribution system. The company is also counting on Super Kmart stores, which combine discount merchandise and groceries.

WHEN

Sebastian Kresge and John McCrory opened five-and-dime stores in Memphis and Detroit in 1897. When the partners split in 1899, Kresge got Detroit and McCrory took Memphis. By the time Kresge incorporated as the S. S. Kresge Company in 1912, the company had become the 2nd largest dimestore chain in the US. Kresge expanded rapidly in the next several decades, forming S. S. Kresge, Ltd., in 1929 to operate stores in Canada. In the late 1920s and 1930s the company began opening stores in suburban shopping centers. By the 1950s Kresge was one of the largest general merchandise retailers in the US.

In 1958 a marketing study prompted management to enter discount retailing, and 3 unprofitable locations were transformed into Jupiter Discount stores in 1961. The company judged this a success and opened the first Kmart discount store in Detroit in 1962. Kresge formed a joint venture with G. J. Coles & Coy Ltd. (later Coles Myer Ltd.) to operate Kmart stores in Australia (1968).

The company built up the Kmart format swiftly in the 1970s and changed its corporate name to Kmart in 1977. Diversifications begun in 1980 led to the purchase of Furr's Cafeterias and Bishop Buffets (in 1980 and 1983, respectively; sold 1986). In 1984 Kmart bought Walden Book Company and Builders Square, formerly Home Centers of America.

In 1985 the company acquired Oregon-based PayLess Drug Stores Northwest and Bargain Harold's Discount Outlets, a Canadian retailer (sold in 1990), and in 1987 most of its remaining Kresge and Jupiter locations in the US were sold to McCrory's, the chain started by Sebastian Kresge's former partner. Kmart also

entered the warehouse club business in 1988 with Makro (which it merged with Colorado-based PACE Club) and in 1990 added the 17 Price Savers clubs. (It sold the PACE operations to Wal-Mart in 1994.) Also in 1988 Kmart opened American Fare — a hypermarket, or combination food and general merchandise store — in partnership with Alabama food retailer Bruno's. In 1990 Kmart acquired the Sports Authority.

Kmart passed Sears in retail revenue in 1990, but both were soon overtaken by Wal-Mart. By 1991 Kmart trailed Wal-Mart in sales and market share. Most of Kmart's stores were older, smaller, and less attractive.

In 1991 the company acquired a majority interest in the Cleveland-based OfficeMax. In 1992 Kmart bought 76% of Maj, a Czechoslovak department store, and announced that it would open up to 100 stores in Mexico with Grupo Liverpool. Kmart also bought the Borders chain of book superstores that year, and its OfficeMax segment purchased the 105-store chain Bizmart from Intelligent Electronics.

In 1994, as earnings continued to fall, management proposed to offer stock in the specialty businesses it had amassed. While not exactly a spinoff, the proposal aimed at financing Kmart's renovations by selling shares that reflected the performance of the specialty stores. The proposal was defeated by stockholders, and a few months later the company spun off OfficeMax and the Sports Authority, retaining stakes of about 25% and 30%, respectively. Also in 1994 Kmart sold its 21.5% interest in Australian retailer Coles Meyer.

In 1995 Kmart spun off the Borders Group to the public.

NYSE symbol: KM
Fiscal year ends: Last Wednesday in January

WHO

Chairman and CEO: Floyd Hall, age 56
EVP Special Projects: Joseph R. Thomas, age 59, $500,000 pay
EVP and CFO: Thomas F. Murasky, age 49, $383,000 pay
EVP; President, Super Kmart Centers: Ronald J. Floto, age 52
EVP Store Operations: Donald W. Keeble, age 46
EVP Merchandising: Charles Chinni, age 51
EVP Strategic Planning, Finance, and Administration: Marvin P. Rich, age 49
EVP Marketing and Product Development: Kenneth W. Watson, age 52
EVP and General Counsel: Anthony N. Palizzi, age 52
SVP Sales and Operations: Paul J. Hueber, age 46
SVP International Operations: Thomas W. Watkins, age 49
SVP and Chief Information Officer: Virginia G. Rago, age 43
VP Human Resources — US Kmart Stores: Michael T. Macik, age 48
Auditors: Price Waterhouse LLP

WHERE

HQ: 3100 W. Big Beaver Rd., Troy, MI 48084
Phone: 810-643-1000
Fax: 810-643-5249

Kmart operates retail stores in Canada, the Czech Republic, Mexico, Puerto Rico, Singapore, Slovakia, and the US.

1995 Kmart Group Sales

	$ mil.	% of total
US	28,386	96
Other countries	1,177	4
Adjustments	285	—
Total	**29,848**	**100**

WHAT

	1995 Sales		1995 Operating Income	
	$ mil.	% of total	$ mil.	% of total
Kmart Group	29,848	87	704	89
Builders Square	2,951	9	56	7
Borders Group	1,514	4	28	4
Total	**34,313**	**100**	**788**	**100**

	1995 Stores
	No.
Kmart Group	2,462
Builders Square	166
Total	**2,628**

Kmart Group Stores
Kmart Stores (general merchandise)
Super Kmart Centers (general merchandise/ supermarkets)

Builders Square (home improvement centers)

KEY COMPETITORS

84 Lumber	Melville
Ace Hardware	Montgomery Ward
Ames	Price/Costco
Broadway Stores	Sears
Caldor	Service Merchandise
Circuit City	Staples
Cotter & Co.	Stop & Shop
Dayton Hudson	Toys "R" Us
Eagle Hardware & Garden	Vendex
Fred Meyer	Venture Stores
Home Depot	Waban
J. C. Penney	Walgreen
Lowe's	Wal-Mart
McCoy	Woolworth

HOW MUCH

	9-Year Growth	1986	1987	1988	1989	1990	1991	1992	1993	1994	1995
Sales ($ mil.)	4.9%	22,357	24,152	25,978	27,688	29,992	32,462	34,580	37,724	34,557	34,313
Net income ($ mil.)	3.3%	221	582	692	803	323	756	859	941	(940)	296
Income as % of sales	—	1.0%	2.4%	2.7%	2.9%	1.1%	2.3%	2.5%	2.5%	—	0.9%
Earnings per share ($)	1.1%	0.57	1.49	1.70	2.00	1.07	1.26	2.02	2.06	(2.07)	0.63
Stock price – high ($)[1]	—	13.84	19.14	24.19	19.88	22.44	18.63	24.75	28.13	25.75	22.00
Stock price – low ($)[1]	—	10.22	11.22	10.81	14.50	16.25	11.69	12.81	20.88	19.50	12.50
Stock price – close ($)[1]	1.1%	11.80	14.63	14.88	17.56	17.50	14.19	23.88	24.50	21.50	13.00
P/E – high	—	24	13	14	10	21	15	12	14	—	35
P/E – low	—	18	8	6	7	15	9	6	10	—	20
Dividends per share ($)	8.5%	0.46	0.49	0.56	0.64	0.78	0.85	0.88	0.91	0.95	0.96
Book value per share ($)	4.3%	8.66	9.77	10.83	12.56	16.20	8.77	14.67	15.38	11.88	12.70
Employees	0.3%	340,000	320,000	330,000	350,000	365,000	373,000	349,000	358,000	344,000	348,000

1995 Year-end:
Debt ratio: 43.6%
Return on equity: 5.5%
Cash (mil.): $480
Current ratio: 1.63
Long-term debt (mil.): $3,788
No. of shares (mil.): 465
Dividends
  Yield: 7.4%
  Payout: 152.4%
Market value (mil.): $6,039

**Stock Price History[1]
High/Low 1986–95**

[1] Stock prices are for the prior calendar year.

KNIGHT-RIDDER, INC.

OVERVIEW

Knight-Ridder is the US's #2 newspaper publisher and an international communications powerhouse. The Miami, Florida–based company publishes 29 daily newspapers in 16 US states (major metropolitan papers include the *Detroit Free Press*, *Philadelphia Inquirer*, *Miami Herald*, and *San Jose Mercury News*). Its reporting and editorial quality have won Knight-Ridder 62 Pulitzer Prizes (the latest was in 1994). The company also supplies stories, graphics, and photos to news organizations worldwide. Newspapers generated more than 80% of the company's 1994 revenues.

Knight-Ridder also provides business news (from 18 national and 41 overseas bureaus) and an array of financial news and services to customers worldwide. It is a heavyweight in the electronic information industry, operating a leading on-line information database

(DIALOG). The company's databases (more than 600) are used by thousands of customers in over 100 countries. Joint ventures give the company stakes in cable TV, newsprint mills, and the *Seattle Times* (49.5%).

One of the pioneers of the information autobahn, Knight-Ridder is revving up its business offerings. The company now uses fax, Internet, and e-mail to deliver a wide range of information. It recently introduced SourceOne (patents and business articles); created DIALOG Direct (drugs, health care, and agrochemical news); acquired Technimetrics (global investor information); and agreed to provide Apple's eWorld with business information. In 1995 Knight-Ridder joined with 8 other top newspaper companies to create a national on-line information and advertising service called New Century Network.

WHEN

Knight-Ridder began as a 1974 merger between Knight Newspapers, the #2 newspaper group by circulation, and #3 Ridder Publications. Knight swapped stock worth nearly $160 million for 77,000 Ridder shares (both companies had gone public in 1969) and dominated the new board of directors.

Knight Newspapers had begun in 1903 when Charles Knight, a lawyer turned editor, purchased the *Akron Beacon Journal* and became a publisher. Knight died in 1933, leaving the paper to his sons, Jack and Jim. With their guidance the company grew to include 16 metropolitan dailies, including the *Miami Herald* (1937), *Detroit Free Press* (1940), and *Philadelphia Inquirer* (1969).

Ridder Publications had begun in 1892 when Herman Ridder bought a New York German-language newspaper, the *Staats-Zeitung*. He expanded in 1926 with the purchase of the *Journal of Commerce*, a New York shipping daily founded in 1827. Over the next 5 decades, the company grew to 19 dailies and 8 weeklies, mostly in the West.

After the Knight-Ridder merger, Knight's Lee Hills became chairman and CEO. Ridder's Bernard Ridder Jr. became VC.

During the 1970s and 1980s, Knight-Ridder expanded into television, radio, and book publishing. In 1978 the company purchased VHF stations in 3 states. The company bought HP Books in 1979 and formed TKR Cable with Tele-Communications, Inc., in 1981. A year later Knight-Ridder launched VU/TEXT (online news retrieval, now a provider of library

systems to newspapers), followed in 1983 by Viewtron, America's first consumer videotext system. In 1988 the company bought DIALOG, the world's largest on-line, full-text service, from Lockheed. Broadcast properties were sold in 1989.

During the 1980s Knight-Ridder's *Detroit Free Press* lost over $90 million in a newspaper war against Gannett's *Detroit News*. After a 43-month court battle, the 2 papers signed a joint operating agreement in 1989.

Knight-Ridder joined the Tribune Co. (with whom it operates a news service) in 1992 to deliver business news electronically to PC users. In 1993 Knight-Ridder's *San Jose Mercury News*, working with America Online, became the first newspaper to integrate on-line services with the daily paper. Also, Knight-Ridder and Andrews and McMeel began to publish books using material from Knight-Ridder newspapers. Knight-Ridder bought Data-Star (European on-line service), Equinet (Australian on-line service), the Dataline Asia-Pacific Database (Hong Kong), and EFECOM (Spain, financial news; renamed KRF/Iberia) in 1993.

In 1995 the company sold the 168-year-old *Journal of Commerce*, along with its print and electronic products, to the Economist Group (UK) and bought a small stake in Netscape Communications, an Internet software developer. Chairman and CEO James Batten died of cancer in mid-1995 and was succeeded in both positions by Anthony Ridder, who was succeeded as president by EVP John Fontaine.

NYSE symbol: KRI
Fiscal year ends: Last Sunday in December

WHO

Chairman and CEO: P. Anthony Ridder, age 54,
$833,000 pay (prior to promotion)
President: John C. Fontaine, age 63, $695,180 pay (prior
to promotion)
SVP and CFO: Ross Jones, age 52, $560,625 pay
VP; President, Business Information Services Division:
David K. Ray, age 53, $479,744 pay
VP Operations: Frank McComas, age 49
VP Operations: Peter E. Pitz, age 53
VP News: Clark Hoyt, age 52
VP News: Marty Claus, age 46
VP Marketing: Jerome S. Tilis, age 52
VP New Media: Robert D. Ingle, age 55
VP and General Counsel: Cristina L. Mendoza, age 48
VP Human Resources: Mary Jean Connors, age 42
Auditors: Ernst & Young LLP

WHERE

HQ: One Herald Plaza, Miami, FL 33132-1693
Phone: 305-376-3800
Fax: 305-376-3828

Knight-Ridder publishes newspapers in 26 cities in 16
states and maintains news bureaus and business
information service facilities worldwide.

WHAT

	1994 Sales		1994 Operating Income	
	$ mil.	% of total	$ mil.	% of total
Newspapers	2,135	81	351	94
Business information svcs.	514	19	23	6
Adjustments	—	—	(43)	—
Total	**2,649**	**100**	**331**	**100**

Major Newspapers	Daily Circulation (Average)
Detroit Free Press	552,603
Philadelphia Inquirer	486,291
Miami Herald and *El Nuevo Herald*	395,725
San Jose Mercury News	284,414
Charlotte Observer	234,860
St. Paul Pioneer Press	212,648
Philadelphia Daily News	198,809

Selected Business Information Services
Article Express International (document supplier)
DIALOG (on-line and CD-ROM information services)
Knight-Ridder Financial (on-line and print news, price
information, and market commentary)
Knight-Ridder Information, Inc. (fax, e-mail, and on-line
delivery of titles, business articles, and patents)
PIERS (Port Import/Export Reporting Service)
Technimetrics (investor information)

Selected Investments and Joint Ventures
Data-Star (on-line medical and business information)
Infomart DIALOG (50%, electronic business
information, Canada)
Knight-Ridder/Tribune Information Services (50%)
Netscape Communications Corp. (minority stake,
communications software)
Newspapers First (33%, advertising sales)
Ponderay Newsprint Co. (13.5%)
Seattle Times Co. (49% voting interest, newspapers)
Southeast Paper Manufacturing Co. (33%)
TKR Cable Co. (joint venture with Tele-Communications,
Inc.; cable TV systems in NJ and NY)

KEY COMPETITORS

Advance Publications	Dow Jones	Reed Elsevier
American Business Information	Dun & Bradstreet	Reuters
	E.W. Scripps	Thomson Corp.
Associated Press	Gannett	Times Mirror
Bertelsmann	Hearst	Tribune
Bloomberg	McGraw-Hill	United Press
CCH	Media General	International
Cox	New York Times	Washington Post
	Pearson	West Publishing

HOW MUCH

	9-Year Growth	1985	1986	1987	1988	1989	1990	1991	1992	1993	1994
Sales ($ mil.)	4.9%	1,730	1,911	2,073	2,083	2,268	2,305	2,237	2,330	2,451	2,649
Net income ($ mil.)	2.9%	133	140	155	156	180	149	132	146	148	171
Income as % of sales	—	7.7%	7.3%	7.5%	7.5%	7.9%	6.5%	5.9%	6.3%	6.0%	6.5%
Earnings per share ($)	4.1%	2.19	2.41	2.65	2.76	3.44	2.94	2.55	2.65	2.68	3.15
Stock price – high ($)	—	41.38	57.88	61.25	47.75	58.38	58.00	57.50	64.13	65.00	61.00
Stock price – low ($)	—	28.00	37.50	33.25	35.75	42.88	37.00	43.75	51.50	50.63	46.50
Stock price – close ($)	2.7%	39.88	46.88	40.13	45.38	58.38	45.75	52.88	58.00	59.75	50.50
P/E – high	—	19	24	23	17	17	20	23	24	24	19
P/E – low	—	13	16	13	13	13	13	17	19	19	15
Dividends per share ($)	7.4%	0.76	0.88	1.00	1.12	1.22	1.32	1.40	1.40	1.40	1.44
Book value per share ($)	7.2%	12.38	14.28	15.85	15.47	17.83	18.09	21.44	21.50	22.66	23.15
Employees	(0.5%)	22,000	24,000	24,000	22,000	21,000	21,000	20,000	20,000	20,000	21,000

1994 Year-end:
Debt ratio: 25.2%
Return on equity: 13.9%
Cash (mil.): $9
Current ratio: 1.01
Long-term debt (mil.): $412
No. of shares (mil.): 53
Dividends
　Yield: 2.9%
　Payout: 45.7%
Market value (mil.): $2,671

Stock Price History
High/Low 1985–94

KOCH INDUSTRIES, INC.

OVERVIEW

Family feuds notwithstanding, Koch (pro-nounced "coke") has consolidated its position as the 2nd largest privately held, family-run company in the US after grain merchant Cargill. The Wichita, Kansas–based company is an energy giant, posting estimated sales in excess of $23 billion, with refineries, gas pipelines, and operations in oil trading, chemical technology, cattle ranches, minerals, and financial services. Koch is a raw material provider and has no retail profile, but its product reach is extensive (it makes the surface material of the tennis courts at the site of the US Open).

The company's refineries have a combined capacity of 440,000 barrels/day and can produce a broad range of petroleum products. Koch operates a liquid pipeline network from Texas to Canada and a worldwide distribution system of storage facilities, terminals, trucks, and barges. Koch's agricultural business controls 450,000 acres of ranchland in Kansas, Montana, and Texas and is one of the 10 largest calf producers in the US. The company's trading operations are based in Wichita, London, and Singapore.

Koch is controlled by Charles and David Koch, owners of 80% of the company's stock. As part of a long-running family feud, their brother William (of America's Cup fame) is suing them for $1 billion. James Howard Marshall, a former executive at Ashland Oil and former partner of founder Fred Koch, owns approximately 16% of the company. Marshall added to the Koch intrigue with his marriage in 1994 (at age 89) to 26-year-old *Playboy* centerfold Anna Nicole Smith.

WHEN

In 1928 Fred Koch developed a process to refine more gasoline from crude oil, but when he tried to market his invention, he was sued by the major oil companies for patent infringement. Although Koch eventually won the lawsuits, the controversy left him unable to attract many customers at home, so in 1929 he took his process abroad to the USSR. Disenchanted with Stalin's brand of communism, he returned to the US and eventually became a founding member of the anticommunist John Birch Society.

Koch launched Wood River Oil & Refining in Illinois (1940) and bought the Rock Island refinery in Duncan, Oklahoma (1946). Though he would later sell the refineries, he folded the remaining purchasing and gathering network into Rock Island Oil & Refining.

After Koch's death in 1967, his 32-year-old son Charles took the helm and renamed the company Koch Industries in honor of his father. With the help of his father's confidant, Sterling Varner, Koch began a series of acquisitions, adding petrochemical and oil trading services operations.

During the 1980s Koch was thrust into various arenas, legal and political. Charles's brother David, also a Koch Industries executive, ran for US vice-president on the Libertarian ticket in 1980. Also in 1980 the other 2 Koch brothers, Frederick and William, launched a proxy fight for the company. Charles, with the help of David, William's twin, retained control, and William was fired from his job as vice-president. The brothers traded lawsuits, and in a 1983 settlement

Charles and David bought out the dissident family members for just over $1 billion. William, though, continued to challenge his brothers in court, claiming he had been shortchanged in the deal. One 1987 suit listed his mother as a defendant.

Despite the family's legal wrangling, Koch Industries continued to expand. In 1981 it purchased Sun Company's Corpus Christi, Texas, refinery for $265 million and its Massachusetts-based Koch Process Systems subsidiary bought Helix Process Systems. It expanded its pipeline system, buying Bigheart Pipe Line in Oklahoma in 1986 and 2 systems from Santa Fe Southern Pacific in 1988.

In 1991 Koch purchased Scurlock Permian's (a unit of Ashland Oil) Corpus Christi marine terminal, pipelines, and gathering systems for $21 million. The company bought United Gas Pipe Line (renamed Koch Gateway Pipeline Co.) and its 9,721-mile pipeline system, extending from Texas to Florida, in 1992. In 1993 Koch bought Trident NGL's fractionation complex in Hutchinson, Kansas.

In 1994 the Federal Energy Regulatory Commission gave permission to Koch Gateway Pipeline to charge market-based storage rates on its system, making it the first interstate pipeline to use such a rate system.

Koch acquired a municipal equipment leasing portfolio from the financial arm of Chrysler in 1994 for $100 million.

In 1995 Koch expanded its number of refineries to 3 with the purchase of Kerr-McGee's Corpus Christi facility for an undisclosed amount.

Private company
Fiscal year ends: December 31

Chairman and CEO: Charles G. Koch, age 59
President and COO: Bill W. Hanna
EVP Chemical Technology Group: David H. Koch, age 54
EVP Finance and Administration: F. Lynn Markel
EVP and Chief Legal Officer: Donald L. Cordes
EVP Supply, Trading, and Transportation: Joe W. Moeller
EVP Hydrocarbon Group: Chris C. McCampbell
SVP Corporate and Management Development: Paul W. Brooks
SVP Refining and Chemical Group: Cy S. Nobles
SVP Government and Public Affairs: Richard H. Fink
SVP Transportation and Operations: Bill R. Caffey
SVP Refining and Engineering: John M. Ehlen
SVP Financial Services Group: Corky J. Nelson
SVP Refining and Chemicals: Kyle D. Vann
VP Chemical Technology: John M. Van Gelder
VP Environment, Health, and Safety: Art F. Pope
VP Information Technology: M. Brad Hall
Controller: Diana M. Kidd
Secretary: H. Allan Caldwell
Director Human Resources: R. A. Pohlman
Auditors: KPMG Peat Marwick LLP

WHERE

HQ: 4111 E. 37th St. North, PO Box 2256, Wichita, KS 67220-3203
Phone: 316-832-5500
Fax: 316-832-5739 (Public Affairs)

Koch's Refining and Chemical Group has operations in 35 states and 5 Canadian provinces. It has 3 refineries (2 in Corpus Christi, Texas, and one in Rosemount, Minnesota). Koch's Hydrocarbon Group has facilities in 22 states. Its Materials Group markets asphalt through 110 plants and terminals in the US and Canada. Its Chemical Technology Group operates 15 facilities in the US, Canada, and Europe. The company's Agriculture Group has operations throughout the Midwest and West. Koch Minerals Group has facilities in the US and Canada. Its Supply, Trading, and Transportation Group trades commodities worldwide from its offices in Wichita, London, and Singapore.

WHAT

Agriculture Group
Cattle ranches
Feedlots
Fertilizer and agricultural chemicals distribution
Grain storage and merchandising
Oil seed and feed processing

Chemical Technology Group
Automotive sealants
Combustion and vapor recovery equipment
Distillation, mixing, and mist elimination
Gamma ray scanning and radioactive tracer services
Heat exchangers
Membrane separation systems
Specialty coatings

Financial Services Group
Diversified real estate
Domestic and international instruments
Foreign exchange trading
Leasing

Hydrocarbon Group
Anhydrous ammonia
Carbon dioxide
Natural gas and gas liquids
Nitrogen products
Sulfur products

Materials Group
Industrial asphalt
Paving asphalt
Recreational surfaces
Waterproofing products

Minerals Group
GranCem cement
Lime
Slag aggregate and slag-based specialty products

Refining and Chemical Group
Commodity and specialty chemicals
Crude oil
Sulfur and sulfur-based chemicals

Supply, Trading, and Transportation Group
Ammonia
Chemicals
Coal and petroleum coke
Crude oil
Intermediate feedstocks
Natural gas and gas liquids
Refined products

KEY COMPETITORS

Amerada Hess	Exxon	Pennzoil
Amoco	General	Petrobrás
ASARCO	Dynamics	Petrofina
Ashland, Inc.	Hearst	Phillips Petroleum
Atlantic Richfield	Imperial Oil	PPG
British Petroleum	King Ranch	Repsol
Broken Hill	Lyondell	Royal Dutch/Shell
Cargill	Petrochemical	Salomon
Chevron	Mobil	Sun Company
Coastal	Norsk Hydro	Tenneco
Continental Grain	Occidental	Texaco
DuPont	Oryx	TOTAL
Elf Aquitaine	PDVSA	Unocal
Enron	PEMEX	USX–Marathon

HOW MUCH

	9-Year Growth	1985	1986	1987	1988	1989	1990	1991	1992	1993	1994
Estimated sales ($ mil.)	7.9%	12,000	16,000	13,000	16,000	16,000	17,190	19,250	19,914	20,000	23,725
Employees	7.0%	6,500	6,500	7,000	7,500	8,000	9,300	10,000	12,000	12,000	12,000

Estimated Sales ($ mil.) 1985–94

KOCH

KPMG

OVERVIEW

Klynveld Peat Marwick Goerdeler (KPMG) is the most international of the Big 6 accounting firms, doing more than 2/3 of its business outside the US. It is also the one that is still most tied to its auditing business. The combination of overseas recessions, exchange imbalances, and increased price competition in auditing in the 1990s has brought repeated rounds of layoffs and cost cutting, including the firing of 65 junior auditors just in time for the glad new fiscal year of 1995.

But in 1995 the firm began a counteroffensive designed to remind potential clients of its preeminence overseas and to change the nature of its relationship with its clients. The firm launched *Worldbusiness,* a new magazine version of its quarterly newsletter. KPMG Peat Marwick, the US affiliate, admitted 127 new partners, each of whom will specialize in a specific area. The firm believes clients will appreciate the advantage of using auditors who actually know something about the industries they are dealing with.

KPMG has also made a number of strategic alliances with producers of computer hardware and software, which the company believes will contribute to both its accounting and consulting work.

WHEN

KPMG was formed in 1987 when Peat, Marwick, Mitchell, & Copartners joined KMG, an international federation of accounting firms. The combined firms immediately jumped to #1 in worldwide revenues.

Peat Marwick was founded in 1911, when William Peat, a respected London accountant, met James Marwick on a westbound crossing of the Atlantic. Marwick and fellow University of Glasgow alumnus S. Roger Mitchell had formed Marwick, Mitchell & Company in New York in 1897. Peat and Marwick agreed to join their firms under an agreement that was to terminate in 1919. In 1925 they merged permanently as Peat, Marwick, Mitchell, & Copartners.

In 1947 William Black became senior partner, a position he held until 1965. He guided the firm's 1950 merger with Barrow, Wade, Guthrie, the oldest and most prestigious US firm, and built up the firm's management consulting practice. Peat Marwick restructured its international practice as PMM&Co. (International) in 1972 and reformed it as Peat Marwick International in 1978.

In 1979 a group of European accounting firms led by Klynveld Kraayenhoff (the Netherlands) and Deutsche Treuhand (Germany) discussed the formation of an international accounting federation to serve multinationals. At that time 2 American firms that had been founded around the turn of the century, Main Lafrentz and Hurdman Cranstoun, agreed to merge in order to combat the growing reach of the Big 8. The Europeans needed an American member for their federation and encouraged the formation of the new firm, Main Hurdman & Cranstoun. By 1980 Main Hurdman had joined the Europeans to form Klynveld Main Goerdeler (KMG), named after

2 of the member firms and the chairman of Deutsche Treuhand, Dr. Reinhard Goerdeler. Other federation members were C. Jespersen (Denmark), Thorne Riddel (Canada), Thomson McLintok (UK), and Fides Revision (Switzerland). KMG immediately became one of the world's largest accounting firms, breaking dominance of the Anglo-US firms.

In 1987 Peat Marwick merged with KMG to form Klynveld Peat Marwick Goerdeler (KPMG). As a result of the merger, KPMG lost 10% of its business owing to the departure of competing companies that had formerly been clients of Peat Marwick or KMG; the firm nevertheless jumped into the #1 position worldwide in 1987.

KPMG in 1992 established the first joint accounting venture in China and opened an office in Estonia. In that same year the RTC sued KPMG Peat Marwick for alleged negligence and breach of contract in auditing Pennsylvania-based Hill Financial S&L. There were several other such suits. In 1994 the firm settled its S&L/banking suits with the US government for $187 million.

In 1993 the firm was named by the Agency for International Development to head a consortium providing technical assistance to 12 countries of the former Soviet Union, as those countries attempt to privatize their economies.

KPMG's Australian affiliate agreed to pay $97 million in 1994 to settle a suit brought by the Australian state of Victoria. The state claimed that faulty audits were to blame in the collapse of Tricontinental Group, a subsidiary of the State Bank of Victoria.

As part of its drive to improve the quality of both its auditing and consulting, in 1995 KPMG allied with both Integral and Hyperion for the promotion of client/server software.

International partnership
Fiscal year ends: September 30

WHO

Chairman: Hans Havermann
US Chairman and CEO: Jon C. Madonna
Administration and Finance Partner, KPMG Peat Marwick LLP: Joseph E. Heintz
General Counsel, KPMG Peat Marwick LLP: Ed Scott
Human Resources Partner, KPMG Peat Marwick LLP: Mary L. Dupont

WHERE

HQ: Klynveld Peat Marwick Goerdeler, PO Box 74555, 1070 BC Amsterdam, The Netherlands
Phone: +31-20-656-7890
Fax: +31-20-656-7000
US HQ: KPMG Peat Marwick LLP, 767 Fifth Ave., New York, NY 10153
US Phone: 212-909-5000
US Fax: 212-909-5299

KPMG has offices in 134 countries. KPMG Peat Marwick LLP has 130 offices in the US.

	1994 Sales % of total
US	32
Other countries	68
Total	**100**

WHAT

	1994 Sales % of total
Accounting & auditing	55
Management consulting/tax	45
Total	**100**

Selected Services
Financial services
Health care and life sciences
Information, communications, and entertainment
Manufacturing, retailing, and distribution
Public services

Representative Clients
Aetna
American Cyanamid
BMW
British Aerospace
Citicorp
Daimler-Benz
First Union
General Mills
Gillette
Hasbro
Heineken
J. C. Penney
Kemper Corp.
Koch Industries
Motorola
Nestlé
Norfolk Southern
PepsiCo
Pfizer
Polaroid
Ryder
Siemens
TCI
Union Carbide
USAir
Wells Fargo
Xerox

Affiliated Firms
Century Audit Corp. (Japan)
KPMG Deutsche Treuhand-Gesellschaft (Germany)
KPMG Klynveld (The Netherlands)
KPMG Peat Marwick (Belgium)
KPMG Peat Marwick (UK)
KPMG Peat Marwick (US)
KPMG Peat Marwick Huazhen (China)
KPMG Peat Marwick Thorne (Canada)
KPMG Reviconsult (Russia)

KEY COMPETITORS

Arthur Andersen
Arthur D. Little
Bain & Co.
Booz, Allen
Boston Consulting
Carlson
Coopers & Lybrand
Deloitte & Touche
Delta Consulting
EDS
Ernst & Young
Gemini Consulting
H&R Block
IBM
Marsh & McLennan
McKinsey & Co.
Perot Systems
Price Waterhouse
Wyatt Co.

HOW MUCH

	9-Year Growth	1985	1986	1987	1988	1989	1990	1991	1992	1993	1994
Sales ($ mil.)	17.3%	1,446	1,672	3,250	3,900	4,300	5,368	6,011	6,150	6,000	6,100
Offices	14.1%	335	342	620	637	700	800	820	819	1,100	1,100
Partners	10.4%	2,507	2,726	5,150	5,050	5,300	6,300	6,100	6,004	6,100	6,100
Employees	11.0%	29,864	32,183	60,000	63,700	68,000	77,300	75,000	73,488	76,200	76,200

1994 Year-end:
Sales per partner: $1,000,000

Sales ($ mil.) 1985–94

KPMG

Note: Figures prior to 1987 are for Peat Marwick only.

THE KROGER CO.

Kroger rings up more sales each year than any other supermarket chain in the country. The Cincinnati-based company, including its Dillon Companies unit, operates 1,301 supermarkets in 16 Midwest and Sunbelt states as well as 816 convenience stores. In addition to Kroger stores, the company's supermarkets carry such names as King Soopers and Sav-Mor, while its convenience stores operate under the Turkey Hill and Kwik Shop names, among others. Kroger has 37 food processing facilities that provide milk, ice cream, juice, bread, deli items, and other grocery products.

In 1994 the company built 45 stores, expanded 17, and bought 20, with greater expansion and renovation planned for 1995 and thereafter. Kroger spent $69 million on technological improvements in 1994 and has another $100 million earmarked for such projects over the next 3 years. Sales of private-label goods (Kroger has 6,000 such items) account for 20% of the company's grocery business and are growing faster than overall sales. Kroger's main competition is super-centers offering both groceries and general merchandise, although the impact from such stores is not as great as Kroger had feared.

Like many supermarket chains, Kroger has been trying out various innovations in grocery shopping. In Houston it has constructed large Signature stores that offer Taco Bell and KFC outlets, extensive arrays of produce, and — in at least one store — a staff rabbi to select kosher items. Kroger is testing its shop-at-home service through an interactive cable TV network in the Dallas area. And in Ohio the company is expanding its offering of self-service checkout lanes.

Bernard Kroger was 22 when he started the Great Western Tea Company in 1883 in Cincinnati. He quickly turned a profit and added new stores. Kroger was the first grocer to advertise in newspapers and to add bakeries to his grocery stores.

In 1902 the company became Kroger Grocery and Baking Company, with 40 stores in Cincinnati and northern Kentucky. Two years later Kroger became the first company to offer in-store butcher shops. Mr. Kroger had a reputation as a demanding boss and a tough competitor, keeping overhead low and discounting prices. The company spread to St. Louis in 1912. Kroger sold his holdings in the company for $28 million in 1928, the year before the stock market crash, and retired.

In the late 1920s the company acquired Piggly Wiggly stores in Ohio, Tennessee, Michigan, Kentucky, Missouri, and Oklahoma and bought most of Piggly Wiggly's corporate stock (now controlled by Bruno's), which it held until the early 1940s. In 1930 Kroger manager Michael Cullen suggested opening self-service, low-price supermarkets, but company executives demurred. Cullen left Kroger and began King Kullen, the first supermarket. If he was ahead of his time at Kroger, it wasn't by much; within 5 years, the company itself had 50 supermarkets.

During the 1950s Kroger acquired companies with stores in Texas, Georgia, and Washington, DC. With its purchase of Sav-on drugstores (1960, New Jersey) and its opening of the first SupeRx drugstore (1961, Ohio), Kroger broadened its sales. In 1983 it bought Kansas-based Dillon Food Stores and Kwik Shop convenience stores.

In 1987 Kroger sold most of its interests in the Hook and SupeRx drug chains (which became Hook-SupeRx) and focused on its food-and-drug stores. The next year Kroger faced takeover bids from the Herbert Haft family and from Kohlberg Kravis Roberts. Then-CEO Lyle Everingham warded off the raiders by borrowing $4.1 billion to pay a special dividend to shareholders and to buy shares for an employee stock plan.

To reduce debt, Kroger sold most of its equity in Price Saver Membership Wholesale Clubs, 95 food stores, 29 liquor stores, and its Fry's California stores. In 1990 the company made its first major acquisition since the 1988 restructuring by buying 29 Great Scott! supermarkets in Michigan.

In 1992 Kroger, about to further lower its stake in Hook-SupeRx, instead raised it, becoming the largest shareholder; Kroger cited long-term investment potential as the reason for the reversal. Also in 1992 a 10-week strike in Michigan and a work stoppage in Tennessee hit the company hard.

In 1994 Kroger joined with Bank South (Atlanta) to promote the bank's debit card; for 6 months shoppers using the card at Kroger stores received a 5% discount. The next year the company sold its Time Saver Stores unit (which operated or franchised 116 convenience stores in the New Orleans area) to E-Z Serve Corp. of Houston.

NYSE symbol: KR
Fiscal year ends: Saturday nearest December 31

WHO

Chairman and CEO: Joseph A. Pichler, age 55,
$1,114,832 pay
President and COO: Richard L. Bere, age 63,
$770,330 pay
EVP and CFO: William J. Sinkula, age 64, $573,832 pay
EVP; President, Dillon Companies: David B. Dillon,
age 43, $571,059 pay
SVP: Patrick J. Kenney, age 58, $527,959 pay
SVP and Chief Information Officer: Michael S. Heschel,
age 53
SVP Manufacturing: Ronald R. Rice, age 59
Group VP Labor Relations and Human Resources:
Thomas E. Murphy, age 52
VP, Secretary, and General Counsel: Paul W. Heldman,
age 43
Auditors: Coopers & Lybrand L.L.P.

WHERE

HQ: 1014 Vine St., Cincinnati, OH 45202
Phone: 513-762-4000
Fax: 513-762-4454

The company operates 1,061 supermarkets, primarily in
the Midwest, South, Southeast, and Southwest, under
the Kroger name. It operates 240 additional
supermarkets under a variety of names through its
Dillon Companies subsidiary. The company also operates
816 convenience stores in 15 states.

WHAT

	1994 Sales	
	$ mil.	% of total
Grocery stores	21,442	93
Convenience stores	898	4
Other	619	3
Total	**22,959**	**100**

Grocery Stores
City Market
Dillon Food Stores
Fry's Food Stores
Gerbes Supermarkets
King Soopers
Kroger
Sav-Mor

Convenience Stores
Kwik Shop
Loaf 'N Jug
Mini-Mart
Quik Stop Markets
Tom Thumb Food Stores
Turkey Hill Minit Markets

Joint Venture
Foodland Distributors (grocery and general merchandise
wholesaling and support services, with SUPERVALU)

KEY COMPETITORS

Albertson's	IGA
American Stores	Longs
Associated Wholesale	Megafoods Stores
Grocers	Meijer
Bashas'	National Convenience
Big B	Phar-Mor
Bruno's	Price/Costco
Buttrey Food and Drug	Publix
Casey's General Stores	Randall's
Circle K	Revco
Delchamps	Rite Aid
Eckerd	Roundy's
FFP Partners	Safeway
Food Lion	Smith's Food & Drug
George Weston	Southland
Great A&P	Walgreen
H. E. Butt	Wal-Mart
Holiday Cos.	Winn-Dixie
Hy-Vee Food Stores	Yucaipa

HOW MUCH

	9-Year Growth	1985	1986	1987	1988	1989	1990	1991	1992	1993	1994
Sales ($ mil.)	3.3%	17,124	17,123	17,660	19,053	19,104	20,261	21,351	22,145	22,384	22,959
Net income ($ mil.)	4.5%	181	52	183	35	(16)	83	101	101	171	269
Income as % of sales	—	1.1%	0.3%	1.0%	0.2%	—	0.4%	0.5%	0.5%	0.8%	1.2%
Earnings per share ($)	0.7%	2.05	0.55	2.20	0.24	(0.23)	0.96	1.12	1.11	1.50	2.19
Stock price – high ($)	—	25.00	35.00	41.50	59.00	19.75	17.00	24.50	21.13	21.75	26.88
Stock price – low ($)	—	18.88	21.38	23.38	7.25	8.38	10.63	12.63	11.25	14.00	19.38
Stock price – close ($)	0.1%	23.94	29.88	24.75	8.88	14.75	14.25	19.75	14.63	20.13	24.13
P/E – high	—	12	64	19	77	—	18	22	19	15	12
P/E – low	—	9	39	11	30	—	11	11	10	10	9
Dividends per share ($)	(100.0%)	1.00	1.03	1.05	40.82	0.00	0.00	0.00	0.00	0.00	0.00
Book value per share ($)	—	12.30	12.25	12.82	(36.20)	(36.35)	(33.43)	(31.36)	(29.52)	(22.85)	(19.40)
Employees	1.3%	178,200	173,900	170,000	160,000	170,000	170,000	170,000	190,000	190,000	200,000

1994 Year-end:
Debt ratio: 100.0%
Return on equity: —
Cash (mil.): $27
Current ratio: 0.90
Long-term debt (mil.): $3,889
No. of shares (mil.): 111
Dividends
  Yield: —
  Payout: —
Market value (mil.): $2,678

**Stock Price History
High/Low 1985–94**

LANDS' END, INC.

OVERVIEW

"Take care of your people, take care of your customers, and the rest will take care of itself," says Lands' End's founder and chairman Gary Comer. Comer owns 52% of the company, headquartered in Dodgeville, Wisconsin (population 3,882), and he built Lands' End following a people-first philosophy.

With about 8.2 million customers in the US and a 20 million–member mailing list, Lands' End markets men's and women's apparel and soft goods such as luggage and home furnishings through its folksy flagship catalog (12 issues in 1994) and 5 specialty catalogs (*Kids, Coming Home, Beyond Buttondowns, The Territory Ahead,* and *Textures*). The company's ware is highly traditional and generally unaffected by fashion trends. The company also has a generous no-questions-asked return policy.

Lands' End has grown rapidly and Comer decided to bring in some new blood to help manage the expansion. William End, a former executive with L.L. Bean, was named CEO in 1993. He added modern touches to the company's management style, including a teamwork system and numerical employee performance evaluations. End also set the company's sights on international expansion and diversification. While End's strategy won many outsiders' hearts, company employees, raised on Comer's homespun management style, balked at the new controls. In late 1994 Comer, unhappy with the direction his company was headed, asked for End's resignation and replaced him with 34-year-old Michael Smith.

Lands' End's profits dropped in fiscal 1995 as the company wrestled with the costs of expanding internationally and improving its distribution system. The company, which launched a catalog business in Japan in 1994, plans to continue its overseas expansion.

WHEN

High school–educated copywriter Gary Comer decided to leave his job at Young & Rubicam in 1962, opting to pursue his passion for sailing. At first he worked as a salesman for a sailmaker. Then, in 1963, Comer launched Lands' End, a Chicago-based mail-order supplier of sailboat hardware and equipment that produced one catalog annually in its early years (the misplaced apostrophe in the company's name is the result of a typographical error in an early catalog). Responding to customer inquiries, Comer began carrying new items in his catalog. First came duffel bags, then luggage, later clothing for boating, and, finally, general clothing lines.

In 1976 Comer began to emphasize clothing and soft luggage, and by the next year he had eliminated sailboat hardware from Lands' End's catalogs. By 1979 the company had moved its warehouse and fulfillment operations to rural Dodgeville, Wisconsin.

Lands' End launched a national advertising campaign in 1981 to promote the company's brand name. In the world of mail-order advertising, the campaign was unusual in that it focused on the company's quality image rather than on specific product offerings. The company prospered, using folksy catalog copy to sell basic clothing in basic colors.

Lands' End briefly experimented with more expensive, dressy clothes in the mid-1980s, creating the Charter Collection for men. A separate Charter Collection catalog emerged but was discontinued, deemed a distraction despite its profitability.

Lands' End went public in 1986. A year later the company launched a line of children's clothing. In 1988 Comer passed the CEO job to Richard Anderson (now VC).

After several years of sustained growth, earnings fell in 1989 as an increase in pages and mailings of Lands' End's catalogs failed to generate enough incremental business to offset their cost.

In 1990 sales of basic clothes appeared to weaken, and the company reacted by releasing new products and slashing inventory. When Christmas orders surged, Lands' End was unable to ship 1/4 of its orders on its promised same-day basis. The company lost sales and incurred heavy freight costs by shipping back orders at its own expense.

Results improved in 1991 as higher inventory levels allowed Lands' End to increase its fulfillment rate. That same year the company launched its first catalog in the UK.

In 1993 Lands' End made its first acquisition: Territory Ahead, a $6 million men's and women's apparel retailer. Also in 1993 it opened a telephone order and distribution center in Oakham, England. In 1994 it began small mailings of native language, native currency catalogs in France, Germany, and the Netherlands from its UK distribution center.

In 1995 Lands' End opened a 2,000-square-foot outlet store in the UK.

NYSE symbol: LE
Fiscal year ends: Friday nearest January 31

WHO

Chairman: Gary C. Comer, age 67
VC: Richard C. Anderson, age 65
President and CEO: Michael J. Smith, age 34,
 $187,590 pay (prior to promotion)
EVP, COO, and CFO: Stephen A. Orum, age 49,
 $299,200 pay (prior to promotion)
SVP Merchandising: Mindy C. Meads, age 43,
 $374,321 pay (prior to promotion)
SVP Operations: Francis P. Schaecher, age 47,
 $273,885 pay
SVP and Creative Director: Al Shackelford
VP Marketing: Michael P. Atkin
VP Quality Assurance: Joan T. Brown
VP New Business Development: Ronald T. Campo
VP International: Frank A. Buettner, age 40
VP Human Resources: Kelly A. Ritchie
Auditors: Arthur Andersen & Co, SC

WHERE

HQ: Lands' End Lane, Dodgeville, WI 53595
Phone: 608-935-9341
Fax: 608-935-4260

The company's manufacturing facilities are located in
Elkader and West Union, Iowa.

Outlet Stores

Brookfield, WI	Madison, WI (2)
Chicago, IL	Niles, IL
Dodgeville, WI	Oakham, England
Evanston, IL	Oshkosh, WI
Fox Point, WI	Pismo Beach, CA
Gurnee, IL	Santa Cruz, CA
Iowa City, IA	Schaumburg, IL
Lombard, IL	West Des Moines, IA

WHAT

Catalogs
Primary
Prospect
Specialty
 Beyond Buttondowns
 Coming Home
 Kids
 Textures
 The Territory Ahead

Products
Accessories
Children's clothing
Domestic products
Holiday gifts
Men's clothing
Soft luggage
Women's clothing

KEY COMPETITORS

Bed Bath & Beyond	Liz Claiborne
Benetton	L.L. Bean
Blair	Luxottica
Broadway Stores	Marks and Spencer
Calvin Klein	May
Dayton Hudson	Melville
Dillard	Men's Wearhouse
DM Management	Mercantile Stores
Edison Brothers	Montgomery Ward
Federated	NIKE
The Gap	Nordstrom
Harcourt General	Oshkosh B'Gosh
INTERCO	Polo/Ralph Lauren
J. Crew	Reebok
J. C. Penney	Sears
Jos. A. Bank	Spiegel
L.A. Gear	Talbots
Levi Strauss	TJX
The Limited	

HOW MUCH

	Annual Growth	1986	1987	1988	1989	1990	1991	1992	1993	1994	1995
Sales ($ mil.)	17.8%	227	265	336	456	545	604	683	734	870	992
Net income ($ mil.)	13.8%	11	15	22	32	29	15	29	34	42	36
Income as % of sales	—	5.0%	5.5%	6.6%	7.1%	5.3%	2.4%	4.2%	4.6%	4.9%	3.6%
Earnings per share ($)	15.1%	0.29	0.37	0.56	0.81	0.73	0.38	0.77	0.93	1.18	1.03
Stock price – high ($)[1]	—	—	7.44	14.75	15.44	17.88	10.50	15.25	18.94	23.69	27.75
Stock price – low ($)[1]	—	—	5.81	6.19	8.75	9.50	4.50	6.69	11.50	11.63	13.63
Stock price – close ($)[1]	10.8%	—	6.06	10.19	14.00	10.13	6.94	14.81	14.25	23.00	13.75
P/E – high	—	—	20	26	19	25	28	20	20	20	27
P/E – low	—	—	16	11	11	13	12	9	12	10	13
Dividends per share ($)	—	—	0.00	0.10	0.10	0.10	0.10	0.10	0.10	0.10	0.00
Book value per share ($)	24.3%	—	0.95	1.41	2.29	2.88	2.94	3.43	3.87	4.94	5.43
Employees	18.7%	—	2,000	2,700	3,700	4,900	5,600	6,500	6,500	6,400	7,900

1995 Year-end:
Debt ratio: 3.9%
Return on equity: 19.7%
Cash (mil.): $5
Current ratio: 1.93
Long-term debt (mil.): $0
No. of shares (mil.): 35
Dividends
 Yield: —
 Payout: —
Market value (mil.): $479

**Stock Price History[1]
High/Low 1987–95**

[1] Stock prices are for the prior calendar year.

LEHMAN BROTHERS HOLDINGS INC.

OVERVIEW

"Free at last, free at last, thank God almighty, free at last." That was how most people at New York–based Lehman Brothers felt in May of 1994, when American Express spun off the venerable investment bank to stockholders and the public. After more than 10 years with American Express, the company is making its way as a public company for the first time in its 145-year history.

Lehman Brothers is a leading investment bank, with offices in the US, Latin America, Europe, the Middle East, and Asia. It raises money for corporate, institutional, and government clients through underwriting and placing securities, and it provides a variety of advisory and investment management services to its clientele of corporations, governments and individuals. Lehman also trades stocks, currency, derivatives, and commodities.

Lehman gained its independence in one of the worst years in recent memory for the financial industry, as the Federal Reserve raised interest rates 6 times in 1994 alone. This played havoc with the firm's bond business (it is one of the US's leading corporate debt underwriters).

But a severe round of cost cutting, including massive layoffs, lifted Lehman into the black for the year. Simultaneously with its cost cutting, the firm is expanding into such emerging markets as China and India. It is also targeting markets in Europe: Lehman was authorized as a primary trader in Italian government bonds in 1994.

Lehman's share price got off to a rocky start (but insiders have bought stock on the open market). Nippon Life, which lent the firm money in 1987, owns 11.5% of the stock.

WHEN

Henry Lehman came to the US in 1844. After a year in New York, he moved to Montgomery, Alabama, and opened a dry goods store. His 2 younger brothers, Emanuel and Mayer, had joined him by 1850. Their Lehman Brothers store prospered on the strength of the pre–Civil War cotton boom. The brothers often accepted raw cotton instead of cash in return for merchandise, and they developed a thriving cotton business on the side. Soon cotton trading dominated the firm, and in 1858 (2 years after Henry's death) the company opened a New York office.

Despite the effects of the Civil War, in 1862 the remaining Lehman brothers joined with another cotton merchant, John Durr, to form Lehman, Durr & Co. This company helped finance Alabama's postwar reconstruction. In 1870 Lehman Brothers led in the formation of the New York Cotton Exchange.

Lehman Brothers continued to grow and diversify, underwriting its first IPO in 1899 for the International Steam Pump Company. Seven years later Lehman joined with Goldman Sachs to take Sears public. In the 1920s and even during the Depression, Lehman continued its investment operations, pioneering private placements during the long eclipse of the stock market in the 1930s.

The firm remained under family management until the death of Robert Lehman (Emanuel's grandson) in 1969. There followed a period of drifting.

In 1977 Lehman Brothers merged with Kuhn Loeb & Co., a firm of similar vintage, which had helped finance the development of the railroad industry. Kuhn Loeb had significant business overseas dating from the turn of the century, when it had helped the Japanese government to finance the Russo-Japanese War (which the Japanese won).

But the late 1970s were a precarious time in the financial world; in addition the 2 firms did not meld well. By 1984 Lehman Brothers Kuhn Loeb was rent by infighting among its partners and managers and ripe for a sellout to the right suitor. Along came Sanford Weill, who had sold out his Shearson brokerage to American Express and become that company's president. He was attempting to assemble a financial supermarket and needed an investment banking firm.

Lehman Brothers Kuhn Loeb had trouble adjusting to Shearson, and there were mass defections. Shearson instilled a more go-getting ethos than Lehman had previously known, and results improved. But they remained spotty, and Lehman was notoriously free-spending on employee perks.

In 1992 American Express began to refocus on its core businesses and divest financial services, splitting the unit by business lines. Lehman Brothers kept investment banking but lost brokerage, with its network of sales offices, and mutual funds. American Express gave it $1 billion to shore up its balance sheet.

In 1995 Lehman made plans to enter the mutual funds field, with its potentially lucrative (and steady) fee income, and began beefing up its equities trading operations.

NYSE symbol: LEH
Fiscal year ends: November 30

WHO

Chairman and CEO: Richard S. Fuld Jr., age 48,
$1,425,000 pay
President and COO: T. Christopher Pettit, age 49,
$1,237,500 pay
Chief Administrative Officer: John L. Cecil, age 40,
$1,600,000 pay
Chief Legal Officer: Thomas A. Russo, age 51,
$1,275, 000 pay
CFO: Robert Matza, age 38, $900,000 pay
**Managing Director Fixed Income Division, Lehman
Brothers:** Joseph M. Gregory
**Managing Director Investment Banking Division,
Lehman Brothers:** Mel A. Shaftel
Managing Director Lehman Brothers: Bruce R.
Lakefield
Managing Director Human Resources: Maryanne
Rasmussen
Auditors: Ernst & Young LLP

WHERE

HQ: 3 World Financial Center, New York, NY 10285
Phone: 212-526-7000
Fax: 212-526-3738

Lehman Brothers has 46 offices in Argentina, Bahrain,
Canada, Chile, China, Dubai, France, Germany, Hong
Kong, Israel, Italy, Japan, Korea, Mexico, Singapore,
Switzerland, Taiwan, the UK, the US, and Venezuela.

	1994 Sales		1994 Pretax Income	
	$ mil.	% of total	$ mil.	% of total
US	8,020	87	225	95
Europe	846	9	(43)	—
Asia/Pacific	324	4	11	5
Total	**9,190**	**100**	**193**	**100**

WHAT

	1994 Sales	
	$ mil.	% of total
Interest & dividends	6,761	74
Principal transactions	1,345	15
Investment banking	572	6
Commissions	445	5
Other	67	0
Total	**9,190**	**100**

Services
Asset management
Commodities and futures trading
Derivatives origination and trading
Foreign exchange services
Merchant banking
Research
Securities trading and underwriting

KEY COMPETITORS

Bankers Trust
Bear Stearns
Brown Brothers Harriman
Chemical Banking
CS Holding
Dai-Ichi Kangyo
Dean Witter, Discover
Deutsche Bank
Equitable
Fannie Mae
Goldman Sachs
Industrial Bank of Japan
J.P. Morgan
Merrill Lynch
Morgan Stanley
Nomura Securities
Paine Webber
Royal Bank of Canada
Salomon
Travelers

HOW MUCH

	Annual Growth	1985	1986	1987	1988	1989	1990	1991	1992	1993	1994[1]
Sales ($ mil.)	(3.1%)	—	—	—	—	10,776	8,750	9,830	10,611	10,586	9,190
Net income ($ mil.)	(4.4%)	—	—	—	—	110	(809)	207	(116)	(102)	88
Income as % of sales	—	—	—	—	—	1.0%	—	2.1%	—	—	1.0%
Earnings per share ($)	—	—	—	—	—	—	—	—	—	—	0.81
Stock price – high ($)	—	—	—	—	—	—	—	—	—	—	20.88
Stock price – low ($)	—	—	—	—	—	—	—	—	—	—	13.75
Stock price – close ($)	—	—	—	—	—	—	—	—	—	—	14.75
P/E – high	—	—	—	—	—	—	—	—	—	—	26
P/E – low	—	—	—	—	—	—	—	—	—	—	17
Dividends per share ($)	—	—	—	—	—	—	—	—	—	—	0.18
Book value per share ($)	—	—	—	—	—	—	—	—	—	—	25.70
Employees	(25.3%)	—	—	—	—	—	—	—	—	9,300	6,950

1994 Year-end:
Debt ratio: 84.4%
Return on equity: 4.4%
Cash (mil.): $2,384
Current ratio: 1.15
Long-term debt (mil.): $11,321
No. of shares (mil.): 105
Dividends
  Yield: 1.2%
  Payout: 21.6%
Market value (mil.): $1,542

Stock Price History
High/Low 1994

[1] 11-month fiscal year

LEVI STRAUSS ASSOCIATES INC.

OVERVIEW

Not content with inventing and manufacturing the global uniform of the young (blue jeans), Levi Strauss, the world's largest clothing maker, is expanding its business operations and its product line. Of the company's $6.1 billion in sales, approximately 72% comes from jeans and jeans-related products under the brand names Levi's and Brittania. Levi Strauss ranks 2nd in US jean sales, after V. F. Corp. (Wrangler, Lee).

Levi Strauss is pushing its domestically successful Dockers line of casualwear (about 30% of US sales) in foreign markets such as Europe, Hong Kong, New Zealand, and the Philippines. Levi's is promoting custom-fit jeans in the US and plans to introduce a new line of men's dress pants to bridge the gap between casual clothing (such as Dockers) and formal businesswear.

The company got a boost in 1994 when the Federal Trade Commission dropped a 16-year ban that prevented Levi Strauss from selling its own products in the US. While management is scotching any rumors of "store wars" with its well-established casualwear retail rivals, such as the Gap and V. F., it plans to open up to 200 retail stores nationwide over the next 5 years.

Haas family members, descendants of founder Levi Strauss, own most of the company's stock.

WHEN

Levi Strauss arrived in New York City from Bavaria in 1847 to join his 2 brothers' dry goods business. In 1853 he moved to San Francisco to sell dry goods (particularly tent canvas) to the gold rush miners.

Shortly after Strauss arrived, a prospector told him of miners' problems in finding sufficiently sturdy pants. Strauss made a pair out of canvas for the prospector, and word of the rugged pants spread quickly.

Strauss made a few more pairs of canvas pants before switching to a durable French fabric called serge de Nimes, soon known as "denim." Strauss colored the fabric with indigo dye and adopted the idea of Nevada tailor Jacob Davis of reinforcing the pants with copper rivets. In 1873 Strauss and Davis produced their first pair of Levi's Patent Riveted 501 Waist High Overalls (501 was the lot number). The pants, which soon became the standard attire of lumberjacks, cowboys, railroad workers, oil drillers, and farmers, are the same today as they were in 1873 (minus the rivets on the crotch and on the back pockets). The 2-horse logo was introduced in 1886.

Strauss continued to build his pants and wholesaling business until his death in 1902, when the company passed to his 4 nephews, who continued to produce their uncle's blue jeans (the term *jeans* traces its roots to the cotton trousers worn by ancient Genoese sailors) while maintaining the company's reputation for philanthropy.

After WWII Walter Haas Jr. and Peter Haas (a 4th-generation Strauss family member) assumed leadership and in 1948 discontinued the wholesale segment (then most of the company) to concentrate solely on Levi's clothing.

Levi's jeans became popular in the 1950s and were soon the uniform of youth everywhere. In the 1960s the company added women's attire and expanded overseas.

In 1971 Levi Strauss went public and diversified, buying Koret sportswear (sold in 1984), adding a women's career line, and making a licensing agreement with Perry Ellis. By the mid-1980s profits had declined and the firm was losing its family business tradition. The Haas family took it private again in 1985.

In 1987 the company acquired Brittania. In 1989 Levi Strauss publicly offered shares of Levi Strauss Japan (its subsidiary in Tokyo).

Although the basic jeans business declined in the 1980s, sales began rising again in 1991 as consumers forsook designer fashions for more traditional and practical clothes.

Under Robert Haas (the founder's great-great-grandnephew), Levi Strauss has been an innovator in employee-management relations. In 1991, in order to contain costs and keep jobs in the US, Levi Strauss instituted a team approach to production, in which the workers divide work within the unit. In 1993 the company's sewing plants adopted Japanese-style production techniques that encourage more worker responsibility. These changes have increased flexibility and production and reduced errors.

In 1994 Heath Rackley won a Levi Strauss contest to find the oldest pair of 501 jeans: a discarded pair of 1920s jeans he discovered in a mine shaft. Also that year, Levi Strauss opened its first company-owned retail outlet, on London's fashionable Regent Street.

In 1995 the company tested a line of clothing made from recycled beverage containers.

Private company
Fiscal year ends: Last Sunday in November

WHO

Honorary Chairman: Walter A. Haas Sr., age 79
Chairman of the Executive Committee of the Board:
Peter E. Haas Sr., age 76
Chairman and CEO: Robert D. Haas, age 52,
$2,418,242 pay
President and COO: Thomas W. Tusher, age 53,
$1,495,805 pay
SVP; President, Levi Strauss North America: Robert D.
Rockey Jr., age 53, $853,462 pay
SVP and CFO: George B. James, age 57, $743,229 pay
SVP; President, Levi Strauss International: Peter A.
Jacobi, age 51, $712,812 pay
SVP and Chief Information Officer: R. William
Eaton Jr., age 51
SVP and General Counsel, and Secretary: Thomas J.
Bauch, age 51
SVP Human Resources: Donna J. Goya, age 47
President, Levi's USA: George Porter
President, Dockers USA: James Capon
Marketing Director, Levi's USA: Steve Goldstein
Marketing Director, Dockers USA: Robert Hanson
Auditors: Arthur Andersen & Co, SC

WHERE

HQ: 1155 Battery St., San Francisco, CA 94111-1230
Phone: 415-544-6000
Fax: 415-544-3939

The company operates production/warehouse and
distribution facilities around the world. Levi Strauss has
operations in 74 countries.

	1994 Sales	
	$ mil.	% of total
US	3,721	62
Europe	1,543	25
Asia/Pacific	514	8
Canada	184	3
Mexico	82	1
Latin America	30	1
Total	**6,074**	**100**

WHAT

	1994 Sales
	% of total
Jeans & related products	72
Other products	28
Total	**100**

Products	Orange Tab
Fleece	Red Tab
Jackets	silverTab
Jeans	
Shirts	**Operating Divisions**
Skirts	Levi Strauss North America
Slacks	Brittania Sportswear Ltd.
Sportswear	Canada
Tops	Dockers
	Levi's
Brand Names	Mexico
501 jeans	Levi Strauss International
Brittania	Asia Pacific
Brittgear	Europe
Dockers	Latin America
Levi's Action	
Levi's Traveler	**Company-owned Retail and**
Levi's Youth	**Outlet Stores**
Little Levi's	Dockers Shops
	Original Levi's Stores

KEY COMPETITORS

Calvin Klein	Liz Claiborne
County Seat	L.L. Bean
Farah	Nautica Enterprises
Fruit of the Loom	Oxford Industries
The Gap	Oshkosh B'Gosh
Guess	Miller's Outpost
Haggar	Polo/Ralph Lauren
Hartmarx	Russell Corp.
J. Crew	Tommy Hilfiger
J. C. Penney	Urban Outfitters
Jordache	V. F.
Lands' End	Yes Clothing
The Limited	

HOW MUCH

	Annual Growth	1985	1986	1987	1988	1989	1990	1991	1992	1993	1994
Sales ($ mil.)	10.0%	2,584	2,762	2,867	3,117	3,628	4,247	4,903	5,570	5,892	6,074
Net income ($ mil.)	—	(19)	49	116	85	272	265	367	362	492	321
Income as % of sales	—	—	1.8%	4.0%	2.7%	7.5%	6.2%	7.5%	6.5%	8.4%	5.3%
Employees	3.3%	—	—	—	—	31,000	31,000	32,100	34,200	36,400	36,500

1994 Year-end:
Debt ratio: 4.3%
Return on equity: 23.6%
Cash (mil.): $813
Current ratio: 2.43
Long-term debt (mil.): $17
Shareholders'
equity (mil.): $1,472
Total assets (mil.): $3,925

LEVI'S

Net Income
($ mil.)
1985–94

THE LIMITED, INC.

OVERVIEW

Thinking that keeping all its eggs in one basket is too limiting, Columbus, Ohio–based the Limited is planning to make some new baskets. Sales have been slipping in the company's flagship the Limited stores, as well as in its other women's stores, and booming at its other outlets, so in 1995 the company announced plans to split into 3 separate companies.

One company will consist of the Limited's women's apparel stores (the Limited, Express, Lerner, Henri Bendel, and Lane Bryant), which had sales of $4.3 billion in fiscal 1995. A 2nd company will hold Victoria's Secret's catalogs and stores (lingerie, fragrances, and gifts), Cacique (lingerie), Bath & Body Works,

and Penhaligon's (perfumes and toiletries), which had sales of $2.1 billion in fiscal 1995.

The Limited will retain 85% of each of these companies and sell the rest to the public. It will also hold the company's other businesses, including retailers Abercrombie & Fitch (sportswear), Structure (men's sportswear), and the Limited Too (girls' clothing), which had sales of $895 million in fiscal 1995.

The Limited is hoping the parts are worth more than the sum. The reorganization is designed to boost its stock value by separating the slow-growing women's apparel business from the faster-growing lingerie and toiletries businesses. Founder and CEO Leslie Wexner owns about 19% of the Limited's stock.

WHEN

In 1963, after a disagreement with his father over the operation of the family store (Leslie's), Leslie Wexner, then 26, opened the first the Limited store in Columbus, Ohio, with $5,000 borrowed from his aunt. The store sold moderately priced fashions to teenagers and young women. When the Limited went public in 1969, it had only 5 stores, but the rapid development of large, covered malls spurred growth to 100 stores by 1976. The Limited acquired Mast Industries, an international apparel purchasing and importing company, in 1978. Two years later Wexner created Express, with a format aimed at younger girls; it has since widened its product line.

In 1982 the Limited began an acquisitions program, beginning with Lane Bryant, which was founded in 1900 and specializes in large-sized fashions. The Brylane fashion catalog division was formed when the company acquired Roaman's, a catalog merchandiser, that same year. Also in 1982 the Limited bought Victoria's Secret, a chain of 4 stores and a catalog specializing in women's lingerie. Meanwhile, new decor and the introduction of the company's Forenza and Outback Red lines helped increase the Limited's sales.

Beginning in 1984 Wexner made unsuccessful takeover bids for Carter Hawley Hale, Federated Department Stores, and R.H. Macy.

The Limited acquired Lerner Stores and Henri Bendel (1985) as well as Abercrombie & Fitch (1988) and London-based perfumer Penhaligon's (1990). Since 1987 the company has introduced several new shops, including Cacique (French lingerie), the Limited Too (girls' fashions), Structure (men's sportwear), and Bath & Body Works (toiletries) shops.

In 1989 it sold its Lerner Woman division to a new company (United Retail Group, Inc.), in which it took a 1/3 interest (reduced to 20% in 1993). All of these stores were based in malls, frequently clustered together so that their synergy would yield department store–levels of sales.

In 1990 and 1991 organizational problems caused late delivery of new season merchandise to some the Limited stores. There were also quality problems with some of Victoria's Secret's merchandise. The failure of the Paul et Duffier line and the retail downturn depressed profit growth and reduced same-store sales. In an effort to boost sagging profits at the budget-priced Lerner stores, the company introduced the popular Forenza line, which had previously been offered exclusively at the Limited. In addition, the Limited Too, Cacique, Structure, and Bath & Body Works divisions were restructured. In 1991 and 1992 a group of insiders that included Wexner sold off large numbers of shares.

The Limited began to restructure itself in 1993, closing or downsizing its overwhelmingly mall-based collection of the Limited and Lerner stores. That same year the company launched its own credit card.

The next year the company concluded an agreement with Next PLC to open 4 Bath & Body Works stores in the UK (its first non-US stores), with more to come once they become established on the home turf of natural-toiletries rival the Body Shop.

In 1995 the Limited moved into sporting goods with the acquisition of Indianapolis-based retailer Galyan's Trading, which operates a chain of sporting goods superstores.

NYSE symbol: LTD
Fiscal year ends: Saturday nearest January 31

WHO

Chairman, CEO, and President: Leslie H. Wexner, age 57, $1,982,370 pay
VC: Michael A. Weiss, age 53, $1,369,904 pay
VC and CFO: Kenneth B. Gilman, age 48, $1,369,904 pay
EVP and Director Human Resources: Arnold F. Kanarick, age 54
President, Mast Industries: Martin Trust, age 60, $864,268 pay
President, Store Planning: Charles W. Hinson, age 58, $825,978 pay
VP Taxes: Timothy B. Lyons, age 48
VP Internal Audit: Wade H. Buff, age 60
VP Finance: William K. Gerber, age 40
VP and General Counsel: Samuel Fried, age 43
VP and Director of Marketing: Edward G. Razek, age 46
VP Financial and Public Relations: Alfred S. Dietzel, age 63
VP and Corporate Controller: Barry Erdos, age 50
VP and Chief Sourcing and Production Officer: Jack Listanowsky, age 47
VP: Bruce A. Soll, age 37
Treasurer: Patrick C. Hectorne, age 42
Secretary: Bella Wexner
Auditors: Coopers & Lybrand L.L.P.

WHERE

HQ: 3 Limited Pkwy., PO Box 16000, Columbus, OH 43216
Phone: 614-479-7000
Fax: 614-479-7080

The Limited operates 4,867 stores (with 25.6 million square feet of selling space) nationwide. The company also operates distribution and shipping facilities in Columbus, Ohio.

WHAT

	1995 Stores
	No.
Lerner New York	846
Lane Bryant	812
Express	716
The Limited	709
Victoria's Secret Stores	601
Structure	466
Bath & Body Works	318
The Limited Too	210
Cacique	114
Abercrombie & Fitch	67
Henri Bendel	4
Penhaligon's	4
Total	**4,867**

Other Operations
Gryphon Development, Inc. (bath and personal care products)
Mast Industries, Inc. (contract clothing manufacturing)
Victoria's Secret Catalogue
World Financial Network/Limited Credit Services (credit card bank)

KEY COMPETITORS

Benetton	J. C. Penney
Body Shop	Lands' End
Broadway Stores	Levi Strauss
Charming Shoppes	L.L. Bean
Clothestime	Marks and Spencer
CML Group	May
Dayton Hudson	Melville
Dillard	Montgomery Ward
Dress Barn	Nordstrom
Edison Brothers	Sears
Federated	Spiegel
The Gap	TJX
Harcourt General	U.S. Shoe
J. Crew	Woolworth

HOW MUCH

	9-Year Growth	1986	1987	1988	1989	1990	1991	1992	1993	1994	1995
Sales ($ mil.)	13.3%	2,387	3,143	3,528	4,071	4,648	5,254	6,149	6,944	7,245	7,321
Net income ($ mil.)	13.4%	145	228	235	245	347	398	403	456	391	448
Income as % of sales	—	6.1%	7.2%	6.7%	6.0%	7.5%	7.6%	6.6%	6.6%	5.4%	6.1%
Earnings per share ($)	13.5%	0.40	0.61	0.63	0.68	0.96	1.10	1.11	1.25	1.08	1.25
Stock price – high ($)[1]	—	10.63	17.25	26.44	13.94	19.94	25.56	31.63	32.88	30.00	22.38
Stock price – low ($)[1]	—	4.33	10.25	7.94	8.19	12.63	11.75	17.63	19.25	16.63	16.75
Stock price – close ($)[1]	6.3%	10.42	15.88	8.63	13.63	17.44	18.00	28.75	27.00	17.00	18.13
P/E – high	—	27	28	42	21	21	23	29	26	28	18
P/E – low	—	11	17	13	12	13	11	16	15	15	13
Dividends per share ($)	31.8%	0.03	0.08	0.12	0.12	0.12	0.16	0.24	0.28	0.28	0.36
Book value per share ($)	23.9%	1.12	2.07	2.04	2.64	3.45	4.57	5.19	6.22	6.82	7.72
Employees	13.6%	33,600	43,200	50,200	56,700	63,000	72,500	83,800	100,700	97,500	105,600

1995 Year-end:
Debt ratio: 19.1%
Return on equity: 17.2%
Cash (mil.): $243
Current ratio: 3.19
Long-term debt (mil.): $650
No. of shares (mil.): 358
Dividends
  Yield: 2.0%
  Payout: 28.8%
Market value (mil.): $6,482

Stock Price History[1]
High/Low 1986–95

[1] Stock prices are for the prior calendar year.

LITTON INDUSTRIES, INC.

OVERVIEW

Things are shipshape at Litton now that the company has spun off its nondefense businesses and repositioned itself as an aerospace and defense company. In 1994 Litton's oil and industrial automation segments were spun off as Western Atlas. Litton, which earned 73% of 1994 revenues from the US government, is now focused on building advanced electronics and warships for the US and allied militaries.

Litton's military sales are strong despite cuts in the defense budget. In 1995 the US Navy gave the nod for Litton's Ingalls Shipbuilding subsidiary to build 2 more Aegis guided missile destroyers (the company already has several Aegis ships under construction) for nearly $740 million.

Litton fortified its defense electronics niche in 1995 by buying Teledyne's Electronic Systems subsidiary, a manufacturer of airborne computers, avionics, doppler radar, and other aircraft systems, and Imo Industries' Electro-Optical Systems, which develops laser and night vision systems for the military. The company has promised more strategic acquisitions as the defense industry continues to consolidate.

Litton's spinoff of Western Atlas and the settlement of a false claims lawsuit resulted in a net loss for fiscal 1994, even though the company's operating income was positive. The Chicago-based insurance firm Unitrin owns over 27% of Litton.

WHEN

Charles "Tex" Thornton, head of the Statistical Control Department of the army air force during WWII, was responsible for predicting manufacturing needs in the war effort. He foresaw a growing demand for new, technologically advanced military products in the postwar years. In 1953, after working for Ford and for Howard Hughes, he organized his own company (Electro Dynamics) to reap the benefits of this new market. Thornton began by borrowing $1.5 million and buying Litton Industries, which made microwave tubes for the navy. He had added 8 other small firms by the end of his company's first 9 months. Litton stock went public in 1954, and the cash generated was invested in R&D and expansion, which were to be the priorities for Litton for nearly 2 decades. In 1958 Litton bought privately owned Monroe Calculating Machines. Sales topped $100 million that year.

After 1959 Litton continued to expand internally as well as by acquisition, buying over 50 companies during the next decade. These purchases included Svenska Dataregister (Sweden, cash registers, 1959), Western Geophysical (seismic oil exploration, 1960), Ingalls Shipbuilding (1961), Cole Steel Equipment (office furniture, 1961), Winchester Electronics (1963), and Fitchburg Paper (1964). With the acquisition of Royal McBee (typewriters) and Hewitt-Robbins (office equipment) in 1965, Litton's annual sales topped $1 billion. Litton continued to expand worldwide, acquiring Kester Solder, Rust Engineering, Business Equipment Holdings (Australia), Stouffer Foods, and Eureka X-Ray Tube in 1967; Landis Tool in 1968; and Triumph Werke Nürmburg (Germany,

typewriters) in 1969. Litton's annual sales passed the $2 billion mark in 1968, but that year also saw the first quarterly decline in earnings in the company's history. Litton stock quickly dropped from over $120 to around $60.

During the 1970s and 1980s, Litton management restructured the company. Although acquisitions continued, they were coupled with consolidations as well as major divestitures, including Rust Engineering (1972), Stouffer Foods food divisions (1973), and Triumph Werke Nürmburg (1980). During the 1970s Litton's sales and net earnings fluctuated as the company reorganized.

In the 1980s Litton focused on its core business segments, selling its unrelated and unprofitable businesses. The Department of Defense temporarily suspended business with Litton after the company admitted to 300 counts of fraud.

Litton bought Intermec (a barcode systems maker) and General Instrument's defense electronics business in 1991. In 1993 the company won a $1.2 billion patent infringement judgment against Honeywell involving the companies' aircraft navigation systems (the award was set aside by a California court in 1995). Also in 1993 Litton won contracts worth $230 million to equip a variety of US military aircraft with threat-warning equipment. In 1994 Litton won contracts for laser transmitters for Stealth bombers and early warning system upgrades for Germany's F-4 aircraft.

In 1995 Litton moved its headquarters from Beverly Hills to Woodland Hills in the "technology corridor" north of Los Angeles.

NYSE symbol: LIT
Fiscal year ends: July 31

WHO

Chairman: Alton J. Brann, age 52, $730,915 pay
President and CEO: John M. Leonis, age 61, $801,351 pay
SVP; President, Ingalls Shipbuilding, Inc.: Gerald J. St. Pé, age 54, $622,616 pay
SVP and CFO: Rudolph E. Lang Jr., age 58, $610,198 pay
SVP; Group Executive, Electronic Warfare Systems Group: Michael R. Brown, age 53, $462,706 pay
SVP; Group Executive, Command, Control, and Communications Systems Group: Richard D. Fleck, age 64, $438,392 pay
SVP; Group Executive, Navigation, Guidance, and Control Systems Group: Larry A. Frame, age 58
SVP and General Counsel: John E. Preston, age 53
VP and Treasurer: Timothy G. Paulson, age 47
VP and Controller: Carol A. Wiesner, age 55
VP Corporate Communications and Investor Relations: Kathleen M. Wailes
VP Human Resources: Mathias J. Diederich
Auditors: Deloitte & Touche LLP

WHERE

HQ: 21240 Burbank Blvd., Woodland Hills, CA 91367-6675
Phone: 818-598-5000
Fax: 818-598-5940

Litton's principal operations are located in Canada, Germany, Italy, and the US.

	1994 Sales		1994 Operating Income	
	$ mil.	% of total	$ mil.	% of total
US	3,160	92	185	—
Other countries	286	8	(4)	—
Adjustments	—	—	(90)	—
Total	**3,446**	**100**	**91**	—

WHAT

	1994 Sales		1994 Operating Income	
	$ mil.	% of total	$ mil.	% of total
Advanced Electronics	1,732	50	36	20
Marine Engineering	1,484	42	141	76
Interconnect Products	289	8	8	4
Adjustments	(59)	—	(94)	—
Total	**3,446**	**100**	**91**	**100**

Advanced Electronics
Command, control, communications, and intelligence systems
Computer services
Electronic components
Electronic warfare systems
Inertial navigation and guidance systems for commercial and military aircraft

Marine Engineering and Production
Amphibious assault ships, cruisers, and destroyers for the US Navy (Ingalls Shipbuilding, Inc.)

Interconnect Products
Back panels
Card cages (assemblies to hold multiple computer cards)
Electronic and electrical connectors
Interconnection subsystems
Printed circuit boards
Solder products

KEY COMPETITORS

Altron	Kollmorgen	Samsung
Daewoo	Lockheed Martin	Schlumberger
GATX	Loral	SCI Systems
General Dynamics	Micron	Siemens
General Electric	Technology	Teledyne
General Motors	Mitsui	Thomson SA
Halliburton	Motorola	Thorn EMI
Honeywell	Raytheon	United
Hyundai	Rockwell	Technologies
Ingersoll-Rand	Rogers Corp.	Westinghouse

HOW MUCH

	9-Year Growth	1985	1986	1987	1988	1989	1990	1991	1992	1993	1994
Sales ($ mil.)	(3.1%)	4,585	4,521	4,420	4,864	5,023	5,156	5,219	5,693	3,474	3,446
Net income ($ mil.)	—	299	71	138	167	178	179	64	174	182	(122)
Income as % of sales	—	6.5%	1.6%	3.1%	3.4%	3.5%	3.5%	1.2%	3.1%	5.2%	—
Earnings per share ($)	—	3.62	1.26	2.58	3.17	3.53	3.63	1.45	3.94	4.41	(2.69)
Stock price – high ($)	—	46.75	46.13	54.13	43.63	49.00	40.63	46.13	49.75	71.38	40.00
Stock price – low ($)	—	32.13	35.88	32.00	33.75	35.75	34.38	36.88	39.50	42.75	28.25
Stock price – close ($)	(1.4%)	41.88	37.00	36.13	35.88	38.63	38.75	43.88	44.88	64.50	37.00
P/E – high	—	13	37	21	14	14	11	32	13	16	—
P/E – low	—	9	28	13	11	10	9	25	10	10	—
Dividends per share ($)	(100.0%)	0.75	0.00	0.00	0.00	0.00	0.00	0.00	0.00	0.00	0.00
Book value per share ($)	(2.8%)	17.08	18.55	20.14	22.91	25.82	28.82	29.12	33.67	36.58	13.25
Employees	(7.4%)	58,200	55,000	54,200	55,000	50,700	50,600	36,700	34,700	32,300	29,000

1994 Year-end:
Debt ratio: 25.0%
Return on equity: —
Cash (mil.): $117
Current ratio: 1.03
Long-term debt (mil.): $106
No. of shares (mil.): 46
Dividends
  Yield: —
  Payout: —
Market value (mil.): $1,699

**Stock Price History
High/Low 1985–94**

LIZ CLAIBORNE, INC.

OVERVIEW

Liz Claiborne is weaving itself a new look. The New York–based company, one of the nation's largest makers of women's clothing, has not liked what it has seen in the mirror lately. The biggest problem at the company has been the weak sales of its core women's sportswear line. Analysts claim the company saturated its main market, department stores, with products that were too much alike.

Liz Claiborne designs and sells sportswear and professional clothing at prices lower than designer lines. Brands include Liz Claiborne, Liz & Co., Elisabeth, Dana Buchman, and the men's label, Claiborne. Other products include fashion jewelry, shoes, accessories, cosmetics, and fragrance. To correct the company's problems, its divisions (which formerly were run independently) are now sharing information so they don't bring out similar lines.

Liz Claiborne is also taking on problems in its retailing business. In late 1994 it announced plans to phase out its chain of 77 First Issue women's clothing stores. The company is closing many of the stores and converting others (where it has long-term leases) into its other retail formats.

The company is looking overseas for a boost, opening franchised stores in Asia, Latin America, and the Middle East. Slated for openings in 1995 or 1996 are operations in Brazil, Ecuador, Taiwan, and Thailand.

In 1995 COO Paul Charron was named CEO, a post that had been vacant since Liz Claiborne retired in 1989. Chairman Jerome Chazen had handled the duties.

WHEN

In 1975 Liz Claiborne, a dress designer in Jonathan Logan's Youth Guild division, had a vision of stylish, sporty, and affordable clothes for America's working woman. Unable to sell the concept to her employer, Claiborne left the company and joined her husband, Arthur Ortenberg, and 2 other partners, Jerome Chazen and Leonard Boxer, to found Liz Claiborne, Inc., in 1976. With a starting investment of $250,000, the company was an immediate success. It showed a profit its first year and became the fastest-growing, most profitable US apparel company in the 1980s.

In 1981 Liz Claiborne went public at $19 per share, raising $6.1 million. By 1986 the company was on *FORTUNE*'s list of the top 500 industrial companies. Revenues that year were over $800 million.

Until her retirement Claiborne maintained close control over the design side of the business, overseeing and "editing" the work of the designers. The company produced 4 to 6 new collections a year, which gave consumers new styles every 2 to 3 months. These short cycles allowed more frequent updates of new styles and put clothes on the racks in the appropriate seasons. An automated inventory network allowed quick response to market demand.

Liz Claiborne expanded into men's clothing (Claiborne, 1985), cosmetics (Liz Claiborne, a 1986 joint venture with Avon; in 1988 the company regained full rights to the line), a clothing line for larger women (Elisabeth, 1989), and a line of knit sportswear (Liz & Co., 1989). A new label of higher-priced sportswear by in-house designer Dana Buchman was introduced in 1987, by which time a 1984 foray into girls' clothing had failed.

The company moved into the retail apparel business in 1988 when it opened its first stores, offering the First Issue brand of casual sportswear. It expanded with Liz Claiborne and Claiborne stores in 1989 — a "store-within-a-store" located inside department stores. These areas are jointly managed.

Liz Claiborne and Arthur Ortenberg retired from management in 1989 and from the board in 1990. Also in 1990 the company established a separate shoe division.

In 1992 Liz Claiborne acquired the Crazy Horse, Russ Togs, Villager, and Red Horse brand names and took over 16 outlet stores from bankrupt Russ Togs.

In 1993 the company's earnings plunged 42% because of excess inventories. Sales of the sportswear collections, its core business, fell for the first time in its history. The company also discontinued its line of athletic sneakers and consolidated its suit and dress divisions following a 25% drop in sales. Also in 1993 VC Jay Margolis resigned abruptly and was replaced by Paul Charron, a former executive with V.F.

In 1994 the company announced it would stop making and buying goods in Myanmar (formerly Burma) because of human rights violations by that country's authoritarian government.

In 1995 the company introduced a new line of bedding and accessories, including sheets, pillowcases, comforters, candlesticks, and wastebaskets.

NYSE symbol: LIZ
Fiscal year ends: Last Saturday in December

WHO

Chairman: Jerome A. Chazen, age 68, $600,000 pay
President and CEO: Paul R. Charron, age 52,
$669,200 pay (prior to promotion)
President, Collection Division: Glenn S. Palmer
President, Lizsport Division: Linda Larsen-German
President, Lizwear Division: James C. Lewis
President, Elisabeth Division: Karen R. Greenberg
President, Menswear Division: Jay Friedman
President, Retail Division: H. James Metscher
SVP Finance, CFO, and Chief Accounting Officer:
Samuel M. Miller, age 57, $444,700 pay
**SVP Service, Systems, and Reengineering and Chief
Information Officer:** John R. Thompson, age 43
SVP Operations and Manufacturing – Far East:
Rosemary Chang
SVP Distribution: Kenneth S. Ganz
SVP Human Resources: Jorge L. Figueredo
Secretary: Kenneth P. Kopelman
Auditors: Arthur Andersen & Co, SC

WHERE

HQ: 1441 Broadway, New York, NY 10018
Phone: 212-354-4900
Fax: 212-626-3416

Liz Claiborne's products are produced in more than 50
countries, mainly the US, China, Indonesia, Hong Kong,
South Korea, and Sri Lanka. The company also operates
29 Liz Claiborne stores, 21 Elisabeth stores, one Dana
Buchman store, and 70 outlet shops.

	1994 Sales	
	$ mil.	% of total
US	2,040	94
Other countries	123	6
Total	**2,163**	**100**

WHAT

	1994 Sales	
	$ mil.	% of total
Misses sportswear	772	33
Petite women's sportswear	228	10
Accessories	187	8
Retail specialty stores	150	7
Outlet stores	140	6
Elisabeth	137	6
Dresses & suits	122	5
Dana Buchman	113	5
Moderate sportswear	112	5
Men's sportswear & furnishings	102	4
Cosmetics	84	4
Liz & Co.	76	3
Shoes	63	3
Jewelry & watches	31	1
Licensing	3	—
Adjustments	(157)	—
Total	**2,163**	**100**

Selected Brand Names

Women's Apparel, Cosmetics, and Accessories

Collection	Liz Claiborne	Russ
Crazy Horse	Lizsport	The Villager
Dana Buchman	Lizwear	Vivid (fragrance)
Elisabeth	Realities (fragrance)	
Liz & Co.		

Men's Clothing and Accessories
Claiborne
Claiborne for Men

KEY COMPETITORS

Anne Klein	L.A. Gear	LVMH
AnnTaylor	Lands' End	Marks and
Benetton	Leslie Fay	Spencer
Calvin Klein	Levi Strauss	Polo/Ralph
Donna Karan	The Limited	Lauren
Fruit of the Loom	L'Oréal	Spiegel
J. Crew		

HOW MUCH

	9-Year Growth	1985	1986	1987	1988	1989	1990	1991	1992	1993	1994
Sales ($ mil.)	16.3%	557	814	1,053	1,184	1,411	1,729	2,007	2,194	2,204	2,163
Net income ($ mil.)	3.5%	61	86	114	110	165	206	223	219	125	83
Income as % of sales	—	10.9%	10.6%	10.9%	9.3%	11.7%	11.9%	11.1%	10.0%	5.7%	3.8%
Earnings per share ($)	4.6%	0.71	1.00	1.32	1.26	1.87	2.37	2.61	2.61	1.54	1.06
Stock price – high ($)	—	12.31	23.75	38.50	19.75	27.50	35.00	50.75	47.88	42.88	26.63
Stock price – low ($)	—	5.88	11.88	12.75	13.50	16.75	20.25	28.25	31.88	18.00	15.38
Stock price – close ($)	3.8%	12.13	21.38	16.50	17.25	24.00	29.75	42.25	41.63	22.63	17.00
P/E – high	—	17	24	29	16	15	15	19	18	28	25
P/E – low	—	8	12	10	11	9	9	11	12	12	15
Dividends per share ($)	19.6%	0.09	0.12	0.16	0.18	0.19	0.24	0.33	0.39	0.44	0.45
Book value per share ($)	23.6%	1.90	2.86	4.10	5.22	6.94	8.08	10.67	12.05	12.41	12.77
Employees	15.4%	2,200	3,000	3,400	4,800	5,400	6,000	7,000	7,400	7,900	8,000

1994 Year-End:
Debt ratio: 0.1%
Return on equity: 8.4%
Cash (mil.): $330
Current ratio: 3.37
Long-term debt (mil.): $1
No. of shares (mil.): 77
Dividends:
  Yield: 2.6%
  Payout: 42.5%
Market value (mil.): $1,309

**Stock Price History
High/Low 1985–94**

LOCKHEED MARTIN CORPORATION

OVERVIEW

Lockheed Martin was formed in 1995 with the merger of Lockheed (the US's 2nd largest defense contractor, with $13 billion in sales in 1994) and Martin Marietta (the 3rd largest, with about $10 billion in sales). The new company, based in Bethesda, Maryland, leapfrogged McDonnell Douglas to become the largest defense contractor in the US.

Lockheed Martin products include the Trident II submarine–launched ballistic missile and systems for the space station *Freedom,* as well as night navigation systems, external fuel tanks for the space shuttle, and the Titan IV space launch vehicle. Lockheed Martin's commercial products include spacecraft for Motorola's IRIDIUM satellite communication network and information systems for state and local governments.

As part of the consolidation of the 2 companies, Lockheed Martin plans to lay off between 15,000 and 20,000 workers. With US defense budgets dwindling, Lockheed Martin is looking to get more contracts in the Middle East and Asia.

WHEN

Brothers Allan and Malcolm Loughead (pronounced "Lockheed") teamed with Fred Keeler in 1926 to form Lockheed Aircraft. John Northrop (who founded Northrop Corporation) designed Lockheed's first airplane, the famous Vega (flown by such pilots as Wiley Post and Amelia Earhart).

Robert Gross, Carl Squier, and Lloyd Stearman bought Lockheed in 1932. With designer Clarence "Kelly" Johnson, the company produced a long series of successes: the P-38 Lightning fighter of WWII, the U-2 spyplane (1955), and the SR-71 Blackbird. It also produced submarine-launched ballistic missiles, beginning with the Polaris (1958), military transports (C-5 Galaxy, 1968), and the L-1011 TriStar airliner (1970).

In the late 1960s and early 1970s, the company suffered the cancellation of its Cheyenne attack helicopter, the C-5A cost-overrun scandal, and financial problems with the L-1011. Government-sponsored loans saved the company from bankruptcy in 1971. In the 1970s and 1980s, Lockheed developed the Hubble Space Telescope and the F-117A stealth fighter. However, in 1981 Lockheed discontinued production of the L-1011 Tristar.

In 1990 Lockheed's main aircraft plant in Burbank, California, was closed, eliminating 5,500 jobs. Disappointing postlaunch performance of the Hubble telescope added to the company's woes. In 1990 and 1991 billionaire Harold Simmons led 2 proxy battles aimed at stopping the company's expansion into nondefense operations. Lockheed emerged intact, and Simmons sold most of his 19.8% stake in the company at a $42 million loss.

Lockheed signed a deal with Motorola to provide satellites for its IRIDIUM project in 1992 and the next year provided mission support for NASA's repair work on the Hubble telescope. In 1994 Lockheed-Khrunichev-Energia, Lockheed's joint venture with 2 Russian aerospace firms, won a contract to launch radio and television satellites for Société Européenne des Satellites.

In 1917 Glenn Martin, a barnstormer and aircraft designer, founded the Glenn L. Martin Company in Cleveland. The company, which moved to Baltimore in 1929, produced the first US-built bombers as well as military and commercial flying boats, including the M-130, the famous Pan Am "Clipper" that made transpacific air service practical (1935). Martin also designed the WWII-era B-26 Marauder bomber.

During the 1950s Martin began reducing aircraft production in favor of missiles, electronics, and nuclear systems. In 1953 it began designing the Titan, an ICBM that evolved into a versatile space launch vehicle. In 1961 Martin merged with the American-Marietta Company, a supplier of construction materials and chemical products, formed in 1913.

With a mix of aerospace, chemicals, electronics, building materials, and aluminum production, Martin Marietta began a period of growth in the 1970s. It defeated a hostile takeover bid by Bendix in 1982. To reduce the $1.34 billion debt incurred during the takeover battle, the company sold many of its businesses, including cement, chemical, and aluminum operations.

In 1992 Martin Marietta almost doubled in size when it acquired General Electric's aerospace business for $3.05 billion. In 1994 the company spun off its Materials unit, selling about 20% of the newly created Martin Marietta Materials, Inc., to the public.

The 1995 merger of Lockheed and Martin Marietta came as the defense industry continued to consolidate to ward off the effects of shrinking defense budgets.

NYSE symbol: LMT
Fiscal year ends: Last Sunday in December

WHO

Chairman and CEO: Daniel M. Tellep, age 63,
$1,470,000 pay (prior to merger)
President: Norman R. Augustine, age 59, $1,830,000 pay
(prior to merger)
EVP: Vincent N. Marafino, age 64, $1,168,750 pay (prior
to merger)
EVP: A. Thomas Young, age 56, $1,185,000 pay (prior to
merger)
Sector President, Aeronautics: Kenneth W. Cannestra,
age 64, $641,750 pay
Sector President, Space and Strategic Missiles: Vance
D. Coffman, age 50, $711,250 pay
Sector President, Electronics: Thomas A. Corcoran,
age 50, $586,336 pay
**Sector President, Information and Technology
Services:** Peter B. Teets, age 53, $724,231 pay
SVP and CFO: Marcus C. Bennett, age 59
VP and General Counsel: Frank H. Menaker Jr.
VP Human Resources: Robert B. Corlett, age 55
Auditors: Ernst & Young LLP

WHERE

HQ: 6801 Rockledge Dr., Bethesda, MD 20817
Phone: 301-897-6000
Fax: 301-897-6704

	1994 Sales		1994 Operating Income	
	$ mil.	% of total	$ mil.	% of total
US	12,790	97	836	98
Other countries	340	3	19	2
Total	**13,130**	**100**	**855**	**100**

WHAT

	1994 Sales	
	$ mil.	% of total
Aeronautical systems	6,573	50
Missiles & space systems	3,608	27
Electronic systems	1,650	13
Technology services	1,299	10
Total	**13,130**	**100**

	1994 Sales
	% of total
US government	73
Other governments	16
Commercial	11
Total	**100**

Selected Products and Services
Aggregates
Aircraft
Armaments
Communication systems
Engineering services
Guidance, navigation, detection, and tracking systems
Information systems
Satellite systems
Space shuttle processing
Surveillance systems
Titan rockets

KEY COMPETITORS

AlliedSignal	General Dynamics	Raytheon
Ariane	General Electric	Rockwell
Boeing	Hughes Electronics	Siemens
British Aerospace	Loral	Textron
Ceridian	McDonnell Douglas	Thiokol
Daimler-Benz	Northrop Grumman	Thomson SA
GEC	Orbital Sciences	TRW

HOW MUCH

	9-Year Growth	1985	1986	1987	1988	1989	1990	1991	1992	1993	1994
Sales ($ mil.)	3.6%	9,535	10,273	11,321	10,590	9,891	9,958	9,809	10,100	13,071	13,130
Net income ($ mil.)	1.2%	401	408	421	624	2	335	308	348	422	445
Income as % of sales	—	4.2%	4.0%	3.7%	5.9%	0.0%	3.4%	3.1%	3.4%	3.2%	3.4%
Earnings per share ($)	1.6%	6.09	6.18	6.41	10.37	0.03	5.30	4.86	5.65	6.70	7.00
Stock price – high ($)	—	58.00	60.25	61.50	48.00	54.75	41.50	47.75	58.38	72.38	79.50
Stock price – low ($)	—	40.75	43.00	28.75	34.75	35.75	24.75	31.25	39.63	54.25	58.75
Stock price – close ($)	4.4%	49.13	50.13	34.38	41.25	39.00	33.63	45.00	56.50	68.25	72.63
P/E – high	—	10	10	10	5	—	8	10	10	11	11
P/E – low	—	7	7	5	3	—	5	6	7	8	8
Dividends per share ($)	12.9%	0.75	0.95	1.30	1.55	1.75	1.80	1.95	2.09	2.12	2.24
Book value per share ($)	7.5%	23.17	28.45	33.29	41.75	32.63	36.53	39.86	33.42	38.96	44.41
Employees	(0.3%)	84,500	94,200	97,200	85,600	82,500	73,000	72,300	71,700	83,500	82,500

1994 Year-end:
Debt ratio: 44.6%
Return on equity: 17.0%
Cash (mil.): $452
Current ratio: 1.52
Long-term debt (mil.): $2,248
No. of shares (mil.): 63
Dividends
  Yield: 3.1%
  Payout: 32.0%
Market value (mil.): $4,590

Stock Price History
High/Low 1985–94

Note: Financial information is for Lockheed Corporation only.

LOEWS CORPORATION

OVERVIEW

Larry Tisch got upstaged by a rodent in 1995. Loews, the holding company run by Tisch and his brother Bob, owns 18% of CBS and was at the center of the decision to sell the network to Westinghouse for $5.4 billion. Network chairman Larry's announcement of the sale, however, came one day after Walt Disney agreed to buy Capital Cities/ABC for $19 billion — making the CBS deal look rather Mickey Mouse by comparison.

Most of Loews's revenue comes from insurance. The company's 84%-owned CNA Financial holding company provides health, life, and professional insurance; 36% of premiums are from workers' compensation. Catastrophic losses related to the Northridge earthquake in California and severe winter weather hurt CNA's profits in 1994. CNA acquired the Conti-

nental Corp. in 1994 and Alexsis in 1995, making it the US's 7th largest insurance provider.

A discount pricing strategy is firing up sales at wholly owned Lorillard, which makes the Kent, Newport, and True cigarette brands. Lorillard, the US's 4th largest cigarette maker, had 7.5% of the US cigarette market in 1994.

Smaller Loews holdings include Loews Hotels, which has 12 US hotels plus one each in Canada and Monaco; Bulova, the watch and clock maker; and 49-rig Diamond Offshore Drilling. (Loews announced in 1995 that it would offer 26% of Diamond Offshore to the public.) Loews owns 49% of Hellespont, which operates 6 crude oil tankers.

The Tisch brothers each own 16% of the company and have involved their sons — a total of 5 Tisches sit on the company's board.

WHEN

In 1946 Larry Tisch, who had received an NYU business degree at age 18, dropped out of Harvard Law and with his younger brother Bob bought a Lakewood, New Jersey, resort hotel, with help from their parents. Tisch Hotels, the new entity, bought Atlantic City's Traymore and Ambassador Hotels in the early 1950s and 10 others by 1955. In the early 1960s the brothers erected 6 hotels simultaneously in New York City.

Moving beyond hotels, the brothers bought money-losing companies saddled with poor management. Discarding the management along with underperforming divisions, they quickly tightened operational control and eliminated frills such as fancy offices, company planes, and even memos.

In 1960 Tisch Hotels gained control of MGM's ailing Loew's Theaters division and sold the real estate underneath many of the elegant one-screen theaters to developers. The company name became Loews in 1971; it sold its remaining theater operations in 1985.

In 1968 the company bought Lorillard, shed pet food and candy operations, and regained its slipping tobacco market share by introducing low-tar brands (Kent III, True). CNA Financial (bought in 1974) was next: the Tisch method turned losses of $208 million in 1974 to $110 million in profits the next year.

Bulova Watch (acquired in 1979), guided by Larry's son Andrew, combated a nagging image problem with sleek new watch styles; profitability returned in 1984.

In 1985 Loews helped CBS fend off a takeover attempt by Ted Turner and ended up with

almost 25% of the company (7% was later sold); Larry became president of CBS.

Loews's deep pockets allowed the purchase of 6 used tankers for $5.5 million apiece (average construction cost: $60 million) during a period of depressed supertanker prices in the early 1980s. In 1990 Loews sold 3 of the tankers for $133 million to Hellespont and exchanged the other 3 for 49% interest in that company. Loews bought offshore drilling rig operator Diamond M in 1989.

Loews's caution during the hotel overexpansion of the 1980s later enabled the company to purchase some bargains (e.g., Loews Giorgio, Denver; 1989). In 1989 Loews also entered a joint venture with Covia, a United Airlines affiliate, to create a new computer reservation service for hotels. Diamond M bought Odeco Drilling for $372 million in 1992. CNA Financial increased its reserves for asbestos claims to $1.5 billion in 1993, in part to cover claims associated with asbestos producer Fireboard, which CNA insured from 1957 to 1959. Also in 1993 CNA's drilling activities were grouped as Diamond Offshore Drilling. In 1994, 5 US tobacco companies, including Lorillard, were hit with a $5 billion lawsuit following allegations that cigarette manufacturers manipulated nicotine levels.

In 1995 Bulova sold its industrial and defense products segment (36% of 1994 revenues) for about $21 million. That same year a West Virginia judge dismissed 8 of 10 counts in a suit against Lorillard and other cigarette makers seeking recovery of that state's Medicaid payments for smokers' health problems.

NYSE symbol: LTR
Fiscal year ends: December 31

WHO

Co-chairman and Co-CEO: Laurence A. Tisch, age 72, $601,660 pay
Co-chairman and Co-CEO: Preston Robert Tisch, age 68, $1,555,448 pay
President and COO: James S. Tisch, age 42, $697,443 pay
Chairman and CEO, Lorillard Tobacco: Alexander Spears III
VP; President and CEO, Loews Hotels: Jonathan M. Tisch, age 41, $696,432 pay
Chairman, CNA Insurance: Dennis H. Chookaszian
President, Diamond Offshore Drilling: Robert E. Rose
SVP and CFO: Roy E. Posner, age 61
SVP; President, Bulova: Herbert C. Hofmann, age 52
VP Personnel: Kenneth Abrams, age 61
Auditors: Deloitte & Touche LLP

WHERE

HQ: 667 Madison Ave., New York, NY 10021-8087
Phone: 212-545-2000
Fax: 212-545-2498

WHAT

	1994 Sales		1994 Operating Income	
	$ mil.	% of total	$ mil.	% of total
Insurance	10,992	81	(14)	—
Cigarettes	1,916	14	584	86
Drilling	304	2	(14)	—
Hotels	217	2	49	7
Watches & clocks	151	1	4	0
CBS	—	—	46	7
Investments	(90)	—	(94)	—
Adjustments & other	25	—	(16)	—
Total	**13,515**	**100**	**545**	**100**

Major Holdings

CNA Financial (84%)
Alexsis
Continental Assurance
Continental Casualty
Continental Corporation

Lorillard, Inc. (Cigarette Brands)
Kent
Newport
Old Gold
Style
True

Diamond Offshore Drilling, Inc.
Drilling rigs

Loews Hotels
Days Hotel (NYC)
Howard Johnson Hotel (NYC)
Loews Anatole (Dallas)
Loews Annapolis
Loews Coronado Bay Resort (San Diego)
Loews Giorgio (Denver)
Loews Le Concorde (Quebec City)
Loews L'Enfant Plaza (DC)
Loews Monte Carlo
Loews New York
Loews Santa Monica Beach
Loews Vanderbilt Plaza (Nashville)
Loews Ventana Canyon Resort (Tucson)
Regency (NYC)

Bulova Corporation (97%)
Clocks
Jewelry
Watches

CBS Inc. (18%)

Hellespont (49%)
Crude oil tankers

KEY COMPETITORS

Accor	Halliburton	Nestlé
Aetna	Hanson	North American
Allstate	Helmsley	Watch
Baker Hughes	Hilton	Philip Morris
Bass	Home Holdings	Promus Hotels
B.A.T	Hyatt	Prudential
Brown &	Imasco	Rank
Williamson	Ingram	Ritz-Carlton
Canadian Pacific	ITT Corp.	RJR Nabisco
Carlson	ITT Hartford	SAFECO
Casio	ITT Industries	Seiko
Chubb	Kemper National	SMH Group
CIGNA	Insurance	Tidewater
Citizen Watch	Liggett	Travelers
Fossil	Marriott Intl.	USF&G
GEICO	MetLife	Westin Hotel

HOW MUCH

	9-Year Growth	1985	1986	1987	1988	1989	1990	1991	1992	1993	1994
Sales ($ mil.)	8.5%	6,475	8,405	9,254	10,514	11,437	12,637	13,620	13,691	13,687	13,515
Net income ($ mil.)	(8.4%)	589	546	696	909	907	805	904	(22)	594	268
Income as % of sales	—	3.7%	2.9%	3.1%	3.5%	2.8%	2.3%	2.3%	—	4.3%	2.0%
Earnings per share ($)	(5.2%)	7.23	6.69	8.92	11.94	12.07	11.01	13.14	(0.33)	9.27	4.45
Stock price – high ($)	—	56.25	72.38	96.25	83.13	135.00	126.88	112.88	126.50	120.25	102.75
Stock price – low ($)	—	32.97	53.75	58.00	62.00	77.00	75.00	88.50	103.50	86.75	84.50
Stock price – close ($)	5.3%	54.50	58.25	66.63	78.88	124.25	98.13	109.50	120.13	93.00	86.88
P/E – high	—	8	11	11	7	11	12	9	—	13	23
P/E – low	—	5	8	7	5	6	7	7	—	9	19
Dividends per share ($)	(11.5%)	3.00	1.00	1.00	1.00	1.00	1.00	1.00	1.00	1.00	1.00
Book value per share ($)	13.2%	29.96	36.07	42.56	53.20	64.09	72.10	84.18	84.90	99.59	91.67
Employees	1.7%	21,900	22,950	23,900	24,500	26,800	26,600	26,800	28,100	27,100	25,400

1994 Year-end:
Debt ratio: 28.4%
Return on equity: 4.6%
Cash (mil.): $8,598
Current ratio: —
Long-term debt (mil.): $2,144
No. of shares (mil.): 59
Dividends
  Yield: 1.2%
  Payout: 22.5%
Market value (mil.): $5,123

Stock Price History
High/Low 1985–94

LONGS DRUG STORES CORPORATION

OVERVIEW

One of the largest drugstore chains in the US, Walnut Creek, California–based Longs operates 324 stores in 5 western states, with a majority located in California.

Longs prides itself on its decentralized management style. The company gives store managers considerable independence in running their stores and ties managers' salaries to each location's performance. Consequently, managers, who are referred to as "entrepreneurs," can tailor their stores to local preferences or flair (the Newport Beach store features a soda fountain/cappuccino bar).

Longs's decentralized system has made it something of an anachronism in the drugstore industry, where centralized buying, distribution, and promotion have become the norm. Some analysts have suggested that the company must change its management style to compete, not only with the large drug chains,

but also with megaretailers, such as Wal-Mart, which can out-price Longs.

However, Longs does not normally attempt to compete on price with discounters. Instead, it stresses service and more upscale products than the traditional drugstore. Longs stores are also larger than the industry average, allowing for more nonpharmacy merchandise, which represents a large percentage of the company's sales (70%). Longs has begun to concentrate more intensively on its pharmacy operations, which are not as vulnerable to consumer buying cycles. The company is also experimenting with some new marketing concepts, including hiring teenage girls to do in-store makeovers and sell cosmetics to their peers. However, the biggest boost for Longs could be a rebounding California economy.

The Long family owns about 30% of the company's stock.

WHEN

Joseph Long (son-in-law of Safeway founder Marion Skaggs) and his brother Thomas opened their first store, Longs Self-Service Drug Store, in Oakland, California, in 1938; their 2nd store opened in nearby Alameda in 1939. The Oakland store (still operating today) was the first to introduce the then-new retailing idea of self-service to drugstores. The brothers believed that the manager of each store should make the decisions regarding its operation. The stores offered the lowest prices in their neighborhoods.

By 1950 the company had 6 stores in the Oakland area and one in Fresno. Longs opened 10 more stores during the 1950s in California and Hawaii. In 1969 the chain went public. In 1975 Joseph Long became chairman and his son, Robert, president. The company continued to add stores. In the late 1970s it expanded into other western states. By 1980 Longs had 132 outlets.

Longs continued its decentralized philosophy in the late 1980s despite its growing number of locations. Unlike most chain stores, where stocking and operations decisions are made at headquarters, Longs gave each store manager extraordinary freedom in price setting, inventory selection, and sales promotion.

In 1987 the company departed from its habit of growing through new openings by acquiring one Osco Drug store in Denver and 11 in California from American Stores, increasing its market share in California to 20%.

At the same time it sold all 15 Longs locations in Arizona to Osco.

The pharmacy of each store remains the core of Longs. In late 1989 a pharmacy distribution center was opened in Southern California. And to speed up prescription dispensing, some high-volume stores have been upgraded to "superpharmacy" status. Joseph Long died in 1990 and was succeeded as chairman by Robert. In 1993 cofounder Thomas Long died at the age of 82.

The company is also trying to position itself for the growth potential it foresees as the elderly population increases. Part of this strategy has been to offer free blood pressure and cholesterol screenings and to promote its pharmacists as health care advisors through informational advertising.

In 1993 state and federal agencies began investigating Longs for inaccurate Medicaid billings in Hawaii and Nevada. Longs admitted the mistakes, saying that the inaccuracies were a result of billing procedures no longer used by the company. A settlement was reached with Nevada for $750,000 in 1993 and with Hawaii for $2.4 million in 1994. Also in 1993 the company acquired the 21-store Bill's Drugs for $12 million. In 1994 the company completed installation of a point-of-sale scanning system that should increase efficiency and time of response to customer demand.

In 1995 Longs bought 6 drugstores in Hawaii from Thrifty PayLess.

NYSE symbol: LDG
Fiscal year ends: Last Thursday in January

WHO

Chairman and CEO: Robert M. Long, age 56, $355,670 pay
President: Stephen D. Roath, age 54, $355,372 pay
SVP Development: Ronald A. Plomgren, age 61, $250,980 pay
SVP Properties and Secretary: Orlo D. Jones, age 56, $232,040 pay
SVP: Bill M. Brandon, age 56, $203,090 pay
SVP Marketing: Dan R. Wilson, age 53
SVP: George A. Duey, age 62
VP Controller: Grover L. White, age 54
VP Administration: William G. Combs, age 64
VP Construction, Longs Drugs Stores California: Al A. Arrigoni
VP Personnel, Longs Drug Stores California: Les C. Anderson
Treasurer (Principal Financial Officer): Clay E. Selland, age 38
Auditors: Deloitte & Touche LLP

WHERE

HQ: 141 N. Civic Dr., PO Box 5222, Walnut Creek, CA 94596
Phone: 510-937-1170
Fax: 510-210-6886

Longs operates 324 drugstores in 5 western states, primarily in California.

	1995 Stores	
	No.	% of total
California	278	86
Hawaii	32	10
Colorado	6	2
Nevada	6	2
Alaska	2	0
Total	**324**	**100**

WHAT

1995 Estimated Product Mix	% of Total
Photo, cosmetics, greeting cards & other products	70
Pharmacy	30
Total	**100**

Divisions
Cosmetics
Pharmacy
Photography
Greeting cards (cards, gifts, remembrances)

KEY COMPETITORS

Albertson's
American Stores
Dayton Hudson
Edward J. DeBartolo
Eli Lilly
Hughes Markets
Kmart
Kroger
J. C. Penney
Melville
Merck
Price/Costco
Raley's
Safeway
Stater Bros.
Thrifty PayLess
Venture Stores
Vons
Walgreen
Wal-Mart
Yucaipa

HOW MUCH

	9-Year Growth	1986	1987	1988	1989	1990	1991	1992	1993	1994	1995
Sales ($ mil.)	6.3%	1,481	1,635	1,773	1,926	2,111	2,334	2,366	2,476	2,499	2,558
Net income ($ mil.)	2.8%	38	39	49	56	61	60	55	53	50	49
Income as % of sales	—	2.5%	2.4%	2.8%	2.9%	2.9%	2.6%	2.3%	2.1%	2.0%	1.9%
Earnings per share ($)[1]	3.4%	1.74	1.78	2.33	2.75	3.01	2.94	2.71	2.58	2.41	2.35
Stock price – high ($)[1]	—	31.75	38.75	41.00	37.38	48.50	44.88	44.38	40.00	37.88	39.88
Stock price – low ($)[1]	—	21.63	26.63	25.13	29.38	34.50	33.25	30.88	32.50	31.25	30.25
Stock price – close ($)[1]	0.4%	30.63	29.50	30.38	35.50	44.63	37.38	39.13	35.75	32.88	31.75
P/E – high	—	18	22	18	14	16	15	16	16	16	17
P/E – low	—	12	15	11	11	12	11	11	13	13	13
Dividends per share ($)	5.4%	0.70	0.75	0.79	0.86	0.94	1.02	1.07	1.11	1.12	1.12
Book value per share ($)	7.5%	13.33	13.74	14.59	15.46	16.68	18.81	20.70	22.45	24.19	25.49
Employees	4.0%	11,000	12,000	12,000	12,400	14,200	15,100	15,000	15,200	15,600	15,600

1995 Year-end:
Debt ratio: 2.5%
Return on equity: 9.5%
Cash (mil.): $58
Current ratio: 1.65
Long-term debt (mil.): $11
No. of shares (mil.): 21
Dividends
  Yield: 3.5%
  Payout: 47.7%
Market value (mil.): $653

**Stock Price History[1]
High/Low 1986–95**

[1] Stock prices are for the prior calendar year.

LORAL CORPORATION

OVERVIEW

Loral is a leading manufacturer of defense electronics and telecommunications and space systems, and with its 1995 acquisition of the defense systems business of Unisys, the New York–based company continues to beef up its systems integration business as well. The $800 million purchase of the Unisys unit (which includes air traffic control; command, control, and communications; and naval computers) follows the company's 1994 purchase of IBM's Federal Systems unit. The moves are part of CEO Bernard Schwartz's strategy of diversifying within defense- and government contract–related businesses. While more than 80% of the company's sales go to the US government, no program represents more than 6% of sales,

and Loral plans to continue to diversify its operations.

Loral's defense electronics business includes a variety of high-tech military equipment, from radar-jamming devices to weapons guidance systems. The company also provides electronic reconnaissance and satellite tracking systems for the DOD, and mission and operations support for NASA. Loral affiliate Space Systems/Loral builds telecommunications satellites.

Loral also holds a 32% interest in Globalstar, a wireless telephone system joint venture with Qualcomm, Alcatel-Alsthom, and other investors. Globalstar plans to have worldwide voice and data service by 1998.

WHEN

Loral was founded in 1948 by William Lorenz and Leon Alpert (the "Lor" and "Al" in Loral). Lorenz and Alpert set about creating a conglomerate, acquiring a variety of companies, including a toymaker, a copper wire business, and an industrial meter manufacturer. However, many of the acquisitions proved less than successful, and by the early 1970s the company was floundering. In 1972 the company was in the process of posting a $3 million loss, was in default on its loans, and was being threatened with delisting by the New York Stock Exchange. That's when Bernard Schwartz stepped in.

Schwartz, who had been president of computer leasing company Leasco, came on board as Loral's chairman and president. He worked out new agreements with Loral's creditors and sold off its weaker subsidiaries. Within a year Schwartz had the company back in the black and focused on defense electronics systems. To attract the talented engineers he needed to move Loral up among the leaders in electronic warfare, Schwartz offered stock options in the company.

Schwartz's timing proved impeccable. When Egypt shot down nearly 100 Israeli planes with Soviet-made radar-guided weapons during the 1973 Yom Kippur War, the US and its allies took notice, and the electronic defense industry took off.

Loral's breakthrough came with the ALR56 radar-warning receiver for the F-15 fighter plane. Previously, when a radar receiver was updated to cope with new enemy radar signals, the system had to be rewired, which took over 3 weeks. Loral's system, which used programmable software, took only 20 minutes. The

company also took its business overseas, signing a deal to develop an integrated system that provided radar warning and jamming for the Belgian Air Force in 1975. It was the first such system designed and manufactured by a single company.

While Loral has had its share of technological breakthroughs, its growth has been spurred through acquisitions. Led by Schwartz it acquired 13 companies between 1980 and 1992, including Xerox's electrooptical defense and aerospace business (1983), Rolm's military computer unit (1985), and Goodyear Aerospace (1987). Schwartz's biggest deal came in 1990 when he bought Ford Aerospace (annual sales of $1.8 billion) for $715 million, more than doubling Loral's size.

Like many defense contractors, Loral was swept up in the General Accounting Office's Operation Ill Wind investigation of defense procurements, and in 1989 it pleaded guilty to 3 charges and had to give up part of a contract to provide radar warning systems for the F-16 fighter plane.

In 1991 Loral sold 49% of Space Systems/Loral to a consortium of European space system manufacturers. Loral bought LTV's missile business in 1992 for $254 million.

In 1994 Loral moved into systems integration with its $1.5 billion acquisition of IBM's Federal Systems unit. Federal Systems, which had sales of about $2.2 billion in 1993, builds large computer systems for government agencies, including the FAA and the IRS.

In 1995 Loral Air Traffic Control won a $955 million contract with the US Department of Transportation to upgrade the FAA's air traffic control system.

NYSE symbol: LOR
Fiscal year ends: March 31

WHO

Chairman and CEO: Bernard L. Schwartz, age 69,
$6,244,191 pay
President and COO: Frank C. Lanza, age 63,
$3,247,179 pay
SVP Finance: Michael P. DeBlasio, age 58, $954,633 pay
SVP and Controller: Robert V. LaPenta, age 49,
$883,979 pay
SVP and Secretary: Michael B. Targoff, age 50,
$874,427 pay
Group VP Telemetry: Hugh Bennett, age 63
Group VP Missiles: Felix W. Fenter, age 68
Group VP; President, Federal Systems: Arthur E.
Johnson, age 48
**Group VP Microwave; President, Loral Microwave-
Narda:** Bernard Leibowitz, age 65
VP Washington Operations: Jimmie V. Adams, age 59
VP Technology: Lawrence H. Schwartz, age 57
VP Special Projects: William F. Gates, age 73
VP Communications: Joanne Hvala, age 44
VP and Treasurer: Nicholas C. Moren, age 48
VP and General Counsel: Eric J. Zahler, age 44
VP Administration (HR): Stephen L. Jackson, age 53
Auditors: Coopers & Lybrand L.L.P.

WHERE

HQ: 600 Third Ave., New York, NY 10016
Phone: 212-697-1105
Fax: 212-661-8988

	1995 Sales	
	$ mil.	% of total
US	4,463	81
Europe	616	11
Asia	234	4
Middle East	151	3
Other regions	20	1
Total	**5,484**	**100**

WHAT

	1995 Sales	
	$ mil.	% of total
US government agencies	3,548	64
Foreign and export	1,021	19
Other	915	17
Total	**5,484**	**100**

**Command, Control,
Communications, and
Intelligence/
Reconnaissance**
Data and voice recorders
("black boxes")
Information processing
and display hardware
Satellite communication
terminals

Electronic Combat
Electronic jamming and
radar warning systems
Forward-Looking Infrared
(FLIR) targeting and
weapon delivery pod

Systems Integration
Display System
Replacement (air traffic
control)
Document Processing
System (for the IRS)
NEXRAD weather-
detection system

Tactical Weapons
Digital Scene Matching Area
Correlation guidance
system
Extended Range Interceptor
missile
Multiple Launch Rocket
System (MLRS)

**Telecommunications and
Space Systems**
Mission control and
operations support
Telecommunications
satellites

Training and Simulation
Close Combat Tactical
Trainer (computer-based
trainer)
Flight and weapons
simulators for F-15 and
F-15E
Multiple Integrated Laser
Engagement System
(MILES)

KEY COMPETITORS

AlliedSignal
Boeing
EDS
EG&G
GEC
General Electric

Hughes Electronics
Lockheed Martin
McDonnell Douglas
Motorola
Northrop
Grumman

Orbital Sciences
Raytheon
Rockwell
Thomson SA

HOW MUCH

	9-Year Growth	1986	1987	1988	1989	1990	1991	1992	1993	1994	1995
Sales ($ mil.)	26.4%	664	690	1,441	1,187	1,274	2,127	2,882	3,335	4,009	5,484
Net income ($ mil.)	20.7%	53	58	74	88	78	90	122	159	228	288
Income as % of sales	—	8.0%	8.3%	5.2%	7.4%	6.1%	4.3%	4.2%	4.8%	5.7%	5.3%
Earnings per share ($)[1]	13.5%	1.08	1.14	1.46	1.69	1.51	1.71	1.93	2.02	2.72	3.38
Stock price – high ($)[1]	—	19.50	24.38	24.63	20.25	18.94	17.44	22.75	23.69	38.75	42.75
Stock price – low ($)[1]	—	12.13	16.94	12.50	15.25	13.75	12.06	16.06	15.38	22.25	33.50
Stock price – close ($)[1]	8.5%	18.25	19.19	15.75	16.13	14.81	16.75	19.69	23.00	37.75	37.88
P/E – high	—	18	21	17	12	13	10	12	12	14	13
P/E – low	—	11	15	9	9	9	7	8	8	8	10
Dividends per share ($)	9.5%	0.26	0.29	0.24	0.35	0.39	0.43	0.47	0.50	0.55	0.59
Book value per share ($)	13.2%	6.53	7.56	8.66	10.15	11.41	12.95	15.64	14.39	16.57	19.86
Employees	15.2%	8,100	14,500	13,700	13,700	12,700	23,750	22,000	24,500	32,600	28,900

1995 Year-end:
Debt ratio: 43.8%
Return on equity: 18.8%
Cash (mil.): $126
Current ratio: 1.53
Long-term debt (mil.): $1,316
No. of shares (mil.): 85
Dividends
  Yield: 1.6%
  Payout: 17.5%
Market value (mil.): $3,219

**Stock Price History[1]
High/Low 1986–95**

[1] Stock prices are for the prior calendar year.

LOWE'S COMPANIES, INC.

OVERVIEW

If there were a phone booth on Retail Avenue, Lowe's would be in it, doing a quick change from its mild-mannered, small-store, street clothes into its superstore retailer suit. The North Carolina–based company has transformed itself from a chain of small showroom stores to one of giant home improvement centers, each with up to 114,000 square feet of sales space. Lowe's is the #2 US building supplies/home center chain (after Home Depot).

A pioneer in do-it-yourself retailing, the company sells hardware, building supplies, home decoration materials, major appliances, and consumer electronics in 21 states through 336 stores, mostly in the southeastern US. Employees own 15% of the company's stock.

Lowe's sales and net income have shot up like a speeding bullet as the company has added larger stores. In the past 4 years, the large stores have grown from 13% to 57% of total stores and from 16% to 69% of sales. Most of the company's stores are located in small towns, where mom-and-pop stores have trouble competing with the large selection and low prices at Lowe's.

The company continues to add more stores and plans to reach 600 by the year 2000. From its stronghold in the Southeast, Lowe's is eyeing a major expansion in the Midwest, but it could find some kryptonite in the form of rival Home Depot, which is also planning a big move into that area.

WHEN

Lowe's was founded in 1921 as Mr. I. S. Lowe's North Wilkesboro Hardware in North Wilkesboro, North Carolina. A family operation by 1945, Mr. Lowe's store was run by his son Jim and his son-in-law Carl Buchan. Jim Lowe and Buchan opened a 2nd store in Sparta, North Carolina, (about 40 miles from North Wilkesboro) in 1949. Buchan bought Jim Lowe's share in the company in 1952. Incorporating as Lowe's North Wilkesboro Hardware, Buchan kept Lowe's as part of the company name because he liked the slogan "Lowe's Low Prices." Sales in 1952 were $4 million. By 1960 Buchan had 15 stores in North Carolina, Virginia, Tennessee, and South Carolina and sales of $31 million.

Buchan planned to create a profit-sharing plan for Lowe's employees, but he died in 1960. In 1961 Lowe's management and the executors of Buchan's estate established the Lowe's Employees Profit Sharing and Trust, which bought Buchan's 89% of the company (later renamed Lowe's Companies). They financed the transaction through a public offering in 1961, which diluted the employees' stock. Lowe's was listed on the NYSE in 1979.

Harvard MBA Robert Strickland, who had joined the company directly out of business school in 1957, became chairman in 1978. Revenues increased from $170 million in 1971 to more than $900 million, with net income of $25 million, in 1979. Traditionally the majority of Lowe's business was in sales to professional home builders, but in 1980 housing starts fell to 1.3 million, and Lowe's profits dropped. Concurrently, Home Depot introduced its low-price warehouse concept, which Strickland initially rejected. Instead he reorganized his stores' layouts and by 1982 had redesigned half of the 229 stores to be more oriented toward do-it-yourself consumers. The new designs featured softer lighting and displays of entire room layouts to appeal to women, who made up over half of all do-it-yourself customers. In 1982 Lowe's made more than half of its sales to consumers for the first time in its history.

In 1984 Lowe's got on the warehouse bandwagon, announcing that it would increase its total store floor space through new store construction and relocation. By 1989, however, Home Depot had overtaken Lowe's, which had continued to target contractors as well as do-it-yourselfers.

In 1993 Lowe's opened 57 large stores (half were replacements for existing stores), almost doubling its total floor space; 3 were in new markets — Maryland, Indiana, and Illinois. Lowe's also pared its Texas operations from 7 to 2. Lowe's agreed to selectively carry personal computers, software, accessories, and peripherals in 1994 to take advantage of the expected growth in home office products.

In 1995 Lowe's announced plans to rebuild its presence in Texas, opening 10 stores in the next 2 years. That same year Sutherland Building Materials, a Missouri-based retailer, filed suit against Lowe's, claiming employees from a Lowe's store in Joplin, Missouri, on orders from their supervisors, deliberately disrupted business at a Sutherland's store across the street. Sutherland said the Lowe's employees moved merchandise, switched price tags, parked in Sutherland's best parking spots, stole shopping carts, and spit tobacco juice on the store's floor. Lowe's denied the charges.

NYSE symbol: LOW
Fiscal year ends: January 31

WHO

Chairman: Robert L. Strickland, age 64, $892,500 pay
President and CEO: Leonard G. Herring, age 67,
$977,500 pay
SEVP and COO: Robert L. Tillman, age 51,
$545,385 pay
EVP Sales/Store Operations: R. Michael Rouleau,
age 56, $540,096 pay
SVP and Treasurer (CFO): Harry B. Underwood II,
age 52, $352,000 pay
SVP Real Estate/Engineering and Construction:
J. Gregory Dodge, age 47
SVP Management Information Services: William L.
Irons, age 51
SVP, General Counsel, and Secretary: William C.
Warden Jr., age 42
VP Human Resources: Perry G. Jennings
Auditors: Deloitte & Touche LLP

WHERE

HQ: PO Box 1111, North Wilkesboro, NC 28656-0001
Phone: 910-651-4000
Fax: 910-651-4766

	1995 Stores
	No.
North Carolina	71
Virginia	35
Tennessee	26
South Carolina	24
Georgia	20
Kentucky	19
Ohio	19
Indiana	16
West Virginia	16
Florida	15
Others	75
Total	**336**

WHAT

	1995 Sales	
	$ mil.	% of total
Building commodities & millwork	1,225	20
Home decorating & lighting	1,195	20
Structural lumber	911	15
Yard, patio & garden	736	12
Kitchen, bathroom & laundry fixtures	701	11
Tools	382	6
Heating, cooling & water systems	348	6
Special order sales	342	6
Home entertainment	271	4
Total	**6,111**	**100**

Selected Services
In-store CAD programs
In-store interactive video demonstrations
Special Order System (S.O.S.)

Subsidiaries
The Contractor Yards, Inc.
LF Corp.
Lowe's Home Centers, Inc.
Sterling Advertising, Ltd.

KEY COMPETITORS

84 Lumber	Payless Cashways
Ace Hardware	Price/Costco
Cotter & Co.	Sears
Hechinger	Servistar
Home Depot	Sherwin-Williams
Kmart	Waban
Lechters	Wal-Mart
McCoy	Wickes Lumber
Menard	

HOW MUCH

	9-Year Growth	1986	1987	1988	1989	1990	1991	1992	1993	1994	1995
Sales ($ mil.)	12.8%	2,073	2,284	2,442	2,517	2,651	2,833	3,056	3,846	4,538	6,111
Net income ($ mil.)	15.8%	60	55	56	69	75	71	7	85	132	224
Income as % of sales	—	2.9%	2.4%	2.3%	2.7%	2.8%	2.5%	0.2%	2.2%	2.9%	3.7%
Earnings per share ($)	14.5%	0.41	0.36	0.39	0.46	0.51	0.48	0.05	0.58	0.89	1.39
Stock price – high ($)[1]	—	7.78	10.38	8.19	6.09	8.03	12.41	9.28	12.69	31.00	41.38
Stock price – low ($)[1]	—	5.19	5.63	3.81	4.06	5.19	4.59	5.75	8.00	13.32	26.50
Stock price – close ($)[1]	20.5%	6.47	6.50	4.03	5.25	7.38	6.13	8.53	12.06	29.75	34.75
P/E – high	—	19	29	21	13	16	26	—	22	35	30
P/E – low	—	13	16	10	9	10	10	—	14	15	19
Dividends per share ($)	8.0%	0.09	0.10	0.11	0.12	0.13	0.13	0.14	0.15	0.16	0.18
Book value per share ($)	13.9%	2.75	3.41	3.70	3.95	4.33	4.68	4.59	5.02	5.91	8.90
Employees	12.2%	13,317	14,783	14,761	14,774	15,271	15,556	18,368	21,269	28,843	37,555

1995 Year-end:
Debt ratio: 33.3%
Return on equity: 19.5%
Cash (mil.): $268
Current ratio: 1.65
Long-term debt (mil.): $681
No. of shares (mil.): 160
Dividends
  Yield: 0.5%
  Payout: 12.6%
Market value (mil.): $5,544

**Stock Price History[1]
High/Low 1986–95**

[1]Stock prices are for the prior calendar year.

THE LTV CORPORATION

OVERVIEW

After one of the longest and largest bankruptcies in history, LTV, once one of the US's largest conglomerates, is back on its feet, in the black, and ready to grow again. The 3rd largest US steelmaker (after USX–U.S. Steel and Bethlehem Steel), Cleveland-based LTV is teaming up with Japan's Sumitomo Metal Industries (which is also a minority stakeholder in the company) and British Steel to build its first US minimill — which produces high-quality steel at a lower cost than conventional steelmaking technology.

Expected to open in 1996, the plant will be located in the southeastern US, where demand for construction steel is growing. It will use modern technology and nonunion labor, once spurned by big steelmakers, to keep costs down. With US demand at record levels in 1994, LTV is positioning itself to absorb the excess that is usually filled by imports and to extend its reach into international markets. Recovering economies in Europe, Asia, and Latin America are expected to boost a growing worldwide demand for steel.

A leading supplier to the automotive, appliance, and electrical equipment industries, LTV produces mostly sheet and tubular steel (93% of 1994 sales); General Motors is LTV's largest customer (11% of revenues). The balance of the company sales is from LTV's energy company, Continental Emsco, which is one of the largest oil- and gas-drilling equipment suppliers in North America.

In 1995 LTV retained consultants to decide whether to sell or possibly merge its energy products business with another company.

WHEN

LTV was the result of a series of mergers and acquisitions orchestrated by James Ling. Ling had taken his company (Ling Electric) public in 1955, aggressively marketing his stock, even distributing its prospectus at the Texas State Fair. LTV began with the purchase of L. M. Electronics by Ling Electric in 1956. Ling Electric bought Altec Electronics (1959) and merged with Temco (electronics and missiles, 1960). In 1961 Ling-Temco bought Chance Vought (well-known maker of navy planes), becoming Ling-Temco-Vought (LTV).

In 1964 Ling made LTV a holding company and broke out its operations into 3 public companies: LTV Aerospace, LTV Ling Altec, and LTV Electrosystems. LTV maintained majority interest in all 3. This strategy drove up the price of each subsidiary's stock and subsequently raised the value of LTV's assets. LTV then used its shares in the 3 companies as collateral for further acquisitions.

With borrowed funds LTV continued its acquisition campaign, buying Okonite (copper wire and cable, 1965), Wilson (meatpacking, pharmaceuticals, and sporting goods; 1967), Greatamerica (parent of Braniff Airlines and National Car Rental, 1968), and Jones & Laughlin Steel (1968). In 1969 LTV's finances began to deteriorate, made worse by a declining stock market. LTV reported a $38.1 million net loss that year and was forced to sell divisions to pay its debt. In 1970 the LTV board demoted Ling to president; he quit 6 weeks later. In 1971 LTV sold Braniff and Okonite as part of an antitrust settlement.

In 1977 LTV bought Lykes (petroleum equipment) and Youngstown Sheet & Tube (steel). After selling Wilson in 1981, LTV was left with LTV Steel, LTV Aerospace & Defense, and LTV Energy Products. In 1984 LTV bought Republic Steel for $770 million.

By 1986 lower-priced steel imported from Japan, Europe, and Canada was flooding the US market. To pare costs, LTV sold Gulf States Steel, most of its nonsteel assets, and its Specialty Products division. But after 5 years of losses and with steel and oil prices low, LTV filed for bankruptcy protection in July — the largest industrial filing as of that date. The company subsequently closed several plants, modernized others, and laid off more than 30,000 employees. LTV went through a radical restructuring to reduce expenses. It planned to sell its defense operations to France's Thomson-CSF, but the US government nixed the deal because of national security concerns; LTV's aircraft business was sold to a consortium of US-based Loral and Northrop/Carlyle in 1992.

In 1993 LTV emerged from bankruptcy after creditors, shareholders, and the bankruptcy court approved a reorganization plan that would settle most debts through a stock offering in the new company. Sumitomo Metal Industries (Japan) also invested $200 million in the company for a 10% stake. In late 1994 LTV agreed to form a joint venture with Sumitomo and British Steel, called Trico Steel Company, which expects to start building its new minimill in 1995.

NYSE symbol: LTV
Fiscal year ends: December 31

WHO

Chairman, President, and CEO: David H. Hoag, age 55, $910,000 pay
Group VP — Steel: J. Peter Kelly, age 53, $512,500 pay
Group VP — Energy: David E. Althoff, age 53
SVP and CFO: Arthur W. Huge, age 49, $387,500 pay
SVP, General Counsel, and Secretary: Glenn J. Moran, age 47, $350,004 pay
SVP Technology and Business Ventures; President and CEO, Trico Steel: William G. Wiley, $331,125 pay
SVP Personnel and Corporate Affairs: Frank Filipovitz
VP and Controller: William C. Armbruster, age 48
Auditors: Ernst & Young LLP

WHERE

HQ: 25 W. Prospect Ave., Cleveland, OH 44115
Phone: 216-622-5000
Fax: 216-622-4610

LTV operates 2 integrated steel plants, the Cleveland Works and Indiana Harbor Works (East Chicago, IN); 2 electrogalvanizing plants; various finishing and processing facilities; and tubular and tin mill operations. LTV has offices in Mexico and Japan.

WHAT

	1994 Sales		1994 Operating Income	
	$ mil.	% of total	$ mil.	% of total
Steel	4,233	93	201	—
Energy products	299	7	(1)	—
Adjustments	(3)	—	(11)	—
Total	**4,529**	**100**	**189**	**—**

1994 Steel Market	% of tons shipped
Steel service centers	28
Automotive	26
Converters & processors	13
Electrical, agricultural & other machinery	9
Household appliances & office equipment	8
Containers & packaging	8
Construction	6
Other	2
Total	**100**

Subsidiaries and Affiliates
Continental Emsco Co. (energy products)
Empire Iron Mining Partnership (25%, iron ore mine)
LTV Steel Mining Co. (iron ore mine)
Presque Isle Corp. (53.5%, limestone quarry)
Processing Technology Inc. (33%, steel processing and warehousing)
Trico Steel Co., LLC (50%; joint venture with British Steel plc and Sumitomo Metal Industries, Ltd.)

KEY COMPETITORS

AK Steel	Kawasaki
Armco	Kobe Steel
Baker Hughes	Koch
Bethlehem Steel	Mitsubishi
Broken Hill	National Steel
Cargill	Nippon Steel
Dresser	NKK
FMC	Nucor
Friedrich Krupp	Oregon Steel Mills
Gallatin Steel	Ormet
Halliburton	Schlumberger
Hitachi Metals	Tata
Hyundai	Thyssen
Ingram	USX–U.S. Steel
Inland Steel	Weirton Steel
IRI	Wheeling-Pittsburgh

HOW MUCH

	Annual Growth	1985	1986	1987	1988	1989	1990	1991	1992	1993	1994
Sales ($ mil.)	(3.0%)	5,944	4,752	5,062	5,163	4,354	4,178	3,702	3,826	4,163	4,529
Net income ($ mil.)	—	(724)	(3,268)	503	(3,154)	265	71	74	599	387	127
Income as % of sales	—	—	—	9.9%	—	6.1%	1.7%	2.0%	—	9.3%	2.8%
Earnings per share ($)	(57.8%)	—	—	—	—	—	—	—	—	3.01	1.27
Stock price – high ($)	—	—	—	—	—	—	—	—	—	16.25	21.25
Stock price – low ($)	—	—	—	—	—	—	—	—	—	10.00	14.00
Stock price – close ($)	2.3%	—	—	—	—	—	—	—	—	16.13	16.50
P/E – high	—	—	—	—	—	—	—	—	—	5	17
P/E – low	—	—	—	—	—	—	—	—	—	3	11
Dividends per share ($)	—	—	—	—	—	—	—	—	—	0.00	0.00
Book value per share ($)	109.3%	—	—	—	—	—	—	—	—	5.78	12.10
Employees	(12.8%)	56,800	48,300	48,200	38,800	38,000	35,300	34,600	17,900	17,000	16,500

1994 Year-end:
Debt ratio: 12.9%
Return on equity: 14.4%
Cash (mil.): $693
Current ratio: 2.35
Long-term debt (mil.): $190
No. of shares (mil.): 106
Dividends
  Yield: —
  Payout: —
Market value (mil.): $1,749

Stock Price History
High/Low 1993–94

LYONDELL PETROCHEMICAL COMPANY

OVERVIEW

Formerly a subsidiary of oil giant Atlantic Richfield (ARCO), Houston-based Lyondell Petrochemical was spun off to the public in 1989 and is still 49.9%–owned by ARCO. One of the US's largest petrochemical companies, (it has reported a net income of over $2 billion since 1985). Lyondell is an integrated petrochemical and petroleum processor and manufacturer.

Lyondell's Channelview, Texas, petrochemical complex produces ethylene, propylene, butadiene, methanol, specialty chemicals, and other products used in everything from trash bags and milk containers to paints and tires. The company conducts some of its refining operations through LYONDELL-CITGO Refining, a joint venture with CITGO Petroleum (a subsidiary of Petróleos de Venezuela), in which it holds an approximate 90% stake. LYONDELL-CITGO refines a number of petrochemical products, including aromatics, gasoline, heating oil, jet fuel, and motor oil. The raw material for this processing — Venezuelan crude oil — is supplied by LAGOVEN, a Petróleos de Venezuela affiliate.

An improving US economy fueled demand for petrochemical products in 1994. The company's methanol sales were particularly strong. In response, the firm increased its unit capacity 6%, to 248 million gallons per year.

WHEN

It wasn't exactly a model of efficiency. Located 16 miles apart on the Texas Gulf Coast, Atlantic Richfield's Houston refinery and its Channelview petrochemical complex were run by offices in Los Angeles and Philadelphia, respectively.

The operations were losing ground in the competitive Gulf Coast market, and ARCO Chemical was contemplating selling the petrochemical complex. However, Bob Gower, SVP of planning, convinced the company that the 2 Houston-area properties could be run together. In 1985 ARCO set up Lyondell Petrochemical Corporation (soon changed to Lyondell Petrochemical Company) as a wholly owned division, with Gower as CEO.

The refining facility that Gower and Lyondell got dated back to 1919, when Sinclair Oil & Refining Company had built a crude oil refinery in Houston. What was to become Lyondell's petrochemical complex was a petrochemical plant built on the Lyondell Country Club in Channelview by Texas Butadiene and Chemical Corporation in 1955. Sinclair Petrochemical, a subsidiary of Sinclair Oil, which had become a subsidiary of Richfield Oil Corporation in 1936, bought the petrochemical plant in 1962.

In 1966 Richfield and Atlantic Refining Company merged. Following the merger, the refinery became part of ARCO Products Company and the petrochemicals plant joined ARCO Chemical Company.

When ARCO Chemical was considering selling the petrochemical complex, Gower argued that there were synergies between the refinery and the petrochemical plant that could be exploited. The plant used inputs such as gas oil produced at the refinery, and the refinery used byproducts such as gasoline produced by the plant.

Gower proved to be right. By the 4th quarter of its first year, Lyondell was showing a profit. From the beginning Gower focused on making Lyondell flexible and efficient. The company upgraded its refinery so it could handle any kind of crude oil in the world. Gower also reduced Lyondell's work force by over 1,000 workers (including 75% of its executive staff) through voluntary layoffs in 1985.

With Lyondell's profits jumping over 340% between 1987 and 1988, ARCO decided to sell the company to the public. In 1989 ARCO sold 50.1% of Lyondell in an IPO worth $1.4 billion. However, before the sale ARCO had Lyondell pay it $500 million, leaving the fledgling company saddled with debt.

Lyondell persevered, and during 1989 the company upgraded its petrochemical facilities to increase capacity. In 1990 the firm acquired 2 chemical plants from Rexene Products Company. In 1992 Lyondell became the first major US refiner to recycle used motor oil into gasoline. In 1993 the company entered into an agreement with CDTECH to develop petrochemical technologies.

In 1994 ARCO completed a 3-year, $1 billion debt offering that gives ARCO the option to reduce its stake in Lyondell. Also that year Lyondell began upgrading its Houston refinery to increase its processing capacity from 130,000 to 200,000 barrels per day.

In 1995 the company signed an agreement to acquire Occidental Chemical Corp.'s Alathon high-density polyethylene business.

NYSE symbol: LYO
Fiscal year ends: December 31

WHO

Chairman and CEO: Robert G. Gower, age 57, $1,258,203 pay
President and COO: Dan F. Smith, age 48, $792,175 pay
SVP, General Counsel, and Secretary: Jeffrey R. Pendergraft, age 46, $381,830 pay
SVP, CFO, and Treasurer: Russell S. Young, age 46, $374,456 pay
SVP Petrochemicals Business Management and Marketing: Debra L. Starnes, age 42, $328,634 pay
VP; VP Marketing, Supply, and Evaluations, LYONDELL-CITGO Refining Company Ltd.: Robert H. Isé
VP Quality, Supply, and Planning: John R. Beard, age 42
VP Channelview Operations: W. Norman Phillips Jr., age 40
VP Olefins: Clifton B. Currin Jr., age 40
VP and Controller: Joseph M. Putz, age 54
VP Human Resources: Richard W. Park, age 55
Auditors: Coopers & Lybrand L.L.P.

WHERE

HQ: 1221 McKinney St., Ste. 1600, Houston, TX 77010
Phone: 713-652-7200
Fax: 713-652-7430

Lyondell operates a petrochemical complex in Channelview, Texas. LYONDELL-CITGO operates a refinery on the Houston ship channel, a storage facility at Mont Belvieu, Texas, and a lube oil blending and packaging plant in Birmingport, Alabama.

WHAT

	1994 Sales		1994 Operating Income	
	$ mil.	% of total	$ mil.	% of total
Refined products	2,074	54	54	12
Petrochemicals	1,783	46	413	88
Adjustments	—	—	(43)	—
Total	**3,857**	**100**	**424**	**100**

Refining
Aromatics (benzene, paraxylene, orthoxylene, toluene)
Industrial products (coke, residual fuel, sulfur)
Light products (diesel fuel, gasoline, heating oil, jet fuel)
Lubricants (base oils, industrial lubricants, motor oils, process oils, white oils)

Petrochemicals
Aromatics (benzene, toluene)
Olefins (butadiene, ethylene, propylene)
Oxygenated products (methanol, MTBE)
Polymers (low-density polyethylene, polypropylene)
Specialty products (DCPD, isoprene, piperylenes, resin oil)

Subsidiaries
Lyondell Refining Company
LYONDELL-CITGO Refining Company Ltd. (90%)

KEY COMPETITORS

A. Schulman	Formosa	Petrobrás
Amerada Hess	Plastics	Petrofina
Amoco	Hanson	Phillips
Ashland, Inc.	Huntsman	Petroleum
British Petroleum	Chemical	Repsol
Broken Hill	Imperial Oil	Royal Dutch/
Chevron	Koch	Shell
Coastal	Mobil	Sun Energy
Dow Chemical	Norsk Hydro	Texaco
DuPont	Occidental	TOTAL
Eastman Chemical	Oryx	Unocal
Elf Aquitaine	PEMEX	USX–Marathon
Exxon	Pennzoil	

HOW MUCH

	Annual Growth	1985	1986	1987	1988	1989	1990	1991	1992	1993	1994
Sales ($ mil.)	3.1%	—	3,010	3,931	4,696	5,361	6,499	5,735	4,809	3,850	3,857
Net income ($ mil.)	7.2%	—	128	123	543	374	356	222	26	4	223
Income as % of sales	—	—	4.2%	3.1%	11.6%	7.0%	5.5%	3.9%	0.5%	0.1%	5.8%
Earnings per share ($)	(9.9%)	—	—	—	—	4.67	4.45	2.78	0.32	0.06	2.78
Stock price – high ($)	—	—	—	—	—	33.50	21.50	26.13	25.88	29.50	33.00
Stock price – low ($)	—	—	—	—	—	16.75	13.13	14.63	21.13	16.75	20.63
Stock price – close ($)	3.8%	—	—	—	—	21.50	14.63	22.63	24.63	21.25	25.88
P/E – high	—	—	—	—	—	7	5	9	81	—	12
P/E – low	—	—	—	—	—	4	3	5	66	—	7
Dividends per share ($)	(5.6%)	—	—	—	—	1.20	4.10	1.75	1.80	1.35	0.90
Book value per share ($)	48.3%	—	—	—	—	0.11	0.48	1.53	(0.08)	(1.10)	0.79
Employees	4.8%	—	1,911	1,874	2,000	2,070	2,250	2,270	2,312	2,283	2,263

1994 Year-end:
Debt ratio: 92.1%
Return on equity: —
Cash (mil.): $52
Current ratio: 1.61
Long-term debt (mil.): $707
No. of shares (mil.): 80
Dividends
  Yield: 3.5%
  Payout: 32.4%
Market value (mil.): $2,070

Stock Price History
High/Low 1989–94

MACANDREWS & FORBES HOLDINGS, INC.

OVERVIEW

Murdoch has it; Ted Turner, too. So why shouldn't fellow billionaire Ronald Perelman have the media bug? Perelman, whose MacAndrews & Forbes holding company is one of the US's largest private firms, spent the last few years creating his own media empire. MacAndrews & Forbes (i.e., Perelman) oversees an eclectic portfolio of public and private companies, including Coleman (camping gear), Marvel (the US's top comic book publisher), and Revlon (cosmetics).

In 1993 MacAndrews & Forbes acquired 37.5% of TV infomercial producer Guthy-Renker and SCI Television's 7 stations, merging them to create New World Television. That company was combined with TV syndicator Genesis Entertainment and TV production house New World Entertainment to create New

World Communications Group, which Perelman took public in 1994.

New World Communications has since purchased 4 TV stations from Great American Communications and, as part of a deal that brought a $500 million investment from Rupert Murdoch in exchange for switching its stations to Fox, bought 4 stations from Argyle Television. In 1995 former NBC executive Brandon Tartikoff became chairman of New World Entertainment. The company also bought Cannell Television, a producer of television programming.

In mid-1995 rumors surfaced of an upcoming Revlon IPO. Revlon has lost money since 1991, and Perelman has sold several of the cosmetics maker's product lines and drastically cut its work force.

WHEN

Ron Perelman grew up working in his father's Philadelphia-based conglomerate, Belmont Industries, but left it at the age of 35 to seek his fortune in New York. In 1978 he bought 40% of jewelry store operator Cohen-Hatfield Industries. In 1979 Cohen-Hatfield bought a minority interest in MacAndrews & Forbes (licorice flavoring). It acquired the rest of the company the next year, then took MacAndrews & Forbes Group as its name.

In 1982 MacAndrews & Forbes bought 82% of Technicolor, a motion picture processor (sold in 1988). After going private in 1983, the company bought control of video production company Compact Video. In 1984 Perelman reshuffled his assets, creating MacAndrews & Forbes Holdings and making it the owner of MacAndrews & Forbes Group. Perelman's holding company acquired control of Pantry Pride, a Florida-based supermarket chain, in 1985. Later that year Pantry Pride announced a $1.8 billion hostile takeover bid for Revlon.

Revlon had been #1 in US cosmetics until founder Charles Revson died in 1975. His successor, Michel Bergerac, cut R&D spending and used beauty division earnings to buy health care and pharmaceutical companies. After Perelman acquired Revlon in 1985, he sold all its health care businesses except for National Health Laboratories. In the late 1980s he added several other cosmetics vendors (including Max Factor and Yves Saint Laurent's fragrance and cosmetic lines). MacAndrews & Forbes took Revlon private in 1987.

In 1988 MacAndrews & Forbes Holdings agreed to invest $315 million in 5 failing Texas

S&Ls, which Perelman combined and named First Gibraltar (sold to BankAmerica in 1993, when Perelman sold 2.6 million shares of BankAmerica). The next year MacAndrews & Forbes bought the Coleman Company.

The company bought a controlling interest in Marvel Entertainment Group from New World Entertainment in 1988, buying the rest of New World in 1989. Between 1988 and 1992 MacAndrews & Forbes sold 80% of National Health Laboratories. In 1991 Perelman took Marvel public and sold Revlon's Max Factor and Betrix units to Procter & Gamble for over $1 billion. In 1992 he sold the Halston and Princess Marcella Borghese brands.

MacAndrews & Forbes increased its stake in Marvel from 60% to 80% in 1993. That same year New World Communications was formed. In 1994 its First Madison Bank bought Ford's First Nationwide, the US's 5th largest S&L.

In 1995 MacAndrews & Forbes subsidiaries Mafco Worldwide Corp. and Consolidated Cigar Corp. merged with Abex (aircraft parts) to create Mafco Consolidated Group; New World Communications and Hachette Filipacchi joined forces to buy the entertainment magazine *Premiere*; and National Health Laboratories merged with Roche's clinical laboratory to create Laboratory Corp. of America, the US's largest operator of medical testing labs.

Also in 1995 former CFO Fred Tepperman accused Perelman of firing him for taking time off to care for his wife, who suffers from Alzheimer's disease. After early trial testimony painted less than flattering portraits of the parties, the case was settled.

Private company
Fiscal year ends: December 31

WHO

Chairman and CEO: Ronald O. Perelman, age 51
VC: Howard Gittis
VC: Donald G. Drapkin
President: Bruce Slovin
EVP: Meyer Laskin
EVP and General Counsel: Barry F. Schwartz
CFO: Erwin Engelman
Auditors: KPMG Peat Marwick LLP

WHERE

HQ: 35 E. 62nd St., New York, NY 10021
Phone: 212-688-9000
Fax: 212-572-8400

MacAndrews & Forbes's entertainment and consumer
products operations are principally in the US.

WHAT

Groups

Entertainment and Publishing
New World Communications Group, Inc. (37%)
  Genesis Entertainment (TV syndication)
Guthy-Renker Corp. (37%, infomercial production)
Marvel Entertainment Group (81%, comic book
  publishing)
    Fleer Trading Cards
    Toy Biz (46%, toys)
New World Entertainment, Ltd. (TV production and
  distribution)
New World Sales and Marketing, Inc. (advertising
  representation)
New World Television, Inc. (TV broadcasting)
    Four Star International (film library)

Industrial and Consumer Products
MacAndrews & Forbes Group, Inc.
  Mafco Consolidated Group (80%, cigars and licorice
    flavoring used in cigarettes)
  NWL Aerospace (10%, aerospace products)
Revlon Group, Inc.
  Revlon, Inc. (cosmetics and fragrances)
    Almay, Inc. (cosmetics)
    Charles of the Ritz Group Ltd. (cosmetics and
      fragrances)
    Germaine Monteil Cosmetiques (cosmetics)
  Laboratory Corporation of America (12%, medical
    testing services)

Financial Services
First Nationwide Bank (based in San Francisco; over 150
  branches in 8 states)

Recreation Products Companies
Coleman Co., Inc. (83%; camping equipment, portable
  generators, power washers, and recreational
  accessories)
Meridian Sports, Inc. (65%)
  Boston Whaler (boats)
  Mastercraft Boats
  O'Brien International (water skis and accessories)
  Skeeter Products (boats)
  Wet Jet International

KEY COMPETITORS

Actava	Helene Curtis
Alberto-Culver	Honda
Amway	Igloo
Avon	Jean Philippe Fragrances
Banc One	Johnson Publishing
BancFlorida Financial	Kellwood
BankAmerica	Liz Claiborne
Bayer	L'Oréal
Black & Decker	LVMH
Body Shop	Mary Kay
Bristol-Myers Squibb	McGraw-Hill
Brunswick	NationsBank
Capital Bancorp	Nature's Sunshine
Chattem	Outboard Marine
Chemical Banking	Procter & Gamble
Citicorp	RJR Nabisco
Cosmair	Rubbermaid
Colgate-Palmolive	Shiseido
Cox	Suzuki
Dayton Hudson	Time Warner
Estée Lauder	Tribune
First Chicago	Turner Broadcasting
First Interstate	Unilever
Fleetwood	Union Bank
Fountain Powerboat	Yamaha
Gannett	Warner-Lambert
General Electric	Washington Post
Hearst	Wells Fargo

HOW MUCH

	9-Year Growth	1985	1986	1987	1988	1989	1990	1991	1992	1993	1994
Estimated sales ($ mil.)	16.8%	750	552	2,440	2,500	5,325	5,381	4,521	3,496	2,748	3,030
Employees	25.0%	3,000	3,000	28,000	24,582	44,000	44,000	38,100	25,700	23,500	22,328

Estimated Sales ($ mil.) 1985–94

MANPOWER INC.

OVERVIEW

Manpower, based in Milwaukee, is the world's largest temporary-employment company, with operations spanning the globe and employing more than one million people. In addition to temporary services, the company provides permanent-employment services, including employee testing and training. One of Manpower's advantages is that it can fulfill the worldwide staffing needs of multinational companies on a contract basis. Such contracts constitute about 50% of business.

The company has been significantly restructured since 1989, when it was the object of a vicious struggle between the head of its former UK parent, Blue Arrow, and Mitchell Fromstein, its US chief. Fromstein won, bringing Manpower back to the US in 1991.

Although Manpower has suffered in the recessions that hammered the US, Europe, and Japan, much of its wretched-looking results have been the result of amortized write-offs of goodwill (the difference between the actual value of the company and its purchase price) related to the Blue Arrow purchase. The company was profitable in 1994 with $84 million in net earnings.

WHEN

Manpower was founded by 2 Milwaukee lawyers, Elmer Winter and Aaron Scheinfeld, in 1948. In the beginning Manpower concentrated on supplying temporary help to industry during the first flush of the postwar boom. In the next few years, the company expanded, and in 1956 it began growing through franchising. During the 1960s the company began opening franchises in Europe, Asia, and South America. It continued to emphasize blue-collar placements, however, unlike many of its competitors.

Manpower's growth into a powerhouse was orchestrated by Mitchell Fromstein, whose connection with the company began when he was Manpower's advertising account executive in the 1960s. Fromstein joined Manpower's board in 1971 and became president and CEO in 1976.

In the 1970s Manpower embarked on a series of acquisitions and began to shift its emphasis from industrial to clerical placements. In the mid-1970s, with Scheinfeld deceased and Winter eager to sell out, Parker Pen came along. Parker, also based in Wisconsin, was trying to re-energize its fading fortunes after the arrival of the disposable pen. In 1976 Parker bought Manpower, which sold the pen business 10 years later and became Manpower Inc. Fromstein continued as president and CEO, with a 20% interest in the company.

In the late 1970s Manpower entered the computer age, instituting a computer training program for its temporary employees. The company grew as the character of employment in the US changed from the norm of career-long employment with one company to a series of shorter-term jobs with many employers. In addition to providing short-term workers, Manpower began offering hiring and training services for permanent employees, thus saving companies in-house recruitment and training costs.

In 1987 Manpower was acquired by Blue Arrow, a temporary-employment agency based in the UK, with the combined companies operating as Manpower. Almost immediately tensions arose between Fromstein and his new boss, Antony Berry, who accused Fromstein of obstructing efforts to unite the 2 companies. Fromstein was fired in 1988, but he did not go away quietly.

Manpower's worldwide franchisees revolted against Berry, and the UK began an investigation of how the acquisition of Manpower was financed (a $1.5 billion stock sale by NatWest). Berry was ousted in 1989, and Fromstein regained control. A push by American interests (particularly Southeastern Asset Management, of Memphis) changed the composition of Manpower's ownership during that year from just 9% American in January to over 60% by the end of the year. This gave Fromstein the support he needed to move Manpower back to Wisconsin in 1991.

Since then Fromstein has worked to disentangle the 2 companies by selling off Blue Arrow holdings not related to employment.

With its management trauma behind it, Manpower has reset its sights on growth. Its bottom line has been aided by the shift toward more use of temporary employees. And more important, the goodwill write-offs have ended. In 1994 Manpower opened 113 new offices in the US and abroad. Also in 1994 the company had 250 on-site contracts (with an on-site manager who is responsible for the recruitment, orientation, and deployment of all temporary workers at that work site) in the US and Canada and 80 in the UK. In 1995 the company planned offices in Italy, Russia, Singapore, and Sweden.

NYSE symbol: MAN
Fiscal year ends: December 31

WHO

Chairman, President, and CEO: Mitchell S. Fromstein, age 67, $2,606,998 pay
EVP, Principal Financial Officer, and Secretary: Jon F. Chait, age 44, $786,750 pay
EVP US Temporary Services: Terry A. Hueneke
SVP and General Counsel: Walt Koslowski
VP, Treasurer, and Principal Accounting Officer: Michael J. Van Handel, age 35
VP North American Administration (HR): David Wescoe
Managing Director (UK and Ireland): Maureen Miffling
General Manager (Japan): Hiroshi Ono
Gérant (France): Michael Grunelius
General Manager (Israel): Yoav Michaely
Geschaftsfuhrer (Germany): Diethelm Bender
Managing Director, Brook Street Bureau PLC (UK): Anthony J. Howard
Auditors: Arthur Andersen & Co, SC

WHERE

HQ: 5301 North Ironwood Rd., Milwaukee, WI 53217
Phone: 414-961-1000
Fax: 414-961-7081

	1994 Manpower Worldwide Offices	
	Owned	Franchise or other
Europe outside UK	752	—
US	561	442
UK	138	5
Israel	40	—
South America	19	18
Japan	26	—
Mexico	20	—
Canada	9	48
Australia	—	7
Other countries	26	—
Total	**1,591**	**520**

	1994 Sales		1994 Pretax Income	
	$ mil.	% of total	$ mil.	% of total
France	1,707	40	47	26
US	1,339	31	83	46
UK	642	15	25	14
Other Europe	310	7	17	10
Other countries	298	7	8	4
Adjustments	—	—	(44)	—
Total	**4,296**	**100**	**136**	**100**

WHAT

Services
Employee testing and training
Industrial trades temporary staffing
Medical staffing services
Office and clerical temporary staffing
Permanent employment agency services

KEY COMPETITORS

Adia
Alternative Resources
BIS
Butler International
CDI
Diversified Human Resources
Eastridge Group
ECCO
Harcourt General
Heidrick & Struggles
Hooper Holmes
Interim Services
Kelly Services
MacTemps
NRI Staffing
Olsten
Randstad
Right Management Consultants
Source Services
Vendex
Watsco

HOW MUCH

	Annual Growth	1985	1986	1987	1988	1989	1990	1991	1992	1993	1994
Sales ($ mil.)	31.4%	—	—	635	2,457	2,729	3,054	2,800	3,187	3,180	4,296
Net income ($ mil.)	32.0%	—	—	12	2	(1,208)	(82)	(53)	(47)	(49)	84
Income as % of sales	—	—	—	1.9%	0.1%	—	—	—	—	—	2.0%
Earnings per share ($)	13.6%	—	—	0.46	0.03	(16.75)	(1.13)	(0.73)	(0.54)	(0.66)	1.12
Stock price – high ($)	—	—	—	—	—	—	—	15.13	17.13	17.88	29.88
Stock price – low ($)	—	—	—	—	—	—	—	11.13	13.25	13.50	16.88
Stock price – close ($)	24.0%	—	—	—	—	—	—	14.75	14.50	17.63	28.13
P/E – high	—	—	—	—	—	—	—	—	—	—	27
P/E – low	—	—	—	—	—	—	—	—	—	—	15
Dividends per share ($)	—	—	—	—	—	—	—	0.00	0.00	0.00	0.00
Book value per share ($)	(3.5%)	—	—	—	—	—	—	3.05	2.17	1.39	2.74
Employees	0.0%	—	—	—	—	—	1,507,600	1,506,500	1,206,600	1,206,700	1,507,400

1994 Year-end:
Debt ratio: 47.9%
Return on equity: 54.8%
Cash (mil.): $82
Current ratio: 1.51
Long-term debt (mil.): $131
No. of shares (mil.): 74
Dividends
  Yield: —
  Payout: —
Market value (mil.): $2,089

Stock Price History High/Low 1991–94

MANVILLE CORPORATION

Holding company Manville's strong financial performance rests on the solid revenues of its paper and fiber companies. Manville's 81.5%-owned Riverwood International subsidiary (paper and packaging) accounted for 49% of 1994 sales. Schuller International (fiberglass building and engineered products) accounted for the balance.

Riverwood, the leading maker of linerboard packaging for beer and soft drinks (with 50% of the US market and 14% of the market outside the US), has bounced back from a price slump in the early 1990s on the back of resurgent paper prices and innovative products. Manville's 3rd business, Stillwater Mining (27% owned), is a Montana-based firm

engaged in the mining and production of palladium, platinum, and associated metals.

The ghost of asbestos litigation still haunts the banquet of Manville's improving revenues and income. Once the world's largest producer of asbestos, Manville has a backlog of 210,000 unsettled claims and as many as 350,000 additional claims still to come in before the deadline of 2047. To handle this drain on assets, the company has built up a liability trust fund, currently estimated at $750 million.

Riverwood raised $100 million in 1994 with the sale of just under 50% of its Brazilian operations. That year Schuller introduced several promising new products, including improved fiberglass and polymer materials.

In 1858 H. W. Johns founded a roofing materials business in Brooklyn. In 1868 he patented a line of products containing asbestos, a substance that would cost the company dearly more than a century later. In 1901 the company merged with Manville Covering Co. (begun in 1886 in Milwaukee to produce pipe coverings and insulation materials).

Thomas Manville headed the new company, named Johns-Manville, until his death in 1925. His brother Hiram purchased most of the stock and in 1927 sold 53% of the company to J.P. Morgan & Co. for about $20 million. Under Morgan the company focused on building materials, moving away from earlier diversification ventures such as automobile horns, fire extinguishers, and spark plugs.

Johns-Manville had moved to Colorado by 1973 and in 1979 bought paper producer Olinkraft. Manville took its present name in 1981.

In 1974, 448 WWII shipyard workers filed the first major asbestos health suits against Manville. By 1982 Manville had settled more than 4,100 suits yet faced a backlog of nearly 17,000. Bankruptcy followed that same year. While in Chapter 11, Manville closed its plastic pipe and residential roofing operations and terminated all activities related to asbestos. In 1985 Manville acquired Eastex Packaging (forest products).

The reorganization plan finalized in 1988 created a trust fund to cover asbestos-related claims filed before mid-1985 and bar any party from future claims against Manville. This personal injury trust, which has faced liquidity problems since 1989, owns 80% of Manville

common stock. As part of the settlement, Manville began paying the trust $75 million a year. But in 1992 a court tossed out this method of funding the plan. Manville has said it intends to fulfill its obligation to fund the trust while the legal wrangling continues.

In 1990 the company purchased carton and paperboard companies in 3 countries. In 1991 Manville's US and European filtration and minerals groups were combined and named Celite Corp. Alleghany Corp. bought Celite for about $140 million later that year.

In 1991 Manville converted to a holding company. Its 2 divisions, Manville Forest Products Corp. and Manville Sales Corp., were renamed Riverwood International Corp. and Schuller International and became subsidiaries. That same year Riverwood purchased packaging, equipment, and marketing companies in Brazil (M.E.A.D.), Spain (Jorba and Syspack), Minnesota (Minnesota Automation), and New Jersey (Jak-et-Pak). In 1992 the company acquired a 525,000-ton-capacity linerboard mill from Macon Kraft and initiated a $250 million project to modernize and convert the plant to coated-board production. Also that year Manville sold 19.5% of Riverwood International in a $172 million public offering. In 1993 Manville acquired Steinachglas, a glass-mat maker in eastern Germany, and swapped its residential roofing business for Corning's commercial roofing unit. In 1994 Riverwood introduced the Twin-Stack package (a 2-layer carton) for the beverage market.

Manville was looking to sell its Riverwood unit in 1995. Georgia-Pacific was seriously considering the $1.3 billion asking price.

NYSE symbol: MVL
Fiscal year ends: December 31

WHO

Chairman, President, and CEO: W. Thomas Stephens,
 age 52, $1,250,000 pay
President, Schuller International: Richard A. Kashnow,
 age 53, $708,000 pay
President and CEO, Riverwood International Corp.:
 Thomas H. Johnson
SVP, General Counsel, and Secretary: Richard B. Von
 Wald, age 52, $520,833 pay
SVP and CFO: Robert E. Cole, age 45, $500,000 pay
SVP Paperboard Operations Group, Riverwood
 International Corp.: Robert C. Hart
SVP Coated Board Systems and Service Group,
 Riverwood International Corp.: Octavio Orta
SVP Human Resources, Riverwood International Corp.:
 Robert H. Burg
SVP Strategic Planning, Schuller International:
 William J. Ehner
SVP Human Resources & Purchasing, Schuller
 International: Ron L. Hammons
Auditors: Coopers & Lybrand L.L.P.

WHERE

HQ: 717 17th St., Denver, CO 80202
Phone: 303-978-2000
Fax: 303-978-2363

Manville owns or leases about 540,000 acres of
timberland in the US and another 176,000 acres in
Brazil.

	1994 Sales		1994 Operating Income	
	$ mil.	% of total	$ mil.	% of total
US	2,008	77	285	79
Brazil	161	6	32	9
Other countries	433	17	43	12
Adjustments	(42)	—	(63)	—
Total	**2,560**	**100**	**297**	**100**

WHAT

	1994 Sales		1994 Operating Income	
	$ mil.	% of total	$ mil.	% of total
Paperboard & packaging prods.	1,283	49	154	45
Building prods.	744	29	110	32
Engineered prods.	558	22	77	23
Adjustments	(25)	—	(44)	—
Total	**2,560**	**100**	**297**	**100**

Principal Products

Riverwood International Corp.	Schuller International, Inc.
Carrierboard	Aerospace insulation
Cartonboard	Air duct components
Corrugated boxes	Air filtration media
Corrugating medium	Aircraft insulation
Folding cartons	Automotive molding
Kraft board and paper	Building insulation
Kraft linerboard	Equipment insulation
Lumber	Filter cartridges
Packaging machinery	Liquid filtration parts
Plywood	Pipe insulation
Preprint linerboard	Roofing mat
Recycled paperboard	Roofing products
	Specialty fibers and mat

KEY COMPETITORS

Aracruz Celulose	Jefferson Smurfit
Boise Cascade	Jim Walter Corp.
Bridgestone	Longview Fibre
Carlisle Cos.	Mead
Champion International	Owens-Corning
Consolidated Papers	PPG
Fletcher Challenge	St.-Gobain
GAF Corp.	Stone Container
Georgia-Pacific	Tamko Asphalt
IKPC	USG
International Paper	Weyerhaeuser
James River	Willamette Industries

HOW MUCH

	Annual Growth	1985	1986	1987	1988	1989	1990	1991	1992	1993	1994
Sales ($ mil.)	3.5%	1,880	1,920	2,063	2,062	2,192	2,245	2,025	2,224	2,276	2,560
Net income ($ mil.)	(7.6%)	75	108	164	96	197	111	(13)	36	62	37
Income as % of sales	—	4.0%	5.6%	9.0%	4.7%	9.0%	4.9%	—	2.1%	2.7%	1.4%
Earnings per share ($)	(29.1%)	—	—	—	0.79	1.39	0.79	(0.24)	0.22	0.31	0.10
Stock price – high ($)	—	—	—	—	8.88	10.50	9.38	8.50	10.88	9.75	10.88
Stock price – low ($)	—	—	—	—	6.38	6.88	4.38	4.00	7.63	6.50	7.00
Stock price – close ($)	4.0%	—	—	—	7.13	9.13	4.63	7.88	8.63	8.50	9.00
P/E – high	—	—	—	—	11	8	12	—	50	31	—
P/E – low	—	—	—	—	8	5	6	—	35	21	—
Dividends per share ($)	—	—	—	—	0.00	0.00	0.00	0.00	1.04	1.04	0.00
Book value per share ($)	(0.4%)	—	—	—	7.39	9.87	12.57	5.39	5.98	6.05	7.20
Employees	(4.7%)	21,000	19,400	18,600	18,200	17,000	18,000	16,000	15,800	16,000	13,600

1994 Year-end:
Debt ratio: 58.8%
Return on equity: 4.6%
Cash (mil.): $342
Current ratio: 1.57
Long-term debt (mil.): $1,424
No. of shares (mil.): 123
Dividends
 Yield: —
 Payout: —
Market value (mil.): $1,105

**Stock Price History
High/Low 1988–94**

MARRIOTT INTERNATIONAL, INC.

OVERVIEW

Things are getting ritzy at Marriott International these days. One of the world's leading hotel operators, with a focus on middle- and upper–middle-level hotels, the Bethesda, Maryland–based company is moving into the luxury end of the hospitality business. In 1995 it paid about $200 million for 49% of Ritz-Carlton Hotel Company, which manages 31 luxury hotels around the world. The deal creates a Marriott-Ritz Carlton joint venture that owns the Ritz-Carlton name and assets but no real estate; Marriott has the right to purchase the remaining 51% of the Ritz-Carlton holdings over the next several years.

Marriott International is the larger and more profitable of 2 companies formed when Marriott Corporation divided itself in late 1993, creating Host Marriott (from the debt-ridden segment that owned the company's real estate) and Marriott International (from the profitable hotel management division). An ongoing strategic alliance exists between the 2 companies, with Host Marriott buying properties and Marriott International managing them.

Marriott International operates or franchises more than 850 hotels and is one of the largest US providers of food and services management to businesses, hospitals, and schools. The company also manages retirement communities and golf courses. Marriott is looking to expand its time-share resort and retirement community businesses.

The company's investment in Ritz-Carlton is part of Marriott's strategy to expand into higher-margin luxury hotels now that the hospitality business is rebounding following a downturn during the late 1980s and early 1990s. Marriott also has been rumored to be eyeing the Four Seasons chain.

WHEN

In 1927 John Marriott and his wife, Alice, opened a root beer stand in Washington, DC. They soon added hot food and called their restaurant The Hot Shoppe. In 1929 they incorporated their business as Hot Shoppes, Inc., and began to build it into a regional chain. The company entered the airline food service business in 1937, providing food for Eastern, American, and Capital Airlines flights out of Washington, DC.

In 1957 the company opened its first hotel, the Twin Bridges Marriott Motor Hotel in Arlington, Virginia. When the Marriotts' son Bill became president (1964), the company had sales of $85 million from 4 hotels, 45 Hot Shoppes, and airline catering. Bill concentrated on expanding the company's hotel business, and by 1971 it had 14 hotels.

In 1967 the company changed its name to Marriott Corporation. That same year it bought Bob's Big Boy restaurants. It started Roy Rogers restaurants in 1968 and bought an Athens cruise line (Oceanic) and a 45% interest in another (Sun) in 1971.

Bill Marriott became CEO in 1972, and during the 1970s the company continued to expand its hotel business, concentrating primarily on business travelers. With the growth in airline travel, the company began to build a number of hotels near airports.

By 1977 sales had topped $1 billion, and Marriott operated 1,335 restaurants, 34 full-service hotels, and 14 franchised inns. As part of a plan to manage rather than own,

Marriott sold 8 hotels to Equitable Life Assurance for $92 million (1978). The company introduced its moderately priced Courtyard hotels in 1983. In 1985 Marriott paid $531 million for competitor Howard Johnson (the hotels, later sold, are now owned by Hospitality Franchise Systems) and in 1986 bought Saga (contract food service and restaurants) for $694 million.

Marriott sold its cruise ships in 1987 and entered 3 new market segments: full-service suites (Marriott Suites), moderately priced suites (Residence Inn, acquired for $260 million), and economy hotels (Fairfield Inn). In 1988 Marriott began developing "life-care" communities, providing apartments, meals, and limited nursing care to the elderly. It sold its airline catering businesses to management in 1989 and Roy Rogers to Hardee's in 1990.

Marriott bought the Duna Intercontinental, a major Hungarian hotel, in 1992. That same year Marriott recruited Stephen Bollenbach, formerly Donald Trump's right-hand financial man, to lead Marriott's debt reduction as the new CFO. In 1993, when Marriott International and Host Marriott were created, Bollenbach remained with Host Marriott as president and CEO.

Marriott International entered the gourmet coffee business in 1994, operating a chain of coffee bars, carts, and kiosks. In 1995 it announced plans to build a luxury time-share resort on top of the Beach Place entertainment and retail complex in Fort Lauderdale.

NYSE symbol: MAR
Fiscal year ends: Friday nearest December 31

WHO

Chairman, President, and CEO: J. W. "Bill" Marriott Jr., age 62, $1,434,375 pay
EVP; President, Marriott Service Group: William J. Shaw, age 49, $835,000 pay
EVP; President, Marriott Lodging Group: William R. Tiefel, age 60, $792,775 pay
EVP and CFO: Michael A. Stein, age 45, $490,500 pay
EVP and General Counsel: Joseph Ryan, age 53
EVP and Managing Director, Mariott Lodging International: Edwin D. Fuller
EVP and General Manager, Marriott Senior Living Services: Paul E. Johnson Jr.
SVP Corporate Relations: R. A. Rankin Jr.
SVP Finance and Treasurer: Raymond G. Murphy
SVP New Ventures: Michael R. Ruffer
SVP Human Resources: Clifford J. Ehrlich, age 56
Secretary: Joan R. McGlockton
Auditors: Arthur Andersen & Co, SC

WHERE

HQ: 10400 Fernwood Rd., Bethesda, MD 20817
Phone: 301-380-3000
Fax: 301-897-9014 (Public Relations)
Reservations: 800-228-9290

Marriott International operates over 3,800 units in 50 states and 22 countries. The company controls more than 180,000 hotel rooms through its 851 domestic and international hotels. It also provides contract services to thousands of businesses and industrial operations.

	1994 Sales	
	$ mil.	% of total
US	8,120	96
Other countries	295	4
Total	**8,415**	**100**

WHAT

	1994 Sales		1994 Operating Income	
	$ mil.	% of total	$ mil.	% of total
Lodging	4,848	58	297	72
Contract services	3,567	42	116	28
Total	**8,415**	**100**	**413**	**100**

	1994 Hotels	
	Hotels	Rooms
Marriott hotels, resorts & suites	259	106,254
Courtyard	231	33,593
Residence Inn	189	23,064
Fairfield Inn	172	17,475
Total	**851**	**180,386**

Lodging Under Management

Hotels	Retirement Communities
Courtyard	Brighton Gardens
Fairfield Inn	Independent retirement
Marriott Hotels and Resorts	communities
Marriott Suites	
Residence Inn	

Contract Services
Marriott Distribution Services (food distribution)
Marriott Golf (provides management for 16 golf courses)
Marriott Management Services (provides food service and facilities management to 3,000 clients)

KEY COMPETITORS

Accor	Doubletree	La Quinta Inns
Advocat	Four Seasons	Loews
ARAMARK	Helmsley	Nestlé
Bass	Hilton	Ogden
Canadian Pacific	Hospitality	Rank
Carlson	Franchise	SYSCO
Club Corp.	Hyatt	Westin Hotel
Dial	ITT Corp.	Wyndham Hotel

HOW MUCH

	Annual Growth	1985	1986	1987	1988	1989	1990	1991	1992	1993	1994
Sales ($ mil.)	7.9%	—	—	—	—	—	—	6,707	6,971	7,430	8,415
Net income ($ mil.)	14.6%	—	—	—	—	—	—	133	134	159	200
Income as % of sales	—	—	—	—	—	—	—	2.0%	1.9%	2.1%	2.4%
Earnings per share ($)	19.8%	—	—	—	—	—	—	—	—	1.26	1.51
Stock price – high ($)	—	—	—	—	—	—	—	—	—	29.00	32.13
Stock price – low ($)	—	—	—	—	—	—	—	—	—	22.75	25.63
Stock price – close ($)	(3.0%)	—	—	—	—	—	—	—	—	29.00	28.13
P/E – high	—	—	—	—	—	—	—	—	—	23	21
P/E – low	—	—	—	—	—	—	—	—	—	18	17
Dividends per share ($)	300.0%	—	—	—	—	—	—	—	—	0.07	0.28
Book value per share ($)	13.0%	—	—	—	—	—	—	—	—	5.54	6.26
Employees	(1.5%)	—	—	—	—	—	—	—	—	166,000	163,440

1994 Year-end:
Debt ratio: 39.7%
Return on equity: 27.3%
Cash (mil.): $204
Current ratio: 0.88
Long-term debt (mil.): $506
No. of shares (mil.): 123
Dividends
  Yield: 1.0%
  Payout: 18.5%
Market value (mil.): $3,445

**Stock Price History
High/Low 1993–94**

MARS, INC.

OVERVIEW

The McLean, Virginia–based Mars company manufactures the well-known candy brands M&M's, Snickers, and Milky Way. Mars also produces pet food (Kal Kan), rice (Uncle Ben's, the world's leading parboiled rice brand), and ice cream bars. Estimates place Mars as the 5th largest private company in the US. Having lost market share for the last 3 years, Mars now holds about 29% of the US candy market to Hershey's nearly 35%. Analysts suggest the lack of new products and the loner strategy at Mars has contributed to its market share losses.

Company heads Forrest Mars Jr. and younger brother John are well known for their imperious natures. With the company worth at least $15 billion, the Mars family is one of the richest in the US and one of the most secretive about its company operations. Some say that the CIA, whose headquarters is just a scant 2 miles from Mars's, is only the 2nd most mysterious organization in Virginia.

Mars has 52 plants in 31 countries. Its products are sold worldwide, from South Africa to China. The company does a brisk business in Russia and other former Soviet states through Masterfoods, its Russian arm. In 1995 Mars ushered in its blue period — replacing its tan-colored coating of M&M's with a bright blue which was chosen as the new color by 55% of the 10 million people "voting" in Mars's much publicized effort.

WHEN

Franklin (Frank) Mars invented the Milky Way candy bar in 1923 after his previous 3 efforts at the candy business left him bankrupt. After his estranged son Forrest graduated from Yale, Mars hired him to work at his candy operation. When Forrest demanded 1/3 control of the company and Frank refused, Forrest moved to England with the foreign rights to Milky Way and started his own company (Food Manufacturers) in the 1930s. He made a sweeter version of Milky Way for his English audience and called it a Mars bar. Forrest also began making pet food and at one point controlled 55% of the British pet food market.

During WWII Forrest returned to the US and introduced Uncle Ben's rice and M&M's. The idea for M&M's was borrowed from British Smarties, for which he obtained rights (from Rowntree Mackintosh) by relinquishing similar rights for the Snickers bar in some foreign markets. The ad slogan "Melts in your mouth, not in your hand" elevated the company to industry leader.

Little is known about Mars between the mid-1940s and 1964, when Forrest merged his firm with his deceased father's company after buying his dying half-sister's controlling interest in Mars. (But Mars was one of the first candy companies to sponsor a television show — *Howdy Doody* in the 1950s.) In 1968 Mars bought Kal Kan and followed with Puppy Palace pet shops in 1969 (sold in 1976). Mars claims that Forrest (born in 1904) is still alive but that he delegated his company responsibility to sons Forrest Jr. and John in 1973.

By 1978 the brothers, looking for snacks to offset dwindling candy revenues from a more diet-conscious America, brought out Twix, a chocolate-covered cookie. In 1987 they bought Dove Bar International, an ice cream bar manufacturer that was started by Greek immigrant Leo Stefanos in his Chicago candy store in 1939 (to keep his children from buying ice cream bars from trucks) and had grown to making 40,000 bars per day by 1985.

Around 1988 the brothers purchased Ethel M Chocolates, producer of liqueur-flavored chocolates, a business their father had begun in his retirement. Unlike the other secretive Mars plants, the Ethel M plant is open to the public for conducted tours.

Hershey's passed Mars as the US's largest candy maker in 1988 when it acquired Cadbury Schweppes's US division (Mounds and Almond Joy). In 1989 Mars introduced Bounty Bars and PB Max. In response to the success of Hershey's Symphony Bar, Mars introduced a new dark chocolate candy bar, Dove, in 1991. Other recent introductions include peanut butter, mint, and almond M&M's; Milky Way Dark; Snickers Peanut Butter; and Milky Way II.

In 1993 the company announced its entry into the Indian confectionery market with the establishment of a $10 million factory there. Also that year Procter & Gamble sued Mars for failure to meet a purchasing agreement (of caprenin, a low-calorie substance used in the poorly selling Milky Way II).

In 1994 Forrest Mars was named "Worst Marketer" by *The Delaney Report* for letting Mars lose market share to Hershey (for the 3rd year in a row). Company reaction to lost market share is unclear. In 1995 Houston Rockets basketball star Hakeem Olajuwon agreed to be a spokesperson for Uncle Ben's.

Private company
Fiscal year ends: December 31

WHO

Chairman, CEO, and Co-President: Forrest E. Mars Jr.,
age 63
Co-President: John F. Mars, age 58
Director External Relations: Jim Conlan
Secretary: E. J. Stegeman
VP Marketing, M&M/Mars: Paul Michaels

WHERE

HQ: 6885 Elm St., McLean, VA 22101-3810
Phone: 703-821-4900
Fax: 703-448-9678

Mars owns candy plants in Albany, GA; Chicago;
Cleveland, TN; Hackettstown, NJ; and Waco, TX. It owns
a pet food plant in Vernon, CA, and a rice plant in
Houston.

The company has over 50 operating plants worldwide.

WHAT

Brand Names

Candy
3 Musketeers
Bounty
Dove
Ethel M Chocolates
M&M's Almond
M&M's Peanut
M&M's Peanut Butter
M&M's Plain
Mars Almond
Milky Way
Milky Way II
Milky Way Dark
Mint M&M's
PB Max Real Peanut Butter Snack
Peanut Butter Snickers
Skittles
Snickers
Starburst

Ice Cream Bar Products
3 Musketeers
DoveBars
Milky Way
Snickers

Pet Food
Kal Kan
Mealtime
Pedigree
Sheba
Whiskas

Rice
Uncle Ben's Converted Rice
Uncle Ben's Country Inn Rice
Uncle Ben's Long Grain & Wild Rice

Snacks
Combos
Kudos
Twix

Other Products
Coin changers
Handheld scanning devices

Major Subsidiaries

Kal Kan Foods, Inc.
M&M/Mars
Uncle Ben's, Inc.

KEY COMPETITORS

ADM
Allied Domecq
Anheuser-Busch
Ben & Jerry's
Berkshire Hathaway
Borden
Cadbury Schweppes
Campbell Soup
Carter-Wallace
Colgate-Palmolive
ConAgra
General Mills
Hartz Group
Heinz

Hershey
Hormel
Kellogg
Nestlé
PepsiCo
Pet Ventures
Philip Morris
Ralston Purina Group
Reynolds Metals
Riceland Foods
RJR Nabisco
Tootsie Roll
Tyson Foods
Unilever

HOW MUCH

	9-Year Growth	1985	1986	1987	1988	1989	1990	1991	1992	1993	1994
Estimated sales ($ mil.)	6.7%	7,000	7,700	8,000	8,541	8,450	9,100	11,000	12,500	13,000	12,500
Ad expenses ($ mil.)	2.8%	313	379	340	293	272	254	255	320	338	400
Employees	2.7%	22,000	22,000	22,000	22,000	23,000	26,000	28,000	28,000	27,000	28,000

Estimated Sales
($ mil.) 1985–94

MARSH & MCLENNAN COMPANIES, INC.

OVERVIEW

It's a good news/bad news situation for Marsh & McLennan Companies. Its Marsh & McLennan unit is the world's top insurance brokerage service. Other units include Guy Carpenter & Company (reinsurance), the Mercer Consulting Group (management consulting), and Putnam Investments (money management, with over $95 billion in assets in 1994). Its Frizzell Financial Services is the UK's leading provider of group insurance programs; Seabury & Smith is the same in the US.

The good news for Marsh & McLennan is that as companies move to improve competitiveness and operating efficiency, Mercer Consulting Group is seeing consulting revenues increase. The bad news is that insurance premiums are declining and competition is intense, keeping insurance revenues depressed. Meanwhile, the volatile financial markets are dampening investors' appetite for risk.

Marsh & McLennan is looking overseas for relief. In 1994 Mercer Consulting expanded in the Netherlands and Latin America, while Marsh & McLennan improved operations in Germany and the UK. In 1995 Mercer acquired MID SA, a French consulting firm.

The Trident Partnership, an investment partnership formed by Marsh & McLennan Risk Capital, had won over $600 million in capital commitments by the end of 1994.

WHEN

Marsh & McLennan evolved from 3 turn-of-the-century midwestern firms: Marsh Ullmann & Co. (led by Henry Marsh, who pioneered insurance brokering and in 1901 set up U.S. Steel's self-insurance program), Manley-McLennan of Duluth (specialists in railroad insurance), and D.W. Burrows (a small Chicago-based railroad insurance firm).

In 1904, after discovering that they had both been promised the Burlington Northern Railroad account, Donald McLennan and Marsh joined forces with Daniel Burrows to form the world's largest insurance brokerage, with $3 million in premiums. In 1906 the firm became Marsh & McLennan, with Marsh as the chief, McLennan overseeing the railroad business, and a new partner, Charles Seabury, handling technical and support services.

In the early 20th century, Marsh won AT&T's business by arranging to meet the company's president on an Atlantic crossing; McLennan landed the Armour Meat Packing account by chatting with P. D. Armour while on a commuter train to Chicago.

In 1923 Marsh & McLennan became a closely held corporation. As the business became more technical, Marsh lost interest; he sold out to McLennan in 1935. The company weathered the Depression without major layoffs by cutting pay and branching into life insurance and employee-benefits consulting after passage of the Social Security Act (1935).

Until the late 1930s the company never billed for consulting services that were expected to lead to insurance placements. This changed when the president of American Can insisted on paying for the time of the company's employees. In 1946 the company won Ford Motor Company's business.

In the 1950s, as the company grew through acquisitions, interoffice rivalries developed. In 1962 it went public and in 1969 it organized a holding company that became Marsh & McLennan Companies. In the 1970s the company began to diversify, buying The Putnam Cos. (investment management).

Marsh & McLennan set up its employee-benefits consulting business in 1975 as a separate subsidiary, William M. Mercer, and in 1980 acquired a foothold in the UK with C.T. Bowring Reinsurance. In 1982 Marsh & McLennan formed Seabury & Smith to manage its insurance programs.

As the insurance business stagnated in the 1980s, the financial and consulting fields grew. In 1992 the company formed Mercer Consulting Group to encompass its various consulting companies.

Also in 1992 Marsh & McLennan continued its expansion program, acquiring The Frizzell Group of the UK. It also added Marsh & McLennan Risk Capital Corp., which oversees investments in insurance companies.

The company formed Mid Ocean Reinsurance and Underwriters Capital (Merrett) Ltd. with J.P. Morgan in 1993.

In 1994 the Trident Fund (also formed with J.P. Morgan) began accepting subscriptions for investments that capitalize on the restructuring occurring in the insurance industry.

In 1994 Putnam president Lawrence Lasser was awarded a $10.5 million bonus based on that company's successful growth. However, early in 1995 Putnam and Alliance Capital Management, who together own $50 million in Orange County notes, lost a court ruling to have the bankrupt California county set aside payments for notes coming due.

NYSE symbol: MMC
Fiscal year ends: December 31

Chairman and CEO: A. J. C. Smith, age 60,
$1,825,000 pay
VC: Philip L. Wroughton, age 61
Chairman and CEO, Guy Carpenter & Company, Inc.:
Richard H. Blum, age 56, $850,000 pay
Chairman, Marsh & McLennan, Inc.: David D.
Holbrook, age 56, $840,000 pay
President and CEO, Putnam Investments, Inc.:
Lawrence J. Lasser, age 52, $11,320,000 pay
President, Mercer Consulting Group, Inc.: Peter Coster,
age 55, $875,000 pay
President and CEO, Marsh & McLennan, Inc.: John T.
Sinnott, age 55, $840,000 pay
SVP and CFO: Frank J. Borelli, age 59
SVP Human Resources and Administration: Francis N.
Bonsignore, age 48
General Counsel and Secretary: Gregory F. Van Gundy,
age 49
Auditors: Deloitte & Touche LLP

WHERE

HQ: 1166 Avenue of the Americas, New York, NY
10036-2774
Phone: 212-345-5000
Fax: 212-345-4838 (Public Affairs)

Marsh & McLennan operates in more than 80 countries.

	1994 Sales		1994 Operating Income	
	$ mil.	% of total	$ mil.	% of total
US	2,227	65	478	67
Europe	910	26	181	25
Canada	165	5	35	5
Other regions	133	4	16	2
Adjustments	—	—	(40)	—
Total	**3,435**	**100**	**670**	**100**

WHAT

	1994 Sales		1994 Operating Income	
	$ mil.	% of total	$ mil.	% of total
Insurance services	1,887	55	406	57
Consulting	933	27	96	14
Investment mgmt.	615	18	208	29
Other	—	—	(40)	—
Total	**3,435**	**100**	**670**	**100**

Selected Subsidiaries
The Frizzell Group Limited (insurance, finance, and
financial planning programs for affinity groups; UK)
Guy Carpenter & Co., Inc. (reinsurance)
Marsh & McLennan, Inc. (insurance brokerage)
Marsh & McLennan Risk Capital Corp. (insurance
industry investments and advisory services)
Mercer Consulting Group, Inc. (management
consulting, Europe and North America)
Putnam Investments, Inc. (investment management)
Seabury & Smith, Inc. (insurance program management
services; Canada, the UK, and the US)

KEY COMPETITORS

AIG	General Electric
Alexander & Alexander	General Re
Allianz	Johnson & Higgins
American Express	Kemper Corp.
American Re	KPMG
Arthur Andersen	Lloyd's of London
Arthur Gallagher	McKinsey & Co.
Booz, Allen	MDC Holding
Charles Schwab	Merrill Lynch
Chubb	Nomura Securities
CIGNA	Paine Webber
Coopers & Lybrand	Price Waterhouse
Deloitte & Touche	Prudential
Ernst & Young	T. Rowe Price
First Fidelity	Tokio Marine and Fire
FMR	Transnational Re
Franklin Resources	USF&G

HOW MUCH

	9-Year Growth	1985	1986	1987	1988	1989	1990	1991	1992	1993	1994
Sales ($ mil.)	10.8%	1,368	1,804	2,147	2,272	2,428	2,723	2,779	2,937	3,163	3,435
Net income ($ mil.)	9.9%	163	243	302	296	295	304	306	304	332	382
Income as % of sales	—	11.9%	13.5%	14.1%	13.0%	12.1%	11.2%	11.0%	10.3%	10.5%	11.1%
Earnings per share ($)	9.8%	2.23	3.30	4.06	4.09	4.10	4.15	4.18	4.21	4.52	5.19
Stock price – high ($)	—	41.75	76.75	72.00	59.75	89.75	81.00	87.25	94.50	97.63	88.75
Stock price – low ($)	—	28.25	40.63	43.75	45.25	55.13	59.75	69.13	71.25	77.00	71.25
Stock price – close ($)	7.7%	40.75	60.75	49.50	56.25	78.00	78.00	81.38	91.38	81.25	79.25
P/E – high	—	19	23	18	15	22	20	21	22	22	17
P/E – low	—	13	12	11	11	13	14	17	17	17	14
Dividends per share ($)	9.5%	1.24	1.57	2.15	2.43	2.50	2.55	2.60	2.65	2.70	2.80
Book value per share ($)	12.3%	7.02	8.64	10.71	10.56	12.06	14.77	14.41	15.05	18.47	19.95
Employees	4.4%	17,700	19,900	22,700	22,800	23,600	24,400	23,400	25,800	25,600	26,000

1994 Year-end:
Debt ratio: 21.9%
Return on equity: 27.0%
Cash (mil.): $295
Current ratio: 1.04%
Long-term debt (mil.): $409
No. of shares (mil.): 73
Dividends
Yield: 3.5%
Payout: 53.9%
Market value (mil.): $5,801

**Stock Price History
High/Low 1985–94**

MASCO CORPORATION

OVERVIEW

Masco Corporation, the US's leading manufacturer of faucets (Brass-Craft, Delta), tapped its legal resources in 1994 to flush out a competitor (Price Pfister) that had infringed on its Delta lavatory faucet patent. The erring company was docked $1.4 million in damages. Masco is a major US manufacturer of home furnishings and kitchen and bathroom products. It produces more than one out of every 3 faucets made in the US. It is also the nation's largest manufacturer of cabinets (KraftMaid, Fieldstone, Merillat, StarMark), producing 20 lines and claiming a 14% share of the domestic market. In addition, it is the US's largest furniture maker (Bench Craft, Berkline, Drexel Heritage, Lexington, Universal), with a 9% market share.

Flush with successful products and leading brands in a number of markets, Masco claims that 96% of its sales represent brands that hold leadership positions in their respective markets. In recent years the company has taken advantage of the expanded sales opportunities that have opened up with the increasing popularity of high-volume home center retail chains and superstores.

Masco has also benefited from the health of the US housing market. Historically low interest rates has meant a surge in mortgage refinancing and home improvement activities.

WHEN

Alex Manoogian, Masco's founder, came to the US at age 19 in 1920. With partners Harry Adjemian and Charles Saunders, he started the Masco Screw Products Company a mere 8 days before the crash of 1929. Masco derived its name from the first letters of the partners' last names plus "co" for company. Manoogian's 2 partners left the company within the year.

Largely dependent on Detroit's auto industry, Masco grew slowly during the Depression, producing custom parts for Chrysler, Ford, Hudson Motor Co., and Spicer Manufacturing. By 1937, with sales of over $200,000, it offered shares to the public and was listed on the Detroit Stock Exchange. During WWII Masco devoted its production to defense, and in 1942 sales topped $1 million. A new plant, opened in 1948 in Dearborn, Michigan, expanded production space to nearly 100,000 square feet. Masco resumed peacetime business, primarily with the auto industry, although the Korean War prompted a return to defense production.

In 1954 Masco began producing and selling Manoogian's version of an efficient one-handle kitchen faucet (Delta). Delta sales had exceeded $1 million by 1958, and Masco opened a new faucet factory in Greensburg, Indiana.

Under Manoogian's son Richard's direction, Masco Corporation (renamed in 1961) diversified its product line and began buying companies. In 1962 it was listed on the AMEX.

Between 1964 and 1980 Masco acquired more than 50 companies, concentrating on tool and metal casting, energy exploration, and other industrial products such as pumping equipment and air compressors. The company continued to focus on both industrial and consumer products until 1984, when it underwent a major corporate restructuring that split it into 2 entities. Masco Corporation pursued the course set by its successful faucet sales, expanding its interests in home improvement and home furnishings companies. The company spun off its industrial products business, creating Masco Industries, a separate public corporation in which Masco maintained a sizable stake. (Masco Industries later became MascoTech.)

Masco Corporation became the largest US furniture manufacturer in the 1980s by buying several leading North Carolina furniture makers, including Henredon and Drexel Heritage (1986), Hickorycraft and Lexington Furniture (1987), and Universal Furniture (1989).

Despite the 1990–91 recession, Masco expanded market share (though profits declined). In 1990 Masco acquired KraftMaid cabinets (in exchange for stock), repurchased 9 million Masco shares, launched its Lineage furniture line, and opened 3 wood products plants in China. In 1991 Masco bought British fabric supplier Ramm, Son & Crocker. In 1992, following its strategy to simplify its firm and build on positions of market leadership, Masco sold its interests in Mechanical Technology, Emco Limited of Canada, and Payless Cashways. In 1993 Masco reduced its stake in MascoTech (parts maker for the transportation industry) from 47% to 35%.

The company acquired both kitchen cabinetmaker Alma Küchen Aloys (Germany) and hand-held shower maker NewTeam Group (UK) in 1994 for a total of $104 million.

In 1995 the firm's Delta Faucet subsidiary opened a Pacific Rim Distribution and Business Center in the Philippines.

NYSE symbol: MAS
Fiscal year ends: December 31

WHO

Chairman Emeritus: Alex Manoogian, age 93
Chairman and CEO: Richard A. Manoogian, age 58,
$1,407,000 pay
President and COO: Wayne B. Lyon, age 62,
$1,111,000 pay
President, Building Products: Raymond F. Kennedy,
age 52, $876,000 pay
President, Home Furnishings Products: Ronald L.
Jones, age 52, $723,000 pay
SVP Finance: Richard G. Mosteller, age 62, $741,000 pay
SVP Home Furnishings Products: Frank W. Burr
VP and General Counsel: John R. Leekley, age 51
VP Marketing: Robert H. Schirmer
VP Technology and Support Services: John F. Ullrich
VP Investments: Samuel Valenti III, age 49
VP Taxes: David A. Doran, age 53
VP Controller: Robert B. Rosowski, age 54
VP and Secretary: Eugene A. Gargaro Jr., age 52
VP Human Resources: David G. Wesenberg, age 64
VP: Gerald Bright, age 72
Treasurer: John C. Nicholls Jr., age 61
Auditors: Coopers & Lybrand L.L.P.

WHERE

HQ: 21001 Van Born Rd., Taylor, MI 48180
Phone: 313-274-7400
Fax: 313-374-6787 (Executive Offices)

Masco Corporation has about 152 manufacturing plants
in 23 states and 17 countries.

	1994 Sales		1994 Operating Income	
	$ mil.	% of total	$ mil.	% of total
US	3,741	84	480	81
Europe	404	9	73	12
Other regions	323	7	40	7
Total	**4,468**	**100**	**593**	**100**

WHAT

	1994 Sales		1994 Operating Income	
	$ mil.	% of total	$ mil.	% of total
Building & home improvement products	2,523	56	504	85
Home furnishings & specialty prods.	1,945	44	89	15
Total	**4,468**	**100**	**593**	**100**

Selected Subsidiaries and Brand Names

Furnishings
Ametex Fabrics
Benchcraft
Drexel Heritage
Frederick Edward
Gebhardt
Henredon
Henry Link
Hickorycraft
LaBarge/Marbro
Lexington
Lineage
Maitland-Smith
Marge Carson
Marvel
Ramm, Son & Crocker

Robert Allen
Fabrics
Sunbury Textile
Mills
Universal

Plumbing Products
Alsons
Aqua Glass
Artistic Brass
Brass-Craft
Damixa
Delta
Epic
HotSpring Spa
Hüppe
Jung Pumpen

Peerless Faucet
PlumbShop
Sherle Wagner

Cabinets
Fieldstone
KraftMaid
Merillat
StarMark

Hardware
Baldwin
Saflok
Weiser
Winfield

Appliances
Thermador

KEY COMPETITORS

American Brands
American Standard
American Woodmark
Armstrong World Industries
Bassett Furniture

Black & Decker
Cooper Industries
Eljer Industries
Hanson
Herman Miller
INTERCO
Jones Plumbing
Klaussner

Kohler
Ladd Furniture
La-Z-Boy Chair
Leggett & Platt
Newell Co.
Triangle Pacific
Waxman

HOW MUCH

	9-Year Growth	1985	1986	1987	1988	1989	1990	1991	1992	1993	1994
Sales ($ mil.)	16.2%	1,154	1,452	2,023	2,439	3,151	3,209	3,141	3,525	3,886	4,468
Net income ($ mil.)	1.8%	165	203	219	288	221	139	45	183	221	194
Income as % of sales	—	14.3%	14.0%	10.8%	11.8%	7.0%	4.3%	1.4%	5.2%	5.7%	4.3%
Earnings per share ($)	(0.5%)	1.28	1.56	1.65	2.10	1.42	0.91	0.30	1.21	1.45	1.22
Stock price – high ($)	—	21.19	34.50	40.88	30.38	31.13	26.75	26.50	30.00	38.88	39.88
Stock price – low ($)	—	13.00	19.50	18.75	22.00	23.75	14.25	17.00	22.00	25.50	21.25
Stock price – close ($)	1.3%	20.13	29.00	21.63	25.38	24.38	17.13	23.50	29.63	37.00	22.63
P/E – high	—	17	22	25	15	22	29	—	25	27	33
P/E – low	—	10	13	11	11	17	16	—	18	18	17
Dividends per share ($)	14.1%	0.22	0.34	0.38	0.44	0.50	0.54	0.57	0.61	0.65	0.72
Book value per share ($)	6.6%	7.60	8.84	10.33	11.30	11.94	12.01	11.91	12.56	13.07	13.46
Employees	16.0%	13,500	21,000	27,000	27,500	42,000	41,300	40,000	43,100	45,000	51,300

1994 Year-end:
Debt ratio: 43.7%
Return on equity: 9.4%
Cash (mil.): $71
Current ratio: 3.15
Long-term debt (mil.): $1,593
No. of shares (mil.): 157.0
Dividends
  Yield: 3.2%
  Payout: 59.0%
Market value (mil.): $3,552

**Stock Price History
High/Low 1985–94**

MASSACHUSETTS MUTUAL LIFE

OVERVIEW

MassMutual, based in Springfield, Massachusetts, has 4 core business areas. Insurance and Financial Management includes investment and asset management services as well as life insurance. The Life and Health Benefits Management unit provides health coverage and managed care and case review services in more than 100 US markets. MassMutual's Pension Management administers 401(k) and other pension programs. The Investment Management unit (through its ownership of Concert Capital and a controlling interest in Oppenheimer Management) manages income from the company and outside clients.

The company's traditional policy of financial conservatism helped it weather 1994, one of the worst years in recent memory for the financial industry because of the collapse of the bond market (from which MassMutual derives significant revenue).

MassMutual has invested heavily in technology recently. One of its projects was to install an optical disk storage system that allows customer service workers to access noncurrent information instantly, rather than having to search through old files or on microfiche. In 1995 the company opened a web site at http://www.massmutual.com.

WHEN

Massachusetts Mutual was formed in Springfield by George Rice, an insurance agent, in 1851. It started as a stock company but in 1867 converted to a mutual company. By 1868 MassMutual had opened a San Francisco office. For its first 50 years the company sold only individual life insurance, but after 1900 it branched out, offering annuities (1917) and disability coverage (1918).

Though WWI forced the company to adopt higher premiums on new policies, the 1918 flu epidemic was much more costly. MassMutual endured the Great Depression despite policy terminations and expanded its products to include income insurance. In 1946 MassMutual wrote its first group policy, for Brown-Forman Distillers (Louisville), makers of Jack Daniel's. By 1950 the company had more than 200 employees in its group sector and had diversified into medical insurance.

MassMutual began investing in stocks in the 1950s, switching over from reliance upon fixed-return bonds and mortgages, to receive a higher return. It also decentralized and in 1961 began automating operations. By 1970 MassMutual had installed a computer network that linked it to its independent agents. In this period, whole life insurance remained the dominant product. The company was also responsive to social needs, investing in and anchoring commercial development that helped in the redevelopment of Springfield.

After the interest rate increases of the late 1970s, many insurers began to diversify, offering high-yield products, like guaranteed investment contracts, funded by high-risk investments. MassMutual resisted as long as it could, but as interest rates soared to 20%, the company experienced a rash of policy loans (policyholders taking low-rate loans on their

policies to invest the money at higher rates), which led to a cash crunch. In 1981, with its policy growth rate trailing the rest of the industry, MassMutual sought new products. Fearing that a rush into universal life would hurt agents' earnings, the company instead developed UPDATE, which offered whole life holders higher dividends in return for adjustable interest on policy loans. Over 750,000 policyholders converted to UPDATE. Though the competition began diversifying into financial services, MassMutual stuck to its core business for the time being and avoided risky investments.

In the 1980s MassMutual reduced its investment in stocks (to about 5% of total investments by 1987), allowing the company to emerge virtually unscathed from the 1987 stock market crash.

In 1990 MassMutual changed its course and entered financial services. The company bought a controlling interest in mutual fund manager Oppenheimer Management, paying $21.6 million for stock in the parent company and loaning it $44.4 million.

In 1993 MassMutual announced that, because of state legislation limiting rates, it would stop writing new individual and small-group policies in New York.

The next year, the company announced a plan to target the neglected niche of family-owned businesses. It continued this policy in 1995 by becoming a founding sponsor of the American Alliance of Family-Owned Businesses. It also brought out new whole life products aimed at small businesses.

In 1995 MassMutual began to explore the possibility of buying Cambridge, Massachusetts–based investment management firm David L. Babson, which was founded in 1940.

Mutual company
Fiscal year ends: December 31

WHO

President and CEO: Thomas B. Wheeler
EVP Corporate Financial Operations: Daniel J. Fitzgerald
EVP and Chief Investment Officer: Gary E. Wendlandt
EVP Operations: John J. Pajak
EVP Insurance and Financial Management: John B. Davies
EVP Insurance and Financial Management: Lawrence L. Grypp
EVP Life and Health Benefits Management: James E. Miller
EVP Pension Management: John M. Naughton
EVP and General Counsel: Lawrence V. Burkett Jr.
SVP Financial Services: Kenneth D. Cardwell
SVP Government Relations: Barry H. Gottehrer
SVP Insurance and Financial Management: Paul D. Adornato
SVP Life and Health Benefits: William J. Burton
SVP Corporate Human Resources: Susan A. Alfano
Auditors: Coopers & Lybrand L.L.P.

WHERE

HQ: Massachusetts Mutual Life Insurance Company, 1295 State St., Springfield, MA 01111-0001
Phone: 413-788-8411
Fax: 413-744-8889

Massachusetts Mutual serves more than 2 million individual and group policyholders and other clients in the US.

WHAT

	1994 Sales	
	$ mil.	% of total
Individual policy premiums	1,646	24
Life & health premiums	526	8
Pension premiums	703	10
Net investment income	2,207	33
Other	1,700	25
Total	**6,782**	**100**

	1994 Assets	
	$ mil.	% of total
Cash & equivalents	2,228	6
Treasury & agency securities	5,723	16
Mortgage-backed securities	3,425	10
State & municipal bonds	128	0
Utility bonds	914	3
Corporate bonds	7,751	21
Stocks	203	1
Mortgage loans	2,990	8
Real estate	1,346	4
Policy loans	2,705	8
Other investments	681	2
Separate account assets	6,659	18
Other	967	3
Total	**35,720**	**100**

Services
Health insurance
Investment management
Life insurance
Pension management

Subsidiaries
Concert Capital Management, Inc.
Cornerstone Real Estate Advisers, Inc.
MML Investors Services, Inc.
Oppenheimer Management Corp.

KEY COMPETITORS

Aetna	Kaiser Foundation
AIG	Kemper National
Allianz	Insurance
Allstate	Liberty Mutual
American Financial	Mellon Bank
American General	Merrill Lynch
Blue Cross	MetLife
Charles Schwab	New York Life
Chubb	Paine Webber
CIGNA	Prudential
CNA Financial	Sierra Health Services
Conseco	State Farm
Equitable	T. Rowe Price
FMR	Teachers Insurance
Foundation Health	Torchmark
Guaranty National	Transamerica
Jefferson-Pilot	Travelers
ITT Hartford	USF&G
John Hancock	

HOW MUCH

	9-Year Growth	1985	1986	1987	1988	1989	1990	1991	1992	1993	1994
Assets ($ mil.)	9.6%	15,716	18,182	20,042	22,589	25,062	27,507	29,582	31,495	34,699	35,720
Net income ($ mil.)	2.4%	75	288	51	50	142	101	180	116	139	93
Income as % of assets	—	0.5%	1.6%	0.3%	0.2%	0.6%	0.4%	0.6%	0.4%	0.4%	0.3%
Employees	(1.1%)	10,007	9,860	10,515	10,947	11,244	11,000	10,463	9,314	8,888	9,049

1994 Year-end:
Equity as % of assets: 5.4%
Return on equity: 5.0%
Sales (mil.): $6,782

MassMutual®

Net Income ($ mil.)
1985–94

MATTEL, INC.

OVERVIEW

Barbie now comes with brain and concern for the community included. Mattel's recent versions of its flagship doll, which represents over 1/3 of company sales, include Dr. Barbie and Teacher Barbie. The company has overtaken Hasbro as the #1 toy maker in the US, achieving over $3 billion in sales in 1994. That year Mattel's earnings nearly doubled to $256 million, despite a $70 million charge related to the company's 1993 acquisition of Fisher-Price, maker of preschool toys.

Mattel focuses on its 4 principal brands (Barbie, Fisher-Price, Disney entertainment lines, and Hot Wheels), which together account for 80% of the company's sales. Mattel's other toy brands include Cabbage Patch Kids, Wham-O (frisbees), and Hacky Sack.

Mattel is restructuring its operations in order to cut costs. The plan, which calls for the elimination of about 1,000 jobs, is expected to save the company $25 million initially and even more in future years. Mattel hopes the savings will protect it from rising raw material costs.

Mattel believes that children's play patterns are the same wherever they live. The company designs its products to have worldwide appeal and markets them in a total of 36 countries.

WHEN

Mattel began in 1945 as a small California toy manufacturer operating out of a converted garage and producing toy furniture. Harold Matson and Elliot Handler named their new company Mattel, using letters from their last and first names. Matson soon sold his share to Handler and his wife, Ruth, who incorporated the business in 1948, with headquarters in Culver City, California.

By 1952 the company's toy line had expanded to include burp guns and musical toys, and sales exceeded $5 million. Sponsorship of Walt Disney's *Mickey Mouse Club* (1955), a first in toy advertising, was a shrewd marketing step for Mattel, providing direct, year-round access to millions of young potential customers.

In 1959 Mattel introduced the Barbie doll, named after the Handlers' daughter, Barbara, and later introduced Ken, named after their son. Barbie, with her fashionable wardrobe and extensive accessories, was an instant hit and in the past 30 years has become the most successful brand-name toy ever sold.

Mattel went public in 1960, and within 2 years sales had jumped from $25 million to $75 million. The company began its purchase of smaller toy companies and nontoy businesses, such as the Dee & Cee Toy Company (1962), the A&A Die Casting Company (1968), Western Printing (1979), and the Ringling Brothers–Barnum & Bailey Combined Shows circus (1979).

The Handlers were ousted from management in 1974 after an investigation by the SEC found irregularities in reports of the company's profits. The company was ordered to restructure its board, and the Handlers, with 29% of the company's stock, could no longer direct Mattel's activities.

By the 1980s Mattel was a high-volume business with heavy overhead expenses and high development costs. In an effort to recapitalize, Mattel sold all its nontoy assets by 1983. In 1987 sales were over $1 billion, but Mattel showed a $93 million net loss. In that year John Amerman, the newly appointed chairman, closed down 40% of Mattel's manufacturing capacity and fired 22% of the corporate staff. The results were positive: the following year Mattel's net income was $36 million and in 1989 it showed an $80 million profit.

In 1991 Mattel bought Aviva Sport, a San Francisco–based producer of toys and sports equipment. It also established a Japanese subsidiary and purchased Auritel, a Mexican toy company, 40% of which it already controlled. Mattel established its presence in the game market in early 1992 with the purchase of International Games, maker of the popular UNO and Skip-Bo games.

In 1992 Mattel also opened a Barbie boutique in New York City toy store FAO Schwarz and a toy shop at Disneyland. The latter move gave Mattel outlets for its products at all three Disney theme parks. Mattel lost the 1993 summer movie merchandising melee to Hasbro, which held the licensing rights for *Jurassic Park*.

In 1994 Mattel countered by producing merchandising tie-ins for Disney's summer sensation, *The Lion King*. That same year the company acquired Kransco, a maker of battery powered ride-on vehicles, for $260 million, and Britain's J. W. Spear & Sons, which owns the rights to Scrabble in markets outside the US (Hasbro owns US rights), for $95 million.

In 1995 Mattel introduced the River Rowing Pocahontas doll, based on Disney's latest animated adventure film.

NYSE symbol: MAT
Fiscal year ends: December 31

Chairman and CEO: John W. Amerman, age 63,
$1,783,164 pay
President and COO: Jill E. Barad, age 43, $1,360,810 pay
Group President, US-Mattel and Fisher-Price, Inc.:
James A. Eskridge, age 52, $980,786 pay (prior to
promotion)
President, Mattel International: Lindsey F. Williams,
age 58, $870,006 pay
President, Mattel Operations: Joseph C. Gandolfo,
age 52, $690,000 pay
President, Fisher-Price, Inc.: Byron Davis, age 47
EVP Finance: Francesca Luzuriaga, age 40
**EVP, Chief Administrative Officer, General Counsel,
and Secretary:** Ned Mansour, age 46
SVP and Controller: Gary P. Rolfes, age 43
SVP Human Resources and Administration:
E. Joseph McKay, age 54
VP and Treasurer: William Stavro, age 55
Auditors: Price Waterhouse LLP

WHERE

HQ: 333 Continental Blvd., El Segundo, CA 90245-5012
Phone: 310-252-2000
Fax: 310-524-3861

Mattel's primary manufacturing facilities are in China,
Indonesia, Italy, Malaysia, and Mexico.

	1994 Sales		1994 Operating Income	
	$ mil.	% of total	$ mil.	% of total
US	2,316	49	306	53
Asia & Latin America	1,288	28	130	22
Canada & Europe	1,066	23	144	25
Adjustments	(1,465)	—	(186)	—
Total	**3,205**	**100**	**394**	**100**

WHAT

	1994 Sales	
	$ mil.	% of total
Barbie	1,100	34
Fisher-Price	828	26
Disney toys	442	14
Kransco & Spear	179	6
Hot Wheels	177	6
Other toys	479	14
Total	**3,205**	**100**

Selected Brand Names

Action Toys
Corgi
Hot Wheels

Activity Toys
Aviva
Nickelodeon

Dolls
Aladdin
Barbie
Lion King
Pocahontas

Games
Scrabble (foreign rights)
Skip-Bo
UNO

Infant/Preschool Toys
Disney (dolls)
Disney (plush toys)
See 'N Say

KEY COMPETITORS

Acclaim Entertainment
Dakin
Equity Marketing
Hasbro
Just Toys
Lewis Galoob Toys
Lincoln Logs
Monarch Avalon
Nintendo
Ohio Art

Pleasant
Revell Monogram
Rubbermaid
Sega
SLM International
T-HQ
Time Warner
Toy Biz
Tyco Toys
Vermont Teddy Bear

HOW MUCH

	9-Year Growth	1985	1986	1987	1988	1989	1990	1991	1992	1993	1994
Sales ($ mil.)	13.2%	1,051	1,059	1,020	990	1,237	1,471	1,622	1,848	2,704	3,205
Net income ($ mil.)	17.9%	58	(1)	(93)	36	80	91	118	144	121	256
Income as % of sales	—	5.5%	—	—	3.6%	6.4%	6.2%	7.3%	7.8%	5.0%	8.0%
Earnings per share ($)	14.0%	0.34	(0.07)	(0.78)	0.26	0.54	0.62	0.78	0.88	0.60	1.11
Stock price – high ($)	—	5.85	5.29	5.42	3.67	7.13	9.01	14.25	17.28	19.68	23.60
Stock price – low ($)	—	3.37	2.65	2.18	2.09	3.20	5.29	6.23	12.70	13.12	16.56
Stock price – close ($)	19.1%	4.18	2.82	2.35	3.24	6.74	6.87	14.14	16.24	17.68	20.10
P/E – high	—	17	—	—	14	13	15	18	20	33	21
P/E – low	—	10	—	—	8	6	9	8	14	22	15
Dividends per share ($)	—	0.00	0.00	0.00	0.00	0.00	0.02	0.06	0.11	0.14	0.18
Book value per share ($)	11.1%	1.91	1.36	0.75	0.93	1.50	2.28	2.96	3.50	3.85	4.91
Employees	1.6%	19,000	17,500	12,700	11,000	11,000	12,500	12,500	15,000	21,000	22,000

1994 Year-end:
Debt ratio: 29.8%
Return on equity: 26.9%
Cash (mil.): $250
Current ratio: 1.69
Long-term debt (mil.): $355
No. of shares (mil.): 221
Dividends
  Yield: 0.9%
  Payout: 16.2%
Market value (mil.): $4,440

**Stock Price History
High/Low 1985–94**

THE MAY DEPARTMENT STORES CO.

OVERVIEW

May Department Stores is one of the US's leading upmarket department store owners, operating 314 stores under such well-known names as Lord & Taylor, Foley's, Filene's, Hecht's, and Kaufmann's. The St. Louis–based company also runs Payless ShoeSource, the nation's #1 self-service family shoe store chain, with more than 4,400 Payless and Payless Kids stores.

May chalked up its 20th consecutive year of record sales and income per share in fiscal 1994. Same-store sales were up 4.4%. To ensure more records in the future, May continues to expand. The company added 19 new

department stores in 1994 — a company record, but one that probably won't last. The company plans to open 23 new stores in 1995. Overall May plans to spend $5 billion over the next 5 years to add 125 new department stores, remodel 100 department stores, and open 1,200 new Payless stores.

May has invested in upgrading its information and inventory systems, a move that has promoted better communication and greater efficiency in restocking its stores. The company is also working to improve its department store services, including bridal and baby gift registries.

WHEN

David May, age 15, arrived in New York from Germany in 1863. After working in the Midwest, he tried mining in Colorado, unsuccessfully. He finally tried retailing, opening a clothing store in Leadville in 1877 and expanding to Denver in 1888. In 1892 he and 3 other investors bought the Famous in St. Louis, and in 1898 they bought a store in Cleveland.

Having moved headquarters to St. Louis in 1905, the partners bought competitor Barr's in 1911 when that store's owners ran out of money trying to construct the Railway Exchange Building. The building still serves as May's headquarters and is the site of the flagship Famous-Barr store.

The company continued to buy other operations, including O'Neil's (Akron, 1912), Hamburger & Sons (Los Angeles, 1923), Bernheimer-Leader (Baltimore, 1927), Kaufmann's (Pittsburgh, 1946), Daniels & Fischer (Denver, 1957), Hecht's (Washington, DC; 1959), G. Fox (Hartford, 1965), and Meier & Frank (Portland, Oregon; 1966).

Meanwhile, 2 other companies, the Associated Merchants Company and the United Dry Goods Companies, had reorganized in 1916 to form Associated Dry Goods. Their core businesses were Lord & Taylor in New York, Hahne's in Newark, and Hengerer's in Buffalo. This company bought out numerous family-owned stores: J. W. Robinson (Los Angeles, 1955); Sibley's (Rochester, 1957); Pogue's (Cincinnati, 1961); Goldwater's (Phoenix, 1962); Stix, Baer (St. Louis, 1963); Denver Dry Goods (1965); Horne's (Pittsburgh, 1966); and Ayres (Indianapolis, 1972). Associated also created Robinson's in Florida in the 1970s.

But the 1970s were a difficult time for the US economy. High inflation eroded earning

power while incomes stagnated. This drove people away from the department stores and into the arms of discounters and specialty retailers. May got on the bandwagon with Venture Stores, as did Associated with Caldor and Loehmann's. May also became heavily involved in the development and management of regional mall shopping centers. In 1979 it acquired the Volume Shoe Corporation (now Payless ShoeSource).

The corporate restructuring that swept America in the 1980s affected the big retailers as well; in 1986 May bought Associated. In 1988 May also bought Foley's (Houston) and Filene's (Boston) from Federated Department Stores (when Federated was acquired by Campeau). May consolidated, closed, sold, or spun off operations (Caldor and Venture are now public companies). In late 1990 May bought Thalhimers from Carter Hawley Hale (now Broadway Stores).

To help control marketing and administrative expenses, May consolidated L. S. Ayres with Famous-Barr in 1991 and Thalhimers with Hecht's in early 1992.

In 1994 May expanded its discount shoe operations with the purchase of 550 stores from 2 Columbus, Ohio, chains (Kobacker Company and the Shoe Works). The company also added Payless Kids stores next to existing Payless ShoeSource stores. Also in 1994 May began talks with Mercantile Stores to acquire the Fairfield, Ohio–based department store company, but the 2 sides could not reach an agreement.

In 1995 May and J. C. Penney outbid Federated Department Stores for stores being sold by bankrupt Washington, DC–based retailer Woodward & Lothrop. May came away with 14 stores in Philadelphia and 3 in Washington.

NYSE symbol: MA
Fiscal year ends: Saturday nearest January 31

Chairman and CEO: David C. Farrell, age 61,
$1,632,820 pay
Deputy Chairman: Thomas A. Hays, age 62,
$1,197,386 pay
VC: Richard L. Battram, age 60, $889,338 pay
President and CFO: Jerome T. Loeb, age 54,
$1,012,307 pay
President and CEO, May Merchandising Co.: Anthony J.
Torcasio, age 49, $695,314 pay
EVP and General Counsel: Louis J. Garr Jr., age 55
EVP Real Estate: R. Dean Wolfe, age 51
SVP Strategic Planning: William D. Edkins, age 42
SVP Planning and Reporting: Lonny J. Jay, age 53
SVP and Treasurer: Jan R. Kniffen, age 46
SVP Data Processing: John F. Danahy
SVP Customer Service and Operations: James F.
Harner
SVP Human Resources: Douglas J. Giles
VP, Secretary, and Senior Counsel: Richard A. Brickson,
age 47
VP Taxes: Martin M. Doerr, age 40
VP Accounting and Reporting: Andrew T. Hall, age 34
VP Corporate Communications: James Abrams
VP Merchandise and Consumer Research: Laurence M.
Hellman
Auditors: Arthur Andersen & Co, SC

WHERE

HQ: The May Department Stores Company,
611 Olive St., St. Louis, MO 63101
Phone: 314-342-6300
Fax: 314-342-4461

May operates 314 upmarket department stores in 29
states and Washington, DC. Payless ShoeSource has
4,435 stores in 49 states and Washington, DC, and in
Puerto Rico and the Virgin Islands.

WHAT

	1995 Sales	1995 Stores
	$ mil.	No.
Payless ShoeSource (Topeka)	2,116	4,435
Foley's (Houston)	1,633	49
Robinsons-May (Los Angeles)	1,494	52
Lord & Taylor (New York)	1,452	54
Hecht's (Washington, DC)	1,423	45
Kaufmann's (Pittsburgh)	1,303	40
Filene's (Boston)	1,162	36
Famous-Barr (St. Louis)	947	30
Meier & Frank (Portland, OR)	347	8
Adjustments	346	—
Total	**12,223**	**4,749**

	1995 Sales		1995 Operating Income	
	$ mil.	% of total	$ mil.	% of total
Department stores	9,761	80	1,400	86
Payless ShoeSource	2,116	20	219	14
Adjustments	346	—	—	—
Total	**12,223**	**100**	**1,619**	**100**

KEY COMPETITORS

Ames	Melville
Benetton	Men's Wearhouse
Broadway Stores	Mercantile Stores
Brown Group	Montgomery Ward
Dayton Hudson	Nine West
Dillard	Nordstrom
Edison Brothers	Saks
Federated	Sears
The Gap	Service Merchandise
Harcourt General	Shoe Carnival
INTERCO	Spiegel
J. C. Penney	Stein Mart
Jos. A. Bank	Talbot's
Lands' End	TJX
The Limited	Toys "R" Us
L.L. Bean	Woolworth

HOW MUCH

	9-Year Growth	1986	1987	1988	1989	1990	1991	1992	1993	1994	1995
Sales ($ mil.)	2.8%	9,542	10,376	10,581	11,742	9,602	10,066	10,615	11,150	11,529	12,223
Net income ($ mil.)	9.4%	347	381	444	534	498	500	515	603	711	782
Income as % of sales	—	3.6%	3.7%	4.2%	4.5%	5.2%	5.0%	4.9%	5.4%	6.2%	6.4%
Earnings per share ($)	11.5%	1.10	1.22	1.45	1.82	1.76	1.87	1.94	2.26	2.65	2.92
Stock price – high ($)[1]	—	16.25	22.06	25.44	20.00	26.31	29.56	30.19	37.25	46.50	45.13
Stock price – low ($)[1]	—	9.53	15.00	11.13	14.38	17.31	18.81	18.69	25.81	33.38	32.25
Stock price – close ($)[1]	8.9%	15.63	17.75	14.56	18.13	23.94	21.38	26.25	35.31	39.38	33.75
P/E – high	—	15	18	18	11	15	16	16	17	18	15
P/E – low	—	9	12	8	8	10	10	10	11	13	11
Dividends per share ($)	9.5%	0.46	0.51	0.56	0.63	0.70	0.77	0.81	0.83	0.90	1.04
Book value per share ($)	8.0%	8.31	8.50	9.13	11.11	9.32	10.04	11.26	12.88	14.55	16.65
Employees	4.6%	79,500	151,700	143,000	152,000	115,000	116,000	115,000	111,000	113,000	119,000

1995 Year-end:
Debt ratio: 42.4%
Return on equity: 20.1%
Cash (mil.): $55
Current ratio: 2.59
Long-term debt (mil.): $2,875
No. of shares (mil.): 248
Dividends
  Yield: 3.1%
  Payout: 35.6%
Market value (mil.): $8,384

**Stock Price History[1]
High/Low 1986–95**

[1] Stock prices are for the prior calendar year.

MAYTAG CORPORATION

OVERVIEW

Who wants the baby boomers to buy before they get old? Maytag, for one. The Newton, Iowa–based manufacturer is counting on the aging, affluent members of the post-WWII generation to replace older home appliances with new, high-end Maytag models. Results in 1994 suggest that it's a solid strategy, as shipments of premium Maytag and Jenn-Air brand appliances grew twice as fast as the company's total sales.

Maytag is the 4th largest US manufacturer of large appliances such as ovens, dishwashers, refrigerators, and washing machines; its midprice brand names include Magic Chef and Admiral. Hoover, the top brand of vacuum cleaners, belongs to Maytag, as does Dixie-Narco, a maker of vending machines and equipment.

About 80% of Maytag's 1994 sales came from its North American Appliance Group. In late 1994 the manufacturer sold Hoover Australia to Southcorp Holdings for $84 million. And although Maytag's Hoover Europe unit had its first profit in 5 years in 1994, the company sold it to Italy's Candy for $170 million in 1995. Also in 1995 Maytag began implementing a unified regional distribution network in the US to speed up product delivery.

WHEN

In 1893 F. L. Maytag and 3 associates formed the Parsons Bandcutter and Self Feeder Company in Newton, Iowa, to manufacture feeder attachments for grain threshing machines. In 1903 the firm changed its name to the Maytag Co. In 1907 Maytag produced its first washing machine, a hand-cranked wooden tub model. At about the same time, F. L. Maytag became sole owner of the firm. The company introduced a washer with an electric motor in 1911, brought out a gasoline-powered washer in 1914, and in 1919 cast the first aluminum washer tub. L. B. Maytag, son of F. L. and president of the company from 1920 to 1926, along with Howard Snyder, head of Maytag's development department, designed and produced the first vaned agitator washer in 1922. The agitator washer was very successful, and Maytag concentrated on washing machine production, producing one million by 1927.

In 1925 the company's stock began trading on the NYSE. In 1929 Maytag's earnings reached a prewar high of $6.8 million on sales of $25.6 million. The company survived the Great Depression without a loss. During the war years, 1941 to 1945, Maytag suspended production of washers and made components for military airplanes.

In 1949 the company built a 2nd plant to produce a new line of automatic washing machines. During the Korean War Maytag built tank parts and other military hardware while continuing production of washers. Clothes dryers went into production in 1953. In the late 1950s Maytag began to make products for the commercial laundry field. In 1966 the company entered the kitchen appliance field, introducing dishwashers and, in 1968, food waste disposers.

Maytag expanded in the 1980s, purchasing Hardwick Stove and Jenn-Air (cooking appliances) in 1981 and the Magic Chef group of companies, including Magic Chef, Toastmaster, Admiral, and Dixie-Narco (a vending machine manufacturer), in 1986. The company sold Toastmaster in 1987 and in 1988 consolidated Admiral into the company's other divisions. Maytag sold Magic Chef air conditioning (1988) and bought Chicago Pacific (furniture manufacturing and Hoover appliances, 1989) for $960 million, doubling Maytag's debt. The company sold the furniture companies to Ladd Furniture for $213.4 million (1989), retaining Hoover. In 1989 the company introduced its first line of Maytag brand refrigerators.

Heavy debt, recession, and tough competition all contributed to Maytag's declining profits between 1988 and 1992. After a weak 1990 showing in its European markets, Maytag consolidated its European operations. It also forged an alliance with Bosch-Siemens Hausgeräte GmbH in hopes of improving its market share.

In 1993 a UK promotion offering free airline tickets to Hoover buyers resulted in nearly 200,000 consumers seeking tickets ($49 million beyond what had been budgeted). Maytag fired its Hoover UK managing director (and president of Hoover Europe) and reviewed its European operations, cutting nearly 40% of its work force, replacing most of its management team, and closing a French plant.

Maytag plans to unveil an energy-efficient, horizontal-axis washer in 1996 on the heels of its new TimeSavor oven (which combines aspects of conventional and microwave ovens) and IntelliSense dishwasher (which measures how much washing each load needs).

NYSE symbol: MYG
Fiscal year ends: December 31

WHO

Chairman and CEO: Leonard A. Hadley, age 60, $1,068,800 pay
EVP; President, North American Appliance Group: Joseph F. Fogliano, age 55, $640,594 pay
EVP and CFO: John P. Cunningham Jr., age 57, $550,225 pay
SVP Planning and Business Development: Carleton F. Zacheis, age 61, $275,889 pay
SVP Human Resources: Jon O. Nicholas, age 55
VP and General Counsel: Edward H. Graham, age 59, $281,344 pay
VP, Controller, and Chief Accounting Officer: Mark A. Garth, age 35
VP and Treasurer: David D. Urbani, age 50
VP Public Affairs: Janis C. Cooper
VP Technology: John H. Jansen
Auditors: Ernst & Young LLP

WHERE

HQ: 403 W. Fourth St. North, Newton, IA 50208
Phone: 515-792-8000
Fax: 515-791-8395

Maytag has manufacturing operations in Illinois, Indiana, Iowa, Ohio, South Carolina, Tennessee, and Texas. The company also has facilities in Canada, Mexico, Portugal, and the UK.

	1994 Sales		1994 Pretax Income	
	$ mil.	% of total	$ mil.	% of total
North America	2,832	84	343	96
Europe	399	12	0	0
Other countries	142	4	13	4
Adjustments	—	—	(115)	—
Total	**3,373**	**100**	**241**	**100**

WHAT

	1994 Sales		1994 Pretax Income	
	$ mil.	% of total	$ mil.	% of total
Home appliances	3,181	94	334	94
Vending equipment	192	6	22	6
Adjustments	—	—	(115)	—
Total	**3,373**	**100**	**241**	**100**

Home Appliances
Admiral (midrange and private-label laundry equipment, dishwashers, refrigerators, and cooking appliances)
Hoover North America (vacuum cleaners, utility cleaners, floor polishers, and shampooers)
Jenn-Air (high-end cooking appliances, dishwashers, and refrigerators)
Magic Chef (midrange and private-label cooking appliances, refrigerators, dishwashers, laundry equipment, and microwave ovens)
Maytag (high-end laundry equipment, dishwashers, refrigerators, and cooking appliances)

Vending Equipment
Dixie-Narco, Inc.

Other Businesses
Maytag Customer Service (service and parts distribution)
Maytag International Inc. (international marketing)

KEY COMPETITORS

Amway	Figgie Intl.	Royal Appliance
Berkshire	General Electric	Sanyo
Hathaway	Hitachi	Sharp
Black & Decker	HMI Industries	Siemens
Daimler-Benz	Raytheon	Toshiba
AB Electrolux	Robert Bosch	Whirlpool

HOW MUCH

	9-Year Growth	1985	1986	1987	1988	1989	1990	1991	1992	1993	1994
Sales ($ mil.)	19.4%	684	1,724	1,909	1,886	3,089	3,057	2,971	3,041	2,987	3,373
Net income ($ mil.)	8.6%	72	117	153	159	132	99	79	(8)	51	151
Income as % of sales	—	10.5%	6.8%	8.0%	8.4%	4.3%	3.2%	2.7%	—	1.7%	4.5%
Earnings per share ($)	(6.7%)	2.65	1.35	1.91	2.07	1.27	0.94	0.75	(0.08)	0.48	1.42
Stock price – high ($)	—	19.94	27.44	32.31	27.63	26.75	20.63	16.50	20.63	18.63	20.13
Stock price – low ($)	—	10.88	18.00	17.00	18.88	18.88	9.88	10.38	12.50	13.00	14.00
Stock price – close ($)	(2.9%)	19.47	23.63	22.38	19.38	19.50	10.63	15.38	14.88	18.00	15.00
P/E – high	—	8	20	17	13	21	22	22	—	39	14
P/E – low	—	4	13	9	9	15	11	14	—	27	10
Dividends per share ($)	(12.4%)	1.65	0.85	0.95	0.98	0.95	0.95	0.50	0.50	0.50	0.50
Book value per share ($)	4.2%	4.72	6.53	5.43	6.55	8.89	9.60	9.50	5.62	5.50	6.82
Employees	16.6%	4,930	12,205	13,072	12,913	26,019	24,000	22,533	21,407	20,951	19,604

1994 Year-end:
Debt ratio: 50.7%
Return on equity: 22.9%
Cash (mil.): $110
Current ratio: 2.11
Long-term debt (mil.): $663
No. of shares (mil.): 107
Dividends
  Yield: 3.3%
  Payout: 35.2%
Market value (mil.): $1,610

**Stock Price History
High/Low 1985–94**

MCDERMOTT INTERNATIONAL, INC.

OVERVIEW

It's forward to the past for McDermott International, which in 1995 revived its original name, J. Ray McDermott. In a sweeping reorganization the company consolidated all its marine construction operations into a wholly-owned subsidiary, J. Ray McDermott, and then merged the new company with Offshore Pipeline, Inc., which will change its name.

The new company, of which McDermott International owns 61%, is the largest marine construction company in the world, with a market share of over 50%.

Prospects for the company's other operations (power generation facilities and equipment, nuclear submarine services, and

shipbuilding), which had seemed so bleak a few years ago, are looking up. To meet greater demand for new power sources, the company is leveraging its nuclear submarine technology into new power-storage applications. Also, the aging of the world's commercial fleet may mean a renaissance for the shipbuilding industry. The company is also expanding its land-based construction operations; in 1994 it was awarded the contract for a new paper and pulp mill, to be built for Domtar, a Canadian forest products company. To cut its risk and reduce its costs, McDermott is pursuing many of these opportunities within the framework of alliances and joint ventures.

WHEN

In 1923, when R. Thomas McDermott won a contract to supply drilling rigs to a Texas wildcatter, he started a new company, J. Ray McDermott & Co., named after his father. In the 1930s the oil industry expanded to Louisiana, and the McDermotts followed, making New Orleans their headquarters. When the company incorporated in 1946, it supplied services for oil and natural gas production.

After WWII McDermott became a pioneer in the construction of offshore drilling platforms. Spurred by increased demand for oil in the 1960s and by the price rises of the 1970s, the company's offshore business boomed. McDermott also supplied the US Navy and the salvage and subsea markets.

By 1978, when 86% of revenues were from marine construction, McDermott had diversified into other energy areas, buying Babcock & Wilcox, which manufactured energy generation equipment and provided maintenance, repair, and other services. In 1980 the company became McDermott Inc., and in 1983, McDermott International.

Babcock & Wilcox (B&W) started as a boilermaker in 1867 when Stephen Wilcox and George Babcock patented an improved boiler. B&W built the boilers for the US's first 2 electrical stations. It incorporated in 1881. In 1889 B&W began building marine boilers and formed a relationship with the US Navy. B&W supplied 75% of major US military vessels' boilers in WWII. After the war B&W focused on nuclear energy, building the reactor for the first nuclear-powered merchant ship. In the 1950s B&W made significant contributions to the navy's nuclear program and then branched into nuclear power plants and waste-disposal and emission-control systems.

In 1978 the combination of McDermott and B&W seemed ideal: oil and gas services, as well as electrical and nuclear energy generation. Then came the oil gluts of the 1980s, the price collapse of 1986, and reduced demand for exploration equipment. Like much of corporate America, McDermott wandered into the recession of the late 1980s ingrown, sales-oriented, and unprepared for a fast-changing world.

Between 1979 and 1988 McDermott's work force shrank by 57%, and a number of plants were closed or sold. The company sold its insulating, controls, trading, and seamless tube production operations between 1988 and 1990.

Rescuing the company from its financial free fall in the late 1980s required radical strategies. When Robert Howson took over as chairman in 1988, he consolidated operations, focusing on McDermott's core businesses and reducing the company's debt. McDermott went into joint ventures (for the first time) with some of its biggest foreign competitors, such as French giant EPTM.

Diversification was another strategy, with the company taking on profitable smaller-scale projects (e.g., components for bridge girders and water mains) as opposed to keeping a single focus on the giant, often loss-making power plant constructions of the past.

In 1994 Offshore Pipeline proposed an alliance to McDermott, which resulted in the merger that made the new company a formidable world power in marine construction. The next year the company completed its acquisition of Delta Catalytic Corp., a construction company that provides McDermott with footing on dry land. In the field of energy the company is targeting developing countries and focusing on pollution control in the US.

NYSE symbol: MDR
Fiscal year ends: March 31

Chairman and CEO: Robert E. Howson, age 63,
$1,109,278 pay
President and COO, J. Ray McDermott, SA: James J.
Wildasin, age 60, $474,306 pay
**EVP and Chief Project Management Officer; President,
Babcock & Wilcox Government Group:** Joe J. Stewart,
age 57, $458,863 pay
**EVP and CFO; President, Engineering and
Construction Group:** Brock A. Hattox, age 47,
$409,775 pay
EVP and Chief Administrative Officer: Richard E.
Woolbert, age 61, $378,633 pay
SVP, General Counsel, and Secretary: Lawrence R.
Purtell, age 48
SVP and Chief Technical Officer: Edgar A.
Womack Jr., age 52
Director Human Resources: L. J. Sannino
Auditors: Ernst & Young LLP

WHERE

HQ: 1450 Poydras St., New Orleans, LA 70112-6050
Phone: 504-587-5400
Fax: 504-587-6433

McDermott's power generation equipment and marine
services are sold worldwide.

	1995 Sales		1995 Operating Income	
	$ mil.	% of total	$ mil.	% of total
US	1,500	49	(39)	—
Canada	740	25	28	26
Europe & Africa	349	11	30	28
Far East	326	11	39	36
Middle East	129	4	11	10
Other regions	0	0	(4)	—
Total	**3,044**	**100**	**65**	**100**

WHAT

	1995 Sales		1995 Operating Income	
	$ mil.	% of total	$ mil.	% of total
Power systems	1,663	54	21	32
Marine construction services	1,391	46	44	68
Adjustments	(10)	—	—	—
Total	**3,044**	**100**	**65**	**100**

Power Generation Systems and Equipment
Air-cooled heat exchangers
Nuclear fuel assemblies
Nuclear reactor components
Pollution control systems
Process recovery boilers
Utility plant construction and repair

Marine Construction Services
Construction of petrochemical, gas, and mineral plants
Engineering services
Marine pipelines
Offshore platforms
Shipyard operation
Vessel chartering operations

Selected Operations
Babcock & Wilcox Government Group
Babcock & Wilcox Power Generation Group
Engineering and Construction Group
J. Ray McDermott, SA (61%)
Technical and Shipbuilding Operations

KEY COMPETITORS

ABB	Fluor	Rolls-Royce
Alcatel Alsthom	General Electric	Schlumberger
Ashland, Inc.	Halliburton	Westinghouse
Baker Hughes	Michael Baker	WMX
Bechtel	Morrison Knudsen	Technologies
Dresser	Parsons	
Duke Power	Peter Kiewit Sons'	

HOW MUCH

	9-Year Growth	1986	1987	1988	1989	1990	1991	1992	1993	1994	1995
Sales ($ mil.)	(0.7%)	3,257	3,289	2,352	2,423	2,645	3,136	3,525	3,173	3,060	3,044
Net income ($ mil.)	(16.5%)	56	(133)	(266)	(144)	(10)	(70)	77	67	90	11
Income as % of sales	—	1.7%	—	—	—	—	—	2.2%	2.1%	2.9%	0.4%
Earnings per share ($)	(31.6%)	1.52	(3.60)	(7.16)	(3.88)	(0.27)	(1.58)	1.67	1.29	1.57	0.05
Stock price – high ($)[1]	—	30.13	23.38	33.13	21.50	26.25	34.50	28.50	26.00	32.88	27.50
Stock price – low ($)[1]	—	16.38	13.63	13.00	13.75	14.63	21.63	15.25	16.00	22.25	19.38
Stock price – close ($)[1]	3.4%	18.25	21.75	14.75	14.75	23.13	24.63	17.13	23.13	26.50	24.75
P/E – high	—	20	—	—	—	—	—	17	20	21	—
P/E – low	—	11	—	—	—	—	—	9	12	14	—
Dividends per share ($)	(6.3%)	1.80	1.80	1.80	1.60	1.00	1.00	1.00	1.00	1.00	1.00
Book value per share ($)	(9.6%)	32.57	27.94	19.95	16.00	15.25	12.88	13.71	8.82	10.09	13.12
Employees	(3.6%)	35,000	29,000	26,000	28,000	30,000	34,000	29,500	26,000	23,000	25,200

1995 Year-end:
Debt ratio: 44.9%
Return on equity: 1.7%
Cash (mil.): $219
Current ratio: 0.97
Long-term debt (mil.): $579
No. of shares (mil.): 54
Dividends
  Yield: 4.0%
  Payout: —
Market value (mil.): $1,336

**Stock Price History[1]
High/Low 1986–95**

[1]Stock prices are for the prior calendar year.

MCDONALD'S CORPORATION

OVERVIEW

If old McDonald had this farm, he'd be singing M-O-N-E-Y. Based in Oak Brook, Illinois, McDonald's is the largest global food service retailer and the US's most profitable retailer over the past decade. The company's brand name is the world's 2nd most recognized (after Coca-Cola).

McDonald's operates more than 15,000 restaurants (2nd only to PepsiCo) and has a 21% share of the US fast-food restaurant business. It has responded to the competitive US fast-food marketplace by redesigning its menus to stress value and choice. An annual advertising budget of over $1.4 billion keeps product awareness high, while movie tie-ins (including

one with *Batman Forever* in 1995) and video offerings add merchandising to the mix.

With profits in the US climbing slowly, McDonald's continues to look abroad for growth. It plans to open between 1,200 and 1,500 new restaurants in 1995, most outside the US, where less competition, lighter market saturation, and high name recognition have already brought success. The company's overseas restaurants (a little more than 1/3 of its total) account for half its profits.

The company and its affiliates operate only about 30% of all McDonald's restaurants. Franchisees control the rest under agreements that generally last 20 years.

WHEN

The first McDonald's opened in 1948 in San Bernardino, California. In 1954 owners Dick and Mac McDonald signed a franchise agreement with 52-year-old Ray Kroc (a malt machine salesman). A year later Kroc opened his first restaurant in Des Plaines, Illinois. By 1957 Kroc was operating 14 McDonald's restaurants in Illinois, Indiana, and California. The company sold its 100 millionth hamburger in 1958 and opened its 100th restaurant in 1959. Kroc bought out the McDonald brothers for $2.7 million in 1961.

In 1962 McDonald's adopted the golden arches as its company trademark. The company served its billionth hamburger live on the "Art Linkletter Show" in 1963. Ronald McDonald made his debut that year, as did the company's first new menu item — the Filet-O-Fish sandwich. In 1965 McDonald's went public, and Kroc ran the first McDonald's TV ads. In 1967 the company opened its first stores outside the US (in Canada).

In 1968 McDonald's added the Big Mac to its menu and opened its 1,000th restaurant. The company's advertising began featuring the slogan "You deserve a break today — so get up and get away to McDonald's" in 1970.

During the 1970s McDonald's grew at the rate of about 500 restaurants per year. New menu items included the Quarter Pounder (1972), the Egg McMuffin (pioneering breakfast fast food, 1973), and Happy Meals (1979). The first Ronald McDonald House (residence for families of hospitalized children) opened in 1974. That year Fred Turner, longtime operations chief and Kroc protégé, was named CEO. (Turner became chairman in 1977, with Kroc staying on as senior chairman until his death in 1984.) In 1975, the year the drive-thru ap-

peared, McDonald's formed the National Operators Advisory Board (NOAB) in response to operators unhappy with the franchising system. (NOAB gave some power back to them.) By 1978 McDonald's had over 5,000 restaurants, with sales exceeding $3 billion.

After introducing Chicken McNuggets in 1983, McDonald's became the first fast-food chain to provide customers with a list of its products' ingredients (1986). In 1987 it started serving salads, and in 1989 McDonald's served its 75 billionth hamburger.

At the end of the 1980s, growing competition in the domestic market slowed the company's US sales growth to about 5% per year. McDonald's responded by adding "value menus" and the unsuccessful McLean Deluxe, a low-fat hamburger (1991). Franchisees were also granted leeway to experiment with decor and new menu items.

In 1993 McDonald's opened its first restaurants inside Wal-Mart stores, an experimental joint venture between the 2 US business giants. By 1994 more than 30 Wal-Marts shared space with McDonald's.

Also in 1994 Hospitality Franchise Systems, which operates Days Inn, Ramada, and Howard Johnson hotels, among others, joined with McDonald's to test fast-food deliveries to 40 hotels in 20 cities. That same year a jury awarded Stella Liebeck about $2.7 million after she sued McDonald's for severe burns she received when she spilled hot coffee on herself. The award was later reduced to less than $600,000 following a settlement.

In 1995 McDonald's announced plans to open its first restaurants in India. Menus will include chicken and fish sandwiches and vegetable nuggets but no beef.

NYSE symbol: MCD
Fiscal year ends: December 31

WHO

Senior Chairman: Fred L. Turner, age 62
Chairman and CEO: Michael R. Quinlan, age 51,
$1,948,875 pay
VC and CFO: Jack M. Greenberg, age 53, $1,142,353 pay
President and CEO, USA: Edward H. Rensi, age 51,
$1,196,837 pay
President and CEO, International: James R. Cantalupo,
age 52, $1,183,219 pay
SEVP and Chief Marketing Officer: Paul D. Schrage,
age 60, $755,872 pay
EVP and Chief Operations Officer: Thomas W. Glasgow
Jr., age 48
SVP, General Counsel, and Secretary: Shelby Yastrow
SVP (Personnel): Stanley R. Stein
Auditors: Ernst & Young LLP

WHERE

HQ: McDonald's Plaza, Oak Brook, IL 60521
Phone: 708-575-3000
Fax: 708-575-3392 (Stockholder Relations)

McDonald's has restaurants in 79 countries.

	1994 No. of Restaurants
US	9,744
Japan	1,133
Canada	717
Germany	570
England	526
Australia	454
France	350
Brazil	149
The Netherlands	110
Mexico	102
Other countries	1,350
Total	**15,205**

	1994 Sales		1994 Operating Income	
	$ mil.	% of total	$ mil.	% of total
US	4,155	50	1,130	50
Europe/Africa/ Middle East	2,605	31	672	30
Asia/Pacific	731	9	243	11
Canada	546	7	117	5
Latin America	284	3	79	4
Total	**8,321**	**100**	**2,241**	**100**

WHAT

	1994 Restaurants	
	No.	% of total
Operated by franchisees	10,458	69
Operated by the company	3,083	20
Operated by affiliates	1,664	11
Total	**15,205**	**100**

	1994 Sales	
	$ mil.	% of total
Company restaurants	5,793	70
Fees from franchised restaurants	2,528	30
Total	**8,321**	**100**

Major Products

Big Mac	French fries
Chicken McNuggets	Milkshakes
Egg McMuffin	Quarter Pounder
Filet-O-Fish	Salads

KEY COMPETITORS

Blimpie	Grand	Shoney's
Checkers	Metropolitan	Sonic Corp.
Drive-In	Imasco	Subway
CKE Restaurants	Krystal	Tennessee
Dairy Queen	Little Caesars	Restaurant
Domino's Pizza	PepsiCo	Triarc
Flagstar	Rally's	Wendy's
Foodmaker	ShowBiz Pizza	Whataburger

HOW MUCH

	9-Year Growth	1985	1986	1987	1988	1989	1990	1991	1992	1993	1994
Sales ($ mil.)	9.4%	3,695	4,144	4,894	5,566	6,142	6,640	6,695	7,133	7,408	8,321
Net income ($ mil.)	12.2%	433	480	549	646	727	802	860	959	1,083	1,224
Income as % of sales	—	11.7%	11.6%	11.2%	11.6%	11.8%	12.1%	12.8%	13.4%	14.6%	14.7%
Earnings per share ($)	13.0%	0.56	0.63	0.73	0.86	0.98	1.10	1.18	1.30	1.46	1.68
Stock price – high ($)	—	9.09	12.80	15.28	12.75	17.44	19.25	19.94	25.19	29.56	31.38
Stock price – low ($)	—	5.69	8.13	7.84	10.19	11.50	12.50	13.06	19.13	22.75	25.56
Stock price – close ($)	14.0%	9.00	10.16	11.00	12.03	17.25	14.56	19.00	24.38	28.50	29.25
P/E – high	—	16	20	21	15	18	18	17	19	20	19
P/E – low	—	10	13	11	12	12	11	11	15	16	15
Dividends per share ($)	9.7%	0.10	0.11	0.12	0.14	0.16	0.17	0.18	0.20	0.21	0.23
Book value per share ($)	13.6%	2.84	3.22	3.86	4.54	4.63	5.55	6.33	7.30	7.91	8.95
Employees	2.4%	148,000	159,000	159,000	169,000	176,000	174,000	168,000	166,000	169,000	183,000

1994 Year-end:
Debt ratio: 41.2%
Return on equity: 20.7%
Cash (mil.): $180
Current ratio: 0.30
Long-term debt (mil.): $2,935
No. of shares (mil.): 694
Dividends
  Yield: 0.8%
  Payout: 13.7%
Market value (mil.): $20,291

**Stock Price History
High/Low 1985–94**

MCDONNELL DOUGLAS CORPORATION

OVERVIEW

McDonnell Douglas has a new pilot these days, but his license doesn't say McDonnell or Douglas. Harry Stonecipher became the first non-family member to run the St. Louis–based aerospace company when he became CEO in 1994. McDonnell Douglas is the world's 3rd largest maker of commercial airplanes (after Boeing and Airbus), and it fell to #2 among US defense contractors in 1995 after the merger of Lockheed and Martin Marietta.

The company remains the world's #1 maker of military aircraft. Among its products are the F/A-18 Hornet, the F-15 Eagle, and the AV-8B Harrier II Plus. It also makes the C-17 transport plane. However, the C-17 has suffered cost overruns, and the Pentagon will decide in late 1995 whether it will extend the contract.

The company's commercial aircraft unit builds MD-80s, MD-90s, and MD-11s. Its missile, space, and electronics unit's projects include components for space station *Alpha* and Delta launch vehicles.

Stonecipher replaces John McDonnell, who stepped down as CEO but remains chairman. McDonnell had spent the last few years slashing costs by closing plants and cutting employment. With the company now sporting healthy profits, Stonecipher is focusing on building its commercial aircraft business, taking orders for the MD-95, a proposed 100-seat jet for short- and medium-range flights. He has also not ruled out a possible merger with a defense rival in this era of defense contractor consolidation.

WHEN

Donald Douglas started the Davis-Douglas Company in the back of a Los Angeles barbershop in 1920 to build the Cloudster biplane for David Davis, who planned to fly it in the first nonstop transcontinental flight in 1921. When the attempt failed, Davis left the firm, which then became the Douglas Company. Many records were set in Douglas airplanes, including the first round-the-world flight (in 1924 by the US Army). The company was renamed Douglas Aircraft in 1928.

In 1935 Douglas introduced the twin-engine DC-3 airliner. Fast, rugged, and economical, the legendary DC-3 revolutionized air travel, and the company built more than 10,000 as military transports during WWII. Douglas also built attack aircraft, such as the Dauntless dive bomber.

The DC-3 and its descendants enabled Douglas to dominate the airliner market until the advent of the Boeing 707 jetliner in the late 1950s. The DC-8 (1958) proved unable to compete with the 707, but the smaller DC-9 (1965) became Douglas's top seller and one of the world's most popular airliners.

Despite the DC-9's success, its development costs and slow sales of the DC-8 resulted in losses in 1966, leading Douglas to invite merger proposals from healthier companies. McDonnell Aircraft made the winning offer of $68.7 million in 1967.

James McDonnell had started his company in 1939 mainly as a supplier of aircraft parts. A series of fighters included the US Navy's first jet, the FH-1 (1945), and culminated in the F-4 Phantom II (1958). Like Douglas, which produced an upper stage for the Saturn moon rocket (1961) as well as the Delta expendable launch vehicle (1960), McDonnell also built missiles and spacecraft, including the Mercury and Gemini capsules of the early 1960s.

After the merger the new McDonnell Douglas Corporation produced the DC-10 airliner (1970), Skylab (1973), and fighter/attack aircraft (F-15, 1972; F/A-18, 1978; AV-8B, 1978). With the 1984 purchase of Hughes Helicopter, the company inherited production of the AH-64 Apache attack helicopter.

Although orders for airliners hit record levels in 1988 and 1989, the transport segment of McDonnell Douglas in 1989 endured a $222 million loss because of a reorganization and a production buildup for the MD-80 and the MD-11. In 1991 the company announced a plan to sell 40% of its commercial aircraft business to Taiwan Aerospace to provide capital for developing the MD-12, a double-deck jumbo jet, but the deal fell through in 1992.

The company's military aircraft business got a boost in 1993 when Switzerland ordered 34 F/A-18s (valued at $2.5 billion) and in 1994 when Israel ordered 20 F-15s (valued at $2 billion). Also in 1994 McDonnell Douglas won a $400 million contract to launch 40 satellites for the Iridium system, a project led by Motorola that will provide worldwide mobile phone service.

With production of the Tomahawk cruise missile winding down, the company announced in 1995 that it would close its Titusville, Florida, plant and lay off about 1,000 workers by the end of the year.

WHO

Chairman: John F. McDonnell, age 56, $1,105,485 pay
President and CEO: Harry C. Stonecipher, age 58, $206,250 pay
President, McDonnell Douglas Aerospace: John P. Capellupo, age 60, $653,269 pay
President, Douglas Aircraft Company: Robert H. Hood Jr., age 62, $628,071 pay
EVP and CFO: Herbert J. Lanese, age 49, $642,493 pay
EVP: Kenneth A. Francis, age 61
SVP Space and Defense Systems: Willard P. Olson, age 55
SVP New Aircraft and Missile Products: James M. Sinnett, age 55
SVP and C-17 Program Manager: Donald R. Kozlowski, age 57
SVP Administration and General Counsel: F. Mark Kuhlmann, age 46
SVP Total Quality Management: James H. MacDonald, age 58
SVP Washington Operations: Stanley Ebner, age 61
VP Human Resources: Laurie A. Broedling, age 49
Auditors: Ernst & Young LLP

WHERE

HQ: PO Box 516, St. Louis, MO 63166-0516
Phone: 314-232-0232
Fax: 314-234-3826

McDonnell Douglas conducts principal operations in 6 states and Canada.

	1994 Sales	
	$ mil.	% of total
US	8,941	68
Other countries	4,235	32
Total	**13,176**	**100**

WHAT

	1994 Sales		1994 Operating Income	
	$ mil.	% of total	$ mil.	% of total
Military aircraft	7,804	59	708	66
Commercial aircraft	3,155	24	47	4
Missiles, space & electronic sys.	1,877	14	262	25
Financial services & other	340	3	50	5
Total	**13,176**	**100**	**1,067**	**100**

Military Aircraft
AH-64 Apache
AV-8B Harrier II
C-17 Globemaster III
F-15 Eagle
F/A-18 Hornet
MD 500 (helicopter)
MD Explorer (helicopter)
T-45 Training System

Commercial Aircraft
MD-11 (trijet)
MD-80 and MD-90 (twin jet)

Missiles, Space, and Electronic Systems
Delta rockets
Harpoon/Standoff Land Attack Missiles (SLAM)
Mast Mounted Sight (targeting system)
Space station *Alpha* components
Tomahawk missiles

KEY COMPETITORS

Airbus
AlliedSignal
Boeing
British Aerospace
Daimler-Benz
FlightSafety
General Dynamics
General Electric
General Motors
GM Hughes Electronics
Harris Corp.
Honeywell
Koor
Lockheed Martin
Loral
Nissan
Northrop Grumman
Orbital Sciences
Raytheon
Rockwell
Siemens
Textron
Thomson SA
Thorn EMI
United Technologies

HOW MUCH

	9-Year Growth	1985	1986	1987	1988	1989	1990	1991	1992	1993	1994
Sales ($ mil.)	1.5%	11,478	12,661	13,146	15,072	14,589	16,255	18,448	17,384	14,487	13,176
Net income ($ mil.)	6.3%	346	278	313	350	40	306	423	755	396	598
Income as % of sales	—	3.0%	2.2%	2.4%	2.3%	0.3%	1.9%	2.3%	4.3%	2.7%	4.5%
Earnings per share ($)	6.5%	2.86	2.28	2.58	3.04	0.35	2.66	3.67	6.47	3.36	5.05
Stock price – high ($)	—	28.97	30.34	26.93	26.43	31.47	21.19	26.81	25.97	39.42	48.53
Stock price – low ($)	—	21.40	23.64	13.65	19.65	19.86	11.32	8.82	11.41	16.15	34.13
Stock price – close ($)	7.5%	24.73	23.73	19.81	25.06	20.40	12.95	24.39	16.07	35.63	47.29
P/E – high	—	10	13	10	9	90	8	7	4	12	10
P/E – low	—	8	10	5	7	57	4	2	2	5	7
Dividends per share ($)	(2.7%)	0.60	0.67	0.75	0.83	0.92	0.94	0.59	0.47	0.47	0.47
Book value per share ($)	4.8%	21.76	23.35	25.54	27.78	28.58	30.55	33.62	25.70	28.92	33.18
Employees	(4.2%)	97,067	105,696	112,400	121,421	127,926	121,190	109,123	87,377	70,016	65,760

1994 Year-end:
Debt ratio: 39.9%
Return on equity: 16.4%
Cash (mil.): $421
Current ratio: 3.66
Long-term debt (mil.): $5,790
No. of shares (mil.): 117
Dividends
  Yield: 1.0%
  Payout: 9.3%
Market value (mil.): $5,519

**Stock Price History
High/Low 1985–94**

THE MCGRAW-HILL COMPANIES, INC.

OVERVIEW

If this is, indeed, the Information Age, then McGraw-Hill is in the right place at the right time. The New York City–based company's commodity is information, served up a variety of ways for the ever-expanding assortment of media humans keep inventing to communicate. McGraw-Hill serves customers ranging from elementary school students to corporate executives. It serves the business, professional, consumer, government, and education markets through print (books, magazines, newsletters), via digital formats (electronic networks, software, CD-ROMs), and over the air (the company owns 4 TV stations).

McGraw-Hill's sales have blossomed thanks to its 1993 acquisition of full control of joint venture Macmillan/McGraw-Hill School Pub-

lishing from Macmillan. The company, now part of McGraw-Hill's Educational and Professional Publishing division, has helped to make McGraw-Hill the US's #1 schoolbook publisher.

Subsidiary Standard & Poor's (S&P) is a leading provider of credit ratings and also publishes directories of corporate information. The company's Information and Media Services division publishes *Business Week, BYTE,* and other consumer and trade magazines.

McGraw-Hill is focusing on paying down the debt left over from its Macmillan/McGraw acquisition, and it is also looking to expand internationally. It hopes to have about 30% of its revenue come from outside the US by the end of the decade, up from 18% in 1994.

WHEN

In 1909 magazine publishers James McGraw (*Street Railway Journal*) and John Hill (*American Machinist, Locomotive Engineer*) formed the McGraw-Hill Book Company to publish scientific and technical books. Initially the 2 kept their magazines separate, but following Hill's death in 1916 the magazine segments were merged with McGraw-Hill.

In the 1920s McGraw-Hill pioneered the risky but successful "send-no-money" plan, giving customers a free 10-day examination of its books. In 1929, 2 months before the stock market crash, McGraw-Hill started *Business Week* magazine, in which it expressed concerns about the economy's health — a view contrary to general opinion.

During the 1930s and 1940s, McGraw-Hill continued to expand as a publisher of trade journals and college textbooks. It had entered trade publishing in 1930 under the Whittlesey House name (changed to McGraw-Hill in 1950), but it was not until the 1950s that the trade division earned some distinction. Its biggest commercial success was *Betty Crocker's Picture Cook Book* (1947), which sold 2.3 million copies in its first 2 years.

In the 1960s and 1970s, McGraw-Hill acquired Standard & Poor's (S&P), an investment information service (1966); 4 TV stations from Time Inc. (1972); Datapro Research Corporation, a product information service (1976); and Data Resources Inc. (DRI), an economic forecasting service (1979). In 1979 it successfully fended off American Express's attempt at an $830 million takeover.

In the 1980s McGraw-Hill expanded its electronic information services and acquired

small, industry-specific publishing and information service companies. In 1989 it sold its trade books division, and S&P downgraded its parent company's common stock rating to A⁻ because of a restructuring charge associated with McGraw-Hill's reorganization.

Also in 1989 McGraw-Hill (in partnership with Kodak and R. R. Donnelley) produced the first computerized college textbook, which allows instructors to select contents for custom publications from McGraw-Hill's Primis database.

In 1990 the company bought J.J. Kenny, a provider of municipal securities information. In 1991 its joint venture Macmillan/McGraw-Hill acquired Computer Systems Research and its integrated learning system for instruction in basic mathematics, reading, and writing.

In 1993 McGraw-Hill bought Macmillan's half of the 1989 Macmillan/McGraw-Hill School Publishing Co. textbook and educational software joint venture, sold for $337.5 million as part of Macmillan parent Maxwell Communication's bankruptcy. Also in 1993 McGraw-Hill bought 25% of Liberty Brokerage, Inc. (New York), which gave McGraw-Hill access to US Treasury securities pricing information.

Reflecting the growing interest in overseas markets, S&P Ratings Group opened a branch in Hong Kong in 1994 and announced plans to open one in Singapore in 1995.

In 1995 the company established a new information services group to focus on the development of the company's information products and publications and of new media opportunities.

NYSE symbol: MHP
Fiscal year ends: December 31

WHO

Chairman and CEO: Joseph L. Dionne, age 61,
$1,539,480 pay
President and COO: Harold W. "Terry" McGraw III, age
46, $929,404 pay
EVP and CFO: Robert J. Bahash, age 49, $638,368 pay
EVP Administration: Thomas J. Sullivan, age 59,
$586,934 pay
EVP New Ventures: Michael K. Hehir, age 47,
$483,268 pay
SVP Taxes: Frank J. Kaufman, age 50
SVP and Executive Assistant to the Chairman: Barbara
A. Munder, age 49
SVP Treasury Operations: Frank D. Penglase, age 54
SVP and General Counsel: Kenneth M. Vittor
VP Human Resources: Patrick Pavelski
Auditors: Ernst & Young LLP

WHERE

HQ: 1221 Avenue of the Americas, New York, NY 10020
Phone: 212-512-2000
Fax: 212-512-4871

McGraw-Hill has operations worldwide.

WHAT

	1994 Sales		1994 Operating Income	
	$ mil.	% of total	$ mil.	% of total
Educational & professional pub.	1,162	42	126	28
Info. & media svcs.	853	31	108	24
Financial services	746	27	217	48
Total	**2,761**	**100**	**451**	**100**

Selected Operations and Publications

Educational and Professional Publishing
Macmillan/McGraw School Division
McGraw-Hill Continuing Education Center
McGraw-Hill Home Software
Osborne Books
Primis Custom Publishing (college publishing)
Schaum (college publishing)
Shepard's/McGraw-Hill (legal information)
TAB Books

Financial Services
DRI/McGraw-Hill (business and financial advising)
Equity Services
J.J. Kenny Drake (securities information)
Kenny S&P Information Services (securities and commodities data)
Liberty Brokerage Investment Corp. (25%)
Standard & Poor's Ratings Group (financial information & credit ratings)

Information and Media Services
Architectural Record
Aviation Week & Space Technology
Business & Commercial Aviation
Business Week
Business Week International
BYTE
Chemical Engineering
Datapro Information Services (database)
Electrical World
Engineering News-Record
F.W. Dodge (construction information)
KERO-TV (Bakersfield)
KGTV (San Diego)
KMGH-TV (Denver)
Newsletters/On-line
Postgraduate Medicine
Power
Tower Group International (custom broker, freight forwarder, trade-related services)
World Aviation Directory
WRTV (Indianapolis)

KEY COMPETITORS

Advance Publications
Bertelsmann
Bloomberg
CCH
Dow Jones
Dun & Bradstreet
Forbes
Harcourt General
Houghton Mifflin
John Wiley
Knight-Ridder
Media General
Morningstar
News Corp.
Pearson
Primark
Reed Elsevier
Reuters
Thomson Corp.
Time Warner
Times Mirror
TRW
Value Line
Viacom
West Publishing

HOW MUCH

	9-Year Growth	1985	1986	1987	1988	1989	1990	1991	1992	1993	1994
Sales ($ mil.)	7.1%	1,491	1,577	1,751	1,818	1,789	1,939	1,943	2,051	2,196	2,761
Net income ($ mil.)	3.6%	147	154	165	186	40	173	148	153	11	203
Income as % of sales	—	9.9%	9.8%	9.4%	10.2%	2.2%	8.9%	7.6%	7.5%	0.5%	7.4%
Earnings per share ($)	3.8%	2.92	3.04	3.27	3.83	0.82	3.53	3.03	3.13	0.23	4.10
Stock price – high ($)	—	52.00	64.00	84.50	76.00	86.13	61.13	64.75	66.50	75.25	77.25
Stock price – low ($)	—	39.75	46.50	43.00	46.75	53.50	39.88	49.75	53.00	55.25	62.50
Stock price – close ($)	3.8%	48.00	54.63	48.25	62.25	56.75	52.63	57.38	61.38	67.63	66.88
P/E – high	—	18	21	26	20	—	17	21	21	—	19
P/E – low	—	14	15	13	12	—	11	16	17	—	15
Dividends per share ($)	5.8%	1.40	1.52	1.68	1.84	2.05	2.16	2.20	2.24	2.28	2.32
Book value per share ($)	2.0%	15.40	17.04	16.33	17.94	18.08	19.50	20.37	18.58	16.66	18.38
Employees	0.7%	14,345	15,232	15,892	16,255	14,461	13,868	13,539	13,393	15,661	15,339

1994 Year-end:
Debt ratio: 45.5%
Return on equity: 23.4%
Cash (mil.): $8
Current ratio: 1.12
Long-term debt (mil.): $658
No. of shares (mil.): 50
Dividends
  Yield: 3.5%
  Payout: 56.6%
Market value (mil.): $3,322

**Stock Price History
High/Low 1985–94**

MCI COMMUNICATIONS CORPORATION

MCI Communications is no longer content to be called simply the 2nd largest long distance supplier in the US. Based in Washington, DC, MCI has agreed to invest up to $2 billion in Rupert Murdoch's News Corp. and has been broadening its communications product line with paging and Internet services. MCI has also recently launched a business communications software package, called networkMCI BUSINESS, integrating e-mail, fax messaging, and desktop videoconferencing, among other services.

The belief among MCI's senior executives is that the company's strengths lie in providing the basic network circuits, software, and hard-ware for on-demand information and entertainment services of the future. With MCI's investment in News Corp., the companies will form a joint venture to develop and distribute communications products that potentially may include pay-per-view movies and computer information services for business customers. News Corp.'s on-line computer service, Delphi Internet Services, will likely be incorporated into networkMCI.

In the highly competitive long distance business, MCI has been losing ground to its archrival, AT&T. MCI lost 1.1 million customers to AT&T in 1994 — thus, MCI's strategy to develop more profitable services.

MCI's history is tied to legal actions against AT&T. In 1963 John Goeken wanted to build a microwave radio system between St. Louis and Chicago for his mobile radio company. AT&T was then acting as a monopoly, and any company wishing to compete with AT&T had to obtain FCC authorization.

In 1966 the FCC ruled that MCI (Microwave Communications, Inc.) was qualified to provide services. In 1968 William McGowan, a consultant, obtained new financing for the company and founded MCI Communications. Goeken left the company and went on to found Airfone, which provides air-to-ground service. In 1969 the FCC ruled that MCI could operate but gave no assurances that it could expand its network or connect to the Bell companies. After appealing, AT&T withdrew its arguments, and MCI began service in 1972.

By 1973 MCI's network reached more than 40 cities but could not provide switched services, which had to be connected to the Bell system. MCI provided dedicated services between switches owned by users. Execunet became a switched service with interconnection rights at AT&T facilities in 1973. MCI won interconnection rights at its own facilities in 1976, but AT&T filed tariffs that eliminated MCI's cost savings. In 1978 MCI began antitrust proceedings against this practice, but in 1983 a US court of appeals held that AT&T had not been engaging in predatory practices. McGowan often referred to MCI as a "law firm with an antenna on top" during this period as the company sought to break AT&T's monopoly through the courts.

MCI has continued to offer services that compete directly with AT&T and to acquire new divisions. Major acquisitions include Western Union International (1982), a telex provider; Satellite Business Systems (1986), a satellite-based long distance carrier; and RCA Global Communications (1988), a data communications service provider. In 1990 MCI bought Telecom*USA, which had slightly more than 1% of the long distance market, and agreed to build a transatlantic fiber-optic cable with British Telecom.

Heavy investment in digital upgrades and back-office computer systems has enabled MCI to beat its competition in customized billing and calling plans. By 1991 MCI's nationwide network was fully digital. MCI launched a highly successful marketing campaign (Friends & Family) that offered residential customers a 20% discount on calls to 20 named MCI subscribers in 1991. By the beginning of 1993, the program had signed up over 10 million customers. McGowan, a heart transplant patient, retired as CEO in 1991 and died in mid-1992; his replacement as CEO, Bert Roberts, also succeeded him as chairman.

In 1993 British Telecom bought 20% of MCI and formed a joint venture to sell communications services globally. In 1994 MCI announced that it would develop a long distance network in Mexico with Grupo Financiero Banamex-Accival. MCI will own 45% of the business.

In 1995 MCI unveiled internetMCI, a line of products and services including software and dial-up access; its World Wide Web site; and marketplaceMCI for electronic shopping. MCI also named former Prodigy EVP Scott Kurnit as president of its Information Services Company, which will market on-line services. Also that year MCI said it would buy reseller Nationwide Cellular for about $190 million.

Nasdaq symbol: MCIC
Fiscal year ends: December 31

WHO

Chairman and CEO: Bert C. Roberts Jr., age 52, $1,750,000 pay
President and COO: Gerald H. Taylor, age 53, $957,885 pay
President, MCI International, Inc.: Seth D. Blumenfeld, age 54
EVP; Group President, MCI Telecommunications Corporation: Timothy F. Price, age 41, $600,635 pay
EVP, MCI Global Access Corporation: Daniel E. Crawford, age 55, $442,775 pay
EVP and CFO: Douglas L. Maine, age 46, $427,000 pay
EVP, MCI Telecommunications Corporation: Angela O. Dunlap, age 38
EVP, MCI Telecommunications Corporation: John W. Gerdelman, age 42
EVP, MCI Telecommunications Corporation: Scott B. Ross, age 43
EVP, MCI Telecommunications Corporation: Michael J. Rowny, age 44
SVP, MCI Telecommunications Corporation: Fred M. Briggs, age 46
SVP, MCI Telecommunications Corporation: Laurence E. Harris, age 58
SVP and General Counsel: John R. Worthington, age 64
VP and Controller: Bradley E. Sparks, age 48
Chief Human Resources Officer: John H. Zimmerman
Auditors: Price Waterhouse LLP

WHERE

HQ: 1801 Pennsylvania Ave. NW, Washington, DC 20006
Phone: 202-872-1600
Fax: 202-887-3140

MCI operates throughout the US. The company and its affiliates operate globally.

WHAT

Selected Services
1-800-COLLECT
Custom Language Card (voice-prompted calling instructions in 6 languages)
Friends & Family Connections (integrated consumer communications services including paging, electronic mail, personal 800 service, and calling card)
Friends & Family Paging
Friends & Family Worldwide (flexible consumer overseas call plan)
Friends of the Firm (flexible small business call plan)
In-Flight Phone Corporation
internetMCI
marketplaceMCI
MCI VideoPhone
MCImetro
networkMCI BUSINESS
networkMCI PAGING
NEW Friends & Family (flexible consumer call plan)
Personal 800 (inbound WATS-like service)
Proof Positive (periodic business account reviews and recommendations for savings)

Major Alliances
AVANTEL, SA (joint venture with Grupo Financiero Banamex-Accival; long distance network in Mexico)
Concert (joint venture with British Telecom to provide global voice and data network services)
Stentor (extension of MCI network to Canada)

KEY COMPETITORS

America Online	GPT Holdings	Sprint
Ameritech	GTE	Telephone and
AT&T	MFS	Data Systems
Bell Atlantic	Communications	Teleport
BellSouth	NYNEX	U.S. Long
Cable & Wireless	Pacific Telesis	Distance
Century Telephone	Prodigy	U S WEST
CompuServe	SBC	WorldCom
Goeken Group	Communications	

HOW MUCH

	9-Year Growth	1985	1986	1987	1988	1989	1990	1991	1992	1993	1994
Sales ($ mil.)	20.2%	2,542	3,592	3,939	5,137	6,471	7,680	8,433	10,562	11,921	13,338
Net income ($ mil.)	21.3%	140	(431)	85	356	603	299	551	609	627	795
Income as % of sales	—	5.5%	—	2.2%	6.9%	9.3%	3.9%	6.5%	5.8%	5.3%	6.0%
Earnings per share ($)	17.9%	0.30	(0.79)	0.15	0.64	1.13	0.53	1.01	1.11	1.12	1.32
Stock price – high ($)	—	5.63	6.56	5.94	12.19	23.88	22.44	15.94	20.44	29.88	29.00
Stock price – low ($)	—	3.69	3.06	2.56	4.88	10.88	9.25	8.94	14.75	18.81	17.25
Stock price – close ($)	14.0%	5.63	3.13	4.69	11.31	22.00	9.94	15.13	19.81	28.25	18.38
P/E – high	—	19	—	40	19	21	42	16	18	27	22
P/E – low	—	12	—	17	8	10	18	9	13	17	13%
Dividends per share ($)	—	0.00	0.00	0.00	0.00	0.00	0.05	0.05	0.05	0.05	0.05
Book value per share ($)	18.8%	2.80	2.21	2.37	2.79	3.99	4.60	5.71	5.99	8.71	13.24
Employees	14.2%	12,445	13,650	14,236	17,596	19,198	24,509	27,857	30,964	36,235	41,000

1994 Year-end:
Debt ratio: 25.8%
Return on equity: 11.6%
Cash (mil.): $1,429
Current ratio: 1.56
Long-term debt (mil.): $2,997
No. of shares (mil.): 680
Dividends
    Yield: 0.3%
    Payout: 3.8%
Market value (mil.): $12,498

Stock Price History High/Low 1985–94

MCKESSON CORPORATION

OVERVIEW

The largest wholesale drug distributor in the US and Canada, McKesson provides pharmaceuticals as well as health and beauty products to drugstores, hospitals, food stores, and mass merchandisers. The company also owns 22.7% of Nadro S.A. de C.V., Mexico's leading drug distributor.

The San Francisco–based company's other holdings include Armor All Products Corporation (55% owned), which manufactures automotive and household finish-protection products. Its flagship brand, Armor All Protectant, is the nation's #1 automotive protectant. McKesson Water Products is the 2nd largest bottled water company in the US (after Perrier Group).

McKesson reorganized in late 1994 as part of its sale of PCS Health Systems. It sold PCS, the US's #1 3rd-party prescription claims processor, to Eli Lilly for about $4 billion in 1994. As part of the deal, McKesson distributed about $3.4 billion, or $76 per share, to its shareholders. The company restructured its remaining businesses, and shareholders were issued stock in the "New McKesson."

The profitable and fast-growing PCS was McKesson's main growth business. What's left is a slow-growth, low-margin distribution business that McKesson plans to improve using over $600 million in cash from the PCS sale. It is already working to improve its health care services operations. In 1995 it created McKesson Health Systems to provide pharmaceutical products, computer services, and delivery services to hospitals, long-term care facilities, and other health care providers.

WHEN

John McKesson opened a Manhattan drug store in 1833. Daniel Robbins joined him as a partner in 1840, and in 1853 the company was renamed McKesson-Robbins. They expanded into chemical and drug production, and the enterprise grew steadily; however, differences arose between the descendants of McKesson and Robbins, and in 1926 the company was sold to Donald Coster.

Coster was actually twice-convicted felon Philip Musica, who purchased McKesson-Robbins with fraudulently obtained bank loans. For over a decade his real identity was a secret — from all but a single blackmailer. By 1930 McKesson-Robbins had wholesale drug operations in 33 states serving more than 15,000 retail druggists and employing more than 6,000 people. The company appeared to be growing, but a treasurer discovered a Musica-orchestrated accounting scam and a cash shortfall of $3 million. Faced with certain exposure, Musica committed suicide in 1939; bankruptcy followed.

McKesson-Robbins emerged from bankruptcy in 1941. By the early 1960s it was acquiring drug suppliers. In a 1967 hostile takeover, San Francisco–based Foremost Dairies bought McKesson-Robbins to form Foremost-McKesson. Over the next 20 years, it bought wholesalers in the liquor, chemical, and software industries and several bottled water companies; entered and exited homebuilding; and sold Foremost Dairies (1983) in order to focus on distribution. The company changed its name to McKesson in 1984.

McKesson continued to build its drug wholesaling business through acquisitions. By 1985 it was the US's largest distributor of drug and medical equipment, wine and liquor, bottled water, and car waxes and polishes. A 1988 antitrust action blocked McKesson's acquisition of drug and consumer goods wholesaler Alco Health Services on the basis that the combined companies would control 90% of drug distribution in some states.

After becoming CEO in 1986, Thomas Field sold McKesson's liquor and chemical distributors to narrow the company's focus. The drug distribution business grew stronger in 1989 when McKesson won the contract to supply all Wal-Mart stores and again in 1990 when it acquired 50% of Medis, a leading Canadian drug distributor, buying the remaining 50% in 1991.

The company continued to improve and automate its 45 distribution facilities in 1992 (there had been 110 in the 1970s) and to stress price and value in its services. In 1993 McKesson was awarded a 3-year, $100 million contract with Franciscan Health System. Also in 1993 McKesson acquired a stake in Mexican drug distributor Nadro S.A. de C.V.

In 1994 the company sold $180 million in debt exchangeable for 6.9 million shares in Armor All, which could reduce the company's stake to 22%.

In 1995 McKesson signed a $1 billion contract with Albertson's to provide the supermarket chain with pharmaceuticals and other drugstore items.

WHO

Chairman and CEO: Alan J. Seelenfreund, age 58, $1,725,000 pay
President and COO: David E. McDowell, age 52, $1,230,000 pay
VP; President, Healthcare Delivery Systems: David L. Mahoney, age 40, $587,500 pay
VP Human Resources and Administration: William A. Armstrong, age 54, $480,000 pay
VP; President, McKesson Drug Co.: James H. Smith, age 51, $440,000 pay
VP; President, McKesson Water Products Co.: Charles A. Norris, age 50
VP and CFO: Kevin B. Ferrell, age 47
VP Finance: Garret A. Scholz, age 55
VP Strategic Planning: Michael T. Dalby, age 49
VP and Corporate Secretary: Nancy A. Miller, age 51
VP and General Counsel: Ivan D. Meyerson, age 50
Auditors: Deloitte & Touche LLP

WHERE

HQ: McKesson Plaza, One Post St., San Francisco, CA 94104
Phone: 415-983-8300
Fax: 415-983-7160

McKesson and its subsidiaries operate throughout Canada, Mexico, and the US.

	1995 Sales		1995 Operating Income	
	$ mil.	% of total	$ mil.	% of total
US	11,805	90	44	59
Other countries	1,384	10	31	41
Total	**13,189**	**100**	**75**	**100**

WHAT

	1995 Sales		1995 Operating Income	
	$ mil.	% of total	$ mil.	% of total
Health care services	12,711	96	20	27
Water products	246	2	15	19
Armor All	217	2	40	54
Other	15	—	—	—
Total	**13,189**	**100**	**75**	**100**

Selected Health Care Services
Econolink and Economost (inventory management and ordering systems)
Millbrook Distribution Services (health and beauty products, general merchandise, and specialty food distribution)
Sunmark (home health care products)
Valu-Rite pharmacy program (cooperative marketing)
Zee Medical, Inc. (first-aid supplies to industry)

Bottled Water
Alhambra   Crystal
Aqua-Vend   Sparkletts

Armor All
Armor All protectants and cleaners
Rain Dance car polishes

KEY COMPETITORS

Abbott Labs	Coca-Cola
Alco Health Services	Culligan
Allou	Danone
Amway	First Brands
Avon	Glacier Water Services
Baxter	Humiston-Keeling
Behrens	Johnson & Johnson
Bergen Brunswig	National Intergroup
Bindley Western	Nestlé
Cardinal Health	Teledyne

HOW MUCH

	9-Year Growth	1986	1987	1988	1989	1990	1991	1992	1993	1994	1995
Sales ($ mil.)	8.6%	6,285	6,660	7,283	7,046	7,791	8,421	10,313	11,669	12,428	13,189
Net income ($ mil.)	20.1%	78	90	95	101	99	101	32	115	157	405
Income as % of sales	—	1.2%	1.4%	1.3%	1.4%	1.3%	1.2%	0.3%	1.0%	1.0%	3.1%
Earnings per share ($)	18.1%	1.98	1.95	2.14	2.28	2.10	2.21	0.65	2.51	3.48	8.86
Stock price – high ($)[1]	—	26.75	35.25	39.63	35.88	39.75	38.38	40.13	44.25	57.25	33.50
Stock price – low ($)[1]	—	18.50	24.75	23.25	25.75	29.63	26.88	30.38	30.25	38.63	30.13
Stock price – close ($)[1]	2.5%	26.19	31.75	26.50	31.13	35.63	34.00	36.50	42.50	54.00	32.63
P/E – high	—	14	18	19	16	19	17	62	18	21	4
P/E – low	—	9	13	11	11	14	12	47	12	14	3
Dividends per share ($)	1.2%	1.20	1.24	1.28	1.40	1.44	1.56	1.60	1.60	1.66	1.34
Book value per share ($)	4.1%	15.92	17.73	16.43	17.01	14.02	14.27	10.94	12.15	13.63	22.83
Employees	(3.7%)	17,200	17,000	16,700	14,800	13,800	13,300	14,150	14,000	14,500	12,200

1995 Year-end:
Debt ratio: 39.9%
Return on equity: 51.6%
Cash (mil.): $693
Current ratio: 1.55
Long-term debt (mil.): $459
No. of shares (mil.): 44
Dividends
  Yield: 4.1%
  Payout: 15.1%
Market value (mil.): $1,448

Stock Price History[1]
High/Low 1986–95

[1]Stock prices are for the prior calendar year.

MCKINSEY & COMPANY

OVERVIEW

Members of McKinsey & Co., the world's best-known business consulting firm, like to compare their institution to the marines and the Catholic Church. But the frequency with which its consultants join the firms that they have advised is more suggestive of a very expensive employment agency with tryout privileges. Alumni include business theorist Tom Peters, American Express chairman and CEO Harvey Golub, IBM chairman and CEO Louis Gerstner, and, internationally, high-ranking executives of Bull, Deutsche Bundespost and Deutsche Telekom, Grand Metropolitan, Swiss Bank, and Swiss Re.

McKinsey is one of the US's oldest consulting firms. Its meticulous methods of gathering data, its discretion, and its cultivated mystique have given it a reputation as the ultimate source of reliable, objective advice. And while the recent histories of some of its client companies (IBM and GM) are hardly a recommen-

dation, McKinsey maintains that the quality of its advice is tempered by the determination of the client to take it.

A McKinsey study, in which consultants observe a company for several months and provide a report on topics of the client's choosing, may cost $1 million or more, depending on its scope and complexity.

Some in the industry (including Tom Peters) believe that McKinsey, whose practice is geared largely toward strategy, may be out of step with the consulting business, which has recently focused on information technology.

McKinsey is owned by its partners (who survive a rigorous weeding process described as "up or out," in which failure to advance to ever-higher levels means dismissal). It is led by a managing director elected triennially. In 1994 the firm elected its first managing director of non-European descent — India-born, US-educated Rajat Gupta.

WHEN

McKinsey & Co. was founded in Chicago in 1926 by University of Chicago accounting professor James McKinsey, an early pioneer in the field of management. At first the firm did little more than audit clients' books, but this provided McKinsey and his partners, who included Marvin Bower and A. T. Kearney, with a wealth of basic information that they could use in their analyses of business and industry. Two years after McKinsey's death in 1937, Bower, who headed the New York office, and Kearney, in Chicago, split up the firm. Kearney renamed the Chicago office A. T. Kearney & Co. Bower kept the McKinsey name and built up a collegial practice structured like a law firm.

By 1950 billings were at $2 million, partly due to Bower's policy of emphasizing the "big picture" rather than specific operating problems. He hired staff straight out of the most prestigious business schools, a recruiting model still followed today by the company. Bower also implemented the "up or out" policy that requires employees who are not continually promoted to leave the firm. Only 20% of associates become partners, and only 10% ever become directors.

Before becoming US president in 1953, Dwight Eisenhower asked McKinsey to find what it was exactly that the government did.

By 1959 Bower had opened the first overseas office in London, followed by others in Europe. When Bower retired in 1967, sales

were $20 million, and McKinsey was the preeminent management consulting firm. By 1976 the firm faced stiff competition from other firms with newer approaches. McKinsey lost market share until managing director Ronald Daniel instituted specialty practices and expanded McKinsey's foreign business.

Much of the boom in consulting in the 1980s was spurred by the wave of corporate restructurings as executives looked to firms such as McKinsey to guide them through their transitions. By 1988, when Frederick Gluck, an engineer with no MBA, became managing director, the firm had 1,800 consultants, sales were $620 million, and 50% of billings came from overseas.

The recession of the early 1990s hit white-collar workers, including consultants. As McKinsey scrambled to upgrade its technical side, it bought the Information Consulting Group (ICG), its first acquisition. But there was a considerable clash of corporate cultures, and most ICG people left by 1993. McKinsey has also begun to capitalize on the information contained in its internal database, PDNet.

Some of the firm's jobs have come full circle. In 1994 Anglo Dutch/Shell brought McKinsey in to help it cut costs partly attributable to a decentralized structure that the firm had recommended in the 1950s.

Also in 1994 McKinsey (UK) consultant Norman Blackwell was named to Prime Minister John Major's policy unit.

Private company
Fiscal year ends: December 31

WHO

Managing Director: Rajat Gupta
CFO: James Rogers
General Counsel: Jean Molino
Director, Tokyo: Gunter Rommel
Director, London: Norman Sanson
Director, Stockholm: Christian Caspar
Principal and Director of Personnel: Jerome Vascellaro

WHERE

HQ: 55 E. 52nd St., New York, NY 10022
Phone: 212-446-7000
Fax: 212-446-8575

McKinsey has 66 offices in 35 countries.

	1994 Sales % of total
US	40
Other countries	60
Total	**100**

WHAT

Areas of Practice
Corporate finance
Corporate organization
Corporate strategy
Customer satisfaction and service
Information technology/systems
Logistics
Marketing
Marketing organization
M&A/change of ownership
New product development
Operations
Organization
Post-merger management
Pricing
Purchasing and supply management
Services marketing and management
Strategic planning
Technology management

Representative Clients
(past and present)
Alcoa
American Express
AT&T
British Airways
Citicorp
Deutsche Bank
Eastman Kodak
First Interstate Bank
Ford
General Electric
General Motors
Guinness
Hewlett-Packard
IBM
Johnson & Johnson
Levi Strauss
LVMH
Merrill Lynch
Mobil
Nestlé
New York City Transit
  Authority
Nissan
Pacific Gas & Electric
PepsiCo
Royal Dutch/Shell
Sears
Time Warner
USF&G
The Vatican
Wells Fargo Bank

Pro Bono Clients
Cleveland Foundation
Golden Gate National Park
  Association
Greater Cleveland Regional
  Transit Authority
San Francisco Symphony

KEY COMPETITORS

Arthur Andersen
Arthur Little
Bain & Co.
Booz, Allen
Boston Consulting
Carlson
Coopers & Lybrand
DEC
Deloitte & Touche
Earnings Performance
  Group
EDS
Ernst & Young
Gemini Consulting
Hewitt Associates
IBM
KPMG
Maritz
Marsh & McLennan
NYNEX
Perot Systems
Price Waterhouse
Towers Perrin
Wyatt Co.

HOW MUCH

	Annual Growth	1985	1986	1987	1988	1989	1990	1991	1992	1993	1994
Estimated sales ($ mil.)	17.6%	350	400	510	620	635	900	1,050	1,200	1,300	1,500
Employees	8.4 %	—	—	—	—	4,000	4,500	4,500	5,500	5,560	6,000

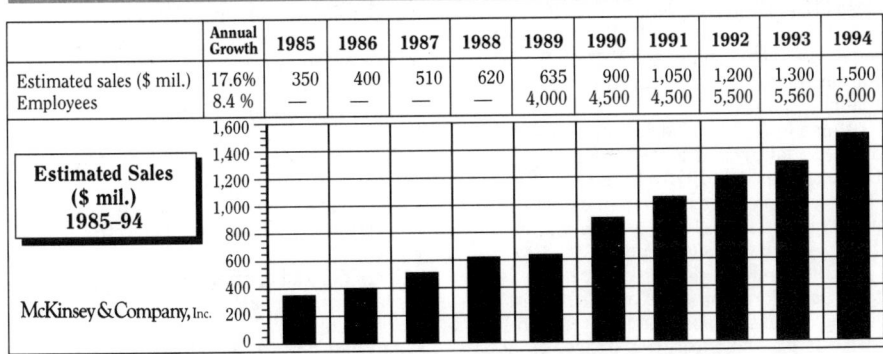

Estimated Sales
($ mil.)
1985–94

McKinsey & Company, Inc.

THE MEAD CORPORATION

OVERVIEW

Mead Corporation is going back to school and to its other paper businesses. Choosing Gutenberg over Gates, the Ohio-based pulp and paper giant and #1 manufacturer and distributor of school supplies has exited its electronic media business in order to get back to basics. In 1994 Mead sold its Data Central electronic services unit (including the well-known LEXIS-NEXIS service, the nation's largest online electronic data retrieval unit) to Reed Elsevier for $1.5 billion. The cash is helping Mead to focus on its core paper and packaging businesses and to pay off debt accumulated during the slump in pulp and paper prices in the early 1990s.

The company, one of the world's largest manufacturers of paper (1.3 million tons

annually), produces corrugated containers, coated paperboard, and multiple packaging as well as printing, writing, and specialty papers. It is a major distributor of paper, plastic products, packaging equipment, and supplies in addition to school and office supplies. The firm controls 1.35 million acres of US timberlands and holds a 50% interest in Northwood Forest, a lumber and pulp producer.

Mead made 2 strategic purchases in 1994. In Canada it acquired the assets of Hilroy (a division of Abitibi-Price), a leading manufacturer of paper-based school supplies, giving the firm an opportunity to expand in the Canadian market. In a move to grow its global packaging business, Mead also acquired IBE, a Spanish converter of beverage packaging.

WHEN

Daniel Mead established Mead Paper in 1882 when he became the sole owner of a small Dayton, Ohio, paper mill. The company faltered after his death in 1891 until a grandson, George Mead, took over in 1905. The company raised cash by going public in 1906 and was profitable by 1915. Over the next 40 years, Mead expanded by buying and building pulp and paper mills in the East and the South.

After WWII Mead continued to grow by acquiring other paper companies and packaging firms in the US and Europe. Jackson Box of Cincinnati (1955) was the beginning of Mead's container division; Atlanta Paper (1957) began the packaging division, which originated the 6-pack carrier. Mead began diversifying in the 1960s, buying coal, furniture, fabric, and steel and rubber products companies. The 1966 purchase of Westab of Dayton, Ohio, began the school and office supply division. In 1968 Mead bought Data Corporation, which became the company's electronic publishing division (Mead Data Central). In the mid-1970s Mead Data Central introduced LEXIS, the largest legal research database, and NEXIS, the largest full-text database of news and business information.

After a long public battle for control, Mead avoided a takeover attempt by Occidental Petroleum in the late 1970s. In the early 1980s the recession caused a slump in demand for paper products, and Mead lost $62 million in 1982 — its first loss in 44 years.

In 1982 and 1983 Mead shed many divisions to focus on forest products and electronic publishing. Mead's school products were top sellers in the 1980s; those featuring images of the

Smurfs and Garfield the Cat accounted for about 30% of the division's earnings in 1983. Acquisitions included Micromedex (medical database, 1985; sold 1992), Ampad (office supplies, 1986), Dataline (financial information, 1987), Zellerbach (paper distribution, 1988), and Michie (legal publishing, 1989). In 1988 Mead introduced Cycolor, a copier paper that reproduces color by an inexpensive technique. Because growth in this sector was much slower than expected, in 1990 Mead wrote down its investment in color imaging. This, and write-downs of other nonproductive assets (totaling $88.5 million), contributed to a 51% decline in earnings for that year. Mead reduced capital spending by 29% in 1991 and postponed plans for a new pulp and paper-making plant.

In 1992 the company experienced a changing of the guard when Burnell Roberts retired after 10 years as chairman. He was succeeded by former vice-chairman Steve Mason. Also that year Mead sold Ampad, its commercial office products business. Mead Data Central sold its Micromedex medical information company and acquired Folio, a Provo, Utah–based developer of information software used by commercial publishers.

In 1993 Mead trimmed 800 people from its work force (following a 1,200-person cut in 1992), and in 1994 Mead made a major cash-generating move by selling its electronic data services.

In 1995 Mead continued its cost reduction strategy with the sale of its Kingsport, Tennessee paper mill (which had been losing $10 million a year) to Willamette Industries.

NYSE symbol: MEA
Fiscal year ends: December 31

WHO

Chairman, President, and CEO: Steven C. Mason, age 58, $1,349,472 pay
VP and Operating Officer: Elias M. Karter, age 54, $450,748 pay
VP and Operating Officer: Raymond W. Lane, age 46, $425,799 pay
VP and General Counsel: Thomas E. Palmer, age 55, $429,196 pay
VP and Operating Officer: Jerome F. Tatar, age 48, $394,575 pay
VP and CFO: William R. Graber, age 51, $394,200 pay
VP Purchasing and Logistics: Wallace O. Nugent, age 56
VP Information Resources: John K. Langenbahn
VP Strategy and Planning: Cynthia A. Niekamp, age 52
VP Human Resources: Charles J. Mazza, age 52
Auditors: Deloitte & Touche LLP

WHERE

HQ: Mead World Headquarters, Courthouse Plaza NE, Dayton, OH 45463
Phone: 513-495-6323
Fax: 513-461-2424

Mead operates 18 paper and packaging mills throughout the US, 7 manufacturing and distribution locations for school products, and 48 wholesale locations. Mead's foreign plants and offices are located in Argentina, Canada, Chile, France, Germany, Hong Kong, Italy, Japan, Mexico, the Netherlands, Spain, and the UK.

WHAT

US Timberlands	Acres (thou.)
Long-term lease	107
Owned & other	1,243
Total	**1,350**

	1994 Sales		1994 Operating Income	
	$ mil.	% of total	$ mil.	% of total
Distrib. & school & office prods.	2,146	47	21	10
Packaging & paperboard	1,255	28	124	57
Paper	1,157	25	72	33
Other	—	—	(164)	—
Total	**4,558**	**100**	**52**	**100**

Distribution and School and Office Products
Envelopes
Filler paper
Legal pads
Loose-leaf binders
Portfolios
Stationery
Wire-bound notebooks

Packaging and Paperboard
Coated natural kraft packaging board
Corrugated shipping containers
Multiple packaging systems

Paper
Carbonless paper
Coated and uncoated printing papers
Copy paper
Greeting card stock
Market pulp
Premium text paper
Specialty papers

Forest Products Affiliates
Northwood Forest Industries Ltd. (50%, joint venture with Noranda Forest Inc.)
Northwood Panelboard Co. (50%, joint venture with Noranda Forest Inc.)

KEY COMPETITORS

Akzo Nobel
Alco Standard
Boise Cascade
Bowater
Burhmann-Tetterode
Champion International
Fletcher Challenge
Fort Howard
General Binding
Georgia-Pacific
International Paper
James River
Jefferson Smurfit
Kimberly-Clark
Manville
Newell Co.
Scott
Stone Container
Stora
Weyerhaeuser
Willamette Industries

HOW MUCH

	9-Year Growth	1985	1986	1987	1988	1989	1990	1991	1992	1993	1994
Sales ($ mil.)	5.8%	2,740	3,218	4,209	4,464	4,612	4,772	4,579	4,703	4,790	4,558
Net income ($ mil.)	24.9%	94	46	218	353	216	39	66	38	124	696
Income as % of sales	—	3.4%	1.3%	5.2%	7.9%	4.7%	0.7%	1.4%	0.8%	2.6%	16.4%
Earnings per share ($)	25.0%	1.51	0.09	3.47	5.37	3.33	0.62	1.12	0.63	2.08	11.21
Stock price – high ($)	—	22.44	30.44	48.38	49.50	46.63	39.50	37.25	41.63	48.50	53.75
Stock price – low ($)	—	16.81	21.25	21.00	29.00	34.25	19.50	24.50	33.13	37.50	29.13
Stock price – close ($)	9.1%	22.19	27.31	33.88	39.00	36.75	25.75	34.50	38.25	45.00	48.63
P/E – high	—	15	—	14	9	14	64	33	66	23	5
P/E – low	—	11	—	6	5	10	31	22	53	18	3
Dividends per share ($)	5.8%	0.60	0.60	0.65	0.74	0.85	0.97	1.00	1.00	1.00	1.00
Book value per share ($)	9.4%	16.63	16.91	19.85	24.83	26.55	26.28	25.34	25.46	26.66	37.21
Employees	(0.9%)	17,500	20,600	20,500	21,000	21,800	21,600	21,600	20,400	19,600	16,100

1994 Year-end:
Debt ratio: 30.9%
Return on equity: 37.0%
Cash (mil.): $484
Current ratio: 1.74
Long-term debt (mil.): $958
No. of shares (mil.): 59
Dividends
  Yield: 2.1%
  Payout: 8.9%
Market value (mil.): $2,852

Stock Price History
High/Low 1985–94

MEIJER, INC.

OVERVIEW

With sprawling stores that occupy up to 250,000 square feet, grocery and general merchandise retailer Meijer covers relatively little ground geographically. In 1995 the Grand Rapids, Michigan–based company opened its first store in Illinois, complementing 99 others located in Michigan, Ohio, and Indiana. The company, which also operates about 80 gas stations in the Midwest, is known by its competitors as a relentless advertiser.

A pioneer of the hypermarket format in the 1960s, Meijer today is privately held and chaired by the founder's son, Fred Meijer. The company's giant stores are open 24 hours a day and are noted for competitive pricing and high-quality food. Where competitors Wal-Mart and Kmart have tried to lure customers into their hypermarket grocery departments through the stores' general merchandise selections, Meijer has done just the opposite and has had more success with the format.

Meijer in 1995 scrapped plans to enter the Cleveland market with 10 stores by 1999. The company had earlier stirred protests by would-be neighbors when it announced that it would open a $10 million store in an upscale housing development there. Meanwhile, the chain affirmed its plans to open 3 stores in Cincinnati in 1996.

The first labor strike in Meijer's history hit 4 stores in Toledo, Ohio, in mid-1994; the strike led to pickets at 14 other stores. After 9 weeks, the company agreed to recognize the newly attained union affiliation of its workers.

WHEN

In 1934 Dutch immigrant and barber Hendrik Meijer opened Thrift Market in Greenville, Michigan, with the help of his wife, Gezina; son, Fred; and daughter, Johanna. Next to his barbershop was a vacant storefront space that he owned but, because of the Depression, was unable to rent. He bought $338.76 worth of merchandise on credit and started his own grocery store. Meijer had 22 competitors in Greenville alone, but his dedication to low prices (he and Fred often traveled long distances to find bargains) attracted customers. In 1935, to encourage self-service, Meijer placed 12 wicker baskets at the front of the store and posted signs that read, "Take a basket. Help yourself."

A 2nd store was opened in 1942. The company continued to grow: 4 stores were opened in the 1950s. In the 1960s Meijer pioneered the one-stop shopping concept with the first Meijer Thrifty Acres stores. By 1964, the year that Hendrik died and Fred took over, 3 of these general merchandise stores were operating. In the late 1960s the company entered markets in Ohio.

In the 1970s many of the company's Meijer Thrifty Acres stores were equipped with gasoline pumps. However, a 1978 law that prohibited the sale of gasoline and alcohol at the same site forced the company to separate the 2 operations.

Meijer bought 14 Twin Fair stores in Ohio for more than $20 million in the early 1980s. The company renamed the stores, 10 of which were located in Cincinnati, Meijer Square. But in 1987 most of these stores were divested (Zayre was a major buyer) after disappointing results, signaling Meijer's egress from Cincinnati. The company had greater success in Columbus. It entered that city in 1987 and immediately captured 20% of the market with only one store. By 1993 Meijer was operating 4 stores in Columbus.

In 1988 the company began operating most of its stores on round-the-clock schedules. The next year Meijer began an environmental awareness program that emphasized recycling, among other measures.

In 1991 Meijer annihilated competitors in Dayton, Ohio, when it opened 4 stores in a one-year period. Rumors circulated about a possible Meijer/Kmart merger in 1992.

Meijer entered the Toledo market in 1993 with 4 stores; after one year, the company had taken 11.5% of the local grocery market. Also in 1993 Meijer abandoned its foray into the membership warehouse market, announcing that all 7 of its SourceClub warehouses would soon be closed. Readers of *Consumer Reports* that year rated Meijer the #1 grocer in competitive pricing in the US.

Meijer aggressively entered Indiana in 1994, opening 16 stores in less than 2 years; it also reached an agreement with McDonald's to open restaurants in several stores. During the Toledo strike, union officials said they were intimidated by Meijer's hiring of large, uniformed men in flak jackets and combat boots.

In 1995 Wal-Mart and Kmart prepared hypermarts that resembled Meijer's stores more than their previous efforts had. Now with one store in Illinois, Meijer is expected by some in the retail industry to make a push toward the Chicago market.

HOOVER'S HANDBOOK OF AMERICAN COMPANIES 1996

Private company
Fiscal year ends: December 31

Chairman of the Executive Committee: Fred Meijer,
  age 75
Co-Chairman: Doug Meijer, age 40
Co-Chairman: Hank Meijer, age 42
President: Earl Holton
EVP Retail Operations/Merchandising: Harold Hans
EVP Distribution and Logistics: Paul Boyer
**SVP Real Estate, Properties, and Information
  Technology and Services:** Jim McLean
SVP Finance and Administration: Fritz Kolk
SVP, General Counsel, and Secretary: Bob Riley
SVP Personnel: Windy Ray

WHERE

HQ: 2929 Walker Ave. NW, Grand Rapids, MI
  49504-9428
Phone: 616-453-6711
Fax: 616-791-2572

Meijer operates 100 combination stores and about 80 gas
stations in Illinois, Indiana, Kentucky, Michigan, and
Ohio. The company has 3 offices in Michigan and one in
Ohio; operates 12 distribution centers in Michigan and 4
in Ohio; and has a property services facility in Michigan.

	1994 Combination Stores
	No.
Michigan	57
Ohio	26
Indiana	16
Illinois	1
Total	**100**

Distribution Facilities
Grand Rapids, Michigan (central marking, general
  merchandise [2])
Lansing, Michigan (cold storage, general
  merchandise [2], grocery, perishables, retail support
  center)
Newport, Michigan (regional distribution center)
Tipp City, Ohio (cold storage, general merchandise,
  perishables, retail support center)

WHAT

Selected Meijer Store Departments
Bakery
Bulk foods
Cafe
Delicatessen
Gas station
The Grand Food Fair (food court)
  Fred's American Grill
  The Pizza Pan
  Wonton's
McDonald's
Pharmacy
Photo lab
Service meat and seafood
Video shop

Selected Services and Programs
Alcohol awareness programs
Meijer Reclamation Center (collection for food banks)
We Care about the Earth We Share (environmental
  awareness)

KEY COMPETITORS

American Stores
Amoco
Dayton Hudson
Dollar General
Eagle Food
F&M Distributors
Fred Albrecht Grocery
Great A&P
IGA
Kmart
Kroger
Marsh Supermarkets
Melville
Phar-Mor
Price/Costco
Revco
Riser Foods
Rite Aid
Roundy's
Seaway Food Town
Thriftway Food & Drug
Walgreen
Wal-Mart
Woolworth
Yucaipa

HOW MUCH

	Annual Growth	1985	1986	1987	1988	1989	1990	1991	1992	1993	1994
Estimated sales ($ mil.)	17.1%	—	—	—	2,000	3,000	3,700	5,370	5,390	4,250	5,160
No. of combo. stores	11.2%	—	—	—	53	56	—	63	72	85	100
Employees	17.3%	—	—	—	—	—	37,000	42,700	50,000	60,000	70,000

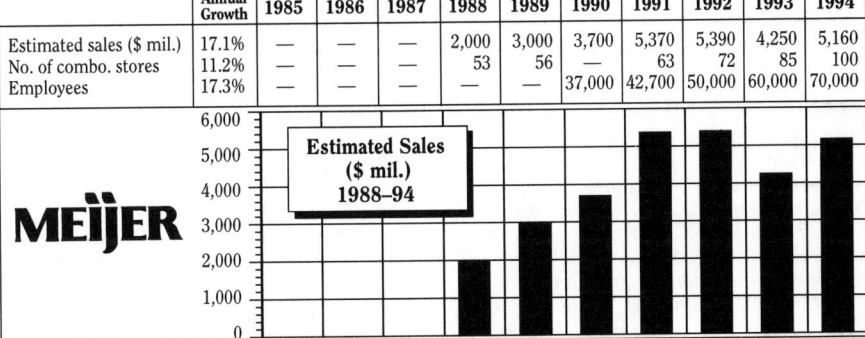

Estimated Sales
($ mil.)
1988–94

MEiJER

6,000
5,000
4,000
3,000
2,000
1,000
0

MELLON BANK CORPORATION

OVERVIEW

What we've got here is, failure to communicate. Mellon Bank's heralded entry into the high-flying world of investment services has faltered over culture clashes between the staid bank and its new subsidiaries, the informally managed Dreyfus mutual fund group and the daredevil asset manager Boston Company. The new companies were expected to fit well with Mellon's consumer banking business, but philosophical differences over management and investment styles (in addition to a downward blip in the mutual funds field relating to the rising interest rates of 1994) have brought declining results and staff defections for both operations. As managers have left the Boston Company and Dreyfus, Pittsburgh-based Mellon has installed its own people.

Mellon's other primary businesses are retail financial services (individual consumer banking services) and wholesale banking (corporate and middle-market banking services and selected international services, like foreign exchange). Mellon Mortgage is one of the US's largest mortgage servicers.

Warburg, Pincus entities own 9% of the company's stock.

WHEN

Judge Thomas Mellon founded a bank, T. Mellon and Sons, in Pittsburgh in 1869. A few years later his sons Andrew and Richard B. opened their own bank. In 1882, at age 69, the judge gave control of his bank to his son Andrew, who 5 years later gave half to his brother Richard B. In the late 1800s the Mellons set up Fidelity Title and Trust, as well as the Union Trust Company. In 1902 T. Mellon and Sons became Mellon National Bank. Thomas died in 1908, the same year the bank opened its first foreign bureau.

Under Andrew the bank was instrumental in financing Pittsburgh businesses. Mellon investments included Alcoa, Westinghouse, Bethlehem Steel, Pullman, Pittsburgh Coal, Pittsburgh Plate Glass, Koppers, and Carborundum. The bank's most successful investment was in a start-up oil company that became Gulf Oil.

In 1921 Andrew became treasury secretary under President Harding and was retained in that post by Coolidge and Hoover. Richard B. became Mellon National's president.

In 1929 Richard B. formed Mellbank, a holding company for various banks in which the Mellons had a stake. Such was the Mellon mystique in Pennsylvania that the Mellon Banks gained depositors during the Depression. Richard B. died at the age of 75, and a few months later in 1934, his son, Richard K., became president of Mellon National Bank. In 1946 Mellon merged with Union Trust Co. to form Mellon National Bank & Trust. In 1955 Mellon became the world's first computerized bank when it purchased an IBM computer.

In 1967 Richard K. retired from active duties, ending the Mellons' near-century-long management of the bank. In 1972 the bank created a holding company, Mellon National Corp. (the current name was adopted in 1984).

In the 1980s, under CEO J. David Barnes, Mellon made millions of dollars of high-risk loans to developing countries, oil companies, and real estate developers. This house of cards collapsed in 1987, when Mellon's first loss ever forced the bank to cut dividends. Barnes was forced out, and outsider Frank Cahouet came from Fannie Mae to be CEO.

Cahouet turned the bank around. In 1988 he dumped most of Mellon's bad loans into a new entity, Grant Street National, and spun it off. Freed of these liabilities, Mellon was able to recapitalize, and Grant Street sold most of the bad loans ahead of schedule.

In the 1990s Mellon has followed a core region/core lines strategy, selling businesses in noncore regions and business lines and making acquisitions within its core areas. It also formed a joint venture with Canada's Royal Trustco to provide stock transfer services in Canada and started an investment advisory firm, Pareto Partners, in London.

In 1993 Mellon completed its purchase of the Boston Company from American Express. The next year Mellon bought the Dreyfus Corp. (just in time for a slowdown in the mutual fund market). The expense control measures Mellon introduced were unpopular, but deemed necessary by some. Meanwhile, management was struggling with the Boston Company. Simmering resentments over control came to a boil in late 1994, when Mellon closed out a derivatives position (taking a loss) against the wishes of Boston Company's management. In 1995 Boston Company's president, Desmond Heathwood, and 5 others quit to form their own firm. Several clients followed them, and Mellon sued the defectors. More departures followed when Mellon tried to induce key Boston Company staff members to sign long-term contracts.

NYSE symbol: MEL
Fiscal year ends: December 31

WHO

Chairman, President, and CEO: Frank V. Cahouet, age 62, $1,068,542 pay
VC; Chairman, President, and CEO, Mellon PSFS: Thomas F. Donovan, age 61, $404,188 pay
VC Retail Financial Services: Martin G. McGuinn, age 52, $380,500 pay
VC, CFO, and Treasurer: Steven G. Elliott, age 48, $380,250 pay
VC Corporate Strategy and Development: David R. Lovejoy, age 46
VC Corporate Banking: Jamie B. Stewart Jr.
VC Wholesale Banking: Jeffrey L. Morby, age 57
VC and Chief Risk and Credit Officer: Keith P. Russell, age 49
Chairman and CEO, The Boston Company: W. Keith Smith, age 60, $478,750 pay
EVP Institutional Banking and Canada: Frederick K. Beard
EVP Mellon Information Services: Allan P. Woods
EVP and Chief Compliance Officer: John T. Chesko
EVP Human Resources: D. Michael Roark
SVP Economics and Chief Economist: Richard B. Berner
Secretary: James M. Gockley
General Counsel: Michael E. Bleier
Auditors: KPMG Peat Marwick LLP

WHERE

HQ: One Mellon Bank Center, Pittsburgh, PA 15258-0001
Phone: 412-234-5000
Fax: 412-234-6265

Mellon engages in retail and wholesale banking, trust and investment management, information services, and mortgage servicing operations in 15 states and 5 foreign countries.

WHAT

	1994 Assets	
	$ mil.	% of total
Cash & equivalents	3,145	8
Treasury & agency securities	1,282	3
Mortgage-backed securities	3,559	9
Net loans	26,126	68
Other	4,532	12
Total	**38,644**	**100**

	1994 Sales	
	$ mil.	% of total
Loan interest & fees	1,926	49
Other interest	384	10
Service fees	1,652	41
Total	**3,962**	**100**

Services
Credit cards
Leasing
Money and stock transfers
Real estate loans
Retail and corporate banking
Trust and investment management

Subsidiaries
The Boston Company
The Boston Safe Deposit and Trust Company
The Dreyfus Corp.
The Glendale Banks
Mellon Bank, FSB
Mellon PSFS

KEY COMPETITORS

AT&T
Banc One
Bank of Boston
Bank of New York
BankAmerica
Barnett Banks
Canadian Imperial
Chase Manhattan
Chemical Banking
Citicorp
CoreStates Financial
Countrywide Credit
First Chicago
Fleet
General Electric
H.F. Ahmanson
J.P. Morgan
Merrill Lynch
PNC Bank
State Street Boston

HOW MUCH

	9-Year Growth	1985	1986	1987	1988	1989	1990	1991	1992	1993	1994
Assets ($ mil.)	1.6%	33,406	34,499	30,525	31,153	31,467	28,762	29,355	31,574	36,139	38,644
Net income ($ mil.)	8.9%	202	183	(844)	(65)	181	174	280	437	361	433
Income as % of assets	—	0.6%	0.5%	—	—	0.6%	0.6%	1.0%	1.4%	1.0%	1.1%
Earnings per share ($)	(7.2%)	4.76	4.14	(20.80)	(2.43)	2.22	1.89	3.11	4.64	3.09	2.42
Stock price – high ($)	—	37.68	48.35	38.68	22.17	25.43	20.01	25.43	37.01	44.93	40.35
Stock price – low ($)	—	29.68	34.59	16.76	15.17	16.67	11.75	14.42	22.51	34.18	30.00
Stock price – close ($)	(1.4%)	34.76	36.93	18.01	16.67	19.09	15.84	23.26	35.35	35.35	30.63
P/E – high	—	8	12	—	—	12	11	8	8	15	17
P/E – low	—	6	8	—	—	8	6	5	5	11	12
Dividends per share ($)	(1.4%)	1.79	1.84	1.16	0.93	0.93	0.93	0.93	0.93	1.01	1.57
Book value per share ($)	(5.1%)	40.28	42.47	20.23	27.64	22.32	19.63	21.49	25.48	28.59	25.05
Employees	5.2%	15,807	18,400	16,650	16,500	16,500	16,400	16,900	18,000	21,400	25,000

1994 Year-end:
Equity as % of assets: 10.7%
Return on assets: 1.1%
Return on equity: 13.5%
Long-term debt (mil.): $2,135
No. of shares (mil.): 147
Dividends
　Yield: 5.1%
　Payout: 64.9%
Market value (mil.): $4,508
Sales (mil.): $3,962

Stock Price History
High/Low 1985–94

MELVILLE CORPORATION

OVERVIEW

One of the largest diversified specialty retailers in the US, Melville Corporation operates more than 7,000 stores worldwide. Melville's stores, almost all of which are located in "strip" shopping centers or malls, include CVS drugstores, Marshalls (apparel and home products), Thom McAn (shoes), Kay-Bee (toys), and Linens 'n Things (housewares). The Rye, New York–based company focuses on being a low-cost provider for value-conscious customers.

Melville operates 4 divisions. Its largest unit, prescription drugs, health, and beauty aids, which includes CVS, is the company's biggest revenue generator. Melville has worked to improve CVS's operations by investing in new computer systems. The company's apparel unit, which includes Marshalls, has been hurt by a downturn in the apparel industry. In response Marshalls is broadening its mix of home products. Melville's footwear division includes FootAction, which is growing rapidly, and Thom McAn, which has struggled. Its toys and home furnishings unit is developing larger store formats.

Melville has shed several underperforming businesses and stores as part of its strategic realignment program launched in 1992, and the company began a strategic review in 1994 to discover how to get the most out of its broadly diversified retail operations.

WHEN

In 1892 shoe supplier Frank Melville formed Melville Shoe by taking over 3 New York shoe stores when their owner left town owing him money. During WWI Ward Melville, Frank's son and vice-president of the firm, served in the Quartermaster Corps's shoe and leather division under shoe manufacturer J. Frank McElwain. The 2 men devised the merchandising scheme of mass-producing shoes for distribution through a chain of low-price stores. Melville opened the first of its Thom McAn (named after a Scottish professional golfer) stores, for which McElwain provided the shoes, in New York in 1922. There were 370 stores in the chain by 1927.

By 1931 Melville operated 476 shoe stores and had income of $1.2 million on sales of over $26 million. In 1939 Melville bought the McElwain factory, consolidating production and distribution into one corporation. By 1958 Melville was operating 1,034 stores, 796 of them Thom McAn stores, but profits were declining because of changes in customer tastes and shifting populations.

Melville met the challenge of change, moving stores from urban areas to the suburbs and adding more fashionable merchandise to existing lines. Its Meldisco division began leasing space for shoe sales in S. S. Kresge's Kmart discount department stores in 1961. In 1968 the company launched Chess King (young men's apparel) and bought Foxwood (young women's apparel, renamed Foxmoor) stores. Melville bought the Consumer Value Stores (CVS) drugstore chain in 1969.

In 1975 Kresge demanded a 49% equity interest in all Meldisco subsidiaries operating in Kmart stores. Melville accepted the terms of the new agreement rather than lose one of its largest divisions. The company purchased Marshalls (discount department stores, 1976), Mack Drug (1977), Kay-Bee Toy and Hobby Shops (1981), Freddy's (deep-discount drugstores, 1984), Prints Plus (1985), This End Up Furniture (1985), and Accessory Lady (1987), and it sold Foxmoor (1985).

In 1990 Melville added 823 stores by buying Bob's Stores (apparel and footwear "superstores"), People's Drug Stores (merged with CVS), and Circus World toys (merged with Kay-Bee). The acquisitions made Melville the 5th largest drugstore operator in the US and one of the largest toy retailers.

In 1991 the company acquired the 128-store FootAction chain and the 136-store K&K toy store chain. The acquisitions strengthened Melville's presence in the Southeast and the Sunbelt.

In 1992 Melville initiated a massive restructuring aimed at sharpening its focusing on its most successful operations. Targeted for downsizing were the company's Thom McAn and Kay-Bee stores. The company also announced plans to convert many of its Linens 'n Things stores to a larger format.

Melville sold its Prints Plus framing stores to CPI Corporation and the men's clothier Chess King to Merry-Go-Round Enterprises in 1993. It sold its 114 Accessory Lady stores to Woolworth Corp. later that year.

In 1994 Melville created PharmaCare Management Services to provide pharmacy services and managed-care drug programs.

In 1995 Warren Feldberg resigned as chairman and CEO of Marshalls.

NYSE symbol: MES
Fiscal year ends: December 31

WHO

Chairman and CEO: Stanley P. Goldstein, age 60, $1,541,400 pay
President and COO: Harvey Rosenthal, age 52, $1,042,500 pay
EVP: Jerald S. Politzer, age 49, $829,750 pay
SVP Human Resources: Jerald L. Mauer, age 52, $343,640 pay
SVP and Acting CFO: Gary L. Crittenden, age 41
SVP; President, Melville Realty: Daniel B. Katz, age 49
VP and Treasurer: Philip C. Galbo, age 44
VP and Corporate Secretary: Arthur V. Richards, age 56
Auditors: KPMG Peat Marwick LLP

WHERE

HQ: One Theall Rd., Rye, NY 10580
Phone: 914-925-4000
Fax: 914-925-4026

Melville operates 7,378 stores in all 50 states and Washington DC, and in Canada, the Czech Republic, Mexico, Puerto Rico, Singapore, Slovakia, the UK, and the US Virgin Islands.

	No. of Stores	1994 Sales ($ mil.)
Meldisco (footwear)	2,778	1,281
CVS (drugstores)	1,328	4,330
Kay-Bee (toys)	996	1,012
Wilsons (leather apparel)	628	475
Marshalls (apparel)	484	2,775
FootAction	439	332
Thom McAn (footwear)	323	227
This End Up (furniture)	237	125
Linens 'n Things	145	440
Bob's (apparel & footwear)	20	289
Total	**7,378**	**11,286**

KEY COMPETITORS

50-Off Stores	The Limited
American Stores	Liz Claiborne
Arbor Drugs	Longs
The Athlete's Foot	Luxottica
Bed Bath & Beyond	May
Big B	Men's Wearhouse
Broadway Stores	Merck
Brown Group	Merry-Go-Round
Dayton Hudson	NIKE
Eckerd	Nine West
Edison Brothers	Reebok
The Gap	Revco
Genovese Drug Stores	Rite Aid
Harcourt General	Sports Authority
INTERCO	Thriftway Food & Drug
J. C. Penney	Toys "R" Us
Jos. A. Bank	V. F.
Just For Feet	Walgreen
Kmart	Wal-Mart
L.A. Gear	Woolworth
Lands' End	

WHAT

	1994 Sales		1994 Operating Income	
	$ mil.	% of total	$ mil.	% of total
Prescription drugs, health & beauty aids	4,330	38	228	35
Apparel	3,539	31	161	25
Footwear	1,840	16	159	25
Toys & household furnishings	1,577	14	99	15
Total	**11,286**	**100**	**647**	**100**

HOW MUCH

	9-Year Growth	1985	1986	1987	1988	1989	1990	1991	1992	1993	1994
Sales ($ mil.)	10.0%	4,775	5,262	5,930	6,780	7,554	8,687	9,886	10,433	10,435	11,286
Net income ($ mil.)	4.3%	210	238	285	355	398	385	347	156	332	307
Income as % of sales	—	4.4%	4.5%	4.8%	5.2%	5.3%	4.4%	3.5%	1.5%	3.2%	2.7%
Earnings per share ($)	3.9%	1.95	2.20	2.63	1.63	3.56	3.59	3.20	1.34	3.00	2.75
Stock price – high ($)	—	26.44	36.88	42.00	38.31	53.63	57.75	55.25	55.00	54.75	41.63
Stock price – low ($)	—	17.63	24.63	22.13	26.63	36.88	32.75	38.25	42.50	38.88	29.50
Stock price – close ($)	2.3%	25.25	27.00	26.50	37.19	44.63	42.00	44.50	53.13	40.63	30.88
P/E – high	—	14	17	16	24	15	16	17	41	18	15
P/E – low	—	9	11	8	16	10	9	12	32	13	11
Dividends per share ($)	8.7%	0.72	0.78	0.88	1.05	1.30	1.42	1.44	1.48	1.52	1.52
Book value per share ($)	9.1%	10.20	11.64	13.41	15.66	12.11	15.65	19.93	19.67	21.15	22.42
Employees	4.9%	76,011	80,394	90,500	96,554	100,541	119,590	110,148	115,644	111,082	117,000

1994 Year-end:
Debt ratio: 18.2%
Return on equity: 13.4%
Cash (mil.): $117
Current ratio: 1.61
Long-term debt (mil.): $331
No. of shares (mil.): 106
Dividends
  Yield: 4.9%
  Payout: 55.3%
Market value (mil.): $3,262

Stock Price History
High/Low 1985–94

MERCANTILE STORES COMPANY, INC.

OVERVIEW

Mercantile Stores's ears must be burning. The company has been at the center of takeover rumors, with both May Department Stores and Dillard Department Stores named as possible suitors, but in 1995 the company announced it was not in merger talks with anyone.

Based in Fairfield, Ohio, Mercantile is a department store retailer operating 13 separate chains (totaling 103 stores) located in 17 states, mostly in the South and the Midwest. Mercantile's stores specialize in fashion apparel, accessories, and fashion home furnishings, catering, in general, to the middle and upper-middle classes. Some of the larger and better-known of Mercantile's chains are Gayfers (Alabama), Maison Blanche (Louisiana), Castner Knott (Nashville), and McAlpin's (Cincinnati). It also is a partner in a joint venture with interests in 5 shopping centers where the company operates stores.

After remaining flat during fiscal 1994, Mercantile's net income jumped 20% in fiscal 1995 thanks to a series of cost cutting measures the company has implemented over the last few years. It has restructured its corporate and field organizations in an attempt to eliminate redundant operations. Store groups, which numbered 11 at one time, have now been reduced to 5. The company merged the McAlpin's and Bacons (Midwest) divisions and the Joslins (Colorado) and Jones (Missouri and Kansas) divisions. Mercantile wants to continue adding stores to its roster. It plans to open up to 5 department stores by 1996.

Most analysts still think the company is ripe for takeover. A deciding factor could be a capital gains tax cut, which could persuade the Milliken family of South Carolina, which owns about 40% of the company's stock, to approve a deal.

WHEN

H. B. Claflin Company, a large New York dry goods wholesaler, expanded into retailing around the turn of the century with the acquisitions of such major names as Lord & Taylor of New York and Hahne's of Newark. In 1914 the company collapsed into bankruptcy and eventually emerged as 2 creditor-controlled firms: Associated Dry Goods got Lord & Taylor and other premier, primarily northeastern names, while Mercantile Stores got the smaller and less attractive names. Mercantile's lead creditor was Milliken & Company, the textile giant. While Associated became part of May Department Stores Company in 1986, Mercantile has remained a public company under Milliken control.

With weak positions in their markets, the company's divisions barely survived the Great Depression. The chief executive ordered them to sell off inventory to raise cash but did it in person because he didn't trust the telephone. After WWII, management adopted a 2-part merchandising strategy. First, local buyers selected fashion merchandise to remain in tune with local markets, as did other department stores. Second, centralized buyers in New York bought commodity items such as sheets and socks to minimize costs and passed savings on to the customer (a strategy similar to that of Sears and J. C. Penney). The company also established a tradition of excellent expense control. Mercantile bought the Glass Block in Duluth (1944) and de Lendrecie's in Fargo (1955).

In the 1980s, in conjunction with Milliken, Mercantile began experimenting with quick-response inventory replenishment, in which sales data are sent immediately to manufacturers and suppliers.

Mercantile sold its Canadian operations in 1987. During the late 1980s, while many of its competitors were buying up or merging with weaker department store chains, Mercantile focused on renovating its existing stores rather than buying other chains' stores. In 1990 the company moved its headquarters from New York to Fairfield, Ohio.

In early 1992 the company bought the 16-store Maison Blanche chain, its largest purchase ever. The company decided to consolidate Hennessy's, de Lendrecie's, and Glass Block into the Denver-based Joslins.

The company encourages initiative in its employees and has set up Entrepreneurial Centers in each of its stores. Although it opened no stores throughout 1992 (it had planned to open several), Mercantile managed to open a McAlpin's in Kentucky in early 1993.

In 1994 Mercantile opened 4 new stores: a Maison Blanche store in New Orleans, a Joslins in Denver, a Gayfers in Hattiesburg, Mississippi, and a McAlpin's in Crestview Hills, Kentucky. The Maison Blanche and Joslins stores replaced older, smaller stores.

In 1995 Mercantile restructured its operations, creating a Mercantile Merchandise Group.

NYSE symbol: MST
Fiscal year ends: Saturday nearest January 31

WHO

Chairman and CEO: David L. Nichols, age 53,
$999,025 pay
SVP and CFO: James M. McVicker, age 48, $481,187 pay
VP Merchandising: Paul E. McLynch, age 53,
$476,163 pay
VP Administration: James D. Cain, age 59, $434,858 pay
VP Real Estate: Randolph L. Burnette, age 53,
$345,484 pay
Treasurer: William A. Carr, age 56
Controller: Kathryn M. Muldowney, age 36
Secretary: Dennis F. Murphy
Director Human Resources: Lou Ripley
Auditors: Arthur Andersen & Co, SC

WHERE

HQ: 9450 Seward Rd., Fairfield, OH 45014
Phone: 513-881-8000
Fax: 513-881-8689

	No. of Stores
Florida	14
Kentucky	12
Ohio	11
Alabama	10
Colorado	10
Tennessee	9
Louisiana	8
Georgia	5
Missouri	5
South Carolina	4
Mississippi	4
Kansas	3
Montana	3
Indiana	2
Other states	3
Total	**103**

WHAT

	No. of Stores
Gayfers	27
Castner Knott Co.	13
McAlpin's	12
Joslins	11
Maison Blanche	8
The Jones Store Co.	8
Bacons	7
J.B. White	7
Lion	4
Hennessy's	3
de Lendrecie's	1
Glass Block	1
Root's	1
Total	**103**

KEY COMPETITORS

Bombay Company
Broadway Stores
Brown Group
Dayton Hudson
Dillard
Edison Brothers
Federated
The Gap
Lands' End
The Limited
Luxottica
May
Meijer
Melville
Men's Wearhouse
Montgomery Ward
J. C. Penney
Sears
Spiegel
TJX
Wal-Mart
Woolworth

HOW MUCH

	9-Year Growth	1986	1987	1988	1989	1990	1991	1992	1993	1994	1995
Sales ($ mil.)	4.6%	1,880	2,028	2,156	2,266	2,313	2,367	2,442	2,732	2,730	2,820
Net income ($ mil.)	0.2%	102	111	130	145	130	124	114	87	87	105
Income as % of sales	—	5.4%	5.5%	6.0%	6.4%	5.6%	5.2%	4.7%	3.2%	3.2%	3.7%
Earnings per share ($)	0.2%	2.78	3.02	3.52	3.92	3.54	3.36	3.10	2.36	2.35	2.84
Stock price – high ($)[1]	—	31.25	46.81	53.38	46.50	50.50	45.38	42.50	42.13	37.25	57.00
Stock price – low ($)[1]	—	21.81	29.09	30.63	34.75	37.50	24.25	26.75	29.38	29.88	30.50
Stock price – close ($)[1]	2.6%	31.25	38.31	37.00	42.75	39.13	30.00	38.38	36.25	36.25	39.50
P/E – high	—	11	16	15	12	14	14	14	18	16	20
P/E – low	—	8	10	9	9	11	7	9	12	13	11
Dividends per share ($)	8.0%	0.51	0.58	0.68	0.78	0.89	0.96	1.01	1.02	1.02	1.02
Book value per share ($)	8.4%	18.40	20.84	23.68	26.62	29.24	31.83	33.95	34.81	36.18	38.01
Employees	4.0%	21,400	23,000	24,000	25,800	26,500	27,500	28,850	30,000	30,000	30,500

1995 Year-end:
Debt ratio: 16.0%
Return on equity: 7.6%
Cash (mil.): $114
Current ratio: 4.66
Long-term debt (mil.): $261
No. of shares (mil.): 37
Dividends
  Yield: 2.6%
  Payout: 35.9%
Market value (mil.): $1,455

Stock Price History[1]
High/Low 1986–95

[1] Stock prices are for the prior calendar year.

MERCK & CO., INC.

OVERVIEW

With the merger of competitors Glaxo and Wellcome, Merck is now only the 2nd largest pharmaceutical company in the world. Vasotec, its biggest-selling drug (with sales of $2.2 billion), is the world's leading cardiovascular treatment. Two of the company's cholesterol-lowering drugs, Mevacor and Zocor, each has sales of over $1 billion.

The New Jersey–based company also makes pesticides and animal health products, but it sold its specialty chemical concerns to Bristol-Myers and Monsanto to concentrate on core businesses. In 1993 Merck bought Medco Containment Services, the largest pharmacy benefits management company in the US. Medco, which processes and ships the prescriptions of more than 41 million Americans, is helping Merck capture a larger share of the growing managed-care market. Merck drugs account for about 12% of Medco's available pharmaceuticals, up from 10%.

Merck spends about 8.2% of sales on R&D. Among the drugs Merck has in the research pipeline are treatments for schizophrenia (with Swedish partner Astra), osteoporosis, and asthma. It expects growth to come from new drugs and expansion of Medco, not from acquisition. Chairman Raymond Gilmartin says that Merck's goal is to again be the world's largest pharmaceutical company.

WHEN

Merck was started in 1887 when chemist Theodore Weicker came to the US from Germany to set up an American branch of E. Merck AG of Germany. George Merck (grandson of the German company's founder) came in 1891 and entered into a partnership with Weicker. At first the firm imported and sold drugs and chemicals from Germany, but in 1903 it opened a plant in Rahway, New Jersey, to manufacture alkaloids. Weicker sold out to Merck in 1904 and bought a controlling interest in competitor Squibb. During WWI Merck gave the US government the 80% of company stock owned by family in Germany (George kept his shares). After the war the stock was sold to the public.

Merck merged with Powers-Weightman-Rosengarten of Philadelphia (a producer of the antimalarial quinine) in 1927. At its first research lab, established in 1933, Merck scientists did pioneering work on vitamin B-12 and developed the first steroid (cortisone, 1944). Five Merck scientists received Nobel prizes in the 1940s and 1950s. In 1953 Merck merged with Sharp & Dohme of Philadelphia, which brought with it a strong sales force.

Merck introduced Diuril (antihypertensive) in 1958 and other drugs in the early 1960s (Indocin, Aldomet), but for nearly 10 years there were few new drugs. John Horan, who took over in 1976, accelerated R&D in an effort to create new products. By the late 1970s the company had produced Clinoril (antiarthritic), Flexeril (muscle relaxant), and Timoptic (for glaucoma).

Biochemist Roy Vagelos, who joined Merck in 1976 as head of research and became CEO in 1985, continued the commitment to R&D. Merck introduced 10 major new drugs in the 1980s, including Mevacor for high cholesterol and Vasotec for high blood pressure.

In 1990 Merck bought the nonprescription drug segment of ICI Americas, whose drugs it markets through a joint venture with Johnson & Johnson. Merck and DuPont formed a joint venture in 1991 to market drugs in the US and Europe.

In 1993 Merck paid $6.6 billion in stock and cash for Medco Containment Services. Medco traces its roots to National Pharmacies, a mail order pharmacy founded in 1969. Investor Martin Wygod bought National Pharmacies from corporate raider Victor Posner in 1983 for about $30 million. A year later Wygod sold 20% of the company to the public and changed its name to Medco Containment.

In 1985 Medco bought retail drug claim processor Paid Prescriptions for $29 million. The acquisition gave Medco access to information from a network of more than 40,000 drugstores. To attract more customers, Medco introduced its Prescriber's Choice program in 1991. The program tracks its clients' prescriptions. When Medco finds a cheaper equivalent (such as a generic version) that could be prescribed, it contacts the doctor, notifying him or her of the cheaper alternative. About 40% of the doctors contacted prescribe the cheaper version.

In 1994 the company established new subsidiaries in Cyprus, Germany, Holland, Peru, and South Korea and began a joint venture in China to manufacture and sell Merck products. Also that year the FDA cleared Trusopt as the first topical treatment for elevated intraocular pressure in patients with ocular hypertension or glaucoma. In 1995 the FDA issued a license for Merck's chicken pox vaccine, Varivax.

WHO

Chairman, President, and CEO: Raymond V. Gilmartin, age 54, $1,541,671 pay
EVP Science and Technology; President, Merck Research Laboratories: Edward M. Scolnick, age 54, $1,209,996 pay
EVP: Jerry T. Jackson, $1,135,004 pay
EVP: Francis H. Spiegel Jr., $1,009,749 pay
EVP Worldwide Basic Research, Merck Research Laboratories: Bennett M. Shapiro, age 55, $633,946 pay
President, Human Health US and Canada: David W. Anstice, age 46, $681,589 pay
President, Merck Vaccines: R. Gordon Douglas Jr., age 60
SVP and CFO: Judy C. Lewent, age 46, $684,996 pay
SVP and General Counsel: Mary M. McDonald, age 50
VP Planning and Development: Clifford S. Cramer, age 43
VP Human Resources: Steven M. Darien, age 52
Auditors: Arthur Andersen & Co, SC

WHERE

HQ: PO Box 100, Whitehouse Station, NJ 08889-0100
Phone: 908-423-1000
Fax: 908-594-4662

Merck has operations around the world.

	1994 Sales	
	$ mil.	% of total
North America	10,561	70
Europe	2,553	17
Asia/Pacific	1,587	11
Other regions	269	2
Total	**14,970**	**100**

WHAT

	1994 Sales	
	$ mil.	% of total
Cardiovasculars	5,352	36
Anti-ulcerants	1,566	10
Animal health/ crop protection	1,027	7
Antibiotics	827	6
Vaccines/biologicals	485	3
Ophthalmologicals	482	3
Specialty chemicals	422	3
Anti-inflammatories/ analgesics	271	2
Other Merck human health	433	3
Other human health	4,104	27
Total	**14,970**	**100**

Selected Products

Heartgard (canine heartworm prevention)
Indocin (anti-inflammatory)
Mevacor (cardiovascular)
M-M-R II (measles, mumps, and rubella virus vaccine)
Pepcid (anti-ulcerant)
Primaxin (antibiotic)
Prinivil (cardiovascular)
Proscar (benign prostate enlargement)
Recombivax HB (hepatitis B vaccine recombinant)
Vasotec (cardiovascular)
Zocor (cardiovascular)

KEY COMPETITORS

Abbott Labs
American Home Products
American Stores
Amgen
Baxter
Bayer
Bristol-Myers Squibb
Ciba-Geigy
Eli Lilly
FoxMeyer Health
Genentech
Glaxo
Wellcome
Hoechst
J. C. Penney
Johnson & Johnson
Longs
McKesson
Melville
Monsanto
Pfizer
Procter & Gamble
Rhône-Poulenc
Rite Aid
Roche
Sandoz
Schering-Plough
SmithKline Beecham
Upjohn
Walgreen
Wal-Mart
Warner-Lambert

HOW MUCH

	9-Year Growth	1985	1986	1987	1988	1989	1990	1991	1992	1993	1994
Sales ($ mil.)	17.3%	3,548	4,129	5,061	5,940	6,551	7,672	8,603	9,663	10,498	14,970
Net income ($ mil.)	21.0%	540	676	906	1,207	1,495	1,781	2,122	2,447	2,166	2,997
Income as % of sales	—	15.2%	16.4%	17.9%	20.3%	22.8%	23.2%	24.7%	25.3%	20.6%	20.0%
Earnings per share ($)	21.3%	0.42	0.54	0.74	1.02	1.26	1.52	1.83	2.12	1.87	2.38
Stock price – high ($)	—	7.65	14.39	24.78	19.88	26.92	30.38	55.67	56.58	44.13	39.50
Stock price – low ($)	—	5.01	7.46	13.56	16.00	18.75	22.33	27.33	40.50	28.63	28.13
Stock price – close ($)	19.6%	7.61	13.76	17.61	19.25	25.83	29.96	55.50	43.38	34.38	38.13
P/E – high	—	18	27	34	19	21	20	30	27	24	17
P/E – low	—	12	14	18	16	15	15	15	19	15	12
Dividends per share ($)	22.8%	0.18	0.21	0.27	0.43	0.55	0.64	0.77	0.92	1.03	1.14
Book value per share ($)	17.9%	2.03	2.03	1.73	2.41	2.96	3.27	4.24	4.34	7.99	8.93
Employees	4.9%	30,900	30,700	31,100	32,000	34,400	36,900	37,700	38,400	47,100	47,500

1994 Year-end:
Debt ratio: 10.4%
Return on equity: 28.3%
Cash (mil.): $2,270
Current ratio: 1.27
Long-term debt (mil.): $1,146
No. of shares (mil.): 1,248
Dividends
  Yield: 3.0%
  Payout: 47.9%
Market value (mil.): $47,573

Stock Price History High/Low 1985–94

MERISEL, INC.

OVERVIEW

The world's #1 publicly held wholesale computer hardware and software distributor, Merisel sells a line of 25,000 products from more than 900 manufacturers, including Apple, DEC, Hewlett-Packard, and IBM.

With competition in the distribution business rising, Merisel is looking to gain an edge by broadening its operations. In 1994 Merisel became what it calls a Master Distributor, both a distributor and a reseller, when it acquired the franchise and distribution operations of ComputerLand (now Vanstar) for $110 million. The deal allows Merisel to provide about $1 billion a year in merchandise to its more than 750 ComputerLand franchisees and Datago resellers. It also acquired ComputerLand's aggregator business, which puts together complete computer systems for customers. However, the move has ruffled the feathers of some of Merisel's customers who now see their distributor competing with them on the retail level via its ComputerLand franchisees. In order to keep its clients, Merisel has lowered prices, which has cut into its profits.

To attract more business, Merisel is customizing its service levels, allowing it to charge less to clients who need bare-bones service and more to those who are looking for expanded service.

WHEN

Robert Leff, a software developer for Citibank's Transaction Technologies subsidiary, got started in the distribution business in 1980 when he bought $1,700 worth of game and entertainment software and began selling it in his spare time. He and co-worker David Wagman quit their day jobs and founded Softsel Computer Products to sell software full-time.

Working out of Leff's house and using a list of authorized Apple Computer distributors as a prospect sheet, the pair had sales of $350,000 in their first year. By the end of 1981, sales had jumped to $7 million. Softsel expanded its operations, moving into Europe in 1983, and becoming one of the first computer distributors to expand overseas. Also in 1983 Softsel introduced Softeach, a series of training seminars for purchasers of computer products.

In 1985, looking for new opportunities for expansion, the company moved into mass-market software. However, the computer industry slumped, and Softsel had to take back millions of dollars in returns on unsold products, leading to the first loss in the company's history. To lower its costs the company sold its software publishing division and its unprofitable German subsidiary, saving about $10 million.

Softsel rebounded and in 1988 it went public. That same year Softsel promoted Mike Pickett, who as COO had helped guide the company back into the black, to CEO. By 1989 the company had sales of more than $600 million, but it had its eyes on bigger things.

In late 1989 it announced plans to acquire hardware distributor Microamerica for about $80 million, making it the largest computer products distributor in the world, with sales of more than $1 billion. The acquisition, which included Microamerica's warehouses in Europe and Latin America, also helped the company to expand its overseas operations.

In 1990, when the deal was completed, the companies combined their names to create Merisel. While merging the 2 names just meant moving a few letters around, merging the 2 corporate cultures proved to be more difficult. California-based Softsel had a laid-back atmosphere (Leff's taste ran to Hawaiian shirts), while Boston-based Microamerica was more button-down in dress and atmosphere. However, employees choosing what to wear to work each day was the least of the company's problems. Its costs soared as it struggled to meld decentralized Microamerica with the centralized operations of Softsel, and its profits plummeted.

By 1991 profits began to rise. That same year Merisel made another push into mass-market channels, this time with much better results, as the computer industry shifted away from traditional computer retailers toward big chains and warehouse stores.

As part of its increased concentration on mass merchandising, in 1993 the company reorganized its sales department, creating a unit that served only mass merchants. By the end of 1994, half of the North American warehouses were automated, cutting shipping and receiving errors by 1/2.

In 1995 co-chairman Bob Leff and VC David Wagman both retired. Pickett, the other co-chairman, became chairman. Also in 1995 Merisel signed distribution agreements with Mustang Software, Microdyne, and Cirrus Logic.

Nasdaq symbol: MSEL
Fiscal year ends: December 31

WHO

Chairman, President, and CEO: Michael D. Pickett,
age 47, $579,068 pay
SVP European Operations: Susan J. Miller-Smith,
age 42, $252,342 pay
**SVP Worldwide Information Services and Chief
Information Officer:** Paul M. Lemerise, age 49,
$242,592 pay
SVP Finance, CFO, and Secretary: James L. Brill,
age 43, $237,205 pay
SVP Worldwide Operations: John F. Thompson, age 50
SVP Canadian Operations: Thomas P. Reeves, age 33
**SVP Franchise and Aggregator Operations and
Asia/Pacific Operations:** Verilyn Smith, age 42
SVP: Martin D. Wolf, age 36
Acting VP Human Resources: Carol Baker
President, Merisel Latin America: Cliff Dyer
Managing Director, Merisel Australia: Patrick Woods
Managing Director, Merisel UK: Derek Anderson
General Counsel: Kelly Martin
Auditors: Deloitte & Touche LLP

WHERE

HQ: 200 Continental Blvd., El Segundo, CA 90245-0948
Phone: 310-615-3080
Fax: 310-615-1238

Merisel has offices in Australia, Europe, and North and
South America.

	1994 Sales		1994 Operating Income	
	$ mil.	% of total	$ mil.	% of total
US	3,413	68	52	78
Europe	784	16	(6)	—
Canada	517	10	10	15
Other regions	305	6	5	7
Total	**5,019**	**100**	**61**	**100**

WHAT

	1994 Sales
	% of total
Hardware & accessories	75
Software	25
Total	**100**

Hardware	Selected Suppliers
Computer systems	Apple
Disk drives	AST
Modems	Compaq
Monitors	DEC
Plug-in boards	Hewlett-Packard
Printers	IBM
	Intel
Software	Lotus
Desktop publishing	Microsoft
and graphics	NEC
Operating systems	Novell
Spreadsheets	Sun Microsystems
Word processing	Texas Instruments

KEY COMPETITORS

Arrow Electronics	Ingram
ASCII	Intelligent Electronics
Avnet	Jaco Electronics
Baker & Taylor	Marshall Industries
Bell Industries	Micro Warehouse
Bell Microproducts	MicroAge
CompuCom	Pioneer-Standard
CompUSA	Electronics
Corporate Software	Premier Industrial
D&H Distributing	Software Spectrum
Dell	Stream International
Entex	Tandy
Gates F/A Distributing	Tech Data
Gateway 2000	Technology Solutions
Graybar Electric	TTI
InaCom	Wyle Labs

HOW MUCH

	Annual Growth	1985	1986	1987	1988	1989	1990	1991	1992	1993	1994
Sales ($ mil.)	48.2%	—	—	319	465	629	1,192	1,585	2,239	3,086	5,019
Net income ($ mil.)	8.0%	—	—	7	8	10	1	11	20	30	12
Income as % of sales	—	—	—	2.1%	1.7%	1.6%	0.1%	0.7%	0.9%	1.0%	0.2%
Earnings per share ($)	(6.8%)	—	—	0.62	0.70	0.81	0.03	0.43	0.67	1.00	0.38
Stock price – high ($)	—	—	—	—	6.25	7.88	6.38	9.38	14.88	18.50	22.50
Stock price – low ($)	—	—	—	—	5.13	5.50	1.63	1.75	6.63	9.75	6.25
Stock price – close ($)	4.9%	—	—	—	6.00	6.13	2.38	9.13	10.13	18.38	8.00
P/E – high	—	—	—	—	9	10	—	22	22	19	59
P/E – low	—	—	—	—	7	7	54	4	10	10	16
Dividends per share ($)	—	—	—	—	0.00	0.00	0.00	0.00	0.00	0.00	0.00
Book value per share ($)	17.0%	—	—	—	3.10	4.08	4.71	5.13	6.79	7.56	7.95
Employees	31.9%	—	—	442	538	629	1,282	1,450	1,939	2,502	3,072

1994 Year-end:
Debt ratio: 62.6%
Return on equity: 5.0%
Cash (mil.): $4
Current ratio: 1.67
Long-term debt (mil.): $358
No. of shares (mil.): 30
Dividends
  Yield: —
  Payout: —
Market value (mil.): $238

**Stock Price History
High/Low 1988–94**

MERRILL LYNCH & CO., INC.

OVERVIEW

Merrill Lynch managed to keep its income above the $1 billion mark despite turbulent markets that brought earnings declines in its foreign operations and static-to-declining revenues in 3 of its 4 major business categories (brokerage, proprietary trading, and investment banking). The firm had rising results in asset and portfolio management. Merrill Lynch, the US's largest brokerage firm and the leader in US and foreign equities underwriting, is unique in combining a retail brokerage and cash management business with investment banking. Other lines include clearing services, retail banking, and insurance.

In 1994 and 1995 Merrill Lynch was hit with at least a dozen suits related to the bankruptcy of Orange County, California, because it had sold the county the derivatives whose loss in value had precipitated the bankruptcy. In addition to suits alleging misconduct in the sale of the instruments to the county, the firm is named as a defendant in suits by investors who bought Merrill Lynch's California and other municipal bond funds or the county bonds themselves, and in suits by Merrill Lynch stockholders because of the firm's potential liability in all these suits. In turn, Merrill Lynch sued several ex-employees.

WHEN

Wall Street bond salesman Charles Merrill opened an underwriting firm in 1914 and within 6 months took on his friend Edmund Lynch as partner. In the 1920s the new firm pursued nontraditional investors (i.e., the small investor) by stressing personal service. Merrill became known as the man who brought Wall Street to Main Street. During the 1920s the firm took a lead in financing the new supermarkets that were providing consumers with more service and variety.

In 1930 the company sold its retail business to Wall Street's largest brokerage firm, E. A. Pierce, and survived the Depression as an investment banking firm. Merrill Lynch reacquired the retail business in a 1940 merger with Pierce, and in 1941 the company merged with Fenner and Beane. Winthrop Smith, an employee transferred to Pierce in 1930, became a partner in 1958.

The company continued to grow by pursuing new investor groups, aiming information and advertising campaigns at small investors. Merrill Lynch was the first NYSE member to incorporate (1959) and go public (1971). In the 1960s it diversified into government securities, real estate financing (and sales in the 1970s), and asset management and consulting. In the 1970s, under Donald Regan (Ronald Reagan's secretary of the treasury and chief of staff), the company introduced the patented Cash Management Account and built up its investment banking, insurance, and foreign operations.

In the 1980s Merrill Lynch's underwriting business boomed. It became the global leader in offerings and advised on the largest of them all, Kohlberg Kravis Roberts's LBO of RJR Nabisco.

After the 1987 crash, Merrill Lynch retrenched and reorganized, jettisoning or trimming less profitable segments (merchant banking, real estate, and its mortgage insurance business) and closing some overseas offices. In addition to increasing the proportion of earnings from management and other fees and reducing dependence on commissions, Merrill Lynch moved to reduce its holdings of junk bonds and curtail its granting of bridge loans to ailing companies. In 1990, to reduce staff turnover (14–15% of its professional staff annually), the company introduced new training and pay procedures to reward long service and reduce dependency by inexperienced staff members on commission earnings. In 1991 Merrill Lynch received permission to buy a seat on the Seoul exchange.

In 1990 the stock market rebounded, followed in 1991 and 1992 by a recovery in merchant and investment banking, with a record number of new issues worldwide. Many of the issues were related to the privatization of formerly state-owned companies in Eastern and southern Europe and in South America, as well as to a burgeoning number of US IPOs.

Although Merrill Lynch cut back its Japanese operations because of the recession there, it has continued to expand in Asia, opening offices in Beijing and Thailand. In 1995 it entered into a joint venture with India's largest investment bank, DSP Financial Consultants. However, its operations in Latin America, where it is a major underwriter of new issues, were hurt in late 1994 and into 1995 by the effects of the collapse of the Mexican peso.

In 1995, in order to boost brokerage sales and compete with regional full-service brokerages, Merrill Lynch announced that it would open up to 250 new branches in small towns throughout the US to bring personal service to wealthy individuals in smaller markets.

NYSE symbol: MER
Fiscal year ends: Last Friday in December

WHO

Chairman and CEO: Daniel P. Tully, age 63, $4,840,000 pay
President and COO: David H. Komansky, age 55, $3,200,000 pay
VC and General Counsel: Stephen L. Hammerman, age 56, $2,800,000 pay
EVP Private Client Group: John L. Steffens, age 53, $3,200,000 pay
EVP Corporate and Institutional Business Group: Herbert M. Allison Jr., age 51, $3,200,000 pay
EVP Asset Management Group: Arthur Zeikel, age 62, $2,800,000 pay
EVP International: Winthrop H. Smith Jr., age 45
EVP; Chairman, Investment Banking: Barry S. Friedberg
SVP and CFO: Joseph T. Willet, age 43
SVP Human Resources: Patrick J. Walsh
Auditors: Deloitte & Touche LLP

WHERE

HQ: World Financial Center, North Tower, 250 Vesey St., New York, NY 10281-1332
Phone: 212-449-1000
Fax: 212-236-4384

	1994 Sales		1994 Pretax Income	
	$ mil.	% of total	$ mil.	% of total
US	13,754	73	1,342	78
Europe & Middle East	3,464	19	176	10
Asia/Pacific	963	5	75	4
Canada & Latin America	617	3	137	8
Adjustments	(565)	—	—	—
Total	**18,233**	**100**	**1,730**	**100**

WHAT

	1994 Sales	
	$ mil.	% of total
Commissions	2,871	16
Interest & dividends	9,578	52
Trading	2,335	13
Investment banking	1,239	7
Asset management & portfolio service fees	1,739	9
Other	471	3
Total	**18,233**	**100**

Selected Subsidiaries	Financial Services
Merrill Lynch Asset Management, L.P.	Cash management accounts
ML Bank & Trust Co.	Commodity futures
ML Capital Services, Inc.	Government and
ML Derivative Products, Inc.	municipal securities
ML Futures Investment Partners Inc.	Investment banking and underwriting
ML Government Securities Inc.	Life insurance and annuity products
ML International Inc.	Mutual funds
ML Money Markets Inc.	Securities and
ML, Pierce, Fenner & Smith Inc.	economic research
	Securities brokerage

KEY COMPETITORS

A. G. Edwards	Edward Jones	Paine Webber
Alex. Brown	Equitable	Piper Jaffray
Bankers Trust	FMR	Prudential
Bear Stearns	Goldman Sachs	Quick & Reilly
Brown Brothers Harriman	Hambrecht & Quist	Raymond James Financial
Charles Schwab	ING Bank	
CS Holding	J.P. Morgan	Salomon
Dean Witter, Discover	Lehman Brothers	S. G. Warburg
Deutsche Bank	Mellon Bank	T. Rowe Price
	Morgan Stanley	Travelers
	Nomura Securities	

HOW MUCH

	9-Year Growth	1985	1986	1987	1988	1989	1990	1991	1992	1993	1994
Sales ($ mil.)	11.0%	7,117	9,475	11,036	10,547	11,273	11,147	12,353	13,413	16,588	18,233
Net income ($ mil.)	18.3%	224	469	391	463	(213)	192	696	952	1,394	1,017
Income as % of sales	—	3.2%	5.0%	3.5%	4.4%	—	1.7%	5.6%	7.1%	8.4%	5.6%
Earnings per share ($)	17.5%	1.11	2.14	1.76	2.11	(1.16)	0.80	2.95	4.17	6.11	4.74
Stock price – high ($)	—	18.38	21.88	23.38	14.19	18.38	13.63	30.44	33.38	51.13	45.63
Stock price – low ($)	—	12.75	16.19	9.75	11.06	11.75	8.06	9.56	22.19	28.00	32.25
Stock price – close ($)	8.5%	17.19	18.25	11.19	12.00	13.13	10.38	29.56	29.75	42.00	35.75
P/E – high	—	17	10	13	7	—	17	10	8	8	10
P/E – low	—	12	8	6	5	—	10	3	5	5	7
Dividends per share ($)	9.3%	0.40	0.40	0.48	0.50	0.50	0.50	0.50	0.58	0.70	0.89
Book value per share ($)	10.3%	11.49	13.28	15.83	17.65	15.34	14.95	17.43	20.92	24.85	27.67
Employees	(0.3%)	44,900	47,900	43,400	41,800	41,200	39,000	38,300	40,100	41,900	43,800

1994 Year-end:
Debt ratio: 95.7%
Return on equity: 18.0%
Cash (mil.): $9,590
Long-term debt (mil.): $14,863
No. of shares (mil.): 188
Dividends
  Yield: 2.5%
  Payout: 18.8%
Market value (mil.): $6,718
Assets (mil.): $163,749

Stock Price History High/Low 1985–94

METROPOLITAN LIFE INSURANCE CO.

OVERVIEW

Get Met — It pays. New York–based Metropolitan Life Insurance uses this motto to assure customers that its insurance (and annuity products) will pay off as expected. In recent years, however, it has seemed like the slogan of insurance regulators investigating the sales practices of some of MetLife's agents and levying fines against the company for not policing itself. The over $100 million in fines and restitution payments to customers in 13 states (who had bought insurance after being told that it was a retirement investment) adversely affected 1994's results and shook customer confidence.

MetLife (the largest North American life insurer, with over $1.2 trillion of life insurance in force) is trying to end such abuses, possibly by making agents less dependent on commissions. It has also begun to refocus on life insurance and related financial services.

In 1995 MetLife announced that it would merge with Boston-based New England Mutual, whose upper-income clientele would complement MetLife's middle-class customer base. MetLife's financial strength, meanwhile, would help reduce the effects of New England's portfolio of troubled real estate and commercial mortgages.

WHEN

Simeon Draper, a New York merchant, tried to form National Union Life and Limb Insurance to cover Union soldiers in the Civil War, but investors were scared off by heavy casualties. After several reorganizations and name changes, the company emerged in 1868 as Metropolitan Life Insurance, a stock company.

Sustained at first by business from mutual assistance societies for German immigrants, Metropolitan went into industrial insurance with workers' burial policies. Metropolitan agents combed working-class neighborhoods, collecting small premiums. This nickel-and-dime business could be particularly profitable during the recessions of the late 19th century because if a worker missed one payment the company could cancel the policy and keep all premiums paid, a practice outlawed in 1900.

Aggressive sales were a Metropolitan hallmark. The company even imported polished British salesmen when no suitable Americans could be found.

Metropolitan became a mutual company, owned by policyholders, in 1915 and in 1917 offered group insurance. Metropolitan expanded to Canada in 1924.

After being led by the conservative Frederick Eckers and his son Frederick Jr. from 1929 to 1963, Metropolitan began to change, dropping industrial insurance in 1964. In 1974 Metropolitan began offering automobile and homeowner's insurance.

The company began to diversify in the 1980s (along with most insurers). It bought State Street Research & Management (1983), which founded the first US mutual fund; Century 21 Real Estate (1985); London-based Albany Life Assurance (1985); and Allstate's group life and health business (1988). In 1987 Metropolitan took over the annuities segment

of the failed Baldwin United Co. and expanded into Spain and Taiwan in 1988.

In 1989 MetLife bought J. C. Penney's casualty insurance portfolio, United Resources Insurance Services (retirement and financial programs), and Texas Life Insurance. Metropolitan also launched a "Family Reunion" program to contact holders of old industrial insurance policies still in force.

With the economy in recession in the early 1990s, Metropolitan began to cut costs, trimming jobs and transferring thousands of others from New York City. The company also reemphasized insurance products and added new ones, such as long-term care insurance.

In 1992 Metropolitan continued expanding despite the costs of natural disasters like Hurricane Andrew. In addition to joint ventures in Mexico and Portugal, MetLife added the 30,000 policyholders of United Mutual Life Insurance Company, which, until its merger into MetLife, was New York's only African-American life insurance company.

The next year MetLife was hit by charges of improper sales practices by agents in 13 states. Improprieties included misrepresentation of life insurance policies as retirement accounts and churning (persuading policyholders to buy more expensive policies to replace old ones). Legal fees, fines, and refunds in these cases exceeded $100 million, and bad publicity had a chilling effect on policy sales in 1994.

MetLife has added an array of services, including mutual funds and employee benefits administration, and has subtracted other operations. In 1993 it combined its health plans with Travelers's to form MetraHealth, but in 1995 this joint venture was bought by United Health. Also sold were Century 21 and MetLife's Canadian trust business.

Mutual company
Fiscal year ends: December 31

Chairman and CEO: Harry P. Kamen
President and COO: Ted Athanassiades
SEVP and CFO: Stewart G. Nagler
EVP and Chief Investment Officer: Gerald Clark
EVP and Chief Legal Officer: Gary A. Beller
EVP: Robert J. Crimmins
EVP: John D. Moynahan Jr.
EVP: William G. Poortvliet
EVP: Anthony C. Cannatella
EVP: C. Robert Henrikson
SVP and General Counsel: Richard M. Blackwell
SVP Human Resources: Anne E. Hayden
Auditors: Deloitte & Touche LLP

WHERE

HQ: Metropolitan Life Insurance Company,
One Madison Ave., New York, NY 10010-3690
Phone: 212-578-2211
Fax: 212-578-3320

MetLife and its affiliated companies operate in Canada, Mexico, Portugal, South Korea, Spain, Taiwan, the UK, and the US.

	1994 Life Insurance Premiums	
	$ mil.	% of total
New York	877	14
California	471	8
Illinois	372	6
Michigan	359	6
New Jersey	361	6
Pennsylvania	351	6
Texas	332	5
Florida	251	4
Ohio	243	4
Connecticut	127	3
Massachusetts	191	3
Missouri	109	2
Other US	1,766	29
Canada	259	4
Total	**6,069**	**100**

WHAT

	1994 Assets	
	$ mil.	% of total
Cash & equivalents	2,334	2
Treasury & agency securities	9,807	7
Foreign government securities	1,931	2
Mortgage-backed securities	17,485	13
Corporate bonds	31,262	24
State & municipal bonds	1,483	1
Stocks	3,672	3
Mortgage loans	14,524	11
Real estate	10,417	8
Policy loans	3,964	3
Separate account assets	25,424	19
Other	8,874	7
Total	**131,177**	**100**

	1994 Sales	
	$ mil.	% of total
Premiums & deposits	19,881	66
Investments	7,143	24
Supplementary contracts & dividends	2,879	10
Other	80	0
Total	**29,983**	**100**

Selected Affiliates
Albany Life Assurance Company Ltd. (UK)
Farmers National Co.
GFM International Investors Ltd. (UK)
MetLife HealthCare Management Corp.
MetLife (UK) Limited
MetLife Securities, Inc.
Metropolitan Property and Casualty Insurance Co.
Metropolitan Tower Life Insurance Co.
Metropolitan Trust Company of Canada
Seguros Génesis, S.A. (Mexico)

KEY COMPETITORS

Aetna	ITT Hartford	Pacific Mutual
Allstate	John Hancock	Life
Berkshire Hathaway	Kemper Corp.	Prudential
Blue Cross	MassMutual	State Farm
Equitable	Mutual of Omaha	Tokio Marine
GEICO	New York Life	and Fire
Guardian Life	Northwestern	Travelers
Insurance	Mutual	USAA

HOW MUCH

	Annual Growth	1985	1986	1987	1988	1989	1990	1991	1992	1993	1994
Assets ($ mil.)	6.6%	73,803	78,773	88,140	94,232	98,740	103,228	110,799	118,178	128,225	131,177
Net income ($ mil.)	(25.2%)	—	—	809	836	494	360	237	225	133	106
Income as % of assets	—	—	—	—	0.9%	0.9%	0.5%	0.3%	0.2%	0.1%	0.0%
Employees	4.7%	35,000	33,000	33,000	37,000	42,464	45,342	58,000	57,000	55,000	53,000

1994 Year-end:
Equity as % of assets: 4.8%
Return on equity: 1.7%
Sales (mil.): $29,983

Net Income ($ mil.)
1987–94

MetLife

MICROSOFT CORPORATION

OVERVIEW

Microsoft has macro plans, including the release of Windows 95, its upgraded operating system; startup of the Microsoft Network, its on-line service; and (since its plans to acquire Intuit fizzled) rollout of the revamped *Money* personal finance software to compete with Intuit's popular *Quicken*. With more than 70 consumer products, Microsoft is the world's #1 independent software company. The company's Windows operating system is installed on 60 million computers, its MS-DOS on even more.

Microsoft is moving ahead despite Justice Department roadblocks. Current inquiries concern contract provisions that prohibit Windows 95 licensees from suing Microsoft for patent infringement and whether the inclusion of Microsoft Network software with Windows 95 would give the company an unfair advantage among on-line providers. Microsoft itself has a suit against Apple alleging deceptive business practices regarding video software.

In an effort to expand its multimedia products and services, in 1995 Microsoft signed development deals with the Children's Television Workshop, NBC, Reader's Digest, and SOFTBANK (Japan's largest software distributor). The company also acquired Rendermorphics, a leader in 3-D programming tools and technology for PCs, and formed a joint venture with DreamWorks SKG to establish DreamWorks Interactive, a software company set to capitalize on entertainment properties.

CEO Bill Gates, the richest person in the world, owns about 25% of Microsoft.

WHEN

Microsoft (originally Micro-soft) was founded in 1975 after 19-year-old William Gates dropped out of Harvard and teamed with high school friend Paul Allen to sell a version of the programming language BASIC. While Gates was at Harvard, the pair had written the language for the Altair, the first commercial microcomputer (sold by Albuquerque-based MITS, a maker of electronic kits). Gates and Allen moved to Albuquerque and set up Microsoft in a hotel room to produce the program. Although MITS folded in 1979, Microsoft continued to grow by modifying its BASIC program for other computers.

Microsoft moved to Gates's native Seattle area (Bellevue) in 1979 and developed software that enabled others to write programs for PCs. Microsoft's big break came in 1980, when it was chosen by IBM, over Gary Kildall's Digital Research, to write the operating system (software that controls a computer's basic functions) for IBM's new PC. Faced with a complex task and a tight deadline, Microsoft bought the rights to QDOS (short for "quick and dirty operating system") for $50,000 from Seattle programmer Tim Paterson and renamed it the Microsoft Disk Operating System (MS-DOS).

The popularity of IBM's PC made MS-DOS an instant monopoly because other PC makers wanted to be compatible with IBM. It became the standard PC operating system in the 1980s. Microsoft went on to develop software for IBM, Apple, and Radio Shack computers. In the meantime, Allen fell ill with Hodgkin's disease; he left Microsoft in 1983. Allen later started his own software company, Asymetrix, and acquired or invested in several other companies,

including Starwave, Telescan, and Ticketmaster. Allen owns about 10% of Microsoft's stock and still serves on its board.

In the mid-1980s Microsoft introduced Windows. When the company went public in 1986, Gates retained 45% of the shares, becoming, in 1987, the PC industry's first billionaire. In 1989 Microsoft bought a minority stake (now 14%) in UNIX developer Santa Cruz Operation. In 1992 Microsoft acquired Fox Software (database management system) and released *Access*, a Windows-compatible database program.

In 1993 Microsoft introduced Windows NT, a client/server product. Windows 95 (which is to replace DOS and Windows) was scheduled for release in 1994 but was delayed into late 1995. Ironically, Windows 95's main competitor, OS/2, is made by the company that ensured Microsoft's success — IBM.

Microsoft agreed in July 1994 to modify its marketing practices in order to settle an antitrust investigation by the US Department of Justice. When the settlement moved to judicial review, it was ruled unconducive to the public good and set aside. In a victory for Microsoft, a federal appeals court in mid-1995 reinstated the 1994 antitrust settlement between Microsoft and the Justice Department.

Targeting the Internet, Microsoft bought a *Mosaic* (Web browser) license from Spyglass in 1995. Also in 1995 the company released advanced programming technologies to boost its presence in databases and other forms of server-based computing for corporate clients; it also began offering on-site consulting and service for its large business customers.

Nasdaq symbol: MSFT
Fiscal year ends: June 30

WHO

Chairman and CEO: William H. Gates, age 38, $457,545 pay
EVP and COO: Robert J. Herbold, age 52
EVP Sales and Support: Steven A. Ballmer, age 38, $426,862 pay
SVP; President, Microsoft Europe: Bernard P. Vergnes, age 49, $497,366 pay
SVP Applications and Technology Group: Nathan P. Myhrvold, age 35
SVP Applications and Technology Group: Frank M. (Pete) Higgins, age 37
SVP Law and Corporate Affairs and Secretary: William H. Neukom, age 52
SVP Consumer Systems Division: Craig J. Mundie, age 45
SVP Developer Division: Roger J. Heinen Jr., age 43
SVP OEM Sales Division: Joachim Kempin, age 52
VP Research: Richard Rashid, age 42
VP Finance and CFO: Michael W. Brown, age 48
VP Human Resources: Michael R. Murray, age 39
Auditors: Deloitte & Touche LLP

WHERE

HQ: One Microsoft Way, Redmond, WA 98052-6399
Phone: 206-882-8080
Fax: 206-883-8101

Microsoft has marketing and support subsidiaries in 47 countries and sells its products worldwide.

	1994 Sales		1994 Operating Income	
	$ mil.	% of total	$ mil.	% of total
US	3,472	66	1,394	79
Europe	1,401	27	346	19
Other regions	375	7	31	2
Adjustments	(599)	—	(45)	—
Total	**4,649**	**100**	**1,726**	**100**

WHAT

	1994 Sales	
	$ mil.	% of total
Applications products	2,927	63
Operating systems	1,519	33
Hardware	203	4
Total	**4,649**	**100**

Selected Products

Business Systems
Microsoft Access
Microsoft at Work
Microsoft Excel
Microsoft LAN Manager
Microsoft Mail
Microsoft PowerPoint
Microsoft Project
Microsoft Schedule+
Microsoft SQL Server
Microsoft Word

Consumer Products
Microsoft Ancient Lands
Microsoft Bookshelf
Microsoft Cinemania
Microsoft Dinosaurs
Microsoft Encarta
Microsoft Flight Simulator

Microsoft Mouse
Microsoft Publisher
Microsoft Works

Developer Products
Microsoft FoxPro
Microsoft Visual Basic & C++

Operating Systems
Microsoft MS-DOS
Microsoft Windows
Microsot Windows 95
Microsoft Windows for Workgroups
Microsoft Windows NT

Other
Computer books
Microsoft Network

KEY COMPETITORS

America Online
Apple
AT&T
Borland
CompuServe
Computer Associates
Davidson & Associates
Delphi Internet
Electronic Arts
eWorld
GE Information Systems
General Magic
Gupta
IBM
Learning Co.
MCI
NeXT
Novell
Oracle
Pearson
Prodigy
Sierra On-Line
Silicon Graphics
Softkey
Sony
Stac Electronics
Sybase
Symantec
Tribune
Wind River Systems

HOW MUCH

	Annual Growth	1985	1986	1987	1988	1989	1990	1991	1992	1993	1994
Sales ($ mil.)	47.6%	140	198	346	591	804	1,183	1,843	2,759	3,753	4,649
Net income ($ mil.)	53.7%	24	39	72	124	171	279	463	708	953	1,146
Income as % of sales	—	17.2%	19.9%	20.8%	21.0%	21.2%	23.6%	25.1%	25.7%	25.4%	24.7%
Earnings per share ($)	46.6%	0.06	0.09	0.15	0.25	0.34	0.52	0.83	1.21	1.58	1.88
Stock price – high ($)	—	—	2.84	8.79	7.74	9.84	17.96	37.35	47.50	49.00	65.13
Stock price – low ($)	—	—	1.42	2.66	5.12	5.17	9.34	16.24	32.75	35.19	39.00
Stock price – close ($)	47.8%	—	2.68	6.03	5.92	9.68	16.74	37.10	42.69	40.31	61.13
P/E – high	—	—	32	59	31	29	35	45	39	31	35
P/E – low	—	—	16	18	21	15	18	20	27	22	21
Dividends per share ($)	—	—	0.00	0.00	0.00	0.00	0.00	0.00	0.00	0.00	0.00
Book value per share ($)	49.9%	—	0.30	0.50	0.78	1.14	1.80	2.59	4.03	5.75	7.66
Employees	38.1%	—	1,153	1,816	2,793	4,037	5,635	8,226	11,542	14,430	15,257

1994 Year-end:
Debt ratio: 0.0%
Return on equity: 29.8%
Cash (mil.): $3,614
Current ratio: 4.72
Long-term debt (mil.): $0
No. of shares (mil.): 581
Dividends
  Yield: —
  Payout: —
Market value (mil.): $35,514

Stock Price History
High/Low 1986–94

MINNESOTA MINING AND MANUFACTURING

OVERVIEW

While mining its product development expertise and international markets, Minnesota Mining and Manufacturing (3M) has been manufacturing strong earnings growth.

St. Paul–based 3M is a diversified manufacturer with 3 main sectors: Industrial and Consumer; Information, Imaging, and Electronics; and Life Sciences.

3M spends heavily on R&D (over $1 billion and 7% of sales in 1994). The company encourages creativity in its technical and engineering staff, allowing them to spend about 15% of their workday (called "bootleg time") tinkering with new products. The company has halved the time it takes to introduce many new products by allowing its manufacturing, marketing, and service areas to work in parallel with product development. 3M is also shifting its emphasis in R&D from research to development. With about 16% of the scouring-pad market, the Never Rust Wool Soap Pad (made of recycled plastic bottles) has been one of 3M's most successful new products.

Deriving 50% of its sales from overseas, 3M continues to expand outside the US, particularly in the Pacific Rim. In 1995 3M opened a $24.7 million plant to produce vinyl tape and telecommunications products near Shanghai and a $1.3 million assembly line for hard-disk drive filters in Bangkok.

WHEN

In 1902, 3M was started by 5 businessmen in Two Harbors, Minnesota, to sell corundum to manufacturers for grinding wheels. When they made only one sale, one of the founders, John Dwan, asked his friend Edgar Ober for working capital in exchange for 60% of 3M's stock. Convinced of the need for a company to make sandpaper and abrasive wheels, Ober persuaded Lucius Ordway, vice-president of a plumbing company, to underwrite 3M. At the 3rd annual meeting (May 1905), Ober and Ordway took over the company. They moved 3M to Duluth and converted an old flour mill to a sandpaper factory.

Orders began arriving by January 1906, but expenses exceeded sales, and Ordway's investment reached $200,000. In 1907 William McKnight (future CEO) joined 3M as a bookkeeper. In 1910 the plant moved to St. Paul to escape Duluth's high humidity.

In 2 years sales doubled, and the board of directors declared a dividend to stockholders in the last quarter of 1916. The company has not missed a quarterly dividend since. The next 2 products 3M developed — Scotch brand masking tape (1925) and Scotch brand cellophane tape (1930) — assured 3M's future.

In 1931 McKnight introduced one of the first employee pension plans. In 1944 McKnight issued his historic challenge to management: "Management that is destructively critical when mistakes are made kills initiative, and it's essential that we have many people with initiative if we're to continue to grow." In the late 1940s McKnight reorganized the company around a vertical management structure and introduced his autonomy-for-performance philosophy. In 1947, 3M introduced the first commercially viable magnetic recording tape.

In 1950, after a decade of work and $1 million in development costs, 3M employee Carl Miller completed the Thermo-Fax copying machine. The machine was the beginning of 3M's Duplicating Division, a group that produced such image-related products as microfilm, overhead-projection transparencies, carbonless papers, and facsimile and word processing equipment.

The company developed Post-it notes (1980) when a 3M scientist wanted to attach page markers to his church hymnal. Recalling that a colleague had developed an adhesive that wasn't very sticky, he brushed some on paper and began a product line that now generates sales of hundreds of millions of dollars a year.

In 1990, 3M bought O-Cel-O, a sponge manufacturer. That same year it opened a tape and telecommunication products plant in India and purchased an Australian advertising company. In late 1992, 3M introduced the Scotch-Brite Never Rust Wool Soap Pad.

New products for 1993 included a tiny anti-theft device that doubles as a price tag, a privacy filter for personal computers, and a line of overhead projectors. In 1994, 3M introduced brightness-enhancing plastic sheeting for portable computer displays.

In 1995 3M won its case against Mitsui Petrochemical Industries for patent infringement on filters for air conditioners and air purifiers (although the patent was to expire within days of the ruling). Along with Bristol-Myers Squibb and Baxter Healthcare, 3M has also agreed to renegotiate the global settlement over silicone breast implants.

NYSE symbol: MMM
Fiscal year ends: December 31

WHO

Chairman and CEO: Livio D. DeSimone, age 58, $1,161,808 pay
EVP Industrial and Consumer Sector: Ronald A. Mitsch, age 60, $658,278 pay
EVP Information, Imaging, and Electronic Sector: Lawrence E. Eaton, age 57, $641,544 pay
EVP International Operations: Harry A. Hammerly, age 61
EVP Life Science Sector: W.G. Meredith, age 52
SVP Finance: Giulio Agostini, age 59, $544,248 pay
SVP Engineering, Quality, and Manufacturing Services: Charles E. Kiester, age 58
VP Marketing: J.M. Adam, age 57
VP Legal Affairs and General Counsel: John J. Ursu, age 55
VP Research and Development: William E. Coyne, age 58
VP Human Resources: Richard A. Lidstad, age 58
Auditors: Coopers & Lybrand L.L.P.

WHERE

HQ: Minnesota Mining and Manufacturing Company, 3M Center, St. Paul, MN 55144-1000
Phone: 612-733-1110
Fax: 612-733-9973

3M has 297 sales offices and distribution centers worldwide. The company has operations in the US and 60 foreign countries.

	1994 Sales		1994 Operating Income	
	$ mil.	% of total	$ mil.	% of total
US	7,511	50	1,107	49
Europe & Middle East	3,870	26	401	18
Asia/Pacific	2,469	16	515	23
Other regions	1,229	8	228	10
Total	**15,079**	**100**	**2,251**	**100**

WHAT

	1994 Sales		1994 Operating Income	
	$ mil.	% of total	$ mil.	% of total
Industrial & Consumer	5,875	39	994	44
Info., Imaging & Electronic	4,635	31	292	13
Life Sciences	4,553	30	954	43
Adjustments	16	—	11	—
Total	**15,079**	**100**	**2,251**	**100**

Industrial and Consumer Sector
Abrasive, chemical, and film products
Automotive systems
Consumer markets
Office markets
Tape (Scotch brand)

Information, Imaging, and Electronic Sector
Electro and communications systems
Imaging systems
Memory technologies

Life Sciences Sector
Medical products
Pharmaceuticals, dental and personal care products
Traffic and personal safety products

KEY COMPETITORS

Alco Standard	Dial	Motorola
Allied Healthcare Products	Eastman Kodak	Pfizer
ALZA	Fuji Photo	Polaroid
AMP	General Electric	PPG
Armstrong World	Henkel	S.C. Johnson
BASF	Hitachi	Siemens
Bayer	Illinois Tool Works	Sony
Bell & Howell	International Paper	Tyco Intl.
Boise Cascade	Johnson & Johnson	USG
		Xerox

HOW MUCH

	9-Year Growth	1985	1986	1987	1988	1989	1990	1991	1992	1993	1994
Sales ($ mil.)	7.1%	8,117	9,056	10,004	11,323	11,990	13,021	13,340	13,883	14,020	15,079
Net income ($ mil.)	8.0%	664	779	918	1,154	1,244	1,308	1,154	1,236	1,263	1,322
Income as % of sales	—	8.2%	8.6%	9.2%	10.2%	10.4%	10.0%	8.7%	8.9%	9.0%	8.8%
Earnings per share ($)	9.0%	1.45	1.70	2.01	2.55	2.80	2.96	2.63	2.83	2.91	3.13
Stock price – high ($)	—	22.91	29.72	41.75	33.75	40.94	45.69	48.75	53.50	58.50	57.13
Stock price – low ($)	—	18.41	21.50	22.50	27.63	30.07	36.82	39.13	42.75	48.63	46.38
Stock price – close ($)	10.1%	22.44	29.16	32.19	31.00	39.82	42.88	47.63	50.32	54.38	53.38
P/E – high	—	16	17	21	13	15	15	19	19	20	18
P/E – low	—	13	13	11	11	11	12	15	15	17	15
Dividends per share ($)	8.1%	0.88	0.90	0.93	1.06	1.30	1.46	1.56	1.60	1.66	1.76
Book value per share ($)	7.0%	8.75	9.77	11.12	12.29	12.08	13.90	14.36	15.07	15.16	16.04
Employees	(0.4%)	88,093	84,498	85,144	85,569	87,584	89,601	88,477	87,292	86,168	85,166

1994 Year-end:
Debt ratio: 22.4%
Return on equity: 20.0%
Cash (mil.): $491
Current ratio: 1.92
Long-term debt (mil.): $1,031
No. of shares (mil.): 420
Dividends
  Yield: 3.3%
  Payout: 56.2%
Market value (mil.): $22,406

Stock Price History
High/Low 1985–94

MOBIL CORPORATION

OVERVIEW

Mobil is the 2nd largest oil company in the US (after Exxon) and 3rd largest in the world (Royal Dutch/Shell holds the #1 slot). The 130-year-old Fairfax, Virginia–based company has reserves of 6.6 billion barrels of oil equivalent and is seeking new exploration and production opportunities in 34 countries on 6 continents. It owns all or part of 21 refineries in 12 countries, markets its petroleum products in 120 countries, and sells its motor fuels in 19,500 Mobil-branded service stations in more than 50 countries.

Mobil also operates a fully integrated chemicals operation, which produces petrochemicals, packaging films, plastics, Baggies food bags, Tucker housewares, Hefty and Cinch Sak garbage bags, and Trex wood/poly-mer composite building material. Mobil Chemicals is the world's #1 producer of oriented polypropylene flexible packaging film products. Mobil subsidiaries are also involved in mining (the company is a major producer of phosphate rock) and real estate development.

Mobil is continuing to cut costs and restructure its operations to become more profitable. In 1995 the company announced plans to save approximately $1 billion in costs by eliminating 4,700 jobs (8% of its global work force), primarily from its domestic businesses.

But Mobil's international operations will not be spared the ax. The company also plans to close a German refinery and cut staff at 2 plants in England and France, for a savings of $80 million a year.

WHEN

Mobil is yet another of the companies flung into orbit after the Big Bang breakup of John D. Rockefeller's Standard Oil. The pieces that would eventually form Mobil's cosmos were Rochester, New York–based Vacuum Oil and Standard Oil of New York. Vacuum, under founders Hiram Bond Everest and Matthew Ewing, had developed a way to make kerosene by distilling crude oil in a vacuum; Rockefeller bought 75% of Vacuum in 1879. Standard Oil Company of New York, nicknamed Socony, was founded in 1882. Vacuum and Socony were 2 of the 33 subsidiaries cut loose by the 1911 Supreme Court order to dissolve Standard Oil of New Jersey.

After the breakup, Socony, which had depended on its Standard Oil sisters for oil to sell in New York, New England, and overseas, quickly cast about for supplies of its own. The company bought control of Texas-based Magnolia Petroleum (1918) and acquired California-based General Petroleum (1926).

Vacuum, which had grown to 1,500 service stations in the Midwest, and Socony reunited in 1931 as Socony-Vacuum. Shortly thereafter, it adopted the Flying Red Horse (Pegasus) as a trademark. Representing speed and power, the symbol was first used by company operations in South Africa.

Socony-Vacuum still needed crude, so in 1933 it joined with Standard Oil (New Jersey) to form Stanvac and began drilling in the Far East. Socony-Vacuum added crude supplies, buying a 10% stake in Aramco (Arabian American Oil Company) in 1948.

The company changed its name to Socony Mobil Oil in 1955, shortened to Mobil Oil in 1966. In 1974 it gained control of Marcor, the Chicago-based parent of retail chain Montgomery Ward, and of Container Corporation of America, maker of paper packaging.

Although it dropped "oil" from its name in 1976, Mobil continued as an outspoken defender of the petroleum industry, purchasing editorial-type ads in major publications. It bought Superior Oil (1984) for $5.7 billion. To refocus and reduce debt, Mobil sold $7 billion in assets, including Container Corp. (1986) and Montgomery Ward (1988).

Mobil upgraded its refinery operations in the early 1990s, spending $300 million on its Beaumont, Texas, facility and $100 million in Singapore. Sales of assets such as its Wyoming coal mine and hundreds of West Texas oil wells brought in $570 million in 1991.

In 1992 Mobil signed a joint venture with Qatar General Petroleum Corporation (with Mobil taking a 30% interest) to set up a liquefied natural gas project. Mobil also sold its polystyrene-resin business to Germany's BASF AG for $300 million. The next year Mobil signed a deal with Malaysia's national oil company, PETRONAS, to explore an area off the coast of Borneo.

In 1994 Mobil signed a production-sharing agreement with state-owned PetroVietnam to develop the Blue Dragon field off the coast of Vietnam. That same year chairman and CEO Allen Murray retired. He was succeeded by COO Lucio Noto.

In 1995 Mobil teamed up with British Gas, British Petroleum, and Mott Ewbank Preece to prepare a master plan for the development of Vietnam's fledgling natural gas industry.

WHO

Chairman and CEO: Lucio A. Noto, age 56,
$1,295,833 pay
EVP, Mobil Oil Corp.: Paul J. Hoenmans, age 62,
$1,105,000 pay
EVP, Mobil Oil Corp.: Eugene A. Renna, age 50,
$1,016,667 pay
SVP: Robert O. Swanson, age 58, $882,500 pay
SVP and CFO: Thomas C. DeLoach Jr., age 47,
$671,250 pay
VP Administration: Rex D. Adams, age 54
VP Corporate Public Affairs: James T. Mann, age 52
VP Planning and Economics: Walter R. Arnheim,
age 50
Controller: Robert C. Musser, age 54
Treasurer: R. Hartwell Gardner, age 60
General Counsel: Samuel H. Gillespie III, age 52
Manager Human Resources: Douglas O. Fitzsimmons
Auditors: Ernst & Young LLP

WHERE

HQ: 3225 Gallows Rd., Fairfax, VA 22037-0001
Phone: 703-846-3000
Fax: 703-846-4669

Mobil has operations in more than 120 countries,
including 21 refineries located in 12 countries.

	1994 Sales		1994 Net Income	
	$ mil.	% of total	$ mil.	% of total
US	22,388	33	302	15
Europe	21,094	32	380	18
Pacific Rim	15,411	23	1,029	50
Other countries	7,906	12	355	17
Adjustments	584	—	(307)	—
Total	**67,383**	**100**	**1,759**	**100**

WHAT

	1994 Sales		1994 Operating Income	
	$ mil.	% of total	$ mil.	% of total
Marketing & refining	56,230	84	1,359	33
Exploration & production	6,374	10	2,737	65
Chemicals	4,195	6	82	2
Adjustments	584	—	—	—
Total	**67,383**	**100**	**4,178**	**100**

Principal Products and Activities
Crude oil and natural gas production
Lubricants
Petrochemicals and plastics
Petroleum refining and marketing
Phosphate rock mining
Plastic film and other packaging materials
Service stations

Selected Brand Names

Baggies	Hefty	Mobil 1
Cinch Sak	MicroView	Tucker

KEY COMPETITORS

Amerada Hess	Elf Aquitaine	Phillips
Amoco	Enron	Petroleum
Ashland, Inc.	Exxon	Quaker State
Atlantic Richfield	First Brands	Repsol
British Gas	Imperial Oil	Reynolds Metals
British	Koch	Royal Dutch/
Petroleum	Lyondell	Shell
Broken Hill	Petrochemical	Southland
Caltex Enterprise	Norsk Hydro	Star Petroleum
Chevron	Occidental	Sun Company
Circle K	Oryx	Texaco
Coastal	PDVSA	TOTAL
Diamond Shamrock	PEMEX	Union Carbide
Dow Chemical	Pennzoil	Unocal
DuPont	Petrobrás	USX–Marathon
Eastman Chemical	Petrofina	YPF

HOW MUCH

	9-Year Growth	1985	1986	1987	1988	1989	1990	1991	1992	1993	1994
Sales ($ mil.)	2.4%	54,606	44,936	51,678	54,740	56,388	64,774	63,311	64,456	63,975	67,383
Net income ($ mil.)	6.0%	1,040	1,612	1,448	1,893	1,809	1,929	1,920	1,308	2,084	1,759
Income as % of sales	—	1.9%	3.6%	2.8%	3.5%	3.2%	2.9%	3.0%	2.0%	3.3%	2.6%
Earnings per share ($)	1.7%	3.69	5.04	2.96	4.93	4.40	4.60	4.65	3.13	5.07	4.28
Stock price – high ($)	—	34.38	40.88	55.00	49.13	63.25	69.50	73.13	69.75	84.75	87.13
Stock price – low ($)	—	25.50	26.25	32.00	38.63	45.25	55.88	55.13	57.88	59.50	72.00
Stock price – close ($)	12.1%	30.25	40.13	39.13	45.50	62.63	58.00	67.88	63.13	79.13	84.25
P/E – high	—	9	8	19	10	14	15	16	22	17	20
P/E – low	—	7	5	11	8	10	12	12	18	12	17
Dividends per share ($)	5.0%	2.20	2.20	2.20	2.35	2.55	2.83	3.13	3.20	3.25	3.40
Book value per share ($)	2.1%	34.50	32.86	36.46	38.19	39.84	42.44	43.74	41.06	42.74	41.42
Employees	(10.8%)	163,600	127,400	120,600	69,600	67,900	67,300	67,500	63,700	61,900	58,500

1994 Year-end:
Debt ratio: 31.1%
Return on equity: 10.7%
Cash (mil.): $531
Current ratio: 0.83
Long-term debt (mil.): $4,714
No. of shares (mil.): 396
Dividends
  Yield: 4.0%
  Payout: 79.4%
Market value (mil.): $33,362

Stock Price History
High/Low 1985–94

MONSANTO COMPANY

Monsanto is one of the US's chemical giants. The # 4 chemical company (after DuPont, Dow, and Occidental Petroleum) makes a wide range of products. The St. Louis, Missouri–based company's output includes aspartame, control valves, detergents, fibers, pharmaceuticals, phosphates, plastics, resins, rubbers, and specialty chemicals.

Monsanto's underperforming Searle pharmaceuticals division manufactures anti-inflammatories (Arthrotec), cardiovasculars (Aldactone), oral contraceptives, and other drugs. The company's chemicals unit makes detergents, nylon carpet fiber, plastic interlayer for laminated glass (Saflex), plastics, and other chemicals. Its NutraSweet unit holds 62% of the US tabletop sweeteners market and makes low-calorie sweeteners (Equal) and a fat substitute (Simplesse).

After several years of cost cutting, restructuring, and struggling to make Searle a success, the company is looking for growth from new product investments, including agricultural biotechnology products. In 1994 it began marketing Posilac, which improves milk production in cows. Within a year the product had been used by owners of 30% of the US dairy herd. During 1994 the company worked on developing a range of agricultural products that it plans to put on the market in 1996. These biotechnology crop applications will help produce crops that are tolerant of Monsanto's Roundup herbicide and crops that are internally resistant to pests.

Richard Mahoney retired in 1995 after 12 years as CEO and 33 years with the company; he was replaced as top executive by president and COO Robert Shapiro.

John Queeny, a buyer for a St. Louis drug company, had only one source for saccharin in 1900 — Germany. He believed that this sweetener (derived from coal tar) had a growing market in the US. Thus, in 1901 in St. Louis, with $5,000 and using his wife's maiden name of Monsanto, Queeny founded Monsanto Chemical Works to manufacture saccharin. The German competition cut prices to drive Monsanto from the marketplace but failed. Monsanto soon diversified with caffeine (1904), vanillin (1905), phenol (antiseptic used in WWI, 1916), and, when Bayer's German patent expired, aspirin (1917). Monsanto Chemical went public in 1927.

In 1928 Edgar Monsanto Queeny, only son of the founder, became president. Edgar recognized the potential of rubber additives, buying Rubber Service Laboratories (Akron, Ohio; 1929), and plastics, buying Fiberloid (Springfield, Massachusetts; 1938). In 1943 Monsanto began production of styrene monomer (used in synthetic rubber) for the army's first synthetic tires in WWII.

Monsanto entered the synthetic fiber market in a joint venture with American Viscose, forming Chemstrand (1949; buying the whole company in 1961); it developed Acrilan fibers (1952) and the synthetic surface AstroTurf (first used commercially in the Houston Astrodome in 1966). In 1952 Monsanto marketed "all" (detergent) but in 1957 abandoned consumer products and sold "all" to Unilever. In 1954 Monsanto and Bayer (Germany) entered into a joint venture (Mobay Chemical) for the

R&D of urethane foams. Bayer bought Mobay in 1967.

In 1960 Edgar resigned as chairman. In 1964 the company changed its name to Monsanto Company to emphasize its diversity. Monsanto introduced new products, including the herbicides Lasso (1969) and Roundup (1973). In 1969 Monsanto bought 67% of Fisher Governor (valves and control systems; Marshalltown, Iowa), changing its name to Fisher Controls (buying the other 33% in 1983). Monsanto abandoned saccharin production in 1972 because of competition from Japan.

In 1985 Monsanto acquired G. D. Searle (pharmaceuticals, founded 1868) and, consequently, the lawsuits resulting from Searle's Copper-7 IUD (introduced in 1974). Through Searle, Monsanto also bought the licensing rights to produce NutraSweet (artificial sweetener). Monsanto sold its animal feed business in 1991.

The company sold its Fisher Controls unit, a leading worldwide manufacturer of process control gear, to Emerson Electric in 1992.

In 1993 Monsanto acquired Chevron's Ortho lawn and garden products business for $416 million. The company received EPA approval in 1994 to market Harness Plus, a corn herbicide.

The company shelled out $1.1 billion in 1995 to acquire Kelco, the specialty chemicals division of Merck. Kelco is the worldwide leader in the development and production of alginates and biogums.

WHO

Chairman and CEO: Robert B. Shapiro, age 56,
$1,461,405 pay (prior to promotion)
VC: Nicholas L. Reding, age 60, $1,246,408 pay
EVP: Robert G. Potter, age 55, $1,102,387 pay
Chairman and CEO, G. D. Searle & Co.: Richard U.
De Schutter, age 54
Chairman and CEO, The NutraSweet Company: Robert
E. Flynn, age 60
SVP, Secretary, and General Counsel: Richard W.
Duesenberg, age 64
SVP and CFO: Robert B. Hoffman, age 58
**SVP R&D and Chief Scientist; President,
G. D. Searle & Co.:** Philip Needleman, age 56
SVP Public Policy: Virginia V. Weldon
VP International Operations and Development: Robert
W. Reynolds
VP; President, Growth Enterprises Business Unit:
Pierre Hochuli, age 47
VP Human Resources: Teresa E. McCaslin, age 45
Auditors: Deloitte & Touche LLP

WHERE

HQ: 800 N. Lindbergh Blvd., St. Louis, MO 63167
Phone: 314-694-1000
Fax: 314-694-7625

	1994 Sales		1994 Operating Income	
	$ mil.	% of total	$ mil.	% of total
US	5,376	65	507	51
Europe & Africa	1,653	20	340	34
Asia/Pacific	552	7	39	4
Latin America	373	4	65	7
Canada	318	4	37	4
Adjustments	—	—	(65)	—
Total	**8,272**	**100**	**923**	**100**

WHAT

	1994 Sales		1994 Operating Income	
	$ mil.	% of total	$ mil.	% of total
Chemicals	3,715	45	304	31
Agricultural prods.	2,224	27	476	48
Searle	1,681	20	72	7
NutraSweet	652	8	139	14
Adjustments	—	—	(68)	—
Total	**8,272**	**100**	**923**	**100**

Chemical Group
Acrylic fibers (Acrilan)
Food additives
Industrial phosphates
Plastic interlayer
Polymers
Resins
Rubber and process
chemicals
Water treatment
chemicals

Agricultural Group
Biotechnology products
(Posilac)
Herbicides (Avadex,
Lasso, Roundup)
Lawn and garden
products (Ortho)

Searle
Anti-infective (Maxaquin)
Anti-inflammatory
(Arthrotec, Daypro)
Cardiovascular (Aldactazide,
Aldactone, Calan)
Central nervous system drug
(Ambien)
Gastrointestinal (Cytotec)
Oral contraceptives

NutraSweet
Fat substitute (Simplesse)
High-intensity sweetener
(NutraSweet)
Low-calorie tabletop
sweeteners (Equal,
NutraSweet Spoonful)

KEY COMPETITORS

Abbott Labs	Dow Chemical	Occidental
Alberto-Culver	DuPont	Pfizer
ALZA	Elf Aquitaine	Procter & Gamble
American	Eli Lilly	Purepac
Home Products	Genentech	Rhône-Poulenc
BASF	Henkel	Sandoz
Bayer	Hercules	Syntex
Bristol-Myers	Hoechst	Union Carbide
Squibb	Imperial Chemical	W. R. Grace
Ciba-Geigy	Koor	

HOW MUCH

	9-Year Growth	1985	1986	1987	1988	1989	1990	1991	1992	1993	1994
Sales ($ mil.)	1.4%	7,304	6,879	7,639	8,293	8,681	8,995	8,864	7,763	7,902	8,272
Net income ($ mil.)	—	(128)	433	436	591	679	546	296	452	494	622
Income as % of sales	—	—	6.3%	5.7%	7.1%	7.8%	6.1%	3.3%	5.8%	6.3%	7.5%
Earnings per share ($)	—	(0.84)	2.78	2.82	4.14	5.02	4.23	2.33	3.67	4.10	5.32
Stock price – high ($)	—	27.69	40.75	50.13	46.19	62.13	60.13	76.00	71.25	75.00	86.50
Stock price – low ($)	—	20.31	22.38	28.50	36.75	40.25	38.75	46.00	49.75	48.88	66.50
Stock price – close ($)	12.8%	23.88	38.25	41.50	40.88	57.69	48.25	67.88	57.63	73.38	70.50
P/E – high	—	—	15	18	11	12	14	33	19	18	16
P/E – low	—	—	8	10	9	8	9	20	14	12	13
Dividends per share ($)	8.1%	1.23	1.29	1.38	1.48	1.65	1.91	2.05	2.20	2.30	2.47
Book value per share ($)	2.0%	22.19	24.34	26.32	27.60	29.79	32.51	29.72	24.95	24.62	26.43
Employees	(6.9%)	56,103	51,703	49,734	45,635	42,179	41,081	39,281	33,797	30,019	29,354

1994 Year-end:
Debt ratio: 36.8%
Return on equity: 21.4%
Cash (mil.): $507
Current ratio: 1.59
Long-term debt (mil.): $1,405
No. of shares (mil.): 112
Dividends
  Yield: 3.5%
  Payout: 46.4%
Market value (mil.): $7,863

**Stock Price History
High/Low 1985–94**

MONTGOMERY WARD HOLDING CORP.

OVERVIEW

One of the largest department store operators in the US, Chicago-based Montgomery Ward operates 402 Montgomery Ward department stores and Lechmere superstores in 43 states. The company also runs Montgomery Ward Direct (a catalog company) and 13 outlet stores that sell overstocked items.

Led by CEO and firebrand Bernard Brennan — who owns about 40% of Ward's stock and whose brother, Edward, chairs crosstown rival Sears — Montgomery Ward saw profits rise 14% in 1994 after 2 years in the doldrums. Brennan reformulated the company's strategy in the late 1980s, when insiders took the company private in a $3.8 billion LBO, one of the largest in US history. Brennan introduced brand-name merchandise to the stores and established specialty departments, including Electric Avenue (appliances and electronics) and Home Ideas (home furnishings). These departments are distinct and often have separate entrances.

The company is entering the home-shopping business. In 1994 it introduced "The Electric Avenue & More," a home-shopping TV program. That same year the company bought a 4.7% stake in Value Vision International. Montgomery Ward has an option to buy up to 49% of the home-shopping cable company.

WHEN

Aaron Montgomery Ward started the Chicago company that bears his name in 1872. It was the world's first general merchandise mail-order concern. Before, farmers had bought goods from general stores or peddlers. Ward provided them with an inexpensive way to shop. In 1873 brother-in-law George Thorne became Ward's partner. In 1875 the company pioneered the "Satisfaction Guaranteed or Your Money Back" policy.

In 1893 Thorne bought a controlling interest in the company. By 1900 Ward's sales had fallen behind flamboyant Chicago rival Sears (founded in 1893). In 1904 Ward introduced what is believed to be the first company magazine edited by employees without a company-dictated policy. Profits surpassed $1 million for the first time in 1909, and the following year George Thorne retired, leaving 5 sons in control of the company. In 1913 Ward died; Charles Thorne became president. He moved to chairman 3 years later, and his brother Robert became president. In 1919 Ward went public; Robert Wood took over.

From 1920 to 1924 Ward's sales grew by 48%, versus Sears's 16% decrease. Wood wanted Ward to develop retail stores, but the company wanted to remain in the mail-order business, so in 1924 Wood left and went to work for Sears. In 1926 Ward opened its first retail store in Plymouth, Indiana.

In 1931 Sewell Avery became CEO; he ended 4 years of losses with a profitable 1934. Avery refused to turn over the company to federal control during a WWII labor dispute, and President Franklin Roosevelt had National Guardsmen carry Avery out of his office. Avery, who had correctly predicted the Great Depression, was convinced a recession would follow WWII and canceled expansion plans, so Ward missed the postwar boom.

After Avery's departure (1955), Ward started an expansion program that included new stores in Alaska and the company's first major distribution center (1958). In 1968 the company merged with Container Corporation of America. In 1974 Mobil Oil acquired 54% control of Ward, acquiring 100% by 1976. Mobil made huge loans to the company in hopes of making Ward profitable.

In 1985 Mobil put Ward up for sale and brought in Bernard Brennan — who had worked for Sears before 1976, joined Ward in 1982, and quit after disputes with then-CEO Stephen Pistner in 1983 — to lead the company. Brennan and other senior managers led a $3.8 billion LBO in 1988. Brennan sold Ward's credit card business to General Electric Capital for $716 million in cash and assumption of $1.7 billion in debt. In 1990 president Bernard Andrews left Ward and joined consumer electronics retailer Circuit City.

In 1994 Ward agreed to buy Lechmere, an appliance and consumer electronics retailer founded in 1913, with 24 stores in the Northeast and $800 million in annual sales.

Between 1993 and 1994, 3 people held the post of president, and Brennan's fiery temper is said to be the cause of the turnover. Brennan finally talked Bernard Andrews into returning to Ward as president.

However, in 1995 Andrews resigned from the company. Some insiders say Brennan's intrusive management style forced Andrews to leave again, but because former executives are offered lucrative severance packages to keep quiet, little is known about the revolving door in Montgomery Ward's executive offices.

Private company
Fiscal year ends: Saturday nearest December 31

WHO

Chairman and CEO: Bernard F. Brennan, age 56,
$1,515,600 pay
VC Operations and Catalog: Richard M. Bergel, age 59,
$762,500 pay
Chairman and CEO, Signature Financial Marketing:
G. Joseph Reddington, age 53, $660,000 pay
EVP, Secretary, and General Counsel: Spencer H.
Heine, age 52, $468,447 pay
EVP, CFO, and Assistant Secretary: John L. Workman,
age 43
EVP Merchandise and Store Operations: Edwin G.
Pohlmann, age 47
**EVP Marketing, Sales Promotion, and Business
Development:** Gene C. McCaffery, age 49
EVP Apparel: Robert F. Connolly, age 51
EVP Human Resources, Montgomery Ward: Robert A.
Kasenter, age 48
Auditors: Arthur Andersen & Co, SC

WHERE

HQ: One Montgomery Ward Plaza, Chicago, IL
60671-0042
Phone: 312-467-2000
Fax: 312-467-3975

	No. of Stores
California	57
Texas	45
Illinois	36
Florida	22
New York	18
Virginia	17
Maryland	16
Michigan	16
Pennsylvania	14
Colorado	13
Massachusetts	13
Arizona	11
Other states	124
Total	**402**

WHAT

	1994 Sales	
	$ mil.	% of total
Retail merchandising	6,573	93
Direct marketing	465	7
Total	**7,038**	**100**

Retail Specialties
The Apparel Store (includes the Kids Store)
Auto Express (tires, batteries, parts, and service)
Electric Avenue (electronics and major appliances)
Gold 'N Gems (jewelry)
Home Ideas (home furnishings)
Rooms & More (home furnishings)

Subsidiaries
Lechmere, Inc. (retailer with stores in the Northeast)
Montgomery Ward Direct L.P. (50% partnership with
Fingerhut Cos., Inc., specialty catalog)
Signature Group
(Montgomery Ward Auto Club, life/health
insurance, and direct-mail marketing)

KEY COMPETITORS

50-Off Stores	Levitz
AAA	L.L. Bean
Ames	May
AutoZone	Melville
Best Buy	Men's Wearhouse
Best Products	Pennzoil
Circuit City	Pep Boys
Damark Intl.	Price/Costco
Dayton Hudson	Schottenstein
Dillard	Sears
Federated	Service Merchandise
The Gap	Spiegel
Good Guys	Sun Television & Appliance
Hanover Direct	TJX
J. C. Penney	Venture Stores
Kmart	Wal-Mart
Lands' End	Woolworth

HOW MUCH

	Annual Growth	1985	1986	1987	1988	1989	1990	1991	1992	1993	1994
Sales ($ mil.)	3.0%	5,388	4,870	5,024	5,567	5,461	5,584	5,654	5,781	6,002	7,038
Net income ($ mil.)	—	(298)	110	130	146	151	153	135	100	101	115
Income as % of sales	—	—	2.3%	2.6%	2.6%	2.8%	2.7%	2.4%	1.7%	1.7%	1.6%
Earnings per share ($)	(0.4%)	—	—	—	2.74	2.71	2.79	2.40	2.01	2.29	2.68
Dividends per share ($)	—	—	—	—	—	—	—	—	0.25	0.50	0.50
Book value per share ($)[1]	19.2%	—	—	—	—	5.74	8.61	10.39	12.11	13.61	13.82
Employees	(2.1%)	71,200	56,300	52,300	65,000	67,000	66,300	62,400	62,300	51,350	58,600

1994 Year-end:
Debt ratio: 39.7%
Return on equity: 18.9%
Cash (mil.): $350
Current ratio: —
Long-term debt (mil.): $309
No. of shares (mil.): 44
Dividend payout
  Class A: 18.7%
  Class B: 21.7%
Total assets (mil.): $4,540

Net Income ($ mil.)
1985–94

[1] Approximate for both class A and class B

MORGAN STANLEY GROUP INC.

OVERVIEW

Morgan Stanley is hiring. In one of the worst years this decade for the financial industry, the New York–based investment banking and brokerage house added another 17% to its head count, primarily overseas. It also added new offices in Beijing, Montreal, Sydney, and Geneva as well as Johannesburg (in the former pariah nation South Africa). The firm expanded its established operations in other nations, too, upgrading its status in Germany, Italy, and France and winning authorization for brokerage operations in Mexico.

All this in a year in which the Fed raised interest rates 6 times, casting a pall over the bond business. The Mexican peso crash late in the year and a weakening dollar were also problems that contributed to a 50% decline in earnings in fiscal year 1995. On the other hand, Morgan Stanley's mergers and acquisitions, merchant banking, custody and clearing, and asset management businesses performed well.

The firm is making several changes in 1995. In addition to consolidating most of its New York operations in one office building, it is changing its fiscal year end to November 30 so that year-end accounting does not coincide with its budget and compensation planning.

WHEN

Morgan Stanley split from the J.P. Morgan banking company after the 1934 Glass-Steagall Act required banks to separate commercial banking (deposit taking and lending) from investment banking activities (issuing and trading securities).

In 1935 Henry Morgan, Harold Stanley, and others established Morgan Stanley as an investment banking firm. Capitalizing on its old ties to major corporations, the company handled $1 billion in issues in its first year.

By the time Morgan Stanley became a partnership in 1941 so it could join the New York Stock Exchange, it had managed 25% of all bond issues underwritten since the Glass-Steagall Act took effect.

In the 1950s Morgan Stanley was known as a well-managed firm that handled issues by itself and rarely participated with other firms. Despite having only $3 million in capital, the partnership was the investment bank for such major US corporations as General Motors, U.S. Steel, General Electric, and DuPont.

Morgan Stanley chose not to help finance the merger wave of the 1960s, since its blue-chip clients were not involved. But in the early 1970s it entered the mergers and acquisitions world, forming Wall Street's first M&A department. In 1974 Morgan Stanley handled its first hostile takeover, International Nickel's takeover of ESB, the world's largest battery manufacturer. Competing investment banking firms then became involved in hostile takeovers.

When Morgan Stanley went public in 1986, its managing directors and principals retained 81% of its stock. The firm amassed a $1.6 billion investment pool and bought Burlington Industries for $46.3 million in cash and $2.2 billion in debt (1987). Burlington's best assets were sold to service the debt, and Morgan Stanley reaped over $176 million in fees and dividends.

Although the 1987 crash sent the financial world into a tailspin and tipped the Northeast into recession, Morgan Stanley escaped virtually unscathed. It was, in fact, the only one of its New York peers to see its earnings rise in 1987, and it was not forced to lay off any employees.

In the 1990s Morgan Stanley became mired in numerous lawsuits arising from investor dissatisfaction with its M&A and LBO activities in the 1980s. In 1991 a jury awarded investors a $16 million settlement for the firm's role in the 1987 formation of First RepublicBank Corp, whose collapse was the costliest in US history. In a suit arising from the 1987 stock crash, Morgan Stanley was ordered in 1995 to reimburse West Virginia over $32 million in pension fund losses. The firm was West Virginia's financial advisor, and the losses arose from prohibited speculative trades by the state. The firm has appealed the judgment.

In 1992 Morgan Stanley's Real Estate Fund bought interests in resorts in California and Colorado. In 1994 the firm unsuccessfully engaged in merger talks with London-based S. G. Warburg Group, an investment bank.

During the 1990s Morgan Stanley has lost market share, slipping out of the top 5 in its class. The 1993 defection of star banker Robert Greenhill and several others (to the Travelers's Smith Barney) was a blow, and the firm began taking corrective action, bringing in Joseph Perella (formerly of Wasserstein Perella) and otherwise upgrading its operations. By 1995 Morgan Stanley was able to lure other high-profile staff, raiding 6 members of CS First Boston's Houston office to help beef up its energy banking capacities.

NYSE symbol: MS
Fiscal year ends: January 31

WHO

Chairman and Managing Director: Richard B. Fisher, age 58, $2,637,500 pay
President and Managing Director: John J. Mack, age 50, $2,575,000 pay
Managing Director: Peter F. Karches, age 43, $2,325,000 pay
Managing Director: Barton M. Biggs, age 62, $2,150,000 pay
Managing Director and CFO: Philip N. Duff, age 38
Managing Director, General Counsel, and Secretary: Jonathan M. Clark, age 57
Treasurer: Charles B. Hintz
Director Human Resources: William Higgins
Auditors: Ernst & Young LLP

WHERE

HQ: 1585 Broadway, New York, NY 10036
Phone: 212-703-4000
Fax: 212-703-6503

Morgan Stanley operates in Chicago, Los Angeles, New York, and San Francisco and has offices in Beijing, Bombay, Frankfurt, Geneva, Hong Kong, Johannesburg, London, Luxembourg, Madrid, Melbourne, Milan, Montreal, Moscow, Paris, Seoul, Shanghai, Singapore, Sydney, Taipei, Tokyo, Toronto, and Zurich.

	1995 Sales		1995 Pretax Income	
	$ mil.	% of total	$ mil.	% of total
North America	8,332	65	527	89
Europe	3,942	30	11	2
Asia	603	5	56	9
Adjustments	(3,501)	—	—	—
Total	**9,376**	**100**	**594**	**100**

WHAT

	1995 Sales	
	$ mil.	% of total
Interest & dividends	6,406	68
Trading & investing	1,243	13
Investment banking	919	10
Commissions	449	5
Asset management	350	4
Other	9	—
Total	**9,376**	**100**

Financial Services
Asset management
Corporate finance
Futures, option, foreign exchange, and commodities trading
Investment banking
Securities distribution and trading
Securities underwriting
Stock brokerage and research

KEY COMPETITORS

Alex. Brown	FMR
Alliance Capital	General Electric
Bankers Trust	Goldman Sachs
Barclays	HSBC
Bear Stearns	John Nuveen
Brown Brothers	ING Group
Harriman	Lehman Brothers
Canadian Imperial	Mellon Bank
Charles Schwab	Merrill Lynch
Chase Manhattan	Nomura Securities
Citicorp	Paine Webber
CS Holding	Prudential
Daiwa Securities	Salomon
Dean Witter, Discover	T. Rowe Price
Deutsche Bank	Travelers
Equitable	

HOW MUCH

	Annual Growth	1986	1987	1988	1989	1990	1991	1992	1993	1994	1995
Sales ($ mil.)	20.2%	1,795	2,463	3,148	4,109	5,831	5,869	6,785	7,382	9,176	9,376
Net income ($ mil.)	15.8%	106	201	231	395	443	270	475	511	786	395
Income as % of sales	—	5.9%	8.2%	7.3%	9.6%	7.6%	4.6%	7.0%	6.9%	8.6%	4.2%
Earnings per share ($)	9.5%	1.78	2.81	3.00	5.13	5.61	3.38	5.61	5.71	9.16	4.03
Stock price – high ($)[1]	—	—	27.34	28.64	28.31	39.75	37.75	65.00	67.88	89.63	80.38
Stock price – low ($)[1]	—	—	20.47	12.75	15.59	27.44	23.56	26.00	45.88	54.00	55.00
Stock price – close ($)[1]	13.4%	—	21.64	17.09	27.69	32.31	27.19	63.75	55.75	70.75	59.00
P/E – high	—	—	10	10	6	7	11	12	12	10	20
P/E – low	—	—	7	4	3	5	7	5	8	6	14
Dividends per share ($)	33.4%	—	0.12	0.27	0.48	0.50	0.75	0.80	0.96	1.08	1.20
Book value per share ($)	28.7%	5.11	10.53	13.44	19.09	23.92	24.48	30.13	37.71	49.03	49.62
Employees	10.0%	4,100	7,000	6,517	6,414	6,640	7,122	7,053	7,421	8,273	9,685

1995 Year-end:
Debt ratio: 94.1%
Return on equity: 10.7%
Cash (mil.): $4,626
Long-term debt (mil.): $8,814
No. of shares (mil.): 75
Dividends
  Yield: 2.0%
  Payout: 29.8%
Market value (mil.): $4,443
Assets (mil.): $116,694

Stock Price History[1]
High/Low 1987–95

[1] Stock prices are for the prior calendar year.

MORTON INTERNATIONAL, INC.

OVERVIEW

Morton International's successful diversification has rubbed salt into the wounds of its competitors. The salt maker, whose "Umbrella Girl" logo is one of the most famous brand icons in the US, also manufactures specialty chemicals for a variety of applications. Products include adhesives for food packaging, liquid plastic coatings for autos, electronic materials used in printed circuit boards, and dyes used in inks.

The company's Automotive Safety Products division is the US's leading air bag maker. US legislation requiring air bags on both the passenger's and the driver's sides by 1999 helped boost division sales in 1994 by 79%. The division produced over 11 million air bags that year and won major contracts to provide air bags for cars sold in Europe and Japan. In

addition to these contracts, favorable conditions in the US have Morton executives anticipating further solid sales gains.

The company's salt unit is a consistent cash generator. Morton's table salt remains the #1 seller in the US. The company also sells table salt under the Windsor label in Canada and sells salt for water conditioning, highway/ice control, and industrial and chemical uses. Recurring storms in the Ohio Valley and the eastern US in 1994 created a strong demand for the firm's highway/ice control salt.

The company's largest business segment, Specialty Chemicals, has benefited from an improving US economy, opportunities in Europe and Southeast Asia, and lower costs from streamlined operations; it posted a 7% increase in sales in 1994.

WHEN

Alonzo Richmond started Richmond & Company, agents for Onondaga Salt, in Chicago in 1848. During the first year Richmond received 36,656 barrels of salt for packing from Onondaga Lake near Syracuse.

In 1867 the company became Haskins, Martin & Wheeler, and the salt supply came by boat from lumber towns in northern Michigan. In 1886 Joy Morton became the controlling owner of Haskins, Martin & Wheeler (renamed Joy Morton & Company). The company remained a sales agency until 1890, when it built its first salt evaporation plant in Wyandotte, Michigan. In 1910 the company was renamed Morton Salt Company. In 1914, after 3 years of advertisements featuring the Morton Salt girl holding an umbrella, the company added its now-well-known slogan: "When it rains it pours."

Morton expanded nationwide with 8 production centers in the 1940s. It also bought a Louisiana salt plant (1947) for salt cake (paper making) and muriatic acid (steel production). In 1951 the company purchased Edwal Laboratories, an Illinois manufacturer of photographic chemicals, and introduced Morton Pellets, salt for recharging home water softeners. In 1954 Morton purchased the Canadian Salt Company Ltd.

In the 1960s Morton diversified by purchasing Adcote Chemicals (1964, commercial adhesives); Simoniz (1965, waxes); and Williams Hounslow (1967, food and cosmetic dyes). In 1969 Morton merged with Norwich Pharmacal, maker of drugs (Pepto-Bismol, Chloraseptic) and household cleaners (Fantastik,

Spray'N Wash), to form Morton-Norwich Products, Inc. During the 1970s the company organized into 4 divisions: salts, pharmaceuticals, household products, and specialty chemicals. In 1982 the company sold its Norwich-Eaton Pharmaceuticals division to Procter & Gamble for $371 million. Later that year Morton-Norwich bought Thiokol, Inc., a rocket and chemical manufacturer, to form Morton Thiokol, Inc.

The company successfully applied Thiokol's propulsion knowledge to develop automobile air bags. However, then-CEO Charles Locke was concerned that aerospace represented about 45% of sales but only 28% of profits in 1987. By 1989 salt and specialty chemicals outperformed aerospace by an even wider margin, and the company spun off the aerospace division into a new company, Thiokol Corporation. Morton International retained the salt, chemical, and air bag businesses.

In 1990 Morton bought Whitaker Corporation (coatings, adhesives). Morton formed a joint venture with Germany's Robert Bosch to produce air bags for the European market, and it sold its food and cosmetic colors business in 1991. In 1992 Morton Bendix, a joint venture with the Bendix Safety Restraints Group of AlliedSignal, opened an air bag module assembly plant in Tennessee.

To support the rapid growth in the European air bag market, the company acquired air bag production facilities in Germany and Amsterdam in 1994.

In 1995 Morton won a contract to supply passenger-side airbags for GM's C/K trucks.

NYSE symbol: MII
Fiscal year ends: June 30

WHO

Chairman and CEO: S. Jay Stewart, age 55,
$1,063,750 pay
EVP Administration: William E. Johnston Jr., age 53,
$612,667 pay
VP; President, Coatings: Stephen A. Gerow, age 51,
$425,333 pay
VP Legal Affairs and General Counsel: James R. Stanley,
age 62, $423,767 pay
VP; President, Salt: Walter W. Becky II, age 51
VP; President, Electronic Materials: Daniel D. Feinberg,
age 51
VP; President, Specialty Chemical Products: James J.
Fuerholzer, age 58
VP; President, Adhesives and Specialty Polymers:
Thomas S. Russell, age 49
VP Finance and CFO: Thomas F. McDevitt, age 54
VP Human Resources: John C. Hedley, age 64
President, Automotive Safety Products: Fred J. Musone,
age 50
Auditors: Ernst & Young LLP

WHERE

HQ: 100 N. Riverside Plaza, Chicago, IL 60606-1596
Phone: 312-807-2000
Fax: 312-807-2241

Morton operates facilities in the US, the Bahamas,
Belgium, Canada, France, Germany, Italy, Japan, Mexico,
the Netherlands, and the UK.

	1994 Sales		1994 Operating Income	
	$ mil.	% of total	$ mil.	% of total
US	2,281	80	384	81
Europe	341	12	44	9
Canada/Bahamas	198	7	46	10
Other regions	30	1	3	—
Total	**2,850**	**100**	**477**	**100**

WHAT

	1994 Sales		1994 Operating Income	
	$ mil.	% of total	$ mil.	% of total
Specialty chemicals	1,370	48	194	41
Automobile safety products	938	33	119	25
Salt	542	19	164	34
Total	**2,850**	**100**	**477**	**100**

Specialty Chemicals
Automotive coatings
Industrial adhesives
Industrial coatings
Liquid and dry film
  photoresists
Liquid colorants
Organic specialties
Packaging adhesives
Performance chemicals
Plastic additives
Polymers and sealants
Powder coatings
Process chemicals and
  ancillary products for
  printed circuit boards
Specialty dyes
Thermoplastic
  polyurethanes

Traffic markings
Water-based polymers

Automotive Safety Products
Driver-side and passenger-
  side air bag inflators and
  modules

Salt
Agricultural salt
Food/chemical processing
  salt
Highway/ice control salt
  (SAFE-T-SALT)
Morton and Windsor table
  salts
Private-label table salt
Water conditioning salt

KEY COMPETITORS

American Home
  Products
ARCO
Ashland Inc.
Atlantic Richfield
BASF
Bayer
Breed Technologies
Cargill
Ciba-Geigy

Dow Chemical
DuPont
FMC
Hercules
Hitachi
Hoechst
Imperial Chemical
3M
Mobil

PPG
Rhône-Poulenc
Safety
  Components
Sherwin-
  Williams
TRW
Union Carbide
W.R. Grace

HOW MUCH

	Annual Growth	1985	1986	1987	1988	1989	1990	1991	1992	1993	1994
Sales ($ mil.)	12.7%	970	1,023	1,094	1,248	1,407	1,639	1,906	2,044	2,310	2,850
Net income ($ mil.)	12.0%	82	90	105	116	97	135	138	145	127	227
Income as % of sales	—	8.5%	8.8%	9.6%	9.3%	6.9%	8.2%	7.2%	7.1%	5.5%	7.9%
Earnings per share ($)	11.9%	0.55	0.63	0.74	0.81	0.68	0.93	0.95	0.98	0.86	1.51
Stock price – high ($)	—	—	—	—	—	13.96	15.83	19.42	21.63	33.54	37.25
Stock price – low ($)	—	—	—	—	—	10.50	11.17	12.88	16.92	19.25	25.50
Stock price – close ($)	19.0%	—	—	—	—	11.96	15.21	19.38	20.29	31.17	28.50
P/E – high	—	—	—	—	—	21	17	20	22	39	25
P/E – low	—	—	—	—	—	16	12	14	17	22	17
Dividends per share ($)	6.3%	—	—	—	—	—	0.29	0.31	0.32	0.32	0.37
Book value per share ($)	8.6%	—	—	—	—	6.27	7.00	7.61	8.40	8.20	9.48
Employees	5.9%	7,800	7,700	7,700	7,800	8,400	9,700	10,200	10,700	11,900	13,100

1994 Year-end:
Debt ratio: 16.0%
Return on equity: 17.4%
Cash (mil.): $59
Current ratio: 1.79
Long-term debt (mil.): $199
No. of shares (mil.): 147.6
Dividends
  Yield: 1.3%
  Payout: 24.5%
Market value (mil.): $4,207

Stock Price History
High/Low 1989–94

MOTOROLA, INC.

OVERVIEW

Motorola is leading a consortium that will ring the planet with low-orbit satellites. By 1997 the system will provide instant global telecommunications services such as faxes, paging, and mobile telephones. Motorola owns 30% of the project, called Iridium, which also involves Bell Canada, Ericsson, Lockheed, Raytheon, and Sprint.

Schaumburg, Illinois–based Motorola manufactures a wide range of products. Semiconductors and integrated circuits are at the core of the company's businesses, which include computers and microcomputer boards, cellular telephones, data communications equipment, and pagers. The company also makes electronic systems and controls for aerospace, automotive, communications, lighting, military, navigation, and transportation industry customers.

In 1994 Motorola joined with Apple and IBM to develop the PowerPC microprocessor. It also began shipping computers and servers based on the PowerPC chip. The company is a leader in technology development, with 940 patents granted in 1994. That year Motorola spent 8.4% of revenues on R&D.

With contracts in countries such as China, Colombia, India, and Malaysia, Motorola is taking wireless phone service to areas where traditional wired service is underdeveloped and revenue potential is enormous. The company is also supplying pagers and paging infrastructure to India's first commercial paging service, which started in early 1995.

WHEN

Two individuals share primary responsibility for shaping Motorola. The first, Paul Galvin, founded Galvin Manufacturing in 1928. Basing his company in Chicago, Galvin began producing car radio receivers in 1929 and began speculating as to whether he could make a mobile radio for the police. The 2nd key figure, Daniel Noble, was a professor working on mobile design when he met Galvin, who persuaded him to join the company in 1940. That same year Motorola developed the first hand-held 2-way radio for the US Army.

In 1947 Galvin renamed the company Motorola, after its car radios. That same year Noble established an Arizona research laboratory to pursue defense contracts for radio communications. Radios and TVs required vacuum tubes, which Motorola had to purchase. Noble persuaded Galvin to invest R&D dollars in solid-state devices, and in the late 1950s Motorola turned to semiconductors. The company began manufacturing integrated circuits and microprocessors, which allowed it to market outside its auto industry mainstay. Galvin died in 1959, and his son Robert became CEO. Noble continued as chairman of the science committee. In 1965 Motorola debuted the 8-track tape player for automobiles.

Motorola changed focus in the 1970s. In 1974 the company launched its microprocessor, the 6800 chip, and sold its TV business to Matsushita (Japan). The company began investing in the data communications market for hardware (such as modems) through the acquisitions of Codex (1977) and Universal Data Systems (1978). In 1987 Motorola made its last car radio.

Robert Galvin's chosen successor, George Fisher, took over in 1990. That same year Motorola organized the $3.4 billion Iridium project, an ambitious scheme to create a global satellite system capable of handling digital service to hand-held telephones, faxes, and pagers without using land-based stations; commercial service is expected in 1998. In 1991 Motorola formed a partnership with IBM and Apple to develop the PowerPC chip. That same year Motorola started making electronic ballasts for lighting systems.

In 1993 the company acquired Lexicus (handwriting-recognition software for pen-based computers) and purchased a 40% interest in Monterrey, Mexico–based CedeTel, a regional cellular phone service.

Robert Galvin's son Christopher was widely expected to be Fisher's successor until Fisher jumped to Eastman Kodak in 1993 after only 3 years at Motorola's helm. Though Gary Tooker became CEO, Christopher was promoted to the #2 spot. In 1993 William Weisz was elected chairman, a position now separate from management.

In 1994 Motorola sold its US 800MHz mobile radio business to Nextel for a minority stake in the company valued at $1.7 billion.

In 1995 Motorola began shipping its Envoy wireless communicator, a hand-held device used to exchange electronic messages and receive stock updates. Also in 1995 the company completed a DRAM facility in Japan (a joint venture with Toshiba) and signed 4 technology agreements for projects in China, including joint ventures with Leshan Radio Company and Panda Electronics Group.

NYSE symbol: MOT
Fiscal year ends: December 31

WHO

Chairman: William J. Weisz, age 67
VC: John F. Mitchell, age 66, $1,320,000 pay
VC and CEO: Gary L. Tooker, age 55, $1,980,000 pay
President and COO: Christopher B. Galvin, age 44, $1,488,667 pay
EVP; President and General Manager, General Systems Sector: Edward F. Staiano, age 58, $1,263,000 pay
EVP and CFO: Carl F. Koenemann, age 56
EVP; Manager, Semiconductor Products Sector: Thomas D. George, age 54
EVP; President and General Manager, Land Mobile Products Sector: Merle Gilmore, age 46
EVP; President and General Manager, Messaging, Information, and Media Sector: Robert L. Growney, age 52
EVP; President and General Manager, Government and Space Technology Group: David G. Wolfe, age 59
EVP and Director, Automotive, Energy, and Controls Group: Frederick T. Tucker, age 54
EVP; Director Human Resources: James Donnelly, age 55
Auditors: KPMG Peat Marwick LLP

WHERE

HQ: 1303 E. Algonquin Rd., Schaumburg, IL 60196
Phone: 708-576-5000
Fax: 708-576-8003

Motorola has manufacturing facilities in the US and 18 foreign countries.

	1994 Sales		1994 Operating Income	
	$ mil.	% of total	$ mil.	% of total
US	16,297	56	1,932	60
Other countries	12,758	44	1,292	40
Adjustments	(6,810)	—	(353)	—
Total	**22,245**	**100**	**2,871**	**100**

WHAT

	1994 Sales		1994 Operating Income	
	$ mil.	% of total	$ mil.	% of total
General systems	8,613	35	1,214	41
Semiconductors	6,936	28	996	34
Communications	5,776	24	589	20
Govt. & systems technology	829	3	(55)	—
Other products	2,434	10	156	5
Adjustments	(2,343)	—	(29)	—
Total	**22,245**	**100**	**2,871**	**100**

Selected Products
Cellular infrastructure equipment systems
Computers and microcomputers
Electronic ballasts for fluorescent lighting
High-speed leased-line and dial modems
Microprocessors, microcontrollers, gate arrays, and motherboards
Radio-telephone products (cellular and cordless telephones)
Two-way radios (mobile and portable), radio paging products and services, and wireless data systems
X.25 networking equipment

KEY COMPETITORS

AMD	Hitachi	Robert Bosch
Analog Devices	Hyundai	Samsung
Apple	IBM	Siemens
AT&T	Intel	Silicon Graphics
Chips and Technologies	LG Group	Texas Instruments
Cirrus Logic	Matsushita	Thomson SA
Cyrix	Mitsubishi	Toshiba
DEC	National Semiconductor	Trimble
Eaton	NEC	Navigation
Ericsson	Nokia	U.S. Robotics
Fujitsu	Oki	Westinghouse
Harris	Philips	Zoom
Hewlett-Packard	Pioneer	Telephonics

HOW MUCH

	9-Year Growth	1985	1986	1987	1988	1989	1990	1991	1992	1993	1994
Sales ($ mil.)	16.9%	5,443	5,888	6,707	8,250	9,620	10,885	11,341	13,303	16,963	22,245
Net income ($ mil.)	40.7%	72	194	308	445	498	499	454	576	1,022	1,560
Income as % of sales	—	1.3%	3.3%	4.6%	5.4%	5.2%	4.6%	4.0%	4.3%	6.0%	7.0%
Earnings per share ($)	36.6%	0.16	0.39	0.60	0.86	0.96	0.95	0.86	1.08	1.78	2.65
Stock price – high ($)	—	10.19	12.50	18.50	13.66	15.63	22.09	17.81	26.59	53.75	61.13
Stock price – low ($)	—	7.28	8.41	8.75	8.97	9.88	12.28	11.44	16.06	24.38	42.13
Stock price – close ($)	22.0%	9.72	8.91	12.44	10.50	14.59	13.09	16.31	26.13	46.13	58.00
P/E – high	—	64	33	31	16	16	23	21	25	30	23
P/E – low	—	46	22	15	10	10	13	13	15	14	16
Dividends per share ($)	7.6%	0.16	0.16	0.16	0.16	0.19	0.19	0.19	0.19	0.22	0.31
Book value per share ($)	13.9%	4.79	5.37	5.83	6.51	7.29	8.08	8.76	9.54	11.50	15.47
Employees	4.3%	90,200	94,400	97,700	102,000	104,000	105,000	103,000	107,000	120,000	132,000

1994 Year-end:
Debt ratio: 18.3%
Return on equity: 20.1%
Cash (mil.): $1,059
Current ratio: 1.51
Long-term debt (mil.): $1,127
No. of shares (mil.): 588
Dividends
  Yield: 0.5%
  Payout: 11.7%
Market value (mil.): $34,104

Stock Price History
High/Low 1985–94

NATIONAL RAILROAD PASSENGER CORP.

OVERVIEW

The National Railroad Passenger Corporation, better known as Amtrak, is a private, for-profit company. However, it is almost wholly owned by the US DOT and receives nearly $1 billion in subsidies from the federal government. In 1994 Amtrak carried 54 million passengers over 25,000 miles of track in 45 states. It also provides commuter service in 7 major metro areas. Amtrak has recently reorganized into 3 business units: Northeast Corridor, Intercity Rail Services, and Amtrak West.

Established by Congress in 1970, Amtrak (whose name is derived from "American travel by track") also receives large subsidies from state and local governments: in its 25-year history it hasn't once turned a profit. Its

9-member board includes the secretary of transportation and 5 presidential appointees.

Facing a $200 million shortfall, in late 1994 and 1995 the company cut service by 21% — eliminating entire runs, trimming service on other runs' frequency, and cutting close to 20% of its workers. It has offered to reinstate certain routes if states will pick up more of the costs.

Chairman Graham Claytor retired in 1993 after almost 12 years. During his tenure Amtrak's operating loss lessened considerably. The company's goal is to become profitable by the year 2000 — if it's around that long. With the Republicans winning control of Congress in 1994, talk of privatizing or just shutting down the money-losing railroad has increased.

WHEN

US passenger train travel peaked in 1929. That year there were 20,000 passenger trains in operation. But the spread of automobiles, bus service, and air travel cut sharply into business, especially short-distance travel (the industry's most profitable), and by the late 1960s there were only about 500 passenger trains operating in the US. Railroad company CEOs who saw the demise of the industry looming let service and equipment decay dramatically. In 1970 the combined losses of all private train operations exceeded $1.8 billion in today's dollars. That year Congress passed the Rail Passenger Service Act to preserve America's passenger railroad system. Although railroads were offered stock in Amtrak for their passenger equipment, the majority of accepting companies just wrote off the loss. Track, stations, yards, and service staff remained with the individual railroads.

Amtrak began operating in 1971 with 1,200 cars, most of which had been built in the 1950s. Although Amtrak lost money from the get-go ($153 million in 1972), it continued to be bankrolled by Uncle Sam, despite much criticism. One economist claimed that there weren't enough train enthusiasts to support an operational museum line, let alone an entire national system.

Amtrak ordered its first new equipment in 1973; that year it also began taking over stations, yards, and service staff. By 1976 most of the staff that served Amtrak's passengers were the company's own. Amtrak didn't own any track until 1975, after 2 acts of Congress enabled it to purchase hundreds of miles of right-of-way track in several areas of the US.

In 1978 Amtrak lost $544 million. The following year Amtrak reduced its route mileage by 13% at the secretary of transportation's suggestion (although he had hoped for a greater reduction). After a 1979 study showed Amtrak passengers to be by far the most heavily subsidized travelers in the US, Congress mandated Amtrak to better maximize resources. This resulted in some diversification and better use of resources.

Graham Claytor, who had served as navy secretary and deputy defense secretary, took the helm in 1982. He has steadfastly maintained that profitability is attainable, despite never achieving it himself.

In 1992 Amtrak ordered new cars and locomotives for delivery over the next several years. The following year the company reduced its work force and adjusted services in the name of cost cutting. But flooding in the Midwest during the peak travel season and continuing airfare wars hurt Amtrak. The 1993 wreck of the Sunset Limited did not help the situation: 47 people died near Mobile, Alabama, in the worst accident in Amtrak's history. Although a barge that had run into a bridge moments before the Sunset crossed it was thought to be at fault, the public remained jittery. Adding insult to injury, just months after the Mobile derailment, a train near Kissimmee, Florida, derailed in December 1993, injuring 63.

In December 1994 Amtrak completed the final phase of testing for higher-speed trains that will run from New York to Washington. Four companies have been authorized to bid to manufacture 26 of the fast trains; the first is expected in 1997.

US government-owned corporation
Fiscal year ends: September 30

Chairman and President: Thomas M. Downs
EVP: Dennis F. Sullivan
CFO: Elizabeth C. Reveal
CEO Intercity Rail Service: Arthur F. McMahon
CEO West Coast SBU: Gilbert O. Mallery
CEO Northeast Corridor SBU: George D. Warrington
VP Customer Service: Robert C. VanderClute
VP Marketing and Sales: Robert K. Wehrmann
VP Information Systems Technology: Donald G. Gentry
VP Government and Public Affairs: Thomas J.
  Gillespie Jr.
VP Reengineering: Norris W. Overton
General Counsel: Stephen C. Rogers
VP HR and Labor Relations: Dennis R. Wright
VP Corporate Management and Secretary: Anne W.
  Hoey
Assistant VP Contract Services: Ronald J. Hartman
Auditors: Price Waterhouse LLP

WHERE

HQ: National Railroad Passenger Corporation,
  60 Massachusetts Ave. NE, Washington, DC 20002
Phone: 202-906-3860
Fax: 202-906-3865

Amtrak operates trains in 45 states, running on 25,000
miles of track.

WHAT

	1994 Sales	
	$ mil.	% of total
Passenger-related	880	63
Commuter operating	184	13
Commuter fees	87	6
Mail & express	60	4
State-supported services	33	2
Nontransportation (includes freight fees)	169	12
Total	**1,413**	**100**

	1994 Ridership	
	No. (mil.)	% of total
Amtrak system		
Northeast Corridor	11	21
Short Distance	5	9
Long Distance	5	9
Contract commuter	32	59
Other	1	2
Total	**54**	**100**

	1994 Passenger Car Fleet	
	No.	% of total
Amfleet I	490	28
Superliner	407	23
Heritage	273	15
Amfleet II	148	8
Horizon	103	6
Turboliner	50	3
Low-level cab	30	2
Self-propelled	19	1
Other	240	14
Total	**1,760**	**100**

KEY COMPETITORS

Alaska Air
America West
AMR
Atlantic Coast Airlines
Atlantic Southeast Airlines
Continental Airlines
Delta
Greyhound
Kiwi Intl. Airlines
Mesa Air
Northwest Airlines
Peter Pan Bus Lines
Port Authority of NY & NJ
Reno Air
SkyWest Airlines
Southwest Airlines
TWA
UAL
USAir Group
ValuJet Airlines

HOW MUCH

	Annual Growth	1985	1986	1987	1988	1989	1990	1991	1992	1993	1994
Sales ($ mil.)	6.1%	826	861	974	1,107	1,269	1,308	1,359	1,325	1,403	1,413
Net income ($ mil.)	—	(774)	(702)	(699)	(650)	(665)	(703)	(722)	(712)	(731)	(986)
Ridership (mil.)	11.1%	21	21	31	37	39	40	40	42	51	54
Passenger miles (mil.)	2.3%	4,825	5,013	5,221	5,678	5,859	6,057	6,273	6,091	6,199	5,921
Employees	0.9%	—	—	—	—	23,000	—	23,741	24,000	24,000	24,000

1994 Year-end:
Cash (mil.): $24
Current ratio: 0.47

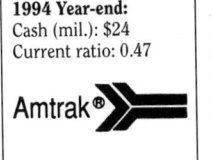

Net Income ($ mil.)
1985–94

NATIONAL SEMICONDUCTOR

OVERVIEW

National Semiconductor is getting into shape. The company has spent most of the 1990s firming up its product focus and cumbersome corporate structure. In 1994 National began shifting its product mix away from overcrowded microprocessor markets already owned by Intel and AMD to niche analog- and mixed-signal markets. In mid-1995 the company shed part of its management hierarchy to come up with 7 units that report directly to the president's office.

With its management structure now leaner, National is pumping up its manufacturing facilities. Earlier in the decade, as chip sales and technological advances surged, the company had trouble meeting shifting customer demands. During 1995 it increased production at its plants in Maine, Texas, and Scotland. That same year National committed nearly

$400 million to expand its facilities in Maine, Texas, the Philippines, and Singapore. The company will also build a $100 million R&D facility in Santa Clara, California.

National is also using strategic acquisitions to develop more muscle in its core markets. In 1994 and 1995 the company added Comlinear Corporation (integrated circuits; Fort Collins, Colorado) and minority interests in 2 closely held California companies: Synaptics (mixed-signal computer control systems, San Jose) and Integrated Information Technology (chip designs, Santa Clara).

National, which spent over 11% of 1994 revenues on R&D, announced several new products in 1994 and 1995, including advanced Ethernet adapter cards and flash memory devices as well as a battery charger that greatly reduces charging time.

WHEN

National, a transistor company founded in 1959 in Danbury, Connecticut, was by 1967 struggling on only $7 million in sales. That year Peter Sprague, heir to the Sprague electric fortune, took over as chairman and hired manufacturing expert Charles Sporck away from Fairchild Semiconductor.

Sporck transferred operations to the Silicon Valley, halved the transistor work force, and plowed the savings into developing linear and digital logic chips. During the 1970s National's mass manufacturing of low-cost chips made the company the leading US semiconductor maker for a time, while its no-frills management approach led to its employees being dubbed "the animals of Silicon Valley."

The company then bought National Advanced Systems (NAS, a distributor/servicer of Hitachi mainframes; 1979) and Data Terminal Systems (point-of-sale terminals, 1983), which became Datachecker. When Japanese manufacturers dumped digital memory chips on the market in 1984 and 1985, National pulled out of the memory business. Its logic chips also suffered price squeezes, and in 1986 the company lost $148 million.

Sporck then moved to transform his low-cost commodity chipmaker into a higher-margin supplier of niche products. National bought troubled Fairchild Semiconductor in 1987 to gain superior logic chip designs and custom linear circuits for the US military.

Sluggish mainframe demand, coupled with mounting mainframe competition from IBM and Amdahl, prompted National in 1989 to sell

NAS for $386 million (to a joint venture between Hitachi and Electronic Data Systems) and Datachecker for $126 million (to ICL). It also consolidated plants and laid off 5% of its work force.

Also in 1989, as sales continued to decline, Sporck implemented a restructuring plan that grouped the company into 3 market-based divisions to better respond to customer needs, but the changes failed to improve results. National left the high-speed, high-density SRAM business, and in early 1991 Sporck retired after 24 years as National's president. Former Rockwell International executive Gilbert Amelio was hired as CEO and undertook another restructuring.

Late in 1992 the company obtained flash memory technology from Toshiba. By early 1993 National had ended large-scale chip production in the Silicon Valley, having shifted production to Arlington, Texas. Also that year the company signed an agreement with Adaptive to develop asynchronous transfer mode technology for computer networks.

In 1994 the company introduced a data-security microchip for use in pocket-size cards. The cards can be used in place of passwords to access computers and can meter transactions and keep billing records, enabling users to shop on computer networks.

National's sales for fiscal 1995 totaled almost $2.4 billion, yielding net income of $264 million. The company has joined an industry alliance to develop a standard for isochronous (same time) network communication.

NYSE symbol: NSM
Fiscal year ends: Last Sunday in May

WHO

President and CEO: Gilbert F. Amelio, age 51,
$1,441,862 pay
EVP and COO: Kirk P. Pond, age 49, $710,199 pay
EVP and COO: Richard M. Beyer, age 45, $617,797 pay
(prior to promotion)
EVP Finance and CFO: Donald MacLeod, age 45
SVP Business Process Improvement: R. Thomas Odell,
age 45, $523,519 pay
SVP and Chief Administrative Officer: George M.
Scalise, age 60, $519,094 pay
**SVP Intellectual Property Protection and Business
Development:** Richard L. Sanquini, age 59
SVP and Chief Technical Officer: Charles P. Carinalli,
age 46
SVP, General Counsel, and Secretary: John M. Clark III,
age 44
President, International Business Group: Patrick J.
Brockett, age 46
VP Human Resources: Robert G. MacLean, age 50
Auditors: KPMG Peat Marwick LLP

WHERE

HQ: National Semiconductor Corporation, 2900
Semiconductor Dr., PO Box 58090, Santa Clara, CA
95052-8090
Phone: 408-721-5000
Fax: 408-739-9803

Manufacturing facilities are located in Malaysia, the
Philippines, Singapore, the UK, and the US.

	1994 Sales	
	$ mil.	% of total
Americas	1,010	44
Asia	788	34
Europe	497	22
Total	**2,295**	**100**

WHAT

Operating Groups and Divisions
Analog Products Division (amplifiers, data acquisition
circuits, voltage regulators, variable function controls)
Data Management Division (data manipulation,
switching, mass storage products)
Embedded Technologies Division (microcontrollers,
microprocessors for imaging peripherals, input/output
devices for personal systems, and voice processors)
LAN (Local Area Network) Division (LAN Ethernet
controller chipsets)
Mixed Signal Systems Division (products for systems
that require analog and digital signals on the same
chip)
Personal Systems Division (products for small computer
systems such as PDAs, laptops, and desktops)
WAN (Wide Area Network) Division (wireless
communications products)

KEY COMPETITORS

AMD	LG Group
Analog Devices	Linear Technology
Apple	LSI Logic
AT&T	Micron Technology
Brooktree	Mitsubishi
Chips and Technologies	Motorola
Cypress Semiconductor	NEC
Cyrix	Oki
Daewoo	Philips
Dallas Semiconductor	Pioneer
Fujitsu	Samsung
General Signal	Siemens
Harris Corp.	Silicon Graphics
Hitachi	Sony
Hyundai	Texas Instruments
IBM	Toshiba
Intel	Unitrode

HOW MUCH

	9-Year Growth	1985	1986	1987	1988	1989	1990	1991	1992	1993	1994
Sales ($ mil.)	2.8%	1,788	1,478	1,868	2,470	1,648	1,675	1,702	1,718	2,014	2,295
Net income ($ mil.)	25.2%	34	(148)	(29)	63	(23)	(25)	(150)	(120)	130	259
Income as % of sales	—	1.9%	—	—	2.5%	—	—	—	—	6.5%	11.3%
Earnings per share ($)	19.2%	0.38	(1.73)	(0.42)	0.48	(0.32)	(0.34)	(1.55)	(1.24)	0.96	1.84
Stock price – high ($)	—	15.13	15.63	22.25	15.00	10.00	8.88	9.00	14.13	21.75	25.00
Stock price – low ($)	—	10.13	8.25	9.75	8.13	6.38	3.00	3.88	6.38	10.13	14.38
Stock price – close ($)	4.9%	12.63	10.63	12.00	9.75	7.25	4.38	6.50	10.63	16.25	19.50
P/E – high	—	40	—	—	31	—	—	—	—	23	14
P/E – low	—	27	—	—	17	—	—	—	—	11	8
Dividends per share ($)	—	0.00	0.00	0.00	0.00	0.00	0.00	0.00	0.00	0.00	0.00
Book value per share ($)	1.9%	7.64	7.91	8.69	9.43	8.28	7.91	6.34	5.07	7.63	9.04
Employees	(5.5%)	37,100	30,800	29,200	37,700	32,200	32,700	29,800	27,200	23,400	22,300

1994 Year-end:
Debt ratio: —
Return on equity: 26.7%
Cash (mil.): $398
Current ratio: 1.76
Long-term debt (mil.): $15
No. of shares (mil.): 122
Dividends
Yield: —
Payout: —
Market value (mil.): $2,385

**Stock Price History
High/Low 1985–94**

NATIONSBANK CORPORATION

OVERVIEW

The shark is on the move again. Charlotte, North Carolina–based NationsBank snacked on 4 small banks and 4 mortgage servicing operations (including KeyCorp's) in 1994 and 1995 before announcing in July 1995 that it would gobble up CSF Holdings (Florida's largest S&L) for $516 million. It has also expressed interest in even larger acquisitions, possibly Chase Manhattan or First Chicago.

NationsBank is a superregional bank, with strong operations in Georgia, North Carolina, South Carolina, and Virginia. It is also one of the strongest banks in Texas and Florida. And its aspirations appear to be national. In addition, it is placing heavy emphasis on the mortgage business and striving to increase its financial services segment. To this end it has raced to add investment and brokerage services, insurance, and mutual funds.

The combination of the bank's drive for profit with its new focus on financial services has resulted in an increase in fee and commission income. It has also led to customer litigation and SEC investigations of the brokerage subsidiary, NationSecurities (originally a joint venture with Dean Witter, Discover from which Dean Witter withdrew in disagreement over sales policies). Allegations of high-pressure sales tactics included rebates to banking personnel referring clients to brokers and pushing proprietary investment products without telling investors of potential risks.

WHEN

In 1874 several Charlotte, North Carolina, citizens organized Commercial National Bank, and in 1901 Charlotte's George Stephens and Word Wood started Southern States Trust Co. (renamed American Trust Co. in 1907). Commercial National and American Trust merged in 1957 to become American Commercial Bank and 2 years later merged with First National of Raleigh to begin forming a statewide banking system. In 1960 American Commercial merged with Security National (founded in Greensboro in 1933) to form North Carolina National Bank, with 40 offices in 20 North Carolina cities.

In the 1960s the bank continued to expand, and it formed NCNB Corp., a holding company, in 1968. By 1970 NCNB had 91 offices in 27 cities. By the end of that decade NCNB was the largest bank in North Carolina.

NCNB became the first non-Florida bank to expand its retail banking into Florida by buying First National Bank of Lake City in 1982 (winning approval of the interstate move by announcing its intention to move its corporate headquarters to Florida). By 1984 NCNB had acquired banks in Boca Raton, Tampa, Miami, and Bradenton. In 1985 NCNB bought Miami's Pan American, and by 1988 it was the 4th largest bank in Florida, with 200 offices.

With the addition between 1985 and 1987 of Southern National Bankshares, Inc., of Atlanta; Bankers Trust of South Carolina; Prince William Bank of Dumfries, Virginia; and CentraBank of Baltimore, NCNB became the first Southern banking organization to operate in 6 states.

NCNB profited hugely from the S&L crisis of the late 1980s and early 1990s, both through management of assets and branches and through acquisition of defunct thrifts for bargain-basement prices. It nearly doubled its assets in 1988, when the FDIC chose it to manage the restructured banks of First Republicbank Corp. (closed by the FDIC earlier in 1988), Texas's largest bank. NCNB bought 20% of that company in 1988 and the rest in 1989. Also in 1989 NCNB bought University Federal Savings (Texas) and Freedom Savings and Loan Association (Florida) from the RTC. Other FDIC/RTC transactions included a contract to manage the problem loans and real estate of Bright Banc Savings (Texas).

In 1991 NCNB took over C&S/Sovran, the product of a 1990 merger between Georgia-based Citizens & Southern and Virginia-based Sovran, in a $4.26 billion deal that made it the 4th largest bank in the US. After this acquisition the company was renamed NationsBank.

In 1993 the company diversified with the purchase of Chicago Research & Trading (CRT), a government securities, derivatives, and options dealer and the largest US provider of oil and gas financing.

The next year the bank made an initial move into Mexico with the acquisition of 10% of Grupo Financiero Bancomer's factoring business. It also continued acquiring financial businesses in the US, folding the new banks and mortgage companies into the corporation in its usual efficient manner by centralizing processing and back-office functions.

In 1995 the bank settled several customer suits arising from nondisclosure of risk in some investment products by reimbursing the customers for their losses.

NYSE symbol: NB
Fiscal year ends: December 31

WHO

Chairman and CEO: Hugh L. McColl Jr., age 59, $3,000,000 pay
VC and CFO: James H. Hance Jr., age 50, $1,700,000 pay
VC; Chairman, NationsBank East: James W. Thompson, age 55, $1,700,000 pay
President: Kenneth D. Lewis, age 47, $1,750,000 pay
Chairman, Corporate Risk Policy: Fredric J. Figge II, age 58, $1,400,000 pay
Chairman, NationsBank South: Hugh M. Chapman
President, NationsBank Mid-Atlantic Banking Group: R. Eugene Taylor
President, NationsBank N.A. (Carolinas): Joel A. Smith III
President, Institutional Bank: F. William Vandiver Jr.
President, NationsBank of Delaware: Edgar S. Lanham II
President, NationsBank of Florida: Adelaide A. Sink
Principal Corporate Officer for Personnel: Charles J. Cooley
Auditors: Price Waterhouse LLP

WHERE

HQ: NationsBank Corporate Center, Charlotte, NC 28255
Phone: 704-386-5000
Fax: 704-386-6444

NationsBank has 1,929 banking centers in Florida, Georgia, Kentucky, Maryland, North Carolina, South Carolina, Tennessee, Texas, Virginia, and Washington, DC. Its NationsCredit and Greyrock Capital subsidiaries operate 288 consumer finance offices in 34 states, and NationsBank maintains offices in Frankfurt, Grand Cayman, Hong Kong, London, Mexico City, Nassau, Osaka, Paris, Singapore, and Tokyo.

WHAT

	1994 Assets	
	$ mil.	% of total
Cash & equivalents	22,853	13
Treasury & agency securities	32,188	19
Derivatives	1,577	1
Net loans	100,181	59
Other	12,805	8
Total	**169,604**	**100**

	1994 Sales	
	$ mil.	% of total
Loan interest	7,577	58
Other interest	2,952	23
Service charges on deposits	797	6
Trust fees	435	3
Credit cards	280	2
Trading	273	2
Other	812	6
Total	**13,126**	**100**

Selected Services
Bank credit cards
Commercial, corporate, and retail banking
Corporate finance
Home mortgage loans
Insurance
Investment banking
Mergers and acquisitions
Retail brokerage
Trust services

Selected Subsidiaries
NationsBanc Commercial Capital Corp.
NationsBanc Discount Brokerage
NationsBanc Leasing Corp.
NationsBanc Mortgage Corp.
NationsBank Dealer Financial Services
Panmure Gordon & Co.

KEY COMPETITORS

Banc One
Bank of New York
BankAmerica
Bankers Trust
Barnett Banks
CCB Financial
Chase Manhattan
Chemical Banking
Citicorp
Countrywide Credit
First Chicago
First Interstate
First Union
General Electric
H.F. Ahmanson
J.P. Morgan
Mellon Bank
SunTrust
Wachovia

HOW MUCH

	9-Year Growth	1985	1986	1987	1988	1989	1990	1991	1992	1993	1994
Assets ($ mil.)	27.0%	19,754	27,472	28,915	29,848	66,191	65,285	110,319	118,059	157,686	169,604
Net income ($ mil.)	29.5%	165	199	167	253	563	366	202	1,145	1,301	1,690
Income as % of assets	—	0.8%	0.7%	0.6%	0.8%	0.9%	0.6%	0.2%	1.0%	1.0%	1.0%
Earnings per share ($)	11.4%	2.30	2.53	2.03	2.90	4.44	3.34	0.76	4.52	4.95	6.06
Stock price – high ($)	—	23.56	27.75	29.13	29.13	55.00	47.25	42.75	53.38	58.00	57.38
Stock price – low ($)	—	16.94	20.00	15.50	17.50	27.00	16.88	21.50	39.63	44.50	43.38
Stock price – close ($)	8.0%	22.63	21.50	17.25	27.25	46.25	22.88	40.63	51.38	49.00	45.13
P/E – high	—	10	11	14	10	12	14	56	12	12	10
P/E – low	—	7	8	8	6	6	5	28	9	9	7
Dividends per share ($)	11.8%	0.69	0.78	0.86	0.94	1.10	1.42	1.48	1.51	1.68	1.88
Book value per share ($)	12.0%	14.23	16.42	17.87	22.43	29.21	31.18	26.57	30.42	36.39	39.43
Employees	22.4%	9,981	12,107	39,936	42,786	57,069	58,449	58,449	50,828	57,463	61,484

1994 Year-end:
Equity as % of assets: 6.5%
Return on assets: 1.0%
Return on equity: 16.4%
Long-term debt (mil.): $11,007
No. of shares (mil.): 276
Dividends
 Yield: 4.2%
 Payout: 31.0%
Market value (mil.): $12,470
Sales (mil.): $13,126

Stock Price History
High/Low 1985–94

NATIONWIDE INSURANCE ENTERPRISE

OVERVIEW

Nationwide Insurance is going halfway around the world to return to its roots — farm insurance. In 1994 the company announced a program to assist Podderzhka, a Russian farm insurance company, in improving its operations. As part of the program it will host employees from the Russian company, and some of its staff will travel to Russia to observe Podderzhka's operations.

Columbus-based Nationwide provides property/casualty insurance, life and health insurance, and financial services. It operates in 4 core areas: exclusive agency lines (proprietary insurance policies sold through its own agencies), long-term savings (annuities and pension plans for individuals and groups),

commercial services (insurance for businesses), and investments (companies in which it owns interests).

The group's larger operating companies include Nationwide Mutual (auto insurance), Nationwide Mutual Fire, and the Wausau Group. Nationwide also has interests in radio (12 stations in 7 states) and real estate.

After 43 years with Nationwide, during which the company grew into a nationwide force, John Fisher retired as chairman in 1994, relinquishing the post to CEO Richard McFerson. McFerson is focusing on loss reduction programs, keeping a lid on expenses, and installing state-of-the-art technology to improve customer service.

WHEN

Nationwide traces its origins to 1919, when members of the Ohio Farm Bureau Federation, a farmers' consumer group, decided to establish their own automobile insurance company. They reasoned that because they were all rural drivers they shouldn't be made to pay the same for auto insurance as city drivers. In order to get a license from the state, the company had to have at least 100 policyholders. More than 1,000 policies were gathered by 1926 with only 3 employees and 20 volunteer agents. The company began as Farm Bureau Mutual. Murray Lincoln, a founder, headed the young company from its birth until 1964.

The company expanded across state lines in 1928 to Delaware, Maryland, North Carolina, and Vermont, and in 1931 it began selling auto insurance to city dwellers. The company expanded into fire insurance in 1934 and into life insurance in 1935 (buying American Insurance Union, which had been established in 1931) with $100,000 in capital and $50,000 in surplus.

During WWII growth slowed; nonetheless, the company had operations in 12 states and Washington, DC, by 1943. The company diversified out of insurance for the first time in 1946, when it bought a Columbus radio station. A few years later it moved into real estate. By 1952 the company had resumed expansion; to reflect this growth Farm Bureau Mutual changed its name to Nationwide. Nationwide was one of the first auto insurance companies to use its agents to sell other financial products, adding life insurance and mutual funds in the mid-1950s. Another subsidiary, Nationwide General, the country's

first merit-rated auto insurance company, was formed in 1956.

Nationwide established Neckura, its first overseas venture, in Germany in 1965 to sell auto and fire insurance. Four years later the company bought GatesMcDonald, a provider of risk, tax, benefit, and health care management services. The company organized its property and casualty insurers into Nationwide Property & Casualty in 1979.

Nationwide experienced solid growth throughout the 1980s by establishing or purchasing insurance companies, among them Colonial Insurance of California (1980), Financial Horizons Life (1981, investment-oriented life insurance products), Scottsdale (1982, excess and surplus lines underwriter), and, the largest, Employer Insurance of Wausau (1985). Wausau, widely known for its "Spelling Bee" ("Wausau . . . it has a USA in the middle") and "Where's Wausau?" commercials and its sponsorship of the TV program *60 Minutes*, wrote the country's first workmen's compensation policy in 1911. Nationwide has infused Wausau, which had been plagued by high loss ratios, with $400 million since 1985, including $100 million in 1992.

In 1994 the company issued $500 million in "surplus notes" (debt that is subordinate to policyholders' claims and other liabilities), which will help beef up its life and annuity and property/casualty operations.

As part of Nationwide's reorganization, the company has consolidated its data centers (at a 3-year savings of $27 million), instituted a state-by-state rather than regional structure, set up an ethics office, and made a concerted effort to hire more women as agents.

Mutual company
Fiscal year ends: December 31

WHO

Chairman, President, and CEO: D. Richard McFerson, age 57, $239,239 pay
EVP Investments; President and COO, Nationwide Life and Financial Horizons Life Insurance Companies: Peter F. Frenzer, age 60, $608,301 pay
EVP Law and Corporate Services and Secretary: Gordon E. McCutchan, age 59
SVP Sales, Financial Products: Richard A. Karas, age 52, $250,764 pay
SVP and CFO: Robert A. Oakley, age 48
SVP Investment Product Operations: James E. Brock
SVP and General Counsel: W. Sidney Druen, age 52
VP Human Resources: Susan A. Wolken
Auditors: KPMG Peat Marwick LLP

WHERE

HQ: One Nationwide Plaza, Columbus, OH 43215-2220
Phone: 614-249-7111
Fax: 614-249-9071

Nationwide is licensed in all 50 states, the District of Columbia, Puerto Rico, and Germany. It operates service centers in Connecticut, Florida, Maryland, North Carolina, Ohio, Oregon, Pennsylvania, Tennessee, Texas, and Virginia.

WHAT

	1994 Assets	
	$ mil.	% of total
Cash	125	0
Bonds	24,308	50
Stocks	2,287	5
Mortgage loans & real estate	4,898	10
Other investments	851	2
Premiums receivable	1,256	3
Separate account assets	12,227	26
Other	1,745	4
Total	**47,696**	**100**

	1994 Sales	
	$ mil.	% of total
Property/casualty	7,414	45
Health, life & annuity	6,587	40
Net investment income	2,359	14
Other	147	1
Total	**16,507**	**100**

	1994 Sales	
	$ mil.	% of total
Life companies	7,891	47
Nationwide P/C cos.	5,945	36
Wausau companies	1,617	10
Other property/casualty cos.	788	5
Noninsurance cos.	266	2
Total	**16,507**	**100**

Selected Subsidiaries
Colonial Insurance of California
Farmland Life Insurance
Farmland Mutual Insurance
GatesMcDonald
Nationwide Agribusiness Insurance
Nationwide Communications Inc.
Nationwide Financial Services
NEA ValueBuilder Investor Services, Inc.
Neckura Insurance Cos. (Germany)
Public Employees Benefit Services Corp.
Scottsdale Insurance
Wausau Insurance Cos.
West Coast Life Insurance

KEY COMPETITORS

Aetna	MetLife
Allianz	New York Life
Allstate	Northwestern Mutual
American Financial Group	Pacific Mutual
CIGNA	PacifiCare
Equitable	Principal Financial
Foundation Health	Prudential
Guardian Life Insurance	Sierra Health Services
ITT Hartford	State Farm
John Hancock	Transamerica
Liberty Mutual	USAA
MassMutual	USF&G

HOW MUCH

	Annual Growth	1985	1986	1987	1988	1989	1990	1991	1992	1993	1994
Assets ($ mil.)	14.0%	14,700	17,500	—	22,349	25,044	27,848	32,779	37,582	42,213	47,696
Net income ($ mil.)	1.7%	—	—	—	403	261	148	393	69	501	445
Income as % of assets	—	—	—	—	1.8%	1.0%	0.5%	1.2%	0.2%	1.2%	0.9%
Employees	7.3%	23,400	24,100	24,900	24,800	25,000	26,000	27,000	32,500	32,583	44,000

1994 Year-end:
Equity as % of assets: 10.1%
Return on equity: 10.1%
Sales (mil.): $16,507

Net Income ($ mil.)
1988–94

NAVISTAR INTERNATIONAL

OVERVIEW

Chicago-based Navistar is the US's #1 maker of heavy- and medium-sized trucks (27% of the 1994 market) and the leading supplier of school bus chassis. The company also builds diesel engines for its vehicles and sells engines to original equipment makers. In addition, Navistar provides financing and insurance to both dealers and customers.

After years of losses, Navistar is starting to rally. In 1994 the company made its first profit since 1989. Navistar has been adding new shifts, overtime, and more employees at some of its manufacturing plants to match an upsurge in demand. The company also rolled out

some improved products in 1994, such as new engines and larger sleeping compartments — amenities trucking companies want in order to attract drivers. Also that year Navistar produced its first fully electronic diesel engine. The company is continuing to upgrade its engines, which it started doing in 1993.

However, Navistar is still hobbled by the expense of retiree health care costs, although it cut its health and operational costs $280 million over the last 2 years. The company has set cost reduction goals that include simplifying its products, using fewer parts, and reducing development times.

WHEN

Cyrus McCormick, the Virginia-born inventor who perfected the reaper in 1831, moved west and set up his first factory in Chicago in 1846. To compete with other manufacturers, McCormick offered such innovations as the installment plan, a written guarantee, and factory-trained repairmen. In 1886 a strike at the Chicago works in favor of the 8-hour workday led to the infamous Haymarket Square riot. In 1902, with the backing of J. P. Morgan, McCormick merged with Deering and several smaller firms to form International Harvester (IH). The new enterprise controlled 85% of US harvester production.

IH set up its first overseas factory in 1905 in Sweden. In 1906 Harvester entered the tractor industry and in 1907 began production of the Auto Buggy, forerunner of the truck. By 1910 the firm was annually producing 1,300 trucks and 1,400 tractors and had reached over $100 million in sales.

In 1913 Cyrus Jr. (Cyrus Sr. had died in 1884) borrowed $5 million from John D. Rockefeller and gained control of the company. The new general manager, Alexander Legge (also president from 1922 to 1929), introduced the Farmall, the first all-purpose tractor, in 1924. In 1928 IH began production of a heavy truck with a 4-cylinder engine, and by 1937 it was the top US producer of medium and heavy trucks.

In the post-WWII industry boom, IH's neglect of product development and capital improvement, combined with the effects of overdiversification, caused market share to decline for most of its products. The company sold more trucks than agricultural equipment for the first time in 1955. IH lost its lead in agricultural equipment to John Deere in 1958. During the 1960s IH lost its medium industry

sales leadership to Ford, and the company's construction equipment business, although buoyed by the 1952 acquisition of the Payloader, consistently lost market share.

A 6-month strike by the UAW in 1980, coupled with a recession, sent IH to the edge of bankruptcy. Between 1980 and 1982 the company lost $2.3 billion. Restructuring, IH sold the construction equipment division to Dresser Industries in 1982. In 1985 Tenneco bought the agricultural equipment business and the International Harvester name. By 1986 the number of employees had dropped 85%, and plants had decreased from 48 worldwide to 6 in North America.

The company was renamed Navistar in 1986. By 1987 it had redesigned 85% of its truck line. In 1989 Navistar introduced a 9-speed heavy truck transmission (developed jointly with Dana), the first all-new design in more than 25 years. In 1991 Navistar raised its stake in Mexican truck maker Dina Camiones to 17% and inked OEM deals for its engines with Perkins Group (UK) and Perkins's North American distributor, Detroit Diesel. The next year Navistar announced it would recall up to 185,000 school buses after one failed a federal safety test.

A boom in demand for heavy trucks in 1992 and 1993 resulted in Navistar's retail deliveries rising nearly 33%. Also in 1993 the company started a program to increase fuel efficiency and torque in its engines. That same year Navistar introduced 3 new 6-cylinder engines for its line of medium trucks. In 1994 Navistar was the first truck maker to offer a one-million-mile warranty for its heavy trucks.

In early 1995 chairman and CEO James Cotting stepped down, relinquishing his posts to John Horne, Navistar's president and COO.

NYSE symbol: NAV
Fiscal year ends: October 31

WHO

Chairman, President, and CEO: John R. Horne, age 56,
$543,000 pay (prior to promotion)
EVP and CFO: Robert C. Lannert, age 54, $393,833 pay
Group VP; General Manager Financial Services: John J.
Bongiorno, $313,420 pay
Group VP Truck Businesses: David J. Johanneson
Group VP Sales and Distribution: James T. O'Dare Jr.
Group VP; General Manager Engine and Foundry:
Daniel C. Ustian
Group VP International Operations: Dennis W. Webb
SVP and General Counsel: Robert A. Boardman, age 47,
$310,510 pay
SVP Employee Relations and Administration: John M.
Sheahin
VP Truck Engineering: Kirk A. Gutmann
VP and Treasurer: Thomas M. Hough
VP and Controller: Robert I. Morrison
Auditors: Deloitte & Touche LLP

WHERE

HQ: Navistar International Corporation,
455 N. Cityfront Plaza Dr., Chicago, IL 60611
Phone: 312-836-2000
Fax: 312-836-2192

Navistar has 7 manufacturing and assembly plants in the
US and one in Canada. The company sells its products
through approximately 951 dealers in North America
and exports trucks and parts to more than 77 countries
around the world.

	1994 Sales	
	$ mil.	% of total
US	4,670	91
Canada	483	9
Adjustments	184	—
Total	**5,337**	**100**

WHAT

	1994 Sales	
	$ mil.	% of total
Manufacturing	5,153	96
Financial services	152	3
Other	32	1
Total	**5,337**	**100**

	1994 Sales
	% of total
Heavy trucks	42
Medium trucks	32
Replacement parts	14
Engines	12
Total	**100**

Navistar International Transportation Corp.
Diesel engines
Replacement parts
School bus chassis
Trucks

Navistar Financial Corporation
Customer financing
Dealer financing
Insurance

KEY COMPETITORS

Blue Bird	Mitsubishi
Caterpillar	Nissan
Cummins Engine	Oshkosh Truck
Daimler-Benz	PACCAR
Fiat	Peugeot
Ford	Renault
General Motors	Saab-Scania
Harley-Davidson	Tata
Hino	Volvo
Isuzu	

HOW MUCH

	9-Year Growth	1985	1986	1987	1988	1989	1990	1991	1992	1993	1994
Sales ($ mil.)	4.7%	3,508	3,357	3,530	4,080	4,023	3,643	3,259	3,875	4,694	5,337
Net income ($ mil.)	—	(463)	(2)	146	244	87	(11)	(165)	(212)	(273)	82
Income as % of sales	—	—	—	4.1%	6.0%	2.2%	—	—	—	—	1.5%
Earnings per share ($)	—	(36.70)	(1.80)	5.00	8.40	2.30	(1.60)	(7.70)	(9.50)	(8.63)	0.72
Stock price – high ($)	—	112.50	116.25	87.50	73.75	70.00	46.25	42.50	41.25	33.75	26.63
Stock price – low ($)	—	65.00	41.25	30.00	31.25	32.50	20.00	21.25	17.50	19.25	12.25
Stock price – close ($)	(17.5%)	85.00	47.50	42.50	53.75	38.75	22.50	26.25	22.50	23.63	15.13
P/E – high	—	—	—	18	9	30	—	—	—	—	37
P/E – low	—	—	—	6	4	14	—	—	—	—	17
Dividends per share ($)	—	0.00	0.00	0.00	0.00	0.00	0.00	0.00	0.00	0.00	0.00
Book value per share ($)	(1.3%)	(138.07)	(27.76)	14.98	24.10	26.43	22.80	13.27	3.66	7.09	7.71
Employees		16,836	14,997	14,918	15,719	14,118	14,071	13,472	13,945	13,612	14,910

1994 Year-end:
Debt ratio: 59.9%
Return on equity: 14.9%
Cash (mil.): $557
Current ratio: 1.59
Long-term debt (mil.): $696
No. of shares (mil.): 74
Dividends
  Yield: —
  Payout: —
Market value (mil.): $1,125

Stock Price History
High/Low 1985–94

NEW YORK LIFE INSURANCE COMPANY

OVERVIEW

New York Life has taken the high road in addressing the problem of deceptive sales practices. It had to, after a Texas jury awarded $21 million to an aggrieved customer and Florida also began investigating the company. But unlike some of the other insurers involved in such cases, New York Life, one of the largest US life insurers, moved decisively to forestall further problems by ordering a comprehensive review of all sales materials in use throughout the country. As a result, it issued standardized materials and prohibited any other from being used to make sales.

New York Life offers a wide variety of life, health, and disability insurance policies; annuities; mutual funds and other investments; and health care management services. In 1995 it was authorized to open a trust bank, which will aid its benefits and mutual funds operations.

Although New York Life closed its operations in Canada in 1994, it is expanding elsewhere in the world, opening a representative office in Shanghai. It expects its business in Mexico to grow, fueled by demand in a country where only 2% of the people are insured.

WHEN

In 1841 actuary Pliny Freeman and 56 New York businessmen founded Nautilus Insurance Co., the 3rd US mutual (policyholder-owned) company. It began operating in 1845 and became New York Life in 1849.

In 1846 the company had the first life insurance agent west of the Mississippi River. Although cut off from its southern business by the Civil War, New York Life honored all its obligations and renewed lapsed policies when the war ended. By 1887 the company had developed its branch office system.

By 1900 the company had established the NYLIC Plan for compensating agents, which featured a lifetime income after 20 years of service. New York Life had moved into Europe in the late 1800s but withdrew after WWI.

Much of the company's growth and product development has occurred since WWII. In the early 1950s the company simplified insurance policy forms, slashed premiums, and replaced mortality tables of the 1860s with more up-to-date data. These actions resulted in new company sales records and were widely copied by competitors. In 1956 the company became the first life insurance firm to use data processing equipment on a large scale.

In the 1960s New York Life was instrumental in developing variable life insurance, a new product with variable benefits and level premiums. In 1968 the company added variable annuities. Steady growth continued until the late 1970s, when high interest rates led to heavy policyholder borrowing. Jarred by the outflow of money, the company sought to make its products more competitive as investments.

In 1981 the company offered single- and flexible-premium deferred annuities, and in 1982 it added a universal life product. New York Life also formed New York Life and Health Insurance Co. in 1982.

The company acquired MacKay-Shields Financial, which now oversees its MainStay mutual funds, in 1984. This, along with a modernization program, caused income to plummet. Also in 1984 NYLIFE Realty offered the company's first pure investment product, a real estate limited partnership.

Expansion continued in 1987 with the purchase of a controlling interest in Hillhouse Associates Insurance (3rd-party administrator of insurance plans) and Madison Benefits Administrators (group insurance programs). The company also acquired Sanus Corp. Health Systems, the largest privately held manager of health care programs in the US. It returned to Europe in 1988, opening an office in Ireland.

New York Life entered a joint venture to provide insurance in Indonesia in 1992, when it also began operations in Korea and Taiwan. The next year it bought Aetna UK's life insurance operations.

In a climate of increased scrutiny of insurance industry sales practices in 1993 and 1994, New York Life was investigated by the state of Florida and faced several suits in Texas. The company also launched its own investigations, which won praise from the state regulators involved. In late 1994 it increased its health care holdings, adding ETHIX Corp. (utilization review) and Avanti Health Systems (physician practice management).

In early 1995 president George Bundschuh announced his retirement in October. He will be succeeded by current EVP Seymour Sternberg. As part of the expansion of its overseas business, New York Life entered into a joint venture with St. James's Place Capital, PLC, to form Life Assurance Holding Corp. That same year New York Life and Oracle Systems began developing client/server database software specifically for the insurance industry.

Mutual company
Fiscal year ends: December 31

Chairman and CEO: Harry G. Hohn
VC and EVP: Lee M. Gammill Jr., age 61
EVP Human Resources: George J. Trapp, age 47
EVP: Seymour Sternberg, age 51
EVP: Frederick J. Sievert, age 47
SVP and General Counsel: Alfred J. T. Byrne
SVP and Chief Information Officer: Lee Lapioli, age 53
SVP and Chief Actuary: Stephen N. Steinig
SVP Corporate Office of Business Conduct: Richard A. Hansen
SVP, Deputy General Counsel, and Secretary: Melbourne Nunes
VP and Controller: Marc J. Chalfin
VP and Treasurer: Jay S. Calhoun
VP and General Auditor: Thomas J. Warga
Auditors: Price Waterhouse LLP

WHERE

HQ: 51 Madison Ave., New York, NY 10010
Phone: 212-576-7000
Fax: 212-576-8145

New York Life operates in Argentina, Bermuda, China, Hong Kong, Indonesia, Korea, Mexico, Taiwan, the UK, and the US.

WHAT

	1994 Assets	
	$ mil.	% of total
Cash & equivalents	2,506	4
Treasury & agency securities	6,682	10
Municipal bonds	11,992	18
Foreign governments' securities	1,699	2
Corporate bonds	22,740	33
Other bonds	2,187	3
Stocks	1,789	2
Mortgage loans	5,990	9
Real estate	1,290	2
Policy loans	5,380	8
Separate account assets	3,580	5
Other	3,091	4
Total	**68,926**	**100**

	1994 Sales	
1994 Sales	$ mil.	% of total
Premiums	10,255	65
Net investment income	4,679	30
Other income	873	5
Total	**15,807**	**100**

Business Units
Asset Management
Group Operations
Individual Operations
Investments

Selected Products
Annuities
Disability insurance
Group pensions
Life insurance
MainStay (mutual funds)

Selected Subsidiaries
Las Buenos Aires New York Life
New York Life and Health Insurance Co.
New York Life Insurance and Annuity Corp.
New York Life Worldwide (Bermuda) Ltd.
New York Life Worldwide Holding, Inc.
NYL Benefit Services, Inc. (employee benefit consulting)
NYLIFE Distributors, Inc. (brokerage)
NYLIFE Insurance Company of Arizona
Sanus Corp. Health Systems (HMO)

KEY COMPETITORS

Aetna
Allstate
American National Insurance
Berkshire Hathaway
Blue Cross
Charles Schwab
Chubb
CIGNA
CNA Financial
Dean Witter, Discover
Equitable
Guardian Life Insurance
ITT Hartford
John Alden Financial
John Hancock
Kaiser Foundation Health Plan
Kemper Corp.
MassMutual
Mellon Bank
Merrill Lynch
MetLife
Mutual of Omaha
Northwestern Mutual
Oxford Health Plans
Paine Webber
Prudential
State Farm
T. Rowe Price
Transamerica
USF&G

HOW MUCH

	Annual Growth	1985	1986	1987	1988	1989	1990	1991	1992	1993	1994
Assets ($ mil.)	9.0%	31,740	35,087	38,877	43,417	46,648	50,126	54,066	59,169	66,791	68,926
Net income ($ mil.)	32.5%	32	194	92	204	57	290	280	271	368	404
Income as % of assets	—	0.1%	0.6%	0.2%	0.5%	0.1%	0.6%	0.5%	0.5%	0.6%	0.6%
Employees	(4.4%)	—	—	—	—	19,438	18,200	18,848	17,406	17,169	15,534

1994 Year-end:
Equity as % of assets: 5.4%
Return on equity: 11.3%
Sales (mil.): $15,807

Net Income ($ mil.)
1985–94

THE NEW YORK TIMES COMPANY

OVERVIEW

The New York Times Company is a sprawling, $2.4 billion media and communications conglomerate with interests in newspapers, magazines, broadcasting, and information services. It publishes one of the world's most respected newspapers, the *New York Times*, which is also the US's #1 metropolitan daily. The company owns the *Boston Globe*, 23 smaller daily newspapers (plus 5 weeklies) in 10 states, half of the *International Herald Tribune*, 2 newspaper distributors, and a stake in 2 US and Canadian paper mills. Newspapers represented 83% of 1994 revenues. The company also operates 5 TV stations and 2 New York radio stations; publishes 10 sports and leisure magazines; sells wire and photo services (it is the world's largest supplemental news service); repackages information and news for fax, CD-ROM, microform, and on-line services; and licenses trademarks and copyrighted material from the *Times*.

A traditional print publisher (90% of its profits are from print properties), the Times Co. is now moving quickly into multimedia. Previously hamstrung by an exclusive contract with on-line information provider LEXIS/NEXIS, the company regained control of the electronic rights to the *Times* in late 1994. In 1995 the company teamed up with 8 other major newspaper companies to distribute the *Times* on-line through a new service, New Century Network, which is expected to be operational by late 1995. The company intends to further explore other news outlets, especially TV, and look for opportunities in local TV stations and national cable TV programming.

WHEN

In 1851 George Jones and Henry Raymond, 2 former *New York Tribune* staffers, started the *New York Times*. The paper began a long tradition of political coverage during the Civil War and of investigative reporting with the Tammany Hall scandals, but by the late 1800s it had lost popularity to the yellow journalism of the Hearst and Pulitzer papers.

In 1896 Adolph Ochs, a newspaperman from Chattanooga, bought the *Times*. Continuing hard news and business coverage and eschewing diversification, Ochs added the newspaper's now-famous slogan: "All the News That's Fit to Print." Ochs's son-in-law Arthur Sulzberger, who ran the paper from 1935 to 1961, diversified the company with the purchase of 2 New York City radio stations (1944). Sulzberger's son-in-law Orvil Dryfoos was publisher until his death in 1963, leaving Adolph's grandson Arthur Ochs "Punch" Sulzberger in charge.

In the 1960s declining ad revenues from Manhattan stores and a newspaper strike sent the company into the red. To regain strength Punch built the largest news-gathering staff of any newspaper. The *Times*'s coverage of the Vietnam War helped change public sentiment, and the newspaper won a Pulitzer Prize in 1972 for publishing the Pentagon Papers.

In the meantime Punch had taken the company public (1967), though the family retained solid control through ownership of most of the Class B stock. In the 1970s the Times Co. bought magazines, publishing houses, television stations, smaller newspapers, and cable TV systems and began copublishing, with the Washington Post Co., the *International Herald Tribune*. To contain costs the company bought interests in 3 pulp and paper companies.

In the 1980s the *Times* added feature sections to compete with suburban papers. The company bought *Golf World* in 1988, and in 1989 it bought *McCall's* (sold 1994) and sold its cable systems. In 1990 the company started *TimesFax*, a summary of the *Times* sent to subscribers' fax machines worldwide.

Family members are still active on the board and in publishing activities. In 1992 Arthur Ochs Sulzberger Jr. succeeded his father as *Times* publisher; Punch remained Times Co. chairman and CEO.

In 1993 the Times Co. bought Affiliated Publications, owner of the *Boston Globe*, for a record $1.1 billion. Started in 1872, the *Globe* found its footing in 1878 under the financing of Eben Jordan (one of 6 *Globe* cofounders and founder of Jordan Marsh department stores) and the management of Charles Taylor. By selling to the Times Co., Affiliated avoided a possible hostile takeover in 1996, the year the Jordan and Taylor family trusts were to expire. In 1994 the Times Co. sold the 1/3 interest in BPI Communications (specialty magazines) that had come with the Affiliated purchase.

In 1994 the company started building a state-of-the-art printing plant, which should add more color and allow later deadlines. The company also sold its women's and 3 UK golf magazines. In 1995 the Times Co. agreed to buy a majority stake in Video News International, a video news-gathering company, and launched 2 cable news channels in Arkansas.

AMEX symbol: NYT.A
Fiscal year ends: December 31

WHO

Chairman and CEO: Arthur Ochs "Punch" Sulzberger, age 69, $962,200 pay
President and COO: Lance R. Primis, age 48, $1,100,800 pay
Publisher, *The New York Times*: Arthur Ochs Sulzberger Jr., age 43, $918,200 pay
SVP and CFO: David L. Gorham, age 62, $683,400 pay
Publisher, *The Boston Globe*: William O. Taylor, age 62, $550,451 pay
SVP Broadcasting, Corporate Development, and Human Resources: Katharine P. Darrow, age 51
VP Operations and Planning: Gordon Medenica, age 43
VP and General Counsel: Solomon B. Watson IV, age 50
Auditors: Deloitte & Touche LLP

WHERE

HQ: 229 W. 43rd St., New York, NY 10036
Phone: 212-556-1234
Fax: 212-556-3722

WHAT

	1994 Sales	
	$ mil.	% of total
Newspapers	1,969	83
Magazines	280	12
Broadcasting & information svcs.	109	5
Total	**2,358**	**100**

Major Newspapers
Boston Globe (504,500 average daily circulation)
International Herald Tribune (50%, with the Washington Post Co.)
New York Times (1,149,700 average daily circulation)

Magazines

Cruising World	*Sailing World*
Golf Digest	*Snow Country*
Golf Shop Operations	*Snow Country Business*
Golf World	*Tennis*
Sailing Business	*Tennis Buyer's Guide*

Broadcasting

KFSM-TV, Fort Smith, AR	WQAD-TV, Moline, IL
WHNT-TV, Huntsville, AL	WQEW (AM), New York
WNEP-TV, Wilkes-Barre/ Scranton, PA	WQXR (FM), New York
	WREG-TV, Memphis

Information Services
The New York Times Syndication Sales Corp.
  The New York Times News Service (650 newspaper and magazine customers)
  Special Features (supplemental news and information)
  TimesFax (fax-, satellite-, and PC-delivered *Times* summary)
NYT Business Information Services
  The New York Times Index
  New York Times on Dow Jones News/Retrieval and LEXIS/NEXIS
NYT New Media/New Products
  @*times* on America Online
  NYT Custom Publishing (custom magazines)

Forest Products
Donohue Malbaie Inc. (49%, Canada)
Northern SC Paper Corp. (80%)
  Madison Paper Industries

KEY COMPETITORS

Advance Publications	Gannett	Pearson
Associated Press	Hearst	Reuters
Bloomberg	Herald Media	Thomson Corp.
Cox	Knight-Ridder	Time Warner
Daily News	Lagardère	Times Mirror
Dow Jones	Media General	Tribune
E.W. Scripps	Meredith Corp.	Viacom
	News Corp.	Washington Post

HOW MUCH

	9-Year Growth	1985	1986	1987	1988	1989	1990	1991	1992	1993	1994
Sales ($ mil.)	6.0%	1,394	1,565	1,690	1,700	1,769	1,777	1,703	1,774	2,020	2,358
Net income ($ mil.)	7.0%	116	132	160	168	267	65	47	(11)	6	213
Income as % of sales	—	8.3%	8.4%	9.5%	9.9%	15.1%	3.6%	2.8%	—	0.3%	9.0%
Earnings per share ($)	3.9%	1.45	1.63	1.96	2.08	3.39	0.85	0.61	(0.14)	0.07	2.05
Stock price – high ($)	—	25.44	42.00	49.63	32.75	34.75	27.50	25.25	32.13	31.25	29.50
Stock price – low ($)	—	17.50	23.31	24.75	24.38	24.50	16.88	18.25	22.63	22.38	21.25
Stock price – close ($)	(1.1%)	24.50	35.50	31.00	26.88	26.50	20.63	23.63	26.38	26.25	22.13
P/E – high	—	18	26	25	16	10	32	41	—	—	14
P/E – low	—	12	14	13	12	7	20	30	—	—	10
Dividends per share ($)	8.0%	0.28	0.32	0.38	0.45	0.49	0.67	0.42	0.70	0.56	0.56
Book value per share ($)	9.0%	7.24	8.64	10.04	10.44	13.63	13.68	13.70	12.53	14.96	15.71
Employees	2.4%	10,350	10,000	10,500	10,700	10,600	10,400	10,100	10,100	13,000	12,800

1994 Year-end:
Debt ratio: 25.4%
Return on equity: 13.6%
Cash (mil.): $41
Current ratio: 0.91
Long-term debt (mil.): $523
No. of shares (mil.): 98
Dividends
  Yield: 2.5%
  Payout: 27.3%
Market value (mil.): $2,174

Stock Price History High/Low 1985–94

NIKE, INC.

NIKE, the world's biggest shoe company, has a reputation for fancy footwork, especially in the arena of marketing. With both Forrest Gump and Michael Jordan sporting NIKE's athletic shoes, NIKE's appeal is wide ranging. But despite a $120 million advertising outlay in 1994, NIKE stumbled in the footrace for US market share. Although the shoe giant still holds nearly 30% of the US market, its stake slipped 2 points, while #2 Reebok gained ground, climbing nearly one point to over 21% on an advertising budget of $70 million.

NIKE — a powerhouse in the world of sports, the designer and international marketer of athletic shoes, casual footwear, apparel, and accessories — is looking for new growth opportunities. Faced with a softening US market for its traditional athletic products, in recent years NIKE has diversified its products and expanded its international operations. NIKE bought capmaker Sports Specialties in 1994, and in 1995 it entered the in-line skates market by purchasing Canstar Sports, the world's largest hockey equipment maker, for $395 million. The company acquired 100% of its subsidiaries in Japan and Korea in 1994. It also set up a joint venture in Argentina.

NIKE founder, chairman, and owner Phil Knight holds approximately 34% of the company's stock.

WHEN

In 1958 Phil Knight, an undergraduate business student at the University of Oregon and a good miler, often spoke with his coach Bill Bowerman about the lack of a good American running shoe. Bowerman, resolving to create a better shoe, sent an original design to several leading sporting goods companies. Turned down by all of them, Bowerman decided to make the shoe himself.

In 1964 Knight and Bowerman formed their own athletic shoe company, Blue Ribbon Sports, each putting up $300 for the first order of 300 pairs of shoes, manufactured by Onitsuka Tiger, a Japanese shoe manufacturer. They stored the shoes in the basement of Knight's father's house and sold them out of cars at track meets.

In 1968 the 2 men formed NIKE, named for the Greek goddess of victory invoked by the legendary runner from Marathon. The NIKE "swoosh" logo was designed by a graduate student named Carolyn Davidson, who was paid $35. In 1972 NIKE broke with Onitsuka in a dispute over distribution rights.

At the 1972 Olympic Trials in Eugene, Oregon, Knight and Bowerman persuaded some of the marathoners to wear NIKE shoes. When some of these runners placed, the 2 men quickly advertised that NIKEs were worn by "four of the top seven finishers."

In 1975 Bowerman had an idea for a new sole, which he tested by stuffing a piece of rubber into a waffle iron. The result was the waffle sole, which NIKE added to its running shoes. When running became popular in the 1970s, NIKE improved its line of running shoes to appeal to the new market.

When enthusiasm for running faded, rival Reebok forged ahead with its aerobic lines, and NIKE responded with shoes for other sports. NIKE introduced Air Jordan (a basketball shoe named for basketball star Michael Jordan) in 1985, the Cross Trainer in 1987, the "Just Do It" slogan in 1988, Air Pressure (basketball shoes with inflatable soles) in 1989, and Aqua Sock (water shoes) in 1990. In the meantime NIKE bought Cole Haan (dress shoes, 1988).

With Air Raid, the company in 1992 introduced yet another successful athletic shoe. Also in 1992 NIKE and competitor Avia came to undisclosed terms in a patent infringement lawsuit. Avia had accused NIKE of swiping a design for shoe cushioning, and NIKE had responded with similar charges. That same year the firm opened the first NIKE Concept Shop, a 2,000-square-foot "store within a store" at Macy's in San Francisco. The company also launched NIKE TOWN, a concept retail store that combines innovative products with endorsements and image selling by top athletes, in Portland, Oregon.

In 1993 chief NIKE icon Jordan, having led the Chicago Bulls to their 3rd consecutive NBA championship, retired from professional basketball to try his hand at baseball. Handing the company an unexpected boost, Jordan (whose NIKE ads outperformed Shaquille O'Neal's Pepsi ads by 6-to-1, according to Sports Marketing Letter's poll of 3,000 readers) returned to play professional basketball in 1995 and starred in a new series of NIKE ads.

By 1995 the company's 2nd NIKE TOWN, in Chicago, was the city's #1 retail tourist attraction. NIKE plans to open more NIKE TOWNs in several US cities, including Boston, New York, Seattle, and San Francisco. Net income for fiscal 1995 hit nearly $400 million.

NYSE symbol: NKE
Fiscal year ends: May 31

WHO

Chairman and CEO: Philip H. Knight, age 56, $900,000 pay
VC: Richard K. Donahue, age 67, $720,000 pay (prior to promotion)
Deputy Chairman and SVP: William J. Bowerman, age 83
President and COO: Thomas E. Clarke, age 43, $483,271 pay
EVP: Delbert J. Hayes, age 59
VP and General Manager, Sports and Fitness: Harry C. Carsh, age 55, $375,562 pay
VP and General Manager, International Division: David Kottkamp, age 52
VP and General Manager, Consumer Product Marketing: Mark G. Parker, age 38
VP, General Counsel, and Assistant Secretary: Lindsay D. Stewart, age 47
VP and CFO: Robert S. Falcone, age 47
Director Human Resources: Jim Fredericks
Auditors: Price Waterhouse LLP

WHERE

HQ: One Bowerman Dr., Beaverton, OR 97005-6453
Phone: 503-671-6453
Fax: 503-671-6300

NIKE sells its products in 82 countries, operates 61 retail outlets, and has administrative offices in Austria, Canada, Hong Kong, the Netherlands, and the US.

	1994 Sales		1994 Operating Income	
	$ mil.	% of total	$ mil.	% of total
US	2,433	64	345	65
Europe	927	25	124	23
Other countries	430	11	66	12
Adjustments	—	—	(44)	—
Total	**3,790**	**100**	**491**	**100**

WHAT

	1994 Sales	
	$ mil.	% of total
Domestic footwear	1,869	49
International footwear	998	26
International apparel	359	10
Domestic apparel	339	9
Other domestic prods.	225	6
Total	**3,790**	**100**

Athletic Shoes

Aquatic	Fitness	Running
Baseball	Football	Soccer
Basketball	Golf	Tennis
Bicycling	Hockey	Volleyball
Cheerleading	Roller skates	Wrestling

Athletic Wear

Accessories	Jackets	Shorts
Athletic bags	Leotards	Skirts
Caps	Pants	Socks
Fitness wear	Running	Vests
Gloves	clothes	Uniforms
Headwear	Shirts	Unitards

Selected Subsidiaries
Canstar Sports (hockey equipment and in-line skates)
Cole Haan Holdings Inc. (footwear and accessories)
Sports Specialties, Corp. (headwear and licensed team logos)
Tetra Plastics, Inc. (plastic footwear components)

KEY COMPETITORS

Adidas	The Limited	Russell Corp.
Converse	Nautica	Stride Rite
Deckers Outdoor	New Balance	Timberland
First Team	Puma	Variflex
The Gap	Reebok	V. F. Corp.
L.A. Gear	Rÿka	Wolverine
Lands' End	Rollerblade	World Wide
Levi Strauss		

HOW MUCH

	9-Year Growth	1985	1986	1987	1988	1989	1990	1991	1992	1993	1994
Sales ($ mil.)	16.7%	946	1,069	877	1,203	1,711	2,235	3,004	3,405	3,931	3,790
Net income ($ mil.)	45.4%	10	59	36	102	167	243	287	329	365	299
Income as % of sales	—	1.1%	5.5%	4.1%	8.5%	9.8%	10.9%	9.6%	9.7%	9.3%	7.9%
Earnings per share ($)	45.0%	0.14	0.78	0.47	1.35	2.23	3.21	3.77	4.30	4.74	3.96
Stock price – high ($)	—	7.25	10.06	12.25	17.00	34.00	47.94	75.75	90.25	89.25	76.50
Stock price – low ($)	—	3.94	5.31	5.81	8.81	12.94	24.00	35.13	55.00	43.13	46.25
Stock price – close ($)	30.0%	7.06	5.88	9.75	13.25	26.63	40.25	72.38	83.00	46.25	74.63
P/E – high	—	52	13	26	13	15	15	20	21	19	19
P/E – low	—	28	7	12	7	6	8	9	13	9	12
Dividends per share ($)	16.7%	0.20	0.20	0.20	0.20	0.20	0.25	0.35	0.48	0.58	0.75	0.80
Book value per share ($)	14.9%	6.54	4.19	4.45	5.55	7.53	10.51	13.72	17.64	21.70	22.85
Employees	9.8%	4,100	3,400	3,000	3,450	4,700	3,400	4,515	7,800	9,600	9,500

1994 Year-end:
Debt ratio: 7.6%
Return on equity: 17.6%
Cash (mil.): $519
Current ratio: 3.15
Long-term debt (mil.): $12
No. of shares (mil.): 76
Dividends
  Yield: 1.1%
  Payout: 20.2%
Market value (mil.): $5,687

Stock Price History High/Low 1985–94

HOOVER'S HANDBOOK OF AMERICAN COMPANIES 1996   **639**

NORDSTROM, INC.

OVERVIEW

Based in Seattle, Nordstrom is a leading up-scale apparel and shoe chain. The company, known as "Nordy's," has built a loyal customer base and a strong reputation thanks to its emphasis on customer service. Nordstrom sells clothes, shoes, and accessories to an affluent clientele through 55 department stores in 10 states. It also leases shoe departments in 12 department stores in Hawaii and Guam and operates 19 clearance stores (Last Chance and Nordstrom Rack). The chain is closely supervised by a 3rd generation of the Nordstrom family, which owns about 26% of the stock.

After flat earnings the last few years, Nordstrom rebounded in fiscal 1995. Profits were up 45% thanks to contributions from 4 new stores, remodeled stores, and a new inventory management system that has helped cut costs. Same-store sales were up 4.4% in fiscal 1995.

Nordstrom is concentrating its efforts on geographic expansion. From its strong base on the West Coast, the company is moving into other parts of the US. It has already opened several stores in the Washington, DC, area, and it continues to expand in the New York area (where it plans to have 10 stores by the year 2000) and in Chicago. The company plans to open stores in Dallas, Philadelphia, Detroit, and Denver in 1996; in Ohio, Connecticut, Virginia, and Georgia in 1997; and in Arizona in 1998.

Nordstrom has also introduced a catalog, which attracted 300,000 shoppers in its first year, and Nordstrom Personal Touch America, an on-line shopping service.

WHEN

In 1901 John Nordstrom, a lumberjack and successful gold miner from Sweden, opened Wallin & Nordstrom shoe store in Seattle with shoemaker Carl Wallin. In 1928 Nordstrom retired and sold his half of the business, which included a 2nd store, to his sons Everett and Elmer. In 1929 Wallin sold out to the Nordstroms; a 3rd Nordstrom son, Lloyd, joined in 1933. The shoe chain thrived and incorporated as Nordstrom's, Inc., in 1946.

By 1963 Nordstrom's was the largest independent shoe chain in the country. The company decided to diversify into apparel retailing and that year acquired Best Apparel, which had a store in Seattle and another in Portland. In 1966 Nordstrom's bought Portland's Nicholas Ungar, a fashion retailer, which Nordstrom's merged with one of its shoe stores, in Portland, under the name Nordstrom Best.

Renamed Nordstrom Best in 1966, the company went public in 1971; in 1973 the name was changed to Nordstrom. The retailer grew steadily throughout the 1970s, opening new stores, boosting sales in existing stores, and diversifying.

In 1976 Nordstrom started Place Two, featuring apparel and shoes in smaller stores than its traditional department stores. The foray into Southern California began with the opening of a store in Orange County (1978). Buoyed by almost $300 million in new sales, Nordstrom executives planned an aggressive expansion effort.

The chain's biggest growth area was California, but in 1988 the primarily West Coast retailer opened its first store on the East Coast in an affluent Virginia suburb. This store had the highest first-day sales in the company's history — $1 million. Nordstrom continued to expand in the East as well as in California. The chain continued to open more stores in Northern California (the San Francisco store was its largest) and in the Virginia suburbs around Washington, DC.

The 1989 San Francisco earthquake, along with a general national downturn, hurt retail sales significantly. In 1990 the company was investigated for not paying employees for some of the exceptional personal service they gave to customers, which included delivering merchandise. The company continued to expand in the East and Midwest, opening its first store in the metropolitan New York area in Paramus, New Jersey (1991), and one in the Chicago suburb Oak Brook (1992).

In 1993 Nordstrom set aside $15 million in a reserve fund to pay back wages to employees who had performed off-the-clock services. That same year the retailer opened a men's boutique in New York (Façonnable). Looking for new ways to attract customers, the company introduced a mail-order catalog and a proprietary Visa credit card in 1994.

In 1995 Nordstrom signed a deal with the Andy Johns International unit of Biscayne Apparel to produce a line of private-label outerwear. Also in 1995 the company opened its first store in the state of New York (in White Plains), as well as a store in Schaumberg, Illinois, near Chicago.

Nasdaq symbol: NOBE
Fiscal year ends: January 31

Co-chairman: Bruce A. Nordstrom, age 61, $580,000 pay
Co-chairman: John N. Nordstrom, age 57, $580,000 pay
Co-chairman: James F. Nordstrom, age 55, $580,000 pay
Co-chairman: John A. McMillan, age 63, $580,000 pay
Co-president: Raymond A. Johnson, age 53,
  $630,000 pay
Co-president: John J. Whitacre, age 42, $630,000 pay
EVP Finance and Treasurer: John A. Goesling,
  $615,000 pay
EVP; Manager, Men's Wear Merchandise: Jack F. Irving,
  age 50
EVP; General Manager, Southern California: Jammie
  Baugh, age 41
EVP Product Development: Gail A. Cottle, age 43
EVP; Manager, Shoe Merchandise: Robert T. Nunn,
  age 55
EVP; Manager, Better Apparel Merchandise: Cynthia C.
  Paur, age 44
VP Human Resources: Charles L. Dudley, age 44
Auditors: Deloitte & Touche LLP

HQ: 1501 Fifth Ave., Seattle, WA 98101-1603
Phone: 206-628-2111
Fax: 206-628-1795

	1995 Retail Locations
	No.
Southern California	20
Washington	13
Hawaii and Guam (shoe departments)	12
Northern California	12
Washington, DC, area	9
Oregon	8
Utah	4
Other	11
Total	**89**

	1995 Retail Sales
	% of total
Women's apparel	38
Shoes	20
Women's accessories	20
Men's apparel & furnishings	16
Children's apparel & accessories	4
Other	2
Total	**100**

	1995 Stores
	No.
Nordstrom (large department stores)	55
Nordstrom Rack (discount/clearance stores)	19
Leased shoe departments	12
Other	3
Total	**89**

American Retail	Lands' End
AnnTaylor	The Limited
Basic Living Products	Liz Claiborne
Benetton	L.L. Bean
Blair	Luxottica
Bombay Co.	Marks and Spencer
Broadway Stores	May
Brown Group	Melville
Charming Shoppes	Men's Wearhouse
Dayton Hudson	Mercantile Stores
Dillard	Montgomery Ward
Edison Brothers	Ross Stores
Federated	Saks
Fred Meyer	Sears
The Gap	Spiegel
Gottschalks	Stein Mart
Harcourt General	Talbots
J. Crew	Tanger Factory Outlet
J. C. Penney	TJX

	9-Year Growth	1986	1987	1988	1989	1990	1991	1992	1993	1994	1995
Sales ($ mil.)	12.9%	1,302	1,630	1,920	2,328	2,671	2,894	3,180	3,422	3,590	3,894
Net income ($ mil.)	16.8%	50	73	93	123	115	116	136	137	140	203
Income as % of sales	—	3.8%	4.5%	4.8%	5.3%	4.3%	4.0%	4.3%	4.0%	3.9%	5.2%
Earnings per share ($)	15.8%	0.66	0.91	1.13	1.51	1.41	1.42	1.66	1.67	1.71	2.47
Stock price – high ($)[1]	—	12.94	25.50	40.50	33.50	42.25	39.25	53.00	42.75	43.50	49.75
Stock price – low ($)[1]	—	7.06	11.88	17.75	20.50	30.00	17.25	22.00	25.50	22.25	31.00
Stock price – close ($)[1]	15.0%	11.94	20.88	19.75	30.25	37.25	22.25	36.00	38.75	33.00	42.00
P/E – high	—	20	28	36	22	30	28	32	26	25	20
P/E – low	—	11	13	16	14	21	12	13	15	15	13
Dividends per share ($)	15.1%	0.11	0.13	0.18	0.22	0.28	0.30	0.31	0.32	0.34	0.39
Book value per share ($)	17.3%	3.88	5.57	6.55	7.85	8.99	10.11	11.48	12.84	14.22	16.34
Employees	6.7%	19,600	23,600	28,000	33,000	28,000	29,000	31,000	33,000	33,000	35,000

1995 Year-end:
Debt ratio: 10.8%
Return on equity: 16.2%
Cash (mil.): $33
Current ratio: 2.02
Long-term debt (mil.): $298
No. of shares (mil.): 82
Dividends
  Yield: 0.9%
  Payout: 15.8%
Market value (mil.): $3,454

**Stock Price History[1]
High/Low 1986–95**

[1]Stock prices are for the prior calendar year.

NORFOLK SOUTHERN CORPORATION

OVERVIEW

Norfolk Southern Corporation owns a major freight railway (Norfolk Southern Railway), which competes with long-haul truckers by forming joint ventures and providing complete freight transportation; a motor carrier (North American Van Lines, purchased 1985, partially divested 1993); and Appalachian coal, natural gas, and timber holdings (Pocahontas Land). The Norfolk, Virginia–based company continues to exemplify what observers call the "Railroad Renaissance" of higher earnings and improved efficiency and service. After entertaining a buyout of Conrail (which would have created the 2nd largest railroad in the US), Norfolk no longer seems interested in such a combination.

The railroad has 14,652 miles of track in 20 midwestern and southeastern states and Ontario, Canada. Norfolk Southern Railway's intermodal programs (freight transported in the same container by train, truck, or ship) have experienced strong growth (9% in 1994). The intermodal concerns include Triple Crown Services (a joint venture with Conrail), which uses RoadRailers, freight containers that can be hauled on highways by trucks and over the rails by locomotives. Norfolk Southern Railway has teamed with rival Conrail to operate a comprehensive new intermodal service that covers the entire eastern seaboard. During 1995 double-stack railcars will be added to this intermodal service.

WHEN

Norfolk Southern Corporation is the result of the 1982 merger of 2 major US railroads: Norfolk & Western Railway Company (N&W) and Southern Railway Company.

N&W dates to 1838, when a single track connected Petersburg, Virginia, to City Point (now Hopewell). This 8-mile stretch became part of the Atlantic, Mississippi & Ohio (AM&O), which was created by consolidating 3 Virginia railways in 1870. In 1881 the Philadelphia banking firm E. W. Clark bought the AM&O, renamed it the Norfolk & Western, and established headquarters at Roanoke, Virginia. N&W rolled into Ohio by purchasing 2 other railroads (1892, 1901). In 1959 the company took over the Virginian Railway, a coal carrier with trackage paralleling much of its own. In 1964 N&W acquired the New York, Chicago & St. Louis Railroad (a freight line nicknamed the Nickel Plate Road) and the Pennsylvania Railroad's line between Columbus and Sandusky, Ohio, and leased the Wabash Railroad, with lines from Detroit and Chicago to Kansas City and St. Louis.

The Southern Railway can be traced back to the South Carolina Canal & Rail Road, a 9-mile line chartered in 1827 and built by Horatio Allen to win trade for the port of Charleston. It became the longest railway in the world when it opened a 136-mile line to Hamburg, South Carolina (1833). Soon other railroads sprang up throughout the South, including the Richmond & Danville (Virginia, 1847) and the East Tennessee, Virginia & Georgia (1869), which were combined to form the Southern Railway System in 1894. Southern eventually controlled more than 100 railroads,

forging a system from Washington, DC, to St. Louis and New Orleans.

The 1982 merger of Southern and N&W created an extensive rail system operating throughout the East, South, and Midwest. Norfolk Southern (a holding company created for the 2 railroads) bought North American Van Lines in 1985 and attempted (unsuccessfully) to buy Consolidated Rail in 1986. Triple Crown Services, the company's intermodal subsidiary, started in 1986. The company attempted to take over Piedmont Aviation in 1987 but sold its 17% stake when Piedmont agreed to merge with USAir. Arnold McKinnon (named CEO in 1987) retired in 1992, and president David Goode replaced him as chairman and CEO. Norfolk Southern revived North American Van Lines (which lost nearly $40 million in 1992) by selling its refrigerator truck operation, Tran-star (1993), and suspending its poorly performing commercial trucking line operation.

In 1993 Norfolk Southern's Triple Crown Services began its intermodal joint venture with Conrail, linking 23 Conrail terminals with 12 Norfolk Southern facilities (in the South and Midwest). In 1993 the High Value Products Division of North American Van Lines formed a logistics services unit focusing on customer needs, including emergency parts order fulfillment, freight transportation deadlines, returns, and recycling. Bad weather in the winter of 1994 seriously disrupted the company's services. Following discussions in 1994 to buy Conrail, in 1995 Norfolk Southern appeared uninterested in doing such a deal. In April 1995 the company added 125 efficient diesel locomotives to its fleet.

NYSE symbol: NSC
Fiscal year ends: December 31

WHO

Chairman, President, and CEO: David R. Goode, age 54, $1,082,250 pay
VC: John R. Turbyfill, age 63, $765,000 pay
EVP Marketing: D. Henry Watts, age 63, $647,500 pay
EVP Law: John S. Shannon, age 64, $647,500 pay
EVP Operations: Stephen C. Tobias, age 50, $468,125 pay
EVP Finance (Principal Financial Officer): Henry C. Wolf, age 52, $468,125 pay
EVP Transportation Logistics; President, North American Van Lines: R. Alan Brogan, age 54
VP Personnel: Paul N. Austin, age 51
VP Intermodal: Thomas L. Finkbiner, age 42
VP Transportation: Jon L. Manetta, age 57
VP Engineering: Phillip R. Ogden, age 54
Auditors: KPMG Peat Marwick LLP

WHERE

HQ: 3 Commercial Place, Norfolk, VA 23510-2191
Phone: 804-629-2680
Fax: 804-629-2798

Norfolk Southern operates a 14,652-mile rail system in Alabama, Florida, Georgia, Illinois, Indiana, Iowa, Kentucky, Louisiana, Maryland, Michigan, Mississippi, Missouri, New York, North Carolina, Ohio, Pennsylvania, South Carolina, Tennessee, Virginia, and West Virginia and in Ontario, Canada.

North American Van Lines offers services through 696 US locations and agents in Canada, Germany, Panama, and the UK.

WHAT

	1994 Equipment Owned
	No.
Freight cars	100,579
Locomotives	2,055
Total	**102,634**

	1994 Sales	
	$ mil.	% of total
Railway operations		
Coal	1,263	28
Chemicals	512	11
Paper/forest	505	11
Automotive	432	9
Intermodal	426	9
Agriculture	348	8
Metals/construction	321	7
Motor carrier	663	15
Other revenues — primarily switching & demurrage	111	2
Total	**4,581**	**100**

Major Subsidiaries and Affiliates
Norfolk Southern Railway Co. (railroad)
North American Van Lines, Inc. (motor carrier)
Pocahontas Land Corp. (coal mines and other energy-related properties)
Triple Crown Services, Inc. (50%, intermodal services with Conrail)

KEY COMPETITORS

American Freightways	C.H. Robinson	Illinois Central
	Conrail	J.B. Hunt
American President	Consolidated	Roadway
AMERCO	Freightways	Ryder
Bekins	CSX	Schneider Group
Burlington	Cyprus Amax	Union Pacific
Northern	Global Van Lines	United Van Lines
Canadian Pacific	Hub Group	Yellow Corp.

HOW MUCH

	9-Year Growth	1985	1986	1987	1988	1989	1990	1991	1992	1993	1994
Sales ($ mil.)	2.0%	3,825	4,076	4,113	4,462	4,536	4,617	4,451	4,607	4,460	4,581
Net income ($ mil.)	3.3%	500	519	172	635	606	556	30	558	549	668
Income as % of sales	—	13.1%	12.7%	4.2%	14.2%	13.4%	12.0%	0.7%	12.1%	12.3%	14.6%
Earnings per share ($)	7.1%	2.65	2.74	0.91	3.51	3.48	3.43	0.20	3.94	3.94	4.90
Stock price – high ($)	—	27.06	33.06	38.25	32.88	41.25	47.25	65.75	67.50	72.38	74.75
Stock price – low ($)	—	19.22	24.59	21.00	24.50	30.25	35.00	39.75	53.25	59.25	58.50
Stock price – close ($)	9.4%	27.06	28.13	26.25	31.38	40.50	41.75	59.38	61.25	70.50	60.63
P/E – high	—	10	12	42	9	12	14	—	17	18	15
P/E – low	—	7	9	23	7	9	10	199	14	15	12
Dividends per share ($)	6.1%	1.13	1.13	1.20	1.26	1.38	1.52	1.60	1.80	1.86	1.92
Book value per share ($)	3.8%	25.17	26.76	26.48	28.74	30.43	31.57	28.64	30.16	33.36	35.19
Employees	(2.9%)	39,794	38,297	36,102	34,539	34,312	33,281	31,952	30,135	29,304	27,168

1994 Year-end:
Debt ratio: 26.2%
Return on equity: 14.4%
Cash (mil.): $307
Current ratio: 1.18
Long-term debt (mil.): $1,548
No. of shares (mil.): 133
Dividends
  Yield: 3.2%
  Payout: 39.2%
Market value (mil.): $8,072

**Stock Price History
High/Low 1985–94**

NORTHROP GRUMMAN CORPORATION

OVERVIEW

Northrop Grumman is thinking big. The Los Angeles–based company, one of the largest defense contractors in the US, was created from the 1994 merger of Northrop Corporation and Grumman Corporation as Northrop outbid rivals and paid $2.1 billion for Grumman. Later that same year Northrop Grumman paid $130 million for the remaining 51% it did not already own of Vought Aircraft. The deals are part of an ongoing consolidation in the defense industry as weapons makers seek to grab a bigger slice of the shrinking defense budget.

Northrop Grumman manufactures military aircraft, electronics, and commercial jet parts. Its products include the B-2 Stealth bomber, subassemblies for the F/A-18 and the 747, and radar equipment. The company also develops computer systems for scientific and management applications.

The company is focusing on consolidating its operations and plans to cut its work force by more than 5,000 over the next year. The cuts are part of a drive to increase efficiency as Northrop Grumman pays down the debt from its recent acquisitions.

WHEN

John "Jack" Northrop, cofounder of Lockheed Aircraft (1927) and designer of that company's record-setting Vega monoplane, founded Northrop Aircraft in California in 1939. Northrop had previously established 2 other companies, Avion Corporation (formed in 1928 and bought by United Aircraft and Transportation) and Northrop Corporation (formed in 1932 in cooperation with Douglas Aircraft, which absorbed it in 1938).

During WWII Northrop produced the P-61 fighter. It also built the famous Flying Wing bombers, which advanced the state of aeronautical engineering but failed to win a production contract. In the 1950s Northrop's income depended heavily on the F-89 fighter and the Snark missile, making the company sensitive to fluctuations in government funding. When Thomas Jones succeeded Jack Northrop as president in 1959, he moved the company away from risky prime contracts in favor of numerous subcontracts and bought Page Communications Engineers (telecommunications, 1959) and Hallicrafters (electronics, 1966) to help reduce Northrop's dependence on government contracts. Jones also promoted its inexpensive F-5 fighter for export to developing countries.

Northrop was hit with a bribery scandal and the disclosure of illegal payments to Richard Nixon's 1972 campaign fund. During the 1970s Northrop developed the F-20 fighter, but none sold even after years of marketing overseas. In 1981 it won the contract to develop the B-2 Stealth bomber.

Jones retired at 70 in 1990. That year, under the leadership of Kent Kresa, the company pleaded guilty to 34 counts related to falsifying test results on some government projects and paid a $17 million fine. In a related shareholders' suit, Northrop agreed to pay $18 million

in damages in 1991. That same year it won a $2.2 billion contract to develop a new missile (Brilliant Anti-Tank) for the army.

In 1992 Northrop and the Carlyle Group bought LTV's aircraft divison (Vought Aircraft). The company filed suit against the Canadian government and Bristol Aerospace in 1993 for allegedly selling spare parts for F-5 fighter jets without making royalty payments to Northrop. In 1994 Northrop paid $2.1 billion for Grumman.

Grumman was founded in 1929 by Jake Swirbul, Bill Schwendler, and Roy Grumman, and within 3 months they had a contract to design a navy fighter. In 1937, a year before going public, it completed its first commercial aircraft (the Grumman Goose). The company soared during WWII on the wings of Wildcat and Hellcat fighter planes.

Grumman built its first corporate jet (Gulfstream) in 1958 and began work on the Lunar Module for the Apollo space program in 1963. Grumman inched near bankruptcy during the 1970s because of costs related to the F-14 Tomcat fighter. It rebuilt its military business in the 1980s, achieving its greatest success in electronic systems. During the 1990s a number of its aircraft production contracts were cut as the US government slashed military budgets.

In 1994 Northrop Grumman agreed to buy Hexcel's electromagnetically tailored materials plant in Chandler, Arizona, for $30 million.

In 1995 federal agents raided 6 of Northrop Grumman's buildings in California, seizing documents and interviewing employees as part of an investigation of false testing and improper billing. The company allegedly mixed commercial work with military contracts, improperly billed for F/A-18 parts, and submitted false or negligent tests of metal bulkheads.

NYSE symbol: NOC
Fiscal year ends: December 31

WHO

Chairman, President, and CEO: Kent Kresa, age 56,
$1,550,833 pay
Corporate VP and General Counsel: Richard R. Molleur,
age 62, $620,000 pay
**Corporate VP; General Manager, Military Aircraft
Division:** Wallace C. Solberg, age 63, $605,833 pay
Corporate VP and CFO: Richard B. Waugh Jr., age 51,
$605,833 pay
Corporate VP; General Manager, B-2 Division: Ralph D.
Crosby Jr., age 47
**Corporate VP; General Manager, Commercial Aircraft
Division:** Gordon L. Williams, age 62
**Corporate VP; General Manager, Electronics and
Systems Integration Division:** John E. Harrison,
age 59
**Corporate VP; General Manager, Data Systems and
Services Division:** Herbert W. Anderson, age 55
**Corporate VP and Chief Advanced Development,
Planning, and Public Affairs Officer:** James G. Roche,
age 55
Corporate VP Government Relations: Robert W. Helm,
age 43
**Corporate VP and Chief Human Resources and
Administrative Officer:** Marvin Elkin, age 58
Auditors: Deloitte & Touche LLP

WHERE

HQ: 1840 Century Park East, Los Angeles, CA 90067
Phone: 310-553-6262
Fax: 310-553-2076

The company has operations in California, Florida,
Georgia, Illinois, Louisiana, Maine, Maryland,
Massachusetts, Michigan, New York, North Dakota,
Ohio, Oklahoma, Pennsylvania, Texas, Virginia,
Washington, and West Virginia.

WHAT

	1994 Sales		1994 Operating Income	
	$ mil.	% of total	$ mil.	% of total
Aircraft	4,583	68	463	78
Electronics	1,441	22	122	20
Missiles & unmanned vehicle systems	339	5	(18)	—
Data systems & other services	348	5	14	2
Total	**6,711**	**100**	**581**	**100**

Selected Products and Services

Aircraft components and major subassemblies (Airbus,
Boeing, Fokker, Gulfstream, McDonnell Douglas)
B-2 Spirit Stealth bomber
BAT antiarmor submunition
C-17 airlifter subassemblies
E-2C Hawkeye early warning aircraft
E-8 Joint Surveillance Target Attack Radar System (E-8
Joint STARS)
Electronic countermeasures systems (ECM, radar
jamming)
F-14 Tomcat modification kits
F/A-18 Hornet strike fighter subassemblies
Service Center Recognition Image Processing System
(SCRIPS) for Internal Revenue Service
Systems integration for governments and private
industry

KEY COMPETITORS

Akzo Nobel	Litton Industries	Siemens
AlliedSignal	Lockheed Martin	Textron
British Aerospace	Loral	Thomson SA
Daimler-Benz	LTV	Thorn EMI
FMC	McDonnell	Tracor
General Dynamics	Douglas	United
General Electric	Raytheon	Technologies
Hughes Electronics	Rockwell	Westinghouse

HOW MUCH

	9-Year Growth	1985	1986	1987	1988	1989	1990	1991	1992	1993	1994
Sales ($ mil.)	3.2%	5,057	5,608	6,053	5,797	5,248	5,490	5,694	5,550	5,063	6,711
Net income ($ mil.)	(18.2%)	214	41	94	(31)	(81)	210	268	121	96	35
Income as % of sales	—	4.2%	0.7%	1.6%	—	—	3.8%	4.7%	2.2%	1.9%	0.5%
Earnings per share ($)	(18.7%)	4.63	0.89	2.01	(0.65)	(1.71)	4.48	5.69	2.56	1.99	0.72
Stock price – high ($)	—	56.63	51.63	52.63	35.88	29.75	20.25	31.25	34.88	42.63	47.38
Stock price – low ($)	—	31.63	36.88	24.75	25.13	16.00	13.75	16.50	22.50	30.50	34.50
Stock price – close ($)	(0.5%)	44.13	39.25	25.50	27.75	17.50	17.38	26.25	34.13	37.38	42.00
P/E – high	—	12	58	26	—	—	5	6	14	21	66
P/E – low	—	7	41	12	—	—	3	3	9	15	48
Dividends per share ($)	3.2%	1.20	1.20	1.20	1.20	1.20	1.20	1.20	1.20	1.60	1.60
Book value per share ($)	3.4%	19.42	19.29	20.23	21.40	18.65	22.00	25.11	26.46	27.03	26.20
Employees	(1.1%)	46,900	46,800	48,200	44,600	41,357	38,200	36,200	33,600	29,800	42,400

1994 Year-end:
Debt ratio: 60.0%
Return on equity: 2.7%
Cash (mil.): $17
Current ratio: 1.24
Long-term debt (mil.): $1,633
No. of shares (mil.): 49
Dividends
  Yield: 3.8%
  Payout: 222.0%
Market value (mil.): $2,068

Stock Price History
High/Low 1985–94

NORTHWEST AIRLINES CORPORATION

OVERVIEW

A Dutch treat and increased efficiency have lifted Minnesota-based Northwest Airlines from a prolonged financial tailspin.

Plagued by heavy debt and difficult competitive conditions since a 1989 LBO, the company came close to crashing into bankruptcy in 1993. But pay concessions from its unions, cancellations of orders for new aircraft, and a breather from fare wars allowed the #4 world carrier (in terms of revenue passenger miles) to lift clear of trouble in 1994. KLM Royal Dutch Airlines, Bankers Trust, and some suppliers provided the company with a $250 million emergency loan, but the key to the company's bailout was the $886 million in wage concessions by Northwest unions, in return for 26% of company stock. Original LBO investors and current co-chairmen Alfred Checchi and Gary Wilson each own 12.7% of Northwest, and KLM owns 25%.

Northwest went public again in 1994 and has returned to a profitable cruising altitude, posting a net profit of $236 million that year following 4 years of losses. The company combines its services with KLM in a joint venture arrangement serving 88 locations in North America and 29 outside the US.

The company is also uniquely positioned among US carriers as the world's 9th largest air cargo company.

WHEN

A group of Detroit, Minneapolis, and St. Paul businessmen, led by Colonel Louis Brittin, founded Northwest Airways in 1926 to provide air mail service between Minneapolis and Chicago. In 1928 it became the first US airline to offer coordinated airline and railroad service. In 1934 the company changed its name to Northwest Airlines. It expanded its air routes to Seattle the same year, and service to New York completed the airline's transcontinental route in 1945. Northwest started flying to the Far East in 1947, pioneering a Great Circle route (over Alaska and the Aleutians) to the Orient.

Former Civil Aeronautics Board chairman Donald Nyrop became Northwest's president in 1954. Famous for his thrift, Nyrop held debt to 10% of capital, the lowest proportion in the airline industry. When Nyrop retired in 1978, his successor, Joseph Lapensky, continued Nyrop's fiscal policies, keeping Northwest profitable throughout his tenure.

In 1984 the company formed NWA, a holding company. In 1986 NWA bought Republic Airlines. That same year Northwest bought 50% of PARS (TWA's computer reservation system, which merged with Delta's DATAS II in 1990, forming WORLDSPAN).

Northwest's failure to reach an agreement with its unions after the Republic acquisition resulted in low employee morale. Northwest's pilots still had no contract in 1989 when Wings Holdings — an investment group that included KLM and was led by former Marriott executive Alfred Checchi — took NWA private in a $3.65 billion LBO, after which Checchi became chairman.

In 1990 NWA bought a 25% stake in HAL (Hawaiian Airlines), gaining 3 Pacific routes.

The high fuel prices and decreased travel that accompanied Iraq's invasion of Kuwait produced huge losses for NWA in 1990 and 1991. In 1991 Northwest needed money and persuaded Minnesota to back a new bond issue.

In 1991 it bought Eastern's Washington, DC, landing slots and arranged $20 million in debtor-in-possession financing for America West, gaining the option to buy the ailing Phoenix-based carrier's route from Honolulu to Nagoya, Japan. After paying $20 million for Midway Airlines's 21 gates and other facilities at Chicago's Midway Airport, NWA backed out of a broader deal to buy the bankrupt Chicago-based carrier. NWA then sold 18 of its Midway Airport gates and other assets to Southwest Airlines for $15 million in 1992. That year NWA released its interest in HAL.

In 1993 it initiated service to Raleigh/Durham, North Carolina; Greenville/Spartanburg, South Carolina; and Reno as part of its strategy of expanding by assuming low-traffic routes and allying with smaller airlines to act as feeders into its hubs.

After the IPO, NWA renamed itself Northwest Airlines Corporation and kept searching for ways to save or raise money. KLM increased its stake in Northwest (from 20% to 25%) with the acquisition of the Australia-based Foster's Brewing Group's stake in Northwest. KLM shelled out approximately $180 million for Foster's roughly 5% stake in Northwest.

In 1994 Northwest inaugurated service from Osaka's new Kansai International Airport and formed a code-sharing agreement with Asiana Airlines, of Korea. It also doubled its service to China, planning to add 5 more weekly flights to that country in 1995.

Nasdaq symbol: NWAC
Fiscal year ends: December 31

WHO

Co-chairman: Alfred A. Checchi, age 46
Co-chairman: Gary L. Wilson, age 55
President and CEO: John H. Dasburg, age 52, $853,751 pay
EVP and CFO: Mickey Foret, age 49, $549,312 pay
EVP Marketing and International: Michael E. Levine, age 53, $549,312 pay
EVP; President, Northwest Cargo: William D. Slattery, age 51, $517,812 pay
EVP Customer Service and Operations: Donald A. Washburn, age 50, $508,676 pay
SVP Sales and Chief Information Officer: Barry A. Kotar, age 49
SVP Operations and Chief Safety Officer: John S. Kern, age 52
SVP Corporate Affairs: Richard B. Hirst, age 50
SVP, General Counsel, and Secretary: Douglas M. Steenland, age 43
SVP Communications, Advertising, and Human Resources: Christopher E. Clouser, age 42
Auditors: Ernst & Young LLP

WHERE

HQ: 2700 Lone Oak Pkwy., Eagan, MN 55121
Phone: 612-726-2111
Fax: 612-726-3942
Reservations: 800-225-2525

Northwest Airlines serves 150 cities worldwide, with hubs at Detroit, Memphis, Minneapolis/St. Paul, and Tokyo.

	1994 Passenger Sales
	% of total
North America	61
Pacific	33
Atlantic	6
Total	**100**

WHAT

	1994 Sales	
	$ mil.	% of total
Passenger service	7,731	85
Cargo	756	8
Other	656	7
Total	**9,143**	**100**

Aircraft	No. Owned	No. Leased
A320	22	28
Boeing 727-200	22	33
Boeing 747	23	18
Boeing 757	9	24
DC-9	105	40
DC-10	24	5
MD-80	6	2
Total	**211**	**150**

Selected Subsidiaries and Affiliates
MLT Inc. (wholesale travel and tour programs)
Northwest Aerospace Training Corp. (pilot training)
Northwest PARS, Inc. (32% partner in WORLDSPAN computer reservations system joint venture with Delta, TWA, and ABACUS)

KEY COMPETITORS

Air France	Kiwi Int'l Airlines
Alaska Air	Korean Air
All Nippon Airways	Lufthansa
America West	Qantas
American Express	SAS
AMR	Singapore Airlines
British Airways	Southwest Airlines
Carlson	Swire Pacific
Continental Airlines	Swissair
Delta	TWA
FlightSafety	UAL
HAL	USAir
IRI	Virgin Group
JAL	

HOW MUCH

	Annual Growth	1985	1986	1987	1988	1989	1990	1991	1992	1993	1994
Sales ($ mil.)	14.7%	2,655	3,589	5,142	5,650	6,576	7,426	7,683	8,128	8,649	9,143
Net income ($ mil.)	13.9%	73	77	103	135	75	(361)	(388)	(1,046)	(207)	236
Income as % of sales	—	2.7%	2.1%	2.0%	2.4%	1.1%	—	—	—	—	2.6%
Earnings per share ($)	—	—	—	—	—	—	—	—	—	—	2.87
Stock price – high ($)	—	—	—	—	—	—	—	—	—	—	21.38
Stock price – low ($)	—	—	—	—	—	—	—	—	—	—	11.50
Stock price – close ($)	—	—	—	—	—	—	—	—	—	—	15.75
P/E – high	—	—	—	—	—	—	—	—	—	—	7
P/E – low	—	—	—	—	—	—	—	—	—	—	4
Dividends per share ($)	—	—	—	—	—	—	—	—	—	—	0.00
Book value per share ($)	—	—	—	—	—	—	—	—	—	—	(16.25)
Employees	11.4%	16,641	33,427	33,742	35,532	39,422	43,385	45,620	44,455	43,358	44,079

1994 Year-end:
Debt ratio: 100.0%
Return on equity: —
Cash (mil.): $1,070
Current ratio: 0.86
Long-term debt (mil.): $3,679
No. of shares (mil.): 84
Dividends
  Yield: —
  Payout: —
Market value (mil.): $1,328

**Stock Price History
High/Low 1994**

NORTHWESTERN MUTUAL LIFE

OVERVIEW

Northwestern Mutual is the quintessential insurance company: solid, reliable, fiscally sound, honest. Boring. At a time when many insurers have been subject to investigations of sales practices or have found themselves buffeted by turbulent financial markets, Northwestern just keeps chugging away, winning awards for its sales force and socking away an ever-growing surplus. In 1994 the company's financial picture improved because its investment portfolio was flexible enough to allow it to take advantage of rising interest rates when almost everyone else in the financial industry was caught in the bond market crash.

Northwestern markets its life, health, and retirement products and services through a network of 7,300 exclusive agents. The company is renowned for its training programs, both for agents (including an innovative internship program that funnels young agents into the company directly from college) and underwriters (who receive training in medical issues so that they can make informed decisions on undertaking risks).

Northwestern has been one of the industry's lowest-cost providers for 50 years and also has excellent retention rates for agents and policyholders.

WHEN

In 1854 at age 72, John Johnston, a successful New York insurance agent, moved to Wisconsin to become a farmer. Three years later Johnston returned to the insurance business when he and 36 leading Wisconsin citizens founded Mutual Life Insurance Co.

When the company became Northwestern Mutual Life Insurance Co. in 1865, it was already the 14th largest company in total amount of insurance in force. As early as the 1880s, however, Northwestern Mutual's commitment was to serve policyholders rather than simply to achieve size.

In 1907 Northwestern appointed policyholders to evaluate the entire company's operations. This 5-person committee, whose members change every year, still operates, and a summary of its report is published in the company's annual report.

The company continued to offer level-premium life insurance in the 1920s while competitors offered new types of products. As a result of its conservatism, Northwestern's insurance-in-force ranking fell between 1918 and 1946.

The company began to develop the most comprehensive computer system in the industry in the late 1950s. One result was the 1962 introduction of the Insurance Service Account (ISA), in which all policies owned by a family or business could be combined into one premium with monthly payments made by preauthorized checks.

Northwestern was one of the first major life insurance companies to give women a lower premium rate than men because they live longer on average.

Northwestern in 1968 introduced Extra Ordinary Life (EOL), which combined whole life with term insurance, using dividends to convert term to paid-up whole life each year. In less than a year, EOL became the company's most popular policy.

Northwestern became a major advertiser in 1972 by introducing "The Quiet Company" campaign to sponsor ABC's coverage of the summer Olympics. The result was a phenomenal jump in the public's awareness of Northwestern.

In the 1980s Northwestern began financing leveraged buyouts. In return, Northwestern gained ownership shares and stock options in addition to loan payments. The company and other insurers bought a 2/3 interest in Congoleum, a flooring manufacturer, and majority interests in Robert W. Baird, a Milwaukee securities firm (1982), and Mortgage Guaranty Insurance (MGIC, 1985).

Despite these modest purchases, the company remained largely immune to the 1980s' mania for fast money and high-risk diversification. Unlike many insurers the company has no aspirations to become a financial services supermarket. Instead, the company continues to devote itself, with an almost religious fervor, primarily to its core business, despite predictions by some that it is a shrinking market.

Certainly new life policy purchases were down in 1994. (The effect of this on current results is negligible since most of the first year's premiums are earmarked for agents' commissions; the company makes its premium income on retained policies, so a reduction in sales bodes ill for the future.) Also, agent recruitment is down.

In keeping with Northwestern's technological innovations of past years, the company intends to invest in new systems, including 24-hour telephone service and on-line services so that customers have access to policy data.

Mutual company
Fiscal year ends: December 31

WHO

President and CEO: James D. Ericson, age 59
EVP: Robert E. Carlson, age 59
EVP Operations and Administration: Peter W. Bruce, age 49
EVP Finance and Investments and CFO: Edward J. Zore, age 49
SVP, General Counsel, and Secretary: John M. Bremer, age 47
SVP Government Relations: Frederic H. Sweet, age 51
SVP and Treasurer: Mark G. Doll, age 45
SVP New Business: Deborah A. Beck, age 47
SVP Agencies: Dennis Tamcsin, age 56
SVP Corporate Planning: Richard L. Hall, age 49
VP Communications: W. Ward White, age 55
VP Compliance and Sales Practices: Meridee J. Sagadin, age 39
VP Corporate Development: Martha M. Valerio, age 48
VP Human Resources: Susan A. Lueger, age 41
Auditors: Price Waterhouse LLP

WHERE

HQ: The Northwestern Mutual Life Insurance Company, 720 E. Wisconsin Ave., Milwaukee, WI 53202
Phone: 414-271-1444
Fax: 414-299-7022

Northwestern Mutual operates through more than 7,300 agents in all 50 states and the District of Columbia, with more than 100 general agency offices and 240 district agencies.

WHAT

	1994 Sales	
	$ mil.	% of total
Premiums	5,743	61
Net investment income	3,106	33
Other	636	6
Total	**9,485**	**100**

	1994 Assets	
	$ mil.	% of total
Cash & equivalents	803	2
Treasury & agency securities	3,501	7
Other bonds	19,232	40
Stocks	3,207	7
Mortgage loans	7,099	14
Real estate	1,213	3
Policy loans	6,144	12
Other investments	1,301	3
Separate accounts	3,806	8
Other assets	1,806	4
Total	**48,112**	**100**

Insurance Products
Annuities
Disability insurance
Mortgage insurance
Permanent and term life insurance
Securities brokerage

Selected Subsidiaries and Affiliates
Carlisle Ventures, Inc.
MGIC Investment Corp.
Northwestern Mutual Investment Services, Inc.
Northwestern Mutual Series Fund, Inc.
Robert W. Baird and Co. Inc.

KEY COMPETITORS

Aetna	ITT Hartford
Alliance Capital	John Hancock
American Financial	Kemper Corp.
American Bankers Insurance	Liberty Mutual
	MassMutual
Berkshire Hathaway	Mellon Bank
Charles Schwab	Merrill Lynch
Chubb	MetLife
CIGNA	Mutual of Omaha
CNA Financial	New York Life
Colonial Group	Prudential
Dean Witter, Discover	State Farm
Eaton Vance	Teachers Insurance
Equitable	Transamerica
FMR	Travelers
Guardian Life	USF&G

HOW MUCH

	9-Year Growth	1985	1986	1987	1988	1989	1990	1991	1992	1993	1994
Assets ($ mil.)	11.5%	18,087	20,196	22,613	25,362	28,515	31,389	35,757	39,679	44,061	48,112
Net income ($ mil.)	40.6%	13	18	40	118	372	143	227	244	330	279
Income as % of assets	—	0.1%	0.1%	0.2%	0.5%	1.3%	0.5%	0.6%	0.6%	0.7%	0.6%
Employees	3.4%	2,432	2,468	2,761	2,840	2,970	3,050	3,100	3,298	3,500	3,300

1994 Year-end:
Equity as % of assets: 4.6%
Return on equity: 13.1%
Sales (mil.): $9,485

Northwestern Mutual Life

Net Income ($ mil.) 1985–94

NOVELL, INC.

OVERVIEW

Novell wants to be the software company that connects the world into one big WAN (wide-area network). Orem, Utah–based Novell is the leading provider of networking software with 66% of that market; NetWare is its flagship product. The company's NEST (Novell Embedded Systems Technology) software allows a variety of products (faxes, printers, phones — even cars) to plug into a network. More than 100 companies, including Canon, Xerox, and 2 auto makers, are gearing up to provide NEST connectivity with their products.

With the mid-1994 acquisition of #2 word processing software vendor WordPerfect, Novell solidified its place among the top software companies. Its PerfectOffice business applications suite (including *WordPerfect* and another recent purchase, Borland's *Quattro*

Pro spreadsheet) is battling rivals Microsoft and Lotus for market share. The spiffed-up NetWare version 4, shipped in late 1994, is winning rave reviews. The company is also set to release its SuperNOS network operating system, which lets one network integrate both NetWare- and UNIX-based systems.

Novell's latest contribution to connectivity is a host of Internet access products, including the *Corsair* 3D navigational interface and *Ferret* Web browser. Novell and AT&T are working together on the AT&T NetWare Connect Services (ANCS), which will allow LANs to connect yet remain secure. Novell spent 17% of 1994 revenues on R&D.

Former Novell CEO Ray Noorda owns 7.8%; WordPerfect founders Alan Ashton and Bruce Bastian own about 6% and 7%, respectively.

WHEN

Novell Data Systems started out in 1980 as a Provo, Utah–based maker of PC peripherals. In 1981 Safeguard Scientifics, a high-tech venture capital firm, bought a 55% stake in Novell (raised to 88% in 1982). By 1983 Novell, which had had 8 presidents, was nearly defunct. Safeguard provided 51% of the capital needed for revival and brought in as CEO turnaround artist Raymond Noorda, who invested $125,000 of his own money in the new Novell (then equal to a 33% stake).

When Noorda took over, Novell was already working on solutions to PC networking. Noorda approached the challenge by designating one machine in the network as a file server to manage the network and to control access to shared devices, such as disk drives and printers. As a result of Noorda's vision, Novell introduced NetWare, the first LAN software based on file server technology, in 1983.

After going public in 1985, Novell began acquiring other companies to enhance and expand its product line. In 1987 Novell bought Santa Clara Systems (microcomputer workstations), CXI (computer products), and SoftCraft (programming tools). The company bought 60% of Indisy Software (electronic messaging systems, 1988), Excelan (networking software and related equipment, 1989), a minority stake in Gupta Technologies (database servers, 1990), and the remaining 40% of Indisy (1990). In 1988 Novell announced it would drop production of most hardware. In 1989 it released NetWare 386, which could take advantage of Intel's 386 chip and run on UNIX and Macintosh operating systems.

In 1990 Lotus, at Noorda's instigation, announced it would acquire Novell for $1.5 billion in Lotus stock. However, Novell's directors nixed the deal. (Lotus itself was acquired by IBM in 1995.) In 1991 Novell acquired a number of software companies, including Digital Research (PC operating software) and Univel (UNIX products). That same year Novell bought interests in former AT&T unit UNIX Systems Laboratories and object-oriented software tool developer Serius. Novell acquired the remaining shares of both UNIX Systems Laboratories and Serius in 1993.

Noorda stepped down in 1994 and was succeeded by Robert Frankenberg, an experienced Hewlett-Packard executive. Also in 1994 Novell transferred its database products (NetWare SQL, Xtrieve) to Btrieve Technologies, a company in which Novell holds a minority stake. Novell acquired Borland's *Quattro Pro* spreadsheet for $120 million and WordPerfect Corp. for shares and options worth about $1.4 billion.

WordPerfect was founded in 1978 as Satellite Software International. Brigham Young University professor Alan Ashton and his student Bruce Bastian created the company to market their word processing program *WP*. They introduced a PC version in 1982. In 1986 the company (which, like Novell, is based in Orem, Utah) took the name WordPerfect.

In 1995 Frankenberg said Novell is working with communications equipment manufacturer General Instrument to develop cable systems (such as cable television) into 2-way networks.

Nasdaq symbol: NOVL
Fiscal year ends: Last Saturday in October

WHO

Chairman, President, and CEO: Robert J. Frankenberg, age 47, $288,462 pay
EVP Worldwide Sales: Joseph A. Marengi, age 41, $496,336 pay
EVP and COO: Mary M. Burnside, age 47, $394,717 pay
EVP and CFO: James R. Tolonen, age 45, $383,829 pay
EVP Corporate Technology: Kanwal S. Rekhi, $322,247 pay
EVP UNIX Systems Group: Michael J. DeFazio, age 48
EVP NetWare Systems Group: Richard W. King, age 38
EVP Information Access and Management Group: Steven Markman, age 49
EVP and General Manager Novell Applications Group: Jeff Waxman
SVP, General Counsel, and Corporate Secretary: David R. Bradford, age 44
SVP Development, Applications Group: David C. Moon, age 36
SVP Services and Support: John C. Lewis, age 40
SVP Corporate Marketing: Christine G. Hughes, age 48
SVP Corporate Development: R. Duff Thompson, age 43
SVP Human Resources: Ernest J. Harris, age 47
Auditors: Ernst & Young LLP

WHERE

HQ: 1555 N. Technology Way, Orem, UT 84057
Phone: 801-429-7000
Fax: 801-429-5775

Novell markets its products worldwide through 40 offices in the US and 56 offices in foreign countries.

	1994 Sales	
	$ mil.	% of total
US	1,137	57
Other countries	861	43
Total	**1,998**	**100**

WHAT

	1994 Sales
	% of total
NetWare network operating systems	46
Business applications	25
Connectivity & management software	11
UNIX system products	9
Education & service	4
GroupWare & other applications	5
Total	**100**

Product Groups and Selected Products

Information Access and Management Group
LAN WorkPlace TCP/IP software
Novell Distributed Management Services software

NetWare Systems Group
AppWare software development tools
NetWare networking software
Novell Embedded Systems Technology (NEST)

Novell Applications Group
GroupWise electronic mail
Main Street consumer software
PerfectOffice software suite
Quattro Pro spreadsheet
SoftSolutions document management
WordPerfect word processing

UNIX Systems Group
TUXEDO secure on-line transaction processing software
UnixWare network application server platform

KEY COMPETITORS

3Com
Apple
Artisoft
Banyan Systems
Bay Networks
Cheyenne Software
Computer Associates
DEC
Digi International
Hewlett-Packard
IBM
Madge
Microsoft
Oracle
PLATINUM technology
Proteon
Retix
Software Publishing
Sun Microsystems
Wang

HOW MUCH

	9-Year Growth	1985	1986	1987	1988	1989	1990	1991	1992	1993	1994
Sales ($ mil.)	57.2%	34	82	183	281	422	498	640	933	1,123	1,998
Net income ($ mil.)	55.0%	4	10	20	30	49	94	163	249	(35)	207
Income as % of sales	—	12.5%	12.4%	11.1%	10.8%	11.5%	19.0%	25.4%	26.7%	—	10.3%
Earnings per share ($)	38.4%	0.03	0.06	0.10	0.14	0.19	0.34	0.55	0.81	(0.11)	0.56
Stock price – high ($)	—	1.23	1.64	3.69	4.02	4.72	8.50	32.38	33.50	35.25	26.25
Stock price – low ($)	—	0.28	0.88	1.50	2.22	3.03	3.44	7.63	22.50	17.00	13.75
Stock price – close ($)	34.4%	1.20	1.61	3.00	3.75	3.88	8.25	30.00	28.50	20.75	17.13
P/E – high	—	41	27	37	29	25	25	59	41	—	47
P/E – low	—	9	15	15	16	16	10	14	28	—	25
Dividends per share ($)	—	0.00	0.00	0.00	0.00	0.00	0.00	0.00	0.00	0.00	0.00
Book value per share ($)	72.6%	0.03	0.40	0.47	0.62	0.89	1.41	2.08	3.12	3.23	4.08
Employees	47.7%	236	507	1,138	1,584	2,120	2,419	2,843	3,637	4,335	7,914

1994 Year-end:
Debt ratio: 0.0%
Return on equity: 16.6%
Cash (mil.): $862
Current ratio: 3.14
Long-term debt (mil.): $0
No. of shares (mil.): 364
Dividends
  Yield: —
  Payout: —
Market value (mil.): $6,240

Stock Price History High/Low 1985–94

NUCOR CORPORATION

OVERVIEW

North Carolina–based Nucor is a maverick in the competitive and cyclical steel industry. The entrepreneurial company pioneered minimills, which make steel at a fraction of the time and cost of conventional steelmaking. Nucor uses new technology, nonunion labor, and hefty bonuses to keep its mills running 7 days a week at close to 100% capacity. Nucor is the US's 4th largest steelmaker and one of the lowest-cost steel producers in the world. Low production costs is a key to its success.

Unlike conventional steelmaking, which dates back more than 100 years, minimills melt scrap metal in electric arc furnaces to make steel. Integrated steelmakers are adopting Nucor's state-of-the-art technology, however, and a spate of new minimills are underway. For its part Nucor is teaming up with longtime rival USX–U.S. Steel to create a revolutionary, although untested, way to make steel. The partnership depends on the success of Nucor's experimental Trinidad plant, which will produce iron carbide, a substitute for scrap (which is in tight supply and steadily increasing in price). Plans are to perfect the technology over the next year and then build a demonstration plant.

With steel prices and profits up in 1994, thanks to rebounding economies worldwide, Nucor had record sales and earnings. The company is building its 8th steel mill, which should come on-line in 1997.

WHEN

Nucor started as the 2nd car-making venture of Ransom E. Olds, who had built his first gasoline-powered car in 1897. In 1899 Samuel Smith, a Detroit copper and lumber magnate, put up $199,600 to finance Olds Motor Works. A fire destroyed the company's Detroit plant in 1901, so Olds moved production to Lansing, where he built America's first mass-produced car — the Oldsmobile. In 1904 Olds left the company (which was bought by General Motors in 1908) and formed Reo Car Company (renamed Reo Motor Car, 1906). In addition to cars, Reo eventually made trucks and buses.

By the end of the depression, Ford, General Motors, and Chrysler commanded 85–90% of the US passenger car market. Reo stopped making cars in 1936 and sold its truck manufacturing operations to White Motor Company in 1957. Meanwhile, it had formed Reo Holding, which in 1955 merged with Nuclear Consultants to form Nuclear Corporation of America. Nuclear Corporation offered services such as radiation studies and made nuclear instruments and electronics.

In 1962 Nuclear Corporation bought Vulcraft, a maker of steel joists (used in construction), gaining at the same time the services of Kenneth Iverson. Although diverse, Nuclear Corporation was unprofitable, losing $2 million on $22 million in sales in 1965, when Iverson took over as CEO. He moved the company's headquarters to Charlotte, North Carolina, shut down or sold about half the company's businesses, and focused on its profitable steel joist operations. By the end of 1966 the company was operating in the black.

By 1968 Nuclear Corporation was the leader in steel joists, with a 20% market share.

Because the company depended on imports for 80% of its steel needs, Iverson decided to move Nuclear Corporation into steel production, building its first minimill in 1969.

The company (renamed Nucor in 1972) started making steel deck in 1977 and cold-finished steel bars in 1979. Production tripled and sales more than doubled between 1974 and 1979. Nucor began to diversify its products, producing grinding balls (used in the mining industry to process ores, 1981), steel bolts (1986), steel bearings and machined steel parts (1986), and metal buildings and components (1987). The company and Japanese steelmaker Yamato Kogyo built a mill near Blytheville, Arkansas, to produce heavy structural steel products (Nucor-Yamato, 1988). In 1989 Nucor opened a state-of-the-art mill in Crawfordsville, Indiana, and opened a 2nd mill near Hickman, Arkansas, in 1992. Nucor also agreed that year to produce sheet steel (used in construction) with Oregon Steel. Nucor has a 60% stake in the West Coast operation.

In 1993 Nucor modernized its South Carolina steel mill and, with rising scrap prices, announced its intention to produce its own raw materials by building an iron carbide plant in the West Indies. That same year Crawfordsville plant manager Keith Busse, who helped pioneer the company, quit to start his own minimill, Steel Dynamics.

The West Indies iron carbide plant was completed in late 1994 but suffered from start-up problems. In 1995 Nucor began constructing another flat-rolled steel mill in South Carolina, which will boost capacity to nearly 10 million tons per year.

WHO

Chairman and CEO: F. Kenneth Iverson, age 69, $1,155,232 pay
VC, CFO, Treasurer, and Secretary: Samuel Siegel, age 64, $868,020 pay
President and COO: John D. Correnti, age 47, $868,020 pay
VP and Corporate Controller: Terry S. Lisenby
VP Steel Technologies Operations: Leroy C. Prichard
VP; General Manager, Nucor-Yamato Steel Co.: Daniel R. DiMicco, age 44, $582,750 pay
VP; General Manager, Nucor Steel Division (Crawfordsville, IN): Larry A. Roos, age 53, $206,813 pay
VP; General Manager, Nucor Building Systems Division: Harry R. Lowe
VP; General Manager, Vulcraft Division (Grapeland, TX): Kenneth F. Huff
VP; General Manager, Nucor Steel Division (Hickman, AR): Rodney B. Mott
VP; General Manager, Nucor Steel Division (Norfolk, NE): John A. Doherty
VP; General Manager, Nucor Steel Division (Plymouth, UT): A. Jay Bowcutt
General Manager, Nucor Iron Carbide, Inc. (Trinidad and Tobago, West Indies): Douglas R. Schad
Manager Personnel Services: Jim Coblin
Auditors: Coopers & Lybrand L.L.P.

WHERE

HQ: 2100 Rexford Rd., Charlotte, NC 28211
Phone: 704-366-7000
Fax: 704-362-4208

Nucor has operations in Alabama, Arkansas, Indiana, Nebraska, North Carolina, Nebraska, South Carolina, Texas, and Utah, and in the Republic of Trinidad and Tobago, West Indies.

WHAT

Nucor Bearing Products
Steel bearing components

Nucor Building Systems
Metal buildings and components

Nucor Cold Finis
Cold-finished steel bars
Turned, ground, and polished steel bars

Nucor Fastener
Hex bolts
Hexhead cap screws
Socket-head cap screws
Structural bolts

Nucor Grinding Balls
Steel grinding balls

Nucor Steel
Flat-rolled steel
Light structural carbon and alloy steels
Steel angles and bars

Nucor-Yamato Steel (51%, with Yamato Kogyo, Japan)
Heavy structural steel products
Pilings
Wide-flange steel beams

Vulcraft
Joist girders
Steel deck
Steel joists

KEY COMPETITORS

AK Steel
Allegheny Ludlum
Armco
Bethlehem Steel
Birmingham Steel
Broken Hill
Cargill
Chaparral Steel
Daewoo
Fried. Krupp
Gallatin Steel
Hylsa
Hyundai
Inland Steel
IPSCO

IRI
LTV
Lukens
Mitsubishi
Mitsui
National Steel
Nippon Steel
Ormet
Steel Dynamics
Tata
Thyssen
Trico Steel
Usinor Sacilor
USX–U.S. Steel

HOW MUCH

	9-Year Growth	1985	1986	1987	1988	1989	1990	1991	1992	1993	1994
Sales ($ mil.)	16.4%	759	755	851	1,061	1,269	1,482	1,466	1,619	2,254	2,976
Net income ($ mil.)	16.2%	59	46	51	71	58	75	65	79	124	227
Income as % of sales	—	7.7%	6.1%	5.9%	6.7%	4.6%	5.1%	4.4%	4.9%	5.5%	7.6%
Earnings per share ($)	15.9%	0.69	0.55	0.60	0.84	0.68	0.88	0.75	0.92	1.42	2.60
Stock price – high ($)	—	9.30	11.55	12.38	12.19	16.88	20.44	22.38	39.94	57.25	72.00
Stock price – low ($)	—	5.17	7.28	7.38	9.13	11.22	12.06	14.25	20.94	38.00	48.75
Stock price – close ($)	22.4%	8.98	7.63	9.91	11.94	15.06	15.50	22.34	39.19	53.00	55.38
P/E – high	—	14	21	21	15	25	23	30	43	40	28
P/E – low	—	8	13	12	11	17	14	19	23	27	19
Dividends per share ($)	11.1%	0.07	0.09	0.09	0.09	0.10	0.11	0.12	0.13	0.14	0.18
Book value per share ($)	13.4%	4.16	4.54	5.05	6.27	6.83	7.70	8.23	9.04	10.36	12.85
Employees	4.7%	3,900	4,400	4,600	5,100	5,400	5,500	5,600	5,800	5,900	5,900

1994 Year-end:
Debt ratio: 13.4%
Return on equity: 22.4%
Cash (mil.): $102
Current ratio: 1.67
Long-term debt (mil.): $173
No. of shares (mil.): 87
Dividends
  Yield: 0.3%
  Payout: 6.9%
Market value (mil.): $4,837

Stock Price History
High/Low 1985–94

NYNEX CORPORATION

OVERVIEW

Based in New York City, NYNEX provides local telecommunications services in New York and New England. With one of the oldest telephone networks in the US, NYNEX has been busy defending its lucrative New York City market from competitors. In preparation for the competitive future of telecommunications, NYNEX has begun improving both its cost structure, by cutting 16,800 positions through 1996, and its system, by spending $2.5 billion in 1994 on capital improvements.

NYNEX also is combining its cellular telephone operations with those of Bell Atlantic. Due to its smaller customer base, NYNEX will own approximately 38% of the combined business. The NYNEX-Bell Atlantic partnership also has joined forces with U S WEST and AirTouch Communications (formerly the cellular operations of Pacific Telesis), to develop a national brand and marketing strategy for their cellular operations. The foursome has successfully acquired licenses to offer personal communications services in 11 markets.

NYNEX also has been developing ways of obtaining the content as well as the means of delivering entertainment and information services to its customers. Along with Bell Alantic and Pacific Telesis, NYNEX has formed a new media company with the assistance of Creative Artists Agency to purchase and develop the content for its network. In addition, NYNEX and Bell Atlantic are investing $100 million in CAI Wireless Systems, a wireless cable provider in Albany, Buffalo, New York City, Rochester, Syracuse, NY; Boston, MA; Hartford, CT; Norfolk, VA; and Providence, RI. NYNEX has chosen Ivan Seidenberg as its new chairman, president, and CEO.

WHEN

NYNEX's 2 telephone divisions, New York Telephone and New England Telephone and Telegraph, began as arms of AT&T. New York Telephone was incorporated in 1896 and grew out of 2 small, independent telephone companies, Metropolitan Telephone & Telegraph and Westchester Telephone. Gardiner Hubbard, Alexander Bell's father-in-law, formed New England Telephone Company in 1878 with a plan to offer switching hardware. Half interest was later sold to a group that included Colonel William Forbes, who merged New England Telephone into the Bell system.

In 1984 the Bell companies were split from AT&T as part of the AT&T antitrust suit settlement, and NYNEX became a separate operating entity. At the time, NYNEX received 1/7 of Bell Communications Research (Bellcore) and cellular rights for its telephone territory.

In 1986 NYNEX purchased IBM's computer retailing operations. It then invested in financial services software, buying Business Intelligence Services (1987) and AGS Computers (1988). NYNEX tried to enter the international long distance market between 1986 and 1988 but failed to receive the necessary approvals.

NYNEX has suffered a number of setbacks since its formation. Over 60,000 laborers went on strike in 1989, and NYNEX Materiel Enterprises came in for regulatory scrutiny in 1990. While a Massachusetts audit found no improprieties, an FCC inquiry led to $35.5 million being paid in customer rebates and $1.4 million being paid to the government. NYNEX Materiel and NYNEX Service merged in late 1990, forming Telesector Resources. NYNEX sold its 77 computer stores in 1991.

In 1992 NYNEX bought an interest in TelecomAsia, which is expanding Bangkok's telephone network by 2 million lines. NYNEX joined with Dow Jones that year to form a model to provide programming and information services over NYNEX's telephone system.

In 1993 NYNEX and the leading European electronics company (Philips) formed a joint venture to develop information services for residential use on visual display telephones. In 1993 and 1994 NYNEX sold its UK software unit, BIS Group, and AGS Computers, Inc. Also in those years, NYNEX invested heavily in NYNEX CableComms, which is building a telecommunications and cable network in the United Kingdom.

In 1993 NYNEX bought $1.2 billion of Viacom preferred stock in support of Viacom's successful battle to buy Paramount Communications. In 1994 NYNEX and Times Mirror formed a joint venture to offer electronic shopping services in New York City by combining the company's directory listings and the newspaper group's advertising and news services. In the same year NYNEX changed the names of its New England Telephone and New York Telephone companies to NYNEX.

In 1995 NYNEX established a joint venture with Reliance Industries to acquire licenses for basic and cellular telephone services in India. The company also made its Yellow Pages accessible over the Internet to 7500 universities and public libraries in the US.

NYSE symbol: NYN
Fiscal year ends: December 31

WHO

Chairman, President, and CEO: Ivan G. Seidenberg,
age 48, $729,000 pay (prior to promotion)
VC Finance and Business Development: Frederic V.
Salerno, age 51, $769,000 pay
EVP, General Counsel and Secretary: Raymond F.
Burke, age 61, $609,000 pay
EVP and CFO: Alan Z. Senter, age 53
EVP and General Counsel: Morrison DeS. Webb, age 47
President and Group Executive - NYNEX
Telecommunications: Richard A. Jalkut, age 50
President and Group Executive - NYNEX Worldwide
Services Group: Richard W. Blackburn, age 52
President and Group Executive - NYNEX External
Affairs and Corporate Communications: Donald B.
Reed, age 50
EVP and Group Executive - Network Services: Arnold J.
Eckelman, age 51
VP Human Resources: Donald J. Sacco, age 53,
$445,300 pay
Auditors: Coopers & Lybrand L.L.P.

WHERE

HQ: 1095 Avenue of the Americas, New York, NY 10036
Phone: 212-395-2121
Fax: 212-921-2684 (Investor Relations)

NYNEX offers telecommunications services in
Connecticut, Maine, Massachusetts, New Hampshire,
New York, Rhode Island, and Vermont. Cellular service
is provided throughout the northeastern US. Major
international operations and investments are located in
the Czech Republic, Gibraltar, Greece, Indonesia, Japan,
Poland, Slovakia, Thailand, and the UK.

WHAT

	1994 Sales		1994 Operating Income	
	$ mil.	% of total	$ mil.	% of total
Telecommunications	11,511	86	1,875	91
Publishing	894	7	66	3
Cellular	720	5	51	3
Financial services	89	1	69	3
Other	93	1	(135)	—
Adjustments	—	—	(170)	—
Total	**13,307**	**100**	**1,756**	**100**

Major Subsidiaries

Telecommunications
Bell Communications
Research, Inc. (1/7)
NYNEX New England
Telephone
NYNEX New York
Telephone
NYNEX Science &
Technology, Inc.
Telesector Resources
Group, Inc.

Publishing
NYNEX Information
Resources Co.

Cellular
NYNEX Mobile
Communications Co.

Financial Services
NYNEX Capital Funding Co.
NYNEX Credit Co.
NYNEX Trade Finance Co.

Other Diversified
Operations
NYNEX CableComms Ltd.
NYNEX Network Systems Co.

KEY COMPETITORS

American Business
Information
Ameritech
AT&T
BellSouth
BT
Cable & Wireless
Cellular Communications,
Inc.
Century Communications
GTE

MCI
MFS Communications
Nextel
Pacific Telesis
SBC Communications
Sprint
Teleport
U.S. Long Distance
U S WEST
WorldCom

HOW MUCH

	9-Year Growth	1985	1986	1987	1988	1989	1990	1991	1992	1993	1994
Sales ($ mil.)	2.9%	10,314	11,342	12,084	12,661	13,211	13,582	13,229	13,155	13,408	13,307
Net income ($ mil.)	(3.5%)	1,095	1,215	1,277	1,315	808	949	601	1,311	(272)	793
Income as % of sales	—	10.6%	10.7%	10.6%	10.4%	6.1%	7.0%	4.5%	10.0%	—	6.0%
Earnings per share ($)	(4.0%)	2.72	3.01	3.13	3.32	2.05	2.39	1.49	3.20	(0.66)	1.89
Stock price – high ($)	—	24.63	36.63	39.19	35.44	46.00	45.50	40.38	44.25	48.88	41.38
Stock price – low ($)	—	18.22	23.22	29.00	30.44	32.63	33.56	33.50	34.56	40.13	33.25
Stock price – close ($)	4.6%	24.44	32.06	32.13	33.00	45.69	35.56	40.38	41.94	40.13	36.75
P/E – high	—	9	12	13	11	22	19	27	14	—	22
P/E – low	—	7	8	9	9	16	14	23	11	—	18
Dividends per share ($)	4.6%	1.58	1.71	1.86	1.99	2.14	2.26	2.28	2.48	2.35	2.36
Book value per share ($)	1.2%	18.18	21.88	22.82	23.91	23.78	22.86	22.48	24.61	20.39	20.26
Employees	(3.4%)	89,600	90,200	95,300	97,400	95,400	93,800	83,900	82,500	76,200	65,400

1994 Year-end:
Debt ratio: 59.5%
Return on equity: 9.3%
Cash (mil.): $138
Current ratio: 0.65
Long-term debt (mil.): $7,785
No. of shares (mil.): 424
Dividends
Yield: 6.4%
Payout: 124.9%
Market value (mil.): $15,567

Stock Price History
High/Low 1985–94

OCCIDENTAL PETROLEUM CORPORATION

OVERVIEW

The improved sales picture at Occidental Petroleum (Oxy) has been far from accidental. Boasting oil reserves of 918 million barrels and gas reserves of 2.3 trillion cubic feet, Oxy has been following a plan of noncore asset disposition and strategic acquisition. The Los Angeles–based company explores, produces, and markets crude oil and natural gas; engages in interstate and intrastate natural gas transmission and marketing; and makes a variety of industrial chemicals, fertilizers, and plastics.

MidCon, Oxy's natural gas subsidiary, carries about 10% of the gas used in the US through its 16,000 miles of pipelines. The company is looking to expand its markets to take advantage of opportunities created by the deregulation of the natural gas industry. In 1994 MidCon moved into the international arena with the formation of a new subsidiary, Occidental Energy Ventures Corp., to serve the growing gas demands of Asia. The subsidiary set up an office in Manila.

Oxy's chemical subsidiary, Occidental Chemical Corporation (OxyChem), is one of the largest chemical companies in the US. The nation's #6 producer of ethylene, OxyChem uses it and related products to make a broad range of plastics, solvents, fibers, and detergents.

In 1994 Oxy acquired closely held Placid Oil (with extensive reserves in the North Sea and the US) for $250 million.

WHEN

The Occidental Petroleum Corporation was founded in 1920 but remained small until 1956, when Dr. Armand Hammer, seeking a tax shelter, sank $100,000 into the company (whose net worth was $34,000). Two wells were drilled using the investment; both came in. Hammer acquired more stock and, eventually, control of the company.

Oxy's discovery of California's 2nd largest gas field (1959) was followed by its biggest coup: a concession from Libya's King Idris (1966) and the discovery of a billion-barrel Libyan oil field. In 1968 Oxy purchased Signal Oil's European refining and marketing organization as an outlet for the Libyan crude and diversified, buying Island Creek Coal and Hooker Chemical (owner of the notorious Love Canal toxic waste disposal site).

In 1969 Oxy sold, under duress, 51% of its Libyan production to the Libyan government (after Colonel Qaddafi ousted Idris). Oxy started oil exploration in Latin America (1971) and in the North Sea (1972–73), where it discovered the lucrative Piper field. Other projects included a 20-year fertilizer-for-ammonia deal with the USSR (1974) and a coal joint venture with China (1985).

In the 1980s Occidental opted for safer domestic shores by selling parts of its foreign operations and buying Cities Service for almost $4 billion (US oil and gas exploration, 1982; sold Citgo refining and marketing unit to Southland, 1983) and MidCon for $2.6 billion (US natural gas pipelines, 1986). Oxy also bought Iowa Beef Processors (IBP) for stock worth $750 million (1981); Oxy spun off 49% of IBP in 1987 for $960 million.

In 1983 Hammer hired Ray Irani to revive Oxy's ailing chemicals business (losses that year: $38 million). Irani integrated operations to ensure high margins during industry downturns, purchasing Diamond Shamrock Chemicals for $850 million (1986), Shell's vinyl chloride monomer unit (1987), a DuPont chloralkali facility (1987), and Cain Chemical (1988). Oxychem's profits reached almost $1.1 billion by 1989.

The colorful Hammer died at the end of 1990, and Irani took the CEO post. In 1991, to reduce debt, Oxy exited the Chinese coal business, sold North Sea oil properties to France's Elf Aquitaine (for $1.5 billion), and sold half of its US natural gas liquids business to its joint venture with Dallas investment firm Hicks, Muse & Co. ($700 million).

Also in 1991 Oxy spun off IBP, the largest US red meat producer, to its shareholders, reducing debt $760 million. In 1992 Oxy sold 12 million shares of Canadian Occidental Petroleum (CanadianOxy) for $241 million, reducing its interest from 48% to 30%.

In 1993 Occidental exited the US natural gas liquids business by selling its interest in Trident NGL. That same year the company sold its Island Creek Coal operations to CONSOL Energy.

In 1994 Oxy acquired interests in 17 Gulf Coast oil and gas properties from Agip Petroleum, a subsidiary of Italy's national energy company, ENI, for $195 million.

In 1995 Occidental established a wholly owned petroleum subsidiary in Tokyo as part of its strategy to expand operations in Japan and neighboring countries.

WHO

Chairman, President, and CEO: Ray R. Irani, age 60, $2,866,233 pay
EVP and Senior Operating Officer: Dale R. Laurance, age 49, $1,205,439 pay
EVP; President and CEO, Occidental Oil and Gas Corporation: David R. Martin, age 63, $814,527 pay
EVP; President and CEO, Occidental Chemical Corporation: J. Roger Hirl, age 63, $740,000 pay
EVP; President and CEO, MidCon Corp.: John F. Riordan, age 59, $735,000 pay
EVP and CFO: Anthony R. Leach, age 55
EVP Corporate Development: Stephen I. Chazen, age 48
EVP, General Counsel, and Secretary: Donald P. de Brier, age 54
EVP Human Resources: Richard W. Hallock, age 50
VP; President, Occidental International Corp.: Robert M. McGee, age 48
Auditors: Arthur Andersen & Co, SC

WHERE

HQ: 10889 Wilshire Blvd., Los Angeles, CA 90024
Phone: 310-208-8800
Fax: 310-824-2372

Occidental operates worldwide.

	1994 Sales	
	$ mil.	% of total
US	8,263	89
Other Western Hemisphere	626	7
Other regions	421	4
Adjustments	106	—
Total	**9,416**	**100**

WHAT

	1994 Sales		1994 Operating Income	
	$ mil.	% of total	$ mil.	% of total
Chemicals	4,681	50	368	47
Oil & gas	2,494	26	128	17
Natural gas transmission	2,135	23	281	36
Corporate	106	1	(670)	—
Total	**9,416**	**100**	**107**	**100**

Selected Subsidiaries and Affiliates
Canadian Occidental Petroleum Ltd. (30%, exploration and production)
MidCon Corp. (interstate and intrastate natural gas transmission and marketing)
 Natural Gas Pipeline Company of America (interstate pipeline transmission systems)
 Occidental Energy Ventures Corp. (pipelines, Asia)
Occidental Chemical Corp. (chemicals, petrochemicals, polymers, and plastics)
Occidental Oil and Gas Corp. (exploration and production)

KEY COMPETITORS

Amerada Hess	Huntsman	PPG
Amoco	Chemical	Repsol
Ashland, Inc.	Imperial Oil	Royal Dutch/
Atlantic Richfield	Koch	Shell
Chevron	Lyondell	Sinclair Oil
Coastal	Petrochemical	Sun Company
Columbia Gas	Mobil	Tenneco
Dow Chemical	Monsanto	Texaco
DuPont	NGC	TOTAL
Eastman	Oryx	Union Pacific
Chemical	Panhandle	Unocal
Enron	Eastern	USX–Delhi
Exxon	Pennzoil	USX–Marathon
Hanson	Phillips	
Hoechst	Petroleum	

HOW MUCH

	9-Year Growth	1985	1986	1987	1988	1989	1990	1991	1992	1993	1994
Sales ($ mil.)	(14.3%)	15,644	16,028	17,746	19,933	20,364	22,060	11,499	9,177	8,544	9,416
Net income ($ mil.)	—	696	181	240	302	285	(1,695)	460	(498)	283	(36)
Income as % of sales	—	4.4%	1.1%	1.4%	1.5%	1.4%	—	4.0%	—	3.3%	—
Earnings per share ($)	—	4.53	0.72	1.06	1.21	1.03	(5.82)	1.52	(1.66)	0.80	(0.36)
Stock price – high ($)	—	36.75	31.25	39.63	29.00	31.00	30.25	25.38	23.00	23.00	22.38
Stock price – low ($)	—	23.13	22.63	22.25	23.50	25.13	17.75	16.50	15.75	15.75	15.13
Stock price – close ($)	(8.3%)	31.00	27.50	24.38	25.38	29.63	18.38	17.88	17.00	17.00	19.25
P/E – high	—	8	43	37	24	30	—	17	—	29	—
P/E – low	—	5	31	21	19	24	—	11	—	20	—
Dividends per share ($)	(9.7%)	2.50	2.50	2.50	2.50	2.50	2.50	1.38	1.00	1.00	1.00
Book value per share ($)	(10.4%)	26.59	24.10	23.98	23.08	21.68	13.74	14.33	11.33	11.07	9.88
Employees	(8.3%)	43,000	51,000	50,300	52,500	53,500	55,000	24,700	23,600	19,860	19,660

1994 Year-end:
Debt ratio: 57.0%
Return on equity: —
Cash (mil.): $129
Current ratio: 1.03
Long-term debt (mil.): $5,823
No. of shares (mil.): 316.9
Dividends
 Yield: 5.2%
 Payout: —
Market value (mil.): $6,099

Stock Price History
High/Low 1985–94

OFFICE DEPOT, INC.

OVERVIEW

Described by one analyst as the "runaway train of retail," Florida-based Office Depot is the largest office supply retail chain in the US. A pioneer in retail discount office supplies, it has grown explosively since its founding in 1986 and has over 400 stores in the US and Canada.

The company buys high-quality, brand-name products in large volume and at steep discounts and then sells them through warehouse-style superstores. Once the privilege of large companies that could buy in quantity, low-priced office supplies became available to small and medium-sized businesses, Office Depot's main customers.

The stores feature a wide selection of merchandise, such as general office supplies, business machines, telephones and fax machines, computer hardware and software, and art and engineering supplies. Each store offers an array of services, which include printing, faxing, copying, business cards and personalized checks, discount long-distance service, and engraving.

Office Depot continues to expand, with plans to open about 200 stores in the next 3 years. The company is also expanding into new areas. In 1995 it launched a Business Services Division, providing a nationwide delivery network with a focus on large companies. The company also introduced its first Images outlet, offering a one-stop shop of printing, graphic design, layout, and mailing services.

WHEN

In 1986 Pat Scher, Stephen Dougherty, and Jack Kopkin opened the first Office Depot, one of the first office supply superstores, in Lauderdale Lakes, Florida. Scher was selected as chairman, and the company spent its early months searching for new markets, raising money, hiring personnel, and creating an efficient management information system. By the end of the year, 2 additional stores had been opened in Miami and West Palm Beach.

Office Depot opened 7 more stores (in Georgia and Florida) in 1987. When Scher died of leukemia that same year, the company recruited David Fuente, the former president of Sherwin-Williams's Paint Store Division, as his successor. Office Depot continued its breakneck expansion under Fuente. In 1988 the company opened 16 stores and broke into new markets in 4 states.

Of the original office discount chains, Office Depot was the first to turn a profit for 4 consecutive quarters. In 1988 Office Depot made its initial public offering. Its rivals Staples and Office Club, which also helped pioneer the fledgling industry, and newcomer BizMart (bought by Kmart in 1993) went public around the same time.

The company stepped up its pace in 1989 by adding 41 new stores and breaking into the South and Midwest. Fifty-five new stores in several other states followed in 1990. Also that year Office Depot introduced computers and peripherals into its product line and opened its first delivery center to coordinate shipments to customers of its busy southern Florida stores.

In 1991 the company expanded its presence in the West almost overnight through the acquisition of former rival Office Club, another warehouse-type office supply chain with 59 stores, most of them in California. Fuente remained chairman while former Office Club CEO Mark Begelman became president and COO.

Begelman, a former executive with British American Tobacco, founded Office Club in 1987, opening his first store in Concord, California. While Office Depot was growing east of the Mississippi, Office Club was expanding through the West. Office Club went public in 1989. The acquisition of Office Club made Office Depot North America's #1 office products retailer.

The company entered the Canadian market through its 1992 purchase of H. Q. Office International. In 1993 the company signed licensing agreements with overseas partners which opened stores in Colombia and Israel. That same year Office Depot bought Houston-based Wilson Stationery & Printing Company and Eastman Office Products, the West Coast's #1 contract office supplier, with combined annual revenues of $345 million.

Office Depot bought 4 more contract stationers in 1994: Yorkship Press, which serves New Jersey and Philadelphia; Boston-based L.E. Muran; Cincinnati's J.A. Kindel; and Tampa-based Allstate Office Products. That same year Office Depot opened 16 stores in Michigan and in the Toronto area.

In 1995 Begelman, citing personal reasons, resigned as president and COO. Fuente took over his duties. That same year the company announced plans to open an experimental 17,000-square-foot store near Dallas that will sell only furniture.

NYSE symbol: ODP
Fiscal year ends: Last Saturday in December

WHO

Chairman, President, CEO, and COO: David I. Fuente, age 49, $1,875,000 pay
EVP Marketing: Gary D. Foss, age 52, $708,000 pay
EVP Retail Division: Richard M. Bennington, age 54, $696,600 pay
EVP Finance, CFO, and Secretary: Barry J. Goldstein, age 52, $693,600 pay
EVP Systems and Distribution: William Seltzer, age 56
EVP Merchandising: Harry S. Brown, age 48
EVP Business Services Division: Judith A. Rogala, age 53
EVP Human Resources: F. Terry Bean, age 47
Auditors: Deloitte & Touche LLP

WHERE

HQ: 2200 Old Germantown Rd., Delray Beach, FL 33445
Phone: 407-278-4800
Fax: 407-265-4403 (Public Relations)

	1994 Stores
	No.
California	82
Florida	60
Texas	47
Canada	21
Georgia	20
Illinois	19
North Carolina	15
Michigan	13
Colorado	12
Missouri	12
Washington	12
Louisiana	10
Maryland	10
Ohio	10
Other states & District of Columbia	89
Total	**432**

WHAT

	1994 Sales
	% of total
General office supplies	48
Business machines	39
Office furniture	13
Total	**100**

General Office Supplies
Art supplies
Binders
Books
Business forms
Calendars
Desktop accessories
Engineering and janitorial supplies
Filing supplies
Mailing supplies
Organizers
Writing instruments

Business Machines
Adding machines
Calculators
Cash registers
Computers
Copiers
Fax machines
Safes
Telephones
Typewriters

Office Furniture
Chairs
Desks
Filing cabinets
Partitions
Storage cabinets
Tables

KEY COMPETITORS

Best Buy
Boise Cascade
Circuit City
CompUSA
Corporate Express
Kinko's
Moore Products
Nashua
OfficeMax
Daisytek
Price/Costco
Quill
Staples
Tandy
United Stationers
Viking Office Products
Wal-Mart

HOW MUCH

	Annual Growth	1985	1986[1]	1987	1988	1989	1990	1991	1992	1993	1994
Sales ($ mil.)	99.8%	—	2	34	132	315	626	1,301	1,733	2,579	4,266
Net income ($ mil.)	—	—	—	(2)	3	6	10	14	38	63	105
Income as % of sales	—	—	—	—	2.3%	1.9%	1.6%	1.1%	2.2%	2.5%	2.5%
Earnings per share ($)	46.4%	—	—	—	0.07	0.09	0.13	0.12	0.27	0.45	0.69
Stock price – high ($)	—	—	—	—	2.71	5.84	4.78	12.01	15.52	23.93	27.00
Stock price – low ($)	—	—	—	—	1.87	2.39	2.45	3.17	8.34	11.90	18.88
Stock price – close ($)	46.5%	—	—	—	2.38	4.00	3.48	11.23	15.07	22.43	23.53
P/E – high	—	—	—	—	39	65	37	100	58	53	39
P/E – low	—	—	—	—	27	27	19	26	31	26	27
Dividends per share ($)	—	—	—	—	0.00	0.00	0.00	0.00	0.00	0.00	0.00
Book value per share ($)	42.6%	—	—	—	0.57	1.46	1.60	2.38	2.85	3.93	4.79
Employees	54.0%	—	—	—	1,950	3,800	5,600	9,000	11,300	20,400	26,000

1994 Year-end:
Debt ratio: 35.7%
Return on equity: 16.5%
Cash (mil.): $32
Current ratio: 1.62
Long-term debt (mil.): $394
No. of shares (mil.): 149
Dividends
    Yield: —
    Payout: —
Market value (mil.): $3,515

**Stock Price History
High/Low 1988–94**

[1] Less than a 12-month fiscal year

OGDEN CORPORATION

OVERVIEW

New York City–based Ogden offers a wide range of management and waste disposal services through its 2 operating groups.

Its services group provides management services (including engineering and consultation, catering, promotion, and facility management) to airlines, industrial plants, governments, and other major organizations. Its Ogden Entertainment unit is one of the world's top providers of services to entertainment and sports venues. The long baseball strike in 1994 hurt the performance of this group, but the company is looking to make up this ground at a number of Ogden-contracted venues opening in 1995. Ogden's Aviation unit provides catering services, cargo handling, and refueling facilities and is cashing in on the industry-wide growth in passenger and cargo traffic.

Ogden Projects, Inc., is the largest US developer of waste-to-energy (WTE) facilities and provides waste disposal and wastewater services. It also invests in alternative energy power plants and in construction services.

WHEN

Ogden Corporation has reinvented itself many times since its founding in 1939 as a holding company for a failing public utilities company. The new company liquidated most of the utility's assets and was about to dissolve when Allen & Co. bought 80% of the stock between 1949 and 1951. Allen transformed it into a nondiversified investment company.

Some companies remained part of the organization. One was Luria Brothers (scrap metal dealer, 1955), whose president, Ralph Ablon, became head of Ogden in 1962. Under Ablon the company became a collection of industrial companies whose centerpiece was Luria's scrap metal operation. The company acquired Better Built Machinery in 1965 and also invested heavily in Avondale shipyard (Louisiana, 1959) and shipping services, such as International Terminal Operating (cargo handling, 1962). But in the late 1960s, scrap prices declined, and Ablon added food services with the purchase of Tillie Lewis Foods (1966), Wilson Foods (1967), International Products (1967), and Chef's Orchid (airline catering, 1968). Expansion in the food industry continued in 1969 with Doggie Diner restaurants (Oakland) and Schreibers Catering (Cleveland).

The company grew at an annually compounded rate of more than 60% in Allen's first 10 years. In the 1970s Ogden consolidated the 3 areas of scrap metal, shipping services, and food and divested businesses that did not fit in, including a number of racetracks. The company weathered the uncertainties of the 1970s with continued steady growth. In the 1980s it took a new turn — into services.

In 1982 the company bought Allied Maintenance (janitorial services). In 1984 it obtained the US rights to a WTE process developed by Martin GmbH of Germany and established Ogden Projects, the waste disposal group. Throughout the decade the company divested most of its industrial and shipping interests, selling its shipbuilding and industrial companies to a new employee-owned company, Avondale Industries (1985), and its food services to IC Industries (1986).

In an effort to concentrate on its core businesses, Ogden left the financial services and child care businesses in 1990. It expanded its aviation services and by 1991 was established in over 80 airports worldwide. In the same year, Ogden paid $39 million for the 39% of ERC Environmental & Energy Services that it did not already own and renamed it Ogden Environmental and Energy Services.

Ogden Projects continued to acquire waste disposal and WTE companies (Catalyst New Martinsville Hydroelectric, Blount Energy Resource, and Qualtec). Ogden touts WTE technology as a practical addition to city waste disposal programs that usually consist of landfills and recycling programs. With the entertainment sector struggling in 1992, the aviation services sector came to the rescue with record revenues and new locations in Australia, Europe, and Latin America.

In early 1993 Ogden reconfirmed its commitment to a long-term WTE strategy with the acquisition of Asea Brown Boveri's entire WTE business in the US.

In 1994 Ogden Projects signed a joint venture agreement with Yorkshire Water Enterprises to own and operate municipal water and wastewater facilities. Also that year the company ended its management contract with Millwall Soccer Stadium (its first UK contract, and venue of arguably the most violent soccer fans in Europe), citing breach of contract.

In 1995 Ogden won an 11-year contract to redevelop and manage one of New York's tourist attractions, the 107th Floor Observation Deck of the World Trade Center.

NYSE symbol: OG
Fiscal year ends: December 31

WHO

Chairman: Ralph E. Ablon, age 78
VC: Abraham Zaleznik
President and CEO: R. Richard Ablon, age 45,
$1,800,000 pay
President and COO, Ogden Projects: Scott G. Mackin,
age 38, $750,000 pay
EVP and Chief Administrative Officer: Constantine G.
Caras, age 56, $420,000 pay
SVP, CFO, and Treasurer: Philip G. Husby, age 48,
$376,250 pay
SVP and General Counsel: Lynde H. Coit, age 40,
$347,500 pay
SVP Business Development, Asia: David L. Hahn,
age 43
SVP Business Development, Latin America: Rodrigo
Arboleda, age 54
VP Investor Relations: Nancy R. Christal, age 36
VP, Controller, and Chief Accounting Officer: Robert M.
DiGia, age 70
VP and Secretary: Kathleen Ritch, age 52
VP Human Resources: David Belka
Assistant Secretary: James L. Efflinger
Assistant Secretary: Bruce W. Stone
Assistant Treasurer: Wayne A. Francis
Auditors: Deloitte & Touche LLP

WHERE

HQ: 2 Pennsylvania Plaza, New York, NY 10121
Phone: 212-868-6100
Fax: 212-868-5714

Ogden performs a wide range of management services
for clients located throughout the US and in Aruba,
Brazil, Canada, Chile, Germany, Great Britain, Japan,
Mexico, Pakistan, Panama, Peru, Puerto Rico, Spain,
Turkey, and Venezuela. Ogden Projects operates 27
waste-to-energy facilities in 15 US states.

WHAT

	1994 Sales		1994 Operating Income	
	$ mil.	% of total	$ mil.	% of total
Services	1,379	65	53	33
Projects	731	35	110	67
Total	2,110	100	163	100

Services
Aviation Services (aircraft catering, handling, and
fueling)
Entertainment Services (entertainment facility
management)
Environmental Services (consulting, engineering, and
design services)
Facility Management Services (facility management,
maintenance, and manufacturing support)
Technology Services
    ADTI (air combat maneuvering instrumentation))
    Atlantic Design Co., Inc. (engineering design,
    technical services, electronics contract
    manufacturing, and medical products)
    Universal Ogden Services (remote facility support)
    WJSA (technical and engineering support for US
    government defense projects)

Projects
Construction Activities (construction of Ogden plants)
Independent Power (alternative energy projects)
Waste-To-Energy (waste disposal and energy production
services)
Water and Wastewater (water and wastewater mgmt.)

KEY COMPETITORS

Accor	Flagstar	Waste
ARAMARK	Halliburton	Onex
Browning	Host	Peter Kiewit Sons'
Ferris	Marriott	Safety-Kleen
Catalyst Energy	Hyatt	SCI Systems
Corning	Matsushita	Union Pacific
Delaware North	Michael Baker	USA Waste Services
Dial	Mid-American	WMX Technologies

HOW MUCH

	9-Year Growth	1985	1986	1987	1988	1989	1990	1991	1992	1993	1994
Sales ($ mil.)	8.3%	1,026	800	858	1,088	1,369	1,563	1,568	1,769	2,039	2,110
Net income ($ mil.)	—	(22)	120	54	58	67	56	44	61	57	68
Income as % of sales	—	—	14.9%	6.3%	5.3%	4.9%	3.6%	2.8%	3.4%	2.8%	3.2%
Earnings per share ($)	—	(0.58)	2.98	1.32	1.41	1.66	1.29	1.00	1.41	1.42	1.54
Stock price – high ($)	—	17.31	24.00	44.63	32.38	34.75	32.88	23.25	24.38	27.00	24.38
Stock price – low ($)	—	13.25	13.75	17.50	25.13	25.50	15.00	17.63	17.13	21.50	17.75
Stock price – close ($)	1.4%	16.56	20.00	27.75	29.38	31.88	18.75	20.25	22.75	22.75	18.75
P/E – high	—	—	8	34	23	21	26	23	17	18	16
P/E – low	—	—	5	13	18	15	12	18	12	15	12
Dividends per share ($)	3.7%	0.90	0.90	0.98	1.08	1.21	1.25	1.25	1.31	1.25	1.25
Book value per share ($)	4.8%	8.00	10.25	10.63	10.74	8.99	11.30	11.12	11.14	11.18	12.24
Employees	1.6%	39,000	38,000	38,000	37,000	45,000	45,000	42,000	43,000	41,800	45,000

1994 Year-end:
Debt ratio: 77.8%
Return on equity: 12.5%
Cash (mil.): $204
Current ratio: 1.94
Long-term debt (mil.): $1,594
No. of shares (mil.): 49
Dividends
    Yield: 6.7%
    Payout: 81.2%
Market value (mil.): $915

Stock Price History
High/Low 1985–94

ORACLE CORPORATION

Oracle is one of the world's top software vendors and the leading developer of database management systems (DBMS) software, which allows multiple users and applications to access the same data at the same time. Such accessibility is the basis of client/server computing and of complex data manipulation tasks used, for example, in tracking sales and inventory. The company's flagship software, Oracle7, runs on everything from notebook computers to mainframes and accounts for 70% of revenues. Digital Equipment Corp. (DEC), IBM, and Unisys use Oracle software to sell their network hardware.

After a rough period, Oracle is on a roll. Several factors are helping boost the company's bottom line, including the migration from mainframes to networks of smaller computers, Oracle's recent upgrades of its applications software, and its introduction of low-end products and workgroup software. The

company is also nurturing its consulting business and is developing multimedia projects. A recent alliance with DEC for a hardware/software package based on DEC's new Alpha microprocessor is expected to speed up data processing. Oracle will also help IBM's Lotus subsidiary expand the capabilities of its *Notes* workgroup software to access large databases.

Oracle's success is funding CEO Lawrence Ellison's attempts to kick-start what he calls the "I-Way" — a global information and entertainment network. Ellison has lined up nearly 60 companies (including Apple, Hitachi, and Samsung) in an alliance to develop a standard for set-top boxes for interactive television. British Telecom and Bell Atlantic are testing Oracle's digitized video-on-demand software.

Ellison, softwaredom's 2nd richest CEO after Bill Gates, owns over 23% of Oracle and a majority interest in nCUBE, a maker of massively parallel computers.

Lawrence Ellison, Robert Miner, and Edward Oates founded Oracle in 1977 to create a relational database management system for minicomputers according to theoretical specifications published by IBM. Ellison, who grew up on Chicago's South Side, studied physics at the University of Chicago and dropped out to seek his fortune in Silicon Valley in the 1960s. Working first for Ampex and then Amdahl, he was part of the team that developed the first IBM-compatible mainframe. Miner, a programmer with more than 14 years of experience, was mostly responsible for developing Oracle DBMS, introduced in 1979. One of Oracle's early advantages was its ability to tailor its products to run on many brands of computers of all sizes — from PCs to mainframes.

Oracle went public in 1986 and started making inroads into government circles in 1986. Within 2 years Oracle had a healthy 36% share of the government PC database market. The company also added software products, including financial management, graphics, and human resource management programs.

Oracle's rapid growth came at a great cost. Responding to Ellison's call for a doubling of sales each year, management was sloppy. Oracle developed a reputation as a leader in "vaporware," products announced but never developed. Products were released prematurely, bug ridden, and lacking promised features. Oracle also offered generous payment terms, which led to uncollectible receivables.

Duplicate billings and the booking of unconsummated sales inflated revenues. Profits were further increased by capitalizing, rather than expensing, R&D costs.

The company recorded a loss for fiscal 1991, accompanied by a downward restate for past years. Its stock nosedived. Oracle laid off 400 employees, including 6 executives, and revised its growth estimates.

Recognizing (with a little push from the board) that Oracle had passed the entrepreneurial stage, Ellison got company funding on solid ground by granting Nippon Steel an option to buy 25% of its Japanese operations. He also brought in Raymond Lane, formerly of Booz-Allen, giving him 6 months to reorganize the company. Lane streamlined and centralized the company and imposed strict performance standards. In 1992, solidly convalescent, Oracle launched Oracle7, a network database featuring simplified information access.

Sales at Oracle hit the $2 billion mark in fiscal 1994, helping to secure its position as the #1 maker and distributor of DBMS software. Also in 1994, British Telecom chose Oracle to provide software for its London cable network and nCUBE to provide the servers.

In 1995 the company said it would use the Internet to distribute Personal Oracle7, a desktop version of the business database software. Also in 1995, the company had its first $1 billion quarter and ended the year with nearly $3 billion in revenues.

Nasdaq symbol: ORCL
Fiscal year ends: May 31

WHO

Chairman: James A. Abrahamson, age 61, $847,962 pay
President and CEO: Lawrence J. Ellison, age 49, $2,409,618 pay
EVP; President, Worldwide Operations: Raymond J. Lane, age 47, $1,222,602 pay
EVP and CFO: Jeffrey O. Henley, age 49, $866,502 pay
SVP, General Counsel, and Corporate Secretary: Raymond L. Ocampo Jr., age 41, $318,758 pay
SVP Worldwide Customer Support: Randy Baker
SVP Worldwide Marketing: André Boisvert
SVP Server Technologies: Derry Kabcenell
SVP Worldwide Consulting and Education: Robert Shaw
SVP Interactive Multimedia and Document Automation Division: Jerry Held
SVP CDE Product Division: Sohaib Abbasi
SVP Product Line Division: Jerry Baker
SVP Applications Division: Ron Wohl
SVP Human Resources: Phillip E. Wilson
VP and Corporate Controller: Thomas A. Williams, age 42
Senior Architect: Edward Screven
Auditors: Arthur Andersen & Co, SC

WHERE

HQ: 500 Oracle Pkwy., Redwood City, CA 94065
Phone: 415-506-7000
Fax: 415-506-7200

Oracle has operations in 90 countries worldwide.

	1994 Sales		1994 Operating Income	
	$ mil.	% of total	$ mil.	% of total
US	815	41	309	74
Europe	800	40	76	18
Other countries	386	19	35	8
Total	**2,001**	**100**	**420**	**100**

WHAT

	1994 Sales	
	$ mil.	% of total
Licenses & other	1,164	58
Services	837	42
Total	**2,001**	**100**

Selected Products and Services

Cooperative Development Environment
Applications development productivity tools
Computer-Automated Software Engineering (CASE) products
Document automation products

Cooperative Server Technology
Oracle relational DBMS software

Distributed Database Integration Products
Oracle Procedural Developer's Kit
Oracle Procedural Gateways
Oracle Transparent Gateways

End-User Accounting Applications Products
Oracle Government Financials
Oracle Human Resources
Oracle Manufacturing

Services
Consulting
Education
Support
Systems Integration

KEY COMPETITORS

American Software	Gupta	PeopleSoft
BMC Software	H&R Block	SAP
Borland	Hyperion	Silicon Graphics
Computer Associates	Software	Sybase
DEC	IBM	System Software
Dun & Bradstreet	Informix	Associates
Fourth Shift	Microsoft	Wang
	Novell	

HOW MUCH

	Annual Growth	1985	1986	1987	1988	1989	1990	1991	1992	1993	1994
Sales ($ mil.)	64.2%	23	55	131	282	584	971	1,028	1,179	1,503	2,001
Net income ($ mil.)	73.4%	2	6	16	43	82	117	(12)	62	98	284
Income as % of sales	—	6.9%	10.6%	11.9%	15.2%	14.0%	12.1%	—	5.2%	6.5%	14.2%
Earnings per share ($)	66.1%	0.01	0.03	0.07	0.17	0.31	0.43	(0.05)	0.22	0.34	0.96
Stock price – high ($)	—	—	1.78	4.66	5.56	12.88	14.19	8.31	14.31	37.75	46.50
Stock price – low ($)	—	—	0.84	1.30	2.94	4.75	2.44	2.75	6.00	13.25	26.25
Stock price – close ($)	55.4%	—	1.30	3.63	4.88	11.69	3.94	7.25	14.19	28.75	44.13
P/E – high	—	—	59	67	33	42	33	—	65	113	48
P/E – low	—	—	28	19	17	15	6	—	27	40	27
Dividends per share ($)	—	—	0.00	0.00	0.00	0.00	0.00	0.00	0.00	0.00	0.00
Book value per share ($)	44.0%	—	0.14	0.36	0.56	0.91	1.48	1.26	1.55	1.86	2.59
Employees	40.9%	—	776	1,072	2,207	4,148	6,811	7,466	8,160	9,247	12,058

1994 Year-end:
Debt ratio: 10.8%
Return on equity: 44.7%
Cash (mil.): $465
Current ratio: 1.58
Long-term debt (mil.): $83
No. of shares (mil.): 286
Dividends
  Yield: —
  Payout: —
Market value (mil.): $12,636

Stock Price History High/Low 1986–94

OWENS-CORNING FIBERGLAS

OVERVIEW

Owens-Corning hopes that when you see the Pink Panther character, you will think of the company instead of Peter Sellers. The world's #1 maker of (mainly pink) glass fiber materials (many of which are sold under the trade name Fiberglas) and a major producer of polyester resins, the company launched an identity campaign in 1994 using its Pink Panther logo. The Toledo, Ohio–based firm has been on the rebound since 1991, when it took a huge loss to cover its liability for asbestos products it no longer makes. Strong demand in the US housing market has boosted sales of its fiberglass insulation products.

The firm's 11 units are Asia/Pacific, Building Products–Europe, Composite, Insulation–North America, Latin America, Miraflex, Pipe, Retail/Distribution, Roofing/Asphalt, Specialty & Foam, and Western Fiberglass.

Glen Hiner (CEO since 1992) has refocused the company on R&D, with an eye to speeding up the time between the research and production stages. The innovations that have resulted from Hiner's strategy (including AURA, a new insulation that has tested up to an R-factor of 94, and Fibron, an insulating liner for windows and patios), coupled with highly effective cost-cutting measures, have put the company back on the competitive frontier. In 1994 Owens-Corning introduced its first new fiberglass in 60 years, Miraflex fiber, sold under the brand name PinkPlus (attic insulation).

Increased demand from the growing European economies helped lift revenue in 1994. Also that year Owens-Corning expanded the capacity of its Visé, Belgium, plant by 50%, and it acquired Pilkington's insulation and industrial supply business for $110 million.

WHEN

In the 1930s Corning Glass Works and Owens-Illinois Glass independently found that glass has special resilience and strength. Hoping for a large market, they formed Owens-Corning Fiberglas as a joint venture (1938). The 2 glass companies expanded rapidly in the 1940s and 1950s, establishing several US plants and one in Ontario. Their products included fine fibers, thermal wool, textiles, and continuous filaments.

In 1949 a US antitrust decree denied the 2 founding firms control over Owens-Corning or any claim to its earnings. They each retained 1/3 ownership (later reduced) when the company went public in 1952. During the 1950s Owens-Corning developed new uses for glass fibers in automobile bodies, shingles, and insulation. In the 1960s the company expanded overseas. Glass fiber uses multiplied as applications developed in aerospace, tires, and noncorrosive underground tanks.

In 1977 Owens-Corning bought Lloyd Fry (roofing and asphalt) for $108 million. By 1980 the company had invested over $700 million in acquisitions and in internal efforts to strengthen its roofing materials position, and the Pink Panther had become its advertising "spokesman." Owens-Corning introduced a rolled insulation in 1982.

A takeover attempt by Wickes Companies in 1986 was successfully fended off, but the effort necessitated taking on $2.6 billion in debt and forced Owens-Corning to redirect its strategy. It sold 10 businesses, halved its research budget, laid off or lost to divestitures 46% of its work force, and mothballed 14% of productive capacity by 1987.

In 1989 Owens-Corning bought Fiberglas Canada, Canada's largest glass fiber insulation maker, for $195 million. To expand globally, the company formed alliances in 1990 with BASF, Lucky-Goldstar, and Siam Cement.

In 1991 Owens-Corning spent $65 million on restructuring, closing one plant and mothballing another. A new products division was formed to make window products for the home. David Devonshire, formerly with Honeywell, became CFO at Owens in 1993. That same year the company demonstrated its commitment to the restructuring initiated by new CEO Hiner in 1992: In addition to selling several assets, the company established a new division (Asia/Pacific) to capitalize on the emerging markets in the Far East and exchanged its commercial roofing business for the residential roofing business of Schuller International.

In 1994 Owens-Corning acquired UC Industries, a privately held foam board insulation maker, for $45 million. It also completed the formation of the Alpha/Owens-Corning joint venture, the largest polyester resin producer in North America.

The company formed 2 new Latin American companies in 1995: a service center in Colombia and a pipe manufacturer in Argentina. The company is also actively exploring joint ventures in other South American countries, including Brazil and Chile.

NYSE symbol: OCF
Fiscal year ends: December 31

WHO

Chairman and CEO: Glen H. Hiner, age 60,
$1,826,076 pay
EVP Development/Planning/Sourcing: Charles H. Dana,
age 55, $607,500 pay
SVP and CFO: David W. Devonshire, age 49,
$568,333 pay
SVP, General Counsel, and Secretary: Christian L.
Campbell, age 44
SVP Human Resources: Gregory M. Thomson, age 47
VP; President, Miraflex: Paula H. J. Cholmondeley,
age 48
VP; President, Western Fiberglass Group: Robert D.
Heddens
VP; President, Building Products Europe: Warren D.
Knowlton
VP; President, Latin America: Scott K. Koepke
VP Science and Technology: Robert C. Lonergan, age 51
Auditors: Arthur Andersen & Co, SC

WHERE

HQ: Owens-Corning Fiberglas Corporation, Fiberglas
Tower, Toledo, OH 43659
Phone: 419-248-8000
Fax: 419-248-5337 (Public Relations)

Owens-Corning operates manufacturing facilities in the
US and 11 foreign countries.

	1994 Sales		1994 Operating Income	
	$ mil.	% of total	$ mil.	% of total
US	2,547	76	253	85
Europe	537	16	18	6
Other regions	267	8	27	9
Adjustments	—	—	(72)	—
Total	**3,351**	**100**	**226**	**100**

WHAT

	1994 Sales		1994 Operating Income	
	$ mil.	% of total	$ mil.	% of total
Construction prods.	2,273	68	189	63
Industrial materials	1,078	32	109	37
Other	—	—	(72)	—
Total	**3,351**	**100**	**226**	**100**

Strategic Business Segments
Asia/Pacific (operates facilities and develops
opportunities in the region)
Building Products–Europe (manufactures, markets, and
sells building products in Europe)
Composites (manufactures, markets, and sells
reinforcements, textile yarns, and wet-chop strands/
mats and veils)
Insulation–North America (handles insulation
contractors, mechanical insulation, AURA insulation,
and insulation plants)
Latin America (operates facilities and develops
opportunities in Latin America)
Miraflex Products (sells Miraflex residential insulation
fiber)
Pipe (develops pipe business worldwide)
Retail/Distribution (distributes and sells insulation,
roofing, windows, and patio doors)
Roofing/Asphalt (manufactures residential roofing
products and industrial asphalt)
Specialty and Foam Products (produces and sells foam
insulation and foam products)
Western Fiberglass Group (develops residential and
commercial building insulation)

KEY COMPETITORS

Andersen Corp.	Elcor	Manville
Armstrong World	Fletcher	Pella
Bird Corp.	Challenge	PPG
Boise Cascade	Georgia-Pacific	St. Gobain
Bridgestone	Guardian	U.S. Intec
Dalmine	Industries	

HOW MUCH

	9-Year Growth	1985	1986	1987	1988	1989	1990	1991	1992	1993	1994
Sales ($ mil.)	0.2%	3,305	3,644	2,891	2,831	3,000	3,111	2,783	2,878	2,944	3,351
Net income ($ mil.)	(6.1%)	131	16	220	197	172	75	(515)	72	105	74
Income as % of sales	—	4.0%	0.4%	7.6%	7.0%	5.7%	2.4%	—	2.5%	3.6%	2.2%
Earnings per share ($)	(10.3%)	4.42	0.49	5.30	4.71	4.08	1.78	(12.58)	1.68	2.28	1.66
Stock price – high ($)	—	38.75	82.50	32.38	26.50	36.88	26.50	35.50	39.75	49.13	46.00
Stock price – low ($)	—	30.50	8.88	9.00	15.88	22.25	13.63	15.00	22.38	34.38	27.75
Stock price – close ($)	(1.8%)	37.50	13.75	16.38	22.25	25.13	16.00	22.38	36.00	44.38	31.88
P/E – high	—	9	—	6	6	9	15	—	24	22	28
P/E – low	—	7	18	2	3	6	8	—	13	15	17
Dividends per share ($)	(100.0%)	1.40	1.05	0.00	0.00	0.00	0.00	0.00	0.00	0.00	0.00
Book value per share ($)	—	29.80	39.53	(20.23)	(15.18)	(10.78)	(8.62)	(25.83)	(23.72)	(20.12)	(15.38)
Employees	(4.2%)	25,000	30,000	21,000	20,000	20,000	18,000	17,000	16,400	16,200	17,000

1994 Year-end:
Debt ratio: 100.0%
Return on equity: —
Cash (mil.): $59
Current ratio: 0.87
Long-term debt (mil.): $1,037
No. of shares (mil.): 44
Dividends
  Yield: —
  Payout: —
Market value (mil.): $1,409

Stock Price History
High/Low 1985–94

OWENS-ILLINOIS, INC.

OVERVIEW

Toledo-based Owens-Illinois has been sending its message in a bottle for most of this century. The world's leading producer of glass containers, with a nearly 50% share of the world market, is growing internationally, betting on the bottled-up demand for glass containers from emerging markets in India, Latin America, and Eastern Europe to lift sales.

The company is also one of the world's largest manufacturers of packaging products (27% of 1994 sales). Owens-Illinois's range of major products includes glass beverage and food containers, plastic containers and closures, and glass pharmaceutical containers and packaging material.

Faced with a mature market for glass bottles in the US, Owens-Illinois has been focusing on restructuring operations by selling noncore businesses, closing plants, and cutting jobs, in addition to ramping up its overseas manufacturing and marketing.

The company has sold off assets within its specialty glass segment over the past 2 years. Libbey Glass (tableware) was spun off as a separate public firm, and the company sold 51% of its interest in Kimble Glass (specialty packaging and laboratory ware) as well as its 50% interest in OI-NEG TV Products (television specialty glass).

The company is beefing up its plastic packaging business as part of its strategy for growth. Owens-Illinois is adding manufacturing capacity to its existing plants to meet the growing demand for custom-molded polyethylene terephthalate (PET) containers for personal care and health care products. The firm is also exploring strategic acquisitions to broaden its packaging line.

WHEN

The Owens Bottle Machine Corp. was incorporated in Toledo in 1907 as the successor to a 4-year-old New Jersey company of the same name. The company grew by acquiring small glass companies. In 1929 Owens bought the Illinois Glass Co. (medical and pharmaceutical glass) and became Owens-Illinois Glass.

Owens-Illinois bought Libbey Glass (tableware) in 1935. In 1938 the company and Corning Glass, which were both studying glass fiber uses, began Owens-Corning Fiberglas, a joint venture with a virtual industry monopoly. After it went public in 1952, founders retained less than 1/3 of the company.

After WWII Owens-Illinois started to diversify beyond glass. In 1956 the company bought National Container (cardboard boxes). During the 1950s Owens-Illinois created a semirigid plastic container that was adopted by numerous bleach and detergent companies during 1958.

The introduction of the nonreturnable bottle in the 1960s gave new life to Owens-Illinois and the glass industry. During the late 1960s Owens-Illinois bought Lily Tulip Cups (paper products, 1968; sold to KKR in 1981) and entered ventures such as Bahamas sugar cane farming and Florida phosphate mining. In the 1970s the company started producing specialty optical and TV glass.

With the glass industry floundering at the beginning of the 1980s under pressure from increased use of alternate packaging materials, Owens-Illinois invested over $600 million to realign and modernize its glass operations. In 1981 the company entered the health care field with a minority interest in Health Group, Inc. In 1984 Owens-Illinois bought the Health Care and Retirement Corp.

In 1986 KKR offered to purchase Owens-Illinois. The company initially refused, but when KKR raised the offer to $60 per share, Owens-Illinois sold for $4.6 billion and went private. Total debt after the LBO was $4.4 billion. The following year the company bought Brockway (glass and plastic containers).

In the years following the LBO, Owens-Illinois sold its forest products and mortgage banking businesses. In August 1991 the company sold its health care business for $369 million. Owens-Illinois went public in 1991, ending its 5 years as a private company. Capital raised by the sale of shares was used to pay down LBO debt, among other things.

In 1992 the firm greatly expanded its plastics business with the purchase of Specialty Packaging Products, allowing it to add trigger sprayers and finger pumps to its line.

In 1993 the company expanded its South American operations, buying a controlling interest in a Peruvian glass firm and increasing its investment in its Bolivian affiliate.

Ongoing litigation related to the firm's pre-1960 use of asbestos forced Owens-Illinois to write down $100 million in 1994.

In 1995 Owens-Illinois acquired a majority share in Ballarpur Industries (a subsidiary of the Thapar conglomerate), one of India's largest glass container makers, with 3 glass manufacturing plants.

NYSE symbol: OI
Fiscal year ends: December 31

WHO

Chairman and CEO: Joseph H. Lemieux, age 64,
$1,240,000 pay
EVP Domestic Packaging Operations: Terry L.
Wilkison, age 53, $445,000 pay
EVP International Operations: R. Scott Trumbull,
age 46, $440,000 pay
**EVP Operations, Administration, General Counsel, and
Secretary:** Thomas L. Young, age 51, $420,000 pay
SVP and CFO: Lee A. Wesselmann, age 59, $459,000 pay
VP; General Manager, Plastic Operations: Russell C.
Berkoben, age 53
VP; General Manager, International Operations: Gary R.
Clinard, age 56
VP; General Manager, Kimble: Larry A. Griffith,
age 49
Director Human Resources Management: Gary
Benjamin
Auditors: Ernst & Young LLP

WHERE

HQ: One SeaGate, Toledo, OH 43666
Phone: 419-247-5000
Fax: 419-247-2839

Owens-Illinois has facilities in over 60 cities in the US
and affiliates in 11 foreign countries and Puerto Rico.

	1994 Sales		1994 Operating Income	
	$ mil.	% of total	$ mil.	% of total
US	2,860	78	395	74
Other Western Hemisphere	510	14	114	21
Europe	283	8	26	5
Adjustments	—	—	(127)	—
Total	**3,653**	**100**	**408**	**100**

WHAT

	1994 Sales		1994 Operating Income	
	$ mil.	% of total	$ mil.	% of total
Glass containers	2,590	71	393	74
Plastics & closures	976	27	140	26
Other	87	2	(125)	—
Total	**3,653**	**100**	**408**	**100**

Glass Containers
Bottles
Jars

Plastics and Closures
Carriers (for beverage containers)
Closures (bottle tops and container lids)
Containers
Prescription medicine containers
Trigger sprayers, finger pumps

Specialized Glass (Kimble, 49% interest)
Laboratory ware (beakers, culture tubes, flasks, and
pipets)
Pharmaceutical products (ampuls, syringe barrels and
cartridges, and vials)

KEY COMPETITORS

Amway
Ball Corp.
Bemis
Brown-Forman
Carlisle Plastics
Carlsberg
Continental Can
Corning
Crown Cork & Seal
Danone
Dart Container
Gallo

Johnson Controls
Liqui-Box
Myers Industries
Pechiney SA
Premark
Reynolds Metals
Rubbermaid
Sealright
Silgan
Stone Container
Sun Coast Industries
Wheaton

HOW MUCH

	Annual Growth	1985	1986	1987	1988	1989	1990	1991	1992	1993	1994
Sales ($ mil.)	2.5%	2,931	2,891	3,098	3,374	3,389	3,739	3,628	3,474	3,662	3,653
Net income ($ mil.)	(7.4%)	156	179	(23)	(59)	(68)	(56)	(130)	91	18	78
Income as % of sales	—	5.3%	6.2%	—	—	—	—	—	2.8%	0.5%	2.1%
Earnings per share ($)	—	—	—	—	—	—	—	(3.25)	0.81	0.13	0.64
Stock price - high ($)	—	—	—	—	—	—	—	12.13	14.50	12.38	13.63
Stock price - low ($)	—	—	—	—	—	—	—	9.75	7.88	9.00	10.25
Stock price - close ($)	(2.9%)	—	—	—	—	—	—	12.00	10.00	12.38	11.00
P/E - high	—	—	—	—	—	—	—	—	18	95	21
P/E - low	—	—	—	—	—	—	—	—	10	69	16
Dividends per share ($)	—	—	—	—	—	—	—	0.00	0.00	0.00	0.00
Book value per share ($)	(5.6%)	—	—	—	—	—	—	3.49	2.29	2.26	2.94
Employees	(5.4%)	44,048	45,000	31,900	46,500	47,000	47,000	34,300	33,400	28,900	26,700

1994 Year-end:
Debt ratio: 88.5%
Return on equity: 25.3%
Cash (mil.): $142
Current ratio: 1.18
Long-term debt (mil.): $2,625
No. of shares (mil.): 119
Dividends
  Yield: —
  Payout: —
Market value (mil.): $1,310

**Stock Price History
High/Low 1991–94**

PACCAR INC

OVERVIEW

PACCAR is the world's 3rd largest heavy-duty truck maker (after Freightliner and Navistar International). The Bellevue, Washington, company makes and sells worldwide Kenworth, Peterbilt, and Foden trucks, which altogether accounted for 90% of 1994 revenues. PACCAR's other businesses include truck leasing and financing services, oilfield pumps and equipment, winches, and medium-duty trucks. The company also sells automotive parts and accessories in the western US through 121 Al's Auto Supply and Grand Auto retailers.

The 1994 upswing in the US economy and low interest rates fueled record demand for PACCAR's trucks. The timely recent opening of a Washington plant has positioned the company to meet new orders; truck sales grew 28% in 1994. A $3.2 billion backlog in orders is expected to carry over well into 1996.

PACCAR is looking at new geographical markets and ways to increase production. In addition, it is discussing a 2nd joint venture with ZiL, Russia's largest truck manufacturer, to build Kenworth trucks and has agreed to distribute winches worldwide. The company may build a 3rd Peterbilt factory in the US.

Brothers Charles and James Pigott, descendants of PACCAR's founder, own 10.0% of the company, and BankAmerica owns 10.7%.

WHEN

William Pigott founded the Seattle Car Manufacturing Company in 1905 to produce railroad cars for timber transport. Meeting with immediate success, Pigott expanded production to other kinds of rail cars in 1906. The Seattle plant burned in 1907, and the company moved to near Renton, Washington. In 1911 Pigott renamed the company Seattle Car & Foundry.

In 1917 Seattle Car merged with the Twohy Brothers of Portland, and the new company, Pacific Car & Foundry, was sold to American Car & Foundry in 1924. Pacific Car then diversified into bus manufacturing, structural steel fabrications, and metal technology. A company metallurgist developed a strong, lightweight steel called Carcometal that was used in tractor equipment and winches.

When Pacific Car was in decline in 1934, the original founder's son, Paul Pigott, bought it; the company has remained under family management. Pigott added Hofius Steel and Equipment, as well as Tricoach, a bus manufacturer, in 1936. The company entered the truck manufacturing business with the 1945 purchase of Seattle-based Kenworth. It proved to be a shrewd move, as growth in the western US during the late 1940s and early 1950s led to an increased demand for trucks.

In the 1950s Pacific Car became the industry leader in mechanical refrigerator car production, began producing off-road, heavy trucks, and acquired Peterbilt Trucks of Oakland (1958). To augment its winch business, Pacific Car bought Canada's Gearmatic in 1963.

The company moved its headquarters to Bellevue in 1969 and changed its name to PACCAR in 1971. Acquisitions in the 1970s included those of Wagner Mining Equipment (1973); International Car, the largest US caboose producer (1975); and Braden Winch (1977). In 1980 PACCAR acquired Foden trucks of the UK.

A shift in demand toward smaller trucks caused heavy truck sales to drop 35% between 1979 and 1986, leading PACCAR to experiment with new markets and close 2 factories, the first closures in 41 years. In 1987 PACCAR built its first medium-duty truck, bought Trico Industries (oil drilling equipment), and entered the auto parts sales market.

In 1989 PACCAR surpassed Navistar as the industry leader in heavy truck sales, with 24.5% of the market. In 1990 truck demand hit a 9-year low. PACCAR responded by cutting its work force by 11% in 1990 and withdrawing from the auto parts wholesale market in 1991. The company lost leadership of the US heavy truck market to Navistar in 1991. In the following year PACCAR acquired a 21% interest in Wood Group ESP, a maker and servicer of oilfield equipment.

PACCAR formed a joint venture in 1993 with Caterpillar and ZiL to build trucks in Russia. That same year the company completed construction of a plant in Washington State and bought Caterpillar's line of winches.

In 1994 the company raised its stake in its joint venture VILPAC, owner of Mexico's leading heavy-duty truck maker, Kenworth Mexicana, from 49% to 55%. Also that year the company added new sales representation in Central and South America, Asia, and New Zealand, which expanded its coverage to over 40 countries.

In 1995 PACCAR started exploring business opportunities in China.

Nasdaq symbol: PCAR
Fiscal year ends: December 31

WHO

Chairman and CEO: Charles M. Pigott, age 65,
$897,116 pay
VC: Michael A. Tembreull, age 48, $329,385 pay
VC: Mark C. Pigott, age 40, $298,269 pay
President: David J. Hovind, age 54, $476,808 pay
EVP: William E. Boisvert, age 52, $320,000 pay
SVP: Gary S. Moore, age 51
VP and Controller: G. Don Hatchel, age 50
VP, General Counsel, and Secretary: G. Glen Morie,
age 52
VP Employee Relations (HR): Laurie L. Baker
VP: Louis J. Cattaneo
Treasurer: John J. Waggoner
Auditors: Ernst & Young LLP

WHERE

HQ: 777 106th Ave. NE, Bellevue, WA 98004
Phone: 206-455-7400
Fax: 206-453-4900

PACCAR has 15 manufacturing plants in California,
Ohio, Oklahoma, Pennsylvania, Tennessee, Texas, and
Washington as well as Australia, Canada, Mexico, and the
UK. Its 2 auto supply houses operate in 121 locations.

	1994 Sales		1994 Pretax Income	
	$ mil.	% of total	$ mil.	% of total
US	3,543	79	278	76
Canada	364	8	22	6
Other countries	591	13	67	18
Adjustments	(8)	—	(47)	—
Total	**4,490**	**100**	**320**	**100**

WHAT

	1994 Sales		1994 Pretax Income	
	$ mil.	% of total	$ mil.	% of total
Trucks	4,029	89	299	77
Financial services	205	5	58	15
Auto parts	172	4	4	1
Other	93	2	28	7
Adjustments	(9)	—	(69)	—
Total	**4,490**	**100**	**320**	**100**

Product Lines
Auto supply retailing (Al's Auto Supply, Grand Auto)
Financing and leasing programs for trucks
Heavy-duty trucks (Foden, Kenworth, Peterbilt)
Industrial winches (Braden, Carco, Gearmatic)
Medium-duty trucks
Oilfield extraction pumps (Kobe, Trico)
Truck parts

Selected Divisions, Subsidiaries, and Affiliates
Dynacraft (truck and automotive parts and supplies)
Kenworth Truck Company
PACCAR Automotive, Inc. (auto parts retailing)
PACCAR Financial Corp.
PACCAR International (export sales)
PACCAR Leasing Corp. (full-service truck leasing)
PACCAR Parts
PACCAR Technical Center (R&D and testing)
PACCAR U.K. Ltd. (Foden trucks)
PACCAR Winch Division
Peterbilt Motors Company
Trico Industries, Inc. (oilfield equipment)

KEY COMPETITORS

AutoZone	Fiat	Oshkosh Truck
Baker Hughes	Ford	Pep Boys
Cooper Industries	General Motors	Renault
DAF	McDermott	Sears
Daimler-Benz	Montgomery Ward	Trak Auto
Dresser	Navistar	Volvo

HOW MUCH

	9-Year Growth	1985	1986	1987	1988	1989	1990	1991	1992	1993	1994
Sales ($ mil.)	10.1%	1,893	1,796	2,448	3,112	3,523	2,778	2,339	2,735	3,542	4,490
Net income ($ mil.)	12.2%	73	54	113	176	242	64	40	65	142	205
Income as % of sales	—	3.9%	3.0%	4.6%	5.6%	6.9%	2.3%	1.7%	2.4%	4.0%	4.6%
Earnings per share ($)	13.0%	1.75	1.31	2.72	4.26	6.00	1.59	1.02	1.68	3.66	5.26
Stock price – high ($)	—	22.95	25.23	33.93	38.28	45.02	39.80	43.72	54.81	61.12	61.75
Stock price – low ($)	—	17.29	17.94	19.25	23.93	33.28	23.27	27.30	41.54	46.55	40.00
Stock price – close ($)	9.1%	20.23	20.34	24.80	35.67	37.19	28.06	42.20	49.81	53.29	45.25
P/E – high	—	13	19	13	9	8	25	43	33	19	12
P/E – low	—	10	14	7	6	6	15	27	25	15	8
Dividends per share ($)	0.5%	0.96	1.04	0.74	1.44	2.18	2.18	0.87	0.96	1.74	1.00
Book value per share ($)	6.5%	17.14	17.64	19.43	21.91	25.12	26.23	26.55	26.71	28.50	30.22
Employees	5.9%	8,683	8,323	11,090	13,709	13,077	11,586	10,191	10,977	11,800	14,600

1994 Year-end:
Debt ratio: 46.3%
Return on equity: 17.9%
Cash (mil.): $532
Current ratio: 1.53
Long-term debt (mil.): $1,011
No. of shares (mil.): 39
Dividends
  Yield: 2.3%
  Payout: 19.0%
Market value (mil.): $1,720

Stock Price History
High/Low 1985–94

PACIFIC ENTERPRISES

OVERVIEW

Based in Los Angeles, Pacific Enterprises is the holding company for Southern California Gas (SoCalGas), the US's largest natural gas distribution utility, which serves about 4.7 million customers in 535 cities and communities in Central and Southern California. Through its subsidiaries Pacific also operates interstate and offshore natural gas pipelines and builds electric generation plants that use alternative forms of energy (hydropower, geothermal).

In response to the deregulation of the natural gas industry, Pacific is restructuring its utility operations to make them more flexible. It has divided SoCalGas into 2 business units, separating residential and smaller business customers from major accounts. The company has also formed a new product development unit, an energy management services unit, and an international unit that will look for opportunities in Latin America and Asia.

In early 1995 Pacific Enterprises began layoffs of 480 employees as part of a cost-cutting plan designed to reduce expenses by $59 million a year.

WHEN

In 1886 Walter Cline and C. O. G. Miller started Pacific Lighting Company, a San Francisco gas lamp rental business. Competition from the increasingly popular electric lamp led them to expand into gas distribution. In 1889 they bought 3 Los Angeles gas and electric utilities, including Los Angeles Gas Company, and in 1890 added Los Angeles Electric Company to Pacific Lighting's growing list of utility properties. Cline then opened an office in Los Angeles to manage the company's activities in Southern California, while Miller remained in San Francisco.

Pacific Lighting consolidated in the 1920s, buying Southern Counties Gas and Industrial Fuel Supply in 1925, Santa Maria Gas in 1928, and a majority stake in Southern California Gas in 1929. In 1937 the company sold its Los Angeles electric properties to the city of Los Angeles in exchange for a long-term gas utility franchise agreement.

During WWII Pacific Lighting put idle gas plants to use making butadiene, an essential ingredient in the production of synthetic rubber. Population growth in Southern California doubled the number of the company's gas customers to almost 3 million between 1950 and 1965. Miller's son Robert served as CEO during this period and was succeeded by his son Paul in 1968.

The company diversified into oil and gas exploration and development in 1960. In 1967 it moved to Los Angeles and, marking its move into land development, bought Blackfield Hawaii Corporation (1969). Pacific Lighting's gas properties were merged in 1970, forming SoCalGas.

In the 1970s it got into and out of fruit growing and agriculture management. It bought Terra Resources in 1983, increasing its participation in oil and gas exploration, and more than doubled its land development operations by buying the Presley Companies (1984). Oil and gas prices fell, resulting in a $227 million charge in 1986. The company sold its land development businesses in 1987.

Pacific Lighting spent $900 million for Thrifty Corporation (drugstores, 1986) and $700 million for Sabine Corporation (oil and gas, 1988). In 1988 the company became Pacific Enterprises and bought Pay'n Save and Bi-Mart drugstores for $234 million. Following the company's $81 million loss in 1991, CEO Willis Wood began a radical restructuring. The company sold its North Sea oil and gas interests to 2 Dutch companies for $50 million.

In 1992 Pacific sold its Pay'n Save drugstore chain to Pay Less Drug Stores, a division of Kmart. Later that year Pacific sold Thrifty Corporation — which included 602 Thrifty Drug Stores — and its Big 5 Sporting Goods stores for $275 million to a group led by investment firm Leonard Green & Partners. It also sold its Canadian oil and gas exploration operations to Canada's Enerplus Group in 1992 and in 1993 sold its US oil and gas subsidiary to Hunt Oil for $371 million.

In 1994 the Northridge earthquake caused about 500 leaks in Pacific's distribution pipelines, cutting service to about 150,000 customers for up to 12 days. Also in 1994 Pacific settled 2 class-action lawsuits brought by shareholders angry with the company's failed diversification strategy. The $45 million settlement included $17 million from Pacific and the rest from auditors Deloitte and Touche and Pacific's insurers.

In 1995 the company and the U.S. Department of Energy's Argonne Lab announced that they had developed an environmentally friendly chemical that can help fight bacteria that create corrosion in pipes. Pacific Enterprises expects the treatment to save millions of dollars a year in operating costs.

NYSE symbol: PET
Fiscal year ends: December 31

WHO

Chairman and CEO: Willis B. Wood Jr., age 60,
$1,069,626 pay
President and COO: Richard D. Farman, age 59,
$726,250 pay
President, Southern California Gas Company: Warren I.
Mitchell, age 57, $462,000 pay
SVP Public Policy: Fredrick E. John, age 49
SVP Energy Management Services: Christopher R.
Sherman, age 42
**SVP Energy Distribution Services, Southern California
Gas Company:** Debra L. Reed, age 38
**SVP Energy Transportation Services, Southern
California Gas Company:** Lee M. Stewart, age 49
VP and General Counsel: Leslie E. LoBaugh Jr., age 49,
$361,250 pay
VP and Controller: Ralph Todaro, age 44
VP Human Resources: G. Joyce Rowland
Auditors: Deloitte & Touche LLP

WHERE

HQ: 555 W. Fifth St., Los Angeles, CA 90031-1001
Phone: 213-895-5000
Fax: 213-629-1225

Pacific Enterprises distributes natural gas in Southern
and Central California.

Selected Cities Served
Bakersfield
Burbank
Los Angeles
Palm Springs
San Bernadino
San Luis Obispo
Santa Barbara
Visalia

WHAT

	1994 Sales	
	$ mil.	% of total
Residential	1,713	63
Commercial & industrial	799	29
Utility electric generation	118	4
Wholesale	98	4
Adjustments	(64)	—
Total	**2,664**	**100**

Selected Subsidiaries
Pacific Energy (renewable energy source power plants
and facilities, centralized heating and air conditioning
plants)
Pacific Enterprises International (overseas power plant
operations)
Pacific Interstate Co. (natural gas transmission)
Pacific Interstate Offshore Co.
Pacific Interstate Transmission Co.
Pacific Offshore Pipeline Co.
Southern California Gas Co. (SoCalGas)
Southern California Gas Tower (15% limited partnership
interest in Los Angeles office building)

KEY COMPETITORS

AES	Pacific Gas and Electric
California Energy	Panhandle Eastern
Catalyst Energy	SCEcorp
Destec Energy	Southern Co.
Duke Power	Tenneco
Enron	Transco Energy
FPL	Unocal
General Electric	USX–Delhi
NGC	Westinghouse
Occidental	Wheelabrator
Ogden	Williams Cos.

HOW MUCH

	9-Year Growth	1985	1986	1987	1988	1989	1990	1991	1992	1993	1994
Sales ($ mil.)	(6.9%)	5,083	5,324	5,339	5,932	6,762	6,923	6,599	2,900	2,899	2,664
Net income ($ mil.)	1.1%	156	84	476	222	211	(43)	(88)	(550)	181	172
Income as % of sales	—	3.0%	1.5%	8.8%	3.7%	3.1%	—	—	—	6.2%	6.5%
Earnings per share ($)	(7.1%)	3.80	1.34	4.14	3.51	3.05	(0.86)	(1.45)	(7.57)	2.06	1.95
Stock price – high ($)	—	48.75	57.50	61.25	52.88	53.75	52.00	43.38	27.38	27.38	24.50
Stock price – low ($)	—	39.00	45.00	45.75	35.63	37.13	34.25	23.25	17.38	18.50	19.25
Stock price – close ($)	(8.8%)	48.50	49.00	49.75	37.50	50.50	38.88	26.25	18.50	23.75	21.25
P/E – high	—	13	43	15	15	18	—	—	—	13	13
P/E – low	—	10	34	11	10	12	—	—	—	9	10
Dividends per share ($)	(10.3%)	3.36	3.48	3.48	3.48	3.48	3.48	2.62	0.44	0.60	1.26
Book value per share ($)	(9.3%)	35.52	28.12	29.03	31.22	27.55	27.41	23.27	12.87	12.19	14.74
Employees	(11.9%)	26,550	26,571	27,928	40,538	43,891	42,370	40,953	9,884	9,300	8,500

1994 Year-end:
Debt ratio: 57.8%
Return on equity: 15.4%
Cash (mil.): $287
Current ratio: 1.15
Long-term debt (mil.): $1,420
No. of shares (mil.): 82
Dividends
  Yield: 5.9%
  Payout: 64.6%
Market value (mil.): $1,745

Stock Price History
High/Low 1985–94

PACIFIC GAS AND ELECTRIC COMPANY

OVERVIEW

Pacific Gas & Electric (PG&E) is the largest publicly owned electric and gas utility in the US, serving approximately 4.4 million electric customers and 3.5 million gas customers throughout a 94,000-square-mile territory in Northern and central California.

Based in San Francisco, the company obtains electricity from a number of sources, including its Diablo Canyon nuclear power plant, fossil-fuel plants, hydroelectric and geothermal systems, and such renewable sources as wind power and solar power. PG&E pipes its natural gas in from Canada, the southwestern US, and California.

The company's PG&E Enterprises subsidiary manages nonutility projects that range from real estate development (PG&E Properties) to the operation and maintenance of independent power facilities and the operation of independent power plants (U.S. Operating Services Company). The company is also becoming a major player in the independent power market through U.S. Generating Company (USGen), a partnership with Bechtel Group. In the US, USGen has interests in 12 power plants and is building 5 more. PG&E is also working with Bechtel to pursue power projects in Europe, Asia, and Latin America.

With California leading the charge for deregulation of the power industry and with the recent deregulation of the natural gas industry by the federal government, PG&E is facing increased competition. In response it has focused on cutting costs and increasing efficiency. The company also put a freeze on retail electric prices through 1996.

WHEN

Peter Donahue founded the first gas company in the western US, San Francisco Gas, in 1852. This company became San Francisco Gas & Electric (SFG&E) in 1896 after merging with Edison Light & Power.

Meanwhile, in San Francisco, money broker George Roe and other investors founded California Electric Light (1879), the first electric utility in the US, predating Edison's New York Pearl Street Station by 3 years. California Electric and SFG&E consolidated in 1905 to form Pacific Gas and Electric (PG&E).

In 1928 PG&E discovered natural gas reserves in California's Kings County, and in 1930 it began converting more than 2.5 million appliances to burn this fuel — the largest conversion in history. The company began exploring for out-of-state gas supplies in the 1950s, first in Texas and New Mexico and then in western Canada.

PG&E operated the world's first private atomic power plant (Vallecitos) in 1957 and developed the first geothermal plant (the Geysers) to operate in North America in 1960. PG&E's Humboldt Bay facility (completed in 1963) was one of the world's first nuclear plants to produce electricity at a cost comparable to conventional plants.

From its inception through the late 1970s, PG&E bought about 500 utilities (water, gas, and electric) and by 1978 was serving about 9 million customers. The company sold the last of its water systems by 1985, the same year Unit 1 of the Diablo Canyon nuclear facility went on line. Diablo Canyon, begun in 1968, had been plagued by delays and cost overruns (a design problem discovered in 1981 resulted in a 15-month review of construction plans and methods). Unit 2 was in operation by 1986. In 1988, instead of utilizing traditional rate structures, PG&E started basing revenues chiefly on how much electricity Diablo Canyon generates, creating a direct relationship between the plant's performance and the company's earnings. Settlement of the Diablo Canyon rate issues in 1988 and an unscheduled refueling outage resulted in negative earnings for that year.

Under natural gas deregulation, customers began to bypass PG&E in the mid-1980s (finding it cheaper to generate their own electricity or buy gas directly from suppliers). PG&E responded by eliminating about 2,500 jobs in 1987; in 1990 it announced a 3-year phaseout of about 300 management jobs.

In 1991 PG&E launched a 10-year initiative to conserve energy and formed a joint venture with Chevron to install natural gas pumps at certain California Chevron filling stations.

Three major Canadian gas producers filed suit against PG&E in 1992 for failure to fulfill contractual gas purchases. PG&E, which had bought gas under contract from a pool of Canadian producers for decades, suddenly needed less gas because of deregulation. In 1993 PG&E settled the claims brought by the gas producers for $210 million.

In 1995, after severe winter storms damaged several of its facilities, PG&E cancelled a planned layoff of about 800 employees in order to accelerate its maintenance program.

NYSE symbol: PCG
Fiscal year ends: December 31

WHO

Chairman and CEO: Stanley T. Skinner, age 57,
$684,173 pay (prior to promotion)
President and COO: Robert D. Glynn Jr., age 52,
$294,817 pay (prior to promotion)
EVP: James D. Shiffer, age 56, $371,776 pay
**SVP and General Manager, Nuclear Power Generation
Business Unit:** Gregory M. Rueger, age 44,
$280,358 pay
SVP and General Counsel: Bruce R. Worthington,
age 45
SVP and CFO: Gordon R. Smith, age 46
SVP Corporate Services (HR): Thomas W. High, age 47
Auditors: Arthur Andersen & Co, SC

WHERE

HQ: 77 Beale St., PO Box 770000, San Francisco, CA
94177
Phone: 415-973-7000
Fax: 415-543-7813

Generating Facilities

Fossil Fueled
Contra Costa (Contra Costa County)
Humboldt Bay (Humboldt County)
Hunters Point (San Francisco County)
Morro Bay (San Luis Obispo County)
Moss Landing (Monterey County)
Oakland (Alameda County)
Pittsburg (Contra Costa County)
Potrero (San Francisco County)

Geothermal
The Geysers (Sonoma and Lake Counties)

Hydroelectric
Conventional plants (16 counties)
Helms Pumped Storage Plant (Fresno County)

Nuclear
Diablo Canyon (San Luis Obispo County)

WHAT

	1994 Sales	
	$ mil.	% of total
Electric	8,028	77
Gas	2,419	23
Total	**10,447**	**100**

	1994 Power Sources
	% of total
Generation from others	45
Fossil fuels	28
Nuclear	14
Hydroelectric	7
Geothermal	6
Total	**100**

Subsidiaries
Alberta and Southern Gas Co. Ltd. (Canada-based gas supplier)
Pacific Gas Transmission Co.
PG&E Enterprises
DALEN Resources Corp. (natural gas and oil exploration)
PG&E Properties, Inc. (real estate development)
U.S. Generating Co. (partnership with Bechtel Group; builds, owns, and manages independent power projects)
U.S. Operating Services Co. (partnership with Bechtel Group, provides power facilities with operations and maintenance services)

KEY COMPETITORS

AES	FPL
California Energy	General Electric
Coastal	Koch
Columbia Gas	Occidental
Destec Energy	Pacific Enterprises
Duke Power	Panhandle Eastern
El Paso Natural Gas	Tenneco
Enron	Transco Energy

HOW MUCH

	9-Year Growth	1985	1986	1987	1988	1989	1990	1991	1992	1993	1994
Sales ($ mil.)	2.4%	8,431	7,817	7,186	7,646	8,588	9,470	9,778	10,296	10,582	10,447
Net income ($ mil.)	(0.3%)	1,031	1,081	597	62	901	987	1,026	1,171	1,065	1,008
Income as % of sales	—	12.2%	13.8%	8.3%	0.8%	10.5%	10.4%	10.5%	11.4%	10.1%	9.6%
Earnings per share ($)	(2.0%)	2.65	2.60	1.29	(0.10)	1.90	2.10	2.24	2.58	2.33	2.21
Stock price – high ($)	—	20.38	27.50	27.88	18.38	22.00	25.63	32.63	34.63	36.75	35.00
Stock price – low ($)	—	16.00	18.75	15.00	14.00	17.25	20.00	24.00	29.00	31.75	21.38
Stock price – close ($)	2.2%	20.00	24.25	16.25	17.50	22.00	25.00	32.50	33.13	35.13	24.38
P/E – high	—	8	11	22	—	12	12	15	13	16	16
P/E – low	—	6	7	12	—	9	10	11	11	14	10
Dividends per share ($)	1.0%	1.78	1.88	1.92	1.79	1.40	1.49	1.61	1.73	1.85	1.94
Book value per share ($)	1.2%	18.04	19.06	19.70	16.79	17.38	17.86	18.40	19.41	19.77	20.07
Employees	(3.7%)	29,600	29,200	27,300	26,600	26,200	26,200	26,700	26,600	23,000	21,000

1994 Year-end:
Debt ratio: 50.4%
Return on equity: 11.8%
Cash (mil.): $137
Current ratio: 0.99
Long-term debt (mil.): $8,675
No. of shares (mil.): 430
Dividends
  Yield: 8.0%
  Payout: 87.8%
Market value (mil.): $10,489

Stock Price History
High/Low 1985–94

PACIFIC TELESIS GROUP

OVERVIEW

Based in San Francisco, Pacific Telesis provides local and medium distance telecommunications services and access to long distance service in California and Nevada.

Since January 1, 1995, the California Public Utilities Commission has permitted AT&T, MCI, and other companies to compete against Pacific Bell (one of the company's Bell operating companies) in its medium distance (toll) market. As a result, Pacific Bell has reduced its toll rates by about 40%. Pacific Bell is also facing a similar fate in its local telecommunications market later this year, but for now it has increased its basic (local) service rate from $8.35 to $11.25 per month. Separately, the Public Utilities Commission enacted a new

regulatory framework based on a price-cap formula. As a result, Pacific Bell is facing price reductions of about $230 million in 1995.

Pacific Telesis is focusing on new communications and information services in California. The company is building a $16 billion statewide interactive video network and owns licenses for wireless video services in Southern California (from purchasing Cross Country Wireless). Pacific Telesis is also developing new video programming and channels with Bell Atlantic, NYNEX, and Creative Artists Agency. In addition, Pacific Telesis expects to offer personal communications services in 1997 with its purchase of 2 licenses (costing $700 million) in California and Nevada.

WHEN

The Pacific and Nevada Bell companies, owned by Pacific Telesis, were formerly 2 of AT&T's 22 operating companies. California's first exchange was opened in 1878 in San Francisco, the city that in 1915 was one end (with New York as the other) of the first coast-to-coast telephone call.

By 1980 AT&T was rumored to be considering Pacific Bell's sale. Pacific Bell's battles with the California Public Utilities Commission (CPUC) had soured relations with AT&T to the point that it claimed AT&T had denied it equity capital. But during 1980 and 1981, instead of selling, AT&T hired a new management team for the company. Donald Guinn, CEO of Pacific Bell (and chairman and CEO of Pacific Telesis from 1984 to 1988), and new CFO John Hulse took steps to cut spending and improve relations with the CPUC.

Pacific Bell was folded into parent Pacific Telesis Group in 1984 after divestiture from AT&T. Pacific Telesis gained California and Nevada phone territories, 1/7 interest in Bell Communications Research (R&D arm shared by the Bell companies), and PacTel Cellular.

In 1986 the CPUC ordered Pacific Bell to refund subscribers for fees derived from deceptive marketing practices and ordered a rate refund instead of the requested hike. But unregulated enterprises began to fuel Pacific Telesis's growth. The 1986 purchase of Communications Industries made Pacific Telesis a top player in cellular radio and paging, giving it 5 cellular and 14 paging operations outside its territory. In 1988 Guinn retired. The next year Pacific Telesis bought 8.5% of International Digital Communications, which was formed with several Japanese companies con-

structing a transpacific fiber-optic cable. Pacific Telesis owns 26% of Mannesmann Mobilfunk, a group licensed in 1989 to supply Germany with its first privately owned cellular phone system.

The company agreed to buy an option for 75% of TC Cable, a Chicago cable TV franchise, and ventured into the UK cable market. In 1990 the company agreed to combine its Ohio and Michigan cellular units with those of Cellular Communications (CCI), gaining the option to acquire CCI over several years.

Pacific Telesis sold its interest in UK's Microtel to British Aerospace in 1991. Also in 1991 it agreed to combine cellular services in San Francisco, San Jose, Dallas, and Kansas City with those of McCaw Cellular. In 1992 Pacific Telesis bought 20% of a French mobile radio business that it will operate jointly with construction firm Bouygues.

In 1993 the company acquired a 51% interest in NordicTel Holdings, a Swedish provider of cellular services under the name Europolitan.

Pacific Telesis spun off its AirTouch wireless communications unit and sold the last of its UK cable operations in 1994. That same year it partnered with Sony to pipe movies into theaters on fiber-optic cable. Also in 1994, David Dorman joined the company as president of Pacific Bell, and Michael Fitzpatrick became president of Pacific Telesis Enterprises.

In 1995 Pacific Telesis announced plans to offer businesses and consumers access to the Internet. Pacific Telesis formed a marketing partnership with Sun Microsystems, Cisco Systems, and Netscape Communications to offer this service.

NYSE symbol: PAC
Fiscal year ends: December 31

Chairman, President, and CEO: Philip J. Quigley, age 52, $933,196 pay
President and CEO, Pacific Bell: David W. Dorman, age 41, $808,750 pay
President and CEO, Pacific Telesis Enterprises: Michael J. Fitzpatrick, age 46, $606,675 pay
EVP General Counsel, External Affairs, and Secretary: Richard W. Odgers, age 58, $519,425 pay
EVP Human Resources: Jim R. Moberg, age 59, $519,425 pay
EVP, CFO, and Treasurer: William E. Downing, age 55
VP Corporate Strategy and Development: Robert L. Barada, age 50
VP Government Relations, Public Affairs, and Corporate Communications: Thomas O. Moulton Jr.
VP Pacific Telesis Group — Washington: Ronald F. Stowe
President and CEO, Nevada Bell: MacLellan E. King Jr.
President and CEO Video and Information Services, Pacific Telesis Enterprises: Lee G. Camp
President and CEO Mobile Services, Pacific Telesis Enterprises: Lyndon R. Daniels
President and CEO Directory Services, Pacific Telesis Enterprises: Forrest E. Miller
EVP Technology and Services Group, Pacific Bell: Martin A. Kaplan
EVP California Markets, Pacific Bell: Robert Lee
Auditors: Coopers & Lybrand L.L.P.

WHERE

HQ: 130 Kearny St., San Francisco, CA 94108
Phone: 415-394-3000
Fax: 415-362-2913 (External Affairs)

Pacific Telesis provides communications and information services in California and Nevada.

WHAT

	1994 Sales	
	$ mil.	% of total
Local service	3,455	37
Toll service	2,006	22
Network access — interstate	1,612	18
Network access — intrastate	734	8
Other service	1,428	15
Total	**9,235**	**100**

Major Subsidiaries
Bell Communications Research, Inc. (1/7)
Nevada Bell
Pacific Bell
Pacific Bell Directory (directory publishing)
Pacific Bell Information Services (voice mail, call management)
Pacific Bell Mobile Services (personal communications services)
Pacific Telesis Electronic Publishing Services
Pacific Telesis Video Services (interactive video services)
Pacific Telesis Wireless Broadband Services (wireless video services)
PacTel Cable (option to purchase 75% of Prime Cable of Chicago)
PacTel Capital Resources (corporate funding)
PacTel Re Insurance Co., Inc.
Telesis Foundation (charitable grants)
Telesis Technologies Laboratory (wireless video distribution)

KEY COMPETITORS

American Business	MCI	TCI Intl.
Information	MFS	Time Warner
Ameritech	Communications	U.S. Long
AT&T	NYNEX	Distance
Bell Atlantic	SBC	U S WEST
BellSouth	Communications	Viacom
Cable & Wireless	Sprint	

HOW MUCH

	9-Year Growth	1985	1986	1987	1988	1989	1990	1991	1992	1993	1994
Sales ($ mil.)	0.5%	8,836	9,337	9,503	9,483	9,593	9,716	9,895	9,935	9,244	9,235
Net income ($ mil.)	2.5%	929	1,079	950	1,188	1,242	1,030	1,015	1,142	220	1,159
Income as % of sales	—	10.5%	11.6%	10.0%	12.5%	12.9%	10.6%	10.3%	11.5%	2.4%	12.6%
Earnings per share ($)	2.1%	2.27	2.51	2.21	2.81	3.02	2.59	2.58	2.83	0.53	2.73
Stock price – high ($)	—	12.92	18.74	20.32	19.57	30.78	31.00	27.39	28.29	35.67	34.92
Stock price – low ($)	—	10.03	11.66	5.42	14.97	18.29	21.82	23.18	22.20	26.04	28.25
Stock price – close ($)	9.4%	12.74	16.03	16.03	18.59	30.33	27.24	26.86	26.71	32.66	28.50
P/E – high	—	6	8	9	7	10	12	11	10	67	13
P/E – low	—	4	5	3	5	6	8	9	8	49	10
Dividends per share ($)	5.0%	1.41	1.50	1.61	1.73	1.85	1.99	2.11	2.17	2.18	2.18
Book value per share ($)	(3.5%)	17.04	18.01	18.72	19.96	18.92	18.53	19.27	21.87	18.40	12.34
Employees	(3.6%)	71,488	74,939	71,877	69,696	68,452	65,829	62,236	61,346	60,050	51,590

1994 Year-end:
Debt ratio: 49.6%
Return on equity: 17.8%
Cash (mil.): $135
Current ratio: 0.83
Long-term debt (mil.): $4,897
No. of shares (mil.): 424
Dividends
  Yield: 7.6%
  Payout: 79.9%
Market value (mil.): $12,086

**Stock Price History
High/Low 1985–94**

PACIFICARE HEALTH SYSTEMS, INC.

OVERVIEW

A more accurate name ought to be in store for PacifiCare Health Systems, a Cypress, California–based company that is becoming a nationwide health care operator. Though most of its nearly 1.4 million members reside on the West Coast, PacifiCare has turned its attention to the rest of the US. In 1994 the company agreed with Affordable Medical Networks to form a preferred provider organization (PPO) for multistate employers in 46 states.

As employers strive to cut insurance costs, more businesses are turning to health maintenance organizations (HMOs), which pay set amounts per person or per procedure rather than all or part of the bill. The ranks of HMO providers are thinning, however, as larger companies gobble up their smaller competitors. PacifiCare is one of the 10 largest HMO

providers in the US, and like many of its major rivals, the company is loaded with cash. Combined with a $250 million line of credit obtained in late 1994, that money has PacifiCare poised for a major shopping spree.

PacifiCare, which has never declared even a quarterly loss since going public in 1985, gets 56% of its $2.9 billion in revenues from its Secure Horizons Medicare program. Based on a fee-per-member premium, Secure Horizons is the largest risk-contract Medicare program in the nation. Only 2 million of the 36 million Medicare beneficiaries are in risk plans, and PacifiCare sees substantial growth in that area.

In December 1994 PacifiCare's pharmacy benefit management subsidiary bought Preferred Solutions, a PBM company serving about 1 million members.

WHEN

PacifiCare was formed as a nonprofit health care corporation in 1975 by the Lutheran Hospital Society (founded 1920; one of the largest health care systems in Los Angeles). In 1978 the company began operating as a federally qualified HMO. HMOs outside California received stiff physician resistance, and they were illegal in 38 states. In 1981 PacifiCare started a Medicare program, Secure Horizons.

Lutheran Hospital Society converted PacifiCare from a nonprofit to a for-profit corporation in 1984 and took the company public in 1985, retaining a 66% interest in the new company. (Lutheran Health Services later merged with HealthWest Foundation, also of Los Angeles, to form UniHealth, one of the US's largest nonprofit health care companies.) Also that year PacifiCare expanded into Oregon, although to conform to Oregon's regulations it had to form a nonprofit HMO and award itself a management contract for its administration.

The company expanded rapidly, moving into Oklahoma, Oregon, and Texas in 1986 and buying a life insurance company, Columbia General Life, in Indiana. The company used the 1987 stock market crash to repurchase shares. That same year it expanded its Texas operations from San Antonio to Austin.

In 1988 PacifiCare expanded its Oklahoma operations by purchasing an existing HMO, Multi-Med, in Oklahoma City. Within 2 years the company found itself so large that it moved to new quarters in Cypress, California. In 1991 it received permission from the state

to begin operating in the Northern California market, Kaiser's home turf.

As it grew, PacifiCare moved into new fields within the health care industry, forming a subsidiary to offer centralized billing and account services to multistate employers, opening staff-model pharmacies (in which the staff is employed by PacifiCare), and buying ExecuFit, a wellness and health education provider.

PacifiCare has pursued alliances with other health care–related companies and increased the amount of business it does with federal and state government agencies. To facilitate this expansion by allowing the company to offer stock for new purchases, UniHealth has gradually decreased its interest, and in 1993 its ownership of PacifiCare fell below 50%.

In 1993 the company began venturing beyond its traditional geographic area. First, PacifiCare purchased a Miami-area HMO; then it went on to win a CHAMPUS (Civilian Health and Medical Program for the Uniformed Services) contract to provide care to military personnel and dependents in 19 northeastern and midwestern states.

The company also expanded its scope in 1994 by contracting to provide Medi-Cal (California's Medicaid system) with HMO services that will give beneficiaries access to routine and preventive care as an alternative to expensive, time-consuming emergency room visits. In addition, PacifiCare forged an alliance with Liberty Mutual, the US's foremost workers' compensation insurance company, to provide managed care for injured workers.

Nasdaq symbol: PHSYA
Fiscal year ends: September 30

WHO

Chairman: Terry Hartshorn, age 49
President and CEO: Alan R. Hoops, age 47,
$847,803 pay
EVP and Chief Medical Officer: Roger S. Taylor, age 49,
$450,108 pay
EVP and COO: Jeffrey M. Folick, age 47, $429,904 pay
EVP and CFO: Wayne B. Lowell, age 39, $406,004 pay
SVP and Corporate Controller: Fred V. Ryder, age 38
SVP and Chief Information Officer: James Williams,
age 48
SVP Corporate Marketing: William L. Young, age 49
SVP Human Resources: Wanda Lee, age 53
General Counsel and Secretary: Joseph S. Konowiecki,
age 41
Auditors: Ernst & Young LLP

WHERE

HQ: 5995 Plaza Dr., Cypress, CA 90630-5028
Phone: 714-952-1121
Fax: 714-220-3725

PacifiCare operates health maintenance organizations
(HMOs) in California, Florida, Oklahoma, Oregon, Texas,
and Washington and manages health care programs for
Medicare and Medicaid members.

	1994 Membership	
	No. of members	% of total
California	922,284	68
Oklahoma	125,050	9
Texas	99,154	7
Oregon	97,128	7
Florida	68,604	5
Washington	45,999	4
Total	**1,358,219**	**100**

WHAT

	1994 Membership	
	No. of members	% of total
Commercial	949,124	70
Medicare & Medicaid	409,095	30
Total	**1,358,219**	**100**

	1994 Sales	
	$ mil.	% of total
Medicare & Medicaid premiums	1,618	56
Commercial premiums	1,237	43
Other	38	1
Total	**2,893**	**100**

Selected Services

Dental and vision care	Physical therapy
Hospital care	Prescription drugs
Laboratory and radiology services	Primary care
Medicare risk management	Psychological counseling
Military health care management	Skilled nursing care
Pharmacy benefit management	Specialty physician care

KEY COMPETITORS

Aetna	Humana
Blue Cross	John Hancock
Chubb	Kaiser Foundation Health
CIGNA	Plan
Columbia/HCA	Maxicare Health Plans
Coventry	Prudential
FHP International	Ramsay Health Care
Foundation	United HealthCare
Group Health Co-op	U.S. Healthcare
of Puget Sound	Value Health
Health Systems	WellPoint Health Networks

HOW MUCH

	9-Year Growth	1985	1986	1987	1988	1989	1990	1991	1992	1993	1994
Sales ($ mil.)	42.6%	90	172	306	428	650	976	1,242	1,686	2,221	2,893
Net income ($ mil.)	34.9%	6	3	3	6	11	18	26	44	63	85
Income as % of assets	—	6.3%	1.8%	0.1%	1.4%	1.2%	1.8%	2.1%	2.6%	2.8%	2.9%
Earnings per share ($)	21.3%	0.53	0.25	0.25	0.57	0.96	1.48	2.20	1.78	2.25	3.02
Stock price – high ($)	—	5.75	4.31	3.41	3.13	15.13	13.75	21.25	51.00	57.50	79.50
Stock price – low ($)	—	3.81	2.56	1.31	1.53	3.13	6.00	7.25	18.63	25.50	37.25
Stock price – close ($)	35.2%	4.31	2.56	1.44	3.06	12.75	8.13	19.75	51.00	37.38	65.13
P/E – high	—	11	17	14	6	16	9	10	29	26	26
P/E – low	—	7	10	5	3	3	4	3	11	11	12
Dividends per share ($)	—	0.00	0.00	0.00	0.00	0.00	0.00	0.00	0.00	0.00	0.00
Book value per share ($)	23.1%	2.31	2.54	2.76	3.26	4.08	6.55	8.76	7.76	11.71	15.02
Employees	36.1%	241	397	478	616	1,024	1,393	1,647	2,186	2,603	3,856

1994 Year-end:
Debt ratio: 20.9%
Return on equity: 23.1%
Cash (mil.): $711
Current ratio: 1.39
Long-term debt (mil.): $101
No. of shares (mil.): 28
Dividends
  Yield: —
  Payout: —
Market value (mil.): $1,793

**Stock Price History
High/Low 1985–94**

PACKARD BELL ELECTRONICS, INC.

OVERVIEW

Westlake Village, California–based Packard Bell is the #1 seller of PCs in mass-market retail channels, with a 48% market share, and in late 1994 Packard Bell became the largest PC maker in the US. The company has embraced the new Pentium chip, selling a higher percentage of Pentium-based machines than any other manufacturer. Despite its name the entrepreneurial company is not related to either computer giant Hewlett-Packard or the once mighty telephone behemoth Ma Bell.

Led by CEO Beny Alagem, the company pioneered the idea of selling personal computers to consumers through retail chains. Packard Bell's retail distributors include Wal-Mart, Sears, Price/Costco, and Montgomery Ward. Packard Bell overtook former market share leaders IBM and Compaq (which relied on selling largely to corporations) thanks to the surge in the sales of computers for home use. With its big presence in retail outlets, Packard Bell has been the computer of choice for novice buyers who don't want to go to computer stores for fear of being overwhelmed by tech-talk. Packard Bell makes its products as user-friendly as possible; it color-codes cables for easy setup and provides software, called *Navigator*, that helps new users learn to use Windows. However, the company offers only a one-year warranty, compared with an industry standard of 3 years.

Packard Bell hopes to increase international sales from 15% to as much as 50% in the next few years.

In 1995 the company announced that it would sell a 20% interest to Japanese computer maker NEC for $170 million. The move was widely seen as confirming industry views that, despite its huge market share, Packard Bell has been struggling financially. As part of the deal, France's Groupe Bull paid $30 million to maintain its 19.9% stake.

Founders Beny Alagem, Alex Sandel, and Jason Barzilay, along with a number of senior executives, own the remainder of the privately held company.

WHEN

Israeli immigrants Beny Alagem, Jason Barzilay, and Alex Sandel owned Cal Circuit Abco, a computer component distribution company, when they decided to get into the PC business in the mid-1980s. With so many upstarts doing the same thing, they wanted something to set their company apart, something that would give a prospective buyer the feeling that the company would be around for a while to provide service.

They found what they were looking for in late 1985 when Alagem acquired the Packard Bell name from Teledyne for less than $100,000. The original Packard Bell made radios beginning in the 1920s and later moved into TV manufacturing, but by the mid-1980s it was defunct. Having the name of a company that had been around since the 1920s gave their products an instant heritage, and the inferences consumers might make with respect to the better-known Hewlett-Packard and Bell Telephone didn't hurt either. Alagem, Barzilay, and Sandel founded their computer company, Packard Bell, in 1986.

The next year the new company shipped its first PCs to mass-market retail stores, a channel its competitors had avoided because of the risks of high return rates. As part of its strategy of making its products as user-friendly as possible, Packard Bell preloaded its machines with operating systems, applications, and entertainment software. In 1988 the firm became the first PC maker to offer toll-free technical support, and in 1989 it became the first to provide on-site service in customers' homes.

By 1990 the company had more than $500 million in sales and was earning high marks for the reliability of its machines. It earned low marks for technical support, however, in part because its users tended to need more help, which overloaded phone lines. In response, the company beefed up its technical staff. In 1991 Packard Bell moved into Europe, opening a marketing headquarters in Paris and a factory in the Netherlands.

In 1992, with multimedia just beginning to make waves, Packard Bell began offering fully configured multimedia systems. Also in 1992 the company announced plans to go public, but when it posted less-than-stellar financial numbers (partly because of a high number of returns), investors balked and the IPO was withdrawn. However, to compete with the likes of IBM and Compaq, who were beginning to move in on its turf, Packard Bell needed cash, so in 1993 it sold 19.9% of the company to Groupe Bull.

The company expanded its product lines in 1994, adding several software products, including children's storybook titles. In 1995 Packard Bell launched Spectria, a multimedia PC with a built-in monitor.

Private company
Fiscal year ends: December 31

WHO

Chairman, President, and CEO: Beny Alagem, age 42
COO: Brent Cohen
VC Finance and Strategic Planning: Jeffrey Scheinrock
VP Marketing: Mal D. Ransom
VP Treasury and Planning: Michael Burney
VP Human Resources: Larry Levinsohn

WHERE

HQ: 31717 La Tienda Dr., Westlake Village, CA 91362
Phone: 818-865-1555
Fax: 818-865-0379

Offices
Argentina
Australia
Austria
Brazil
Canada
Chile
China
Czech Republic
Denmark
Finland
France
Germany
Hong Kong
Hungary
India
Israel
Italy
Japan
Mexico
The Netherlands
New Zealand
Norway
Poland
Portugal
Russia
South Africa
Spain
Sweden
Switzerland
UK
US

WHAT

Selected Brand Names
Axcel
Executive
Force
Legend
Packard Bell
Packmate

Products
Monitors
Multimedia PCs
PCs
Software
  Navigator

KEY COMPETITORS

Acer
Advanced Logic Research
Amstrad
Apple
AST
Compaq
CompuAdd
CompuCom
Data General
DEC
Dell
Fujitsu
Gateway 2000
Hewlett-Packard
Hitachi
Honeywell
Hyundai
IBM
Matsushita
Micron Technology
NEC
Oki
Olivetti
Power Computing
Sharp
Siemens
Toshiba
Vobis

HOW MUCH

	Annual Growth	1985	1986	1987	1988	1989	1990	1991	1992	1993	1994
Estimated sales ($ mil.)	58.7%	—	—	—	188	338	518	676	925	1,250	3,000
Est. net income ($ mil.)	170.5%	—	—	—	—	—	—	5	—	48	99
Income as % of sales	—	—	—	—	—	—	—	0.7%	—	3.8%	3.3%
Employees	41.4%	—	—	—	—	—	—	—	2,000	2,600	4,000

PACKARD BELL ▆ Estimated Sales ($ mil.) 1988–94

PAINE WEBBER GROUP INC.

OVERVIEW

It was a quiet wedding for Wall Street. In 1994 Paine Webber and Kidder, Peabody joined forces. The bride, Kidder, Peabody, was given away by GE and will take the groom's name. In this way Paine Webber's less-than-stellar investment banking operations will receive a boost and GE rids itself of a drag on earnings.

New York–based Paine Webber serves a varied clientele, offering retail brokerage services, investment banking, municipal securities underwriting, real estate services, institutional stock and bond trading, asset management (through its Mitchell Hutchins subsidiaries), and transaction services.

The cost of the Kidder, Peabody transaction, though a relatively modest $670 million (plus GE's acquisition of 21.6% of Paine Webber's stock), contributed to an 87% decline in earnings for 1994 (to $32 million). But the primary factor in this stunning reduction was the bond market crash and the subsequently reduced volume of bond and equity issues. The effect of the crash was so severe for one of Paine Webber's bond mutual funds (primarily because of derivatives-related losses) that the company felt forced to support the fund's value, at a cost of a $34 million charge against earnings.

WHEN

William Paine and Wallace Webber, 2 former clerks at Boston's Blackstone National Bank, opened a brokerage house in 1880. The firm joined the New York Stock Exchange in 1890 and bought seats on the Chicago Board of Trade in 1909 and the Chicago Stock Exchange in 1916.

The company opened its first branch in 1899, in Houghton, Michigan, the headquarters of copper companies that Paine Webber had helped underwrite. After WWI the company expanded rapidly during the bull market of the 1920s. The Depression forced the firm to eliminate offices.

In 1942 Paine Webber merged with another Boston brokerage house, Jackson and Curtis, formed by Charles Cabot Jackson and Laurence Curtis in 1879. Paine, Webber, Jackson & Curtis moved its offices from Boston to New York in 1963 and broadened its national scope by buying Kansas City brokerage Barret Fitch North (1967) and Richmond, Virginia–based Abbott, Proctor & Paine (no relation; 1970). The firm also launched overseas offices in London and Tokyo (1973).

Paine Webber converted from a partnership to a corporation in 1970 and went public in 1972, creating a holding company for its operations — Paine Webber Group Inc. The company added Mitchell Hutchins (equity research, 1977) and Blyth Eastman Dillon (investment banking, 1979). Blyth executives defected, taking customers with them, and Paine Webber was late bringing its new bank into play during the M&A craze of the 1980s.

Donald Marron, named CEO in 1980, continued to expand the company, buying Houston-based Rotan Mosle and First Mid America, a Nebraska company. After the 1987 stock market crash, Marron, who had begun his career running his own investment bank at age 25, aggressively restructured the company and sold operations, including the commercial paper business (1987) and its venture capital unit (1988). In late 1987 Japanese insurance company Yasuda injected capital for an equity stake that grew to 20% by 1990. A bridge loan to financially beleaguered Federated Department Stores (1988) dogged Paine Webber into 1990, when the company curtailed merchant banking and increased reserves against bad loans.

In the early 1990s the stock market bounced back with a vengeance, and Paine Webber Inc. expanded its sales force, hiring 350 new brokers in 1991.

Since the 1987 crash the company has diversified to reduce its dependence on commissions and increase the amount of money it derives from fee-producing services.

The company was hit in 1993 by the departure of key personnel from Mitchell Hutchins Institutional Investors. It suffered still more personnel problems that year when it was directed by NASD arbitrators to pay an award to 5 brokers who said they had been forced from their jobs for refusing to direct investors into inappropriate proprietary mutual funds.

The 1994 bond crash and its aftermath had a profound effect on the company's bottom line and led to layoffs of a projected 5% of its staff just months after the company had spent heavily on compensation for personnel from Kidder, Peabody, the investment banking firm it acquired in 1994.

Paine Webber has spent heavily on technology recently, introducing an in-house system in 1995 to monitor trading activities as they occur on its state-of-the-art workstation system.

NYSE symbol: PWJ
Fiscal year ends: December 31

WHO

Chairman and CEO: Donald B. Marron, age 60,
$2,525,000 pay
Chairman, PaineWebber International: John A. Bult,
age 58
President, PaineWebber International: Joseph J.
Grano Jr., age 47, $1,320,000 pay
EVP Administration (HR): Ronald M. Schwartz
VP, General Counsel, and Secretary: Theodore
A. Levine, age 50, $850,000 pay
VP and CFO: Regina A. Dolan, age 40, $655,000 pay
Treasurer: Pierce R. Smith, age 51
Auditors: Ernst & Young LLP

WHERE

HQ: 1285 Avenue of the Americas, New York, NY 10019
Phone: 212-713-2000
Fax: 212-713-4924

Paine Webber Group operates 295 offices in the US and
Puerto Rico, France, Hong Kong, Japan, Switzerland,
and the UK.

	1994 Offices
	No.
Southern US	75
Western US	63
Central US	59
Mid-Atlantic US	59
Northeast US	31
Outside US	8
Total	**295**

WHAT

	1994 Sales	
	$ mil.	% of total
Interest	1,695	43
Commissions	970	24
Principal transactions	519	13
Investment banking	285	7
Asset management	356	9
Other	139	4
Total	**3,964**	**100**

Selected Services	Selected Subsidiaries
Asset management	Mitchell Hutchins Asset
Commodities	Management Inc.
Corporate and government	Mitchell Hutchins
bonds	Institutional Investors
Insurance	Inc.
Investment banking	PaineWebber Capital Inc.
Listed securities	PaineWebber Incorporated
Mortgage securities	PaineWebber International
Municipal securities	Bank Ltd.
Mutual funds	PaineWebber International
Options and futures	(UK) Ltd.
Research services	PaineWebber Life Insurance
Retail brokerage	PW Trust Company

KEY COMPETITORS

A.G. Edwards	Dean Witter,	Merrill Lynch
Alex. Brown	Discover	Morgan Stanley
Alliance Capital	Equitable	Nomura
Bankers Trust	Fannie Mae	Securities
Bear Stearns	FMR	Prudential
Brown Brothers	General Electric	Royal Bank of
Harriman	Goldman Sachs	Canada
Canadian Imperial	Hambrect &	Salomon
Charles Schwab	Quist	Stephens
Chase Manhattan	J. P. Morgan	T. Rowe Price
Citicorp	Kemper Corp.	Transamerica
CS Holding	Lehman	Travelers
Dai-Ichi Kangyo	Brothers	USAA

HOW MUCH

	Annual Growth	1985	1986	1987	1988	1989	1990	1991	1992	1993	1994
Sales ($ mil.)	8.6%	1,885	2,385	2,437	2,512	2,926	2,979	3,166	3,364	4,005	3,964
Net income ($ mil.)	(0.7%)	34	72	75	42	52	(57)	151	213	246	32
Income as % of sales	—	1.8%	3.0%	3.1%	1.7%	1.8%	—	4.8%	6.3%	6.1%	0.8%
Earnings per share ($)	(4.3%)	0.61	1.09	1.00	0.26	0.47	(1.43)	1.67	2.37	2.95	0.41
Stock price – high ($)	—	15.35	17.41	17.41	8.40	10.51	9.18	16.51	17.84	23.09	19.76
Stock price – low ($)	—	8.98	11.30	5.84	6.40	6.95	5.12	4.89	10.51	14.08	12.75
Stock price – close ($)	2.1%	12.46	14.01	6.40	7.17	7.51	6.12	15.59	16.26	18.01	15.00
P/E – high	—	25	16	17	32	22	—	10	8	8	48
P/E – low	—	15	10	6	25	15	—	3	4	5	31
Dividends per share ($)	9.1%	0.21	0.21	0.29	0.23	0.23	0.23	0.23	0.29	0.36	0.46
Book value per share ($)	8.3%	7.49	9.17	10.58	11.06	11.61	10.06	16.58	13.51	15.51	15.41
Employees	4.5%	—	—	12,000	13,000	12,900	12,700	12,900	13,600	14,400	16,300

1994 Year-end:
Debt ratio: 93.5%
Return on equity: 2.3%
Cash (mil.): $629
Long-term debt (mil.): $2,315
No. of shares (mil.): 99
Dividends
  Yield: 3.1%
  Payout: 112.2%
Market value (mil.): $1,490
Assets (mil.): $35,856

**Stock Price History
High/Low 1985–94**

PANHANDLE EASTERN CORPORATION

OVERVIEW

Houston-based Panhandle Eastern operates one of the US's largest natural gas transmission systems. Its more than 34,000 miles of pipeline stretch from gas gathering areas in the southeastern and western US and in Canada to markets in the Upper Midwest and Northeast. With its 1994 merger with gas gathering company Associated Natural Gas, Panhandle Eastern has become one of the largest gas gatherers and marketers in the US.

Panhandle Eastern's 4 transmission subsidiaries deliver nearly 2.5 trillion cubic feet of natural gas a year (roughly 12% of the US's gas consumption). The company also imports and re-gasifies Algerian liquefied natural gas for sale in the US through its subsidiary Trunkline LNG.

The deregulation of the gas industry, which requires companies to "unbundle" their services — separating out sales, transportation, and gathering and storage functions — was a major reason for Panhandle's merger with Associated Natural Gas. While Panhandle had a strong business in transportation, where rates remain regulated, it wanted to expand into the less regulated business of gas gathering. The addition of Associated brings more than 9,000 miles of gathering pipelines and a presence in western markets.

The company plans to continue building its supply-area activities, including gathering, storage, and marketing, and to expand into new markets, including the UK and South America.

WHEN

Panhandle Eastern first appeared in 1929 as Interstate Pipe Line Company. Renamed Panhandle Eastern Pipe Line Company in 1930, it completed its first pipeline in 1931, which extended 2,100 miles from the Texas Panhandle to eastern Illinois by the end of 1939.

In 1951 the company started building its 2nd major pipeline system (Trunkline Gas Company), linking the Gulf Coast to Panhandle Eastern's system in Illinois.

In 1959 Panhandle Eastern bought Anadarko Production Company, an oil-and-gas exploration firm. It then joined National Distillers and Chemical to form National Helium in 1961, which built a helium extraction plant near Liberal, Kansas, in 1963.

Trunkline extended its system to the Indiana-Michigan border through 2 more pipelines, and by the end of 1969 the combined Panhandle-Trunkline system supplied natural gas to 12 states and Canada.

Hoping to reduce the effects of gas shortages, Panhandle Eastern entered into a 20-year contract for liquefied natural gas (LNG) with Algerian supplier Sonatrach in 1975. It also bought a coal mining firm (Youghiogheny and Ohio Coal, 1976) and an oil drilling firm (Dixilyn Corporation, 1977), which owned 1/3 of an offshore contractor, Dixilyn Godager Company (renamed Dixilyn-Field Godager, 1979). Panhandle Eastern completed its acquisition of Dixilyn-Field in 1980.

The company adopted the name Panhandle Eastern Corporation in 1981 and, in response to falling gas prices, suspended its Algerian LNG contract in 1983. Sonatrach subsequently filed for international arbitration.

In 1986, after rejecting a takeover bid from Wagner and Brown (a Midland, Texas–based oil and gas firm), Panhandle Eastern spun off Anadarko to its stockholders. In 1987 the company charged $460 million against earnings as part of its settlement with Sonatrach (which included a 20-year contract to buy LNG from Sonatrach). Also in 1987 the company shut down Youghiogheny and Ohio Coal and Dixilyn-Field (both were sold in 1990).

In 1989, when Texas Eastern Corporation (TEC, another Houston-based pipeline company) faced a hostile takeover by Coastal Corporation, Panhandle Eastern agreed to buy the company for $3.2 billion. Founded in 1947, Texas Eastern operated a gas pipeline extending from the Gulf Coast to the eastern seaboard. Panhandle Eastern took on $2.6 billion of debt to finance the TEC acquisition ($1.7 billion was retired that year through the sale of TEC's nonpipeline assets).

In 1991 the company's Texas Eastern Transmission Corporation (TETCO) joined 2 other pipeline operators to form Liberty Pipeline Company, a project designed to connect existing lines to high-need areas of Long Island and New York City.

Panhandle Eastern formed a new subsidiary in 1993, 1 Source Corporation, to provide customized gas transportation management services. In 1994 Panhandle subsidiary Centana Energy acquired several assets from a unit of Texas-based Mitchell Energy & Development, including a pipeline, a storage facility, and a processing plant.

In 1995 Paul Anderson succeeded Dennis Hendrix as CEO. Hendrix remains chairman.

WHO

Chairman: Dennis R. Hendrix, age 55
VC: George L. Mazanec, age 59, $529,414 pay
President and CEO: Paul M. Anderson, age 50,
$531,964 pay (prior to promotion)
President, Algonquin Gas Transmission Co.: Joseph T.
Hydok, age 67
President, Associated Natural Gas Corp.: Donald H.
Anderson, age 47
President, Panhandle Eastern Pipeline Co.: Steven M.
Roverud, age 56
President, Texas Eastern Transmission Corp.: Fred J.
Fowler, age 49
President, Trunkline Gas Co.: L. B. Gatewood, age 48
SVP and CFO: James B. Hipple, age 61, $403,827 pay
SVP and General Counsel: Carl B. King, age 52,
$390,333 pay
VP Finance, Accounting, and Treasurer: Paul F.
Ferguson, age 46
VP Human Resources: Dan R. Hennig, age 54
Corporate Secretary: Robert W. Reed, age 51
Auditors: KPMG Peat Marwick LLP

WHERE

HQ: 5400 Westheimer Ct., PO Box 1642, Houston, TX
77251-1642
Phone: 713-627-5400
Fax: 713-627-4145

Primary Market Areas

Connecticut	Missouri
Delaware	New Jersey
Illinois	New York
Indiana	Ohio
Iowa	Pennsylvania
Kentucky	Rhode Island
Maryland	Vermont
Massachusetts	Virginia
Michigan	West Virginia

WHAT

	1994 Sales	
	$ mil.	% of total
Market and supply services	2,893	63
Natural gas transmission	1,637	36
Other	55	1
Total	**4,585**	**100**

Market and Supply Services Group
Associated Natural Gas Corp.
Associated Natural Gas Inc. (ANGI)
Associated Transport and Trading Co. (ATTCO)
Centana Energy Corp. (gas extraction, gathering,
processing, and marketing)

Natural Gas Transmission Group
1Source Development Co.
1Source Information Services Co.
Algonquin Gas Transmission Co.
Panhandle Eastern Pipe Line Co. (PEPL)
Texas Eastern Transmission Corp. (TETCO)
Trunkline Gas Co.

Other Activities
Midland Cogeneration Venture (14.3%)
National Methanol Co. (25%, Saudi Arabia)
Northern Border Partners, L.P. (8.5%, gas transmission
system extending from Canada through Montana to
Iowa)
TEPPCO Partners, L.P. (transportation and storage of
petroleum products)
Trunkline LNG Co. (storage and regasification terminal
for liquefied natural gas)

KEY COMPETITORS

Amoco	Exxon	Sun Company
Ashland	Koch	Tenneco
Chevron	NGC	USX–Delhi
Coastal	Occidental	Williams Cos.
Columbia Gas	Phillips	
Enron	Petroleum	
ENSERCH Corp.		

HOW MUCH

	9-Year Growth	1985	1986	1987	1988	1989	1990	1991	1992	1993	1994
Sales ($ mil.)	5.3%	2,889	2,250	1,653	1,307	2,781	2,988	2,454	2,342	2,121	4,585
Net income ($ mil.)	6.8%	125	(542)	108	(172)	58	(218)	85	187	148	225
Income as % of sales	—	4.3%	—	6.5%	—	2.1%	—	3.5%	8.0%	7.0%	4.9%
Earnings per share ($)	(6.7%)	2.83	(11.06)	2.04	(3.13)	0.82	(2.46)	0.86	1.74	1.29	1.51
Stock price – high ($)	—	41.50	50.25	34.75	27.38	30.75	29.75	16.50	19.75	27.25	25.50
Stock price – low ($)	—	32.38	24.25	18.25	21.00	20.50	10.38	9.88	12.88	16.75	18.25
Stock price – close ($)	(7.0%)	38.00	27.75	20.75	25.63	29.88	12.50	15.38	16.75	23.75	19.75
P/E – high	—	15	—	17	—	38	—	19	11	21	17
P/E – low	—	11	—	9	—	25	—	12	7	13	12
Dividends per share ($)	(10.6%)	2.31	2.23	2.00	2.00	2.00	1.40	0.80	0.80	0.80	0.84
Book value per share ($)	(10.9%)	38.42	18.93	19.40	14.06	16.21	12.80	12.32	12.65	13.88	13.65
Employees	(0.4%)	5,700	4,250	3,800	3,170	6,078	6,000	5,300	5,000	4,900	5,500

1994 Year-end:
Debt ratio: 53.8%
Return on equity: 12.2%
Cash (mil.): $33
Current ratio: 0.86
Long-term debt (mil.): $2,364
No. of shares (mil.): 149
Dividends
  Yield: 4.3%
  Payout: 55.6%
Market value (mil.): $2,945

**Stock Price History
High/Low 1985–94**

PATHMARK STORES, INC.

OVERVIEW

Grocery shoppers in the New York, New Jersey, and Philadelphia metro areas know well the path to Pathmark. The Woodbridge, New Jersey–based chain, operated by Pathmark Stores, has 143 supermarkets in the Northeast and is one of the region's most dominant grocery retailers.

Pathmark also operates pharmacies. However, the company is now limiting that business mainly to its food stores, most of which already have pharmacies. In 1995 Pathmark agreed to sell its 30 New York City–area freestanding drugstores to Rite Aid. Pathmark has 6 discount drugstores in Connecticut.

Pathmark is benefiting from the growing willingness of urbanites to shop at large grocery superstores, such as the chain's 62,000-square-foot Super Centers. The latest twist to Pathmark's Super Centers is the upscale Pathmark 2000 store format, which emphasizes produce selection and offers wider aisles, better access to information, and more in-store help. The chain expects to have 50 Pathmark 2000 stores by the end of 1995.

This upscale emphasis extends to Pathmark's 3,300-item private-label grocery program, which the company believes is one of the biggest in the nation. Pathmark has introduced its first premium private-label brand, Pathmark Preferred, to go with its established Pathmark and No Frills brands.

In 1994 Pathmark began offering free home delivery of health, beauty, and pharmacy products as well as general merchandise.

WHEN

After WWII, supermarket operators in New York and New Jersey banded together to form a cooperative to combat chain grocers, and the Wakefern Cooperative was born. Members enjoyed enhanced buying power and, with some stores sharing the name Shop-Rite, extended advertising reach.

Three participants in the cooperative — Alex Aidekman, Herbert Brody, and Milton Perlmutter — combined in a smaller group to form Supermarkets Operating Company in 1956. Supermarkets Operating's stores continued to use the Shop-Rite name and the Wakefern Cooperative's services.

In 1966 Supermarkets Operating merged with General Super Markets to become Supermarkets General Corporation.

Supermarkets General left Wakefern in 1968 and renamed its stores Pathmark. The company branched into small-town department stores with the purchase of Genung's, which operated chains under the names Steinbach (New Jersey) and Howland (New York and New England). In 1969 the company added to its department store holdings with the purchase of Baltimore retailer Hochschild, Kohn & Co. and entered the home improvement market by purchasing the 6-store Rickel chain. The company grew steadily in the 1970s, pioneering large supermarket and grocery/drug combinations in densely populated areas of New York, New Jersey, and Connecticut. The company's aggressive discounting and experimentation gained it a reputation as one of the US's best-run supermarket chains.

Value House, a catalog showroom that grew to 20 locations, was sold in 1978. In 1983 Leonard Lieberman became CEO. Supermarkets General acquired Boston's Purity Supreme, operator of Purity Supreme and Heartland grocery stores and Li'l Peach convenience stores, for $80 million (1984; sold 1991). In 1985 the company opened superstores, under both the Pathmark and Purity Supreme names, which offered a great variety of merchandise. The company boosted its New England market share when it bought Angelo's Supermarkets in 1986. Also that year it sold its department store operations, and Aidekman stepped down as chairman.

Supermarkets General's expansion slowed when the Haft family's Dart Group made a $1.62 billion raid on the company in 1987. Merrill Lynch Capital Partners stepped in with an LBO, retaining control of Supermarkets General after the company was taken private. In 1989 CEO Kenneth Peskin, who had replaced Lieberman, resigned, and Jack Futterman took his place.

In 1991 the company sold its Purity Operations to Freeman Spogli & Co. for about $265 million, retaining a 10% interest in Purity.

Pathmark Stores, Inc., became the successor company to Supermarkets General in 1993, but a plan to go public was shelved when executives did not believe shares would garner a worthy price. Instead, the company was recapitalized, with ownership of Pathmark transferred to a newly formed holding company, Newco, and the Rickel Home Center chain spun off to a new entity, Plainbridge, Inc.

In early 1995 president Anthony Cuti said he expected Pathmark to go public before the end of the year.

Private company
Fiscal year ends: Saturday nearest January 31

WHO

Chairman and CEO: Jack Futterman, age 61,
$583,473 pay
President and CFO: Anthony J. Cuti, age 49,
$364,266 pay
EVP Marketing: Neill Crowley, age 52
EVP and CFO: Ron Marshall, age 41
SVP Merchandising: Ronald Rallo, age 57, $221,526 pay
SVP Operations: Robert Joyce, age 49, $199,183 pay
SVP Retail Development: Harvey M. Gutman, age 49,
$189,801 pay
VP and Controller: Joseph W. Adelhardt, age 48
VP, General Counsel, and Secretary: Marc A. Strassler,
age 46
VP and General Counsel, Real Estate: Myron D.
Waxberg, age 61
VP Human Resources: Maureen McGurl, age 47
Auditors: Deloitte & Touche LLP

WHERE

HQ: 301 Blair Rd., PO Box 5301, Woodbridge, NJ
07095-0915
Phone: 908-499-3000
Fax: 908-499-3072

The company operates 143 Pathmark supermarkets in
Connecticut, Delaware, New Jersey, New York, and
Pennsylvania and 6 deep-discount drugstores in
Connecticut. The company also has distribution or
processing facilities in the New Jersey cities of Avenel,
Dayton, Edison, Somerset, and Woodbridge.

WHAT

	1995 Sales	
	$ mil.	% of total
Supermarkets	4,006	96
Other	176	4
Total	**4,182**	**100**

Supermarkets and Drugstores
Deep-discount drugstores (6)
Supermarkets (143)
  Super Centers (108)
  Pathmark 2000 (29)
  Conventional supermarkets (6)

Distribution Facilities
Dry grocery (Woodbridge, NJ)
Frozen food (Dayton, NJ)
General merchandise (health and beauty care products,
  pharmaceuticals, tobacco; Edison, NJ)
Meat, dairy, deli, produce (Woodbridge, NJ)

Processing Facilities
Banana ripening (Avenel, NJ)
Delicatessen products (Somerset, NJ)

Private-Label Brands
No Frills
Pathmark
Pathmark Preferred

KEY COMPETITORS

American Stores
Big V Supermarkets
Circle K
Eckerd
Fay's
Genovese Drug Stores
Giant Eagle
Golub
Grand Union
Great A&P
Inserra Supermarkets
J Sainsbury
Key Food
King Kullen Grocery
Kmart
Mayfair Supermarkets
Melville
Penn Traffic
Red Apple Group
Rite Aid
Southland
Stop & Shop
Vendex
Victory Markets
Village Supermarkets
Walgreen
Wal-Mart
Wegmans Food Markets
Weis Markets

HOW MUCH

	9-Year Growth	1986	1987	1988	1989	1990	1991	1992	1993	1994	1995
Sales ($ mil.)	(2.2%)	5,123	5,508	5,767	5,962	5,475	4,481	4,378	4,340	4,207	4,182
Net income ($ mil.)	(7.7%)	64	63	(66)	(59)	(74)	(18)	(197)	(623)	(132)	31
Income as % of sales	—	1.2%	1.1%	—	—	—	—	—	—	—	0.7%
Employees	(6.3%)	52,000	53,000	53,000	52,000	51,000	46,000	31,000	27,000	28,000	29,000

1995 Year-end:
Debt ratio: 100%
Return on equity: —
Cash (mil.): $7
Current ratio: 0.57
Long-term debt (mil.): $1,399
Shareholder deficit (mil.): ($1,210)
Total assets (mil.): $776

Net Income ($ mil.)
1986–95

PENNZOIL COMPANY

OVERVIEW

Under the leadership of CEO James Pate, Houston-based Pennzoil has sold ailing businesses and refocused on 3 core areas: oil and gas exploration, motor oils, and Jiffy Lube oil change outlets. The company still has an interest in the sulfur business internationally but sold its domestic operations to Freeport-McMoRan in 1995.

Pennzoil owns Jiffy Lube International, the world's largest franchiser of quick lube centers with 52% of the US market. Its motor oil (which promises to act like liquid ball bearings) is the top-selling motor oil in the US. The company is taking advantage of the prominence of its market-leading brands with some strategic alliances. In 1995 it teamed up with Prestone, the #1-selling antifreeze in the US, in a joint marketing agreement. In an arrangement with Sears it plans to expand its Jiffy Lube quick oil change operation by opening units in over half of the Sears Auto Center locations across the US (approximately 456) over the next 3 years.

The company is looking for growth in oil and exploration from major international projects. Pennzoil signed an agreement with Azerbaijan in 1994 to develop the Guneshli oil field in the Caspian Sea. Pennzoil Canada acquired Canadian oil and gas company Co-enerco Resources that year, increasing Pennzoil's presence in the North American natural gas market. Also that year the company signed contracts for oil and gas projects in Egypt and Qatar.

WHEN

The post-WWII oil boom in West Texas attracted brothers J. Hugh and Bill Liedtke and a Connecticut scion named George Bush. Eager to make their fortunes, they formed Zapata Petroleum. Zapata hit big, with more than 120 producing wells in its Jameson Field.

Zapata expanded with a subsidiary that drilled in the Gulf of Mexico. In 1959 Bush bought out the subsidiary and moved to Houston, where he later embarked on a political career that eventually took him to the White House. The Liedtkes set their sights on South Penn Oil of Oil City, Pennsylvania — a rusty relic from the 1911 dissolution of Standard Oil. Enlisting the support of J. Paul Getty, they took control of South Penn in 1963, merged it with Zapata, renamed it Pennzoil in honor of the lubricant it sold, and moved the headquarters to Houston.

In 1965 J. Hugh Liedtke engineered the historic takeover of Shreveport-based United Gas Pipeline, 5 times the size of Pennzoil. Though blessed with a large pipeline system and vast mineral interests, United Gas was hampered by lethargic management.

Using a takeover tactic that would break ground for a generation of corporate raiding, Liedtke launched a hostile cash tender offer. Pennzoil invited United Gas shareholders to sell their shares at a price higher than the market price. Shareholders tendered 5 times the number of shares that Pennzoil wanted to buy. Undaunted, the Liedtkes raised the additional funds to buy 42% of United Gas stock. They spun off a scaled-down United in 1974.

In the late 1960s Pennzoil financed speculative drilling by selling, directly to the public, stock in subsidiary companies. Shareholders in the subsidiaries were given some security, with rights to Pennzoil stock if the risky drilling proved unsuccessful.

In 1983 J. Hugh Liedtke hoped to purchase Getty Oil, the company begun by his old benefactor, and thought he had a deal. Texaco bought Getty instead. Pennzoil sued, and in 1985 a Texas jury awarded a record $10.5 billion in damages. Texaco sought refuge in bankruptcy court, emerging after settling with Pennzoil for $3 billion.

Liedtke stepped down as CEO in 1988 but remained chairman as Pennzoil determined how to spend its booty. In 1989 Pennzoil spent $2.1 billion for 8.8% of Chevron, but Liedtke denied that his company had a takeover in mind. Chevron wasn't convinced and filed suit in 1989 to keep him at bay. Much of the suit was dismissed in 1990, and by year's end Pennzoil had increased its stake to 9.4%, just under Chevron's poison pill threshold.

In 1992 Pennzoil swapped $1.2 billion of its Chevron stock for 266 of Chevron's oil and gas properties primarily located in the Gulf of Mexico and along the Gulf Coast. The swap ended litigation between the 2 companies. Also in 1992 Pennzoil spun off filter maker Purolator, raising about $206 million.

In 1994 Pennzoil signed a joint venture agreement with Conoco to build a lube oil hydrocracker at Conoco's refinery in Louisiana. Pennzoil's weak 1994 results included a $500 million write-down on back taxes and losses on the sale of its sulfur subsidiary.

In 1995 Pennzoil teamed up with Citicorp to set up loans for lube center operators.

NYSE symbol: PZL
Fiscal year ends: December 31

WHO

Chairman, President, and CEO: James L. Pate, age 59, $830,500 pay
Group VP, Oil and Gas: Thomas M. Hamilton, age 51, $395,100 pay
Group VP Finance and Treasurer (CFO): David P. Alderson II, age 45, $290,700 pay
Group VP Accounting and Controller: Mark A. Malinski, age 39, $289,800 pay
Group VP Administration (HR): Terry Hemeyer, age 56
Group VP Products Manufacturing: William M. Robb, age 50
Group VP Products Marketing: William E. Welcher, age 62
General Counsel: James W. Shaddix, age 48, $294,900 pay
Corporate Secretary: Linda F. Condit, age 47
Auditors: Arthur Andersen & Co, SC

WHERE

HQ: Pennzoil Place, PO Box 2967, Houston, TX 77252-2967
Phone: 713-546-4000
Fax: 713-546-6639

Exploration and Production: Drilling in the US (primarily in California, Louisiana, Pennsylvania, Texas, and Utah) and in Canada, Indonesia, and Qatar.

Products: 2 refineries — Oil City, Pennsylvania, and Shreveport, Louisiana. Pennzoil motor oil and lubricants are sold in 60 countries.

Franchise Operations: 1,132 Jiffy Lube service centers in the US; 9 overseas.

Sulfur: Pennzoil operates an international sulfur business. It owns and operates a sulfur terminal in Antwerp, Belgium.

WHAT

	1994 Sales		1994 Operating Income	
	$ mil.	% of total	$ mil.	% of total
Motor oil & refined products	1,510	56	42	—
Oil & gas	834	32	(5)	—
Franchise ops.	258	10	3	—
Sulfur	72	2	(57)	—
Other	(111)	—	55	—
Total	**2,563**	**100**	**38**	**—**

Selected Subsidiaries
Jiffy Lube International, Inc. (quick lubrication shops)
Pennzoil Exploration and Production Co. (oil and gas)
  Pennzoil Gas Marketing Co.
Pennzoil Products Co. (refining, processing, and marketing of automotive products, industrial specialties, and motor oil)
Richland Development Corp. (real estate)
  Inco Real Estate Co.

Selected Brand Names
Gumout car care products
Pennzoil gasoline (7 US states)
Pennzoil motor oil and lubricants
Wolf's Head lubricants

KEY COMPETITORS

Amerada Hess	Exxon	Phillips Petroleum
Amoco	Imperial Oil	Quaker State
Ashland, Inc.	Koch	Repsol
Atlantic Richfield	Mobil	Royal Dutch/Shell
British Petroleum	Norsk Hydro	Sinclair Oil
Broken Hill	Occidental	Sun Company
Chevron	Oryx	Texaco
Coastal	PDVSA	TOTAL
Diamond Shamrock	PEMEX	Unocal
DuPont	Petrobrás	USX-Marathon
Elf Aquitaine	Petrofina	

HOW MUCH

	9-Year Growth	1985	1986	1987	1988	1989	1990	1991	1992	1993	1994
Sales ($ mil.)	1.5%	2,239	1,889	1,809	2,274	2,215	2,367	2,685	2,357	2,782	2,563
Net income ($ mil.)	—	113	69	44	(187)	104	94	70	29	160	(284)
Income as % of sales	—	5.0%	3.7%	2.4%	—	4.7%	4.0%	2.6%	1.2%	5.8%	—
Earnings per share ($)	—	2.20	1.28	0.69	(5.22)	2.42	2.37	1.73	0.71	3.80	(6.16)
Stock price – high ($)	—	72.00	91.00	95.00	79.13	88.88	89.50	76.50	57.50	70.75	56.38
Stock price – low ($)	—	40.50	48.13	38.50	65.25	71.63	61.75	52.13	43.13	49.38	43.00
Stock price – close ($)	(4.0%)	64.00	67.00	71.00	71.75	88.63	66.00	56.38	50.00	53.38	44.13
P/E – high	—	33	71	138	—	37	38	44	81	19	—
P/E – low	—	18	38	56	—	30	26	30	61	13	—
Dividends per share ($)	3.5%	2.20	2.20	2.20	2.70	3.00	3.00	3.00	3.00	3.00	3.00
Book value per share ($)	4.1%	18.23	16.78	15.06	35.67	35.23	31.10	28.79	28.99	32.80	26.11
Employees	2.7%	8,320	6,257	6,153	10,021	6,103	7,859	8,145	9,125	9,901	10,501

1994 Year-end:
Debt ratio: 67.6%
Return on equity: —
Cash (mil.): $25
Current ratio: 1.08
Long-term debt (mil.): $2,175
No. of shares (mil.): 46
Dividends
  Yield: 6.8%
  Payout: —
Market value (mil.): $2,036

Stock Price History High/Low 1985–94

PEPSICO, INC.

OVERVIEW

Long-time #2 player in the cola wars, PepsiCo is widening the playing field. Over the last 3 years, the company has invested more than $2 billion in its worldwide bottling operations. Although dominated by Coca-Cola (Coke brands have 42% of the market, to Pepsi's 32%), international markets are less saturated and offer a huge potential for growth.

In 1994 Pepsi-Cola International (PCI) formed a joint venture with Brazil's BAESA to market products in South America. The following year PCI launched Atlantis bottled water in Asia and Mexico. Other recent investments include plants in China and India. Pepsi Max, which contains an artificial sweetener not available in the US, is marketed in over 50 countries.

Pepsi is also diversifying its product line. In a joint venture with Lipton, it has won over 30% of the ready-to-drink tea market, a part of the so-called "new age" beverage segment. The company also has a pact with Ocean Spray to market fruit juices. In 1995 Pepsi began testing Mazagran, a coffee-based drink codeveloped with Starbucks.

The fast-food industry (PepsiCo owns KFC, Taco Bell, and Pizza Hut, among others) is also ripe for PepsiCo's aggressive innovations. In 1995 Pizza Hut, the top pizza chain with $4.6 billion in 1994 sales, introduced "stuffed crust" pizza and quickly began setting sales records. Pizza Hut is now set to enter India. In mid-1995 Taco Bell gave away $12 million worth of food to push its "border light" menu. Not long after, KFC began adding Taco Bell units to 50 of its restaurants.

Sales from PepsiCo's other segment, salty snack foods, jumped 7% in 1994 on the strong performance of Frito-Lay, which has 43% of its market. The chip maker is investing $225 million to develop reduced-fat snacks, including baked chips and fat-free pretzels.

WHEN

In New Bern, North Carolina, pharmacist Caleb Bradham invented Pepsi in 1898. He named his new drink Pepsi-Cola (claiming it cured dyspepsia) and registered the trademark in 1903.

Following Coca-Cola's example, Bradham developed a system of bottling franchises. By WWI 300 bottlers had signed up. After the war Bradham stockpiled sugar to safeguard against rising costs. In 1920 sugar prices plunged, forcing Bradham to sell the company in 1923.

Pepsi existed on the brink of ruin under various owners for the next decade, until the Loft Candy Company bought it in 1931. The company's fortunes took a turn for the better in 1934 when, in the midst of the Depression, it doubled the size of its bottles to 12 ounces without raising the 5¢ price. In 1939 Pepsi introduced the world's first radio jingle. In 1941 Loft Candy merged with its Pepsi subsidiary and became the Pepsi-Cola Company.

Pepsi started to produce drinks in cans in 1948. Former Coca-Cola executive Alfred Steele became president 2 years later. Steele introduced the slogan "Be Sociable, Have a Pepsi" and in 1954 put his wife, actress Joan Crawford, to work as a Pepsi spokesperson.

Donald Kendall, who became president of Pepsi in 1963, persuaded Soviet premier Nikita Khrushchev to down a Pepsi for the cameras at the Moscow Trade Fair and turned Pepsi's attention to young people ("The Pepsi Generation").

In 1965 Pepsi acquired Frito-Lay and became PepsiCo. Dallas-based Frito-Lay had been created when Elmer Doolin (who had discovered Fritos at a cafe near the Mexican border in 1932) and Herman Lay (HW Lay & Company) joined efforts in 1960.

During the early 1970s Kendall broke into the Soviet market by agreeing to distribute Stolichnaya vodka in the US in exchange for Pepsi distribution in the USSR. With the purchases of Pizza Hut (1977), Taco Bell (1978), and Kentucky Fried Chicken (1986), PepsiCo became a major force in the fast-food industry.

When Coca-Cola changed its formula in 1985, Pepsi stepped up the competition with its longtime archrival, claiming victory in the cola wars. Coke and Pepsi expanded their rivalry to tea in 1991 when they formed a venture with #1 Lipton in response to Coke's announced venture with Nestlé (Nestea).

In 1993 the company successfully refuted claims that syringes had been found in Pepsi cans. After slow sales Pepsi began scaling back plans for its double drive-through Hot 'n Now burger stands in 1994. Also that year Mountain Dew, the #6 carbonated beverage, grew more than any of its competitors, topping 500 million cases sold.

Courting the interest of Generation X, in 1995 Pepsi began US testing of Pepsi XL, which has 50% sugar and 50% aspartame, a combination that supposedly masks aspartame's bitter taste while still cutting calories.

NYSE symbol: PEP
Fiscal year ends: Last Saturday in December

WHO

Chairman and CEO: D. Wayne Calloway, age 59, $2,943,269 pay
VC; Chairman, PepsiCo Worldwide Restaurants: Roger A. Enrico, age 50, $1,347,134 pay
EVP and CFO: Robert G. Dettmer, age 63, $830,163 pay
SVP, General Counsel, and Secretary: Edward V. Lahey Jr., age 56, $600,642 pay
SVP and Controller: Robert L. Carleton, age 54, $485,460 pay
SVP Personnel: J. Roger King, age 54
Chairman and CEO, Taco Bell Corp.: John E. Martin
President and CEO, Frito-Lay, Inc.: Steven S. Reinemund, age 46
President and CEO, Pepsi-Cola North America: Craig E. Weatherup, age 49
President and CEO, PepsiCo Foods and Beverages International: Christopher A. Sinclair, age 44
President and CEO, Pizza Hut Inc.: Allan S. Huston
President and CEO, Kentucky Fried Chicken Corp.: David C. Novak, age 42
Auditors: KPMG Peat Marwick LLP

WHERE

HQ: Purchase, NY 10577-1444
Phone: 914-253-2000
Fax: 914-253-2070

PepsiCo's beverages, snack foods, and fast foods are sold worldwide.

	1994 Sales		1994 Operating Income	
	$ mil.	% of total	$ mil.	% of total
US	20,246	71	2,706	81
Canada & Mexico	3,267	11	343	10
Europe	2,177	8	17	1
Other regions	2,782	10	258	8
Total	**28,472**	**100**	**3,324**	**100**

WHAT

	1994 Sales		1994 Operating Income	
	$ mil.	% of total	$ mil.	% of total
Restaurants	10,521	37	730	22
Beverages	9,687	34	1,217	37
Snack foods	8,264	29	1,377	41
Total	**28,472**	**100**	**3,324**	**100**

Selected Subsidiaries

Frito-Lay North America (snack foods, including Chee•tos, Doritos, Fritos, Lay's, Ruffles, and Tostitos brands)

KFC Corp. (2,250 restaurants, 100 licensed outlets, and 3,600 franchises in the US and Canada)

PepsiCo Foods International (snack food manufacturing and marketing outside the US and Canada, including Chee•tos, Doritos, Fritos, Gamesa, Ruffles, Sabritas, Sonric's, Sunchips, and Walkers Crisps brands)

Pepsi-Cola International (beverage bottling and marketing outside the US and Canada, including Pepsi-Cola, Mirinda, Pepsi Max, and 7Up brands)

Pepsi-Cola North America (beverage bottling and marketing, including Pepsi-Cola, Mountain Dew, Slice, Mug, and, in Canada, 7Up, brands)

Pizza Hut, Inc. (5,990 restaurants and other outlets and 2,650 franchises in the US and Canada)

Taco Bell Corp. (3,270 restaurants, 960 specialty outlets, and 1,500 franchises in the US and Canada)

KEY COMPETITORS

Anheuser-Busch	Dairy Queen	Procter &
Borden	Domino's Pizza	Gamble
Boston Chicken	Ferolito, Vultaggio	Quaker Oats
Cadbury Schweppes	Flagstar	Rally's
Celestial	Grand	RJR Nabisco
Seasonings	Metropolitan	Seagram
Checker's Drive-In	Lance	Sonic Corp.
Clearly Canadian	Little Caesars	Triarc
Coca-Cola	McDonald's	Virgin
Cott	Nestlé	Wendy's

HOW MUCH

	9-Year Growth	1985	1986	1987	1988	1989	1990	1991	1992	1993	1994
Sales ($ mil.)	15.1%	8,057	9,291	11,485	13,007	15,242	17,803	19,608	21,970	25,021	28,472
Net income ($ mil.)	14.1%	544	458	595	762	901	1,077	1,080	1,302	1,588	1,784
Income as % of sales	—	6.7%	4.9%	5.2%	5.9%	5.9%	6.0%	5.5%	5.9%	6.3%	6.3%
Earnings per share ($)	14.6%	0.65	0.58	0.76	0.97	1.13	1.35	1.35	1.61	1.96	2.22
Stock price – high ($)	—	8.36	11.86	14.07	14.53	21.94	27.88	35.63	43.38	43.63	41.13
Stock price – low ($)	—	4.51	7.32	6.83	9.99	12.57	17.98	23.50	30.50	34.50	29.25
Stock price – close ($)	18.2%	8.06	8.66	11.11	13.15	21.31	26.00	33.88	41.50	40.88	36.25
P/E – high	—	13	20	19	15	19	21	26	27	22	19
P/E – low	—	7	13	9	10	11	13	17	19	18	13
Dividends per share ($)	18.3%	0.15	0.21	0.22	0.25	0.31	0.37	0.44	0.50	0.58	0.68
Book value per share ($)	15.8%	2.32	2.63	3.21	4.02	4.91	6.22	7.03	7.94	8.68
Employees	13.6%	150,000	214,000	225,000	235,000	266,000	308,000	338,000	372,000	423,000	471,000

1994 Year-end:
Debt ratio: 58.1%
Return on equity: 27.0%
Cash (mil.): $1,488
Current ratio: 0.96
Long-term debt (mil.): $8,841
No. of shares (mil.): 790
Dividends
  Yield: 1.9%
  Payout: 30.6%
Market value (mil.): $28,634

Stock Price History High/Low 1985–94

PFIZER INC.

Pfizer's relies on its pharmaceuticals for 70% of its net sales. It concentrates on cardiovascular agents, anti-infectives, central nervous system drugs, anti-inflammatories, and diabetes treatments. Procardia XL remains a leading US heart drug, with sales of $1.2 billion in 1994. Pfizer also manufactures medical products (pumps and catheters), consumer health products (Visine), food science products (such as the bulking agent polydextrose for dietetic foods), and veterinary drugs.

In 1994 Pfizer agreed to buy Smith-Kline Beecham's animal health business for $1.45 billion in cash. The acquisition will create the largest animal drug maker, controlling about 10% of the market, and will overtake Merck.

The company continues its commitment to pharmaceutical health care products; it has a number of drugs in the late trial phases and expects to enlarge its product pipeline through a 20% increase in the 1995 research budget, to about $1.4 billion. Also in 1995 Pfizer announced investments of about $115 million in 2 small US-based biotechnology firms (Myco Pharmaceuticals and Immusol) and in 2 UK-based ones (AEA Technology and Oxford Asymmetry).

Pfizer's US pharmaceutical marketing division is organized along disease category lines to improve relations with the powerful US managed-care sector.

Charles Pfizer and his cousin, confectioner Charles Erhart, started to manufacture chemicals in Brooklyn in 1849. Pfizer's products included camphor, citric acid (business sold in 1990), and santonin (an early antiparasitic). The company was incorporated in 1900 as Chas. Pfizer & Co. Pfizer was propelled into the modern drug business when the company was asked to mass-produce penicillin for the war effort in 1941.

After WWII Pfizer continued to make penicillin as well as streptomycin, most of which it sold to other companies. Pfizer researchers discovered Terramycin, which the company introduced in 1950. Pfizer bought the drug firm Roerig in 1953, its first major acquisition. In the early 1950s the company opened branches in Canada, Mexico, Cuba, the UK, and Belgium and began manufacturing in Europe, Japan, and South America. By the mid-1960s Pfizer had worldwide sales of over $200 million in 100 countries.

Beginning in the late 1950s, Pfizer made Salk and Sabin polio vaccines and added new pharmaceuticals, including Diabinese (antidiabetic, 1958) and Vibramycin (antibiotic, 1967). Pfizer acquired 14 other companies in the early 1960s, including makers of specialty metals, consumer products (Ben-Gay, Desitin), and cosmetics (Coty, sold in 1992). The company bought its first hospital products company, Howmedica, in 1972 and heart-valve maker Shiley in 1979.

Growth slowed during the 1970s, although sales had reached $2 billion by 1977. A new chairman, Edmund Pratt, increased R&D expenditures, which resulted in several new

drugs, including Minipress (antihypertensive, 1975), Feldene (arthritis pain reliever, 1982), and Glucotrol (antidiabetic, 1984). Licensing agreements with foreign companies allowed Pfizer to sell Procardia (for angina and hypertension, developed by Bayer in Germany) and Cefobid (antibiotic, from Japan). In the 1980s Pfizer expanded its hospital products division, buying 18 product lines or companies. It bought Plax (mouthwash) in 1988, of which it sold the international part in 1991. In 1990 Pfizer acquired the license to market the anticancer drug D-99 being developed by the Liposome Company.

In 1991 Pfizer established a joint venture with Hungarian drug company Biogal to market drugs in Europe. Suits filed over the failure of about 500 Shiley heart valves and the alleged falsification of quality-control records led Pfizer to divest Shiley in 1992. Drugs released in 1992 included the antidepressant Zoloft, the antibiotic Zithromax, and the cardiovascular agent Norvasc.

In 1993 Pfizer collaborated with 14 other leading drug makers to work on finding an AIDS cure. That year the company expanded distribution capabilities by purchasing Charwell Pharmaceuticals, an over-the-counter drug distributor in the UK, and by buying an interest in Koshin Medical Corporation, a Japanese hospital products distributor.

In 1994 Pfizer began a jointly owned managed care unit with Connecticut-based Value Health, Inc. In 1995 a team of Pfizer scientists discovered a genetic technique that may help in developing better methods to prevent Type II (adult-onset) diabetes.

NYSE symbol: PFE
Fiscal year ends: December 31

WHO

Chairman and CEO: William C. Steere Jr., age 58, $2,941,667 pay
VC: Edward C. Bessey, age 60, $1,206,000 pay
EVP; President, Hospital Products Group: Henry A. McKinnell Jr., age 52, $1,049,333 pay
EVP Research and Development: John F. Niblack, age 56, $947,000 pay
EVP; President, International Pharmaceuticals Group: Robert Neimeth, age 59, $946,500 pay
President, US Pharmaceuticals Group: Karen L. Katen, age 46
SVP Corporate Affairs, Secretary, and Corporate Counsel: C. L. Clemente
SVP and General Counsel: Paul S. Miller, age 56
CFO: David Shedlarz, age 47
VP Personnel: Bruce R. Ellig, age 58
Auditors: KPMG Peat Marwick LLP

WHERE

HQ: 235 E. 42nd St., New York, NY 10017-5755
Phone: 212-573-2323
Fax: 212-573-7851

The company's products are manufactured in 30 countries and are available in more than 140 countries.

	1994 Sales		1994 Operating Income	
	$ mil.	% of total	$ mil.	% of total
US	4,411	53	1,427	67
Europe	1,817	22	535	25
Asia	1,249	15	115	5
Canada/Latin Amer.	619	8	45	2
Africa/Mid. East	185	2	12	1
Adjustments	—	—	(45)	—
Total	**8,281**	**100**	**2,089**	**100**

WHAT

	1994 Sales		1994 Operating Income	
	$ mil.	% of total	$ mil.	% of total
Health care	6,963	84	1,977	95
Animal health	605	7	47	2
Consumer products	409	5	34	2
Food science	304	4	31	1
Total	**8,281**	**100**	**2,089**	**100**

Selected Drugs
Cardura (cardiovascular)
Cefobid (antibiotic)
Diflucan (antifungal)
Feldene (antiarthritic)
Glucotrol (antidiabetic)
Minipress (antihypertensive)
Norvasc (cardiovascular)
Procardia XL (cardiovascular)
Unasyn (antibiotic)
Zithromax (antibiotic)
Zoloft (antidepressive)

Hospital Products Group Division
American Medical Systems (penile implants)
Schneider (angioplasty devices)

Consumer Products
Barbasol (shaving creams)
Ben-Gay (analgesic cream)
Desitin (diaper rash cream)
Plax (dental rinse)
Rid (antilice products)
Visine (eye drops)

KEY COMPETITORS

Abbott Labs
American Home Products
Amgen
Ballard Medical
Bausch & Lomb
Baxter
Bayer
Becton, Dickinson
Biogen
Bristol-Myers Squibb
Carter-Wallace
Ciba-Geigy
Colgate-Palmolive
C. R. Bard
Dow Chemical
DuPont
Eli Lilly
Genentech
Gillette
Glaxo Wellcome
Hoechst
Immunex
Johnson & Johnson
LVMH
Medtronic
Merck
Monsanto
Novo Nordisk
Rhône-Poulenc
Roche
St. Jude Medical
Sandoz
Schering-Plough
SmithKline Beecham
Unilever
Upjohn
U.S. Surgical
Warner-Lambert

HOW MUCH

	9-Year Growth	1985	1986	1987	1988	1989	1990	1991	1992	1993	1994
Sales ($ mil.)	8.3%	4,025	4,476	4,920	5,385	5,672	6,406	6,950	7,230	7,478	8,281
Net income ($ mil.)	9.4%	580	660	690	791	681	801	722	1,094	658	1,298
Income as % of sales	—	14.4%	14.7%	14.0%	14.7%	12.0%	12.5%	10.4%	15.1%	8.8%	15.7%
Earnings per share ($)	10.4%	1.72	1.95	2.04	2.35	2.02	2.38	2.13	3.25	2.05	4.19
Stock price – high ($)	—	28.13	36.44	38.50	30.13	37.88	40.88	86.13	87.00	75.63	79.38
Stock price – low ($)	—	18.81	23.13	20.63	23.69	27.00	27.25	36.75	65.13	52.50	53.13
Stock price – close ($)	13.2%	25.31	30.50	23.31	29.00	34.75	40.38	84.00	72.50	69.00	77.25
P/E – high	—	16	19	19	13	19	17	40	27	37	19
P/E – low	—	11	12	10	10	13	11	17	20	26	13
Dividends per share ($)	10.9%	0.74	0.82	0.90	1.00	1.10	1.20	1.32	1.48	1.68	1.88
Book value per share ($)	4.9%	8.93	10.35	11.80	13.00	13.72	15.42	15.25	14.51	12.04	13.76
Employees	0.4%	39,200	40,000	40,700	40,900	42,100	42,500	44,100	40,700	40,500	40,800

1994 Year-end:
Debt ratio: 39.5%
Return on equity: 31.7%
Cash (mil.): $2,019
Current ratio: 1.20
Long-term debt (mil.): $604
No. of shares (mil.): 314
Dividends
  Yield: 2.4%
  Payout: 44.9%
Market value (mil.): $24,274

Stock Price History
High/Low 1985–94

PHELPS DODGE CORPORATION

OVERVIEW

International mining giant Phelps Dodge is on a roll. One of the world's lowest-cost copper producers, the Phoenix-based company posted new production and sales records in 1994 with an upturn in demand and higher copper prices. Overall production is expected to increase 20% with the recent startup of a low-cost South American copper mine.

On the verge of bankruptcy in the early 1980s, Phelps Dodge gambled on a new, untested extraction process — solvent extraction/electrowinning (SX/EW), which produces copper without smelting — and slashed its production costs. To offset the cyclical swings in copper prices, Phelps Dodge also diversified out of copper by buying manufacturing businesses. Now almost half of its sales are from manufacturing operations, which include Columbian Chemicals (the world's 2nd largest

producer of carbon black, used in tires), Hudson International Conductors (the world's leading maker of high-performance conductors, used in aerospace, automobiles, and electronics), and Accuride (North America's biggest truck wheel and rim company). Phelps Dodge is the world's #1 maker of magnet wire, used in electrical equipment, and a producer of gold, silver, molybdenum, and other minerals. The company also makes electrical and telecommunication cables through joint ventures in 14 countries.

By 2007 the company wants to double its copper production and, through strategic purchases, modernization, and product development, double its cash flow from manufacturing by the end of the century. In 1994 Phelps Dodge bought 2 magnet wire plants in the US and a carbon black plant in Spain.

WHEN

In 1821 Anson Greene Phelps formed a trading business between New York and England, exporting cotton and importing metals. In 1834 Phelps formed a partnership with sons-in-law William Dodge and Daniel James, founding the firm Phelps Dodge & Company. In the 1830s Phelps Dodge invested in coal, iron, and timber in Pennsylvania. It established 2 metal manufacturers in Connecticut in the 1840s: Ansonia Brass & Battery and Ansonia Manufacturing. Their products included the soft copper wire used for the first transcontinental telegraph (1861). Anson Phelps died in 1853.

Although primarily an East Coast mercantile business, Phelps Dodge bought 2 copper mines near Bisbee, Arizona: the Atlanta (1881) and the Copper Queen (1885). The company expanded its mining operations into northern Mexico (founding Moctezuma Copper, 1895), eastern Arizona (buying Detroit Copper Mining, 1897), and New Mexico (buying coal miner Stag Canon Fuel).

Phelps Dodge built a copper smelter near Bisbee in 1901. The town of Douglas (named for a company geologist) grew up around the site. The company also built railroad connections to haul its copper, including the El Paso and Southwestern (1903). Copper mining was so successful that Phelps Dodge closed its original East Coast businesses in 1906.

The company bought Arizona Copper (1921); Nichols Copper, which had a modern refinery in El Paso (1930); Calumet & Arizona Mining (with properties in Bisbee and Ajo, Arizona; 1931); and mines in the Rio Verde

Valley near Jerome, Arizona. In the 1950s the company expanded into other countries. In 1971 Phelps Dodge bought Western Nuclear (uranium mining) and a 40% share in Consolidated Aluminum.

Amid depressed copper prices in the early 1980s and $400 million in losses, Phelps Dodge moved its headquarters from New York to Phoenix to reduce costs. The company also restructured, cut staff by 56%, and diversified, buying Columbian Chemicals (1986), Accuride (1988), and Hudson International Conductors (1989). In 1991 the company's Accuride unit joined Goodyear to form the first-ever commercial tire and wheel assembly joint venture.

In 1992 Phelps Dodge sold a 20% interest in its La Candelaria project (copper and gold mining, Chile) to a subsidiary of Sumitomo Metal Mining and announced that its 72%-owned Seven-Up Pete mine (Montana) had discovered a major gold deposit. Phelps Dodge also acquired 3 Venezuelan wire and cable makers and opened a wire and cable plant in Thailand.

In 1993 Hudson International Conductors consolidated 3 manufacturing plants into one South Carolina plant. In 1994 Phelps Dodge announced a $200 million expansion of its Morenci mine (Arizona), which is the world's 2nd largest copper producing operation, and opened its largest copper mine in Chile. In 1995 Phelps Dodge added to its copper properties in Arizona and formed a joint venture in Mexico with Canadian mining concern AZCO.

WHO

Chairman, President, and CEO: Douglas C. Yearley, age 59, $1,120,000 pay
SVP; President, Phelps Dodge Mining Co.: J. Steven Whisler, age 40, $541,100 pay
SVP; President, Phelps Dodge Industries: Manuel J. Iraola, age 46
SVP and CFO: Thomas M. St. Clair, age 59, $457,200 pay
VP and General Counsel: Scott A. Crozier
VP Human Resources: John C. Replogle
Auditors: Price Waterhouse LLP

WHERE

HQ: 2600 N. Central Ave., Phoenix, AZ 85004-3089
Phone: 602-234-8100
Fax: 602-234-8337

Phelps Dodge has facilities in 25 countries.

	1994 Sales		Operating Income	
	$ mil.	% of total	$ mil.	% of total
US	2,659	81	359	90
Latin America	347	10	30	7
Other regions	283	9	11	3
Total	**3,289**	**100**	**400**	**100**

WHAT

	1994 Sales		1994 Operating Income	
	$ mil.	% of total	$ mil.	% of total
Primary metal	1,821	55	326	75
Manufacturing & specialty chemicals	1,468	45	106	25
Adjustments	—	—	(32)	—
Total	**3,289**	**100**	**400**	**100**

Phelps Dodge Mining Company
Black Mountain Mineral Development Co. (Pte.) Ltd. (45%; lead, silver, zinc, and copper mining; South Africa)
Chino Mines Co. (67%, copper mining)
Compañía Contractual Minera Candelaria (80%, copper and gold mining, Chile)
Compañía Contractual Minera Ojos del Salado, S.A. (copper, Chile)
Phelps Dodge Copper Products Co. (copper rod production)
Phelps Dodge Development Corp.
Phelps Dodge Exploration Corp.
Phelps Dodge Hidalgo, Inc. (copper smelting)
Phelps Dodge Mining (Pty.) Ltd. (fluorspar mining, South Africa)
Phelps Dodge Morenci, Inc. (85%, copper mining)
Phelps Dodge Refining Corp. (copper refining)
Phelps Dodge Sales Co., Inc.
Phelps Dodge Tyrone, Inc. (copper mining)
Southern Peru Copper Corp. (16%; copper mining, smelting, and refining)

Phelps Dodge Industries
Accuride Corp. (wheels and rims)
Columbian Chemicals Co. (carbon black, synthetic iron oxide)
Hudson International Conductors (alloy, silver-, nickel-, and tin-plated copper conductors)
Phelps Dodge International Corp. (interests in foreign wire and cable producers)
Phelps Dodge Magnet Wire Co. (copper and aluminum wire)

KEY COMPETITORS

ABB	FMC	International Nickel
Alcan	Freeport-McMoRan	
Alcoa	Copper & Gold	Magma Copper
Anglo American	General Cable	Newmont Mining
ASARCO	Hanson	Reynolds Metals
Broken Hill	Homestake Mining	RTZ
Cyprus Amax	Inco	Southwire
Essex Group		

HOW MUCH

	9-Year Growth	1985	1986	1987	1988	1989	1990	1991	1992	1993	1994
Sales ($ mil.)	15.7%	887	846	1,612	2,320	2,700	2,636	2,434	2,579	2,596	3,289
Net income ($ mil.)	34.4%	19	42	151	420	267	455	273	302	188	271
Income as % of sales	—	2.1%	4.9%	9.3%	18.1%	9.9%	17.3%	11.2%	11.7%	7.2%	8.2%
Earnings per share ($)	48.3%	0.11	0.53	2.09	5.64	3.73	6.56	3.93	4.28	2.66	3.81
Stock price – high ($)	—	12.00	16.25	28.00	26.88	39.31	35.81	39.63	53.00	55.63	65.00
Stock price – low ($)	—	6.75	8.00	10.31	16.25	25.69	23.06	26.19	32.00	39.13	47.63
Stock price – close ($)	20.6%	11.50	10.38	23.50	26.50	29.56	28.31	33.50	48.50	48.75	61.88
P/E – high	—	109	31	13	5	11	6	10	12	21	17
P/E – low	—	61	15	5	3	7	4	7	8	15	13
Dividends per share ($)	—	0.00	0.00	0.08	0.48	6.43	1.50	1.50	1.61	1.65	1.69
Book value per share ($)	8.9%	14.39	15.18	17.68	23.55	19.50	24.43	26.71	28.03	28.67	30.95
Employees	10.3%	6,427	8,787	8,680	10,752	13,288	14,066	13,931	14,750	14,799	15,498

1994 Year-end:
Debt ratio: 23.5%
Return on equity: 12.9%
Cash (mil.): $287
Current ratio: 1.86
Long-term debt (mil.): $622
No. of shares (mil.): 71
Dividends
  Yield: 2.7%
  Payout: 44.4%
Market value (mil.): $4,373

Stock Price History High/Low 1985–94

PHILIP MORRIS COMPANIES INC.

OVERVIEW

There's a new Marlboro Man in town — he's Geoff Bible, a smoker and drinker who was recently named CEO of Philip Morris. Bible has already made heroic strides to revive the sagging tobacco-and-food giant. Now he's standing tall against forces attacking the tobacco industry.

In addition to top tobacco brands, Philip Morris owns Kraft Foods, the US's #2 food business (after ConAgra), and Miller Brewing, the world's #3 beer producer (after Anheuser-Busch and Heineken). Its Philip Morris Capital Corporation subsidiary is involved in financial services and real estate investment.

After several years of slowing growth, in early 1995 Philip Morris streamlined its North American food business by merging Kraft and General Foods, now called Kraft Foods. It has also been selling off low-margin subsidiaries, including Kraft Foodservice to buyout firm Clayton, Dubilier & Rice.

Bible is fighting to redeem smokers. Suits filed by Philip Morris challenge the EPA's findings regarding secondhand smoke and challenge Florida and San Francisco's antismoking regulations. Meanwhile, a 1995 recall of more than 7 billion cigarettes contaminated with an irritant cost the company $100 million.

WHEN

Philip Morris opened a London tobacco store in 1847; by 1854 he was making his own cigarettes. When Morris died in 1873, the company passed to his brother and widow, who sold it to William Thomson just before the turn of the century. In 1902 Thomson introduced his company's cigarettes to the US. American investors purchased the rights to the Philip Morris Cambridge, Oxford Blues, English Ovals, Marlboro, and Players brands in 1919 and 10 years later began manufacturing cigarettes in Richmond, Virginia.

When the original members of the old Tobacco Trust (broken up by the federal government in 1911) raised their prices in 1930, Philip Morris countered by introducing inexpensive cigarettes popular with Depression-weary consumers. A popular ad campaign in 1933 featured bellhop Johnny Roventini chanting the slogan "Call for Philip Morris."

In 1954 Philip Morris acquired Benson & Hedges and its president, Joseph Cullman III. Cullman, assigned to market the filtered Marlboro brand, enlisted the help of advertiser Leo Burnett, who created a simple red-and-white box and the hugely successful Marlboro Man. In 1968 the company introduced Virginia Slims, a cigarette targeted at women. Under Cullman, Philip Morris experienced tremendous overseas expansion.

In 1970 Philip Morris purchased Miller Brewing Company (formed in 1855 by Frederic Miller) and with aggressive marketing vaulted it from the #7 world position in beer to the #2 position by 1980.

In 1985 Philip Morris paid $5.6 billion for food and coffee giant General Foods. General Foods traces its roots back to acquisitions made by C.W. Post's cereal company, including Jell-O (1925) and Maxwell House Coffee (1928). The Post company then acquired the General Foods Company from frozen foods pioneer Clarence Birdseye, and changed its own name to General Foods, in 1929.

In 1988 Philip Morris spent $12.9 billion to purchase Kraft, which had been created in 1930 when Thomas McInnerney's National Dairy Products bought Kraft-Phenix (formed in 1903 by cheese wholesaler James Kraft). In 1991 chairman Hamish Maxwell retired, and Kraft executive Michael Miles became the first nontobacco man to fill the post.

In 1993 the company acquired RJR Nabisco's North American cold cereal operation for $448 million, chocolatier Terry's Group from the UK's United Biscuits Holdings for $295 million, Scandinavian candy maker Freia Marabou for $1.3 billion, and a 20% interest in Molson (Canada's largest brewer) and 100% of Molson Breweries USA for $320 million. That same year it sold Bird's Eye frozen foods to Dean Foods for $140 million.

Also in 1993 Philip Morris cut the price on Marlboro cigarettes to fend off low-priced competitors. The 40¢-per-pack price cut resulted in a 46% drop in domestic tobacco profits but boosted market share for Marlboro and other Philip Morris brands in the US. The profit decline in domestic tobacco was partially offset by stronger 1993 earnings on food, beer, and international cigarette sales.

Amid price pressures and political attacks, CEO Michael Miles suddenly stepped down in mid-1994, shortly after the board rejected a proposal to split Philip Morris into separate tobacco and food companies.

WHO

Chairman and CEO: Geoffrey C. Bible, age 57,
$1,875,000 pay
EVP Worldwide Foods: James M. Kilts, age 47,
$1,178,077 pay
EVP and CFO: Hans G. Storr, age 63, $1,200,000 pay
SVP Human Resources and Administration: Lawrence
A. Gates, age 57
Auditors: Coopers & Lybrand L.L.P.

WHERE

HQ: 120 Park Ave., New York, NY 10017
Phone: 212-880-5000
Fax: 212-878-2167

	1994 Sales		1994 Operating Income	
	$ mil.	% of total	$ mil.	% of total
US	35,936	55	7,306	74
Europe	19,888	31	1,914	19
Other regions	9,301	14	671	7
Adjustments	—	—	(442)	—
Total	**65,125**	**100**	**9,449**	**100**

WHAT

	1994 Sales		1994 Operating Income	
	$ mil.	% of total	$ mil.	% of total
Food	31,669	48	3,108	32
Tobacco	28,671	44	6,162	62
Beer	4,297	7	413	4
Finance/real estate	488	1	208	2
Adjustments	—	—	(442)	—
Total	**65,125**	**100**	**9,449**	**100**

Selected Brands

Kraft Foods	Philadelphia	Suchard
Breakstone's	Brand	Terry's of York
Bull's-Eye	Post	Tobler
Cheez Whiz	Sanka	Toblerone
Chiffon	Seven Seas	Vegemite
Claussen	Shake 'N Bake	**Miller Brewing**
Cool Whip	Tombstone	Löwenbräu
Country Time	Velveeta	Meister Bräu
Cracker Barrel	Yuban	Miller
DiGiorno		Milwaukee's Best
Entenmann's	**Kraft Foods International**	Molson
Freihofer's	Callard & Bowser	Red Dog
Jell-O	Côte d'Or	Sharp's
Knudsen	Daim	
Lender's	Dairylea	**Philip Morris**
Log Cabin	El Caserío	Alpine
Louis Rich	Estrella	Basic
Lunchables	Freia	Benson & Hedges
Maxim	Frisco	Bristol
Maxwell House	Hollywood	Cambridge
Minute	Kibon	Chesterfield
Miracle Whip	Marabou	Marlboro
Oroweat	Milka	Merit
Oscar Mayer	Mirácoli	Parliament
Parkay	Q-Refres-Ko	Players
		Virginia Slims

KEY COMPETITORS

Adolph Coors	CPC	Kellogg
Allied Domecq	Danone	Kirin
American Brands	Foster's Brewing	Loews
Anheuser-Busch	George Weston	Mars
Bass	Grand Metropolitan	Nestlé
B.A.T	Guinness	Procter & Gamble
Ben & Jerry's	Heileman	Quaker Oats
Boston Beer	Heineken	RJR Nabisco
Cadbury	Heinz	S&P
Schweppes	Hershey	Sara Lee
Carlsberg	Hormel	Starbucks
Clorox	Imasco	Stroh
Coca-Cola	John Labatt	Unilever

HOW MUCH

	9-Year Growth	1985	1986	1987	1988	1989	1990	1991	1992	1993	1994
Sales ($ mil.)	16.9%	15,964	25,409	27,695	31,742	44,759	51,169	56,458	59,131	60,901	65,125
Net income ($ mil.)	15.9%	1,255	1,478	1,842	2,337	2,946	3,540	3,972	4,939	3,568	4,725
Income as % of sales	—	7.9%	5.8%	6.7%	7.4%	6.6%	6.9%	7.0%	8.4%	5.9%	7.3%
Earnings per share ($)	17.2%	1.31	1.55	1.94	2.51	3.18	3.83	4.24	5.45	4.06	5.45
Stock price – high ($)	—	11.91	19.50	31.13	25.50	45.50	52.00	81.75	86.63	77.63	64.50
Stock price – low ($)	—	9.00	11.00	17.25	20.13	25.00	36.00	41.75	69.50	45.00	47.25
Stock price – close ($)	20.1%	11.06	17.97	21.34	25.47	41.63	51.75	80.25	77.13	55.63	57.50
P/E – high	—	9	13	16	10	14	14	19	16	19	12
P/E – low	—	7	7	9	8	8	9	10	13	11	9
Dividends per share ($)	22.1%	0.48	0.56	0.75	0.96	1.19	1.46	1.82	2.23	2.60	2.86
Book value per share ($)	13.1%	4.96	5.94	7.21	8.31	10.31	12.90	13.60	14.07	13.26	14.99
Employees	4.2%	114,000	111,000	113,000	155,000	157,000	168,000	166,000	161,000	173,000	165,000

1994 Year-end:
Debt ratio: 56.3%
Return on equity: 38.7%
Cash (mil.): $184
Current ratio: 1.07
Long-term debt (mil.): $14,975
No. of shares (mil.): 853
Dividends
  Yield: 5.0%
  Payout: 52.5%
Market value (mil.): $49,039

**Stock Price History
High/Low 1985–94**

PHILLIPS PETROLEUM COMPANY

OVERVIEW

One of the world's largest fully integrated petroleum companies, with operations in exploration, production, refining, and marketing, Phillips Petroleum is on the move again. The Bartlesville, Oklahoma–based company, which also processes and markets natural gas liquids and produces petrochemicals and plastics, increased its oil production for the first time since 1988 and doubled its profits in 1994. It also ended the year with reserves of oil and gas at their highest levels since 1979, more than 2.1 billion barrels-equivalent.

The company has benefited from its booming gas and chemicals sectors. Phillips's gas production has risen by more than 1/3 in the last 7 years. Its chemicals unit produces petrochemicals and plastics, including polyethylene, polypropylene, and K-Resin, and is a leading producer of cyclohexane (feedstock for nylon). New production capacity, plus higher demand, led to record sales of ethylene and polyethylene in 1994. The company is continuing to invest in its chemical money-maker in 1995; it plans to upgrade and expand its petrochemical complex in Puerto Rico.

The company conducts refining, marketing, and transportation operations under the Phillips 66 trademark. It owns 3 US oil refineries and sells Phillips 66 gasoline through 8,500 service stations in 26 states.

Phillips's employees own approximately 23% of the company stock.

WHEN

Frank Phillips was a prosperous Iowa barber who, after marrying a banker's daughter in 1897, turned to selling bonds. He met a Methodist missionary (assigned to Native Americans in Oklahoma) who regaled him with stories of opportunities in the oil patch.

Phillips migrated to Bartlesville, Oklahoma, and established Anchor Oil (1903). Anchor's first 2 wells were dry holes, but the next one — the Anna Anderson No. 1 — began a string of 81 successfully producing wells. Phillips and his brother L. E., who doubled as bankers in Bartlesville, transformed Anchor into Phillips Petroleum (1917).

With continued success, particularly on Native American lands in Oklahoma, Phillips branched out into refining and marketing. In 1927 the company opened its first filling station in Wichita, Kansas. The Phillips 66 name for the company's gasoline was a salute both to Route 66 (hence the highway-sign shape of the logo) and to the speed reached during a test drive using the gasoline. Frank Phillips retired after WWII and was succeeded as chairman by William Keeler, a Cherokee known as Tsula Westa Nehi ("worker who doesn't sit down") to his tribesmen.

In 1951, 2 Phillips chemists stumbled onto a petrochemical compound eventually marketed as Marlex, the building block for many modern plastic products. In the 1950s the hula hoop spurred demand for the new substance, saving it from a rocky debut and earning the toy a place in the Phillips president's office.

In the 1970s Phillips was rocked by disclosure of illegal campaign contributions. Settlement of the resulting stockholder-initiated suit required the appointment of 6 new directors from outside the cloistered executive boardroom.

To fend off corporate raiders T. Boone Pickens (1984) and Carl Icahn (1985) in separate takeover attempts, Phillips repurchased stock and ran its debt up to $9 billion. At one point it was spending more on interest than on oil exploration. It then beefed up the employee stock ownership plan, cut 8,300 jobs, and sold billions of dollars' worth of assets.

Leaner after the takeover tries, Phillips saw its stock and profits rebound but suffered another blow when its Houston Chemical Complex exploded in 1989, killing 23 people and shutting down US polyethylene production.

In 1990 Phillips won rights to explore 700,000 acres off the Australian coast as it pressed to replace reserves in low-cost areas. In 1992 Phillips restored complete capacity to its Houston Chemical Complex.

In 1993 Phillips and its partners announced plans to spend $3–$4 billion rebuilding Ekofisk, an oil and gas production facility in the Norwegian sector of the North Sea. In 1994 the Norwegian government, which had threatened to shut down the operation because of safety concerns, approved the plans and agreed to extend the facilities' pipeline licenses through 2028. Phillips, through Phillips Petroleum Company Norway, owns 37% of the Scandinavian project.

Also in 1994 Wayne Allen succeeded Pete Silas as chairman and CEO of Phillips.

In 1995 Phillips declared the commercial viability of the Gulf of Mexico's first subsalt oil discovery (in about 370 feet of water) and announced plans to begin production from its Gulf subsalt oil fields by the end of 1996.

NYSE symbol: P
Fiscal year ends: December 31

WHO

Chairman and CEO: Wayne W. Allen, age 58,
$1,581,099 pay
President and COO: James J. Mulva, age 48,
$927,460 pay
EVP: J. L. Whitmire, age 54, $660,747 pay
**EVP Planning and Corporate Relations and Services
(HR):** Charles L. Bowerman, age 55, $597,354 pay
SVP and General Counsel: William G. Paul, age 64,
$652,002 pay
SVP Refining, Marketing, and Transportation: Kirby L.
Hedrick, age 42
SVP Natural Gas Liquids, Chemicals, and Plastics:
J. L. Howe, age 50
SVP Corporate Technology: J. C. Mihm, age 52
SVP, CFO, and Treasurer: Tom C. Morris, age 54
President and CEO, Phillips Gas Company: Mike J.
Panatier, age 46
Auditors: Ernst & Young LLP

WHERE

HQ: Phillips Bldg., Bartlesville, OK 74004
Phone: 918-661-6600
Fax: 918-661-7636

Phillips conducts exploration and production activities
primarily in the US, Nigeria, Norway, and the UK.

	1994 Sales		1994 Operating Income	
	$ mil.	% of total	$ mil.	% of total
US	10,233	84	784	63
UK	979	8	16	1
Norway	426	4	352	28
Africa	165	1	64	5
Other regions	408	3	40	3
Adjustments	156	—	—	—
Total	**12,367**	**100**	**1,256**	**100**

WHAT

	1994 Sales		1994 Operating Income	
	$ mil.	% of total	$ mil.	% of total
Refining, marketing & transportation	7,029	57	187	15
Chemicals	2,793	23	323	26
Exploration & production	1,787	14	708	56
Gas gathering, processing & marketing	595	5	45	3
Corporate & other	163	1	(7)	—
Total	**12,367**	**100**	**1,256**	**100**

Business Lines

Refining, Marketing, and Transportation (crude oil
refining, gasoline marketing, and transportation)
Chemicals (petrochemicals and plastics)
Exploration and Production (oil, natural gas, gas liquids)
Gas Gathering, Processing, and Marketing (natural gas
liquids processing and marketing)

KEY COMPETITORS

Amerada Hess	Formosa	PEMEX
Amoco	Plastics	Pennzoil
Ashland, Inc.	Hoechst	Petrobrás
Atlantic	Huntsman	Petrofina
Richfield	Chemical	Repsol
BASF	Imperial	Royal Dutch/
British	Chemical	Shell
Petroleum	Imperial Oil	Sinclair Oil
Broken Hill	Koch	Southland
Chevron	Lyondell	Sun Co.
Coastal	Petrochemical	Texaco
Dow Chemical	Mobil	TOTAL
DuPont	Monsanto	Union
Eastman	Norsk Hydro	Carbide
Chemical	Occidental	Unocal
Elf Aquitaine	Oryx	USX–
Exxon	PDVSA	Marathon

HOW MUCH

	9-Year Growth	1985	1986	1987	1988	1989	1990	1991	1992	1993	1994
Sales ($ mil.)	(2.6%)	15,676	9,788	10,721	11,304	12,384	13,603	13,259	12,140	12,545	12,367
Net income ($ mil.)	1.6%	418	228	35	650	219	541	98	270	243	484
Income as % of sales	—	2.7%	2.3%	0.3%	5.8%	1.8%	4.0%	0.7%	2.2%	1.9%	3.9%
Earnings per share ($)	2.8%	1.44	0.89	0.06	2.72	0.90	2.18	0.38	1.04	0.94	1.85
Stock price – high ($)	—	17.17	12.75	18.75	22.38	30.13	31.13	29.50	28.88	37.38	37.25
Stock price – low ($)	—	11.00	8.25	10.00	12.13	19.13	22.50	21.88	22.00	24.50	25.50
Stock price – close ($)	11.7%	12.13	11.75	14.00	19.50	25.25	26.13	24.00	25.13	29.00	32.75
P/E – high	—	12	14	—	8	33	14	78	28	40	20
P/E – low	—	8	9	—	4	21	10	58	21	26	14
Dividends per share ($)	1.8%	0.95	0.70	0.60	0.66	0.94	1.03	1.12	1.12	1.12	1.12
Book value per share ($)	5.1%	7.24	7.55	7.08	8.69	8.74	10.51	10.61	10.37	10.28	11.29
Employees	(3.5%)	25,300	21,800	22,500	21,000	21,800	22,400	22,700	21,400	19,400	18,400

1994 Year-end:
Debt ratio: 51.4%
Return on equity: 17.2%
Cash (mil.): $193
Current ratio: 1.01
Long-term debt (mil.): $3,106
No. of shares (mil.): 262
Dividends
  Yield: 3.4%
  Payout: 60.5%
Market value (mil.): $8,569

**Stock Price History
High/Low 1985–94**

PITNEY BOWES INC.

OVERVIEW

Based in Connecticut, Pitney Bowes is the world's largest producer of mailing equipment and postage meters. The company is restructuring its operations to focus on its core business of mailing systems and office products. As part of this program, Pitney Bowes plans to sell its Dictaphone Corp. (voice processing systems) to Stonington Partners, a New York investment group, for $450 million. The company is also selling its Monarch Marking Systems subsidiary (bar code equipment) and reorganizing its German operations.

Pitney Bowes is trimming costs by eliminating about 2,000 nontechnical positions and adding around 850 skilled employees to serve its new software-driven equipment and systems. These new products were developed through Pitney Bowes's own research and joint ventures with partners such as IBM. Although businesses are increasingly using electronic mail, business-to-consumer correspondence is still delivered via the traditional mail channels. As a result, Pitney Bowes is pursuing opportunities as a contractor of outsourced mailroom services.

Pitney Bowes is planning for the eventual retirement of George Harvey, the company's chairman, president, and CEO. The company named Michael Critelli and Marc Breslawsky as vice-chairmen in 1994. They will eventually assume the roles of chairman and CEO, and president and COO, respectively.

WHEN

In 1912 English-born Walter Bowes, an addressing machine salesman, obtained control of the Universal Stamping Machine Company (Stamford, Connecticut), which became a major producer of post office stamp canceling machines. In 1920 Bowes formed a partnership with Arthur Pitney, who had been developing a postage metering machine for 14 years. In 1921 Pitney received his final patent, congressional legislation authorizing the use of his invention was passed, and the Pitney-Bowes Postage Meter Company began leasing its new machines to customers.

In 1929 Pitney-Bowes expanded to overseas markets, and by 1932 revenues totaled almost $1.5 million. In 1945 the company adopted its current name. It continued to grow in the postage meter and letter handling business throughout the 1940s and 1950s.

In the 1960s, with a focus on accelerated growth and diversification, Pitney Bowes began marketing a new line of internally produced copiers (1967) and bought Monarch Marking Systems (price marking and inventory control products, 1968) and Malco Plastics (credit and ID cards, 1968). The company wrote off its 4-year joint venture with Alpex (point-of-sale terminals) in 1973, resulting in its first loss in 54 years. In 1979 Pitney Bowes bought Dictaphone Corporation, including subsidiaries Data Documents (computer supplies) and Grayarc (office supplies), for $124 million. In 1981 it consolidated Grayarc with the Drawing Board (office supply catalog, 1980) to form the Wheeler Group, a direct-mail marketer of office supplies.

To support the financing needs of its US customers, Pitney Bowes set up a leasing organization, Pitney Bowes Financial Services (PBFS), in 1977. As Pitney Bowes grew, so did PBFS, extending its coverage to Canada, the UK, Australia, France, and Germany. PBFS broke even in its 2nd year of business and has increased its profits every year since.

In 1982 Pitney Bowes began designing, marketing, and selling high-end, sophisticated facsimile machines to corporate customers. By 1991 its sales force and extensive support network had brought the company approximately 45% of the large corporate market for fax machines. The machines are serviced by Pitney Bowes's Facsimile Systems' National Diagnostic Centers, which handle most customer problems via telephone.

Pitney Bowes stopped remanufacturing old copiers in 1990 and started selling new, higher-margin copiers (such as its 9000 series, introduced in 1991) to larger businesses. The same year it decided to sell the Wheeler Group, completing the sale in 1992.

New products for 1991 included automated freight management software programs, address and mail list management software, and a medical records transcription network. In 1993 Pitney Bowes's contribution to US postal history was featured in the new National Postal Museum in Washington, DC.

In 1994 the company's successful Paragon mailing system was introduced in Germany, the world's 2nd largest postage meter market. In addition, Pitney Bowes signed an agreement with the Chinese Ministry of Telecommunications and Posts and the Mexican Post Office to assist in the modernization of their postal systems. In 1995 Pitney Bowes opened sales and service offices in France and Spain.

NYSE symbol: PBI
Fiscal year ends: December 31

WHO

Chairman, President, and CEO: George B. Harvey,
age 63, $1,390,417 pay
VC: Marc C. Breslawsky, age 52, $888,825 pay
VC: Michael J. Critelli, age 46, $632,610 pay
President and CEO, Pitney Bowes Business Services:
Carole F. St. Mark, age 52, $667,317 pay
VP Finance and Administration and Treasurer:
Carmine F. Adimando, age 50, $593,850 pay
VP Controller: Steven J. Green, age 43
**VP Communications and Planning, Secretary, and
General Counsel:** Douglas A. Riggs, age 50
VP Personnel: Johnna G. Torsone, age 44
Auditors: Price Waterhouse LLP

WHERE

HQ: One Elmcroft Rd., Stamford, CT 06926-0700
Phone: 203-356-5000
Fax: 203-351-6303 (Public Relations)

Pitney Bowes products are sold worldwide. The company
has manufacturing facilities in Connecticut and the UK.

	1994 Sales		1994 Operating Income	
	$ mil.	% of total	$ mil.	% of total
US	2,851	84	655	97
Europe	293	9	(13)	—
Other countries	231	7	19	3
Adjustments	(104)	—	(9)	—
Total	**3,271**	**100**	**652**	**100**

WHAT

	1994 Sales		1994 Operating Income	
	$ mil.	% of total	$ mil.	% of total
Business equip. & services	2,586	79	425	65
Financial services	685	21	227	35
Total	**3,271**	**100**	**652**	**100**

Business Equipment and Services
Copier systems (SmartTouch, Value Added Maintenance
System [VAMS] 2)
Facsimile systems (PrintScan software for Model 9720)
Mailing systems (Addressright, Business Basics, E530
and E540, PARAGON, Postage by Phone)
Management services (image-based litigation support,
records management, document services)
Production mail systems (SPECTRUM and 7 and 8 Series
inserting systems)
Shipping and weighing systems (ARRIVAL, SEND-IT,
STAR 460/470)

Financial Services
Pitney Bowes financial services (lease financing
programs for Pitney Bowes and other products)

KEY COMPETITORS

Alcatel Alsthom	Matsushita
AM Intl.	Merrill Corp.
Bell & Howell	3M
Brother	Minolta
Canon	Moore Products
Copifax	NEC
Eastman Kodak	Oki
Fuji Photo	Olivetti
GEC	Sharp
Harris Corp.	Smith Corona
Hewlett-Packard	Varitronic
Hitachi	Xerox
IBM	Zebra Technologies

HOW MUCH

	9-Year Growth	1986	1987	1988	1989	1990	1991	1992	1993	1994	1995
Sales ($ mil.)	6.7%	1,832	1,987	2,251	2,650	2,876	3,196	3,333	3,434	3,543	3,271
Net income ($ mil.)	11.3%	150	168	199	243	187	213	295	315	353	394
Income as % of sales	—	8.2%	8.5%	8.9%	9.2%	6.5%	6.7%	8.9%	9.2%	10.0%	12.0%
Earnings per share ($)	11.2%	0.96	1.06	1.27	1.54	1.19	1.34	1.85	1.98	2.22	2.50
Stock price – high ($)	—	12.47	19.13	25.13	23.75	27.38	26.75	32.75	41.00	44.50	46.38
Stock price – low ($)	—	8.41	11.38	14.81	16.88	20.44	13.50	19.00	28.00	36.25	29.25
Stock price – close ($)	11.3%	12.13	18.31	19.13	21.38	23.75	19.88	31.56	39.88	41.38	31.75
P/E – high	—	13	18	20	15	23	20	18	21	20	19
P/E – low	—	9	11	12	11	17	10	10	14	16	12
Dividends per share ($)	14.8%	0.30	0.33	0.38	0.46	0.52	0.60	0.68	0.78	0.90	1.04
Book value per share ($)	9.3%	5.17	4.83	6.48	8.09	9.07	9.93	11.31	10.50	11.81	11.52
Employees	1.4%	28,995	29,166	29,460	29,316	31,404	29,942	29,421	28,958	32,539	32,792

1994 Year-end:
Debt ratio: 66.1%
Return on equity: 21.8%
Cash (mil.): $76
Current ratio: 0.52
Long-term debt (mil.): $779
No. of shares (mil.): 151
Dividends
Yield: 3.3%
Payout: 41.6%
Market value (mil.): $4,803

**Stock Price History
High/Low 1986–95**

PNC BANK CORP.

OVERVIEW

PNC's growth strategy is taking a new turn. For years it pursued a strategy of expansion through branching, acquiring banks in Pennsylvania and neighboring states and standardizing its product offerings. Now the company has begun to reduce its more than 600 branches by as much as 30% and to centralize as many operations as possible, phasing in telebanking where appropriate. This will save operating and personnel costs, allow customers to conduct their banking around the clock, and pave the way for electronic banking in the

future. PNC has also begun unifying its operations, merging 2 subsidiaries in Ohio and northern Kentucky into one unit (legislation allowing interstate banking was passed in 1994). PNC offers credit cards, leasing, and trust services as well.

The interest rate increases of 1994 hit PNC especially hard, helping to drag earnings down 18%. In order to reduce the risk of further interest rate hikes, the bank sold a sizable percentage of its securities investments and hedged its positions with swaps.

WHEN

First National Bank of Pittsburgh, chartered under the National Bank Act, opened in 1863. Ten years later it had $2 million in deposits. In 1913 the bank consolidated with Second National Bank of Pittsburgh (chartered in 1864) as First-Second National and 5 years later became First National in Pittsburgh. Three years later it bought Peoples National.

The company weathered the Depression and WWII and began a long period of postwar expansion. In the 1940s and 1950s First National bought Peoples–Pittsburgh Trust, Sewickley Valley Trust, Monongahela Trust, and 12 other Pennsylvania banks. First National then changed its name to Pittsburgh National.

Pittsburgh National entered the bank credit card business in 1965 and joined the BankAmericard program 4 years later. The bank formed Pittsburgh National Corp., a holding company, in 1968.

In the inflationary 1970s Pittsburgh National began to diversify, establishing new operations in commercial paper financing (1972), insurance on consumer loans (1972), lease financing (1979), and credit life, health, and accident reinsurance (1979).

In 1983, in the largest US banking merger up to that time, Pittsburgh National merged with Provident National of Philadelphia (which had been founded in 1865 as Provident Life & Trust) to form PNC Corp. The merger, made possible by the easing of banking rules, combined Pittsburgh National's corporate lending strength with Provident's money management and trust operations.

The PNC network expanded through the 1980s by buying banks across Pennsylvania, including Marine (1984), Northeastern (1985), and Hershey (1986). Much of this growth and

the interstate expansion that followed was directed by Thomas O'Brien, who was named CEO in 1985. PNC bought Citizen's Fidelity of Louisville (1987) and Central Bancorp (Cincinnati, 1988). In 1987 PNC, with $37 billion in assets, passed Mellon as Pennsylvania's largest bank.

PNC continued to expand in 1988 by starting PNC National of Cherry Hill (New Jersey). In 1989 PNC moved into Delaware with the acquisition of Bank of Delaware.

This growth was accompanied by investment in risky commercial mortgages, so when the market unraveled in 1989 and 1990, PNC was caught with millions in problem loans. It bit the bullet and began selling off its bad loans and property and tightening underwriting standards, but it kept making acquisitions.

In 1991 PNC reorganized itself, beginning to operate as if it were a single entity and refocusing on its core businesses: corporate and retail banking, investment and trust management, and investment banking.

Despite the company's heavy program of acquisitions, PNC has continued to emphasize cost containment. Although the 1993 acquisition of Sears Mortgage (which made PNC the 15th largest mortgage servicer in the US) caused an upward blip, staff levels have remained nearly flat.

In 1995 PNC completed its purchase of BlackRock Financial Management, an asset management company that will provide a boost for PNC's own asset management operations. The company also continued to buy branches, taking over 84 locations from Chemical Bank in central and southern New Jersey, affluent areas that are contiguous to PNC's current business region.

NYSE symbol: PNC
Fiscal year ends: December 31

WHO

Chairman and CEO: Thomas H. O'Brien, age 58, $1,099,900 pay
President: James E. Rohr, age 46, $628,558 pay
EVP Finance and Administration: Walter E. Gregg Jr., age 53, $446,663 pay
EVP Corporate Banking: Bruce E. Robbins, age 50, $378,810 pay
EVP Investment Management and Trust: Richard C. Caldwell, age 50, $378,810 pay
EVP Corporate Development and Communications: Susan B. Bohn, age 50
SVP and CFO: Robert L. Haunschild, age 45
SVP and General Counsel: Helen P. Pudlin, age 45
SVP Human Resources: Daniel F. Gillis, age 54
Auditors: Ernst & Young LLP

WHERE

HQ: One PNC Plaza, 5th Ave. and Wood St., Pittsburgh, PA 15265
Phone: 412-762-3900
Fax: 412-762-6238

PNC operates 10 banking subsidiaries in Delaware, Indiana, Kentucky, Ohio, Massachusetts, New Jersey, and Pennsylvania and over 80 nonbanking subsidiaries.

| | 1994 Deposits | |
	$ mil.	% of total
Pennsylvania	24,700	71
Kentucky	3,400	9
Ohio	4,900	14
Delaware	1,700	6
Other states	311	0
Total	**35,011**	**100**

WHAT

| | 1994 Assets | |
	$ mil.	% of total
Cash & equivalents	3,401	5
Mortgage-backed securities	14,470	23
Government bonds	4,444	7
Private placements	1,597	2
Net loans	34,405	54
Other	5,828	9
Total	**64,145**	**100**

| | 1994 Sales | |
	$ mil.	% of total
Loan interest & fees	2,479	51
Other interest	1,382	29
Service charges & fees	370	8
Investment mgmt. & trust	292	6
Mortgage banking	199	4
Other	97	2
Total	**4,819**	**100**

Selected Subsidiaries
BlackRock Financial Management L.P.
PFPC Inc. (mutual fund management)
PNC Bank International, New York
PNC Leasing Corp
PNC Mortgage Corp.
PNC National Bank (credit card services)
PNC Securities Corp
Provident Capital Management, Inc. (institutional investment management)

KEY COMPETITORS

Banc One	Countrywide	KeyCorp
BankAmerica	Credit	Keystone
Chase Manhattan	Equitable	Financial
Chemical	First Fidelity	Mellon Bank
Banking	Fleet	NSD Bancorp
Citicorp	FMR	T. Rowe Price
CoreStates	Household Intl.	Transamerica
Financial	Integra Financial	

HOW MUCH

	9-Year Growth	1985	1986	1987	1988	1989	1990	1991	1992	1993	1994
Assets ($ mil.)	14.6%	18,778	22,199	36,504	40,811	45,661	45,534	44,892	51,380	62,080	64,145
Net income ($ mil.)	14.0%	188	237	256	443	377	71	390	529	745	610
Income as % of assets	—	1.0%	1.1%	0.7%	1.1%	0.8%	0.2%	0.9%	1.0%	1.2%	1.0%
Earnings per share ($)	3.9%	1.82	2.25	1.47	2.48	1.96	0.37	1.95	2.34	3.13	2.56
Stock price – high ($)	—	17.75	25.38	25.44	23.25	24.50	22.06	24.13	29.25	36.38	31.63
Stock price – low ($)	—	11.41	17.44	16.63	18.25	19.25	7.88	9.44	23.13	27.00	20.00
Stock price – close ($)	2.1%	17.50	20.63	18.63	19.88	20.81	10.81	23.56	28.50	29.00	21.13
P/E – high	—	10	11	17	9	13	60	12	13	12	12
P/E – low	—	6	8	11	7	10	21	5	10	9	8
Dividends per share ($)	8.7%	0.62	0.71	0.80	0.89	1.00	1.06	1.06	1.08	1.18	1.31
Book value per share ($)	4.9%	12.24	8.57	12.82	14.49	15.08	13.61	15.43	16.10	18.43	18.84
Employees	7.3%	9,531	11,381	15,666	15,600	17,681	18,100	16,900	17,800	21,100	18,000

1994 Year-end:
Equity as % of assets: 6.9%
Return on assets: 1.0%
Return on equity: 14.0%
Long-term debt (mil.): $1,454
No. of shares (mil.): 233
Dividends
  Yield: 6.2%
  Payout: 51.2%
Market value (mil.): $4,929
Sales (mil.): $4,819

Stock Price History
High/Low 1985–94

POLAROID CORPORATION

OVERVIEW

Polaroid zoomed in on the world's imaging market by inventing and marketing instant photography. Based in Cambridge, Massachusetts, the company designs, manufactures, and markets cameras and films, electronic imaging devices, and filters and lenses.

Polaroid is focusing on 2 new businesses — high-resolution imaging and electronic imaging — for its future growth (despite division losses of more than $150 million in 1994). The company's Helios Laser Imaging System produces high-quality medical images by using a laser system with a digitally responsive, carbon-based film. Polaroid is also venturing into the graphic arts business with the introduction of 2 new products — Dry Tech Imagesetting System (producing high-quality separation films with a dry processing method) and DryJet Color Proofing System (providing high-quality proofs using printing ink and coated and uncoated papers).

Polaroid is streamlining its US operations and increasingly targeting international markets for its core photographic business. Polaroid consolidated its distribution and manufacturing facilities and retired 900 employees (8% of the work force) in 1995. In China the company is establishing 3 regional sales offices and focusing on sales of cameras and instant film where there are few photo processors. Sales in Russia already account for 13% of international sales.

WHEN

In the late 1920s Harvard University undergraduate Edwin Land began the research that led him to develop the world's first synthetic light-polarizing material, which he named Polaroid. In 1932, just months before he would have graduated, Land left Harvard to establish a company exploiting the new material. He was 23 years old.

During the 1930s the company licensed the use of the new material, using the resulting cash to fund further research and development. Polaroid prospered during WWII, developing a number of military uses for its basic product. The company's sales rose from $1 million in 1941 to over $15 million by 1945. Although sales dropped back to about $1.5 million in 1947, Land unveiled his instant-picture camera that year, and the course of the company was set.

Polaroid introduced the $14 Swinger in 1965; by 1968 it had sold 7 million of the cameras. But its SX-70 camera, introduced in 1972, sold sluggishly, and Polaroid's net income foundered until 1975, when it introduced the Pronto, which set an annual sales record of 6 million cameras. That same year Eastman Kodak began selling a line of instant cameras. Polaroid filed suit for patent infringement in 1976.

Introduction of the new, high-quality Spectra camera and film in 1986 boosted sales, but Polaroid spent most of the 1980s streamlining operations in pursuit of profits and in the face of a hostile takeover bid (1988–89) by Shamrock Holdings.

Polaroid introduced conventional film in 1989. The opening of the Eastern European markets, particularly the demand for passport images, increased sales in that region in the early 1990s. In 1991 Polaroid won an $873 million award in its 15-year-old patent infringement suit against Eastman Kodak. Also that year I. MacAllister Booth replaced retiring chairman William McCune, and Edwin Land, Polaroid's founder, died at the age of 81 after having retired in 1982.

Polaroid expanded into the imaging industry, which includes photocopying, printing, and video as well as photography. Helios, a system for recording diagnostic images with no chemical processing or toxic fluids, was named one of the top 10 innovative products of 1991 by *Radiology Today*. (Helios was released in 1993, 2 years behind schedule.)

In 1992 Polaroid introduced documentation cameras (for emergency medical services and the construction business) and photo credit cards for banks. That same year Polaroid released its first-ever single-lens reflex instant camera as Polaroid Vision in Germany. It was launched in the US in 1993 under the brand name Captiva. Also in 1993 Polaroid and IBM demonstrated a project involving digital camera systems and mobile computers at the Consumer Electronics Show in Las Vegas.

In 1994 Gerald Knudson, formerly of General Electric Medical Systems, and Henry Ancona from Digital Equipment were hired to manage the high-resolution imaging and electronic imaging businesses, respectively.

With its expertise in image science, laser optics, and digital technology, Polaroid introduced 3 new technologies in 1995 — a new lithographic printing plate, a direct digital color proofer, and direct digital plates — at the DRUPA95 International Printing Fair.

NYSE symbol: PRD
Fiscal year ends: December 31

Chairman, President, and CEO: I. MacAllister Booth, age 63, $577,506 pay
EVP Photographic Imaging: Joseph R. Oldfield, age 54, $296,250 pay
EVP and CFO: William J. O'Neill Jr., age 52, $275,004 pay
EVP Electronic Imaging: Enrico I. "Henry" Ancona, age 49, $157,293 pay
SVP Business Development: Peter O. Kliem, age 57
SVP Photographic Imaging, Americas: Robert M. Delahunt, age 60
SVP Photographic Imaging, Europe: Lee C. Brewer, age 59
VP and Chief Technology Officer: Satish C. Agrawal, age 51
VP Secretary, and General Counsel: Richard F. deLima, age 64
VP Human Resources: Joseph G. Parham Jr., age 45
Auditors: KPMG Peat Marwick LLP

WHERE

HQ: 549 Technology Sq., Cambridge, MA 02139
Phone: 617-386-2000
Fax: 617-386-3118

Polaroid sells its products worldwide. US manufacturing and primary office facilities are in Massachusetts, with other manufacturing facilities in Mexico, the Netherlands, and Scotland.

	1994 Sales		1994 Operating Income	
	$ mil.	% of total	$ mil.	% of total
US	1,160	50	101	44
Europe	705	31	82	36
Other regions	448	19	45	20
Adjustments	—	—	(28)	—
Total	**2,313**	**100**	**200**	**100**

WHAT

Selected Products
Conventional cameras
  SideKick
  Talking SideKick
Digital scanners
  SprintScan 35 (35mm color slides)
Film recorders
Films
  Conventional
  Instant
Filters
Graphic imaging
Instant cameras
  Captiva (single-lens reflex)
  OneStep
  Spectra
LCD panels and projectors
Lenses
Medical imaging systems
  Helios Model 810 and 1417
Photo card systems
Professional cameras
  MicroCam SLR (microscopic photography)
  ProCam
Security ID systems
  ID-4000
Videotapes

KEY COMPETITORS

Acuson	Eastman Kodak	Medtronic
BASF	Fuji Photo	3M
Bausch & Lomb	GEC	Minolta
Baxter	General Electric	Mitsubishi
Bayer	Hewlett-Packard	Philips
Canon	Hitachi	Siemens
Concord Camera	Honeywell	Sony
CPI Corp.	Johnson Controls	Xerox
C.R. Bard	Matsushita	

HOW MUCH

	9-Year Growth	1985	1986	1987	1988	1989	1990	1991	1992	1993	1994
Sales ($ mil.)	6.7%	1,295	1,629	1,764	1,863	1,905	1,972	2,071	2,152	2,245	2,313
Net income ($ mil.)	13.7%	37	104	116	(23)	145	151	684	99	68	117
Income as % of sales	—	2.8%	6.4%	6.6%	—	7.6%	7.7%	33.0%	4.6%	3.0%	5.1%
Earnings per share ($)	16.8%	0.60	1.67	1.88	(0.34)	1.96	2.20	10.88	2.02	1.45	2.42
Stock price – high ($)	—	22.63	37.38	42.75	44.13	50.38	48.25	29.00	35.00	38.75	36.75
Stock price – low ($)	—	12.13	21.13	16.50	21.50	35.13	20.25	19.63	23.63	25.75	29.25
Stock price – close ($)	4.6%	21.63	33.25	23.63	36.88	45.75	23.38	26.63	31.13	33.50	32.50
P/E – high	—	38	22	23	—	26	22	3	17	27	15
P/E – low	—	20	13	9	—	18	9	2	12	18	12
Dividends per share ($)	2.0%	0.50	0.50	0.60	0.60	0.60	0.60	0.60	0.60	0.60	0.60
Book value per share ($)	2.7%	14.89	16.06	17.34	14.12	2.86	4.03	15.44	16.54	16.39	18.85
Employees	(0.7%)	12,932	14,765	13,662	11,613	11,441	11,768	12,003	12,359	12,048	12,104

1994 Year-end:
Debt ratio: 45.4%
Return on equity: 14.4%
Cash (mil.): $229
Current ratio: 2.47
Long-term debt (mil.): $566
No. of shares (mil.): 46
Dividends
  Yield: 1.8%
  Payout: 24.8%
Market value (mil.): $1,491

**Stock Price History
High/Low 1985–94**

PPG INDUSTRIES, INC.

OVERVIEW

With its headquarters appropriately located in a glass tower, Pittsburgh, Pennsylvania–based PPG Industries towers above other US glass makers. The nation's leading glass manufacturer produces windows for homes and businesses and windshields for autos and jets. PPG is also the world leader in supplying automotive and industrial paints, as well as a leader in the residential and commercial coatings business. The firm is the world's leading producer of optical resins, the #2 producer of continuous-strand fiberglass, and the 3rd largest producer of chlorine and caustic soda. PPG also makes a range of other chemicals.

Under Jerry Dempsey, the first outsider to head PPG in its history (appointed chairman and CEO in 1993), PPG has focused on geographical expansion, the introduction of new products, strategic alliances, and acquisitions. PPG has also divested itself of a number of noncore assets; it sold its medical electronics unit to Enhanced Imaging Technologies for about $55 million in 1993 and its biomedical systems unit in 1994 and 1995.

PPG and Vista Chemical (a US subsidiary of RWE AG) signed an agreement in 1995 to form a joint-venture production company to manufacture vinyl chloride monomer. In the Asia-Pacific region, the priority growth area for the company, PPG is building Chinese silicas plants and is planning to make contact lenses in Australia.

WHEN

After the failure of 2 previous plants, John Ford persuaded former railroad superintendent John Pitcairn to invest $200,000 in a 3rd plate glass factory in 1883 in Creighton, Pennsylvania. Named Pittsburgh Plate Glass, the enterprise became the first commercially successful US plate glass factory.

Ford left in 1896 when Pitcairn pushed through a plan to set up a company distribution system, replacing glass jobbers. (Ford went on to found a predecessor of competitor Libbey-Owens-Ford, now owned by Pilkington [UK].) Expanding the existing business, Pitcairn built a soda ash plant in 1899, bought a Milwaukee paint company in 1900, and began producing window glass in 1908.

Strong automobile and construction markets in the early part of the century increased demand for the company's products. Pitcairn died in 1916 and left his stock (31% of the total) to his sons. In 1924 PPG revolutionized the glass production process with the introduction of a straight-line conveyor manufacturing method. In the 1930s and 1940s, PPG successfully promoted structural glass for use in the commercial construction industry.

PPG was listed on the NYSE in 1945. In 1952 it began making fiberglass, and in 1968 the company adopted its present name.

Vincent Sarni (CEO from 1984–93) saw that PPG's markets (85% of sales were to the construction and automobile industries) were maturing. Sarni wrote a document entitled Blueprint for the Decade, 1985–1994, which spelled out his vision for the company. Principal among the goals were global expansion and an average ROE of 18%. The average ROE over the 10 years of the Blueprint was 16.7%.

In 1986 PPG spent $154 million on acquisitions, the most important of which were the worldwide medical electronics units of Litton Industries and Honeywell, which gave PPG its first entry into the high-technology instrumentation business. PPG acquired the medical technology business of Allegheny International in 1987 for $100 million. In 1989 the company bought Casco Nobel, a coatings distributor, and the Olympic and Lucite paint lines from Clorox for $134 million.

PPG, which owned 1/3 of Dutch fiberglass producer Silenka BV, acquired the remaining 2/3 and purchased or expanded facilities in 3 other countries in 1991. The company's Florida lens-making facility (joint venture with Essilor International) started operations in 1991. In 1992 the company acquired a silica plant in the Netherlands, the company's first in Europe. In its continuing effort to expand overseas, PPG purchased a 20% interest in a coatings and resins subsidiary in Italy in 1993. In 1994 the company acquired the European original automotive coatings business of Netherlands-based Akzo Nobel.

Also in 1994 PPG broke ground for an automotive coatings facility in China and began operation of a 2nd Chinese silicas manufacturing plant. In 1994 sales growth was 12%, and for the 10-year period ending in 1994 it averaged 4% a year.

With an eye to environmental protection, PPG cut the waste from its North American facilities by more than 152,000 tons, or 40%, between 1988 and 1994.

The firm launched its Blueprint for the Future in 1995. PPG's new sales goal is to achieve 5% nominal sales growth.

NYSE symbol: PPG
Fiscal year ends: December 31

WHO

Chairman and CEO: Jerry E. Dempsey, age 62, $1,976,667 pay
EVP: Robert D. Duncan, age 55, $964,983 pay
EVP: Raymond W. LeBoeuf, age 48, $935,483 pay
SVP Chemicals: Peter R. Heinze, age 52, $727,617 pay
SVP Fiber Glass: John J. Horgan, age 52, $622,867 pay
SVP and General Counsel: Guy A. Zoghby, age 60
SVP Finance: William H. Hernandez, age 46
SVP Human Resources and Administration: Russell L. Crane, age 54
VP Coatings & Resins: E. Kears Pollock
VP Specialty Chemicals: Donald W. Bogus
VP Glass: Frank A. Archinaco
Controller: Dan W. Kiener
Secretary: H. Kennedy Linge
Auditors: Deloitte & Touche LLP

WHERE

HQ: One PPG Place, Pittsburgh, PA 15272
Phone: 412-434-3131
Fax: 412-434-2448

PPG has 68 major plants in the US, Canada, China, France, Germany, Italy, Mexico, the Netherlands, Portugal, Spain, Taiwan, and the UK.

	1994 Sales		1994 Pretax Income	
	$ mil.	% of total	$ mil.	% of total
US	4,332	68	771	80
Europe	1,405	22	88	9
Canada	413	7	72	8
Other countries	181	3	30	3
Adjustments	—	—	(105)	—
Total	**6,331**	**100**	**856**	**100**

WHAT

	1994 Sales		1994 Pretax Income	
	$ mil.	% of total	$ mil.	% of total
Coatings & resins	2,647	42	497	48
Glass	2,388	38	315	29
Chemicals	1,296	20	227	23
Other	—	—	(78)	—
Adjustments	—	—	(105)	—
Total	**6,331**	**100**	**856**	**100**

Chemicals
Caustic soda
Chlorine
Flame retardants
Industrial applications
Optical resins
Phosgene derivatives
Pool treatment chemicals
Silica products
Sulfur chemicals
Surfactants
Vinyl chloride monomer
Water treatment chemicals

Coatings and Resins
Adhesives
Architectural finishes
Automotive coatings
Industrial coatings
Metal pretreatment chemicals
Sealants

Glass
Aircraft glass
Architectural glass
Automotive glass
Coated glass products
Fiberglass
Flat glass

KEY COMPETITORS

AFG Industries	General Electric	Occidental
Akzo Nobel	Guardian	Olin
Apogee	Industries	Owens-Corning
Asahi Glass	Hewlett-Packard	Philips
BASF	Hoechst	Pilkington
Bausch & Lomb	Huntsman	Pratt & Lambert
Berkshire	Chemical	St.-Gobain
Hathaway	Imperial	Sherwin-Williams
C. R. Bard	Chemical	Siemens
Dow Chemical	Manville	Sumitomo
DuPont	Mitsubishi	USG
Ford	Morton	Vulcan Materials

HOW MUCH

	9-Year Growth	1985	1986	1987	1988	1989	1990	1991	1992	1993	1994
Sales ($ mil.)	4.3%	4,346	4,687	5,183	5,617	5,734	6,021	5,673	5,814	5,754	6,331
Net income ($ mil.)	6.1%	303	316	377	468	465	475	201	319	295	515
Income as % of sales	—	7.0%	6.7%	7.3%	8.3%	8.1%	7.9%	3.5%	5.5%	5.1%	8.1%
Earnings per share ($)	8.9%	1.13	1.33	1.60	2.13	2.09	2.22	0.95	1.51	1.39	2.43
Stock price – high ($)	—	12.75	19.38	26.75	23.38	23.00	27.63	29.63	34.13	38.13	42.13
Stock price – low ($)	—	8.13	11.25	13.75	15.63	18.50	17.25	20.75	25.00	29.63	33.75
Stock price – close ($)	12.6%	12.75	18.13	16.50	20.13	19.88	23.50	25.25	32.88	37.88	37.13
P/E – high	—	11	15	17	11	11	12	31	23	27	17
P/E – low	—	7	8	9	7	9	8	22	17	21	14
Dividends per share ($)	12.2%	0.41	0.47	0.56	0.64	0.74	0.82	0.86	0.94	1.04	1.16
Book value per share ($)	6.2%	7.19	8.28	9.22	10.24	10.49	12.01	12.50	12.71	11.57	12.34
Employees	(2.2%)	37,500	36,500	36,800	36,300	35,500	35,100	33,700	32,300	31,400	30,800

1994 Year-end:
Debt ratio: 30.4%
Return on equity: 20.5%
Cash (mil.): $62
Current ratio: 1.52
Long-term debt (mil.): $745
No. of shares (mil.): 290.6
Dividends
 Yield: 3.1%
 Payout: 47.7%
Market value (mil.): $10,788

Stock Price History High/Low 1985–94

PREMARK INTERNATIONAL, INC.

The party is not over at Premark. The company's Tupperware division, which accounts for about 56% of profits, still markets its plastic food-storage containers through "Tupperware parties," 12 million of which were held last year at homes, offices, and social clubs worldwide. Tupperware gets around 80% of its sales in foreign countries where cheaper imitations are more difficult to find.

Premark's other divisions include its Food Equipment Group, which sells commercial food products under the brand names Vulcan, Foster, and Adamatic; and the Consumer and Decorative Products division, which sells laminates, floor tile, hardwood flooring, small appliances, and physical fitness equipment.

Premark, which stands for "premier trademarks," considers its brands to be its principal asset. Besides Tupperware, the company's Hobart (commercial food equipment) and West Bend (small appliances) remain 2 of the best-known brand names in their categories. Premark hopes to make more of its brands available internationally.

The company still considers Latin America and Asia to be prime areas for growth despite losses due to the peso devaluation and the Kobe earthquake. The 1995 quake in Japan knocked out many Tupperware distributors. However, increased sales volume in that country and a strong yen have more than offset the losses from the quake.

WHEN

Premark's story begins with Justin Dart, a native of Illinois who, after graduating from Northwestern in the 1920s, married (and then divorced) the daughter of Walgreen Company's founder, Charles Walgreen. When Walgreen died in 1939, Dart became general manager of the company but left in 1941 to join United Drugs, a Boston-based drug company started in 1903. Dart took control of United Drugs in 1943, moving its headquarters from Boston to Los Angeles in 1945.

Boasting Rexall as a major brand, the company adopted the name Rexall Drug in 1947. Dart led Rexall through a series of acquisitions, including Tupper Corporation, former DuPont chemist Earl Tupper's plastic container company (Tupperware, 1958); Ralph Wilson Plastics, a decorative laminated plastics manufacturer (Wilsonart, 1966); and West Bend, a cookware maker (1968). The company adopted the name Dart Industries in 1969.

Dart sold its Rexall division, the last vestige of the original drug company, in 1977 and bought P. R. Mallory and Company, maker of Duracell batteries, in 1978.

In 1980 the company merged with Kraft, the Chicago food conglomerate, to form Dart & Kraft. Founded in 1903 by cheese wholesaler James Kraft, Kraft merged with rival cheesemaker Phenix Cheese in 1928 to form Kraft-Phenix. In 1930 the company was acquired by National Dairy Products Corporation, which adopted the name Kraftco (1969) and then Kraft, Inc. (1976) to take advantage of the name value of its best-known products. After the Dart-Kraft merger, John Richman, CEO of Kraft since 1979, became chairman

and CEO of Dart & Kraft. Dart acted as an advisor to the company until his death in 1984.

Warren Batts, former CEO of Mead, became president and COO of Dart & Kraft in 1981. That year the company bought Hobart Corporation, maker of commercial kitchen equipment, including KitchenAid appliances (sold in 1986). Other purchases included Precor (fitness equipment, 1984) and Vulcan-Hart (gas stoves, 1986).

In 1986 the company decided to spin off its nonfood divisions. Tupperware, Hobart, Vulcan-Hart, Ralph Wilson Plastics, and West Bend became Premark International, a new company headed by Batts. Kraft kept all of its pre-1980 assets and Duracell batteries. Premark has since acquired several businesses, including Tibbals (oak flooring, 1988) and Florida Tile (decorative tiles, 1990).

Premark sought to expand its marketing options by starting Tupperware Express, which delivered (and eventually would have sold) merchandise directly to customers. In 1992, however, Premark announced that shipping costs for Tupperware Express were prohibitive and began trying out other delivery systems. Domestic Tupperware sales, which had been sluggish, began to turn around in 1993 as the company expanded its sales force by 27% and improved its use of promotions. Sales continued to improve in 1994. That year Tupperware introduced about 100 new products worldwide and started TupperKids, an extension of its toy business that includes lunch boxes, educational games, and a series of tapes and books.

Premark intends to introduce Tupperware in India in 1997–98.

NYSE symbol: PMI
Fiscal year ends: Last Saturday in December

Chairman and CEO: Warren L. Batts, age 62,
$2,365,833 pay
President and COO: James M. Ringler, $1,429,500 pay
EVP; President, Tupperware Worldwide: E. V. Goings,
age 49, $1,676,763 pay
SVP and CFO: Lawrence B. Skatoff, age 55,
$827,500 pay
SVP, General Counsel, and Secretary: John M. Costigan,
age 52
SVP Human Resources: James C. Coleman, age 55
Group VP and President, Food Equipment Group:
Joseph W. Deering, age 54, $818,565 pay
Corporate VP and President, The West Bend Company:
Thomas W. Kieckhafer, age 56
VP Planning: Isabelle C. Goossen, age 43
VP and Treasurer: Lisa Kearns Richardson, age 42
Auditors: Price Waterhouse LLP

WHERE

HQ: 1717 Deerfield Rd., Deerfield, IL 60015
Phone: 708-405-6000
Fax: 708-405-6013

Premark manufactures products in 15 countries and
markets them in over 100.

	1994 Sales		1994 Operating Income	
	$ mil.	% of total	$ mil.	% of total
US	1,898	55	151	42
Europe	939	27	139	39
Asia/Pacific	378	11	48	14
Latin America & Canada	236	7	18	5
Total	**3,451**	**100**	**356**	**100**

WHAT

	1994 Sales		1994 Operating Income	
	$ mil.	% of total	$ mil.	% of total
Tupperware	1,333	39	199	56
Food equipment	1,135	33	81	23
Other	983	28	76	21
Total	**3,451**	**100**	**356**	**100**

Operations and Selected Brand Names

Tupperware	Consumer and
TupperCare	**Decorative Products**
TupperKids	Florida Tile (decorative tile)
Tuppertoys	Gibraltar (surfacing
Tupperware	products)
Tupperwave	Hartco (flooring installation)
	Precor (fitness equipment)
Food Equipment	West Bend (appliances)
Adamatic	Wilsonart (laminates)
Foster	
Hobart	**Principal Subsidiaries**
Still	Dart Industries Inc.
Tasselli	(Tupperware)
Vulcan	Florida Tile Industries, Inc.
Wolf	Precor, Inc.
	Premark FEG Corp.
	Ralph Wilson Plastics Co.
	The West Bend Co.

KEY COMPETITORS

Amway	Gillette	Acquisition
Armstrong World	Hasbro	Owens-Illinois
Avon	Home	Rubbermaid
Black & Decker	Interiors &	Soloflex
CML Group	Gifts	Sunbeam-Oster
Color Tile	Mattel	Toastmaster
Corning	3M	Tyco Toys
Dal-Tile	Mobil	U. S. Industries
AB Electrolux	Nautilus	

HOW MUCH

	Annual Growth	1985	1986	1987	1988	1989	1990	1991	1992	1993	1994
Sales ($ mil.)	7.7%	1,763	1,959	2,197	2,397	2,592	2,721	2,816	2,946	3,097	3,451
Net income ($ mil.)	13.9%	70	(98)	72	121	78	52	102	5	173	226
Income as % of sales	—	4.0%	—	3.3%	5.1%	3.0%	1.9%	3.6%	0.2%	5.6%	6.5%
Earnings per share ($)	17.1%	0.82	(1.44)	1.04	1.75	1.12	0.82	1.63	0.07	2.58	3.39
Stock price – high ($)	—	—	10.75	15.88	18.13	21.00	15.50	20.31	25.63	41.88	48.00
Stock price – low ($)	—	—	8.75	9.25	11.06	14.69	6.38	8.13	14.88	19.13	33.50
Stock price – close ($)	20.9%	—	9.81	11.19	15.75	15.38	8.69	20.31	20.31	40.13	44.75
P/E – high	—	—	—	15	10	19	19	13	—	16	14
P/E – low	—	—	—	9	6	13	8	5	—	7	10
Dividends per share ($)	—	—	0.00	0.13	0.23	0.36	0.42	0.42	0.46	0.53	0.74
Book value per share ($)	7.7%	—	8.42	9.84	11.14	11.76	12.33	13.44	11.17	12.72	15.22
Employees	1.1%	—	22,000	22,800	24,000	24,700	25,400	24,000	24,000	24,000	24,000

1994 Year-end:
Debt ratio: 17.5%
Return on equity: 25.3%
Cash (mil.): $121
Current ratio: 1.38
Long-term debt (mil.): $122
No. of shares (mil.): 64
Dividends
  Yield: 1.7%
  Payout: 21.8%
Market value (mil.): $2,859

**Stock Price History
High/Low 1986–94**

PRICE WATERHOUSE LLP

OVERVIEW

Price Waterhouse (PW) is the smallest of the Big 6 accounting firms, the best known (thanks to decades of tallying the votes for the Academy Awards), and traditionally the most prestigious. But in the 1990s the firm's luster has been tarnished by the involvement of its UK branch with the Bank of Credit & Commerce Intl. (BCCI), which failed spectacularly in 1992 amid charges of fraud and double-dealing throughout the world. The UK branch faces suits for billions of dollars in damages brought by BCCI's liquidator, Touche Ross (the UK branch of Big 6 rival Deloitte Touche Tohmatsu). Other world partners would not be liable for monetary payment in a judgment

against the UK firm, but full recovery of damages could put an important link in PW's operations out of business.

In addition to auditing, PW offers a full range of management consulting services.

In 1995 the firm embarked on a sweeping restructuring, separating the offices of US and world chairpersons, rooting out a layer of middle management, and reorganizing its practice along business lines, to ensure that auditors and consultants are specialists in the fields they work in. New areas of specialization include entertainment, media, and communications; high tech; energy; and individual product groups like food and health.

WHEN

In 1850 Samuel Lowell Price founded an accounting firm in London, and in 1865 he took on Edwin Waterhouse as a partner. The firm quickly attracted several important accounts and a group of prestigious partners that included 4 Knights of the British Empire. Aided by the explosive industrial growth in Britain and the rest of the world, Price Waterhouse expanded rapidly (as did the accounting industry as a whole) and by the late 1800s had established itself as the most prestigious accounting firm in the world, providing its services in accounting, auditing, and business consulting.

By the 1890s the firm's dealings in America (where it kept tabs on the US investments of Britons) had grown sufficiently to warrant permanent representation, so Lewis Jones and William Caesar were sent to open offices in New York City and Chicago. United States Steel chose Price Waterhouse as its auditors in 1902.

Through the next several decades, PW's London office initiated tremendous expansion into other countries. By the 1930s, 57 PW offices boasting 2,500 employees operated globally. The growth of PW in New York was largely due to the Herculean efforts of partner Joseph Sterrett, and PW, along with other accounting firms, benefited from SEC audit requirements. The firm's reputation was enhanced further in 1935 when it was chosen to handle the Academy Awards balloting. Its prestige attracted several important clients, notably large oil and steel interests.

During WWII, PW recruited and trained women with college experience to fill its depleted ranks for the duration; some remained with the firm after the end of the hostilities. In

1946 the firm started a management consulting service.

While PW tried to coordinate and expand its international offices after the war, the firm lost its dominance in the 1960s. The company came to be viewed as the most traditional and formal of the major firms. PW tried to show more aggressiveness in the 1980s.

In 1989 the firm made plans to merge with Arthur Andersen, but the 2 managements were unable to come to terms. When the deal fell through, the firm expanded internationally, merging with Swiss firm Revisuisse and opening an office Budapest that same year.

In 1992 PW lost a $338 million judgment in a suit brought by Standard Chartered PLC (UK). Standard Chartered had sued the firm for negligence in its audits of Arizona-based United Bank, which Standard Chartered had bought in 1987. The judgment was thrown out in late 1992 and a new trial was ordered.

In 1993 PW achieved some notoriety when it was revealed that it had charged US thrift regulators 67 cents a page for copying more than 10 million documents in reviewing the assets of a failed S&L. But it remained the only Big 6 firm not sued by the FDIC or RTC.

It was not so lucky overseas. In addition to the BCCI litigation, in 1994 the firm was sued by stockholders in Banco Español de Crédito, charging that PW did not reveal the bank's financial problems. Similar complaints were made after the near bankruptcy of Italy's Montedison, a food and chemical conglomerate. Yet another suit, arising from the bankruptcy of a Hong Kong property company, was settled out of court. Also in 1994 the firm was granted a license to start up operations in Vietnam.

Limited liability partnership
Fiscal year ends: June 30

WHO

US Chairman: James J. Schiro, age 49
World Chairman: Dominic A. Tarantino, age 63
Deputy World Chairman; Europe Chairman: Jermyn
Brooks
VC, Audit, Tax, and Consulting Groups: Willard W.
Brittain Jr.
VC Human Resources: Richard P. Kearns
VC Management Consulting Services: Tom Beyer
General Counsel: Eldon Olson

WHERE

HQ: Southwark Towers, 32 London Bridge St.,
London SE1 9SY, UK
Phone: +44-(01)71-939-3000
Fax: +44-(01)71-378-0647
US HQ: 1251 Avenue of the Americas, New York, NY
10020
US Phone: 212-819-5000
US Fax: 212-790-6620

Price Waterhouse maintains 447 offices in 118 countries
and territories.

	1994 Revenues	
	$ mil.	% of total
US	1,570	39
Other countries	2,410	61
Total	**3,980**	**100**

WHAT

	1994 US Revenues
	% of total
Auditing & accounting	43
Management consulting	32
Tax	25
Total	**100**

Selected Services
Audit and business advisory services
Employee benefits services
Government services
Industry services
International business development services
International trade services
Inventory services
Investment management and securities operations
consulting
Litigation and reorganization
consulting
Management consulting services
Merger and acquisition services
Partnership services
Personal financial services
Tax services
Valuation services

Representative Clients

AlliedSignal	Exxon
Amoco	Goodyear
Anheuser-Busch	Hewlett-Packard
Baxter	IBM
Bristol-Myers Squibb	J. P. Morgan
Campbell Soup	Kellogg
Caterpillar	Kmart
Chase Manhattan	NIKE
Chemical Banking	Ralston Purina
Chevron	United Technologies
CIGNA	Walt Disney
Compaq	Warner-Lambert
Dresser	Washington Post
DuPont	W. R. Grace
Eastman Kodak	

KEY COMPETITORS

Arthur Andersen	H&R Block
Bain & Co.	Hewitt
Booz, Allen	IBM
Boston Consulting Group	KPMG
Coopers & Lybrand	Marsh & McLennan
Deloitte & Touche	McKinsey & Co.
EDS	Perot Systems
Ernst & Young	SHL Systemhouse
Gemini Consulting	Towers Perrin
Grant Thornton	Wyatt Co.

HOW MUCH

	9-Year Growth	1985	1986	1987	1988	1989	1990	1991	1992	1993	1994
Sales ($ mil.)	14.6%	1,170	1,488	1,804	2,097	2,468	2,900	3,603	3,781	3,890	3,980
Offices	2.4%	360	381	400	412	420	448	458	453	448	447
Partners	4.2%	2,100	2,300	2,297	2,526	2,680	3,007	3,227	3,221	3,242	3,045
Employees	5.7%	30,372	32,794	33,236	37,120	40,869	46,406	49,461	48,600	48,781	50,122

1994 Year-end:
Sales per partner:
$1,307,061

Price Waterhouse

Sales ($ mil.)
1985–94

PRICE/COSTCO, INC.

OVERVIEW

Based in Kirkland, Washington, Price/Costco is the 2nd largest wholesale club operator in the US, after Wal-Mart's Sam's Clubs. The company operates more than 230 warehouse stores using the Price Club and Costco Wholesale names, serving more than 9.7 million members. The warehouses, which average about 120,000 square feet, offer discount prices on a limited number of products (3,500 to 4,000 items, versus 40,000 to 60,000 at discount retailers) but sell everything from fresh foods and cosmetics to major appliances and clothing.

Price/Costco was created from the merger of the Price Company and Costco Wholesale in 1993, and the new company has concentrated on consolidating the operations of its predecessors. In 1994 the company took a charge for the costs of the merger, which resulted in a net loss. With more than 1/3 of its stores located in California, Price/Costco was hurt by that state's weak economy.

The company plans to open 25 new stores during 1995 in the US and abroad. Its international operations include stores in Canada and the UK, as well as a licensee in Korea.

WHEN

Sol Price, who from 1954 to 1974 built Fedmart into a $300 million chain selling general merchandise at a discount to government employees, sold his company to German Hugo Mann in 1975. With son Robert, Rick Libenson, and Giles Bateman, Price opened the first Price Club warehouse in San Diego in 1976 to sell in volume to small businesses at steep discounts. Several former Fedmart employees added $500,000 to Sol's $800,000 to help get the venture going.

The company posted a large loss its first year, prompting the decision to expand membership to include government, utility, and hospital employees, as well as credit union members. In 1978 Price Club opened a 2nd store, in Phoenix. Laurence Price, Sol's other son, who had declined to join the start-up company, began a chain of tire-mounting stores with the help of his father. The stores, located adjacent to Price Club locations on land leased from the company, mounted tires sold by the Price Clubs.

Price Company went public in 1980 with 4 stores in California and Arizona. The company expanded into Albuquerque and Richmond, Virginia, the first eastern location (1984), and Glen Burnie, Maryland (1985). Canadian retailer Steinberg and Price formed a joint venture in 1986 to operate stores in Canada. The first Canadian warehouse opened that year in Montreal. Also in 1986 a quarrel between Sol and Laurence led Price Company to cancel the leases for the son's business. Laurence won a $3.7 million arbitration award. In 1987 Price opened stores in New York.

In 1988 Price acquired A. M. Lewis (grocery distributor, Southern California and Arizona). In 1989 the company started a delivery service to better serve its one million small business customers and opened Price Club Furnishings,

a home and office furniture extension of the company's discount format, at 2 locations. Price bought out Steinberg's interest in the Canadian locations in 1990. That same year Bateman left the company to pursue other interests, and Price added stores on the East Coast and in California, Colorado, and British Columbia. Price had trouble in the East, however. Competition from ensconced rivals like Sam's and PACE forced the closure of 2 stores (in New York and Pennsylvania) in 1992.

In 1991 Price announced a 50-50 joint venture with retailer Controladora Comercial Mexicana to open Price Clubs in Mexico City, the first of which opened in 1992. Price bolstered its presence in that country in 1993, opening its 2nd store in Mexico's capital.

Price merged with Costco Wholesale Corporation in 1993. Costco was founded in 1983 by Jeffrey Brotman and James Sinegal, a former EVP of Price Company. The company opened its first warehouse stores in Seattle, Portland, and Spokane. In 1985 Costco went public and expanded into Canada. The company continued to add warehouse stores and by 1988 had reached $2 billion in sales. In 1990 Costco expanded its merchandise mix to include do-it-yourself home improvement items.

Price/Costco opened its first warehouse outside North America in a suburb of London in 1993 in a joint venture with UK retailer Littlewoods and French retailer Carrefour.

In 1994 Price/Costco spun off its commercial real estate operations to its shareholders as Price Enterprises. That same year Price/Costco agreed to sell its 10 Mexican warehouses to Controladora Comercial Mexicana for $95 million. However, in early 1995, following the devaluation of the peso, Controladora withdrew its offer.

Nasdaq symbol: PCCW
Fiscal year ends: Sunday nearest August 31

Chairman: Jeffrey H. Brotman, age 52, $300,000 pay
President and CEO: James D. Sinegal, age 58,
$300,000 pay
**EVP Merchandising, Distribution, Construction, and
Marketing:** Richard D. DiCerchio, age 51,
$296,923 pay
EVP and CFO: Richard A. Galanti, age 38
SVP Human Resources/Risk Management: John
Matthews
Auditors: Arthur Andersen & Co, SC

WHERE

HQ: 10809 120th Ave. NE, Kirkland, WA 98033
Phone: 206-828-8100
Fax: 206-313-8103

	1994 Sales		1994 Operating Income	
	$ mil.	% of total	$ mil.	% of total
US	13,770	84	298	83
Other countries	2,711	16	62	17
Total	**16,481**	**100**	**360**	**100**

	1994 Stores
	No.
California	82
Washington	16
Florida	11
Oregon	9
Arizona	7
New Jersey	7
New York	7
Other states	43
Canada	37
UK	2
Total	**221**

WHAT

	1994 Sales	
	$ mil.	% of total
Sales	16,161	98
Membership fees & other	320	2
Total	**16,481**	**100**

	1994 Merchandise Sales
	% of total
Sundries	32
Food	31
Hardlines	22
Softlines	12
Other	3
Total	**100**

Selected Products

Alcoholic beverages	Furniture
Apparel	Health and beauty aids
Appliances	Housewares
Automotive supplies	Jewelry
Cameras	Linens
Candy	Office supplies
Cleaning and institutional	Pharmaceuticals
supplies	Tobacco
Dry and fresh foods	Tools
Electronics	Video and audio tape

KEY COMPETITORS

Albertson's	Lechters	Staples
American Stores	Longs	Stop & Shop
Ames	Megafoods Stores	Thrifty PayLess
Best Buy	Office Depot	Venture Stores
Bruno's	OfficeMax	Vons
Circuit City	Pathmark	Waban
Dayton Hudson	Safeway	Walgreen
Fred Meyer	Save Mart	Wal-Mart
Home Depot	Supermarkets	Winn-Dixie
Kmart	Service	
Kroger	Merchandise	

HOW MUCH

	9-Year Growth	1985	1986	1987	1988	1989	1990	1991	1992	1993	1994
Sales ($ mil.)	27.6%	1,834	2,649	3,306	4,053	4,901	5,287	6,598	7,320	15,498	16,481
Net income ($ mil.)	—	46	59	73	95	117	125	134	129	223	(112)
Income as % of sales	—	2.5%	2.2%	2.2%	2.3%	2.4%	2.4%	2.0%	1.8%	1.4%	—
Earnings per share ($)	—	0.48	0.59	0.70	0.91	1.08	1.16	1.23	1.19	1.00	(0.51)
Stock price – high ($)	—	16.83	25.80	24.62	19.58	23.10	22.63	30.60	25.80	21.38	21.63
Stock price – low ($)	—	9.56	13.84	11.02	14.89	16.53	12.43	17.70	13.84	13.25	12.50
Stock price – close ($)	(2.7%)	16.42	15.36	15.36	17.59	21.69	18.41	23.57	17.00	19.25	12.88
P/E – high	—	35	44	35	22	21	20	25	22	21	—
P/E – low	—	20	24	16	16	15	11	14	12	13	—
Dividends per share ($)	—	0.00	0.00	0.00	0.00	0.70	0.00	0.00	0.00	0.00	0.00
Book value per share ($)	18.6%	1.67	2.90	3.63	4.56	5.04	5.95	7.34	8.14	8.28	7.74
Employees	27.2%	5,404	7,294	9,236	11,077	12,545	13,336	19,142	20,777	43,000	47,000

1994 Year-end:
Debt ratio: 35.9%
Return on equity: —
Cash (mil.): $63
Current ratio: 0.93
Long-term debt (mil.): $796
No. of shares (mil.): 218
Dividends
  Yield: —
  Payout: —
Market value (mil.): $2,805

Stock Price History
High/Low 1985–94

THE PROCTER & GAMBLE COMPANY

OVERVIEW

With over half of its sales from outside the US, Procter & Gamble is adopting a corporate structure that reflects that fact. The Cincinnati-based household products company is reorganizing its worldwide operations under 4 regional executive vice-presidents for North America; Europe, the Middle East, and Africa; Asia; and Latin America. With the retirement of chairman Edwin Artzt, P&G has given the posts of chairman and CEO to John Pepper and those of president and COO to Durk Jager.

P&G plans to continue its strategy of building consumer value, globalizing, and cutting costs and is beginning to realize the effects of its completed restructuring program. The turnaround has been particularly pronounced in its food and beverage business, led by the

success of Pringles potato chips and Sunny Delight juice drink. P&G has also revitalized its Duncan Hines brand, introduced Reduced Fat Jif, and tested new products like Sunny Delight Solar Surge and Ultra Folgers.

P&G is also using new ways of marketing its products. Historically the company promoted the different benefits of each product in a category. P&G is now promoting benefits across categories. In 2 advertisements P&G touts the reduced packaging of 6 of its concentrated "ultra" laundry brands and the sanitary power of its dishwashing detergents.

In addition P&G has announced plans to sell about 10 of its brands, including Fisher Nut and Bain de Soleil. The 10 brands account for less than $160 million of P&G's sales.

WHEN

In 1837 candlemaker William Procter and soapmaker James Gamble merged their small Cincinnati businesses, creating Procter & Gamble. By 1859 P&G had become one of the largest companies in Cincinnati, with sales of $1 million. In 1879 the company introduced Ivory, a floating soap. The campaign for the product, a forerunner of P&G's advertising of later years, was one of the first to advertise directly to the consumer. P&G introduced Crisco shortening in 1911.

Family members headed the company until 1930, when William Deupree became president. In the 29 years that Deupree served as president and then chairman, P&G became the largest US seller of packaged consumer goods. P&G advertising innovations included sponsorship of daytime dramas, the first being *The Puddle Family*, a 1932 radio show. P&G introduced Tide detergent in 1947 after years of research to determine how to make a cleanser work well in hard water.

P&G acquired Spic and Span (1945), Duncan Hines (1956), Charmin Paper Mills (1957), Clorox (1957), and Folgers Coffee (1963). P&G sold Clorox in 1968. Crest (introduced in 1955) was the first fluoride toothpaste that was endorsed by the American Dental Association. In 1961 P&G rolled out Head & Shoulders shampoo and Pampers disposable diapers.

A few brands haven't fared so well: P&G bought Crush soft drinks in 1980 and sold it in 1989; Duncan Hines lost out to Nabisco in the "cookie wars" of the early 1980s; Rely tampons had to be removed from the market in 1980 when investigators linked them to toxic shock

syndrome. Several P&G products had lost market share by the mid-1980s.

In 1985 P&G suffered its first profit decline in 33 years, but under CEO John Smale it improved existing products and introduced new ones. Product improvements led to P&G's dominance of the US diaper market.

In the 1980s P&G moved into health care: Norwich-Eaton (1982, pharmaceuticals), Richardson-Vicks (1985; Nyquil, Formula 44), and G.D. Searle's nonprescription drug division (1985, Metamucil). In 1990 P&G bought the rights from Rorer to sell Maalox. The acquisitions of Noxell (1989; Cover Girl, Noxzema) and Max Factor (1991) made P&G the biggest cosmetics company in America, with 32% of the market.

The 1990s have been an eventful time for the secretive company. In 1990 Edwin Artzt was appointed CEO. In 1992 P&G initiated an everyday low-pricing policy that reduced its reliance on coupons and trade promotions. The move eliminated inefficient production demands and allowed P&G to cut prices on major brands. In 1993 P&G began a major restructuring program, cutting 13,000 jobs and closing 30 manufacturing plants. P&G also sued a former top executive, Neil DeFeo, for defecting to rival Clorox. Also in 1993 P&G took one-time charges of almost $3 billion to cover the disposal of its Citrus Hill juice business and restructuring efforts.

In 1995 P&G formed an alliance with Paramount Television to develop television programming. P&G hopes to ensure that it has an advertising medium after television is transformed by the telecommunications revolution.

NYSE symbol: PG
Fiscal year ends: June 30

WHO

Chairman and CEO: John E. Pepper, age 56,
$1,614,000 pay (prior to promotion)
President and COO: Durk I. Jager, age 51,
$1,247,100 pay (prior to promotion)
EVP North America: Wolfgang C. Berndt, age 53
EVP Europe, the Middle East, and Africa: Harald
Einsmann, age 60, $1,028,800 pay (prior to promotion)
EVP Asia: A. G. Lafley, age 48
EVP Latin America: Jorge G. Montoya, age 49
SVP and CFO: Erik G. Nelson, age 54
SVP and General Counsel: James J. Johnson, age 47
SVP Human Resources: Benjamin L. Bethell, age 54
Auditors: Deloitte & Touche LLP

WHERE

HQ: One Procter & Gamble Plaza, Cincinnati, OH 45202
Phone: 513-983-1100
Fax: 513-983-9369

	1994 Sales		1994 Net Income	
	$ mil.	% of total	$ mil.	% of total
US	15,019	48	1,691	69
Other countries	16,058	52	767	31
Adjustments	(781)	—	(247)	—
Total	**30,296**	**100**	**2,211**	**100**

WHAT

	1994 Sales		1994 Operating Income	
	$ mil.	% of total	$ mil.	% of total
Personal care	16,640	55	1,946	51
Laundry/cleaning	9,762	32	1,483	38
Food & beverage	3,290	11	371	10
Pulp & chemicals	750	2	26	1
Adjustments	(146)	—	(480)	—
Total	**30,296**	**100**	**3,346**	**100**

Selected Brand Names

Personal Care	Old Spice	Cheer
Aleve	Pampers	Comet
Always	Pantene	Dash
Attends	Pepto-Bismol	Dawn
Camay	Pert	Downy
Charmin	Puffs	Dreft
Chloraseptic	Red	Era
Clearasil	Safeguard	Formula 44
Coast	Scope	Gain
Cover Girl	Secret	Joy
Crest	Sure	Mr. Clean
Fixodent	Vicks	Spic and Span
Giorgio	Vidal Sassoon	Tide
Head & Shoulders	Zest	
Hugo Boss		**Food and**
Ivory	**Laundry and**	**Beverage**
Lava	**Cleaning**	Crisco
le Jardin	Ariel	Duncan Hines
Luvs	Biz	Folgers
Max Factor	Bold	Hawaiian Punch
Metamucil	Bounce	Jif
NyQuil	Bounty	Pringles
Oil of Olay	Cascade	Sunny Delight

KEY COMPETITORS

Alberto-Culver	Gillette	Monsanto
American Home	Grand	Nestlé
Products	Metropolitan	Neutrogena
Amway	Helene Curtis	PepsiCo
Avon	Henkel	Pfizer
Body Shop	James River	Philip Morris
Carter-Wallace	Johnson &	Quaker Oats
Chattem	Johnson	Rhône-Poulenc
Church & Dwight	Kimberly-Clark	RJR Nabisco
Clorox	L'Oréal	S.C. Johnson
Coca-Cola	LVMH	Seagram
Colgate-Palmolive	MacAndrews &	Tambrands
ConAgra	Forbes	Unilever
CPC	Mary Kay	Warner-Lambert
Dial	Maybelline	Weyerhaeuser
Estée Lauder		

HOW MUCH

	9-Year Growth	1985	1986	1987	1988	1989	1990	1991	1992	1993	1994
Sales ($ mil.)	9.4%	13,552	15,439	17,000	19,336	21,398	24,081	27,026	29,362	30,433	30,296
Net income ($ mil.)	14.9%	635	709	327	1,020	1,206	1,602	1,773	1,872	269	2,211
Income as % of sales	—	4.7%	4.6%	1.9%	5.3%	5.6%	6.7%	6.6%	6.4%	0.9%	7.3%
Earnings per share ($)	14.0%	0.95	1.05	0.47	1.49	1.78	2.25	2.46	2.62	0.25	3.09
Stock price – high ($)	—	17.88	20.63	25.88	22.00	35.13	45.63	47.63	55.75	58.88	64.63
Stock price – low ($)	—	12.63	15.88	15.00	17.63	21.13	30.88	38.00	45.13	45.25	51.25
Stock price – close ($)	15.1%	17.44	19.09	21.34	21.75	35.13	43.31	46.94	53.63	57.00	62.00
P/E – high	—	19	20	55	15	20	20	19	21	—	21
P/E – low	—	13	15	32	12	12	14	15	17	—	17
Dividends per share ($)	7.4%	0.65	0.66	0.68	0.69	0.75	0.88	0.98	1.03	1.10	1.24
Book value per share ($)	2.8%	7.87	8.47	8.49	9.35	8.05	9.41	8.41	10.44	8.03	10.07
Employees	5.0%	62,000	76,200	73,000	77,000	79,000	89,000	94,000	106,000	103,500	96,500

1994 Year-end:
Debt ratio: 48.0%
Return on equity: 35.8%
Cash (mil.): $2,373
Current ratio: 1.24
Long-term debt (mil.): $4,980
No. of shares (mil.): 684
Dividends
  Yield: 2.0%
  Payout: 40.1%
Market value (mil.): $42,430

Stock Price History
High/Low 1985–94

THE PRUDENTIAL INSURANCE CO.

OVERVIEW

A few million in fines here, a few million in customer restitution there, and pretty soon it adds up to real money, enough to send Prudential into the red, especially when combined with a year for disasters (like 1994, with the Northridge earthquake in California).

Since 1991 the company has paid more than $1 billion in fines, restitution, and legal fees resulting from the sale of risky real estate partnerships wrongly represented by employees of Prudential Securities as low-risk investments. The company has also been stung by allegations of systematic misrepresentation of insurance policies as retirement accounts and of account churning. Many of these investigations are still open and may result in even more fines and charges.

The effects on Prudential's business have been widespread: the company is re-examining its quest for leadership in the worldwide financial services field; Prudential Securities is operating at reduced strength because of staff departures; and Prudential has also decided to shed some other financial businesses, including Residential Services Corp., its residential mortgage operation, and Prudential Reinsurance, which it hopes to take public.

On the plus side, Prudential's health care segment (which underwrites the AARP's health insurance products) is doing well.

Guiding the company through these changes is a new CEO, Arthur Ryan, formerly of Chase Manhattan, who replaced Robert Winters upon his retirement.

WHEN

In 1873 John Dryden founded the Widows and Orphans Friendly Society in New Jersey to sell workers industrial insurance (life insurance with small face values and premiums paid weekly). In 1875 he changed the name to the Prudential Friendly Society, naming it after the successful Prudential Assurance Co. of England. In 1876 he visited the English company and copied some of its methods, such as recruiting agents from neighborhoods where insurance was to be sold. In 1877 the company adopted its current name.

Prudential began issuing ordinary whole life insurance in addition to industrial insurance in 1886 and by the end of 1890 was selling more than 2,000 ordinary life policies a year. By this time the company had 3,000 field agents in 8 states. In 1896 Dryden commissioned the J. Walter Thompson advertising agency to design a company trademark. The product was the famed Rock of Gibraltar logo.

Prudential issued its first group life policy in 1916 (the company became a major group life insurer in the 1940s). In the 1920s it was a pioneer in shifting the burden of group life record keeping to the client company.

In 1928 Prudential introduced 3 new insurance policies. An Intermediate Monthly Premium Plan combined some features of the industrial and ordinary life policies. The Modified 3 policy was a whole life policy with a rate change after 3 years. The addition of an Accidental Death Benefit to weekly premium policies cost the company an extra $3 million in benefits in the next year alone.

In 1943 Prudential became a mutual insurance company (owned by the policyholders).

In the 1940s President Carroll Shanks began to decentralize the company's operations. When the system proved successful, other companies copied Prudential. Later the company introduced a Property Investment Separate Account (PRISA), which gave pension plans a real estate investment option. By 1974, 20 of the country's largest 100 corporations were PRISA contract holders, and Prudential was the US's group pension leader.

Prudential acquired the Bache Group (renamed Prudential Securities), a securities brokerage, for $385 million in 1981. Bache's forte was retail investments, an area expected to blend well with Prudential's insurance business. Under George Ball the company tried to become a major investment banker — but failed. In 1991, after losing almost $260 million and facing lawsuits relating to the sale of real estate limited partnerships, Ball resigned.

In 1993 losses caused by Hurricane Andrew led Prudential to seek permission from the state of Florida to allow 25,000 homeowners' policies to lapse.

Despite the 1992 settlement of the real estate partnership suit, Prudential found itself under increasing scrutiny in 1993 and 1994. There were several state investigations into its insurance sales practices, including allegations of churning (persuading policyholders to buy costlier policies, thus generating a large new commission). In 1995 Prudential was hit by new suits in Connecticut and Florida.

In 1995 Prudential Securities opened a representative office in Shanghai, and Prudential joined with Wausau Insurance to provide a workers' compensation managed care plan.

Mutual company
Fiscal year ends: December 31

WHO

Chairman, President, and CEO: Arthur F. Ryan
VC: Garnett L. Keith Jr.
CFO: Mark Grier, age 43
Chairman and CEO Group Operations: William P. Link
President and CEO, Prudential Securities Inc.:
Hardwick Simmons
**President and CEO, Prudential Asset Management
Group:** Eric A. Simonson
Operations and Systems Executive Officer: John V.
Scicutella
Chief Communications Officer: Elizabeth R. Krupnick
SVP and Chief Ethics Officer: Stephen R. Braswell
SVP and General Counsel: James R. Gillen
SVP Human Resources: Donald C. Mann
Auditors: Deloitte & Touche LLP

WHERE

HQ: The Prudential Insurance Company of America,
751 Broad St., Newark, NJ 07102-3777
Phone: 201-802-6000
Fax: 201-802-6092

Prudential operates in Canada, China, Italy, Japan,
South Korea, Spain, Taiwan, the UK, and the US.

WHAT

	1994 Assets	
	$ mil.	% of total
Cash & equivalents	11,739	6
Trading account	6,218	3
Treasury & agency		
securities	13,624	7
Foreign govt. securities	3,101	1
Mortgage-backed securities	4,889	2
State & municipal bonds	2,776	1
Corporate bonds	54,144	26
Stocks	2,327	1
Broker-dealer receivables	7,311	3
Mortgage loans		
& real estate	27,799	13
Policy loans	6,631	3
Other investments	10,947	5
Separate account assets	48,633	23
Other	11,763	6
Total	**211,902**	**100**

	1994 Sales	
	$ mil.	% of total
Premiums & annuities	29,698	68
Net investment income	9,595	22
Broker-dealer revenues	3,677	8
Realized investment losses	(450)	—
Other	1,037	2
Total	**43,557**	**100**

Product Lines
Annuities
Asset management
Credit card services
Deposit accounts
Estate and financial planning
Life, health, and property insurance
Reinsurance
Residential real estate services

Selected Subsidiaries
Capital Management Group
Prudential Asset Management Group
Prudential Health Care System
Prudential International Insurance
Prudential Preferred Financial Services
The Prudential Realty Group
Prudential Securities, Inc.
Prudential Select

KEY COMPETITORS

Aetna	FMR	Northwestern
AIG	Foundation Health	Mutual
Alliance Capital	General Electric	Oxford Health
Management	General Re	Plans
Allianz	Goldman Sachs	Paine Webber
Allstate	Guardian Life	RE/MAX
American	Insurance	Salomon
Financial	Health Systems	Sierra Health
Bankers Trust	ITT Hartford	Services
Bear Stearns	John Hancock	State Farm
Blue Cross	John Nuveen	T. Rowe Price
Coldwell Banker	Kaiser	Trammell
Canadian Imperial	Foundation	Crow
Charles Schwab	Health Care	Residential
Chase Manhattan	Liberty Mutual	Transamerica
Chubb	MassMutual	Travelers
CIGNA	Merrill Lynch	United
Citicorp	MetLife	HealthCare
Equitable	Morgan Stanley	USF&G
First Chicago	New York Life	

HOW MUCH

	Annual Growth	1985	1986	1987	1988	1989	1990	1991	1992	1993	1994
Assets ($ mil.)	9.8%	91,706	133,733	140,931	153,023	163,967	169,046	189,148	199,625	218,440	211,902
Net income ($ mil.)	—	—	—	967	829	743	113	2,280	347	879	(1,175)
Income as % of assets	—	—	—	0.7%	0.5%	0.5%	0.1%	1.2%	0.2%	0.4%	—
Employees	2.2%	81,634	85,503	93,290	98,009	105,063	104,847	103,284	101,000	105,534	99,386

1994 Year-end:
Equity as % of assets: 3.5%
Return on equity: —
Sales (mil.): $43,557

Net Income
($ mil.) 1987–94

PUBLIC SERVICE ENTERPRISE GROUP

OVERVIEW

Public Service Enterprise Group (Enterprise) is the parent company of Public Service Electric and Gas Company (PSE&G), New Jersey's largest electric and natural gas utility.

PSE&G provides services to about 300 cities and towns, including Newark, Trenton, and Camden. Through its subsidiary, Enterprise Diversified Holdings (EDHI), the company is also involved in nonutility businesses, including oil and gas exploration, independent power projects, and commercial real estate development in several states.

With deregulation of the utility industry increasing competition, Enterprise has reorganized PSE&G, creating separate business units for generation, transmission, and customer service. It also formed a new subsidiary, Enterprise Ventures and Services, to develop products and services that it can sell outside its traditional boundaries. The changes are part of a strategy focused on improving efficiency and increasing flexibility.

Since the passage of the Energy Policy Act, which opens the utility market up to independent power producers, Enterprise (along with other utilities) has had to compete for large corporate accounts. In 1995 the company requested a rate decrease of about $7.3 million annually for its 2nd largest customer, Co-Steel Raritan.

WHEN

Newark, New Jersey, was the scene of a tragedy in 1903 when a trolley car full of high school students collided with a Delaware, Lackawanna and Western train. While investigating the accident, state attorney general Thomas McCarter discovered the underlying financial weakness of the trolley company and many of New Jersey's other transportation, gas, and electric companies. Planning to buy and consolidate these companies, McCarter resigned as attorney general. He and several colleagues then established the Public Service Corporation (1903).

The company originally formed separate divisions for gas utilities, trolley and other transportation companies, and electric utilities. Management spent most of its energies on the trolley company, reasoning that these operations would be the most profitable. Indeed, during its first full year of operation, the trolley company generated almost half of Public Service's total sales.

In 1924 the gas and electric companies consolidated as Public Service Electric and Gas (PSE&G). A new company formed to operate buses that year and merged with the trolley company in 1928 to form Public Service Coordinated Transport (later Transport of New Jersey). PSE&G signed interconnection agreements with 2 Pennsylvania electric companies in 1928 to form the world's first integrated power pool — later known as the Pennsylvania–New Jersey–Maryland (PJM) Interconnection when Baltimore Gas & Electric joined in 1956. Four more companies joined in 1965.

PSE&G began exploring new gas fields in Texas and Louisiana in response to the 1972 Arab oil embargo and formed a research subsidiary in 1977 to develop solar and other non–fossil fuel energy sources.

The state of New Jersey, which had been subsidizing Transport of New Jersey, bought it from PSE&G in 1980. Public Service Enterprise Group, a holding company, was formed in 1985 to allow PSE&G to diversify into nonutility enterprises. A new subsidiary, Enterprise Diversified Holdings, was formed in 1989 to handle these activities, which included commercial real estate development (Enterprise Group Development) and 94 oil- and gas-producing properties in West Texas and the Gulf of Mexico (Energy Development Corporation). In 1989 Energy Development bought Pelto Oil Company (oil and gas exploration) from Houston-based Southdown.

Community Energy Alternatives, Enterprise's independent power production subsidiary, and 3 partners acquired a 650-megawatt power station near Buenos Aires, Argentina, in 1993. In 1994 Energy Development announced an agreement with the Chinese government to evaluate and analyze an oil block in the East China Sea.

In 1995 PSE&G and AT&T said they planned to develop an interactive customer communications system that will provide services such as automatic and remote meter reading and energy-use monitoring. After a test in New Jersey, the 2 companies plan to market the system worldwide. Also in 1995 PSE&G's Salem Generating Station nuclear plant agreed to pay the state of Delaware $10.5 million to offset the costs of damage to aquatic life caused by the plant's use of water from the Delaware River.

NYSE symbol: PEG
Fiscal year ends: December 31

WHO

Chairman, President, and CEO: E. James Ferland,
age 52, $652,492 pay
President and COO, PSE&G: Lawrence R. Codey,
age 50, $398,468 pay
President and COO, EDHI: Paul H. Way, age 57,
$308,813 pay
SVP Electric, PSE&G: Robert J. Dougherty Jr., age 43,
$273,946 pay
SVP Customer Operations, PSE&G: Thomas M.
Crimmins Jr., age 51
SVP External Affairs, PSE&G: Howard W. Borden Jr.,
age 50
**Chief Nuclear Officer and President Nuclear Business
Unit, PSE&G:** Leon R. Eliason, age 55
VP and CFO: Robert C. Murray, age 49, $353,832 pay
VP and General Counsel: R. Edwin Selover, age 49
VP Human Resources, PSE&G: Martin P. Mellet
Auditors: Deloitte & Touche LLP

WHERE

HQ: Public Service Enterprise Group Incorporated,
80 Park Plaza, PO Box 1171, Newark, NJ 07101-1171
Phone: 201-430-7000
Fax: 201-430-5983

Selected Generating Facilities

Oil and Gas
Bayonne (NJ)
Bergen (NJ)
Burlington (NJ)
Conemaugh (22.5%, PA)
Edison (NJ)
Essex (NJ)
Hudson (NJ)
Kearny (NJ)
Keystone (22.8%, PA)
Linden (NJ)

Mercer (NJ)
National Park (NJ)
Salem (NJ)
Sewaren (NJ)

Nuclear
Hope Creek (95.0%, NJ)
Peach Bottom (42.5%, PA)
Salem (42.6%, NJ)

Pumped Storage
Yards Creek (50.0%, NJ)

WHAT

	1994 Sales	
	$ mil.	% of total
Electric	3,733	63
Gas	1,779	30
Nonutility activities	404	7
Total	**5,916**	**100**

	1994 Electricity Fuel Sources
	% of total
Nuclear	45
Interchange & 2-party purchases	27
Coal	19
Natural gas	7
Residual oil	2
Total	**100**

Selected Subsidiaries

Enterprise Diversified Holdings Incorporated
Community Energy Alternatives Inc. (investment in and
development of cogeneration and small power plants)
Energy Development Corporation (oil and gas
exploration, development, and production)
Enterprise Group Development Corporation
(commercial real estate development)

Enterprise Ventures and Services Corporation
Public Service Conservation Resources Corporation
(energy management products and services)
U.S. Energy Partners (gas marketing partnership with
Cincinnati Gas and Electric Company)

Public Service Electric and Gas Company

KEY COMPETITORS

AES	Columbia Gas	Koch
Associated Natural	Consolidated	Occidental
Gas	Edison	Panhandle
California Energy	Destec Energy	Eastern
Coastal	Enron	Tenneco

HOW MUCH

	9-Year Growth	1985	1986	1987	1988	1989	1990	1991	1992	1993	1994
Sales ($ mil.)	3.3%	4,428	4,498	4,211	4,395	4,805	5,357	5,092	5,357	5,706	5,916
Net income ($ mil.)	6.1%	400	378	520	529	523	404	543	504	596	679
Income as % of sales	—	9.0%	8.4%	12.3%	12.0%	11.0%	8.4%	10.7%	9.4%	10.4%	11.5%
Earnings per share ($)	2.7%	2.18	1.90	2.55	2.57	2.53	1.90	2.43	2.17	2.48	2.78
Stock price – high ($)	—	22.08	32.20	30.50	26.88	29.38	29.75	29.38	31.38	36.13	32.00
Stock price – low ($)	—	16.92	20.50	20.00	22.00	23.00	22.50	25.25	25.38	30.00	23.88
Stock price – close ($)	2.6%	21.08	26.83	23.88	24.50	29.25	26.38	29.38	30.88	32.00	26.50
P/E – high	—	10	17	12	10	12	16	12	14	15	12
P/E – low	—	8	11	8	9	9	12	10	12	12	9
Dividends per share ($)	1.6%	1.87	1.95	1.99	2.01	2.05	2.09	2.13	2.16	2.16	2.16
Book value per share ($)	2.2%	17.87	17.92	18.54	19.11	19.48	19.44	20.04	20.32	21.07	21.70
Employees	(0.9%)	13,500	13,800	13,800	12,832	13,113	13,383	13,116	13,115	13,115	12,390

1994 Year-end:
Debt ratio: 54.0%
Return on equity: 13.0%
Cash (mil.): $68
Current ratio: 0.73
Long-term debt (mil.): $5,234
No. of shares (mil.): 245
Dividends
  Yield: 8.2%
  Payout: 77.7%
Market value (mil.): $6,484

**Stock Price History
High/Low 1985–94**

PUBLIX SUPER MARKETS, INC.

OVERVIEW

To ever more grocery stores in the Southeast, Publix is enemy #1. The Lakeland, Florida–based company — one of the nation's 10 largest supermarket chains — has 488 stores and is expanding rapidly, especially in Georgia and South Carolina. Publix is private: relatives of its founder own 35% of the company, while the other 65% is owned by employees. Ninety-nine percent of the Publix management team rose from within the company.

The chain is poised for massive growth both within and beyond its current region. A 3-million-square-foot dairy processing and grocery distribution facility scheduled to open near Atlanta in 1995 will allow Publix to serve stores in cities within a 300-mile radius, in-cluding Birmingham, Alabama; Charlotte, North Carolina; and Nashville, Tennessee. The company intends to open 59 new stores and hit $10 billion in sales by the end of the year.

Publix, which produces its own deli, bakery, and dairy goods, has built its reputation on cleanliness, service, and product variety while maintaining reasonable prices. Satisfaction among customers, however, isn't matched by enthusiasm from the United Food and Commercial Workers Union. The UFCW in 1994 began a campaign against alleged gender and racial discrimination in Publix's hiring, promotion, and compensation policies. The Equal Employment Opportunity Commission is investigating the charges.

WHEN

In 1930 George Jenkins, age 22, resigned as manager of the Piggly Wiggly grocery store in Winter Haven, Florida. With money he had saved to buy a car, he opened his own grocery store, the first Publix, next door to his old employer. Despite the Depression the small store prospered, and in 1935 Jenkins opened another Publix in Winter Haven.

In 1940, after the supermarket format became popular, Jenkins closed his 2 smaller locations and opened a new Publix Market, a modern marble, tile, and stucco edifice. With pastel colors and electric-eye doors, it was also the first US store to feature air conditioning.

In 1944 Publix bought the All-American chain of Lakeland, Florida (19 stores), and moved its corporate headquarters to Lakeland, where it also built a warehouse (1950). The company began offering S&H Green Stamps (1953) and replaced its original Winter Haven supermarket with a mall featuring an enlarged Publix and a Green Stamp redemption center (1956). Publix expanded into southeastern Florida, opening a store in Miami and then buying and converting 7 former Grand Union stores (1959).

As Florida's population grew, Publix continued to expand and opened its 100th store in 1964. The company launched a discount chain, Food World, in 1970 (sold in the mid-1980s). Publix was the first grocery chain in Florida to use bar code scanners; all Publix stores had scanners by 1981. The company beat Florida banks in installing ATMs and during the 1980s opened debit card stations.

Publix continued to grow in the 1980s, safe from takeovers because of its employee ownership. In 1988 the company bought stores from takeover refugee Kroger and installed the first automated checkout systems in South Florida, giving patrons an always-open checkout lane.

The company completed its withdrawal from offering Green Stamps in 1989, and most of the $19 million decrease in Publix advertising expenditures was attributed to the end of the 36-year promotion. Also in 1989, after almost 60 years, "Mr. George" — as founder Jenkins is known — stepped down as chairman in favor of his son Howard.

In 1991 Publix opened its first store outside of Florida, in Savannah, Georgia, as part of its plan to become a major player throughout the Southeast. The company's latest vehicle toward this end is a store prototype that offers ready-to-eat foods and a cafe. The chain is now designing other formats.

In 1992 Hurricane Andrew destroyed 3 stores. Publix entered South Carolina in 1993 with one supermarket; it also tripled its presence in Georgia to 15 stores. In 1993 Publix's supermarkets were rated #1 in the US by *Consumer Reports* readers in terms of overall customer satisfaction. The company received top ratings in every survey category — which included cleanliness, courtesy, checkout efficiency, and brand variety — except prices.

Publix and Selectrak Family Video began testing a video rental department in an Atlanta store in 1994; though not the grocery chain's first such test, it was the first time Publix had used a nationally known video supplier.

In a highly favorable profile of Publix in April 1995, the *New York Times* referred to "its late founder, George Jenkins." Days later, a correction confirmed that Jenkins was still alive at 87 and serving as chairman emeritus.

Private company
Fiscal year ends: Last Saturday in December

WHO

Chairman Emeritus: George Jenkins, age 87
Chairman and CEO: Howard M. Jenkins, age 43,
$412,934 pay
Chairman of the Executive Committee:
Charles H. Jenkins Jr., age 51, $311,767 pay
President and COO: Mark C. Hollis, age 60,
$412,521 pay
EVP and CFO: William H. Vass, age 45, $327,245 pay
EVP: Hoyt R. Barnett, age 51, $278,894 pay
EVP: W. Edwin Crenshaw, age 44
VP: Jesse L. Benton, age 52
VP: Bennie F. Brown, age 53
VP: R. Scott Charlton, age 36
VP: William R. Curry, age 54
VP: Glenn J. Eschrich, age 50
VP: M. Clayton Hollis Jr., age 38
VP: Mark R. Irby, age 39
VP: James J. Lobinsky, age 55
VP: Thomas M. McLaughlin, age 44
VP: Robert H. Moore, age 52
VP: Thomas M. O'Connor, age 47
VP Human Resources: James H. Rhodes, age 50
Auditors: KPMG Peat Marwick LLP

WHERE

HQ: 1936 George Jenkins Blvd., Lakeland, FL 33801
Phone: 813-688-1188
Fax: 813-680-5257 (Public Relations)

Publix Super Markets operates 488 grocery stores in
Florida, Georgia, and South Carolina. In Florida, the
company also operates dairy processing plants at
Deerfield Beach and Lakeland and bakery and deli plants
in Lakeland. Publix operates 7 distribution centers in
Florida (in Boynton Beach, Deerfield Beach, Jacksonville,
Lakeland, Miami, and Sarasota) and one in Georgia (in
Lawrenceville).

	Stores
Florida	435
Georgia	45
South Carolina	8
Total	**488**

WHAT

	1994 Sales
	% of total
Existing stores	87
New/closed stores	12
Other	1
Total	**100**

Supermarket Departments
Bakery
Deli
Floral
Groceries
Health and beauty care
Housewares
Meat
Pharmacy
Photo processing
Produce
Seafood

Foods Processed
Baked goods
Dairy products
Deli items

KEY COMPETITORS

Albertson's	Kmart
Big B	Kroger
Bruno's	Price/Costco
Delchamps	Pueblo Xtra
Eckerd	Revco
Fleming	Rite Aid
Food Lion	Ruddick
Great A&P	Sedano's Supermarkets
Harry's Farmers Market	Walgreen
Ingles Markets	Wal-Mart
Kash n' Karry	Winn-Dixie

HOW MUCH

	9-Year Growth	1985	1986	1987	1988	1989	1990	1991	1992	1993	1994[1]
Sales ($ mil.)	10.8%	3,446	3,760	4,152	4,848	5,386	5,821	6,214	6,729	7,554	8,665
Net income ($ mil.)	14.3%	72	84	87	102	129	149	158	167	184	239
Income as % of sales	—	2.1%	2.2%	2.1%	2.1%	2.4%	2.6%	2.5%	2.5%	2.4%	2.8%
Employees	9.4%	40,098	44,813	50,123	57,791	64,037	66,756	68,606	73,000	82,000	90,000

1994 Year-end:
Debt ratio: 0.3%
Return on equity: 17.2%
Cash (mil.): $266
Current ratio: 1.24
Long-term debt (mil.): $3
Total assets (mil.): $2,302

Net Income ($ mil.)
1985–94

[1] 53-week fiscal year

THE QUAKER OATS COMPANY

OVERVIEW

Does Passion Supreme go well with oatmeal? Can the staid Quaker Man and the flamboyant Snapple Lady find true happiness together? And how does Gatorade spokesman Michael Jordan fit into it? These were the questions on everyone's lips when Quaker Oats (the grain products and good-for-you-drinks company) paid a whopping $1.7 billion for the new-age noncarbonated drinks pioneer Snapple.

The Snapple purchase in 1994 stretched Quaker's resources because, in addition to the purchase price itself, the entrepreneurial Snapple needed an overhaul in its distribution and marketing operations. Problems in these areas, as well as increased competition in its field, had contributed to a falling market share. Quaker expects that its strength in supermarket distribution (gained through Gatorade's dominance of the sports drink area)

will mean increased sales in the long run. However, Snapple's greatest distribution was in single-serving bottles for cooler-case sales, with which Quaker has little experience but which it hopes will provide a new outlet for marketing Gatorade.

To help pay for the purchase, Quaker decided in 1995 to exit several businesses, including its European and US pet foods (which it sold to Dalgety of the UK and to Heinz); Van Camp's beans and Wolf Brand chili (sold to ConAgra); and its Mexican chocolate business (which it sold to Nestlé). The remaining focus is on grain-based foods and noncarbonated drinks.

In 1994 and 1995 Quaker has been consolidating operations not intended for sale, and the costs of the restructuring helped depress earnings in 1994.

WHEN

The familiar, friendly Quaker Man of the Quaker Oats Company was first used as a trademark in 1877 by Henry Crowell at his Quaker Mill in Ravenna, Ohio. Crowell was one of 7 prominent millers who formed the American Cereal Company of Chicago in 1891. Called by some the "oatmeal trust," the company changed its name to the Quaker Oats Company in 1901 and adopted Crowell's Quaker Man as its logo.

The company was an immediate success. Crowell's creative marketing practices and powerful sales staff covered the nation with the image of the Quaker Man — on billboards, in magazines, in newspapers, on cards on subways and streetcars, and in coupon promotions and miniature samples left on doorsteps — extolling the virtues of oatmeal to a newly health conscious public. Crowell was an early advertising innovator.

Robert Stuart, another founder, consolidated mill operations to 2 locations: a large mill in Akron, Ohio, and his own mill in Cedar Rapids, Iowa, which he modernized and expanded. The company prospered and by 1911 was diversifying its product line with such purchases as animal feed and grocery items. Sales reached $123 million in 1918. In 1925 Quaker bought Aunt Jemima pancake flour, one of its most successful brands.

The company remained under Stuart family management until 1953. Cap'n Crunch cereal was introduced in 1963. Robert Stuart, son of a previous president, became CEO in 1966 and embarked on a program of diversification.

Acquisitions included Fisher-Price toys (1969, sold 1991), restaurants, and candies.

William Smithburg became CEO in 1979 and continued to diversify (clothiers, opticians). The company bought Stokely-Van Camp in 1983 for $238 million and kept its top brands of canned beans and Gatorade sports beverage. In 1986 the company paid $801 million for Anderson, Clayton & Company, a Houston food products company with such brands as Seven Seas salad dressings, Chiffon margarine, and Igloo ice chests (all later sold), as well as Gaines dog food. Smithburg began to refocus the company on foods.

Following a down year in 1990, Quaker reinforced its back-to-basics food strategy by increasing its advertising budget, reformulating its dog foods, and launching new products. Continuing to emphasize its core food categories, in 1993 Quaker sold Sutherland Foods, a British maker of sandwich filling products, and purchased the Chico-San rice cake brand from the Heinz Company. In 1994 the company announced a plan to consolidate manufacturing and cut employment. The costs of these actions were dwarfed by those associated with the Snapple purchase later that year. The company also formed a joint venture with a Taiwanese firm to sell All-In-One cereal and Mighty pudding in China.

The restructuring continued in 1995 when Quaker combined its cereal, snack, and convenience food divisions into one organization and eliminated duplicate administration, marketing, and supply functions.

WHO

Chairman and CEO: William D. Smithburg, age 56,
$1,395,006 pay
President and COO: Philip A. Marineau, age 47,
$1,010,834 pay
SVP Gatorade Worldwide Division: James F. Doyle,
age 42, $554,008 pay
SVP Law, Corporate Affairs, and Corporate Secretary:
Luther C. McKinney, age 63, $553,978 pay
SVP International Grocery Products: Robert S.
Thomason, age 49, $512,368 pay
SVP Finance and CFO: Terry G. Westbrook, age 48
SVP Human Resources: Douglas J. Ralston, age 49
VP Investor Relations and Corporate Communications:
Margaret M. Eichman
VP Corporate Planning: Barbara A. Allen, age 41
VP Government Relations: Penelope C. Cate
Auditors: Arthur Andersen & Co, SC

WHERE

HQ: Quaker Tower, PO Box 049001, 321 N. Clark St.,
Chicago, IL 60604-9001
Phone: 312-222-7111
Fax: 312-222-8304

Quaker operates in Argentina, the Benelux countries,
Brazil, Colombia, France, Germany, Italy, Mexico, the
UK, the US, and Venezuela, and its products are sold
through marketing agreements throughout the world.

	1994 Sales		1994 Operating Income	
	$ mil.	% of total	$ mil.	% of total
US	4,029	67	432	80
Europe	1,164	20	17	3
Canada	224	4	(1)	—
Other regions	538	9	89	17
Total	**5,955**	**100**	**537**	**100**

WHAT

	1994 Sales	
	$ mil.	% of total
International grocery products	1,702	29
Breakfast foods	1,573	26
Convenience foods	924	16
Gatorade	906	15
Pet foods	539	9
Golden grain	305	5
Other	6	—
Total	**5,955**	**100**

Selected Brand Names

Cereals
Cap'n Crunch
Life
Quaker 100% Natural
Quaker Kids' Choice
Quaker MultiGrain
Quaker Oat Squares
Quaker Oatmeal
Quaker Oats
Quaker Toasted Oatmeal

Other Food Products
Ardmore Farms
(citrus juice)
Arnie's Bagelicious
Bagels
Aunt Jemima
Burry (cookies and
crackers)

Celeste (pizza)
Chico-San (rice cakes)
Continental Coffee
Gatorade
Golden Grain (pasta)
Maryland Club (food service
coffee)
Near East (grain-based dishes)
Nile Spice
Noodle Roni
Petrofsky's bagels
Proof & Bake (frozen foods)
Quaker Caramel Corn Cakes
Quaker Chewy Granola Bars
Quaker Rice Cakes
Rice-A-Roni
Snapple

KEY COMPETITORS

Borden	General Mills	Mars
Cadbury	Grand	Nestlé
Schweppes	Metropolitan	PepsiCo
Celestial	Ferolito,	Philip Morris
Seasonings	Vultaggio	Proctor & Gamble
Coca-Cola	Heinz	Ralcorp
ConAgra	Hershey	RJR Nabisco
Dole	Kellogg	TLC Beatrice

HOW MUCH

	9-Year Growth	1985	1986	1987	1988	1989	1990	1991	1992	1993	1994
Sales ($ mil.)	6.0%	3,520	3,671	4,421	5,330	5,724	5,031	5,491	5,576	5,731	5,955
Net income ($ mil.)	4.4%	157	180	244	256	203	169	206	248	287	232
Income as % of sales	—	4.4%	4.9%	5.5%	4.8%	3.5%	3.4%	3.7%	4.4%	5.0%	4.0%
Earnings per share ($)	6.7%	0.94	1.13	1.55	1.60	1.28	1.08	1.33	1.63	1.97	1.68
Stock price – high ($)	—	15.75	22.44	28.81	30.75	34.44	29.75	37.88	37.19	38.50	42.50
Stock price – low ($)	—	8.25	13.69	15.88	19.25	24.81	20.50	23.88	25.13	30.19	29.69
Stock price – close ($)	8.9%	14.31	20.00	20.81	26.56	28.88	26.44	37.44	32.50	35.50	30.75
P/E – high	—	17	20	19	19	27	28	29	23	20	25
P/E – low	—	9	12	10	12	19	19	18	16	15	18
Dividends per share ($)	14.4%	0.31	0.34	0.39	0.48	0.58	0.68	0.76	0.84	0.94	11.04
Book value per share ($)	(4.1%)	4.88	4.95	6.47	7.88	7.22	6.73	5.90	5.52	3.97	3.34
Employees	(3.9%)	28,700	29,500	30,800	31,300	31,700	28,200	20,900	21,100	20,200	20,000

1994 Year-end:
Debt ratio: 69.5%
Return on equity: 46.4%
Cash (mil.): $140
Current ratio: 1.00
Long-term debt (mil.): $760
No. of shares (mil.): 134
Dividends
Yield: 3.4%
Payout: 61.9%
Market value (mil.): $4,109

Stock Price History
High/Low 1985–94

QUANTUM CORPORATION

OVERVIEW

Quantum, the leading global supplier of computer hard disks with 23% of the market, took a quantum leap in late 1994 with one strategic purchase. The Silicon Valley–based company bought the disk, tape, and solid-state drive and thin film head operations of Digital Equipment Corp. (DEC). The acquisition frees Quantum from its dependence on outside sources (Japanese firm Matsushita-Kotobuki Electronics [MKE] manufactured 80% of Quantum's 1995 production). It also expands the company's mainframe and minicomputer product lines. The $348 million purchase (which also included DEC's cutting-edge magneto-resistive recording head technology) bit into Quantum's 1995 earnings, although sales increased 58%.

Quantum — which sells its hard drives through OEMs and commercial and industrial distribution channels — expanded its distribution in 1995 when Compaq and Silicon Graphics both added Quantum storage as an optional feature on their high-end systems. That same year Quantum and software developer Symantec agreed to codevelop S.M.A.R.T. (self-monitoring analysis and reporting technology) storage and software products.

In early 1995 Quantum rolled out the "next-generation" additions to its 3.5" drive family, including the Trailblazer for low-end PCs and the Fireball for high-performance PCs. It also introduced 2 high-capacity drives, the Atlas II and Empire II; both have 10-disk arrays with 9.1 gigabytes of memory.

Compaq accounted for 16% of Quantum's 1995 sales; Apple Computer accounted for 12%. The company's La Cie subsidiary also sells products directly to Apple users.

WHEN

Founded in 1980 by a group including David Brown and James Patterson, Quantum was almost immediately successful. It began manufacturing 8" hard disk drives in early 1981 and, in its first year of business, reported $186,000 in profits on almost $14 million in sales. Plus Development was founded in 1983 as Quantum's sales, marketing, and R&D arm. A 1986 litigation settlement with Computer Memories cost $6 million in write-offs. Apple became a customer during that year as well.

Plus Development was awarded a patent for its Hardcard, a "hard-disk-on-a-card" that slides into floppy disk drives, in 1987. Hardcard revenues had risen from about $10 million in 1986 to more than $60 million in 1987. However, Quantum fell behind in the hard disk drive market in 1987, losing 8" and 5.25" drive sales as the industry began looking to 3.5" models. CEO Stephen Berkley, who majored in economics and art history in college, repositioned the company to concentrate on this emerging market. By turning over manufacturing to Japan's MKE, a leader in robotics manufacturing and a subsidiary of Matsushita Electric, Quantum saved time and money in getting its first 3.5" models, the ProDrive Series, to market in 1988.

On the strength of its 3.5" drives, Quantum acquired a host of new customers, including Sun Microsystems, AT&T, Hewlett-Packard, Unisys, Intel, and Zenith.

NEC paid almost $3 million to the company in a patent infringement settlement in 1988. Another suit was settled in 1990, and this time Quantum received from Western Digital net proceeds of $3.7 million. By 1990, 3.5" disk drives were accounting for almost 90% of Quantum's sales. The company joined the ranks of the *FORTUNE* 500 in 1991.

In 1992 William Miller, formerly with Control Data, succeeded Berkley as CEO. Quantum and MKE renewed their long-term agreement whereby Quantum has the exclusive right to design and market worldwide and MKE has the exclusive right to manufacture worldwide. Also in 1992 Quantum folded Plus Development into Quantum Commercial Products, a new unit established to better meet buyers' needs.

Quantum lost market share as demand exceeded supply in 1992. Less than a year later, though — in true industry spirit — demand had faltered again, and the worst price wars in the industry's history had begun. In 1993 the company purchased a minority interest in SST, a flash memory company, and sold its Passport XL line of removable disk drives to MountainGate Data Systems. The following year it opened an international repair center in Malaysia.

In 1995 Quantum announced it would build a state-of-the-art research and development facility in Colorado. That same year the company opened PT Quantum Peripherals Indonesia to manufacture thin film recording heads (the plant had belonged to DEC). Quantum has contracted with Lafe Computer Magnetics of China as a supplier for that operation.

Nasdaq symbol: QNTM
Fiscal year ends: March 31

WHO

Chairman and CEO: William J. Miller, age 49
President, Desktop and Portable Storage Group:
Michael A. Brown, age 36
President, High-Capacity Storage Group: Robert K.
Maeser, age 55
EVP Finance, CFO, and Secretary: Joseph T. Rodgers,
age 52
EVP Worldwide Sales: William F. Roach, age 51
**EVP Engineering and Technology and Chief Technical
Officer; VP, Recording Heads Group:** Kenneth Lee,
age 57
**VP Corporate Development and Planning; VP and
General Manager, Specialty Storage Products Group:**
Gina M. Bornino, age 34
VP Human Resources: Deborah E. Barber, age 55
Auditors: Ernst & Young LLP

WHERE

HQ: 500 McCarthy Blvd., Milpitas, CA 95035
Phone: 408-894-4000
Fax: 408-894-3218

Quantum has manufacturing facilities in California,
Colorado, and Massachusetts and overseas plants in
Indonesia and Malaysia. Its manufacturing partner,
Matsushita-Kotobuki Electronics, has facilities in
Ireland, Japan, and Singapore.

	1995 Sales		1995 Operating Income	
	$ mil.	% of total	$ mil.	% of total
US	1,908	51	56	16
Europe	1,738	46	294	84
Other regions	109	3	(3)	—
Adjustments	(387)	—	(186)	—
Total	**3,368**	**100**	**161**	**100**

WHAT

Selected Products

Disks
3.5" disks
5.25" disks

Disk drives
2.5" hard drives for notebook systems
Daytona
3.5" hard drives for desktop PCs

Fireball	Maverick
Lightning	Trailblazer

3.5" hard drives for disk arrays, minicomputers, servers,
and workstations

Atlas	Empire
Capella	Grand Prix

3.5" and 5.25" solid-state disks
ESP

Memory Cards
QCard flash memory cards with embedded drivers

Mini-libraries
DLT 2500/2700/4500/4700 mini-libraries for high-
capacity data backup

Tape drives
DLT 2000 and DLT 4000 tape drives

KEY COMPETITORS

Centennial	Fujitsu	Sequel
Technologies	Hewlett-Packard	Sharp
Chinon America	Hitachi	Stac Electronics
Conner Peripherals	IBM	Sundisk
Cray Research	Maxtor	SyQuest
Drexler	Micropolis	Toshiba
Technology	MiniStor	Western Digital
EMC Corp.	Seagate	

HOW MUCH

	9-Year Growth	1986	1987	1988	1989	1990	1991	1992	1993	1994	1995
Sales ($ mil.)	44.7%	121	121	189	208	446	878	1,128	1,697	2,131	3,368
Net income ($ mil.)	15.7%	22	9	(3)	13	47	74	47	94	3	-82
Income as % of sales	—	18.3%	7.3%	—	6.2%	10.6%	8.4%	4.2%	5.5%	0.1%	2.4%
Earnings per share ($)	12.9%	0.51	0.21	(0.08)	0.30	1.14	1.69	1.05	1.12	0.06	1.52
Stock price – high ($)[1]	—	6.67	6.00	7.50	3.06	10.67	17.18	18.18	18.00	17.75	20.25
Stock price – low ($)[1]	—	4.00	3.56	1.81	2.17	2.90	5.92	8.88	11.13	9.38	11.63
Stock price – close ($)[1]	10.9%	5.96	4.63	2.81	2.96	7.25	12.42	11.38	15.25	14.13	15.13
P/E – high	—	13	29	—	10	9	10	17	10	296	13
P/E – low	—	8	17	—	7	3	4	9	6	156	8
Dividends per share ($)	—	0.00	0.00	0.00	0.00	0.00	0.00	0.00	0.00	0.00	0.00
Book value per share ($)	18.0%	2.49	2.65	2.59	2.82	4.14	6.09	7.19	9.19	9.22	11.04
Employees	29.8%	696	696	508	531	763	1,445	1,752	2,455	2,984	7,265

1994 Year-end:
Debt ratio: 42.6%
Return on equity: 17.7%
Cash (mil.): $188
Current ratio: 1.69
Long-term debt (mil.): $328
No. of shares (mil.): 46
Dividends
　Yield: —
　Payout: —
Market value (mil.): $698

**Stock Price History[1]
High/Low 1986–95**

[1]Stock prices are for the prior calendar year.

RALSTON PURINA GROUP

OVERVIEW

Ralston Purina Group (RPG) is fighting to remain top dog of its 2 core markets. St. Louis–based RPG is the world's #1 maker of dry cat and dog foods (Cat Chow and Dog Chow) as well as the world's top maker of dry cell batteries (Eveready). The company's Protein Technologies International segment produces soy proteins and fibers used in animal and human foods as well as polymers used in the manufacture of paper.

Faced with increased competition and shifting consumer trends, in 1994 the Ralston Purina Company spun off its baby food and cereal businesses (as Ralcorp Holdings) and reorganized as Ralston Purina Group and the Continental Baking Group (sold in 1995).

RPG continues to refine its focus, selling off noncore businesses and acquiring complementary ones. In 1994 the company created a global pet food organization by merging its international pet food and pet products businesses. In 1995 that segment acquired Golden Cat Corp., a producer of cat litter.

RPG's Eveready Battery Company faces a rapidly changing marketplace in which high-tech devices have new battery requirements. The company has already seen sales of carbon zinc batteries give way to demand for alkaline batteries. In 1994 Eveready and National Semiconductor codeveloped a "smart battery" for products such as portable computers. The smart battery is rechargeable and can "communicate" with its host computer to control its charge and to signal when its charge is low.

Agricultural giant Archer-Daniels-Midland owns more than 5.5% of RPG.

WHEN

In 1894 William Danforth founded the Robinson-Danforth Commission Company, a small St. Louis feed producer. The company's slogan, "Where Purity is Paramount," inspired Danforth to name a new whole wheat cereal product Purina (1898). The popularity of Danforth's cereal was enhanced by the endorsement of Everett Ralston, a well-known advocate of whole grain foods. In return, Ralston's name was included, and the cereal became Ralston health breakfast food. Trading on the cereal's popularity, Danforth renamed his company Ralston Purina in 1902.

Danforth proved to be a skillful marketer, introducing slogans and logos that would support Ralston Purina's image and products for many years. In 1900 he introduced the distinctive checkerboard design used on packages, grain elevators, and delivery trucks. The pattern was based on his childhood memory of a family who dressed in red-and-white checks. He changed the word "feed" to "chow" in the company's brands after returning from the front lines of WWI, where he noted the soldiers' eager response to each evening's "chow call." Ralston's animal foods have used the word "chow" ever since.

Danforth retired in 1932 and devoted his next 20 years to a variety of philanthropic activities. His book, *I Dare You*, shows his philosophy of enthusiasm and hard work.

During the 1950s the company decided to apply its knowledge of animal feeds to producing a domestic dog food. Purina Dog Chow, introduced in 1957, quickly became the nation's leading brand of dry dog food.

In 1962 the company experienced the worst disaster in its history when a dust explosion and fire demolished its St. Louis mill. Nevertheless, Ralston embarked on a major diversification program in the 1960s, buying Van Camp Seafood, with its Chicken of the Sea brands (1963, sold in 1988), and Foodmaker (1968), which included Jack-in-the-Box hamburger restaurants (sold in 1985).

The company became the nation's largest baker following the 1984 purchase of Continental Baking Company (Wonder Bread and Hostess Twinkies and Cupcakes) from ITT for approximately $475 million. Two years later it became the #1 battery producer in the world with the acquisition of the Eveready and Energizer brands from Union Carbide. In 1986 Ralston sold its domestic livestock feed business (Purina Mills) to British Petroleum but kept its international feed business intact. In 1989 the company bought Beech-Nut baby foods from Nestlé. In 1992 Ralston bought Ever Ready (UK) from Hanson.

In 1993 Ralston distributed 55% of Continental Baking to shareholders, retaining a 45% stake. The following year the company spun off its cereals and baby food businesses, hoping its new focus on pet food and batteries would energize revenues.

In 1995 Eveready signed an agreement with General Motors and Valence Technology to develop rechargeable lithium polymer batteries. That same year the company's Energizer bunny commercials (produced by Chiat/Day) ranked among the top 10 television spots according to a consumer survey.

WHO

Chairman, President, and CEO: William P. Stiritz,
age 60, $1,325,000 pay
VP; President and CEO, Grocery Products Group:
W. Patrick McGinnis, age 47, $532,500 pay
**VP; Chairman, President, and CEO, Eveready Battery
Co.:** J. Patrick Mulcahy, age 50, $444,000 pay
**VP; President and CEO, Protein Technologies
International:** Paul H. Hatfield, age 58, $407,500 pay
VP; CEO, Ralston Purina International: Franklin J.
Cornwell Jr., age 52
VP; EVP, Eveready, International: Patrick C. Mannix,
age 49
VP and CFO: James R. Elsesser, age 50
VP and Controller: Anita M. Wray, age 40
VP, General Counsel, and Secretary: James M. Neville,
age 55
VP; Robert W. Bracken, age 56
VP Director of Administration (HR): Charles Sommer
Auditors: Price Waterhouse LLP

WHERE

HQ: Checkerboard Square, St. Louis, MO 63164
Phone: 314-982-1000
Fax: 314-982-2134

Ralston Purina Group has 21 manufacturing plants for
human and pet foods and 37 battery plants worldwide.

	1994 Sales		1994 Operating Income	
	$ mil.	% of total	$ mil.	% of total
US	3,167	55	602	86
Europe	949	16	1	0
South & Central America	722	13	26	4
Asia/Pacific	683	12	69	10
Other regions	238	4	5	0
Total	**5,759**	**100**	**703**	**100**

WHAT

	1994 Sales		1994 Operating Income	
	$ mil.	% of total	$ mil.	% of total
Human & pet foods	2,215	37	367	52
Batteries	2,113	37	189	27
Agricultural prods. & other	1,431	26	147	21
Total	**5,759**	**100**	**703**	**100**

Selected Brand Names

Pet Foods	Batteries
Alley Cat	Energizer
Cat Chow Special Care	Eveready
CNM Clinical Nutrition Management	**Protein Technologies International (soybean products)**
Deli-Cat	
Dog Chow Senior	Fibrim
Meow Mix	Pro-Cote
Pro Plan	Solka-Floc
Purina Cat Chow	Supro
Purina Dog Chow	Supro Plus
Purina Fit & Trim	
Purina Hi Pro	
Purina Kibbles	
Purina O.N.E.	
Purina Puppy Chow	

KEY COMPETITORS

ADM	Mars
Ag Processing	Matsushita
Colgate-Palmolive	Moorman Manufacturing
Dalgety	Nestlé
Duracell	Pet Ventures
Eastman Kodak	Philips
Hartz Group	Rayovac
Heinz	Sony

HOW MUCH

	9-Year Growth	1985	1986	1987	1988	1989	1990	1991	1992	1993	1994
Sales ($ mil.)	(0.2%)	5,864	5,515	5,868	5,876	6,658	7,101	7,376	7,752	5,915	5,759
Net income ($ mil.)	(2.5%)	256	264	526	363	351	396	392	321	278	205
Income as % of sales	—	4.4%	4.8%	9.0%	6.2%	5.3%	5.6%	5.3%	4.1%	4.6%	3.6%
Earnings per share ($)	2.8%	1.54	1.69	3.58	2.61	2.52	3.03	3.13	2.65	2.35	1.98
Stock price – high ($)	—	25.31	38.50	47.00	44.19	50.75	54.19	60.13	58.88	49.88	46.38
Stock price – low ($)	—	16.88	21.88	28.81	31.88	39.38	38.88	46.00	40.88	33.50	33.50
Stock price – close ($)	7.4%	23.50	35.38	31.94	40.94	41.50	51.25	56.38	47.63	39.75	44.63
P/E – high	—	16	23	13	17	20	18	19	22	21	23
P/E – low	—	11	13	8	12	16	13	15	15	14	17
Dividends per share ($)	10.5%	0.49	0.54	0.60	0.72	0.81	0.90	1.04	1.17	1.20	1.20
Book value per share ($)	(14.2%)	5.76	6.55	6.85	7.88	2.92	1.34	3.50	6.32	2.04	1.45
Employees	(6.6%)	59,100	62,508	58,298	56,734	56,219	56,127	57,996	59,222	31,703	32,039

1994 Year-end:
Debt ratio: 71.5%
Return on equity: —
Cash (mil.): $112
Current ratio: 1.09
Long-term debt (mil.): $1,252
No. of shares (mil.): 100
Dividends
  Yield: 2.7%
  Payout: 60.6%
Market value (mil.): $4,463

Stock Price History
High/Low 1985–94

RAYTHEON COMPANY

OVERVIEW

Raytheon is proving the leopard can indeed change its spots. The missile maker's commercial operations (including Amana appliances and Beech aircraft) surpassed military sales in 1993 and grew to 65% in 1994. Massachusetts-based Raytheon has consolidated its operations into 4 segments: aircraft, appliances, electronics, and engineering and construction.

As recent purchases indicate, Raytheon intends to balance its commercial and military operations as it grows through acquisitions. The company bought Xyplex (computer networking products) and UniMac (commercial washing machines) in 1994, E-Systems (military electronics) and Anschütz (marine electronics) in 1995.

Raytheon, which took in nearly $4 billion from DOD sales in 1994, plans to remain a leader in military technology but is facing the reality of decreased defense spending by turning its military know-how to commercial uses. Cross-technology products include electronic controls for high-speed trains, weather warning systems, and components for wireless communications.

In 1995 Raytheon said it might spin off its engineering and construction unit to bolster its stock prices, which have been held back by defense cuts. Raytheon Engineers & Constructors has recently won contracts for industrial construction projects in China, the Dominican Republic, Norway, Portugal, and Thailand.

WHEN

In 1922 Laurence Marshall and several others started the American Appliance Company to manufacture C. G. Smith's new home refrigerator. When Smith's invention failed, Marshall began producing radio tubes under the brand name Raytheon, which in 1925 became the company's name.

Raytheon bought the radio division of Chicago's Q. R. S. Company in 1928 and formed the Raytheon Production Company with National Carbon Company (the makers of the Eveready battery) to market Eveready Raytheon tubes in 1929.

While enjoying a period of unprecedented growth during WWII, Raytheon became the first company to produce magnetrons (tubes used in both radar and microwave ovens). Wartime sales peaked at $173 million but had dwindled by 1947. With rumors of bankruptcy in the air, Charles Adams became president (he is still a company director). Adams sold Raytheon's unprofitable radio and TV business to Admiral Corporation in 1956.

Military orders stemming from the Korean conflict boosted sales in the mid-1950s. In 1964 Adams (then chairman) named missile engineer Thomas Phillips president. Phillips oversaw a series of acquisitions designed to equalize Raytheon's commercial and military earnings, beginning with Amana Refrigeration in 1965. Raytheon added D.C. Heath (textbook publishing, 1966), Caloric (stoves, 1967), and 3 companies involved in petrochemical construction and exploration (1966, 1968, 1969). Raytheon started making computer terminals in 1971, but unable to compete, it left the business in 1984. In 1980 the company bought Grumman's Beech Aircraft division and began making single- and twin-engine planes.

But in spite of its diversification efforts, Raytheon still depended on missiles, radar, and communications systems for 90% of its earnings in 1987. A 1990 government investigation revealed that Raytheon and other defense contractors had been trading in Pentagon secrets; Raytheon pled guilty and agreed to pay a $1 million fine. In 1991 the US Army, pleased with the success of the company's Patriot missile in the Persian Gulf War, awarded Raytheon an $800 million R&D contract to upgrade the missile and other programs. Tom Phillips retired as chairman in 1991 after 43 years with the company and was succeeded by president Dennis Picard.

In 1993 the company reorganized its construction businesses into Raytheon Engineers & Constructors International and merged Caloric's operations into Amana. That same year the company paid out $566 million for acquisitions; most were in the civilian jet and construction businesses. Purchases included Applied Remote Technology (unmanned underwater vehicles and sensor systems) from TRW; the Menumaster line of commercial microwave ovens from Litton; the business jet division of British Aerospace; and assets of Ebasco Services (power plants and infrastructure construction) from ENSERCH. The following year Raytheon won a Brazilian contract, worth over $1 billion, to build an environmental surveillance and air traffic control system in the Amazon region.

After losing a bid for Unisys's military units, in 1995 Raytheon purchased E-Systems, Inc., a maker of advanced electronic and surveillance equipment. The $2.3 billion acquisition helps Raytheon remain competitive as the defense industry continues to consolidate.

NYSE symbol: RTN
Fiscal year ends: December 31

WHO

Chairman and CEO: Dennis J. Picard, age 62,
$1,835,754 pay
EVP; General Manager, Raytheon Electronic Systems:
William H. Swanson, age 46, $701,450 pay
**EVP; Chairman and CEO, Raytheon Engineers &
Constructors:** Charles Q. Miller, age 49
EVP; Chairman and CEO, Raytheon Aircraft: Arthur E.
Wegner, age 57
**EVP Law, Human Resources, and Corporate
Administration, and Secretary:** Christoph L.
Hoffmann, age 50
EVP; Group Executive, Appliance Group: Robert L.
Swam, age 54
EVP, CFO, and Controller: Peter R. D'Angelo, age 56
SVP and Treasurer: Herbert Deitcher, age 61
**President, Home Appliance Division, Raytheon
Appliances:** Thomas F. L'Esperance
VP Engineering: Frank Kendall, age 46
VP and General Counsel: Thomas D. Hyde, age 46
VP Human Resources: Gail Philip Anderson, age 52
Auditors: Coopers & Lybrand L.L.P.

WHERE

HQ: 141 Spring St., Lexington, MA 02173
Phone: 617-862-6600
Fax: 617-860-2172

Raytheon operates globally, principally in the Americas,
Europe, the Middle East, and the Pacific Rim countries.

	1994 Sales		1994 Net Income	
	$ mil.	% of total	$ mil.	% of total
US	9,224	92	547	92
Other countries	789	8	50	8
Total	**10,013**	**100**	**597**	**100**

WHAT

	1994 Sales		1994 Operating Income	
	$ mil.	% of total	$ mil.	% of total
Electronics	4,068	41	683	54
Engineers & constructors	2,821	28	259	21
Aircraft	1,722	17	233	18
Appliances	1,402	14	84	7
Total	**10,013**	**100**	**1,259**	**100**

Selected Products

Electronics
Air traffic control systems
Educational materials
Electronic controls for
autos and appliances
Environmental
monitoring systems
Marine electronics
Patriot air defense systems
Radar and sonar systems
Semiconductors

**Engineers and
Constructors**
Design, construction, and
maintenance of heavy
industrial plants
Facility and site planning

Aircraft
Baron twin-engine aircraft
Beech passenger aircraft
Beechcraft Bonanza
single-engine aircraft
Beechjet business jet
Hawker business jets
King Air jetprop
Starship jetprop
T-1A Jayhawk Trainer

Appliances
Amana
Caloric
Menumaster
Modern Maid
Speed Queen
UniMac

KEY COMPETITORS

AMP
Bombardier
Daimler-Benz
AB Electrolux
Emerson
Fluor
General Electric
Gulfstream
Aerospace
Halliburton
Harris Corp.
Intel
Lockheed
Martin
Loral
Maytag
McDermott
Mitsubishi
Northrop Grumman
Peter Kiewit Sons'
Rockwell
Samsung
Textron
Thomson SA
United
Technologies
Whirlpool

HOW MUCH

	9-Year Growth	1985	1986	1987	1988	1989	1990	1991	1992	1993	1994
Sales ($ mil.)	5.1%	6,409	7,308	7,659	8,192	8,796	9,268	9,274	9,058	9,201	10,013
Net income ($ mil.)	5.3%	376	393	445	490	529	557	592	635	693	597
Income as % of sales	—	5.9%	5.4%	5.8%	6.0%	6.0%	6.0%	6.4%	7.0%	7.5%	6.0%
Earnings per share ($)	7.7%	2.30	2.55	3.03	3.66	3.98	4.25	4.45	4.72	5.07	4.48
Stock price – high ($)	—	27.81	35.88	42.44	36.94	42.50	35.63	44.13	53.50	68.50	68.88
Stock price – low ($)	—	19.69	26.19	28.63	30.50	32.31	28.88	32.88	51.25	50.50	60.50
Stock price – close ($)	10.1%	26.81	33.63	33.31	33.50	34.75	35.06	41.56	51.25	66.00	63.88
P/E – high	—	12	14	14	10	11	8	10	11	14	15
P/E – low	—	9	10	9	8	8	7	7	9	10	14
Dividends per share ($)	7.1%	0.80	0.85	0.90	1.00	1.08	1.18	1.20	1.30	1.40	1.48
Book value per share ($)	11.0%	12.42	13.19	13.66	15.98	18.49	21.78	24.91	28.33	31.79	31.85
Employees	(2.1%)	73,000	75,000	76,500	76,200	77,600	76,700	71,600	63,900	63,800	60,200

1994 Year-end:
Debt ratio: 21.2%
Return on equity: 14.5%
Cash (mil.): $202
Current ratio: 1.52
Long-term debt (mil.): $25
No. of shares (mil.): 123.3
Dividends
Yield: 2.3%
Payout: 32.9%
Market value (mil.): $7,877

**Stock Price History
High/Low 1985–94**

THE READER'S DIGEST ASSOCIATION, INC.

OVERVIEW

The Reader's Digest Association is the company that parlayed condensed reprints of journal articles into a global publishing and entertainment empire with nearly $3 billion in sales. Its flagship publication, *Reader's Digest*, is the world's most widely read magazine; 47 editions are published in 18 languages and read by 100 million people. The New York–based company also produces a wide range of books, music, videos, and special-interest magazines whose traditional values inspire, inform, and entertain legions of worldwide customers. Reader's Digest is one of the leading European book and magazine publishers. In 1994, 60% of the company's revenues were from international sales. Reader's Digest markets its products through sophisticated direct

mailings and an extensive consumer database that is considered one of the best in the world.

The company, which published 56 million copies of cookbooks and reference, do-it-yourself, series, and condensed books in 1994, is moving into multimedia. A new director was hired in 1994 to expand the company's video operations; its history, travel, and comedy videos have won 3 Emmys and 26 awards for excellence since the business line was launched in 1986. Reader's Digest has teamed up with software giant Microsoft to produce a line of CD-ROM products. It already has put 2 magazines, *Family Handyman* and *Travel Holiday*, on-line, and the company intends to expand its presence in the electronic publishing marketplace.

WHEN

The first edition of DeWitt ("Wally") and Lila Wallace's monthly *Reader's Digest* appeared in 1922 and was an immediate success. Within 3 years circulation had almost quintupled, and the Wallaces moved from New York City to Pleasantville, New York. The idea of condensing material from other magazines into a compact, readable form proved to be popular, and the *Digest* grew enormously. It expanded from mail subscriptions only to newsstand sales in 1929 and reached a circulation of one million by 1935. In 1939 the company moved to Chappaqua, New York, but kept Pleasantville as a mailing address.

In the 1940s the *Digest* expanded internationally (the first overseas edition started in England in 1938), opening company offices on 5 continents and providing foreign-language translations. During that decade Wally began to write his own articles (partly because some magazines had stopped allowing him reprint rights), giving the *Digest* its conservative, optimistic style.

In 1950 the first Reader's Digest Condensed Book was published. In 1955 the *Digest* accepted its first advertising but did not carry liquor ads until 1978 and has never carried cigarette ads. The *Digest* published articles in the mid-1950s examining the link between smoking and cancer.

The company added the Recorded Music Division in 1959 and General Books in 1963. Reader's Digest was the first publisher to use direct-mail advertising with "personalized" letters to promote its products. Its huge mailing list was later used for promotions such as the Reader's Digest Sweepstakes.

The Wallaces continued to manage the company until 1973. Wally died in 1981; Lila died 3 years later. Their voting stock in the company passed to trust funds, and about 6 million nonvoting shares were given to 10 organizations, including Lincoln Center, the Metropolitan Museum of Art, and the New York Zoological Society.

George Grune took over as chairman and CEO in 1984. He cut staff by 20% and disposed of unprofitable subsidiaries, ushering in an era of increased profitability for the company. Reader's Digest added a line of specialty magazines by purchasing *Travel Holiday* in 1986, *Family Handyman* in 1988, *50 Plus* (renamed *New Choices for Retirement Living*) in 1988, and *American Health* in 1990. The company bought 50% of British publisher Dorling Kindersley in 1987.

Following a 1990 public offering, Reader's Digest made a transition from nearly a public trust to a profit-oriented company. Most of the voting shares are owned by the DeWitt Wallace–Reader's Digest Fund and the Lila Wallace–Reader's Digest Fund (36% each).

In 1993 "Reader's Digest: On Television" aired on network TV. The one-hour special was the company's first venture into TV (excepting home video production) since 1955.

In 1994 James Schadt took over as CEO. Grune, a 34-year veteran of the company, remained chairman. In 1995 the company launched a Polish edition of *Reader's Digest*, upping to 18 the number of local-language editions. Former RJR Nabisco CFO Stephen Wilson joined Reader's Digest after SVP and CFO Anthony Ruggiero resigned.

NYSE symbol: RDA
Fiscal year ends: June 30

WHO

Chairman: George V. Grune, age 65, $1,537,308 pay
President and CEO: James P. Schadt, age 56, $1,058,846 pay
EVP; President, Reader's Digest USA: Kenneth A. H. Gordon, age 57, $688,077 pay (prior to promotion)
EVP and CFO: Stephen R. Wilson, age 48
SVP Global Direct Marketing: Peter J. C. Davenport, age 54
SVP Human Resources: Joseph M. Grecky, age 55
VP; President, US Magazine Publishing: Thomas M. Kenney, age 47, $540,000 pay
VP; President, Reader's Digest Europe: Heikki K. Helenius, age 52
VP; President, Reader's Digest Pacific: Martin J. Pearson, age 47
VP; President, Special Markets Group: William H. Willis, age 43
VP Public Relations and Communications Policy: Carole M. Howard, age 49
VP Operations: Bruce G. Koe, age 51
VP; Editor-in-Chief, General Books: John A. Pope Jr., age 61
Auditors: KPMG Peat Marwick LLP

WHERE

HQ: Reader's Digest Rd., Pleasantville, NY 10570-7000
Phone: 914-238-1000
Fax: 914-238-4559

	1994 Sales		1994 Operating Income	
	$ mil.	% of total	$ mil.	% of total
Europe	1,301	46	160	39
US	1,118	40	229	55
Other regions	397	14	24	6
Adjustments	(10)	—	(19)	—
Total	**2,806**	**100**	**394**	**100**

WHAT

	1994 Sales		1994 Operating Income	
	$ mil.	% of total	$ mil.	% of total
Books, CDs, cassettes, videos	1,900	68	311	75
Reader's Digest	689	25	79	19
Special-interest magazines	91	3	(3)	—
Other	130	4	26	6
Adjustments	(4)	—	(19)	—
Total	**2,806**	**100**	**394**	**100**

Books and Home Entertainment Products
General-interest books and CDs (how-to and reference books, cookbooks, and songbooks; 12 languages)
Reader's Digest Condensed Books (popular fiction; 15 editions in 12 languages)
Recorded music (original and licensed recordings)
Series books (multiple volumes; 9 languages)
Videocassettes and original video productions

Magazines
American Health
The Family Handyman
Moneywise (UK)
New Choices for Retirement Living
Reader's Digest (47 editions in 18 languages)
Travel Holiday

Other Operations
Fundraising products and services for school and youth groups (QSP, Inc.)
Sweepstakes direct-mail promotion
Other direct marketing (language courses, globes)

KEY COMPETITORS

AARP	Hearst	Sony
Advance Publications	Lagardère	Thomson Corp.
	New York Times	Time Warner
Bertelsmann	News Corp.	Viacom
Cox	Reed Elsevier	Virgin Group

HOW MUCH

	Annual Growth	1985	1986	1987	1988	1989	1990	1991	1992	1993	1994
Sales ($ mil.)	8.6%	1,217	1,255	1,420	1,712	1,832	2,010	2,345	2,614	2,869	2,806
Net income ($ mil.)	11.6%	52	73	95	141	152	176	209	234	258	272
Income as % of sales	—	4.3%	5.8%	7.6%	8.2%	8.3%	8.8%	8.9%	9.0%	9.0%	9.7%
Earnings per share ($)	12.1%	0.41	0.59	0.78	1.18	1.28	1.48	1.74	1.95	2.16	2.34
Stock price–high ($)	—	—	—	—	—	—	29.50	49.00	56.38	55.88	49.38
Stock price–low ($)	—	—	—	—	—	—	21.00	26.13	43.00	36.13	39.88
Stock price–close ($)	13.6%	—	—	—	—	—	29.50	48.38	54.00	45.00	49.13
P/E–high	—	—	—	—	—	—	20	28	29	26	21
P/E–low	—	—	—	—	—	—	14	15	22	17	17
Dividends per share ($)	83.1%	—	—	—	—	—	0.12	0.57	0.80	1.15	1.35
Book value per share ($)	8.2%	—	—	—	—	—	5.07	6.36	7.79	6.72	6.95
Employees	(2.0%)	—	—	—	—	7,400	7,400	7,400	7,400	7,300	6,700

1994 Year-end:
Debt ratio: 1.1%
Return on equity: 34.1%
Cash (mil.): $183
Current ratio: 1.15
Long-term debt (mil.): $9
No. of shares (mil.): 114
Dividends
  Yield: 2.7%
  Payout: 57.7%
Market value (mil.): $5,588

Stock Price History
High/Low 1990–94

REEBOK INTERNATIONAL LTD.

OVERVIEW

Stoughton, Massachusetts–based Reebok is the 2nd largest athletic shoemaker in the US, a couple of steps behind NIKE (21.3% and 29.7%, respectively). The company makes a variety of athletic shoes for everything from basketball and volleyball to aerobics and rock climbing and manufactures athletic apparel and accessories. The company's Rockport subsidiary makes casual and dress shoes.

In an effort to catch NIKE, CEO Paul Fireman, who with his wife owns 14.5% of the company, has aggressively pursued endorsements from sports stars (including Shaquille O'Neal, Emmitt Smith, and Greg Norman), boosted international sales, and licensed Reebok's technology or name for various sporting goods or products. In 1995 the company signed a licensing deal with the NFL to make sideline apparel with NFL team logos. The company is also looking for major growth from Rockport, which targets baby boomers.

The company suffered a pair of shocks in 1995 when the 2 top executives at its Reebok Division, Roberto Muller and John Duerden, resigned within 2 months of each other. Each cited "personal reasons" for leaving.

WHEN

English runner Joseph Foster invented a spiked running shoe in 1894. Other runners liked the shoe so much that Foster started his own shoe company (JW Foster and Sons). In 1924 Foster supplied the shoes for the British Olympic team (of *Chariots of Fire* fame). Two of Foster's grandsons formed a companion company, Reebok (named for a speedy African antelope), in 1958 that eventually absorbed JW Foster and Sons.

Reebok remained a small British shoe company until 1979, when Paul Fireman, a distributor of fishing and camping supplies, noticed the shoes at a Chicago international trade show. Fireman quickly acquired the exclusive North American license to sell Reebok shoes. Pentland Industries, another British company, agreed to finance Fireman for 55.5% ownership of Reebok USA. Fireman acquired 40% of the new venture, with the remainder going to a group of US investors. Reebok established its headquarters in Massachusetts and started production in Korea.

Sales executives at Reebok USA realized the difficulty the company would have competing with the running shoes of established competitors NIKE and Adidas; therefore, they looked to the aerobic shoe market. In 1982 Reebok introduced Freestyle, a women's oxford-style sneaker, following with a line of men's fitness shoes in 1983. The introduction of these new aerobic shoe lines coincided with a rise in the popularity of aerobics, and the Freestyle became one of the largest-selling shoes in history. Sales went from $3.5 million in 1982 to $919 million in 1986, giving Reebok the lead over NIKE in the athletic shoe industry.

In 1985 Reebok USA acquired the original British Reebok company. That year Reebok went public, acquiring Rockport (walking and casual shoes, 1986), Avia (athletic shoes, 1987), Frye (boots, 1987; sold 1989), and Boston Whaler (recreational boats, 1989; sold 1993). The Pump (a hot-selling inflatable basketball shoe) was introduced in 1989.

Facing a mature US market, Reebok turned its emphasis to Europe. In 1990 Reebok bought out its European distributor and reorganized its US and international operations into a single division.

The company has been a leader in athletic shoe technology, with such innovations as the Pump, Energy Return System (ERS), Hexalite, Energaire, and Avia's cantilever sole. In 1992 Reebok received a patent for the Pump's technology and promptly filed an infringement lawsuit against L.A. Gear, which paid a $1 million settlement.

Also in 1992 Reebok developed a new line of cleated athletic shoes and successfully introduced Boks casual footwear. Reebok also added to its apparel business by purchasing California brands Above the Rim and Tinley. Reebok sold off Ellesse (apparel and footwear) as well as Boston Whaler in 1993 to concentrate on core businesses.

In 1994 Reebok signed a deal with NBC to be an official sponsor of NBC's broadcast of the 1996 Summer Olympics in Atlanta. That same year the company began operations, through a joint venture, in China.

In 1995 Reebok settled a price-fixing suit with the FTC and the attorneys general of all 50 states. The FTC claimed Reebok and Rockport had conspired to keep prices artificially high by threatening to stop supplying any retailers who discounted their shoes below a certain price. Reebok agreed to pay the states $9.5 million.

NYSE symbol: RBK
Fiscal year ends: December 31

WHO

Chairman, President, and CEO: Paul B. Fireman,
age 51, $2,000,012 pay
EVP; COO, Reebok Division: Paul R. Duncan, age 54,
$1,107,716 pay
EVP; President, Specialty Business Group: Robert
Meers, age 51, $572,019 pay
EVP; President and CEO, The Rockport Company:
Angel R. Martinez, age 39
EVP and CFO: Kenneth I. Watchmaker, age 52
SVP North American Operations, Reebok Division:
Tom Carmody
SVP European Operations, Reebok Division: Bruce
Nevins
SVP Law and Human Resources and General Counsel:
John B. Douglas III, age 41
Treasurer: Leo S. Vannoni
Auditors: Ernst & Young LLP

WHERE

HQ: 100 Technology Center Dr., Stoughton, MA 02072
Phone: 617-341-5000
Fax: 617-341-5087

The company sells its products in 120 countries;
operates retail "concept" stores in California,
Massachusetts, and New York; and sells footwear,
apparel, and accessories from more than 50 factory
outlets.

	1994 Sales		1994 Net Income	
	$ mil.	% of total	$ mil.	% of total
US	1,975	61	127	50
UK	506	15	63	25
Other Europe	502	15	28	11
Other regions	297	9	37	14
Total	**3,280**	**100**	**255**	**100**

WHAT

	1994 Sales	
	$ mil.	% of total
Reebok	2,813	86
Rockport	314	10
Avia	153	4
Total	**3,280**	**100**

Selected Products and Brands

Shoes
Avia
Boks
Greg Norman
Reebok
  BlackTop
  DynaMaX
  Instapump
  The Kamikaze
  Preseason
  The Pump
  Shaq
  The Transcender
  Weebok
Rockport

Apparel
Active wear
Children's clothing
Golf wear

Related Products
Slide Reebok (training
  equipment)
Sports and fitness videos

Trademark Licensing
Athletic gloves
Basketballs
Bicycle helmets
Gymnastic apparel
Sunglasses and protective
  eyewear

KEY COMPETITORS

Adidas
Bausch & Lomb
Berkshire
  Hathaway
Birkenstock
Converse
Deckers
  Outdoors
Edison Brothers
Fruit of the Loom

The Gap
J. Crew
K-Swiss
L.A. Gear
Lands' End
Levi Strauss
L.L. Bean
New Balance
NIKE
Oshkosh B'Gosh

Puma
Russell Corp.
Rykä
Starter
Stride Rite
Timberland
V. F.
Wolverine
World Wide

HOW MUCH

	Annual Growth	1985	1986	1987	1988	1989	1990	1991	1992	1993	1994
Sales ($ mil.)	30.1%	307	919	1,389	1,786	1,822	2,159	2,735	3,023	2,894	3,280
Net income ($ mil.)	23.2%	39	132	165	137	175	177	235	115	223	255
Income as % of sales	—	12.7%	14.4%	11.9%	7.7%	9.6%	8.2%	8.6%	3.8%	7.7%	7.8%
Earnings per share ($)	23.3%	0.46	1.28	1.49	1.20	1.53	1.54	2.37	1.24	2.53	3.02
Stock price – high ($)	—	4.88	16.50	25.19	18.38	19.63	20.00	35.13	35.63	38.63	40.25
Stock price – low ($)	—	3.28	4.31	7.00	9.50	11.13	8.13	10.75	21.38	23.00	28.38
Stock price – close ($)	26.8%	4.66	11.69	10.63	12.25	19.00	11.50	33.13	34.00	30.00	39.50
P/E – high	—	11	13	17	15	13	13	15	29	15	13
P/E – low	—	7	3	5	8	7	5	5	17	9	9
Dividends per share ($)	—	0.00	0.00	0.15	0.28	0.30	0.30	0.30	0.30	0.30	0.30
Book value per share ($)	33.3%	0.92	2.82	5.20	6.12	7.42	8.71	9.05	9.22	10.12	12.24
Employees	30.7%	—	—	1,000	2,234	3,000	3,800	4,200	4,500	4,700	6,500

1994 Year-end:
Debt ratio: 16.9%
Return on equity: 27.7%
Cash (mil.): $84
Current ratio: 2.65
Long-term debt (mil.): $132
No. of shares (mil.): 81
Dividends
  Yield: 0.8%
  Payout: 9.9%
Market value (mil.): $3,197

**Stock Price History
High/Low 1985–94**

REYNOLDS METALS COMPANY

OVERVIEW

Virginia-based Reynolds Metals is one of the world's top aluminum producers (after Canada's Alcan and the US's Alcoa). An integrated aluminum producer, Reynolds makes aluminum cans and aluminum foil (Reynolds Wrap); nonaluminum products, such as plastics for packaging and consumer markets; and materials for the construction industry. It also processes gold.

With aluminum prices at new highs, Reynolds is rebounding from years of sluggish demand, low prices, and overcapacity. During this time Reynolds, like other aluminum producers, reorganized, cut employment, closed its more costly facilities, and sold noncore assets. Reynolds sold off some of its gold mining operations in 1994 and may sell more.

Reynolds is exploring new markets and products having higher profit margins. Through joint ventures in South America, the company hopes to boost its production of aluminum packaging (26% of 1994 revenues), which was given a lift when Reynolds bought Bev-Pak, a key supplier to the soft-drink industry. The company also intends to make more products for the automotive industry and explore new markets around the world (especially in Asia, Central America, and South America) and in the growing building supply and infrastructure industry. But some of Reynolds's continued well-being depends on the success of an uneasy truce among major aluminum producing countries that agreed in 1994 to cut back production for 2 years.

WHEN

Richard Reynolds began his business career under the tutelage of his uncle R. J. Reynolds, of tobacco industry fame and fortune. In 1912 Richard returned to Bristol, Tennessee, to run his father's Reynolds Company (silica-based cleansers). Near the end of WWI, the company changed from producing cleansers to making waterproof gunpowder canisters (from tin, asphalt, and asphalt felt paper).

After the war the company needed a peacetime product. In 1919 Reynolds entered a joint venture with R.J. Reynolds Tobacco, forming United States Foil Company to roll tinfoil for cigarette packaging. Reynolds Tobacco sold its shares of US Foil to outsiders in 1924. That same year US Foil bought the company that made Eskimo Pies, the ice cream product wrapped in foil.

In 1928 Richard bought Robertshaw Thermostat, Fulton Sylphon, and part of Beechnut Foil, adding the companies to US Foil to form Reynolds Metals. By 1929 Reynolds Metals was using both tin and the lighter-weight aluminum. In the late 1930s Richard foresaw that the US need for aluminum would dramatically increase if it became involved in WWII, so the company began mining bauxite (aluminum ore) in Arkansas in 1940. The next year Reynolds Metals built its first aluminum plant (near Sheffield, Alabama) and quickly built other plants in Alabama and Washington.

In 1946 the US government forced Alcoa to give up the patent rights to Alcoa's process of obtaining aluminum from bauxite. Thus Reynolds Metals received this process gratis when it bought 6 surplus government aluminum plants (which used Alcoa's patented pro-

cess) after WWII. Reynolds Metals developed many of the innovative uses of aluminum, including siding (1945) and aluminum foil (1947). The company began to search for bauxite in Jamaica (1949) and British Guyana (1952, mines nationalized 1975). In 1959 the company bought British Aluminum jointly with Tube Investments (sold to Tube, 1978). Reynolds developed the aluminum beverage can (1963) and began the recycling of it (1968). The company bought Industrial Metals (1969) and May Aluminum (1971).

In 1982 the company introduced Reynolds Plastic Wrap. In 1986 it began mining gold in Australia and made a major strike in 1987; other gold operations were bought in 1991. In 1988 the company acquired Presto Products (plastic bags, food wrap). In 1992 Reynolds sold its wire and cable operations and, after nearly 70 years of ownership, spun off its 84% interest in Eskimo Pie. Also in 1992 the company announced it would dismiss up to 12% of its salaried work force to cut costs.

In 1993 Reynolds restructured the company to redirect resources to more profitable market areas, reduced its production of alumina, and cut aluminum production by 21%. That same year Reynolds sold its Benton Harbor, Michigan, aluminum reclamation plant.

In 1994 Reynolds bought the aluminum and stainless steel products distribution business of Prime Metals and sold its 40% stake in the Boddington Gold Mine (Australia). From U.S. Shoe that same year it bought a Wisconsin plant that will be converted to manufacturing aluminum automobile wheels.

NYSE symbol: RLM
Fiscal year ends: December 31

WHO

Chairman and CEO: Richard G. Holder, age 63,
$975,000 pay
VC: Yale M. Brandt, age 64, $530,000 pay
VC; President and CEO, Reynolds International:
Randolph N. Reynolds, age 53, $507,083 pay
President and COO: Jeremiah J. Sheehan, age 56,
$553,750 pay
EVP and CFO: Henry S. Savedge Jr., age 61,
$410,000 pay
EVP Raw Materials, Metals, and Industrial Products:
J. Wilt Wagner, age 53, $410,000 pay
EVP Human Resources and External Affairs: Donald T.
Cowles, age 47
VP, General Counsel, and Secretary: D. Michael Jones,
age 41
VP, Flexible Packaging Division: Thomas P. Christino,
age 55
VP: James R. Aitken, age 60
VP: Eugene M. Desvernine, age 53
Auditors: Ernst & Young LLP

WHERE

HQ: 6601 W. Broad St., PO Box 27003, Richmond, VA
23261-7003
Phone: 804-281-2000
Fax: 804-281-3695

Reynolds has operations in 22 countries.

	1994 Sales		1994 Operating Income	
	$ mil.	% of total	$ mil.	% of total
US	4,507	77	55	25
Canada	375	6	105	47
Europe & other regions	998	17	63	28
Adjustments	133	—	(11)	—
Total	**6,013**	**100**	**212**	**100**

WHAT

	1994 Sales	
	$ mil.	% of total
Aluminum finished products	2,032	34
Other finished products	1,008	17
Flat-rolled	1,003	17
Other production & processing	1,836	30
Other	134	2
Total	**6,013**	**100**

Major Products

Consumer Goods	Finished Products
Baker's Choice (baking cups)	Aluminum cans and containers
Cut-Rite wax paper and sandwich bags	Building products Packaging products
Presto disposer bags	Plastic lids and containers
Reynolds Crystal Color Plastic Wrap	Printing cylinders and machinery
Reynolds Freezer Paper	
Reynolds Oven Bags	**Other**
Reynolds Plastic Wrap	Auto parts (wheels,
Reynolds Wrap (aluminum foil)	bumpers,drive shafts, heat exchanger tubing)
	Gold
	Reclaimed aluminum

KEY COMPETITORS

ACX Technologies	Dow Chemical	Mobil
Alcan	First Brands	Norsk Hydro
Alcoa	FMC	Ormet
Alumax	Hayes Wheels	Owens-Illinois
ASARCO	Inland Steel	Phelps Dodge
Bethlehem Steel	James River	Rubbermaid
Broken Hill	Johnson Controls	Superior Industries
Crown Cork & Seal	Kaiser Aluminum	Thyssen U.S. Can
Cyprus Amax	LTV	USX–U.S. Steel
	MAXXAM	

HOW MUCH

	9-Year Growth	1985	1986	1987	1988	1989	1990	1991	1992	1993	1994
Sales ($ mil.)	5.9%	3,578	3,903	4,317	5,619	6,211	6,076	5,785	5,656	5,294	6,013
Net income ($ mil.)	—	(298)	102	201	482	533	297	154	(109)	(322)	88
Income as % of sales	—	—	2.6%	4.7%	8.6%	8.6%	4.9%	2.7%	—	—	1.5%
Earnings per share ($)	—	(6.96)	2.04	3.95	9.01	9.20	5.01	2.60	(1.83)	(5.38)	1.42
Stock price – high ($)	—	20.63	26.38	61.75	58.00	62.75	70.00	65.38	64.38	58.88	59.38
Stock price – low ($)	—	15.13	18.13	20.13	34.00	49.00	48.50	46.00	47.00	41.13	40.38
Stock price – close ($)	11.2%	18.88	20.00	47.63	53.75	53.63	57.00	55.00	53.13	45.38	49.00
P/E – high	—	—	13	16	6	7	14	25	—	—	42
P/E – low	—	—	9	5	4	5	10	18	—	—	28
Dividends per share ($)	8.0%	0.50	0.50	0.58	0.90	1.70	1.80	1.80	1.80	1.20	1.00
Book value per share ($)	2.4%	22.92	27.05	29.69	37.77	45.24	49.22	49.66	34.47	26.83	28.42
Employees	0.3%	28,200	26,800	27,300	29,000	30,500	30,800	30,900	29,300	29,000	29,000

1994 Year-end:
Debt ratio: 52.9%
Return on equity: 5.2%
Cash (mil.): $434
Current ratio: 1.63
Long-term debt (mil.): $1,848
No. of shares (mil.): 62
Dividends
Yield: 2.0%
Payout: 70.4%
Market value (mil.): $3,046

Stock Price History
High/Low 1985–94

RITE AID CORPORATION

OVERVIEW

Rite Aid won't sell you an exhaust manifold or dry-clean your suit anymore, but if you need a prescription, they will be glad to help. The Camp Hill, Pennsylvania–based company is the largest operator of retail drugstores in the US (by store count), with more than 2,800 stores in 23 eastern states. The company has sold off most of its other businesses to focus on its drugstore and pharmacy operations.

In addition to prescription drugs, which account for over 50% of drugstore sales, each store offers a wide selection of health and beauty care products and seasonal merchandise, as well as a large private-label product line. Rite Aid also operates Eagle Managed Care Corp., a wholly owned subsidiary, which is designed to market prescription benefit programs.

As part of its 1994 restructuring Rite Aid sold Sera-Tec Biologicals, which operates a chain of 33 plasma collection centers; a 93-unit chain of bookstores, Encore Books; a chain of 168 dry cleaners, Concord Custom Cleaners; and ADAP, a 96-store auto parts chain. Rite Aid also closed about 200 underperforming stores.

Since its restructuring Rite Aid has been on a buying spree, with a particular taste for the Big Apple. Among several recent deals in the New York City area, the company agreed to buy 30 drugstores from Pathmark, making it the largest drugstore chain in the city.

In 1995 founder Alex Grass was succeeded by his son, Martin, as chairman and CEO. The Grass family owns about 4% of Rite Aid's stock.

WHEN

In 1958 wholesale grocer Alex Grass established Rack Rite Distributors in Harrisburg, Pennsylvania, to provide health and beauty aids and other nonfood products to grocery stores. Grass offered these same products at his first discount drugstore, Thrif D Discount Center, which he opened in 1962 in Scranton, Pennsylvania. By 1966 the company had 36 drugstores, and that same year it began installing pharmacies in drugstores. In 1967 the company introduced a line of private-label products. Rite Aid adopted its current name and went public in 1968 and in 1969 bought Daw Drug (47 stores), Blue Ridge Nursing Homes, and plasma suppliers Immuno Serums and Sero Genics.

In 1971 the company bought Sera-Tec Biologicals of New Jersey (blood plasma); the 40 stores of Cohen Drug of Charleston, West Virginia; and 50% of Superdrug Stores, Ltd., a UK-based chain. Rite Aid filled over 5 million prescriptions that year. In 1973 the company bought 2 Philadelphia-area chains (50-store Warner and 49-store Thomas Holmes) and in 1976, the 52-store Keystone Centers, which had drugstores in Pennsylvania and New Jersey. In 1977 it bought the Read chain, adding 99 Baltimore drugstores, and in 1978 Rite Aid sold its nursing homes.

By 1981 acquisitions had made Rite Aid the 3rd largest drugstore chain, and sales had exceeded $1 billion. Diversifying, Rite Aid bought American Discount Auto Parts's 32-store chain and Encore Books's 19-store discount chain in 1984. The company spun off

its wholesale grocery operation as Super Rite, retaining a 47% stake (sold 1989).

In 1987 Rite Aid bought 113 SupeRx drugstores in Florida, Georgia, and Alabama and 94 Gray Drug Fair stores and sold its share in Superdrug to Woolworth Holdings, netting about $68 million. The company bought the rest of the 356-store Gray Drug Fair operation in 1988. By 1989 the costs associated with rapid expansion had eroded Rite Aid's profit margins from 4.0% in 1986 to 3.3%. During 1990 the company focused on integrating all its acquisitions.

In 1991 Rite Aid added 68 stores and bought the prescription records from 65 drugstores in Washington, DC. In 1993 Rite Aid acquired 34 Wellby Super Drug stores and 35 Reliable Drugs stores the next year.

In 1994 the company acquired LaVerdiere's Enterprises, a chain of 67 drugstores based in Maine. That same year, as part of its massive restructuring, Rite Aid acquired Pharmacy Card Inc. and Intell-Rx and merged the 2 to form Eagle Managed Care. During its first year of operation Eagle signed up several groups to its pharmacy plans, including the Hotel Employees and Restaurant Employees International Union.

Also in 1994 Rite Aid joined a group of 7 national drugstore chains to form Pharmacy Direct Network to compete with Merck's Medco Containment Services and PCS Health Systems for 3rd-party prescription drug sales.

In 1995 Rite Aid acquired Michigan-based Perry Drug Stores for $132 million.

NYSE symbol: RAD
Fiscal year ends: Saturday nearest March 1

WHO

Honorary Chairman: Alex Grass, age 67, $1,537,100 pay
Chairman and CEO: Martin L. Grass, age 41,
$1,092,000 pay (prior to promotion)
President and COO: Timothy J. Noonan, age 53,
$382,354 pay (prior to promotion)
EVP and Chief Legal Counsel: Franklin C. Brown,
age 67, $500,346 pay
EVP and CFO: Frank M. Bergonzi, age 49
EVP Marketing: Kevin J. Mann, age 42
SVP Information Services: Dennis J. Bowman, age 41
SVP Eagle Managed Care: Joel F. Feldman, age 41
SVP Planning: Wayne Gibson, age 36
SVP Drugstore Operations: Charles R. Kibler, age 48
SVP Corporate Real Estate: Philip D. Markovitz, age 54
SVP Distribution: Ronald A. Miller, age 55
SVP Human Resources: Robert R. Souder, age 55
VP and Treasurer: Thomas R. Coogan, age 39
VP Government and Trade Relations: James E.
Krahulec, age 49
VP Risk Management: James O. Lott, age 56
VP Corporate Communications: Suzanne Mead, age 43
VP Corporate Security: W. Michael Knievel, age 47
Assistant VP and Secretary: I. Lawrence Gelman, age 48
Auditors: KPMG Peat Marwick LLP

WHERE

HQ: 30 Hunter Ln., Camp Hill, PA 17011
Phone: 717-761-2633
Fax: 717-975-5871

Rite Aid operates 2,829 drugstores in 23 states and in
the District of Columbia. The company also has
distribution centers in Florida, Michigan, New York,
Pennsylvania, South Carolina, and West Virginia.

	No. of Stores
Pennsylvania	386
Michigan	347
Ohio	329
New York	270
New Jersey	184
Maryland	180
Virginia	163
Florida	141
West Virginia	135
Kentucky	117
North Carolina	111
South Carolina	81
Maine	77
Georgia	56
Connecticut	47
Massachusetts	47
Other states	158
Total	**2,829**

WHAT

Selected Subsidiaries

Eagle Managed Care Corp.	Name Rite, Inc.
Gray Drug Fair, Inc.	Rack Rite Distributors, Inc.
Lane Drug Co.	Rite Aid Realty Corp.
Life-Aid Services, Inc.	Rite Investments, Inc.

KEY COMPETITORS

American Stores	Genovese Drug	Publix
Ames	Stores	Revco
Arbor Drugs	Giant Food	Safeway
Big B	Great A&P	Sears
Bruno's	J. C. Penney	Southland
Circle K	Kmart	Stop & Shop
Drug Emporium	Kroger	Thriftway Food
Duane Reade	Melville	& Drug
Eckerd	Merck	Walgreen
Eli Lilly	Montgomery Ward	Wal-Mart
Fay's	Pathmark	Winn-Dixie
Food Lion	Price/Costco	Woolworth

HOW MUCH

	9-Year Growth	1986	1987	1988	1989	1990	1991	1992	1993	1994	1995
Sales ($ mil.)	12.6%	1,564	1,757	2,486	2,868	3,173	3,448	3,748	4,085	4,059	4,534
Net income ($ mil.)	9.5%	63	78	141	95	102	107	124	132	9	141
Income as % of sales	—	4.0%	4.4%	5.7%	3.3%	3.2%	3.1%	3.3%	3.2%	0.2%	3.1%
Earnings per share ($)	9.1%	0.76	0.95	1.71	1.15	1.24	1.30	1.43	1.51	0.11	1.67
Stock price – high ($)[1]	—	16.75	17.75	23.13	20.44	20.56	19.31	23.88	24.13	22.25	24.00
Stock price – low ($)[1]	—	10.75	12.13	14.25	14.56	14.75	14.75	17.25	19.25	15.25	15.75
Stock price – close ($)[1]	6.8%	12.94	14.75	18.00	16.31	16.69	18.44	21.50	21.38	15.88	23.38
P/E – high	—	22	19	14	18	17	15	17	16	—	14
P/E – low	—	14	13	8	13	12	11	12	13	—	9
Dividends per share ($)	10.1%	0.26	0.30	0.34	0.38	0.42	0.46	0.51	0.56	0.60	0.62
Book value per share ($)	10.7%	4.82	5.48	6.90	7.48	8.49	9.32	10.83	11.79	11.10	12.02
Employees	9.5%	16,217	19,454	26,703	27,347	26,935	27,290	27,607	27,750	27,364	36,700

1995 Year-end:
Debt ratio: 48.3%
Return on equity: 14.4%
Cash (mil.): $7
Current ratio: 2.38
Long-term debt (mil.): $806
No. of shares (mil.): 84
Dividends
  Yield: 2.7%
  Payout: 37.1%
Market value (mil.): $1,968

Stock Price History[1]
High/Low 1986–95

[1]Stock prices are for the prior calendar year.

RJR NABISCO HOLDINGS CORP.

OVERVIEW

With the split of its food and tobacco companies and the departure of the LBO firm Kohlberg Kravis Roberts (KKR), RJR Nabisco Holdings has recently undergone major structural and ownership changes. Based in New York, RJR Nabisco separated its 2 companies by selling 19.5% of Nabisco to the public in early 1995. The resulting $1 billion will likely be used to pay down debt and begin an annual common stock dividend. The split of its food and tobacco companies will also help to shield Nabisco from litigation resulting from RJR's tobacco business. KKR concluded the final episode of its historic LBO of RJR Nabisco, which took place in 1989, by selling its $4 billion stake in the company for what, in the end, was only a modest profit of about 11 cents a share for KKR shareholders.

With sales growth of 10% in 1994, Nabisco generated sales of $7.7 billion with such strong food brands as Oreo, A.1. Steak Sauce, Life Savers, and SnackWell's (its successful reduced-fat and fat-free snack line). In contrast, RJR is experiencing both operational and legal troubles. Its leading brand of cigarettes (Winston) is losing market share in the US, declining by about a point to 5.8%. Along with other cigarette makers, RJR is also facing an increasingly hostile regulatory and legal environment. As a result, RJR plans to rely on its 81% ownership in Nabisco and a rapidly growing international tobacco market. In addition, the company announced a 1-for-5 reverse stock split in February 1995 and hopes the higher price per share will enhance interest among institutional investors.

WHEN

R. J. Reynolds formed the R.J. Reynolds Tobacco Company in 1875 in Winston, North Carolina, to produce chewing tobacco. In the late 1890s James Duke of the American Tobacco trust forced Reynolds to sell out to him for $3 million. Reynolds regained control in 1911 after Duke's trust was dismantled by the government. In 1913 the company introduced Camel, its best-selling cigarette. After Reynolds died in 1918, leadership passed to Bowman Gray, whose family ran the company for the next 50 years.

With the success of Camel, R.J. Reynolds became the largest domestic cigarette company. During the 1930s and 1940s, Camel and Lucky Strike (American Tobacco Company) vied for the #1 cigarette position. In response to growing health concerns in the 1950s, the company introduced its filtered Winston (1954) and Salem (1956) brands.

Growing antismoking sentiment led to diversification in the 1960s and 1970s. Acquisitions included Chun King (1966; sold 1989), Patio Foods (1967), American Independent Oil (1970; sold 1984), and Del Monte (processed foods, 1979; sold 1990). In 1970 the company became R.J. Reynolds Industries and acquired Heublein in 1982. Heublein's Kentucky Fried Chicken chain was sold to PepsiCo in 1986 and its liquor business to Grand Metropolitan in 1987.

In 1985 the company bought Nabisco Brands for $4.9 billion and renamed itself RJR Nabisco. The National Biscuit Company had been formed by the 1898 consolidation of several baking companies by Adolphus Green,

Nabisco's first president. Products included Fig Newtons, Oreo, and Premium Saltines. Nabisco acquired Shredded Wheat (1929), Milk-Bone (1931), Dromedary (1954), Cream of Wheat (1961), James Welch (candy, 1963), and Standard Brands (Planters nuts, Blue Bonnet margarine, beer, wine; 1981). Standard Brands's CEO, Ross Johnson, became CEO of Nabisco and then of RJR Nabisco.

In 1987 Johnson attempted an LBO that backfired when KKR outbid him and acquired the company for $29.6 billion in 1989. Former American Express president Louis Gerstner became CEO. To reduce the LBO debt, the company sold many of its holdings, including Nabisco's European food business (1989).

After an American Medical Association report determined that RJR Nabisco's controversial 1991 cigarette–ad campaign featuring Joe Camel, a cartoon character, appealed to children (implying the ad encouraged children to smoke), the FTC considered banning the spokescamel altogether in 1993.

In 1992 the company acquired Stella D'oro (pastries) and New York Style Bagel Chips. In 1993 RJR sold its cold cereal business to Kraft and brought new tobacco processing plants on line in Poland and Turkey. Former ConAgra CEO Charles Harper replaced Gerstner, who left to become head of IBM.

In a series of transactions in late 1994 and early 1995, KKR unloaded its 35% stake in RJR Nabisco. KKR exchanged approximately 3/4 of its stake in RJR Nabisco to acquire 100% of Borden and subsequently sold off its remaining 8%.

WHO

Chairman and CEO: Charles M. Harper, age 67, $3,010,000 pay
VC: James W. Johnston, age 49, $2,425,000 pay (prior to promotion)
President and CEO; President and CEO, Nabisco, Inc.: H. John Greeniaus, age 50, $1,683,430 pay
SVP and Treasurer: John J. Delucca, age 51
President and CEO, R.J. Reynolds Tobacco International: Anthony J. Butterworth, age 57
President and CEO, Nabisco International: James J. Postl, age 49
CFO: Robert S. Roath, age 52
SVP and Controller: Richard G. Russell, age 49
SVP and Deputy Head, Human Resources and Administration: Gerald Angowitz, age 45
Auditors: Deloitte & Touche LLP

WHERE

HQ: 1301 Avenue of the Americas, New York, NY 10019
Phone: 212-258-5600
Fax: 212-969-9173

The company sells its products in more than 160 countries around the world.

	1994 Sales		1994 Operating Income	
	$ mil.	% of total	$ mil.	% of total
US	11,144	69	2,159	78
Europe	1,934	12	272	10
Other regions	3,039	19	326	12
Adjustments	(751)	—	(207)	—
Total	**15,366**	**100**	**2,550**	**100**

WHAT

	1994 Sales		1994 Operating Income	
	$ mil.	% of total	$ mil.	% of total
Tobacco	7,667	50	1,826	66
Food	7,699	50	931	34
Adjustments	—	—	(207)	—
Total	**15,366**	**100**	**2,550**	**100**

Selected Product Names

Cigarettes	Cookies, Crackers, and Cereals	Teddy Grahams
Camel	Barnum's Animal	Triscuit
Century	Crackers	Wheat Thins
Doral	Better Cheddar	
Gold Coast	Cheese Nips	**Other**
Magna	Chicken in a Biskit	A.1. Steak Sauce
More	Chips Ahoy!	Blue Bonnet
NOW	Cream of Wheat	College Inn
Salem	Granola Bars	Fleischmann's
Sterling	Harvest Crisps	Grey Poupon
Vantage	Mr. Phipps	Knox
Winston	Nabisco Honey Maid	Milk-Bone
	Grahams	Move Over
Candy, Gum, and Nuts	Newtons	Butter
Beech-Nut	Nilla Wafers	My*T*Fine
Breath Savers	Nutter Butter	New York
Bubble Yum	Oreo	Style Bagel
Care*Free	Premium	Ortega
Life Savers	Ritz	Pita Chips
Now and Later	SnackWell's	Regina
Planters	Stella D'oro	Royal
		Vermont Maid

KEY COMPETITORS

Anheuser-Busch	General Mills	Philip Morris
B.A.T	Heinz	Procter & Gamble
Borden	Hershey	Quaker Oats
Campbell Soup	Imasco	Tootsie Roll
ConAgra	Loews	Unilever
CPC	Mars	Wrigley
Danone		

HOW MUCH

	Annual Growth	1985	1986	1987	1988	1989	1990	1991	1992	1993	1994
Sales ($ mil.)	1.4%	13,533	15,978	15,766	16,956	12,764	13,879	14,989	15,734	15,104	15,366
Net income ($ mil.)	(9.0%)	910	962	1,179	1,378	(976)	(429)	195	268	(213)	388
Income as % of sales	—	6.7%	6.0%	7.5%	8.1%	—	—	1.3%	1.7%	—	2.5%
Earnings per share ($)	—	—	—	—	—	(3.21)	(1.19)	0.22	0.20	(0.15)	0.25
Stock price – high ($)	—	—	—	—	—	—	—	12.88	11.75	9.25	8.13
Stock price – low ($)	—	—	—	—	—	—	—	5.50	7.88	4.38	5.38
Stock price – close ($)	(20.0%)	—	—	—	—	—	—	10.75	8.63	6.38	5.50
P/E – high	—	—	—	—	—	—	—	59	59	—	33
P/E – low	—	—	—	—	—	—	—	25	39	—	22
Dividends per share ($)	—	—	—	—	—	—	—	0.00	0.00	0.00	0.00
Book value per share ($)	(2.7%)	—	—	—	—	—	—	7.51	7.38	6.65	6.91
Employees	(7.9%)	147,513	124,617	120,334	116,881	48,000	55,000	56,000	63,000	66,500	70,600

1994 Year-end:
Debt ratio: 54.2%
Return on equity: 4.6%
Cash (mil.): $423
Current ratio: 0.78
Long-term debt (mil.): $8,883
No. of shares (mil.): 1,362
Dividends
  Yield: —
  Payout: —
Market value (mil.): $7,489

Stock Price History
High/Low 1991–94

ROADWAY SERVICES, INC.

OVERVIEW

Roadway Services, originally a US long-haul trucking company, is now a holding company specializing in transporting freight and packages worldwide.

Roadway Express, the Akron, Ohio–based company's biggest subsidiary, specializes in less-than-truckload shipments (LTL, less than 10,000 pounds). It offers export service from North America to Asia, Europe, and Latin America. Roadway also has a US LTL company, Roadway Regional Group. Another subsidiary, Roberts Express, expedites high-security, hazardous, and fragile shipments in North America and Europe.

Roadway Package System (RPS) offers small package pickup and delivery to 96% of the US and 86% of Canada's population. RPS is expanding its ground delivery market and ex-

pects to extend service to the entire US in 1996. In Mexico it offers expedited deliveries of shipments from the US to Mexico City, Guadalajara, and Monterrey. Roadway Global Air (RGA) provides air freight service. RGA, started in 1993, uses airline and charter flights to transport freight weighing 25 pounds or more to the US, Europe, and Asia. Roadway continues to have big start-up costs associated with RGA, and revenue for higher-priced overnight services has been lower than expected.

Roadway's use of state-of-the-art technology for its logistics services continues to serve it well. Its systems enhancements include tracking satellites and onboard computers to estimate miles to go and arrival times. Over 21% of Roadway's stock is owned by the founding Roush family.

WHEN

Brothers Galen and Carroll Roush founded Roadway Express in 1930. Based in Akron, Ohio, the company started with 10 owner-operated trucks and terminals in Chicago, Houston, and Kansas City. By 1935 Roadway was moving freight over 20 states.

In 1945 the company began converting from owner-operators to a company-owned fleet. This process, completed in 1956, coincided with the Roushes' decision (1950) to specialize in LTL shipments. Although LTLs cost more to operate than full truckloads (one truck carrying multiple shipments to and from various destinations), rates were proportionately higher.

In 1956 Carroll Roush sold his half of the company to the public and went on to buy ONC Fast Freight (later part of ROCOR). Galen Roush remained Roadway's chairman until his retirement in 1974. By 1975 Roadway was operating 300 terminals in 40 states, with coast-to-coast operations by 1977.

During the recession of the mid-1970s, Roadway fared better than most trucking companies by cutting labor costs, thereby sustaining profits even though tonnage dropped 15% between 1974 and 1975. The company was also (and remains) debt free. In the early 1980s Roadway expanded its network in the West, concentrating on the Pacific Northwest (traditionally dominated by Consolidated Freightways), and established service to Alaska, Hawaii, Canada, Mexico, and Puerto Rico. In 1984 Roadway bought Roberts Express, which specialized in direct (from shipper to consignee) express delivery. The company also

bought 2 regional trucking companies: Spartan Express, (Greer, South Carolina), which enhanced operations in the South (1984), and Viking Freight, (San Jose, California), which served 10 western states and Guam (1988).

However, increased competition in the LTL market made diversification necessary. In 1985 Roadway Express fell from its position as America's #1 freight carrier to #3 (after Yellow Freight and Consolidated Freightways). The company entered the small-package shipping market in 1985 by establishing Roadway Package System, which used owner-operated trucks to deliver packages weighing up to 100 pounds. In 1989 Roadway formed Roadway Logistics Systems to design transportation and distribution systems based on customer needs. Roadway introduced service to Mexico City in 1990 and to Europe in 1991.

The company expanded through the acquisitions of Coles Express (1992, a 75-year-old New England carrier) and Central Freight Lines (1993, the largest regional truck line in Texas). Roadway began its worldwide air freight service, Roadway Global Air (RGA), in 1993.

In 1994 the company suffered a 24-day strike (18 working days) at Roadway Express that reduced yearly revenues by 24%, and it took a charge of $25 million in a settlement with the IRS over employment taxes. Despite these and other difficulties the company made a profit.

In 1995 computer giant Dell outsourced its worldwide shipping needs through a contract with Roadway Logistics.

Nasdaq symbol: ROAD
Fiscal year ends: December 31

WHO

Chairman and CEO: Joseph M. Clapp, age 58, $607,539 pay
President and COO: Daniel J. Sullivan, age 48, $577,366 pay
SVP Finance and Planning, CFO, and Secretary: D. A. Wilson, age 50, $367,483 pay
VP Administration and Treasurer (HR): John P. Chandler, age 51, $402,387 pay
VP and General Counsel: John M. Glenn, age 63, $247,850 pay
VP Corporate Support Services: Donald C. Brown, age 39
VP Real Estate and Environmental Services: William F. Klug, age 55
VP and Group Executive: Rodger G. Marticke, age 46
VP and Controller: Roy E. Griggs, age 58
Auditors: Ernst & Young LLP

WHERE

HQ: 1077 Gorge Blvd., PO Box 88, Akron, OH 44309-0088
Phone: 216-384-8184
Fax: 216-258-6042

Roadway Express operates in Asia, Australia, Canada, Europe, Mexico, South America, and the US through 577 terminals.

WHAT

	1994 Freight	
	Tons	% of total
Less-than-truckload	11,712	75
Truckload	3,872	25
Total	**15,584**	**100**

Selected Business Units

Roadway Express, Inc. (Akron, OH; long-haul LTL carrier in North America, Europe, Puerto Rico, and the Pacific Rim)
Roadway Express (Canada) Inc.
TNL-Roadway S.A. de C.V. (Mexico)

Roadway Global Air International (Indianapolis, IN; integrated air carrier with subsidiaries in France, Hong Kong, Italy, and Spain)

Roadway Logistics Systems, Inc. (Hudson, OH; contract logistics services)

Roadway Package System, Inc. (Pittsburgh, PA; small-package shipping)
Roadway Package System, Ltd. (Toronto, Canada)
Roadway Package System S.A. de C.V. (Mexico)

Roadway Regional Group, Inc. (San Jose, CA; LTL trucking)
Central Freight Lines, Inc. (Waco, TX; LTL carrier in 6 southwestern states and Mexico)
Coles Express, Inc. (Bangor, ME; LTL carrier in 10 northeastern states)
Spartan Express, Inc. (18 southern and central states)
Viking Freight System, Inc. (11 western states)

Roberts Transportation Services, Inc. (Akron, OH; specialized express service in US and Europe)
Roberts Express, Inc. (companies in France, Germany, and the Netherlands)

KEY COMPETITORS

Air Express	Consolidated	Pittston Services
Airborne	Freightways	Schneider
Freight	CSX	National
American	DHL Worldwide	Southern Pacific
President	Express	Rail
Burlington	FedEx	Union Pacific
Northern	Harper Group	UPS
Canadian	Hub Group	U.S. Postal
Pacific	J.B. Hunt	Service
C.H. Robinson	Norfolk Southern	Yellow Corp.

HOW MUCH

	9-Year Growth	1985	1986	1987	1988	1989	1990	1991	1992	1993	1994
Sales ($ mil.)	12.5%	1,580	1,718	1,909	2,185	2,661	2,971	3,177	3,578	4,156	4,572
Net income ($ mil.)	(14.0%)	76	77	51	80	96	119	127	147	119	20
Income as % of sales	—	4.8%	4.5%	2.6%	3.7%	3.6%	4.0%	4.0%	4.1%	2.9%	0.4%
Earnings per share ($)	(13.8%)	1.90	1.91	1.26	2.00	2.44	3.05	3.27	3.73	3.02	0.50
Stock price – high ($)	—	35.50	45.00	42.75	34.75	43.00	43.00	61.75	77.75	72.50	74.25
Stock price – low ($)	—	24.75	30.75	23.25	27.00	28.00	27.25	38.00	55.25	51.75	46.00
Stock price – close ($)	5.6%	34.75	34.50	32.00	30.75	42.25	38.50	61.75	68.00	60.00	56.75
P/E – high	—	19	24	34	17	18	14	19	21	24	149
P/E – low	—	13	16	19	14	12	9	12	15	17	92
Dividends per share ($)	3.8%	1.00	1.10	1.10	1.10	1.10	1.10	1.15	1.25	1.35	1.40
Book value per share ($)	5.5%	15.37	16.28	16.18	16.73	18.35	20.15	22.72	25.71	26.60	24.83
Employees	9.9%	21,610	23,500	30,000	32,500	34,500	36,000	37,900	39,000	46,600	50,600

1994 Year-end:
Debt ratio: 0.0%
Return on equity: 1.9%
Cash (mil.): $37
Current ratio: 0.92
Long-term debt: $0
No. of shares (mil.): 41
Dividends
  Yield: 2.5%
  Payout: 280.0%
Market value (mil.): $2,321

Stock Price History
High/Low 1985–94

ROCKWELL INTERNATIONAL CORP.

OVERVIEW

With about 1/3 of its sales going to the US government, Rockwell International is still endorsing plenty of checks from Uncle Sam, but the company continues to boost its commercial businesses. To increase its reliance on nongovernment business, the Seal Beach, California–based company acquired Reliance Electric for $1.6 billion in late 1994.

Rockwell merged Reliance with its automation unit, Allen-Bradley, creating the US's largest industrial automation company. The new unit, which makes programmable controllers, worker-machine interface devices, industrial motors, and power transmission products, is expected to have annual sales of around $3.5 billion.

Rockwell is the world's #1 maker of chips and chip sets for fax and data modems, with an 80% market share for fax modems and a 60% share for PC data modems. It is the world leader in web offset press equipment for commercial and newspaper printing and is a leading supplier of components for light and heavy vehicles. For the government Rockwell builds the space shuttle orbiter, provides support and modification for the B-1B bomber, makes defense electronics systems, and is designing the power system for space station *Alpha*.

Rockwell posted its first sales gain in 3 years, thanks to strong performances from its industrial automation, telecommunications, and heavy vehicle businesses.

WHEN

Rockwell International is the legacy of 2 early 20th-century entrepreneurs: Willard Rockwell and Clement Melville Keys.

Willard Rockwell gained control of Wisconsin Parts Company, an Oshkosh maker of automotive axles, in 1919. He went on to acquire a number of industrial manufacturers, merging them in 1953 to create Rockwell Spring & Axle. Renamed Rockwell-Standard (1958), by 1967 this company led the world in the production of mechanical automotive parts.

In 1928 Keys founded North American Aviation (NAA) as a holding company for his aviation interests. General Motors bought North American in 1934 and installed James Kindelberger as its president. In 1935 the company moved from Dundalk, Maryland, to Inglewood, California, where it built military training planes. North American built over 15,000 AT-6 trainers during WWII and produced the B-25 bomber (1940) and the P-51 fighter (1940). By the end of WWII, the company had built nearly 43,000 aircraft, more than any other US manufacturer.

North American's sales plunged at the end of WWII. In 1948 GM took its subsidiary public; Kindelberger revitalized the company, opening new factories in Downey, California (1948), and Columbus, Ohio (1950). Major products included the F-86 (1948), a highly successful jet fighter of the Korean War, and its successor, the F-100 (1953), America's first production supersonic aircraft. The company also produced the X-15 rocket plane (1959) and the XB-70 bomber (1964).

In the 1960s North American built rocket engines and spacecraft for the Apollo program. In 1967 the company merged with Rockwell

Standard, creating North American Rockwell (changed to the current name in 1973).

Rockwell won the prime contracts for the B-1 bomber (1970) and the space shuttle orbiter (1972). In 1973 Rockwell bought Collins Radio, which would form the backbone of its avionics segment. The company ventured into consumer goods briefly, buying Admiral in 1974 and selling it in 1979.

Rockwell invested its B-1 proceeds in industrial electronics, acquiring Allen-Bradley for $1.7 billion in 1985. Facing declining defense-related revenues as B-1 production ended, Don Beall, who had become CEO in 1988, spent billions on plant modernization and R&D for Rockwell's electronics and graphics segments. In 1989 Rockwell sold its Measurement & Flow Control Division and bought Baker Perkins, a UK-based printing machinery company. In 1991 it sold its fiber-optic transmission equipment unit to Alcatel Alsthom.

In 1993 it bought a computer chip–making plant from Western Digital for $115 million and also acquired industrial automation supplier Sprecher + Schuh for $105 million.

In 1994 Rockwell agreed to sell its automotive plastics unit to Plastics Acquisition, a subsidiary of Cambridge Industries. Also in 1994 Rockwell signed an agreement with software developer Zexel USA to provide the hardware for an in-vehicle navigation system for Oldsmobiles. In 1995 Rockwell signed a joint venture agreement with the Guangdong Science Research Institute to manufacture telecommunications test equipment in China.

Also in 1995 COO Don Davis became Rockwell's first president in 7 years.

NYSE symbol: ROK
Fiscal year ends: September 30

WHO

Chairman and CEO: Donald R. Beall, age 56,
$2,115,000 pay
President and COO: Don H. Davis Jr., age 55,
$920,000 pay (prior to promotion)
EVP and COO: Kent M. Black, age 55, $1,025,833 pay
EVP and Deputy Chairman for Major Programs: Sam F.
Iacobellis, age 65, $843,000 pay
SVP, General Counsel, and Secretary: William J.
Calise Jr., age 56
SVP Finance and Planning and CFO: W. Michael
Barnes, age 52
**SVP and Technical Advisor to the Office of the
Chairman:** Robert L. Cattoi, age 68
SVP Organization and Human Resources: Robert H.
Murphy, age 56
Auditors: Deloitte & Touche LLP

WHERE

HQ: Rockwell International Corporation, 2201 Seal
Beach Blvd., Seal Beach, CA 90740-8250
Phone: 310-797-3311
Fax: 310-797-5690 (Public Relations)

Rockwell operates manufacturing and R&D facilities
around the world.

	1994 Sales		1994 Operating Income	
	$ mil.	% of total	$ mil.	% of total
US	8,918	75	1,012	82
Europe	1,649	14	92	8
Asia/Pacific	455	4	9	1
Canada	455	4	84	7
Latin America	352	3	25	2
Adjustments	(624)	—	—	—
Total	**11,205**	**100**	**1,222**	**100**

WHAT

	1994 Sales		1994 Operating Income	
	$ mil.	% of total	$ mil.	% of total
Electronics	5,016	45	688	56
Automotive	2,826	25	131	11
Aerospace	2,627	23	372	30
Graphics	655	6	31	3
Other	81	1	—	—
Total	**11,205**	**100**	**1,222**	**100**

Electronics
Avionics
Defense electronics
Industrial automation
Telecommunications

Automotive
Heavy vehicles systems
(antilock brakes, axles
clutches, transmissions)
Light vehicles systems
(door components,
suspension systems,
sunroofs, wheels)

Aerospace
B-1B bomber support
National Aero-Space
Plane (NASP)
Propulsion system for
Atlas and Delta rockets
Space shuttle orbiter and
main engines

Graphics
Web offset presses for
newspaper and
commercial presses

KEY COMPETITORS

Alcatel Alsthom
AlliedSignal
AM Intl.
Apple
Baldwin Technology
Boeing
Borg-Warner
Automotive
British Aerospace
Cummins Engine
Dana
Eaton
FlightSafety
General Dynamics
General Signal
Harris Corp.
Hitachi
Honeywell
IBM
Intel
Lockheed Martin
Loral
Matsushita
McDonnell
Douglas
Motorola
Northrop
Grumman
Orbital Sciences
Raytheon
Rolls-Royce
Groupe
Schneider
Siemens
Texas
Instruments
Textron
Thiokol
Thomson SA
Unisys
United
Technologies
Westinghouse

HOW MUCH

	9-Year Growth	1985	1986	1987	1988	1989	1990	1991	1992	1993	1994
Sales ($ mil.)	(0.1%)	11,338	12,296	12,123	11,946	12,518	12,379	11,927	10,910	10,840	11,205
Net income ($ mil.)	0.7%	595	611	635	812	735	624	601	483	562	634
Income as % of sales	—	5.3%	5.0%	5.2%	6.8%	5.9%	5.0%	5.0%	4.4%	5.2%	5.7%
Earnings per share ($)	4.4%	1.91	1.98	2.23	3.01	2.84	2.53	2.54	2.14	2.51	2.82
Stock price – high ($)	—	20.34	23.81	30.13	23.50	27.13	28.75	29.25	29.38	38.50	44.13
Stock price – low ($)	—	14.56	15.28	14.25	16.13	19.75	20.50	22.75	22.25	27.88	33.50
Stock price – close ($)	8.3%	17.41	22.09	19.00	21.75	23.75	27.75	27.38	29.00	37.13	35.75
P/E – high	—	11	12	14	8	10	11	12	14	15	16
P/E – low	—	8	8	6	5	7	8	9	10	11	12
Dividends per share ($)	7.8%	0.52	0.58	0.65	0.71	0.75	0.80	0.86	0.92	0.96	1.02
Book value per share ($)	4.9%	9.99	10.70	11.85	13.20	15.91	17.51	18.50	12.55	13.17	15.34
Employees	(5.8%)	123,266	121,194	116,418	112,160	108,715	101,923	87,004	78,685	77,028	71,891

1994 Year-end:
Debt ratio: 22.8%
Return on equity: 20.1%
Cash (mil.): $628
Current ratio: 1.63
Long-term debt (mil.): $831
No. of shares (mil.): 219
Dividends
Yield: 2.9%
Payout: 36.2%
Market value (mil.): $7,815

**Stock Price History
High/Low 1985–94**

R. R. DONNELLEY & SONS COMPANY

OVERVIEW

Chicago-based R. R. Donnelley & Sons is the largest supplier of commercial print and related services in the US. Although its prepress, presswork, and binding operations now account for over 90% of revenues, Donnelley stays in the forefront of printing technology by creating integrated manufacturing platforms. Donnelley's view is that electronics and print coexist, and that each spurs the other's growth — computer documentation involves more than just printed manuals; Donnelley also reproduces the accompanying software.

The company operates 3 sectors. Commercial Print (61% of sales) covers magazine, catalog, newspaper insert, and directory printing, as well as their digital versions. Networked Services (32% of sales) controls the

company's book publishing, computer documentation, CD-ROM and diskette replication, and financial printing. This sector's software services unit is the world's #1 provider of software distribution services.

The 3rd sector is Information Resources (7% of sales). Its Metromail unit provides, enhances, and manages consumer mailing lists and offers cross-reference and on-line services, while its information services unit offers digital and on-demand printing, sophisticated graphics design and management, and CD-ROM production, among other services.

Donnelley is the #1 supplier of Microsoft's printed matter and handles disk duplication and order fulfillment for other software companies.

WHEN

In 1864 Richard Robert Donnelley, an emigre Canadian printer, joined Chicago publishers Edward Goodman and Leroy Church. Their partnership became the Lakeside Publishing and Printing Co. in 1870. The company produced a variety of periodicals and some of the first inexpensive paperback books. The new Lakeside Building was destroyed in the 1871 Chicago Fire, but by 1873 it had reopened.

By 1877 Lakeside no longer existed, but its paperback subsidiary survived as Donnelley, Loyd & Co. Donnelley bought out his partners in 1879 and separated the printing component (reorganized as R. R. Donnelley & Sons in 1882) from publishing (Chicago Directory Co.). Chicago Directory became the Reuben H. Donnelley Corp. (1916), named for a Donnelley son. In 1961 Dun & Bradstreet bought Reuben H. Donnelley Corp.

Before 1900 Donnelley had printed telephone books and the Montgomery Ward catalog. In 1910 it began printing the *Encyclopædia Britannica*. In 1927 it won the contract to print *Time*. The firm's innovation in high-speed printing was a major factor in Henry Luce's 1936 decision to begin *Life*.

For most of Donnelley's history, family members have served as chairman and president. An in-law, Charles Haffner (chairman, 1952–1964), took the company public in 1956. The first outsider to become chairman was Charles Lake (1975). Family members are still active in the company.

In the last 2 decades, Donnelley acquired printing companies in the UK (Ben Johnson, 1978; Index Press and Thompson Photo Litho, 1985), Japan (Dowa Insatsu, 1988), and Ire-

land (Irish Printers, 1989). During the 1980s Donnelley developed the Selectronic process, which can tailor editions of magazines and catalogs to small target audiences. In 1987 it bought Metromail, the largest US mailing list business, which in 1991 generated a national telephone directory with 77 million names and addresses on 9 CD-ROMs. In 1990 it acquired high-quality printer Meredith/Burda and Business Mail Data Services, a UK equivalent of Metromail.

A 1991 partnership with French publisher Hachette brought Donnelley into the continental European market. A Singapore plant, opened in 1991, made it possible to offer a full range of computer hardware and software documentation services. A new plant in Mexico allowed Donnelley to enter the lucrative children's book business, and its Japanese unit produced a video catalog of US direct-mail products for Japanese customers.

The company closed its Southside Chicago plant — its oldest — in 1993 when one customer, Sears, canceled its catalog.

In 1994 Donnelley invested in Nimbus CD International (CD-ROM manufacturing) to expand its software fulfillment abilities. The company also bought 51% of Chilean printer Editorial Lord Cochrane. In late 1994 Donnelley won a 10-year, $2.5 billion contract to print telephone directories for SBC Communications, Southwestern Bell's parent.

In 1995, to further expand its capacity, Donnelley merged its software operations with Corporate Software to form the $1.3 billion company Stream International, a mail-order software retailer.

NYSE symbol: DNY
Fiscal year ends: December 31

WHO

Chairman and CEO: John R. Walter, age 48,
$1,294,316 pay
VC: James R. Donnelley, age 59
EVP; Sector President, Information Resources: Rory J.
Cowan, age 42, $564,772 pay
EVP and CFO: Frank R. Jarc, age 52, $508,295 pay
EVP; Sector President, Commercial Print: Jonathan P.
Ward, age 40, $433,891 pay
EVP; Sector President, Networked Services: W. Ed
Tyler, age 42, $385,503 pay
SVP and General Counsel: T. J. Quarles, age 45
SVP Strategy, Human Resources, and Communication:
Steven J. Baumgartner, age 43
President, Telecommunications Unit: E. Patrick Duffy,
age 53
Auditors: Arthur Andersen & Co, SC

WHERE

HQ: 77 W. Wacker Dr., Chicago, IL 60601
Phone: 312-326-8000
Fax: 312-326-8543

WHAT

	1994 Sales
	% of total
Catalogs, inserts & specialty products	31
Magazines	18
Global software services	14
Books	13
Directories	12
Financial printing	5
Other	7
Total	**100**

Commercial Print Sector
Magazine publishing services (consumer and trade
magazine printing, prepress services, editorial and
advertorial versioning, and pool shipping distribution)
Merchandise media (catalog and retail printing, prepress
services, specialty printing, direct marketing services,
customized versioning, and distribution)
Telecommunications (telephone directory printing,
digital directories, and digital ad-production systems)

Information Resources Sector
Information services (marketing communication,
database management and digital printing services,
creative design, interactive services, and graphics
management services)
Metromail (information for direct marketing; mailing
list and database development, management, and
enhancement; cross-reference products; and on-line
services)

Networked Services Sector
Book publishing services (book printing and binding,
distribution and fulfillment, and direct marketing)
Financial services (corporate and municipal financial
printing, mutual fund marketing and distribution
support, personalized on-demand printing, and equity
and debt issue typesetting and printing)
Global software services (computer documentation
localization, printing and binding; CD-ROM and
diskette replication, packaging, licensing, fulfillment,
and distribution; and mail-order software)

KEY COMPETITORS

ADVO	Graphic	Taylor Corp.
American Business	Industries	Treasure Chest
Information	Merrill Corp.	Advertising
Banta	Moore	U S WEST
Bertelsmann	NYNEX	Valassis Comm.
Bowne	Quad/Graphics	Webcraft
Cadmus Comm.	Quebecor	Technologies
Courier	Ringier	World Color Press
Dun & Bradstreet	Sullivan Graphics	

HOW MUCH

	9-Year Growth	1985	1986	1987	1988	1989	1990	1991	1992	1993	1994
Sales ($ mil.)	10.2%	2,038	2,234	2,483	2,878	3,122	3,498	3,915	4,193	4,388	4,889
Net income ($ mil.)	6.9%	148	158	178	205	222	226	205	235	121	269
Income as % of sales	—	7.3%	7.1%	7.2%	7.1%	7.1%	6.5%	5.2%	5.6%	2.8%	5.5%
Earnings per share ($)	6.8%	0.97	1.01	1.15	1.32	1.43	1.45	1.32	1.51	0.79	1.75
Stock price – high ($)	—	16.13	20.00	22.63	19.38	25.63	26.25	25.63	33.75	32.75	32.50
Stock price – low ($)	—	11.50	14.63	12.75	14.88	17.13	17.13	19.38	23.75	26.13	26.88
Stock price – close ($)	7.1%	15.88	15.38	16.31	17.31	25.63	19.88	25.00	32.75	31.13	29.50
P/E – high	—	17	20	20	15	18	18	19	22	41	19
P/E – low	—	12	15	11	11	12	12	15	16	33	15
Dividends per share ($)	8.4%	0.29	0.32	0.35	0.39	0.44	0.48	0.50	0.51	0.54	0.60
Book value per share ($)	8.9%	5.87	6.34	7.45	8.34	9.28	10.30	11.14	11.93	11.96	12.63
Employees	8.3%	19,100	20,600	22,000	24,500	26,100	27,500	29,100	30,400	32,100	39,000

1994 Year-end:
Debt ratio: 38.6%
Return on equity: 27.2%
Cash (mil.): $21
Current ratio: 1.69
Long-term debt (mil.): $1,212
No. of shares (mil.): 153
Dividends
Yield: 2.2%
Payout: 36.6%
Market value (mil.): $4,516

Stock Price History
High/Low 1985–94

RUBBERMAID INCORPORATED

OVERVIEW

Ohio-based Rubbermaid is bouncing back. The company is combating sluggish sales and a dwindling market share by widening its product line, cutting costs, and stepping up international marketing efforts. Rubbermaid boasts 43 years of sales growth and 57 years of profits. In 1994 sales edged past $2.1 billion, but the company wants to double that to $4 billion by 1998.

Rubbermaid has bought several companies to expand geographically and complement its wide range of products, which include gardening accessories, housewares, furniture, decorations, toys, office products, and leisure items.

In 1994 it picked up Empire Brushes (brushes, brooms, and mops), Carex (home health care products), and Australia-based Glenwood Systems (commercial playground equipment). The company also created Rubbermaid Japan, a joint venture with Richell, a leading housewares maker in Japan. In 1995 Rubbermaid formed a joint venture with Canada-based Royal Plastics Group to make modular, plastic components and storage sheds, and it bought Injectaplastic, a French company, which will provide a way to reenter the European housewares market.

State Farm owns 6.2% of the company.

WHEN

In 1920, 5 local businessmen formed The Wooster Rubber Company in a rented building in Wooster, Ohio, to manufacture toy balloons. Horatio Ebert and Errett Grable purchased the company in the mid-1920s.

Sales fell during the Depression. In the early 1930s Ebert noticed a line of housewares that had been developed by James Caldwell. Caldwell's product line (which he named Rubbermaid) included rubber dustpans, drainboard mats, soap dishes, and sink stoppers. Ebert contacted Caldwell, and the 2 men agreed to join their businesses. In 1934 Wooster Rubber began producing Rubbermaid brand products.

In 1942 the government froze civilian use of rubber because of WWII. The Wooster Rubber Company was forced to halt its production of housewares but was able to survive the war by producing self-sealing fuel tanks, life jackets, and tourniquets for the government.

At the end of WWII, Wooster Rubber resumed production of housewares. In 1950 the company established a Canadian manufacturing facility. During the mid-1950s the company produced its first plastic product (a dishpan) and introduced a line of commercial goods for hotels, motels, restaurants, and institutions. In 1955 the company made its first public stock offering and 2 years later changed its name to Rubbermaid. In 1958 Caldwell stepped down as president. Donald Noble became CEO in 1959, and the company was listed on the New York Stock Exchange.

During the 1960s the company bought its first overseas company (Dupol, West Germany). Rubbermaid introduced the sales party as a marketing technique in 1969.

When Noble retired in 1980, Rubbermaid recruited General Electric executive Stanley

Gault, the son of one of Wooster's 5 founders, as its chairman and CEO. Gault immediately restructured the company and led it through a decade of phenomenal growth in which sales more than quadrupled, from just over $300 million to over $1.5 billion.

Rubbermaid acquired Con-Tact (decorative coverings, 1981), Little Tikes (plastic toys, 1984), Gott (leisure and recreational products, 1985), SECO (floor products, 1986), Micro-Computer Accessories (1986), and Viking Brush (cleaning supplies, 1987). In 1985 Rubbermaid was listed as one of *FORTUNE*'s most admired companies in America.

In 1989 Rubbermaid formed a joint venture with French company Allibert to produce resin furniture. The following year it entered into a joint venture with the Curver group of the Dutch chemical company DSM to market housewares (dissolved in 1994). Also in 1990 the company purchased EWU AG (floor care supplies, Switzerland) and Eldon Industries (office accessories).

In 1991 Stanley Gault retired from Rubbermaid and became CEO of Goodyear. That year the company formed a joint venture with Pannonplast, a Hungarian group, to sell housewares in Eastern Europe. In 1992 Rubbermaid bought CIPSA, the #1 housewares firm in Mexico, and scaled down its venture with Allibert to a strategic alliance. Also in 1992 Rubbermaid purchased Iron Mountain Forge, a manufacturer of playground equipment.

In 1994 Rubbermaid sold its casual outdoor furniture operations to Sunbeam-Oster; later that year the company increased its stake in Rubbermaid Japan from 40% to 51%. In 1995 *FORTUNE* tapped Rubbermaid as the most admired company in the US.

NYSE symbol: RBD
Fiscal year ends: December 31

WHO

Chairman and CEO: Wolfgang R. Schmitt, age 51, $1,051,183 pay
President and COO: Charles A. Carroll, age 45, $643,233 pay
President and General Manager, Rubbermaid Commercial Products Inc.: Joseph M. Ramos, age 53, $360,624 pay
President and General Manager, The Little Tikes Company: Gary E. Kleinjan, age 46
SVP, General Counsel, and Secretary: James A. Morgan, age 59
SVP and CFO: George C. Weigand, age 43
SVP Human Resources: David L. Robertson, age 49
Auditors: KPMG Peat Marwick LLP

WHERE

HQ: 1147 Akron Rd., Wooster, OH 44691-6000
Phone: 216-264-6464
Fax: 216-287-2739

The company operates major manufacturing and/or warehousing facilities in 14 US states and 9 foreign countries.

	1994 Sales		1994 Operating Income	
	$ mil.	% of total	$ mil.	% of total
US	1,906	88	330	93
Other countries	263	12	26	7
Total	**2,169**	**100**	**356**	**100**

WHAT

	1994 Sales % of total
Consumer	79
Institutional	21
Total	**100**

Selected Products

Aprons	Lab coats
Ash/trash containers	Liquid dispensers
Bags	Measuring cups and scoops
Beverage containers	Mops
Bins (storage)	Office furniture
Bottles	Packing materials
Boxes (storage)	Playground equipment
Buckets	Sealing tape
Cabinets	Service carts
Carpet mats and sweepers	Shelf bins
Chair mats	Shipping containers
Clothing (disposable)	Shovels
Dispensers	Spray bottles
Dustpans	Storage sheds
Floor sweepers	Tape
Gloves	Toys
Hoppers (self-dumping)	Trash liners
Infectious-waste bags	Utility carts
Insulated coolers	Wall racks
Janitorial supplies	Wastebaskets
Jars (covered)	Wheelbarrows
Jugs (plastic)	Workbenches

KEY COMPETITORS

American Brands	First Brands	Owens-Illinois
Amway	Hasbro	Sandoz
Avon	Mattel	Tyco Toys
Boise Cascade	Mobil	U.S. Industries
Carlisle Plastics	Myers	Westinghouse
Coleman	Industries	
Corning		

HOW MUCH

	9-Year Growth	1985	1986	1987	1988	1989	1990	1991	1992	1993	1994
Sales ($ mil.)	13.7%	684	795	1,015	1,194	1,344	1,534	1,667	1,805	1,960	2,169
Net income ($ mil.)	16.4%	58	70	85	99	116	144	163	167	211	228
Income as % of sales	—	8.5%	8.8%	8.3%	8.3%	8.7%	9.4%	9.8%	9.2%	10.8%	10.5%
Earnings per share ($)	15.1%	0.40	0.48	0.58	0.68	0.79	0.90	1.02	1.04	1.32	1.42
Stock price – high ($)	—	8.75	14.25	17.50	13.50	18.88	22.50	38.25	37.25	37.38	35.75
Stock price – low ($)	—	5.50	8.25	9.50	10.50	12.50	15.50	18.50	27.00	27.63	23.63
Stock price – close ($)	14.3%	8.63	12.13	12.44	12.56	18.38	21.00	38.25	31.75	34.75	28.75
P/E – high	—	22	30	30	20	24	25	38	36	28	25
P/E – low	—	14	17	16	15	16	17	18	26	21	17
Dividends per share ($)	17.3%	0.11	0.13	0.16	0.19	0.23	0.27	0.31	0.35	0.41	0.46
Book value per share ($)	16.1%	2.08	2.45	2.97	3.48	4.06	4.80	5.53	6.16	7.05	8.00
Employees	9.0%	5,934	6,509	7,512	8,643	9,098	9,304	9,754	11,296	11,978	12,939

1994 Year-end:
Debt ratio: 2.6%
Return on equity: 18.9%
Cash (mil.): $151
Current ratio: 3.13
Long-term debt (mil.): $12
No. of shares (mil.): 161
Dividends
  Yield: 1.6%
  Payout: 32.6%
Market value (mil.): $4,623

**Stock Price History
High/Low 1985–94**

RYDER SYSTEM, INC.

OVERVIEW

Ryder System provides full-service leasing, as well as short-term rental of trucks, tractors, and trailers. The company, best-known for its bright yellow rental trucks, continues as the #1 provider of commercial truck rentals and of full-service truck leasing, supplying clients such as Home Depot and GM (GM accounted for 10% of company revenues in 1994) with everything from vehicles made to transport specific cargoes to vehicle maintenance.

Miami-based Ryder, the leading North American transporter of new cars and trucks, also hauls materials under contract for companies such as Chrysler, Ford, GM, Toyota, and Honda (GM is Ryder's biggest customer for vehicle transportation services, accounting for 54% of revenues for that service). The company transports over 440,000 students by school bus in 20 states and manages or operates 89 public transit systems. Ryder also operates a fast-growing dedicated logistics services segment for transportation that has state-of-the-art technology for information systems and logistics tracking. This segment was the company's 2nd largest revenue generator in 1994. Logistics customers include Saturn, Xerox, Northern Telecom, and the *Wall Street Journal*.

Ryder is committed to expanding its foreign operations from less than 10% of revenues to 25% by 2005. Expansion efforts are concentrating on Europe and Mexico.

WHEN

Ryder Truck Rental, founded in Miami by Jim Ryder in 1933, was the US's first truck leasing firm. The company rented trucks in 4 southern states until 1952, when it bought Great Southern Trucking (renamed Ryder Truck Lines), doubling Ryder's size. In 1955 the company went public as Ryder System.

That year Ryder bought Carolina Fleets (a South Carolina trucking company) and Yellow Rental (a northeastern leasing service). More purchases over the next decade extended services (called Ryder Truck Rentals) across the US and into Canada. Ryder Truck Lines, which had expanded service throughout the South, East, and Midwest, was sold to International Utilities in 1965.

After establishing One-Way truck rental services for self-movers in 1968, Ryder entered several new markets, including new automobile transport (1968), truck driver and heavy equipment operator training (1969), temporary services (1969), insurance (1970), truck stops (1971), and oil refining (1974). Profits reached $20 million in 1973, but because of its debt load ($500 million), the company was hard hit when interest rates soared in 1974.

In 1975 former Allegheny Airlines (USAir) president Leslie Barnes replaced Jim Ryder as Ryder's CEO. By selling the oil refinery and other assets, Barnes had the company in the black by the end of the year. Jim Ryder (who had moved into the chairmanship) left Ryder in 1978 and founded Jartran that year.

Anthony Burns became Ryder's president in 1979 (and CEO in 1983, when Barnes retired). Burns sold Ryder's truck stops (1984) and, through 65 acquisitions, moved the company into aviation sales and service (1982), freight hauling (1983), aircraft leasing (1984), aircraft engine overhauling (1985), and school busing (1985). By 1987 Ryder was the US leader in truck leasing and automobile hauling, the world's largest nonairline provider of aviation maintenance and parts, and 2nd only to Canada's Laidlaw in school bus fleet management. It also briefly surpassed U-Haul as the US leader in one-way moving services in 1987.

In 1989 Ryder sold Ryder Freight System (full truckload freight hauling) and most of its insurance interests. In response to the weak economy and financial turmoil in the airline industry, the company discontinued its aircraft leasing business in 1991. Also in 1991 persistent problems in Ryder's truck leasing division led to a shakeup when Burns ousted president David Parker (who was widely considered Burns's heir apparent) and took over the division's management temporarily. The division, Ryder's largest, had been losing market share to #2 U-Haul.

Ryder's headquarters served as a relief center in 1992 when Hurricane Andrew ransacked South Florida. In 1993 the company created an international division and spun off its aviation division, Aviall. In 1994 Ryder acquired LogiCorp, expanding its logistical services; acquired 2 UK logistical businesses from FedEx; and announced plans to invest $250 million to increase its business in Mexico. Ryder suffered from bad publicity when its vehicles were used in recent terrorist acts. In 1993 a Ryder truck was used in the World Trade Center bombing in New York, and in 1995 Ryder stock suffered temporarily after one of the company's trucks was used in the Oklahoma City federal building bombing.

NYSE symbol: R
Fiscal year ends: December 31

WHO

Chairman, President, and CEO: M. Anthony Burns,
age 52, $1,585,000 pay
SEVP Finance and CFO: Edwin A. Huston, age 56,
$919,167 pay
SEVP and General Counsel: James M. Herron, age 60,
$761,000 pay
President, Ryder Commercial Leasing and Services:
Dwight D. Denny, age 51, $615,000 pay
President, Ryder Dedicated Logistics: Larry S. Mulkey,
age 51, $565,833 pay
**President, Ryder Consumer Truck Rental and Ryder
Public Transportation Services:** Gerald R. Riordan,
age 46
President, Ryder Automotive Carrier Group: James B.
Griffin, age 40
EVP Marketing: J. Ernest Riddle, age 53
EVP Human Resources and Administration: Thomas E.
McKinnon, age 50
SVP Public Affairs: R. Ray Goode, age 58
SVP MIS and Chief Information Officer: Bruce D.
Parker
Auditors: KPMG Peat Marwick LLP

WHERE

HQ: 3600 NW 82nd Ave., Miami, FL 33166
Phone: 305-593-3726
Fax: 305-593-3336

Ryder offers truck rentals through locations in Canada,
Germany, Mexico, Poland, the UK, and the US. Ryder
operates a fleet of 188,831 vehicles.

	1994 Sales	
	$ mil.	% of total
US	4,338	93
Other countries	348	7
Total	**4,686**	**100**

WHAT

	1994 Sales		1994 Operating Income	
	$ mil.	% of total	$ mil.	% of total
Vehicle leasing				
& services	3,710	79	359	82
Automotive carriers	645	14	50	11
International	348	7	30	7
Adjustments	(17)	—	—	—
Total	**4,686**	**100**	**439**	**100**

Divisions

Vehicle Leasing and Services
Managed Logistics System, Inc.
Ryder Commerical Leasing & Services
Ryder Consumer Truck Rental
Ryder Dedicated Logistics, Inc.
Ryder Public Transportation Services
Ryder Student Transportation Servies, Inc.
Ryder Truck Rental Canada Ltd.

Automotive Carriers
A.T.G. Automotive Transport Group, Inc.
Blazer Truck Lines, Inc.
Ryder Automotive Carrier Group, Inc.
Ryder Automotive Operations, Inc.

International
Ryder de México,   Ryder Polska Spz oo (Poland)
  SA de CV   Ryder Transport Services GmbH
Ryder Plc (UK)   (Germany)

KEY COMPETITORS

Allied Holdings	Leaseway Transportation
American Freightways	Norfolk Southern
American President	Penske
Budget Rent a Car	Roadway
Canadian Pacific	Rollins Leasing
CH Robinson	U-Haul
Conrail	Union Pacific
CSX	Yellow Corp.
Hub Group	

HOW MUCH

	9-Year Growth	1985	1986	1987	1988	1989	1990	1991	1992	1993	1994
Sales ($ mil.)	5.5%	2,905	3,768	4,609	5,030	5,073	5,162	5,061	5,192	4,217	4,686
Net income ($ mil.)	2.3%	125	161	187	135	52	43	14	124	(36)	154
Income as % of sales	—	4.3%	4.3%	4.1%	2.7%	1.0%	0.8%	0.3%	2.4%	—	3.3%
Earnings per share ($)	1.3%	1.73	2.09	2.29	1.61	0.58	0.43	0.05	1.51	(0.51)	1.95
Stock price – high ($)	—	21.40	30.77	37.27	28.17	26.98	20.26	18.74	25.03	29.13	28.00
Stock price – low ($)	—	12.73	18.63	13.00	19.61	17.12	10.62	12.13	17.01	22.75	19.88
Stock price – close ($)	1.5%	19.28	28.93	22.97	22.53	17.66	13.00	17.55	23.83	26.50	22.00
P/E – high	—	12	15	16	18	47	47	—	17	—	14
P/E – low	—	7	9	6	12	30	25	—	11	—	10
Dividends per share ($)	4.6%	0.40	0.44	0.52	0.56	0.60	0.60	0.60	0.60	0.60	0.60
Book value per share ($)	1.8%	12.21	14.72	16.75	18.75	18.24	18.06	17.50	18.26	12.81	14.33
Employees	6.4%	24,624	30,865	36,811	40,625	37,628	35,591	35,566	37,336	37,949	43,095

1994 Year-end:
Debt ratio: 62.9%
Return on equity: 14.5%
Cash (mil.): $76
Current ratio: 0.69
Long-term debt (mil.): $1,795
No. of shares (mil.): 79
Dividends
  Yield: 2.7%
  Payout: 30.8%
Market value (mil.): $1,733

Stock Price History
High/Low 1985–94

SAFEWAY INC.

OVERVIEW

Safeway has reformed into a dangerous competitor after being considered stagnant and noncompetitive a decade ago. The grocer is one of the world's largest food retailers with 1,059 stores, located mostly in the western and mid-Atlantic regions of the US and western Canada. The company owns 35% of The Vons Companies, the largest supermarket chain in Southern California, and 49% of Casa Ley, S.A. de C.V., which operates food/variety and wholesale stores in western Mexico. Safeway also manufactures and sells private-label merchandise under well-known brand names, including its Safeway SELECT line, which encompasses about 350 items.

Safeway has achieved its comeback mostly by cutting costs. In the last few years, the company has reduced its corporate staff by 25%, consolidated its distribution centers, and restructured its debt (Safeway is still strapped

with a heavy debt load from its 1986 LBO, orchestrated by Kohlberg Kravis Roberts [KKR]). The company is also reducing costs by cutting employee health benefits and avoiding wage increases. In 1995 supermarket employees began picketing more than 200 Safeway stores in Northern California after their request for higher pay was denied. Safeway quickly hired replacement workers for some of the stores.

Safeway is building larger stores and remodeling its older stores to accommodate a wider selection of both food and general merchandise. The company is also adding more specialty departments, such as deli/bakery counters, which generally earn higher margins than general grocery sales.

Safeway is over 61% owned by KKR Associates, which took the company public once again in 1990.

WHEN

Marion Skaggs bought a grocery from his father in American Falls, Idaho, in 1915, founding Skaggs United Stores. Unlike other stores of the day, where merchandise was kept in barrels or stacked on tables, Skaggs made goods easy to reach by utilizing shelves. In 1926 Safeway, a grocer with 338 stores in California and Hawaii, merged with Skaggs United (then at 428 stores) to form Safeway Stores. M. B. Skaggs, son of the founder, became president, and his brother L. S. Skaggs (founder of what is now American Stores) became vice-president.

Safeway bought Arizona Grocery, Piggly Wiggly Pacific, and Eastern Stores in 1928 and Piggly Wiggly Western States, a grocer operating in California, Texas, and Nevada, in 1929. Since that time the company has made numerous acquisitions, expanding nationwide. In 1931 the company had its greatest number of stores (3,527); this number was reduced as Safeway eliminated smaller stores and adopted the supermarket format. In addition, the company expanded internationally, into western Canada, the UK, and Australia. Safeway sold its Australian and German operations in 1985.

The Magowan family has been important to Safeway. Robert Magowan, a former Macy's executive, was chairman of Safeway in the 1950s, retiring in 1970. Robert's son Peter (the current chairman) has been a key executive in the company since 1979.

In 1986 Safeway received an unsolicited buyout bid from the Dart Group. In response,

Magowan and takeover specialist KKR took Safeway private in a leveraged deal, paying Dart a $159 million profit on its shares. The company sold some 1,200 locations in Utah, Oklahoma, Kansas, Arkansas, and the UK in 1987 and in Texas in 1988. Safeway sold stores in Southern California to The Vons Companies for 35% of Vons's stock.

In 1990 Safeway reemerged as a public company by selling 10% of its stock. The proceeds were earmarked for store expansion and remodeling. In April 1991 the company made a public offering of 17.5 million shares of stock. Safeway received about $341 million in net proceeds from the offering, and the company's bank credit was removed from highly leveraged status.

In 1993 Safeway was losing customers in Alberta, Canada (where it has 87 stores), to competitors with lower labor costs (and therefore lower prices). To lower prices to competitive levels, the company renegotiated union contracts to allow for lower wages. However, related severance that was paid for a voluntary employee buyout reduced income by over $30 million.

In 1994 the company remodeled 71 stores, opened 20, and closed 36. In 1995 Safeway signed an agreement with Bergen Brunswig, whereby the company will supply Safeway with pharmaceuticals. The deal is expected to generate more than $1 billion in revenue over the next 5 years for Bergen.

NYSE symbol: SWY
Fiscal year ends: Saturday nearest December 31

	1994 Sales		1994 Operating Income	
	$ mil.	% of total	$ mil.	% of total
US	12,240	78	491	80
Canada	3,387	22	121	20
Total	**15,627**	**100**	**612**	**100**

WHO

Chairman: Peter A. Magowan, age 52
President and CEO: Steven A. Burd, age 45, $1,263,000 pay
EVP Labor Relations, Human Resources, Law, and Public Affairs: Kenneth W. Oder, age 47, $814,000 pay
EVP Supply Operations: E. Richard Jones, age 50, $727,000 pay
EVP and CFO: Julian C. Day, age 42, $667,000 pay
Group VP Finance: Frithjof J. Dale, age 50, $477,000 pay
SVP, Secretary, and General Counsel: Michael C. Ross, age 47
SVP Corporate Retail Operations: Larree M. Renda, age 36
SVP and Chief Information Officer: David T. Ching, age 42
SVP and Director Marketing: Wilber L. Schinner, age 54
SVP Finance and Public Affairs: Melissa C. Plaisance, age 35
Auditors: Deloitte & Touche LLP

WHERE

HQ: 4th and Jackson Sts., Oakland, CA 94660
Phone: 510-891-3000
Fax: 510-891-3603

Safeway has 31 factories in the US and 17 in Canada.

US/Canada Divisions	No. of Stores
Northern California	252
Canada	223
Seattle	172
Eastern US	125
Denver	113
Portland	102
Phoenix	72
Total	**1,059**

WHAT

Selected Brand Names
Bel-air
Lucerne
SELECT
TownHouse

Stores with Specialty Departments	
	% of stores
Floral	92
Deli	89
Bakery	73
Pharmacy	52
Seafood	47

KEY COMPETITORS

Albertson's
American Stores
Associated Wholesale Grocers
Bashas'
Certified Grocers
Eckerd
Fred Meyer
Furr's Supermarkets
Giant Food
Great A&P
J Sainsbury
Kmart
Kroger
Loblaw
Megafoods Stores
Melville
Oshawa
Price/Costco
Rite Aid
Royal Ahold
Vons
Walgreen
Wal-Mart
Whole Foods Market
Yucaipa

HOW MUCH

	Annual Growth	1985	1986	1987	1988	1989	1990	1991	1992	1993	1994
Sales ($ mil.)	(2.5%)	19,651	20,311	18,301	13,612	14,325	14,874	15,119	15,152	15,215	15,627
Net income ($ mil.)	0.4%	231	(14)	(112)	31	3	87	79	98	123	240
Income as % of sales	—	1.2%	—	—	0.2%	0.0%	0.6%	0.5%	0.6%	0.8%	1.5%
Earnings per share ($)	31.2%	—	—	—	0.38	0.03	0.91	0.69	0.83	1.00	1.94
Stock price – high ($)	—	—	—	—	—	—	16.88	21.63	20.25	22.75	31.88
Stock price – low ($)	—	—	—	—	—	—	10.25	11.75	9.63	10.88	19.25
Stock price – close ($)	27.0%	—	—	—	—	—	12.25	17.75	13.00	21.25	31.88
P/E – high	—	—	—	—	—	—	19	31	24	23	16
P/E – low	—	—	—	—	—	—	11	17	12	11	10
Dividends per share ($)	—	—	—	—	—	—	0.00	0.00	0.00	0.00	0.00
Book value per share ($)	—	—	—	—	—	—	(2.31)	2.19	2.46	3.77	6.14
Employees	(4.4%)	164,385	174,412	130,922	107,200	110,100	114,500	110,100	104,900	105,900	110,000

1994 Year-end:
Debt ratio: 77.3%
Return on equity: 46.7%
Cash (mil.): $61
Current ratio: 0.79
Long-term debt (mil.): $2,024
No. of shares (mil.): 105
Dividends
  Yield: —
  Payout: —
Market value (mil.): $3,341

**Stock Price History
High/Low 1990–94**

SALOMON INC

OVERVIEW

Management descriptions of last year's results at Salomon ran the gamut from "awful" to "appalling." And 1994's $399 million loss was just the tip of the iceberg of the New York–based investment bank's problems. Although the firm remained profitable even after the 1991 Treasury bond scandal, Salomon has experienced low morale and a steady stream of high-level defections as Warren Buffett (who owns about 20% of the company) and his handpicked management team have tried to make the firm's "me first" culture more communal and client oriented. A 1994 attempt to link compensation with firm performance for client-driven operations led to more depar-

tures (including that of founding-family member Robert Salomon) and a reorganization of the operating committee.

Other contributors to the firm's sorry results included the bond market crash and resulting slowdown in securities activity and the discovery, when Salomon updated its accounting systems, of errors dating to the 1980s. Reconciling the discrepancies cost the firm more than $140 million in after-tax charges.

Salomon's primary income source is trading (its Phibro operations are petroleum and commodities oriented); many stockholders wondered in 1995 whether the firm can survive the loss of so many staff members.

WHEN

Arthur, Herbert, and Percy Salomon founded Salomon Brothers as a money brokerage firm in 1910. In 1917 the company became a US government securities dealer. Until the 1960s it specialized in bond trading.

In the 1950s and 1960s, Salomon expanded its research and trading departments and entered stock underwriting. It added a corporate finance department in the 1960s and in 1970 opened branches in London and Tokyo.

In 1978 John Gutfreund, head of corporate finance, became managing partner. He sought capital in 1981 through a merger with Phibro Corporation, an international oil and commodities trader. The 2 companies remained autonomous, and Gutfreund and Phibro's John Tendler became co-CEOs. Gutfreund became sole CEO in 1984. As the economy boomed in the 1980s, Salomon's staff grew exponentially.

When Salomon suffered losses in mortgage-backed securities and in the stock market crash, Gutfreund sought capital from Warren Buffett. Salomon withdrew from municipal bonds and commercial paper and went into LBOs. Two LBOs, Southland and Revco, ended in Chapter 11. Salomon sold its interest in the 3rd, Grand Union, in 1992.

In 1991 rumors circulated that Salomon was manipulating US Treasurys auctions (at which no company may buy more than 35% of an issue); in April, Gutfreund and others became aware that the 35% limit had been violated in February through unauthorized bids on a client's behalf. Complaints prompted an SEC investigation, which found that Salomon had bought 94% of the May auction issue on its own behalf or for clients and bought back the excess.

When this became public, Gutfreund resigned. Investor Warren Buffett became chairman and installed Robert Denham (Buffett's lawyer) and Deryck Maughan (a Salomon administrator) as the top executives. Buffett made a full revelation of Salomon's actions and took disciplinary action in the company. During the ensuing scandal, the company sold assets to continue operating as credit became more difficult to obtain. Morale plunged and employees left.

After the scandal the company's brokerage business rebounded, but Salomon's energy business became a major problem. In 1992 the company broke up Phibro Energy. It turned the commodities business into a division of Salomon, grouped the refineries operations together as Phibro USA, and separated a joint venture with Russia (the largest US venture in Russia) into Phibro Energy Production, Inc. (PEPI). After the joint venture was begun, Russia imposed new taxes. Although PEPI received an exemption from these taxes in 1994, the question of whether Salomon will ever recoup its investment, despite the fact that the project's oil production has increased significantly, remains open. Phibro USA, which operates oil refineries, is subject to the fluctuations of the oil market. The company as a whole also retains an undetermined amount of potential environmental liability attributable to Phibro's former smelting (and current refinery) operations.

In 1995, after announcing with much fanfare a new, stricter compensation plan for client-side personnel (while leaving the firm's proprietary traders untouched), Maughan was forced to modify it after the departure of nearly 10% of the firm's 200 managing directors.

NYSE symbol: SB
Fiscal year ends: December 31

WHO

Chairman and CEO: Robert E. Denham, age 49,
$1,000,000 pay
EVP; Chairman and CEO, Salomon Brothers Inc:
Deryck C. Maughan, age 47, $838,000 pay
EVP and General Counsel: Robert H. Mundheim,
age 62, $1,048,000 pay
President, Phibro Division: Andrew J. Hall,
$1,000,000 pay
Treasurer: John G. Macfarlane, age 40, $1,000,000 pay
CFO: Jerome H. Bailey, age 42, $1,000,000 pay
**Managing Director Planning and Resources (Human
Resources):** Matthew Levitan
Auditors: Arthur Andersen & Co, SC

WHERE

HQ: 7 World Trade Center, New York, NY 10048
Phone: 212-783-7000
Fax: 212-783-2110

	1994 Sales		1994 Pretax Income	
	$ mil.	% of total	$ mil.	% of total
North America	4,449	71	(119)	—
Europe	1,332	21	(841)	—
Asia & other	497	8	129	—
Total	**6,278**	**100**	**(831)**	**—**

WHAT

	1994 Sales		1994 Pretax Income	
	$ mil.	% of total	$ mil.	% of total
Salomon Brothers	5,751	92	(963)	—
Phibro Division	208	3	81	—
Phibro USA	87	1	18	—
Corporate & other	232	4	33	—
Total	**6,278**	**100**	**(831)**	**—**

	1994 Sales	
	$ mil.	% of total
Interest & dividends	5,902	86
Investment banking	486	7
Commissions	336	5
Principal transactions	(560)	—
Other	114	2
Total	**6,278**	**100**

Salomon Brothers
Asset and money
management
Financial research and
advice
Investment banking
Mutual funds
Securities and
currency trading
Securities underwriting

Phibro USA
Oil refining

Phibro Division
Commodities trading

**Phibro Energy Production,
Inc. (PEPI)**
Russian oil joint venture

The Mortage Corp. (UK)

Salomon Swapco Inc
Derivatives subsidiary

KEY COMPETITORS

ADM	Dean Witter,	Pennzoil
Alex. Brown	Discover	Phillips
Amerada Hess	Equitable	Petroleum
American Express	Exxon	Prudential
Amoco	Goldman Sachs	Raymond
Ashland, Inc.	Hambrecht &	James
Atlantic Richfield	Quist	Financial
Bear Stearns	ING Group	Rothschilds
Brown Brothers	KKR	Stephens
Harriman	Koch	Sun Company
Cargill	Lehman Brothers	Swiss Bank
Chevron	Merrill Lynch	Texaco
Coastal	Mobil	Transamerica
ConAgra	Morgan Stanley	Travelers
Continental	Nomura Securities	Unocal
Grain	Occidental	USX–Marathon
CS Holding	Oryx	Yamaichi
Daiwa Securities	Paine Webber	Securities

HOW MUCH

	9-Year Growth	1985	1986	1987	1988	1989	1990	1991	1992	1993	1994
Sales ($ mil.)	1.1%	5,701	6,789	6,003	6,146	8,999	8,946	9,175	8,183	8,799	6,278
Net income ($ mil.)	—	557	516	142	280	470	303	507	550	864	(399)
Income as % of sales	—	9.8%	6.7%	2.4%	4.6%	5.2%	3.4%	5.5%	6.7%	9.8%	—
Earnings per share ($)	—	3.60	3.32	0.86	1.63	3.20	2.05	3.79	4.05	6.57	(4.31)
Stock price – high ($)	—	46.75	59.38	44.50	28.38	29.38	27.00	37.00	39.00	51.88	52.75
Stock price – low ($)	—	30.00	37.38	16.63	19.38	20.50	20.00	20.75	26.63	34.38	35.00
Stock price – close ($)	(1.6%)	43.50	38.38	19.63	24.13	23.38	24.38	30.63	38.13	47.63	37.50
P/E – high	—	13	18	52	17	9	13	10	10	8	—
P/E – low	—	8	11	19	12	6	10	6	7	5	—
Dividends per share ($)	1.9%	0.54	0.62	0.64	0.64	0.64	0.64	0.64	0.64	0.64	0.64
Book value per share ($)	5.7%	20.02	22.72	21.15	21.82	24.08	25.68	28.31	32.34	39.06	32.88
Employees	4.1%	6,300	7,800	8,000	8,400	8,924	8,883	8,917	8,631	8,640	9,077

1994 Year-end:
Debt ratio: 96.5%
Return on equity: —
Cash (mil.): $3,539
Long-term debt (mil.): $18,228
No. of shares (mil.): 106
Dividends
  Yield: 1.7%
  Payout: —
Market value (mil.): $3,969
Assets (mil.): $172,732

**Stock Price History
High/Low 1985–94**

SARA LEE CORPORATION

OVERVIEW

If you've had one too many slices of Sara Lee's yummy cheesecake, don't despair. Just head on over to your supermarket meat case and pick up some fat-free Ball Park hot dogs, and then on to sundries for some Hanes Her Way Smooth Illusions pantyhose (they'll hide those extra few pounds) and a pair of Hanes Briefs for your significant other. If you have time, you can stop at the department store for a Playtex 18-Hour Bra (lingering to wonder who in the real world needs a Wonderbra to create curves), some Isotoner gloves, and a new Coach bag. When you're done shopping, Chicago-based Sara Lee Corp. will be a little richer.

Although Sara Lee is best known for its frozen baked goods and other foods, its businesses include personal and household goods, food services (through its PYA/Monarch operations), and direct sales of toiletries, jewelry, and other personal items.

Most of the company's operations have grown in recent years, but sheer hosiery has gotten snagged by the recent worldwide trend toward a more casual lifestyle. The change has been so devastating that a restructuring (to consolidate operations and shift production to trouser socks and tights) of the personal products division dragged down earnings for the whole company in 1994.

WHEN

Sara Lee Corporation began in 1939 when businessman Nathan Cummings bought the C. D. Kenny Company, a Baltimore wholesaler of coffee, tea, and sugar. Cummings soon purchased several grocery firms and later changed the company's name to Consolidated Grocers (1945). In 1946 the company's stock was listed on the New York Stock Exchange. The company was renamed Consolidated Foods Corporation (CFC) in 1954.

In 1956 CFC purchased the Kitchens of Sara Lee, a Chicago bakery founded by Charles Lubin in 1951. Lubin had introduced Sara Lee cheesecake (named after his daughter) in 1949, and it became his most popular product. He remained with Consolidated Foods, successfully building the frozen desserts market under the Sara Lee brand name.

Focusing primarily on food and grocery concerns, Cummings broadened his investments by buying and selling an array of food companies, grocery stores, and producers of personal care and consumer products. Purchases included Piggly Wiggly Midwest supermarkets (1956) and Eagle Food Centers (1961). The company's Eagle Complex, which included Piggly Wiggly and Eagle stores, drugstores, and photo supply stores, was sold in 1968. The company also bought Shasta Water Company in 1960 (sold in 1985), Chicken Delight food franchises (bought in 1965, sold in 1979), and Electrolux Corporation (bought in 1968, sold in 1987). Cummings served as president until 1970.

The company continued to buy and sell a long list of businesses in the US and Europe. Its operations have included foods, beverages, grocery stores, apparel, appliances, food services, and chemicals. In 1962 Consolidated

Foods made its first European acquisition and began to build its international markets. Some of its major purchases included Douwe Egberts (coffee, tea, and tobacco; Holland; 1978), Nicholas Kiwi (shoe care and pharmaceuticals, Australia, 1984), Akzo Consumenten Produkten (food, household, and personal care products; Holland; 1987), Dim (hosiery and underwear, France, 1989), and Pretty Polly (hosiery, UK, 1991).

Some major US company purchases were Hanes Corporation (1979), Jimmy Dean Meat Company (1984), and Champion Products (athletic knitwear, 1989).

Consolidated Foods changed its name to Sara Lee Corporation in 1985, using one of its most respected brand names to enhance the public's awareness of the company.

In the 1990s Sara Lee bought Playtex Apparel, kosher meat producer Bessin, the European bath and body care lines of SmithKline Beecham, the consumer food group of BP Nutrition, and the Filodoro Group, an Italian hosiery maker. The company also signed basketball superstar Michael Jordan to promote Hanes knit products and Ball Park franks.

After years of acquisitions, Sara Lee found itself (like some of its most devoted customers) just a bit overweight. In 1993 the company embarked on a plan to trim operations and cut more than 8,000 employees.

The next year it entered into a joint venture with Mexican meat processor Kir Alimentos, a major producer of ham and luncheon meats.

As part of its restructuring, the company has upgraded some of its technical systems. In 1995 it agreed to replace several information systems in its bakery division with a single manufacturing management system by Oracle.

NYSE symbol: SLE
Fiscal year ends: Saturday nearest June 30

WHO

Chairman and CEO: John H. Bryan, age 58,
$1,569,015 pay
VC, CFO, and Administrative Officer: Michael E.
Murphy, age 58, $924,105 pay
EVP: C. Steven McMillan, age 48, $916,750 pay
EVP: Donald J. Franceschini, age 59, $703,367 pay
SVP: Gordon H. Newman, $579,000 pay
SVP, Secretary, and General Counsel: Janet L. Kelly,
age 37
SVP: Jan H. Konings, age 52
SVP Corporate Development: Mark J. McCarville, age 48
SVP Human Resources: Gary C. Grom, age 47
VP Investor Relations and Corporate Affairs: Janet E.
Bergman, age 35
VP Public Responsibility: Elynor A. Williams, age 47
Auditors: Arthur Andersen & Co, SC

WHERE

HQ: 3 First National Plaza, Chicago, IL 60602-4260
Phone: 312-726-2600
Fax: 312-726-3712

Sara Lee operates 310 food and consumer product plants
in 27 states and 35 other nations.

	1994 Sales		1994 Operating Income	
	$ mil.	% of total	$ mil.	% of total
US	9,782	63	330	52
Europe	4,433	29	193	31
Asia/Latin America	1,006	6	65	10
Other regions	348	2	44	7
Adjustments	(33)	—	—	—
Total	**15,536**	**100**	**632**	**100**

WHAT

	1994 Sales		1994 Operating Income	
	$ mil.	% of total	$ mil.	% of total
Personal products	6,049	40	(71)	—
Meats & bakery	5,472	36	318	45
Coffee & grocery	2,090	14	274	39
Home/personal care	1,539	10	111	16
Adjustments	386	—	—	—
Total	**15,536**	**100**	**632**	**100**

Selected Brand Names

Foods	Shoe Care	Home/Personal Care
Ball Park	Kiwi	Ambi-Pur
Bryan	Tana	Behold
Duyvis		Biotex
Hillshire Farm	**Clothing/**	Bloo Ultra 5
Jimmy Dean	**Hosiery**	Bloom
Mr. Turkey	Bali	Brylcreem
Sara Lee	Champion	Catch
Sinai 48	Dim	Endust
	Donna Karan	Sanex
Coffee/Tea	Hanes	Vapona
Douwe Egberts	L'eggs	Zwitsal
Marcilla	Liz Claiborne	
Merrild	Playtex	**Leather Goods**
Pickwick	Princesa	Coach

KEY COMPETITORS

American Home	Fruit of the Loom	Philip Morris
Products	General Mills	Procter &
Amway	Gillette	Gamble
Anheuser-Busch	Hormel	Quaker Oats
Bristol-Myers	IBP	RJR Nabisco
Squibb	Johnson &	S.C. Johnson
Campbell Soup	Johnson	TLC Beatrice
Coca-Cola	Kellogg	Vendôme
Colgate-Palmolive	LVMH	Warnaco Group
CPC	Nestlé	Warner-Lambert
Danskin	PepsiCo	

HOW MUCH

	9-Year Growth	1985	1986	1987	1988	1989	1990	1991	1992	1993	1994
Sales ($ mil.)	7.5%	8,117	7,938	9,155	10,424	11,718	11,606	12,382	13,243	14,580	15,536
Net income ($ mil.)	1.4%	206	224	267	325	411	470	535	761	704	234
Income as % of sales	—	2.5%	2.8%	2.9%	3.1%	3.5%	4.1%	4.3%	5.7%	4.8%	1.5%
Earnings per share ($)	(0.5%)	0.45	0.51	0.59	0.71	0.88	0.94	1.05	1.50	1.37	0.43
Stock price – high ($)	—	6.50	9.20	12.28	12.88	16.88	16.69	29.06	32.44	31.13	26.00
Stock price – low ($)	—	3.89	5.89	6.63	8.22	10.72	12.06	14.81	23.31	21.00	19.38
Stock price – close ($)	16.6%	6.36	8.47	8.81	10.50	16.75	15.88	28.94	30.00	25.00	25.25
P/E – high	—	14	18	21	18	19	18	28	22	23	61
P/E – low	—	9	12	11	12	12	13	14	16	15	45
Dividends per share ($)	14.5%	0.18	0.19	0.23	0.28	0.33	0.39	0.45	0.61	0.54	0.61
Book value per share ($)	12.9%	2.32	2.70	3.20	3.56	4.21	4.97	5.48	7.05	7.31	6.92
Employees	5.2%	92,800	87,000	92,400	85,700	101,800	107,800	113,400	128,000	138,000	145,900

1994 Year-end:
Debt ratio: 46.2%
Return on equity: 6.8%
Cash (mil.): $189
Current ratio: 0.91
Long-term debt (mil.): $1,496
No. of shares (mil.): 481
Dividends
  Yield: 2.4%
  Payout: 141.9%
Market value (mil.): $12,134

Stock Price History
High/Low 1985–94

SBC COMMUNICATIONS INC.

SBC Communications (formerly Southwestern Bell) continues to place calls outside of its traditional telephone business. Based in San Antonio, SBC has cellular operations in Boston, Chicago, Dallas/Fort Worth, St. Louis, and Washington, DC. SBC has expanded its cellular operations in Texas (Austin, El Paso, and Houston) through an alliance with GTE and purchased cellular systems in New York State (Albany, Buffalo, Glens Falls, Ithaca, Rochester, Syracuse, and Utica).

Internationally, the company has acquired a 10% stake in a national cellular carrier in France and a 40% stake in a Chilean telecommunications company. SBC also provides other telecommunications services and products and directory advertising. In 1994 nontraditional telephone operations accounted for 35% of the company's earnings.

SBC is adjusting its strategy for the future interactive television market. Even though the company is trying to sell its 2 cable systems in the Washington, DC, area, SBC has formed an alliance with Microsoft to develop the software for SBC's interactive video trial in Richardson, Texas, in late 1995. The company also formed a venture with Walt Disney and 2 other Baby Bells, Ameritech and BellSouth, to provide television programming, including on-demand videos, interactive games, and shopping over telephone lines.

In addition, SBC provides voice messaging services called CallNotes in selected markets and has introduced its own VISA credit card.

WHEN

Southwestern Bell was once an arm of AT&T, providing local communications services in its present region. Telephone service first arrived in Southwestern Bell territory in 1878, just 2 years after the telephone was invented. One man responsible for early growth of telephony in this region was George Durant, who located 12 customers for St. Louis's first telephone exchange. This grew into Bell Telephone Company of Missouri.

Meanwhile, the Missouri and Kansas Telephone Company had also been established. The first president of Southwestern Bell, Eugene Nims, negotiated the merger of Missouri and Kansas and Southwestern Bell into the Southwestern Telephone System around 1912. Southwestern Bell became part of AT&T in 1917; Nims served as president from 1919 to 1929. After WWII, demand for new telephone lines grew rapidly. By 1945 Southwestern Bell was providing service to one million telephones; by the 1980s this number had grown nearly tenfold.

In 1983 AT&T was split from the Bell Operating Companies, and Southwestern Bell became a separate legal entity; it began operations in 1984. At the time of the breakup, Southwestern Bell received local phone service rights in 5 states, Southwestern Bell Mobile Systems (cellular service provider), the directory advertising business, and a 1/7 share in Bell Communications Research (Bellcore), the R&D arm shared by the Bell companies. The company set up its telecommunications and publishing groups later.

Southwestern Bell concentrated much of its diversification effort in mobile communications. The company purchased operations from Metromedia (1987), which included paging in 19 cities and 6 major cellular franchises. Southwestern Bell also bought paging assets from Omni Communications (1988).

By 1988 the company had deployed more lines than any other for an integrated voice and data phone service known as ISDN.

In 1990 Southwestern Bell joined with France Télécom and Grupo Carso (mining, manufacturing, and tobacco) to purchase 20.4% of Teléfonos de México (Telmex), the previously state-owned telephone monopoly, for a total of $1.76 billion. The company's stake in the venture represents about 10% of Telmex.

In 1993 Southwestern Bell sold a 25% (it's now up to 50%) interest in its UK cable television and telephone operations to Cox Cable; it also sold its Metromedia Paging unit. That same year Southwestern Bell and Panasonic offered a new wireless telephone called FreedomLink, which can be used as a cellular phone outside of an office and as a cordless phone inside the office. In 1994 Southwestern Bell acquired 2 Washington, DC–area cable systems from Hauser Communications for $650 million. Also in 1994 Southwestern Bell and Cox Communications canceled their planned cable TV partnership, blaming cuts in cable rates and other new regulations issued by the FCC. That same year Southwestern Bell changed its name to SBC Communications and ceased printing operations.

In 1995 SBC plans to expand its messaging service, CallNotes, to El Paso and Corpus Christi, Texas.

WHO

Chairman and CEO: Edward E. Whitacre Jr., age 53, $1,952,000 pay
Group President: James R. Adams, age 55, $753,000 pay
Group President: Charles E. Foster, age 58, $607,600 pay
President and CEO, Southwestern Bell Telephone: Royce S. Caldwell, age 56, $695,100 pay
SEVP External Affairs: William E. Dreyer, age 56, $628,500 pay
SEVP and General Counsel: James D. Ellis, age 51
SVP Corporate Communications: Robert A. Dickemper, age 51
SVP Strategic Planning and Corporate Development: James S. Kahan, age 47
SVP Federal Relations: Thomas M. Barry, age 50
SVP, Treasurer, and CFO: Donald E. Kiernan, age 54
SVP Human Resources: Cassandra C. Carr, age 50
President and CEO, Mobile Systems: John T. Stupka, age 45
President and CEO, Southwestern Bell Yellow Pages: R. McRae Geschwind, age 53
President and CEO, Telecom: Dick G. Boerger, age 54
President, SBC International (Telmex): John H. Atterbury III, age 46
Auditors: Ernst & Young LLP

WHERE

HQ: 175 E. Houston, San Antonio, TX 78205-2233
Phone: 210-821-4105
Fax: 210-351-2071 (Investor Relations)

SBC Communications provides telephone services in Arkansas, Kansas, Missouri, Oklahoma, and Texas and cellular service in 61 domestic markets. The company owns interests in operations in Australia, Chile, France, Israel, Mexico, South Korea, and the UK.

WHAT

	1994 Sales	
	$ mil.	% of total
Local service	5,788	50
Network access	2,857	25
Directory advertising	947	8
Long distance service	917	8
Other	1,110	9
Total	**11,619**	**100**

Subsidiaries and Affiliates
Associated Directory Services, Inc.
Bell Communications Research, Inc. (1/7)
SBC International, Inc. (holding company)
SBC Media Ventures, Inc. (cable TV)
SFR (10%, France)
Southwestern Bell Messaging Services (automated voice messaging services under brand name CallNotes)
Southwestern Bell Mobile Systems, Inc. (cellular phone services)
Southwestern Bell Technology Resources (research, development, and technology assessment)
Southwestern Bell Telecommunications, Inc. (communications equipment)
Southwestern Bell Telephone Company
Teléfonos de México, SA de CV (Telmex, 10%)
VTR SA (telecommunications company, 40%, Chile)

KEY COMPETITORS

Alcatel Alsthom	Dun & Bradstreet	TCI
American Business	GTE	Teléfonos de
Information	MCI	Chile
Ameritech	Metromedia	Telephone and
AT&T	MFS	Data Systems
Bell Atlantic	Communications	U.S. Long
BellSouth	Motorola	Distance
BT	NYNEX	U S WEST
Cable & Wireless	Pacific Telesis	WorldCom
Century Telephone	Sprint	

HOW MUCH

	9-Year Growth	1985	1986	1987	1988	1989	1990	1991	1992	1993	1994
Sales ($ mil.)	3.6%	8,460	7,902	8,003	7,259	8,730	9,113	9,332	10,015	10,690	11,619
Net income ($ mil.)	5.8%	996	1,023	1,047	1,013	1,093	1,101	1,157	1,302	1,282	1,649
Income as % of sales	—	11.8%	12.9%	13.1%	14.0%	12.5%	12.1%	12.4%	13.0%	12.0%	14.2%
Earnings per share ($)	5.7%	1.67	1.71	1.74	1.76	1.82	1.84	1.93	2.17	2.14	2.74
Stock price – high ($)	—	14.73	19.38	22.75	21.31	32.19	32.38	32.94	37.38	47.00	44.38
Stock price – low ($)	—	11.39	13.16	10.75	16.50	19.44	23.63	24.50	28.31	34.19	36.75
Stock price – close ($)	12.3%	14.23	18.69	17.19	20.19	31.94	28.00	32.31	37.00	41.50	40.38
P/E – high	—	9	11	13	12	18	18	17	17	22	16
P/E – low	—	7	8	6	9	11	13	13	13	16	13
Dividends per share ($)	5.3%	0.98	1.05	1.14	1.22	1.29	1.36	1.41	1.45	1.51	1.56
Book value per share ($)	1.2%	12.36	12.99	13.62	11.80	13.92	14.31	14.76	15.51	12.68	13.72
Employees	(2.1%)	71,000	61,770	67,100	64,930	66,200	66,690	61,218	59,500	58,400	58,750

1994 Year-end:
Debt ratio: 47.4%
Return on equity: 20.7%
Cash (mil.): $365
Current ratio: 0.67
Long-term debt (mil.): $5,848
No. of shares (mil.): 609
Dividends
  Yield: 3.9%
  Payout: 56.9%
Market value (mil.): $24,595

**Stock Price History
High/Low 1985–94**

S.C. JOHNSON & SON, INC.

OVERVIEW

Commonly known as Johnson Wax because of its popular floor wax products, S.C. Johnson & Son is one of the largest makers of consumer chemical specialty products in the world. The company's products include some of the best-known consumer brands in the US, such as Edge shaving gel, Raid household insecticide, OFF! insect repellent, Windex cleaner, and Glade air freshener.

The Racine, Wisconsin–based company also has interests in real estate, sanitation services, commercial pest control, and venture capital financing.

S.C. Johnson continues to expand its overseas operations and has offices in 48 foreign countries.

The company operates a charitable foundation and gives 5% of pretax profits to charity. It has been recognized as a leader in corporate environmental responsibility for its recycling, toxic waste emission reduction, and other programs. Chairman Samuel Johnson, who is listed by *Forbes* as one of the US's richest people, is the great-grandson of the company's founder. Johnson controls about 60% of the family-owned company.

WHEN

S.C. Johnson & Son was founded in Racine, Wisconsin, in 1886 by Samuel C. Johnson, a carpenter whose customers were as interested in his floor wax product as in his parquet floors. Forsaking carpentry, Johnson began to manufacture floor care products. By the time his son and successor, Herbert Johnson, died in 1928, annual sales were $5 million. A dispute over Herbert's estate was later settled, with his son, Herbert Jr., and his daughter, Henrietta Louis, receiving 60% and 40% of the company, respectively.

In 1954, when annual sales were $45 million, Herbert Jr.'s son Samuel Curtis Johnson joined the company. As new products director, Samuel turned his attention in 1955 to insect control. In 1956 the company introduced Raid, the first indoor/outdoor insecticide, and soon thereafter an insect repellent, OFF!. Each became a leader in its market. The 1950s and 1960s saw unsuccessful diversification efforts into the paint, chemical, and lawn care businesses. The home care products section prospered, however, with the introduction of Pledge aerosol furniture polish and Glade aerosol air freshener.

Herbert Jr. suffered a stroke in 1965, and Samuel became president. Sales were $200 million that year. Herbert Jr. lived 13 more years, spending much of that time ensuring continued family ownership of the business. Samuel, also determined to maintain family ownership, decided in 1965 to develop a recreational products business that could eventually be sold to pay estate taxes. This new company acquired boating, fishing, and camping gear companies and an ink stamping equipment maker. When the company went public in 1987 as Johnson Worldwide Associates, Inc., the family retained a large ownership interest and effective voting control.

In 1975, following a report that chlorofluorocarbons (CFCs) were harmful to the ozone layer (and after Johnson's own researchers checked out the theory), the company banned the use of the chemicals in its products, 3 years before CFCs were banned by the US government.

In the 1970s successful product launches included Edge shaving gel and Agree hair products. In the 1980s, however, the company made few successful product launches. Also in the 1970s the company had moved into real estate with Johnson Wax Development (JWD). However, in 1989, with a portfolio worth $600 million, Johnson began winding JWD down, selling its portfolio.

S. Curtis Johnson, Samuel's son, joined the company in 1983 (all 4 of the chairman's children work there) and was instrumental in the company's investment in Wind Point Partners I, a $36 million venture capital fund, and, later, in Wind Point Partners II. In 1986 S.C. Johnson bought Bugs Burger Bug Killers, moving into commercial pest control; 4 years later it entered into an agreement with Mycogen Corporation to develop biological pesticides for household use. Also in 1990 the company began selling a line of children's shampoos under the Fisher-Price (a toy maker spun off by Quaker Oats) label.

In 1993 the company bought Drackett, bringing Drano and Windex to its product roster, but also bringing increased competition from heavyweights like Procter & Gamble and Clorox. That same year the company sold the Agree and Halsa hair care lines to Dep Corporation.

Constantly on the lookout for ways to extend its brands, S.C. Johnson introduced a potpourri-scented Windex in 1995.

Private company
Fiscal year ends: Friday nearest June 30

WHO

Chairman: Samuel Curtis Johnson, age 67
President and CEO: William D. George Jr., age 63
President and COO, Worldwide Consumer Products: William D. Perez
President and COO, Worldwide Professional Products: Barry P. Harris
EVP; Regional Director, Consumer Products, Europe: Gianni C. Montezemolo
EVP; Regional Director, Consumer Products, Asia/Pacific: John R. Buerr
SVP Worldwide Consumer Products, Research, Development, and Engineering: James F. DiMarco
SVP, Secretary, and General Counsel: Robert C. Hart
SVP and CFO: Neal R. Nottleson
SVP Human Resources and Corporate Communications Worldwide: M. Garvin Shankster
VP Strategic Sales Development: Larry L. Beebe
VP; Group Director, Europe: Philippe Darquier
Auditors: Coopers & Lybrand L.L.P.

WHERE

HQ: 1525 Howe St., Racine, WI 53403-2236
Phone: 414-631-2000
Fax: 414-631-2133

	1994 Employees	
	No.	% of total
US	3,300	25
Other countries	9,800	75
Total	**13,100**	**100**

Selected Countries of Operation

Argentina	Korea
Australia	Mexico
Brazil	The Netherlands
Canada	New Zealand
Chile	Nigeria
China	Philippines
Colombia	Saudi Arabia
Egypt	South Africa
Ghana	Spain
Greece	Taiwan
Indonesia	UK
Japan	Ukraine
Kenya	Venezuela

WHAT

Principal US Subsidiaries
Johnson Venture Capital, Inc. (Chicago, major limited partner in venture capital fund, Wind Point Partners LP)
Micro-Gen Equipment Corp. (San Antonio, pest control equipment and chemicals)
PRISM (Miami, sanitation services for restaurants and hotels)

Principal US Brand Names

Home Care

Brite	Toilet Duck
Drano	Vanish
Favor	Windex
Fine Wood	
Future	**Insect Control**
Glade	OFF!
Glo-Coat	Raid
Glory	
Jubilee	**Personal Care**
Klean 'n Shine	Aveeno (bath products)
Klear	Edge (shaving products)
Pledge	Rhuli (skin care products)
Shout	Skintimate (shaving gel for
Step Saver	women)

KEY COMPETITORS

Amway
Bayer
Bristol-Myers Squibb
Carter-Wallace
Church & Dwight
Clorox
Colgate-Palmolive
Dial
Dow Chemical
DuPont
Eastman Kodak
First Brands
Gillette
Henkel
Johnson & Johnson
NCH
Pfizer
Procter & Gamble
Unilever

HOW MUCH

	9-Year Growth	1985	1986	1987	1988	1989	1990	1991	1992	1993	1994
Estimated sales ($ mil.)	7.4%	2,000	2,000	2,000	2,400	2,500	3,000	3,400	3,300	3,550	3,800
Employees	1.0%	12,000	11,000	11,000	11,500	12,000	13,000	13,600	13,400	13,100	13,100

Estimated Sales ($ mil.) 1985–94

SCECORP

SCEcorp is the parent company of Southern California Edison, the 2nd largest electric utility in the US (after Pacific Gas and Electric, based on number of customers). Based in Rosemead, California, Edison provides electricity to more than 4.1 million customers in a 50,0000 square mile service area covering central and Southern California (excluding Los Angeles).

The company is also involved in nonutility businesses, including real estate development and the engineering and construction of generating plants and transmission systems. Mission Energy, one of the US's largest independent power producers, owns about 2,000

megawatts in 34 projects in the US and abroad. With little new demand for power in the US, Mission is focusing on providing power projects for developing countries. A 500-megawatt plant it is building in Australia is scheduled to go on-line in 1996.

Many businesses have threatened to leave California because of high energy costs, and the state has been a leader in the push for deregulation of the power industry. To prepare for an onslaught of competition, Edison has announced a rate freeze through 1996. The company has also said it will reduce real electricity rates (adjusted for inflation) by 25% by the year 2000.

In 1896 Elmer Peck, Walter Wright, William Staats, and George Barker organized the West Side Lighting Company to provide electricity to the growing number of Los Angeles residents. Barker (of Barker Brothers furniture stores) became the company's first president.

In 1897 West Side Lighting agreed to merge with the Edison Electric Company of Los Angeles, which owned the rights to use Thomas Edison's name and patents in Los Angeles and the surrounding area. Barker continued as president of the company (which kept the Edison company's name), overseeing the installation of the first underground electrical conduits in the Southwest.

John Barnes Miller became president in 1901. Known as the "Great Amalgamator," Miller bought numerous utilities in Southern California and constructed several generating facilities, including 3 hydroelectric plants. By 1909, when the company adopted the name Southern California Edison, it served 5 counties from Santa Barbara to Redlands.

In 1917 Henry Huntington (founder of Pacific Light & Power) sold his Southern California electrical interests, including 2 utilities in the San Joaquin Valley and the Big Creek generating complex, to Edison, doubling the company's assets. However, in 1912 the city of Los Angeles decided to develop its own power distribution system, and by 1922 Edison's authority inside the city had ended.

A 1925 earthquake destroyed the company's Santa Barbara station, and the 1928 collapse of the St. Francis Dam washed out substations in the Santa Clara River valley and caused extensive damage throughout the Los Angeles area. But Edison survived; it later consolidated its service area in Southern

California when it assimilated California Electric Power (1964).

Although the company built 11 oil- and gas-fueled power stations (1948–73), it also diversified beyond fossil fuels. In 1963 Edison broke ground on the San Onofre nuclear plant with San Diego Gas & Electric Company. In the late 1970s Edison began to build power plants using less conventional generation techniques, including solar, geothermal, and wind generators. In 1987 SCEcorp was formed as a holding company for Edison and a group of nonutility subsidiaries collectively named The Mission Group.

In 1988 Edison agreed to buy San Diego Gas & Electric, a purchase that, if approved by California regulators, would have added about one million customers and 4,100 square miles of service territory to Edison's system, creating America's largest investor-owned electric utility. However, in 1991 regulators shot down the proposal as anticompetitive. Later that year the company reached an agreement to shutter its San Onofre Nuclear Station Unit 1, permanently retiring it in 1992.

In 1994 the Northridge earthquake cut power to more than a million customers, but Edison was able to restore most service within a day. That same year Mission Energy brought gas-fired plants in Florida and Virginia on-line. Also in 1994 a consortium led by Mission Energy signed a deal to build a 1,230-megawatt coal-fired plant in Indonesia.

In 1995 Mission Energy signed a $400 million deal with Indian industrial giant Tata Group to build a coal-fired plant in Jamshedpur, India. The plant will provide electricity to Tata Iron and Steel.

WHO

Chairman and CEO: John E. Bryson, age 51,
$664,000 pay
President and CEO, Mission Energy Company: Edward
R. Muller, age 42, $510,000 pay
President and CEO, Mission First Financial: Thomas R.
McDaniel, age 45, $327,500 pay
SVP and General Counsel: Bryant C. Danner, age 57,
$335,000 pay
SVP, Treasurer, and CFO: Alan J. Fohrer, age 44,
$262,000 pay
SVP Power Systems, Southern California Edison:
Harold B. Ray, age 54, $260,000 pay
**VP Health Care and Employee Services, Southern
California Edison:** Margaret H. Jordan, age 51
Auditors: Arthur Andersen & Co, SC

WHERE

HQ: 2244 Walnut Grove Ave., Rosemead, CA 91770
Phone: 818-302-2222
Fax: 818-302-8984

Generating Facilities

Coal
Four Corners Units 4
and 5 (48%, NM)
Mohave (56%, NV)

Hydroelectric
38 plants in central and
Southern California

Nuclear
Palo Verde (15.8%, AZ)
San Onofre Units 2
and 3 (75%, CA)

Fossil Fuels
Alamitos (CA)
Axis (CA)
Cool Water (CA)
El Segundo (CA)
Etiwanda (CA)
Highgrove (CA)
Huntington Beach (CA)
Long Beach (CA)
Mandalay (CA)
Ormond Beach (CA)
Pebble Beach (CA)
Redondo (CA)
San Bernardino (CA)

WHAT

	1994 Sales
	% of total
Electricity	
Commercial	35
Residential	34
Industrial	12
Public authorities	7
Other electric	6
Diversified operations	6
Total	**100**

	1994 Fuel Source
	% of total
Purchases: nonutility producers	34
Natural gas	26
Nuclear	20
Coal	13
Hydro	4
Purchases: other utilities	3
Total	**100**

Subsidiaries

Mission Energy Co. (cogeneration, geothermal, and
other energy-related projects)
Mission First Financial (project financing, cash
management, and venture capital)
Southern California Edison Co.

KEY COMPETITORS

AES	NIPSCO Industries
California Energy	Pacific Enterprises
Destec Energy	Pacific Gas and Electric
Duke Power	Southern Co.
FPL	Westinghouse
Kenetech	

HOW MUCH

	9-Year Growth	1985	1986	1987	1988	1989	1990	1991	1992	1993	1994
Sales ($ mil.)	5.5%	5,171	5,313	5,494	6,253	6,904	7,199	7,503	7,984	7,821	8,345
Net income ($ mil.)	(1.4%)	774	769	721	809	823	830	745	781	639	681
Income as % of sales	—	15.0%	14.5%	13.1%	12.9%	11.9%	11.5%	9.9%	9.8%	8.2%	8.2%
Earnings per share ($)	(0.6%)	1.61	1.64	1.54	1.75	1.78	1.80	1.61	1.66	1.43	1.52
Stock price – high ($)	—	14.25	19.38	19.13	18.63	20.50	20.13	23.69	23.81	25.75	20.50
Stock price – low ($)	—	11.06	12.63	13.81	14.56	15.50	16.75	18.00	20.13	19.88	12.38
Stock price – close ($)	1.1%	13.31	16.94	15.25	16.19	19.69	18.94	23.38	22.00	20.00	14.63
P/E – high	—	9	12	12	11	12	11	15	14	18	13
P/E – low	—	7	8	9	8	9	9	11	12	14	8
Dividends per share ($)	1.4%	1.05	1.13	1.17	1.23	1.26	1.30	1.34	1.38	1.42	1.21
Book value per share ($)	3.0%	10.56	11.05	11.57	11.59	12.10	12.59	12.91	13.30	13.30	13.72
Employees	0.0%	17,182	17,553	17,264	17,025	17,010	16,925	17,511	17,259	17,193	17,074

1994 Year-end:
Debt ratio: 54.7%
Return on equity: 11.3%
Cash (mil.): $534
Current ratio: 0.68
Long-term debt (mil.): $6,347
No. of shares (mil.): 448
Dividends
  Yield: 8.3%
  Payout: 79.6%
Market value (mil.): $6,551

**Stock Price History
High/Low 1985–94**

SCHERING-PLOUGH CORPORATION

Schering-Plough produces pharmaceuticals, consumer health products, and animal health products. The company's top-selling product is Claritin, with worldwide sales that increased 71% in 1994. Claritin is #1 in the US for new prescriptions for plain antihistamines. The Madison, New Jersey–based company also makes such top-selling drugs as Proventil (an antiasthmatic that is experiencing generic competition) and Eulexin (treatment for advanced prostate cancer). Over-the-counter products include Coricidin, Afrin, Dr. Scholl's, Coppertone, and Solarcaine.

Schering-Plough spends about 1/4 of its R&D expenditures on biotechnology research. The company believes the key to cost-effective quality medical care is continued biomedical innovation. It has developed a joint venture with Canji Inc. to research new cancer treatments based on Canji's new p53 gene therapy technology. The company has an agreement with Corvas to develop oral antithrombotic drugs to treat cardiovascular disorders. Schering-Plough has more products in the early development stages and fewer ones close to the production stage.

Chairman Robert Luciano's continual restructuring, downsizing efforts, and increased attention to managed care organizations have resulted in a lean and well-managed company. Schering-Plough is expanding worldwide (almost 1/2 of its sales are foreign). It has built new plants in Ireland and is working on plants in China, Mexico, and Singapore.

WHEN

Schering takes its name from Ernst Schering, a Berlin chemist who formed the company in 1864 to sell chemicals to apothecary shops. By 1880 the German company was exporting pharmaceuticals to the US. An American subsidiary was established in 1928, and during the 1930s it developed processes for the mass production of sex hormones. At the outbreak of WWII the US government seized the subsidiary and appointed government attorney Francis Brown director. Brown put together a research team whose efforts led to development of new postwar drugs, including Chlor-Trimeton, one of the first antihistamines, and the cold medicine Coricidin.

In 1952 the government sold Schering to Merrill Lynch, which took it public. Its most profitable products in the 1950s were new steroids. In 1957 Schering bought White Labs. In the 1960s the company introduced Tinactin (antifungal, 1965), Garamycin (antibiotic, 1964), and Afrin (decongestant, 1967).

The 1971 merger with Plough, Inc., expanded the product line to include cosmetics and consumer items such as Coppertone and Di-Gel. Plough had originated in Memphis, Tennessee, in 1908. Abe Plough, its founder, borrowed $125 from his father to create an "antiseptic healing oil" consisting of cottonseed oil, carbolic acid, and camphor. Plough sold his concoction door-to-door and went on to acquire 28 companies. He served as chairman of newly merged Schering-Plough until 1976. Known for his philanthropy in Memphis, Plough died in 1984 at the age of 92.

Schering-Plough introduced many products after the merger, including Lotrimin AF (anti-fungal, 1975), Drixoral (cold remedy, made nonprescription in 1982), and the anti-asthmatics Vanceril (1976) and Proventil (1981). When Garamycin's patent expired in 1980, the company introduced a similar antibiotic, Netromycin.

Schering-Plough was one of the first of the drug giants to make significant investments in biotechnology: it owns a portion of Biogen of Cambridge, Massachusetts, and acquired DNAX Research Institute of Palo Alto, California, in 1982. In 1993 Intron A, a biotechnology drug to treat chronic hepatitis C, was the company's top-selling product.

Acquisitions in the late 1970s and 1980s included Scholl (foot care, 1979), Key Pharmaceuticals (cardiovascular drugs, 1986), and Cooper Companies (eye care, 1988). The company sold Maybelline (cosmetics) to Playtex in 1990 and received FDA approval to sell Gyne-Lotrimin (a treatment for yeast infections) as an over-the-counter product.

In April 1993 Schering-Plough began marketing its nonsedating antihistamine, Claritin, in the US. By year's end domestic sales had reached an impressive $130 million. In 1994 the company gained FDA approval to market the first colored disposable contact lenses. In late 1994 the company received FDA permission for Claritin-D, which adds a decongestant to the top-selling product.

In 1995 Schering-Plough's Robert Luciano announced that he would resign as CEO at year's end but would retain his chairmanship until his contract expires in 1998. Company president and COO Richard Kogan is expected to succeed Luciano as CEO.

NYSE symbol: SGP
Fiscal year ends: December 31

WHO

Chairman and CEO: Robert P. Luciano, age 61,
$2,274,100 pay
President and COO: Richard J. Kogan, age 53,
$1,366,500 pay
EVP Administration: Hugh A. D'Andrade, age 56,
$879,125 pay
EVP; President, Schering-Plough HealthCare Products:
Donald R. Conklin, age 58, $880,000 pay
EVP Finance (Principal Financial Officer): Harold R.
Hiser Jr., age 63, $754,475 pay
EVP; President, Schering-Plough Pharmaceuticals:
Raul E. Cesan, age 47
**SVP Investor Relations and Corporate
Communications:** Geraldine U. Foster, age 52
SVP Taxes: Daniel A. Nichols, age 54
SVP Human Resources: Gordon C. O'Brien, age 54
SVP and General Counsel: Joseph C. Connors, age 46
VP Administration and Business Development:
J. Martin Comey, age 60
VP Corporate Information Services: Robert S. Lyons
Auditors: Deloitte & Touche LLP

WHERE

HQ: One Giralda Farms, Madison, NJ 07940-1000
Phone: 201-822-7000
Fax: 201-822-7447

	1994 Sales		1994 Operating Income	
	$ mil.	% of total	$ mil.	% of total
US	2,553	55	878	65
Europe, Middle East & Africa	1,064	23	232	17
Canada & Asia/ Pacific	646	14	138	10
Latin America	394	8	102	8
Total	**4,657**	**100**	**1,350**	**100**

WHAT

	1994 Sales		1994 Operating Income	
	$ mil.	% of total	$ mil.	% of total
Pharmaceuticals	4,001	86	1,191	88
Health care prods.	656	14	159	12
Total	**4,657**	**100**	**1,350**	**100**

Selected Pharmaceuticals
Celestone (anti-inflammatory)
Claritin (antihistamine)
Elocon (dermatological)
Eulexin (for prostate cancer)
Garamycin (antibiotic)
Intron A (cancer treatment)
Nitro-Dur (antianginal)
Normodyne
  (antihypertensive)
Proventil (antiasthmatic)
Theo-Dur (antiasthmatic)
Vancenase AQ (antiallergy)
Vanceril (antiasthmatic)

**Selected Consumer
Health Care**
Afrin (decongestant)
Coppertone (suncare)
Coricidin (decongestant)
Dr. Scholl's (foot care)
Drixoral (decongestant)
Durasoft (contact lenses)
Gyne-Lotrimin
  (antifungal)
Lotrimin AF (antifungal)
Solarcaine (sunburn pain)
Tinactin (antifungal)

Holiday Products
Paas (egg coloring)

KEY COMPETITORS

Abbott Labs
ALZA
American Home Products
Amgen
Bausch & Lomb
Bayer
Biogen
Bristol-Myers Squibb
Carter-Wallace
Chiron Corp.
Ciba-Geigy
Dow Chemical
Eli Lilly
Genentech
Glaxo

Hoechst
Johnson & Johnson
Merck
Nestlé
Novo Nordisk
Pfizer
Procter &
  Gamble
Rhône-Poulenc
Roche
Sandoz
SmithKline
  Beecham
Upjohn
Warner-Lambert

HOW MUCH

	9-Year Growth	1985	1986	1987	1988	1989	1990	1991	1992	1993	1994
Sales ($ mil.)	9.4%	2,079	2,399	2,699	2,969	3,158	3,323	3,616	4,056	4,341	4,657
Net income ($ mil.)	19.1%	192	266	316	390	471	565	646	720	825	922
Income as % of sales	—	9.2%	11.1%	11.7%	13.1%	14.9%	17.0%	17.9%	17.8%	19.0%	19.8%
Earnings per share ($)	22.1%	0.80	1.09	1.37	1.74	2.09	2.50	3.01	3.60	4.23	4.82
Stock price – high ($)	—	16.63	22.00	27.63	29.69	43.00	50.75	67.13	70.13	71.00	75.88
Stock price – low ($)	—	8.81	14.00	15.63	22.63	27.69	36.94	40.75	49.88	51.75	54.50
Stock price – close ($)	19.8%	14.53	19.75	23.50	28.38	42.75	44.38	65.75	63.63	68.50	74.00
P/E – high	—	21	20	20	17	21	20	22	20	17	16
P/E – low	—	11	13	11	13	13	15	14	14	12	11
Dividends per share ($)	18.8%	0.42	0.45	0.51	0.70	0.89	1.07	1.27	1.50	1.74	1.98
Book value per share ($)	1.9%	7.15	6.24	6.17	7.46	8.64	9.37	6.67	8.00	8.17	8.46
Employees	(1.0%)	23,200	23,500	21,700	22,400	21,300	19,700	20,200	21,100	21,600	21,200

1994 Year-end:
Debt ratio: 38.1%
Return on equity: 58.4%
Cash (mil.): $161
Current ratio: 0.86
Long-term debt (mil.): $186
No. of shares (mil.): 186
Dividends
  Yield: 2.7%
  Payout: 41.1%
Market value (mil.): $13,765

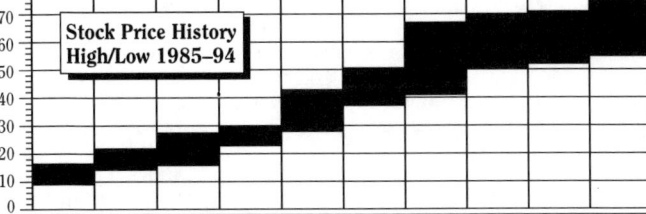
Stock Price History
High/Low 1985–94

SCHLUMBERGER N.V.

OVERVIEW

New York–based Schlumberger packs a one-two punch, combining oil field services and exploration with a sophisticated electronics and technology business. With extensive operations worldwide and 75% of sales and income derived from business outside the US, Schlumberger discovered that the world was a dangerous place in 1994. In Algeria 2 of its engineers were killed by terrorists. Political unrest caused the company to curtail its activities in Algeria and Nigeria, while political confusion in the former Soviet Union forced the company to pull back on investment plans in that region, leading to a 22-year low in the number of active drilling rigs outside North America.

Schlumberger's Oilfield Services unit includes wireline logging, well testing, seismic surveying, geoscience software and computing services, drilling and pumping services, and cementing and stimulation services for enhanced well productivity.

Schlumberger's Measurement & Systems unit makes such diverse products as utility meters, automatic testing equipment for the semiconductor industry, fuel dispensing systems for gas stations, point-of-sale payment systems, and parking management systems. Schlumberger Technology's ATE Division is the world leader in engineering-based electron beam probing systems (used in the testing of integrated circuits).

WHEN

Conrad and Marcel Schlumberger were Alsatian scientists who believed that electrical resistance could be used to measure the earth's subsurface. Paul Schlumberger, their father and fellow scientist, thought a business would follow and offered capital for the venture (1919); the brothers' Paris home became the site of Schlumberger.

Their theories were proven by the mid-1920s, but no application developed until 1927, when Pechelbronn Oil became interested in using their technique to search for oil. Conrad asked his son-in-law, Henri Doll, to design a tool for the purpose, and the process of wireline logging, akin to an X-ray for charting where oil and gas lie in a well, was born. Doll turned out to be a tremendous asset — upon his 1967 retirement it was estimated that 40% of Schlumberger revenues stemmed from his inventions.

Conrad died in 1936, leaving Marcel in charge until 1953; Marcel's death resulted in factionalism. Different family members controlled the 4 divisions (North American, South American/Middle Eastern, European, and Doll's US technical development), creating disorganization. Marcel's son Pierre took the company public, merged foreign operations with North American headquarters in Houston, and restructured the company in 1956 as Schlumberger Ltd, incorporated in the Netherlands Antilles. In 1965 Pierre ended nepotism, giving leadership of Schlumberger to another Frenchman, Jean Riboud. That year Riboud moved the headquarters to New York, where it remains today.

Riboud began a series of acquisitions, including the Compagnie des Compteurs, a

French electric-meter manufacturer (1970). Envisioning a company that would provide information as well as oil field services, he purchased Fairchild Camera & Instrument in 1979, believing that semiconductors would play an important future role. Today 35% of revenues are derived from non–oil field products and services. Riboud bought Applicon, a producer of computer-aided design and manufacturing software, in 1982.

Through a series of acquisitions, Schlumberger invested in artificial intelligence technology, which it introduced in 1982. Known for providing state-of-the-art equipment to the oil industry, Schlumberger in 1986 bought GECO, a Norwegian geophysical company noted for marine seismic analysis. In 1991 Schlumberger acquired 51% of Prakla Seismos (and the remaining 49% in 1993), which had strong onshore seismic operations, from the German government and folded it into its GECO unit.

In 1992 Schlumberger acquired oil field service businesses Seismograph Service Limited and GeoQuest Systems from Raytheon. The next year the company acquired semiconductor manufacturing supplier TLA Technology. Also in 1993 Schlumberger acquired Dow Chemical's half of well cementing and stimulation joint venture Dowell Schlumberger, giving it full ownership.

In 1994 GeoQuest acquired CPS, which makes mapping software for oil and gas exploration and production.

In 1995 the company announced that it had teamed up with Cable and Wireless to form Omnes, a global communications and information system for the oil and gas industry.

WHO

Chairman, President, and CEO: D. Euan Baird, age 57,
$1,600,000 pay
EVP Oilfield Services: Victor E. Grijalva, age 56,
$830,000 pay
EVP Measurement and Systems: Clermont A. Matton,
age 53, $660,000 pay
EVP Finance and CFO: Arthur Lindenauer, age 57,
$650,000 pay
EVP Health, Safety, and Environment: Alain Roger,
age 64, $520,646 pay
EVP Technology and Communication: Ian Strecker,
age 55
VP Business Development and Treasurer: Michel
Soublin, age 49
VP Personnel: Pierre E. Bismuth, age 50
VP: Patrick J. B. Corser, age 51
VP: Jean-Marc Perraud, age 47
Secretary and General Counsel: David S. Browning,
age 55
Auditors: Price Waterhouse LLP

WHERE

HQ: 277 Park Ave., New York, NY 10172-0266
Phone: 212-350-9400
Fax: 212-350-9564

Schlumberger operates 930 facilities in 100 countries.

	1994 Sales		1994 Operating Income	
	$ mil.	% of total	$ mil.	% of total
US	1,650	25	177	27
France	690	10	58	10
Other Europe	1,609	24	(9)	—
Other countries	2,748	41	410	63
Adjustments	—	—	(43)	—
Total	**6,697**	**100**	**593**	**100**

WHAT

	1994 Sales		1994 Operating Income	
	$ mil.	% of total	$ mil.	% of total
Oilfield Services	4,362	65	495	80
Measurement & Systems	2,335	35	121	20
Adjustments	—	—	(23)	—
Total	**6,697**	**100**	**593**	**100**

Oilfield Services
Anadrill (directional drilling, logging while drilling,
measurements while drilling)
Dowell (coiled tubing services, drilling fluid services,
pumping services, well cementing and stimulation)
GECO-Prakla (exploration services, marine and land
seismic acquisition, seismic data processing)
GeoQuest (data services and software products)
Sedco Forex (contract drilling and operation)
Wireline & Testing (borehole measurements, corrosion
evaluation services, production monitoring services,
well testing)

Measurement and Systems
Automatic test equipment (semiconductors and circuit
boards test systems)
Electricity management (electricity meters,
management services)
Electronic transactions (fuel dispensing systems,
parking management systems, public pay phones)
Gas management (gas meters, management services)
Water management (water meters, management
services)

KEY COMPETITORS

Ashland, Inc.	Hewlett-Packard	McDermott
Baker Hughes	Ingram	Nabors Industries
BJ Services	Intergraph	Teledyne
Dresser	Kaneb Services	Teradyne
Emerson	Litton	Vishay
Fluor	Industries	Intertechnology
Halliburton	LTV	Western Atlas

HOW MUCH

	9-Year Growth	1985	1986	1987	1988	1989	1990	1991	1992	1993	1994
Sales ($ mil.)	1.0%	6,119	4,568	4,402	4,925	4,686	5,306	6,145	6,332	6,706	6,697
Net income ($ mil.)	4.8%	351	(2,018)	283	454	420	570	816	662	583	536
Income as % of sales	—	5.7%	—	6.4%	9.2%	9.0%	10.7%	13.3%	10.4%	8.7%	8.0%
Earnings per share ($)	7.3%	1.17	(7.02)	1.02	1.72	1.77	2.40	3.42	2.75	2.40	2.21
Stock price – high ($)	—	43.88	37.75	51.00	38.75	50.50	69.88	74.00	70.63	68.88	63.00
Stock price – low ($)	—	32.38	27.25	26.00	28.50	32.00	43.50	50.50	52.63	55.38	50.00
Stock price – close ($)	3.6%	36.50	31.75	28.75	32.63	49.13	57.88	62.38	57.25	59.13	50.38
P/E – high	—	38	—	50	23	29	29	22	26	26	29
P/E – low	—	28	—	26	17	18	18	15	19	19	23
Dividends per share ($)	0.0%	1.20	1.20	1.20	1.20	1.20	1.20	1.20	1.20	1.20	1.20
Book value per share ($)	(2.3%)	23.24	14.67	14.09	11.59	12.19	13.67	16.06	17.50	18.09	18.92
Employees	(2.6%)	61,000	50,000	50,000	48,000	46,000	50,000	53,000	51,000	48,000	48,000

1994 Year-end:
Debt ratio: 19.4%
Return on equity: 11.9%
Cash (mil.): $1,232
Current ratio: 1.37
Long-term debt (mil.): $394
No. of shares (mil.): 242
Dividends
  Yield: 2.4%
  Payout: 54.3%
Market value (mil.): $12,204

**Stock Price History
High/Low 1985–94**

SCI SYSTEMS, INC.

OVERVIEW

Call SCI the unknown computer company. Although it is one of the largest computer manufacturers, SCI isn't well known because it contracts its services to big-name companies. Among the logos on SCI-made machines are those of Dell, Conner Peripherals, Hewlett-Packard (HP), and IBM. In 1994 HP alone accounted for 24% of the company's business.

SCI builds computers and hundreds of other electronic products and parts for a long list of mostly anonymous customers. The company runs one of the world's largest surface-mount technology operations (SMT fixes components to both sides of a circuit

board, instead of a single side). Its flexible and superefficient assembly lines can build a PC in 45 seconds.

With PC sales booming and HP hustling to become a top vendor, in 1995 SCI's order backlog doubled to nearly $2 billion.

Also in 1995 SCI agreed to acquire the contract manufacturing business of Digital Equipment Corp. (DEC), including DEC's Maine plant and contract accounts. SCI will also supply DEC with networking electronics products DEC had previously made at the plant.

Founder and CEO Olin King owns 4.4% of the company.

WHEN

Olin King (a former employee at Wernher von Braun's army rocket center) and 2 friends started Space Craft Inc., later SCI Systems, in 1961 in Huntsville, Alabama. The 3 men combined their $21,000 in savings with $300,000 in venture capital and started the company to do contract engineering for NASA.

Initially the company specialized in building electronics systems for the Saturn rocket and later for other NASA and military missile and satellite programs. Its product line expanded to include subsystems for military aircraft (e.g., cockpit controls for the F-15 fighter plane) and military surface systems.

SCI's major breakthrough came in 1976 with a contract from IBM to produce subassemblies for IBM terminals. The contract helped the company get its start in subcontracting for OEMs. SCI continued to do work for the US government, but it also began to build everything from white blood cell analyzers to coin sorters.

When IBM went to work on its personal computer, introduced in 1981, it turned to SCI with a $30 million contract for the PC's first batch of circuit boards. IBM shipped 100,000 PCs in 1981. In 1984 that number had grown to 2.3 million — all outfitted with SCI boards. SCI's contracts with IBM, which extended to other parts and subassemblies for the PC, accelerated SCI's sales. The company was ranked as the 8th fastest-growing electronics company in the US in 1985, based on its sales growth between 1981 and 1985. SCI's 1985 sales totaled $538 million.

In an attempt to reduce its reliance on IBM contracts, which accounted for 60% of sales in 1982–83, SCI expanded into making entire microcomputers (1984) and selling them to companies like Kodak, which resold them

under its label. However, microcomputer sales could not compensate for SCI's loss when IBM cut its orders for circuit boards in 1985. SCI's sales dropped 12% in 1986.

The company's sales bounced back in 1987 after SCI negotiated a new contract with IBM for circuit boards for IBM's PS/2 computers, but the experience of a dropoff in IBM contracts sent SCI looking for new customers.

SCI built additional facilities in the US and overseas and moved quickly into a leadership position among SMT manufacturers. Because of the high cost of surface-mount production, companies rely on subcontractors such as SCI to supply surface-mount boards.

In 1990 SCI added capacity by increasing to 100% its holdings in Adelantos de Tecnología (Mexico) and Cambridge Computer (UK). The following year, responding to a decline in demand for its circuit board services and the cancellation of the US Navy's A-12 aircraft program (for which SCI was a subcontractor), the company closed plants and lowered staffing levels.

SCI opened a new plant in Canada and acquired a California manufacturing facility from Tandem Computers in 1992, and the next year it expanded its plant in Guadalajara, Mexico, to meet increased demand.

In 1994 SCI bought Hewlett-Packard's Surface Mount Centre in Grenoble, France. Also in 1994 the company reached an agreement to sell Cambridge Computer for around $7 million.

NEC signed up SCI in 1995 for a contract worth over $100 million to provide a family of computer products. That same year SCI completed an expansion and began production at its Grenoble manufacturing facility. The company also added a new plant in Asia.

Nasdaq symbol: SCIS
Fiscal year ends: June 30

WHO

Chairman and CEO: Olin B. King, age 60, $611,183 pay
President and COO: A. Eugene Sapp Jr., age 58, $446,347 pay
SVP Commercial Division, Western Region: David F. Jenkins, age 57, $232,774 pay
SVP Commercial Division, Central Region: Jerry F. Thomas, age 53, $209,581 pay
SVP Government Division: Richard A. Holloway, age 52, $179,357 pay
SVP Commercial Division, Eastern Region: Jeffrey L. Nesbitt, age 43
SVP Commercial Division, Asian Region: Peter M. Scheffler, age 43
SVP Commercial Division, European Region: Alexander A. C. Wilson, age 57
VP: Bruce R. Anderson
VP: C.T. Chua
VP: George J. King
VP Personnel: Francis X. Henry
Auditors: Ernst & Young LLP

WHERE

HQ: 2101 W. Clinton Ave., Huntsville, AL 35805
Phone: 205-882-4601
Fax: 205-882-4804

The company has plants in Canada, France, Hong Kong, Ireland, Mexico, Scotland, Singapore, Thailand, and the US.

	1994 Sales		1994 Operating Income	
	$ mil.	% of total	$ mil.	% of total
US	1,155	62	60	99
Other countries	697	38	1	1
Total	**1,852**	**100**	**61**	**100**

WHAT

Commercial Division
Component testing
Computer-aided design services
Engineering support
Pin-in-hole circuit board assembly
Surface-mount circuit board assembly

Government Division
Advanced Airborne Test Instrumentation System
Apache Longbow helicopter weapons, systems computers, and communication interface units
Digital Non-Secure Voice Terminal
Distributed Data Acquisition System for the Titan IV Launch Vehicle

Selected Subsidiaries
Adelantos de Tecnología S.A. de C.V. (Mexico)
Cambridge Computer, Ltd. (UK)
Consolidated Communications Corp. (50%)
Norlite Technology, Inc. (Canada)
SCI Ireland Limited
SCI Manufacturing Singapore Pte. Ltd.
SCI Systems (Thailand) Limited
SCI Technology, Inc.

KEY COMPETITORS

AlliedSignal	Intel
AMP	Loral
AST	Oki
Benchmark Electronics	PCI Ltd
Comptronix	Raytheon
DOVatron	Rockwell
General Signal	Sanmina
GM Hughes	SigmaTron International
Group Technologies	Solectron
Harris Corp.	Teledyne
Hitachi	Texas Instruments
Honeywell	Thomson SA
IEC Electronics	Tyco International

HOW MUCH

	9-Year Growth	1985	1986	1987	1988	1989	1990	1991	1992	1993	1994
Sales ($ mil.)	14.7%	538	470	553	774	987	1,179	1,129	1,045	1,697	1,852
Net income ($ mil.)	4.6%	14	14	16	19	21	2	4	4	27	21
Income as % of sales	—	2.5%	2.9%	2.9%	2.5%	2.1%	0.2%	0.3%	0.4%	1.6%	1.1%
Earnings per share ($)	1.4%	0.67	0.67	0.77	0.91	1.00	0.11	0.16	0.18	1.07	0.76
Stock price – high ($)	—	10.44	13.84	22.75	15.00	15.88	13.13	10.13	18.50	23.38	22.25
Stock price – low ($)	—	6.91	9.00	11.50	10.88	8.00	5.25	5.88	6.50	14.38	12.63
Stock price – close ($)	6.6%	10.09	11.75	13.25	15.00	8.63	8.25	6.50	18.25	17.63	18.00
P/E – high	—	16	21	30	17	16	119	63	103	22	29
P/E – low	—	10	13	15	12	8	48	37	36	13	17
Dividends per share ($)	—	0.00	0.00	0.00	0.00	0.00	0.00	0.00	0.00	0.00	0.00
Book value per share ($)	10.0%	4.78	5.53	6.39	7.27	8.11	8.42	8.87	9.17	10.27	11.27
Employees	12.1%	4,290	5,185	6,660	8,970	8,578	10,694	9,762	9,512	10,811	12,027

1994 Year-end:
Debt ratio: 48.3%
Return on equity: 7.3%
Cash (mil.): $36
Current ratio: 2.21
Long-term debt (mil.): $278
No. of shares (mil.): 27
Dividends
  Yield: —
  Payout: —
Market value (mil.): $487

Stock Price History High/Low 1985–94

SCOTT PAPER COMPANY

OVERVIEW

Great Scott! After just more than a year under the leadership of Albert Dunlap, a paper industry veteran, former paratrooper, and self-described "Rambo in pinstripes," Scott Paper has tidied up the mess caused by some losing years in the early 1990s. With its employee rolls slashed and its stock price more than doubled, the cleaned-up company caught the eye of rival tissue maker Kimberly-Clark, which agreed in July 1995 to buy Scott for $7.4 billion.

Scott is the world's #1 producer of consumer tissue products and operates in 22 countries. Its brands include Cottonelle bathroom tissue, Viva paper towels, and Scotties facial tissue. The company is also a major US producer of baby wipes (Baby Fresh and Wash a-bye Baby).

Like baby wipes, Scott has been getting to the bottom of its problems (debt overload) and in 1994 wiped away much of its accumulated debt through the sale of noncore assets. It sold its S. D. Warren division, one of America's top makers of coated printing and publishing pa-

pers, to Sappi Limited for $1.6 billion; its Mobile-based energy and recovery complex to a subsidiary of the Southern Company; and its 50%-owned joint venture, Scott Health Care, maker of adult incontinence care and wound care products, to Molnlycke AB of Sweden (the other owner of the venture) for $65.7 million. Scott also made arrangements to dispose of its US and UK food service business operations.

In addition, Scott has been boosting its core tissue-making activities. In 1994 the company signed an agreement with Shanghai Paper Company to become the first major international tissue producer to have operations in China. Scott also announced plans for a $148 million Mexican expansion program and secured an agreement to set up operations in Indonesia.

Dunlap continued to cut away in 1995. Scott announced plans to divest additional assets, including its remaining US timberlands and several pulp mills.

WHEN

Founded in Pennsylvania in 1879 by brothers Irvin and Clarence Scott, the Scott Paper Company was the first to market rolls of tissue for use as toilet paper. Irvin's son Arthur (president until 1927) came up with the advertising slogan "Soft as old linen." Scott began making paper towels in 1907 and went public in 1915.

Before WWII, Scott expanded overseas (it credits its global success to its 50-50 formula: Scott would own up to 50% of a foreign venture, and a local company would own the rest). Sanyo Scott produced Japan's top paper towel brand. Other joint ventures included Spain's Gureola-Scott, Australia's Bowater-Scott, and Italy's Burgo-Scott.

Until the 1960s Scott was the leader in the so-called "Great Toilet Paper War." In 1957 Procter & Gamble introduced Charmin toilet tissue, which soon outsold Scott's brand. Between 1960 and 1971 Scott's market share of consumer paper products dropped from 45% to 33%. The firm diversified in 1967, buying S. D. Warren (printing and publishing papers, sold in 1994) and Plastic Coating Corporation.

Under CEO Charles Dickey Jr. (1971–79), the company made major changes, reducing administrative expenses by about 20% and withdrawing unsuccessful items from the consumer market in order to concentrate on household and industrial paper products such as towels, napkins, cups, and plates. In 1976 Scott introduced Cottonelle to compete with

Charmin. Cottonelle captured about 35% of the 4-roll-pack market within several months of its introduction.

Scott invested in a 5-year, $1.6 billion US plant upgrade (1981); a 3-year, $250 million European plant upgrade (1988); and a $475 million upgrade to 3 S. D. Warren plants (1988). In 1989 the company bought the White Swan Tissue Division (sanitary products) of E. B. Eddy Forest Products (Canada).

Scott sold its interest in Sanyo Scott (1991) and its food service container and nonwoven fabrics businesses (1992). In 1993 the company agreed to pay $3 million to settle a shareholder group's suit accusing then-chairman Philip Lippincott and then-SVP Ashok Bakhru of mishandling the disclosure of Scott's 1990 earnings.

In 1994 Scott bought the remaining stake in Scott-Feldmuhle, a tissue maker in Germany and the Netherlands owned jointly since 1990 with Stora Feldmuhle AG. The 8,300 job cuts announced in 1994 included 3,800 positions in the US, 1,900 in Mexico, and 2,600 in other countries.

In 1995 Scott opened a $240 million plant in Owensboro, Kentucky, that houses a state-of-the-art tissue-making machine. It also agreed to sell its corporate headquarters to California-based real estate investor Koll for $39 million, relocating its executive offices to Boca Raton, Florida.

NYSE symbol: SPP
Fiscal year ends: Last Saturday in December

WHO

Chairman and CEO: Albert J. Dunlap, age 57,
$3,205,753 pay
SVP Worldwide Away-from-Home Business:
P. Newton White, age 52, $622,178 pay
SVP European Consumer Business: Paolo Forlin,
$563,584 pay
SVP Finance and Administration: Russell A. Kersh,
age 41, $489,849 pay
SVP, General Counsel, and Secretary: John P. Murtagh,
age 46, $365,767 pay
SVP Worldwide Consumer Business: Richard R.
Nicolosi, age 47
VP, Treasurer, and CFO: Basil L. Anderson, age 49,
$421,752 pay
VP and Controller: Edward B. Betz, age 60
VP Human Resources: John P. Nee
Auditors: Coopers & Lybrand L.L.P.

WHERE

HQ: The Scott Center, 2650 N. Military Tr., Ste. 300,
Boca Raton, FL 33431-6394
Phone: 407-989-2300
Fax: 407-989-2453

Scott manufactures and markets consumer tissue
products in 22 countries.

	1994 Sales		1994 Operating Income	
	$ mil.	% of total	$ mil.	% of total
US	2,170	61	350	68
Europe	1,128	31	122	24
Other regions	283	8	42	8
Adjustments	—	—	(134)	—
Total	**3,581**	**100**	**380**	**100**

WHAT

Major Products
Baby wipes (Baby Fresh, Wash a-bye Baby)
Bathroom tissue (Cottonelle, Family Scott, JRT,
Natural, Pétalo, ScotTissue)
Cleaning and wiping products (Cleanworks, EconoMizer,
Micro-Wipes, Sani-Prep, Scottcloth, Scottpure,
WypAll)
Cloths (Ultra Scrub)
Dispensing systems for bathroom tissues, towels, toilet
seat covers, facial tissue, napkins, and wiping products
(Windows, In-Sight, Reflections)
Disposable auto and home maintenance products (Rags
in a Box, Shop Towels on a Roll)
Disposable towels (Job Squad, ScotTowels, White Swan,
Viva)
Drop cloths (Gotcha Covered)
Facial tissues (Scotties, White Swan)
Industrial garments (Durafab)
Napkins (Scott, Scottex, Viva, Viva Accents)
Premoistened cleansing cloths (KidFresh, Sofkins)
Sanitary protection products (Confort, Saba)
Soap dispensers (Sani-Fresh, Sani-Tuff, SureTouch)
Special task systems (Cleanworks chemical dispensing
system, WetTask cleaning system)
Tabletop ensembles (Viva)
Toilet seat covers (P.S. Personal Seats)

KEY COMPETITORS

Boise Cascade	Johnson & Johnson
Canadian Pacific	Mead
Champion Intl.	Procter & Gamble
Fletcher Challenge	Rayonier
Fort Howard	Sandoz
Georgia-Pacific	Stone Container
International Paper	Weyerhaeuser
James River	

HOW MUCH

	9-Year Growth	1985	1986	1987	1988	1989	1990	1991	1992	1993	1994
Sales ($ mil.)	1.8%	3,050	3,437	4,122	4,726	5,066	5,356	4,977	4,886	4,749	3,581
Net income ($ mil.)	0.5%	201	187	234	401	376	148	(70)	167	(308)	210
Income as % of sales	—	6.6%	5.4%	5.7%	8.5%	7.4%	2.8%	—	3.4%	—	7.6%
Earnings per share ($)	2.5%	1.13	1.24	1.53	2.61	2.56	1.01	(0.48)	1.13	(1.96)	1.41
Stock price – high ($)	—	13.06	16.66	21.75	21.38	26.25	25.69	23.31	23.00	20.63	35.31
Stock price – low ($)	—	8.34	12.00	13.75	16.19	19.19	15.00	14.75	17.25	15.50	18.63
Stock price – close ($)	11.8%	12.66	15.69	17.63	19.63	24.06	18.94	17.44	17.88	20.56	34.56
P/E – high	—	12	13	14	8	10	25	—	20	—	25
P/E – low	—	7	10	9	6	8	15	—	15	—	13
Dividends per share ($)	2.9%	0.31	0.32	0.34	0.38	0.40	0.40	0.40	0.40	0.40	0.40
Book value per share ($)	4.6%	8.15	9.31	10.72	13.30	14.01	14.77	13.44	13.65	10.59	12.21
Employees	(1.2%)	22,200	24,900	25,400	27,000	29,400	30,800	29,100	26,500	25,900	19,900

1994 Year-end:
Debt ratio: 51.5%
Return on equity: 12.7%
Cash (mil.): $1,114
Current ratio: 1.19
Long-term debt (mil.): $1,093
No. of shares (mil.): 143
Dividends
  Yield: 1.2%
  Payout: 22.0%
Market value (mil.): $4,941

Stock Price History
High/Low 1985–94

SEAGATE TECHNOLOGY, INC.

OVERVIEW

Seagate helps drive the computer industry — the California-based company manufactures more than 100 hard drive models for notebook and desktop computers, workstations, and supercomputers. Seagate is #2 among drive makers (after Quantum) with nearly 19% of the market. The company's products are sold primarily to OEMs, distributors, and VARs. Now Seagate hopes to leverage its expertise into an extended product range. In 1995 the company reorganized its operations into units for storage products, components, and software.

One key area that Seagate is pursuing is software. In 1994 it acquired software companies Palindrome and Crystal Computer Services; in 1995 it added Network Computing

and NetLabs. CEO Alan Shugart's goal is to build a $1 billion software firm by 1999.

Seagate, which spent about 4.9% of 1994 sales on R&D, is also exploring new ways to expand its core business with high-margin products for high-end systems such as network and client/server computing, data management, and digital audio and video. Seagate continues to develop flash memory products, especially for mobile computing, through its SunDisk subsidiary. In 1994 the company purchased a 25% stake in Dragon Systems, a developer of speech recognition products for PCs, and expanded its components manufacturing capabilities when it bought the magnetic head operations of Applied Magnetics.

WHEN

Seagate Technology was founded in 1979 by Alan Shugart, an 18-year IBMer who had made floppy disks standard on microcomputers at Shugart Associates; manufacturing expert Tom Mitchell, formerly of Commodore and Memorex; design engineer Douglas Mahon; and Finis Conner. Seagate pioneered the downsizing of mainframe hard disk drives for PCs; the resulting drive had 30 times more storage than floppy disks, faster access times, and much higher long-term reliability.

Seagate's first product, the ST506 (a 5.25" hard disk, 1980), sold briskly. With IBM as a customer, Seagate had grabbed half of the market for small disk drives by 1982; by 1984 sales had reached $344 million. Soon, though, Seagate's heavy dependence on IBM showed its double edge, as eroding IBM PC demand prompted it to cut orders. Sales in 1985 dropped to $215 million and profits to $1 million (from $42 million the year before).

Having distinguished itself through high-volume, low-cost, reliable manufacturing, Seagate now hastened the transfer of manufacturing to Singapore (and later Thailand); its California work force was halved.

The company also accelerated its vertical integration to ensure availability of critical components and reduce time to market. Seagate purchased Grenex (thin-film magnetic media, 1984), Aeon (aluminum substrates, 1987), and Integrated Power Systems (custom semiconductors, 1987). Seagate also succeeded in luring back computer giant IBM, which had turned to an alternate supplier in the interim.

With revenues more than doubling in 1986 and again in 1987 (to $958 million), Seagate

spent $290 million and doubled its work force to 30,000 to increase 5.25" production, ignoring signs of a coming 3.5" standard for hard disk drives. The strong market in 1988 for 3.5" drives, coupled with IBM's decision to produce more drives in-house, prompted Seagate to reduce its work force by almost 4,000 and shift quickly to 3.5" production.

Seagate purchased Imprimis from Control Data (1989), thus making itself the world's premier independent drive maker. The acquisition nearly doubled Seagate's size and made it a leader in high-capacity (greater than one gigabyte) drives. Imprimis's strengths in R&D and high-capacity drives for large computers (sold to OEMs), combined with Seagate's manufacturing talent, resulted in a formidable competitor to both Asian and domestic drive producers. Concern over Seagate's late (1990) introduction of 2.5" drives faded as demand for the drives failed to match expectations.

In 1991 a sudden slowdown in PC sales led to an inventory buildup and a drop in profits. But soon plummeting PC prices fueled an upswing in PC sales, and Seagate ended the year struggling to meet demand.

In 1993 Seagate acquired a 25% interest in SunDisk, a leader in flash memory storage systems. That year, when Sun Microsystems accounted for 11% of sales, Seagate was the only independent disk drive company that made a profit.

In 1994 Seagate and Hitachi signed an agreement to share their mass-storage technologies. The following year the company announced that it would set up a 50,000-square-foot disk manufacturing plant in Jiangsu Province, China.

NYSE symbol: SEG
Fiscal year ends: Friday nearest June 30

WHO

Chairman, President, CEO, and COO: Alan F. Shugart, age 63, $938,058 pay
EVP, Chief Administrative Officer, and CFO: Donald L. Waite, age 61, $606,047 pay (prior to promotion)
EVP and COO, Components Group: Brendan C. Hegarty, age 51, $577,544 pay (prior to promotion)
EVP Worldwide Sales and Marketing: Bernardo A. Carballo, age 44, $551,728 pay (prior to promotion)
EVP and COO, Storage Products Group: Ronald D. Verdoon, age 43, $551,532 pay (prior to promotion)
EVP Corporate Development; COO, Software Group: Stephen J. Luczo, age 37
SVP and Chief Technical Officer, Data Storage Products: Hossein M. Moghadam, age 50
SVP Quality and Customer Service and Repair: Stephen B. Greenspan, age 53
SVP Corporate Materials: Robert A. Sandie, age 58
SVP Administration (HR): Robert A. Kundtz, age 53
Auditors: Ernst & Young LLP

WHERE

HQ: 920 Disc Dr., Scotts Valley, CA 95066
Phone: 408-438-6550
Fax: 408-438-6172

Seagate has sales offices in 17 countries. The company's primary manufacturing facilities are located in China, Malaysia, Singapore, Thailand, the UK, and the US.

	1994 Sales		1994 Operating Income	
	$ mil.	% of total	$ mil.	% of total
US	1,827	52	51	16
Far East	1,673	48	260	84
Total	**3,500**	**100**	**311**	**100**

WHAT

	1994 Sales
	% of total
OEMs	68
Systems integrators & distributors	32
Total	**100**

Products
Mainframe and supercomputer applications
Rigid disk drives
  1.8" drives for pen-based and hand-held computers
  2.5" drives for notebook computers; 131 MB to 455 MB
  3.5" drives for PCs, workstations, arrays, and servers;
    214 MB to 4 GB (gigabytes)
  5.25" drives for mainframes and enterprise and
    departmental servers; 2.9 GB to 9 GB
Solid-state flash memory devices

Selected Cross-Licensing Agreements
Areal Technology
Ceridian
Hewlett-Packard
Hitachi
Machines Bull
Quantum Corp.
Unisys
Western Digital

KEY COMPETITORS

BCE	Matsushita
Canon	Maxtor
Conner Peripherals	Micropolis
Data General	Mitsubishi
DEC	NEC
Fujitsu	Quantum Corp.
Hewlett-Packard	Storage Technology
Hitachi	Toshiba
IBM	Unisys
Komag	Western Digital

HOW MUCH

	9-Year Growth	1985	1986	1987	1988	1989	1990	1991	1992	1993	1994
Sales ($ mil.)	36.3%	215	460	958	1,266	1,372	2,413	2,677	2,875	3,044	3,500
Net income ($ mil.)	82.5%	1	35	140	77	0	117	63	63	195	225
Income as % of sales	—	0.5%	7.5%	14.6%	6.1%	0.0%	4.9%	2.3%	2.2%	6.4%	6.4%
Earnings per share ($)	73.4%	0.02	0.72	2.81	1.54	0.01	1.92	0.95	0.92	2.71	2.83
Stock price – high ($)	—	8.50	20.75	45.13	23.00	15.50	19.75	19.88	22.38	25.13	28.75
Stock price – low ($)	—	4.75	7.13	10.13	6.63	8.88	5.63	7.13	9.00	13.13	18.63
Stock price – close ($)	14.2%	7.25	19.13	14.88	8.63	15.00	11.75	9.13	19.63	23.75	24.00
P/E – high	—	—	29	16	15	—	10	21	24	9	10
P/E – low	—	—	10	4	4	—	3	8	10	5	7
Dividends per share ($)	—	0.00	0.00	0.00	0.00	0.00	0.00	0.00	0.00	0.00	0.00
Book value per share ($)	19.5%	3.66	4.41	7.36	8.89	8.85	10.64	11.76	12.63	15.34	18.24
Employees	30.9%	4,700	8,900	16,000	30,000	40,000	38,000	42,000	43,000	43,000	53,000

1994 Year-end:
Debt ratio: 29.3%
Return on equity: 19.0%
Cash (mil.): $1,334
Current ratio: 3.20
Long-term debt (mil.): $549
No. of shares (mil.): 73
Dividends
  Yield: —
  Payout: —
Market value (mil.): $1,748

Stock Price History
High/Low 1985–94

SEARS, ROEBUCK AND CO.

OVERVIEW

Sears single-handedly lessened the nation's landfill "crisis" when it discontinued its "Great American Wish Book" catalog in 1993. Since then the company has been shedding its other weighty operations, including Dean Witter, Discover, as part of a plan to focus on its core Merchandise Group, which operates a network of mall-based department stores and free-standing stores in the US, Canada, and Mexico.

In 1995 Sears spun off Allstate (it owned 80%), the nation's largest publicly held property and casualty insurance company, with over 20 million customers and over $20 billion in sales. Allstate has suffered heavy losses because of the recent floods and earthquakes in California. Sears does plan on keeping its 50% stake in Prodigy, an on-line computer network, and its automotive division, which includes Western Auto, an operator of 633 stores (including 118 Tire America and 125 NTW stores). Sears also operates hardware stores and Homelife furniture stores.

The company's commitment to its retail operations is paying off. Same-store sales climbed 8.3% in 1994, due in part to improved apparel sales. Sears is continuing to remodel many of its stores to make more room for higher-margin clothing.

In 1995 Sears agreed to have Jiffy Lube (a Pennzoil unit) open oil change centers inside Sears Auto Centers. Also, CEO Edward Brennan announced his retirement. Arthur Martinez, chairman and CEO of the Sears Merchandise Group, will replace Brennan.

WHEN

In 1886 Richard W. Sears, a railway agent in Minnesota, bought a shipment of watches being returned to the maker. He started the R. W. Sears Watch Company 6 months later, moved to Chicago (home of mail order pioneer Montgomery Ward), and in 1887 hired watchmaker Alvah C. Roebuck. Sears sold the watch business in 1889 and 2 years later formed another mail order business that became Sears, Roebuck, and Company in 1893. The company issued its first general catalog in 1896, offering low prices and money-back guarantees to the farmers who were Sears's principal customers.

Roebuck left the company in 1895, and Sears found 2 new partners: Aaron Nussbaum (who left in 1901) and Julius Rosenwald. In 1906 Sears went public to raise money for expansion. Differences soon arose between Sears and Rosenwald; Sears departed in 1908 and Rosenwald became president.

Anticipating the changes that the automobile would bring to rural life, Sears opened its first retail store in 1924 so that farmers could drive to town to buy merchandise; in 1925 Sears brought out a line of tires under the name Allstate. Auto insurance (named after the tire) followed in 1931.

The company bought Homart Development (shopping centers, 1959) and several savings and loans. The Sears Tower — the world's tallest building — opened in 1973.

After struggling through the high interest rates and low growth of the late 1970s, Sears decided to diversify into financial services and in 1981 acquired Coldwell Banker (real estate sales) and Dean Witter Reynolds (stock brokerage). Under the Dean Witter umbrella, Sears launched the Discover Card in 1985. But the financial operations never created any synergy for Sears and detracted from retailing.

In reaction to falling market share in the 1980s, Sears lurched from retail strategy to retail strategy, going up and down market, diversifying into auto supplies and repairs, and neglecting its department stores.

In 1992 Sears Auto Centers in California came under fire when it was alleged that salespeople sold unneeded auto parts and services in order to build their commissions. Sears tried to change the commission system, but some salespeople remained on commission, and the system was quietly revamped.

In 1992 Sears entered into a joint venture with IBM, its partner in the on-line service Prodigy, to form Advantis, a voice-and-data network services company. In 1993 Sears agreed to sell its Eye Care Centers of America stores, sold the last part of Coldwell Banker that it owned, and disposed of Dean Witter, Discover in a combination IPO and spinoff.

In 1994 the company transferred ownership of the Sears Tower, in Chicago, to a trust. The deal, which will enable a 3rd party to become owner of the building in 2003, relieved Sears of about $850 million in debt. That same year the company added 3.4 million square feet of apparel space to its stores. Sears also introduced national brands to go along with its own private-label clothing.

In 1995 the company announced its intention to divest Homart, its real estate subsidiary with about $2 billion in assets.

NYSE symbol: S
Fiscal year ends: Saturday nearest December 31

WHO

Chairman, President, and CEO: Edward A. Brennan, age 61, $1,483,805 pay
VC and Acting CFO: James M. Denny, age 62, $973,455 pay
Chairman and CEO, Sears Merchandise Group: Arthur C. Martinez, age 55, $2,050,746 pay
EVP Administration (HR): Anthony J. Rucci
SVP, General Counsel, and Secretary: David Shute, age 64
VP and Treasurer: Alice M. Peterson, age 42
VP Public Affairs: Gerald E. Buldak, age 50
Auditors: Deloitte & Touche LLP

WHERE

HQ: Sears Tower, Chicago, IL 60684
Phone: 312-875-2500
Fax: 312-875-8351

Sears operates 1,940 Homelife, Sears, Western Auto, and other retail stores in the US; 1,548 Sears and catalog stores in Canada; and 47 stores in Mexico.

	1994 Sales		1994 Operating Income	
	$ mil.	% of total	$ mil.	% of total
Merchandising				
US	29,376	54	1,484	84
Other countries	3,649	7	60	3
Allstate	21,464	39	227	13
Other	110	—	(59)	—
Adjustments	(40)	—	—	—
Total	**54,559**	**100**	**1,712**	**100**

WHAT

	1994 Sales		1994 Pretax Income	
	$ mil.	% of total	$ mil.	% of total
Merchandising	33,025	61	1,544	78
Property & liability insurance	18,607	34	108	5
Life insurance	2,856	5	334	17
Corporate	110	—	(59)	—
Adjustments	(39)	—	(215)	—
Total	**54,559**	**100**	**1,712**	**100**

Selected Stores

Sears catalog stores
Sears department stores
Sears Hardware stores
Sears Homelife furniture stores
Western Auto Supply Co.
　NTW
　Tire America

KEY COMPETITORS

Ace Hardware	Harcourt	Montgomery
Ames	General	Ward
AutoZone	Home Depot	Nordstrom
Best Products	Hudson's Bay	Office Depot
Black & Decker	J. C. Penney	Service
Broadway Stores	Kmart	Merchandise
Caldor	L. Luria	Servistar
Carson Pirie Scott	Levitz	Sherwin-Williams
Circuit City	Lowe's	Spiegel
Cotter & Company	May	Waban
Dayton Hudson	Maytag	Wal-Mart
Edison Brothers	Mercantile	Woolworth
Federated	Stores	
The Gap		

HOW MUCH

	9-Year Growth	1985	1986	1987	1988	1989	1990	1991	1992	1993	1994
Sales ($ mil.)	3.3%	40,715	44,282	48,440	50,251	53,794	55,972	57,242	52,345	50,838	54,559
Net income ($ mil.)	1.2%	1,303	1,351	1,649	1,032	1,446	892	1,279	(2,059)	2,374	1,454
Income as % of sales	—	3.2%	3.1%	3.4%	2.1%	2.7%	1.6%	2.2%	—	4.7%	2.7%
Earnings per share ($)	0.4%	3.53	3.62	4.30	2.71	4.30	2.63	3.71	(5.65)	6.13	3.66
Stock price – high ($)	—	41.13	50.38	59.50	46.25	48.13	41.88	43.50	48.00	60.13	55.13
Stock price – low ($)	—	30.88	35.88	26.00	32.25	36.50	22.00	24.38	37.00	39.88	42.13
Stock price – close ($)	1.9%	39.00	39.75	33.50	40.88	38.13	25.38	37.88	45.50	52.88	46.00
P/E – high	—	12	14	14	17	11	16	12	—	10	15
P/E – low	—	9	10	6	12	9	8	7	—	7	12
Dividends per share ($)	(1.1%)	1.76	1.76	1.94	2.00	2.00	2.00	2.00	2.00	1.60	1.60
Book value per share ($)	(1.8%)	31.70	33.98	35.76	37.75	39.77	34.10	40.29	27.89	29.58	26.91
Employees	(2.8%)	466,000	485,400	501,100	520,000	500,000	460,000	450,000	403,000	359,000	360,570

1994 Year-end:
Debt ratio: 61.2%
Return on equity: 12.9%
Cash (mil.): $1,421
Current ratio: —
Long-term debt (mil.): $10,854
No. of shares (mil.): 352
Dividends
　Yield: 2.2%
　Payout: 43.7%
Market value (mil.): $16,178

Stock Price History
High/Low 1985–94

SERVICE MERCHANDISE COMPANY, INC.

OVERVIEW

Service Merchandise is the nation's largest catalog showroom retailer, with 406 stores (averaging 50,000 square feet) located in 37 states. The company also sells more jewelry, cameras, and electric razors than anyone else in the US and is 2nd only to J. C. Penney in the sale of luggage. Service Merchandise's other products include housewares; small appliances; TVs; patio, lawn, and garden accessories; sporting goods; and toys. Most customers preselect their purchases in the company's catalog, which is distributed each fall to approximately 16 million households. In addition, Service Merchandise publishes spring and holiday catalogs and over 45 special sales flyers and newspaper inserts.

Over the past several years, Service Merchandise has cut back on customer service. It says the lack of sales staff coupled with a very competitive retail environment caused the company's earnings to drop last year. In response, Service Merchandise has revamped the cash register computer system to make transactions quicker and smoother and has added sales staff to all its stores to reestablish a sense of customer service. Analysts believe that besides enhancing customer service, the additional salespeople should be useful in guiding customers to the higher-margin items.

Under the tutelage of its new president and COO, Gary Witkin, Service Merchandise is adding more promotional items and displaying its products to create more opportunities for impulse buying. Witkin, who is known for his marketing savvy and experience, hopes to do this without taking away from the company's main focus: its catalog operations.

CEO Raymond Zimmerman owns just over 7% of the company's stock.

WHEN

Harry and Mary K. Zimmerman and their son Raymond started Service Merchandise in 1960. Until 1967 they operated one Service Merchandise catalog showroom, located in Nashville, Tennessee. The idea was simple: the Zimmermans displayed samples of merchandise such as jewelry, toys, and appliances (almost no soft goods) on the showroom floor from which customers made their selections and then ordered, paid, and waited while their merchandise was brought in from the adjoining warehouse. Service Merchandise went public in 1971, operating 5 showrooms in Tennessee by 1972. Raymond Zimmerman became president in 1973.

In 1974 the company acquired the catalog showroom operations of Malone & Hyde, which operated stores in Arkansas, Missouri, and Tennessee. By the end of the 1970s, Service Merchandise was a leader in the increasingly popular catalog showroom shopping business. Harry and Mary K. Zimmerman retired as chairman and secretary, respectively, in 1980, leaving the operation of the company to Raymond, who began expanding into other formats to complement Service Merchandise's main business. The company opened Toy Store units — large discount stores stocking children's games, toys, and furniture — in Nashville and Louisville (1980) but abandoned the concept within a few years.

In the 1980s Service Merchandise went on an acquisitions binge, adding both compatible (Sam Solomon Company, a catalog showroom operator based in Charleston, South Carolina; 1982) and incompatible (the Computer Shoppe, a computer retailer; 1983) operations. One of its biggest acquisitions was Florida-based Home Owners Warehouse (1983). The company changed the name of Home Owners Warehouse to Mr. HOW and tried to market it as a do-it-yourself discount home improvement center. The company disposed of the 22 Mr. HOW stores in 1986 following 3 years of poor sales.

Service Merchandise's growth, as well as operation and disposal of its noncore acquisitions, depressed earnings so that shares sank to under $2 in 1987. In 1988 the company's largest catalog competitor, Best Products, was bought by New York investment firm Adler and Shaykin. In order to discourage any potential takeovers, Service Merchandise took on approximately $1 billion of debt in 1989, using part of the funds to pay a special dividend to its stockholders.

After pulling through the recession and lackluster sales in the 1990s, the company decided to reemphasize jewelry, which has become its most important line.

The company opened 15 stores in 1994, concentrating on markets in Texas and southern Florida. Service Merchandise's plans for 1995 include a realignment of its districts so that each district manager will be in charge of fewer stores. The company hopes this action will allow the managers more time for "people development."

NYSE symbol: SME
Fiscal year ends: Sunday nearest December 31

WHO

Chairman and CEO: Raymond Zimmerman, age 62, $751,677 pay
President and COO: Gary M. Witkin, age 46
Divisional SVP Hardlines Merchandising: Frank X. Bisceglia, $296,936 pay
Divisional SVP Jewelry Merchandising: Charles Septer, age 43, $287,491 pay
SVP Human Resources: Robert C. Eimers, age 47
VP and CFO: S. Cusano, age 41, $301,680 pay
VP, General Counsel, and Secretary: Glen A. Bodzy, age 42, $292,204 pay
Treasurer: Michael E. Hogrefe, age 34
Auditors: Deloitte & Touche LLP

WHERE

HQ: 7100 Service Merchandise Dr., Brentwood, TN 37027; P.O. Box 24600, Nashville, TN 37202-4600
Phone: 615-660-6000
Fax: 615-660-7912

	1994 Stores	
	No.	**% of total**
Florida	48	12
Texas	48	12
Illinois	24	6
New York	23	6
California	22	5
Tennessee	18	4
Georgia	16	4
Indiana	16	4
Ohio	16	4
Louisiana	14	3
Michigan	14	3
Other states	147	37
Total	**406**	**100**

WHAT

Major Product Lines
Cameras
Crystal
Fine jewelry
Giftware
Home electronics
Housewares
Lawn and garden accessories
Luggage
Silverware
Small appliances
Sporting goods
Toys

KEY COMPETITORS

Ames	Kmart
Barry's Jewelers	L. Luria
Ben Franklin Retail	Lechters
Best Buy	May
Best Products	Mayor's Jewelers
Broadway Stores	McCrory
Caldor	Montgomery Ward
Circuit City	Oshman's Sporting Goods
Claire's Stores	Price/Costco
Comcast	Reeds Jewelers
Consolidated Stores	Sears
Dayton Hudson	TJX
Federated	Toys "R" Us
Friedman's	Venture Stores
Home Depot	Vons
Home Shopping Network	Wal-Mart
	Woolworth
Jan Bell Marketing	Zale
J. C. Penney	

HOW MUCH

	9-Year Growth	1985	1986	1987	1988	1989	1990	1991	1992	1993	1994
Sales ($ mil.)	5.4%	2,527	2,527	2,719	3,093	3,307	3,435	3,400	3,713	3,815	4,050
Net income ($ mil.)	21.2%	11	(47)	25	77	72	61	76	85	82	62
Income as % of sales	—	0.4%	—	0.9%	2.5%	2.2%	1.8%	2.2%	2.3%	2.2%	1.5%
Earnings per share ($)	15.3%	0.17	(0.75)	0.40	0.81	0.74	0.62	0.76	0.83	0.80	0.61
Stock price – high ($)	—	5.83	5.38	3.38	6.67	6.94	5.27	9.00	14.88	15.38	10.00
Stock price – low ($)	—	3.91	2.63	1.06	1.25	4.07	2.00	2.73	6.50	9.75	4.25
Stock price – close ($)	0.8%	4.41	2.75	1.25	6.36	5.00	3.27	7.17	14.50	10.00	4.75
P/E – high	—	34	—	8	8	9	9	12	18	19	18
P/E – low	—	23	—	3	2	6	3	4	8	12	8
Dividends per share ($)	(100.0%)	0.04	0.04	0.04	0.04	5.35	0.00	0.00	0.00	0.00	0.00
Book value per share ($)	(4.7%)	5.19	4.46	4.91	4.07	(0.43)	0.26	1.06	1.96	2.81	3.37
Employees	(1.6%)	33,300	29,300	21,200	19,800	20,200	22,800	22,400	22,200	22,879	28,836

1994 Year-end:
Debt ratio: 65.5%
Return on equity: 18.2%
Cash (mil.): $173
Current ratio: 1.30
Long-term debt (mil.): $618
No. of shares (mil.): 100
Dividends
  Yield: —
  Payout: —
Market value (mil.): $474

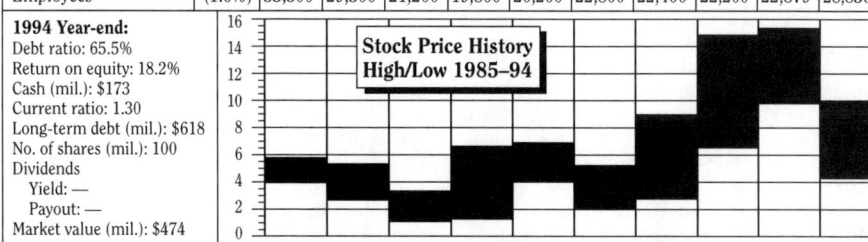

Stock Price History
High/Low 1985–94

THE SHERWIN-WILLIAMS COMPANY

OVERVIEW

Next time you paint the town red, you'll undoubtedly use a Sherwin-Williams shade; the company is North America's largest manufacturer of paints and varnishes, with 35% of the market. It also makes chemical and automotive coatings as well as equipment for applying paint. The company produces such top-selling brands as Dutch Boy, Kem-Tone, Martin Senour, and Sherwin-Williams. Its private-label paints include Sears's Weatherbeater brand and Kmart's store brand.

Sales from the company's 2,046 Paint Stores segment increased 8.5% in 1994. About 50 new stores are expected to open in 1995. Sherwin-Williams is continuing its "America's Paint Company" theme, despite an ill-timed 1994 advertising push centered on major-league baseball. The company is also promoting its Dutch Boy brand via a tie-in with the

NBA, Healthy Families America (a nonprofit group), and *USA Today*.

Management initiated a 5% price increase for the company's Coatings Segment in 1995 to offset the rising cost of raw materials as the building industry began bouncing back from the recession.

In 1995 Sherwin-Williams and American Business Computers introduced a computerized paint-tinting system designed for retail paint stores and chain stores. The new system uses either bar codes or color-matching equipment to custom tint small amounts of paint.

Also that year the company, which has based its growth partly on strong acquisitions, purchased Florida-based FLR Paints, a private maker of specialty stains and sealers, including the H&C, Runway Pavement Stain, and Shark Skin brands.

WHEN

In 1870 Henry Sherwin bought out paint materials distributor Truman Dunham and joined with Edward Williams and A.T. Osborn to form Sherwin, Williams & Company in Cleveland. The company began making paints in 1871, becoming the leader in its industry after it improved the paint-grinding mill in the mid-1870s, patented a reclosable can in 1877, and introduced an improved liquid paint in 1880. In 1884 the Sherwin-Williams Company incorporated.

In 1874 Sherwin-Williams introduced a special paint for carriages, beginning the concept of specific-purpose paint. (By 1900 the company had paints for floors, roofs, barns, metal bridges, railroad cars, and automobiles.) In 1891 a dealership opened in Massachusetts that was the forerunner of the company-run retail stores. In 1895 the company obtained its "Cover the Earth" trademark.

Before the Depression Sherwin-Williams acquired a number of smaller paint manufacturers: Detroit White Lead (1910), Martin-Senour (1917), Acme Quality Paints (1920), and The Lowe Brothers (1929). Responding to wartime restrictions, the company developed a new paint, fast drying and water reducible, called Kem-Tone, and the forerunner of the paint roller, the Roller-Koater.

Sales doubled during the 1960s as the company made acquisitions, including a chemical company and Sprayon (aerosol paint, 1966), but rising expenses kept earnings flat. In 1972 the company expanded its stores to include carpeting, draperies, and other decorating

items. But long-term debt ballooned from $80 million in 1974 to $196 million by 1977, when the company lost $8.2 million and suspended dividends for the first time since 1885.

Present CEO John Breen joined the company in 1979, reinstated the dividend, purged over half of the top management positions, and closed inefficient plants. He concentrated company stores' products on paint and wallpaper and purchased Dutch Boy (1980).

During 1990 Sherwin-Williams began selling Dutch Boy in Sears and Kem-Tone in Wal-Mart. Acquisitions that year included the Borden's Krylon and Illinois Bronze aerosol operations and DeSoto's architectural coatings segment, which made private-label paints for chains such as Sears and Home Depot. In 1991 Sherwin-Williams bought 2 coatings business units from Cook Paint and Varnish and the Cuprinol brand of coatings.

In 1993 the company settled a complaint by the State of California charging that the firm had failed to inform consumers that its products contained a birth defect–causing chemical. An EPA suit for alleged hazardous waste disposal violations, also filed in 1993, is pending.

Sherwin-Williams purchased the California-based Old Quaker Paint Company in 1994. The following year the company's home decorating program, *Room by Room*, began broadcasting on the Home and Garden cable TV network. Also that year golfer Chi Chi Rodriguez became a spokesman for Martin-Senour brand paints.

NYSE symbol: SHW
Fiscal year ends: December 31

WHO

Chairman and CEO: John G. Breen, age 60,
$1,383,888 pay
President and COO: Thomas A. Commes, age 52,
$912,038 pay
President and General Manager, Coatings Division:
F. E. Butler, age 59, $461,340 pay
President, Paint Stores Group: J. C. Macatee, age 43,
$447,845 pay
SVP Finance, Treasurer, and CFO: Larry J. Pitorak,
age 48, $430,024 pay
VP, General Counsel, and Secretary: Louis E. Stellato,
age 44
VP Corporate Planning and Development: Conway G.
Ivy, age 53
VP Administration: Robert E. Kinney, age 59
VP Human Resources: Thomas Kroeger, age 46
Auditors: Ernst & Young LLP

WHERE

HQ: 101 Prospect Ave. NW, Cleveland, OH 44115-1075
Phone: 216-566-2000
Fax: 216-566-3310

Sherwin-Williams operates 2,046 specialty paint stores
and 139 automotive branches in the US, Canada, and
Puerto Rico. In addition to 44 licensing agreements in
36 foreign countries, the company has subsidiaries in
Brazil, Canada, Curaçao, Grand Cayman, Jamaica,
Mexico, and the Virgin Islands.

WHAT

	1994 Sales		1994 Operating Income	
	$ mil.	% of total	$ mil.	% of total
Paint Stores	1,986	64	141	40
Coatings	1,100	35	201	58
Other	14	1	8	2
Adjustments	—	—	(51)	—
Total	**3,100**	**100**	**299**	**100**

Business Segments
Coatings Segment (manufactures, distributes, and sells
  paints and related products)
  Automotive Division (coatings for vehicles)
  Coatings Division (paint and paint-related products)
  Consumer Brands Division (sales and distribution to
    unaffiliated and independent distributors)
  Specialty Division (aerosol paints and paint
    applicators)
  Transportation Services Division (warehousing and
    distribution for the company and by contract)
Paint Stores Segment (retail stores selling Sherwin-
  Williams brand paints plus wallpaper, floor coverings,
  painting equipment, and other decorating products)

Selected Paint and Coating Brands

Acme	Illinois Bronze	Pro Mar
Color Works	Kem-Tone	Rubberset
Cuprinol	Kid's Room	Rust Tough
Dupli-Color	Krylon	Sherwin-Williams
Dutch Boy	Martin-Senour	Standox
EverClean	Old Quaker	SuperPaint
Glas-Clad	Perma-Clad	

KEY COMPETITORS

Ace Hardware	Home Depot	Morton
Akzo Nobel	Imperial Chemical	PPG
BASF	Kmart	Pratt & Lambert
Benjamin Moore	Loctite	Rhône-Poulenc
Dayton Hudson	Lowes	Valspar
DuPont	Montgomery	Wal-Mart
Hoechst	Ward	

HOW MUCH

	9-Year Growth	1985	1986	1987	1988	1989	1990	1991	1992	1993	1994
Sales ($ mil.)	3.9%	2,195	1,553	1,793	1,951	2,124	2,267	2,541	2,748	2,949	3,100
Net income ($ mil.)	10.7%	75	106	97	101	109	123	128	145	165	187
Income as % of sales	—	3.4%	6.8%	5.4%	5.2%	5.1%	5.4%	5.0%	5.3%	5.6%	6.0%
Earnings per share ($)	11.5%	0.81	1.16	1.08	1.15	1.26	1.41	1.45	1.63	1.85	2.15
Stock price – high ($)	—	11.75	16.13	19.25	15.81	17.88	21.06	27.75	32.88	37.50	35.75
Stock price – low ($)	—	6.97	10.66	10.06	12.00	12.50	15.06	17.63	25.38	29.88	29.50
Stock price – close ($)	13.1%	11.06	13.81	12.19	12.69	17.19	18.69	26.75	30.63	35.75	33.38
P/E – high	—	15	14	18	14	14	15	19	20	20	17
P/E – low	—	9	9	9	10	10	11	12	16	16	14
Dividends per share ($)	10.4%	0.23	0.25	0.28	0.32	0.35	0.38	0.42	0.44	0.50	0.56
Book value per share ($)	10.5%	5.05	5.58	6.29	6.99	7.74	8.80	9.90	10.17	11.67	12.42
Employees	(0.9%)	19,458	13,706	15,901	16,607	16,726	16,397	16,682	16,947	17,200	17,900

1994 Year-end:
Debt ratio: 1.9%
Return on equity: 17.9%
Cash (mil.): $251
Current ratio: 1.99
Long-term debt (mil.): $21
No. of shares (mil.): 85
Dividends
  Yield: 1.7%
  Payout: 26.0%
Market value (mil.): $2,831

Stock Price History
High/Low 1985–94

SILICON GRAPHICS, INC.

OVERVIEW

Silicon Graphics conquered Hollywood with the eye-popping special effects in *Forrest Gump* and *Jurassic Park*. Now the Mountain View, California–based maker of high-end graphics computers wants to conquer cyberspace as well; the company's WebFORCE line of workstations and servers and WebSpace 3-D graphics software targets designers creating visual content for the World Wide Web.

So far the company has been most visible as the leading manufacturer of 3-D graphics modeling and animation systems; 15% of the company's 1994 revenues came from users in the entertainment industry. In 1995 it moved to consolidate its position in Hollywood with the purchase of Alias Research, a Canadian developer of digital effects software (seen in

The Terminator), and California-based Wavefront Technologies, known for its 2-D and 3-D imaging and animation software (used in making *StarTrek Generations*). The merged Alias/Wavefront's software runs exclusively on Silicon Graphics's hardware.

In 1995 the company's MIPS Technologies subsidiary debuted Magic Carpet, its first multimedia chip set designed for games and other interactive consumer products. Silicon Graphics spends 12% of revenues on R&D.

A less visible but significant part of Silicon Graphics's revenues comes from more mundane businesses: the company is the leading seller of mid-range, high-performance computers and supercomputers, with installations at BMW, Texaco, and the University of Illinois.

WHEN

In 1981 Professor James Clark left Stanford University to develop and market 3-D computer graphics technology. In 1982 he formed Silicon Graphics, introducing the first 3-D terminal (IRIS 1000) and IRIS Graphics Library in 1983; he had chosen the name IRIS because it related to color and vision. In 1984 Clark developed the first 3-D workstation, which retailed for $75,000. Former Hewlett-Packard executive Edward McCracken joined Silicon Graphics as president in that year. By 1986 (the year it went public), Silicon Graphics led in its niche — making high-end 3-D workstations for technical and scientific markets. But McCracken knew the company would have to broaden its product line, offering lower-priced workstations, to compete with heavyweights such as Sun Microsystems.

In 1987 Silicon Graphics pioneered the use of RISC chips, developed by MIPS Computer Systems. That year the workstation market grew 63%. Although Silicon Graphics's sales doubled, its share of the workstation market was a tiny 4%. In 1988 the company released the Personal IRIS and the IRIS POWER series of workstations and supercomputers and raised $68.4 million for R&D by selling a 20% stake to Control Data (buying back most of it for $53.3 million in 1989). After hoarding its 3-D technology for 6 years, Silicon Graphics licensed IRIS Graphics Library to IBM in 1988, hoping to encourage developers to write software for Silicon Graphics machines.

In 1990 the company's share of the workstation market reached 5.4%. To develop its fast-growing Japanese market, Silicon Graphics formed an alliance with steel maker NKK

in 1990, under which NKK distributed Silicon Graphics's products in Japan in return for an ownership interest in the company.

In 1991 Silicon Graphics introduced the first RISC-based PC, the IRIS Indigo. It licensed IRIS General Library to Microsoft and joined Compaq in a product development agreement, selling the PC maker 13% of its convertible preferred stock for $135 million. That year the company joined Compaq and 29 other companies to form Advanced Computing Environment (ACE), a consortium to set workstation standards. In 1992 Compaq left ACE, its technology deal with Silicon Graphics fell apart, and Silicon Graphics repurchased Compaq's stake in SG for $150 million. That same year the company acquired MIPS.

In search of diversity and greater market penetration, in 1993 Silicon Graphics introduced smaller, less expensive ($10,000 and under) systems, including the Indy (a desktop system with a digital color video camera), the Onyx (an advanced graphics supercomputer), and the Indigo^2 (a workstation).

Unable to direct the future of the company he founded, in 1994 Jim Clark left to start Netscape with Marc Andreessen, originator of the Mosaic Web browser. That same year Silicon Graphics and AT&T agreed to codevelop an interactive communications system.

In 1995 Silicon Graphics and Dreamworks SKG teamed up to create a $50 million state-of-the-art digital animation studio that will accommodate 500 animators. The company also formed an alliance with Rocket Science Games to develop authoring tools for the next generation of computer games.

NYSE symbol: SGI
Fiscal year ends: June 30

WHO

Chairman and CEO: Edward R. McCracken, age 50, $1,256,375 pay
President and COO: Thomas A. Jermoluk, age 38, $911,169 pay
President, Alias/Wavefront: Robert K. Burgess, age 36
VP Marketing, Alias/Wavefront: Penny R. Wilson, age 36
Head of Research and Development, Alias/Wavefront: Martin Plaehn
President, MIPS Technologies: Tom Whiteside
President, Silicon Studio: Michael Ramsay
SVP Finance and CFO: Stanley J. Meresman, age 47
SVP Research and Development and Chief Technical Officer: Forest Baskett, age 51
VP Business Development, General Counsel, and Secretary: William M. Kelly
VP and Chief Information Officer: Michael Graves
VP Employee Relations: Leilani Gayles
Auditors: Ernst & Young LLP

WHERE

HQ: 2011 N. Shoreline Blvd., Mountain View, CA 94043-1389
Phone: 415-960-1980
Fax: 415-390-6220

Silicon Graphics has 63 offices in North America and 55 offices in 29 other countries.

	1994 Sales $ mil.	1994 Sales % of total	1994 Operating Income $ mil.	1994 Operating Income % of total
US	872	59	92	47
Europe	369	25	70	35
Pacific/Americas	241	16	35	18
Adjustments	—	—	(4)	—
Total	**1,482**	**100**	**193**	**100**

WHAT

	1994 Sales % of total
Products	89
Service	11
Total	**100**

Selected Products

Microprocessors
MIPS Magic Carpet (multimedia chip set)

Software
Alias/Wavefront
 ArcVision (architectural 3-D graphics)
 Alias AutoStudio (3-D design)
 Alias Eclipse (2-D digital photo imaging)
 Alias PowerAnimator (3-D animation)
 Alias Sketch! (3-D modeling/rendering)
 Alias StudioPaint (2-D sketching)

DesignVision (3-D design for engineering)
Explore (modeling and animation)
Silicon Graphics, Inc.
 Firewalker (graphical user interface)
 IndigoMagic (user environment)
 InPerson (network)
 IRIX (operating system)
 WebSpace (animation for Web pages)

Systems and Servers
Challenge   IRIS Indigo
Indigo²   Onyx
Indy   WebFORCE

KEY COMPETITORS

3DO
Apple
AT&T
Concurrent Computer
Cray Research
Data General
DEC
Fujitsu
Hewlett-Packard

Hitachi
IBM
Intel
Intergraph
Machines Bull
Microsoft
Motorola
National Semiconductor
NEC
NeXT
Novell

Olivetti
Oracle
Pixar
Siemens
Sun Microsystems
Tandem
Texas Instruments
Toshiba
Unisys
Wang

HOW MUCH

	Annual Growth	1985	1986	1987	1988	1989	1990	1991	1992	1993	1994
Sales ($ mil.)	60.0%	22	42	86	153	264	420	550	867	1,091	1,482
Net income ($ mil.)	—	(5)	2	6	12	12	32	33	(118)	88	141
Income as % of sales	—	—	4.6%	6.5%	8.0%	4.4%	7.7%	6.0%	—	8.0%	9.5%
Earnings per share ($)	—	(0.14)	0.05	0.12	0.22	0.17	0.40	0.37	(1.10)	0.60	0.91
Stock price – high ($)	—	—	3.56	6.88	6.13	7.31	10.22	12.19	14.88	24.75	33.13
Stock price – low ($)	—	—	3.00	2.81	3.44	3.56	4.50	5.56	7.06	11.75	18.75
Stock price – close ($)	32.7%	—	3.25	4.06	4.69	7.31	6.75	11.31	14.31	24.75	31.16
P/E – high	—	—	71	57	28	43	26	33	—	41	36
P/E – low	—	—	60	23	16	21	11	15	—	20	21
Dividends per share ($)	—	—	0.00	0.00	0.00	0.00	0.00	0.00	0.00	0.00	0.00
Book value per share ($)	—	—	(1.03)	1.06	2.24	2.45	3.01	3.97	3.61	4.56	6.37
Employees	38.0%	—	331	605	1,055	1,483	2,099	2,500	3,575	3,750	4,357

1994 Year-end:
Debt ratio: 21.3%
Return on equity: 18.3%
Cash (mil.): $401
Current ratio: 2.88
Long-term debt (mil.): $230
No. of shares (mil.): 139
Dividends
  Yield: —
  Payout: —
Market value (mil.): $4,337

Stock Price History High/Low 1986–94

SMITHSONIAN INSTITUTION

OVERVIEW

The Smithsonian Institution is having some problems, but if you were 150 years old, you'd probably be falling apart and suffering from addled judgment, too. Celebrating its sesquicentennial in 1996, the Washington, DC–based treasury of US artifacts needs $500 million in repairs over the next 10 years.

The timing couldn't be worse for the Smithsonian, a nonprofit organization that gets about half of its funding from the federal government. Congress is in a budget cutting mood, and the institution outraged many Americans by planning an atomic bomb exhibit that was seen as historically dubious.

Known as "the nation's attic" for the 140 million items housed in its many facilities, the Smithsonian is the world's largest museum. Among its pieces are the flag that inspired Francis Scott Key to write *The Star-Spangled Banner* and the chair used by Archie Bunker on TV's *All in the Family*. The Smithsonian also stores fossils and paintings, conducts research worldwide, and runs the National Zoo.

The Smithsonian Institution is headed by a Board of Regents that includes the vice-president of the US, the chief justice of the Supreme Court, 3 senators, 3 US representatives, and 8 private citizens.

WHEN

In 1826 James Smithson, an English chemist, wrote a proviso to his will that would lead to the creation of the Smithsonian Institution. When Smithson died in 1829, his will bequeathed his estate to his nephew, Henry James Hungerford, with the stipulation that if Hungerford died without heirs, the estate would go to the US to create "an Establishment for the increase and diffusion of knowledge among men." When Hungerford died in 1835 without any heirs, the US government inherited more than $500,000 in gold.

Although the 105 bags of gold coins didn't arrive in the US until 1838, Congress still hadn't decided exactly what to do with them. While they were deciding they invested most of the money in State of Arkansas bonds. When Arkansas defaulted, Congress, perhaps feeling pangs of guilt for having lost the "increase of knowledge" endowment, made an appropriation to cover the loss.

In 1846 Congress finally created the institution and named Princeton physicist Joseph Henry as its first secretary. That same year the Smithsonian established the Museum of Natural History, the Museum of History and Technology, and the National Gallery of Art. In 1855 the Smithsonian's first building, a red stone, medieval-style castle designed by Thomas Renwick, was completed.

In 1858 the collection of the US Patent Office was turned over to the Smithsonian, and Stephen Baird, who succeeded Henry in 1878, developed the National Museum around the Patent Office's collection. The Smithsonian continued to expand, adding the National Zoological Park in 1889 and the Smithsonian Astrophysical Observatory in 1890.

The Freer Gallery, a gift of industrialist Charles Freer, opened in 1923. In 1937 the National Gallery was renamed the National Collection of Fine Arts. A new National Gallery, created with Andrew Mellon's gift of his art collection and a building, opened in 1941. In 1946 the Air and Space Museum was established, and the Smithsonian began directing the Tropical Research Bureau in Panama.

More museums were added in the 1960s, including the National Portrait Gallery (1962) and the Anacostia Museum (exhibits and materials on African-American history, 1967). The Kennedy Center for the Performing Arts was opened in 1971. In 1980 the Collection of Fine Arts was renamed the National Museum of American Art, and the Museum of History and Technology was renamed the National Museum of American History.

In 1992 a scandal erupted when the institution paid $351,000 in legal fees for a zoologist who was charged with helping hunters stalk endangered species. The Smithsonian placed its first-ever contribution boxes in 4 of its museums in 1993.

A planned exhibit featuring the *Enola Gay* — the plane that dropped the atomic bomb on Hiroshima — created a firestorm for the Smithsonian in 1994. Critics charged that the exhibit rewrote history by downplaying Japanese aggression and US casualties in WWII. In 1995 the original exhibit was cancelled, the director of the Air and Space Museum resigned, and a scaled-down version of the exhibit opened without the controversial historical context.

The Smithsonian received its 2 largest cash donations ever in 1994 and 1995. The Mashantucket Pequot tribe gave $10 million from its casino operations for a planned American Indian museum, and prolific electronics inventor Jerome Lemelson donated $10.4 million.

Nonprofit organization
Fiscal year ends: September 30

WHO

Secretary: I. Michael Heyman
Under Secretary: Constance B. Newman
Assistant Secretary for Institutional Initiatives: Alice G. Burnette
Assistant Secretary for Education and Public Service: James C. Early
Assistant Secretary for the Arts and Humanities: Tom L. Freudenheim
Assistant Secretary for the Sciences: Robert S. Hoffmann
Assistant Secretary for Environmental and External Affairs: Thomas E. Lovejoy
Assistant Secretary for Finance and Administration and CFO: Nancy D. Suttenfield
Director, Office of Government Relations: Mark W. Rodgers
Acting Director, Office of Public Affairs: Linda St. Thomas
Acting Director, Office of Human Resources: Susan G. Roehmer
General Counsel: Peter C. Powers
Auditors: KPMG Peat Marwick LLP

WHERE

HQ: 1000 Jefferson Dr. SW, Washington, DC 20560
Phone: 202-357-2700
Fax: 202-786-2515

The Smithsonian Institution runs museums, publishing operations, and a zoo in the US and oversees research projects around the world. Most of the Smithsonian's holdings are in Washington, DC.

WHAT

	1994 Revenues	
	$ mil.	% of total
Appropriations	302	50
Sales & membership revenue	198	33
Government grants & contracts	46	8
Gifts & nongovernment grants	32	5
Investment income	18	3
Other	9	1
Total	**605**	**100**

Selected Organizations

Arts and Humanities
Anacostia Museum
Archives of American Art
Arthur M. Sackler Gallery
Cooper-Hewitt, National Design Museum
Freer Gallery of Art
Hirshhorn Museum and Sculpture Garden
International Gallery
National Air and Space Museum
National Museum of African Art
National Museum of American Art
National Museum of American History
National Museum of the American Indian
National Portrait Gallery

Education and Public Service
Center for Folklife Programs and Cultural Studies
Natural Science Resources Center

Environmental and External Affairs
Air & Space/Smithsonian magazine
Smithsonian magazine

Sciences
National Museum of Natural History
National Zoological Park
Smithsonian Astrophysical Observatory
Smithsonian Environmental Research Center

Independently Governed Affiliates

John F. Kennedy Center for the Performing Arts
National Gallery of Art
Woodrow Wilson International Center for Scholars

HOW MUCH

	9-Year Growth	1985	1986	1987	1988	1989	1990	1991	1992	1993	1994
Revenues ($ mil.)	3.9%	430	443	501	506	578	595	656	714	729	605
Assets ($ mil.)[1]	7.4%	595	644	732	777	838	887	941	1,030	1,077	1,130
Appropriations ($ mil.)	5.2%	191	191	211	230	246	267	326	332	344	302
Employees	(0.4%)	6,900	6,800	7,100	—	6,000	6,300	6,700	6,800	6,800	6,671

1994 Year-end:
Debt ratio: 0.3%
Return on trust fund: 3.1%
Cash (mil.): $2
Long-term debt (mil.): $3

SMITHSONIAN INSTITUTION

Revenues ($ mil.) 1985–94

[1]Not including collections

THE SOUTHERN COMPANY

OVERVIEW

Based in Atlanta, the Southern Company is a holding company for a group of utilities providing service to more than 3.5 million customers in 4 southeastern states. Southern provides electricity through 5 operating companies: Alabama Power Company, Georgia Power Company, Gulf Power Company, Mississippi Power Company, and Savannah Electric and Power Company.

Southern Electric Generating Company (SEGCO), a subsidiary of Alabama Power and Georgia Power, operates generating plants on Alabama's Coosa River, with its 2 parents each entitled to half of the power SEGCO generates. Southern Company subsidiary Southern Elec-

tric International designs, builds, and runs cogeneration power plants and provides power for the independent power market both in the US and abroad.

The company is also broadening its reach beyond power systems. Its Southern Communication Services subsidary will provide wireless communications services to company subsidiaries and also plans to begin marketing its services to businesses.

With deregulation opening up the electric power industry to more competition, Southern is focusing on cutting costs and improving efficiency, and it continues to aggressively seek overseas power projects.

WHEN

Steamboat captain W. P. Lay founded the Alabama Power Company in 1906 to develop electric power on the Coosa River. James Mitchell took over the company in 1912, moving its headquarters from Montgomery to Birmingham. From 1912 until his death in 1920, he bought a number of Alabama's utilities, consolidating them with Alabama Power under his Canadian holding company Alabama Traction Light & Power (ATL&P).

Tom Martin, Alabama Power's legal counsel, became president in 1920 and reorganized ATL&P into Southeastern Power & Light. Southeastern formed Mississippi Power Company to take over electric utilities in Mississippi (1924) and Gulf Power Company to do the same in northern Florida (1925). In 1926 Southeastern bought several Georgia utilities, which were consolidated as Georgia Power Company in 1927.

In 1929 B. C. Cobb acquired Southeastern, combining its assets with those of Penn–Ohio Edison to form Commonwealth & Southern Corporation, a New York holding company that owned about 165 utilities. Martin served as president of Commonwealth & Southern until 1933 and was replaced by Wendell Willkie (the Republican nominee for president in 1940).

In 1942 Commonwealth & Southern was dissolved by the SEC. Four of its southern holdings (Alabama Power, Georgia Power, Gulf Power, and Mississippi Power) were placed under the authority of the Southern Company (a new holding company) in 1949.

During the energy shortages of the 1970s, both Alabama Power and Georgia Power faced an anti-utility political environment, led by Alabama's governor, George Wallace. In late

1974 and early 1975, Georgia Power approached bankruptcy. Alabama Power suspended its $700 million construction program and laid off 4,000 employees in 1978. Wallace left office that year, and state regulators allowed much-needed rate relief, ushering in a period of moderate growth for the Southern Company as a whole. In 1988 Southern added Savannah Electric and Power to its system.

In 1990 Georgia Power took a $218 million charge, which contributed to Southern's 28.6% drop in earnings for that year. The charge was related to a Georgia Supreme Court decision preventing the company from passing on to its customers certain costs related to the construction of the Vogtle nuclear plant (on-line since 1989). Also in 1990 Georgia Power agreed to sell unit 4 of its Scherer plant to Florida Power and Light and Jacksonville Electric Authority for $805 million. In 1992 it bought 50% of Freeport Power Co., a Bahamian electric utility.

In 1994 Southern Electric International began construction of a 220-megawatt coal-fired power plant in Virginia. That same year Southern Electric received a permit to construct a power plant in Mexico, paid $350 million for a 105-megawatt energy and chemical recovery complex in Mobile, Alabama, and, in partnership with an Amoco subsidiary, paid over $100 million for a 49% stake in 3 power plants in Trinidad and Tobago.

In 1995 Southern was ordered to pay $2 million in legal fees related to a defamation and breach of contract suit by a former executive who earlier had won $2.7 million in compensatory damages. Also that year, British utility South Western Electricity agreed to be bought by Southern for $1.7 billion.

NYSE symbol: SO
Fiscal year ends: December 31

WHO

Chairman, President, and CEO: A. W. Dahlberg, age 54, $720,441 pay
EVP; President and CEO, Alabama Power: Elmer B. Harris, age 55, $532,991 pay
EVP; President and CEO, Georgia Power: H. Allen Franklin, age 50, $503,717 pay
EVP; President and CEO, Southern Company Services: Paul J. DeNicola, age 46, $435,912 pay
VP Finance and CFO: W. L. Westbrook, age 55
VP Human Resources: Alan Martin, age 46
Auditors: Arthur Andersen & Co, SC

WHERE

HQ: 64 Perimeter Center East, Atlanta, GA 30346
Phone: 404-393-0650
Fax: 404-668-3559

The Southern Company operates in Alabama, Florida, Georgia, and Mississippi.

Selected Generating Facilities

Alabama Power Co.
Barry (fossil fueled)
Bouldin (hydroelectric)
Farley (nuclear)
Gorgas (fossil fueled)
Jordan (hydroelectric)
Lay (hydroelectric)
Miller (fossil fueled)
Mitchell (hydroelectric)

Georgia Power Co.
Bowen (fossil fueled)
Branch (fossil fueled)
Hatch (nuclear, 50.1%)
Tallulah Falls (hydroelectric)
Vogtle (nuclear, 45.7%)
Wallace Dam (hydroelectric)

Wansley (53.5%, fossil fueled)
Yates (fossil fueled)

Gulf Power Co.
Crist (fossil fueled)
Daniel (fossil fueled, 50%)

Mississippi Power Co.
Daniel (fossil fueled, 50%)
Watson (fossil fueled)

Savannah Electric and Power Co.
Boulevard (fossil fueled)
McIntosh Units 5&6 (fossil fueled)

WHAT

	1994 Sales	
	$ mil.	% of total
Electricity		
Residential	2,560	31
Commercial	2,357	29
Industrial	2,162	26
Sales for resale	360	4
Nonterritorial & other	575	7
Other	283	3
Total	**8,297**	**100**

	1994 Energy Sources
	% of total
Coal	71
Nuclear	18
Hydroelectric	5
Oil & gas	1
Purchased power	5
Total	**100**

System Companies
Alabama Power Co.
Georgia Power Co.
Gulf Power Co.
Mississippi Power Co.
Savannah Electric and Power Co.
Southern Electric Generating Co.
Southern Nuclear Operating Co., Inc.

Engineering and Technical Services
Southern Company Services, Inc.
Southern Electric International, Inc.

Other
Hidroeléctrica Alicurá, S.A. (55%, Argentina)
Southern Communications Services Project (mobile communications)

KEY COMPETITORS

AES
AT&T
Bechtel
Duke Power
FPL

General Electric
NIPSCO
Pacific Enterprises
Pacific Gas and Electric

Peter Kiewit Sons'
SCEcorp
Westinghouse

HOW MUCH

	9-Year Growth	1985	1986	1987	1988	1989	1990	1991	1992	1993	1994
Sales ($ mil.)	2.2%	6,814	6,847	7,010	7,235	7,492	7,975	8,050	8,073	8,489	8,297
Net income ($ mil.)	2.0%	830	883	554	846	846	604	876	953	1,002	989
Income as % of sales	—	12.2%	12.9%	7.9%	11.7%	11.3%	7.6%	10.9%	11.8%	11.8%	11.9%
Earnings per share ($)	(0.6%)	1.60	1.59	0.96	1.36	1.34	0.96	1.39	1.51	1.57	1.52
Stock price – high ($)	—	11.63	13.63	14.50	12.13	14.88	14.69	17.38	19.56	23.63	22.06
Stock price – low ($)	—	8.94	10.19	8.94	10.19	11.00	11.50	12.88	15.19	18.44	17.00
Stock price – close ($)	6.7%	11.13	12.69	11.19	11.19	14.56	13.94	17.19	19.25	22.06	20.00
P/E – high	—	7	9	15	9	11	15	13	13	15	15
P/E – low	—	6	6	9	8	8	12	9	10	12	11
Dividends per share ($)	2.1%	0.98	1.04	1.07	1.07	1.07	1.07	1.07	1.10	1.14	1.18
Book value per share ($)	2.6%	9.92	10.55	12.26	10.61	10.87	10.74	11.05	11.05	12.06	12.47
Employees	(1.7%)	32,354	32,358	32,612	32,523	30,530	30,263	30,402	29,085	28,743	27,826

1994 Year-end:
Debt ratio: 47.6%
Return on equity: 12.5%
Cash (mil.): $139
Current ratio: 0.85
Long-term debt (mil.): $7,593
No. of shares (mil.): 657
Dividends
  Yield: 5.9%
  Payout: 77.6%
Market value (mil.): $13,131

Stock Price History
High/Low 1985–94

SOUTHERN PACIFIC RAIL CORPORATION

OVERVIEW

Southern Pacific Rail Corporation (SP), the 6th largest US freight rail company, has 5 main routes, with about 14,500 miles of primary track, through 15 states in the West and Southwest. The San Francisco–based company's main subsidiaries are the Denver and Rio Grande Western Railroad (D&RGW) and Southern Pacific Transportation Company (SPT). In August 1995 chairman Philip Anschutz agreed to sell the railroad to Union Pacific, which would create the biggest railroad in the US. The $3.9 billion deal is subject to ICC approval.

The corporation is the leading carrier of intermodal (truck-to-train and truck- or train-to-ship) freight in the US. Its intermodal business continues to grow, and its international container yard in Southern California is the US's largest. SPT also serves 6 US cities on the Mexican border, the most of any US railroad.

Railway industry veteran Jerry Davis replaced retiring Ed Moyers as CEO and president in early 1995. Davis has his work cut out for him; the railroad needs to slash its costs. Toward this end SP has added more-efficient locomotives and reconditioned others (about 500 in 1994 and 1995) and thinned employee ranks (by nearly 5,000 in 1993 and 1994).

In 1995 Southern Pacific agreed not to challenge the merger of the Burlington Northern and Santa Fe Pacific railroads. The agreement followed negotiation between Burlington Northern and Southern Pacific on a package of track rights and hauling service privileges for SP on Burlington Northern track.

Southern Pacific went public in 1993 after 5 years of control by RGI, a holding company owned by Denver billionaire Anschutz. Anschutz owns about 32% of the recapitalized company.

WHEN

Southern Pacific dates back to 1861, when 4 Sacramento merchants founded the Central Pacific Railroad. Construction began in Sacramento in 1863. In 1869 Central Pacific reached Promontory, Utah, where its rails were spiked to those of the Union Pacific (which had built westward from Omaha), thus completing the first transcontinental railway.

By building new track and buying other railroads, including the Southern Pacific (1868), a San Francisco–to–San Jose line founded in 1865, the Central Pacific expanded throughout California, Texas, and Oregon by 1887. The 2 railroads officially merged in 1885 under a holding company called Southern Pacific Company.

Union Pacific bought control of Southern Pacific in 1901 but, on antitrust grounds, was ordered by the Supreme Court to sell its stake in 1913. In 1932 Southern Pacific bought control of the St. Louis Southwestern Railway, gaining an entrance to St. Louis.

Facing competition from behemoths Union Pacific and Burlington Northern, Southern Pacific merged with competitor Atchison, Topeka & Santa Fe Railway in 1983 to form Santa Fe Southern Pacific Corporation. In 1987 the ICC deemed the merger anticompetitive. In 1988 Santa Fe Southern Pacific sold Southern Pacific to RGI — the Rio Grande railroad's holding company controlled by the Anschutz Corporation (owned by Denver billionaire Philip Anschutz) for $1 billion

in mostly borrowed money. A public stock offering in 1993 raised cash to reduce RGI's debt.

The Rio Grande was founded as the Denver and Rio Grande in 1871 by General William Jackson Palmer to build a line from Denver to Mexico City. The company entered Salt Lake City in 1882, but an attempt to build on to San Francisco resulted in bankruptcy. Renamed the Denver and Rio Grande Western, the railroad emerged from receivership in 1924. In 1934 it finally placed Denver on a transcontinental main line.

The combined Southern Pacific and Rio Grande improved Chicago's transportation access in 1989, when SPCSL Corporation (an RGI subsidiary) bought 282 track miles between East St. Louis and Chicago from the trustees of bankrupt Chicago, Missouri & Western Railway.

In 1991 a SP train derailed in California, spilling weed killer into the Sacramento River. In 1993 most of the spill-related lawsuits were brought in a class action, and most claims from that suit were settled at a cost of about $14 million. Also in 1993 the rail union agreed to stabilize wages through 1997 to assist in restoring the railroad for the long term.

In 1994 intermodal traffic revenue grew by 16.4% and total earnings set a record. Revenues for 1995 will be seriously affected by the heavy rains, flooding, and mud slides in California, which have damaged track and forced major rerouting of many SP trains.

WHO

Chairman: Philip F. Anschutz, age 55
VC; VC, SPT and D&RGW: Robert F. Starzel, age 54, $345,000 pay
President and CEO; Chairman, President, and CEO, SPT and D&RGW: Jerry R. Davis, age 56
President, SPT and D&RGW: Donald C. Orris, age 53, $345,000 pay
EVP Finance and Law and General Counsel; EVP Finance and Law and General Counsel, SPT and D&RGW: Cannon Y. Harvey, age 54
EVP Operations and Distribution Services: L. R. Parsons
SVP Administration; SVP Administration, SPT and D&RGW: Thomas J. Matthews, age 54, $345,000 pay
VP Finance; VP Finance, SPT and D&RGW: Lawrence C. Yarberry, age 52
Secretary; Secretary, SPT and D&RGW: Thomas F. O'Donnell, age 52
Treasurer; Treasurer, SPT and D&RGW: Lynn K. Ducken, age 51
VP Human Resources: Judy Holm
Auditors: KPMG Peat Marwick LLP

WHERE

HQ: Southern Pacific Bldg., One Market Plaza, San Francisco, CA 94105
Phone: 415-541-1000
Fax: 415-541-1256

Southern Pacific and its subsidiaries operate more than 14,500 route miles of track in 15 states.

WHAT

	1994 Sales	
	$ mil.	% of total
Railroad	3,056	97
Other	87	3
Total	**3,143**	**100**

Principal Subsidiaries
Denver and Rio Grande Western Railroad Co. (D&RGW)
Southern Pacific Transportation Co. (SPT)

	1994 Gross Freight Revenues	
Items transported	$ mil.	% of total
Intermodal	852	26
Chemical & petroleum products	615	19
Forest products	432	13
Food & agricultural products	415	13
Coal	299	9
Metals & ores	275	9
Automotive	189	6
Construction materials & minerals	172	5
Total	**3,249**	**100**

KEY COMPETITORS

American Freightways
American President
Arkansas Best
Burlington Northern
Conrail
Consolidated Freightways
Crowley Maritime
CSX
J. B. Hunt
Leaseway Transportation
Norfolk Southern
Roadway
Schneider National
UPS
Yellow Corp.

HOW MUCH

	Annual Growth	1985	1986	1987	1988	1989	1990	1991	1992	1993	1994
Sales ($ mil.)	3.1%	—	—	—	—	2,702	2,822	2,786	2,878	2,919	3,143
Net income ($ mil.)	115.0%	—	—	—	—	5	(34)	(185)	24	(51)	248
Income as % of sales	—	—	—	—	—	0.2%	—	—	0.8%	—	7.9%
Earnings per share ($)	100.7%	—	—	—	—	0.05	(0.34)	(1.85)	0.24	(0.46)	1.63
Stock price – high ($)	—	—	—	—	—	—	—	—	—	21.38	24.38
Stock price – low ($)	—	—	—	—	—	—	—	—	—	14.25	16.63
Stock price – close ($)	(8.2%)	—	—	—	—	—	—	—	—	19.75	18.13
P/E – high	—	—	—	—	—	—	—	—	—	—	15
P/E – low	—	—	—	—	—	—	—	—	—	—	10
Dividends per share ($)	—	—	—	—	—	—	—	—	—	0.00	0.00
Book value per share ($)	184.3%	—	—	—	—	—	—	—	—	2.39	6.79
Employees	(6.2%)	—	—	—	—	24,775	23,814	23,396	22,793	18,982	18,010

1994 Year-end:
Debt ratio: 52.1%
Return on equity: 36.1%
Cash (mil.): $241
Current ratio: 0.66
Long-term debt (mil.): $1,089
No. of shares (mil.): 156
Dividends
  Yield: —
  Payout: —
Market value (mil.): $2,824

**Stock Price History
High/Low 1993–94**

THE SOUTHLAND CORPORATION

OVERVIEW

Seller of Slurpees, Big Gulps, and more lottery tickets than any other US retailer, Dallas-based Southland Corporation owns 7-Eleven, the #1 convenience store chain in the world. Even with hundreds of store closings in recent years, the company still operates or franchises more than 5,600 US and Canadian stores under the 7-Eleven banner and other names. Through a licensing agreement, Seven-Eleven Japan runs more than 5,800 7-Elevens, while licensees in the US and 19 other countries operate more than 3,200 stores.

In 1994 the company saw its first increase in same-store merchandise sales since 1988.

That may be a sign that 7-Eleven's efforts to rejuvenate its stores are paying off. The chain's stores now offer fresh baked goods, dairy products, and fruits and vegetables in an attempt to snag working customers who want healthy basics for their families at reasonable prices but don't have time to spend at the supermarket. The company has also been improving the lighting inside and outside its stores and has been installing new security systems. New store openings are expected to exceed closings by 1997.

Japanese retailer Ito-Yokado owns 64% of Southland's stock.

WHEN

Claude Dawley, son of an ice company pioneer, formed the Southland Ice Company in Dallas in 1927 to buy 4 other Texas ice plant operations. Ice was both a rare commodity and a basic necessity during Texas summers for storing and transporting food and, especially, beer. Dawley was backed in his bid by Chicago utility magnate Martin Insull.

One of the ice operations Dawley bought was Consumers Ice, where a young employee, Joe Thompson, had made the firm some money with his idea of selling chilled watermelons off the truck docks.

After the Dawley enterprise was underway, an ice dock manager in Dallas began stocking a few food items for customers. He demonstrated the idea to Thompson, who was by then running the ice operation, and the practice was adopted at all company locations.

Thompson promoted the grocery operations by calling them Tote'm Stores and erecting Alaska-made totem poles by the docks. In 1928 he arranged for the construction of gas stations at some stores.

Insull bought out Dawley in 1930, and Thompson became president. He expanded Southland's operations even as the Depression-hurt company operated briefly under the direction of bankruptcy court (1932–34). It began a dairy, Oak Farms, to meet its needs as the largest dairy retailer in the Dallas–Fort Worth area (1936). By 1946 the company had bought other Texas ice-retail operations, changed its name to the Southland Corporation, and adopted for its stores the name 7-Eleven, a reference to its store hours.

After Thompson died in 1961, his eldest son, John, became president and opened new stores in Colorado, New Jersey, and Arizona in 1962 and in Utah, California, and Missouri in

1963. The company purchased Gristede Brothers (1968), a New York grocer; Baricini Stores (1969), a candy chain; and Hudgins Truck Rental (1971; sold in 1980).

Southland franchised the 7-Eleven format in the UK (1971) and in Japan (1973). In 1983 the company purchased Citgo, a gasoline refining and marketing business, later selling 50% of the company to Petróleos de Venezuela, a Venezuelan oil company (1986).

In 1988 John Thompson and his 2 brothers borrowed heavily to buy 70% of Southland's stock in an LBO. The company defaulted on $1.8 billion in publicly traded debt in mid-1990. Southland filed for bankruptcy protection that year; the company persuaded bondholders to restructure its debt and take 25% of the company stock, clearing the way for the purchase of 70% of Southland in 1991 by its Japanese partner, Ito-Yokado.

In 1992 the company contracted with Wal-Mart's McLane subsidiary to provide wholesale distribution services to its stores and sold to McLane 2 distribution centers and 3 food processing plants. From 1991 through 1993 the company closed about 600 underperforming 7-Elevens. In 1993 Southland realized its first annual profit since 1986.

In 1994 Southland broke off relations with the National Coalition of Associations of 7-Elevens, a franchisee group. That year, 9 7-Eleven franchisees sued the company for more than $1 billion on charges of fraud and breach of contract, claiming that Southland had not spent enough money on store maintenance and remodeling, advertising, and other services.

Southland opened 18 stores and closed 184 in 1994; the company planned to close another 150 stores in 1995.

Nasdaq symbol: SLCMC
Fiscal year ends: December 31

WHO

Chairman: Masatoshi Ito, age 70
VC: Toshifumi Suzuki, age 62
President and CEO: Clark J. Matthews II, age 58, $567,840 pay
EVP and COO: Stephen B. Krumholz, age 45, $383,980 pay
SVP Distribution and Foodservice: Rodney A. Brehm, age 47, $259,280 pay
SVP Finance: James W. Keyes, age 39
VP and Controller: Vernon P. Lotman, age 55
VP and General Counsel: Bryan F. Smith Jr., age 42
VP Human Resources: David M. Finley, age 54
Auditors: Coopers & Lybrand L.L.P.

WHERE

HQ: 2711 N. Haskell Ave., PO Box 711, Dallas, TX 75221-0711
Phone: 214-828-7011
Fax: 214-822-7848

	1994 Owned/Franchised Stores	
	No.	% of total
California	1,196	21
Virginia	639	11
Florida	447	8
Maryland	346	6
Texas	308	5
Washington	253	5
Colorado	244	4
New York	222	4
New Jersey	203	4
Nevada	187	3
Pennsylvania	174	3
Illinois	151	3
Oregon	137	3
Other states	662	12
Canada	461	8
Total	**5,630**	**100**

WHAT

	1994 Stores – US and Canada	
	No.	% of total
Franchised	2,962	53
Company-operated	2,668	47
Total	**5,630**	**100**

	1994 Stores – US and Canada	
	No.	% of total
7-Eleven	5,541	98
Quik Mart/Super-7	51	1
High's Dairy Stores	38	1
Total	**5,630**	**100**

	1994 Sales
	% of total
Gasoline	24
Tobacco products	17
Groceries	10
Beer/wine	9
Soft drinks	9
Food service	8
Nonfoods	6
Dairy products	5
Baked goods	4
Candy	4
Customer services	2
Health/beauty aids	2
Total	**100**

KEY COMPETITORS

Albertson's	Exxon	Safeway
American Stores	Kroger	Shell Oil
Atlantic Richfield	Mobil	Sun Co.
British Petroleum	National	Texaco
Chevron	Convenience	Thrifty Oil
Circle K	Publix	Unocal
Cumberland	QuikTrip	Wal-Mart
Farms	Racetrac	Wawa
Dairy Mart	Petroleum	Winn-Dixie

HOW MUCH

	Annual Growth	1985	1986	1987	1988	1989	1990	1991	1992	1993	1994
Sales ($ mil.)	(2.7%)	—	7,783	8,076	7,950	8,275	8,348	8,010	7,426	6,814	6,760
Net income ($ mil.)	(9.3%)	—	200	(60)	(216)	(1,251)	(302)	(74)	(131)	99	92
Income as % of sales	—	—	2.6%	—	—	—	—	—	—	1.3%	1.4%
Earnings per share ($)	—	—	—	—	—	—	—	(0.22)	(0.32)	0.21	0.22
Stock price – high ($)	—	—	—	—	—	—	—	3.03	4.25	7.69	6.75
Stock price – low ($)	—	—	—	—	—	—	—	0.94	1.19	2.97	3.81
Stock price – close ($)	33.8%	—	—	—	—	—	—	1.88	3.03	6.75	4.50
P/E – high	—	—	—	—	—	—	—	—	—	37	31
P/E – low	—	—	—	—	—	—	—	—	—	14	17
Dividends per share ($)	—	—	—	—	—	—	—	0.00	0.00	0.00	0.00
Book value per share ($)	—	—	—	—	—	—	—	(2.95)	(3.22)	(3.05)	(2.82)
Employees	(9.4%)	—	67,174	65,800	50,724	48,114	45,665	42,616	35,646	32,406	30,417

1994 Year-end:
Debt ratio: 100.0%
Return on equity: —
Cash (mil.): $59
Current ratio: 0.44
Long-term debt (mil.): $2,227
No. of shares (mil.): 410
Dividends
  Yield: —
  Payout: —
Market value (mil.): $1,845

Stock Price History
High/Low 1991–94

SOUTHWEST AIRLINES CO.

OVERVIEW

For several years Southwest Airlines's successful low-cost, on-time, no-frills, no-allocated seats, no-meals approach to air travel has helped the company fly high above its competitors with hefty profit gains. In contrast with the industry as a whole, which has lost billions of dollars, Southwest's lean, mean flying machine has carved out 22 consecutive years of profits and has risen to become the #8 US airline.

However, its days of flying solo may be over. USAir, Continental, United, and Delta are muscling into the low-frills, short-haul market. In particular, United's shuttle service in the West (introduced in October 1994) is taking a bite out of the company's profits. Starting with 184, United increased its daily flights to 304 by the end of the year. Continen-

tal gave over about half of its 2,000 flights to low-fare, short-haul operations (but recently made plans to pull out of its "Continental Lite" strategy, which had cost the carrier millions of dollars and led to the exit of its CEO). Competitors have also resorted to electronic warfare. Citing Southwest's refusal to pay for service, 3 airline reservation systems partially owned by rivals bumped Southwest off their computer systems, making it more difficult for travel agents to write tickets for Southwest.

The company, which operates a fleet of 199 Boeing 737s, acquired Morris Air in 1994. The Salt Lake City–based carrier (also a Boeing 737 operator) had a strong route system in the Pacific Northwest. The acquisition gave the company more planes to counter the United shuttle incursion in the West.

WHEN

Texas businessman Rollin King and lawyer Herb Kelleher founded Air Southwest Company in 1967 as an intrastate airline, linking Dallas, Houston, and San Antonio. Braniff and Texas International sued the company, questioning whether the region needed another airline, but the Texas Supreme Court ruled in Southwest's favor. In 1971 the company (renamed Southwest Airlines) made its first scheduled flight, from Dallas Love Field to San Antonio.

Capitalizing on its home base at Love Field, Southwest adopted love as the theme of its early ad campaigns, complete with stewardesses wearing hot pants and serving love potions (drinks) and love bites (peanuts). To curb maintenance costs, the airline uses only fuel-efficient Boeing 737s. When other airlines moved to the Dallas–Fort Worth (D/FW) airport in 1974, Southwest stayed at Love Field, gaining a virtual monopoly at the airfield. This monopoly proved to be limiting, however, with adoption of the Wright Amendment in 1979. This federal law prevents airlines operating out of Love Field from providing direct service to states other than those neighboring Texas. Southwest's customers can fly from Love Field to New Mexico, Oklahoma, Arkansas, and Louisiana but must buy new tickets and board different Southwest flights to points beyond.

When Lamar Muse, Southwest's president, resigned in 1978 because of differences with King, Kelleher became president. Muse later took over his son Michael's nearly bankrupt airline, Muse Air Corporation, and in 1985 sold it to Southwest. Kelleher operated the

Houston-based airline as TranStar but liquidated it in 1987.

Regarded as something of an industry maverick, Kelleher went on to introduce advance-purchase "Fun Fares" in 1986 and a frequent-flyer program based on the number of flights rather than mileage in 1987. He often stars in Southwest's unconventional TV commercials, and, when Southwest became the official airline of Sea World (Texas) in 1988, Kelleher had a 737 painted to resemble Shamu, the park's killer whale.

Southwest established an operating base at Phoenix Sky Harbor Airport in 1990. The airline continues to add destinations, especially on the West Coast, with service to Oakland and Indianapolis (1989), Burbank and Reno (1990), Sacramento (1991), San Jose (1993), and Spokane (1994).

In 1992 Southwest assumed the leased operations of Northwest Airlines at Chicago Midway Airport and Detroit Metropolitan Airport and in 1993 initiated service to Baltimore, its first East Coast destination. The airline also won the first annual Triple Crown for the best on-time performances, best baggage handling record, and best customer satisfaction in 1992 (winning again in 1993). In 1994 the company acquired Morris Air in a stock swap.

In 1995 Southwest launched a "ticketless" travel system to trim travel agent commissions and announced that it would begin flights to Ft. Lauderdale, Orlando, and Tampa in 1996. The company is also using a new computer reservation system for automated booking of passengers.

NYSE symbol: LUV
Fiscal year ends: December 31

WHO

Chairman, President, and CEO: Herbert D. Kelleher, age 63, $567,000 pay
EVP and COO: Gary A. Barron, age 50, $322,209 pay
EVP Customers and Corporate Secretary: Colleen C. Barrett, age 50, $305,361 pay
EVP Corporate Services: John G. Denison, age 50, $300,754 pay
VP and General Counsel: James F. Parker, age 48, $240,680 pay
VP Finance and CFO: Gary C. Kelly, age 39
VP Governmental Affairs: Ron Ricks, age 45
VP Ground Operations: James C. Wimberly, age 42
VP People: Elizabeth P. Sartain, age 40
Auditors: Ernst & Young LLP

WHERE

HQ: PO Box 36611, Love Field, Dallas, TX 75235-1611
Phone: 214-904-4000
Fax: 214-904-4200
Reservations: 800-435-9792

Cities Served

Albuquerque, NM	Houston, TX	Orange County, CA
Amarillo, TX	Indianapolis, IN	Phoenix, AZ
Austin, TX	Kansas City, MO	Portland, OR
Baltimore, MD	Las Vegas, NV	Reno, NV
Birmingham, AL	Little Rock, AR	Sacramento, CA
Boise, ID	Los Angeles, CA	St. Louis, MO
Burbank, CA	Louisville, KY	Salt Lake City, UT
Chicago, IL	Lubbock, TX	San Antonio, TX
Cleveland, OH	Midland, TX	San Diego, CA
Columbus, OH	Nashville, TN	San Francisco, CA
Corpus Christi, TX	New Orleans, LA	San Jose, CA
Dallas, TX	Oakland, CA	Seattle, WA
Detroit, MI	Oklahoma City, OK	Spokane, WA
El Paso, TX	Omaha, NE	Tucson, AZ
Harlingen, TX	Ontario, CA	Tulsa, OK

WHAT

	1994 Sales	
	$ mil.	% of total
Passengers	2,498	96
Freight	54	2
Other	40	2
Total	**2,592**	**100**

Services
The Company Club (frequent-flyer program based on trips rather than mileage)

1994 Flight Equipment	No.	Orders & Options
Boeing 737-30	124	66
Boeing 737-200	50	—
Boeing 737-500	25	—
Boeing 737-700	—	126
Total	**199**	**192**

1994 Statistics	No. (bil.)
Revenue passengers carried	42.7
Revenue passenger miles	21.6
Available seat miles	32.1

KEY COMPETITORS

Alaska Air
America West
AMR
Continental Airlines
Delta
Kimberly-Clark
Mesa Air
Northwest Airlines
Reno Air
TWA
UAL
USAir

HOW MUCH

	9-Year Growth	1985	1986	1987	1988	1989	1990	1991	1992	1993	1994
Sales ($ mil.)	16.0%	680	769	778	860	1,058	1,237	1,379	1,803	2,297	2,592
Net income ($ mil.)	16.0%	47	50	20	58	75	51	33	97	154	179
Income as % of sales	—	7.0%	6.5%	2.6%	6.7%	7.0%	4.1%	2.4%	5.4%	6.7%	6.9%
Earnings per share ($)	15.3%	0.34	0.34	0.14	0.41	0.54	0.39	0.25	0.68	1.05	1.22
Stock price – high ($)	—	6.89	6.11	5.61	4.64	6.83	6.67	11.67	19.92	37.63	39.00
Stock price – low ($)	—	4.72	4.06	2.61	2.92	4.36	4.25	5.45	10.80	18.13	15.50
Stock price – close ($)	12.1%	5.97	4.58	2.97	4.50	5.33	5.83	11.38	19.67	37.38	16.75
P/E – high	—	20	18	40	11	13	17	47	29	36	32
P/E – low	—	14	12	19	7	8	11	22	16	17	13
Dividends per share ($)	3.7%	0.03	0.03	0.03	0.03	0.03	0.03	0.03	0.04	0.04	0.04
Book value per share ($)	11.6%	3.21	3.53	3.65	4.03	4.47	4.78	4.96	6.16	7.38	8.65
Employees	13.8%	5,271	5,819	5,765	6,467	7,760	8,620	9,778	11,397	15,175	16,818

1994 Year-end:
Debt ratio: 32.4%
Return on equity: 15.6%
Cash (mil.): $175
Current ratio: 0.60
Long-term debt (mil.): $583
No. of shares (mil.): 143
Dividends
Yield: 0.2%
Payout: 3.3%
Market value (mil.): $2,400

Stock Price History
High/Low 1985–94

SPIEGEL, INC.

OVERVIEW

Spiegel is one of the largest specialty retailers in the US. Although largely known for its flagship catalog, the company also sells clothes through its Newport News catalog (moderately priced women's apparel) and its Eddie Bauer subsidiary, which operates 356 stores in the US, Canada, and Japan, as well as its own catalogs (Eddie Bauer, Eddie Bauer Home, AKA Eddie Bauer, and The Complete Resource [combining the 3 concepts]). In sum, Spiegel's catalog circulation neared 340 million in 1994. The company operates 13 Spiegel outlet stores as well.

Spiegel saw its earnings drop by nearly 1/2 in 1994. The disappointing results were due to unseasonably warm weather, and thus weak demand for winter apparel, and start-up costs

for its new common catalog distribution center. Spiegel plans to fill orders from all its separate catalogs through this center, bringing the company closer to its long-term goal: to be a low-cost operator.

Spiegel no longer depends on demographics for marketing and merchandising decisions but rather on its sophisticated database of customer buying habits. Besides being used to predict customers' future purchases, the database helps Spiegel decide where to place new stores, targeting areas with high concentrations of its catalog customers.

Spiegel is expanding internationally. In 1994 Eddie Bauer began distributing catalogs in Germany and opened 3 stores in Tokyo.

WHEN

A few weeks after his release from a Confederate prison, Joseph Spiegel established a home furnishings store in Chicago in 1865. New railroads and an influx of immigrants contributed to the city's bustle and to the burgeoning sales of Spiegel's enterprise. In 1871 Spiegel's store was razed in the Great Chicago Fire, but because he had stored much of his wares in his backyard, he was soon back in business. Spiegel's business grew quickly and in 1905, at his son Arthur's suggestion, and probably to compete with the other 2 local mail order giants, Montgomery Ward and Sears, he began offering mail order sales to customers in rural areas.

Arthur soon took over, and in 1912 the company began selling women's clothing. Spiegel's focus shifted to its catalog business, and during the Depression it sold its retail operations. The company pioneered many catalog innovations: it was the first to use photographs in catalogs, to publish a Christmas catalog, and to offer credit, a novel service that was the main driver behind Spiegel's mail order business.

Credit restrictions during WWII brought the company back to retailing. While the stores increased sales, they were not as profitable as the catalogs, and in 1953 Spiegel once again returned to solely mail order sales.

Spiegel was bought by Beneficial Corporation in 1965. By the mid-1970s the company was facing tough competition from 4 other catalogers: Sears, J. C. Penney, Montgomery Ward, and Aldens, each virtually identical. To set itself apart, Spiegel targeted more upscale consumers, shifting from "mass to class." By

1985 it was selling apparel by Liz Claiborne, Calvin Klein, and Ralph Lauren.

In 1982 Spiegel was acquired by European catalog company Otto Versand. Sales tripled in 4 years. Although the company went public in 1987, Otto Versand chairman Michael Otto controlled the voting stock.

Spiegel bought Eddie Bauer in 1988. Eddie Bauer had founded his business in 1928 after a bout with hypothermia, when the wool clothing he had worn on a fishing trip proved inadequate. Upon his return he invented the Skyline, a goose down–insulated jacket, which was so popular that the air force contracted Bauer to provide down-insulated flight suits during WWII. Mail order operations began in 1946, and the company grew into a network of retail stores.

In 1990 Spiegel acquired First Consumer National Bank, the basis of its credit card operations. In 1993 it bought New Hampton (now Newport News), which publishes catalogs aimed at lower-middle-market shoppers.

Spiegel joined with Time Warner in 1993 to create a new shopping channel, Catalog 1, offering goods to a more affluent clientele than most such services. It began test marketing in 4 areas in early 1994. However, after disappointing sales results, the company discontinued television production of Catalog 1 in 1995 and reduced its programming from 24 hours a day to just 2 hours on Saturday.

Also in 1995 Eddie Bauer launched a new line of stores called AKA Eddie Bauer, specializing in upscale dress for men and women. This new concept feature's its own specialty catalogs.

WHO

Chairman: Michael Otto, age 51
VC, President, and CEO: John J. Shea, age 56,
$836,250 pay
President, Eddie Bauer: Richard T. Fersch,
$550,000 pay
EVP Merchandise: David C. Moon, age 52, $310,900 pay
SVP Operations and Information Services: Kenneth A.
Bochenski, age 52, $314,500 pay
SVP Human Resources: Harold S. Dahlstrand,
age 50
VP Manufacturing: Alois J. Lohn, age 60, $370,500 pay
VP Finance and CFO: James W. Sievers, age 52
VP Corporate Planning: Stanley D. Leibowitz, age 43
VP Advertising: Davia L. Kimmey, age 41
VP, Secretary, and General Counsel: Michael R. Moran,
age 48
Treasurer: John R. Steele, age 42
Auditors: KPMG Peat Marwick LLP

WHERE

HQ: 3500 Lacey Rd., Downers Grove, IL 60515-5432
Phone: 708-986-8800
Fax: 708-769-3101

In addition to catalog sales, Spiegel operates 356 Eddie
Bauer stores in Canada, Japan, and the US and 13
Spiegel outlet stores.

WHAT

| | 1994 Sales | |
	$ mil.	% of total
Catalog	1,742	58
Retail	965	32
Finance & other	309	10
Total	**3,016**	**100**

| | 1994 Sales |
	% of total
Apparel	68
Household furnishings & other general merchandise	32
Total	**100**

| | 1994 Stores |
	No.
Eddie Bauer — retail	318
Eddie Bauer — outlet	38
Spiegel outlet	13
Total	**369**

Selected Subsidiaries
Cara Corp. (information management)
Eddie Bauer, Inc.
First Consumers National Bank (credit cards)
Newport News, Inc. (moderately priced women's
apparel)
Spiegel Credit Corporation
Spiegel Properties Inc.

KEY COMPETITORS

50-Off Stores	Harcourt General	Montgomery
L. L. Bean	Home Shopping	Ward
Blair	Network	Nordstrom
Broadway Stores	J. Crew	Polo/Ralph
Brown Group	J. C. Penney	Lauren
Comcast	Kmart	REI
Dayton Hudson	Lands' End	Ross Stores
Dillard	Lechters	SearsStein Mart
Edison Brothers	The Limited	Talbots
Federated	Luxottica	Wal-Mart
Fingerhut	May	Woolworth
The Gap	Melville	
Hanover Direct	Mercantile Stores	

HOW MUCH

	Annual Growth	1985	1986	1987	1988	1989	1990	1991	1992	1993	1994
Sales ($ mil.)	15.3%	836	985	927	1,402	1,696	1,993	1,976	2,219	2,596	3,016
Net income ($ mil.)	7.5%	13	36	41	57	73	62	17	39	48	25
Income as % of sales	—	1.6%	3.7%	4.4%	4.1%	4.3%	3.1%	0.9%	1.8%	1.9%	0.8%
Earnings per share ($)	3.4%	0.17	0.46	0.51	0.59	0.71	0.59	0.17	0.38	0.47	0.23
Stock price – high ($)	—	—	—	7.63	5.63	11.56	13.50	10.50	9.00	23.38	26.75
Stock price – low ($)	—	—	—	3.50	3.88	4.44	4.88	5.38	5.00	7.75	8.75
Stock price – close ($)	13.4%	—	—	4.19	4.56	10.13	6.75	6.63	8.50	22.50	10.13
P/E – high	—	—	—	15	10	16	23	62	24	50	116
P/E – low	—	—	—	7	7	6	8	32	13	16	38
Dividends per share ($)	—	—	—	0.00	0.12	0.18	0.18	0.18	0.18	0.20	0.20
Book value per share ($)	16.2%	1.39	1.66	2.67	3.44	3.97	4.38	4.31	4.55	5.32	5.35
Employees	15.2%	5,500	—	6,000	9,000	10,500	12,300	12,000	13,500	11,104	19,700

1994 Year-end:
Debt ratio: 70.4%
Return on equity: 4.4%
Cash (mil.): $33
Current ratio: 3.04
Long-term debt (mil.): $1,300
No. of shares (mil.): 108
Dividends
  Yield: 2.0%
  Payout: 87.0%
Market value (mil.): $1,096

Stock Price History
High/Low 1987–94

SPRINGS INDUSTRIES, INC.

OVERVIEW

Based in Fort Mill, South Carolina, Springs Industries is one of the largest manufacturers of home furnishings and specialty fabrics in the US. The company produces bed and bath products, including sheets, pillowcases, bedspreads, shower curtains, and bath rugs, under such well-known brand names as Wamsutta, Springmaid, and Wabasso. It also makes decorative window treatments under names including Bali and Graber, apparel fabrics such as Ultrasuede, and fire-resistant and other industrial fabrics sold under the Clark-Schwebel label. It has licenses to put charac-

ters from the *Mighty Morphin Power Rangers* and *The Lion King* on its bedding products.

In 1995 Springs expanded its product line with the acquisition of towel maker Dundee Mills for about $118 million in stock and cash. Springs had long been on the lookout for a towel company to expand its bath products line. (It earlier lost out in a bid to buy Fieldcrest Cannon, the US's largest towel maker.)

The Close family, descendants of one of the founders, Leroy Springs, still controls 75% of the voting stock of the company.

WHEN

Springs Industries began in 1887 as Fort Mill Manufacturing Company, organized by Samuel Elliott White and 15 others, including Leroy Springs, his future son-in-law. Springs, a self-made millionaire, obtained control of Fort Mill Manufacturing in the late 1890s.

In 1931 Elliott Springs, Leroy's only son, became president when his father died leaving massive debts and declining plants. Elliott saved the company by modernizing mill equipment and consolidating the plants into the Springs Cotton Mills (1933). During WWII the company's 7 mills made fabric for military use (up to 6 million yards a week).

In 1945 Springs started the Springmaid line of bedding and fabrics. Elliott Springs's satiric, risqué, but effective ads (beginning in 1948) helped the company become the world's biggest producer of sheets.

In 1959 Elliott died and his son-in-law H. William Close became president. Close oversaw construction of the Springs Building, current New York sales headquarters (1962), and a $200 million program to expand product lines and modernize plants. With profits sharply declining, the company went public as Springs Mills, Inc. (1966).

In 1969 the first nonfamily member, Peter Scotese from Federated Department Stores, was hired as president. Springs diversified into synthetic fabrics, buying a minority interest in a Japanese textile plant to produce Ultrasuede (apparel fabric and car upholstery, 1971), and into frozen foods, buying Seabrook Foods (1973, sold in 1981).

Along with a name change to Springs Industries in 1982, subsequent acquisitions and mergers reflected the company's focus on home furnishings and industrial textiles:

Lawtex Industries (bedspreads, draperies; 1979), Graber Industries (window decorating products, 1979), M. Lowenstein (Wamsutta home furnishings and industrial textiles, 1985), Clark-Schwebel Fiber Glass (industrial fabrics, 1985), and Carey-McFall (Bali blinds, 1989).

Declining economic conditions throughout the textile industry forced Springs to implement an $18 million restructuring in 1988 and to take a further $70 million charge in 1990, with the company closing plants, offering early retirements, and trimming its weakened finished-fabrics segment. The 1990 charge led to Springs reporting a $7 million loss, its first in 25 years as a public company. Springs's downsizing of its finished-fabrics line continued into 1993.

In 1991 the company established a bath group with the purchase of C. S. Brooks for about $30 million. In 1992 the company quickly became a leading seller of home textiles in Canada by buying 2 companies: C. S. Brooks Canada's marketing and sales arms and Springmaid distributor Griffiths-Kerr.

Springs was rebuffed by rival Fieldcrest Cannon in a hostile takeover bid in 1993. That same year one of Springs's subsidiaries, Clark-Schwebel, traded its UK and Belgian outfits to German fiberglass manufacturer CS-Interglas AG in return for a minority stake in Interglas.

In 1994 Springs raised prices on its bedding products for the first time in 6 years. Also in 1994 the company restructured and Clark-Schwebel sold its subsidiary, Clark-Schwebel Distribution.

In 1995 Springs signed a deal to acquire Dawson Home Fashions, a manufacturer of shower curtains and other bath products.

NYSE symbol: SMI
Fiscal year ends: Saturday nearest December 31

WHO

Chairman, President, and CEO: Walter Y. Elisha, age 62, $1,125,000 pay
EVP; President, Specialty Fabrics Group: Stephen P. Kelbley, age 52, $445,004 pay
EVP; President, Home Fashions Group: Thomas P. O'Connor, age 49, $380,004 pay
EVP: Robert W. Móser, age 56, $380,004 pay
EVP; President, Textile Manufacturing Group: Crandall C. Bowles, age 47, $350,000 pay
SVP, Growth and Development: J. Spratt White, age 53
VP Finance and Treasurer (CFO): James F. Zahrn, age 44
VP, General Counsel, and Corporate Secretary: C. Powers Dorsett, age 50
VP and Controller: James C. McKelvey, age 50
VP Public Affairs: Robert L. Thompson, age 58
VP Corporate Engineering: Charles L. Abrams Jr.
VP Environmental Services: R. A. Odom Jr.
VP Information Systems: James H. Wood
VP Springs Quality System: Jennifer L. Scott
VP Human Resources: Richard D. Foster, age 55
Assistant Treasurer: George B. Gambrell
Assistant Treasurer: Samuel J. Ilardo
Associate General Counsel and Assistant Secretary: Robert W. Sullivan
Auditors: Deloitte & Touche LLP

WHERE

HQ: 205 N. White St., Fort Mill, SC 29715
Phone: 803-547-1500
Fax: 803-547-1636

Springs operates 39 US manufacturing plants in 9 states. Twenty-four are in South Carolina, 4 in North Carolina, 3 in Georgia, 2 each in Alabama and California, and one each in Nevada, Pennsylvania, Tennessee, and Wisconsin. Springs also has operations in Asia, Canada, and Mexico.

WHAT

	1994 Sales		1994 Operating Income	
	$ mil.	% of total	$ mil.	% of total
Home furnishings	1,460	71	98	72
Specialty fabrics	609	29	38	28
Total	**2,069**	**100**	**136**	**100**

Home Furnishings	Specialty Fabrics
Bed and bath products	Finished fabrics
Performance	Springmaid
Springmaid	Ultrasuede
Supercale	Wamsutta
Texmade	Fire-retardant fabrics
Wabasso	Woven fiberglass fabrics
Wamsutta	Clark-Schwebel
Window furnishings	
Bali	
CrystalPleat	
FashionPleat	
Graber	

Selected Subsidiaries
Catawba Trucking, Inc.
Clark-Schwebel, Inc. (woven fiberglass, industrial fabrics)
Springs Canada, Inc.
Springs de Mexico, S.A. de C.V.
Springs Industries (Asia) Inc.

KEY COMPETITORS

Avondale Mills
Burlington Industries
Collins & Aikman
DuPont
Fieldcrest Cannon
Greenwood Mills
Guilford Mills
Interface
Milliken
Unifi
WestPoint Stevens

HOW MUCH

	9-Year Growth	1985	1986	1987	1988	1989	1990	1991	1992	1993	1994
Sales ($ mil.)	8.2%	1,014	1,505	1,661	1,825	1,909	1,878	1,890	1,976	2,023	2,069
Net income ($ mil.)	19.0%	13	33	56	53	65	(7)	27	45	47	62
Income as % of sales	—	1.3%	2.2%	3.4%	2.9%	3.4%	—	1.4%	2.3%	2.3%	3.0%
Earnings per share ($)	18.7%	0.75	1.83	3.13	2.98	3.64	(0.39)	1.53	2.50	2.65	3.50
Stock price – high ($)	—	23.00	28.44	38.25	38.75	45.25	39.50	36.25	43.88	49.00	41.00
Stock price – low ($)	—	15.63	20.50	20.75	27.00	30.50	16.88	21.25	30.50	33.50	29.25
Stock price – close ($)	5.9%	22.00	24.94	30.25	31.50	38.25	22.63	31.50	36.13	37.75	37.00
P/E – high	—	31	16	12	13	12	—	24	18	18	12
P/E – low	—	21	11	7	9	8	—	14	12	13	8
Dividends per share ($)	5.2%	0.76	0.57	0.80	.92	1.20	1.20	1.20	1.20	1.20	1.20
Book value per share ($)	3.2%	25.03	26.24	28.63	30.67	33.08	32.05	32.39	33.48	30.90	33.20
Employees	2.0%	17,000	23,500	23,100	23,400	24,100	23,200	21,700	20,900	20,300	20,300

1994 Year-end:
Debt ratio: 33.8%
Return on equity: 11.0%
Cash (mil.): $1
Current ratio: 2.53
Long-term debt (mil.): $265
No. of shares (mil.): 18
Dividends
  Yield: 3.2%
  Payout: 34.3%
Market value (mil.): $651

Stock Price History High/Low 1985–94

SPRINT CORPORATION

OVERVIEW

Best known as a long distance provider, Sprint is enhancing its services in the other 2 domestic telecommunications markets — local and wireless services. Based in Westwood, Kansas, Sprint recently signed an agreement with 3 cable companies — Tele-Communications, Comcast Corp., and Cox Communications — to provide local telecommunications services on a national basis. Sprint will own 40% of the new company. Shortly afterwards, Sprint and its cable partners purchased licenses from the federal government to provide wireless "personal communication services" and acquired a 49% stake in American Personal Communications, a recipient of a "pioneer preference" license for personal communications services (PCS). Sprint and its partners are planning to

offer a complete line of wireless and wired telecommunications services over phone and cable networks.

Sprint has also accomplished another step in its pursuit of international partners. Sprint, France Telecom, and Deutsche Telekom have agreed on the final terms of their joint venture to create a global telecommunications network. France Telecom and Deutsche Telekom together will buy a 20% stake in Sprint for up to $4.1 billion; however, the purchase remains subject to regulatory approval.

Sprint reported healthy revenue growth in all 4 of its business segments, ranging from 7% in local communications services to 51% in cellular and wireless communications services.

WHEN

In 1899 Jacob Brown and son Cleyson received a franchise from the city of Abilene, Kansas, for one of the first non-Bell telephone companies in the West. Using poles from their electric utility, the men had their telephone company operational within 3 months. By 1903 they had 1,400 subscribers.

Cleyson formed Union Electric Company to sell telephone equipment (1905) and a long distance company, Home Telephone and Telegraph (1910). In 1911 he consolidated with other Kansas independents as United Telephone Company. That year he obtained capital from his fiercest competitor, Missouri and Kansas Telephone (later Southwestern Bell), which bought 60% of United's stock.

WWI brought labor and materials shortages that curtailed growth until the war's end, when Cleyson resumed acquisitions in Kansas. In 1925 he sold his electric utility to finance telephony and incorporated United Telephone and Electric. Cleyson acquired more exchanges, even during the Great Depression while he was losing subscribers. He retired in 1934. Wartime shortages created several years of order backlog during WWII, and acquisitions ceased until 1952, when United bought control of Investors Telephone; further purchases followed.

In 1959 Carl Scupin took over the company and updated equipment and services. After Scupin's retirement (1964), president Paul Henson focused on satellite communications, nuclear power plants, and cable TV. He bought North Electric (1965), the oldest independent telephone equipment manufacturer in the US; Automated Data Service (1967) to offer batch

processing and time sharing; and United Business Communications (1970) to sell telephone and data hardware (sold to Stromberg-Carlson in 1974). He renamed the company United Telecommunications in 1971 and purchased Florida Telephone in 1974. United prospered through industry deregulation in the 1970s and the 1983 AT&T breakup. In 1985 United bought 50% of GTE's long distance provider, GTE Sprint (started in 1970 by Southern Pacific; acquired by GTE in 1983). United bought another 30.1% in 1989.

In 1990 competition among long distance services heated up and ate into United's profits. Sprint countered with a new focus on the residential and small-business markets and with TV's Candice Bergen as spokesperson. In 1992 United bought GTE's remaining 19.9% of Sprint and officially adopted Sprint as its name. That year Sprint joined the state-owned telephone companies of Sweden and the Netherlands to form a 50-50 venture (Unisource) that will provide telecommunications networks for European-based multinational corporations.

In 1993 Sprint received permission to join Bell Communications Research (Bellcore), the research consortium for the regional Bell operating companies. In the same year Sprint announced plans to participate in Motorola's Iridium project and to begin a public video conferencing network with Kinko's.

In 1995 Sprint announced plans to spin off its rapidly growing Sprint Cellular unit. The company also signed agreements with Teléfonos de México (Telmex) and China United Telecommunications (Unicom).

NYSE symbol: FON
Fiscal year ends: December 31

WHO

Chairman and CEO: William T. Esrey, age 55,
$1,949,487 pay
President and COO, Local Telecommunications Division: D. Wayne Peterson, age 59, $652,982 pay
President and COO, Long Distance Division: Ronald T. LeMay, age 49, $1,193,975 pay
President and COO, Cellular and Wireless Division: Dennis E. Foster, age 54
EVP and CFO: Arthur B. Krause, age 53, $614,349 pay
EVP Law and External Affairs: J. Richard Devlin, age 44, $554,578 pay
SVP Corporate Finance: Gene M. Betts, age 42
SVP and Controller: John P. Meyer, age 44
SVP Strategic Planning and Corporate Development: Theodore H. Schell, age 50
SVP Quality Development and Public Relations: Richard C. Smith Jr., age 53
SVP Human Resources: I. Benjamin Watson, age 46
VP and Secretary: Don A. Jensen, age 59
Auditors: Ernst & Young LLP

WHERE

HQ: 2330 Shawnee Mission Pkwy., Westwood, KS 66205
P.O. Box 11315, Kansas City, MO 64112
Phone: 913-624-3000
Fax: 913-624-3281

Sprint provides long distance, cellular, and local telephone services in these states:

Florida	Nevada	South Carolina
Illinois	New Jersey	Tennessee
Indiana	North Carolina	Texas
Kansas	Ohio	Virginia
Minnesota	Oregon	Washington
Missouri	Pennsylvania	Wyoming
Nebraska		

WHAT

	1994 Sales		1994 Operating Income	
	$ mil.	% of total	$ mil.	% of total
Long distance svcs.	6,805	52	605	34
Local services	4,413	34	1,022	57
Product distribution, directory publishing	1,109	9	76	4
Cellular & wireless	702	5	85	5
Adjustments	(367)	—	—	—
Total	**12,662**	**100**	**1,788**	**100**

Selected Telephone Companies
Centel Corp.
United Telephone Co. of the Northwest
United Telephone Co. of the West
United Telephone-Southeast, Inc.

Selected Subsidiaries
Centel Corp.
  Sprint Cellular Co.
  Telespectrum, Inc.
DirectoriesAmerica, Inc.
  Sprint Publishing & Advertising, Inc.
North Supply Co. (wholesale distributor of telecommunications, security and alarm systems, and electrical products)
US Telecom, Inc.
  Sprint International Inc.

KEY COMPETITORS

American Business Information	Cable & Wireless Century Telephone	SBC Communications
Ameritech	Dun & Bradstreet	Telephone and Data Systems
AT&T	GTE	U.S. Long Distance
BCE	MCI	U S WEST
Bell Atlantic	NYNEX	WorldCom
BellSouth	Pacific Telesis	
BT	R. R. Donnelley	

HOW MUCH

	9-Year Growth	1985	1986	1987	1988	1989	1990	1991	1992	1993	1994
Sales ($ mil.)	15.8%	3,376	2,372	3,064	6,493	7,549	8,345	8,780	9,230	11,368	12,662
Net income ($ mil.)	51.6%	21	181	(52)	509	363	309	368	427	439	888
Income as % of sales	—	0.6%	7.6%	—	7.8%	4.8%	3.7%	4.2%	4.6%	3.9%	7.0%
Earnings per share ($)	45.0%	0.09	0.90	(0.28)	2.48	1.72	1.43	1.68	1.93	1.27	2.55
Stock price – high ($)	—	12.50	15.63	16.69	23.94	43.75	46.38	31.50	26.73	40.25	40.13
Stock price – low ($)	—	10.06	11.63	11.75	12.13	22.00	20.63	21.25	20.75	25.50	26.13
Stock price – close ($)	9.8%	11.88	12.75	12.31	23.19	38.00	23.25	23.75	25.50	34.75	27.63
P/E – high	—	139	17	—	10	25	32	19	14	32	16
P/E – low	—	112	13	—	5	13	14	13	11	20	10
Dividends per share ($)	0.5%	0.96	0.96	0.96	0.96	1.00	1.00	1.00	1.00	1.00	1.00
Book value per share ($)	4.4%	8.80	8.75	6.52	9.15	10.03	10.70	11.56	12.77	12.15	12.98
Employees	7.3%	27,415	23,245	23,325	37,661	41,359	43,100	43,200	52,200	50,000	51,600

1994 Year-end:
Debt ratio: 52.2%
Return on equity: 21.1%
Cash (mil.): $123
Current ratio: 0.72
Long-term debt (mil.): $4,605
No. of shares (mil.): 349
Dividends
  Yield: 3.6%
  Payout: 39.2%
Market value (mil.): $9,632

**Stock Price History
High/Low 1985–94**

THE STANLEY WORKS

OVERVIEW

New Britain, Connecticut–based Stanley Works boasts a record unparalleled by any other industrial company listed on the New York Stock Exchange — 128 consecutive years of annual dividend payments.

Stanley's 11 businesses (including Stanley Tools, Stanley Door Systems, and MAC Tools) make a comprehensive range of hardware and tools. Its major product lines are consumer tools (carpentry tools, toolboxes, and masonry tools), industrial tools (hand tools, electronic diagnostic tools, and cabinets), engineered tools (pneumatic nailers, staplers, and office products), hardware (hinges, hasps, brackets, and bolts), and specialty hardware (residential door systems, power-operated gates, and garage door openers). Stanley leads in several markets, including the manufacture of industrial cabinets, fasteners, and hinges.

The company operates globally under a variety of brand names, including Bostitch, Goldblatt, Jensen, MAC Tools, Proto, and Vidmar.

Stanley has had international operations since the 1920s and currently has 114 manufacturing and distribution centers worldwide. The firm is pursuing expanding international sales as a key strategy for growth. By 1994 50% of the company's consumer tool sales came from outside the US.

WHEN

In 1843 Frederick T. Stanley opened a bolt shop in a converted War of 1812–era armory in New Britain, Connecticut. With the first steam engine used in New Britain industry, he produced bolts and house trimmings. In 1852 he teamed with his brother and 5 friends to form The Stanley Works to cast, form, and manufacture various types of metal.

The business prospered during the 1860s when the Civil War and westward migration created a need for hardware and tools. When Stanley started to devote less time to the business to concentrate on political and civic affairs, management of the company fell to William H. Hart.

Hart quickly demonstrated his competitive business ability. He expanded the company, engaging in a "knuckles-bared" fight with Stanley's 4 leading (and larger) competitors. Through a combination of innovation, efficiency, quality, and marketing, Hart emerged as the sole survivor. He led the company into steel strapping production, which would become a major element in Stanley's operations. Hart was named president in 1884.

Stanley entered a period of rapid expansion in the early 20th century. During WWI the company produced belt buckles and rifle and gas mask parts. In addition to making numerous domestic acquisitions, Stanley established operations in Canada (1914) and Germany (1926). In 1920 it merged with Stanley Rule and Level (a local tool company formed in 1857 by a cousin of Frederick Stanley) and in 1925 opened a new hydroelectric plant near Windsor to provide power for all its operations. In 1929 Stanley organized its electric tool division.

After a difficult decade caused by the Great Depression, Stanley geared up production in the early 1940s. Following WWII the company embarked on a massive period of expansion that lasted 4 decades. Staying within its traditional product line, Stanley acquired a myriad of companies, including Berry Industries (garage doors, 1965); Ackley Manufacturing and Sales (hydraulic tools, 1972), Mac Tools (1980), and National Hand Tool Corporation (1986). In the late 1980s the company grew globally by establishing high-tech plants in Europe and the Far East.

Newell Company made a brief bid in 1991 to buy as much as 25% of Stanley. To fend off a takeover, Stanley sued Newell on antitrust grounds and stoked the employee stock plan with about 25% of the outstanding stock. Newell backed off momentarily but in late 1991 returned with the new intention of buying up to 15% of Stanley stock, prompting company to renew its defensive measures.

In 1992 Stanley acquired LaBounty Manufacturing (large hydraulic tools), American Brush (paint brushes and decorator tools), Mail Media (Jensen Tools precision tool kits and Direct Safety safety equipment), Goldblatt Tool (masonry and drywall tools), and a controlling interest in Tona a.s. Pecky, a major Czech maker of mechanic's tools.

In 1993 the company sold its Taylor Rental subsidiary, the largest system of general rental centers in the US, to SERVISTAR. Stanley is exploring expanding its business to the huge markets of China and India. In 1994 the company set up a small fastener joint venture in China. Stanley is also expanding its sales presence in Eastern Europe and Latin America.

NYSE symbol: SWK
Fiscal year ends: Saturday nearest December 31

WHO

Chairman and CEO: Richard H. Ayers, age 52,
$950,674 pay
President and COO: R. Alan Hunter, age 48,
$557,400 pay
VP, General Counsel, and Secretary: Stephen S. Weddle,
age 56, $354,918 pay
VP Finance and CFO: Richard Huck, age 50,
$343,615 pay
VP Corporate Development: Thomas K. Clarke, age 63,
$323,947 pay
**VP Marketing Development; President and General
Manager, Stanley Customer Support Division:** James
S. Amtmann, age 47
VP Information Systems: James B. Gustafson, age 52
VP and Controller: Theresa F. Yerkes, age 39
VP Taxes: John P. Callahan, age 49
VP Human Resources: Barbara W. Bennett, age 51
Auditors: Ernst & Young LLP

WHERE

HQ: 1000 Stanley Dr., New Britain, CT 06053
Phone: 203-225-5111
Fax: 203-827-3895

The company operates 114 manufacturing and
major distribution facilities in the US and 19 other
countries.

	1994 Sales		1994 Operating Income	
	$ mil.	% of total	$ mil.	% of total
US	1,808	72	215	79
Europe	358	14	32	11
Other regions	345	14	27	10
Total	**2,511**	**100**	**274**	**100**

WHAT

	1994 Sales		1994 Operating Income	
	$ mil.	% of total	$ mil.	% of total
Tools	1,884	75	217	79
Specialty hardware	316	13	24	9
Hardware	311	12	33	12
Total	**2,511**	**100**	**274**	**100**

Selected Products	Selected Brand Names
Air tools	Bostitch
Automatic parking gates	Direct Safety
Bolts and brackets	Friess
Chisels	Goldblatt
Closet organizers	Jensen
Door hardware	Jet-Cut
Electronic controls	LaBounty
Fasteners	Leverlock
Garage doors and openers	MAC Tools
Hammers	Mastertech
Hasps	Monarch
Hinges	Mosley-Stone
Hydraulic tools	Nirva
Knives	Powerlock
Planes	Professional
Power-operated doors	Proto
Rules	Sidchrome
Saws	Stanley
Screwdrivers	Tona
Shelving	Vidmar
Sockets	
Wrenches	

KEY COMPETITORS

Black & Decker	Illinois Tool Works	Overhead Door
Cooper Industries	Ingersoll-Rand	Robert Bosch
Emerson	Makita	Rubbermaid
Esstar	Masco	Snap-on Tools
Hillenbrand	Newell Co.	Textron

HOW MUCH

	9-Year Growth	1985	1986	1987	1988	1989	1990	1991	1992	1993	1994
Sales ($ mil.)	8.5%	1,208	1,371	1,763	1,909	1,972	1,977	1,962	2,218	2,273	2,511
Net income ($ mil.)	5.4%	78	79	87	104	118	107	95	98	93	125
Income as % of sales	—	6.5%	5.7%	4.9%	5.4%	6.0%	5.4%	4.8%	4.4%	4.1%	5.0%
Earnings per share ($)	4.4%	1.90	1.86	2.00	2.40	2.71	2.53	2.31	2.15	2.06	2.80
Stock price – high ($)	—	22.50	30.84	36.63	31.75	39.25	40.00	44.00	48.13	47.88	44.88
Stock price – low ($)	—	16.34	20.50	21.25	23.63	27.50	26.38	26.00	32.50	37.88	34.88
Stock price – close ($)	5.9%	21.34	25.50	25.88	28.50	39.00	29.00	40.88	42.50	44.50	35.75
P/E – high	—	12	17	18	13	15	16	19	22	23	16
P/E – low	—	9	11	11	10	10	10	11	15	18	13
Dividends per share ($)	8.4%	0.67	0.73	0.82	0.92	1.02	1.14	1.22	1.28	1.34	1.38
Book value per share ($)	3.7%	12.04	13.05	14.59	16.31	15.67	16.92	15.59	15.32	15.23	16.74
Employees	4.8%	13,069	16,128	19,142	18,988	18,464	17,784	17,420	18,650	18,988	20,000

1994 Year-end:
Debt ratio: 39.2%
Return on equity: 17.6%
Cash (mil.): $69
Current ratio: 2.11
Long-term debt (mil.): $387
No. of shares (mil.): 44
Dividends
  Yield: 3.9%
  Payout: 49.3%
Market value (mil.): $1,589

**Stock Price History
High/Low 1985–94**

STATE FARM

OVERVIEW

"Like a good neighbor, State Farm is there." But in recent years its neighborhood has shrunk, as the company has limited, reduced, or withdrawn its operations in specific regions and business lines, including auto, home-owners, and individual and small group health in markets such as California, Florida, Texas, New Jersey, and Kentucky.

Bloomington, Illinois–based State Farm Mutual has been the nation's largest auto insurance company almost since its founding. Owned by policyholders, the company has been run by executives from only 2 families, the Mecherles (1922–54) and the Rusts (1954–present).

In addition to its flagship auto operations, the company has wholly owned but not consolidated property/casualty affiliates such as State Farm Fire & Casualty Co. (which provides the parent with reinsurance coverage). The 1994 Northridge earthquake in California caused the P/C segment to lose almost $1 billion, which was in large part responsible for the 72% decrease in 1994 earnings. The life insurance affiliates made a modest profit.

State Farm began trying to recruit home-owners insurance customers in 1995 by targeting 40 Los Angeles inner-city zip codes for new business despite the demonstrated risk of natural disasters and 1992's urban unrest.

WHEN

Retired farmer George Mecherle founded State Farm Mutual Automobile Insurance Co. in Bloomington, Illinois, in 1922. State Farm restricted membership, primarily to members of farm bureaus and farm mutual insurance companies, and charged a one-time member-ship fee and a premium to protect an automobile against loss or damage.

From the beginning State Farm, unlike most of its competitors, offered 6-month premium payments. State Farm also billed and collected renewal premiums from its home office, relieving the agent of the task. Another State Farm feature was a simplified 7-class system for charging auto rates instead of charging separate rates for each auto model, as most other companies did.

Before the end of its first year, State Farm had placed policies in 46 Illinois counties. To insure nonfarmers' autos, the company in 1926 started City and Village Mutual Automobile Insurance, which became part of State Farm in 1927. Between 1927 and 1931 State Farm introduced borrowed-car protection, wind coverage, and insurance for buses or cars used in transporting schoolchildren.

State Farm expanded to Berkeley, California, in 1928 and started State Farm Life Insurance, a wholly owned subsidiary, in 1929. In 1935 the company established State Farm Fire Insurance. George Mecherle moved up to chairman in 1937, and his son Ramond assumed the presidency. Yet George remained active, challenging agents in 1939 to write "A Million or More (auto policies) by '44." State Farm met the deadline with a 110% increase in policies.

In the 1940s State Farm began to focus on metropolitan areas after most of the farm bureaus formed their own insurance companies. By 1941 State Farm was the largest auto insurer in total automobile premiums written. In the late 1940s and 1950s, it moved to a full-time agency force.

Adlai Rust led State Farm from 1954 to 1958, when Edward Rust took over, running the company until his death in 1985. His son, Edward Rust Jr., now holds the top spot.

Between 1974 and 1987 the company was hit by several sex discrimination suits (a 1992 settlement awarded $157 million to 814 California women). The company has since tried to hire more women and minorities.

Facing increasing state regulation, the company in 1990 stopped writing new auto business in Pennsylvania. After legislation in other states prompted some insurers to stop insuring in those states, State Farm faced the dilemma of either using the exodus to pick up market share or avoiding risk. By 1993 it seemed to be resolving the problem in favor of the bottom line and stopped writing new auto policies in Texas.

In recent years State Farm has been cited by state regulators for various infractions, including failing to give state-mandated discounts for air bags and automatic safety belts.

In recent years a string of disasters such as Hurricane Andrew, the Los Angeles riot, and the Northridge earthquake have been very costly for the company. The Northridge earthquake alone generated more than $2.5 billion in claims. It also brought class action suits in 1995 by policyholders who claimed that their policies had been changed from full replacement value to a dollar amount without proper notice. There are more than 100,000 potential class members.

Mutual company
Fiscal year ends: December 31

Chairman, President, and CEO: Edward B. Rust Jr.
VC and EVP: Vincent J. Trosino
SVP and Treasurer: Roger S. Joslin
VP Health: Glenn A. Britt
VP Property/Casualty: Harold D. Covey
VP and General Counsel: William A. Montgomery
VP Investments: Kurt G. Moser
VP Claims: Frank R. Haines
VP Personnel: John P. Coffey
Auditors: Coopers & Lybrand L.L.P.

WHERE

HQ: State Farm Mutual Automobile Insurance
Company, One State Farm Plaza, Bloomington, IL
61710-0001
Phone: 309-766-2311
Fax: 309-766-6169

State Farm has operations in all 50 states, the District of
Columbia, and Canada.

	1994 Premiums	
	$ mil.	% of total
California	2,542	12
Texas	2,232	8
Florida	1,466	7
Illinois	1,417	7
New York	1,005	5
Michigan	988	5
Pennsylvania	960	5
Ohio	746	4
Georgia	664	3
Louisiana	621	3
Missouri	535	2
Minnesota	521	2
Indiana	485	2
Virginia	480	2
Colorado	441	2
Maryland	422	2
Tennessee	416	2
Other states	5,367	25
Canada	507	2
Total	**21,815**	**100**

WHAT

	1994 Assets	
	$ mil.	% of total
Cash & equivalents	487	1
Government securities	13,504	28
State & municipal bonds	5,183	11
Public utility bonds	2,137	4
Other bonds	3,463	7
Stocks	17,392	35
Mortgage loans & real estate	1,840	4
Other investments	519	1
Other	4,317	9
Total	**48,842**	**100**

	1994 Sales	
	$ mil.	% of total
Premiums & membership	23,216	91
Net investments	2,233	8
Finance & service charges	142	1
Other	7	0
Total	**25,598**	**100**

Lines of Business
Accident and health
Automobile insurance
Reinsurance

Affiliates and Subsidiaries
Amberjack, Ltd. (real estate)
Fiesta Jack, Ltd. (real estate)
State Farm County Mutual Insurance Co. of Texas
(common management)
State Farm Fire and Casualty Co.
State Farm General Insurance Co.
State Farm Indemnity Co.
State Farm International Services, Inc.
State Farm Investment Management Corp.
State Farm Life & Accident Assurance Co.
State Farm Life Insurance Co.
State Farm Lloyds, Inc.

KEY COMPETITORS

20th Century	CIGNA	Liberty Mutual
Industries	CNA Financial	Nationwide
Aetna	GEICO	Insurance
Allstate	General Re	Prudential
Chubb	ITT Hartford	Travelers
		USAA

HOW MUCH

	9-Year Growth	1985	1986	1987	1988	1989	1990	1991	1992	1993	1994
Assets ($ mil.)	10.6%	19,695	23,679	27,101	30,922	35,493	37,508	42,676	43,603	47,537	48,842
Net income ($ mil.)	(3.5%)	666	1,033	1,041	721	419	372	1,317	1,780	1,742	485
Income as % of assets	—	3.4%	4.4%	3.8%	2.3%	1.2%	1.0%	3.1%	4.1%	3.7%	1.0%
Employees	7.2%	37,543	40,748	44,086	48,082	52,236	55,133	58,113	60,786	64,520	70,220

1994 Year-end:
Equity as % of assets:
20.2%
Return on equity: 4.9%
Sales (mil.): $25,598

Net Income ($ mil.)
1985–94

STEELCASE INC.

Steelcase rested its case early in the O. J. Simpson trial — both Robert Shapiro's and Johnnie Cochran's specially requested and comfortable courtroom chairs are made by the company. Headquartered in Grand Rapids, Michigan, closely held Steelcase is the world's largest office furniture manufacturer. It makes a wide variety of products — from swivel tilt chairs and filing cabinets to entire office furniture systems. The furniture maker's nearest rival, Herman Miller, is only about half its size.

In the wake of the slowdown in furniture industry sales in the early 1990s, the firm has been diversifying its services beyond its core office furniture business. It currently has operations in construction products, low-priced home office furniture, consultant services, and products for the health care market.

Steelcase is also engaged in a number of alliances to boost product sales. In 1995 it teamed up with AT&T and Marriott to improve hotel office services for business travelers.

WHEN

In the early 1900s offices were still heated with wood stoves and lighted with gas lamps, so when a pensive executive leaned back in his wooden chair and put his feet up on his wooden desk, he was taking a calculated risk. Enter Peter Wege, a sheet-metal designer who espoused the fireproof benefits of steel furniture. Wege persuaded a group of investors led by Grand Rapids banker Henry Idema to sink $75,000 into his idea, and in 1912 the Metal Office Furniture Company was born.

The company's first big hit, however, wasn't a desk or a chair: it was a metal wastepaper basket, much less flammable than the wicker wastebaskets popular at the time.

Despite the company's innovative ideas, businesses were slow to switch from wood to the more expensive metal furniture. However, US government architects, concerned with fire safety, began specifying metal furniture in their designs, and in 1915 the company won the first of many government contracts.

In 1921 Wege hired media consultant Jim Turner to tout the benefits of metal furniture. Turner came up with a trademark to describe the indestructible nature of the company's products — Steelcase. During the 1930s Metal Office Furniture continued to create innovative designs, patenting the suspension cabinet in 1934 and teaming with Frank Lloyd Wright in 1937 to create office furniture for the Johnson Wax headquarters building.

WWII brought a cutback in steel available for use by furniture manufacturers, but the company was able to weather the storm thanks to a contract to provide the US Navy with shipboard furniture. After the war, the company introduced modular furniture based on designs learned in building furniture with interchangeable parts for the navy.

The company changed its name to Steelcase Inc. in 1954 and in 1959 introduced Convertibles and Convertiwalls, a system of frames, cabinets, and panels that could tailor a work area to an individual worker's needs. By 1968 the company had become the largest metal office-furniture maker in the world.

During the early 1970s Steelcase entered into a pair of joint ventures in order to boost its presence overseas, signing deals with Kurogane Kosakusho (creating Steelcase Japan) in 1973 and Strafor Facom (creating Steelcase Strafor) in 1974. In 1978 Steelcase began a series of acquisitions, fueling growth that helped to triple its sales during the 1980s.

In 1987, in an effort to position itself as a more design-oriented company, Steelcase created the Steelcase Design Partnership, made up of 7 companies providing products for special market niches such as wood office furniture (Stow Davis) and fabrics (DesignTex).

Steelcase was hit hard by the early 1990s recession as many businesses postponed buying new office furniture. The firm, long known for its job security, was forced to fire 300 staff and lay off hourly workers, but by 1992 it was able to recall all the hourly employees.

Also in 1992 Steelcase fought off an effort by outsiders — who had obtained company stock after it had passed to a brokerage firm following the death of an heir of one of the founders — to force the company to go public. Through a reverse stock split, the outsiders were forced to sell their stock to Steelcase.

Steelcase launched 2 new companies in 1993: Turnstone, which serves small businesses and home office workers; and Continuum, which commissions work from minority designers. In 1994 the firm's first annual loss prompted the resignations of Robert Pew III, grandson of one of the founders, as president of Steelcase North America and of CEO Jerry Myers.

In 1995 Steelcase gained access to the huge Indian market when it signed a manufacturing joint venture deal with Godrej & Boyce.

Private company
Fiscal year ends: Last day of February

WHO

Chairman: Robert Pew, age 70
President and CEO: James P. Hackett, age 39
EVP; President, Steelcase Design Partnership: William P. Crawford, age 51
SVP Operations: Robert Ballard
CFO: Alwyn Rougier-Chapman
SVP Sales, Marketing, and Dealer Alliances: James Mitchell
VP, Secretary, and General Counsel: David S. Fry
Marketing Manager, New Business Development: Jeannie Bouchet
Director Human Resources: Dan Wiljanen
Auditors: BDO Seidman

WHERE

HQ: 901 44th St. SE, Grand Rapids, MI 49508-7575
Phone: 616-247-2710
Fax: 616-246-9015

Steelcase has manufacturing plants in Belgium, Canada, France, Germany, Japan, Ivory Coast, Morocco, Portugal, Spain, the UK, and the US. It sells its products worldwide through a network of over 900 independent dealers.

WHAT

Products

Desks and Tables	Seating
Chancellor	Criterion
Edgewood	Player
Ellipse	Protegé
Paladin	Rally
	Sensor
Filing and Storage	
Bookcases	**Systems Furniture**
Lateral files	Activity
Modular storage	Avenir
cabinets	Context
Vertical files	Elective Elements
	Valencia

Other Operations

Joint Ventures
KSM (office furniture manufacture, Japan)
Steelcase Japan KK. (marketing and sales; 75%-owned, Kurogane Kosakusho owns 25%)
Steelcase Strafor (France, with Strafor Facom)
Steelcase/Godrej & Boyce (office furniture manufacture, India)

Selected Subsidiaries
Attwood Corporation
Continuum Inc.
Steelcase Design Partnership
 Atelier International Ltd. (designer seating manufacture)
 Brayton International, Inc.
 DesignTex Fabrics, Inc. (textiles manufacture)
 Details (desktop and computer accessory manufacture)
 Health Design (subsidiary of Brayton International)
 Metropolitan Furniture Corporation
 Stow Davis (wood cabinets)
 Vecta ((designer seating manufacture)
Steelcase Export
Steelcase North America
Tangerine (consultant services)
Turnstone

Strategic Alliance
Marriott /AT&T/Steelcase — a collaborative agreement to jointly research, develop, and produce a new generation of products and service for the business traveler. Prototype "Room That Works" at selected Marriott hotels includes a large console table, mobile writing desk, 2 power outlets, fully adjustable chair, PC modem jack, and movable task light.

KEY COMPETITORS

Allsteel
American Brands
Globe Furniture
Hanson
Haworth
Herman Miller
HON Industries
Krueger International
Masco
O'Sullivan Industries
Rubbermaid
Shelby Williams
United Stationers
Westinghouse

HOW MUCH

	9-Year Growth	1986	1987	1988	1989	1990	1991	1992	1993	1994	1995
Sales ($ mil.)	6.7%	1,393	1,506	1,624	1,810	1,896	1,945	2,300	2,400	2,500	2,500
Employees	2.8%	15,000	16,000	14,000	18,500	21,500	21,000	20,500	19,000	17,800	19,200

Sales ($ mil.)
1986–95

Steelcase

STONE CONTAINER CORPORATION

OVERVIEW

After overexpansion and slumping paper prices almost broke Stone Container in the early 1990s, Stone is on a roll again. The 1994 surge in paper prices is lifting the once-sinking Stone toward profitability.

The company is the world's largest producer of paperboard and paper packaging; it is the #1 producer of containerboard and corrugated containers as well as bags and sacks (such as those used in supermarkets and 20-pound bags of Purina dog food). In addition, Stone Container is major producer of newsprint, uncoated groundwood paper, and market pulp and makes lumber, plywood, and veneer at 16 North American mills. The company operates in Latin America, Europe, Australia, and the Far East as well. Foreign sales accounted for 27% of total 1994 revenue.

Stone Container's financial problems stem from its 1989 purchase of Consolidated-Bathhurst (renamed Stone-Consolidated) for $2.2 billion. Shortly after the acquisition, prices for newsprint produced by Stone-Consolidated softened, and the company began negotiating with lenders. In recent years the company has taken measures to lighten its debt load, including selling off assets, issuing new debt, and selling stock.

The Stone family, which holds several key executive positions, owns about 15% of the company's common stock. Led by Roger Stone's unsinkable optimism, the company reckons to make $1 billion in net profit on $10 billion sales in 1998.

The company is leaving no stone unturned in its twin strategies of decreasing debt and increasing sales. In 1994 the company restructured $2.5 billion of its debt, and CEO Stone is looking to the expanding demand for boxes in Europe and Asia to keep sales growing.

WHEN

Go to America, Joseph Stone's mother told him in 1888. There's nothing for you in Russia, she said.

Stone moved to the US, first to Philadelphia, then to Chicago. In 1926, with $2,300 he scraped together from savings and from sons Norman and Marvin, he launched J.H. Stone & Sons as a jobber for shipping supplies such as wrapping paper and tissue. A 3rd son, Jerome, joined the business in 1928, the same year the little company (first year sales: $68,000) began jobbing corrugated boxes. During the Depression the Stone firm suffered a shortage of corrugated boxes, and when a supplier offered to sell the Stones used box-making equipment, they paid $7,200 for it. In 1938 the Stones built a 150,000-square-foot plant to manufacture corrugated boxes. They paid the $382,000, 20-year note off in 3 years, because, as Marvin Stone would recall later, "we . . . did not view business debt as virtue."

Stone bought a Philadelphia corrugated box company (1943), incorporated as Stone Container Corp. (1945), and went public (1947). In the early 1960s the company launched its South Carolina Industries affiliate to manufacture kraft linerboard.

Roger Stone, Marvin's son, became president in 1975. In 1979 Stone Container's board of directors turned down a $125 million purchase offer from Boise Cascade. Under Roger the company shifted from target to marksman, picking off distressed companies during industry slumps. Using junk bond financing, Stone Container paid $509 million for Continental Group's forest products unit (1983), $426 million for the brown paper business of Champion (1986), and $760 million for Southwest Forest Industries (1987).

In 1989 Stone Container bought Consolidated-Bathhurst of Canada, a leading maker of newsprint, in an all-cash $2.2 billion deal, seeing in Consolidated-Bathhurst's European subsidiaries a beachhead for gaining entry into the European market. But when prices slumped and interest expense skyrocketed, Stone Container suffered. In 1993 Stone sold to the public 25% of its stake in the Canadian subsidiary, raising $462 million.

In 1990 the company pushed into the recycling market, entering a joint venture with WMX (Paper Recycling International) and beefing up its recycling capacity at plants in Germany, Connecticut, and Montana. In 1993, as part of its effort to shore up its balance sheet, the company sold its interest in Titan, a Mexican corrugated container firm, and 2 short-line railroads for $125 million. In 1994 the company raised $962 million by selling 16.5 million shares of common stock and another $710 million by issuing debt.

The company sold 2 Detroit area container plants in 1994 to Laimbeer Packaging and closed 3 solid wood products operations in the Pacific Northwest.

NYSE symbol: STO
Fiscal year ends: December 31

WHO

Chairman, President, and CEO: Roger W. Stone, age 60, $730,000 pay
President and CEO, Stone-Consolidated: James Doughan, age 61, $678,412 pay
EVP Corporate Administration: Morty Rosenkranz, age 67, $420,000 pay
EVP, CFO, and Chief Planning Officer: Arnold F. Brookstone, age 65, $322,000 pay
SVP and General Manager, North American Containerboard, Paper and Pulp: James B. Heider, age 51, $285,000 pay
SVP and General Manager, Industrial and Retail Packaging Division: Thomas W. Cadden Sr., age 61
SVP and General Manager, Forest Products Division: Gerald M. Freeman, age 58
VP, Secretary, and Counsel: Leslie T. Lederer, age 47
VP Human Resources and Benefits Administration: Gayle M. Sparapani
Auditors: Price Waterhouse LLP

WHERE

HQ: 150 N. Michigan Ave., Chicago, IL 60601-7568
Phone: 312-346-6600
Fax: 312-580-4919

Stone Container has more than 125 plants in the US, 27 in Canada, 16 in Germany, 2 in Australia, 2 in Belgium, 2 in Costa Rica, 2 in the UK, 6 in France, and one each in Mexico, the Netherlands, and Venezuela.

	1994 Sales		1994 Operating Income	
	$ mil.	% of total	$ mil.	% of total
US	4,188	73	344	91
Canada	942	16	20	5
Europe	619	11	15	4
Total	**5,749**	**100**	**379**	**100**

WHAT

	1994 Sales		1994 Operating Income	
	$ mil.	% of total	$ mil.	% of total
Paperboard & paper packaging	4,199	73	354	94
White paper & pulp	1,550	27	25	6
Adjustments	—	—	—	—
Total	**5,749**	**100**	**379**	**100**

Paperboard and Paper Packaging
Bags and sacks
Boxboard
Containerboard
Corrugated containers
Folding cartons
Kraft paper

White Paper and Pulp
Market pulp
Newsprint
Uncoated paper

Wood Products
Lumber
Plywood
Veneer

KEY COMPETITORS

Arjo Wiggins
Appleton
Boise Cascade
Bowater
Burhmann-
Tetterode
Champion Intl.
Consolidated
Papers
Fletcher Challenge
Fort Howard
Georgia-Pacific
International
Paper
James River

Jefferson Smurfit
Kimberly-Clark
Longview Fibre
Manville
Mead
Potlach
Scott
Stora
Temple-Inland
Union Camp
Westvaco
Weyerhaeuser
Willamette
Industries

HOW MUCH

	9-Year Growth	1985	1986	1987	1988	1989	1990	1991	1992	1993	1994
Sales ($ mil.)	18.7%	1,229	2,032	3,233	3,743	5,330	5,756	5,384	5,521	5,060	5,749
Net income ($ mil.)	—	4	35	161	342	286	95	(49)	(170)	(319)	(190)
Income as % of sales	—	0.3%	1.7%	5.0%	9.1%	5.4%	1.7%	—	—	—	—
Earnings per share ($)	—	0.09	0.73	2.65	5.58	4.67	1.56	(0.78)	(2.59)	(4.59)	(2.30)
Stock price – high ($)	—	13.17	20.00	38.83	39.50	36.38	25.25	26.00	32.63	19.50	21.13
Stock price – low ($)	—	8.00	11.38	15.33	20.67	22.13	8.13	9.00	12.50	6.38	9.63
Stock price – close ($)	3.8%	12.38	18.95	24.02	31.37	23.41	11.27	25.37	16.75	9.63	17.38
P/E – high	—	—	27	15	7	8	16	—	—	—	—
P/E – low	—	—	16	6	4	5	5	—	—	—	—
Dividends per share ($)	(100.0%)	0.19	0.19	0.25	0.35	0.70	0.71	0.71	0.35	0.00	0.00
Book value per share ($)	(2.0%)	7.08	9.92	12.40	17.73	22.50	24.34	22.12	13.91	6.91	5.90
Employees	13.4%	9,400	15,500	18,800	20,700	32,600	32,300	31,800	31,200	29,000	29,100

1994 Year-end:
Debt ratio: 89.9%
Return on equity: —
Cash (mil.): $109
Current ratio: 1.76
Long-term debt (mil.): $4,432
No. of shares (mil.): 90
Dividends
  Yield: —
  Payout: —
Market value (mil.): $1,571

Stock Price History High/Low 1985–94

STORAGE TECHNOLOGY CORPORATION

OVERVIEW

Storage Technology hopes Iceberg will keep it afloat. In 1995 the company, known as StorageTek, shipped its 500th Iceberg disk array. Iceberg, an advanced mainframe storage system, is the linchpin in the company's ongoing corporate makeover.

Louisville, Colorado–based StorageTek manufactures information storage systems — including disk arrays, tape libraries, and enterprise backup and recovery software products — for high-performance computers. It has about 8% of the market for high-end direct access storage devices (DASDs) and is the world leader in robotic library systems.

StorageTek, which spent 10% of 1994 revenues on R&D, had 90 new products on the drawing board to be introduced in 1995. Recent rollouts include the Arctic Fox DASD;

TimberLine, the world's fastest 1/2" tape transport subsystem; and Central Archive Management (CAM) software. In 1995 the company announced development of a high-performance, high-capacity mass storage cartridge subsystem called RedWood.

StorageTek acquired Minneapolis-based Network Systems Corp. (NSC) in 1995. The addition of NSC's computer networking products broadens StorageTek's presence in the booming network computing marketplace. Among NSC's 11 subsidiaries are Bytex (networking hardware), Bus-Tech (circuit testing equipment), and TMD (software).

In 1995 StorageTek opened its new manufacturing and R&D center in Toulouse, France. The plant manufactures the TimberLine tape subsystems.

WHEN

A group of 4 former IBM engineers founded Storage Technology in Colorado in 1969 to fill a niche in tape drives for IBM-compatible mainframe computers. One of the founders, a Palestinian refugee named Jesse Aweida, led the company to the top of its industry.

Heady growth inspired StorageTek to become a full-line supplier of peripherals. Acquisitions included Promodata (1973), Disk Systems (1974), Microtechnology (1979), and Documation (1980). The company also began developing an IBM-compatible mainframe computer and an optical laser disk. Sales leaped from $4 million in 1971 to $922 million in 1981, making StorageTek the world's leading supplier of tape drives (with a 55% market share for IBM-compatible tape drives) and disk drives (35%) and the 9th largest company in the computer industry.

In 1982, however, delayed expansion projects ate capital while providing no return. In addition, malfunctions on disk drives installed earlier resulted in costly replacements and damage to the company's reputation. Aweida's termination of several product lines could not prevent a cash-flow crisis, and in late 1984 StorageTek filed for bankruptcy.

Aweida stepped down, and turnaround artist Ryal Poppa (who became CEO in 1985) sliced $85 million in expenses by eliminating 2 layers of management, 5,000 workers, and the mainframe and optical disk projects. Although the company was still awash in red ink, Poppa persuaded creditors to fund his vision of automated tape storage at a fraction of disk drive prices. The resulting 4400 ACS (Automated

Cartridge System) was instrumental to the company's success after its 1987 emergence from bankruptcy. The company's Library Server software allowed the ACS to work with most high-performance computers, reducing StorageTek's dependence on IBM machines.

In 1989 the company purchased Aspen Peripherals to enter the mid-range tape market. Aspen president Jesse Aweida did not rejoin the company he had helped found.

In 1991 StorageTek merged its nonimpact printer operations into a venture with Siemens Nixdorf (sold to Siemens Nixdorf, 1994) and bought troubled computer distributor XL/Datacomp. In 1992 the company agreed to buy Swedish storage system distributor Edata. Later in the year StorageTek expanded its mid-range computer (AS/400) product line by acquiring Lago Systems and Prime Solutions. Also in 1992 DEC and StorageTek established Rocky Mountain Magnetics (with StorageTek owning 19%) to develop magneto-resistive thin-film heads.

Poor European results, heavy price competition in the mid-range market, and new product development expenses pushed StorageTek over $100 million into the red in 1993. The company restructured, reorganized its distribution and service operations, and overhauled its product line, returning to profitability in 1994.

In early 1995 StorageTek shares rose on rumors of a takeover bid by chief competitor IBM. That same year the company said it would sell its computer-leasing business to AT&T Capital and use the profits to offset downsizing costs.

NYSE symbol: STK
Fiscal year ends: Last Friday in December

WHO

Chairman, President, and CEO: Ryal R. Poppa, age 61, $692,500 pay
EVP Worldwide Field Operations: John V. Williams, age 51, $311,972 pay
EVP Operations: Lowell Thomas Gooch, age 50, $287,500 pay
EVP Systems Development and COO: David E. Weiss, age 50
President and COO, Network Systems, Inc.: Michael Ashby
VP and Interim CFO: David E. Lacey, age 48
VP, Treasurer, and Interim Controller: Mark D. McGregor, age 53
VP Sourcing: Gary R. Anderson
VP Business Development and Support: Lynn A. Leier
VP International Manufacturing: Victor M. Perez
VP, General Counsel, and Secretary: W. Russell Wayman, age 50
VP Human Resources: Sewell I. Sleek
Auditors: Price Waterhouse LLP

WHERE

HQ: 2270 S. 88th St., Louisville, CO 80028-4309
Phone: 303-673-5151
Fax: 303-673-5019

StorageTek has manufacturing facilities in California, Colorado, Florida, Puerto Rico, and the UK. The company sells its products worldwide.

	1994 Sales		1994 Operating Income	
	$ mil.	% of total	$ mil.	% of total
US	1,055	65	100	—
Europe	446	27	(16)	—
Other countries	124	8	4	—
Adjustments	—	—	(11)	—
Total	**1,625**	**100**	**77**	**—**

WHAT

	1994 Sales	
	$ mil.	% of total
Sales	1,116	69
Rental & service	509	31
Total	**1,625**	**100**

	1994 Sales	
	$ mil.	% of total
Serial-access subsystems	1,033	64
Random-access subsystems	254	16
Mid-range systems	252	15
Other	86	5
Total	**1,625**	**100**

Serial-Access Subsystems
4480 18-track cartridge drives
PowderHorn
RedWood
Silverton
TimberLine
View Direct software
WolfCreek

Random-Access Subsystems
Arctic Fox
Iceberg Disk Array
Kodiak
Nordique

Mid-range Systems
Alpine 9600 Storage Manager
Highlands
Northfield
Twin Peaks

Other Products
NearNet networking hardware and software

Selected Subsidiaries
Amperif Corp.
Network Systems Corporation
XL/Datacomp, Inc.

KEY COMPETITORS

3Com	Data General	Micropolis
Amdahl	DEC	MTI Technology
AT&T	EMC Corp.	NEC
Cabletron	Exabyte	Siemens
Colorado Memory Systems	Fujitsu	SyQuest
Conner Peripherals	Hitachi	Tandem
	IBM	

HOW MUCH

	9-Year Growth	1985	1986	1987	1988	1989	1990	1991	1992	1993	1994
Sales ($ mil.)	10.3%	673	696	750	874	983	1,141	1,585	1,522	1,405	1,625
Net income ($ mil.)	—	(44)	17	19	44	36	71	93	16	(128)	29
Income as % of sales	—	—	2.4%	2.5%	5.1%	3.7%	6.2%	5.9%	1.0%	—	1.8%
Earnings per share ($)	—	(12.60)	4.80	1.30	1.90	1.40	2.22	2.33	0.37	(2.98)	0.66
Stock price – high ($)	—	38.75	73.75	50.00	36.25	22.50	35.25	51.50	78.00	45.00	41.50
Stock price – low ($)	—	10.00	17.50	11.25	12.50	9.25	11.00	17.75	18.38	18.00	25.00
Stock price – close ($)	5.8%	17.50	35.00	18.75	17.50	11.75	21.50	39.88	20.75	31.88	29.00
P/E – high	—	—	15	39	—	16	16	22	—	—	63
P/E – low	—	—	4	9	—	7	5	8	—	—	38
Dividends per share ($)	—	0.00	0.00	0.00	0.00	0.00	0.00	0.00	0.00	0.00	0.00
Book value per share ($)	—	(15.69)	(5.21)	10.23	1.25	13.12	16.14	21.80	22.25	23.62	24.13
Employees	2.1%	8,540	8,608	8,865	8,498	9,300	9,100	10,100	10,100	10,100	10,300

1994 Year-end:
Debt ratio: 30.1%
Return on equity: 2.8%
Cash (mil.): $206
Current ratio: 2.06
Long-term debt (mil.): $357
No. of shares (mil.): 45
Dividends
  Yield: —
  Payout: —
Market value (mil.): $1,291

Stock Price History High/Low 1985–94

STUDENT LOAN MARKETING ASSN.

OVERVIEW

The travails of the Student Loan Marketing Association (Sallie Mae) may illustrate some of the difficulties of privatizing government services. On the one hand, the company is being squeezed by the effects of legislation designed to phase out much of its function (to buy student loans from originators), and, on the other, many stockholders of the government-sponsored enterprise oppose management's plan to fully privatize and diversify Sallie Mae.

Like Fannie Mae (the Federal National Mortgage Association), Sallie Mae is a publicly mandated private company, designed to keep loan money flowing and protect student loans from the vagaries of the credit market. The company also lends money to colleges for capital equipment and facilities.

Sallie Mae enjoys advantages its private competitors lack, including an implicit guarantee of US government support and protection from the costs of defaulted loans by state and federal guarantees. But legislation enacted in 1993 provides for the government to take over up to 60% of student loan originations by 1998.

In response Sallie Mae sought to sever its link to the government and give up its preferential position, which would allow it to diversify into new areas. It would also free Sallie Mae of a burdensome 0.3% surcharge designed to eliminate the bottom-line effects of its advantages in the interest market.

But Sallie Mae has been impeded in this effort by a group of dissident stockholders led by former COO Albert Lord (who resigned after being passed over for promotion) and including the Capital Group, which owns 11.5% of the company. In 1995, after the dissidents staged a proxy battle to pack the board, Sallie Mae sued. The dissidents in turn sued the company, alleging that it had closed the polls early, thus preventing them from gaining the seats to which they believed they were entitled.

WHEN

The Student Loan Marketing Association was chartered in 1972 in response to problems in the Guaranteed Student Loan Program of 1965. For years the program had tinkered with rates to induce banks to make loans, but servicing the small loans (processing payment) was expensive and troublesome. Sallie Mae began operations in 1973, buying loans from their originators and providing liquidity to the student loan market. Its size offered economies of scale in servicing the loans.

Originally, only educational or student loan lending institutions were allowed to own stock; this was later changed so that anyone could buy nonvoting stock. In 1993 voting stock was listed on the NYSE.

Sallie Mae has always been a political football, having been changed again and again to reflect the opinions of the parties in power at a given time. When it was founded during the Nixon administration, its loans were restricted by a needs test, which was repealed during the Carter years. The Reagan administration reimposed the needs test, while at the same time speeding up the schedule under which the company was to become self-supporting. The first year of the Reagan administration was the last year Sallie Mae asked for a handout. It became self-supporting in 1981.

Forced onto its own resources, Sallie Mae turned to creative financing. One of the company's traditional advantages is that its loan interest rates are linked to Treasury bills, traditionally about 3% above the T-bill rate. The company became a master at riding the spread between its cost of funds and the interest rates it charges. In recent years the company has had success with securitizing the loans it buys (packaging them together and selling them like bonds).

Between 1983 and 1992 Sallie Mae's assets grew over 400%, and its income rose by almost 500%. As it grew, management became more visible, with high pay and extravagant benefits and perks. Although salaries were not inconsistent with those of executives at corporations of comparable size, the remuneration level and perks irked members of Congress and other politicians.

Sallie Mae kept growing, adding new programs to service loans and assist banks in servicing them. In 1992 it expanded its facilities and added 900 new staff members.

The Clinton administration's 1993 Omnibus Budget Reconciliation Act, with its transfer of the student loan program directly to the government and its surcharge on Sallie Mae, had already begun to have an adverse effect on earnings by 1994. Pending permission to alter its charter, the company has stepped up its marketing efforts (primarily to school loan officers, who advise students on loan options), and in 1995 it acquired HICA Holding, one of 2 private insurers of education loans.

NYSE symbol: SLM
Fiscal year ends: December 31

WHO

Chairman: William Arceneaux, age 53
President and CEO: Lawrence A. Hough, age 50, $655,025 pay
EVP and CFO: Denise B. McGlone, age 42, $503,846 pay
EVP and General Counsel: Timothy G. Greene, age 55, $443,000 pay
EVP Servicing: Robert D. Friedhoff, age 40, $410,000 pay
EVP Marketing: Lydia M. Marshall, age 45, $400,000 pay
EVP; Chairman, President, and CEO, CyberMark, Inc.: Dennis A. Kernahan, age 47
EVP Systems and Chief Technology Officer: Edith W. Martin, age 49
SVP Credit: William L. Wingate Jr., age 57
SVP Personnel and Administration: Gerald Cohen, age 59
VP and Treasurer: Robert R. Levine
VP Product Development: Robert W. Jackson
VP Marketing and Lender Products: Barry W. Goulding
VP Regional Servicing: Richard J. Boyle
VP Regional Servicing: J. Barry Morrow
VP Investments: Robert J. Ruggero-Lavin
VP Product Management and Business Development: Jeffrey W. Salinger
Auditors: Ernst & Young LLP

WHERE

HQ: Student Loan Marketing Association, 1050 Thomas Jefferson St. NW, Washington, DC 20007
Phone: 202-333-8000
Fax: 202-298-3160

The company buys student loans and lends funds for student loans to banks and other institutions throughout the US. It also offers an array of loan management services and finances capital equipment for educational institutions.

WHAT

	1994 Assets	
	$ mil.	% of total
Cash & investments	12,697	24
Student loans, net	30,371	58
Warehousing advances	7,032	13
Academic facilities financings	1,548	3
Other	1,313	2
Total	**52,961**	**100**

	1994 Sales	
	$ mil.	% of total
Interest income		
Student loans	2,109	69
Warehousing advances	346	11
Academic facilities financings	102	4
Investment income	500	16
Total	**3,057**	**100**

Lending and Payment Products
ExportSS (loan management support)
Great Rewards (payment incentives)
LineSS (loan processing automation software)
PortSS (client/server software for lenders)
Select your Terms (repayment plan)
Smart Rewards (payment plan)

Subsidiary
CyberMark, Inc. (electronic information delivery systems)

KEY COMPETITORS

Chase Manhattan
Chemical Banking
Citicorp
Other banks and institutions that buy or service student loans

HOW MUCH

	9-Year Growth	1985	1986	1987	1988	1989	1990	1991	1992	1993	1994
Assets ($ mil.)	15.5%	14,450	18,232	22,864	28,628	35,488	41,124	45,320	46,621	46,509	52,961
Net income ($ mil.)	14.1%	123	145	181	225	258	301	345	394	430	403
Income as % of assets	—	0.9%	0.8%	0.8%	0.8%	0.7%	0.7%	0.8%	0.8%	0.9%	0.8%
Earnings per share ($)	19.6%	0.98	1.23	1.66	2.14	2.53	2.96	3.55	4.21	4.83	4.91
Stock price – high ($)	—	15.34	27.44	35.81	34.59	53.50	56.50	76.00	76.00	75.25	49.88
Stock price – low ($)	—	9.94	14.09	24.41	28.00	33.25	32.75	43.63	59.00	39.88	31.25
Stock price – close ($)	9.1%	14.81	26.44	28.19	33.84	48.00	46.25	74.00	68.88	44.88	32.50
P/E – high	—	16	22	22	16	21	19	21	18	16	10
P/E – low	—	10	12	15	13	16	11	12	14	8	6
Dividends per share ($)	39.7%	0.07	0.07	0.16	0.24	0.41	0.59	0.85	0.75	1.25	1.42
Book value per share ($)	19.2%	4.13	4.31	4.97	6.42	8.35	9.35	12.40	13.65	15.23	20.01
Employees	22.1%	820	1,000	1,200	1,550	2,100	2,450	3,425	4,350	4,510	4,948

1994 Year-end:
Equity as % of assets: 2.8%
Return on assets: 1.5%
Return on equity: 29.3%
Long-term debt (mil.): $34,319
No. of shares (mil.): 74
Dividends
 Yield: 4.4%
 Payout: 28.9%
Market value (mil.): $2,389
Sales (mil.): $3,057

**Stock Price History
High/Low 1985–94**

SUN COMPANY, INC.

OVERVIEW

Operating 5 refineries in the US, Philadelphia-based Sun markets SUNOCO gasoline in 17 states. The oil company also sells petrochemicals worldwide, operates domestic pipelines and terminals, and produces crude oil and natural gas internationally. Sluggish refined oil prices in 1994 pulled down Sun's financial performance, which had begun to pick up momentum after the company lost money in the early 1990s.

The company has limited its exploration activities to Canada, while development, production, and marketing activities are conducted in Canada and the North Sea. Sun's subsidiary Sun Company, Inc. (R&M) manages refining, marketing, chemicals, lubricants, and pipeline and terminal operations. Its chemical operations make petrochemicals for use in plastics and other industries.

Sun has interests in coal, real estate, and leasing operations but is planning to dispose of them as nonstrategic businesses.

In line with the company's strategy to focus on its profitable business lines, Sun sold its 33.3% interest in a Colombian oil field in 1994 for $25 million. In 1995 Sun sold its 55% interest in Suncor, its Canadian oil and gas exploration and oil sands mining subsidiary, to a group of Canadian underwriters for approximately $855 million.

WHEN

Joseph Newton Pew began his energy career in 1876 in a Pennsylvania natural gas pipeline partnership. One arm of his enterprise supplied Pittsburgh with the first natural gas system for a major city's home and industrial use. When oil discoveries in northwest Ohio sparked an 1886 boom, Pew organized Sun Oil Line, consolidated in 1890 as Sun Oil (Ohio). In 1894 Sun created Diamond Oil to purchase a Toledo refinery; Sun traces its trademark diamond pierced by an arrow to that short-lived Diamond subsidiary.

With the 1901 Spindletop gusher, Pew dispatched nephew J. Edgar Pew to Texas, where he bought land for a storage terminal and at a 1902 auction bought the oil-rich properties of a bankrupt firm. Back East, the elder Pew bought Delaware River acreage in Pennsylvania for a shipping terminal and refinery to process Texas crude into Red Stock. The lubricating oil carved Sun a place in the Standard Oil–dominated petroleum industry.

Joseph Newton Pew died in 1912 and was succeeded by sons J. Howard, 30, and Joseph Newton Jr., 26. The young Pews launched the company into shipbuilding (1916) and gasoline stations (1920). Sun's gasoline was dyed blue (legend says it matched a Chinese tile chip Joseph Pew Jr. and his wife had received on their honeymoon) and sold as Blue Sunoco.

When Howard Pew retired in 1947, brother Joe became chairman and Robert Dunlop became the first non-Pew president of Sun. Dunlop led the company to its first major foreign oil strike, in Venezuela's Lake Maracaibo in 1957.

In 1967 Dunlop's chance meeting with a Sunray DX executive in Midland, Texas, led Sun to acquire Sunray DX the next year. The addition of Sunray DX diluted the Pew family's stake in the company. In the 1970s president Robert Sharbaugh diversified the company away from its energy roots. The company dropped "oil" from its name in 1976. Sharbaugh left in 1978 after Sun's foray into the medical supply business.

To refocus on the oil business, the company purchased Seagram's Texas Pacific Oil for $2.3 billion in 1980, sold its venerable shipbuilding arm in 1982, and sold the medical supply business in 1985. In 1988 Sun acquired Atlantic Petroleum and its more than 1,000 service stations. Sun decided to forsake drilling in the US when it spun off its domestic oil and gas properties into Oryx Energy in 1988, but it retained its international exploration and production business.

In 1992 Sun settled a dispute with the Iranian government and the National Iranian Oil Company over lands the company had lost following the Iranian Revolution. The settlement required Iran to pay Sun more than $130 million. In 1993 the company sold its Cordero Mining Co. to Kennecott for $120 million and cut its interest in Suncor, a Canadian petroleum company (sold in 1995), from 68% to 55% through a stock offering. In 1994 Sun agreed to pay Chevron $170 million for a refinery in Philadelphia and a 1/3 interest in a pipeline connecting the refinery to the New York Harbor. Also that year the company won a 5-year contract to operate 16 service stations on the Ohio Turnpike. Sun also operates or supplies 51 service plazas on major highways in New Jersey, New York, and Pennsylvania.

Sun announced plans for an extensive operational and financial restructuring in 1995, including cutting its workforce by 800.

NYSE symbol: SUN
Fiscal year ends: December 31

WHO

Chairman, CEO, and President: Robert H. Campbell, age 57, $771,745 pay
SVP Corporate Development: David E. Knoll, age 51, $354,026 pay
SVP and CFO: Robert M. Aiken Jr., age 52, $342,430 pay
SVP Operations: Harwood S. Roe Jr., age 50, $286,281 pay
SVP and Chief Administrative Officer: Sheldon L. Thompson, age 56, $261,151 pay
SVP Marketing: John G. Driscoll, age 48
SVP Logistics: Deborah M. Fretz, age 46
SVP Corporate Development: David E. Knoll, age 51
VP and General Counsel: Jack L. Foltz, age 59
VP Human Resources: Albert Little
Comptroller: Richard L. Cartlidge, age 40
Treasurer: Malcolm I. Ruddock, age 52
Auditors: Coopers & Lybrand L.L.P.

WHERE

HQ: 10 Penn Center, 1801 Market St., Philadelphia, PA 19103-1699
Phone: 215-977-3000
Fax: 215-977-3409

Sun operates primarily in the US, Canada, and the UK North Sea.

	1994 Sales		1994 Operating Income	
	$ mil.	% of total	$ mil.	% of total
US	7,963	81	21	13
Canada	1,397	14	45	28
Other countries	447	5	94	59
Adjustments	11	—	54	—
Total	**9,818**	**100**	**214**	**100**

WHAT

	1994 Sales		1994 Operating Income	
	$ mil.	% of total	$ mil.	% of total
Refining & marketing	9,651	98	36	15
Exploration & production	156	2	144	58
Oil sands mining	—	—	68	27
Corp.	11	0	(34)	—
Total	**9,818**	**100**	**214**	**100**

Selected Subsidiaries
Sun Company, Inc. (R&M) (refining and marketing operations)
Sun Oil Britain Ltd. (production outside North America)
Sun Pipe Line Co.
Sun Pipeline Services Co.

Selected Brand Names
APLUS convenience stores
OPTIMA gasoline
SUNOCO service stations
SUNOCO Super C diesel engine oil
SUNSPRAY ULTRA-FINE pesticide spray oil
ULTRA gasoline
ULTRA SERVICE CENTER service stations

KEY COMPETITORS

Amerada Hess	Elf Aquitaine	Phillips
Amoco	Exxon	Petroleum
Ashland, Inc.	Imperial Oil	Quaker State
Atlantic Richfield	Mobil	Repsol
British	Norsk Hydro	Royal Dutch/Shell
Petroleum	Occidental	Sinclair Oil
Chevron	Oryx	Southland
Circle K	PDVSA	Star Enterprise
Coastal	PEMEX	Texaco
Diamond	Pennzoil	TOTAL
Shamrock	Petrobrás	Unocal
DuPont	Petrofina	USX–Marathon

HOW MUCH

	9-Year Growth	1985	1986	1987	1988	1989	1990	1991	1992	1993	1994
Sales ($ mil.)	(6.5%)	14,369	9,603	8,824	11,128	12,723	12,573	11,493	10,445	9,180	9,818
Net income ($ mil.)	(17.1%)	527	385	348	7	98	199	(387)	(298)	283	97
Income as % of sales	—	3.7%	4.0%	3.9%	0.1%	0.8%	1.6%	—	—	3.1%	1.0%
Earnings per share ($)	(16.7%)	4.72	3.54	3.21	0.06	0.92	1.86	(3.65)	(2.80)	2.65	0.91
Stock price – high ($)	—	56.25	59.50	73.13	61.75	43.25	41.88	35.75	30.75	32.75	35.25
Stock price – low ($)	—	43.63	42.25	34.00	28.00	31.38	25.75	25.75	22.50	22.25	25.13
Stock price – close ($)	(1.8%)	51.75	54.25	51.38	32.13	40.88	27.88	30.50	28.00	29.38	28.75
P/E – high	—	12	17	23	—	47	23	—	—	12	39
P/E – low	—	9	12	11	—	34	14	—	—	8	28
Dividends per share ($)	(2.7%)	2.30	3.00	3.00	2.70	1.80	1.80	1.80	1.80	1.80	1.80
Book value per share ($)	(10.8%)	48.71	49.03	49.36	31.24	30.50	30.83	25.41	17.82	18.60	17.42
Employees	(10.1%)	37,818	23,645	22,600	21,309	21,608	20,926	17,000	14,219	14,500	14,568

1994 Year-end:
Debt ratio: 42.8%
Return on equity: 5.0%
Cash (mil.): $117
Current ratio: 0.79
Long-term debt (mil.): $1,073
No. of shares (mil.): 107
Dividends
 Yield: 6.3%
 Payout: 197.8%
Market value (mil.): $3,074

**Stock Price History
High/Low 1985–94**

SUN MICROSYSTEMS, INC.

OVERVIEW

What's hot? Sun Microsystems and its suite of new Internet solutions are. In mid-1995 Sun unveiled the Hot Java browser and a new Internet server called Netra. It also introduced Internet solutions for the x86 platform (Internet Gateway) and for PCs (SolarNet).

Sun, which already provides more than half of all Internet servers, developed the infrastructure for Time Warner's Pathfinder site on the World Wide Web and an Internet presence for the San Jose Sharks pro hockey team. In 1995 Pacific Bell said it had chosen Sun servers for its Internet Services network.

Sun, the leading manufacturer of network-based distributed computing systems, is the #1 maker of UNIX-based workstations, with 38% of that market. Its top-to-bottom product line includes microprocessors (UltraSPARC), software (Solaris, SunLink), systems (SPARCserver, SPARCstation), and service.

Sun's success is due partly to its early adoption of an open system architecture, which encouraged software developers to create programs for its machines — over 9,300 by 1994. The company has been able to attract corporate clients by offering UNIX-based computing at a lower cost than mainframes. In 1994 Sun and IBM began modifying Solaris software (the leading UNIX operating system) for PowerPC-based machines.

The company expects its UltraSPARC microprocessor to rival Intel's P6 (now under development) and the PowerPC chip when it debuts in late 1995.

WHEN

The four 27-year-olds who founded Sun Microsystems in 1982 saw great market potential for workstations able to share data using the UNIX operating system so popular with scientists and engineers.

German-born Andreas Bechtolsheim, a Stanford engineering graduate student, had built a workstation from spare parts for his numerical problems. Two Stanford MBA graduates, Scott McNealy and India-born Vinod Khosla, liked Bechtolsheim's creation, and they tapped Berkeley's UNIX guru William Joy to supply the software. Khosla was president and McNealy was director of manufacturing of the new company.

By adopting AT&T's UNIX operating system, Sun's workstations, unlike those of industry pioneer Apollo, from the outset networked easily with the hardware and software of other vendors. Sun, with lower prices made possible by its use of existing technologies, zoomed to more than $500 million in sales in just 5 years. In 1984 Khosla retired; he was succeeded by McNealy. Sun went public in 1986.

The engineering market devoured such Sun offerings as the Sun-3 family (1985) and the 386i (1987). Sun hooked its workstations into networks with its NFS (a widely used file access system), SunNet, and SunLink.

In 1987 Sun signed with AT&T to develop an enhanced UNIX operating system; AT&T took a 19% equity investment in Sun the following year but sold it in 1991. The product that emerged in late 1989 established a de facto high-end UNIX standard (System V, Release 4.0). Sun's development of the fast and highly adaptable SPARC microprocessor (which uses a simplified RISC design) gave its SPARCstation 2 (1990) minicomputer power.

Sun licensed SPARC to stimulate low-cost, high-volume production of SPARC systems and thus increase the number of 3rd-party applications available. PC programs such as *Lotus 1-2-3*, *WordPerfect*, and Borland's *dBASE IV* for Sun systems have broadened Sun's commercial market.

In 1991 the company introduced the SPARCserver 600MP line of multiprocessor network servers. In 1993 Sun announced plans to sell microprocessors and other computer chips in an effort to become a one-stop technology shop. It also signed deals with NeXT (to develop easier-to-use operating systems for workstations) and Amdahl (to develop software for mainframe computers). Sun began producing a video server with software maker Starlight Networks in 1994. Rather than focus on video-on-demand for consumers, it is targeting corporate customers who want to transmit training videos, news conferences, and other visuals over private networks.

In 1995 Sun introduced 2 new versions of its SPARCstation Voyager portable workstations. That same year the US Army tapped Sun to supply about 28,000 workstations and servers over a 10-year-period for a new tactical command and control system. Also in 1995 the South African Constitutional Assembly chose SPARCserver to help that country write its new constitution. Using SPARCserver, the South Africans are creating the first interactive, on-line constitutional process, with committee reports, expert opinions, and citizens' comments accessible via the Internet.

Nasdaq symbol: SUNW
Fiscal year ends: June 30

WHO

Chairman, President, and CEO: Scott G. McNealy, age 39, $651,304 pay
President, Sun Microsystems Computer Co.: Edward J. Zander, age 47, $495,688 pay (prior to promotion)
President, SPARC Technology Business: Chester J. Silvestri, age 45
President, SunExpress: Dorothy A. Terrell, age 49
President, SunService: Lawrence W. Hambly, age 48
President, SunSoft: Jon Kannegaard
VP Corporate Planning and Development and Chief Information Officer: William J. Raduchel, age 48, $436,977 pay
VP and CFO: Michael E. Lehman, age 44
VP and Chief Technology Officer: Eric E. Schmidt, age 39
VP Research and Development: William N. Joy, age 39
VP Technology: Andreas Bechtolsheim
VP, General Counsel, and Secretary: Michael H. Morris, age 46
VP Human Resources: Kenneth M. Alvares, age 50, $428,033 pay
Auditors: Ernst & Young LLP

WHERE

HQ: 2550 Garcia Ave., Mountain View, CA 94043-1100
Phone: 415-960-1300
Fax: 415-969-9131

Sun products are distributed in more than 125 countries worldwide.

	1994 Sales	
	$ mil.	**% of total**
US	2,483	53
Europe	1,171	25
Other regions	1,036	22
Total	**4,690**	**100**

WHAT

Systems

Servers	Workstations
Netra	SPARCclassic
SPARCserver 20	SPARCclassic X
SPARCserver 1000	SPARCstation 5
SPARCcenter 2000	SPARCstation 10
Storage	SPARCstation 20
SPARCstorage Array series	

Software
Developer products
Enterprise management products
Networking products
PC desktop integration products
Server products (Solaris)

Operating Companies
SPARC Technology Business (microprocessors)
Sun Microsystems Computer Co. (systems)
SunExpress, Inc. (distribution of nonsystems products)
SunSoft, Inc. (UNIX software environments)
SunService (service and support)

KEY COMPETITORS

Advanced Logic Research	LG Group
AMD	Machines Bull
Apple	Microsoft
AST	National Semiconductor
AT&T	NEC
Ceridian	Netscape
Compaq	NeXT
CompuServe	Novell
Data General	Samsung
DEC	Sequent
Fujitsu	Siemens
Harris	Silicon Graphics
Hewlett-Packard	Sony
Hitachi	Tandem
IBM	Toshiba
Intel	Unisys
Intergraph	Wang

HOW MUCH

	Annual Growth	1985	1986	1987	1988	1989	1990	1991	1992	1993	1994
Sales ($ mil.)	51.0%	115	210	538	1,052	1,765	2,466	3,221	3,589	4,309	4,690
Net income ($ mil.)	40.8%	9	12	36	66	61	111	190	173	157	196
Income as % of sales	—	7.4%	5.7%	6.8%	6.3%	3.4%	4.5%	5.9%	4.8%	3.6%	4.2%
Earnings per share ($)	30.8%	0.18	0.23	0.56	0.90	0.76	1.21	1.85	1.71	1.49	2.02
Stock price – high ($)	—	—	12.06	22.19	20.25	22.75	37.13	38.63	36.13	41.00	37.63
Stock price – low ($)	—	—	5.63	12.00	13.38	13.63	15.00	20.75	22.50	21.13	18.25
Stock price – close ($)	14.5%	—	12.00	16.75	16.63	17.25	21.38	28.38	33.63	29.13	35.50
P/E – high	—	—	52	40	23	30	31	21	21	28	19
P/E – low	—	—	25	21	15	18	12	11	13	14	9
Dividends per share ($)	—	—	0.00	0.00	0.00	0.00	0.00	0.00	0.00	0.00	0.00
Book value per share ($)	31.3%	—	1.97	3.58	5.11	7.88	10.01	11.96	14.85	16.09	17.35
Employees	30.3%	1,223	4,200	7,100	7,090	10,208	11,500	12,480	12,800	13,253	13,282

1994 Year-end:
Debt ratio: 12.8%
Return on equity: 12.0%
Cash (mil.): $883
Current ratio: 2.01
Long-term debt (mil.): $122
No. of shares (mil.): 94
Dividends
　Yield: —
　Payout: —
Market value (mil.): $3,332

**Stock Price History
High/Low 1986–94**

SUNTRUST BANKS, INC.

OVERVIEW

Despite the poor performance of its asset management group, Atlanta-based SunTrust Banks has had another banner year. The company has grown through the acquisition of banks in the affluent retirement markets of Florida (where it does more business than in its home state, Georgia). It also does business in Tennessee and Alabama. In all, SunTrust operates 29 banking subsidiaries in 4 southeastern states. Until 1995 the company's subsidiaries operated under the names of its local subsidiaries (SunBanks in Florida, Trust Company of

Georgia, and Third National Corporation in Tennessee and Alabama). But in that year they started operating under the SunTrust name.

In addition to standard retail and commercial banking services, SunTrust offers credit cards, mortgage banking, mutual funds, asset and investment management, and securities underwriting and dealing (for which it received approval in 1994). The new unit, SunTrust Capital Markets, will focus on corporate and institutional markets, particularly in the area of municipal financing.

WHEN

SunTrust was born from the union of old-money Georgia and new-money Florida. Founded in 1891 as the Commercial Traveler's Savings Bank, the Trust Company of Georgia served Atlanta's oldest and richest institutions. It helped underwrite Coca-Cola's first public stock sale in 1919; the only written copy of the Coke formula lies in a Trust vault. The company still retains ownership of about $1 billion in Coke stock, the value of the shares it received for acting as underwriter.

Beginning in 1933 Trust acquired controlling interests in 5 other Georgia banks. As regulation of multibank ownership relaxed in the 1970s, Trust acquired the remaining interests in its original banks and bought 25 more. At the height of the Sunbelt boom in 1984, Trust was the most profitable bank in the nation, with a low ratio of nonperforming assets.

Sun Banks began in 1934 as the First National Bank at Orlando. It grew into a holding company in 1967, and the Sun name was adopted in 1973. In the early 1970s the bank helped assemble the land for Orlando's Walt Disney World.

Under Joel Wells, then president and CEO, Sun Banks acquired Florida's Century Banks (1982) and the Flagship Banks group (1984). Sun Banks grew from $1.9 billion to $9.4 billion in assets in only 8 years (1976–84) and increased the number of its branches more than fivefold (51 to 274).

After a lingering courtship, Sun and Trust executives agreed in 1984 to marry the 2 companies, forming a super holding company over the 2 organizations. The union followed state legislation in Georgia and Florida that permitted multistate bank holding companies, and, when the marriage was consummated in 1985, Sun brought a dowry of $9.4 billion in assets and Trust contributed $6.2 billion. Trust's chairman, Bob Strickland, became chairman

and CEO for the new Atlanta-based SunTrust, and Wells became president.

In 1986 SunTrust bought Nashville-based Third National Bank, the 2nd largest bank holding company in Tennessee, with assets of $5 billion. But problems with Tennessee real estate loans increasingly plagued SunTrust. In 1990 it increased the amount of loans it wrote off, and a credit-rating service lowered SunTrust's ratings in light of nonperforming loans for properties in overbuilt Florida. In 1991 nonperforming assets in Tennessee decreased by $28 million; however, bad real estate loans in Florida and Georgia were up.

Strickland stepped down as chairman and CEO in 1990 but remained chairman of the board's executive committee until his 1992 retirement. Wells died in 1991, and James Williams, a conservative banker who instilled strict fiscal management in the Trust banks, became chairman and CEO.

In 1992 and 1993 SunTrust continued its growth pattern while steadily reducing its portfolio of nonperforming loans and increasing the amount of income attributable to noninterest sources.

In 1993 the bank adopted accounting rules that caused it to revalue its long-held Coca-Cola stock from its historic value of $110,000 to almost $1.1 billion. The dividends from these holdings (now over $1.2 billion) contribute about $20 million to the bottom line and are often used to repurchase its stock.

Although SunTrust is prosperous, many consider it behind the curve of banking evolution because so much of its revenues (62%) come from loans. Service income, which helps cushion the effect of lending downturns, is about 20%. To remedy this, SunTrust has begun to offer securities brokerage and underwriting and is attempting to boost its credit card business with a PGA Tour affinity card.

NYSE symbol: STI
Fiscal year ends: December 31

WHO

Chairman and CEO: James B. Williams, age 61,
$967,790 pay
President: L. Phillip Humann, age 49, $580,674 pay
EVP and CFO: John W. Spiegel, age 53, $439,228 pay
Chairman, Trust Company of Georgia: Edward P.
Gould, age 64, $375,126 pay
Chairman, President, and CEO, SunBanks, Inc.:
Wendell H. Colson, age 64, $350,883 pay
EVP Trust and Investment Services: E. Jenner
Wood III, age 43
SVP Legal and Corporate Secretary: Raymond D. Fortin
SVP Marketing: Dennis M. Patterson
SVP Corporate/International: Gianfranco
Rossi-Espagnet
SVP Credit Card Services: William J. Moore
SVP Investment Services: Bert C. Madden
SVP Human Resources: Robert H. Bowen
Auditors: Arthur Andersen & Co, SC

WHERE

HQ: 25 Park Place NE, PO Box 4418, Atlanta, GA
30302-4418
Phone: 404-588-7711
Fax: 404-827-6001

SunTrust operates 658 offices in Alabama, Florida,
Georgia, and Tennessee.

	1994 Net Income	
	$ mil.	% of total
Florida	212	41
Georgia	159	30
Tennessee & Alabama	68	13
Nonbanking net income	84	16
Total	**523**	**100**

WHAT

	1994 Assets	
	$ mil.	% of total
Cash & equivalents	3,592	9
Bonds	4,358	10
Mortgage-backed securities	3,500	8
Coca-Cola stock	1,243	3
Net loans	27,902	65
Other	2,114	5
Total	**42,709**	**100**

	1994 Sales	
	$ mil.	% of total
Interest & fees on loans	2,018	62
Other interest	535	16
Trust fees	250	8
Deposit svc. charges	218	7
Other	234	7
Total	**3,255**	**100**

Selected Services	Selected Subsidiaries
Consumer and	SunTrust Banks of
commercial banking	Florida, Inc.
Corporate banking	SunTrust Banks of
Corporate finance	Georgia, Inc.
Insurance	SunTrust Banks of
Investment services	Tennessee, Inc.
Loans	SunTrust Capital
Mortgage banking	Markets, Inc.
Trust services	

KEY COMPETITORS

Banc One	Chase Manhattan
BancFlorida Financial	Chemical Banking
Bank South	Citicorp
BankAmerica	Countrywide Credit
BankAtlantic	First Tennessee National
Barnett Banks	First Union
Capitol Bancorp	Merrill Lynch
Charles Schwab	NationsBank

HOW MUCH

	9-Year Growth	1985	1986	1987	1988	1989	1990	1991	1992	1993	1994
Assets ($ mil.)	9.2%	19,406	26,166	27,188	29,177	31,044	33,411	34,554	36,649	40,728	42,709
Net income ($ mil.)	13.5%	167	245	283	309	337	350	371	413	474	523
Income as % of assets	—	0.9%	0.9%	1.0%	1.1%	1.1%	1.0%	1.1%	1.1%	1.2%	1.2%
Earnings per share ($)	11.3%	1.67	1.86	2.17	2.38	2.61	2.75	2.90	3.28	3.77	4.37
Stock price – high ($)	—	20.00	27.75	27.75	24.50	26.88	24.25	40.00	45.63	49.63	51.38
Stock price – low ($)	—	15.50	17.31	17.00	18.50	19.75	16.50	20.50	33.50	41.38	43.50
Stock price – close ($)	10.7%	19.13	20.00	18.25	19.88	22.88	22.75	39.88	43.75	45.00	47.75
P/E – high	—	12	15	13	10	10	9	14	14	13	12
P/E – low	—	9	9	8	8	8	6	7	10	11	10
Dividends per share ($)	17.9%	0.30	0.61	0.65	0.70	0.78	0.86	0.94	1.03	1.16	1.32
Book value per share ($)	12.6%	10.23	11.59	12.83	14.53	16.32	17.67	20.34	22.67	28.73	29.85
Employees	2.3%	15,873	19,711	20,047	19,936	20,023	19,739	19,103	18,956	19,532	19,400

1994 Year-end:
Equity as % of assets: 8.1%
Return on assets: 1.3%
Return on equity: 14.8%
Long-term debt (mil.): $930
No. of shares (mil.): 116
Dividends
Yield: 2.8%
Payout: 30.2%
Market value (mil.): $5,524
Sales (mil.): $3,255

Stock Price History
High/Low 1985–94

SUPERVALU INC.

Like many middlemen, grocery wholesaler SUPERVALU is caught between the profit margins of manufacturers and retailers. To counter this squeeze, the company is turning to "value added" services such as store design, insurance, and payroll services to keep customers happy. It is also streamlining its operations, cutting its work force by 10%. SUPERVALU, which operates nearly 300 of its own retail stores, is closing or selling unprofitable stores while expanding profitable ones.

The company is among the US's top food distributors, supplying its 4,600 primarily independent customers with thousands of grocery and nongrocery items — produce, meat, dairy products, sundries, paper goods, household items, and even clothing — plus the buying clout to compete against large chains.

In 1992 SUPERVALU began its ADVANTAGE restructuring program designed to increase the company's competitiveness. The program calls for the company to realign its operations into 4 logistical and 6 marketing regions. In 1995 SUPERVALU began building regional distribution centers in Colorado, Illinois, Pennsylvania, and the Northwest, with a new Anniston, Alabama, center serving as its distribution prototype.

The tough marketplace for distributors plus the cost of implementing the ADVANTAGE program spoiled SUPERVALU's profitability in 1995 — the company's first decline in earnings in 20 years. But SUPERVALU believes ADVANTAGE is laying the foundation for increased operating efficiency and profitability into the next century.

WHEN

SUPERVALU was formed as Winston & Newell of Minneapolis in 1926 through the combination of the 2 largest grocery distributors in the Midwest: Winston, Harper, Fisher and George R. Newell, both founded in Minneapolis in the 1870s. The company's purpose was to help independent grocers compete with the new chain stores then becoming prevalent.

The company adopted its SUPERVALU name in 1954 and began expanding, acquiring Joannes Brothers of Green Bay (1955) and Piggly-Wiggly Midland of La Crosse, Wisconsin (1958). It continued making acquisitions and expanding its territory through the 1960s.

In 1971 SUPERVALU entered nonfood retailing by acquiring ShopKo, a discount department store chain in Minnesota, Michigan, and Wisconsin. SUPERVALU also added a new format to its food operations by purchasing Cub Stores warehouse-style groceries in 1980.

The company formed a Bermuda-based reinsurance company, SUVACO, in 1979 to provide insurance to hundreds of independent grocers. SUPERVALU acquired West Coast Grocery Company, a large distributor in Oregon and Washington (1985), and West Coast Fruit & Produce (1986). In 1986 the company bought assets of Southern Supermarket Services of Louisiana and acquired Food Giant, a large Atlanta grocery chain, from Delhaize Frères, the Belgian owner of Food Lion. SUPERVALU then either closed Food Giant stores and reopened them as new businesses or sold them to independents. In 1989 and 1990 the company combined its Cub Stores and ShopKo formats and opened 2

supercenters in the Cleveland area under the Twin Valu name. In 1991 the company acquired Scott's, an Indiana food store chain.

SUPERVALU's acquisitions and internal growth almost tripled sales levels from $4.2 billion in 1980 to $11.6 billion in 1991. In 1991 SUPERVALU sold a 54% interest in ShopKo to the public, netting the company around $420 million. SUPERVALU's chairman, Michael Wright, stated that the ShopKo offering reflects the company's belief that the marketplace will more accurately value the businesses as 2 distinctly capitalized entities.

The sale also freed enough capital to allow the purchase of food wholesaler Wetterau in 1992 for $1.1 billion. Wetterau had 1991 sales of $5.7 billion and distributed products to about 2,800 retailers. The acquisition also brought more than 150 retail food stores to the company.

After leaping past Fleming to become the #1 independent food distributor in the US following its 1992 acquisition of Wetterau, SUPERVALU fell to #2 when Fleming acquired Scrivner in 1994. That same year the company added Sweet Life Foods (280 stores) and Hyper Shoppes (7 stores) and introduced its Preferred Selection premium brand. It also began a pilot program to convert its fleet of refrigerated trucks to CFC-free refrigeration systems.

In 1995 SUPERVALU closed its 4 experimental MAX Club stores and sold part of its Preferred Products Inc. subsidiary. That same year the company eliminated 2,600 jobs and took a $244 million restructuring charge as part of the ADVANTAGE program.

NYSE symbol: SVU
Fiscal year ends: Last Saturday in February

WHO

Chairman, CEO, and President: Michael W. Wright, age 56, $780,000 pay
EVP; President and CEO, Retail Food Companies: Laurence L. Anderson, age 53, $406,350 pay
EVP and CFO: Jeffrey C. Girard, age 47, $357,000 pay
EVP; President, Retail Services and Corporate Strategies Group: Phillip A. Dabill, age 52, $354,900 pay
EVP; President and COO, Wholesale Food Companies: Jeffrey Noddle, age 48, $343,353 pay
SVP Distribution: Gregory C. Heying, age 46
SVP Information Services: H. S. Smith III, age 48
SVP Human Resources: Ronald C. Tortelli, age 49
VP; President and CEO, Cub Foods: John H. Hooley, age 43
Auditors: Deloitte & Touche LLP

WHERE

HQ: 11840 Valley View Rd., Eden Prairie, MN 55344
Phone: 612-828-4000
Fax: 612-828-8998

SUPERVALU's 29 distribution centers serve 4,600 stores in 48 states, and its military operations serve more than 130 military bases. SUPERVALU also operates 296 retail and discount food stores in 31 states.

WHAT

	1995 Sales		1995 Operating Income	
	$ mil.	% of total	$ mil.	% of total
Food distribution	14,820	78	257	—
Retail food	4,219	22	(104)	—
Adjustments	(2,476)	—	—	—
Total	**16,564**	**100**	**153**	**—**

Selected Operations

Private Label Brands	Retail Food Stores
Bi-Rite	bigg's
Chateau	County Market
Flav-O-Rite	Cub Foods
Foodland	Foodland
Home Best	Hornbacher's
IGA	IGA
Nature's Best	Laneco
Preferred Selection	Save-A-Lot
Shop 'N Save	Scott's Foods
Shoppers Value	Shop 'n Save
Super Valu	SUPERVALU
Sweet Life	
Why Pay More	

Services
Accounting and tax services
Advertising, merchandising, and promotion assistance
Commercial and group insurance
Consumer research
Inventory control and ordering services
Payroll services
Personnel management
Retail operations counseling
Store design and construction
Store layout and equipment planning
Store management assistance

KEY COMPETITORS

ADP	McKesson
Albertson's	Meijer
Allou	Nash Finch
American Stores	Pathmark
Bergen Brunswig	Paychex
C&S Wholesale	Safeway
Fleming	Services Group
Food Lion	Spartan Stores
Great A&P	Wakefern Food
Grocers Supply	Wal-Mart
Kroger	Winn-Dixie

HOW MUCH

	9-Year Growth	1986	1987	1988	1989	1990	1991	1992	1993	1994	1995
Sales ($ mil.)	8.6%	7,905	9,066	9,372	10,296	11,136	11,612	10,632	12,568	15,937	16,564
Net income ($ mil.)	(7.9%)	91	89	112	135	148	155	208	165	185	43
Income as % of sales	—	1.2%	1.0%	1.2%	1.3%	1.3%	1.3%	2.0%	1.3%	1.2%	0.3%
Earnings per share ($)	(7.5%)	1.23	1.20	1.50	1.81	2.06	2.78	2.31	2.58	0.61
Stock price – high ($)[1]	—	23.88	27.88	30.38	26.38	30.13	29.00	30.25	34.88	37.88	40.13
Stock price – low ($)[1]	—	15.13	19.75	16.00	17.00	22.63	21.75	21.63	23.38	29.50	22.00
Stock price – close ($)[1]	1.0%	22.38	24.50	17.88	24.50	29.00	23.75	27.25	31.13	36.25	24.38
P/E – high	—	19	23	20	15	15	14	11	15	15	66
P/E – low	—	12	17	11	9	12	11	8	10	11	36
Dividends per share ($)	10.9%	0.36	0.40	0.43	0.47	0.56	0.63	0.69	0.75	0.93	0.91
Book value per share ($)	10.0%	7.20	8.00	9.07	10.40	11.59	13.01	14.35	15.84	17.62	16.92
Employees	5.6%	26,575	30,350	35,595	39,700	41,150	42,905	24,400	42,000	42,500	43,500

1995 Year-end:
Debt ratio: 72.3%
Return on equity: 3.5%
Cash (mil.): $5
Current ratio: 1.14
Long-term debt (mil.): $1,460
No. of shares (mil.): 70
Dividends
  Yield: 3.7%
  Payout: 149.2%
Market value (mil.): $1,711

**Stock Price History[1]
High/Low 1986–95**

[1] Stock prices are for the prior calendar year.

SYSCO CORPORATION

OVERVIEW

Be it frozen or fresh, served on paper plates or china, eaten in a restaurant, hospital, or hotel, there's a lot of food out there that SYSCO helped put on the table. The Houston company is the #1 food service distributor in the US, providing products and services to 245,000 dining sites outside the home. Although SYSCO's share of the market is less than 10% — the food service industry is dominated by local operators — the company is bigger than its 6 closest competitors put together.

SYSCO's market area includes the entire United States, Mexico, and the Pacific Coast region of Canada. The company distributes frozen foods, canned and dry goods, fresh meat and produce, imported specialties, paper products, and tableware to customers including hotels, schools, industrial caterers, and hospi-

tals. Its SYGMA subsidiary services 22 restaurant chains.

A variety of brand names appear on the products SYSCO distributes, including not only national name brands but also SYSCO's Imperial, Classic, and Reliance labels. The company has introduced new brand names for its ethnic food products, with Arrezzio appearing on Italian food, the Casa Solana on Mexican food, and Jade Mountain and Imperial Dynasty on Chinese food.

Other products distributed by SYSCO include restaurant and kitchen equipment and supplies, cleaning supplies, and medical and surgical supplies. SYSCO plans to expand the number of its subsidiaries distributing medical and personal care supplies. Currently, 17 SYSCO units have medical departments.

WHEN

SYSCO was founded in 1969 when John Baugh, a Houston wholesale foods distributor, convinced the owners of 8 other US wholesalers that they should combine and form a national distribution company. Joining Baugh's Zero Foods of Houston to form SYSCO were Frost-Pack Distributing (Grand Rapids, Michigan), Louisville Grocery (Louisville, Kentucky), Plantation Foods (Miami), Thomas Foods and its Justrite subsidiary (Cincinnati), Wicker (Dallas), Houston's Food Service Company (Houston), Global Frozen Foods (New York), and Texas Wholesale Grocery (Dallas). The company went public in 1970. SYSCO, which derives its name from Systems and Services Company, benefited from Baugh's recognition of the trend toward dining out in American society. Until SYSCO was formed, food distribution to restaurants, hotels, and other nongrocers was provided almost exclusively by thousands of small, independent, regional operators.

Since SYSCO's inception the company has expanded to 96 times its original size through internal growth and the acquisitions of strong local distributors. SYSCO has ensured the success of its acquisitions through buyout agreements requiring the seller to continue managing the company and earn a portion of the sale price with future profits.

In 1988, when SYSCO was already the largest food service distributor, it purchased Olewine's, a Harrisburg, Pennsylvania, distributor. It also acquired CFS Continental, the 3rd largest food distributor at the time, for $750 million. The CFS acquisition added sev-

eral warehouses and a large truck fleet and increased the company's penetration along the West Coast of the US and Canada. In 1990 SYSCO acquired the Oklahoma City–based food service distribution business of Scrivner (renamed SYSCO Food Services of Oklahoma).

In 1991 SYSCO's Houston subsidiary pleaded guilty to one count of conspiring to rig contract bids for sales to schools in southeastern Texas. SYSCO reorganized its school-bid department and added controls to prevent any recurrences.

SYSCO acquired Collin's Foodservice and Benjamin Polakoff & Son in 1992. It also acquired Philadelphia-based Perloff Brothers, which operated Tartan Foods, and created a new subsidiary, Tartan Sysco Food Services. SYSCO sold its last remaining retail business, consumer-size frozen food distributor Global Sysco, that same year.

In 1993 SYSCO acquired St. Louis–based Clark Foodservice and New Jersey's Ritter Food Corporation.

In 1994 SYSCO announced the acquisition of Woodhaven Foods, a distributor owned by ARA (now ARAMARK), one of the nation's largest cafeteria and concession operators. SYSCO expects the deal to result in a significant increase in business with ARAMARK. Also that year, SYSCO's SYGMA unit entered a distribution agreement with 71-unit Pancho's Mexican Buffet.

SYSCO's newest distribution facilities, all scheduled to open by the end of 1995, include sites in Hartford, Connecticut; in Milwaukee, Wisconsin; and on Florida's west coast.

NYSE symbol: SYY
Fiscal year ends: Saturday nearest June 30

WHO

Chairman: John F. Woodhouse, age 63, $1,015,129 pay
President and CEO: Bill M. Lindig, age 57, $886,663 pay
(prior to promotion)
EVP and COO; President, Foodservice Operations:
Charles H. Cotros, age 57, $701,840 pay (prior to
promotion)
SVP Multi-Unit Sales; CEO, SYGMA Network, Inc.:
Gregory K. Marshall, age 47, $423,195 pay
SVP, CFO, and Controller: John K. Stubblefield Jr.
SVP Merchandising Services: Richard J. Schnieders
VP Employee Relations/Management Development:
Michael C. Nichols
Auditors: Arthur Andersen & Co, SC

WHERE

HQ: 1390 Enclave Pkwy., Houston, TX 77077-2099
Phone: 713-584-1390
Fax: 713-584-1245

SYSCO has 106 facilities in 38 states and 2 in Canada.

State	1994 Facilities No.
California	9
New York	9
Texas	9
Ohio	7
Pennsylvania	6
Colorado	5
Tennessee	5
Maryland	4
Michigan	4
Florida	3
Georgia	3
Massachusetts	3
Other states	39
Canada	2
Total	**108**

WHAT

Customers	1994 Sales % of total
Restaurants	60
Hospitals & nursing homes	13
Schools & colleges	7
Hotels & motels	6
Other	14
Total	**100**

Products	1994 Sales % of total
Canned & dry products	25
Fresh & frozen meats	16
Poultry	9
Dairy products	8
Paper & disposable products	7
Fresh produce	6
Seafoods	6
Beverage products	3
Equipment & smallwares	3
Janitorial products	2
Medical supplies	1
Other frozen products	14
Total	**100**

KEY COMPETITORS

Alex Lee
AmeriServ Food
Cagle's
Gordon Food Service
Heinz
JP Foodservice
Performance Food
Rykoff-Sexton
Services Group
US Foodservice

HOW MUCH

	9-Year Growth	1985	1986	1987	1988	1989	1990	1991	1992	1993	1994
Sales ($ mil.)	17.2%	2,628	3,172	3,656	4,385	6,851	7,591	8,150	8,893	10,022	10,942
Net income ($ mil.)	17.6%	50	58	62	80	108	133	154	172	202	217
Income as % of sales	—	1.9%	1.8%	1.7%	1.8%	1.6%	1.7%	1.9%	1.9%	2.0%	2.0%
Earnings per share ($)	16.4%	0.30	0.34	0.35	0.45	0.30	0.73	0.84	0.93	1.08	1.18
Stock price – high ($)	—	5.81	8.47	10.38	9.72	16.00	19.19	23.69	27.75	31.00	29.25
Stock price – low ($)	—	3.97	5.59	5.63	6.50	9.16	12.81	15.00	20.56	22.25	21.13
Stock price – close ($)	18.5%	5.59	7.50	6.78	9.63	15.81	16.81	23.31	26.38	29.25	25.75
P/E – high	—	19	25	30	22	53	26	28	30	29	25
P/E – low	—	13	16	16	14	31	18	18	22	21	18
Dividends per share ($)	22.9%	0.05	0.06	0.07	0.08	0.09	0.10	0.12	0.17	0.26	0.32
Book value per share ($)	14.7%	1.97	2.25	2.55	3.01	3.93	4.20	4.96	5.69	6.17	6.78
Employees	12.5%	9,100	10,700	12,000	13,000	18,700	19,600	21,000	22,500	24,200	26,200

1994 Year-end:
Debt ratio: 30.7%
Return on equity: 18.2%
Cash (mil.): $87
Current ratio: 1.89
Long-term debt (mil.): $539
No. of shares (mil.): 183
Dividends
  Yield: 1.2%
  Payout: 27.1%
Market value (mil.): $4,714

Stock Price History
High/Low 1985–94

TANDEM COMPUTERS

Absolute reliability — that's what Tandem guarantees to computer users (e.g., the communications and financial industries) who cannot afford systems failures. Cupertino, California–based Tandem is a leading provider of fault-tolerant computers that use a parallel architecture to ensure uninterrupted performance. An estimated 75% of the world's automatic teller transactions and 66% of all credit card transactions run on Tandem computers. The company markets hardware, software, and peripherals such as add-on storage modules, printers, and, through its UB Networks subsidiary, networking products.

Tandem got its start selling expensive proprietary systems but saw sales drop off as networked computing gained popularity. In 1993 the company cut prices and adopted an "open strategy" based on the widely used UNIX operating system and RISC microprocessor. Staff cuts and a corporate reorganization followed. The tactic worked, and the company returned to profitability in 1994.

That year Tandem introduced Himalaya, a new line of lower-priced computer servers. Available in entry-level, mid-range, and high-end models, Himalaya's capabilities can be expanded as an operation grows.

Tandem is back on technology's leading edge, teaming up with Silicon Graphics and with Spyglass to provide financial transaction security on the Internet and with Sage Communications to develop data warehousing solutions.

Tandem Computers was started in Cupertino, California, in 1974 by James Treybig, a former marketing manager at Hewlett-Packard and limited partner in venture capital firm Kleiner, Perkins, Caufield & Byers (KPCB). Along with 2 computer engineers, and with an initial $1 million from KPCB, Treybig pioneered a way to link computers to work in tandem so that if one failed, another would take over without interruption. Tandem introduced its first fail-safe minicomputer, the NonStop16, in 1976.

Tandem's computers quickly became a success. Revenues doubled each year from 1976 to 1981. Designed to process continuous, on-line transactions quickly, the computers were popular with banks, brokerage firms, manufacturers, and hospitals. By 1987 Tandem was a $1 billion company with 130 offices worldwide.

Although Tandem dominated the fail-safe computer market in the 1970s, it faced stiff competition in the early 1980s from companies like Stratus Computer. From 1982 to 1985 Tandem's earnings were flat. Tandem, long noted for its unorthodox, people-oriented management, was forced to reassess both its product line and its business methods. By 1987 Tandem had tightened its management control and substantially revamped and expanded its product line. That year sales grew 35%. Contributing to the rise in sales were Tandem's 1987 introduction of a smaller CLX minicomputer and announcement of a more versatile database software product, NonStop SQL.

Tandem expanded into complementary specialty areas through acquisition of Atalla

(1987, data security products), Integrated Technology (1988, telecommunications software), and Ungermann-Bass (1988, network specialists; now UB Networks). The 1989 introduction of the NonStop Cyclone moved Tandem into the mainframe market, enabling it to compete head-on with IBM's comparable machine at 1/3 the cost.

In 1990 Tandem bought Array Technology (sold 1994), which made fault-tolerant mass storage systems by using redundant disks. The next year Tandem acquired Applied Communications (finance and telecommunications software, sold 1994), MPACT EDI (software developer for Tandem products, sold 1993), and 50% of NetWorth (LAN software and hardware, sold 1994). But the company refused to make its systems compatible with other operating systems, forcing its clients to use only Tandem's software. Eventually this stance brought client defections, falling profits, and losses in 1992 and 1993. In order to turn the company around, Tandem underwent a major restructuring, divesting noncore operations, switching to open-system technologies, and recording more than $500 million in restructuring charges.

After delays and cost overruns, in 1994 California state officials terminated a contract with Tandem to modernize the state's huge Department of Motor Vehicles database.

In 1995 NEC, Japan's #1 maker of PCs, said it would use Tandem computers as part of NEC-packaged systems designed to process large databases. Also in 1995 Tandem opened its first sales office in Russia and formed several strategic partnerships in China.

NYSE symbol: TDM
Fiscal year ends: September 30

WHO

Chairman: Thomas J. Perkins, age 62
President and CEO: James G. Treybig, age 54,
$933,057 pay
SVP; President and CEO, UB Networks: Roel Pieper,
age 38, $469,498 pay
SVP and COO: Robert C. Marshall, age 63, $450,432 pay
SVP; General Manager, Systems Development Group:
Kurt L. Friedrich, age 45, $436,902 pay
SVP and CFO: David J. Rynne, age 54, $409,672 pay
SVP; General Manager, Solutions Products Group:
Donald E. Fowler, age 56
SVP; General Manager, Sales and Support Group:
Gerald L. Peterson, age 49
VP Systems Development: Lawrence A. Laurich, age 51
VP, General Counsel, and Secretary: Josephine T. Parry,
age 46
VP Human Resources: Susan J. Cook
Auditors: Ernst & Young LLP

WHERE

HQ: Tandem Computers Incorporated,
19333 Vallco Pkwy., Cupertino, CA 95014-2599
Phone: 408-285-6000
Fax: 408-285-4545

Tandem has manufacturing facilities in Scotland and the
US and customer support services worldwide.

	1994 Sales		1994 Pretax Income	
	$ mil.	% of total	$ mil.	% of total
US	1,128	53	140	77
Europe	512	24	29	16
Japan	265	13	13	7
Other regions	203	10	(2)	—
Adjustments	—	—	1	—
Total	**2,108**	**100**	**181**	**100**

WHAT

	1994 Sales	
	$ mil.	% of total
Computer systems	1,731	82
Networking	377	18
Total	**2,108**	**100**

Selected Products

Industry Platform Systems	NonStop Systems and Servers
Banking and securities	Cyclone/R hardware
Electronic commerce	Himalaya hardware
Telecommunications	NonStop CLX/800
	hardware
Integrity Systems	NonStop Kernel software
Integrity FT	NonStop SQL/MP
Integrity NR	software
	NonStop Transaction
Networking, Communications, and Network Management	Manager/MP software
Distributed Systems management	**Peripherals**
	Servers
Virtual network architecture	Storage subsystems
	Terminals
	Workstations

KEY COMPETITORS

3Com	Data General	Pyramid
Amdahl	DEC	Technology
Apple	Deluxe Corp.	Sequent
Asanté	Fujitsu	Silicon Graphics
AT&T	Hewlett-Packard	Storage
Bay Networks	Hitachi	Technology
Cabletron	IBM	Stratus Computer
Cisco Systems	Machines Bull	Sun Microsystems
Concurrent	NEC	Unisys
Computer	Proteon	

HOW MUCH

	9-Year Growth	1985	1986	1987	1988	1989	1990	1991	1992	1993	1994
Sales ($ mil.)	14.5%	624	768	1,036	1,315	1,633	1,866	1,922	2,037	2,031	2,108
Net income ($ mil.)	19.6%	34	64	106	95	118	122	(41)	(530)	170
Income as % of sales	—	5.5%	8.3%	10.2%	7.2%	7.2%	6.5%	1.8%	—	—	8.1%
Earnings per share ($)	15.5%	0.41	0.72	1.08	0.96	1.17	1.13	0.33	(0.38)	(4.72)	1.50
Stock price – high ($)	—	14.25	19.63	37.38	29.50	26.38	30.13	17.63	15.88	16.88	19.13
Stock price – low ($)	—	6.44	9.75	17.56	12.38	14.75	8.88	9.13	9.88	8.50	10.50
Stock price – close ($)	4.9%	11.13	17.13	27.50	16.88	23.00	11.63	11.25	15.00	10.88	17.13
P/E – high	—	35	27	35	31	23	27	53	—	—	13
P/E – low	—	16	14	16	13	13	8	28	—	—	7
Dividends per share ($)	—	0.00	0.00	0.00	0.00	0.00	0.00	0.00	0.00	0.00	0.00
Book value per share ($)	5.4%	5.08	6.09	7.74	8.92	9.69	11.41	11.54	11.18	6.48	8.13
Employees	4.9%	5,494	5,719	7,007	8,624	9,548	10,936	11,167	10,784	9,963	8,466

1994 Year-end:
Debt ratio: 13.3%
Return on equity: 20.3%
Cash (mil.): $124
Current ratio: 1.26
Long-term debt (mil.): $86
No. of shares (mil.): 116
Dividends
  Yield: —
  Payout: —
Market value (mil.): $1,979

**Stock Price History
High/Low 1985–94**

TANDY CORPORATION

OVERVIEW

One of the US's leading electronics retailers, Fort Worth–based Tandy has sold off most of its computer manufacturing operations to focus on its core retail business. But not just manufacturing has fallen by the wayside; some of Tandy's other retail operations are being discontinued as well. In 1995 the company announced plans to close all of its VideoConcepts mall stores and more than half of its McDuff electronics stores. The company is concentrating on 3 retail formats: Radio Shack, Computer City, and Incredible Universe.

The newest is Incredible Universe, a chain of "gigastores" each the size of 3 football fields, which sells an array of electronics (including appliances, cameras, and computers) and software and other accessories. The stores also offer child-care facilities, fast food, live entertainment, and a recording studio. Sales at the first 9 gigastores have grown rapidly, and Tandy plans to add 8 new stores during 1995.

Tandy is also expanding Computer City. It planned to add 30 stores in 1995 to the chain, which had 1994 sales of $1.2 billion, double the previous year's sales.

Tandy still gets most of its sales from its Radio Shack chain, but the balance is shifting. Radio Shack sales accounted for 58% of 1994 company revenues, down from about 66% in 1993. Analysts see Radio Shack as an important anchor to Tandy's retailing scheme since its products tend to be less price sensitive than the higher-end products at its other 2 chains.

WHEN

During the 1950s Charles Tandy expanded his family's small Fort Worth leather business (founded in 1919) into a nationwide chain of leathercraft and hobby stores. By 1960 Tandy Corporation stock was being traded on the NYSE. In the early 1960s Tandy began to expand into other retail areas, buying Leonard's, a Fort Worth department store.

In 1963 Tandy purchased Radio Shack, a nearly bankrupt electronic parts supplier with a mail-order business and 9 retail stores in the Boston area. Tandy collected part of the $800,000 owed the company and began expanding, stocking the stores with quick turnover items and putting 8–9% of sales revenue into advertising. Between 1961 and 1969 Tandy's sales grew from $16 million to $180 million, and earnings rose from $720,000 to $7.7 million, with the bulk of the growth due to the expansion of Radio Shack. Between 1968 and 1973 Tandy expanded from 172 to 2,294 stores; Radio Shack provided over 50% of Tandy's sales and 80% of earnings in 1973.

The company sold its department store operations to Dillard in 1974. The next year Tandy spun off to shareholders its leather products business as Tandy Brands and its hobby and handicraft business as Tandycrafts, focusing Tandy Corporation on the consumer electronics business. During 1976 the boom in CB radio sales pushed income up 125% as Tandy opened 1,200 stores. In 1977 it introduced the first mass-marketed personal computer, the TRS-80, which became the #1 PC on the market. In 1979, the year after Charles Tandy died, there were 5,530 McDonald's, 6,805 7-Elevens, and 7,353 Radio Shacks.

The company in 1984 introduced the Tandy 1000, the first IBM-compatible PC priced under $1,000. Since 1984 Tandy has expanded through acquisitions — Scott/McDuff and VideoConcepts in 1985, GRiD Systems in 1988, and Victor Technologies in 1990.

In 1987 Tandy spun off its foreign retail operations as InterTAN. Realizing that Radio Shack had nearly exhausted its expansion possibilities, the company focused on alternate retail formats such as GRiD Systems Centers and in 1991 opened Computer City and the Edge in Electronics. That same year Tandy announced the introduction of name-brand products into Radio Shack stores. The company also increased its manufacturing and R&D capacity and focused on such emerging technologies as digital audio recording and multimedia computing.

Tandy sold Memtek Products (magnetic tape), O'Sullivan Industries (ready-to-assemble furniture), LIKA (printed circuit boards), and its computer manufacturing and marketing operations in 1993. As part of the restructuring, Tandy scaled back 2 mall retail operations, VideoConcepts and McDuff Electronics.

In 1994 Radio Shack stores began offering repair services under the name the Repair Shop at Radio Shack. The service fixes VCRs, audio equipment, and computers that are no longer under manufacturer warranty.

The company announced plans in 1995 to sell its credit card business to SPS Services — a subsidiary of Dean Witter, Discover — for $710 million. Also in 1995 Radio Shack introduced an expanded in-store catalog for hard-to-find electronic equipment and parts.

NYSE symbol: TAN
Fiscal year ends: December 31

WHO

Chairman, President, and CEO: John V. Roach, age 56, $1,050,028 pay
President, Radio Shack: Leonard H. Roberts, age 46, $814,291 pay
President, Computer City: Alan C. Bush
SVP and Secretary: Herschel C. Winn, age 63, $389,670 pay
SVP, Tandy Retail Services: Robert M. McClure, age 59, $360,023 pay
SVP and CFO: Dwain H. Hughes, age 47
VP and General Manager, Incredible Universe: Rich Hollander
VP and Controller: Richard L. Ramsey, age 49
VP Law and Assistant Secretary: Frederick W. Padden, age 62
VP and Treasurer: Loren K. Jensen
VP Tax: Mark W. Barfield, age 37
VP Corporate Relations: Lou Ann Blaylock, age 56
VP Corporate Development: Ronald L. Parrish, age 52
VP Human Resources: George Berger
Auditors: Price Waterhouse LLP

WHERE

HQ: 1800 One Tandy Center, Fort Worth, TX 76102
Phone: 817-390-3700
Fax: 817-390-2774

Tandy operates or franchises more than 6,600 Radio Shacks throughout the US; operates 69 Computer City stores in the US, Canada, and Europe; and has 9 Incredible Universe stores in the US. The company also operates 15 distribution centers and 128 service centers in the US. Tandy has 9 manufacturing plants in the US and 2 manufacturing plants in China and Taiwan.

WHAT

	1994 Retail Outlets
	No.
Radio Shack	
Company-owned	4,598
Dealer/franchise	2,005
Tandy Name Brand Retail Group	
VideoConcepts (mall stores)	219
McDuff Supercenters	71
The Edge in Electronics	16
Computer City SuperCenters	69
Incredible Universe	9
Total	**6,987**

	1994 Sales
	% of total
Consumer electronics	45
Electronic parts, accessories & specialty equipment	36
PCs, peripherals, software & accessories	12
Other	7
Total	**100**

KEY COMPETITORS

Anam Group	Intelligent	Sanyo
Best Buy	Electronics	Sears
Circuit City	Kmart	Service
CompuCom	LG Group	Merchandise
CompUSA	Matsushita	Sharper Image
Egghead	MicroAge	Sony
ELEK-TEK	Montgomery	Sun Television &
Entex	Ward	Appliances
Fretter	NeoStar	Toshiba
Fry's	Office Depot	Toys "R" Us
Electronics	Philips	Vanstar
Good Guys	Price/Costco	Wal-Mart
InaCom	Samsung	

HOW MUCH

	9-Year Growth	1985	1986	1987	1988	1989	1990	1991	1992	1993	1994
Sales ($ mil.)	6.3%	2,841	3,036	3,452	3,794	4,181	4,500	4,562	4,680	4,103	4,944
Net income ($ mil.)	1.6%	189	198	242	316	324	290	206	184	84	218
Income as % of sales	—	6.7%	6.5%	7.0%	8.3%	7.7%	6.5%	4.5%	3.9%	2.1%	4.4%
Earnings per share ($)	3.6%	2.11	2.22	2.70	3.54	3.64	3.54	2.58	2.24	1.01	2.91
Stock price – high ($)	—	42.13	45.00	56.50	48.63	48.75	41.13	36.50	31.75	50.75	50.63
Stock price – low ($)	—	24.00	30.50	28.00	31.50	37.00	23.50	23.38	22.25	24.63	30.75
Stock price – close ($)	2.3%	40.75	42.50	33.00	41.00	39.13	29.25	28.88	29.75	49.50	50.00
P/E – high	—	20	20	21	14	13	12	14	14	50	17
P/E – low	—	11	14	10	9	10	7	9	10	24	11
Dividends per share ($)	—	0.00	0.00	0.25	0.55	0.60	0.60	0.60	0.60	0.60	0.63
Book value per share ($)	7.3%	12.00	14.57	15.38	18.10	20.13	21.78	23.56	22.17	22.22	22.66
Employees	3.0%	35,000	36,000	39,000	37,000	38,000	40,000	40,000	37,000	42,000	45,800

1994 Year-end:
Debt ratio: 19.6%
Return on equity: 15.9%
Cash (mil.): $206
Current ratio: 2.12
Long-term debt (mil.): $153
No. of shares (mil.): 58
Dividends
  Yield: 1.3%
  Payout: 21.6%
Market value (mil.): $2,913

Stock Price History
High/Low 1985–94

TEACHERS INSURANCE

OVERVIEW

The giant is stirring. Teachers Insurance and Annuity Association–College Retirement Equities Fund (TIAA-CREF) is beginning to use its investment might to influence the management of the companies in which it invests. As one of the US's largest insurance companies and the world's largest private pension system, TIAA-CREF has the muscle to succeed in this endeavor: it is estimated that the association owns about 1% of US stocks. In 1994 the association used its influence to help oust the chairman of W.R. Grace. It also started a corporate assessment program, headed by Kenneth West, formerly of Harris Bancorp in

Chicago, to further good corporate governance procedures.

TIAA-CREF provides portable insurance and retirement benefits to the often-transient employees of educational and research organizations. It gains new clients primarily through the adoption of its services by new institutions, as part of an increasing menu of benefit plans available to a formerly underserved group. In recent years the organization has increased its scope to include public school teachers.

One of TIAA-CREF's strengths is its unusually low overhead: about 0.25% for TIAA and 0.4% for CREF.

WHEN

The Carnegie Foundation for the Advancement of Teaching established TIAA in New York City in 1905 with an endowment of $15 million to provide retirement benefits and other forms of financial security to employees of educational and research organizations. The original endowment was found to be insufficient, and in 1918 the fund was reorganized into a defined contribution plan with another $1 million from Carnegie. TIAA, now the major pension system of higher education in the US, was the first portable pension plan, allowing participants to move between institutions without losing retirement benefits and offering a fixed annuity. But the fund kept requiring cash from the foundation until 1947.

In 1952 CEO William Greenough pioneered the first variable annuity, based on common stock investments, and established the College Retirement Equities Fund (CREF) to offer it. Designed to supplement TIAA's fixed-dollar annuity, CREF invested participants' premiums in stocks. CREF, like TIAA, was subject to New York insurance regulations but not SEC regulation.

In the 1950s TIAA led the fight for Social Security benefits for university employees and began offering group total disability coverage (1957) and group life insurance (1958).

In 1971 TIAA-CREF established the Common Fund to help colleges boost investment returns from their endowments; TIAA went on to help manage endowments. TIAA facilitated the establishment in 1972 of the Investor Responsibility Research Center, which provides objective information on making socially responsible investments.

For 70 years TIAA-CREF members had no way to exit the system other than retirement. Members had only 2 investment choices:

stocks through CREF or a one-way transfer into TIAA's annuity accounts based on long-term bond, real estate, and mortgage investments. In the 1980s CREF indexed its funds to the S&P average. By the 1987 stock crash, the organization had one million members, many of whom wanted protection from stock market fluctuations and more investment options. In 1988 CREF added a money market fund, but this required SEC oversight, and the SEC required complete transferability, even outside of TIAA-CREF.

Since transferability made TIAA-CREF vulnerable to competition, it began to add investment options (the TIAA Interest Payment Retirement Option; CREF Bond Market and Social Choice accounts; and Global Equities, Growth, and Equity Index accounts) and to offer long-term care plans.

With about 40% of its investments in mortgages and real estate, TIAA was somewhat affected by the cycles of the commercial real estate sector, but less so than other insurers because of its policy of direct investment in such projects as the Mall of America.

In 1993 chairman and CEO Clifton Wharton resigned after being named US deputy secretary of state and was replaced by John Biggs.

In addition to investment activism, in 1994 TIAA-CREF began a major educational campaign to acquaint its members with basic principles of retirement planning and investment. One the most important elements in the campaign is its emphasis on long-term results. This may help persuade members not to switch their funds to flashy short-term investments outside the TIAA-CREF system and not to panic during cyclical events like the 1994 bond crash, which depressed income.

HOOVER'S HANDBOOK OF AMERICAN COMPANIES 1996

Nonprofit organization
Fiscal year ends: December 31

Chairman and CEO: John H. Biggs
President and COO: Thomas W. Jones
EVP Finance and Planning: Richard L. Gibbs
EVP Law and General Counsel: Charles H. Stamm
EVP TIAA Investments: J. Daniel Lee Jr.
EVP CREF Investments: James S. Martin
EVP Pension and Annuity Services: John J. McCormack
EVP Insurance Services: Thomas G. Walsh
EVP Operations Support: John A. Putney Jr.
EVP External Affairs: Don W. Harrell
EVP Human Resources: Matina S. Horner
Auditors: Deloitte & Touche LLP

WHERE

HQ: Teachers Insurance and Annuity Association–
College Retirement Equities Fund, 730 Third Ave.,
New York, NY 10017-3206
Phone: 212-490-9000
Fax: 212-916-6231

TIAA-CREF is licensed in 33 states, is exempt from
licensing in 17 states, and is licensed in Canada.

WHAT

	1994 TIAA Assets	
	$ mil.	% of total
Cash & equivalents	432	1
US, Canadian & other		
government bonds	2,424	3
Utility bonds	8,016	11
Corporate bonds	19,022	26
Mortgage- & asset-		
backed securities	13,911	19
Stocks	163	0
Mortgage loans	20,217	27
Real estate	7,075	10
Other	2,088	3
Total	**73,348**	**100**

	1994 CREF Assets	
	$ mil.	% of total
Stock account	54,761	88
Money Market account	2,919	5
Bond Market account	619	1
Social Choice account	782	1
Global Equities	2,745	4
Growth fund	309	1
Equity Index	72	0
Total	**62,207**	**100**

CREF Investment Accounts
Bond Market account
Global Equities account
Money Market account
Social Choice account
Stock account

Selected TIAA Investments

African Development Bank	J. C. Penney
Alco Standard	Kmart
AT&T	May Stores
BankAmerica	MCI
Circus Circus	Panhandle Eastern
Coca Cola	Pipeline Co.
Cox Enterprises	Sears
Enron	Sprint
Federal Express	Sun Microsystems
First Union Corp.	Time Warner
General Mills	Viacom

TIAA Insurance Products
Group life insurance
Group total disability insurance
Individual life insurance
Long-term care insurance
Retirement and group retirement annuities

KEY COMPETITORS

Aetna	MassMutual
American Express	Merrill Lynch
Berkshire Hathaway	MetLife
Chubb	New York Life
CIGNA	Northwestern Mutual
Citicorp	Prudential
Equitable	T. Rowe Price
Fleet	Transamerica
FMR	Travelers
John Hancock	USAA

HOW MUCH

	Annual Growth	1985	1986	1987	1988	1989	1990	1991	1992	1993	1994
TIAA assets ($ mil.)	13.7%	23,159	27,887	33,210	38,631	44,374	49,894	55,576	61,777	67,483	73,348
TIAA sales ($ mil.)	6.8%	5,774	6,839	7,735	8,414	9,046	9,370	10,067	10,300	10,400	10,413
TIAA increase in reserves ($ mil.)	2.7%	—	—	—	—	—	240	232	178	(63)	268
CREF assets ($ mil.)	12.4%	21,651	26,191	25,510	31,700	39,515	38,055	48,450	52,064	60,737	62,207
Employees	4.9%	2,600	2,800	3,200	3,500	3,500	3,700	3,800	3,800	4,000	4,000

1994 Year-end:
TIAA equity
as % of assets: 4.7%

TIAA CREF

TIAA Assets
($ mil.) 1985–94

TELE-COMMUNICATIONS, INC.

Tele-Communications, Inc. (TCI), is the largest US cable TV systems operator, serving about 11.7 million basic subscribers. TCI and Liberty Media, which it spun off in 1991, are back together after a 1994 merger.

Under the leadership of 22-year company veteran and consummate deal maker John Malone, TCI has a stable of multimedia interests, both in the US and internationally. TCI has joined with other businesses, including media and telephone companies, to develop the technology of 500-channel, interactive TV systems integrated with telephone service.

TCI is undertaking a major restructuring, splitting itself into 4 separately traded units and creating a holding company to house them. Each of the separate businesses — which cover cable, programming, new technology, and foreign operations — will have its own class of stock tied only to that unit's performance. TCI believes separate units will be better able to focus on their individual businesses and finance their operations.

TCI Communications handles cable TV services in the US; Liberty Media invests in entertainment, educational, and informational programs for TV and other media; Tele-Communications International is a leading operator of broadband cable TV and telephony networks outside the US; and TCI Technology Ventures develops new technologies such as digitally compressed video services, interactive television, and electronic games.

In July 1995 Viacom agreed to sell its cable operations (1.2 million subscribers) to TCI for $2.25 billion, which would give TCI almost 14 million total subscribers. Executives and directors control 7.8% of TCI's stock.

Tele-Communications began in 1956 when rancher Bob Magness sold some cattle to build his first cable TV system in the Texas Panhandle. In 1965 he moved the company to Denver to serve small Rocky Mountain towns.

TCI went public in 1970 just as the capital-intensive cable TV industry was taking off. Magness hired 32-year-old John Malone in 1973. The deal-making Malone stabilized the company and extended its reach. Malone's first battle was with the city of Vail, Colorado, over services and rates. For one weekend Malone showed nothing on the cable system but the names and phone numbers of city officials. The city backed down.

In 1977 Malone restructured TCI's debt. He then sat out the bidding for big-city franchises and bought them later at hefty discounts after bigger competitors stumbled.

The cable industry was deregulated in 1984, and TCI aggressively bought more than 150 cable companies in the late 1980s. In 1986 it won control of United Artists Communications (later UAE), the largest movie theater operator. TCI purchased Heritage Communications, which included a Dallas system, in 1987. Debt led to losses in late 1989.

Cable programmers kept prices low to curry favor with the giant TCI. Malone, recognizing that his systems needed a variety of programming, financed nascent channels in exchange for stock. He helped to save the debt-plagued Turner Broadcasting in 1987; TCI came away with substantial Turner stock. TCI also invested in Black Entertainment Television (1979), Discovery Channel (1986), and American Movie Classics (1987).

In a complex 1991 transaction, TCI spun off its interests in QVC Network (shopping), other networks, and various cable systems as Liberty Media, with Malone as chairman and principal shareholder. (Liberty retained many links to TCI, and it went back to TCI's fold in a 1994 merger.) TCI, U S WEST, and AT&T began testing video on demand in Denver.

Also in 1991 UAE became a wholly owned subsidiary of TCI. TCI sold the UAE theater division in 1992 and kept the cable division. TCI acquired 49.9% of Teleport Communications Group, a specialized telecommunications services company and competitor of regional telephone companies, in 1992.

In 1993 TCI joined with Microsoft and Time Warner to form Cablesoft, a venture exploring interactive cable TV.

After much-publicized merger preparations with Bell Atlantic in late 1993 and early 1994, TCI went its own way. In 1994 TCI was mentioned in merger speculations that had QVC joining with CBS. No such deal was concluded; instead, TCI and Comcast Corp. bought the 65% of QVC that they didn't already own. Also in 1994 TCI set up a center for digitizing audio and video channels.

TCI entered the telephony market in a big way when the FCC auctioned the next generation of telephone services in 1995 (30-MHz licenses for personal communications service). TCI's partnership gained licenses for 29 of the 51 major trading areas auctioned.

Nasdaq symbol: TCOMA
Fiscal year ends: December 31

WHO

Chairman: Bob Magness, age 71, $830,769 pay
President and CEO: John C. Malone, age 54,
$501,731 pay
EVP: J. C. Sparkman, age 63, $568,750 pay
EVP: Brendan R. Clouston, age 42, $525,000 pay
EVP: Fred A. Vierra, age 64, $419,613 pay
EVP, General Counsel, and Secretary: Stephen M. Brett,
age 55
EVP and Treasurer: Donne F. Fisher, age 57
EVP: Peter R. Barton, age 44
EVP: Larry E. Romrell, age 55
Auditors: KPMG Peat Marwick LLP

WHERE

HQ: 5619 DTC Pkwy., Englewood, CO 80111
Phone: 303-267-5500
Fax: 303-779-1228

Tele-Communications operates cable television systems
and provides telecommunications services throughout
the US. The company also has ownership interests in
cable operations in other countries.

WHAT

	1994 Sales		1994 Operating Income	
	$ mil.	% of total	$ mil.	% of total
Cable & communications services	4,247	86	865	99
Electronic retailing services	482	10	9	1
Other programming services	207	4	(86)	—
Total	**4,936**	**100**	**788**	**100**

Operating Groups and Selected Subsidiaries and Affiliates

Liberty Media Corp.
BET Holdings, Inc. (18%; BET Cable Network, BET
Action Pay-Per-View)
Courtroom Television Network (33%, Court TV)
Discovery Communications, Inc. (49%, cable networks)
Encore Media Corp. (90%; Encore)
Home Shopping Network (42%, home shopping
channels)
International Cable Channels Partnership Ltd. (45%)
Prime SportsChannel Networks Associates (34%; Prime
Network, NewSport)
QVC Inc. (43%, home shopping channels)
Turner Broadcasting System, Inc. (23%, 6 US and other
international cable networks)

TCI Communications, Inc.
Primestar (direct satellite service)

TCI Technology Ventures, Inc.
Netscape (2.4% ownership; World Wide Web software)
The Sega Channel (interactive games)

Tele-Communications International, Inc.
Flextech PLC (60%, UK, European cable programming)
Jupiter Telecommunications (Japan, cable multisystem
operator)
TeleWest Communications PLC (UK cable and telephone
distribution)
Videopole (France, cable)

KEY COMPETITORS

3DO	General Electric
Advance Publications	GTE
Bell Atlantic	Hearst
BT	Motorola
Cable & Wireless	News Corp.
Cablevision	Nintendo
Capital Cities/ABC	Rogers Communications
CBS	Time Warner
Comcast	U S WEST
Continental Cablevision	Viacom
Cox	Walt Disney
Davidson & Associates	

HOW MUCH

	9-Year Growth	1985	1986	1987	1988	1989	1990	1991	1992	1993	1994
Sales ($ mil.)	18.9%	1,042	973	3,016	4,284	3,026	3,625	3,827	3,574	4,153	4,936
Net income ($ mil.)	20.9%	10	95	6	56	(257)	(287)	(102)	(34)	(7)	55
Income as % of sales	—	1.0%	9.7%	0.2%	1.3%	—	—	—	—	—	1.1%
Earnings per share ($)	9.4%	0.04	0.31	0.02	0.16	(0.73)	(0.81)	(0.28)	(0.12)	(0.02)	0.09
Stock price – high ($)	—	6.50	9.72	14.81	13.88	21.38	18.50	17.50	22.00	33.25	30.25
Stock price – low ($)	—	3.75	5.88	8.09	10.31	12.81	8.38	11.63	15.38	17.50	18.25
Stock price – close ($)	15.1%	6.13	7.63	11.81	13.06	17.88	13.25	17.00	21.25	30.25	21.75
P/E – high	—	163	31	—	87	—	—	—	—	—	336
P/E – low	—	94	19	—	64	—	—	—	—	—	203
Dividends per share ($)	—	0.00	0.00	0.00	0.00	0.00	0.00	0.00	0.00	0.00	0.00
Book value per share ($)	16.6%	1.30	2.44	2.40	3.41	2.54	1.74	3.44	3.46	4.70	5.16
Employees	23.7%	4,716	14,800	22,000	28,300	34,000	33,000	33,000	22,000	24,000	32,000

1994 Year-end:
Debt ratio: 79.0%
Return on equity: 2.2%
Cash (mil.): $74
Current ratio: —
Long-term debt (mil.): $11,162
No. of shares (mil.): 576
Dividends
  Yield: —
  Payout: —
Market value (mil.): $12,529

Stock Price History
High/Low 1985–94

TELEDYNE, INC.

OVERVIEW

In the wake of the end of the Cold War, Los Angeles–based Teledyne continues to redefine itself as the federal government continues to limit defense spending. It is seeking to expand its international business (21% of total sales in 1994) and to develop commercial products from its defense technologies.

The company has cast about for ways to adapt its military products to civilian consumer use (applying its pilot ejection technology to auto air bags or introducing a mini mass spectrometer for commercial lab use). But Teledyne is also shrinking. By 1994 management had sold more than 25 companies and had cut the number of operating companies from 65 to 18 in order to focus on areas where it can attain market leadership. Also, the restructuring led to eliminating over 1,000 administrative jobs.

Teledyne has had much legal trouble arising from its defense business, including suits related to improper testing, overbilling, defective parts, and bribery. The company has spent millions settling these suits, including one in 1994 settled for $112.5 million.

In 1994 WHX attempted a hostile takeover of Teledyne. Although the attempt failed, WHX chairman Ron LaBow was elected to the Teledyne board in 1995. While Teledyne's leaders have indicated a willingness to sell part or all of the company, they believe the company's earning potential is greater than currently indicated, and they are not willing to sell the company for less than they feel it is worth.

Former board chair Henry Singleton owns 13.1% of company stock. Cofounder George Kozmetsky owns 5.2% of Teledyne stock.

WHEN

Teledyne is the creation of Henry Singleton. The son of a Texas rancher, Singleton earned a PhD in electrical engineering from MIT and learned business management while working at Hughes Aircraft, North American Aviation, and Litton Industries in the 1950s.

Singleton and another Litton executive, George Kozmetsky, each invested $225,000 in 1960 to found Teledyne to make electronic components for aircraft. The company's sales grew from $4.5 million its first year to nearly $90 million 4 years later. It beat out IBM and Texas Instruments to win the contract for an avionics system for a navy helicopter in 1965. Kozmetsky, laden with Teledyne stock, left in 1966 to become dean of the University of Texas at Austin's business school and later founded a think tank, the Institute for Constructive Capitalism (IC²), at UT.

Under Singleton, Teledyne grew into a conglomerate, buying over 100 companies, mostly small, successful manufacturing and technology companies, primarily in defense-related areas such as engines, unmanned aircraft, specialty metals, computers, and semiconductors. The company also moved into offshore oil drilling equipment, insurance and finance, and the Water Pik line of bathroom hardware. The company usually left incumbent management in place.

By 1969 sales passed $1 billion. But in 1970 Singleton stopped buying companies, and Teledyne lost favor with investors. Earnings flattened and then dropped in 1974, when one of its insurance divisions lost money on doctors' malpractice insurance.

Singleton bought Teledyne shares back from stockholders between 1972 and 1976, when they sold for as little as $7.88 a share. Yet Teledyne continued to grow as the Cold War continued. Sales grew from $1.2 billion in 1970 to $2.7 billion in 1979, and profits increased 315% from 1969 to 1978. Earnings per share skyrocketed 1,226%. By 1979 Teledyne stock sold for over $100 a share.

In 1986 Teledyne spun off its Argonaut Insurance unit and left the insurance business entirely with its 1990 spinoff of Unitrin, which owned 25% of the stock of Litton Industries and 44% of Curtiss-Wright Corporation. Teledyne's defense businesses were caught in a 1989 FBI fraud probe, and the company paid $4.4 million in restitution.

Teledyne began its drastic consolidation process in 1991. In 1993 Teledyne was indicted on charges of knowingly selling zirconium (used in bombs) to a Chilean arms manufacturer for use in cluster bombs sold to Iraq. The company had certified that it was for peaceful uses and maintains that the US government knew of and approved of the Chilean arms maker's intentions because the US was then tacitly supporting Iraq in its war with Iran. In 1995 Teledyne agreed to pay $13 million and plead guilty to the charges.

Despite Teledyne's rebuff of WHX's takeover offer, WHX is still interested in acquiring the company. Teledyne appears to still be up for sale, but it is waiting for a better deal.

NYSE symbol: TDY
Fiscal year ends: December 31

WHO

Chairman and CEO: William P. Rutledge, age 53, $680,000 pay
President and COO: Donald B. Rice, age 55, $870,290 pay
SVP: Hudson B. Drake, age 60, $500,000 pay
VP: Gary L. Riley, age 57, $405,000 pay
VP: Gordon J. Bean, age 57, $315,000 pay
General Counsel and Secretary: Judith R. Nelson, age 54
Treasurer: Douglas J. Grant, age 44
Director Human Resources: Dan Lucasik
Auditors: Arthur Andersen & Co, SC

WHERE

HQ: 2049 Century Park East, Los Angeles, CA 90067-3101
Phone: 310-277-3311
Fax: 310-551-4369

Teledyne operates manufacturing facilities in 10 US states.

WHAT

	1994 Sales		1994 Pretax Income	
	$ mil.	% of total	$ mil.	% of total
Aviation & electronics	1,048	44	(38)	—
Specialty metals	685	29	30	—
Industrial products	342	14	12	—
Consumer products	316	13	19	—
Other	—	—	(27)	—
Total	**2,391**	**100**	**(4)**	**—**

Aviation and Electronics
Aircraft engines
Aircraft, military tank, and truck batteries
Airframe structures
Cable and wire
Electronic counter-measure equipment
Microcircuitry and components
Microwave devices
Remotely piloted aircraft
Seismometers
Spectrometers
Systems engineering for military, space shuttle
Telemetry equipment

Specialty Metals
Molybdenum
Niobium
Tantalum
Titanium
Tungsten
Zirconium

Industrial Products
Engines
Forklifts
Machine tools and dies
Mining equipment
Valves

Commercial and Consumer Products
Dentist and dental lab equipment
Instapure water and air filters
Laars swimming pool and spa heaters
Plastic cups and containers
Specialty metals joint implants
Water Pik oral hygiene products
Water Pik shower massage

KEY COMPETITORS

Akzo Nobel	Gillette	Northrop
Alcan	Hewlett-Packard	Grumman
AlliedSignal	Honeywell	Raytheon
Amway	Ingersoll-Rand	Reynolds Metals
Andrew Corp.	ITT Industries	Rockwell
Bausch & Lomb	James River	Rolls-Royce
Clorox	Keystone	Siemens
Cyprus Amax	International	Texas
Dart Container	Litton	Instruments
Dentsply	Industries	Textron
Emerson	Lockheed Martin	Thomson SA
FMC	Loral	Trimble
Fried. Krupp	Masco	Navigation
General Dynamics	McDonnell	TRW
General Electric	Douglas	United
General Motors	Morton	Technologies
General Signal		

HOW MUCH

	9-Year Growth	1985	1986	1987	1988	1989	1990	1991	1992	1993	1994
Sales ($ mil.)	(3.4%)	3,256	3,241	3,217	3,535	3,531	3,446	3,207	2,888	2,492	2,391
Net income ($ mil.)	—	546	238	371	392	259	95	(25)	46	73	(8)
Income as % of sales	—	16.8%	7.3%	11.5%	11.1%	7.3%	2.8%	—	1.6%	2.9%	—
Earnings per share ($)	—	9.33	4.07	6.34	6.81	4.66	1.71	(0.46)	0.83	1.31	(0.15)
Stock price – high ($)	—	67.63	73.63	78.00	69.70	76.13	31.75	24.38	28.75	27.75	26.63
Stock price – low ($)	—	45.38	58.13	48.38	58.13	63.50	12.00	14.88	17.00	18.50	14.25
Stock price – close ($)	(12.4%)	66.13	60.25	60.75	66.45	68.63	14.75	19.63	20.38	26.00	20.13
P/E – high	—	7	18	12	10	16	19	—	35	21	—
P/E – low	—	5	14	8	9	14	7	—	21	14	—
Dividends per share ($)	—	0.00	0.00	0.80	0.80	0.80	0.80	0.80	0.80	0.80	0.00
Book value per share ($)	(17.2%)	26.94	27.95	33.87	38.22	41.99	9.45	8.19	7.96	5.06	4.92
Employees	(10.2%)	47,200	44,800	44,400	43,800	43,200	33,200	29,400	23,800	21,000	18,000

1994 Year-end:
Debt ratio: 56.6%
Return on equity: —
Cash (mil.): $30
Current ratio: 1.63
Long-term debt (mil.): $357
No. of shares (mil.): 55
Dividends
  Yield: —
  Payout: —
Market value (mil.): $1,116

Stock Price History High/Low 1985–94

TENET HEALTHCARE CORPORATION

OVERVIEW

Tenet, anyone? Previously known as National Medical Enterprises (NME), the Santa Monica, California–based health care provider bought American Medical International and took the name Tenet Healthcare Corporation in March 1995. With the $3.3 billion deal, Tenet became the nation's #2 hospital chain (at 1/3 the size of leader Columbia/HCA). Tenet operates 70 US hospitals (concentrated largely in California, Florida, and Texas) as well as long-term care facilities. It also runs psychiatric and rehabilitation facilities but has sold off most of its operations in those areas.

The company chose its new name in hopes of evoking certain principles and values — the sort lacking in its later years as NME, when it had to cough up almost $380 million in state and federal fines stemming from kickback and fraud charges. Even before the name change, Tenet established a companywide ethics program — including a toll-free ethics hot line — in an effort to avoid the problems that existed under previous management.

Singapore health care group Parkway announced in 1995 that it would pay $337 million (and take on $78 million of Tenet's massive debt) for Tenet's dozen or so hospitals in Asia and Australia. Tenet was left with a Zurich construction project and a Barcelona hospital as its sole foreign hospital operations.

WHEN

Hospital attorney and financial consultant Richard Eamer, along with attorneys Leonard Cohen and John Bedrosian, founded National Medical Enterprises in 1969. With $23 million from the sale of public stock, NME bought 10 general hospitals, nursing homes, an office building, and potential hospital sites in California. Within 6 years the company owned, operated, and managed 23 hospitals, owned a home health care business, sold medical equipment and bottled oxygen, and provided training for vocational nurses.

The company bought Stolte (hospital construction, 1977) and Medfield's 5 Florida hospitals (1979). In 1980 the company acquired the Hillhaven Corporation (long-term care), expanding services to 33 states. NME also signed a 5-year, billion-dollar health care contract with Saudi Arabia and by 1981 had become the 3rd largest health care company in the US, owning or managing 193 hospitals and nursing homes. Total revenues exceeded $1 billion for the first time in 1982.

NME continued to expand in the early 1980s, buying National Health Enterprises's 66 long-term homes (1982); Psychiatric Institutes of America (PIA), operator of 21 mental health centers (1983); and Rehabilitation Hospital Services Corporation (RHSC, 1985). In 1983 the company formed Recovery Centers of America (RCA), opening 8 substance abuse treatment programs. By 1985 the company had become the 2nd largest publicly owned health care company. Before the end of the 1980s, NME's Specialty Hospital Group (PIA, RCA, and RHSC) was bringing in more than 50% of the company's net operating revenues.

In 1990 NME spun off most of its long-term care businesses (including 345 long-term care units, 120 Medi-$ave Pharmacies, and 24 retirement homes) to its shareholders as the Hillhaven Corporation. NME kept 14% of the Hillhaven stock and about 1/3 of the nursing home real estate, leasing the property to Hillhaven until selling it to Hillhaven in 1993. NME also kept the 19 long-term care facilities operated in the UK by its Westminster Health Care subsidiary. In 1991 NME opened a teaching hospital at the University of Southern California. In 1992 the company acquired a controlling interest in Markalinga, an Australian hospital management company.

Also that year several large insurance companies sued NME, alleging hundreds of millions of dollars in fraudulent psychiatric claims; NME settled for $215 million in 1993. In June 1993 investment banker Jeff Barbakow took over as CEO, forcing the resignations of Eamer and Cohen and ousting other senior management. Two months later 600 federal agents raided company headquarters, seizing papers related to the suspected fraud.

In 1993 and 1994 NME sold almost all of its psychiatric facilities and rehabilitation hospitals. The proceeds helped pay $363 million in federal penalties to conclude a sweeping 3-year federal criminal and civil investigation into allegations of insurance fraud, kickbacks, and patient abuse at its psychiatric hospitals. NME paid another $16 million in related state fines.

The company's name change from NME to Tenet coincided with its acquisition of Dallas-based American Medical, which was incorporated in 1957 and became the first investor-owned hospital company 3 years later. Tenet's net income for fiscal 1995 (including American Medical's results during the period) was $165 million on sales of $3.3 billion.

WHO

Chairman and CEO: Jeffrey C. Barbakow, age 50,
$1,742,500 pay
Co-VC: Robert W. O'Leary, age 51, $1,280,991 pay
(prior to promotion)
Co-VC and EVP: John T. Casey, age 49, $772,380 pay
(prior to promotion)
President and COO: Michael H. Focht Sr., age 52,
$1,018,750 pay
EVP Operations: Barry P. Schochet, age 43,
$700,000 pay
EVP Eastern Operations: W. Randolph Smith, age 46,
$434,873 pay
EVP Western Operations: Thomas B. Mackey, age 46
SVP and CFO: Raymond L. Mathiasen, age 51,
$523,964 pay
SVP and Treasurer: Maris Andersons, age 58
SVP and General Counsel: Scott M. Brown, age 49
SVP Human Resources: Alan R. Ewalt, age 50
Auditors: KPMG Peat Marwick LLP

WHERE

HQ: 2700 Colorado Ave., PO Box 4070, Santa Monica, CA
90411-4070
Phone: 310-998-8000
Fax: 310-998-6293

Tenet's hospital operations include 70 facilities in 13
states and one in Barcelona, Spain.

	1995 Hospitals
	No.
California	22
Texas	11
Florida	10
Louisiana	6
Missouri	4
Other states	17
Total	**70**

WHAT

	1994 Sales		1994 Operating Income	
	$ mil.	% of total	$ mil.	% of total
Hospitals	2,807	95	358	90
Other	160	5	42	10
Total	**2,967**	**100**	**400**	**100**

Selected Services
Acute care
Clinical laboratories
Coronary care
Intensive care
Long-term care
Outpatient
Pharmacies
Physical therapy
Psychiatry
Radiology
Recovery
Rehabilitation
Surgery

Long-Term Care Affiliates
The Hillhaven Corporation (33% owned)
Westminster Health Care Holdings PLC (42% owned)

KEY COMPETITORS

Adventist Health
Apria Healthcare
Beverly Enterprises
Catholic Healthcare West
Charter Medical
Columbia/HCA
Healthsouth
Holy Cross Health System
Horizon/CMS Healthcare
Kaiser Foundation Health Plan
Mayo Foundation
Merck
OrNda HealthCorp
Sisters of Charity Health Care

HOW MUCH

	9-Year Growth	1985	1986	1987	1988	1989	1990	1991	1992	1993	1994
Sales ($ mil.)	(0.2%)	3,034	3,595	2,881	3,202	3,676	3,935	3,806	3,982	3,762	2,967
Net income ($ mil.)	—	149	94	63	148	143	242	277	133	(485)	
Income as % of sales	—	4.9%	2.6%	2.2%	4.6%	3.9%	6.1%	7.3%	3.3%	4.3%	—
Earnings per share ($)	—	0.99	0.59	0.41	0.92	0.90	1.34	1.54	0.75	0.91	(2.87)
Stock price – high ($)	—	16.44	13.38	15.44	12.38	19.50	20.13	25.81	18.13	14.38	19.50
Stock price – low ($)	—	9.38	9.63	8.06	8.81	10.69	14.63	12.63	9.63	6.50	12.50
Stock price – close ($)	2.6%	11.19	11.25	9.44	10.75	19.38	18.75	16.88	12.38	14.00	14.13
P/E – high	—	17	23	38	14	22	15	17	24	16	—
P/E – low	—	10	16	20	10	12	11	8	13	7	—
Dividends per share ($)	(7.4%)	0.24	0.27	0.29	0.31	0.34	0.36	0.39	0.45	0.48	0.12
Book value per share ($)	2.8%	6.18	6.42	6.23	6.55	7.40	7.97	10.08	10.03	10.56	7.95
Employees	(6.2%)	69,000	80,900	79,800	71,600	74,600	45,300	48,540	51,906	50,423	38,800

1994 Year-end:
Debt ratio: 38.7%
Return on equity: —
Cash (mil.): $313
Current ratio: 0.88
Long-term debt (mil.): $223
No. of shares (mil.): 166
Dividends
  Yield: 0.8%
  Payout: —
Market value (mil.): $2,347

**Stock Price History
High/Low 1985–94**

TENNECO INC.

Houston-based Tenneco had a 2nd profitable year in 1994 following 2 years of losses. This diversified company's operations include natural gas pipelines, shipbuilding, automotive parts, packaging, and chemicals. The sale of 56% of Case, its suffering, Wisconsin-based farm and construction equipment manufacturer, helped improve Tenneco's financial picture.

Tenneco's best-known, most profitable business is gas pipelines. In the past 10 years, as federal energy regulations have changed, Tenneco has gone from being primarily a seller of the gas its pipelines transport (which made the company subject to a maze of federal regulations and tariff restrictions) to a transporter of gas to be bought and sold by others (a business subject to less regulation, which is therefore more profitable).

Tenneco's Newport News Shipbuilding and Dry Dock Co., the US's #1 privately owned shipbuilder, once specialized in nuclear submarines. With the end of the Cold War, Newport News Shipbuilding faced a declining nuclear business; to compensate it has diversified into designing, building, repairing, and overhauling conventional ships for both domestic and foreign governments and commercial entities. Tenneco's Packaging Corporation of America subsidiary is the 5th largest supplier of corrugated containers in the US.

In 1994 chairman Michael Walsh died at age 51 from brain cancer. Also in 1994 Tenneco announced a strategy to build its value by focusing on higher-return, less-cyclical businesses, including packaging, automotive parts, and nonregulated natural gas operations, and by continuing to sell its cyclical businesses.

Tennessee Gas and Transmission began in 1943 as a division of The Chicago Corporation, headed by Gardiner Symonds and authorized to construct a 1,265-mile pipeline between the Gulf of Mexico and West Virginia. As the US faced WWII fuel shortages, the group finished the project in a record 11 months, obtaining right-of-way from thousands of landowners and crossing 67 rivers.

After WWII, Tennessee Gas went public with Symonds as president. The company expanded its pipeline and merged its oil and gas exploration interests into Tennessee Production Company (1954), which, with Bay Petroleum (bought 1955), became Tenneco Oil (1961). Symonds entered the chemical industry by acquiring 50% of Petro-Tex Chemical (1955).

In 1963 Tennessee Gas moved to its present Houston headquarters and in 1966 adopted the Tenneco name. In 1967 Tenneco bought Kern County Land Company, which owned 2.5 million acres of California farmland and mineral rights. The purchase thrust Tenneco into the farming business; by 1984 Tenneco was the US's largest grower/shipper of table grapes and 2nd largest almond processor. The Kern purchase also included 2 Racine, Wisconsin–based manufacturers: J. I. Case, known for tractors and construction digging equipment, and Walker Manufacturing, which entered the automotive field in 1912 by producing jacks.

Symonds bought Packaging Corporation of America, a maker of shipping containers, pulp, and paperboard products, in 1965. In 1968 he acquired Newport News Shipbuilding, founded by Collis Huntington in 1886. Newport News began building submarines and nuclear-powered aircraft carriers in the 1960s.

After Symonds's death in 1971, Tenneco bought shock absorber manufacturer Monroe of Monroe, Michigan (1977), and Philadelphia Life Insurance Company (1977; sold to ICH Corporation in 1986). In 1985 Tenneco bought UK chemical company Albright & Wilson (which administered all the company's chemical operations until its sale in 1995), and Case bought International Harvester's farm equipment operations. Tenneco sold its agricultural production operations in 1987 and its oil exploration and production operations in 1988.

Restructuring in the 1990s included the sale of Tenneco's natural gas liquids business to Enron ($632 million), the sale of its pulp chemicals business to Sterling Chemicals ($202 million), the sale of a US soda ash plant to Belgium's Solvay ($500 million), and the purchase of EnTrade Corp., a gas marketer.

As the company continued to reposition its segments (Newport News Shipbuilding, for example, raised its commercial repair business from zero contracts in 1991 to 38 contracts in 1993), it came to the conclusion that Tenneco's poorly performing farm and construction equipment company, Case, no longer fit in with its long-term plans. It sold 56% of Case stock in 1994. Tenneco's UK-based chemical company, Albright & Wilson, went public in 1995, netting about $670 million.

NYSE symbol: TEN
Fiscal year ends: December 31

WHO

Chairman and CEO: Dana G. Mead, age 59,
$1,778,177 pay
CEO and President, Tenneco Gas: Stephen D.
Chesebro', age 53, $647,880 pay
**Chairman and CEO, Newport News Shipbuilding and
Dry Dock Company:** W. R. Phillips Jr., age 63
General Counsel: Theodore R. Tetzlaff, age 50,
$700,000 pay
SVP and CFO: Robert T. Blakely, age 53, $637,640 pay
SVP Strategy: Stacy S. Dick, age 38, $578,560 pay
SVP Government Relations: John J. Castellani, age 43
SVP Corporate Affairs: Arthur H. House, age 52
SVP: Peter Menikoff, age 53
SVP Human Resources: Barry R. Schuman, age 53
VP Operations: Ilene S. Gordon, age 41
VP Investor Relations: Jack Lascar, age 40
VP Financial Analysis and Planning: Mark A. McCollum
VP: Kenneth D. Allen, age 55
Auditors: Arthur Andersen & Co, SC

WHERE

HQ: Tenneco Bldg., PO Box 2511, Houston, TX
77252-2511
Phone: 713-757-2131
Fax: 713-757-1410

	1994 Sales		1994 Operating Income	
	$ mil.	% of total	$ mil.	% of total
US	9,492	78	1,165	84
European Community	1,656	14	74	5
Canada	532	4	82	6
Other regions	494	4	72	5
Total	**12,174**	**100**	**1,393**	**100**

WHAT

	1994 Sales		1994 Operating Income	
	$ mil.	% of total	$ mil.	% of total
Farm & const. equip.	3,881	32	326	24
Nat. gas pipelines	2,378	20	415	30
Packaging	2,184	18	209	15
Automotive parts	1,989	16	223	16
Shipbuilding	1,753	14	200	15
Other & adjustments	(11)	—	6	—
Total	**12,174**	**100**	**1,379**	**100**

Selected Pipeline Concerns
Channel Industries Gas Co. (50%)
East Tennessee Natural Gas Co.
Iroquois Gas Transmission Co. (13.2%)
Kern River Gas Transmission Co. (50%)
Midwestern Gas Transmission Co.
Tennessee Gas Pipeline

Manufacturing Companies
Case Corp. (farm and construction equipment, 44%)
Newport News Shipbuilding and Dry Dock Co.
Packaging Corp. of America
Tenneco Automotive
Tenneco Gas

KEY COMPETITORS

AGCO
Allied Products
AlliedSignal
American Oil and Gas
American Standard
Bath Iron Works
Borg-Warner Automotive
Caterpillar
Coastal
Columbia Gas
Daewoo
Deere
Eaton
Fiat
General Dynamics
Hyundai
Johnson Controls
Komatsu
Kubota
Litton Industries
Occidental
Owens-Illinois
Panhandle Eastern
Reynolds Metals
Stone Container
USX–Delhi

HOW MUCH

	9-Year Growth	1985	1986	1987	1988	1989	1990	1991	1992	1993	1994
Sales ($ mil.)	(2.4%)	15,200	14,529	14,790	13,234	14,083	14,511	13,662	13,139	13,255	12,174
Net income ($ mil.)	10.9%	172	7	(218)	822	584	561	(732)	(612)	451	437
Income as % of sales	—	1.1%	0.0%	—	6.2%	4.1%	3.9%	—	—	3.4%	3.6%
Earnings per share ($)	14.1%	0.75	(0.40)	(1.81)	5.48	4.46	4.37	(6.09)	(4.35)	2.59	2.45
Stock price – high ($)	—	45.25	43.13	62.50	51.00	64.25	71.00	52.00	46.00	55.00	58.75
Stock price – low ($)	—	36.50	34.50	36.13	38.25	46.88	40.00	27.38	31.25	39.13	37.00
Stock price – close ($)	0.7%	39.75	38.25	39.75	48.88	62.25	47.50	31.38	40.63	52.63	42.50
P/E – high	—	60	—	—	9	14	16	—	—	21	24
P/E – low	—	49	—	—	7	11	9	—	—	15	15
Dividends per share ($)	(6.6%)	2.95	3.04	3.04	3.04	3.04	3.12	2.80	1.60	1.60	1.60
Book value per share ($)	(10.1%)	40.22	30.04	25.67	24.93	26.02	27.60	22.40	9.11	15.32	15.45
Employees	(7.5%)	111,000	101,000	104,000	94,000	90,000	92,000	89,000	79,000	75,000	55,000

1994 Year-end:
Debt ratio: 58.7%
Return on equity: 16.4%
Cash (mil.): $405
Current ratio: 1.28
Long-term debt (mil.): $3,570
No. of shares (mil.): 188
Dividends
  Yield: 3.8%
  Payout: 65.3%
Market value (mil.): $7,978

Stock Price History
High/Low 1985–94

TENNESSEE VALLEY AUTHORITY

OVERVIEW

The Tennessee Valley Authority (TVA) is a federally owned corporation set up by Congress to provide power and nonpower programs to the Tennessee River valley.

The TVA's power programs, although originally financed by congressional appropriations, are now required to be self-supporting. They supply electricity to power companies serving 7 million people in a region covering Tennessee and parts of Alabama, Georgia, Kentucky, Mississippi, North Carolina, and Virginia through a power network consisting of nuclear, coal-fired, and hydroelectric plants.

Nonpower programs, including flood control and river management, agricultural and industrial development, and forestry services, are funded primarily by congressional appropriations ($143 million in 1995). The agency is run by a 3-member board appointed by the US president and approved by the Senate.

Chairman Craven Crowell has called for Congress to end the restrictions that limit the TVA's service area, saying that the agency must compete in the open market to survive in a deregulated power industry. Some members of Congress have proposed privatization.

WHEN

In 1924 the Army Corps of Engineers completed construction (begun in 1918) of the Wilson Dam on the Tennessee River at Muscle Shoals, Alabama. The dam was built to provide power for 2 nitrate plants that were to manufacture munitions for WWI. With the war long since ended, the question of what to do with the facilities became a political football during the 1920s.

Sen. George Norris, head of the Senate Committee on Agriculture and Forestry, got 2 bills (to create a regional federal agency to take control of the plants, 1928; and to manage the waterways of the Tennessee Valley, 1931) through Congress, but both were vetoed. It wasn't until 1933, after Franklin Roosevelt became president, that the Tennessee Valley Authority was created by an act of Congress. New Dealers saw the TVA as a way to revitalize the economy of the region through flood control, improved navigation, and electric generation.

From the beginning the TVA faced opposition. Power companies claimed the agency was unconstitutional, but in 1939 a special 3-judge federal court ruled against them. By 1939 the agency had 5 hydroelectric facilities in operation and 5 others under construction. That same year the TVA bought the Tennessee Electric Power Company's power plants and transmission lines.

During the 1940s the TVA supplied power for the war effort, including the Manhattan Project in Oak Ridge, Tennessee. Between 1945 and 1950 power usage in the Tennessee Valley nearly doubled as postwar industries sprang up in the region, but even though it continued to add dams to provide hydroelectric power, it couldn't keep up with demand, so in 1949 it began construction of its first coal-fired plant.

The TVA's move into coal-fired power generation brought more controversy as some members of Congress questioned whether the new (nonhydroelectric) plants fit in with the agency's mission. In 1955 a task force headed by former President Herbert Hoover recommended the TVA be dissolved. The agency survived that salvo but saw its funding cut back.

In 1959 the TVA Act was amended so that the TVA could sell bonds. It no longer received government appropriations and was also required to pay back the funds it had received from the government.

During the 1960s the TVA passed 2 million in number of electric customers. As its customer base grew, it continued to add generating capacity. In 1967 it began construction of its first nuclear plant, Browns Ferry in Alabama. The agency undertook an ambitious nuclear program, planning a total of 17 units. However, costs skyrocketed, forcing the TVA to raise rates and cut maintenance to its coal-burning plants, which led to breakdowns. Construction on 8 of the units was canceled, and in 1985, 5 reactors that had come on-line had to be shut down because of safety concerns.

In 1988 former auto industry executive Marvin Runyon was appointed chairman of the agency. Nicknamed "Carvin' Marvin," he eliminated layers of management, sold 3 airplanes, and got rid of peripheral businesses, saving $400 million a year. Runyon left the TVA to become US postmaster general in 1992. He was replaced by Craven Crowell in 1993.

In 1995 the TVA's board voted to stop building any new nuclear plants. The TVA plans to finish Watts Bar Unit 1 near Spring City, Tennessee, but said it "will not, by itself" complete a 2nd unit at Watts Bar or 2 units near Hollywood, Alabama.

US government–owned corporation
Fiscal year ends: September 30

WHO

Chairman: Craven Crowell, $123,100 pay
Director: Johnny H. Hayes, $115,700 pay
Director: William H. Kennoy, $115,700 pay
President and Chief Nuclear Officer: Oliver D.
  Kingsley Jr.
Chief Operating Officer: Joseph W. Dickey
Chief Administrative Officer: Norman A. Zigrossi
CFO: David Smith
SVP Human Resources: Eva D. Hall
General Counsel: Edward S. Christenbury
Auditors: Coopers & Lybrand L.L.P.

WHERE

HQ: 400 W. Summit Hill Dr., Knoxville, TN 37902-1499
Phone: 615-632-2101
Fax: 615-632-6783

The Tennessee Valley Authority operates through 160
municipal and cooperative power distributors in 7 states.

Major Substations

Alcoa SW Sta. (TN)	McMinnville (TN)
Bowling Green (KY)	Milan (TN)
Charleston (TN)	Montgomery (TN)
Clarksville (TN)	Morristown (TN)
Columbia (TN)	Murfreesboro (TN)
Columbus (MS)	North Nashville (TN)
Cordova (TN)	Philadelphia (MS)
Corinth (MS)	Phipps Bend (TN)
Covington (TN)	Pigeon Forge (TN)
Davidson (TN)	Radnor (TN)
Decatur (AL)	Roane (TN)
Franklin (KY)	Rockwood (TN)
Franklin (TN)	Shelby (TN)
Freeport (TN)	Starkville (MS)
Harriman (TN)	Sullivan (TN)
Holly Springs (MS)	Trinity (AL)
Jackson (TN)	Tupelo (MS)
Lawrenceburg (TN)	Union (MS)
Lebanon (TN)	Volunteer (TN)
Madison (AL)	Weakley (TN)
Manchester (TN)	West Nashville (TN)
Marshall (KY)	West Point (MS)
Maury (TN)	Wilson (TN)
Mayfield (KY)	

WHAT

	1994 Power Generation
	% of total
Coal	70
Hydro	16
Nuclear	14
Total	**100**

	1994 Sales	
	$ mil.	% of total
Municipalities & cooperatives	4,582	85
Industries	452	8
Federal agencies	296	6
Other	71	1
Total	**5,401**	**100**

Nonpower Programs
Environmental Research Center
Land Between the Lakes (national outdoor recreation
  area in Kentucky and Tennessee)
Rural development
Stewardship
Water and land

HOW MUCH

	9-Year Growth	1985	1986	1987	1988	1989	1990	1991	1992	1993	1994
Sales ($ mil.)	1.9%	4,547	4,639	5,156	5,322	5,287	5,339	5,136	5,065	5,276	5,401
Net income ($ mil.)	(10.9%)	426	274	451	413	559	(387)	286	120	311	151
Income as % of sales	—	9.4%	5.9%	8.7%	7.8%	10.6%	—	5.6%	2.4%	5.9%	2.8%
Employees	(6.0%)	33,238	31,189	33,031	30,131	26,700	28,392	24,870	19,493	18,974	19,027

1994 Year-end:
Debt ratio: 83.5%
Cash (mil.): $152
Current ratio: 0.26
Long-term debt (mil.): $22,427

**Net Income
($ mil.)
1985–94**

TEXACO INC.

OVERVIEW

White Plains, New York–based Texaco is an integrated petroleum company with worldwide operations. Over the past 2 years, the oil giant has reorganized its operations in order to focus on its core oil and gas businesses. Texaco sold its chemical operations to a joint venture controlled by John Huntsman (of Huntsman Chemical) and Kerry Packer (owner of Australia's Consolidated Press Holdings) in 1993. Texaco also cut overhead costs by almost $200 million in 1994 and disposed of 300 scattered, nonstrategic US oil and gas producing properties in early 1995.

Despite a sluggish market for oil and gas and a drop in sales in 1994, the company is actively investing in developing new fields and upgrading old ones. In 1994 the company increased worldwide oil production by 66,000 barrels a day and plans to pour $19 billion into its oil and gas businesses over the next 5 years.

Internationally, the company is exploring high-potential areas in Russia, China, and Colombia. It is also investing in high technology to increase its output in oil fields in the North Sea, and it is continuing to develop fields in the Gulf of Martaban, the Gulf of Mexico, and the Permian Basin of Texas.

Caltex Petroleum, Texaco's 50-50 refining and marketing joint venture with Chevron, operates in 61 countries. It is currently upgrading refineries and expanding its retail outlets; in 1994 Caltex renovated 177 existing service stations and built an additional 119.

WHEN

"Buckskin Joe" Cullinan came to Texas in 1897 and, relying on sales to old friends from his days as a Standard Oil worker in Pennsylvania, began his own oil company.

When the Spindletop gusher hit in 1901, some 200 "oil companies" swarmed onto the scene. Cullinan decided the way to make money was to sell oil other people had found. He enlisted the support of Arnold Schlaet, who managed investments for 2 New York leather merchants. Cullinan and the Schlaet interests formed Texas Fuel in 1902. In a few months they changed the name to the Texas Company, selling under the Texaco brand.

The colorful Cullinan was deposed in a 1916 fight with New York executives. From its New York base, the Texas Company quickly expanded across the globe. When Standard of California's discoveries in Saudi Arabia proved more than it could handle, it summoned the Texas Company, and the 2 companies spawned Caltex for overseas marketing in 1936.

In the 1930s the Texas Company, partly through a company controlled by political boss Huey Long's family, leased a million acres of state-owned, oil-rich marshland in Louisiana. With such resources it became the only oil company with service stations in all states. In the 1940s it began sponsoring radio opera and Milton Berle's TV show. Its ads urged, "You can trust your car to the man who wears the star," a reference to the company logo. But Texaco (renamed in 1959) fell from atop the oil industry in the 1960s and 1970s as US wells dried up. Also it passed up drilling in Alaska's Prudhoe Bay and lost overseas supplies to nationalizations by developing countries.

Texaco thought it had found a source of oil in the $8.6 billion purchase of Getty Oil in 1983, but Getty had already agreed to be acquired by Pennzoil. A Texas court ordered Texaco to pay Pennzoil $10.53 billion in damages, and Texaco sought bankruptcy protection in 1987. After a $3 billion settlement with Pennzoil later that year, Texaco emerged from bankruptcy — just in time to fend off raider Carl Icahn. After those battles, Texaco raised about $7 billion, partly by selling its West German subsidiary and Texaco Canada (1988). It shucked 2,500 unprofitable gas stations, pulling out of 11 states.

In 1989 it launched a joint venture, Star Enterprise, with Saudi Arabia. Texaco put in 60% of its US refining and marketing operations, and the Saudis chipped in $812 million in cash and a steady flow of crude. The Persian Gulf War highlighted the weakness in that arrangement: 60% of Texaco's refinery output relied on Saudi crude.

In 1993 James Kinnear, who had led Texaco back from bankruptcy and streamlined the company's operations, retired. He was succeeded by Alfred DeCrane.

In 1994, hoping to take advantage of the deregulation of the natural gas industry, Texaco created the Gulf Coast Star Center, a natural gas system with transportation, storage, processing, and marketing operations providing a "one-stop shop" for customers.

In 1995 Texaco and Huntsman announced plans to form a joint venture to run Texaco's worldwide lubricant additives line. Texaco also launched a major advertising campaign to promote its gas, oil, and antifreeze products.

NYSE symbol: TX
Fiscal year ends: December 31

Chairman and CEO: Alfred C. DeCrane Jr., age 63,
$1,522,635 pay
VC: Allen J. Krowe, age 62, $1,023,705 pay
SVP: James L. Dunlap, age 57, $581,723 pay
SVP: Peter I. Bijur, age 52, $523,379 pay
SVP: C. Robert Black, age 59, $514,212 pay
SVP and CFO: William C. Bousquette, age 58
SVP: William K. Tell Jr., age 61
SVP and General Counsel: Stephen M. Turner, age 56
VP Human Resources: John D. Ambler, age 60
VP and Secretary: Carl B. Davidson, age 61
VP Investor Relations and Shareholder Services:
Elizabeth P. Smith, age 45
General Tax Counsel: Michael N. Ambler, age 58
Treasurer: James F. Link, age 50
Comptroller: Robert C. Oelkers, age 50
Auditors: Arthur Andersen & Co, SC

WHERE

HQ: 2000 Westchester Ave., White Plains, NY 10650
Phone: 914-253-4000
Fax: 914-253-7753

Texaco conducts exploration and production activities in
the US, Europe, Latin America, western Africa, the
Middle East, and the Far East.

	1994 Sales		1994 Operating Income	
	$ mil.	% of total	$ mil.	% of total
US	15,936	49	522	69
Europe	8,479	26	65	9
Other countries	8,125	25	171	22
Total	**32,540**	**100**	**758**	**100**

WHAT

	1994 Sales % of total
Refined products	54
Crude oil	30
Natural gas	8
Other	8
Total	**100**

Selected Subsidiaries and Affiliates
Caltex Petroleum Corp. (50%, refining and marketing
venture with Chevron, Asia-Pacific region and Africa)
Star Enterprise (50%, refining and marketing venture
with Saudi Arabian Oil, 26 eastern and Gulf
Coast states)
Texaco Oil Trading and Supply Company
Texaco Refining and Marketing Inc. (gas stations,
23 midwestern and western states)
Texaco Trading and Transportation Inc. (pipeline and
trucking operations)
Timan Pechora Co. LLC (Russian oil exploration
partnership with Amoco, Exxon, and Norsk Hydro)

KEY COMPETITORS

Amerada Hess	E-Z Serve	Petrofina
Amoco	Imperial Oil	Phillips
Ashland, Inc.	Kerr-McGee	Petroleum
Atlantic Richfield	Koch	Racetrac
British Gas	Kroger	Petroleum
British Petroleum	Mobil	Repsol
Broken Hill	National	Royal Dutch/Shell
Chevron	Convenience	Sinclair Oil
Circle K	Norsk Hydro	Southland
Coastal	Occidental	Sun Company
Columbia Gas	Panhandle	TOTAL
Diamond	Eastern	Unocal
Shamrock	PDVSA	USA Petroleum
Elf Aquitaine	PEMEX	USX–Marathon
Enron	Pennzoil	World Oil
Exxon	Petrobrás	

HOW MUCH

	9-Year Growth	1985	1986	1987	1988	1989	1990	1991	1992	1993	1994
Sales ($ mil.)	(3.8%)	46,297	31,613	34,372	33,544	32,416	40,899	37,271	36,812	33,245	32,540
Net income ($ mil.)	(3.3%)	1,233	725	(4,407)	1,304	2,413	1,450	1,294	1,012	1,068	910
Income as % of sales	—	2.7%	2.3%	—	3.8%	7.3%	3.5%	3.4%	2.7%	3.2%	2.8%
Earnings per share ($)	(4.6%)	4.85	3.01	(18.15)	5.19	8.74	5.08	4.55	3.53	3.74	3.17
Stock price – high ($)	—	40.88	37.13	47.50	52.75	59.00	68.50	70.00	66.88	69.50	68.13
Stock price – low ($)	—	27.00	26.00	23.50	35.63	48.50	55.00	55.50	56.13	57.63	58.13
Stock price – close ($)	8.0%	30.00	35.88	37.25	51.13	58.88	60.50	61.25	59.75	64.75	59.88
P/E – high	—	8	12	—	10	7	14	15	19	19	21
P/E – low	—	6	9	—	7	6	11	12	16	15	18
Dividends per share ($)	0.7%	3.00	3.00	0.75	2.25	10.10	3.05	3.20	3.20	3.20	3.20
Book value per share ($)	(5.5%)	57.04	56.71	37.76	33.27	34.65	33.84	35.51	36.04	37.18	34.42
Employees	(6.5%)	54,481	51,978	50,164	41,820	37,067	39,199	40,181	37,582	32,514	29,713

1994 Year-end:
Debt ratio: 42.0%
Return on equity: 10.3%
Cash (mil.): $464
Current ratio: 1.20
Long-term debt (mil.): $5,564
No. of shares (mil.): 260
Dividends
  Yield: 5.3%
  Payout: 100.9%
Market value (mil.): $15,541

**Stock Price History
High/Low 1985–94**

TEXAS INSTRUMENTS INCORPORATED

OVERVIEW

Texas Instruments (TI) dazzled technology fans in mid-1995 when it unveiled DMD. The Dallas-based company's patented "digital mirror device" gives big-screen TVs, computer monitors, and other display panels a super-clear picture.

TI, the #5 manufacturer of computer chips, is riding the industry's boom — income was up nearly 50% in 1994. The company's chip menu includes DSPs (digital signal processors, used in computer sound cards and cellular phones) and DRAMs (dynamic random-access memory chips). TI also makes computers, defense electronics, personal productivity products such as calculators and printers, and electrical control devices.

TI's marketing failures and defense cutbacks (in 1994 the US government accounted for 10% of revenues, down from 12% in 1993) prompted a recent company restructuring.

DMD is just one of many recent advances developed by TI, which has been known for thinking up new gizmos (the company spends about 7% of revenues on R&D) but not for getting them to consumers. Notebook computers, one area where TI has fallen short, are now the focus of a renewed marketing effort. The company has several joint ventures, including a new Dallas plant (with Hitachi) and 2 Asian fabs (with Acer and Kobe Steel).

In 1995 Northern California chip makers Cypress Semiconductor, LSI Logic, and VLSI Technology were ordered to pay $51.8 million to TI for infringement of a patented process for encasing chips in plastic. The defendants plan to appeal.

WHEN

"Doc" Karcher and Eugene McDermott founded Geophysical Service Inc. (GSI) in Newark, New Jersey, in 1930. The company specialized in reflective seismology, a new technology used to explore for oil and gas deposits. In 1934 GSI moved its headquarters to Dallas.

GSI started making defense electronics during WWII, when it made submarine detectors for the US Navy, and established a defense division in 1946. The company changed its name to Texas Instruments in 1951 and was listed on the NYSE in 1953.

TI started manufacturing transistors in 1952 after buying a license from Western Electric. TI invested about $2 million in an effort to reduce the price of the germanium transistor, which expanded the market for its uses and made possible the pocket transistor radio (1954). TI produced the first commercial silicon transistor in 1954, and TI engineer Jack Kilby (with Intel founder Bob Noyce) invented the integrated circuit in 1958. By 1959 TI's semiconductor manufacturing division accounted for half of its total sales.

TI's technological know-how led to other firsts in microelectronics, including terrain-following airborne radar (1958), forward-looking infrared (FLIR) systems (1964), hand-held calculators (1967), single-chip microcomputers (1971), and the LISP (list processing language) chip, a 32-bit microcomputer for artificial intelligence applications (1987).

TI moved from defense and semiconductors into consumer products in the 1970s with calculators, digital watches, and home computers. Although TI developed the basic technologies for these products, its inability to follow through in the face of low-cost foreign competition led it to lose money and then abandon its digital watch and PC businesses. Attempts to meet competitors' prices, as well as plunging semiconductor prices, led to TI's first annual loss in 1983.

TI's Kilby patent for the integrated circuit (named after the coinventor of the IC) was upheld in Japan in 1989, and all major Japanese electronics firms except Fujitsu pay royalties to TI.

In 1991 TI sold its remaining interest in GSI to Halliburton; Hewlett-Packard bought its industrial controls business (1991) and multiuser minicomputer business (1992). In 1991 TI signed a licensing pact with chip maker Cyrix for its design of a clone of Intel's 486. TI introduced the TI486 in 1992.

In tough times TI leveraged its DRAM know-how in a number of strategic alliances that include a joint venture (26%) with Canon, Hewlett-Packard, and the Singapore Economic Development Board to make 4-megabit DRAMs (TECH, 1991) and an agreement with Hitachi to research and develop 256-megabit DRAM chips (1993).

The company posted record profits and sales in 1994 thanks in large part to a strong performance from its semiconductor business. That same year TI and Hitachi announced plans to form a joint venture and build a $500 million DRAM chip plant in Richardson, Texas.

In 1995 the company sold its line of educational toys, including Speak & Spell and Speak & Math, to Tiger Electronics.

NYSE symbol: TXN
Fiscal year ends: December 31

Chairman, President, and CEO: Jerry R. Junkins,
age 57, $1,927,800 pay
VC: William P. Weber, age 54, $995,000 pay
VC: William B. Mitchell, age 59, $859,100 pay
EVP; President, Semiconductor Group: Thomas J.
Engibous, age 42, $906,000 pay
EVP: William F. Hayes, age 51, $831,350 pay
**EVP; President, Defense Systems and Electronics
Group:** Gary D. Clubb, age 48
SVP, Treasurer, and CFO: William A. Aylesworth,
age 52
SVP, Secretary, and General Counsel: Richard J.
Agnich, age 51
VP; President, Materials and Controls Group: Nicholas
K. Brookes, age 47
VP: Elwin L. Skiles Jr., age 53
VP and Corporate Controller: Marvin M. Lane Jr., age 60
VP Human Resources: Charles F. Nielson, age 57
Auditors: Ernst & Young LLP

WHERE

HQ: 13500 N. Central Expwy., PO Box 655474, Dallas,
TX 75265
Phone: 214-995-2551
Fax: 214-995-4360

Texas Instruments has manufacturing operations in 18
countries.

	1994 Sales		1994 Pretax Income	
	$ mil.	% of total	$ mil.	% of total
US	5,943	58	1,018	82
East Asia	2,729	26	(12)	—
Europe	1,574	15	219	18
Other regions	69	1	5	0
Adjustments	—	—	(188)	—
Total	**10,315**	**100**	**1,042**	**100**

WHAT

	1994 Sales		1994 Pretax Income	
	$ mil.	% of total	$ mil.	% of total
Components	6,787	66	1,101	82
Defense electronics	1,710	17	172	13
Digital products	1,661	16	62	5
Metallurgical matls.	152	1	(8)	—
Adjustments	5	—	(285)	—
Total	**10,315**	**100**	**1,042**	**100**

Selected Products
Audio decoders
Avionics systems
Digital mirror devices (DMD)
Digital signal processors (DSP)
Dynamic random-access memory (DRAM) chips
Electrical and electronic control devices
Electronic connectors
microLaser Pro E printers
Missile guidance and control systems
Multimedia video processors
Navigation systems
Notebook computers
Radar systems
Speech recognition products
Thermal Vision infrared imaging systems

KEY COMPETITORS

AMD	General Dynamics	National
Apple	General Electric	Semiconductor
AST	Harris Corp.	NEC
Canon	Hewlett-Packard	Oki
Casio	Hitachi	Raytheon
Chips and	Honeywell	Rockwell
Technologies	Hyundai	Samsung
Compaq	IBM	Sharp
EG&G	Intel	Siemens
Emerson	LG Group	Thomson SA
Fujitsu	Micron Technology	Thorn EMI
Gateway 2000	Motorola	Toshiba

HOW MUCH

	9-Year Growth	1985	1986	1987	1988	1989	1990	1991	1992	1993	1994
Sales ($ mil.)	8.6%	4,925	4,974	5,595	6,295	6,522	6,567	6,784	7,440	8,523	10,315
Net income ($ mil.)	—	(119)	40	257	366	292	(39)	(409)	247	476	691
Income as % of sales	—	—	0.8%	4.6%	5.8%	4.5%	—	—	3.3%	5.6%	6.7%
Earnings per share ($)	—	(1.59)	0.38	2.96	4.05	3.04	(0.92)	(5.40)	2.50	5.07	7.27
Stock price – high ($)	—	43.88	49.38	80.25	60.00	46.75	44.00	47.63	52.25	84.25	89.50
Stock price – low ($)	—	28.72	34.22	36.25	34.50	28.13	22.50	26.00	30.00	45.75	61.00
Stock price – close ($)	8.8%	35.13	39.34	55.75	41.00	35.88	38.00	30.75	46.63	63.50	74.88
P/E – high	—	—	—	27	15	15	—	—	21	17	12
P/E – low	—	—	—	12	9	9	—	—	12	9	8
Dividends per share ($)	3.7%	0.67	0.67	0.69	0.72	0.72	0.72	0.72	0.72	0.72	0.93
Book value per share ($)	6.3%	18.89	22.49	21.95	21.36	24.10	22.46	19.36	20.92	25.49	32.79
Employees	(3.5%)	77,872	77,270	77,984	75,685	73,854	70,318	62,939	60,577	59,048	56,333

1994 Year-end:
Debt ratio: 21.2%
Return on equity: 25.8%
Cash (mil.): $1,290
Current ratio: 1.83
Long-term debt (mil.): $808
No. of shares (mil.): 93
Dividends
  Yield: 1.2%
  Payout: 12.8%
Market value (mil.): $6,940

**Stock Price History
High/Low 1985–94**

TEXAS UTILITIES COMPANY

OVERVIEW

Dallas-based Texas Utilities is one of the largest electric utilities in the US. Through its principal subsidiary, Texas Utilities Electric Company (TU Electric), it provides electric service to about 5.7 million people, about 1/3 of the state's population. TU Electric's service area covers 372 cities and towns (including the Dallas–Fort Worth metroplex) in north-central, eastern, and western Texas.

Other TU subsidiaries support TU Electric by providing the lignite coal (Texas Utilities Mining Company) and natural gas and oil (Texas Utilities Fuel Company) for the company's generating plants. TU Fuel Company owns a 50% interest in a 395-mile natural gas pipeline linking the Dallas–Fort Worth area to West Texas producing fields, and Chaco Energy owns coal reserves totaling some 120 million recoverable tons.

Increased competition in the power industry has hurt Texas Utilities. The company has lost about 380 megawatts of wholesale business to competitors, equal to about 4% of TU's revenues. It has focused on improving efficiency in order to compete more effectively. TU is also moving into new areas. In 1995 the company paid $200 million for a 20% stake in the Texas operations of PCS PrimeCo, a wireless telecommunications firm created by Bell Atlantic, U S West, and NYNEX.

WHEN

The first electric power company in North Texas was founded in Dallas in 1883. Another was built in 1885 in Fort Worth. From these and other small power plants grew 3 companies to serve the north-central, western, and eastern regions of the state: Texas Power and Light (1912), Dallas Power and Light (1917), and Texas Electric Service Company (1929). By 1932 a network of transmission lines connecting these 3 utilities was virtually complete. Texas Utilities Company was formed in 1945 as a holding company to enable the 3 utilities to raise capital and obtain construction financing at lower cost.

Beginning in the 1940s TU moved away from strict dependence on natural gas, which was cheap and abundant, and began to lease large lignite coal reserves. In 1952 it formed Industrial Generating Company to mine lignite and operate an early coal-fired generating plant. It pioneered new lignite coal–burning technology during the 1960s, building larger boilers than had ever been used in the US. The first of 9 large lignite plants went into use in 1971, and TU began construction of the Comanche Peak nuclear plant, 45 miles southwest of Fort Worth, in 1974.

In 1984 Dallas Power and Light, Texas Electric Service, Texas Power and Light, and Texas Utilities Generating Company were combined as Texas Utilities Electric. The mining company was renamed Texas Utilities Mining.

In 1985 the Nuclear Regulatory Commission suspended licensing of the Comanche Peak nuclear plant, citing both design and construction faults. Further negotiations with the NRC resulted in the granting of a license to operate the plant at 5% of capacity in 1990, followed by a full-power license in the spring of that year. In the interim TU lost its 3 construction partners over the issue of multibillion-dollar cost overruns and bought their interests for $984.5 million.

In 1990 Santa Fe Pacific Corporation agreed to settle an antitrust suit brought by TU in 1981 over a 1977 lease agreement granting TU the right to mine about 228 million tons of coal owned by Santa Fe. TU won substantial royalty and lease agreement concessions from Santa Fe in a new agreement, running from 1990 through 2017.

In 1991 the Public Utilities Commission of Texas (PUC) authorized a 10.2% rate increase (worth about $442 million in revenues) but disallowed $1.4 billion in costs related to the construction of its Comanche Peak nuclear facility and the buyout of a former minority interest in the project.

In 1993 Texas Utilities acquired Southwestern Electric Service Company for approximately $65 million in stock and cash. That same year TU Electric received a low-power license for Unit 2 at Comanche Peak. Also in 1993 Texas Utilities' profits suffered a power outage after the PUC disallowed $250 million in costs related to construction of TU's Comanche Peak nuclear plant and approved only an 8.7% rate increase instead of the 15.3% rate increase TU had requested. As a result, in 1994 Texas Utilities failed to raise its dividend for the first time since 1948.

In 1994 TU bought Atlantic Richfield's I. M. Pei–designed office tower in Dallas for $29 million; critics claimed the price was unusually low because TU is one of Atlantic Richfield's major customers.

In 1995 Erle Nye succeeded Jerry Farrington (who remains chairman) as CEO.

NYSE symbol: TXU
Fiscal year ends: December 31

WHO

Chairman: Jerry S. Farrington, age 60, $804,167 pay
President and CEO: Erle Nye, age 57, $618,750 pay
(prior to promotion)
EVP, TU Services: Michael D. Spence, $302,000 pay
EVP, TU Electric: W. M. Taylor, $289,333 pay
VP and Principal Financial Officer: H. Jarrell Gibbs,
age 57, $285,167 pay
Controller and Principal Accounting Officer: H. Dan
Farell
Treasurer and Assistant Secretary: Cathryn C. Hulen
Secretary and Assistant Treasurer: Peter B. Tinkham
VP Personnel: Pitt Pittman
Auditors: Deloitte & Touche LLP

WHERE

HQ: Energy Plaza, 1601 Bryan Tower, Dallas, TX 75201
Phone: 214-812-4600
Fax: 214-812-4079

Generating Facilities

Oil and Gas

Collin	Rivercrest
Decordova	Stryker Creek
Eagle Mountain	Tradinghouse
Graham	Trinidad
Handley	Valley
Lake Creek	
Lake Hubbard	**Lignite**
Main	Big Brown
Morgan Creek	Martin Lake
Mountain Creek	Monticello
North Main	Sandow
Northlake	
Parkdale	**Nuclear**
Permian Basin	Comanche Peak

WHAT

	1994 Sales	
	$ mil.	% of total
Residential	2,490	43
Commercial	1,707	29
Industrial	987	17
Government & municipal	400	7
Other electric utilities	216	4
Adjustments	(136)	—
Total	**5,664**	**100**

	1994 Fuel Sources
	% of total
Lignite	37
Oil & gas	34
Nuclear	16
Purchased power	13
Total	**100**

Subsidiaries

Basic Resources Inc. (resource development and related
technology and services)
Chaco Energy Co. (coal production, sale, and delivery)
Southwestern Electric Service Co. (SESCO, electric
utility serving customers in eastern and central Texas)
Texas Utilities Electric Co. (TU Electric, electric utility
serving customers in north-central, eastern, and
western Texas)
Texas Utilities Fuel Co. (natural gas pipeline; acquires,
stores, and delivers gas fuel)
Texas Utilities Mining Co. (surface mining for lignite)
Texas Utilities Properties Inc. (property ownership,
leasing, and management)
Texas Utilities Services Inc. (accounting and
administrative services)

KEY COMPETITORS

Entergy
Houston Industries
Southwestern Public Service

HOW MUCH

	9-Year Growth	1985	1986	1987	1988	1989	1990	1991	1992	1993	1994
Sales ($ mil.)	3.5%	4,170	3,932	4,083	4,154	4,321	4,543	4,893	4,908	5,435	5,664
Net income ($ mil.)	(0.9%)	588	627	680	643	779	851	(410)	619	369	543
Income as % of sales	—	14.1%	15.9%	16.7%	15.5%	18.0%	18.7%	—	12.6%	6.8%	9.6%
Earnings per share ($)	(6.4%)	4.35	4.45	4.55	4.00	4.44	4.40	(1.98)	2.88	1.66	2.40
Stock price – high ($)	—	31.88	37.50	36.63	30.63	37.63	39.00	43.00	43.75	49.75	43.13
Stock price – low ($)	—	25.13	29.50	25.50	24.63	27.75	32.00	34.13	37.00	41.63	29.63
Stock price – close ($)	0.8%	29.88	31.50	27.00	28.13	35.13	36.63	41.75	42.50	43.25	32.00
P/E – high	—	7	8	8	8	9	9	—	15	30	18
P/E – low	—	6	7	6	6	6	7	—	13	25	12
Dividends per share ($)	2.4%	2.52	2.68	2.80	2.88	2.92	2.96	3.00	3.04	3.08	3.08
Book value per share ($)	(0.3%)	29.46	31.24	33.02	33.38	34.56	34.66	29.82	30.33	29.29	28.74
Employees	(4.6%)	16,528	16,927	16,086	15,669	15,248	15,216	15,262	10,687	10,859	10,798

1994 Year-end:
Debt ratio: 51.9%
Return on equity: 8.3%
Cash (mil.): $8
Current ratio: 0.48
Long-term debt (mil.): $7,888
No. of shares (mil.): 226
Dividends
  Yield: 9.6%
  Payout: 128.3%
Market value (mil.): $7,227

Stock Price History
High/Low 1985–94

TEXTRON INC.

OVERVIEW

After shedding unwanted businesses, Providence-based Textron, one of America's oldest industrial companies and a major defense contractor, is posting solid revenue growth. Subsidiary Bell Helicopter is scheduled to deliver 35 helicopters to Canada in 1995 as the first part of a 3-year contract to deliver 100 units to that country (at $4–$5 million apiece).

The company's automotive division (which was relocated to Detroit in 1994) is the largest supplier of automotive interiors in the US, with a 25% market share, and its sales have been lifted by the recent boom in the auto market. Cessna, another subsidiary, is the world leader in light and mid-size business jets, with a 60% share.

Textron is still a widely diversified company (with 6 business segments and 29 operating companies in 1994), but CEO James Hardymon is pushing for focus and operational efficiency in response to shrinking government contracts (40% of total revenues in 1988, 20% in 1992, and 17% in 1994).

The company's manufacturing units make such diverse products as auto interiors, Cone Drive gear motors, E-Z-GO golf carts, Greenlee electrical test equipment, McCord Winn windshield washer systems, and Speidel watchbands. The conglomerate's other main businesses are in finance (Avco Financial Services and Textron Financial Corp.) and insurance (Paul Revere).

WHEN

Pioneer conglomerate builder Royal Little founded Special Yarns Corporation, a Boston textile business, in 1923. To save the company from bankruptcy, he merged it with the Franklin Rayon Dyeing Company in 1928. The resulting company, Franklin Rayon Corporation, moved its headquarters to Providence, Rhode Island, in 1930 and changed its name to Atlantic Rayon in 1938.

The company expanded during WWII to keep up with government orders for parachutes and in 1944 adopted the name Textron (connoting "textile products made from synthetics"). But Textron failed in its postwar efforts to distribute Textron-brand consumer products. In 1952 Little convinced Textron's shareholders to allow the company to diversify beyond the textile industry, and between 1953 and 1960 he bought more than 40 different companies, including Randall (auto parts, 1959) and E-Z-GO (golf carts, 1960). Before turning over the company to banker Rupert "Rupe" Thompson in 1960, Little bought Bell Helicopter. Within 6 years defense-related sales accounted for 41% of Textron's revenues.

Under Thompson, businesses deemed incapable of earning a 20% ROE were sold, including Amerotron, Textron's last textile business (1963). Known on Wall Street as "Miscellaneous, Inc.," Textron bought 20 companies between 1960 and 1965, mostly to enhance its existing business divisions. By 1968, when former Wall Street attorney William Miller stepped up to replace Thompson as CEO, Textron made products ranging from Homelite chain saws (acquired 1955) to Speidel watchbands (acquired 1964).

Miller tried unsuccessfully to make several large acquisitions, including Lockheed (1974). He sold several companies and bought Jacobsen Manufacturers (lawn care equipment, 1978) before leaving Textron in 1978 to head the Federal Reserve and become President Carter's treasury secretary.

B. F. Dolan, who became president in 1980, sold Textron's least-profitable businesses, including its zipper and snowmobile makers (1980) and machine tool manufacturer Jones & Lamson (1985). Textron bought Avco Corporation (aerospace and financial services, 1985) and Ex-Cell-O (defense and auto parts, 1986), financing these acquisitions by selling nondefense companies and increasing debt. Textron's purchase of UK-based Avdel (metal fastening systems, 1989) remained held up in 1992 by the FTC's claim that the deal would limit competition.

In 1992 Textron bought Cessna Aircraft, the world leader in light and mid-size business jets, from General Dynamics. In 1994 Textron completed its acquisition of Avdel (which had revenues of $153 million in 1993), improving its access to the Asian and European fastener markets. Between 1990 and 1994 the company restructured 11 commercial aerospace and defense businesses, which included the closing or selling of 24 plants.

In 1994 Textron sold its Lycoming Turbine Engine division to AlliedSignal for $375 million. Later that year Textron acquired Orag Inter AG of Switzerland, Europe's #1 distributor of golf and turf care equipment.

In 1995 Textron bought Household Finance of Australia.

NYSE symbol: TXT
Fiscal year ends: December 31

Chairman and CEO: James F. Hardymon, age 60, $1,825,000 pay
President and COO: Lewis B. Campbell, age 48, $980,000 pay
EVP and General Counsel: Wayne W. Juchatz, age 48
EVP and CFO: Stephen L. Key, age 51
EVP Corporate Development: Thomas P. Hollowell, age 51
EVP Administration and Chief Human Resources Officer: William F. Wayland, age 59, $700,000 pay
SVP Government and International Relations: Mary L. Howell, age 42
VP Communications and Risk Management: Edward C. Arditte
VP and Treasurer: Brian T. Downing
Staff VP Corporate Information Management and Chief Information Officer: William B. Gauld
Auditors: Ernst & Young LLP

WHERE

HQ: 40 Westminster St., Providence, RI 02903
Phone: 401-421-2800
Fax: 401-421-2878

Textron operates 138 plants within the US and 9 plants outside the US.

	1994 Sales		1994 Operating Income	
	$ mil.	% of total	$ mil.	% of total
US	7,103	73	825	80
Canada	1,085	11	119	12
Europe	745	8	46	4
Asia/Pacific	392	4	46	4
Mexico	146	2	—	
Other regions	212	2	—	—
Total	**9,683**	**100**	**1,036**	**100**

WHAT

	1994 Sales		1994 Operating Income	
	$ mil.	% of total	$ mil.	% of total
Aircraft	2,186	23	194	19
Finance	1,672	17	331	32
Automotive	1,557	16	139	13
Sys. & components	1,540	16	99	9
Industrial	1,395	14	142	14
Paul Revere	1,331	14	131	13
Adjustments	2		—	
Total	**9,683**	**100**	**1,036**	**100**

Aircraft
Business jets (Cessna)
Helicopters (Bell)

Finance
Commercial finance
Consumer loans (Avco)

Automotive
Auto parts (McCord Winn)
Camshafts (CWC Castings)
Metal parts (Randall)
Textron Automotive Exteriors
Textron Automotive Interiors

Systems and Components
Aircraft wings and parts (Textron Aerostructures)
Assault landing craft

Control systems (HR)
Fuel systems
Logistics support (Avco)
Rotors (Airfoil)
Specialty materials
Weapons systems

Industrial
Fastening systems
Gears and components (Cone Drive)
Golf and specialty carts (E-Z-GO, Orag)
Hand tools, power tools, machine tools (Greenlee, Micromatic)
Lawnmowers (Jacobsen)
Watch attachments and fashion jewelry (Speidel)

Insurance (Paul Revere, Avco)

KEY COMPETITORS

21 International
Aetna
AlliedSignal
Bombardier
General Electric
Gulfstream Aerospace
Lear Seating
Litton Industries
Lockheed Martin
Raytheon
United Technologies

HOW MUCH

	9-Year Growth	1985	1986	1987	1988	1989	1990	1991	1992	1993	1994
Sales ($ mil.)	10.2%	4,039	5,023	5,388	7,286	6,432	7,918	7,840	8,348	9,078	9,683
Net income ($ mil.)	7.6%	224	246	264	272	269	283	300	324	379	433
Income as % of sales	—	5.5%	4.9%	4.9%	3.7%	4.2%	3.6%	3.8%	3.9%	4.2%	4.5%
Earnings per share ($)	5.4%	3.00	2.98	3.27	3.10	3.02	3.18	3.42	3.66	4.21	4.80
Stock price – high ($)	—	29.88	35.00	39.75	30.00	29.38	27.63	40.25	44.88	58.88	60.63
Stock price – low ($)	—	16.19	24.31	17.25	20.00	22.63	18.75	24.25	33.63	40.38	46.50
Stock price – close ($)	8.3%	24.50	31.50	22.63	23.75	24.63	27.38	39.63	44.75	58.25	50.38
P/E – high	—	10	12	12	10	10	9	12	12	14	13
P/E – low	—	5	8	5	7	8	6	7	9	10	10
Dividends per share ($)	4.7%	0.90	0.90	0.95	1.00	1.00	1.00	1.00	1.12	1.21	1.36
Book value per share ($)	5.7%	20.38	22.19	26.38	27.79	28.39	31.16	33.78	28.20	31.26	33.52
Employees	(0.6%)	56,000	72,000	61,000	60,000	58,000	54,000	52,000	54,000	56,000	53,000

1994 Year-end:
Debt ratio: 76.5%
Return on equity: 15.4%
Cash (mil.): $49
Current ratio: 5.21
Long-term debt (mil.): $9,364
No. of shares (mil.): 85
Dividends
  Yield: 2.7%
  Payout: 28.3%
Market value (mil.): $4,307

Stock Price History High/Low 1985–94

TIME WARNER INC.

OVERVIEW

With $15.9 billion in total sales, Time Warner is the world's #1 media company (at least until Disney's merger with Capital Cities/ABC). Known for its formidable assets and famous brand names, the New York City–based company's portfolio contains such industry giants as Time Inc. (the US's #1 magazine publisher); Warner Bros. (the world's #1 producer and distributor of movies, TV programs, and videos); Warner Music Group (the world's #1 music publisher, Warner/Chappell, plus 49 record labels); Home Box Office (the #1 pay cable TV service); Little, Brown and Co. and Warner Books (leading book publishers); and Time Warner Cable (the #2 US cable system).

Time Warner also owns stakes in cable TV programming through Turner Broadcasting (19.6%) and other networks such as Cinemax, Court TV (55%), Comedy Central (50%), and the Sega Channel (33%, video games). The company considered buying NBC but instead launched WB Network in 1995 as an outlet for its library of films, TV programs, and cartoons.

The company has pledged to reduce the debt assumed for the 1989 merger of Time and Warner. In 1995 it sold a 51% stake in its Six Flags amusement parks as part of its plan to sell $2–$3 billion in noncore businesses over the next year.

Time Warner is investing heavily in cable as that industry consolidates. The company's recent expansion in New York, Ohio, Florida, Texas, and North Carolina widens its reach to 11.5 million subscribers — enough to vie with Tele-Communications, Inc., for #1. It is also investing in Japan's fledgling cable industry. Concentrated in major metropolitan and suburban areas, Time Warner's cable operation expects to provide a wide range of services (pay-per-view, interactive TV, and telephone) as well as on-line outlets for its treasury of magazines, movies, TV programs, and books.

WHEN

Time Warner was created in 1989 when Time Inc. merged with Warner Communications Inc. Henry Luce had founded Time Inc. with Briton Hadden in 1922. Their first magazine, *Time*, summarized a week's worth of news. In the 1930s they added *FORTUNE*, *Life*, and other magazines. Luce, a controversial business manager, stepped down as editor-in-chief in 1964; he died in 1967.

During the 1970s and 1980s Time Inc. explored new ventures. It entered the cable TV market with Home Box Office (1972) and bought Book-of-the-Month Club (1977). In magazines, *Money* (1972) was a moderate success and *People* (1974) was a hit, but *TV-Cable Week* lasted only 5 months.

Warner Brothers, founded by Harry, Albert (Abe), Jack, and Sam Warner, was one of Hollywood's largest movie studios. Warner Brothers made such classics as *Little Caesar* (1930), *Casablanca* (1942), and *Rebel Without a Cause* (1955). Sam died in 1927; Harry and Abe retired in 1951; and Jack remained until 1967, when Seven Arts Ltd. bought the studio. Steven Ross's Kinney National Services, owner of Famous Agency (talent) and National Periodical Publications (*Superman* and *Batman* comics and *Mad* magazine), bought the studio in 1969.

Kinney sold the pre-1948 movies to United Artists and shared the studios with Columbia. The company changed its name to Warner Communications Inc. in 1972. During the 1970s and early 1980s, Warner made most of its money with its game subsidiary, Atari (1976), but losses in this field led Warner to sell most of Atari in 1984.

Under the pressure of a possible takeover, Time agreed to merge with Warner, effective in 1990, at a cost of $14 billion, most of it in debt. During the 1990s the new conglomerate launched *Entertainment Weekly*, *Martha Stewart Living*, *In Style*, and *Vibe*. In 1992 the company created Time Warner Entertainment, a limited partnership for its film, TV programming, and cable businesses. Time Warner retained a 63% stake but sold interests to U S WEST, a regional Bell telephone company, and 2 Japanese companies, ITOCHU and Toshiba.

In 1993 Gerald Levin, former Time Inc. VC and one of the architects of the merger, became chairman, shortly after Ross's death from cancer. Time Warner announced plans to start a US network of broadcast stations in some markets and cable systems in others.

When Canadian spirits maker Seagram increased its holdings in Time Warner in 1994 to 14.9%, the company adopted a "poison pill" plan to discourage more purchases. Also that year the Warner Books unit of Time Warner bought a stake in The Reference Press, publisher of this profile.

In 1995 Seagram, the company's largest shareholder, bought rival studio MCA. That August, Time Warner offered to buy the portion of Turner Broadcasting it doesn't already own.

NYSE symbol: TWX
Fiscal year ends: December 31

WHO

Chairman and CEO: Gerald M. Levin, age 55,
$5,050,000 pay
President: Richard D. Parsons, age 46
EVP, General Counsel, and Secretary: Peter R. Haje,
age 60, $1,650,000 pay
SVP and CFO: Richard J. Bressler, age 37
Editor in Chief: Norman Pearlstine, age 52
President and CEO, Time Inc.: Don Logan, age 51
**Chairman and CEO, Warner Music Group; Chairman,
Home Box Office:** Michael J. Fuchs, age 49
CEO, Home Box Office: Jeffrey Bewkes
Chairman and Co-CEO, Warner Bros.: Robert A. Daly
Chairman and Co-CEO, Warner Bros.: Terry S. Semel
Chairman and CEO, Time Warner Cable: Joseph J.
Collins, age 50
VP Administration (HR): Carolyn McCandless
Auditors: Ernst & Young LLP

WHERE

HQ: 75 Rockefeller Plaza, New York, NY 10019
Phone: 212-484-8000
Fax: 212-484-8734 (Corporate Communications)

	1994 Sales		1994 Operating Income	
	$ mil.	% of total	$ mil.	% of total
Time Warner Inc.				
US	4,944	31	494	32
Europe	1,445	9	108	7
Pacific Rim	724	5	74	5
Other regions	283	2	37	2
Subtotal	**7,396**	**47**	**713**	**46**
Entertainment Group	—	—	852	54
US	6,816	43	—	—
Other countries	1,693	10	—	—
Total	**15,905**	**100**	**1,565**	**100**

WHAT

	1994 Sales		1994 Operating Income	
	$ mil.	% of total	$ mil.	% of total
Time Warner Inc.				
Music	3,986	25	366	23
Publishing	3,433	21	347	22
Adjustments	(23)	—	—	—
Subtotal	**7,396**	**46**	**713**	**45**
Entertainment Group				
Films/TV	5,041	31	275	18
Cable	2,242	14	340	22
Programming/HBO	1,513	9	237	15
Adjustments	(287)	—	—	—
Total	**15,905**	**100**	**1,565**	**100**

Selected Operations

Cable
Time Warner Cable

Film
Warner Bros.
Warner Home Video

Music
The Atlantic Group
Elektra Entertainment

Publishing
FORTUNE

Little, Brown and Co.
People
Sports Illustrated
Time
Warner Books, Inc.

Other Interests
Columbia House (50%,
music/video club)
Pathfinder (on-line services)
Six Flags Entertainment (49%)
Turner Broadcasting (19.6%)

KEY COMPETITORS

Advance Publications	Cox Communications	Sony TCI
Anheuser-Busch	Forbes	Thorn EMI
Bertelsmann	General Electric	Times Mirror
Cablevision Systems	Lagardère	U.S. News &
Capital Cities/ABC	MCA	World
CBS	McGraw-Hill	Report
Comcast	News Corp.	Viacom
Continental Cablevision	Philips	Walt Disney

HOW MUCH

	9-Year Growth	1985	1986	1987	1988	1989	1990	1991	1992	1993	1994
Sales ($ mil.)	9.0%	3,404	3,762	4,193	4,507	7,642	11,517	12,021	13,560	6,581[1]	7,396[1]
Net income ($ mil.)	—	200	376	250	289	(256)	(786)	(692)	(542)	(339)	(104)
Income as % of sales	—	5.9%	10.0%	6.0%	6.4%	—	—	—	—	—	—
Earnings per share ($)	—	0.79	1.49	1.05	1.25	(1.08)	(3.42)	(2.40)	(1.46)	(0.90)	(0.27)
Stock price – high ($)	—	16.31	22.84	29.22	30.63	45.69	31.16	31.25	29.75	46.88	44.25
Stock price – low ($)	—	10.63	14.38	16.44	19.69	25.91	16.53	19.44	21.63	28.75	31.50
Stock price – close ($)	9.5%	15.53	17.50	20.56	26.75	30.16	21.44	21.88	29.25	44.25	35.13
P/E – high	—	21	15	28	24	—	—	—	—	—	—
P/E – low	—	14	10	16	16	—	—	—	—	—	—
Dividends per share ($)	4.1%	0.25	0.25	0.25	0.25	0.25	0.25	0.26	0.27	0.31	0.36
Book value per share ($)	(5.1%)	4.82	5.40	5.98	5.99	—	—	—	—	3.62	3.02
Employees	12.1%	19,000	21,500	20,000	21,000	34,700	41,000	41,700	44,000	50,000	53,300

1994 Year-end:
Debt ratio: 88.9%
Return on equity: —
Cash (mil.): $282
Current ratio: 0.95
Long-term debt (mil.): $8,839
No. of shares (mil.): 379
Dividends
  Yield: 1.0%
  Payout: —
Market value (mil.): $13,323

**Stock Price History
High/Low 1985–94**

[1] The company stopped consolidating Time Warner Entertainment Group sales.

THE TIMES MIRROR COMPANY

OVERVIEW

The nation's 3rd largest newspaper company is having to change with the times. The $3.4 billion Times Mirror Co. is closing down some of its operations, cutting costs and staff, and reorganizing to remedy disappointing earnings. Unlike other top media and information companies, Times Mirror, whose diversified holdings include newspapers, magazines, book publishers, information services, and educational products, is scaling back to survive in a changing industry. Veteran newsman Robert Erburu has relinquished his posts as president and CEO to outsider Mark Willes, a former General Mills VC known as a cost cutter, who will also succeed Erburu as chairman in January 1996.

Times Mirror publishes the venerable *Los Angeles Times* and *Newsday*, 2 of the nation's largest metropolitan daily newspapers; other daily and weekly newspapers; and specialty magazines (such as *Field & Stream, Popular Science,* and *Outdoor Life*). The California-based company also owns several specialty book publishers (Richard D. Irwin, Matthew Bender, and Mosby-Year Book), and is in a cable TV joint venture with Cox Enterprises.

Times Mirror already has shuttered the evening edition of the *Sun* (Baltimore) and *New York Newsday,* and hundreds of other newspaper jobs are on the line as the company reins in its flagship Los Angeles newspaper, other papers, and nonessential businesses. Willes intends to retain the company's newspapers and magazines but close down its multimedia group, sell stakes in its cable operations and TV programming ventures, and trim corporate staff.

Times Mirror is controlled by descendants of cofounder Harry Chandler, who own 57% of the company's voting stock.

WHEN

Union Army general Harrison Gray Otis moved to California after the Civil War and became rich from the 1880s land boom. Among his acquisitions was the *Los Angeles Times* (started 1881). Son-in-law Harry Chandler controlled circulation routes to destroy rivals. In 1884 Otis and Chandler formed Times Mirror to own the *Los Angeles Times*. Chandler took over after Otis's death in 1917, and by the 1930s he had amassed a fortune in shipping, road building, oil, and land.

The *Los Angeles Times* had a reputation for serving Otis's and Chandler's political and economic interests. The paper successfully prevented unionization long after unions had become strong in the East. The paper faked photos in its campaign against 1935 gubernatorial candidate Upton Sinclair. For years the paper was known for its right-wing slant.

In 1960 Otis Chandler, grandson of Harry, was named *Times* publisher and began to give the paper a more balanced character. He hired better journalists and transformed the paper into one of the nation's finest. During his tenure the paper was awarded 7 Pulitzer Prizes.

The 1960s also marked the beginning of diversification under president and CEO Norman Chandler, Harry's son and Otis's father. Times Mirror acquired Jeppesen Sanderson (publisher of pilot information, 1961); Matthew Bender & Company (legal publisher, 1963); C.V. Mosby (medical publisher, 1967); Long Island Cablevision (1970); KDFW-TV, Dallas–Fort Worth (1970); and *Newsday* (1970). Times Mirror entered the magazine field by buying *Popular Science* (1967), *Outdoor Life* (1967), *Golf Magazine* (1972), and *Ski Magazine* (1972).

In the 1980s the company experimented with an on-line service that failed to generate consumer interest. Times Mirror sold the New American Library (1984), the *Dallas Times Herald* (1986), and the *Denver Post* (1987).

In the late 1980s Times Mirror spent $1.5 billion on acquisitions of TV stations, cable TV systems, newspapers (the *Sun* [Baltimore], 1986), magazines (*Yachting, Skiing, Field & Stream, Home Mechanix;* 1987), and publishers (CRC Press, 1986; Richard D. Irwin, 1988). New divisions included training systems Zenger-Miller and Kaset (1989). In 1990 the company bought 50% of *La Opinion*, the #1 US Spanish-language newspaper, and in 1991 it sold *Broadcasting* magazine at a loss. Times Mirror bought Wm. C. Brown Publishers, a textbook publisher, in 1992.

In 1993 Matthew Bender & Company sold its federal and state tax services to Commerce Clearing House. Also in 1993 Times Mirror sold its 4 remaining broadcast TV stations.

In 1994 Times Mirror agreed to sell 80% of its cable TV systems (Dimension Cable Services) to Cox Enterprises for $2.3 billion in a move that would form the #4 US cable operator. The 1995 restructuring will end funding for the Times Mirror Center for the People and the Press, a media research group based in Washington.

NYSE symbol: TMC
Fiscal year ends: December 31

WHO

Chairman: Robert F. Erburu, age 64, $1,923,077 pay
President and CEO: Mark H. Willes, age 54
Editor-at-Large: David Laventhol, age 61
EVP; Publisher, *Los Angeles Times*: Richard T. Schlosberg III, age 50, $922,115 pay
EVP: Curtis A. Hessler, age 51, $898,078 pay
SVP and General Counsel: Thomas Unterman, age 50, $612,020 pay
SVP: Donald F. Wright, age 60, $609,231 pay
SVP: Edward E. Johnson, age 51
VP and CFO: James F. Guthrie, age 50
VP Human Resources: James R. Simpson, age 54
Auditors: Ernst & Young LLP

WHERE

HQ: Times Mirror Square, Los Angeles, CA 90053
Phone: 213-237-3700
Fax: 213-237-3800

Times Mirror operates throughout the US.

WHAT

	1994 Sales		1994 Operating Income	
	$ mil.	% of total	$ mil.	% of total
Newspaper publishing	2,063	61	194	53
Professional information	1,005	30	174	47
Consumer media	290	9	(5)	—
Adjustments	(1)	—	(69)	—
Total	**3,357**	**100**	**294**	**100**

Newspapers and Selected News Organizations

The Advocate (Stamford, CT; 29,314 daily circulation)
Greenwich Times (CT; 13,054 daily circulation)
The Hartford Courant (CT; 228,807 daily circulation)
Los Angeles Times (1,077,277 daily circulation)
Los Angeles Times Syndicate
Los Angeles Times–Washington Post News Service (50%)
The Morning Call (Allentown, PA; 134,449 daily circulation)
Newsday (Long Island, NY; daily)
The Sun (Baltimore; 252,094 daily circulation)
TimesLink (on-line interactive newspaper service)
Other daily and weekly newspapers in California and Maryland

Selected Magazines	Book Publishing
Field & Stream	CRC Press (science, technical)
Golf Magazine	
Government Executive	Harry N. Abrams (art)
Home Mechanix	Jeppesen Sanderson (aeronautical)
National Journal	
Outdoor Life	Matthew Bender & Co. (legal)
Popular Science	
Salt Water Sportsman	Mosby-Year Book (health)
Ski Magazine	Richard D. Irwin (business)
Skiing	Wm. C. Brown Publishers (texts)
Skiing Trade News	
The Sporting Goods DEALER	**Professional Training**
The Sporting News	Kaset
Yachting	Learning International
	Zenger-Miller

KEY COMPETITORS

Advance Publications	Gannett	Thomson Corp.
ADVO	Harcourt General	Time Warner
Bertelsmann	Hearst	Tribune
CCH	John Wiley	Viacom
Daily News	Knight-Ridder	Washington Post
Dow Jones	McGraw-Hill	West Publishing
Dun & Bradstreet	New York Times	Wolters Kluwer
E.W. Scripps	News Corp.	
	Reed Elsevier	

HOW MUCH

	9-Year Growth	1985	1986	1987	1988	1989	1990	1991	1992	1993	1994
Sales ($ mil.)	1.9%	2,831	2,821	3,032	3,234	3,415	3,516	3,520	3,594	3,714	3,357
Net income ($ mil.)	(3.4%)	237	408	267	332	298	181	82	57	317	173
Income as % of sales	—	8.4%	14.5%	8.8%	10.3%	8.7%	5.1%	2.3%	1.6%	8.5%	5.2%
Earnings per share ($)	(2.8%)	1.75	3.16	2.06	2.58	2.30	1.40	0.64	0.44	2.46	1.35
Stock price – high ($)	—	29.50	36.94	52.94	40.25	45.00	39.38	32.63	38.38	35.25	37.13
Stock price – low ($)	—	19.00	25.06	30.19	29.00	32.38	21.25	25.50	28.50	28.25	28.75
Stock price – close ($)	1.0%	28.81	31.75	35.88	32.88	35.75	26.75	31.00	31.25	33.38	31.38
P/E – high	—	17	12	26	16	20	28	—	—	14	28
P/E – low	—	11	8	15	11	14	15	—	—	11	21
Dividends per share ($)	5.3%	0.68	0.75	0.82	0.92	1.00	1.08	1.08	1.08	1.08	1.08
Book value per share ($)	8.1%	7.56	10.09	11.31	13.11	14.54	14.92	14.66	13.23	14.77	15.22
Employees	(1.4%)	30,585	27,941	27,915	27,963	29,066	29,121	27,732	28,313	26,936	26,902

1994 Year-end:
Debt ratio: 31.3%
Return on equity: 9.0%
Cash (mil.): $82
Current ratio: 1.03
Long-term debt (mil.): $246
No. of shares (mil.): 129
Dividends
  Yield: 3.4%
  Payout: 80.0%
Market value (mil.): $4,035

Stock Price History High/Low 1985–94

THE TJX COMPANIES, INC.

OVERVIEW

TJX is the #1 off-price specialty apparel retailer in North America. The Framingham, Massachusetts–based company's largest chain is T.J. Maxx, which sells family apparel, accessories, women's shoes, domestics, giftware, and jewelry at 20% to 60% off full price. The company also operates Hit or Miss, a chain of off-price women's apparel stores; Winners Apparel, a Canadian chain of family clothing stores; and Chadwick's of Boston, a women's apparel catalog company.

TJX struggled during 1994. Net income fell over 33%, hurt by increased competition, a weak clothing market (because there was no hot, new fashion trend), and a shift to less-expensive casual clothes. In particular, Chadwick's has had trouble as its success put a strain on distribution and hurt customer service. It is concentrating on improving operations and service.

Hit or Miss has also struggled with image troubles, waffling between career and casual clothing and sometimes carrying merchandise too expensive for the company's trademark strip mall locations and clientele. It has addressed this problem by closing underperforming stores and revamping inventory.

While TJX has been tweaking its apparel chains' operations, it is also broadening its retail lineup. Hoping to take advantage of the growing retail home furnishing market, the company is expanding its HomeGoods chain of off-price home fashions stores. It plans to add 10–12 HomeGoods stores in 1995.

WHEN

Cousins Stanley and Sumner Feldberg opened the first Zayre (Yiddish for "very good") store in Hyannis, Massachusetts, in 1956. Sales increased and in the next 15 years the number of stores grew to nearly 200.

In 1969 Zayre purchased the Hit or Miss chain, another Massachusetts company, founded in 1965. Hit or Miss stores sold upscale women's clothing at discounted prices. Immediately following the purchase, the early-1970s recession hit, and superb results at Hit or Miss prompted Zayre to look for further opportunities in the off-price apparel marketplace. Zayre hired Ben Cammarata (now president and CEO) to create a new store concept, and in March 1977 he opened the first T.J. Maxx, in Auburn, Massachusetts, to market discounted upscale clothing to the whole family. Six years later Zayre formed the catalog retailer Chadwick's of Boston to sell Hit or Miss apparel by mail.

Zayre came to rely increasingly on its specialty operations to provide consistent sales and income as its flagship general merchandise stores often struggled. By 1983 the specialty chains were producing almost half of Zayre's sales.

In the 2nd half of the 1980s Zayre's fashionable and upscale (yet still off-priced) retailers' sales began to surge, while its general merchandise stores (targeting lower-income earners) dropped. To keep its specialty stores unhindered by its flagging Zayre stores, it established the TJX Companies as a public company in 1987. Zayre sold over 9 million shares, about 17%, of its new subsidiary to the public.

In 1988 Zayre sold its 400 general merchandise stores to Ames for about $430 million in cash, $140 million in Ames's stock, and a receivable note. The next year the company spun off its warehouse club operations (which were acquired in 1984) and merged with its subsidiary, TJX Companies, taking its name.

The company moved north of the border in 1990 when it acquired Winners Apparel, a Toronto-based 5-store apparel chain. Also in 1990, in the same month that Ames declared bankruptcy, TJX established a $185 million reserve against losses it might suffer through its ownership of Ames's stock. Ames emerged from bankruptcy 2 years later, and TJX was left with 4% of Ames's voting shares and over 100 empty Ames stores. By the spring of 1992, TJX has sold or leased most of them.

In 1992 TJX began testing the first of its HomeGoods gift and houseware stores, opening outlets in 3 of its remaining Ames stores. TJX closed about 70 Hit or Miss stores that year. Also in 1992 TJX paid off about $128 million of its long-term debt, and T.J. Maxx stores entered the metropolitan New York market.

Encouraged by the success of its off-price operations in Canada, TJX decided to leap the pond, and in 1994 it opened 5 T.K. Maxx stores (with a concept similar to T.J. Maxx and Winners) in Great Britain.

In 1995 Sumner Feldberg retired as chairman. He was succeeded by board member John Nelson, who is also chairman of aerospace manufacturer Wyman-Gordon.

NYSE symbol: TJX
Fiscal year ends: Last Saturday in January

WHO

Chairman: John M. Nelson, age 63
President and CEO: Bernard "Ben" Cammarata, age 55, $1,136,132 pay
EVP and COO: Richard Lesser, age 60, $786,315 pay
SVP Finance and CFO: Donald G. Campbell, age 43, $460,636 pay
SVP Property Development: Joseph K. Birmingham
SVP General Counsel and Secretary: Jay H. Meltzer
VP Human Services: Mark O. Jacobson
Auditors: Coopers & Lybrand L.L.P.

WHERE

HQ: 770 Cochituate Rd., Framingham, MA 01701
Phone: 508-390-1000
Fax: 508-390-3635

TJX operates 1,041 T.J. Maxx and Hit or Miss stores and 15 HomeGoods stores in the US, 37 Winners Apparel stores in Canada, and 5 T.K. Maxx stores in the UK.

	No. of Stores	
	T.J. Maxx	**Hit or Miss**
California	46	37
Florida	40	43
New York	38	28
Illinois	36	31
Massachusetts	36	38
Ohio	31	18
Pennsylvania	28	30
Texas	25	26
Michigan	23	25
Virginia	22	18
Connecticut	21	20
Other states	205	176
Total	**551**	**490**

WHAT

	1995 Sales		1995 Operating Income	
	$ mil.	% of total	$ mil.	% of total
Family apparel	3,056	80	209	97
Women's specialty stores	354	9	(5)	—
Mail-order operations	434	11	6	3
Total	**3,843**	**100**	**210**	**100**

	1995 Sales	
	$ mil.	% of total
T.J. Maxx	2,932	77
Chadwick's	433	11
Hit or Miss	354	9
Winners Apparel Ltd.	124	3
Total	**3,843**	**100**

KEY COMPETITORS

50-Off Stores	Kmart
Ames	Lands' End
Bombay Company	Lechters
Bradlees	Levi Strauss
Broadway Stores	The Limited
Brown Group	Luxottica
Dayton Hudson	May
Dress Barn	Melville
Edison Brothers	Mercantile Stores
Federated	Montgomery Ward
Filene's Basement	Paul Harris Stores
Fingerhut	Ross Stores
Fred Meyer	Sears
The Gap	Spiegel
Hills Department Stores	Stein Mart
INTERCO	Thomson Corp.
J Sainsbury	Tuesday Morning
J. Crew	Wal-Mart
J. C. Penney	Woolworth

HOW MUCH

	Annual Growth	1986	1987	1988	1989	1990	1991	1992	1993	1994	1995
Sales ($ mil.)	13.5%	1,194	1,395	1,644	1,921	2,149	2,446	2,758	3,261	3,627	3,843
Net income ($ mil.)	5.9%	44	52	67	(168)	(78)	74	20	103	120	83
Income as % of sales	—	3.7%	3.7%	4.1%	—	—	3.0%	0.7%	3.2%	3.3%	2.1%
Earnings per share ($)	(4.4%)	1.55	2.10	1.35	(2.97)	(1.10)	1.06	0.29	1.40	1.62	1.03
Stock price – high ($)[1]	—	33.06	43.88	37.00	27.13	30.50	17.75	20.38	29.00	34.25	29.38
Stock price – low ($)[1]	—	16.22	20.75	13.50	14.25	13.88	8.75	9.63	15.38	24.50	14.25
Stock price – close ($)[1]	(7.3%)	30.81	24.00	14.00	25.50	15.38	10.88	16.88	28.25	29.13	15.63
P/E – high	—	21	21	27	—	—	17	70	21	21	29
P/E – low	—	10	10	10	—	—	8	33	11	15	14
Dividends per share ($)	8.0%	0.28	0.24	0.38	0.41	3.90	0.45	0.46	0.46	0.50	0.56
Book value per share ($)	(4.8%)	10.31	11.24	13.03	9.67	3.27	3.88	3.73	5.43	6.57	6.65
Employees	7.7%	—	21,000	22,000	26,000	32,000	28,000	30,000	33,000	36,000	38,000

1995 Year-end:
Debt ratio: 32.4%
Return on equity: 16.8%
Cash (mil.): $42
Current ratio: 1.38
Long-term debt (mil.): $240
No. of shares (mil.): 72
Dividends
  Yield: 3.6%
  Payout: 54.4%
Market value (mil.): $1,132

**Stock Price History[1]
High/Low 1986–95**

[1] Stock prices are for the prior calendar year.

TOYS "R" US, INC.

OVERVIEW

Although Toys "R" Us is the world's #1 toy retailer, it is not all fun and games at the Paramus, New Jersey–based chain. The company, which operates 618 toy superstores and 204 Kids "R" Us children's clothing stores in the US and 293 toy stores overseas, is feeling the heat from major competitors, such as Wal-Mart, that have expanded their toy businesses to attract more young families.

Toys "R" Us, which holds a 22% share of the US toy market, saw domestic same-store sales rise only 2% in fiscal 1995. It struggled with both competition and a weak video game market, which has slumped as video game buyers wait for the new 64-bit game systems that are scheduled to be released for the 1995 Christmas season.

The company's sales and net income have continued to grow as it adds more stores, but with the US market saturated, the company is looking for growth overseas. In addition to opening corporate-owned stores, Toys "R" Us has begun making franchise arrangements in other countries. Its success overseas is due to both the popularity of things American and the fact that toys know no language.

To compete more effectively against the big US discounters, Toys "R" Us is cutting prices, increasing advertising and promotions, and adding computer software to its product mix. It is also establishing several in-store specialty shops, including Books "R" Us bookstores, the Lego Store, and the Learning Center, which carries learning aids and PC software.

WHEN

Charles Lazarus entered retailing in 1948, adding his $2,000 savings to a $2,000 bank loan to convert his father's Washington, DC, bicycle-repair shop into a children's furniture store. Customers persuaded him to add toys. He renamed the store Children's Supermart. Lazarus added a 2nd store, which he later converted to cash-and-carry self-service, but it was with his 3rd store that he established the pattern for his success. Opened in 1958, this 25,000-square-foot discount toy store offered a wider variety of toys than other retailers at 20–50% lower prices.

By 1966 sales had reached $12 million, but Lazarus had added only one store and needed cash to expand, so he sold his company to discount-store operator Interstate Stores for $7.5 million with the condition that he would retain control of the toy operation. Initially the arrangement worked, but after a 1969 high of $11 million profit on $589 million in sales, Interstate began to feel the competition from stronger chains like Kmart. By 1974, although Lazarus had expanded to 47 stores and $130 million yearly sales, the parent had lost $92 million and filed for bankruptcy.

Lazarus kept increasing sales in the toy division. His approach of selling toys year-round (not just during the Christmas season) was encouraged by toy manufacturers in the form of generous credit terms. By 1978 he had generated enough profit to pull Interstate out of bankruptcy. Now under his control, the company adopted a new name: Toys "R" Us, with the R backwards to grab attention. With 72 toy stores (and 10 department stores

remaining from Interstate) and a 5% share of the toy market, Toys "R" Us posted a $36 million pretax profit on $349 million in sales that year.

From 1978 to 1983 net earnings grew at an annual rate of 40%, market share climbed to 12.5%, and the number of toy stores grew to 169. The company diversified by opening 2 Kids "R" Us children's clothing stores in 1983, copying the toy stores' success formula of huge discount stores.

In 1991 the company won a major victory when it successfully penetrated the notoriously bureaucratic and xenophobic Japanese retail market.

Stiff competition from Toys "R" Us was partially responsible for causing rivals Child World and Lionel to seek Chapter 11 bankruptcy in 1992. In 1993 Kids Central, Service Merchandise's experiment in the children's apparel and accessory market, also folded. That same year Toys "R" Us continued its international expansion, opening more stores outside the US than in it, including its first stores in Australia, Belgium, the Netherlands, Portugal, and Switzerland.

In 1994 Lazarus retired from daily involvement with Toys "R" Us, giving up his CEO hat but remaining chairman. He will continue to work with the company on a consulting basis. Also in 1994, to boost its sales outside the Christmas rush, Toys "R" Us circulated a mid-year coupon catalog.

In 1995 the company opened its first franchise store, in Dubai, United Arab Emirates.

NYSE symbol: TOY
Fiscal year ends: Saturday nearest January 31

WHO

Chairman: Charles Lazarus, age 71, $7,862,530 pay
VC and CEO: Michael Goldstein, age 53, $1,202,700 pay
President and COO: Robert C. Nakasone, age 47, $1,202,700 pay
EVP; General Merchandise Manager, Toys "R" Us US: Roger V. Goddu, age 44, $516,574 pay
SVP Finance and CFO: Louis Lipschitz, age 50
SVP Human Resources: Jeffrey S. Wells
VP; President, Toys "R" Us International: Larry D. Bouts, age 46, $569,667 pay
VP; President, Kids "R" Us Division: Richard L. Markee, age 42, $516,420 pay
Auditors: Ernst & Young LLP

WHERE

HQ: 461 From Rd., Paramus, NJ 07652
Phone: 201-262-7800
Fax: 201-262-7606

| | No. of US Stores | |
	Toys "R" Us	Kids "R" Us
California	77	25
Texas	50	7
New York	41	20
Florida	39	8
Illinois	34	20
Pennsylvania	29	14
Ohio	28	19
Michigan	23	13
New Jersey	21	17
Virginia	18	7
Maryland	17	8
North Carolina	16	—
Georgia	14	4
Other states	211	42
Total	**618**	**204**

| | No. of Stores |
	Toys "R" Us
US	618
Canada	56
Germany	53
UK	49
France	29
Japan	24
Spain	20
Other countries	62
Total	**911**

| | 1995 Sales | | 1995 Pretax Income | |
	$ mil.	% of total	$ mil.	% of total
US	6,645	76	779	85
Other countries	2,101	24	141	15
Adjustments	—	—	(76)	—
Total	**8,746**	**100**	**844**	**100**

WHAT

Books "R" Us (bookstores located within company toy stores)
Kids "R" Us (children's apparel)
Toys "R" Us (toys, games, sporting goods)

KEY COMPETITORS

Ames	Melville
Barnes & Noble	Mercantile Stores
Bradlee	Montgomery Ward
Caldor	Sears
CompUSA	Service Merchandise
Crown Books	Sports Authority
Dayton Hudson	Tandy
The Gap	Time Warner
Gymboree	Wal-Mart
Hills Stores	Walt Disney
Kmart	Woolworth
May	Zany Brainy

HOW MUCH

	9-Year Growth	1986	1987	1988	1989	1990	1991	1992	1993	1994	1995
Sales ($ mil.)	18.0%	1,976	2,445	3,137	4,000	4,788	5,510	6,124	7,169	7,946	8,746
Net income ($ mil.)	18.0%	120	152	204	268	321	326	340	438	483	532
Income as % of sales	—	6.1%	6.2%	6.5%	6.7%	6.7%	5.9%	5.5%	6.1%	6.1%	6.1%
Earnings per share ($)	18.2%	0.41	0.52	0.69	0.91	1.09	1.11	1.15	1.47	1.63	1.85
Stock price – high ($)[1]	—	12.24	15.32	19.01	18.01	26.85	35.00	36.00	41.00	42.88	40.88
Stock price – low ($)[1]	—	7.50	9.75	9.80	13.34	16.01	19.88	22.00	30.38	32.38	29.63
Stock price – close ($)[1]	12.7%	10.42	12.80	14.01	16.51	23.93	22.50	32.75	40.13	40.88	30.63
P/E – high	—	30	30	28	20	25	32	31	28	26	22
P/E – low	—	18	19	14	15	15	18	19	21	20	16
Dividends per share ($)	—	0.00	0.00	0.00	0.00	0.00	0.00	0.00	0.00	0.00	0.00
Book value per share ($)	18.9%	2.58	3.22	3.95	4.95	5.95	7.11	8.39	9.87	10.66	12.21
Employees	2.8%	45,200	54,000	52,000	63,200	73,400	73,000	78,000	87,000	55,000	58,000

1995 Year-end:
Debt ratio: 20.9%
Return on equity: 16.2%
Cash (mil.): $370
Current ratio: 1.18
Long-term debt (mil.): $785
No. of shares (mil.): 281
Dividends
  Yield: —
  Payout: —
Market value (mil.): $8,604

Stock Price History[1]
High/Low 1986–95

[1] Stock prices are for the prior calendar year.

TRANS WORLD AIRLINES, INC.

OVERVIEW

Trans World Airlines, once the leader in transatlantic flights, is finding it hard to live up to its name, as it is shrinking its international routes in order to save costs. But TWA is running out of ballast to throw out of its rapidly sinking balloon. Not even the dropping of several European routes; the sale of subsidiaries World Marketing Services, Travel Marketing Services, and Midcoast Aviation; and employee wage and work-rule concessions could prevent TWA from making its 2nd visit to bankruptcy court in 4 years, in 1995.

TWA moved its corporate headquarters from Mt. Kisco, New York, to St. Louis in 1994 for a savings of an estimated $1 million a year in rent. It also reduced its flight operations in Atlanta, where intense competition from Delta had resulted in low passenger revenues, and relocated its Atlanta-based aircraft to St. Louis.

Donald Craib, an insurance executive, was chosen as chairman in 1994, replacing William Howard, but Craib quit for "personal reasons" only a few months later. Former British Aerospace chairman John Cahill was brought in as chairman in 1995 in an attempt to bring an end to the high turnover of top executives that had followed a 1993 bankruptcy settlement.

TWA was better prepared for its 1995 trip to bankruptcy court, having secured the support of Carl Icahn and other key creditors for its prepackaged reorganization plan.

WHEN

Western Air Express (WAE), founded in 1925 by Los Angeles businessmen Harry Chandler and James Talbot, began flying from Los Angeles to Salt Lake City in 1926. In its early years it was primarily a mail carrier, and Charles Lindbergh scouted its routes. It merged with Transcontinental Air Transport (TAT) in 1930 to form Transcontinental and Western Air (TWA), America's first coast-to-coast airline.

Airline magnate Clement Keys had formed TAT in 1928, coordinating operations with the Pennsylvania and Santa Fe Railroads to establish air-rail service from New York to the West Coast. The service lost money and was terminated after the WAE-TAT merger.

Howard Hughes bought TWA in 1939. The company (then based in Kansas City) introduced transatlantic service (New York–Paris) in 1946, moved its headquarters to New York in 1947, and changed its name to Trans World Airlines in 1950, reflecting its expansion to over 21,000 international route miles.

In 1956 Hughes ordered 63 jets, with long-term financing through a New York investment banker. When he was unable to meet the terms of the loan in 1960, the bank placed Hughes's TWA stock in a voting trust. Hughes sold his interest to the public in 1966.

TWA tried to stabilize earnings through acquisitions (consolidated under Trans World Corporation in 1979). These included Hilton International (hotels, 1967), the Canteen Corporation (food services and vending machines, 1973), Spartan Food Systems (Hardee's restaurants, 1979), and Century 21 (real estate, 1979). However, in 1984 TWA's problems led to a split from Trans World Corporation, which became TW Services in 1986 after selling its hotels to United Air Lines.

In 1986 Carl Icahn took over TWA after winning a takeover battle with airline raider Frank Lorenzo. Icahn, as CEO, bought Ozark Air Lines (TWA's main competitor at its St. Louis hub) in 1987. By 1988, when he took TWA private (recouping his $356 million investment), Icahn owned 90% of TWA, with the other 10% owned by its employees. TWA, Delta, and NWA formed the computer reservation system WORLDSPAN in 1990.

Late in 1990 Icahn proposed merging TWA with financially beleaguered Pan Am. Talks failed when Pan Am sold its London routes to United. Fearing transatlantic competition from United, TWA agreed to sell its London routes (to Heathrow Airport) to American Airlines, planning to use the proceeds to buy Pan Am, which then entered bankruptcy. Delta outbid TWA for Pan Am in 1991. After filing for bankruptcy protection itself in 1992, TWA sold most of its cable television subsidiary (the Travel Channel); it also sold its routes from Philadelphia and Baltimore to London's Gatwick Airport to USAir.

TWA's attempt to open a hub in Atlanta in 1992 failed because it lacked the fleet to compete in that busy market.

In 1993, as part of its bankruptcy reorganization, TWA made preparations to sell its stake in WORLDSPAN, and in 1994 the airline further reduced its network by reducing service in the Northeast and cutting back service to Europe. In an attempt to boost ticket sales in 1995, TWA broke ranks with other airlines by rejecting the $50 commission cap for travel agents, adopted by its rivals. The company also launched a major advertising campaign.

WHO

Chairman: John C. Cahill, age 65
President and CEO: Jeffrey H. Erickson, age 50, $345,398 pay
EVP Finance and CFO: Robert A. Peiser, age 46, $106,110 pay
SVP Employee Relations: Charles J. Thibaudeau, age 48, $150,801 pay
SVP and General Counsel: Richard P. Magurno, age 51
SVP Operations: Don Monteath, age 53
SVP Marketing: Mark J. Coleman, age 48
Auditors: KPMG Peat Marwick LLP

WHERE

HQ: One City Centre, 515 N. 6th St., St. Louis, MO 63101
Phone: 314-589-3000
Fax: 314-589-3129

TWA flies to cities in the US, Europe, and the Middle East.

Hub Locations
New York
St. Louis

Selected International Destinations

Athens	Lisbon
Barcelona	London
Cairo	Riyadh
Frankfurt	

	1994 Sales		1994 Operating Income	
	$ mil.	% of total	$ mil.	% of total
US	2,614	77	(141)	—
Other countries	794	23	(139)	—
Total	**3,408**	**100**	**(280)**	**—**

WHAT

	1994 Sales	
	$ mil.	% of total
Passenger	2,876	84
Freight & mail	150	4
Other	382	12
Total	**3,408**	**100**

Subsidiary
Trans World Express, Inc. (regional airline service)

	1994 Sales
	% of total
Trans World Airline	98
Trans World Express	2
Total	**100**

	1994 Aircraft	
	Owned	Leased
Boeing 727	33	8
Boeing 747	8	3
Boeing 767	4	10
Douglas DC-9	—	58
Douglas MD-80	—	45
Lockheed 1011	8	8
Total	**53**	**132**

KEY COMPETITORS

Air France	KLM
Alaska Air	Lufthansa
America West	Mesa Air
AMR	Northwest Airlines
Austrian Airlines	SABENA
British Airways	SAS
Continental Airlines	Southwest Airlines
Delta	TowerAir
IRI	UAL
Kimberly-Clark	USAir
Kiwi Intl. Airlines	Virgin Group

HOW MUCH

	Annual Growth	1985	1986	1987	1988	1989	1990	1991	1992	1993	1994
Sales ($ mil.)	(1.4%)	3,867	3,185	4,056	4,361	4,507	4,606	3,660	3,634	3,157	3,408
Net income ($ mil.)	—	(208)	(106)	45	250	(287)	(274)	(11)	(318)	(452)	(451)
Income as % of sales	—	—	—	1.1%	5.7%	—	—	—	—	(4.52)	(22.44)
Earnings per share	—	—	—	—	—	—	—	—	—		
Stock price – high ($)	—	—	—	—	—	—	—	—	—	6.88	5.50
Stock price – low ($)	—	—	—	—	—	—	—	—	—	4.13	0.50
Stock price – close ($)	(85.6%)	—	—	—	—	—	—	—	—	5.63	0.81
P/E – high	—	—	—	—	—	—	—	—	—	—	—
P/E – low	—	—	—	—	—	—	—	—	—	—	—
Dividends per share ($)	—	—	—	—	—	—	—	—	—	0.00	0.00
Book value per share ($)	—	—	—	—	—	—	—	—	—	0.94	(20.88)
Employees	(2.7%)	29,080	27,442	29,919	30,817	32,895	33,725	29,463	25,500	26,100	22,800

1994 Year-end:
Debt ratio: 100.0%
Return on equity: —
Cash (mil.): $121
Current ratio: 0.31
Long-term debt (mil.): $340
No. of shares (mil.): 20
Dividends
 Yield: —
 Payment: —
Market value (mil.): $16

Stock Price History
High/Low 1993–94

TRANSAMERICA CORPORATION

OVERVIEW

The success of Transamerica's effort to focus its business on specific insurance and financial services was shown in 1994 by record income.

Transamerica Finance Group encompasses consumer lending (home equity and unsecured loans), commercial lending (financing inventories and consumer goods), and leasing (it has one of the world's largest fleets of transportation equipment for rail, motor, and steamship carriers and is the world's 2nd largest container lessor). The company also offers real estate services (property tax monitoring and real estate development and management). Transamerica is one of the largest life insurers in North America and the continent's largest life reinsurer.

Since reducing from a diversified holding company with over 30,000 employees to a svelte insurance and finance company with 10,800 staffers, Transamerica has reorganized its management to reflect a more centralized strategy. This strategy is reflected in the company's recent purchases and divestitures.

In 1994 Transamerica bought the container operations of Tiphook PLC to beef up its leasing capacities and began selling its remaining asset management interests (the final 21% of insurance broker Sedgwick Group and Transamerica Fund Management in 1994 and Criterion Investment Management in 1995). The company intends to make only those acquisitions that fit in with its business lines.

WHEN

A. P. Giannini's Bank of Italy (founded 1904) rose from the ruins of the San Francisco earthquake to become one of California's largest banks. In 1918 Giannini formed Bancitaly, hoping to create a national branch banking system. By 1928 Bancitaly had bought 5 banks, including the Bank of America (BOA). Giannini formed Transamerica in 1928 as a national holding company for Bancitaly, BOA, and other new nonbanking businesses.

Despite the Depression, management infighting, and regulatory investigations which dashed its hopes of becoming a truly nationwide bank, Transamerica kept buying banks; by 1936 it had 475 offices in 294 cities and had diversified into insurance (Occidental Life) and real estate foreclosures (subsidiaries Capital Company and California Lands).

In 1937 regulators forced the company to sell 58% of BOA, but it was allowed to keep 54 other banks.

By 1953 SEC antitrust action had resulted in divestiture of all BOA stock. After a period of banking expansion was ended by the 1956 Bank Holding Company Act, Transamerica divested its banks and focused on its insurance operations, which it had acquired in the 1920s, 1930s, and 1940s.

In the 1960s, under chairman John Beckett's leadership, Transamerica diversified indiscriminately, entering such diverse fields as financial services (Pacific Financial, 1961), title insurance (City Title, 1962; renamed Transamerica Title), manufacturing (Delaval Turbine, 1962), entertainment (United Artists, 1967), transportation (Budget Rent a Car, 1968; TransInternational Airlines, 1968), and leasing (Interway, 1979).

James Harvey (who became CEO in 1981) made strategic subtractions and additions aimed to reposition the company as a financial services company. He sold UA to MGM in 1981 and in 1986 spun off Delaval to shareholders, sold Budget, and closed TransInternational. Transamerica Title was sold in 1990. Purchases included insurance brokers (Fred S. James, 1982; exchanged for 39% of Sedgwick Group, UK, 1985; sold 1994), consumer and commercial finance companies (the Money Stores, 1983; BWAC, 1987; TIFCO, 1988), a worker's compensation insurer (Fairmont Financial, 1987), and an investment management company (Criterion Group, 1989).

Harvey had exchanged $1.5 billion worth of old businesses for $1.7 billion worth of new businesses, to great effect: between 1985 and 1987 alone, net income more than tripled. In 1989 the company reduced costs by merging lending and leasing operations into the financial division.

Harvey stepped down as president and CEO but remained chairman, and Frank Herringer became president and CEO in 1991. Herringer continued to refine the company's strategic focus in 1992 by restructuring its commercial lending segment, closing branches, and increasing its sales force.

Although overall sales and income were up in 1994, many of the company's segments were victims of the continuing recession in California (which hurt commercial lending) and overseas (which affected its leasing operations in Japan and Europe).

In 1995 Transamerica bought ITT's home equity loan portfolio, increasing its own $3 billion loan portfolio by about 1/3.

NYSE symbol: TA
Fiscal year ends: December 31

WHO

Chairman: James R. Harvey, age 60
President and CEO: Frank C. Herringer, age 52, $1,536,566 pay
EVP; President and CEO, Transamerica Finance Group: Richard H. Finn, age 60, $1,002,167 pay
EVP and CFO: Edgar H. Grubb, age 55, $593,094 pay
President, Transamerica Occidental Life Insurance: John Fibiger, age 62
SVP and Chief Investment Officer; President and CEO, Transamerica Investment Services: Richard N. Latzer, age 58, $625,825 pay
SVP, General Counsel, and Secretary: Shirley H. Buccieri, age 43
SVP: Thomas J. Cusack, age 39
VP and General Auditor: Maureen B. Evans, age 40
VP and Treasurer: Robert R. Lindberg, age 54
VP Public Affairs: James B. Lockhart, age 59
VP Corporate Communications: William H. McClave, age 52
VP Corporate Relations: Richard J. Olsen, age 56
VP Investor Relations: Ronald C. Petrunoff, age 31
VP Human Resources: Rona King Pehrson, age 47
Auditors: Ernst & Young LLP

WHERE

HQ: 600 Montgomery St., San Francisco, CA 94111
Phone: 415-983-4000
Fax: 415-983-4234

Transamerica Life Companies operate 597 agencies in the US and Canada; its consumer lending services have 549 branches in the US, 13 in Canada, and 6 in the UK. Its leasing business has branches in 50 countries, and its commercial finance business has branches in 6 countries. The real estate and real estate tax services operate 36 offices in the US.

WHAT

	1994 Assets	
	$ mil.	% of total
Cash & equivalents	64	0
Mortgage-backed securities	7,368	18
Corporate bonds	12,920	32
Other investments	1,341	4
Net receivables	6,070	15
Other assets	12,631	31
Total	**40,394**	**100**

	1994 Sales	
	$ mil.	% of total
Life insurance	1,495	28
Investments	1,783	33
Finance charges & other fees	1,042	19
Leasing	621	12
Real estate & tax services	256	5
Other	158	3
Total	**5,355**	**100**

Selected Subsidiaries and Affiliates
Transamerica Commercial Finance (lending)
Transamerica Financial Services (consumer lending)
Transamerica Leasing (intermodal leasing)
Transamerica Life Companies (life insurance)
Transamerica Real Estate Tax Service (property tax monitoring and management)
Transamerica Realty Services (real estate investment and loan and property management)

KEY COMPETITORS

Aetna	Itel	PLM Intl.
AT&T	John Hancock	Prudential
Avondale Industries	MassMutual	Travelers
Chubb	MetLife	Trinity
CIGNA	New York Life	Industries
Equitable	Northwestern	USAA
Household Intl.	Mutual	USF&G

HOW MUCH

	9-Year Growth	1985	1986	1987	1988	1989	1990	1991	1992	1993	1994
Sales ($ mil.)	(0.5%)	5,590	6,076	7,175	7,879	6,834	6,703	6,815	4,988	4,833	5,355
Net income ($ mil.)	14.6%	126	268	427	346	332	266	99	243	401	427
Income as % of sales	—	2.3%	4.4%	5.6%	4.4%	4.9%	4.0%	1.5%	4.9%	8.3%	8.0%
Earnings per share ($)	12.8%	1.84	2.97	5.47	4.42	4.18	3.29	1.14	2.83	4.80	5.45
Stock price – high ($)	—	36.25	40.13	51.50	36.75	48.00	44.63	40.00	50.50	62.38	57.63
Stock price – low ($)	—	26.00	31.75	17.13	29.75	32.75	23.25	29.63	37.13	45.63	46.25
Stock price – close ($)	4.4%	33.75	32.63	29.88	33.88	44.25	32.63	39.88	48.00	56.75	49.75
P/E – high	—	20	14	9	8	12	14	35	18	13	11
P/E – low	—	14	11	3	7	8	7	26	13	10	9
Dividends per share ($)	2.2%	1.65	1.70	1.78	1.85	1.89	1.93	1.97	2.00	2.00	2.00
Book value per share ($)	2.0%	29.12	28.61	31.84	34.54	36.03	36.56	36.28	36.32	38.46	34.87
Employees	(4.0%)	15,600	15,200	17,600	17,400	17,600	16,100	15,000	10,700	10,700	10,800

1994 Year-end:
Debt ratio: 71.4%
Return on equity: 15.9%
Cash (mil.): $214
Long-term debt (mil.): $9,005
No. of shares (mil.): 69
Dividends
  Yield: 4.0%
  Payout: 36.7%
Market value (mil.): $3,452
Assets (mil.): $40,394

Stock Price History
High/Low 1985–94

THE TRAVELERS INC.

OVERVIEW

Last year was one of consolidation and adjustment for Travelers following the 1993 acquisition of the venerable company by Sanford Weill's Primerica (Primerica took the Travelers name and its distinctive red umbrella logo) and the addition of Smith Barney, the US's 2nd largest brokerage and investment bank (after Merrill Lynch), which Primerica also bought in 1993.

The company devoted 1994 to the process of streamlining itself along business lines. These include investment services (Smith Barney), consumer finance (Commercial Credit), credit cards (Travelers Bank, formerly Primerica Bank), and mutual funds (Primerica Financial Services). Insurance operations include Travelers Insurance (insurance and retirement products) and Travelers Indemnity (property/casualty insurance, commercial and personal lines).

In the process, Travelers jettisoned several businesses, including mutual fund manager American Capital Management and specialty auto insurer Shippers Insurance Company.

At the time of the merger Travelers's health insurance operations were unfocused and poorly positioned. After examining several possibilities, the company entered into a health insurance and managed care joint venture with MetLife, called MetraHealth.

WHEN

In 1864 James Batterson and 9 other Hartford businessmen founded Travelers as the first accident insurance company in the US. The company began using its red umbrella logo as early as 1870.

The company diversified into life insurance (1865), annuities (1884), and liability insurance (1889). In 1897 it issued the first auto policy, and in 1919 it sold President Woodrow Wilson the first air travel policy.

The company added group life insurance coverage in 1913, with the Victor Co. (later part of RCA) as one of its first clients.

A decision on the eve of the 1929 crash to sell gold stocks and buy federal bonds helped the company survive the Depression. In 1940 the company began insuring government projects carried out by civilian contractors.

Travelers prospered during the post-WWII boom and issued the first space travel accident insurance, covering the Apollo 11 astronauts in their historic lunar landing.

In the late 1970s and early 1980s, the company bought Keystone (mutual funds, 1979; sold 1989) and Dillon, Read (investment banking, 1986; sold 1991). As the real estate market, in which the company had invested heavily, turned sour in the late 1980s and early 1990s, Travelers sold Travelers Mortgage Services (home mortgage and relocation business) in 1990 to focus on its investment and insurance business.

In the 1990s Travelers began cutting jobs and withdrawing from unprofitable business areas. These and other cost-control measures made Travelers attractive to the profit-driven management of Primerica.

One of Primerica's antecedents, American Can, had started life in 1901 as a canning company in New Jersey. By the 1930s it was an industry leader, but by the 1960s it had to diversify into other areas (paper and forest products). In the 1970s it went still farther afield and bought Musicland (record stores, sold 1988) and Fingerhut (catalog sales). In 1981 American Can bought life insurance company Associated Madison. Five years later it jettisoned its container operations and became a financial services company. In 1987 it became Primerica.

The next year Primerica was bought by Sanford Weill's much smaller company, Commercial Credit. Weill had started out by building Shearson Loeb Rhoades and selling it to American Express, of which he later became president. Later still, he engineered a buyout of Control Data. Commercial Credit had been founded in 1912 to deal in commercial acceptances and receivables.

When Weill bought Primerica, he got rid of the noncore businesses; finding no buyer for Fingerhut, Primerica gradually reduced its share of the company, selling its last 2% interest in 1993. Weill soon began the same process at Travelers.

The $4 billion merger of Primerica and Travelers was no union of equals. Primerica dominated. New management members included Weill's son Marc (as chief investment officer) and Robert Greenhill (whom Weill hired from J.P. Morgan to lead Smith Barney).

The consolidation of Smith Barney has been rocky. Not only were the brokerage unit's results hit by the 1994 bond market crash, but there were also whispers that the compensation packages negotiated by Greenhill and his new recruits had inspired bad feelings among Smith Barney's veterans.

NYSE symbol: TRV
Fiscal year ends: December 31

Chairman and CEO: Sanford I. Weill, age 61,
$3,678,750 pay
VC; Group Chief Executive, Travelers Insurance:
Robert I. Lipp, age 56, $2,189,375 pay
**VC; Group Chief Executive, Primerica Financial
Services:** Joseph J. Plumeri II, age 51, $1,960,375 pay
President, COO, and CFO: James Dimon, age 38,
$2,774,375 pay
Chairman and CEO, Smith Barney Inc.: Robert F.
Greenhill, age 58, $5,029,755 pay
EVP Marketing: Edwin M. Cooperman, age 51
EVP Strategic Planning: Michael A. Carpenter, age 47
SVP, General Counsel, and Secretary: Charles O.
Prince III, age 45
**SVP Corporate Communications and Investor
Relations:** Mary McDermott
SVP and Chief Information Officer: Richard F.
Morrison
SVP Human Resources: Barry L. Mannes
Auditors: KPMG Peat Marwick LLP

HQ: 65 E. 55th St., New York, NY 10022
Phone: 212-891-8900
Fax: 212-891-8999

	1994 Sales	
	$ mil.	% of total
Premiums	7,590	41
Investment income	3,637	19
Commissions & fees	2,691	15
Other charges & fees	2,725	15
Other	1,822	10
Total	**18,465**	**100**

	1994 Assets	
	$ mil.	% of total
Cash & equivalents	1,227	1
Treasury & agency securities	7,900	7
Mortgage-backed securities	4,913	4
Corporate bonds	15,567	14
Other securities	10,270	9
Securities under		
resale agreements	25,655	22
Receivables & recoverables	20,010	17
Mortgage & policy loans	6,997	6
Other assets	22,758	20
Total	**115,297**	**100**

Selected Services	Selected Subsidiaries
Brokerage services	Commercial Credit
Consumer finance	The MetraHealth
Credit cards	Companies
Investment banking	Primerica Financial
Life insurance	Services, Inc.
Mutual funds	RCM Capital Management
Property/casualty	Travelers Bank
insurance	Travelers Insurance
	Company

ADVANTA	CNA Financial	New York Life
Aetna	CS Holding	Nomura
AFLAC	Dean Witter,	Securities
Alex. Brown	Discover	Northwestern
Allstate	Equitable	Mutual
American	FMR	Paine Webber
Express	GEICO	Prudential
American	Goldman Sachs	Raymond James
Financial	ING Group	Financial
Bear Stearns	ITT Hartford	Rothschilds
Berkshire	John Hancock	Salomon
Hathaway	Kemper Corp.	State Farm
Brown Brothers	Lehman Brothers	Swiss Bank
Harriman	MassMutual	T. Rowe Price
Chubb	Merrill Lynch	Transamerica
CIGNA	MetLife	USAA
Citicorp	Morgan Stanley	USF&G

	Annual Growth	1985	1986	1987	1988	1989	1990	1991	1992	1993	1994
Assets ($ mil.)	38.3%	6,235	4,864	4,306	14,435	17,955	19,689	21,561	23,397	101,360	115,297
Net income ($ mil.)	—	(5)	46	24	162	289	373	479	756	951	1,326
Income as % of assets	—	—	0.9%	0.6%	1.1%	1.6%	1.9%	2.2%	3.2%	0.9%	1.2%
Earnings per share ($)	—	(0.07)	0.59	0.24	1.81	1.43	1.64	2.14	3.34	3.88	3.86
Stock price – high ($)	—	—	11.38	17.32	14.51	15.01	18.88	20.07	24.95	49.50	43.13
Stock price – low ($)	—	—	9.88	8.50	10.26	10.13	8.44	10.94	17.88	24.07	30.38
Stock price – close ($)	13.6%	—	10.26	11.19	10.88	14.26	11.44	19.70	24.20	38.88	32.38
P/E – high	—	—	19	72	8	11	12	9	8	13	11
P/E – low	—	—	17	35	6	7	5	5	5	6	8
Dividends per share ($)	43.8%	—	0.03	0.12	0.14	0.14	0.18	0.23	0.36	0.49	0.55
Book value per share ($)	11.5%	—	9.20	7.67	10.14	11.77	13.21	15.10	17.70	25.68	24.46
Employees	6.4%	29,822	33,353	33,000	36,000	35,000	34,000	32,000	30,000	65,000	52,000

1994 Year-end:
Equity as % of assets: 6.8%
Return on assets: 1.2%
Return on equity: 16.4%
Long-term debt (mil.): $7,075
No. of shares (mil.): 317
Dividends
  Yield: 1.7%
  Payout: 14.2%
Market value (mil.): $10,249
Sales (mil.): $18,465

Stock Price History
High/Low 1986–94

TRIBUNE COMPANY

OVERVIEW

Chicago's Tribune Company is a multimedia information and entertainment giant. It gathers, packages, and delivers information to 60% of US households via newspapers, radio, TV, and, lately, cyberspace. Tribune is the US's 13th largest media company, with 3 major daily newspapers (*Chicago Tribune*, Ft. Lauderdale's *Sun-Sentinel*, and the *Orlando Sentinel*); 8 TV stations (in Los Angeles, New York, Philadelphia, Chicago, and other cities); and 6 radio stations (in New York, Chicago, and other cities). Publishing accounted for 60% of sales and 68% of operating profits in 1994. The company also owns various book publishing companies (including Compton's and Contemporary Books), produces and syndicates TV, radio, and on-line programming, and owns a major league baseball team (Chicago Cubs). Tribune has radio and TV

broadcast rights for 7 of the 28 major league baseball teams. It also owns other daily and weekly newspapers and has a stake in cable TV.

Tribune continues to extend its reach for new markets and information sources. In 1994 the company bought Farm Journal Inc., publisher of the country's leading farm magazine and 4 other agribusiness magazines; acquired a minority stake in Qwest Broadcasting, which buys TV and radio stations; bought The Wright Group, a publisher of educational materials; took a minority stake in Checkfree, an on-line bill-paying and collection service; and bought Boston's leading TV newscast and movie station, WLVI. To focus on information and entertainment, Tribune reduced its stake to 34% in QUNO, one of the largest Canadian newsprint suppliers, at a time when newsprint prices are skyrocketing.

WHEN

Tribune Company had its beginnings as the *Chicago Tribune*, which produced 400 newspapers on its first day in 1847. Joseph Medill, a promoter who, some say, gave the Republican party its name, became part owner and editor in 1855. He spent the next 44 years building the *Tribune* into a conservative newspaper.

Medill reportedly warned that Chicago was a fire hazard just a month before the Great Fire of 1871. He rallied his employees to publish the paper despite being burned out of their building. Medill died in 1899 and was succeeded by son-in-law Robert Patterson and grandson Medill McCormick. In 1914 his other 2 grandsons, Robert McCormick and Joseph Patterson, took over the newspaper.

McCormick, great-nephew of the inventor of the harvest machine, built the *Tribune* into the self-proclaimed "World's Greatest Newspaper," whose acronym, WGN, became part of the company's subsequent radio and TV station call letters. Patterson left for New York in 1919 to found the *News*, later the *Daily News*.

In 1924 the company branched into radio by starting WGN, which became the first radio station to broadcast the World Series, Indianapolis 500, and Kentucky Derby. WGN moved into TV broadcasting in 1948, the same year the paper prematurely published its "Dewey Defeats Truman" headline .

McCormick took over the *Daily News* when Patterson died in 1946 and ran both papers from Chicago. He remained at that post until his death in 1955.

Tribune expanded its radio and TV broadcasting outside of Chicago. It founded WPIX-TV in New York (1948) and bought TV stations in Denver (1965), New Orleans (1983), Atlanta (1984), Los Angeles (1985), Philadelphia (1992), and Boston (1994). The company also bought newspapers in Florida (Ft. Lauderdale, 1963; Orlando, 1965), California (Los Angeles, 1973, sold 1985; Escondido, 1977; Palo Alto, 1978, closed 1993), and Virginia (Newport News, 1986).

Tribune diversified with news and entertainment programming, beginning Independent Network News in 1980 (shut down, 1990) and the Tribune Broadcasting Co. in 1981. That same year it bought the Chicago Cubs baseball team from chewing gum maker Wm. Wrigley. Tribune went public in 1983.

A protracted strike at the *Daily News* prompted Tribune to sell the newspaper in 1991. Also that year Tribune began a series of investments in on-line technology companies, buying a stake in America Online, with which it launched the local Chicago Online.

In 1993 Tribune bought Compton's Multimedia Publishing Group and print-based Contemporary Books. In 1994 it acquired The Wright Group for its New Media & Education group and joined with Time Warner to form a prime-time network.

Also that year John Madigan was named Tribune president and heir apparent to chairman Charles Brumback. Madigan, a former investment banker before joining Tribune in 1975, was named CEO in 1995.

NYSE symbol: TRB
Fiscal year ends: Last Sunday in December

WHO

Chairman: Charles T. Brumback, age 66, $1,261,806 pay
President and CEO: John W. Madigan, age 57,
$839,616 pay (prior to promotion)
EVP Media Operations: James C. Dowdle, age 61,
$770,000 pay
EVP Tribune Broadcasting Co.: Dennis J. FitzSimons,
age 44, $600,431 pay
EVP Tribune Publishing Co.: Joseph D. Cantrell, age 50
EVP and General Manager, New Media/Education:
Robert D. Bosau, age 48
SVP Development: David D. Hiller, age 41, $454,923 pay
SVP and CFO: Donald C. Grenesko, age 46
SVP Information Systems: John S. Kazik, age 52
SVP Administration (HR): John T. Sloan, age 43
VP and General Counsel: James E. Cushing Jr.
Auditors: Price Waterhouse LLP

WHERE

HQ: 435 N. Michigan Ave., Chicago, IL 60611
Phone: 312-222-9100
Fax: 312-222-0449

Tribune media properties are located in 11 states.

WHAT

	1994 Sales		1994 Operating Income	
	$ mil.	% of total	$ mil.	% of total
Publishing	1,293	60	288	68
Broadcasting &				
Entertainment	764	35	132	31
New Media/Education	98	5	3	1
Other	—	—	(26)	—
Total	**2,155**	**100**	**397**	**100**

Selected Publishing Operations

Alternate Postal Delivery (private mail delivery)
America Online (6%) and Chicago Online
Chicago Tribune (682,000 daily circulation)
Knight-Ridder/Tribune Information Services (50%)
The Orlando Sentinel (269,000 daily circulation)
The Orlando Sentinel Online (electronic publishing)
Peapod (minority stake; grocery shopping by computer)
Picture Network International (52%; electronic photo
archive marketing system)
Real Estate Information Connection (50%)
StarSight Telecast (TV guide and VCR recording)
Sun-Sentinel (Ft. Lauderdale; 266,000 daily circulation)
Tribune Interactive Network Services
Tribune Media Services

Selected Broadcasting and Entertainment Operations

Chicago National League	Tribune Entertainment
Ball Club, Inc. (baseball)	Co. (TV programming)
CLTV News (cable TV news)	TV Food Network (31%)
Farm Journal Inc.	WGN (AM), Chicago
(agribusiness magazine)	WGN-TV, Chicago
KCTC (AM), Sacramento	WGNO-TV, New Orleans
KEZW (AM), Denver	WGNX-TV, Atlanta
KOSI (FM), Denver	WLVI-TV, Boston
KTLA-TV, Los Angeles	WPHL-TV, Philadelphia
KWGN-TV, Denver	WPIX-TV, New York
KYMX (FM), Sacramento	WQCD (FM), New York

New Media/Education

Compton's Multimedia Publishing Group (CD-ROMs)
Contemporary Books, Inc. (trade book publisher)
The Wright Group (educational materials)

KEY COMPETITORS

Advance	Encyclopædia	News Corp.
Publications	Britannica	Reuters
Associated Press	Gannett	Sony
Capital Cities/ABC	General Electric	Time Warner
CBS	Hearst	Times Mirror
Chris-Craft	Lagardère	UPI
Cox	Microsoft	Viacom
Dow Jones	New York Times	Washington Post

HOW MUCH

	9-Year Growth	1985	1986	1987	1988	1989	1990	1991	1992	1993	1994
Sales ($ mil.)	1.2%	1,938	2,030	2,160	2,335	2,455	2,353	2,035	2,109	1,953	2,155
Net income ($ mil.)	7.7%	124	293	142	210	242	(64)	142	137	189	242
Income as % of sales	—	6.4%	14.4%	6.6%	9.0%	9.9%	—	7.0%	6.5%	9.7%	11.2%
Earnings per share ($)	8.0%	1.53	3.63	1.80	2.78	3.00	(1.22)	1.83	1.70	2.36	3.07
Stock price – high ($)	—	28.94	39.00	49.75	43.00	63.13	48.25	48.38	50.75	61.25	64.50
Stock price – low ($)	—	16.00	24.75	28.63	33.75	36.38	31.25	33.13	38.75	48.00	48.88
Stock price – close ($)	7.8%	27.88	28.50	41.00	38.88	47.38	35.25	41.00	48.00	60.13	54.75
P/E – high	—	19	11	28	16	21	—	26	30	26	21
P/E – low	—	11	7	16	12	12	—	18	23	20	16
Dividends per share ($)	10.6%	0.42	0.50	0.60	1.00	0.88	0.96	0.96	0.96	0.96	1.04
Book value per share ($)	6.7%	11.19	13.91	14.35	15.88	10.63	6.49	7.84	8.72	16.36	19.98
Employees	(6.2%)	18,700	17,300	16,800	16,800	17,100	16,100	12,900	12,400	9,900	10,500

1994 Year-end:
Debt ratio: 24.8%
Return on equity: 19.9%
Cash (mil.): $22
Current ratio: 1.03
Long-term debt (mil.): $411
No. of shares (mil.): 67
Dividends
  Yield: 1.9%
  Payout: 33.9%
Market value (mil.): $3,652

Stock Price History
High/Low 1985–94

TRW INC.

OVERVIEW

Based in Cleveland, TRW provides advanced technology products and services in the automotive, space and defense, and commercial and consumer information systems markets.

With the increased popularity of air bags, power rack-and-pinion steering, and multivalve engines, TRW expects its products to be used in more vehicles. The company increased its production of air bags from 4.6 million in 1993 to 9.5 million in 1994. TRW also signed a long-term agreement in 1994 with Briggs & Stratton Corp. to supply 75% of the valves for its large engines and all of the valves for its small engines. Overseas, TRW sees tremendous opportunities in China and has signed a memorandum of understanding with Jinan Auto-Accessories Works to make engine valves for the Chinese automotive market.

In its space and defense business, TRW plans to develop a $2 billion, 12-satellite communications network called Odyssey with its Montreal-based partner Teleglobe. Odyssey will be competing in the satellite phone business against Motorola's Iridium project and Globalstar, led by Loral Corp. and Qualcomm.

In its information systems and services business, TRW sold its Credentials Services International (which allows consumers to monitor credit reports) to the New York–based Lincolnshire Equity Fund. TRW continues to provide consumer and business credit, real estate, and other information services.

WHEN

TRW got its start in 1901 as Cleveland Cap Screw Company. In 1904 company welder Charles Thompson devised an improved method for assembling automobile valves, similar to the methods used to make cap screws. Within 4 years the firm (renamed Electric Welding Company) was making most of the engine valves for the mushrooming automobile industry. After changing its name again to Steel Products Company (1915), it made valves for American and French aircraft used in WWI.

In 1921 the company produced the Silcrome metal valve, which allowed aircraft to fly longer distances. A similar Thompson valve was used in Lindbergh's plane on the first transatlantic flight. Charles Thompson had become president in 1915; the company became Thompson Products in 1926.

Thompson suffered losses during the Great Depression, but under the leadership of new president Frederick Crawford, it avoided major plant closings and layoffs. (Crawford died in 1994 at the age of 103.) Diversification began in the 1930s, especially into products for the aviation industry (the company developed an improved fuel pump that prevented vapor lock at high altitudes). At the government-built Tapco plant (Thompson Aircraft Products Company) in Cleveland, the company hired up to 16,000 workers during WWII. By 1945 sales were 7 times those in 1939.

In 1953 the company provided fiscal support for the Ramo-Wooldridge Corporation, founded by former Hughes Aircraft engineers Simon Ramo and Dean Wooldridge to build the intercontinental ballistic missile. In one of the first uses of "systems engineering," the company coordinated the work of 220 prime contractors to build the Atlas ICBM, which was launched 5 years later. In 1958 the companies merged to form Thompson Ramo Wooldridge (officially renamed TRW in 1965).

In the 1960s TRW's space and defense, automotive, and information systems segments were formed through internal development and acquisitions. The company participated in numerous space and defense projects, including building satellites, missiles, and Apollo rocket engines.

In the 1980s TRW sold its marginal operations and focused on its core businesses. Ford designated TRW as its sole air bag supplier (a contract worth $1 billion) in 1989, but TRW's image was blemished when Ford recalled 55,000 vehicles for defective air bag systems in 1990 and 8,600 vehicles in 1995.

TRW sold its once-profitable computer repair business in 1990. The company expanded its European manufacturing capacity in 1991 and opened automotive plants in France, England, and Brazil the following year. In 1992 the company acquired a 92% stake in the Czech Republic's largest auto engine valve and steering systems maker. The first Milstar satellite, whose military communications system was built by TRW, was launched in 1994. Also in that year TRW initiated a joint venture credit operation in Mexico, where the company planned to begin operations in mid-1995.

In 1995 TRW sold a controlling stake in its TRW PhonePrint unit, which was renamed Corsair Communications, to a group of venture capitalists. The company produces a control system that blocks unauthorized cellular telephone calls by counterfeiters.

NYSE symbol: TRW
Fiscal year ends: December 31

WHO

Chairman and CEO: Joseph T. Gorman, age 57, $4,003,133 pay
President and COO: Peter S. Hellman, age 45, $2,083,605 pay
EVP and General Manager, Steering, Suspension, and Engine Group: Chester O. Macey, age 57, $1,342,375 pay
EVP, General Counsel, and Secretary: Martin A. Coyle, age 53, $1,313,317 pay
EVP and General Manager, Occupant Restraint Systems Group: John A. Janitz, age 52, $1,287,142 pay
EVP and General Manager, Automotive Electronics Group: Philippe Lemaitre, age 45
EVP and General Manager, Avionics and Surveillance Group: Robert J. Kohler, age 57
EVP and General Manager, Information Systems and Services Group: D. Van Skilling, age 61
EVP and General Manager, Space and Electronics Group: Timothy W. Hannemann, age 52
EVP and CFO: Ronald D. Sugar, age 46
EVP Human Resources and Communications: Howard V. Knicely, age 59
Auditors: Ernst & Young LLP

WHERE

HQ: 1900 Richmond Rd., Cleveland, OH 44124
Phone: 216-291-7000
Fax: 216-291-7629

TRW has 93 manufacturing, R&D, and other facilities in 25 states and 82 facilities in 19 other countries.

	1994 Sales	
	$ mil.	% of total
US	6,290	69
Europe	1,965	22
Other regions	832	9
Total	**9,087**	**100**

WHAT

	1994 Sales		1994 Operating Income	
	$ mil.	% of total	$ mil.	% of total
Automotive	5,679	62	476	64
Space & defense	2,812	31	175	23
Info. sys. & svcs.	596	7	96	13
Total	**9,087**	**100**	**747**	**100**

Automotive
Electromechanical assemblies
Electronic monitoring and control systems
Engine and chassis parts
Engine valves
Occupant safety systems (seat belts and air bags)
Steering gears
Suspension components

Space and Defense
Electronic systems, equipment, and services
Electro-optical and instrument systems
High-energy lasers
Propulsion subsystems
Software and systems engineering support services
Spacecraft equipment and payloads

Information Systems and Services
Credit information
Direct marketing services
Imaging systems engineering and integration services
Real estate information

KEY COMPETITORS

ABS Industries
AlliedSignal
Arvin Industries
Borg-Warner Automotive
Breed
Dana
Dun & Bradstreet
Eaton
AB Electrolux
Equifax
General Electric
Harris Corp.
ITT Industries
Litton Industries
Lockheed Martin
Loral
Morton
Motorola
OEA
Orbital Sciences
Robert Bosch
Safety Components
Siemens
Simula
Teledyne
Textron
Thiokol
WMX Technologies

HOW MUCH

	9-Year Growth	1985	1986	1987	1988	1989	1990	1991	1992	1993	1994
Sales ($ mil.)	4.9%	5,917	6,036	6,821	6,982	7,340	8,169	7,913	8,311	7,948	9,087
Net income ($ mil.)	10.7%	134	218	243	261	263	208	(140)	194	220	333
Income as % of sales	—	2.3%	3.6%	3.6%	3.7%	3.6%	2.5%	—	2.3%	2.8%	3.7%
Earnings per share ($)	12.9%	1.68	3.56	3.95	4.23	4.25	3.36	(2.30)	3.09	3.35	5.01
Stock price – high ($)	—	48.50	55.00	70.00	54.00	49.88	51.75	46.25	60.25	70.25	77.50
Stock price – low ($)	—	34.50	41.13	37.00	40.63	41.25	30.75	34.50	41.00	52.50	61.00
Stock price – close ($)	4.6%	44.00	42.25	47.63	41.63	49.38	37.88	42.00	57.50	69.25	66.00
P/E – high	—	29	15	18	13	12	15	—	20	21	16
P/E – low	—	21	12	9	10	10	9	—	13	16	12
Dividends per share ($)	2.9%	1.50	1.53	1.60	1.63	1.77	1.74	1.80	1.82	1.88	1.94
Book value per share ($)	5.4%	17.46	20.31	24.54	26.01	28.84	31.35	27.40	22.50	23.92	28.06
Employees	(4.1%)	93,186	78,556	77,931	73,211	74,300	75,600	71,300	64,100	61,200	64,200

1994 Year-end:
Debt ratio: 34.8%
Return on equity: 19.9%
Cash (mil.): $109
Current ratio: 1.12
Long-term debt (mil.): $694
No. of shares (mil.): 65
Dividends:
  Yield: 2.9%
  Payout: 38.7%
Market value (mil.): $4,283

Stock Price History High/Low 1985–94

TURNER BROADCASTING SYSTEM, INC.

OVERVIEW

Turner Broadcasting System (TBS) is a $2.8 billion global entertainment and news company built around cable TV. TBS owns 4 cable TV entertainment networks (Turner Network Television, TBS SuperStation, the Cartoon Network, and Turner Classic Movies) in the US and 4 abroad (TNT Latin America, TNT & Cartoon Network Europe, TNT & Cartoon Network Asia, and Cartoon Network Latin America). The Atlanta-based company supplies its 24-hour entertainment networks with programming from the world's largest film and animation library (which includes thousands of MGM, RKO, and Warner Bros. films, TV shows, and cartoons), programming rights from the NFL and NBA, and the animation library of Hanna-Barbera.

TBS's ownership of Cable News Network (CNN), an international cable TV network with 29 bureaus worldwide, makes it a major international news source. TBS also owns a profes-

sional baseball team (Atlanta Braves), a professional basketball team (Atlanta Hawks), interests in wrestling, and stakes in cable networks SportSouth and n-tv (news, Germany).

Visionary CEO Ted Turner is diving deeper into the entertainment business. The acquisition of New Line Cinema (*The Mask*) and Castle Rock Entertainment (*The Shawshank Redemption*) has catapulted TBS into 5th place among major film producers. With New Line, Turner Pictures (*Gettysburg*), and Fine Line Features, Turner hopes to create the top Hollywood studio plus more programming for cable TV. TBS recently teamed up with Rhino Records to create a new record label, which will initially distribute soundtracks from its MGM/Warner Bros. film library. In mid-1995 the company was considering buying syndicated TV distributor King World Productions (*The Oprah Winfrey Show*, *Wheel of Fortune*) and possibly a major TV network.

WHEN

In 1970 Ted Turner, using profits from his billboard advertising business, bought Rice Broadcasting, a small Atlanta TV station, and formed Turner Communications Corp. In its first year the station lost $689,000, but its prospects were considered good enough to justify keeping it on the air. The following year WTSG (which stood for "watch this station grow," according to staffers) was the #1 independent TV station in the South. Turner spun the billboard business off in 1975.

Discovering he could reach cable systems around the country by satellite, in 1979 Turner turned WTSG into "superstation" WTBS (for Turner Broadcasting System) and broadcast older TV shows, movies, and Atlanta Braves and Hawks games (teams Turner had bought in 1976 and 1977, respectively). In 1979 the station reached 5.8 million homes.

Turner launched the first serious challenge to broadcast network TV news, the 24-hour Cable News Network (CNN), in 1980. CNN frequently "scooped" the competition, reporting first on the 1981 attempt to assassinate President Reagan and broadcasting live the space shuttle explosion in 1986. CNN2 (later Headline News) was introduced in 1982. CNN began European distribution in 1985 and added Headline News in Spanish in 1988.

In 1986, after failing to take over CBS, Turner bought MGM/UA. The $1.4 billion price nearly caused Turner to founder, but cable operators who saw Turner's importance to

their systems bailed the company out. Turner formed Turner Network Television (TNT) in 1988 to air the MGM/UA films, many in colorized versions criticized by purists.

In 1990 a subsidiary of the company bought a stake in SportSouth, a regional sports network serving the Southeast. Turner and an investment company bought the Hanna-Barbera cartoon library in 1991; in 1993 Turner acquired 100%. Included were licensing rights to the characters. The Cartoon Network, launched in 1992 (US) and 1993 (Latin America), quickly equaled and then surpassed CNN's ratings.

TNT started Latin American operations in 1991. Though Turner's 2-year-old Checkout Channel (news and information in supermarkets) checked out in 1992, the year-old Airport Channel kept its boarding pass. Also in 1992 Turner set up the first independent TV station in Moscow in a joint venture, and in 1993 the company bought 40% of a St. Petersburg, Russia, TV station.

In 1993 Turner released *Gettysburg* in theaters and bought Castle Rock Entertainment (movies and TV) and a stake in n-tv, a German-language cable TV news network. In 1994 Turner bought New Line Cinema, the #1 independent US movie producer and distributor, and launched its 4th US entertainment network, Turner Classic Movies. In August 1995 major shareholder Time Warner offered to buy the 80% of TBS it doesn't already own.

AMEX symbol: TBS.A
Fiscal year ends: December 31

WHO

Chairman, President, and CEO: Robert Edward "Ted"
Turner III, age 56, $1,541,030 pay
EVP: Terence F. McGuirk, age 43, $1,452,328 pay
VP, Turner Entertainment Group: Scott M. Sassa,
age 36, $1,401,030 pay
VP News: W. Thomas Johnson, age 53, $1,027,922 pay
VP Finance and CFO: Wayne H. Pace, age 48
VP, General Counsel, and Secretary: Steven W. Korn,
age 41
VP and Treasurer: Christian L. Becken, age 41
VP Worldwide Distribution: William H. Grumbles,
age 45
VP Advertising Sales and Marketing: Steven J. Heyer,
age 42
VP Administration (Personnel): William M. Shaw,
age 50
Auditors: Price Waterhouse LLP

WHERE

HQ: One CNN Center, Atlanta, GA 30303
Phone: 404-827-1700
Fax: 404-827-2437

Turner Broadcasting operates worldwide, but most of its
activities are centered in Atlanta.

WHAT

	1994 Sales		1994 Operating Income	
	$ mil.	% of total	$ mil.	% of total
Entertainment	2,001	70	119	33
News	667	24	227	63
Other	164	6	(71)	—
Adjustments	(23)	—	13	4
Total	**2,809**	**100**	**288**	**100**

Entertainment

Networks
Cartoon Network (animation programming)
Cartoon Network Latin America
TBS SuperStation (Atlanta TV station on cable systems)
TNT (Turner Network Television; sports and
entertainment)
TNT & Cartoon Network Asia
TNT & Cartoon Network Europe
TNT Latin America (trilingual entertainment service)
Turner Classic Movies (TCM)
Production and Distribution
Castle Rock Entertainment (film production)
Fine Line Features (film production)
Hanna-Barbera Inc. (new animation products)
New Line Cinema (film production)
Turner Entertainment Co. (film/TV/cartoon library)
Turner Home Entertainment (distributes home video
and pay-per-view programs; licenses merchandise)
Turner Interactive (video games)
Turner Publishing (book publisher)
Turner Pictures Worldwide, Inc. (film production)

News
Cable News Network (CNN, US newscasts)
CNN Airport Network (newscasts at airports)
CNN Headline News (30-minute newscasts)
CNN International (news for a worldwide audience)
n-tv (30.3%, Germany)

Selected Other Interests
Atlanta Hawks L.P. (96%, basketball)
Atlanta National League Baseball Club, Inc. (Braves)
SportSouth Network, Ltd. (44%, regional sports network)
Turner Classic Movies Music (movie soundtracks)
World Championship Wrestling (wrestling programming
and live matches)

KEY COMPETITORS

Capital Cities/ABC	Metromedia	TCI
Carolco Pictures	News Corp.	Time Warner
CBS	Samuel Goldwyn	Tribune
DreamWorks SKG	Seagram	Viacom
General Electric	Sony	Walt Disney

HOW MUCH

	9-Year Growth	1985	1986	1987	1988	1989	1990	1991	1992	1993	1994
Sales ($ mil.)	26.0%	352	557	652	807	1,065	1,394	1,480	1,770	1,922	2,809
Net income ($ mil.)	2.4%	17	(187)	(131)	(95)	28	(16)	43	34	72	21
Income as % of sales	—	4.9%	—	—	—	2.6%	—	2.9%	1.9%	3.8%	0.7%
Earnings per share ($)	(12.3%)	0.26	(3.65)	(1.47)	(1.06)	(0.13)	(0.42)	0.06	0.13	0.27	0.08
Stock price – high ($)	—	4.20	4.87	4.50	5.62	21.31	17.90	23.75	27.50	29.75	27.75
Stock price – low ($)	—	1.79	1.91	2.29	3.50	5.66	8.25	10.75	18.63	19.38	14.50
Stock price – close ($)	24.1%	2.35	2.31	3.62	5.62	16.82	11.38	23.13	21.38	27.25	16.38
P/E – high	—	16	—	—	—	—	—	—	—	110	173
P/E – low	—	7	—	—	—	—	—	179	143	72	91
Dividends per share ($)	—	0.00	0.00	0.00	0.00	0.00	0.00	0.00	0.05	0.07	0.07
Book value per share ($)	(1.8%)	0.47	(3.20)	(2.16)	(4.57)	(4.65)	(4.98)	(1.69)	(0.15)	(1.38)	0.40
Employees	12.6%	2,062	1,600	2,774	3,187	3,466	3,802	4,370	5,239	5,317	6,000

1994 Year-end:
Debt ratio: 88%
Return on equity: —
Cash (mil.): $53
Current ratio: 1.99
Long-term debt (mil.): $2,518
No. of shares (mil.): 206
Dividends
  Yield: 0.4%
  Payout: 87.5%
Market value (mil.): $3,370

Stock Price History
High/Low 1985–94

TYCO INTERNATIONAL LTD.

OVERVIEW

Posting sales of over $3 billion and operating in 50 countries, Tyco International (based in Exeter, New Hampshire) is the world's #1 manufacturer and provider of fire protection systems. It also holds leadership positions in its markets for electrical and electronic components; disposable medical, adhesive, and other related packaging products; and flow control materials.

Tyco's Wormald and 145-year-old Grinnell subsidiaries, along with other fire protection units, bring in the bulk of the company's total revenues (47% in 1994). Tyco's fire protection products include explosion suppression systems, automatic sprinklers, fire extinguishers, fire hydrants, and fire detection systems.

Flow control products (valves, pipes, couplings, fittings, meters, and tubing) accounted for 28% of 1994 revenues.

Tyco's Simplex subsidiary is the world's leading producer of undersea fiber-optic cable.

The company expanded its disposable and specialty products capacity in 1994 with the $1.4 billion acquisition of Kendall, a maker of medical supplies and adhesive products.

International expansion and a growing fire safety consciousness are expected to lift the sales of Tyco products over the next few years.

WHEN

Tyco Laboratories started in the 1960s, but its roots extend back to the 1880s.

Arthur Rosenberg founded Tyco Laboratories in the early 1960s to conduct experimental research for the government and commercial sectors. The company successfully developed the Dynalux battery charger, the first blue-light laser, and the first laser with a nonstop beam. An explosion of acquisitions in the mid-1960s boosted sales from under $1 million in 1963 to over $41 million by 1969. Rosenberg left the company the following year.

Joseph Gaziano became CEO in 1973 and increased the scale of Tyco Laboratories' acquisitions. In 1974 Tyco Laboratories acquired Simplex Wire & Cable, a firm specializing in undersea cables and whose predecessor had been founded by Charles Morss. During the 1880s Morss switched from making wire bird cages to manufacturing insulated wire for electrical products. In the 1920s company scientists developed water-resistant Anhydrex cables, and during WWII the company made submarine cable for the US Navy and Coast Guard. In 1966 the company began installing undersea cables.

Tyco Laboratories almost tripled its sales in 1975 by acquiring Grinnell from ITT, which had been ordered to divest Grinnell on antitrust grounds. Grinnell got its start in 1882, when Frederick Grinnell obtained a patent for an automatic valve sprinkler; he started licensing his fire protection systems the next year to Mather and Platt (which later became part of Wormald International).

Tyco Laboratories acquired Armin, a polyethylene producer, in 1979 and Ludlow, a producer of packaging materials, 2 years later. The pace of Tyco Laboratories' acquisitions slowed after Gaziano's death in 1982 at the age of 47.

The company acquired Grinnell Flow Control, a valve distributor, from ITT in 1986 and the next year bought Allied Pipe & Tube, a pipe manufacturer. In 1988 Tyco Laboratories acquired Mueller, a water and gas pipe provider. Hieronymous Mueller had founded H. Mueller & Son in 1885. He invented the water stop and water main tapping systems, which remain the standard means of installing water service today. Other inventions by the Mueller family include the spark plug, the variable-speed auto transmission, and the roller skate.

In 1990 Tyco Laboratories expanded its fire protection operations by acquiring Wormald International, which had a strong presence in Asia, Australia, Europe, and New Zealand. The company acquired NeoTecha, a Swiss valve manufacturer, in 1992. In 1993 Tyco Laboratories acquired the Industrial Valves Division of Suter and agreed to acquire Classic Medical Group.

In 1993 Tyco decided to drop "Laboratories" from its name (which had been tied to its research lab origins) and replace it with "International" to reflect its operations in over 25 countries (expanded to 50 by 1995). In 1994 Simplex Wire & Cable also changed its name, to Simplex Technologies, to better describe its range of services.

In 1994 Simplex received a boost with a $250 million 2-year extension of its contract with AT&T Submarine Systems for undersea fiber-optic cable. Simplex also signed a $35 million contract in 1995 with Schahin Cury Engenharia to manufacture an undersea fiber-optic cable for the Brazilian domestic telephone system. The system will interconnect with the UNISUR undersea cable.

WHO

Chairman, President, and CEO: L. Dennis Kozlowski,
age 47, $1,350,000 pay
VP; President, Ludlow Corporation: John C. Armacost,
age 58, $1,058,833 pay
VP; President, Flow Control Division, Grinnell Corp.:
Robert P. Mead, age 43, $909,917 pay
SVP: Irving Gutin, age 62, $550,000 pay
SVP; President, Kendall International: Richard A.
Gilleland, age 50
VP and CFO: Terry L. Hall, age 40, $497,917 pay
VP: Robert F. Sharpe Jr., age 42
VP: Vincent R. Gatto, age 56
VP and Corporate Controller: John R. Guarnieri, age 44
Treasurer: William G. Gardner
President, Grinnell Fire Protection: Jerry R. Boggess
President, Simplex Technologies: Peter L. Bergeron
President, Armin Plastics: Armin Kaufman
**VP Worldwide Marketing, Advertising/Public Relations,
Government Affairs, and Human Resources:** David P.
Brownell, age 50
Auditors: Coopers & Lybrand L.L.P.

WHERE

HQ: One Tyco Park, Exeter, NH 03833
Phone: 603-778-9700
Fax: 603-778-7700

Tyco International operates 250 offices on 5 continents.

	1994 Sales		1994 Operating Income	
	$ mil.	% of total	$ mil.	% of total
North America	2,311	71	236	89
Europe	622	19	22	9
Asia/Pacific	330	10	6	2
Total	**3,263**	**100**	**264**	**100**

WHAT

	1994 Sales		1994 Operating Income	
	$ mil.	% of total	$ mil.	% of total
Fire protection	1,526	47	69	26
Flow control	914	28	70	26
Electrical & electronic comp.	437	13	71	27
Disposal and specialty prods.	386	12	54	21
Total	**3,263**	**100**	**264**	**100**

Fire Protection
Ansul Fire Protection
Grinnell Corp. (fire protection and detection systems,
automatic sprinklers)
Wormald

Flow Control
Allied Tube and Conduit
Grinnell Corp.
Mueller Co.

Electrical and Electronic Components
Allied Tube and Conduit (electrical conduit)
Simplex Technologies, Inc. (transoceanic fiber-optic
telecommunications cable, underwater power and data
gathering systems)
Tyco Printed Circuit Group (high-precision printed
circuit boards, backplane assemblies)

Disposable and Specialty Products
Accurate Forming
Armin Plastics (polyethylene films)
Kendall (medical products)
Ludlow Corp. (protective packaging)

KEY COMPETITORS

Alcatel Alsthom	Honeywell	Mobil
Cable & Wireless	Illinois Tool Works	SCI Systems
Ericsson	Johnson Controls	Siemens
Hanson	3M	Thorn EMI

HOW MUCH

	9-Year Growth	1985	1986	1987	1988	1989	1990	1991	1992	1993	1994
Sales ($ mil.)	19.2%	674	796	1,062	1,575	1,971	2,103	3,108	3,067	3,115	3,263
Net income ($ mil.)	15.1%	35	35	27	67	91	119	118	95	72	125
Income as % of sales	—	5.2%	4.4%	2.5%	4.2%	4.6%	5.7%	3.8%	3.1%	2.3%	3.8%
Earnings per share ($)	12.4%	0.94	1.02	0.75	1.75	2.26	2.90	2.57	2.06	1.58	2.70
Stock price – high ($)	—	12.16	21.25	28.13	38.38	53.75	65.75	52.25	43.13	51.75	55.25
Stock price – low ($)	—	8.31	11.69	15.75	21.00	32.25	37.13	28.00	30.63	37.38	42.50
Stock price – close ($)	16.8%	11.78	20.38	22.75	35.75	50.38	43.00	34.38	41.38	51.63	47.50
P/E – high	—	13	21	38	22	24	23	20	21	33	21
P/E – low	—	9	12	21	12	14	13	11	15	24	16
Dividends per share ($)	8.0%	0.20	0.20	0.20	0.23	0.26	0.30	0.34	0.36	0.38	0.40
Book value per share ($)	18.6%	5.00	5.76	6.45	8.15	11.69	14.45	19.24	22.14	19.85	23.28
Employees	9.1%	11,000	10,000	10,000	10,600	12,000	14,000	24,700	23,000	24,000	24,000

1994 Year-end:
Debt ratio: 32.9%
Return on equity: 12.5%
Cash (mil.): $62
Current ratio: 1.29
Long-term debt (mil.): $413
No. of shares (mil.): 46
Dividends
  Yield: 0.8%
  Payout: 14.8%
Market value (mil.): $2,202

**Stock Price History
High/Low 1985–94**

TYSON FOODS, INC.

OVERVIEW

After years of laying gold, Tyson Foods laid an egg by reporting a net loss of $2 million in 1994. However, Tyson still has plenty to crow about; it controls 18% of the domestic chicken market, exports to 43 countries, and controls 70% of the chickens exported to Japan. Almost half of sales are to food service (catering accounts) and clients such as Kentucky Fried Chicken and McDonald's. The company breeds, raises, processes, and markets chickens and produces beef, pork, and Cornish game hens. It also sells Mexican food products (under the Mexican Original brand) and seafood, raises swine, and produces animal feed and pet food.

Seafood, added to the company's table in 1992 and expanded in 1994, already nets 5% of Tyson's total sales. The company will expand its chicken processing capacity from 30 million to 37 million a week by the end of 1997.

Tyson, the undisputed heavyweight champion of poultry, has been on the ropes because of ties to the Clinton administration. Tyson is accused of giving favors to Department of Agriculture officials in exchange for "favorable treatment" for the company by poultry inspectors. The allegations led to an investigation that contributed to the resignation of secretary of agriculture Mike Espy. Senior chairman Don Tyson owns 90% of total shares.

WHEN

During the Great Depression, Arkansas poultry farmer John Tyson supported his family by buying, transporting, and selling vegetables and poultry. In 1935 he developed a method for transporting live poultry (he installed a food-and-water trough and nailed small feed cups on a trailer) and bought 500 Arkansas chickens that he sold in Chicago.

For the next decade Tyson bought, sold, and transported chickens exclusively. By 1947, the year Tyson incorporated his company as Tyson Feed & Hatchery, he was raising the chickens himself. Tyson emphasized chicken production significantly more during the early 1950s. In 1958 Tyson opened his first processing plant in Springdale, Arkansas, at which he implemented an ice-packing system allowing the company to send its chicken products greater distances.

In 1960 Tyson's son Don took over as manager of the company. In 1962 the company began processing Rock Cornish game hens, and the following year it went public under its current name. The company introduced Tyson Country Fresh Chicken (packaged chicken that would become the company's mainstay) in 1967. In 1969 Tyson underwent an expansion and modification program, buying Prospect Farms (precooked chicken for the food service industry).

During the early 1970s Tyson experienced rapid expansion that included a new egg processing building (1970), a new plant and computerized feed mill (1971), and the acquisition of the Ocoma Foods Division (poultry, 1972) from Consolidated Foods (now Sara Lee). This time of growth ended with the purchase of a Creswell, North Carolina, hog company and Wilson Foods's Poultry Division.

During the 1980s health-conscious consumers increasingly turned away from red meats to poultry, causing phenomenal growth in the industry and at Tyson. In 1985 the company reached $1 billion in annual sales. Tyson became the industry leader with several key poultry operation acquisitions that included the Tastybird division of Valmac (1985), Lane Processing (1986), and Heritage Valley (1986).

In 1989, after a lengthy bidding struggle with ConAgra, Tyson purchased Holly Farms for $1.5 billion. The acquisition contributed to Tyson's 51% sales increase in 1990 and greatly strengthened its lead in the poultry industry. In 1992 Tyson increased its presence in Mexico through a joint venture with Trasgo. The company also acquired 2 seafood companies, a pork processing plant in Marshall, Missouri, and value-enhanced poultry producer Brandywine Foods.

In 1992 Tyson plunged into seafood with the purchase of Arctic Alaska Fisheries, a Seattle-based fish processor; it also netted Louis Kemp Seafood, a leading US producer of lobster and crab products.

In 1994 Tyson bought Culinary Foods (frozen foods, $70 million in annual sales) and Mexico's Trasgo (poultry, $140 million in sales). It also pulled out of a $330 million hostile takeover bid of WLR Foods, a leading Virginia turkey producer, citing the extreme resistance of the WLR management. During 1994 the company announced plans to build 4 new poultry processing plants.

International Multifoods Corp. announced in 1995 that it had reached an agreement to sell its seafood division to Tyson. A Multifoods division makes surimi seafood that imitates crab, lobster, and other seafood.

Nasdaq symbol: TYSNA
Fiscal year ends: Saturday nearest September 30

WHO

Senior Chairman: Don Tyson, age 65
Chairman and CEO: Leland E. Tollett, age 57,
$1,173,750 pay (prior to promotion)
President and COO: Donald E. Wray, age 57,
$547,495 pay (prior to promotion)
EVP Operations: David S. Purtle, age 50, $397,413 pay
(prior to promotion)
EVP Finance: Gerald Johnston, age 52, $395,080 pay
EVP Sales, Marketing, R&D, and Quality Assurance:
Greg Lee, age 47
SVP International Sales and Marketing: Wayne Britt,
age 45
SVP Seafood Division: Roy Brown, age 42
Group VP Swine Division: Bill Moeller, age 44
Group VP Research and Quality Assurance: Ellis
Brunton, age 52
Group VP Human Resources: William P. Jaycox, age 48
President, Beef and Pork Division: John H. Tyson,
age 41
Secretary and Director of Investor Relations: Mary
Rush, age 60
Treasurer: Dennis Leatherby, age 34
Corporate Controller: Gary Johnson, age 50
Auditors: Ernst & Young LLP

WHERE

HQ: 2210 W. Oaklawn Dr., Springdale, AR 72762-6999
Phone: 501-756-4000
Fax: 800-643-3410

The company operates production and distribution
facilities in 20 states and 12 other countries, and it
participates in joint ventures in China and Mexico. Its
products are sold in Canada, Hong Kong, Japan, Russia,
and the US and in several Asian, Caribbean, Far Eastern,
and Latin American countries.

WHAT

	1994 Sales
	% of total
Value-enhanced poultry	65
Beef, pork, Mexican food, live swine & prepared foods	18
Basic poultry	10
Seafood	5
Animal foods, by-products & other	2
Total	**100**

Selected Products and Brand Names

Chicken
Holly Farms (roasted)
Tastybasted
Tastybird
Tyson (fresh and frozen)
Weaver
Wing Stingers
W.W. Flyers

Lunch Meat and Entrees
Quick-to-Fix (chicken
fried steak)
Tyson (ham, bacon,
sausage, pork)
Weaver (hot dogs)

Mexican Food
Mexican Original
(tortillas and chips)

Seafood
Arctic Ice
Crab Delights
Lobster Delights
Louis Kemp
Ocean Master

KEY COMPETITORS

America Foods
BeefAmerica
Bob Evans
Campbell Soup
Cargill
Chiquita Brands
ConAgra
Continental Grain
Foster Poultry
Gold Kist
Heinz

Hormel
Hudson Foods
IBP
Keystone Foods
Perdue
Pilgrim's Pride
Sara Lee
Schreiber Foods
Seaboard Corp.
Smithfield Foods
WLR Foods

HOW MUCH

	9-Year Growth	1985	1986	1987	1988	1989	1990	1991	1992	1993	1994
Sales ($ mil.)	18.2%	1,136	1,504	1,786	1,936	2,538	3,825	3,922	4,169	4,707	5,110
Net income ($ mil.)	—	35	50	68	81	101	120	146	161	180	(2)
Income as % of sales	—	3.1%	3.3%	3.8%	4.2%	4.0%	3.1%	3.7%	3.9%	3.8%	—
Earnings per share ($)	—	0.30	0.40	0.53	0.64	0.78	0.91	1.05	1.16	1.22	(0.01)
Stock price – high ($)	—	4.70	12.59	11.75	10.06	13.00	17.69	23.25	24.88	27.13	25.00
Stock price – low ($)	—	1.83	4.20	5.50	5.63	7.38	11.38	14.00	15.25	19.25	18.75
Stock price – close ($)	18.6%	4.58	9.09	6.44	8.63	12.44	15.50	20.13	24.25	24.00	21.25
P/E – high	—	16	32	22	16	17	19	22	21	22	—
P/E – low	—	6	11	10	9	10	13	13	13	16	—
Dividends per share ($)	24.1%	0.01	0.01	0.02	0.02	0.02	0.02	0.03	0.04	0.04	0.07
Book value per share ($)	24.8%	1.21	1.59	2.10	2.62	3.46	4.85	5.99	7.13	9.24	8.88
Employees	14.1%	17,000	25,000	25,500	26,000	42,000	44,000	47,000	47,950	50,358	55,800

1994 Year-end:
Debt ratio: 53.0%
Return on equity: —
Cash (mil.): $27
Current ratio: 2.34
Long-term debt (mil.): $1,382
No. of shares (mil.): 145
Dividends
  Yield: 0.3%
  Payout: —
Market value (mil.): $3,086

Stock Price History
High/Low 1985–94

UAL CORPORATION

OVERVIEW

Shuttle, not subtle. United Airlines (the operational arm of UAL Corporation) and the #2 US airline (after American) has challenged #8 Southwest Airlines at its own game by introducing a no-frills shuttle service in the western US. United began in October 1994 with 184 daily flights; its service jumped to 304 by the end of the year and is putting the squeeze on Southwest's profits.

United Airlines serves 152 airports in 30 countries and operates a fleet of 543 aircraft. Its major hub airports are at Chicago; Denver; San Francisco; Washington, DC; London; and Tokyo.

On July 12, 1994, United Airlines's stockholders approved a plan ceding 55% of the company to its employees in exchange for $4.8 billion in wage concessions and changes in work rules. The radical restructuring worked. Since the buyout the firm has reduced its costs and improved its efficiency; on-time performances have reached a record level.

The buyout came after 3 years of losses totaling more than $800 million, caused in part by fare wars with competitors and the growth of a generation of small, short-haul airlines.

In 1994 United formed a joint service agreement with Lufthansa German Airlines, giving United passengers connections on Lufthansa flights (and vice versa) to 40 destinations worldwide.

In an expansive mode since the 1994 buyout, United inaugurated service to its 12th Latin American destination — Lima, Peru — in 1995. United also plans to initiate nonstop service to a number of Canadian cities.

WHEN

In 1929 aircraft designer Bill Boeing (Boeing Airplane and Transport) and engine designer Fred Rentschler (Pratt & Whitney) merged their companies to form United Aircraft and Transport. Renamed United Air Lines in 1931, the New York–based company offered one of America's first coast-to-coast airline services. In 1934 United's manufacturing and transportation divisions split, and former banker Bill Patterson became president of the latter (United Airlines), moving it to Chicago.

Under Patterson (1934–63), United was slow to use new technology, offering jet service in 1959, later than American, its leading rival. Still, in 1961 United became the US's #1 airline after buying Capital Airlines, which added Washington, DC, and points along the Great Lakes and in Florida to its network.

The company bought the Westin Hotel Company in 1970 and named Westin president Eddie Carlson as United's CEO in 1971. Another hotelier, Richard Ferris, became CEO in 1979. Hoping to build United into a travel conglomerate, Ferris spent $2.3 billion buying Hertz Corporation (1985), Pan Am's Australian and Asian routes (1986), and Transworld's Hilton International (1987). In 1987, after spending an additional $7.3 million to change United's name to Allegis Corporation, Ferris resigned when Coniston Partners, the company's largest shareholder, threatened to oust the board and liquidate the company. Assuming its old name under Stephen Wolf (former Flying Tigers chief), United sold its hotels and car rental business as well as 50% of its computer reservation partnership (Covia).

A 1989 takeover bid by Los Angeles billionaire Marvin Davis led to a management and union buyout plan, which failed in 1989. Another union buyout attempt failed the next year. United then reached an accord with Coniston, which sold most of its stake in UAL in exchange for 2 seats on the board.

In 1990 United received DOT permission to fly from Chicago to Tokyo. In 1991 and 1992 United bought Pan Am's London and Paris routes, most of Pan Am's Latin American routes, and its Los Angeles–Mexico City route. UAL bought Air Wis (owner of Air Wisconsin, one of its feeders) in 1992.

Throughout 1993 United sought to negotiate a buyout with its unions. Early in the year it canceled plans to hire 1,900 new employees, instead laying off 2,800 and cutting US management salaries and directors' fees.

Finally, the 1993 sale of United's kitchen operations to Dial's Dobbs Houses (eliminating 5,800 union jobs) and the announcement of plans to start up a subsidiary short-haul airline brought the pilots and machinists (but not the flight attendants) back to the table.

Despite improved job performance after the buyout, the company is not out of the woods yet. United expects to incur $124 million in costs caused by overruns and delays at the new Denver International Airport. Even so, United has ambitious expansion plans; while its rivals are shrinking services, United plans to increase its capacity by 3% in 1995.

NYSE symbol: UAL
Fiscal year ends: December 31

WHO

Chairman and CEO, UAL and United Airlines: Gerald
Greenwald, age 59, $3,975,821 pay
President, UAL and United Airlines: John A.
Edwardson, age 45, $2,372,094 pay
**EVP Corporate Affairs and General Counsel, UAL and
United Airlines:** Stuart I. Oran, age 44, $1,687,865 pay
EVP; EVP Operations, United Airlines: Joseph R.
O'Gorman Jr., age 51, $556,945 pay
EVP; EVP Marketing and Planning, United Airlines:
James M. Guyette, age 50, $555,296 pay
SVP Finance and CFO; SVP Finance, United Airlines:
Douglas A. Hacker, age 39
SVP International, United Airlines: James E. Goodwin
SVP, United Airlines; President, Shuttle by United:
Alan B. Magary
SVP People, United Airlines: Paul G. George, age 43
Auditors: Arthur Andersen & Co, SC

WHERE

HQ: 1200 Algonquin Rd., Elk Grove Township,
IL 60007; PO Box 66919, Chicago, IL 60666
Phone: 708-952-4000
Fax: 708-952-7578
Reservations: 800-241-6522

United serves 152 airports in 30 countries.

Hub Locations

Chicago, IL	San Francisco, CA
Denver, CO	Tokyo, Japan
London, UK	Washington, DC

	1994 Sales	
	$ mil.	% of total
US	9,030	65
Other countries	4,920	35
Total	**13,950**	**100**

WHAT

	1994 Sales	
	$ mil.	% of total
Passengers	12,295	88
Cargo	685	5
Contract services & other	970	7
Total	**13,950**	**100**

Major Subsidiaries and Affiliates
Air Wis Services, Inc.
Apollo Travel Services Partnership (77%)
Four Star Insurance Company, Ltd.
Galileo International Partnership (38%)
Mileage Plus, Inc.
UAL Leasing Corporation
U-C Corp.
United Airlines, Inc.

	Aircraft	
	Owned	Leased
A320	—	21
Boeing 727	50	25
Boeing 737	82	145
Boeing 747	23	28
Boeing 757	33	55
Boeing 767	22	20
DC-10	18	21
Total	**228**	**315**

KEY COMPETITORS

Air Canada	Delta	Airlines
Air China	HAL	Qantas
Air France	IRI	SAS
Alaska Air	JAL	Singapore Airlines
All Nippon Airways	Kiwi Int'l	Southwest Airlines
America West	Airlines	Swire Pacific
AMR	KLM	TWA
British Airways	Korean Air	USAir
Continental	Mesa Air	Virgin Group
Airlines	Northwest	

HOW MUCH

	9-Year Growth	1985	1986	1987	1988	1989	1990	1991	1992	1993	1994
Sales ($ mil.)	9.1%	6,383	9,196	8,292	8,982	9,794	11,037	11,663	12,890	14,511	13,950
Net income ($ mil.)	—	(49)	12	(4)	600	324	94	(332)	(417)	(50)	77
Income as % of sales	—	—	0.2%	—	6.7%	3.3%	0.9%	—	—	—	0.6%
Earnings per share ($)	—	(3.43)	0.25	(0.08)	20.20	14.96	4.33	(14.13)	(17.34)	(3.40)	0.76
Stock price – high ($)	—	59.50	64.38	105.88	110.00	294.00	171.00	161.50	159.00	155.50	150.00
Stock price – low ($)	—	39.75	46.25	52.25	68.50	105.25	84.25	109.00	103.00	110.75	83.13
Stock price – close ($)	6.5%	49.75	52.25	71.50	109.50	171.25	110.13	145.75	126.13	146.00	87.38
P/E – high	—	—	—	—	6	20	40	—	—	—	—
P/E – low	—	—	—	—	3	7	20	—	—	—	—
Dividends per share ($)	(100.0%)	1.00	1.00	0.75	0.00	0.00	0.00	0.00	0.00	0.00	0.00
Book value per share ($)	—	44.50	45.69	51.50	56.76	71.64	76.34	67.21	29.11	24.55	(99.94)
Employees	5.8%	47,000	59,000	64,000	66,000	69,000	74,000	79,000	84,000	83,400	77,900

1994 Year-end:
Debt ratio: 100.0%
Return on equity: —
Cash (mil.): $1,532
Current ratio: 0.65
Long-term debt (mil.): $2,887
No. of shares (mil.): 12
Dividends
  Yield: —
  Payout: —
Market value (mil.): $1,087

**Stock Price History
High/Low 1985–94**

UNICOM CORPORATION

OVERVIEW

Unicom is the holding company for Commonwealth Edison (ComEd), the 4th largest publicly owned electric utility in the US. ComEd's service area covers the northern portion of Illinois (including Chicago) — representing about 70% of the state's population. Nuclear power plants are the company's main source of power, generating about 71% of its electricity in 1994.

Unicom was formed in 1994 as a holding company for all of ComEd's operations in order to provide more flexibility as the company prepares to deal with increased competition created by deregulation. The company formed Unicom Enterprises to handle its unregulated businesses, including Unicom Thermal, which provides cooling services to large buildings in downtown Chicago. Unicom Enterprises also plans to offer power plant design and construction services and energy consulting services. Its R&D department is developing large-scale energy storage technology.

Unicom's profits rebounded in 1994 after settlements of Illinois Supreme Court rate orders led to an annual rate reduction of more than $300 million and customer refunds totaling more than $1.3 billion. In 1994 the company filed for a $469 million increase, and in 1995 the Illinois Commerce Commission granted a $303 million increase. However, with deregulation on the horizon, ComEd's rates, which are 30% higher than neighboring utilities, could put the company at a competitive disadvantage.

WHEN

A group of Chicago businessmen formed Western Edison Light in 1882. It was reorganized as Chicago Edison by its 39 shareholders in 1887, and under the leadership of Samuel Insull, it bought its main competitor, Chicago Arc Light & Power, in 1893. In 1898 the company created a holding company, Commonwealth Electric, to buy other power companies in the Chicago area. Commonwealth and Chicago Edison merged in 1907 to form Commonwealth Edison.

In 1912 ComEd finished its Northwest Station — then the largest steam generator ever built — and followed it with the even more powerful Crawford Station in 1924. ComEd also continued to buy other utilities and by 1933 consisted of 77 separate companies.

ComEd bought the Public Service Company of Northern Illinois (1937) and Chicago District Electric Generating Corporation (1939), which, combined with Western United Gas & Electric and Illinois Northern Utility (both bought in 1950), created one unit providing power in northern Illinois (outside Chicago). ComEd consolidated its position in Chicago through other purchases, including Produce Terminal Corporation (1956) and Central Illinois Electric and Gas (1966).

In 1960 ComEd opened the world's first full-scale, privately owned nuclear facility (Dresden Station) and by 1974 had built 7 nuclear plants. That year the company bought the Cotter Corporation, a Colorado uranium mining company, to provide low-cost fuel for its nuclear plants. In 1976 ComEd bought mining rights to 8,200 coal-rich acres in Wyoming, and in 1979 the company formed Edison Development Canada to explore for uranium deposits in Newfoundland.

Although touted as one of the US's best-run nuclear utilities during the mid-1980s, ComEd drew criticism in later years from environmental and consumer groups for its heavy investment in nuclear construction, which has resulted in some of the highest utility bills in the US. In 1984 and 1985, 2 nuclear plants went on-line, but when construction costs skyrocketed in 1986, the Illinois Commerce Commission (ICC) threatened to revoke licenses for 2 other nuclear plants (Byron 2 and Braidwood 1 & 2) still under construction. These went into service in 1987 and 1988, costing a total of $7.1 billion.

ComEd applied to the ICC for rate increases to pay for the new plants, but the ICC deemed the plants not 100% "used and useful." In 1991 ComEd received a rate increase, to be phased in over 3 years; however, later that year the Illinois Supreme Court remanded the increase and suspended the 2nd and 3rd phases.

In 1993 ComEd reached 2 settlements involving 6 rate- and fuel-related cases, including the Byron and Braidwood rate matters. The company agreed to cut its annual electric rates by $339 million and to refund $1.37 billion to customers — the largest refund in utility history.

In 1995 the Nuclear Regulatory Commission (NRC) announced it would levy a $100,000 fine against ComEd. The NRC said workers at the company's Braidwood nuclear power plant left a monitoring system used to detect hydrogen gas leaks disconnected for 3 months.

NYSE symbol: UCM
Fiscal year ends: December 31

WHO

Chairman and CEO: James J. O'Connor, age 58,
$1,258,642 pay
President: Samuel K. Skinner, age 56, $1,146,086 pay
SVP: Thomas J. Maiman, age 56, $423,378 pay
SVP: Michael J. Wallace, age 47, $393,492 pay
SVP: Cordell Reed, age 57, $356,937 pay
SVP: Robert J. Manning, age 52
SVP: Donald A. Petkus, age 53
VP and CFO: John C. Bukovski, age 52
VP and General Counsel: Pamela B. Strobel, age 42
VP Customer Service: K. Edward Bartels
Treasurer: Dennis F. O'Brien, age 49
Secretary: David A. Scholz, age 53
Comptroller: Roger F. Kovak, age 46
Director Human Resources: Ted Horwath
Auditors: Arthur Andersen & Co, SC

WHERE

HQ: One First National Plaza, 37th Fl., 10 S. Dearborn
St., PO Box 767, Chicago, IL 60690-0767
Phone: 312-394-4321
Fax: 312-394-3110

Generating Facilities

Fossil Fuels
Collins (near Morris, IL)
Crawford (Chicago)
Fisk (Chicago)
Joliet 6, 7 & 8 (near Joliet, IL)
Kincaid (near Taylorville, IL)
Powerton (near Pekin, IL)
State Line (Hammond, IN)
Waukegan (Waukegan, IL)
Will County (near Lockport, IL)

Nuclear
Braidwood (near
 Braidwood, IL)
Byron (near Byron, IL)
Dresden (near
 Morris, IL)
LaSalle County (near
 Seneca, IL)
Quad-Cities (75%, near
 Cordova, IL)
Zion (Zion, IL)

WHAT

	1994 Sales	
	$ mil.	% of total
Residential	2,274	36
Small commercial & industrial	1,917	31
Large commercial & industrial	1,381	22
Public authorities	453	7
Sales for resale	187	3
Electric railroads	26	—
Provisions for refunds	(16)	—
Other	56	1
Total	**6,278**	**100**

	1994 Fuel Sources
	% of total
Nuclear	71
Coal	25
Natural gas	3
Oil	1
Total	**100**

Subsidiaries
Commonwealth Edison Co.
Commonwealth Edison Co. of Indiana, Inc.
Cotter Corp.
Edison Development Co.
Unicom Enterprises Inc.
Unicom Thermal Technologies Inc.

KEY COMPETITORS

Bechtel
Duke Power
Fluor
General Electric
Peter Kiewiet Sons'
Southern Co.
Westinghouse

HOW MUCH

	9-Year Growth	1985	1986	1987	1988	1989	1990	1991	1992	1993	1994
Sales ($ mil.)	2.6%	4,964	5,479	5,674	5,613	5,751	5,262	6,276	6,026	5,260	6,278
Net income ($ mil.)	(10.4%)	956	1,050	1,086	738	694	128	95	514	103	355
Income as % of sales	—	19.3%	19.2%	19.1%	13.1%	12.1%	2.4%	1.5%	8.5%	2.0%	5.7%
Earnings per share ($)	(10.4%)	4.45	4.69	4.73	3.01	2.83	0.22	0.08	2.08	0.17	1.66
Stock price – high ($)	—	32.88	35.75	38.00	33.38	40.75	37.88	42.63	40.13	31.63	28.75
Stock price – low ($)	—	27.00	28.63	25.25	22.75	32.13	27.25	33.63	21.75	22.88	20.63
Stock price – close ($)	(2.2%)	29.38	33.88	27.50	33.00	37.63	34.75	39.88	23.25	28.13	24.00
P/E – high	—	7	8	8	11	14	—	—	19	—	17
P/E – low	—	6	6	5	8	11	—	—	11	—	12
Dividends per share ($)	(6.7%)	3.00	3.00	3.00	3.00	3.00	3.00	3.00	2.65	1.60	1.60
Book value per share ($)	(1.8%)	29.96	31.60	33.27	32.85	32.68	29.97	26.98	26.76	25.40	25.42
Employees	(0.1%)	18,634	18,429	17,898	17,867	17,649	18,087	19,551	19870	19,265	18,460

1994 Year-end:
Debt ratio: 59.6%
Return on equity: 6.5%
Cash (mil.): $126
Current ratio: 0.91
Long term debt (mil.): $7,453
No. of shares (mil.): 214
Dividends
 Yield: 6.7%
 Payout: 96.4%
Market value (mil.): $5,144

**Stock Price History
High/Low 1985–94**

Note: Figures for 1985–93 are for Commonwealth Edison.

UNION CARBIDE CORPORATION

OVERVIEW

Like the gas cloud that once lingered over Bhopal, India, Union Carbide's financial woes have dissipated. The world's #1 producer of ethylene oxide and ethylene glycol (used to make antifreeze and polyester fibers), Union Carbide is also one of the largest manufacturers of polyethylene, the most widely used plastic in the world, and is a maker of solvents, coatings, latex, resins, emulsions, and plasticizers. The company is emerging profitably from a troubled decade in which it was buffeted by the Bhopal disaster and an abortive takeover by Samuel Heyman's GAF Corp.

In the 1980s, as the company was reeling under heavy debt, CEO Robert Kennedy (1986–1995) took the ax to the organization,

slashing nearly 90% of the work force and selling a number of businesses, including its Eveready battery, Praxair industrial gases, and consumer products units.

The company is positioning itself to make major inroads into the Asian plastics market with the building of a $1.5 billion petrochemical complex in Kuwait with the Kuwaiti government. In close proximity to the Asian markets, the plant, the firm claims, which will have access to the low-cost oil needed to compete against Saudi Arabian petrochemical firms, will produce the world's cheapest plastic when it comes onstream in 1997.

Kennedy stepped down as CEO in 1995, and president and COO William Joyce took over.

WHEN

Union Carbide Corporation traces its origins back to 2 chemical companies: National Carbon Company (1886), which manufactured carbons for street lights and began the Eveready trademark, and Union Carbide (1898), which manufactured calcium carbide. In 1917 the 2 companies — along with Linde Air Products (oxygen), Prest-O-Lite (calcium carbide), and Electro Metallurgical (metals) — joined to form Union Carbide & Carbon Corporation (UCC).

In 1919 the company began forming subsidiaries in Canada and in 1925 expanded overseas with the purchase of a Norwegian hydroelectric power plant. UCC expanded into chemical manufacturing and in 1920 established its own chemicals division, which developed ethylene glycol (antifreeze), eventually marketed as Prestone. The company bought vanadium interests in Colorado from U.S. Vanadium in 1926. UCC continued to grow with further purchases, including Acheson Graphite (1928) and Bakelite (an early developer of plastics, 1939). In the 1940s the company entered the atomic field and ran the US government's nuclear laboratories in Oak Ridge, Tennessee, and in Paducah, Kentucky, until 1984.

UCC bought Visking (food casings) in 1956. In 1957 the company changed its name to Union Carbide Corporation and in the early 1960s introduced Glad plastic household products (sold in 1985).

In 1975 the company built a pesticide plant in Bhopal, India, and kept 51% ownership (giving 49% to Indian companies). In 1984 a tank at the plant leaked 5 tons of poisonous methyl isocyanate gas, killing more than 3,000

people and permanently injuring 50,000 — the world's worst recorded industrial accident. Resulting legal action against Union Carbide led to a $470 million settlement in India's Supreme Court in 1989.

In 1985 GAF (chemicals and roofing materials) tried to take over Union Carbide; in response the company went into debt by $3 billion, which it used to buy back 55% of its stock to defeat the attempt. In 1986 Union Carbide sold its battery division (including Eveready) to Ralston Purina, its agricultural products business to Rhône-Poulenc, and its home and auto products business to First Brands in order to concentrate on its 3 core businesses: chemicals and plastics, industrial gases, and carbon products.

In 1992 the company spun off its industrial gases unit, Praxair, to shareholders. That same year, in legal proceedings related to the Bhopal case, a court in India seized the assets of Union Carbide's Indian operations. In 1993 an Indian court ordered 8 employees of the firm's Indian subsidiary, plus its Hong Kong subsidiary, the parent company, and former chairman Warren Anderson, to stand trial for "culpable homicide." With the case still pending, the firm sold its Indian subsidiary in 1994 for $92 million.

In 1994 Union Carbide announced plans to build a rubber manufacturing plant in Seadrift, Texas. The plant (estimated to cost $94 million) will have an annual capacity of 200 million pounds of ethylene-propylene rubber. In 1995 Union Carbide set up a joint venture with Elf Aquitaine (in Europe) to produce specialty polyethylene resins and products for the cable and wire, pipe, and other industries.

NYSE symbol: UK
Fiscal year ends: December 31

WHO

Chairman: Robert D. Kennedy, age 62, $1,715,000 pay
President and CEO: William H. Joyce, age 59,
$910,833 pay (prior to promotion)
VP, General Counsel, and Secretary: Joseph E.
Geoghan, age 57, $615,000 pay
VP Corporate Ventures & Purchasing: Joseph C.
Soviero, age 56, $503,333 pay
VP; General Manager - UNIPOL: Roger B. Staub, age 60,
$470,000 pay
VP, Controller, and Principal Accounting Officer: John
K. Wulff, age 46, $444,167 pay
VP; General Manager, Solvents and Intermediates:
James F. Flynn, age 52
VP; General Manager, Ethylene Oxide/Glycol: Lee P.
McMaster, age 52
VP and Principal Financial Officer: Gilbert E. Playford,
age 47
VP Human Resources: Malcolm A. Kessinger, age 51
Auditors: KPMG Peat Marwick LLP

WHERE

HQ: 39 Old Ridgebury Rd., Danbury, CT 06817
Phone: 203-794-2000
Fax: 203-794-4336

Union Carbide operates in 14 countries.

	1994 Sales		1994 Operating Income	
	$ mil.	% of total	$ mil.	% of total
US	3,535	73	433	88
Europe	474	10	12	2
Latin America	218	4	16	3
Canada	136	3	14	3
Far East & other	502	10	17	13
Adjustments	—	—	59	—
Total	**4,865**	**100**	**551**	**100**

WHAT

	1994 Sales	
	$ mil.	% of total
Polyolefins	1,562	32
Solvents, intermediates & emulsion systems	1,344	27
Olefins, ethylene oxide, glycol & derivatives	1,253	26
Specialty polymers & prods.	706	15
Total	**4,865**	**100**

Selected Products

Polyolefins
Polyethylenes
Recycled plastics
(Curbside Blend)
Resins
Wire insulation,
semiconducting, and
jacketing compounds

**Solvents, Intermediates,
and Emulsion Systems**
Acids
Acrylics
Alcohols
Esters
Glycol ethers
Latex products (UCAR)

**Olefins, Ethylene Oxide,
Glycol, and Derivatives**
Aircraft and runway de-icing
fluids (UCAR)
Fluids and lubricants (UCON)
Specialty surfactants
(TERGITOL, TRITON)

**Specialty Polymers and
Products**
Hydroxyethyl cellulose
(CELLOSIZE)
Plasticizers (FLEXOL)
Polyester modifiers
(NEULON)
Water-soluble resins
(POLYOX)

KEY COMPETITORS

Akzo Nobel
Atlantic
 Richfield
BASF
Bayer
British
 Petroleum
Chevron
Dow Chemical
DuPont

Eastman Chemical
Exxon
Formosa Plastics
Hanson
Hercules
Hoechst
Huntsman Chemical
Imperial Chemical
Lyondell
 Petrochemical

Mitsubishi
Mobil
Monsanto
Occidental
Phillips
 Petroleum
Rhône-Poulenc
Royal Dutch/
 Shell
Texaco

HOW MUCH

	9-Year Growth	1985	1986	1987	1988	1989	1990	1991	1992	1993	1994
Sales ($ mil.)	(6.6%)	9,003	6,244	6,914	8,324	8,744	5,238	4,877	4,872	4,640	4,865
Net income ($ mil.)	—	(599)	135	232	662	573	308	(9)	186	165	389
Income as % of sales	—	—	2.2%	3.4%	8.0%	6.6%	5.9%	—	3.8%	3.6%	8.0%
Earnings per share ($)	—	(2.86)	1.30	1.76	4.66	3.92	2.13	(0.22)	1.27	1.00	2.27
Stock price – high ($)	—	10.28	13.78	13.52	11.80	13.83	10.35	10.09	17.13	23.13	35.88
Stock price – low ($)	—	4.99	7.80	6.45	7.07	9.46	5.88	6.40	8.37	16.00	21.50
Stock price – close ($)	12.9%	9.82	9.36	9.05	10.66	9.67	6.81	8.42	16.63	22.38	29.38
P/E – high	—	—	11	8	3	4	5	—	14	23	16
P/E – low	—	—	6	4	2	2	3	—	7	16	10
Dividends per share ($)	(4.5%)	1.13	1.50	1.50	1.15	1.00	1.00	1.00	0.88	0.75	0.75
Book value per share ($)	(6.9%)	19.82	7.87	9.35	13.34	16.83	16.06	17.55	9.32	9.49	10.45
Employees	(20.2%)	91,459	50,292	43,119	43,992	45,987	37,756	16,705	15,075	13,051	12,004

1994 Year-end:
Debt ratio: 38.5%
Return on equity: 26.5%
Cash (mil.): $109
Current ratio: 1.26
Long-term debt (mil.): $899
No. of shares (mil.): 144
Dividends
 Yield: 2.6%
 Payout: 33.0%
Market value (mil.): $4,243

**Stock Price History
High/Low 1985–94**

UNION PACIFIC CORPORATION

OVERVIEW

Union Pacific (UP) is a diversified transportation corporation that has a "seamless" network for moving goods across North America by various transportation modes. The company operates the nation's youngest locomotive fleet across a nearly 23,600-mile network spanning the West, Midwest, and Gulf Coast regions. In August 1995 UP agreed to acquire the Southern Pacific Rail Corp. for $3.9 billion in cash and stock. If approved, the purchase will create the biggest US railroad, with 35,000 miles of track in 25 states.

Bethlehem, Pennsylvania–based UP has a growing intermodal (truck-to-train) business and strong ties to Mexico's national railway. In addition to railroads the company is invested in other transportation efforts and related industries. Overnite Transportation, UP's trucking subsidiary, focuses on the fast-growing and lucrative less-than-truckload (LTL) business in the US.

UP's oil and gas subsidiary (Union Pacific Resources) was the most active US oil driller in 1994. The company is drilling gas in Wyoming, where it has a pipeline serving the giant Southern California market. Union Pacific Technologies provides computer technology to UP and other shippers. The company sold its hazardous waste management company, USPCI, in 1994.

In early 1995 UP withdrew a hostile bid for Santa Fe Pacific.

WHEN

In 1862 Congress chartered the Union Pacific Railroad to build part of the first transcontinental railway. The driving of the Golden Spike at Promontory, Utah, in 1869 marked the linking of the East and West Coasts as the UP's rails met those of the Central Pacific (which had been built east from Sacramento).

In 1872 the *New York Sun* revealed UP's role in the Credit Mobilier scandal. The chief promoters had taken excess profits during the railroad's construction. UP continued to expand, but the lingering effects of the scandal, further mismanagement, and deepening debt forced it into bankruptcy in 1893.

A syndicate headed by E. H. Harriman bought UP in 1897. Improvements tripled UP's earnings within 3 years. After reacquiring Oregon branches lost in the bankruptcy, UP gained control of the Southern Pacific (1901) and the Chicago & Alton (1904). The Supreme Court ordered UP to sell its Southern Pacific holdings in 1913 on antitrust grounds.

In the 1930s UP diversified into trucking. It continued to expand its rail holdings (buying Spokane International Railway in 1958) and moved into energy in 1970 when it bought Champlin Petroleum and Pontiac Refining. In 1982 UP purchased the 11,547-mile Missouri Pacific railroad. Other acquisitions included Overnite Transportation (1986) and USPCI (1988, sold in 1994). To remain competitive in the 1980s, UP cut about 40% of its work force, improved service, and bought equipment.

When Drew Lewis (transportation secretary under President Reagan) became CEO in 1987, UP began focusing on core businesses. UP joined certain Chicago and North Western (CNW) managers to form Blackstone Capital Partners, a limited partnership that bought CNW for $1.6 billion in 1989.

Chicago's first mayor, W. B. Ogden, had founded the Galena & Chicago Union Railroad company in 1836. In 1864 it consolidated with Chicago & North Western Railway. By 1925 the North Western (as it was then known) had tracks throughout the Midwest.

Ben Heineman became company president in 1956 and became famous for making the railroad's Chicago commuter trains run on time. It acquired the Minneapolis & St. Louis (1960) and the Chicago Great Western (1968).

Heineman put the railroad up for sale in 1969 because of financial and labor problems. A group of employees bought CNW in 1972, making it the first employee-owned major US railroad. The railroad created a new holding company, CNW Corporation, in 1985.

In 1991 UP planned to reduce its crews from 3 to 2 on 90% of its rail lines by the following year. An agreement by CNW's railroad union to cut crews by that much resulted in CNW paying over $36 million in severance pay. To fund this and other debts, CNW went public again in 1992. UP's CNW investment assured continued access to Chicago rail yards. Also in 1992, UP entered an intermodal venture with Schneider National truck lines.

In 1994 UP purchased the oil and gas assets of Cyprus Amax Minerals for $725 million. In early 1995, following its unsuccessful bid for Santa Fe Pacific, UP bought the rest of CNW for $1.2 billion. This acquisition gives UP ownership of its main freight link to the eastern part of the US. The purchase also brings the company into the passenger transportation business.

NYSE symbol: UNP
Fiscal year ends: December 31

WHO

Chairman and CEO: Drew Lewis, age 63, $2,380,000 pay
President; Chairman and CEO, Union Pacific Railroad: Richard K. Davidson, age 53, $1,337,450 pay
President and CEO, Union Pacific Resources: Jack L. Messman, age 55, $1,145,000 pay
President and COO, Overnite Transportation: James D. Douglas, age 45
President and CEO, Union Pacific Technologies: L. Merill Bryan Jr.
President and CEO, Skyway Freight Systems: Kip Hawley
EVP Finance: L. White Matthews III, age 49, $960,000 pay
SVP and General Counsel: Carl W. von Bernuth, age 51, $767,500 pay
SVP Human Resources: Ursula F. Fairbairn, age 52
VP and Controller: Charles E. Billingsley, age 61
VP Corporate Development: John E. Dowling, age 47
VP Taxes: John B. Gremillion Jr., age 48
VP External Relations: Mary E. McAuliffe, age 49
VP Corporate Relations: Gary F. Schuster, age 53
VP and Treasurer: Gary M. Stuart, age 54
VP and Corporate Secretary: Judy L. Swantak, age 39
Auditors: Deloitte & Touche LLP

WHERE

HQ: Martin Tower, Eighth and Eaton Aves., Bethlehem, PA 18018
Phone: 610-861-3200
Fax: 610-861-3111

UP has railroads serving the western 2/3 of the US; trucking operations in all 50 states and in Montreal and Toronto; and oil, gas, and mining operations primarily in Canada, the Gulf of Mexico, and the US.

WHAT

	1994 Sales		1994 Operating Income	
	$ mil.	% of total	$ mil.	% of total
Railroad	5,318	68	1,173	74
Natural resources	1,306	17	351	22
Trucking	1,037	13	67	4
Other	137	2	4	—
Total	**7,798**	**100**	**1,595**	**100**

Major Subsidiaries and Affiliates
Missouri Pacific Railroad Co.
Overnite Transportation Co. (trucking)
Skyway Freight Systems, Inc.
Union Pacific Minerals, Inc.
   Black Butte Coal Co. (50%, coal-mining joint venture)
   Rhône-Poulenc of Wyoming
      (49%, trona-mining and soda ash–production joint venture with Rhône-Poulenc)
Union Pacific Railroad Co.
Union Pacific Resources Co. (oil and natural gas)
Union Pacific Technologies (technological support)

KEY COMPETITORS

American Freightways	Chevron	Leaseway Transportation
American President	Coastal	Mobil
Amoco	Conrail	Norfolk Southern
Arkansas Best	Consolidated Freightways	Occidental
Ashland Coal	CSX	Phillips Petroleum
Atlantic Richfield	Cyprus Amax	Roadway
Bechtel	Exxon	Sun Company
Broken Hill	Illinois Central	Tenneco
Burlington Northern	J.B. Hunt	Texaco
Canadian Pacific	Kansas City Southern	TNT Freightways
Carolina Freight	Kerr-McGee	Unocal
	Koch	Yellow Corp.

HOW MUCH

	9-Year Growth	1985	1986	1987	1988	1989	1990	1991	1992	1993	1994
Sales ($ mil.)	(0.3%)	7,985	6,719	6,099	6,214	6,639	7,146	7,227	7,452	7,561	7,798
Net income ($ mil.)	1.0%	501	(460)	583	644	595	618	64	728	705	546
Income as % of sales	—	6.3%	—	9.6%	10.4%	9.0%	8.6%	0.9%	9.8%	9.3%	7.0%
Earnings per share ($)	2.7%	2.09	(2.29)	2.60	2.83	2.81	3.09	0.31	3.57	3.43	2.66
Stock price – high ($)	—	27.63	33.69	43.31	35.06	40.50	39.88	51.75	60.50	67.00	67.13
Stock price – low ($)	—	19.88	23.25	22.56	25.50	31.63	30.69	32.63	44.38	56.88	43.75
Stock price – close ($)	6.0%	26.94	31.13	27.00	32.13	38.31	35.31	51.75	58.50	62.63	45.38
P/E – high	—	13	—	17	12	14	13	167	17	20	25
P/E – low	—	10	—	9	9	11	10	105	12	17	16
Dividends per share ($)	6.8%	0.90	0.90	1.00	1.03	1.10	1.16	1.28	1.39	1.51	1.63
Book value per share ($)	2.6%	19.83	16.23	15.29	19.84	19.50	21.36	20.52	22.75	23.81	24.92
Employees	0.6%	44,419	39,476	46,559	47,259	48,126	48,323	47,090	46,039	47,126	46,900

1994 Year-end:
Debt ratio: 47.1%
Return on equity: 10.9%
Cash (mil.): $121
Current ratio: 0.73
Long-term debt (mil.): $4,090
No. of shares (mil.): 206
Dividends
   Yield: 3.6%
   Payout: 61.3%
Market value (mil.): $9,345

Stock Price History
High/Low 1985–94

UNISYS CORPORATION

OVERVIEW

Unisys is hoping OPUS will be music to its descending bottom line. The veteran defense technology contractor unveiled its new OPUS megacomputer (the name is an acronym for Open Parallel Unisys Servers) in mid-1995. Codeveloped with Intel and priced beginning around $700,000, OPUS uses parallel processing technology to speed computations.

Unisys, one of the world's largest computer companies, provides computer systems, software, and services to commercial and government clients. As the computer market has shifted from mainframes to client/server computing, Unisys has turned to manufacturing and servicing the smaller systems. While the resurgence in mainframe sales bypassed

Unisys, OPUS signals its renewed faith in large systems.

In 1995 Unisys sold its defense unit to Loral Corp. for $862 million in cash that will be used to boost its commercial business. The company also formed USoft, a subsidiary funded with $50 million to acquire small companies in an attempt to bolster Unisys's presence in the client/server software market. USoft's first purchase was TopSystems, a Dutch business analysis software developer.

Unisys isn't abandoning government work. In 1995 it won contracts worth $119 million to provide data storage for the IRS, voice mail for a Colombian state, and an oil spill management system for Texas A&M University.

WHEN

Unisys was formed in 1986 when struggling mainframe computer giant Burroughs swallowed fellow mainframe manufacturer Sperry Corporation. Burroughs traces its roots back to American Arithmometer (St. Louis, 1886), later Burroughs Adding Machine (Detroit, 1905) and Burroughs Corporation (1953). Burroughs entered data processing by purchasing Electrodata (1956) and many others, including Memorex (1982).

Sperry was the product of a 1955 merger of Sperry Gyroscope (founded in 1910 by Elmer Sperry) and Remington Rand, an old-line typewriter manufacturer and maker of the first commercially viable computer, the UNIVAC. Sperry bought RCA's faltering computer unit in 1971.

In 1986 Burroughs president Michael Blumenthal (a treasury secretary under President Jimmy Carter) sought to achieve efficiency in parts and development by merging Burroughs's small database managers with Sperry's defense-related number crunchers. The new company was called Unisys, a condensation of "United Information Systems."

As president of Unisys, Blumenthal quickly disposed of $1.8 billion in assets (Sperry Aerospace and Marine divisions, Memorex), closed plants, and cut the combined work force of 120,000 by 24,000. He also promised continued support for Sperry's flagship 1100 line of mainframes and nurtured Burroughs's prized A series of computers. The initial results were positive, with 1986's $43 million loss followed by 1987's $578 million profit.

Amidst an industry trend toward stronger, smaller systems, Unisys in 1988 equipped its U line of servers with the open UNIX operating

system, sponsored 4th-generation languages (4GLs) to connect its new 2200 and A mainframe series, and moved to networked smaller systems, spending $650 million to buy Timeplex (voice/data networks) and Convergent (UNIX-based workstations).

The Justice Department in 1988 launched an investigation of unethical and illegal defense procurement practices committed by Sperry prior to its merger with Burroughs. Unisys settled the charges in 1991 by agreeing to pay $54 million over 5 years, forgo $46 million in fees and profits, and make contingency payments of up to $90 million through 1997, based on asset sales and net income.

Plummeting mainframe demand in 1989 and 1990 caught Unisys in transition, leading to heavy losses over the next few years. Blumenthal left Unisys in 1990. Continuing heavy losses prompted a new round of layoffs in 1991 and further consolidation. The company's product line was pared, as Unisys closed 7 of its 15 plants and shed noncore assets.

Unisys and Intel entered a joint venture in 1993 to develop a parallel processing computer using Intel's Pentium chip. The following year the company was awarded a $127 million contract by the Savings Bank of the Russian Federation to provide an information management system.

In 1995 Unisys said it would back off from its demand that developers of software released prior to 1995 honor an old patent for code used in the graphics interchange format (GIF). The format is commonly used to view on-line graphics. That same year Unisys cut another 4,000 jobs from the payrolls.

NYSE symbol: UIS
Fiscal year ends: December 31

WHO

Chairman and CEO: James A. Unruh, age 53, $1,213,336 pay
EVP; President, Government Systems Group: Albert F. Zettlemoyer, age 60, $440,004 pay
EVP; President, Information Services and Systems Group: Stephen A. Carns, age 49
EVP; President, Computer Systems Group: Alan G. Lutz, age 49
SVP; President, Europe/Africa Division: Malcolm D. Coster, age 50, $472,109 pay
SVP; President, United States/Canada Division: Edward A. Blechschmidt, age 42
SVP and CFO: George T. Robson, age 47, $465,002 pay
SVP, General Counsel, and Secretary: Harold S. Barron, age 58
VP; President, Client/Server Systems: Frank G. Brandenberg, age 48
VP; President, Communications Line of Business: Patricia L. Higgins, age 45
VP and Chief Information Officer: William G. Rowan
VP Human Resources: Thomas E. McKinnon, age 50
Auditors: Ernst & Young LLP

WHERE

HQ: PO Box 500, Blue Bell, PA 19424-0001
Phone: 215-986-4011
Fax: 215-986-6850

Unisys has over 60,000 clients in 100 countries

	1994 Sales		1994 Operating Income	
	$ mil.	% of total	$ mil.	% of total
US	3,635	49	130	23
Europe	1,940	26	(82)	—
Americas/Pacific	1,825	25	434	77
Adjustments	—	—	(176)	—
Total	**7,400**	**100**	**306**	**100**

WHAT

	1994 Sales	
	$ mil.	% of total
Products	4,078	55
Services	1,980	27
Equipment maintenance	1,342	18
Total	**7,400**	**100**

Selected Products and Services

Departmental Servers and Desktop Systems
CTOS networked servers and workstations
OPUS parallel processing computer
PW^2 networked personal computers
U 6000 UNIX network and document imaging servers

Enterprise Systems and Servers
2200 series and A series mainframes
2200/500, A11, and A7 servers
Peripherals

Equipment Maintenance
A la Carte (outside US)
Surety 2000

Information Services and Systems Integration
Application development
Desktop services
Education
Information planning
Outsourcing services
Systems integration

Software
Applications development
Database management
Networking
Systems management
Transaction processing

KEY COMPETITORS

Amdahl	Gupta	Silicon
Apple	Hewlett-Packard	Graphics
Arthur Andersen	Hitachi	Sony
AT&T	IBM	Storage
Computer	Machines Bull	Technology
Associates	Microsoft	Stratus
Data General	NEC	Computer
DEC	Oracle	Sun
Dun &	Perot Systems	Microsystems
Bradstreet	Sequent	Tandem
EDS	Siemens	Wang
Fujitsu		

HOW MUCH

	9-Year Growth	1985	1986	1987	1988	1989	1990	1991	1992	1993	1994
Sales ($ mil.)	4.4%	5,038	7,432	9,713	9,902	10,097	10,111	8,696	8,422	7,743	7,400
Net income ($ mil.)	—	248	(43)	578	681	(639)	(437)	(1,393)	296	214	(20)
Income as % of sales	—	4.9%	—	6.0%	6.9%	—	—	—	3.5%	2.8%	—
Earnings per share ($)	—	1.82	(0.54)	2.93	3.27	(4.71)	(3.45)	(9.37)	1.04	1.37	(0.11)
Stock price – high ($)	—	22.66	28.81	48.38	39.00	30.50	17.13	6.88	11.75	13.88	16.50
Stock price – low ($)	—	17.31	19.16	24.00	25.00	12.38	1.75	2.13	4.13	9.88	8.25
Stock price – close ($)	(9.5%)	21.09	26.63	33.63	28.13	14.75	2.50	4.13	10.13	12.63	8.63
P/E – high	—	13	—	17	12	—	—	—	11	10	—
P/E – low	—	10	—	8	8	—	—	—	4	7	—
Dividends per share ($)	(100.0%)	0.87	0.87	0.89	0.96	1.00	0.75	0.00	0.00	0.00	0.00
Book value per share ($)	(11.6%)	18.22	17.43	20.90	22.23	15.49	11.79	2.69	4.12	6.57	6.02
Employees	(2.9%)	60,500	98,300	92,500	93,000	82,300	75,300	60,300	54,300	49,000	46,300

1994 Year-end:
Debt ratio: 42.7%
Return on equity: —
Cash (mil.): $885
Current ratio: 1.25
Long-term debt (mil.): $1,864
No. of shares (mil.): 172
Dividends
  Yield: —
  Payout: —
Market value (mil.): $1,482

Stock Price History High/Low 1985–94

UNITED HEALTHCARE CORPORATION

OVERVIEW

CEO and butterfly aficionado William McGuire sure has a way with a net — just watch the way he scoops up HMOs and adds them to his collection. As head of United HealthCare (UHC), he has overseen the rapid growth of the Minnetonka, Minnesota–based company into one of the US's largest, most geographically diverse providers of managed care. Offering services from Alaska to Puerto Rico, UHC owns or manages more than 20 HMOs serving more than 3 million members. Most UHC-owned HMOs are #1 or #2 in their markets.

UHC also offers a variety of specialized services, such as geriatric care programs, managed mental health and substance abuse services, and workers' compensation and casualty services. The company is known for low premiums and rapid enrollment growth in a fiercely competitive industry. UHC topped *FORTUNE*'s list of the most admired health care companies in 1995.

The company's recent run of acquisitions has been impressive. In 1995 UHC completed purchases of HMOs GenCare (#1 in St. Louis) and Group Sales and Service of Puerto Rico and announced an agreement to buy MetraHealth (a joint venture between MetLife and Travelers) for $2.4 billion.

UHC's Center for Health Care Policy and Evaluation, which researches industry issues, received a DOD contract in 1995 to help reorganize the military's managed care.

WHEN

Dr. Paul Ellwood became known as "Father of the HMO" for his role as an early champion of the health care concept. In the 1950s as a medical school neurology student, Ellwood first got the idea to make health care more affordable by applying business principles to medicine and minimizing costs. In 1970, although the HMO was still considered a radical approach to health care reform, Ellwood got Congress and the Nixon administration to approve his HMO model; the next year he hired Richard Burke to put the model into action. In 1974 Burke established United HealthCare to manage the nonprofit Physicians Health Plan of Minnesota (PHP). UHC incorporated in 1977.

UHC bought HMOs and began managing others, operating 11 HMOs in 10 states by 1984, the year it went public. UHC's expansion continued with the purchases of Share Development Corp. (1985) and Peak Health Care (1986), HMOs with members in more than one state. Unfortunately, acquisitions and startups began to eat away at UHC's financial health. Meanwhile Burke, CEO of both UHC and PHP, was accused by PHP doctors of having a conflict of interest after a change in the HMO's Medicare policy threatened to cut off patients from some member hospitals. He resigned as head of both organizations in 1987 and was replaced as CEO of UHC by Kennett Simmons, formerly president of Peak.

That year investment firm Warburg, Pincus bought 39.5% of UHC, providing it with much-needed cash. UHC lost nearly $16 million in 1987, largely from a restructuring that axed UHC's Phoenix HMO as well as startups in 6 other markets. UHC sold several other businesses in 1988, including its share of Peak Health Care. The divestitures soon paid off, taking UHC out of the red and putting it back in the pink.

In the late 1980s the company adopted a new strategy of holding down costs by acquiring specialty companies that provided expensive health care services. One key subsidiary was its Diversified Pharmaceutical Services drug management unit. UHC also bought up other HMOs, including PrimeCare Health Plan (Wisconsin, 1990), Ocean State Physicians Health Plan (New England, 1991), and Physicians Health Plan of Ohio (1992). Another approach employed by UHC was to offer supplementary services to clients of other HMOs. UHC was the biggest independent provider of managed care by the end of 1990.

McGuire, another former Peak president, became UHC's CEO in 1991. That year, PHP and Share merged into Medica, and Warburg, Pincus distributed its UHC shares to several pension funds and financial institutions. In 1993 the company bought Western Ohio HealthCare Corporation (now part of United HealthCare of Ohio) and HMO America (Chicago's #2 HMO, now part of United HealthCare of Illinois). UHC picked up Complete Health Services and Ramsay-HMO (together adding 449,000 members in the South) in 1994. Also that year UHC sold its Diversified Pharmaceutical Services subsidiary to SmithKline Beecham for $2.3 billion, providing cash for further HMO acquisitions.

In 1995 McGuire announced that UHC planned to expand its Medicaid coverage into several states now enrolling Medicaid-eligible patients in HMOs.

NYSE symbol: UNH
Fiscal year ends: December 31

WHO

Chairman, President, and CEO: William W. McGuire,
age 46, $2,686,731 pay
EVP Health Plan Operations: Jeannine M. Rivet, age 46,
$345,082 pay
EVP: Marshall V. Rozzi
SVP Specialty Operations: Travers H. Wills, age 51,
$1,244,971 pay
SVP International Development: Brian S. Gould, age 47,
$357,212 pay
SVP Sales, Marketing, and Development: William W.
Pogue, age 48, $306,278 pay
**President, Center for Health Care Policy and
Evaluation:** Sheila T. Leatherman, age 43
VP, Treasurer, and CFO: David P. Koppe, age 38
**VP Human Resources and Administrative Support
Services:** Robert J. Backes
General Counsel and Secretary: Kevin H. Roché, age 44
Auditors: Arthur Andersen & Co, SC

WHERE

HQ: 300 Opus Center, 9900 Bren Rd. East, Minnetonka,
MN 55343
Phone: 612-936-1300
Fax: 612-935-1471

WHAT

	1994 Sales		1994 Operating Income	
	$ mil.	% of total	$ mil.	% of total
Owned health plans	3,359	88	352	70
Managed plans & specialty care	456	12	72	14
Adjustments	(46)	—	82	16
Total	**3,769**	**100**	**506**	**100**

Owned Health Plans
CAC-Ramsay Health Plans, Inc. (Miami)
Community Health Network of Louisiana, Inc. (Baton
  Rouge)
Complete Health, Inc. (Birmingham, AL)
Complete Health of Arkansas, Inc. (Little Rock)
Complete Health of Georgia, Inc. (Atlanta)
Complete Health of Mississippi, Inc. (Jackson)
Complete Health of Tennessee, Inc. (Chattanooga)
GenCare Health Systems, Inc. (St. Louis)
Group Sales and Service of Puerto Rico, Inc. (San Juan)
Physicians Health Plan of Greater St. Louis, Inc.
PrimeCare Health Plan, Inc. (Milwaukee)
United Health Plans New England, Inc. (Warwick, RI)
United HealthCare of Georgia, Inc. (Atlanta)
United HealthCare of Illinois (Chicago)
United HealthCare of Ohio, Inc. (Columbus and Dayton)
United HealthCare of the Midlands, Inc. (Omaha)
United HealthCare of Utah (Salt Lake City)

Minority-Owned or -Managed Health Plans
Medica (Minneapolis)
Physicians Health Plan of North Carolina (Greensboro)
Physicians Health Plan of Mid Michigan (Lansing)
Physicians Health Plan of Northern Indiana (Ft. Wayne)
Physicians Health Plan of South Carolina (Columbia)
Physicians Health Plan of South Michigan (Jackson)
Physicians Health Plan of Southwestern Michigan
  (Kalamazoo)
Physicians Health Plan of Western Michigan (Muskegon)
Physicians Plus Insurance Co. (Madison, WI)

KEY COMPETITORS

Aetna	PacifiCare
AFLAC	Prudential
Blue Cross	State Farm
CIGNA	U.S. Healthcare
FHP Intl.	Value Health
HealthCare Compare	WellPoint Health
Humana	Networks
Kaiser Foundation	
Health Plan	

HOW MUCH

	Annual Growth	1985	1986	1987	1988	1989	1990	1991	1992	1993	1994
Sales ($ mil.)	49.5%	101	216	440	440	412	605	847	1,442	2,527	3,769
Net income ($ mil.)	110.0%	2	3	(16)	(37)	14	34	75	114	195	1,665
Income as % of sales	—	2.1%	1.2%	—	—	3.3%	5.6%	8.8%	7.9%	7.7%	44.2%
Earnings per share ($)	83.6%	0.04	0.04	(0.25)	(0.57)	0.15	0.30	0.61	0.82	1.24	9.50
Stock price – high ($)	—	2.72	4.00	2.25	1.34	5.16	6.00	19.56	29.19	39.38	55.38
Stock price – low ($)	—	1.94	1.88	0.66	0.88	1.03	2.00	5.00	17.13	20.00	37.25
Stock price – close ($)	37.5%	2.56	2.09	0.91	1.13	1.03	5.81	18.63	28.44	38.00	45.13
P/E – high	—	68	100	—	—	34	20	32	36	32	6
P/E – low	—	48	47	—	—	7	7	8	21	16	4
Dividends per share ($)	—	0.00	0.00	0.00	0.00	0.00	0.01	0.01	0.01	0.02	0.03
Book value per share ($)	54.6%	0.32	0.89	0.65	0.24	0.78	1.16	2.53	4.73	6.22	16.17
Employees	20.9%	1700	2700	2900	2500	2437	2900	3,200	5,431	6,502	9,400

1994 Year-end:
Debt ratio: 0.9%
Return on equity: 88.7%
Cash (mil.): $1,654
Current ratio: 2.87
Long-term debt (mil.): $24
No. of shares (mil.): 173
Dividends
  Yield: 0.1%
  Payout: 0.3%
Market value (mil.): $7,799

Stock Price History
High/Low 1985–94

UNITED PARCEL SERVICE

OVERVIEW

Atlanta-based UPS is the world's #1 package delivery company and the 3rd largest private company in the US. But increased competition from rivals such as Federal Express and Roadway Package System has forced the company to add a few modern touches to attract customers. Known for its chocolate-colored delivery trucks, UPS is trying to accommodate the growing demand for logistics services. "Big Brown" has strengthened its logistics subsidiary, UPS Worldwide Logistics, by incorporating 4 other previously separate subsidiaries into it — UPS Truck Leasing, RoadNet, Inventory Express, and MarTrac. The company has also launched same-day and next-flight-out delivery services through the acquisition of

the same-day shipper SonicAir. The new same-day delivery prices start from $160 a package (depending on package weight). Ironically, this new delivery service was matched on the same day by competitor FedEx.

Despite continual losses in overseas services, UPS continues to look for new foreign opportunities and ways to improve current services. It has expanded its air service to 200 countries (up from 41 countries in 1988).

UPS stock is owned primarily by its employees and their families and heirs. The company is noted for its philanthropy. The UPS Foundation supported efforts to stock soup kitchens and has collected relief supplies for Bosnian refugee schoolchildren.

WHEN

Seattle teenagers Jim Casey and Claude Ryan started American Messenger Company, a telephone message service, in 1907. They were soon making small-parcel deliveries for local department stores and in 1913 changed the company's name to Merchants Parcel Delivery. By 1915 the company had a staff of 20 messengers, and 2 important events had already occurred — Casey, who led the company for the next 47 years, had established a policy of manager ownership, and Charlie Soderstrom (one of the company's 4 stockholders) had chosen the brown paint still used on the company's delivery vehicles.

Service expanded outside Seattle in 1919 when Merchants Parcel bought Oakland-based Motor Parcel Delivery. Renamed United Parcel Service, the company by 1930 served residents in New York City (its headquarters from 1930 to 1975); Newark, New Jersey; and Greenwich, Connecticut.

UPS expanded small-package delivery to include addresses within a 150-mile radius of certain metropolitan areas, starting with Los Angeles in 1952. Expanding westward from the East Coast and eastward from the West, it served all the US mainland by 1975.

The company had already gained heightened public awareness when in 1972 the US Postal Service, in an effort to improve its own public image, cited UPS as a competitor. Up to this time UPS had developed in relative obscurity, with most of its stock owned by managers, their families, heirs, or estates.

After moving its headquarters to Greenwich in 1975, UPS expanded to Europe in 1976 with service to West Germany and in the late 1970s established a base at Standiford Airfield in

Louisville, Kentucky, to start an air express delivery service. By 1982 UPS Blue Label Air Service (now UPS 2nd Day Air) guaranteed delivery anywhere on the mainland US and Oahu, Hawaii, within 48 hours. Overnight service (UPS Next Day Air) began in 1982, expanding nationwide and to Puerto Rico by 1985. In the late 1980s, when UPS adopted the slogan "We run the tightest ship in the shipping business" for its first TV advertising campaign, it was already one of America's most profitable transportation companies.

To ensure a market for its services, in 1990 UPS bought a 9.5% stake (since increased to 14.8%) in Mail Boxes Etc., America's leading neighborhood mailing and business service center franchise. Also that year UPS expanded service into Eastern Europe and, with Japan's Yamato Transport, formed a joint venture (UniStar Air Cargo) to gain a foothold in the Japanese market. To cut costs, UPS moved from Connecticut to Atlanta in 1991.

To expand its presence in Europe, the company acquired Prost Transports (France) in 1991 and, in 1992, Carryfast (UK), Star Air Parcel (Austria), and Beemsterboer (the Netherlands). In 1993 UPS announced plans to spend $400 million to lower the noise levels of its fleet of 727-100s.

In 1994 Teamsters staged a one-day strike to protest UPS's new per-package weight limit, which was raised from 70 pounds to 150 pounds. UPS claimed the walkout cost it over $50 million. Also in 1994 UPS began offering next-day delivery by 8:30 a.m., with same-day delivery added in 1995. UPS landed a 5-year, $1 billion contract with J. C. Penney in 1995, the biggest pact ever in the delivery industry.

Private company
Fiscal year ends: December 31

WHO

Chairman and CEO: Kent C. Nelson, age 57
EVP and COO: James P. Kelly, age 51
President and CEO, UPS Worldwide Logistics: Dick Bogen
SVP Business Development: John W. Alden
SVP and CFO: Robert J. Clanin, age 51
SVP Engineering: Charles L. Schaffer, age 49
SVP Legal and Public Affairs and Secretary: Joseph Moderow, age 46
SVP Human Resources: John J. Kelley, age 59
SVP and Chief Information Officer: Francis J. Erbrick
SVP Air Operations: Thomas H. Weidemeyer
SVP International Operations: Edward L. Schroeder
SVP US Operations: Calvin E. Tyler Jr.
SVP US Operations: Clinton L. Yard
SVP and COO, UPS Worldwide Logistics: Dan DiMaggio
Auditors: Deloitte & Touche LLP

WHERE

HQ: United Parcel Service of America, Inc.,
55 Glenlake Pkwy., Atlanta, GA 30328
Phone: 404-828-6000
Fax: 404-828-6593

UPS operates in more than 200 countries and territories worldwide. The company owns and operates 135,000 automotive delivery vehicles.

Air Hub Locations

Cologne/Bonn, Germany	Miami, FL
Columbia, SC	Montreal, Quebec
Dallas, TX	Ontario, CA
Hamilton, Ontario	Philadelphia, PA
Hong Kong	Rockford, IL
Louisville, KY	Singapore

	1994 Sales		1994 Operating Income	
	$ mil.	% of total	$ mil.	% of total
US	17,298	88	1,902	—
Other countries	2,278	12	(327)	—
Total	**19,576**	**100**	**1,575**	**—**

WHAT

Air Delivery Services
Early A.M. Service
Next-Flight-Out
UPS 2nd Day Air
UPS Customs & Brokerage
UPS Next Day Air
UPS SonicAir Service (same day)
UPS Worldwide Expedited
UPS Worldwide Express

Ground Delivery Services
3 Day Select
Authorized Return Service
Consignee Billing
UPS GroundTrac
UPS Hundredweight Service

Major Subsidiaries and Affiliates
II Morrow (technological support)
Mail Boxes Etc. (14.8%)
UniStar Air Cargo, Inc.
UPS Properties, Inc.
UPS SonciAir
UPS Telecommunications (cellular network)
UPS Worldwide Logistics, Inc.

KEY COMPETITORS

Air Express
Airborne Freight
American Freightways
American President
AMR
Consolidated Freightways
Continental Airlines
Delta
DHL Worldwide Express
FedEx
Harper Group
Heartland Express
KLM
Lufthansa
Northwest Airlines
Pittston Services
Qantas
Roadway
SAS
Singapore Airlines
Skynet Worldwide Courier
UAL
U.S. Postal Service
USAir Group
Yellow Corp.

HOW MUCH

	Annual Growth	1985	1986	1987	1988	1989	1990	1991	1992	1993	1994
Sales ($ mil.)	10.9%	7,687	8,620	9,682	11,032	12,358	13,606	15,020	16,519	17,782	19,576
Net income ($ mil.)	5.8%	568	669	625	759	693	597	700	765	810	943
Income as % of sales	—	7.4%	7.8%	6.5%	6.9%	5.6%	4.4%	4.7%	4.6%	4.6%	4.8%
Earnings per share ($)	8.8%	—	—	—	—	1.07	0.95	1.14	1.29	1.40	1.63
Dividends per share ($)	2.8%	—	—	—	—	0.48	0.48	0.48	0.50	0.50	0.55
Book value per share ($)	8.5%	—	—	—	—	—	5.77	6.29	6.25	6.80	8.01
Employees	8.6%	152,400	168,200	191,600	219,400	237,700	246,800	256,000	267,000	286,000	320,000

1994 Year-end:
Debt ratio: 19.5%
Return on equity: 22.0%
Cash (mil.): $261
Current ratio: 1.04
Long-term debt (mil.): $1,127
No. of shares (mil.): 580
Total assets (mil.): $11,182

Net Income ($ mil.) 1985–94

UNITED STATES POSTAL SERVICE

OVERVIEW

The United States Postal Service (USPS) processed and delivered more than 177 billion pieces of mail in 1994 — that is about 40% of the world's mail. If the post office were private, it would be one of the US's largest companies. An 11-member board of governors sets policy, and a Postal Rate Commission recommends postage rates. USPS continues its mission, "universal service at a uniform price," aided by its monopoly on first-class mail.

Despite competition from an increasing number of communication services and devices (fax, telephone, overnight services, electronic transfers, video shopping, and tele-

marketing), mail volume increased by almost 3.5% in 1994. To keep up with the Joneses' communication alternatives, USPS is developing systems that will use message encryption to authenticate E-mail. Other services will include time stamps and guaranteed return-receipts. The FAA is test piloting USPS's new electronic systems.

CEO Marvin Runyon, known variously as "Onion Runyon" (he peels until you cry) and "Carvin' Marvin" because of his reputation for cutting costs, continues to eliminate bureaucracy, improve productivity, and focus on customer service.

WHEN

The 2nd oldest agency of the US government (after Indian Affairs), the Post Office was created by the Continental Congress in 1775, with Benjamin Franklin as its first postmaster general. Since then, the postal system has played a vital role in the development of transportation in the US.

When the Post Office first began operation, mail service consisted of men riding on horses on muddy roads delivering letters with no stamps and no envelopes. Postal rates varied, depending on distance and number of pages in a letter. Letters were taken to the post office for mailing and picked up at the recipient's post office. Congress approved the first official postal policy in 1792: rates ranged from 6¢ for less than 30 miles to 25¢ for more than 450 miles. Letter carriers began delivering mail in cities in 1794. Instead of a salary, they collected 2¢ from each recipient.

The Post Office was headquartered in Philadelphia until 1800. That year, all postal records, furniture, and supplies were loaded into 2 wagons and transferred to Washington, DC. In 1829 Andrew Jackson elevated the postmaster general to cabinet rank and transformed the office into a means for rewarding political cronies. The first adhesive postage stamp appeared in the US in 1847. Mail contracts subsidized the early development of US railroads.

Uniform postal rates that did not vary with distance were instituted in 1863. That same year free city delivery began. Rural free delivery started in 1896, and its implementation stimulated the construction of roads for the delivery of mail to isolated parts of the US.

Parcel post was inaugurated in 1913, providing the means for mail-order houses such as Montgomery Ward and Sears, Roebuck to

flourish. Scheduled airmail service between Washington and New York began in 1918, stimulating the development of commercial air travel.

The zip code was introduced in 1963. In 1966 the Chicago post office, then the world's largest postal facility, ceased to function for 3 weeks until a backlog of 10 million pieces of mail was eliminated. Postal workers grew increasingly militant under the stress of the working environment. A work stoppage in the New York City post office in 1970 spread within 9 days to 670 other post offices, and the US Army was deployed to handle the mail. Later that year the Postal Reorganization Act was passed. The new law pulled the postmaster general out of the president's cabinet and made the position the CEO of an independent agency, the US Postal Service. The next year the new agency entered the first US government labor contract negotiated through collective bargaining. Express Mail Service, which guaranteed either same day or next day delivery, was instituted in 1977 to counter the growth of Federal Express and similar businesses. In 1978, 4 digits were added to existing zip codes.

In 1991 the cost of mailing a first-class letter was raised from 25¢ to 29¢. In 1992 the service began a reorganization that included streamlining management. Although USPS had a net loss of $914 million in 1994, that figure was $430 million less than expected. After 4 years with no rate increase, first-class rates were raised by 3 cents on January 1, 1995.

In 1995 the US General Accounting Office issued a scathing report stating that USPS continued to have very tense relations between labor and management.

Government agency
Fiscal year ends: September 30

WHO

Chairman: Sam Winters
VC: Tirso del Junco
Postmaster General and CEO: Marvin Runyon
Deputy Postmaster General: Michael S. Coughlin
EVP and COO: William J. Henderson
Chief Postal Inspector: Kenneth J. Hunter
SVP and CFO: Michael J. Riley
SVP and Chief Marketing Officer: Loren E. Smith
SVP and General Counsel: Mary S. Elcano
VP Engineering: William J. Dowling
VP Operations Support: Allen R. Kane
VP Quality: Norman E. Lorentz
VP Labor Relations: Joseph J. Mahon Jr.
VP Employee Relations: Gail G. Sonnenberg
VP Information Systems: Richard D. Weirich
VP Technology Applications: Robert A. F. Reisner
VP and Consumer Advocate: Ann McK. Robinson
Auditors: Ernst & Young LLP

WHERE

HQ: 475 L'Enfant Plaza SW, Washington, DC
20260-0010
Phone: 202-268-2000
Fax: 202-268-2392

The US Postal Service is the largest independent agency
of the executive branch of the US government.

WHAT

	1994 Sales	
	$ mil.	% of total
First-Class	29,395	60
Second-Class	1,757	4
Third-Class	10,511	21
Fourth-Class	1,351	3
Priority Mail	2,649	5
Express Mail	671	1
Mailgram	2	0
International Surface	204	1
International Air	1,206	2
Special Services	1,505	3
Total	**49,251**	**100**

Services
First-Class Mail (letters)
Second-Class Mail (classroom, nonprofit, and regular-
rate publications)
Third-Class Mail (nonprofit, regular bulk, and single-
piece)
Fourth-Class Mail (bound printed matter, library
materials, and parcels)
Priority Mail (2-day delivery between major business
centers in the US)
Express Mail (overnight delivery every day of the year)
Mailgram (combination letter-telegram)
International Surface
International Air
Special Services
  Box rentals
  Certified mail
  Collection-on-Delivery
  Insurance
  Money orders
  Registry
  Special Delivery
  Stamped envelopes

KEY COMPETITORS

Airborne Freight
Consolidated Freightways
DHL Worldwide Express
FedEx
Harper Group
Pittston Services
Roadway
Skynet Worldwide Courier
UPS

HOW MUCH

	9-Year Growth	1985	1986	1987	1988	1989	1990	1991	1992	1993	1994
Sales ($ mil.)	6.1%	28,956	31,021	32,297	35,036	37,979	39,201	43,323	46,151	47,418	49,252
Net income ($ mil.)	—	(251)	305	(223)	(597)	61	(874)	(1,469)	(536)	(1,765)	(914)
Income as % of sales	—	—	1.0%	—	—	0.2%	—	—	—	—	—
Pieces of mail (mil.)	2.6%	140,098	147,400	153,900	160,954	161,603	166,301	165,851	166,443	171,220	177,062
Employees	(0.2%)	744,000	785,000	791,000	779,083	777,715	760,668	748,961	725,290	691,723	728,944

1994 Year-end:
Cash (mil.): $1,421
Current ratio: 0.23
Long-term debt (mil.):
$7,727
Total assets (mil.): $46,416

Net Income
($ mil.)
1985–94

UNITED TECHNOLOGIES CORPORATION

OVERVIEW

CEO George David is showing progress in reshaping the $21 billion Goliath of United Technologies Corporation with a little help from Otis. Based in Hartford, Connecticut, United Technologies is a conglomerate with such well-known units as Carrier (#1 manufacturer of heating and air-conditioning systems), Hamilton Standard (flight systems), Otis (#1 manufacturer of elevators and escalators), Pratt & Whitney (aircraft engines), Sikorsky (helicopters), and UT Automotive.

United Technologies (UTC) is betting that the modernization of the developing world will mean more elevators, air-conditioning systems, and airline travel. David is using the international, entrepreneurial, and customer-driven Otis to transform the rest of United Technologies — in particular, hierarchical, inflexible Pratt & Whitney.

Otis generated 88% of its revenues abroad in 1994 and has been particularly successful in Asia. Otis, which re-entered the Chinese market in 1984, generated sales of $250 million in China. In addition Otis plans a joint venture in Vietnam. Following its lead, UT Automotive is forming a joint venture in China to produce electrical distribution systems.

The once-dominant Pratt & Whitney has undergone a massive restructuring. Its work force has been cut by 40% since late 1992. David believes that Pratt & Whitney can no longer produce jet engines only in the US and is working on a venture to supply engines to a Russian airframe maker.

WHEN

In Hartford, Connecticut, in 1925, Frederick Rentschler and engine designer George Mead founded Pratt & Whitney Aircraft (P&W), precursor of United Technologies, to develop aircraft engines. Rentschler merged P&W with Seattle-based Boeing Airplane Company and with Chance Vought Corporation in 1929 to form United Aircraft & Transport. United Aircraft soon acquired other aviation manufacturers, including Hamilton Aero, Standard Steel Propeller, and Sikorsky.

In 1934, after congressional investigations led to new antitrust laws, United Aircraft's management split the corporation into 3 independent companies: United Airlines, Boeing Airplane Company, and United Aircraft. United Aircraft retained P&W and several of Rentschler's other manufacturing interests.

During WWII United Aircraft produced half of all engines used by US warplanes. Igor Sikorsky developed helicopters, and Vought produced the Corsair and Cutlass airplanes. After an initial postwar decline in sales, the company retooled for production of jet engines. United Aircraft spun off Chance Vought in 1954 and in 1958 bought Norden-Ketay, a manufacturer of aeronautical electronics.

In the late 1960s engines produced for the Boeing 747 proved costly for P&W when a design flaw sparked an expensive return to the drawing board. A concerned board of directors appointed Harry Gray, a 17-year Litton Industries executive, as president in 1971. Gray turned the company into a conglomerate, renaming it United Technologies Corporation in 1975. To decrease the company's dependence on government business, Gray diversified UTC with numerous purchases, including Otis Elevator (1975) and Carrier (1979). By 1986 Gray's acquisitions had expanded the company's sales to $15.7 billion. Gray, under pressure from his board, tapped Bob Daniell in 1986 and retired a year later.

Daniell, a 25-year Sikorsky veteran, emphasized profitability rather than growth, selling many businesses (such as Mostek, a semiconductor firm) and implementing layoffs and management changes. After a year of record earnings in 1990, UTC initiated cost-cutting measures in 1991 in response to reduced military orders, slumps in the auto and building industries, and slack demand for commercial airline parts. UTC took a $1.3 billion restructuring charge in 1991, which contributed to its first operating loss in 20 years. As part of its restructuring efforts, the company said in 1992 it would close 100 facilities by 1995, reducing worldwide manufacturing capacity by 16%. The company took a $700 million write-off in 1992, mostly for Pratt & Whitney.

In 1992 UTC paid a $6 million fine after admitting that it had hired advisors to illegally inform the company about competitors' bids for Pentagon contracts. Also that year Carrier bought a controlling stake in China's Tianjin Uni-Air Conditioning Co., its 4th Chinese joint venture in 5 years. In 1993 Pratt & Whitney lost out to GE for a China Southern Airlines Boeing 777 engine contract (worth $120 million). In 1994 UTC raised $200 million by selling its Norden radar unit (to Westinghouse) and its stake in the Westland helicopter firm. Sikorsky laid off 370 employees in 1995 because of declining defense contracts.

NYSE symbol: UTX
Fiscal year ends: December 31

WHO

Chairman: Robert F. Daniell, age 61, $1,422,916 pay
President and CEO: George David, age 52,
$1,606,250 pay
President, Pratt & Whitney: Karl J. Krapek, age 46,
$987,500 pay
EVP and General Counsel: Irving B. Yoskowitz, age 49,
$790,000 pay
EVP and CFO: Stephen F. Page, age 55, $783,750 pay
President, Carrier Corporation: John R. Lord, age 51
President, Hamilton Standard: Raymond P. Kurlak
President, Otis Elevator: Jean-Pierre van Rooy, age 60
President, Sikorsky Aircraft: Eugene Buckley, age 64
President, UT Automotive: Norman R. Bodine, age 52
SVP Human Resources and Organization: William L.
Bucknall Jr., age 52
Auditors: Price Waterhouse LLP

WHERE

HQ: United Technologies Bldg., Hartford, CT 06101
Phone: 203-728-7000
Fax: 203-728-7979

United Technologies has manufacturing operations in
Africa, Asia, Australia, Canada, Europe, Latin America,
Mexico, the Middle East, and the US.

	1994 Sales		1994 Operating Income	
	$ mil.	% of total	$ mil.	% of total
US	13,384	61	746	48
Europe	4,119	19	399	26
Asia/Pacific	2,415	11	200	13
Other regions	2,069	9	204	13
Adjustments	(790)	—	(5)	—
Total	**21,197**	**100**	**1,544**	**100**

WHAT

	1994 Sales		1994 Operating Income	
	$ mil.	% of total	$ mil.	% of total
Pratt & Whitney	5,846	27	380	25
Carrier	4,919	23	278	18
Otis	4,644	22	421	27
Flight Systems	3,218	15	282	18
Automotive	2,683	13	182	12
Adjustments	(113)	—	1	—
Total	**21,197**	**100**	**1,544**	**100**

Selected Brand Names
Carrier (heating, ventilating, air conditioning, and
refrigeration)
Hamilton Standard (engine controls, environmental
systems, propellers, and other flight systems)
Otis (elevators, escalators, and service)
Pratt & Whitney (engines and space propulsion)
Sikorsky (helicopters and parts)

Selected Aircraft Engines	Selected Helicopters
F100 and F117 (for military	Black Hawk
aircraft)	CH-53E Super Stallion
JT8D-200, PW2000,	HH-60 Jayhawk
PW4000, IAE V2500 (for	S-76
commercial aircraft)	Seahawk

KEY COMPETITORS

American Standard	Lockheed Martin
Boeing	Loral
British Aerospace	McDonnell Douglas
AB Electrolux	Raytheon
Fedders	Rockwell
General Dynamics	Rolls-Royce
General Electric	Teledyne
Hyundai	Thiokol
Kaman	Watsco
Lennox	Westinghouse
Litton Industries	York International

HOW MUCH

	9-Year Growth	1985	1986	1987	1988	1989	1990	1991	1992	1993	1994
Sales ($ mil.)	3.9%	14,992	15,669	17,170	18,000	19,532	21,783	21,262	22,032	21,081	21,197
Net income ($ mil.)	7.2%	313	73	592	659	702	751	(1,021)	35	487	585
Income as % of sales	—	2.1%	0.5%	3.4%	3.7%	3.6%	3.4%	—	0.2%	2.3%	2.8%
Earnings per share ($)	7.7%	2.25	0.54	4.52	5.05	5.20	5.53	(8.91)	(0.05)	3.30	4.40
Stock price – high ($)	—	46.50	56.25	60.50	42.63	57.38	62.50	54.50	57.88	66.13	72.00
Stock price – low ($)	—	34.50	39.25	30.00	33.00	39.88	40.13	42.13	41.50	43.75	55.00
Stock price – close ($)	4.1%	43.75	46.00	33.88	41.13	54.25	47.88	54.25	48.13	62.00	62.88
P/E – high	—	21	104	13	8	11	11	—	—	20	16
P/E – low	—	15	73	7	7	8	7	—	—	13	13
Dividends per share ($)	3.5%	1.40	1.40	1.40	1.55	1.60	1.80	1.80	1.90	1.80	1.90
Book value per share ($)	(0.3%)	31.29	29.14	32.90	36.88	39.14	44.10	32.49	27.23	28.54	30.47
Employees	(0.8%)	184,800	193,500	190,000	187,000	201,400	192,600	185,100	178,000	168,600	171,500

1994 Year-end:
Debt ratio: 39.4%
Return on equity: 15.9%
Cash (mil.): $386
Current ratio: 1.26
Long-term debt (mil.): $1,885
No. of shares (mil.): 123
Dividends
  Yield: 3.0%
  Payout: 43.2%
Market value (mil.): $7,743

Stock Price History
High/Low 1985–94

UNIVERSAL CORPORATION

OVERVIEW

Poor-quality US tobacco and a worldwide glut caused a dip in Universal Corporation's earnings in 1994 but weren't enough to snuff out profits entirely. The Richmond, Virginia–based company — the world's largest buyer and processor of leaf tobacco — may just be blowing smoke, but it believes those problems were temporary and hopes that it can puff its earnings back up to record levels. And while the antismoking attitude in the US may be giving the company something to chew on, executives' eyes are lighting up as the habit picks up elsewhere in the world, ensuring that Universal will have new customers in the pipeline for quite some time.

Tobacco — from selecting to shipping to packing to financing — is Universal's primary business. The company does not produce any consumer tobacco products but makes most of its money off of those who do. Cigarette maker

Philip Morris (Marlboro, Virginia Slims) accounts for 41% of Universal's sales. Universal's other operations (through its Deli Universal division) include lumber (a market leader in the Netherlands) and agricultural products such as rubber, tea, dried fruit, and sunflower seeds. And while there are those who believe coffee and cigarettes were made for each other, Universal is no longer one of them; the company withdrew from the java trade in 1994.

Universal's tobacco buyers can be found in markets throughout the eastern half of the US, from Wisconsin to Florida, from Kentucky to Connecticut. The company also has a presence in 32 foreign countries, from Argentina to Zimbabwe. In fiscal 1994 Universal bought a controlling share of Nyiregyhaza Tobacco Processing Company, Hungary's largest leaf processor, and agreed to equip a processing facility in China's Anhui Province.

WHEN

In 1918 the American tobacco industry was booming because of increased cigarette demand and the recent invention of a cigar-making machine. Universal Leaf was formed that year to consolidate and expand the J.P. Taylor Company (tobacco buyer, incorporated in North Carolina in 1904). Universal quickly acquired interests in a number of other competitors.

During the 1930s Philip Morris became a customer. Universal financed the tobacco for Philip Morris, which was trying to increase its market share. By 1940 Universal was purchasing as much leaf tobacco as any other domestic company. That year the US government filed antitrust charges against Universal and 7 other tobacco companies. American, Liggett & Myers, and Reynolds stood trial for the whole group, and 4 years later each of the 8 was fined $15,000.

Universal grew during the next several decades by concentrating on buying and selling tobacco. It diversified in 1968, buying Inta-Roto Machine (packaging machinery and steel cylinders for printing fabrics) and Overton Container (tobacco containers). Universal also acquired a division of Usry Inc. (modular buildings).

The company diversified further in 1980 by purchasing Royster (fertilizer; sold in 1984 after poor returns). In 1984 Universal purchased Lawyers Title and Continental Land Title together for $115 million. In 1986 the company acquired Netherlands-based Deli

(timber and building products) for $48 million.

Two years later Universal bought Thorpe and Ricks (tobacco processor), and in 1990 it purchased Gebreder Kulenkampffag, a German tobacco company, giving Universal a greater presence in the opening East European market.

In 1991 the company acquired Kliemann SA, a tobacco supplier headquartered in Brazil, ensuring access to Brazilian flue-cured tobacco. Later that year the company spun off its title insurance operation (Lawyers Title) to shareholders. Also that year chairman Gordon Crenshaw retired, passing the position to Henry Harrell. Allen King was promoted to president.

In 1992 the company sold its Blakely, Georgia, peanut shelling operations. Also that year Universal's Brazilian operations began to gain steam, contributing heavily to the year's earnings, as Brazil's political landscape began to stabilize.

In 1993 the company sold its flat-board finishing company, Universal Woods. Universal also bought the Casalee Group SA, a UK tobacco processor with key operations in Brazil and Africa and trading operations in Europe and the Far East, for about $100 million. In 1994 Universal announced a major restructuring of its world operations.

Universal blamed lower-than-expected sales in 1995 on struggling Eastern European economies.

NYSE symbol: UVV
Fiscal year ends: June 30

WHO

Chairman and CEO: Henry H. Harrell, age 55,
$659,210 pay
President and COO: Allen B. King, age 48, $458,263 pay
President and Chairman, Deli Universal: Jaap Godthelp,
age 60, $513,920 pay
SVP, Universal Leaf Tobacco: Robert J. Zalneck, age 48
VP and Chief Administrative Officer: William L. Taylor,
age 53, $340,070 pay
VP and CFO: Hartwell H. Roper, age 46, $251,590 pay
VP and Treasurer: Karen M. L. Whelan, age 47
VP (HR): Mike Oberschmidt Jr.
Secretary and General Counsel: James M. White III,
age 55
Controller: William J. Coronado, age 40
Auditors: Ernst & Young LLP

WHERE

HQ: PO Box 25099, Hamilton St. at Broad, Richmond,
VA 23260
Phone: 804-359-9311
Fax: 804-254-3584

The company has tobacco operations in 33 countries.

	1994 Sales		1994 Operating Income	
	$ mil.	% of total	$ mil.	% of total
US	1,534	48	45	39
Europe	1,123	36	49	43
South/Central America	341	11	21	18
Other regions	171	5	(4)	—
Adjustments	(195)	—	—	—
Total	**2,975**	**100**	**111**	**100**

WHAT

	1994 Sales		1994 Operating Income	
	$ mil.	% of total	$ mil.	% of total
Tobacco	2,176	73	83	75
Agri-products	431	15	9	8
Lumber & building products	368	12	19	17
Total	**2,975**	**100**	**111**	**100**

Tobacco Products

Air-cured	Dark air-cured
Burley	Dark fired
Chewing	Flue-cured
Cigar	Maryland

Agricultural Products

Canned meats	Seasonings
Dried fruit	Spices
Nuts	Sunflower seeds
Rubber	Tea

Lumber and Building Materials

KEY COMPETITORS

Agway	Louisiana-Pacific
American Home Products	McCormick
Campbell Soup	North Pacific Lumber
Cargill	PET
Chiquita Brands	Riverwood International
ConAgra	Simpson Investment
DiMon	Standard Commercial
Dole	Universal Forest Products
Farmer Bros.	Weyerhaeuser
Georgia-Pacific	Wickes Lumber
Goya	

HOW MUCH

	9-Year Growth	1985	1986	1987	1988	1989	1990	1991	1992	1993	1994
Sales ($ mil.)	13.7%	938	1,129	2,104	2,414	2,920	2,815	2,897	2,989	3,047	2,975
Net income ($ mil.)	(2.0%)	46	47	56	61	54	37	24	71	80	39
Income as % of sales	—	4.9%	4.2%	2.7%	2.5%	1.8%	1.3%	0.8%	2.4%	2.6%	1.3%
Earnings per share ($)	(2.3%)	1.35	1.37	1.63	1.78	1.60	1.11	0.73	2.15	2.39	1.09
Stock price – high ($)	—	12.25	15.50	18.38	16.88	19.50	18.06	34.00	34.25	33.75	26.25
Stock price – low ($)	—	9.38	11.63	12.81	13.94	16.50	11.00	11.81	22.25	21.75	17.50
Stock price – close ($)	5.6%	12.13	13.44	15.44	16.50	17.75	11.88	34.00	34.13	25.63	19.88
P/E – high	—	9	11	11	10	12	16	47	16	14	24
P/E – low	—	7	9	8	8	10	10	16	10	9	16
Dividends per share ($)	7.7%	0.47	0.52	0.56	0.67	0.59	0.72	0.75	0.78	0.84	0.92
Book value per share ($)	4.0%	7.58	8.54	9.47	10.52	11.41	12.08	11.89	9.18	11.73	10.79
Employees	6.7%	14,000	14,000	20,000	20,000	20,000	20,000	25,000	25,000	25,000	25,000

1994 Year-end:
Debt ratio: 45.0%
Return on equity: 9.7%
Cash (mil.): $165
Current ratio: 1.37
Long-term debt (mil.): $298
No. of shares (mil.): 35
Dividends
  Yield: 4.6%
  Payout: 84.4%
Market value (mil.): $696

Stock Price History High/Low 1985–94

UNOCAL CORPORATION

OVERVIEW

Already one of the largest petroleum companies in the US, Los Angeles–based Unocal has its eyes set on becoming a significant player among the world's leading energy companies in the next 5 years. Unocal is principally engaged in the exploration and production of crude oil and natural gas. The company is also the world's #1 producer of geothermal energy and manufactures chemicals for agricultural and industrial uses. In addition, it has interests in specialty minerals and real estate.

In the past 2 years, lower gas prices and asset divestments, including the closing of its retail marketing line in the Southeast, pushed sales down sharply.

Unocal has extensive exploration and development projects (oil, gas, and geothermal) in North and South America, the Middle East, and Asia. In particular, the company is developing its Southeast Asia operations in response to the energy demand in the region. The company is ramping up production in Indonesia, Myanmar, the Philippines, and Thailand and has recently opened new offices in Cambodia, China, Singapore, and Vietnam.

Unocal owns 3 refineries in California and is co-owner of another in Chicago (as part of a joint venture with Petróleos de Venezuela, UNO-VEN). It markets gasoline and other products under the Unocal 76 brand name.

WHEN

In 1859, not far from the Pennsylvania well that ushered in the modern oil industry, Lyman Stewart, just 19, hoped to finance Presbyterian evangelism by joining the boom. He plunked down $124 for a 1/8 interest in a Pennsylvania oil lease.

By the 1880s Stewart had put aside a religious career in favor of the oil business. He and partner Wallace Hardison headed for Southern California. When they united 3 oil companies in 1890, the result was Union Oil of California.

The fledgling company boasted a petroleum laboratory — the West's first — at its Santa Paula refinery. In 1901 one of its geologists discovered a trove of prehistoric bones in the La Brea tar pits. In 1903 Union Oil built the world's first oil tanker, a wooden ship outfitted with steel tanks.

As Union service stations multiplied in the 1930s, the company cast about for a new name for its gasoline. Lead in the gas added a reddish tinge and made the old brand name, White Magic, obsolete. An executive suggested 76 to conjure the spirit of America.

During WWII the company provided US Navy ships in the Pacific with fuel. After the war was over, while many of Union's competitors were developing crude oil supplies overseas, the company focused its operations in North America, and by the end of the 1950s the company was still getting 2/3 of its production from its California holdings.

In an effort to expand its distribution network, Union Oil acquired Pure Oil in 1965. Pure Oil was formed in New Jersey in 1895 when independent refiners bristled at the dictates of Standard Oil. The merger with Pure Oil doubled Union's size.

Union operated the offshore well that produced the infamous 1969 Santa Barbara oil spill. The damage became a rallying point for the fledgling US environmental movement. During the 1970s Fred Hartley, named CEO in 1964, steered the company to develop alternative energy sources. Geothermal development proved profitable, but extracting oil from Colorado shale, a process underwritten by federal subsidies, did not live up to expectations.

The company adopted its Unocal nickname as the name for its corporate umbrella in 1983. In 1985 takeover artist T. Boone Pickens targeted Unocal, and the tenacious Hartley ran debt to more than $5.5 billion to repurchase almost 1/3 of Unocal's outstanding stock.

Unocal has continued to struggle with the debt. Hartley's successor, Richard Stegemeier, sold the Los Angeles headquarters complex (1988). In 1989 Unocal raised cash by transferring midwestern refining and marketing operations to UNO-VEN, a joint venture with a Petróleos de Venezuela subsidiary. In 1992 Unocal bought Chevron's nitrogen fertilizer plant in Washington.

In 1993 the company sold its network of 140 auto/truckstops to National Auto/Truckstops for approximately $180 million.

In 1994 Unocal pleaded no contest to criminal charges that it had inadvertently contaminated groundwater in California. The company agreed to pay at least $5.5 million to settle the criminal charges.

In 1995 Unocal opened new offices in Caracas, Venezuela, and Islamabad, Pakistan to develop long-term business opportunities in those markets.

Also that year, Stegemeier was succeeded as chairman by CEO Roger Beach.

NYSE symbol: UCL
Fiscal year ends: December 31

WHO

Chairman and CEO: Roger C. Beach, age 58,
$811,709 pay (prior to promotion)
President: John F. Imle Jr., age 54, $610,195 pay
CFO: Neal E. Schmale, age 48, $405,000 pay
**VP, General Counsel, Chief Legal Officer, and
Corporate Secretary:** Dennis P. Codon, age 46,
$287,127 pay
Group VP Oil and Gas Operations: John W. Schanck,
age 43, $280,520 pay
Group VP and President, 76 Products Company:
Lawrence M. Higby, age 49
VP Washington, DC, Office: Thomas F. Hairston
VP External Affairs: Karen A. Sikkema
VP Organization Development: Fielding L. Walker
VP Health, Environment, and Safety: George A. Walker
VP Planning and Information Services: Charles R.
Williamson
VP Technology and Operations Support: Paul J.
Durning
VP Exploration: Graydon H. Laughbaum Jr.
VP Human Resources: Charles O. Strathman
Auditors: Coopers & Lybrand L.L.P.

WHERE

HQ: 1201 W. Fifth St., Los Angeles, CA 90017
Phone: 213-977-7600
Fax: 213-977-5362 (Personnel)

Unocal produces oil and gas in the US and 6 foreign
countries.

	1994 Sales		1994 Pretax Income	
	$ mil.	% of total	$ mil.	% of total
US	6,533	83	522	53
Other countries	1,342	17	470	47
Adjustments	90	—	(698)	—
Total	**7,965**	**100**	**294**	**100**

WHAT

	1994 Sales		1994 Pretax Income	
	$ mil.	% of total	$ mil.	% of total
Refining, mktg. & trans.	5,766	62	144	14
Exploration & production	2,641	29	719	72
Chemicals	484	5	81	8
Geothermal	139	2	58	6
Corporate & other	198	2	(708)	—
Adjustments	(1,263)	—	—	—
Total	**7,965**	**100**	**294**	**100**

Subsidiaries and Affiliates
76 Products Co. (refining and marketing)
Molycorp, Inc. (lanthanide mining)
Union Oil Company of California (integrated petroleum)
Unocal Britain Limited
Unocal Indonesia, Ltd.
Unocal Land & Development Company
Unocal Netherlands B.V.
Unocal Pipeline Company
Unocal Thailand, Ltd.
UNO-VEN (50%, refining and marketing)

KEY COMPETITORS

Amerada Hess	Dow Chemical	PEMEX
Amoco	DuPont	Pennzoil
Ashland, Inc.	Enron Corp.	Petrobrás
Atlantic	Exxon	Petrofina
Richfield	Imperial Oil	Phillips
British	Koch	Petroleum
Petroleum	Lyondell	Royal Dutch/
California	Petrochemical	Shell
Energy	Mobil	Sinclair Oil
Chevron	Norsk Hydro	Sun Company
Coastal	Occidental	Texaco
Diamond	Oryx	TOTAL
Shamrock	PDVSA	USX–Marathon

HOW MUCH

	9-Year Growth	1985	1986	1987	1988	1989	1990	1991	1992	1993	1994
Sales ($ mil.)	(4.2%)	11,693	8,408	9,457	10,142	11,353	11,808	10,895	10,061	8,344	7,965
Net income ($ mil.)	(10.2%)	326	176	181	24	260	401	73	203	343	124
Income as % of sales	—	2.8%	2.1%	1.9%	0.2%	2.3%	3.4%	0.7%	2.0%	4.1%	1.6%
Earnings per share ($)	(12.4%)	1.18	0.76	0.78	0.11	1.11	1.71	0.31	0.75	1.27	0.36
Stock price – high ($)	—	26.50	14.13	22.50	20.19	31.25	34.50	29.50	28.88	32.63	30.75
Stock price – low ($)	—	13.06	7.81	10.50	14.25	18.69	24.63	20.63	20.25	23.50	24.38
Stock price – close ($)	8.2%	13.44	13.31	14.13	18.94	29.75	26.25	23.38	25.50	27.88	27.25
P/E – high	—	23	19	29	184	28	20	95	39	26	85
P/E – low	—	11	10	14	130	17	14	67	27	19	68
Dividends per share ($)	3.6%	0.58	0.55	0.50	0.50	0.55	0.70	0.70	0.70	0.73	0.80
Book value per share ($)	3.3%	7.01	7.23	7.58	9.26	9.83	10.87	10.50	10.88	10.84	9.43
Employees	(4.7%)	20,214	18,005	18,130	18,235	17,286	17,518	17,248	14,687	13,613	13,127

1994 Year-end:
Debt ratio: 55.1%
Return on equity: 5.0%
Cash (mil.): $148
Current ratio: 1.22
Long-term debt (mil.): $3,461
No. of shares (mil.): 244
Dividends
  Yield: 2.9%
  Payout: —
Market value (mil.): $6,654

**Stock Price History
High/Low 1985–94**

THE UPJOHN COMPANY

OVERVIEW

To restore its long-term economic health, Upjohn has prescribed itself a merger with Sweden's Pharmacia. Announced in August 1995, the merger would create one of the 10 biggest pharmaceutical companies in the world. Upjohn could use the boost. Over the last 2 years, it lost patent protection on 4 of its top-selling pharmaceuticals: Ansaid (arthritis drug), Xanax and Halcion (tranquilizers), and Micronase (diabetic drug). Patent protection will also expire on its Depo-Provera (contraceptive injection) in late 1995 and on Rogaine (hair growth restorer) in 1996. The company, based in Kalamazoo, Michigan, is also known for its consumer products (which include Motrin and Kaopectate).

To counter the inevitable drop in sales from patent losses, Upjohn joined Geneva Pharmaceuticals in making generic versions of some of these drugs. In 1994 the company sold off its nondrug-related assets, including a seed business and its 50% interest in a chicken breeding venture. In late 1994, clinical trials of its drug Freedox (a treatment for strokes and head and spinal injuries) were suspended because the death rate for participants who took the drug was higher than for those who took a placebo. Controversy over Halcion (including a jury's placing partial blame on the drug for a murder) remains. Though Halcion is banned in several European countries, Upjohn maintains that the drug is safe.

R&D is now 18.5% of sales. Upjohn will maintain its R&D spending and expects to reduce its drug development time. In 1995 the company launched a disease-management unit, Greenstone Healthcare Solutions, to assist health care organizations such as hospitals and managed care groups in overseeing treatment of chronically ill individuals.

WHEN

Dr. William Upjohn formed the Upjohn Pill and Granule Company in partnership with his brothers in Kalamazoo, Michigan, in 1886. William's patented "friable" pill (which disintegrated readily after being swallowed) was the basis for the company's early success. (Some pills of the day would not disintegrate when struck with a hammer.) Upjohn took its current name in 1902. Its most successful products around the turn of the century were antimalarial quinine and the Phenolax wafer, a candy-type laxative.

By 1912 annual sales had passed $1 million. Research initiated the following year led to the development of several new products, including Citrocarbonate, an effervescent antacid, which had sales of over $1 million in 1926. Other products included Cheracol cough syrup (1924), Kaopectate antidiarrheal (1936), and Unicap multivitamins (1940).

During WWII the company produced large amounts of penicillin and sulfanilamide. Research on steroids after the war eventually yielded important medicines for treating a variety of inflammatory conditions, including Medrol (methylprednisolone, 1956), which had fewer side effects than others.

Completion of a new manufacturing plant near Kalamazoo in 1951 increased production by 1/3 and consolidated operations in one location. Increasing demand for the company's products overseas led to the formation of the Upjohn International Division in 1952. By 1955 annual sales had reached $100 million.

In 1957 Upjohn introduced Orinase, the first oral agent for diabetes. The company went public in 1958 and in 1959 introduced Depo-Provera, a contraceptive that was sold all over the world. In the 1960s Upjohn combined its plant and animal health operations and acquired companies involved in agricultural products (sold in 1994), home health care, and medical testing labs.

Motrin (ibuprofen), an analgesic introduced in 1974, achieved greater first-year sales than any other drug and continued its success into the 1980s. The diabetic drug Micronase (1984) and the tranquilizers Xanax (1982) and Halcion (1983) also sold well in the 1980s. In 1988 Upjohn began marketing Rogaine, the first FDA-approved treatment for baldness.

In 1990 the company sold its health care services business. Upjohn was dealt a blow in 1991 when an appeals court ruled that Genetics Institute's version of the drug EPO (marketed in the US by Upjohn under the name Marogen) violated Amgen's patent. That same year Upjohn bought drug companies Delta West (Australia), Sanorania OHG (Germany), Cheminex Laboratories (UK), and Kurran Chemical Company (Pakistan), among others.

In 1992 Upjohn got approval to sell an injectable form of its birth control method, Depo-Provera, in the US.

In 1994 Xanax, Upjohn's version of the generic drug alprazolam, was dispensed for 83% of new prescriptions for the tranquilizer.

NYSE symbol: UPJ
Fiscal year ends: December 31

WHO

Chairman and CEO: John L. Zabriskie, age 55,
$1,385,018 pay
VC; President, Upjohn Laboratories: Jerry R. Mitchell,
age 53, $658,588 pay
President and COO: Ley S. Smith, age 60, $825,010 pay
EVP and CFO: Robert C. Salisbury, age 51, $464,453 pay
EVP Administration: Donald R. Parfet, age 42,
$429,026 pay
EVP, Secretary, and General Counsel: Kenneth M.
Cyrus, age 56
SVP US and Canadian Pharmaceutical Operations: Jack
J. Jackson
SVP International Pharmaceutical Operations:
Fernando A. Leal
SVP Technical Operations: Carlos A. Salvagni
VP Clinical Development and Medical Affairs: Arthur J.
Atkinson Jr.
VP Human Resources: Robert B. Hughes
Auditors: Coopers & Lybrand L.L.P.

WHERE

HQ: 7000 Portage Rd., Kalamazoo, MI 49001
Phone: 616-323-4000
Fax: 616-323-4077

Upjohn has facilities for manufacturing, research, sales,
and distribution throughout the world.

	1994 Sales		1994 Operating Income	
	$ mil.	% of total	$ mil.	% of total
US	1,948	59	533	83
Europe	639	20	43	7
Japan & Pacific	426	13	23	3
Other regions	262	8	44	7
Adjustments	70	—	—	—
Total	**3,345**	**100**	**643**	**100**

WHAT

	1994 Sales	
	$ mil.	% of total
Human health care	2,231	67
Animal health care	336	10
Other products	778	23
Total	**3,345**	**100**

Selected Brand Names

Major Prescription Drugs
Ansaid (arthritis drug)
Cleocin T (topical
antibiotic)
Colestid (cholesterol-
lowering drug)
Depo-Provera (injectable
contraceptive)
Glynase (diabetic drug)
Halcion (tranquilizer)
Lincocin (antibiotic)
Micronase (diabetic drug)
Provera (hormonal drug)
Rogaine (baldness
treatment)
Xanax (tranquilizer)

Animal Drugs
Lincomix (antibiotic)
Naxcel (bovine and swine
antibiotic)

Consumer Products
Cortaid (anti-inflammatory
ointment)
Doxidan (laxative)
Dramamine (antimotion
sickness)
Kaopectate
(antidiarrheal drug)
Motrin IB (analgesic)
Mycitracin (antibiotic
ointment)
Surfak (laxative)
Unicap (vitamin)

KEY COMPETITORS

Abbott Labs
American
 Home Products
Amgen
Baxter
Bayer
Bristol-Myers
 Squibb
Carter-Wallace
Chiron Corp.
Ciba-Geigy
DuPont

Elf Aquitaine
Eli Lilly
Genentech
Glaxo Wellcome
Herbalife Intl.
Hoechst
Johnson
 & Johnson
Merck
Monsanto
Nature's Sunshine
NBTY

Novo Nordisk
Pfizer
Procter
 & Gamble
Rexall Sundown
Rhône-Poulenc
Roche
Sandoz
Schering-Plough
SmithKline
 Beecham
Warner-Lambert

HOW MUCH

	9-Year Growth	1985	1986	1987	1988	1989	1990	1991	1992	1993	1994
Sales ($ mil.)	5.8%	2,017	2,291	2,521	2,746	2,916	3,033	3,426	3,669	3,653	3,345
Net income ($ mil.)	10.0%	203	253	305	353	176	443	525	535	399	478
Income as % of sales	—	10.1%	11.0%	12.1%	12.9%	6.0%	14.6%	15.3%	14.6%	10.9%	14.3%
Earnings per share ($)	10.4%	1.10	1.35	1.63	1.90	0.95	2.40	2.87	2.95	2.23	2.68
Stock price – high ($)	—	23.56	35.38	53.75	35.25	42.13	44.63	49.25	45.88	35.00	37.13
Stock price – low ($)	—	11.13	20.56	22.63	26.88	27.63	33.00	34.75	29.63	25.63	25.75
Stock price – close ($)	3.7%	22.22	31.06	30.00	28.75	38.50	38.00	41.00	32.25	29.00	30.75
P/E – high	—	21	26	33	19	44	19	17	16	16	14
P/E – low	—	10	15	14	14	29	14	12	10	12	10
Dividends per share ($)	14.4%	0.44	0.50	0.58	0.76	0.91	1.00	1.21	1.39	1.48	1.48
Book value per share ($)	6.3%	6.95	7.85	8.95	9.83	9.44	10.07	9.73	9.84	10.31	12.06
Employees	(1.6%)	19,600	19,600	19,600	19,400	18,800	18,400	19,000	18,800	18,600	16,900

1994 Year-end:
Debt ratio: 26.0%
Return on equity: 25.3%
Cash (mil.): $502
Current ratio: 1.90
Long-term debt (mil.): $796
No. of shares (mil.): 173
Dividends
 Yield: 4.8%
 Payout: 55.2%
Market value (mil.): $5,324

Stock Price History
High/Low 1985–94

U S WEST, INC.

OVERVIEW

Once seen as the least likely to succeed of the 7 Baby Bells (it had the least-populated region), Englewood, Colorado–based U S WEST is ahead of its telephone siblings in the charge toward a multimedia future. U S WEST was the first of the Bells to diversify into cable TV on a large scale through its 25.5% investment in Time Warner Entertainment (a joint venture with Time Warner, Toshiba, and ITOCHU), which is constructing interactive networks combining entertainment and information with communications.

U S WEST does not plan to limit its new services to the 14 western US states it currently provides with local phone lines. With Tele-Communications, Inc., it has formed TeleWest Communications, the largest provider of combined cable TV/telephone services

in the UK. The company also owns interests in cable TV systems in France, Hungary, Norway, and Sweden; in cellular operations in the Czech Republic, Hungary, Russia, and Slovakia; and in the world's first commercial personal communications network, in the UK.

U S WEST bought 2 cable TV systems in Atlanta in 1994, setting up possible competition with BellSouth and its Atlanta experiment with interactive TV. Also that year the company started a trial of interactive TV services in Omaha.

Diversification and the company's cost-cutting campaign of the past 2 years have affected the product quality of its core business, telephone service. Colorado, Idaho, and Utah regulators have slapped fines on the company in 1994 and 1995 for poor service.

WHEN

Incorporated in 1983 as one of 7 regional operating companies formed when AT&T was split, U S WEST is rooted in AT&T's Mountain Bell, Northwestern Bell, and Pacific Northwest Bell companies. The CEO of Northwestern Bell, a maverick named Jack MacAllister, became CEO of U S WEST and promptly moved the company into such risky fields as cable TV and equipment financing.

At divestiture U S WEST was composed of phone operations in 14 states; 1/7 interest in Bell Communications Research (Bellcore, the R&D arm shared by the Bell companies); and NewVector, a cellular service provider eventually traded publicly. The company's primary business, local phone service, was growing only 3–5% annually. Hoping to expand its ability to enter unregulated markets, U S WEST was the first Bell company to seek changes in the divestiture agreement.

Within a few days of independence, MacAllister moved *Yellow Pages* operations to a new subsidiary, Landmark Communication (now part of U S WEST Marketing Resources), which has added about 20 smaller directory publishers. In 1984 U S WEST set up U S WEST Financial Services. Other new subsidiaries included BetaWest Properties (1986), a developer of commercial real estate, and Applied Communications (1987), which provides software to the banking industry.

MacAllister stunned the industry in 1988 when he removed Bell's name, synonymous with telecommunications since the phone was invented, from the U S WEST telephone companies, consolidating them as U S WEST Com-

munications. Also in 1988 U S WEST invested in a French cable TV company, made plans to offer cable billing and maintenance services domestically, and broke ground on a $45 million R&D facility in Boulder, Colorado, after expressing dissatisfaction with Bellcore. The company began expanding internationally with projects in the UK, France, Czechoslovakia, Hungary, and Russia.

In 1990 U S WEST bought the 19% of NewVector that it didn't own. MacAllister retired and was succeeded by Richard McCormick. The company and Tele-Communications, Inc., agreed to combine their European cable TV and telephone operations in a 50/50 venture in 1991.

In 1992 the company formed a 10-year alliance with Motorola to upgrade U S WEST's cellular operations. In 1993 the company paid $2.5 billion for a 25.5% stake in Time Warner Entertainment, the media giant's cable and entertainment unit. U S WEST also received 12.75% of Time Warner Entertainment Japan and an option to increase its ownership in the US unit to 31.8%. U S WEST began disposing of its Capital Assets segment (finance and real estate interests) in 1993.

In 1994 the company bought Thomson Directories, a UK publisher, from Thomson Corporation and Dun & Bradstreet. That same year U S WEST formed a cellular joint venture with AirTouch Communications.

In 1995 Apple Computer entered discussions with U S WEST aimed at securing the company's investment in Apple's poorly performing on-line computer service, eWorld.

NYSE symbol: USW
Fiscal year ends: December 31

Chairman, President, and CEO: Richard D.
McCormick, age 54, $1,260,000 pay
President and CEO, U S WEST Communications:
A. Gary Ames, age 50, $740,000 pay
President and CEO, U S WEST Multimedia Group:
Thomas E. Pardun
**President and CEO, U S WEST Marketing Resources
Group:** Solomon D. Trujillo
**EVP; President and CEO, U S WEST Diversified
Group:** Charles M. Lillis, age 53, $748,333 pay
**EVP; President, U S WEST International and Business
Development Group:** Richard J. Callahan, age 53,
$665,000 pay
EVP, General Counsel, and Secretary: Charles P.
Russ III, age 50, $531,667 pay
EVP and CFO: James M. Osterhoff, age 58
EVP and Acting Chief Human Resources Officer:
James H. Stever, age 51
Acting EVP, Public Policy: C. Scott McClellan, age 46
VP Quality: Lorne G. Rubis
VP and Treasurer: James T. Anderson
VP Public Relations: Judith A. Servoss
VP Federal Relations: H. Laird Walker
Auditors: Coopers & Lybrand L.L.P.

WHERE

HQ: 7800 E. Orchard Rd., Englewood, CO 80111
Phone: 303-793-6500
Fax: 303-793-6654

U S WEST provides telephone exchange service in 14
states (Arizona, Colorado, Idaho, Iowa, Minnesota,
Montana, Nebraska, New Mexico, North Dakota, Oregon,
South Dakota, Utah, Washington, and Wyoming) and
has overseas ventures in the Czech Republic, France,
Hungary, Japan, Norway, Poland, Russia, Slovakia,
Sweden, and the UK.

WHAT

	1994 Sales		1994 Net Income	
	$ mil.	% of total	$ mil.	% of total
U S WEST				
Communications	8,998	82	1,175	82
Publishing & other	1,077	10	232	16
Cellular & other	878	8	19	2
Total	**10,953**	**100**	**1,426**	**100**

	1994 Sales	
	$ mil.	% of total
Local service	4,067	37
Access charges (interstate)	2,269	21
Long-distance network svc.	1,329	12
Publishing & other	1,077	10
Domestic cellular	781	7
Access charges (intrastate)	729	7
International directories	79	1
Other telecommunications	622	5
Total	**10,953**	**100**

Major Subsidiaries and Affiliates
U S WEST Communications (telephone services)
U S WEST International and Business Development
Group (overseas telephone, cable, and wireless
services)
U S WEST Marketing Resources Group (*Yellow Pages*
and specialty directory publishing)
U S WEST Multimedia Group (multimedia services
outside U S WEST's region)
U S WEST NewVector Group (cellular services)

KEY COMPETITORS

Ameritech	GTE	SBC
AT&T	MCI	Communications
Bell Atlantic	MFS	Sprint
BellSouth	Communications	Telephone and
BT	NYNEX	Data Systems
Cable &	Pacific Telesis	U.S. Long Distance
Wireless	R. R. Donnelley	WorldCom

HOW MUCH

	9-Year Growth	1985	1986	1987	1988	1989	1990	1991	1992	1993	1994
Sales ($ mil.)	3.8%	7,813	8,308	8,445	9,221	9,691	9,957	10,577	10,281	10,294	10,953
Net income ($ mil.)	4.9%	926	924	1,006	1,132	1,111	1,199	553	1,179	394	1,426
Income as % of sales	—	11.8%	11.1%	11.9%	12.3%	11.5%	12.0%	5.2%	11.5%	3.8%	13.0%
Earnings per share ($)	2.9%	2.42	2.43	2.66	3.09	3.01	3.11	1.38	2.86	0.94	3.14
Stock price – high ($)	—	22.25	31.00	30.13	29.81	40.31	40.50	40.75	40.00	50.75	46.25
Stock price – low ($)	—	17.13	20.81	21.25	24.38	28.38	32.38	33.75	32.88	37.75	34.63
Stock price – close ($)	5.4%	22.25	27.00	25.56	28.88	40.06	38.88	37.88	38.38	45.88	35.63
P/E – high	—	9	13	11	10	13	13	30	14	54	15
P/E – low	—	7	9	8	8	9	10	25	12	40	11
Dividends per share ($)	4.7%	1.41	1.50	1.61	1.73	1.85	1.97	2.06	2.11	2.14	2.14
Book value per share ($)	(1.6%)	18.24	19.16	20.09	21.31	21.60	23.48	23.39	19.95	13.29	15.73
Employees	(1.5%)	70,202	69,375	68,523	69,765	70,587	65,469	65,829	63,707	60,778	61,505

1994 Year-end:
Debt ratio: 51.8%
Return on equity: 21.5%
Cash (mil.): $209
Current ratio: 0.46
Long-term debt (mil.): $5,101
No. of shares (mil.): 469
Dividends
  Yield: 6.0%
  Payout: 68.2%
Market value (mil.): $16,723

**Stock Price History
High/Low 1985–94**

USAA

OVERVIEW

San Antonio–based USAA is the stealth bomber of the insurance and financial industry. The company started out providing services only to active or retired military personnel (its property/casualty insurance and buying services are still open only to people affiliated with the military). But USAA has developed an avid following among civilians for its other insurance, annuity, and investment products and has won high respect among professionals in the industry for its stability and value.

In addition to military officers, USAA membership includes Secret Service and FBI agents and other selected government officials and their families. The company has more than 2.5 million members, including over 90% of active-duty US military officers.

In addition to auto and homeowners insurance and investments, the company provides health insurance, credit cards, a travel agency, and a buying service that allows members to buy discount merchandise.

The company has no field agents. Instead it finds its members through direct marketing as well as through the military grapevine. In 1994, however, it began advertising through the media to generate new contacts, particularly for investment products. The company's data processing functions are highly sophisticated and are frequently upgraded to provide better service.

In 1995 USAA was considering setting up a mutual fund service to allow account holders to move between its own and other funds without incurring transaction fees.

WHEN

In 1922 a group of US Army officers gathered in a San Antonio hotel and formed their own automobile insurance association. The reason? As military officers they often moved from one post to another, and they had a hard time getting insurance because they were considered "transient." So the 26 officers who met that day decided to insure each other. Led by Major William Garrison, who became the company's first president, they formed the United States Army Automobile Insurance Association.

In 1924, when navy and marine corps officers were allowed to join, the company changed its name to United Services Automobile Association. By the mid-1950s the company had more than 200,000 members.

During the 1960s the company added to its insurance lines when it formed USAA Life Insurance Company (1963) and USAA Casualty Insurance Company (1968).

In 1969 Robert McDermott, a retired air force brigadier general and a former dean of the Air Force Academy, became president. He cut employment through attrition (USAA has never had a layoff), established education and training seminars for employees, and invested heavily in computers and telecommunications. A new computer system cut automobile policy processing time from 13 days to 3 days.

McDermott also added new products and services, such as mutual funds, real estate investments, and banking services. Under McDermott, USAA's membership grew from 653,000 in 1969 to over 2.5 million in 1993.

In 1974 USAA began to move into its huge new headquarters facilities on a 286-acre cam-

pus featuring subsidized cafeterias, 2 walk-in medical clinics, and 2 physical fitness centers.

During the 1970s, as part of McDermott's goal to make USAA a completely paperless company, USAA switched most of its business from mail to toll-free telephone, becoming one of the insurance industry's first companies to use 800 numbers.

In the early 1980s the company introduced USAA Buying Services, allowing members to buy merchandise at a discount. In 1985 it opened the USAA Federal Savings Bank next door to its headquarters. In the late 1980s USAA began installing an optical storage system, automating some customer service operations.

McDermott retired in 1993 and was succeeded by Robert Herres, a former vice-chairman of the Joint Chiefs of Staff. USAA continues to add new services. In 1994 USAA Federal Savings Bank began developing a home banking system, providing members with information and services over advanced screen telephones provided by IBM.

In 1994 winter storms and the Northridge earthquake in California cost USAA more than $250 million in claims. The crash of the bond market was another blow.

The company has also suffered disappointment in its real estate investments. In 1995 USAA announced that it would henceforth concentrate on previously developed properties in geographically diverse areas. It sought to restructure its interest in Fiesta Texas, a theme park in San Antonio that it had helped develop.

Mutual company
Fiscal year ends: December 31

WHO

Chairman and CEO: Robert T. Herres
VC; President, USAA Capital Corporation: Hansford T. Johnson
EVP Information Services: M. Staser Holcomb
SVP, CFO, and Controller: Josue Robles Jr.
SVP Corporate Communications: John R. Cook
SVP and General Counsel: William McCrae
SVP Human Resources: William B. Tracy
President, Property and Casualty Insurance Group: Wilson C. Cooney
President, USAA Life Insurance Co.: Edwin L. Rosane
President, USAA Investment Management Co.: Michael J. C. Roth
President, USAA Federal Savings Bank: Jack M. Antonini
President, USAA Real Estate Co. and La Cantera Development Co.: Edward B. Kelley
President, USAA Buying Services, Inc.: Bobby W. Presley
Auditors: KPMG Peat Marwick LLP

WHERE

HQ: 9800 Fredericksburg Rd., USAA Bldg., San Antonio, TX 78288
Phone: 210-498-2211
Fax: 210-498-9940

USAA provides services worldwide.

Regional Offices

Colorado Springs, CO	Reston, VA
Frankfurt, Germany	Sacramento, CA
London, England	Seattle, WA
Norfolk, VA	Tampa, FL

WHAT

	1994 Sales	
	$ mil.	% of total
Premiums	4,564	74
Net investment income	757	12
Other	860	14
Total	**6,181**	**100**

	1994 Assets	
	$ mil.	% of total
Cash & equivalents	501	3
Investments	12,025	61
Net bank loans	4,037	21
Premiums receivable	660	3
Other	2,325	12
Total	**19,548**	**100**

Selected Products and Services
Auto insurance
Brokerage services
Buying services
Car rental discounts
Credit card services
Life, health, and homeowners insurance
Mutual funds and other investments
Pension and retirement services
Travel services
USAA Floral Service
USAA Parklane West (health care facility)
USAA Road & Travel Plan
USAA Towers (retirement community)
USAA/Sprint Long-Distance Program

KEY COMPETITORS

20th Century Industries	ITT Hartford
AAA	John Hancock
AARP	Kemper Corp.
Aetna	Liberty Mutual
Allstate	MassMutual
American Express	MetLife
American Financial	Mutual of Omaha
American General	Nationwide Insurance
Berkshire Hathaway	New York Life
Charles Schwab	Northwestern Mutual
Chubb	Pacific Mutual Life
CIGNA	Paine Webber
CNA Financial	Prudential
Dean Witter, Discover	State Farm
Equitable	T. Rowe Price
FMR	Transamerica
FTD, Inc.	Travelers
GEICO	USF&G
Guardian Life Insurance	

HOW MUCH

	9-Year Growth	1985	1986	1987	1988	1989	1990	1991	1992	1993	1994
Assets ($ mil.)	18.9%	4,121	5,740	7,168	8,866	10,562	12,258	14,520	16,235	18,494	19,548
Net income ($ mil.)	11.8%	207	294	482	430	424	321	413	140	676	564
Income as % of assets	—	5.0%	5.1%	6.7%	4.8%	4.0%	2.6%	2.8%	0.9%	3.7%	2.9%
Employees	7.6%	7,896	8,355	9,274	11,226	12,515	13,884	14,222	14,667	15,905	15,233

1994 Year-end:
Equity as % of assets: 20.8%
Return on equity: 13.6%
Sales (mil.): $6,181

Net Income
($ mil.)
1985–94

USAA

USAIR GROUP, INC.

OVERVIEW

USAir's hopes to climb out of 6 consecutive years of losses came crashing to the ground in 1994 with the double blow of 2 air crashes and intense competition in its core East Coast markets. A holding company, USAir Group, owns USAir, Allegheny Airlines, and other aviation subsidiaries. USAir accounted for approximately 93% of the company's 1994 sales, and with 59 million passengers a year it is the 6th largest US airline in terms of revenue per passenger miles flown.

However, the company is hemorrhaging cash, and despite a commitment to cut costs by over $1 billion a year by reducing labor costs and increasing productivity, the airline has yet to reach a long-term cost-cutting deal with all of its employee groups.

The entry of lower-fare competitors, especially Continental, in nearly half of USAir's major markets in 1994 (primarily on the East Coast) forced the company to cut its own fares to fight off the challenge.

British Airways (BA) holds about 20% of USAir, but the American carrier's losses forced BA to write off half this investment in 1995. USAir and BA have a "code sharing" agreement, which gives each airline access to the other's markets by making them appear as one airline to customers.

Rumors of a slide into bankruptcy forced CEO Seth Schofield to publicly denounce this notion in 1995. USAir made plans to cut 240 underperforming daily flights in 1995 and defer the acquisition of 8 new aircraft.

WHEN

Pilot Richard du Pont (of the du Pont chemical dynasty) founded All American Aviation, a Washington, DC–based airmail service, in 1937. Serving small northeastern communities, All American picked up and delivered mail "on the fly," using a system of hooks and ropes. Passenger service commenced in 1949.

The company (renamed Allegheny Airlines in 1953) developed by serving communities too remote for major airline service, in an area bounded by Boston, Washington, Cleveland, and Detroit. Allegheny Commuters (now USAir Express) began offering commuter links with Allegheny's route system in 1967.

The airline gained routes in the Great Lakes area, in New York, and on the East Coast by buying Lake Central Airlines (1968) and Mohawk Airlines (1972). Company president Edwin Colodny became chairman in 1978. He reemphasized service to smaller cities and extended service to the South. In 1979 he renamed the company USAir.

USAir augmented its commuter service by buying Pennsylvania Commuter Airlines (1985) and Suburban Airlines (1986). After rebuffing a takeover bid by TWA in 1987, USAir acquired Piedmont Aviation (which operated primarily in the Southeast) and Los Angeles–based Pacific Southwest Airlines.

In 1988 USAir bought 11% of Covia Partnership, which operated the Apollo computerized reservations system (Covia merged with the European CRS operator Galileo in 1992, forming Galileo International, of which USAir owns 11%).

USAir offered its first transatlantic flight (Charlotte to London) in 1989. In that year

difficulty in integrating USAir and Piedmont (one of the largest airline mergers in history), combined with the rising cost of jet fuel, resulted in USAir's only loss during the 1980s and ended 12 consecutive years of profitability. As losses continued into 1990 and 1991, the company cut jobs and sold its engine maintenance and general aviation units. Colodny retired in 1991, leaving Seth Schofield as the top executive.

USAir spent $50 million in 1991 for TWA's London routes and $16.2 million in 1992 for a 40% equity stake (and an option to buy) in the Trump Shuttle (which it operates as USAir Shuttle). The losses continued in 1992, with a 5-day-long mechanics' strike, which stranded passengers, and the construction of new terminals at LaGuardia and Pittsburgh.

Early in 1993 the company started using the term USAir Florida Shuttle to denote its USAir and USAir Express flights within that state. Later in 1993 USAir initiated Philadelphia–Frankfurt service. Sporadic fare wars broke out during the year in the heavily traveled California and Northeast shuttle markets.

The airline found itself hard pressed to compete with lower-cost competitors like Continental's new CALite services. In 1994 president and chief of operations Michael Schwab resigned after receiving criticism from unions. The firm sought further concessions from its unions under pressure from director Warren Buffett (who was forced to write down his investment in USAir).

In 1995 USAir and several of its employee unions reached an agreement on wage concessions.

WHO

Chairman and CEO: Seth E. Schofield, age 55,
$500,000 pay
President and COO: Frank L. Salizzoni, age 56,
$385,769 pay
EVP Marketing, USAir, Inc.: W. Thomas Lagow, age 53,
$325,000 pay
EVP, General Counsel, and Secretary: James T. Lloyd,
age 53, $275,000 pay
EVP Customer Services, USAir, Inc.: John R. Long III,
age 46
SVP Human Resources, USAir, Inc.: John P. Frestel Jr.,
age 55, $275,000 pay
SVP Finance and CFO, USAir Group and USAir, Inc.:
John W. Harper, age 54
SVP Planning, USAir, Inc.: Robert L. Fornaro, age 42
SVP Maintenance Operations, USAir, Inc.: Bruce R.
Aubin, age 64
SVP Public and Community Relations: Nancy R.
Rohrbach, age 48
VP Flight Operations, USAir, Inc.: Gene F. Sharp
VP USAir Express Division: Keith D. Houk
Auditors: KPMG Peat Marwick LLP

WHERE

HQ: 2345 Crystal Dr., Arlington, VA 22227
Phone: 703-418-5306
Fax: 703-418-5307 (Investor Relations)
Reservations: 800-428-4322

USAir serves cities in the US, the Bahamas, Bermuda,
Canada, France, Germany, and the West Indies. It
operates worldwide in partnership with British Airways.

Hub Locations
Baltimore, MD/Washington, DC
Charlotte, NC
Philadelphia, PA
Pittsburgh, PA

WHAT

	1994 Sales	
	$ mil.	% of total
Passenger transportation	6,357	91
Cargo & freight	164	2
Other	476	7
Total	**6,997**	**100**

Major Subsidiaries and Affiliates
Allegheny Airlines, Inc.
Jetstream International Airlines, Inc.
Material Services Co., Inc.
Piedmont Airlines, Inc.
USAir Fuel Corporation
USAir, Inc.
USAir Leasing and Services, Inc.
USAM Corp. (owns 11% of Galileo International,
owner of Galileo Computer Reservations System,
and 21% of Apollo Travel Services)

Aircraft		
	Owned	Leased
Boeing 727	—	6
Boeing 737	87	129
Boeing 757	19	11
Boeing 767	4	5
DC-9	58	14
MD-80	15	16
Other	40	19
Total	**223**	**200**

KEY COMPETITORS

Air Canada
Air France
Air South
Alaska Air
America West
AMR
Continental
Airlines
Delta
Kiwi Air
KLM
Lufthansa
Mesa Air
Northwest
Airlines
Southwest
Airlines
TWA
UAL
Virgin Group

HOW MUCH

	9-Year Growth	1985	1986	1987	1988	1989	1990	1991	1992	1993	1994
Sales ($ mil.)	16.5%	1,765	1,835	3,001	5,707	6,252	6,559	6,514	6,686	7,083	6,997
Net income ($ mil.)	—	117	98	195	165	(63)	(454)	(305)	(601)	(349)	(763)
Income as % of sales	—	6.6%	5.4%	6.5%	2.9%	—	—	—	—	—	—
Earnings per share ($)	—	3.98	3.33	5.27	3.81	(1.73)	(10.89)	(7.62)	(13.88)	(7.68)	(12.73)
Stock price – high ($)	—	38.50	41.00	53.50	40.13	54.75	33.75	24.50	18.38	24.75	15.38
Stock price – low ($)	—	27.25	30.13	22.00	28.00	30.63	12.63	7.00	10.50	11.13	3.88
Stock price – close ($)	(20.7%)	34.38	36.25	33.75	34.50	33.38	15.75	12.13	12.75	12.88	4.25
P/E – high	—	10	12	10	11	—	—	—	—	—	—
P/E – low	—	7	9	4	7	—	—	—	—	—	—
Dividends per share ($)	(100.0%)	0.12	0.12	0.12	0.12	0.15	0.09	0.00	0.00	0.00	0.00
Book value per share ($)	—	35.47	38.78	43.89	47.27	42.86	31.50	28.95	(3.58)	(7.19)	(18.17)
Employees	14.2%	13,789	14,976	16,509	24,337	50,600	53,000	48,700	48,900	48,500	45,500

1994 Year-end:
Debt ratio: 100.0%
Return on equity: —
Cash (mil.): $452
Current ratio: 0.49
Long-term debt (mil.): $2,895
No. of shares (mil.): 61
Dividends
  Yield: —
  Payout: —
Market value (mil.): $260

**Stock Price History
High/Low 1985–94**

USF&G CORPORATION

OVERVIEW

Baltimore-based USF&G has a new strategy for building its business: it wants to play in an area in which it has an unfair advantage. The area it has staked out is small- and middle-market business and personal lines. To gain that advantage, the company has rethought its business and devised a number of new products designed to appeal to that audience. In 1995 it even formed a new business group, the Family and Business Insurance Group, to concentrate on the market.

USF&G provides property/casualty insurance and life insurance. Its largest subsidiary, United States Fidelity and Guaranty, is one of the largest US property/casualty insurers, handling both commercial and personal property/casualty insurance, reinsurance, and fidelity-surety lines. Fidelity and Guaranty Life Insurance offers life insurance and individual and annuity insurance products.

This refinement of focus follows on the heels of a radical 3-year restructuring undertaken by chairman and CEO Norman Blake. He oversaw the dismantling of a network of noncore businesses. And although costs have decreased thanks to that effort, USF&G still has not met the goal (elusive in the industry in recent years) of achieving an underwriting profit.

WHEN

In 1896 Baltimore businessman John Bland had the idea of selling businesses a list of attorneys bonded as collection agents by a surety company. He formed United States Fidelity and Guaranty to write surety bonds guaranteeing prompt remittance of money collected by attorneys for mercantile houses.

In 1900 the company added burglary insurance to its operations, which already covered the entire country. USF&G grew through a network of independent agents, many of whom were personally selected by Bland. By 1903 the company was also doing business in Alaska, Canada, and Hawaii. A short foray into Europe ended in failure that same year.

After the introduction of the automobile and enactment of workers' compensation laws, the company added casualty and health insurance. Within 5 years casualty premiums equaled the combined premiums of fidelity (bonds covering employee dishonesty), surety, and burglary insurance. Aided by insurance business with the government in WWI, casualty premiums soon contributed twice as much to sales as did sureties. In 1920 the company began offering fire and inland marine insurance.

In the early 1930s, hit by the Depression, the company reduced the par value of its stock to replenish its surplus fund, and by 1935 it was in the black again.

With the 1952 purchase of Fidelity and Guaranty Fire Insurance, the company was able to write all lines of property insurance. In the 1950s USF&G established new branches and further developed its agency force. In 1960 it formed F&G Life and in 1962 bought Merchants Fire Assurance and Merchants Indemnity. In 1969 USF&G bought Thomas Jefferson Life Insurance from First Executive.

The company centralized operations in Baltimore in the 1970s. Hard times hit the insurance industry in the early 1970s, and USF&G lost about $1 million per month in 1973 and 1974 but by 1978 was back on track with the highest underwriting profits of any stock insurance company.

In 1981 the life insurance and property/casualty operations became part of the holding company USF&G. Hit by losses in the 1980s, the company diversified into financial services, acquiring 40 subsidiaries worldwide. In 1985 USF&G created USF&G Financial Services to provide investment management services to corporate and institutional clients worldwide. Other new operations included foreign currency and bond trading, travel services, and oil and gas operations. In 1988 USF&G bought Citicorp Investment Management (renamed Chancellor Capital Management) and stopped writing workers' compensation insurance.

In 1990, with the company facing recession, declining profits, a portfolio of problem bonds and real estate investments, and increasing expenses, the entire management team was replaced by a new group led by Norman Blake. More than 85% of the management was replaced after 1990. Blake slashed dividends and established loss reserves for junk bonds and real estate. He also sold $1.2 billion in non-performing assets. In 1991 USF&G raised funds through a private stock offering and targeted 12 companies for disposal, including all of the financial services units, in order to focus on property/casualty and life insurance.

This entailed cutting personnel by 48% and structural expenses by 31% between 1991 and 1994. The next year USF&G acquired specialty auto insurer Victoria Financial and property/casualty company Discover Re.

NYSE symbol: FG
Fiscal year ends: December 31

WHO

Chairman, President, and CEO: Norman P. Blake Jr., age 53, $1,894,362 pay
EVP and CFO: Dan L. Hale, age 50, $752,188 pay
EVP Field Operations: Gary C. Dunton, age 39, $496,428 pay
SVP Human Resources and General Counsel: John A. MacColl, age 45, $494,654 pay
SVP and Chief Investment Officer; Chairman, Falcon Asset Management: John C. Sweeney, age 50, $436,300 pay
SVP Personal Lines: James R. Lewis, age 46
SVP and Chief Information Officer: Thomas K. Lewis Jr., age 42
SVP Strategic Planning/Corporate Marketing: Andrew A. Stern, age 37
Auditors: Ernst & Young LLP

WHERE

HQ: 100 Light St., Baltimore, MD 21202
Phone: 410-547-3000
Fax: 410-625-5682

USF&G sells property/casualty and life insurance throughout the US. It maintains 5 regional and 30 branch offices.

	1994 Premiums (% of total)	
	Life	Property/casualty
Northeast	41	29
Northwest	21	—
Southeast	—	24
South	14	—
Southwest	13	—
Midwest	11	21
West	—	18
Mississippi	—	8
Total	**100**	**100**

WHAT

	1994 Assets	
	$ mil.	% of total
Cash & equivalents	488	4
Mortgage-backed securities	2,798	20
Corporate bonds	4,917	36
High-yield bonds	597	4
Mortgages & real estate	1,011	7
Receivables	1,957	14
Other	2,006	15
Total	**13,774**	**100**

	1994 Sales		1994 Pretax Income	
	$ mil.	% of total	$ mil.	% of total
P&C insurance	2,697	86	213	94
Life insurance	470	14	14	6
Adjustments	54	—	(276)	—
Total	**3,221**	**100**	**(49)**	**100**

Property/Casualty Insurance
Auto
Business
Home
Reinsurance

Life Insurance
Annuities
Individuals
Universal life

Major Subsidiaries
F&G Re, Inc.
Fidelity and Guaranty Life Insurance Co.
United States Fidelity and Guaranty Co.

KEY COMPETITORS

20th Century Industries	CIGNA	Lloyd's of London
Aetna	CNA Financial	MetLife
AFLAC	Equitable	New York Life
AIG	GEICO	Northwestern
Allianz	General Electric	Mutual
Allstate	General Re	State Farm
American General	Guardian Life	Transamerica
BankAmerica	ITT Hartford	Travelers
Chubb	John Hancock	USAA
	Kemper	

HOW MUCH

	9-Year Growth	1985	1986	1987	1988	1989	1990	1991	1992	1993	1994
Assets ($ mil.)	6.7%	7,674	8,936	10,141	12,361	13,604	13,910	14,456	13,134	14,335	13,774
Net income ($ mil.)	—	(258)	243	265	232	117	(569)	(176)	28	127	232
Income as % of assets	—	—	2.7%	2.6%	1.9%	0.9%	—	—	0.2%	0.9%	1.7%
Earnings per share ($)	—	(4.43)	3.61	3.28	2.66	1.21	(6.99)	(2.53)	(0.24)	0.98	1.86
Stock price – high ($)	—	41.50	46.75	48.75	34.38	34.00	30.38	12.50	15.00	19.63	16.13
Stock price – low ($)	—	25.50	36.25	26.25	28.50	28.25	7.00	5.63	7.13	11.13	11.69
Stock price – close ($))	(11.0%)	39.00	39.75	28.38	28.50	29.00	7.50	7.25	12.38	14.75	13.63
P/E – high	—	—	13	15	13	28	—	—	—	20	9
P/E – low	—	—	10	8	11	23	—	—	—	11	6
Dividends per share ($)	(23.3%)	2.17	2.29	2.44	2.60	2.76	2.89	0.40	0.20	0.20	0.20
Book value per share ($)	(6.0%)	18.91	23.13	18.85	22.57	21.60	14.35	10.30	9.64	12.42	10.86
Employees	(4.0%)	9,100	9,700	10,500	11,800	12,600	12,500	8,000	7,500	6,500	6,300

1994 Year-end:
Equity as % of assets: 9.9%
Return on assets: 1.7%
Return on equity: 22.2%
Long-term debt (mil.): $616
No. of shares (mil.): 96
Dividends
  Yield: 1.5%
  Payout: 10.8%
Market value (mil.): $1,303
Sales (mil.): $3,221

**Stock Price History
High/Low 1985–94**

USX–MARATHON GROUP

OVERVIEW

USX–Marathon Group is a business unit of USX Corporation, along with USX–U.S. Steel Group and USX–Delhi Group. The Marathon Group is a medium-sized, fully integrated oil company. Its largest holding is Houston-based Marathon Oil; other subsidiaries include Emro Marketing and Carnegie Natural Gas.

Marathon's operations range from exploration to marketing. It explores for oil in 17 countries, principally in Argentina, Bolivia, China, Egypt, Gabon, Ireland, the Netherlands, Tunisia, the UK, and the US. It produces oil and natural gas in 8 countries and operates 4 refineries in the US. The company sells its products through Marathon-brand retailers and other outlets, including Bonded, Starvin'

Marvin, and Speedway. The group's companies are also involved in natural gas transportation and liquefied natural gas operations.

On the retail side of its business, Marathon has been boosting the number of gas stations it operates, acquiring 133 service stations in 1994 and expanding its market reach to a 16-state area. On the production side, the company finished its first full year of production in the East Brae fields in the UK's North Sea in 1994 and completed the SAGE gas pipeline from the East Brae fields to the UK. The North Sea schemes, plus significant projects in the Gulf of Mexico and Indonesia, have boosted Marathon's oil and gas production by approximately 30% over the past 2 years.

WHEN

Marathon was founded in 1887 as the Ohio Oil Company by a group of 14 independent Ohio oil producers who joined together to better compete with the dominant purchaser of the time, Standard Oil. The partnership worked so well that within 2 years Ohio Oil was the largest producer in the state, a fact that did not go unnoticed at Standard Oil headquarters. Standard Oil bought out Ohio Oil in 1889.

When Standard Oil was ordered broken up by the US Supreme Court in 1911, Ohio Oil became independent once again. Led by new president James Donnell, the company soon began to expand its exploration activities to Wyoming, Kansas, Louisiana, and Texas.

One major discovery in Texas almost never happened. In 1924 Ohio Oil agreed to drill 3 wells on leases west of the Pecos River. By mistake it drilled 3 dry holes on leases east of the river. Ohio Oil planned to abandon the properties, until a geologist reported the error. Drilled in the right area, the wells flowed voluminously. Also in 1924 the company acquired Lincoln Oil Refining — its first venture outside crude oil production.

O. D. Donnell became president of the company following his father's death in 1927 and continued the company's expansion into refining and marketing operations. Following WWII, a 3rd generation of Donnells took the helm of the company. J. C. Donnell II led Ohio Oil's foray into international exploration. Through Conorada Petroleum Corporation, a partnership with Continental Oil (now Conoco) and Amerada Hess, the company explored Africa and South and Central America. Conorada's biggest overseas deal came in

1955, when it acquired concessions on over 60 million acres in Libya.

In 1962 Ohio Oil acquired Plymouth Oil, including its producing properties, a refinery in Texas City, and transportation, distribution, and marketing facilities, for over $100 million. Also in 1962 the company changed its name to Marathon Oil Company; it had been using the Marathon name in its marketing activities since the late 1930s.

In 1976 Marathon added a 200,000-barrel-a-day refinery in Louisiana to its operations when it acquired ECOL Ltd. for $403 million.

Following a battle with Mobil, U.S. Steel acquired Marathon in 1982 for $6.5 billion. In 1986 U.S. Steel changed its name to USX and acquired Texas Oil & Gas for $3.6 billion. Also that year the US government introduced economic sanctions against Libya, putting Marathon's Libyan holdings in suspension.

In 1990 USX consolidated Texas Oil with Marathon. Following a protracted battle with corporate raider Carl Icahn, USX split Marathon and U.S. Steel into 2 separate stock classes in 1991. In 1992 USX created a 3rd offering, USX–Delhi Group. The pipeline operator had previously been a part of the Marathon Group.

In 1994 a consortium led by Marathon Oil signed an agreement with the Russian government to develop oil and gas fields off Sakhalin Island (the site of a devastating 1995 earthquake). These fields contain 750 million barrels of oil and 14 trillion cubic feet of gas.

In 1995 Marathon introduced reformulated gasoline to its various terminals to meet the requirements of the EPA.

NYSE symbol: MRO
Fiscal year ends: December 31

WHO

VC, Marathon Group; President, Marathon Oil: Victor G. Beghini, age 60, $1,109,167 pay
EVP Refining, Marketing, and Transportation, Marathon Oil: J. Louis Frank, age 58, $589,000 pay
EVP Exploration and Production, Marathon Oil: Carl P. Giardini, age 59
SVP Finance and Accounting, Marathon Oil: Jimmy D. Low, age 57
VP Administration and Services, Marathon Oil: William F. Madison, age 52
VP Worldwide Exploration, Marathon Oil: Ron S. Keisler
VP Marketing, Marathon Oil: Richard E. White
VP Human Resources and Environment, Marathon Oil: Kenneth L. Matheny
General Counsel and Secretary, Marathon Oil: William F. Schwind Jr., age 50
Auditors: Price Waterhouse LLP

WHERE

HQ: 600 Grant St., Pittsburgh, PA 15219-4776
Phone: 412-433-1121
Fax: 412-433-5733

Marathon conducts exploration and development activities in 17 countries. The group sells petroleum products in 2,356 Marathon-brand retail outlets and over 1,700 retail outlets operated by Emro Marketing Company.

	1994 Sales		1994 Operating Income	
	$ mil.	% of total	$ mil.	% of total
US	12,270	96	537	85
Europe	456	4	96	15
Other regions	31	0	(49)	—
Total	**12,757**	**100**	**584**	**100**

WHAT

	1994 Sales	
	$ mil.	% of total
Refined products & merchandise	6,491	51
Excise taxes	2,542	20
Buy/sell agreements	2,071	16
Liquid hydrocarbons	800	6
Natural gas	670	5
Other	183	2
Total	**12,757**	**100**

Selected Subsidiaries and Affiliates
Carnegie Natural Gas Co.
CLAM Petroleum Co. (The Netherlands, 50%)
Emro Marketing Co.
FWA Drilling Co., Inc.
LOCAP INC. (pipeline & storage facilities, 37%)
LOOP INC. (offshore oil port, 32%)
Kenai LNG Corp. (30%)
Marathon Oil Co.
Marathon Pipe Line Co.
Sakhalin Energy Investment Co. Ltd (Russia, 30%)

Selected Brand Names

Bonded	Starvin' Marvin
Marathon	United
Speedway	Wake Up

KEY COMPETITORS

Amerada Hess	Exxon	Pennzoil
Amoco	Kerr-McGee	Phillips
Ashland, Inc.	Koch	Petroleum
British Petroleum	Mobil	Repsol
Chevron	Norsk Hydro	Royal Dutch/Shell
Circle K	Occidental	Sinclair Oil
Coastal	Oryx	Southland
Diamond	Panhandle	Sun Co.
Shamrock	Eastern	Texaco
Elf Aquitaine	PDVSA	TOTAL
Enron	PEMEX	Unocal

HOW MUCH

	Annual Growth	1985	1986	1987	1988[1]	1989[1]	1990[1]	1991	1992	1993	1994
Sales ($ mil.)	4.2%	—	—	—	9,949	12,264	14,616	13,975	12,782	11,962	12,757
Net income ($ mil.)	35.0%	—	—	—	53	425	508	(71)	109	(6)	312
Income as % of sales	—	—	—	—	0.5%	3.5%	3.5%	—	0.9%	—	2.5%
Earnings per share ($)	(5.9%)	—	—	—	—	1.49	1.94	(0.31)	0.37	(0.04)	1.10
Stock price – high ($)	—	—	—	—	—	—	—	33.13	24.75	20.63	19.13
Stock price – low ($)	—	—	—	—	—	—	—	20.88	15.75	16.38	15.63
Stock price – close ($)	(12.6%)	—	—	—	—	—	—	24.50	17.25	16.50	16.38
P/E – high	—	—	—	—	—	—	—	—	67	—	17
P/E – low	—	—	—	—	—	—	—	—	43	—	14
Dividends per share ($)	(1.0%)	—	—	—	—	—	—	0.70	1.22	0.68	0.68
Book value per share ($)	(3.6%)	—	—	—	—	13.25	13.92	12.45	11.37	10.58	11.01
Employees	(2.0%)	—	—	—	23,772	25,762	26,200	24,762	22,810	21,914	21,005

1994 Year-end:
Debt ratio: 56.1%
Return on equity: 10.4%
Cash (mil.): $28
Current ratio: 1.01
Long-term debt (mil.): $3,983
No. of shares (mil.): 287
Dividends
   Yield: 4.2%
   Payout: 61.8%
Market value (mil.): $4,703

Stock Price History
High/Low 1991–94

[1] Pro forma for USX energy group

USX–U.S. STEEL GROUP

OVERVIEW

Venerable U.S. Steel is one of the nation's oldest and largest steelmakers. Its Pennsylvania steel mill, the first steel plant built by Andrew Carnegie, is considered "the birthplace of American steel." Today the company is still the US's #1 integrated steelmaker, producing about 11% of the 1994 domestic total.

U.S. Steel is one of 3 publicly traded companies that make up the giant, international, diversified energy conglomerate USX Corporation and accounts for about 31% of USX's revenues. The steelmaker also produces domestic coal and iron ore and provides engineering, consulting, mineral resource management, and real estate management services.

For almost a decade, low steel prices and stiff competition from foreign steelmakers and low-cost US minimills have forced U.S. Steel and other steelmakers to slash production, jobs, and costs. In addition to closing less-efficient facilities (7 out of 10 raw steel production facilities were closed), U.S. Steel has diversified through joint ventures and is concentrating on products that are more profitable, such as coated and laminated steel.

In October 1994 U.S. Steel teamed up with rival Nucor — developer of the low-cost technology used by minimills — to explore a new technology, based on iron carbide instead of iron ore, that would reduce much of the cost and pollution of the steelmaking process. The 2 companies will first conduct a feasibility study and, if the method is viable, build a demonstration plant to evaluate commercializing the new process. Industrial gas maker Praxair has a small stake in the new company.

WHEN

United States Steel Corporation was conceived in a 1901 merger of 10 steel companies that combined their furnaces, ore deposits, railroad companies, and shipping lines. The merger, still the largest in US corporate history, involved industrial pioneers such as Andrew Carnegie, Charles Schwab, Elbert Gary, and J. P. Morgan.

Morgan, who had helped organize the Federal Steel Company in 1898, wanted to create a centralized trust to dominate the steel market, which was soaring at the turn of the century. Carnegie owned the largest US steel company at the time, Carnegie Steel, but wanted to retire. When Morgan attended a dinner in 1900, he met Schwab, Carnegie Steel's president, who outlined the idea of the steel trust based on a merger of the Carnegie and Federal steel companies. Morgan asked Schwab to persuade Carnegie to sell his mills and name his price. He did. Morgan didn't haggle when Carnegie asked for almost a half billion dollars.

The Carnegie-Morgan combination created the world's first billion-dollar company. It produced 67% of the country's steel in its first year (its huge steel complex and the Indiana company town where it was located were named after Gary, who was CEO until 1927). Generally profitable, the company has been known throughout its history for its acquisitions, divestitures, reorganizations, consolidations, and labor disputes.

The company boomed during WWI and WWII, but its market share fell to about 30% by the 1950s. It set new profit records in 1955, but during the 1970s the prospects for long-term growth in steel became dismal in light of rising costs, foreign competition, and competitive pricing.

In a move that doubled the company's size, U.S. Steel purchased Marathon Oil in 1982, a major integrated energy company with huge oil and gas reserves. It continued to cut back its steelmaking capacity, laying off 100,000 employees, closing steel mills, and selling off assets worth billions of dollars.

In 1986 U.S. Steel bought Texas Oil & Gas and was renamed USX Corporation to reflect the decreasing role of steel. Also that year corporate raider Carl Icahn, USX's largest single shareholder, unsuccessfully tried to get the company to sell its steel operations. In 1991 stockholders approved splitting the company into 2 separate entities under the USX umbrella: U.S. Steel and Marathon. A 3rd group, USX–Delhi Group, was created in 1992 to hold the company's natural gas operations.

During the 1990s U.S. Steel continued to close steel-producing facilities. In 1992 USX joined 5 other leading US steel companies in a suit against subsidized foreign steelmakers; an unfavorable decision in 1993 is under appeal. Also in 1993 the company formed 2 joint ventures in the US with Japan's Kobe Steel.

In 1994 U.S. Steel ratified 2 long-term labor contracts that cover 80% of its employees. In April 1995 USX chairman Charles Corry retired earlier than expected; former U.S. Steel chief Thomas Usher, who had been named USX president and COO months earlier, was appointed his successor.

WHO

Chairman and CEO, USX Corporation: Thomas J. Usher, age 52, $1,028,500 pay (prior to promotion)
President, U.S. Steel Group: Paul J. Wilhelm, age 52
EVP Raw Materials and Diversified Businesses: Charles C. Gedeon, age 54
EVP Commercial: Reuben L. Perin Jr., age 56
VP Environmental Affairs: Charles G. Carson III, age 52
VP International Business; President, USX Engineers and Consultants, Inc.: John J. Connelly
VP Operations: Roy G. Dorrance, age 49
VP Accounting and Finance: Edward F. Guna, age 46
VP Technology and Management Services: Bruce A. Haines, age 50
VP Employee Relations: Thomas W. Sterling III, age 47
General Counsel: Donald M. Laws, age 59
President, U.S. Steel Mining Co., Inc.: John F. Dickinson II
President, USX Realty Development: Albert E. Ferrara Jr.
Auditors: Price Waterhouse LLP

WHERE

HQ: 600 Grant St., Pittsburgh, PA 15219-4776
Phone: 412-433-1121
Fax: 412-433-4818

USX–U.S. Steel operates 3 raw steel manufacturing plants: Gary Works in Indiana, Mon Valley Works in Pennsylvania, and Fairfield Works in Alabama.

	1994 Sales		1994 Operating Income	
	$ mil.	% of total	$ mil.	% of total
US	5,989	99	311	99
International	77	1	2	1
Total	**6,066**	**100**	**313**	**100**

WHAT

1994 Steel Shipments		
	Net tons (thou.)	% of total
Steel service centers	2,795	27
Further conversions	2,390	23
Transportation	2,023	19
Containers	995	9
Construction	738	7
Export, appliances & other	623	6
Machinery	570	5
Oil & gas drilling	434	4
Total	**10,568**	**100**

Principal Subsidiaries and Affiliates
Double Eagle Steel Coating Co. (50%, steel processing)
National-Oilwell (50%; oil well equipment, supplies)
PRO-TEC Coating Co. (50%, steel galvanizing)
RMI Titanium Co. (54%, titanium metal products)
Transtar (46%; railroads, shipping, docks)
U.S. Steel Mining Co. (coal reserves and mining)
USS/Kobe Steel Company (50%, tubular and bar steel)
USS-POSCO Industries (50%, sheet and tin products)
USX Engineers and Consultants, Inc. (engineering and consulting services)
USX Realty Development (management services)
Worthington Specialty Processing (50%, steel coils and blanks)

KEY COMPETITORS

AK Steel	Inland Steel	Pohang Iron & Steel
Allegheny Ludlum	J&L Specialty Steel	Republic Engineered Steels
Armco	LTV	
ASARCO	Mitsubishi	
Bechtel	Mitsui	Rouge Steel
Bethlehem Steel	National Steel	Thyssen
Birmingham Steel	Nippon Steel	WCI Steel
Broken Hill	Nucor	Weirton Steel
Cargill	Oregon Steel Mills	WHX
Cyprus Amax		
Fried. Krupp		
Hyundai	Peter Kiewit Sons'	

HOW MUCH

	Annual Growth	1985	1986	1987	1988	1989	1990	1991	1992	1993	1994
Sales ($ mil.)	(2.3%)	—	—	—	6,996	6,509	6,073	4,864	4,919	5,612	6,066
Net income ($ mil.)	(18.1%)	—	—	—	664	540	310	(509)	(274)	(190)	201
Income as % of sales	—	—	—	—	9.5%	8.3%	5.1%	—	—	—	3.3%
Earnings per share ($)	(23.9%)	—	—	—	12.09	10.17	6.00	(10.00)	(4.92)	(2.96)	2.35
Stock price – high ($)	—	—	—	—	—	—	—	30.25	34.38	46.00	45.63
Stock price – low ($)	—	—	—	—	—	—	—	20.00	22.13	27.50	30.25
Stock price – close ($)	9.0%	—	—	—	—	—	—	27.38	34.00	43.25	35.50
P/E – high	—	—	—	—	—	—	—	—	—	—	19
P/E – low	—	—	—	—	—	—	—	—	—	—	13
Dividends per share ($)	26.0%	—	—	—	—	—	—	0.50	1.00	1.00	1.00
Book value per share ($)	(28.4%)	—	—	—	—	—	—	32.70	3.98	8.32	12.02
Employees	(5.3%)	—	—	—	—	27,173	24,664	22,234	21,479	21,527	20,711

1994 Year-end:
Debt ratio: 60.6%
Return on equity: 26.8%
Cash (mil.): $20
Current ratio: 1.4
Long-term debt (mil.): $1,432
No. of shares (mil.): 76
Dividends
  Yield: 2.8%
  Payout: 42.6%
Market value (mil.): $2,697

Stock Price History
High/Low 1991–94

V. F. CORPORATION

OVERVIEW

V. F. makes its money by putting its pants on one leg at a time. The nation's largest maker of denim jeans with a 30% market share, the Wyomissing, Pennsylvania–based company gets more than half its revenues from its Jeanswear division, which makes Lee, Rustler, and Wrangler brands. Other apparel brands include Vanity Fair (lingerie and loungewear), Jantzen (sportswear), Red Kap (industrial work clothes), and Healthtex (infants' and children's clothes).

Rather than take his chances with the roller-coaster world of high fashion, CEO Lawrence Pugh prefers to keep his feet on the ground, concentrating more on apparel staples. The company has spent heavily to create a state-of-the art distribution system to restock its major customers, such as Wal-Mart and J. C. Penney, in as little as 3 days. (It used to take up to 3 months).

V. F. has made a number of acquisitions to build up its brands — most recently in sports apparel — but Pugh is concentrating now on internal expansion. He plans to spend about $200 million to build V. F.'s existing businesses. The company is also making a major push overseas, having launched its Vanity Fair line in Europe in late 1994.

WHEN

In 1899, 6 partners, including banker John Barbey, started the Reading Glove and Mitten Manufacturing Company. Barbey bought out his 5 partners in 1911 and changed the name of the Reading, Pennsylvania, company to Schuylkill Silk Mills in 1913.

Barbey expanded the mills' production to underwear and, in the 1920s, discontinued glove manufacturing. A company contest with a $25 prize produced the brand name Vanity Fair in 1917. Barbey changed the mills' name to Vanity Fair Silk Mills in 1919.

Barbey and his son J. E. led their lingerie company (Barbey banned the word underwear) to national prominence. The mills made only silk garments until the 1920s, when synthetics such as rayon and acetate were developed. In response to the US embargo on silk in 1941, Vanity Fair converted to rayon, finally converting all production to the new wonder fabric, nylon tricot, in 1948.

Vanity Fair opened its first Alabama production plant in 1937 (opening 5 more by 1962). By 1948 Vanity Fair manufactured all stages of its nylon products, from filament to finished garment. It expanded its color offerings and introduced permanent pleating and printed lingerie, including leopard and mermaid prints. The company won awards for its innovative advertising with photographs of live models in Vanity Fair lingerie.

J. E. Barbey owned all of Vanity Fair's stock until 1951, when he sold 1/3 of his holdings to the public. In 1966 the stock, previously traded OTC, was listed on the NYSE.

After changing its name to V. F. Corporation in 1969, the company used acquisitions to expand its lingerie business and to begin producing sportswear and blue jeans. It bought Berkshire International (hosiery, 1969), H.D. Lee (jeans, 1969), and Kay Windsor (lingerie, 1971). V. F. sold Berkshire International's US operations in 1976, but the site of the division's Reading, Pennsylvania, hosiery mill now houses the original VF Factory Outlet.

More acquisitions followed, including Modern Globe (lingerie, 1984) and Bassett-Walker (fleecewear, 1984). In 1986 V. F. bought Blue Bell, a North Carolina maker of blue jeans (Wrangler and Rustler), sportswear (Jantzen and JanSport), and occupational clothing (Red Kap and Big Ben). The company bought the Vassarette brand name (lingerie) from Munsingwear in 1990. The following year V. F. added Healthtex (infant's and children's apparel), WorkWear (occupational clothing), and the Barbizon brand of lingerie.

The company obtained 3 European producers of lingerie (Valero, Vivesa, and Jean Bellanger Enterprises) in 1992 for a total of 8 new international lingerie brands. In 1993 V. F. moved its Lee brand products from discount chains to department and specialty stores and introduced a lower-cost Rider brand for discount outlets; Shopko and Target retaliated by boycotting V. F. sportswear.

To compete in the rapidly growing sports-apparel business, V. F. bought Nutmeg Industries and H.H. Cutler in 1994. Nutmeg is licensed by the 4 major US professional sports leagues and most US colleges and universities; Cutler is the exclusive licensee of Fisher-Price children's wear in the US and one of the largest children's wear licensees of Walt Disney products.

In 1995 V. F. introduced a new brand of licensed team apparel, Lee Sport, that will include T-shirts, fleecewear, and headwear.

NYSE symbol: VFC
Fiscal year ends: Saturday nearest December 31

WHO

Chairman and CEO: Lawrence R. Pugh, age 62, $1,760,000 pay
President and COO: Mackey J. McDonald, age 48, $1,225,000 pay
Chairman, Decorated Knitwear Coalition: Daniel G. Mac Farlan, age 44
Chairman, Jeanswear Coalition: John P. Schamberger, age 46
VP Finance and CFO: Gerard G. Johnson, age 54, $683,000 pay
VP Human Resources and Administration: Harold E. Addis, age 64, $412,000 pay
VP and Controller: Robert K. Shearer, age 43, $324,133 pay
VP Business Systems: Thomas H. Scott, age 38
VP Private Label/Intimate Apparel: Janet J. Peters, age 64
VP and Secretary: Lori M. Tarnoski, age 55
VP and Treasurer: Frank C. Pickard III, age 50
VP and General Counsel: Candace S. Cummings, age 47
Auditors: Ernst & Young LLP

WHERE

HQ: 1047 North Park Rd., Wyomissing, PA 19610
Phone: 610-378-1151
Fax: 610-375-9371

V. F. sells its products around the world.

	1994 Sales		1994 Operating Income	
	$ mil.	% of total	$ mil.	% of total
US	4,209	85	497	86
International	763	15	80	14
Total	**4,972**	**100**	**577**	**100**

WHAT

	1994 Sales		1994 Operating Profit	
	$ mil.	% of total	$ mil.	% of total
Jeanswear	2,547	51	372	65
Intimate apparel	725	15	60	10
Specialty apparel	709	14	76	13
Decorated knitwear	623	13	32	6
Playwear	368	7	37	6
Total	**4,972**	**100**	**577**	**100**

Selected Brand Names

Jeanswear	Intima Cherry	Decorated Knitwear
Lee	Lou	
Marithé & François	Silhouette	Jansport
Girbaud (license)	Siltex	Lee
Riders	Vanity Fair	Lee Sport
Rustler	Variance	Nutmeg
Timber Creek	Vassarette	Riders
Wrangler		
	Specialty Apparel	**Playwear**
Intimate Apparel	Jansport	Fisher-Price
Belcor	Jantzen	(licensed)
Bolero	Red Kap	Healthtex
Carina		Lee
Eileen West		Nike (licensed)
Gemma		Wrangler

KEY COMPETITORS

Berkshire Hathaway	Melville
Bugle Boy	NIKE
Fruit of the Loom	Oshkosh B'Gosh
The Gap	Oxford Industries
Guess?	Polo/Ralph Lauren
Gymboree	Reebok
Hartmarx	Russell Corp.
Levi Strauss	Sandoz
The Limited	Sara Lee
Liz Claiborne	Starter
Marks and Spencer	Warnaco Group

HOW MUCH

	9-Year Growth	1985	1986	1987	1988	1989	1990	1991	1992	1993	1994
Sales ($ mil.)	14.4%	1,481	1,545	2,574	2,516	2,533	2,613	2,952	3,824	4,320	4,972
Net income ($ mil.)	7.9%	139	129	180	174	176	81	161	237	246	275
Income as % of sales	—	9.4%	8.4%	7.0%	6.9%	6.9%	3.1%	5.5%	6.2%	5.7%	5.5%
Earnings per share ($)	6.9%	2.25	2.05	2.65	2.55	2.72	1.33	2.62	3.85	3.71	4.10
Stock price – high ($)	—	27.00	36.00	48.25	33.88	38.38	34.25	41.50	57.50	56.50	53.75
Stock price – low ($)	—	12.94	24.00	22.00	24.75	27.75	11.63	17.63	38.50	39.50	44.25
Stock price – close ($)	7.2%	25.94	30.88	24.50	28.75	31.88	18.38	39.63	53.25	46.13	48.63
P/E – high	—	12	18	18	13	14	26	16	15	15	13
P/E – low	—	6	12	8	10	10	9	7	10	11	11
Dividends per share ($)	9.9%	0.58	0.66	0.75	0.85	0.91	1.00	1.02	1.11	1.22	1.36
Book value per share ($)	13.1%	8.91	12.20	14.40	16.09	14.14	14.44	16.26	19.39	23.99	27.02
Employees	8.7%	32,000	50,000	49,000	43,000	44,500	40,300	49,000	57,000	62,000	68,000

1994 Year-end:
Debt ratio: 32.7%
Return on equity: 16.7%
Cash (mil.): $60
Current ratio: 1.70
Long-term debt (mil.): $517
No. of shares (mil.): 64
Dividends
  Yield: 2.8%
  Payout: 33.2%
Market value (mil.): $3,120

Stock Price History
High/Low 1985–94

VIACOM INC.

Viacom, one of the world's largest media companies, is the medium *and* the message. The New York–based company is a major force in TV, owning such cable channels as MTV, VH1, Nickelodeon/Nick at Nite, pay movie channels (Showtime, The Movie Channel, and Flix), and 50% of USA Network, Comedy Central, the Sci-Fi Channel, and the All News Channel. It is a major producer of leading TV shows (*Entertainment Tonight* and *Frasier*, among others, and *Melrose Place* and *Beverly Hills 90210* through Spelling Entertainment); a syndicator of popular TV programs (the *Star Trek* series, *Cheers*, and *Taxi*); a major movie producer (*Forrest Gump*); a leading book publisher (Simon & Schuster); and the world's top video and music retailer (Blockbuster Video and Blockbuster Music). The diversified entertainment giant also owns a score of radio and TV stations, presides over a library of TV programs and feature films, operates regional theme parks, and owns movie theaters in the US, Canada, and Europe.

Viacom emerged as a world-class company in 1994 when its chairman, Sumner Redstone, won a bidding war for Paramount and subsequently bought Blockbuster Video (Redstone owns about 1/2 of Viacom's common stock through his company, National Amusements). To offset the debt incurred for the Paramount purchase, Redstone sold off Madison Square Garden, along with the Knicks (basketball), the Rangers (hockey), the Paramount Theater, and a cable sports station, and agreed in principle to sell Viacom's cable system.

Other noncore assets may be put on the block to reduce debt and enable the company to exploit its many copyrights in movies, TV, toys, games, and books, and to enter the fast-growing music business.

CBS formed Viacom in 1970 after the FCC ruled that TV networks could not own cable systems and TV stations in the same market. Viacom took over CBS's program syndication division. In the early 1970s Viacom bought cable systems in 5 states. In 1978 it formed Showtime, a subscription TV service, with Teleprompter, becoming full owner in 1982.

Paramount was started in 1912 by Adolph Zukor, becoming Paramount Pictures after merging with Famous Players-Lasky, a studio formed by Jesse Lasky, Samuel Goldwyn (né Goldfish), and Cecil B. DeMille. In the 1940s the government forced Paramount to divest its theater holdings. Movie attendance slipped as TV grew, and in 1966 Gulf + Western bought the struggling Paramount Pictures.

Gulf + Western began in 1956 when Charles G. Bluhdorn bought Michigan Plating and Stamping (Studebaker rear bumpers). Two years later he merged his company with Beard & Stone Electric and in 1959 adopted the name Gulf + Western Industries. The company acquired many diverse firms. When Bluhdorn died in 1983, his successor, Martin Davis, sold off all the other businesses except Associates Investment (auto loans, later sold in 1989), Simon & Schuster (1975), and Madison Square Garden (1977, sold 1995). In 1989 Gulf + Western became Paramount Communications, the same year it made an unsuccessful $200-per-share bid for Time.

In the late 1970s and early 1980s, Viacom purchased TV and radio stations in 5 states.

Viacom and Warner/Amex combined Showtime with The Movie Channel to form Showtime Networks in 1983. American Express left the Warner/Amex venture in 1986, and Viacom bought Warner's share of Showtime Networks and MTV Networks, including cable's first all-music video channel. Viacom also began producing series for network TV and bought a St. Louis TV station.

Sumner Redstone's National Amusements, a movie theater chain, bought 83% of Viacom for $3.4 billion in 1987 after a bidding war against Carl Icahn and a Viacom management group. In 1988 Viacom tried unsuccessfully to buy Orion Pictures.

In the early 1990s Paramount bought TV station operator TVX, King's Entertainment (theme parks), and a Detroit TV station. In 1993 Viacom bought ICOM Simulations (CD-ROM and video game software).

The 1994 acquisition of Paramount ultimately could bring Viacom $200 million in profits from Academy Award–winner *Forrest Gump*'s stunning box office success. In early 1995 Viacom launched a new TV network (United Paramount Network) with New York–based Chris-Craft. Congress's repeal of an FCC tax credit program for minorities killed Viacom's planned sale of its cable system (Viacom Cable Television) to Mitgo, a partnership with a black entrepreneur and major institutional investors. Viacom now will sell the system to an affiliate of Tele-Communications.

AMEX symbol: VIA
Fiscal year ends: December 31

WHO

Chairman: Sumner M. Redstone, age 71
VC; Chairman, Blockbuster Entertainment Group: H. Wayne Huizenga, age 57
President and CEO: Frank J. Biondi Jr., age 50, $3,991,895 pay
EVP, General Counsel, Chief Administrative Officer, and Secretary: Philippe P. Dauman, age 41, $2,159,465 pay
EVP Finance, Corporate Development, and Communications: Thomas E. Dooley, age 38, $2,155,912 pay
SVP and CFO: George S. Smith Jr., age 46
SVP; Chairman and CEO, Viacom Interactive Media: Edward D. Horowitz, age 47, $938,400 pay
SVP Human Resources and Administration: William A. Roskin, age 52
Auditors: Price Waterhouse LLP

WHERE

HQ: 1515 Broadway, New York, NY 10036
Phone: 212-258-6000
Fax: 212-258-6597

WHAT

	1994 Sales		1994 Operating Income	
	$ mil.	% of total	$ mil.	% of total
Entertainment	2,285	31	(88)	—
Networks	1,855	25	357	43
Publishing	1,787	24	194	23
Video/music/parks	1,070	15	199	24
Cable TV	406	5	79	10
Adjustments	(40)	—	(133)	—
Total	**7,363**	**100**	**608**	**100**

Selected Holdings

Entertainment
Movie theaters in the US, Canada, and Europe, mostly as joint ventures
Paramount Pictures
Paramount Television
Spelling Entertainment Group (77%)
  Republic Pictures
  Spelling Television
Virgin Interactive Entertainment (90%)
Worldvision Enterprises
Viacom Interactive Media

Networks and Broadcasting
All News Channel (50%)
Comedy Central (50%)
MTV Networks
  MTV: Music Television
  Nickelodeon/Nick at Nite
  VH1 Music First
Showtime Networks
  Flix
  The Movie Channel
  Showtime

USA Networks (50%)
  Sci-Fi Channel
  USA Network

Publishing
Simon & Schuster
  Allyn and Bacon
  Educational Management Group, Inc.
  MacMillan Publishing USA
  Pocket Books
  Prentice Hall
  Scribner
  Simon & Schuster

Video/Music/Theme Parks
Block Party (entertainment centers)
Blockbuster Music
Blockbuster Video
Discovery Zone, Inc. (49.6%)
Paramount Parks (5 theme parks in US and Canada)

KEY COMPETITORS

Advance Publications	Hearst	Sony
Anheuser-Busch	Heritage Media	TCI Intl.
Bertelsmann	K-III	Thomson Corp.
Capital Cities/ABC	King World	Thorn EMI
CBS	McGraw-Hill	Ticketmaster
Comcast	Metromedia	Time Warner
DreamWorks SKG	MTS	Tribune
Gaylord Entertainment	Music Land	Turner Broadcasting
General Electric	News Corp.	Walt Disney
Harcourt General	Pearson	Washington Post
	Reed Elsevier	
	Seagram	

HOW MUCH

	Annual Growth	1985	1986	1987	1988	1989	1990	1991	1992	1993	1994
Sales ($ mil.)	36.6%	444	919	1,011	1,259	1,436	1,600	1,712	1,865	2,005	7,363
Net income ($ mil.)	(9.5%)	37	(10)	(124)	(123)	131	(90)	(50)	49	158	15
Income as % of sales	—	8.3%	—	—	—	9.1%	—	—	2.6%	7.9%	0.2%
Earnings per share ($)	—	—	(0.13)	(1.64)	(1.77)	1.07	(0.84)	(0.44)	0.41	1.23	0.07
Stock price – high ($)	—	—	—	14.25	15.69	32.62	29.56	35.38	44.00	67.50	49.75
Stock price – low ($)	—	—	—	5.00	8.87	15.25	15.63	23.50	28.13	37.13	24.50
Stock price – close ($)	24.3%	—	—	9.06	15.56	28.75	26.25	34.25	44.00	48.88	41.63
P/E – high	—	—	—	—	—	31	—	—	104	55	—
P/E – low	—	—	—	—	—	14	—	—	69	30	—
Dividends per share ($)	—	—	—	0.00	0.00	0.00	0.00	0.00	0.00	0.00	0.00
Book value per share ($)	28.9%	—	—	4.98	3.21	4.27	3.43	5.82	6.28	7.60	29.45
Employees	37.8%	3,900	4,700	4,800	4,400	4,900	5,000	4,900	5,000	17,500	70,000

1994 Year-end:
Debt ratio: 46.9%
Return on equity: 1.9%
Cash (mil.): $598
Current ratio: 1.27
Long-term debt (mil.): $10,402
No. of shares (mil.): 360
Dividends
  Yield: —
  Payout: —
Market value (mil.): $14,972

Stock Price History
High/Low 1987–94

THE VONS COMPANIES, INC.

OVERVIEW

Vons, one of the biggest grocery retailers in Southern California, has been trying to pull itself out of a slump in recent years and may finally be having some luck. Although sales and earnings were down — again — in 1994, the Arcadia, California–based chain's same-store sales improved slightly as the company cleaned up the financial rubble caused by the Northridge earthquake early that year.

One of the largest US supermarket chains, Vons operates more than 320 stores from central California to the state's Mexican border and into the Las Vegas area. More than half of its stores offer separate service departments for floral, bakery, and deli products, and the company operates its own facilities for producing milk, ice cream, and baked goods. Vons offers 1,500 private-label store-brand items, which accounted for 14% of 1994 sales; the company wants such items to make up 20% of sales and in 1994 introduced its Select premium private-label line to help reach that goal.

Vons has been cutting jobs, closing stores, and consolidating its stores under 2 names, Vons and Pavilions. Vons has phased out its Mexican-style Tianguis stores and closed all 8 EXPO discount warehouse stores. The company plans to open 15 more upscale Pavilions stores over the next 3 years and to remodel 65 stores in 1995.

A subsidiary of Kohlberg Kravis Roberts–controlled Safeway owns nearly 35% of Vons.

WHEN

Charles Von der Ahe opened a small grocery market in Los Angeles in 1906 with $1,200. Prior to the 1929 stock market crash, Von der Ahe sold his 87 stores to McMarr Stores (eventually bought by Safeway) and soon retired. His 2 sons, Ted and Wil, restarted Vons stores with their father's financing.

In 1948 Vons opened a 50,300-square-foot store in Los Angeles that was the first US grocery to feature self-service produce, meat, and delicatessen sections. In 1960 Vons bought Shopping Bag Food Stores but 7 years later was forced by the US government to divest. The company opened 10 stores in 1968, bringing the total to 80 stores. In 1969 Household Finance (now Household International) bought Vons. In the 1970s Vons expanded into the San Diego area and sold products wholesale to retailers and fast-food restaurants.

A management team led by Roger Stangeland bought Vons supermarkets and other retail units from Household International in a 1985 LBO. The next year Vons opened its first Pavilions, a huge store featuring a wide selection of merchandise and specialty items, and bought the 10-store Pantry Food Markets of California. In 1987 Vons built its first Tianguis superstore, which resembled a Mexican market and provided signs in Spanish and bilingual employees.

Also in 1987 Vons merged with publicly owned, Michigan-based Allied Supermarkets (Great Scott! Supermarkets in Detroit), creating the Vons Companies, Inc. At that time Allied's former management bought Allied's Michigan operations, leaving newly public Vons with its Southern California locations intact and $100 million in cash.

Vons bought Safeway's 162 Southern California locations in 1988, doubling its size. As part of the transaction, Kohlberg Kravis Roberts (which had executed an LBO of Safeway in 1986) acquired a 31.3% interest in Vons.

Vons bought the 18-store central California chain Williams Bros. in 1992. Later that year several Vons stores were damaged and looted in the Los Angeles riots. In 1993 Vons supplied the fast-food chain Jack-In-The-Box with the frozen beef patties that later made many ill. Inspectors awarded Vons a clean bill of health soon after, but the company in 1995 remained both a defendant and a plaintiff in lawsuits arising from the episode.

Also in 1993 Vons introduced 2 new store types: EXPOs (no-frills, warehouse-type discount stores where customers bagged their own groceries; closed in 1995) and Vons Super Combo stores (offering food and drug services, video rental, dry cleaning, and banking).

In early 1994, 4 days after the company introduced "Vons Value," a new pricing strategy, the Northridge earthquake occurred, forcing not only the brief closure of 45 stores but also a costly relaunching of the promotional campaign. To boost postquake sales, the company moved up price cuts that had been scheduled for later in the year. Also in 1994 Stangeland was replaced as CEO by Lawrence Del Santo, who had previously been with Vons before becoming an executive with American Stores.

Del Santo succeeded Stangeland again in 1995, this time as chairman. Del Santo himself plans to retire in 1997 and will likely be replaced as CEO by president Richard Goodspeed, who followed him from American Stores.

NYSE symbol: VON
Fiscal year ends: Sunday nearest December 31

WHO

Chairman and CEO: Lawrence A. Del Santo, age 61, $598,917 pay (prior to promotion)
President and COO: Richard E. Goodspeed, age 58, $405,231 pay
EVP Retailing: Robert J. Kelly, age 50, $274,426 pay
EVP, General Counsel, and Secretary: Terrence J. Wallock, age 50, $243,600 pay
SVP and CFO: Pamela K. Knous, age 40
SVP Vons: Phillip E. Hawkins
SVP Real Estate and Construction: Donald J. Howard
SVP Marketing: Susan M. Klug
SVP Retail Purchasing: Harold E. Rudnick
Group VP Distribution: Warren D. Cox
Group VP Grocery/Frozen/Liquor: William M. Gensemer
Group VP Human Resources: Dick W. Gonzales
VP Corporate Communications: Mary M. McAboy
Auditors: KPMG Peat Marwick LLP

WHERE

HQ: 618 Michillinda Ave., Arcadia, CA 91007-6300
Phone: 818-821-7000
Fax: 818-821-7933

Vons operates most of its more than 320 stores in central and Southern California, primarily in Los Angeles, Orange, San Diego, Ventura, and other oceanside counties. The company also operates stores in the Las Vegas area.

WHAT

	Store Formats	
	No. of stores	% of total
Vons	293	90
Pavilions	33	10
Total	**326**	**100**

Store Formats and Selected Departments

Pavilions
  Bagel shops
  Cosmetics
  General merchandise
  Health and beauty care
  Hot bakeries
  Party shops
  Pharmacies
  Prepared foods
  Produce
  Sausage and smoke shops
  Service floral
  Service meat
  Service seafood
  Sushi bars
  Wines
Vons
  Bakeries
  Dairy products
  General merchandise
  Health and beauty care
  Meat departments
  Pharmacies
  Produce
  Service delicatessens
  Service floral
  Service seafood
  Wine and liquor

Private Labels
Select
Vons

KEY COMPETITORS

Albertson's
American Stores
Certified Grocers
Circle K
Hughes Markets
Kroger
Longs
Melville
Price/Costco
Raley's
Save Mart Supermarkets
Smart & Final
Smith's Food & Drug
Southland
Stater Bros.
Thrifty Payless
Walgreen
Yucaipa

HOW MUCH

	Annual Growth	1985	1986	1987	1988	1989	1990	1991	1992	1993	1994
Sales ($ mil.)	32.9%	386	222	3,276	3,917	5,221	5,334	5,350	5,596	5,075	4,997
Net income ($ mil.)	23.6%	4	1	(4)	(24)	(25)	50	65	82	32	27
Income as % of sales	—	1.1%	0.3%	—	—	—	0.9%	1.2%	1.5%	0.6%	0.5%
Earnings per share ($)	6.7%	0.34	0.04	(0.14)	(0.77)	(0.65)	1.28	1.56	1.89	0.73	0.61
Stock price – high ($)	—	10.13	10.13	13.75	13.50	23.75	23.88	34.13	29.13	26.38	21.50
Stock price – low ($)	—	6.25	6.25	6.00	6.75	11.38	14.75	19.75	19.50	15.38	15.13
Stock price – close ($)	10.8%	7.13	7.13	7.38	11.50	19.50	22.50	23.75	25.50	16.00	18.00
P/E – high	—	30	—	—	—	—	19	22	15	36	35
P/E – low	—	18	—	—	—	—	12	13	10	21	25
Dividends per share ($)	—	0.00	0.00	0.00	0.00	0.00	0.00	0.00	0.00	0.00	0.00
Book value per share ($)	18.2%	2.83	—	5.69	5.53	4.91	7.04	11.05	11.38	12.12	12.73
Employees	3.5%	—	—	22,000	35,000	35,000	33,900	34,000	32,300	30,000	28,000

1994 Year-end:
Debt ratio: 59.5%
Return on equity: 4.9%
Cash (mil.): $9
Current ratio: 0.83
Long-term debt (mil.): $804
No. of shares (mil.): 43
Dividends
  Yield: —
  Payout: —
Market value (mil.): $781

Stock Price History
High/Low 1985–94

WALGREEN CO.

OVERVIEW

Apparently Walgreen has prescribed itself a growth hormone. The Deerfield, Illinois–based company is the largest drugstore chain in the US, filling more prescriptions than any other retailer. But it is looking to get even bigger.

Led by CEO Daniel Jorndt, Walgreen plans to open 200 stores a year through the end of the decade and to be operating 3,000 stores by the year 2000. The company has momentum on its side — 20 straight years of record sales and earnings — with sales up 11% to $9.2 billion in 1994. That year Walgreen was named to *FORTUNE* magazine's list of "Most Admired Corporations in America" for the first time.

To compete more effectively, the company has spent more than $1 billion over the last 5 years on remodeling its stores, adding new technology, and improving its distribution systems. It recently introduced Intercom Plus, which allows customers to request refills 24 hours a day via a touch-tone telephone. The orders are automatically entered into the store's computer system. Walgreen hopes the new system will boost orders per day by as much as 60%.

Walgreen has used changes in the retail pharmacy industry to its advantage over the last few years. As more and more customers use managed care or drug benefit plans, the company has worked to sign up these providers (even the money-losing ones) to increase its customer base and sales of its nonprescription items, such as cosmetics, cigarettes, and liquor. Now, with its position as the dominant player in the retail prescription business, Walgreen is renegotiating contracts with many managed care providers in order to boost its profits.

WHEN

In 1901 Chicago pharmacist Charles Walgreen borrowed $2,000 from his father for a down payment on his first drugstore. In 1909 Walgreen sold a half interest in his first store and bought a 2nd, where he installed a large soda fountain and began serving lunches. In 1916, 9 stores consolidated under the corporate name Walgreen Co. By 1920 there were 20 stores in Chicago, with sales of $1.55 million. The firm was first listed on the NYSE in 1927. In 1929 the chain's 397 stores in 87 cities had sales of $47 million.

During the Great Depression the company did comparatively well. Although average sales per store dropped between 1931 and 1935, per-store earnings went up, thanks to a chainwide emphasis on efficiency. By 1940 Walgreen had 489 stores, but the chain shrank during WWII when unprofitable stores were closed.

The 1950s saw a major change in the way retailers did business. Walgreen was an early leader in self-service merchandising. The company opened its first self-serve store in 1952 and had 22 by the end of 1953, leading the industry. Between 1950 and 1960, as small, older stores were replaced with larger, more efficient, self-service units, the total number of stores in the chain increased only about 10%, but sales grew by more than 90%.

By 1960 Walgreen had 451 stores, half of which were self-service. In 1962 the company bought 3 Globe discount department stores in Houston. By 1966 there were 13 Globes in the Southwest doing over $120 million in annual sales, but these survived only 11 years. During the 1960s soda fountains in the stores proved unprofitable and were phased out.

The 1970s and 1980s saw rapid growth and modernization in the chain. In 1973 company management organized a planning committee to boost Walgreen's sagging return on investment. After a customer survey characterized the stores as "junky, disorganized, and hard-to-shop," Walgreen modernized them and emphasized health aid and pharmacy business. In 1986 the company purchased Medi Mart.

Responding to the public's demand for convenient shopping and its own desire for greater efficiency, Walgreen began linking its stores through a satellite network in 1989.

The company began Pharmacy Mail services to serve the growing mail-order drug business in 1991. In 1992 it completed the installation of point-of-sale inventory tracking equipment in all of its stores.

In 1993 the company organized a subsidiary, Healthcare Plus, and established a $15 million distribution center to focus on large, national accounts with state-of-the-art mail service capabilities.

Walgreen and an alliance of independent drugstores helped set up Pharmacy Direct Network in 1994 to compete with Merck and others for the fast-growing market in the management of prescription drug programs for employers' health care plans. Also in 1994 it opened its 2,000th store, in Cleveland.

In 1995 Walgreen opened a $60 million distribution center in Woodland, California, to serve its California and Washington stores.

NYSE symbol: WAG
Fiscal year ends: August 31

WHO

Chairman and CEO: Charles R. Walgreen III, age 58,
$1,130,489 pay
President and COO: L. Daniel Jorndt, age 53,
$816,756 pay
EVP Store Operations: Glenn S. Kraiss, age 61,
$465,970 pay
EVP Marketing: Vernon A. Brunner, age 54,
$465,970 pay
SVP and CFO: Roger Polark, age 46
SVP Distribution: John R. Brown, age 58
SVP Facilities Development: William A. Shiel, age 43
SVP Human Resources: John A. Rubino, age 53
VP and Treasurer: W. Lynn Earnest, age 51
VP, General Counsel, and Secretary: Julian A. Oettinger,
age 55
Auditors: Arthur Andersen & Co, SC

WHERE

HQ: 200 Wilmot Rd., Deerfield, IL 60015
Phone: 708-940-2500
Fax: 708-940-2804

	1994 Stores	
	No.	% of total
Florida	326	17
Illinois	313	16
Texas	189	10
California	117	6
Arizona	110	6
Wisconsin	108	5
Indiana	94	5
Tennessee	69	3
Massachusetts	67	3
Other states & Puerto Rico	575	29
Total	**1,968**	**100**

1994 Sales by Geographical Area	
	% of total
South & Southeast	28
Midwest (except Chicago)	21
Southwest	18
Chicago & suburbs	14
West	10
East	9
Total	**100**

WHAT

Estimated 1994 Sales by Product Class	
	% of total
Prescription drugs	41
General merchandise	24
Nonprescription drugs	13
Liquor & beverages	9
Cosmetics & toiletries	9
Tobacco products	4
Total	**100**

Subsidiary
Walgreens Healthcare Plus (mail-order pharmacy)

KEY COMPETITORS

Albertson's	National Convenience
American Stores	Pathmark
Bruno's	Phar-Mor
Circle K	Price/Costco
Eckerd	Publix
Eli Lilly	Pueblo Xtra
Fiesta Mart	Randall's
Fred Meyer	Revco
H. E. Butt	Rite Aid
J. C. Penney	Safeway
Kmart	Southland
Kroger	Thrifty PayLess
Longs	Vons
Meijer	Wal-Mart
Melville	Whole Foods Market
Merck	Winn-Dixie

HOW MUCH

	9-Year Growth	1985	1986	1987	1988	1989	1990	1991	1992	1993	1994
Sales ($ mil.)	12.6%	3,162	3,661	4,282	4,884	5,380	6,048	6,733	7,475	8,295	9,235
Net income ($ mil.)	13.0%	94	103	104	129	154	175	195	221	245	282
Income as % of sales	—	3.0%	2.8%	2.4%	2.6%	2.9%	2.9%	2.9%	3.0%	3.0%	3.1%
Earnings per share ($)	12.8%	0.77	0.84	0.84	1.05	1.25	1.42	1.58	1.78	1.98	2.28
Stock price – high ($)	—	15.13	19.75	22.44	18.69	25.13	26.63	38.63	44.50	44.63	45.38
Stock price – low ($)	—	10.75	12.13	12.38	13.56	15.00	19.94	24.69	30.38	35.38	33.75
Stock price – close ($)	13.4%	14.06	16.19	15.38	15.13	23.38	25.69	38.00	43.63	40.88	43.63
P/E – high	—	20	24	27	18	20	19	24	25	23	20
P/E – low	—	14	14	15	13	12	14	16	17	18	15
Dividends per share ($)	13.6%	0.21	0.24	0.27	0.29	0.33	0.39	0.45	0.51	0.60	0.66
Book value per share ($)	14.0%	3.92	4.50	5.06	5.79	6.69	7.70	8.79	10.02	11.20	12.79
Employees	5.8%	37,200	42,100	45,300	43,800	46,500	48,500	51,000	53,500	57,700	61,900

1994 Year-end:
Debt ratio: 0.0%
Return on equity: 19.1%
Cash (mil.): $108
Current ratio: 1.59
Long-term debt (mil.): $0
No. of shares (mil.): 123
Dividends
  Yield: 1.5%
  Payout: 28.9%
Market value (mil.): $5,370

Stock Price History
High/Low 1985–94

WAL-MART STORES, INC.

OVERVIEW

Wal-Mart is taking its title as the world's largest retailer seriously. In the US it operates nearly 2,000 Wal-Marts and more than 400 Sam's Clubs, but these days the Bentonville, Arkansas–based company is learning to say "buy" in some new languages. Wal-Mart operates more than 200 stores in Canada, Mexico, and Hong Kong, and it plans to add another 100 stores during 1996, with new locations in Argentina, Brazil, and China.
Wal-Mart continues to grow rapidly. Its sales were up more than 22% in fiscal 1995.

The company's basic discount stores remain its biggest profit generators. Same-store sales at these outlets were up 10% in fiscal 1995. However, its Sam's Clubs discount warehouses have struggled, with same-store sales dropping 2.2% in fiscal 1995. To combat this trend

Wal-Mart is reemphasizing the clubs' role as a commercial supply source rather than as a consumer store. Wal-Mart also continues to develop its Supercenter format (large Wal-Marts with supermarkets). The company added 75 of these stores in 1995, raising the total to 143, and it plans to add another 90–100 in 1996.

As it has grown, Wal-Mart has added layers of management that make it more difficult to maintain Sam Walton's personal touch. Wal-Mart is no longer the "little store that could" and is sometimes perceived as a "model of savage capitalism" by towns it seeks to enter. Communities in Maine, Massachusetts, and New Hampshire have voted to keep Wal-Mart out. Members of the Walton family control about 38% of the company's stock.

WHEN

Sam Walton began his retail career as a J. C. Penney management trainee and later leased a Ben Franklin franchised dime store in Newport, Arkansas (1945). In 1950 he relocated to Bentonville, Arkansas, and opened a Walton 5&10. By 1962 Walton owned 15 Ben Franklin stores under the Walton 5&10 name.

After Ben Franklin management rejected his suggestion to open discount stores in small towns, Walton, with his brother James "Bud" Walton, opened the first Wal-Mart Discount City in Rogers, Arkansas (1962). Growth was slow at first. Wal-Mart Stores went public (1970) with 18 stores and sales of $44 million.

In the 1970s growth accelerated because of 2 key developments: Wal-Mart established highly automated distribution centers, which cut shipping costs and time, and it implemented a computerized inventory system that sped up checkout and reordering. By 1980 the 276 stores had sales of $1.2 billion.

Acquisitions included Mohr Value (1977), Hutchinson Wholesale Shoe (1978), Kuhn's Big-K Stores (1981), and Super Saver Warehouse Club (1987). Wal-Mart phased out Ben Franklin stores (1976) and sold 15 Dot Discount Drugstores (1989).

In 1983 Wal-Mart opened Sam's Wholesale Club, modeled on the successful cash-and-carry, membership-only warehouse format pioneered by the Price Company of California. Sam's lured small-business owners in metropolitan areas with extremely slim profit margins on large quantities. A large percentage of Sam's shoppers, however, were ordinary consumers paying annual membership fees.

In 1987 Wal-Mart started Hypermart*USA, originally a joint venture with Cullum Companies, a Dallas-based supermarket chain (Wal-Mart bought out Cullum's interest in 1989). The hypermarket, a European hybrid of the discount store and supermarket, features over 200,000 square feet of shopping in a mall-like setting, including ancillary businesses like branch banks, fast food outlets, photo developers, and playrooms for shoppers' children.

In 1990 the company bought McLane Company, a grocery and retail distributor, and Western Merchandise, a music, book, and video distributor. In 1991 the company acquired Wholesale Club (warehouse stores).

Wal-Mart expanded into Mexico in 1992 through a joint venture with Cifra, Mexico's largest retailer. That same year an NBC news program suggested that Wal-Mart sold merchandise that was labeled US-made but actually wasn't. It was an embarrassment for a company with a "Buy American" campaign (which it has repeated with its "Hecho en México" campaign). Also in 1992 Sam Walton died.

The company introduced a line of private-label packaged food products, called Great Value, for its supercenters in 1993. In 1994 Wal-Mart acquired 122 former Woolco stores from Woolworth in Canada and began to convert them. In 1995 cofounder Bud Walton died. That same year the company announced plans to open a scaled-down version of its typical discount store in Bennington, Vermont, which will give Wal-Mart a presence in all 50 states.

NYSE symbol: WMT
Fiscal year ends: January 31

WHO

Chairman: S. Robson Walton, age 50
VC and COO: Donald G. Soderquist, age 61,
  $790,000 pay
President and CEO: David D. Glass, age 59,
  $985,000 pay
EVP; President and CEO, Wal-Mart Stores Division:
  William R. Fields, age 45, $590,000 pay
EVP; President and CEO, Sam's Club Division: Dean L.
  Sanders, age 44, $590,000 pay
EVP; COO, Wal-Mart Stores Division: Joseph S.
  Hardin Jr., age 49, $500,000 pay
**EVP; President and CEO, Wal-Mart International
  Division:** Bob L. Martin, age 46
EVP and CFO: Paul R. Carter, age 54
EVP Supercenter Division: Nicholas J. White, age 50
SVP, General Counsel, and Secretary: Robert K.
  Rhoads, age 40
SVP Human Resources: Cole Petersen
Auditors: Ernst & Young LLP

WHERE

HQ: Bentonville, AR 72716
Phone: 501-273-4000
Fax: 501-273-8650

	1995 Stores
	No.
Texas	288
Florida	162
Illinois	128
Missouri	118
California	104
Georgia	99
Tennessee	95
Other US states	1,567
Other countries	222
Total	**2,783**

WHAT

	1995 Sales
	% of total
Softgoods/domestics	26
Hardgoods (hardware, housewares, auto supplies, small appliances)	24
Stationery & candy	11
Records & electronics	10
Sporting goods & toys	9
Pharmaceuticals	9
Health & beauty aids	7
Jewelry	2
Shoes	2
Total	**100**

Operating Units
Sam's Clubs (membership warehouse clubs)
Supercenters (large combination general merchandise
  and food stores)
Wal-Mart Stores (general merchandise)

Support Divisions
Distribution centers (30 regional and food distribution
  centers)
International (foreign operations)
McClane Co. (food and merchandise distribution to
  convenience stores and selected Sam's Clubs,
  Supercenters, and Wal-Marts)

KEY COMPETITORS

Ace Hardware	Hill Stores	Price/Costco
Ames	Home Depot	Sears
AutoZone	Hudson's Bay	Service
Best Buy	J. C. Penney	Merchandise
Best Products	Kmart	TJX
Bradlees	Lechters	Toys "R" Us
Caldor	Lowe's	Venture Stores
Circuit City	McCrory	Waban
Cotter & Co.	Montgomery	Walgreen
Dayton Hudson	Ward	Winn-Dixie
The Gap	Pep Boys	Woolworth

HOW MUCH

	9-Year Growth	1986	1987	1988	1989	1990	1991	1992	1993	1994	1995
Sales ($ mil.)	28.8%	8,465	11,909	15,959	20,649	25,811	32,602	43,887	55,484	67,344	82,494
Net income ($ mil.)	26.3%	328	450	628	837	1,076	1,291	1,609	1,995	2,333	2,681
Income as % of sales	—	3.9%	3.8%	3.9%	4.1%	4.2%	4.0%	3.7%	3.6%	3.5%	3.2%
Earnings per share ($)	25.6%	0.15	0.20	0.28	0.37	0.48	0.57	0.70	0.87	1.02	1.17
Stock price – high ($)[1]	—	4.31	6.73	10.72	8.47	11.22	18.38	29.94	32.94	34.13	29.25
Stock price – low ($)[1]	—	2.37	3.64	5.00	6.06	7.50	10.09	14.00	25.06	23.00	21.00
Stock price – close ($)[1]	20.4%	3.98	5.81	6.50	7.84	11.22	15.13	29.44	32.00	25.00	21.25
P/E – high	—	29	34	38	23	23	32	43	38	33	25
P/E – low	—	16	18	18	16	16	18	20	29	23	18
Dividends per share ($)	26.8%	0.02	0.02	0.04	0.04	0.06	0.07	0.09	0.11	0.13	0.17
Book value per share ($)	28.7%	0.57	0.75	1.00	1.33	1.75	2.35	3.04	3.81	4.68	5.54
Employees	22.0%	104,000	141,000	183,000	223,000	271,000	328,000	371,000	434,000	528,000	622,000

1995 Year-end:
Debt ratio: 43.5%
Return on equity: 22.8%
Cash (mil.): $45
Current ratio: 1.54
Long-term debt (mil.): $9,709
No. of shares (mil.): 2,297
Dividends
  Yield: 0.8%
  Payout: 14.5%
Market value (mil.): $48,811

Stock Price History[1]
High/Low 1986–95

[1] Stock prices are for the prior calendar year.

THE WALT DISNEY COMPANY

To Disney's extensive list of cuddly, well-known characters, add Ted Koppel and Roseanne. In July 1995 the company that built a far-flung empire on the backs of a talking mouse and duck announced it was buying Capital Cities/ABC for $19 billion. The purchase — making it the biggest entertainment company in the world — will give Disney the top-rated TV network, several TV and radio stations, large shares of 3 cable channels, and extensive holdings in publishing, on top of theme parks and hotels; movie, TV, and audio production; a hockey team; and the licensing, production, and retailing of merchandise. "We have a good brand, and we know how to manage it," says Disney CEO Michael Eisner.

Prior to the ABC deal, the company had suffered a series of trials and tribulations. Eisner underwent heart bypass surgery, president Frank Wells died in a helicopter crash, and Jeffrey Katzenberg, chairman of Disney's film unit, quit after Eisner refused to give him Wells's job. Disney restructured its ownership of Disneyland Paris (formerly Euro Disney), cutting its ownership from 49% to 39%. So far the company has written off $625 million from its investment in the theme park, which has lost almost $2 billion since it opened in 1992. In addition the company halted plans for a US history theme park in Virginia because of public resistance to Disney's locating the park near a Civil War battlefield.

None of this has deterred Eisner from continuing to build on the Disney brand. He has assembled a new management team and continues to look for new ways to extend the company's reach, such as increasing its presence in the music business. The company bought a stake in the California Angels baseball team in 1995.

Disney plans to release 25 films a year, looking for a success like *The Lion King*, which has earned nearly $750 million at the box office and $1 billion in retail merchandise sales. *Pocahontas*, released in 1995, is expected to earn roughly $1 billion over the next 3 years.

After his first animated film business failed, artist Walt Disney and his brother Roy started a film studio in 1923 in Hollywood. Walt directed the first Mickey Mouse cartoon, *Plane Crazy*, in 1928 (the 3rd, *Steamboat Willie*, was the first cartoon with a soundtrack). Disney's studio created short animated cartoons such as *The Three Little Pigs*.

The studio produced its first animated feature film, *Snow White*, in 1937 and *Fantasia* and *Pinocchio* in the 1940s. Disney produced *The Mickey Mouse Club* (1955–59) and a weekly network series (under a number of titles) that ran for 29 straight years. Disneyland opened in 1955 in Anaheim, California.

Walt Disney died in 1966 of lung cancer, and Roy became chairman. Disney World opened in Florida in 1971, and Roy died the same year. His son Roy E. Disney, then animation VP, became the company's principal individual shareholder. Without Walt's and Roy's leadership and creativity, Disney films went from producing over 50% of company revenues in 1971 to only 20% in 1979.

In 1980 Walt's son-in-law Ron Miller became president. In 1982 Epcot Center opened in Florida. Miller started Touchstone Pictures in order to produce films like *Splash* (1984), Disney's first hit since *The Love Bug* (1969).

In 1984 Texas's Bass family, in alliance with Roy E. Disney, bought a controlling interest in the company. New CEO Michael Eisner (from Paramount) and president Frank Wells (from Warner Bros.) ushered in a new era of innovation, prosperity, and high executive salaries.

The company started the Disney Channel (cable TV) and opened retail stores in the 1980s. A Japanese corporation paying royalties to Disney opened Tokyo Disneyland in 1984. Disney opened the Disney–MGM Studios Theme Park in Florida in 1989.

Disney established Hollywood Records, a mainstream label, in 1990. The company agreed to distribute Jim Henson's Muppet videos in 1991. Disney wanted to buy Henson out and bring his Muppets into Disney's fold, but the deal went sour after Henson's death.

In 1992 Euro Disney opened near Paris amid French concern over the park's possible effects on the nation's culture. In 1993 Disney bought Miramax Film Corp. Disney also spent $50 million for an NHL expansion team, which it named the Mighty Ducks of Anaheim, after the 1992 Disney movie.

In 1995 Disney entered into a joint venture with BellSouth, SBC Communications, and Ameritech to develop, market, and deliver video programming. In August 1995 Disney followed its purchase of Capital Cities/ABC with another Hollywood-shaking surprise: the naming of Creative Artists Agency chairman Michael Ovitz as the new Disney president.

NYSE symbol: DIS
Fiscal year ends: September 30

WHO

Chairman and CEO: Michael D. Eisner, age 53, $8,018,807 pay
VC; Chairman, Walt Disney Feature Animation: Roy E. Disney, age 64, $850,000 pay
President: Michael Ovitz, age 48
SEVP and Chief of Corporate Operations (HR): Sanford M. Litvack, age 58, $2,100,000 pay
SEVP and CFO: Stephen F. Bollenbach, age 52
EVP Strategic Planning and Development: Lawrence P. Murphy, age 42, $1,236,846 pay
Chairman, Walt Disney Attractions: Richard A. Nunis
CEO, Walt Disney Motion Pictures: Joseph E. Roth
President, Disney Consumer Products: Barton K. Boyd
President, Disney Design and Development: Peter S. Rummell
President, Walt Disney Imagineering: Martin A. Sklar
Auditors: Price Waterhouse LLP

WHERE

HQ: 500 S. Buena Vista St., Burbank, CA 91521
Phone: 818-560-1000
Fax: 818-560-1930

The Walt Disney Company is a US-based conglomerate of theme parks, production studios, retail stores, and other entertainment-related ventures.

	1994 Sales		1994 Operating Income	
	$ mil.	% of total	$ mil.	% of total
US	8,155	81	1,393	69
Europe	1,345	13	405	20
Other regions	555	6	226	11
Adjustments	—	—	(58)	—
Total	**10,055**	**100**	**1,966**	**100**

WHAT

	1994 Sales		1994 Operating Income	
	$ mil.	% of total	$ mil.	% of total
Film	4,793	48	856	43
Theme parks	3,464	34	684	35
Consumer prods.	1,798	18	426	22
Total	**10,055**	**100**	**1,966**	**100**

Film, Television, Records
Buena Vista Home Video
Buena Vista Television
The Disney Channel
Hollywood Pictures
Hollywood Records
KCAL-TV, Los Angeles
Miramax Film Corp.
Touchstone Pictures
Touchstone Television
Walt Disney Pictures
Walt Disney Records
Walt Disney Television

Major Parks
Disneyland Park (CA)
Disneyland Paris (39%, France)
The Disney–MGM Studios Theme Park
Epcot Center
Tokyo Disneyland (royalty earnings, Japan)
Walt Disney World (FL)

Selected Sales, Sports, Publishing
Childcraft direct-marketed catalog
Discover magazine
Disney Adventures magazine
Disney Interactive
Disney Press
The Disney Stores
FamilyFun magazine
Hyperion Press
Mighty Ducks of Anaheim (hockey team)

KEY COMPETITORS

Accor
Addison-Wesley
Anheuser-Busch
Bertelsmann
Boston Ventures
Carolco Pictures
CBS
Crédit Lyonnais
DreamWorks SKG
Electronic Arts
General Electric
Hearst
King World
Knowledge Adventure
MCA
News Corp.
Samuel Goldwyn
Savoy Pictures
Scholastic
Sony
Thorn EMI
Time Warner
Turner Broadcasting
Viacom
Virgin Group
Western Publishing

HOW MUCH

	9-Year Growth	1985	1986	1987	1988	1989	1990	1991	1992	1993	1994
Sales ($ mil.)	19.6%	2,015	2,471	2,877	3,438	4,594	5,844	6,182	7,504	8,529	10,055
Net income ($ mil.)	22.9%	174	247	445	522	703	824	637	817	671	1,110
Income as % of sales	—	8.6%	10.0%	15.5%	15.2%	15.3%	14.1%	10.3%	10.9%	7.9%	11.0%
Earnings per share ($)	16.1%	0.32	0.46	0.81	0.95	1.28	1.50	1.20	1.52	1.23	2.04
Stock price – high ($)	—	7.34	13.72	20.63	17.09	34.06	34.13	32.44	45.25	47.88	48.63
Stock price – low ($)	—	3.70	7.02	7.94	13.50	16.22	21.50	23.41	28.47	36.00	37.75
Stock price – close ($)	23.2%	7.05	10.78	14.81	16.44	28.00	25.38	28.63	43.00	42.63	46.00
P/E – high	—	23	30	26	18	27	23	27	30	39	24
P/E – low	—	12	15	10	14	13	14	20	19	29	19
Dividends per share ($)	13.0%	0.08	0.08	0.08	0.07	0.11	0.13	0.16	0.19	0.24	0.28
Book value per share ($)	18.4%	2.29	2.71	3.50	4.43	5.62	6.62	7.43	8.97	9.39	10.51
Employees	9.8%	28,000	32,000	30,000	39,000	47,000	52,000	58,000	58,000	62,000	65,000

1994 Year-end:
Debt ratio: 34.8%
Return on equity: 21.1%
Cash (mil.): $1,510
Current ratio: 1.57
Long-term debt (mil.): $1,985
No. of shares (mil.): 524
Dividends
  Yield: 0.6%
  Payout: 13.7%
Market value (mil.): $24,104

Stock Price History
High/Low 1985–94

WARNER-LAMBERT COMPANY

OVERVIEW

Diversified Warner-Lambert is committed to becoming the world's leading provider of consumer health care products (54% of sales in 1994 were international) and keeping its pharmaceutical pipeline full. Through an initial $30 million, 3-year investment, Warner-Lambert will establish a confectionery and consumer health care products operation in China. With a Chinese partner the company will build and run a manufacturing plant in Guangzhou (formerly Canton).

The Morris Plains, New Jersey–based company has numerous drugs in various development phases. Most brands are marketed under the Parke-Davis and Goedecke names. Warner-Lambert's 72 generic drugs (including the generic equivalent of its former blockbuster cholesterol reducer Lopid) are produced by its Warner Chillcott Laboratories Division. Warner spent 7% of 1994 sales on R&D.

Domestically, the company estimates that more than 50% of its pharmaceutical sales are to managed-care organizations, including governmental units and hospitals. Warner-Lambert has plans to develop a marketing group to deal exclusively with managed-care organizations' specific needs.

Neurontin (a drug for treating epilepsy) received FDA approval in 1993 and contributed to overall sales growth in 1994. Worldwide sales of cardiovascular drug Accupril increased by 36% in 1994.

WHEN

In 1856 pharmacist William Warner opened a drugstore in Philadelphia and soon made his mark by sugar-coating pills and tablets. In 1886 he began drug production by opening William R. Warner & Co. In 1908 St. Louis–based Pfeiffer Chemical bought the company, adopted the Warner name, and moved it to New York in 1916. By 1945 the company had several overseas operations and over 50 businesses, including Sloan's (liniment), Corn Husker's (lotion), and Hudnut (cosmetics).

In 1950 the company, under the leadership of Elmer Bobst, changed its name to Warner-Hudnut and went public. Two years later Warner bought Chilcott Labs (founded in 1874 as the Maltine Company). Warner Chilcott is now the part of Warner-Lambert responsible for producing generic drugs. In 1955 the company assumed its current name following the purchase of Lambert Pharmacal (founded in 1884 by Jordan Lambert after he acquired the formula for Listerine antiseptic).

Acquisitions continued throughout the next 2 decades and included Emerson Drugs (Bromo-Seltzer, 1956), Nepera Chemical (antihistamines, 1956), American Chicle (chewing gum, 1962), and Schick (razors, 1970). The purchase of Parke-Davis in 1970 resulted in an antitrust investigation and the selling of certain product lines in 1976 (thyroid preparations, blood products, vaccines, and others). Founded in Detroit in 1866, Parke-Davis was the first company to make "biologicals" (vaccines). It later introduced Dilantin (anticonvulsant, 1938), Benadryl (antihistamine, 1946), and Chloromycetin (antibiotic, 1949), all still sold today.

Because of slipping profits in the 1970s, unprofitable divisions were sold and others consolidated in the early 1980s. In 1985 the divestitures and restructuring caused the company to take a $553 million write-down. The restructuring, however, along with new, efficient robotic manufacturing methods, resulted in annual savings of over $300 million and led to generally profitable bottom lines throughout the rest of the 1980s. In 1992 Warner-Lambert introduced Cool Mint Listerine and formed a partnership with British company Xenova to test and develop pharmaceuticals from natural compounds. Also that year Accupril's market numbers grew.

In 1993, to sharpen its consumer health care products line, Warner-Lambert purchased Wilkinson Sword, the razor and toiletries maker, to augment its Schick razor line (#2, after Gillette). In that year the company began research partnerships with biotechnology firms Ribozyme and Neurex. Also in 1993 the company agreed to buy consumer health care products concern Fisons PLC, with operations in Australia and New Zealand, for $23 million.

In 1994 the company began joint ventures with Wellcome and Glaxo to market over-the-counter versions of their products (including Sudafed, Actifed, and Zantac) in the US, Australia, and Europe. Also that year the Parke-Davis Division restructured to improve relationships with managed care organizations and address patent expirations. How Glaxo's 1995 buyout of Wellcome will affect Warner's joint operations with Wellcome is unclear. Warner continues its worldwide expansion, especially in China, India, and eastern Europe.

NYSE symbol: WLA
Fiscal year ends: December 31

WHO

Chairman and CEO: Melvin R. Goodes, age 59, $1,686,250 pay
President and COO: Lodewijk J. R. de Vink, age 50, $1,116,500 pay
EVP; President, Consumer Healthcare Sector: John F. Walsh, age 52, $718,333 pay
VP External Relations: Joseph E. Smith, age 55, $573,000 pay
VP and CFO: Ernest J. Larini, age 52, $543,967 pay
VP; President, Confectionery Sector: J. Frank Lazo, age 47
VP; Chairman, Parke-Davis Research: Ronald M. Cresswell, age 60
VP; President, Parke-Davis Research: Pedro M. Cuatrecasas, age 58
VP and General Counsel: Gregory L. Johnson, age 48
VP Human Resources: Raymond M. Fino, age 52
Auditors: Price Waterhouse LLP

WHERE

HQ: 201 Tabor Rd., Morris Plains, NJ 07950-2693
Phone: 201-540-2000
Fax: 201-540-3761

The company has 72 production facilities in 34 countries.

	1994 Sales		1994 Operating Income	
	$ mil.	% of total	$ mil.	% of total
US	2,954	46	844	50
Americas & Far East	1,845	29	422	25
Europe, Middle East & Africa	1,618	25	428	25
Adjustments	—	—	(456)	—
Total	**6,417**	**100**	**1,238**	**100**

WHAT

	1994 Sales		1994 Operating Income	
	$ mil.	% of total	$ mil.	% of total
Consumer health care	2,970	46	649	53
Pharmaceuticals	2,079	33	241	19
Confectionery	1,368	21	348	28
Total	**6,417**	**100**	**1,238**	**100**

Consumer Health Care
Benadryl (antihistamine)
Benylin (cough syrup)
Halls (cough tablets)
Listerine (mouthwash)
Lubriderm (skin lotion)
Rolaids (antacid)

Pharmaceuticals
Accupril (cardiovascular product)
Chloromycetin (antibiotic)
Cognex (treatment for Alzheimer's)
Dilantin (anticonvulsant)
ERYC (erythromycin, antibiotic)
Gemfibrozil (generic of Lopid, lipid regulator)

Loestrin (contraceptive)
Neurontin (anticonvulsant)

Confectionery
Bubblicious
Certs
Chiclets
Cinn*A*Burst
Clorets
Dentyne
Trident

Other
Capsugel (empty gelatin capsules)
Schick (razors)
Tetra (aquarium supplies)
Wilkinson Sword (razors)

KEY COMPETITORS

ALZA	Eastman	Procter & Gamble
American Home Products	Chemical	Rhône-Poulenc
Amway	Gillette	Nabisco Holdings
Bausch & Lomb	Hoechst	Schering-
Bristol-Myers	Hershey	Plough
Squibb	Johnson &	SmithKline
Carter-Wallace	Johnson	Beecham
Colgate-Palmolive	Merck	Unilever
Dow Chemical	Nestlé	Upjohn
	Novo Nordisk	Wrigley

HOW MUCH

	9-Year Growth	1985	1986	1987	1988	1989	1990	1991	1992	1993	1994
Sales ($ mil.)	8.0%	3,200	3,103	3,485	3,908	4,196	4,687	5,059	5,598	5,794	6,417
Net income ($ mil.)	12.7%	237	262	296	340	413	485	141	644	285	694
Income as % of sales	—	7.4%	8.4%	8.5%	8.7%	9.8%	10.3%	2.8%	11.5%	4.9%	10.8%
Earnings per share ($)	14.5%	1.53	1.77	2.08	2.50	3.05	3.61	1.05	4.78	2.11	5.17
Stock price – high ($)	—	24.63	31.63	43.75	39.75	59.38	70.38	82.25	79.25	76.38	86.75
Stock price – low ($)	—	16.63	22.50	24.13	29.94	37.25	49.63	61.75	58.38	59.75	60.00
Stock price – close ($)	14.0%	23.75	29.31	33.75	39.19	57.75	67.50	77.63	69.13	67.50	77.00
P/E – high	—	16	18	21	16	19	19	78	17	36	17
P/E – low	—	11	13	12	12	12	14	59	12	28	12
Dividends per share ($)	14.0%	0.75	0.80	0.89	1.08	1.28	1.52	1.76	2.04	2.28	2.44
Book value per share ($)	6.4%	5.89	6.32	6.37	7.36	8.38	10.44	8.70	11.29	10.36	10.32
Employees	(0.9%)	39,000	33,200	33,500	33,000	33,000	34,000	34,000	34,000	35,000	36,000

1994 Year-end:
Debt ratio: 51.2%
Return on equity: 49.9%
Cash (mil.): $465
Current ratio: 1.07
Long-term debt (mil.): $535
No. of shares (mil.): 134
Dividends
  Yield: 3.2%
  Payout: 47.2%
Market value (mil.): $10,364

Stock Price History High/Low 1985–94

THE WASHINGTON POST COMPANY

OVERVIEW

The Washington Post Company is a diversified, $1.6 billion national media company with major stakes in 4 areas: newspaper publishing, magazine publishing, TV broadcasting, and cable TV. Controlled by the Graham family, it presides over the highly respected *Washington Post*, the leading editorial voice in the DC area, and the #2 weekly news magazine, *Newsweek*, published in 3 languages and distributed worldwide in 9 editions. The Post Company's portfolio includes 13 Maryland community newspapers, a national weekly edition of the *Post*, a writers' and cartoonists' syndicate, and half of the English-language *International Herald Tribune* (Paris), which is distributed in more than 180 countries. It has a growing presence in TV with 6 top-ranked stations in major urban areas (Detroit, Hartford, Houston, Jacksonville, Miami, and San Antonio), a regional sports cable system based in Detroit,

and a regional cable system in 15 western, midwestern, and southern states that serves mostly small towns and rural areas — a niche where the Post Company would be willing to buy other cable systems at the right price.

A 1990 foray into personal communications services was foiled by subsequent FCC decisions, which led the company to sell almost all of its 70% stake in American Personal Communications in 1995. Like other publishers, the Post Company is cruising the infobahn. In 1995 it joined with other top newspaper chains to form the New Century Network, which will put advertising, sports, entertainment, tickets, and newspapers on-line — for a price.

Revenues from the company's TV stations jumped 46% in 1994, but the Post Company is facing much higher newsprint and postage costs in 1995.

WHEN

Stilson Hutchins, journalist and politician, published the first edition of the *Washington Post* in 1877. Strong reporting made the *Post* successful. Hutchins retired in 1889 and sold the *Post* to banker/politician Beriah Wilkins and journalist Frank Hatton. Hatton died in 1894, and the *Post* took on Wilkins's conservative leanings. In 1905 John McLean, an Ohio Democratic politician and inheritor of the *Cincinnati Enquirer*, bought the *Post*.

McLean focused on society columns and added color comics and sensationalist headlines. Hard news coverage took a back page to crime and scandal. By McLean's death (1916), the *Post* had resorted to yellow journalism.

McLean's son Ned took over the *Post* and the *Enquirer*. Ned ruined the *Post*'s integrity by lying to a Senate committee (1924) about his involvement in the Teapot Dome oil scandal. He yielded *Post* management in 1932.

Wealthy, conservative banker Eugene Meyer bought the bankrupt *Post* for $825,000 in 1933. Meyer spent the next 12 years building a first-class news staff. By 1946, when Meyer's son-in-law Philip Graham took over as publisher, the *Post* was in the black again. In 1948 Meyer transferred his stock to his daughter Katharine and Philip.

Graham bought radio and TV stations and established overseas bureaus. In 1961 he bought *Newsweek* magazine and started a news service with the *Los Angeles Times*. In 1963 Philip Graham lost a struggle with manic depression and killed himself.

An editor since 1939, Katharine Graham became publisher after her husband's death. In 1971 the *Post* went public, though the Graham family retained control of the company. In 1972 Bob Woodward and Carl Bernstein broke the Pulitzer Prize–winning Watergate story, which led to President Richard Nixon's resignation. In the 1970s and 1980s, Graham bought TV and radio stations, databases, cable TV companies, newspapers, newsprint mills, and Stanley H. Kaplan Educational Centers.

The guard changed at the *Post* in 1991. Katharine Graham's son Donald became CEO, and longtime executive editor Ben Bradlee retired. Also that year the *Post* and the *New York Times* bought out Whitcom's 1/3 interest in the *International Herald Tribune*. In 1992 the *Post* invested in ACTV, Inc. (interactive television), bought 84% of Gaithersburg Gazette, Inc. (community newspapers, upped to 100% in 1993), and a sports cable TV system.

Donald Graham became chairman when his mother stepped down in 1993. Also that year the company sold its UK cable holdings. It began publishing a CD-ROM version of *Newsweek* and created Digital Ink to explore interactive electronic publishing.

In 1994 the Post Company bought TV stations in Houston and San Antonio and an 80% stake in Mammoth Micro Productions, a CD-ROM producer. In 1995 the *Post* announced it would build a new $250 million offset printing plant that is expected to produce a full-color newspaper by 1998.

NYSE symbol: WPO
Fiscal year ends: Sunday nearest December 31

WHO

Chairman and CEO; Publisher, *The Washington Post*:
Donald E. Graham, age 49, $399,996 pay
President and COO: Alan G. Spoon, age 43,
$753,141 pay
VP; President and CEO, Post-Newsweek Stations, Inc.:
G. William Ryan, age 54, $1,232,998 pay
**VP; President, Newsweek, Inc.; Editor-in-Chief,
Newsweek:** Richard M. Smith, age 49, $400,000
VP; President, *The Washington Post*: Boisfeuillet
Jones Jr., age 48
VP; President and CEO, Post-Newsweek Cable: Thomas
O. Might, age 43
VP, General Counsel, and Secretary: Diana M. Daniels,
age 45
VP Finance: John B. Morse Jr., age 48
VP Human Resources: Beverly R. Keil, age 48
Controller: Hal S. Jones, age 42
Auditors: Price Waterhouse LLP

WHERE

HQ: 1150 15th St. NW, Washington, DC 20071
Phone: 202-334-6000
Fax: 202-334-1031

WHAT

	1994 Sales		1994 Operating Income	
	$ mil.	% of total	$ mil.	% of total
Newspaper Division	717	45	134	45
Newsweek	338	21	14	5
Broadcast Division	260	16	108	36
Cable Division	182	11	41	14
Other	117	7	(23)	—
Total	**1,614**	**100**	**274**	**100**

News Publications and Organizations
Cowles Media Co. (28%, Minneapolis–St. Paul *Star
Tribune*)
The Daily Herald Co. (*The Herald*; Everett, WA)
The Gazette Newspapers, Inc. (one newspaper and 13
weekly community papers in Maryland)
Hankuk Pan (Korean-language edition of *Newsweek*)
International Herald Tribune (50%, New York Times Co.)
Los Angeles Times–Washington Post News Service (50%)
Newsweek, Newsweek Business Plus, and *Newsweek
Woman*
Newsweek InterActive (on-line magazine and CD-ROM)
Newsweek International (3 English-language editions)
Nihon Ban (Japanese-language edition of *Newsweek*)
The Washington Post (821,956 daily circulation)
The Washington Post National Weekly Edition
The Washington Post Writers Group (features syndicate)

Television
PASS Sports (regional sports cable network, Detroit)
Post-Newsweek Cable (systems in 15 states)
Post-Newsweek Stations (KPRC-TV, Houston; KSAT-TV,
San Antonio; WDIV-TV, Detroit; WFSB-TV, Hartford,
CT; WJXT-TV, Jacksonville; WPLG-TV, Miami)

Selected Other Businesses and Holdings
Bear Island Paper Co. (35%, newsprint)
Bowater Mersey Paper Co. Ltd. (49%, newsprint, Canada)
Digital Ink Co. (audiotext and on-line services)
Kaplan Educational Centers
Legi-Slate, Inc. (on-line database and legal publishing)
Mammoth Micro Productions (80%, CD-ROM producer)
Moffett, Larson & Johnson (71%, telecommunications)

KEY COMPETITORS

Advance	Hearst	Thomson Corp.
Publications	Knight-Ridder	Time Warner
Bloomberg	McGraw-Hill	Times Mirror
Capital Cities/ABC	New York Times	Tribune
CBS	News Corp.	US News
Cox	Pearson	Viacom
Dow Jones	Reed Elsevier	Washington
E.W. Scripps	Reuters	Times
Gannett	TCI	West Publishing

HOW MUCH

	9-Year Growth	1985	1986	1987	1988	1989	1990	1991	1992	1993	1994
Sales ($ mil.)	4.6%	1,079	1,215	1,315	1,368	1,444	1,439	1,380	1,451	1,498	1,614
Net income ($ mil.)	4.5%	114	100	187	269	198	175	119	128	154	170
Income as % of sales	—	10.6%	8.2%	14.2%	19.7%	13.7%	12.1%	8.6%	8.8%	10.3%	10.5%
Earnings per share ($)	6.0%	8.66	7.80	14.52	20.91	15.50	14.45	10.00	10.80	13.10	14.65
Stock price – high ($)	—	130.00	184.50	269.00	229.00	311.00	295.50	251.00	246.00	256.50	284.00
Stock price – low ($)	—	77.75	115.00	150.00	186.50	204.00	167.00	169.00	191.50	212.00	221.75
Stock price – close ($)	8.3%	118.75	156.00	187.00	210.75	281.50	198.00	194.50	229.75	254.75	242.50
P/E – high	—	15	24	19	11	20	20	25	23	20	19
P/E – low	—	9	15	10	9	13	12	17	18	16	15
Dividends per share ($)	17.8%	0.96	1.12	1.28	1.56	1.84	4.00	4.20	4.20	4.20	4.20
Book value per share ($)	13.3%	32.90	34.04	47.80	67.49	75.40	76.31	77.84	84.17	92.84	101.08
Employees	0.9%	6,300	6,400	6,400	6,300	6,200	6,200	6,100	6,400	6,600	6,800

1994 Year-end:
Debt ratio: 4.3%
Return on equity: 15.3%
Cash (mil.): $142
Current ratio: 1.38
Long-term debt (mil.): $50
No. of shares (mil.): 11
Dividends
  Yield: 1.7%
  Payout: 28.7%
Market value (mil.): $2,704

**Stock Price History
High/Low 1985–94**

WELLS FARGO & COMPANY

OVERVIEW

Wells Fargo has finally recovered from its real estate bust hangover. With earnings at an all-time high, nonperforming assets below 3% of total loans, and the California economy seemingly on the mend, the 2nd largest bank in California (after BankAmerica) is on the move.

One of its priorities is to prevent a recurrence of the real estate woes it experienced in the late 1980s and early 1990s. It is doing this, in part, by abandoning its mortgage loan business. In place of an in-house mortgage operation, Wells Fargo entered into a joint venture with Norwest Corp.'s Norwest Mortgage company in 1995, removing the company from direct participation in an increasingly competitive industry. Instead, Wells Fargo intends to concentrate its lending activities on commercial loans.

The company also deepened its relationship with Hong Kong & Shanghai Bank (HSBC) in 1995, when HSBC decided to close several US branches and consign their business to a joint venture, the Wells Fargo HSBC Trade Bank.

But Wells Fargo's bread-and-butter business is in consumer retail banking, and the company announced that it was expanding its coverage in Southern California by opening offices in selected Vons supermarkets.

In 1994 the interests of the bank's 2 largest stockholders, Walter Annenberg and Warren Buffett, increased to 8.8% and 13.3%, respectively, primarily because of stock repurchases.

WHEN

Henry Wells and William G. Fargo were among the founders of the American Express Company (1850). When the 2 men were denied board permission to extend the company's delivery network to California to take advantage of the gold-shipping business, they started their own business, Wells Fargo and Company, in San Francisco in 1852. Thereafter the 2 related but unaffiliated companies divided their US shipping business along the Mississippi. Wells Fargo became famous for its short-lived Pony Express and its stagecoach lines. Wells Fargo separated its banking and express businesses in 1905, and the latter, with its Cuban and Mexican subsidiaries, later fell under the control of American Express.

In 1905 Wells Fargo & Co. Bank merged with Nevada National Bank. The new institution, Wells Fargo Nevada National Bank, grew and in 1923 merged with Union Trust Company to form Wells Fargo Bank & Union Trust. The bank maintained this form until it merged with American Trust, one of the oldest western banks, in 1960. The current name was adopted in 1962.

The bank added branch operations in the 1960s and grew by acquiring smaller banks in California. When it formed a bank holding company in 1969, Wells Fargo had more than 250 branches in the state, a total that almost doubled by the end of 1988.

In 1970 Carl Reichardt and Paul Hazen joined the bank's real estate investment trust section and in 1983 took over management of the bank, which was suffering the effects of overheated growth and a $21 million employee embezzlement scandal. Reichardt sold underperforming operations, cut costs, and made important acquisitions. He transformed the bank into a regional institution focused on retail and middle-market banking.

The first major acquisition by Reichardt was Crocker National Bank (San Francisco, 1986), whose assets made Wells Fargo the 11th largest bank company in the US. It went on to buy Bank of America's personal trust business (1987) and Barclays Bank of California (1988). By 1989 the bank had eliminated loans to developing countries and was 2nd only to Citicorp in leveraged buyout loans. This involvement in LBO loans and its overexposure in the booming commercial real estate market became heavy liabilities when California slid into recession.

In 1990 (when Warren Buffett invested in the company) Wells Fargo merged its investment advisory business with a unit of Japan's Nikko Securities. It also bought 4 California banks and part of California's Great American Bank (completing the purchase in 1991).

By December 1991 the bubble had burst. Wells Fargo cut its dividend to help finance a 432% increase in loan-loss reserves. Nonperforming asset levels peaked in September 1992 but have fallen steadily since. By 1994 it appeared that the bank had exceeded its regulatory reserve levels, which would further increase its profit levels.

Although many banks rid themselves of their problem real estate assets through bulk sales, Wells Fargo has held most of its assets, selling them or returning many of them to accrual status as the economy improves.

In 1995, as Wells Fargo continued to improve, Carl Reichardt retired and was replaced as chairman and CEO by Hazen.

NYSE symbol: WFC
Fiscal year ends: December 31

WHO

Chairman and CEO: Paul Hazen, age 53, $1,987,500 pay (prior to promotion)
President and COO: William F. Zuendt, age 48, $1,325,000 pay (prior to promotion)
VC: Clyde W. Ostler, age 48, $850,000 pay
VC and CFO: Rodney L. Jacobs, age 54, $845,833 pay
VC: Michael J. Gillfillan, age 46
VC: Charles M. Johnson, age 53
EVP, Chief Counsel, and Secretary: Guy Rounsaville Jr., age 51
EVP and Controller: Frank A. Moeslein, age 51
EVP and Personnel Director: Patricia R. Callahan, age 41
SVP and Director Investor Relations: Leslie L. Altick
Auditors: KPMG Peat Marwick LLP

WHERE

HQ: 420 Montgomery St., San Francisco, CA 94163
Phone: 415-477-1000
Fax: 415-362-6958

Wells Fargo operates 344 branches in Northern California and 290 in Southern California.

WHAT

| | 1994 Assets | |
	$ mil.	% of total
Cash & equivalents	3,234	6
Treasurys	2,134	4
Mortgage-backed securities	6,774	13
Private CMOs	2,484	5
Net loans	34,265	64
Other	4,483	8
Total	**53,374**	**100**

| | 1994 Sales | |
	$ mil.	% of total
Loan interest	3,015	61
Other interest	750	15
Service charges on deposit accounts	473	9
Fees & commissions	387	8
Trust & investment fees	203	4
Other	137	3
Total	**4,965**	**100**

Selected Services
Asset and cash management
Commercial real estate loans
Consumer, commercial, and corporate banking
Credit cards
Mutual funds

Subsidiaries and Operating Units
Business Banking Group
Consumer Lending Group
Investment Group
Real Estate Group
Retail Distribution Group
Wholesale Products Group
Wells Fargo Nikko Investment Advisors (50%)

KEY COMPETITORS

Bank of the West	Glendale Federal
BankAmerica	Golden West Financial
CalFed	Great Western
California Bancshares	H.F. Ahmanson
Chemical Banking	Household International
Citicorp	Pacific Bank
City National	Redwood Empire Bancorp
Dai-Ichi Kangyo	Silicon Valley Bancshares
First Interstate	Sumitomo
First Republic	Union Bank
General Electric	WestAmerica Corp.

HOW MUCH

	9-Year Growth	1985	1986	1987	1988	1989	1990	1991	1992	1993	1994
Assets ($ mil.)	6.8%	29,429	44,577	44,183	46,617	48,737	56,199	53,547	52,537	52,513	53,374
Net income ($ mil.)	18.0%	190	274	51	513	601	712	21	283	612	841
Income as % of assets	—	0.6%	0.6%	0.1%	1.1%	1.2%	1.3%	0.0%	0.5%	1.2%	1.6%
Earnings per share ($)	15.2%	4.15	5.03	0.52	9.20	11.02	13.39	0.04	4.44	10.10	14.78
Stock price – high ($)	—	32.50	57.50	60.13	71.25	87.50	86.00	98.75	86.38	133.50	169.75
Stock price – low ($)	—	22.75	30.50	37.50	43.13	59.00	41.25	48.00	56.38	74.75	127.13
Stock price – close ($)	18.4%	31.69	50.75	43.00	60.38	74.13	57.88	58.00	76.38	129.39	145.00
P/E – high	—	8	11	—	8	8	6	—	20	13	11
P/E – low	—	6	6	—	5	5	3	—	13	7	9
Dividends per share ($)	14.6%	1.17	1.36	1.56	2.20	3.15	3.80	4.00	2.00	2.25	4.00
Book value per share ($)	8.9%	30.94	36.11	42.60	41.45	48.08	57.44	54.00	57.44	65.86	66.77
Employees	3.8%	14,000	21,500	20,100	19,700	19,500	21,800	21,000	21,100	20,800	19,598

1994 Year-end:
Equity as % of assets: 7.3%
Return on assets: 1.6%
Return on equity: 23.7%
Long-term debt (mil.): $2,853
No. of shares (mil.): 51
Dividends
  Yield: 2.8%
  Payout: 27.1%
Market value (mil.): $7,432
Sales (mil.): $4,965

**Stock Price History
High/Low 1985–94**

WESTINGHOUSE ELECTRIC CORPORATION

OVERVIEW

Michael Jordan doesn't slam-dunk in this company. But CEO Jordan of Westinghouse, the Pittsburgh-based broadcasting, defense electronics, and power behemoth, has at least gotten his team on the offensive again; in 1994 the company made its first profit since 1990, and in 1995 its $5.4 billion bid to buy CBS was accepted by the ailing 3rd-place network.

Westinghouse has 8 business segments: electronic systems (radar, space, and military equipment), government and environmental services (hazardous waste disposal), power generation (power plants), energy systems (nuclear fuel and power plant services), mobile refrigeration units (Thermo King), broadcasting (Westinghouse Broadcasting — Group W), real estate (WCI Communities), and office furniture and equipment (the Knoll Group).

Under Jordan's leadership, since 1993, the company has been selling off noncore busi-nesses (including Westinghouse Electric Supply Company) and cutting costs. The firm has also liquidated much of the real estate assets of its ailing financial services unit. To help finance the CBS purchase, Westinghouse plans to unload up to $2 billion more in assets, possibly including Knoll and Thermo King.

In 1994 Westinghouse purchased United Technologies Corp.'s $220 million radar unit, Norden Systems, and secured a $400 million contract to improve a nuclear power plant in the Czech Republic. Westinghouse's non-nuclear power generation business has grown 50% in the past 5 years and has obtained contracts in Asia and Latin America.

In 1994 Westinghouse Broadcasting (Group W) produced record sales and profits and signed a joint venture with CBS that increased from 5 to 8 the number of television companies under the control of Group W.

WHEN

George Westinghouse, inventor of the train air brake, founded Westinghouse Electric in Pittsburgh in 1886. He entered the newly developing electric industry after having devised a method for transmitting electric current over long distances. The success of his system was due to his choice of using alternating current (AC) as opposed to the direct current (DC) favored by Thomas Edison. He paid Nikola Tesla, an eccentric Croatian inventor, $1 million for his AC patents and installed the first AC power system in Telluride, Colorado, in 1891. One of the company's early successes was powering the 1893 Chicago World's Fair. In 1896 Westinghouse and rival General Electric formed a patent pool that allowed the 2 companies to continue further development of electrical generation and distribution technology without the threat of being sued by the other for patent infringement.

Westinghouse expanded into manufacturing electrical products — from light bulbs (1890s) to radios (1920) to major appliances. In 1920 the company set up KDKA, the nation's first radio broadcasting station, in East Pittsburgh.

By concentrating on the market for huge turbines and generators, as well as nuclear reactors for ship propulsion, Westinghouse got a late start and was 2nd to GE in the post–World War II home appliances market.

In the mid-1970s Westinghouse lost a large part of its main business (utility generators) to GE when its turbine generators were found to be defective. And after years as an also-ran, Westinghouse sold its appliance business to White Consolidated in 1975.

The 1980s were a period of restructuring for Westinghouse. It dropped its unprofitable businesses (selling 70 businesses between 1985 and 1987), acquired complementary ones, and entered into joint ventures with foreign companies (Mitsubishi Electric, Siemens, Asea Brown Boveri, and AEG).

In 1990 Westinghouse placed $3.2 billion of its problem loans and properties up for sale and froze much of its new lending.

In 1992 the company settled a suit brought against it in 1988 by the Philippine government, alleging bribery to win a contract to build a nuclear power plant. In 1993 Westinghouse sold $1 billion worth of commercial property loans to a partnership it formed with Lehman Brothers and completed the sale of its electrical distribution and control business to Eaton for $1.1 billion in 1994. It also agreed to an alliance with New World Power to develop, market, and construct renewable energy power systems worldwide.

The company's Government and Environmental Services division achieved a 15% sales increase in 1994; it also secured its biggest contracts to date, at the Savannah River (South Carolina) and Hanford (Washington) DOE waste sites.

In 1995 Westinghouse tied up a deal with Harbin Turbine to jointly manufacture and supply 2 steam turbines to a nuclear power plant in China.

NYSE symbol: WX
Fiscal year ends: December 31

WHO

Chairman and CEO: Michael H. Jordan, age 58,
$1,356,554 pay
President: Gary M. Clark, age 59, $813,359 pay
EVP and CFO: Fredric G. Reynolds, age 44,
$469,410 pay
Chairman and CEO, Westinghouse Broadcasting:
Willard C. Korn, age 52, $917,917 pay
Chairman, Electronic Systems: Richard A. Linder,
$561,500 pay
Chairman and CEO, The Knoll Group: Burton B.
Staniar
President, WCI Communities: Byron R. Koste
**President, Westinghouse Government and
Environmental Services:** James S. Moore
President, Thermo King Corporation: James F.
Watson Jr.
President, Energy Systems: Nathaniel D. Woodson
SVP and General Counsel: Louis J. Briskman
Director of Human Resources (Acting): Ardie
Tennyson
Auditors: Price Waterhouse LLP

WHERE

HQ: Westinghouse Building, 11 Stanwix St., Pittsburgh,
PA 15222-1384
Phone: 412-244-2000
Fax: 412-642-3404

Westinghouse has operations in 902 locations in the US
and 32 other countries.

	1994 Sales	
	$ mil.	% of total
US	7,875	89
Other countries	973	11
Total	**8,848**	**100**

WHAT

	1994 Sales		1994 Operating Income	
	$ mil.	% of total	$ mil.	% of total
Electronic Systems	2,467	27	165	—
Power generation	1,715	19	110	—
Energy Systems	1,235	14	7	—
Thermo King	877	10	130	—
Broadcasting	870	10	203	—
Knoll Group	567	6	(67)	—
Govt. and Environ. Services	389	4	58	—
WCI Communities	248	3	68	—
Other	645	7	(55)	—
Adjustments	(165)	—	—	—
Total	**8,848**	**100**	**619**	**—**

Selected Subsidiaries
Aptus, Inc. (environmental services)
Electronic Systems (advanced electronics)
Energy Systems (waste-to-energy projects)
The Knoll Group (office furniture)
Thermo King Corporation (refrigerated transport)
WCI Communities, Inc. (real estate development)
Westinghouse Broadcasting Company (Group W; TV and
radio stations, cable TV)
Westinghouse Government and Environmental Services
Company (DOE facility cleanup)

KEY COMPETITORS

ABB	Haworth Intl.	Raytheon
Alcatel Alsthom	Herman Miller	Steelcase
AlliedSignal	Hon Industries	TCI Intl.
Capital Cities/ABC	Litton Industries	Time Warner
Dresser	Lockheed Martin	TRW
Duke Power	Loral	United
Fluor	Mitsui	Technologies
FMC	Motorola	Viacom
General Electric	News Corp.	WMX
General Signal	Ogden	Technologies
Halliburton	Peter Kiewit Sons'	

HOW MUCH

	9-Year Growth	1985	1986	1987	1988	1989	1990	1991	1992	1993	1994
Sales ($ mil.)	(2.1%)	10,700	10,731	10,679	12,500	12,844	12,915	12,794	8,447	8,875	8,848
Net income ($ mil.)	(20.5%)	605	671	739	823	922	268	(1,086)	(953)	(270)	77
Income as % of sales	—	5.7%	6.3%	6.9%	6.6%	7.2%	2.1%	—	4.1%	—	0.9%
Earnings per share ($)	(30.0%)	1.73	2.16	2.52	2.83	3.15	0.91	(3.46)	(2.82)	(0.91)	0.07
Stock price – high ($)	—	23.38	31.25	37.50	28.69	38.13	39.38	31.00	21.13	17.13	15.25
Stock price – low ($)	—	12.69	21.00	20.00	23.81	25.63	24.25	13.75	9.38	12.75	10.88
Stock price – close ($)	(6.4%)	22.25	27.88	24.88	26.31	37.00	28.50	18.00	13.38	14.13	12.25
P/E – high	—	14	15	15	10	12	43	—	—	—	—
P/E – low	—	7	10	8	8	8	27	—	—	—	—
Dividends per share ($)	(11.2%)	0.58	0.68	0.82	0.97	1.15	1.35	1.40	0.72	0.40	0.20
Book value per share ($)	(8.9%)	10.52	10.56	12.46	13.22	15.10	13.43	11.04	6.77	2.66	4.56
Employees	(4.3%)	124,935	117,267	112,478	119,640	121,963	115,774	113,664	109,050	101,654	84,400

1994 Year-end:
Debt ratio: 58.9%
Return on equity: 5.4%
Cash (mil.): $344
Current ratio: 1.27
Long-term debt (mil.): $1,886
No. of shares (mil.): 393
Dividends
  Yield: 1.6%
  Payout: 285.7%
Market value (mil.): $4,814

**Stock Price History
High/Low 1985–94**

WEYERHAEUSER COMPANY

OVERVIEW

Tacoma,Washington–based forest products giant Weyerhaeuser is the world's largest private owner of softwood timber. Its forest products include logs, lumber, plywood, paneling and particleboard. It also makes a range of paper products, including pulp, newsprint, uncoated and coated papers, shipping containers, and containerboard. The company owns approximately 5.7 million acres of US timberland and has cutting rights on about 18 million acres of timberland in Canada.

Under the leadership of John Creighton (appointed CEO in 1991, the first from outside the company's 16 founding families), Weyerhaeuser has returned to profitability. He retained its profitable real estate and mortgage subsidiaries but lopped off other operations such as nursery and garden supplies, using the cash to upgrade paper and lumber mills. He set a goal of adding $700 million to operating earnings by 1995, a goal he met a year ahead of schedule, in part by squeezing $100 million out of corporate overhead.

Weyerhaeuser is increasing its overseas operations. It is a leading supplier of logs and newsprint to Japan and has signed a deal with a South African forest products company to distribute logs internationally.

The spotted owl still haunts the company's Pacific Northwest timberlands, but in 1995 Weyerhaeuser reached terms with federal authorities for selected harvesting in the region.

WHEN

Frederick Weyerhaeuser, a 24-year-old German immigrant, bought his first lumberyard (in Illinois) in 1858. He participated in several joint logging ventures, particularly in Illinois, Wisconsin, and Minnesota. In 1900 he and 15 partners bought 900,000 timbered acres near Tacoma, Washington, from the Northern Pacific Railway. The venture was named Weyerhaeuser Timber Company.

During the Great Depression the company recouped losses in the deflated lumber market through the sale of wood pulp. Frederick's grandson J. P. "Phil" Weyerhaeuser Jr. took over as CEO in 1933. Phil championed the reforestation and management of cutover timberlands, proposing a visionary replanting program in Grays Harbor County, Washington. Clemons Tree Farm, America's first tree farm, was dedicated in 1941.

Diversification into the production of containerboard (1949), particleboard (1955), paper (1956), and other products led the company to drop "timber" from its name in 1959. In 1963 Weyerhaeuser went public and opened its first overseas office, in Tokyo.

In the 1970s George Weyerhaeuser (Phil's son) presided over another diversification effort, this time to insulate the company from the cyclical nature of the forest products industry. Weyerhaeuser ended up with a mishmash of businesses and products, from disposable diapers to pet supplies.

The eruption of Mount St. Helens in 1980 killed 68,000 acres of Weyerhaeuser timber. The costs of this disaster and the soft US lumber market depressed the company's earnings through 1982. To cut costs Weyerhaeuser reduced its salaried work force by 25% during this period. In 1983 the company bought GNA Corporation, a seller of annuities through financial institutions. The following year Weyerhaeuser opened an office in Beijing to tap the growing Chinese wood and paper products market.

Under John Creighton (president since 1988 and CEO since 1991), Weyerhaeuser refocused on forest products, organizing along product lines rather than by geographic region, while putting less successful ventures up for sale, including its milk carton plant (1989), a hardwood plant (1989), and a gypsum board plant (1989). The company took a $497 million pretax charge in 1989 related to the decision to close unprofitable operations. Earnings improved in 1990 but dropped again in 1991, reflecting the recession in the US and plant closures in the Pacific Northwest.

Weyerhaeuser dissolved its Republic Federal Savings & Loan Association in 1992. Also that year the company outbid Georgia-Pacific to pay $600 million for 2 pulp mills, 3 sawmills, and over 200,000 acres of Georgia forestland, boosting its market pulp capacity by 40%.

In 1993 the company sold its disposable diaper business through a public offering in a new company, Paragon Trade Brands. Also that year Weyerhaeuser sold GNA Corporation to a General Electric subsidiary (GE Capital) for $525 million. In 1994 the company bought a Phoenix paper recycling plant, its 23rd recycling facility in North America.

In 1995 Weyerhaeuser began discussions with private investors to establish a $1.5 billion fund to help it diversify beyond North America, including exploring the purchase of timberland in New Zealand.

NYSE symbol: WY
Fiscal year ends: Last Sunday in December

WHO

Chairman: George H. Weyerhaeuser, age 68
President and CEO: John W. Creighton Jr., age 62, $1,314,357 pay
EVP Timberlands, Raw Materials, and External Affairs: Charles W. Bingham, age 61, $636,477 pay
EVP Wood Products: William R. Corbin, age 53, $541,789 pay
EVP Pulp, Paper, and Packaging: Richard C. Gozon, age 56
SVP and CFO: William C. Stivers, age 56, $459,398 pay
SVP Technology: Norman E. Johnson, age 61, $406,995 pay
SVP Human Resources: Steven R. Hill, age 47
VP and General Counsel: Robert C. Lane
VP Strategic Planning: Darien E. Roseen
VP and Controller: Kenneth J. Stancato
Auditors: Arthur Andersen & Co, SC

WHERE

HQ: Tacoma, WA 98477
Phone: 206-924-2345
Fax: 206-924-7407

Owned or Leased Timberland	Acres (thou.)
Washington	1,522
Oregon	1,210
Alabama, Arkansas, Georgia, Mississippi, North Carolina & Oklahoma	3,011
Canada	17,861
Total	**23,604**

	1994 Sales	
	$ mil.	% of total
US	8,858	85
Other countries	1,540	15
Total	**10,398**	**100**

WHAT

	1994 Sales		1994 Operating Income	
	$ mil.	% of total	$ mil.	% of total
Timberlands & wood products	4,992	48	1,034	82
Pulp & paper	4,066	39	211	16
Real estate	911	9	7	1
Financial services	206	2	11	1
Corporate & other	223	2	(142)	—
Total	**10,398**	**100**	**1,121**	**100**

Wood Products
Doors
Fiber-based specialty products
Hardwood and softwood lumber and logs
Particleboard
Plywood and veneer

Pulp and Paper Products and Services
Bleached paperboard
Coated and uncoated papers
Containerboard packaging
Corrugated shipping containers
Corrugating medium
Linerboard
Newsprint
Papermaking chemicals
Pulp
Wastepaper recycling

Real Estate
Building and development of commercial and residential properties

Financial Services
Mortgage loans and mortgage-backed securities

KEY COMPETITORS

Boise Cascade
Canadian Pacific
Champion Intl.
Fletcher Challenge
Georgia-Pacific
International Paper
James River
Jefferson Smurfit
Kimberly-Clark
Louisiana-Pacific
Mead
Plum Creek Timber
Ply Gem
Rayonier
Scott
Stone Container
Temple-Inland
Willamette Industries

HOW MUCH

	9-Year Growth	1985	1986	1987	1988	1989	1990	1991	1992	1993	1994
Sales ($ mil.)	5.8%	6,270	6,891	8,385	9,328	10,181	9,066	8,773	9,266	9,545	10,398
Net income ($ mil.)	12.8%	200	277	446	566	341	394	(101)	372	579	589
Income as % of sales	—	3.2%	4.0%	5.3%	6.1%	3.3%	4.3%	—	4.0%	6.0%	5.7%
Earnings per share ($)	14.0%	0.88	1.27	2.12	2.68	1.56	1.87	(0.50)	1.83	2.83	2.86
Stock price – high ($)	—	22.67	27.50	40.00	29.50	32.75	28.38	30.38	39.25	46.50	51.25
Stock price – low ($)	—	16.50	19.75	19.92	23.50	24.50	17.38	20.13	26.63	36.25	35.75
Stock price – close ($)	6.9%	20.50	25.17	25.83	25.13	27.63	21.88	27.50	36.88	44.63	37.50
P/E – high	—	26	22	19	11	21	15	—	21	16	18
P/E – low	—	19	16	9	9	16	9	—	15	13	13
Dividends per share ($)	3.6%	0.87	0.87	0.90	1.15	1.20	1.20	1.20	1.20	1.20	1.20
Book value per share ($)	4.2%	14.42	14.82	16.54	18.14	18.55	19.21	17.25	17.85	19.34	20.86
Employees	(0.7%)	38,922	41,757	45,123	46,976	45,214	40,621	38,669	39,022	36,748	36,665

1994 Year-end:
Debt ratio: 41.5%
Return on equity: 14.3%
Cash (mil.): $39
Current ratio: 1.19
Long-term debt (mil.): $2,713
No. of shares (mil.): 206
Dividends
  Yield: 3.2%
  Payout: 42.0%
Market value (mil.): $7,711

**Stock Price History
High/Low 1985–94**

WHIRLPOOL CORPORATION

OVERVIEW

As much time as Whirlpool has spent in other countries lately, romancing new partners and courting new customers, you might think there was trouble at home. Not so. The Benton Harbor, Michigan–based appliance manufacturer is still the top maker of washers and dryers in the US and ranks among the domestic leaders in refrigerators, room air conditioning equipment, and dishwashers.

Nonetheless, Whirlpool has a wandering eye. The company sees unlimited sales potential in Asia and Latin America, where the numbers of consumers are growing quickly and the appliance markets remain fragmented among 50–65 manufacturers. In 1994 and 1995 the

company discussed or entered at least 4 joint ventures in China, and the number of Whirlpool employees in Asia was expected to jump from 800 in 1994 to as many as 10,000 by the end of 1995.

The company is restructuring its North American and European operations, slashing 3,200 jobs for a savings of $150 million a year by 1997. Whirlpool is the #3 appliance maker (13% share) in Europe, behind Electrolux and Bosch-Siemens. Whirlpool's shipments of appliances to Sears (under the Sears and Kenmore brand names) have dwindled somewhat following the retailer's shutdown of its catalog business and closing of several stores.

WHEN

The Upton Machine Company was founded in St. Joseph, Michigan, in 1911 by brothers Fred and Lou Upton and their uncle, Emory Upton. The company made hand-operated washing machines. In 1916 Sears, Roebuck began buying washing machines from the Uptons, and by 1925 the company was supplying all of Sears's washers. The Uptons combined their company with the Nineteen Hundred Washer Company in 1929 to form the Nineteen Hundred Corporation, the world's largest washing machine company. Sears and Nineteen Hundred continued to prosper through the Great Depression. During WWII Nineteen Hundred's factories produced war materials. Sears was still Nineteen Hundred's main customer in 1947 when the company decided to market a washing machine under the brand name Whirlpool. The machine was a success, and the company took its current name in 1950.

During the 1950s and 1960s, Whirlpool became a full-line appliance manufacturer while continuing as Sears's principal Kenmore appliance supplier. The company bought Seeger Refrigerator Company and the stove and air conditioning interests of RCA (1955); the gas refrigeration and ice-maker manufacturing facilities of Servel (1958); a majority interest in Heil-Quaker, makers of central heaters and space heaters (1964); Sears's major television set supplier, Warwick Electronics (1966); and 33% of Canadian appliance manufacturer/distributor John Inglis Company (1969). The company entered into an agreement with Sony in 1973 to distribute Whirlpool brand products in Japan. Whirlpool sold its television manufacturing business to Sanyo of Japan in 1976.

Between 1981 and 1991, in a static US market, Whirlpool net sales nearly tripled from $2.4 billion to almost $6.6 billion. In 1986 Whirlpool bought top-end appliance manufacturer KitchenAid from Dart and Kraft, kitchen cabinet maker St. Charles Manufacturing, and 65% of Italian cooling compressor manufacturer Aspera. Also in 1986 it sold its Heil-Quaker central heating business for $156 million to Inter City Gas and closed much of its original St. Joseph, Michigan, manufacturing facility. The company increased its ownership of Inglis to 100% in 1990.

Whirlpool Europe resulted from a $500 million joint venture with Philips Electronics in 1989; for $600 million, Whirlpool bought full ownership of the unit in 1991. The company took control of appliance marketer SAGAD of Argentina (formerly controlled by Philips) in early 1992. A joint venture with Slovakia's Tatramat was created in 1992; Whirlpool acquired majority interest in 1994.

In 1993 Whirlpool set up offices in Singapore and Tokyo. That same year the company won a $30 million prize in a competition among US appliance manufacturers to develop a superefficient refrigerator. In 1994 Whirlpool acquired controlling interest in Kelvinator of India for $120 million. Also that year Whirlpool was questioned in a Justice Department investigation into appliance pricing tactics. News of the inquiry coincided with Best Buy's announcement that Whirlpool had ended its relationship with the retailer.

Whirlpool has begun building a $100 million gas and electric range factory in Tulsa; the facility, scheduled to open in 1996, may eventually employ as many as 1,300 workers.

NYSE symbol: WHR
Fiscal year ends: December 31

WHO

Chairman and CEO: David R. Whitwam, age 52, $2,350,000 pay
President and COO: William D. Marohn, age 54, $830,250 pay
EVP and Chief Technology Officer: Ronald L. Kerber, age 51, $551,000 pay
EVP North American Appliance Group: Ralph F. Hake, age 45, $546,067 pay
EVP and Chief Administrative Officer: James R. Samartini, age 59, $534,067 pay
EVP; President, Whirlpool Europe: Jeff M. Fettig, age 37
EVP; Chairman and CEO, Whirlpool Asia Appliance Group: Robert I. Frey, age 51
EVP Latin American Appliance Group: P. Daniel Miller
VP Human Resources and Assistant Secretary: E. R. Dunn
Auditors: Ernst & Young LLP

WHERE

HQ: 2000 M-63, Benton Harbor, MI 49022-2692
Phone: 616-923-5000
Fax: 616-923-5486

Whirlpool has manufacturing facilities in Arkansas, Indiana, Michigan, Mississippi, Ohio, and Tennessee and in Argentina, Brazil, Canada, China, France, Germany, India, Italy, Mexico, Slovakia, and Sweden.

	1994 Sales		1994 Operating Income	
	$ mil.	% of total	$ mil.	% of total
North America	5,048	63	522	71
Europe	2,373	30	163	22
Latin America	329	4	49	7
Asia	205	3	(22)	—
Adjustments	149	—	(315)	—
Total	**8,104**	**100**	**397**	**100**

WHAT

	1994 Sales	
	$ mil.	% of total
Major home appliances	7,949	98
Financial services	155	2
Total	**8,104**	**100**

	1994 Sales	
	$ mil.	% of total
Refrigeration & air conditioning	2,900	36
Home laundry appliances	2,610	32
Other home appliances	2,439	30
Financial services	155	2
Total	**8,104**	**100**

Selected Products and Services	Selected Brand Names
Air conditioners	Admiral
Automatic dryers	Bauknecht
Automatic washers	Coolerator
Consumer financing services	Eslabon de Lujo
Dehumidifiers	Estate
Dishwashers	Ignis
Freezers	Inglis
Ice makers	Kenmore
Manufacturer, dealer, and distributor financing	KitchenAid
	Laden
Microwave ovens	Roper
Ranges	Sears
Refrigerators	Speed Queen
Trash compactors	Whirlpool

KEY COMPETITORS

Dako	Madosa	Refripar
Electrolux	Masco	Rival
Elfi/Brandt	Maytag	Robert Bosch
GEC	Merloni	Sanyo
Hitachi	Raytheon	Sharp

HOW MUCH

	9-Year Growth	1985	1986	1987	1988	1989	1990	1991	1992	1993	1994
Sales ($ mil.)	9.9%	3,475	4,009	4,179	4,315	6,289	6,434	6,550	7,301	7,533	8,104
Net income ($ mil.)	(1.6%)	182	200	181	94	187	72	170	205	231	158
Income as % of sales	—	5.2%	5.0%	4.3%	2.2%	3.0%	1.1%	2.6%	2.8%	3.1%	1.9%
Earnings per share ($)	(1.9%)	2.49	2.70	2.53	1.36	2.70	1.04	2.45	2.79	3.11	2.09
Stock price – high ($)	—	25.38	41.50	40.88	29.88	33.25	33.50	41.00	48.88	68.00	73.50
Stock price – low ($)	—	20.25	24.25	20.25	23.50	24.25	17.50	19.88	34.50	43.25	44.63
Stock price – close ($)	8.2%	24.69	33.88	24.38	24.75	33.00	23.50	38.88	44.63	66.50	50.25
P/E – high	—	10	15	16	22	12	32	17	18	22	35
P/E – low	—	8	9	8	17	9	17	8	12	14	21
Dividends per share ($)	2.2%	1.00	1.03	1.10	1.10	1.10	1.10	1.10	1.10	1.19	1.22
Book value per share ($)	3.9%	16.46	18.21	18.83	19.06	20.49	20.49	21.76	22.89	22.58	23.28
Employees	4.8%	25,573	30,520	30,301	29,110	39,411	36,157	37,886	38,520	39,590	39,016

1994 Year-end:
Debt ratio: 54.8%
Return on equity: 9.4%
Cash (mil.): $72
Current ratio: 1.03
Long-term debt (mil.): $885
No. of shares (mil.): 74
Dividends
  Yield: 2.4%
  Payout: 58.4%
Market value (mil.): $3,719

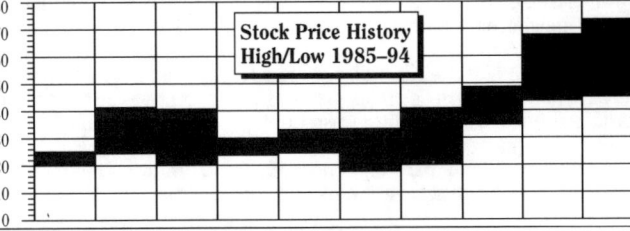

Stock Price History
High/Low 1985–94

WHITMAN CORPORATION

OVERVIEW

Combining the bottling of Pepsi-Cola with the manufacture of mufflers and walk-in refrigerators sounds like a difficult challenge, but Chicago-based Whitman Corporation has made a success of it. Its Pepsi-Cola General Bottlers is the largest independent Pepsi bottler in the US; its Midas International is the largest franchised network for servicing mufflers in the world; and its Hussmann Corp. produces merchandising and refrigeration systems for the commercial food industry.

The bottling division operates in 12 states in the Midwest and Southeast. It has grown by acquisition and by the increase of Pepsi's share of the US soft drink market. Some 34% of the division's sales come from noncola product distribution. In 1994 it expanded its operations to Poland. Midas is also expanding in Europe and plans to double its European chain to 600 units by the year 2000.

Southeastern Asset Management, an investment firm, owns 9.5% of Whitman.

WHEN

Whitman Corporation is a very different business from its grandparent company, the Illinois Central Railroad. Started in 1851 with a 3.6 million–acre land grant, Illinois Central became one of the nation's 10 largest rail systems. In 1901, its 50th year, it boasted 4,200 rail miles, a $32 million income, and freight and passenger service in 13 states. Its famous passenger trains included the Green Diamond (Chicago to St. Louis) and the Diamond Special and City of New Orleans (Chicago to New Orleans). Passenger service, no longer profitable, was sold to Amtrak in 1971. In 1972 the company (renamed Illinois Central Industries in 1962) acquired the Gulf, Mobile and Ohio Railroad (Chicago to Mobile, Alabama), and the railroad was renamed Illinois Central Gulf (ICG).

The company maintained its focus on railroads until William Johnson, former president of Railway Express Agency, became president in 1966. Johnson served as president for 21 years, transforming it into a multinational conglomerate that was renamed IC Industries in 1975. IC bought numerous companies, including Pepsi-Cola General Bottlers (1970); Midas International auto muffler shops (1972); and the venerable St. Louis company, Pet Inc. (1978). Pet had begun in 1885 as an evaporated milk company and had made substantial diverse purchases of its own, including Hussmann Refrigeration, a leading producer of refrigeration systems for grocery stores; Downyflake Foods; Stuckey roadside candy stores; and chocolate company Stuart F. Whitman and Son.

By the late 1970s the ICG railroad provided only 1% of the company's pretax profits. IC was determined to sell it, but it wasn't until 1989 that IC spun off ICG to its stockholders. In the interim IC sold many of its real estate holdings, and ICG's trackage shrank by 2/3.

A private concern, Prospect Group, bought the railroad within a month of the spinoff.

The company changed its name in 1988 to Whitman Corporation (after Pet's well-known chocolate brand) to reflect its concentration on consumer goods and services. In the 1980s Whitman sold 65 companies, including its Pneumo Abex aerospace operations (for $1.2 billion, 1988). In the same time period, Whitman has bought 98 companies, including Orval Kent (refrigerated salad products, 1988) and Van de Kamp's Frozen Seafoods (1989). In 1989 Whitman announced plans to sell Hussmann but, lacking an acceptable offer, decided in 1990 to keep the unit.

In an attempt to restructure, the company spun off its Pet food unit to shareholders, losing such brands as Old El Paso (Mexican foods), Progresso (Italian foods), and Whitman Chocolates (sold to Russell Stover Candies in 1993). The company also pared jobs to reduce debt. Whitman purchased 39 European muffler shops and 3 Pepsi franchises in the early 1990s.

In 1993 Pepsi General began work on a $7.5 million line at its Munster, Indiana, plant for production of Lipton Original Tea. Hussmann introduced Protocol, a refrigeration system that doesn't use CFCs, and continued to upgrade its largest plant (in Bridgeton, Missouri). In 1993 and 1994 Whitman took steps to reduce its heavy debt, refinancing $360 million that is expected to cut annual interest costs by $12 million.

In 1994 Hussmann completed development of medium-temperature refrigerated cases, as part of its new product line called Impact. That same year Hussmann set up a joint venture with Luoyang Refrigeration Machinery Factory, China's #1 maker of commercial refrigerators. Hussmann plans to begin production there in 1995.

NYSE symbol: WH
Fiscal year ends: December 31

WHO

Chairman and CEO: Bruce S. Chelberg, age 60,
$1,160,417 pay
EVP (CFO): Thomas L. Bindley, age 51,
$657,500 pay
SVP and Controller: Frank T. Westover
SVP Human Resources: Lawrence J. Pilon, age 46
VP; President and CEO, Pepsi-Cola General Bottlers:
Gerald A. McGuire, age 63, $560,250 pay
VP; President and CEO, Midas Intl Corp.: John R.
Moore, age 59, $531,000 pay
VP; President and CEO, Hussmann Corp.: J. Larry
Vowell, age 54, $405,166 pay
VP Secretary and General Counsel: William B. Moore
VP and Treasurer: Kathleen R. Gannon
VP Taxes: Louis J. Corna
Auditors: KPMG Peat Marwick LLP

WHERE

HQ: 3501 Algonquin Rd., Rolling Meadows, IL 60008
Phone: 708-818-5000
Fax: 708-818-5045 (Corporate Affairs)

Whitman's Pepsi operations are located in 12
midwestern and southeastern states and in Poland.
Midas has 2,575 shops in the US and 13 other countries.
Hussmann has operations in Canada, Mexico, the UK,
and the US and joint ventures in Asia and Europe.

	1994 Sales		1994 Operating Income	
	$ mil.	% of total	$ mil.	% of total
US	2,236	83	312	91
Other countries	472	17	31	9
Adjustments	(49)	—	(16)	—
Total	**2,659**	**100**	**327**	**100**

WHAT

	1994 Sales		1994 Operating Income	
	$ mil.	% of total	$ mil.	% of total
Pepsi General	1,256	47	185	54
Hussmann	860	32	83	24
Midas	543	21	75	22
Other	—	—	(16)	—
Total	**2,659**	**100**	**327**	**100**

Pepsi-Cola General Bottlers, Inc.
All-Sport
A&W Root Beer
Caffeine Free Pepsi
Canada Dry
Dad's Root Beer
Diet Pepsi
Dr Pepper
Hawaiian Punch
Lipton's Tea
Mountain Dew
Ocean Spray
Pepsi
Seven-Up
Slice
Wild Cherry Pepsi

Hussmann Corporation
Bottle coolers
Commercial/industrial
refrigeration systems
HVAC equipment
Refrigerated display cases
Storage coolers
Walk-in coolers

Midas International Corporation
Auto service shops

KEY COMPETITORS

American Standard
Bridgestone
Cadbury Schweppes
Celestial Seasonings
Coca-Cola
Coca-Cola Bottling
of Chicago
Coca-Cola Enterprises
Cott
AB Electrolux
Fedders
Ferolito, Vultaggio
GKN
Goodyear
Lennox Intl.
Meineke
Montgomery Ward
National Beverage
Nestlé
Quaker Oats
Scotsman Industries
Sears
Triarc
United Technologies
York Intl.

HOW MUCH

	9-Year Growth	1985	1986	1987	1988	1989	1990	1991	1992	1993	1994
Sales ($ mil.)	(5.5%)	4,405	4,222	4,027	3,583	3,986	2,305	2,393	2,388	2,530	2,659
Net income ($ mil.)	(4.9%)	163	(126)	252	210	191	19	98	60	106	103
Income as % of sales	—	3.7%	—	6.3%	5.9%	4.8%	0.8%	4.1%	2.5%	4.2%	3.9%
Earnings per share ($)	3.5%	0.71	(0.54)	1.03	0.91	0.70	(0.08)	0.92	0.56	0.99	0.97
Stock price – high ($)	—	9.40	14.06	19.10	17.25	17.71	13.77	14.13	16.38	17.00	18.00
Stock price – low ($)	—	6.22	8.25	10.36	13.72	12.73	7.87	8.22	12.25	12.75	14.75
Stock price – close ($)	7.7%	8.88	10.65	15.22	16.55	13.31	8.33	13.38	14.75	16.25	17.25
P/E – high	—	13	—	19	19	25	—	15	29	17	19
P/E – low	—	9	—	10	15	18	—	9	22	13	15
Dividends per share ($)	0.0%	0.32	0.35	0.39	0.43	0.46	0.48	0.37	0.25	0.28	0.32
Book value per share ($)	(3.8%)	7.40	6.30	6.79	3.91	1.78	1.61	4.32	4.47	4.83	5.24
Employees	(10.9%)	43,050	38,162	15,174	15,099	15,165	15,219	14,703	14,374	14,868	15,271

1994 Year-end:
Debt ratio: 59.5%
Return on equity: 19.3%
Cash (mil.): $71
Current ratio: 1.46
Long-term debt (mil.): $723
No. of shares (mil.): 106
Dividends
  Yield: 1.9%
  Payout: 33.0%
Market value (mil.): $1,820

**Stock Price History
High/Low 1985–94**

WM. WRIGLEY JR. COMPANY

OVERVIEW

Chicago-based Wm. Wrigley Jr. is the world's #1 chewing gum maker and a giant in the US, commanding a 49% share of the domestic gum market. Wrigley derives 90% of its revenues from gum. Its products include such popular brands as Juicy Fruit, Doublemint, Freedent, and top seller Extra sugar-free gum. Overseas, these and other brands are manufactured in 9 factories and sold in more than 120 countries. International sales accounted for 44% of 1994 revenues.

Wrigley has maintained low prices to foil competitors and increase its customer base. The company also has benefited from automation and declining costs of such materials as gum base and corn syrup. It is building new plants in Poland and India and expanding its Alsace manufacturing plant in France to meet the demand in Eastern Europe and Russia, which accounts for almost half of its sales growth. Sales of sugar-free gum, overseas and at home, outpaced shipments of regular gum for the first time in 1994. Wrigley's success, however, has attracted imitators. Japanese confectionary Sun Kotobuki plans to make a knockoff of Wrigley's Doublemint gum in Vietnam.

Wrigley still has no long-term debt. CEO William Wrigley, grandson of the founder, owns roughly 1/4 of the company.

WHEN

William Wrigley Jr. started his career at 13 when, following his expulsion from school, his father put him to work at the family's soap factory in Philadelphia. After a year Wrigley was promoted to the sales staff, where he was very successful selling door-to-door.

In 1891 he opened, in Chicago, an office of his father's soap company. Wrigley learned to promote his products with free premiums, such as cookbooks. When he began offering customers chewing gum made of spruce gum and paraffin by Zeno Manufacturing (1892), he received numerous requests to buy the gum. At the time chicle (a naturally sweet gum base from Central America) was being imported for the rubber industry. Wrigley successfully gambled on the idea that chicle would work as a main ingredient in chewing gum.

By 1893 Wrigley had introduced Spearmint and Juicy Fruit and was selling only gum. He offered dealers sales incentives such as counter scales, cash registers, and display cases for volume purchases. In 1898 he merged with Zeno to form Wm. Wrigley, Jr. & Co. By 1910 Spearmint gum was the leading US brand, and Wrigley began to expand into Canada (1910), Australia (1915), and Great Britain (1927).

The Wrigley family bought real estate, including Catalina Island (1919) and the Arizona Biltmore Hotel (1931); built the Wrigley Building (1924); and purchased the Chicago Cubs (1924, sold 1981). Wrigley was keen on advertising. He plastered simple messages on huge billboards and used twins to promote Doublemint gum in the 1930s. By the time of his death in 1932, when son Philip took over, the company was the largest single-product advertiser.

For over 75 years Wrigley made 3 gums: Spearmint, Juicy Fruit, and Doublemint (introduced in 1914). Unable to obtain the proper ingredients during WWII, Wrigley produced inferior gum under a different label but kept the Wrigley brand alive with a picture of his former gum and the ad slogan "Remember this Wrapper." It worked: After the war Wrigley's popularity increased. The company did not raise its original 5¢ price until 1971, when management grudgingly went to 7¢.

By 1974 Wrigley faced competition from sugar-free gums. Despite declining market share, management refused to bring out a sugar-free gum at that time, instead introducing Freedent for denture wearers. Later the company introduced Big Red (1975); Orbit, a sugar-free gum (1977); and Hubba Bubba (1978; through Amurol, bought in 1958). Philip died in 1977, and a 3rd-generation Wrigley (William) took over.

In 1984 Wrigley introduced a new sugar-free gum, Extra. In 1991 the company launched Michael Jordan Hang Time shredded bubble gum, a sugar-free version of Freedent, and a bubble gum version of Extra.

The company has made rapid inroads overseas, particularly in Eastern Europe, establishing operations in Hungary, Slovenia, and the Czech Republic. In 1993 the company opened a new chewing gum factory in China.

In 1994 Wrigley began an ambitious construction program to build new factories in the US and abroad and sold its Singapore affiliate for a $38 million profit. Wrigley also launched its first new sugar-based chewing gum in nearly 20 years, Winterfresh, which has been very successful without undermining sales of other company brands.

NYSE symbol: WWY
Fiscal year ends: December 31

WHO

President and CEO: William Wrigley, age 61,
$475,000 pay
EVP: R. Darrell Ewers, age 61, $376,500 pay
Group VP International: Douglas S. Barrie, age 61,
$324,833 pay
Group VP Marketing: Ronald O. Cox, age 56,
$276,500 pay
SVP and CFO: John F. Bard, age 53, $261,000 pay
SVP Manufacturing: Martin J. Geraghty, age 58
VP Treasurer: Dushan Petrovich, age 41
VP Personnel: David E. Boxell, age 53
Auditors: Ernst & Young LLP

WHERE

HQ: 410 N. Michigan Ave., Chicago, IL 60611
Phone: 312-644-2121
Fax: 312-644-0097 (Marketing)

The company has operations in 27 countries.

	1994 Sales		1994 Operating Income	
	$ mil.	% of total	$ mil.	% of total
North America	938	55	177	50
Europe	573	33	107	30
Other regions	200	12	70	20
Adjustments	(50)	—	1	—
Total	**1,661**	**100**	**356**	**100**

WHAT

US Brands (Gum)	Non-US Brands (Gum)
Big Red	Arrowmint
Doublemint	Big Boy
Extra	Big G
Freedent	Cool Crunch
Juicy Fruit	Dulce 16
Spearmint	Freedent
Winterfresh	Hubba Bubba
	Juicy Fruit

Amurol Products — Orbit
Co. Brands — P.K.
Big League Chew
Bubble Tape — **Real Estate**
Hubba Bubba — Wrigley Building, Chicago

US Subsidiaries and Divisions
Amurol Confections Co. (children's bubble gum and
candy)
Four-Ten Corporation
L.A. Dreyfus Co. (chewing gum base)
Northwestern Flavors, Inc. (flavorings)
Wrico Packaging (wrapping supplies)

KEY COMPETITORS

Cadbury Schweppes
Hauser Chemical
Hercules
Hershey
IFF
Mars
Marvel
Nabisco Holdings
Roche
Sun Kotobuki
Tootsie Roll
Warner-Lambert

HOW MUCH

	9-Year Growth	1985	1986	1987	1988	1989	1990	1991	1992	1993	1994
Sales ($ mil.)	11.6%	620	699	781	891	993	1,111	1,149	1,287	1,429	1,661
Net income ($ mil.)	20.4%	44	54	70	87	106	117	129	149	175	231
Income as % of sales	—	7.0%	7.7%	9.0%	9.8%	10.7%	10.6%	11.2%	11.5%	12.2%	13.9%
Earnings per share ($)	21.6%	0.34	0.43	0.56	0.73	0.90	1.00	1.09	1.27	1.50	1.98
Stock price – high ($)	—	5.27	8.66	11.82	13.65	17.90	19.73	26.97	39.88	46.13	53.88
Stock price – low ($)	—	3.19	4.58	6.49	10.66	11.82	14.57	16.36	22.10	29.50	38.13
Stock price – close ($)	28.5%	5.16	7.62	11.51	12.03	17.86	17.07	26.89	32.63	44.13	49.38
P/E – high	—	16	20	21	19	20	20	25	31	31	27
P/E – low	—	9	11	12	15	13	15	15	17	20	19
Dividends per share ($)	20.3%	0.17	0.21	0.28	0.36	0.45	0.49	0.55	0.62	0.75	0.90
Book value per share ($)	12.6%	2.04	2.31	2.39	2.59	2.91	3.41	3.94	4.27	4.94	5.92
Employees	2.5%	5,600	5,500	5,500	5,500	5,750	5,850	6,250	6,400	6,700	7,000

1994 Year-end:
Debt ratio: 0.0%
Return on equity: 36.5%
Cash (mil.): $128
Current ratio: 2.97
Long-term debt (mil.): $0
No. of shares (mil.): 116
Dividends
  Yield: 1.8%
  Payout: 45.5%
Market value (mil.): $5,738

**Stock Price History
High/Low 1985–94**

WINN-DIXIE STORES, INC.

OVERVIEW

You can learn a lot about a company by considering its name. Take supermarket chain Winn-Dixie, for example. The Jacksonville, Florida–based company's moniker evokes not only its success (51 consecutive stockholder dividends — an NYSE record) but also its market area (primarily the South). With more than 1,150 stores in 13 states and the Bahamas, Winn-Dixie is one of the 10 biggest grocery retailers in the US. The company also manufactures items ranging from peanut butter to pizza to paper bags.

Winn-Dixie operates its domestic stores under the Winn-Dixie, Marketplace, and Buddies names. The Marketplace stores, which are 44,000 square feet and larger, count deli-cafes among their newest features. The company's stores, for the most part, compete on price, with a chainwide policy (adopted in 1991) of having the lowest prices in each of its markets.

In recent years Winn-Dixie has closed small or unprofitable stores and replaced them with larger models; the company has also enlarged or remodeled many of its locations. In fiscal 1995 Winn-Dixie closed about 60 stores while opening or renovating more than twice as many. The company also has been installing in each store computers that will connect them to the main office via satellite and save over $2.5 million annually on phone bills.

The heirs of founder William Davis control 41% of the company's stock.

WHEN

In 1925 William Davis borrowed $10,000 to open the cash-and-carry Rockmoor Grocery in Lemon City near Miami. After a slow start Davis expanded his chain of Table Supply Stores to 34 by the time of his death in 1934, when his 4 sons took control. In 1939 they purchased control of Winn & Lovett Grocery Company, which operated 78 stores in Florida and Georgia. The company, incorporated in 1928, was a leader in the 1930s in building new supermarket-type stores. In 1944 the combined company settled in Jacksonville and formally took the name Winn & Lovett.

After WWII the company, still controlled by the Davis family, acquired grocery chains throughout the South, including the Steiden Stores in Kentucky, Margaret Ann Stores in Florida, Wylie Company Stores in Alabama, Penney Stores in Mississippi, King Stores in Georgia, and the Eden and Ballentine Stores in South Carolina. In 1955 the company consolidated with Dixie Home Stores of the Carolinas and changed its name to Winn-Dixie Stores, Inc. During the 1950s and early 1960s, Winn-Dixie continued to expand by acquisitions, adding the Ketner and Milner Stores in the Carolinas and the Hill Stores of Louisiana and Alabama. Also in the 1960s Winn-Dixie entered manufacturing, processing, and distribution.

By 1966, under the leadership of chairman J. E. Davis (one of the founder's sons), the company controlled so much of the grocery business in the South that, for antitrust reasons, the FTC imposed a 10-year moratorium on its buying stores. The company responded by buying 9 stores outside the US, in Nassau and Freeport in the Bahama Islands. When the moratorium ended in 1976, the company bought Kimbell of Texas, adding stores and extensive support facilities in Texas, Oklahoma, and New Mexico. Winn-Dixie refused to deal with the workers' union in New Mexico, and when a pro-union boycott was organized in 1979, the company sold its 23 stores there.

William Davis's grandson Robert Davis took control of the company as chairman in 1983. He was succeeded 5 years later by his cousin and current chairman, Dano Davis.

Winn-Dixie began converting all of its stores to its Low-Price-Leader marketing program in 1991. This approach lowers gross margins but raises sales per store and spreads corporate overhead across a larger sales base. In 1992 Winn-Dixie employed a novel advertising technique to lure shoppers in — it sent a videotaped, 10-minute commercial describing newly renovated stores' amenities to infrequent Winn-Dixie shoppers.

In 1993 Winn-Dixie unveiled its one-stop-shopping concept stores, called the Marketplace and Food Pavilion, which feature more space (50,000 square feet), more products, and more services (photo developing, dry cleaning, and a complete pharmacy).

In 1994 the company agreed to participate in a test of ShopperVision, an interactive service on Time Warner's Full Service Network in Orlando, which allows shoppers to order groceries for home delivery via TV. Also that year Winn-Dixie began testing home shopping services via America Online. The company's shop-at-home services were already available through phone and fax.

Winn-Dixie bought the 25-store Cincinnati supermarket chain Thriftway in 1995.

NYSE symbol: WIN
Fiscal year ends: Last Wednesday in June

WHO

Chairman and Principal Executive Officer: A. Dano
Davis, age 50, $717,500 pay
President: James Kufeldt, age 57, $717,500 pay
EVP Operations: Charles H. McKellar, age 57,
$588,093 pay
SVP and Regional Director: E. T. Walters, age 61,
$329,045 pay
SVP and Regional Director: Charles E. Winge, age 50,
$309,737 pay
SVP and Regional Director: H. E. Hess, age 55
SVP and Regional Director: T. E. McDonald, age 58
VP, General Counsel, and Secretary: W. E. Ripley Jr.
Financial VP and Principal Financial Officer: Richard P.
McCook, age 42
**VP and Director of Associate Relations/Human
Resources:** L. H. May, age 50
Auditors: KPMG Peat Marwick LLP

WHERE

HQ: 5050 Edgewood Ct., PO Box B, Jacksonville, FL
32203-0297
Phone: 904-783-5000
Fax: 904-783-5294

State	1994 Stores No.
Florida	439
North Carolina	129
Georgia	126
South Carolina	86
Alabama	84
Louisiana	78
Texas	72
Kentucky	53
Virginia	30
Other states & Bahamas	62
Total	**1,159**

WHAT

Store Names
Buddies (1)
The City Meat Markets
(11; Bahamas)
Marketplace (286)
Winn-Dixie (858)
Winn-Dixie Stores
(3; Bahamas)

Subsidiaries
Astor Products
Deep South Products
Dixie Packers
Fairway Food Stores
First Northern Supply
Monterey Canning Co.
Save Rite Foods
Second Northern Supply
Sunbelt Products
Superior Food Company
Third Northern Supply
W-D (Bahamas) Ltd.
Bahamas Supermarkets Ltd.
The City Meat Markets Ltd.
Winn-Dixie Atlanta
Winn-Dixie Charlotte
Winn-Dixie Greenville
Winn-Dixie Louisiana

Winn-Dixie Louisville
Winn-Dixie
Montgomery
Winn-Dixie Raleigh
Winn-Dixie Texas

**Items Produced or
Processed**
Carbonated beverages
Cheese
Coffee and tea
Condiments
Cookies
Cottage cheese
Crackers
Detergents
Eggs
Frozen pizza
Ice cream
Jams and jellies
Meats
Milk
Oleomargarine
Paper bags
Peanut butter
Snacks
Spices
Yogurt

KEY COMPETITORS

Albertson's	Ingles Markets	Pueblo Xtra
Bruno's	Kash n' Karry	Randall's
Circle K	Kmart	Ruddick
Delchamps	Kroger	Schwegmann
Food Lion	Minyard Food	Sedano's
George Weston	Stores	Supermarkets
Goodings	Penn Traffic	Southland
Supermarkets	Price/Costco	SUPERVALU
Great A&P	Publix	Wal-Mart

HOW MUCH

	9-Year Growth	1985	1986	1987	1988	1989	1990	1991	1992	1993	1994
Sales ($ mil.)	4.0%	7,775	8,225	8,804	9,008	9,151	9,744	10,074	10,337	10,832	11,082
Net income ($ mil.)	8.0%	108	116	112	117	135	153	171	216	236	216
Income as % of sales	—	1.4%	1.4%	1.3%	1.3%	1.5%	1.6%	1.7%	2.1%	2.2%	1.9%
Earnings per share ($)	9.1%	1.32	1.42	1.36	1.44	1.68	1.93	2.20	2.82	3.11	2.90
Stock price – high ($)	—	19.44	29.50	26.00	23.50	32.50	38.63	41.25	79.50	79.75	58.38
Stock price – low ($)	—	15.75	17.44	18.75	18.75	21.44	28.38	29.75	35.75	52.75	42.63
Stock price – close ($)	11.6%	19.19	22.94	22.13	22.00	32.50	32.38	37.50	76.63	53.63	51.38
P/E – high	—	15	21	19	16	19	20	19	28	26	20
P/E – low	—	12	12	14	13	13	15	14	13	17	15
Dividends per share ($)	7.0%	0.84	0.87	0.90	0.93	0.88	0.99	1.07	1.19	1.31	1.55
Book value per share ($)	6.8%	7.90	8.53	8.97	8.59	9.81	10.38	11.15	12.39	13.14	14.26
Employees	4.7%	74,300	76,900	80,000	83,800	94,000	101,000	106,000	102,000	105,000	112,000

1994 Year-end:
Debt ratio: 8.5%
Return on equity: 21.2%
Cash (mil.): $32
Current ratio: 1.56
Long-term debt (mil.): $85
No. of shares (mil.): 74
Dividends
Yield: 3.0%
Payout: 53.4%
Market value (mil.): $3,811

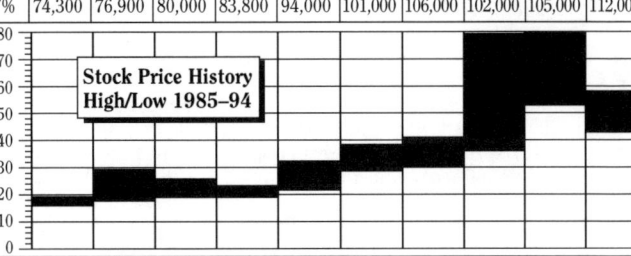

Stock Price History
High/Low 1985–94

WMX TECHNOLOGIES, INC.

OVERVIEW

Too many irons in the incinerator has management reeling at WMX, the world's largest waste collection and disposal company. To rescue its fragmented worldwide operations, WMX is taking a long look at its components, acquiring new businesses that complement the company's core segments (spending nearly $173 million for 46 businesses in 1994), and shedding weak units (about 10 in 1994).

To boost its share of the growing recycling market, WMX bought Resource Recycling Technologies, an East Coast operator of recycling facilities, in 1995. The addition could also help WMX win municipal refuse contracts.

In a move to tighten its operations, the company purchased the outstanding shares of spinoff Chemical Waste Management in 1994.

It also repurchased the publicly held shares of Rust International in 1995. WMX still has 2 public subsidiaries: Wheelabrator Technologies and Waste Management International.

Also in 1995 WMX agreed to sell Rust's hazardous waste and nuclear remediation business to OHM Corp., an Ohio-based pollution services company. The transaction gives Rust about 37% of OHM's stock. WMX's hazardous waste segment has been especially troublesome, with capacity outstripping volume. The company took a $91 million charge in the first quarter of 1995 to write down its investments in hazardous waste–handling equipment.

In 1995 WMX's North American operations served 11.3 million residential and 1 million commercial and industrial customers.

WHEN

In 1956 Dean L. Buntrock joined Ace Scavenger Service (Illinois), which had 12 collection trucks and $750,000 per year in revenues. Under Buntrock's leadership the company expanded into Wisconsin.

In the early 1970s a growing number of waste service companies were forming. In 1971 Waste Management, Inc., emerged when Buntrock joined forces with H. Wayne Huizenga, who had bought 2 waste routes in Broward County, Florida, in 1962. Both companies had grown rapidly during the 1960s, as concern with air quality prompted bans on residential and industrial on-site waste burning. Waste Management, with customers in Florida, Illinois, Indiana, Minnesota, Ohio, and Wisconsin, reported earnings of $1.2 million its first year. In the 1970s it made acquisitions in Michigan, New York, Ohio, Pennsylvania, and Canada.

In 1975 the company bid on and won a contract in Riyadh, Saudi Arabia (service started in 1978), and formed its international subsidiary. Other foreign contracts followed, and the company now operates in 20 foreign countries, including Argentina, Australia, Germany, Italy, the Netherlands, New Zealand, and Venezuela. Waste Management also divided into specialty areas, forming Chemical Waste Management (1975) and offering site cleanup services (ENRAC, 1980) and low-level nuclear waste disposal (Chem-Nuclear Systems, 1982). Expansion in this period included a great coup — the acquisition of 60% of competitor SCA of Boston (1984).

Huizenga retired from his trash-hauling business in 1983 and soon purchased Block-

buster Video, the #1 video rental chain in the country (now a unit of Viacom, Inc.).

During the 1980s the company established joint ventures for the sale of recyclable materials with DuPont, Stone Container Corporation, and American National Can. Its partnership with the Henley Group created Wheelabrator Technologies (22% owned in 1988, now 57% owned). In 1989 Waste Management contracted to dispose of approximately 90% of the waste from the *Exxon Valdez* oil spill. In 1991 Waste Management International and Wessex Waste Management, a UK-based water company, formed a joint venture, creating UK Waste Management Ltd.

For many years the company has been targeted, and in some cases fined, for violation of antitrust laws and pollution ordinances. The company has also challenged ordinances, including an Alabama tax charging $72 per ton on waste brought into a company-owned site from out-of-state. In 1992 the court found in Chemical Waste Management's favor.

In 1993 Waste Management became WMX Technologies and opened the most modern hazardous-waste treatment plant in the world: a $150 million plant in Hong Kong. That same year the company spun off Rust International.

Wheelabrator's Air Pollution Control unit was awarded a $40 million contract in 1994 to build a trio of 750-foot chimneys for the Salt River Project in Page, Arizona.

In a move aimed at breaking into New York City's lucrative refuse market, in 1995 WMX agreed to purchase a majority interest in a 14-acre solid-waste transfer station located in the Bronx.

NYSE symbol: WMX
Fiscal year ends: December 31

WHO

Chairman and CEO: Dean L. Buntrock, age 63,
$2,520,000 pay
President and COO: Phillip B. Rooney, age 50,
$2,029,280 pay
SVP, Treasurer, and CFO: James E. Koenig, age 47,
$750,000 pay
SVP Corporate and Public Affairs: D. P. Payne, age 52
VP, General Counsel, and Secretary: Herbert A. Getz,
age 39, $502,500 pay
VP, Controller, and Principal Accounting Officer:
Thomas C. Hau, age 59
VP and Chief Environmental Officer: Donald A.
Wallgren, age 53
**VP Technology Development and Management;
President and CEO, Rust, International, Inc.:** Rodney
C. Gilbert, age 55
VP Communications: William J. Plunkett
VP Human Resources: Edward Kalebich
Auditors: Arthur Andersen & Co, SC

WHERE

HQ: 3003 Butterfield Rd., Oak Brook, IL 60521
Phone: 708-572-8800
Fax: 708-572-3094

The company has over 12 million residential clients and
municipal and commercial accounts in the US and 21
foreign countries.

	1994 Sales		1994 Operating Income	
	$ mil.	% of total	$ mil.	% of total
US	7,947	79	1,496	85
Europe	1,504	15	198	11
Other regions	646	6	74	4
Total	**10,097**	**100**	**1,768**	**100**

WHAT

	1994 Sales		1994 Operating Income	
	$ mil.	% of total	$ mil.	% of total
Solid waste	5,118	49	1,066	60
Intl. waste mgmt.	1,711	16	236	13
Engineering/ construction	1,683	16	97	6
Water treatment/ air quality	1,324	13	290	16
Hazardous waste	649	6	89	5
Adjustments	(388)	—	(10)	—
Total	**10,097**	**100**	**1,768**	**100**

Selected Services
Air quality (pollution control technologies)
Chemical waste (transport, treatment, and disposal)
Hazardous and low-level radioactive waste (collection,
transportation, treatment, and resource recovery)
Solid waste (collection, transport, disposal, recycling,
and energy recovery)
Trash-to-energy (power facilities)
Water and wastewater (treatment facilities)

Selected Subsidiaries
Chemical Waste Management (CWM; 100%, hazardous
waste management services)
Rust International (100% [CWM owns 56%,
Wheelabrator owns 40%]; engineering, construction,
and environmental and infrastructure consulting
services; remediation and related on-site services)
Waste Management International (56%; collection,
processing, transfer, and disposal services)
Wheelabrator Technologies (57%; air, energy, and water
treatment services)

KEY COMPETITORS

Allwaste	CSX	Ogden
Bechtel	EnviroSource	Safety-Kleen
Browning-Ferris	Halliburton	TRW
Canadian	Mid-American	USA Waste
Pacific	Waste	Services

HOW MUCH

	9-Year Growth	1985	1986	1987	1988	1989	1990	1991	1992	1993	1994
Sales ($ mil.)	22.5%	1,625	2,018	2,758	3,566	4,459	6,034	7,551	8,661	9,136	10,097
Net income ($ mil.)	18.4%	172	371	327	464	562	709	606	921	453	784
Income as % of sales	—	10.6%	18.4%	11.9%	13.0%	12.6%	11.8%	8.0%	10.6%	5.0%	7.8%
Earnings per share ($)	15.9%	0.43	0.88	0.73	1.03	1.22	1.49	1.23	1.86	0.93	1.62
Stock price – high ($)	—	9.50	14.94	24.25	21.38	35.88	45.50	44.38	46.63	40.25	30.75
Stock price – low ($)	—	5.44	8.63	13.50	15.75	20.38	28.63	32.63	32.00	23.00	22.63
Stock price – close ($)	12.7%	8.88	13.91	18.81	20.69	35.00	35.00	42.13	40.00	26.38	26.13
P/E – high	—	22	17	33	21	29	31	36	25	43	19
P/E – low	—	13	10	19	15	17	19	27	17	25	14
Dividends per share ($)	20.7%	0.11	0.13	0.17	0.21	0.27	0.34	0.40	0.48	0.58	0.60
Book value per share ($)	14.4%	2.79	3.67	4.19	4.82	5.88	7.52	8.37	8.81	8.60	9.38
Employees	15.8%	19,800	24,485	30,650	36,750	42,640	62,050	63,040	67,200	72,600	74,400

1994 Year-end:
Debt ratio: 60.4%
Return on equity: 18.0%
Cash (mil.): $142
Current ratio: 0.97
Long-term debt (mil.): $6,044
No. of shares (mil.): 484
Dividends
  Yield: 2.3%
  Payout: 37.0%
Market value (mil.): $12,645

Stock Price History
High/Low 1985–94

WOOLWORTH CORPORATION

OVERVIEW

The question remains: what is Woolworth? Founded as a general merchandiser, the company is abandoning its roots to concentrate on building its eclectic collection of specialty stores. Based in New York City, Woolworth has struggled mightily to reinvent itself. The company's revenues dropped more than 13% in fiscal 1995, reflecting the closure of many of its US five-and-dimes and the sale of 122 Canadian Woolco stores to Wal-Mart.

Leading the charge into specialty retailing is new CEO Roger Farah, a former executive with R. H. Macy. Farah is the first non-Woolworth executive to be named CEO of the company.

Farah plans to continue the company's shift to specialty retailing, which includes athletic and dress shoes, costume jewelry and accessories, casual apparel, and home furnishings and accessories. He also plans to sell some underperforming specialty chains and is looking for other ways to cut costs. In 1995 the company announced plans to reduce employment by 2,000, and it eliminated the dividend on its common stock for the first time in 92 years.

WHEN

With the idea of selling merchandise priced at no more than 5 cents, Frank Woolworth opened The Great Five Cent Store in Utica, New York, in 1879. It failed. That same year he moved to Lancaster, Pennsylvania, and created the first five-and-dime.

Woolworth moved his headquarters to New York City (1886) and spent the rest of the century acquiring other dime-store chains. He later expanded to Canada (1897), England (1909), France (1922), and Germany (1927).

With $10 million in sales, the 120-store chain incorporated as F.W. Woolworth & Company in 1905, with Frank Woolworth as president. In 1912 Woolworth merged with 5 rival chains and went public with 596 stores, making $52 million in sales the first year.

Frank Woolworth built lavish homes and corporate headquarters. In 1913, paying $13.5 million in cash, he finished construction of the Woolworth Building, then the world's tallest building (792 feet). When Woolworth died in 1919, the chain had 1,081 stores, with sales of $119 million.

Woolworth became more competitive after WWII by advertising, establishing revolving credit and self-service, moving stores to the suburbs, and expanding merchandise selections. In 1962 Woolworth opened Woolco, a US and Canadian discount chain. The US stores were closed in 1982.

Since the 1960s the company has become a specialty retailer, growing by acquiring and expanding US, Canadian, Australian, and European chains. Acquisitions included G.R. Kinney (shoes, 1963), Richman Brothers (men's clothing, 1969), Holtzman's Little Folk Shop (children's clothing, 1983), Champs (sporting goods, 1987), Moderna Shuh Center (shoes, Germany, 1988), Mathers (shoes, Australia, 1988), and Profoot (the Netherlands and Belgium, 1990).

In 1974 the company introduced Foot Locker, the athletic-shoe chain, later developing Lady Foot Locker (1982) and Kids Foot Locker (1987). Woolworth Express (1987) was a smaller version of the original dime store that has since been discontinued.

Since 1980 Woolworth's specialty stores have increased dramatically, while general merchandise stores have decreased sharply. In 1990 the company "reopened" a German store, in Halle, that it had operated before WWII. It was the first opened by any US retailer in eastern Germany.

In 1993 CFO William Lavin replaced retiring CEO Harold Sells. Lavin launched an ambitious restructuring plan, abandoning general merchandise in favor of becoming a diverse collection of specialty stores (primarily apparel and shoes). Although the company had been heading in this direction for years, in 1993 it took important steps to cut its general merchandise segment in half, closing 400 stores in the US and selling 122 Canadian Woolco stores to Wal-Mart. It also closed about 300 underperforming shoe stores.

The realignment was interrupted by an accounting scandal in 1994, when it was discovered that quarterly results had been overstated. An investigation found no intentional wrongdoing and no effect on annual results but noted that accountants were under pressure by management to show good results. CFO Charles Young was fired. The scandal prompted a deluge of shareholders lawsuits and an SEC investigation. The lawsuits and the investigation are pending. Later in 1994 Lavin was forced to resign by the board of directors, which was dissatisfied with the turnaround of the company.

In June 1995 Woolworth sold its Kids Mart/Little Folks children's wear chain to investor group LFS Acquisition.

NYSE symbol: Z
Fiscal year ends: Last Saturday in January

WHO

Chairman and CEO: Roger N. Farah, age 42,
$2,000,000 pay
President and COO: Dale W. Hilpert, age 52
VC, Kinney Shoe Corporation: Harold C. Rowen,
$330,000 pay
EVP Worldwide Specialty Operations: Ronald J. Berens,
age 55, $375,630 pay
SVP and Chief Administrative Officer: W. Barry
Thomson, age 42, $280,000 pay
SVP and CFO: Andrew P. Hines, age 55
SVP Corporate Planning and Development: C. Jackson
Gray, age 47
VP and Treasurer: John H. Cannon, age 53
VP Real Property: Gary H. Brown, age 55
VP Public Affairs: Frances E. Trachter, age 49
VP, General Counsel, and Secretary: Gary M. Bahler,
age 43
VP Human Resources: Patricia A. Peck, age 44
Auditors: Price Waterhouse LLP

WHERE

HQ: 233 Broadway, New York, NY 10279-0003
Phone: 212-553-2000
Fax: 212-553-2042

Woolworth operates over 8,000 specialty and general
merchandise stores in 23 countries worldwide.

	1995 Sales		1995 Operating Income	
	$ mil.	% of total	$ mil.	% of total
US	5,444	66	266	91
Europe	1,745	21	20	7
Canada	772	9	(16)	—
Pacific Rim	222	3	5	2
Mexico	110	1	(1)	—
Total	**8,293**	**100**	**274**	**100**

WHAT

	1995 Sales		1995 Operating Income	
	$ mil.	% of total	$ mil.	% of total
Specialty stores	5,017	60	258	94
General merch.	3,276	40	16	6
Total	**8,293**	**100**	**274**	**100**

1995 Specialty Stores	No.
Foot Locker (athletic footwear)	1,828
AfterThoughts/Carimar/Rubin/ Reflexions (boutiques)	1,082
Kinney (shoes)	826
Lady Foot Locker (athletic footwear)	595
Champs Sports (sporting goods)	539
Northern Reflections (women's casual wear)	466
Other formats	1,889
Total	**7,225**

1995 General Merchandise Stores	No.
Woolworth	812
The Bargain! Shop (low-priced apparel & household items	194
Other formats	65
Total	**1,071**

KEY COMPETITORS

50-Off Stores	J. C. Penney	Montgomery
Ames	Kmart	Ward
Broadway Stores	The Limited	NIKE
Brown Group	Longs	Nine West
Dayton Hudson	Luxottica	Price/Costco
Dillard	May	Reebok
Edison Brothers	Melville	Sears
Federated	Men's Wearhouse	TJX
The Gap	Merry-Go-Round	Wal-Mart
Gymboree		

HOW MUCH

	9-Year Growth	1986	1987	1988	1989	1990	1991	1992	1993	1994	1995
Sales ($ mil.)	3.7%	5,958	6,501	7,134	8,088	8,820	9,789	9,914	9,962	9,626	8,293
Net income ($ mil.)	(13.7%)	177	214	251	288	329	317	(53)	280	(495)	47
Income as % of sales	—	3.0%	3.3%	3.5%	3.6%	3.7%	3.2%	—	2.8%	—	0.6%
Earnings per share ($)	(13.9%)	1.38	1.63	1.91	2.24	2.56	2.45	(0.41)	2.14	(3.76)	0.36
Stock price – high ($)[1]	—	15.63	24.50	29.81	30.38	36.13	36.63	36.38	35.00	32.75	26.25
Stock price – low ($)[1]	—	9.16	14.53	14.75	17.06	24.19	22.88	23.50	26.00	20.50	12.88
Stock price – close ($)[1]	0.0%	15.00	19.31	17.25	25.88	31.94	30.25	26.50	31.63	25.38	15.00
P/E – high	—	11	15	16	14	14	15	—	16	—	73
P/E – low	—	7	9	8	8	9	9	—	12	—	36
Dividends per share ($)	6.7%	0.49	0.55	0.66	0.78	0.91	1.02	1.07	1.11	1.15	0.88
Book value per share ($)	0.8%	9.55	11.32	13.01	14.41	16.08	18.04	15.57	15.67	10.22	10.25
Employees	0.0%	119,000	121,000	125,000	132,000	138,000	141,000	142,000	145,000	111,000	119,000

1995 Year-end:
Debt ratio: 46.7%
Return on equity: 3.5%
Cash (mil.): $72
Current ratio: 1.21
Long-term debt (mil.): $309
No. of shares (mil.): 133
Dividends
Yield: 5.9%
Payout: —
Market value (mil.): $1,988

Stock Price History[1]
High/Low 1986–95

[1] Stock prices are for the prior calendar year.

W. R. GRACE & CO.

OVERVIEW

CEO J. P. Bolduc fell from grace in 1995. Bolduc's forced departure on the grounds that he sexually harassed female employees was only one scene in a long-running soap opera of boardroom power plays and revolts that have tended to obscure the operational success of W. R. Grace. The Boca Raton, Florida–based company is the world's largest specialty chemicals manufacturer; its $3.2 billion in specialty chemicals sales accounted for 63% of the firm's 1994 revenue. Grace also holds a leadership position in specialized health care; its National Medical Care subsidiary is the US's #1 provider of kidney dialysis products and related services, operating 550 kidney dialysis centers around the world.

The firm operates 6 divisions: Construction Products, Container Products (sealants and specialty polymers), Davison (petroleum fluid cracking catalysts), Dearborn (water treatment chemicals), Packaging (plastics), and Health Care. Since 1991, Grace has sold noncore assets worth $2.1 billion, including interests in oil and gas services; book, video, and software distribution; food industry hygiene services; and other business lines.

In 1994 the firm acquired Home Nutritional Services (for $131.8 million) and several other kidney dialysis and health care businesses.

Albert Costello, a 37-year veteran with American Cyanamid (bought by American Home Products in 1994), succeeded Bolduc.

WHEN

W. R. Grace & Co. grew from the Peruvian business activities of Irishman William R. Grace. Grace, who had left Ireland because of the potato famine, was in Peru in 1854 chartering ships to trade guano (bird dung), a natural fertilizer. In 1866 he moved his headquarters to New York and established 3-way shipping routes from New York to South America to Europe, trading fertilizer, agricultural products, and US manufactured goods.

W. R. Grace, who served as mayor of New York City in the 1880s, died in 1904. His brother Michael took over until 1907, when W. R.'s son Joseph became president. Under Joseph's direction the shipping business grew, powered first by sail, then by steam, and became known as the Grace Line. Joseph expanded the company's investments in South America, eventually buying cotton mills, sugar plantations, and sugar refineries in Peru and nitrate production facilities in Chile. In 1916 he started the W. R. Grace & Company's Bank (later the Grace National Bank). The company entered aviation in 1928 in a joint venture with Pan American Airlines, forming Pan American–Grace Airways, called Panagra, which served Latin America.

In 1945 J. Peter Grace, Joseph's son, took the helm at the age of 32. To capitalize his planned diversification, Peter took the company public in 1953. In 1954 Grace expanded into chemicals with the purchases of Davison Chemical (industrial and agricultural chemicals, silica gels) and Dewey & Almy Chemical (can sealants, batteries). Peter also sold Grace National Bank (1965), Panagra (to Braniff, 1967), and the Grace Line (1969), 3 of the company's oldest businesses.

Purchases during the 1960s and 1970s also illustrated Grace's changing nature: American Breeders Service (1967); Herman's (sporting goods, 56% interest, 1970); Sheplers (western wear, 1976); El Torito–La Fiesta Restaurants (1976); and home improvement stores Handy City (1976) and Channel (1977). It also bought Baker & Taylor book wholesalers (1970). Peru nationalized Grace's paper and chemical outfits in 1974.

In 1986 Grace sold virtually all of its full-service restaurants, Sheplers, and its interest in Herman's. In 1988 the company sold its agricultural and fertilizer businesses. Grace added 3 European water treatment businesses to its holdings in 1990. In 1992 the company sold Baker & Taylor and bought the North American food service packaging operation of DuPont Canada.

In 1993 J. Peter Grace stepped down after nearly 50 years as CEO. He was succeeded by COO J. P. Bolduc. That same year the company acquired Riggers Medizintechnik of Germany (dialysis products) and Florida-based Home Intensive Care (home health care). Grace sold its oil field services business and its liquid storage and terminal business in 1993.

In 1994 Grace sold Colowyo Coal to Kennecott for $233 million. That same year Grace's dialysis services and products unit, National Medical Care (NMC), was ordered by the FDA to correct quality control problems at its US manufacturing facilities.

In an eventful 1995, J. Peter Grace and a number of senior directors were forced to retire from the board in a Bolduc-engineered coup. Bolduc's March exit was followed in April by J. Peter's death.

NYSE symbol: GRA
Fiscal year ends: December 31

WHO

President and CEO: Albert J. Costello, age 59
EVP Grace Health Care: Constantine L. Hampers, age 62, $1,506,250 pay
EVP and Chief of Staff: Donald H. Kohnken, age 60, $767,000 pay
EVP Grace Packaging: Jean-Louis Grèze, age 63, $723,333 pay
EVP and General Counsel: Robert H. Beber, age 61
EVP and Chief Technical Officer: F. Peter Boer, age 54
EVP and Assistant to the CEO: Hugh L. Carey
EVP Corporate Investments: James P. Neeves
SVP Grace Latin America: J. Murfree Butler
SVP Grace Ventures: Christian F. Horn
SVP Grace Container Products: Fred Lempereur, age 57
SVP Grace Cocoa: Pedro F. Mata
SVP and CFO: Peter D. Houchin
SVP Corporate Administration: W. Brian McGowan
SVP Human Resources: Pamela J. Hamilton
Auditors: Price Waterhouse LLP

WHERE

HQ: One Town Center Rd., Boca Raton, FL 33486-1010
Phone: 407-362-2000
Fax: 407-362-2193

Grace has operations worldwide.

	1994 Sales		1994 Operating Income	
	$ mil.	% of total	$ mil.	% of total
US/Canada	3,431	67	432	74
Europe	1,058	21	74	13
Asia/Pacific	378	7	58	10
Latin America	226	5	23	3
Total	**5,093**	**100**	**587**	**100**

WHAT

	1994 Sales		1994 Operating Income	
	$ mil.	% of total	$ mil.	% of total
Specialty chemicals	3,218	63	338	58
Health care	1,875	37	249	42
Total	**5,093**	**100**	**587**	**100**

Specialty Chemicals
Construction Products (concrete and cement additives, fireproofing and waterproofing systems)
Container Products (closure sealant systems and specialty polymers used in printed circuit board manufacture and component assembly)
Davison (petroleum fluid cracking catalysts, polyolefin catalysts, silica and zeolite absorbents)
Dearborn water treatment and process chemicals (corrosion, scale, and microbiotic growth inhibitors; process chemicals for paper and other industries)
Packaging (shrink wrap, foam trays, plastic containers)

Grace Health Care
Dialysis services (outpatient dialysis clinics)
Homecare services (home infusion and respiratory services)
Medical products (dialysis products and medical supplies)

KEY COMPETITORS

ARAMARK	Eastman	Medicore
BASF	Chemical	Monsanto
Baxter	Henkel	Morton
Bayer	Hercules	Renal Treatment
Cargill	Hoechst	Centers
Columbia/HCA	Hormel	Rhône-Poulenc
Dow Chemical	Imperial	TRW
DuPont	Chemical	Union Carbide
	In Home Health	Vivra

HOW MUCH

	9-Year Growth	1985	1986	1987	1988	1989	1990	1991	1992	1993	1994
Sales ($ mil.)	(0.2%)	5,193	3,726	4,515	5,786	6,115	6,754	6,049	5,518	4,408	5,093
Net income ($ mil.)	(6.2%)	147	(472)	161	229	253	203	219	(105)	26	83
Income as % of sales	—	2.8%	—	3.6%	4.0%	4.1%	3.0%	3.6%	—	0.5%	1.6%
Earnings per share ($)	(12.1%)	2.82	(5.63)	1.89	2.62	2.82	2.36	2.40	(1.17)	0.28	0.88
Stock price – high ($)	—	24.75	30.38	37.31	29.88	39.13	33.63	40.75	45.00	41.25	46.75
Stock price – low ($)	—	17.75	22.63	19.13	23.50	25.13	17.00	23.38	32.00	34.38	35.25
Stock price – close ($)	5.5%	23.94	24.19	24.00	26.00	32.75	23.88	39.50	40.25	40.63	38.63
P/E – high	—	9	—	20	11	14	14	17	—	—	53
P/E – low	—	6	—	10	9	9	7	10	—	—	40
Dividends per share ($)	0.0%	1.40	1.40	1.40	1.40	1.40	1.40	1.40	1.40	1.40	1.40
Book value per share ($)	(3.4%)	21.70	15.66	17.25	18.24	20.16	22.29	22.77	17.10	16.16	15.91
Employees	(9.6%)	94,000	41,400	39,400	45,700	49,700	52,000	49,000	44,100	34,000	38,000

1994 Year-end:
Debt ratio: 50.5%
Return on equity: 5.5%
Cash (mil.): $78
Current ratio: 1.00
Long-term debt (mil.): $1,099
No. of shares (mil.): 94
Dividends
  Yield: 3.6%
  Payout: 159.1%
Market value (mil.): $3,634

**Stock Price History
High/Low 1985–94**

XEROX CORPORATION

OVERVIEW

The Document Company — Xerox — focuses on the intersection of the paper and digital worlds by producing, marketing, servicing, and financing a wide range of copiers, scanners, printers, and document processing software. Based in Stamford, Connecticut, Xerox sold its Xerox Financial Services Life Insurance Company to General American Life Insurance Company in 1995 and is in the process of selling its remaining nondocument processing companies, primarily in the insurance sector.

Xerox is also adjusting its ownership in one of its international joint ventures and the division of its global markets. Xerox has raised its stake in Rank Xerox, its European subsidiary, from 51% to 71% by purchasing additional shares from the Rank Organisation for $960 million. Also, Xerox is now forming a production venture in China with Fuji Xerox that would allow Fuji Xerox to compete directly with its Japanese rivals already in China. Xerox has historically controlled the production and sales operations in China along with North and South America.

Xerox's $900 million R&D program is concentrating on 3 developing markets: digital printing, color systems, and network systems.

WHEN

The Haloid Company was incorporated in 1906 to make and sell photographic paper. In 1935 it bought the Rectigraph Company (photocopiers). This purchase led Haloid to acquire a license for a new process called electrophotography (later renamed xerography from the ancient Greek words for *dry* and *writing*) from the Battelle Memorial Institute in 1947. Battelle had backed inventor Chester Carlson, who had labored since 1937 to perfect a process of transferring electrostatic images from a photoconductive surface to paper.

Haloid commercialized the process, introducing the Model A copier in 1949 and the Xerox Copyflo in 1955. By 1956 xerographic products represented 40% of the company's sales. The company became Haloid Xerox in 1958 and in 1959 introduced the Xerox 914, the first simplified office copier. The 914 took the world by storm, beating out such competing technologies as mimeograph (A.B. Dick), thermal paper (3M), and damp copy (Kodak). Xerox's revenues soared from $37 million in 1960 to $268 million in 1965. The firm dropped Haloid from its name in 1961.

Xerox branched out in the 1960s, buying 3 publishing firms and one computer company, all of which were subsequently sold or discontinued.

In the 1970s Xerox bought companies that made printers (Diablo, 1972), plotters (Versatec, 1975), and disk drives (Shugart, 1977; sold in 1984); it also bought record carrier Western Union International (1979; sold in 1982). In 1974 the FTC, believing Xerox was too dominant in its market, forced the company to license its xerographic technology to other manufacturers.

In the 1980s Xerox bought companies in optical character recognition (Kurzweil,

1980), scanning and fax (Datacopy, 1988), and desktop publishing (Ventura, 1990). It also diversified into financial services, buying insurance companies (Crum and Forster, 1983) and investment banking companies (Van Kampen Merritt, 1984), among others.

After becoming CEO in 1990, Paul Allaire embarked on a major restructuring program to focus Xerox's operations on its core document processing business. In 1992 Xerox reorganized into 9 independent business divisions and 3 geographical customer operations units. Also in 1992 the company eliminated 2,500 jobs, with savings of $150 million. With an eye to future alliances, Xerox signed agreements to supply print engines to computer companies Compaq (1992) and Apple (1993). The Apple contract was a particular coup, as Canon, a chief US competitor, had been Apple's sole print engine supplier since 1985.

In 1993 Xerox sold 2 financial companies, Van Kampen Merritt for $360 million and Furman Selz for $99 million. In late 1993 Xerox announced plans to cut an additional 10,000 jobs by 1996 (more than 10% of its total work force). A surge of new products accompanied the cost cutting, indicating better use of its R&D centers. Xerox's R&D had a reputation for great inventions (the laser printer, PC networking, the graphical computer screen) but slow implementation. Xerox also formed partnerships with Lotus, Microsoft, and Novell to market its technology faster.

In 1995 Xerox introduced a new family of networked color laser printers and a host of software products. These products include DocuWeb and InterDoc, which allow documents to be printed via the Internet and the World Wide Web. Xerox also announced a multiple-site printing service with AT&T.

NYSE symbol: XRX
Fiscal year ends: December 31

WHO

Chairman and CEO: Paul A. Allaire, age 56,
$3,294,284 pay
EVP and CFO: Barry D. Romeril, age 51, $1,920,904 pay
EVP Operations: A. Berry Rand, age 50, $1,539,055 pay
EVP Operations: Peter van Cuylenburg, age 47,
$1,402,498 pay
EVP; Chairman and CEO, Xerox Financial Services:
Stuart B. Ross, age 57
SVP Corporate Strategic Services: Allan E. Dugan,
age 54, $1,273,371 pay
SVP Corporate Research and Technology: Mark B.
Myers, age 56
SVP and Chief Staff Officer: William F. Buehler, age 55
SVP and General Counsel: Richard S. Paul, age 53
VP Treasurer and Secretary: Eunice M. Filter, age 54
VP Controller: Philip D. Fishbach, age 53
VP Human Resources: Anne M. Mulcahy
Auditors: KPMG Peat Marwick LLP

WHERE

HQ: 800 Long Ridge Rd., PO Box 1600,
Stamford, CT 06904
Phone: 203-968-3000
Fax: 203-968-4312 (Public Relations)

Xerox, in conjunction with jointly owned subsidiaries
Rank Xerox and Fuji Xerox, operates offices,
manufacturing plants, and other facilities worldwide.

	1994 Sales		1994 Net Income	
	$ mil.	% of total	$ mil.	% of total
US	10,571	59	386	49
Europe	4,633	26	215	27
Other regions	2,633	15	193	24
Total	**17,837**	**100**	**794**	**100**

WHAT

	1994 Sales	
	$ mil.	% of total
Sales	7,853	44
Service & rentals	6,229	35
Insurance	2,749	15
Equipment financing	1,006	6
Total	**17,837**	**100**

Business Divisions
Desktop Document Systems (digital desktop devices)
Office Document Products (copiers)
Office Document Systems (laser and ink-jet printers)
Personal Document Products (personal/convenience
copiers)
Xerox Business Services (document management
services)
Xerox Engineering Systems (document systems for
engineering and scientific applications)
Xerox Production Systems (publishing and printing
systems)
XSoft (software for document management and other
applications)

Other
Insurance services

KEY COMPETITORS

Alco Standard	Matsushita
AM Intl.	3M
Canon	Minolta
Casio	Mitsubishi
Copifax	Moore Corp.
Eastman Kodak	NEC
GEC	Olivetti
General Binding	Pitney Bowes
Harris Corp.	Polaroid
Hewlett-Packard	Sharp
Hitachi	Siemens
Machines Bull	

HOW MUCH

	9-Year Growth	1985	1986	1987	1988	1989	1990	1991	1992	1993	1994
Sales ($ mil.)	8.1%	8,838	9,355	10,320	31,234	33,148	17,973	17,830	18,261	17,410	17,837
Net income ($ mil.)	5.9%	475	423	578	388	704	243	454	(1,074)	(126)	794
Income as % of sales	—	5.4%	4.5%	5.6%	1.2%	2.1%	1.4%	2.5%	—	—	4.5%
Earnings per share ($)	4.2%	4.44	3.85	5.35	3.50	6.41	1.66	3.86	(3.32)	(1.84)	6.44
Stock price – high ($)	—	60.50	72.25	85.00	63.00	69.00	58.88	69.75	82.25	90.00	112.75
Stock price – low ($)	—	37.25	48.63	50.00	50.25	54.38	29.00	35.25	66.50	69.88	87.75
Stock price – close ($)	5.8%	59.75	60.00	56.63	58.38	57.25	35.50	68.50	79.25	89.38	99.00
P/E – high	—	14	19	16	18	11	36	18	—	—	18
P/E – low	—	8	13	9	14	9	18	9	—	—	14
Dividends per share ($)	0.0%	3.00	3.00	3.00	3.00	3.00	3.00	3.00	3.00	3.00	3.00
Book value per share ($)	(1.6%)	45.47	48.00	51.00	52.22	54.66	54.76	55.36	40.76	38.15	39.41
Employees	(1.7%)	102,396	100,400	99,200	100,000	99,000	99,000	100,900	99,300	97,000	87,600

1994 Year-end:
Debt ratio: 72.0%
Return on equity: 19.5%
Cash (mil.): $35
Current ratio: 1.35
Long-term debt (mil.): $7,596
No. of shares (mil.): 106
Dividends
  Yield: 3.0%
  Payout: 46.6%
Market value (mil.): $10,493

**Stock Price History
High/Low 1985–94**

YELLOW CORPORATION

OVERVIEW

Yellow Corporation, based near Kansas City in Overland Park, Kansas, is one of the nation's biggest trucking companies. Traditionally a long-haul company, it has expanded into regional LTL — less than truckload (shipments weighing less than 10,000 pounds) — trucking because of potential growth opportunities. Yellow acquired Preston Corporation, owner of 3 regional trucking lines, in 1993 and acquired LTL company Johnson's Freightlines in 1994. The company's new acquisition, renamed WestEx, serves portions of the Southwest.

Yellow Freight System, the corporation's biggest subsidiary, is the largest provider of LTL transportation in the US. Yellow Freight is responsible for 77% of corporate sales. This subsidiary has direct service to over 35,000 points in all 50 states as well as in Canada, Mexico, and Puerto Rico. It also makes shipments to Europe through an alliance with the Royal Frans Maas Group based in the Netherlands.

Another subsidiary, Yellow Logistics Services, provides a range of integrated logistic management services and warehousing for a number of industries.

Since 1952, 3 generations of the Powells have managed Yellow Corporation's daily affairs. The Powell family and the Powell Family Foundation control 9.3% of Yellow Corporation stock.

WHEN

In 1924 A. J. Harrell established a trucking company in conjunction with his Oklahoma City bus line and Yellow Cab franchise. Operating as Yellow Transit, Harrell's trucking company hauled LTL shipments between Oklahoma City and Tulsa. By 1944 Yellow was operating in Illinois, Indiana, Kansas, Kentucky, Missouri, and Texas through 51 independent subsidiaries. However, its policy of paying high dividends stunted growth, and by 1951 Yellow faced bankruptcy.

The company was losing about $75,000 a month in 1952 when George Powell, formerly of Riss & Company (a then-leading trucking company), took over. Within 5 months he had turned Yellow around.

Powell focused the company on long-haul interstate shipments (i.e., from Chicago to Los Angeles) rather than shorter hauls of a few hundred miles. To accomplish this, Yellow needed a more extensive route network, so Powell established a central dispatch office in Kansas City and started to buy other trucking companies to extend Yellow's operations.

In 1965 the company expanded to the West Coast and to the Southeast by buying Watson-Wilson Transportation System. After changing its name to Yellow Freight System (1968), the company acquired part of Norwalk Truck Lines, with routes in the Northeast (1970), and Adley Express (1973), connecting Yellow's eastern US routes.

The company then extended routes into the Pacific Northwest by purchasing Republic Freight Systems in 1975. It bought Braswell Motor Freight, consolidating its routes in California, Texas, and the Southeast in 1977. Yellow's only deviation from route acquisitions was its $4 million investment in Overland Energy (oil and gas exploration) in 1976, which it dissolved in the early 1980s.

Yellow was unprepared, however, when Congress deregulated trucking routes and shipping rates in 1980. Yellow upgraded its aging depots and terminals, but it still experienced a decline in profits between 1980 and 1983. In 1987 the company opened a terminal in Alaska, thereby extending service to all 50 states.

In 1990 Yellow introduced *EDIPartners*, software allowing customers to use their PCs to access information in Yellow's computer regarding their shipments. In the following year the company formed Yellow Freight Mexicana and expanded its Canadian service to the Maritime Provinces. In 1992 Yellow launched Metroliner 2-day service and Express Lane guaranteed expedited delivery.

Preston Trucking's Teamsters voted in 1993 to accept a temporary 9% wage cut to improve profitability. In 1994 Yellow Freight experienced a 24-day strike by the Teamsters; Preston was only affected for 6 days. The strike did not negatively affect the year's revenue figure. Yellow Corporation also suffered significant losses from harsh winter weather, which slowed freight transportation.

In early 1995 Yellow's Smalley subsidiary was merged into a larger subsidiary, Saia, which began serving the Carolinas. Also in 1995 Yellow raised its hauling rates. The rate hike is expected to improve earnings for the year. The company plans in 1995 to launch services to the Pacific Rim and begin shipping by air to add to its current service to Europe.

Nasdaq symbol: YELL
Fiscal year ends: December 31

WHO

Chairman: George E. Powell Jr., age 68
President and CEO: George E. Powell III, age 46,
$420,109 pay
President, Yellow Freight System: M. Reid Armstrong,
age 57, $343,639 pay
President, Preston Trucking Company: Leo H. Suggs,
age 55, $252,850 pay
President, Saia Motor Freight Line: Jimmy D. Crisp
SVP Corporate Development/Public Affairs: Robert W.
Burdick, age 52, $261,565 pay
SVP Operations, Yellow Freight System: Robert L.
Bostick, age 54, $236,251 pay
SVP Finance and CFO: H. A. Trucksess III, age 45
SVP and Legal/Corporate Secretary: William F.
Martin Jr., age 47
SVP Administration, Yellow Freight System: Gail A.
Parris, age 43
SVP Marketing and Sales, Yellow Freight System:
J. Kevin Grimsley, age 47
SVP Operations and Sales, Preston Trucking Company:
Gordon S. MacKenzie
VP and Treasurer: Phillip A. Spangler, age 54
VP Taxation: J. Michael Golden, age 47
Director Employees and Benefits (HR): Harold
Marshall
Auditors: Arthur Andersen & Co, SC

WHERE

HQ: 10777 Barkley, PO Box 7563,
Overland Park, KS 66207
Phone: 913-967-4300
Fax: 913-344-3433

Yellow Freight operates 671 freight terminals (314
owned, 357 leased) in Canada, Mexico, Puerto Rico, and
throughout the US. The company owns 59,842 trucks,
tractors, and trailers.

WHAT

	1994 Sales	
	$ mil.	% of total
Yellow Freight System	2,221	77
Preston Trucking	417	15
Saia Motor Freight	178	6
CSI/Reeves	36	1
WestEx	17	1
Adjustments	(2)	—
Total	**2,867**	**100**

Major Subsidiaries
CSI/Reeves, Inc. (specialty carrier and warehousing for
carpet and floor covering industry)
Preston Trucking Co., Inc. (regional LTL carrier serving
the Northeast and the Midwest)
Saia Motor Freight Line, Inc. (regional LTL carrier
serving the South)
WestEx, Inc. (regional LTL carrier serving the
Southwest)
Yellow Freight System, Inc. (motor freight transport in
the US, Canada, Mexico, and Puerto Rico)
Yellow Logistics Services, Inc. (logistics, packaging, and
distribution consultant)
Yellow Technology Services, Inc. (information supplier
to Yellow subsidiaries)

KEY COMPETITORS

Airborne Freight	Harper Group
American Freightways	Hub Group
American President	J.B. Hunt
Arkansas Best	Norfolk Southern
Burlington Northern	Roadway
Canadian Pacific	Schneider National
C.H. Robinson	Southern Pacific Rail
Conrail	TNT Freightways
Consolidated Freightways	U-Haul
CSX	Union Pacific
DHL	UPS
FedEx	U.S. Postal Service

HOW MUCH

	9-Year Growth	1985	1986	1987	1988	1989	1990	1991	1992	1993	1994
Sales ($ mil.)	7.3%	1,579	1,770	1,822	2,085	2,295	2,378	2,429	2,347	2,961	2,867
Net income ($ mil.)	—	56	67	41	69	19	65	27	41	19	(8)
Income as % of sales	—	3.5%	3.8%	2.3%	3.3%	0.8%	2.7%	1.1%	1.7%	0.6%	—
Earnings per share ($)	—	1.95	2.35	1.44	2.40	0.65	2.31	0.95	1.46	0.67	(0.28)
Stock price – high ($)	—	29.50	41.13	42.50	33.63	32.63	31.25	33.50	32.38	29.88	30.25
Stock price – low ($)	—	15.81	27.50	20.88	23.88	24.38	18.75	23.75	21.75	16.88	16.75
Stock price – close ($)	(2.1%)	29.00	36.88	27.88	31.63	26.75	26.50	26.63	27.38	24.88	23.88
P/E – high	—	15	18	30	14	50	14	35	22	45	—
P/E – low	—	8	12	15	10	38	8	25	15	25	—
Dividends per share ($)	6.8%	0.52	0.58	0.62	0.66	0.73	0.82	0.94	0.94	0.94	0.94
Book value per share ($)	4.3%	11.27	13.14	13.66	14.21	15.24	16.69	16.94	17.28	17.31	16.40
Employees	6.7%	20,750	23,400	25,500	27,200	29,200	28,900	28,700	26,800	35,000	33,400

1994 Year-end:
Debt ratio: 35.0%
Return on equity: —
Cash (mil.): $25
Current ratio: 1.07
Long-term debt (mil.): $240
No. of shares (mil.): 28
Dividends
Yield: 3.9%
Payout: —
Market value (mil.): $671

Stock Price History
High/Low 1985–94

YOUNG & RUBICAM INC.

OVERVIEW

Young & Rubicam Inc. (Y&R) has cut the apron strings, setting up a separate management group for its flagship subsidiary, Young & Rubicam Advertising. This move, part of a nearly year-long reorganization in 1994, indicates a recognition that administering one of the largest worldwide federations of advertising agencies was distracting the company from the actual business of advertising.

In recent years overall billings and sales have declined and the company has lost market share. In addition to the reorganization of the US operations (which include a number of new executive hires despite general staff cuts),

Y&R has trimmed operations elsewhere in 1995, cutting staff in France and closing its Rio de Janeiro office (another local affiliate will handle business there).

The company operates in 5 areas: advertising, public relations, sales promotion/direct marketing, corporate and product identity consulting, and health care communications.

Y&R is employee-owned and maintains a lower public profile than many of its more flamboyant competitors. In 1994 it was thrust into the spotlight when one of its top executives, Thomas Mosser, was killed by a mail bomb sent by the Unabomber.

WHEN

In 1923 Raymond Rubicam and John Orr Young founded their Philadelphia advertising agency literally on a shoestring — their first client was Presto Quick Tip Shoelaces. Y&R got its first major client, General Foods, when it asked for and received the account for the company's least-successful product, Postum. Its success in increasing sales of that beverage led to more business with General Foods and to a 1926 move to New York at that client's request. With its informal atmosphere and tolerance for eccentric behavior, the agency soon became a haven for the leading creative people in the industry.

In 1931 the firm opened an office in Chicago. In the early 1930s Rubicam, who by then dominated the firm, recruited George Gallup to create advertising's first research department. In 1934 Young was forced out; the firm, despite its unconventional working environment, had become a hard-driving place.

The Great Depression put many agencies out of business, but Y&R billings grew from $6 million in 1927 to $22 million in 1937; Y&R became the 2nd largest agency after J. Walter Thompson.

WWII brought surprising prosperity to the advertising industry. By 1945 Y&R's billings had reached $53 million. Rubicam retired to Arizona in 1944 at age 52.

During the 1950s the agency prospered; billings reached $212 million in 1960. In the 1960s Y&R produced the first color television commercials and a series of notable campaigns. Rubicam's emphasis on creativity, teamwork, and group management continued to work. During this period, however, growth slowed, and expenses and staff grew.

In 1970 Edward Ney became CEO, cut staff, and installed Alex Kroll as creative director.

Kroll required that creativity be controlled and disciplined and that it produce sales results. Ney expanded the agency through acquisitions, which included Wunderman Worldwide (direct marketing, 1973), Cato Johnson (sales promotion, 1976), and Burson-Marsteller (public relations, 1979).

By 1975, when Kroll became president of US operations, billings of $477 million had made Y&R the #1 US agency. Since 1979 it has been the largest independent agency in the US. The 1980s saw challenges to Y&R's dominance from the growth of such holding company agencies as the UK's Saatchi & Saatchi. Y&R's size and bureaucracy also threatened its reputation for creativity. Kroll became CEO in 1985 (he is now chairman emeritus).

In 1990 Y&R pleaded guilty to bribery charges in connection with a Jamaican tourism account. HDM Worldwide, a partnership with Dentsu (Japan) and Eurocom (France), fell apart when Eurocom withdrew. Y&R and Dentsu, partners for 30 years, regrouped as Dentsu, Young & Rubicam Partnerships.

In 1993 Y&R announced its 4th restructuring in 8 years, spending $50–$80 million to install a new communications system. That year the managing director of Y&R's Italian subsidiary was arrested for allegedly making kickbacks to win a government-sponsored anti-AIDS campaign contract.

In 1994 Y&R's Dentsu, Young & Rubicam Partnerships announced its purchase of 40% of Bombay-based Rediffusion Advertising.

As part of the technological upgrading undertaken by the company, in 1994 Y&R introduced the Brand/Asset Valuator, a statistical tool to help its clients evaluate the strength of their brands and the effectiveness of their advertising.

Private company
Fiscal year ends: December 31

WHO

Chairman Emeritus: Alexander S. Kroll, age 56
Chairman and CEO: Peter A. Georgescu, age 54
VC and Worldwide Creative Director: Ted Bell
EVP and CFO: Dave Greene
EVP and General Counsel: Stephanie Abramson
Chairman and CEO, Young & Rubicam Advertising:
John McGarry, age 54
President, Young & Rubicam Advertising: Ed Vick
**Director Research and Planning, Young & Rubicam
Advertising:** Stephanie Kugelman
Director Media and New Technology: Michael Samet
Director Human Resources: Raquel Suarez
Auditors: Price Waterhouse LLP

WHERE

HQ: 285 Madison Ave., New York, NY 10017-6486
Phone: 212-210-3000
Fax: 212-370-3796

Young & Rubicam has 331 offices in 64 countries
worldwide. Its Burson-Marsteller public relations arm
operates 63 offices in 32 countries.

WHAT

Selected Divisions

Burson-Marsteller (public relations)
The Advocacy Communications Team (communications
services)
Black, Manafort, Stone & Kelly (lobbying and public
affairs)
Cohn & Wolfe (public relations)
Executive Consultants Ltd. (public affairs consultants,
Canada)
Gold & Liebengood (lobbying and public affairs)
Robinson Linton Associates (government relations,
Belgium)

Special Communications Group
Chapman Direct Advertising
Landor Associates (corporate identity management)
Sudler & Hennessey (health care communications)

Wunderman Cato Johnson (sales promotion)

Young & Rubicam Advertising

Joint Ventures

Dentsu Wunderman Direct (Japanese direct marketing)
Dentsu, Young & Rubicam Partnerships (advertising)
Dentsu/Burson-Marsteller (public relations)

Representative Clients

American Express
American Home Products
AT&T
Clorox
Colgate-Palmolive
DuPont
Eastman Kodak
Ford
Grand Metropolitan
MetLife
PepsiCo
Philip Morris
Sears
Tandy
Time Warner
US Army
US Postal Service
Xerox

KEY COMPETITORS

Bozell
Carlson
Cordiant
D'Arcy Masius
Grey Advertising
Heritage Media
Interpublic Group
Leo Burnett
N W Ayer
Omnicom Group
WPP Group

HOW MUCH

	9-Year Growth	1985	1986	1987	1988	1989	1990	1991	1992	1993	1994
Total billings ($ mil.)	9.3%	3,575	4,191	4,905	5,390	6,251	8,001	7,840	7,781	7,559	7,990
Total sales ($ mil.)	7.9%	536	628	736	758	865	1,074	1,057	1,059	1,009	1,060
Sales as % of billings	—	15.0%	15.0%	15.0%	14.1%	13.8%	13.4%	13.5%	13.6%	13.3%	13.3%
US billings ($ mil.)	6.1%	2,272	2,389	2,577	2,792	3,115	3,937	3,739	3,637	3,670	3,865
US sales ($ mil.)	3.5%	341	358	386	373	410	487	466	458	445	463
Employees	1.1%	9,030	10,844	11,634	12,311	10,473	11,133	10,324	10,122	9,846	9,932

Young&Rubicam Inc.

Total Sales
($ mil.)
1985–94

1,200
1,000
800
600
400
200
0

ZENITH ELECTRONICS CORPORATION

OVERVIEW

Zenith is one company that's never going to overlook the Big Picture — especially not with the large-screen television market expected to explode over the next few years. The Glenview, Illinois, company sold a record number of TVs in 1994, outstripping the industry's overall unit sales growth of 10% and recording a near-doubling of sales of large-screen models. However, Zenith's 6-year money-losing streak continued, like a never-ending rerun.

The channel changed in July 1995 with the announcement that Zenith — the last US manufacturer of color televisions and picture tubes — was selling a majority stake to South Korea's LG Electronics for $350 million.

In addition to standard TVs, VCRs, and cable boxes, Zenith is pushing projection TVs, high-definition televisions (HDTV, to be introduced

to the US in 1997), and newly developed sets that operate in the 3 major broadcast systems used throughout North and South America. The company is tuning in to opportunities offered by cable and telephone companies, too. In 1996 it plans to offer TVs incorporating services available through the AT&T Home Information Center, and Zenith's *ScreenPlay* software now allows cable operators to create custom video displays for their customers.

Opportunities outside the US beckon also. NAFTA has created higher demand for picture tubes, and in 1995 the company struck a deal for a Canadian cable operator to use its HomeWorks Universal high-speed modem for an IBM work-at-home program in Ontario.

In 1995 Zenith president Albin Moschner replaced Jerry Pearlman as CEO.

WHEN

In 1915 Karl Hassel and R. H. G. Mathews, 2 ham radio operators, formed Chicago Radio Laboratory. In 1918 they began manufacturing radio equipment. In 1921 they were joined by Eugene McDonald Jr., a wealthy investor, who formed Zenith Radio Corporation (named after the call letters 9ZN of Hassel's amateur radio station) in 1923 to act as the sales agent for Chicago Radio Laboratory. Zenith was an early innovator in radio, developing the first portable radio (1924), the first home receiver to run on alternating current (1926), and the first push-button radio (1927). The Great Depression caused sales to drop 80%, but the company survived. It started a radio station and a TV station and began making hearing aids prior to WWII. During the war the company produced radar and communications equipment.

In 1948 Zenith bought the Rauland Corporation, which manufactured picture tubes, and produced its first black-and-white television sets. In 1956 Zenith's Robert Adler invented the first practical television remote control device. By 1959 the company was the black-and-white sales leader. In 1961 Zenith introduced its first line of color televisions. In the same year the FCC adopted Zenith's system for broadcasting FM radio in stereo.

During the 1970s and 1980s, Zenith faced the challenge of low-priced Japanese imports. Though it led the market in color television sales from 1972 to 1978, prices were held down by the Japanese "dumping" of television sets in the US market (selling sets in America for less than their cost). Under the pressure of

falling prices, the company moved some manufacturing operations to Mexico and Taiwan. Zenith chairman John Nevin lobbied Congress and filed suits against the Japanese TV manufacturers, eventually winning the battle but losing market share.

In 1979, moving away from radio and TV, Zenith acquired the Heath Company, makers of microcomputers and do-it-yourself electronics kits. Zenith's Data Systems subsidiary grew from sales of $10 million in 1980 to over $1 billion in 1989 on the strength of government and university contracts for its IBM-compatible personal computers; during that time, in 1984, the company changed its name to Zenith Electronics Corporation. In 1989 Zenith sold all computer operations, including the industry-leading laptop computer business, to Groupe Bull of France, using the proceeds to retire much of its debt. That year Zenith entered a joint venture with AT&T to develop an HDTV broadcast system.

In 1992 the company began consolidating its Mexican manufacturing operations, reorganizing its distribution, and cutting employment by about 1/5. Zenith sold its high-resolution monochrome monitor business in 1993 and its switch-mode power supply business in 1994. Its HDTV system was chosen in 1994 as the industry standard by a coalition of 3 groups that developed the systems. The company has benefited from the passage of NAFTA, which has lowered the duty on parts going to and from its Mexican manufacturing facilities.

Zenith plans to offer its first digital video disc (DVD) players in mid-1996.

WHO

Chairman: Jerry K. Pearlman, age 55, $458,333 pay
CEO and President: Albin F. Moschner, age 42,
$276,667 pay (prior to promotion)
**EVP Sales and Marketing; President, Zenith Sales
Company:** Gerald M. McCarthy, age 53, $212,000 pay
SVP Finance and CFO: Kell B. Benson, age 47,
$157,833 pay
SVP Operations: Philip S. Thompson, age 45
SVP and General Counsel: Richard F. Vitkus, age 55
VP Human Resources: Michael J. Kaplan, age 55,
$137,167 pay
VP and Controller: Richard C. Lueck, age 51
**VP Research and Development and Network Systems
Engineering:** John W. Bowler
VP Consumer Products Sales: Larry G. Cockrell
Auditors: Arthur Andersen LLP

WHERE

HQ: 1000 Milwaukee Ave., Glenview, IL 60025-2493
Phone: 708-391-7000
Fax: 708-391-8334 (Public Relations)

Zenith operates from 20 locations in the US: 6 production, research, and administration facilities in the Chicago area, 5 warehouses in Texas, one warehouse in Arizona, and 8 domestic distribution centers throughout the country. The company also has 15 locations in Mexico, 3 in Canada, and one purchasing office in Taiwan.

	1994 Sales		1994 Pretax Income	
	$ mil.	% of total	$ mil.	% of total
US	1,365	93	(8.4)	—
Other countries	104	7	(6.1)	—
Total	**1,469**	**100**	**(14.5)**	**—**

WHAT

Selected Products
Analog set-top boxes
Digital set-top boxes
High-definition television systems
HomeWorks high-speed cable modems
Large-screen televisions
Multistandard televisions
Picture tubes
Projection televisions
Remote controls
ScreenPlay software
StarSight interactive on-screen program guide
Television cabinets
Television/videocassette recorder combinations
Videocassette recorders

KEY COMPETITORS

ADC Telecommunications	NEC
Antec	Philips
Bose	Pioneer
Compaq	Recoton
Curtis Mathes	Samsung
DEC	Sanyo
Gemstar	Scientific-Atlanta
General Electric	Sharp
General Instrument	Siemens
Harman Intl.	Sony
Hitachi	Sun Microsystems
IBM	Thomson S.A.
International Jensen	Toshiba
Matsushita	Universal Electronics
Mitsubishi	Yamaha
Motorola	

HOW MUCH

	9-Year Growth	1985	1986	1987	1988	1989	1990	1991	1992	1993	1994
Sales ($ mil.)	(1.1%)	1,624	1,892	2,363	2,686	1,549	1,410	1,322	1,244	1,228	1,469
Net income ($ mil.)	7.0%	(8)	(10)	(19)	5	(68)	(63)	(52)	(106)	(97)	(14)
Income as % of sales	—	—	—	—	0.2%	—	—	—	—	—	—
Earnings per share ($)	0.3%	(0.33)	(0.43)	(0.78)	(0.20)	(2.56)	(2.36)	(1.79)	(3.59)	(3.01)	(0.34)
Stock price – high ($)	—	25.00	29.88	33.63	30.00	21.50	13.63	9.38	11.13	10.50	14.13
Stock price – low ($)	—	16.25	17.88	10.00	13.50	11.50	4.00	5.13	5.00	5.75	7.00
Stock price – close ($)	(6.1%)	20.50	21.88	14.75	19.00	12.75	6.63	7.38	5.88	7.00	11.63
P/E – high	—	—	—	—	150	—	—	—	—	—	—
P/E – low	—	—	—	—	68	—	—	—	—	—	—
Dividends per share ($)	—	0.00	0.00	0.00	0.00	0.00	0.00	0.00	0.00	0.00	0.00
Book value per share ($)	(13.7%)	18.90	18.49	18.45	18.84	14.90	12.33	10.60	6.94	4.25	5.00
Employees	(4.2%)	33,000	37,000	35,000	36,000	32,000	27,000	27,700	25,000	22,100	22,500

1994 Year-end:
Debt ratio: 44.4%
Return on equity: —
Cash (mil.): $9
Current ratio: 1.94
Long-term debt (mil.): $182
No. of shares (mil.): 46
Dividends
 Yield: —
 Payout: —
Market value (mil.): $531

**Stock Price History
High/Low 1985–94**

3

INDEXES

A

ALABAMA

Huntsville
SCI Systems, Inc. **764**

ARIZONA

Phoenix
The Circle K Corporation
228
The Dial Corp **302**
Phelps Dodge Corporation
692

ARKANSAS

Bentonville
Wal-Mart Stores, Inc. **908**

Fort Smith
Beverly Enterprises, Inc.
164

Little Rock
Dillard Department
Stores, Inc. **306**

Springdale
Tyson Foods, Inc. **862**

C

CALIFORNIA

Arcadia
The Vons Companies, Inc.
904

Beverly Hills
Hilton Hotels Corporation
450

Burbank
The Walt Disney Company
910

Chatsworth
Great Western Financial
Corporation **422**

Cupertino
Apple Computer, Inc. **100**
Tandem Computers **816**

Cypress
PacifiCare Health
Systems, Inc. **676**

El Segundo
Mattel, Inc. **570**
Merisel, Inc. **602**

Irvine
AST Research, Inc. **116**
Fluor Corporation **376**

Irwindale
H.F. Ahmanson &
Company **448**

Los Angeles
Atlantic Richfield
Company **120**
First Interstate Bancorp
364
Hughes Electronics Corp.
462
Northrop Grumman
Corporation **644**
Occidental Petroleum
Corporation **656**
Pacific Enterprises **670**
Teledyne, Inc. **824**
The Times Mirror
Company **842**
Unocal Corporation **884**

Milpitas
Quantum Corporation
722

Modesto
E. & J. Gallo Winery **322**

Mountain View
Silicon Graphics, Inc.
776
Sun Microsystems, Inc.
808

Oakland
American President
Companies, Ltd. **82**
The Clorox Company **234**
Kaiser Foundation Health
Plan, Inc. **504**
Safeway Inc. **748**

Orange
Bergen Brunswig
Corporation **156**

Palo Alto
Consolidated Freightways,
Inc. **262**
Hewlett-Packard Company
446

Rancho Cordova
Foundation Health
Corporation **384**

Redwood City
Oracle Corporation **662**

Riverside
Fleetwood Enterprises,
Inc. **372**

Rosemead
SCEcorp **758**

San Francisco
BankAmerica Corporation
136
Bechtel Group, Inc. **148**
The Charles Schwab
Corporation **212**
Chevron Corporation **218**
The Gap, Inc. **394**
Levi Strauss Associates
Inc. **532**
McKesson Corporation
586
Pacific Gas and Electric
Company **672**
Pacific Telesis Group **674**
Southern Pacific Rail
Corporation **782**
Transamerica Corporation
850
Wells Fargo & Company
916

San Jose
Conner Peripherals, Inc.
256

Santa Clara
Intel Corporation **476**
National Semiconductor
Corporation **626**

Santa Monica
Tenet Healthcare
Corporation **826**

Scotts Valley
Seagate Technology, Inc.
768

Seal Beach
Rockwell International
Corporation **740**

South San Francisco
Genentech, Inc. **400**

Sunnyvale
Advanced Micro Devices,
Inc. **50**
Amdahl Corporation **66**

Thousand Oaks
Amgen Inc. **90**

Walnut Creek
Longs Drug Stores
Corporation **544**

Westlake Village
Dole Food Company, Inc.
308
Packard Bell Electronics,
Inc. **678**

Note: Page numbers in **boldface** indicate the company's profile. Lightface numbers indicate references to other profiles.

Symbols

1 Source Corporation 682, 683
1-2-3 Baseball 439
1-2-3 spreadsheet 480
1-2-3 Swing 439
1-800-COLLECT service 585
3 Musketeers 563
3M. *See* Minnesota Mining and Manufacturing Company
5th Avenue (candy bar) 445
7-Eleven 784, 785, 818
7Up 689
9-Lives 453
20 Mule Team 302
20th Century Fox 194
20th Century Industries 80
50 Plus magazine 728
59th Street Station generating facility 261
60 Minutes 370, 630
74th Street Station generating facility 261
76 Products Co. 884, 885
386 chip 650
501 jeans 532, 533
727 jet 301, 355, 647
737 jet 786, 787
747 jet 644, 647, 880
757 jet 647
767 jet 300
777 jet 404
1897 Corp. 237
1911 Corp. 237
1986 Tax Reform Act 432
1993 Omnibus Budget Reconciliation Act 804
3333 Holding Corp. 208

A

A & K Petroleum 510
A+ Audit Software System 298
A.1. Steak Sauce 736, 737
A-12 aircraft 764
A320 aircraft 647
AAdvantage frequent flyer program 96
A&A Die Casting Company 570
A&E Network 195

A&P. *See* Great Atlantic & Pacific Tea Company, Inc.
A&W Root Beer 220, 925
AARP. *See* American Association of Retired Persons
A.B. Dick 936
ABACUS 647
Abbasi, Sohaib 663
Abbokinase 45
Abbott Alkaloidal Company 44
Abbott Laboratories **44–45**, 90
Abbott, Proctor & Paine 680
Abbott, Wallace 44
Abboud, Robert 360
ABC. *See* American Broadcasting Companies
Abercrombie & Fitch 534, 535
Abex 378, 554
Abex Friction Products 268
Abitibi-Price 590
Ables, Clinton E. 317
Ablon, Ralph E. 660, 661
Ablon, R. Richard 661
Aborn, Foster L. 497
Above the Rim apparel 730
Abraham & Straus 358
Abrahamson, James A. 663
Abrahamson, James R. 451
Abrams, Charles L. Jr. 791
Abrams, James 573
Abrams, Kenneth 543
Abrams, Robert 506
Abramson, Stephanie 941
Abu Al Bu Khoosh 510
A.C. Nielsen Co. 320, 321
Academy Awards 708, 902
ACB Business Services 363
AccelGraphics 304
Accent paints 172
Access database program 608
Access Technology 433
Accessory Lady 596
ACCO office products 70, 71
Acco World Corp. 71
Accor 198
Accupril 912, 913
Accurate Forming 861
Accuride Corp. 692, 693
AccuSource 156
Ace Scavenger Service 930
Acer 834
Acheson Graphite 868
ACI electric motors 269
Ackerman, F. Duane 154, 155
Ackerman, Roger G. 273
Ackley Manufacturing and Sales 794
Acme Boot Company 390

Acme Quality Paints 774, 775
Acme Supermarkets 87
Acme Tea 86
Acrilan fibers 614, 615
Act II brand 255
Actifed 912
Actimmune 400, 401
Activase 400, 401
Activity furniture 799
ACTV, Inc. 914
Acushnet Co. 70, 71
Acuvue 498, 499
ACX Technologies 46
Adalet 159
Adam, J. M. 611
Adamatic food equipment 706, 707
Adams, Austin A. 367
Adams, Charles 726
Adams, James R. 755
Adams, Rex D. 613
Adams, William G. 325
Adamson, James B. 368, 369
Adaptive 626
Adcote Chemicals 620
Adderley, Terence E. 508, 509
Addis, Harold E. 901
Addressright 699
ADD-Vantage 45
Adelantos de Tecnología S.A. de C.V. 764, 765
Adelhardt, Joseph W. 685
Adidas 730
Adimando, Carmine F. 699
Adjemian, Harry 566
Adjemian, Vart 267
Adler and Shaykin 772
Adley Express 938
ADM Chemical 112
Admiral Corporation 574, 575, 726, 923
Adolph Coors Company **46–47**
Adornato, Paul D. 569
ADP Credit Corp. 123
Adrean, Lee 363
ADTI 661
Advance Magazine 473
Advance Publications, Inc. **48–49**
Advanced Airborne Test Instrumentation System 765
Advanced Computer Environment 248
Advanced Computing Environment (ACE) 776
Advanced Micro Devices, Inc. **50–51**, 476, 626
Advantage! 116, 117
Advantis 480
Adventure Island 99

Callahan, John P. 795
Callahan, Michael J. 379
Callahan, Patricia R. 917
Callahan, Richard J. 889
Callard & Bowser 695
Calle, Craig R. L. 279
CallNotes 754, 755
Calloway, D. Wayne 689
Caloric stoves 726, 727
Caltex Petroleum
    Corporation 190–191, 218,
    219, 832, 833
Calumet & Arizona Mining
    692
Camarata, G. J. 191
Cambria brand 372
Cambridge cigarettes 694,
    695
Cambridge Computer, Ltd.
    764, 765
Cambridge Industries 740
Cambridge Soundworks 160
Camdat Corp. 441
Camden, Carl T. 509
Camel cigarettes 736, 737
Cameo 303
Cameron Brown 366
Cameron Financial
    Corporation 366
Cameron Forged Products
    268
Cameron Iron Works 268
Camex 152
Cammarata, Bernard 844,
    845
Camp, Lee G. 675
Campbell, C. Robert 369
Campbell, Christian L. 665
Campbell, Donald G. 845
Campbell, Ian D. 423
Campbell, Joseph 192
Campbell Kids 192
Campbell, Lewis B. 839
Campbell, Robert H. 807
Campbell Soup Company
    192–193, 709
Campbell Taggart 98, 99
Campbell, Terry M. 353
Campbell, Van C. 273
Campbell, Victor L. 247
Campbell, W. Patrick 89
Campeau 572
Campeau, Robert 358
Campfire marshmallows 172
Campo, Ronald T. 529
Camstra, William A. 507
Canada Cup paper products
    493
Canada Dry 925
Canadair 402
Canadian Freightways 263
Canadian International Paper
    482

Canadian Mist whiskey 180,
    181
Canadian Occidental
    Petroleum Ltd. 657
Canadian Salt Company Ltd.
    620
Candler, Asa 240
C&S/Sovran 628
Candy Land 438, 439
Candy Man 193
Canion, Joseph R. 248, 256
Canji Inc. 760
Cannatella, Anthony C. 607
Cannavino, James 480
Cannell Television 554
Cannestra, Kenneth W. 541
Cannon, Charles H. 379
Cannon Electric 490
Cannon, John H. 933
Cannon, W. Stephen 231
Canon 326, 650, 834, 936
Cansica 354
Canstar Sports 638
Cantalupo, James R. 579
Canteen Corporation 848
Canteen food services 368
Cantrell, Joseph D. 855
Cantrell, Wesley E. 437
CA-OpenIngres/Desktop
    software 252
Cape Canaveral generating
    facility 387
Capella disk drives 723
Capellupo, John P. 581
Capital Airlines 560, 864
Capital Area Permanente
    Medical Group, P.C. 505
Capital Cities/ABC, Inc. 158,
    159, 194–195, 440
Capital Company 850
Capital Financial Services
    236
Capital Group 804
Capital Management Group
    346, 715
Capitol Finance Group 422
Capitol Software, Inc. 433
Capon, James 533
Capoten 178, 179
Cappello, Juan C. 487
Cappy, Joseph E. 223
Capstaff, Diane M. 497
Capsugel 913
Captiva instant camera 702,
    703
Cara Corp. 789
Caramello 444, 445
Carano, Richard D. 377
Caras, Constantine G. 661
Carballo, Bernardo A. 769
Carbone, Anthony J. 313
Carbones del Zulia 284
Carborundum 594

Carco winches 669
Carcometal steel 668
Cardinal Distribution 156
Cardinal generating facility
    73
Cardinal Health 156
Cardura 691
Cardwell, Kenneth D. 569
CareFlorida Health Systems
    384
Care*Free gum 737
Caremark medical products
    144
CareVue medical information
    system 446
Carex 744
Carey, Hugh L. 935
Carey-McFall 790
Cargill, Edna 196
Cargill, Incorporated 104,
    196–197, 522
Cargill, James 196
Cargill, Sam 196
Cargill, William Jr. 196
Cargill, William Sr. 196
Cargo Carriers, Inc. 197
Cariboo Pulp & Paper Co.
    211
Carimar stores 933
Carina apparel 901
Carinalli, Charles P. 627
Carl, John L. 93
Carleton, Robert L. 689
Carley, John B. 57
Carlisle Ventures, Inc. 649
Carlo Rossi wine 322, 323
Carlsberg 99, 254
Carlson, Arleen 198
Carlson, Chester 936
Carlson Companies, Inc.
    198–199
Carlson, Curtis L. 198, 199
Carlson, Eddie 864
Carlson, Robert E. 649
Carlson Wagonlit Travel 199
Carlton cigarettes 70
Carlyle Group 402
CarMax 230
Carmen Vineyards 181
Carmody, Tom 731
Carnaud Metalbox 278
Carnegie, Andrew 896
Carnegie Foundation for the
    Advancement of Teaching
    820
Carnegie Group 168
Carnegie Natural Gas Co.
    896, 897
Carney, Thomas D. 175
Carney, W. Peter 437
Carnival Corporation **200–**
    201
Carnivale cruise ship 200

Goodwin, James K. 493
Goodwin, Larry D. 265
Goodwin, Leo 398
Goodwin, Lillian 398
Goodyear Aerospace 418
Goodyear, Charles 418
The Goodyear Tire & Rubber Company **418–419**, 692, 709, 744
Gookin, Burt 452
Goonrey, Charles W. 95
Goossen, Isabelle C. 707
Gordon, Bruce S. 153
Gordon, Harold P. 439
Gordon, Ilene S. 829
Gordon, Kenneth A. H. 729
Gorgas generating facility 781
Gorham 180, 181
Gorham, David L. 637
Gorjat, Jean 95
Gorman, Joseph T. 857
Gorman, Lillian R. 365
Gorton's seafood 406
Goslee, Dwight J. 255
Goss, Rebecca O. 337
Gossage, Thomas L. 443
Gotcha Covered 767
Gott 744
Gottehrer, Barry H. 569
Gottschalk, Thomas A. 409
Gould, Brian S. 875
Gould, Edward P. 811
Gould, Jay 88
Goulding, Barry W. 805
Gourmet 49
Government Employees Insurance Co. 398, 399
Government Executive 843
Government National Mortgage Association 356
Gower, Robert G. 552, 553
Goya, Donna J. 533
Gozon, Richard C. 921
gp120 (immunotherapy) 400, 401
GQ 49
G.R. Kinney shoes 932
Graber Industries 790, 791
Graber, William R. 591
Grable, Errett 744
Grace, Joseph 934
Grace Line shipping 934
Grace, Michael 934
Grace National Bank 934
Grace, William R. 934
Grace, W. R. *See* W. R. Grace & Co.
Graf, Alan B. Jr. 355
Graham, Alexander Bell 118
Graham, Benjamin 158
Graham, Donald E. 914, 915
Graham, Edward H. 575

Graham generating facility 837
Graham, George 421
Graham-Newman Corp. 398
Graham, Philip 914
Graham, Robert W. 373
Graham, William B. 144, 145
Graham, William H. 163
Grainger Brothers 374
Granadillo, Pedro P. 337
Granath, Herbert A. 195
Grand Auto retailers 668, 669
Grand Central chain 388
Grand Coulee Dam 504
The Grand Food Fair 593
Grand Gulf Nuclear Station 342, 343
Grand Hyatt hotels 465
Grand Metropolitan 736, 941
Grand Prix (disk drives) 723
Grand Teton Lodge Co. 280, 281
Grand Union 518, 750
Granger, Gordon F. 277
Granite Management Corp. 382, 383
Granny's (food) 193
Grano, Joseph J. Jr. 681
Granola Bars 737
Grant, Douglas J. 825
Grant, Joseph M. 335
Grant Street National 594
Grant, Ulysses S. 320
Graphic Scanning Corp. 154
Graphika! paper 493
Grass, Alex 734, 735
Grass, Martin L. 734, 735
Graves, Michael 777
Gravy Train 453
Gray, Bowman 736
Gray, C. Jackson 933
Gray, C. William 435
Gray Drug Fair, Inc. 734, 735
Gray, Elisha 118
Gray, Harry 880
Gray, Rodney L. 734
Gray Security Service 330
Grayarc 698
Grayson, Edward D. 457
Graziano, Joseph A. 101
Grazier, George E. 353
Great American Bank 916
Great American Communications 76, 554
Great American Insurance Group 76, 77
Great American Software, Inc. 433
The Great Atlantic & Pacific Tea Company, Inc. 299, **420–421**
Great Chicago Fire 788

The Great Five Cent Store 932
Great Northern Ins. Co. 225
Great Northern Nekoosa 412
Great Northern Paper 412
Great Northern Railway 188
Great Scott! Supermarkets 526, 904
Great Southern Trucking 746
Great Starts 193
Great Value 908
Great Western Financial Corporation **422–423**
Great Western Tea Company 526
Greatamerica 550
Greater All American Markets 56
Grebow, Edward 207
Grecky, Joseph M. 729
Greco, Samuel A. 247
Greeley, Horace 512
The Green Bay Packers, Inc. **424–425**
Green Bay Press-Gazette 424
Green Diamond train 924
Green Frog luncheonette 288
Green, Adolphus 736
Green, Cyril K. 389
Green, Steven J. 699
Green, Thomas B. 297
Greenberg, Alan C. 146, 147
Greenberg, Evan 81
Greenberg, Frank S. 186, 187
Greenberg, Jack M. 579
Greenberg, Karen R. 539
Greenberg, Maurice R. 80, 81
The Greenbrier 280, 281
Greene, Anson Phelps 692
Greene, Carl W. 261
Greene, Dave 941
Greene, Timothy G. 805
Greenfield Healthy Foods 192
Greenhill, Robert F. 852, 853
Greenhill, Robert 618
Greeniaus, H. John 737
Greenlee 839
Greenough, William 820
Greenspan, Stephen B. 769
Greenstone Healthcare Solutions 886
Greenwald, Gerald 865
Greenwich Times 843
Greenwood Trust Company 62, 293
Greer, George C. 453
Greg Norman shoes 731
Gregg, Michael W. 469
Gregg, Walter E. Jr. 701
Gregory, George G. 449

U.S. Department of
Transportation 96, 864
US DOT 624
U.S. Electrical Motors 339
US General Accounting Office
878
U.S. Generating Company
149, 672, 673
US Industrial Chemicals 104
US Intermodal Services 323
US Marine (boats) 185
US Maritime Administration
82
US Navy 168, 446, 462, 536,
537, 576, 764, 798, 834
US Open 522
U.S. Operating Services
Company 672, 673
US Patent Office 778
US Plywood 210
US Postal Service 262, 292,
300, 500, 941
U.S. Satellite Broadcasting
314
U.S. Shoe 732
US Sprint long-distance
service 426
U.S. Steel 416, 502, 564, 618
U.S. Steel Mining Co. 899
US Supreme Court 292, 778,
870, 896
US Telecom, Inc. 793
US Treasury 582, 804
U.S. Vanadium 868
U S WEST, Inc. 152, 836,
840, 654, **888–889**
US Zinc 110
USA Network 902, 903
USA TODAY 158, 392, 393,
774
USAA **890–891**
USAA Buying Services, Inc.
891
USAA Capital Corporation
891
USAA Federal Savings Bank
890, 891
USAir Group, Inc. 158, 525,
642, 746, 786, 848, **892–
893**
USAM Corp. 893
USDA 466
USF&G Corporation 349,
894–895
Usher, Thomas J. 899
Usher's scotch 181
USL Capital Corp. 383
USoft 872
USPCI 870
Usry Inc. 882
Ustian, Daniel C. 633
USTravel 335
USX Corporation 120, 898

USX–Delhi Group 896, 898
USX–Marathon Group **896–
897**
USX–U.S. Steel Group 162,
550, 652, 896, **898–899**
UT Automotive 880
Utah Oil Refining 92
Utilimaster delivery vehicles
434
UtoteM 76, 228

V

V & V Associates 58
V8 juice 192
VAC 336
Vac'N'Mulch outdoor
appliances 167
Vacutainer blood collection
system 150
Vacuum Oil 612
Vadasz, Leslie L. 477
Vagelos, Roy 600
Vail, Theodore 118, 154
Valade, Gary C. 223
Valence Technology 724
Valencia furniture 799
Valencia, Luis E. 213
Valens, Ritchie 484
Valenti, Carl M. 315
Valenti, Samuel III 567
Valentines of Dundee 431
Valerio, Martha M. 649
Valero apparel 900
Valero Energy 238
Vallecitos atomic power plant
672
Valley Forge Insurance Co.
237
Valley Gas Production 340
Valley generating facility 837
Valley Line 280
Valley National 130
Valmac 862
Val-Pak Direct Marketing
274
Value Added Maintenance
System 699
Value Health, Inc. 690
Value House 684
Value Vision International
616
Value Wise products 86
Valu-Rite pharmacy program
587
The Valvoline Company 112,
113
Van Camp Seafood 724
van Cuylenburg, Peter 937
Van de Kamp's Frozen
Seafoods 924
Van Dorn 278
Van Gelder, John M. 523
Van Gilder, George T. 225

Van Graafeiland, Gary P. 327
Van, Gregory F. Gundy 565
Van Handel, Michael J. 557
Van, John A. Steenberg 515
Van Kampen Merritt 936
van Rooy, Jean-Pierre 881
van Schijndel, Anton 167
Van Voorhis, Gerald D. 111
Vancenase AQ 761
Vanceril 760, 761
Vancocin 337
Vanderbilt, Cornelius 82, 258
Vanderclute, Robert C. 625
Vandewater, David T. 247
VanErden, Donald L. 469
VanEssendelft, Richard C.
399
Vanish 757
Vanity Fair 48, 49
Vanity Fair apparel 900, 901
Vanity Fair paper napkins
493
Vann, Kyle D. 523
Vannoni, Leo S. 731
Vanstar 602
Vantage cigarettes 737
Vanzura, Cedric J. 175
Vapnek, Daniel 91
Vapona 753
Vapor Corporation 184
Varec 338
Variance apparel 901
Varivax 600
Varner, Michael O. 111
Varner, Sterling 522
Varney Speed Lines 264
Varta 500
Vasotec 600, 601
Vass, William H. 719
Vassarette apparel 900, 901
Vaughn, Donald C. 317
VAX computers 304
V-Crest 122
Veale, Tinkham II 58
Vecta 799
VectoBac 45
Vega airplane 540, 644
Vegemite 695
Velcro 514
Velsicol Chemical 390
Velveeta 695
Vendamerica BV 306
Vendex International 140,
306
Vent, Richard H. 103
Ventura 936
Venture Stores 572
VePesid 179
Veratec fabrics 483
Verbatim 326
Verdoon, Ronald D. 769
Vergnes, Bernard P. 609
Verkerke Reprodukties 431

INTRODUCING
HOOVER'S COMPANY
PROFILES ON DEMAND

A new fax delivery service that puts detailed company profiles from the

Hoover's Company Database at your fingertips

WHY WAIT? Get invaluable information immediately on more than 1,000 public and private companies.

The information is arranged in the same easy-to-use format as the company profiles found in *Hoover's Handbooks* and includes company overviews and histories, up to 10 years of key financial and employment data, lists of products and key competitors, names of key officers, addresses, and phone and fax numbers.

IT'S SIMPLE.

1. Choose any number of companies from the index on the following pages.*

2. Then call *800-510-4452*, 24 hours a day, 7 days a week to receive a detailed profile for only $2.95* for each company you choose. Have your fax number and the five-digit company code number ready.

3. A voice-automated system will guide you through your order, and you'll receive your company profiles via fax within minutes.

*American Express, MasterCard, and VISA accepted.

FASTEST-GROWING COMPANIES IN SECONDS.

3Com Corporation	12475	Andersen Consulting	43516	Borg-Warner Automotive, Inc.	14127
3D Systems Corporation	15229	Anglo American Corporation	41809	Borland International, Inc.	14730
The 3DO Company	16077	Applebee's International, Inc.	13585	Boston Beer Company	40674
50-OFF Stores, Inc.	15159	Applied Materials, Inc.	12647	Boston Chicken, Inc.	16244
7th Level, Inc.	42268	Arctco, Inc.	13346	Breed Technologies, Inc.	11296
AAON, Inc.	16562	Argosy Gaming Company	14601	Bridgestone Corporation	41861
ABB Asea Brown Boveri Ltd.	43750	Army & Air Force Exchange Service	40039	Brinker International, Inc.	10330
Acclaim Entertainment, Inc.	10544	Arrow Electronics, Inc.	10130	British Aerospace PLC	40681
Accor SA	43751	Artisoft, Inc.	15359	British Airways PLC	41761
Ace Hardware Corporation	40005	Asante Technologies, Inc.	16624	The British Petroleum Company p.l.c.	41759
Acer Incorporated	42451	Ascend Communications, Inc.	41997	British Telecommunications plc	41763
ACT Manufacturing, Inc.	43463	Aspect Telecommunications Corporation	14113	Broadway Stores Inc.	10300
Active Voice Corporation	16684	AT&T Global Information Solutions	43707	Broderbund Software, Inc.	11907
Acuson Corporation	10034	Atmel Corporation	14420	The Broken Hill Proprietary Co. Ltd.	41757
Adaptec, Inc.	12515	Attachmate Corporation	42453	Brooktrout Technology, Inc.	11719
Addison-Wesley Longman/Penguin	43656	Auspex Systems, Inc.	16036	Brown Group, Inc.	10242
Adia S.A.	12517	Austin Ventures	43266	Bruno's, Inc.	12812
Adobe Systems Incorporated	12518	Authentic Fitness Corporation	15727	BTR plc	42398
Advance Ross Corporation	12522	Autocam Corporation	15442	Buffets, Inc.	12815
Advanced Marketing Services, Inc.	12525	Autodesk, Inc.	12689	Cable and Wireless Public Limited Company	41766
ADVO, Inc.	12490	Autotote Corporation	15023	Cabletron Systems, Inc.	10276
AFL-CIO	40565	AutoZone, Inc.	11376	Cadbury Schweppes PLC	41767
AGCO Corporation	15593	Avid Technology, Inc.	15999	Cadence Design Systems, Inc.	12867
Agway Inc.	40013	Avnet, Inc.	10151	Caere Corporation	11430
Airbus Industrie	43752	Baby Superstore, Inc.	42110	Calgene, Inc.	12871
Airgas, Inc.	10044	Bacardi Imports, Inc.	40051	Callaway Golf Company	15521
Akzo Nobel N.V.	43753	Baker & McKenzie	40052	Cambex Corporation	15396
Alaska Air Group, Inc.	10046	Baker & Taylor Inc.	40053	Cameron Ashley Inc.	17198
Alcan Aluminium Limited	42408	Bally Entertainment Corporation	10166	Canadian Imperial Bank of Commerce	40707
Alcatel Alsthom	43754	Bank of Montreal	42380	Canadian Pacific Limited	41851
Alex. Brown Incorporated	12547	Bantam Doubleday Dell Publishing Group Inc.	43616	CANAL+	41802
All Nippon Airways Co, Ltd.	43755	Banyan Systems Incorporated	15842	Canandaigua Wine Company, Inc.	11800
Allegro New Media, Inc.	43500	Barclays PLC	41754	Canon Inc.	41862
Alliance Semiconductor Corp.	16807	Bard, Inc., C. R.	10253	Cap Gemini Sogeti SA	42454
Allianz AG Holding	43756	Barefoot, Inc.	15449	Carlsberg A/S	40715
Allied Domecq PLC	50001	BASF AG	41755	Carmike Cinemas, Inc.	12900
The Alpine Group, Inc.	11695	Bass PLC	41788	Carrefour SA	40719
Alpine Lace Brands, Inc.	13478	B.A.T Industries PLC	41762	Cascade Communications Corp.	42090
Altera Corporation	12568	Battelle Memorial Institute	40057	Casino America, Inc.	16032
Alternative Resources Corporation	20015	Bausch & Lomb Incorporated	10187	Casio Computer Co., Ltd.	41863
ALZA Corporation	11677	Bay Networks, Inc.	15419	Castle Energy Corporation	12908
America Online, Inc.	15558	Bayer AG	41808	Catalina Marketing Corporation	15571
America West Airlines, Inc.	41891	Bayerische Motoren Werke AG	41758	Catholic Healthcare West Inc.	40083
American Association of Retired Persons	40003	BCE Inc.	43059	CBI Industries, Inc.	10255
American Business Information	15513	Bed Bath & Beyond Inc.	14933	CDW Computer Centers, Inc.	16199
American Cancer Society	43092	Bell Microproducts Inc.	16410	Cellstar Corporation	41895
American Classic Voyages Co.	15544	Benetton Group S.p.A	41756	Ceridian Corporation	10402
American Freightways Corporation	12657	Benson Eyecare Corporation	11905	Checkpoint Systems, Inc.	12955
American General Corporation	10087	Bertelsmann AG	40661	The Cheesecake Factory Incorporated	15835
American Greetings Corporation	12591	Bertucci's Inc.	13144	Cheyenne Software, Inc.	12967
American HomePatient, Inc.	13121	BET Holdings, Inc.	10916	Chipcom Corporation	11002
American Management Systems, Inc.	12600	Biogen, Inc.	12776	Chiron Corporation	12972
American Medical Response, Inc.	15818	Birkenstock	42138	Ciba-Geigy Limited	41771
American Power Conversion Corporation	12609	The BISYS Group, Inc.	14874	Cidco Incorporated	17123
American Red Cross	40025	Blockbuster Entertainment Corporation	10218	Cifra, S.A. de C.V.	42411
American Software, Inc.	12614	Bloomberg L.P.	40671	Circus Circus Enterprises, Inc.	10344
American Stock Exchange, Inc.	40590	Blue Cross and Blue Shield Association	40067	Cirrus Logic, Inc.	12986
Ameridata Technologies, Inc.	16433	The Body Shop International PLC	41856	Cisco Systems, Inc.	13494
AmeriSource	40016	Bolt Beranek and Newman Inc.	10223	Clear Channel Communications, Inc.	11824
Ames Department Stores, Inc.	42031	Bombardier Inc.	42381	Club Mediterranee SA	42391
Ampex Incorporated	15804	The Bombay Company, Inc.	16119	CML Group, Inc.	10262
Amway Corporation	40031	Books-A-Million, Inc.	14665	CMP Publications, Inc.	42455
Analog Devices, Inc.	10112	Boole & Babbage, Inc.	12791	Coastal Healthcare Group, Inc.	12837
Anam Group	43398	The Boots Company PLC	42397	Cody's Books Inc.	41897

CALL TODAY FOR A FREE CATALOG FEATURING OVER 140 BUSINESS SOURCES

The 100 Best Companies to Work for in America	$27.95
1995 American Stock Exchange Fact Book	$14.95
1995 Information Please Business Almanac & Desk Reference	$21.95
1995 Nasdaq Fact Book & Company Directory	$19.95
The 1995 National Directory of Addresses and Telephone Numbers	$94.95
The 1995 What Color Is Your Parachute?	$14.95
The Almanac of American Employers 1994–95	$109.95
The American Forecaster Almanac	$14.95
Association Directories 1995 — 2-volume set	$134.95
The Best Business Schools	$14.95
Bond's Franchise Guide	$29.95
Built to Last	$24.95
The Burwell World Directory of Information Brokers	$99.95
Business Information Sources	$34.95
Competing for the Future	$24.95
The Computer Industry Almanac 1994–1995	$59.95
Cover Letters	$10.95
Customers As Partners	$24.95
Data Sources for Business and Market Analysis	$54.95
The Discipline of Market Leaders	$24.95
The Ernst & Young Almanac and Guide to U.S. Business Cities	$16.95
First Things First	$22.95
The Fitzroy Dearborn Directory of Venture Capital Funds	$64.95
Forbes MediaGuide 500	$19.95
The FORTUNE Encyclopedia of Economics	$49.95
Guide to Information Access	$18.95
Hollywood Financial Directory	$44.95
The Inc. 100 Handbook	$19.95
The Internet Business Book	$22.95
Interviewing	$10.95
Living Logos: How U.S. Corporations Revitalize Their Trademarks	$22.95
Logos of America's Fastest Growing Corporations	$39.95
Logos of America's Largest Corporations	$39.95
Logos of Major World Corporations	$39.95
The National Book of Lists	$19.95
National Directory of Corporate Public Affairs 1995	$89.95
Net Guide	$26.95
Net Money	$18.95
Networking	$10.95
The New Competitor Intelligence	$24.95
The New Rules	$24.95
New York Stock Exchange Fact Book	$9.95
The Official Guide to American Incomes	$69.95
The Official Guide to Household Spending	$69.95
The Official Guide to the American Marketplace	$79.95
The On-line Job Search Companion	$14.95
Plunkett's Health Care Industry Almanac	$124.95
Quantum Companies	$21.95
Reengineering Management	$24.95
Resumes	$10.95
Standard & Poor's 500 Guide 1995	$19.95
Standard & Poor's Midcap 400 Guide 1995	$19.95
Standard & Poor's Smallcap 600 Guide 1995	$24.95
Standard & Poor's Stock and Bond Guide 1995	$19.95
Statistical Abstract of the United States 1994	$24.95
Stop Selling Start Partnering	$21.95
The Universal Almanac 1995	$19.95
U.S. Industrial Outlook 1994	$27.95
Who Knows What	$27.95
Zapp! The Lightning of Empowerment	$19.95

ALSO INCLUDES COMPANY INFORMATION FROM AROUND THE WORLD

LATIN AMERICA

1995 Trade Directory of Mexico	$89.95
American Companies	$94.95
Argentina Company Handbook	
1995/96	$34.95
Brazil Company Handbook 1994/95	$34.95
Cracking Latin America	$44.95
Mexico Business	$24.95
Mexico Company Handbook 1994/95	$34.95
Venezuela Company Handbook	
1992/93	$29.95

ASIA/PACIFIC

Access Nippon 1994	$34.95
Asia Pacific Securities	
Handbook 1994–95	$99.95
Asian and Australasian Companies	$94.95
Australian Company Handbook	$69.95
China Business	$24.95
China Securities Handbook 1995–96	$99.95
Cracking the Pacific Rim	$44.95
Hong Kong Business	$24.95
Japan Business	$24.95
Korea Business	$24.95
Philippines Business	$24.95
Singapore Business	$24.95
Taiwan Business	$24.95
Thailand 1995	$46.95
Vietnam Business Directory	
1994–95	$49.95

EUROPE

Company Handbook Spain 1995	$84.95
Cracking Eastern Europe	$44.95
Directory of East European Businesses	$74.95
The European 5000 4-volume set	$359.95
European Companies	$89.95
French Company Handbook 1995	$59.95
Germany's Top 500 1995	$49.95
The Guardian Guide to the UK's	
Top Companies 1995	$49.95
Nordic Stock Guide 1994	$34.95
The Times 1000 1995	$49.95
Weissmann Travel Planner for	
Western and Eastern Europe	$49.95

OTHER GLOBAL INFORMATION

The African Business Handbook	$34.95
Canada Company Handbook 1995	$49.95
The Complete American Depositary	
Receipt Directory	$24.95
The Dow Jones Guide to the	
World Stock Market 1995–1996	$34.95
Emerging Markets Analyst 1995	$49.95
Importers Manual USA 1995–96	$86.95
International Investing with ADRs	$24.95
The McGraw-Hill Handbook of	
American Depositary Receipts	$59.95
Russia 1994	$64.95
The Statesman's Year-Book 1994–95	$89.95
World Trade Almanac 1995–1996	$86.95
The World's Emerging Stock Markets	$64.95

TRY IT FREE

Includes software and 10 free hours on America Online!*

WHERE you'll find *Hoover's Business Resources*:

- ☛ in the "Personal Finance" and the "Reference Desk" sections, under "Hoover's Business Resources"
- ☛ Or for quick access, type keyword: Hoovers

WHAT you'll find in *Hoover's Business Resources*:

- ☛ Over 1,500 company profiles
- ☛ Searchable MasterList of more than 8,500 companies
- ☛ Gateway to Hoover's Online on the Internet with special free access to areas that non-AOL customers must pay for

OTHER BUSINESS INFORMATION ON AMERICA ONLINE INCLUDES:

- ☛ Stock quotes
- ☛ On-line stock trading
- ☛ Small Business Center
- ☛ Career Center
- ☛ *Business Week* magazine
- ☛ *New York Times*
- ☛ Reuters News
- ☛ BankAmerica – banking online
- ☛ *Time* magazine
- ☛ ABC News

Is your America Online for WINDOWS software missing? Need DOS or Macintosh? No problem. Call 1-800-827-6364 ext. 17592 for a replacement kit.**